Women in Particular:

An Index to American Women

by Kali Herman

ORYX PRESS
1984

The rare Arabian Oryx is believed to have inspired the myth of the unicorn. This desert antelope became virtually extinct in the early 1960s. At that time several groups of international conservationists arranged to have 9 animals sent to the Phoenix Zoo to be the nucleus of a captive breeding herd. Today the Oryx population is over 400 and herds have been returned to reserves in Israel, Jordan, and Oman.

Copyright © 1984 by
The Oryx Press
2214 North Central at Encanto
Phoenix, AZ 85004-1483

Published simultaneously in Canada

Printed and Bound in the United States of America

Library of Congress Cataloging in Publication Data

Herman, Kali
   Women in particular.

   Includes index.
   1. Women—United States—Biography—Indexes.
2. Women—United States—Registers.   I. Title.
HQ1412.H47   1984   016.3054'0973   84-1019
ISBN 0-89774-088-2

This book is dedicated
to my grandmother,
Sydney J. Berkey.

Table of Contents

Preface

The inspiration for this project arose from the realization that while growing up I had been exposed to few women who did not fit into "traditional" roles—wife, mother, teacher of small children, social ornament, and helpmeet to men pursuing "serious" work. In the media and in literature, women were rarely portrayed otherwise. Aviator, archaeologist, physician, scientist, artist, police officer, fire fighter, entrepreneur: These were roles women were not seen capable of filling.

The exceptions were few: Susan B. Anthony the suffragist, Elizabeth Blackwell the doctor, Amelia Earhart the pilot. *The* suffragist. *The* soldier. *The* doctor. *The* pilot. Yet, as I was to discover, this depiction—that women of accomplishment were rare exceptions—does not jibe with the reality of American women's lives. Throughout American history there have always been significant numbers of women who chose to live their lives outside the strictures of "female roles."

My aim in compiling this research into a reference work was to bring these women out of obscurity.

Over the last two decades there has been a great rise in interest in the field of women's history, the study of what happened to the "other half" of the human race over the course of time. As researchers have discovered, the history of women is often quite difficult to trace: Sources are hard to uncover, facts hard to find, patterns hard to define. This is especially true when one is researching the contributions of women in a given field, or of a given ethnicity or geographic location. Information about such women is scattered throughout hundreds of sources, often buried in places one would never think to examine, or in places which, if thoroughly examined, would cost the researcher thousands of hours of valuable time.

This discourages all but the most serious women's historian and makes it difficult for the writer of a general text or article to include relevant women. There are women's indexes and bibliographies, but too many of these are ogranized only alphabetically; in order to use them you first must know for whom you are looking. Such rich sources of information as Hinding's *Women's History Sources* are often untapped due to such difficulties.

What is needed is one reference volume that gathers the scattered information about individual women and notes their contributions, listing them chronologically; an in-depth reference that includes minority women, who are usually ignored; an index cross-referenced by occupation, ethnicity, and by such other factors as religion and geographic location; a work that recovers the notable women who have somehow slipped between the cracks and have been "lost" to history. This book attempts to fill that gap.

The rediscovery of these "lost" women may alter our view of the role of women throughout American history; indeed, that is one of the intents of this work. For example, today's business world is considered male turf, territory women have only begun to break into. Yet that view demands rethinking when it emerges that significant numbers of women have always been involved in American business, in positions of influence and power, from the iron manufacturers and indigo traders of the 1600s to the industrialists of the 1900s.

The aim of *Women in Particular* is not simply to *list* women and their accomplishments. Because of its arrangement by career, ethnicity, geography, religion, and chronology, it is meant to encourage interdisciplinary thought, to provide a roadmap for the questioning mind. The ways in which one might use the information in this index include exploring the contribution of women in various fields; verifying their presence in professions where their contribution has usually been discounted, such as business or the military; recognizing the influence of women of various ethnic and racial groups; and noting the chronological development of women's roles in different fields. *Women in Particular* can also be used to contrast such group analyses, to point out the limitations of such studies and remind the researcher that a description of the average condition or representation of women in a field is not necessarily the whole story.

A work of this sort is necessarily subjective; every act of inclusion or exclusion is at some level a political decision. Included in the reference are women who have, through their own efforts, achieved note or prominence in their fields of endeavor and women who are notable because they were involved in professions not generally open to women—our "firsts." Also included are women who have a special importance to the study of an era: women pioneers or women relief workers in the Civil War, for example, who may not have been individually significant but whose collective experience helps the historian recreate the attitudes and flavors of a period in American history.

There are also women I deliberately did not include. Because this work was undertaken in the hope that it would help encourage the creation of role models for women, there are cateogries I omitted. I was not interested in listing courtesans unless they had other pursuits that would suit them for inclusion; if, for example, they wrote poetry, too. Women noted solely for their beauty or for their social position were also excluded—these attributes did not seem to me to be suitable reasons for fame or remembrance. Those famous only for marrying or being related to famous men are also not mentioned unless there was an indication that they had accomplished something themselves. Hence, you will find Abigail Adams listed, but not Mary Todd Lincoln.

Also, because *Women in Particular* was meant to provide a historical perspective and because I did not wish to flood the work with material on women easily located elsewhere, the majority of women in this book are not contemporary. I did not, for example, use the current *Who's Who* to research this book.

Though I believe this reference is the most complete and comprehensive listing of American women extant, it is not to be regarded as definitive. The discovery of lost women will continue for a long time to come. The information is also not without its limitations. Certain birth and death dates have been difficult to ascertain. Some women may be listed more than once in this reference because of my inability to distinguish between a real name and a pseudonym or a maiden name and a married name. At times a single listing may turn out to be more than one woman—a mother and daughter who have been reduced to a single entity in the literature, or two women of the same name who lived at the same time. This is unavoidable due to the nature of this sort of research. It is my hope that the scholars who use this work will sift through these errors and inform me of them so that an addendum can be compiled to make these corrections available to everyone. This index, culled from some of the most well-known and generally available indexes and biographical collections, is one more tool to aid in the work of recovering women's history.

What I have learned in the last four years as I compiled this index has given me great pride in being a woman. I have learned to exult in the many and varied accomplishments of my sex. I have also grown angry that these accomplishments were kept hidden from me, that no one ever told me about the important roles women played in such "male" fields as medicine, aviation, the military, and business. It gives me tremendous satisfaction to present this work to the public, helping to penetrate the veil of obscurity that hangs over the history of women in America.

Acknowledgments

Though I am solely responsible for selecting, compiling, and arranging the contents of this work, I gratefully acknowledge the moral and financial support of the following people:

My parents, Dorothy and Michael Herman, made the completion of *Women in Particular* possible when they provided the computer system I used to cross-reference the entries and type the manuscript. They also provided warmth, humor, and unfaltering faith in my competence. My brother Tal, the recipient of a number of late-night phone calls, was always ready with understanding and encouragement.

Several of my professors at the University of California–Santa Cruz also offered support. Marge Frantz granted an independent study so that I could recieve academic credit for my work. J. Herman Blake served as friend, counselor, and mentor. The entire reference staff at the McHenry Library went out of their way to be kind and helpful.

My friends were also there when needed: Roger Stone, Dan Wolf, Ariane Shapero, Jonathan Amsterdam, Wendy Meyer, Mark Daley, April Green, Linda Angeloni, Cindy Ashbrook, Debby Harlow, Barbara Blau, Joe Barsugli, Brian Diamond, Kim Philips, Jennifer Memhard, Yvette Huginnie, Margaret Mary Daley, Christiane Tarney, and Kiera Edelstein.

Finally, my deepest thanks to Ray Chester Imel III, who has stayed with me since the beginning of this project, from California to Colorado to Connecticut, and who has shown grace, compassion, patience, courage and fortitude.

Introduction

Women in Particular: An Index to American Women is actually five indexes. The first four—Field and Career (I), Religious Affiliation (II), Ethnic and Racial (III), and Geographical (IV)—are chronological listings that follow the same format, described here. The fifth, an alphabetical guide to the other four, is described below.

Each of the first four indexes is divided into subcategories: e.g., Business and Economics is a subdivision of Index I; Methodist, of Index II; Black, of Index III; and New York, of Index IV. Within each of these subcategories, women are listed chronologically, by birth date. (Those born in the same year appear alphabetically under that year.) Women for whom no birth date is known are listed at the end of each subcategory, under the heading "No Dates."

Within each index, entries have been assigned consecutive Arabic accession numbers.

Sample Entries

FIRST 4 INDEXES

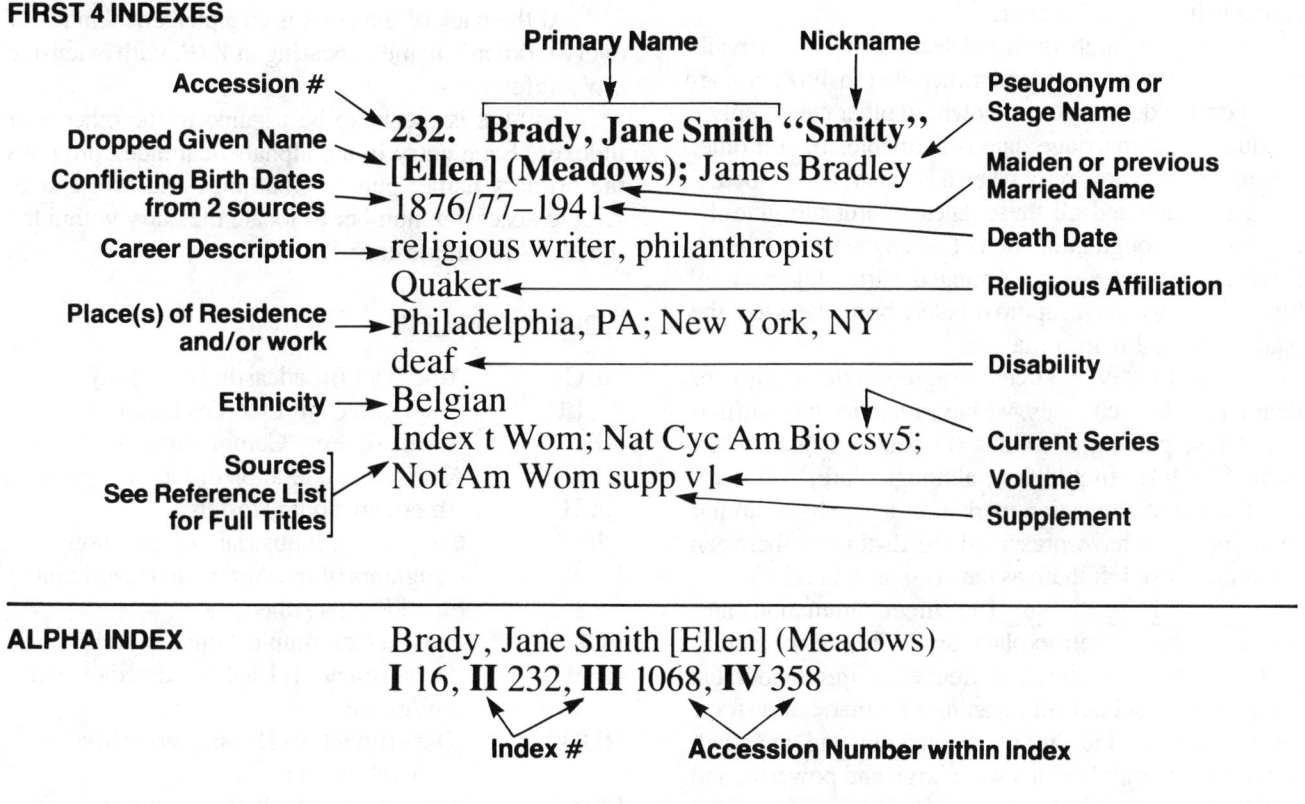

ALPHA INDEX

Brady, Jane Smith [Ellen] (Meadows)
I 16, **II** 232, **III** 1068, **IV** 358

Index #   Accession Number within Index

CROSS-REFERENCE

Bradley, James. *See* Brady, Jane.

THE ENTRIES

The following information appears in every entry: name, relevant dates, career description, and the sources of the information in abbreviated form. Optional data include: religious affiliation, state or territory where the woman lived and/or worked, race and/or ethnicity, and disability, when applicable. Thus, eight descriptions may be included in a single entry; each appears on a separate line.

Names. As the reader will soon discover, the name of a woman often consists of several names. An entry may include, aside from a primary name—or name used most often in private life—a maiden or previous married name, a nickname, and a pseudonym or stage name. A variety of punctuation and typefaces have been used in *WIP* to differentiate between these names. The primary name appears first and may be followed by a nickname in quotation marks; it may also be followed by maiden or previous married names in parentheses. A stage name or pseudonym—often identical to the married or maiden name—comes after a semicolon. If a nickname replaced a given name, it is placed directly before the semicolon; otherwise it stands before the maiden name.

At times a rarely used given name is included. These names appear in brackets; for example: Roosevelt, [Anna] Eleanor.

Dates. Accurate birth and death dates are not available for many of the women included in *WIP*. Sometimes only a death date is known; in other cases, only a graduation or marriage date is available. In still other instances, we know only when a woman "flourished." We have included all these dates in order to give the researcher a rough indication of when the woman lived. Because the indexes are arranged chronologically by birth date, we have approximated birth dates on the basis of available information.

Occasionally, sources disagree about a birth or death date. In such cases, we have included the conflicting dates, placing a solidus (/) between them; e.g., 1858/62–1931. In addition, although "pre," "circa" and the use of a question mark after a date have similar meanings, we have preserved the distinction between these and have left them as the original sources did.

Career Descriptions. The career summations are, on the whole, self-explanatory. The term "clubwoman," used with some frequency throughout the book, has a specialized meaning in American history. During one period, in the nineteenth and twentieth centuries, women's clubs were large and powerful and constituted a women's movement. When it is known which club a woman belonged to, that information is included in the career description; often all that is known is that she was active in the club movement.

Due to the length of the work, familiar acronyms have been used to save space. A list of these is included at the front of the book.

Religious Affiliation. The reader will find that "religion" has been used flexibly. Many movements elsewhere characterized as philosophical (Transcendentalism, Theosophy) are included here under religion. It was felt that many of these "quasi-religions" had a strong influence on American and women's history.

Geography. With one exception, "geography" means state or territory (including District of Columbia and Puerto Rico) and, when available, the city or area of the state in which the woman lived and/or worked. The exception is New England. Because of its distinct role in American history and because some of the women lived when boundaries between the states had not yet been drawn, New England has been included as a separate category.

Sources. Sources appear in shortened form; a full reference list precedes the indexes.

ALPHABETICAL INDEX

At the back of the book is an alphabetical index of every woman's name appearing in *WIP*, with extensive cross-references.

The list is meant to be a guide to the other four indexes. Each entry in the alphabetical index provides the primary name, plus a roman index number and an Arabic accession number to locate the entry within the index. (See sample entry.)

ACRONYMS LIST

ABC	American Broadcasting Company
ACLU	American Civil Liberties Union
AEC	Atomic Energy Commission
AFL	American Federation of Labor
AYH	American Youth Hostels
CIO	Congress of Industrial Organizations
DAR	Daughters of the American Revolution
ERA	Equal Rights Amendment
FCC	Federal Communications Commission
HEW	(Department of) Health, Education and Welfare
HUD	(Department of) Housing and Urban Development
IBM	International Business Machines
MIT	Massachusetts Institute of Technology

NAACP	National Association for the Advancement of Colored People	UNESCO	United Nations Educational, Scientific, and Cultural Organization
NBC	National Broadcasting Company	UNICEF	United Nations International Children's Emergency Fund
NOW	National Organization for Women	UPI	United Press International
PTA	Parent-Teacher Association	WAC	Women's Army Corps
SPCA	Society for the Prevention of Cruelty to Animals	WAF	Women in the Air Force
UMW	United Mine Workers	WCTU	Women's Christian Temperance Union
UN	United Nations	YWCA	Young Women's Christian Association

Source List

Am Bio Dict: *The American Biographical Dictionary,* 3d edition, by William Allen. Boston: John P. Jewett & Co. Originally published Cleveland, OH: Henry P. B. Jewett, 1857.

Am Bio New Cyc: *American Biography, A New Cyclopedia.* New York: American Historical Society, Inc., 1931.

Appl Cyc Am Bio: *Appleton's Cyclopedia of American Biography,* edited by James Grant Wilson and John Fiske. New York: D. Appleton & Co., 1888.

Aust Dict Bio: *Australian Dictionary of Biography. Volume 1.* Melbourne, Australia: Melbourne University Press. Vol. 2–8 published by Cambridge University Press, Cambridge: 1966.

Bio Dict Am Lab: *Biographical Dictionary of American Labor,* edited by Gary M. Fink. Westport, CT: Greenwood Press, 1974.

Bio Dict Confed: *Biographical Dictionary of the Confederacy,* by John L. Akelyn. Westport, CT: Greenwood Press, 1977.

Bio Dict Sudan: *A Biographical Dictionary of the Sudan,* by Richard Hill. London: Frank Cass & Co., Ltd., 1967.

Cur Biog: *Current Biography,* 1969–1982, edited by Charles Moritz. New York: H. W. Wilson & Co.

Cyc Am Bio: *The Cyclopedia of American Biography,* originally edited by James Grant Wilson and John Fiske. Revision to 1914 edited by Charles Dick and James E. Homans. New York: Press Association Compilers, Inc., 1915.

Dict Am Auth: *Dictionary of American Authors,* 5th edition, by Oscar Fay Adams. Detroit, MI: Gale Research Co., 1969. Originally published New York: Houghton Mifflin Co., 1904.

Dict Am Bio: *Dictionary of American Biography,* 1927–1957, edited by Allen Johnson. New York: Charles Scribner's Sons.

Dict Am Bio Men Time: *Dictionary of American Biography Including Men of the Time,* by Francis S. Drake. Boston: Houghton, Osgood & Co., n.d. Originally published Cambridge, MA: Riverside Press, 1879.

Dict Am Rel Bio: *Dictionary of American Religious Biography,* by Henry Warner Bowden. Westport, CT: Greenwood Press, 1977.

Dict Aust Bio: *Dictionary of Australian Biography,* by Percival Serle. Sydney, Australia: Angus and Robertson, 1949.

Dict Ind Bio: *Dictionary of Indian Biography,* by C. E. Buckland. Detroit, MI: Gale Research Co., 1968. Originally published London: Swan Sonnenschein & Co., Ltd., 1906.

Dict Irish Bio: *A Dictionary of Irish Biography,* by Henry Boylan. Dublin, Ireland: Gill & Macmillian, Ltd., 1978; New York: Harper & Row, 1978.

Dict Lit Bio: *Dictionary of Literary Biography,* edited by Joel Myerson. Detroit, MI: Gale Research Co., 1978.

Dict Mex Am Hist: *Dictionary of Mexican American History,* by Matt S. Meier and Feliciano Rivera. Westport, CT: Greenwood Press, 1981.

Dict Nat Bio: *Dictionary of National Biography,* 1900–1960, edited by Sir Leslie Stephen and Sir Sidney Lee. London: Oxford Press.

Dict Phil: *Dictionary of Philosophy,* edited by Dagobert D. Runes. Paterson, NJ: Littlefield, Adams & Co., 1961.

Dict South Af Bio: *Dictionary of South African Biography,* edited by W. J. deKock. Capetown, South Africa: Nasionale Boekhandel Beperk, 1968.

Encyc Black Am: *Encyclopedia of Black America,* edited by W. Augustus Low. New York: McGraw-Hill, 1981.

Encyc South Hist: *Encyclopedia of Southern History,* edited by David G. Roller and Robert W. Twyman. Baton Rouge, LA: Louisiana State University Press, 1979.

Encyc Third Reich: *Encyclopedia of the Third Reich,* by Louis L. Snyder. New York: McGraw-Hill, 1976.

Eng Wom: *English Women,* by Edith Sitwell. London: William Collins, 1942.

Esk Art: *Eskimo Artists,* by Philip Howard Gray. Bozeman, MT: Montana State University Press, 1974.

Great North Am Ind: *Great North American Indians: Profiles in Life and Leadership,* by Frederick J. Dockstader. New York: Van Nostrand Reinhold Co., 1977.

Great Sov Encyc: *Great Soviet Encyclopedia,* 3d edition, edited by A. M. Projhorov. New York: Macmillan Co., 1973.

Hall Fame Sport: *Halls of Fame in the U.S. and Canada: Sports.* New York: R. R. Bowker & Co., 1977.

Ill Encyc Myst: *An Illustrated Encyclopedia of Mysticism,* by John Ferguson. London: Thames & Gudson, 1976.

Index t Wom: *Index to Women of the World from Ancient to Modern Times: Biographies and Portraits,* by Norma Olin Ireland. Westwood, MA: F. W. Faxon Co., Inc., 1970.

Ind Today: *Indians of Today,* edited by Marion E. Gridley. n.p., I.C.F.P., Inc., 1971.

Nat Cyc Am Bio: *The National Cyclopedia of American Biography.* Ann Arbor, MI: University Microfilms, Xerox Co., 1967. Originally published New York: James White & Co., 1898, 1899, 1921.

Negro Alman: *The Negro Almanac: A Reference Work on the Afro-American,* edited by Harry A. Ploski and Warren Marr II. New York: Bellweather Co., 1976.

Negro Her Lib: *Negro Heritage Library: Negroes in Public Affairs and Government,* by Walter Christman. Yonkers, NY: Educational Heritage, Inc., 1966.

New Cath Encyc: *New Catholic Encyclopedia,* issued by the Catholic University of America. New York: McGraw-Hill, 1967.

Nort Anth Poet: *The Norton Anthology of Modern Poetry,* edited by Richard Ellman and Robert O'Clair. New York: W. W. Norton & Co., 1973.

Not Am Wom: *Notable American Women 1607-1950. A Biographical Dictionary,* edited by Edward T. James. Cambridge, MA: Harvard Press, Belknap Press, 1973. Supplementary volume edited by Barbara Sickerman and Carol Hurd Green.

Obit File: *Obituaries on File,* compiled by Felice Levy. New York: Facts on File, 1979.

Our Count: *Our Countrymen, or Brief Memoirs of Eminent Americans,* by Benson J. Lossing. New York: Ensign, Bridgman & Fanning, 1855.

Prof Negro Wom: *Profiles of Negro Womanhood,* by Sylvia G. L. Dannett. New York: M. W. Lads, 1964.

Read Encyc Am West: *Reader's Encyclopedia of the American West,* edited by Howard R. Lamarr. New York: Thomas Y. Crowell Co., 1977.

Slavon Encyc: *Slavonic Encyclopedia,* edited by Joseph Rocek. New York: Philosophy Publishing, 1949.

South Af Dict Nat Bio: *Southern African Dictionary of National Biography,* compiled by Eric Rosenthal. New York: Frederick Warne & Co., 1966.

Twent Cen Bio Dict Not Am: *Twentieth Century Biographical Dictionary of Notable Americans,* edited by Rossiter Johnson and John Howard Brown. Detroit, MI: Gale Research Co. Originally published Boston, MA: Biographical Society, 1904.

Who Who Dur Am Rev: *Who Was Who during the American Revolution,* edited by Who's Who with Jerry Kail. New York: Bobbs-Merrill, 1976.

Who Who Jew Hist: *Who's Who in Jewish History,* by Joan Comay. New York: David Mckay Co., 1974.

Who Who Phil: *Whos's Who in Philosophy,* edited by Dagobert D. Runes. New York: Philosophical Library, Inc., 1962.

Who Who Egypt: *Who Was Who in Egyptology,* by Warren R. Dawson and Eric P. Uphill. London: Egypt Exploration Society, 1972.

Wom Cent: *A Woman of the Century: Leading American Women,* edited by Frances Willard and Mary Livermore. Detroit, MI: Gale Research Co., 1967. Originally published New York: Charles Wells Moulton, 1893.

Wom Cour: *Women of Courage,* by Margaret Truman. New York: William Morrow & Co., 1976.

Wom Lit: *Women in Literature: Criticism of the '70's* by Carol Myers. Metuchen, NJ: Scarecrow Press, 1976.

Wom Lit, More: *More Women in Literature: Criticism of the '70's,* by Carol Meyers. Metuchen, NJ: Scarecrow Press, 1979.

World Great Men Col: *World's Great Men of Color,* by J. A. Rogers. New York, NY: 1947.

Women
in Particular:
An Index to
American Women

I. Field and Career Index

ANTHROPOLOGY, ETHNOLOGY, AND ARCHAEOLOGY

1. Dawson-Damer, Mary Georgiana Emma
died 1848
Egyptologist, diarist
Who Who Egypt

2. William, Caroline Louise (Ransom)
died 1852
Egyptologist
Who Who Egypt

3. Eastman, Mary (Henderson)
1817/18–1887
author, scholar of Native American life and culture, ethnologist, Native American folklorist
Virginia
Cyc Am Bio; Dict Am Auth; Dict Am Bio Men Time; Not Am Wom; Twent Cen Bio Dict Not Am

4. Hemenway, Mary Porter (Tileston)
1820/22–1894
philanthropist, patron of archaeology and education
Dict Am Bio; Index t Wom; Not Am Wom; Twent Cen Bio Dict Not Am

5. Robertson, Ann Eliza Worcester
1826–1905
missionary, educator, student of Native American languages
Not Am Wom

6. Harris, Selima
circa 1830–circa 1895
Egyptologist
Black
Who Who Egypt

7. Converse, Harriet Maxwell; Ya-ie-wah-no; Salome; Musidora
1836–1903
Seneca rights advocate, Seneca tribal leader, author, folklorist, Native American scholar, poet
New York
Native American (Seneca by adoption)
Dict Am Auth; Not Am Wom; Twent Cen Bio Dict Not Am; Wom Cent

8. Smith, Erminnie Adele (Platt)
1836/37–1886
ethnologist, geologist, geographer
Cyc Am Bio; Dict Am Auth; Dict Am Bio; Index t Wom; Nat Cyc Am Bio v13; Not Am Wom

9. Emerson, Ellen (Russell)
1837–1907
author, ethnologist, writer on Native American art and mythology
Boston, MA
Dict Am Auth; Dict Am Bio; Twent Cen Bio Dict Not Am; Wom Cent

10. Fletcher, Alice Cunningham
1838/45–1923
ethnologist, Native American rights worker, writer on Native American music
Dict Am Auth; Dict Am Bio; Index t Wom; Nat Cyc Am Bio v5; Not Am Wom; Twent Cen Bio Dict Not Am; Wom Cent

11. Hearst, Phoebe Apperson
1842–1919
philanthropist, patron of education and anthropology, Egyptologist
Dict Am Bio; Index t Wom; Nat Cyc Am Bio v25; Not Am Wom; Who Who Egypt

12. Mitchell, Lucy Myers Wright
1845–88
archaeologist, historian of ancient art, writer on Greek art
Dict Am Auth; Dict Am Bio; Nat Cyc Am Bio v6; Twent Cen Bio Dict Not Am

13. Stevenson, Sarah (Yorke)
1847–1921
archaeologist, writer on archaeology
Philadelphia, PA
Dict Am Auth; Dict Am Bio; Index t Wom; Nat Cyc Am Bio v13; Twent Cen Bio Dict Not Am

14. Stevenson, Matilda Coxe Evans
1849/50–1915
Native American ethnologist, anthropologist
Dict Am Bio; Index t Wom; Nat Cyc Am Bio v20; Not Am Wom; Read Encyc Am West; Twent Cen Bio Dict Not Am

15. Peck, Annie Smith
1850–1933/35
mountain climber, musician, archaeologist, lecturer, educator
Rhode Island
Index t Wom; Nat Cyc Am Bio v15; Not Am Wom; Wom Cent

16. Coronel, Mariana W. de, Senora
born 1851
collector of Native American artifacts
Los Angeles, CA
Wom Cent

17. Porter, Bertha
1852–1941
bibliographer, Egyptologist
Who Who Egypt

18. Murray, Louise Shipman Welles
1854–1931

19. Nuttall, Zelia Maria Magdalena
1857/58–1933
archaeologist, student of Mexican history
Index t Wom; Not Am Wom; Twent Cen Bio Dict Not Am

20. Owen, Mary Alicia; Julia Scott
born 1858
folklorist, ethnologist, children's folklore writer, ghost story and short story writer
Dict Am Auth; Index t Wom; Nat Cyc Am Bio v13; Wom Cent

21. Buttles, Janet
flourished 1890s–1913
author, Egyptologist
Who Who Egypt

22. Lummis, Dorothea
born 1860
physician, music critic, journalist, newspaper editor, Native American artifacts collector
Los Angeles, CA
Index t Wom; Wom Cent

23. Horsford, Cornelia
born 1861
archaeologist, writer on archaeology
Cambridge, MA
Dict Am Auth; Index t Wom; Twent Cen Bio Dict Not Am

24. van Deman, Esther Boise
1862–1937
Roman archaeologist
Dict Am Bio supp v2; Not Am Wom

25. Eastman, Elaine (Goodale); Elaine Hall
1863–1953

historian, Native American archaeologist
Dict Am Bio

educator of Native Americans, poet, short story writer, humorist, editor, scholar of Native American culture
South Dakota
Cyc Am Bio; Dict Am Auth; Index t Wom; Nat Cyc Am Bio v8; Twent Cen Bio Dict Not Am; Wom Cent

26. Semple, Ellen Churchill
1863–1932
geographer, writer on geography, anthropologist, anthropogeographer
Louisville, KY
Dict Am Auth; Dict Am Bio; Encyc South Hist; Index t Wom; Nat Cyc Am Bio v35 and csv1; Not Am Wom

27. Eckstorm, Fannie Pearson Hardy
1865–1946
ornithologist, writer on ornithology, scholar of the Native Americans of Maine, historian of Maine folk songs
Episcopalian
Brewer, ME
Dict Am Auth; Dict Am Bio supp v4; Nat Cyc Am Bio v36; Not Am Wom

28. Austin, Mary (Hunter)
1866/68–1934
novelist, folklorist, short story writer, journalist, conservationist, feminist, worker for Native American rights
California
Dict Am Auth; Dict Am Bio supp v1; Dict Lit Bio v9; Not Am Wom; Read Encyc Am West; Wom Lit; Wom Lit, More

29. Densmore, Frances Theresa
1867–1957
ethnomusicologist, musician, scholar of Native American culture
Dict Am Bio supp v6; Index t Wom; Not Am Wom supp v1; Read Encyc Am West

30. King, Lida Shaw
1868–1932
classical scholar, archaeologist, educator, college administrator
Pennsylvania
Nat Cyc Am Bio v23; Not Am Wom

31. McClure, Mary Louise Dora
died 1918
translator, Egyptologist
Who Who Egypt

32. Wolcott, Ann Louise
born 1868

archaeologist, educator
Index t Wom

33. Young, Ella
1868–1956
poet, authority on Celtic folklore
Irish
Obit File

34. Wier, Jeanne Elizabeth
1870–1950
historian of Nevada and the state's Native Americans, educator, suffragist
Nevada
Nat Cyc Am Bio v51 and csv1; Obit File; Read Encyc Am West

35. Hawes, Harriet Ann Boyd
1871–1945
classical archaeologist, war nurse in the Greco-Turkish and Spanish-American wars and in World War I
Dict Am Bio supp v3; Not Am Wom

36. Pound, Louise
1872–1958
university educator, writer on literature, folklorist, tennis player, bicyclist, golfer
Nebraska
Nat Cyc Am Bio v45, csv2, and csv5; Not Am Wom supp v1; Obit File

37. Griffith, Nora Christina Cobban
1873–1937
Egyptologist
Who Who Egypt

38. Burlin, Natalie (Curtis)
1875–1921
ethnomusicologist specializing in Native American and Afro-American music, worker for Native American rights, composer, pianist, lecturer
Dict Am Bio; Not Am Wom; Index t Wom

39. Parsons, Elsie Clews
1875–1941
sociologist, anthropologist, folklorist, Native American ethnologist, president of the American Anthropology Association
Dict Am Bio supp v3; Index t Wom; Not Am Wom; Obit File; Read Encyc Am West

40. Burchenal, Elizabeth
1876–1959
folklorist, folk dance educator, cofounder of the American Folk Dance Society, originator of the New York Folk Dance Festival
New York
Index t Wom; Not Am Wom supp v1; Obit File

41. Tanzer, Helen Henrietta
born 1876
archaeologist
Episcopalian
Nat Cyc Am Bio csv7

42. Dohan, Edith Hayward Hall
1877–1943
classical archaeologist
Not Am Wom

43. Lawson, Roberta Campbell
1878–1940
clubwoman, student of Native American music and culture, ethnologist, Native American leader, singer, songwriter
Presbyterian
Native American (Delaware)
Great North Am Ind; Nat Cyc Am Bio v36; Not Am Wom

44. Scarborough, Dorothy
1878–1935
novelist, English teacher, folklorist
Dict Am Bio supp v1; Index t Wom; Wom Lit

45. Wheelwright, Mary Cabot
1878–1958
anthropologist
Dict Am Bio supp v6

46. Bieber, Margarete
1880–1978
historian, author, archaeologist, educator, authority on Greek and Roman art
German
Obit File

47. Goldman, Hettie
1881–1972
archaeologist, nurse in the Greek-Balkan war
Jewish
Nat Cyc Am Bio v56; Not Am Wom supp v1

48. Richter, Gisela Marie Augusta
1882–1972
classical archaeologist, museum curator, author
English
Index t Wom; Not Am Wom supp v1

49. Swindler, Mary Hamilton
1884–1967
archaeologist, classicist
Nat Cyc Am Bio v54; Not Am Wom supp v1

50. Underhill, Ruth Murray
born 1884
anthropologist
Index t Wom

51. Greenfield, Edith Mary
died 1935
patron of Egyptology
Who Who Egypt

52. Rourke, Constance Mayfield
1885–1941
student of American culture, historian, folklorist, author, critic, educator
Dict Am Bio supp v3; Index t Wom; Nat Cyc Am Bio v32; Not Am Wom

53. Cadilla de Martinez, Maria; Liana
1886–1951
educator, folklorist, author, feminist
Not Am Wom supp v1

54. Benedict, Ruth Fulton
1887–1948
anthropologist, author, philosopher, educator
Dict Am Bio supp v4; Index t Wom; Nat Cyc Am Bio v36; Not Am Wom; Who Who Phil

55. Deloria, Ella Carla; Anpetu Wastewin
1888–1971
interpreter, linguist, ethnologist, anthropologist, lecturer
Native American (Yankton Sioux-Dakota)
Great North Am Ind; Ind Today; Not Am Wom supp v1

56. Seymour, Flora Warren
born 1888
author, lawyer, Native American scholar
Index t Wom

57. Toor, Frances
1890–1956
anthropologist, scholar of Mexican folklore, children's author
Obit File

58. Richard, Gladys Amanda
1893–1955
anthropologist
Not Am Wom supp v1

59. Powdermaker, Hortense
1896/1900–1970
anthropologist, ethnologist, educator, author
California
Cur Biog '70; Index t Wom; Nat Cyc Am Bio v55 and csv10; Not Am Wom supp v1

60. Robeson, Eslanda Cardoza Goode
1896–1965
author, civil rights reformer, anthropologist

Black
Index t Wom; Not Am Wom
   supp v1

61. Bunzel, Ruth
born 1898
philosopher, anthropologist
Index t Wom; Who Who Phil

62. Wolle, Muriel Sibell
1898–1977
artist, art educator, Native American art scholar and collector, western history writer, conservationist
Episcopalian
Boulder, CO
Nat Cyc Am Bio v60

63. Hansen, Hazel Dorothy
1899–1962
archaeologist, editor
California
Nat Cyc Am Bio v49

64. Talcott, Lucy
1899–1970
archaeologist, archaeological author
Congregationalist
Nat Cyc Am Bio v54

65. Tantaquidgeon, Gladys
born 1899
anthropologist
Native American (Mohegan)
Ind Today

66. Steedman, Elsie V.
flourished 1930s
anthropologist
Index t Wom

67. Hurston, Zora Neale
1901/03–1960
author, novelist, folklorist, cultural anthropologist
Black
Dict Am Bio supp v6; Encyc Black Am; Index t Wom; Negro Alman; Not Am Wom; Obit File; Prof Negro Wom v2; Wom Lit; Wom Lit, More

68. Mead, Margaret; Margaret Bateson
1901/02–1978
anthropologist, writer of popular books on anthropology, autobiographer
Episcopalian
Cur Biog '79; Index t Wom; Nat Cyc Am Bio csv9; Obit File

69. Dunham, Katherine
born 1910
dancer, choreographer, anthropologist
Black
Encyc Black Am; Index t Wom; Negro Alman; Prof Negro Wom v2

70. Marriott, Alice Lee
born 1910
ethnologist
Index t Wom

71. Pomerance, Harriet Kline
1916–72
archaeologist
Obit File

72. Brown, Ina Corinne
flourished 1950s
educator, anthropologist
Index t Wom

73. Meggers, Betty Jane
born 1921
cultural anthropologist
Index t Wom

74. Ritchie, Jean
born 1922
folksinger, folklorist, author
Index t Wom

75. Medicine, Beatrice
born 1924
anthropologist
Native American (Dakota-Standing Rock)
Ind Today

76. Moore, Joan W.
born 1929
sociologist, student of Mexican American culture, author, educator
Dict Mex Am Hist

77. Monture, Ethel Brant
flourished 1960s
author, specialist in Native American culture
Native American (Mohawk)
Ind Today

78. Morris, Christine
born 1932
sociologist, anthropologist
Native American (Blackfoot)
Ind Today

BUSINESS AND ECONOMICS

79. Viart, Guyonne
flourished sixteenth century
pioneer printer
Index t Wom

80. Penalosa, Eufemia
flourished circa 1590s
American colony cosponsor
Spanish
Index t Wom

81. Pole, Elizabeth; Elizabeth Poole
1588–1654
pioneer; founder of the town of Taunton, New Jersey
Taunton, NJ; Massachusetts
English
Am Bio Dict; Index t Wom; Nat Cyc Am Bio v4

82. Brent, Margaret
1600/01–1670/71
landowner, business agent, executor for the governor of Maryland
Maryland
Dict Am Bio; Index t Wom; Not Am Wom

83. Bull, Sarah Wells
flourished 1630s
pioneer landowner
Index t Wom

84. Glover, Elizabeth
flourished 1630s
printer
Index t Wom

85. Brent, Mary
flourished 1638–50s
colonial land proprietor, colonizer
Index t Wom

86. Clark, Katherine
flourished 1640s
colonial businessperson
Index t Wom

87. Coffin, Dionis Stevens
flourished 1640s–60s
colonial businessperson
Index t Wom

88. Goose, Mrs.
flourished 1640s
colonial grocer
Index t Wom

89. Davenport, Elizabeth Wooley
flourished 1650s
colonial property manager, businessperson
Index t Wom

90. Philipse, Margaret Hardenbrook de Vries
flourished 1659; died 1690
colonial merchant, ship owner
Index t Wom; Not Am Wom

91. Prentiss, John, Mrs.
died 1691
colonial proprietor
Index t Wom

92. Papegoija, Armegot
died 1695
pioneer landowner
Index t Wom

93. Printz, Aregot
died 1695

landowner
Swedish
Index t Wom

94. Diggs, Elizabeth
died 1699
colonial planter, plantation owner and manager
Index t Wom

95. Nuthead, Dinah
flourished 1680s–90s
pioneer printer
Index t Wom

96. Provoost, Maria de Peyster Schrick Spratt; Maria Spratt; Maria de Peyster
died 1700
colonial merchant
Index t Wom

97. Smith, Martha Turnstall
flourished 1680s–1700s
colonial businessperson
Index t Wom

98. Philipse, Catharine Duval van Cortland
flourished 1690s
colonial property manager, philanthropist
Index t Wom

99. Ferree, Mary Warenbuer
died 1716
colonial property manager
Index t Wom

100. Knight, Sarah Kemble
1666–1725/27
diarist, educator, hotel keeper, traveler, merchant
Boston, MA
Cyc Am Bio; Dict Am Auth; Dict Am Bio; Dict Am Bio Men Time; Index t Wom; Not Am Wom; Wom Lit, More

101. Baker, Rhoda
flourished eighteenth century
colonial leather worker
Index t Wom

102. Ducoudray, Madame
flourished eighteenth century
inventor
Index t Wom

103. Duncan, Margaret
flourished eighteenth century
colonial merchant, church builder
Index t Wom

104. Schuyler, Cornelia
flourished 1700s
colonial property owner, patriot
Index t Wom

105. de Peyster, Cornelia Lubbetse
died 1725

colonial property manager
Index t Wom

106. Perry, Joanna
died 1725
colonial bookseller
Index t Wom

107. Estaugh, Elizabeth Haddon
1680/83–1762
colonial proprietor; founder of
Haddonfield, New Jersey; pioneer
Quaker
New Jersey
Cyc Am Bio; Dict Am Bio; Index
t Wom; Nat Cyc Am Bio v17;
Not Am Wom

108. Masters, Sybilla
flourished circa 1710s
colonial inventor
Index t Wom

109. Nutt, Anna Rutter Savage
1686–1760
colonial manufacturer
Index t Wom

110. Craighton, Elizabeth
flourished 1720s
printer
Index t Wom

111. Franklin, Ann Smith
1696–1763
printer
Index t Wom; Not Am Wom

112. Wright, Susanna
1697–1784
poet, colonial frontiersperson, businessperson
Index t Wom; Not Am Wom

113. Bosomworth, Mary Musgrove
1700–1760
colonial land negotiator
Index t Wom

114. Byrd, Mary Willing
flourished eighteenth century
colonial business executive, plantation manager
Index t Wom

115. Crabb, Mary
flourished 1730s
colonial needleworker, businessperson
Index t Wom

116. Gazley, Martha
flourished 1730s
colonial manufacturer, needleworker, educator
Index t Wom

117. Goddard, Sarah Updike
circa 1700–70

printer, editor, publisher
Index t Wom; Not Am Wom

118. Macklewain, Margaret
flourished 1730s
educator, businessperson
Index t Wom

119. Musgrove, Mary; Coosaponakeesa
circa 1770–circa 1763
Native American leader in colonial Georgia, interpreter, trader
Georgia
Native American (Creek)
Great North Am Ind; Not Am
Wom

120. Russell, Ezekiel, Mrs.
flourished eighteenth century
colonial printer, ballad writer
Index t Wom

121. Smith, Cornelia
flourished eighteenth century
printer
Index t Wom

122. Minis, Abigail
1701–94
planter
Jewish
Index t Wom

123. Marriott, Elizabeth
died 1755
colonial merchant, innkeeper
Index t Wom

124. Brasher, Judith
flourished 1737
colonial businessperson
Index t Wom

125. Timothy, Elizabeth
died 1757
printer, newspaper publisher and
editor, journalist
Index t Wom; Not Am Wom

126. Cahill, Mary
flourished 1740s
colonial dressmaker
Index t Wom

127. Goodwin, Sarah
flourished 1740s
colonial businessperson
Index t Wom

128. Grant, Sueton
flourished 1740s
colonial merchant, importer
Index t Wom

129. Jackson, Mary
flourished 1740s
colonial merchant
Index t Wom

130. Netmaker, Bendicta
flourished 1740s

colonial merchant
Index t Wom

131. Pratt, Margaret
flourished 1740s–60s
colonial proprietor
Index t Wom

132. Roberts, Widow
flourished 1740s
colonial inn proprietor
Index t Wom

133. Blakeway, Sarah
flourished 1741
colonial planter, businessperson
Index t Wom

134. Cowley, Mary
flourished 1741
colonial businessperson
Index t Wom

135. Deimer, Catherine
died 1761/62
colonial businessperson
Index t Wom

136. Coffin, Keziah Folger
married 1740
merchant during American Revolution
Index t Wom

137. Bottomshaw, Mrs.
flourished 1746
inventor
Index t Wom

138. Breintnall, Hannah
flourished 1750s
colonial merchant
Index t Wom

139. Brown, Sarah
flourished 1750s
colonial businessperson
Index t Wom

140. Franklin, Elizabeth
flourished 1750s
colonial merchant, manufacturer
Index t Wom

141. Green, Anna Catherine Hoof
circa 1720–75
printer
Not Am Wom

142. Matthews, Anne
flourished 1750s
merchant
Index t Wom

143. Purcell, Mary
flourished 1750s–70s
colonial merchant
Index t Wom

144. Quick, Alice
flourished 1750s–60s

colonial merchant
Index t Wom

145. Salmon, Mary
flourished 1750s
colonial blacksmith
Index t Wom

146. Todd, Sarah
flourished 1750s–70s
colonial merchant
Index t Wom

147. Wells, Rebecca
flourished 1750s
colonial realtor
Index t Wom

148. Bradford, Cornelia Smith
died 1772/75
colonial publisher
Index t Wom; Not Am Wom

149. Pinckney, Elizabeth Lucas "Eliza"
1722/23–1793
plantation manager identified
with the development of indigo
as a staple of the colonial South,
textile manufacturer, agriculturist, author
South Carolina
Dict Am Bio; Encyc South Hist;
Index t Wom; Not Am Wom;
Who Who Dur Am Rev

150. Ballard, Mary
flourished 1755
colonial hotelier
Index t Wom

151. Bird, Clementine
died 1775
printer
Index t Wom

152. Eustis, Jane
flourished 1755–59
colonial merchant
Index t Wom

153. Green, Anne Catherine
died 1775
colonial printer, publisher
Index t Wom

154. Kitchin, Hannah Chapman
married 1751
colonial manufacturer
Index t Wom

155. Timothy, Ann Donovan
circa 1727–92
printer, newspaper publisher and
editor, journalist
Index t Wom; Not Am Wom

156. Beales, Hannah
flourished 1760s
colonial businessperson
Index t Wom

157. Boyleston, Sarah
flourished 1760s
colonial businessperson
Index t Wom

158. Crathorne, Mary
flourished 1760s
colonial manufacturer
Index t Wom

159. Draper, Margaret Green
circa 1730–1807
publisher, printer, journalist
Massachusetts
Dict Am Bio; Index t Wom; Who Who Dur Am Rev

160. Ducray, Anne
flourished 1760s
colonial businessperson, needle-worker
Index t Wom

161. East, Henrietta Maria
flourished 1760s
colonial businessperson, needle-worker
Index t Wom

162. Emerson, Mary
flourished 1760s
colonial merchant
Index t Wom

163. Moorland, Jane; Jane Morland
flourished 1760s
colonial caterer, grocer
Index t Wom

164. Morcomb, Mary
flourished 1760s
colonial dressmaker
Index t Wom

165. Stoneman, Abigail
flourished 1760s; died 1777
innkeeper of colonial Rhode Island
Rhode Island
Not Am Wom

166. Treby, Bridget
flourished 1760s
colonial merchant
Index t Wom

167. Tucker, Ann
flourished 1760s
colonial merchant
Index t Wom

168. Greene, Catherine
1731–circa 1794
inventor, landholder
Index t Wom

169. Cannan, Mary
flourished 1763
colonial businessperson
Index t Wom

170. Perkins, Elizabeth Peck
1735/36–1807
businessperson, philanthropist, merchant
Index t Wom; Not Am Wom

171. Goddard, Mary Katherine
1738–1816
printer, newspaper publisher, postmaster of Baltimore, merchant
Catholic
Baltimore, MD
Index t Wom; Not Am Wom

172. Copley, Mary Singleton
died 1789
colonial merchant
Irish
Index t Wom

173. Brown, Hannah
flourished 1770s
innkeeper
Index t Wom

174. Downs, Jane Douglas
flourished 1770s
planter
Index t Wom

175. Goddard, Anna
flourished 1770s
printer, publisher
Index t Wom

176. Hoit, Mary
flourished 1770s
publisher
Index t Wom

177. Keith, Franklin, Mrs.
flourished 1770s–80s
theater operator
Index t Wom

178. Phillips, Elizabeth
flourished 1770s
colonial producer, businessperson
Index t Wom

179. Rind, Clementina
circa 1740–74
printer, newspaper editor, publisher
Index t Wom; Not Am Wom

180. Russell, Penelope
flourished 1770s
printer
Index t Wom

181. Sheafe, Susannah Child
flourished 1770s
colonial grocer
Index t Wom

182. Harnet, Mary
died 1792
colonial plantation manager
Index t Wom

183. Hudson, Hester
died circa 1796
innkeeper
Index t Wom

184. Ferguson, Catherine
circa 1749–1854
religious and welfare worker, baker
New York
Black
Index t Wom; Our Count

185. Crouch, Mary
flourished 1780s
colonial printer
Index t Wom

186. Morier
flourished 1780s
baker, confectioner
Black; African
Prof Negro Wom v1

187. Hathorne, Mary
died 1802
merchant
Index t Wom

188. Ross, Betsy Griscom;
Elizabeth Claypool; Elizabeth Grimke
1752–1832/36
flag maker
Pennsylvania
Dict Am Bio; Index t Wom; Not Am Wom; Who Who Dur Am Rev

189. Smith, Susan Hayes
married 1784
pioneer, telegraph operator
Index t Wom

190. Cabot, Lydia Dodge
flourished 1790s
landowner
Index t Wom

191. Oswald, Elizabeth Holt
flourished 1790s
printer
Index t Wom

192. Russell, Sarah
flourished 1790s
printer, publisher
Index t Wom

193. Ryan, Harriet
flourished 1790s
hairdresser
Index t Wom

194. Withy, Mary
died 1810
innkeeper
Index t Wom

195. Hillhouse, Sarah Porter
born 1763

colonial editor, publisher
Index t Wom

196. Aitken, Jane
1764–1832
printer, bookbinder, bookseller
Index t Wom; Not Am Wom

197. Bent, Ann
1768–1857
merchant
Index t Wom

198. Merry, Ann Brunton
1769–1808
actor, tragedian, theater manager
Cyc Am Bio; Dict Am Bio; Index t Wom; Not Am Wom

199. Royall, Anne Newport
1769–1854
traveler, journalist, newspaper editor and publisher, novelist
Washington, DC; Virginia
Am Bio Dict; Cyc Am Bio; Dict Am Auth; Dict Am Bio; Dict Am Bio Men Time; Encyc South Hist; Index t Wom; Not Am Wom

200. Barber, Ann
flourished 1800s
publisher
Index t Wom

201. Harrison, Margaret
flourished 1800s
printer
Index t Wom

202. Kies, Mary
flourished 1800s
inventor
Index t Wom

203. Marshall, Elizabeth
flourished 1800s
pharmacist
Index t Wom

204. Swallow, Frances
flourished eighteenth century
colonial educator, businessperson
Index t Wom

205. Bradstreet, Martha
married 1799
landholder
Index t Wom

206. Jennison, Mary
died 1825/30
landholder
Index t Wom

207. Bailey, Lydia R.
1779–1869
printer
Index t Wom; Twent Cen Bio Dict Not Am

208. Engle, Mary
flourished 1810s–20s
innkeeper
Index t Wom

209. Low, Esther
flourished 1810s
printer, bookseller
Index t Wom

210. Pickersgill, Caroline
flourished 1810s
flag maker
Index t Wom

211. Ware, Mary Pickard
flourished 1810s
merchant, importer
Index t Wom

212. Woodhouse, Sophia
flourished 1810s
inventor
Index t Wom

213. Holt, Elizabeth Hunter
1781–85 [sic]
printer, publisher
Index t Wom

214. Holley, Mary Phelps Austin
1784–1846
Texas historian, historical author, biographer, miscellaneous writer, land speculator
Texas
Am Bio Dict; Dict Am Auth; Not Am Wom

215. Eldridge, Elleonor
1785–1845
author, amateur lawyer, dairy farmer
Black
Negro Alman; Prof Negro Wom v1

216. Johnson, Lucy
circa 1789–1867
inventor
Index t Wom

217. Baxter, Susan Phinney
flourished 1820s
tailor
Index t Wom

218. Dickson, Mary
flourished 1820s
printer, publisher, bookseller
Index t Wom

219. Gould, Beulah H.
1790–1856
milliner
Am Bio Dict

220. Parsons, Augustina
flourished 1820s
publisher
Index t Wom

221. Tytler, Jane
flourished 1820s
pharmacist
Scottish
Index t Wom

222. Lukens, Rebecca Webb Pennock
1794–1854
iron manufacturer, shipwright
Pennsylvania
Dict Am Bio; Index t Wom; Nat Cyc Am Bio v15; Not Am Wom

223. Anthony, Sarah Porter Williams
flourished 1830s
businessperson
Index t Wom

224. Davis, Hannah
flourished 1830s
businessperson, manufacturer
Index t Wom

225. Peabody, Elizabeth
circa 1800–94
bookseller
Index t Wom

226. Bagley, Sarah G.
flourished 1835–47
labor leader, pioneer telegrapher
Bio Dict Am Lab; Index t Wom; Not Am Wom

227. Cazneau, Jane Maria Eliza McManus Storms
1807–78
journalist, publicist, expansionist
Not Am Wom

228. Elsworth, Annie
flourished 1840s
telegrapher
Index t Wom

229. McCord, Louisa Susannah (Cheves)
1810–1879/80
miscellaneous author, poet, political writer, translator, Confederate essayist, Black welfare worker, feminist, plantation manager
South Carolina
Cyc Am Bio; Dict Am Auth; Dict Am Bio; Dict Am Bio Men Time; Index t Wom; Nat Cyc Am Bio v9; Not Am Wom; Twent Cen Bio Dict Not Am

230. Sproat, Florantha Thompson
born 1811
western pioneer, innkeeper
Index t Wom

231. Farley, Harriet
1813/17–1907
millworker, writer on women in the textile mills, children's author, editor
New Hampshire
Cyc Am Bio; Dict Am Auth; Dict Am Bio; Dict Am Bio Men Time; Nat Cyc Am Bio v11; Not Am Wom

232. Handlin, Mary Flug
1813–1976
economist, American historian
Jewish
Nat Cyc Am Bio v59

233. Haughery, Margaret Gaffney; The Bread Woman of New Orleans
1813/25–1882
charitable worker, philanthropist, dairy farmer, bakery operator and owner
Cyc Am Bio; Dict Am Bio; Index t Wom; Not Am Wom; Twent Cen Bio Dict Not Am

234. Pleasant, Mary Ellen "Mammy"
1814?–1904
pioneer, boardinghouse keeper, civil rights advocate
California
Black
Not Am Wom

235. Wells, Charlotte Fowler
1814–1901
phrenologist, patron of women's medical education, educator, publisher, lecturer, businessperson
New York
Cyc Am Bio; Index t Wom; Not Am Wom; Wom Cent

236. Ottendorfer, Anna Sartorius (Behr) Uhl
1815–84
newspaper publisher, philanthropist
Dict Am Bio; Nat Cyc Am Bio v8; Not Am Wom; Twent Cen Bio Dict Not Am

237. Swisshelm, Jane (Grey) (Cannon)
1815/16–1884
journalist, author, editor, publisher, abolitionist, women's rights worker, Civil War nurse
Cyc Am Bio; Dict Am Auth; Dict Am Bio; Dict Am Bio Men Time; Index t Wom; Nat Cyc Am Bio v2; Not Am Wom

238. Keckley, Elizabeth Hobbs
1818/20–1907
dressmaker, author
Black
Index t Wom; Not Am Wom; Prof Negro Wom v1

239. Pinkham, Lydia Estes
1819–83
patent medicine proprietor, abolitionist, temperance worker, women's rights worker
Quaker
Dict Am Bio; Not Am Wom

240. Davis, Sarah Iliff
born 1820
philanthropist, temperance worker, women's prison reformer, milliner, sanitation worker for the Union army during the Civil War, Freedmen's Aid worker
Wom Cent

241. Drew, Louisa Lane
1820–97
actor, theater manager
English
Cyc Am Bio; Dict Am Bio; Index t Wom; Nat Cyc Am Bio v8; Not Am Wom; Twent Cen Bio Dict Not Am; Wom Cent

242. Keene, Laura
1820/26–1873
actor, theater manager
English
Cyc Am Bio; Dict Am Bio; Dict Am Bio Men Time; Index t Wom; Nat Cyc Am Bio v8; Not Am Wom; Twent Cen Bio Dict Not Am

243. St. Clair, Catherine N.
flourished 1850s
actor, theatrical builder, manager
Index t Wom

244. Washburn, Florinda
flourished 1850s
pioneer, milliner, businessperson
Index t Wom

245. Filley, Mary A. Powers
born 1821
suffragist, dairy stock farmer
New Hampshire
Wom Cent

246. Thomas, M. Louise (Palmer)
born 1822
president of Sorosis, farmer, agriculturist, apiarist
Index t Wom; Nat Cyc Am Bio v13

247. Bateman, Sidney Frances Cowell
1823–81
dramatist, theater manager, actor
Dict Am Bio

248. Demorest, Ellen Louise Curtis
1824–98
businessperson
Not Am Wom

249. Soule, Caroline Augusta (White)
1824–1903/04
author, publisher, editor, church worker, Universalist minister, foreign missionary, social reformer, lecturer
Universalist
Cyc Am Bio; Dict Am Auth; Dict Am Bio Men Time; Index t Wom; Not Am Wom; Twent Cen Bio Dict Not Am

250. Adsit, Nancy
born 1825
insurance agent
Index t Wom

251. Gaffney, Margaret
1825–82
philanthropist, dairy farmer
Nat Cyc Am Bio v2

252. Long, Ellen Call
1825–1905
civic leader, author, planter
Florida
Read Encyc Am West

253. Robinson, Harriet Jane (Hanson)
1825–1911
suffragist, women's rights worker, feminist, abolitionist, author, poet, dramatist, journalist, merchant
Malden, MA
Cyc Am Bio; Dict Am Auth; Dict Am Bio; Index t Wom; Nat Cyc Am Bio v3; Not Am Wom; Wom Cent

254. Ruggles, Emily
born 1827
businessperson
Index t Wom

255. Wheeler, Candace (Thurber)
1827–1923
pioneer in American textile design, interior decorator, artist, needleworker, writer on artistic technique, fairy tale writer
New York, NY
Dict Am Auth; Index t Wom; Not Am Wom

256. Beaumont, Betty Bentley
born 1828
author, milliner, merchant
Wom Cent

257. Chandler, Lucinda Banister
born 1828
political author, temperance worker, political economist
Wom Cent

258. Coston, Martha J.
1828–86
inventor of navy night signals from ship to ship
Twent Cen Bio Dict Not Am

259. Robinson, Abbie C. B.
born 1828
editor, Democratic newspaper publisher, political author
Wisconsin
Index t Wom; Wom Cent

260. Waite, Catharine (Van Valkenburg)
1829–1913
suffragist, women's rights advocate, lawyer, legal journalist, financier, real estate and building executive, writer on Mormonism
Chicago, IL
Cyc Am Bio; Dict Am Auth; Not Am Wom; Wom Cent

261. Carter, Mary Adaline Edwards
flourished 1860s–80s
industrial arts instructor and designer, embroiderer, painter, china painter, plastics artist, temperance worker
Wom Cent

262. Dulany, Ida
flourished 1860s
plantation manager, Civil War patriot
Index t Wom

263. Elmore, Ellen
flourished 1860s
plantation manager
Index t Wom

264. Elmore, Grace
flourished 1860s
plantation manager
Index t Wom

265. Gillett, Sisters
flourished 1860s–80s
farm managers, businesspeople
Index t Wom

266. Leonard, Willard A., Mrs.
flourished 1860s
government employee, money specialist
Index t Wom

267. Stearns, Betsey Ann (Goward)
born 1830
inventor of a mechanical dress cutter
Index t Wom; Wom Cent

268. Terhune, Mary Virginia (Hawes); Marian Harland
1830/35–1922
popular novelist, writer on household affairs, historian, cookbook author, editor, publisher
New York, NY
Cyc Am Bio; Dict Am Auth; Dict Am Bio; Dict Am Bio Men Time; Index t Wom; Nat Cyc Am Bio v1; Not Am Wom; Twent Cen Bio Dict Not Am; Wom Cent

269. Grant, Bridget
1831–1923
pioneer, innkeeper
Irish
Index t Wom

270. Lyman, Laura Elizabeth Baker
born 1831
journalist, business executive
Cyc Am Bio; Index t Wom

271. Culver, Helen
1832–1925
philanthropist, Black welfare worker, patron of science, hospital administrator, educator, real estate businessperson
Index t Wom; Nat Cyc Am Bio v17; Twent Cen Bio Dict Not Am

272. King, Henrietta Maria Morse Chamberlain
1832–1925
cattle rancher
Texas
Nat Cyc Am Bio v20

273. Walker, Mary Edwards
1832–1919
physician, Civil War medical worker, hospital founder, army war surgeon, Union spy during the Civil War; women's rights worker, suffragist, dress reformer, inventor, lecturer, winner of the Congressional Medal of Honor
Dict Am Bio; Index t Wom; Nat Cyc Am Bio v13; Not Am Wom; Wom Cent

274. Churchill, Caroline M.
born 1833
newspaper editor, publisher, journalist, political activist
Wom Cent

275. Reed, Virginia
born 1833
western pioneer, realtor
Index t Wom

276. Cary, Mary Stockley
born 1834
businessperson, investor, philanthropist
Cleveland, OH
Wom Cent

277. Conway, Sarah G. Crocker
1834–1874/75
actor, theater manager
Cyc Am Bio; Nat Cyc Am Bio v11

278. Green, Henrietta Howland (Robinson) "Hettie"
1834/35–1916
entrepreneur, financier
Dict Am Bio; Index t Wom; Nat Cyc Am Bio v15; Not Am Wom

279. Gregory, Elizabeth Goadby
born 1834
author, translator of French and German literature, journalist, writer on industrial and social topics
Wom Cent

280. Carse, Matilda Bradley
1835–1917
temperance worker, child care worker, welfare worker, philanthropist, financier
Chicago, IL
Index t Wom; Not Am Wom; Twent Cen Bio Dict Not Am; Wom Cent

281. Jones, Amanda Theodosia
1835–1914
author, inventor of an improved process for canning food, poet, educator
Spiritualist
Chicago, IL
Cyc Am Bio; Dict Am Auth; Dict Am Bio; Nat Cyc Am Bio v7; Not Am Wom; Wom Cent

282. McCormick, Nancy Maria Fowler "Nettie"
1835–1923
patron of education in China, philanthropist, businessperson
Presbyterian
Index t Wom; Nat Cyc Am Bio v21; Not Am Wom

283. Whiting, Mary Collins
born 1835
lawyer, businessperson
Michigan
Wom Cent

284. Doe, Mary L.
born 1836
suffragist, temperance reformer, merchant
Methodist
Iowa
Wom Cent

285. Leslie, Miriam Florence (Folline); Frank K. Leslie
1836/51–1914
magazine editor, publisher, feminist, philanthropist

New York
Cyc Am Bio; Dict Am Bio; Index t Wom; Nat Cyc Am Bio v25; Not Am Wom; Twent Cen Bio Dict Not Am; Wom Cent

286. Scripps, Ellen Browning
1836–1932
philanthropist, newspaper writer and publisher, patron of marine science, founder of Scripps Marine Lab, pacifist, feminist, temperance worker
La Jolla, CA
Dict Am Bio; Index t Wom; Nat Cyc Am Bio v27; Not Am Wom

287. Dye, Mary Irene Clark
born 1837
telegrapher, welfare worker, temperance worker
Wom Cent

288. Hughes, Kate Duval
born 1837
author, inventor
Catholic
Washington, DC
Wom Cent

289. Spencer, Sara Andrews
born 1837
suffragist, women's rights worker, business educator, author
Washington, DC
Cyc Am Bio; Dict Am Auth

290. Knight, Margaret E.
1838–1914
inventor
Index t Wom; Not Am Wom

291. Scott, Mary Sophie
born 1838
author, businessperson
Index t Wom; Wom Cent

292. Woodhull, Victoria Claflin;
Victoria Martin
1838–1927
social reformer, political reformer, stockbroker, feminist
English (American expatriate to England)
Dict Am Auth; Dict Am Bio; Index t Wom; Not Am Wom

293. Molloy, Emma
born 1839
social reformer, editor, printer
Index t Wom

294. Barton, Kate
flourished 1870s
inventor
Index t Wom

295. Conise, Annette
flourished 1870s
notary public
Index t Wom

296. Dudley, Sarah Marie
flourished 1870s–90s
merchant, investor, inventor, architect, designer, builder
Detroit, MI
Wom Cent

297. Gill, Elizabeth Mary
flourished 1870s–80s
businessperson
Index t Wom

298. Hawley, Maria
flourished 1870s
publisher
Index t Wom

299. Hill, Eliza Trask
born 1840
suffragist, women's welfare worker, journalist, newspaper publisher, political activist, Prohibitionist
Massachusetts
Wom Cent

300. Jeffery, Isador Gilbert
born 184?
poet, stenographer
Chicago, IL
Wom Cent

301. MacDowell, Annie A. E.
flourished 1870s
editor, publisher
Index t Wom

302. McPherson, Lydia Starr
flourished 1870s–90s
poet, author, journalist, newspaper publisher
Texas
Wom Cent

303. Miller, August A.
flourished 1870s
printer
Index t Wom

304. Miller, Harriet Granger
flourished 1870s
printer
Index t Wom

305. Newton, Charlotte
flourished 1870s–80s
businessperson
Index t Wom

306. Rathbun, Harriet M.
born 1840
author, businessperson, journalist, magazine publisher and editor
Wom Cent

307. Remington, Mather, Mrs.
flourished 1870s
businessperson
Index t Wom

308. Rodger, Augusta M.
flourished 1870s–80s
inventor
Index t Wom

309. Sawyer, Lucy
flourished 1870s–80s
inventor
Index t Wom

310. Slocum, Lillia
flourished 1870s
businessperson
Index t Wom

311. Taylor, Elizabeth
flourished 1870s–80s
printer
Index t Wom

312. Weaver, Anna K.
flourished 1870s
businessperson
Index t Wom

313. Wellington, Margaret
flourished 1870s–80s
printer
Index t Wom

314. White, Callie
flourished 1870s
printer
Index t Wom

315. White, Nettie L.
flourished 1870s–90s
stenographer, government employee
Washington, DC
Index t Wom; Wom Cent

316. la Forge, Margaret Getchell
1841–80
business executive
Not Am Wom

317. Oberholtzer, Sara Louisa (Vikers)
1841–1930
poet, author, novelist, temperance worker, leader in school savings movement, economist
Quaker
Norristown, PA
Cyc Am Bio; Dict Am Auth; Dict Am Bio; Index t Wom; Nat Cyc Am Bio v7; Wom Cent

318. Plumb, L. H.
born 1841
social reformer, temperance worker, financier, banker
Illinois
Index t Wom; Wom Cent

319. Sinclair, Catherine
died 1891
actor, manager
English
Index t Wom

320. Thomas, Mary Ann (Lane)
born 1841
journalist, newspaper editor and publisher
Tennessee
Wom Cent

321. Todd, Marion Marsh
1841–post 1913
lawyer, Greenback party worker, political economist, labor leader, author, lecturer
Not Am Wom; Wom Cent

322. Conant, Frances Augusta
born 1842
journalist, businessperson, founder of a women's employment company
Wom Cent

323. Hill, Agnes Leonard (Scanland); Molly Myrtle
1842–1917
poet, author, newspaper publisher, religious writer, novelist, prisoner's welfare worker, Universalist pastor
Universalist
Colorado
Dict Am Auth; Index t Wom; Nat Cyc Am Bio v17; Wom Cent

324. Stone, Mary Perry
born 1842
businessperson, railroad station agent, suffragist
Oregon
Wom Cent

325. Thompson, Eva Griffith
born 1842
temperance worker, Presbyterian missionary worker, newspaper editor and publisher
Presbyterian
Pennsylvania
Wom Cent

326. Cluff, Ann (Whipple)
born 1843
entrepreneur
Nat Cyc Am Bio v17

327. Rose, Ellen Alida
born 1843
feminist, agriculturist, businessperson, Grange worker, suffragist
Index t Wom; Wom Cent

328. Thorp, Mandana Coleman
born 1843
Union patriot during the Civil War, pioneer, deputy clerk and register of deeds in northern Michigan, sheep and wool farmer
Michigan
Wom Cent

329. Brown, Harriet A.
born 1844
inventor of pattern-cutting system
   for sewing
Wom Cent

330. Collins, Libby Smith
1844–1921
western pioneer, cattle rancher
Index t Wom

331. Loud, Hulda Barker
born 1844
editor, publisher, women's rights
   worker, suffragist, labor worker,
   lecturer
Index t Wom; Wom Cent

332. Stevens, Alzina Parsons
1844/49–1900
labor leader, industrial reformer,
   settlement house worker, social
   reformer, newspaper editor and
   publisher, journalist, author
Chicago, IL
Index t Wom; Not Am Wom;
   Wom Cent

333. Barrows, Isabel C.
1845–1913
pioneer stenographic reporter
Index t Wom

334. Claflin, Tennessee Celeste
1845/46–1923
social reformer, feminist, stockbroker, newspaper editor, journalist
Index t Wom; Not Am Wom

**335. Pringle, Elizabeth Waties
Allston**
1845–1921
rice planter, author
Not Am Wom

**336. Shepherd, Theodosia Burr
Hall**
1845–1906
florist, business executive
Index t Wom

337. Blanchard, Helen Augusta
flourished 1876
inventor of zigzag attachment for
   sewing machines and of textile,
   sewing, and manufacturing
   equipment
Index t Wom; Wom Cent

338. Gutelius, Jean Harrower
born 1846
artist, bookstore proprietor
Scottish
Wom Cent

339. Reid, Margaret E.
1846–1923
innkeeper
Index t Wom

340. Seymour, Mary Foot
1846–93
stenographer, businessperson,
   journalist, law reporter, suffragist, women's labor worker
Not Am Wom; Wom Cent

341. Trott, Novella Jewell
born 1846
author, editor
Wom Cent

**342. Hammond, Mary Virginia
Spitler**
born 1847; flourished 1890s
manager of the 1899 Chicago
   World's Fair
Indiana
Wom Cent

343. Rodgers, Elizabeth Flynn
1847–1939
labor leader, insurance society executive
Not Am Wom

344. Wynne, Madelene (Yale)
born 1847
author, short story writer, silversmith, artist
Index t Wom

345. Alexander, Jane Grace
born 1848
banker
Wom Cent

346. Dow, Mary E. H. G.
born 1848
financier, president of the Dover
   Horse Railway
Wom Cent

**347. Frackleton, Susan Stuart
(Goodrich)**
born 1848/51
artist, ceramicist, inventor of a
   gas kiln, writer on ceramic technique
Dict Am Auth; Index t Wom;
   Twent Cen Bio Dict Not Am;
   Wom Cent

348. Marshall, Clara
circa 1848–1931
physician, pharmacist, medical
   educator
Dict Am Bio; Index t Wom

**349. Moore, Susanne Bande-
grift**
born 1848
editor and publisher
Missouri
Wom Cent

350. Ayer, Harriet (Hubbard)
1849/54–1903
businessperson, realtor, manufacturer, journalist, suffragist
Dict Am Auth; Nat Cyc Am Bio
   v43; Not Am Wom; Wom Cent

351. Boit, Elizabeth Eaton
1849–1932
textile manufacturer
Nat Cyc Am Bio v15; Not Am
   Wom

352. Chandler, Mary Alderson
born 1849
educator, stenographic educator
Wom Cent

353. Foltz, Clara Shortridge;
   The Portia of the Pacific
1849–1934
lawyer, political activist, women's
   rights worker, suffragist, newspaper publisher, orator
California
Cyc Am Bio; Nat Cyc Am Bio
   csv3; Not Am Wom; Twent Cen
   Bio Dict Not Am; Wom Cent

354. Hayward, Mary E. Smith
born 1849
oil and mercantile businessperson,
   suffragist
Nebraska
Wom Cent

355. Houghton, Alice
born 1849
real estate broker, insurance and
   investment counselor
Washington, DC
Wom Cent

**356. Nicholson, Eliza Jane
(Poitevent) Holbrook; Pearl
Rivers**
1849–96
poet, journalist, editor, publisher
   and owner of the New Orleans
   Picayune-Times
New Orleans, LA
Dict Am Auth; Dict Am Bio;
   Index t Wom; Nat Cyc Am Bio
   v1; Not Am Wom; Twent Cen
   Bio Dict Not Am; Wom Cent

357. Sandes, Margaret Isabelle
born 1849
industrial reformer, club leader
Scottish
Wom Cent

358. Saunders, Mary A.
born 1849
inventor, businessperson
New York
Index t Wom; Wom Cent

**359. Shoaff, Carrie M.; Carrie
Shoff**
born 1849
artist, ceramicist, inventor
Index t Wom; Wom Cent

360. Allison, Emma
flourished 1880s
inventor
Index t Wom

361. Bailey, Ellen Alice
flourished 1880s–90s
inventor, businessperson
Wom Cent

362. Burke, B. Ellen
born 1850
educator, lecturer, editor, publisher
Index t Wom

363. Coyriere, E. Miriam
flourished 1880s
school furniture businessperson,
   founder and manager of a
   teacher's agency
Wom Cent

364. Fryatt, Frances Elizabeth
flourished 1880s–90s
author, specialist in household
   art, interior decorator
New York
Wom Cent

365. Hughes, Caroline
flourished 1880s–90s
philanthropist, realtor
Chicago, IL
Wom Cent

366. King, Susan
flourished 1880s
businessperson
Index t Wom

367. Lane, Columbia
flourished 1880s
businessperson
Index t Wom

**368. Maxwell, Kate; Cattle
Kate**
flourished 1880s–90s
western cattle rancher
Index t Wom

369. Monmouth, L. N., Mrs.
flourished 1880s
businessperson
Index t Wom

370. Peasley, Mrs.
flourished 1880s
businessperson
Index t Wom

371. Pugh, Esther
flourished 1880s
social reformer, temperance reformer, publisher
Index t Wom; Wom Cent

372. Richmond, Lizzie R.
born 1850
businessperson, insurance agent
Illinois
Wom Cent

373. Wood, Frances Fisher
flourished 1880s–90s

educator, lecturer, scientist, dress reformer, dairy farmer, businessperson
Wom Cent

374. Cory, Florence Elizabeth
born 1851
industrial designer, industrial design teacher
Wom Cent

375. Gilbert, Ruby I.
born 1851
temperance worker, businessperson
Wom Cent

376. Harriman, Mary Williamson (Averall)
1851–1932
philanthropist, businessperson
New York
Index t Wom; Nat Cyc Am Bio v23; Not Am Wom

377. Kimball, Jennie
born 1851
actor, theatrical manager
Index t Wom; Wom Cent

378. Whipple, M. Ella
born 1851
physician, temperance worker, suffragist, Methodist Episcopal church worker, politician, educator, inventor
Methodist Episcopal
Wom Cent

379. Wupperman, Josephine Wright (Hancox)
1851–1936
manufacturer
New York
Nat Cyc Am Bio v27

380. Balbach, Julia Anna
born 1852
inventor, philanthropist, suffragist
Nat Cyc Am Bio v17

381. Ballore, Ella Maria
born 1852
stenographer, women's rights worker
Wom Cent

382. Davidson, Hannah Amelia
1852–1919
author of study guides, educator, editor, lecturer, publisher
Index t Wom; Nat Cyc Am Bio v19

383. Gordon, Anna Adams
1853–1931
temperance reformer, financier, children's author
Index t Wom; Nat Cyc Am Bio csv1; Not Am Wom; Wom Cent

384. Monoghan, Josephine; Little Jo
died 1903
pioneer, rancher
Index t Wom

385. Sweet, Ada Celeste
1853–1928
journalist, editor, author, social reformer, philanthropist, pension agent
Chicago, IL
Index t Wom; Wom Cent

386. Brauenlich, Sophia (Toepken)
1854–98
journalist, business manager of Scientific Publishing Co., fellow of the Imperial Institute of Great Britain
Nat Cyc Am Bio v9

387. Cohen, Mary M.
born 1854
social economist
Jewish
Wom Cent

388. Proctor, Mary Virginia
born 1854
journalist, newspaper publisher, philanthropist
Methodist Episcopal
Virginia
Wom Cent

389. Washington, Olivia Davidson
1854/59–1889
fund-raiser
Black
Negro Alman; Prof Negro Wom v1

390. Goodrich, Frances Louisa
born 1856
author, weaver, business executive
Index t Wom

391. Marbury, Elizabeth
1856–1933
theatrical and author's agent
Dict Am Bio supp v1; Index t Wom

392. Willard, Mary Hatch
1856–1926
businessperson, chef, social worker
Dict Am Bio

393. Coman, Katharine
1857–1915
economic historian, writer on history, social reformer, educator
Ohio
Dict Am Auth; Index t Wom; Not Am Wom

394. Cummings, Alma Carrie
born 1857
journalist, newspaper editor and publisher
New Hampshire
Wom Cent

395. Harper, Martha Matilda; Mrs. Robert Arthur MacBain
1857/68–1950
cosmetics executive, founder of the Harper Beauty Culture Method
Nat Cyc Am Bio v39; Obit File

396. Kelly, Ella Maynard
born 1857
railroad operator, telegrapher
Index t Wom

397. Knox, Rose Markward
1857–1950
businessperson, manufacturer of gelatin, industrialist
Dict Am Bio supp v4; Index t Wom; Not Am Wom

398. Lamson, Lucy Stedman
born 1857
educator, realtor
Washington
Index t Wom; Wom Cent

399. MacDowell, Marian Griswold Nevins
1857–1956/57
patron of music, musician, pianist, founder of the MacDowell Artists Colony, lecturer
New Hampshire
Index t Wom; Not Am Wom supp v1; Obit File

400. Roby, Ida Hall
born 1857/67
pharmacist
Chicago, IL
Index t Wom; Wom Cent

401. Thayer, Lizzie E. D.
born 1857
train dispatcher, telegraph operator
Connecticut
Index t Wom; Wom Cent

402. Alden, Cynthia May; Sunshine
1858/62–1931
journalist, editor, linguist, author, inventor, social worker, philanthropist, humanitarian
New York, NY
Dict Am Bio supp v1; Index t Wom; Nat Cyc Am Bio v14 and v22

403. Beer, Rachel "Richa"
1858–1927
newspaper editor, publisher, composer

Jewish
Who Who Jew Hist

404. Helmer, Bessie Bradwell
1858–1927
lawyer, editor, publisher
Dict Am Bio; Index t Wom

405. Murdock, Louise Caldwell
1858–1915
interior designer, art patron
Kansas
Not Am Wom

406. Westover, Cynthia M.
born 1858
scientist, naturalist, inventor, businessperson, linguist
Wom Cent

407. Baker, Ida Wickoff
born 1859
stock company owner, temperance worker, women's rights worker
Wom Cent

408. Blair, Emily Jane Newell
1859/77–1933
suffragist, feminist, author, vice-president of the Democratic National Committee, chairperson of the Consumer's Advisory Board of the National Recovery Administration
Dict Am Bio supp v5; Not Am Wom supp v1; Obit File

409. Churchill, Lide A.
born 1859
telegrapher, stenographer, author
Wom Cent

410. Dauvray, Helen; Little Nell; The California Diamond
born 1859
actor, theatrical manager
Cyc Am Bio; Index t Wom; Wom Cent

411. Kelley, Ella Maynard
born 1859
telegraph operator
Wom Cent

412. Miller, Addie Dickman
born 1859
educator, temperance worker, inventor of the dishwasher
Oregon
Wom Cent

413. Miller, Annie (Jenness)
born 1859/84
dress reformer, fashion designer, magazine publisher, author, novelist, essayist, lecturer
New York, NY
Dict Am Auth; Index t Wom; Wom Cent

Minneapolis, MN
Index t Wom; Wom Cent

455. Balch, Emily Greene
1867–1961
pacifist, social reformer, sociologist, economist, winner of the Nobel Peace Prize
Quaker
Index t Wom; Nat Cyc Am Bio csv7; Not Am Wom; Obit File

456. MacDougall, Alice Foote
1867–1945
businessperson, restaurateur, entrepreneur
New York
Index t Wom; Obit File

457. Miller, Bina West
1867–1954
insurance executive, founder of the Women's Benefit Association
Nat Cyc Am Bio v44; Obit File

458. Newbury, Mollie Netcher;
Mollie Neuberger
1867–1954
owner and operator of the Boston Store
Chicago, IL
Obit File

459. Randall, Minnie Josephine Smith
1867–1955
industrialist, founder of the Vacuum Can Co., philanthropist
Catholic
Chicago, IL
Nat Cyc Am Bio v42; Obit File

460. Shelton, Louise
1867–1934
author, businessperson
Index t Wom

461. Walker, Sarah McWilliams Breedlove "Madame C. J."
1867/69–1919
cosmetics executive and manufacturer, millionaire entrepreneur
Black
Dict Am Bio; Encyc Black Am; Index t Wom; Negro Alman; Not Am Wom; Prof Negro Wom v1

462. Bates, Eda Tibbles
1868–1950
suffragist, economist
Catholic
Nat Cyc Am Bio v37

463. Dortch, Ellen J.
born 1868
newspaper editor, publisher, Farmers Alliance party worker
Georgia
Wom Cent

464. Follet, Mary Parker
1868–1933
writer and lecturer on political science, group psychology, and industrial management
Dict Am Auth; Dict Am Bio supp v1; Not Am Wom

465. Percival, Olive May Graves
born 1868
underwriter, travel writer
Los Angeles, CA
Dict Am Auth

466. Robins, Margaret Dreier
1868/69–1945
labor reformer, woman- and child-labor welfare worker, suffragist, feminist, social economist, founder of the Municipal League
Bio Dict Am Lab; Dict Am Bio supp v3; Index t Wom; Nat Cyc Am Bio v33; Not Am Wom; Obit File

467. Andrews, Harriet White Fisher
born 1869
disaster relief nurse, dairy farmer, anvil manufacturer
Nat Cyc Am Bio csv2

468. Best, Gertrude Delprat
1869–1947
newspaper publisher
Washington
Nat Cyc Am Bio v41

469. Francis, Louise E.
born 1869
journalist, newspaper editor and publisher
California
Wom Cent

470. Goldman, Emma
1869–1940
political anarchist, lecturer, publicist, agitator for free speech, popularizer of the arts, feminist, pioneer advocate of birth control, politician
Jewish
Russian
Dict Am Bio supp v2; Index t Wom; Not Am Wom; Who Who Jew Hist

471. Graser, Hilda Regina
born 1869
customhouse broker
Chicago, IL
Canadian
Wom Cent

472. Hughes, Adella Prentiss
1869–1950
concert manager, founder of the Cleveland Symphony Orchestra

Cleveland, OH
Nat Cyc Am Bio csv3; Not Am Wom; Obit File

473. Lowell, Ettie Lois; Mrs. George Fl.
born 1869
suffragist, composer, alto singer, owner and director of the bond and investment firm of E. L. Lowell of Boston
Boston, MA
Nat Cyc Am Bio v14

474. Ringling, Edith Conway
1869–1953
chairperson of the Ringling Bros. and Barnum and Bailey Circus
Obit File

475. Schaffer, Margaret Eliza
born 1869
insurance agent
Wom Cent

476. Cook, Myrtle Foster
1870–1951
educator, civic leader, financier, Black civil rights worker
Kansas City, KS
Black; Canadian
Negro Alman; Prof Negro Wom

477. Kingsbury, Susan Myra
1870–1949
social investigator, social work educator, social economist, feminist
Pennsylvania
Not Am Wom; Obit File

478. Mallone, Annie M. Turnbo; Annie Turnbo-Mallone
1870–1957
business executive, philanthropist
Black
Encyc Black Am; Not Am Wom supp v1

479. Rubenstein, Helena
1870/71–1965
cosmetics manufacturer, entrepreneur, art collector, philanthropist
Jewish
Polish
Index t Wom; Nat Cyc Am Bio v50; Not Am Wom supp v1; Obit File; Who Who Jew Hist

480. Spurr, Elizabeth Albright
1870–1934
rubber manufacturer, philanthropist
Newark, NJ
Nat Cyc Am Bio v27

481. Starr, Stella
flourished 1900s
milliner
Index t Wom

482. Williams, Molly
flourished pre-1900
fire fighter
New York
Black
Prof Negro Wom v1

483. Bonstelle, Justine Laura "Jessie"
1871–1932
stage actor, director, producer, theater manager
Dict Am Bio supp v1; Nat Cyc Am Bio v25; Not Am Wom

484. Eudy, Mary Cummings Paine
1871–... dress manufactur...
Presbyterian
Kentucky
Nat Cyc Am Bio v41; Obit File

485. Harvey, Kate Benedict Hanna
1871–1936
public health worker, patron of nursing, cattle breeder
Protestant Episcopal
Cleveland, OH
Nat Cyc Am Bio v34

486. Smith, Ida B. Wise
1871–1952
president of WCTU, educator, businessperson
Index t Wom; Obit File

487. Wood, Edith (Elmer)
1871–1945
housing reformer, housing economist, novelist
Washington, DC
Dict Am Auth; Dict Am Bio supp v3; Index t Wom; Not Am Wom

488. Dreyfuss, Florence Wolf
1872–1958
owner of the Pittsburgh Pirates baseball team
Obit File

489. Jones, Jesse Homan
1872–1962
philanthropist, publisher of the *Houston Chronicle*
Houston, TX
Obit File

490. Morgan, Alice Bell
1872–1958
educator, financial expert
Obit File

491. Patino, Albina Rodriguez
1872–1953
mine owner and operator, dairy farmer, philanthropist
Bolivian
Nat Cyc Am Bio v40

Canadian
Index t Wom; Not Am Wom
supp v1; Obit File

492. ...
1872...
chem...
tion...
tor...
Index...
supp...

493. R...
Nellie...
1872–195...
journalist,
publicist,
World re...
tator and...
Dict Am B...
Wom; Obi...

494. Seton, ... Thompson;
1872–1959
suffragist, fem...
grapher, aut...
er, bookmak...
popular song...
founder of the...
Dict Am Auth;
supp v6; Index t...
Am Bio v47; ...
Wom supp v1; ...

495. Tyler, Helen
1872–1950
Broadway stage pro...
New York
Obit File

496. Curry, Anne Og...
flourished 1903
cosmetic executive
Index t Wom

497. Fisher, Harriet Wl...
married 1898
business manager, author
Index t Wom

498. Kellor, Frances [Alice]
Frances Kellar
1873–1952
social investigator and ref...
arbitration specialist,
grant-welfare worker,
mist, author, sociolog...
Dict Am Bio supp v...
Wom; Nat Cyc A...
Not Am Wom s...
File

499. Livingston...
Hutchins
1873–1957
speakeasy ope...
Obit File

500. Ba... Knight...
1874–...
busi...
Obi...

539. Dodge, Lillian Sef...
1879–1960
cosmetics manufactur...
Episcopalian
Nat Cyc Am Bio...

540. Fisher, Welt... Honsinger...
1879/80–1980...
Methodist...
and Chi...
cator...
Meth...
Cu...

530. Chess, Mary Grace; Mrs. Avery Robinson
1878–1964
perfumer, flower sculptor
New York
Nat Cyc Am Bio v52

531. Gilbreth, Lillian Evelyn (Moller)
1878–1972
industrial engineer and psychologist, household efficiency and labor efficiency expert, management consultant
Cur Biog '72; Index t Wom; Not Am Wom supp v1; Obit File

532. Kalmus, Natalie M.
1878–1965
codeveloper of Technic...
Obit File

533. McKesson, ... ka
born 1878
business exe...
Toledo, Oh...
Nat Cyc...

534. ...

Black
Encyc Black Am; Index t Wom; Negro Alman; Not Am Wom supp v1; Obit File; Prof Negro Wom v1 and v2

567. Colcord, Joanna Carver (Bruno)
1882–1960
social worker, director of the Russell Sage Foundation, author
Index t Wom; Not Am Wom supp v1; Obit File

568. Cook, Susan Glaspell
1882–1948
novelist, playwright, stage producer, Pulitzer Prize winner
Obit File

569. Guggenheim, Minnie
1882–1966
patron of music, founder and manager of the Lewisohn Stadium Outdoor Concerts, philanthropist
Jewish
New York
Index t Wom; Obit File

570. Jasie, Tillie Leblang
1882–1945
theater ticket agent
New York
Obit File

571. Laimbeer, Nathalie Schenk
1882–1929
banker, financial writer
Dict Am Bio

572. Mason, Lucy Randolph
1882–1959
labor publicist, public relations officer for the CIO, southern trade union organizer, social worker and reformer, suffragist
Episcopalian
Virginia
Bio Dict Am Lab; Dict Am Bio supp v6; Encyc South Hist; Not Am Wom supp v1; Obit File

573. Miller, Bertha Everett Mahony
1882–1969
bookseller, children's literature specialist, editor
Not Am Wom supp v1

574. Reid, Helen Miles Rogers
1882–1970
publisher of *The New York Herald-Tribune* newspaper, journalist, suffragist, philanthropist
Episcopalian
New York
Cur Biog '70; Index t Wom; Nat Cyc Am Bio v56; Not Am Wom supp v1; Obit File

575. Traphagen, Ethel; Mrs. William R. Leigh
1882–1963
fashion designer, founder of the first school of fashion design in the United States, pacifist
Index t Wom; Nat Cyc Am Bio v54 and csv9; Obit File

576. Woodward, Helen
born 1882
advertising executive
Index t Wom

577. Cowl, Jane Cowles
1883/84–1950
stage actor, playwright, theatrical producer and director
Dict Am Bio supp v4; Index t Wom; Nat Cyc Am Bio csv2 and csv5; Not Am Wom; Obit File

578. Frederick, Christine McGaffey
1883–1970
household efficiency expert, home economist, author, businessperson
Index t Wom; Not Am Wom supp v1

579. Haynes, Elizabeth A. Ross
1883–1953
YWCA official, social researcher, social worker, author, businessperson, community leader
Index t Wom; Not Am Wom supp v1

580. Maxwell, Elsa
1883–1963
professional party giver
Obit File

581. Morse, [Alfreda] Theodora Strandberg "Dolly"
1883–1953
popular song lyricist, music publisher
Obit File; Index t Wom

582. Phipps, Henry Carnegie, Mrs.
1883–1970
owner of Wheatly Racing Stables
Obit File

583. Watson, Jeannette Kittredge
1883–1966
philanthropist, founder and director of International Business Machines
Nat Cyc Am Bio v51

584. Wilson, Matilda Rausch
1883–1967
philanthropist, Detroit civic worker, chairperson of the board of directors of Fidelity Bank & Trust, member of the state board of agriculture, lieutenant governor of Michigan, Salvation Army worker
Presbyterian
Detroit, MI
Nat Cyc Am Bio v59

585. Andrus, Ethel Percy
1884–1967
founder of retirement organizations, educator, executive
Not Am Wom supp v1

586. Broadhurst, Lillian Trimble Bradley
1884–1959
Broadway theatrical director, playwright
Obit File

587. Emery, Mary Muhlenberk Hopkins
1884–1927
philanthropist, founder of Mariemont, a model town near Cincinnati
Protestant Episcopal
Ohio
Nat Cyc Am Bio v24

588. MacDonald, Lillie Ann Neal
1884–1966
candy manufacturer
Mormon
Utah
Nat Cyc Am Bio v53

589. Mars, Ethel Veronica
1884–1945
president of the Mars Candy Co.
Chicago, IL
Obit File

590. Neiman, Carrie
1884–1953
cofounder of Neiman Marcus department stores
Dallas, TX
Obit File

591. Tolstoy, Mary Koutouzow
1884–1976
author, fashion director, World War I and II nurse
Obit File

592. Ames, Elizabeth
1885–1977
executive director of Yaddo, an artists retreat
Saratoga Springs, NY
Obit File

593. Baker, Elizabeth Bradford Faulkner
born 1885
educator, economist
Index t Wom

594. Dennis, Olive Wetzel
1885–1957
engineer, inventor, railroad executive
Index t Wom

595. Dillon, Mary Elizabeth
born 1885
business executive
Index t Wom

596. Harding, Margaret Snodgrass
born 1885
editor, publisher
Index t Wom

597. Ogilvie, Jessica
1885–1943
cosmetician, business executive
Index t Wom; Obit File

598. Waldo, Ruth Fanshaw
1885–1975
advertising executive
Not Am Wom supp v1

599. Clark, Pearl Franklin
1886–1962
dramatist, international management consultant, business executive
Christian Scientist
New York
Nat Cyc Am Bio v47

600. Hardwick, Katharine Davis
1886–1974
pianist, newspaper publisher
Christian Scientist
Indiana
Nat Cyc Am Bio v58

601. Kyrk, Hazel
1886–1957
consumer economist
Not Am Wom supp v1

602. Lane, Rose Wilder
1886/87–1968
novelist, telegrapher, World War I Red Cross worker in Europe, Vietnam war correspondent
Index t Wom; Nat Cyc Am Bio v54

603. Roche, Josephine Aspinwall
1886–1976
industrialist, lecturer, UMW executive
Index t Wom; Obit File

604. Rosenthal, Ida Cohen
1886–1973
manufacturing executive, director of Maidenform Co., inventor of the brassiere
Jewish

New York
Nat Cyc Am Bio v57; Not Am
Wom supp v1

605. Westropp, Clara Elizabeth
1886–1965
banker
Catholic
Ohio
Nat Cyc Am Bio v51

606. Allison, Marjorie
1887–1961
banker
Episcopalian
Pennsylvania
Nat Cyc Am Bio v49

607. Auerbach, Beatrice
1887–1968
philanthropist, businessperson
Not Am Wom supp v1

608. Beach, Sylvia Woodbridge
1887–1962
bookshop proprietor, publisher of
James Joyce, lending library
owner
French (American expatriate to
Paris)
Dict Lit Bio v4; Nat Cyc Am Bio
v47; Not Am Wom supp v1;
Obit File

609. Deardorff, Neva R.
1887–1958
social welfare statistical expert,
president of the Child Welfare
League of America, cofounder
of the Health Insurance Plan of
Greater New York
New York
Obit File

610. Fawcett, Claire
1887–1960
cofounder of Fawcett Publications, Inc.
Obit File

**611. Helburn, Therese (Op-
dyke)**
1887–1959
theatrical producer, dramatist,
codirector and administrator of
New York City's theater guild
New York, NY
Dict Am Bio supp v6; Index t
Wom; Not Am Wom supp v1;
Obit File

**612. May, Marjorie Merri-
weather Post Close Hutton
Davies**
born 1887
financier
Index t Wom

**613. Meyer, Agnes Elizabeth
(Ernst)**
1887–1970

author, journalist, vice-president
and co-owner of *The Washington Post*, World War II correspondent, autobiographer,
lecturer, social worker, Republican party worker, crusader for
social services and education
causes
Lutheran
New York
Cur Biog '70; Index t Wom; Nat
Cyc Am Bio v56; Obit File

614. Muller, Gertrude Agnes
1887–1954
businessperson, inventor
Not Am Wom supp v1

**615. Pedder, Alice Pratt Ber-
dell**
1887–1947
realtor, business executive
Episcopalian
California
Nat Cyc Am Bio v36

**616. Post, Marjorie Merri-
weather**
1887–1973
philanthropist, antique collector,
suffragist, director of National
Savings and Trust, founder and
director of General Foods
Christian Scientist
Washington, DC
Nat Cyc Am Bio v58; Not Am
Wom supp v1; Obit File

**617. Sabin, Pauline Morton;
Mrs. Charles**
1887–1955
Prohibition repeal leader, Republican party official, interior decorator
Index t Wom; Not Am Wom
supp v1

618. Steloff, Frances [Ida]
born 1887
bookseller
Index t Wom

619. Valdo, Pat
born 1887
circus personnel director
Index t Wom

620. Blakeslee, Myra Allen
circa 1888–1953
advertising executive, social welfare worker
Index t Wom

621. Cobb, Beatrice
1888–1959
newspaper editor, publisher of the
Morganton, North Carolina,
News-Herald
Methodist
Morganton, NC
Nat Cyc Am Bio v45; Obit File

**622. McMein, Neysa; Mrs.
John Gordon Baragwanath**
1888/90–1949
illustrator, magazine illustrator,
painter, portraitist, commercial
artist, author
Episcopalian
Index t Wom; Nat Cyc Am Bio
v36; Not Am Wom; Obit File

**623. Perry, Antoinette
(Frueauff)**
1888–1946
actor, theatrical director and pro-
ducer
Dict Am Bio supp v4; Index t
Wom; Nat Cyc Am Bio v37;
Not Am Wom

**624. Phillips, Luba Galanchi-
koff (Philpoff)**
1888–1959
pioneer aviator, pre–World War I
test pilot, early altitude and distance record holder, taxi driver
New York
Russian
Obit File

625. Alexander, Mary Louise
1889–1976
librarian
Connecticut
Nat Cyc Am Bio v59

626. Bonfils, Helen Gertrude
1889–1962
newspaper executive, chairperson
of the board of the *Denver Post*,
theatrical producer
Catholic
Denver, CO
Nat Cyc Am Bio v56; Obit File

627. Dowd, Alice Casey
circa 1889–1964
fashion consultant, publicist
Index t Wom

**628. Draper, Dorothy Tucker-
man**
1889–1969
interior decorator, inventor,
newspaper columnist
Cur Biog '69; Index t Wom; Obit
File

629. Mesta, Perle
1889/91–1975
businessperson, US diplomat,
feminist
Index t Wom; Not Am Wom
supp v1

630. Morrison, Adrienne
1889–1940
actor, literary agent
Index t Wom

631. Shaw, Lois Kenyon
1889–1958

founder of Portraits, Inc.,
painters'and sculptors'agents
Obit File

**632. Wallace, Lila Bell Ache-
son**
born 1889
editor, publisher
Canadian
Index t Wom

633. Wallace, Mildred White
born 1889
composer, singer, publisher, author
Index t Wom

634. Waller, Judith Carey
1889–1973
broadcasting executive
Not Am Wom supp v1

635. Ward, Maisie
1889–1975
book publisher, author, lecturer,
Catholic church worker
Catholic
English
Cur Biog '75; Index t Wom

**636. Butler, Kate Maddux
Robinson**
circa 1890–1974
publisher, philanthropist, patron
of French relief in World War
II
Buffalo, NY
Nat Cyc Am Bio v58

637. Carr, Charlotte E.
1890–1956
personnel manager, social worker,
settlement house director
Dict Nat Bio supp v6; Index t
Wom; Obit File

638. Charlick, Edith
flourished 1920s–30s
nurse, business executive
Index t Wom

639. Cuthbert, Margaret Ross
1890–1968
program director of NBC
Canadian
Index t Wom; Obit File

640. Devereux, Margaret Green
flourished 1920s–30s
interior decorator, editor
Index t Wom

**641. Flanagan, Hallie Mae Fer-
guson (Davis); Hallie Davis**
189?–1969
theater educator, theater administrator and director, playwright
Not Am Wom supp v1, Obit File

642. Gaddis, Edith
flourished 1920s–30s

purchasing agent
Index t Wom

643. Gilliam, Florence
flourished 1920s–40s
journalist, theater critic, magazine publisher
French (American expatriate to Paris)
Dict Lit Bio v4

644. Mideladze, Ketto
flourished 1920s–30s
dancer, fashion designer
Russian
Index t Wom

645. Perry, Margaret
flourished 1920s
aviator, airport operator
Index t Wom

646. Sternbergh, Katharine Eleanor Cornell
1890–1950
Reading, Pennsylvania, civic worker; owner and manager of the American Tool and Die Co.
Reading, PA
Nat Cyc Am Bio v39

647. Susong, Edith (Ingles) O'Keefe
1890–1974
newspaper publisher
Episcopalian
Greenville, TN
Nat Cyc Am Bio v59

648. Wall, Florence Emeline
flourished 1920s–30s
industrial chemist, cosmetician
Index t Wom

649. Weekes, Marie
flourished 1920s
publisher, journalist
Index t Wom

650. Woodham, Eva Esther Dowling
1890–1962
insurance executive, floriculturist
Methodist
South Carolina
Nat Cyc Am Bio v46

651. Woodhouse, Margaret Chase Going
born 1890
representative to Congress, economist, educator, author
Index t Wom

652. Mack, Nila; Nila Mac-Laughlin
1891–1953
radio producer, writer, director, actor
Index t Wom; Not Am Wom supp v1; Obit File

653. Mears, Henrietta C.
1891–1963
founder of Gospel Light Church Publications
Obit File

654. Newcomer, Mabel
born 1891
economist, educator
Index t Wom

655. Stewart, Dorothy M.
1891/97–1954
theatrical agent, composer, pianist, author
Australian
Index t Wom

656. Street, Margaret Berry
1891–1967
cattle farmer, lawyer, Civil Air Regulations executive, suffragist, Black welfare worker
Presbyterian
North Carolina
Nat Cyc Am Bio v54

657. Vestey, Evelyn
died 1941
executive of Union Cold Storage and Blue Star Steamship companies
Obit File

658. Crosby, Caresse; Polly Jacob
1892–1970
poet, patron of the arts, cofounder of the Black Sun Press
French (American expatriate to Paris)
Dict Lit Bio v4

659. Grant, Jane
1892–1972
journalist, cofounder of *The New Yorker*, feminist
Index t Wom; Obit File

660. Grossinger, Jennie
1892–1972
philanthropist; hotel executive, owner, and manager; country club owner
Jewish
Catskill Mountains, NY
Austrian
Cur Biog '73; Index t Wom; Not Am Wom supp v1; Obit File

661. Pattee, Alida Frances
died 1942
dietician, lecturer, publisher, author
Index t Wom

662. Boothe, Viva Belle
1893–1964
business researcher, economist, educator
Methodist

Ohio
Nat Cyc Am Bio v51

663. Comiskey, Grace Elizabeth Reidy
1893–1956
co-owner of the Chicago White Sox baseball team
Obit File

664. Cornell, Katharine
1893/98–1973
stage actor, theatrical producer
Cur Biog '74; Index t Wom; Nat Cyc Am Bio csv4; Not Am Wom supp v1; Obit File

665. Davis, Tobe Collier
born circa 1893
fashion designer, business executive
Index t Wom

666. Fitz-Gibbon, Bernice; Mrs. Herman Block
graduated 1918
advertising executive
Catholic
New York
Nat Cyc Am Bio csv9

667. Kirchwey, Mary Fredrika "Freda"; Mrs. Evans Clark
1893–1976
editor, publisher of *The Nation*, Socialist party worker, feminist
Cur Biog '76; Index t Wom; Obit File

668. Kirkus, Virginia
1893–1980
literary critic, book preview company founder, author
Cur Biog '80; Index t Wom

669. Stover, Clara [Mae] Lewis
born 1893
candy manufacturer
Presbyterian
Nat Cyc Am Bio csv12

670. Whitman, Lucile Mara de Vescovi, Countess
born 1893
fashion designer, businessperson
Italian
Index t Wom

671. Williams, Faith Moors; Mrs. Frank W. Lorimer
1893–1958
economist, US Bureau of Labor Statistics economist, chief of the Office of Labor Economics
Nat Cyc Am Bio v49; Obit File

672. Anderson, Gertrude E. Fisher
born 1894
business executive
Index t Wom

673. Barker, Ellen Frye
died 1944
advertising copywriter, dramatic critic, genealogist, publisher
Index t Wom; Obit File

674. Johnson, Osa Helen Leighty
1894–1952/53
explorer, geographer, big game hunter, filmmaker and film producer, aviator, author
Index t Wom; Nat Cyc Am Bio v39; Obit File

675. Knopf, Blanche Wolf
1894–1966
editor, publisher, president of Alfred A. Knopf Inc.
New York
Index t Wom; Not Am Wom supp v1; Obit File

676. Smith, Blanche Hixson
1894–1974
newspaper publisher and editor
Congregationalist
Connecticut
Nat Cyc Am Bio v58

677. Alexander, Beatrice
born 1895
doll maker
Index t Wom

678. Alexander, Ruth Wilbur; Mrs. Raymond L. Redhefer
born 1895
economist, editorial columnist, lecturer, pianist
Buddhist
Index t Wom; Nat Cyc Am Bio csv12

679. Bryant, Lane; Lena Himmelstein; Mrs. Albert Malsin
1881/1895–1951
dress merchant, mail order businessperson, maternity and special sizes designer
Jewish
New York
Lithuanian
Nat Cyc Am Bio v47; Index t Wom; Who Who Jew Hist

680. Cheney, Margaret Aneline
born 1895
banker
Methodist Episcopal
Lafayette, IN
Nat Cyc Am Bio csv2

681. Dulles, Eleanor Lansing
born 1895
government worker, economist
Index t Wom

682. Erb, Leticia H.
born 1895
chamber of commerce executive
Index t Wom

683. Gordon, Mazie P.
born circa 1895
theater owner
Index t Wom

684. Smith, Ada; Bricktop
born 1895
singer, dancer, cabaret owner
Index t Wom

685. Victor, Sally (Josephs)
1895/1905–1977
hat designer
Jewish
New York
Cur Biog '77; Index t Wom; Nat
Cyc Am Bio v49

686. Bowman, Geline MacDonald
died 1946
women's business worker, head of
the National Federation of
Business and Professional
Women
Obit File

687. Frantz, Virginia Kneeland
1896–1967
surgical pathologist, medical educator, cancer researcher, dairy
farmer
Episcopalian
New York
Nat Cyc Am Bio v53; Not Am
Wom supp v1

688. Gabor, Jolie
born 1896
businessperson
Hungarian
Index t Wom

689. Kellems, Vivien
1896–1975
industrialist, engineer, president
of the Kellems Co.
Connecticut
Cur Biog '69; Index t Wom

690. Remsen, Alice
born 1896
composer, author, publisher
English
Index t Wom

**691. Russell, Helen Victoria
Crocker**
1896–1966
bank director, UNESCO execu-
tive, philanthropist
Episcopalian
San Francisco, CA
Nat Cyc Am Bio v53

692. St. George, Katharine
born 1896
representative to Congress, business executive
Index t Wom

**693. Blodgett, Katherine Burr
(Seibert)**
1897/98–1979
physicist, chemist, inventor of scientific equipment
Cur Biog '80; Eng Wom; Index t
Wom

694. Gentry, Helen
graduated 1922
printer
Index t Wom

695. Hayden, Saint Clare Okie
born 1897
industrialist
Episcopalian
Colorado
Nat Cyc Am Bio csv7

**696. Hughes, Arleen Florence
Wilson**
born 1897
investment counselor
Christian Scientist
Colorado
Nat Cyc Am Bio csv9

697. Lewis, Mary
born 1897
fashion designer
Index t Wom

**698. Liebes, Dorothy Katharine
(Wright)**
1897/99–1972
textile designer, businessperson,
weaver
Cur Biog '72; Index t Wom; Not
Am Wom supp v1

699. Rosenstein, Nettie
born 1897
fashion designer, philanthropist,
business executive
Australian
Index t Wom

700. Rudkin, Margaret Fogarty
1897–1967
businessperson, bakery executive,
founder of Pepperidge Farms,
Inc.
Index t Wom; Not Am Wom
supp v1; Obit File

701. Shaver, Dorothy (Yeiser)
1897–1959
business executive, merchandising
executive, president of Lord and
Taylor department stores
Episcopalian
New York
Index t Wom; Nat Cyc Am Bio
v56 and csv8; Not Am Wom
supp v1; Obit File

702. Sloane, Isabel Dodge
circa 1897–1962
racehorse breeder, owner of
Brookemeade Stables
Obit File

703. Talmadge, Norma
1897–1957
silent-screen actor, producer
California
Dict Am Bio supp v6; Index t
Wom; Nat Cyc Am Bio v48;
Obit File

704. Wilder, Frances Farmer
born 1897
radio executive
Index t Wom

705. Wolfson, Theresa
1897–1972
labor economist, educator
Not Am Wom supp v1

706. Campbell, Persia Crawford
1898–1974
economist, consumer advocate
Not Am Wom supp v1

**707. Langner, Armina Mar-
shall; Isabelle Louden**
born 1898
playwright, producer
Index t Wom

708. Warburton, Amber Arthun
1898–1976
economist, educational guidance
consultant
Unitarian
Nat Cyc Am Bio v59

709. Kaminska, Ida
1899–1980
stage actor, producer, director of
Yiddish theater
Jewish
New York, NY
Cur Biog '69 and '80

710. le Gallienne, Eva
born 1899
stage actor and producer
English
Nat Cyc Am Bio csv3

711. Amen, Marion Clevelan
flourished 1930s
business executive
Index t Wom

712. Archibald, Anne
flourished 1930s
business executive
Index t Wom

713. Askwith, Margaret Long
flourished 1930s
educator, businessperson
Index t Wom

714. Babcock, Lucille
flourished 1930s
advertising executive, fashion expert, editor
Index t Wom

715. Bailey, Florence
flourished 1930s
advertising executive, jewelry designer
Index t Wom

**716. Bay, Josephine Holt Per-
fect**
born 1900
financier, philanthropist
Index t Wom

717. Beaupre, Enid
flourished 1930s
advertising executive
Welsh
Index t Wom

718. Beechman, Maria A.
flourished 1930s
railroad worker
Index t Wom

719. Berliner, Constance Hope
flourished 1930s
business executive
Index t Wom

720. Bernie, Rose L.
flourished 1930s
realtor, health expert
Index t Wom

721. Bickum, Dorothy
flourished 1930s
salesperson
Index t Wom

722. Binger, Delphine
flourished 1930s
business executive
Index t Wom

723. Binner, Madam
flourished 1930s
business executive
Australian
Index t Wom

724. Bleicher, Blanche O.
flourished 1930s
businessperson
Index t Wom

725. Blondin, Catharine F.
flourished 1930s
designer, business executive
Index t Wom

726. Bloodworth, Bess
flourished 1930s
business executive, personnel and
production expert
Index t Wom

727. Boehm, Mildred Witt
flourished 1930s
businessperson
Index t Wom

728. Bollman, Mary O'R.
flourished 1930s

business executive, broker
Index t Wom

729. Bonfield, Lida
flourished 1930s
business executive
Index t Wom

730. Bossidy, Mary
flourished 1930s
advertising executive
Index t Wom

731. Brandwein, Gertrude
flourished 1930s
insurance company executive
Index t Wom

732. Briant, Nila Mack
flourished 1930s
radio director
Index t Wom

733. Brooks, G. Anne
flourished 1930s
playwright, stage producer
Index t Wom

734. Brosnan, Mary
flourished 1930s
business executive, window display designer
Index t Wom

735. Brown, Eleanor Stockstrom
flourished 1930s
interior decorator, business executive
Index t Wom

736. Brown, Katharine
flourished 1930s
motion picture executive, editor
Index t Wom

737. Brown, Sarah J.
flourished 1930s
sales manager
Index t Wom

738. Browning, Marge
flourished 1930s
milliner
Index t Wom

739. Brupbacher, Alice
flourished 1930s
business executive
Swiss
Index t Wom

740. Burt, Alene
flourished 1930s
business executive
Index t Wom

741. Campbell, Amelia M.
flourished 1930s
businessperson
Index t Wom

742. Carothers, Mina Hall
flourished 1930s
advertising executive
Index t Wom

743. Carter, Mabel Ogilvie
flourished 1930s
cosmetics executive
Index t Wom

744. Clair, Joan
flourished 1930s
cosmetic business executive
Index t Wom

745. Clarahan, Virg Binns
flourished 1930s
public relations worker
Index t Wom

746. Clark, Verne
flourished 1930s
cosmetics business executive
Index t Wom

747. Clarke, Alva J.
flourished 1930s
employment agency manager
Index t Wom

748. Clements, Hall-Kane
flourished 1930s
journalist, publicist
Index t Wom

749. Close, Elizabeth Stuart
flourished 1930s
fashion designer
Index t Wom

750. Coale, Virginia
flourished 1930s
retail executive
Index t Wom

751. Coit, Elizabeth
flourished 1930s
architectural executive
Index t Wom

752. Colburn, Joan
flourished 1930s
fashion commentator, radio broadcasting executive
Index t Wom

753. Cole, Helen D.
flourished 1930s
fashion designer
Index t Wom

754. Connor, Emily E.
flourished 1930s
printer, typographer
Index t Wom

755. Connor, Marcia
flourished 1930s
journalist, advertising specialist
Index t Wom

756. Converse, Thelma; Lady Furness
flourished 1930s–40s
businessperson
Index t Wom

757. Cookman, Helen Cramp
flourished 1930s
fashion designer, business executive
Index t Wom

758. Coppage, Grace
flourished 1930s
cosmetician
Index t Wom

759. Crowley, Mary M.
flourished 1930s
business executive
Index t Wom

760. Cumming, Rose Stuart
flourished 1930s
business executive, interior decorator
Index t Wom

761. Daniels, Angela B.
flourished 1930s
production manager, business executive
Index t Wom

762. Davis, Louise Taylor
flourished 1930s–40s
advertising executive
Index t Wom

763. de Barker, Lorraine
flourished 1930s
cosmetician, businessperson
Index t Wom

764. de Mott, Marjorie Mahon
flourished 1930s
businessperson
Index t Wom

765. Delafield, Ann
flourished 1930s
cosmetician, dietician, educator
Index t Wom

766. Diehl, Mary
flourished 1930s
educator, business executive, personnel director
Index t Wom

767. Dingman, Margaret Christian
flourished 1930s
retail buyer
Canadian
Index t Wom

768. Dodd, Carolyn G.
flourished 1930s
interior decorator, employment agency executive
Index t Wom

769. Dolson, Hildegarde
flourished 1930s
fashion designer
Index t Wom

770. Donner, Vyvyan
flourished 1930s
journalist, fashion designer, artist
Index t Wom

771. Doty, Katharine S.
flourished 1930s
personnel worker
Index t Wom

772. Dublin, Mary
flourished 1930s
economist, humanitarian
Index t Wom

773. Edgerly, Anne R.
flourished 1930s
business executive
Index t Wom

774. Eggleston, Marjorie E.
flourished 1930s
security salesperson
Index t Wom

775. Elliot, Rebekah Ward
flourished 1930s
hotel executive
Index t Wom

776. Fairman, Agnes Rowe
flourished 1930s
interior decorator
Index t Wom

777. Feigenblatt, Ann
flourished 1930s
actor, retailer
Polish
Index t Wom

778. Forbes, Jessica L.
flourished 1930s
publisher
Index t Wom

779. Ford, Gertrude H.
flourished 1930s
business executive, importer
Index t Wom

780. Ford, Kathryn
flourished 1930s
clubwoman, insurance agent
Index t Wom

781. Fuchs, Henriette J.
flourished 1930s
trust officer
Index t Wom

782. Gammons, Ethel Thirza
flourished 1930s
banker
Index t Wom

783. **Gilmore, Gladys Chase**
flourished 1930s
educator, businessperson
Index t Wom

784. **Gordon, Edith Frances**
flourished 1930s
business executive
Index t Wom

785. **Grandstaff, Grace M.**
flourished 1930s
personnel worker
Index t Wom

786. **Grew, Agnes Mengel**
flourished 1930s
motion picture executive
Index t Wom

787. **Hall, Marian Wells**
flourished 1930s
interior decorator
Index t Wom

788. **Halpert, Edith Gregor**
1900?–70
art dealer and collector
Russian
Cur Biog '70; Index t Wom; Not
Am Wom supp v1

789. **Hamill, Virginia**
flourished 1930s
interior decorator
Index t Wom

790. **Hanssen, Hertha I.**
flourished 1930s
business executive
Index t Wom

791. **Hayes, Irene**
flourished 1930s
florist
Index t Wom

792. **Haywood, Rosemary**
flourished 1930s
editor, publisher
Index t Wom

793. **Heiman, Gertrude**
flourished 1930s
hotel executive
Index t Wom

794. **Helvarg, Sue**
flourished 1930s
photographer's agent
Russian
Index t Wom

795. **Hentz, Eta**
flourished 1930s
business executive
Hungarian
Index t Wom

796. **Herman, Mollie C.**
flourished 1930s

advertising executive
Index t Wom

797. **Hilder, Vera Gertrude**
flourished 1930s
actor, business executive
English
Index t Wom

798. **Hill, Carol**
flourished 1930s
author, literary agent
Index t Wom

799. **Hill, Dorothy Lampe**
flourished 1930s
advertising manager
Index t Wom

800. **Hines, Eleanor Culton**
flourished 1930s
business executive, realtor
Index t Wom

801. **Hoederlin, Lillina Ottilie**
flourished 1930s
business executive
Index t Wom

802. **Holland, Clara Helena**
flourished 1930s
personnel director
Canadian
Index t Wom

803. **Holley, Bertha Delbert**
flourished 1930s
fashion designer, artist
Index t Wom

804. **Horn, Berta**
flourished 1930s
business executive
Index t Wom

805. **Hough, Maude Clark**
flourished 1930s
poet, telegraph operator
Index t Wom

806. **Howard, Lulu Smith**
flourished 1930s
investment analyst
Index t Wom

807. **Hoyt, Peggy**
flourished 1930s
designer
Index t Wom

808. **Hudson, Hortense Imboden**
flourished 1930s
personnel worker
Index t Wom

809. **Hulse, Anne Elizabeth**
flourished 1930s
educator, economist
Index t Wom

810. **Humert, Anne Schumacher**
flourished 1930s–40s
advertising executive, radio producer
Index t Wom

811. **Hyde, Helen Smith**
flourished 1930s
businessperson, employment
manager
Index t Wom

812. **Johnson, Sonya Bortin**
flourished 1930s
businessperson, advertising executive
Index t Wom

813. **Jordan, Alice Boyer**
flourished 1930s
nurse, business executive
Index t Wom

814. **Joseph, Nannine**
flourished 1930s
business executive
Index t Wom

815. **Kayshus, Effie**
flourished 1930s
businessperson
Index t Wom

816. **Kimball, Josephine**
flourished 1930s
bookseller, business executive
Index t Wom

817. **King, Frances Rockefeller**
flourished 1930s
press agent, radio agent
Index t Wom

818. **Knox, Helen**
flourished 1930s
banker
Index t Wom

819. **Koch, Marion**
flourished 1930s
retail buyer
Index t Wom

820. **Koernig, Anna Mabel**
flourished 1930s
business executive
Index t Wom

821. **Kops, Margot de Bruyn**
flourished 1930s
fashion designer
Index t Wom

822. **Kramer, Maria**
flourished 1930s
hotel owner and operator
Index t Wom

823. **Kretschmar, Alice Ann**
flourished 1930s
personnel director
Index t Wom

810. **Humert, Anne Schumacher**
flourished 1930s–40s
advertising executive, radio producer
Index t Wom

824. **Laslett, Dixie L.**
flourished 1930s
personnel executive
Index t Wom

825. **Law, Helen Lynch**
flourished 1930s
radio advertising executive
Index t Wom

826. **le Grange, Ann**
flourished 1930s
fashion designer
Index t Wom

827. **Leahy, Agnes Berkeley**
flourished 1930s
personnel worker
Index t Wom

828. **Lee, Rosamond**
flourished 1930s
business executive, journalist, advertising director
Index t Wom

829. **Leis, B. Eugenia**
flourished 1930s
retailer
Index t Wom

830. **Lelash, Ethelyn L.**
flourished 1930s
business school executive
Index t Wom

831. **Lenart, Marian F.**
flourished 1930s
business executive
Index t Wom

832. **Lewis, Ethel**
flourished 1930s
interior decorator
Index t Wom

833. **Lewis, Mary Carlile**
flourished 1930s
business executive
Index t Wom

834. **Lewis, Rosa Ovenden**
flourished 1930s
hotel manager
Index t Wom

835. **Lobdell, Avis**
flourished 1930s
railroad public relations expert,
editor
Index t Wom

836. **Logan, Charlotte**
flourished 1930s
commercial artist, fashion designer, inventor
Index t Wom

837. **Loughlin, Mary**
flourished 1930s
advertising executive
Index t Wom

838. Lyman, Esther
flourished 1930s
fashion editor, advertising manager
Index t Wom

839. Mabry, Beatrice
flourished 1930s
advertising executive
Index t Wom

840. Macy, Margaret
flourished 1930s
advertising executive
Index t Wom

841. Maneck, Margaret Brown
flourished 1930s
business executive
Index t Wom

842. McClung, Mary J.
flourished 1930s
journalist, advertising executive, personnel director
Index t Wom

843. McCrea, Vera T.
flourished 1930s
businessperson
Index t Wom

844. McFadden, Dorothy L.
flourished 1930s
business executive
German
Index t Wom

845. McInnis, Clara Ogilvie
flourished 1930s
cosmetic executive
Index t Wom

846. McKay, Isabel
flourished 1930s
fashion executive
Index t Wom

847. Mears, Virginia
flourished 1930s
advertising executive
Index t Wom

848. Mendelsohn, Celia
flourished 1930s
artist, business executive
Index t Wom

849. Mercereau, Ethel F.
flourished 1930s
business executive
Index t Wom

850. Merzon, Ruth
flourished 1930s
businessperson
Polish
Index t Wom

851. Miles, Allie Lowe
flourished 1930s
cosmetician, radio personality, advertising writer
Index t Wom

852. Miller, Gladys
flourished 1930s
interior decorator, retail executive
Index t Wom

853. Mistrot, Ethel Reed
flourished 1930s
businessperson
Index t Wom

854. Morgan, Therese E.
flourished 1930s
retailer
Index t Wom

855. Morse, Fanny
flourished 1930s
businessperson
Index t Wom

856. Morse, Ruth V.
flourished 1930s
travel specialist
Index t Wom

857. Munro, Beatrice Loundsbery
flourished 1930s
business executive
Index t Wom

858. Myers, Ella Burns
flourished 1930s
business executive
Index t Wom

859. Newman, Henriette
flourished 1930s
business executive, antique dealer
Index t Wom

860. Norton, Katherine Byrd Rodgers
flourished 1930s
business executive
Index t Wom

861. Nosworthy, Meta
flourished 1930s
cosmetician, business executive
Index t Wom

862. Noyes, Dorothy
flourished 1930s
business executive, advertising writer
Index t Wom

863. O'Brien, Paulyna J.
flourished 1930s
publicity director
Index t Wom

864. Odlum, Hortense
flourished 1930s–40s
merchant
Index t Wom

865. Ogilvie, Elizabeth
flourished 1930s
cosmetician, business executive
Index t Wom

866. Ogilvie, Gladys
flourished 1930s
cosmetician, business executive
Index t Wom

867. O'Leary, Lydia
flourished 1930s
cosmetologist
Index t Wom

868. Olivier, Frances
flourished 1930s
cosmetician, business executive
Index t Wom

869. Olney, Dorothy McGrayne
flourished 1930s
concert manager
Index t Wom

870. Olsen, Leonora Emelie
flourished 1930s
insurance executive
Index t Wom

871. Paige, Richard E., Mrs.
flourished 1930s–50s
businessperson
Index t Wom

872. Patterson, Lillian D.
flourished 1930s
business executive
Index t Wom

873. Paul, Josephine Bay
1900–62
brokerage and shipping business executive
Reformed Church
Nat Cyc Am Bio csv9; Obit File

874. Paul, Nora Vincent
flourished 1930s
insurance executive, journalist
Index t Wom

875. Peirce, Isabel
flourished 1930s
businessperson
Index t Wom

876. Perlman, Phyllis
flourished 1930s
publicity director, journalist
Index t Wom

877. Pettit, Polly
flourished 1930s
business executive
Index t Wom

878. Polykoff, Shirley
flourished 1930s
advertising executive
Index t Wom

879. Reed, Helena D.
flourished 1930s
banker
Index t Wom

880. Rice, Laura W.
flourished 1930s
designer
Hungarian
Index t Wom

881. Richards, Henrietta King
flourished 1930s
business executive
Index t Wom

882. Roman, Mae
flourished 1930s
interior decorator, business executive
Index t Wom

883. Rosenberg, Beatrice
flourished 1930s
merchandise counselor
Index t Wom

884. Ryan, Mary P. van Buren
flourished 1930s
singer, music educator, accountant
Index t Wom

885. Saruya, Julia Salinger
flourished 1930s
milliner, business executive
Index t Wom

886. Schupack, May
flourished 1930s
journalist, publicity director
Index t Wom

887. Schuyler, Margaretta
flourished 1930s
retail manager
Canadian
Index t Wom

888. Scovil, Cora
flourished 1930s
inventor, business executive
Index t Wom

889. Shatford, Vera V.
flourished 1930s
interior decorator
Index t Wom

890. Sherman, Florence A.
flourished 1930s
fashion designer, doll designer
Index t Wom

891. Shook, Virginia Nelson
flourished 1930s
advertising manager
Index t Wom

892. Singer, Betty
flourished 1930s

businessperson
Index t Wom

893. Sioussat, Helen J.
flourished 1930s
business executive
Index t Wom

894. Slator, Helen M.
flourished 1930s
public relations expert
Index t Wom

895. Slocum, Caroline Edna
flourished 1930s
businessperson, club leader
Index t Wom

896. Sparks, Sarah
flourished 1930s
personnel director
Canadian
Index t Wom

897. Stuerm, Ruza Lukavaska
flourished 1930s
railroad executive, lecturer
Czechoslovak
Index t Wom

898. Sullivan, Marie
flourished 1930s
aviation inspector, decorator
Index t Wom

899. Summer, Quinneth C.
flourished 1930s
business executive
Index t Wom

900. Sweeney, Edith Igoe
flourished 1930s
fashion designer
Index t Wom

901. Taylor, Kathleen Devere
flourished 1930s
feminist, stockbroker
Index t Wom

902. Thal, Augusta
flourished 1930s
businessperson
Index t Wom

903. Tuttle, Marguerite
flourished 1930s
business executive
Index t Wom

904. Tweddle, Georgina Ogilvie
flourished 1930s
cosmetician
Index t Wom

905. Vanderlip, Candace Alig
flourished 1930s
humanitarian, business executive
Index t Wom

906. Vaupel, Ouise
flourished 1930s

fashion designer, realtor, singer,
  author
Index t Wom

907. Vigon, Anne
flourished 1930s
retail buyer
Index t Wom

908. Watson, Louise
flourished 1930s
businessperson
Index t Wom

909. Westgate, Elizabeth
flourished 1930s
personnel director, retailer
Index t Wom

910. Wilson, Mabel K.
flourished 1930s
aviator, airport manager
Index t Wom

911. Witt, Estelle E.
flourished 1930s
retail executive
Index t Wom

912. Wright, Jessie
1900–70
orthopedist, orthopedic inventor,
  medical educator
English
Nat Cyc Am Bio v55

913. Cohen, Barbara
born 1901
recording company executive
Index t Wom

914. Leser, Tina
born 1901
fashion designer
Index t Wom

915. Lewis, Tillie [Myrtle]
1901–77
cannery owner and executive
Jewish
California
Nat Cyc Am Bio v60

916. Maxwell, Vera (Huppe)
born 1901
fashion designer
Cur Biog '77

917. Schneider, Alma Kittredge
1901–75
superintendent of the Denver
  Mint
Denver, CO
Index t Wom; Obit File

918. Wickens, Aryness Joy
born 1901
government official, economist
Index t Wom

919. Abbell, Fannie Edelman
born 1902

business executive, philanthropist
Jewish
Chicago, IL
Nat Cyc Am Bio csv11

920. Crawford, Cheryl
born 1902
theatrical producer
Index t Wom

921. Dawson, Mary Cardwell
1902–62
founder of the National Negro
  Opera Company, soprano concert singer
Black
Obit File

922. Duncan, Vivian
born 1902
composer, author, publisher
Index t Wom

923. Eddy, Lillian E.
circa 1902–66
industrial designer
New Zealand
Index t Wom

**924. Freudenthal, Elsbeth Es-
telle**
circa 1902–53
economist, aviation writer
Index t Wom

925. Gimbel, Sophie
born 1902
fashion designer
Index t Wom

926. Hickey, Margaret E.
born 1902
editor, government employee,
  personnel worker
Index t Wom

927. Soss, Wilma Porter
born circa 1902
public relations expert, economist, organization official
Index t Wom

928. Beech, Olive Ann Mellor
born 1903
aviation executive, industrialist
Index t Wom

929. Copeland, Jo
born 1903
fashion designer
Index t Wom

930. Dickason, Gladys Marie
1903–71
labor economist, labor organizer
Not Am Wom supp v1

931. Hawes, Elizabeth
1903–71
fashion designer, author, feminist
Index t Wom; Not Am Wom
  supp v1

**932. Neuschaefer, Helen Ah-
rens**
1903–61
inventor of colored nail polish,
  business executive
Lutheran
New York
Nat Cyc Am Bio v46

933. Nin, Anais
1903–77
author, novelist, diarist, printer,
  feminist
French
Cur Biog '75 and '77; Dict Lit
  Bio v2 and v4; Index t Wom;
  Wom Lit; Wom Lit, More

934. Payson, Joan Whitney
1903–75
philanthropist, race horse breeder, owner of the New York
  Mets, patron of medicine, art
  collector and investor, founder
  of the Museum of Modern Art
  in New York
Episcopalian
New York
Cur Biog '72 and '75; Index t
  Wom; Nat Cyc Am Bio v58 and
  csv10; Obit File

935. Shaw, Carolyn Hagner
born circa 1903
publisher
Index t Wom

936. Simpson, Adele Smithline
born 1903
fashion designer
Cur Biog '70; Index t Wom

937. Thackrey, Dorothy (Schiff)
born 1903
journalist, publisher
Index t Wom

938. Dache, Lilly
born 1904
milliner, fashion designer
French
Index t Wom

939. Fenner, Beatrice
born 1904
composer, author, publisher
Index t Wom

940. Mann, Elizabeth
died 1954
printer
Index t Wom

941. Poletti, Jean Ellis
1904–74
advertising executive, New York
  civic worker, UNICEF worker
Presbyterian
Nat Cyc Am Bio v58

942. Valentina
born 1904

fashion designer
Russian
Index t Wom

943. Klein, Anne; Hannah Golofsky
1905/23–1974
fashion designer
Jewish
New York
Nat Cyc Am Bio v58; Obit File

944. McCardell, Claire (Harris)
1905–58
fashion designer
Dict Am Bio supp v6; Index t
  Wom; Not Am Wom supp v1;
  Obit File

945. Roebling, Mary Gindhart
born 1905/06
banker
Episcopalian
Trenton, NJ
Index t Wom; Nat Cyc Am Bio
  csv9

946. Webster, Margaret
1905–72
theatrical director, actor, author,
  producer
Cur Biog '73; Index t Wom; Not
  Am Wom supp v1

947. Wurster, Catherine Bauer
1905–64
advertising executive, international consultant on housing and
  city planning, journalist
Nat Cyc Am Bio v51

948. Zorbaugh, Geraldine Bone
born 1905
radio and television executive,
  lawyer
Index t Wom

949. Bishop, Hazel
born 1906
industrial chemist, manufacturer
Index t Wom

950. Brady, Mildred Edie
1906–65
consumer advocate, editor, journalist
Not Am Wom supp v1

951. Cochran, Jacqueline; Mrs.
  Floyd B. Odlum
1906/10–1980
aviator, director of the Women's
  Air Force Service Pilots, flight
  captain in the US Air Force,
  colonel in the Air Force Reserve, World War II correspondent, business executive,
  cosmetician
Cur Biog '80; Index t Wom; Nat
  Cyc Am Bio csv10

952. Custin, Mildred
born 1906
business executive
Index t Wom

953. Dunnigan, Alice Allison
born 1906
journalist, educator, economist
Index t Wom

954. Jackson, Martha Kellogg
1906–69
art dealer
Nat Cyc Am Bio v55

955. Patterson, Alicia; Alice
  Guggenheim
1906–63
Newsday founder, newspaper editor and publisher
Index t Wom; Not Am Wom
  supp vl; Obit File

956. Chase, Lucia
born 1907
ballet dancer, director of the
  American Ballet Theater
Cur Biog '75; Index t Wom

957. Irene
1907–62
fashion designer
Index t Wom

**958. Carey, Ernestine Moller
  Gilbreth**
born 1908
author, retail executive
Index t Wom

959. Crawford, Joan
1908–77
screen actor, director of the Pepsi-Cola Co.
Hollywood, CA
Cur Biog '77; Index t Wom; Obit
  File

960. Fisher, Katherine A.
died 1958
home economist, director of the
  Good Housekeeping Institute
Canadian
Obit File

961. Hall, Marjory
born 1908
author, businessperson
Index t Wom

962. Harrison, Joan Mary
circa 1908
producer, scenarist
English
Index t Wom

963. Rosenthal, Jean
1908/12–1969
theatrical lighting designer, specialist and consultant
Index t Wom; Not Am Wom
  supp vl; Obit File

**964. Schnurer, Carolyn Gold-
  sand**
born 1908
fashion designer
Index t Wom

965. Thompson, Helen Muford
1908–74
orchestra manager, executive of
  the American Symphony Orchestra League
Not Am Wom supp v1

**966. Winters, Jeannette Epler
  McPheeters**
born 1908
manufacturer
Presbyterian
Indiana
Nat Cyc Am Bio csv8

**967. Barnes, Florence Lowe
  "Pancho"**
1909–75
aviator, motion-picture stunt pilot, resort owner
Index t Wom; Obit File

968. Parnis, Mollie
born 1909
fashion designer, businessperson
Index t Wom

969. Barbour, Ella
flourished 1940s
home economist, restaurateur
Index t Wom

970. Cowles, Fleur Fenton
born 1910
painter, editor, author, businessperson
Index t Wom

971. Cullman, Marguerite
married 1935
theatrical producer
Index t Wom

972. Dalrymple, Jean
born 1910
theatrical publicist, producer, director
Index t Wom

973. Edwards, Ester Gordy
flourished 1940s–70s
publishing executive, vice-president of Motown Records
Black
Encyc Black Am

974. Evans, Margaret B.
flourished 1940s–50s
printer
Index t Wom

975. Fitzgerald, Pegeen
born 1910
advertising, sales, and fashion director
Index t Wom

976. Kahane, Melanie
born 1910
interior decorator, industrial engineer
Index t Wom

977. Milgrim, Sally
flourished 1940s
fashion designer
Index t Wom

978. Murray, Evelyn
flourished 1940s
employment consultant
Index t Wom

979. Palmer, Bernice
flourished 1940s
aircraft inventor
Index t Wom

980. Parker, Gladys
1910–66
fashion designer, cartoonist
Index t Wom; Obit File

981. Pennoyer, Sara
flourished 1940s
retail executive
Index t Wom

982. Schain, Josephine
flourished 1940s
consultant, social worker, lecturer
Index t Wom

983. Selznick, Irene
born 1910
theatrical producer
Index t Wom

984. Showalter, Edna Blanche
flourished 1940s
singer, music educator, pianist,
  manager
Index t Wom

985. Smith, Quincy
flourished 1940s
aircraft inventor
Index t Wom

986. Stein, Camille L.
flourished 1940s
airline executive
Index t Wom

987. Stewart, Ellen
flourished 1940s–70s
off-off-Broadway theatrical producer
Black
Cur Biog '73

988. Wilson, Elva
flourished 1940s
aircraft inventor
Index t Wom

989. Armstrong, Alice Catt
born 1911
biographer, book publisher

Religious Scientist
California
Nat Cyc Am Bio csv10

990. Briney, Nancy Wells
born 1911
publisher, editor
Index t Wom

991. Gibbons, Irene
died 1962
movie fashion designer
Hollywood, CA
Obit File

992. Jones, Margo
1912–55
Broadway stage producer and director, founder of the modern American concept of theater-in-the-round
Not Am Wom supp v1; Obit File

993. Reid, Rose Marie
1912–78
fashion designer
Obit File

994. Trigere, Pauline
born 1912
fashion designer
French
Index t Wom

995. Bondy, Elizabeth Jeanne Hale
1913–69
literary agent, book editor
Congregationalist
New York
Nat Cyc Am Bio v54

996. Gerlette, Anne
1913–58
actor, director, producer, dramatics teacher
Canadian
Obit File

997. Heywood, Anne
circa 1913–61
businessperson, vocational counselor
Index t Wom

998. Porter, Sylvia Field Feldman
born 1913
economics journalist, financial columnist, author
Jewish
Cur Biog '80; Index t Wom

999. Colby, Anita
born 1914
actor, technical adviser, journalist, editor
Index t Wom

1000. Culver, Agnes Moe
1914–75
illustration dealer, historian

Congregationalist
New York
Nat Cyc Am Bio v58 and v59

1001. Davis, Arlene Palsgraff
died 1964
aviator, business executive
Index t Wom

1002. May, Catherine Dean
born 1914
representative to Congress, radio commentator, radio producer
Index t Wom

1003. Smith, Hazel Brannon
born 1914
publisher and editor of Mississippi daily newspapers, Pulitzer Prize winner, civil rights worker
Mississippi
Cur Biog '73

1004. Twomey, Kathleen "Kay"

born 1914
author, designer, songwriter
Index t Wom

1005. Fisher, Doris
born 1915
composer, singer, producer, author
Index t Wom

1006. Knauer, Virginia Harrington (Wright)
born 1915
consumer affairs worker, special assistant for consumer affairs to President Nixon
Cur Biog '70

1007. Sokolow, Anna
born 1915
choreographer, director, dancer, dance educator
Jewish
Cur Biog '69

1008. Leach, Ruth Marian
born 1916
business executive
Index t Wom

1009. Graham, Katharine (Meyer)
born 1917
president of the Washington Post Co.
Cur Biog '70

1010. Moss, Elizabeth Murphy
born 1917
business executive, World War II correspondent
Black
Encyc Black Am

1011. Raedler, Dorothy Florence
born 1917

theatrical producer
Index t Wom

1012. Smith, Mary Elizabeth Leinen
born 1917
business executive, worker for the welfare of the handicapped, philanthropist
Nat Cyc Am Bio csv13

1013. Frankfurt, Elsie
born 1918
fashion designer
Index t Wom

1014. Fogarty, Anne
1919–80
fashion designer
Cur Biog '80; Index t Wom

1015. Gillis, Ann; Ann Slocum
1919–57
NBC radio and television producer
Obit File

1016. Leigh, Dorian
born 1919
business executive
Index t Wom

1017. Chambers, Yolande Hargrave
flourished 1950s–60s
lawyer, business executive
Black
Encyc Black Am

1018. Guest, Barbara
born 1920
poet, theatrical producer
New York
Dict Lit Bio v5

1019. Hershman, Aleene
flourished 1950s
businessperson
Index t Wom

1020. Hoyle, Ethel
flourished 1950s
printer, type designer
Index t Wom

1021. Lee, Frances Marron
flourished 1950s–60s
rancher, politician
Index t Wom

1022. Lee, Peggy; Peggy Lee Barbour
born 1920
singer, composer, actor, businessperson
Index t Wom

1023. Shera, Florence B.
flourished 1950s
printer, club leader
Index t Wom

1024. Thompson, Myrtle Grey
flourished 1950s–60s
aviator, airport operator
Index t Wom

1025. Willis, Gertrude Geddes
died 1970
business executive
Black
Encyc Black Am

1026. Worman, Donna
flourished 1950s
businessperson
Index t Wom

1027. Comiskey, Grace Lou
1921–52
co-owner of the Chicago White Sox baseball team
Chicago, IL
Obit File

1028. Kreps, Juanita M(orris)
born 1921
US secretary of commerce, university educator, economist
Cur Biog '77

1029. Luckenbach, Andrea
1921–62
vice-president of the Luckenbach Steamship Co.
Obit File

1030. McClendon, Ernestine
born 1921
theatrical agent
Black
Negro Alman

1031. Ford, Eileen (Otte)
born 1922
founder and president of the Ford Modeling Agency
Cur Biog '70

1032. McWhinney, Adeline H(ouston)
born 1922
banking executive, founder and president of the First Women's Bank
New York, NY
Cur Biog '76

1033. Bentley, Helen Delich
born 1923
newspaper journalist, chairperson of the Federal Maritime Commission, marine shipping expert, television documentary producer
Cur Biog '71

1034. Davis, Georgia M.
born 1923
business executive, Kentucky state senator, Black civil rights worker
Kentucky

Black
Encyc Black Am

1035. Williams, Esther
born 1923
aquacade and screen swimmer, actor, businessperson
Hall Fame Sport; Index t Wom

1036. Cook, Celestine Strode
born 1924
business executive, civic leader
New Orleans, LA
Black
Encyc Black Am

1037. Ford, Mary
1924–77
popular singer, guitarist, codeveloper of the recording technique of multiple harmonies
Index t Wom; Obit File

1038. Henderson, Vivian
1924–76
president of Clark College, labor economist
Atlanta, GA
Obit File

1039. Smith, Virginia Beatrice
born 1924
president of Vassar College, economist
Cur Biog '78

1040. Stutz, Geraldine
born 1924
businessperson, fashion expert
Index t Wom

1041. Banuelos, Ramona Acosta
born 1925
US treasurer, banker
Los Angeles, CA
Mexican
Dict Mex Am Hist

1042. Brennan, Ella
born 1925
restaurateur
Index t Wom

1043. Jones, Candy
born 1925
businessperson
Index t Wom

1044. Fox, Carol
1926–81
producer and manager of the Chicago Opera
Chicago, IL
Cur Biog '78 and '81

1045. Peden, Katherine Graham
born 1926
organization official, business executive
Index t Wom

1046. Olivarez, Graciela
born 1928
lawyer, United Way executive, civil rights worker
Mexican
Dict Mex Am Hist

1047. Wells, Mary Georgene Berg
born 1928
advertising executive
Index t Wom

1048. Cooney, Joan Ganz
born 1929
television executive, educational-television programer
Cur Biog '70

1049. Lind, Shirley Motter
born 1929
editor, publisher
Black
Encyc Black Am

1050. Bowen, Ruth
born 1930
businessperson, founder of a talent booking agency
Black
Encyc Black Am; Negro Alman

1051. Clayton, Xernona
1930/33–post 1952
television producer, television personality, television host
Black
Encyc Black Am; Negro Alman

1052. Fornes, Maria Irene
born 1930
playwright, theatrical director
New York
Cuban
Dict Lit Bio v7

1053. Massey, Edna Hogner
flourished 1960s
interior designer, arts and crafts specialist
Native American (Cherokee)
Ind Today

1054. Wallace, Gladys Sky
flourished 1960s
stockbroker
Native American (Peoria)
Ind Today

1055. Sanders, Marlene
born 1931
television broadcast journalist, ABC News executive, director of television documentaries
Cur Biog '81

1056. Pfeiffer, Jane (Cahill)
born 1932
chairperson of the board of NBC, IBM executive
Cur Biog '80

1057. Radziwill, Lee (Bouvier)
born 1933
interior decorator
Cur Biog '77

1058. Verdy, Violette
born 1933
ballet dancer, manager of the Boston Ballet
French
Cur Biog '69 and '80

1059. Whitman, Marina von Neumann
born 1935
international economist, university educator, member of the Council of Economic Advisors
Cur Biog '73

1060. Turnure, Pamela
born 1937
press secretary
Index t Wom

1061. Bryant, Hazel J.
born 1939
singer, actor, producer
Black
Encyc Black Am

1062. Taylor, Lynette Dobbins
flourished 1970s
editor, executive
Black
Negro Alman

1063. Barry, Mary Treadwell
born 1941
executive and cofounder of Pride Corp.
Black
Negro Alman

1064. Murray, Joan
born 1941
television newscaster, advertising executive
Black
Encyc Black Am; Negro Alman

1065. Lagace, Sherry
1944–75
strip miner
Kentucky
Obit File

1066. Lansing, Sherry
born 1944
president of production at Twentieth Century–Fox
Cur Biog '81

1067. Davis, Christine R.
flourished 1976
publishing executive; staff director, US House Committee on Government Operations, 1949
Black
Negro Alman; Negro Her Lib v1

1068. von Furstenberg, Diane
born 1946
fashion designer, business executive
Cur Biog '76

1069. Onassis, Christina
born 1950
shipping magnate
Cur Biog '76

1070. Swados, Elizabeth
born 1951
play score writer, avant-garde composer, theatrical director, playwright
Jewish
New York
Cur Biog '79

No Dates

1071. Benjamin, Mary A.
autograph dealer
Index t Wom

1072. Carter, Amy
aircraft factory instructor
Index t Wom

1073. Mark, Joyce
pioneer airline radio operator
Index t Wom

1074. Parsons, Harriet Oettinger
motion picture producer, writer
Index t Wom

1075. Woolsey, Betty
skier and skisport builder
Hall Fame Sport

CIVIL RIGHTS

1076. Brant, Mary; Molly Brant; Deganiwadonte
circa 1736–96
British advocate, worker for Native American rights
Native American (Mohawk-Iroquois)
Great North Am Ind; Not Am Wom; Read Encyc Am West

1077. Ward, Nancy; Nanye hi; The Pocahontas of the West
circa 1738/40–1822
Native American leader and civil rights advocate
Native American (Cherokee)
Cyc Am Bio; Great North Am Ind; Not Am Wom; Who Who Dur Am Rev

1078. Sanders, Elizabeth (Elkins)
1762–1851/54

social critic, pamphleteer, author, history writer on Massachusetts, Native American rights worker
Salem, MA
Cyc Am Bio; Dict Am Auth; Dict Am Bio; Dict Am Bio Men Time; Not Am Wom

1079. Truth, Sojourner; Isabel Baumfree
1775/97–1883/85
social reformer, abolitionist, feminist, lecturer, temperance writer
Black
Cyc Am Bio; Dict Am Rel Bio; Encyc Black Am; Index t Wom; Negro Alman; Not Am Wom; Prof Negro Wom v1

1080. Follen, Eliza Lee (Cabot)
1787–1859/60
children's author, poet, abolitionist
Cyc Am Bio; Dict Am Auth; Dict Am Bio; Dict Am Bio Men Time; Index t Wom; Not Am Wom; Twent Cen Bio Dict Not Am; Dict Lit Bio v1

1081. d'Arusmont, Frances Wright
1789–1852
abolitionist, political essayist, author
Scottish
Am Bio Dict; Dict Am Auth

1082. Minor, Jane
flourished 1820s
nurse, liberator of slaves
Black
Prof Negro Wom v1

1083. Folsom, Abby
circa 1792–1867
abolitionist
Cyc Am Bio; Nat Cyc Am Bio v2

1084. Grimke, Sarah Moore
1792/93–1873
abolitionist, women's rights worker, writer on social problems, political author, lecturer
Quaker
Cyc Am Bio; Dict Am Auth; Dict Am Bio; Dict Am Rel Bio; Index t Wom; Nat Cyc Am Bio v2; Twent Cen Bio Dict Not Am; Wom Cent

1085. Smith, Julia Evelina
1792–1886/92
suffragist, women's rights worker, abolitionist, Biblical translator
Connecticut
Cyc Am Bio; Dict Am Bio; Nat Cyc Am Bio v7; Not Am Wom

1086. Mott, Lucretia (Coffin)
1793–1880

abolitionist, feminist, Quaker minister, pacifist
Quaker
Cyc Am Bio; Dict Am Bio; Dict Am Bio Men Time; Dict Am Rel Bio; Index t Wom; Nat Cyc Am Bio v2; Not Am Wom; Twent Cen Bio Dict Not Am; Wom Cent

1087. Wright, Frances (d'Arusmont) "Fanny"; Fanny d'Arusmont
1795–1852
author, abolitionist, feminist, philanthropist, lecturer
Scottish
Am Bio Dict; Cyc Am Bio; Dict Am Bio; Dict Am Bio Men Time; Index t Wom; Nat Cyc Am Bio v2; Not Am Wom

1088. Cox, Hannah
1796/97–1876
abolitionist, temperance worker, pacifist, women's rights worker
Quaker
Cyc Am Bio; Dict Am Bio; Index t Wom

1089. Smith, Abigail Hadassah "Abby"
1796/97–1878
suffragist, women's rights worker, abolitionist
Connecticut
Cyc Am Bio; Dict Am Bio; Nat Cyc Am Bio v7; Not Am Wom

1090. Forten, Harriet
flourished 1830s
abolitionist
Philadelphia, PA
Black
Prof Negro Wom v1

1091. Forten, Margaretta
flourished 1830s
abolitionist
Philadelphia, PA
Black
Prof Negro Wom v1

1092. Forten, Sarah Louisa
flourished 1830s
abolitionist
Philadelphia, PA
Black
Prof Negro Wom v1

1093. Pugh, Sarah
1800–84
educator, abolitionist, suffragist
Not Am Wom

1094. Seward, Maria
flourished 1830s; died 188?
Black women's rights worker
Black
Index t Wom

1095. Gibbons, Abigail Hopper "Abby"
1801–93
abolitionist, prison reformer, feminist, women's welfare worker, Civil War nurse, philanthropist, journalist
Quaker
Cyc Am Bio; Dict Am Bio; Index t Wom; Nat Cyc Am Bio v7; Not Am Wom; Twent Cen Bio Dict Not Am; Wom Cent

1096. Child, Lydia Maria (Francis)
1802–80
author, philanthropist, abolitionist, editor, social reformer
Quaker
Massachusetts
Cyc Am Bio; Dict Am Auth; Dict Am Bio; Dict Am Bio Men Time; Dict Lit Bio v1; Index t Wom; Nat Cyc Am Bio v2; Not Am Wom; Twent Cen Bio Dict Not Am; Wom Cent

1097. Fayerweather, Sarah Harris
1802/20–1870
Underground Railroad worker, abolitionist
Black
Index t Wom; Negro Alman; Prof Negro Wom v1

1098. Crandall, Prudence (Philles)
1803–1889/90
educator of Blacks, abolitionist, philanthropist
Quaker
English
Cyc Am Bio; Dict Am Bio; Eng Wom; Index t Wom; Nat Cyc Am Bio v2; Not Am Wom; Twent Cen Bio Dict Not Am

1099. Green, Frances Harriet (Whipple)
1805–78
author, poet, abolitionist, botanist
Cyc Am Bio; Dict Am Bio; Dict Am Bio Men Time

1100. Grimke, Angelina Emily; Angelina Emily Grimke Weld
1805/38–1879
abolitionist, feminist, lecturer
Quaker
Cyc Am Bio; Dict Am Auth; Dict Am Rel Bio; Index t Wom; Nat Cyc Am Bio v2; Twent Cen Bio Dict Not Am

1101. Martin, Sarah Towne (Smith); Sarah Martyn
1805–79
historian, religious and historical writer for children, editor, abolitionist, temperance worker

New York, NY
Cyc Am Bio; Dict Am Auth; Dict Am Bio; Twent Cen Bio Dict Not Am

1102. Chace, Elizabeth Buffum
1806–99
abolitionist, suffragist, women's rights worker, prison reformer, temperance worker
Quaker
Dict Am Bio; Not Am Wom; Twent Cen Bio Dict Not Am; Wom Cent

1103. Chapman, Maria Weston
1806–85
abolitionist, feminist, philanthropist
Dict Am Bio; Index t Wom; Nat Cyc Am Bio v2; Not Am Wom; Twent Cen Bio Dict Not Am

1104. Cook, Martha Elizabeth Duncan Walker
1806–74
magazine editor, author, linguist, translator, abolitionist, patron of Polish arts and artists
Cyc Am Bio; Dict Am Bio

1105. Douglass, Sarah Mapps Douglass
1806–82
educator, abolitionist
Philadelphia, PA
Black
Negro Alman; Not Am Wom; Prof Negro Wom v1

1106. Pyles, Charlotta Gordon
1806–80
abolitionist, social reformer
Black
Index t Wom; Negro Alman

1107. Chandler, Elizabeth Margaret
1807–1834/35
author, poet, abolitionist
Delaware
Cyc Am Bio; Dict Am Auth; Dict Am Bio; Dict Am Bio Men Time; Index t Wom; Not Am Wom; Twent Cen Bio Dict Not Am

1108. Gage, Frances Dana (Barker); Aunt Fanny
1808–84
lecturer, author, temperance worker, abolitionist, suffragist, women's rights worker, Civil War relief worker
Cyc Am Bio; Dict Am Auth; Dict Am Bio; Dict Am Bio Men Time; Index t Wom; Nat Cyc Am Bio v2; Not Am Wom; Twent Cen Bio Dict Not Am; Wom Cent

1109. Haviland, Laura Smith
1808–98
abolitionist, freedmen's welfare worker, philanthropist
Quaker
Cyc Am Bio; Not Am Wom

1110. Kemble, Frances Anne "Fanny"; Fanny Kemble Butler
1809/11–1893
actor, diarist, author, abolitionist
Georgia
English
Cyc Am Bio; Dict Am Bio; Dict Am Bio Men Time; Dict Nat Bio supp; Encyc South Hist; Index t Wom; Nat Cyc Am Bio v3; Not Am Wom

1111. Foster, Abigail (Kelley) "Abby"
1810/11–1887
abolitionist, feminist, Prohibitionist, lecturer, suffragist, temperance worker
Quaker
Cyc Am Bio; Dict Am Bio; Index t Wom; Nat Cyc Am Bio v2; Not Am Wom; Twent Cen Bio Dict Not Am

1112. Rose, Ernestine Louise Lasmond Siismondi Potowski
1810–92
feminist, women's rights worker, temperance worker, abolitionist
Jewish
Polish
Cyc Am Bio; Dict Am Bio; Not Am Wom

1113. Ball, Martha Violet
born 1811
abolitionist, philanthropist, educator of Black women
Baptist
Wom Cent

1114. Stowe, Harriet Elizabeth Beecher
1811/12–1896
author, abolitionist, social reformer, theologian
Connecticut
Cyc Am Bio; Dict Am Auth; Dict Am Bio; Dict Am Bio Men Time; Dict Am Rel Bio; Dict Lit Bio v1; Nat Cyc Am Bio v1; Not Am Wom; Twent Cen Bio Dict Not Am; Wom Cent; Wom Lit; Wom Lit, More

1115. Davis, Pauline Kellog Wright
1813–76
feminist, women's rights worker, suffragist, abolitionist, temper-

ance worker, journalist, editor, lecturer
Cyc Am Bio; Dict Am Bio; Index t Wom; Nat Cyc Am Bio v22; Not Am Wom

1116. Grew, Mary
1813–96
abolitionist, suffragist, feminist, Unitarian preacher, lecturer
Unitarian
Index t Wom; Not Am Wom; Wom Cent

1117. Jones, Jane Elizabeth Hitchcock
1813–96
antislavery and women's rights advocate, lecturer
Index t Wom; Not Am Wom

1118. Collins, Emily Parmely
born 1814
suffragist, abolitionist, political writer, Civil War nurse
Hartford, CT
Wom Cent

1119. Griffing, Josephine Sophia White
1814–72
abolitionist, feminist, suffragist, welfare worker
Dict Am Bio; Index t Wom; Not Am Wom

1120. Pleasant, Mary Ellen "Mammy"
1814?–1904
pioneer, boardinghouse keeper, civil rights advocate
California
Black
Not Am Wom

1121. Spear, Catherine Swan Brown
born 1814
educator, abolitionist, Underground Railroad worker, prison reformer, suffragist
Wom Cent

1122. Comstock, Elizabeth Leslie Rous
1815–1891/92
social reformer, abolitionist, Underground Railroad worker, pacifist, freed slave's welfare worker, temperance reformer, women's rights worker, Quaker minister, prison reformer, Civil War nurse
Quaker
Dict Am Bio; Index t Wom; Nat Cyc Am Bio v22; Not Am Wom

1123. Miner, Myrtilla
1815–64

educator, pioneer in teacher education for Black women, abolitionist, philanthropist
Cyc Am Bio; Dict Am Bio; Not Am Wom

1124. Remond, Sarah Parker
1815/26–post 1887
abolitionist, antislavery lecturer, physician
Black
Negro Alman; Not Am Wom; Prof Negro Wom v1

1125. Swisshelm, Jane (Grey) (Cannon)
1815/16–1884
journalist, author, editor, publisher, abolitionist, women's rights worker, Civil War nurse
Cyc Am Bio; Dict Am Auth; Dict Am Bio; Dict Am Bio Men Time; Index t Wom; Nat Cyc Am Bio v2; Not Am Wom

1126. Whittier, Elizabeth Hussey
1815–64
poet, abolitionist, religious worker
Quaker
Cyc Am Bio; Index t Wom; Nat Cyc Am Bio v8

1127. Bonney, Mary Lucinda
1816–1900
Native American rights advocate, educator
Not Am Wom

1128. Gardner, Anna
born 1816
abolitionist, educator of freedmen, women's rights worker
Wom Cent

1129. Rambaut, Mary Lucinda Bonney
1816–1900
Native American rights worker, educator
Baptist
Dict Am Bio; Index t Wom; Nat Cyc Am Bio v6; Twent Cen Bio Dict Not Am; Wom Cent

1130. Coleman, Lucy Newhall; Lucy Colman
1817–1906
abolitionist, educator of Blacks, women's rights worker, suffragist, lecturer, health reformer
Universalist
Dict Am Bio; Nat Cyc Am Bio v4, Wom Cent

1131. Holley, Sallie
1818–93
abolitionist, educator of freedmen, feminist, lecturer
Index t Wom; Not Am Wom

1132. Stone, Lucy; Mrs. Henry Brown Blackwell
1818–93
feminist, suffragist, women's rights worker, abolitionist, social reformer, editor, lecturer
Massachusetts
Cyc Am Bio; Dict Am Bio; Dict Am Bio Men Time; Index t Wom; Nat Cyc Am Bio v2 and v29; Not Am Wom; Twent Cen Bio Dict Not Am; Wom Cent

1133. Cutter, Eunice Powers
1819–93
lecturer, health reformer, abolitionist, historian
Twent Cen Bio Dict Not Am

1134. Greene, Louisa Morton
born 1819
author, abolitionist, suffragist, women's rights worker, temperance worker, Civil War relief worker
Wom Cent

1135. Howe, Julia Ward
1819–1910
poet, dramatist, songwriter, lecturer, suffrage and women's club leader, feminist, abolitionist, pacifist, prison reformer, Union patriot during the Civil War, philanthropist, traveler
Boston, MA
Cyc Am Bio; Dict Am Auth; Dict Am Bio; Dict Am Bio Men Time; Dict Lit Bio v1; Index t Wom; Nat Cyc Am Bio v1; Not Am Wom; Twent Cen Bio Dict Not Am; Wom Cent

1136. Pinkham, Lydia Estes
1819–83
patent medicine proprietor, abolitionist, temperance worker, women's rights worker
Quaker
Dict Am Bio; Not Am Wom

1137. Sewall, Harriet (Winslow)
1819–89
suffragist, poet, religious poet, abolitionist
Transcendentalist
Boston, MA
Dict Am Auth; Nat Cyc Am Bio v10

1138. Anthony, Susan Brownell
1820–1906
women's suffrage leader, feminist, abolitionist, newspaper publisher, editor

Quaker
Appl Cyc Am Bio; Cyc Am Bio;
Dict Am Bio; Dict Am Bio Men
Time; Index t Wom; Nat Cyc
Am Bio v4; Not Am Wom;
Twent Cen Bio Dict Not Am;
Wom Cent

1139. Gleason, Rachel Brooks
1820–1905
physician, medical author, abolitionist, patron of freedmen's education, dress reformer,
women's rights worker
Dict Am Auth; Index t Wom;
Wom Cent

**1140. Livermore, Mary Ashton
(Rice)**
1820/21–1905
health reformer, hospital adminis-
trator, suffragist, temperance
worker, abolitionist, Civil War
patriot, miscellaneous author
Universalist
Melrose, MA
Cyc Am Bio; Dict Am Auth; Dict
Am Bio Men Time; Dict Am
Rel Bio; Index t Wom; Nat Cyc
Am Bio v1; Not Am Wom;
Twent Cen Bio Dict Not Am;
Wom Cent

1141. Mather, Sarah Ann
born 1820
philanthropist, patron of Black
education, educator, author
South Carolina
Index t Wom; Wom Cent

**1142. Severance, Carolina Ma-
ria (Seymour)**
1820–1914
social reformer, women's club
leader, women's rights worker,
feminist, abolitionist
Dict Am Bio; Index t Wom; Nat
Cyc Am Bio v8; Not Am Wom;
Wom Cent

1143. Tubman, Harriet Ross
1820/26–1913
hero of the Underground Railroad, liberator of slaves, abolitionist, Union spy during the
Civil War, Civil War nurse, lecturer
Black
Cyc Am Bio; Dict Am Bio; Encyc
Black Am; Encyc South Hist;
Index t Wom; Nat Cyc Am Bio
v9; Negro Alman; Not Am
Wom; Prof Negro Wom v1

1144. Diaz, Abby (Morton)
1821–1904
author, children's author, essayist, social reformer, suffragist,
abolitionist, lecturer

Boston, MA
Dict Am Auth; Nat Cyc Am Bio
v11; Not Am Wom; Twent Cen
Bio Dict Not Am; Wom Cent

**1145. Morse, Rebecca A.; Ruth
Moza; R. A. Kidder; R. A.
K.**
born 1821
clubwoman, Sorosis member, suffragist, patron of art, abolitionist, author
New York
Index t Wom; Wom Cent

1146. Whitney, Anne
1821–1915
sculptor, artist, poet, abolitionist,
suffragist
Boston, MA
Cyc Am Bio; Dict Am Auth; Dict
Am Bio; Index t Wom; Nat Cyc
Am Bio v7; Not Am Wom;
Wom Cent

1147. Delaney, Catherine A.
1822–94
Black civil rights leader
Black
Index t Wom

1148. Dixon, Mary J. Scarlett
born 1822
physician, abolitionist
Pennsylvania
Wom Cent

1149. Cary, Mary Ann Shad
1823–93
educator, lawyer, journalist, editor, abolitionist, Canadian pioneer
Black; Canadian
Index t Wom; Negro Alman; Not
Am Wom; Prof Negro Wom

**1150. Douglass, Margaret Crit-
tenden**
flourished 1853
educator, founder of a school for
Black children that was closed
by authorities
Cyc Am Bio

1151. Kemp, Agnes Nininger
born 1823
physician, abolitionist, temperance worker, lecturer
Wom Cent

**1152. Peake, Mary Smith Kel-
sey**
1823–62
educator of freedmen, Union patriot in the Civil War
Black
Index t Wom; Negro Alman; Prof
Negro Wom v1

1153. Stebbins, Catherine A. F.
1823–post 1880

social reformer, abolitionist, feminist, suffragist
Index t Wom; Wom Cent

**1154. Cheney, Endah Dow (Lit-
tlehale)**
1824–1904
philanthropist, author, abolitionist, suffragist, women's rights
worker, Black civil rights worker, lecturer, philosopher
Transcendentalist
Boston, MA
Cyc Am Bio; Dict Am Auth; Dict
Am Bio; Dict Lit Bio v1; Index
t Wom; Nat Cyc Am Bio v9;
Not Am Wom; Twent Cen Bio
Dict Not Am; Wom Cent

1155. Packard, Sophia B.
1824–91
founder of Spelman College,
church worker, educator of
Blacks
Baptist
Atlanta, GA
Nat Cyc Am Bio v2; Not Am
Wom

**1156. Blackwell, Antoinette
Louisa (Brown)**
1825–1921
Universalist minister, author, lec-
turer, temperance worker, aboli-
tionist, suffragist, women's
rights worker, philosopher,
poet, novelist
Unitarian; Congregationalist
Appl Cyc Am Bio; Cyc Am Bio;
Dict Am Bio; Dict Am Bio Men
Time; Index t Wom; Nat Cyc
Am Bio v9 and v29; Not Am
Wom; Twent Cen Bio Dict Not
Am; Wom Cent

**1157. Harper, Frances Ellen
Watkins**
1825–1911
poet, lecturer, author, abolitionist
Black
Dict Am Rel Bio; Encyc Black
Am; Index t Wom; Negro Alman; Not Am Wom; Prof Ne-
gro Wom v1

**1158. Robinson, Harriet Jane
(Hanson)**
1825–1911
suffragist, women's rights worker,
feminist, abolitionist, author,
poet, dramatist, journalist, mer-
chant
Malden, MA
Cyc Am Bio; Dict Am Auth; Dict
Am Bio; Index t Wom; Nat Cyc
Am Bio v3; Not Am Wom;
Wom Cent

1159. Towne, Laura Matilda
1825–1901
educator of freedmen
Not Am Wom

1160. Craft, Ellen
circa 1826–circa 1897
fugitive slave, abolitionist, lecturer
Black
Index t Wom; Not Am Wom

1161. Gage, Matilda Joslyn
1826–98
feminist, suffragist, abolitionist,
author, lecturer
Cyc Am Bio; Dict Am Auth; Dict
Am Bio; Index t Wom; Nat Cyc
Am Bio v2; Not Am Wom;
Twent Cen Bio Dict Not Am;
Wom Cent

1162. Howland, Emily
1827–1929
educator, educator of Blacks, abolitionist, suffragist, pacifist, temperance worker, philanthropist
Quaker
New York
Dict Am Bio; Nat Cyc Am Bio
v25; Not Am Wom; Wom Cent

**1163. Slenker, Elmina (Drake);
Aunt Elmina**
born 1827
miscellaneous author, abolitionist
Snowville, VA
Cyc Am Bio; Dict Am Auth; Nat
Cyc Am Bio v7

**1164. Hill, Caroline Sherman
Andrews**
1829–1914
civil rights leader
Black
Index t Wom

1165. May, Abigail Williams
1829–88
Boston social reformer, abolitionist, suffragist, education commissioner, Civil War relief
worker
Boston, MA
Index t Wom; Not Am Wom;
Twent Cen Bio Dict Not Am

**1166. Patton, Abigail Jemima;
Abby Hutchinson**
1829–92
alto singer, composer, poet, social
reformer, abolitionist, suffragist,
hymn writer, feminist
New York; New Hampshire
Nat Cyc Am Bio v10; Wom Cent;
Not Am Wom; Index t Wom

**1167. Avery, Rosa Miller; Sue
Smith**
1830–94
author, abolitionist, suffragist
Index t Wom; Nat Cyc Am Bio
v6; Wom Cent

**1168. Dodge, Mary Abigail
"Abby"; Gail Hamilton**
1830/36–1896

author, essayist, humorist, magazine writer, editor, abolitionist, suffragist, women's rights worker
Massachusetts
Cyc Am Bio; Dict Am Auth; Dict Am Bio; Dict Am Bio Men Time; Index t Wom; Nat Cyc Am Bio v9; Not Am Wom; Twent Cen Bio Dict Not Am; Wom Cent

1169. Granson, Milla
flourished pre-1860s
educator of slaves
Mississippi
Black
Prof Negro Wom v1

1170. Jackson, Helen Maria (Fiske) (Hunt); Saxe Holme; H. H.
1830/31–1881/85
author, poet, novelist, crusader for Native American rights, philanthropist
Quaker
Cyc Am Bio; Dict Am Auth; Dict Am Bio; Index t Wom; Nat Cyc Am Bio v1; Not Am Wom; Read Encyc Am West; Twent Cen Bio Dict Not Am; Wom Cent; Wom Lit, More

1171. Wells, Mary Fletcher
flourished 1860s–90s
philanthropist, educator of freedmen
Alabama
Wom Cent

1172. Doolittle, Lucy Salisbury
born 1832
philanthropist, reformer of women's prisons, suffragist, educator of freedwomen
Wom Cent

1173. Douglass, Anna Murray
died 1882
Underground Railroad worker, abolitionist
Black
Index t Wom; Negro Alman; Prof Negro Wom v1

1174. Russell, Elizabeth Augusta
born 1832
philanthropist, Freedmen's Bureau worker, temperance worker
Wom Cent

1175. Quinton, Amelia Stone
1833–1926
Native American reform and rights worker, temperance

worker, club leader, humanitarian
Index t Wom; Not Am Wom; Twent Cen Bio Dict Not Am; Wom Cent

1176. Severance, Juliet H.
born 1833
physician, abolitionist, feminist, temperance worker, political activist
Spiritualist
Wom Cent

1177. Grubb, Sophronia Farrington Naylor
born 1834
temperance worker, freedmen's welfare worker
Wom Cent

1178. Howe, Mary Ann
1835–70
educator of Blacks, philanthropist
Nat Cyc Am Bio v8

1179. Converse, Harriet Maxwell; Ya-ie-wah-no; Salome; Musidora
1836–1903
Seneca rights advocate, Seneca tribal leader, author, folklorist, Native American scholar, poet
New York
Native American (Seneca by adoption)
Dict Am Auth; Not Am Wom; Twent Cen Bio Dict Not Am; Wom Cent

1180. Stearns, Sarah Burger
1836–post 1899
suffragist, women's rights worker, philanthropist, Civil War humanitarian, temperance worker, social reformer, educator of freedmen
Unitarian
Cyc Am Bio; Index t Wom; Nat Cyc Am Bio v10; Twent Cen Bio Dict Not Am; Wom Cent

1181. Dickey, Sarah Ann
1838–1904
educator of freedmen
Not Am Wom

1182. Fletcher, Alice Cunningham
1838/45–1923
ethnologist, Native American rights worker, writer on Native American music
Dict Am Auth; Dict Am Bio; Index t Wom; Nat Cyc Am Bio v5; Not Am Wom; Twent Cen Bio Dict Not Am; Wom Cent

1183. Freeman, Mattie A.
born 1839

abolitionist, suffragist, women's rights worker, lecturer, journalist
Chicago, IL
Wom Cent

1184. Hancock, Cornelia
1839/40–1927
Civil War nurse, educator of freedmen, charity worker, housing reformer
Quaker
Index t Wom; Not Am Wom

1185. Morse, Lucy (Gibbons)
1839–1936
author, novelist, abolitionist, Black welfare worker
New York, NY
Dict Am Auth; Nat Cyc Am Bio

1186. Schofield, Martha
1839–1916
educator of freedmen
Quaker
Not Am Wom

1187. Baldwin, Esther E.
born 1840
missionary to China, worker for the rights of Chinese Americans, temperance worker
Wom Cent

1188. Bond, Elizabeth Powell
1841–1926
abolitionist, educator of Blacks, women's rights worker, pacifist, civil rights and temperance worker, dean of Swarthmore College
Pennsylvania
Dict Am Bio; Index t Wom; Nat Cyc Am Bio v6; Wom Cent

1189. Dickinson, Anna Elizabeth
1842–1932
Civil War orator, lyceum lecturer, abolitionist, women's rights worker, suffragist, political activist, Republican party worker, author, actor, philanthropist
Quaker
Cyc Am Bio; Dict Am Auth; Dict Am Bio supp v1; Dict Am Bio Men Time; Index t Wom; Nat Cyc Am Bio v3; Not Am Wom; Twent Cen Bio Dict Not Am; Wom Cent

1190. Lowman, Mary D.
born 1842
educator of Blacks; deputy register of deeds and mayor of Oskaloosa, Kansas
Presbyterian
Oskaloosa, KS
Index t Wom; Wom Cent

1191. Ruffin, Josephine St. Pierre
1842–1924
clubwoman, Black leader, Black welfare and rights worker, president of the National Federation of Afro-American Women, Union patriot in the Civil War
Black
Index t Wom; Negro Alman; Not Am Wom; Prof Negro Wom v1

1192. Slocum, Jane Mariah
born 1842
educator of freedmen
Wom Cent

1193. Ripley, Martha George Rogers
1843–1912
physician, humanitarian, feminist, abolitionist, temperance worker, suffragist
Index t Wom; Not Am Wom; Wom Cent

1194. Villard, Helen Frances Garrison "Fanny"
1844–1928
philanthropist, suffragist, pacifist, worker for Black civil rights
Dict Am Bio; Not Am Wom

1195. Winnemucca, Sarah (Thocmetony)
circa 1844–91
hero, Native American rights worker
Native American (Paviotsu Paiute)
Dict Am Bio; Eng Wom; Great North Am Ind; Not Am Wom

1196. Brown, Hallie Quinn
1845/50–1949
educator, elocutionist, lecturer, Black women's leader
Index t Wom; Negro Alman; Not Am Wom; Prof Negro Wom v1

1197. Mallory, Lucy A.
born 1846
editor, educator of Blacks
Oregon
Index t Wom; Wom Cent

1198. Holmes, Mary Emilie
born 1850
educator, zoologist, herbalist, educator of Black women
Presbyterian
Illinois
Wom Cent

1199. Mattingly, Sarah Irwin
1852–1934
educator of Blacks, suffragist
Nat Cyc Am Bio v30

1200. McDowell, Mary Eliza
1854–1936

settlement house director and founder, social welfare reformer and worker, NAACP member
Methodist
Dict Am Bio supp v2; Index t Wom; Nat Cyc Am Bio csv2; Not Am Wom

1201. Tibbles, Susette Laflesche; Inshtatheumba; Bright Eyes
1854–1903
spokesperson for Native American rights
Native American (Osage); French
Great North Am Ind; Not Am Wom

1202. Mead, Lucia True (Ames)
1856–1936
pacifist, internationalist, suffragist, Black welfare and education worker, author
Unitarian
Nat Cyc Am Bio v28; Not Am Wom; Twent Cen Bio Dict Not Am

1203. Drexel, Katharine Mary; Mother Mary Katharine
1858–1955
founder of the Catholic Sisters of the Most Blessed Sacrament for Indians and Colored People, educator of Blacks, missionary, philanthropist
Catholic
Dict Am Bio supp v5; Dict Am Rel Bio; Index t Wom; Not Am Wom supp v1; Obit File; Read Encyc Am West

1204. Talbert, Mary Burnett
1862/66–1923
educator, social reformer, prison reformer, Black rights worker, club leader
Black
Index t Wom; Negro Alman; Prof Negro Wom v1

1205. Wells-Barnett, Ida Bell; Iola
1862/64–1931
Black equal rights advocate, journalist, newspaper publisher, clubwoman, lecturer, antilynching reformer
Black
Encyc Black Am; Encyc South Hist; Eng Wom; Index t Wom; Negro Alman; Not Am Wom; Prof Negro Wom v1 and v2

1206. Terrell, Mary Eliza Church
1863–1954
community leader, social reformer, suffragist, feminist, civil rights leader, NAACP organizer, lecturer, educator

Congregationalist
Washington, DC
Dict Am Bio supp v5; Encyc Black Am; Encyc South Hist; Index t Wom; Nat Cyc Am Bio v52; Negro Alman; Not Am Wom; Prof Negro Wom v1; World Great Men Col v2

1207. Gannett, Mary Thorn Lewis
1864–1952
suffragist, civil rights worker
Obit File

1208. Ovington, Mary White
1865–1951
civil rights reformer, a founder of the NAACP
Not Am Wom supp vl; Obit File

1209. Austin, Mary (Hunter)
1866/68–1934
novelist, folklorist, short story writer, journalist, conservationist, feminist, worker for Native American rights
California
Dict Am Auth; Dict Am Bio supp v1; Dict Lit Bio v9; Not Am Wom; Read Encyc Am West; Wom Lit; Wom Lit, More

1210. Martin, Georgia May; George Madden Martin
1866–1946
author, civil rights and antilynching worker
Episcopalian
Nat Cyc Am Bio v33

1211. Wesley, Rachel Parker
died 1918
litigant who sued for her freedom from slavery and won
Maryland
Black
Prof Negro Wom v1

1212. Cook, Myrtle Foster
1870–1951
educator, civic leader, financier, Black civil rights worker
Kansas City, KS
Black; Canadian
Negro Alman; Prof Negro Wom

1213. Williams, Lulu Margaret Roberts
1874/75–1945
educator, social reformer, Black student aid worker
Black
Negro Alman; Prof Negro Wom v1

1214. Barnard, Kate
1875–1930
Democratic political reformer, Native American rights advo-

cate, child welfare leader, philanthropist
Oklahoma
Index t Wom; Nat Cyc Am Bio v15, Not Am Wom; Read Encyc Am West

1215. Bethune, Mary McLeod
1875–1955
educator, founder and president of Bethune-Cookman College, director of the Negro Affairs National Youth Council, civil rights worker, women's rights worker
Daytona Beach, FL
Black
Dict Am Bio supp v5; Dict Am Rel Bio; Encyc Black Am; Encyc South Hist; Index t Wom; Nat Cyc Am Bio v49; Negro Alman; Negro Her Lib v1; Not Am Wom supp v1; Prof Negro Wom; Obit File

1216. Bonnin, Gertrude Simmons; Zitkala-sa
1875–1938
author, Native American rights worker
Native American (Yankton Sioux)
Great North Am Ind; Not Am Wom

1217. Burlin, Natalie (Curtis)
1875–1921
ethnomusicologist specializing in Native American and Afro-American music, worker for Native American rights, composer, pianist, lecturer
Dict Am Bio; Not Am Wom; Index t Wom

1218. Huntington, Addie D. Waites
1875–1943
civil rights worker, YWCA official
Black
Not Am Wom

1219. Cleghorn, Sarah Norcliffe
1876–1959
poet, novelist, educator, suffragist, civil rights worker, labor worker, pacifist, antivivisectionist, Socialist party member
Vermont
Index t Wom; Nat Cyc Am Bio v46; Obit File; Dict Am Bio supp v5

1220. Brown, Sue M.
1877–1941
clubwoman, educator, author, suffragist, women's rights worker, Black civil rights worker
Black
Negro Alman; Prof Negro Wom

1221. Jenckes, Virginia Ellis
1878–1975
representative to Congress from Indiana, anticommunist activist
Indiana
Index t Wom; Obit File

1222. Lawson, Roberta Campbell
1878–1940
clubwoman, student of Native American music and culture, ethnologist, Native American leader, singer, songwriter
Presbyterian
Native American (Delaware)
Great North Am Ind; Nat Cyc Am Bio v36; Not Am Wom

1223. Mitchell, Lucy Sprague
1878–1967
educator, college administrator, Black education worker, children's author
New York
Nat Cyc Am Bio v53; Not Am Wom supp v1

1224. Bass, Charlotta A. Spears
1880/90–1969
Progressive party vice-presidential candidate in 1952, civil rights reformer, editor
Black
Negro Alman; Not Am Wom supp v1

1225. Ames, Jessie Daniel
1883–1972
Progressive party politician, Black civil rights worker, antilynching reformer, suffragist
Texas
Encyc South Hist; Not Am Wom supp v1

1226. Lampkin, Daisy Elizabeth Adams
1883?–1965
civil rights reformer, suffragist, community leader
Not Am Wom supp v1

1227. Tilly, Dorothy Eugenia Rogers
1883–1970
civil rights reformer
Not Am Wom supp v1

1228. Kenyon, Dorothy
1888–1972
lawyer, feminist, suffragist, women's rights worker, prochoice abortion lobbyist, civil libertarian, director of the ACLU, UN official
New York
Cur Biog '72; Index t Wom; Nat Cyc Am Bio v56; Not Am Wom supp v1

1229. Clark, Septima Poinsette
flourished 1920s–80s
civil rights leader
Black
Prof Negro Wom v2

1230. Gaines, Irene McCoy
1892?–1964
civil rights worker, community
leader, clubwoman
Not Am Wom supp v1

**1231. Fauset, Crystal Dreda
Bird**
1893–1965
race relations specialist, state legislator
Black
Not Am Wom supp v1

1232. King, Carol Weiss
1895–1952
lawyer with specialty in immigration law, civil libertarian, specialist in deportation and civil
rights cases, counsel for American Communist party leaders
Dict Am Bio supp v5; Index t
Wom; Not Am Wom supp v1;
Obit File

**1233. Robeson, Eslanda Cardo-
za Goode**
1896–1965
author, civil rights reformer, anthropologist
Black
Index t Wom; Not Am Wom
supp v1

1234. Smith, Lilian Eugenia
1897–1966
novelist, newspaper columnist,
writer on race relations, civil
rights worker, editor, social
worker, educator, lecturer
Florida
Encyc South Hist; Index t Wom;
Not Am Wom supp v1; Obit
File; Wom Lit; Wom Lit, More

1235. Carter, Lillian "Bessie"
born 1898
nurse, social service worker,
peace worker, civil rights worker
Georgia
Cur Biog '78

1236. Freeman, Frankie Muse
flourished 1930s–60s
lawyer, Black civil rights leader
Black
Encyc Black Am

1237. Jackson, Juanita A.
flourished 1930s–60s
lawyer, civil rights worker
Black
Encyc Black Am

**1238. Kuhn, Margaret E.
"Maggie"**
born 1905
founder of the Gray Panthers,
fighter against age discrimination
Cur Biog '78

1239. Baker, Josephine
1906–75
actor, dancer, singer, civil rights
worker
Black
Cur Biog '75; Encyc Black Am;
Index t Wom; Negro Alman;
Not Am Wom

**1240. du Bois, Shirley Lola
Graham**
1906–77
children's author, biographer,
composer, stage director, civil
rights worker
Black
Cur Biog '77; Encyc Black Am

1241. Weed, Ethel Berenice
1906–75
military officer, Japanese wom-
en's rights advocate
Not Am Wom supp v1

1242. Murray, Paule
born 1910
educator, author, lawyer, civil
rights activist
Black
Encyc Black Am

1243. Height, Dorothy Irene
born 1912/13
social worker, YWCA executive,
civil rights worker, president of
the National Council of Negro
Women
Cur Biog '72; Encyc Black Am;
Negro Alman

1244. Smith, Hazel Brannon
born 1914
publisher and editor of Mississippi daily newspapers, Pulitzer
Prize winner, civil rights worker
Mississippi
Cur Biog '73

1245. Parks, Rosa
born 1915
civil rights activist
Black
Negro Alman; Prof Negro Wom
v2

1246. Peterson, Helen White
born 1915
assistant to the commissioner of
the Bureau of Indian affairs,
race relations worker
Colorado
Native American (Dakota-
Oglala)
Ind Today; Read Encyc Am West

1247. Calloway, Deverne Lee
born 1916
Missouri state legislator, Black
civil rights worker, women's
rights worker
Encyc Black Am

**1248. Tenayuca (Brooks),
Emma**
born 1916
civil rights worker, labor leader,
Communist party worker
Mexican
Dict Mex Am Hist

1249. Hamer, Fannie Lou
1917–77
civil rights worker, founder of the
Mississippi Freedom Democrat-
ic party, worker for Student
Nonviolent Coordinating Com-
mittee, farmer
Mississippi
Black
Encyc Black Am; Obit File

1250. Elliott, Daisy
born 1919
Michigan state legislator from
Detroit, civil rights worker
Detroit, MI
Black
Encyc Black Am

1251. Jordan, June
flourished 1950s–1980s
poet, essayist, political writer, civil rights worker, educator
Black
Wom Lit; Wom Lit, More

1252. Bates, Daisy Lee Gatson
born 1922
civil rights leader
Little Rock, AR
Black
Encyc Black Am; Index t Wom;
Negro Alman; Prof Negro
Wom v2

1253. Richardson, Gloria Hays
born 1922
civil rights activist
Black
Encyc Black Am

1254. Davis, Georgia M.
born 1923
business executive, Kentucky
state senator, Black civil rights
worker
Kentucky
Black
Encyc Black Am

1255. Sipuel, Ada Lois
born 1924
lawyer, educator, civil rights activist
Black
Encyc Black Am

1256. Hernandez, Aileen Clarke
born 1926
public affairs consultant; commissioner of Equal Employment
Opportunities Committee, 1965;
president of NOW; labor worker; civil rights worker; feminist
Black
Cur Biog '71; Negro Alman; Negro Her Lib v1

1257. King, Coretta Scott
born 1927
singer, civil rights leader
Atlanta, GA
Black
Cur Biog '69; Encyc Black Am;
Negro Alman

1258. Liuzzo, Viola Gregg
1927–66
civil rights worker
Obit File

1259. Olivarez, Graciela
born 1928
lawyer, United Way executive,
civil rights worker
Mexican
Dict Mex Am Hist

1260. Hansberry, Lorraine
1930–65
playwright, civil rights reformer,
Socialist party worker
New York
Black
Dict Lit Bio v7; Encyc Black Am;
Index t Wom; Nat Cyc Am Bio
v60; Negro Alman; Not Am
Wom supp v1; Obit File; Prof
Negro Wom v2; Wom Lit;
Wom Lit, More

1261. Hayden, Iola Pohucsucut
born 1934
Native American rights worker,
educator
Native American (Comanche)
Ind Today

1262. Deer, Ada
born 1935
social worker, worker for Native
American rights
Native American (Menominee)
Ind Today

1263. Norton, Eleanor Holmes
born 1937
lawyer, chairperson of the Equal
Opportunities Committee, New
York City Human Rights com-
missioner, civil rights worker
New York
Black
Cur Biog '76; Encyc Black Am;
Negro Alman

1264. Bryant, Anita
born 1940

singer, television personality, antifeminist, antiabortion worker, antihomosexual crusader; Baptist religious worker
Baptist
Florida
Cur Biog '75

1265. Hernandez, Maria L.
flourished 1970s–80s
Mexican American community leader, civil rights worker
Texas
Mexican
Dict Mex Am Hist

1266. Robinson, Ruby Doris Smith
1942–67
civil rights reformer, founder and executive of the Student Nonviolent Coordinating Committee
Black
Not Am Wom supp v1; Obit File

1267. Davis, Angela [Yvonne]
born 1944
civil rights worker, politician, Communist party presidential candidate, political writer, university educator
Black
Cur Biog '72; Encyc Black Am; Negro Alman

1268. Mercer, Margaret
1771/92–1845
abolitionist, philanthropist, author
Cyc Am Bio; Dict Am Bio; Dict Am Bio Men Time; Index t Wom

CLUBS, ORGANIZATIONS, AND CIVIC WORK

1269. Bradford, Alice
circa 1590–1670
Pilgrim, Plymouth Colony civic worker, patron of education
Puritan
Massachusetts
English
Am Bio Dict; Index t Wom

1270. Delafield, Elizabeth Hanenkamp
flourished 1800s
clubwoman
Index t Wom

1271. Merrill, Margaret Manton
born 18?
journalist, temperance worker, Sorosis member
English
Wom Cent

1272. Prout, Mary Ann
born 1801
burial society founder
Black
Prof Negro Wom v1

1273. Ripley, Sophia Willard
1803–61
leading spirit in the Brook Farm commune experiment
Transcendentalist
Not Am Wom

1274. Parton, Sarah Payson (Willis); Fanny Fern
1811–72
author, newspaper columnist, magazine writer, novelist, clubwoman
Cyc Am Bio; Dict Am Auth; Dict Am Bio; Dict Am Bio Men Time; Index t Wom; Nat Cyc Am Bio v1; Not Am Wom; Twent Cen Bio Dict Not Am; Wom Cent; Wom Lit; Wom Lit, More

1275. Curtis, Harriot F.
1813–89
magazine editor, novelist, journalist, club leader
Dict Am Auth; Index t Wom

1276. Walworth, Ellen Hardin
1813–1915
author, clubwoman
Not Am Wom

1277. Goodrich, Mary Hopkins
born 1814
originator of village improvement association cooperatives
Massachusetts
Wom Cent

1278. Stone, Lucinda Hinsdale
1814–1900
educator, clubwoman, women's club organizer, women's educator, feminist
Index t Wom; Nat Cyc Am Bio v13; Not Am Wom; Wom Cent

1279. Cunningham, Ann Pamela
1816–75
pioneer southern clubwoman, founder and regent of the Mt. Vernon Ladies Association of the Union; preserver of Mt. Vernon
Dict Am Bio; Index t Wom; Not Am Wom

1280. Howe, Julia Ward
1819–1910
poet, dramatist, songwriter, lecturer, suffrage and women's club leader, feminist, abolitionist, pacifist, prison reformer, Union patriot during the Civil War, philanthropist, traveler

Boston, MA
Cyc Am Bio; Dict Am Auth; Dict Am Bio; Dict Am Bio Men Time; Dict Lit Bio v1; Index t Wom; Nat Cyc Am Bio v1; Not Am Wom; Twent Cen Bio Dict Not Am; Wom Cent

1281. Blavatsky, Helena Petrovna (Hahn-Hahn)
1820/31–1891
occultist, mystic, founder of the semireligious Theosophical Society
Theosophist
Russian
Appl Cyc Am Bio; Cyc Am Bio; Dict Am Auth; Dict Am Bio; Dict Am Rel Bio; Nat Cyc Am Bio v15; Not Am Wom; Twent Cen Bio Dict Not Am; Wom Cent

1282. Colt, Miriam Davis
flourished 1850s
author, clubwoman
Index t Wom

1283. Severance, Carolina Maria (Seymour)
1820–1914
social reformer, women's club leader, women's rights worker, feminist, abolitionist
Dict Am Bio; Index t Wom; Nat Cyc Am Bio v8; Not Am Wom; Wom Cent

1284. Barton, Clara; Clarissa Harlowe
1821/30–1912
founder of the American Red Cross, Civil War hospital founder, expert on organizing military hospitals, philanthropist, nurse
Appl Cyc Am Bio; Cyc Am Bio; Dict Am Bio; Dict Am Rel Bio; Index t Wom; Nat Cyc Am Bio v3 and v15; Not Am Wom; Twent Cen Bio Dict Not Am; Wom Cent

1285. Morse, Rebecca A.; Ruth Moza; R. A. Kidder; R. A. K.
born 1821
clubwoman, Sorosis member, suffragist, patron of art, abolitionist, author
New York
Index t Wom; Wom Cent

1286. Thomas, M. Louise (Palmer)
born 1822
president of Sorosis, farmer, agriculturist, apiarist
Index t Wom; Nat Cyc Am Bio v13

1287. Sanders, Sue A. Pike
1824–post 1910
club leader, president of the Women's Relief Corps
Illinois
Index t Wom; Wom Cent

1288. Hoffman, Sophia Curtiss
born 1825
philanthropist, Sorosis member
Index t Wom; Wom Cent

1289. Long, Ellen Call
1825–1905
civic leader, author, planter
Florida
Read Encyc Am West

1290. Turner, Eliza L. Sproat Randolph
1826–1903
author, poet, suffragist, women's club leader
Pennsylvania
Dict Am Auth; Not Am Wom

1291. Bottome, Margaret (McDonald)
1827–1906
health reformer, religious author, founder of King's Daughters, a religious society
Dict Am Bio; Nat Cyc Am Bio v13; Twent Cen Bio Dict Not Am

1292. Croly, Jane Cunningham "Jean" "Jennie"; Jennie June
1829/31–1901
journalist, magazine editor, women's club leader, Sorosis member
Cyc Am Bio; Dict Am Auth; Dict Am Bio; Index t Wom; Nat Cyc Am Bio v6; Not Am Wom; Twent Cen Bio Dict Not Am; Wom Cent

1293. Kerfoot, Annie Warfield
born 1829
clubwoman
Index t Wom

1294. Doyle, Sarah Elizabeth
1830–1922
educator, clubwoman, women's rights worker
Dict Am Bio; Not Am Wom

1295. Kinne, Elizabeth d'Arcy
flourished 1860s–1900s
clubwoman
Index t Wom

1296. Smith, Emily L. Goodrich; Peter Parley
born 1830
club leader, newspaper foreign correspondent
Index t Wom; Wom Cent

1297. Gardner, Eliza Ann
1831–1922
clubwoman
Index t Wom

1298. Garnett, Sarah J. Smith Thompson
1831–1911
educator, civic worker
New York
Black
Index t Wom; Not Am Wom; Prof Negro Wom v1

1299. Geer, Augusta Danforth
married 1856
clubwoman
Index t Wom

1300. Lockwood, Mary Smith
born 1831
editor, clubwoman, patriot, writer on art and architecture
Dict Am Auth; Index t Wom; Nat Cyc Am Bio v3

1301. Allen, Elizabeth Anne Chase (Akers); Florence Percyips
1832–1911
poet, journalist, author, Sorosis Club member
Appl Cyc Am Bio; Cyc Am Bio; Dict Am Auth; Index t Wom; Nat Cyc Am Bio v6; Not Am Wom; Twent Cen Bio Dict Not Am; Wom Cent

1302. Poole, Hester Martha (Hunt)
born 1833/43
author, poet, writer on social and domestic issues, art critic, artist, women's rights worker, Sorosis member
Metuchen, NJ
Dict Am Auth; Nat Cyc Am Bio v11; Wom Cent

1303. Quinton, Amelia Stone
1833–1926
Native American reform and rights worker, temperance worker, club leader, humanitarian
Index t Wom; Not Am Wom; Twent Cen Bio Dict Not Am; Wom Cent

1304. Wilbour, Charlotte Beebee
1833–1914
women's rights worker, dress reformer, lecturer, president of Sorosis
Cyc Am Bio and ad; Index t Wom; Nat Cyc Am Bio v13

1305. McHenry, Mary Sears
born 1834
president of the National Women's Relief Corps, clubwoman

Illinois
Index t Wom; Wom Cent

1306. Rose, Martha E. (Parmelee)
born 1834
women's labor welfare worker, social reformer, sociologist, author, art patron, journalist, Sorosis member
Cleveland, OH
Index t Wom; Nat Cyc Am Bio v11; Wom Cent

1307. Nash, Mary McKinlay
born 1835
club leader
Index t Wom

1308. Vaughan, Sue Landon (Adams)
born 1835
founder of Decoration Day
Nat Cyc Am Bio v14

1309. Peirce, Melusina [Fay]
born 1836
author, community organizer, co-op advocate, writer on domestic science
Newport, RI
Dict Am Auth; Twent Cen Bio Dict Not Am

1310. Runcie, Constance (Faunt le Roy)
1836–1911
composer, pianist, club leader, poet, children's author, biographer
St. Joseph, MO
Dict Am Auth; Dict Am Bio; Index t Wom; Nat Cyc Am Bio v7; Wom Cent

1311. Deer, Mary Little Dickinson
married 1862
clubwoman
Index t Wom

1312. Keatinge, Harriet Charlotte
born 1837
physician, Sorosis member
New Orleans, LA
Nat Cyc Am Bio v18

1313. Langworthy, Elizabeth
born 1837
philanthropist; civic worker in Monticello, Iowa, and Seward, Nebraska; clubwoman
Monticello, IA; Seward, NE
Index t Wom; Wom Cent

1314. Brown, Charlotte Emerson
1838–95

president of the General Federation of Women's Literary Clubs, patron of missionaries
Dict Am Bio; Wom Cent

1315. Bryan, Mary (Edwards)
1838/46–1913
journalist, author, editor, poet, clubwoman
Atlanta, GA; New York, NY
Cyc Am Bio; Dict Am Bio; Index t Wom; Nat Cyc Am Bio v8; Not Am Wom; Twent Cen Bio Dict Not Am; Wom Cent

1316. McCrackin, Josephine Woempner Clifford
1838/46–1920
author, journalist, clubwoman, conservationist
German
Index t Wom; Not Am Wom

1317. Ransford, Nettie
born 1838
clubleader, general grand matron of the Order of the Eastern Star
Episcopalian
Index t Wom; Wom Cent

1318. Rude, Ellen (Sargent)
born 1838
poet, author, temperance worker, Worthy Chief Templar of the Order of Good Templars
Duluth, MN
Dict Am Auth; Index t Wom; Wom Cent

1319. Sullivan, Mary Mildred Hammond
1838–1933
philanthropist, Civil War patriot, New York civic leader
Presbyterian
New York
Index t Wom; Nat Cyc Am Bio v31

1320. Woods, Kate Tannatt
1838–1910
club leader, editor, poet, children's author
Salem, MA
Dict Am Auth; Index t Wom; Wom Cent

1321. George, Lydia A.
born 1839
army nurse in Civil War, Women's Relief Corps worker, philanthropist
Wom Cent

1322. Telford, Mary Jewett
born 1839
army nurse, Civil War nurse, Women's Relief Corps organizer, church worker, children's author
Quaker
Wom Cent

1323. Avery, Nina Horton
circa 1840–1930
clubwoman
Index t Wom

1324. Barker, Eliza Harris
flourished 1870s
clubwoman
Index t Wom

1325. Darling, Flora (Adams)
1840–1910
fiction writer, novelist, founder of the Daughters of the Revolution patriotic society
Dict Am Auth; Dict Am Bio; Index t Wom; Nat Cyc Am Bio v19; Not Am Wom; Wom Cent

1326. Foster, John W., Mrs.
flourished 1870s
clubwoman
Index t Wom

1327. Imen, Loraine
born 1840
elocutionist, clubwoman
Wom Cent

1328. Martin, Sarah J.
1840–1900
clubwoman
Index t Wom

1329. Ruprecht, Jenny Terrill
born 1840
author, children's author, Sorosis member
Cleveland, OH
Wom Cent

1330. Stone, Cornelia Branch
born 1840
Civil War patriot, club leader
Index t Wom

1331. Conklin, Jennie Maria (Drinkwater); Maria Drinkwater
1841–1900
children's author, philanthropist, clubwoman, founder of the Shut-in Society for Invalids
Dict Am Auth; Index t Wom; Dict Am Bio

1332. Oberholtzer, Sara Louisa (Vikers)
1841–1930
poet, author, novelist, temperance worker, leader in school savings movement, economist
Quaker
Norristown, PA
Cyc Am Bio; Dict Am Auth; Dict Am Bio; Index t Wom; Nat Cyc Am Bio v7; Wom Cent

1333. Plimpton, Hannah R. Cope
born 1841

club leader, Women's Relief Corps worker, Civil War nurse
Index t Wom; Wom Cent

1334. Sherwood, Katharine Margaret (Brownlee) "Kate"
1841/43–1914
journalist, newspaper editor, poet, author, clubwoman, suffragist
Canton, OH
Dict Am Auth; Dict Am Bio; Index t Wom; Nat Cyc Am Bio v1; Not Am Wom; Twent Cen Bio Dict Not Am; Wom Cent

1335. Wallace, Emma R. (Gilson)
1841–1911
club leader, philanthropist
Universalist
Chicago, IL
Index t Wom; Wom Cent

1336. Dailey, Charlotte Field
born 1842
World's Columbian Exposition official
Wom Cent

1337. Mumford, Mary Eno Bassett
1842–1935
education and civic leader, clubwoman
Philadelphia, PA
Not Am Wom

1338. Ruffin, Josephine St. Pierre
1842–1924
clubwoman, Black leader, Black welfare and rights worker, president of the National Federation of Afro-American Women, Union patriot in the Civil War
Black
Index t Wom; Negro Alman; Not Am Wom; Prof Negro Wom v1

1339. Fethers, Frances Conkey
married 1868
clubwoman
Index t Wom

1340. Roebling, Emily Warren
1843–1903
Civil War patriot, philanthropist, club leader, author, lawyer
Index t Wom

1341. Rose, Ellen Alida
born 1843
feminist, agriculturist, businessperson, Grange worker, suffragist
Index t Wom; Wom Cent

1342. Wickens, Margaret R.
born 1843

Women's Relief Corps worker, temperance worker, clubwoman
Wom Cent

1343. Cramsie, Mary Isabel
born 1844
clubwoman
Index t Wom

1344. Sewall, Mary Eliza Wright
1844–1920
educator, suffragist, women's rights worker, feminist, Sorosis member, clubwoman, pacifist
Dict Am Bio; Index t Wom; Nat Cyc Am Bio v19; Not Am Wom; Wom Cent

1345. Strong, Harriet Williams Russell
1844–1926/29
agriculturist, student of water supply problems, horticulturist, engineer, civic leader
Los Angeles, CA
Dict Am Bio; Nat Cyc Am Bio v17; Not Am Wom

1346. Blankenburg, Lucretia M. Longshore
1845–1937
suffragist, women's rights worker, clubwoman, civic worker
Pennsylvania
Nat Cyc Am Bio csv2; Not Am Wom

1347. Brown, Hallie Quinn
1845/50–1949
educator, elocutionist, lecturer, Black women's leader
Index t Wom; Negro Alman; Not Am Wom; Prof Negro Wom v1

1348. Comfort, Anna (Manning)
born 1845
gynecologist, medical author, suffragist, women's rights worker, Sorosis member
Dict Am Auth; Nat Cyc Am Bio v3; Wom Cent

1349. Mayo, Mary Anne Bryant
1845–1903
Grange and Farmers Institute worker
Dict Am Bio

1350. Richardson, Ellen A.
1845–1911
artist, editor, author, club leader
Index t Wom

1351. Cotten, Sallie Sims Southall
1846–1929
leader in North Carolina women's club movement
North Carolina
Encyc South Hist; Not Am Wom

1352. Gibbons, Marie Raymond
married 1871
clubwoman
Index t Wom

1353. Mink, Sarah C.
died 1896
clubwoman
Index t Wom

1354. Barker, E. Florence
died 1897
officer in Women's Relief Corps
Index t Wom

1355. Glynes, Ella Maria (Dietz); Ella Maria (Dietz) Glynes-Clymer
born 1847
author, actor, founder of Sorosis
Nat Cyc Am Bio v13

1356. Henrotin, Ellen M. Martin
1847–1922
women's club leader, labor and social reformer, philanthropist
Index t Wom; Not Am Wom

1357. Lakey, Alice
1847–1935
clubwoman, leader in the pure food movement
Not Am Wom

1358. Lawless, Margaret H. Wynne
born 1847
poet, religious worker, clubwoman
Wom Cent

1359. Tingley, Katherine Augusta Westcott
1847/52–1929
founder of the Point Loma Community in California, pacifist
Theosophist
Point Loma, CA
Dict Am Bio; Index t Wom; Nat Cyc Am Bio v15; Not Am Wom

1360. Hall, Mary, Dame
born 1848
president of Sorosis
Nat Cyc Am Bio v12

1361. Hamlin, Frances Bacon
married 1873
clubwoman
Index t Wom

1362. Mee, Cassie Ward
born 1848
labor leader, Knights of Labor worker, temperance worker, lecturer
Quaker
Canadian
Index t Wom; Wom Cent

1363. Roby, Lelia P.
born 1848
philanthropist, founder of the Ladies of the Grand Army of the Republic, veteran's welfare worker
Index t Wom; Wom Cent

1364. Gannett, Mary Chase
married 1874
clubwoman
Index t Wom

1365. Harbee, Lee (Cohen)
born 1849
author, Texas historian, Sorosis member
Texas; New York
Dict Am Auth; Wom Cent

1366. Knight, Sarah (Harrison)
1849–1928
philanthropist, Minneapolis civic leader, Methodist church worker, hospital founder, patron of nurse's training
Methodist
Minneapolis, MN
Am Bio New Cyc

1367. Minot, Fannie E.
married 1874
clubwoman
Index t Wom

1368. Palmer, Bertha Honore
1849/51–1918
clubwoman, philanthropist, women's rights worker, art collector
Chicago, IL
Dict Am Bio; Index t Wom; Twent Cen Bio Dict Not Am; Wom Cent

1369. Sandes, Margaret Isabelle
born 1849
industrial reformer, club leader
Scottish
Wom Cent

1370. Thurman, Lucy Smith
1849–1918
social worker, club leader
Index t Wom

1371. Ames, Minerva Ross
married 1875
clubwoman
Index t Wom

1372. Bancroft, Jane M.
flourished 1880s
clubwoman
Index t Wom

1373. Burrows, Frances L. Peck
flourished 1880s
clubwoman
Index t Wom

1374. Doremus, R. Ogden, Mrs.
flourished 1880s–90s
clubwoman
Index t Wom

1375. Fuller, Sarah R.
flourished 1880s–90s
clubwoman
Index t Wom

1376. Hall, Herman J., Mrs.
flourished 1880s
clubwoman
Index t Wom

1377. Halvey, Margaret Mary Brophy
flourished 1880s
clubwoman, educator, poet
Irish
Index t Wom

1378. Horton, John Miller, Mrs.
flourished 1880s–1900s
philanthropist, clubwoman
Index t Wom

1379. Jackson, Lily Irene
flourished 1880s–90s
sculptor, artist, designer, clubwoman
Virginia
Index t Wom; Wom Cent

1380. Lozier, Jennie de la Montagnie
born 1850
physician, president of Sorosis, clubwoman, lecturer
Index t Wom; Nat Cyc Am Bio v13; Wom Cent

1381. Mussey, Ellen (Persis) Spencer
1850–1936
international lawyer, law educator, feminist, women's rights worker, clubwoman, child welfare worker, Red Cross worker, social reformer
Swedenborgian
Washington, DC
Dict Am Bio supp v2; Index t Wom; Nat Cyc Am Bio v47 and csv1; Not Am Wom; Twent Cen Bio Dict Not Am

1382. Washington, Eugenie
died 1900
patriot, club leader
Index t Wom

1383. Doyle, John H., Mrs.
born 1851
clubwoman
Index t Wom

1384. Winslow, Helen Maria
1851–1938
clubwoman, author, journalist, editor, publisher
Boston, MA
Dict Am Auth; Index t Wom; Nat Cyc Am Bio csv2; Wom Cent

1385. Decker, Sarah Sophia Chase Platt
1852–1912
civic and social reformer, educator
Index t Wom; Not Am Wom

1386. Draper, Amos G., Mrs.
graduated 1877
clubwoman
Index t Wom

1387. Gonzales Parsons, Lucia
circa 1852–1942
feminist, labor leader, a founder of International Labor Defense and of Industrial Workers of the World, Socialist party worker
Mexican
Dict Mex Am Hist

1388. Holcombe, Emily Seymour Goodwin
1852–1923
civic worker
Connecticut
Nat Cyc Am Bio v16 and v18

1389. Moore, Eva Perry
1852–post 1900
club leader, pacifist
Index t Wom; Nat Cyc Am Bio csv1

1390. Stoddard, Anna Elizabeth
born 1852
journalist, anti–secret society agitator, temperance worker, suffragist
Baptist
Wom Cent

1391. Logan, Sallie
born 1853
clubwoman
Index t Wom

1392. Noyes, Ida E. Smith
1853–1912
artist, photographer, philanthropist, club leader
Index t Wom; Nat Cyc Am Bio v17

1393. Ward, May (Alden)
born 1853
historical author, biographer, editor, lecturer, club leader, president of the Massachusetts State Federation of Women's Clubs
Dict Am Auth; Index t Wom; Twent Cen Bio Dict Not Am; Wom Cent

1394. Brauenlich, Sophia (Toepken)
1854–98
journalist, business manager of Scientific Publishing Co., fellow of the Imperial Institute of Great Britain
Nat Cyc Am Bio v9

1395. Keith, Eliza D.; Erie Douglas; Di Vernon
born 1854
author, journalist, worker for the SPCA
California
Nat Cyc Am Bio v2; Wom Cent

1396. McDowell, Mary Eliza
1854–1936
settlement house director and founder, social welfare reformer and worker, NAACP member
Methodist
Dict Am Bio supp v2; Index t Wom; Nat Cyc Am Bio csv2; Not Am Wom

1397. Perkins, Angie Villette
1854–1921
educator, clubwoman, philanthropist
Nat Cyc Am Bio v19

1398. Straus, Lina Gutherz
1854–1930
patron of Hadassah medical work in Palestine
Jewish
German
Nat Cyc Am Bio v22

1399. Washington, Olivia Davidson
1854/59–1889
fund-raiser
Black
Negro Alman; Prof Negro Wom v1

1400. Burdette, Clara Bradley
1855–1954
clubwoman, founder of women's clubs, philanthropist
Los Angeles, CA
Index t Wom; Nat Cyc Am Bio csv2; Obit File

1401. Davis, Elizabeth Lindsay
born 1855
author, clubwoman
Illinois
Black
Prof Negro Wom v1

1402. Laws, Annie
1855–1927
kindergarten and education worker, clubwoman, civic leader, patron of nursing
Ohio
Nat Cyc Am Bio v22; Not Am Wom

1403. Williams, Fannie Barrier
1855–1944
lecturer, civic leader, librarian, clubwoman
Chicago, IL
Black
Dict Am Bio supp v3; Not Am Wom; Prof Negro Wom v1

1404. Baldwin, Mary Louise "Maria Louisa"
1856–1919/22
educator, civic leader
Massachusetts
Black
Index t Wom; Negro Alman; Not Am Wom; Prof Negro Wom

1405. Bishop, Ella Matilda Clark
1856–1926
clubwoman
Michigan
Nat Cyc Am Bio v21

1406. Clymer, Ella Maria (Dietz)
1856–post 1880
poet, actor, president of Sorosis
New York
Dict Am Auth; Wom Cent

1407. MacLeish, Martha Hillard
1856–1947
educator, leader in church and community work, second president of Rockford College
Not Am Wom; Obit File

1408. Taylor, Lodusky J., Mrs.
born 1856
organization official
Index t Wom

1409. Hay, Mary Garret
1857–1928
suffragist, temperance worker, New York civic worker
New York, NY
Dict Am Bio; Index t Wom; Not Am Wom

1410. Trumbull, Annie Eliot
1857–1949
novelist, poet, playwright, short story writer, first president of the Town and Country Club
Hartford, CT
Dict Am Auth; Obit File

1411. Turner, Lizabeth A.
died 1907
club leader
Index t Wom

1412. Adams, Agnes Jones
1858–1923
clubwoman
Index t Wom

1413. Boole, Ella Alexander
1858–1952
temperance leader, president of WCTU, suffragist, pacifist, Presbyterian deacon
Presbyterian
Dict Am Bio supp v5; Index t Wom; Nat Cyc Am Bio v38 and csv2; Not Am Wom supp v1; Obit File

1414. Earle, Mary Orr
born 1858
clubwoman
Index t Wom

1415. Judd, Ida Benfy
1858–1952
founder of the Mark Twain Association, monologuist, speech educator
Obit File

1416. Solomon, Hannah Greenebaum
1858–1942
clubwoman, founder of the National Council of Jewish Women, welfare worker
Jewish
Chicago, IL
Nat Cyc Am Bio v36; Not Am Wom

1417. Steedman, Mary Balch Lippitt
born 1858
Providence, Rhode Island, civic worker
Unitarian
Providence, RI
Nat Cyc Am Bio csv2

1418. Wright, S. J., Mrs.
married 1883
club leader
Index t Wom

1419. Cropper, Anna McLane
born 1859
clubwoman
Index t Wom

1420. Herrick, Christine Terhune
1859–1944
writer on household affairs, home economist, domestic scientist, Sorosis member
New York, NY; New Jersey
Dict Am Auth; Index t Wom; Nat Cyc Am Bio v8; Not Am Wom; Wom Cent

1421. Manning, Mary Margaret Fryer
married 1884
clubwoman
Index t Wom

1422. Stevens, Anna Evans (Shipman)
1859–1939
women's club worker
Detroit, MI
Nat Cyc Am Bio v17 and v32

1423. Boardman, Mabel Thorp
1860–1946
nurse, Red Cross leader
Dict Am Bio supp v4; Index t Wom; Not Am Wom; Obit File

1424. Booth-Tucker, Emma Moss
1860–1903
consul of the Salvation Army
Salvationist
Dict Am Bio

1425. Brown, Elizabeth Carolyn Seymour
flourished 1890s–1900s
clubwoman
Index t Wom

1426. Buchanan, Robert, Mrs.
flourished 1890s
clubwoman
Index t Wom

1427. Buchwalter, Edward L., Mrs.
flourished 1890s
clubwoman
Index t Wom

1428. Davis, M. E.
flourished 1890
clubwoman
Index t Wom

1429. Ely, Gertrude S.
flourished 1890s; died 1970
two-time recipient of the French Croix de Guerre for bravery in operating a YWCA canteen in World War I while under fire
Obit File

1430. Harris, Belle C.
flourished 1890s–1900s
clubwoman
Index t Wom

1431. Heaton, Eliza Putnam
born 1860
journalist, photojournalist, newspaper editor, Sorosis member
Wom Cent

1432. Hichborn, Jennie Franklin
flourished 1890s
clubwoman
Index t Wom

1433. Hitt, Agnes
flourished 1890s–1900s
clubwoman
Index t Wom

1434. Knott, A. Leo
flourished 1890s
clubwoman
Index t Wom

1435. Low, Juliette Magill Kinzie (Gordon)
1860–1927
founder of the Girl Scouts of America, clubwoman
Protestant Episcopal
Dict Am Bio; Index t Wom; Nat Cyc Am Bio v24; Not Am Wom

1436. Main, Charlotte Emerson
flourished 1890s–1910s
clubwoman
Index t Wom

1437. Mendes, Grace P.
flourished 1890s–1910s
clubwoman
Index t Wom

1438. Nobles, Catherine
flourished 1890s
club leader, author
Louisiana
Index t Wom; Wom Cent

1439. Pope, Sarah Lloyd Moore Ewing
flourished 1890s
club leader
Index t Wom

1440. Rice, Alice Caldwell (Hegan)
1860/70–1942
author, novelist, children's author, civic worker
New York; Louisville, KY
Dict Am Auth; Dict Am Bio supp v3; Index t Wom; Nat Cyc Am Bio v14; Not Am Wom; Obit File

1441. Ritchie, John, Mrs.
flourished 1890s
club leader
Index t Wom

1442. Shippen, William Watson, Mrs.
flourished 1890s
club leader
Index t Wom

1443. Taylor, Emily Drayton
1860–1952
miniature painter, founder of the Philadelphia Arts Alliance
Philadelphia, PA
Obit File

1444. Trout, Grace Wilbur
flourished 1890s; died 1955
suffragist, feminist, club leader, author, lecturer
Illinois
Index t Wom; Nat Cyc Am Bio csv2

1445. van Meter, Pattie Field
flourished 1890s–1910s
club leader
Index t Wom

1446. Gordon, Kate M.
1861–1932
suffrage leader, civic leader
Not Am Wom

1447. Haley, Margaret Angela
1861–1939
educator, civic reformer, labor leader
Catholic
Illinois
Bio Dict Am Lab; Not Am Wom

1448. Matthews, Victoria Earle
1861–98
social worker, mission society founder, clubwoman
Fort Valley, GA
Black
Index t Wom; Negro Alman; Prof Negro Wom v1

1449. Montgomery, Helen Barrett
1861–1934
civic reformer, churchperson, foreign missions worker, translator, author
Baptist
Index t Wom; Nat Cyc Am Bio csv1; Not Am Wom

1450. Pennypacker, Anna J. Hardwicke
born 1861
clubwoman
Index t Wom; Nat Cyc Am Bio csv1

1451. Taft, Helen Herron
1861–1943
founder and patron of the Cincinnati Orchestra Association, musician, music educator
Index t Wom; Nat Cyc Am Bio v14

1452. American, Sadie
1862–1944
lecturer, clubwoman, founder of the National Council of Jewish Women
Jewish
Index t Wom; Obit File

1453. Booth, Florence Eleanor Soper
1862–1957
Salvation Army leader
Salvationist
Obit File

1454. Delano, Jane Arminda
1862–1919

nurse, Red Cross worker, nurse in the Mexican-American War, nursing educator
Dict Am Bio; Index t Wom; Nat Cyc Am Bio v19; Not Am Wom

1455. Mason, Harriet Lawrence
born 1862
writer on English language and English literature
Twent Cen Bio Dict Not Am

1456. Rose, Laura Martin
born 1862
club leader
Index t Wom

1457. Sherman, Mary Belle King
1862–1935
clubwoman, champion of national parks
Not Am Wom

1458. Shuler, Nettie Rogers
1862–1939
suffragist, clubwoman
Not Am Wom

1459. Talbert, Mary Burnett
1862/66–1923
educator, social reformer, prison reformer, Black rights worker, club leader
Black
Index t Wom; Negro Alman; Prof Negro Wom v1

1460. Wells-Barnett, Ida Bell; Iola
1862/64–1931
Black equal rights advocate, journalist, newspaper publisher, clubwoman, lecturer, antilynching reformer
Black
Encyc Black Am; Encyc South Hist; Eng Wom; Index t Wom; Negro Alman; Not Am Wom; Prof Negro Wom v1 and v2

1461. Beaver, Mary (Miller)
died 1913
San Francisco civic leader
San Francisco, CA
Am Bio New Cyc

1462. Danner, Louise Rutledge
circa 1863–1943
welfare worker, YWCA official
Index t Wom

1463. Elkers, Bertha Kahn
born 1863
Red Cross worker, clubwoman
Index t Wom

1464. Fairbanks, Cornelia Cole
died 1913
clubwoman
Index t Wom

1465. King, Louisa Boyd Yeomans
1863–1948
writer on gardening, pioneer of the garden club movement
Not Am Wom

1466. Smith, Minnie Louise
1863–1927
educator, Sorosis member
Methodist Episcopal
Illinois
Nat Cyc Am Bio v21

1467. Terrell, Mary Eliza Church
1863–1954
community leader, social reformer, suffragist, feminist, civil rights leader, NAACP organizer, lecturer, educator
Congregationalist
Washington, DC
Dict Am Bio supp v5; Encyc Black Am; Encyc South Hist; Index t Wom; Nat Cyc Am Bio v52; Negro Alman; Not Am Wom; Prof Negro Wom v1; World Great Men Col v2

1468. Boswell, Helen Varick
1864–1942
suffrage leader, founder and president of the Women's Forum
New York
Obit File

1469. Frazier, Susan Elizabeth
1864/66–1909/24
educator, president of the 369th Infantry of the New York National Guard's Women's Auxiliary
Black
Index t Wom; Negro Alman; Prof Negro Wom v1

1470. Hatcher, Georgia H. Stockton
born 1864
clubwoman
Index t Wom

1471. Jarvis, Anna M.
1864–1948
founder of Mother's Day
Obit File

1472. Martin, Elizabeth Price
1864–1932
civic leader
Philadelphia, PA
Dict Am Bio supp v1

1473. Minor, Anne Rogers
1864–1947
president general of DAR
Obit File

1474. Barnum, Charlotte P. Acer
born 1865

clubwoman
Index t Wom

1475. Booth, Evangeline Cory
1865–1950
fourth general of the Salvation Army, orator, musician, poet
Salvationist
English
Dict Am Bio supp v4; Dict Am Rel Bio; Index t Wom; Nat Cyc Am Bio csv2; Not Am Wom; Obit File

1476. Booth, Maud Ballington (Charlesworth)
1865–1948
Salvation Army leader, evangelist, philanthropist, prison reformer, author, founder of PTA
Salvationist
English
Dict Am Auth; Index t Wom; Nat Cyc Am Bio v14 and v38; Not Am Wom; Obit File

1477. Dawes, Helen B. Palmer
married 1890s
educator, clubwoman
Index t Wom

1478. Heindel, Augusta Foss
1865–1949
cofounder of the Rosicrucian Fellowship
Obit File

1479. Hepburn, Emily [Louisa] Eaton
1865–1956
clubwoman, philanthropist
New York
Index t Wom; Nat Cyc Am Bio v46

1480. Locke, Bessie
1865–1952
kindergarten educator, founder and executive secretary of the National Kindergarten Association
Dict Am Bio supp v5; Index t Wom; Nat Cyc Am Bio v39; Obit File

1481. Munford, Mary Cooke Branch
1865–1938
education reformer, civic leader
Virginia
Index t Wom; Not Am Wom

1482. Ovington, Mary White
1865–1951
civil rights reformer, a founder of the NAACP
Not Am Wom supp vl; Obit File

1483. Rauh, Bertha
born 1865
club leader
Index t Wom

1484. Swormstedt, Mabel Godfrey
graduated 1890
educator, club leader
Index t Wom

1485. Winter, Alice Vivian Ames
1865–1944
women's club leader, author
Not Am Wom

1486. Carpenter, Fanny Hallock (Rouse)
flourished 1896–1900s
lawyer, Sorosis member
New England
Nat Cyc Am Bio v14

1487. Jordan, Jessie Knight
born 1866
clubwoman
Index t Wom

1488. Lawrence, Ruth Woodhull
1866–1956
founder of the National Society of Colonial Dames, authority on colonial families
Obit File

1489. Merrick, Mary Virginia
1866–1955
social worker, philanthropist, founder of the Christ Child Society to aid crippled children
Index t Wom; Obit File

1490. Poppenheim, Mary B.
1866–1936
organization official
Index t Wom

1491. Brown, Helen
1867–1942
president of the Women's Land Army (volunteer farm labor workers) during World War I
Obit File

1492. Capps, Effa Caroline
born 1867
San Diego civic worker
San Diego, CA
Nat Cyc Am Bio csv6

1493. Mason, Maud M.
1867/77–1957
artist, floral painter, president of the National Association of Women Sculptors and Painters
Index t Wom; Obit File

1494. Meyer, Annie Florence Nathan
1867–1950/51
publicist, author, playwright, novelist, educationist, founder of Barnard College, antisuffragist, patron of Black music education, clubwoman

Jewish
New York
Dict Am Auth; Dict Am Bio; Index t Wom; Nat Cyc Am Bio v42; Not Am Wom supp v1; Obit File; Twent Cen Bio Dict Not Am; Wom Cent

1495. Ogden, Esther Gracie
1867–1956
suffragist, secretary of the Foreign Policy Association
Obit File

1496. Sippel, Betty Manro
1867–1943
president of the General Federation of Women's Clubs
Obit File

1497. Woodruff, Caroline
1867–1949
educator, president of the National Education Association
Obit File

1498. Butler, Ida Fatio
1868–1949
Red Cross nurse
Index t Wom

1499. Cratty, Mabel
1868–1928
YWCA leader, social worker
Methodist
Dict Am Bio; Nat Cyc Am Bio v22; Not Am Wom

1500. Heard, Marie Bartlett
born 1868
clubwoman
Index t Wom

1501. Landes, Bertha Ethel Knight
1868–1943
clubwoman, civic reformer, mayor of Seattle
Seattle, WA
Index t Wom; Not Am Wom; Obit File

1502. Laughlin, Gail
1868–1952
lawyer, suffragist, feminist, state legislator, leader of the National Women's party
Not Am Wom supp v1; Obit File

1503. Robins, Margaret Dreier
1868/69–1945
labor reformer, woman- and child-labor welfare worker, suffragist, feminist, social economist, founder of the Municipal League
Bio Dict Am Lab; Dict Am Bio supp v3; Index t Wom; Nat Cyc Am Bio v33; Not Am Wom; Obit File

1504. Sherwin, Belle
1868–1955
suffragist, president of the National League of Women Voters, civic leader
Ohio
Nat Cyc Am Bio csv3; Not Am Wom supp v1; Obit File

1505. Spurgeon, Caroline Frances Eleanor
1868–1942
authority on Shakespeare and Chaucer, educator, founder of the International Federation of University Women
Obit File

1506. Barnum, Mary Gilmore
born 1869
educator, social worker, Los Angeles civic worker
Congregationalist
Los Angeles, CA
Nat Cyc Am Bio csv7

1507. Bullowa, Emilie M.
1869–1942
lawyer, World War II relief worker, Sorosis member
Jewish
New York
Nat Cyc Am Bio v31

1508. Dyar, Clara
born 1869
suffragist, Detroit civic worker
Detroit, MI
Nat Cyc Am Bio csv1

1509. Evans, Anne
1869/71–1941
civil leader, patron of the arts
Colorado
Index t Wom; Not Am Wom

1510. Higgins, Edward J., Mrs.
1869–1952
Salvation Army pioneer
Obit File

1511. Kussy, Sarah
1869–1956
cofounder of Hadassah
Jewish
Obit File

1512. Lovejoy, Esther Clayson Pohl
1869/70–1967
physician; director of the Portland, Oregon, health department; World War I Red Cross worker in France; feminist
Protestant Episcopal
Portland, OR
Index t Wom; Nat Cyc Am Bio csv1; Not Am Wom supp v1

1513. Baxter, Alice
flourished 1900s

clubwoman
Index t Wom

1514. Block, Anna Scott
flourished 1900s
clubwoman
Index t Wom

1515. Carpenter, Phillip, Mrs.
flourished 1900s
clubwoman, lawyer
Index t Wom

1516. Conger, Al, Mrs.
flourished 1900s
humanitarian, clubwoman
Index t Wom

1517. Cook, Myrtle Foster
1870–1951
educator, civic leader, financier, Black civil rights worker
Kansas City, KS
Black; Canadian
Negro Alman; Prof Negro Wom

1518. Dirbell, Ella Dancy
flourished 1900s
clubwoman
Index t Wom

1519. Gadsby, James Eakin, Mrs.
flourished 1900s
clubwoman, author
Index t Wom

1520. Gilman, Mary C.
flourished 1900s
clubwoman
Index t Wom

1521. Graham, Nellie Dean; Vosey
born 1870
short story writer, magazine writer, philanthropist, clubwoman, Republican party worker, Los Angeles civic leader
Los Angeles, CA
Am Bio New Cyc

1522. Harriman, Florence Jaffray (Hurst)
1870–1967
Democratic party official, diplomat, minister to Norway, politician, journalist, suffragist, clubwoman, social rights worker, Red Cross worker in World War I, World War II relief worker in Norway
Washington, DC
Index t Wom; Nat Cyc Am Bio v53 and csv6; Not Am Wom supp v1; Obit File

1523. Hunton, Addie Waites
born 1870
Red Cross worker, World War I relief worker

Black
Prof Negro Wom v2

1524. Johnson, Mary Katharine
flourished 1900s
clubwoman
Index t Wom

1525. Jones, Kate E.
flourished 1900s
clubwoman, poet
Index t Wom

1526. Karnes, Matilda Theresa
flourished 1900s
educator, clubwoman
Index t Wom

1527. Kumler, Charles H., Mrs.
flourished 1900s
clubwoman
Index t Wom

1528. Ludington, Katherine
1870–1953
suffrage leader, cofounder of the National League of Women Voters
Obit File

1529. Michael, Moina; The Poppy Lady
circa 1870–1944
educator, originator of Poppy Day as a memorial to war dead
Index t Wom; Obit File

1530. Pitkin, Louisa Rochester
flourished 1900s–10s
clubwoman
Index t Wom

1531. Walker, Alice Brendard Ewing
flourished 1900s
club leader
Index t Wom

1532. Bjerkoe, Ethel Hall
1871–1978
antiques authority and author, clubwoman
Connecticut; Maine
Nat Cyc Am Bio v60

1533. Chase, Kate Fowler
1871–1951
educator, lecturer, clubwoman
Index t Wom

1534. Draper, Helen Fidelia
1871–1951
Red Cross nurse, World War I relief worker, social worker
Episcopalian
New York
Index t Wom; Nat Cyc Am Bio v39

1535. Gabriel, Olive Stott
1871–1944

suffrage leader, lawyer, president of the National Association of Women Lawyers
Obit File

1536. Park, Maud May Wood;
C. J. Maywood
1871–1955
suffragist, feminist, civic leader, social worker, police reformer, pacifist
Dict Am Bio supp v5; Index t Wom; Nat Cyc Am Bio csv1; Not Am Wom supp v1

1537. Sabin, Florence Rena
1871–1953
physician, medical researcher and educator, anatomist, public health worker, first woman life member of the American Academy of Sciences, author
Colorado
Dict Am Bio supp v5; Index t Wom; Nat Cyc Am Bio v40 and csv3; Not Am Wom supp v1; Obit File

1538. Smith, Ida B. Wise
1871–1952
president of WCTU, educator, businessperson
Index t Wom; Obit File

1539. Wood, Louise
1871–1943
Red Cross leader
Obit File

1540. Blum, Florence A.
circa 1872–1959
clubwoman
Index t Wom

1541. Brosseau, Grace Lincoln Hall
1872–1959
president general of DAR
Congregationalist
Illinois
Nat Cyc Am Bio csv4; Obit File

1542. Butler, Selena Sloan
1872?–1964
community leader, founder of the National Congress of Colored Parents and Teachers Association
Black
Not Am Wom supp v1

1543. Dennett, Mary Coffin Ware
1872–1947
suffragist, birth control and sex education advocate, founder of the National Birth Control League, pacifist
Not Am Wom; Obit File

1544. Howard, Helen Margaret Willard
born 1872
clubwoman, composer
Massachusetts
Nat Cyc Am Bio v29

1545. Langworthy, Mary Lewis
born 1872
clubwoman, drama director
Nat Cyc Am Bio csv2

1546. Moore, Emmeline
1872–1963
biologist, fishery scientist, president of the American Fisheries Association, conservationist
Obit File

1547. Seton, Grace Gallatin Thompson; Dorothy Dodge
1872–1959
suffragist, feminist, explorer, geographer, author, book designer, bookmaker, composer of popular songs, historian, cofounder of the Campfire Girls
Dict Am Auth; Dict Am Bio supp v6; Index t Wom; Nat Cyc Am Bio v47 and csv5; Not Am Wom supp v1; Obit File

1548. Speers, Emma (Doll) Bailey
1872–1961
YWCA executive
Presbyterian
Pennsylvania
Nat Cyc Am Bio v52

1549. Vonnoh, Bessie Onahotema (Potter); Bessie Keyes
1872–1955
sculptor, member of the National Institute of Arts and Letters
Index t Wom; Nat Cyc Am Bio v11; Obit File

1550. Wells, Marguerite Milton
1872–1959
suffragist, civic leader
Not Am Wom supp v1

1551. Crane, Josephine (Porter) Boardman
1873–1972
New York civic leader, patron of the arts
Episcopalian
New York
Nat Cyc Am Bio v57

1552. Fitzgerald, Alice
1873–1962
chief nurse of the American Red Cross in Europe
Italian
Obit File

1553. Hanks, Mary Esther Vilas
1873–1959

Madison civic leader
Episcopalian
Madison, WI
Nat Cyc Am Bio v49

1554. Irwin, Inez Leonore Haynes Gillmore
1873–1970
suffragist, feminist, head of the World Center for Women's Archives, author, first woman president of the Authors League of America
Brazilian
Index t Wom; Nat Cyc Am Bio csv6; Not Am Wom supp v1; Obit File

1555. Laidlaw, Harriet Davenport Wright Burton
1873–1949
suffragist, author, educator, lecturer, clubwoman
Presbyterian
Index t Wom; Nat Cyc Am Bio v38; Not Am Wom

1556. Lingelbach, Anna Lane
1873–1954
historian, educator, civic leader, feminist
Presbyterian
Pennsylvania
Dict Am Bio supp v5; Nat Cyc Am Bio v44; Obit File

1557. Neilson, Nellie
1873–1947
English historian, first woman president of the American Historical Association, educator, author
Episcopalian
Nat Cyc Am Bio v36; Not Am Wom; Obit File

1558. Prentiss, Harriet Doan
flourished 1903
poet, club leader
Index t Wom

1559. Seligsberg, Alice Lillie
1873–1940
social worker, developer of Hadassah's medical program, Zionist
Jewish
Who Who Jew Hist

1560. Simms, Daisy Florence
1873–1923
YWCA executive
Not Am Wom

1561. Ashley, Grace Bosley
born 1874
politician, clubwoman
Index t Wom

1562. Best, Marjorie Ayres;
Mrs. A. Starr Best
born 1874

founder of the Drama League of America
Nat Cyc Am Bio v16

1563. Bloodgood, Edith Holt
1874–1961
cofounder of the New York Association for the Blind and of *Searchlight*, a Braille magazine
New York
Obit File

1564. Brown, Laura A.
1874–1924
politician, clubwoman
Index t Wom

1565. Hammand, Emily Vanderbilt Sloane
1874–1907
philanthropist, social worker, Moral Rearmament Society member
Presbyterian
New York
Nat Cyc Am Bio v55 and csv8

1566. McKee, Ruth Karr
1874–1951
clubwoman
Index t Wom

1567. Pouch, Helena R. Hellwig
1874–1960
humanitarian, president of DAR, tennis champion
Index t Wom; Obit File

1568. Smith, Jane Norman
1874–1953
feminist, leader of the National Women's Party
Index t Wom; Obit File

1569. Wise, Louise Waterman
1874–1947
charitable worker, founder and president of the women's division of the American Jewish Congress, Zionist
Jewish
New York
Not Am Wom

1570. Ball, Bertha
born 1875
philanthropist, civic worker
Universalist
Muncie, IN
Nat Cyc Am Bio csv6

1571. Batchelder, Evelyn Beatrice Longman
1875–1954
sculptor, first woman elected to the National Academy of Design
Obit File

1572. Bowles, Eva Del Vakia
1875–1943

YWCA leader
Not Am Wom

1573. Dreier, Mary Elisabeth
1875–1963
labor reformer, suffragist, New York civic leader, Bull Moose party politician
Presbyterian
New York
Nat Cyc Am Bio csv9; Not Am Wom supp v1

1574. Hull, Rose Frances Witz Whitney
1875–1954
founder of the Women's National Democratic Club
Obit File

1575. Huntington, Addie D. Waites
1875–1943
civil rights worker, YWCA official
Black
Not Am Wom

1576. Morris, Dave Hennen, Mrs.
1875–1950
founder of the International Auxiliary Language Association
Obit File

1577. Parsons, Elsie Clews
1875–1941
sociologist, anthropologist, folklorist, Native American ethnologist, president of the American Anthropology Association
Dict Am Bio supp v3; Index t Wom; Not Am Wom; Obit File; Read Encyc Am West

1578. Prisk, Laura B.; The Mother of Flag Day
1875–1950
patriot, proponent of Flag Day
Obit File

1579. Tiffany, Katrina Brandes Ely
1875–1927
civic worker, suffragist
Dict Am Bio

1580. Westley, Helen; Henrietta Remsen Meserole Manney
1875–1942
stage and screen actor, founder of the Theater Guild
Dict Am Bio supp v3; Index t Wom; Not Am Wom; Obit File

1581. Bacon, Josephine Dodge Daskam
1876–1961
humorist, children's author, short story writer, Girl Scout executive

Stamford, CT
Dict Am Auth; Index t Wom

1582. Beard, Mary
1876–1946
administrator and educator in nursing and public health, Rockefeller Foundation administrator, director of American Red Cross Nursing Service
Dict Am Bio supp v4; Index t Wom; Nat Cyc Am Bio v35; Obit File

1583. Burchenal, Elizabeth
1876–1959
folklorist, folk dance educator, cofounder of the American Folk Dance Society, originator of the New York Folk Dance Festival
New York
Index t Wom; Not Am Wom supp v1; Obit File

1584. Cushman, Vera Charlotte Scott
1876–1946
YWCA leader
Dict Am Bio v4; Not Am Wom

1585. Vanamee, Grace Davis
1876–1946
club leader, lecturer, educator, author
Index t Wom

1586. White, Eartha Mary Magdalene
1876–1974
social welfare worker, community leader, businessperson
Black
Not Am Wom supp v1

1587. Bancroft, Jane Wallis Waldron
1877–1949
publisher of the *Wall Street Journal*, president of the Dow Jones & Co. newsgathering organization, Boston civic worker, equestrian
Boston, MA
Nat Cyc Am Bio v38; Obit File

1588. Berry, Harriet Morehead
1877–1940
civic worker, public official
Not Am Wom

1589. Brown, Sue M.
1877–1941
clubwoman, educator, author, suffragist, women's rights worker, Black civil rights worker
Black
Negro Alman; Prof Negro Wom

1590. Gildersleeve, Virginia Crocheron
1877–1965

educator, dean emeritus of Barnard College, US delegate to the 1945 San Francisco conference to draft the UN charter, creator of UNESCO
New York
Index t Wom; Nat Cyc Am Bio csv1 and csv7; Not Am Wom supp v1; Obit File

1591. Hayes, Mary Sanders
1877–1959
president of the Women's National Republican Club
Obit File

1592. Marvin, Adelaide Camilla Hoffman
born 1877
New York civic leader
Congregationalist
New York, NY
Nat Cyc Am Bio csv8

1593. Miller, Daisy Orr
1877–1955
editor, dog specialist, president of the Animal Protection Union
Index t Wom; Obit File

1594. Sapp, Ruth Bent
1877–1951
clubwoman
Congregationalist
Illinois
Nat Cyc Am Bio v47

1595. Walrath, Florence Dahl
1877–1958
founder of adoption societies
Obit File

1596. Warbasse, Agnes Louise Dyer
1877–1945
cooperative manufacturer, cooperative housing expert, suffragist, pacifist
Nat Cyc Am Bio v34

1597. Bancroft, Elizabeth McQueen
1878–1958
founder of the Women's International Association of Aeronautics
Obit File

1598. Batcheller, Tryophosa Bates
born 1878
clubwoman, singer
Index t Wom

1599. Gellhorn, Edna Fischel
1878–1970
community leader, suffragist
Not Am Wom supp v1

1600. Good, Alice Campbell
1878–1956

Democratic party worker, New York civic worker
Catholic
New York
Nat Cyc Am Bio v42

1601. Kitt, Edith O.
born 1878
clubwoman
Index t Wom

1602. Lawson, Roberta Campbell
1878–1940
clubwoman, student of Native American music and culture, ethnologist, Native American leader, singer, songwriter
Presbyterian
Native American (Delaware)
Great North Am Ind; Nat Cyc Am Bio v36; Not Am Wom

1603. Stearns, Clark D., Mrs.
1878–1958
founder and president of the Pan-American League
Obit File

1604. Parker, Valeria Hopkins
1879–1959
physician, public health worker, Sorosis member
Index t Wom; Nat Cyc Am Bio csv1

1605. Sporborg, Constance Amberg
1879–1961
organization official
Index t Wom

1606. Stovall, Kate Bradley
married 1904
club leader
Index t Wom

1607. Wilcox, Elsie Hart
1879–1954
Kauai, Hawaii, civic worker; territorial senator from Hawaii; politician; business executive
Congregationalist
Hawaii
Nat Cyc Am Bio v48

1608. Achelis, Elisabeth
born 1880
clubwoman, calendar reformer
Index t Wom; Nat Cyc Am Bio csv9

1609. Foerster, Alma
flourished 1910
Red Cross nurse
Index t Wom

1610. Fromenson, Ruth Bernard
1880–1953
cofounder of Hadassah

Jewish
Obit File

1611. Glass, Meta
1880–1967
president of Sweet Briar College, educator, YWCA executive, World War I and II relief worker, defense worker
Episcopalian
Virginia
Nat Cyc Am Bio v53 and csv7; Obit File

1612. Hale, Florence
1880–1959
president of the National Education Association, rural education director of Maine
Maine
Obit File

1613. Johnson, Florence Merriam
flourished 1910s
Red Cross nurse
Index t Wom

1614. Lawrence, Charlotte Louise
flourished 1910s
clubwoman
Index t Wom

1615. Maxwell, Lawrence
flourished 1910s
clubwoman
Index t Wom

1616. McBride, Lucia McCurdy
1880–1970
Cleveland civic leader, suffragist
Episcopalian
Cleveland, OH
Nat Cyc Am Bio v57 and csv7

1617. McCartney, Katharine Searle
flourished 1910s
clubwoman
Index t Wom

1618. McClellan, Aurora Pryor
flourished 1910s
clubwoman
Index t Wom

1619. Miller, Flo Jamison
flourished 1910s
clubwoman
Index t Wom

1620. Morgan, Sarah Berrien Casey
flourished 1910s
clubwoman
Index t Wom

1621. Nestor, Agnes
1880–1948
trade union leader, president of the Chicago Women's Trade Union League
Bio Dict Am Lab; Dict Am Bio supp v4; Not Am Wom; Obit File

1622. Noble, Esther Frothingham
flourished 1910s
club leader
Index t Wom

1623. O'Mahoney, Katherine A.
flourished 1910s
publisher, editor, lecturer, club leader
Irish
Index t Wom

1624. Page, Lucy Gaston
flourished 1910s
social reformer, club leader
Index t Wom

1625. Patterson, Lindsay, Mrs.
flourished 1910s
club leader
Index t Wom

1626. Pierce, Elizabeth F.
flourished 1910s
club leader
Index t Wom

1627. Putnam, Mary Steiner
flourished 1910s
club leader
Index t Wom

1628. Read, Carrie R.
flourished 1910s
club leader
Index t Wom

1629. Roelefs, Henrietta
circa 1880–1942
organization official
Index t Wom

1630. Rosenbery, Millie R. M.
flourished 1910s
club leader, philanthropist
Index t Wom

1631. Scott, Matthew T., Mrs.
flourished 1910s
club leader
Index t Wom

1632. Sherman, Minna E.
flourished 1910s
agriculturist, club leader, lecturer, author
Index t Wom

1633. Smallwood, Delia Graeme
flourished 1910s
club leader
Index t Wom

1634. Smith, J. Morgan, Mrs.
flourished 1910s
club leader
Index t Wom

1635. Spilman, Baldwin Day, Mrs.
flourished 1910s
club leader
Index t Wom

1636. Wadsworth, Alice Hay
born 1880
New York civic worker, suffragist
Presbyterian
New York
Nat Cyc Am Bio csv8

1637. Wickins, Margaret Ray
flourished 1910s
club leader
Index t Wom

1638. Wilcox, Mary R.
flourished 1910s
club leader
Index t Wom

1639. Winans, Sarah D.
flourished 1910s
club leader
Index t Wom

1640. Blossom, Elizabeth Beardsley Bingham
1881–1970
Cleveland civic worker, philanthropist
Cleveland, OH
Nat Cyc Am Bio v58

1641. Driscoll, Clara
1881–1945
clubwoman, philanthropist, politician, political activist
Texas
Not Am Wom; Obit File

1642. Evans, Alice Catherine
1881–1975
microbiologist, bacteriologist, president of the Society of American Bacteriologists
Cur Biog '75; Index t Wom; Not Am Wom supp v1

1643. Gruenberg, Sidonie Matsner
1881–1974
parent education leader; director of the Child Study Association of America, specialist in child guidance, parent education, and family relationships; nonfiction writer; lecturer
Austrian
Cur Biog '74; Index t Wom; Not Am Wom supp v1; Obit File

1644. McClellan, Irene Moulton Ward
1881–1967

philanthropist, World War I Red Cross relief worker in England, patent medicine manufacturer, dairy and chicken farmer
Episcopalian
New York
Nat Cyc Am Bio v53

1645. Phillips, Lena Madesin
1881–1955
feminist, founder of the National and International Federations of Business and Professional Women's Clubs, author, editor, lecturer, politician
Dict Am Bio supp v5; Index t Wom; Not Am Wom supp v1; Obit File

1646. Rumsey, Mary Harriman
1881–1934
social welfare leader, New York civic worker, spokesperson for consumer interests, chairperson of the Consumer Advisory Board, defense worker during World War I
New York
Dict Am Bio supp v1; Nat Cyc Am Bio v24 and csv4; Not Am Wom

1647. Smith, Anne R.
1881–1949
cofounder of Alcoholics Anonymous
Obit File

1648. Smith, Gertrude Robinson
1881–1963
New York civic worker, World War I relief worker, founder of the Tanglewood music festival, music patron
Nat Cyc Am Bio v48; Obit File

1649. Stein, Beatrice Borg
1881–1958
welfare leader, philanthropist, founder of the Play School Association
Jewish
New York
Nat Cyc Am Bio v47; Obit File

1650. Stewart, Sallie W.
1881–1951
educator, clubwoman, realtor, lecturer, Black women's welfare worker
Indiana
Black
Negro Alman; Prof Negro Wom v1

1651. Brown, Charlotte Eugenia Hawkins
1882/83–1961
educator, founder of the Palmer Memorial Institute, YWCA national board member

North Carolina
Black
Encyc Black Am; Index t Wom;
Negro Alman; Not Am Wom
supp v1; Obit File; Prof Negro
Wom v1 and v2

1652. Davis, Frances Eliott
1882?–1965
nurse, community leader
Not Am Wom supp v1

**1653. Dickinson, Lucy Jennings
Dickinson**
born 1882
clubwoman
Index t Wom

1654. Hay, Helen
died 1932
Red Cross nurse
Index t Wom

1655. Hunter, Jane Edna
1882–1971
social worker, nurse, educator,
clubwoman
Cleveland, OH
Black
Index t Wom; Negro Alman; Prof
Negro Wom v1

1656. Mason, Lucy Randolph
1882–1959
labor publicist, public relations
officer for the CIO, southern
trade union organizer, social
worker and reformer, suffragist
Episcopalian
Virginia
Bio Dict Am Lab; Dict Am Bio
supp v6; Encyc South Hist; Not
Am Wom supp v1; Obit File

**1657. Mitchell, Ruth Comfort;
Mrs. Sanborn Young**
1882–1954
author, poet, novelist, leader in
Republican Organizations for
Women
California
Index t Wom; Nat Cyc Am Bio
v44; Obit File

**1658. Rippen, Jane Parker
Deeter**
1882–1953
social worker, journalist, Girl
Scouts of America executive
Not Am Wom supp v1; Obit File

1659. Schneiderman, Rose
1882/84–1972
labor organizer, Women's Trade
Union leader, secretary of the
New York State Labor Depart-
ment, social reformer, suffragist
Jewish
Polish; Russian
Bio Dict Am Lab; Cur Biog '72;
Index t Wom; Not Am Wom
supp v1; Obit File

1660. Townshend, Anna Draper
born 1882
suffragist, Connecticut state legis-
lator from New Haven, New
Haven civic worker
Unitarian
New Haven, CT
Nat Cyc Am Bio csv6

1661. Balz, Arcada Stark
1883–1973
Indiana state senator, Indianapo-
lis civic worker
Methodist
Indianapolis, IN
Nat Cyc Am Bio v57

**1662. Carter, Alice (Olin)
Draper**
born 1883
YWCA executive, world war re-
lief worker, welfare worker
Episcopalian
New York
Nat Cyc Am Bio v55

1663. Colvin, Mamie White
1883–1955
WCTU president
Obit File

**1664. Haynes, Elizabeth A.
Ross**
1883–1953
YWCA official, social researcher,
social worker, author, businessperson, community leader
Index t Wom; Not Am Wom
supp v1

**1665. Lampkin, Daisy
Elizabeth Adams**
1883?–1965
civil rights reformer, suffragist,
community leader
Not Am Wom supp v1

**1666. Lamson, Armene Tashiji-
an**
1883–1970
medical illustrator, physician,
UNICEF worker, medical au-
thor
Episcopalian
Seattle, WA
Turkish
Nat Cyc Am Bio v56

**1667. Springs, Lena Joan
Jones**
1883–1942
Democratic National Committee
member, Democratic vice-presi-
dential nominee at the 1924
convention, suffrage leader,
World War I Red Cross worker
South Carolina
Nat Cyc Am Bio csv2; Obit File

1668. Wilson, Matilda Rausch
1883–1967

philanthropist, Detroit civic
worker, chairperson of the
board of directors of Fidelity
Bank & Trust, member of the
state board of agriculture, lieu-
tenant governor of Michigan,
Salvation Army worker
Presbyterian
Detroit, MI
Nat Cyc Am Bio v59

1669. Woodsmall, Ruth Frances
1883–1963
YWCA leader, government official, author
Index t Wom; Not Am Wom
supp v1

1670. Andrus, Ethel Percy
1884–1967
founder of retirement organizations, educator, executive
Not Am Wom supp v1

1671. Finney, Ruth Elbright
1884–1955
journalist, editor, author, clubwoman
Index t Wom

1672. Fox, Elizabeth Gordon
1884–1958
nurse, director of the Red Cross
Public Health Nursing Pro-
gram, president of the National
Organization for Public Health
Nursing
Index t Wom; Obit File

1673. Gross, M. Louise
1884–1951
founder and president of the
Women's Moderation Unit, an
anti-Prohibition group
Obit File

1674. Hill, Elsie
1884–1970
suffrage leader, chairperson of the
National Women's party
Obit File

**1675. Jordan, Sarah Claudia
Murray**
1884–1959
gastroenterologist, cofounder of
the Lahey Clinic, president of
the American Gastroenterological Association
Index t Wom; Not Am Wom
supp v1; Obit File

1676. Bowser, Rosa Dixon
1885–1931
educator, clubwoman
Richmond, VA
Black
Negro Alman; Prof Negro Wom

1677. Bremer, Edith Terry
1885–1964

social worker, founder of the International Institute movement
Not Am Wom supp v1

**1678. Challinor, Mercedes
Crimmins (Clara)**
1885–1966
Red Cross official, World War I
relief worker
Catholic
Nat Cyc Am Bio v52

**1679. Clowes, Edith Whitehill
(Hinkel)**
1885–1967
Indianapolis civic leader, patron
of music
Episcopalian
Indianapolis, IN
Nat Cyc Am Bio v53

**1680. Curtis, Namahyoke Soc-
kum**
died 1935
Des Moines civic leader, nurse
Des Moines, IA
Black
Prof Negro Wom v2

**1681. Everett, Flora Pierce
Morris**
born 1885
Cleveland civic worker
Episcopalian
Cleveland, OH
Nat Cyc Am Bio csv6

1682. Kaplan, Lena
1885–1958
cofounder of Hadassah
Jewish
Obit File

1683. Kelman, Sarah R.
circa 1885–1969
psychiatrist, psychoanalyst,
founder of the Association for
the Advancement of Psychoanalysis, the American Institute
for Psychoanalysis, and the
American Academy of Psychoanalysis
Russian
Obit File

1684. Magna, Edith Scott
1885–1960
executive of DAR
Congregationalist
Massachusetts
Nat Cyc Am Bio v49

1685. Natelson, Rachel
1885–1943
cofounder of Hadassah
Jewish
Obit File

1686. Paul, Alice
1885–1977

feminist, founder of the National
Women's Party, co-author of
the ERA, suffragist, lawyer
Quaker
Cur Biog '77; Index t Wom; Obit
File

1687. Stokes, Lilia Woodruff
1885–1973
Philadelphia civic worker, worker
for Women's International
League for Peace and Freedom,
conservationist
Quaker
Pennsylvania
Nat Cyc Am Bio v58

1688. Clothier, Anita Porter
1886–1955
Philadelphia civic worker, eques-
trian
Philadelphia, PA
Nat Cyc Am Bio v50

1689. Lane, Rose Wilder
1886/87–1968
novelist, telegrapher, World War
I Red Cross worker in Europe,
Vietnam war correspondent
Index t Wom; Nat Cyc Am Bio
v54

1690. Lindheim, Irma
born 1886
clubwoman, author
Index t Wom

1691. Maher, Frances
1886–1958
supreme regent of the Catholic
Daughters of America
Catholic
Obit File

**1692. McLean, Alice Throck-
morton**
1886–1968
organization official
Index t Wom

**1693. Slade, Caroline McCor-
mick**
1886–1951
novelist, social worker, civic
worker, suffragist, founder of
the National League of Women
Voters
New York
Index t Wom

1694. Deardorff, Neva R.
1887–1958
social welfare statistical expert,
president of the Child Welfare
League of America, cofounder
of the Health Insurance Plan of
Greater New York
New York
Obit File

**1695. Helburn, Therese (Op-
dyke)**
1887–1959
theatrical producer, dramatist,
codirector and administrator of
New York City's theater guild
New York, NY
Dict Am Bio supp v6; Index t
Wom; Not Am Wom supp v1;
Obit File

1696. Ladd, Mary Babbott
1887–1964
New York civic worker, worker
for the welfare of the aged
Nat Cyc Am Bio v51

1697. Rehan, Mary
1887–1963
lawyer, a founder of the International Bar Association
Obit File

1698. Abel, Hazel Hempel
1888–1966
US senator, civic leader, educator
Index t Wom

**1699. Aldrich, Harriet Alexan-
der**
1888–1972
New York civic worker, World
War II relief worker
New York, NY
Nat Cyc Am Bio v60

**1700. Beasley, Victoria Louise
Dowling**
1888–1956
Hartsville, South Carolina, civic
worker
Hartsville, SC
Nat Cyc Am Bio v46

1701. Bussey, Gertrude C.
1888–1961
president of the Women's International League for Peace and
Freedom, philosopher, educator
Obit File

1702. Bussey, Ruth Carman
1888–1961
educator, worker for Women's
International League for Peace
and Freedom party
Episcopalian
Maryland
Nat Cyc Am Bio v49

1703. Franklin, Pearl
circa 1888–1958
playwright, lawyer, Zionist, Hadassah leader
Jewish
Index t Wom; Obit File

1704. Hall, Florence Louise
born 1888
director of the Women's Land
Army
Index t Wom

1705. Kenyon, Dorothy
1888–1972
lawyer, feminist, suffragist, wom-
en's rights worker, prochoice
abortion lobbyist, civil libertarian, director of the ACLU, UN
official
New York
Cur Biog '72; Index t Wom; Nat
Cyc Am Bio v56; Not Am Wom
supp v1

1706. Lasker, Loula Davis
1888–1961
New York civic worker, Zionist,
Hadassah member
Jewish
New York
Nat Cyc Am Bio v48

1707. Peck, Lillie
1888–1957
leader in the settlement house
movement, social worker, president of the International Federation of Settlements, German
welfare worker after World War
II
Dict Am Bio supp v6; Obit File

**1708. Claytor, Gertrude
(Harris) Boatwright**
1889–1973
poet, Red Cross worker in World
War I
Christian Scientist
Virginia
Nat Cyc Am Bio v57

**1709. Hayward, Mildred Mar-
shal**
1889–1967
artist, Moral Rearmament worker
Nat Cyc Am Bio v53

**1710. Hillman, Bessie Abra-
mowitz**
1889–1970
labor leader, president of the
Amalgamated Clothing Work-
ers of America
Jewish
New York, NY
Russian
Nat Cyc Am Bio v56; Obit File

1711. McHale, Kathryn
1889/90–1956
educator, psychologist, general
director of the American Association of University Women
Dict Am Bio supp v6; Index t
Wom; Nat Cyc Am Bio v46;
Obit File

**1712. Myrin, Mabel (Anderson)
Pew**
1889–1972
Philadelphia civic leader
Presbyterian
Philadelphia, PA
Nat Cyc Am Bio v57

**1713. Patton, Marguerite
Courtright**
born 1889
organization official
Index t Wom

1714. Smith, Eliza Kennedy
born 1889
suffragist, executive of the League
of Women Voters
Nat Cyc Am Bio csv4

1715. Boyer, Sophia Ames
flourished 1920s
clubwoman
Index t Wom

1716. Brown, Annie Florence
flourished 1920s
clubwoman
Index t Wom

1717. Dreier, Ethel E.
flourished 1920s–30s
humanitarian, club leader
Index t Wom

1718. Hay, Regina Deem
born 1890
politician, clubwoman
Index t Wom

1719. Hurd, Muriel Jeffries
1890–1958
poet, editor, president of the National League of American Pen
Women
Obit File

1720. Marshall, Bernice C.
flourished 1920s–30s
clubwoman
Index t Wom

1721. Morris, Alice V. Shepard
flourished 1920s–30s
clubwoman
Index t Wom

1722. Scott, Kate Frances
born 1890
physician, organization official
Index t Wom

**1723. Sternbergh, Katharine El-
eanor Cornell**
1890–1950
Reading, Pennsylvania, civic
worker; owner and manager of
the American Tool and Die Co.
Reading, PA
Nat Cyc Am Bio v39

1724. Williams, Mattie
flourished 1920s–30s
club leader
Index t Wom

1725. Bearden, Bessye J.
1891–1943

educator, first female member of the New York City school board, clubwoman
New York, NY
Black
Encyc Black Am; Index t Wom

1726. Eliot, Martha May
1891–1978
pediatrician, public health official, president of the American Health Association, UNICEF member, US Children's Bureau official
Unitarian
Massachusetts
Cur Biog '78; Index t Wom; Nat Cyc Am Bio v60

1727. Mudd, Mildred Hardy Esterbrook
1891–1958
national president of the Girl Scouts of America
Episcopalian
Nat Cyc Am Bio csv8; Obit File

1728. Parsons, Rose Peabody
born 1891
organization official
Cur Biog '59; Index t Wom

1729. Romm, May E.
1891–1977
psychiatrist, president of the Los Angeles and Southern California psychoanalytic societies, motion picture technical adviser
Los Angeles, CA
Obit File

1730. Street, Margaret Berry
1891–1967
cattle farmer, lawyer, Civil Air Regulations executive, suffragist, Black welfare worker
Presbyterian
North Carolina
Nat Cyc Am Bio v54

1731. Barus, Jane Garey
1892–1977
suffragist; political activist; prison reformer; Montclair, New Jersey, civic worker; antinuclear activist; anti–Vietnam war worker
Unitarian
Montclair, NJ
Nat Cyc Am Bio v60

1732. Gaines, Irene McCoy
1892?–1964
civil rights worker, community leader, clubwoman
Not Am Wom supp v1

1733. Harrison, Gertrude [Alice] Gordon Grayson
1892–1961

Washington, DC, civic leader; patron of medicine; racehorse breeder
Episcopalian
Nat Cyc Am Bio v51

1734. Dodge, Pauline Morgan
1893–1971
YWCA executive, philanthropist
Presbyterian
New York
Nat Cyc Am Bio v56

1735. Garrett, Eileen Jeanette; Jean Lyttle
1893–1970
parapsychologist, novelist, founder of the Parapsychology Foundation
Anglican
Irish
Nat Cyc Am Bio v55; Obit File

1736. Levy, Adele Rosenwald
1893–1960
philanthropist, chairperson of the United Jewish Appeal National Women's Division, art collector
Jewish
New York
Obit File

1737. Speers, Helen Barrett
died 1943
YWCA national president
Obit File

1738. Swing, Betty Gram
1893–1969
feminist, leader of the National Women's Party
Obit File

1739. Bellanca, Dorothy Jacobs
1894–1946
trade union organizer, founder and only woman vice-president of the Amalgamated Clothing Workers union, social reformer, politician
Jewish
Russian
Bio Dict Am Lab; Dict Am Bio supp v3; Not Am Wom; Obit File

1740. Ireland, Margaret Allen
1894–1961
public health worker, Cleveland civic worker, welfare worker
Episcopalian
Cleveland, OH
Nat Cyc Am Bio v50

1741. Lloyd, Alice C.
1894–1950
dean of women of the University of Michigan, president of the National Association of Deans of Women
Michigan
Obit File

1742. McHugh, Bernard, Mrs.
born 1894
clubwoman
Index t Wom

1743. O'Hara, Joyce
circa 1894–1953
executive vice-president of the Motion Picture Association of America
Obit File

1744. Parker, Karla van Ostrand
born 1894
organization official
Index t Wom

1745. Porter, Elizabeth Kerr
born 1894
organization official, nurse
Index t Wom

1746. Alexander, Helen M.
died 1945
New York civic leader
New York, NY
Obit File

1747. Howorth, Lucy Somerville
born 1895
government official, clubwoman
Index t Wom

1748. Lewisohn, Margaret Seligman
1895–1954
educator, art patron, clubwoman
New York
Index t Wom; Nat Cyc Am Bio v44

1749. Bowman, Geline MacDonald
died 1946
women's business worker, head of the National Federation of Business and Professional Women
Obit File

1750. Clapper, Olive Ewing
1896–1968
author, lecturer, radio commentator, autobiographer, director of the Washington, DC, bureau of CARE
Washington, DC
Cur Biog '69; Index t Wom

1751. Halprin, Rose
1896–1978
president of Hadassah, Zionist
Jewish
Obit File

1752. Riley, Susan B.
born 1896
educator, organization official
Index t Wom

1753. Sayre, Ruth Buxton
born 1896
organization official
Index t Wom

1754. Woolley, Alice Stone
died 1946
physician, president of the American Medical Women's Association
New York
Obit File

1755. Bogan, Louise
1897–1970
lyric poet, poetry critic, holder of Library of Congress Chair of Poetry, member of the American Academy of Arts and Letters
Index t Wom; Not Am Wom supp v1; Wom Lit; Wom Cent

1756. Bronson, Ruth Muskrat
born 1897
Cherokee government official, field representative of Save the Children Federation
Oklahoma
Native American (Cherokee)
Ind Today; Read Encyc Am West

1757. Layton, Olivia (Cameron) Higgins
1897–1975
Girl Scout executive
Index t Wom; Nat Cyc Am Bio v59

1758. Lowry, Edith Elizabeth
1897–1970
religious leader, Protestant Organization executive of the Council of Women
Protestant
Not Am Wom supp v1

1759. Marshall, Lenore Guinzburg
1897–1971
author, poet, novelist, antinuclear worker, cofounder of the Committee for a Sane Nuclear Policy, worker for Women's International League for Peace and Freedom
Nat Cyc Am Bio v55; Obit File

1760. Prince, Mildred Mallon
1897–1961
lawyer, social legislation agitator, San Francisco civic worker
Catholic
San Francisco, CA
Nat Cyc Am Bio v47

1761. Daniels, Anna Kleegman
born 1898
gynecologist, medical director of Planned Parenthood
Jewish

1855. Height, Dorothy Irene
born 1912/13
social worker, YWCA executive, civil rights worker, president of the National Council of Negro Women
Cur Biog '72; Encyc Black Am; Negro Alman

1856. Jones, Clara Stanton
born 1913
librarian, president of the American Library Association
Detroit, MI
Black
Cur Biog '76; Encyc Black Am

1857. Sink, Mary Virginia
born 1913
engineer, organization official
Index t Wom

1858. Martin, Allie Beth (Dent)
1914–76
librarian, president of the American Library Association
Cur Biog '75

1859. Usher, Elizabeth Reuter
born 1914
librarian, organization official
Index t Wom

1860. Bradshaw, Lillian Moore
born 1915
librarian, president of the American Library Association
Cur Biog '70

1861. Oltman, Florine
born 1915
military librarian, president of the Special Libraries Association
Cur Biog '70

1862. Deming, Louise Mac-Pherson
1916–76
international educator, author, civic worker in Okinawa, Japan
Episcopalian
Nat Cyc Am Bio v58

1863. Hooper, Virginia Fite
born 1917
politician, clubwoman
Index t Wom

1864. Kabis, Dorothy Andrews
1917–71
US treasurer, Republican party activist, president of the National Federation of Republican Women
Washington, DC
Obit File

1865. Sewell, Winifred [Emma]
born 1917
librarian, organization official
Index t Wom

1866. Lowrie, Jean E[lisabeth]
born 1918
librarian, president of the American Library Association, library educator
Cur Biog '73

1867. Gadsden, Marie Davis
born 1919
Peace Corps training officer
Black
Index t Wom

1868. Wilson, Margaret Berenice Bush
born 1919
lawyer, civic leader, chairperson of the national board of the NAACP
St. Louis, MO
Black
Cur Biog '75; Encyc Black Am

1869. Blanchard, Hazel Ann
born 1920
educator, organization official
Index t Wom

1870. Irwin, Helen
flourished 1950s–60s
librarian, clubwoman
Index t Wom

1871. Johnson, Olivia
flourished 1950s–60s
clubwoman
Index t Wom

1872. Ohlson, Agnes
flourished 1950s
nurse, organization official
Index t Wom

1873. Rawalt, Marguerite
flourished 1950s
organization official
Index t Wom

1874. Robinson, Martha Gilmore
flourished 1950s–60s
club leader
Index t Wom

1875. Shera, Florence B.
flourished 1950s
printer, club leader
Index t Wom

1876. Trulock, Mussette Langford
flourished 1950s
organization official, lecturer
Index t Wom

1877. White, Doris Pike
flourished 1950s
club leader
Index t Wom

1878. Friedan, Betty
born 1921
feminist, founder and president of NOW, writer on the condition of women, women's rights worker
Cur Biog '70

1879. Nidetch, Jean
born 1923
founder and president of Weight Watchers International
Cur Biog '73

1880. Cook, Celestine Strode
born 1924
business executive, civic leader
New Orleans, LA
Black
Encyc Black Am

1881. Smith, Elizabeth Bacheler "Isabel"
born 1924
founder of AYH
Not Am Wom

1882. Weafer, Elizabeth
born 1924
organization official
Index t Wom

1883. Hernandez, Aileen Clarke
born 1926
public affairs consultant; commissioner of Equal Employment Opportunities Committee, 1965; president of NOW; labor worker; civil rights worker; feminist
Black
Cur Biog '71; Negro Alman; Negro Her Lib v1

1884. Peden, Katherine Graham
born 1926
organization official, business executive
Index t Wom

1885. Walker, Cora T.
born 1926
lawyer, civic leader, co-op founder
Harlem, NY
Black
Encyc Black Am; Negro Alman; Prof Negro Wom v2

1886. Olivarez, Graciela
born 1928
lawyer, United Way executive, civil rights worker
Mexican
Dict Mex Am Hist

1887. Huerta, Dolores Fernandez
1930–post 1970
United Farm Workers executive
Catholic
California
Mexican
Bio Dict Am Lab; Dict Mex Am Hist

1888. Shabazz, Betty
born 1936
community activist
Black Muslim
Black
Negro Alman

1889. Smeal, Eleanor [Marie] Cutri
born 1939
president of NOW
Cur Biog '80

1890. Hernandez, Maria L.
flourished 1970s–80s
Mexican American community leader, civil rights worker
Texas
Mexican
Dict Mex Am Hist

1891. Robinson, Ruby Doris Smith
1942–67
civil rights reformer, founder and executive of the Student Nonviolent Coordinating Committee
Black
Not Am Wom supp v1; Obit File

No Dates

1892. King, Louise Woodward
founder of the Georgia SPCA, philanthropist
Georgia
Cyc Am Bio

DANCE

1893. Stagg, Mary
flourished 1710s–30s
colonial actor, dancer, dancing teacher
Index t Wom

1894. Hallam, Sarah
flourished 1760s–70s
actor, dancer
Index t Wom

1895. Douvillier, Suzanne Theodore Vaillande; Madame Placide
1778–1826
dancer, pantomimist
Not Am Wom

1896. Ellsler, Fanny
1810–84
dancer
Cyc Am Bio

1897. Celeste, Madame; Celeste-Elliott
1814?–82
actor, dancer
Cyc Am Bio

**1898. Montez, Maria "Lola"
Dolores Eliza Rosanna
Gilbert Porris y; Marie Do-
lores Eliza Rosanna Gilbert;
Countess of Landsfeld**
1818/24–1861
dancer, western pioneer, adven-
turer
Irish
Aust Dict Bio; Cyc Am Bio; Dict
Am Bio Men Time; Dict Irish
Bio; Dict Nat Bio; Index t
Wom; Read Encyc Am West

**1899. Gilbert, Anne Jane Hart-
ley**
1821–1904
dancer, actor, autobiographer
Dict Am Auth; Dict Am Bio;
Index t Wom; Not Am Wom;
Twent Cen Bio Dict Not Am

1900. Turnbull, Julia Anna
1822–87
ballet dancer
Not Am Wom

1901. Lee, Mary Ann
1824/26–1899
ballet dancer
Index t Wom; Not Am Wom

1902. Maywood, Augusta
1825–76
ballet dancer
Index t Wom; Not Am Wom

**1903. Williams, Maria Pray
Mestayer**
born 1828
dancer, actor
Cyc Am Bio; Index t Wom

1904. Florence, Malvina Pray
1830–1906
dancer, comic actor
Index t Wom; Not Am Wom

1905. Morlacchi, Giuseppina
1836–88
dancer
Not Am Wom

1906. Bonfanti, Marie
circa 1847–1921
ballet dancer
Not Am Wom

1907. Collins, Laura Sedgwick
flourished 1880s–90s
actor, musician, composer, pianist, dancer, dramatic reader
Wom Cent

1908. Cooke, Kate Walsh
died 1903
dancer
Index t Wom

1909. Fuller, Loie
1862–1928

actor, dancer, innovator in stage
lighting
Dict Am Bio; Index t Wom; Not
Am Wom

1910. Hopper, Edna Wallace
1864?–1959
stage actor, singer, dancer, broker
Dict Am Bio supp v6; Index t
Wom; Obit File

1911. Burchenal, Elizabeth
1876–1959
folklorist, folk dance educator,
cofounder of the American Folk
Dance Society, originator of the
New York Folk Dance Festival
New York
Index t Wom; Not Am Wom
supp v1; Obit File

1912. Hartman, Grace (Abbott)
1876/1907–1955
dancer, comedian
Index t Wom; Obit File

1913. Duncan, Isadora
1878–1927
dancer
Dict Am Bio; Index t Wom; Nat
Cyc Am Bio v22; Not Am Wom

1914. St. Denis, Ruth
1878/80–1968
dancer, pioneer of American
modern dance, co-creator of the
Denishawn Dance Company,
choreographer
Index t Wom; Not Am Wom
supp v1; Obit File

1915. Suratt, Valeska
flourished 1910s
dancer
Index t Wom

1916. Tan Eyk, Melissa
flourished 1910s
vaudeville dancer
Index t Wom

**1917. van Duren, Kate Rock-
well Waner Matson; Klondike
Kate**
1881–1957
dancer, Alaska financier
Alaska
Obit File

1918. Patterson, Nan
born circa 1882
actor, dancer
Index t Wom

**1919. Orstein, Honora;
Diamond Tooth Lil**
1883–1975
dance hall actor during the Alaska gold rush
Alaska
Obit File

**1920. Nesbit, Evelyn; Evelyn
Thaw**
circa 1885–1967
dancer
Index t Wom; Obit File

1921. Karinska, Barbara
born 1886
ballet costume designer and maker
Russian
Cur Biog '71

**1922. Stirling, Mrs.; Lady
Cholmondeley**
married 1911
dancer
English
Index t Wom

1923. Brummer, Ethel Serly
1888–1952
vaudeville dancer
Austrian
Obit File

**1924. Janis, Elisie (Bierbower)
(Wilson)**
1889/93–1956
mimic, stage actor, singer, dancer,
vaudevillian, author, songwriter, World War I entertainer
Dict Am Bio supp v6; Index t
Wom; Nat Cyc Am Bio csv1;
Obit File

1925. Mideladze, Ketto
flourished 1920s–30s
dancer, fashion designer
Russian
Index t Wom

**1926. Murray, Mae; Marie An-
drienne Koenig**
circa 1890–1965
dancer, silent-screen actor
Index t Wom; Obit File

**1927. Page, Ruth; Mrs.
Thomas Hart Fisher**
flourished 1920s
choreographer
Nat Cyc Am Bio csv5

1928. Cannell, Kathleen
1891–1974
journalist, fashion editor, ballet
critic, autobiographer
French (American expatriate to
Paris)
Dict Lit Bio v4

1929. Nijinska, Bronislava
1891–1972
choreographer, ballet dancer
Russian
Obit File

1930. Dolly, Jenny
1892–1941
dancer

California
Index t Wom; Obit File

1931. Castle, Irene (Foote)
1893–1969
ballroom dancer, animal welfare
worker
Index t Wom; Not Am Wom
supp v1; Obit File

1932. Dolly, Rosie
1893–1970
dancer
Obit File

1933. Gadd, May
born 1894
folk dance teacher, organizer
Index t Wom

1934. Graham, Martha
born circa 1894
modern dancer, choreographer
Index t Wom

1935. Pennington, Anne
1894–1971
dancer
Obit File

1936. Humphrey, Doris
1895–1958
choreographer, dancer
Dict Am Bio supp v6; Index t
Wom; Not Am Wom supp v1

1937. Mills, Florence
1895–1927
singer, dancer, stage comedian
Black
Encyc Black Am; Index t Wom;
Negro Alman; Not Am Wom

1938. Smith, Ada; Bricktop
born 1895
singer, dancer, cabaret owner
Index t Wom

1939. Chace, Marian
1896–1970
creator of dance therapy, dancer
Not Am Wom supp v1

1940. Galli, Rosina
1896–1940
dancer
Index t Wom

1941. Duncan, Irma
1897–1977
modern dancer
German
Index t Wom; Obit File

1942. Clayton, Bessie
died 1948
vaudeville dancer
Index t Wom

1943. Astaire, Adele
born 1899

dancer
Index t Wom

1944. Gray, Gilda
1899/1901–1959
dancer, singer
Polish
Dict Am Bio supp v6; Index t
Wom; Obit File

1945. Vanderbilt, Gertrude
circa 1899–1960
actor, dancer, vaudevillian
Index t Wom

1946. Ewing, Lucia Chase
flourished 1930s
ballet dancer
Index t Wom

1947. Field, Laura
flourished 1930s
ballet dancer, pianist
Index t Wom

1948. Goya, Carola
flourished 1930s
dancer
Index t Wom

1949. La Meri
flourished 1930s
dancer
Index t Wom

1950. Marsh, Lucille
flourished 1930s
educator, dancer
Index t Wom

1951. Richards, Rosa Coates
flourished 1930s
dancer, poet
Index t Wom

**1952. Sweeney, Genevieve Eve-
lyn**
flourished 1930s
dancer
Index t Wom

1953. van Cleve, Edith
flourished 1930s
dancer, actor
Index t Wom

1954. Hastings, Mary Hay
1901–57
screen dancer
Obit File

1955. Mielziner, Jo
1902–76
set and lighting designer for dramas, musicals, operas, and ballets
Obit File

**1956. Pleydel-Bouverie, Ava
Alice Muriel Astor**
1902–56

patron of art, patron of ballet
Obit File

1957. Tamaris, Helen; Helen
Becker
1902/05–1966
dancer, choreographer
Index t Wom; Not Am Wom
supp v1

1958. Williams, Frances;
Frances Jelinek
1902–59
musical comedy actor, dancer
who introduced the Charleston
Obit File

1959. Chamie, Tatiana
died 1953
ballet dancer, soloist
Obit File

**1960. MacDonald, Jeanette
Anna**
1903/07–1965
screen actor, soprano singer,
dancer
Index t Wom; Not Am Wom
supp v1; Obit File

1961. Page, Ruth; Mrs.
Thomas Hart Fisher
born circa 1903
ballet dancer, choreographer
Index t Wom

1962. Littlefield, Catherine
1904–51
ballet dancer, choreographer
Obit File

1963. Rand, Sally
born 1904
dancer
Index t Wom

1964. Cassiday, Claudia
born circa 1905
music, ballet, and drama critic
Index t Wom

1965. de Mille, Agnes George
born circa 1905
dancer, choreographer
Index t Wom

1966. Losch, Tilly
1905/07–1975
stage and screen dancer, choreographer
Austrian
Cur Biog '76; Obit File

1967. Baker, Josephine
1906–75
actor, dancer, singer, civil rights
worker
Black
Cur Biog '75; Encyc Black Am;
Index t Wom; Negro Alman;
Not Am Wom

1968. Murray, Kathryn
born 1906
dancer
Index t Wom

1969. Chase, Lucia
born 1907
ballet dancer, director of the
American Ballet Theater
Cur Biog '75; Index t Wom

1970. Enters, Angna
born 1907
dancer, painter, author
Index t Wom

1971. Shannon, Peggy
1907/10–1941
screen actor, dancer
Index t Wom; Obit File

1972. Keeler, Ruby
born 1909/10
Broadway stage actor and dancer,
screen actor
Canadian
Cur Biog '71; Index t Wom

1973. de Marco, Renee
flourished 1940s
dancer
Index t Wom

1974. Dunham, Katherine
born 1910
dancer, choreographer, anthro-
pologist
Black
Encyc Black Am; Index t Wom;
Negro Alman; Prof Negro
Wom v2

1975. Miller Sisters
flourished 1940s
dancers
Index t Wom

1976. Reed, Janet
flourished 1940s
ballet dancer
Index t Wom

1977. Rees, Rosemary
flourished 1940s
ballet dancer, aviator
Index t Wom

1978. Souther, Marguerite
flourished 1940s
basketball coach, dance teacher
Index t Wom

1979. Rogers, Ginger; Virginia
Katherine McMath
born 1911
screen actor, dancer
Index t Wom; Nat Cyc Am Bio
csv6

1980. Kitchell, Iva
born 1912

dancer, comedian
Index t Wom

1981. Koner, Pauline
born circa 1912
dancer, choreographer
Index t Wom

1982. Marcci, Carmelia
born circa 1912
dancer
Index t Wom

1983. Moore, Lillian
1912–67
ballet dancer, educator, dance historian and critic
Obit File

1984. Powell, Eleanor; Mrs.
Glenn Ford
born 1912/13
dancer, actor, television personality
Index t Wom; Nat Cyc Am Bio
csv7

**1985. Harkness, Rebekah
(West)**
born 1915
patron of dance, semiclassical
composer, popular composer
Cur Biog '74

1986. Luahine, Iolana
1915–78
traditional sacred hula dancer
Hawaii
Polynesian
Obit File

1987. Sokolow, Anna
born 1915
choreographer, director, dancer,
dance educator
Jewish
Cur Biog '69

1988. Erdman, Jean
born circa 1917
modern dancer, choreographer
Cur Biog '70

1989. Zorina, Vera
born 1917
dancer
German
Index t Wom

1990. Boris, Ruthanna
born 1918
choreographer, ballet dancer
Index t Wom

1991. Bettis, Valerie Elizabeth
born 1919
ballet dancer
Index t Wom

1992. Miller, Ann; Lucille Ann
Collier
born 1919/23

tap dancer, stage actor
Cur Biog '80; Index t Wom

1993. Osato, Sono
born 1919
dancer, actor
Japanese
Index t Wom

1994. Primus, Pearl
born 1919
dancer
Black; West Indian (Trinidad)
Negro Alman

1995. Gollner, Nana
born 1920
ballet dancer
Index t Wom

1996. Hightower, Rosella
born 1920
ballet dancer, choreographer
Native American (Choctaw)
Index t Wom; Ind Today

1997. Kay, Nora
born 1920
ballet dancer
Index t Wom

1998. Alonso, Alicia; Alicia Ernestina de la Caridad del Cobre Martinez
born 1921?
ballet dancer
Cuban
Cur Biog '77

1999. Lang, Pearl
born 1922
modern dancer, choreographer
Cur Biog '70

2000. McCraken, Joan
1922–61
actor, dancer
Index t Wom; Obit File

2001. Charisse, Cyd
born 1923
dancer
Index t Wom

2002. Collins, Janet
born 1923
dancer
Black
Encyc Black Am

2003. Paige, Janis
born 1923
dancer, actor, comedian
Index t Wom

2004. Haney, Carol
1924–64
dancer, choreographer, musical
stage and screen actor
Index t Wom; Obit File

**2005. Champion, Marge Ce-
leste;** Marjorie Celeste Belcher
born 1925
dancer
Index t Wom

2006. Larkin, Moscelyne
born 1925
ballet dancer and teacher, choreographer, lecturer
Native American (Shawnee-Ploria)
Ind Today

2007. Tallchief, Maria
born 1925
ballet dancer
Native American (Osage)
Index t Wom; Ind Today

2008. Verdon, Gwen
born 1925
dancer, actor
Index t Wom

2009. Vollmar, Jocelyn
born 1925
ballet dancer
Index t Wom

2010. Adams, Diana
born 1926
ballet dancer
Index t Wom

2011. Garroway, Pamela
1926–61
actor, ballet dancer
Obit File

2012. Linn, Bambi
born 1926
ballet dancer
Index t Wom

2013. Moylan, Mary Ellen
born 1926
ballet dancer
Index t Wom

2014. Vera-Ellen; Vera-Ellen
Rohe
1926–81
stage actor, dancer
Cur Biog '81; Index t Wom

2015. Tallchief, Marjorie
born 1927
ballet dancer
Native American (Osage)
Index t Wom; Ind Today

2016. Angelou, Maya
born 1928
poet, autobiographer, dancer,
producer
Black
Cur Biog '74; Encyc Black Am;
Wom Lit; Wom Lit, More

2017. Kitt, Eartha
born 1928
singer, actor, dancer
Black
Encyc Black Am; Index t Wom

2018. Wilde, Patricia
born 1928
ballet dancer and teacher, choreographer
Index t Wom

2019. Chouteau, Yvonne
born 1929
ballet dancer
Index t Wom

2020. Calkin, Laurie Archer
flourished 1960s
dancer, choreographer, costume
designer, actor
Native American (Cherokee)
Ind Today

2021. Rivera, Chita
flourished 1960s–80s
singer, dancer, stage and screen
comedian
Puerto Rican
Index t Wom

2022. Baker, Carroll
born 1931
dancer, actor
Index t Wom

2023. de Lavallade, Carmen
born 1931
dancer
Index t Wom

2024. North, Sheree
born circa 1932
dancer, actor
Index t Wom

2025. Verdy, Violette
born 1933
ballet dancer, manager of the Boston Ballet
French
Cur Biog '69 and '80

2026. Chase, Barrie
born 1934
dancer
Index t Wom

2027. Lawrence, Carol
born 1934
actor, singer, dancer
Index t Wom

2028. MacLaine, Shirley
born 1934
stage and screen actor, dancer,
autobiographer, feminist, Democratic party worker, political
activist, world traveler
Cur Biog '78; Index t Wom

2029. Newmar, Julie
born 1935
dancer, director
Index t Wom

2030. Provine, Dorothy
born 1937
dancer, singer, television personality
Index t Wom

2031. Kent, Allegra
born 1938
ballet dancer
Cur Biog '70

2032. Makarova, Natalia
born 1940
ballet dancer
Russian
Cur Biog '72

2033. Tharp, Twyla
born 1941
modern dancer, choreographer
Cur Biog '75

2034. Funicello, Annette
born 1942
singer, actor, dancer
Index t Wom

2035. McBride, Patricia
born 1942
ballet dancer
Index t Wom

2036. Jamison, Judith
born 1943/44
modern dancer
Black
Cur Biog '73; Encyc Black Am;
Negro Alman

2037. Perrine, Valerie
born 1943
stage actor, dancer
Cur Biog '75

2038. Farrell, Suzanne
born 1945
ballet dancer
Index t Wom

2039. van Hamel, Martine
born 1945
ballet dancer
Dutch
Cur Biog '79

2040. Gregory, Cynthia
born 1946
ballet dancer
Cur Biog '77

2041. Mazzo, Kay
born 1947
ballet dancer
Cur Biog '71

2042. Ashley, Merril
born 1950

ballet dancer
Cur Biog '81

2043. Kirkland, Gelsey
born 1952
ballet dancer
Cur Biog '75

DOMESTIC SCIENCE AND HOME ECONOMICS

2044. Randolph, Mary Randolph
1762–1828
cookbook author
Not Am Wom

2045. Leslie, Eliza
1787–1858
cookbook writer, children's author, humorist, short story writer, editor
Philadelphia, PA
Cyc Am Bio; Dict Am Auth; Dict Am Bio; Dict Am Bio Men Time; Index t Wom; Nat Cyc Am Bio v7; Not Am Wom

2046. Gilman, Caroline (Howard)
1794–1888
author, poet, editor, domestic novelist
Charleston, SC
Cyc Am Bio; Dict Am Auth; Dict Am Bio; Dict Am Bio Men Time; Dict Lit Bio v3; Index t Wom; Nat Cyc Am Bio v6; Not Am Wom; Twent Cen Bio Dict Not Am

2047. Nitsch, Helen Alice (Matthews); Catherine Owen
18?–1889
domestic scientist, writer on domestic science
Plainfield, NJ

Dict Am Auth

2048. Beecher, Eunice White (Bullard); A Minister's Wife
1812–97
author on domestic subjects
Appl Cyc Am Bio; Cyc Am Bio; Dict Am Auth; Twent Cen Bio Dict Am Auth

2049. Dewey, Mary Elizabeth
1821; died post 1871
author, translator, educator, biographer
Cyc Am Bio; Dict Am Auth; Index t Wom; Twent Cen Bio Dict Not Am

2050. Stephens, Harriet Marion
1823–1850/58

author, domestic writer, novelist, editor
Cyc Am Bio; Dict Am Auth; Dict Am Bio Men Time

2051. Youmans, Eliza Ann
born 1826
botanist, writer on botany, cookbook author
Cyc Am Bio; Dict Am Auth; Nat Cyc Am Bio v5

2052. Doten, Lizzie
born 1829
poet
Spiritualist
Boston, MA
Cyc Am Bio; Dict Am Auth

2053. Terhune, Mary Virginia (Hawes); Marian Harland
1830/35–1922
popular novelist, writer on household affairs, historian, cookbook author, editor, publisher
New York, NY
Cyc Am Bio; Dict Am Auth; Dict Am Bio; Dict Am Bio Men Time; Index t Wom; Nat Cyc Am Bio v1; Not Am Wom; Twent Cen Bio Dict Not Am; Wom Cent

2054. Poole, Hester Martha (Hunt)
born 1833/43
author, poet, writer on social and domestic issues, art critic, artist, women's rights worker, Sorosis member
Metuchen, NJ
Dict Am Auth; Nat Cyc Am Bio v11; Wom Cent

2055. Peirce, Melusina [Fay]
born 1836
author, community organizer, co-op advocate, writer on domestic science
Newport, RI
Dict Am Auth; Twent Cen Bio Dict Not Am

2056. Ewing, Emma Pike
born 1838
home economics teacher, cooking teacher
Twent Cen Bio Dict Not Am; Wom Cent

2057. Campbell, Helen (Stuart)
1839–1918
journalist, children's author, social reformer, home economist, educator, philanthropist
New York
Cyc Am Bio; Dict Am Auth; Nat Cyc Am Bio v9; Not Am Wom; Twent Cen Bio Dict Not Am; Wom Cent

2058. Corson, Juliet
1841/42–1897
culinary educator, cookbook writer
New York
Cyc Am Bio; Dict Am Auth; Dict Am Bio; Index t Wom; Nat Cyc Am Bio v8; Not Am Wom; Twent Cen Bio Dict Not Am

2059. Lemcke, Gesine
born 1841
domestic science educator, cookbook author
New York
Dict Am Auth

2060. Dare, Ella
born 1842
lecturer, journalist, Civil War relief worker, sanitarian
Wom Cent

2061. Henderson, Mary Foote
born 1842/46
suffragist, home economist, cooking and nutrition writer
St. Louis, MO
Dict Am Auth; Twent Cen Bio Dict Not Am

2062. Richards, Ellen Henrietta (Swallow)
1842–1911
sanitation chemist and engineer, mineralogist, leader in applied and domestic science, writer on domestic science, professor at MIT, educator
Massachusetts
Cyc Am Bio; Dict Am Auth; Dict Am Bio; Index t Wom; Nat Cyc Am Bio v7; Not Am Wom; Twent Cen Bio Dict Not Am; Wom Cent

2063. Parloa, Maria
1843–1909
home economics educator, writer on cooking and domestic economy, lecturer
Dict Am Auth; Index t Wom; Not Am Wom

2064. Arnold, Augusta Foote
born 1844
cookbook writer, author
New York
Dict Am Auth

2065. Colby, H. Maria George; H. Maria George
born 1844
children's author, domestic writer, women's rights and temperance worker
Wom Cent

2066. Lincoln, Mary Johnson (Bailey)
1844–1921

educator, writer and lecturer on cookery, culinary educator, home economist
Boston, MA
Dict Am Auth; Dict Am Bio; Index t Wom; Nat Cyc Am Bio v24; Not Am Wom

2067. Rorer, Sarah Tyson (Heston)
1849–1937
cooking teacher, cookbook author, home economist, dietician
Dict Am Auth; Nat Cyc Am Bio v16; Not Am Wom; Twent Cen Bio Dict Not Am

2068. Hogan, Louise E. (Shimer)
born 1855
writer on domestic science
Dict Am Auth

2069. Willard, Mary Hatch
1856–1926
businessperson, chef, social worker
Dict Am Bio

2070. Farmer, Fannie Merrit
1857–1915
culinary expert, home economist, cookbook author
Dict Am Bio; Index t Wom; Nat Cyc Am Bio v22; Not Am Wom

2071. Kander, Lizzie Black
1858–1950
settlement house founder, cookbook author, social worker
Index t Wom; Not Am Wom

2072. Talbot, Marion
1858–1948
first dean of women of the University of Chicago, professor of household administration
Chicago, IL
Not Am Wom; Obit File

2073. Herrick, Christine Terhune
1859–1944
writer on household affairs, home economist, domestic scientist, Sorosis member
New York, NY; New Jersey
Dict Am Auth; Index t Wom; Nat Cyc Am Bio v8; Not Am Wom; Wom Cent

2074. Bevier, Isabel
1860–1942
educator, author, lecturer, home economist
Dict Am Bio supp v3; Index t Wom; Not Am Wom

2075. Norton, Mary Alice Peloubet
1860–1928

home economics educator
Dict Am Bio; Not Am Wom

2076. Woolman, Mary Raphael Schenck
1860–1940
home economist, textile specialist, vocational educator, author, lecturer
Nat Cyc Am Bio csv1; Not Am Wom

2077. Wilson, Margaret Barclay
1863–1945
physician, domestic scientist, medical educator
Nat Cyc Am Bio v34

2078. van Rensselaer, Martha
1864–1932
home economist, educator
Methodist
New York
Dict Am Bio; Nat Cyc Am Bio v23; Not Am Wom

2079. Calvin, Henrietta Willard
1865–1947
home economist
Baptist
Nat Cyc Am Bio v41

2080. Marlatt, Aby Lillian
1869–1943
home economist
Dict Am Bio supp v3

2081. Stern, Frances
1873–1947
social worker, dietician
Not Am Wom

2082. Cooley, Anna Maria
1874–1955
home economist, author
Index t Wom

2083. Graves, Lulu Grace
1874/78–1949
dietician, home economist
Index t Wom

2084. Parker, Eleanor R.
born 1874
home economist, editor, author
Index t Wom

2085. Rose, Mary Davies Swartz
1874–1941
pioneer nutritionist, director of the Bureau of Conservation of the Federal Food Board during World War I
Dict Am Bio supp v3; Index t Wom; Not Am Wom; Obit File

2086. Bradley, Alice
born 1875
home economics educator
Methodist

Massachusetts
Nat Cyc Am Bio csv2

2087. Atwater, Helen Woodard
1876–1947
US Department of Agriculture official, home economist
Nat Cyc Am Bio v46 and csv12; Not Am Wom; Obit File

2088. Blunt, Katharine
1876–1954
college administrator, home economics educator, nutritionist, chemist
Index t Wom; Nat Cyc Am Bio csv2; Not Am Wom supp v1

2089. Rombauer, Irma Louise von Starkloff
1877–1962
writer on food, cookbook author
Index t Wom; Not Am Wom supp v1; Obit File

2090. Toklas, Alice Babette
1877/97–1967
writer, cookbook author
Jewish
French (American expatriate to Paris)
Dict Lit Bio v4; Index t Wom; Not Am Wom supp v1; Obit File

2091. Wheeler, Ruth
1877–1948
home economist, nutritionist, dietician
Not Am Wom

2092. Gilbreth, Lillian Evelyn (Moller)
1878–1972
industrial engineer and psychologist, household efficiency and labor efficiency expert, management consultant
Cur Biog '72; Index t Wom; Not Am Wom supp v1; Obit File

2093. McLeod, Grace
1878–1962
nutritionist, nutrition educator, editor
Congregationalist
Scottish
Index t Wom; Nat Cyc Am Bio v50

2094. Roberts, Lydia Jane
1879–1965
nutritionist, home economics educator
Not Am Wom supp v1

2095. White, Edna Noble
1879–1954
educator, home economist
Not Am Wom supp v1

2096. Batchelder, Ann
1883–1955
food editor, poet
Obit File

2097. Frederick, Christine McGaffey
1883–1970
household efficiency expert, home economist, author, businessperson
Index t Wom; Not Am Wom supp v1

2098. Richardson, Anna Euretta
1883–1931
home economist
Dict Am Bio

2099. Stanley, Louise
1883–1954
home economist, first chief of the Agriculture Department Bureau of Human Nutrition
Not Am Wom supp v1; Obit File

2100. Morgan, Agnes Fay
1884–1968
biochemist, nutritionist
Index t Wom; Not Am Wom supp v1

2101. Picken, Mary Brooks
born 1886
home economist
Index t Wom

2102. Bane, Juliet Lita
1887–1957
home economics educator
Illinois
Nat Cyc Am Bio v43

2103. Taylor, Marion Sayle
1889–1942
radio adviser on domestic affairs
Obit File

2104. Strahan, Elsie T.
flourished 1920s–30s
dietician, home economist
Index t Wom

2105. Dye, Marie
born 1891
educator, nutrition researcher
Index t Wom

2106. Barber, Edith Michael
1892–1963
home economist, author
Index t Wom

2107. Bond, Helen Judy
born 1892
home economist
Index t Wom

2108. Pattee, Alida Frances
died 1942

dietician, lecturer, publisher, author
Index t Wom

2109. Godfrey, Grace
1893–1944
home economics educator
Philadelphia, PA
Obit File

2110. Metzelthin, Pearl Violette
1894–1947
dietician, author, editor, health worker
Index t Wom

2111. van Deman, Ruth
died 1948
information director of the Agriculture Department's Nutrition and Home Economics Bureau
Obit File

2112. Herbert, Elizabeth Sweeney
born 1899
editor, home economist
Index t Wom

2113. Davison, Eloise
flourished 1930s–40s
home economist
Index t Wom

2114. Flager, Alicia Mayre
flourished 1930s
nutritionist
Index t Wom

2115. Gilmore, Marion Sprague
flourished 1930s
dietician
Index t Wom

2116. Hager, Alice Mayre
flourished 1930s
dietician
Index t Wom

2117. Haines, Edith Key
flourished 1930s
cookery author
Index t Wom

2118. Lord, Isabel Ely
flourished 1930s
librarian, home economist
Index t Wom

2119. Paddleford, Clementine Haskin
1900–67
journalist, food editor
Index t Wom

2120. Stark, Elsie
flourished 1930s
home economist
Index t Wom

2121. Tisdale, Doris H.
flourished 1930s
home economist, educator
Index t Wom

2122. Winning, Freda J. Gerwin
flourished 1930s
educator, home economist
Index t Wom

2123. de Lany, Dorothy Celia
1901–60
home economics educator
Ithaca, NY
Nat Cyc Am Bio v47

2124. Davis, Adelle
1904–74
food writer, nutritionist
California
Cur Biog '73 and '74; Not Am Wom supp v1; Obit File

2125. Goldsmith, Grace Arabell
1904–75
physician, public health educator, nutritionist
Episcopalian
Louisiana
Nat Cyc Am Bio csv10; Not Am Wom supp v10

2126. Braucher, Pela Fay
1905–66
nutritionist, educator
Evangelical Lutheran
Nat Cyc Am Bio v52

2127. White, Poppy Cannon
1906–75
food columnist, cookbook author
Obit File

2128. Fisher, Katherine A.
died 1958
home economist, director of the Good Housekeeping Institute
Canadian
Obit File

2129. Barbour, Ella
flourished 1940s
home economist, restaurateur
Index t Wom

2130. Beeuwkes, Adelia Marie
1910–66
nutritionist, educator
Episcopalian
Michigan
Nat Cyc Am Bio v52

2131. Child, Julia McWilliams
born 1912
home economist, cookbook author, chef, TV personality
Index t Wom

2132. Jackson, Shirley Hardie
1916/19–1965

short story writer, novelist, ghost story writer, playwright, television scriptwriter, writer on domestic subjects, children's author
Dict Lit Bio v6; Index t Wom; Not Am Wom supp v1; Obit File; Wom Lit; Wom Lit, More

2133. Bowles, Heloise; Heloise
1919–77
syndicated newspaper columnist on household affairs
Obit File; Index t Wom

2134. Vanocur, Edith C.
1924–75
cookbook author, food columnist for The *Washington Post*
Obit File

2135. Widmark, Emma G.
flourished 1960s
home economist
Native American (Tlinget)
Ind Today

No Dates

2136. Cannon, Poppy
food columnist
South African
Index t Wom

EDUCATION

2137. Hicks, Margaret
flourished 1600s
colonial educator, pioneer
Index t Wom

2138. Bradford, Alice
circa 1590–1670
Pilgrim, Plymouth Colony civic worker, patron of education
Puritan
Massachusetts
English
Am Bio Dict; Index t Wom

2139. l'Incarnation, Maria de, Mother
1599–1672
Catholic nun, educator, founder of the Ursuline Convent in Quebec, student of Native American languages
Catholic
Canadian
Cyc Am Bio

2140. la Peltrie, Marie Madeleine de
1603–71
educator
Canadian (French Canada)
Cyc Am Bio

2141. Walker, Robert, Mrs.
died 1695
colonial educator
Index t Wom

2142. Walker, Widow
flourished 1680s
colonial educator
Index t Wom

2143. Knight, Sarah Kemble
1666–1725/27
diarist, educator, hotel keeper, traveler, merchant
Boston, MA
Cyc Am Bio; Dict Am Auth; Dict Am Bio; Dict Am Bio Men Time; Index t Wom; Not Am Wom; Wom Lit, More

2144. Stagg, Mary
flourished 1710s–30s
colonial actor, dancer, dancing teacher
Index t Wom

2145. Tranchepain de Saint Augustine, Marie De, Sister
died 1733
Catholic nun, mother superior and founder of the Ursuline convents, hospital administrator, educator
Catholic
Cyc Am Bio; Index t Wom

2146. Rhodes, Mrs.
flourished 1720s
colonial educator
Index t Wom

2147. Hoskens, Jane
born 1694
colonial clergyperson, educator
Index t Wom

2148. Domment, John, Mrs.
flourished circa 1730
colonial educator
Index t Wom

2149. Gazley, Martha
flourished 1730s
colonial manufacturer, needleworker, educator
Index t Wom

2150. Macklewain, Margaret
flourished 1730s
educator, businessperson
Index t Wom

2151. Todd, Sarah
flourished 1730s
colonial educator
Index t Wom

2152. Logan, Martha Daniell
1702/04–1779

educator, gardener, botanist, florist, horticulturist
Am Bio Dict; Index t Wom; Not Am Wom

2153. Hiller, Mrs.
flourished 1740s
colonial educator
Index t Wom

2154. Voyer, Jane
flourished 1740s
colonial educator
Index t Wom

2155. Brittano, Susannah
died 1764
colonial educator, philanthropist
Index t Wom

2156. Brownlow, Kate
flourished 1745
colonial educator
Irish
Index t Wom

2157. Zinzendorff, Anna Carita Nitschmann
1715–60
colonial educator
Index t Wom

2158. Jacintha do San Jose
1716–68
Catholic nun, school and hospital founder
Catholic
Brazilian
Cyc Am Bio

2159. Fraser, Matilda
flourished 1750s
educator
Index t Wom

2160. Green, Mary
flourished 1750s
colonial educator
Index t Wom

2161. Purcell, Elinor
flourished 1750s
colonial art educator
Index t Wom

2162. Watteville, Benigna [Henrietta] Justine Zinzendorf von
1725–89
educator, a founder of the Moravian Seminary and College for Women
Moravian
Moravian
Index t Wom; Not Am Wom

2163. Ellis, Mehetable
flourished 1760s
colonial educator
Index t Wom

2164. Scharibrook, Elizabeth
flourished 1760s
colonial educator
Index t Wom

2165. Hay, Sarah
flourished 1770s
educator
Index t Wom

2166. Graham, Isabella Marshall
1742–1814/15
educator, charity worker, philanthropist
New York
Scottish
Am Bio Dict; Cyc Am Bio; Dict Am Bio; Dict Am Bio Men Time; Index t Wom; Nat Cyc Am Bio v4; Not Am Wom; Our Count; Who Who Dur Am Rev

2167. Lake, Mary
1742–1802
western pioneer, religious worker, educator
English
Am Bio Dict; Index t Wom

2168. Southgate, Eliza
flourished eighteenth to nineteenth century
educator
Index t Wom

2169. Parrish, Anne
1760–1800
colonial philanthropist for women's causes, educator
Pennsylvania
Dict Am Bio; Index t Wom; Who Who Dur Am Rev

2170. Rogers, Abigail Dodge
flourished 1790s
educator
Index t Wom

2171. Rogers, Mrs.
flourished 1790s
educator
Index t Wom

2172. Rowson, Susanna (Haswell)
1762/67–1824
novelist, dramatist, poet, educator, actor
Boston, MA
English
Cyc Am Bio; Dict Am Auth; Dict Am Bio; Dict Am Bio Men Time; Dict Nat Bio; Index t Wom; Nat Cyc Am Bio v9; Not Am Wom; Wom Lit; Wom Lit, More

2173. Lalor, Alice Teresa;
Mother Teresa
1766–1846
mother superior and founder of the Convent and Academy of the Visitation, the first Roman Catholic female academy in the United States, educator
Catholic
Irish
Cyc Am Bio; Twent Cen Bio Dict Not Am; Who Who Dur Am Rev

2174. Pierce, Sarah "Sally"
1767–1852
educator
Litchfield, PA
Am Bio Dict; Index t Wom; Not Am Wom

2175. Phillips, Phoebe Foxcraft
died 1818
cofounder of the Andover Theological Seminary, philanthropist
Cyc Am Bio; Index t Wom

2176. Duchesne, Rose Philippine
1769–1852
missionary, Catholic nun, founder of the American Convents of the Sacred Heart, pioneer, educator
Catholic
Kansas
Cyc Am Bio; Dict Am Rel Bio; Not Am Wom; Read Encyc Am West; Twent Cen Bio Dict Not Am

2177. Hinsdale, Nancy
1769–1851
educator of women
Am Bio Dict

2178. Chiles, Marietta
flourished 1800s
educator
Index t Wom

2179. Hurley, Catharine
flourished 1800s–10s
educator
Index t Wom

2180. Swallow, Frances
flourished eighteenth century
colonial educator, businessperson
Index t Wom

2181. Greenwood, Mary Langdon
1775–1855
writer on women's education
Am Bio Dict

2182. Fiske, Catharine
1776–1837
educator, scientist, farmer
New Hampshire
Am Bio Dict; Index t Wom

2183. Gratz, Rebecca
1781/82–1869
charity worker, philanthropist, educator
Jewish
Dict Am Bio; Index t Wom; Nat Cyc Am Bio v10; Not Am Wom

2184. Stetson, Ellen
1783–1848
missionary to the Cherokee people, educator
Am Bio Dict

2185. Robbins, Eliza
1786–1853
educator, historian, author
Boston, MA
Dict Am Auth

2186. Gould, M. Woodbridge
1787–1838
scholar of classical languages, educator
Am Bio Dict

2187. Willard, Emma C. (Hart)
1787–1870/76
educator, textbook writer, poet
Troy, NY
Cyc Am Bio; Dict Am Auth; Dict Am Bio; Dict Am Bio Men Time; Index t Wom; Nat Cyc Am Bio v1; Not Am Wom; Twent Cen Bio Dict Not Am; Wom Cent

2188. Ricord, Elizabeth (Stryker)
1788–1865
educator, poet
New York; New Jersey
Cyc Am Bio; Dict Am Auth; Dict Am Bio Men Time

2189. Whittlesey, Abigail Goodrich
1788–1858
educator, magazine editor, author
Connecticut
Cyc Am Bio; Dict Am Bio; Not Am Wom

2190. Barber, Mary Augustine
1789–1860
educator, convent founder
Catholic
Appl Cyc Am Bio; Cyc Am Bio; Wom Cent

2191. Sedgwick, Catharine Maria
1789–1867
novelist, writer of moral tales for juveniles, educator
Stockbridge, MA
Cyc Am Bio; Dict Am Auth; Dict Am Bio; Dict Am Bio Men Time; Dict Lit Bio v1; Index t Wom; Nat Cyc Am Bio v1; Not Am Wom; Twent Cen Bio Dict Not Am; Wom Cent; Wom Lit; Wom Lit, More

2192. Abbot, Sarah
flourished 1820s–30s
educator
Index t Wom

2193. Garnett, James M., Mrs.
flourished 1820s
educator
Index t Wom

2194. Mitchell, Maria
1791/1818–1889
astronomer, women's rights worker, educator, novelist, poet
Quaker
Massachusetts
Cyc Am Bio; Dict Am Bio; Dict Am Bio Men Time; Index t Wom; Nat Cyc Am Bio v5; Not Am Wom; Twent Cen Bio Dict Not Am; Wom Cent

2195. Sedgwick, Elizabeth Buckminster (Dwight)
1791–1864
educator, writer of Sunday school tales
Dict Am Auth

2196. Hyde, Nancy Maria
1792–1816
educator, author
Connecticut
Am Bio Dict; Cyc Am Bio; Dict Am Bio Men Time

2197. Putnam, Katharine Hunt (Palmer)
1792–1861
religious textbook writer
Boston, MA
Dict Am Auth

2198. Phelps, Almira (Hart) (Lincoln)
1793–1884
educator, botanist, chemist, textbook author
Baltimore, MD
Cyc Am Bio; Dict Am Auth; Dict Am Bio; Dict Am Bio Men Time; Index t Wom; Nat Cyc Am Bio v11; Not Am Wom; Twent Cen Bio Dict Not Am

2199. Ripley, Sarah Alden Bradford
1793–1867
scholar, educator
Index t Wom; Not Am Wom

2200. Dumont, Julia Louisa (Carey)
1794–1857
poet, author, educator
Vevay, IN
Cyc Am Bio; Dict Am Auth

2201. Grant, Zilpah Polly
1794–1874
educator
Index t Wom; Not Am Wom

2202. Page, Elizabeth Whitredge
died 1845
educator, religious worker
Index t Wom

2203. Whiting, Martha
born 1795
educator
Index t Wom

2204. Smith, Sophia
1796–1870
founder of Smith College, educationist, philanthropist
Dict Am Bio; Index t Wom; Nat Cyc Am Bio v7; Not Am Wom; Twent Cen Bio Dict Not Am

2205. Winslow, Harriet W. (Lathrop)
1796–1833
missionary and educator in Ceylon
Am Bio Dict; Cyc Am Bio

2206. Lyon, Mary
1797–1844/49
educator and founder of Mt. Holyoke Female Seminary (now Mt. Holyoke College)
Mt. Holyoke, MA
Am Bio Dict; Cyc Am Bio; Dict Am Bio; Dict Am Bio Men Time; Index t Wom; Nat Cyc Am Bio v4; Not Am Wom; Twent Cen Bio Dict Not Am; Wom Cent

2207. Guerin, Anne-Theresa; Mother Theodore
1798–1856
educator, Catholic nun, founder of the Sisters of Providence of St. Mary-of-the-Woods
Indiana
French
Dict Am Bio; Nat Cyc Am Bio v23

2208. Hill, Frances Maria Mulligan
1799/1807–1884
Episcopal missionary and pioneer educator of women in Greece
Episcopalian
Cyc Am Bio; Index t Wom; Not Am Wom

2209. Beecher, Catherine Esther
1800–78
educator of women, education writer, social reformer, poet
Episcopalian
New York
Appl Cyc Am Bio; Cyc Am Bio; Dict Am Bio; Dict Am Bio Men Time; Dict Lit Bio v1; Index t Wom; Nat Cyc Am Bio v3; Not Am Wom; Twent Cen Bio Dict Not Am; Wom Cent

2210. Coxe, Margaret
born 1800
historical author, botanist, feminist, educator
Cyc Am Bio; Dict Am Auth; Dict Am Bio Men Time; Index t Wom

2211. Crandall, Almira
flourished 1830s
educator
Index t Wom

2212. Cruse, Mary Anne
born 18?
author, educator
Alabama
Dict Am Auth

2213. Dow, Betsy
flourished 1830s
religious educator
Index t Wom

2214. Guerber, Helen Adeline
born 18?
educator, textbook writer, historical author
Nyack, NY
Dict Am Auth

2215. Hentz, Caroline Lee (Whiting)
1800–56
novelist, dramatist, poet, romance writer, educator
Episcopalian
Am Bio Dict; Cyc Am Bio; Dict Am Bio; Dict Am Bio Men Time; Dict Lit Bio v3; Index t Wom; Nat Cyc Am Bio v6; Not Am Wom; Twent Cen Bio Dict Not Am; Wom Lit, More

2216. McLeod, Georgiana A. (Hulse)
18?–1890
educator, short story writer
Baltimore, MD
Dict Am Auth

2217. Meeker, Eleanor Richardson
flourished 1830s–50s
missionary, educator
Index t Wom

2218. Peter, Sarah Anne (Worthington) King
1800–77
charity worker, philanthropist, founder of art school for women, hospital founder, Civil War nurse, pioneer industrial arts educator, church worker
Catholic
Ohio
Dict Am Bio; Index t Wom; Not Am Wom; Twent Cen Bio Dict Not Am

2219. Pugh, Sarah
1800–84
educator, abolitionist, suffragist
Not Am Wom

2220. Hall, Arethusa
1802–91
literary educator, author
Massachusetts
Cyc Am Bio; Dict Am Auth; Dict Am Bio; Nat Cyc Am Bio v22; Twent Cen Bio Dict Not Am

2221. Jackson, Mercy Ruggles Bisbee
1802–77
homeopathic physician, temperance and suffrage worker, educator
Cyc Am Bio; Dict Am Bio; Index t Wom

2222. Whittlesey, Anna L.
died 1852
missionary educator to Beirut
Am Bio Dict

2223. Crandall, Prudence (Philles)
1803–1889/90
educator of Blacks, abolitionist, philanthropist
Quaker
English
Cyc Am Bio; Dict Am Bio; Eng Wom; Index t Wom; Nat Cyc Am Bio v2; Not Am Wom; Twent Cen Bio Dict Not Am

2224. Stewart, Maria [Frances] W. Miller
1803–79
educator, lecturer, social reformer
Black
Index t Wom; Not Am Wom

2225. Dwight, Margarette
1804–45
educator
Northampton, MA
Am Bio Dict

2226. Peabody, Elizabeth Palmer
1804–94
educator, writer on education, educational reformer, kindergartner
Transcendentalist
Boston, MA
Cyc Am Bio; Dict Am Auth; Dict Am Bio; Dict Am Bio Men Time; Dict Lit Bio v1; Index t Wom; Not Am Wom; Twent Cen Bio Dict Not Am; Wom Cent

2227. Tanner, Sarah Elizabeth
1804–1914
educator, religious worker
Index t Wom

2228. Becroft, Ann Marie; Sister Aloysius
1805–33
educator, Catholic nun
Catholic
Black
Negro Alman; Prof Negro Wom

2229. Douglass, Sarah Mapps Douglass
1806–82
educator, abolitionist
Philadelphia, PA
Black
Negro Alman; Not Am Wom; Prof Negro Wom v1

2230. Dwight, Mary Ann
1806–58
textbook author, writer on art, artist
New York, NY
Cyc Am Bio; Dict Am Auth; Dict Am Bio Men Time

2231. Embury, Emma Catherine (Manly)
1806–63
author, poet, writer on women's education
Brooklyn, NY
Cyc Am Bio; Dict Am Auth; Dict Am Bio; Dict Am Bio Men Time; Index t Wom; Nat Cyc Am Bio v9

2232. Mann, Mary Tyler (Peabody)
1806–87
miscellaneous author, kindergarten educator
Cyc Am Bio; Dict Am Auth; Dict Am Bio; Twent Cen Bio Dict Not Am

2233. Martin, Margaret Maxwell
born 1807
author, educator, poet
Columbia, SC
Cyc Am Bio; Dict Am Auth

2234. McKeever, Harriet Burn
1807–86
educator
Pennsylvania
Cyc Am Bio

2235. Porter, Eliza Emily Chappell
1807–88
educator, Civil War relief worker
Not Am Wom

2236. Chatfield, Fulia
1809–78
educator
Cyc Am Bio

2237. Hardey, Mary Aloysia Hawley; Mother Mary Aloysia
1809/10–1886
Catholic nun, founder of the Sacred Heart convents and schools in the New World, educator
Catholic
Cyc Am Bio; Dict Am Bio; Index t Wom; Not Am Wom; Twent Cen Bio Dict Not Am

2238. Ladd, Catherine; Minnie Mayflower; Morna; Alida; Arcturus
1809–99
educator, author, Civil War nurse, designer of the Confederate flag
Cyc Am Bio; Dict Am Bio; Nat Cyc Am Bio v24; Twent Cen Bio Dict Not Am

2239. Stafford, Maria Brewster Brooks
born 1809
educator
Alabama
Wom Cent

2240. Cowles, Betsey Mix
1810–76
educator
Not Am Wom

2241. Fuller, Sarah Margaret; Marchioness Ossoli; Sarah Margaret Fuller Ossoli
1810–50
author, critic, educator, feminist, philosopher, journalist, Transcendentalist revolutionary
Transcendentalist
Boston, MA
Cyc Am Bio; Dict Am Auth; Dict Am Bio; Dict Am Bio Men Time; Dict Lit Bio v1; Index t Wom; Nat Cyc Am Bio v3; Not Am Wom; Twent Cen Bio Dict Not Am; Wom Cent

2242. Hale, Mary Whitwell
1810–62
poet, educator, hymn writer
Massachusetts
Dict Am Auth; Index t Wom

2243. Ball, Martha Violet
born 1811
abolitionist, philanthropist, educator of Black women
Baptist
Wom Cent

2244. Fobes, Philena
1811–98
educator
Nat Cyc Am Bio v6

2245. Lowell, Anna Cabot (Jackson)
1811/19–1874
textbook author, educator, writer on conversation
Cyc Am Bio; Dict Am Auth; Dict Am Bio Men Time; Twent Cen Bio Dict Not Am

2246. Lozier, Clemence Sophia
1812/13–1888
physician, founder and dean of the New York Women's Medical College and Hospital for Women, suffragist, feminist
Cyc Am Bio; Dict Am Bio; Index t Wom; Not Am Wom; Twent Cen Bio Dict Not Am

2247. Osborne, Phoebe Ann Sayre
1812–97
educator
Twent Cen Bio Dict Not Am

2248. Porter, Sarah
1813–1900
educator, school founder
Cyc Am Bio; Dict Am Bio; Nat Cyc Am Bio v10; Not Am Wom; Twent Cen Bio Dict Not Am

2249. Preston, Ann
1813–72
physician, hospital founder, college administrator, educator
Pennsylvania
Cyc Am Bio; Dict Am Bio; Index t Wom; Nat Cyc Am Bio v10; Not Am Wom; Twent Cen Bio Dict Not Am; Wom Cent

2250. Hayden, Mary Bridget, Mother
1814–90
Catholic nun, missionary, educator of Native Americans
Not Am Wom

2251. Spear, Catherine Swan Brown
born 1814
educator, abolitionist, Underground Railroad worker, prison reformer, suffragist
Wom Cent

2252. Stone, Lucinda Hinsdale
1814–1900
educator, clubwoman, women's club organizer, women's educator, feminist
Index t Wom; Nat Cyc Am Bio v13; Not Am Wom; Wom Cent

2253. Wells, Charlotte Fowler
1814–1901
phrenologist, patron of women's medical education, educator, publisher, lecturer, businessperson

New York
Cyc Am Bio; Index t Wom; Not Am Wom; Wom Cent

2254. Botta, Anne Charlotte Lynch
1815/20–1891
author, literary host, educator, poet
New York
Cyc Am Bio; Dict Am Auth; Dict Am Bio; Dict Am Bio Men Time; Dict Lit Bio v3; Nat Cyc Am Bio v7; Not Am Wom; Twent Cen Bio Dict Not Am; Wom Cent

2255. Mason, Emily Virginia
1815–1909
Civil War hospital matron, Confederate army Civil War nurse, author, biographer, educator
Cyc Am Bio; Dict Am Auth; Index t Wom; Nat Cyc Am Bio v5

2256. Miner, Myrtilla
1815–64
educator, pioneer in teacher education for Black women, abolitionist, philanthropist
Cyc Am Bio; Dict Am Bio; Not Am Wom

2257. Bonney, Mary Lucinda
1816–1900
Native American rights advocate, educator
Not Am Wom

2258. Fiske, Fidelia
1816–1864/84
Congregationalist missionary to Persia, educator
Congregationalist
Cyc Am Bio; Dict Am Bio; Dict Am Bio Men Time; Index t Wom; Nat Cyc Am Bio v3; Not Am Wom; Wom Cent

2259. Gardner, Anna
born 1816
abolitionist, educator of freedmen, women's rights worker
Wom Cent

2260. Mortimer, Mary
1816/18–1877
educator, women's educator, founder of the Milwaukee Female College
Wisconsin
English
Dict Am Bio; Index t Wom; Nat Cyc Am Bio v7; Not Am Wom; Wom Cent

2261. Newcomb, Josephine Louise le Monnier
1816–1901

philanthropist, patron of women's education
Dict Am Bio; Not Am Wom

2262. Porter, Lydia Ann (Emerson)
born 1816
author, educator
Springfield, VT
Cyc Am Bio; Dict Am Auth

2263. Rambaut, Mary Lucinda Bonney
1816–1900
Native American rights worker, educator
Baptist
Dict Am Bio; Index t Wom; Nat Cyc Am Bio v6; Twent Cen Bio Dict Not Am; Wom Cent

2264. Sill, Anna Peck
1816–89
educator, founder of the Rockford Female Seminary
Dict Am Bio; Not Am Wom

2265. Anneke, Mathilde Franziska Giesler
1817–84
author, educator, women's rights worker
Dict Am Bio; Nat Cyc Am Bio v4; Not Am Wom

2266. Atkins, Mary
1817/19–1882
educator
Index t Wom; Not Am Wom

2267. Bishop, Harriet E.
1817–83
educator, missionary
Index t Wom; Not Am Wom

2268. Coleman, Lucy Newhall; Lucy Colman
1817–1906
abolitionist, educator of Blacks, women's rights worker, suffragist, lecturer, health reformer
Universalist
Dict Am Bio; Nat Cyc Am Bio v4, Wom Cent

2269. Bean, Mary J.
circa 1818–75
educator
Nat Cyc Am Bio v4

2270. Burnham, Sarah Maria
1818–1901
educator, historical author, writer on geology and travel
Cambridge, MA
Dict Am Auth

2271. Holley, Sallie
1818–93
abolitionist, educator of freedmen, feminist, lecturer
Index t Wom; Not Am Wom

2272. Marwedel, Emma Jacobina Christiana
1818–93
kindergarten educator
Dict Am Bio

2273. Arey, Harriet Ellen (Grannis)
1819–post 1888
poet, education writer, educator, magazine editor
Appl Cyc Am Bio; Cyc Am Bio; Dict Am Auth; Dict Am Bio Men Time; Wom Cent

2274. Clapp, Louise Amelia Knapp Smith; Dame Shirley; Amelia Knapp Smith
1819–1906
author, educator, letter writer during the California gold rush, gold rush pioneer
California
Index t Wom; Not Am Wom; Read Encyc Am West

2275. Haven, Mary Emerson
born 1819
educator
Wom Cent

2276. Johnson, Ellen Cheney
1819/29–1899
prison reformer, prison superintendent, educator
Dict Am Bio; Not Am Wom; Twent Cen Bio Dict Not Am

2277. Lord, Elizabeth W. Russell
born 1819
educator, philanthropist, educator of the blind
Index t Wom; Wom Cent

2278. Gleason, Rachel Brooks
1820–1905
physician, medical author, abolitionist, patron of freedmen's education, dress reformer, women's rights worker
Dict Am Auth; Index t Wom; Wom Cent

2279. Hemenway, Mary Porter (Tileston)
1820/22–1894
philanthropist, patron of archaeology and education
Dict Am Bio; Index t Wom; Not Am Wom; Twent Cen Bio Dict Not Am

2280. Mather, Sarah Ann
born 1820
philanthropist, patron of Black education, educator, author
South Carolina
Index t Wom; Wom Cent

2281. McHenry, Mary
flourished 1850s–70s
philanthropist, sponsor of Native American children's education
Cyc Am Bio

2282. Scott, Elizabeth Thorn
flourished 1850s
school founder
Index t Wom

2283. Blackwell, Elizabeth
1821–1910
physician, medical author and educator, worker for women's medical education
English
Appl Cyc Am Bio; Cyc Am Bio and ad; Dict Am Auth; Dict Am Bio; Dict Am Bio Men Time; Eng Wom; Nat Cyc Am Bio v9; Not Am Wom; Twent Cen Bio Dict Not Am; Wom Cent

2284. Dewey, Mary Elizabeth
1821; died post 1871
author, translator, educator, biographer
Cyc Am Bio; Dict Am Auth; Index t Wom; Twent Cen Bio Dict Not Am

2285. Dodge, Hannah P.
born 1821
educator, temperance worker
Wom Cent

2286. Graves, Adelia Cleopatra (Spencer); Aunt Alice
1821–95
author, children's author, rhetorician, linguist, educator, president of Mary Sharp College
Tennessee
Cyc Am Bio; Dict Am Auth; Twent Cen Bio Dict Not Am; Wom Cent

2287. Richards, Maria Tolman
born 1821
author, educator, lecturer
Providence, RI
Cyc Am Bio; Dict Am Auth

2288. Thompson, Elizabeth Rowell
1821–99
philanthropist, temperance worker, patron of science and of women's medical education, suffragist, political philosopher
Cyc Am Bio; Index t Wom; Nat Cyc Am Bio v5; Not Am Wom; Twent Cen Bio Dict Not Am; Wom Cent

2289. Agassiz, Elizabeth Cabot Carrie
1822–1907
founder and president of Radcliffe College, educator, biographer, naturalist, science writer
Boston, MA
Dict Am Auth; Dict Am Bio; Index t Wom; Not Am Wom; Wom Cent

2290. Dall, Caroline Wells (Healey)
1822–1912
author, essayist, women's rights worker, women's labor reformer, educator
Boston, MA
Cyc Am Bio; Dict Am Auth; Dict Am Bio; Dict Lit Bio v1; Index t Wom; Nat Cyc Am Bio v9; Not Am Wom; Twent Cen Bio Dict Not Am; Wom Cent

2291. Ewing, Catherine A. Fay
born 1822
educator, philanthropist, missionary to the Choctaw people
Wom Cent

2292. Lamson, Mary (Swift)
born 1822
educator of the blind and deaf, biographer
Dict Am Auth

2293. Latimer, [Mary] Elizabeth (Wormeley)
1822–1904
novelist, educator, historian, writer on history
Baltimore, MD
English
Cyc Am Bio; Dict Am Auth; Dict Am Bio; Dict Am Bio Men Time; Index t Wom; Nat Cyc Am Bio v9; Wom Cent

2294. Shattuck, Lydia White
1822–89
naturalist, botanist, chemist, teacher of science
Not Am Wom; Wom Cent

2295. Bradley, Amy Morris
1823–1904
educator, Civil War nurse, hospital administrator
Index t Wom; Not Am Wom; Wom Cent

2296. Burnz, Eliza Boardman
1823–1903
educator, phonetician, stenographic educator, spelling reformer
English
Nat Cyc Am Bio v6; Wom Cent

2297. Cary, Mary Ann Shad
1823–93
educator, lawyer, journalist, editor, abolitionist, Canadian pioneer
Black; Canadian
Index t Wom; Negro Alman; Not Am Wom; Prof Negro Wom

2298. Douglass, Margaret Crittenden
flourished 1853
educator, founder of a school for Black children that was closed by authorities
Cyc Am Bio

2299. Peake, Mary Smith Kelsey
1823–62
educator of freedmen, Union patriot in the Civil War
Black
Index t Wom; Negro Alman; Prof Negro Wom v1

2300. Very, Lydia Louise Ann
1823–1901/07
poet, children's author, illustrator, educator
Salem, MA
Cyc Am Bio; Dict Am Auth; Dict Am Bio; Index t Wom; Nat Cyc Am Bio v6; Wom Cent

2301. Worthen, Augusta Harvey
born 1823
educator, author, historian of New Hampshire
New Hampshire
Wom Cent

2302. Brigham, Mary Ann
1824/29–1889
university educator
Dict Am Bio and supp v4

2303. Gillespie, Eliza Maria; Mother Mary of St. Angela
1824–87
mother superior and founder of the American Sisters of the Holy Cross, educator, Civil War hospital administrator
Catholic
Cyc Am Bio; Dict Am Bio; Index t Wom; Not Am Wom; Twent Cen Bio Dict Not Am; Wom Cent

2304. Ketchum, Annie Chambers
1824–1904
poet, novelist, educator, lecturer
Cyc Am Bio; Dict Am Auth

2305. Larcom, Lucy
1824/26–1893
millworker, author, poet, magazine editor, seminary teacher
Beverly, MA
Cyc Am Bio; Dict Am Auth; Dict Am Bio Men Time; Index t Wom; Nat Cyc Am Bio v1; Not Am Wom; Twent Cen Bio Dict Not Am; Wom Cent

2306. Merrill, Catherine
1824–1900
educator, writer on Indiana

Indianapolis, IN
Dict Am Auth

2307. Packard, Sophia B.
1824–91
founder of Spelman College,
church worker, educator of
Blacks
Baptist
Atlanta, GA
Nat Cyc Am Bio v2; Not Am
Wom

2308. Starr, Eliza Allen
1824–1901
writer and lecturer on art and
religion, poet, author, artist, ed-
ucator
Chicago, IL
Cyc Am Bio; Dict Am Auth; Dict
Am Bio; Nat Cyc Am Bio v13;
Not Am Wom; Twent Cen Bio
Dict Not Am; Wom Cent

**2309. Walton, Electa Noble
Lincoln**
born 1824
educator, lecturer, suffragist, feminist
Massachusetts
Wom Cent

**2310. Beauchamp, Mary
Elizabeth; Filia Ecclesiae**
born 1825
religious author, educator
Wom Cent

**2311. Chesebro, Caroline; Che-
sebrough, Caroline**
1825/28–1873
short story writer, novelist, col-
lege educator
New York
Cyc Am Bio; Dict Am Auth; Dict
Am Bio; Dict Am Bio Men
Time; Nat Cyc Am Bio v22;
Twent Cen Bio Dict Not Am

**2312. Cooper, Sarah Brown In-
gersoll**
1825/36–1896
kindergartner, Bible teacher, philanthropist
California
Dict Am Bio; Nat Cyc Am Bio
v3; Not Am Wom; Wom Cent

**2313. French, Lucy Virginia
(Smith)**
1825/30–1881
poet, author, editor, educator
Memphis, TN
Cyc Am Bio; Dict Am Auth; Dict
Am Bio; Nat Cyc Am Bio v7

**2314. Mills, Susan Lincoln
Tolman**
1825/26–1912

missionary educator, college pres-
ident
Dict Am Bio; Index t Wom; Not
Am Wom; Twent Cen Bio Dict
Not Am

**2315. Stanford, Jane Eliza La-
throp**
1825/28–1905
cofounder of Stanford University,
patron of education, philanthropist
Index t Wom; Nat Cyc Am Bio
v24; Not Am Wom; Twent Cen
Bio Dict Not Am; Wom Cent

2316. Towne, Laura Matilda
1825–1901
educator of freedmen
Not Am Wom

2317. White, Catherine Ann
1825–78
writer on religions, superior of the
Convent of the Sacred Heart,
Catholic nun, classicist
Catholic
Dict Am Auth

2318. Frazier, Martha M.
born 1826
educator, temperance worker
Wisconsin
Wom Cent

2319. Nash, Mary Louise
born 1826
educator, author, humorist, botanist, geologist
Wom Cent

2320. Penny, Virginia
born 1826
author, educator, women's labor
reform worker, feminist
Cyc Am Bio; Dict Am Auth; Dict
Am Bio Men Time

**2321. Robertson, Ann Eliza
Worcester**
1826–1905
missionary, educator, student of
Native American languages
Not Am Wom

2322. Doggett, Kate Newell
1827/28–1884
suffragist, educator, art critic,
translator
Cyc Am Bio; Index t Wom

2323. Howland, Emily
1827–1929
educator, educator of Blacks, abolitionist, suffragist, pacifist, temperance worker, philanthropist
Quaker
New York
Dict Am Bio; Nat Cyc Am Bio
v25; Not Am Wom; Wom Cent

2324. Kennedy, Kate
1827–90
educator, educational reformer,
champion of equal pay for
women, women's rights worker,
women's labor worker
Oakland, CA
Irish
Nat Cyc Am Bio v30; Not Am
Wom

2325. McGroarty, Julia, Sister
1827–1901
Catholic nun, educator
Catholic
Not Am Wom

2326. Brinkerhoff, Clara M.
born 1828
soprano singer, composer, music
educator
English
Wom Cent

2327. Coe, Emily M.
graduated 1853; died post 1870
kindergarten educator
Wom Cent

**2328. Kirkland, Elizabeth
Stansbury**
1828–96
miscellaneous writer, educator
Dict Am Auth; Twent Cen Bio
Dict Not Am

2329. Woolsey, Abby Howland
1828–93
Civil War relief worker, hospital
worker, charity and educational
worker, author on public
health, philanthropist
Dict Am Auth; Index t Wom;
Not Am Wom

**2330. Cady, Sarah Louise (En-
sign)**
1829–1912
educator, kindergartner, founder
of Mrs. Cady's School for Girls
(now the West End Institute)
New Haven, CT
Dict Am Bio; Nat Cyc Am Bio v9

**2331. Cleveland, Emeline Hor-
ton**
1829–78
surgeon, medical educator, lecturer
Index t Wom; Not Am Wom

2332. Crocker, Lucretia
1829–86
educator, school administrator
Index t Wom; Not Am Wom

2333. Howard, Ada Lydia
1829–1907

educator, first president of
Wellesley College
Dict Am Bio; Nat Cyc Am Bio
v7; Twent Cen Bio Dict Not
Am

2334. May, Abigail Williams
1829–88
Boston social reformer, abolitionist, suffragist, education commissioner, Civil War relief
worker
Boston, MA
Index t Wom; Not Am Wom;
Twent Cen Bio Dict Not Am

2335. Oakey, Emily Sullivan
1829–83
author, poet, educator
Albany, NY
Cyc Am Bio; Dict Am Auth

**2336. Rogers, Elizabeth Ann;
Sister Beatrice**
1829–1921
educator, Anglican nun
Anglican
Not Am Wom

2337. Botume, Elizabeth Hyde
flourished 1860s
Civil War patriot, educator
Index t Wom

2338. Bucklin, Sophronia
flourished 1860s
Civil War relief worker, educator,
nurse
Index t Wom

2339. Calahan, Mary A.
flourished 1860s
educator
Index t Wom

2340. Cappiani, Luisa
flourished 1860s–80s
opera singer, music educator
Austrian
Wom Cent

2341. Carter, Hannah Johnson
flourished 1860s–90s
art educator
Wom Cent

**2342. Carter, Mary Adaline
Edwards**
flourished 1860s–80s
industrial arts instructor and designer, embroiderer, painter,
china painter, plastics artist,
temperance worker
Wom Cent

2343. Clapp, Anna L.
flourished 1860s
Civil War relief worker, educator
Index t Wom

2344. Collins, Delia
born 1830

educator, temperance worker, philanthropist, welfare worker
Wom Cent

2345. Doyle, Sarah Elizabeth
1830–1922
educator, clubwoman, women's rights worker
Dict Am Bio; Not Am Wom

2346. Eddy, Sara Hershey
flourished 1860s–70s
music educator, singer
Index t Wom; Wom Cent

2347. Granson, Milla
flourished pre-1860s
educator of slaves
Mississippi
Black
Prof Negro Wom v1

2348. Hunt, Mary Hannah Hanchett
1830–1906
leader of the campaign for temperance education in the schools, educator
Dict Am Bio; Not Am Wom; Wom Cent

2349. Leavitt, Mary Greenleaf Clement
1830–1912
educator, temperance missionary, traveler
Dict Am Bio; Nat Cyc Am Bio v5; Not Am Wom; Twent Cen Bio Dict Not Am; Wom Cent

2350. Louis, Minnie Dessau
flourished 1860s–90s
Jewish welfare worker, educator
Jewish
New York
Nat Cyc Am Bio v18

2351. MacKaye, Maria Ellery (Goodwin)
born 1830
educator, author
Cambridge, MA
Dict Am Auth

2352. Mann, Maria R.
flourished 1860s
Civil War philanthropist, educator
Index t Wom

2353. McNall, B. A.
flourished 1860s
educator, lawyer
Index t Wom

2354. Miller, Dora Richards
flourished 1860s–80s
author, Civil War diarist, journalist, educator
West Indian (Danish West Indies)
Index t Wom; Wom Cent

2355. Park, Lucia Darling
flourished 1860s
western pioneer, educator, vigilante
Index t Wom

2356. Rullmann, Maria
flourished 1860s
educator, philanthropist
Index t Wom

2357. Russell, E. J.
flourished 1860s
Civil War nurse, educator
Index t Wom

2358. Smith, Rebecca S.
flourished 1860s
educator, Civil War nurse
Index t Wom

2359. Springer, C. R., Mrs.
flourished 1860s
Civil War humanitarian, educator
Index t Wom

2360. Stevens, Emily Pitt
flourished 1860s–90s
educator, temperance worker, feminist, suffragist
Presbyterian
California
Wom Cent

2361. Wells, Mary Fletcher
flourished 1860s–90s
philanthropist, educator of freedmen
Alabama
Wom Cent

2362. Woolsey, Jane Stuart
1830–91
Civil War relief and hospital worker, charity and educational worker, nurse, author
Index t Wom; Not Am Wom

2363. Bodley, Rachel Littler
1831–88
chemist, botanist, physician, naturalist, dean of the Women's Medical College of Pennsylvania
Pennsylvania
Not Am Wom; Wom Cent

2364. Dean, Rebecca Pennell
1831–90
educator
Index t Wom

2365. Deane, Margaret
born 1831
educator
Index t Wom

2366. Garnett, Sarah J. Smith Thompson
1831–1911
educator, civic worker
New York

Black
Index t Wom; Not Am Wom; Prof Negro Wom v1

2367. Hallowell, Anna
1831–1905
welfare worker, educational reformer, kindergarten leader
Not Am Wom

2368. Nutting, Mary Olivia
1831–1910
author, historian, educator, librarian, autobiographer
Dict Am Auth; Index t Wom

2369. Ripley, Mary A.
born 1831
poet, educator, lecturer, author
Index t Wom; Wom Cent

2370. Culver, Helen
1832–1925
philanthropist, Black welfare worker, patron of science, hospital administrator, educator, real estate businessperson
Index t Wom; Nat Cyc Am Bio v17; Twent Cen Bio Dict Not Am

2371. Doolittle, Lucy Salisbury
born 1832
philanthropist, reformer of women's prisons, suffragist, educator of freedwomen
Wom Cent

2372. Fussell, Susan
1832–89
educator, army nurse in the Civil War, Civil War relief worker, philanthropist
Quaker
Wom Cent

2373. Knowlton, Helen Mary
1832–1918
painter, art educator, writer on art and art technique
Boston, MA
Cyc Am Bio; Dict Am Auth; Not Am Wom; Twent Cen Bio Dict Not Am

2374. Lawton, Elizabeth Tillinghast
1832–1904
educator
Index t Wom

2375. Magill, Mary Tucker
1832–99
fiction writer, journalist, educator
Winchester, VA
Cyc Am Bio; Dict Am Auth; Twent Cen Bio Dict Not Am

2376. McKinney, Jane Army
born 1832

educator, temperance worker, suffragist, kindergartner
Wom Cent

2377. Mead, Elizabeth Storrs (Billings)
1832–1917
president of Mt. Holyoke College, educator
Nat Cyc Am Bio v4; Not Am Wom; Twent Cen Bio Dict Not Am

2378. Pollock, Louise
born 1832
kindergarten educator
Prussian
Index t Wom; Wom Cent

2379. Aiken, Amanda L.
1833–92
philanthropist, editor, patron of women's education
Index t Wom; Wom Cent

2380. Andrews, Jane
1833–87
educator, children's author
Dict Am Auth; Index t Wom; Not Am Wom

2381. Boya, Ellen Wright
born 1833
educator, author on religious education, writer on art and architecture
Albany, NY
Dict Am Auth

2382. Carson, Delia E.
born 1833
educator of women, traveler
Madison, WI
Wom Cent

2383. Goodwin, Lavinia Stella (Tyler)
born 1833
author, children's author, poet, educator
Dict Am Auth; Wom Cent

2384. Hooker, Ellen Kelley
born 1833
college educator
Nat Cyc Am Bio v4; Twent Cen Bio Dict Not Am

2385. Miller, Emily Clark Huntington
1833–1913
author, children's author, journalist, editor, poet, semireligious-fiction writer, church worker, temperance worker, educator
Evanston, IL
Dict Am Auth; Dict Am Bio; Index t Wom; Not Am Wom; Twent Cen Bio Dict Not Am; Wom Cent

2386. Otis, Eliza Ann (Wetherby)
1833–1904
poet, journalist
Nat Cyc Am Bio v14; Wom Cent

2387. Schurz, Margarethe Meyer
1833–76
early kindergarten advocate, educator
Index t Wom; Not Am Wom

2388. Woolsey, Georgeanne Muirson
1833–1906
Civil War relief and hospital worker, charity and educational worker
Index t Wom; Not Am Wom

2389. Beasley, Matilda, Mother
1834–1903
educator, social worker, Catholic nun
Catholic
Georgia
Black
Negro Alman; Prof Negro Wom

2390. Hopkins, Louisa Parsons (Stone)
1834–95
educator, writer on education, poet
Boston, MA
Dict Am Auth

2391. Leonowens, Anna Harriette (Crawford)
born 1834
author on Siam, kindergarten educator, missionary educator in Siam
New York
English
Cyc Am Bio; Dict Am Bio

2392. Rogers, Harriet Burbank
1834–1919
educator of the deaf
Not Am Wom

2393. Willing, Jennie Fowler
1834–1916
Methodist local preacher, church worker, temperance reformer, lecturer, author, educator
Methodist
Canadian
Index t Wom; Not Am Wom; Wom Cent

2394. Bristol, Augusta (Cooper)
1835–1910
educator, writer on education, author, poet, sociologist, lecturer on philosophic and scientific topics
Cyc Am Bio and ad; Dict Am Auth; Twent Cen Bio Dict Not Am; Wom Cent

2395. Coppin, Fanny Marion Jackson
1835/37–1912/18
educator, foreign missionary, social worker, lecturer, women's rights worker
Black
Encyc Black Am; Index t Wom; Negro Alman; Not Am Wom; Prof Negro Wom

2396. Edwards, Anna Cheney
born 1835
geologist, botanist, educator
Wom Cent

2397. Eytinge, Rose
1835/38–1911
actor, author, drama teacher
Cyc Am Bio; Dict Am Bio; Index t Wom; Not Am Wom; Twent Cen Bio Dict Not Am

2398. Haskell, Harriet Newell
1835–1907
educator
Nat Cyc Am Bio v6; Wom Cent

2399. Howe, Mary Ann
1835–70
educator of Blacks, philanthropist
Nat Cyc Am Bio v8

2400. Jones, Amanda Theodosia
1835–1914
author, inventor of an improved process for canning food, poet, educator
Spiritualist
Chicago, IL
Cyc Am Bio; Dict Am Auth; Dict Am Bio; Nat Cyc Am Bio v7; Not Am Wom; Wom Cent

2401. McCormick, Nancy Maria Fowler "Nettie"
1835–1923
patron of education in China, philanthropist, businessperson
Presbyterian
Index t Wom; Nat Cyc Am Bio v21; Not Am Wom

2402. Meech, Jeannette du Bois
born 1835
evangelist, missionary worker, Baptist preacher, temperance worker, industrial educator of women
Baptist
New Jersey
Index t Wom; Wom Cent

2403. Miles, Ellen E.
born 1835
poet, educator
Index t Wom

2404. Tutwiler, Julia Strudwick
1835/41–1916

educator, women's educator, temperance worker, prison reformer
Alabama
Dict Am Bio; Encyc South Hist; Index t Wom; Nat Cyc Am Bio v15; Not Am Wom; Wom Cent

2405. Wilhorst, Cora de (Withers)
born 1835
concert and opera singer, voice teacher
Cyc Am Bio

2406. Brackett, Anna Callender
1836–1911
women's educator, women's rights worker, author
Dict Am Auth; Dict Am Bio; Nat Cyc Am Bio v21; Not Am Wom

2407. Brownell, Helen M. Davis
born 1836
educator
Wom Cent

2408. Bullock, Helen Louise
born 1836
temperance worker, music educator, women's prison reformer
Wom Cent

2409. Fuller, Sarah
1836–1927
educator of the deaf
Not Am Wom

2410. Kilgore, Caroline Burnham "Carrie"
1836/38–1909
educator, lawyer, women's rights advocate
Index t Wom; Nat Cyc Am Bio v5; Not Am Wom

2411. Kraus-Boelte, Maria
1836–1918
kindergarten educator
German
Dict Am Bio; Nat Cyc Am Bio v13; Not Am Wom

2412. Picken, Lillian Hoxie
born 1836
educator
Wom Cent

2413. Prang, Mary Amelia [Dana] Hicks
1836–1927
art educator, writer on art, editor
Dict Am Bio; Index t Wom; Nat Cyc Am Bio v27; Not Am Wom; Twent Cen Bio Dict Not Am

2414. Reignolds, Catherine Mary "Kate"
1836–1911

actor, dramatic reader, educator
Not Am Wom

2415. Sanford, Maria Louise
1836–1920
educator, college professor
Nat Cyc Am Bio v20; Not Am Wom

2416. Stearns, Sarah Burger
1836–post 1899
suffragist, women's rights worker, philanthropist, Civil War humanitarian, temperance worker, social reformer, educator of freedmen
Unitarian
Cyc Am Bio; Index t Wom; Nat Cyc Am Bio v10; Twent Cen Bio Dict Not Am; Wom Cent

2417. Talcott, Eliza
1836–1911
missionary educator and nurse in Japan
Dict Am Bio; Not Am Wom

2418. Wright, Hannah Amelia
born 1836
gynecologist, medical educator
New York
Wom Cent

2419. Dike, Jeannie Dean Scott
1837–1920
music educator, Congregationalist missionary
Congregationalist
New York
Twent Cen Bio Dict Not Am; Wom Cent

2420. Ferguson, Abbie Park
1837–1919
educator, president of Huguenot University in South Africa
Dict South Af Bio v2; Not Am Wom; South Af Dict Nat Bio

2421. Flower, Lucy Louisa (Coues)
1837–1921
social welfare worker, philanthropist, patron of education, president of the Illinois Training School for Nurses, member of the Chicago school board, trustee of the University of Illinois, Republican party worker
Episcopalian
Dict Am Bio; Nat Cyc Am Bio v9; Not Am Wom

2422. Fonda, Mary Alice Ives; Octavia Hensel
born 1837
linguist, author, musician, music educator, writer on music
Wom Cent

2423. Grimke, Charlotte L. Forten
1837/38–1914
educator, author, poet
Black
Index t Wom; Negro Alman; Not Am Wom; Prof Negro Wom v1

2424. Johnston, Adelia Antoinette Field
born 1837
educator
Wom Cent

2425. Mountcastle, Clara H.
born 1837
author, elocutionist
Canadian
Cyc Am Bio; Wom Cent

2426. Norton, Minerva (Brace)
born 1837
educator, author, missionary worker
Beloit, WI
Dict Am Auth; Wom Cent

2427. Richardson, Abby (Sage)
1837–1900
author, actor, historian, lecturer on history, writer on literature, educator
Dict Am Auth; Index t Wom; Nat Cyc Am Bio v5; Twent Cen Bio Dict Not Am

2428. Spencer, Sara Andrews
born 1837
suffragist, women's rights worker, business educator, author
Washington, DC
Cyc Am Bio; Dict Am Auth

2429. Truitt, Anna Augusta
born 1837
temperance reformer, suffragist, patron of industrial education
Muncie, IN
Wom Cent

2430. Wait, Anna C.
born 1837
suffragist, educator, politician
Kansas
Wom Cent

2431. West, Mary Allen
1837–92
educator, temperance worker, writer on education and child care, journalist
Illinois
Cyc Am Bio; Dict Am Auth; Index t Wom; Wom Cent

2432. Cobb, Mary Emilie
born 1838
educator, philanthropist, juvenile-prison reformer
Wom Cent

2433. Dickey, Sarah Ann
1838–1904
educator of freedmen
Not Am Wom

2434. Edwards, Emma Atwood
born 1838
educator
Wom Cent

2435. Ewing, Emma Pike
born 1838
home economics teacher, cooking teacher
Twent Cen Bio Dict Not Am; Wom Cent

2436. Foster, Theodosia Maria (Toll); Faye Huntington
born 1838
author, children's author, educator
Vermont
Twent Cen Bio Dict Not Am

2437. Lippincott, Esther J. (Trimble)
1838–88
educator, author on literature, temperance reformer, convalescent-hospital reformer
Quaker
Pennsylvania
Dict Am Auth; Wom Cent

2438. Little, Sarah F. Cowles
born 1838
educator of the blind
Index t Wom; Wom Cent

2439. Roge, Charlotte Fiske (Bates)
born 1838
author, poet, literary critic, educator
New York
Dict Am Auth; Wom Cent

2440. Stokes, Missouri H.
1838–post 1860
Civil War diarist, educator, temperance worker
Presbyterian
Georgia
Index t Wom; Wom Cent

2441. Vashon, Susan Paul
1838–1912
educator, nurse, Civil War relief organizer
Black
Index t Wom; Negro Alman; Prof Negro Wom v1

2442. Wells, Catharine Boott (Gannett)
born 1838
author, religious writer, essayist, novelist, educator
Boston, MA
Dict Am Auth; Twent Cen Bio Dict Not Am

2443. Woods, Kate Tannatt
1838–1910
club leader, editor, poet, children's author
Salem, MA
Dict Am Auth; Index t Wom; Wom Cent

2444. Woolson, Abba Louisa (Goold)
1838–1921
educator, author, lecturer, dress reformer
Boston, MA
Cyc Am Bio; Dict Am Auth; Dict Am Bio; Index t Wom; Nat Cyc Am Bio v9; Not Am Wom; Wom Cent

2445. Campbell, Helen (Stuart)
1839–1918
journalist, children's author, social reformer, home economist, educator, philanthropist
New York
Cyc Am Bio; Dict Am Auth; Nat Cyc Am Bio v9; Not Am Wom; Twent Cen Bio Dict Not Am; Wom Cent

2446. Cooper-Pucher, Matilda S.
1839–1900
secondary educator
Dict Am Bio

2447. Dickinson, Mary Lowe
1839–1914
author, educator, short story writer, poet
New York, NY
Dict Am Auth; Index t Wom

2448. Garrett, Mary Smith
1839–1925
educator of the deaf, child welfare worker
Not Am Wom

2449. Hancock, Cornelia
1839/40–1927
Civil War nurse, educator of freedmen, charity worker, housing reformer
Quaker
Index t Wom; Not Am Wom

2450. Kidd, Lucy Ann
1839–1916
educator, president of the North Texas Female College
Texas
Index t Wom; Nat Cyc Am Bio v117; Wom Cent

2451. Nixon, Jennie Caldwell
born 1839
educator
Louisiana
Wom Cent

2452. Putnam, Georgianna Frances
1839–1914
educator, school principal
Black
Index t Wom; Negro Alman; Prof Negro Wom v1

2453. Randolph, Sarah Nicholas (Jefferson)
1839–92
author, educator, biographer
Baltimore, MD
Cyc Am Bio; Dict Am Auth; Dict Am Bio; Twent Cen Bio Dict Not Am

2454. Sanborn, Katharine Abbott "Kate"
1839–1917
miscellaneous author, educator, lecturer, essayist, literary professor, agriculturist
New Hampshire
Cyc Am Bio; Dict Am Auth; Dict Am Bio; Index t Wom; Nat Cyc Am Bio v9; Twent Cen Bio Dict Not Am

2455. Schofield, Martha
1839–1916
educator of freedmen
Quaker
Not Am Wom

2456. Shafer, Helen Almira
1839–94
mathematician, educator, third president of Wellesley College
Cyc Am Bio; Dict Am Bio; Index t Wom; Nat Cyc Am Bio v7; Twent Cen Bio Dict Not Am; Wom Cent

2457. Willard, Frances Elizabeth Caroline
1839–98
educator, educational philosopher, suffragist, feminist, women's rights worker, temperance leader, naturalist, philanthropist, newspaper editor, traveler
Methodist Episcopal
Cyc Am Bio; Dict Am Auth; Dict Am Bio; Dict Am Bio Men Time; Dict Am Rel Bio; Index t Wom; Nat Cyc Am Bio v1; Not Am Wom; Twent Cen Bio Dict Not Am; Wom Cent

2458. Adams, Mary (Mathews)
1840–1902
educator, poet
Madison, WI
Irish
Dict Am Auth; Wom Cent

2459. Andrews, Eliza Frances
1840/47–1931
journalist, Civil War diarist, educator, botanist

Georgia
Dict Am Auth; Index t Wom;
Nat Cyc Am Bio v6; Not Am
Wom; Wom Cent

2460. Baggett, Alice
born 184?
educator
Wom Cent

2461. Burnett, Cynthia S.
born 1840
educator, temperance worker
Index t Wom; Wom Cent

2462. Carpenter, Caroline A.
flourished 1870s–80s
educator
Index t Wom

2463. Chapin, Mary E.
flourished 1870s–80s
educator
Index t Wom

2464. Coolidge, Harriet Abbot Lincoln
flourished 1870s–80s
philanthropist, sanitary educator,
worker for women's education,
author
Wom Cent

2465. Dargan, Clara Victoria (MacLean); Claudia
born 1840
poet, fiction writer, educator
South Carolina
Cyc Am Bio; Dict Am Auth; Nat
Cyc Am Bio v7

2466. de Fere, A. Litsner
flourished 1870s–80s
classical singer, voice trainer
Hungarian
Wom Cent

2467. Gibbs, Eleanor Churchill
flourished 1870s–90s
educator
Alabama
Wom Cent

2468. Hall, Sarah Elizabeth
flourished 1870s–80s
educator
New York
Wom Cent

2469. Hardin, Julia Carlin
flourished 1870s
religious educator
Index t Wom

2470. Hawes, Charlotte W.
flourished 1870s–80s
composer, lecturer, music educator
Wom Cent

2471. Hopper, Anna M.
flourished 1870s

educator
Index t Wom

2472. Howard, Ida Tinsley
flourished 1870s
pioneer, educator
Index t Wom

2473. Hubbard, Emma
flourished 1870s–80s
lawyer, educator
Index t Wom

2474. Imen, Loraine
born 1840
elocutionist, clubwoman
Wom Cent

2475. Leland, Caroline Weaver
born 1840
philanthropist, educator
Presbyterian
Michigan
Wom Cent

2476. McLaughlin, Mary Louise M.
flourished 1870s–1900s
ceramic artist, writer on art techniques
Cincinnati, OH
Dict Am Auth; Index t Wom

2477. O'Keefe, Katharine A.
flourished 1870s–90s
educator, lecturer
Massachusetts
Irish
Wom Cent

2478. Patterson, Mary Jane
1840–94
educator
Philadelphia, PA
Black
Index t Wom; Negro Alman; Prof
Negro Wom vl

2479. Polyblank, Ellen Albertina; Sister Albertina
1840–1930
Anglican sister, educator
Anglican
Not Am Wom

2480. Pritchard, Esther Tuttle
born 1840
editor, educator, minister, temperance worker, missionary
Index t Wom; Wom Cent

2481. Raymond, Sarah E.
flourished 1870s–80s
educator
Index t Wom

2482. Richards, Fannie M.
1840–1923
educator
Index t Wom

2483. Robinson, Leora (Bettison)
born 1840
fiction writer, educator
Baptist
Tallahassee, TN
Dict Am Auth; Wom Cent

2484. Shaw, Quincy A., Mrs.
flourished 1870s
pioneer kindergarten educator
Index t Wom

2485. Smedes, Susan (Dabney)
born 1840
author, missionary to the Sioux
people, educator, historian of
the antebellum South
Mississippi
Cyc Am Bio; Dict Am Auth;
Wom Cent

2486. Starrett, Helen (Ekin)
born 1840
nonfiction author, educator
Chicago, IL
Dict Am Auth; Twent Cen Bio
Dict Not Am

2487. Strickland, S. E.
flourished 1870s
feminist, lecturer, educator
Index t Wom

2488. Thoburn, Isabella
1840–1901
Methodist missionary to India,
educator
Canadian
Dict Am Bio; Index t Wom; Nat
Cyc Am Bio v19; Not Am Wom

2489. Trott, Lois E.
flourished 1870s–90s
educator, philanthropist, temperance worker
Wom Cent

2490. Washington, Rachel M.
flourished 1870s
music educator, pianist
Black
Index t Wom

2491. Wixon, Susan Helen
flourished 1870s–90s
author, children's editor, educator, feminist
Massachusetts
Wom Cent

2492. Woodbury, Anna Lowell
flourished 1870s–80s
humanitarian, educator
Index t Wom

2493. Amies, Olive Pond
flourished 1871
temperance worker, educator
Universalist
Wom Cent

2494. Bond, Elizabeth Powell
1841–1926
abolitionist, educator of Blacks,
women's rights worker, pacifist,
civil rights and temperance
worker, dean of Swarthmore
College
Pennsylvania
Dict Am Bio; Index t Wom; Nat
Cyc Am Bio v6; Wom Cent

2495. Clerc, Henrietta Fannie Virginie
born 1841
educator
French
Wom Cent

2496. Corson, Juliet
1841/42–1897
culinary educator, cookbook writer
New York
Cyc Am Bio; Dict Am Auth; Dict
Am Bio; Index t Wom; Nat Cyc
Am Bio v8; Not Am Wom;
Twent Cen Bio Dict Not Am

2497. Lemcke, Gesine
born 1841
domestic science educator, cookbook author
New York
Dict Am Auth

2498. Oberholtzer, Sara Louisa (Vikers)
1841–1930
poet, author, novelist, temperance
worker, leader in school savings
movement, economist
Quaker
Norristown, PA
Cyc Am Bio; Dict Am Auth; Dict
Am Bio; Index t Wom; Nat Cyc
Am Bio v7; Wom Cent

2499. Putnam, Alice Harvey Whiting
1841–1919
pioneer kindergarten educator
Not Am Wom

2500. Richards, Melinda Ann "Linda"
1841–1930
pioneer nursing educator
Index t Wom; Not Am Wom

2501. Sartain, Emily
1841–1927
painter, mezzotint engraver, etcher, illustrator, art educator
Philadelphia, PA
English
Cyc Am Bio; Dict Am Bio; Index
t Wom; Nat Cyc Am Bio v13;
Not Am Wom; Twent Cen Bio
Dict Not Am; Wom Cent

2502. Scott, Mary Augusta
1841–1916

author, educator
Index t Wom

2503. Willard, Mary Bannister
born 1841
temperance worker, educator,
newspaper editor
Methodist
Wom Cent

**2504. Wilson, Lettie Luella
Melissa (Little)**
born 1841
educator
Nat Cyc Am Bio v10

2505. Cunningham, Susan Jane
1842–1921
suffragist, educator, mathematician, astronomer
Pennsylvania
Nat Cyc Am Bio v6; Wom Cent

2506. Edgar, Elizabeth
born 1842
educator
Presbyterian
Pennsylvania
Wom Cent

2507. Halcott, Elizabeth Lente
1842–1943
music educator
Obit File

2508. Hearst, Phoebe Apperson
1842–1919
philanthropist, patron of education and anthropology, Egyptologist
Dict Am Bio; Index t Wom; Nat
Cyc Am Bio v25; Not Am
Wom; Who Who Egypt

**2509. Huntington, Margaret
Jane Evans**
1842–1926
educator
Dict Am Bio

**2510. Jacobi, Mary Corinna
Putnam**
1842–1906
physician, medical author, phar-
macist, educator, feminist
New York, NY
Cyc Am Bio; Dict Am Auth; Dict
Am Bio; Index t Wom; Nat Cyc
Am Bio v8; Not Am Wom;
Twent Cen Bio Dict Not Am;
Wom Cent

2511. Lowman, Mary D.
born 1842
educator of Blacks; deputy register of deeds and mayor of Oskaloosa, Kansas
Presbyterian
Oskaloosa, KS
Index t Wom; Wom Cent

2512. Monroe, Harriet Earhart
born 1842
lecturer, educator, journalist
Kansas; Washington, DC
Dict Am Auth; Wom Cent

**2513. Mumford, Mary Eno
Bassett**
1842–1935
education and civic leader, clubwoman
Philadelphia, PA
Not Am Wom

**2514. Richards, Ellen Henrietta
(Swallow)**
1842–1911
sanitation chemist and engineer,
mineralogist, leader in applied
and domestic science, writer on
domestic science, professor at
MIT, educator
Massachusetts
Cyc Am Bio; Dict Am Auth; Dict
Am Bio; Index t Wom; Nat Cyc
Am Bio v7; Not Am Wom;
Twent Cen Bio Dict Not Am;
Wom Cent

2515. Slocum, Jane Mariah
born 1842
educator of freedmen
Wom Cent

2516. Blow, Susan Elizabeth
1843–1916
kindergarten educator
Dict Am Bio; Not Am Wom

2517. le Row, Caroline Bigelow
born 1843
educator, writer on education
Brooklyn, NY
Dict Am Auth

2518. Moore, Lizzie
1843–1915
educator
Index t Wom

2519. Parloa, Maria
1843–1909
home economics educator, writer
on cooking and domestic economy, lecturer
Dict Am Auth; Index t Wom;
Not Am Wom

2520. Phillips, Elizabeth Buford
1843–1925
educator, litterateur
Nat Cyc Am Bio v20

2521. Weatherby, Delia L.
born 1843
temperance reformer, author, politician, educator
Kansas
Wom Cent

**2522. Avery, Catharine
Hitchcock Tilden**
born 1844
author, educator
Wom Cent

**2523. Butts, Annice E.
Bradford**
born 1844
educator
Nat Cyc Am Bio v11

2524. Gilman, Stella (Scott)
born 1844
founder of Radcliffe College, author
Dict Am Auth; Nat Cyc Am Bio
v10; Not Am Wom

**2525. Harrell, Sarah Carmicha-
el**
born 1844
educator, temperance worker
Indiana
Wom Cent

2526. Hazen, Frances Mary
1844–1925
educator
Nat Cyc Am Bio v6

2527. Howe, Julia Romana
1844–86
educator
Cyc Am Bio

2528. Lawton, Henrietta Beebe
born 1844
musician, vocal music educator
Wom Cent

**2529. Lincoln, Mary Johnson
(Bailey)**
1844–1921
educator, writer and lecturer on
cookery, culinary educator,
home economist
Boston, MA
Dict Am Auth; Dict Am Bio;
Index t Wom; Nat Cyc Am Bio
v24; Not Am Wom

2530. Lozier, Charlotte Irene
1844–70
physician, women's rights worker, suffragist, medical educator
Cyc Am Bio

2531. Merrick, Sarah Newcomb
born 1844
educator, educational missionary
to Nova Scotia
Texas
Canadian
Wom Cent

2532. Orum, Julia Anna
born 1844
educator, elocutionist
Pennsylvania
Wom Cent

2533. Preston, Frances E. L.
1844–1929
temperance lecturer, organist, elocutionist
Black
Negro Alman; Prof Negro Wom
v1

**2534. Sewall, Mary Eliza
Wright**
1844–1920
educator, suffragist, women's
rights worker, feminist, Sorosis
member, clubwoman, pacifist
Dict Am Bio; Index t Wom; Nat
Cyc Am Bio v19; Not Am
Wom; Wom Cent

2535. Swarthout, M. French
born 1844
educator, mathematics textbook
author
Illinois
Wom Cent

2536. Tanner, Mero L. White
born 1844
educator, humanitarian
Index t Wom

2537. Alrich, Emma B.
born 1845
journalist, author, educator
Wom Cent

2538. Barboza, Mary (Garnet)
1845–90
educator, missionary
Black
Nat Cyc Am Bio v5

2539. Brown, Hallie Quinn
1845/50–1949
educator, elocutionist, lecturer,
Black women's leader
Index t Wom; Negro Alman; Not
Am Wom; Prof Negro Wom v1

2540. Carhart, Clara Sully
born 1845
educator, temperance worker,
women's labor welfare worker
Methodist Episcopal
New York
Canadian
Wom Cent

2541. Dorsey, Susan M.
1845–1919
educator
Index t Wom

2542. Garner, Eliza A.
born 1845
educator, politician
South Carolina
Wom Cent

2543. Haygood, Laura Askew
1845–1900

educator, school administrator, missionary educator in China
Dict Am Bio; Not Am Wom

2544. Hough, Emma E. (Smith-Payne)
1845–1907
soprano concert and light opera soloist, patron of music education, philanthropist
California
Am Bio New Cyc

2545. Knowles, Mary Henrietta
1845–1926
educator
Chicago, IL
Nat Cyc Am Bio v22

2546. Mitchell, Nellie Brown
1845?–1924
singer, music educator
New Hampshire
Black
Index t Wom; Prof Negro Wom v1

2547. Morgan, Anne Eugenia Felicia
1845–1909
philosopher, classicist, educator, author
Dict Am Auth; Index t Wom; Wom Cent

2548. Morgan, Helen Clarissa
born 1845
educator
Cyc Am Bio

2549. Paine, Harriet Eliza; Eliza Chester
1845–1910
author, educator
Boston, MA
Dict Am Auth; Index t Wom; Twent Cen Bio Dict Not Am

2550. Thursby, Emma Cecelia
1845/57–1931
soprano concert singer, music educator
Cyc Am Bio; Dict Am Bio; Index t Wom; Nat Cyc Am Bio v22; Not Am Wom; Twent Cen Bio Dict Not Am

2551. Young, Ella (Flagg)
1845–1918
university educator and administrator, writer on education, suffragist
Chicago, IL
Dict Am Auth; Dict Am Bio; Index t Wom; Nat Cyc Am Bio v19; Not Am Wom

2552. Bergen, Fanny (Dickerson)
born 1846/48

educator, botanist, naturalist, science writer
Appl Cyc Am Bio; Cyc Am Bio; Dict Am Auth

2553. Chenoweth, Caroline van Duesen
born 1846
author, university literary educator, military clerk during Civil War, US vice-consul in China
Dict Am Auth; Index t Wom; Twent Cen Bio Dict Not Am; Wom Cent

2554. Garrett, Emma
circa 1846–93
educator of the deaf
Not Am Wom

2555. Hodgkins, Louise Manning
born 1846
author, university educator in literature, writer on literature
Massachusetts
Dict Am Auth; Wom Cent

2556. Mallory, Lucy A.
born 1846
editor, educator of Blacks
Oregon
Index t Wom; Wom Cent

2557. Noble, Edna Chaffee
born 1846
educator, elocutionist
Michigan
Index t Wom; Wom Cent

2558. Woody, Mary Williams Chawner
born 1846
philanthropist, educator, temperance worker
Wom Cent

2559. Broomall, Anna Elizabeth
1847–1931
obstetrician, medical educator
Pennsylvania
Index t Wom; Nat Cyc Am Bio v24; Not Am Wom

2560. Dorsey, Susan Almira Miller
1847–1946
educator
Not Am Wom

2561. Hanna, Sarah Jackson
born 1847
musical educator
Georgia
Wom Cent

2562. Leonard, Mary Hall
1847–1921
educator
Massachusetts
Nat Cyc Am Bio v20

2563. Robinson, Fannie Ruth
born 1847
poet, educator
Index t Wom; Wom Cent

2564. Robinson, Jane Marie Bancroft
1847–1932
Methodist educator, deaconess leader, author, historian, philanthropist
Methodist
Index t Wom; Not Am Wom; Wom Cent

2565. Smith, Jane Luella Dowd
born 1847
educator, author, poet, children's author, suffragist, temperance worker
Hudson, NY
Cyc Am Bio; Dict Am Auth; Nat Cyc Am Bio v1; Twent Cen Bio Dict Not Am; Wom Cent

2566. Whitney, Mary Watson
1847–1920/21
astronomer, educator
Dict Am Bio; Not Am Wom

2567. Blondner, Aline Reese
flourished 1878
pianist, organist, music educator
Wom Cent

2568. Gould, Elizabeth Porter
born 1848
author, essayist on education, journalist, lecturer, social critic
Wom Cent

2569. Homans, Amy Morris
1848–1933
educator, physical education director
Index t Wom

2570. Irvine, Julia Josephine (Thomas)
1848–post 1886
classical scholar, fourth president of Wellesley College
Nat Cyc Am Bio v12; Twent Cen Bio Dict Not Am

2571. Kollock, Florence E.
born 1848
Universalist minister, suffragist, temperance worker, kindergarten educator, missionary
Index t Wom; Wom Cent

2572. Lipscomb, Mary Ann (Rutherford)
born 1848
academic administrator of the Lucy Cobb Institute
Twent Cen Bio Dict Not Am

2573. Marshall, Clara
circa 1848–1931

physician, pharmacist, medical educator
Dict Am Bio; Index t Wom

2574. Norris, Mary Harriot
born 1848
author, novelist, literary editor, university educator
New York; Illinois
Dict Am Auth; Twent Cen Bio Dict Not Am

2575. Spray, Ruth Hinshaw
born 1848
educator, philanthropist
Index t Wom

2576. Taylor, Susie Baker King
born 1848
educator, Civil War nurse
Black
Prof Negro Wom v1

2577. Yale, Caroline Ardelia
1848–1933
educator of the deaf
Congregationalist
Vermont
Dict Am Bio; Nat Cyc Am Bio v31; Not Am Wom

2578. Atherton, Mary Alderson Chandler
born 1849
suffragist, educator, author
Massachusetts
Nat Cyc Am Bio v18

2579. Bowen, Ariel Serena Hedges
1849–1904
musician, music educator
Black
Index t Wom; Prof Negro Wom

2580. Brown, Corinne Stubbs
born 1849
Socialist party member, labor activist, sociologist, educator
Index t Wom; Wom Cent

2581. Chandler, Mary Alderson
born 1849
educator, stenographic educator
Wom Cent

2582. Harrison, Elizabeth
1849–1927
kindergarten educator
Dict Am Bio; Nat Cyc Am Bio v21; Not Am Wom

2583. Knight, Sarah (Harrison)
1849–1928
philanthropist, Minneapolis civic leader, Methodist church worker, hospital founder, patron of nurse's training
Methodist
Minneapolis, MN
Am Bio New Cyc

2584. Rorer, Sarah Tyson (Heston)
1849–1937
cooking teacher, cookbook author, home economist, dietician
Dict Am Auth; Nat Cyc Am Bio v16; Not Am Wom; Twent Cen Bio Dict Not Am

2585. Bacon, Rebecca Taylor
flourished 1880s–90s
philanthropist, patron of nursing education
Appl Cyc Am Bio

2586. Barnes, Mary Downing Sheldon
1850–98
educator, historian, textbook author
California
Dict Am Auth; Dict Am Bio; Not Am Wom; Wom Cent

2587. Booth, Almida
flourished 1880s
educator
Index t Wom

2588. Burke, B. Ellen
born 1850
educator, lecturer, editor, publisher
Index t Wom

2589. Burt, Mary Elizabeth
1850–1919
primary school educator, author
Dict Am Bio

2590. Butler, Clarissa
flourished 1880s
educator, historian
Index t Wom

2591. Conway, Clara
flourished 1880s
founder of the Clara Conway School
Tennessee
Wom Cent

2592. Coyriere, E. Miriam
flourished 1880s
school furniture businessperson, founder and manager of a teacher's agency
Wom Cent

2593. Crane, Ogden, Mrs.
born 1850
concert singer, music educator
Wom Cent

2594. Durley, Ella Hamilton
flourished 1880s
educator, journalist
Des Moines, IA
Wom Cent

2595. Farnham, Mary Frances
flourished 1880s–1900s

educator
Index t Wom

2596. Goodrich, Florence Ada (Backus)
1850–1928
composer, organ teacher
Index t Wom; Nat Cyc Am Bio v23

2597. Hahr, Emma
flourished 1880s
pianist, composer, musical educator
Georgia
Wom Cent

2598. Hall, Frances M.
flourished 1880s
western pioneer, educator
Index t Wom

2599. Halvey, Margaret Mary Brophy
flourished 1880s
clubwoman, educator, poet
Irish
Index t Wom

2600. Holbrook, Florence
born 185?
textbook author, educator
Chicago, IL
Dict Am Auth

2601. Holmes, Mary Emilie
born 1850
educator, zoologist, herbalist, educator of Black women
Presbyterian
Illinois
Wom Cent

2602. Howard, Mary M.
flourished 1880s
organist, music educator
Wom Cent

2603. Keating, Josephine E.
flourished 1880s–90s
literary critic, musician, music educator
Tennessee
Wom Cent

2604. Kempin, Emile
flourished 1880s–90s
lawyer, educator
Swiss
Index t Wom

2605. Marble, Ella M. S.
born 1850
journalist, educator, suffragist, temperance worker, dress reformer
Wom Cent

2606. Mussey, Ellen (Persis) Spencer
1850–1936

international lawyer, law educator, feminist, women's rights worker, clubwoman, child welfare worker, Red Cross worker, social reformer
Swedenborgian
Washington, DC
Dict Am Bio supp v2; Index t Wom; Nat Cyc Am Bio v47 and csv1; Not Am Wom; Twent Cen Bio Dict Not Am

2607. Patrick, Mary Mills
1850–1940
educator in Turkey
Index t Wom; Nat Cyc Am Bio csv1

2608. Peck, Annie Smith
1850–1933/35
mountain climber, musician, archaeologist, lecturer, educator
Rhode Island
Index t Wom; Nat Cyc Am Bio v15; Not Am Wom; Wom Cent

2609. Sabin, Ellen Clara
1850–1949
school administrator, college president, educator
Not Am Wom; Wom Cent

2610. Seaver, Nancy B.
flourished 1880s
educator
Index t Wom

2611. Sheldon, Mary Downing
1850–98
historian, professor at Wellesley College
Cyc Am Bio

2612. Sommerfield, Rose
flourished 1880s–90s
religious worker, educator
Index t Wom

2613. Stowell, Louisa Maria (Reed)
born 1850
microscopist, botanist, author on microscopal botany, educator, editor
Cyc Am Bio and ad; Dict Am Auth; Index t Wom; Wom Cent

2614. Thurber, Jeannette Meyers
1850–1946
patron of music, founder of the National Conservatory of Music of America
Dict Am Bio supp v4; Nat Cyc Am Bio csv4; Not Am Wom

2615. Todd, Adah J.
flourished 1880s–90s
author, educator, physiologist
Wom Cent

2616. Wood, Frances Fisher
flourished 1880s–90s
educator, lecturer, scientist, dress reformer, dairy farmer, businessperson
Wom Cent

2617. Cory, Florence Elizabeth
born 1851
industrial designer, industrial design teacher
Wom Cent

2618. Crane, Sibylla (Bailey)
1851–1902
vocalist, composer, music educator, writer on music
Boston, MA
Dict Am Auth; Nat Cyc Am Bio v7; Twent Cen Bio Dict Not Am; Wom Cent

2619. Hayes, Ellen
born 1851
mathematician, geologist, educator, author
Index t Wom; Twent Cen Bio Dict Not Am

2620. Martin, Lillian Jane
1851–1943
psychologist, gerontologist, worker for the welfare of the aged, suffragist, university educator
Index t Wom; Nat Cyc Am Bio v16; Obit File; Twent Cen Bio Dict Not Am

2621. Mergler, Marie Josepha
1851–1901
physician, surgeon, medical educator
Dict Am Bio; Index t Wom; Not Am Wom

2622. Morgan, Anna
1851–1936
speech teacher, drama coach, elocutionist
Chicago, IL
Nat Cyc Am Bio v17; Not Am Wom

2623. Moten, Lucy Ella
1851–1933
educator
Not Am Wom

2624. Rutherford, Mildred Lewis
1851/52–1928
educator, textbook author, apologist for the Old South
Athens, GA
Dict Am Auth; Nat Cyc Am Bio v10; Not Am Wom; Twent Cen Bio Dict Not Am

2625. Spencer, Anna Carpenter (Garlin)
1851–1931

Unitarian minister, journalist, educator, temperance worker, suffragist, pacifist, child-labor reformer, philanthropist
Unitarian
Dict Am Bio; Nat Cyc Am Bio v9 and csv2; Not Am Wom

2626. Whipple, M. Ella
born 1851
physician, temperance worker, suffragist, Methodist Episcopal church worker, politician, educator, inventor
Methodist Episcopal
Wom Cent

2627. Adams, Jane Kelley
born 1852
educator
Index t Wom; Wom Cent

2628. Brace, Maria Porter
born 1852
educator, elocutionist
New York
Wom Cent

2629. Davidson, Hannah Amelia
1852–1919
author of study guides, educator, editor, lecturer, publisher
Index t Wom; Nat Cyc Am Bio v19

2630. Decker, Sarah Sophia Chase Platt
1852–1912
civic and social reformer, educator
Index t Wom; Not Am Wom

2631. Durrell, Irene Clark
born 1852
educator
Methodist
New Hampshire
Wom Cent

2632. Foxworthy, Alice S.
born 1852
educator
Tennessee
Wom Cent

2633. Fuller, Clara Cornelia
1852–1940
educator
Index t Wom

2634. Gillett, Emma Millinda
1852–1927
lawyer, educator, feminist
Nat Cyc Am Bio v17; Not Am Wom

2635. Krout, Mary Hannah
1852/57–1927
poet, author, educator, journalist

Denver, CO
Dict Am Auth; Index t Wom; Wom Cent

2636. Mattingly, Sarah Irwin
1852–1934
educator of Blacks, suffragist
Nat Cyc Am Bio v30

2637. Millar, Clara Smart
born 1852
singer, music educator
Wom Cent

2638. Morton, Eliza Happy
1852–1916
author, songwriter, educator, geographer
Maine
Index t Wom; Wom Cent

2639. Robertson, Georgia Trowbridge; Marcia
born 1852
educator, author
Wom Cent

2640. van Hook, Loretta C.
born 1852
missionary, educator in Persia
Wom Cent

2641. Yates, Josephine Silone; R. K. Potter
1852–1912
educator, author
Missouri
Black
Index t Wom; Negro Alman; Prof Negro Wom v1

2642. Avann, Ella H. Brockway
born 1853
educator
Wom Cent

2643. Call, Annie Payson
born 1853
author, teacher of nerve training
Dict Am Auth; Index t Wom

2644. Cheney, Abbey Perkins
born 1853
music educator, pianist
Wom Cent

2645. Cooke, Anna Charlotte Rice
1853–1934
founder of the Honolulu Academy of the Arts
Honolulu, HI
Not Am Wom

2646. Kelley, Catherine Bishop
1853–1944
educator, religious worker
Index t Wom

2647. Kotzschmar, Hermann, Mrs.
born 1853
pianist, music educator
Index t Wom

2648. McMurry, Lida Brown
born 1853
children's author, educator
Nat Cyc Am Bio csv2

2649. Mossell, Mary Ella
1853–86
educator, missionary to Haiti
Black
Index t Wom; Negro Alman; Prof Negro Wom v1

2650. Parrish, Celestia Susannah
1853–1918
educator, psychologist
Dict Am Bio; Not Am Wom; Twent Cen Bio Dict Not Am

2651. Poulsson, Anne Emilie
1853–1939
children's author, writer on children, editor, illustrator, kindergarten educator
Boston, MA
Dict Am Auth; Index t Wom; Nat Cyc Am Bio v10; Twent Cen Bio Dict Not Am

2652. Reynolds, Myra
1853–1936
scholar of English literature, educator
Not Am Wom

2653. Salmon, Lucy Maynard
1853–1927
historian, writer on history, university educator
Dict Am Auth; Dict Am Bio; Not Am Wom

2654. Scribner, Lucy Skidmore
1853–1931
founder of Skidmore College, educator
New York
Nat Cyc Am Bio v23

2655. Webster, Helen Livermore
1853–post 1890
writer on philology, philologist, university educator
Dict Am Auth; Wom Cent

2656. Weed, Ella
1853–94
educator, leading figure in the formative years of Barnard College
Not Am Wom

2657. Wenckebach, Anna Doris Amalie Catharina Carla
born 1853

educator, author on German language and literature
Prussian
Nat Cyc Am Bio v10

2658. White, Helen Magill
1853–1944
educator, first American woman to receive a PhD
Not Am Wom

2659. Woods, Katharine Pearson
1853–1923
fiction author, educator, social service worker
Dict Am Auth; Not Am Wom

2660. Blaker, Eliza Ann Cooper
1854–1926
educator
Not Am Wom

2661. Boughton, Caroline Greenbank
born 1854
educator, suffragist, philanthropist
Wom Cent

2662. Case, Mary Sophia
born 1854
college educator
Twent Cen Bio Dict Not Am

2663. Comstock, Anna (Botsford)
1854–1930
naturalist, scientific illustrator, insect artist, leader in the nature study movement, wood engraver, educator
New York
Index t Wom; Nat Cyc Am Bio v11 and v22; Not Am Wom; Twent Cen Bio Dict Not Am

2664. Crow, Martha Emilie Foote
1854–1924
college educator, author
Nat Cyc Am Bio v22; Twent Cen Bio Dict Not Am

2665. Cummins, Mary Stuart
born 1854
educator, temperance worker
Presbyterian
Montana
Wom Cent

2666. Fulton, Mary Hannah
1854–1927
medical missionary to China, pioneer in medical education of Chinese women
Not Am Wom

2667. Hall, Margaret Thompson
born 1854

educator, newspaper correspondent
Wom Cent

2668. Laney, Lucy Craft
1854–1933
educator, founder of the Haines Normal Institute
Georgia
Black
Index t Wom; Negro Alman; Not Am Wom; Prof Negro Wom v1

2669. Miller, Louise Klein
1854–1943
horticulturist, landscape architect, educator
Index t Wom

2670. Nicholls, Rhoda Holmes
1854–1930
artist, educator, painter
English
Dict Am Bio; Index t Wom; Nat Cyc Am Bio v7; Wom Cent

2671. Perkins, Angie Villette
1854–1921
educator, clubwoman, philanthropist
Nat Cyc Am Bio v19

2672. Rive-King, Julie; Julie King
1854/57–1937
pianist, piano educator
Index t Wom; Not Am Wom; Wom Cent

2673. Robertson, Alice Mary
1854–1931
educator of Native Americans, representative to Congress from Oklahoma, educator, social worker, postmaster
Oklahoma
Dict Am Bio; Index t Wom; Not Am Wom

2674. Tappan, Eva March
1854–1930
educator, children's author, history text writer
Worcester, MA
Dict Am Auth; Dict Am Bio; Not Am Wom; Twent Cen Bio Dict Not Am

2675. Babcock, Hannah Almy
1855–1931
music educator and director for the blind, suffragist, temperance worker
Nat Cyc Am Bio v16

2676. Cocke, Martha Louise
1855–1938
president of Hollins College
Enon Baptist
Virginia
Nat Cyc Am Bio v29

2677. Crane, Julia Ettie
1855–1923
musician, music educator
Index t Wom; Nat Cyc Am Bio v6

2678. Dowd, Mary Alice
born 1855
poet, educator
Connecticut
Dict Am Auth; Wom Cent

2679. Dunlap, Laura Comstock
1855–1947
religious writer, textbook author
Obit File

2680. Galpin, Kate Tuppe
born 1855
educator
Wom Cent

2681. Hersey, Heloise Edwina
born 1855
educator, writer on education
Boston, MA
Dict Am Auth

2682. Laws, Annie
1855–1927
kindergarten and education worker, clubwoman, civic leader, patron of nursing
Ohio
Nat Cyc Am Bio v22; Not Am Wom

2683. Leach, Abby
1855–1918
professor of Greek, philologist
Nat Cyc Am Bio v12; Not Am Wom

2684. Palmer, Alice Elvira Freeman
1855–1902
educator, second president of Wellesley College
Cyc Am Bio v3; Dict Am Bio; Index t Wom; Nat Cyc Am Bio v7; Not Am Wom; Twent Cen Bio Dict Not Am; Wom Cent

2685. Richman, Julia
1855–1912
educator
Not Am Wom

2686. Rogers, Effie Louise Hoffman
born 1855
educator; superintendent of schools of Mahaska County, Iowa; newspaper editor; temperance worker
Mahaska County, IA
Wom Cent

2687. Bailey, Sarah Lord
born 1856
elocutionist
Massachusetts

British
Wom Cent

2688. Baldwin, Mary Louise "Maria Louisa"
1856–1919/22
educator, civic leader
Massachusetts
Black
Index t Wom; Negro Alman; Not Am Wom; Prof Negro Wom

2689. Bradford, Mary Carroll Craig
born 1856/60
magazine and newspaper correspondent, educator, labor union leader
Christian Scientist
Colorado
Nat Cyc Am Bio csv2; Wom Cent

2690. Carson, Luella Clay
born 1856
educator
Index t Wom

2691. Conner, Elizabeth Marney; Paul Veronique
born 1856
dramatic reader, educator, actor
Wom Cent

2692. Dodge, Grace Hoadley
1856–1914
social welfare and charity worker, philanthropist, educator
New York
Cyc Am Bio; Dict Am Bio; Index t Wom; Nat Cyc Am Bio v18; Not Am Wom; Wom Cent

2693. Gates, Susa Young
1856–1933
Mormon author, educator, suffragist
Mormon
Nat Cyc Am Bio csv2; Read Encyc Am West

2694. Gill, Emily Frances Lombard Abbey
1856–1950
patron of college education
Obit File

2695. Gulliver, Julia Henrietta
1856–1940
philosopher, educator
Not Am Wom

2696. Hazard, Caroline
1856–1945
fifth president of Wellesley College, historian, historical author
Congregationalist
Dict Am Auth; Index t Wom; Nat Cyc Am Bio v12, v34, and csv43; Not Am Wom; Twent Cen Bio Dict Not Am

2697. Hogue, Lydia Evans
born 1856
educator
Wom Cent

2698. Hopekirk, Helene; Helene Wilson
1856–1945
concert pianist, composer, educator
Not Am Wom; Obit File

2699. MacLeish, Martha Hillard
1856–1947
educator, leader in church and community work, second president of Rockford College
Not Am Wom; Obit File

2700. Mead, Lucia True (Ames)
1856–1936
pacifist, internationalist, suffragist, Black welfare and education worker, author
Unitarian
Nat Cyc Am Bio v28; Not Am Wom; Twent Cen Bio Dict Not Am

2701. Reese, Lizette Woodworth
1856–1935
lyric poet, English literature teacher
Baltimore, MD
Dict Am Auth; Dict Am Bio supp v1; Index t Wom; Nat Cyc Am Bio csv3; Not Am Wom; Wom Cent; Wom Lit, More

2702. Street, Ida Maria
born 1856
educator, art criticism author
Milwaukee, WI
Dict Am Auth

2703. Walter, Carrie Stevens
born 1856
educator, poet
Catholic
California
Wom Cent

2704. Wiggin, Kate Douglas Smith
1856/59–1923
author, children's author, kindergarten educator, philanthropist
California
Dict Am Bio; Index t Wom; Nat Cyc Am Bio v6; Not Am Wom; Wom Cent

2705. Willcox, Mary Alice
1856–1953
zoologist, writer on zoology, college educator
Dict Am Auth; Index t Wom

2706. Benedict, Emma Lee
born 1857
author, educator, temperance worker
New York
Wom Cent

2707. Blake, Katherine Devereux
1857–1950
educator, suffragist, international peace movement leader
New York
Index t Wom; Obit File

2708. Brown, Katherine "Kate" Louise
1857–1921
children's author, composer, educator
Boston, MA
Dict Am Auth; Index t Wom

2709. Case, Mary Emily
born 1857
university educator, classical languages scholar
New York
Dict Am Auth

2710. Coman, Katharine
1857–1915
economic historian, writer on history, social reformer, educator
Ohio
Dict Am Auth; Index t Wom; Not Am Wom

2711. Denton, Mary Florence
1857–1947
missionary educator in Japan
Not Am Wom

2712. Greene, Mary A.
born 1857
lawyer, law educator
Rhode Island
Index t Wom; Wom Cent

2713. Lamson, Lucy Stedman
born 1857
educator, realtor
Washington
Index t Wom; Wom Cent

2714. Manley, Fanny Louisa
born 1857
educator, history author
Twent Cen Bio Dict Not Am

2715. Oldham, Marie Augusta
born 1857
missionary to India, educator, temperance worker
Methodist Episcopal
Wom Cent

2716. Peirce, Frances Elizabeth
born 1857
elocutionist, educator
Wom Cent

2717. Putnam, Helen Cordelia
1857–1951
physician, health educator, suffragist
Dict Am Bio supp v5

2718. Raymond, Carrie Isabelle Rice
born 1857
musician, educator, organist, music director, conductor
Nebraska
Wom Cent

2719. Thomas, Martha Carey
1857–1935
university educator, second president of Bryn Mawr College, author, feminist
Quaker
Dict Am Auth; Dict Am Bio supp v1; Index t Wom; Nat Cyc Am Bio v13; Not Am Wom; Twent Cen Bio Dict Not Am

2720. Wergeland, Agnes Mathilde
1857–1914
historian, educator
Dict Am Bio

2721. Wheelock, Lucy
1857–1946
kindergarten educator, founder of Wheelock College, lecturer, author
Boston, MA
Dict Am Bio supp v4; Not Am Wom; Wom Cent

2722. Whiton, Mary Bartlett
born 1857
educator
Cyc Am Bio

2723. Adams, Juliette Aurelia Graves
born 1858
composer, pianist, music educator, author, lecturer
Index t Wom

2724. Bacon, Alice Mable
1858–1918
authority on Japan, author on Japanese culture, lecturer, educator of Blacks
Virginia
Dict Am Auth; Dict Am Bio; Not Am Wom

2725. Bender, Ida Catherine
1858–1916
educator
Buffalo, NY
Nat Cyc Am Bio v21

2726. Bishop, Emily Mulkin Montague
born 1858
Delsartean lecturer and instructor in dress, expression, and physical culture
Index t Wom; Wom Cent

2727. Bryan, Anna E.
1858–1901
kindergarten educator
Not Am Wom

2728. Cobb, Sarah M. Maxson
born 1858
artist, art educator, photographer, microscopist
Wom Cent

2729. Cooper, Anna Julia Haywood
1858/68–1964
educator, scholar
Black
Negro Alman; Not Am Wom supp v1; Prof Negro Wom v1

2730. Corr, Mary Bernadine
born 1858
author, educator
Index t Wom

2731. Dewey, Alice Chipman
1858–1927
educator
Not Am Wom

2732. Drexel, Katharine Mary; Mother Mary Katharine
1858–1955
founder of the Catholic Sisters of the Most Blessed Sacrament for Indians and Colored People, educator of Blacks, missionary, philanthropist
Catholic
Dict Am Bio supp v5; Dict Am Rel Bio; Index t Wom; Not Am Wom supp v1; Obit File; Read Encyc Am West

2733. Fisher, Anna A.
born 1858
educator
Wom Cent

2734. Fisher, Mary
born 1858
textbook author, educator, novelist
Kansas City, MO
Dict Am Auth; Twent Cen Bio Dict Not Am

2735. Granger, Lottie E.
born 1858
temperance worker, educator
Wom Cent

2736. Hatcher, Orie Latham
1858–1946
English scholar, pioneer in vocational guidance
Not Am Wom

2737. Hibler, Nellie
born 1858
music educator, soprano singer
Wom Cent

2738. Judd, Ida Benfy
1858–1952
founder of the Mark Twain Association, monologuist, speech educator
Obit File

2739. Meleney, Carolyn Coit
1858–1934
kindergarten educator
Nat Cyc Am Bio v29

2740. Morley, Margaret Warner
1858–1923
educator, author, writer on sex education, naturalist, botanist, zoologist
Boston, MA
Dict Am Auth; Dict Am Bio

2741. Morrison, May Treat
1858–1939
patron of the University of California, philanthropist
San Francisco, CA
Nat Cyc Am Bio v31

2742. Nutting, Mary Adelaide
1858–1948
leader in professional nursing and nursing education, writer on nursing
Dict Am Bio supp v4; Index t Wom; Not Am Wom; Obit File

2743. Slosson, May Genevieve Preston
1858–1943
educator, suffragist
Congregationalist
Nat Cyc Am Bio v35

2744. Smith, Eleanor
1858–1942
music educator, composer, songwriter
Episcopalian
Index t Wom; Nat Cyc Am Bio v35

2745. Talbot, Marion
1858–1948
first dean of women of the University of Chicago, professor of household administration
Chicago, IL
Not Am Wom; Obit File

2746. Welsch, Lilian
1858–1938
physician, educator
Not Am Wom

2747. Adams, Carrie B.
1859–1940

composer, music educator, organist
Index t Wom

2748. Arnold, Sarah Louise
born 1859
educator, education writer
Boston, MA
Dict Am Auth; Index t Wom

2749. Baker, Charlotte Sanford
1859–1932
educator
New York
Nat Cyc Am Bio v23

2750. Bates, Katharine Lee
1859–1929
poet, author, professor of English
literature
Massachusetts
Dict Am Auth; Dict Am Bio;
Index t Wom; Nat Cyc Am Bio
v1, v9, and v42; Not Am Wom;
Twent Cen Bio Dict Not Am;
Wom Cent

2751. Brain, Belle M.
born 1859
temperance author, educator
Springfield, OH
Dict Am Auth

2752. Cone, Helen Gray
1859–1934
educator, poet
New York
Dict Am Auth; Index t Wom;
Wom Cent

2753. Dickerman, Julia Elida
born 1859
teacher, organist
Index t Wom

2754. Dicklow, Adelaide Lynn
born 1859
educator
Wom Cent

2755. Grisham, Sadie Park
born 1859
educator; city councilperson in
Cottonwood Falls, Kansas
Cottonwood Falls, KS
Wom Cent

**2756. Kehew, Mary Morton
Kimball**
1859–1918
social reformer in education and
employment for women, labor
organizer, worker for the welfare of children and the blind
Dict Am Bio; Not Am Wom

2757. Lutz, Edelia Armstrong
born 1859
artist, art educator
Knoxville, TN
Wom Cent

2758. Miller, Addie Dickman
born 1859
educator, temperance worker, inventor of the dishwasher
Oregon
Wom Cent

**2759. Moody, Helen (Water-
son)**
1859/60–1928
author, journalist, educator
Ohio; New York, NY
Dict Am Auth; Index t Wom;
Nat Cyc Am Bio v22; Wom
Cent

**2760. Sheardown, Annie Fill-
more**
born 1859
singer, voice teacher, writer on
voice teaching
Wom Cent

2761. Shorter, Susie
1859–1912
educator, author, businessperson
Black
Index t Wom; Negro Alman

2762. Smith, Nora Archibald
1859–1934
kindergarten educator, children's
author
Dict Am Bio; Nat Cyc Am Bio
v26 and csv2

**2763. Sutliff, Phebe Temper-
ance**
born 1859
educator, historian
Twent Cen Bio Dict Not Am

2764. Tapper, Bertha Feiring
1859–1915
pianist, music educator
Norwegian
Dict Am Bio; Index t Wom

**2765. Thompson, Adaline Emer-
son**
born 1859
educational worker, women's education reformer
Wom Cent

2766. Thompson, Mary Sophia
born 1859
Delsartean acting-method instructor, elocutionist
Wom Cent

2767. Tyler, Alice Sarah
1859–1944
librarian, educator
Index t Wom; Nat Cyc Am Bio
v33; Not Am Wom

2768. Ahern, Mary Eileen
1860/65–1938
librarian, editor, educator
Index t Wom; Nat Cyc Am Bio
csv1; Not Am Wom

2769. Bevier, Isabel
1860–1942
educator, author, lecturer, home
economist
Dict Am Bio supp v3; Index t
Wom; Not Am Wom

**2770. Butler, Marie Joseph,
Mother**
1860–1940
founder of Marymount Schools,
Catholic nun
Catholic
Not Am Wom

2771. Clark, Frances Eliot
1860–1958
music educator
Index t Wom

2772. Desha, Mary
died 1910
educator
Index t Wom

2773. Dunning, Carrie Louise
1860–1929
music educator
Index t Wom

2774. Dussuchal, Eugenie
born 1860
musical educator
St. Louis, MO
Wom Cent

**2775. Franklin, Gertrude; Vir-
ginia H. Beatty**
flourished 1890s
singer, music educator
Wom Cent

2776. Furman, Myrtie E.
born 1860
professor of elocution, orator
blind
Wom Cent

2777. Gale, Ada Iddings
flourished 1890s
author, educator
Michigan
Wom Cent

2778. Gill, Laura Drake
1860–1926
vocational educator
Dict Am Bio; Nat Cyc Am Bio
v24

**2779. Goessmann, Helena The-
resa**
flourished 1890s–1900s
educator, lecturer
Index t Wom

**2780. Greene, Frances Nimmo;
Dixie**
born 186?
educator, author
Alabama
Wom Cent

2781. Hamilton, Anna J.
born 1860
educator, journalist
Kentucky
Wom Cent

2782. Jones, Julia L.
flourished 1890s
western pioneer, educator
Index t Wom

2783. Keysor, Jennie Ellis
born 1860
educator
Omaha, NE
Wom Cent

**2784. Lee, Jeanette Barbour
(Perry)**
1860–1951
educator, novelist
Northampton, MA
Dict Am Auth; Index t Wom;
Nat Cyc Am Bio csv1; Obit File

2785. Lord, Eleanor Louise
flourished 1890s–1900s
educator
Index t Wom

**2786. Merritt, Emma Frances
Grayson**
1860–1933
educator
Black
Encyc Black Am; Negro Alman;
Prof Negro Wom v1

**2787. Norton, Mary Alice Pel-
oubet**
1860–1928
home economics educator
Dict Am Bio; Not Am Wom

2788. Parker, Helen Almena
graduated 1885
educator, dramatic reader, impersonator
Index t Wom; Wom Cent

2789. Phelps, Maude Gilette
born 1860
educator, writer of texts on English literature
Dict Am Auth

2790. Plummer, Nellie Arnold
1860–1924
educator
Black
Encyc Black Am

**2791. Robb, Isabella Adams
(Hampton)**
1860/63–1910
professional nurse, educator, writer on nursing
Cleveland, OH
Index t Wom; Not Am Wom

2792. Smith, Ella May
1860–1934

composer, pianist, organist, music
educator, author
Index t Wom

2793. Spencer, Fannie M.
born circa 1860
organist, composer, music educator
Nat Cyc Am Bio v11

**2794. Starkweather, Amelia
Minerva**
flourished 1890s
educator, author, poet, temperance worker, Methodist Episcopal deaconess
Methodist Episcopal
Wom Cent

**2795. van Benschoten, Mary
Crowell**
flourished 1890s
author, writer on industrial education
Illinois
Wom Cent

**2796. Wilson, Ellen Louise Ax-
son; Mrs. Woodrow Wilson**
1860–1914
welfare worker, education worker
for southern mountain people
Nat Cyc Am Bio v19

**2797. Woolman, Mary Raphael
Schenck**
1860–1940
home economist, textile specialist,
vocational educator, author,
lecturer
Nat Cyc Am Bio csv1; Not Am
Wom

2798. Bagg, Clara B.
born 1861
pianist, music educator
Wom Cent

**2799. Bailey, Eliza Randall
Simmons**
1861–1939
educator, textbook author, education writer
Congregationalist
Nat Cyc Am Bio v29

**2800. Benjamin, Caroline Shev-
elson**
1861–1951
founder of the Benjamin Dean
School for Girls, educator
New York
Obit File

2801. Biggart, Mabelle
born 1861
educator, dramatic reader
Wom Cent

**2802. Fensham, Florence
Amanda**
born 1861

religious educator
Index t Wom

2803. Haley, Margaret Angela
1861–1939
educator, civic reformer, labor
leader
Catholic
Illinois
Bio Dict Am Lab; Not Am Wom

2804. Hazelrigg, Clara H.
born 1861
author, educator, temperance
worker
Wom Cent

2805. Hebard, Grace Raymond
1861–1936
educator, feminist historian, author
Wyoming
Index t Wom; Read Encyc Am
West

2806. Jewett, Sophie
born 1861
university educator, writer on literature
Dict Am Auth

2807. Luce, Alice Hanson
born 1861
dean of women of Oberlin College, English literature professor, educator
Twent Cen Bio Dict Not Am

**2808. Magoun, Martha Roberts
(Mann)**
born 1861
botanist, biologist, educator
Twent Cen Bio Dict Not Am

**2809. Marshall, Nina (Caroline)
Lovering**
born 1861
educator
New York, NY
Dict Am Auth

2810. Martin, Myra Belle
born 1861
educator, financier
Nat Cyc Am Bio v14

2811. Miner, Sarah Luella
1861–1935
Congregationalist missionary and
educator in China
Congregationalist
Not Am Wom

2812. Morgan, Mary Kimball
1861–1948
Christian Science educator
Christian Scientist
Not Am Wom

2813. Ryan, Mary M.
1861–1955

cofounder of the Katherine Gibbs
Secretarial Schools
Obit File

2814. Scudder, Vida Dutton
1861–1954
social reformer, writer on English
literature, author, university ed-
ucator
Christian Scientist
Massachusetts
Cyc Am Bio; Dict Am Auth; Dict
Am Bio supp v5; Index t Wom;
Not Am Wom supp v1; Twent
Cen Bio Dict Not Am; Wom
Lit, More

2815. Taft, Helen Herron
1861–1943
founder and patron of the Cincinnati Orchestra Association, musician, music educator
Index t Wom; Nat Cyc Am Bio
v14

2816. Taney, Mary Florence
born 1861
educator, journalist, author, editor
Index t Wom

**2817. Timlow, Elizabeth Wes-
tyn**
born 1861
educator, children's author
Dict Am Auth

**2818. Washington, Josephine
Turpin**
1861–1949
journalist, educator
Black
Negro Alman; Prof Negro Wom
v1

2819. Bauer, Bertha
1862–1940
music educator
Cincinnati, OH
German
Index t Wom; Nat Cyc Am Bio
v31

2820. Baur, Clara
died 1912
music educator
Ohio
German
Nat Cyc Am Bio v26

2821. Beck, Leonora
born 1862
educator, founder of Leonora
Beck College
Atlanta, GA
Wom Cent

**2822. Brown, Alice van Vecht-
en**
1862–1949
art educator
Not Am Wom

2823. Buckland, Fanny
1862–1939
pioneer in women's education,
first headmistress of the Witwatersrand School in South Africa
Not Am Wom supp v1

**2824. Chamberlain, Georgia
Louise**
1862–1943
educator, author
Index t Wom

2825. Delano, Jane Arminda
1862–1919
nurse, Red Cross worker, nurse in
the Mexican-American War,
nursing educator
Dict Am Bio; Index t Wom; Nat
Cyc Am Bio v19; Not Am Wom

**2826. Evans, Helen (Schlie-
mann)**
born 1862
educator
Nat Cyc Am Bio csv3

2827. Hicks, Mary Dana
born 1862
art educator
Wom Cent

**2828. Merrill, Winifred Edger-
ton**
1862–1951
women's educator
Episcopalian
Nat Cyc Am Bio v41

2829. Peirce, Mary Bisbing
born 1862
educator, principal of the Peirce
School of Business
Cyc Am Bio

**2830. Richardson, Hester Dor-
sey**
born 1862
educator, author
Baltimore, MD
Index t Wom; Wom Cent

2831. Sherman, Marietta R.
born 1862
musical educator, orchestral conductor
Wom Cent

2832. Smith, Mary Belle
born 1862
educator, temperance worker
Methodist Episcopal
Connecticut
Wom Cent

2833. Spence, Clara Beebe
1862–1923
educator of women, World War I
patriot
Nat Cyc Am Bio v20

2834. Talbert, Mary Burnett
1862/66–1923
educator, social reformer, prison reformer, Black rights worker, club leader
Black
Index t Wom; Negro Alman; Prof Negro Wom v1

2835. Weir, Irene
1862–1944
painter, art educator, writer on art, founder of the New York School of Design and Liberal Arts
New York
Not Am Wom; Obit File

2836. Wright, Carrie Douglas
born 1862
music educator, biographer
Chicago, IL
Dict Am Auth

2837. Bailey, Florence Augusta (Merriam)
1863–1948
ornithologist, nature writer, educator
Dict Am Auth; Dict Am Bio supp v4; Index t Wom; Nat Cyc Am Bio v13 and csv1; Not Am Wom

2838. Calkins, Mary Whiton
1863–1930
philosopher, psychologist, educator, author
Dict Am Bio supp v1; Dict Phil; Index t Wom; Nat Cyc Am Bio v13; Not Am Wom; Who Who Phil

2839. Claghorn, Kate Holladay
born 1863
writer on women's education
New York
Dict Am Auth; Twent Cen Bio Dict Not Am

2840. Dopp, Katherine Elizabeth
born 1863
educator
Index t Wom

2841. Eastman, Elaine (Goodale); Elaine Hall
1863–1953
educator of Native Americans, poet, short story writer, humorist, editor, scholar of Native American culture
South Dakota
Cyc Am Bio; Dict Am Auth; Index t Wom; Nat Cyc Am Bio v8; Twent Cen Bio Dict Not Am; Wom Cent

2842. Hurll, Estelle May
born 1863

educator, lecturer and writer on art
Dict Am Auth; Index t Wom

2843. Logan, Adelle Hunt
1863–1915
educator, a founder of Tuskegee Institute
Black
Negro Alman; Prof Negro Wom v1

2844. Mosher, Clelia
born 1863
physician, educator
Index t Wom

2845. Perley, Mary Elizabeth
born 1863
educator, poet
New Hampshire
Wom Cent

2846. Smith, Minnie Louise
1863–1927
educator, Sorosis member
Methodist Episcopal
Illinois
Nat Cyc Am Bio v21

2847. Terrell, Mary Eliza Church
1863–1954
community leader, social reformer, suffragist, feminist, civil rights leader, NAACP organizer, lecturer, educator
Congregationalist
Washington, DC
Dict Am Bio supp v5; Encyc Black Am; Encyc South Hist; Index t Wom; Nat Cyc Am Bio v52; Negro Alman; Not Am Wom; Prof Negro Wom v1; World Great Men Col v2

2848. Wilson, Margaret Barclay
1863–1945
physician, domestic scientist, medical educator
Nat Cyc Am Bio v34

2849. Woolley, Mary Emma
1863–1947
second president of Mt. Holyoke College, educator, pacifist, suffragist
Congregationalist
Dict Am Bio supp v4; Index t Wom; Nat Cyc Am Bio v13, v37, and csv4; Not Am Wom

2850. Brant, Cornelia Chase
1864–1959
physician, dean of New York Medical College
Obit File

2851. Buck, Henriette
born 1864
educator

French; English; Canadian
Wom Cent

2852. Cooke, Flora Juliette
1864–1953
educator
Not Am Wom supp v1

2853. Frazier, Susan Elizabeth
1864/66–1909/24
educator, president of the 369th Infantry of the New York National Guard's Women's Auxiliary
Black
Index t Wom; Negro Alman; Prof Negro Wom v1

2854. Fuld, Carrie Bamberger Frank
1864–1944
philanthropist, cofounder of the Institute for Advanced Study at Princeton University
Princeton, NJ
Not Am Wom

2855. Kellas, Eliza
1864–1943
educator, cofounder and president of Russell Sage College, president of the Emma Willard School
New York
Index t Wom; Not Am Wom; Obit File

2856. Kohut, Rebekah Bettelheim
1864–1951
social welfare leader, educator, suffragist, lecturer, author, Jewish welfare worker
Jewish
Hungarian
Index t Wom; Nat Cyc Am Bio v41 and csv5; Not Am Wom supp v1

2857. Kroeger, Alice Bertha
1864–1909
librarian, library school director
Index t Wom; Not Am Wom

2858. Merrill, Helen Abbot
1864–1949
educator, mathematician
Congregationalist
Nat Cyc Am Bio v42

2859. Peixotto, Jessica Blanche
1864–1941
social economist, university educator
Not Am Wom

2860. Pendleton, Ellen Fitz
1864–1936

sixth president of Wellesley College, educator
Dict Am Bio supp v2; Index t Wom; Nat Cyc Am Bio csv1; Not Am Wom

2861. Sherwood, Margaret Pollock; Elizabeth Hastings
1864–1955
writer on literature, college educator
Dict Am Auth; Index t Wom

2862. Smith, Lura Eugenie (Brown)
born 1864
journalist
Little Rock, AR
Dict Am Auth; Wom Cent

2863. Smith, Mabell Shippie Clarke
1864–1942
educator, lecturer, author
Index t Wom

2864. Thorp, Louisa Elizabeth Garden McLeod
1864–1944
artist, founder of the first recognized art school in Los Angeles
Los Angeles, CA
Obit File

2865. van Rensselaer, Martha
1864–1932
home economist, educator
Methodist
New York
Dict Am Bio; Nat Cyc Am Bio v23; Not Am Wom

2866. Waite, Alice Vinton
1864–1943
educator, dean of Wellesley College
Index t Wom; Obit File

2867. Wilson, Lucy Langdon Williams
1864–1937
educator
Philadelphia, PA
Nat Cyc Am Bio v29

2868. Woods, Virna
1864–1903
educator, novelist, dramatist
Sacramento, CA
Dict Am Auth

2869. Barrett, Janie Porter
1865–1948
social welfare leader, educator
Virginia
Black
Dict Am Bio supp v4; Negro Alman; Index t Wom; Not Am Wom; Prof Negro Wom

2870. Bartlett, Maud White-head
born 1865
educator
Methodist Episcopal
Colorado
Index t Wom

2871. Booth, Maud Ballington (Charlesworth)
1865–1948
Salvation Army leader, evange-list, philanthropist, prison re-former, author, founder of PTA
Salvationist
English
Dict Am Auth; Index t Wom; Nat Cyc Am Bio v14 and v38; Not Am Wom; Obit File

2872. Chase, Jessie Anderson
born 1865
author, textbook writer
Brookline, MA
Dict Am Auth

2873. Dawes, Helen B. Palmer
married 1890s
educator, clubwoman
Index t Wom

2874. Emerson, Mary Alice
1865–1922
educator
Boston, MA
Nat Cyc Am Bio v20

2875. Fearn, Anne Walter
1865/71–1939
physician, surgeon, hospital ad-ministrator, medical educator in China
Berkeley, CA
Index t Wom; Nat Cyc Am Bio v31 and csv4; Not Am Wom

2876. Kendall, Elizabeth Kem-ball
1865–1952
historian, university educator, world traveler
Obit File

2877. Locke, Bessie
1865–1952
kindergarten educator, founder and executive secretary of the National Kindergarten Associa-tion
Dict Am Bio supp v5; Index t Wom; Nat Cyc Am Bio v39; Obit File

2878. McKane, Alice Woodby
born 1865
physician, hospital and nursing school founder
Black
Encyc Black Am

2879. Munford, Mary Cooke Branch
1865–1938
education reformer, civic leader
Virginia
Index t Wom; Not Am Wom

2880. Putnam, Emily James Smith
1865–1944
author, educator, first dean of Barnard College, lecturer
Index t Wom; Not Am Wom; Obit File; Twent Cen Bio Dict Not Am

2881. Roach, Aurelia
born 1865
educator
Atlanta, GA
Wom Cent

2882. Sharp, Katharine Lucinda
1865–1914
librarian, library school director
Dict Am Bio; Not Am Wom; Twent Cen Bio Dict Not Am

2883. Smith, Clara Eliza
circa 1865–1943
mathematician, educator
Index t Wom

2884. Swormstedt, Mabel God-frey
graduated 1890
educator, club leader
Index t Wom

2885. Valentine, Lila Hardaway Meade
1865–1921
suffragist, educational reformer, public health worker
Virginia
Encyc South Hist; Not Am Wom

2886. Washington, Margaret Murry
1865–1925
women's organizer, Tuskegee College dean of women, author
Black
Index t Wom; Negro Alman; Prof Negro Wom v1

2887. Berry, Martha McChes-ney; Sunday Lady of the Pos-sum Trot
1866–1942
educator, founder of the Berry School for underprivileged mountain children, philanthro-pist
Episcopalian
Georgia
Dict Am Bio supp v3; Encyc South Hist; Index t Wom; Nat Cyc Am Bio csv3; Not Am Wom; Obit File

2888. Blaine, Anita [Eugenie] McCormick
1866–1954
philanthropist, pacifist, patron of education and child welfare, pa-tron of the League of Nations
Chicago, IL
Dict Am Bio supp v5; Nat Cyc Am Bio v44; Not Am Wom supp v1; Obit File

2889. Breckinridge, Sophonisba Preston
1866–1948
social worker, social economist, immigrant welfare worker, writ-er on social issues, educator, lawyer
Presbyterian
Dict Am Bio supp v4; Nat Cyc Am Bio v37; Not Am Wom

2890. Burnham, Bertha H.
born 1866
author, educator
Wom Cent

2891. Chiles, Rosa Pendleton
born 1866
educator, author
Presbyterian
Nat Cyc Am Bio csv4

2892. Dowd, Mary Hickey
born 1866
educator, lecturer
Index t Wom

2893. Goodrich, Annie Warbur-ton
1866–1954
World War I nurse, director of the Army School of Nursing, nursing educator, suffragist
Dict Am Bio supp v5; Index t Wom; Nat Cyc Am Bio v42; Not Am Wom supp v1

2894. Gordon, Nora Antonia
1866–1901
educator, missionary to Africa
Black
Negro Alman; Prof Negro Wom v1

2895. Hovey, Harriette Spof-ford
died 1916
educator
Nat Cyc Am Bio v6

2896. Reed, Clare Osborn
born 1866
musician, pianist, music educator
Nat Cyc Am Bio csv7

2897. Simpson, Georgianna R.
1866–1944
professor, linguist
Black
Negro Alman; Prof Negro Wom v1

2898. Sullivan, Anne; Anne Sullivan Macy
1866–1936
educator of the blind
Index t Wom; Not Am Wom

2899. Wright, Sophie Bell
1866–1912
educator, night school founder, welfare worker, temperance worker
Nat Cyc Am Bio v10; Not Am Wom

2900. Young, Mary Vance
1866–1946
educator, linguist, World War I relief worker
Presbyterian
Index t Wom; Nat Cyc Am Bio v33

2901. Bancroft, Jessie Hubbell
1867–1952
physical education specialist
Not Am Wom supp v1

2902. Brown, Gertrude Foster
1867–1956
suffragist, concert pianist, music educator
Dict Am Bio supp v6; Obit File

2903. Bugbee, L. A.
died 1917
composer, music educator
Index t Wom

2904. Hamilton, Edith
1867–1963
author, classicist, educator, head-master of Bryn Mawr College
German
Index t Wom; Nat Cyc Am Bio v52; Not Am Wom supp v1; Obit File

2905. Hathaway, Maggie Smith
born 1867
educator, welfare worker, politi-cian
Index t Wom

2906. Hinman, Alice Hamlin
1867–1934
educator
Turkish
Nat Cyc Am Bio v26

2907. McVea, Emilie Watts
1867–1928
president of Sweet Briar College
Episcopalian
Virginia
Nat Cyc Am Bio v21

2908. Meyer, Annie Florence Nathan
1867–1950/51
publicist, author, playwright, novelist, educationist, founder of Barnard College, antisuffrag-

ist, patron of Black music education, clubwoman
Jewish
New York
Dict Am Auth; Dict Am Bio; Index t Wom; Nat Cyc Am Bio v42; Not Am Wom supp v1; Obit File; Twent Cen Bio Dict Not Am; Wom Cent

2909. O'Donnell, Nellie
born 1867
educator
Tennessee
Index t Wom; Wom Cent

2910. Potter, Frances Squire
1867–1914
suffragist, educator
Nat Cyc Am Bio v15

2911. Robertson, Ina Law
1867–1916
educator, philanthropist
Nat Cyc Am Bio v17

2912. Seymour, Harriet Ayer
1867/76–1944
pianist, music educator, pioneer of music therapy, music author
Index t Wom; Nat Cyc Am Bio v33; Obit File

2913. Shipley, Katherine Morris
1867–1929
educator
Pennsylvania
Nat Cyc Am Bio v23

2914. Sitgreaves, Beverley
1867–1943
actor, dramatic coach
Index t Wom; Obit File

2915. Talbot, Ellen Bliss
1867–1968
philosopher, educator, author
Congregationalist
Index t Wom; Nat Cyc Am Bio v54; Who Who Phil

2916. Walker, Edythe
1867/70–1950
opera singer, voice teacher
Index t Wom; Not Am Wom

2917. Wilder, Laura Ingalls
1867–1957
children's author, educator, editor
Dict Am Bio supp v6; Index t Wom; Not Am Wom supp v1; Obit File; Read Encyc Am West

2918. Woodruff, Caroline
1867–1949
educator, president of the National Education Association
Obit File

2919. Berenson, Senda
1868–1954
basketball player, gymnast, physical education authority
Jewish
Lithuanian
Dict Am Bio supp v5

2920. Chase, Mary Wood
born 1868
pianist, educator, author
Index t Wom

2921. Fryberger, Agnes Moore
born 1868
music educator, lecturer, author
Index t Wom

2922. Grenfell, Helen Loring
born 1868
educator, penologist
Index t Wom

2923. Hill, Patty Smith
1868–1946
educator, leader in kindergarten reform
Dict Am Bio supp v4; Index t Wom; Not Am Wom; Obit File

2924. King, Lida Shaw
1868–1932
classical scholar, archaeologist, educator, college administrator
Pennsylvania
Nat Cyc Am Bio v23; Not Am Wom

2925. Miller, Mary Rogers
born 1868
educator, author
New York, NY
Dict Am Auth

2926. Spurgeon, Caroline Frances Eleanor
1868–1942
authority on Shakespeare and Chaucer, educator, founder of the International Federation of University Women
Obit File

2927. Talbot, Anna Charlotte Hedges
born 1868
women's educator
Unitarian
New York
Nat Cyc Am Bio v30

2928. Wolcott, Ann Louise
born 1868
archaeologist, educator
Index t Wom

2929. Arnold, Cornelia Eliza Macmullan
1869–1945
educator, author
Episcopalian
Nat Cyc Am Bio v33

2930. Barnum, Mary Gilmore
born 1869
educator, social worker, Los Angeles civic worker
Congregationalist
Los Angeles, CA
Nat Cyc Am Bio csv7

2931. Brower, Harriette
1869–1928
pianist, music educator, author
Index t Wom

2932. Hamilton, Alice
1869–1970
industrial physician and toxicologist, pioneer in industrial medicine, medical educator, medical author, social reformer
Cur Biog '70; Index t Wom; Nat Cyc Am Bio csv7; Not Am Wom supp v1

2933. Kelley, Jessie Stillman
born 1869
pianist, piano educator
Nat Cyc Am Bio csv3

2934. Mannes, Clara Domrosch
1869–1948
pianist, music educator
Lutheran
German
Dict Am Bio supp v4; Index t Wom

2935. Marshall, Harriet Gibbs
1869–1941
pianist, music educator
Black
Encyc Black Am; Index t Wom

2936. Mehan, Caroline Eleanore Catharine
born 1869
singer, music educator, voice coach
Nat Cyc Am Bio csv2

2937. Noyes, Clara Dutton
1869/70–1936
nurse, nursing educator, field nurse in World War I, author
Dict Am Bio supp v2; Index t Wom; Nat Cyc Am Bio csv2

2938. Regan, Agnes Gertrude
1869–1943
Catholic social welfare leader, educator, women's rights worker
Catholic
Dict Am Bio supp v3; Not Am Wom

2939. Schoonhoven, Helen Butterfield
born 1869
lecturer, educator
Index t Wom

2940. Stair, Patty
1869–1926
composer, pianist, organist, music educator
Index t Wom

2941. Woodbury, Rosa Louise
born 1869
journalist, educator
Georgia
Wom Cent

2942. Buell, Edith May
born 1870
educator of the deaf
Congregationalist
Nat Cyc Am Bio csv6

2943. Byington, Margaret
born 1870s; died 1952
educator, social worker
Bulgarian
Obit File

2944. Colgan, Eleanor
flourished 1900s
educator
Index t Wom

2945. Cook, Myrtle Foster
1870–1951
educator, civic leader, financier, Black civil rights worker
Kansas City, KS
Black; Canadian
Negro Alman; Prof Negro Wom

2946. Davenport, Frances Gardiner
born 1870
historian, educator
Index t Wom

2947. Donnelly, Lucy Martin
1870–1948
English professor
Not Am Wom

2948. Goodsell, Willystine
born 1870
educator, author
Index t Wom

2949. Hathaway, Winifred Phillips
circa 1870–1954
educator of the partially blind
Index t Wom; Obit File

2950. Jenkins, Cora W.
circa 1870–1947
composer, music educator
Index t Wom

2951. Karnes, Matilda Theresa
flourished 1900s
educator, clubwoman
Index t Wom

2952. Kingsbury, Susan Myra
1870–1949
social investigator, social work educator, social economist, feminist

Pennsylvania
Not Am Wom; Obit File

2953. Lacey, Margaret E.
flourished 1900s–30s
educator, songwriter
Index t Wom

2954. Levy, Florence Nightingale
1870–1947
art administrator, art educator
Nat Cyc Am Bio csv2; Not Am Wom

2955. Marshall, Florence M.
flourished 1900s–30s
vocational educator
Index t Wom

2956. Michael, Moina; The Poppy Lady
circa 1870–1944
educator, originator of Poppy Day as a memorial to war dead
Index t Wom; Obit File

2957. Mosher, Edith R.
flourished 1900s–10s
educator, author
Index t Wom

2958. Page, Fannie Pender
1870–1942
missionary, educator
Index t Wom

2959. Pape, Nina
1870–1944
educator
Savannah, GA
Obit File

2960. Stevens, Georgia Lydia, Mother
1870–1946
musician, cofounder of the Piux X School of Liturgical Music, educator, Catholic nun
Catholic
Not Am Wom; Obit File

2961. Strachan, Grace Charlotte
flourished 1900s
educator, philanthropist
Index t Wom

2962. Wier, Jeanne Elizabeth
1870–1950
historian of Nevada and the state's Native Americans, educator, suffragist
Nevada
Nat Cyc Am Bio v51 and csv1; Obit File; Read Encyc Am West

2963. Allinson, Anne Crosby Emery
1871–1931

educator, college administrator, author
Dict Am Bio supp v1

2964. Chase, Kate Fowler
1871–1951
educator, lecturer, clubwoman
Index t Wom

2965. Holland, Annie Wealthy
1871–1934
educator
North Carolina
Black
Negro Alman; Prof Negro Wom v1

2966. Morse, Ednah Anne Rich
1871–1945
educator
California
Nat Cyc Am Bio v38

2967. Pearson, Elizabeth Ware Winson
1871–1960
nursery school training pioneer
Obit File

2968. Perrin, Ethel
1871–1962
physical education specialist
Not Am Wom supp v1

2969. Powell, Louise Mathilde
1871–1943
nursing educator
Not Am Wom

2970. Reed, Anna Yeomans
born 1871
educator
Index t Wom; Nat Cyc Am Bio csv4

2971. Rickert, Martha Edith
1871–1938
medievalist, professor of English, philologist, novelist
Dict Am Auth; Dict Am Bio supp v2; Not Am Wom

2972. Sabin, Florence Rena
1871–1953
physician, medical researcher and educator, anatomist, public health worker, first woman life member of the American Academy of Sciences, author
Colorado
Dict Am Bio supp v5; Index t Wom; Nat Cyc Am Bio v40 and csv3; Not Am Wom supp v1; Obit File

2973. Smith, Ida B. Wise
1871–1952
president of WCTU, educator, businessperson
Index t Wom; Obit File

2974. Stocker, Corinne
born 1871
elocutionist, journalist
Georgia
Wom Cent

2975. Adams, Elizabeth Kemper
1872–1948
educator, editor
Index t Wom

2976. Butler, Selena Sloan
1872?–1964
community leader, founder of the National Congress of Colored Parents and Teachers Association
Black
Not Am Wom supp v1

2977. Colton, Elizabeth Avery
1872–1924
professor of English, crusader for better women's colleges
Dict Am Bio; Not Am Wom

2978. Haines, Helen Elizabeth
1872–1961
librarian, author, editor, educator
Index t Wom; Not Am Wom supp v1

2979. Morgan, Alice Bell
1872–1958
educator, financial expert
Obit File

2980. Phelan, Marie Gerard
1872–1960
superior general of the Institute of the Religious of the Sacred Heart of Mary, cofounder of Marymount College
Catholic
California
Obit File

2981. Pound, Louise
1872–1958
university educator, writer on literature, folklorist, tennis player, bicyclist, golfer
Nebraska
Nat Cyc Am Bio v45, csv2, and csv5; Not Am Wom supp v1; Obit File

2982. Putnam, Bertha Haven
1872–1960
historian, history writer, authority on medieval history and criminology, educator
Unitarian
Nat Cyc Am Bio v43; Not Am Wom supp v1; Obit File

2983. Abel-Anderson, Annie Heloise
1873–1947
historian, educator
Dict Am Bio supp v4; Not Am Wom

2984. Baker, Caroline Tilden
1873–1931
educator
Quaker
New York
Nat Cyc Am Bio v22

2985. Bolton, Margaret
1873–1943
religious educator, author
Catholic
Obit File

2986. Broadhurst, Jean
1873–1954
author, educator, bacteriologist
Index t Wom

2987. Cromwell, Otelia
1873–1972
educator, author
Black
Encyc Black Am

2988. Dammann, Grace Cowardin
1873–1945
president of Manhattanville College of the Sacred Heart
Catholic
Obit File

2989. Laidlaw, Harriet Davenport Wright Burton
1873–1949
suffragist, author, educator, lecturer, clubwoman
Presbyterian
Index t Wom; Nat Cyc Am Bio v38; Not Am Wom

2990. Lamkin, Nina Belle
born 1873
educator, child welfare worker
Nat Cyc Am Bio v18

2991. Lingelbach, Anna Lane
1873–1954
historian, educator, civic leader, feminist
Presbyterian
Pennsylvania
Dict Am Bio supp v5; Nat Cyc Am Bio v44; Obit File

2992. Morrow, Elizabeth Cutter
1873–1955
author, educator
Index t Wom; Obit File

2993. Neilson, Nellie
1873–1947
English historian, first woman president of the American Historical Association, educator, author
Episcopalian
Nat Cyc Am Bio v36; Not Am Wom; Obit File

2994. Reynolds, Alice Louise
born 1873

educator
Index t Wom

2995. Sloop, Mary T. Martin
1873–1962
physician, educator, social worker
Index t Wom

2996. van Duyn, Sarah Elizabeth
born 1873
physician, medical educator
Nat Cyc Am Bio csv2

2997. Vernon, Weston, Mrs.
born 1873
educator
Index t Wom

2998. Flexner, Anne Crawford
1874–1955
playwright, director of the Institute for Advanced Studies at Princeton University
Princeton, NJ
Index t Wom; Obit File

2999. Greaves, Jessie Royer
1874–1967
educator of the blind
United Church of Christ
Pennsylvania
Nat Cyc Am Bio v53

3000. Mather, Winifred Holt
1874–1945
sculptor, patron of welfare of the blind, founder of a school for the blind, author
Episcopalian
Nat Cyc Am Bio v34 and csv6

3001. Ogilvie, Ida Helen
born 1874
geologist, educator
Nat Cyc Am Bio v16

3002. Randolph, Virginia Estelle
1874/76–1958
social worker, educator
Virginia
Black
Index t Wom; Negro Alman; Prof Negro Wom v1

3003. Robinson, Mabel Louise
1874–1962
author, children's author, educator
Index t Wom; Nat Cyc Am Bio v47

3004. Starr, Sarah Logan Wister
1874–1956
physician, president of the Women's Medical College of Pennsylvania
Pennsylvania
Obit File

3005. Williams, Lulu Margaret Roberts
1874/75–1945
educator, social reformer, Black student aid worker
Black
Negro Alman; Prof Negro Wom v1

3006. Benedict, Mary Kendrick
1875–1956
president of Sweet Briar College
Pennsylvania
Obit File

3007. Bethune, Mary McLeod
1875–1955
educator, founder and president of Bethune-Cookman College, director of the Negro Affairs National Youth Council, civil rights worker, women's rights worker
Daytona Beach, FL
Black
Dict Am Bio supp v5; Dict Am Rel Bio; Encyc Black Am; Encyc South Hist; Index t Wom; Nat Cyc Am Bio v49; Negro Alman; Negro Her Lib v1; Not Am Wom supp v1; Prof Negro Wom; Obit File

3008. Bradley, Alice
born 1875
home economics educator
Methodist
Massachusetts
Nat Cyc Am Bio csv2

3009. Cahier, Sarah Jane Layton-Walker
1875–1951
contralto singer, vocal coach
Index t Wom; Obit File

3010. Cornell, Sophia S.
born 1875
educator, author
Index t Wom

3011. Dickinson, Helena Adall Snyder
1875–1975
nonfiction writer, educator
Presbyterian
Canadian
Nat Cyc Am Bio v54

3012. Fitch, Florency Mary
1875–1959
Biblical literature authority, university educator, religious writer for children
Oberlin, OH
Obit File

3013. Holton, Susan May
circa 1875–1951
business executive, author, educator
Index t Wom

3014. Hughan, Jessie Wallace
1875–1955
pacifist, Socialist party worker, politician, educator, author
Index t Wom; Not Am Wom supp v1

3015. Humphrey, Caroline Louise
born 1875
educator
Unitarian
Boston, MA
Nat Cyc Am Bio csv2 and csv5

3016. Kelly, Myra
1875/76–1910
author, humorist, social reformer, educator
Irish
Dict Am Auth; Dict Am Bio; Index t Wom; Nat Cyc Am Bio v24; Wom Lit, More

3017. Marks, Jeannette Augustus
1875–1964
poet, children's author, educator, Socialist party worker
Index t Wom; Nat Cyc Am Bio csv2

3018. Nelson, Alice Ruth Dunbar (Moore)
1875–1935
author, editor, social worker
Louisiana
Black
Encyc Black Am; Negro Alman; Not Am Wom; Prof Negro Wom v1

3019. Noyes-Greene, Edith Rowens
born 1875
composer, music educator, pianist
Index t Wom

3020. Park, Marion Edwards
1875–1960
president of Bryn Mawr College, dean of Simmons College and Radcliffe College
Nat Cyc Am Bio csv1; Obit File

3021. Risher, Anne Priscilla
born 1875
composer, organist, music educator, composer
Index t Wom

3022. Stanwood, Cornelia Terry McKinne
born 1875
educator
Episcopalian
California
Nat Cyc Am Bio csv7

3023. Thurston, Matilda Smynell Calder
1875–1958

missionary educator in Turkey and China, founder and president of Ginling College in Nanking, China
Congregationalist
Not Am Wom supp v1; Obit File

3024. Wick, Frances Gertrude
1875–1941
physicist, educator
Presbyterian
Index t Wom; Nat Cyc Am Bio v34; Obit File

3025. Abbott, Edith
1876–1957
social reformer, social work educator, author
Nebraska
Dict Am Bio supp v6; Index t Wom; Nat Cyc Am Bio csv3; Not Am Wom; Obit File

3026. Beard, Mary
1876–1946
administrator and educator in nursing and public health, Rockefeller Foundation administrator, director of American Red Cross Nursing Service
Dict Am Bio supp v4; Index t Wom; Nat Cyc Am Bio v35; Obit File

3027. Blunt, Katharine
1876–1954
college administrator, home economics educator, nutritionist, chemist
Index t Wom; Nat Cyc Am Bio csv2; Not Am Wom supp v1

3028. Bole, Roberta Holden
1876–1950
philanthropist; patron of art, science, and education
Unitarian
Nat Cyc Am Bio v38

3029. Burchenal, Elizabeth
1876–1959
folklorist, folk dance educator, cofounder of the American Folk Dance Society, originator of the New York Folk Dance Festival
New York
Index t Wom; Not Am Wom supp v1; Obit File

3030. Cleghorn, Sarah Norcliffe
1876–1959
poet, novelist, educator, suffragist, civil rights worker, labor worker, pacifist, antivivisectionist, Socialist party member
Vermont
Index t Wom; Nat Cyc Am Bio v46; Obit File; Dict Am Bio supp v5

3031. Comstock, Ada Louise;
Ada Notestein
1876–1973
college administrator, president of
Radcliffe College
Boston, MA
Nat Cyc Am Bio csv3; Not Am
Wom supp v1; Obit File

3032. Cornish, Nellie Centennial
1876–1956
music educator, patron of music,
music school founder
Washington
Index t Wom; Read Encyc Am
West

3033. Dickenson, Helena A.
1876–1957
cofounder of the Sacred Heart
Music School at Union Theological Seminary
Catholic
Obit File

3034. Eckel, Berenice Long
born 1876
pianist, violinist, music educator
Presbyterian
Nat Cyc Am Bio csv5

3035. Hartman, Gertrude
1876–1955
author of school texts, educator,
writer on education
Obit File

3036. Hockaday, Ela
1876–1956
educator
Texas
Nat Cyc Am Bio v42

3037. Lloyd, Alice Spencer Geddes
1876–1972
educator
Not Am Wom supp v1

3038. Lynch, Ella Frances
1876–1945
educator
Obit File

3039. MacChesney, Norma Gertrude
born 1876
music educator
Index t Wom

3040. Ouspenskaya, Maria
1876–1949
dramatic teacher, character actor
Russian
Index t Wom; Obit File

3041. Peters, Iva (Lowther)
born 1876
educator, author on education
Methodist Episcopal
Nat Cyc Am Bio csv1

3042. Phelps, Ruth Shepherd;
Mme. Paul Morand
born 1876
educator, writer on Romance languages
Nat Cyc Am Bio csv2 and csv5

3043. Prichard, Maude Hancock
born 1876
educator
Index t Wom

3044. Ryder, Theodora Sturkow
born 1876
composer, pianist, music educator
Index t Wom

3045. Tracy, Martha
1876–1942
physician, public health expert,
dean of the Women's Medical
College of Pennsylvania
Philadelphia, PA
Index t Wom; Nat Cyc Am Bio
v31; Not Am Wom

3046. Vanamee, Grace Davis
1876–1946
club leader, lecturer, educator,
author
Index t Wom

3047. Venable, Mary Elizabeth
died 1926
pianist, music educator, author
Index t Wom

3048. Wells, Agnes Ermina
1876–1959
mathematician, astronomer, educator
Index t Wom

3049. Williams, Amelia Worthington
1876–1958
educator, historian of Texas
Presbyterian
Texas
Nat Cyc Am Bio v44

3050. Barrows, Alice Prentiss
1877–1954
educator, school building specialist
Dict Am Bio supp v5

3051. Brown, Sue M.
1877–1941
clubwoman, educator, author,
suffragist, women's rights worker, Black civil rights worker
Black
Negro Alman; Prof Negro Wom

3052. Burgess, Elizabeth Chamberlain
1877–1949
nurse, educator
Index t Wom

3053. Cunningham, Kate (Richards) (O'Hare)
1877–1948
Socialist party presidential nominee, community organizer, prison reformer, anti–World War I
activist, lecturer, educator
Index t Wom; Not Am Wom;
Obit File; Dict Am Bio v4

3054. Diller, Angela
1877–1968
music educator
Index t Wom; Not Am Wom
supp v1

3055. Douglass, Mabel Smith
1877–1933
founder and dean of the New
Jersey College for Women
(Douglass College)
New Jersey
Not Am Wom

3056. Franklin, Lucy Jenkins
born 1877
university educator
Methodist Episcopal
Boston, MA
Nat Cyc Am Bio csv4

3057. Gildersleeve, Virginia Crocheron
1877–1965
educator, dean emeritus of Barnard College, US delegate to the
1945 San Francisco conference
to draft the UN charter, creator
of UNESCO
New York
Index t Wom; Nat Cyc Am Bio
csv1 and csv7; Not Am Wom
supp v1; Obit File

3058. Hutchison, Ida Jones Seymour
1877–1950
educator, philanthropist
Index t Wom

3059. Jarrett, Mary Cromwell
1877–1961
social worker, social work educator
Not Am Wom supp v1

3060. Landowska, Wanda (Lew)
1877/79–1959
harpsichordist, pianist, composer,
musicologist, music educator,
writer on music
Jewish
Polish
Dict Am Bio supp v6; Obit File;
Slavon Encyc; Who Who Jew
Hist

3061. Norsworthy, Naomi
1877–1916
psychologist, educator
Dict Am Bio

3062. Redfield, Ethel
born 1877
educator, author
Index t Wom

3063. Reinhardt, Aurelia Isabelle Henry
1877–1948
president of Mills College, educator, religious worker, Unitarian
minister
Unitarian
Oakland, CA
Dict Am Bio supp v4; Index t
Wom; Not Am Wom; Obit File

3064. Roberts, Mary May
1877–1959
nurse, nursing magazine editor,
nursing educator, chief nurse of
the World War II army nurse
corps
Index t Wom; Not Am Wom
supp v1; Obit File

3065. Robinson-Duff, Frances
1877–1951
dramatic coach
Index t Wom; Obit File

3066. Sullivan, Mary Josephine Quinn
1877–1939
art teacher and collector, a founder of the New York Museum of
Modern Art
Not Am Wom

3067. Akeley, Mary Lee Jobe
1878/86–1966
explorer, photographer, educator,
author, botanist
Index t Wom; Not Am Wom

3068. Burroughs, Nannie Helen
1878/83–1961
educator, founder of the National
Trade and Professional School
for Women and Girls, women's
rights worker
Baptist
Black
Index t Wom; Negro Alman; Not
Am Wom supp v1; Prof Negro
Wom

3069. Center, Stella Steward
born 1878
educator, lecturer
Index t Wom

3070. Collier, Constance; Laura
Constance Hardie
1878–1955
stage and screen actor, drama
coach
English
Dict Am Bio supp v5; Obit File

3071. Frame, Alice Seymour Browne
1878–1941

Congregationalist missionary and
    educator in China
Congregationalist
Dict Am Bio supp v3; Not Am
    Wom

3072. Gardner, Helen
1878–1946
art historian, educator
Dict Am Bio supp v4; Index t
    Wom; Not Am Wom

3073. Harcum, Edith H.
1878–1958
cofounder and president of Har-
    cum Junior College
Philadelphia, PA
Obit File

3074. Jean, Sally Lucas
born 1878
nurse, educator
Index t Wom

3075. Lawton, Thais
1878–1956
stage actor, dramatic coach
Obit File

3076. McKinstry, Helen May
1878–1949
president of Russell Sage College,
    physical education expert
Presbyterian
New York
Nat Cyc Am Bio v37; Obit File

3077. McLeod, Grace
1878–1962
nutritionist, nutrition educator,
    editor
Congregationalist
Scottish
Index t Wom; Nat Cyc Am Bio
    v50

3078. Mitchell, Lucy Sprague
1878–1967
educator, college administrator,
    Black education worker, chil-
    dren's author
New York
Nat Cyc Am Bio v53; Not Am
    Wom supp v1

3079. Robyn, Louise
circa 1878–1949
composer, author, music educator
Index t Wom

3080. Scarborough, Dorothy
1878–1935
novelist, English teacher, folklor-
    ist
Dict Am Bio supp v1; Index t
    Wom; Wom Lit

3081. Stewart, Isabel Maitland
1878–1963
nursing educator

Canadian
Index t Wom; Not Am Wom
    supp v1

3082. Vengerova, Isabelle
1878–1956
pianist, piano teacher
Obit File

3083. Baker, Mary Cornelia
1879–1963
labor leader, educator
Not Am Wom supp v1

3084. Boyd, Anna Tomlinson
born 1879
pianist, music educator
Index t Wom; Nat Cyc Am Bio
    v11

3085. Cabot, Ella Lyman
graduated 1904
educator, author
Index t Wom

3086. Chapin, Alice Delafield
1879–1964
educator, social welfare leader
Episcopalian
New York
Index t Wom; Nat Cyc Am Bio
    v52

3087. Cleophas, Mary
1879–1946
president of Rosemont College
Pennsylvania
Obit File

3088. Fisher, Dorothy Canfield;
    Dorothea Frances Canfield
1879–1958
novelist, writer on education, es-
    sayist
Cyc Am Bio; Dict Am Bio supp
    v6; Dict Lit Bio v9; Index t
    Wom; Nat Cyc Am Bio v18 and
    v44; Not Am Wom supp v1;
    Obit File

**3089. Fisher, Welthy (Blakes-
    ley) Honsinger**
1879/80–1980
Methodist missionary to India
    and China, social worker, edu-
    cator, president of World Edu-
    cation, Inc.
Methodist
Cur Biog '69 and '81; Index t
    Wom

3090. Nash, Alice Morrison
born circa 1879
educator
Index t Wom

3091. Reilly, Marion
1879–1928
educator, suffragist, philanthro-
    pist
Dict Am Bio

3092. Roberts, Lydia Jane
1879–1965
nutritionist, home economics edu-
    cator
Not Am Wom supp v1

3093. White, Edna Noble
1879–1954
educator, home economist
Not Am Wom supp v1

3094. Williams, Blanche Colton
1879–1926/44
educator, writer on writing, an-
    thology editor
Index t Wom; Nat Cyc Am Bio
    csv2

3095. Bieber, Margarete
1880–1978
historian, author, archaeologist,
    educator, authority on Greek
    and Roman art
German
Obit File

3096. Bilbro, Mathilde (Anne)
flourished 1910s–50s
composer, music educator, author
Index t Wom

3097. Bliss, Ethel House
circa 1880–1946
educator
Index t Wom

3098. Branch, Hazel E.
flourished 1910s–20s
entomologist, educator
Index t Wom

**3099. Brownson, Josephine van
    Dyke**
1880–1942
educator, catechist
Index t Wom

3100. Chandler, Anna Curtis
flourished 1910s–30s
educator
Index t Wom

3101. Coulter, Edith Margaret
1880–1963
librarian, library educator
Presbyterian
California
Nat Cyc Am Bio v50

3102. Fernald, Grace M.
1880–1950
educator, psychologist specializ-
    ing in retarded children
Obit File

3103. Glass, Meta
1880–1967
president of Sweet Briar College,
    educator, YWCA executive,
    World War I and II relief work-
    er, defense worker
Episcopalian

Virginia
Nat Cyc Am Bio v53 and csv7;
    Obit File

3104. Griffith, Emily
1880?–1947
educator
Not Am Wom

3105. Hale, Florence
1880–1959
president of the National Educa-
    tion Association, rural educa-
    tion director of Maine
Maine
Obit File

3106. Hickman, Emily Gregory
1880–1947
educator
Index t Wom

**3107. Irwin, Elisabeth Antoin-
    ette**
1880–1942
progressive educator
Dict Am Bio supp v3; Index t
    Wom; Not Am Wom

3108. Keller, Helen Adams
1880–1968
author, feminist, suffragist, edu-
    cator, advocate for the handi-
    capped, pacifist, Socialist party
    worker
Swedenborgian
Alabama
blind, deaf
Encyc South Hist; Index t Wom;
    Nat Cyc Am Bio v15 and v57;
    Not Am Wom supp v1; Obit
    File

**3109. Kelley, Edgar Stillman,
    Mrs.**
flourished 1910s–30s
pianist, music educator
Index t Wom

3110. Kluegel, Anne Jennings
born 1880
author, educator
Index t Wom

3111. Lhevinne, Rosina
1880–1976
classical pianist, piano educator
Russian
Cur Biog '77; Index t Wom; Obit
    File

3112. Martin, Gertrude
flourished 1910s
educator
Index t Wom

3113. Mary de Sales, Mother;
    Wilhelmina Tredow
flourished 1910s
educator, Catholic nun
Catholic
Index t Wom

3114. Masland, Mary Elizabeth
flourished 1910s–30s
educator
Index t Wom

3115. Molloy, Mary Aloysia
born 1880
educator, author, Franciscan nun
Catholic
Nat Cyc Am Bio csv3

3116. Prentice, Marion
flourished 1910s–20s
composer, director, music educator
Index t Wom

3117. Prentiss, Henrietta
1880–1940
educator, speech authority
Index t Wom

3118. Warren, Constance
born 1880
educator
Index t Wom

3119. Wellington, Violet Irene
flourished 1910s
dramatic reader, drama teacher, suffragist, pacifist
Nat Cyc Am Bio v19

3120. Burlingame, Anne Elizabeth
born 1881
author, educator
Nat Cyc Am Bio csvl

3121. Frazier, Maude
1881–1963
educator, state legislator
Not Am Wom supp v1

3122. Gruenberg, Sidonie Matsner
1881–1974
parent education leader; director of the Child Study Association of America, specialist in child guidance, parent education, and family relationships; nonfiction writer; lecturer
Austrian
Cur Biog '74; Index t Wom; Not Am Wom supp v1; Obit File

3123. Harrison, Hazel Lucile
1881/83–1969
pianist, music educator
Black
Encyc Black Am; Index t Wom; Not Am Wom supp v1

3124. Shambaugh, Jessie Field
1881–1971
rural educator
Not Am Wom supp v1

3125. Stein, Beatrice Borg
1881–1958

welfare leader, philanthropist, founder of the Play School Association
Jewish
New York
Nat Cyc Am Bio v47; Obit File

3126. Stewart, Sallie W.
1881–1951
educator, clubwoman, realtor, lecturer, Black women's welfare worker
Indiana
Black
Negro Alman; Prof Negro Wom v1

3127. Stimson, Julia Catherine
1881–1948
professional nurse, World War I nurse, superintendent of the Army Nursing Corps, nursing educator, colonel in the US Army
Dict Am Bio supp v4; Index t Wom; Nat Cyc Am Bio csv2; Not Am Wom; Obit File

3128. Atwood, Elizabeth Gordon
born 1882
educator
Index t Wom

3129. Branch, Mary E.
1882–1945
educator
Black
Encyc Black Am

3130. Brown, Charlotte Eugenia Hawkins
1882/83–1961
educator, founder of the Palmer Memorial Institute, YWCA national board member
North Carolina
Black
Encyc Black Am; Index t Wom; Negro Alman; Not Am Wom supp v1; Obit File; Prof Negro Wom v1 and v2

3131. Dodd, Katharine
1882–1965
pediatrician, medical educator and author
Episcopalian
Nat Cyc Am Bio v53

3132. Fauset, Jessie Redmon
1882/86–1961
author, novelist, editor, educator
Encyc Black Am; Index t Wom; Negro Alman; Not Am Wom supp v1; Prof Negro Wom v2; Wom Lit; Wom Lit, More

3133. Gulliver, Lucile
born 1882
social studies text author
Nat Cyc Am Bio csv2

3134. Harris, Mary Ormerod
born 1882
philanthropist, patron of the University of Southern California
Congregationalist
California
Nat Cyc Am Bio csv6

3135. Hunter, Jane Edna
1882–1971
social worker, nurse, educator, clubwoman
Cleveland, OH
Black
Index t Wom; Negro Alman; Prof Negro Wom v1

3136. Mathews, Blanche Dingley
died 1932
composer, author, music educator
Index t Wom

3137. Samaroff, Olga; Olga Stokowski
1882–1948
concert pianist, music educator
Dict Am Bio supp v4; Index t Wom; Not Am Wom; Nat Cyc Am Bio v36; Obit File

3138. Scott, Miriam Finn
1882–1944
pioneer child diagnostician, educator, lecturer, author
Russian
Index t Wom; Nat Cyc Am Bio v36

3139. Taft, Jessie
1882–1960
psychologist, social work educator
Not Am Wom supp v1

3140. Traphagen, Ethel; Mrs. William R. Leigh
1882–1963
fashion designer, founder of the first school of fashion design in the United States, pacifist
Index t Wom; Nat Cyc Am Bio v54 and csv9; Obit File

3141. Baker, Edna Dean
1883–1956
kindergarten educator
Methodist
Nat Cyc Am Bio v43

3142. Cane, Florence Naumburg
1883–1952
artist, educator, author
Obit File

3143. Joseph, Mary, Sister
born 1883
educator, Catholic nun
Catholic
Index t Wom

3144. Meredith, Florence Lyndon
1883–1951
physician, medical educator
Massachusetts
Nat Cyc Am Bio v45 and csv1

3145. Shaver, Mary Mumpere
1883–1942
librarian, educator
Index t Wom

3146. Stauffer, Edna Pennypacker
1883–1956
painter, lithographer, art educator
Obit File

3147. Winn, Edith L.
died 1933
violinist, music educator, author
Index t Wom

3148. Andrus, Ethel Percy
1884–1967
founder of retirement organizations, educator, executive
Not Am Wom supp v1

3149. Arbuthnot, May Hill
1884–1969
educator, specialist in children's literature
Not Am Wom supp v1

3150. Copp, Laura Remick
died 1934
pianist, music educator
Index t Wom

3151. Elliott, Harriet Wiseman
1884–1947
educator, dean of women's college at the University of North Carolina, suffragist, women's rights worker, political organizer, public official
North Carolina
Encyc South Hist; Index t Wom; Not Am Wom; Obit File

3152. Gulesian, Grace Warner
born 1884
composer, pianist, music educator, choral director
Index t Wom

3153. Haake, Gail Martin
born 1884
pianist, music educator
Index t Wom

3154. Hatch, Edith
born 1884
organist, composer, piano educator
Index t Wom

3155. Liebling, Estelle
born 1884/86

composer, singer, music educator, editor
Index t Wom

3156. Messenger, Ruth Ellis
1884–1964
hymnologist, educator
Protestant Episcopal
New York
Nat Cyc Am Bio v51

3157. Olcott, Virginia
graduated 1909
social worker, educator, author
Index t Wom

3158. Bailey, Margaret Emerson
1885–1949
educator, journalist, novelist, magazine writer, police commissioner
Episcopalian
New Canaan, CT
Nat Cyc Am Bio csv6; Obit File

3159. Baker, Elizabeth Bradford Faulkner
born 1885
educator, economist
Index t Wom

3160. Bowser, Rosa Dixon
1885–1931
educator, clubwoman
Richmond, VA
Black
Negro Alman; Prof Negro Wom

3161. Brooker, Mary Isaphene Ives
born 1885
elocutionist
Nat Cyc Am Bio csv3

3162. Cohn, Fannie Mary
1885/88–1962
labor leader and organizer, labor educator
Jewish
Russian
Cyc Am Bio; Bio Dict Am Lab; Not Am Wom supp v1

3163. Graves, Marion Coates
born 1885
college educator
Nat Cyc Am Bio csv4

3164. Ilsley, Marjorie [Louise] Henry
1885–1961
educator
Massachusetts
Nat Cyc Am Bio v52

3165. Kelman, Sarah R.
circa 1885–1969
psychiatrist, psychoanalyst, founder of the Association for the Advancement of Psychoanalysis, the American Institute

for Psychoanalysis, and the American Academy of Psychoanalysis
Russian
Obit File

3166. Lucke, Marion Hague Rea
1885–1946
physician, medical educator
Nat Cyc Am Bio v36

3167. McLaren, Louise Leonard
1885–1968
labor educator
Not Am Wom supp v1

3168. Randolph, Bessie Carter
1885–1966
political scientist, international law and affairs expert, president of Hollins College
Episcopalian
Virginia
Nat Cyc Am Bio v52 and csv6

3169. Reel, Estell
married 1910
educator
Index t Wom

3170. Rourke, Constance Mayfield
1885–1941
student of American culture, historian, folklorist, author, critic, educator
Dict Am Bio supp v3; Index t Wom; Nat Cyc Am Bio v32; Not Am Wom

3171. Siddall, Louise
died 1935
composer, educator
Index t Wom

3172. Slowe, Lucy Diggs
1885–1937
educator, school administrator, college dean
Not Am Wom

3173. Appleton, Adeline Carola
born 1886
composer, music educator
Index t Wom

3174. Bridgman, Olga Louise
born 1886
psychiatrist, medical educator and author
Episcopalian
California
Nat Cyc Am Bio csv6

3175. Cadilla de Martinez, Maria; Liana
1886–1951
educator, folklorist, author, feminist
Not Am Wom supp v1

3176. Conrad, Elisabeth Whiting
1886–1964
educator
Presbyterian
Nat Cyc Am Bio v52

3177. Fitzu, Anna (Powell)
circa 1886–1967
soprano opera singer, voice teacher
Index t Wom; Obit File

3178. Gilbert, Katharine Everett
1886–1952
philosopher, philosophy educator
Nat Cyc Am Bio v49; Who Who Phil

3179. Griggs, Mary Amerman
1886–1962
chemist, chemistry educator
Dutch Reformed
Nat Cyc Am Bio v49

3180. Hollingworth, Leta Anna Stetter
1886–1939
educational psychologist
Dict Am Bio supp v2; Not Am Wom

3181. Mary Julia, Sister; Elizabeth Ann Dullea
born 1886
educator, Catholic nun
Catholic
Index t Wom

3182. Schmitt, Bernadotte Everly
1886–1969
author on modern European history, educator, historian
Cur Biog '69

3183. Vautrin, Minnie
1886–1941
missionary educator in China
Not Am Wom

3184. Addition, Henrietta Silvis
born 1887
social worker, educator
Index t Wom

3185. Baker, Martha Atwood
1887–1950
soprano opera singer, music educator
Obit File

3186. Bane, Juliet Lita
1887–1957
home economics educator
Illinois
Nat Cyc Am Bio v43

3187. Bauer, Marion Eugenia
1887–1955

music educator, writer on music history, composer, editor, music critic
Index t Wom; Nat Cyc Am Bio v43, Not Am Wom supp v1; Obit File

3188. Beam, Lura
born 1887
educator, author
Index t Wom

3189. Benedict, Ruth Fulton
1887–1948
anthropologist, author, philosopher, educator
Dict Am Bio supp v4; Index t Wom; Nat Cyc Am Bio v36; Not Am Wom; Who Who Phil

3190. Biddle, Mary Duke
1887–1960
humanitarian, philanthropist, patron of Duke University
Methodist Episcopal
North Carolina
Index t Wom; Nat Cyc Am Bio v49

3191. Boulanger, Nadia
1887–1979
composer, pianist, music educator, conductor
French
Cur Biog '80

3192. Chase, Mary Ellen
1887–1973
novelist, biographer, short story writer, literary critic, writer on the Bible, university educator
Episcopalian
Cur Biog '73; Index t Wom; Nat Cyc Am Bio csv9; Obit File; Wom Lit, More

3193. Dobie, Edith
1887–1975
historian, educator
Methodist
Washington
Nat Cyc Am Bio v58

3194. Fairbank, Ruth Eldred
1887–1972
psychiatrist, psychiatric educator
Congregationalist
Massachusetts
Nat Cyc Am Bio v58

3195. Franklin, Elizabeth Jennings
1887–1967
founder of Bennington College and chairperson of the board of trustees
Presbyterian
Vermont; New York
Nat Cyc Am Bio v53; Obit File

3196. Lyman, Mary Ely
1887–1975

theologian, university educator
Not Am Wom supp v1; Obit File

3197. Madelva, Mary Eveline Wolff, Sister
1887–1964
president of St. Mary's College, medievalist, educator, author, poet, Catholic nun
Catholic
Index t Wom; Nat Cyc Am Bio v51; Obit File

3198. Meyer, Agnes Elizabeth (Ernst)
1887–1970
author, journalist, vice-president and co-owner of *The Washington Post*, World War II correspondent, autobiographer, lecturer, social worker, Republican party worker, crusader for social services and education causes
Lutheran
New York
Cur Biog '70; Index t Wom; Nat Cyc Am Bio v56; Obit File

3199. Parkhurst, Helen
1887–1973
educator, author
Obit File

3200. Parkhurst, Helen Huss
1887–1959
philosopher, educator, aesthetician
Index t Wom; Obit File; Who Who Phil

3201. Snyder, Alice Dorothea
1887–1943
professor of English literature, author
Index t Wom; Not Am Wom; Obit File

3202. Spofford, Grace Harriet
1887–1974
music educator, music administrator
Index t Wom; Not Am Wom supp v1

3203. Starbuck, Kathryn Helene
1887–1965
lawyer, women's rights worker, educator
Baptist
New York
Nat Cyc Am Bio v53

3204. Waring, Laura Wheeler
1887–1948
painter, educator
Black
Encyc Black Am; Negro Alman

3205. Williamson, Pauline Brooks
1887–1972
educator
Virginia
Nat Cyc Am Bio v56

3206. Willkie, Julia E.
1887–1943
bacteriologist, educator, linguist
Obit File

3207. Wolff, Mary Evaline "Madelva", Sister
1887–1964
college administrator, Catholic nun, religious educator, poet
Catholic
Not Am Wom supp v1

3208. Abel, Hazel Hempel
1888–1966
US senator, civic leader, educator
Index t Wom

3209. Ashton, Dorothy Laing
1888–1958
surgeon, obstetrician/gynecologist, medical educator
Pennsylvania
Nat Cyc Am Bio v49

3210. Barker, Tommie Dora
born 1888
librarian, author, educator
Index t Wom

3211. Blakeslee, Myra Allen
circa 1888–1953
advertising executive, social welfare worker
Index t Wom

3212. Bussey, Gertrude C.
1888–1961
president of the Women's International League for Peace and Freedom, philosopher, educator
Obit File

3213. Bussey, Ruth Carman
1888–1961
educator, worker for Women's International League for Peace and Freedom party
Episcopalian
Maryland
Nat Cyc Am Bio v49

3214. Hull, Helen Rose
1888–1971
novelist, short story writer, university educator
New York
Cur Biog '71; Index t Wom; Nat Cyc Am Bio v60; Obit File

3215. Pitts, Carol Marhoff
born 1888
composer, conductor, educator
Index t Wom

3216. Price, Florence Beatrice Smith
1888–1953
composer, instrumentalist, pianist, organist, music educator
Black
Index t Wom; Not Am Wom supp v1

3217. Smith, Lucy Harth
1888–1955
educator, educational administrator
Kentucky
Black
Dict Am Bio supp v5

3218. Akers, Susan Grey
born 1889
librarian, educator, author
Index t Wom

3219. Burns, Annelu
1889–1942
violinist, composer, music educator
Index t Wom

3220. Coit, Dorothy
born 1889
drama coach, director, educator
Index t Wom

3221. Cramm, Helen L.
died 1939
composer, music educator
Index t Wom

3222. Fromm-Reichman, Frieda
1889–1957
psychiatrist, psychoanalyst, authority on schizophrenia, faculty chairperson of the Washington School of Psychiatry
Jewish
Washington, DC
German
Dict Am Bio supp v5; Not Am Wom supp v1; Obit File

3223. Hier, Ethel Glenn
born 1889
pianist, composer, music educator
Index t Wom

3224. Marcial-Dorado, Caroline
1889–1941
educator
Spanish
Index t Wom

3225. McHale, Kathryn
1889/90–1956
educator, psychologist, general director of the American Association of University Women
Dict Am Bio supp v6; Index t Wom; Nat Cyc Am Bio v46; Obit File

3226. Morgan, Lucy Calista
born 1889
educator
Index t Wom

3227. Smith, Hannah
died 1939
composer, music educator, author
Index t Wom

3228. Virgil, Antha Minerva
died 1939
composer, pianist, educator
Index t Wom

3229. Andrews, Emily Russell
1890–1973
physical education authority
Congregationalist
Nat Cyc Am Bio v57

3230. Bell, Ruth Moench
flourished 1920s
educator
Index t Wom

3231. Bertola, Mariana
flourished 1920s
physician, child welfare worker, educator
Index t Wom

3232. Boehringer, Cora Louise
flourished 1920s
educator, journalist
Index t Wom

3233. Chandor, Valentine
flourished 1920s–30s
educator
Index t Wom

3234. Corbett, Margaret Darst
born 1890
visual-correction instructor
Nat Cyc Am Bio csv7

3235. Dawley, Almira
1890–1956
sociologist, educator
Dict Nat Bio supp v6

3236. Densford, Katharine Jane
born 1890
nurse, educator
Index t Wom

3237. Eads, Laura Krieger
flourished 1920s–30s
educator, psychologist
Index t Wom

3238. Flanagan, Hallie Mae Ferguson (Davis); Hallie Davis
189?–1969
theater educator, theater administrator and director, playwright
Not Am Wom supp v1, Obit File

3239. Griffin, Clementina de Forest
born 1890
high school educator, aviator
Los Angeles, CA
Nat Cyc Am Bio csv9

3240. Hawkes, Anna Lorette Rose
born 1890
educator
Index t Wom

3241. Hawkinson, Nellie X.
flourished 1920s–30s
nurse, educator
Index t Wom

3242. Logan, Laura R.
flourished 1920s–30s
nurse, educator
Index t Wom

3243. McGauley, Minna Hoppe
flourished 1920s
author, dramatic coach
Index t Wom

3244. Murray, Charlotte Wallace
married 1915
singer, music educator
Black
Index t Wom

3245. Muse, Maude B.
flourished 1920s–30s
nurse, educator
Index t Wom

3246. Plumb, Alma E.
flourished 1920s
educator
Index t Wom

3247. Stuart, Cora Wilson
flourished 1920s
educator, social reformer
Index t Wom

3248. Taylor, Effie J.
flourished 1920s–30s
nurse, educator
Canadian
Index t Wom

3249. Woodhouse, Margaret Chase Going
born 1890
representative to Congress, economist, educator, author
Index t Wom

3250. Armstrong, Barbara
1891–1976
lawyer, law professor
Obit File

3251. Bearden, Bessye J.
1891–1943
educator, first female member of the New York City school board, clubwoman
New York, NY
Black
Encyc Black Am; Index t Wom

3252. Coolidge, Mary Lowell
1891–1958
philosopher, educator, dean of Wellesley College
Massachusetts
Obit File; Who Who Phil

3253. Dye, Marie
born 1891
educator, nutrition researcher
Index t Wom

3254. Grooms, Jessie Macy Roberts
1891–1955
artist, art educator
Ohio
Nat Cyc Am Bio v46

3255. Harkness, Georgia Elma
1891–1974
philosopher, theologian, religious educator, author
Dict Am Rel Bio; Index t Wom; Not Am Wom supp v1; Who Who Phil

3256. Johnson, Edith Christina
1891–1954
educator
Massachusetts
Nat Cyc Am Bio v41

3257. Newcomer, Mabel
born 1891
economist, educator
Index t Wom

3258. Quimby, Edith Hinckley
born 1891
biophysicist, educator
Index t Wom

3259. Carroll, Consolata; Sister Mary Consolata
born 1892
author, educator, Catholic nun
Catholic
Index t Wom

3260. Combs, Helen
1892–1944
physician, physiologist, medical educator
Obit File

3261. Coyle, Grace Longwell
1892–1962
social work educator
Not Am Wom supp v1

3262. Davis, Fay Simmons
died 1942
pianist, composer, music educator
Index t Wom

3263. Hamilton, Gordon
1892–1967
social worker, educator
Not Am Wom supp v1

3264. Haupt, Alma Cecelia
1892–1956
authority of public health nursing, administrative educator
Dict Am Bio supp v6

3265. Kaucher, Dorothy Wanita
1892–1972
educator, author, writer on aviation
California
Nat Cyc Am Bio v57

3266. Link, Adeline Desale
1892–1943
chemist, university educator
Obit File

3267. McCollin, Frances
1892–1960
composer, educator, lecturer, Socialist party worker
Episcopalian
Pennsylvania
blind
Index t Wom; Nat Cyc Am Bio v45

3268. Boothe, Viva Belle
1893–1964
business researcher, economist, educator
Methodist
Ohio
Nat Cyc Am Bio v51

3269. Godfrey, Grace
1893–1944
home economics educator
Philadelphia, PA
Obit File

3270. Hagan, Helen Eugenia
1893–1964
pianist, music educator
Black
Encyc Black Am; Index t Wom; Prof Negro Wom v2

3271. Lusk, Georgia Lee Witt
1893–1971
educator, Democratic representative to Congress from New Mexico
New Mexico
Cur Biog '71; Index t Wom; Not Am Wom supp v1

3272. Manner, Jane; Jennie Mannheimer
died 1943
dramatic coach
Index t Wom

3273. Peabody, May E.
died 1943
authority on child training
Obit File

3274. Sutley, Margaret Hutchinson
1893–1947
physician, surgeon, medical educator in Japan, venereal disease clinic founder
Nat Cyc Am Bio v35

3275. Wanstrum, Ruth Cecilia
1893–1971
pathologist, medical educator
Episcopalian
Michigan
Nat Cyc Am Bio v57

3276. Ainsworth, Dorothy Sears
born 1894
physical education authority
Congregationalist
Nat Cyc Am Bio csv12

3277. Gadd, May
born 1894
folk dance teacher, organizer
Index t Wom

3278. Groves, Gladys Hoagland
1894–1980
educator, marriage and sex counselor, writer on marriage and sex
Cur Biog '80; Index t Wom

3279. Hoisington, May Folwell
born 1894
poet, educator
Index t Wom

3280. Lloyd, Alice C.
1894–1950
dean of women of the University of Michigan, president of the National Association of Deans of Women
Michigan
Obit File

3281. Nicholson, Marjorie Hope
1894–1981
university educator, writer on literature
Cur Biog '81; Index t Wom; Nat Cyc Am Bio csv7

3282. Schulze, Margaret
1894–1943
gynecologist, surgeon, pathologist, medical educator, medical author
California
Nat Cyc Am Bio v34

3283. Stern, Catherine Brieger "Kathe"
1894–1973
educator, child education specialist, writer on child education

Lutheran
German
Nat Cyc Am Bio v57; Not Am
Wom supp v1

3284. Stewart, Isabella Hilda
born 1894
educator
Massachusetts
Canadian
Nat Cyc Am Bio csv8

3285. Taggard, Genevieve
1894–1948
poet, educator, biographer of Emily Dickinson, literature professor
Dict Am Bio supp v4; Index t Wom; Not Am Wom; Obit File

3286. Todd, Lois Pendleton
1894–1968
physician, medical educator in China
Congregationalist
California
Nat Cyc Am Bio v54

3287. Zachary, Caroline Beaumont
1894–1945
educational psychologist
Not Am Wom

3288. Amidon, Beulah
1895–1958
labor and education authority
Obit File

3289. Blanshard, Frances Bradshaw
1895–1966
educator
Quaker
Connecticut
Nat Cyc Am Bio v54

3290. Borchardt, Selma Munter
1895/1900–1968
educator, lawyer, labor leader, lobbyist
Washington, DC
Bio Dict Am Lab; Not Am Wom supp v1

3291. Bragdon, Helen Dalton
born 1895
educator
Index t Wom

3292. Copp, Evelyn Fletcher
died 1945
music educator
Index t Wom

3293. Emerson, Sybil
born 1895
illustrator, painter, educator
Index t Wom

3294. Langer, Susanne Katherina Knauth
born 1895
philosopher, author, educator
Index t Wom; Who Who Phil

3295. Lewisohn, Margaret Seligman
1895–1954
educator, art patron, clubwoman
New York
Index t Wom; Nat Cyc Am Bio v44

3296. Strang, Ruth [May]
1895–1971
educator, writer on education, education teacher
Cur Biog '71; Index t Wom; Not Am Wom supp v1

3297. Cori, Gerty Theresa Radnitz
1896–1957
biochemist, physician, medical educator, Nobel Prize winner
Czechoslovak
Dict Am Bio supp v6; Index t Wom; Nat Cyc Am Bio v48 and csv8; Not Am Wom supp v1; Obit File

3298. Dodge, Eva Francette
born 1896
obstetrician, medical educator, birth control and Planned Parenthood worker, public health worker
Baptist
Nat Cyc Am Bio csv12

3299. Fay, Marion (Spencer)
born 1896
educator, physiological chemist
Episcopalian
Pennsylvania
Nat Cyc Am Bio csv12

3300. Frantz, Virginia Kneeland
1896–1967
surgical pathologist, medical educator, cancer researcher, dairy farmer
Episcopalian
New York
Nat Cyc Am Bio v53; Not Am Wom supp v1

3301. Jarrell, Helen Ira
1896–1973
school superintendent, union leader
Not Am Wom supp v1

3302. Powdermaker, Hortense
1896/1900–1970
anthropologist, ethnologist, educator, author
California
Cur Biog '70; Index t Wom; Nat Cyc Am Bio v55 and csv10; Not Am Wom supp v1

3303. Riley, Susan B.
born 1896
educator, organization official
Index t Wom

3304. Rowe, Lucretia Olin
born 1896
missionary to Africa, educator
Index t Wom

3305. Towle, Charlotte Helen
1896–1966
social work educator
Not Am Wom supp v1

3306. White, Helen Constance
1896–1967
educator, historial novelist, religious historian, UNESCO member
Catholic
Index t Wom; Nat Cyc Am Bio v53; Not Am Wom supp v1

3307. Bixby, Allene K.
died 1947
organist, composer, music educator
Index t Wom

3308. Derricotte, Juliette
1897–1931
educator, dean of women at Fiske University
Black
Encyc Black Am; Prof Negro Wom v1

3309. Jessye, Eva Alberta
1897–post 1930s
music director, educator, writer on music, conductor
Black
Encyc Black Am; Index t Wom

3310. Pryor, Helen Brenton
1897–1972
pediatrician, medical educator
Methodist
California
Nat Cyc Am Bio v57

3311. Robinson, Ophelia
born 1897
educator, poet
Index t Wom

3312. Smith, Lilian Eugenia
1897–1966
novelist, newspaper columnist, writer on race relations, civil rights worker, editor, social worker, educator, lecturer
Florida
Encyc South Hist; Index t Wom; Not Am Wom supp v1; Obit File; Wom Lit; Wom Lit, More

3313. Thomas, Anna Perry
born 1897
educator

Black
Encyc Black Am

3314. Wolfson, Theresa
1897–1972
labor economist, educator
Not Am Wom supp v1

3315. Blanding, Sarah Gibson
born 1898
educator, president of Vassar College
Index t Wom; Nat Cyc Am Bio csv7

3316. Gambrell, Mary Latimer
1898–1974
educator, president of Hunter College
Presbyterian
New York
Nat Cyc Am Bio v59; Obit File

3317. Glueck, Eleanor (Touroff)
1898–1972
research criminologist, Harvard Law School criminologist, pioneer in the study of juvenile delinquency, social worker
New York; Massachusetts
Cur Biog '72; Index t Wom; Nat Cyc Am Bio v57; Not Am Wom supp v1; Obit File

3318. Kelly, Regina Zimmerman
born 1898
author, educator
Index t Wom

3319. McIntosh, Millicent [Margaret]
born 1898
educator, dean
Index t Wom

3320. Mudd, Emily Hatshore
born 1898
educator, author, marriage counselor
Index t Wom

3321. Pickel, Mary Barnard
1898–1955
educator, dean of women at Columbia University
New York
Obit File

3322. Roseborough, Melanie Rohrer; Mrs. Adolph J. Radosta
born 1898
German language educator
Lutheran
Florida
Nat Cyc Am Bio csv13

3323. Schlaugh, Margaret
born 1898
educator, author, philologist
Index t Wom

3324. Warburton, Amber Arthun
1898–1976
economist, educational guidance consultant
Unitarian
Nat Cyc Am Bio v59

3325. Wolle, Muriel Sibell
1898–1977
artist, art educator, Native American art scholar and collector, western history writer, conservationist
Episcopalian
Boulder, CO
Nat Cyc Am Bio v60

3326. Barrett, S. Ruth
1899–1961
educator of the blind
Obit File

3327. Cosgrave, Jessica Garretson Finch
died 1949
educator
Index t Wom

3328. Schenck, Rachel Katherine
born 1899
librarian, educator
Index t Wom

3329. Strauss, Anna Lord
1899–1979
editor, club leader, feminist, political activist, New York civic worker, internationalist
Quaker
New York
Cur Biog '79; Index t Wom; Nat Cyc Am Bio csv10

3330. Wanamaker, Pearl Aderson
born 1899
educator
Index t Wom

3331. White, Olive Bernadine
born 1899
author, educator
Index t Wom

3332. Achilles, Edith Mulhall
flourished 1930s
educator
Index t Wom

3333. Ames, Elinor
flourished 1930s
lecturer, educator, editor
Index t Wom

3334. Askwith, Margaret Long
flourished 1930s
educator, businessperson
Index t Wom

3335. Bailey, Edna Watson
flourished 1930s
educator
Index t Wom

3336. Baker, Helen
1900–55
industrial relations expert, university educator
Obit File

3337. Bildersee, Adele
flourished 1930s
educator
Index t Wom

3338. Braddock, Amelia
flourished 1930s
singer, music educator
English
Index t Wom

3339. Bradley, Ora Lewis
flourished 1930s
educator, artist, author
Index t Wom

3340. Brown, Winnifred
flourished 1930s
educator
Index t Wom

3341. Burke, Marion E.
flourished 1930s
aviator, flying school owner
Index t Wom

3342. Butterfield, Frances W.
flourished 1930s
educator
Index t Wom

3343. Cahill, Mary F.
flourished 1930s
educator
Index t Wom

3344. Carden, Mae
flourished 1930s
educator
Index t Wom

3345. Carey, Helen A.
flourished 1930s
educator, author
Index t Wom

3346. Carey, Ocean Daily
flourished 1930s
educator
Index t Wom

3347. Carpara, Clara H.
flourished 1930s
music educator
Index t Wom

3348. Cassiday, Mary
flourished 1930s
educator
Index t Wom

3349. Cavis, Helen
flourished 1930s
aviator, aviation instructor
Index t Wom

3350. Chase, Helen Frances
flourished 1930s
musician, music educator
Index t Wom

3351. Cleaver, Ethelyn Hardesty
flourished 1930s
educator, clubwoman
Index t Wom

3352. Coffey, Phyllis C.
flourished 1930s
educator, humanitarian
Index t Wom

3353. Collver, Nathalie S.
flourished 1930s
educator
Index t Wom

3354. Crawford, Gretchen C.
flourished 1930s
educator
Index t Wom

3355. Crowell, Annie L.
flourished 1930s
pianist, music educator
Index t Wom

3356. Crowley, Teresa M.
flourished 1930s
educator
Index t Wom

3357. de Pina, May Frances
flourished 1930s
modeling-school director
Venezualan
Index t Wom

3358. Delafield, Ann
flourished 1930s
cosmetician, dietician, educator
Index t Wom

3359. Dickerman, Marion
flourished 1930s
educator
Index t Wom

3360. Diehl, Mary
flourished 1930s
educator, business executive, personnel director
Index t Wom

3361. Dithridge, Rachel L.
flourished 1930s
poet, educator
Index t Wom

3362. Downing, Eleanor
flourished 1930s
author, educator
Index t Wom

3363. Dyhrenfurth, Hettie
flourished 1930s
educator, author
Index t Wom

3364. Erickson, Barbara Jane
flourished 1930s
aviator, flying instructor
Index t Wom

3365. Estelle, Helen G. H.
flourished 1930s
educator, social reformer
Index t Wom

3366. Farr, Virginia
flourished 1930s
aviation instructor
Index t Wom

3367. Fetter, Ellen Cole
flourished 1930s
educator
Index t Wom

3368. Flagg, Marion
flourished 1930s
music educator
Index t Wom

3369. Forbes, Grace Springer
flourished 1930s
educator, zoologist
Index t Wom

3370. Fries, Constance
flourished 1930s
physician, educator
Index t Wom

3371. Galajikian, Florence Grandland
born 1900
composer, pianist, music educator
Index t Wom

3372. Gates, Edith Mildred
flourished 1930s
educator
Index t Wom

3373. Getchell, Donnie Campbell
flourished 1930s
educator
Index t Wom

3374. Gilmore, Gladys Chase
flourished 1930s
educator, businessperson
Index t Wom

3375. Gipson, Elsie
flourished 1930s
aviation instructor
Index t Wom

3376. Gross, Miriam Zeller
flourished 1930s
educator, public relations worker
Index t Wom

3377. Hager, Carol
flourished 1930s
aviation instructor
Index t Wom

3378. Hallady, Bessie G.
flourished 1930s
aviation instructor
Index t Wom

3379. Harmon, Ruth J.
flourished 1930s
aviation instructor
Index t Wom

3380. Harvitt, Helene
flourished 1930s
editor, educator
Index t Wom

3381. Hayes, Evelyn Carroll
flourished 1930s
educator
Index t Wom

3382. Hensel, Ruth
flourished 1930s
educator
Index t Wom

3383. Horton, Mildred Helen McAfee
born 1900
president of Wellesley College, director of the WAVES
Presbyterian
Index t Wom

3384. Hubbard, Charlotte Moton
flourished 1930s–70s
US deputy assistant secretary of state for public affairs, educator
Black
Encyc Black Am; Negro Alman; Negro Her Lib v1

3385. Hulse, Anne Elizabeth
flourished 1930s
educator, economist
Index t Wom

3386. Irvine, Theodore Ursula
flourished 1930s; died 1952
educator, dramatic coach
Canadian
Index t Wom; Obit File

3387. Johnston, Agnes M.
flourished 1930s
educator
Index t Wom

3388. Kilgore, Evelyn
flourished 1930s
aviator, head of a training school for aviators
Index t Wom

3389. Lape, Esther Everett
flourished 1930s

educator, editor
Index t Wom

3390. Lelash, Ethelyn L.
flourished 1930s
business school executive
Index t Wom

3391. Lennox, Peggy
flourished 1930s–40s
aviator, flying instructor
Index t Wom

3392. Lipman, Miriam Hillman
flourished 1930s
educator
Index t Wom

3393. Loeber, L. Elsa
flourished 1930s
educator, librarian
Index t Wom

3394. Lynn, Meda C.
flourished 1930s
educator, humanitarian
Index t Wom

3395. MacVay, Anna Pearl
flourished 1930s
educator
Index t Wom

3396. Marsh, Lucille
flourished 1930s
educator, dancer
Index t Wom

3397. McElroy, Lenore
flourished 1930s
aviator instructor
Index t Wom

3398. McLean, Margaret
flourished 1930s
dramatic coach, speech teacher
Index t Wom

3399. Monasterio, Lillian
flourished 1930s
aviation instructor
Index t Wom

3400. Moor, Anne
flourished 1930s
physiologist, dramatic teacher
Index t Wom

3401. Morgan, Charlotte E.
flourished 1930s
educator, author
Index t Wom

3402. Newby, Ruby Warren
flourished 1930s
artist, educator
Index t Wom

3403. Nichols, Edith Elizabeth
flourished 1930s
singer, voice teacher
Index t Wom

3404. Nickerson, Camille L.
flourished 1930s
pianist, music educator
Black
Index t Wom

3405. Odencrantz, Louise Christine
flourished 1930s
vocational guidance director
Index t Wom

3406. Ovens, Florence Jane
flourished 1930s
child specialist, editor
English
Index t Wom

3407. Paxton, Ethel
flourished 1930s
artist, educator, lecturer, author
Index t Wom

3408. Paxton, Jean Gregory
flourished 1930s
editor, author
Index t Wom

3409. Payne-Gaposchkin, Ceilia Helena
born 1900
astronomer, educator, author
English
Index t Wom

3410. Plant, Jane
flourished 1930s
aviation instructor
Index t Wom

3411. Platt, Estelle Gertrude
flourished 1930s
singer, educator, musical director
Index t Wom

3412. Reutiman, Gladys Harriet
flourished 1930s
educator
Index t Wom

3413. Robbins, Sarah Franklin
flourished 1930s
psychologist, adult education pioneer
Index t Wom

3414. Rusk, Evelyn Carroll
1900–64
mathematician, educator
Catholic
New York
Nat Cyc Am Bio v51

3415. Ryan, Mary P. van Buren
flourished 1930s
singer, music educator, accountant
Index t Wom

3416. Samuels, Margaret
flourished 1930s
educator, librarian, author
Index t Wom

3417. Scharr, Adela Rick
flourished 1930s
aviation instructor
Index t Wom

3418. Scott, Helen Jo
flourished 1930s
educator
Index t Wom

3419. Seitz, Helen
flourished 1930s
educator, journalist
Index t Wom

3420. Silberta, Rhea
born 1900
composer, singer, educator
Index t Wom

3421. Spirito, Yolanda
flourished 1930s–40s
aviation instructor
Index t Wom

3422. Stark, Mary B.
flourished 1930s
physician, educator
Index t Wom

3423. Stillings, Kemp
flourished 1930s
violinist, educator
Index t Wom

3424. Stilson, Ruth
flourished 1930s
aviation instructor
Index t Wom

3425. Syrkin, Marie
born 1900
editor, educator, author
Swiss
Index t Wom

3426. Taylor, Pauline
flourished 1930s
educator
Index t Wom

3427. Tead, Ordway, Mrs.
flourished 1930s
educator
Index t Wom

3428. Thomas, Patricia
flourished 1930s
aviation instructor
Index t Wom

3429. Tisdale, Doris H.
flourished 1930s
home economist, educator
Index t Wom

3430. Ulmer, Edith Ann
flourished 1930s
educator, author
Index t Wom

3431. von Hesse, Elizabeth F.
flourished 1930s
educator, author, lecturer
Index t Wom

3432. Wandling, Arlita R.
flourished 1930s
child research worker
Index t Wom

3433. Welcome, Verda Freeman
flourished 1930s–60s
educator, Maryland state legislator
Maryland
Black
Encyc Black Am

**3434. Wells, Margaret
Elizabeth**
flourished 1930s
educator
Index t Wom

3435. Wilder, Jessie
flourished 1930s
poet, educator, critic, lecturer
English
Index t Wom

**3436. Winning, Freda J. Ger-
win**
flourished 1930s
educator, home economist
Index t Wom

3437. Wolter, Annett
flourished 1930s
dramatics educator
Index t Wom

3438. Wright, Jessie
1900–70
orthopedist, orthopedic inventor,
medical educator
English
Nat Cyc Am Bio v55

**3439. Brunauer, Esther Delia
Caukin**
1901–59
international affairs specialist,
UN official, textbook editor
Index t Wom; Not Am Wom
supp v1

**3440. Crawford-Seeger, Ruth
Porter**
1901–53
composer, folk music scholar,
music educator, pianist
Index t Wom; Not Am Wom
supp v1

3441. de Lany, Dorothy Celia
1901–60
home economics educator

Ithaca, NY
Nat Cyc Am Bio v47

3442. Delany, Clarissa Scott
1901–27
poet, educator
Black
Encyc Black Am

3443. Osborne, Estelle Massey
1901–post 1976
nurse, nursing educator, army
nurse in World War II
Black
Negro Alman; Prof Negro Wom
v2

3444. Reid, Helen Dwight
1901–65
international political scientist,
educator, pacifist
Christian Scientist
Washington, DC
Scottish
Nat Cyc Am Bio v51

3445. Studebaker, Mabel
born 1901
educator, organization official
Index t Wom

3446. Williams, Bertye Young
died 1951
poet, editor of *Taleria*
Index t Wom; Obit File

3447. Block, Virginia Lee
1902–70
psychologist, educator
California
Nat Cyc Am Bio v56

3448. Brico, Antonia
born 1902
conductor, pianist, music educator
Index t Wom

**3449. Forman, Julie (Rose)
Ripley**
1902–75
educator
Christian Scientist
Connecticut
Nat Cyc Am Bio v59

3450. Goodnow, Minnie
died 1952
nurse, author, educator
Index t Wom

3451. Gray, Elizabeth Janet
born 1902
author, librarian, educator
Index t Wom

3452. Hardy, Kay
born 1902
artist, lecturer, educator
Index t Wom

3453. Ilg, Frances Lillian
1902–81
pediatrician, medical educator
and author
Cur Biog '81; Index t Wom

3454. Lamont, Florence Corliss
died 1952
patron of education
Obit File

3455. MacLean, Bernice
1902–46
zoologist, educator
Obit File

**3456. Omlie, Phoebe Jane
Fairgrave**
1902–75
aviator, aviation instructor
Index t Wom; Not Am Wom
supp v1

**3457. Overstrett, Bonaro Wil-
kinson**
born 1902
educator, lecturer, author
Congregationalist
California
Index t Wom; Nat Cyc Am Bio
csv11

3458. Rees, Mina S.
born 1902
mathematician, educator, government official
Index t Wom

**3459. Shelley, Mary
J[osephine]**
1902–76
aviator, air force colonel, head of
the navy education program for
women during World War II,
commander of women in the air
force during the Korean War
Cur Biog '76; Index t Wom; Obit
File

3460. Shull, Martha Arvesta
born 1902
organization official, educator
Index t Wom

3461. Taba, Hilda
1902–67
educator, UNESCO consultant
Estonian
Nat Cyc Am Bio v54; Not Am
Wom supp v1

3462. Bicking, Ada Elizabeth
died 1953
music educator
Index t Wom

3463. Dodds, Bernice Lee
1903–59
dean of the University of Illinois
College of Education, head of
the education department of
Purdue University

Illinois
Obit File

3464. Petry, Lucile
born 1903
nurse, educator
Index t Wom

3465. Ross, Margaret Wheeler
died 1953
pianist, music teacher, club leader
Index t Wom

**3466. Thackrey, Dorothy
(Schiff)**
born 1903
journalist, publisher
Index t Wom

3467. Tuve, Rosemond
1903–64
literary scholar, educator
Not Am Wom supp v1

3468. Alter, Martha
born 1904
composer, pianist, music educator
Index t Wom

3469. Arnstein, Margaret Gene
1904–72
public health nurse, nursing educator
Not Am Wom supp v1

3470. Caldwell, Sarah Campbell
born 1904
educator
Index t Wom

**3471. Emch, Minna Elizabeth
Libman**
1904–58
psychiatrist, psychiatric educator
and author
Chicago, IL
Lithuanian
Nat Cyc Am Bio v47

3472. Goldsmith, Grace Arabell
1904–75
physician, public health educator,
nutritionist
Episcopalian
Louisiana
Nat Cyc Am Bio csv10; Not Am
Wom supp v10

**3473. Hennock, Frieda Barkin
(Simmons)**
1904–60
criminal lawyer, FCC member,
advocate of educational televi-
sion
Jewish
New York
Polish
Index t Wom; Nat Cyc Am Bio
csv8; Not Am Wom supp v1;
Obit File

3474. McBride, Katharine Elizabeth
1904–76
psychologist, university educator, president of Bryn Mawr College
Bryn Mawr, PA
Cur Biog '76; Index t Wom; Obit File

3475. Morton, Florrinell Frances
born 1904
librarian, educator
Index t Wom

3476. Anderson, Gertrude Maynard
1905–53
actor, theatrical trainer
Obit File

3477. Bartlett, Phyllis (Brooks); Mrs. John A. Pollard
1905–73
educator, scholar of English literature
Episcopalian
New York
Nat Cyc Am Bio v58

3478. Black, Marian Watkins
1905–75
educator
Methodist
Florida
Twent Cen Bio Dict Not Am

3479. Braucher, Pela Fay
1905–66
nutritionist, educator
Evangelical Lutheran
Nat Cyc Am Bio v52

3480. Dodd, Bella V.
1905–69
lawyer, educator, Communist party worker
Obit File

3481. Jones, Lois Mailore
born 1905
painter, art educator
Black
Index t Wom; Negro Alman

3482. Ambrose, Alice
born 1906
philosopher, educator
Who Who Phil

3483. Black, Irma Simonton
1906–72
preschool director, children's author
New York
Nat Cyc Am Bio v58

3484. Carter, Gwendolyn Margaret
born 1906
political scientist, writer on political science, educator

Black
Encyc Black Am

3485. Cunningham, Ruth Marion
1906–56
college educator, authority on child development
Nat Cyc Am Bio v46; Obit File

3486. Dunnigan, Alice Allison
born 1906
journalist, educator, economist
Index t Wom

3487. Gaver, Mary Virginia
born 1906
librarian, educator
Index t Wom

3488. Komarovsky, Mirra
born 1906
educator, sociologist
Russian
Index t Wom

3489. Mayer, Marie Gertrude Goeppert
1906–72
theoretical physicist, Nobel Prize winner in physics, educator, author
German; Polish
Cur Biog '72; Index t Wom; Nat Cyc Am Bio v58; Not Am Wom supp v1; Obit File

3490. Newstead, Helaine
born 1906
educator
Index t Wom

3491. Blake, Florence G.
born 1907
nurse, nursing educator
Index t Wom

3492. Farrell, Muriel; Mrs. Thomas Ward
1907–74
preschool education specialist
Nat Cyc Am Bio v58

3493. Hamilton, Grace Towns
born 1907
educator, Georgia state legislator from Atlanta
Atlanta, GA
Black
Encyc Black Am

3494. Hofmann, Melita Cecelia
1907–76
artist, art educator, book illustrator and designer, author, conservationist
Congregationalist
New York
Nat Cyc Am Bio v60

3495. Hottel, Althea Hallowell Kratz
born 1907
educator
Index t Wom

3496. Lorenz, Ellen Jane
born 1907
composer, editor, educator
Index t Wom

3497. Park, Rosemary
born 1907
educator, president of Barnard College
Congregationalist
Connecticut
Index t Wom; Nat Cyc Am Bio csv10

3498. Rosenstein, Sophie
1907–52
drama coach
Hollywood, CA
Obit File

3499. Sartain, Harriet
died 1957
artist, dean of Moore Institute of Art, Science and Industry, educator
Philadelphia, PA
Index t Wom; Obit File

3500. Wachtel, Erna
born 1907
gymnastics coach
Hall Fame Sport

3501. Anastasi, Anne
born 1908
philosopher, educator
Who Who Phil

3502. Baldwin, Janet Sterling; Mrs. Herbert C. Maier
1908–58
pediatrician, medical educator
Episcopalian
New York
Nat Cyc Am Bio v59

3503. Horwich, Frances Rappaport
born 1908
educator, television personality
Index t Wom

3504. Mallory, Arenia Cornelia
born 1908
educator
Black
Encyc Black Am

3505. Crary, Catherine Snell
1909–74
historian, educator
Presbyterian
New York
Nat Cyc Am Bio v58

3506. Dickens, Helen Octavia
born 1909
obstetrician/gynecologist, medical educator
Black
Encyc Black Am; Prof Negro Wom v2

3507. Horne, Esther Burnett
born 1909
educator
Native American (Shoshone)
Ind Today

3508. Konheim, Beatrice Goldstein
1909–73
science educator, member of the ACLU
Jewish
New York
Nat Cyc Am Bio v58

3509. Player, Willa Beatrice
born 1909
educator
Black
Encyc Black Am; Index t Wom

3510. Resnick, Rose
graduated 1934
educator of the blind, humanitarian
Index t Wom

3511. Schmitt, Gladys Leonore; Gladys Goldfield
1909–72
author, historical novelist, poet, editor, university educator
Cur Biog '72; Index t Wom; Obit File

3512. Beeuwkes, Adelia Marie
1910–66
nutritionist, educator
Episcopalian
Michigan
Nat Cyc Am Bio v52

3513. Blake, Dorothy Gaynor
flourished 1940s
composer, music educator
Index t Wom

3514. Brown, Esther Lucille
flourished 1940s
nurse, nursing educator
Index t Wom

3515. Bunting, Mary Ingraham
born 1910
microbiologist, bacteriologist, educator, president of Radcliffe College
Massachusetts
Index t Wom; Nat Cyc Am Bio csv10

3516. Carrick, Jean Warren
flourished 1940s

pianist, music editor, author
Index t Wom

3517. Clapp, Margaret (Antoinette)
1910–74
president of Wellesley College, historian, biographer, US cultural attaché to India
Nat Cyc Am Bio; Index t Wom

3518. Coit, Lottie Ellsworth
flourished 1940s
music educator, violinist
Index t Wom

3519. Copeland, Bernice Rose
flourished 1940s
composer, music educator
Index t Wom

3520. Crosby, Marie
flourished 1940s
composer, music educator
Index t Wom

3521. Dargans, Louise M.
flourished 1940s–70s
chief clerk, US House Committee on Education and Labor, 1946
Black
Negro Alman; Negro Her Lib v1

3522. Dodge, Mary Hewes
flourished 1940s
violinist, pianist, music educator, composer
Index t Wom

3523. Erb, Mae-Aileen Gerhart
flourished 1940s
composer, music educator
Index t Wom

3524. Foster, Bertha M.
flourished 1940s
organist, music educator, choirmaster
Index t Wom

3525. Franklin, Eleonor I.
flourished 1940s–70s
endocrinologist, educator
Black
Encyc Black Am

3526. Glenn, Mabelle
flourished 1940s
music educator, author
Index t Wom

3527. Gober, Belle Biard
flourished 1940s
composer, pianist, music educator
Index t Wom

3528. Goff, Anna Chandler
flourished 1940s
music educator
Index t Wom

3529. Hamilton, Anna Havermann
flourished 1940s
piano educator
Index t Wom

3530. Hammond, Fanny Reed
flourished 1940s
composer, pianist, music educator
Index t Wom

3531. Hathaway, Ann
flourished 1940s
violinist, author, educator
Index t Wom

3532. Holst, Marie Seuel
flourished 1940s
composer, pianist, music educator
Index t Wom

3533. Howe, Helen
flourished 1940s
music educator
Index t Wom

3534. Hudson, Octavia
flourished 1940s
composer, pianist, music educator, author
Index t Wom

3535. Huss, Hildegarde Hoffman
flourished 1940s
singer, lecturer, music educator
Index t Wom

3536. Inskeep, Alice Carey
flourished 1940s
music educator and director
Index t Wom

3537. Kinscella, Hazel Gertrude
flourished 1940s
musician, composer, music educator
Index t Wom

3538. Knouss, Isabelle G.
flourished 1940s
composer, pianist, music educator
Index t Wom

3539. Laich, Katherine; Wilhelmina Schlegel
born 1910
librarian, president of the American Library Association, library science educator
California
Cur Biog '72

3540. Lang, Edith
flourished 1940s
organist, music educator
Index t Wom

3541. Leonard, Florence
flourished 1940s

musician, pianist, music educator, author
Index t Wom

3542. Lewyn, Helena
flourished 1940s
pianist, music educator
Index t Wom

3543. Liszniewska, Marguerite Melville
flourished 1940s
pianist, music educator, composer
Index t Wom

3544. Lockwood, Charlotte
flourished 1940s
organist, educator
Index t Wom

3545. McGuire, Rosalie J.
born 1910
educator
Black
Negro Alman

3546. Moore, Luella Lockwood
flourished 1940s
composer, pianist, music educator
Index t Wom

3547. Murray, Paule
born 1910
educator, author, lawyer, civil rights activist
Black
Encyc Black Am

3548. Owen, Julia D.
flourished 1940s
composer, singer, music educator
Index t Wom

3549. Paldi, Mari
flourished 1940s
composer, music educator
Index t Wom

3550. Pannell, Anne Thomas Gary
born 1910
educator, president of Sweet Briar College
Protestant Episcopal
Virginia
Index t Wom; Nat Cyc Am Bio csv10

3551. Patterson, Elizabeth Kelso
flourished 1940s
singer, music educator
Index t Wom

3552. Pease, Jessie L.
flourished 1940s
composer, pianist, music educator
Index t Wom

3553. Perfield, Effa Ellis
flourished 1940s

educator, author, organist
Index t Wom

3554. Peterson, Edna Gunnar
flourished 1940s
pianist, music educator
Index t Wom

3555. Phippen, Laud German
flourished 1940s
composer, pianist, music educator
Index t Wom

3556. Pray, Ada Jordan
flourished 1940s
composer, pianist, educator, lecturer
Index t Wom

3557. Ralston, F. Marion
flourished 1940s
composer, pianist, music educator
Index t Wom

3558. Rebe, Louise Christine
flourished 1940s
composer, pianist, educator
Index t Wom

3559. Ritter, Irene Marschand
flourished 1940s
composer, organist, pianist, educator
Index t Wom

3560. Sammis-MacDermid, Sybil
flourished 1940s
singer, educator
Index t Wom

3561. Schmitt, Susan
flourished 1940s
composer, pianist, educator
Index t Wom

3562. Showalter, Edna Blanche
flourished 1940s
singer, music educator, pianist, manager
Index t Wom

3563. Sibley, Harper, Mrs.
flourished 1940s
religious worker, educator
Index t Wom

3564. Simpson, Elizabeth
flourished 1940s
composer, pianist, music educator, lecturer, author
Index t Wom

3565. Souther, Marguerite
flourished 1940s
basketball coach, dance teacher
Index t Wom

3566. Stairs, Louise E.
flourished 1940s

composer, pianist, organist, music
educator
Index t Wom

3567. Stewart, Sylvia
flourished 1940s
aircraft engine instructor
Index t Wom

3568. Stout, Ruth Albertine
born 1910
educator, organization official
Index t Wom

3569. Strong, May A.
flourished 1940s
composer, singer, educator
Index t Wom

3570. Sutor, Adele
flourished 1940s
composer, piano educator
Index t Wom

3571. Tracey, Cateau Stegeman
flourished 1940s
pianist, music educator, author,
critic, lecturer
Index t Wom

3572. Vandevere, J. Lilian
flourished 1940s
composer, music educator
Index t Wom

3573. Watson, Mabel Madison
flourished 1940s
composer, pianist, violin teacher
Index t Wom

3574. Weston, Mildred
flourished 1940s
composer, music educator
Index t Wom

3575. Wilson, Frances M.
1910–59
director of child guidance for the
New York City board of education
New York
Obit File

3576. Wood, Louise Aletha
born 1910
educator
Index t Wom

3577. Wright, N. Louise
flourished 1940s
composer, pianist, music educator
Index t Wom

3578. Edmonds, Helen Grey
born 1911
historian, educator
Black
Encyc Black Am

**3579. Ingalls, Mildred Dodge
Jeramy**
born 1911

poet, educator
Index t Wom

**3580. Strasberg, Paula; Paula
Miller**
1911–66
actor, drama coach
Obit File

**3581. Walker, Waurine
Elizabeth**
born 1911
educator, organization official
Index t Wom

3582. Wolfenstein, Martha
1911–76
psychiatrist, child psychology
specialist, educator
Jewish
Obit File

3583. Brooks, Gwendolyn
born 1912/17
poet, educator, autobiographer,
lecturer, poet laureate of Illinois
Chicago, IL
Black
Cur Biog '77; Dict Lit Bio v5;
Encyc Black Am; Index t Wom;
Negro Alman; Nort Anth Poet;
Prof Negro Wom; Wom Lit;
Wom Lit, More

**3584. Carnegie, Dorothy Reed-
er Price**
born 1912
educator, author
Index t Wom

3585. Fortune, Hilda O.
born circa 1912
educator
Black
Encyc Black Am

3586. Holbrook, Sabra Rollins
born 1912
educator, youth worker
Index t Wom

3587. Jones, Virginia Lacy
born 1912/14
librarian, educator
Black
Encyc Black Am; Index t Wom

3588. Kline, Clarice Lenore
born 1912
educator
Index t Wom

3589. Lucas, Martha Bob
born 1912
educator, president of Sweet Briar
College
Episcopalian
Virginia
Index t Wom; Nat Cyc Am Bio
csv7

3590. McCarthy, Mary Therese
born 1912
author, novelist, autobiographer,
short story writer, essayist, educator
Cur Biog '69; Dict Lit Bio v2;
Index t Wom; Wom Lit; Wom
Lit, More

3591. Moore, Lillian
1912–67
ballet dancer, educator, dance historian and critic
Obit File

3592. Robinson, Wilhelmina S.
born 1912
educator, historian
Black
Encyc Black Am

3593. Gerlette, Anne
1913–58
actor, director, producer, dramatics teacher
Canadian
Obit File

**3594. Rickard, Montana Hop-
kins**
born 1913
professor of humanities
Native American (Cherokee)
Ind Today

3595. Andrews, Marie Scherer
1914–73
orthopedic nurse, nursing educator
Catholic
Massachusetts
Nat Cyc Am Bio v57

**3596. Cartwright, Marguerite
Dorsey**
born 1914
educator, journalist
Black
Encyc Black Am

3597. Clark, Mary Gail
born 1914
composer, music educator
Index t Wom

**3598. Graves, Helen (Louise)
Pierson**
born 1914
physician, medical educator
Methodist
Ohio
Nat Cyc Am Bio csv13

3599. Schlotfeldt, Rozella May
born 1914
nurse, nursing educator, women's
rights worker, feminist
Nat Cyc Am Bio csv13

**3600. Alexander, Margaret
(Walker)**
born 1915

poet, novelist, college administra-
tor
Black
Encyc Black Am; Encyc South
Hist; Index t Wom; Negro Al-
man; Wom Lit; Wom Lit, More

3601. Brown, Letitia Woods
1915–76
historian, educator
Black
Encyc Black Am

**3602. Hurlburt, Margaret
"Marge"**
circa 1915–47
aviator, speed flyer, educator
Index t Wom; Obit File

3603. Morgan, Edith Galt
1915–68
psychiatric nursing educator
Presbyterian
Nat Cyc Am Bio v55

3604. Sokolow, Anna
born 1915
choreographer, director, dancer,
dance educator
Jewish
Cur Biog '69

**3605. Deming, Louise Mac-
Pherson**
1916–76
international educator, author,
civic worker in Okinawa, Japan
Episcopalian
Nat Cyc Am Bio v58

**3606. Peterson, Martha
Elizabeth**
born 1916
president of Barnard College
Cur Biog '69

3607. Putney, Martha Settle
born 1916
historian, educator
Black
Encyc Black Am

**3608. Wolfe, Deborah Cannon
Partridge**
born 1916
educator, government consultant
Index t Wom

3609. Goff, Regina
born 1917
educator; consultant to the Ministry of Education of Iran, 1955;
assistant commissioner of
HEW's Office of Education
Black
Negro Alman; Negro Her Lib v1

3610. Wright, Mary Clabaugh
1917–70
historian, scholar of Chinese history, university educator

Connecticut
Not Am Wom supp v1; Obit File

3611. Guzman, Jessie P.
born 1918
educator
Black
Negro Alman

3612. Hewell, Grace
born 1918
educator; social worker; HEW official; chief of education, House Committee on Education and Labor
Washington, DC
Black
Encyc Black Am; Negro Her Lib v1

3613. Loehrke, Leah Marie
1918–71
psychologist, psychological educator
Lutheran
Ohio
Nat Cyc Am Bio v57

3614. Lowrie, Jean E[lisabeth]
born 1918
librarian, president of the American Library Association, library educator
Cur Biog '73

3615. Rogers, Lettie Hamlett
1918–57
educator, author
Obit File

3616. Koontz, Elizabeth Duncan
born 1919
director of the US Department of Labor Women's Bureau, US delegate to the Commission on the Status of Women, labor organizer, educator
Black
Cur Biog '69; Encyc Black Am; Index t Wom; Negro Alman

3617. Watson, Virginia
1919–51
swimming instructor, swimmer
Hollywood, CA
Obit File

3618. Blanchard, Hazel Ann
born 1920
educator, organization official
Index t Wom

3619. Brown, Ina Corinne
flourished 1950s
educator, anthropologist
Index t Wom

3620. Cobbs, Susan Parker
flourished 1950s
educator
Index t Wom

3621. Crosson, Wilhelmina
flourished 1950s
educator, president of Palmer Memorial Institute
Black
Prof Negro Wom v2

3622. Cushman, Beulah
flourished 1950s
physician, educator
Index t Wom

3623. Drewry, Cecelia Hodges
flourished 1950s–60s
educator
New Jersey
Black
Prof Negro Wom v2

3624. Hastings, Alicia E.
flourished 1950s–60s
physician, medical educator
Black
Encyc Black Am

3625. Hixon, Jean
flourished 1950s
educator, aviator
Index t Wom

3626. Jordan, June
flourished 1950s–1980s
poet, essayist, political writer, civil rights worker, educator
Black
Wom Lit; Wom Lit, More

3627. Sawyer, Helen Alice
flourished 1950s
artist, educator
Index t Wom

3628. Smart, Alice McGee
flourished 1950s
sociologist, poet, educator
Index t Wom

3629. Southern, Eileen Jackson
born 1920
musicologist, educator
Black
Encyc Black Am

3630. Webster, Augusta
flourished 1950s
physician, educator
Index t Wom

3631. Kreps, Juanita M(orris)
born 1921
US secretary of commerce, university educator, economist
Cur Biog '77

3632. Saxl, Eva R.
born circa 1921
educator, traveler, lecturer, author
Czechoslovak
Index t Wom

3633. Spurlock, Jeanne
born 1921
psychiatrist, educator
Black
Encyc Black Am

3634. Gaines, Edyth J.
born 1922
educator
Black
Encyc Black Am

3635. Gunter, Laurie Martin
born 1922
nurse, nursing educator
Black
Encyc Black Am

3636. Smith, Constance Elizabeth
1922–70
college educator and administrator
Episcopalian
Massachusetts
Nat Cyc Am Bio

3637. Rapoport, Lydia
1923–71
social work educator
Not Am Wom supp v1

3638. Williams, Lorraine Anderson
born 1923
educator, author
Index t Wom

3639. Harris, Patricia Roberts
born 1924
lawyer, educator, ambassador to Luxembourg
Black
Encyc Black Am; Index t Wom; Negro Alman; Negro Her Lib v1; Prof Negro Wom v2

3640. Henderson, Vivian
1924–76
president of Clark College, labor economist
Atlanta, GA
Obit File

3641. Martin, Julia M.
born 1924
chemist, educator
Black
Encyc Black Am

3642. Sipuel, Ada Lois
born 1924
lawyer, educator, civil rights activist
Black
Encyc Black Am

3643. Smith, Virginia Beatrice
born 1924
president of Vassar College, economist
Cur Biog '78

3644. Hufstedler, Shirley [Ann] Mount
born 1925
US secretary of education
Cur Biog '80

3645. Larkin, Moscelyne
born 1925
ballet dancer and teacher, choreographer, lecturer
Native American (Shawnee-Ploria)
Ind Today

3646. Buckley, Mary Lorraine; Mrs. Joseph M. Parriott
born 1926
artist, art educator
Nat Cyc Am Bio csv13

3647. Chewiwi, Louise Abeita
born 1926
children's author, educator
Native American (Pueblo-Laguna)
Ind Today

3648. Kirkpatrick, Jeanne
born 1926
permanent representative to the UN, political scientist, university educator
Cur Biog '81

3649. Lawrence, Annie L.
born 1926
nurse, educator
Black
Encyc Black Am

3650. Noble, Jeanne Lavetta
born 1926
educator
Index t Wom

3651. Wexler, Jacqueline Grennan
born 1926
president of Hunter College
Catholic
New York
Cur Biog '70

3652. Hinderas, Natalie
born 1927
concert pianist, music educator
Black
Encyc Black Am

3653. Jones, Edith Irby
born 1927
physician, medical educator
Black
Encyc Black Am

3654. Arnez, Nancy Levi
born 1928
educator, poet, author
Black
Encyc Black Am

3655. Crowe, Amanda M.
born 1928
wood sculptor, carving teacher
Native American (Cherokee)
Ind Today

3656. Jaramillo, Mari-Luci
born 1928
educator, US ambassador to Honduras
Mexican
Dict Mex Am Hist

3657. Wilde, Patricia
born 1928
ballet dancer and teacher, choreographer
Index t Wom

3658. Cooney, Joan Ganz
born 1929
television executive, educational-television programer
Cur Biog '70

3659. Moore, Joan W.
born 1929
sociologist, student of Mexican American culture, author, educator
Dict Mex Am Hist

3660. Rich, Adrienne [Cecile]
born 1929
poet, educator
Cur Biog '76; Dict Lit Bio v5; Nort Anth Poet; Wom Lit; Wom Lit, More

3661. Walker, Tillie
born 1929
specialist in Native American education
North Dakota
Native American (Mandan-Hidatsa)
Read Encyc Am West

3662. Bates, Lila Curtis
flourished 1930s
pianist, poet, educator
Index t Wom

3663. Davids, Dorothy W.
flourished 1960s
educator
Native American (Stockbridge-Munsee)
Ind Today

3664. Gray, Hannah Holborn
born 1930
president of the University of Chicago, historian
Chicago, IL
German
Cur Biog '79

3665. Smith, Jessie Carney
born 1930
librarian, educator

Black
Encyc Black Am

3666. Veronica, M., Sister
flourished 1960s
educator, Catholic nun
Catholic
Index t Wom

3667. Victor, Wilma L.
flourished 1960s
educational administrator
Native American (Choctaw)
Ind Today

3668. Burke, Yvonne Watson Brathwaite
born 1932
lawyer, representative to Congress from California, regent of the University of California, environmentalist, feminist
California
Black
Cur Biog '75; Encyc Black Am; Negro Alman

3669. Chennault, Madelyn
born 1932
psychologist, educator
Black
Negro Alman

3670. Crockett, Gwendolyn
born 1932
lawyer, educator
Louisiana
Black
Encyc Black Am

3671. Drake, Debra Bella "Debbie"
born 1932
physical education teacher, author
Index t Wom

3672. Jackson, Jaquelyn Johnson
born 1932
sociologist, educator
Black
Encyc Black Am

3673. Davis, Gloria Ann, Sister
born 1933
Catholic nun, educator
Catholic
Native American (Navaho-Chocktaw)
Ind Today

3674. Nelson, Mary
born 1933
educator, sculptor
Native American (Colville-Cree-Mohawk)
Ind Today

3675. Sinkford, Jeanne Craig
born 1933
dentist, dental educator

Black
Encyc Black Am

3676. Hayden, Iola Pohucsucut
born 1934
Native American rights worker, educator
Native American (Comanche)
Ind Today

3677. Young, Lois A.
born 1934
ophthalmologist, educator
Black
Encyc Black Am

3678. Scheirbeck, Helen Maynor
born 1935
director of the Education for American Indians Office of HEW
Native American (Lumbee)
Ind Today

3679. Whitman, Marina von Neumann
born 1935
international economist, university educator, member of the Council of Economic Advisors
Cur Biog '73

3680. Berry, Mary Frances
born 1938
historian, educator
Black
Encyc Black Am

3681. Oates, Joyce Carol
born 1938
poet, novelist, short story writer, university educator
Cur Biog '70; Dict Lit Bio v2 and v5; Wom Lit; Wom Lit, More

3682. Bambara, Toni Cade
born 1939
short story writer, novelist, educator
Black
Encyc Black Am; Wom Lit; Wom Lit, More

3683. Cabell, Mary Virginia Ellet
born 1939
educator
Virginia
Wom Cent

3684. Edelman, Marian Wright
born 1939
lawyer, member of the Yale University board of trustees
Black
Encyc Black Am; Negro Alman

3685. Horner, Matina Souretis
born 1939

psychologist, president of Radcliffe College, college educator
Cur Biog '73

3686. Noble, Jeanne
flourished 1970s
educator
Black
Negro Alman

3687. Saunders, Sally; Sally Love Saunders Craigie
born 1940
poet, educator
Episcopalian
Pennsylvania
Nat Cyc Am Bio csv12

3688. Davis, Angela [Yvonne]
born 1944
civil rights worker, politician, Communist party presidential candidate, political writer, university educator
Black
Cur Biog '72; Encyc Black Am; Negro Alman

3689. Richter, Ada
born 1944
composer, educator, lecturer
Index t Wom

No Dates

3690. Becker, Angela
pianist, composer, music educator, organist
Index t Wom

3691. Briggs, Cora S.
composer, organist, music educator
Index t Wom

3692. Bristol, Margaret
composer, singer, conductor, music educator, writer on music
Index t Wom

3693. Broughton, Julia
organist, music educator
Index t Wom

3694. Carter, Amy
aircraft factory instructor
Index t Wom

3695. Hall, Ilizabeth
aviation instructor
Index t Wom

3696. Jorgensen, Evelyn
aircraft instructor
Index t Wom

3697. Mallette, Dorothy
aircraft instructor
Index t Wom

3733. Fairfax, Beatrice; Marie M. Gasch
circa 1878–1945
journalist, advice columnist
Index t Wom; Obit File

3734. Dodge, Lillian Sefton
1879–1960
cosmetics manufacturer
Episcopalian
Nat Cyc Am Bio v47

3735. Howard, Kathleen
1879–1956
opera singer, screen actor, fashion editor
Obit File

3736. Bodine, Helen K.
flourished 1910s–30s
fashion editor
Index t Wom

3737. Phillips, Bessie I.
circa 1880–1954
journalist, society editor of *The New York Times*
Index t Wom; Obit File

3738. Woods, Mary A.
flourished 1910s
dressmaker, flag maker
Index t Wom

3739. Lowe, Corinne Martin
1882–1952
journalist, fashion editor, author
Index t Wom

3740. Traphagen, Ethel; Mrs. William R. Leigh
1882–1963
fashion designer, founder of the first school of fashion design in the United States, pacifist
Index t Wom; Nat Cyc Am Bio v54 and csv9; Obit File

3741. Tolstoy, Mary Koutouzow
1884–1976
author, fashion director, World War I and II nurse
Obit File

3742. Ogilvie, Jessica
1885–1943
cosmetician, business executive
Index t Wom; Obit File

3743. Karinska, Barbara
born 1886
ballet costume designer and maker
Russian
Cur Biog '71

3744. Rosenthal, Ida Cohen
1886–1973
manufacturing executive, director of Maidenform Co., inventor of the brassiere

Jewish
New York
Nat Cyc Am Bio v57; Not Am Wom supp v1

3745. Vanderbilt, Amy; Mrs. Hans Knopf
1888/1908–1974
journalist, syndicated columnist, author, etiquette authority
Cur Biog '75; Index t Wom; Obit File

3746. Dowd, Alice Casey
circa 1889–1964
fashion consultant, publicist
Index t Wom

3747. Roulston, Margorie Hillis
1889–1971
editor of *Vogue*
Obit File

3748. Little, Ethel Holland
flourished 1920s–30s
fashion editor
Index t Wom

3749. Mideladze, Ketto
flourished 1920s–30s
dancer, fashion designer
Russian
Index t Wom

3750. Snow, Carmel White
1890–1961
editor of *Harper's Bazaar*, journalist, fashion expert
Irish
Index t Wom; Obit File

3751. Wall, Florence Emeline
flourished 1920s–30s
industrial chemist, cosmetician
Index t Wom

3752. Cannell, Kathleen
1891–1974
journalist, fashion editor, ballet critic, autobiographer
French (American expatriate to Paris)
Dict Lit Bio v4

3753. McCarroll, Marion Clyde; Beatrice Fairfax
1891–1977
journalist, syndicated advice columnist, author
Nat Cyc Am Bio v60; Obit File

3754. Davis, Tobe Collier
born circa 1893
fashion designer, business executive
Index t Wom

3755. Whitman, Lucile Mara de Vescovi, Countess
born 1893
fashion designer, businessperson

Italian
Index t Wom

3756. Groves, Gladys Hoagland
1894–1980
educator, marriage and sex counselor, writer on marriage and sex
Cur Biog '80; Index t Wom

3757. Bryant, Lane; Lena Himmelstein; Mrs. Albert Malsin
1881/1895–1951
dress merchant, mail order businessperson, maternity and special sizes designer
Jewish
New York
Lithuanian
Nat Cyc Am Bio v47; Index t Wom; Who Who Jew Hist

3758. Victor, Sally (Josephs)
1895/1905–1977
hat designer
Jewish
New York
Cur Biog '77; Index t Wom; Nat Cyc Am Bio v49

3759. Lewis, Mary
born 1897
fashion designer
Index t Wom

3760. Rosenstein, Nettie
born 1897
fashion designer, philanthropist, business executive
Australian
Index t Wom

3761. Archer, Alma
flourished 1930s
fashion expert, editor, author
Index t Wom

3762. Ashley, Grace
flourished 1930s
fashion designer
Index t Wom

3763. Babcock, Lucille
flourished 1930s
advertising executive, fashion expert, editor
Index t Wom

3764. Bennett, Eve
flourished 1930s
fashion designer, editor
Index t Wom

3765. Bernard, Marie
flourished 1930s
fashion designer
Index t Wom

3766. Carter, Mabel Ogilvie
flourished 1930s
cosmetics executive
Index t Wom

3767. Clair, Joan
flourished 1930s
cosmetic business executive
Index t Wom

3768. Clark, Verne
flourished 1930s
cosmetics business executive
Index t Wom

3769. Close, Elizabeth Stuart
flourished 1930s
fashion designer
Index t Wom

3770. Colburn, Joan
flourished 1930s
fashion commentator, radio broadcasting executive
Index t Wom

3771. Cole, Helen D.
flourished 1930s
fashion designer
Index t Wom

3772. Cookman, Helen Cramp
flourished 1930s
fashion designer, business executive
Index t Wom

3773. Coppage, Grace
flourished 1930s
cosmetician
Index t Wom

3774. de Barker, Lorraine
flourished 1930s
cosmetician, businessperson
Index t Wom

3775. de Pina, May Frances
flourished 1930s
modeling-school director
Venezualan
Index t Wom

3776. Delafield, Ann
flourished 1930s
cosmetician, dietician, educator
Index t Wom

3777. Dill, Marie
flourished 1930s
fashion expert
Index t Wom

3778. Dolson, Hildegarde
flourished 1930s
fashion designer
Index t Wom

3779. Donner, Vyvyan
flourished 1930s
journalist, fashion designer, artist
Index t Wom

3780. Fitzwater, Fanny Fern
flourished 1930s
editor, fashion expert
Index t Wom

3831. Reid, Rose Marie
1912–78
fashion designer
Obit File

3832. Trigere, Pauline
born 1912
fashion designer
French
Index t Wom

3833. Cashin, Bonnie
born 1915
fashion designer, costume designer
Cur Biog '70; Index t Wom

3834. Frankfurt, Elsie
born 1918
fashion designer
Index t Wom

3835. Landers, Ann
born 1918
advice columnist, journalist
Index t Wom

3836. Fogarty, Anne
1919–80
fashion designer
Cur Biog '80; Index t Wom

3837. Ford, Eileen (Otte)
born 1922
founder and president of the Ford
  Modeling Agency
Cur Biog '70

3838. Stutz, Geraldine
born 1924
businessperson, fashion expert
Index t Wom

3839. von Furstenberg, Diane
born 1946
fashion designer, business executive
Cur Biog '76

FINE ARTS AND ARCHITECTURE

3840. Merian, Marie Sibylle
1647–1717
naturalist, botanist, entomologist,
  botanical and entomological illustrator
Cyc Am Bio

3841. Johnston, Henrietta
pre-1670–1728/29
pastel painter
Dict Am Bio; Index t Wom; Not
  Am Wom

3842. Crabb, Mary
flourished 1730s
colonial needleworker, businessperson
Index t Wom

3843. Gazley, Martha
flourished 1730s
colonial manufacturer, needleworker, educator
Index t Wom

3844. Lancaster, Sarah
flourished 1730s
colonial needleworker
Index t Wom

3845. Sargent, Mary Forward Kooser
flourished eighteenth century
artist
Quaker
Nat Cyc Am Bio v50

3846. Roberts, Mary
died 1761
colonial painter
Index t Wom

3847. Jones, Anne Scotton
flourished 1750s
colonial needleworker
Index t Wom

3848. Purcell, Elinor
flourished 1750s
colonial art educator
Index t Wom

3849. Wright, Patience Lovell
1725–1785/86
wax modeler, spy during American Revolution
Quaker
New Jersey
Dict Am Bio; Dict Nat Bio; Index
  t Wom; Nat Cyc Am Bio v8;
  Not Am Wom; Who Who Dur
  Am Rev

3850. Ducray, Anne
flourished 1760s
colonial businessperson, needleworker
Index t Wom

3851. East, Henrietta Maria
flourished 1760s
colonial businessperson, needleworker
Index t Wom

3852. Benbridge, Letitia Sage
1770–87
painter
Index t Wom

3853. Pinney, Eunice Griswold
1770–1849
folk artist, painter
Index t Wom; Not Am Wom

3854. Bascom, Ruth Henshaw
circa 1772–1841
artist
Index t Wom

3855. Derby, Mary
flourished 1810s
pioneer, artist
Index t Wom

3856. Lee, Hannah Farnham (Sawyer)
1780/89–1865
writer on history and art
Boston, MA
Cyc Am Bio; Dict Am Auth; Dict
  Am Bio; Dict Am Bio Men
  Time; Index t Wom; Nat Cyc
  Am Bio v25

3857. Willson, Mary Ann
flourished 1810s–20s
primitive painter
Index t Wom

3858. Wirt, Elizabeth Washington (Gamble)
1784–1857
children's author, illustrator, botanist
Cyc Am Bio; Dict Am Auth

3859. Honeywell, Martha Ann
born circa 1787
artist
Index t Wom

3860. Goodridge, Sarah
1788–1853
painter
Dict Am Bio

3861. Peale, Anna Claypoole
1791–1878
still life and portrait painter
Cyc Am Bio; Dict Am Bio; Index
  t Wom; Not Am Wom

3862. Hall, Anne
1792–1863
miniaturist painter
Index t Wom; Nat Cyc Am Bio
  v10; Not Am Wom

3863. Peale, Margaretta Angelica
1795–1882
still life and portrait painter
Not Am Wom

3864. Martin, Maria
1796–1863
botanical artist
Index t Wom

3865. Quiner, Joanna
1796–1869
sculptor
Index t Wom

3866. Myers, Sarah Ann (Irwin)
1800–76
children's author, artist
Carlisle, PA
Cyc Am Bio; Dict Am Auth

3867. Peale, Sarah Miriam
1800–85
still life and portrait painter
Cyc Am Bio; Dict Am Bio; Index
  t Wom; Not Am Wom

3868. Peter, Sarah Anne (Worthington) King
1800–77
charity worker, philanthropist,
  founder of art school for women, hospital founder, Civil War
  nurse, pioneer industrial arts
  educator, church worker
Catholic
Ohio
Dict Am Bio; Index t Wom; Not
  Am Wom; Twent Cen Bio Dict
  Not Am

3869. Potter, Mary Knight
born 18?
writer on art, author
Boston, MA
Dict Am Auth

3870. Weeden, Howard
born 18?
artist, poet
Huntsville, AL
Dict Am Auth

3871. Ward, Emily Elizabeth
born circa 1805
illustrator
Cyc Am Bio

3872. Cook, Martha Elizabeth Duncan Walker
1806–74
magazine editor, author, linguist,
  translator, abolitionist, patron
  of Polish arts and artists
Cyc Am Bio; Dict Am Bio

3873. Dwight, Mary Ann
1806–58
textbook author, writer on art,
  artist
New York, NY
Cyc Am Bio; Dict Am Auth; Dict
  Am Bio Men Time

3874. Taylor, Charlotte de Bernier
1806–61
entomologist, author, illustrator
Dict Am Bio; Nat Cyc Am Bio v1

3875. Dassel, Herminie
died 1857
painter
German
Index t Wom

3876. Clarke, Sarah
1808–96
painter
Index t Wom

3877. Goldsmith, Deborah
1808–36

painter
Index t Wom

3878. Hawthorne, Sophia Amelia Peabody
1809–71
artist, illustrator, travel writer
Cyc Am Bio; Dict Am Auth; Not
Am Wom

3879. Hawley, Margaret Foote
1810–1963
painter
Index t Wom

3880. Legare, Mary Swinton
flourished 1840s
artist
Index t Wom

3881. Stuart, Jane
1810–88
portrait painter
Cyc Am Bio; Index t Wom

3882. Peterson, Hannah Mary (Bouvier)
1811–70
astronomer, author, illustrator, writer on astronomy
Cyc Am Bio; Dict Am Auth

3883. Whitcher, Frances Miriam (Berry); Widow Bedott
1811/14–1857/67
author, humorist, caricaturist
New York
Cyc Am Bio; Dict Am Auth; Dict Am Bio; Index t Wom; Nat Cyc Am Bio v6; Not Am Wom; Twent Cen Bio Dict Not Am

3884. Palmer, Frances Flora Bond "Fanny"
1812–76
draftsperson, lithographer
Not Am Wom

3885. Stebbins, Emma
1815–82
painter, sculptor, biographer of Charlotte Cushman
New York
Cyc Am Bio; Dict Am Auth; Index t Wom; Nat Cyc Am Bio v8; Not Am Wom; Twent Cen Bio Dict Not Am

3886. Ames, Sarah Fisher
1817–1901
sculptor
Index t Wom

3887. Peabody, Sophia
married 1842
artist
Index t Wom

3888. Mitchell, Martha Reed
born 1818

patron of art, traveler, philanthropist
Index t Wom; Wom Cent

3889. Greatorex, Eliza (Pratt)
1819/20–1897
artist, painter
Irish
Cyc Am Bio; Index t Wom; Nat Cyc Am Bio v3; Not Am Wom; Wom Cent

3890. Liddell, Mary
born 1819
illustrator
Index t Wom

3891. Morrell, Imogene Robinson
flourished 1850s–80s
artist
Cyc Am Bio

3892. Lewis, Grace Anna
born 1821
naturalist, scientific illustrator, science writer, conservationist, ornithologist, abolitionist, Underground Railroad operator, pacifist, suffragist, philanthropist
Quaker
Index t Wom; Nat Cyc Am Bio v9; Twent Cen Bio Dict Not Am; Wom Cent

3893. Morse, Rebecca A.; Ruth Moza; R. A. Kidder; R. A. K.
born 1821
clubwoman, Sorosis member, suffragist, patron of art, abolitionist, author
New York
Index t Wom; Wom Cent

3894. Whitney, Anne
1821–1915
sculptor, artist, poet, abolitionist, suffragist
Boston, MA
Cyc Am Bio; Dict Am Auth; Dict Am Bio; Index t Wom; Nat Cyc Am Bio v7; Not Am Wom; Wom Cent

3895. Very, Lydia Louise Ann
1823–1901/07
poet, children's author, illustrator, educator
Salem, MA
Cyc Am Bio; Dict Am Auth; Dict Am Bio; Index t Wom; Nat Cyc Am Bio v6; Wom Cent

3896. Starr, Eliza Allen
1824–1901
writer and lecturer on art and religion, poet, author, artist, educator

Chicago, IL
Cyc Am Bio; Dict Am Auth; Dict Am Bio; Nat Cyc Am Bio v13; Not Am Wom; Twent Cen Bio Dict Not Am; Wom Cent

3897. Adsit, Mary H.
born 1825
art lecturer
Wom Cent

3898. Freeman, Horatia Augusta Latilla
born 1826
sculptor
Cyc Am Bio

3899. Lander, Louisa
born 1826/35
sculptor
Cyc Am Bio; Dict Am Bio Men Time; Index t Wom

3900. Doggett, Kate Newell
1827/28–1884
suffragist, educator, art critic, translator
Cyc Am Bio; Index t Wom

3901. Foley, Margaret E.
died 1877
artist, sculptor, woodcarver
Cyc Am Bio; Index t Wom; Nat Cyc Am Bio v9; Wom Cent

3902. Jones, Virginia (Smith)
born 1827
naturalist, ornithologist, ornithological illustrator
Dict Am Auth; Twent Cen Bio Dict Not Am

3903. Wheeler, Candace (Thurber)
1827–1923
pioneer in American textile design, interior decorator, artist, needleworker, writer on artistic technique, fairy tale writer
New York, NY
Dict Am Auth; Index t Wom; Not Am Wom

3904. Blackwell, Sarah Ellen
born 1828
artist, author, suffragist, land and labor reformer, antivivisectionist
Nat Cyc Am Bio v9; Wom Cent

3905. Woodward, Caroline Marshall
1828–90
author, artist
Indiana
Wom Cent

3906. Badger, Mrs.
flourished 1859
artist, author
Index t Wom

3907. Fuller, Sarah E.
1829–1901
artist, wood engraver
Index t Wom

3908. Ballou, Addie L.
flourished 1860s
Civil War nurse, author, artist, lawyer
Index t Wom

3909. Carpenter, Ellen M.
born 1830/36
artist
Boston, MA
Cyc Am Bio; Twent Cen Bio Dict Not Am; Wom Cent

3910. Carter, Hannah Johnson
flourished 1860s–90s
art educator
Wom Cent

3911. Carter, Mary Adaline Edwards
flourished 1860s–80s
industrial arts instructor and designer, embroiderer, painter, china painter, plastics artist, temperance worker
Wom Cent

3912. Hosmer, Harriet Goodhue
1830–1908
sculptor
Cyc Am Bio; Dict Am Bio; Dict Am Bio Men Time; Index t Wom; Nat Cyc Am Bio v1 and v8; Not Am Wom; Twent Cen Bio Dict Not Am; Wom Cent

3913. Pattison, Helen Searle
flourished 1860s–80s
painter
Index t Wom

3914. Post, Cornelia S.
flourished 1860s
artist
Index t Wom

3915. Stranahan, Clara Harrison
183?–post 1890
writer on art
Boston, MA
Dict Am Auth; Wom Cent

3916. Fassett, Cornelia Adele (Strong)
1831–98
artist, painter, author
Cyc Am Bio; Dict Am Bio; Index t Wom; Twent Cen Bio Dict Not Am

3917. Lakey, Emily Jane
1831–96
artist
Index t Wom; Twent Cen Bio Dict Not Am

3918. Lockwood, Mary Smith
born 1831
editor, clubwoman, patriot, writer
on art and architecture
Dict Am Auth; Index t Wom;
Nat Cyc Am Bio v3

3919. Knowlton, Helen Mary
1832–1918
painter, art educator, writer on
art and art technique
Boston, MA
Cyc Am Bio; Dict Am Auth; Not
Am Wom; Twent Cen Bio Dict
Not Am

3920. Kollock, Mary
1832/40–1911
artist, painter
Cyc Am Bio; Index t Wom; Nat
Cyc Am Bio v10; Twent Cen
Bio Dict Not Am

**3921. Scott, Emily Maria (Spa-
ford)**
1832–1915
artist, flower painter
Index t Wom; Nat Cyc Am Bio
v11; Wom Cent

3922. Boya, Ellen Wright
born 1833
educator, author on religious education, writer on art and architecture
Albany, NY
Dict Am Auth

3923. Coman, Charlotte Buell
1833/45–1924
painter
Christian Scientist
New York
Cyc Am Bio; Dict Am Bio; Index
t Wom; Nat Cyc Am Bio v22

3924. Hale, Susan
1833/38–1910
author, children's author, travel
writer, artist, painter
Cyc Am Bio; Dict Am Auth;
Index t Wom; Not Am Wom;
Twent Cen Bio Dict Not Am

3925. Ney, Elizabeth
1833/45–1907
sculptor
German
Dict Am Bio; Index t Wom; Nat
Cyc Am Bio v13; Not Am Wom

**3926. Poole, Hester Martha
(Hunt)**
born 1833/43
author, poet, writer on social and
domestic issues, art critic, artist,
women's rights worker, Sorosis
member
Metuchen, NJ
Dict Am Auth; Nat Cyc Am Bio
v11; Wom Cent

3927. Bridges, Fidelia
1834/35–1923
painter
Cyc Am Bio; Index t Wom; Not
Am Wom; Twent Cen Bio Dict
Not Am

**3928. Rose, Martha E. (Parme-
lee)**
born 1834
women's labor welfare worker,
social reformer, sociologist, author, art patron, journalist, Sorosis member
Cleveland, OH
Index t Wom; Nat Cyc Am Bio
v11; Wom Cent

3929. Shedd, Julia Ann (Clark)
1834–97
writer on art
Cyc Am Bio; Dict Am Auth

**3930. Waters, Clara (Erskine)
(Clement); Clara Clement**
1834–1916
author, writer on art, art histori-
an, world traveler
Boston, MA
Dict Am Auth; Index t Wom;
Not Am Wom; Wom Cent;
Wom Lit, More

**3931. Brigham, Sarah J. (Lath-
bury)**
born 1835
children's author, illustrator
Dict Am Auth

**3932. Weiss, Susan Archer
(Talley)**
born 1835
poet, artist
Virginia; New York, NY
Cyc Am Bio; Dict Am Auth;
Wom Cent

**3933. Boyd, Kate Parker
(Scott)**
born 1836
artist, temperance worker
Wom Cent

3934. Freeman, Florence
1836–83
sculptor
Cyc Am Bio; Index t Wom

**3935. Prang, Mary Amelia
[Dana] Hicks**
1836–1927
art educator, writer on art, editor
Dict Am Bio; Index t Wom; Nat
Cyc Am Bio v27; Not Am
Wom; Twent Cen Bio Dict Not
Am

**3936. Alexander, Esther
Frances "Francesca"**
1837–1917
artist, illustrator, author, translator, philanthropist

Italian (American expatriate to
Italy)
Dict Am Auth; Not Am Wom

3937. Emerson, Ellen (Russell)
1837–1907
author, ethnologist, writer on Native American art and mythology
Boston, MA
Dict Am Auth; Dict Am Bio;
Twent Cen Bio Dict Not Am;
Wom Cent

**3938. Jamison, Cecelia Viets
(Dakin) (Hamilton)**
1837/48–1909
author, artist
Dict Am Auth; Dict Am Bio;
Twent Cen Bio Dict Not Am

3939. Hardy, Anna Eliza
1839–1934
artist
Not Am Wom

3940. Boott, Elizabeth
flourished 1870s; died post 1914
painter
Cyc Am Bio; Index t Wom

3941. Brooks, Caroline Shawk
born 1840
sculptor
Twent Cen Bio Dict Not Am

3942. Cory, Fanny Young
flourished 1870s
illustrator, cartoonist
Index t Wom

3943. Curtis, Jessie
flourished 1870s–80s
illustrator
Index t Wom

3944. de Kay, Helena
flourished 1870s
painter
Index t Wom

3945. Dudley, Sarah Marie
flourished 1870s–90s
merchant, investor, inventor, architect, designer, builder
Detroit, MI
Wom Cent

3946. Gardner, Isabella Stewart
1840–1924
art collector
Dict Am Bio; Index t Wom; Not
Am Wom

3947. Granberry, Virginia
flourished 1870s–80s
artist, portraitist
Wom Cent

**3948. Harrison, Margaritta
Willetts**
flourished 1870s–80s

artist
Index t Wom

3949. Hicks, Margaret
flourished 1870s–80s
architect
Index t Wom

3950. Hoyt, Deristha Lavinta
born 184?
lecturer on the history of painting, writer on art
Massachusetts
Dict Am Auth

3951. Lamb, Rose
flourished 1870s–80s
painter
Index t Wom

**3952. Loop, Jennette Shepherd
(Harrison)**
1840–1909
artist, painter
New York
Cyc Am Bio; Index t Wom;
Twent Cen Bio Dict Not Am;
Wom Cent

**3953. McLaughlin, Mary Lou-
ise M.**
flourished 1870s–1900s
ceramic artist, writer on art techniques
Cincinnati, OH
Dict Am Auth; Index t Wom

3954. Nieriker, May (Alcott)
1840–79
artist, author, still life painter
Appl Cyc Am Bio; Cyc Am Bio;
Dict Am Auth; Index t Wom;
Twent Cen Bio Dict Not Am;
Wom Cent

**3955. Normandie, Elizabeth K.
de**
flourished 1870s–80s
artist
Index t Wom

3956. Orvis, Mrs.
flourished 1870s–80s
artist
Index t Wom

3957. Ransom, Sarah
flourished 1870s–80s
artist
Index t Wom

**3958. Robinson, Imogene Mor-
rell**
flourished 1870s
painter
Index t Wom

3959. Sawyer, A. R.
flourished 1870s–80s
artist
Index t Wom

3960. Smallwood, Hannah T.
flourished 1870s
scientific illustrator
Index t Wom

3961. Warner, Harriet E.
flourished 1870s–80s
architect
Index t Wom

3962. Weston, Mary Pillsbury
flourished 1870s–90s
artist
Index t Wom

3963. Wormly, Mrs.
flourished 1870s–80s
artist, steel engraver
Index t Wom

3964. Janvier, Catharine Ann
1841–1922
painter, author
Dict Am Bio

3965. Nevin, Blanche
born 1841
sculptor
Cyc Am Bio; Twent Cen Bio Dict
Not Am

3966. Sartain, Emily
1841–1927
painter, mezzotint engraver, etch-
er, illustrator, art educator
Philadelphia, PA
English
Cyc Am Bio; Dict Am Bio; Index
t Wom; Nat Cyc Am Bio v13;
Not Am Wom; Twent Cen Bio
Dict Not Am; Wom Cent

**3967. Brush, Christine (Chap-
lin)**
1842–92
watercolorist, novelist
Dict Am Auth

3968. Gardner, Elizabeth Jane
born 1842
artist
Cyc Am Bio

3969. Moran, Mary Nimmo
1842–99
painter, etcher
Scottish
Cyc Am Bio; Index t Wom; Nat
Cyc Am Bio v22; Not Am
Wom; Twent Cen Bio Dict Not
Am

3970. Pike, Maria Louisa
died 1892
naturalist, illustrator
Twent Cen Bio Dict Not Am

**3971. Thayer, Emma (Homan)
(Graves)**
born 1842
author, novelist, artist, botanical
illustrator

Salida, CO
Dict Am Auth; Twent Cen Bio
Dict Not Am; Wom Cent

**3972. Vanderpoel, Emily Caro-
line Noyes**
1842–1939
painter, author
New York
Nat Cyc Am Bio v29

**3973. Westinghouse, Marguerite
Erskine Walker**
1842–1914
sculptor, philanthropist
Nat Cyc Am Bio v15

**3974. Whitman, Sarah de St.
Crix**
1842–1904
painter
Index t Wom

**3975. Cadwalader-Guild, Emma
Marie; Emma Guild**
born 1843
painter, sculptor
Index t Wom

**3976. Cassat, Marie (Steven-
son)**
1844/45–1926
artist, painter
Dict Am Bio; Index t Wom; Nat
Cyc Am Bio v33; Not Am Wom

3977. Fletcher, Lisa Anne
born 1844
poet, flower painter
New Hampshire
Wom Cent

3978. Goff, Eugenia Wheeler
born 1844
historian, designer of historical
maps
Nat Cyc Am Bio v17

**3979. Merriman, Helen (Bige-
low)**
born 1844
artist, writer on art, religious author
Worcester, MA
Dict Am Auth; Index t Wom;
Twent Cen Bio Dict Not Am

**3980. Merritt, Anna Massey
Lea**
1844–1908/30
artist, painter, etcher
Cyc Am Bio and ad; Dict Am
Bio; Index t Wom; Twent Cen
Bio Dict Not Am

3981. Walton, Sarah Stokes
born 1844
poet, artist
Protestant Episcopal
Wom Cent

3982. Brooks, Maria
1845–1913
artist
Nat Cyc Am Bio v8

**3983. Dewing, Maria Richards
(Oakey)**
1845/55–1927
artist, painter
Dict Am Auth; Index t Wom;
Twent Cen Bio Dict Not Am

3984. Lewis, Edmonia [Mary]
1845–90
sculptor
Native American (Chippewa);
Black
Cyc Am Bio; Encyc Black Am;
Index t Wom; Nat Cyc Am Bio
v5; Negro Alman; Not Am
Wom; Prof Negro Wom v1;
Twent Cen Bio Dict Not Am

**3985. Mitchell, Lucy Myers
Wright**
1845–88
archaeologist, historian of ancient
art, writer on Greek art
Dict Am Auth; Dict Am Bio; Nat
Cyc Am Bio v6; Twent Cen Bio
Dict Not Am

3986. Richardson, Ellen A.
1845–1911
artist, editor, author, club leader
Index t Wom

3987. Smith, Isabel Elizabeth
1845–1938
painter
Ohio
Index t Wom; Wom Cent

**3988. Tillinghast, Mary
Elizabeth**
1845–1912
stained glass artist, tapestry weaver, painter
Index t Wom; Nat Cyc Am Bio
v19

**3989. Ward, Lydia Arms
(Avery) (Coonley)**
1845–1924
author, poet, patron of the arts,
suffragist, philanthropist
Chicago, IL
Dict Am Auth; Dict Am Bio;
Index t Wom; Nat Cyc Am Bio
v34

3990. Wright, Emma Scholfield
born 1845
artist
English
Index t Wom

3991. Donlevy, Alice Heighes
1846–1929
artist, illuminator, china painter,
wood engraver

English
Index t Wom; Wom Cent

3992. Gregory, Mary Rogers
born 1846
artist
Wom Cent

3993. Gutelius, Jean Harrower
born 1846
artist, bookstore proprietor
Scottish
Wom Cent

3994. Hoxie, Vinnie (Ream)
1846/50–1914/19
sculptor
Cyc Am Bio; Dict Am Bio; Index
t Wom; Nat Cyc Am Bio v1;
Not Am Wom; Twent Cen Bio
Dict Not Am

**3995. Ketcham, Harriet Ann
(McDivitt)**
1846–90
sculptor
Nat Cyc Am Bio v9

3996. Moore, Sarah Wool
born 1846
artist, journalist
Nebraska
Index t Wom; Wom Cent

3997. Abbatt, Agnes Dean
1847–1917
artist
Index t Wom; Nat Cyc Am Bio
v8; Wom Cent

**3998. Dodson, Sarah Paxton
Ball**
1847–1907
painter
Index t Wom

**3999. Foote, Mary Anna (Hal-
lock)**
1847–1938
author, novelist, artist, illustrator
Dict Am Auth; Index t Wom;
Nat Cyc Am Bio v6; Not Am
Wom; Read Encyc Am West;
Twent Cen Bio Dict Not Am;
Wom Lit, More

4000. Irwin, Harriet
died 1897
architect
Index t Wom

**4001. Jenks, Phoebe A. Picker-
ing Hoyt**
1847–1907
artist, portraitist
Cyc Am Bio; Index t Wom; Nat
Cyc Am Bio v12; Twent Cen
Bio Dict Not Am

4002. Johnson, Adelaide
1847/49–1955

sculptor, feminist, women's rights worker
Index t Wom; Not Am Wom supp v1; Obit File

4003. Wynne, Madelene (Yale)
born 1847
author, short story writer, silversmith, artist
Index t Wom

4004. Durgin, Harriet Thayer
born 1848
artist
Wom Cent

4005. Frackleton, Susan Stuart (Goodrich)
born 1848/51
artist, ceramicist, inventor of a gas kiln, writer on ceramic technique
Dict Am Auth; Index t Wom; Twent Cen Bio Dict Not Am; Wom Cent

4006. Perry, Lilla Cabot
1848–1933
artist, painter, poet
Dict Am Auth; Index t Wom; Nat Cyc Am Bio v26

4007. Bohan, Elizabeth Baker
born 1849
painter, author, poet
Wom Cent

4008. Dyer, Clara L. Brown
born 1849
artist
Wom Cent

4009. Palmer, Bertha Honore
1849/51–1918
clubwoman, philanthropist, women's rights worker, art collector
Chicago, IL
Dict Am Bio; Index t Wom; Twent Cen Bio Dict Not Am; Wom Cent

4010. Shoaff, Carrie M.; Carrie Shoff
born 1849
artist, ceramicist, inventor
Index t Wom; Wom Cent

4011. Solari, Mary M.
born 1849
artist
Memphis, TN
Italian
Wom Cent

4012. Storer, Maria Longworth Nichols
1849–1932
patron of music, ceramicist, sculptor
Index t Wom; Nat Cyc Am Bio v11; Not Am Wom

4013. Tuttle, Mary McArthur (Thompson)
born 1849/59
artist, writer and lecturer on art, art historian, novelist
Methodist
Dict Am Bio; Nat Cyc Am Bio v10

4014. Bartlett, Jennie E.
flourished 1880s
artist
Index t Wom

4015. Brownscombe, Jennie Augusta
1850–1936
painter
Index t Wom; Nat Cyc Am Bio v16; Not Am Wom; Wom Cent

4016. Dabney, Julia Parker
born 1850
author, artist, novelist
Brookline, MA
Twent Cen Bio Dict Not Am

4017. Dillaye, Blanche
flourished 1880s; died 1931
artist, painter, etcher, sculptor
Philadelphia, PA
Index t Wom; Wom Cent

4018. Durgin, Lyle
born 1850
artist
Wom Cent

4019. Fryatt, Frances Elizabeth
flourished 1880s–90s
author, specialist in household art, interior decorator
New York
Wom Cent

4020. Hawes, Franc P.
flourished 1880s
artist, tapestry weaver, screen painter
Wom Cent

4021. Hawthorn, Mrs.
flourished 1880s
painter, sculptor
Index t Wom

4022. Humphrey, Elizabeth B.
born 1850
artist
Cyc Am Bio

4023. Jackson, Lily Irene
flourished 1880s–90s
sculptor, artist, designer, clubwoman
Virginia
Index t Wom; Wom Cent

4024. Lea, Anna M.
flourished 1880s
artist
Index t Wom

4025. Leslie, Ann
flourished 1880s
artist
Index t Wom

4026. Mellen, Mary B.
flourished 1880s
artist
Index t Wom

4027. Post, Parthenia
flourished 1880s
needlework artist
Index t Wom

4028. Pre, Julia du
flourished 1880s
artist
Index t Wom

4029. Swope, Kate
flourished 1880s–90s
painter
Index t Wom

4030. Barnes, Catharine Wee
born 1851
artist, photographer
Nat Cyc Am Bio; Wom Cent

4031. Bougureau, Elizabeth Jane
1851–1922
painter
Index t Wom

4032. Eddy, Sarah James
born 1851
sculptor
Index t Wom

4033. Greatorex, Kathleen Honora
born 1851
artist
Cyc Am Bio

4034. Lathrop, Rose (Hawthorne); Mother Mary Alphonsa; Rose Hawthorne
1851–1926
author, artist, poet, Catholic nun, founder of the Dominican Congregation of St. Rose of Lima, philanthropist
Catholic
Cyc Am Bio; Dict Am Auth; Dict Am Bio; Index t Wom; Nat Cyc Am Bio v9; Not Am Wom; Twent Cen Bio Dict Not Am; Wom Cent

4035. Rimmer, Caroline Hunt
born 1851
writer on artistic technique
Dict Am Auth

4036. van Rensselaer, Mariana Alley (Griswold); Mrs. Schuyler
1851–1934
writer on art, art critic, art historian
Cyc Am Bio and ad; Dict Am Auth; Dict Am Bio; Index t Wom; Not Am Wom

4037. Owen, Ella Seaver
born 1852
artist, decorator
Vermont
Wom Cent

4038. Rankin, Ellen Houser
born 1852
sculptor
Nat Cyc Am Bio v8

4039. Shaw, Annie Cornelia
1852–87
artist, painter
Cyc Am Bio; Index t Wom; Wom Cent

4040. Butterfield, Mellona Moulton
born 1853
china painter
Wom Cent

4041. Campbell, Georgine
flourished 1883
artist
New Orleans, LA
Wom Cent

4042. Cooke, Anna Charlotte Rice
1853–1934
founder of the Honolulu Academy of the Arts
Honolulu, HI
Not Am Wom

4043. Copp, Helen Rankin
born 1853
sculptor
Chicago, IL
Wom Cent

4044. Poulsson, Anne Emilie
1853–1939
children's author, writer on children, editor, illustrator, kindergarten educator
Boston, MA
Dict Am Auth; Index t Wom; Nat Cyc Am Bio v10; Twent Cen Bio Dict Not Am

4045. Read, Jane Maria
born 1853
poet, artist
Colebrook Springs, MA
Dict Am Auth; Wom Cent

4046. Wentworth, Cecile (Smith) De
circa 1853–1933
painter
Dict Am Bio; Index t Wom

4047. Worden, Sarah A.
born 1853
artist
Wom Cent

4048. Comstock, Anna (Botsford)
1854–1930
naturalist, scientific illustrator, insect artist, leader in the nature study movement, wood engraver, educator
New York
Index t Wom; Nat Cyc Am Bio v11 and v22; Not Am Wom; Twent Cen Bio Dict Not Am

4049. Greatorex, Elizabeth Eleonor
born 1854
artist
Cyc Am Bio

4050. Miller, Louise Klein
1854–1943
horticulturist, landscape architect, educator
Index t Wom

4051. Nicholls, Rhoda Holmes
1854–1930
artist, educator, painter
English
Dict Am Bio; Index t Wom; Nat Cyc Am Bio v7; Wom Cent

4052. Selinger, Emily Harris McGary
born 1854
artist
Wom Cent

4053. Sherwood, Rosina (Emmet)
1854/57–post 1880
illustrator, painter
Cyc Am Bio v3; Index t Wom; Nat Cyc Am Bio v17; Twent Cen Bio Dict Not Am; Wom Cent

4054. Smillie, Nellie Sheldon Jacobs
born 1854
artist
Cyc Am Bio; Twent Cen Bio Dict Not Am

4055. Beaux, Cecelia
1855/63–1942
portrait painter
Dict Am Bio supp v3; Index t Wom; Nat Cyc Am Bio v11 and v40; Not Am Wom; Obit File

4056. Hale, Ellen Day
born 1855
artist, painter
Cyc Am Bio; Index t Wom; Twent Cen Bio Dict Not Am

4057. Havemeyer, Louisine Waldron Elder
1855–1929
art collector, philanthropist, suffragist
Not Am Wom

4058. Pennell, Elizabeth (Robins)
1855–1936
author, travel writer, biographer, art critic, bicycle tourer
Dict Am Auth; Index t Wom; Nat Cyc Am Bio v10; Not Am Wom

4059. Stearns, Nellie George
born 1855
artist
New Hampshire
Wom Cent

4060. Archambault, A. Margaretta
1856–1956
portrait painter, miniaturist
Obit File

4061. Bethune, Louise Blanchard
1856–1913
architect
Index t Wom; Nat Cyc Am Bio v12; Not Am Wom; Wom Cent

4062. Braumuller, Luetta Elmina
born 1856
artist
Wom Cent

4063. Goodrich, Frances Louisa
born 1856
author, weaver, business executive
Index t Wom

4064. Hirschberg, Alice
born 1856
artist
Wom Cent

4065. Klumpke, Anna Elizabeth
1856–1942
painter
San Francisco, CA
Index t Wom; Nat Cyc Am Bio v31

4066. Plummer, Mary Wright
1856–1916
librarian, educator, poet, author
Brooklyn, NY
Dict Am Auth; Dict Am Bio; Index t Wom; Nat Cyc Am Bio v21; Not Am Wom; Twent Cen Bio Dict Not Am

4067. Street, Ida Maria
born 1856
educator, art criticism author

Milwaukee, WI
Dict Am Auth

4068. Woodward, Dewing
1856–1950
painter
Index t Wom

4069. Fry, Laura Ann
born 1857
artist, ceramicist
Ohio
Wom Cent

4070. Hall, Adelaide S.
born 1857
art lecturer, author
Index t Wom

4071. Keith, Dora Wheeler
1857–1940
artist
Index t Wom

4072. Cobb, Sarah M. Maxson
born 1858
artist, art educator, photographer, microscopist
Wom Cent

4073. Cole, Jessie Duncan Savage
1858–1940
painter
Index t Wom

4074. Jerome, Irene Elizabeth
born 1858
artist
Cyc Am Bio

4075. Joy, Ida
born 1858
artist
Cyc Am Bio

4076. Low, Mary Fairchild
1858–1946
painter
Index t Wom; Obit File

4077. Morell, Imogene Robinson
died 1908
artist
Index t Wom

4078. Murdock, Louise Caldwell
1858–1915
interior designer, art patron
Kansas
Not Am Wom

4079. Phillips, L. Vance
born 1858
artist
Nebraska
Wom Cent

4080. Stephens, Alice Barber
1858–1932

illustrator, artist, engraver
Dict Am Bio; Index t Wom; Nat Cyc Am Bio v13 and v23; Not Am Wom; Twent Cen Bio Dict Not Am

4081. Turner, Helen Maria
born 1858
painter
Index t Wom; Nat Cyc Am Bio csv5

4082. Walworth, Ellen Hardin
born 1858
author, artist
Cyc Am Bio and ad; Dict Am Auth; Index t Wom

4083. Wheeler, Doris
born 1858/60
artist, needleworker, designer, decorator
New York
Cyc Am Bio; Nat Cyc Am Bio v1; Wom Cent

4084. Ahrens, Ellen Wetherald
born 1859
painter
Index t Wom

4085. Beck, Carol H.
1859–1908
painter
Index t Wom

4086. Cherry, Emma Robinson
born 1859
painter
Index t Wom

4087. Cohen, Katherine Myrtilla
1859–1914
sculptor
Index t Wom; Nat Cyc Am Bio v10

4088. Hills, Laura Coombs
1859–1952
painter
Index t Wom

4089. Lutz, Edelia Armstrong
born 1859
artist, art educator
Knoxville, TN
Wom Cent

4090. Sewell, Lydia Amanda (Brewster)
born 1859
artist
Nat Cyc Am Bio v13

4091. Wall, Annie (Carpenter)
born 1859
author, poet, artist
Pueblo, CO
Dict Am Auth; Nat Cyc Am Bio v5; Wom Cent

4092. Baker, Elizabeth Gowdy
1860–1927
painter
Index t Wom

4093. Baldwin, Edith Ella
flourished 1890s–1900s
painter
Index t Wom

4094. Brooks, Florence; Mrs. John Marone
1860–1948
artist, author, poet
California
Nat Cyc Am Bio v37

4095. Carl, Katharine Augusta
flourished 1890s–1900s
artist
Index t Wom

4096. Eggleston, Allegra
born 1860
artist, woodcarver, illustrator
Wom Cent

4097. Gray, Sophie de Butts
flourished 1890s
artist
Index t Wom

4098. Hazleton, Mary Brewster
flourished 1890s–1900s
artist
Index t Wom

4099. Huber, Alice
flourished 1890s
nurse, artist
Index t Wom

4100. Kirk, Maria Louise
flourished 1890s
painter, illustrator
Index t Wom

4101. Lamb, Ella Condie
flourished 1890s–1900s
sculptor, illustrator, painter
Index t Wom

4102. Loud, Mary Hallowell
born 1860
painter
Index t Wom

4103. MacChesney, Clara Taggart
flourished 1890s–1900s
painter
Index t Wom

4104. MacMonnies, Mary Fairchild
born circa 1860
painter
Index t Wom

4105. Moses, Anna Mary Robertson "Grandma"
1860–1961

primitive painter
New York
Index t Wom; Nat Cyc Am Bio v45; Not Am Wom supp v1

4106. Mumaugh, Frances Miller
born 1860
artist
Nebraska
Wom Cent

4107. Nourse, Elizabeth
1860–1938
artist, painter
Index t Wom; Nat Cyc Am Bio v11; Twent Cen Bio Dict Not Am

4108. Ostertag, Blanche
flourished 1890s–1900s
artist
Index t Wom

4109. Overstolz, Philippine E. von
flourished 1890s
musician, linguist, artist
Wom Cent

4110. Sears, Sarah C.
flourished 1890s–1900s
painter
Index t Wom

4111. Taylor, Emily Drayton
1860–1952
miniature painter, founder of the Philadelphia Arts Alliance
Philadelphia, PA
Obit File

4112. Thurber, Caroline Nettleton
flourished 1890s–1900s
painter
Index t Wom

4113. Tyler, Alice Kellogg
flourished 1890s–1920s
artist
Index t Wom

4114. Usher, Leila
flourished 1890s–1920s
sculptor
Index t Wom

4115. Walcott, Mary Morris Vaux
1860–1940
artist, naturalist
Wom Cent

4116. Hoke, Martha Harriet
born 1861
artist
Nat Cyc Am Bio v5

4117. Lang, Florence Osgood Rand
1861–1943

patron of art, philanthropist
Congregationalist
Massachusetts
Nat Cyc Am Bio v32 and csv5

4118. Lawson, Louise
born 1861
sculptor, medical journal editor
Cyc Am Bio; Wom Cent

4119. MacKubin, Florence
1861–1918
portrait and miniature painter
Italian
Dict Am Bio; Index t Wom; Nat Cyc Am Bio v15

4120. Macomber, Mary Lizzie
1861–1916
painter of decorative symbolic panels, portraitist
Massachusetts
Dict Am Bio; Index t Wom; Nat Cyc Am Bio v24

4121. Nichols, Minerva Parker
1861/63–1949
architect, lecturer
Index t Wom; Not Am Wom; Wom Cent

4122. Platt, Aletha Hill
1861–1932
painter
Index t Wom

4123. Roberts, Mary Fantan
1861–1956
art magazine editor, journalist, art patron
Index t Wom; Obit File

4124. Allen, Marion
1862–1941
artist
Index t Wom

4125. Brown, Alice van Vechten
1862–1949
art educator
Not Am Wom

4126. Hicks, Mary Dana
born 1862
art educator
Wom Cent

4127. Hurlbut, Harriette Persis
born 1862
artist
Wom Cent

4128. Lippincott, Margarette
1862–1910
painter
Index t Wom

4129. Logan, Josephine Hancock
1862–1943
patron of the arts, author, poet

Chicago, IL
Nat Cyc Am Bio v35

4130. Morse, Alice Cordelia
born 1862
artist, stained glass designer, book designer
New York
Index t Wom; Wom Cent

4131. Pickard, Florence [Martha] Willingham
1862–1930
author, painter
Georgia
Nat Cyc Am Bio v27 and csv2

4132. Rice, Jeannie Durant
1862–1919
ceramic artist
Nat Cyc Am Bio v18

4133. Smith, Letta Crapo
1862–1921
painter
Index t Wom

4134. Weir, Irene
1862–1944
painter, art educator, writer on art, founder of the New York School of Design and Liberal Arts
New York
Not Am Wom; Obit File

4135. Baker, Ellen Kendall
died 1913
painter
Index t Wom

4136. Howland, Edith
circa 1863–1949
sculptor
Index t Wom

4137. Hurll, Estelle May
born 1863
educator, lecturer and writer on art
Dict Am Auth; Index t Wom

4138. Hyde, Helen
1863/68–1919
artist, etcher, engraver, painter
Dict Am Bio; Index t Wom

4139. Smith, Jessie Wilcox
1863–1935
painter, illustrator
Philadelphia, PA
Index t Wom; Nat Cyc Am Bio v26; Not Am Wom

4140. Stein, Evaleen
1863–1923
poet, author, artist
Lafayette, IN
Dict Am Auth; Dict Am Bio; Wom Cent

4141. Bliss, Lizzie Plummer
1864–1931
art collector, philanthropist
Not Am Wom

4142. Cone, Claribel
1864–1929
pathologist, art collector
Nat Cyc Am Bio v4; Not Am
Wom

4143. Gerson, Virginia
circa 1864–1951
illustrator, author
Index t Wom

**4144. Thorp, Louisa Elizabeth
Garden McLeod**
1864–1944
artist, founder of the first recognized art school in Los Angeles
Los Angeles, CA
Obit File

**4145. Cox, Louise Howland
(King)**
1865–1945
painter, sculptor
Index t Wom; Nat Cyc Am Bio
v11; Twent Cen Bio Dict Not
Am

4146. de Wolfe, Elsie Anderson; Lady Mendl
1865/70–1950
actor, stage producer, interior
decorator, World War I relief
worker
Dict Am Bio supp v4; Index t
Wom; Nat Cyc Am Bio csv6;
Not Am Wom

**4147. Fenollosa, Mary
(McNeill); Sidney McCall;
Mrs. Rolfs**
circa 1865–1954
poet, writer on art
Dict Am Auth; Index t Wom

4148. Newcomb, Maria Guise
born 1865
painter
Index t Wom

4149. Perkins, Lucy Fitch
1865–1937
children's author, illustrator
Nat Cyc Am Bio v33; Not Am
Wom

4150. Prellwitz, Edith Mitchell
born 1865
painter
Index t Wom

**4151. Robineau, Adelaide Beers
Alsop; Adelaide Robinson**
1865–1929
ceramicist
Index t Wom; Nat Cyc Am Bio
v36

4152. Singleton, Esther
1865–1930
author, writer on music and architecture, writer on art and
design, editor, music critic
Dict Am Auth; Dict Am Bio;
Twent Cen Bio Dict Not Am

**4153. Stevens, Augusta de
Grasse**
1865–94
novelist, art critic
Belgian
Dict Am Auth; Index t Wom

4154. Tryon, Kate
born 1865
journalist, artist, lecturer
Wom Cent

4155. Woodbury, Marcia Oakes
1865–1913
painter
Index t Wom

4156. Wright, M. Louise Wood
born 1865/75
illustrator, painter
Index t Wom

4157. Emmet, Lydia Field
1866–1952
artist, painter of children's portraits, suffragist, women's rights
worker
Episcopalian
Index t Wom; Nat Cyc Am Bio
v15, cv42, and csv6; Obit File

4158. Johnson, Helen Lossing
1866–1946
artist, children's author
Obit File

4159. Maury, Cornelia Field
born 1866
painter
Index t Wom

4160. Miner, Jean Pond
born 1866
sculptor
Illinois; Wisconsin
Wom Cent

4161. Willet, Anne Lee
1866–1943
artist, stained glass artist and designer
Index t Wom; Nat Cyc Am Bio
v34; Obit File

4162. Wilson, Melva Beatrice
1866/75–1921
sculptor
Index t Wom

**4163. Wolfe, Elsie De; Lady
Mendl**
1866–1950
actor, interior decorator
Index t Wom; Obit File

**4164. Armstrong, Margaret
Neilson**
1867–1944
author, illustrator
Index t Wom; Obit File

4165. Gill, Rosalie Lorraine
born 1867
artist, painter
Nat Cyc Am Bio v7

4166. Hart, Letitia Bennet
born 1867
painter
Index t Wom

4167. Houston, Frances C. Lyons
1867–1906
painter
Index t Wom

**4168. Humphreys, Marie
Champney**
1867–1906
painter
Index t Wom

4169. Mason, Maud M.
1867/77–1957
artist, floral painter, president of
the National Association of
Women Sculptors and Painters
Index t Wom; Obit File

4170. Rogers, Grace Rainey
1867–1943
art collector, philanthropist
Not Am Wom

4171. Beckington, Alice
born 1868
painter
Index t Wom

4172. Chase, Adelaide Cole
born 1868
painter
Index t Wom

4173. Hayden, Sophia Gregoria
1868–1953
architect
Index t Wom; Not Am Wom
supp v1

4174. Humphrey, Maud
born 1868
painter, artist
Wom Cent

4175. Lederer, Charlotte
1868–1955
children's author, illustrator
Hungarian
Obit File

4176. Mayor, Harriet Hyatt
1868–1934
sculptor
Index t Wom

4177. Thayer, Theodora Willard
1868–1905
miniature painter
Index t Wom; Nat Cyc Am Bio
v21

4178. Williams, Adele
born 1868
artist
Wom Cent

4179. Ball, Caroline Peddle
born 1869
sculptor
Index t Wom

4180. Baxter, Martha Wheeler
born 1869
sculptor, painter
Christian Scientist
Index t Wom; Nat Cyc Am Bio
csv8

**4181. Blumenschein, Mary
Shepard Greene**
born 1869
painter, illustrator, sculptor
Index t Wom

4182. Browne, Matilda
born 1869
sculptor, painter
Index t Wom

**4183. Caddy, Alice; Mrs. Ben
Lucien Burman**
1869–1977
artist, illustrator, traveler
Episcopalian
Nat Cyc Am Bio v59

4184. Evans, Anne
1869/71–1941
civil leader, patron of the arts
Colorado
Index t Wom; Not Am Wom

**4185. Fromen, Agnes Valborg
Erica**
1869–1956
sculptor
Swedish
Obit File

4186. Goldman, Emma
1869–1940
political anarchist, lecturer, publicist, agitator for free speech,
popularizer of the arts, feminist,
pioneer advocate of birth control, politician
Jewish
Russian
Dict Am Bio supp v2; Index t
Wom; Not Am Wom; Who
Who Jew Hist

4187. Goldthwaite, Anne Wilson
1869/75–1944

painter, printmaker, etcher, lithographer
Index t Wom; Nat Cyc Am Bio v39; Not Am Wom; Obit File

4188. Grimes, Frances
born 1869
sculptor
Index t Wom

4189. Joy, Josephine
born 1869
artist
Index t Wom

4190. O'Day, Caroline Love Goodwin
1869/75–1943
social welfare worker, Democratic representative to Congress from New York, New Deal supporter, artist
Episcopalian
New York
Index t Wom; Nat Cyc Am Bio csv6; Not Am Wom; Obit File

4191. Page, Marie Danforth
1869/70–1940
painter, artist
Boston, MA
Index t Wom; Nat Cyc Am Bio v29

4192. Scudder, Janet
1869/74–1940
sculptor, painter
Index t Wom; Nat Cyc Am Bio v13 and v15; Not Am Wom

4193. St. Gaudens, Annetta Johnson
born 1869
sculptor
Index t Wom

4194. Waters, Sadie P.
1869–1900
painter
Index t Wom

4195. Young, Jennie B.
born 1869
artist
Kansas
Wom Cent

4196. Bailey, Caroline A. B.
flourished 1900s
artist
Index t Wom

4197. Bonsall, Mary M.
flourished 1900s
painter
Index t Wom

4198. Bracken, Clio Hinton Huneker
1870–1925
sculptor
Index t Wom

4199. Clews, Mary Else Whelen
1870–1959
patron of art
French
Obit File

4200. Cone, Etta
1870–1949
art collector
Nat Cyc Am Bio v4; Not Am Wom

4201. Cooper, Emma Lampert
died 1920
painter
Index t Wom

4202. de Haas, Alice Preble Tucker
flourished 1900
painter
Index t Wom

4203. Fuller, Lucia Fairchild
1870/72–1924
painter, miniaturist
Index t Wom; Not Am Wom

4204. Havens, Belle
flourished 1900s
painter
Index t Wom

4205. Hekking, Avis
flourished 1900s
artist
Index t Wom

4206. Heustis, Louise Lyons
flourished 1900s
painter, illustrator
Index t Wom

4207. Hitchcock, Helen Sanborn (Sargent)
born 1870
social welfare worker, creator of social welfare programs to promote the arts
Episcopalian
Nat Cyc Am Bio v18

4208. Holt, Winifred
1870–1945
leader in work for the blind, sculptor
Dict Am Bio supp v3; Index t Wom; Not Am Wom

4209. Horne, William Henry, Mrs.
flourished 1900s–10s
artist
Index t Wom

4210. Hudson, Grace
flourished 1900s
painter
Index t Wom

4211. Hulbert, Katharine Allmond
flourished 1900s
painter, illustrator, designer
Index t Wom

4212. Jackson, May Howard
1870/77–1931
sculptor
Black
Index t Wom; Negro Alman; Prof Negro Wom v1

4213. James, Alice Archer (Sewall)
born 1870
artist, poet
Dict Am Auth; Index t Wom

4214. Kaula, Lee Lufkin
flourished 1900s
painter
Index t Wom

4215. Levy, Florence Nightingale
1870–1947
art administrator, art educator
Nat Cyc Am Bio csv2; Not Am Wom

4216. Lotz, Matilda
flourished 1900s
painter
Index t Wom

4217. MacManus Mansfield, Blanche
flourished 1900s
illustrator
Index t Wom

4218. O'Reilly, Gertrude
flourished 1900s–10s
artist
Index t Wom

4219. Perry, Clara Greenleaf
flourished 1900s
painter
Index t Wom

4220. Putnam, Sara Goold
flourished 1900s
painter
Index t Wom

4221. Richards, Anna Mary
born 1870
painter
Index t Wom

4222. Rubenstein, Helena
1870/71–1965
cosmetics manufacturer, entrepreneur, art collector, philanthropist
Jewish
Polish
Index t Wom; Nat Cyc Am Bio v50; Not Am Wom supp v1; Obit File; Who Who Jew Hist

4223. Shrimpton, Ada M.
flourished 1900s
painter
Index t Wom

4224. Stacey, Anna Lee
flourished 1900s
painter
Index t Wom

4225. Stumm, Maud
flourished 1900s
painter
Index t Wom

4226. Toro, Petronella
flourished 1900s
artist
Index t Wom

4227. van der Veer, Miss
flourished 1900s
painter
Index t Wom

4228. Ward, E.
flourished 1900s
artist, sculptor
Index t Wom

4229. Wheeler, Janet D.
flourished 1900s–30s
painter
Index t Wom

4230. Willis, Louise Hammond
born 1870
artist, illustrator, needleworker
Wom Cent

4231. Wood, Caroline S.
flourished 1900s
sculptor
Index t Wom

4232. Yandell, Enid
1870–1934
sculptor
Index t Wom

4233. Adams, Winifred Brady
born 1871
painter
Presbyterian
Indiana
Nat Cyc Am Bio csv6

4234. Baker, Martha Susan
1871–1911
miniaturist painter
Index t Wom; Nat Cyc Am Bio v15

4235. Bjerkoe, Ethel Hall
1871–1978
antiques authority and author, clubwoman
Connecticut; Maine
Nat Cyc Am Bio v60

4236. Burroughs, Edith Woodman
1871–1916
sculptor
Index t Wom

4237. Conkling, Mabel Viola Harrs
1871–1966
sculptor
Methodist
Maine
Index t Wom; Nat Cyc Am Bio v53

4238. Corbett, Gail Sherman
1871–1952
sculptor
Index t Wom; Obit File

4239. Cowles, Genevieve Almeda
born 1871
painter, stained glass decorator
Index t Wom

4240. Cowles, Maud Alice
1871–1905
painter, stained glass decorator
Index t Wom

4241. Dietz, Angel de Cora; Hinookmahiw-kilinaka; Fleecy Cloud Floating into Place
circa 1871–1919
artist
Native American (Winnebago)
Great North Am Ind

4242. Green, Elizabeth Shippen; Elizabeth Elliott
1871–1954
illustrator
Index t Wom

4243. Griffin, Marion Lucy Mahony
1871–1961?
architect, delineator
Not Am Wom supp v1

4244. Hering, Elsie Ward
1871–1923
artist
Index t Wom

4245. Kendall, Margaret Stickney
born 1871
painter
Index t Wom

4246. Kitson, Theo Alice (Ruggles)
1871–1932
sculptor
Massachusetts
Index t Wom; Wom Cent

4247. MacNeil, Carol Brooks
born 1871

artist, sculptor
Index t Wom

4248. Murphy, Martha Alice
1871–1909
modern artist
Missouri
Nat Cyc Am Bio v55

4249. Roberts, Elizabeth Wentworth
1871–1927
painter
Dict Am Bio

4250. Torrey, Lillie Gay
born 1871
artist
Episcopalian
Hawaii
Nat Cyc Am Bio csv8

4251. Welch, Mabel R.
1871–1959
painter
Index t Wom

4252. Wendt, Julia M. Bracken
1871–1942
sculptor
Index t Wom; Obit File

4253. Barnard, Elinor M.
1872–1942
artist
Index t Wom

4254. Daviess, Maria Thompson
1872–1924
painter, novelist, author
Dict Am Bio; Index t Wom

4255. Eyre, Louisa
1872–1953
sculptor
Index t Wom

4256. Farrand, Beatrix Cadwalader Jones
1872–1959
landscape architect
Dict Am Bio supp v5; Not Am Wom supp v1

4257. Hale, Louise Closser
1872–1933
actor, author
Dict Am Bio supp v1; Index t Wom

4258. Heller, Helen West
1872–1955
modernist painter, woodcut engraver, poet
Obit File

4259. Kinney, Margaret West
1872–1952
illustrator
Index t Wom

4260. Korzybska, Mina Edgerly
1872–1954
portrait painter
Obit File

4261. Mears, Helen Farnsworth
1872/76–1916
sculptor
Dict Am Bio; Index t Wom; Nat Cyc Am Bio v24; Not Am Wom

4262. Morgan, Julia
1872–1957
architect
California
Dict Am Bio supp v6; Nat Cyc Am Bio csv7; Not Am Wom supp v1

4263. Peixotto, Mary Hutchinson
married 1897
artist
Index t Wom

4264. Seton, Grace Gallatin Thompson; Dorothy Dodge
1872–1959
suffragist, feminist, explorer, geographer, author, book designer, bookmaker, composer of popular songs, historian, cofounder of the Campfire Girls
Dict Am Auth; Dict Am Bio supp v6; Index t Wom; Nat Cyc Am Bio v47 and csv5; Not Am Wom supp v1; Obit File

4265. Southworth, Ella
born 1872
artist
Index t Wom

4266. Vonnoh, Bessie Onahotema (Potter); Bessie Keyes
1872–1955
sculptor, member of the National Institute of Arts and Letters
Index t Wom; Nat Cyc Am Bio v11; Obit File

4267. Clubb, Laura Abigail Rutherford
1873–1952
art collector, rare book collector, philanthropist, cattle rancher
Methodist
Oklahoma
Nat Cyc Am Bio v38

4268. Crane, Josephine (Porter) Boardman
1873–1972
New York civic leader, patron of the arts
Episcopalian
New York
Nat Cyc Am Bio v57

4269. Harding, Charlotte
born 1873

illustrator
Index t Wom

4270. Hollister, Antoinette B.
born 1873
sculptor
Index t Wom

4271. Jewett, Maude Sherwood
born 1873
sculptor
Index t Wom; Nat Cyc Am Bio csv2

4272. Preston, Mary Wilson
1873–1949
illustrator
Not Am Wom

4273. Preston, May Wilson
1873–1949
illustrator
Index t Wom

4274. Smith, Georgine Northrop Wetherill
1873–1955
artist, art patron
Unitarian
Philadelphia, PA
Nat Cyc Am Bio v48

4275. Armer, Laura Adams
1874–1963
author, illustrator
Index t Wom

4276. Beveridge, Kuhue
married 1899
sculptor
Index t Wom

4277. Brooks, Romaine
1874–1970
artist
Not Am Wom supp v1

4278. Clement, Ethel
born 1874
painter
Index t Wom

4279. Longman, Evelyn [Mary] Beatrice; Mrs. Nathanial Horton Batchelder
1874–1954
sculptor
Index t Wom; Nat Cyc Am Bio v40, csv2, and csv5

4280. Mather, Winifred Holt
1874–1945
sculptor, patron of welfare of the blind, founder of a school for the blind, author
Episcopalian
Nat Cyc Am Bio v34 and csv6

4281. Mechlin, Leila
1874–1949

art critic, editor, and administrator
Not Am Wom

4282. Oakley, Violet
1874–1961
illustrator, designer, mural painter
Index t Wom

4283. O'Neill, Rose Cecil
1874–1944
illustrator, author, artist, creator of the Kewpie doll
Dict Am Bio supp v3; Index t Wom; Not Am Wom; Obit File

4284. Rockefeller, Abby Green Aldrich
1874/75–1948
philanthropist, art patron
New York
Dict Am Bio supp v4; Index t Wom; Nat Cyc Am Bio v45; Not Am Wom

4285. Thomas, Elizabeth Finley
1874–1955
portrait painter
Obit File

4286. Voorhees, Henriette Aimee le Prince
1874–1951
ceramicist
Nat Cyc Am Bio v39

4287. Walker, Nellie Verne
born 1874
sculptor
Index t Wom

4288. Batchelder, Evelyn Beatrice Longman
1875–1954
sculptor, first woman elected to the National Academy of Design
Obit File

4289. Bayliss, Lillian
born 1875
painter
Index t Wom

4290. Byne, Mildred Staply
1875–1941
portrait painter, authority on Spanish art and architecture
Obit File

4291. Chanler, Beatrice Ashley Winthrop; Minnie Ashley
1875–1946
actor, sculptor, author, singer
Index t Wom; Nat Cyc Am Bio v36

4292. Dale, Maud Murray Thompson
1875–1953

art collector, artist, designer of automobiles, stage designer
Dict Am Bio supp v5

4293. Lloyd, Caroline Alma
1875–1945
sculptor
Los Angeles, CA
Nat Cyc Am Bio v33

4294. Peabody, Marian Lawrence
born 1875
sculptor
Index t Wom

4295. Rand, Ellen Gertrude Emmet
1875/76–1941
portrait painter
New York
Index t Wom; Nat Cyc Am Bio v40 and csv5; Not Am Wom; Obit File

4296. Stanton, Lucy May
1875–1931
painter
Index t Wom

4297. Watkins, Susan
born 1875
painter
Index t Wom

4298. Whitney, Gertrude Vanderbilt
1875–1942
sculptor, patron of art, patron of opera, museum founder
Dict Am Bio supp v3; Index t Wom; Nat Cyc Am Bio v17, csv2, and csv5; Not Am Wom; Obit File

4299. Apfelbeck, Marie Louise Bailey
born 1876
artist
Index t Wom

4300. Beek, Alice D. Engley
born 1876
painter, author, lecturer
Index t Wom

4301. Bole, Roberta Holden
1876–1950
philanthropist; patron of art, science, and education
Unitarian
Nat Cyc Am Bio v38

4302. Coudert, Amalie Kussner
1876–1932
painter
Index t Wom

4303. Critcher, Catherine Carter
born 1876

artist
Nat Cyc Am Bio csv2

4304. Drayton, Grace (Viola) Gebbie
born 1876
cartoonist, artist
Nat Cyc Am Bio csv2

4305. Farnham, Sally James
1876–1943
sculptor
New York
Index t Wom; Nat Cyc Am Bio v37

4306. Genth, Lillian Matilde
circa 1876–1953
painter
Index t Wom; Nat Cyc Am Bio csv4; Obit File

4307. Huntington, Ann (Vaughan) Hyatt
1876–1973
sculptor, patron of the arts
Cur Biog '73; Index t Wom; Nat Cyc Am Bio v18 and 59; Not Am Wom supp v1; Obit File

4308. Kahn, Addie Wolff
1876–1949
patron of the arts
Obit File

4309. Mora, Jo
1876–1947
sculptor, author
Obit File

4310. Neal, Grace Pruden
born 1876
sculptor
Index t Wom

4311. Pattee, Elsie Dodge
born 1876
artist, illustrator
Index t Wom

4312. Sewell, Amanda Brewster
died 1926
painter
Index t Wom

4313. Sterling, Lindsay Morris
born 1876
sculptor, scientific sculptor, science illustrator
New York
Nat Cyc Am Bio csv3

4314. Stevens, Lucy Beatrice
born 1876
illustrator
Index t Wom

4315. Barrows, Alice Prentiss
1877–1954
educator, school building specialist
Dict Am Bio supp v5

4316. Church, Angelica Schuyler
1877–1954
artist, sculptor
Index t Wom

4317. Dreier, Katherine Sophie
1877–1952
patron of art, painter, early promoter of abstract and surrealist art
Dict Am Bio supp v5; Not Am Wom supp v1; Obit File

4318. Fuller, Meta Vaux Warrick
1877–1967/68
sculptor
Black
Encyc Black Am; Index t Wom; Negro Alman; Not Am Wom supp v1; Prof Negro Wom v2

4319. Magonigle, Edith Marian Day
1877–1949
painter, sculptor
Nat Cyc Am Bio v37

4320. Sahler, Helen Gertrude
1877–1950
sculptor
New York
Index t Wom; Nat Cyc Am Bio v39

4321. Sullivan, Mary Josephine Quinn
1877–1939
art teacher and collector, a founder of the New York Museum of Modern Art
Not Am Wom

4322. Ames, Blanche Ames
1878–1969
botanical illustrator, inventor, feminist, suffragist, birth control advocate
Massachusetts
Nat Cyc Am Bio v53; Not Am Wom; Obit File

4323. Bartlett, Florence Dibell
1878–1954
patron of art
Obit File

4324. Boyle, Gertrude; Gertrude Boyle Kanno; Gertrude Farquharson
1878–1937
sculptor
San Francisco, CA
Nat Cyc Am Bio v34

4325. Chess, Mary Grace; Mrs. Avery Robinson
1878–1964
perfumer, flower sculptor
New York
Nat Cyc Am Bio v52

4326. Dix, Eulabee
1878–1961
artist
Index t Wom

4327. Gardner, Helen
1878–1946
art historian, educator
Dict Am Bio supp v4; Index t Wom; Not Am Wom

4328. Guggenheim, Olga Hersh
1878–1970
philanthropist, patron of the arts
Jewish
New York
Obit File

4329. Hopkins, Edna Boise
born 1878
painter, etcher
Index t Wom

4330. Huntington, Clara
born 1878
sculptor
Index t Wom

4331. Ladd, Anna Coleman
1878–1939
sculptor
Index t Wom

4332. Liquiens, Elizabeth May Bell Kill
born 1878
painter
Nat Cyc Am Bio csv6

4333. MacLane, Jean; Mrs. John C. Johansen
1878–1964
artist, painter
Episcopalian
Index t Wom; Nat Cyc Am Bio v52

4334. Muhlhofer, Mary Elizabeth
1878–1950
painter
Episcopalian
Washington, DC
Nat Cyc Am Bio v38

4335. Neugass, Miriam Dorothy Newman; Isadora Newman
born 1878
author, artist
Jewish
Louisiana
Nat Cyc Am Bio csv3

4336. Parsons, Edith Barretto Stevens
1878–1956
sculptor
Index t Wom

4337. Raugh, Ida; Ida Eastman
1878–1970
feminist, sculptor, painter
Obit File

4338. Stevens, Edith Barretto
born 1878
sculptor
Index t Wom

4339. Stevens, Helen B.
born 1878
etcher
Index t Wom

4340. Drouet, Bessie Clarke
1879–1940
author, painter, sculptor
Index t Wom

4341. Edgerly, Mira; Countess Korzybska
born 1879
painter
Index t Wom

4342. Fiske, Gertrude Horsford
born 1879
artist
Massachusetts
Nat Cyc Am Bio csv2

4343. Hawks, Rachel Marshall
born 1879
sculptor
Index t Wom

4344. Henius, Lillian Grace (Beck)
1879–1926
artist
Pittsburgh, PA
Nat Cyc Am Bio v21

4345. Mead, Marcia
born 1879
architect
Index t Wom

4346. Parke, Jessie Burns
1879–1964
artist
Presbyterian
Nat Cyc Am Bio v50

4347. Taylor, Anna Heyward
1879–1956
artist
Episcopalian
South Carolina
Nat Cyc Am Bio v42

4348. Bernstein, Aline Frankau
1880/82–1955
stage scene and costume designer, author
Jewish
New York
Dict Am Bio supp v5; Index t Wom; Nat Cyc Am Bio v47; Not Am Wom supp v1; Obit File

4349. Bernstein, Theresa; Mrs. William Meyerowitz
flourished 1910s–60s
artist
Jewish
Index t Wom; Nat Cyc Am Bio csv11

4350. Bieber, Margarete
1880–1978
historian, author, archaeologist, educator, authority on Greek and Roman art
German
Obit File

4351. Dunlap, Hope
born 1880
illustrator
Index t Wom

4352. Frishmuth, Harriet Whitney
born 1880
art deco sculptor in brass
Index t Wom; Nat Cyc Am Bio csv2

4353. Grose, Helen Mason
born 1880
illustrator
Index t Wom

4354. Lundborg, Florence
flourished 1910s–30s
painter
Index t Wom

4355. MacRae, Emma Fordyce; Mrs. Homer F. Swift
flourished 1910s
artist
Nat Cyc Am Bio csv2

4356. Manning, Rosalie H.
flourished 1910s–20s
sculptor
Index t Wom

4357. Nitzsche, Else Koenig
1880–1952
artist, author
Unitarian
Pennsylvania
Nat Cyc Am Bio v47

4358. Perrault, I. Marie
flourished 1910s–20s
painter
Index t Wom

4359. Pope, Theodate; Mrs. John Wallace Riddle
flourished 1910s–40s
architect
Nat Cyc Am Bio v30

4360. Roulet, Mary F. Nixon
flourished 1910s
author, journalist, musician, art critic, linguist
Index t Wom

4361. Sage, Cornelia B.
born 1880
art museum director
Nat Cyc Am Bio csv1

4362. Schweppe, Laura Shedd
1880–1937
philanthropist, art patron
Chicago, IL
Nat Cyc Am Bio v50

4363. Tee-Van, Helen Damrosch
flourished 1910s–30s
artist, illustrator
Index t Wom

4364. Venturine, Mario, Countess
flourished 1910s
artist
Index t Wom

4365. Washington, Elizabeth Fisher
flourished 1910s–20s
artist
Nat Cyc Am Bio csv2

4366. Wilde, Jennie
flourished 1910s
artist
Index t Wom

4367. Wood, Ruby Ross
flourished 1910s–20s
decorator
Index t Wom

4368. Cook, Mary Elizabeth
born 1881
sculptor
Index t Wom

4369. Hale, Lilian Westcott
born 1881
artist
Index t Wom

4370. Martinez, Maria Montoya
born 1881/87
ceramicist
New Mexico
Native American (Pueblo-San Ildefonso)
Ind Today; Read Encyc Am West

4371. Myers, Mary Ethel Klinck
1881–1960
sculptor
New York
Nat Cyc Am Bio v45

4372. Spreckels, Alma Emma Charlotte Corday le Normand de Bretteville
1881–1968
patron of art
San Francisco, CA
Obit File

4373. Wright, Alice Morgan
born 1881
sculptor
Index t Wom

4374. Bostelmann, Else W. von Roder
circa 1882–1961
illustrator
German
Index t Wom

4375. Clayburgh, Alma
1882–1958
concert singer, patron of art, philanthropist
Obit File

4376. Green, Florence Topping
circa 1882–1945
painter, portraitist
English
Index t Wom; Obit File

4377. Grosse, Juliet Mary White
born 1882
artist
Nat Cyc Am Bio csv2

4378. Johnson, Grace Mott
born 1882
sculptor
Index t Wom

4379. Richards, Myra Reynolds
born 1882
sculptor
Index t Wom

4380. Barney, Nora Stanton Blatch
1883–1971
civil engineer, architect, suffragist
Not Am Wom supp v1

4381. Bercovici, Naomi Lebrescu
1883–1957
artist, poet
New York
French
Nat Cyc Am Bio v45

4382. Cane, Florence Naumburg
1883–1952
artist, educator, author
Obit File

4383. Daggett, Maud
born 1883
sculptor
Index t Wom

4384. Khoury, Marie Azeez El
1883–1957
jewelry designer
Lebanese
Obit File

4385. Lamson, Armene Tashijian
1883–1970
medical illustrator, physician, UNICEF worker, medical author
Episcopalian
Seattle, WA
Turkish
Nat Cyc Am Bio v56

4386. Redfield, Heloise Guillou
born 1883
painter
Index t Wom

4387. Rorke, Margaret Hayden
1883–1967
color standards expert, suffragist
Catholic
Nat Cyc Am Bio v54

4388. Stauffer, Edna Pennypacker
1883–1956
painter, lithographer, art educator
Obit File

4389. Verner, Elizabeth O'Neill
born 1883
etcher, painter
Episcopalian
South Carolina
Nat Cyc Am Bio csv12

4390. Brown, Margaret Fitzhugh
1884–1972
artist
Episcopalian
Massachusetts
Nat Cyc Am Bio v57

4391. Bulfinch, Ellen Susan
born 1884
artist
Massachusetts
Dict Am Auth

4392. Miller, Evylena Nunn
born 1884
artist
Presbyterian
California
Nat Cyc Am Bio csv6

4393. Peck, Anne Marriman
born 1884
illustrator, author
Index t Wom

4394. Raulston, Marion Churchill
born 1884
painter
California
Nat Cyc Am Bio csv7

4395. Ames, Elizabeth
1885–1977
executive director of Yaddo, an artists retreat
Saratoga Springs, NY
Obit File

4396. Coxe-McCormack, Nancy
born 1885
sculptor
Index t Wom

4397. Donaldson, Alice Willits
circa 1885–1961
artist
Index t Wom

4398. Hoffman, Malvina Cornell
1885/87–1966
sculptor
New York
Index t Wom; Nat Cyc Am Bio v55 and csv6; Not Am Wom supp v1; Obit File

4399. Hutchinson, Mary Amory Hare; Amory Hare
1885–1969
author, novelist, dramatist, painter, poet, thoroughbred-horse breeder
Episcopalian
California
Nat Cyc Am Bio v57, Index t Wom

4400. Kirmse, Marguerite
1885–1954
illustrator, etcher
English
Index t Wom

4401. Lawson, Katherine Stewart
born 1885
sculptor
Index t Wom

4402. Stetson, Katherine Beecher
born 1885
sculptor
Index t Wom

4403. Brinkley, Nell [Ethel]; Mrs. Bruce Moir McRae
1886/88–1944
newspaper artist, cartoonist, illustrator, journalist
Presbyterian
Index t Wom; Nat Cyc Am Bio v33; Obit File

4404. Brock, Emma Lillian
born 1886
author, illustrator
Index t Wom

4405. Gafford, Alice
born 1886
painter
Black
Negro Alman

4406. Ryerson, Margery Austen
born 1886
etcher, painter
Index t Wom

4407. Totten, Vichen von P.
born 1886
sculptor
Swedish
Index t Wom

4408. Bache, Florence Julia
born 1887
artist
Index t Wom

4409. Barney, Maginal Wright
born 1887
illustrator
Index t Wom

4410. Carter, Helene
1887–1961
illustrator
Canadian
Index t Wom

4411. Fenton, Beatrice
born 1887
sculptor
Pennsylvania
Index t Wom; Nat Cyc Am Bio csv6

4412. Hubbard, Theodora Kimball
1887–1935
landscape architect, city planner
Unitarian
Massachusetts
Nat Cyc Am Bio v28 and csv3

4413. O'Keeffe, Georgia
born 1887
painter
Index t Wom

4414. Post, Marjorie Merriweather
1887–1973
philanthropist, antique collector, suffragist, director of National Savings and Trust, founder and director of General Foods
Christian Scientist
Washington, DC
Nat Cyc Am Bio v58; Not Am Wom supp v1; Obit File

4415. Sabin, Pauline Morton; Mrs. Charles
1887–1955
Prohibition repeal leader, Republican party official, interior decorator
Index t Wom; Not Am Wom supp v1

4416. Waring, Laura Wheeler
1887–1948
painter, educator

Black
Encyc Black Am; Negro Alman

4417. Jemne, Elsa Laubach
born 1888
painter
Index t Wom

**4418. McMein, Neysa; Mrs.
John Gordon Baragwanath**
1888/90–1949
illustrator, magazine illustrator,
painter, portraitist, commercial
artist, author
Episcopalian
Index t Wom; Nat Cyc Am Bio
v36; Not Am Wom; Obit File

**4419. Parrish, Anne (Titzell);
Mrs. Charles A. Corliss**
1888–1957
illustrator, novelist, children's author
Index t Wom; Nat Cyc Am Bio
csv4; Obit File

4420. Petersham, Miska
1888–1960
illustrator
Hungarian
Index t Wom

4421. Price, Margaret Evans
born 1888
illustrator
Index t Wom

4422. Pyle, Katherine
died 1938
author, illustrator
Index t Wom

4423. Steere, Lora Woodhead
born 1888
sculptor
Christian Scientist
Los Angeles, CA
Nat Cyc Am Bio csv7

**4424. Wawa Calac Chaw; Keep
from the Water**
1888–1972
author, artist, feminist, lecturer
on Native American and feminist matters
Native American (Luiseno)
Great North Am Ind

4425. Bancroft, Hester
born 1889
sculptor
Index t Wom

4426. Barnhart, Nancy
born 1889
illustrator
Index t Wom

4427. Callender, Bessie Stough
1889–1951
sculptor, mountain climber

Presbyterian
Nat Cyc Am Bio v38

4428. Cresson, Margaret
born 1889
sculptor
Index t Wom

4429. Davis, Marguerite
born 1889
illustrator
Index t Wom

4430. de Angeli, Marguerite
born 1889
illustrator, author
Index t Wom

**4431. Draper, Dorothy Tucker-
man**
1889–1969
interior decorator, inventor,
newspaper columnist
Cur Biog '69; Index t Wom; Obit
File

4432. Fraser, Laura Gardin
born 1889
sculptor
Index t Wom; Nat Cyc Am Bio
csv3

**4433. Hayward, Mildred Mar-
shal**
1889–1967
artist, Moral Rearmament worker
Nat Cyc Am Bio v53

4434. Hodge, Lydia Herrick
born 1889
sculptor
Index t Wom

**4435. Neese, Laura Janvrin Al-
drich**
1889–1967
artist, philanthropist
Congregationalist
Wisconsin
Nat Cyc Am Bio v53

4436. Petersham, Maud Fuller
born 1889
illustrator
Index t Wom

4437. Preston, Alice Bolam
born 1889
illustrator
Index t Wom

4438. Putnam, Brenda
born 1889/90
sculptor
Index t Wom; Nat Cyc Am Bio
csv2 and csv5

4439. Ryan, Anne
1889–1954

abstract artist specializing in
cloth and paper compositions,
author, poet
Not Am Wom supp v1; Obit File

4440. Shaw, Lois Kenyon
1889–1958
founder of Portraits, Inc.,
painters' and sculptors' agents
Obit File

4441. Sherwood, Ruth
born 1889
sculptor
Index t Wom

**4442. Abee, Grace Arnold
(Thurston)**
born 1890
artist
Congregationalist
Rhode Island
Nat Cyc Am Bio csvll

4443. Allen, Louise
flourished 1920s
sculptor
Index t Wom

4444. Ball, Ruth Norton
flourished 1920s
sculptor
Index t Wom

4445. Bartlett, Madeleine A.
flourished 1920s
sculptor
Index t Wom

4446. Bromhall, Winifred
flourished 1920s–40s
illustrator
English
Index t Wom

4447. Brown, Agnes
flourished 1920s
painter
Index t Wom

**4448. Burr, Frances; Mrs. John
Reynolds**
1890–post 1930s
artist, mountaineer, suffragist
Index t Wom; Nat Cyc Am Bio
csv12

4449. Coles, Izabel M.
flourished 1920s–30s
jewelry designer
Index t Wom

**4450. Devereux, Margaret
Green**
flourished 1920s–30s
interior decorator, editor
Index t Wom

4451. Eyre, Elizabeth
flourished 1920s
painter
Index t Wom

4452. Graham, Cecelia B.
flourished 1920s
sculptor
Index t Wom

4453. Grant, Blanche C.
flourished 1920s
artist, author
Index t Wom

4454. Greenwood, Gertrude B.
flourished 1920s
sculptor
Index t Wom

4455. Hader, Berta Hoerner
flourished 1920s–40s
illustrator
Index t Wom

**4456. Johnston, Edith Con-
stance Farrington**
born 1890
painter, illustrator
Index t Wom

4457. Kohn, Estelle Rumbold
flourished 1920s
sculptor
Index t Wom

4458. McLean, Jean
flourished 1920s
painter
Index t Wom

4459. Miles, Emily Winthrop
flourished 1920s
sculptor
Index t Wom

4460. Moore, Mary E.
flourished 1920s
sculptor
Index t Wom

**4461. Mulroney, Regina Win-
ifred**
flourished 1920s
sculptor
Index t Wom

4462. Norton, Clara
flourished 1920s–60s
artist
Index t Wom

4463. Peabody, Amelia
born 1890
sculptor
Index t Wom

4464. Postgate, Margaret J.
flourished 1920s
sculptor
Index t Wom

4465. Rebay, Hilla
1890–1967
museum director, painter
Not Am Wom supp v1

4466. Schille, Alice
flourished 1920s
painter
Index t Wom

4467. Shinn, Florence Scovel
died 1940
illustrator, lecturer, metaphysicist
Index t Wom

4468. Sims, Dorothy Rice
1890–1960
bridge expert, sculptor, poet
Obit File

4469. Southwick, Elsie Whitmore
flourished 1920s
painter
Index t Wom

4470. Stagg, Jessie A.
flourished 1920s
sculptor
Index t Wom

4471. Stillman, Sarah S.
flourished 1920s
illustrator
Index t Wom

4472. Walter, Valerie Harrisse
flourished 1920s
sculptor
Nat Cyc Am Bio csv3

4473. Zilve, Alida
flourished 1920s
sculptor
Dutch
Index t Wom

4474. Ford, Lauren
born 1891
painter
Index t Wom

4475. Grooms, Jessie Macy Roberts
1891–1955
artist, art educator
Ohio
Nat Cyc Am Bio v46

4476. Lathrop, Dorothy Pulis
born 1891
illustrator, author
Index t Wom

4477. Park, Madeleine Fish
1891–1960
animal sculptor
Obit File

4478. Price, Hattie Longstreet
born 1891
illustrator
Index t Wom

4479. Robinson, Irene Bowen
born 1891

painter
Index t Wom

4480. Warner, Nell Walker; Mrs. Emil Shostrum
born 1891
artist
Unitarian
Los Angeles, CA
Nat Cyc Am Bio csv8

4481. Barnes, Djuna
born 1892
novelist, short story writer, poet, playwright, theatrical columnist, illustrator, portrait painter
French (American expatriate to Paris)
Dict Lit Bio v4 and v9; Wom Lit; Wom Lit, More

4482. Best, Allena Champlin; Anne M. Erick-Berry
born 1892
illustrator, author
Index t Wom

4483. Crosby, Caresse; Polly Jacob
1892–1970
poet, patron of the arts, cofounder of the Black Sun Press
French (American expatriate to Paris)
Dict Lit Bio v4

4484. Field, Mary Hickson Matthews
married 1917
artist, philanthropist
Nat Cyc Am Bio v23

4485. Godwin, Frances Bryant
born 1892
sculptor
Index t Wom

4486. Keast, Susette Schultz
1892–1932
artist
Pennsylvania
Nat Cyc Am Bio v25

4487. MacLeary, Bonnie
born 1892
sculptor
Index t Wom

4488. Ochtman, Dorothy; Mrs. William A. del Mar
1892–1971
artist
Congregationalist
Connecticut
Nat Cyc Am Bio v56

4489. Savage, Augusta Christine
1892/1900–1962
sculptor

Black
Encyc Black Am; Index t Wom; Negro Alman; Not Am Wom supp v1

4490. Webb, Aileen Osborn
1892–1949
craft artist
Cur Biog '79; Index t Wom

4491. Chalmers, Audrey
1893/99–1957
illustrator, author
Canadian
Index t Wom

4492. Corte, Fausta Vitorio Mengarini
1893–1952
sculptor
Italian
Obit File

4493. Freeman, Margaret
born 1893
illustrator
Index t Wom

4494. Gag, Wanda [Hazel]
1893–1946
illustrator, painter, children's author
Dict Am Bio supp v4; Index t Wom; Not Am Wom; Obit File

4495. Hokinson, Helen Elna
1893–1949
cartoonist, artist
Christian Scientist
Dict Nat Bio supp v4; Index t Wom; Nat Cyc Am Bio v41; Not Am Wom

4496. Lenski, Lois
born 1893
illustrator, author
Index t Wom

4497. Paeff, Bashka
born 1893
sculptor
Russian
Index t Wom

4498. van Vleck, Natalie Dalton Johnson
1893–1950
portrait painter
Nat Cyc Am Bio v39

4499. Allen, Margaret Newton
born 1894/95
sculptor
Index t Wom

4500. Harbeson, Georgiana Brown
born 1894
industrial artist, designer
Index t Wom

4501. Jackson, Hazel Brill
born 1894
sculptor
Index t Wom

4502. King, Marion P.
born 1894
sculptor
Index t Wom

4503. Mellon, Eleanor M.
born 1894
sculptor
Index t Wom

4504. Milhous, Katherine
born 1894
illustrator
Index t Wom

4505. Phillips, Marjorie Acker
born 1894
artist
Nat Cyc Am Bio csv2

4506. Alexander, Beatrice
born 1895
doll maker
Index t Wom

4507. Bacon, Peggy
born 1895
artist, author
Index t Wom

4508. Barlow, Dorothy Hope Smith
1895–1955
portrait painter
Obit File

4509. Chapin, Helen B.
1895–1950
expert on Far Eastern art and iconography
Obit File

4510. Eastman, Eliena Krylenko
1895–1956
painter
Polish
Obit File

4511. Emerson, Sybil
born 1895
illustrator, painter, educator
Index t Wom

4512. Ets, Marie Hall
born 1895
illustrator, author
Index t Wom

4513. Evatt, Harriet Torrey
born 1895
author, illustrator
Index t Wom

4514. Garner, Elvira Carter
born 1895

illustrator, author
Index t Wom

4515. Laughlin, Alice Denniston
1895–1952
stained glass artist, medieval art expert, wood engraver
Nat Cyc Am Bio v42; Obit File

4516. Lewisohn, Margaret Seligman
1895–1954
educator, art patron, clubwoman
New York
Index t Wom; Nat Cyc Am Bio v44

4517. Thorne, Diana
born 1895
painter
Canadian
Index t Wom

4518. Varian, Dorothy
born 1895
artist
Index t Wom

4519. Dole, Margaret Fernald
1896–1970
portrait painter
Episcopalian
New York
Nat Cyc Am Bio v56

4520. Eberle, Abastenia [Mary] St. Leger
1896–1942
sculptor
Index t Wom; Not Am Wom

4521. Flack, Marjorie
1896–1958
illustrator, children's author
Index t Wom; Obit File

4522. Hamlin, Genevieve Karr
born 1896
sculptor
Index t Wom

4523. Latham, Barbara
born 1896
illustrator, painter
Index t Wom

4524. Lathrop, Gertrude K.
born 1896
sculptor
Index t Wom

4525. Predmore, Jessie
born 1896
artist
Index t Wom

4526. Sewell, Helen Moore
1896–1957
illustrator
Index t Wom

4527. Crosby, Katherine van Rensellaer
born 1897
sculptor
Index t Wom

4528. Davenport, Jane
born 1897
sculptor
Index t Wom

4529. George, Lucy Squirrel
born 1897
basket weaver
Native American (Cherokee)
Ind Today

4530. Liebes, Dorothy Katharine (Wright)
1897/99–1972
textile designer, businessperson, weaver
Cur Biog '72; Index t Wom; Not Am Wom supp v1

4531. Peddle, Juliet
graduated 1922
architect
Index t Wom

4532. Thompson, Helen Victoria Veale
born 1897
artist
Christian Scientist
Detroit, MI
Nat Cyc Am Bio csv9

4533. Brandt, Mary Largent
1898–1962
interior decorator
Nat Cyc Am Bio v45

4534. Guggenheim, Marguerite "Peggy"
born 1898
patron of modern art and music, art collector, author
Jewish
New York
Cur Biog '80; Index t Wom; Who Who Jew Hist

4535. Hare, Jeannette R.
born 1898
sculptor
Belgian
Index t Wom

4536. Keeney, Ana
born 1898
sculptor
Index t Wom

4537. Kent, Rachel Fitch
born 1898
educator
Index t Wom

4538. Maxwell, Coralie Delong
born 1898

sculptor
Index t Wom

4539. Paull, Grace A.
born 1898
illustrator
Index t Wom

4540. Pointer, Augusta L.
born 1898
sculptor
Index t Wom

4541. Tauch, Waldine
born 1898
sculptor
Methodist
Texas
Index t Wom; Nat Cyc Am Bio csv12

4542. Wolle, Muriel Sibell
1898–1977
artist, art educator, Native American art scholar and collector, western history writer, conservationist
Episcopalian
Boulder, CO
Nat Cyc Am Bio v60

4543. Woodward, Hildegard
born 1898
illustrator
Index t Wom

4544. Bachrach, Elise Wald
1899–1940
artist
Index t Wom

4545. Carroll, Ruth Robinson
born 1899
illustrator, author
Index t Wom

4546. Lane, Katherine Ward
born 1899
sculptor
Index t Wom

4547. Ostman, Lempi
born 1899
illustrator
Index t Wom

4548. Ripley, Lucy Fairfield Perkins
died 1949
sculptor, painter
Index t Wom

4549. Sardeau, Helen; Mrs. George Biddle
1899–1969
sculptor
New York
Belgian
Nat Cyc Am Bio v55

4550. Ulreich, Nura Woodson; Nura
1899–1950
illustrator
Index t Wom

4551. Axley, Martha Frances
flourished 1930s
artist
Index t Wom

4552. Aylward, Ida
flourished 1930s
author, painter
Index t Wom

4553. Bailey, Florence
flourished 1930s
advertising executive, jewelry designer
Index t Wom

4554. Bradley, Ora Lewis
flourished 1930s
educator, artist, author
Index t Wom

4555. Brannan, Sophie Marston
flourished 1930s
artist
Index t Wom

4556. Briggs, Berta N.
flourished 1930s
artist
Index t Wom

4557. Brown, Eleanor Stockstrom
flourished 1930s
interior decorator, business executive
Index t Wom

4558. Byard, Dorothy Randolph
flourished 1930s
artist, poet
Index t Wom

4559. Campbell, Helena E. Ogden
flourished 1930s
painter
Index t Wom

4560. Chapin, Cornelia van A.
flourished 1930s
sculptor
Index t Wom

4561. Coit, Elizabeth
flourished 1930s
architectural executive
Index t Wom

4562. Cook, Nancy
flourished 1930s
politician, designer
Index t Wom

4563. Cooper, Alice
flourished 1930s

sculptor
Index t Wom

4564. Cumming, Rose Stuart
flourished 1930s
business executive, interior decorator
Index t Wom

4565. Daggett, Helen M.
flourished 1930s
interior decorator, editor
Index t Wom

4566. Dalmas, Priscilla
flourished 1930s
architect
Index t Wom

4567. Dike, Victoria
flourished 1930s
musical and art director
Index t Wom

4568. Dodd, Carolyn G.
flourished 1930s
interior decorator, employment
agency executive
Index t Wom

4569. Donner, Vyvyan
flourished 1930s
journalist, fashion designer, artist
Index t Wom

4570. du Pre, Grace Annette
flourished 1930s–60s
painter, violinist, tennis player
South Carolina
Nat Cyc Am Bio csv11

4571. Dubois, Yvonne Pene
flourished 1930s
sculptor
Index t Wom

4572. Dwight, Mary Elizabeth
flourished 1930s
artist, clubwoman
Index t Wom

4573. Eliasoph, Paula
flourished 1930s
artist
Index t Wom

4574. Fairman, Agnes Rowe
flourished 1930s
interior decorator
Index t Wom

**4575. Fetherstone, Edith
Hedges**
flourished 1930s
artist
Index t Wom

4576. Ford, Irene de Pendall
flourished 1930s
artist
Index t Wom

4577. Frick, Helen Clay
flourished 1930s
art expert
Index t Wom

4578. Genauer, Emily
flourished 1930s
journalist, art critic, editor
Index t Wom

4579. Goodbar, Octavia Walton
flourished 1930s
artist, journalist
Index t Wom

4580. Hall, Marian Wells
flourished 1930s
interior decorator
Index t Wom

4581. Halpert, Edith Gregor
1900?–70
art dealer and collector
Russian
Cur Biog '70; Index t Wom; Not
Am Wom supp v1

4582. Hamill, Virginia
flourished 1930s
interior decorator
Index t Wom

4583. Harris, Jane Davenport
flourished 1930s
sculptor, explorer
French
Index t Wom

4584. Hobdy, Ann F.
flourished 1930s
needlework designer
Index t Wom

4585. Hogan, Inez
born 1900
illustrator
Index t Wom

4586. Holley, Bertha Delbert
flourished 1930s
fashion designer, artist
Index t Wom

4587. Hoyt, Peggy
flourished 1930s
designer
Index t Wom

4588. Jacobs, Leonebel
flourished 1930s
painter
Index t Wom

4589. Janowszky, Bela
born 1900
sculptor
Hungarian
Index t Wom

4590. Jones, Helen Swift
flourished 1930s

landscape architect
Index t Wom

4591. Lewis, Ethel
flourished 1930s
interior decorator
Index t Wom

4592. Liedloff, Helen
flourished 1930s
sculptor
Index t Wom

4593. Logan, Charlotte
flourished 1930s
commercial artist, fashion designer, inventor
Index t Wom

4594. Marohn, Irma Elaine
flourished 1930s
artist
Index t Wom

4595. Marsh, Alice Randall
flourished 1930s
painter
Index t Wom

4596. Mason, Clara
flourished 1930s
industrial artist
Index t Wom

**4597. McCullough, Esther
Morgan**
flourished 1930s
artist, author
Index t Wom

4598. Mendelsohn, Celia
flourished 1930s
artist, business executive
Index t Wom

4599. Miller, Gladys
flourished 1930s
interior decorator, retail executive
Index t Wom

4600. Miyakawa, Kikuko
flourished 1930s
poet, artist
Japanese
Index t Wom

4601. Neal, Alice (Hartley)
born 1900
painter, portraitist
Cur Biog '76

4602. Nedwill, Rose
flourished 1930s
artist
Index t Wom

4603. Nevelson, Louise
born 1900
sculptor
Russian
Index t Wom

4604. Newby, Ruby Warren
flourished 1930s
artist, educator
Index t Wom

4605. Newman, Henriette
flourished 1930s
business executive, antique dealer
Index t Wom

4606. Newman, Isadora
flourished 1930s
artist, author, sculptor
Index t Wom

4607. Niswonger, Ilse W.
born 1900
sculptor
German
Index t Wom

4608. O'Connor, Mary
1900–64
poet, artist
Obit File

4609. Oehler, Bernice Olivia
flourished 1930s
artist
Index t Wom

4610. Otis, Amy
flourished 1930s
painter
Index t Wom

4611. Paddock, Josephine
flourished 1930s
artist
Index t Wom

4612. Paxton, Ethel
flourished 1930s
artist, educator, lecturer, author
Index t Wom

4613. Peterson, Jane
flourished 1930s
painter
Index t Wom

4614. Robertson, Lucille
flourished 1930s
artist
Index t Wom

4615. Robinson, Maude
flourished 1930s
ceramic artist
Index t Wom

4616. Salomonsky, Verna Cook
flourished 1930s
architect
Index t Wom

4617. Sawyers, Martha
flourished 1930s–40s
illustrator
Index t Wom

4618. Scaravaglione, Concetta Maria
1900–75
sculptor
New York
Nat Cyc Am Bio v59

4619. Schorr, Esther Brann
flourished 1930s
artist, author
Index t Wom

4620. Schwartz, Margaret
born 1900
sculptor
Index t Wom

4621. Sherman, Florence A.
flourished 1930s
fashion designer, doll designer
Index t Wom

4622. Sullivan, Marie
flourished 1930s
aviation inspector, decorator
Index t Wom

4623. Thomas, Clara Fargo
flourished 1930s
painter
Index t Wom

4624. Thorward, Clara Schafer
flourished 1930s
artist
Index t Wom

4625. Tjaden, Olive F.
flourished 1930s
architect
Index t Wom

4626. Walter, Martha
flourished 1930s
painter
Index t Wom

4627. Wamsley, Lillian Barlow
flourished 1930s
artist, ceramicist
Index t Wom

4628. Waugh, Dorothy
flourished 1930s–40s
illustrator, author
Quaker
Index t Wom

4629. Bruce, Ailsa Mellon
1901–69
philanthropist, patron of art, conservationist
Episcopalian
New York
Nat Cyc Am Bio v55; Obit File

4630. Buchanan, Ella
died 1951
sculptor
Index t Wom

4631. Davis, Gladys Rockmore
born 1901
artist
Index t Wom

4632. Eliot, Frances
born 1901
illustrator
Index t Wom

4633. Mullen, Frances Vedder Buell
born 1901
artist
Chicago, IL
Nat Cyc Am Bio csv10

4634. Talbot, Grace Helen
born 1901
sculptor
Index t Wom

4635. Bishop, Isabel
born 1902
painter, etcher
Cur Biog '77

4636. Brall, Ruth Hirsch
1902–57
portrait sculptor
Obit File

4637. Cochran, Dewees
born 1902
artist, doll maker
Index t Wom

4638. Credle, Ellis
born 1902
illustrator
Index t Wom

4639. Derrick-Swindells, Lucy
died 1952
poet, portrait painter
English
Obit File

4640. Hardy, Kay
born 1902
artist, lecturer, educator
Index t Wom

4641. Koussevitzky, Olga
1902–78
patron of the arts
Obit File

4642. Parnell, Eileen
born 1902
sculptor
Irish
Index t Wom

4643. Pleydel-Bouverie, Ava Alice Muriel Astor
1902–56
patron of art, patron of ballet
Obit File

4644. Atkin, Mildred Tommy; Mrs. Fisher Winston
1903–69
artist
Jewish
New York
Nat Cyc Am Bio v53 and csv9

4645. Beer, Lisle; Eloise Crowell Smith
born 1903
artist, author, puppeteer
Unitarian
Nat Cyc Am Bio csv9

4646. Bischoff, Ilse Marthe
born 1903
illustrator
Index t Wom

4647. Brackenridge, Marian
born 1903
sculptor
Index t Wom

4648. Callery, Mary
1903–77
sculptor, ambulance driver in France during World War II
Index t Wom; Nat Cyc Am Bio v60 and csv9

4649. Gregory, Angela
born 1903
sculptor
Index t Wom

4650. Kayne, Hilde
born 1903
artist
Austrian
Index t Wom

4651. Lewis, Flora
born 1903
painter
Index t Wom

4652. Newberry, Clare Turlay
born 1903
illustrator
Index t Wom

4653. Payson, Joan Whitney
1903–75
philanthropist, race horse breeder, owner of the New York Mets, patron of medicine, art collector and investor, founder of the Museum of Modern Art in New York
Episcopalian
New York
Cur Biog '72 and '75; Index t Wom; Nat Cyc Am Bio v58 and csv10; Obit File

4654. Pyne, Mable Mandeville
born 1903
illustrator
Index t Wom

4655. Barber, Muriel Virginia (Kozlay)
1904–71
artist
Presbyterian
New Jersey
Nat Cyc Am Bio v57

4656. Bourgeois, Florence
born 1904
illustrator
Index t Wom

4657. Greene, Gertrude Glass
1904–56
sculptor, abstract painter
New York
Nat Cyc Am Bio v47; Obit File

4658. Honeywell, Annette
born 1904
commercial artist, designer
Index t Wom

4659. Lattimore, Eleanor Frances
born 1904
illustrator
Index t Wom

4660. Miner, Dorothy Eugenia
1904–73
museum curator, librarian, art historian
Not Am Wom supp v1

4661. Stone, Helen
born 1904
illustrator
Index t Wom

4662. Webber, Irma Eleanor Schmidt
born 1904
illustrator
Index t Wom

4663. Wilkin, Eloise Burns
born 1904
illustrator
Index t Wom

4664. Chase, Theodora Larsh
died 1955
portrait painter
Obit File

4665. Darnault, Florence Malcolm
born 1905
sculptor
Episcopalian
Nat Cyc Am Bio

4666. Hammond, Natalie Hays
born 1905
artist, costume designer, stained glass and jewelry designer
Nat Cyc Am Bio csv4

4667. Jackson, Beatrice; Mrs. David Humphreys
born 1905
artist
Episcopalian
New York
English
Nat Cyc Am Bio csv13

4668. Jones, Lois Mailore
born 1905
painter, art educator
Black
Index t Wom; Negro Alman

4669. Lee, Doris Emrick
born 1905
artist
Index t Wom

4670. Ruellan, Andree
born 1905
artist
Index t Wom

4671. Soper, Eileen A.
born 1905
illustrator
Index t Wom

4672. Dalacea Kasudluk
born 1906
sculptor
Port Harrison, AK
Inuit
Esk Art

4673. Doane, Peagie
born 1906
illustrator
Index t Wom

4674. Fosburgh, Mary Cushing
1906–78
patron of the arts
Obit File

4675. Gay, Zhenya
born 1906
illustrator
Index t Wom

4676. Jackson, Martha Kellogg
1906–69
art dealer
Nat Cyc Am Bio v55

4677. MacKay, Frances I.
born 1906
sculptor
Index t Wom

4678. MacKinstry, Elizabeth
died 1956
illustrator, sculptor, violinist
Index t Wom

4679. Messick, Dale
born circa 1906
cartoonist
Index t Wom

4680. Ripley, Elizabeth Blake
born 1906
author, illustrator
Index t Wom

4681. Slocum, Rosalie
born 1906
illustrator
Index t Wom

4682. West, Berenice Delemar; Berenice Delemar Beyers
born 1906
sculptor
Nat Cyc Am Bio csv7

4683. Enters, Angna
born 1907
dancer, painter, author
Index t Wom

4684. Gag, Flavia
born 1907
illustrator
Index t Wom

4685. Hofmann, Melita Cecelia
1907–76
artist, art educator, book illustrator and designer, author, conservationist
Congregationalist
New York
Nat Cyc Am Bio v60

4686. Pereira, Irene Rice
1907–71
abstract painter
Index t Wom; Not Am Wom supp v1; Cur Biog '71

4687. Sartain, Harriet
died 1957
artist, dean of Moore Institute of Art, Science and Industry, educator
Philadelphia, PA
Index t Wom; Obit File

4688. Chastain, Madye Lee
born 1908
author, illustrator
Index t Wom

4689. Knapp, Hazel
born 1908
artist
Index t Wom

4690. Krasner, Lenore "Lee"
born 1908
abstract expressionist painter
Jewish
Cur Biog '74

4691. Perkins, Marion Marche
1908–61
sculptor
Black
Encyc Black Am

4692. Thompson, Helen Muford
1908–74
orchestra manager, executive of the American Symphony Orchestra League
Not Am Wom supp v1

4693. Brooks, Ruth Walker; Mrs. Kenneth L. Hoffman
born 1909
sculptor
New York
Nat Cyc Am Bio csv5

4694. Burton, Virginia Lee
1909–68
author, illustrator
Index t Wom

4695. Cushing, Lily (Dulany)
1909–69
artist, traveler
Nat Cyc Am Bio v60

4696. Enright, Elizabeth
born 1909/10
illustrator, author
Index t Wom

4697. Greenwood, Marion
born 1909
artist
Index t Wom

4698. MacIver, Loren Newman
born 1909
painter
Index t Wom

4699. Rhonie, Aline
born 1909
painter, aviator
Index t Wom

4700. Stern, Mary Simchow; Masha
born 1909
illustrator
Index t Wom

4701. Cowles, Fleur Fenton
born 1910
painter, editor, author, businessperson
Index t Wom

4702. Guion, Molly
born 1910
artist
Episcopalian
Nat Cyc Am Bio csv9

4703. Heyneman, Anne
born 1910
illustrator
Index t Wom

4704. Jones, Elizabeth Orton
born 1910
illustrator
Index t Wom

4705. Kahane, Melanie
born 1910
interior decorator, industrial engineer
Index t Wom

4706. Menard, Nellie Star Boy
born 1910
craft artist, featherworker
Native American (Dakota-Brule)
Ind Today

4707. Rosenthal, Doris
flourished 1940s
artist
Index t Wom

4708. Weil, Lisl
born 1910
artist, author
Austrian
Index t Wom

4709. Turnbull, Ruth
born 1912
sculptor
Index t Wom

4710. Bannon, Laura
died 1963
illustrator, author
Index t Wom

4711. Harmon, Lily
born 1913
artist
Index t Wom

4712. Preminger, Marion Hill; Mrs. Albert Mayer
1913–72
social worker, author, African art collector, missionary to the Congo, philanthropist, screen actor
Catholic
New York
Hungarian
Nat Cyc Am Bio v57; Obit File

4713. Vaughan, Anne
born 1913
illustrator
Index t Wom

4714. Webel, Janet Darling
1913–66
landscape architect
Nat Cyc Am Bio v54

4715. Culver, Agnes Moe
1914–75
illustration dealer, historian
Congregationalist
New York
Nat Cyc Am Bio v58 and v59

4716. Saarinen, Aline Milton Bernstein (Louchheim)
1914–72

art critic, television commentator,
writer on art history
Cur Biog '72; Index t Wom; Not
Am Wom supp v1

4717. Waggoner, Electra
born 1914
sculptor
Texas
Index t Wom; Nat Cyc Am Bio
csv6

4718. Catlett, Elizabeth
born 1915
sculptor, painter
Black
Encyc Black Am

4719. Tudor, Tasha
born 1915
illustrator
Index t Wom

4720. Sterne, Hedda
born 1916
artist
Rumanian
Index t Wom

4721. White, Nancy
born 1916
editor, fashion designer
Index t Wom

4722. Burroughs, Margaret
born 1917
painter, sculptor
Black
Negro Alman

4723. Cooney, Barbara
born 1917
illustrator
Index t Wom

4724. van Doren, Margaret
born 1917
illustrator
Index t Wom

4725. Kent, Corita
born 1918
"op-pop" artist
Catholic
Cur Biog '69

4726. Velarde, Pablita
born 1918
artist
Native American (Pueblo-Santa
Clara)
Ind Today

4727. Annie Weetaluktuk
born 1919
carver
Port Harrison, AK
Inuit
Esk Art

**4728. Hamar, Irene; Mrs. Hen-
ry Peter de Vries**
1919–73
sculptor, skier
New York
Brazilian
Nat Cyc Am Bio v57

4729. Sawyer, Helen Alice
flourished 1950s
artist, educator
Index t Wom

4730. Southern, Eileen Jackson
born 1920
musicologist, educator
Black
Encyc Black Am

4731. Wong, Jeanyee
born 1920
illustrator
Chinese
Index t Wom

**4732. Huxtable, Ada Louise
(Landman)**
born 1921
architecture critic, journalist
New York, NY
Cur Biog '73

4733. Hartigan, Grace
born 1922
painter
Index t Wom

4734. Vanderbilt, Gloria
born 1924
abstract artist, collagist
Cur Biog '72

4735. Whiting, Margaret
born 1924
singer, television personality
Index t Wom

**4736. Buckley, Mary Lorraine;
Mrs. Joseph M. Parriott**
born 1926
artist, art educator
Nat Cyc Am Bio csv13

4737. Hanks, Nancy
born 1927
chairperson of the National Endowment for the Arts and the
National Council for the Arts
Cur Biog '71

4738. Crowe, Amanda M.
born 1928
wood sculptor, carving teacher
Native American (Cherokee)
Ind Today

4739. Frankenthaler, Helen
born 1928
artist
Index t Wom

4740. McCullough, Geraldine
born 1928
sculptor
Black
Negro Alman; Prof Negro Wom
v2

4741. Morgan, Norma Gloria
born 1928
painter, printmaker, engraver
Encyc Black Am; Negro Alman

4742. Billops, Camille
flourished 1960s
ceramic sculptor
Black
Negro Alman

4743. Hill, Joan
flourished 1960s
artist
Native American (Cherokee)
Ind Today

4744. Kimball, Yeffe
flourished 1960s
pioneer painter of outer space
Native American (Osage)
Ind Today

**4745. Loloma, Otellie Sequaf-
enema**
flourished 1960s
ceramic sculptor, painter
Native American (Hopi)
Ind Today

4746. Marisol (Escobar)
born 1930
sculptor, painter
Venezualan
Index t Wom

4747. Massey, Edna Hogner
flourished 1960s
interior designer, arts and crafts
specialist
Native American (Cherokee)
Ind Today

4748. Mondale, Joan (Adams)
born 1930
federal arts consultant, art historian
Cur Biog '80

4749. Waano-Gano, Nunny
flourished 1960s
floral artist
Native American (Karok)
Ind Today

4750. Chryssa (Vardea)
born 1933
sculptor
Greek
Cur Biog '78

4751. Nelson, Mary
born 1933
educator, sculptor

Native American (Colville-Cree-
Mohawk)
Ind Today

4752. Ono, Yoko
born 1933
modern and conceptual artist,
musician
Japanese
Cur Biog '72

4753. Radziwill, Lee (Bouvier)
born 1933
interior decorator
Cur Biog '77

4754. Sontag, Susan
born 1933
cultural and art critic, essayist,
novelist, short story writer,
filmmaker
Cur Biog '69; Dict Lit Bio v2;
Wom Lit, More

4755. Ringgold, Faith
born 1934
painter
Black
Negro Alman

4756. Hesse, Eva
1936–70
sculptor
Not Am Wom supp v1

4757. Chicago, Judy (Cohen)
born 1939
feminist, autobiographer, sculptor, photographer, painter
Cur Biog '81

4758. Graves, Nancy Stevenson
born 1940
sculptor, painter, filmmaker
Cur Biog '81

4759. Maas, Caroline Orr
born 1943
artist
Native American (Colville)
Ind Today

**4760. Hardin, Helen; Tsa-sah-
wee-eh; Little Standing Spruce**
born 1946
artist
Native American (Pueblo-Santa
Clara)
Ind Today

No Dates

4761. Blaisdell, Elinor
illustrator
Index t Wom

4762. Coe, Ethel Louise
artist
Index t Wom

4763. Dunlap, Mary Stewart
painter
Index t Wom

4764. Kinney, Belle
sculptor
Index t Wom

HEROES, PATRIOTISM, AND THE MILITARY

4765. Ludwell, Frances
Culpepper Stephens Berkeley,
Lady
flourished seventeenth century
colonial patriot
Index t Wom

4766. Winthrop, Margaret
1591–1647
colonial patriot
Index t Wom

4767. Yardley, Temperance
Flowerdew Yardley West,
Lady
1593–1636
colonial patriot
Index t Wom

4768. Sayre, Ruth
flourished 1630s–40s
patriot
Index t Wom

4769. Williams, Frances Dighton
married 1632
patriot
Index t Wom

4770. Drummond, Sarah Prescott
flourished 1670s
patriot, politician, lecturer
Cyc Am Bio; Index t Wom

4771. Cadillac, Marie Therese
Guyon
married 1687
patriot of American Revolution
Index t Wom

4772. Grant, Hannah Tracy
flourished 1700s
patriot
Index t Wom

4773. Schuyler, Cornelia
flourished 1700s
colonial property owner, patriot
Index t Wom

4774. Hachard, Marie-Madeliene, Sister
flourished 1710s
pioneer, Catholic nun
Catholic
Index t Wom

4775. Townley, Elizabeth Smith
Carteret
flourished 1710s
colonial patriot
Index t Wom

4776. Wilson, Robert, Mrs.
flourished 1720s–70s
patriot of American Revolution
Index t Wom

4777. Stanley, Esther
1697–1776
patriot of American Revolution
Index t Wom

4778. Hopkins, Sarah Scott
married 1726
patriot
Index t Wom

4779. Schuyler, Margaretta
Schuyler
1701–82
colonial administrator, Tory politician with military influence
New York
Encyc South Hist; Index t Wom

4780. Phelps, Abigail Pettibone
1706–87
patriot
Index t Wom

4781. Adams, Elizabeth Checkley
died 1757
American patriot
Index t Wom

4782. Braxton, Judith Robinson
died 1757
pioneer, patriot of American Revolution
Index t Wom

4783. Cook, Elizabeth
flourished 1740s–70s
patriot of American Revolution
Index t Wom

4784. Sherman, Elizabeth Hartwell
died 1760
patriot
Index t Wom

4785. Humphreys, Sara Riggs
1711–87
patriot of American Revolution
Index t Wom

4786. Taylor, Nancy Savage
married 1739
patriot of American Revolution
Index t Wom

4787. Hart, Deborah Scudder
married 1740
pioneer, patriot
Index t Wom

4788. Thomas, Jane; Jane
Black
married 1740
hero of American Revolution
Cyc Am Bio; Index t Wom

4789. Allen, Elizabeth
born 1716
patriot, western pioneer
Index t Wom

4790. Page, Sarah Carlton
married 1741
patriot
Index t Wom

4791. Lewe, Ann Aylett
died 1767
patriot
Index t Wom

4792. Livingston, Margaret
Beekman
married 1742
patriot of American Revolution
Index t Wom

4793. Draper, Mary Aldis
circa 1718–1810
hero of American Revolution, patriot
Index t Wom

4794. Trumbull, Faith Robinson
1718–80
patriot of American Revolution
Index t Wom

4795. Putnam, Deborah Lothrop
1719–77
patriot of American Revolution
Index t Wom

4796. Lewis, Elizabeth Annesley
married 1745
patriot
Index t Wom

4797. Morton, Anne Justis
married 1745/46
patriot, pioneer
Index t Wom

4798. Murray, Mary Lindley
1720–82
patriot of American Revolution
Index t Wom

4799. Smith, Eleanor Armor
married 1745/46
patriot
Index t Wom

4800. Cooke, Hannah Sabin
born 1722
patriot of American Revolution
Index t Wom

4801. Elderkin, Anne Wood
1722–1804

patriot
Index t Wom

4802. Smith, Elizabeth Quincy
circa 1722–75
patriot of American Revolution
Index t Wom

4803. Wharton, Susannah
Lloyd
died 1772
patriot of American Revolution
Index t Wom

4804. Ludlow, Sarah
died 1773
patriot of American Revolution
Index t Wom

4805. McKean, Mary [Maria]
Borden
died circa 1773
patriot
Index t Wom

4806. Sharpe, Jemima Alexander
married 1748
patriot of American Revolution
Index t Wom

4807. Bailey, Ann; Mad Anne
1725/42–1825
frontier scout and messenger on
the Virginia border, soldier,
Indian fighter, American patriot
Ohio; Virginia
British
Appl Cyc Am Bio; Dict Am Bio;
Encyc South Hist; Who Who
Dur Am Rev; Wom Cent

4808. Caswell, Mary McIlweane
married 1750
patriot of American Revolution
Index t Wom

4809. Chittenden, Elizabeth
Meigs
married 1750
patriot of American Revolution
Index t Wom

4810. Ellery, Ann Ramington
married 1750
patriot, pioneer
Index t Wom

4811. Wright, Patience Lovell
1725–1785/86
wax modeler, spy during American Revolution
Quaker
New Jersey
Dict Am Bio; Dict Nat Bio; Index
t Wom; Nat Cyc Am Bio v8;
Not Am Wom; Who Who Dur
Am Rev

4812. Ross, Anne Lawler
married 1751
patriot
Index t Wom

4813. Winthrop, Hannah
circa 1726–90
patriot of American Revolution
Index t Wom

4814. Wythe, Anne Lewis
born 1726
patriot
Index t Wom

4815. Fitzhugh, Anne
1727–93
patriot of American Revolution
Index t Wom

4816. Warren, Mercy Otis
1727/28–1814
poet, author, dramatist, political
author and satirist, historian,
patriot
Massachusetts
Am Bio Dict; Cyc Am Bio; Dict
Am Auth; Dict Am Bio; Dict
Am Bio Men Time; Index t
Wom; Nat Cyc Am Bio v7; Not
Am Wom; Our Count; Who
Who Dur Am Rev; Wom Lit,
More

4817. Clark, Sarah Hatfield
born 1728
American patriot
Index t Wom

4818. Darragh, Lydia Barring-
ton
1728/29–1789
colonial nurse and midwife, hero
of American Revolution
Pennsylvania
Cyc Am Bio; Index t Wom; Not
Am Wom

4819. Philipse, Mary
circa 1728/30–1822
Tory loyalist in the American
Revolution, hero
Index t Wom; Our Count

4820. Stow, Freelove Baldwin
born 1728
patriot
Index t Wom

4821. Tucker, Frances Bland
Randolph
died 1788
patriot
Index t Wom

4822. Burr, Eunice Dennie
1729–1805
patriot of American Revolution
Index t Wom

4823. Baldwin, Eunice Jennison
flourished 1760s–70s

patriot of American Revolution
Index t Wom

4824. Caldwell, Hannah
died 1780
patriot of American Revolution
Index t Wom

4825. Dissoway, Mrs.
flourished 1770s
patriot of American Revolution
Index t Wom

4826. Green, Alice Kollock
flourished 1770s; died 1832
patriot of American Revolution
Index t Wom

4827. Paca, Anne
died circa 1780
patriot
Index t Wom

4828. Woodruff, Hannah
1730–1815
patriot of American Revolution
Index t Wom

4829. Espy, Jean
died 1781
patriot of American Revolution
Index t Wom

4830. Floyd, Hannah Jones
died 1781
patriot
Index t Wom

4831. Jackson, Elizabeth
Hutchinson
died 1781
hero of American Revolution
Index t Wom

4832. Skinner, Esther
circa 1731–1831
patriot of American Revolution
Index t Wom

4833. Hull, Elizabeth Clarke
1732–1826
patriot of American Revolution
Index t Wom

4834. Arnett, Hannah White
1733–1824
patriot of American Revolution
Index t Wom

4835. Carter, Hannah Benedict
1733–80
patriot of American Revolution
Index t Wom

4836. Hopkins, Anne Smith
died circa 1783
patriot
Index t Wom

4837. Schuyler, Catherine van
Rensselaer
1733–1803/04

patriot of American Revolution
Index t Wom

4838. van Alstine, Nancy
born circa 1733
patriot of American Revolution,
hero
Index t Wom

4839. Bulloch, Mary Deveaux
married circa 1760
patriot of American Revolution
Index t Wom

4840. Gwinnett, Button, Mrs.
married circa 1760
patriot
Index t Wom

4841. Hart, Nancy; Ann
Morgan
1735/55–1830
hero of American Revolution
Georgia
Cyc Am Bio; Encyc South Hist;
Index t Wom; Nat Cyc Am Bio
v13; Not Am Wom

4842. Thornton, Hannah Jack
married 1760
patriot
Index t Wom

4843. Morgan, Abigail Bailey
"Abbie"
1736–1802
pioneer, patriot
Index t Wom

4844. Shelby, Susannah Hart
married 1761
patriot
Index t Wom

4845. Sillman, Mary Fish
1736–1818
hero of American Revolution
Index t Wom

4846. Woodhull, Ruth Floyd
married 1761
patriot of American Revolution
Index t Wom

4847. Chase, Ann Baldwin
married 1762
pioneer, American patriot
Index t Wom

4848. Clarke, Hannah
circa 1737–1827
patriot of American Revolution
Index t Wom

4849. Danielson, Sarah
Williams
born 1737
patriot of American Revolution
Index t Wom

4850. Ferguson, Elizabeth
(Graeme)
1737/39–1801
litterateur, poet, translator, letter
writer, diarist, hero of Ameri-
can Revolution
Philadelphia, PA
Am Bio Dict; Cyc Am Bio; Dict
Am Auth; Dict Am Bio; Dict
Am Bio Men Time; Index t
Wom; Nat Cyc Am Bio v7; Not
Am Wom; Who Who Dur Am
Rev

4851. Keith, Mary Isham
(Marshall)
1737–1809
patriot of American Revolution,
pioneer
Index t Wom

4852. Nelson, Lucy Grymes
married 1762
patriot
Index t Wom

4853. Percival, Mary Fuller
born 1737
patriot of American Revolution
Index t Wom

4854. Ripley, Dorothy Brintnall
1737–1831
patriot of American Revolution
Index t Wom

4855. Shaw, Lucretia
circa 1737–81
patriot of American Revolution
Index t Wom

4856. Stark, Elizabeth Page
"Molly"
circa 1737–1814
patriot of American Revolution
Index t Wom

4857. Stone, Margaret Brown
died 1787
patriot
Index t Wom

4858. Webster, Abigail East-
man
1737–1816
patriot of American Revolution
Index t Wom

4859. Motte, Rebecca Brewton
1738–1815
hero of American Revolution, patriot
Dict Am Bio Men Time; Index t
Wom; Our Count

4860. Paca, Mary Chew
married 1763
patriot
Index t Wom

4861. Read, Gertrude Ross Till
married 1763

patriot
Index t Wom

4862. Sherman, Rebecca Prescott
married 1763
patriot of American Revolution
Index t Wom

4863. Bartlett, Mary
died 1789
patriot of American Revolution
Index t Wom

4864. Caldwell, Rachel
circa 1739–1825
patriot of American Revolution
Am Bio Dict; Index t Wom

4865. Livingston, Susannah French
died 1789
patriot of American Revolution
Index t Wom

4866. Lowrey, Esther Fleming
1739–1814
patriot
Index t Wom

4867. Witherspoon, Elizabeth Montgomery
died 1789
patriot of American Revolution
Index t Wom

4868. Wright, Prudence Cumings
circa 1739–1823
hero of American Revolution
Index t Wom

4869. Adams, Anne
flourished 1770s
patriot of American Revolution
Index t Wom

4870. Adams, Elizabeth Wells
flourished 1770s; died circa 1808
American patriot
Index t Wom

4871. Allen, Maria
flourished 1770s
hero of American Revolution
Index t Wom

4872. Baldwin, Alice
flourished 1770s
writer during American Revolution
Index t Wom

4873. Barlow, Rebecca Sanford
flourished 1770s
patriot of American Revolution
Index t Wom

4874. Barrett, Meliscent "Milly"
flourished 1770s

hero of American Revolution
Index t Wom

4875. Beckham, Mrs.
flourished 1770s
hero of American Revolution
Index t Wom

4876. Berry, Sidney, Mrs.
flourished 1770s
patriot of American Revolution
Index t Wom

4877. Bevier, J.
flourished 1770s
patriot of American Revolution
Index t Wom

4878. Biddle, Rebecca
flourished 1770s
patriot of American Revolution
Index t Wom

4879. Bidlack, Gore, Mrs.
flourished 1770s
patriot of American Revolution
Index t Wom

4880. Borden, Mrs.
flourished 1770s
patriot of American Revolution
Index t Wom

4881. Bowen, Mary
flourished 1770s
patriot of American Revolution
Index t Wom

4882. Braxton, Elizabeth Corbin
flourished 1770s
pioneer, patriot of American Revolution
Index t Wom

4883. Braxton, Mary Carter
flourished 1770s
pioneer, patriot of American Revolution
Index t Wom

4884. Brevard, Mrs.
flourished 1770s
hero of American Revolution
Index t Wom

4885. Brewton, Robert, Mrs.
flourished 1770s
patriot of American Revolution
Index t Wom

4886. Brown, Mary Buckman
1740–1824
hero of American Revolution
Index t Wom

4887. Captain Molly
flourished 1770s
hero of American Revolution
Index t Wom

4888. Channing, Mrs.
flourished 1770s
hero of American Revolution
Index t Wom

4889. Clymer, Elizabeth Meredith
married 1765
patriot of American Revolution
Index t Wom

4890. Cobb, Lydia; Lydia Leonard
flourished 1770s
patriot of American Revolution
Index t Wom

4891. Coffin, Peter, Mrs.
flourished 1770s
patriot of American Revolution
Index t Wom

4892. Conyngham, Anne
flourished 1770s
patriot of American Revolution
Index t Wom

4893. Cranch, Richard, Mrs.
flourished 1770s
patriot of American Revolution
Index t Wom

4894. Cutbert, Susan Stockton
flourished 1770s
patriot, pioneer
Index t Wom

4895. Daggett, Polly
flourished 1770s
hero of American Revolution
Index t Wom

4896. Dana, Mrs.
flourished 1770s
patriot of American Revolution
Index t Wom

4897. Daviess, Mrs.
flourished 1770s
hero of American Revolution
Index t Wom

4898. Dickinson, Sarah
flourished 1770s
patriot of American Revolution
Index t Wom

4899. Dillard, Mrs.
flourished 1770s
hero of American Revolution
Index t Wom

4900. Edgar, Rachel
flourished 1770s
hero of American Revolution
Index t Wom

4901. Elliott, Sabrina
flourished 1770s
patriot of American Revolution
Index t Wom

4902. Farrand, Rhoda Smith
flourished 1770s
patriot of American Revolution
Index t Wom

4903. Floyd, Joanna Strong
flourished 1770s
patriot
Index t Wom

4904. Franks, Rebecca
flourished 1770s; died 1823
hero of American Revolution
Index t Wom

4905. Fulton, Sarah Bradlee
1740–1835
hero of American Revolution
Index t Wom

4906. Gaston, Esther
flourished 1770s–80s
patriot of American Revolution
Index t Wom

4907. Goddard, Hannah
flourished 1770s
patriot, pioneer
Index t Wom

4908. Graydon, Mrs.
flourished 1770s
patriot of American Revolution
Index t Wom

4909. Griswold, Ursula Wolcott
flourished 1770s
patriot of American Revolution
Index t Wom

4910. Hagidorn, Mary
flourished 1770s
patriot of American Revolution
Index t Wom

4911. Hall, Daniel, Mrs.
flourished 1770s
patriot of American Revolution
Index t Wom

4912. Harvey, Mrs.
flourished 1770s
patriot of American Revolution
Index t Wom

4913. Honeyman, Mary Henry
flourished 1770s
patriot of American Revolution
Index t Wom

4914. Hopton, Sarah
flourished 1770s
patriot of American Revolution
Index t Wom

4915. Ives, Lucy
flourished 1770s
patriot of American Revolution
Index t Wom

4916. Jackson, Mrs.
flourished 1770s

hero of American Revolution
Index t Wom

4917. Jones, Willie, Mrs.
flourished 1770s; died 1828
hero of American Revolution
Index t Wom

4918. Lawson, Deborah
flourished 1770s
soldier in American Revolution
Index t Wom

4919. Ledyard, Mary
flourished 1770s
hero of American Revolution,
 philanthropist
Index t Wom

4920. Livingston, Christina Ten Broeck
flourished 1770s
patriot of American Revolution
Index t Wom

4921. Livingston, Susan
flourished 1770s
hero of American Revolution
Index t Wom

4922. Long, Mary M'Kinney
flourished 1770s
patriot of American Revolution
Index t Wom

4923. Mammy Kate
flourished 1770s
hero of American Revolution
Index t Wom

4924. Manter, Parnel
flourished 1770s
hero of American Revolution
Index t Wom

4925. Marshall, Christopher, Mrs.
flourished 1770s
pioneer, patriot of American Revolution
Index t Wom

4926. Martin, Elizabeth Marshall
flourished 1770s
patriot of American Revolution,
 hero
Index t Wom

4927. Martin, Grace
flourished 1770s
hero of American Revolution, patriot
Index t Wom

4928. Martin, Rachel; Rachel Clay
flourished 1770s
hero of American Revolution
Index t Wom

4929. McCalla, Mrs.
flourished 1770s
hero of American Revolution
Index t Wom

4930. McIntosh, Sarah Swinton
flourished 1770s
patriot of American Revolution
Index t Wom

4931. Merrill, John, Mrs.
flourished 1770s–80s
hero of American Revolution, pioneer
Index t Wom

4932. Mersereau, Charity
flourished 1770s
patriot of American Revolution
Index t Wom

4933. Mills, Mary Gills
flourished 1770s
patriot of American Revolution
Index t Wom

4934. Mooney, Hannah Gaunt
flourished 1770s
patriot of American Revolution
Index t Wom

4935. Morris, Ann Eliott
flourished 1770s; died 1848
patriot of American Revolution
Index t Wom

4936. Munro, Mrs.
flourished 1770s
patriot of American Revolution
Index t Wom

4937. Myers, Mrs.
flourished 1770s
patriot of American Revolution
Index t Wom

4938. Newton, Mary
flourished 1770s
patriot
Index t Wom

4939. Otterson, Mrs.
flourished 1770s
hero of American Revolution
Index t Wom

4940. Parker, Ruth
flourished 1770s
patriot of American Revolution
Index t Wom

4941. Potter, Mrs.
flourished 1770s
hero of American Revolution
Index t Wom

4942. Putnam, Susannah French
flourished 1770s
humanitarian of American Revolution
Index t Wom

4943. Redmond, Mary
flourished 1770s
hero of American Revolution, patriot
Index t Wom

4944. Reid, Molly
flourished 1770s
patriot of American Revolution
Index t Wom

4945. Russell, Joseph, Mrs.
flourished 1770s
patriot of American Revolution
Index t Wom

4946. Shattuck, Job, Mrs.
flourished 1770s
soldier in American Revolution
Index t Wom

4947. Shell, Elizabeth Petrie
flourished 1770s–80s
hero of American Revolution
Index t Wom

4948. Shubrick, Richard, Mrs.
flourished 1770s
patriot of American Revolution
Index t Wom

4949. Simms, Sarah Dickinson
flourished 1770s
hero of American Revolution
Index t Wom

4950. Sims, Isabella
flourished 1770s
hero of American Revolution
Index t Wom

4951. Spalding, Mrs.
flourished 1770s
hero of American Revolution
Index t Wom

4952. Steele, Elizabeth Maxwell
flourished 1770s
hero of American Revolution
Index t Wom

4953. Stephens, Martha Stewart Elliot
flourished 1770s
patriot of American Revolution
Index t Wom

4954. Symmes, Susannah
flourished 1770s
patriot
Index t Wom

4955. Varnum, Molly
flourished 1770s
patriot of American Revolution
Index t Wom

4956. Vernoy, Catharine
flourished 1770s
patriot of American Revolution
Index t Wom

4957. Vrooman, Angelica
flourished 1770s
hero of American Revolution
Index t Wom

4958. Walker, John, Mrs.
flourished 1770s
patriot of American Revolution
Index t Wom

4959. Warne, Margaret Violet
flourished 1770s
patriot of American Revolution,
 physician
Index t Wom

4960. Warner, Jemima
flourished 1770s
soldier in American Revolution
Index t Wom

4961. Washington, Jane Elliot
flourished 1770s; died 1830
patriot of American Revolution
Index t Wom

4962. Watts, Mary Stirling
flourished 1770s
patriot
Index t Wom

4963. Whipple, Katharine Moffat
flourished 1770s
patriot of American Revolution
Index t Wom

4964. Whitley, Mrs.
flourished 1770s
patriot of American Revolution
Index t Wom

4965. Wilkinson, Eliza
flourished 1770s
hero of American Revolution
Index t Wom

4966. Williams, Anne Newton
flourished 1770s
patriot of American Revolution
Index t Wom

4967. Woods, Mrs.
flourished 1770s
patriot of American Revolution
Index t Wom

4968. Wright, David, Mrs.
flourished 1770s
hero of American Revolution
Index t Wom

4969. Young, Poyner, Mrs.
flourished 1770s
patriot of American Revolution
French
Index t Wom

4970. Harrison, Elizabeth Bassett
born 1741/42

patriot
Index t Wom

4971. Johnson, Anne Jennings
married 1766
patriot of American Revolution
Index t Wom

4972. Penn, Susan Lyme
born 1741/42
patriot
Index t Wom

4973. Richardson, Dorcas Nelson
circa 1741–1834
hero of American Revolution
Index t Wom

4974. Bissell, Sabra Trumbull
1742–68
American patriot
Index t Wom

4975. Hart, Ruth Cole
1742–1844
patriot of American Revolution
Index t Wom

4976. Heyward, Elizabeth Mathews
married circa 1767/68
patriot of American Revolution
Index t Wom

4977. Hooper, Anne Clark
married 1767
patriot
Index t Wom

4978. Rutledge, Elizabeth Grimke
died 1792
patriot of American Revolution
Index t Wom

4979. Story, Ann; Ann Goodrich
1742–1817
hero of American Revolution
Index t Wom

4980. Wheelock, Deborah Thayer
1742/43–1815
patriot of American Revolution
Index t Wom

4981. Bache, Sarah Franklin
1743/44–1808
relief worker in American Revolution, philanthropist
Philadelphia, PA
Appl Cyc Am Bio; Cyc Am Bio; Dict Am Bio Men Time; Index t Wom; Nat Cyc Am Bio v7; Not Am Wom; Twent Cen Bio Dict Not Am

4982. Campbell, Jane Cannon
1743–1836

patriot of American Revolution
Index t Wom

4983. Ellery, Abigail Carey
died 1793
patriot, pioneer
Index t Wom

4984. Israel, Hannah Erwin
circa 1743–1821
hero of American Revolution
Index t Wom

4985. Adams, Abigail Smith
1744–1818
patriot and relief worker of American Revolution, political mover, letter writer, feminist
Am Bio Dict; Appl Cyc Am Bio; Cyc Am Bio; Dict Am Auth; Dict Am Bio; Dict Am Bio Men Time; Index t Wom; Nat Cyc Am Bio v1; Not Am Wom; Twent Cen Bio Dict Not Am; Wom Cent

4986. Benjamin, Sara Matthews
circa 1744–1861 [*sic*]
patriot of American Revolution, nurse
Index t Wom

4987. Huntington, Martha Devotion
died 1794
patriot of American Revolution
Index t Wom

4988. McCauley, Mary (Ludwig) Hays; Molly Pitcher
1744/54–1832
sergeant in the US Army, hero of American Revolution
Pennsylvania
Dict Am Bio; Index t Wom; Nat Cyc Am Bio v9; Not Am Wom; Twent Cen Bio Dict Not Am; Who Who Dur Am Rev

4989. Quincy, Abigail Phillips
married 1769
patriot
Index t Wom

4990. Clinton, Cornelia Tappen
married 1770
patriot of American Revolution
Index t Wom

4991. Gaylord, Katherine Cole
1745–1840
patriot, hero of American Revolution
Index t Wom

4992. Izard, Alice
circa 1745–1832
patriot of American Revolution
Index t Wom

4993. Paine, Sarah Cobb "Sally"
married 1770
patriot
Index t Wom

4994. Tufts, Susannah Warner
1745–1832
patriot
Index t Wom

4995. Gibbes, Sarah Reeve
1746–1825
hero of American Revolution
Index t Wom

4996. MacDougall, Grace Greenlee
flourished 1776
patriot
Cyc Am Bio

4997. Reed, Esther de Berdt
1746–80
leader of women's relief work during the American Revolution, hero of American Revolution, patriot, philanthropist
Index t Wom; Not Am Wom

4998. Riedesel, Frederica Charlotte Louisa Massow, Baroness de
1746–1808
hero of American Revolution
Index t Wom

4999. Williams, Mary Trumbull
married 1771
patriot
Index t Wom

5000. Wilson, Rachel Bird
married 1771/72
patriot of American Revolution
Index t Wom

5001. Carroll, Mary Darnell
circa 1747–82
patriot of American Revolution
Index t Wom

5002. Lee, Rebecca Tayloe
died 1797
patriot of American Revolution
Index t Wom

5003. Lewis, Elizabeth Washington "Betty"
died 1797
patriot of American Revolution
Index t Wom

5004. Wadsworth, Elizabeth Bartlett
married 1772
patriot
Index t Wom

5005. Whitehall, Ann Cooper
died 1797

patriot
Index t Wom

5006. Wyllys, Ruth Belden
1747–1807
patriot of American Revolution
Index t Wom

5007. Bache, Sarah
died 1798
hero of American Revolution
Index t Wom

5008. Bozarth, Mrs.
flourished 1779
pioneer, hero of American Revolution
Index t Wom

5009. Ackland, Christina Harriet Caroline; Lady Fox
1750–1815
Tory patriot during American Revolution
Appl Cyc Am Bio; Dict Am Bio Men Time

5010. Camp, Milicent Baldwin Porter
1750–1824
patriot of American Revolution
Index t Wom

5011. Clay, Elizabeth
1750–1827
patriot of American Revolution
Index t Wom

5012. Elliott, Susannah Smith
born circa 1750
patriot of American Revolution
Cyc Am Bio; Index t Wom

5013. Hancock, Dorothy Quincy
1750–1828
patriot of American Revolution
Index t Wom

5014. Latham, Eunice Forsyth
flourished 1780s
American patriot
Index t Wom

5015. Peabody, Elizabeth Smith Shaw
1750–circa 1813
patriot of American Revolution
Index t Wom

5016. Pratt, Elizabeth
born 1750
patriot
Index t Wom

5017. Rutledge, Henrietta Middleton
born 1750
patriot of American Revolution
Index t Wom

5018. Shaw, Elizabeth
1750–circa 1816
patriot of American Revolution
Index t Wom

5019. Walton, Dorothy C.
died 1800s
patriot
Index t Wom

5020. Arnold, Margaret Shippen
1751/60–1804/34
Tory patriot during American Revolution
Index t Wom; Nat Cyc Am Bio v7

5021. Corbin, Margaret Cochran
1751–circa 1800
hero of American Revolution, soldier
Pennsylvania
Dict Am Bio; Index t Wom; Nat Cyc Am Bio v6; Not Am Wom; Twent Cen Bio Dict Not Am; Who Who Dur Am Rev

5022. Ross, Betsy Griscom;
Elizabeth Claypool; Elizabeth Grimke
1752–1832/36
flag maker
Pennsylvania
Dict Am Bio; Index t Wom; Not Am Wom; Who Who Dur Am Rev

5023. van Cortlandt, Joanna Livingston; Catharine Clinton
born 1752
patriot
Index t Wom

5024. Fanning, Anne Brewster
1753–1813
patriot of American Revolution
Index t Wom

5025. Greene, Catharine Littlefield
1753–1814
hero of American Revolution, patriot
Index t Wom

5026. Knox, Lucy Flucker
circa 1754/56–1824
political mover, hero of American Revolution, patriot
Cyc Am Bio; Index t Wom

5027. Peters, Fannie Ledyard
circa 1754–1816
hero of American Revolution
Index t Wom

5028. Hull, Sarah
circa 1755–1826
patriot of American Revolution
Index t Wom

5029. Ellsworth, Abigail Wolcott
1756–1818
patriot of American Revolution
Index t Wom

5030. Hamilton, Elizabeth Schuyler
1757–1854
patriot of American Revolution
Index t Wom

5031. Bailey, Anna Warner;
Mother Bailey
1758–1850/51
patriot of American Revolution, colonial hero
Connecticut
Appl Cyc Am Bio; Cyc Am Bio; Dict Am Bio; Index t Wom; Wom Cent

5032. Mattoon, Mary Dickinson
1758–1835
patriot of American Revolution
Index t Wom

5033. Weston, Hannah Watts
1758–1885
hero of American Revolution, patriot
Index t Wom

5034. Wilson, Martha
born 1758
patriot of American Revolution
Index t Wom

5035. Chinn, Sarah Bryan
married circa 1784
western pioneer, American patriot
Index t Wom

5036. Humaston, Abi
circa 1759–1847
hero of American Revolution
Index t Wom

5037. Knight, Mary Worrell
circa 1759–1849
hero of American Revolution
Index t Wom

5038. Rush, Julia Stockton
1759–1848
patriot
Index t Wom

5039. Whetton, Margaret Todd
died 1809
patriot of American Revolution
Index t Wom

5040. Zane, Elizabeth "Betty"
1759/66–1831/47
frontier hero, hero of American Revolution
Cyc Am Bio; Index t Wom; Not Am Wom

5041. Chase, Deborah
born 1760
patriot of American Revolution
Index t Wom

5042. Geiger, Emily
born 1760
hero of American Revolution
Cyc Am Bio; Index t Wom

5043. Hamilton, Anne Kennedy
circa 1760–1836
hero of American Revolution
Index t Wom

5044. Sampson, Deborah; Robert Shirtliffe; Deborah Gannett
1760–1827
soldier and hero of American Revolution, lecturer
Massachusetts
Am Bio Dict; Cyc Am Bio; Dict Am Bio Men Time; Index t Wom; Nat Cyc Am Bio v8; Not Am Wom

5045. Slocum, Mary Hooks
1760–1836
hero of American Revolution
Index t Wom

5046. Springfield, Laodicia Langston "Dicey"
born 1760
hero of American Revolution
Index t Wom

5047. Threrwitz, Emily Geiger
born circa 1760
hero of American Revolution
Index t Wom

5048. Townsend, Sally
1760–1842
hero of American Revolution
Index t Wom

5049. Ludington, Sybil
1761–1839
hero of American Revolution
Index t Wom

5050. Wister, Sarah "Sally"
1761/62–1804
diarist, patriot of American Revolution
Quaker
Pennsylvania
Dict Am Bio; Index t Wom; Who Who Dur Am Rev

5051. Barnum, Lucy Wolcott
1762–99
patriot of American Revolution
Index t Wom

5052. Elliott, Anna
circa 1762–1858

hero of American Revolution, relief worker, nurse
Am Bio Dict; Cyc Am Bio; Index t Wom

5053. Gerry, Ann Thompson
1763–1849
patriot, pioneer
Irish
Index t Wom

5054. Butler, Behethland
born 1764
patriot of American Revolution
Index t Wom

5055. Butler, Rehethland Foote
born 1764
patriot of American Revolution
Index t Wom

5056. Middleton, Mary Izard
died 1814
patriot
Index t Wom

5057. Tallmadge, Mary Floyd
1764–1805
patriot of American Revolution
Index t Wom

5058. Wolcott, Laura Collins
married 1789
Revolutionary War patriot
Index t Wom

5059. Goodrich, Mary Ann;
Mary Ann Wolcott
born 1765
patriot, pioneer
Index t Wom

5060. Bratton, Martha
died 1816
hero of American Revolution, patriot
Cyc Am Bio; Index t Wom

5061. Frietchie, Barbara
1766–1862/65
Union Civil War hero
Maryland
German
Index t Wom; Who Who Dur Am Rev

5062. Morris, Margaret
died 1816
patriot of American Revolution, author
Index t Wom

5063. Leavenworth, Harriet
flourished 1800s
American patriot
Index t Wom

5064. Robb, Louisa St. Clair
born 1773
western pioneer, patriot
Index t Wom

5065. Hopkinson, Ann Borden McKean
died 1827
patriot
Index t Wom

5066. Ellet, Mary
born 1779
war hero
Index t Wom

5067. van Ness, Marcia Burns
1782–1832
philanthropist, patriot
Washington, DC
Cyc Am Bio; Index t Wom

5068. Beekman, Cornelia
1783–1847
patriot of American Revolution
Am Bio Dict

5069. Clay, Susanna Withers
married 1815; died post 1860s
Civil War patriot
Index t Wom

5070. Dix, Dorothea Lynde
1794/1802–1887
crusader for the welfare of the mentally ill, prison reformer, philanthropist, author, essayist, children's author, superintendent of army nurses in the Civil War
Massachusetts
Cyc Am Bio; Dict Am Auth; Dict Am Bio; Dict Am Bio Men Time; Dict Lit Bio v1; Index t Wom; Nat Cyc Am Bio v3; Not Am Wom; Twent Cen Bio Dict Not Am; Wom Cent

5071. Peter, Sarah Anne (Worthington) King
1800–77
charity worker, philanthropist, founder of art school for women, hospital founder, Civil War nurse, pioneer industrial arts educator, church worker
Catholic
Ohio
Dict Am Bio; Index t Wom; Not Am Wom; Twent Cen Bio Dict Not Am

5072. Rouse, Benjamin, Mrs.
born 1800
Civil War humanitarian, social reformer
Index t Wom

5073. Gibbons, Abigail Hopper "Abby"
1801–93
abolitionist, prison reformer, feminist, women's welfare worker, Civil War nurse, philanthropist, journalist
Quaker
Cyc Am Bio; Dict Am Bio; Index t Wom; Nat Cyc Am Bio v7; Not Am Wom; Twent Cen Bio Dict Not Am; Wom Cent

5074. Powers, Eliza Howard
1802–87
philanthropist, patron of army medicine
Cyc Am Bio

5075. Gordon, Sallie Chapman
born 1805
Civil War patriot
Index t Wom

5076. Law, Sallie Chapman Gordon; Mother of the Confederacy
1805–94
Civil War hospital organizer, nurse
Dict Am Bio; Index t Wom; Nat Cyc Am Bio

5077. Morgan, Henrietta Hunt
1805–91
Civil War diarist, pioneer
Index t Wom

5078. Tyler, Adeline Blanchard, Sister
1805–75
Civil War nurse, Episcopalian deaconess
Episcopalian
Not Am Wom

5079. Lee, Mary Randolph Custis
1806–73
Civil War hero
Index t Wom

5080. Porter, Eliza Emily Chappell
1807–88
educator, Civil War relief worker
Not Am Wom

5081. Gage, Frances Dana (Barker); Aunt Fanny
1808–84
lecturer, author, temperance worker, abolitionist, suffragist, women's rights worker, Civil War relief worker
Cyc Am Bio; Dict Am Auth; Dict Am Bio; Dict Am Bio Men Time; Index t Wom; Nat Cyc Am Bio v2; Not Am Wom; Twent Cen Bio Dict Not Am; Wom Cent

5082. Hill, Iley Lawson
born 1808
American patriot
Index t Wom

5083. Cady, Hannah McIntosh
1809–1911

patriot
Index t Wom

5084. Chase, Ann
1809–74
patriot
Index t Wom

5085. Ladd, Catherine; Minnie Mayflower; Morna; Alida; Arcturus
1809–99
educator, author, Civil War nurse, designer of the Confederate flag
Cyc Am Bio; Dict Am Bio; Nat Cyc Am Bio v24; Twent Cen Bio Dict Not Am

5086. le Vert, Octavia Celeste Walton
1810/11–1877
author, Civil War nurse, travel writer
Mobile, AL
Cyc Am Bio; Dict Am Auth; Dict Am Bio Men Time; Index t Wom; Nat Cyc Am Bio v6; Not Am Wom; Twent Cen Bio Dict Not Am

5087. McCord, Louisa Susannah (Cheves)
1810–1879/80
miscellaneous author, poet, political writer, translator, Confederate essayist, Black welfare worker, feminist, plantation manager
South Carolina
Cyc Am Bio; Dict Am Auth; Dict Am Bio; Dict Am Bio Men Time; Index t Wom; Nat Cyc Am Bio v9; Not Am Wom; Twent Cen Bio Dict Not Am

5088. Slidell, Mathilde Deslonde
married 1835
patriot
Index t Wom

5089. Brigham, Susan S.
born 1811
American patriot
Index t Wom

5090. Hoge, Jane Currie Blaike; A. H. Hoge
1811–90
Civil War relief leader, church and welfare worker, sanitation commission worker, author
Index t Wom; Not Am Wom

5091. Nellis, Samantha Stanton
born 1811
patriot
Index t Wom

5092. Colt, Henrietta L. Peckham
1812–post 1860s
Civil War relief worker
Index t Wom

5093. McGuire, Judith Brockenbrough
born 1813
Civil War diarist, patriot
Index t Wom

5094. Pomeroy, Lucy Gaylord
died 1863
Civil War humanitarian
Index t Wom

5095. Collins, Emily Parmely
born 1814
suffragist, abolitionist, political writer, Civil War nurse
Hartford, CT
Wom Cent

5096. Hagar, Sarah J.
died 1864
Civil War nurse
Index t Wom

5097. Howland, Mary Woolsey
died 1864
poet, Civil War nurse
Cyc Am Bio; Index t Wom

5098. O'Connell, Mary; Sister Anthony
1814–97
Catholic nun, Civil War nurse, orphanage and hospital director in Cincinnati
Catholic
Cincinnati, OH
Dict Am Bio; Not Am Wom

5099. Billing, Rose M.
died 1865
Civil War nurse
Index t Wom

5100. Carroll, Anna Ella
1815–1893/94
political pamphleteer, political scientist, Civil War military strategist
Dict Am Auth; Index t Wom; Nat Cyc Am Bio v5; Not Am Wom; Twent Cen Bio Dict Not Am; Wom Cent

5101. Comstock, Elizabeth Leslie Rous
1815–1891/92
social reformer, abolitionist, Underground Railroad worker, pacifist, freed slave's welfare worker, temperance reformer, women's rights worker, Quaker minister, prison reformer, Civil War nurse
Quaker
Dict Am Bio; Index t Wom; Nat Cyc Am Bio v22; Not Am Wom

5102. Greenhow, Rose O'Neal
1815/17–1864
Confederate spy
Catholic
Washington, DC
Bio Dict Confed; Index t Wom;
Not Am Wom; Read Encyc Am
West

5103. Mason, Emily Virginia
1815–1909
Civil War hospital matron, Confederate army Civil War nurse,
author, biographer, educator
Cyc Am Bio; Dict Am Auth;
Index t Wom; Nat Cyc Am Bio
v5

5104. Palmer, Mary E.
died 1865
Civil War humanitarian
Index t Wom

5105. Swisshelm, Jane (Grey) (Cannon)
1815/16–1884
journalist, author, editor, publisher, abolitionist, women's rights
worker, Civil War nurse
Cyc Am Bio; Dict Am Auth; Dict
Am Bio; Dict Am Bio Men
Time; Index t Wom; Nat Cyc
Am Bio v2; Not Am Wom

5106. Walker, Adeline
died 1865
Civil War nurse
Index t Wom

5107. Young, M. A. B.
died 1865
Civil War nurse
Index t Wom

5108. Hopkins, Juliet Ann Opie
1816/18–1890
hospital administrator and founder, Confederate sympathizer
Alabama
Dict Am Bio; Encyc South Hist;
Not Am Wom

5109. Stewart, Eliza Daniel "Mother"
1816–1908
temperance reformer, suffragist,
Civil War relief worker
Illinois
Dict Am Bio; Nat Cyc Am Bio
v7; Not Am Wom; Wom Cent

5110. Stone, Martha Elvira
born 1816
postmaster of North Oxford,
Massachusetts; genealogist; Civil War relief worker
North Oxford, MA
Wom Cent

5111. Bickerdyke, Mary Ann Ball; Mother Bickerdyke
1817–1901
hospital worker, Civil War nurse,
herbalist, philanthropist
Dict Am Bio; Index t Wom; Nat
Cyc Am Bio v21; Not Am
Wom; Wom Cent

5112. Burge, Dolly Sumner Lunt
born 1817
Civil War essayist
Index t Wom

5113. Pomroy, Rebecca Rossignol
1817–84
nurse, war nurse
Massachusetts
Cyc Am Bio

5114. Fales, Almirah L.
died 1868
Civil War relief worker, ambulance nurse, philanthropist
Dict Am Bio Men Time; Index t
Wom

5115. Harding, Elizabeth McGavock
born circa 1818
Civil War diarist
Index t Wom

5116. Olnhausen, Mary Phinney von
1818–1902
Civil War nurse, author
Index t Wom

5117. van Lew, Elizabeth L.
1818–1900
unionist and federal agent during
the Civil War, Civil War spy
Virginia
Index t Wom; Not Am Wom

5118. Greene, Louisa Morton
born 1819
author, abolitionist, suffragist,
women's rights worker, temperance worker, Civil War relief
worker
Wom Cent

5119. Houston, Margaret Moffette Lea
circa 1819–67
Civil War diarist
Index t Wom

5120. Howe, Julia Ward
1819–1910
poet, dramatist, songwriter, lecturer, suffrage and women's
club leader, feminist, abolitionist, pacifist, prison reformer,
Union patriot during the Civil
War, philanthropist, traveler

Boston, MA
Cyc Am Bio; Dict Am Auth; Dict
Am Bio; Dict Am Bio Men
Time; Dict Lit Bio v1; Index t
Wom; Nat Cyc Am Bio v1; Not
Am Wom; Twent Cen Bio Dict
Not Am; Wom Cent

5121. Davis, Sarah Iliff
born 1820
philanthropist, temperance worker, women's prison reformer,
milliner, sanitation worker for
the Union army during the Civil
War, Freedmen's Aid worker
Wom Cent

5122. Harlan, James, Mrs.
married 1845/46
Civil War relief worker
Index t Wom

5123. Livermore, Mary Ashton (Rice)
1820/21–1905
health reformer, hospital administrator, suffragist, temperance
worker, abolitionist, Civil War
patriot, miscellaneous author
Universalist
Melrose, MA
Cyc Am Bio; Dict Am Auth; Dict
Am Bio Men Time; Dict Am
Rel Bio; Index t Wom; Nat Cyc
Am Bio v1; Not Am Wom;
Twent Cen Bio Dict Not Am;
Wom Cent

5124. Preston, Margaret (Junkin)
1820/25–1897
poet, author, novelist, Civil War
letter writer
Lexington, VA
Cyc Am Bio; Dict Am Auth; Dict
Am Bio; Index t Wom; Nat Cyc
Am Bio v7; Not Am Wom;
Twent Cen Bio Dict Not Am;
Wom Cent

5125. Tubman, Harriet Ross
1820/26–1913
hero of the Underground Railroad, liberator of slaves, abolitionist, Union spy during the
Civil War, Civil War nurse, lecturer
Black
Cyc Am Bio; Dict Am Bio; Encyc
Black Am; Encyc South Hist;
Index t Wom; Nat Cyc Am Bio
v9; Negro Alman; Not Am
Wom; Prof Negro Wom v1

5126. Barton, Clara; Clarissa Harlowe
1821/30–1912
founder of the American Red
Cross, Civil War hospital
founder, expert on organizing

military hospitals, philanthropist, nurse
Appl Cyc Am Bio; Cyc Am Bio;
Dict Am Bio; Dict Am Rel Bio;
Index t Wom; Nat Cyc Am Bio
v3 and v15; Not Am Wom;
Twent Cen Bio Dict Not Am;
Wom Cent

5127. Bowser, Mary Elizabeth
flourished 1851
Union spy
Black
Prof Negro Wom

5128. Brady, Mary A.
1821–64
philanthropist, Civil War relief
worker
Irish
Index t Wom

5129. Rishel, Mary Anne
born circa 1821
patriot
Index t Wom

5130. Williams, Mary Ann
1822–74
philanthropist, Civil War relief
worker, Confederate sympathizer
Georgia
Nat Cyc Am Bio v7

5131. Bradley, Amy Morris
1823–1904
educator, Civil War nurse, hospital administrator
Index t Wom; Not Am Wom;
Wom Cent

5132. Chesnut, Mary Boykin Miller
1823–86
Civil War diarist
Not Am Wom

5133. Peake, Mary Smith Kelsey
1823–62
educator of freedmen, Union patriot in the Civil War
Black
Index t Wom; Negro Alman; Prof
Negro Wom v1

5134. Gillespie, Eliza Maria; Mother Mary of St. Angela
1824–87
mother superior and founder of
the American Sisters of the
Holy Cross, educator, Civil War
hospital administrator
Catholic
Cyc Am Bio; Dict Am Bio; Index
t Wom; Not Am Wom; Twent
Cen Bio Dict Not Am; Wom
Cent

5135. Harvey, Cordelia Adelaide Perrine
1824–95
Civil War nurse, relief worker, social welfare leader
Index t Wom

5136. Holstein, Anna
1824–90
author, Civil War nurse
Index t Wom

5137. Minor, Virginia Louisa
1824–94
Civil War relief worker, suffrage leader, women's rights worker
Missouri
Cyc Am Bio; Dict Am Bio; Encyc South Hist; Nat Cyc Am Bio v25; Not Am Wom; Twent Cen Bio Dict Not Am

5138. Moore, Clara Sophia (Jessup); Clara Moreton; Clara Sophia (Jessup) Bloomfield-Moore
1824–99
author, poet, novelist, philanthropist, Civil War relief worker
Philadelphia, PA
Cyc Am Bio; Dict Am Auth; Index t Wom; Nat Cyc Am Bio v9; Not Am Wom; Twent Cen Bio Dict Not Am; Wom Cent

5139. Parsons, Emily Elizabeth
1824–80
Civil War nurse
Index t Wom; Not Am Wom

5140. Sanders, Sue A. Pike
1824–post 1910
club leader, president of the Women's Relief Corps
Illinois
Index t Wom; Wom Cent

5141. Barry, Susan E. (Hare)
born 1826
Civil War nurse
Wom Cent

5142. Davis, Varina Howell
1826–1909
Civil War diarist, journalist, Confederate patriot of Civil War
Bio Dict Confed; Encyc South Hist; Index t Wom; Wom Cent

5143. Denison, Mary Ann Andrews; Mrs. C. W. D.
1826–1911
novelist, short story writer, Civil War nurse
Cyc Am Bio; Dict Am Auth; Dict Am Bio Men Time; Nat Cyc Am Bio v19; Not Am Wom; Twent Cen Bio Dict Not Am

5144. Hazard, Rebecca N.
born 1826

philanthropist, suffragist, Civil War relief worker
Missouri
Wom Cent

5145. Turchin, Nadine
1826–1904
Civil War patriot, soldier, hero
Russian
Index t Wom

5146. Wittenmyer, Annie (Turner)
1827–1900
Civil War relief worker, leader in church and charitable work, philanthropist, temperance worker, lecturer, author
Ohio
Index t Wom; Nat Cyc Am Bio v12; Not Am Wom; Wom Cent

5147. Baker, Delphine P.
born 1828
Civil War relief worker
Index t Wom

5148. Collins, Ellen
1828–1912
philanthropist, housing reformer, Civil War patriot
Index t Wom; Not Am Wom

5149. Coston, Martha J.
1828–86
inventor of navy night signals from ship to ship
Twent Cen Bio Dict Not Am

5150. Cumming, Kate
1828/35–1909
Confederate hospital administrator, diarist, nurse
Alabama
Scottish
Dict Am Auth; Index t Wom; Not Am Wom

5151. Pember, Phoebe Yates Levy
1828–1913
Confederate hospital administrator and nurse, diarist
Index t Wom; Not Am Wom

5152. Woolsey, Abby Howland
1828–93
Civil War relief worker, hospital worker, charity and educational worker, author on public health, philanthropist
Dict Am Auth; Index t Wom; Not Am Wom

5153. Dorsey, Sarah Anne (Ellis); Filia Ecclesiae
1829–79
Civil War nurse, author, novelist, theologian

Mississippi
Cyc Am Bio; Dict Am Auth; Index t Wom; Nat Cyc Am Bio v3; Not Am Wom; Twent Cen Bio Dict Not Am

5154. Gay, Mary Ann Harris
born 1829
Civil War diarist
Index t Wom

5155. May, Abigail Williams
1829–88
Boston social reformer, abolitionist, suffragist, education commissioner, Civil War relief worker
Boston, MA
Index t Wom; Not Am Wom; Twent Cen Bio Dict Not Am

5156. Moon, Charlotte
1829–1912
Civil War spy, hero
Index t Wom

5157. A. M. B., Miss
flourished 1860s
Civil War diarist
Index t Wom

5158. Adams, Martha
flourished 1860s
Civil War nurse
Index t Wom

5159. Agnes
flourished 1860s
Civil War diarist
Index t Wom

5160. Aiken, Lizzie
flourished 1860s
Civil War nurse
Index t Wom

5161. Alder, Emily
flourished 1860s
Civil War nurse
Index t Wom

5162. Allen, Phebe
flourished 1860s
Civil War nurse
Index t Wom

5163. Alter, Belle Thompson
flourished 1860s
Civil War nurse
Index t Wom

5164. Andrews, Emma
flourished 1860s
Civil War relief worker
Index t Wom

5165. Arnold, Mary Ellen
flourished 1860s
Civil War diarist
Index t Wom

5166. Aston, Mary A.
flourished 1860s
Civil War nurse
Index t Wom

5167. Baker, Anna H.
flourished 1860s
Civil War nurse
Index t Wom

5168. Baker, E. H., Mrs.
flourished 1860s
Civil War spy, Pinkerton detective
Index t Wom

5169. Baldridge, Elizabeth Lee
flourished 1860s
Civil War nurse
Index t Wom

5170. Ballou, Addie L.
flourished 1860s
Civil War nurse, author, artist, lawyer
Index t Wom

5171. Barker, Stephen, Mrs.
flourished 1860s
Civil War relief worker, nurse
Index t Wom

5172. Barrows, Ellen B.
flourished 1860s
Civil War patriot
Index t Wom

5173. Barry, Susan E. Hill
flourished 1860s
Civil War nurse
Index t Wom

5174. Baum, A.
flourished 1860s; died 1910
Civil War patriot
German
Index t Wom

5175. Beck, Mrs.
flourished 1860s
Civil War patriot
Index t Wom

5176. Bell, Mary E.
flourished 1860s
Civil War nurse
Index t Wom

5177. Bengless, Catherine H. Griffith
flourished 1860s
Civil War nurse
Index t Wom

5178. Bigelow, R. M.
flourished 1860s
Civil War relief worker
Index t Wom

5179. Bissell, Lucy J.
flourished 1860s

Civil War nurse
Index t Wom

5180. Blackmar, Miss
flourished 1860s
Civil War nurse
Index t Wom

5181. Blalock, L. M., Mrs.
flourished 1860s
Civil War soldier
Index t Wom

5182. Booth, Mrs.
flourished 1860s
Civil War patriot
Index t Wom

5183. Boozer, Mary
flourished 1860s
Civil War patriot
Index t Wom

5184. Boteler, Helen
flourished 1860s
Civil War musician
Index t Wom

5185. Botume, Elizabeth Hyde
flourished 1860s
Civil War patriot, educator
Index t Wom

5186. Boyer, Margaret
flourished 1860s
Civil War patriot
Index t Wom

5187. Boyington, Mary K.
flourished 1860s
Civil War nurse
Index t Wom

5188. Bradford, Charlotte
flourished 1860s
Civil War humanitarian
Index t Wom

5189. Bradford, Mary
flourished 1860s
Civil War hero
Index t Wom

5190. Brayton, Mary Clark
flourished 1860s–80s
Civil War relief worker, social
    reformer
Index t Wom

5191. Breckinridge, Margaret
    Elizabeth
flourished 1860s
Civil War nurse
Index t Wom

5192. Briggs, M. M., Mrs.
flourished 1860s
Civil War nurse
Index t Wom

5193. Brooks, Mary Frances
flourished 1860s

Civil War diarist
Index t Wom

5194. Brown, Nancy M. Nelson
flourished 1860s
Civil War nurse
Index t Wom

5195. Brown, Susan L.
    McLaughlin
flourished 1860s
Civil War nurse
Index t Wom

5196. Buckley, Lettie E. Covell
flourished 1860s
Civil War nurse
Index t Wom

5197. Bucklin, Sophronia
flourished 1860s
Civil War relief worker, educator,
    nurse
Index t Wom

5198. Buie, Mary Ann
flourished 1860s
Civil War patriot
Index t Wom

5199. Bullard, Jennie Matthew-
    son
flourished 1860s
Civil War nurse
Index t Wom

5200. Bunnell, Henrietta S. T.
flourished 1860s
Civil War nurse
Index t Wom

5201. Burnell, Helen M.
flourished 1860s
Civil War nurse
Index t Wom

5202. Byson, Mary
flourished 1860s
Civil War diarist
Index t Wom

5203. Cahal, Mary
flourished 1860s
Civil War diarist
Index t Wom

5204. Campbell, Valeria
flourished 1860s
Civil War relief worker, author
Index t Wom

5205. Canfield, Martha
flourished 1860s
Civil War nurse
Index t Wom

5206. Cartwright, Emily J.
    Avery
flourished 1860s
Civil War nurse
Index t Wom

5207. Cary, Constance
flourished 1860s
Civil War diarist
Index t Wom

5208. Chapin, Hermon, Mrs.
flourished 1860s
Civil War patriot
Index t Wom

5209. Chapman, Elizabeth
flourished 1860s
Civil War nurse
Index t Wom

5210. Chapman, G. D.
flourished 1860s
Civil War patriot
Index t Wom

5211. Chase, Nelly M.
flourished 1860s
Civil War soldier
Index t Wom

5212. Clapp, Anna L.
flourished 1860s
Civil War relief worker, educator
Index t Wom

5213. Clark, Bell Vorse
flourished 1860s
Civil War nurse
Index t Wom

5214. Clarke, Amy
flourished 1860s
Civil War soldier
Index t Wom

5215. Cochran, Nannie M.
flourished 1860s
Civil War nurse
Index t Wom

5216. Cohen, Octavia
flourished 1860s
Civil War patriot
Index t Wom

5217. Cole, Helen Brainard
flourished 1860s
Civil War nurse
Index t Wom

5218. Colfax, Harriet R.
flourished 1860s
Civil War nurse
Index t Wom

5219. Coste, Marie Ravenel de
    la
flourished 1860s
Civil War poet
Index t Wom

5220. Counts, Belle
flourished 1860s
Civil War nurse
Index t Wom

5221. Cox, Lucy Ann
flourished 1860s
Civil War hero
Index t Wom

5222. Cross, Sarah B.
flourished 1860s
Civil War nurse
English
Index t Wom

5223. Crossan, Clarissa Watter
flourished 1860s
Civil War nurse
Index t Wom

5224. Curry, Sadie
flourished 1860s
Civil War nurse
Index t Wom

5225. Dada, Hatte A.
flourished 1860s
Civil War nurse
Index t Wom

5226. Dana, Emily W.
flourished 1860s
Civil War nurse
Index t Wom

5227. Danforth, Ruth
flourished 1860s
Civil War nurse
Index t Wom

5228. Daniels, Frances D.
flourished 1860s
Civil War nurse
Index t Wom

5229. Davis, Clara
flourished 1860s
Civil War nurse
Index t Wom

5230. Davis, G. T. M.
flourished 1860s
Civil War nurse, humanitarian
Index t Wom

5231. Day, Juliana
flourished 1860s
Civil War nurse
Index t Wom

5232. Dieffenbacker, Frances
    A.
flourished 1860s
Civil War nurse
Index t Wom

5233. Divers, Bridget
flourished 1860s
Civil War nurse
Irish
Index t Wom

5234. d'Oremieulx, T., Mrs.
flourished 1860s
Civil War patriot
Index t Wom

5235. Duckett, Elizabeth Waring
flourished 1860s
author, Civil War spy
Index t Wom

5236. Dulany, Evalin
flourished 1860s
Civil War patriot
Index t Wom

5237. Dulany, Ida
flourished 1860s
plantation manager, Civil War patriot
Index t Wom

5238. Dumas, Sarah J. Steady
flourished 1860s
Civil War nurse
Index t Wom

5239. Dupee, Mary A.
flourished 1860s
Civil War nurse
Index t Wom

5240. Duvall, Betty
flourished 1860s
Civil War spy
Index t Wom

5241. Dye, Clarissa F.
flourished 1860s
Civil War nurse
Index t Wom

5242. Eaton, J. S., Mrs.
flourished 1860s
Civil War relief worker
Index t Wom

5243. Eccleston, Sarah Chamberlain
flourished 1860s
Civil War nurse
Index t Wom

5244. Edmondson, Belle
flourished 1860s
Civil War diarist
Index t Wom

5245. Edmondston, Catherine Ann
flourished 1860s
Civil War letter writer
Index t Wom

5246. Edson, Sarah P.
flourished 1860s
Civil War nurse, author
Index t Wom

5247. Eldred, Maria Olmstead
flourished 1860s
Civil War nurse
Index t Wom

5248. Elliott, Melcenia
flourished 1860s

Civil War nurse
Index t Wom

5249. Elmer, Emily Rowell
flourished 1860s
Civil War nurse
Index t Wom

5250. Erving, Anne Princess
flourished 1860s
Civil War nurse
Index t Wom

5251. Etheridge, Annie
flourished 1860s
Civil War hero, nurse, humanitarian
Index t Wom

5252. Ewing, Elizabeth Wendell
flourished 1860s
Civil War nurse
Index t Wom

5253. Farnham, Amanda C.
flourished 1860s
Civil War patriot
Index t Wom

5254. Fay, Delia A. B.
flourished 1860s
Civil War nurse
Index t Wom

5255. Felch, Amanda Farnham
born 183?
Civil War patriot
Index t Wom

5256. Fenn, Curtis T., Mrs.
flourished 1860s
Civil War relief worker
Index t Wom

5257. Fogg, Isabella
flourished 1860s
Civil War nurse, philanthropist
Index t Wom

5258. Ford, Antonia
flourished 1860s
Civil War spy, hero
Index t Wom

5259. Fox, Mary Jane
flourished 1860s
Civil War nurse
Index t Wom

5260. Frick, Rebecca E.
flourished 1860s
Civil War nurse
Index t Wom

5261. Fritcher, Elizabeth L.
flourished 1860s
Civil War nurse
Index t Wom

5262. Gardner, Adaline
flourished 1860s
Civil War patriot

German
Index t Wom

5263. Gardner, Bertha
flourished 1860s
Civil War patriot
Index t Wom

5264. Gardner, Mary Fryer
flourished 1860s
Civil War nurse
Index t Wom

5265. George, E. E., Mrs.
flourished 1860s
Civil War nurse, relief worker
Index t Wom

5266. Gibson, E. O., Mrs.
flourished 1860s
Civil War nurse
Index t Wom

5267. Gilmer, Louisa Fredericka
flourished 1860s
Civil War diarist
Index t Wom

5268. Gilmer, Loulie
flourished 1860s
Civil War diarist
Index t Wom

5269. Goodridge, Ellen
flourished 1860s
Civil War soldier
Index t Wom

5270. Grass, Elizabeth
flourished 1860s
Civil War nurse
Index t Wom

5271. Greble, Susan Virginia
flourished 1860s
Civil War relief worker
Index t Wom

5272. Grier, Maria C.
flourished 1860s
Civil War relief worker
Index t Wom

5273. Griffin, Josephine R.
flourished 1860s
Civil War relief worker, hero, philanthropist
Index t Wom

5274. Griffin, William Preston, Mrs.
flourished 1860s
Civil War patriot
Index t Wom

5275. Hadley, Piety Lucretia
flourished 1860s
Civil War relief worker
Index t Wom

5276. Hahn, Anna
flourished 1860s
Civil War nurse
Index t Wom

5277. Hall, Dorian, Mrs.
flourished 1860s
Civil War diarist
Index t Wom

5278. Hall, Maria M. C.
flourished 1860s
Civil War nurse
Index t Wom

5279. Hall, Susan E.
flourished 1860s
Civil War nurse
Index t Wom

5280. Hallowell, M. M., Mrs.
flourished 1860s
Civil War humanitarian and relief worker
Index t Wom

5281. Harland, Elizabeth Carraway
flourished 1860s
spy
Index t Wom

5282. Harmon, Amelia
flourished 1860s
Civil War hero, patriot
Index t Wom

5283. Harrington, Cornelia
flourished 1860s
Civil War nurse
Index t Wom

5284. Harris, John, Mrs.
flourished 1860s
Civil War relief worker, nurse
Index t Wom

5285. Harris, W. F., Mrs.
flourished 1860s
Civil War nurse
Index t Wom

5286. Hawley, Harriet Foote
flourished 1860s
Civil War nurse
Index t Wom

5287. Hayden, Mary F. Strahan
flourished 1860s
Civil War nurse
Index t Wom

5288. Hayes, Margaret Meserolle
flourished 1860s
Civil War nurse
Index t Wom

5289. Hibbard, Julia A.
flourished 1860s

Civil War nurse
Index t Wom

5290. Hill, Nancy M.
flourished 1860s
Civil War nurse
Index t Wom

5291. Hoisington, Lauretta H. Cutler
flourished 1860s
Civil War nurse
Index t Wom

5292. Holmes, Emma E.
flourished 1860s
Civil War hero
Index t Wom

5293. Hook, Frances
flourished 1860s–70s
soldier, frontier scout
Nat Cyc Am Bio v6

5294. Hosmer, O. E., Mrs.
flourished 1860s
Civil War relief worker
Index t Wom

5295. Howe, Abbie J.
flourished 1860s
Civil War nurse
Index t Wom

5296. Howland, Eliza W.
flourished 1860s
Civil War nurse, author
Index t Wom

5297. Hunt, Elizabeth Pickard
flourished 1860s
Civil War nurse
Index t Wom

5298. Husband, Mary Morris
flourished 1860s
Civil War nurse
Index t Wom

5299. Jackson, Eleanor Noyes
flourished 1860s
Civil War hero
Index t Wom

5300. Jackson, Fannie Oslin
flourished 1860s
Civil War nurse
Index t Wom

5301. Jobes, Mary Adelaide Daugherty
flourished 1860s
Civil War nurse
Index t Wom

5302. Johns, Annie E.
flourished 1860s
Civil War patriot
Index t Wom

5303. Johnson, Ada
flourished 1860s

Civil War nurse
Index t Wom

5304. Johnson, Lydia S.
flourished 1860s
Civil War nurse
Index t Wom

5305. Johnston, John T., Mrs.
flourished 1860s
Civil War patriot
Index t Wom

5306. Johnston, Sarah R.
flourished 1860s
Civil War relief worker
Index t Wom

5307. Johnstone, Mary H.
flourished 1860s
Civil War diarist
Index t Wom

5308. Jones, Calista Robinson
flourished 1860s
Civil War patriot
Index t Wom

5309. Jones, Flora MacDonald
flourished 1860s
Civil War patriot
Index t Wom

5310. Jones, Hetty A.
flourished 1860s
Civil War nurse
Index t Wom

5311. Jordan, Conrelia Jane (Matthews)
1830–98
poet, Confederate sympathizer
Virginia
Cyc Am Bio; Dict Am Auth; Index t Wom; Wom Cent

5312. Kaiser, Lucy L. Campbell
flourished 1860s
Civil War nurse
Index t Wom

5313. Kelly, Amie
flourished 1860s
Civil War diarist
Index t Wom

5314. King, E. M.
flourished 1860s
Civil War nurse
Index t Wom

5315. Kingsbury, Emeline D.
flourished 1860s
Civil War nurse
Index t Wom

5316. Kirby, William, Mrs.
flourished 1860s
Civil War hero
Index t Wom

5317. Kollock, Augusta J.
flourished 1860s
Civil War hero
Index t Wom

5318. Kripps, Susanna
flourished 1860s
Civil War nurse
Index t Wom

5319. Lacey, Mary Roby
flourished 1860s
Civil War nurse
Index t Wom

5320. Lamb, William, Mrs.
flourished 1860s
Civil War diarist
Index t Wom

5321. Lane, Adeline A.
flourished 1860s
Civil War nurse
Index t Wom

5322. Lawton, Hattie
flourished 1860s
Civil War spy
Index t Wom

5323. Lawton, Sarah Alexander
flourished 1860s
Civil War diarist
Index t Wom

5324. Lay, Julia
flourished 1860s
Civil War patriot, author
Index t Wom

5325. le Conte, Emma Florence
flourished 1860s
Civil War diarist
Index t Wom

5326. le Grand, Julia
flourished 1860s
Civil War diarist
Index t Wom

5327. Leaveitt, Adelia
flourished 1860s
Civil War nurse
Index t Wom

5328. Lee, Henrietta Bedinger
flourished 1860s
Civil War letter writer
Index t Wom

5329. Lee, Mary W.
flourished 1860s
Civil War nurse, patriot, philanthropist
Irish
Index t Wom

5330. Loomis, Mary A.
flourished 1860s
Civil War nurse
Index t Wom

5331. Love, Mary
flourished 1860s
Civil War hero
Index t Wom

5332. Lowe, Lucy
flourished 1860s
Civil War diarist
Index t Wom

5333. Lowell, Anna
flourished 1860s
Civil War patriot
Index t Wom

5334. Lowell, Susan R.
flourished 1860s
Civil War nurse
Index t Wom

5335. Lowry, Ellen J.
flourished 1860s
Civil War nurse
Index t Wom

5336. MacKall, Lillie
flourished 1860s
Civil War spy
Index t Wom

5337. Maertz, Louisa
flourished 1860s
Civil War nurse
Index t Wom

5338. Maish, Jennie Gauslin
flourished 1860s
Civil War nurse
Index t Wom

5339. Mann, Maria R.
flourished 1860s
Civil War philanthropist, educator
Index t Wom

5340. Marsh, M. M., Mrs.
flourished 1860s
Civil War relief worker
Index t Wom

5341. Maury, Betty Herdon
flourished 1860s
Civil War diarist
Index t Wom

5342. Maxfield, Mary B.
flourished 1860s
Civil War nurse
Index t Wom

5343. McEwen, Hettie M.
flourished 1860s
Civil War hero, patriot
Index t Wom

5344. McKay, Charlotte E.
flourished 1860s
Civil War nurse
Index t Wom

5345. McLure, Margaret A. E.
flourished 1860s
Civil War patriot
Index t Wom

5346. McMeens, Anna C.
flourished 1860s
Civil War nurse
Index t Wom

5347. McMichael, Margaret T.
flourished 1860s
Civil War patriot
Index t Wom

5348. McPeek, Allie
flourished 1860s
Civil War nurse, patriot
Index t Wom

5349. McSherry, Virginia Faulkner
flourished 1860s
Civil War patriot
Index t Wom

5350. McSweeney, Mattie
flourished 1860s
Civil War patriot
Index t Wom

5351. Meekins, A. M., Mrs.
flourished 1860s
Civil War spy
Index t Wom

5352. Melton, Joann
flourished 1860s
Civil War nurse
Index t Wom

5353. Mendenhall, Elizabeth S.
flourished 1860s
Civil War relief worker, nurse, philanthropist
Index t Wom

5354. Miller, Adaline
flourished 1860s
Civil War nurse
Index t Wom

5355. Miller, Dora Richards
flourished 1860s–80s
author, Civil War diarist, journalist, educator
West Indian (Danish West Indies)
Index t Wom; Wom Cent

5356. Miller, Maria
flourished 1860s
Civil War nurse
Index t Wom

5357. Mills, Susan Carrie
flourished 1860s
Civil War nurse
Index t Wom

5358. Mitchell, Ellen E.
flourished 1860s

Civil War nurse
Index t Wom

5359. Moore, Jane Boswell
flourished 1860s
Civil War relief worker
Index t Wom

5360. Morgan, Martha Ready
flourished 1860s
Civil War diarist
Index t Wom

5361. Morris, Matilda E.
flourished 1860s
Civil War nurse
Index t Wom

5362. Morrison, Mary Anna
flourished 1860s
Civil War hero
Index t Wom

5363. Morton, Jane M.
flourished 1860s
Civil War nurse
Index t Wom

5364. Mott, Mollie C.
flourished 1860s
Civil War nurse
Index t Wom

5365. Munsell, Jane R.
flourished 1860s
Civil War nurse
Index t Wom

5366. Murdock, Ellen E.
flourished 1860s
Civil War patriot
Index t Wom

5367. Newman, Laura A. Mount
flourished 1860s
Civil War nurse
Index t Wom

5368. Newsome, Ella King
circa 1830–circa 1913
Civil War hospital manager, nurse, Confederate sympathizer
Bio Dict Confed; Index t Wom

5369. Nichols, Elizabeth B.
flourished 1860s
Civil War nurse
Index t Wom

5370. Oleson, Rebecca Lemmon
flourished 1860s
Civil War nurse
Index t Wom

5371. Otis, Rebecca
flourished 1860s
Civil War nurse
Index t Wom

5372. Painter, Hettie K.
flourished 1860s

Civil War patriot
Index t Wom

5373. Palmer, Hannah L.
flourished 1860s
Civil War nurse
Index t Wom

5374. Parrish, Lydia G.
flourished 1860s
Civil War humanitarian
Index t Wom

5375. Patterson, Sarepta C. McNall
flourished 1860s
Civil War nurse
Index t Wom

5376. Pearsall, Rachel
flourished 1860s
Civil War patriot
Index t Wom

5377. Perkins, Anne
flourished 1860s
Civil War letter writer
Index t Wom

5378. Pettes, Mary Dwight
flourished 1860s
Civil War nurse
Index t Wom

5379. Phelps, John S., Mrs.
flourished 1860s
Civil War humanitarian
Index t Wom

5380. Phillips, Bettie Taylor
flourished 1860s
Civil War patriot
Index t Wom

5381. Phillips, Emaline
flourished 1860s
Civil War nurse
Index t Wom

5382. Phillips, Eugenia Levy
flourished 1860s
Civil War patriot
Index t Wom

5383. Phillips, Josephine
flourished 1860s
Civil War patriot, author
Index t Wom

5384. Pickens, Lucy Holcombe
flourished 1860s
Civil War hero
Index t Wom

5385. Pierce, Tillie
flourished 1860s
Civil War patriot
Index t Wom

5386. Pigott, Emeline
flourished 1860s

Civil War hero, spy
Dict Am Auth; Index t Wom

5387. Pollard, Carrie Wilkins
flourished 1860s
Civil War nurse
Index t Wom

5388. Pollock, Mary B.
flourished 1860s
Civil War nurse
Index t Wom

5389. Pollock, Roberta
flourished 1860s
Civil War hero
Index t Wom

5390. Poppenheim, C. C.
flourished 1860s
Civil War patriot
Index t Wom

5391. Porter, Eliza C.
flourished 1860s
Civil War nurse
Index t Wom

5392. Powers, Lucy Gaylord
flourished 1860s
Civil War patriot, humanitarian
Index t Wom

5393. Pratt, Malinda A. Miller
flourished 1860s
Civil War nurse
Index t Wom

5394. Price, Rebecca L.
flourished 1860s
Civil War nurse
Index t Wom

5395. Pryor, Sara Agnes Rice
1830–1912
author, Civil War hero
Index t Wom; Not Am Wom

5396. Pugh, Mary Williams
flourished 1860s
Civil War diarist
Index t Wom

5397. Rathnell, Maria L. Moore
flourished 1860s
Civil War nurse
Index t Wom

5398. Ravenel, Charlotte St. Julien
flourished 1860s
Civil War diarist
Index t Wom

5399. Rawson, Mary
flourished 1860s
Civil War diarist
Index t Wom

5400. Reading, Sarah M.
flourished 1860s

Civil War nurse
Index t Wom

5401. Ready, Alice
flourished 1860s
Civil War diarist
Index t Wom

**5402. Richards, Maria M. C.
Hall**
flourished 1860s
Civil War nurse
Index t Wom

**5403. Richardson, Mary A.
Ransorn**
flourished 1860s
Civil War nurse
Index t Wom

5404. Ricketts, Fanny L.
flourished 1860s
Civil War humanitarian
English
Index t Wom

5405. Ridley, Rebeccah C.
flourished 1860s
Civil War diarist
Index t Wom

**5406. Risley, Alice Carey
Farmer**
flourished 1860s
Civil War nurse
Index t Wom

5407. Rogers, Loula Kendall
flourished 1860s
Civil War patriot
Index t Wom

5408. Ross, Anna Maria
flourished 1860s
Civil War philanthropist, nurse
Index t Wom

5409. Russell, E. J.
flourished 1860s
Civil War nurse, educator
Index t Wom

5410. Russell, Lenie
flourished 1860s
Civil War hero
Index t Wom

5411. Russell, Tillie
flourished 1860s
Civil War hero
Index t Wom

**5412. Sackett, Emma A.
French**
flourished 1860s
Civil War nurse
Index t Wom

5413. Salomon, Eliza
flourished 1860s
Civil War philanthropist
Index t Wom

5414. Sansom, Emma
flourished 1860s; died 1900
Civil War hero, diarist
Index t Wom

5415. Scales, Cordelia Lewis
flourished 1860s
Civil War diarist
Index t Wom

5416. Schram, Ann Maria B.
flourished 1860s
Civil War nurse
Index t Wom

5417. Scott, Harriet M.
flourished 1860s
Civil War nurse
Index t Wom

5418. Scott, Kate M.
flourished 1860s; died 1911
Civil War nurse
Index t Wom

5419. Scott, Taylor, Mrs.
flourished 1860s
Civil War patriot
Index t Wom

5420. Seelye, Marie
flourished 1860s
soldier
Index t Wom

5421. Seymour, Horatio, Mrs.
flourished 1860s
Civil War humanitarian
Index t Wom

5422. Sharpless, Hattie R.
flourished 1860s
Civil War nurse
Index t Wom

5423. Sheads, Carrie
flourished 1860s
Civil War hero
Index t Wom

5424. Shelton, A.
flourished 1860s
Civil War nurse
Index t Wom

**5425. Shover, Felicia Lee Car-
ey Thornton**
flourished 1860s
Civil War hero
Index t Wom

5426. Simpson, Annie
flourished 1860s; died 1905
Civil War patriot
Index t Wom

5427. Simpson, Lucy Faucett
flourished 1860s
Civil War patriot
Index t Wom

5428. Sims, Leora
flourished 1860s
Civil War diarist
Index t Wom

5429. Small, Jerusha R.
flourished 1860s
Civil War nurse
Index t Wom

5430. Smith, Lucy
flourished 1860s
Civil War diarist
Index t Wom

5431. Smith, Mary E. Webber
flourished 1860s
Civil War nurse
Index t Wom

5432. Smith, Rebecca S.
flourished 1860s
educator, Civil War nurse
Index t Wom

5433. Smith, S. E. D., Mrs.
flourished 1860s
Civil War patriot
Index t Wom

5434. Smythe, Amanda B.
flourished 1860s
Civil War nurse
Index t Wom

5435. Souder, Emily Bliss
flourished 1860s
Civil War patriot, author
Index t Wom

**5436. Spaulding, Jennie Tile-
ston**
flourished 1860s
Civil War nurse
Index t Wom

5437. Spencer, Emily P.
flourished 1860s
Civil War nurse
Index t Wom

5438. Spencer, R. H., Mrs.
flourished 1860s
Civil War nurse
Index t Wom

**5439. Sprague, Sarah J. Mil-
liken**
flourished 1860s
Civil War nurse
Index t Wom

5440. Sprague, Susannah
flourished 1860s
Civil War nurse
Index t Wom

5441. Springer, C. R., Mrs.
flourished 1860s
Civil War humanitarian, educator
Index t Wom

5442. Squire, Mary E.
flourished 1860s
Civil War nurse
Index t Wom

**5443. Stanley, Cornelia M.
Tomkins**
flourished 1860s
Civil War nurse
Index t Wom

**5444. Starbird, Hannah Jud-
kins**
flourished 1860s
Civil War nurse
Index t Wom

5445. Starr, Lucy E.
flourished 1860s
Civil War nurse
Index t Wom

**5446. Stevens, Mary O. Town-
send**
flourished 1860s
Civil War nurse
Index t Wom

5447. Stevenson, Sophie
flourished 1860s
Civil War nurse
Index t Wom

5448. Stewart, Mary E. Pearce
flourished 1860s
Civil War nurse
Index t Wom

5449. Stewart, Salome M.
flourished 1860s
Civil War nurse
Index t Wom

**5450. Stinson, Virginia McCol-
lum**
flourished 1860s
Civil War diarist
Index t Wom

5451. Stover, Sarah
flourished 1860s
Civil War soldier
Index t Wom

5452. Stranahan, Marianne F.
flourished 1860s
Civil War humanitarian
Index t Wom

5453. Streeter, Elizabeth M.
flourished 1860s
Civil War humanitarian
Index t Wom

5454. Stuart, Flora Cooke
flourished 1860s
Civil War hero
Index t Wom

5455. Stubbs, Annie Bell
flourished 1860s

Civil War nurse
Index t Wom

5456. Sturgis, Mother
flourished 1860s
Civil War nurse
Index t Wom

5457. Sullivan, Betsy "Mother"
flourished 1860s
Civil War patriot
Index t Wom

5458. Sutherlin, W. T., Mrs.
flourished 1860s
Civil War diarist
Index t Wom

5459. Swartz, Vesta M.
flourished 1860s
Civil War nurse
Index t Wom

5460. Tannehill, Arabella
flourished 1860s
Civil War nurse
Index t Wom

5461. Taylor, Alice
flourished 1860s
Civil War patriot
Index t Wom

5462. Taylor, Catherine L.
flourished 1860s
Civil War nurse
Index t Wom

5463. Taylor, Nellie Maria
flourished 1860s
Civil War nurse
Index t Wom

5464. Terry, Ellen F.
flourished 1860s
Civil War humanitarian
Index t Wom

5465. Thomas, E., Mrs.
flourished 1860s
Civil War nurse
Index t Wom

5466. Thompson, Charlotte Marson
flourished 1860s
Civil War nurse
Index t Wom

5467. Titcomb, Louise
flourished 1860s
Civil War nurse
Index t Wom

5468. Titlow, Effie
flourished 1860s
Civil War hero
Index t Wom

5469. Tomkins, Cornelia M.
flourished 1860s

Civil War nurse
Index t Wom

5470. Townsend, Eliza L.
flourished 1860s
Civil War nurse
Index t Wom

5471. Tynes, Mary Elizabeth "Molly"
flourished 1860s
Civil War hero
Index t Wom

5472. Tyson, Laura R. Cotton
flourished 1860s
Civil War nurse
Index t Wom

5473. Usher, Rebecca R.
flourished 1860s
Civil War nurse
Index t Wom

5474. Vance, Mary
flourished 1860s
Civil War nurse
Index t Wom

5475. Wade, Jennie
flourished 1860s
Civil War patriot
Index t Wom

5476. Wade, Mary B.
flourished 1860s
Civil War patriot
Index t Wom

5477. Wadley, Sarah L.
flourished 1860s
Civil War diarist
Index t Wom

5478. Waring, Mary D.
flourished 1860s
Civil War diarist
Index t Wom

5479. Warnock, Susan Mercer
flourished 1860s
Civil War nurse
Index t Wom

5480. Waterbury, Kate E.
flourished 1860s
Civil War patriot
Index t Wom

5481. Wellman, Louisa
flourished 1860s
Civil War soldier
Index t Wom

5482. Wells, Shepard, Mrs.
flourished 1860s
Civil War humanitarian
Index t Wom

5483. Whetton, Harriet Douglas
flourished 1860s

Civil War patriot
Index t Wom

5484. White, Armenia
flourished 1860s
philanthropist, social reformer,
  Civil War patriot
Index t Wom

5485. White, Cynthia Elbin
flourished 1860s
Civil War nurse
Index t Wom

5486. Whiteman, Lydia L.
flourished 1860s
Civil War nurse
Index t Wom

5487. Wilcox, G. Griffin, Mrs.
flourished 1860s
Civil War diarist
Index t Wom

5488. Willard, Electra
flourished 1860s
Civil War nurse
Index t Wom

5489. Willets, Georgiana
flourished 1860s
Civil War nurse
Index t Wom

5490. Willson, Mary Eleanor
flourished 1860s
Civil War nurse
Index t Wom

5491. Windsor, Mary Catherine
1830–1914
Civil War hero, spy
Index t Wom

5492. Wiswall, Hattie
flourished 1860s
Civil War nurse
Index t Wom

5493. Witherall, E. C., Mrs.
flourished 1860s
Civil War nurse
Index t Wom

5494. Woodley, Emily E. Wilson
flourished 1860s
Civil War nurse
Index t Wom

5495. Woodworth, Mary A. E. K.
flourished 1860s
Civil War nurse
Index t Wom

5496. Woolsey, Caroline Caisson
flourished 1860s
Civil War nurse, author
Index t Wom

5497. Woolsey, Harriet Roosevelt "Hatty"
flourished 1860s
Civil War nurse, author
Index t Wom

5498. Woolsey, Jane Newton
flourished 1860s
Civil War nurse
Index t Wom

5499. Woolsey, Jane Stuart
1830–91
Civil War relief and hospital
  worker, charity and educational
  worker, nurse, author
Index t Wom; Not Am Wom

5500. Wormeley, Katharine Prescott
1830/32–1908
Civil War relief and hospital
  worker, writer on sanitation,
  charity worker, philanthropist,
  translator, biographer
Rhode Island
English
Cyc Am Bio; Dict Am Bio; Index
  t Wom; Nat Cyc Am Bio v8;
  Not Am Wom; Twent Cen Bio
  Dict Not Am; Wom Cent

5501. Wright, Crafts J., Mrs.
flourished 1860s
Civil War humanitarian
Index t Wom

5502. Wright, Leonore Smith
flourished 1860s
Civil War nurse
Index t Wom

5503. Young, Lucy A. Newton
flourished 1860s
Civil War nurse
Index t Wom

5504. Bradwell, Myra R. (Colby)
1831–1894/96
lawyer, suffragist, editor, Civil
  War nurse
Chicago, IL
Dict Am Bio; Index t Wom; Nat
  Cyc Am Bio v1; Not Am Wom;
  Twent Cen Bio Dict Not Am;
  Wom Cent

5505. Lockwood, Mary Smith
born 1831
editor, clubwoman, patriot, writer
  on art and architecture
Dict Am Auth; Index t Wom;
  Nat Cyc Am Bio v3

5506. Seacole, Mary
died 1881
war nurse in the Crimea
Black
World Great Men Col v2

5507. Smith, Adelaide W.
born 1831
Civil War nurse
Index t Wom

5508. Tincker, Mary Agnes
1831/37–1907
novelist, Civil War nurse
Catholic
Cyc Am Bio; Dict Am Bio; Nat
Cyc Am Bio v8; Twent Cen Bio
Dict Not Am

5509. Young, Sarah Graham;
Aunt Betty
born 1831
Civil War army nurse, Union
sympathizer
Wom Cent

**5510. Cadwallader, Allice A.
W.**
born 1832
philanthropist, Civil War relief
worker, temperance worker
Wom Cent

5511. Fussell, Susan
1832–89
educator, army nurse in the Civil
War, Civil War relief worker,
philanthropist
Quaker
Wom Cent

5512. Hurd, P. B., Mrs.
married 1857
Civil War hero
Index t Wom

5513. Jackson, Mary Anna
married 1857
Civil War diarist
Index t Wom

5514. Reese, Mary Bynon
born 1832
temperance worker, poet, Civil
War humanitarian, Union sympathizer
Wom Cent

5515. Walker, Mary Edwards
1832–1919
physician, Civil War medical
worker, hospital founder, army
war surgeon, Union spy during
the Civil War; women's rights
worker, suffragist, dress reformer, inventor, lecturer, winner of
the Congressional Medal of
Honor
Dict Am Bio; Index t Wom; Nat
Cyc Am Bio v13; Not Am
Wom; Wom Cent

5516. Walworth, Ellen (Hardin)
1832–1915
author, war nurse, writer on the
history of Saratoga, educator,
poet

Saratoga, NY
Cyc Am Bio and ad; Dict Am
Auth; Index t Wom; Twent Cen
Bio Dict Not Am; Wom Cent

5517. Buckel, Chloe Annette
1833–1912
physician, Civil War nurse
Not Am Wom

5518. Cushman, Pauline
1833/35–1895
Union spy during the Civil War,
actor
Cyc Am Bio; Dict Am Bio; Index
t Wom; Nat Cyc Am Bio v23;
Twent Cen Bio Dict Not Am

**5519. Freeman, Julia S. (Whee-
lock)**
1833–1900
philanthropist, Civil War relief
worker
Nat Cyc Am Bio v7

5520. Pringle, Mary
born 1833
Civil War nurse
Index t Wom

5521. Tompkins, Sally Louisa
1833–1916
Confederate hospital head, cap-
tain of cavalry in the Confeder-
ate army
Virginia
Bio Dict Confed; Dict Am Bio;
Encyc South Hist; Index t
Wom; Not Am Wom

5522. Wheelock, Julia Susan
born 1833
Civil War nurse, hospital nurse,
author
Cyc Am Bio; Index t Wom

**5523. Woolsey, Georgeanne
Muirson**
1833–1906
Civil War relief and hospital
worker, charity and educational
worker
Index t Wom; Not Am Wom

**5524. Brinton, Emma South-
wick**
born 1834
Civil War nurse, traveler
Wom Cent

5525. McHenry, Mary Sears
born 1834
president of the National Wom-
en's Relief Corps, clubwoman
Illinois
Index t Wom; Wom Cent

**5526. Safford, Mary Joanna
Jane**
1834–91
Civil War nurse, physician, surgeon

Boston, MA
Index t Wom; Not Am Wom;
Wom Cent

**5527. Wilson, Martha Eleanor
Loftin**
born 1834
missionary worker, Civil War
nurse
Baptist
Georgia
Wom Cent

**5528. Osgood, Helen Louise
(Gibson/Gilson)**
1835–68
philanthropist, Civil War hospital
administrator, nurse
Cyc Am Bio; Dict Am Bio Men
Time; Index t Wom; Not Am
Wom

**5529. Vaughan, Sue Landon
(Adams)**
born 1835
founder of Decoration Day
Nat Cyc Am Bio v14

**5530. Wilson, Augusta C. Jane
(Evans)**
1835/36–1909
novelist, Confederate author
Methodist
Mobile, AL
Cyc Am Bio; Dict Am Auth; Dict
Am Bio; Dict Am Bio Men
Time; Encyc South Hist; Index
t Wom; Nat Cyc Am Bio v4;
Not Am Wom; Wom Cent;
Wom Lit, More

5531. Woolsey, Sarah Chauncy;
Susan Coolidge
1835/45–1905
children's author, poet, Civil War
nurse
Newport, RI
Dict Am Auth; Dict Am Bio;
Index t Wom; Nat Cyc Am Bio
v11; Not Am Wom; Wom Cent

**5532. Lemmon, Sarah Allen
(Plummer)**
1836–post 1860s
Civil War nurse, botanist, writer
on botany
Dict Am Auth; Index t Wom

**5533. Loughborough, Mary
Ann Webster**
1836–87
author, Civil War diarist
Little Rock, AR
Cyc Am Bio; Dict Am Auth;
Index t Wom

5534. Miller, Elizabeth
born 1836
physician, Civil War nurse
Wom Cent

5535. Smith, Cassie Selden
married 1861
Civil War diarist
Index t Wom

5536. Stearns, Sarah Burger
1836–post 1899
suffragist, women's rights worker,
philanthropist, Civil War humanitarian, temperance worker,
social reformer, educator of
freedmen
Unitarian
Cyc Am Bio; Index t Wom; Nat
Cyc Am Bio v10; Twent Cen
Bio Dict Not Am; Wom Cent

5537. Schuyler, Louisa Lee
1837/40–1926
leader in welfare work, Civil War
philanthropist, patron of nursing, social worker, sanitarian
New York
Dict Am Bio; Index t Wom; Nat
Cyc Am Bio v20; Not Am Wom

5538. Eggleston, Sarah Dabney
born circa 1838
World War I patriot
Index t Wom

**5539. Hague, Parthenia Antoin-
ette (Vardaman)**
born 1838; flourished 1860s
Civil War diarist
Florida
Dict Am Auth; Index t Wom

5540. Proctor, Edna Dean
born 1838
poet, author, Union writer during
Civil War
Cyc Am Bio and ad; Dict Am
Auth; Nat Cyc Am Bio v7

5541. Stokes, Missouri H.
1838–post 1860
Civil War diarist, educator, tem-
perance worker
Presbyterian
Georgia
Index t Wom; Wom Cent

**5542. Sullivan, Mary Mildred
Hammond**
1838–1933
philanthropist, Civil War patriot,
New York civic leader
Presbyterian
New York
Index t Wom; Nat Cyc Am Bio
v31

**5543. Trader, Ella King New-
som**
1838–1919
Confederate hospital administrator, Civil War nurse
Index t Wom; Not Am Wom

5544. Vashon, Susan Paul
1838–1912

educator, nurse, Civil War relief
organizer
Black
Index t Wom; Negro Alman; Prof
Negro Wom v1

5545. Velasquez, Loretta Janeta
born 1838
western pioneer, Civil War diarist, Civil War spy
Index t Wom

5546. Velazquez, Louta Janita;
Velasquez, Loretta Janeta;
Harry T. Buford
born 1838/42
Civil War autobiographer, west-
ern pioneer, Civil War spy
Encyc South Hist; Index t Wom

5547. Walling, Mary Cole; The
Banished Heroine of the
South
born 1838
lecturer, Union patriot during the
Civil War
Texas
Index t Wom; Wom Cent

**5548. Wright, Rebecca
McPherson**
born 1838
Union spy during the Civil War,
Civil War hero
Quaker
Cyc Am Bio; Index t Wom

5549. George, Lydia A.
born 1839
army nurse in Civil War, Wom-
en's Relief Corps worker, philanthropist
Wom Cent

5550. Hancock, Cornelia
1839/40–1927
Civil War nurse, educator of
freedmen, charity worker, housing reformer
Quaker
Index t Wom; Not Am Wom

**5551. Peckham, Mary Chace
(Peck)**
1839–92
author, fiction writer, poet, Civil
War nurse, suffragist, women's
rights worker
Unitarian
Providence, RI
Dict Am Auth; Nat Cyc Am Bio
v9; Twent Cen Bio Dict Not
Am

5552. Telford, Mary Jewett
born 1839
army nurse, Civil War nurse,
Women's Relief Corps organizer, church worker, children's
author

Quaker
Wom Cent

5553. Andrews, Eliza Frances
1840/47–1931
journalist, Civil War diarist, edu-
cator, botanist
Georgia
Dict Am Auth; Index t Wom;
Nat Cyc Am Bio v6; Not Am
Wom; Wom Cent

5554. Darling, Flora (Adams)
1840–1910
fiction writer, novelist, founder of
the Daughters of the Revolution
patriotic society
Dict Am Auth; Dict Am Bio;
Index t Wom; Nat Cyc Am Bio
v19; Not Am Wom; Wom Cent

5555. Hamilton, Margaret
born 1840
Civil War nurse
Index t Wom

5556. Hazen, Fanny Titus
born 1840
Civil War nurse
Index t Wom

**5557. Putnam, Sarah A. Brock
"Sallie";** Virginia Madison
1840/45–post 1900
author, novelist, Civil War writer
New York, NY
Cyc Am Bio; Dict Am Auth; Nat
Cyc Am Bio v10; Twent Cen
Bio Dict Not Am; Wom Cent

5558. Reynolds, Belle
born 1840
Civil War nurse, patriot, author
Index t Wom

**5559. Salm Salm, Agnes
Elizabeth Winona Joy
(Leqlerq), Princess**
1840/42–1881/1912
circus rider, rope dancer, actor,
field hospital worker and organizer, philanthropist
Cyc Am Bio; Dict Am Bio;
Twent Cen Bio Dict Not Am

**5560. Searing, Laura Catherine
(Redden);** Howard Glyndon
1840–1923
author, war correspondent, jour-
nalist, poet
deaf
Cyc Am Bio; Dict Am Auth; Dict
Am Bio; Dict Am Bio Men
Time; Index t Wom; Nat Cyc
Am Bio v9; Wom Cent

**5561. Slemmer, Caroline Lane
Reynolds;** Lady Jebb
born 1840
patriot
Index t Wom

5562. Stone, Cornelia Branch
born 1840
Civil War patriot, club leader
Index t Wom

**5563. Edmonds, Sarah Emma
Evelyn;** Franklin Thompson
1841–98
Civil War soldier, spy, nurse
Canadian
Index t Wom; Not Am Wom

5564. Morgan, Sarah
born 1841
Civil War diarist
Index t Wom

**5565. Plimpton, Hannah R.
Cope**
born 1841
club leader, Women's Relief
Corps worker, Civil War nurse
Index t Wom; Wom Cent

5566. Brownell, Kady
born 1842
Civil War soldier, hero
Index t Wom

5567. Dare, Ella
born 1842
lecturer, journalist, Civil War relief worker, sanitarian
Wom Cent

5568. Dawson, Sarah; Ida Fowler
1842–1909
author, Civil War diarist
Episcopalian
Index t Wom; Nat Cyc Am Bio
v23

**5569. Dickinson, Anna
Elizabeth**
1842–1932
Civil War orator, lyceum lecturer,
abolitionist, women's rights
worker, suffragist, political ac-
tivist, Republican party worker,
author, actor, philanthropist
Quaker
Cyc Am Bio; Dict Am Auth; Dict
Am Bio supp v1; Dict Am Bio
Men Time; Index t Wom; Nat
Cyc Am Bio v3; Not Am Wom;
Twent Cen Bio Dict Not Am;
Wom Cent

**5570. Fowle, Elida Barker
Rumsey**
1842–1919
Civil War relief worker and
nurse, cofounder of a library for
Union soldiers in Washington,
DC
Index t Wom; Not Am Wom

5571. Gist, Malvina Black
born 1842
Civil War diarist
Index t Wom

**5572. Ruffin, Josephine St.
Pierre**
1842–1924
clubwoman, Black leader, Black
welfare and rights worker, president of the National Federation
of Afro-American Women,
Union patriot in the Civil War
Black
Index t Wom; Negro Alman; Not
Am Wom; Prof Negro Wom v1

5573. Boyd, Belle; Belle Hard-
inge
1843/44–1900
Confederate spy, actor, lecturer
Episcopalian
Bio Dict Confed; Dict Am Bio;
Index t Wom; Not Am Wom

5574. Mannon, Mary L.
born 1843
Civil War nurse
Index t Wom

5575. Pickett, Lasalle Carbell
born 1843
Civil War patriot, hero, diarist,
lecturer
Index t Wom; Wom Cent

5576. Roebling, Emily Warren
1843–1903
Civil War patriot, philanthropist,
club leader, author, lawyer
Index t Wom

5577. Simonds, Emma E.
died 1893
Civil War nurse
Index t Wom

5578. Thorp, Mandana Coleman
born 1843
Union patriot during the Civil
War, pioneer, deputy clerk and
register of deeds in northern
Michigan, sheep and wool farm-
er
Michigan
Wom Cent

**5579. Wade, Mary Virginia
"Jenny"**
born 1843
Union hero during the Civil War
Cyc Am Bio v1

5580. Wickens, Margaret R.
born 1843
Women's Relief Corps worker,
temperance worker, clubwoman
Wom Cent

5581. Cheney, Armilla Amanda
born 1845
Civil War relief worker
Detroit, MI
Wom Cent

5582. Dillon, Hester A.
born 1845

American patriot
Index t Wom

5583. Moon, Virginia
1845–1926
Civil War spy, hero
Index t Wom

5584. Tucker, Mary Elizabeth Logan
married 1870
patriot
Index t Wom

5585. Bradford, Susan
born circa 1846
Civil War hero
Index t Wom

5586. Chenoweth, Caroline van Duesen
born 1846
author, university literary educator, military clerk during Civil War, US vice-consul in China
Dict Am Auth; Index t Wom; Twent Cen Bio Dict Not Am; Wom Cent

5587. Waggaman, Mary Teresa McKee
1846–1931
author, Confederate sympathizer
Catholic
Dict Am Bio

5588. Alden, Esther
born 1847
Civil War diarist
Index t Wom

5589. Barker, E. Florence
died 1897
officer in Women's Relief Corps
Index t Wom

5590. Adams, Helen Balfour
1848–1950
Civil War relief worker
Index t Wom

5591. Roby, Lelia P.
born 1848
philanthropist, founder of the Ladies of the Grand Army of the Republic, veteran's welfare worker
Index t Wom; Wom Cent

5592. Taylor, Susie Baker King
born 1848
educator, Civil War nurse
Black
Prof Negro Wom v1

5593. Moore, Marguerite
born 1849
orator, patriot, pacifist
Irish
Wom Cent

5594. Anderson, Elizabeth Milbank
1850–1921
World War I relief worker, philanthropist, patron of social welfare work, patron of Serbian and Yugoslavian welfare, patron of medical missions
Baptist
New York
Dict Am Bio; Nat Cyc Am Bio v23; Not Am Wom

5595. Barlow, Arabella Griffith
flourished 1880s
Civil War nurse
Index t Wom

5596. Washington, Eugenie
died 1900
patriot, club leader
Index t Wom

5597. Craig, Charity Rusk
born 1851
soldier's relief worker
Wom Cent

5598. Scott, Mary Anne
born 1851
patriot
Index t Wom

5599. McGahan, Barbara; Paul Kashirin
born 1852
author, Russian-language journalist, correspondent in the 1874–75 Spanish war, Russo-Turkish Wars correspondent
Wom Cent

5600. Clark, Genevieve Bennett
married 1881
American patriot
Index t Wom

5601. Lamar, Clarinda Huntington Pendleton
1856/77–1943
author, leader of the National Society of Colonial Dames
Nat Cyc Am Bio v32; Obit File

5602. McLean, Emily Nelson Ritchie
1859–1916
patriot
Index t Wom

5603. Thompson, Sarah
died 1909
Civil War spy
Index t Wom

5604. Ely, Gertrude S.
flourished 1890s; died 1970
two-time recipient of the French Croix de Guerre for bravery in operating a YWCA canteen in World War I while under fire
Obit File

5605. Maxon, Hannah W.
died 1910
Civil War nurse
Index t Wom

5606. Parlin, Lucy
flourished 1890s–1910s
patriot
Index t Wom

5607. Delano, Jane Arminda
1862–1919
nurse, Red Cross worker, nurse in the Mexican-American War, nursing educator
Dict Am Bio; Index t Wom; Nat Cyc Am Bio v19; Not Am Wom

5608. Spence, Clara Beebe
1862–1923
educator of women, World War I patriot
Nat Cyc Am Bio v20

5609. McGee, Anita Newcomb
1864–1940
physician, surgeon, founder of the Army Nurse Corps, war doctor, army officer
Index t Wom; Not Am Wom; Twent Cen Bio Dict Not Am

5610. Minor, Anne Rogers
1864–1947
president general of DAR
Obit File

5611. de Wolfe, Elsie Anderson; Lady Mendl
1865/70–1950
actor, stage producer, interior decorator, World War I relief worker
Dict Am Bio supp v4; Index t Wom; Nat Cyc Am Bio csv6; Not Am Wom

5612. Lazarovich-Hrebelianovich, Eleanor (Calhoun), Princess
1865–1957
classical actor, Serbian freedom fighter
Serbian
Index t Wom; Obit File

5613. Merrill, Helen Maud; Samantha Spriggins
born 1865
litterateur, poet, patriotic writer
Maine
Wom Cent

5614. Dellworth, Emma V.
1866–1959
US Army nurse during the Spanish-American War
Obit File

5615. Dorr, Rheta Childe
1866–1948

World War I correspondent, journalist, feminist
Index t Wom; Not Am Wom; Obit File

5616. Goodrich, Annie Warburton
1866–1954
World War I nurse, director of the Army School of Nursing, nursing educator, suffragist
Dict Am Bio supp v5; Index t Wom; Nat Cyc Am Bio v42; Not Am Wom supp v1

5617. Lawrence, Ruth Woodhull
1866–1956
founder of the National Society of Colonial Dames, authority on colonial families
Obit File

5618. Young, Mary Vance
1866–1946
educator, linguist, World War I relief worker
Presbyterian
Index t Wom; Nat Cyc Am Bio v33

5619. Brown, Helen
1867–1942
president of the Women's Land Army (volunteer farm labor workers) during World War I
Obit File

5620. Myers, Harriet Williams
born 1867
author, ornithologist, founder of California Audubon Society, conservationist, animal humane worker, World War II national defense worker
Los Angeles, CA
Am Bio New Cyc

5621. Duryea, Nina Larrey Smith
1868–1951
World War I relief worker, playwright
Obit File

5622. Kittredge, Mabel
1868–1955
World War I relief worker, school lunch crusader
Obit File

5623. Bullowa, Emilie M.
1869–1942
lawyer, World War II relief worker, Sorosis member
Jewish
New York
Nat Cyc Am Bio v31

5624. Lovejoy, Esther Clayson Pohl
1869/70–1967

physician; director of the Portland, Oregon, health department; World War I Red Cross worker in France; feminist
Protestant Episcopal
Portland, OR
Index t Wom; Nat Cyc Am Bio csv1; Not Am Wom supp v1

5625. Noyes, Clara Dutton
1869/70–1936
nurse, nursing educator, field nurse in World War I, author
Dict Am Bio supp v2; Index t Wom; Nat Cyc Am Bio csv2

5626. Granger, Euphrasia Smith
flourished 1900s
patriot
Index t Wom

5627. Harriman, Florence Jaffray (Hurst)
1870–1967
Democratic party official, diplomat, minister to Norway, politician, journalist, suffragist, clubwoman, social rights worker, Red Cross worker in World War I, World War II relief worker in Norway
Washington, DC
Index t Wom; Nat Cyc Am Bio v53 and csv6; Not Am Wom supp v1; Obit File

5628. Hunton, Addie Waites
born 1870
Red Cross worker, World War I relief worker
Black
Prof Negro Wom v2

5629. Kinney, Dita H.
flourished 1900s
army nurse
Index t Wom

5630. Michael, Moina; The Poppy Lady
circa 1870–1944
educator, originator of Poppy Day as a memorial to war dead
Index t Wom; Obit File

5631. Draper, Helen Fidelia
1871–1951
Red Cross nurse, World War I relief worker, social worker
Episcopalian
New York
Index t Wom; Nat Cyc Am Bio v39

5632. Hawes, Harriet Ann Boyd
1871–1945
classical archaeologist, war nurse in the Greco-Turkish and Spanish-American wars and in World War I
Dict Am Bio supp v3; Not Am Wom

5633. Brosseau, Grace Lincoln Hall
1872–1959
president general of DAR
Congregationalist
Illinois
Nat Cyc Am Bio csv4; Obit File

5634. Morgan, Anne Tracy
1873–1952
philanthropist, organizer of relief work in France during World War II, World War I relief worker, social worker
Dict Am Bio supp v5; Index t Wom; Nat Cyc Am Bio csv2 and csv5; Not Am Wom supp v1; Obit File

5635. Pouch, Helena R. Hellwig
1874–1960
humanitarian, president of DAR, tennis champion
Index t Wom; Obit File

5636. Rose, Mary Davies Swartz
1874–1941
pioneer nutritionist, director of the Bureau of Conservation of the Federal Food Board during World War I
Dict Am Bio supp v3; Index t Wom; Not Am Wom; Obit File

5637. Stein, Gertrude
1874–1946
author, novelist, literary salon host, World War I ambulance driver and supply truck driver in France
Jewish
French (American expatriate to Paris)
Dict Am Bio supp v4; Dict Lit Bio v4; Index t Wom; Nat Cyc Am Bio v38 and csv4; Not Am Wom; Obit File; Who Who Jew Hist; Wom Lit; Wom Lit, More

5638. Denning, Delia; Delia (Denning) Akeley Howe
1875–1970
African explorer, big game hunter, geographer, taxidermist, author, lecturer, World War I relief worker
Nat Cyc Am Bio v57; Obit File; Index t Wom

5639. Howe, Delia Akeley (Denning)
1875–1970
African explorer, big game hunter, geographer, taxidermist, author, lecturer, World War I relief worker
Index t Wom; Nat Cyc Am Bio v57; Obit File

5640. Prisk, Laura B.; The Mother of Flag Day
1875–1950
patriot, proponent of Flag Day
Obit File

5641. Morton, Blanche Rosalie Slaughter
born 1876
surgeon, gynecologist, World War I surgeon on Salonica front, major in the US Army
Index t Wom; Nat Cyc Am Bio csv3

5642. Cunningham, Kate (Richards) (O'Hare)
1877–1948
Socialist party presidential nominee, community organizer, prison reformer, anti–World War I activist, lecturer, educator
Index t Wom; Not Am Wom; Obit File; Dict Am Bio v4

5643. Roberts, Mary May
1877–1959
nurse, nursing magazine editor, nursing educator, chief nurse of the World War II army nurse corps
Index t Wom; Not Am Wom supp v1; Obit File

5644. Russell, Edith
1877–1975
fashion writer, World War I correspondent
Obit File

5645. Flikke, Julia Otteson
born circa 1879
army nurse
Index t Wom

5646. Patterson, Hannah Jane
1879–1937
suffragist, World War I defense official
Not Am Wom

5647. Glass, Meta
1880–1967
president of Sweet Briar College, educator, YWCA executive, World War I and II relief worker, defense worker
Episcopalian
Virginia
Nat Cyc Am Bio v53 and csv7; Obit File

5648. Hamblet, Julia E.
flourished 1910s
Marine Corps officer
Index t Wom

5649. Higlsee, Lenah S.
flourished 1910s–20s
navy nurse
Index t Wom

5650. Meirs, Linda
flourished 1910s
war nurse
Index t Wom

5651. Goldman, Hettie
1881–1972
archaeologist, nurse in the Greek-Balkan war
Jewish
Nat Cyc Am Bio v56; Not Am Wom supp v1

5652. McClellan, Irene Moulton Ward
1881–1967
philanthropist, World War I Red Cross relief worker in England, patent medicine manufacturer, dairy and chicken farmer
Episcopalian
New York
Nat Cyc Am Bio v53

5653. McHugh, Rose John
1881–1952
social worker
Dict Am Bio supp v5

5654. Rogers, Edith Nourse
1881–1960
Republican representative to Congress from Massachusetts, sponsor of a bill creating the Women's Army Air Corps, co-author of a bill of rights for World War II veterans, World War I military hospital observer
Massachusetts
Dict Am Bio supp v6; Index t Wom; Nat Cyc Am Bio v44; Not Am Wom supp v1; Obit File

5655. Rumsey, Mary Harriman
1881–1934
social welfare leader, New York civic worker, spokesperson for consumer interests, chairperson of the Consumer Advisory Board, defense worker during World War I
New York
Dict Am Bio supp v1; Nat Cyc Am Bio v24 and csv4; Not Am Wom

5656. Smith, Gertrude Robinson
1881–1963
New York civic worker, World War I relief worker, founder of the Tanglewood music festival, music patron
Nat Cyc Am Bio v48; Obit File

5657. Stimson, Julia Catherine
1881–1948
professional nurse, World War I nurse, superintendent of the Army Nursing Corps, nursing educator, colonel in the US Army
Dict Am Bio supp v4; Index t Wom; Nat Cyc Am Bio csv2; Not Am Wom; Obit File

5658. Blanchfield, Florence Aby
1882/84–1971
nurse, corporal in US Army Nurse Corps, superintendent of Army Nurse Corps during World War II
Cur Biog '71; Index t Wom; Not Am Wom supp v1

5659. Carter, Alice (Olin) Draper
born 1883
YWCA executive, world war relief worker, welfare worker
Episcopalian
New York
Nat Cyc Am Bio v55

5660. Gibbons, Helen Davenport Brown
1883–1960
novelist, founder of Sauvons les Bebes, a World War I orphan aid agency
Obit File

5661. Springs, Lena Joan Jones
1883–1942
Democratic National Committee member, Democratic vice-presidential nominee at the 1924 convention, suffrage leader, World War I Red Cross worker
South Carolina
Nat Cyc Am Bio csv2; Obit File

5662. Booth, Ada Pearl Dunlap; Adeline Dunlap
born 1884
actor, World War I nurse
Michigan
Nat Cyc Am Bio v17

5663. Crawford, Mary Merritt; Mrs. Edward Schuster
1884–1972
surgeon, World War I surgeon in France
Episcopalian
New York
Nat Cyc Am Bio v57

5664. Tolstoy, Mary Koutouzow
1884–1976
author, fashion director, World War I and II nurse
Obit File

5665. Challinor, Mercedes Crimmins (Clara)
1885–1966
Red Cross official, World War I relief worker
Catholic
Nat Cyc Am Bio v52

5666. Jackson, Maude Campbell Davison
1885–1956
US Army major, chief of American nurses on Corregidor in World War II, World War II hero
Obit File

5667. Magna, Edith Scott
1885–1960
executive of DAR
Congregationalist
Massachusetts
Nat Cyc Am Bio v49

5668. Borden, Mary; Lady Spears
1886–1968
novelist, head of a World War II field hospital in France
English (American expatriate to England)
Index t Wom; Obit File

5669. Kauffman, Ruth Hammitt
1886–1952
World War I correspondent, children's author
Obit File

5670. Lane, Rose Wilder
1886/87–1968
novelist, telegrapher, World War I Red Cross worker in Europe, Vietnam war correspondent
Index t Wom; Nat Cyc Am Bio v54

5671. Riach, May Turner
1886–1946
surgeon, eye doctor, World War I doctor, Spanish Loyalist army physician
Methodist
Nat Cyc Am Bio v34

5672. Boyd, Louise Arner
1887–1972
scientific polar explorer, geographer, technical expert for the War Department and the National Bureau of Standards
Episcopalian
Cur Biog '72; Index t Wom; Nat Cyc Am Bio csv7; Obit File

5673. Calverley, Eleanor Jane Taylor
1887–1968
physician, missionary to Kuwait, nurse in the 1920 Kuwait war, birth control advocate, birth control clinic founder

Dutch Reformed
Connecticut
Nat Cyc Am Bio v57

5674. Drake, Dula Heisel Rae
born 1887
philanthropist, patron of World War I relief in Italy
Nat Cyc Am Bio csv2

5675. Lebel, Margaret
1887–1951
World War I hero
Obit File

5676. MacNeil, Marie Stevens Hicks
1887–1952
developer of the British plan for evacuation of bombed-out children in World War II
Obit File

5677. Meyer, Agnes Elizabeth (Ernst)
1887–1970
author, journalist, vice-president and co-owner of *The Washington Post*, World War II correspondent, autobiographer, lecturer, social worker, Republican party worker, crusader for social services and education causes
Lutheran
New York
Cur Biog '70; Index t Wom; Nat Cyc Am Bio v56; Obit File

5678. Aldrich, Harriet Alexander
1888–1972
New York civic worker, World War II relief worker
New York, NY
Nat Cyc Am Bio v60

5679. Hall, Florence Louise
born 1888
director of the Women's Land Army
Index t Wom

5680. Peck, Lillie
1888–1957
leader in the settlement house movement, social worker, president of the International Federation of Settlements, German welfare worker after World War II
Dict Am Bio supp v6; Obit File

5681. Brandstrom-Ulrich, Elsa; The Angel of Siberia
1889–1948
World War I prisoner of war relief worker in Russia and Siberia
Obit File

5682. Chung, Margaret Jessie
1889–1959
plastic surgeon, World War II relief worker
California
Chinese
Nat Cyc Am Bio v48

5683. Claytor, Gertrude (Harris) Boatwright
1889–1973
poet, Red Cross worker in World War I
Christian Scientist
Virginia
Nat Cyc Am Bio v57

5684. Gladwin, Mary E.
died 1939
World War I nurse
Index t Wom

5685. Janis, Elsie (Bierbower) (Wilson)
1889/93–1956
mimic, stage actor, singer, dancer, vaudevillian, author, songwriter, World War I entertainer
Dict Am Bio supp v6; Index t Wom; Nat Cyc Am Bio csv1; Obit File

5686. Butler, Kate Maddux Robinson
circa 1890–1974
publisher, philanthropist, patron of French relief in World War II
Buffalo, NY
Nat Cyc Am Bio v58

5687. Williams, Fannie Ransom
flourished 1920s
constitutionalist, World War I soldier's welfare worker
Presbyterian
North Carolina
Nat Cyc Am Bio v21

5688. Dickinson, Velvalee
born circa 1893
Japanese spy
Index t Wom

5689. Friedman, Elizabeth Smith
born 1894
cryptanalyst in World War I
Nat Cyc Am Bio csv5

5690. May, Geraldine Pratt
born 1895
US military officer, member of WACs and WAFs
Index t Wom

5691. Streeter, Ruth Cheney
born 1895
aviator, marines officer
Index t Wom

5692. Grandma
died 1946
spy
Index t Wom

5693. Bowman, J. Beatrice
graduated 1922
navy nurse
Index t Wom

5694. Marlowe, Helen
died 1947
tennis player, US Marine Corps
captain in World War II
Obit File

5695. Smith, Margaret Chase
born 1897
US senator from Maine, lieutenant colonel in the US Air Force
Reserve
Methodist
Maine
Index t Wom; Nat Cyc Am Bio csv9

5696. Craighill, Margaret D.
born 1898
physician, army medical officer
Index t Wom

5697. Hancock, Joy Bright
born 1898
aviator, lieutenant commander in the US Navy, director of the WAVES
Index t Wom; Nat Cyc Am Bio csv7

5698. Towle, Katherine Amelia
born 1898
marine officer
Index t Wom

5699. Stratton, Dorothy Constance
born 1899
naval officer
Index t Wom

5700. Bailey, Margaret E.
flourished 1930s–60s
lieutenant colonel in US Army, World War I nurse
Black
Encyc Black Am; Prof Negro Wom v2

5701. Buchanan, Annie R.
flourished 1930s
patriot, clubwoman
Index t Wom

5702. Gardner, Elsa
flourished 1930s–40s
navy aeronautical engineer
Index t Wom

5703. Hoffman, Myn M.
flourished 1930s–40s
army nurse
Index t Wom

5704. Horton, Mildred Helen McAfee
born 1900
president of Wellesley College, director of the WAVES
Presbyterian
Index t Wom

5705. Hunton, Hazel
flourished 1930s
patriot, humanitarian
Index t Wom

5706. Ives, Mildred Card
flourished 1930s
patriot, clubwoman
Index t Wom

5707. McAfee, Mildred Helen
born 1900
military officer of WAVES
Index t Wom

5708. Robinson, Nellie C.
flourished 1930s
patriot
Index t Wom

5709. Whyte, Edna Gardner
flourished 1930s
nurse, aviator
Index t Wom

5710. Boyce, Westray Battle
born 1901
director of the WACs
Index t Wom

5711. Osborne, Estelle Massey
1901–post 1976
nurse, nursing educator, army nurse in World War II
Black
Negro Alman; Prof Negro Wom v2

5712. Pell, Isabel Townsend; Frederika; The Girl with Blonde Hair
1901–52
leader of Maquis resistance groups on the French Riviera during World War II
Obit File

5713. Blue, Edna
1902–41
founder and international chairperson of the Foster Parents'Plan for War Children
Obit File

5714. Rosenberg, Anna Marie
born 1902
US assistant secretary of defense
Jewish
Hungarian
Index t Wom; Who Who Jew Hist

5715. Shelley, Mary J[osephine]
1902–76
aviator, air force colonel, head of the navy education program for women during World War II, commander of women in the air force during the Korean War
Cur Biog '76; Index t Wom; Obit File

5716. Strassmann, Antonie
1902–52
aviator, World War II hero, anti-Nazi worker
German
Obit File

5717. Callery, Mary
1903–77
sculptor, ambulance driver in France during World War II
Index t Wom; Nat Cyc Am Bio v60 and csv9

5718. Owen, Maybelle Cochrane
died 1953
first woman in the US Marine Corps
Obit File

5719. Adair, Marion Hopkinson (Barnes)
1904–65
New York civic leader, World War II relief worker, cancer-patient relief worker, patron of cancer research, radio personality, mimic
New York, NY
Nat Cyc Am Bio v51

5720. Hughes, Bernice Gaines
born 1904
military officer
Index t Wom

5721. Parent, Jeanne
1904–57
US Medal of Freedom winner for hiding Allied aviators shot down in Belgium during World War II
Obit File

5722. Hobby, Oveta Culp
born 1905
government official, director of the Women's Army Auxiliary Corps, editor, politician
Texas
Index t Wom; Nat Cyc Am Bio csv6

5723. Packard, Eleanor
1905–72
journalist, World War II correspondent, Rome correspondent
Cur Biog '72; Index t Wom

5724. Cochran, Jacqueline; Mrs. Floyd B. Odlum
1906/10–1980
aviator, director of the Women's Air Force Service Pilots, flight captain in the US Air Force, colonel in the Air Force Reserve, World War II correspondent, business executive, cosmetician
Cur Biog '80; Index t Wom; Nat Cyc Am Bio csv10

5725. Stewart, Wendy
born 1906
lawyer, law journalist
Los Angeles, CA
English
Nat Cyc Am Bio csv7

5726. Weed, Ethel Berenice
1906–75
military officer, Japanese women's rights advocate
Not Am Wom supp v1

5727. Hallaren, Mary Agnes
born 1907
army officer, director of the WACs
Index t Wom

5728. Bentley, Elizabeth Terrill
1908–63
spy for the Soviet Union during World War II
Obit File

5729. Galloway, Irene Otillia
1908–63
colonel in the US Army, director of the Women's Army Corps
Index t Wom; Obit File

5730. Jones, Sarah [Frances] Roddis
1909–75
president general of DAR
Episcopalian
Wisconsin
Nat Cyc Am Bio v59

5731. Freeman, Elizabeth
flourished 1940s
World War II army nurse
Black
Prof Negro Wom v2

5732. Richey, Helen
1910–47
pioneer aviator, wartime ferry pilot
Index t Wom; Obit File

5733. Wilde, Louise Kathleen
born 1910
naval officer
Index t Wom

5734. Milligan, Mary Louise
born 1911

colonel in the US army, Women's Army Air Corps director
Catholic
Index t Wom; Nat Cyc Am Bio csv9

5735. Wilbur, Bernice Marion
born 1911
army nurse
Index t Wom

5736. Oltman, Florine
born 1915
military librarian, president of the Special Libraries Association
Cur Biog '70

5737. Smith, Ruth Camp
born 1916
librarian, director of the scientific document division of the Naval Ship Systems Command
Black
Encyc Black Am

5738. Moss, Elizabeth Murphy
born 1917
business executive, World War II correspondent
Black
Encyc Black Am

5739. Silverstein, Hannah H.
1919–52
navy nurse, experimental cancer cure volunteer
Obit File

5740. Duerk, Alene (Bertha)
born 1920
rear admiral in the US Navy, head of the Navy Nurse Corps
Cur Biog '73

5741. Higgins, Marguerite (Hall)
1920–66
journalist, Korean War correspondent, Pulitzer Prize winner
Index t Wom; Not Am Wom supp v1; Obit File

5742. Jendritza, Loretta S.
flourished 1960s
air force major, war nurse
Native American (Navaho)
Ind Today

5743. Schuyler, Philippa Duke
1932–1967/69
pianist, composer, author, Vietnam war correspondent
Black
Encyc Black Am; Index t Wom; Negro Alman; Obit File

5744. Baez, Joan
born 1941
folk and popular singer, anti–Vietnam war activist, pacifist, worker for Amnesty International

Mexican
Dict Mex Am Hist; Index t Wom

5745. Holtzman, Elizabeth
born 1941
lawyer, Democratic representative to Congress from New York, feminist, anti–Vietnam war protester
New York
Cur Biog '73

5746. Biddleman, Marcia Ann
born 1945
first lieutenant in the US Marine Corps
Native American (Seneca)
Ind Today

No Dates

5747. Cull, Betty
army aerial observer, bomb tester
Index t Wom

HISTORY AND RECORD KEEPING

5748. Capillana
died 1549
author on natural history, historian
Peruvian
Cyc Am Bio

5749. Doughty, Ann Graves Cotton Eaton
flourished circa 1625
historian
Index t Wom

5750. Stone, Verlinda Cotton Burdette Boughton
flourished circa 1650s
colonial journalist, letter writer
Index t Wom

5751. Knight, Sarah Kemble
1666–1725/27
diarist, educator, hotel keeper, traveler, merchant
Boston, MA
Cyc Am Bio; Dict Am Auth; Dict Am Bio; Dict Am Bio Men Time; Index t Wom; Not Am Wom; Wom Lit, More

5752. Alexander, Mary Spratt Provoost "Polly"
1693/94–1760
businessperson
Index t Wom; Not Am Wom

5753. Manigault, Ann
flourished 1750s–80s
diarist, letter writer
Index t Wom

5754. Warren, Mercy Otis
1727/28–1814
poet, author, dramatist, political author and satirist, historian, patriot
Massachusetts
Am Bio Dict; Cyc Am Bio; Dict Am Auth; Dict Am Bio; Dict Am Bio Men Time; Index t Wom; Nat Cyc Am Bio v7; Not Am Wom; Our Count; Who Who Dur Am Rev; Wom Lit, More

5755. Winslow, Anna Green
died 1779
colonial diarist
Index t Wom

5756. Hulton, Ann
flourished 1760s
letter writer
Index t Wom

5757. Ferguson, Elizabeth (Graeme)
1737/39–1801
litterateur, poet, translator, letter writer, diarist, hero of American Revolution
Philadelphia, PA
Am Bio Dict; Cyc Am Bio; Dict Am Auth; Dict Am Bio; Dict Am Bio Men Time; Index t Wom; Nat Cyc Am Bio v7; Not Am Wom; Who Who Dur Am Rev

5758. Drinker, Elizabeth Sandwith
1743–1807
colonial diarist
Quaker
Index t Wom

5759. Adams, Hannah
1755–1831/32
historian, compiler of historical data, religious author
Massachusetts
Am Bio Dict; Appl Cyc Am Bio; Cyc Am Bio; Dict Am Auth; Dict Am Bio; Dict Am Bio Men Time; Index t Wom; Nat Cyc Am Bio v5; Not Am Wom; Wom Cent

5760. Foster, Hannah (Webster)
1758/90–1840
author, novelist, biographer
Massachusetts
Am Bio Dict; Cyc Am Bio; Dict Am Auth; Dict Am Bio; Dict Am Bio Men Time; Index t Wom; Not Am Wom; Who Who Dur Am Rev

5761. Logan, Deborah Norris
1761–1839
collector of historical records, historian

Pennsylvania
Am Bio Dict; Dict Am Bio; Index t Wom; Nat Cyc Am Bio v25; Not Am Wom

5762. Wister, Sarah "Sally"
1761/62–1804
diarist, patriot of American Revolution
Quaker
Pennsylvania
Dict Am Bio; Index t Wom; Who Who Dur Am Rev

5763. Sanders, Elizabeth (Elkins)
1762–1851/54
social critic, pamphleteer, author, history writer on Massachusetts, Native American rights worker
Salem, MA
Cyc Am Bio; Dict Am Auth; Dict Am Bio; Dict Am Bio Men Time; Not Am Wom

5764. White, Tryphena
flourished 1800s
pioneer, diarist
Index t Wom

5765. Smith, Margaret (Bayard)
1778–1844
author, early chronicler of Washington society
Cyc Am Bio; Dict Am Auth; Dict Am Bio; Dict Am Bio Men Time; Index t Wom; Not Am Wom

5766. Lee, Hannah Farnham (Sawyer)
1780/89–1865
writer on history and art
Boston, MA
Cyc Am Bio; Dict Am Auth; Dict Am Bio; Dict Am Bio Men Time; Index t Wom; Nat Cyc Am Bio v25

5767. Burr, Theodosia Alston
1783–1813
letter writer
Cyc Am Bio; Dict Am Bio; Not Am Wom

5768. Holley, Mary Phelps Austin
1784–1846
Texas historian, historical author, biographer, miscellaneous writer, land speculator
Texas
Am Bio Dict; Dict Am Auth; Not Am Wom

5769. Robbins, Eliza
1786–1853
educator, historian, author
Boston, MA
Dict Am Auth

5770. Williams, Catherine Read (Arnold)
1787/90–1872
author, poet, novelist, biographer, historical author
Providence, RI
Cyc Am Bio; Dict Am Auth; Dict Am Bio; Dict Am Bio Men Time

5771. Huntington, Susan Mansfield
1791–1823
religious writer, philanthropist, diarist, poet
Am Bio Dict; Cyc Am Bio; Index t Wom

5772. Campbell, Maria
died 1845
biographer
Am Bio Dict

5773. Caulkins, Frances Manwaring
1795/96–1869
historian, historical author
Connecticut
Cyc Am Bio; Dict Am Bio Men Time; Not Am Wom; Twent Cen Bio Dict Not Am

5774. Robinson, Therese Albertine Louise (von Jakob); Mrs. Edward; Talvi; Talvj
1797–1869/70
author, short story writer, historical writer, translator, linguist, philologist
German
Cyc Am Bio; Dict Am Bio; Dict Am Bio Men Time; Index t Wom; Nat Cyc Am Bio v1

5775. Dawson-Damer, Mary Georgiana Emma
died 1848
Egyptologist, diarist
Who Who Egypt

5776. Colton, Julia M.
born 18?
historical writer
Brooklyn, NY
Dict Am Auth

5777. Coxe, Margaret
born 1800
historical author, botanist, feminist, educator
Cyc Am Bio; Dict Am Auth; Dict Am Bio Men Time; Index t Wom

5778. Guerber, Helen Adeline
born 18?
educator, textbook writer, historical author
Nyack, NY
Dict Am Auth

5779. Tiffany, Nina Moore
born 18?
historical author
St. Paul, MN
Dict Am Auth

5780. Urbino, Lavinia Buoncuore
born 18?
biographer, autobiographer, translator
Boston, MA
Dict Am Auth

5781. Maury, Ann
1803–76
author of histories
Dict Am Auth; Dict Am Bio Men Time; Twent Cen Bio Dict Not Am

5782. Pumpelly, Mary Hollenback (Welles)
1803–79
poet, religious history writer
Cyc Am Bio; Dict Am Auth

5783. Martin, Sarah Towne (Smith); Sarah Martyn
1805–79
historian, religious and historical writer for children, editor, abolitionist, temperance worker
New York, NY
Cyc Am Bio; Dict Am Auth; Dict Am Bio; Twent Cen Bio Dict Not Am

5784. Morgan, Henrietta Hunt
1805–91
Civil War diarist, pioneer
Index t Wom

5785. Kinzie, Juliette Augusta (Magill)
1806–70
historian of the Northwest, novelist
Chicago, IL
Dict Am Auth; Not Am Wom

5786. Conant, Hannah O'Brian (Chaplin)
1809–65
religious worker, translator, Oriental scholar and language expert, magazine editor
Cyc Am Bio; Dict Am Auth; Dict Am Bio; Dict Am Bio Men Time; Nat Cyc Am Bio v22; Not Am Wom; Twent Cen Bio Dict Not Am

5787. Hawthorne, Sophia Amelia Peabody
1809–71
artist, illustrator, travel writer
Cyc Am Bio; Dict Am Auth; Not Am Wom

5788. Kemble, Frances Anne "Fanny"; Fanny Kemble Butler
1809/11–1893
actor, diarist, author, abolitionist
Georgia
English
Cyc Am Bio; Dict Am Bio; Dict Am Bio Men Time; Dict Nat Bio supp; Encyc South Hist; Index t Wom; Nat Cyc Am Bio v3; Not Am Wom

5789. Fairfield, Jane Frazee
born circa 1810
biographer, autobiographer
Dict Am Auth

5790. Lander, Sarah West
1810/19–1872
author of travel books for children
Salem, MA
Cyc Am Bio; Dict Am Auth

5791. le Vert, Octavia Celeste Walton
1810/11–1877
author, Civil War nurse, travel writer
Mobile, AL
Cyc Am Bio; Dict Am Auth; Dict Am Bio Men Time; Index t Wom; Nat Cyc Am Bio v6; Not Am Wom; Twent Cen Bio Dict Not Am

5792. Putnam, Mary Traill Spence (Lowell)
1810–98
author, history writer, translator, linguist, traveler
Boston, MA
Cyc Am Bio; Dict Am Auth; Dict Am Bio Men Time; Index t Wom; Twent Cen Bio Dict Not Am

5793. Cate, Eliza Jane
1812–84
author on New England
New England
Dict Am Auth

5794. Ellett, Elizabeth Fries (Lummis)
1812/18–1877
historian, historical writer
Cyc Am Bio; Dict Am Auth; Dict Am Bio; Dict Am Bio Men Time; Index t Wom; Nat Cyc Am Bio v11; Not Am Wom; Twent Cen Bio Dict Not Am

5795. Silsbee, Marianne Cabot (Devereux)
1812–89
historian of Salem, Massachusetts, poet
Boston, MA
Dict Am Auth

5796. Handlin, Mary Flug
1813–1976
economist, American historian
Jewish
Nat Cyc Am Bio v59

5797. Jacobs, Sarah Sprague
born 1813
children's author, historical author
Cambridge, MA
Cyc Am Bio; Dict Am Auth

5798. McGuire, Judith Brockenbrough
born 1813
Civil War diarist, patriot
Index t Wom

5799. Rea, Julia (de Margueritees) (Foster)
1814–66
opera singer, drama critic, writer on Europe
Philadelphia, PA
English
Cyc Am Bio; Dict Am Auth; Dict Am Bio Men Time

5800. Cheney, Harriet Vaughan (Foster)
born 1815
religious author, historian
Cyc Am Bio; Dict Am Auth; Dict Am Bio Men Time; Index t Wom

5801. Mason, Emily Virginia
1815–1909
Civil War hospital matron, Confederate army Civil War nurse, author, biographer, educator
Cyc Am Bio; Dict Am Auth; Index t Wom; Nat Cyc Am Bio v5

5802. Ord, Augustias de la Guerra
1815–80
historian of California
California
Mexican
Dict Mex Am Hist

5803. Stebbins, Emma
1815–82
painter, sculptor, biographer of Charlotte Cushman
New York
Cyc Am Bio; Dict Am Auth; Index t Wom; Nat Cyc Am Bio v8; Not Am Wom; Twent Cen Bio Dict Not Am

5804. Cunningham, Ann Pamela
1816–75
pioneer southern clubwoman, founder and regent of the Mt. Vernon Ladies Association of

the Union; preserver of Mt. Vernon
Dict Am Bio; Index t Wom; Not Am Wom

5805. Marsh, Caroline Crane
1816–1901
author, translator, poet, biographer
Cyc Am Bio; Dict Am Auth

5806. Stone, Martha Elvira
born 1816
postmaster of North Oxford, Massachusetts; genealogist; Civil War relief worker
North Oxford, MA
Wom Cent

5807. Burge, Dolly Sumner Lunt
born 1817
Civil War essayist
Index t Wom

5808. Dyer, Catherine Cornelia [Joy]
1817–1903
author, genealogist
Cyc Am Bio; Dict Am Auth

5809. Shuck, Henrietta (Hall)
1817–44
missionary to China, writer on China
Cyc Am Bio; Dict Am Auth; Index t Wom

5810. Smith, Elizabeth Lee (Allen)
1817–98
biographical editor, poet, hymn writer
Dict Am Auth

5811. Stewart, Electra Maria (Sheldon); Electra Maria Sheldon
born 1817
writer on Michigan history, writer of religious tales for children
Detroit, MI
Cyc Am Bio; Dict Am Auth

5812. Burnham, Sarah Maria
1818–1901
educator, historical author, writer on geology and travel
Cambridge, MA
Dict Am Auth

5813. Harding, Elizabeth McGavock
born circa 1818
Civil War diarist
Index t Wom

5814. Clapp, Louise Amelia Knapp Smith; Dame Shirley; Amelia Knapp Smith
1819–1906
author, educator, letter writer during the California gold rush, gold rush pioneer
California
Index t Wom; Not Am Wom; Read Encyc Am West

5815. Cutter, Eunice Powers
1819–93
lecturer, health reformer, abolitionist, historian
Twent Cen Bio Dict Not Am

5816. Houston, Margaret Moffette Lea
circa 1819–67
Civil War diarist
Index t Wom

5817. Whitney, Louisa (Goddard)
1819–82
autobiographer, author
Dict Am Auth

5818. Preston, Margaret (Junkin)
1820/25–1897
poet, author, novelist, Civil War letter writer
Lexington, VA
Cyc Am Bio; Dict Am Auth; Dict Am Bio; Index t Wom; Nat Cyc Am Bio v7; Not Am Wom; Twent Cen Bio Dict Not Am; Wom Cent

5819. Dewey, Mary Elizabeth
1821; died post 1871
author, translator, educator, biographer
Cyc Am Bio; Dict Am Auth; Index t Wom; Twent Cen Bio Dict Not Am

5820. Agassiz, Elizabeth Cabot Carrie
1822–1907
founder and president of Radcliffe College, educator, biographer, naturalist, science writer
Boston, MA
Dict Am Auth; Dict Am Bio; Index t Wom; Not Am Wom; Wom Cent

5821. Latimer, [Mary] Elizabeth (Wormeley)
1822–1904
novelist, educator, historian, writer on history
Baltimore, MD
English
Cyc Am Bio; Dict Am Auth; Dict Am Bio; Dict Am Bio Men Time; Index t Wom; Nat Cyc Am Bio v9; Wom Cent

5822. Brittan, Harriet G.
1823–97

missionary to India, writer on India and Africa
Dict Am Auth

5823. Chesnut, Mary Boykin Miller
1823–86
Civil War diarist
Not Am Wom

5824. Leslie, Susan Inches (Lyman)
1823–1904
biographer, autobiographer
Dict Am Auth

5825. Sweat, Margaret Jane (Muzzey)
born 1823
writer on travel
Cyc Am Bio; Dict Am Auth; Dict Am Bio Men Time

5826. Worthen, Augusta Harvey
born 1823
educator, author, historian of New Hampshire
New Hampshire
Wom Cent

5827. Berard, Augusta Blanche
1824–1901
writer on the history of West Point, history text author, historian
West Point, NY
Appl Cyc Am Bio; Cyc Am Bio; Dict Am Auth

5828. Blake, Euphemia Vale
1824/25–1904
author, historian, literary and art critic
Dict Am Auth; Wom Cent

5829. Merrill, Catherine
1824–1900
educator, writer on Indiana
Indianapolis, IN
Dict Am Auth

5830. Larned, Ellen Douglas
born 1825
genealogist, historian
Cyc Am Bio

5831. Merrick, Caroline Elizabeth (Thomas)
1825–1908
suffragist, temperance leader, author on the South
New Orleans, LA
Dict Am Auth; Nat Cyc Am Bio v10; Not Am Wom; Wom Cent

5832. Spencer, Cornelia Ann (Phillips)
1825–1908
historian, history writer, writer on the Civil War era

North Carolina
Dict Am Auth; Dict Am Bio; Not Am Wom

5833. Davis, Varina Howell
1826–1909
Civil War diarist, journalist, Confederate patriot of Civil War
Bio Dict Confed; Encyc South Hist; Index t Wom; Wom Cent

5834. Lamb, Martha Joanna Read (Nash)
1826/29–1893
author, children's author, novelist, New York historian, editor
New York
Cyc Am Bio; Dict Am Auth; Dict Am Bio; Index t Wom; Nat Cyc Am Bio v1; Not Am Wom; Twent Cen Bio Dict Not Am; Wom Cent

5835. Victor, Frances Auretta (Fuller) (Barrett); Florence Fane
1826–1902
author, historian of the Pacific Northwest
Oregon; California
Cyc Am Bio; Dict Am Auth; Dict Am Bio; Nat Cyc Am Bio v13; Not Am Wom; Twent Cen Bio Dict Not Am; Wom Cent

5836. Robinson, Sarah Tappan Doolittle (Lawrence)
born 1827
author, historian of Kansas
Lawrence, KS
Cyc Am Bio; Dict Am Auth; Twent Cen Bio Dict Not Am

5837. Battey, Emily Verdery
born 1828
journalist, women's historian
Wom Cent

5838. Cumming, Kate
1828/35–1909
Confederate hospital administrator, diarist, nurse
Alabama
Scottish
Dict Am Auth; Index t Wom; Not Am Wom

5839. Hemenway, Abby Maria
1828–90
Vermont historian, anthologist, author
Vermont
Dict Am Auth; Not Am Wom; Twent Cen Bio Dict Not Am

5840. Pember, Phoebe Yates Levy
1828–1913
Confederate hospital administrator and nurse, diarist
Index t Wom; Not Am Wom

5841. Wolfe, Catharine Lorillard
1828–87
philanthropist, patron of the Metropolitan Museum of Art, art collector
New York
Cyc Am Bio; Dict Am Bio; Index t Wom; Nat Cyc Am Bio v10; Not Am Wom; Wom Cent

5842. Dixon, Susan (Bullitt)
born 1829
American historian, writer on history
Kentucky
Dict Am Auth; Nat Cyc Am Bio v13

5843. Gay, Mary Ann Harris
born 1829
Civil War diarist
Index t Wom

5844. Hanaford, Phoebe Ann (Coffin)
1829–1921
Universalist minister, historian, journalist, author, feminist, lecturer, chaplain of the Connecticut state legislature
Universalist
New Haven, CT
Cyc Am Bio; Dict Am Auth; Dict Am Bio; Index t Wom; Nat Cyc Am Bio v13; Not Am Wom; Twent Cen Bio Dict Not Am; Wom Cent

5845. Bicknell, Anna Louise
born 183?
historian, biographer
Dict Am Auth

5846. Brooks, Mary Frances
flourished 1860s
Civil War diarist
Index t Wom

5847. Byson, Mary
flourished 1860s
Civil War diarist
Index t Wom

5848. Cahal, Mary
flourished 1860s
Civil War diarist
Index t Wom

5849. Cary, Constance
flourished 1860s
Civil War diarist
Index t Wom

5850. Dickinson, Emily Elizabeth
1830–86
poet, letter writer
Amherst, MA
Dict Am Auth; Dict Lit Bio v1; Index t Wom; Nat Cyc Am Bio v11 and v23; Nort Anth Poet; Not Am Wom; Twent Cen Bio Dict Not Am

5851. Edmondson, Belle
flourished 1860s
Civil War diarist
Index t Wom

5852. Edmondston, Catherine Ann
flourished 1860s
Civil War letter writer
Index t Wom

5853. Gilmer, Louisa Fredericka
flourished 1860s
Civil War diarist
Index t Wom

5854. Gilmer, Loulie
flourished 1860s
Civil War diarist
Index t Wom

5855. Hall, Dorian, Mrs.
flourished 1860s
Civil War diarist
Index t Wom

5856. Johnstone, Mary H.
flourished 1860s
Civil War diarist
Index t Wom

5857. Kelly, Amie
flourished 1860s
Civil War diarist
Index t Wom

5858. Lamb, William, Mrs.
flourished 1860s
Civil War diarist
Index t Wom

5859. Lawton, Sarah Alexander
flourished 1860s
Civil War diarist
Index t Wom

5860. le Conte, Emma Florence
flourished 1860s
Civil War diarist
Index t Wom

5861. le Grand, Julia
flourished 1860s
Civil War diarist
Index t Wom

5862. Lee, Henrietta Bedinger
flourished 1860s
Civil War letter writer
Index t Wom

5863. Lowe, Lucy
flourished 1860s
Civil War diarist
Index t Wom

5864. Maury, Betty Herdon
flourished 1860s
Civil War diarist
Index t Wom

5865. Miller, Dora Richards
flourished 1860s–80s
author, Civil War diarist, journalist, educator
West Indian (Danish West Indies)
Index t Wom; Wom Cent

5866. Morgan, Martha Ready
flourished 1860s
Civil War diarist
Index t Wom

5867. Perkins, Anne
flourished 1860s
Civil War letter writer
Index t Wom

5868. Pugh, Mary Williams
flourished 1860s
Civil War diarist
Index t Wom

5869. Ravenel, Charlotte St. Julien
flourished 1860s
Civil War diarist
Index t Wom

5870. Rawson, Mary
flourished 1860s
Civil War diarist
Index t Wom

5871. Ready, Alice
flourished 1860s
Civil War diarist
Index t Wom

5872. Ridley, Rebeccah C.
flourished 1860s
Civil War diarist
Index t Wom

5873. Ritter, Frances Malone (Raymond) "Fannie"
1830–90
writer on music, song compiler, mezzo-soprano vocalist, poet
Cyc Am Bio; Dict Am Auth; Twent Cen Bio Dict Not Am

5874. Sansom, Emma
flourished 1860s; died 1900
Civil War hero, diarist
Index t Wom

5875. Scales, Cordelia Lewis
flourished 1860s
Civil War diarist
Index t Wom

5876. Sims, Leora
flourished 1860s
Civil War diarist
Index t Wom

5877. Smith, Lucy
flourished 1860s
Civil War diarist
Index t Wom

5878. Stinson, Virginia McCollum
flourished 1860s
Civil War diarist
Index t Wom

5879. Sutherlin, W. T., Mrs.
flourished 1860s
Civil War diarist
Index t Wom

5880. Terhune, Mary Virginia (Hawes); Marian Harland
1830/35–1922
popular novelist, writer on household affairs, historian, cookbook author, editor, publisher
New York, NY
Cyc Am Bio; Dict Am Auth; Dict Am Bio; Dict Am Bio Men Time; Index t Wom; Nat Cyc Am Bio v1; Not Am Wom; Twent Cen Bio Dict Not Am; Wom Cent

5881. Wadley, Sarah L.
flourished 1860s
Civil War diarist
Index t Wom

5882. Waring, Mary D.
flourished 1860s
Civil War diarist
Index t Wom

5883. Wilcox, G. Griffin, Mrs.
flourished 1860s
Civil War diarist
Index t Wom

5884. Wormeley, Katharine Prescott
1830/32–1908
Civil War relief and hospital worker, writer on sanitation, charity worker, philanthropist, translator, biographer
Rhode Island
English
Cyc Am Bio; Dict Am Bio; Index t Wom; Nat Cyc Am Bio v8; Not Am Wom; Twent Cen Bio Dict Not Am; Wom Cent

5885. Ames, Mary E. Clemmer; Mrs. Hudson
1831/40–1884
journalist, biographer, author
Washington, DC
Appl Cyc Am Bio; Cyc Am Bio; Index t Wom; Nat Cyc Am Bio v7; Not Am Wom; Twent Cen Bio Dict Not Am

5886. Austin, Jane Goodwin
1831–94
historical novelist
Boston, MA
Dict Am Auth; Dict Am Bio; Index t Wom; Nat Cyc Am Bio v6; Twent Cen Bio Dict Not Am; Wom Cent

5887. Booth, Mary Louisa
1831–89
historian, journalist, translator, author, editor of *Harper's Bazaar*, women's labor worker
Cyc Am Bio; Dict Am Auth; Dict Am Bio; Dict Am Bio Men Time; Index t Wom; Nat Cyc Am Bio v7; Not Am Wom; Twent Cen Bio Dict Not Am; Wom Cent

5888. Nutting, Mary Olivia
1831–1910
author, historian, educator, librarian, autobiographer
Dict Am Auth; Index t Wom

5889. Rollins, Ellen Chapman (Hobbs); E. H. Arr
1831–81
writer on history
Philadelphia, PA
Cyc Am Bio; Dict Am Auth

5890. Jackson, Mary Anna
married 1857
Civil War diarist
Index t Wom

5891. Ravenel, Harriot Horry (Rutledge)
1832–1912
author, biographer
Charleston, SC
Dict Am Auth; Dict Am Bio

5892. Walworth, Ellen (Hardin)
1832–1915
author, war nurse, writer on the history of Saratoga, educator, poet
Saratoga, NY
Cyc Am Bio and ad; Dict Am Auth; Index t Wom; Twent Cen Bio Dict Not Am; Wom Cent

5893. Woodruff, Julia Louisa Matilda (Curtiss); W. M. L. Jan
born 1832
author, compiler
New York, NY
Dict Am Auth

5894. Hale, Susan
1833/38–1910
author, children's author, travel writer, artist, painter
Cyc Am Bio; Dict Am Auth; Index t Wom; Not Am Wom; Twent Cen Bio Dict Not Am

5895. Stockham, Alice (Bunker)
born 1833
physician, medical author, musician, biographer, suffragist
Dict Am Auth; Wom Cent

5896. Leonowens, Anna Harriette (Crawford)
born 1834
author on Siam, kindergarten educator, missionary educator in Siam
New York
English
Cyc Am Bio; Dict Am Bio

5897. Waters, Clara (Erskine) (Clement); Clara Clement
1834–1916
author, writer on art, art historian, world traveler
Boston, MA
Dict Am Auth; Index t Wom; Not Am Wom; Wom Cent; Wom Lit, More

5898. Bompiani, Sophia van Matre
born 1835
writer about Italy
Dict Am Auth

5899. James, Hannah Packard
1835–1903
librarian
Index t Wom

5900. Ragozin, Zenaide Alexievna
1835–post 1906
traveler, writer of Russian histories
Russian
Cyc Am Bio; Dict Am Auth

5901. Steele, Esther (Baker)
born 1835
historian, history writer
Dict Am Auth; Wom Cent

5902. Loughborough, Mary Ann Webster
1836–87
author, Civil War diarist
Little Rock, AR
Cyc Am Bio; Dict Am Auth; Index t Wom

5903. Preston, Harriet Waters
1836/43–1911
author, literary critic, translator, literary historian
Cyc Am Bio; Dict Am Auth; Dict Am Bio; Nat Cyc Am Bio v8

5904. Runcie, Constance (Faunt le Roy)
1836–1911
composer, pianist, club leader, poet, children's author, biographer

St. Joseph, MO
Dict Am Auth; Dict Am Bio; Index t Wom; Nat Cyc Am Bio v7; Wom Cent

5905. Smith, Cassie Selden
married 1861
Civil War diarist
Index t Wom

5906. Smith, Erminnie Adele (Platt)
1836/37–1886
ethnologist, geologist, geographer
Cyc Am Bio; Dict Am Bio; Index t Wom; Nat Cyc Am Bio v13; Not Am Wom

5907. Furness, Helen Kate (Rogers)
1837–83
Shakespearean scholar, writer on Shakespeare
Cyc Am Bio; Dict Am Auth

5908. Johnson, Sarah (Barclay)
1837–85
author on Syria
Cyc Am Bio; Dict Am Auth; Nat Cyc Am Bio v11

5909. Richardson, Abby (Sage)
1837–1900
author, actor, historian, lecturer on history, writer on literature, educator
Dict Am Auth; Index t Wom; Nat Cyc Am Bio v5; Twent Cen Bio Dict Not Am

5910. Hague, Parthenia Antoinette (Vardaman)
born 1838; flourished 1860s
Civil War diarist
Florida
Dict Am Auth; Index t Wom

5911. Hallowell, Anna Coffin (Davis)
born 1838
biographer of James and Lucretia Mott
Dict Am Auth

5912. Liliuokalani, Lydia Kamekaha; Queen of the Hawaiian Islands
born 1838
writer on Hawaiian history
Hawaii
Polynesian
Dict Am Auth

5913. Stockton, Louise
1838–1914
editor, journalist, novelist, critic, historian, social worker
Philadelphia, PA
Dict Am Auth; Index t Wom; Nat Cyc Am Bio v8; Twent Cen Bio Dict Not Am

5914. Stokes, Missouri H.
1838–post 1860
Civil War diarist, educator, temperance worker
Presbyterian
Georgia
Index t Wom; Wom Cent

5915. Velasquez, Loretta Janeta
born 1838
western pioneer, Civil War diarist, Civil War spy
Index t Wom

5916. Velazquez, Louta Janita; Velasquez, Loretta Janeta; Harry T. Buford
born 1838/42
Civil War autobiographer, western pioneer, Civil War spy
Encyc South Hist; Index t Wom

5917. Fielde, Adele Marion
born 1839
missionary to Siam and China, writer on China, writer in Chinese
Dict Am Auth

5918. Randolph, Sarah Nicholas (Jefferson)
1839–92
author, educator, biographer
Baltimore, MD
Cyc Am Bio; Dict Am Auth; Dict Am Bio; Twent Cen Bio Dict Not Am

5919. Appleton, Mattie H.
flourished 1870s
librarian
Index t Wom

5920. Duffel, Mary Gordon; Mary Duff Gordon
born 1840
poet, writer on the history and geography of Alabama
Alabama
Cyc Am Bio; Dict Am Auth

5921. Gardner, Isabella Stewart
1840–1924
art collector
Dict Am Bio; Index t Wom; Not Am Wom

5922. Glover, Anna
flourished 1870s
genealogist, author
Index t Wom

5923. Haskell, Parola
flourished 1870s
librarian
Index t Wom

5924. Hoyt, Deristha Lavinta
born 184?
lecturer on the history of painting, writer on art

Massachusetts
Dict Am Auth

5925. Johnson, Evangeline Maria
flourished 1870s–80s
translator, poet, bibliographer
Cyc Am Bio

5926. Mason, Amelia (Gere)
184?–1923
author on women's history
Chicago, IL
Dict Am Auth; Index t Wom

5927. Metcalf, Anna
born 1840
librarian
Twent Cen Bio Dict Not Am

5928. Smedes, Susan (Dabney)
born 1840
author, missionary to the Sioux
people, educator, historian of
the antebellum South
Mississippi
Cyc Am Bio; Dict Am Auth;
Wom Cent

5929. Stevens, E. Hebert, Mrs.
flourished 1870s–1910s
agricultural librarian, lecturer
Washington, DC
Index t Wom; Wom Cent

5930. Coolbrith, Ina Donna
1841/42–1928
poet, librarian
California
Dict Am Auth; Dict Am Bio; Nat
Cyc Am Bio v13; Not Am
Wom; Twent Cen Bio Dict Not
Am; Wom Cent; Wom Lit,
More

**5931. Moore, Annie Aubertine
(Woodward); Aubertine Forestier**
1841–1929
pianist, student of Scandinavian
music, music critic, lecturer, author, translator of Scandinavian
languages
Dict Am Auth; Dict Am Bio;
Index t Wom; Twent Cen Bio
Dict Not Am; Wom Cent

5932. Morgan, Sarah
born 1841
Civil War diarist
Index t Wom

5933. Dawson, Sarah; Ida Fowler
1842–1909
author, Civil War diarist
Episcopalian
Index t Wom; Nat Cyc Am Bio
v23

**5934. Fowle, Elida Barker
Rumsey**
1842–1919
Civil War relief worker and
nurse, cofounder of a library for
Union soldiers in Washington,
DC
Index t Wom; Not Am Wom

5935. Garrison, Lucy McKim
1842–77
musician, collector of American
slave songs
Not Am Wom

5936. Gifford, Augusta (Hale)
born 1842
historical author
Portland, ME
Dict Am Auth

5937. Gist, Malvina Black
born 1842
Civil War diarist
Index t Wom

5938. Poree, Caroline E.
born 1842
librarian
Index t Wom

**5939. Reed, Elizabeth
(Armstrong)**
1842–1915
theologist, religious author, philosopher, historian of India and
Persia, writer on Oriental literature, temperance worker, philanthropist
Chicago, IL
Dict Am Auth; Dict Am Bio;
Index t Wom; Nat Cyc Am Bio
v1 and v15; Twent Cen Bio Dict
Not Am

**5940. Vale, Euphemia Vale
Blake**
born 1842
writer on history and science
Cyc Am Bio

5941. Pickett, Lasalle Carbell
born 1843
Civil War patriot, hero, diarist,
lecturer
Index t Wom; Wom Cent

5942. Strohm, Gertrude
born 1843
miscellaneous author, compiler of
information
Dayton, OH
Dict Am Auth; Wom Cent

5943. Goff, Eugenia Wheeler
born 1844
historian, designer of historical
maps
Nat Cyc Am Bio v17

**5944. Oliver, Grace Atkinson
(Little) (Ellis)**
1844–99
author, biographer, story editor
Salem, MA
Cyc Am Bio; Dict Am Auth;
Index t Wom; Twent Cen Bio
Dict Not Am; Wom Cent

**5945. Mitchell, Lucy Myers
Wright**
1845–88
archaeologist, historian of ancient
art, writer on Greek art
Dict Am Auth; Dict Am Bio; Nat
Cyc Am Bio v6; Twent Cen Bio
Dict Not Am

5946. Pealer, Ruth Griswold
married 1869
genealogist
Index t Wom

5947. Porter, Rose
1845–1906
author, religious novelist, compiler
New Haven, CT
Dict Am Auth; Nat Cyc Am Bio
v10; Wom Cent

5948. Wharton, Anne Hollingsworth
1845–1928
author, children's author, biographer, historian, historical writer
Philadelphia, PA
Cyc Am Bio; Dict Am Auth; Dict
Am Bio; Index t Wom; Nat Cyc
Am Bio v13; Twent Cen Bio
Dict Not Am

**5949. Hewins, Caroline Maria
Matilda**
1846–1926
librarian, pioneer in library work
for children, writer on librarianship
Hartford, CT
Dict Am Auth; Index t Wom;
Nat Cyc Am Bio v21; Not Am
Wom; Twent Cen Bio Dict Not
Am

5950. Summerhayes, Martha
1846–1911
western pioneer, memoirist of the
western frontier
Index t Wom; Read Encyc Am
West

5951. Brown, Emma Elizabeth
born 1847
popular biographer, author
Dict Am Auth; Wom Cent

5952. Catherwood, Mary (Hartwell)
1847–1902
novelist, writer of historical romances, children's author
Universalist

Illinois
Dict Am Auth; Dict Am Bio;
Index t Wom; Nat Cyc Am Bio
v9; Not Am Wom; Twent Cen
Bio Dict Not Am; Wom Cent

5953. Kimball, Emma Adeline
born 1847
poet, historical sketch writer
Haverville, MA
Dict Am Auth

**5954. Robinson, Jane Marie
Bancroft**
1847–1932
Methodist educator, deaconess
leader, author, historian, philanthropist
Methodist
Index t Wom; Not Am Wom;
Wom Cent

5955. James, Alice
1848–92
diarist
Index t Wom

**5956. Langford, Laura (Carter)
(Holloway)**
born 1848
author, biographer, journalist
Cyc Am Bio; Dict Am Auth;
Twent Cen Bio Dict Not Am

**5957. van Rensselaer, May
(King)**
born 1848
historical writer on New York
City
New York, NY
Dict Am Auth

5958. Conklin, Viola A. (Peckham)
born 1849
historical writer
Plainfield, NJ
Dict Am Auth

5959. Harbee, Lee (Cohen)
born 1849
author, Texas historian, Sorosis
member
Texas; New York
Dict Am Auth; Wom Cent

5960. Palmer, Bertha Honore
1849/51–1918
clubwoman, philanthropist, women's rights worker, art collector
Chicago, IL
Dict Am Bio; Index t Wom;
Twent Cen Bio Dict Not Am;
Wom Cent

**5961. Tuttle, Mary McArthur
(Thompson)**
born 1849/59
artist, writer and lecturer on art,
art historian, novelist

Methodist
Dict Am Bio; Nat Cyc Am Bio v10

5962. Barnes, Mary Downing Sheldon
1850–98
educator, historian, textbook author
California
Dict Am Auth; Dict Am Bio; Not Am Wom; Wom Cent

5963. Bull, Sarah Chapman (Thorpe)
1850–post 1876
temperance worker, biographer
Dict Am Auth; Wom Cent

5964. Butler, Clarissa
flourished 1880s
educator, historian
Index t Wom

5965. Dieudonne, Florence Carpenter
born 1850
litterateur, letter writer
Wom Cent

5966. Renfrew, Carrie
flourished 1880s–90s
poet, biographer
Nebraska
Wom Cent

5967. Sheldon, Mary Downing
1850–98
historian, professor at Wellesley College
Cyc Am Bio

5968. Coronel, Mariana W. de, Senora
born 1851
collector of Native American artifacts
Los Angeles, CA
Wom Cent

5969. Earle, Alice Morse
1851/53–1911
author, social and domestic historian of colonial New England, writer on history
New England
Dict Am Auth; Dict Am Bio; Index t Wom; Nat Cyc Am Bio v13; Not Am Wom; Twent Cen Bio Dict Not Am

5970. Inglehart, Frances (Chambers) (Gooch)
1851–post 1890
writer on Texas, fiction writer
Austin, TX
Dict Am Auth; Wom Cent

5971. King, Grace Elizabeth
1851/53–1932
historian of New Orleans

New Orleans, LA
Dict Am Auth; Dict Am Bio; Index t Wom; Nat Cyc Am Bio v2; Not Am Wom; Twent Cen Bio Dict Not Am; Wom Lit, More

5972. le Plongeon, Alice (Dixon)
born 1851
explorer, traveler, antiquarian
Dict Am Auth; Index t Wom

5973. Rutherford, Mildred Lewis
1851/52–1928
educator, textbook author, apologist for the Old South
Athens, GA
Dict Am Auth; Nat Cyc Am Bio v10; Not Am Wom; Twent Cen Bio Dict Not Am

5974. van Rensselaer, Mariana Alley (Griswold); Mrs. Schuyler
1851–1934
writer on art, art critic, art historian
Cyc Am Bio and ad; Dict Am Auth; Dict Am Bio; Index t Wom; Not Am Wom

5975. Morton, Eliza Happy
1852–1916
author, songwriter, educator, geographer
Maine
Index t Wom; Wom Cent

5976. Myers, Minnie (Walter)
born 1852
writer on the South
Memphis, TN
Dict Am Auth

5977. Porter, Bertha
1852–1941
bibliographer, Egyptologist
Who Who Egypt

5978. St. John, Cynthia Morgan
1852–1919
author, Wordsworthian expert and collector
New York
Index t Wom; Wom Cent

5979. Wheeler, Cora Stuart
born 1852
poet, author, biographer of notable women
Illinois
Wom Cent

5980. Hager, Lucie Carolyn (Gilson)
born 1853
author, writer on Massachusetts
Massachusetts
Dict Am Auth; Wom Cent

5981. Salmon, Lucy Maynard
1853–1927
historian, writer on history, university educator
Dict Am Auth; Dict Am Bio; Not Am Wom

5982. Stephens, Kate
born 1853
history writer
Nat Cyc Am Bio csv2

5983. Ward, May (Alden)
born 1853
historical author, biographer, editor, lecturer, club leader, president of the Massachusetts State Federation of Women's Clubs
Dict Am Auth; Index t Wom; Twent Cen Bio Dict Not Am; Wom Cent

5984. Carr, Deborah Edith Wallbridge
born 1854
librarian, statistician
Index t Wom

5985. Murray, Louise Shipman Welles
1854–1931
historian, Native American archaeologist
Dict Am Bio

5986. Newberry, Julia
1854–76
diarist
Index t Wom

5987. Sadlier, Anna Theresa
born 1854/56
author, biographer, translator
Catholic
Cyc Am Bio; Dict Am Auth

5988. Tappan, Eva March
1854–1930
educator, children's author, history text writer
Worcester, MA
Dict Am Auth; Dict Am Bio; Not Am Wom; Twent Cen Bio Dict Not Am

5989. Dodd, Anna Bowman (Blake)
1855–post 1890s
travel writer, essayist
New York
Dict Am Auth; Wom Cent

5990. Dye, Eva (Emery)
1855–1947
historian, writer of historical fiction, novelist
Oregon
Dict Am Auth; Index t Wom; Nat Cyc Am Bio v13; Read Encyc Am West

5991. Elmendorf, Theresa Hubbell West
1855–1932
librarian, editor
Buffalo, NY
Index t Wom; Nat Cyc Am Bio v23

5992. Fairchild, Mary Solome Cutler
1855–1921
librarian for the blind, nonfiction writer
New York
Dict Am Auth; Dict Am Bio; Index t Wom; Nat Cyc Am Bio v20; Not Am Wom; Twent Cen Bio Dict Not Am

5993. Havemeyer, Louisine Waldron Elder
1855–1929
art collector, philanthropist, suffragist
Not Am Wom

5994. Pennell, Elizabeth (Robins)
1855–1936
author, travel writer, biographer, art critic, bicycle tourer
Dict Am Auth; Index t Wom; Nat Cyc Am Bio v10; Not Am Wom

5995. Repplier, Agnes
1855/59–1950
essayist, children's author, biographer
Catholic
Philadelphia, PA
Dict Am Auth; Dict Am Bio supp v4; Index t Wom; Nat Cyc Am Bio v4; Not Am Wom; Obit File; Twent Cen Bio Dict Not Am

5996. Williams, Fannie Barrier
1855–1944
lecturer, civic leader, librarian, clubwoman
Chicago, IL
Black
Dict Am Bio supp v3; Not Am Wom; Prof Negro Wom v1

5997. Browning, Eliza Gordon
1856–1927
librarian
Nat Cyc Am Bio v6; Twent Cen Bio Dict Not Am

5998. Forbes, Harriette (Merrifield)
born 1856
historical sketch writer
Westborough, MA
Dict Am Auth

5999. Goodwin, Maud (Wilder)
born 1856
author, historical novelist

New York, NY
Dict Am Auth; Twent Cen Bio
Dict Not Am

6000. Hazard, Caroline
1856–1945
fifth president of Wellesley College, historian, historical author
Congregationalist
Dict Am Auth; Index t Wom;
Nat Cyc Am Bio v12, v34, and
csv43; Not Am Wom; Twent
Cen Bio Dict Not Am

**6001. Lamar, Clarinda
Huntington Pendleton**
1856/77–1943
author, leader of the National
Society of Colonial Dames
Nat Cyc Am Bio v32; Obit File

6002. Plummer, Mary Wright
1856–1916
librarian, educator, poet, author
Brooklyn, NY
Dict Am Auth; Dict Am Bio;
Index t Wom; Nat Cyc Am Bio
v21; Not Am Wom; Twent Cen
Bio Dict Not Am

6003. Putnam, Ruth
1856–1931
author, history writer
Dict Am Auth; Dict Am Bio

**6004. Rathbone, Josephine
Adams**
1856/64–1941
librarian, editor, educator
Index t Wom; Nat Cyc Am Bio
csv4; Not Am Wom

**6005. Scidmore, Eliza Ruham-
ah; Eliza Ruhamah**
1856–1928
geographer, traveler, travel writer, journalist
Washington, DC
Dict Am Auth; Dict Am Bio;
Index t Wom; Twent Cen Bio
Dict Not Am

6006. Smith, Annie Morrill
born 1856
botanist, genealogist
Nat Cyc Am Bio csv2

6007. Todd, Mabel Loomis
1856/58–1932
author, editor of Emily
Dickinson's books and letters,
traveler, lecturer, astronomer
Dict Am Bio; Index t Wom; Nat
Cyc Am Bio v9, v28, and v41;
Not Am Wom; Twent Cen Bio
Dict Not Am; Wom Cent

6008. Coman, Katharine
1857–1915
economic historian, writer on history, social reformer, educator

Ohio
Dict Am Auth; Index t Wom;
Not Am Wom

6009. Manley, Fanny Louisa
born 1857
educator, history author
Twent Cen Bio Dict Not Am

**6010. Nuttall, Zelia Maria
Magdalena**
1857/58–1933
archaeologist, student of Mexican
history
Index t Wom; Not Am Wom;
Twent Cen Bio Dict Not Am

**6011. Sanborn, Helen
Josephine**
born 1857
travel writer
Dict Am Auth

6012. Tarbell, Ida Minerva
1857–1944
investigative journalist, muckraker, lecturer, historian, author,
biographer of Abraham Lincoln
Dict Am Auth; Dict Am Bio
supp v3; Index t Wom; Nat Cyc
Am Bio v14; Not Am Wom;
Obit File

**6013. Wergeland, Agnes Math-
ilde**
1857–1914
historian, educator
Dict Am Bio

6014. Bacon, Alice Mable
1858–1918
authority on Japan, author on
Japanese culture, lecturer, edu-
cator of Blacks
Virginia
Dict Am Auth; Dict Am Bio; Not
Am Wom

6015. Dixon, Zella Allen
born 1858
librarian
Twent Cen Bio Dict Not Am

**6016. Folger, Emily Clara Jor-
dan**
1858–1936
Shakespearean scholar and collector
Not Am Wom

**6017. Seelye, Elizabeth
(Eggleston)**
born 1858
writer on Native American biography and early American history
New York
Dict Am Auth; Wom Cent

6018. Bittinger, Lucy (Forney)
born 1859
historical writer on Pennsylvania

Sweckley, PA
Twent Cen Bio Dict Not Am

**6019. Gilman, Mary Rebecca
Foster**
born 1859
author, religious biographer
Dict Am Auth; Index t Wom

**6020. Klingelsmith, Margaret
Center**
1859–1931
librarian, author, legal authority,
Democratic political activist,
suffragist
Unitarian
Dict Am Bio

6021. Marr, Jane Barron Hope
born 1859
author, history writer
Twent Cen Bio Dict Not Am

**6022. Sutliff, Phebe Temper-
ance**
born 1859
educator, historian
Twent Cen Bio Dict Not Am

6023. Tyler, Alice Sarah
1859–1944
librarian, educator
Index t Wom; Nat Cyc Am Bio
v33; Not Am Wom

6024. Ahern, Mary Eileen
1860/65–1938
librarian, editor, educator
Index t Wom; Nat Cyc Am Bio
csv1; Not Am Wom

6025. Browne, Nina Eliza
born 1860
librarian, editor
Index t Wom; Nat Cyc Am Bio
csv1

6026. Ewell, Alice Maud
born 1860
historical novelist
Virginia
Dict Am Auth

**6027. Jones, Kate Emory San-
born**
born 1860
librarian
Twent Cen Bio Dict Not Am

**6028. MacKaye, Julia
Josephine Gunther**
flourished 1890s
author, librarian
Index t Wom

6029. Orff, Annie L. Y.
flourished 1890s
editor, publisher, women's travel
expert
St. Louis, MO
Wom Cent

6030. Welch, Jane Meade
flourished 1890s
journalist, historical lecturer
New York
Wom Cent

**6031. Bacon, Louise Lee (An-
drews)**
born 1861
travel writer
Dict Am Auth

6032. Doren, Electra Collins
1861–1927
librarian
Index t Wom

6033. Hebard, Grace Raymond
1861–1936
educator, feminist historian, author
Wyoming
Index t Wom; Read Encyc Am
West

6034. Wood, Mary Elizabeth
1861–1931
missionary, librarian in China
Episcopalian
Dict Am Bio; Not Am Wom

6035. Zavala, Adina Emila de
1861–1955
historian of Texas, historical
worker
Mexican
Dict Mex Am Hist

6036. Peattie, Elia Wilkerson
born 1862
author, journalist, novelist, travel
writer
Chicago, IL
Dict Am Auth; Wom Cent

6037. Weir, Irene
1862–1944
painter, art educator, writer on
art, founder of the New York
School of Design and Liberal
Arts
New York
Not Am Wom; Obit File

6038. Wells, Carolyn
1862/69–1942
author, humorist, poet, librarian
Rahway, NJ
Dict Am Auth; Index t Wom;
Nat Cyc Am Bio v13; Not Am
Wom; Twent Cen Bio Dict Not
Am

**6039. Wharton, Edith Newbold
(Jones)**
1862–1937
novelist, short story writer, ghost
story writer, autobiographer,
travel writer, literary critic
New York, NY

French (American expatriate to
Paris)
Dict Am Auth; Dict Am Bio
supp v2; Dict Lit Bio v4 and v9;
Index t Wom; Nat Cyc Am Bio
v14 and csv2; Not Am Wom;
Twent Cen Bio Dict Not Am;
Wom Lit; Wom Lit, More

6040. Wright, Carrie Douglas
born 1862
music educator, biographer
Chicago, IL
Dict Am Auth

6041. Askew, Sarah B.
1863/77–1942
librarian
Index t Wom; Not Am Wom

6042. Giffin, Etta Josselyn
1863–1932
librarian for the blind
Index t Wom

6043. Sears, Clara Endicott
1863–1960
author, antiquarian, cattle breeder
Protestant Episcopal
Massachusetts
Nat Cyc Am Bio v47 and csv1

6044. Semple, Ellen Churchill
1863–1932
geographer, writer on geography,
anthropologist, anthropogeographer
Louisville, KY
Dict Am Auth; Dict Am Bio;
Encyc South Hist; Index t
Wom; Nat Cyc Am Bio v35 and
csv1; Not Am Wom

6045. Cone, Claribel
1864–1929
pathologist, art collector
Nat Cyc Am Bio v4; Not Am
Wom

6046. du Pont, Bessie Gardner
1864–1949
historian
Nat Cyc Am Bio v38

6047. Kroeger, Alice Bertha
1864–1909
librarian, library school director
Index t Wom; Not Am Wom

**6048. Thomas, Edith (Carpen-
ter)**
circa 1864–1901
novelist, biographer
Millville, NJ
Dict Am Auth

6049. Hopkins, Florence May
born 1865
librarian
Detroit, MI
Nat Cyc Am Bio v18

6050. Isom, Mary Frances
1865–1920
librarian
Dict Am Bio; Index t Wom; Not
Am Wom

**6051. Kendall, Elizabeth Kem-
ball**
1865–1952
historian, university educator,
world traveler
Obit File

6052. Madison, Luch (Foster)
born 1865
historical fiction writer
New York, NY
Dict Am Auth

6053. Sharp, Katharine Lucinda
1865–1914
librarian, library school director
Dict Am Bio; Not Am Wom;
Twent Cen Bio Dict Not Am

**6054. Stanard, Mary Mann
Page Newton**
1865–1929
historian of Virginia
Virginia
Dict Am Bio

6055. Wilson, Margaret Stevens
circa 1865–1943
librarian
Index t Wom

6056. Countryman, Gratia Alta
1866–1953
librarian
Minnesota
Index t Wom; Nat Cyc Am Bio
csv5

6057. Foote, Elizabeth Louisa
born 1866
librarian
Methodist Episcopal
Nat Cyc Am Bio csv3

**6058. Lawrence, Ruth Wood-
hull**
1866–1956
founder of the National Society of
Colonial Dames, authority on
colonial families
Obit File

6059. Skinner, Belle
1866–1928
philanthropist, musical instrument collector
Nat Cyc Am Bio v23

6060. Stearns, Lutie Eugenia
1866–1943
librarian, lecturer, social reformer
Index t Wom; Not Am Wom

6061. Eastman, Linda Anne
1867–1963
librarian

Cleveland, OH
Index t Wom; Nat Cyc Am Bio
csv3; Not Am Wom supp v1

**6062. Hurd-Mead, Kate Camp-
bell;** Kate Mead
1867–1941
physician, historian of women in
medicine
Index t Wom; Not Am Wom; Nat
Cyc Am Bio v38

6063. Rogers, Grace Rainey
1867–1943
art collector, philanthropist
Not Am Wom

**6064. Hazeltine, Mary Emo-
gene**
1868–1949
librarian
Index t Wom; Not Am Wom

**6065. Percival, Olive May
Graves**
born 1868
underwriter, travel writer
Los Angeles, CA
Dict Am Auth

**6066. Spurgeon, Caroline
Frances Eleanor**
1868–1942
authority on Shakespeare and
Chaucer, educator, founder of
the International Federation of
University Women
Obit File

6067. Tucker, Rosa Lee
born 1868
state librarian of Mississippi
Mississippi
Wom Cent

6068. Young, Ella
1868–1956
poet, authority on Celtic folklore
Irish
Obit File

6069. Winser, Beatrice
1869–1947
librarian, museum director
Index t Wom; Not Am Wom

**6070. Badcock, Winifred (Ea-
ton);** Onoto Watanna
flourished 1900s
writer on Japan
Dict Am Auth

**6071. Bogle, Sarah Comly
Norris**
1870–1932
librarian
Protestant Episcopal
New York
Index t Wom; Nat Cyc Am Bio
csv3; Not Am Wom

6072. Cone, Etta
1870–1949
art collector
Nat Cyc Am Bio v4; Not Am
Wom

6073. Crowley, Mary Catherine
flourished 1900s
editor, historian, novelist
Detroit, MI
Dict Am Auth; Index t Wom

6074. Culver, Essae Martha
flourished 1900s–30s
librarian
Louisiana
Index t Wom; Nat Cyc Am Bio
csv6

**6075. Davenport, Frances Gar-
diner**
born 1870
historian, educator
Index t Wom

6076. Doyle, Agnes Catherine
flourished 1900s
librarian, author
Index t Wom

6077. Guerrier, Edith
born 1870
librarian
Index t Wom

6078. Lantz, Emily Emerson
flourished 1900s
journalist, genealogist
Index t Wom

6079. Rubenstein, Helena
1870/71–1965
cosmetics manufacturer, entrepreneur, art collector, philanthropist
Jewish
Polish
Index t Wom; Nat Cyc Am Bio
v50; Not Am Wom supp v1;
Obit File; Who Who Jew Hist

6080. Sellers, Kathryn
1870–1939
lawyer, judge, bibliographer, librarian
Index t Wom

6081. Wier, Jeanne Elizabeth
1870–1950
historian of Nevada and the
state's Native Americans, educator, suffragist
Nevada
Nat Cyc Am Bio v51 and csv1;
Obit File; Read Encyc Am West

6082. Wilson, Florence
flourished 1900s–20s
librarian, suffragist
Nat Cyc Am Bio csv3

6083. Beasley, Delilah Leontium
1871–1934
historian, journalist, pacifist
California
Black
Encyc Black Am; Negro Alman; Prof Negro Wom

6084. Bjerkoe, Ethel Hall
1871–1978
antiques authority and author, clubwoman
Connecticut; Maine
Nat Cyc Am Bio v60

6085. Laut, Agnes Christina
1871/72–1936
journalist, novelist, writer on the American West
Canadian
Dict Am Auth; Index t Wom

6086. Moore, Anne Carrol
1871–1961
children's author and librarian
Index t Wom; Not Am Wom supp v1

6087. Oskinson, Hildegarde Hawthorne
1871–1952
author, biographer of literary figures, children's author
Obit File

6088. Rickert, Martha Edith
1871–1938
medievalist, professor of English, philologist, novelist
Dict Am Auth; Dict Am Bio supp v2; Not Am Wom

6089. Anderson, Audentia Smith
born 1872
religious author, genealogist, pioneer
Mormon
Index t Wom

6090. Barnett, Claribel Ruth
1872–1951
librarian
Index t Wom

6091. Colcord, Mabel
born 1872
librarian, bibliographer, entomologist
Index t Wom

6092. Gallup, Anna Billings
1872–1956
museum curator
Index t Wom; Nat Cyc Am Bio csv5

6093. Haines, Helen Elizabeth
1872–1961
librarian, author, editor, educator
Index t Wom; Not Am Wom supp v1

6094. Howard, Minnie F.
born 1872
author, historian, public welfare worker
Index t Wom

6095. Hubbard, Helen Fahnestock
1872–1955
philanthropist, historical collector
Nat Cyc Am Bio v46

6096. Littleton, Martin N., Mrs.
1872–1953
campaigner for historical monuments
Obit File

6097. Putnam, Bertha Haven
1872–1960
historian, history writer, authority on medieval history and criminology, educator
Unitarian
Nat Cyc Am Bio v43; Not Am Wom supp v1; Obit File

6098. Seton, Grace Gallatin Thompson; Dorothy Dodge
1872–1959
suffragist, feminist, explorer, geographer, author, book designer, bookmaker, composer of popular songs, historian, cofounder of the Campfire Girls
Dict Am Auth; Dict Am Bio supp v6; Index t Wom; Nat Cyc Am Bio v47 and csv5; Not Am Wom supp v1; Obit File

6099. Abel-Anderson, Annie Heloise
1873–1947
historian, educator
Dict Am Bio supp v4; Not Am Wom

6100. Bolton, Ethel (Stanwood)
born 1873
genealogist
Brookline, MA
Dict Am Auth

6101. Clubb, Laura Abigail Rutherford
1873–1952
art collector, rare book collector, philanthropist, cattle rancher
Methodist
Oklahoma
Nat Cyc Am Bio v38

6102. Irwin, Inez Leonore Haynes Gillmore
1873–1970
suffragist, feminist, head of the World Center for Women's Archives, author, first woman president of the Authors League of America
Brazilian
Index t Wom; Nat Cyc Am Bio csv6; Not Am Wom supp v1; Obit File

6103. Lingelbach, Anna Lane
1873–1954
historian, educator, civic leader, feminist
Presbyterian
Pennsylvania
Dict Am Bio supp v5; Nat Cyc Am Bio v44; Obit File

6104. Neilson, Nellie
1873–1947
English historian, first woman president of the American Historical Association, educator, author
Episcopalian
Nat Cyc Am Bio v36; Not Am Wom; Obit File

6105. Lowell, Amy
1874–1925
poet, biographer, lecturer, critic
Dict Am Bio; Index t Wom; Nat Cyc Am Bio v19; Not Am Wom; Wom Lit; Wom Lit, More

6106. Monroe, Anne Shannon
1874/77–1942
author, essayist, novelist, magazine writer, Oregon historian, feminist, lecturer, mountain climber
Oregon
Index t Wom; Nat Cyc Am Bio; Obit File

6107. Phillips, Catherine Coffin
1874–1942
author, historian of the Pacific Coast
California
Nat Cyc Am Bio v32 and csv6

6108. Brooks, Geraldine
born 1875
colonial historian, author
New York, NY
Dict Am Auth

6109. Brown, Zaidee Mabel
1875–1950
librarian, editor, lecturer
Index t Wom

6110. Byne, Mildred Staply
1875–1941
portrait painter, authority on Spanish art and architecture
Obit File

6111. Dale, Maud Murray Thompson
1875–1953
art collector, artist, designer of automobiles, stage designer
Dict Am Bio supp v5

6112. Denning, Delia; Delia (Denning) Akeley Howe
1875–1970
African explorer, big game hunter, geographer, taxidermist, author, lecturer, World War I relief worker
Nat Cyc Am Bio v57; Obit File; Index t Wom

6113. Fay, Lucy Ella
1875–1963
librarian
Index t Wom

6114. Howe, Delia Akeley (Denning)
1875–1970
African explorer, big game hunter, geographer, taxidermist, author, lecturer, World War I relief worker
Index t Wom; Nat Cyc Am Bio v57; Obit File

6115. Lacy, Mary Goodwin
1875–1962
librarian, author, government employee
Index t Wom

6116. Mudge, Isodore Gilbert
1875–1957
librarian, bibliographer
Not Am Wom supp v1

6117. Whitney, Gertrude Vanderbilt
1875–1942
sculptor, patron of art, patron of opera, museum founder
Dict Am Bio supp v3; Index t Wom; Nat Cyc Am Bio v17, csv2, and csv5; Not Am Wom; Obit File

6118. Beard, Mary Ritter
1876–1958
historian, writer on history, feminist
Dict Am Bio supp v6; Index t Wom; Not Am Wom supp v1; Obit File

6119. Dix, Beulah Marie
born 1876
historical novelist
Cambridge, MA
Dict Am Auth

6120. Force, Juliana Rieser
1876/88–1948
art museum director
Dict Am Bio supp v4; Index t Wom; Not Am Wom

6121. Slaughter, Elizabeth Vanuxem Kennedy
1876–1960
Confederate historian
Tennessee
Nat Cyc Am Bio v44

6122. Sprague, Harriet Chapman
1876–1969
bibliophile, book collector
Congregationalist
Connecticut
Nat Cyc Am Bio v56

6123. Williams, Amelia Worthington
1876–1958
educator, historian of Texas
Presbyterian
Texas
Nat Cyc Am Bio v44

6124. Woodbury, Helen Laura Sumner
1876–1933
labor historian, social economist, author, government official
Dict Am Auth; Not Am Wom

6125. Anthony, Katharine Susan
1877–1965
author, biographer
New York
Index t Wom; Nat Cyc Am Bio csv6; Obit File

6126. Kerby, Marion
1877–1956
stage actor, folk song singer and collector
Obit File

6127. Kruettner, Caroline McAllister
1877–1957
poet, librarian, poetry editor
Obit File

6128. Skinner, Constance Lindsay
1877–1939
author, poet, novelist, historian
Canadian
Index t Wom; Nat Cyc Am Bio csv2 and csv5; Not Am Wom

6129. Sullivan, Mary Josephine Quinn
1877–1939
art teacher and collector, a founder of the New York Museum of Modern Art
Not Am Wom

6130. Gardner, Helen
1878–1946
art historian, educator
Dict Am Bio supp v4; Index t Wom; Not Am Wom

6131. Howard, Alice Sturtevant
1878–1945
library founder, author, Republican party worker
Episcopalian
Index t Wom; Nat Cyc Am Bio v33

6132. Murray, Elsie
1878–1965
psychologist, color blindness expert, museum director
Presbyterian
Pennsylvania
Nat Cyc Am Bio v53

6133. Williams, Mary Wilhelmine
1878–1944
historian
Not Am Wom

6134. Eastman, Mary Huse
1879–1963
librarian, author
Index t Wom

6135. Olcott, Margaret A.
1879–1949
playwright, biographer
Obit File

6136. Sawyer, Josephine Caroline
born 1879
historical novelist
Watertown, NY
Dict Am Auth

6137. Bieber, Margarete
1880–1978
historian, author, archaeologist, educator, authority on Greek and Roman art
German
Obit File

6138. Bingham, Millicent Todd
1880–1968
geographer, conservationist, author, editor, authority on Emily Dickinson
Episcopalian
Cur Biog '69; Index t Wom; Nat Cyc Am Bio csv9

6139. Coltman, Elizabeth Sweetzer
flourished 1910s–30s
Orientalist, linguist
Index t Wom

6140. Coulter, Edith Margaret
1880–1963
librarian, library educator
Presbyterian
California
Nat Cyc Am Bio v50

6141. Evans, Orrena Louise
flourished 1910s
editor, librarian
Index t Wom

6142. Gunterman, Bertha Lisette
flourished 1910s–30s
librarian, editor
Index t Wom

6143. Morrow, Honore Bryant Willsie
1880–1940
historical novelist
Index t Wom; Nat Cyc Am Bio v29

6144. O'Brien, Margaret
flourished 1910s
librarian
Index t Wom

6145. Sage, Cornelia B.
born 1880
art museum director
Nat Cyc Am Bio csv1

6146. Burnham, Mary
born 1881
editor, librarian
Index t Wom

6147. Thompson, Clara Mildred
born 1881
Reconstruction historian
Georgia
Encyc South Hist

6148. Flexner, Jennie Maas
1882–1944
librarian, scholar of Black literature, author
Jewish
Dict Am Bio supp v3; Index t Wom; Not Am Wom

6149. Metcalf, Eleanor Melville Thomas
1882–1964
editor of biographical data
Obit File

6150. Richter, Gisela Marie Augusta
1882–1972
classical archaeologist, museum curator, author
English
Index t Wom; Not Am Wom supp v1

6151. Greene, Belle da Costa
1883–1950
librarian, library director of the John Pierpont Morgan Library
New York
Dict Am Bio supp v4; Not Am Wom; Obit File

6152. Newman, Frances
1883–1928
librarian, author, novelist
Index t Wom; Not Am Wom; Wom Lit, More

6153. Shaver, Mary Mumpere
1883–1942
librarian, educator
Index t Wom

6154. Werlein, Elizabeth Thomas
1883–1946
leader in preserving the New Orleans French Quarter
New Orleans, LA
Not Am Wom

6155. Darby, Ada Claire
1884–1953
historical author for children
Obit File

6156. Fair, Ethel Marion
born 1884
librarian, editor, author, lecturer
Index t Wom

6157. Bruce, Kathleen Eveleth
1885–1950
historian, author
Nat Cyc Am Bio v42; Obit File

6158. Rourke, Constance Mayfield
1885–1941
student of American culture, historian, folklorist, author, critic, educator
Dict Am Bio supp v3; Index t Wom; Nat Cyc Am Bio v32; Not Am Wom

6159. Winslow, Ola Elizabeth
1885–1977
biographer of Jonathan Edward, historian, Pulitzer Prize winner
Obit File

6160. Schmitt, Bernadotte Everly
1886–1969
author on modern European history, educator, historian
Cur Biog '69

6161. Allis, Marguerite
1887–1958
historical novelist
Index t Wom; Obit File

6162. Bauer, Marion Eugenia
1887–1955
music educator, writer on music history, composer, editor, music critic
Index t Wom; Nat Cyc Am Bio v43, Not Am Wom supp v1; Obit File

6163. Chase, Mary Ellen
1887–1973

novelist, biographer, short story
writer, literary critic, writer on
the Bible, university educator
Episcopalian
Cur Biog '73; Index t Wom; Nat
Cyc Am Bio csv9; Obit File;
Wom Lit, More

6164. Dobie, Edith
1887–1975
historian, educator
Methodist
Washington
Nat Cyc Am Bio v58

**6165. Madelva, Mary Eveline
Wolff, Sister**
1887–1964
president of St. Mary's College,
medievalist, educator, author,
poet, Catholic nun
Catholic
Index t Wom; Nat Cyc Am Bio
v51; Obit File

**6166. Post, Marjorie Merri-
weather**
1887–1973
philanthropist, antique collector,
suffragist, director of National
Savings and Trust, founder and
director of General Foods
Christian Scientist
Washington, DC
Nat Cyc Am Bio v58; Not Am
Wom supp v1; Obit File

**6167. Ratchford, Fannie
Elizabeth**
born 1887
librarian, author, editor
Index t Wom

6168. Stebbins, Lucy Poate
1887–1958
novelist, biographer
Obit File

6169. Barker, Tommie Dora
born 1888
librarian, author, educator
Index t Wom

6170. Akers, Susan Grey
born 1889
librarian, educator, author
Index t Wom

6171. Cranston, Ruth
1889–1956
religious author, biographer, lecturer
Obit File

6172. Furbeck, Mary Elizabeth
flourished 1920s–40s
editor, librarian
Index t Wom

6173. Grant, Frances R.
flourished 1920s–30s

museum director, editor
Index t Wom

6174. Hume, Jessie Fremont
flourished 1920s–30s
librarian
New York
Nat Cyc Am Bio csv1

6175. Jewett, Alice L.
flourished 1920s
librarian, editor
Index t Wom

6176. Petersen, Agnes J.
flourished 1920s–30s
journalist, librarian
Index t Wom

6177. Rebay, Hilla
1890–1967
museum director, painter
Not Am Wom supp v1

6178. Rollins, Charlemae Hill
flourished 1920s–40s
librarian
Black
Encyc Black Am; Index t Wom

6179. Rothrock, Mary Utopia
born 1890
librarian, editor, author
Index t Wom

6180. Saunders, Agnes Kelly
flourished 1920s–30s
museum director
Index t Wom

6181. Winslow, Amy
born 1890
librarian, library director
Index t Wom

6182. Forbes, Esther; Esther
Forbes Hoskins
1891–1967
novelist, children's author, colonial historian, Pulitzer Prize
winner
Congregationalist
Massachusetts
Index t Wom; Nat Cyc Am Bio
v53; Not Am Wom supp v1;
Obit File

6183. Roberts, Kate Louise
died 1941
librarian
Index t Wom

6184. Manley, Marian C.
born 1892
librarian
Index t Wom

6185. Smedley, Agnes
1892/94–1950
author, foreign correspondent,
lecturer, champion of revolu-

tionary China, writer on China
and the Far East
Dict Am Bio supp v4; Index t
Wom; Not Am Wom; Obit File;
Wom Lit, More

**6186. Tomkins, Miriam Down-
ing**
born 1892
librarian, editor
Index t Wom

**6187. Leech, Margaret Kerno-
chan;** Mrs. Ralph Pulitzer
1893–1974
author, novelist, historian
New York
Cur Biog '74; Index t Wom; Nat
Cyc Am Bio csv6

6188. Barker, Ellen Frye
died 1944
advertising copywriter, dramatic
critic, genealogist, publisher
Index t Wom; Obit File

6189. Brown, Alberta Louise
born 1894
librarian
Index t Wom

6190. Fyan, Loleta Dawson
born 1894
librarian, author
Index t Wom

6191. Harsh, Vivian
1894–1960
librarian
Black
Encyc Black Am

6192. Kuhne, Marie Peary
1894–1978
authority on Arctic history, Inuit
welfare worker
Obit File

6193. Moore, Elizabeth Finley
1894–1976
South Carolina historical worker
Episcopalian
South Carolina
Nat Cyc Am Bio v60

6194. Pulitzer, Margaret Leech
1894–1974
historian, Pulitzer Prize winner
Obit File

6195. Savord, Ruth
1894–1966
librarian
Index t Wom

6196. Taggard, Genevieve
1894–1948
poet, educator, biographer of Emily Dickinson, literature professor
Dict Am Bio supp v4; Index t
Wom; Not Am Wom; Obit File

6197. Barry, Iris
1895–1969
film historian and critic
Not Am Wom supp v1

6198. Chapin, Helen B.
1895–1950
expert on Far Eastern art and
iconography
Obit File

6199. Nute, Grace Lee
born 1895
historian
Minnesota
Read Encyc Am West

6200. Vormelker, Rose Lillian
born 1895
librarian, editor, lecturer
Index t Wom

6201. Wright, Zoe Harmon
born 1895
librarian
Index t Wom

**6202. Sandoz, Marie Suzette
"Mari"**
1896/1901–1966
author, novelist, historian
Nebraska
Dict Lit Bio v9; Index t Wom;
Not Am Wom supp v1; Read
Encyc Am West; Wom Lit,
More

6203. White, Helen Constance
1896–1967
educator, historial novelist, religious historian, UNESCO
member
Catholic
Index t Wom; Nat Cyc Am Bio
v53; Not Am Wom supp v1

6204. Winchell, Constance M.
born 1896
librarian
Index t Wom

**6205. Bowen, Catherine (Sho-
ber) Drinker**
1897–1973
biographer, essayist, autobiographer, lecturer
Pennsylvania
Cur Biog '73; Index t Wom; Nat
Cyc Am Bio v58; Not Am Wom
supp v1; Obit File

6206. Goldthwaite, Lucy A.
1897–1957
librarian in the New York Public
Library for the Blind, founder
of the *Braille Book Review*
New York
Obit File

**6207. Green, Constance Winsor
McLaughlin**
1897–1975

historian, Pulitzer Prize winner
Index t Wom; Not Am Wom
supp v1; Obit File

6208. Logasa, Hannah
born 1897
librarian, author
Index t Wom

6209. Ross, Isabel
1897–1975
author, novelist, biographer of
prominent American women
Scottish
Index t Wom; Obit File

6210. Brooks, Juanita
born 1898
historian of Mormonism
Mormon
Read Encyc Am West

**6211. Guggenheim, Marguerite
"Peggy"**
born 1898
patron of modern art and music,
art collector, author
Jewish
New York
Cur Biog '80; Index t Wom; Who
Who Jew Hist

6212. Keck, Lucile Liebermann
born 1898
librarian
Index t Wom

6213. Ludington, Flora Belle
born 1898
librarian
Index t Wom

6214. Wolle, Muriel Sibell
1898–1977
artist, art educator, Native American art scholar and collector,
western history writer, conservationist
Episcopalian
Boulder, CO
Nat Cyc Am Bio v60

6215. Crawford, Phyllis
born 1899
author, librarian, editor
Index t Wom

6216. Hedgeman, Anna Arnold
born 1899
New York civic leader, New
York mayor's cabinet member,
consultant on urban affairs and
Afro-American studies, assis-
tant to the administrator of the
Federal Security Agency
Black
Encyc Black Am; Negro Alman;
Negro Her Lib v1

6217. Hyslop, Beatrice Fry
1899–1973

historian
Not Am Wom supp v1

**6218. Schenck, Rachel Kathe-
rine**
born 1899
librarian, educator
Index t Wom

6219. Wright, Muriel Hazel
1899–1975
historian, community leader
Native American (Choctaw)
Ind Today; Not Am Wom supp
v1

6220. Brode, Mildred Hooker
born 1900
librarian, clubwoman
Index t Wom

6221. Burke, Mildred
flourished 1930s
journalist, librarian
Index t Wom

**6222. Carpenter, Mildred Car-
ver**
flourished 1930s
researcher, genealogist
Index t Wom

6223. Garrison, Jane Wilson
flourished 1930s
museum curator
Index t Wom

6224. Graham, Aubry Lee
flourished 1930s
librarian
Index t Wom

6225. Halpert, Edith Gregor
1900?–70
art dealer and collector
Russian
Cur Biog '70; Index t Wom; Not
Am Wom supp v1

6226. Lindem, Selma Marie
flourished 1930s
librarian
Index t Wom

6227. Loeber, L. Elsa
flourished 1930s
educator, librarian
Index t Wom

6228. Lord, Isabel Ely
flourished 1930s
librarian, home economist
Index t Wom

6229. MacUrm, Adeline
flourished 1930s
librarian
Index t Wom

6230. Meixell, Louise Granville
flourished 1930s

librarian, editor
Index t Wom

6231. Morse, Ruth V.
flourished 1930s
travel specialist
Index t Wom

6232. Pidgeon, Marie Kiersted
flourished 1930s
librarian
Index t Wom

6233. Pratt, Gladys Lynwall
flourished 1930s
explorer, museum patron
Index t Wom

6234. Samuels, Margaret
flourished 1930s
educator, librarian, author
Index t Wom

6235. Singer, Ava Hamilton
flourished 1930s
explorer, geographer
Index t Wom

6236. Towner, Isabel Louise
flourished 1930s
librarian
Index t Wom

6237. Weston, Bertine Emma
flourished 1930s
librarian
Index t Wom

**6238. Robb, Inez (Calloway);
Nancy Randolph**
1901?–79
journalist, columnist, travel writer
Cur Biog '79; Index t Wom

**6239. Skinner, Cornelia Caro-
line Otis**
1901–79
stage actor, monologuist, poet,
essayist, biographer
Cur Biog '79; Index t Wom; Nat
Cyc Am Bio csv6

6240. Gray, Elizabeth Janet
born 1902
author, librarian, educator
Index t Wom

6241. Harris, Christina Phelps
1902–72
Middle East scholar, museum curator
Nat Cyc Am Bio v57

6242. Tremaine, Marie
born 1902
librarian, author, editor
Index t Wom

6243. Nin, Anais
1903–77

author, novelist, diarist, printer,
feminist
French
Cur Biog '75 and '77; Dict Lit
Bio v2 and v4; Index t Wom;
Wom Lit; Wom Lit, More

6244. Payson, Joan Whitney
1903–75
philanthropist, race horse breeder, owner of the New York
Mets, patron of medicine, art
collector and investor, founder
of the Museum of Modern Art
in New York
Episcopalian
New York
Cur Biog '72 and '75; Index t
Wom; Nat Cyc Am Bio v58 and
csv10; Obit File

6245. Spain, Frances Lander
born 1903
librarian, organization official
Episcopalian
Florida
Index t Wom; Nat Cyc Am Bio
csv10

6246. Vreeland, Diana (Dalziel)
born circa 1903
fashion editor, journalist, costume museum consultant
French
Cur Biog '79; Index t Wom

**6247. Baker, Augusta (Alexan-
der)**
flourished 1934–68
children's librarian
Black
Encyc Black Am; Negro Alman

**6248. Fuller, Margaret Hart-
well**
born 1904
librarian
Index t Wom

6249. Graham, Shirley
born 1904/07
musical playwright, biographical
historian, author, composer
Black
Index t Wom; Negro Alman

6250. Miner, Dorothy Eugenia
1904–73
museum curator, librarian, art
historian
Not Am Wom supp v1

**6251. Morton, Florrinell
Frances**
born 1904
librarian, educator
Index t Wom

**6252. Zimmerman, Carma
Russell**
born 1904

librarian, editor
Index t Wom

6253. Brenner, Anita
1905–74
journalist, writer on Mexico
Obit File

6254. Gscheidle, Gertrude E.
born 1905
librarian
Index t Wom

6255. Kimball, Arie Goebel
died 1955
author and authority on Thomas
  Jefferson
Obit File

6256. Klahre, Ethel Susan
born 1905
librarian
Index t Wom

6257. Mann, Erika
1905–69
author, writer on Germany, actor, lecturer
German
Cur Biog '69; Index t Wom

6258. Porter, Dorothy B.
born 1905
librarian, library administrator,
  bibliographer, author
Black
Encyc Black Am; Negro Alman

6259. Scoggin, Margaret Clara
1905–68
librarian
Index t Wom

6260. Tate, Merze
born 1905
historian of the Pacific
Black
Encyc Black Am

6261. Bates, Mary E.
died 1956
librarian, editor
Index t Wom

6262. Charles, Dorothy
1906–56
international index editor of the
  American Library Association
Obit File

6263. Cheney, Frances Neel
born 1906
librarian, author
Index t Wom

6264. du Bois, Shirley Lola
  Graham
1906–77
children's author, biographer,
  composer, stage director, civil
  rights worker

Black
Cur Biog '77; Encyc Black Am

6265. Estes, Eleanor Ruth Ro-
  senfeld
born 1906
librarian, author
Index t Wom

6266. Gaver, Mary Virginia
born 1906
librarian, educator
Index t Wom

6267. MacGregor, Ellen
born 1906
author, librarian
Index t Wom

6268. Morsch, Lucile M.
1906–72
librarian, president of the American Library Association
Cur Biog '72; Index t Wom

6269. Ireland, Norma Olin
born 1907
author, technical indexer, librarian
Index t Wom

6270. Crowinshield, Louise E.
  du Pont
died 1958
philanthropist, patron of historical monuments
Obit File

6271. Crary, Catherine Snell
1909–74
historian, educator
Presbyterian
New York
Nat Cyc Am Bio v58

6272. Schmitt, Gladys Leonore;
  Gladys Goldfield
1909–72
author, historical novelist, poet,
  editor, university educator
Cur Biog '72; Index t Wom; Obit
  File

6273. Shumway, Naomi
born 1909
librarian
Index t Wom

6274. Williams, Ethel
born 1909
librarian, bibliographer, biographer
Black
Encyc Black Am

6275. Clapp, Margaret (Antoin-
  ette)
1910–74
president of Wellesley College,
  historian, biographer, US cultural attaché to India
Nat Cyc Am Bio; Index t Wom

6276. Laich, Katherine; Wilhelmina Schlegel
born 1910
librarian, president of the American Library Association, library
  science educator
California
Cur Biog '72

6277. Penn, Jane Pablo
born 1910
historian, museum director
Native American (Wana-Kik-Cahuilla)
Ind Today

6278. Armstrong, Alice Catt
born 1911
biographer, book publisher
Religious Scientist
California
Nat Cyc Am Bio csv10

6279. Edmonds, Helen Grey
born 1911
historian, educator
Black
Encyc Black Am

6280. Jones, Virginia Lacy
born 1912/14
librarian, educator
Black
Encyc Black Am; Index t Wom

6281. Kinder, Katharine Louise
born 1912
librarian
Index t Wom

6282. Moore, Lillian
1912–67
ballet dancer, educator, dance historian and critic
Obit File

6283. Norton, Alice Mary
  "Andre"
born 1912
speculative fiction writer, children's author, librarian
Dict Lit Bio v8; Index t Wom

6284. Robinson, Wilhelmina S.
born 1912
educator, historian
Black
Encyc Black Am

6285. Tuchman, Barbara Wer-
  theim
born 1912
author, historian
Jewish
Index t Wom; Who Who Jew
  Hist

6286. Jones, Clara Stanton
born 1913
librarian, president of the American Library Association
Detroit, MI

Black
Cur Biog '76; Encyc Black Am

6287. Preminger, Marion Hill;
  Mrs. Albert Mayer
1913–72
social worker, author, African art
  collector, missionary to the
  Congo, philanthropist, screen
  actor
Catholic
New York
Hungarian
Nat Cyc Am Bio v57; Obit File

6288. Culver, Agnes Moe
1914–75
illustration dealer, historian
Congregationalist
New York
Nat Cyc Am Bio v58 and v59

6289. Hudson, Jean Blackwell
born 1914
curator of the Schomburg Collection
Black
Negro Alman

6290. Hutson, Jean Blackwell
born 1914
librarian, curator of the Schom-
  burg Center for Research and
  Black Culture
New York
Black
Encyc Black Am

6291. Martin, Allie Beth
  (Dent)
1914–76
librarian, president of the American Library Association
Cur Biog '75

6292. Saarinen, Aline Milton
  Bernstein (Louchheim)
1914–72
art critic, television commentator,
  writer on art history
Cur Biog '72; Index t Wom; Not
  Am Wom supp v1

6293. Usher, Elizabeth Reuter
born 1914
librarian, organization official
Index t Wom

6294. Bradshaw, Lillian Moore
born 1915
librarian, president of the American Library Association
Cur Biog '70

6295. Brown, Letitia Woods
1915–76
historian, educator
Black
Encyc Black Am

6296. Oltman, Florine
born 1915

military librarian, president of the
   Special Libraries Association
Cur Biog '70

6297. Putney, Martha Settle
born 1916
historian, educator
Black
Encyc Black Am

6298. Smith, Ruth Camp
born 1916
librarian, director of the scientific
   document division of the Naval
   Ship Systems Command
Black
Encyc Black Am

6299. Sewell, Winifred [Emma]
born 1917
librarian, organization official
Index t Wom

6300. Wright, Mary Clabaugh
1917–70
historian, scholar of Chinese history, university educator
Connecticut
Not Am Wom supp v1; Obit File

6301. Lowrie, Jean E[lisabeth]
born 1918
librarian, president of the American Library Association, library
   educator
Cur Biog '73

6302. Early, Eleanor
died 1969
travel guide author
Obit File

6303. Thompson, Alleen
born 1919
librarian
Index t Wom

6304. Irwin, Helen
flourished 1950s–60s
librarian, clubwoman
Index t Wom

6305. Bailey, Minnie T.
born 1922
historian
Black
Encyc Black Am

6306. Atkins, Hannah D.
born 1923
librarian
Black
Encyc Black Am

6307. Chandler, Sue Pinkston
flourished 1953–70s
editor, librarian
Black
Encyc Black Am

6308. Walker, Ernestine
born 1926

historian of England
Black
Encyc Black Am

6309. Gray, Hannah Holborn
born 1930
president of the University of
   Chicago, historian
Chicago, IL
German
Cur Biog '79

6310. Mondale, Joan (Adams)
born 1930
federal arts consultant, art historian
Cur Biog '80

6311. Smith, Jessie Carney
born 1930
librarian, educator
Black
Encyc Black Am

6312. Berry, Mary Frances
born 1938
historian, educator
Black
Encyc Black Am

HUMANITIES

6313. Emerson, Mary Moody
1774–1863
New England intellectual
New England
Not Am Wom

6314. Fuller, Sarah Margaret;
   Marchioness Ossoli; Sarah
   Margaret Fuller Ossoli
1810–50
author, critic, educator, feminist,
   philosopher, journalist, Tran-
   scendentalist revolutionary
Transcendentalist
Boston, MA
Cyc Am Bio; Dict Am Auth; Dict
   Am Bio; Dict Am Bio Men
   Time; Dict Lit Bio v1; Index t
   Wom; Nat Cyc Am Bio v3; Not
   Am Wom; Twent Cen Bio Dict
   Not Am; Wom Cent

6315. Thompson, Elizabeth Ro-
   well
1821–99
philanthropist, temperance worker, patron of science and of
   women's medical education,
   suffragist, political philosopher
Cyc Am Bio; Index t Wom; Nat
   Cyc Am Bio v5; Not Am Wom;
   Twent Cen Bio Dict Not Am;
   Wom Cent

6316. Cheney, Endah Dow (Lit-
   tlehale)
1824–1904

philanthropist, author, abolition-
   ist, suffragist, women's rights
   worker, Black civil rights work-
   er, lecturer, philosopher
Transcendentalist
Boston, MA
Cyc Am Bio; Dict Am Auth; Dict
   Am Bio; Dict Lit Bio v1; Index
   t Wom; Nat Cyc Am Bio v9;
   Not Am Wom; Twent Cen Bio
   Dict Not Am; Wom Cent

6317. Blackwell, Antoinette
   Louisa (Brown)
1825–1921
Universalist minister, author, lec-
   turer, temperance worker, aboli-
   tionist, suffragist, women's
   rights worker, philosopher,
   poet, novelist
Unitarian; Congregationalist
Appl Cyc Am Bio; Cyc Am Bio;
   Dict Am Bio; Dict Am Bio Men
   Time; Index t Wom; Nat Cyc
   Am Bio v9 and v29; Not Am
   Wom; Twent Cen Bio Dict Not
   Am; Wom Cent

6318. Bristol, Augusta (Cooper)
1835–1910
educator, writer on education, author, poet, sociologist, lecturer
   on philosophic and scientific
   topics
Cyc Am Bio and ad; Dict Am
   Auth; Twent Cen Bio Dict Not
   Am; Wom Cent

6319. Sunderland, Eliza Jane
   (Read)
1839–1910
lecturer, author, educator, temperance worker, women's rights
   worker, philosopher
Universalist
Michigan
Dict Am Bio; Nat Cyc Am Bio
   v10; Wom Cent

6320. Willard, Frances
   Elizabeth Caroline
1839–98
educator, educational philoso-
   pher, suffragist, feminist, wom-
   en's rights worker, temperance
   leader, naturalist, philanthro-
   pist, newspaper editor, traveler
Methodist Episcopal
Cyc Am Bio; Dict Am Auth; Dict
   Am Bio; Dict Am Bio Men
   Time; Dict Am Rel Bio; Index t
   Wom; Nat Cyc Am Bio v1; Not
   Am Wom; Twent Cen Bio Dict
   Not Am; Wom Cent

6321. Reed, Elizabeth
   (Armstrong)
1842–1915
theologist, religious author, philosopher, historian of India and
   Persia, writer on Oriental litera-

ture, temperance worker, phi-
   lanthropist
Chicago, IL
Dict Am Auth; Dict Am Bio;
   Index t Wom; Nat Cyc Am Bio
   v1 and v15; Twent Cen Bio Dict
   Not Am

6322. Watson, Elizabeth Lowe
born 1842
lecturer, pastor of the San Francisco Religious and Philosophical Society, fruit farmer
California
Wom Cent

6323. Morgan, Anne Eugenia
   Felicia
1845–1909
philosopher, classicist, educator,
   author
Dict Am Auth; Index t Wom;
   Wom Cent

6324. Gulliver, Julia Henrietta
1856–1940
philosopher, educator
Not Am Wom

6325. Playne, Caroline
   Elizabeth
born 1857
philosopher
Who Who Phil

6326. Giles, Anne H.
born 1860
philanthropist
Presbyterian
Wom Cent

6327. Hughes, Nina Vera B.
flourished 1890s
author, philosopher
Canadian
Wom Cent

6328. Calkins, Mary Whiton
1863–1930
philosopher, psychologist, educator, author
Dict Am Bio supp v1; Dict Phil;
   Index t Wom; Nat Cyc Am Bio
   v13; Not Am Wom; Who Who
   Phil

6329. Stokes, Ella Harrison
born 1863
philosopher
Who Who Phil

6330. Cutler, Anna A.
born 1864
philosopher
Who Who Phil

6331. Carr, Geraldine Wildon
born 1866
philosopher
Who Who Phil

6332. Gildemeister, Theda
born 1866
philosopher
Who Who Phil

6333. Talbot, Ellen Bliss
1867–1968
philosopher, educator, author
Congregationalist
Index t Wom; Nat Cyc Am Bio
v54; Who Who Phil

6334. Dolson, Grace N.
born 1874
philosopher
Who Who Phil

6335. Elkus, Savilla
born 1874
philosopher
Who Who Phil

6336. Delaguna, Grace A.
born 1878
philosopher
Who Who Phil

6337. Gordon, Kate
born 1878
philosopher
Who Who Phil

6338. Neenan, Mary Pius, Sister
born 1878
philosopher, Catholic nun
Catholic
Who Who Phil

6339. Shearer, Edna Aston
born 1881
philosopher
Who Who Phil

6340. McAuliffe, Agnes Teresa
born 1884
philosopher
Who Who Phil

6341. Roesch, Jeanette, Sister
born 1884
philosopher
Who Who Phil

6342. Gilbert, Katharine Everett
1886–1952
philosopher, philosophy educator
Nat Cyc Am Bio v49; Who Who
Phil

6343. Benedict, Ruth Fulton
1887–1948
anthropologist, author, philosopher, educator
Dict Am Bio supp v4; Index t
Wom; Nat Cyc Am Bio v36;
Not Am Wom; Who Who Phil

6344. Morgan, Barbara Spofford
1887–1971

philosopher, psychologist
Congregationalist
New York
Nat Cyc Am Bio v56; Who Who
Phil

6345. Parkhurst, Helen Huss
1887–1959
philosopher, educator, aesthetician
Index t Wom; Obit File; Who
Who Phil

6346. Smith, Ethel Sabin
born 1887
philosopher
Who Who Phil

6347. Verda, Mary (Dorsch), Sister
born 1887
philosopher, Catholic nun
Catholic
Who Who Phil

6348. Bussey, Gertrude C.
1888–1961
president of the Women's International League for Peace and
Freedom, philosopher, educator
Obit File

6349. Garvey, Mary Patricia, Sister
born 1888
Catholic nun, philosopher
Who Who Phil

6350. Block, Marguerite Beck
born 1889
philosopher
Who Who Phil

6351. Harris, Marjorie Silliman
born 1890
philosopher
Who Who Phil

6352. Swabey, Marie Collins
born 1890
philosopher
Who Who Phil

6353. Coolidge, Mary Lowell
1891–1958
philosopher, educator, dean of
Wellesley College
Massachusetts
Obit File; Who Who Phil

6354. Harkness, Georgia Elma
1891–1974
philosopher, theologian, religious
educator, author
Dict Am Rel Bio; Index t Wom;
Not Am Wom supp v1; Who
Who Phil

6355. Liddell, Anna Forbes
born 1891
philosopher
Who Who Phil

6356. McCracken, Anna D.
born 1891
philosopher
Who Who Phil

6357. Pray, Ruth Willis
born 1891
philosopher
Who Who Phil

6358. Healy, Emma Therese, Sister
born 1892
philosopher, Catholic nun
Catholic
Who Who Phil

6359. Melvin, Georgiana
born 1893
philosopher
Who Who Phil

6360. Tilley, Ethel
born 1894
philosopher
Who Who Phil

6361. Langer, Susanne Katherina Knauth
born 1895
philosopher, author, educator
Index t Wom; Who Who Phil

6362. le Boutillier, Cornelia Geer
born 1896
philosopher
Who Who Phil

6363. Brown, Brenda
born 1898
philosopher
Who Who Phil

6364. Bunzel, Ruth
born 1898
philosopher, anthropologist
Index t Wom; Who Who Phil

6365. Heath, Louise Robinson
born 1899
philosopher
Who Who Phil

6366. Kennedy, Gail
born 1900
philosopher
Who Who Phil

6367. McGuigan, Gertrude St. George Congregation de Notre Dame, Sister
born 1900
Catholic nun, philosopher
Catholic
Who Who Phil

6368. Wolfe, Joan of Arc, Sister
born 1900
philosopher, Catholic nun

Catholic
Who Who Phil

6369. Walsh, Dorothy
born 1901
philosopher
Who Who Phil

6370. Hafkesbrink, Hanna
born 1902
philosopher
Who Who Phil

6371. Duffy, Elizabeth
born 1904
philosopher
Who Who Phil

6372. Emmet, Dorothy Mary
born 1904
philosopher
Who Who Phil

6373. Rosenblatt, Louise M.
born 1904
philosopher
Who Who Phil

6374. Patterson, Margaret
born 1905
philosopher
Who Who Phil

6375. Ambrose, Alice
born 1906
philosopher, educator
Who Who Phil

6376. Arendt, Hannah
1906–1975
political theorist, philosopher
Jewish
German
Cur Biog '76; Not Am Wom supp
v1; Obit File

6377. Lam, Elizabeth Paxton
born 1906
philosopher
Who Who Phil

6378. Creed, Isabel Payson
born 1907
philosopher
Who Who Phil

6379. Anastasi, Anne
born 1908
philosopher, educator
Who Who Phil

6380. Johnson, Alison Heart
born 1910
philosopher
Who Who Phil

6381. Jeffery, Harriet
born 1912
philosopher
Who Who Phil

6382. Koch, Adrienne
born 1912
philosopher
Who Who Phil

6383. Flower, Elizabeth
born 1913
philosopher
Who Who Phil

6384. Brodie, Helen
born 1915
philosopher
Who Who Phil

6385. Murphy, Frances Haider
born 1915
philosopher
Who Who Phil

6386. Tracy, Louise
flourished 1960s
humanitarian
Index t Wom

6387. Wunderlich, Frieda
flourished 1960s
philosopher
Who Who Phil

6388. Millett, Kate
born 1934
philosopher, novelist, feminist
leader, writer on sex
Cur Biog '71

No Dates

6389. Rooney, Miriam Theresa
philosopher
Who Who Phil

LABOR WELFARE AND REFORM

6390. Cox, Dinah
1804–1909
Black civil rights leader
Black
Index t Wom

6391. Bagley, Sarah G.
flourished 1835–47
labor leader, pioneer telegrapher
Bio Dict Am Lab; Index t Wom;
Not Am Wom

6392. Farley, Harriet
1813/17–1907
millworker, writer on women in
the textile mills, children's au-
thor, editor
New Hampshire
Cyc Am Bio; Dict Am Auth; Dict
Am Bio; Dict Am Bio Men
Time; Nat Cyc Am Bio v11;
Not Am Wom

6393. Dall, Caroline Wells (Healey)
1822–1912
author, essayist, women's rights
worker, women's labor reformer, educator
Boston, MA
Cyc Am Bio; Dict Am Auth; Dict
Am Bio; Dict Lit Bio v1; Index
t Wom; Nat Cyc Am Bio v9;
Not Am Wom; Twent Cen Bio
Dict Not Am; Wom Cent

6394. Penny, Virginia
born 1826
author, educator, women's labor
reform worker, feminist
Cyc Am Bio; Dict Am Auth; Dict
Am Bio Men Time

6395. Kennedy, Kate
1827–90
educator, educational reformer,
champion of equal pay for
women, women's rights worker,
women's labor worker
Oakland, CA
Irish
Nat Cyc Am Bio v30; Not Am
Wom

6396. Blackwell, Sarah Ellen
born 1828
artist, author, suffragist, land and
labor reformer, antivivisectionist
Nat Cyc Am Bio v9; Wom Cent

6397. Collins, Jennie
1828–87
labor reformer, welfare worker,
philanthropist, suffragist
Massachusetts
Bio Dict Am Lab; Index t Wom;
Not Am Wom; Twent Cen Bio
Dict Not Am

6398. Jones, Mary Harris; Mother Jones
1830–1930
labor leader, union organizer
Irish
Bio Dict Am Lab; Dict Am Bio;
Eng Wom; Index t Wom; Nat
Cyc Am Bio v23

6399. Booth, Mary Louisa
1831–89
historian, journalist, translator,
author, editor of *Harper's Ba-
zaar*, women's labor worker
Cyc Am Bio; Dict Am Auth; Dict
Am Bio; Dict Am Bio Men
Time; Index t Wom; Nat Cyc
Am Bio v7; Not Am Wom;
Twent Cen Bio Dict Not Am;
Wom Cent

6400. Young, Sarah Graham; Aunt Betty
born 1831

Civil War army nurse, Union
sympathizer
Wom Cent

6401. Fray, Ellen Sulley
born 1832
suffragist, feminist, women's labor reformer
Ohio
Wom Cent

6402. Rose, Martha E. (Parme-lee)
born 1834
women's labor welfare worker,
social reformer, sociologist, author, art patron, journalist, Sorosis member
Cleveland, OH
Index t Wom; Nat Cyc Am Bio
v11; Wom Cent

6403. Felton, Rebecca Ann Latimer
1835–1930
senator from Georgia, labor welfare worker, journalist, author,
orator, feminist, women's rights
worker
Georgia
Dict Am Bio; Encyc South Hist;
Index t Wom; Nat Cyc Am Bio
v13 and v36; Not Am Wom;
Wom Cent

6404. Meech, Jeannette du Bois
born 1835
evangelist, missionary worker,
Baptist preacher, temperance
worker, industrial educator of
women
Baptist
New Jersey
Index t Wom; Wom Cent

6405. Wyman, Lillie Buffum Chace
born 1837/47
author, muckraking journalist,
short story writer, philanthropist, suffragist, labor welfare
worker
Georgia
Dict Am Auth; Wom Cent

6406. Ames, Fanny Baker
1840–1931
industrial reformer in public institutions, charity organizer
Index t Wom; Not Am Wom;
Wom Cent

6407. Todd, Marion Marsh
1841–post 1913
lawyer, Greenback party worker,
political economist, labor leader, author, lecturer
Not Am Wom; Wom Cent

6408. Conant, Frances Augusta
born 1842

journalist, businessperson, founder of a women's employment
company
Wom Cent

6409. Lowell, Josephine (Shaw)
1843–1905
charitable worker, philanthropist,
social worker, prison reformer,
labor reformer, writer on philanthropy
New York, NY
Cyc Am Bio; Dict Am Auth; Dict
Am Bio; Index t Wom; Nat Cyc
Am Bio v8; Not Am Wom;
Twent Cen Bio Dict Not Am

6410. Loud, Hulda Barker
born 1844
editor, publisher, women's rights
worker, suffragist, labor worker,
lecturer
Index t Wom; Wom Cent

6411. Stevens, Alzina Parsons
1844/49–1900
labor leader, industrial reformer,
settlement house worker, social
reformer, newspaper editor and
publisher, journalist, author
Chicago, IL
Index t Wom; Not Am Wom;
Wom Cent

6412. Carhart, Clara Sully
born 1845
educator, temperance worker,
women's labor welfare worker
Methodist Episcopal
New York
Canadian
Wom Cent

6413. Seymour, Mary Foot
1846–93
stenographer, businessperson,
journalist, law reporter, suffragist, women's labor worker
Not Am Wom; Wom Cent

6414. Henrotin, Ellen M. Mar-tin
1847–1922
women's club leader, labor and
social reformer, philanthropist
Index t Wom; Not Am Wom

6415. Rodgers, Elizabeth Flynn
1847–1939
labor leader, insurance society executive
Not Am Wom

6416. Mee, Cassie Ward
born 1848
labor leader, Knights of Labor
worker, temperance worker,
lecturer
Quaker
Canadian
Index t Wom; Wom Cent

6417. Troup, Augusta Lewis
circa 1848–1920
labor organizer, journalist
Catholic
Bio Dict Am Lab; Not Am Wom

6418. Barry, Leonore Marie Kearney
1849–1930
labor organizer, lecturer
Not Am Wom

6419. Brown, Corinne Stubbs
born 1849
Socialist party member, labor activist, sociologist, educator
Index t Wom; Wom Cent

6420. de Graffenreid, Mary Clare
1849–1921
social investigator, writer on social conditions, labor authority
Georgia
Encyc South Hist; Not Am Wom

6421. Sandes, Margaret Isabelle
born 1849
industrial reformer, club leader
Scottish
Wom Cent

6422. Spencer, Anna Carpenter (Garlin)
1851–1931
Unitarian minister, journalist, educator, temperance worker, suffragist, pacifist, child-labor reformer, philanthropist
Unitarian
Dict Am Bio; Nat Cyc Am Bio v9 and csv2; Not Am Wom

6423. Bradford, Mary Carroll Craig
born 1856/60
magazine and newspaper correspondent, educator, labor union leader
Christian Scientist
Colorado
Nat Cyc Am Bio csv2; Wom Cent

6424. Henry, Alice
1857–1943
journalist, women's trade union leader, feminist, suffragist, editor
Unitarian
Australian
Bio Dict Am Lab; Dict Am Bio supp v3; Not Am Wom

6425. Kehew, Mary Morton Kimball
1859–1918
social reformer in education and employment for women, labor organizer, worker for the welfare of children and the blind
Dict Am Bio; Not Am Wom

6426. Gilman, Charlotte Anna (Perkins) (Stetson)
1860–1935
author, feminist, lecturer, labor worker
San Francisco, CA
Dict Am Auth; Dict Am Bio supp v1; Index t Wom; Nat Cyc Am Bio v13; Not Am Wom; Twent Cen Bio Dict Not Am; Wom Lit, More

6427. Bissell, Emily Perkins; Priscilla Leonard
1861–1948
welfare and child labor worker, author, inventor of Christmas Seals
Nat Cyc Am Bio v38; Not Am Wom; Obit File

6428. Haley, Margaret Angela
1861–1939
educator, civic reformer, labor leader
Catholic
Illinois
Bio Dict Am Lab; Not Am Wom

6429. Bloor, Ella Reeve; Ella Omholt
1862–1951
radical labor organizer, journalist, suffragist, Socialist and Communist party leader, a founder of the American Communist party
Bio Dict Am Lab; Dict Am Bio supp v5; Not Am Wom supp v1; Obit File

6430. O'Sullivan, Mary Kenney
1864–1943
labor organizer and reformer, factory inspector
Dict Am Bio supp v3; Not Am Wom

6431. Marot, Helen
1865–1940
labor leader
Quaker
Bio Dict Am Lab; Index t Wom

6432. Barnum, Gertrude
1866–1919/48
social worker, labor leader and reformer, government official
Bio Dict Am Lab; Not Am Wom

6433. Valesh, Eva McDonald
born 1866
printer, journalist, social reformer, feminist, labor leader and activist
Minneapolis, MN
Index t Wom; Wom Cent

6434. Gillespie, Mabel [Edna]
1867/77–1923

women's labor reformer, labor leader, social worker
Dict Am Bio; Nat Cyc Am Bio v23; Not Am Wom

6435. Fuller, Minnie Ursula Oliver Scott Rutherford
1868–1946
temperance and child labor worker, suffragist
Arkansas
Encyc South Hist; Not Am Wom

6436. Robins, Margaret Dreier
1868/69–1945
labor reformer, woman- and child-labor welfare worker, suffragist, feminist, social economist, founder of the Municipal League
Bio Dict Am Lab; Dict Am Bio supp v3; Index t Wom; Nat Cyc Am Bio v33; Not Am Wom; Obit File

6437. du Pont, Zara
1869–1946
labor activist
Obit File

6438. Eaves, Lucile
1869–1953
sociologist, labor relations expert
Unitarian
San Francisco, CA
Nat Cyc Am Bio v41 and csv1

6439. Conboy, Sara Agnes McLaughlin
1870–1928
labor reformer
Dict Am Bio

6440. O'Reilly, Leonora
1870–1927
labor leader, labor reformer
Not Am Wom

6441. Younger, Maud
1870–1936
suffragist, labor reformer, trade unionist
Dict Am Bio supp v2; Not Am Wom

6442. Fitzgerald, Susan Grimes Walker
1871–1943
labor worker, trade unionist, suffragist
Unitarian
Boston, MA
Nat Cyc Am Bio v32

6443. Anderson, Mary
1872–1964
director of the US Labor Department Women's Bureau, labor union official

Swedish
Bio Dict Am Lab; Index t Wom; Not Am Wom supp v1; Obit File

6444. Jackson, Alice Hooker Day
1872–1926
labor welfare worker
New York
Nat Cyc Am Bio v21

6445. Mann, Kristine
1873–1945
psychiatrist, women's labor worker
Nat Cyc Am Bio v34

6446. Vorse, Mary Heaton Marvin
1874/81–1960/66
journalist, novelist, labor activist
Bio Dict Am Lab; Index t Wom; Not Am Wom supp v1; Obit File

6447. Dreier, Mary Elisabeth
1875–1963
labor reformer, suffragist, New York civic leader, Bull Moose party politician
Presbyterian
New York
Nat Cyc Am Bio csv9; Not Am Wom supp v1

6448. Jacobs, Pattie Ruffner
1875–1935
Alabama suffrage leader, child labor welfare worker, prison reformer, Prohibition party worker
Encyc South Hist; Not Am Wom

6449. Norton, Mary Teresa Hopkins
1875–1959
representative to Congress from New Jersey, Labor Department aide, first woman Democrat elected to Congress
New Jersey
Dict Am Bio supp v6; Index t Wom; Nat Cyc Am Bio v45; Not Am Wom supp v1; Obit File

6450. Weed, Helen Hill
1875–1958
suffrage leader, pacifist, child labor reformer
Obit File

6451. Brueggeman, Bessie Parker
born 1876
chairperson of the US Employees Compensation Commission
Nat Cyc Am Bio csv2

6452. Cleghorn, Sarah Norcliffe
1876–1959

poet, novelist, educator, suffragist, civil rights worker, labor
worker, pacifist, antivivisectionist, Socialist party member
Vermont
Index t Wom; Nat Cyc Am Bio
v46; Obit File; Dict Am Bio
supp v5

**6453. Woodbury, Helen Laura
Sumner**
1876–1933
labor historian, social economist,
author, government official
Dict Am Auth; Not Am Wom

6454. Thorne, Florence Calvert
1877–1973
labor researcher, editor
Not Am Wom supp v1

6455. Burroughs, Nannie Helen
1878/83–1961
educator, founder of the National
Trade and Professional School
for Women and Girls, women's
rights worker
Baptist
Black
Index t Wom; Negro Alman; Not
Am Wom supp v1; Prof Negro
Wom

**6456. Gilbreth, Lillian Evelyn
(Moller)**
1878–1972
industrial engineer and psychologist, household efficiency and
labor efficiency expert, management consultant
Cur Biog '72; Index t Wom; Not
Am Wom supp v1; Obit File

6457. Baker, Mary Cornelia
1879–1963
labor leader, educator
Not Am Wom supp v1

**6458. Bergoff, Pearl L.; King
of the Strike Breakers**
1879–1947
head of Bergoff Service Bureau
labor suppliers
Obit File

**6459. Stokes, Rose Harriet
Pastor**
1879–1933
Socialist and Communist party
leader, feminist, labor leader,
author
Jewish
Polish
Bio Dict Am Lab; Dict Am Bio;
Not Am Wom

6460. Swartz, Maud O'Farrell
1879–1937
labor leader
Catholic
New York

Irish
Bio Dict Am Lab; Not Am Wom

6461. Nestor, Agnes
1880–1948
trade union leader, president of
the Chicago Women's Trade
Union League
Bio Dict Am Lab; Dict Am Bio
supp v4; Not Am Wom; Obit
File

**6462. Perkins, Frances; Mrs.
Paul C. Wilson**
1880/82–1965
social worker and reformer, US
secretary of labor
Index t Wom; Nat Cyc Am Bio
csv4 and csv6; Not Am Wom
supp v1; Obit File

6463. Christman, Elisabeth
1881–1975
labor organizer, labor reformer
Cyc Am Bio; Bio Dict Am Lab;
Index t Wom; Not Am Wom
supp v1

6464. Mason, Lucy Randolph
1882–1959
labor publicist, public relations
officer for the CIO, southern
trade union organizer, social
worker and reformer, suffragist
Episcopalian
Virginia
Bio Dict Am Lab; Dict Am Bio
supp v6; Encyc South Hist; Not
Am Wom supp v1; Obit File

6465. Schneiderman, Rose
1882/84–1972
labor organizer, Women's Trade
Union leader, secretary of the
New York State Labor Depart-
ment, social reformer, suffragist
Jewish
Polish; Russian
Bio Dict Am Lab; Cur Biog '72;
Index t Wom; Not Am Wom
supp v1; Obit File

6466. Gomper, Gertrude
1883–1953
labor union worker, campaigner
for liberal divorce laws
Obit File

**6467. McCreery, Maria Maud
Leonard**
1883–1938
Wisconsin suffragist, Socialist
party worker, labor organizer
Wisconsin
Not Am Wom

**6468. Bailey, Margaret Emer-
son**
1885–1949
educator, journalist, novelist,
magazine writer, police commissioner

Episcopalian
New Canaan, CT
Nat Cyc Am Bio csv6; Obit File

6469. Cohn, Fannie Mary
1885/88–1962
labor leader and organizer, labor
educator
Jewish
Russian
Cyc Am Bio; Bio Dict Am Lab;
Not Am Wom supp v1

6470. Hutchins, Grace
1885–1969
labor researcher, social reformer
Not Am Wom supp v1

**6471. McLaren, Louise Leon-
ard**
1885–1968
labor educator
Not Am Wom supp v1

**6472. Roche, Josephine
Aspinwall**
1886–1976
industrialist, lecturer, UMW executive
Index t Wom; Obit File

6473. Sender, Toni
born 1888
labor leader
German
Index t Wom

6474. Winslow, Mary N.
1888–1952
women's rights worker, trade
union leader
Obit File

**6475. Hillman, Bessie Abra-
mowitz**
1889–1970
labor leader, president of the
Amalgamated Clothing Work-
ers of America
Jewish
New York, NY
Russian
Nat Cyc Am Bio v56; Obit File

6476. Magee, Elizabeth Stewart
born 1889
social worker, labor leader
Index t Wom

6477. Miller, Frieda S(egelke)
1889/90–1973
labor reformer, director of the US
Department of Labor Women's
Labor Bureau, labor leader
Cur Biog '73; Index t Wom; Not
Am Wom supp v1

6478. Bartlett, Dorothy D.
flourished 1920s
journalist
Index t Wom

6479. Flynn, Elizabeth Gurley
1890–1964
labor organizer, radical politician,
American Communist party
chairperson
Bio Dict Am Lab; Index t Wom;
Not Am Wom supp v1; Obit
File

**6480. Parker, Julia Sarsfied
O'Connor**
1890–1972
labor leader and organizer
Not Am Wom supp v1

6481. Newman, Pauline M.
1891–post 1940s
labor leader, Socialist party work-
er
Jewish
New York
Russian
Bio Dict Am Lab; Index t Wom

**6482. Mandigo, Pauline
Eggleston**
1892–1956
journalist, public relations counsel, counsel to the American
Association for the United Nations, aide to the US Department of Labor Women's Bureau
Index t Wom; Nat Cyc Am Bio
csv7; Obit File

6483. Bellanca, Dorothy Jacobs
1894–1946
trade union organizer, founder
and only woman vice-president
of the Amalgamated Clothing
Workers union, social reformer,
politician
Jewish
Russian
Bio Dict Am Lab; Dict Am Bio
supp v3; Not Am Wom; Obit
File

6484. Amidon, Beulah
1895–1958
labor and education authority
Obit File

6485. Borchardt, Selma Munter
1895/1900–1968
educator, lawyer, labor leader,
lobbyist
Washington, DC
Bio Dict Am Lab; Not Am Wom
supp v1

**6486. Herrick, Elinor More-
house**
1895–1964
labor relations specialist, journalist
Index t Wom; Not Am Wom
supp v1

6487. Jarrell, Helen Ira
1896–1973

school superintendent, union
  leader
Not Am Wom supp v1

6488. Pesotta, Rose
1896–1965
labor organizer and leader
Not Am Wom supp v1

6489. Speare, Dorothy
1897/98–1951
screenwriter, author, novelist,
  opera singer, labor worker
Index t Wom; Nat Cyc Am Bio
  v40; Obit File

6490. Wolfson, Theresa
1897–1972
labor economist, educator
Not Am Wom supp v1

6491. Bambace, Angela
1898–1975
labor organizer, labor leader
Not Am Wom supp v1

6492. Soule, Isobel Walker
1898–1972
author, editor, labor leader, suffragist
Obit File

6493. Lowergan, Anna
flourished 1930s
labor leader
Index t Wom

6494. Moreno, Luisa
flourished 1930s–50s
union organizer
Mexican
Dict Mex Am Hist

6495. Algase, Julia Cohn
1902–75
lawyer, AFL-CIO worker, actor
Jewish
New York, NY
Nat Cyc Am Bio v58

**6496. Biddle, Margret Thomp-
  son**
1902–56
author, keeper of a Paris salon for
  political and literary personalities
French (American expatriate to
  Paris)
Obit File

6497. Dickason, Gladys Marie
1903–71
labor economist, labor organizer
Not Am Wom supp v1

**6498. Peterson, Esther Eggert-
  sen**
born 1906
labor leader, director of the US
  Department of Labor Women's
  Bureau
Mormon

Washington, DC
Bio Dict Am Lab; Index t Wom;
  Nat Cyc Am Bio csv10

6499. Dargans, Louise M.
flourished 1940s–70s
chief clerk, US House Committee
  on Education and Labor, 1946
Black
Negro Alman; Negro Her Lib v1

6500. Kemp, Maida Springer
born 1910
labor leader
Black
Negro Alman

6501. Wolfgang, Myra K.
1915–76
women's labor worker, trade
  union leader
Obit File

**6502. Tenayuca (Brooks),
  Emma**
born 1916
civil rights worker, labor leader,
  Communist party worker
Mexican
Dict Mex Am Hist

6503. Young, Ruth
born 1916
labor union secretary
Index t Wom

**6504. Koontz, Elizabeth Dun-
  can**
born 1919
director of the US Department of
  Labor Women's Bureau, US
  delegate to the Commission on
  the Status of Women, labor organizer, educator
Black
Cur Biog '69; Encyc Black Am;
  Index t Wom; Negro Alman

6505. Abzug, Bella (Savitsky)
born 1920
representative to Congress from
  New York, lawyer with specialty in labor law, lecturer, peace
  worker
Jewish
New York
Cur Biog '71

6506. Rose, Lucille Mason
born 1920
New York City commissioner of
  employment
New York, NY
Black
Negro Alman

6507. Henderson, Vivian
1924–76
president of Clark College, labor
  economist
Atlanta, GA
Obit File

6508. Hernandez, Aileen Clarke
born 1926
public affairs consultant; commissioner of Equal Employment
  Opportunities Committee, 1965;
  president of NOW; labor worker; civil rights worker; feminist
Black
Cur Biog '71; Negro Alman; Negro Her Lib v1

**6509. Huerta, Dolores Fernan-
  dez**
1930–post 1970
United Farm Workers executive
Catholic
California
Mexican
Bio Dict Am Lab; Dict Mex Am
  Hist

**6510. Washington, Bennetta
  Bullock**
flourished 1970s
special assistant, US Department
  of Commerce; director of the
  Women's Job Corps of the Office of Economic Opportunity
Black
Negro Alman; Negro Her Lib v1

6511. Bolden, Dorothy
flourished 1976
labor leader
Black
Negro Alman

LANGUAGES AND TRANSLATION

**6512. l'Incarnation, Maria de,
  Mother**
1599–1672
Catholic nun, educator, founder
  of the Ursuline Convent in Que-
  bec, student of Native Ameri-
  can languages
Catholic
Canadian
Cyc Am Bio

**6513. Stoothoff, Saartze Kiers-
  tede von Borsum**
died 1693
colonial interpreter
Index t Wom

**6514. Montour, Catherine, Ma-
  dame**
circa 1684–circa 1752
interpreter and Native American
  agent for the colonies of New
  York and Pennsylvania
Cyc Am Bio; Not Am Wom

**6515. Musgrove, Mary; Coosa-
  ponakeesa**
circa 1770–circa 1763
Native American leader in colonial Georgia, interpreter, trader

Georgia
Native American (Creek)
Great North Am Ind; Not Am
  Wom

**6516. Lennox, Charlotte Ram-
  sey**
1720–1804
novelist, dramatist, translator
Dict Am Bio; Dict Nat Bio; Index
  t Wom; Nat Cyc Am Bio v6;
  Twent Cen Bio Dict Not Am;
  Wom Lit; Wom Lit, More

**6517. Ferguson, Elizabeth
  (Graeme)**
1737/39–1801
litterateur, poet, translator, letter
  writer, diarist, hero of Ameri-
  can Revolution
Philadelphia, PA
Am Bio Dict; Cyc Am Bio; Dict
  Am Auth; Dict Am Bio; Dict
  Am Bio Men Time; Index t
  Wom; Nat Cyc Am Bio v7; Not
  Am Wom; Who Who Dur Am
  Rev

**6518. Blennerhassett, Adeline
  Agnew**
flourished 1796; died post 1842
linguist, poet
Cyc Am Bio

6519. Murray, Hannah Lindley
1777–1836
translator
Cyc Am Bio

6520. Sacajawea; Bird Woman
1784/87–1812
interpreter, pioneer, guide
Native American (Shoshone)
Dict Am Bio; Great North Am
  Ind; Index t Wom; Not Am
  Wom; Read Encyc Am West

6521. Gould, M. Woodbridge
1787–1838
scholar of classical languages, educator
Am Bio Dict

6522. Lee, Eliza Buckminster
1788/94–1864
novelist, translator
Boston, MA
Cyc Am Bio; Dict Am Auth; Dict
  Am Bio; Dict Am Bio Men
  Time; Index t Wom; Nat Cyc
  Am Bio v25

6523. Smith, Julia Evelina
1792–1886/92
suffragist, women's rights worker,
  abolitionist, Biblical translator
Connecticut
Cyc Am Bio; Dict Am Bio; Nat
  Cyc Am Bio v7; Not Am Wom

6524. Robinson, Therese Albertine Louise (von Jakob); Mrs. Edward; Talvi; Talvj
1797–1869/70
author, short story writer, historical writer, translator, linguist, philologist
German
Cyc Am Bio; Dict Am Bio; Dict Am Bio Men Time; Index t Wom; Nat Cyc Am Bio v1

6525. Rush, Phoebe Ann Ridgway
1797–1857
linguist
Index t Wom

6526. Robinson, Martha Harrison
born 18?
novelist, translator
Philadelphia, PA
Dict Am Auth

6527. Smith, Elizabeth N.
flourished nineteenth century
pianist, linguist
Index t Wom

6528. Urbino, Lavinia Buoncuore
born 18?
biographer, autobiographer, translator
Boston, MA
Dict Am Auth

6529. Canfield, Francesca Anna
1803–23
poet, translator, linguist
Philadelphia, PA
Cyc Am Bio; Dict Am Bio Men Time

6530. Judson, Sarah Hall Boardman
1803–45
missionary to Burma, hymn writer, translator
Cyc Am Bio; Dict Am Bio; Index t Wom; Nat Cyc Am Bio v3, Not Am Wom; Twent Cen Bio Dict Not Am

6531. Cook, Martha Elizabeth Duncan Walker
1806–74
magazine editor, author, linguist, translator, abolitionist, patron of Polish arts and artists
Cyc Am Bio; Dict Am Bio

6532. Conant, Hannah O'Brian (Chaplin)
1809–65

religious worker, translator, Oriental scholar and language expert, magazine editor
Cyc Am Bio; Dict Am Auth; Dict Am Bio; Dict Am Bio Men Time; Nat Cyc Am Bio v22; Not Am Wom; Twent Cen Bio Dict Not Am

6533. McCord, Louisa Susannah (Cheves)
1810–1879/80
miscellaneous author, poet, political writer, translator, Confederate essayist, Black welfare worker, feminist, plantation manager
South Carolina
Cyc Am Bio; Dict Am Auth; Dict Am Bio; Dict Am Bio Men Time; Index t Wom; Nat Cyc Am Bio v9; Not Am Wom; Twent Cen Bio Dict Not Am

6534. Putnam, Mary Traill Spence (Lowell)
1810–98
author, history writer, translator, linguist, traveler
Boston, MA
Cyc Am Bio; Dict Am Auth; Dict Am Bio Men Time; Index t Wom; Twent Cen Bio Dict Not Am

6535. Sawyer, Caroline Mehitabel (Fisher)
1812–94
author, editor, poetry anthologist, poet, translator
Dict Am Auth; Index t Wom; Not Am Wom; Twent Cen Bio Dict Not Am

6536. Coleman, Ann Mary Butler (Crittenden)
1813–91
author, translator
Nat Cyc Am Bio v4; Twent Cen Bio Dict Not Am

6537. Day, Martha
1813–33
scholar of mathematics and language, author
New Haven, CT
Cyc Am Bio; Dict Am Bio Men Time; Index t Wom

6538. Benjamin, Mary Gladding Wheeler
1814–71
translator, poet
Appl Cyc Am Bio; Cyc Am Bio

6539. Marsh, Caroline Crane
1816–1901
author, translator, poet, biographer
Cyc Am Bio; Dict Am Auth

6540. Cross, Jane Tandy (Chinn) (Harding)
1817–70
author, poet, translator
Kentucky
Cyc Am Bio; Dict Am Auth

6541. Henderson, Frances Cox
born 1820
linguist, translator, traveler, philanthropist, suffragist
Episcopalian
Wom Cent

6542. Dewey, Mary Elizabeth
1821; died post 1871
author, translator, educator, biographer
Cyc Am Bio; Dict Am Auth; Index t Wom; Twent Cen Bio Dict Not Am

6543. Graves, Adelia Cleopatra (Spencer); Aunt Alice
1821–95
author, children's author, rhetorician, linguist, educator, president of Mary Sharp College
Tennessee
Cyc Am Bio; Dict Am Auth; Twent Cen Bio Dict Not Am; Wom Cent

6544. Burnz, Eliza Boardman
1823–1903
educator, phoneticist, stenographic educator, spelling reformer
English
Nat Cyc Am Bio v6; Wom Cent

6545. Appleton, Anna E.
born 1825
poet, translator
Index t Wom

6546. Dahlgren, Madeleine Vinton [Sara] (Goodard); Corinne; Cornelia
1825/35–1898
novelist, translator, antisuffragist
Catholic
Washington, DC
Cyc Am Bio; Dict Am Auth; Dict Am Bio; Index t Wom; Nat Cyc Am Bio v22; Twent Cen Bio Dict Not Am; Wom Cent

6547. Robertson, Ann Eliza Worcester
1826–1905
missionary, educator, student of Native American languages
Not Am Wom

6548. Doggett, Kate Newell
1827/28–1884
suffragist, educator, art critic, translator
Cyc Am Bio; Index t Wom

6549. Wister, Annis Lee Furness "Anna"
1830–1908
traveler, translator of German novels
Cyc Am Bio; Dict Am Auth; Index t Wom

6550. Wormeley, Katharine Prescott
1830/32–1908
Civil War relief and hospital worker, writer on sanitation, charity worker, philanthropist, translator, biographer
Rhode Island
English
Cyc Am Bio; Dict Am Bio; Index t Wom; Nat Cyc Am Bio v8; Not Am Wom; Twent Cen Bio Dict Not Am; Wom Cent

6551. Benton, Louisa Dow
born 1831
linguist, lecturer
Index t Wom; Wom Cent

6552. Booth, Mary Louisa
1831–89
historian, journalist, translator, author, editor of *Harper's Bazaar*, women's labor worker
Cyc Am Bio; Dict Am Auth; Dict Am Bio; Dict Am Bio Men Time; Index t Wom; Nat Cyc Am Bio v7; Not Am Wom; Twent Cen Bio Dict Not Am; Wom Cent

6553. Clement, Clara Erskine
born 1834
author, translator
Cyc Am Bio and ad; Twent Cen Bio Dict Not Am

6554. Gregory, Elizabeth Goadby
born 1834
author, translator of French and German literature, journalist, writer on industrial and social topics
Wom Cent

6555. Smith, Mary Stewart (Harrison)
born 1834
author, translator, children's author
Virginia
Dict Am Auth; Wom Cent

6556. Frothingham, Ellen
1835–1902
scholar of German literature, translator, linguist
Boston, MA
Cyc Am Bio; Dict Am Auth; Index t Wom

6557. Wister, Sarah (Butler)
born 1835

poet, translator
Philadelphia, PA
Dict Am Auth

6558. Preston, Harriet Waters
1836/43–1911
author, literary critic, translator, literary historian
Cyc Am Bio; Dict Am Auth; Dict Am Bio; Nat Cyc Am Bio v8

6559. Alexander, Esther Frances "Francesca"
1837–1917
artist, illustrator, author, translator, philanthropist
Italian (American expatriate to Italy)
Dict Am Auth; Not Am Wom

6560. Fonda, Mary Alice Ives; Octavia Hensel
born 1837
linguist, author, musician, music educator, writer on music
Wom Cent

6561. Martin, Elizabeth Gilbert
born 1837
author, translator
Index t Wom

6562. Houghton, Louise Seymour
born 1838
religious magazine editor, translator, religious author
New York, NY
Dict Am Auth

6563. Conant, Helen Charlotte Peters (Stevens)
1839–99
magazine writer, translator, linguist, entomologist
Cyc Am Bio; Dict Am Auth; Index t Wom; Twent Cen Bio Dict Not Am

6564. Fielde, Adele Marion
born 1839
missionary to Siam and China, writer on China, writer in Chinese
Dict Am Auth

6565. Johnson, Evangeline Maria
flourished 1870s–80s
translator, poet, bibliographer
Cyc Am Bio

6566. Smith, Sarah E.
flourished 1870s–80s
botanist, linguist
Index t Wom

6567. Moore, Annie Aubertine (Woodward); Aubertine Forestier
1841–1929
pianist, student of Scandinavian music, music critic, lecturer, author, translator of Scandinavian languages
Dict Am Auth; Dict Am Bio; Index t Wom; Twent Cen Bio Dict Not Am; Wom Cent

6568. Nason, Emma (Huntington)
born 1845
translator, author, poet, children's writer
Augusta, ME
Dict Am Auth; Index t Wom; Wom Cent

6569. Sheldon, Mary French
born 1847
translator, traveler in Africa, author
Wom Cent

6570. Hapgood, Isabel Florence
1850/51–1928
translator, linguist, writer on Russian and European literature, journalist
New York, NY
Dict Am Auth; Dict Am Bio; Nat Cyc Am Bio v21; Not Am Wom; Twent Cen Bio Dict Not Am; Wom Cent

6571. Webster, Helen Livermore
1853–post 1890
writer on philology, philologist, university educator
Dict Am Auth; Wom Cent

6572. Wenckebach, Anna Doris Amalie Catharina Carla
born 1853
educator, author on German language and literature
Prussian
Nat Cyc Am Bio v10

6573. Sadlier, Anna Theresa
born 1854/56
author, biographer, translator
Catholic
Cyc Am Bio; Dict Am Auth

6574. Trail, Florence
born 1854
author, translator
Wom Cent

6575. Leach, Abby
1855–1918
professor of Greek, philologist
Nat Cyc Am Bio v12; Not Am Wom

6576. Case, Mary Emily
born 1857
university educator, classical languages scholar
New York
Dict Am Auth

6577. Alden, Cynthia May; Sunshine
1858/62–1931
journalist, editor, linguist, author, inventor, social worker, philanthropist, humanitarian
New York, NY
Dict Am Bio supp v1; Index t Wom; Nat Cyc Am Bio v14 and v22

6578. Judd, Ida Benfy
1858–1952
founder of the Mark Twain Association, monologuist, speech educator
Obit File

6579. Westover, Cynthia M.
born 1858
scientist, naturalist, inventor, businessperson, linguist
Wom Cent

6580. Overstolz, Philippine E. von
flourished 1890s
musician, linguist, artist
Wom Cent

6581. Rice, Isaac L., Mrs.
born 1860
social reformer, musician, linguist
Index t Wom

6582. Young, Martha; Eli Sheppard
flourished 1890s
author, dialect author, poet
Alabama
Wom Cent

6583. Chanler, Margaret Ward Terry
1861–1952
philanthropist, musician, linguist, author
Index t Wom; Obit File

6584. Montgomery, Helen Barrett
1861–1934
civic reformer, churchperson, foreign missions worker, translator, author
Baptist
Index t Wom; Nat Cyc Am Bio csv1; Not Am Wom

6585. Baker, Joanna
born 1862
linguist
Methodist
Wom Cent

6586. Toussaint, Emma; Portia
born 1862
author, translator
Episcopalian
Massachusetts
Wom Cent

6587. Richardson, Emily Tracey Y.
1863–92
translator, poet
Index t Wom

6588. Brown, Maria J. B.
died post 1914
translator, author
Cyc Am Bio

6589. Bouvet, Marguerite (Marie)
1865–1915
linguist, children's author
Dict Am Auth; Dict Am Bio

6590. Collitz, Klara Hechtenbert
circa 1865–1944
German philologist
German
Index t Wom; Nat Cyc Am Bio csvl

6591. Simpson, Georgianna R.
1866–1944
professor, linguist
Black
Negro Alman; Prof Negro Wom v1

6592. Young, Mary Vance
1866–1946
educator, linguist, World War I relief worker
Presbyterian
Index t Wom; Nat Cyc Am Bio v33

6593. McClure, Mary Louise Dora
died 1918
translator, Egyptologist
Who Who Egypt

6594. Corbin, Edythe Patten
flourished 1900s
linguist
Index t Wom

6595. Rickert, Martha Edith
1871–1938
medievalist, professor of English, philologist, novelist
Dict Am Auth; Dict Am Bio supp v2; Not Am Wom

6596. Colcord, Mabel
born 1872
librarian, bibliographer, entomologist
Index t Wom

6597. Underwood, Edna Worthley
born 1873
author, linguist, translator
Index t Wom

6598. Powell, Alma Webster (Hall), Alma Webster-Powell
1874–1930
musician, economist, linguist, contralto singer, voice teacher
Cyc Am Bio; Dict Am Bio; Index t Wom; Nat Cyc Am Bio v14

6599. Morris, Dave Hennen, Mrs.
1875–1950
founder of the International Auxiliary Language Association
Obit File

6600. Claflin, Edith F.
1876–1953
expert on comparative Indo-European linguistics and on medieval Latin
Obit File

6601. Cooke, Marjorie Benton
1876–1920
author, monologuist
Index t Wom; Wom Lit, More

6602. Lowe-Porter, Helen Tracy
1876–1963
translator of Thomas Mann, poet, author
Not Am Wom supp v1; Obit File

6603. Phelps, Ruth Shepherd; Mme. Paul Morand
born 1876
educator, writer on Romance languages
Nat Cyc Am Bio csv2 and csv5

6604. Branch, Hazel E.
flourished 1910s–20s
entomologist, educator
Index t Wom

6605. Coltman, Elizabeth Sweetzer
flourished 1910s–30s
Orientalist, linguist
Index t Wom

6606. Grabau, Mary Antin
born 188?
autobiographer, translator, writer in Yiddish
Jewish
Dict Am Auth; Dict Am Bio v4; Nat Cyc Am Bio v39 and csv3; Not Am Wom; Obit File

6607. Lupton, Mary Josephine
flourished 1910s
editor, translator, author
Index t Wom

6608. Mary Madalene, Sister; Sarah C. Cox
flourished 1910s
translator, Catholic nun
Catholic
Index t Wom

6609. Mayer, Harriet Wilbur
flourished 1910s–30s
public welfare worker, translator
Index t Wom

6610. McGill, Sarah
flourished 1910s
linguist, translator, philanthropist
Index t Wom

6611. Roulet, Mary F. Nixon
flourished 1910s
author, journalist, musician, art critic, linguist
Index t Wom

6612. Siegrist, Mary
circa 1881–1953
poet, translator
Index t Wom

6613. Braun, Annette Frances
born 1884
entomologist
Index t Wom

6614. Willkie, Julia E.
1887–1943
bacteriologist, educator, linguist
Obit File

6615. Deloria, Ella Carla; Anpetu Wastewin
1888–1971
interpreter, linguist, ethnologist, anthropologist, lecturer
Native American (Yankton Sioux-Dakota)
Great North Am Ind; Ind Today; Not Am Wom supp v1

6616. Goodman, Lillian Rosedale
born 1888
composer, singer, pianist, critic, author, linguist
Index t Wom

6617. Broadbent, Bessie May
born 1895
entomologist
Index t Wom

6618. de Onis, Harrriet Wishnieff
1895/99–1969
translator of Latin American literature, editor
Puerto Rican
Obit File; Cur Biog '69; Index t Wom

6619. Lee, Muna
1895–1965
international affairs specialist, feminist, US State Department aide, poet, novelist, translator
Not Am Wom supp v1; Obit File

6620. Auten, Mary
born 1898

entomologist
Index t Wom

6621. Roseborough, Melanie Rohrer; Mrs. Adolph J. Radosta
born 1898
German language educator
Lutheran
Florida
Nat Cyc Am Bio csv13

6622. Schlaugh, Margaret
born 1898
educator, author, philologist
Index t Wom

6623. Langner, Ruth Livingston
1899–1959
play translator
Obit File

6624. Bayne, Nannette Gude
flourished 1930s
linguist
Index t Wom

6625. Seacombe, Charles M., Mrs.
flourished 1930s
critic, translator, lecturer, actor
Index t Wom

6626. von Klenner, Katherine E.
flourished 1930s
author, translator
Index t Wom

6627. White, Rose Rubin
flourished 1930s
author, translator
Russian
Index t Wom

6628. Zuver, D. DeCourcy
flourished 1930s
linguist, club leader
Index t Wom

6629. Kober, Alice Elizabeth
1906–50
classical scholar, linguist
Not Am Wom

6630. Wollstein, Rose R.
flourished 1940s
pianist, author, linguist
Index t Wom

LAW, POLITICS, AND GOVERNMENT

6631. Marian, Malintzin
early sixteenth century; died post 1550
political mover
Cyc Am Bio

6632. Hutchinson, Anne (Marbury)
1590/91–1642/43
religious and political leader, founder of the Antinomian sect of Puritanism
Puritan
Rhode Island; Massachusetts
English
Am Bio Dict; Cyc Am Bio; Dict Am Bio; Dict Am Bio Men Time; Dict Am Rel Bio; Dict Nat Bio; Index t Wom; Nat Cyc Am Bio v9; Not Am Wom; Twent Cen Bio Dict Not Am

6633. Brent, Margaret
1600/01–1670/71
landowner, business agent, executor for the governor of Maryland
Maryland
Dict Am Bio; Index t Wom; Not Am Wom

6634. Moody, Deborah, Lady
died 1659?
founder of a colony on Long Island, politician
Long Island, NY
Index t Wom; Not Am Wom

6635. Berkeley, Frances, Lady
1634–post 1695
politician
English
Not Am Wom

6636. Chiesman, Lydia
flourished 1670s
colonial politician
Index t Wom

6637. Drummond, Sarah Prescott
flourished 1670s
patriot, politician, lecturer
Cyc Am Bio; Index t Wom

6638. van Rensselaer, Maria van Cortlandt
1645–1688/89
colonial administrator of the Dutch patroonship of Rensselaerwyck
Index t Wom; Not Am Wom

6639. Weetamoo
circa 1650–76
tribal leader
Native American (Pocasset)
Great North Am Ind

6640. Penn, Hannah Callowhill
1671–1726
executor of William Penn
Quaker
Pennsylvania
Cyc Am Bio; Index t Wom; Not Am Wom

6641. Charlotte
flourished 1708
litigant who challenged the legality of slavery in court
Black; Canadian
Prof Negro Wom v1

6642. Montour, Catherine, Madame
circa 1684–circa 1752
interpreter and Native American agent for the colonies of New York and Pennsylvania
Cyc Am Bio; Not Am Wom

6643. Martha
1685–1805 [sic]
agent of the Mohegan people
Connecticut
Native American (Mohegan)
Am Bio Dict

6644. Aubrey, Leticia; Lady Worminghurst
flourished 1730s–40s
owner and ruler of the Barony of Nazareth, a tract of 5,000 acres in Northampton County, Pennsylvania
Pennsylvania
British
Appl Cyc Am Bio

6645. Musgrove, Mary; Coosaponakeesa
circa 1770–circa 1763
Native American leader in colonial Georgia, interpreter, trader
Georgia
Native American (Creek)
Great North Am Ind; Not Am Wom

6646. Schuyler, Margaretta Schuyler
1701–82
colonial administrator, Tory politician with military influence
New York
Encyc South Hist; Index t Wom

6647. Warren, Mercy Otis
1727/28–1814
poet, author, dramatist, political author and satirist, historian, patriot
Massachusetts
Am Bio Dict; Cyc Am Bio; Dict Am Auth; Dict Am Bio; Dict Am Bio Men Time; Index t Wom; Nat Cyc Am Bio v7; Not Am Wom; Our Count; Who Who Dur Am Rev; Wom Lit, More

6648. Freeman, Elizabeth; Mum Bett
1732?–1829
litigant who sued for her freedom and won, midwife
Black
Prof Negro Wom v1

6649. Henry, Anne Wood
1732–99
colonial county treasurer
Index t Wom

6650. Brant, Mary; Molly Brant; Deganiwadonte
circa 1736–96
British advocate, worker for Native American rights
Native American (Mohawk-Iroquois)
Great North Am Ind; Not Am Wom; Read Encyc Am West

6651. Slew, Jenney
flourished 1766
litigant who sued for her freedom from slavery and won
Black
Prof Negro Wom v1

6652. Goddard, Mary Katherine
1738–1816
printer, newspaper publisher, postmaster of Baltimore, merchant
Catholic
Baltimore, MD
Index t Wom; Not Am Wom

6653. Ward, Nancy; Nanye hi; The Pocahontas of the West
circa 1738/40–1822
Native American leader and civil rights advocate
Native American (Cherokee)
Cyc Am Bio; Great North Am Ind; Not Am Wom; Who Who Dur Am Rev

6654. Adams, Abigail Smith
1744–1818
patriot and relief worker of American Revolution, political mover, letter writer, feminist
Am Bio Dict; Appl Cyc Am Bio; Cyc Am Bio; Dict Am Auth; Dict Am Bio; Dict Am Bio Men Time; Index t Wom; Nat Cyc Am Bio v1; Not Am Wom; Twent Cen Bio Dict Not Am; Wom Cent

6655. Montour, Esther
flourished 1778
Seneca leader
Native American (Seneca)
Cyc Am Bio

6656. Knox, Lucy Flucker
circa 1754/56–1824
political mover, hero of American Revolution, patriot
Cyc Am Bio; Index t Wom

6657. Bingham, Anne Willing
1764–1801
Federalist political activist
Pennsylvania
Not Am Wom; Who Who Dur Am Rev

6658. Kapiolani, [Kalakaua]
circa 1781–1841
high chiefess of Hawaii
Cyc Am Bio; Not Am Wom

6659. Kaahumanu
died 1832
Hawaiian ruler, patron of Christianity
Not Am Wom

6660. Eldridge, Elleonor
1785–1845
author, amateur lawyer, dairy farmer
Black
Negro Alman; Prof Negro Wom v1

6661. d'Arusmont, Frances Wright
1789–1852
abolitionist, political essayist, author
Scottish
Am Bio Dict; Dict Am Auth

6662. Grimke, Sarah Moore
1792/93–1873
abolitionist, women's rights worker, writer on social problems, political author, lecturer
Quaker
Cyc Am Bio; Dict Am Auth; Dict Am Bio; Dict Am Rel Bio; Index t Wom; Nat Cyc Am Bio v2; Twent Cen Bio Dict Not Am; Wom Cent

6663. Gaines, Myra Clark
1805–85
litigant
Not Am Wom

6664. Cazneau, Jane Maria Eliza McManus Storms
1807–78
journalist, publicist, expansionist
Not Am Wom

6665. Ferrin, Mary Upton
1810–81
women's legal rights advocate, feminist
Index t Wom; Not Am Wom

6666. Foster, Abigail (Kelley) "Abby"
1810/11–1887
abolitionist, feminist, Prohibitionist, lecturer, suffragist, temperance worker
Quaker
Cyc Am Bio; Dict Am Bio; Index t Wom; Nat Cyc Am Bio v2; Not Am Wom; Twent Cen Bio Dict Not Am

6667. McCord, Louisa Susannah (Cheves)
1810–1879/80

miscellaneous author, poet, political writer, translator, Confederate essayist, Black welfare worker, feminist, plantation manager
South Carolina
Cyc Am Bio; Dict Am Auth; Dict Am Bio; Dict Am Bio Men Time; Index t Wom; Nat Cyc Am Bio v9; Not Am Wom; Twent Cen Bio Dict Not Am

6668. Nichols, Clarinda Irene Howard
1810–85
newspaper editor, political writer, social reformer, lecturer, women's rights leader, suffragist, feminist
Kansas
Cyc Am Bio; Dict Am Bio; Index t Wom; Nat Cyc Am Bio v5; Not Am Wom

6669. Morris, Esther Hobart McQuigg Slack
1813/14–1902
suffragist, feminist, judge, western pioneer, justice of the peace
Wyoming
Index t Wom; Not Am Wom; Read Encyc Am West; Wom Cent

6670. Collins, Emily Parmely
born 1814
suffragist, abolitionist, political writer, Civil War nurse
Hartford, CT
Wom Cent

6671. Carroll, Anna Ella
1815–1893/94
political pamphleteer, political scientist, Civil War military strategist
Dict Am Auth; Index t Wom; Nat Cyc Am Bio v5; Not Am Wom; Twent Cen Bio Dict Not Am; Wom Cent

6672. Dorsey, Annah Hanson McKenney
1815/16–1896
author, dramatist, poet, novelist, essayist, short story writer, political writer
Catholic
Washington, DC
Cyc Am Bio; Dict Am Auth; Dict Am Bio; Index t Wom; Nat Cyc Am Bio v11 Twent Cen Bio Dict Not Am; Wom Cent

6673. Stone, Martha Elvira
born 1816
postmaster of North Oxford, Massachusetts; genealogist; Civil War relief worker
North Oxford, MA
Wom Cent

6674. Kirby, Georgiana (Bruce)
born 1818
feminist, prison matron, autobiographer
Santa Cruz, CA
English
Dict Am Auth

6675. Johnson, Ellen Cheney
1819/29–1899
prison reformer, prison superintendent, educator
Dict Am Bio; Not Am Wom; Twent Cen Bio Dict Not Am

6676. Barkalow, Helena
died 1870
lawyer
Index t Wom

6677. Coe, Emma Robinson
flourished 1850s–60s
lawyer, feminist, lecturer
Index t Wom

6678. Swain, Adeline Morrison
born 1820
suffragist, politician, newspaper political editor, superintendent of public education, Greenback party worker
Iowa
Wom Cent

6679. Swain, Adeline Morrison
born 1820
suffragist, politician, newspaper political editor, superintendent of public education, Greenback party worker
Iowa
Wom Cent

6680. Thompson, Elizabeth Rowell
1821–99
philanthropist, temperance worker, patron of science and of women's medical education, suffragist, political philosopher
Cyc Am Bio; Index t Wom; Nat Cyc Am Bio v5; Not Am Wom; Twent Cen Bio Dict Not Am; Wom Cent

6681. Cary, Mary Ann Shad
1823–93
educator, lawyer, journalist, editor, abolitionist, Canadian pioneer
Black; Canadian
Index t Wom; Negro Alman; Not Am Wom; Prof Negro Wom

6682. Barney, Susan Hammond
flourished 1854–90s
evangelist, Prohibitionist, temperance worker, prison reformer
Rhode Island
Index t Wom; Wom Cent

6683. Meriwether, Elizabeth (Avery)
1824/32–1916
novelist, women's rights worker, suffragist, Prohibition party worker
Memphis, TN
Dict Am Auth; Encyc South Hist

6684. Wood, Julia Amanda A. (Sargent); Minnie Mary Lee
born 1826
author, postmaster, pioneer, Minnesota newspaper editor, Catholic novelist
Catholic
Sauk Rapids, MN
Dict Am Auth; Index t Wom; Not Am Wom; Wom Cent

6685. Chandler, Lucinda Banister
born 1828
political author, temperance worker, political economist
Wom Cent

6686. Robinson, Abbie C. B.
born 1828
editor, Democratic newspaper publisher, political author
Wisconsin
Index t Wom; Wom Cent

6687. Hanaford, Phoebe Ann (Coffin)
1829–1921
Universalist minister, historian, journalist, author, feminist, lecturer, chaplain of the Connecticut state legislature
Universalist
New Haven, CT
Cyc Am Bio; Dict Am Auth; Dict Am Bio; Index t Wom; Nat Cyc Am Bio v13; Not Am Wom; Twent Cen Bio Dict Not Am; Wom Cent

6688. May, Abigail Williams
1829–88
Boston social reformer, abolitionist, suffragist, education commissioner, Civil War relief worker
Boston, MA
Index t Wom; Not Am Wom; Twent Cen Bio Dict Not Am

6689. Waite, Catharine (Van Valkenburg)
1829–1913
suffragist, women's rights advocate, lawyer, legal journalist, financier, real estate and building executive, writer on Mormonism
Chicago, IL
Cyc Am Bio; Dict Am Auth; Not Am Wom; Wom Cent

6690. Baker, E. H., Mrs.
flourished 1860s
Civil War spy, Pinkerton detective
Index t Wom

6691. Ballou, Addie L.
flourished 1860s
Civil War nurse, author, artist, lawyer
Index t Wom

6692. Leonard, Willard A., Mrs.
flourished 1860s
government employee, money specialist
Index t Wom

6693. Lockwood, Belva Ann Bennett McNall
1830/54–1917
lawyer, politician, women's rights worker, suffragist, pacifist
Dict Am Bio; Index t Wom; Nat Cyc Am Bio v1; Not Am Wom; Twent Cen Bio Dict Not Am; Wom Cent

6694. Magoon, Mary E.
flourished 1860s
lawyer
Index t Wom

6695. McNall, B. A.
flourished 1860s
educator, lawyer
Index t Wom

6696. Bradwell, Myra R. (Colby)
1831–1894/96
lawyer, suffragist, editor, Civil War nurse
Chicago, IL
Dict Am Bio; Index t Wom; Nat Cyc Am Bio v1; Not Am Wom; Twent Cen Bio Dict Not Am; Wom Cent

6697. Churchill, Caroline M.
born 1833
newspaper editor, publisher, journalist, political activist
Wom Cent

6698. Severance, Juliet H.
born 1833
physician, abolitionist, feminist, temperance worker, political activist
Spiritualist
Wom Cent

6699. Felton, Rebecca Ann Latimer
1835–1930
senator from Georgia, labor welfare worker, journalist, author, orator, feminist, women's rights worker
Georgia
Dict Am Bio; Encyc South Hist; Index t Wom; Nat Cyc Am Bio v13 and v36; Not Am Wom; Wom Cent

6700. Whiting, Mary Collins
born 1835
lawyer, businessperson
Michigan
Wom Cent

6701. Ahrens, Mary A.
born 1836
philanthropist, suffragist, lawyer
Index t Wom

6702. Converse, Harriet Maxwell; Ya-ie-wah-no; Salome; Musidora
1836–1903
Seneca rights advocate, Seneca tribal leader, author, folklorist, Native American scholar, poet
New York
Native American (Seneca by adoption)
Dict Am Auth; Not Am Wom; Twent Cen Bio Dict Not Am; Wom Cent

6703. Kilgore, Caroline Burnham "Carrie"
1836/38–1909
educator, lawyer, women's rights advocate
Index t Wom; Nat Cyc Am Bio v5; Not Am Wom

6704. Peirce, Melusina [Fay]
born 1836
author, community organizer, co-op advocate, writer on domestic science
Newport, RI
Dict Am Auth; Twent Cen Bio Dict Not Am

6705. Flower, Lucy Louisa (Coues)
1837–1921
social welfare worker, philanthropist, patron of education, president of the Illinois Training School for Nurses, member of the Chicago school board, trustee of the University of Illinois, Republican party worker
Episcopalian
Dict Am Bio; Nat Cyc Am Bio v9; Not Am Wom

6706. Hall, Emma Amelia
1837–84
prison reformer, prison administrator
Not Am Wom

6707. Wait, Anna C.
born 1837
suffragist, educator, politician

Kansas
Wom Cent

6708. Brown, Martha McClellen
1838–1916
founder of the Prohibition party, temperance reformer, suffragist, lecturer
Methodist
Ohio
Index t Wom; Nat Cyc Am Bio v27; Not Am Wom; Wom Cent

6709. Emery, Sarah Elizabeth van de Vort
1838–95
Greenback party and Populist party worker, political journalist
Not Am Wom

6710. Gordon, Laura de Force
1838/40–1907
lawyer, journalist, suffragist, women's rights worker, Democratic politician, orator
California
Dict Am Bio; Index t Wom; Nat Cyc Am Bio v1; Not Am Wom; Wom Cent

6711. Gordon, Laura de Force
1838/40–1907
lawyer, journalist, suffragist, women's rights worker, Democratic politician, orator
California
Dict Am Bio; Index t Wom; Nat Cyc Am Bio v1; Not Am Wom; Wom Cent

6712. Logan, Mary Simmerson Cunningham
1838–1923
political mover, author, magazine editor, pioneer
Cyc Am Bio; Not Am Wom; Wom Cent

6713. Woodhull, Victoria Claflin; Victoria Martin
1838–1927
social reformer, political reformer, stockbroker, feminist
English (American expatriate to England)
Dict Am Auth; Dict Am Bio; Index t Wom; Not Am Wom

6714. Nash, Clara Holmes Hapgood
born 1839
lawyer
Maine
Index t Wom; Wom Cent

6715. Baraloo, Lemma
flourished 1870s
lawyer
Index t Wom

6716. Comb, Helen
flourished 1870s
lawyer
Index t Wom

6717. Conise, Annette
flourished 1870s
notary public
Index t Wom

6718. Foster, Judith Ellen (Horton)
1840–1910
temperance leader, lawyer, Republican party worker, Prohibitionist, suffragist, political writer, lecturer
Iowa
Cyc Am Bio; Dict Am Auth; Dict Am Bio; Index t Wom; Nat Cyc Am Bio v22; Not Am Wom; Twent Cen Bio Dict Not Am; Wom Cent

6719. Goodell, Lavinia
flourished 1870s
lawyer
Index t Wom

6720. Haddock, Emma
flourished 1870s–80s
lawyer
Index t Wom

6721. Hally, Lydia S.
flourished 1870s
lawyer
Index t Wom

6722. Herrick, Mary Elizabeth
flourished 1870s–80s
lawyer, social reformer
Index t Wom

6723. Hill, Eliza Trask
born 1840
suffragist, women's welfare worker, journalist, newspaper publisher, political activist, Prohibitionist
Massachusetts
Wom Cent

6724. Hobbs, Amelia
flourished 1870s
justice of the peace
Index t Wom

6725. Hubbard, Emma
flourished 1870s–80s
lawyer, educator
Index t Wom

6726. Pollard, Marie Antoinette Nathalie Granier-Dowell
flourished 1870s
lecturer, temperance reformer, political activist
Cyc Am Bio

6727. Ricker, Marilla Marks Young
1840–1920
lawyer, suffragist, prison reformer, politician, author, political writer
New Hampshire
Index t Wom; Nat Cyc Am Bio v17; Not Am Wom; Wom Cent

6728. Snow, C. Georgie
flourished 1870s
lawyer
Index t Wom

6729. Stevens, Mary E.
flourished 1870s
justice of the peace
Index t Wom

6730. Wattle, Mary
flourished 1870s
lawyer
Index t Wom

6731. White, Nettie L.
flourished 1870s–90s
stenographer, government employee
Washington, DC
Index t Wom; Wom Cent

6732. Wilson, Zara A.
born 1840
lawyer, suffragist, feminist, temperance worker, missionary worker
Methodist Episcopal
Nebraska
Wom Cent

6733. Robinson-Sawtelle, Lelia
died 1891
lawyer
Index t Wom

6734. Todd, Marion Marsh
1841–post 1913
lawyer, Greenback party worker, political economist, labor leader, author, lecturer
Not Am Wom; Wom Cent

6735. Walker, Harriet Granger
1841–1917
philanthropist, hospital organizer, temperance worker, suffragist, police reformer
Methodist
Minneapolis, MN
Nat Cyc Am Bio v6; Wom Cent

6736. Dickinson, Anna Elizabeth
1842–1932
Civil War orator, lyceum lecturer, abolitionist, women's rights worker, suffragist, political activist, Republican party worker, author, actor, philanthropist

Quaker
Cyc Am Bio; Dict Am Auth; Dict Am Bio supp v1; Dict Am Bio Men Time; Index t Wom; Nat Cyc Am Bio v3; Not Am Wom; Twent Cen Bio Dict Not Am; Wom Cent

6737. Dunham, Marion Howard
born 1842
temperance worker, suffragist, Christian Socialist party worker
Wom Cent

6738. Fry, Elizabeth Turner
born 1842
philanthropist, Prohibitionist, humane worker, suffragist
San Antonio, TX
Wom Cent

6739. Lowman, Mary D.
born 1842
educator of Blacks; deputy register of deeds and mayor of Oskaloosa, Kansas
Presbyterian
Oskaloosa, KS
Index t Wom; Wom Cent

6740. Stone, Mary Perry
born 1842
businessperson, railroad station agent, suffragist
Oregon
Wom Cent

6741. Leonard, Anna Byford
born 1843
sanitation reformer, Chicago health department officer, sociologist
Chicago, IL
Index t Wom; Wom Cent

6742. Roebling, Emily Warren
1843–1903
Civil War patriot, philanthropist, club leader, author, lawyer
Index t Wom

6743. Thorp, Mandana Coleman
born 1843
Union patriot during the Civil War, pioneer, deputy clerk and register of deeds in northern Michigan, sheep and wool farmer
Michigan
Wom Cent

6744. Weatherby, Delia L.
born 1843
temperance reformer, author, politician, educator
Kansas
Wom Cent

6745. Wertman, Sarah Killgore
born 1843
lawyer
Wom Cent

6746. Berry, Martia L. Davis
born 1844
suffragist, temperance worker, politician, political reformer
Index t Wom; Wom Cent

6747. Switzer, Lucy Robbins Messer
born 1844
temperance worker, feminist, suffragist, politician
Wom Cent

6748. Bailey, Lepha Eliza (Dunton)
born 1845
temperance worker, Prohibitionist, suffragist, lecturer, author
Wom Cent

6749. Cleveland, Cynthia Eloise
born 1845
political writer and activist, lawyer, civil service worker, novelist
Washington, DC
Dict Am Auth; Twent Cen Bio Dict Not Am

6750. Garner, Eliza A.
born 1845
educator, politician
South Carolina
Wom Cent

6751. Henry, Josephine Kirby Williamson
born 1845
suffragist, politician, political writer, Prohibitionist
Kentucky
Wom Cent

6752. Pier, Kate Hamilton
1845–1925
lawyer, feminist
Wisconsin
Index t Wom; Nat Cyc Am Bio v21; Wom Cent

6753. Chenoweth, Caroline van Duesen
born 1846
author, university literary educator, military clerk during Civil War, US vice-consul in China
Dict Am Auth; Index t Wom; Twent Cen Bio Dict Not Am; Wom Cent

6754. Milne, Frances Margaret
born 1846
author, journalist, poet, political essayist
California
Irish
Wom Cent

6755. Seymour, Mary Foot
1846–93

stenographer, businessperson, journalist, law reporter, suffragist, women's labor worker
Not Am Wom; Wom Cent

6756. Kepley, Ada Miser
born 1847
lawyer, temperance agitator, Unitarian minister
Unitarian
Index t Wom; Wom Cent

6757. Lakey, Alice
1847–1935
clubwoman, leader in the pure food movement
Not Am Wom

6758. Bittenbender, Ada Matilda Cole
1848–1925
suffragist, temperance leader, political reformer, lawyer admitted to practice before the Supreme Court
Presbyterian
Nebraska
Not Am Wom; Wom Cent

6759. Carroll, Jane Wall
1848–1927
physician, lawyer
Nat Cyc Am Bio v21

6760. Diggs, Annie le Porte
1848/53–1916
Populist party leader, orator, politician, social reformer, temperance worker, journalist
Unitarian
Kansas
Canadian
Not Am Wom; Read Encyc Am West; Wom Cent

6761. Winema, Kaitchkona; Toby Riddle
circa 1848–1932
arbitrator
Native American (Modoc)
Great North Am Ind

6762. Beckwith, Emma (Knight)
born 1849
suffragist, politician
Brooklyn, NY
Wom Cent

6763. Brown, Corinne Stubbs
born 1849
Socialist party member, labor activist, sociologist, educator
Index t Wom; Wom Cent

6764. Foltz, Clara Shortridge; The Portia of the Pacific
1849–1934
lawyer, political activist, women's rights worker, suffragist, newspaper publisher, orator

California
Cyc Am Bio; Nat Cyc Am Bio csv3; Not Am Wom; Twent Cen Bio Dict Not Am; Wom Cent

6765. Kendrick, Ella Bagnell
born 1849
temperance worker, Prohibition party worker
Wom Cent

6766. Braman, Ella Frances
born 1850
lawyer, government official
New York
Index t Wom; Wom Cent

6767. Hall, Mary
born 185?
lawyer, notary public
Congregationalist
Connecticut
Wom Cent

6768. Jones, Melodia Blackmarr
1850–1931
philanthropist, Republican party worker
Episcopalian
Buffalo, NY
Nat Cyc Am Bio v32

6769. Kempin, Emile
flourished 1880s–90s
lawyer, educator
Swiss
Index t Wom

6770. le Valley, Laura A. Woodin
flourished 1880s
lawyer
Congregationalist
New York
Wom Cent

6771. Lease, Mary Elizabeth (Clyens)
1850/53–1933
Populist orator, politician, Prohibition party worker, suffragist, evolutionist, birth control advocate, feminist, political author
Kansas
Dict Am Auth; Dict Am Bio supp v1; Index t Wom; Not Am Wom; Read Encyc Am West

6772. Mussey, Ellen (Persis) Spencer
1850–1936
international lawyer, law educator, feminist, women's rights worker, clubwoman, child welfare worker, Red Cross worker, social reformer
Swedenborgian

Washington, DC
Dict Am Bio supp v2; Index t Wom; Nat Cyc Am Bio v47 and csv1; Not Am Wom; Twent Cen Bio Dict Not Am

6773. Ray, Charlotte E.
1850–1911
lawyer
Index t Wom; Not Am Wom

6774. Sawtelle, Lelia Robinson
1850–91
lawyer
Nat Cyc Am Bio v3

6775. Schoff, Hannah Kent
1850/53–1940
child welfare worker, juvenile court reformer, child aid leader, editor, author
Philadelphia, PA
Index t Wom; Nat Cyc Am Bio v18; Not Am Wom

6776. Shattuck, Harriette Lucy (Robinson)
born 1850
miscellaneous author, legal clerk, writer on parliamentary law, suffragist
Malden, MA
Dict Am Auth; Index t Wom; Twent Cen Bio Dict Not Am; Wom Cent

6777. Smith, Emma Adelia Flint
1850–1946
last executor of the estate of Samuel J. Tilden
Massachusetts
Obit File

6778. Avery, Martha Gallison Moore
1851–1929
Socialist, Catholic lay apostle
Catholic
Not Am Wom

6779. Benneson, Cora Agnes
born 1851
lawyer, author
Cyc Am Bio; Nat Cyc Am Bio v17

6780. Bigelow, Belle G.
born 1851
suffragist, Prohibitionist
Wom Cent

6781. Harper, Ida A. Husted
1851–1931
political journalist, suffragist, feminist, newspaper editor, author
Dict Am Bio; Index t Wom; Nat Cyc Am Bio v25; Not Am Wom; Wom Cent

6782. Johnston, Lizzie Johnston Evans
1851–1934
philanthropist, juvenile-prison reformer, Democratic party worker
Presbyterian
Alabama
Nat Cyc Am Bio v31

6783. Whipple, M. Ella
born 1851
physician, temperance worker, suffragist, Methodist Episcopal church worker, politician, educator, inventor
Methodist Episcopal
Wom Cent

6784. Ballou, Ella Maria
born 1852
court reporter
Index t Wom

6785. Davis, Alice Brown
1852–1935
leader of Seminole people
Native American (Seminole)
Not Am Wom

6786. Gillett, Emma Millinda
1852–1927
lawyer, educator, feminist
Nat Cyc Am Bio v17; Not Am Wom

6787. Gonzales Parsons, Lucia
circa 1852–1942
feminist, labor leader, a founder of International Labor Defense and of Industrial Workers of the World, Socialist party worker
Mexican
Dict Mex Am Hist

6788. Kurt, Katherine
born 1852
homeopathic physician, suffragist, temperance worker, Prohibition party worker
Universalist
Wom Cent

6789. Belmont, Alva Erskin Smith Vanderbilt
1853–1933
suffragist, feminist, politician, philanthropist
Index t Wom; Not Am Wom

6790. Dabbs, Ellen Lawson
born 1853
physician, midwife, women's rights worker, suffragist, temperance worker, journalist, Populist party worker
Texas
Wom Cent

6791. Gardener, Helen Hamilton (Chenoweth)
1853/58–1925

author, novelist, essayist, feminist, suffragist, geneticist, biologist, sociologist, civil service commissioner
Dict Am Bio; Index t Wom; Nat Cyc Am Bio v9; Not Am Wom; Twent Cen Bio Dict Not Am; Wom Cent

6792. Leese, Mary Elizabeth
born 1853
politician
Index t Wom

6793. Strickland, Martha
born 1853
lawyer, feminist, orator
Michigan
Wom Cent

6794. Upton, Harriet Taylor
1853–1945
suffragist, feminist, author, Republican party leader
Index t Wom; Not Am Wom; Obit File

6795. Hulett, Alta M.
1854–77
lawyer
Index t Wom

6796. Pratt, Hannah T.
born 1854
evangelist, temperance worker, chaplain of the Maine Senate
Maine
Wom Cent

6797. Robertson, Alice Mary
1854–1931
educator of Native Americans, representative to Congress from Oklahoma, educator, social worker, postmaster
Oklahoma
Dict Am Bio; Index t Wom; Not Am Wom

6798. Fall, Anna Christy
born 1855
lawyer
Massachusetts
Wom Cent

6799. Iams, Lucy Virginia Dorsey
1855–1924
welfare worker, leader in reform legislation
Not Am Wom

6800. Jones, Minona Stearns Fitts
born 1855
politician, feminist, social reformer
Index t Wom

6801. Rogers, Effie Louise Hoffman
born 1855

educator; superintendent of schools of Mahaska County, Iowa; newspaper editor; temperance worker
Mahaska County, IA
Wom Cent

6802. Bird, Anna Child
born 1856
suffragist, Republican political leader
Nat Cyc Am Bio csv4

6803. Blatch, Harriot Eaton Stanton
1856–1940
leader of the radical wing of the American suffragist movement, author, political activist, Fabian Socialist, lecturer
Dict Am Bio supp v2; Not Am Wom; Obit File

6804. Greene, Mary A.
born 1857
lawyer, law educator
Rhode Island
Index t Wom; Wom Cent

6805. Crane, Caroline Julia Bartlett
1858–1935
Unitarian minister, People's Church minister, urban reformer, suffragist, city planner, sanitation expert
Unitarian
Index t Wom; Nat Cyc Am Bio v15; Not Am Wom

6806. Helmer, Bessie Bradwell
1858–1927
lawyer, editor, publisher
Dict Am Bio; Index t Wom

6807. Lathrop, Julia Edward Clifford
1858–1932
social worker, social reformer, chief of the US Children's Bureau
Dict Am Bio supp v1; Index t Wom; Nat Cyc Am Bio v24 and csv3; Not Am Wom

6808. Moses, Mary Frances Hoyt
1858–1958
first woman appointee to the US Civil Service
Obit File

6809. Bass, George, Mrs.
1859–1950
suffragist, first woman to preside over a national political convention
Obit File

6810. Blair, Emily Jane Newell
1859/77–1933

suffragist, feminist, author, vice-president of the Democratic National Committee, chairperson of the Consumer's Advisory Board of the National Recovery Administration
Dict Am Bio supp v5; Not Am Wom supp v1; Obit File

6811. Grisham, Sadie Park
born 1859
educator; city councilperson in Cottonwood Falls, Kansas
Cottonwood Falls, KS
Wom Cent

6812. Klingelsmith, Margaret Center
1859–1931
librarian, author, legal authority, Democratic political activist, suffragist
Unitarian
Dict Am Bio

6813. la Follette, Belle Case
1859–1931
leader in Wisconsin Progressive movement
Wisconsin
Index t Wom; Not Am Wom; Wom Cent

6814. Parsons, Lucy E.
1859–1942
anarchist
Obit File

6815. Addams, Jane
1860–1935
political activist, social reformer, sociologist, social welfare worker, settlement house founder, peace worker
Chicago, IL
Dict Am Auth; Dict Am Bio supp v1; Index t Wom; Nat Cyc Am Bio v13 and v27; Not Am Wom

6816. Braeunlich, Sophie
born 1860
scientific publisher, government employee
Index t Wom; Wom Cent

6817. Gregory, Ida Leona Sturdavent
born 1860
social worker, juvenile justice worker
Nat Cyc Am Bio v18

6818. Haskell, Ella Louisa (Knowles)
1860/62–1911
lawyer, attorney general of Montana, politician, women's rights advocate, suffragist, Populist party worker

Theosophist
Dict Am Bio; Nat Cyc Am Bio
v11

6819. Rathbun, Mary Jane;
Mary Rathbone
1860–1943
marine zoologist, expert on shells,
author, government employee
Index t Wom; Not Am Wom

6820. Willard, Allie C.
born 1860
journalist, newspaper publisher
and editor, businessperson,
clerk of the Nebraska Senate
Nebraska
Wom Cent

6821. Burlingame, Lettie L.
graduated 1886
lawyer
Index t Wom

6822. Mansfield, Arabella A.
died 1911
lawyer
Index t Wom

6823. Sorin, Sarah Inslee Herring
1861–1914
lawyer
Episcopalian
Arizona
Nat Cyc Am Bio v36

6824. Bloor, Ella Reeve; Ella
Omholt
1862–1951
radical labor organizer, journalist, suffragist, Socialist and
Communist party leader, a
founder of the American Communist party
Bio Dict Am Lab; Dict Am Bio
supp v5; Not Am Wom supp
v1; Obit File

**6825. McCulloch, Catharine
Gouger Waugh**
1862–1945
lawyer, judge, suffragist, temperance worker
Illinois
Not Am Wom; Obit File; Wom
Cent

6826. Fearing, Lillian Blanche
1863–1901
lawyer, poet
Chicago, IL
blind
Dict Am Auth; Wom Cent

**6827. Guggenheim, Florence
Shloss**
1863–1944
philanthropist, patron of music,
Republican party worker
Jewish

New York
Index t Wom; Nat Cyc Am Bio
v33; Obit File

6828. Hawes, Flora Harrod
born 1863
postmaster
Arkansas
Wom Cent

6829. Kearney, Belle
1863–1939
temperance reformer, suffragist,
Mississippi state legislator
Mississippi
Nat Cyc Am Bio v11; Not Am
Wom

6830. Somerville, Nellie Nugent
1863–1952
suffragist, representative to Congress
Not Am Wom supp v1

**6831. Terrell, Mary Eliza
Church**
1863–1954
community leader, social reformer, suffragist, feminist, civil
rights leader, NAACP organizer, lecturer, educator
Congregationalist
Washington, DC
Dict Am Bio supp v5; Encyc
Black Am; Encyc South Hist;
Index t Wom; Nat Cyc Am Bio
v52; Negro Alman; Not Am
Wom; Prof Negro Wom v1;
World Great Men Col v2

6832. Baxter, Annie White
born 1864
county clerk of court, politician
Missouri
Twent Cen Bio Dict Not Am;
Wom Cent

6833. Blake, Alice R. Jordan
born 1864
lawyer
Wom Cent

6834. Frazier, Susan Elizabeth
1864/66–1909/24
educator, president of the 369th
Infantry of the New York National Guard's Women's Auxiliary
Black
Index t Wom; Negro Alman; Prof
Negro Wom v1

6835. Miller, Mary E.
born 1864
lawyer
Index t Wom

6836. Parker, Alice
born 1864
lawyer, feminist
Massachusetts
Index t Wom; Wom Cent

6837. Hilles, Florence Bayard
1865–1954
suffragist, feminist, ERA worker,
pacifist, golfer
Episcopalian
Delaware
Nat Cyc Am Bio v46

**6838. Hooper, Jessie Annette
Jack**
1865–1935
suffragist, Democratic politician,
peace advocate
Wisconsin
Dict Am Bio supp v1; Nat Cyc
Am Bio csv1; Not Am Wom

6839. Lathrop, Mary Florence
1865–1951
lawyer
Index t Wom

6840. Osborn, Alice Dodge
1865–1946
philanthropist, foe of Tammany
Hall
New York
Obit File

**6841. Sutro, Florence Edith
Clinton**
1865–1906
musician, composer, lawyer, traveler
Cyc Am Bio; Nat Cyc Am Bio v5

6842. Barnum, Gertrude
1866–1919/48
social worker, labor leader and
reformer, government official
Bio Dict Am Lab; Not Am Wom

6843. Bartelme, Mary Margaret
1866/69–1954
lawyer, judge, juvenile prison reformer, Chicago juvenile court
judge
Illinois
Index t Wom; Nat Cyc Am Bio;
Not Am Wom; Obit File

**6844. Black, Martha Louise
Munger Purdy**
1866–1957
member of Canadian Parliament,
participant in the Klondike gold
rush
Kansas
Obit File

**6845. Breckinridge, Sophonisba
Preston**
1866–1948
social worker, social economist,
immigrant welfare worker, writer on social issues, educator,
lawyer
Presbyterian
Dict Am Bio supp v4; Nat Cyc
Am Bio v37; Not Am Wom

6846. Carpenter, Fanny Hallock (Rouse)
flourished 1896–1900s
lawyer, Sorosis member
New England
Nat Cyc Am Bio v14

6847. Kahn, Florence Prag
1866/68–1948
Republican representative to
Congress from California
California
Dict Am Bio supp v4; Index t
Wom; Not Am Wom; Obit File

6848. Gilman, Elizabeth
1867–1950
Socialist party worker, social reformer
Not Am Wom

6849. Hamm, Margharita Arlina
1867/71–1907
journalist, author, poet, political
writer
Canadian
Nat Cyc Am Bio v9; Not Am
Wom; Wom Cent

6850. Hathaway, Maggie Smith
born 1867
educator, welfare worker, politician
Index t Wom

6851. Herron, Carrie Rand
1867–1914
patron of socialist causes
Not Am Wom

6852. Ogden, Esther Gracie
1867–1956
suffragist, secretary of the Foreign Policy Association
Obit File

6853. Whitney, Charlotte Anita
1867–1955
suffragist, political activist, Communist party worker, treasurer
of the New York Communist
party
New York
Dict Am Bio supp v5; Obit File

6854. Dortch, Ellen J.
born 1868
newspaper editor, publisher,
Farmers Alliance party worker
Georgia
Wom Cent

6855. Follet, Mary Parker
1868–1933
writer and lecturer on political
science, group psychology, and
industrial management
Dict Am Auth; Dict Am Bio
supp v1; Not Am Wom

6856. Grenfell, Helen Loring
born 1868
educator, penologist
Index t Wom

6857. Landes, Bertha Ethel Knight
1868–1943
clubwoman, civic reformer, mayor of Seattle
Seattle, WA
Index t Wom; Not Am Wom; Obit File

6858. Laughlin, Gail
1868–1952
lawyer, suffragist, feminist, state legislator, leader of the National Women's party
Not Am Wom supp v1; Obit File

6859. Pier, Kate Hamilton
born 1868
lawyer, feminist
Wisconsin
Wom Cent

6860. Sherwin, Belle
1868–1955
suffragist, president of the National League of Women Voters, civic leader
Ohio
Nat Cyc Am Bio csv3; Not Am Wom supp v1; Obit File

6861. Tucker, Rosa Lee
born 1868
state librarian of Mississippi
Mississippi
Wom Cent

6862. Bullowa, Emilie M.
1869–1942
lawyer, World War II relief worker, Sorosis member
Jewish
New York
Nat Cyc Am Bio v31

6863. Diehl, Cora Victoria
born 1869
register of deeds in Great Bend, Kansas; register of deeds for Logan County, Oklahoma; Populist party politician with Democratic endorsement; Farmer's Alliance party worker; Greenback party worker
Kansas; Oklahoma
Wom Cent

6864. Goldman, Emma
1869–1940
political anarchist, lecturer, publicist, agitator for free speech, popularizer of the arts, feminist, pioneer advocate of birth control, politician
Jewish

Russian
Dict Am Bio supp v2; Index t Wom; Not Am Wom; Who Who Jew Hist

6865. Lovejoy, Esther Clayson Pohl
1869/70–1967
physician; director of the Portland, Oregon, health department; World War I Red Cross worker in France; feminist
Protestant Episcopal
Portland, OR
Index t Wom; Nat Cyc Am Bio csv1; Not Am Wom supp v1

6866. McGee, Alice G.
born 1869
lawyer
Pennsylvania
Wom Cent

6867. O'Day, Caroline Love Goodwin
1869/75–1943
social welfare worker, Democratic representative to Congress from New York, New Deal supporter, artist
Episcopalian
New York
Index t Wom; Nat Cyc Am Bio csv6; Not Am Wom; Obit File

6868. Tuttle, Florence Guertin (Onertin)
born 1869
author, feminist, birth control advocate, pacifist, League of Nations worker, politician
Index t Wom; Nat Cyc Am Bio csv2 and csv5

6869. Braddock, Katherine
born 1870
Democratic political leader
Episcopalian
California
Nat Cyc Am Bio csv2

6870. Carpenter, Phillip, Mrs.
flourished 1900s
clubwoman, lawyer
Index t Wom

6871. Edson, Katherine Philips
1870–1933
social reformer, government official
Not Am Wom

6872. Graham, Nellie Dean; Vosey
born 1870
short story writer, magazine writer, philanthropist, clubwoman, Republican party worker, Los Angeles civic leader
Los Angeles, CA
Am Bio New Cyc

6873. Harriman, Florence Jaffray (Hurst)
1870–1967
Democratic party official, diplomat, minister to Norway, politician, journalist, suffragist, clubwoman, social rights worker, Red Cross worker in World War I, World War II relief worker in Norway
Washington, DC
Index t Wom; Nat Cyc Am Bio v53 and csv6; Not Am Wom supp v1; Obit File

6874. Kelly, Margaret V.
flourished 1900s
government employee
Index t Wom

6875. Knowles, Ella L.
born 1870
lawyer, notary public, candidate for attorney general of Montana on the Alliance ticket
Montana
Index t Wom; Wom Cent

6876. Ludington, Katherine
1870–1953
suffrage leader, cofounder of the National League of Women Voters
Obit File

6877. Mack, Harriet Belle Taggart
flourished 1900s–30s
Democratic presidential elector
New York
Nat Cyc Am Bio csv5

6878. Pier, Caroline Hamilton
born 1870
lawyer, feminist
Wisconsin
Wom Cent

6879. Sellers, Kathryn
1870–1939
lawyer, judge, bibliographer, librarian
Index t Wom

6880. Woodruff, Susan Harmons
1870–1953
publisher of the Communist newspaper the *Daily Worker*
Obit File

6881. Gabriel, Olive Stott
1871–1944
suffrage leader, lawyer, president of the National Association of Women Lawyers
Obit File

6882. Park, Maud May Wood; C. J. Maywood
1871–1955

suffragist, feminist, civic leader, social worker, police reformer, pacifist
Dict Am Bio supp v5; Index t Wom; Nat Cyc Am Bio csv1; Not Am Wom supp v1

6883. Reeves, Belle
1871–1948
secretary of state of Washington
Washington
Obit File

6884. Smith, Frances Stanton
1871–1931
journalist, suffragist, member of the New York State Civil Service Commission
New York
Nat Cyc Am Bio v27

6885. Wold, Emma
1871–1950
lawyer, suffragist, women's rights worker, pacifist
Nat Cyc Am Bio v38

6886. Anderson, Mary
1872–1964
director of the US Labor Department Women's Bureau, labor union official
Swedish
Bio Dict Am Lab; Index t Wom; Not Am Wom supp v1; Obit File

6887. Butler, Selena Sloan
1872?–1964
community leader, founder of the National Congress of Colored Parents and Teachers Association
Black
Not Am Wom supp v1

6888. Putnam, Bertha Haven
1872–1960
historian, history writer, authority on medieval history and criminology, educator
Unitarian
Nat Cyc Am Bio v43; Not Am Wom supp v1; Obit File

6889. Ward, Hortense Sparks Malsch
1872–1944
lawyer, social reformer
Texas
Not Am Wom

6890. Baker, Sarah Josephine
1873–1945
physician, public health administrator, child health pioneer
Unitarian
New York, NY
Dict Am Bio supp v3; Index t Wom; Nat Cyc Am Bio v36; Not Am Wom; Obit File

6891. Berger, Meta
1873–1944
Socialist party leader
Obit File

6892. Ickes, Anna Willmarth Thompson
1873–1935
reformer, Illinois state legislator
Illinois
Not Am Wom

6893. O'Reilly, Mary Boyle
born 1873
humanitarian, philanthropist, police commissioner, author
Index t Wom

6894. Welch, Fannie Alma Dixon
1873–1947
suffragist, women's rights worker, political activist
Nat Cyc Am Bio v38

6895. Ashley, Grace Bosley
born 1874
politician, clubwoman
Index t Wom

6896. Brown, Laura A.
1874–1924
politician, clubwoman
Index t Wom

6897. Dewson, Mary Williams
1874–1962
social worker, social reformer, suffragist, economist, politician, Democratic party official
Index t Wom; Not Am Wom supp v1

6898. Fulbright, Roberta Waugh
1874–1953
newspaper publisher, political writer, businessperson, banker
Arkansas
Nat Cyc Am Bio v49

6899. Harris, Mary Belle
1874–1957
prison administrator
Not Am Wom supp v1

6900. Helm, Edith Benham
1874–1962
White House social secretary
Washington, DC
Obit File

6901. Knapp, Florence Elizabeth Smith
1874–1949
New York secretary of state
New York
Obit File

6902. Loeb, Sophia Irene Simon
1874/76–1929
journalist, sponsor of welfare legislation, social reformer, social worker, author
New York
Russian
Dict Am Bio; Index t Wom; Nat Cyc Am Bio v24; Not Am Wom; Slavon Encyc

6903. Miller, Emma Guffey
1874–1970
Democratic party official, suffragist, feminist
Episcopalian
Pennsylvania
Index t Wom; Nat Cyc Am Bio v55; Not Am Wom supp v1

6904. O'Toole, Mary
born 1874
judge, suffragist, banker
Washington, DC
Irish
Nat Cyc Am Bio csv2

6905. Rose, Mary Davies Swartz
1874–1941
pioneer nutritionist, director of the Bureau of Conservation of the Federal Food Board during World War I
Dict Am Bio supp v3; Index t Wom; Not Am Wom; Obit File

6906. Smith, Jane Norman
1874–1953
feminist, leader of the National Women's Party
Index t Wom; Obit File

6907. Barnard, Kate
1875–1930
Democratic political reformer, Native American rights advocate, child welfare leader, philanthropist
Oklahoma
Index t Wom; Nat Cyc Am Bio v15, Not Am Wom; Read Encyc Am West

6908. Bethune, Mary McLeod
1875–1955
educator, founder and president of Bethune-Cookman College, director of the Negro Affairs National Youth Council, civil rights worker, women's rights worker
Daytona Beach, FL
Black
Dict Am Bio supp v5; Dict Am Rel Bio; Encyc Black Am; Encyc South Hist; Index t Wom; Nat Cyc Am Bio v49; Negro Alman; Negro Her Lib v1; Not Am Wom supp v1; Prof Negro Wom; Obit File

6909. Dreier, Mary Elisabeth
1875–1963
labor reformer, suffragist, New York civic leader, Bull Moose party politician
Presbyterian
New York
Nat Cyc Am Bio csv9; Not Am Wom supp v1

6910. Ferguson, Miriam Amanda Wallace "Ma"
1875–1961
twenty-eighth governor of Texas
Episcopalian
Texas
Index t Wom; Nat Cyc Am Bio csv1; Not Am Wom supp v1; Obit File; Encyc South Hist

6911. Hughan, Jessie Wallace
1875–1955
pacifist, Socialist party worker, politician, educator, author
Index t Wom; Not Am Wom supp v1

6912. Hull, Rose Frances Witz Whitney
1875–1954
founder of the Women's National Democratic Club
Obit File

6913. Jacobs, Pattie Ruffner
1875–1935
Alabama suffrage leader, child labor welfare worker, prison reformer, Prohibition party worker
Encyc South Hist; Not Am Wom

6914. Kryszak, Mary Olszewski
1875–1945
Polish American welfare worker, Wisconsin state legislator
Wisconsin
Polish
Not Am Wom

6915. Lacy, Mary Goodwin
1875–1962
librarian, author, government employee
Index t Wom

6916. MacDonald, Marie Bruckmann
1875–1954
Socialist party leader
German
Obit File

6917. Marks, Jeannette Augustus
1875–1964
poet, children's author, educator, Socialist party worker
Index t Wom; Nat Cyc Am Bio csv2

6918. Martin, Anna Henrietta
1875–1951
suffragist, feminist, author, essayist, social critic, pacifist, politician
Nevada
Dict Am Bio supp v5; Not Am Wom supp v1; Read Encyc Am West

6919. Norton, Mary Teresa Hopkins
1875–1959
representative to Congress from New Jersey, Labor Department aide, first woman Democrat elected to Congress
New Jersey
Dict Am Bio supp v6; Index t Wom; Nat Cyc Am Bio v45; Not Am Wom supp v1; Obit File

6920. Paige, Mabeth Hurd
born 1875
Minnesota state legislator, lawyer
Presbyterian
Minnesota
Nat Cyc Am Bio csv2

6921. Atwater, Helen Woodard
1876–1947
US Department of Agriculture official, home economist
Nat Cyc Am Bio v46 and csv12; Not Am Wom; Obit File

6922. Brueggeman, Bessie Parker
born 1876
chairperson of the US Employees Compensation Commission
Nat Cyc Am Bio csv2

6923. Carr, Edith Adele
1876–1965
philanthropist, diplomatic and consular officer
Washington, DC
Nat Cyc Am Bio v51

6924. Cleghorn, Sarah Norcliffe
1876–1959
poet, novelist, educator, suffragist, civil rights worker, labor worker, pacifist, antivivisectionist, Socialist party member
Vermont
Index t Wom; Nat Cyc Am Bio v46; Obit File; Dict Am Bio supp v5

6925. Rembaugh, Bertha
1876–1950
lawyer, author
Index t Wom

6926. Ross, Nellie (Tayloe)
1876/80–1977
thirteenth governor of Wyoming (Democrat)

Wyoming
Cur Biog '78; Index t Wom; Nat Cyc Am Bio csv2 and csv5; Obit File

6927. White, Eartha Mary Magdalene
1876–1974
social welfare worker, community leader, businessperson
Black
Not Am Wom supp v1

6928. Woodbury, Helen Laura Sumner
1876–1933
labor historian, social economist, author, government official
Dict Am Auth; Not Am Wom

6929. Adams, Annette Abbot
1877–1956
lawyer, judge
California
Dict Am Bio supp v6; Index t Wom; Nat Cyc Am Bio v43 and csvl; Not Am Wom supp v1

6930. Berry, Harriet Morehead
1877–1940
civic worker, public official
Not Am Wom

6931. Cunningham, Kate (Richards) (O'Hare)
1877–1948
Socialist party presidential nominee, community organizer, prison reformer, anti–World War I activist, lecturer, educator
Index t Wom; Not Am Wom; Obit File; Dict Am Bio v4

6932. Gildersleeve, Virginia Crocheron
1877–1965
educator, dean emeritus of Barnard College, US delegate to the 1945 San Francisco conference to draft the UN charter, creator of UNESCO
New York
Index t Wom; Nat Cyc Am Bio csv1 and csv7; Not Am Wom supp v1; Obit File

6933. Goldmark, Josephine
1877–1950
social legislation leader
Obit File

6934. Hard, Anne; Annie Marie Nyhan Scribner
1877–1961
author, radio broadcaster, political journalist
Episcopalian
Washington, DC
Nat Cyc Am Bio v57

6935. Hayes, Mary Sanders
1877–1959

president of the Women's National Republican Club
Obit File

6936. Moskowitz, Belle Lindner Israels
1877–1933
social worker, welfare worker, political leader, clubwoman, political adviser to New York governor Alfred E. Smith
Jewish
New York
Dict Am Bio supp v1; Index t Wom; Not Am Wom

6937. Norris, Jean Hortense
born 1877
jurist, international lawyer
New York
Nat Cyc Am Bio csv3

6938. Pratt, Ruth (Sears) Baker
1877–1965
representative to Congress from New York
Episcopalian
New York
Index t Wom; Nat Cyc Am Bio v51

6939. Abbott, Grace
1878–1939
public administrator, child welfare worker, social worker
Unitarian
Dict Am Bio supp v2; Index t Wom; Nat Cyc Am Bio v29 and csv3; Not Am Wom

6940. Caraway, Hattie Ophelia Wyatt
1878–1950
Democratic US senator from Arkansas
Methodist
Arkansas
Australian
Dict Am Bio supp v4; Dict Aust Bio; Encyc South Hist; Eng Wom; Index t Wom; Nat Cyc Am Bio v44 and csv4; Not Am Wom; Obit File

6941. Cline, Genevieve Rose
1878/79–1959
lawyer, judge
Dict Am Bio supp v5; Index t Wom; Not Am Wom supp v1

6942. Gellhorn, Edna Fischel
1878–1970
community leader, suffragist
Not Am Wom supp v1

6943. Good, Alice Campbell
1878–1956
Democratic party worker, New York civic worker
Catholic

New York
Nat Cyc Am Bio v42

6944. Howard, Alice Sturtevant
1878–1945
library founder, author, Republican party worker
Episcopalian
Index t Wom; Nat Cyc Am Bio v33

6945. Jenckes, Virginia Ellis
1878–1975
representative to Congress from Indiana, anticommunist activist
Indiana
Index t Wom; Obit File

6946. Lawson, Roberta Campbell
1878–1940
clubwoman, student of Native American music and culture, ethnologist, Native American leader, singer, songwriter
Presbyterian
Native American (Delaware)
Great North Am Ind; Nat Cyc Am Bio v36; Not Am Wom

6947. Pennypacker, Anna Maria Whitaker
1878–1952
co-owner of *The Daily Worker*, Communist party worker
Obit File

6948. Astor, Nancy Witcher Langhorne Shaw, Lady; Dowager Viscountess
1879–1964
politician, member of the English House of Commons, women's rights worker, temperance worker
British (American expatriate to England)
Index t Wom; Nat Cyc Am Bio csv1; Obit File

6949. Morrisson, Mary (Taylor) Foulke
1879–1971
political economist and activist, suffragist, women's rights worker
Nat Cyc Am Bio v17 and v56

6950. Stokes, Rose Harriet Pastor
1879–1933
Socialist and Communist party leader, feminist, labor leader, author
Jewish
Polish
Bio Dict Am Lab; Dict Am Bio; Not Am Wom

6951. Sullivan, Mary Agnes
circa 1879–1950

police officer, detective
Index t Wom

6952. Wilcox, Elsie Hart
1879–1954
Kauai, Hawaii, civic worker; territorial senator from Hawaii; politician; business executive
Congregationalist
Hawaii
Nat Cyc Am Bio v48

6953. Avary, Myrta Lockett
flourished 1910s
sociologist, politician, editor, author
Index t Wom

6954. Bass, Charlotta A. Spears
1880/90–1969
Progressive party vice-presidential candidate in 1952, civil rights reformer, editor
Black
Negro Alman; Not Am Wom supp v1

6955. Clarke, Marian Williams
1880–1953
representative to Congress
Index t Wom

6956. Garber, Lucy May (Bradley)
1880–1971
US land commissioner in Oklahoma, newspaper publisher
Oklahoma
Nat Cyc Am Bio v58

6957. Hale, Florence
1880–1959
president of the National Education Association, rural education director of Maine
Maine
Obit File

6958. Hamburger, Bessie Snow
1880–1952
lawyer
Index t Wom

6959. Holland, Mary E.
flourished 1910s
fingerprint expert
Index t Wom

6960. Keller, Helen Adams
1880–1968
author, feminist, suffragist, educator, advocate for the handicapped, pacifist, Socialist party worker
Swedenborgian
Alabama
blind, deaf
Encyc South Hist; Index t Wom; Nat Cyc Am Bio v15 and v57; Not Am Wom supp v1; Obit File

6961. Kempfer, Hannah Jensen
1880–1943
Minnesota state legislator
Minnesota
Not Am Wom

6962. McCormick, Anne Elizabeth O'Hare
1880/82–1954
journalist, foreign correspondent, *New York Times* editorialist and writer on world affairs, Pulitzer Prize winner
Dict Am Bio supp v5; Index t Wom; Not Am Wom supp v1; Obit File

6963. Perkins, Frances; Mrs. Paul C. Wilson
1880/82–1965
social worker and reformer, US secretary of labor
Index t Wom; Nat Cyc Am Bio csv4 and csv6; Not Am Wom supp v1; Obit File

6964. Plummer, Edna Covert
flourished 1910s–20s
lawyer, banker
Index t Wom

6965. Pyke, Bernice S.
1880–1964
suffragist, first woman delegate to a national political convention
Obit File

6966. Rankin, Jeannette Pickering
1880–1973
suffragist, feminist, first woman elected to Congress, pacifist
Index t Wom; Not Am Wom supp v1; Obit File

6967. Ranson, Ruth
flourished 1910s–30s
lawyer
Index t Wom

6968. Simms, Ruth Hanna McCormick
1880–1944
representative to Congress from Illinois, political leader, Republican National Committee member from New Mexico, dairy farmer
Quaker
Illinois; New Mexico
Dict Am Bio supp v3; Index t Wom; Nat Cyc Am Bio v34; Not Am Wom; Obit File

6969. van Winkle, Mina Ginger
born 1880
social worker, lieutenant in the police force, suffragist
Nat Cyc Am Bio csv3

6970. Driscoll, Clara
1881–1945
clubwoman, philanthropist, politician, political activist
Texas
Not Am Wom; Obit File

6971. Frazier, Maude
1881–1963
educator, state legislator
Not Am Wom supp v1

6972. Hyde, Elizabeth [Carrie]
1881–1957
lawyer, corporate lawyer for a railroad
Presbyterian
Iowa
Nat Cyc Am Bio v47

6973. Phillips, Lena Madesin
1881–1955
feminist, founder of the National and International Federations of Business and Professional Women's Clubs, author, editor, lecturer, politician
Dict Am Bio supp v5; Index t Wom; Not Am Wom supp v1; Obit File

6974. Pinchot, Cornelia Elizabeth Bryce
1881–1960
politician, suffragist, women's rights worker, worker for the welfare of women and children, advocate of social welfare legislation
Dict Am Bio supp v6; Not Am Wom supp v1

6975. Rogers, Edith Nourse
1881–1960
Republican representative to Congress from Massachusetts, sponsor of a bill creating the Women's Army Air Corps, co-author of a bill of rights for World War II veterans, World War I military hospital observer
Massachusetts
Dict Am Bio supp v6; Index t Wom; Nat Cyc Am Bio v44; Not Am Wom supp v1; Obit File

6976. Rumsey, Mary Harriman
1881–1934
social welfare leader, New York civic worker, spokesperson for consumer interests, chairperson of the Consumer Advisory Board, defense worker during World War I
New York
Dict Am Bio supp v1; Nat Cyc Am Bio v24 and csv4; Not Am Wom

6977. Anderson, Violette
born 1882
lawyer
Chicago, IL
English; Black
Encyc Black Am

6978. Block, Anita
born 1882
author, lecturer, Socialist politician
Nat Cyc Am Bio csv9

6979. Cunningham, Minnie Fisher
1882–1964
suffragist, politician, community leader
Not Am Wom supp v1

6980. Davis, Frances Eliott
1882?–1965
nurse, community leader
Not Am Wom supp v1

6981. Huck, Winnifred Sprague Mason
1882–1936
representative to Congress, journalist
Index t Wom; Not Am Wom

6982. Mitchell, Ruth Comfort; Mrs. Sanborn Young
1882–1954
author, poet, novelist, leader in Republican Organizations for Women
California
Index t Wom; Nat Cyc Am Bio v44; Obit File

6983. Schneiderman, Rose
1882/84–1972
labor organizer, Women's Trade Union leader, secretary of the New York State Labor Department, social reformer, suffragist
Jewish
Polish; Russian
Bio Dict Am Lab; Cur Biog '72; Index t Wom; Not Am Wom supp v1; Obit File

6984. Strunsky, Manya Gordon
1882–1945
leftist author
Obit File

6985. Townshend, Anna Draper
born 1882
suffragist, Connecticut state legislator from New Haven, New Haven civic worker
Unitarian
New Haven, CT
Nat Cyc Am Bio csv6

6986. Wambaugh, Sarah
1882–1955
pacifist, internationalist, authority on plebiscites, author, lecturer, consultant adviser to the League of Nations and the UN
Dict Am Bio supp v5; Index t Wom; Obit File

6987. Ames, Jessie Daniel
1883–1972
Progressive party politician, Black civil rights worker, anti-lynching reformer, suffragist
Texas
Encyc South Hist; Not Am Wom supp v1

6988. Balz, Arcada Stark
1883–1973
Indiana state senator, Indianapolis civic worker
Methodist
Indianapolis, IN
Nat Cyc Am Bio v57

6989. Conkey, Elizabeth A. Louighran
circa 1883–1963
politician
Index t Wom

6990. Earle, Genevieve Beavers
1883–1956
city official, politician
Index t Wom

6991. Esparza, Francisca
1883–1962
litigant
Texas
Mexican
Dict Mex Am Hist

6992. Gomper, Gertrude
1883–1953
labor union worker, campaigner for liberal divorce laws
Obit File

6993. Goode, Edith J.
1883–1970
suffragist, animal humane worker, cofounder of the National Women's party
Obit File

6994. Haynes, Elizabeth A. Ross
1883–1953
YWCA official, social researcher, social worker, author, businessperson, community leader
Index t Wom; Not Am Wom supp v1

6995. Lampkin, Daisy Elizabeth Adams
1883?–1965
civil rights reformer, suffragist, community leader
Not Am Wom supp v1

6996. Langley, Katherine Gudger
1883/88–1948
representative to Congress
Index t Wom; Not Am Wom

6997. McCreery, Maria Maud Leonard
1883–1938
Wisconsin suffragist, Socialist party worker, labor organizer
Wisconsin
Not Am Wom

6998. Springs, Lena Joan Jones
1883–1942
Democratic National Committee member, Democratic vice-presidential nominee at the 1924 convention, suffrage leader, World War I Red Cross worker
South Carolina
Nat Cyc Am Bio csv2; Obit File

6999. Stanley, Louise
1883–1954
home economist, first chief of the Agriculture Department Bureau of Human Nutrition
Not Am Wom supp v1; Obit File

7000. Wilson, Matilda Rausch
1883–1967
philanthropist, Detroit civic worker, chairperson of the board of directors of Fidelity Bank & Trust, member of the state board of agriculture, lieutenant governor of Michigan, Salvation Army worker
Presbyterian
Detroit, MI
Nat Cyc Am Bio v59

7001. Woodsmall, Ruth Frances
1883–1963
YWCA leader, government official, author
Index t Wom; Not Am Wom supp v1

7002. Allen, Florence Ellinwood
1884–1966
lawyer, US Court of Appeals judge, suffragist
Congregationalist
Ohio
Index t Wom; Nat Cyc Am Bio v52 and csv3; Not Am Wom; Obit File

7003. Elliott, Harriet Wiseman
1884–1947
educator, dean of women's college at the University of North Carolina, suffragist, women's rights worker, political organizer, public official
North Carolina
Encyc South Hist; Index t Wom; Not Am Wom; Obit File

7004. Fuller, Willa L.
born 1884
representative to Congress
Index t Wom

7005. Gross, M. Louise
1884–1951
founder and president of the Women's Moderation Unit, an anti-Prohibition group
Obit File

7006. Hill, Elsie
1884–1970
suffrage leader, chairperson of the National Women's party
Obit File

7007. Bailey, Margaret Emerson
1885–1949
educator, journalist, novelist, magazine writer, police commissioner
Episcopalian
New Canaan, CT
Nat Cyc Am Bio csv6; Obit File

7008. Bolton, Frances Payne (Bingham)
1885/86–1977
Republican representative to Congress from Ohio, nurse
Presbyterian
Ohio
Cur Biog '77; Index t Wom; Nat Cyc Am Bio csv11; Obit File

7009. Bryant, Louise Frances Stevens
1885–1959
social researcher, medical editor, feminist, Socialist party worker, physician, public health worker
Dict Am Bio supp v5

7010. King, Isabella Greenway
1885–1953
Democratic representative to Congress from Arizona
Arizona
Obit File

7011. Owen, Ruth Bryan; Ruth Rohde
1885–1954
representative to Congress from Florida, US diplomat, author, lecturer
Dict Am Bio v5; Index t Wom; Nat Cyc Am Bio csvl; Not Am Wom supp v1; Obit File

7012. Paul, Alice
1885–1977
feminist, founder of the National Women's Party, co-author of the ERA, suffragist, lawyer
Quaker
Cur Biog '77; Index t Wom; Obit File

7013. Randolph, Bessie Carter
1885–1966
political scientist, international law and affairs expert, president of Hollins College

Episcopalian
Virginia
Nat Cyc Am Bio v52 and csv6

7014. Shipley, Ruth Bielaski
1885–1966
government official
Index t Wom

7015. Stokes, Lilia Woodruff
1885–1973
Philadelphia civic worker, worker for Women's International League for Peace and Freedom, conservationist
Quaker
Pennsylvania
Nat Cyc Am Bio v58

7016. Strong, Anna Louise
1885–1970
radical journalist, pro–Communist China advocate, author
Cur Biog '70; Index t Wom; Not Am Wom supp v1; Obit File

7017. Boissevain, Inez Milholland
1886–1916
lawyer, feminist, suffragist, Socialist party member
Dict Am Bio; Index t Wom; Not Am Wom

7018. Draper, Muriel Gordon Sanders
1886–1952
feminist, humanitarian, founder of the Pro-Soviet Congress of American Women
Index t Wom; Obit File

7019. Lumpkin, Alva Moore
1886–1941
US senator
Index t Wom

7020. Schaefer, Gertrude Rose Keegan
1886–1944
suffragist, lawyer
Catholic
New York
Nat Cyc Am Bio v34

7021. Slade, Caroline McCormick
1886–1951
novelist, social worker, civic worker, suffragist, founder of the National League of Women Voters
New York
Index t Wom

7022. Sutton, Mary Wooster Munson
born 1886
lawyer
Baptist
Nat Cyc Am Bio csv2

7023. Davis, Pauline Morton Sabin
1887–1955
Republican party women's leader, anti-Prohibition worker
Dict Am Bio supp v5

7024. Hubbard, Theodora Kimball
1887–1935
landscape architect, city planner
Unitarian
Massachusetts
Nat Cyc Am Bio v28 and csv3

7025. Meyer, Agnes Elizabeth (Ernst)
1887–1970
author, journalist, vice-president and co-owner of *The Washington Post*, World War II correspondent, autobiographer, lecturer, social worker, Republican party worker, crusader for social services and education causes
Lutheran
New York
Cur Biog '70; Index t Wom; Nat Cyc Am Bio v56; Obit File

7026. Rehan, Mary
1887–1963
lawyer, a founder of the International Bar Association
Obit File

7027. Sabin, Pauline Morton; Mrs. Charles
1887–1955
Prohibition repeal leader, Republican party official, interior decorator
Index t Wom; Not Am Wom supp v1

7028. Starbuck, Kathryn Helene
1887–1965
lawyer, women's rights worker, educator
Baptist
New York
Nat Cyc Am Bio v53

7029. Thompson, Ruth
born 1887
representative to Congress
Index t Wom

7030. Waln, Nora
1887/95–1964
author, journalist, antifascist worker
Index t Wom; Obit File

7031. White, Sue Shelton
1887–1943
suffragist, lawyer, government official
Not Am Wom

7032. Woodward, Ellen Sullivan
1887–1971
federal official, state legislator, public welfare worker
Encyc South Hist; Not Am Wom supp v1

7033. Abel, Hazel Hempel
1888–1966
US senator, civic leader, educator
Index t Wom

7034. Branham, Sarah E.
1888–1962
bacteriologist, codiscoverer of the cure for one form of meningitis, chief bacteriologist for the US Public Health Service
Obit File

7035. Brill, Jeanette Goodman
circa 1888–1964
judge, lawyer
Index t Wom

7036. Bussey, Gertrude C.
1888–1961
president of the Women's International League for Peace and Freedom, philosopher, educator
Obit File

7037. Bussey, Ruth Carman
1888–1961
educator, worker for Women's International League for Peace and Freedom party
Episcopalian
Maryland
Nat Cyc Am Bio v49

7038. Craig, Elisabeth May Adams
1888–1975
political journalist
Cur Biog '75; Index t Wom; Not Am Wom supp v1

7039. Franklin, Pearl
circa 1888–1958
playwright, lawyer, Zionist, Hadassah leader
Jewish
Index t Wom; Obit File

7040. Kenyon, Dorothy
1888–1972
lawyer, feminist, suffragist, women's rights worker, prochoice abortion lobbyist, civil libertarian, director of the ACLU, UN official
New York
Cur Biog '72; Index t Wom; Nat Cyc Am Bio v56; Not Am Wom supp v1

7041. Seymour, Flora Warren
born 1888

author, lawyer, Native American scholar
Index t Wom

7042. Mesta, Perle
1889/91–1975
businessperson, US diplomat, feminist
Index t Wom; Not Am Wom supp v1

7043. Miller, Frieda S(egelke)
1889/90–1973
labor reformer, director of the US Department of Labor Women's Labor Bureau, labor leader
Cur Biog '73; Index t Wom; Not Am Wom supp v1

7044. Smith, Eliza Kennedy
born 1889
suffragist, executive of the League of Women Voters
Nat Cyc Am Bio csv4

7045. Stern, Elizabeth Gertrude Levin; Eleanor Morton; Elsie-Jeab
1889/90–1954
author, editor, social worker, political activist and antiwar worker
Quaker
Nat Cyc Am Bio v39; Obit File

7046. Willebrandt, Mabel Walker
1889–1963
lawyer, US assistant attorney general
California
Index t Wom; Nat Cyc Am Bio csv2 and csv5; Not Am Wom supp v1

7047. Bryant, Louise
1890–1936
journalist, author, Communist party worker
Great Sov Encyc; Index t Wom

7048. Dayton, Katherine
1890–1945
journalist, playwright, political satirist, humorist
New York
Index t Wom; Nat Cyc Am Bio v34

7049. Flynn, Elizabeth Gurley
1890–1964
labor organizer, radical politician, American Communist party chairperson
Bio Dict Am Lab; Index t Wom; Not Am Wom supp v1; Obit File

7050. Glantzberg, Pinckney L.
flourished 1920s–30s
lawyer
Index t Wom

7051. Hay, Regina Deem
born 1890
politician, clubwoman
Index t Wom

7052. Holtzmann, Fanny
flourished 1920s–30s
lawyer
Index t Wom

7053. Lewinson, Ruth
flourished 1920s–30s
lawyer
Index t Wom

7054. Maltby, Esther Stark
flourished 1920s
park board member
Index t Wom

7055. McLaughlin, Agnes Winifred
flourished 1920s–30s
lawyer
Rhode Island
Nat Cyc Am Bio csv3

7056. Mulliner, Gabrielle
flourished 1920s
lawyer, sociologist
Index t Wom

7057. Nolan, Mae Ella
flourished 1920s
representative to Congress
Index t Wom

7058. Oldfield, Pearl P.
flourished 1920s–30s
representative to Congress
Index t Wom

7059. Rock, Lillian
flourished 1920s–30s
lawyer
Index t Wom

7060. Taft, Martha Bowers
1890–1958
political activist
Obit File

7061. Velhagen, Millicent H.
flourished 1920s
politician
Index t Wom

7062. Whitehead, Reah
flourished 1920s
lawyer
Index t Wom

7063. Williams, Fannie Ransom
flourished 1920s
constitutionalist, World War I soldier's welfare worker
Presbyterian
North Carolina
Nat Cyc Am Bio v21

7064. Woodhouse, Margaret Chase Going
born 1890
representative to Congress, economist, educator, author
Index t Wom

7065. Armstrong, Barbara
1891–1976
lawyer, law professor
Obit File

7066. Barron, Jennie Loitman
1891–1969
judge, lawyer, suffragist, community leader
Not Am Wom supp v1

7067. Bearden, Bessye J.
1891–1943
educator, first female member of the New York City school board, clubwoman
New York, NY
Black
Encyc Black Am; Index t Wom

7068. Eliot, Martha May
1891–1978
pediatrician, public health official, president of the American Health Association, UNICEF member, US Children's Bureau official
Unitarian
Massachusetts
Cur Biog '78; Index t Wom; Nat Cyc Am Bio v60

7069. Kross, Anna Moscowitz
1891–1979
municipal court judge, feminist
New York, NY
Russian
Cur Biog '79; Index t Wom

7070. Lenroot, Katharine Fredrica
born 1891
government official, social worker, child health worker
Congregationalist
Wisconsin
Index t Wom; Nat Cyc Am Bio csv7

7071. Newman, Pauline M.
1891–post 1940s
labor leader, Socialist party worker
Jewish
New York
Russian
Bio Dict Am Lab; Index t Wom

7072. Street, Margaret Berry
1891–1967
cattle farmer, lawyer, Civil Air Regulations executive, suffragist, Black welfare worker
Presbyterian

North Carolina
Nat Cyc Am Bio v54

7073. Barus, Jane Garey
1892–1977
suffragist; political activist; prison reformer; Montclair, New Jersey, civic worker; antinuclear activist; anti–Vietnam war worker
Unitarian
Montclair, NJ
Nat Cyc Am Bio v60

7074. Church, Marguerite Stitt
born 1892
representative to Congress, politician
Index t Wom

7075. Gaines, Irene McCoy
1892?–1964
civil rights worker, community leader, clubwoman
Not Am Wom supp v1

7076. Gifford, Myrnie Ada
1892–1966
public health administrator, pediatrician, conservationist
California
Nat Cyc Am Bio v54

7077. Herbst, Josephine Frey; Josephine Herrmann
1892/99–1962
novelist, reporter of radical social and political movements in the 1930s, member of a European avant-garde writers circle in the 1920s
Dict Lit Bio v9; Index t Wom; Not Am Wom supp v1; Obit File; Wom Lit, More

7078. Hoey, Jane Margueretta
1892–1968
social worker, federal official
Index t Wom; Not Am Wom supp v1

7079. Long, Rose McConnell
1892–1970
US senator
Index t Wom; Obit File

7080. Mandigo, Pauline Eggleston
1892–1956
journalist, public relations counsel, counsel to the American Association for the United Nations, aide to the US Department of Labor Women's Bureau
Index t Wom; Nat Cyc Am Bio csv7; Obit File

7081. McCollin, Frances
1892–1960
composer, educator, lecturer, Socialist party worker
Episcopalian

Pennsylvania
blind
Index t Wom; Nat Cyc Am Bio v45

7082. Potter, Rose Saltonstall
1892–1946
leader in the fight to repeal Prohibition
Obit File

7083. Rienecke, Mabel Eunice (Gilmore)
born 1892
suffragist, internal revenue collector
Protestant
Illinois
Nat Cyc Am Bio csv3

7084. Smedley, Agnes
1892/94–1950
author, foreign correspondent, lecturer, champion of revolutionary China, writer on China and the Far East
Dict Am Bio supp v4; Index t Wom; Not Am Wom; Obit File; Wom Lit, More

7085. Wheaton, Anne (Williams)
1892–1977
journalist, associate press secretary for President Eisenhower, Republican party worker, political activist, public relations expert
Cur Biog '77; Index t Wom; Obit File

7086. Bradley, Florence Kauffman Thacker
born 1893
lawyer, political activist
Methodist
Indiana
Nat Cyc Am Bio csv7

7087. Fauset, Crystal Dreda Bird
1893–1965
race relations specialist, state legislator
Black
Not Am Wom supp v1

7088. Kahn, Dorothy C.
1893–1955
chief of the social services section of the UN Secretariat
Obit File

7089. Kirchwey, Mary Fredrika "Freda"; Mrs. Evans Clark
1893–1976
editor, publisher of *The Nation*, Socialist party worker, feminist
Cur Biog '76; Index t Wom; Obit File

7090. Lusk, Georgia Lee Witt
1893–1971
educator, Democratic representative to Congress from New Mexico
New Mexico
Cur Biog '71; Index t Wom; Not Am Wom supp v1

7091. Mackie, Janet Welch
1893–1959
physician, tropical medicine expert, US Public Health Service adviser
English
Obit File

7092. McIver, Pearl
born 1893
public health worker, nurse, government official
Index t Wom

7093. Reineck, Mabel Gilmore
1893–1958
US collector of internal revenue, first woman to receive a presidential commission to a federal executive position
Obit File

7094. Swing, Betty Gram
1893–1969
feminist, leader of the National Women's Party
Obit File

7095. Williams, Faith Moors; Mrs. Frank W. Lorimer
1893–1958
economist, US Bureau of Labor Statistics economist, chief of the Office of Labor Economics
Nat Cyc Am Bio v49; Obit File

7096. Armstrong, Bess (Furman)
1894/95–1969
journalist, White House correspondent to the *New York Times*, HEW assistant
Washington, DC
Index t Wom; Not Am Wom; Obit File

7097. Bellanca, Dorothy Jacobs
1894–1946
trade union organizer, founder and only woman vice-president of the Amalgamated Clothing Workers union, social reformer, politician
Jewish
Russian
Bio Dict Am Lab; Dict Am Bio supp v3; Not Am Wom; Obit File

7098. Donlon, Mary (Honor)
1894?–1977
US customs court judge, lawyer

New York
Cur Biog '77; Index t Wom

7099. Harden, Cecil Murray, Mrs.
born 1894
US representative to Congress
Index t Wom

7100. Mankin, Helen Douglas
1894/96–1956
lawyer, stage legislator, representative to Congress
Index t Wom; Not Am Wom supp v1

7101. Matthews, Burnita Shelton
born 1894
judge
Index t Wom

7102. McCarthy, Kathryn O'Loughlin
1894–1952
representative to Congress
Index t Wom

7103. Thompson, Dorothy; Mrs. Sinclair Lewis
1894–1961
international journalist, newspaper columnist, magazine writer, anti-Nazi worker, lecturer specializing in foreign affairs, radio commentator
Encyc Third Reich; Index t Wom; Nat Cyc Am Bio csv5; Not Am Wom supp v1; Obit File

7104. Borchardt, Selma Munter
1895/1900–1968
educator, lawyer, labor leader, lobbyist
Washington, DC
Bio Dict Am Lab; Not Am Wom supp v1

7105. Dulles, Eleanor Lansing
born 1895
government worker, economist
Index t Wom

7106. Edwards, India
born 1895/98
journalist, politician
Index t Wom

7107. Fortune, Jennie
born 1895
politician, state official
Index t Wom

7108. Howorth, Lucy Somerville
born 1895
government official, clubwoman
Index t Wom

7109. King, Carol Weiss
1895–1952

lawyer with specialty in immigration law, civil libertarian, specialist in deportation and civil rights cases, counsel for American Communist party leaders
Dict Am Bio supp v5; Index t Wom; Not Am Wom supp v1; Obit File

7110. Lee, Muna
1895–1965
international affairs specialist, feminist, US State Department aide, poet, novelist, translator
Not Am Wom supp v1; Obit File

7111. Williams, Madaline A.
born 1895
register of deeds in Essex County, New Jersey; politician; Democratic party worker
New Jersey
Prof Negro Wom v2

7112. Granahan, Kathryn Elizabeth
1896?–1979
US treasurer, representative to Congress
Cur Biog '79; Index t Wom

7113. Hughes, Sarah Tilghman
born 1896
judge
Index t Wom

7114. Jarrell, Helen Ira
1896–1973
school superintendent, union leader
Not Am Wom supp v1

7115. Russell, Helen Victoria Crocker
1896–1966
bank director, UNESCO executive, philanthropist
Episcopalian
San Francisco, CA
Nat Cyc Am Bio v53

7116. St. George, Katharine
born 1896
representative to Congress, business executive
Index t Wom

7117. Stiebeling, Hazel Katherine
born 1896
physical chemist, government official
Index t Wom

7118. Stoehr, Edith
died 1946
sportswoman, first woman to be a US game warden
Obit File

7119. White, Helen Constance
1896–1967

educator, historial novelist, religious historian, UNESCO member
Catholic
Index t Wom; Nat Cyc Am Bio v53; Not Am Wom supp v1

7120. Bronson, Ruth Muskrat
born 1897
Cherokee government official, field representative of Save the Children Federation
Oklahoma
Native American (Cherokee)
Ind Today; Read Encyc Am West

7121. Clark, Mary Chase; Mrs. Raymond S. Darrenougue
1897–1945
lawyer
Episcopalian
New York
Index t Wom; Nat Cyc Am Bio v32

7122. Day, Dorothy
1897–1980
journalist, social worker, political activist, fiction writer on Catholic life
Catholic
Cur Biog '82; Index t Wom

7123. Marshall, Lenore Guinzburg
1897–1971
author, poet, novelist, antinuclear worker, cofounder of the Committee for a Sane Nuclear Policy, worker for Women's International League for Peace and Freedom
Nat Cyc Am Bio v55; Obit File

7124. Prince, Mildred Mallon
1897–1961
lawyer, social legislation agitator, San Francisco civic worker
Catholic
San Francisco, CA
Nat Cyc Am Bio v47

7125. Smith, Margaret Chase
born 1897
US senator from Maine, lieutenant colonel in the US Air Force Reserve
Methodist
Maine
Index t Wom; Nat Cyc Am Bio csv9

7126. Alexander, Sadie Tanner Mossell
born 1898
lawyer
Black
Encyc Black Am; Negro Alman; Prof Negro Wom

7127. Farrington, Elizabeth [Mary] Pruett
born 1898
representative to Congress
Index t Wom

7128. Glueck, Eleonor (Touroff)
1898–1972
research criminologist, Harvard Law School criminologist, pioneer in the study of juvenile delinquency, social worker
New York; Massachusetts
Cur Biog '72; Index t Wom; Nat Cyc Am Bio v57; Not Am Wom supp v1; Obit File

7129. Howard, Katherine Montague Graham
born 1898
government official, politician
Index t Wom

7130. le Hand, Marguerite Alice
1898–1944
government employee, personal secretary to Franklin D. Roosevelt
Index t Wom; Obit File

7131. Mayes, Rose Gorr
born 1898
politician
Index t Wom

7132. van Deman, Ruth
died 1948
information director of the Agriculture Department's Nutrition and Home Economics Bureau
Obit File

7133. Winter, Ella
1898–1980
journalist, writer on communism, Communist party worker
Australian
Cur Biog '80

7134. Bailey, Consuelo Northrop
born 1899
lieutenant governor of Vermont, lawyer
Episcopalian
Vermont
Index t Wom; Nat Cyc Am Bio csv12

7135. Carter, Eunice Hunton
1899–1970
lawyer, community leader, social worker
New York
Black
Not Am Wom supp v1; Obit File

7136. Douglas, Emily Taft
born 1899

representative to Congress, politician, Red Cross worker
Index t Wom

7137. Hedgeman, Anna Arnold
born 1899
New York civic leader, New York mayor's cabinet member, consultant on urban affairs and Afro-American studies, assistant to the administrator of the Federal Security Agency
Black
Encyc Black Am; Negro Alman; Negro Her Lib v1

7138. Kee, Elizabeth Frazier
born 1899
representative to Congress, politician
Index t Wom

7139. McMillin, Lucille Foster
died 1949
politician, civil service commissioner
Index t Wom; Obit File

7140. Strauss, Anna Lord
1899–1979
editor, club leader, feminist, political activist, New York civic worker, internationalist
Quaker
New York
Cur Biog '79; Index t Wom; Nat Cyc Am Bio csv10

7141. Tucker, Bertha Fain
born 1899
judge
Index t Wom

7142. Willis, Frances Elizabeth
born 1899
US ambassador
Index t Wom

7143. Wright, Muriel Hazel
1899–1975
historian, community leader
Native American (Choctaw)
Ind Today; Not Am Wom supp v1

7144. Bachrach, Marian
1900–57
American Communist party public relations director
Obit File

7145. Baldridge, Alice Boarman
flourished 1930s
lawyer
Index t Wom

7146. Battistella, Sophia L. C.
flourished 1930s
lawyer
Polish
Index t Wom

7147. Breckinridge, Mary Marvin
flourished 1930s
photographer, politician
Index t Wom

7148. Brochester, Ruth
flourished 1930s
lawyer
Index t Wom

7149. Clark, Georgia Neese
born 1900
US treasurer
Index t Wom

7150. Cook, Nancy
flourished 1930s
politician, designer
Index t Wom

7151. Davie, Eugenie M. L.
flourished 1930s
politician
Index t Wom

7152. Davis, Minerva M.
flourished 1930s
lawyer
Index t Wom

7153. Douglas, Helen [Mary] (Gahagan)
1900/05–1980
stage actor, Democratic representative to Congress from California, opera singer
Episcopalian
California
Cur Biog '80; Index t Wom; Nat Cyc Am Bio csvF

7154. Durlach, Theresa Mayer
flourished 1930s
feminist, politician
Index t Wom

7155. Eslick, Willa B.
flourished 1930s
representative to Congress
Index t Wom

7156. Field, Pauline O.
flourished 1930s
lawyer
Index t Wom

7157. Freeman, Frankie Muse
flourished 1930s–60s
lawyer, Black civil rights leader
Black
Encyc Black Am

7158. Frooks, Dorothy
flourished 1930s
lawyer
Index t Wom

7159. Gage, Gloria
flourished 1930s
government official, musician
Index t Wom

7160. Gasque, Bessie Hawley
flourished 1930s
representative to Congress
Index t Wom

7161. Graves, Dixie Bibb
flourished 1930s
US senator
Index t Wom

7162. Greenway, Isabella
flourished 1930s
representative to Congress
Index t Wom

7163. Hollingsworth, Mildred Harvey
flourished 1930s
political scientist
Index t Wom

7164. Honeyman, Nan Wood
flourished 1930s
representative to Congress
Index t Wom

7165. Hubbard, Charlotte Moton
flourished 1930s–70s
US deputy assistant secretary of state for public affairs, educator
Black
Encyc Black Am; Negro Alman; Negro Her Lib v1

7166. Jackson, Juanita A.
flourished 1930s–60s
lawyer, civil rights worker
Black
Encyc Black Am

7167. Kidd, Mae Street
flourished 1930s–70s
Kentucky state legislator
Kentucky
Black
Encyc Black Am

7168. Lippner, Sally Nemerover
flourished 1930s
lawyer
Index t Wom

7169. Lipschitz, Sylvia Steinberg
flourished 1930s
lawyer
Jewish
Index t Wom

7170. Marlatt, Frances Knoche
flourished 1930s
lawyer, editor
Index t Wom

7171. McDannel, Lucy C.
flourished 1930s
lawyer
Index t Wom

7172. McMillan, Clara G.
flourished 1930s

representative to Congress
Index t Wom

7173. Mirenburg, Mary
flourished 1930s
lawyer
Index t Wom

7174. O'Crowley, Irene Rutherford
flourished 1930s
lawyer
Index t Wom

7175. Olmstead, Sophia Amson
flourished 1930s
lawyer
Index t Wom

7176. Pyle, Gladys
flourished 1930s
US senator
Index t Wom

7177. Reavis, Babs H.
flourished 1930s
lecturer, politician, club leader
Index t Wom

7178. Rosenman, Dorothy Reuben
born 1900
housing expert
Index t Wom

7179. Rothenberg, Rose
flourished 1930s
lawyer
Index t Wom

7180. Schmitt, Edwienne
flourished 1930s
lawyer
Index t Wom

7181. Spencer, Ethel
flourished 1930s
lawyer
Index t Wom

7182. Sumner, Jessie
flourished 1930s–40s
representative to Congress, judge
Index t Wom

7183. Switzer, Mary Elizabeth
1900–71
commissioner of welfare and rehabilitation programs for HEW, welfare worker for the disabled
Episcopalian
Index t Wom; Nat Cyc Am Bio v56; Not Am Wom supp v1; Obit File

7184. Todd, Jane Hedges
flourished 1930s
social worker, politician
Index t Wom

7185. Ulm, Mary Josephine
flourished 1930s

aviator, mail pilot
Index t Wom

7186. Welcome, Verda Freeman
flourished 1930s–60s
educator, Maryland state legislator
Maryland
Black
Encyc Black Am

7187. Wingro, Effigene
flourished 1930s
representative to Congress
Index t Wom

7188. Zachs, Anna H.
flourished 1930s
lawyer
Russian
Index t Wom

7189. Brunauer, Esther Delia Caukin
1901–59
international affairs specialist, UN official, textbook editor
Index t Wom; Not Am Wom supp v1

7190. Fleeson, Doris
1901–70
political journalist, syndicated newspaper columnist
Cur Biog '70; Index t Wom; Not Am Wom supp v1; Obit File

7191. Hoan, Gladys
1901–52
Wisconsin Democratic National Committee member
Wisconsin
Obit File

7192. Jemison, Alice Mae Lee
1901–64
Native American political leader, journalist
Not Am Wom supp v1

7193. Lee, Dorothy McCullough
born 1901
mayor, lawyer
Index t Wom

7194. Poynter, Henrietta Malkiel
1901–68
editor and cofounder of Congressional Quarterly, newspaper editor, foreign affairs expert, political journalist
Nat Cyc Am Bio v53

7195. Reid, Helen Dwight
1901–65
international political scientist, educator, pacifist
Christian Scientist
Washington, DC

Scottish
Nat Cyc Am Bio v51

7196. Sampson, Edith (Spurlock)
1901–79
lawyer, judge, alternate delegate to the UN, lecturer
Illinois
Black
Cur Biog '80; Encyc Black Am; Index t Wom; Negro Alman; Negro Her Lib v1

7197. Schwartz, Bertha
1901–61
judge, lawyer, Zionist
Jewish
Austrian
Index t Wom; Nat Cyc Am Bio v51

7198. Weis, Jessica McCullough
1901–63
representative to Congress from New York, president of the National Federation of Republican Women's Clubs
Index t Wom; Obit File

7199. Whaley, Ruth Whitehead
born 1901
lawyer
Black
Encyc Black Am

7200. Wickens, Aryness Joy
born 1901
government official, economist
Index t Wom

7201. Akers, Dolly Smith
born 1902
tribal leader
Native American (Assiniboine)
Ind Today

7202. Algase, Julia Cohn
1902–75
lawyer, AFL-CIO worker, actor
Jewish
New York, NY
Nat Cyc Am Bio v58

7203. Amsterdam, Birdie
born 1902
justice of the peace
Index t Wom

7204. Anderson, Marian
born 1902/08
contralto concert singer, US alternate delegate to the UN, 1958–59
Baptist
Black
Encyc Black Am; Index t Wom; Nat Cyc Am Bio csv9; Negro Alman; Negro Her Lib v1; Prof Negro Wom; World Great Men Col

7205. Baumgartner, Leona; Mrs. Nathaniel M. Elias
born 1902
pediatrician, public health official
Presbyterian
New York, NY
Index t Wom; Nat Cyc Am Bio csv9

7206. Buchanan, Vera D.
1902–55
representative to Congress from Pennsylvania
Pennsylvania
Obit File

7207. Byron, Katharine Edgar
1902–76
Democratic representative to Congress from Maryland
Maryland
Index t Wom; Obit File

7208. Cromwell, Emma Guy
died 1952
secretary of state and treasurer of Kentucky
Kentucky
Obit File

7209. Dwyer, Florence P.
born 1902
representative to Congress, politician
Index t Wom

7210. Hickey, Margaret E.
born 1902
editor, government employee, personnel worker
Index t Wom

7211. Johnson, Marguerite C.
1902–59
public safety director of Dearborn, Michigan; police commissioner
Dearborn, MI
Obit File

7212. Rees, Mina S.
born 1902
mathematician, educator, government official
Index t Wom

7213. Rosenberg, Anna Marie
born 1902
US assistant secretary of defense
Jewish
Hungarian
Index t Wom; Who Who Jew Hist

7214. Serge, Anne Brooks McAdoo
1902–53
chief auditing clerk of the Third District, Internal Revenue Service
New York
Obit File

7215. Strassmann, Antonie
1902–52
aviator, World War II hero, anti-Nazi worker
German
Obit File

7216. Taba, Hilda
1902–67
educator, UNESCO consultant
Estonian
Nat Cyc Am Bio v54; Not Am Wom supp v1

7217. Chambers, Eleanor
1903–72
deputy mayor of Los Angeles
Los Angeles, CA
Obit File

7218. Dean, Vera Micheles
1903–72
international affairs specialist, editor, author, lecturer
Russian
Cur Biog '72; Index t Wom; Not Am Wom supp v1

7219. George, Zelma Watson
1903–post 1960
alternate delegate to the UN, sociologist, singer
Black
Index t Wom; Negro Alman; Negro Her Lib v1

7220. Harron, Marion Janet
born 1903
judge
Index t Wom

7221. Loucheim, Katie Scofield
born 1903
government official, politician
Index t Wom

7222. Luce, Clare (Boothe)
born 1903
playwright, author, journalist, politician, US ambassador
Episcopalian
Index t Wom; Nat Cyc Am Bio csvF; Wom Lit

7223. Oettinger, Katherine Brownell
born 1903
government official
Index t Wom

7224. Palmer, Hazel
born 1903
lawyer
Index t Wom

7225. Hennock, Frieda Barkin (Simmons)
1904–60
criminal lawyer, FCC member, advocate of educational television
Jewish

New York
Polish
Index t Wom; Nat Cyc Am Bio csv8; Not Am Wom supp v1; Obit File

7226. Lord, Mary Stimson Pillsbury
born 1904
social welfare worker, UN representative, humanitarian
Index t Wom

7227. Davie, May Preston
married 1930
politician
Index t Wom

7228. Dodd, Bella V.
1905–69
lawyer, educator, Communist party worker
Obit File

7229. Hall, Ina Beauchamp
born 1905
community leader
Native American (Arikara)
Ind Today

7230. Hobby, Oveta Culp
born 1905
government official, director of the Women's Army Auxiliary Corps, editor, politician
Texas
Index t Wom; Nat Cyc Am Bio csv6

7231. Knight, Frances Gladys
born 1905
government official
Index t Wom

7232. Kuhn, Margaret E. "Maggie"
born 1905
founder of the Gray Panthers, fighter against age discrimination
Cur Biog '78

7233. Murray, Esther Burke Higgins
born 1905
politician
Index t Wom

7234. Priest, Ivy [Maud] Baker; Ivy Maud Baker
1905–75
Republican party worker, US treasurer, politician, treasurer of California
Mormon
California
Cur Biog '75; Index t Wom; Nat Cyc Am Bio v59 and csv9; Not Am Wom supp v1; Obit File

7235. Wurster, Catherine Bauer
1905–64

advertising executive, international consultant on housing and city planning, journalist
Nat Cyc Am Bio v51

7236. Zorbaugh, Geraldine Bone
born 1905
radio and television executive, lawyer
Index t Wom

7237. Adkins, Bertha Sheppard
born 1906
politician, government official
Index t Wom

7238. Arendt, Hannah
1906–1975
political theorist, philosopher
Jewish
German
Cur Biog '76; Not Am Wom supp v1; Obit File

7239. Backus, Louise Laidlaw
1906–73
New York civic worker, UNESCO member, international affairs expert, poet
Episcopalian
New York, NY
Nat Cyc Am Bio v57

7240. Carter, Gwendolyn Margaret
born 1906
political scientist, writer on political science, educator
Black
Encyc Black Am

7241. Kelly, Edna Flannery
born 1906
representative to Congress
Index t Wom

7242. Peterson, Esther Eggertsen
born 1906
labor leader, director of the US Department of Labor Women's Bureau
Mormon
Washington, DC
Bio Dict Am Lab; Index t Wom; Nat Cyc Am Bio csv10

7243. Pfost, Gracie Bowers
1906–65
representative to Congress
Index t Wom

7244. Taueber, Irene Barnes
1906–74
demographer, sociologist, UNESCO member
Nat Cyc Am Bio v58; Not Am Wom supp v1

7245. White, Katherine Elkus
born 1906

US ambassador
Index t Wom

7246. Williams, Clare
graduated 1931
politician
Index t Wom

7247. Austin, Margaretta Stroup
born 1907
government official
Index t Wom

7248. Byrd, Hannah Elizabeth
1907–68
judge
Pennsylvania
Black
Encyc Black Am

7249. Gannett, Betty; Rifke Yawschewsky
1907–70
leader of the American Communist party
Polish
Obit File

7250. Hamilton, Grace Towns
born 1907
educator, Georgia state legislator from Atlanta
Atlanta, GA
Black
Encyc Black Am

7251. Hansen, Julia Butler
born 1907
US representative to Congress, politician
Index t Wom

7252. Neuberger, Maurine
born 1907
US senator from Oregon, politician
Unitarian
Oregon
Index t Wom; Nat Cyc Am Bio csv10

7253. Springer, Adele I.
born 1907
lawyer, organization official
Index t Wom

7254. Adams, Eva Bertrand
born 1908
director of the US Mint, New York politician, lawyer
New York
Index t Wom; Read Encyc Am West

7255. Bolin, Jane Matilda; Mrs. Walter P. Offutt, Jr.
born 1908
lawyer, judge
Black
Encyc Black Am; Index t Wom

7256. Dixon, Margaret Calder Richardson
1908–70
prison reformer, political journalist, newspaper editor
Episcopalian
Baton Rouge, LA
Nat Cyc Am Bio v58; Obit File

7257. Halgarten, Katherine MacArthur Drew
born 1908
government attorney, international lawyer
California
Nat Cyc Am Bio csv13

7258. Jones, Ruth Holoway
born 1908
US customs collector
Black
Negro Her Lib v1

7259. Anderson, Eugenie Moor A.
born 1909
US ambassador
Index t Wom

7260. Humphrey, Helen Florence
1909–63
lawyer, government official
Index t Wom

7261. Konheim, Beatrice Goldstein
1909–73
science educator, member of the ACLU
Jewish
New York
Nat Cyc Am Bio v58

7262. Leopold, Alice Koller
born 1909
government official, politician
Index t Wom

7263. Murrell, Ethel Ernest
born 1909
lawyer
Index t Wom

7264. Stanley, Winifred C.
born 1909
representative to Congress, lawyer
Index t Wom

7265. Byrne, Doris I.
flourished 1940s–50s
politician
Index t Wom

7266. Clapp, Margaret (Antoinette)
1910–74
president of Wellesley College, historian, biographer, US cultural attaché to India
Nat Cyc Am Bio; Index t Wom

7267. Dargans, Louise M.
flourished 1940s–70s
chief clerk, US House Committee on Education and Labor, 1946
Black
Negro Alman; Negro Her Lib v1

7268. Fenwick, Millicent Vernon (Hammond)
born 1910
representative to Congress from New Jersey
New Jersey
Cur Biog '77

7269. Ford, Geraldine Bledsoe
flourished 1940s–70s
lawyer, judge
Black
Encyc Black Am

7270. Gibbs, Florence R.
flourished 1940s
representative to Congress
Index t Wom

7271. Green, Edith Starrett
born 1910
representative to Congress
Index t Wom

7272. Milligan, Lucy Richardson
flourished 1940s–50s
New York civic leader, antifascist, Jewish welfare worker, Hadassah worker, cancer worker
Nat Cyc Am Bio v53

7273. Murray, Paule
born 1910
educator, author, lawyer, civil rights activist
Black
Encyc Black Am

7274. Stout, Ruth Albertine
born 1910
educator, organization official
Index t Wom

7275. Wilson, Frances M.
1910–59
director of child guidance for the New York City board of education
New York
Obit File

7276. Johnson, Thomasina Walker
born 1911
government official, lobbyist
Index t Wom

7277. Smith, Elizabeth Rudel
born 1911
government official
Index t Wom

7278. Blitch, Iris Faircloth
born 1912

representative to Congress
Index t Wom

7279. Cormier, Lucia
born 1912
politician
Index t Wom

7280. Griffiths, Martha
born 1912
representative to Congress
Index t Wom

7281. Knutson, Coya
born 1912
representative to Congress
Index t Wom

7282. Price, Margaret Bayne
1912–68
politician, vice-chairperson of the
Democratic National Committee
Index t Wom; Obit File

7283. Horvath, Stephanie
1913–60
police officer, undercover agent
Austrian
Obit File

7284. Reid, Charlotte (Thompson)
born 1913
representative to Congress from
Illinois, politician, FCC member
Illinois
Cur Biog '75; Index t Wom

7285. Kelsey, Frances
born 1914
physician, government employee
Index t Wom

7286. May, Catherine Dean
born 1914
representative to Congress, radio
commentator, radio producer
Index t Wom

7287. Ray, Dixie Lee
born 1914
marine biologist, chairperson of
the AEC
Cur Biog '73; Index t Wom

7288. Smith, Mary Louise
born 1914
chairperson of the Republican
National Committee
Cur Biog '76

7289. Knauer, Virginia Harrington (Wright)
born 1915
consumer affairs worker, special
assistant for consumer affairs to
President Nixon
Cur Biog '70

7290. Peterson, Helen White
born 1915
assistant to the commissioner of
the Bureau of Indian affairs,
race relations worker
Colorado
Native American (Dakota-Oglala)
Ind Today; Read Encyc Am West

7291. Walz, Erma Hicks
born 1915
chief of tribal relations of the
Bureau of Indian Affairs
Native American (Cherokee)
Ind Today

7292. Burns, Dorothy L.
1916–47
litigator who charged radiation
poisoning in a suit against Westinghouse
Obit File

7293. Calloway, Deverne Lee
born 1916
Missouri state legislator, Black
civil rights worker, women's
rights worker
Encyc Black Am

7294. Diggs, Estella B.
born 1916
New York State legislator
New York
Black
Encyc Black Am

7295. Furness, Betty
born 1916
actor, television personality, government
official
Index t Wom

7296. Gunderson, Barbara Bates
married 1941
government official
Index t Wom

7297. McCauley, Jane Hamilton
born 1916
politician
Index t Wom

7298. Tenayuca (Brooks), Emma
born 1916
civil rights worker, labor leader,
Communist party worker
Mexican
Dict Mex Am Hist

7299. Vredenburgh, Dorothy McElroy
born 1916
politician
Index t Wom

7300. Wolfe, Deborah Cannon Partridge
born 1916
educator, government consultant
Index t Wom

7301. Burke, Lillian W.
born 1917
lawyer, judge
Ohio
Black
Encyc Black Am

7302. Goff, Regina
born 1917
educator; consultant to the Ministry of Education of Iran, 1955;
assistant commissioner of
HEW's Office of Education
Black
Negro Alman; Negro Her Lib v1

7303. Hamer, Fannie Lou
1917–77
civil rights worker, founder of the
Mississippi Freedom Democratic party, worker for Student
Nonviolent Coordinating Committee, farmer
Mississippi
Black
Encyc Black Am; Obit File

7304. Hooper, Virginia Fite
born 1917
politician, clubwoman
Index t Wom

7305. Kabis, Dorothy Andrews
1917–71
US treasurer, Republican party
activist, president of the National Federation of Republican
Women
Washington, DC
Obit File

7306. Tree, Marietta
born 1917
politician
Index t Wom

7307. Hewell, Grace
born 1918
educator; social worker; HEW official; chief of education, House
Committee on Education and
Labor
Washington, DC
Black
Encyc Black Am; Negro Her Lib
v1

7308. Brown, Dorothy
born 1919
surgeon, Tennessee state legislator
Tennessee
Black
Encyc Black Am; Negro Alman

7309. Elliott, Daisy
born 1919
Michigan state legislator from
Detroit, civil rights worker
Detroit, MI
Black
Encyc Black Am

7310. Gadsden, Marie Davis
born 1919
Peace Corps training officer
Black
Index t Wom

7311. Grasso, Ella Tambussi
1919–81
Democratic governor of Connecticut, politician
Connecticut
Cur Biog '75; Index t Wom

7312. Koontz, Elizabeth Duncan
born 1919
director of the US Department of
Labor Women's Bureau, US
delegate to the Commission on
the Status of Women, labor organizer, educator
Black
Cur Biog '69; Encyc Black Am;
Index t Wom; Negro Alman

7313. Lawson, Marjorie
born 1919
lawyer, judge
Pittsburgh, PA
Black
Encyc Black Am; Negro Alman

7314. O'Hair, Madalyn Murray (Mays)
born 1919
lawyer, political activist, fighter
for the separation of church and
state
Cur Biog '77

7315. Stout, Juanita Kidd
1919–post 1976
municipal court judge
Black
Index t Wom; Negro Alman; Prof
Negro Wom v2

7316. Wilson, Margaret Berenice Bush
born 1919
lawyer, civic leader, chairperson
of the national board of the
NAACP
St. Louis, MO
Black
Cur Biog '75; Encyc Black Am

7317. Abzug, Bella (Savitsky)
born 1920
representative to Congress from
New York, lawyer with specialty in labor law, lecturer, peace
worker
Jewish

New York
Cur Biog '71

7318. Carpenter, Leslie
born 1920
government employee, speechwriter
Index t Wom

7319. Chambers, Yolande Hargrave
flourished 1950s–60s
lawyer, business executive
Black
Encyc Black Am

7320. Davis, Katherine McGrath
flourished 1950s
politician
Index t Wom

7321. Ferguson, Rosetta
born 1920
Michigan state legislator
Michigan
Black
Encyc Black Am

7322. Guinn, Nora
born 1920
Alaska district judge
Alaska
Inuit
Ind Today

7323. Jordan, June
flourished 1950s–1980s
poet, essayist, political writer, civil rights worker, educator
Black
Wom Lit; Wom Lit, More

7324. Lee, Frances Marron
flourished 1950s–60s
rancher, politician
Index t Wom

7325. Norrell, Catherine D.
flourished 1950s–60s
representative to Congress
Index t Wom

7326. Paddock, Constance Harper
born 1920
chief clerk of the Alaska House of Representatives
Alaska
Native American (Athabascan)
Ind Today

7327. Poling, Hazel
born 1920
administrator of Indian Health Service
Native American (Ottawa)
Ind Today

7328. Reece, Louise Goff
flourished 1950s–60s

representative to Congress
Index t Wom

7329. Ricklefs, Elsie Gardner
born 1920
tribal leader
Native American (Hoopa)
Ind Today

7330. Rose, Lucille Mason
born 1920
New York City commissioner of employment
New York, NY
Black
Negro Alman

7331. Spaulding, Jane M.
flourished 1950s
assistant to the secretary of HEW
Black
Negro Her Lib v1

7332. Sullivan, Leonore Alice Kretzger
flourished 1950s
representative to Congress
Index t Wom

7333. Tobolowsky, Hermine D.
flourished 1950s–60s
feminist, lawyer
Index t Wom

7334. Kreps, Juanita M(orris)
born 1921
US secretary of commerce, university educator, economist
Cur Biog '77

7335. Marr, Carmell Carrington
born 1921
lawyer, New York State Public Service commissioner, legal adviser to the United Mission of the UN
Black
Encyc Black Am; Negro Alman; Negro Her Lib v1

7336. Motley, Constance Baker
born 1921
lawyer, federal judge, US senator
Black
Encyc Black Am; Index t Wom; Prof Negro Wom v2

7337. Davis, Dorothy
born 1922
politician
Index t Wom

7338. Lafontant, Jewell Stradford
born 1922
lawyer, US deputy soliciter general
Black
Encyc Black Am; Negro Alman

7339. Alexander, Sadie
born 1923
lawyer
Index t Wom

7340. Bentley, Helen Delich
born 1923
newspaper journalist, chairperson of the Federal Maritime Commission, marine shipping expert, television documentary producer
Cur Biog '71

7341. Davis, Georgia M.
born 1923
business executive, Kentucky state senator, Black civil rights worker
Kentucky
Black
Encyc Black Am

7342. Jumper, Betty Mae Tiger
born 1923
tribal chairperson
Native American (Seminole)
Ind Today

7343. Chisholm, Shirley [Anita] (St. Hill)
born 1924/26
New York State legislator, representative to Congress from New York, 1972 presidential candidate in New York Democratic primary
New York
Black
Cur Biog '69; Encyc Black Am; Negro Alman

7344. Harris, Patricia Roberts
born 1924
lawyer, educator, ambassador to Luxembourg
Black
Encyc Black Am; Index t Wom; Negro Alman; Negro Her Lib v1; Prof Negro Wom v2

7345. Sipuel, Ada Lois
born 1924
lawyer, educator, civil rights activist
Black
Encyc Black Am

7346. Banuelos, Ramona Acosta
born 1925
US treasurer, banker
Los Angeles, CA
Mexican
Dict Mex Am Hist

7347. Hufstedler, Shirley [Ann] Mount
born 1925
US secretary of education
Cur Biog '80

7348. Phillips, Velvalea
born 1925
lawyer, politician
Index t Wom

7349. Hernandez, Aileen Clarke
born 1926
public affairs consultant; commissioner of Equal Employment Opportunities Committee, 1965; president of NOW; labor worker; civil rights worker; feminist
Black
Cur Biog '71; Negro Alman; Negro Her Lib v1

7350. Kirkpatrick, Jeanne
born 1926
permanent representative to the UN, political scientist, university educator
Cur Biog '81

7351. Walker, Cora T.
born 1926
lawyer, civic leader, co-op founder
Harlem, NY
Black
Encyc Black Am; Negro Alman; Prof Negro Wom v2

7352. Wallace, Lurleen Burns
1926–68
governor of Alabama, politician
Alabama
Index t Wom; Obit File

7353. Whiting, Willie M.
born 1926
lawyer, judge
Black
Encyc Black Am

7354. Armstrong, Anne (Legedre)
born 1927
US ambassador to Great Britain
Cur Biog '76

7355. Hanks, Nancy
born 1927
chairperson of the National Endowment for the Arts and the National Council for the Arts
Cur Biog '71

7356. Mink, Patsy Takemoto
born 1927
representative to Congress
Japanese
Index t Wom

7357. Tucker, Cynthia Delores Nottage
born 1927
secretary of the Commonwealth of Pennsylvania
Pennsylvania
Black
Encyc Black Am

7358. Black, Shirley Temple
born 1928
child actor, singer, UN representative
Cur Biog '70; Index t Wom

7359. Jaramillo, Mari-Luci
born 1928
educator, US ambassador to Honduras
Mexican
Dict Mex Am Hist

7360. Olivarez, Graciela
born 1928
lawyer, United Way executive, civil rights worker
Mexican
Dict Mex Am Hist

7361. Couzzins, Phoebe Wilson
1929/45–1913
lawyer, US deputy and marshal in Missouri, political author, suffragist
Index t Wom; Nat Cyc Am Bio v15; Not Am Wom; Wom Cent

7362. Lallmang, Sue Sillaway
born 1929
Native American adviser, Republican party worker
Native American (Seneca)
Ind Today

7363. Scott, Ann London
1929–75
feminist, vice-president of NOW, poet
Not Am Wom supp v1; Obit File

7364. Caldwell, Leticia
flourished 1960s
Chippewa tribal leader
Native American (Chippewa)
Ind Today

7365. Gaston, Gloria Laureha
flourished 1960s–70s
development officer for the Agency for International Development's Bureau of Latin America
Black
Negro Alman; Negro Her Lib v1

7366. Hansberry, Lorraine
1930–65
playwright, civil rights reformer, Socialist party worker
New York
Black
Dict Lit Bio v7; Encyc Black Am; Index t Wom; Nat Cyc Am Bio v60; Negro Alman; Not Am Wom supp v1; Obit File; Prof Negro Wom v2; Wom Lit; Wom Lit, More

7367. Miller, Edith
born 1930
lawyer, judge
Black
Encyc Black Am

7368. Mondale, Joan (Adams)
born 1930
federal arts consultant, art historian
Cur Biog '80

7369. Savilla, Agnes
flourished 1960s
tribal leader
Native American (Mohave)
Ind Today

7370. Uccello, Ann
flourished 1960s
mayor, politician
Index t Wom

7371. Wauneka, Annie Dodge
flourished 1960s
tribal leader
Native American (Navaho)
Ind Today

7372. Whittington, Geraldine Delores
born 1931
secretary to Lyndon Johnson
Black
Negro Alman; Negro Her Lib v1

7373. Barrett, Brenetta H.
born 1932
director of the federal Human Resources Administration
Illinois
Black
Negro Alman

7374. Burke, Yvonne Watson Brathwaite
born 1932
lawyer, representative to Congress from California, regent of the University of California, environmentalist, feminist
California
Black
Cur Biog '75; Encyc Black Am; Negro Alman

7375. Costanza, Margaret "Midge"
born 1932
special assistant on women's affairs to President Carter, feminist, human rights worker
Cur Biog '78

7376. Crockett, Gwendolyn
born 1932
lawyer, educator
Louisiana
Black
Encyc Black Am

7377. Krupsak, Mary Anne
born 1932
Democratic lieutenant governor of New York, lawyer, feminist, women's rights worker
New York
Cur Biog '75

7378. Feinstein, Dianne
born 1933
mayor of San Francisco
San Francisco, CA
Cur Biog '79

7379. Byrne, Jane; Margaret Burke
born 1934
Republican mayor of Chicago
Chicago, IL
Cur Biog '80

7380. Hills, Carla Anderson
born 1934
lawyer, secretary of HUD
Cur Biog '75

7381. MacLaine, Shirley
born 1934
stage and screen actor, dancer, autobiographer, feminist, Democratic party worker, political activist, world traveler
Cur Biog '78; Index t Wom

7382. Steinem, Gloria
born 1934/36
journalist, feminist, founder and editor of *Ms.* magazine, political activist
Cur Biog '72

7383. Drew, Elizabeth (Brenner)
born 1935
political journalist, writer on American politics
Cur Biog '79

7384. Scheirbeck, Helen Maynor
born 1935
director of the Education for American Indians Office of HEW
Native American (Lumbee)
Ind Today

7385. Whitman, Marina von Neumann
born 1935
international economist, university educator, member of the Council of Economic Advisors
Cur Biog '73

7386. Jordan, Barbara
born 1936
lawyer, Texas state senator, representative to Congress from Texas
Texas
Black
Cur Biog '74; Encyc Black Am; Negro Alman

7387. Shabazz, Betty
born 1936
community activist
Black Muslim
Black
Negro Alman

7388. Fonda, Jane
born 1937
actor, political activist, antinuclear worker
Index t Wom

7389. Norton, Eleanor Holmes
born 1937
lawyer, chairperson of the Equal Opportunities Committee, New York City Human Rights commissioner, civil rights worker
New York
Black
Cur Biog '76; Encyc Black Am; Negro Alman

7390. Edelman, Marian Wright
born 1939
lawyer, member of the Yale University board of trustees
Black
Encyc Black Am; Negro Alman

7391. Smeal, Eleanor [Marie] Cutri
born 1939
president of NOW
Cur Biog '80

7392. Hernandez, Maria L.
flourished 1970s–80s
Mexican American community leader, civil rights worker
Texas
Mexican
Dict Mex Am Hist

7393. Schroeder, Patricia (Scott)
born 1940
representative to Congress from Colorado, feminist
Colorado
Cur Biog '78

7394. Washington, Bennetta Bullock
flourished 1970s
special assistant, US Department of Commerce; director of the Women's Job Corps of the Office of Economic Opportunity
Black
Negro Alman; Negro Her Lib v1

7395. Baca-Barragan, Polly
born 1941
Colorado state senator, housing reformer
Colorado
Mexican
Dict Mex Am Hist

7396. Holtzman, Elizabeth
born 1941
lawyer, Democratic representative to Congress from New York, feminist, anti–Vietnam war protester
New York
Cur Biog '73

7397. Natches, Millicent Maxine
born 1943
tribal secretary
Native American (Ute)
Ind Today

7398. Davis, Angela [Yvonne]
born 1944
civil rights worker, politician, Communist party presidential candidate, political writer, university educator
Black
Cur Biog '72; Encyc Black Am; Negro Alman

7399. Davis, Christine R.
flourished 1976
publishing executive; staff director, US House Committee on Government Operations, 1949
Black
Negro Alman; Negro Her Lib v1

No Dates

7400. Bosone, Reva Beck
representative to Congress, lawyer
Index t Wom

7401. Boves, Josefina
lawyer, politician
Index t Wom

7402. Byrne, Mabel
politician
Index t Wom

7403. Crews, Julia Lesser
politician
Index t Wom

7404. Heckler, Margaret M.
US representative to Congress
Index t Wom

LITERATURE

7405. Capillana
died 1549
author on natural history, historian
Peruvian
Cyc Am Bio

7406. Bradstreet, Anne Dudley
1612–72
poet
Puritan
English
Am Bio Dict; Cyc Am Bio; Dict Am Auth; Dict Am Bio; Dict Am Bio Men Time; Index t Wom; Nat Cyc Am Bio v7; Not Am Wom; Twent Cen Bio Dict Not Am; Wom Lit; Wom Lit, More

7407. Hutchinson, Lucy Apsley
1620–71
colonial author
Index t Wom

7408. Stone, Verlinda Cotton Burdette Boughton
flourished circa 1650s
colonial journalist, letter writer
Index t Wom

7409. Rowlandson, Mary (White)
circa 1635–circa 1682
author, autobiographer, colonial pioneer
Lancaster, MA
Dict Am Auth; Dict Am Bio; Dict Am Bio Men Time; Index t Wom; Nat Cyc Am Bio v8

7410. Cruz, Juana Inez de la
1651–95
poet
Mexican
Cyc Am Bio; Wom Cour

7411. Knight, Sarah Kemble
1666–1725/27
diarist, educator, hotel keeper, traveler, merchant
Boston, MA
Cyc Am Bio; Dict Am Auth; Dict Am Bio; Dict Am Bio Men Time; Index t Wom; Not Am Wom; Wom Lit, More

7412. Centlivre, Susannah
circa 1667–1723
playwright, actor
Index t Wom

7413. Wright, Susanna
1697–1784
poet, colonial frontiersperson, businessperson
Index t Wom; Not Am Wom

7414. Hume, Sophia Wiginton
1702–74
Quaker minister, religious writer
Index t Wom; Not Am Wom

7415. Turrell, Jane Colman
1708–35
colonial poet
Am Bio Dict; Dict Am Bio; Dict Am Bio Men Time; Index t Wom; Nat Cyc Am Bio v7; Not Am Wom; Wom Lit, More

7416. Fleming, Elizabeth
flourished 1750s
colonial author
Index t Wom

7417. Lennox, Charlotte Ramsey
1720–1804
novelist, dramatist, translator
Dict Am Bio; Dict Nat Bio; Index t Wom; Nat Cyc Am Bio v6; Twent Cen Bio Dict Not Am; Wom Lit; Wom Lit, More

7418. Manigault, Ann
flourished 1750s–80s
diarist, letter writer
Index t Wom

7419. Pinckney, Elizabeth Lucas "Eliza"
1722/23–1793
plantation manager identified with the development of indigo as a staple of the colonial South, textile manufacturer, agriculturist, author
South Carolina
Dict Am Bio; Encyc South Hist; Index t Wom; Not Am Wom; Who Who Dur Am Rev

7420. Anthony, Susanna
1726–91
theologian, religious author
Quaker
Rhode Island
Am Bio Dict; Appl Cyc Am Bio; Cyc Am Bio; Dict Am Bio Men Time

7421. Warren, Mercy Otis
1727/28–1814
poet, author, dramatist, political author and satirist, historian, patriot
Massachusetts
Am Bio Dict; Cyc Am Bio; Dict Am Auth; Dict Am Bio; Dict Am Bio Men Time; Index t Wom; Nat Cyc Am Bio v7; Not Am Wom; Our Count; Who Who Dur Am Rev; Wom Lit, More

7422. Winslow, Anna Green
died 1779
colonial diarist
Index t Wom

7423. Hulton, Ann
flourished 1760s
letter writer
Index t Wom

7424. Terry, Lucy
1730–1821
poet
Black
Negro Alman; Prof Negro Wom v1

7425. Wheatley, Phillis
1735/53–1784
poet
Boston, MA
Black; African
Am Bio Dict; Cyc Am Bio; Dict Am Bio Men Time; Encyc Black Am; Encyc South Hist; Index t Wom; Negro Alman; Nat Cyc Am Bio v1; Not Am Wom; Prof Negro Wom v1; Wom Lit; Wom Lit, More

7426. Stockton, Annis Boudinot
1736–1801
colonial poet
Index t Wom

7427. Ferguson, Elizabeth (Graeme)
1737/39–1801
litterateur, poet, translator, letter writer, diarist, hero of American Revolution
Philadelphia, PA
Am Bio Dict; Cyc Am Bio; Dict Am Auth; Dict Am Bio; Dict Am Bio Men Time; Index t Wom; Nat Cyc Am Bio v7; Not Am Wom; Who Who Dur Am Rev

7428. Baldwin, Alice
flourished 1770s
writer during American Revolution
Index t Wom

7429. Colman, Jane
flourished 1770s
author
Index t Wom

7430. Eve, Sarah
flourished 1770s
colonial author
Index t Wom

7431. Gardner, Anna
flourished 1770s–80s
lecturer, poet
Index t Wom

7432. Drinker, Elizabeth Sandwith
1743–1807
colonial diarist
Quaker
Index t Wom

7433. Adams, Abigail Smith
1744–1818
patriot and relief worker of American Revolution, political mover, letter writer, feminist
Am Bio Dict; Appl Cyc Am Bio; Cyc Am Bio; Dict Am Auth; Dict Am Bio; Dict Am Bio Men Time; Index t Wom; Nat Cyc Am Bio v1; Not Am Wom; Twent Cen Bio Dict Not Am; Wom Cent

7434. Picken, Joanna Belfrage
1748/98–1859
poet
Canadian; Scottish
Cyc Am Bio; Dict Nat Bio

7435. Flintham, Lydia Stirling
flourished 1780s–90s
author, lecturer
Index t Wom

7436. Murray, Judith Sargent Stevens; The Gleaner; Constantia
1751–1820
author, essayist, poet, dramatist, feminist
Massachusetts
Cyc Am Bio; Dict Am Bio; Index t Wom; Not Am Wom; Who Who Dur Am Rev

7437. Bleecker, Ann Eliza (Schuyler)
1752–83
author, poet
New York, NY
Am Bio Dict; Appl Cyc Am Bio; Cyc Am Bio; Dict Am Auth; Dict Am Bio; Dict Am Bio Men Time; Index t Wom; Nat Cyc Am Bio v8; Not Am Wom; Twent Cen Bio Dict Not Am; Wom Lit, More

7438. Crocker, Hannah (Mather)
1752/65–1829/47
author, women's rights worker, pioneer, essayist
Cyc Am Bio; Dict Am Auth; Dict Am Bio; Dict Am Bio Men Time; Index t Wom; Not Am Wom

7439. Wood, Jean (Moncure)
1754–1823
poet
Virginia
Dict Am Auth

7440. Adams, Hannah
1755–1831/32
historian, compiler of historical data, religious author
Massachusetts
Am Bio Dict; Appl Cyc Am Bio; Cyc Am Bio; Dict Am Auth; Dict Am Bio; Dict Am Bio Men Time; Index t Wom; Nat Cyc Am Bio v5; Not Am Wom; Wom Cent

7441. Grant, Anne
1755–1838
author
Scottish
Cyc Am Bio; Dict Am Bio Men Time; Dict Nat Bio

7442. Foster, Hannah (Webster)
1758/90–1840
author, novelist, biographer
Massachusetts
Am Bio Dict; Cyc Am Bio; Dict Am Auth; Dict Am Bio; Dict Am Bio Men Time; Index t Wom; Not Am Wom; Who Who Dur Am Rev

7443. Bowne, Eliza Southgate
died 1809
diarist
Index t Wom

7444. Morton, Sarah Wentworth (Apthorp); Philenia
1759–1846
poet, author
Quincy, MA
Cyc Am Bio; Dict Am Auth; Dict Am Bio; Dict Am Bio Men Time; Nat Cyc Am Bio v8; Not Am Wom; Who Who Dur Am Rev

7445. Ramsay, Martha Laurens
1759–1811
missionary, colonial horticulturist, author, autobiographer
Am Bio Dict; Cyc Am Bio; Index t Wom

7446. Wood, Sarah Sayward (Barrell) (Keating)
1759–1855
writer of sentimental novels
Maine
Am Bio Dict; Dict Am Auth; Dict Am Bio; Not Am Wom

7447. Hall, Sarah (Ewing); Constantia; Florepha
1761–1830
author, essayist, religious writer
Philadelphia, PA
Cyc Am Bio; Dict Am Auth; Dict Am Bio; Index t Wom; Nat Cyc Am Bio v11

7448. Wister, Sarah "Sally"
1761/62–1804
diarist, patriot of American Revolution
Quaker
Pennsylvania
Dict Am Bio; Index t Wom; Who Who Dur Am Rev

7449. Rowson, Susanna (Haswell)
1762/67–1824
novelist, dramatist, poet, educator, actor
Boston, MA
English
Cyc Am Bio; Dict Am Auth; Dict Am Bio; Dict Am Bio Men Time; Dict Nat Bio; Index t Wom; Nat Cyc Am Bio v9; Not Am Wom; Wom Lit; Wom Lit, More

7450. Sanders, Elizabeth (Elkins)
1762–1851/54
social critic, pamphleteer, author, history writer on Massachusetts, Native American rights worker
Salem, MA
Cyc Am Bio; Dict Am Auth; Dict Am Bio; Dict Am Bio Men Time; Not Am Wom

7451. Tenney, Tabitha (Gilman)
1762–1837
satirical novelist
Exeter, NH
Am Bio Dict; Cyc Am Bio; Dict Am Auth; Dict Am Bio; Not Am Wom

7452. Blennerhassett, Adeline Agnew
flourished 1796; died post 1842
linguist, poet
Cyc Am Bio

7453. Morris, Margaret
died 1816
patriot of American Revolution, author
Index t Wom

7454. Royall, Anne Newport
1769–1854
traveler, journalist, newspaper editor and publisher, novelist
Washington, DC; Virginia
Am Bio Dict; Cyc Am Bio; Dict Am Auth; Dict Am Bio; Dict Am Bio Men Time; Encyc South Hist; Index t Wom; Not Am Wom

7455. White, Tryphena
flourished 1800s
pioneer, diarist
Index t Wom

7456. Williams, Cecelia
flourished 1800s
actor, poet
Index t Wom

7457. Faugeres, Margaretta V. (Bleeker)
1771–1801
dramatist, poet
Am Bio Dict; Dict Am Bio Men Time; Index t Wom; Nat Cyc Am Bio v9

7458. Seton, Elizabeth Ann (Bayley), Saint; Mother Seton
1774–1821
Catholic nun, founder and superior of the American Sisters of Charity of St. Vincent de Paul (the first American sisterhood), philanthropist, autobiographer
Catholic

Maryland
Cyc Am Bio; Dict Am Auth; Dict Am Bio; Dict Am Rel Bio; Encyc South Hist; Index t Wom; Nat Cyc Am Bio v2; Not Am Wom; Twent Cen Bio Dict Not Am

7459. Greenwood, Mary Langdon
1775–1855
writer on women's education
Am Bio Dict

7460. de Witt, Susan Linn
1778–1824
author, religious poet
Am Bio Dict; Cyc Am Bio

7461. Smith, Margaret (Bayard)
1778–1844
author, early chronicler of Washington society
Cyc Am Bio; Dict Am Auth; Dict Am Bio; Dict Am Bio Men Time; Index t Wom; Not Am Wom

7462. Lee, Hannah Farnham (Sawyer)
1780/89–1865
writer on history and art
Boston, MA
Cyc Am Bio; Dict Am Auth; Dict Am Bio; Dict Am Bio Men Time; Index t Wom; Nat Cyc Am Bio v25

7463. Trollope, Frances Milton
1780/90–1863
author
English
Cyc Am Bio; Dict Am Bio Men Time

7464. Brown, Phoebe (Hinsdale)
1783–1861
hymn writer, poet
Dict Am Auth; Dict Am Bio; Nat Cyc Am Bio v11

7465. Burr, Theodosia Alston
1783–1813
letter writer
Cyc Am Bio; Dict Am Bio; Not Am Wom

7466. Snyder, Grace McCance
born circa 1783
author
Index t Wom

7467. Holley, Mary Phelps Austin
1784–1846
Texas historian, historical author, biographer, miscellaneous writer, land speculator

Texas
Am Bio Dict; Dict Am Auth; Not
Am Wom

7468. Wirt, Elizabeth Washington (Gamble)
1784–1857
children's author, illustrator, botanist
Cyc Am Bio; Dict Am Auth

7469. Eldridge, Elleonor
1785–1845
author, amateur lawyer, dairy farmer
Black
Negro Alman; Prof Negro Wom v1

7470. Savage, Sarah
1785–1837
author, story writer
Salem, MA
Am Bio Dict

7471. Robbins, Eliza
1786–1853
educator, historian, author
Boston, MA
Dict Am Auth

7472. Follen, Eliza Lee (Cabot)
1787–1859/60
children's author, poet, abolitionist
Cyc Am Bio; Dict Am Auth; Dict Am Bio; Dict Am Bio Men Time; Index t Wom; Not Am Wom; Twent Cen Bio Dict Not Am; Dict Lit Bio v1

7473. Leslie, Eliza
1787–1858
cookbook writer, children's author, humorist, short story writer, editor
Philadelphia, PA
Cyc Am Bio; Dict Am Auth; Dict Am Bio; Dict Am Bio Men Time; Index t Wom; Nat Cyc Am Bio v7; Not Am Wom

7474. Willard, Emma C. (Hart)
1787–1870/76
educator, textbook writer, poet
Troy, NY
Cyc Am Bio; Dict Am Auth; Dict Am Bio; Dict Am Bio Men Time; Index t Wom; Nat Cyc Am Bio v1; Not Am Wom; Twent Cen Bio Dict Not Am; Wom Cent

7475. Williams, Catherine Read (Arnold)
1787/90–1872
author, poet, novelist, biographer, historical author
Providence, RI
Cyc Am Bio; Dict Am Auth; Dict Am Bio; Dict Am Bio Men Time

7476. Hale, Sarah Josepha (Buell)
1788/90–1879/97
magazine editor, author
Philadelphia, PA
Cyc Am Bio; Dict Am Auth; Dict Am Bio; Dict Am Bio Men Time; Dict Lit Bio v1; Index t Wom; Nat Cyc Am Bio v3 and v22; Not Am Wom; Twent Cen Bio Dict Not Am; Wom Lit, More

7477. Lee, Eliza Buckminster
1788/94–1864
novelist, translator
Boston, MA
Cyc Am Bio; Dict Am Auth; Dict Am Bio; Dict Am Bio Men Time; Index t Wom; Nat Cyc Am Bio v25

7478. Livermore, Harriet
1788–1868
preacher, evangelist, religious writer
Index t Wom; Not Am Wom; Twent Cen Bio Dict Not Am

7479. Ricord, Elizabeth (Stryker)
1788–1865
educator, poet
New York; New Jersey
Cyc Am Bio; Dict Am Auth; Dict Am Bio Men Time

7480. Sedgwick, Susan Anne Livingston Ridley; Anne Livingston Ridley
1788/89–1867
children's author
Cyc Am Bio; Dict Am Auth; Twent Cen Bio Dict Not Am

7481. Whittlesey, Abigail Goodrich
1788–1858
educator, magazine editor, author
Connecticut
Cyc Am Bio; Dict Am Bio; Not Am Wom

7482. d'Arusmont, Frances Wright
1789–1852
abolitionist, political essayist, author
Scottish
Am Bio Dict; Dict Am Auth

7483. Gould, Hannah Flagg
1789–1865
poet
Newburyport, VT
Cyc Am Bio; Dict Am Auth; Dict Am Bio; Dict Am Bio Men Time; Index t Wom; Nat Cyc Am Bio v8

7484. Livermore, Sarah White
1789–1874

poet
Index t Wom

7485. Santa Cruz, Maria de las Mercedes; Countess of Merlin
1789–1852
author
Cuban
Cyc Am Bio

7486. Sedgwick, Catharine Maria
1789–1867
novelist, writer of moral tales for juveniles, educator
Stockbridge, MA
Cyc Am Bio; Dict Am Auth; Dict Am Bio; Dict Am Bio Men Time; Dict Lit Bio v1; Index t Wom; Nat Cyc Am Bio v1; Not Am Wom; Twent Cen Bio Dict Not Am; Wom Cent; Wom Lit, More

7487. Townsend, Eliza
1789–1854
poet
Unitarian
Boston, MA
Am Bio Dict; Cyc Am Bio; Dict Am Bio

7488. Buell, Sarah
flourished 1820s
author, editor
Index t Wom

7489. Farrar, Eliza Ware Rotch
1791/1815–1870
children's author
Cambridge, MA
Cyc Am Bio; Dict Am Auth; Dict Am Bio Men Time; Index t Wom; Nat Cyc Am Bio v13; Not Am Wom

7490. Huntington, Susan Mansfield
1791–1823
religious writer, philanthropist, diarist, poet
Am Bio Dict; Cyc Am Bio; Index t Wom

7491. Mitchell, Maria
1791/1818–1889
astronomer, women's rights worker, educator, novelist, poet
Quaker
Massachusetts
Cyc Am Bio; Dict Am Bio; Dict Am Bio Men Time; Index t Wom; Nat Cyc Am Bio v5; Not Am Wom; Twent Cen Bio Dict Not Am; Wom Cent

7492. Moseby, Mary Webster
1791–1844
magazine writer, author

Virginia
Cyc Am Bio; Dict Am Bio Men Time

7493. Sigourney, Lydia Howard (Huntley)
1791–1865
author, poet, philanthropist
Connecticut
Cyc Am Bio; Dict Am Auth; Dict Am Bio; Dict Am Bio Men Time; Dict Lit Bio v1; Index t Wom; Nat Cyc Am Bio v1; Not Am Wom; Twent Cen Bio Dict Not Am; Wom Cent; Wom Lit, More

7494. Grimke, Sarah Moore
1792/93–1873
abolitionist, women's rights worker, writer on social problems, political author, lecturer
Quaker
Cyc Am Bio; Dict Am Auth; Dict Am Bio; Dict Am Rel Bio; Index t Wom; Nat Cyc Am Bio v2; Twent Cen Bio Dict Not Am; Wom Cent

7495. Hyde, Nancy Maria
1792–1816
educator, author
Connecticut
Am Bio Dict; Cyc Am Bio; Dict Am Bio Men Time

7496. Putnam, Katharine Hunt (Palmer)
1792–1861
religious textbook writer
Boston, MA
Dict Am Auth

7497. James, Maria
1793–1868
poet
Cyc Am Bio

7498. Phelps, Almira (Hart) (Lincoln)
1793–1884
educator, botanist, chemist, textbook author
Baltimore, MD
Cyc Am Bio; Dict Am Auth; Dict Am Bio; Dict Am Bio Men Time; Index t Wom; Nat Cyc Am Bio v11; Not Am Wom; Twent Cen Bio Dict Not Am

7499. Brooks, Maria (Gowen); Maria del Occidente
1794/95–1845
poet
Massachusetts
Am Bio Dict; Cyc Am Bio; Dict Am Auth; Dict Am Bio; Dict Am Bio Men Time; Index t Wom; Nat Cyc Am Bio v8; Not Am Wom; Twent Cen Bio Dict Not Am

7500. Dix, Dorothea Lynde
1794/1802–1887
crusader for the welfare of the mentally ill, prison reformer, philanthropist, author, essayist, children's author, superintendent of army nurses in the Civil War
Massachusetts
Cyc Am Bio; Dict Am Auth; Dict Am Bio; Dict Am Bio Men Time; Dict Lit Bio v1; Index t Wom; Nat Cyc Am Bio v3; Not Am Wom; Twent Cen Bio Dict Not Am; Wom Cent

7501. Dumont, Julia Louisa (Carey)
1794–1857
poet, author, educator
Vevay, IN
Cyc Am Bio; Dict Am Auth

7502. Gilman, Caroline (Howard)
1794–1888
author, poet, editor, domestic novelist
Charleston, SC
Cyc Am Bio; Dict Am Auth; Dict Am Bio; Dict Am Bio Men Time; Dict Lit Bio v3; Index t Wom; Nat Cyc Am Bio v6; Not Am Wom; Twent Cen Bio Dict Not Am

7503. Thayer, Caroline Matilda
died 1844
magazine writer, poet
Louisiana
Am Bio Dict

7504. Campbell, Maria
died 1845
biographer
Am Bio Dict

7505. Caulkins, Frances Manwaring
1795/96–1869
historian, historical author
Connecticut
Cyc Am Bio; Dict Am Bio Men Time; Not Am Wom; Twent Cen Bio Dict Not Am

7506. Thornton, Eliza B.
1795–1854
poet
Cyc Am Bio

7507. Wright, Frances (d'Arusmont) "Fanny"; Fanny d'Arusmont
1795–1852
author, abolitionist, feminist, philanthropist, lecturer
Scottish
Am Bio Dict; Cyc Am Bio; Dict Am Bio; Dict Am Bio Men Time; Index t Wom; Nat Cyc Am Bio v2; Not Am Wom

7508. Otis, Eliza Henderson (Boardman)
1796–1873
philanthropist, novelist
Boston, MA
Dict Am Auth; Twent Cen Bio Dict Not Am

7509. Ward, Julia Rush
1796–1824
poet
Cyc Am Bio

7510. Moise, Penina
1797–1880
poet, writer of Jewish hymns
Jewish
Charleston, SC
Cyc Am Bio; Dict Am Auth; Dict Am Bio; Index t Wom; Not Am Wom; Wom Lit, More

7511. Robinson, Therese Albertine Louise (von Jakob); Mrs. Edward; Talvi; Talvj
1797–1869/70
author, short story writer, historical writer, translator, linguist, philologist
German
Cyc Am Bio; Dict Am Bio; Dict Am Bio Men Time; Index t Wom; Nat Cyc Am Bio v1

7512. Walworth, Reubena Hyde
1797–1898
humorist
Dict Am Auth

7513. Ware, Katherine Augusta (Rhodes)
1797–1843
poet
Cyc Am Bio; Dict Am Auth; Dict Am Bio Men Time; Index t Wom; Nat Cyc Am Bio v5

7514. Wells, Ann Maria
born 1797
poet
Index t Wom

7515. Worthington, Jane T. Lomax
died 1847
poet
Index t Wom

7516. Dawson-Damer, Mary Georgiana Emma
died 1848
Egyptologist, diarist
Who Who Egypt

7517. Tuthill, Louisa Cornelia Caroline (Huggins)
1798/99–1879
author, popular writer of moral tales for children

Princeton, NJ
Cyc Am Bio; Dict Am Auth; Dict Am Bio Men Time; Index t Wom; Not Am Wom

7518. Little, Sophia Louise (Robbins)
born 1799
poet, author
Newport, RI
Cyc Am Bio; Dict Am Auth; Dict Am Bio Men Time

7519. Aspinwall, Alicia (Towne)
born 18?
children's author
Brookline, MA
Dict Am Auth

7520. Barbour, A. (Maynard)
born 18?
novelist
Helena, MT
Dict Am Auth

7521. Bates, Josephine W.
born 18?
novelist
Chicago, IL
Dict Am Auth

7522. Beecher, Catherine Esther
1800–78
educator of women, education writer, social reformer, poet
Episcopalian
New York
Appl Cyc Am Bio; Cyc Am Bio; Dict Am Bio; Dict Am Bio Men Time; Dict Lit Bio v1; Index t Wom; Nat Cyc Am Bio v3; Not Am Wom; Twent Cen Bio Dict Not Am; Wom Cent

7523. Bouve, Pauline Carrington (Rust)
born 18?
author
Boston, MA
Dict Am Auth

7524. Brine, Mary Dow (Northam)
born 18?
children's poet
New York, NY
Dict Am Auth

7525. Brodhead, Eva Wilder (McGlasson)
born 18?
poet, magazine writer
Cincinnati, OH
Dict Am Auth

7526. Bugg, Lelia Hardin
born 18?
novelist, religious author
Catholic
Wichita, KS
Dict Am Auth

7527. Cabell, Julia (Mayo)
18?–post 1850
author
Dict Am Auth

7528. Cloud, Virginia Woodward
born 18?
poet
Dict Am Auth

7529. Colton, Julia M.
born 18?
historical writer
Brooklyn, NY
Dict Am Auth

7530. Coxe, Margaret
born 1800
historical author, botanist, feminist, educator
Cyc Am Bio; Dict Am Auth; Dict Am Bio Men Time; Index t Wom

7531. Crane, Elizabeth Green
born 18?
poet, dramatist
Dict Am Auth

7532. Cruse, Mary Anne
born 18?
author, educator
Alabama
Dict Am Auth

7533. Daniels, Gertrude (Potter)
born 18?
novelist
Dict Am Auth

7534. Devereux, Mary (Watson)
born 18?
novelist
Marblehead, MA
Dict Am Auth

7535. Dickinson, Martha Gilbert
born 18?
poet
Amherst, MA
Dict Am Auth

7536. Dodge, Mary Barker (Carter)
born 18?
poet
Dict Am Auth

7537. Drake, Jeanie
born 18?
novelist
Dict Am Auth

7538. du Bois, Constance Goddard
born 18?
novelist

Waterbury, CT
Dict Am Auth

7539. Duer, Catherine King
born 18?
poet
Dict Am Auth

7540. Dunn, Martha Baker
born 18?
novelist
Dict Am Auth

7541. Eliot, Henrietta Robins (Mack)
born 18?
author
Portland, OR
Dict Am Auth

7542. Emerson, Florence (Brooks)
born 18?
poet, prose writer
Dict Am Auth

7543. Fessendon, Laura (Dayton)
born 18?
novelist
Chicago, IL
Dict Am Auth

7544. Foster, Mabel G.
born 18?
author, lecturer
Boston, MA
Dict Am Auth

7545. Gates, Ellen M. (Huntington)
born 18?
poet
East Orange, NJ
Dict Am Auth

7546. Going, Ellen Maud; E. M. Hardinge
born 18?
nature writer
New York
Dict Am Auth

7547. Guerber, Helen Adeline
born 18?
educator, textbook writer, historical author
Nyack, NY
Dict Am Auth

7548. Hall, Violette
born 18?
novelist
Catskill Mountains, NY
Dict Am Auth

7549. Hamilton, Alice King
18?–post 1900
novelist
Dict Am Auth

7550. Hawthorne, Hildegarde
born 18?
novelist
Dict Am Auth

7551. Hentz, Caroline Lee (Whiting)
1800–56
novelist, dramatist, poet, romance writer, educator
Episcopalian
Am Bio Dict; Cyc Am Bio; Dict Am Bio; Dict Am Bio Men Time; Dict Lit Bio v3; Index t Wom; Nat Cyc Am Bio v6; Not Am Wom; Twent Cen Bio Dict Not Am; Wom Lit, More

7552. Hutchinson, Ellen MacKay
born 18?
literary journalist
New York, NY
Dict Am Auth

7553. Kennedy, Sarah Beaumont (Cannon)
born 18?
novelist
Memphis, TN
Dict Am Auth

7554. Krout, Caroline Virginia
born 18?
novelist
Crawfordsville, IN
Dict Am Auth

7555. Lee, Mary Catherine (Jenkins)
born 18?
novelist
Springfield, MA
Dict Am Auth

7556. Loud, Marguerite St. Leon (Barstow)
born circa 1800
poet
Philadelphia, PA
Cyc Am Bio; Dict Am Auth

7557. Lounsberry, Allice
born 18?
botanist, writer on botany
New York
Dict Am Auth

7558. Lund, Mary Dwinnell (Chellis)
born 18?
religious fiction author
Dict Am Auth

7559. MacKubin, Ellen
born 18?
novelist
New York
Dict Am Auth

7560. Mansfield, Blanche (McManus)
born 18?
children's author
Dict Am Auth

7561. Mason, Agnes Louisa (Carter)
born 18?
poet
Montclair, NJ
Dict Am Auth

7562. McElroy, Lucy Cleaver
born 18?
novelist
Dict Am Auth

7563. McLaws, [Emily] Lafayette
born 18?
novelist
Augusta, GA
Dict Am Auth

7564. McLeod, Georgiana A. (Hulse)
18?–1890
educator, short story writer
Baltimore, MD
Dict Am Auth

7565. Merington, Marguerite
born 18?
playwright
New York, NY
Dict Am Auth

7566. Moore, Susan Teakle (Smith)
born 18?
novelist
Brooklyn, NY
Dict Am Auth

7567. Morrison, Sarah Elizabeth
born 18?
children's author
Philadelphia, PA
Dict Am Auth

7568. Myers, Sarah Ann (Irwin)
1800–76
children's author, artist
Carlisle, PA
Cyc Am Bio; Dict Am Auth

7569. Nitsch, Helen Alice (Matthews); Catherine Owen
18?–1889
domestic scientist, writer on domestic science
Plainfield, NJ

Dict Am Auth

7570. Noble, Lucretia Gray
born 18?
novelist

Wilbraham, MA
Dict Am Auth

7571. Orne, Caroline (Chaplin)
18?–1882
magazine story writer
Dict Am Auth

7572. Paddock, Cornelia
born 18?
miscellaneous writer
Dict Am Auth

7573. Pitkin, Helen
born 18?
novelist
New Orleans, LA
Index t Wom

7574. Plympton, Almira George
born 18?
children's author
Massachusetts
Dict Am Auth

7575. Potter, Mary Knight
born 18?
writer on art, author
Boston, MA
Dict Am Auth

7576. Pratt, Anna Marie
born 18?
children's author
Cleveland, OH
Dict Am Auth

7577. Pratt, Cornelia Atwood
born 18?
novelist
Dict Am Auth

7578. Pyle, Katherine
born 18?
children's author
Wilmington, DE
Dict Am Auth

7579. Rayner, Emma
born 18?
novelist
Boston, MA
Dict Am Auth

7580. Robinson, Martha Harrison
born 18?
novelist, translator
Philadelphia, PA
Dict Am Auth

7581. Robinson, Suzanne (Antrobus)
born 18?
novelist
New Orleans, LA
Dict Am Auth

7582. Sanborn, Mary (Farley)
born 18?
novelist

Boston, MA
Dict Am Auth

7583. Shields, Sarah Annie (Frost)
born 18?
writer on etiquette, fashion writer, miscellaneous author
Dict Am Auth

7584. Sibley, Louise Florence Maria (Lyndon)
born 18?
author
Malden, MA
Dict Am Auth

7585. Smith, Alice (Prescott)
born 18?
novelist
California
Dict Am Auth

7586. Spencer, William Loring (Nunez), Mrs.
born 18?
author
Dict Am Auth

7587. Taylor, Mary Imlay
born 18?
novelist
Washington, DC
Dict Am Auth

7588. Ticknor, Caroline
born 18?
short story writer
Boston, MA
Dict Am Auth

7589. Tidball, Mary Langdon
18?–1904
novelist
Virginia
Dict Am Auth

7590. Tiffany, Nina Moore
born 18?
historical author
St. Paul, MN
Dict Am Auth

7591. Urbino, Lavinia Buoncuore
born 18?
biographer, autobiographer, translator
Boston, MA
Dict Am Auth

7592. Walker, Mary Spring
born 18?
miscellaneous author
Boston, MA
Dict Am Auth

7593. Warner, Eliza A.
born 18?
children's author
Northampton, MA
Dict Am Auth

7594. Weeden, Howard
born 18?
artist, poet
Huntsville, AL
Dict Am Auth

7595. Weston, Roxana
1800–91
poet
Skowhegan, ME
Dict Am Auth

7596. White, Rhoda Elizabeth (Waterman)
flourished 1830s–50s
humanitarian, philanthropist, miscellaneous writer
Dict Am Auth; Index t Wom

7597. Whitehouse, Florence Brooks
born 18?
novelist
Portland, ME
Dict Am Auth

7598. Wolfenstein, Martha
born 18?
short story writer
Columbus, OH
Dict Am Auth

7599. Wright, Henrietta Christian
18?–1899
children's story writer
Dict Am Auth

7600. Bremer, Fredrika
1801–65
novelist
Swedish
Dict Am Bio Men Time

7601. Kirkland, Caroline Matilda (Stansbury)
1801–64
miscellaneous writer, editor, journalist, writer on pioneering
New York, NY
Cyc Am Bio; Dict Am Auth; Dict Am Bio; Dict Am Bio Men Time; Dict Lit Bio v3; Index t Wom; Nat Cyc Am Bio v5; Not Am Wom; Twent Cen Bio Dict Not Am

7602. Taggart, Cynthia
1801–49
poet
Rhode Island
Am Bio Dict; Dict Am Bio Men Time

7603. Case, Mary
died 1852
magazine writer
Quaker
New York
Am Bio Dict

7604. Child, Lydia Maria (Francis)
1802–80
author, philanthropist, abolitionist, editor, social reformer
Quaker
Massachusetts
Cyc Am Bio; Dict Am Auth; Dict Am Bio Men Time; Dict Lit Bio v1; Index t Wom; Nat Cyc Am Bio v2; Not Am Wom; Twent Cen Bio Dict Not Am; Wom Cent

7605. Hall, Arethusa
1802–91
literary educator, author
Massachusetts
Cyc Am Bio; Dict Am Auth; Dict Am Bio; Nat Cyc Am Bio v22; Twent Cen Bio Dict Not Am

7606. Hall, Louisa Jane Park
1802–92
poet, author
Providence, RI
Cyc Am Bio; Dict Am Auth; Dict Am Bio Men Time; Index t Wom

7607. Peirson, Lydia Jane (Wheeler)
1802–62
author, poet
Adrian, MI; Pennsylvania
Cyc Am Bio; Dict Am Auth; Dict Am Bio Men Time

7608. Rives, Judith Page (Walker)
1802–82
miscellaneous author
Cyc Am Bio; Dict Am Auth

7609. Traill, Catherine Parr (Strickland)
1802–99
author
Canadian
Cyc Am Bio; Dict Am Bio Men Time

7610. Canfield, Francesca Anna
1803–23
poet, translator, linguist
Philadelphia, PA
Cyc Am Bio; Dict Am Bio Men Time

7611. Maury, Ann
1803–76
author of histories
Dict Am Auth; Dict Am Bio Men Time; Twent Cen Bio Dict Not Am

7612. Maury, Sarah Mytton (Hughes)
1803/08–1948/49
miscellaneous writer

Catholic
Cyc Am Bio; Dict Am Auth; Dict Am Bio Men Time

7613. McIntosh, Maria Jane; Aunt Kitty
1803–78
author, children's author, novelist
New York
Cyc Am Bio; Dict Am Auth; Dict Am Bio Men Time; Index t Wom; Nat Cyc Am Bio v6; Not Am Wom; Twent Cen Bio Dict Not Am

7614. Miles, Anne
born 1803
poet
Index t Wom

7615. Pumpelly, Mary Hollenback (Welles)
1803–79
poet, religious history writer
Cyc Am Bio; Dict Am Auth

7616. Ripley, Sophia Willard
1803–61
leading spirit in the Brook Farm commune experiment
Transcendentalist
Not Am Wom

7617. Whitman, Sarah Helen (Power)
1803/13–1878
poet, essayist, feminist
Spiritualist
Providence, RI
Cyc Am Bio; Dict Am Auth; Dict Am Bio; Dict Am Bio Men Time; Dict Lit Bio v1; Nat Cyc Am Bio v8; Not Am Wom; Wom Cent

7618. Peabody, Elizabeth Palmer
1804–94
educator, writer on education, educational reformer, kindergartner
Transcendentalist
Boston, MA
Cyc Am Bio; Dict Am Auth; Dict Am Bio; Dict Am Bio Men Time; Dict Lit Bio v1; Index t Wom; Not Am Wom; Twent Cen Bio Dict Not Am; Wom Cent

7619. Smith, Eliza Roxey Snow; The Mother of Mormonism
1804–87
Mormon leader, religious poet, hymn writer, women's leader, suffragist, western pioneer
Mormon
Utah
Cyc Am Bio; Dict Am Bio; Index t Wom; Not Am Wom; Read Encyc Am West

7620. Solar, Mercedes Marin De
1804–66
poet
Chilean
Cyc Am Bio

7621. Dinnies, Anna Peyre (Shackelford); Moina
1805/16–1886
poet
New Orleans, LA
Cyc Am Bio; Dict Am Auth; Index t Wom; Nat Cyc Am Bio v13

7622. Green, Frances Harriet (Whipple)
1805–78
author, poet, abolitionist, botanist
Cyc Am Bio; Dict Am Bio; Dict Am Bio Men Time

7623. Locke, Jane Ermina (Starkweather)
1805–59
author, poet
Boston, MA
Cyc Am Bio; Dict Am Auth; Dict Am Bio Men Time; Twent Cen Bio Dict Not Am

7624. Martin, Sarah Towne (Smith); Sarah Martyn
1805–79
historian, religious and historical writer for children, editor, abolitionist, temperance worker
New York, NY
Cyc Am Bio; Dict Am Auth; Dict Am Bio; Twent Cen Bio Dict Not Am

7625. McDougal, Frances Harriet (Whipple) (Greene)
1805–75
poet, miscellaneous writer, suffragist
Rhode Island; California
Dict Am Auth; Cyc Am Bio

7626. Morgan, Henrietta Hunt
1805–91
Civil War diarist, pioneer
Index t Wom

7627. Bogart, Elizabeth; Estelle
1806–18?
poet
New York, NY
Cyc Am Bio; Dict Am Auth; Dict Am Bio Men Time; Wom Lit, More

7628. Cook, Martha Elizabeth Duncan Walker
1806–74
magazine editor, author, linguist, translator, abolitionist, patron of Polish arts and artists
Cyc Am Bio; Dict Am Bio

7629. Dwight, Elizabeth Baker
1806/08–1936
missionary to Constantinople, autobiographer
Am Bio Dict; Index t Wom

7630. Dwight, Mary Ann
1806–58
textbook author, writer on art, artist
New York, NY
Cyc Am Bio; Dict Am Auth; Dict Am Bio Men Time

7631. Embury, Emma Catherine (Manly)
1806–63
author, poet, writer on women's education
Brooklyn, NY
Cyc Am Bio; Dict Am Auth; Dict Am Bio; Dict Am Bio Men Time; Index t Wom; Nat Cyc Am Bio v9

7632. Kinzie, Juliette Augusta (Magill)
1806–70
historian of the Northwest, novelist
Chicago, IL
Dict Am Auth; Not Am Wom

7633. Mann, Mary Tyler (Peabody)
1806–87
miscellaneous author, kindergarten educator
Cyc Am Bio; Dict Am Auth; Dict Am Bio; Twent Cen Bio Dict Not Am

7634. Smith, Elizabeth Oakes (Prince)
1806–93
poet, novelist, lecturer, suffragist, women's rights worker, feminist
Cyc Am Bio; Dict Am Auth; Dict Am Bio; Dict Am Bio Men Time; Dict Lit Bio v1; Index t Wom; Nat Cyc Am Bio v9; Not Am Wom; Twent Cen Bio Dict Not Am; Wom Cent; Wom Lit, More

7635. Taylor, Charlotte de Bernier
1806–61
entomologist, author, illustrator
Dict Am Bio; Nat Cyc Am Bio v1

7636. Chandler, Elizabeth Margaret
1807–1834/35
author, poet, abolitionist
Delaware
Cyc Am Bio; Dict Am Auth; Dict Am Bio; Dict Am Bio Men Time; Index t Wom; Not Am Wom; Twent Cen Bio Dict Not Am

7637. Martin, Margaret Maxwell
born 1807
author, educator, poet
Columbia, SC
Cyc Am Bio; Dict Am Auth

7638. Miles, Sarah E.
born 1807
poet
Index t Wom

7639. Palmer, Phoebe Worrall
1807–74
social reformer, religious writer, Methodist leader, Wesleyan evangelist
Wesleyan
New York, NY
Cyc Am Bio; Dict Am Auth; Dict Am Rel Bio; Index t Wom; Not Am Wom

7640. Davidson, Lucretia Maria
1808–1825/38
poet
New York
Am Bio Dict; Cyc Am Bio; Dict Am Auth; Dict Am Bio; Dict Am Bio Men Time; Index t Wom; Nat Cyc Am Bio v7; Our Count; Twent Cen Bio Dict Not Am; Wom Lit, More

7641. Gage, Frances Dana (Barker); Aunt Fanny
1808–84
lecturer, author, temperance worker, abolitionist, suffragist, women's rights worker, Civil War relief worker
Cyc Am Bio; Dict Am Auth; Dict Am Bio; Dict Am Bio Men Time; Index t Wom; Nat Cyc Am Bio v2; Not Am Wom; Twent Cen Bio Dict Not Am; Wom Cent

7642. Medberry, Rebecca B. (Stetson)
1808–68
author
Cyc Am Bio

7643. Baxter, Lydia
1809–74
poet, hymn writer
Appl Cyc Am Bio; Cyc Am Bio; Dict Am Auth; Twent Cen Bio Dict Not Am

7644. Conant, Hannah O'Brian (Chaplin)
1809–65
religious worker, translator, Oriental scholar and language expert, magazine editor
Cyc Am Bio; Dict Am Auth; Dict Am Bio; Dict Am Bio Men Time; Nat Cyc Am Bio v22; Not Am Wom; Twent Cen Bio Dict Not Am

7645. Hawthorne, Sophia Amelia Peabody
1809–71
artist, illustrator, travel writer
Cyc Am Bio; Dict Am Auth; Not Am Wom

7646. Kemble, Frances Anne "Fanny"; Fanny Kemble Butler
1809/11–1893
actor, diarist, author, abolitionist
Georgia
English
Cyc Am Bio; Dict Am Bio; Dict Am Bio Men Time; Dict Nat Bio supp; Encyc South Hist; Index t Wom; Nat Cyc Am Bio v3; Not Am Wom

7647. Ladd, Catherine; Minnie Mayflower; Morna; Alida; Arcturus
1809–99
educator, author, Civil War nurse, designer of the Confederate flag
Cyc Am Bio; Dict Am Bio; Nat Cyc Am Bio v24; Twent Cen Bio Dict Not Am

7648. Scott, Julia H. (Kinney)
1809–42
poet
Towanda, PA
Dict Am Auth; Dict Am Bio Men Time; Index t Wom

7649. Doolittle, Mary Antoinette
1810–86
lecturer on religious subjects, Shaker eldress, author
Shaker
New York
Cyc Am Bio

7650. Fairfield, Jane Frazee
born circa 1810
biographer, autobiographer
Dict Am Auth

7651. Fuller, Sarah Margaret; Marchioness Ossoli; Sarah Margaret Fuller Ossoli
1810–50
author, critic, educator, feminist, philosopher, journalist, Transcendentalist revolutionary
Transcendentalist
Boston, MA
Cyc Am Bio; Dict Am Auth; Dict Am Bio; Dict Am Bio Men Time; Dict Lit Bio v1; Index t Wom; Nat Cyc Am Bio v3; Not Am Wom; Twent Cen Bio Dict Not Am; Wom Cent

7652. Hale, Mary Whitwell
1810–62
poet, educator, hymn writer

Massachusetts
Dict Am Auth; Index t Wom

7653. Hallock, Mary Angeline A. (Ray) (Lathrop)
born 1810
author of religious tales for children
Cyc Am Bio; Dict Am Auth

7654. Jewett, Susan W.
flourished 1840s–50s
poet
Cyc Am Bio

7655. Kinney, Elizabeth Clemantine (Dodge) (Stedman)
1810–89
poet, essayist
Newark, NJ
Cyc Am Bio; Dict Am Auth; Dict Am Bio; Dict Am Bio Men Time; Nat Cyc Am Bio v13

7656. Lander, Sarah West
1810/19–1872
author of travel books for children
Salem, MA
Cyc Am Bio; Dict Am Auth

7657. le Vert, Octavia Celeste Walton
1810/11–1877
author, Civil War nurse, travel writer
Mobile, AL
Cyc Am Bio; Dict Am Auth; Dict Am Bio Men Time; Index t Wom; Nat Cyc Am Bio v6; Not Am Wom; Twent Cen Bio Dict Not Am

7658. McCord, Louisa Susannah (Cheves)
1810–1879/80
miscellaneous author, poet, political writer, translator, Confederate essayist, Black welfare worker, feminist, plantation manager
South Carolina
Cyc Am Bio; Dict Am Auth; Dict Am Bio; Dict Am Bio Men Time; Index t Wom; Nat Cyc Am Bio v9; Not Am Wom; Twent Cen Bio Dict Not Am

7659. Meigs, Mary Noel
flourished 1840s
poet
Index t Wom

7660. Nichols, Clarinda Irene Howard
1810–85
newspaper editor, political writer, social reformer, lecturer, women's rights leader, suffragist, feminist

Kansas
Cyc Am Bio; Dict Am Bio; Index t Wom; Nat Cyc Am Bio v5; Not Am Wom

7661. Nichols, Mary Sargent (Neal) Gove
1810–84
women's rights worker, feminist, dress and health reformer, medical author, physician, social reformer, temperance reformer, popular author, novelist
Cyc Am Bio; Dict Am Auth; Dict Am Bio Men Time; Dict Lit Bio v1; Index t Wom; Nat Cyc Am Bio v13; Not Am Wom

7662. Pierson, Lydia Jane
flourished 1840s
poet
Index t Wom

7663. Putnam, Mary Traill Spence (Lowell)
1810–98
author, history writer, translator, linguist, traveler
Boston, MA
Cyc Am Bio; Dict Am Auth; Dict Am Bio Men Time; Index t Wom; Twent Cen Bio Dict Not Am

7664. Read, Henrietta Fanning
flourished 1840s
actor, poet
Dict Am Bio Men Time; Wom Lit, More

7665. Shindler, Mary Stanley Bunce (Palmer) (Dana)
1810–83
author, poet, religious writer
Unitarian; Episcopalian
Nacogdoches, TX
Cyc Am Bio; Dict Am Auth; Dict Am Bio Men Time; Index t Wom

7666. Sleight, Mary Breck
flourished 1840s–90s
short story writer
Sag Harbor, NY
Dict Am Auth; Twent Cen Bio Dict Not Am

7667. Steele, Ann
flourished 1840s
author
Index t Wom

7668. Stephens, Anna Sophia (Winterbotham); Jonathan Slick
1810/13–1886
author, poet, novelist, serial fiction writer, editor

New York, NY
Cyc Am Bio; Dict Am Auth; Dict Am Bio; Dict Am Bio Men Time; Dict Lit Bio v8; Index t Wom; Nat Cyc Am Bio v10; Not Am Wom; Twent Cen Bio Dict Not Am; Wom Lit, More

7669. Talley, Susan Archer
flourished 1840s
poet
Index t Wom

7670. Bacon, Delia Salter
1811–95
author, lecturer, originator of the Bacon/Shakespeare theory
Appl Cyc Am Bio; Cyc Am Bio; Dict Am Auth; Dict Am Bio; Dict Lit Bio v1; Index t Wom; Nat Cyc Am Bio v1; Not Am Wom; Twent Cen Bio Dict Not Am

7671. Hoge, Jane Currie Blaikie; A. H. Hoge
1811–90
Civil War relief leader, church and welfare worker, sanitation commission worker, author
Index t Wom; Not Am Wom

7672. Lowell, Anna Cabot (Jackson)
1811/19–1874
textbook author, educator, writer on conversation
Cyc Am Bio; Dict Am Auth; Dict Am Bio Men Time; Twent Cen Bio Dict Not Am

7673. Oliver, Sophia Helen
born 1811
poet
Index t Wom

7674. Osgood, Frances Sargent (Locke)
1811/12–1850
author, poet
Am Bio Dict; Cyc Am Bio; Dict Am Auth; Dict Am Bio; Dict Am Bio Men Time; Index t Wom; Nat Cyc Am Bio v7; Not Am Wom; Twent Cen Bio Dict Not Am

7675. Parton, Sarah Payson (Willis); Fanny Fern
1811–72
author, newspaper columnist, magazine writer, novelist, clubwoman
Cyc Am Bio; Dict Am Auth; Dict Am Bio; Dict Am Bio Men Time; Index t Wom; Nat Cyc Am Bio vl; Not Am Wom; Twent Cen Bio Dict Not Am; Wom Cent; Wom Lit; Wom Lit, More

7676. Peterson, Hannah Mary (Bouvier)
1811–70
astronomer, author, illustrator, writer on astronomy
Cyc Am Bio; Dict Am Auth

7677. Smith, Sarah Louisa P. (Hickman)
1811–32
poet
Cincinnati, OH
Cyc Am Bio; Dict Am Auth; Dict Am Bio Men Time; Index t Wom

7678. Stowe, Harriet Elizabeth Beecher
1811/12–1896
author, abolitionist, social reformer, theologian
Connecticut
Cyc Am Bio; Dict Am Auth; Dict Am Bio; Dict Am Bio Men Time; Dict Am Rel Bio; Dict Lit Bio v1; Nat Cyc Am Bio v1; Not Am Wom; Twent Cen Bio Dict Not Am; Wom Cent; Wom Lit; Wom Lit, More

7679. Whitcher, Frances Miriam (Berry); Widow Bedott
1811/14–1857/67
author, humorist, caricaturist
New York
Cyc Am Bio; Dict Am Auth; Dict Am Bio; Index t Wom; Nat Cyc Am Bio v6; Not Am Wom; Twent Cen Bio Dict Not Am

7680. Bailey, Margaret Jewett
circa 1812–82
pioneer, author
Oregon
Read Encyc Am West

7681. Bailey, Margaret L.
born 1812
poet, journalist
Index t Wom

7682. Beecher, Eunice White (Bullard); A Minister's Wife
1812–97
author on domestic subjects
Appl Cyc Am Bio; Cyc Am Bio; Dict Am Auth; Twent Cen Bio Dict Am Auth

7683. Bolton, Sarah Tittle (Barritt)
1812/15–1893
poet
Cyc Am Bio; Dict Am Auth; Dict Am Bio; Index t Wom; Nat Cyc Am Bio v10; Not Am Wom; Wom Cent

7684. Cate, Eliza Jane
1812–84
author on New England

New England
Dict Am Auth

7685. Eames, Elizabeth Jessup
married 1837
poet
Index t Wom

7686. Ellett, Elizabeth Fries (Lummis)
1812/18–1877
historian, historical writer
Cyc Am Bio; Dict Am Auth; Dict Am Bio; Dict Am Bio Men Time; Index t Wom; Nat Cyc Am Bio v11; Not Am Wom; Twent Cen Bio Dict Not Am

7687. Esling, Catherine Harbeson (Waterman)
born 1812
poet
Philadelphia, PA
Cyc Am Bio; Dict Am Auth

7688. Hawley, Laura M.
1812–42
poet
Index t Wom

7689. Hooper, Ellen Strugis
1812–48
Transcendentalist poet
Transcendentalist
Not Am Wom

7690. Hopkins, Louisa Payson
1812–62
religious writer for children
Cyc Am Bio; Dict Am Auth; Nat Cyc Am Bio v5

7691. Sawyer, Caroline Mehitabel (Fisher)
1812–94
author, editor, poetry anthologist, poet, translator
Dict Am Auth; Index t Wom; Not Am Wom; Twent Cen Bio Dict Not Am

7692. Saxe, Caroline Mehetabel
1812–94
author, editor
Massachusetts
Cyc Am Bio

7693. Silsbee, Marianne Cabot (Devereux)
1812–89
historian of Salem, Massachusetts, poet
Boston, MA
Dict Am Auth

7694. Thurston, Laura M. (Hawley)
1812–42
poet
Cyc Am Bio

7695. Waterston, Anne Cabot Lowell (Quincy)
1812–99
poet
Dict Am Auth

7696. Coleman, Ann Mary Butler (Crittenden)
1813–91
author, translator
Nat Cyc Am Bio v4; Twent Cen Bio Dict Not Am

7697. Cooper, Susan Augusta Fenimore
1813/15–1894
author, philanthropist
Cyc Am Bio; Dict Am Auth; Dict Am Bio; Dict Am Bio Men Time; Index t Wom; Nat Cyc Am Bio v6; Not Am Wom; Twent Cen Bio Dict Not Am

7698. Curtis, Harriot F.
1813–89
magazine editor, novelist, journalist, club leader
Dict Am Auth; Index t Wom

7699. Day, Martha
1813–33
scholar of mathematics and language, author
New Haven, CT
Cyc Am Bio; Dict Am Bio Men Time; Index t Wom

7700. Dodd, Mary Ann Hanmer
born 1813
poet
Cyc Am Bio; Dict Am Bio Men Time; Index t Wom

7701. Farley, Harriet
1813/17–1907
millworker, writer on women in the textile mills, children's author, editor
New Hampshire
Cyc Am Bio; Dict Am Auth; Dict Am Bio; Dict Am Bio Men Time; Nat Cyc Am Bio v11; Not Am Wom

7702. Jacobs, Sarah Sprague
born 1813
children's author, historical author
Cambridge, MA
Cyc Am Bio; Dict Am Auth

7703. Lawrence, Margaret Oliver (Woods); Meta Lander
1813–1901
author
Dict Am Auth

7704. Lee, Mary Elizabeth
1813–49
poet, children's author

Charleston, SC
Cyc Am Bio; Dict Am Auth; Index t Wom; Nat Cyc Am Bio v6

7705. McGuire, Judith Brockenbrough
born 1813
Civil War diarist, patriot
Index t Wom

7706. Poyas, Catherine Gendron
1813–82
poet
Charleston, SC
Dict Am Auth

7707. Rukeyser, Muriel
1913–80
poet
Cur Biog '80; Index t Wom; Wom Lit, More

7708. Walworth, Ellen Hardin
1813–1915
author, clubwoman
Not Am Wom

7709. Benjamin, Mary Gladding Wheeler
1814–71
translator, poet
Appl Cyc Am Bio; Cyc Am Bio

7710. Collins, Emily Parmely
born 1814
suffragist, abolitionist, political writer, Civil War nurse
Hartford, CT
Wom Cent

7711. Conkling, Margaret Cockburn; Mrs. Steele
1814–90
author
Twent Cen Bio Dict Not Am

7712. Daviess, Maria (Thompson)
1814–96
writer on agriculture
Kentucky
Cyc Am Bio; Dict Am Auth; Nat Cyc Am Bio v3

7713. Dupuy, Eliza Ann
1814–1880/81
popular author
Kentucky
Cyc Am Bio; Dict Am Auth; Dict Am Bio; Dict Am Bio Men Time; Nat Cyc Am Bio v6; Not Am Wom

7714. Howland, Mary Woolsey
died 1864
poet, Civil War nurse
Cyc Am Bio; Index t Wom

7715. Olin, Julia Matilda
1814–79

religious author
Cyc Am Bio; Dict Am Auth; Twent Cen Bio Dict Not Am

7716. Perkins, Elmira Johnson
1814–96
missionary to Native Americans in Oregon, poet
Oregon; Boston, MA
Dict Am Auth

7717. Pratt, Louisa Kirby; Bell Smith
died 1864
essayist
Dict Am Bio Men Time

7718. Rea, Julia (de Marguerittes) (Foster)
1814–66
opera singer, drama critic, writer on Europe
Philadelphia, PA
English
Cyc Am Bio; Dict Am Auth; Dict Am Bio Men Time

7719. Baker, Harriette Newell Woods; Mrs. Madeline Leslie; Aunt Hattie
1815–93
religious author, novelist
Appl Cyc Am Bio; Cyc Am Bio; Dict Am Auth; Index t Wom; Nat Cyc Am Bio v14; Wom Cent

7720. Botta, Anne Charlotte Lynch
1815/20–1891
author, literary host, educator, poet
New York
Cyc Am Bio; Dict Am Auth; Dict Am Bio; Dict Am Bio Men Time; Dict Lit Bio v3; Nat Cyc Am Bio v7; Not Am Wom; Twent Cen Bio Dict Not Am; Wom Cent

7721. Carroll, Anna Ella
1815–1893/94
political pamphleteer, political scientist, Civil War military strategist
Dict Am Auth; Index t Wom; Nat Cyc Am Bio v5; Not Am Wom; Twent Cen Bio Dict Not Am; Wom Cent

7722. Cheney, Harriet Vaughan (Foster)
born 1815
religious author, historian
Cyc Am Bio; Dict Am Auth; Dict Am Bio Men Time; Index t Wom

7723. Cutler, Hannah Maria (Conant) (Tracy)
1815–96

women's rights leader, suffragist, physician, journalist, author, lecturer, pacifist
Illinois
Cyc Am Bio ad; Dict Am Auth; Index t Wom; Not Am Wom; Twent Cen Bio Dict Not Am

7724. Dorsey, Annah Hanson McKenney
1815/16–1896
author, dramatist, poet, novelist, essayist, short story writer, political writer
Catholic
Washington, DC
Cyc Am Bio; Dict Am Auth; Dict Am Bio; Index t Wom; Nat Cyc Am Bio v11 Twent Cen Bio Dict Not Am; Wom Cent

7725. Farnham, Eliza Woodson (Burhans)
1815–64
prison reformer, author, lecturer, feminist, suffragist, philanthropist
New York; California
Cyc Am Bio; Dict Am Auth; Dict Am Bio; Dict Am Bio Men Time; Index t Wom; Nat Cyc Am Bio v4; Not Am Wom; Twent Cen Bio Dict Not Am

7726. Hubbell, Martha Elizabeth (Stone)
1815–56
author, religious writer for children
Am Bio Dict; Cyc Am Bio; Dict Am Auth

7727. Mason, Emily Virginia
1815–1909
Civil War hospital matron, Confederate army Civil War nurse, author, biographer, educator
Cyc Am Bio; Dict Am Auth; Index t Wom; Nat Cyc Am Bio v5

7728. Phelps, Elizabeth Wooster (Stuart); H. Trusta
1815–1852/53
novelist, lecturer
Am Bio Dict; Cyc Am Bio; Dict Am Auth; Dict Am Bio Men Time; Index t Wom; Nat Cyc Am Bio v9; Not Am Wom; Twent Cen Bio Dict Not Am

7729. Stanton, Elizabeth Cady
1815/16–1902
feminist, suffragist, women's rights worker, editor, author, social reformer, theologian
Cyc Am Bio; Dict Am Auth; Dict Am Bio; Dict Am Bio Men Time; Dict Am Rel Bio; Index t Wom; Nat Cyc Am Bio v3; Not Am Wom; Twent Cen Bio Dict Not Am; Wom Cent

7730. Stebbins, Emma
1815–82
painter, sculptor, biographer of Charlotte Cushman
New York
Cyc Am Bio; Dict Am Auth; Index t Wom; Nat Cyc Am Bio v8; Not Am Wom; Twent Cen Bio Dict Not Am

7731. Swisshelm, Jane (Grey) (Cannon)
1815/16–1884
journalist, author, editor, publisher, abolitionist, women's rights worker, Civil War nurse
Cyc Am Bio; Dict Am Auth; Dict Am Bio; Dict Am Bio Men Time; Index t Wom; Nat Cyc Am Bio v2; Not Am Wom

7732. Whittier, Elizabeth Hussey
1815–64
poet, abolitionist, religious worker
Quaker
Cyc Am Bio; Index t Wom; Nat Cyc Am Bio v8

7733. Avellanada, Gertrudis Gomez de
1816–64/76
poet, dramatist
Cuban
Appl Cyc Am Bio; Cyc Am Bio

7734. Ayres, Anne
1816–96
pioneer in American Episcopal Sisterhoods, religious author, philanthropist
Dict Am Auth; Dict Am Bio; Not Am Wom

7735. Cushman, Charlotte Saunders
1816–76
actor, author
Cyc Am Bio; Dict Am Bio; Dict Am Bio Men Time; Index t Wom; Nat Cyc Am Bio v4; Not Am Wom; Twent Cen Bio Dict Not Am; Wom Cent

7736. Eames, Jane Anthony
1816–94
author, traveler
New Hampshire; Massachusetts
Cyc Am Bio; Dict Am Auth; Index t Wom; Twent Cen Bio Dict Not Am

7737. Hooper, Lucy
1816–41
poet
Brooklyn, NY
Am Bio Dict; Cyc Am Bio; Dict Am Bio Men Time; Index t Wom

7738. Marsh, Caroline Crane
1816–1901
author, translator, poet, biographer
Cyc Am Bio; Dict Am Auth

7739. Porter, Lydia Ann (Emerson)
born 1816
author, educator
Springfield, VT
Cyc Am Bio; Dict Am Auth

7740. Tillotson, Mary Ella (Tillotson)
1816–190?
writer and lecturer on hygiene, poet
Vineland, NJ
Dict Am Auth

7741. Warfield, Catharine Ann (Ware)
1816/17–1877
author, novelist, poet
Kentucky
Cyc Am Bio; Dict Am Auth; Dict Am Bio; Dict Am Bio Men Time; Nat Cyc Am Bio v5; Twent Cen Bio Dict Not Am

7742. Anneke, Mathilde Franziska Giesler
1817–84
author, educator, women's rights worker
Dict Am Bio; Nat Cyc Am Bio v4; Not Am Wom

7743. Burge, Dolly Sumner Lunt
born 1817
Civil War essayist
Index t Wom

7744. Cross, Jane Tandy (Chinn) (Harding)
1817–70
author, poet, translator
Kentucky
Cyc Am Bio; Dict Am Auth

7745. Dyer, Catherine Cornelia [Joy]
1817–1903
author, genealogist
Cyc Am Bio; Dict Am Auth

7746. Eastman, Mary (Henderson)
1817/18–1887
author, scholar of Native American life and culture, ethnologist, Native American folklorist
Virginia
Cyc Am Bio; Dict Am Auth; Dict Am Bio Men Time; Not Am Wom; Twent Cen Bio Dict Not Am

7747. Judson, Emily (Chubbuck); Fanny Forrester
1817–54
popular author, missionary
Am Bio Dict; Dict Am Auth; Dict Am Bio; Dict Am Bio Men Time; Index t Wom; Nat Cyc Am Bio v3; Not Am Wom; Twent Cen Bio Dict Not Am

7748. Ramsay, Vienna G. (Morrell)
born 1817
poet
Dict Am Auth

7749. Shuck, Henrietta (Hall)
1817–44
missionary to China, writer on China
Cyc Am Bio; Dict Am Auth; Index t Wom

7750. Smith, Elizabeth Lee (Allen)
1817–98
biographical editor, poet, hymn writer
Dict Am Auth

7751. Stewart, Electra Maria (Sheldon); Electra Maria Sheldon
born 1817
writer on Michigan history, writer of religious tales for children
Detroit, MI
Cyc Am Bio; Dict Am Auth

7752. Torrey, Mary (Ide)
1817–69
religious and nonfiction writer
Vermont
Dict Am Auth

7753. Wilbur, Anne Toppan (Wood); Florence Leigh
1817–64
author
Cyc Am Bio; Nat Cyc Am Bio v10

7754. Barnes, Charlotte Mary Sanford
1818–63
actor, dramatist
Twent Cen Bio Dict Not Am

7755. Brewster, Anne M. Hampton
1818–92
author
Italian (American expatriate to Rome)
Dict Am Auth

7756. Burnham, Sarah Maria
1818–1901
educator, historical author, writer on geology and travel
Cambridge, MA
Dict Am Auth

7757. de Kroyft, Sarah Susan Helen (Aldrich)
1818–1915
author, lecturer
New York
blind
Cyc Am Bio; Dict Am Auth; Index t Wom; Nat Cyc Am Bio v11

7758. Evans, Elizabeth Hewlings
1818–55
poet
Cyc Am Bio

7759. Harding, Elizabeth McGavock
born circa 1818
Civil War diarist
Index t Wom

7760. Hewitt, Mary Elizabeth (Stebbins)
born 1818
author
Cyc Am Bio; Dict Am Bio Men Time; Wom Lit, More

7761. Keckley, Elizabeth Hobbs
1818/20–1907
dressmaker, author
Black
Index t Wom; Not Am Wom; Prof Negro Wom v1

7762. Kirby, Georgiana (Bruce)
born 1818
feminist, prison matron, autobiographer
Santa Cruz, CA
English
Dict Am Auth

7763. Olnhausen, Mary Phinney von
1818–1902
Civil War nurse, author
Index t Wom

7764. Orne, Caroline Francis
1818–1906
poet, children's author
Cambridge, MA
Dict Am Auth; Nat Cyc Am Bio v6

7765. Prentiss, Elizabeth (Payson); Elizabeth Prescott
1818–78
children's author, religious fiction writer, hymn writer
Dict Am Auth; Dict Am Bio; Index t Wom; Nat Cyc Am Bio v7; Not Am Wom; Twent Cen Bio Dict Not Am

7766. Southworth, Emma Dorothy Eliza (Nevitte); Dorothy Eliza Nevitte
1818/19–1899
romance novelist

Washington, DC
Cyc Am Bio; Dict Am Auth; Dict Am Bio; Dict Am Bio Men Time; Index t Wom; Nat Cyc Am Bio v1; Not Am Wom; Twent Cen Bio Dict Not Am; Wom Cent; Wom Lit, More

7767. Stebbins, Mary Elizabeth (Moore) (Hewitt)
born 1818
author, poet
Dict Am Auth; Nat Cyc Am Bio v13

7768. Trowbridge, Catherine Maria
born 1818
children's author
South Manchester, CT
Dict Am Auth

7769. Ware, Mary Greene (Chandler)
born 1818
miscellaneous author
Cyc Am Bio; Dict Am Auth

7770. Warner, Susan Bogart; Elizabeth Wetherell
1818/19–1885
author, novelist, religious writer
Highland Falls, NY
Cyc Am Bio; Dict Am Auth; Dict Am Bio; Index t Wom; Nat Cyc Am Bio v5; Not Am Wom; Twent Cen Bio Dict Not Am; Wom Lit; Wom Lit, More

7771. Yale, Catharine (Brooks)
1818–1900
short story writer
Deerfield, MA
Dict Am Auth

7772. Arey, Harriet Ellen (Grannis)
1819–post 1888
poet, education writer, educator, magazine editor
Appl Cyc Am Bio; Cyc Am Bio; Dict Am Auth; Dict Am Bio Men Time; Wom Cent

7773. Chaplin, Jane Dunbar
1819–84
children's author, religious writer
Dict Am Auth; Twent Cen Bio Dict Not Am

7774. Clapp, Louise Amelia Knapp Smith; Dame Shirley; Amelia Knapp Smith
1819–1906
author, educator, letter writer during the California gold rush, gold rush pioneer
California
Index t Wom; Not Am Wom; Read Encyc Am West

7775. Greene, Louisa Morton
born 1819
author, abolitionist, suffragist, women's rights worker, temperance worker, Civil War relief worker
Wom Cent

7776. Houston, Margaret Moffette Lea
circa 1819–67
Civil War diarist
Index t Wom

7777. Howe, Julia Ward
1819–1910
poet, dramatist, songwriter, lecturer, suffrage and women's club leader, feminist, abolitionist, pacifist, prison reformer, Union patriot during the Civil War, philanthropist, traveler
Boston, MA
Cyc Am Bio; Dict Am Auth; Dict Am Bio; Dict Am Bio Men Time; Dict Lit Bio v1; Index t Wom; Nat Cyc Am Bio v1; Not Am Wom; Twent Cen Bio Dict Not Am; Wom Cent

7778. List, Harriet Winslow
born 1819
author, poet
Dict Am Bio Men Time

7779. Mayo, Sarah Carter (Edgarton)
1819–48
miscellaneous author, poet, fiction writer
Cyc Am Bio; Dict Am Auth; Dict Am Bio; Dict Am Bio Men Time; Index t Wom; Nat Cyc Am Bio v2

7780. Mowatt, Anna Cora Ogden (Ritchie); Helen Berkley; Ann Cora Ogden (Mowatt) Ritchie
1819/22–70
author, actor, dramatist, novelist, autobiographer
French
Cyc Am Bio; Dict Am Auth; Dict Am Bio; Dict Am Bio Men Time; Index t Wom; Nat Cyc Am Bio v3 and csvB; Not Am Wom; Obit File; Twent Cen Bio Dict Not Am; Wom Lit, More

7781. Nichols, Rebecca Shepard Reed
1819/20–1903
author, poet
Cyc Am Bio; Dict Am Bio Men Time; Index t Wom

7782. Pike, Frances West (Atherton)
born 1819
religious author, magazine writer
Cyc Am Bio; Dict Am Bio

7783. Royce, Sarah Eleonor Bayliss
1819–91
California pioneer, author
California
English
Index t Wom; Not Am Wom

7784. Sewall, Harriet (Winslow)
1819–89
suffragist, poet, religious poet, abolitionist
Transcendentalist
Boston, MA
Dict Am Auth; Nat Cyc Am Bio v10

7785. Tappan, Caroline Sturgis
1819–88
poet
Transcendentalist
Not Am Wom

7786. Welby, Amelia Ball (Coppuck); Amelie
1819–52
poet, author
Louisville, KY
Am Bio Dict; Cyc Am Bio; Dict Am Bio; Dict Am Bio Men Time; Index t Wom; Nat Cyc Am Bio v6; Wom Cent

7787. Whitney, Louisa (Goddard)
1819–82
autobiographer, author
Dict Am Auth

7788. Bailey, Urania Locke (Stoughton); Una Locke
1820–82
children's author, religious poet
Providence, RI
Dict Am Auth

7789. Cary, Alice
1820–71
poet, novelist
Universalist
New York; Ohio
Cyc Am Bio; Dict Am Auth; Dict Am Bio; Dict Am Bio Men Time; Index t Wom; Nat Cyc Am Bio v1; Not Am Wom; Twent Cen Bio Dict Not Am; Wom Cent; Wom Lit, More

7790. Colt, Miriam Davis
flourished 1850s
author, clubwoman
Index t Wom

7791. Curtiss, Abby (Allin)
born 1820
poet
Madison, WI
Cyc Am Bio; Dict Am Auth; Dict Am Bio Men Time

7792. Dickson, Jeanie A.
flourished circa 1850
author, poet
Cyc Am Bio

7793. Gleason, Rachel Brooks
1820–1905
physician, medical author, abolitionist, patron of freedmen's education, dress reformer, women's rights worker
Dict Am Auth; Index t Wom; Wom Cent

7794. Hale, Lucretia Peabody
1820–1900
children's author, humorist
Cyc Am Bio; Dict Am Auth; Dict Am Bio; Index t Wom; Nat Cyc Am Bio v3; Not Am Wom; Twent Cen Bio Dict Not Am

7795. Herndon, Mary Eliza
born 1820
author
Cyc Am Bio

7796. Howell, Elizabeth (Lloyd)
flourished 1850s–80s
poet
Dict Am Bio Men Time; Index t Wom

7797. Ingersoll, Julia Harriet (Pratt)
182?–98
religious author, religious poet
New Haven, CT
Dict Am Auth

7798. Johnson, Rosa Vertner
flourished 1850s
poet
Dict Am Bio Men Time

7799. Lee, Eleanor Percy (Ware)
circa 1820–circa 1850
poet
Dict Am Bio Men Time

7800. Livermore, Mary Ashton (Rice)
1820/21–1905
health reformer, hospital administrator, suffragist, temperance worker, abolitionist, Civil War patriot, miscellaneous author
Universalist
Melrose, MA
Cyc Am Bio; Dict Am Auth; Dict Am Bio Men Time; Dict Am Rel Bio; Index t Wom; Nat Cyc Am Bio v1; Not Am Wom; Twent Cen Bio Dict Not Am; Wom Cent

7801. Mather, Sarah Ann
born 1820
philanthropist, patron of Black education, educator, author
South Carolina
Index t Wom; Wom Cent

7802. May, Caroline
born 1820
author
Cyc Am Bio

7803. Pierson, Cornelia (Tuthill)
1820–70
moral and religious tale writer
Dict Am Auth

7804. Pindar, Susan
1820–92
story writer
Cyc Am Bio; Dict Am Auth

7805. Preston, Margaret (Junkin)
1820/25–1897
poet, author, novelist, Civil War letter writer
Lexington, VA
Cyc Am Bio; Dict Am Auth; Dict Am Bio; Index t Wom; Nat Cyc Am Bio v7; Not Am Wom; Twent Cen Bio Dict Not Am; Wom Cent

7806. Richards, Helen Dorothy Whiton
flourished 1850s
children's author
Cyc Am Bio

7807. Sadlier, Mary Anne (Madden)
1820–1903
novelist, author, Sunday school story writer
Catholic
Irish
Cyc Am Bio; Dict Am Auth; Dict Am Bio Men Time; Dict Irish Bio; Index t Wom; Not Am Wom

7808. Smith, L. Virginia
flourished 1850s
poet
Index t Wom

7809. Stewart, Priscilla
flourished 1850s
poet
Index t Wom

7810. Tuthill, Cornelia
1820–70
author
Index t Wom

7811. Ullmann, Amelia
flourished 1850s
author
German
Index t Wom

7812. van Allstyne, Frances J[ane] (Crosby) "Fanny"
born 1820
hymn writer, poet, songwriter
New York, NY
Dict Am Auth; Nat Cyc Am Bio v7; Twent Cen Bio Dict Not Am

7813. Warner, Anna Bartlett; Amy Lothrop
1820/27–1915
author, novelist, children's author, religious writer
Cyc Am Bio; Dict Am Auth; Dict Am Bio; Index t Wom; Nat Cyc Am Bio v4; Not Am Wom

7814. Whitaker, Mary Scrimzeour (Furman) (Miller)
1820–post 1867
author, poet, novelist
New Orleans, LA
Cyc Am Bio; Dict Am Auth; Nat Cyc Am Bio v1

7815. Blackwell, Elizabeth
1821–1910
physician, medical author and educator, worker for women's medical education
English
Appl Cyc Am Bio; Cyc Am Bio and ad; Dict Am Auth; Dict Am Bio; Dict Am Bio Men Time; Eng Wom; Nat Cyc Am Bio v9; Not Am Wom; Twent Cen Bio Dict Not Am; Wom Cent

7816. Bloede, Marie
1821–70
author
German
Appl Cyc Am Bio; Cyc Am Bio

7817. Diaz, Abby (Morton)
1821–1904
author, children's author, essayist, social reformer, suffragist, abolitionist, lecturer
Boston, MA
Dict Am Auth; Nat Cyc Am Bio v11; Not Am Wom; Twent Cen Bio Dict Not Am; Wom Cent

7818. Emery, Sarah Anna
born 1821
novelist
West Newbury, MA
Dict Am Auth

7819. Gibbons, Phoebe (Earle)
1821–190?
essayist
Lancaster County, PA
Dict Am Auth

7820. Gilbert, Anne Jane Hartley
1821–1904
dancer, actor, autobiographer
Dict Am Auth; Dict Am Bio; Index t Wom; Not Am Wom; Twent Cen Bio Dict Not Am

7821. Gillespie, Elizabeth (Duane)
1821–1901
autobiographer
Philadelphia, PA
Dict Am Auth

7822. Graves, Adelia Cleopatra (Spencer); Aunt Alice
1821–95
author, children's author, rhetorician, linguist, educator, president of Mary Sharp College
Tennessee
Cyc Am Bio; Dict Am Auth; Twent Cen Bio Dict Not Am; Wom Cent

7823. Hilderburn, Mary Jane (Reed); Marie Roseau
1821–82
author, children's author, religious author
Philadelphia, PA
Cyc Am Bio; Dict Am Auth; Nat Cyc Am Bio v13

7824. Lewis, Grace Anna
born 1821
naturalist, scientific illustrator, science writer, conservationist, ornithologist, abolitionist, Underground Railroad operator, pacifist, suffragist, philanthropist
Quaker
Index t Wom; Nat Cyc Am Bio v9; Twent Cen Bio Dict Not Am; Wom Cent

7825. Lowell, Maria (White)
1821–53
poet
Cyc Am Bio; Dict Am Auth; Nat Cyc Am Bio v8; Not Am Wom

7826. Morse, Rebecca A.; Ruth Moza; R. A. Kidder; R. A. K.
born 1821
clubwoman, Sorosis member, suffragist, patron of art, abolitionist, author
New York
Index t Wom; Wom Cent

7827. Neal, Alice B.
married 1846
author, editor
Index t Wom

7828. Richards, Maria Tolman
born 1821
author, educator, lecturer
Providence, RI
Cyc Am Bio; Dict Am Auth

7829. Whitney, Anne
1821–1915
sculptor, artist, poet, abolitionist, suffragist
Boston, MA
Cyc Am Bio; Dict Am Auth; Dict Am Bio; Index t Wom; Nat Cyc Am Bio v7; Not Am Wom; Wom Cent

7830. Agassiz, Elizabeth Cabot Carrie
1822–1907
founder and president of Radcliffe College, educator, biographer, naturalist, science writer
Boston, MA
Dict Am Auth; Dict Am Bio; Index t Wom; Not Am Wom; Wom Cent

7831. Barrow, Frances Elizabeth (Mease); Aunt Fanny
1822–94
children's author
New York, NY
Appl Cyc Am Bio; Dict Am Auth; Index t Wom; Nat Cyc Am Bio v4; Twent Cen Bio Dict Not Am; Wom Cent

7832. Chase, Mary Maria
1822–1852
botanist, poet
Index t Wom

7833. Clarke, Mary Bayard (Devereaux)
1822/27–1886
author, editor, poet
North Carolina
Cyc Am Bio; Dict Am Auth; Dict Am Bio; Nat Cyc Am Bio v8; Not Am Wom; Twent Cen Bio Dict Not Am

7834. Dall, Caroline Wells (Healey)
1822–1912
author, essayist, women's rights worker, women's labor reformer, educator
Boston, MA
Cyc Am Bio; Dict Am Auth; Dict Am Bio; Dict Lit Bio v1; Index t Wom; Nat Cyc Am Bio v9; Not Am Wom; Twent Cen Bio Dict Not Am; Wom Cent

7835. Dufour, Amanda Louise Ruter
born 1822
poet
Wom Cent

7836. Fowler, Lydia Folger
1822/23–1979

physician, lecturer, social reformer, author, astronomer, science writer
Cyc Am Bio; Dict Am Auth; Index t Wom; Not Am Wom

7837. Latimer, [Mary] Elizabeth (Wormeley)
1822–1904
novelist, educator, historian, writer on history
Baltimore, MD
English
Cyc Am Bio; Dict Am Auth; Dict Am Bio; Dict Am Bio Men Time; Index t Wom; Nat Cyc Am Bio v9; Wom Cent

7838. Linton, Eliza Lynn
1822–98
novelist, author
Cyc Am Bio; Dict Nat Bio 1922–1930; Wom Lit; Wom Lit, More

7839. Marshall, Joanna
born 1822
poet
Maryland
Wom Cent

7840. Richards, Cornelia Holroyd (Bradley); Mrs. Manners
1822–92
miscellaneous writer
Cyc Am Bio; Dict Am Auth; Twent Cen Bio Dict Not Am

7841. Tupper, Ellen Smith
born 1822
apiarist, writer on beekeeping, pioneer
Index t Wom; Wom Cent

7842. Weston, Mary Catharine (North)
1822–82
religious writer
Cyc Am Bio; Dict Am Auth

7843. Brittan, Harriet G.
1823–97
missionary to India, writer on India and Africa
Dict Am Auth

7844. Chesnut, Mary Boykin Miller
1823–86
Civil War diarist
Not Am Wom

7845. Davidson, Margaret Miller
1823–38
poet
Cyc Am Bio; Dict Am Auth; Dict Am Bio; Dict Am Bio Men Time; Index t Wom; Nat Cyc Am Bio v7

7846. Farmer, Hannah Tobey Sharpleigh
1823–91
philanthropist, author, poet, religious worker
Dict Am Bio; Index t Wom; Nat Cyc Am Bio v7; Twent Cen Bio Dict Not Am

7847. Hale, Anne Gardner
born 1823
poet, author
Newburyport, CT
Dict Am Auth

7848. Jervey, Caroline Howard (Gilman) Glover
1823–77
children's author, poet, fiction writer
Dict Am Auth; Twent Cen Bio Dict Not Am

7849. Leslie, Susan Inches (Lyman)
1823–1904
biographer, autobiographer
Dict Am Auth

7850. Lippincott, Sarah Jane (Clarke); Grace Greenwood
1823–1904
newspaper journalist, lecturer, author, editor, novelist, feminist, poet, children's author
Philadelphia, PA
Cyc Am Bio; Dict Am Auth; Dict Am Bio; Dict Am Bio Men Time; Index t Wom; Nat Cyc Am Bio v4; Not Am Wom; Twent Cen Bio Dict Not Am; Wom Cent

7851. Mason, Caroline Atherton (Briggs)
1823–90
poet
Fitchburg, MA
Cyc Am Bio; Dict Am Auth

7852. McAdoo, Mary Faith Floyd
born 1823/32
writer of romances
Cyc Am Bio; Dict Am Auth

7853. McCoy, Catherine (Webb) (Towles)
born 1823
fiction writer
Columbus, GA
Dict Am Auth

7854. Palfrey, Sarah H. Hammond Hamilton; E. Foxton
1823–post 1886
author, poet, novelist
Cambridge, MA
Cyc Am Bio; Dict Am Auth; Nat Cyc Am Bio v7; Twent Cen Bio Dict Not Am

7855. Smith, Emeline Sherman
born 1823
poet
Dict Am Bio Men Time

7856. Smith, Eveline Sherman
born 1823
poet
Index t Wom

7857. Stephens, Harriet Marion
1823–1850/58
author, domestic writer, novelist, editor
Cyc Am Bio; Dict Am Auth; Dict Am Bio Men Time

7858. Stoddard, Elizabeth Drew (Barstow)
1823–1902
poet, novelist, children's author
Cyc Am Bio; Dict Am Auth; Dict Am Bio; Nat Cyc Am Bio v8; Twent Cen Bio Dict Not Am; Wom Cent

7859. Sweat, Margaret Jane (Muzzey)
born 1823
writer on travel
Cyc Am Bio; Dict Am Auth; Dict Am Bio Men Time

7860. Thomas, Martha McCannon
born 1823/25
short story writer
Cyc Am Bio; Dict Am Auth

7861. Towles, Catherine Webb
born 1823
author
Cyc Am Bio

7862. Very, Lydia Louise Ann
1823–1901/07
poet, children's author, illustrator, educator
Salem, MA
Cyc Am Bio; Dict Am Auth; Dict Am Bio; Index t Wom; Nat Cyc Am Bio v6; Wom Cent

7863. Worthen, Augusta Harvey
born 1823
educator, author, historian of New Hampshire
New Hampshire
Wom Cent

7864. Berard, Augusta Blanche
1824–1901
writer on the history of West Point, history text author, historian
West Point, NY
Appl Cyc Am Bio; Cyc Am Bio; Dict Am Auth

7865. Blake, Euphemia Vale
1824/25–1904

author, historian, literary and art
    critic
Dict Am Auth; Wom Cent

**7866. Bowen, Sue (Petrigru)
    (King)**
1824–75
novelist
South Carolina
Dict Am Auth

7867. Cary, Phoebe
1824–71
author, poet
Cyc Am Bio; Dict Am Auth; Dict
    Am Bio; Dict Am Bio Men
    Time; Index t Wom; Nat Cyc
    Am Bio v1; Not Am Wom;
    Twent Cen Bio Dict Not Am;
    Wom Cent

**7868. Cheney, Endah Dow (Lit-
    tlehale)**
1824–1904
philanthropist, author, abolition-
    ist, suffragist, women's rights
    worker, Black civil rights work-
    er, lecturer, philosopher
Transcendentalist
Boston, MA
Cyc Am Bio; Dict Am Auth; Dict
    Am Bio; Dict Lit Bio v1; Index
    t Wom; Nat Cyc Am Bio v9;
    Not Am Wom; Twent Cen Bio
    Dict Not Am; Wom Cent

7869. Chesebro, Frances M.
born 1824
poet
Index t Wom

**7870. Fremont, Jessie Ann
    (Benton)**
1824/25–1902
writer
Los Angeles, CA
Dict Am Auth; Dict Am Bio;
    Index t Wom; Nat Cyc Am Bio
    v4; Not Am Wom; Read Encyc
    Am West; Twent Cen Bio Dict
    Not Am; Wom Cent

7871. Harris, Amanda Bartlett
born 1824
author, children's author, maga-
    zine writer, religious author
Warner, NH
Dict Am Auth; Twent Cen Bio
    Dict Not Am

7872. Holstein, Anna
1824–90
author, Civil War nurse
Index t Wom

**7873. Horsford, Mary
    l'Hommedieu (Gardiner)**
1824–55
poet
Dict Am Auth

**7874. Ketchum, Annie Cham-
    bers**
1824–1904
poet, novelist, educator, lecturer
Cyc Am Bio; Dict Am Auth

**7875. Kimball, Harriet MacEw-
    en**
born 1824/34
religious poet
Portsmouth, NH
Cyc Am Bio; Dict Am Auth; Nat
    Cyc Am Bio v11; Wom Cent

7876. Larcom, Lucy
1824/26–1893
millworker, author, poet, maga-
    zine editor, seminary teacher
Beverly, MA
Cyc Am Bio; Dict Am Auth; Dict
    Am Bio Men Time; Index t
    Wom; Nat Cyc Am Bio v1; Not
    Am Wom; Twent Cen Bio Dict
    Not Am; Wom Cent

**7877. Lewis, Estelle Anna
    Blanche (Robinson); Stella**
1824–80
author, dramatist, poet
Brooklyn, NY
Cyc Am Bio; Dict Am Auth; Dict
    Am Bio; Dict Am Bio Men
    Time; Index t Wom; Nat Cyc
    Am Bio v10

**7878. Lowe, Martha Ann (Per-
    ry)**
1824/29–1902
poet, temperance worker, suffrag-
    ist, author
Somerville, MA
Cyc Am Bio; Dict Am Auth;
    Index t Wom; Nat Cyc Am Bio
    v10; Twent Cen Bio Dict Not
    Am; Wom Cent

**7879. Meriwether, Elizabeth
    (Avery)**
1824/32–1916
novelist, women's rights worker,
    suffragist, Prohibition party
    worker
Memphis, TN
Dict Am Auth; Encyc South Hist

7880. Merrill, Catherine
1824–1900
educator, writer on Indiana
Indianapolis, IN
Dict Am Auth

**7881. Moore, Clara Sophia
    (Jessup); Clara Moreton;
    Clara Sophia (Jessup) Bloom-
    field-Moore**
1824–99
author, poet, novelist, philanthro-
    pist, Civil War relief worker

Philadelphia, PA
Cyc Am Bio; Dict Am Auth;
    Index t Wom; Nat Cyc Am Bio
    v9; Not Am Wom; Twent Cen
    Bio Dict Not Am; Wom Cent

**7882. Pike, Mary Hayden
    (Greene)**
1824/27–1908
author, novelist
Cyc Am Bio; Dict Am Auth; Dict
    Am Bio Men Time; Not Am
    Time; Not Am Wom

7883. Post, Caroline Lathrop
born 1824
poet, author
Illinois
Wom Cent

**7884. Shannon, Mary Eulalie
    Fee**
1824–55
poet
Dict Am Bio Men Time

**7885. Soule, Caroline Augusta
    (White)**
1824–1903/04
author, publisher, editor, church
    worker, Universalist minister,
    foreign missionary, social re-
    former, lecturer
Universalist
Cyc Am Bio; Dict Am Auth; Dict
    Am Bio Men Time; Index t
    Wom; Not Am Wom; Twent
    Cen Bio Dict Not Am

7886. Starr, Eliza Allen
1824–1901
writer and lecturer on art and
    religion, poet, author, artist, ed-
    ucator
Chicago, IL
Cyc Am Bio; Dict Am Auth; Dict
    Am Bio; Nat Cyc Am Bio v13;
    Not Am Wom; Twent Cen Bio
    Dict Not Am; Wom Cent

7887. Steele, Rowena Granice
born 1824
journalist, author
California
Wom Cent

**7888. Whitney, Adeline Dutton
    (Train)**
1824–1906
writer of popular didactic verse
    and fiction
Christian Scientist
Milton, MA
Cyc Am Bio; Dict Am Auth; Dict
    Am Bio Men Time; Index t
    Wom; Nat Cyc Am Bio v1; Not
    Am Wom; Twent Cen Bio Dict
    Not Am; Wom Cent

7889. Appleton, Anna E.
born 1825

poet, translator
Index t Wom

**7890. Auber, Virginia Felicia;
    Felicia**
born 1825
poet
Cuban
Appl Cyc Am Bio

**7891. Beauchamp, Mary
    Elizabeth; Filia Ecclesiae**
born 1825
religious author, educator
Wom Cent

**7892. Blackwell, Antoinette
    Louisa (Brown)**
1825–1921
Universalist minister, author, lec-
    turer, temperance worker, aboli-
    tionist, suffragist, women's
    rights worker, philosopher,
    poet, novelist
Unitarian; Congregationalist
Appl Cyc Am Bio; Cyc Am Bio;
    Dict Am Bio; Dict Am Bio Men
    Time; Index t Wom; Nat Cyc
    Am Bio v9 and v29; Not Am
    Wom; Twent Cen Bio Dict Not
    Am; Wom Cent

**7893. Chesebro, Caroline; Che-
    sebrough, Caroline**
1825/28–1873
short story writer, novelist, col-
    lege educator
New York
Cyc Am Bio; Dict Am Auth; Dict
    Am Bio; Dict Am Bio Men
    Time; Nat Cyc Am Bio v22;
    Twent Cen Bio Dict Not Am

**7894. Claflin, Mary Bucklin
    (Davenport)**
1825–96
author
Boston, MA
Dict Am Auth; Twent Cen Bio
    Dict Not Am

**7895. Dahlgren, Madeleine Vin-
    ton [Sara] (Goodard); Cor-
    inne; Cornelia**
1825/35–1898
novelist, translator, antisuffragist
Catholic
Washington, DC
Cyc Am Bio; Dict Am Auth; Dict
    Am Bio; Index t Wom; Nat Cyc
    Am Bio v22; Twent Cen Bio
    Dict Not Am; Wom Cent

**7896. Dorr, Julia Caroline Rip-
    ley**
1825–1913
poet, author, novelist, essayist
Vermont
Cyc Am Bio; Dict Am Auth; Dict
    Am Bio; Index t Wom; Nat Cyc
    Am Bio v6; Twent Cen Bio Dict
    Not Am; Wom Cent

7897. French, Lucy Virginia (Smith)
1825/30–1881
poet, author, editor, educator
Memphis, TN
Cyc Am Bio; Dict Am Auth; Dict Am Bio; Nat Cyc Am Bio v7

7898. Hanson, Eliza Rice
1825–46
author
Cyc Am Bio

7899. Harper, Frances Ellen Watkins
1825–1911
poet, lecturer, author, abolitionist
Black
Dict Am Rel Bio; Encyc Black Am; Index t Wom; Negro Alman; Not Am Wom; Prof Negro Wom v1

7900. Holmes, Mary Jane (Hawes)
1825–1902/07
writer of sentimental novels
New York
Cyc Am Bio; Dict Am Auth; Dict Am Bio; Index t Wom; Nat Cyc Am Bio v8; Not Am Wom; Wom Cent; Wom Lit, More

7901. Johnson, Laura Winthrop
1825–18?
poet, miscellaneous writer
New York, NY
Dict Am Auth

7902. Long, Ellen Call
1825–1905
civic leader, author, planter
Florida
Read Encyc Am West

7903. Merrick, Caroline Elizabeth (Thomas)
1825–1908
suffragist, temperance leader, author on the South
New Orleans, LA
Dict Am Auth; Nat Cyc Am Bio v10; Not Am Wom; Wom Cent

7904. Olmstead, Elizabeth Martha
born 1825
poet
New York
Index t Wom; Wom Cent

7905. Richmond, Euphemia Johnson (Guernsey)
born 1825
fiction author, temperance advocate
Upton, NY
Dict Am Auth; Nat Cyc Am Bio v4; Wom Cent

7906. Robinson, Harriet Jane (Hanson)
1825–1911
suffragist, women's rights worker, feminist, abolitionist, author, poet, dramatist, journalist, merchant
Malden, MA
Cyc Am Bio; Dict Am Auth; Dict Am Bio; Index t Wom; Nat Cyc Am Bio v3; Not Am Wom; Wom Cent

7907. Spencer, Cornelia Ann (Phillips)
1825–1908
historian, history writer, writer on the Civil War era
North Carolina
Dict Am Auth; Dict Am Bio; Not Am Wom

7908. Thomas, Mary von Erden
born 1825
author, novelist, statistician
Washington, DC
Cyc Am Bio; Dict Am Bio

7909. White, Catherine Ann
1825–78
writer on religions, superior of the Convent of the Sacred Heart, Catholic nun, classicist
Catholic
Dict Am Auth

7910. Whittlesey, Sarah Johnson (Cogswell)
1825–96
author, short story writer
Cyc Am Bio; Dict Am Auth

7911. Winthrop, Laura; Emily Hare
born 1825
children's author
Cyc Am Bio

7912. Barrit, Frances (Fuller)
born 1826
poet
Appl Cyc Am Bio

7913. Bostwick, Helen Louise
born 1826
poet
Cyc Am Bio

7914. Bostwick, Helen Louise (Barrow)
born 1826
poet
Ohio
Dict Am Auth; Dict Am Bio Men Time

7915. Davis, Varina Howell
1826–1909
Civil War diarist, journalist, Confederate patriot of Civil War
Bio Dict Confed; Encyc South Hist; Index t Wom; Wom Cent

7916. Denison, Mary Ann Andrews; Mrs. C. W. D.
1826–1911
novelist, short story writer, Civil War nurse
Cyc Am Bio; Dict Am Auth; Dict Am Bio Men Time; Nat Cyc Am Bio v19; Not Am Wom; Twent Cen Bio Dict Not Am

7917. Dubose, Catherine Anne (Richards)
born 1826
poet, Sunday school story writer
Georgia
Cyc Am Bio; Dict Am Auth

7918. Dunham, Emma Bedelia
born 1826
poet
Universalist
Wom Cent

7919. Ford, Emily Ellsworth (Fowler)
1826–93
author, poet
Brooklyn, NY
Dict Am Auth; Nat Cyc Am Bio v13

7920. Gage, Matilda Joslyn
1826–98
feminist, suffragist, abolitionist, author, lecturer
Cyc Am Bio; Dict Am Auth; Dict Am Bio; Index t Wom; Nat Cyc Am Bio v2; Not Am Wom; Twent Cen Bio Dict Not Am; Wom Cent

7921. Gorton, Cynthia M. R.; Ida Glenwood; The Sweet Singer; The Blind Bard of Michigan
born 1826
poet, author, lecturer
Michigan
blind
Wom Cent

7922. Griswold, Frances Irene (Burge); F. Burge Smith
1826–1900
author, religious writer for children
Brooklyn, NY
Dict Am Auth; Wom Cent

7923. Guernsey, Lucy Ellen
1826–99
children's author
Dict Am Auth; Nat Cyc Am Bio v6

7924. Jeffrey, Rosa Vertner (Griffith) (Johnson); Rosa
1826/28–1894
poet, novelist, dramatist
Lexington, KY
Cyc Am Bio; Dict Am Auth; Dict Am Bio; Nat Cyc Am Bio v11; Wom Cent

7925. Lamb, Martha Joanna Read (Nash)
1826/29–1893
author, children's author, novelist, New York historian, editor
New York
Cyc Am Bio; Dict Am Auth; Dict Am Bio; Index t Wom; Nat Cyc Am Bio v1; Not Am Wom; Twent Cen Bio Dict Not Am; Wom Cent

7926. Nash, Mary Louise
born 1826
educator, author, humorist, botanist, geologist
Wom Cent

7927. Penny, Virginia
born 1826
author, educator, women's labor reform worker, feminist
Cyc Am Bio; Dict Am Auth; Dict Am Bio Men Time

7928. Piatt, Louise Kirby
1826–64
author
Cyc Am Bio

7929. Sherwood, Mary Elizabeth (Wilson); M. E. W. S.
1826/30–1903
short story writer, poet, novelist, miscellaneous writer, patron of literature and science, philanthropist
Washington, DC
Cyc Am Bio; Dict Am Auth; Dict Am Bio; Index t Wom; Nat Cyc Am Bio v5; Wom Cent

7930. Turner, Eliza L. Sproat Randolph
1826–1903
author, poet, suffragist, women's club leader
Pennsylvania
Dict Am Auth; Not Am Wom

7931. Victor, Frances Auretta (Fuller) (Barrett); Florence Fane
1826–1902
author, historian of the Pacific Northwest
Oregon; California
Cyc Am Bio; Dict Am Auth; Dict Am Bio; Nat Cyc Am Bio v13; Not Am Wom; Twent Cen Bio Dict Not Am; Wom Cent

7932. Williams, Mary Busnell
born 1826
author
Cyc Am Bio

**7933. Wood, Julia Amanda A.
(Sargent); Minnie Mary Lee**
born 1826
author, postmaster, pioneer, Minnesota newspaper editor, Catholic novelist
Catholic
Sauk Rapids, MN
Dict Am Auth; Index t Wom;
Not Am Wom; Wom Cent

7934. Youmans, Eliza Ann
born 1826
botanist, writer on botany, cookbook author
Cyc Am Bio; Dict Am Auth; Nat
Cyc Am Bio v5

**7935. Beers, Ethelinda Eliot;
Ethel Lynn**
1827–79
poet, children's author, lyricist
Appl Cyc Am Bio; Cyc Am Bio;
Bio Dict Am Auth; Dict Am
Bio; Index t Wom; Nat Cyc Am
Bio v8; Twent Cen Bio Dict Not
Am

**7936. Boyd, Louise Esther
Vickroy**
born 1827
author
Wom Cent

7937. Cooke, Rose (Terry)
1827–92
author, poet
Connecticut
Cyc Am Bio; Dict Am Auth; Dict
Am Bio; Index t Wom; Nat Cyc
Am Bio v6; Not Am Wom;
Twent Cen Bio Dict Not Am;
Wom Cent; Wom Lit; Wom Lit,
More

7938. Creswell, Julia (Pleasants)
1827–86
poet, novelist
Alabama
Cyc Am Bio; Dict Am Bio

7939. Cummins, Maria Susanna
1827/28–1866
novelist
Massachusetts
Cyc Am Bio; Dict Am Auth; Dict
Am Bio; Dict Am Bio Men
Time; Index t Wom; Nat Cyc
Am Bio v6; Twent Cen Bio Dict
Not Am; Wom Lit; Wom Lit,
More

**7940. Curtis, Caroline Gardiner
(Cary); Carroll Winchester**
born 1827
novelist

Boston, MA
Dict Am Auth

**7941. Drinker, Anne; Edith
May**
born 1827
poet
Montrose, PA
Dict Am Auth; Dict Am Bio Men
Time; Nat Cyc Am Bio v11

**7942. Gillette, Lucia Fidelia
(Woolley); Lyra; Carrie
Russell**
born 1827
Universalist minister, author,
poet
Universalist
Dict Am Auth; Index t Wom;
Wom Cent

**7943. Goodwin, Hannah
Elizabeth (Bradbury)**
1827–93
children's author
Boston, MA
Dict Am Auth; Wom Cent

**7944. Greenough, Sara Dana
(Loring)**
1827–85
fiction writer, poet
Cyc Am Bio; Dict Am Auth

**7945. Guild, Caroline Snowden
(Whitmarsh)**
1827–98
religious author
Boston, MA
Dict Am Auth

**7946. Haven, Alice Bradley;
Emily Bradley Neal Haven;
Alice G. Lee; Cousin Alice**
1827/28–1863
author, children's author, magazine editor
Cyc Am Bio; Dict Am Auth; Dict
Am Bio; Dict Am Bio Men
Time; Nat Cyc Am Bio v5; Not
Am Wom; Twent Cen Bio Dict
Not Am

7947. Howarth, Ellen Clementine (Doran)
1827–99
poet
Trenton, NJ
Dict Am Auth; Nat Cyc Am Bio
v7

**7948. Parker, Helen Eliza
Fitch**
1827–74
miscellaneous writer, marine naturalist
Cyc Am Bio; Dict Am Auth;
Twent Cen Bio Dict Not Am

**7949. Rice, Rosella; Pipsissiway
Pobbs**
1827–18?

author, lecturer, novelist
Cyc Am Bio; Dict Am Auth; Nat
Cyc Am Bio v5

**7950. Rich, Helen (Hinsdale);
The Poet of the Adirondacks**
born 1827
poet, suffragist
Chicago, IL
Dict Am Auth; Index t Wom;
Wom Cent

**7951. Roberts, Anna Smith
(Rickey)**
1827–58
poet
Cyc Am Bio; Dict Am Auth; Dict
Am Bio Men Time

**7952. Robinson, Sarah Tappan
Doolittle (Lawrence)**
born 1827
author, historian of Kansas
Lawrence, KS
Cyc Am Bio; Dict Am Auth;
Twent Cen Bio Dict Not Am

**7953. Slenker, Elmina (Drake);
Aunt Elmina**
born 1827
miscellaneous author, abolitionist
Snowville, VA
Cyc Am Bio; Dict Am Auth; Nat
Cyc Am Bio v7

7954. Terry, Rose
born 1827
poet
Index t Wom

7955. Wheeler, Candace (Thurber)
1827–1923
pioneer in American textile design, interior decorator, artist, needleworker, writer on artistic technique, fairy tale writer
New York, NY
Dict Am Auth; Index t Wom;
Not Am Wom

7956. White, Ellen Gould Harmon
1827–1915
cofounder of the Seventh-Day Adventists, theologian, religious writer
Seventh-Day Adventist
Dict Am Auth; Dict Am Bio;
Dict Am Rel Bio; Index t Wom;
Not Am Wom

**7957. Whitmarsh, Caroline
Snowden**
1827–98
author
Cyc Am Bio

**7958. Wittenmyer, Annie
(Turner)**
1827–1900

Civil War relief worker, leader in church and charitable work, philanthropist, temperance worker, lecturer, author
Ohio
Index t Wom; Nat Cyc Am Bio
v12; Not Am Wom; Wom Cent

7959. Aldrich, Susanna Valentine
born 1828
author
Wom Cent

**7960. Ballard, Julia Perkins
(Pratt)**
1828–94
children's author
Dict Am Auth

7961. Beaumont, Betty Bentley
born 1828
author, milliner, merchant
Wom Cent

7962. Blackwell, Sarah Ellen
born 1828
artist, author, suffragist, land and labor reformer, antivivisectionist
Nat Cyc Am Bio v9; Wom Cent

7963. Bowen, Eliza Andrews
1828–98
newspaper and magazine writer, writer about astronomy
Georgia
Dict Am Auth

7964. Chandler, Lucinda Banister
born 1828
political author, temperance worker, political economist
Wom Cent

7965. Cumming, Kate
1828/35–1909
Confederate hospital administrator, diarist, nurse
Alabama
Scottish
Dict Am Auth; Index t Wom;
Not Am Wom

**7966. Finley, Martha; Martha
Farquharson**
1828–1909
poet, author, children's author, writer of religious and moral tales
Maryland
Cyc Am Bio; Dict Am Auth; Dict
Am Bio; Index t Wom; Nat Cyc
Am Bio v11; Twent Cen Bio
Dict Not Am; Wom Cent

7967. Ford, Sally Rochester
born 1828
author

St. Louis, MO
Cyc Am Bio; Dict Am Auth;
Twent Cen Bio Dict Not Am

7968. Gilchrist, Anne
1828–85
author
Index t Wom

**7969. Goff, Harriet Newell
(Kneeland)**
born 1828
temperance reformer, author, suffragist, women's prison reformer, essayist
Brooklyn, NY
Dict Am Auth; Wom Cent

**7970. Goff, Harriet Newell
(Kneeland)**
born 1828
temperance reformer, author, suffragist, women's prison reformer, essayist
Brooklyn, NY
Dict Am Auth; Wom Cent

7971. Hemenway, Abby Maria
1828–90
Vermont historian, anthologist, author
Vermont
Dict Am Auth; Not Am Wom;
Twent Cen Bio Dict Not Am

**7972. Kirkland, Elizabeth
Stansbury**
1828–96
miscellaneous writer, educator
Dict Am Auth; Twent Cen Bio
Dict Not Am

**7973. Lawson, Mary J.; M. J.
K.; M. J. K. L.**
born 1828
author
Anglican
Wom Cent

**7974. Leonard, Cynthia H. van
Name**
born 1828
philanthropist, author
Illinois
Index t Wom; Wom Cent

**7975. Pember, Phoebe Yates
Levy**
1828–1913
Confederate hospital administrator and nurse, diarist
Index t Wom; Not Am Wom

7976. Ralston, Harriet Newell
born 1828
poet
Wom Cent

**7977. Sturges, Mary Jane
(Upshur) (Stith); Fanny Fielding**
born 1828

novelist, poet
New York, NY
Cyc Am Bio; Dict Am Auth

7978. Ware, Mary (Harris)
born 1828
poet
Alabama
Wom Cent

7979. Wells, Emmeline Blanchard Woodward
1828–1921
leader of Mormon women, feminist, suffragist, editor, poet
Mormon
Utah
Cyc Am Bio; Not Am Wom

**7980. Woodward, Caroline
Marshall**
1828–90
author, artist
Indiana
Wom Cent

7981. Badger, Mrs.
flourished 1859
artist, author
Index t Wom

7982. Brooks, Marie Sears
flourished 1859; died 1893
poet, short story writer, journalist, newspaper editor, suffragist
Index t Wom; Wom Cent

7983. Darden, Fannie (Baker)
born 1829
poet
Dict Am Auth

7984. Dixon, Susan (Bullitt)
born 1829
American historian, writer on history
Kentucky
Dict Am Auth; Nat Cyc Am Bio
v13

7985. Dorsey, Sarah Anne (Ellis); Filia Ecclesiae
1829–79
Civil War nurse, author, novelist, theologian
Mississippi
Cyc Am Bio; Dict Am Auth;
Index t Wom; Nat Cyc Am Bio
v3; Not Am Wom; Twent Cen
Bio Dict Not Am

7986. Gay, Mary Ann Harris
born 1829
Civil War diarist
Index t Wom

**7987. Hanaford, Phoebe Ann
(Coffin)**
1829–1921
Universalist minister, historian, journalist, author, feminist, lec-

turer, chaplain of the Connecticut state legislature
Universalist
New Haven, CT
Cyc Am Bio; Dict Am Auth; Dict
Am Bio; Index t Wom; Nat Cyc
Am Bio v13; Not Am Wom;
Twent Cen Bio Dict Not Am;
Wom Cent

7988. Hentz, Julia L.
1829–79
poet
Cyc Am Bio

**7989. Lincoln, Jane Elizabeth
(Larcombe); Kate Campbell**
born 1829
author
Baptist
Cyc Am Bio

7990. Meriwether, Lide
born 1829
author, lecturer, temperance worker, suffragist
Tennessee
Wom Cent

7991. Oakey, Emily Sullivan
1829–83
author, poet, educator
Albany, NY
Cyc Am Bio; Dict Am Auth

**7992. Patton, Abigail Jemima;
Abby Hutchinson**
1829–92
alto singer, composer, poet, social reformer, abolitionist, suffragist, hymn writer, feminist
New York; New Hampshire
Nat Cyc Am Bio v10; Wom Cent;
Not Am Wom; Index t Wom

**7993. Sherwood, Emily Lee;
Jennie Crayon**
born 1829/43
journalist, novelist, author
Washington, DC
Dict Am Auth; Index t Wom;
Wom Cent

7994. Taylor, Martha Smith
born 1829
author, newspaper correspondent, temperance worker
Wom Cent

**7995. van Deusen, Mary
(Westbrook)**
born 1829
religious writer, novelist, poet
Rondout, NY
Dict Am Auth; Wom Cent

**7996. Waite, Catharine (Van
Valkenburg)**
1829–1913
suffragist, women's rights advocate, lawyer, legal journalist, financier, real estate and building

executive, writer on Mormonism
Chicago, IL
Cyc Am Bio; Dict Am Auth; Not
Am Wom; Wom Cent

7997. Warren, Mary Evalin
born 1829
author, lecturer, temperance worker, suffragist
Baptist
Wisconsin
Wom Cent

7998. A. M. B., Miss
flourished 1860s
Civil War diarist
Index t Wom

7999. Agnes
flourished 1860s
Civil War diarist
Index t Wom

8000. Alder, Emily
flourished 1860s
Civil War nurse
Index t Wom

**8001. Ames, Eleanor Maria
Easterbrook; Eleanor Kirkips**
born 1830
author
New York
Dict Am Auth; Wom Cent

8002. Arnold, Mary Ellen
flourished 1860s
Civil War diarist
Index t Wom

**8003. Avery, Rosa Miller; Sue
Smith**
1830–94
author, abolitionist, suffragist
Index t Wom; Nat Cyc Am Bio
v6; Wom Cent

8004. Ballou, Addie L.
flourished 1860s
Civil War nurse, author, artist, lawyer
Index t Wom

8005. Bicknell, Anna Louise
born 183?
historian, biographer
Dict Am Auth

8006. Brooks, Mary Frances
flourished 1860s
Civil War diarist
Index t Wom

8007. Byson, Mary
flourished 1860s
Civil War diarist
Index t Wom

8008. Cahal, Mary
flourished 1860s

Civil War diarist
Index t Wom

8009. Campbell, Valeria
flourished 1860s
Civil War relief worker, author
Index t Wom

8010. Cary, Constance
flourished 1860s
Civil War diarist
Index t Wom

8011. Coste, Marie Ravenel de la
flourished 1860s
Civil War poet
Index t Wom

8012. Dallas, Mary (Kyle)
1830–97
fiction writer
Philadelphia, PA
Dict Am Auth

8013. Davis, Rebecca (Blaine) Harding
1830/31–1910
children's author, novelist
Cyc Am Bio and ad v2; Dict Am Auth; Dict Am Bio; Index t Wom; Nat Cyc Am Bio v8; Not Am Wom; Twent Cen Bio Dict Not Am; Wom Cent; Wom Lit

8014. Dickinson, Emily Elizabeth
1830–86
poet, letter writer
Amherst, MA
Dict Am Auth; Dict Lit Bio v1; Index t Wom; Nat Cyc Am Bio v11 and v23; Nort Anth Poet; Not Am Wom; Twent Cen Bio Dict Not Am

8015. Dodge, Mary Abigail ''Abby''; Gail Hamilton
1830/36–1896
author, essayist, humorist, magazine writer, editor, abolitionist, suffragist, women's rights worker
Massachusetts
Cyc Am Bio; Dict Am Auth; Dict Am Bio; Dict Am Bio Men Time; Index t Wom; Nat Cyc Am Bio v9; Not Am Wom; Twent Cen Bio Dict Not Am; Wom Cent

8016. Duckett, Elizabeth Waring
flourished 1860s
author, Civil War spy
Index t Wom

8017. Edmondson, Belle
flourished 1860s
Civil War diarist
Index t Wom

8018. Edmondston, Catherine Ann
flourished 1860s
Civil War letter writer
Index t Wom

8019. Edson, Sarah P.
flourished 1860s
Civil War nurse, author
Index t Wom

8020. Ellsworth, Mary Wolcott (Janvrin)
1830–70
magazine writer
Cyc Am Bio; Dict Am Auth; Dict Am Bio Men Time; Nat Cyc Am Bio v11

8021. Gilmer, Louisa Fredericka
flourished 1860s
Civil War diarist
Index t Wom

8022. Gilmer, Loulie
flourished 1860s
Civil War diarist
Index t Wom

8023. Groenevelt, Sara; Stanley M. Bartlett
flourished 1860s
pianist, poet
Wom Cent

8024. Hall, Dorian, Mrs.
flourished 1860s
Civil War diarist
Index t Wom

8025. Holmes, Mary Sophia (Shaw) (Rogers)
born 1830
author, poet
New Orleans, LA
Dict Am Auth

8026. Hosmer, Margaret (Kerr)
1830–97
novelist, religious writer for children
Philadelphia, PA
Cyc Am Bio; Dict Am Auth

8027. Howe, Caroline Dana
born 183?
poet
Portland, ME
Dict Am Auth

8028. Howland, Eliza W.
flourished 1860s
Civil War nurse, author
Index t Wom

8029. Humphreys, Sarah Gibson
born 1830
author, suffragist
Kentucky
Wom Cent

8030. Jackson, Helen Maria (Fiske) (Hunt); Saxe Holme; H. H.
1830/31–1881/85
author, poet, novelist, crusader for Native American rights, philanthropist
Quaker
Cyc Am Bio; Dict Am Auth; Dict Am Bio; Index t Wom; Nat Cyc Am Bio v1; Read Encyc Am West; Twent Cen Bio Dict Not Am; Wom Cent; Wom Lit, More

8031. Janvrin, Mary W. (Ellsworth)
1830–70
author, poet, magazine writer
Dict Am Bio Men Time

8032. Johnstone, Mary H.
flourished 1860s
Civil War diarist
Index t Wom

8033. Jones, Sarah G.
flourished 1860s
poet, physician
Index t Wom

8034. Jordan, Conrelia Jane (Matthews)
1830–98
poet, Confederate sympathizer
Virginia
Cyc Am Bio; Dict Am Auth; Index t Wom; Wom Cent

8035. Kelly, Amie
flourished 1860s
Civil War diarist
Index t Wom

8036. Lamb, William, Mrs.
flourished 1860s
Civil War diarist
Index t Wom

8037. Lawton, Sarah Alexander
flourished 1860s
Civil War diarist
Index t Wom

8038. Lay, Julia
flourished 1860s
Civil War patriot, author
Index t Wom

8039. le Conte, Emma Florence
flourished 1860s
Civil War diarist
Index t Wom

8040. le Grand, Julia
flourished 1860s
Civil War diarist
Index t Wom

8041. Lee, Henrietta Bedinger
flourished 1860s

Civil War letter writer
Index t Wom

8042. Lowe, Lucy
flourished 1860s
Civil War diarist
Index t Wom

8043. MacKaye, Maria Ellery (Goodwin)
born 1830
educator, author
Cambridge, MA
Dict Am Auth

8044. Mathews, Julia A.
born 183?
writer of Sunday school fiction
Dict Am Auth

8045. Maury, Betty Herndon
flourished 1860s
Civil War diarist
Index t Wom

8046. Miller, Dora Richards
flourished 1860s–80s
author, Civil War diarist, journalist, educator
West Indian (Danish West Indies)
Index t Wom; Wom Cent

8047. Morgan, Martha Ready
flourished 1860s
Civil War diarist
Index t Wom

8048. Patterson, Minnie Ward; Zinobar Green
flourished 1860s–90s
poet, author
Michigan
Wom Cent

8049. Perkins, Anne
flourished 1860s
Civil War letter writer
Index t Wom

8050. Phillips, Josephine
flourished 1860s
Civil War patriot, author
Index t Wom

8051. Prichard, Sarah Johnson
born 1830
children's author, fiction writer
Waterbury, CT
Dict Am Auth; Twent Cen Bio Dict Not Am

8052. Pryor, Sara Agnes Rice
1830–1912
author, Civil War hero
Index t Wom; Not Am Wom

8053. Pugh, Mary Williams
flourished 1860s
Civil War diarist
Index t Wom

8054. Ravenel, Charlotte St. Julien
flourished 1860s
Civil War diarist
Index t Wom

8055. Rawson, Mary
flourished 1860s
Civil War diarist
Index t Wom

8056. Ready, Alice
flourished 1860s
Civil War diarist
Index t Wom

8057. Ridley, Rebeccah C.
flourished 1860s
Civil War diarist
Index t Wom

8058. Ritter, Frances Malone (Raymond) "Fannie"
1830–90
writer on music, song compiler, mezzo-soprano vocalist, poet
Cyc Am Bio; Dict Am Auth; Twent Cen Bio Dict Not Am

8059. Sansom, Emma
flourished 1860s; died 1900
Civil War hero, diarist
Index t Wom

8060. Scales, Cordelia Lewis
flourished 1860s
Civil War diarist
Index t Wom

8061. Sedgewick, Elizabeth Dwight
flourished 1860s
author
Cyc Am Bio

8062. Sims, Leora
flourished 1860s
Civil War diarist
Index t Wom

8063. Smiley, Sarah Frances
born 1830
clergyperson, author
Index t Wom

8064. Smith, J. Henry, Mrs.
flourished 1860s
Civil War author
Index t Wom

8065. Smith, Lucy
flourished 1860s
Civil War diarist
Index t Wom

8066. Souder, Emily Bliss
flourished 1860s
Civil War patriot, author
Index t Wom

8067. Stickney, Julia Granby (Noyes)
born 1830
poet
Groveland, MA
Dict Am Auth

8068. Stinson, Virginia McCollum
flourished 1860s
Civil War diarist
Index t Wom

8069. Stranahan, Clara Harrison
183?–post 1890
writer on art
Boston, MA
Dict Am Auth; Wom Cent

8070. Sutherlin, W. T., Mrs.
flourished 1860s
Civil War diarist
Index t Wom

8071. Tenney, Abby Amy Grove
flourished 1860s–70s
naturalist, science writer
Cyc Am Bio

8072. Terhune, Mary Virginia (Hawes); Marian Harland
1830/35–1922
popular novelist, writer on household affairs, historian, cookbook author, editor, publisher
New York, NY
Cyc Am Bio; Dict Am Auth; Dict Am Bio; Dict Am Bio Men Time; Index t Wom; Nat Cyc Am Bio v1; Not Am Wom; Twent Cen Bio Dict Not Am; Wom Cent

8073. Thompson, Ella Mason (Williams)
183?–75
author
Newton, MA
Dict Am Auth

8074. Townsend, Virginia Frances
1830/36–1914/20
author, novelist, children's author, editor
Cyc Am Bio; Dict Am Auth; Dict Am Bio; Index t Wom; Nat Cyc Am Bio v13; Twent Cen Bio Dict Not Am

8075. Treat, Mary Lua Adelia (Davis) (Allen)
born 1830/35
scientific author, naturalist
Vineland, NJ
Dict Am Auth; Index t Wom

8076. Vingut, Gertrude
born 1830

author
Cyc Am Bio

8077. Wadley, Sarah L.
flourished 1860s
Civil War diarist
Index t Wom

8078. Wallace, Susan (Arnold) (Elston)
1830–1907
miscellaneous author, poet, religious writer, philanthropist
Indiana
Cyc Am Bio and ad; Dict Am Auth; Index t Wom; Nat Cyc Am Bio v10; Twent Cen Bio Dict Not Am; Wom Cent

8079. Waring, Mary D.
flourished 1860s
Civil War diarist
Index t Wom

8080. Webber, Mary T.
flourished 1860s
poet
Index t Wom

8081. Wilcox, G. Griffin, Mrs.
flourished 1860s
Civil War diarist
Index t Wom

8082. Wilson, Jane Delaplaine; Mrs. Lawrence
born 1830
author, short story writer
Wom Cent

8083. Wister, Annis Lee Furness "Anna"
1830–1908
traveler, translator of German novels
Cyc Am Bio; Dict Am Auth; Index t Wom

8084. Woolsey, Caroline Caisson
flourished 1860s
Civil War nurse, author
Index t Wom

8085. Woolsey, Harriet Roosevelt "Hatty"
flourished 1860s
Civil War nurse, author
Index t Wom

8086. Woolsey, Jane Stuart
1830–91
Civil War relief and hospital worker, charity and educational worker, nurse, author
Index t Wom; Not Am Wom

8087. Wormeley, Katharine Prescott
1830/32–1908
Civil War relief and hospital worker, writer on sanitation,

charity worker, philanthropist, translator, biographer
Rhode Island
English
Cyc Am Bio; Dict Am Bio; Index t Wom; Nat Cyc Am Bio v8; Not Am Wom; Twent Cen Bio Dict Not Am; Wom Cent

8088. Ames, Mary E. Clemmer; Mrs. Hudson
1831/40–1884
journalist, biographer, author
Washington, DC
Appl Cyc Am Bio; Cyc Am Bio; Index t Wom; Nat Cyc Am Bio v7; Not Am Wom; Twent Cen Bio Dict Not Am

8089. Austin, Jane Goodwin
1831–94
historical novelist
Boston, MA
Dict Am Auth; Dict Am Bio; Index t Wom; Nat Cyc Am Bio v6; Twent Cen Bio Dict Not Am; Wom Cent

8090. Barr, Amelia Edith Huddleston
1831/32–1919
novelist
English
Appl Cyc Am Bio; Cyc Am Bio; Dict Am Auth; Dict Am Bio; Index t Wom; Nat Cyc Am Bio v4; Not Am Wom; Twent Cen Bio Dict Not Am; Wom Cent

8091. Booth, Mary H. C.
1831–65
poet
Cyc Am Bio; Dict Am Bio Men Time

8092. Church, Ella Rodman (MacIlvane)
born 1831
author
Dict Am Auth

8093. Clark, Mary (Latham)
born 1831
Sunday school story writer
Maine
Dict Am Auth

8094. Clarke, Mary Basset; Ida Fairfield
born 1831
author, poet
Seventh-Day Baptist
Wom Cent

8095. Conklin, Jane Elizabeth Dexter
born 1831
poet, religious writer
Binghamton, NY
Wom Cent

8096. Cutler, Lizzie Petit
1831/36–1902
novelist
New York, NY
Cyc Am Bio; Dict Am Auth; Dict
Am Bio

8097. Davis, Caroline E.
born 1831
children's author, religious writer
Cyc Am Bio; Dict Am Auth

**8098. Dodge, Mary Elizabeth
Mapes**
1831/38–1905
children's author, poet, editor
New York
Cyc Am Bio; Dict Am Auth; Dict
Am Bio; Index t Wom; Nat Cyc
Am Bio v1; Not Am Wom;
Twent Cen Bio Dict Not Am;
Wom Cent

8099. Douglas, Amanda Minnie
1831/38–1916
short story writer, novelist, chil-
dren's author
Newark, NJ
Cyc Am Bio; Dict Am Auth; Dict
Am Bio; Index t Wom; Twent
Cen Bio Dict Not Am; Wom
Cent

8100. Dunning, Annie Ketchum;
Nellie Grahame
born 1831
author, Sunday school story writ-
er
Presbyterian
Cyc Am Bio; Dict Am Auth;
Twent Cen Bio Dict Not Am

8101. Eyster, Nellie Blessing
born 1831
author, children's author, temperance reformer, worker for Chinese American welfare
Pennsylvania; California
Cyc Am Bio; Dict Am Auth; Nat
Cyc Am Bio v10; Twent Cen
Bio Dict Not Am; Wom Cent

**8102. Fassett, Cornelia Adele
(Strong)**
1831–98
artist, painter, author
Cyc Am Bio; Dict Am Bio; Index
t Wom; Twent Cen Bio Dict
Not Am

8103. Hunt, Helen Fiske
born 1831
author
Index t Wom

8104. Lockwood, Mary Smith
born 1831
editor, clubwoman, patriot, writer
on art and architecture
Dict Am Auth; Index t Wom;
Nat Cyc Am Bio v3

8105. Miller, Harriet (Mann);
Olive Thorne Miller
1831–1918
author, ornithologist, bird watch-
er, naturalist, nature writer,
conservationist, children's au-
thor, magazine writer
Swedenborgian
Brooklyn, NY
Dict Am Auth; Index t Wom;
Nat Cyc Am Bio v9; Not Am
Wom; Twent Cen Bio Dict Not
Am

8106. Nutting, Mary Olivia
1831–1910
author, historian, educator, librarian, autobiographer
Dict Am Auth; Index t Wom

8107. Perry, Nora
1831/41–1896
poet, children's author, journalist
Boston, MA
Cyc Am Bio; Dict Am Auth; Dict
Am Bio; Index t Wom; Nat Cyc
Am Bio v15; Twent Cen Bio
Dict Not Am; Wom Cent

8108. Ripley, Mary A.
born 1831
poet, educator, lecturer, author
Index t Wom; Wom Cent

**8109. Rollins, Ellen Chapman
(Hobbs); E. H. Arr**
1831–81
writer on history
Philadelphia, PA
Cyc Am Bio; Dict Am Auth

8110. Tincker, Mary Agnes
1831/37–1907
novelist, Civil War nurse
Catholic
Cyc Am Bio; Dict Am Bio; Nat
Cyc Am Bio v8; Twent Cen Bio
Dict Not Am

8111. Torrey, Mary Cutler
born 1831
author
Cyc Am Bio

**8112. Victor, Metta Victoria
(Fuller); Seeley Register; The
Singing Sibyl**
1831/51–1885/86
popular author, novelist, poet
New York, NY
Cyc Am Bio; Dict Am Auth; Dict
Am Bio Men Time; Index t
Wom; Nat Cyc Am Bio v4; Not
Am Wom; Twent Cen Bio Dict
Not Am; Wom Cent

8113. Alcott, Louisa May
1832–88
novelist, children's author, mystery story writer

English
Appl Cyc Am Bio; Cyc Am Bio;
Dict Am Auth; Dict Am Bio;
Dict Lit Bio; Index t Wom; Nat
Cyc Am Bio v1; Not Am Wom;
Wom Lit; Wom Lit, More;
Wom Cent

**8114. Allen, Elizabeth Anne
Chase (Akers); Florence Per-
cyips**
1832–1911
poet, journalist, author, Sorosis
Club member
Appl Cyc Am Bio; Cyc Am Bio;
Dict Am Auth; Index t Wom;
Nat Cyc Am Bio v6; Not Am
Wom; Twent Cen Bio Dict Not
Am; Wom Cent

8115. Chitwood, M. Louisa
1832–55
poet
Dict Am Bio Men Time

**8116. Fairfield, Genevieve Ge-
nevra**
born 1832
novelist
Dict Am Auth; Dict Am Bio Men
Time

8117. Gordon, S. Anna
born 1832
homeopathic physician, Civil War
doctor, author, temperance
worker, meteorologist
Wom Cent

8118. Hiles, Osia Joslyn
born 1832
philanthropist, poet, Native
American welfare worker
Wisconsin
Wom Cent

**8119. Hinsdale, Grace Webster
(Haddock)**
born 1832
hymn writer, religious author
New York, NY
Dict Am Auth; Nat Cyc Am Bio
v9

8120. Ingham, Mary Bigelow;
Anne Hathaway
born 1832
author, temperance worker,
Methodist Episcopal missionary
and religious worker
Methodist Episcopal
Wom Cent

8121. Jackson, Mary Anna
married 1857
Civil War diarist
Index t Wom

8122. Knowlton, Helen Mary
1832–1918
painter, art educator, writer on
art and art technique

Boston, MA
Cyc Am Bio; Dict Am Auth; Not
Am Wom; Twent Cen Bio Dict
Not Am

**8123. Leprohan, Rosanna Eleo-
nora**
1832–79
poet, novelist
Canadian
Cyc Am Bio; Wom Cent

8124. Magill, Mary Tucker
1832–99
fiction writer, journalist, educator
Winchester, VA
Cyc Am Bio; Dict Am Auth;
Twent Cen Bio Dict Not Am

**8125. Morrison, Mary Jane
(Whitney)**
1832–1904
short story writer
Waltham, MA
Dict Am Auth

8126. Nevius, Helen S. (Coan)
born 1832
religious author
Dict Am Auth

8127. Perkins, Jennie Saunders
born 1832
poet
Twent Cen Bio Dict Not Am

**8128. Ravenel, Harriot Horry
(Rutledge)**
1832–1912
author, biographer
Charleston, SC
Dict Am Auth; Dict Am Bio

8129. Reese, Mary Bynon
born 1832
temperance worker, poet, Civil
War humanitarian, Union sympathizer
Wom Cent

8130. Smith, Hannah Whitall
1832–1911
religious author, evangelist, pacifist, temperance worker, wom-
en's rights worker
Quaker
Dict Am Bio; Index t Wom; Not
Am Wom

8131. Springer, Rebecca (Ruter)
1832–1904
novelist, poet
Illinois
Cyc Am Bio; Dict Am Auth;
Index t Wom; Twent Cen Bio
Dict Not Am; Wom Cent

**8132. Townsend, Mary Ashley
(van Voorhees); Xariffa**
1832/36–1901
author, poet

New Orleans, LA
Cyc Am Bio; Dict Am Auth; Dict
Am Bio; Nat Cyc Am Bio v11;
Twent Cen Bio Dict Not Am;
Wom Cent

8133. Walworth, Ellen (Hardin)
1832–1915
author, war nurse, writer on the
history of Saratoga, educator,
poet
Saratoga, NY
Cyc Am Bio and ad; Dict Am
Auth; Index t Wom; Twent Cen
Bio Dict Not Am; Wom Cent

**8134. Woodruff, Julia Louisa
Matilda (Curtiss); W. M. L.
Jan**
born 1832
author, compiler
New York, NY
Dict Am Auth

8135. Andrews, Jane
1833–87
educator, children's author
Dict Am Auth; Index t Wom;
Not Am Wom

**8136. Bianciardi, Elizabeth
Dickinson (Rice)**
circa 1833–85
travel writer
Dict Am Auth

**8137. Blake, Lillie Devereaux
(Umstead)**
1833/35–1913
suffragist, women's rights worker,
magazine writer, short story
writer
Appl Cyc Am Bio; Cyc Am Bio;
Dict Am Auth; Dict Am Bio;
Index t Wom; Nat Cyc Am Bio
v11; Not Am Wom; Twent Cen
Bio Dict Not Am; Wom Cent

8138. Boya, Ellen Wright
born 1833
educator, author on religious education, writer on art and architecture
Albany, NY
Dict Am Auth

8139. Brigham, Sarah Prentice
born 1833
children's author
Dict Am Auth

8140. Carey, Emma Forbes
born 1833
humanitarian, author
Index t Wom

**8141. Clarke, Rebecca Sophia;
Sophie May**
1833–1906
children's author

Maine
Dict Am Auth; Dict Am Bio;
Index t Wom; Nat Cyc Am Bio
v8; Not Am Wom; Twent Cen
Bio Dict Not Am; Wom Cent

**8142. Evans, Elizabeth Edson
(Gibson)**
born 1833
essayist, short story writer
Rhode Island
Cyc Am Bio; Dict Am Auth;
Twent Cen Bio Dict Not Am

**8143. Goodwin, Lavinia Stella
(Tyler)**
born 1833
author, children's author, poet,
educator
Dict Am Auth; Wom Cent

8144. Hale, Susan
1833/38–1910
author, children's author, travel
writer, artist, painter
Cyc Am Bio; Dict Am Auth;
Index t Wom; Not Am Wom;
Twent Cen Bio Dict Not Am

8145. Hentz, Caroline Therese
born 1833
author
Cyc Am Bio

8146. Jones, Jennie E.
born 1833
poet, short story writer
New York
Wom Cent

8147. Lea, Fanny Heaslip
1833–1955
novelist, magazine writer
Nat Cyc Am Bio v42; Obit File

**8148. Miller, Emily Clark
Huntington**
1833–1913
author, children's author, journalist, editor, poet, semireligious-fiction writer, church
worker, temperance worker, educator
Evanston, IL
Dict Am Auth; Dict Am Bio;
Index t Wom; Not Am Wom;
Twent Cen Bio Dict Not Am;
Wom Cent

**8149. Morris, Eugenia Laura
(Tuttle); Alyn Yates Keith**
born 1833
miscellaneous writer
New Haven, CT
Dict Am Auth

**8150. Otis, Eliza Ann (Wether-
by)**
1833–1904
poet, journalist
Nat Cyc Am Bio v14; Wom Cent

**8151. Peebles, Mary Louise
(Parmelee); Lynde Palmer**
1833/34–1915
author of religious tales for children
Cyc Am Bio; Dict Am Auth;
Index t Wom; Nat Cyc Am Bio
v4

**8152. Poole, Hester Martha
(Hunt)**
born 1833/43
author, poet, writer on social and
domestic issues, art critic, artist,
women's rights worker, Sorosis
member
Metuchen, NJ
Dict Am Auth; Nat Cyc Am Bio
v11; Wom Cent

8153. Stockham, Alice (Bunker)
born 1833
physician, medical author, musician, biographer, suffragist
Dict Am Auth; Wom Cent

8154. Wheelock, Julia Susan
born 1833
Civil War nurse, hospital nurse,
author
Cyc Am Bio; Index t Wom

8155. Alden, Emily Gillmore
born 1834
poet
Wom Cent

**8156. Aldrich, Julia Carter; Pe-
tresia Peters**
born 1834
author
Wom Cent

8157. Allen, Esther Lavilla
born 1834
author
Wom Cent

**8158. Banta, Melissa Elizabeth
Riddle**
born 1834
poet
Indiana
Wom Cent

8159. Clement, Clara Erskine
born 1834
author, translator
Cyc Am Bio and ad; Twent Cen
Bio Dict Not Am

8160. Cruger, Mary
born 1834
novelist
New York
Dict Am Auth; Wom Cent

8161. Fields, Annie (Adams)
1834–1915
author, poet, literary host

Boston, MA
Dict Am Auth; Dict Am Bio;
Index t Wom; Nat Cyc Am Bio
v1; Not Am Wom; Twent Cen
Bio Dict Not Am

**8162. Gregory, Elizabeth Goad-
by**
born 1834
author, translator of French and
German literature, journalist,
writer on industrial and social
topics
Wom Cent

8163. Harris, Miriam (Coles)
1834–1925
novelist
New York
Cyc Am Bio; Dict Am Auth; Dict
Am Bio; Nat Cyc Am Bio v11;
Twent Cen Bio Dict Not Am

**8164. Hopkins, Louisa Parsons
(Stone)**
1834–95
educator, writer on education,
poet
Boston, MA
Dict Am Auth

8165. Hoyt, Elizabeth Orpha
born 1834
poet
Cyc Am Bio

**8166. Ireland, Mary E.
(Haines)**
born 1834
children's author
Washington, DC
Dict Am Auth; Wom Cent

**8167. Leonowens, Anna Har-
riette (Crawford)**
born 1834
author on Siam, kindergarten educator, missionary educator in
Siam
New York
English
Cyc Am Bio; Dict Am Bio

**8168. MacConaughy, Julia E.
(Loomis)**
born 1834
religious fiction writer for children
Dict Am Auth

8169. Page, Emily Rebecca
1834–62
poet
Vermont
Cyc Am Bio; Dict Am Auth

8170. Palmer, Henrietta Lee
born 1834
writer on Shakespeare
Cyc Am Bio; Dict Am Auth

8171. Pollard, Josephine
1834/42–1892
children's author, journalist, poet
Cyc Am Bio; Dict Am Auth;
Index t Wom; Twent Cen Bio
Dict Not Am; Wom Cent

8172. Rose, Martha E. (Parmelee)
born 1834
women's labor welfare worker,
social reformer, sociologist, author, art patron, journalist, Sorosis member
Cleveland, OH
Index t Wom; Nat Cyc Am Bio
v11; Wom Cent

8173. Shedd, Julia Ann (Clark)
1834–97
writer on art
Cyc Am Bio; Dict Am Auth

8174. Smith, Mary Stewart (Harrison)
born 1834
author, translator, children's author
Virginia
Dict Am Auth; Wom Cent

8175. Waters, Clara (Erskine) (Clement); Clara Clement
1834–1916
author, writer on art, art historian, world traveler
Boston, MA
Dict Am Auth; Index t Wom;
Not Am Wom; Wom Cent;
Wom Lit, More

8176. Willing, Jennie Fowler
1834–1916
Methodist local preacher, church
worker, temperance reformer,
lecturer, author, educator
Methodist
Canadian
Index t Wom; Not Am Wom;
Wom Cent

8177. Allerton, Ellen Palmer
1835–93
poet
Black
Dict Am Auth; Negro Alman

8178. Bompiani, Sophia van Matre
born 1835
writer about Italy
Dict Am Auth

8179. Booth, Emma Scarr
born 1835
author
English
Wom Cent

8180. Bradley, Mary Emily (Neeley)
1835–98

children's author
Dict Am Auth

8181. Brigham, Sarah J. (Lathbury)
born 1835
children's author, illustrator
Dict Am Auth

8182. Bristol, Augusta (Cooper)
1835–1910
educator, writer on education, author, poet, sociologist, lecturer
on philosophic and scientific
topics
Cyc Am Bio and ad; Dict Am
Auth; Twent Cen Bio Dict Not
Am; Wom Cent

8183. Clare, Ada; Jane McEthenrey
1835/36–1874
author, actor
Nat Cyc Am Bio v6; Not Am
Wom

8184. Clarke, Mary Hannah (Gray); Nina Gray; Nina Gray Clarke
1835–92
author, poet
Nat Cyc Am Bio v6; Wom Cent

8185. Corbin, Caroline Elizabeth (Fairfield)
born 1835
fiction writer
Chicago, IL
Dict Am Auth; Index t Wom

8186. Cornell, Ellen Frances
born 1835
poet, marine shell collector
Swedenborgian
Massachusetts
Wom Cent

8187. Cumming, Kate
born circa 1835
poet
Cyc Am Bio

8188. Dana, Katherine (Floyd)
1835–86
author
New York
Dict Am Auth

8189. Davis, Minnie S.
born 1835
author, temperance worker, suffragist, women's rights worker,
"mental science" healer
Index t Wom; Wom Cent

8190. Dole, Phebe Cobb Larry
born 1835
poet
Maine
Wom Cent

8191. Downing, Frances Murdaugh "Fanny"; Frank Dashmore; Viola
1835–94
poet, author, novelist
Charlottesville, VA; North Carolina
Cyc Am Bio; Dict Am Auth; Nat
Cyc Am Bio v7

8192. Elder, Susan (Blanchard); Hermine
1835–1923
religious author, poet, dramatist,
natural scientist
Catholic
New Orleans, LA
Cyc Am Bio; Dict Am Auth; Dict
Am Bio; Nat Cyc Am Bio v11;
Twent Cen Bio Dict Not Am

8193. Eytinge, Rose
1835/38–1911
actor, author, drama teacher
Cyc Am Bio; Dict Am Bio; Index
t Wom; Not Am Wom; Twent
Cen Bio Dict Not Am

8194. Felton, Rebecca Ann Latimer
1835–1930
senator from Georgia, labor welfare worker, journalist, author,
orator, feminist, women's rights
worker
Georgia
Dict Am Bio; Encyc South Hist;
Index t Wom; Nat Cyc Am Bio
v13 and v36; Not Am Wom;
Wom Cent

8195. Frothingham, Ellen
1835–1902
scholar of German literature,
translator, linguist
Boston, MA
Cyc Am Bio; Dict Am Auth;
Index t Wom

8196. Hamilton, Kate Waterman; Fleeta
born 1835/41
religious author for children, novelist
Illinois
Cyc Am Bio; Dict Am Auth; Nat
Cyc Am Bio v4; Twent Cen Bio
Dict Not Am

8197. Hawks, Annie Sherwood
1835–1918
hymn writer, poet
Baptist
New York
Index t Wom; Nat Cyc Am Bio
v17; Wom Cent

8198. Hooper, Lucy Hamilton
1835–93

poet, dramatist, editor, journalist
Cyc Am Bio; Dict Am Bio; Nat
Cyc Am Bio v8; Twent Cen Bio
Dict Not Am; Wom Cent

8199. Johnston, Maria I.
born 1835
author, newspaper editor, women's rights worker
Mississippi
Index t Wom; Wom Cent

8200. Jones, Amanda Theodosia
1835–1914
author, inventor of an improved
process for canning food, poet,
educator
Spiritualist
Chicago, IL
Cyc Am Bio; Dict Am Auth; Dict
Am Bio; Nat Cyc Am Bio v7;
Not Am Wom; Wom Cent

8201. Jordan, Dulcie (Mason)
1835–95
journalist, poet
Richmond, IN
Dict Am Auth

8202. Larned, Augusta
born 1835
author, journalist, poet, women's
rights worker
New York, NY
Cyc Am Bio; Dict Am Auth; Nat
Cyc Am Bio v13; Twent Cen
Bio Dict Not Am

8203. Marr, Frances Harrison
born 1835
poet
Twent Cen Bio Dict Not Am

8204. Menken, Adah Isaachs; Dolores Adios Fuertes
1835/37–1868
actor, poet
Jewish
English
Cyc Am Bio; Dict Am Auth; Dict
Am Bio; Index t Wom; Nat Cyc
Am Bio v5; Not Am Wom;
Wom Lit, More

8205. Miles, Ellen E.
born 1835
poet, educator
Index t Wom

8206. Moulton, [Ellen] Louise (Chandler)
1835–1908
magazine writer, children's author, poet
Boston, MA
Cyc Am Bio; Dict Am Auth; Dict
Am Bio Men Time; Index t
Wom; Nat Cyc Am Bio v3; Not
Am Wom; Twent Cen Bio Dict
Not Am; Wom Cent

8207. Ragozin, Zenaide Alexievna
1835–post 1906
traveler, writer of Russian histories
Russian
Cyc Am Bio; Dict Am Auth

8208. Rowe, Henrietta Gould
born 1835
short story writer
Bangor, ME
Dict Am Auth

8209. Seymour, Mary Harrison (Browne)
born 1835
children's author
Hartford, CT
Cyc Am Bio; Dict Am Auth; Nat Cyc Am Bio v4; Twent Cen Bio Dict Not Am

8210. Spofford, Harriet Elizabeth (Prescott)
1835–1921
author, novelist, poet
Newburyport, MA
Cyc Am Bio and ad; Dict Am Auth; Dict Am Bio Men Time; Index t Wom; Nat Cyc Am Bio v4; Not Am Wom; Twent Cen Bio Dict Not Am; Wom Cent

8211. Steele, Esther (Baker)
born 1835
historian, history writer
Dict Am Auth; Wom Cent

8212. Taylor, Hannah E.
born 1835
poet, temperance worker
Baptist
Wom Cent

8213. Thaxter, Celia (Laighton)
1835/36–1894
poet, author
New Hampshire
Cyc Am Bio; Dict Am Auth; Dict Am Bio; Index t Wom; Nat Cyc Am Bio v1; Not Am Wom; Twent Cen Bio Dict Not Am; Wom Cent

8214. Todd, Letitia Willey; Alice Afton; Enola
born 1835
poet
Connecticut
Wom Cent

8215. Walworth, Jeanette Ritchie (Hadermann)
1835/37–1906/18
author, novelist
New York, NY
Cyc Am Bio and ad; Dict Am Auth; Dict Am Bio; Nat Cyc Am Bio v8; Wom Cent

8216. Washington, Lucy Hall (Walker)
born 1835
poet, temperance reformer
Port Jervis, NY
Dict Am Auth; Wom Cent

8217. Weiss, Susan Archer (Talley)
born 1835
poet, artist
Virginia; New York, NY
Cyc Am Bio; Dict Am Auth; Wom Cent

8218. Wheeler, Mary Sparks
born 1835
poet, religious author
Philadelphia, PA
Dict Am Auth

8219. Wilson, Augusta C. Jane (Evans)
1835/36–1909
novelist, Confederate author
Methodist
Mobile, AL
Cyc Am Bio; Dict Am Auth; Dict Am Bio Men Time; Encyc South Hist; Index t Wom; Nat Cyc Am Bio v4; Not Am Wom; Wom Cent; Wom Lit, More

8220. Wister, Sarah (Butler)
born 1835
poet, translator
Philadelphia, PA
Dict Am Auth

8221. Woolsey, Sarah Chauncy; Susan Coolidge
1835/45–1905
children's author, poet, Civil War nurse
Newport, RI
Dict Am Auth; Dict Am Bio; Index t Wom; Nat Cyc Am Bio v11; Not Am Wom; Wom Cent

8222. Wormeley, Arianna Randolph
born 1835
author, dramatist
Cyc Am Bio

8223. Alden, Lucy Morris Chaffee
born 1836
author
Wom Cent

8224. Baldwin, Lydia Wood
born 1836
author
Dict Am Auth

8225. Brackett, Anna Callender
1836–1911

women's educator, women's rights worker, author
Dict Am Auth; Dict Am Bio; Nat Cyc Am Bio v21; Not Am Wom

8226. Butts, Mary Frances (Barber)
born 1836
children's author
Dict Am Auth

8227. Comfort, Lucy Randall
1836–1914
novelist
New York
Nat Cyc Am Bio v18

8228. Converse, Harriet Maxwell; Ya-ie-wah-no; Salome; Musidora
1836–1903
Seneca rights advocate, Seneca tribal leader, author, folklorist, Native American scholar, poet
New York
Native American (Seneca by adoption)
Dict Am Auth; Not Am Wom; Twent Cen Bio Dict Not Am; Wom Cent

8229. Davis, August Cordelia
born 1836
poet
Dict Am Auth

8230. Duhring, Julia
1836–92
author of critical essays
Dict Am Auth; Twent Cen Bio Dict Not Am

8231. Holley, Marietta; Josiah Allen's Wife; Jemyma
1836/44–1926
author, humorist, poet, essayist, novelist, popularizer of women's rights and temperance doctrines, feminist
Ellisburg, NY
Dict Am Auth; Dict Am Bio; Index t Wom; Nat Cyc Am Bio v9; Not Am Wom; Twent Cen Bio Dict Not Am; Wom Cent; Wom Lit, More

8232. Hubbell, Mary Elizabeth; Lelia Linwood
1836–56
author
Am Bio Dict

8233. Lemmon, Sarah Allen (Plummer)
1836–post 1860s
Civil War nurse, botanist, writer on botany
Dict Am Auth; Index t Wom

8234. Loughborough, Mary Ann Webster
1836–87

author, Civil War diarist
Little Rock, AR
Cyc Am Bio; Dict Am Auth; Index t Wom

8235. Mace, Frances Parker (Laughton)
1836–99
poet
Maine; San Jose, CA
Cyc Am Bio; Dict Am Auth; Index t Wom; Nat Cyc Am Bio v10; Wom Cent

8236. Mitchell, Marion Juliet
born 1836
poet
New York
Wom Cent

8237. Nourse, Laura A. Sunderlin
born 1836
poet
New York
Wom Cent

8238. Parker, Jane Marsh
1836–1913
author, novelist
Episcopalian
Dict Am Bio; Nat Cyc Am Bio v10; Twent Cen Bio Dict Not Am

8239. Parker, Permelia Jane Marsh
born 1836
children's author, novelist
Rochester, NY
Cyc Am Bio; Dict Am Auth

8240. Peirce, Melusina [Fay]
born 1836
author, community organizer, co-op advocate, writer on domestic science
Newport, RI
Dict Am Auth; Twent Cen Bio Dict Not Am

8241. Piatt, Sarah Morgan (Bryan)
1836–1919
poet
Kentucky
Cyc Am Bio; Dict Am Auth; Dict Am Bio; Index t Wom; Nat Cyc Am Bio v8; Not Am Wom; Twent Cen Bio Dict Not Am; Wom Cent

8242. Prang, Mary Amelia [Dana] Hicks
1836–1927
art educator, writer on art, editor
Dict Am Bio; Index t Wom; Nat Cyc Am Bio v27; Not Am Wom; Twent Cen Bio Dict Not Am

8243. Preston, Harriet Waters
1836/43–1911
author, literary critic, translator, literary historian
Cyc Am Bio; Dict Am Auth; Dict Am Bio; Nat Cyc Am Bio v8

8244. Runcie, Constance (Faunt le Roy)
1836–1911
composer, pianist, club leader, poet, children's author, biographer
St. Joseph, MO
Dict Am Auth; Dict Am Bio; Index t Wom; Nat Cyc Am Bio v7; Wom Cent

8245. Smith, Cassie Selden
married 1861
Civil War diarist
Index t Wom

8246. Smith, Martha Pearson; Mattie May
born 1836
poet, composer
Wom Cent

8247. Tiernana, Mary Spear (Nicholas)
1836–91
novelist
Georgia
Dict Am Auth

8248. Tucker, Margaretta (Ames); Margaret May
born 1836
poet
Boston, MA
Dict Am Auth

8249. Wakefield, Nancy Amelia Woodbury (Priest) "A. C."
1836–70
poet
Massachusetts
Cyc Am Bio; Dict Am Auth; Dict Am Bio Men Time

8250. Alexander, Esther Frances "Francesca"
1837–1917
artist, illustrator, author, translator, philanthropist
Italian (American expatriate to Italy)
Dict Am Auth; Not Am Wom

8251. Allen, Esther Saville
born 1837
author
Wom Cent

8252. Bedford, Lou Singletary
born 1837
poet
Texas
Wom Cent

8253. Bellamy, Emily Elizabeth Whitfield (Croom); A Southern Lady; Kamba Thorpe
1837/39–1900
author, novelist
Mobile, AL; Florida
Appl Cyc Am Bio; Cyc Am Bio; Dict Am Auth; Dict Am Bio; Nat Cyc Am Bio v12; Wom Cent

8254. Eastman, Julia Arabella
1837–1911
children's author, novelist
Massachusetts
Cyc Am Bio; Dict Am Auth; Index t Wom

8255. Emerson, Ellen (Russell)
1837–1907
author, ethnologist, writer on Native American art and mythology
Boston, MA
Dict Am Auth; Dict Am Bio; Twent Cen Bio Dict Not Am; Wom Cent

8256. Festetitts, Kate (Neely)
born 1837
children's author
Washington, DC
Dict Am Auth

8257. Fonda, Mary Alice Ives; Octavia Hensel
born 1837
linguist, author, musician, music educator, writer on music
Wom Cent

8258. Furness, Helen Kate (Rogers)
1837–83
Shakespearean scholar, writer on Shakespeare
Cyc Am Bio; Dict Am Auth

8259. Grimke, Charlotte L. Forten
1837/38–1914
educator, author, poet
Black
Index t Wom; Negro Alman; Not Am Wom; Prof Negro Wom v1

8260. Herrick, Sophia McIlvaine (Bledsoe)
1837–1919
science editor, natural scientist, microscopist, botanist, science writer
Cyc Am Bio; Dict Am Auth; Dict Am Bio; Twent Cen Bio Dict Not Am

8261. Hughes, Kate Duval
born 1837
author, inventor
Catholic
Washington, DC
Wom Cent

8262. Jamison, Cecelia Viets (Dakin) (Hamilton)
1837/48–1909
author, artist
Dict Am Auth; Dict Am Bio; Twent Cen Bio Dict Not Am

8263. Johnson, Sarah (Barclay)
1837–85
author on Syria
Cyc Am Bio; Dict Am Auth; Nat Cyc Am Bio v11

8264. Logan, Celia (Kellog) (Connelly)
1837/40–1904
journalist, author, dramatist
Washington, DC
Cyc Am Bio; Dict Am Auth; Index t Wom; Twent Cen Bio Dict Not Am; Wom Cent

8265. Martin, Elizabeth Gilbert
born 1837
author, translator
Index t Wom

8266. Mountcastle, Clara H.
born 1837
author, elocutionist
Canadian
Cyc Am Bio; Wom Cent

8267. Norton, Minerva (Brace)
born 1837
educator, author, missionary worker
Beloit, WI
Dict Am Auth; Wom Cent

8268. Perez de Zambrana, Luisa
born 1837
author
Cuban
Cyc Am Bio

8269. Pittsinger, Eliza A.
born 1837
poet
San Francisco, CA
Dict Am Auth; Wom Cent

8270. Pratt, Eliza Ella Anna Farman
1837–1907
children's magazine editor, children's author
Dict Am Auth; Dict Am Bio

8271. Richardson, Abby (Sage)
1837–1900
author, actor, historian, lecturer on history, writer on literature, educator
Dict Am Auth; Index t Wom; Nat Cyc Am Bio v5; Twent Cen Bio Dict Not Am

8272. Rothwell, Annie
born 1837
poet
English; Canadian
Wom Cent

8273. Simpson, Corelli C. W.
born 1837
poet
Maine
Wom Cent

8274. Spencer, Sara Andrews
born 1837
suffragist, women's rights worker, business educator, author
Washington, DC
Cyc Am Bio; Dict Am Auth

8275. Swisher, Bella (French)
1837–94
novelist, romance writer
Dict Am Auth

8276. Tucker, Mary Frances Tyler
born 1837
poet
Wom Cent

8277. West, Mary Allen
1837–92
educator, temperance worker, writer on education and child care, journalist
Illinois
Cyc Am Bio; Dict Am Auth; Index t Wom; Wom Cent

8278. Wing, Amelia Kempshall
born 1837
author, philanthropist
New York
Wom Cent

8279. Winslow, Celeste M. A.
born 1837
author
Wom Cent

8280. Wyman, Lillie Buffum Chace
born 1837/47
author, muckraking journalist, short story writer, philanthropist, suffragist, labor welfare worker
Georgia
Dict Am Auth; Wom Cent

8281. Bates, Charlotte Fiske; Madame Roge
1838–1916
poet, poetry editor, author
Appl Cyc Am Bio; Cyc Am Bio; Index t Wom; Twent Cen Bio Dict Not Am

8282. Bates, Clara Doty
1838–95
children's author
Dict Am Auth; Wom Cent

8283. Brown, Charlotte Emerson
1838–95
president of the General Federation of Women's Literary Clubs, patron of missionaries
Dict Am Bio; Wom Cent

8284. Bryan, Mary (Edwards)
1838/46–1913
journalist, author, editor, poet, clubwoman
Atlanta, GA; New York, NY
Cyc Am Bio; Dict Am Bio; Index t Wom; Nat Cyc Am Bio v8; Not Am Wom; Twent Cen Bio Dict Not Am; Wom Cent

8285. Bucknor, Helen Lewis
born 1838
author
Wom Cent

8286. Bullock, Mary Ann
1838–1918
hymn writer, poet
Nat Cyc Am Bio v19

8287. Crane, Anne Moncure (Seemuller)
1838–1872/73
author
Cyc Am Bio; Dict Am Bio; Nat Cyc Am Bio v6

8288. Dannelly, Elizabeth Otis (Marshall)
born 1838
poet
Texas
Dict Am Auth; Wom Cent

8289. Demarest, Mary Augusta Lee
1838–88
poet
Dict Am Auth; Nat Cyc Am Bio v5

8290. Donnelly, Eleonor Cecilia
1838/48–1917
poet, religious author
Catholic
Cyc Am Bio; Dict Am Auth; Dict Am Bio; Nat Cyc Am Bio v2; Twent Cen Bio Dict Not Am

8291. Field, Mary Katherine Kemble "Kate"
1838/54–1896
journalist, actor, playwright, literary critic, lecturer
Washington, DC
Cyc Am Bio; Dict Am Auth; Dict Am Bio; Index t Wom; Nat Cyc Am Bio v6; Not Am Wom; Twent Cen Bio Dict Not Am; Wom Cent

8292. Fletcher, Alice Cunningham
1838/45–1923

ethnologist, Native American rights worker, writer on Native American music
Dict Am Auth; Dict Am Bio; Index t Wom; Nat Cyc Am Bio v5; Not Am Wom; Twent Cen Bio Dict Not Am; Wom Cent

8293. Foster, Theodosia Maria (Toll); Faye Huntington
born 1838
author, children's author, educator
Vermont
Twent Cen Bio Dict Not Am

8294. Greene, Aella
1838–1903
journalist, poet
Springfield, MA
Dict Am Auth

8295. Hague, Parthenia Antoinette (Vardaman)
born 1838; flourished 1860s
Civil War diarist
Florida
Dict Am Auth; Index t Wom

8296. Hallowell, Anna Coffin (Davis)
born 1838
biographer of James and Lucretia Mott
Dict Am Auth

8297. Houghton, Louise Seymour
born 1838
religious magazine editor, translator, religious author
New York, NY
Dict Am Auth

8298. Lambert, Mary Eliza (Perine) (Tucker)
born 1838
poet, author
Philadelphia, PA
Dict Am Auth

8299. Lathrap, Mary Torrans; The Daniel Webster of Prohibition
born 1838
poet, temperance reformer, Congregationalist preacher
Congregationalist
Wom Cent

8300. Liliuokalani, Lydia Kamekaha; Queen of the Hawaiian Islands
born 1838
writer on Hawaiian history
Hawaii
Polynesian
Dict Am Auth

8301. Lincoln, Martha D.; Bessie Beech
born 1838

author, journalist
Wom Cent

8302. Lippincott, Esther J. (Trimble)
1838–88
educator, author on literature, temperance reformer, convalescent-hospital reformer
Quaker
Pennsylvania
Dict Am Auth; Wom Cent

8303. Logan, Mary Simmerson Cunningham
1838–1923
political mover, author, magazine editor, pioneer
Cyc Am Bio; Not Am Wom; Wom Cent

8304. McCrackin, Josephine Woempner Clifford
1838/46–1920
author, journalist, clubwoman, conservationist
German
Index t Wom; Not Am Wom

8305. Proctor, Edna Dean
born 1838
poet, author, Union writer during Civil War
Cyc Am Bio and ad; Dict Am Auth; Nat Cyc Am Bio v7

8306. Roge, Charlotte Fiske (Bates)
born 1838
author, poet, literary critic, educator
New York
Dict Am Auth; Wom Cent

8307. Rude, Ellen (Sargent)
born 1838
poet, author, temperance worker, Worthy Chief Templar of the Order of Good Templars
Duluth, MN
Dict Am Auth; Index t Wom; Wom Cent

8308. Sangster, Margaret Elizabeth (Munson)
1838–1912
editor of *Harper's Bazaar*, author, poet, journalist
New York, NY
Cyc Am Bio and ad; Dict Am Auth; Index t Wom; Nat Cyc Am Bio v6; Not Am Wom; Twent Cen Bio Dict Not Am; Wom Cent

8309. Scott, Mary Sophie
born 1838
author, businessperson
Index t Wom; Wom Cent

8310. Seemuller, Annie Moncure (Crane)
1838–72
novelist
New York, NY
Dict Am Auth

8311. Slosson, Anne (Trumbull)
1838–1926
entomologist, short story writer
New York, NY
Dict Am Auth; Index t Wom

8312. Stockton, Louise
1838–1914
editor, journalist, novelist, critic, historian, social worker
Philadelphia, PA
Dict Am Auth; Index t Wom; Nat Cyc Am Bio v8; Twent Cen Bio Dict Not Am

8313. Stokes, Missouri H.
1838–post 1860
Civil War diarist, educator, temperance worker
Presbyterian
Georgia
Index t Wom; Wom Cent

8314. Tucker, Mary Eliza
born 1838
author
Cyc Am Bio

8315. Underwood, Sara H. (Francis)
born 1838
free thought journal editor, author
Dict Am Auth

8316. Velasquez, Loretta Janeta
born 1838
western pioneer, Civil War diarist, Civil War spy
Index t Wom

8317. Velazquez, Louta Janita; Velasquez, Loretta Janeta; Harry T. Buford
born 1838/42
Civil War autobiographer, western pioneer, Civil War spy
Encyc South Hist; Index t Wom

8318. Ward, Susan Hayes
born 1838
author, religious writer
New York, NY
Dict Am Auth

8319. Washburn, Jean Linsey Bruce
1838–1904
poet
Scottish
Index t Wom

8320. Wells, Catharine Boott (Gannett)
born 1838
author, religious writer, essayist, novelist, educator
Boston, MA
Dict Am Auth; Twent Cen Bio Dict Not Am

8321. Woods, Kate Tannatt
1838–1910
club leader, editor, poet, children's author
Salem, MA
Dict Am Auth; Index t Wom; Wom Cent

8322. Woolson, Abba Louisa (Goold)
1838–1921
educator, author, lecturer, dress reformer
Boston, MA
Cyc Am Bio; Dict Am Auth; Dict Am Bio; Index t Wom; Nat Cyc Am Bio v9; Not Am Wom; Wom Cent

8323. Woolson, Constanta Fennimore
1838/48–1894
author, novelist, poet, traveler
Cyc Am Bio; Dict Am Auth; Dict Am Bio; Index t Wom; Nat Cyc Am Bio v1; Not Am Wom; Twent Cen Bio Dict Not Am; Wom Cent; Wom Lit, More

8324. Campbell, Helen (Stuart)
1839–1918
journalist, children's author, social reformer, home economist, educator, philanthropist
New York
Cyc Am Bio; Dict Am Auth; Nat Cyc Am Bio v9; Not Am Wom; Twent Cen Bio Dict Not Am; Wom Cent

8325. Clemmer, Mary
1839–84
author
Dict Am Bio

8326. Conant, Helen Charlotte Peters (Stevens)
1839–99
magazine writer, translator, linguist, entomologist
Cyc Am Bio; Dict Am Auth; Index t Wom; Twent Cen Bio Dict Not Am

8327. Dickinson, Mary Lowe
1839–1914
author, educator, short story writer, poet
New York, NY
Dict Am Auth; Index t Wom

8328. Easter, Marguerite Elizabeth (Miller)
1839–94
poet
Baltimore, MD
Dict Am Auth

8329. Fenner, Mary Galentine
born 1839
author, poet
New York
Wom Cent

8330. Fernald, M. E.
1839–1919
entomologist, author
Index t Wom

8331. Fielde, Adele Marion
born 1839
missionary to Siam and China, writer on China, writer in Chinese
Dict Am Auth

8332. Graves, Mary H.
born 1839
Unitarian minister, author, lecturer
Unitarian
Index t Wom; Wom Cent

8333. Helm, Lucinda Barbour; Lucile
1839–97
author, religious writer
Methodist Episcopal
Kentucky
Twent Cen Bio Dict Not Am; Wom Cent

8334. Henry, Sarepta Myrenda (Irish)
1839–1900/01
author, religious writer, poet, children's author, temperance worker, evangelist
Evanston, IL
Dict Am Auth; Nat Cyc Am Bio v4; Twent Cen Bio Dict Not Am; Wom Cent

8335. Hudson, Mary (Clemmer) (Ames)
1839/40–1884
journalist, poet
Washington, DC
Dict Am Auth; Wom Cent

8336. Hurd, Helen Marr
born 1839
poet, temperance worker
Maine
Wom Cent

8337. Jack, Annie L. Hayr; Loyal Janet
born 1839
horticulturist, author
Wom Cent

8338. Knapp, Phoebe Palmer
born 1839
musician, author, religious composer
Methodist Episcopal
New York
Wom Cent

8339. Logan, Olive
1839/41–1909
actor, dramatist, lecturer, women's rights reformer, author, journalist
Cyc Am Bio; Dict Am Bio; Dict Am Bio Men Time; Index t Wom; Nat Cyc Am Bio v6; Not Am Wom; Twent Cen Bio Dict Not Am

8340. Manville, Helen Adelia (Wood) "Nellie"
born 1839
poet
La Crosse, WI
Dict Am Auth; Index t Wom; Nat Cyc Am Bio v4

8341. Mordecai, Rose
born 1839
author, religious leader
Index t Wom

8342. Morse, Lucy (Gibbons)
1839–1936
author, novelist, abolitionist, Black welfare worker
New York, NY
Dict Am Auth; Nat Cyc Am Bio

8343. Packard, Charlotte Mellen
born 1839
poet, fiction writer
Dict Am Auth

8344. Palmer, Frances Purdy "Fannie"
1839–1923
author, journalist, lecturer, suffragist, feminist
Providence, RI
Dict Am Auth; Index t Wom; Wom Cent

8345. Peckham, Mary Chace (Peck)
1839–92
author, fiction writer, poet, Civil War nurse, suffragist, women's rights worker
Unitarian
Providence, RI
Dict Am Auth; Nat Cyc Am Bio v9; Twent Cen Bio Dict Not Am

8346. Randolph, Sarah Nicholas (Jefferson)
1839–92
author, educator, biographer

Baltimore, MD
Cyc Am Bio; Dict Am Auth; Dict Am Bio; Twent Cen Bio Dict Not Am

8347. Sanborn, Katharine Abbott "Kate"
1839–1917
miscellaneous author, educator, lecturer, essayist, literary professor, agriculturist
New Hampshire
Cyc Am Bio; Dict Am Auth; Dict Am Bio; Index t Wom; Nat Cyc Am Bio v9; Twent Cen Bio Dict Not Am

8348. Sinclair, Carrie Bell
born 1839
poet
Philadelphia, PA
Cyc Am Bio; Dict Am Auth

8349. Smith, Julia Holmes
born 1839
physician, author
Chicago, IL
Index t Wom; Wom Cent

8350. Sunderland, Eliza Jane (Read)
1839–1910
lecturer, author, educator, temperance worker, women's rights worker, philosopher
Universalist
Michigan
Dict Am Bio; Nat Cyc Am Bio v10; Wom Cent

8351. Tenney, Sarah (Brownsen)
1839–76
miscellaneous author
Cyc Am Bio; Dict Am Auth

8352. Thomas, Carrie A.
1839–83
religious worker, poet, hymn writer
Index t Wom

8353. Tuttle, Emma Rood
born 1839/59
author, poet, lecturer
Berlin Heights, OH
Cyc Am Bio; Dict Am Auth; Wom Cent

8354. Twiggs, Sarah L.
born 1839
poet
Wom Cent

8355. Warner, Marion E. Knowlton
born 1839
poet, story writer
Ohio
Wom Cent

8356. Adams, Mary (Mathews)
1840–1902
educator, poet
Madison, WI
Irish
Dict Am Auth; Wom Cent

8357. Andrews, Eliza Frances
1840/47–1931
journalist, Civil War diarist, educator, botanist
Georgia
Dict Am Auth; Index t Wom; Nat Cyc Am Bio v6; Not Am Wom; Wom Cent

8358. Benjamin, Elizabeth Dundas (Bedell)
died 1890
religious author
Stratford, CT
Dict Am Auth

8359. Blake, Mary Elizabeth McGrath
1840–1907
author, poet
Catholic
Boston, MA
Irish
Dict Am Auth; Dict Am Bio; Wom Cent

8360. Branch, Mary Lydia Bolles
1840–1922
poet, children's author
New York
Cyc Am Bio; Dict Am Auth; Nat Cyc Am Bio v21; Twent Cen Bio Dict Not Am

8361. Brotherton, Alice William
flourished 1870s; died 1930
author, poet, lecturer, magazine writer
Cincinnati, OH
Dict Am Auth; Index t Wom; Wom Cent

8362. Cecil, Elizabeth Frances
flourished 1870s–1900s
author
Catholic
Nat Cyc Am Bio v3

8363. Coffin, Mary Starbuck
flourished 1870s–80s
poet
Index t Wom

8364. Cole, Miriam M.
flourished 1870s–80s
lecturer, feminist, author, journalist
Index t Wom

8365. Conant, Helen C.
flourished 1870s–80s
author
Index t Wom

8366. Cone, Mary
flourished 1870s
author
Index t Wom

8367. Coolidge, Harriet Abbot Lincoln
flourished 1870s–80s
philanthropist, sanitary educator, worker for women's education, author
Wom Cent

8368. Creemer, Lucy M.
flourished 1870s–80s
poet, religious worker
Index t Wom

8369. Dargan, Clara Victoria (MacLean); Claudia
born 1840
poet, fiction writer, educator
South Carolina
Cyc Am Bio; Dict Am Auth; Nat Cyc Am Bio v7

8370. Darling, Flora (Adams)
1840–1910
fiction writer, novelist, founder of the Daughters of the Revolution patriotic society
Dict Am Auth; Dict Am Bio; Index t Wom; Nat Cyc Am Bio v19; Not Am Wom; Wom Cent

8371. Dickinson, Susan E.
flourished 1870s–90s
journalist, author
Quaker
Pennsylvania
Index t Wom; Wom Cent

8372. Duffel, Mary Gordon; Mary Duff Gordon
born 1840
poet, writer on the history and geography of Alabama
Alabama
Cyc Am Bio; Dict Am Auth

8373. Fleming, May Agnes (Early); Cousin May Carleton
1840–80
romance writer
Dict Am Auth

8374. Glover, Anna
flourished 1870s
genealogist, author
Index t Wom

8375. Gordon-Cumming, Constance
flourished 1870s
author
Index t Wom

8376. Griswold, Harriet (Tyng) "Hattie"
1840/42–1910
author, poet

Unitarian
Cyc Am Bio and v3 ad; Dict Am Auth; Nat Cyc Am Bio v10; Twent Cen Bio Dict Not Am; Wom Cent

8377. Harper, Olive
flourished 1870s; died 1907
author
Nat Cyc Am Bio v5

8378. Healey, Mary
flourished 1870s
author
Cyc Am Bio

8379. Higginson, Sarah Jane (Hatfield)
born 1840
novelist
New York, NY
Dict Am Auth

8380. Hoyt, Deristha Lavinta
born 184?
lecturer on the history of painting, writer on art
Massachusetts
Dict Am Auth

8381. Jebb, Caroline Lane Reynolds Slemmer
1840–1930
author
Index t Wom

8382. Jeffery, Isador Gilbert
born 184?
poet, stenographer
Chicago, IL
Wom Cent

8383. Johnson, Evangeline Maria
flourished 1870s–80s
translator, poet, bibliographer
Cyc Am Bio

8384. Killikelly, Sarah Hutchins
1840–1912
author
Pittsburgh, PA
Nat Cyc Am Bio v19

8385. Lee, Margaret
1840–1914
novelist
Brooklyn, NY
Dict Am Auth; Nat Cyc Am Bio v15

8386. Mason, Amelia (Gere)
184?–1923
author on women's history
Chicago, IL
Dict Am Auth; Index t Wom

8387. Mather, Margaret Morgan (Herbert)
184?–1900

writer on polo and fox hunting
Dict Am Auth

8388. Maxwell, Ellen Blackwell
flourished 1870s–90s
author
Twent Cen Bio Dict Not Am

8389. McLaughlin, Mary Louise M.
flourished 1870s–1900s
ceramic artist, writer on art techniques
Cincinnati, OH
Dict Am Auth; Index t Wom

8390. McPherson, Lydia Starr
flourished 1870s–90s
poet, author, journalist, newspaper publisher
Texas
Wom Cent

8391. Morgan, Caroline (Starr)
born 184?
miscellaneous writer
Dict Am Auth

8392. Nieriker, May (Alcott)
1840–79
artist, author, still life painter
Appl Cyc Am Bio; Cyc Am Bio; Dict Am Auth; Index t Wom; Twent Cen Bio Dict Not Am; Wom Cent

8393. Norton, Della Whitney
born 1840
poet, author
Christian Scientist
Wom Cent

8394. Putnam, Sarah A. Brock "Sallie"; Virginia Madison
1840/45–post 1900
author, novelist, Civil War writer
New York, NY
Cyc Am Bio; Dict Am Auth; Nat Cyc Am Bio v10; Twent Cen Bio Dict Not Am; Wom Cent

8395. Rand, Mary Frances (Abbott)
born 1840
writer of Christmas holiday stories
Dict Am Auth

8396. Rathbun, Harriet M.
born 1840
author, businessperson, journalist, magazine publisher and editor
Wom Cent

8397. Reed, Caroline Keating
flourished 1870s–1910s
musician, pianist, author
Index t Wom; Wom Cent

8398. Reed, Rebecca Perley (Page)
born 1840
children's writer
Milwaukee, WI
Dict Am Auth

8399. Reynolds, Belle
born 1840
Civil War nurse, patriot, author
Index t Wom

8400. Rhine, Alice Hyneman
born 1840
author, poet
Cyc Am Bio

8401. Ricker, Marilla Marks Young
1840–1920
lawyer, suffragist, prison reformer, politician, author, political writer
New Hampshire
Index t Wom; Nat Cyc Am Bio v17; Not Am Wom; Wom Cent

8402. Robinson, Leora (Bettison)
born 1840
fiction writer, educator
Baptist
Tallahassee, TN
Dict Am Auth; Wom Cent

8403. Rollston, Adelaide Day
flourished 1870s–90s
author, poet
Kentucky
Wom Cent

8404. Rowland, Kate Mason
flourished 1870s–90s
author
Twent Cen Bio Dict Not Am

8405. Ruprecht, Jenny Terrill
born 1840
author, children's author, Sorosis member
Cleveland, OH
Wom Cent

8406. Schayer, Julia (Thompson) (Von Storch)
born 1840
short story writer
Washington, DC
Dict Am Auth

8407. Searing, Laura Catherine (Redden); Howard Glyndon
1840–1923
author, war correspondent, journalist, poet
deaf
Cyc Am Bio; Dict Am Auth; Dict Am Bio; Dict Am Bio Men Time; Index t Wom; Nat Cyc Am Bio v9; Wom Cent

8408. Smedes, Susan (Dabney)
born 1840
author, missionary to the Sioux people, educator, historian of the antebellum South
Mississippi
Cyc Am Bio; Dict Am Auth; Wom Cent

8409. Smith, Fanny I. Burge
flourished 1870s–80s
author
Index t Wom

8410. Smith, Mary Prudence (Wells); P. Thorne
born 1840
children's author
Cincinnati, OH
Cyc Am Bio and ad; Dict Am Auth

8411. Spencer, Bella Zilfa
born 1840–67
author, novelist
English
Cyc Am Bio; Dict Am Auth; Dict Am Bio Men Time

8412. Starrett, Helen (Ekin)
born 1840
nonfiction author, educator
Chicago, IL
Dict Am Auth; Twent Cen Bio Dict Not Am

8413. Turnbull, Frances Hubbard (Litchfield)
born 184?
novelist
Catholic
Baltimore, MD
Dict Am Auth

8414. Walker, Katherine Kent (Child)
born 1840
religious author
Cyc Am Bio; Dict Am Auth

8415. Wallis, Mary D.
flourished 1870s
traveler, author
Index t Wom

8416. Watson, Annah Robinson
flourished 1870s–90s
author
Episcopalian
Wom Cent

8417. Webster, Mary C.
flourished 1870s
clergyperson, author
Index t Wom

8418. Weitzel, Sophie Winthrop (Shepherd)
1840–92
poet, fiction writer
Dict Am Auth

8419. Wesselhoeft, Elizabeth Foster (Pope)
born 1840
children's author
Boston, MA
Dict Am Auth

8420. West, Maria A.
flourished 1870s–80s
missionary, author
Index t Wom

8421. Williams, Anne (Bolles); Jak
born 1840
children's author
Springfield, MA
Dict Am Auth

8422. Wixon, Susan Helen
flourished 1870s–90s
author, children's editor, educator, feminist
Massachusetts
Wom Cent

8423. Wood, Mary C. Foster; Camilla K. von K.; Mary C. F. Hall-Wood
flourished 1870s–90s
poet, editor, author
California
Wom Cent

8424. Wright, Julia MacNair
1840–1930
author, novelist, temperance writer, temperance worker, anti-Catholic writer
Cyc Am Bio; Dict Am Auth; Index t Wom; Wom Cent

8425. Alden, Isabella (MacDonald); Pansy
1841–1930
religious author, children's author
Appl Cyc Am Bio; Cyc Am Bio; Dict Am Auth; Dict Am Bio; Index t Wom; Nat Cyc Am Bio v10; Not Am Wom; Twent Cen Bio Dict Not Am; Wom Cent

8426. Allen, Mary Wood
born 1841
physician, author, lecturer
Black
Negro Alman

8427. Bennett, Mary E.; Elizabeth Glover
born 1841
miscellaneous author, children's author
New Haven, CT
Dict Am Auth

8428. Bolton, Sarah Knowles
1841–1916
author, temperance worker

Cleveland, OH
Cyc Am Bio and ad; Dict Am Auth; Dict Am Bio; Nat Cyc Am Bio v1; Twent Cen Bio Dict Not Am; Wom Cent

8429. Catlin, Laura Wood
born 1841
philanthropist, author
Wom Cent

8430. Conklin, Jennie Maria (Drinkwater); Maria Drinkwater
1841–1900
children's author, philanthropist, clubwoman, founder of the Shut-in Society for Invalids
Dict Am Auth; Index t Wom; Dict Am Bio

8431. Coolbrith, Ina Donna
1841/42–1928
poet, librarian
California
Dict Am Auth; Dict Am Bio; Nat Cyc Am Bio v13; Not Am Wom; Twent Cen Bio Dict Not Am; Wom Cent; Wom Lit, More

8432. Gustafson, Zadel Barnes (Buddington); Axel Carl Johan Gustafson
born 1841
author, poet, novelist
New York
Cyc Am Bio; Dict Am Auth; Wom Cent

8433. Janvier, Catharine Ann
1841–1922
painter, author
Dict Am Bio

8434. Kleeberg, Minna
1841–1978
poet
Cyc Am Bio

8435. Lathbury, Mary Artemesia; Aunt May
1841–1913
author; psalm, spiritual, and hymn writer; religious writer for children
Dict Am Auth; Dict Am Bio; Nat Cyc Am Bio v10

8436. Lewis, Harriet
1841–78
novelist
Dict Am Auth

8437. McAvoy, Emma
born 1841
author, lecturer
Ohio
Wom Cent

8438. McClain, Louise Bowman
born 1841

author
Methodist Episcopal
Indiana
Wom Cent

8439. Moore, Annie Aubertine (Woodward); Aubertine Forestier
1841–1929
pianist, student of Scandinavian music, music critic, lecturer, author, translator of Scandinavian languages
Dict Am Auth; Dict Am Bio; Index t Wom; Twent Cen Bio Dict Not Am; Wom Cent

8440. Morgan, Sarah
born 1841
Civil War diarist
Index t Wom

8441. Oberholtzer, Sara Louisa (Vikers)
1841–1930
poet, author, novelist, temperance worker, leader in school savings movement, economist
Quaker
Norristown, PA
Cyc Am Bio; Dict Am Auth; Dict Am Bio; Index t Wom; Nat Cyc Am Bio v7; Wom Cent

8442. Osgood, Kate Putnam
born 1841
author
Cyc Am Bio

8443. Patterson, Virginia Sharpe
born 1841
author
Ohio
Wom Cent

8444. Pool, Maria Louisa
1841/45–1898
author, novelist, writer for the *New York Tribune*
Rockland, MA
Dict Am Auth; Index t Wom; Nat Cyc Am Bio v6; Twent Cen Bio Dict Not Am

8445. Pugh, Eliza Lofton (Phillips)
born 1841
author, novelist
Assumption Parish, LA
Cyc Am Bio; Dict Am Auth

8446. Rittenhouse, Laura Jacinta
born 1841
temperance worker, author, poet
Cairo, IL
Wom Cent

8447. Scott, Mary Augusta
1841–1916

author, educator
Index t Wom

8448. Sherwood, Katharine Margaret (Brownlee) "Kate"
1841/43–1914
journalist, newspaper editor, poet, author, clubwoman, suffragist
Canton, OH
Dict Am Auth; Dict Am Bio; Index t Wom; Nat Cyc Am Bio v1; Not Am Wom; Twent Cen Bio Dict Not Am; Wom Cent

8449. Sikes, Olive (Logan)
born 1841
actor, lecturer, author, novelist, autobiographer
Dict Am Auth

8450. Stevenson, Sarah Ann Hackett
1841/49–1909
physician, medical author, science writer
Cyc Am Bio; Dict Am Auth; Index t Wom; Not Am Wom

8451. Stone, Margaret Manson (Barbour)
born 1841
nonfiction writer
St. Louis, MO
Dict Am Auth

8452. Todd, Marion Marsh
1841–post 1913
lawyer, Greenback party worker, political economist, labor leader, author, lecturer
Not Am Wom; Wom Cent

8453. Veeder, Emily Elizabeth (Ferris)
1841–post 1890
author, poet, novelist
Pennsylvania; St. Louis, MO
Dict Am Auth; Wom Cent

8454. Winter, Elizabeth (Campbell)
born 1841
novelist
Staten Island, NY
Dict Am Auth

8455. Wood-Allen, Mary
born 1841
physician, sex education author
Ann Arbor, MI
Dict Am Auth

8456. Alexander, Matilda (Greathouse)
born 1842
author
Nat Cyc Am Bio v4

8457. Baker, Sarah Schoonmaker (Tuthill); Aunt Friendly
born 1842
Sunday school story writer
Dict Am Auth

8458. Britts, Mattie (Dyer)
born 1842
children's author
Dict Am Auth

8459. Brush, Christine (Chaplin)
1842–92
watercolorist, novelist
Dict Am Auth

8460. Chaplin, Ada C.
1842–83
author, Sunday school story writer
Massachusetts
Cyc Am Bio; Dict Am Auth

8461. Custer, Elizabeth Bacon
1842–1933
author, western pioneer, lecturer on frontier life
Cyc Am Bio; Dict Am Auth; Index t Wom; Wom Cent

8462. Dawson, Sarah; Ida Fowler
1842–1909
author, Civil War diarist
Episcopalian
Index t Wom; Nat Cyc Am Bio v23

8463. de Jarnette, Evelyn Magruder
born 1842
author
Virginia
Wom Cent

8464. Dickinson, Anna Elizabeth
1842–1932
Civil War orator, lyceum lecturer, abolitionist, women's rights worker, suffragist, political activist, Republican party worker, author, actor, philanthropist
Quaker
Cyc Am Bio; Dict Am Auth; Dict Am Bio supp v1; Dict Am Bio Men Time; Index t Wom; Nat Cyc Am Bio v3; Not Am Wom; Twent Cen Bio Dict Not Am; Wom Cent

8465. Dyer, Mattie
born 1842
author
Cyc Am Bio

8466. Farmer, Lydia (Hoyt)
1842/43–1903
religious author, journalist

Cleveland, OH
Dict Am Auth; Index t Wom; Nat Cyc Am Bio v8; Twent Cen Bio Dict Not Am; Wom Cent

8467. Fox, Mary Hewins
born 1842
actor, dramatist, poet
Cyc Am Bio

8468. Gifford, Augusta (Hale)
born 1842
historical author
Portland, ME
Dict Am Auth

8469. Gist, Malvina Black
born 1842
Civil War diarist
Index t Wom

8470. Griffith, Harriet Pomroy (Roelofson)
born 1842
author
Nat Cyc Am Bio v11

8471. Henderson, Mary Foote
born 1842/46
suffragist, home economist, cooking and nutrition writer
St. Louis, MO
Dict Am Auth; Twent Cen Bio Dict Not Am

8472. Hill, Agnes Leonard (Scanland); Molly Myrtle
1842–1917
poet, author, newspaper publisher, religious writer, novelist, prisoner's welfare worker, Universalist pastor
Universalist
Colorado
Dict Am Auth; Index t Wom; Nat Cyc Am Bio v17; Wom Cent

8473. Jacobi, Mary Corinna Putnam
1842–1906
physician, medical author, pharmacist, educator, feminist
New York, NY
Cyc Am Bio; Dict Am Auth; Dict Am Bio; Index t Wom; Nat Cyc Am Bio v8; Not Am Wom; Twent Cen Bio Dict Not Am; Wom Cent

8474. Kearney, Martha Eleanor
1842–1930
religious worker, author
Index t Wom

8475. Kirk, Ellen Warner (Olney); Henry Hayes
born 1842/46
author, novelist

Germantown, PA
Cyc Am Bio; Dict Am Auth; Index t Wom; Nat Cyc Am Bio v1; Twent Cen Bio Dict Not Am; Wom Cent

8476. Leonard, Agnes
born 1842
author
Cyc Am Bio

8477. Moran, Jane Warmly (Blackburn)
born 1842
novelist
Charlottesville, VA
Dict Am Auth

8478. Peckham, Lucy Creemer
born 1842
physician, poet
Wom Cent

8479. Poor, Agnes Blake; Dorothy Prescott
1842–1922
author
Brookline, MA
Dict Am Auth; Nat Cyc Am Bio v19

8480. Reed, Elizabeth (Armstrong)
1842–1915
theologist, religious author, philosopher, historian of India and Persia, writer on Oriental literature, temperance worker, philanthropist
Chicago, IL
Dict Am Auth; Dict Am Bio; Index t Wom; Nat Cyc Am Bio v1 and v15; Twent Cen Bio Dict Not Am

8481. Richards, Ellen Henrietta (Swallow)
1842–1911
sanitation chemist and engineer, mineralogist, leader in applied and domestic science, writer on domestic science, professor at MIT, educator
Massachusetts
Cyc Am Bio; Dict Am Auth; Dict Am Bio; Index t Wom; Nat Cyc Am Bio v7; Not Am Wom; Twent Cen Bio Dict Not Am; Wom Cent

8482. Robinson, Annie Douglass Green; Marian Douglas
born 1842
poet, author, children's poet
Briston, NH
Cyc Am Bio; Dict Am Auth; Nat Cyc Am Bio v3

8483. Rollins, Alice Marland (Wellington)
1842/47–1897

author, poet, muckraking journalist
New York, NY
Cyc Am Bio; Dict Am Auth; Dict Am Bio; Nat Cyc Am Bio v8; Twent Cen Bio Dict Not Am; Wom Cent

8484. Smith, Mary Louise (Riley)
born 1842/52
author, poet
New York, NY
Cyc Am Bio; Dict Am Auth; Wom Cent

8485. Thayer, Emma (Homan) (Graves)
born 1842
author, novelist, artist, botanical illustrator
Salida, CO
Dict Am Auth; Twent Cen Bio Dict Not Am; Wom Cent

8486. Vale, Euphemia Vale Blake
born 1842
writer on history and science
Cyc Am Bio

8487. van Fleet, Ellen Oliver
born 1842
poet
Wom Cent

8488. Vanderpoel, Emily Caroline Noyes
1842–1939
painter, author
New York
Nat Cyc Am Bio v29

8489. Whitten, Martha Elizabeth Hotchkiss
born 1842
author, poet
Texas
Wom Cent

8490. Wintermute, Martha (Vandermark)
born 1842
poet, temperance writer
Ohio
Wom Cent

8491. Aldrich, Josephine Cables
born 1843
newspaper publisher, editor, author, philanthropist
Nat Cyc Am Bio v5; Wom Cent

8492. Allyn, Eunice Eloisae Gibbs
flourished 1873
author
Wom Cent

8493. Collier, Ada (Langworthy)
born 1843

poet
Dubuque, IA
Dict Am Auth; Wom Cent

8494. Creevey, Caroline Alathea Stickney
1843–1920
botanist, author, pianist
Nat Cyc Am Bio v30

8495. Downs, George Sheldon, Mrs.
born 1843
author
Index t Wom

8496. Eliot, Charlotte Champe Stearns
1843–1929
author, welfare worker
Not Am Wom

8497. Gougar, Helen Mar Jackson
1843–1907
suffrage and temperance reformer, orator, author
Index t Wom; Not Am Wom; Wom Cent

8498. Harbert, Elizabeth Boynton "Lizzie"
born 1843
author, lecturer, suffragist
Index t Wom; Wom Cent

8499. Harrison, Constance Cary
1843/46–1920
author, novelist, miscellaneous writer, dramatist
New York, NY
Cyc Am Bio; Dict Am Auth; Dict Am Bio; Index t Wom; Nat Cyc Am Bio v4; Not Am Wom; Twent Cen Bio Dict Not Am; Wom Cent; Wom Lit, More

8500. Hawley, Frances Mallette
born 1843
poet, author
Bridgeport, CT
Wom Cent

8501. Johnson, Helen Louise (Kendrick)
1843–1917
miscellaneous writer, children's author, editor
Cyc Am Bio; Dict Am Auth; Dict Am Bio; Nat Cyc Am Bio v1; Twent Cen Bio Dict Not Am

8502. le Row, Caroline Bigelow
born 1843
educator, writer on education
Brooklyn, NY
Dict Am Auth

8503. Lowell, Josephine (Shaw)
1843–1905

charitable worker, philanthropist, social worker, prison reformer, labor reformer, writer on philanthropy
New York, NY
Cyc Am Bio; Dict Am Auth; Dict Am Bio; Index t Wom; Nat Cyc Am Bio v8; Not Am Wom; Twent Cen Bio Dict Not Am

8504. Moore, Idora McClellan (Plowman)
1843–1929
author
Alabama
Index t Wom; Wom Cent

8505. Parloa, Maria
1843–1909
home economics educator, writer on cooking and domestic economy, lecturer
Dict Am Auth; Index t Wom; Not Am Wom

8506. Phillips, Elizabeth Buford
1843–1925
educator, litterateur
Nat Cyc Am Bio v20

8507. Pickett, Lasalle Carbell
born 1843
Civil War patriot, hero, diarist, lecturer
Index t Wom; Wom Cent

8508. Raymond, Evelyn (Hunt)
born 1843
children's author
Baltimore, MD
Dict Am Auth; Twent Cen Bio Dict Not Am

8509. Roebling, Emily Warren
1843–1903
Civil War patriot, philanthropist, club leader, author, lawyer
Index t Wom

8510. Smith, Eva Munson
born 1843
composer, poet
Index t Wom; Wom Cent

8511. Strohm, Gertrude
born 1843
miscellaneous author, compiler of information
Dayton, OH
Dict Am Auth; Wom Cent

8512. Treat, Anna Elizabeth
born 1843
author, poet
Ohio
Wom Cent

8513. Upton, Sara Carr
born 1843
author
Cyc Am Bio

8514. Ward, Mary E.
born 1843
poet
Vermont
Wom Cent

8515. Weatherby, Delia L.
born 1843
temperance reformer, author, politician, educator
Kansas
Wom Cent

8516. Anagnos, Julia Romana (Howe)
1844–86
poet
Dict Am Auth

8517. Arnold, Augusta Foote
born 1844
cookbook writer, author
New York
Dict Am Auth

8518. Austin, Harriet Bunker
born 1844
women's rights worker, author
Wom Cent

8519. Avery, Catharine Hitchcock Tilden
born 1844
author, educator
Wom Cent

8520. Bates, Margaret Holmes (Ernsperger)
born 1844
author, poet
Dict Am Auth; Nat Cyc Am Bio v10; Wom Cent

8521. Burton, Emma
1844–1927
missionary, author
Index t Wom

8522. Colby, H. Maria George; H. Maria George
born 1844
children's author, domestic writer, women's rights and temperance worker
Wom Cent

8523. Davis, Mollie Evelyn Moore
1844/52–1909
poet, author in Black dialect
Not Am Wom; Wom Cent

8524. Fletcher, Lisa Anne
born 1844
poet, flower painter
New Hampshire
Wom Cent

8525. Gilman, Stella (Scott)
born 1844

founder of Radcliffe College, author
Dict Am Auth; Nat Cyc Am Bio v10; Not Am Wom

8526. Greene, Belle Colton
born 1844
author, humorist
Wom Cent

8527. Greene, Isabella Catherine (Colton)
born 1844
novelist, children's author
Nashua, NH
Dict Am Auth

8528. Higginson, Mary Potter (Thacher)
born 1844
short story writer
Dict Am Auth

8529. Howe, Emeline Harriet (Siggins)
born 1844
poet, temperance worker
Pennsylvania
Wom Cent

8530. Janvier, Margaret Thompson; Margaret Vandegrift
1844/45–1913
children's author
Philadelphia, PA
Dict Am Auth; Dict Am Bio; Nat Cyc Am Bio v12

8531. Lothrop, Harriett Mulford (Stone); Margaret Sydney
1844–1924
author, children's author
Concord, MA
Cyc Am Bio; Dict Am Auth; Dict Am Bio; Index t Wom; Nat Cyc Am Bio v8; Not Am Wom; Twent Cen Bio Dict Not Am; Wom Cent

8532. Marshall, Nelly Nichol
1844/45–1898
author
Cyc Am Bio; Twent Cen Bio Dict Not Am

8533. Mason, Clara Stevens Arthur
1844–84
poet
Dict Am Auth

8534. Merriman, Helen (Bigelow)
born 1844
artist, writer on art, religious author
Worcester, MA
Dict Am Auth; Index t Wom; Twent Cen Bio Dict Not Am

8535. Messenger, Lilian Rozell
born 1844/53
journalist, poet
Dict Am Auth; Twent Cen Bio Dict Not Am; Wom Cent

8536. Noble, Annette Lucile
born 1844
fiction writer
Albion, NY
Cyc Am Bio and ad; Dict Am Auth; Twent Cen Bio Dict Not Am

8537. Oliver, Grace Atkinson (Little) (Ellis)
1844–99
author, biographer, story editor
Salem, MA
Cyc Am Bio; Dict Am Auth; Index t Wom; Twent Cen Bio Dict Not Am; Wom Cent

8538. Phelps, Elizabeth Stuart; Mrs. Ward
1844–1911
author, lecturer, women's rights worker, temperance worker
Cyc Am Bio and ad; Dict Am Bio Men Time

8539. Rogers, Clara Kathleen Barnett
1844–1931
singer, author, composer
English
Dict Am Bio; Index t Wom

8540. Runkle, Lucia Isabella
born 1844
author
Cyc Am Bio

8541. Stevens, Alzina Parsons
1844/49–1900
labor leader, industrial reformer, settlement house worker, social reformer, newspaper editor and publisher, journalist, author
Chicago, IL
Index t Wom; Not Am Wom; Wom Cent

8542. Teasdale, Sara; Mrs. Ernst B. Filsinger
1844–1933
lyric poet
Dict Am Bio; Index t Wom; Nat Cyc Am Bio v39 and csv1; Not Am Wom; Wom Lit

8543. Towne, Belle Kellogg
born 1844
author, journalist
Wom Cent

8544. Utter, Rebecca (Palfrey)
born 1844
poet
Unitarian
Dict Am Auth

8545. Walton, Sarah Stokes
born 1844
poet, artist
Protestant Episcopal
Wom Cent

8546. Ward, Elizabeth Stuart (Phelps)
1844–1911
author, popular novelist, women's rights worker, temperance worker, philanthropist
Massachusetts
Cyc Am Bio; Dict Am Auth; Dict Am Bio; Dict Am Bio Men Time; Index t Wom; Nat Cyc Am Bio v9; Not Am Wom; Twent Cen Bio Dict Not Am; Wom Cent; Wom Lit, More

8547. Wynne, Emma (Moffett)
born 1844
novelist
Georgia
Dict Am Auth

8548. Young, Ann Eliza Webb
1844–post 1908
lecturer and writer against Mormon polygamy, feminist, religious worker, pioneer
Index t Wom; Not Am Wom

8549. Alrich, Emma B.
born 1845
journalist, author, educator
Wom Cent

8550. Amory, Estelle (Mendell)
born 1845
author
Wom Cent

8551. Bailey, Lepha Eliza (Dunton)
born 1845
temperance worker, Prohibitionist, suffragist, lecturer, author
Wom Cent

8552. Baines-Miller, Minnie (Willis)
born 1845
author
Springfield, OH
Dict Am Auth

8553. Balch, Elizabeth
1845–90
fiction author
Dict Am Auth

8554. Barrows, Katherine Isabel Hayes Chapin
1845–1913
ophthalmologist, penologist, editor, travel writer
Dict Am Auth; Index t Wom; Not Am Wom

8555. Bloede, Gertrude; Stuart
Sterne
1845–1905
poet
Brooklyn, NY
German
Dict Am Auth; Dict Nat Bio; Nat
Cyc Am Bio v10; Wom Cent

8556. Case, Marietta Stanley
born 1845
author, poet, temperance worker,
home and foreign mission worker
Manchester, OH
Wom Cent

8557. Charles, Emily Thornton;
Emily Thornton
1845–90s
poet, journalist
Dict Am Auth; Twent Cen Bio
Dict Not Am; Wom Cent

8558. Cleveland, Cynthia Eloise
born 1845
political writer and activist, lawyer, civil service worker, novelist
Washington, DC
Dict Am Auth; Twent Cen Bio
Dict Not Am

8559. Comfort, Anna (Manning)
born 1845
gynecologist, medical author, suffragist, women's rights worker,
Sorosis member
Dict Am Auth; Nat Cyc Am Bio
v3; Wom Cent

8560. Dalsheimer, Alice
1845–80
poet
Louisiana
Cyc Am Bio

8561. Engle, Addie C. Strong
born 1845
author
Wom Cent

8562. Gannett, Abbie M.
born 1845
author, women's rights worker
Unitarian
Wom Cent

**8563. Hall, Florence Marion
Howe**
1845–1922
author, essayist, writer on eti-
quette, lecturer, suffragist
Unitarian
Plainfield, NJ
Dict Am Auth; Dict Am Bio; Nat
Cyc Am Bio v19

**8564. Henry, Josephine Kirby
Williamson**
born 1845

suffragist, politician, political
writer, Prohibitionist
Kentucky
Wom Cent

8565. Hobart, Sarah Dyer
born 1845
poet, author
Wisconsin
Wom Cent

8566. Kipp, Josephine
born 1845
author
New York
Wom Cent

8567. Knox, Adeline (Trafton)
born 1845
author, novelist
St. Louis, MO
Dict Am Auth; Index t Wom;
Wom Cent

**8568. MacAfee, Nelly Nichol
(Marshal)**
born 1845
fiction writer
Kentucky
Dict Am Auth

**8569. Miller, Minnie (Willis)
(Baines)**
born 1845
religious author, temperance
worker
Springfield, OH
Dict Am Auth; Wom Cent

**8570. Mitchell, Lucy Myers
Wright**
1845–88
archaeologist, historian of ancient
art, writer on Greek art
Dict Am Auth; Dict Am Bio; Nat
Cyc Am Bio v6; Twent Cen Bio
Dict Not Am

**8571. Morgan, Anne Eugenia
Felicia**
1845–1909
philosopher, classicist, educator,
author
Dict Am Auth; Index t Wom;
Wom Cent

**8572. Murphy, Blanche
Elizabeth Mary Annunciata
Noel, Lady**
1845/50–1881
author, magazine writer
English
Cyc Am Bio; Dict Am Auth; Nat
Cyc Am Bio v11

**8573. Nason, Emma
(Huntington)**
born 1845
translator, author, poet, children's writer

Augusta, ME
Dict Am Auth; Index t Wom;
Wom Cent

8574. Oliver, Martha Capps
born 1845
children's poet
Jacksonville, IL
Dict Am Auth; Wom Cent

8575. Paine, Harriet Eliza; Eliza Chester
1845–1910
author, educator
Boston, MA
Dict Am Auth; Index t Wom;
Twent Cen Bio Dict Not Am

8576. Peters, Alice E. H.
born 1845
church and temperance worker,
suffragist, author
Methodist Episcopal
Ohio
Wom Cent

8577. Porter, Rose
1845–1906
author, religious novelist, compiler
New Haven, CT
Dict Am Auth; Nat Cyc Am Bio
v10; Wom Cent

**8578. Pringle, Elizabeth Waties
Allston**
1845–1921
rice planter, author
Not Am Wom

8579. Richardson, Ellen A.
1845–1911
artist, editor, author, club leader
Index t Wom

**8580. Samuels, Adelaide Flor-
ence Frances**
born 1845
children's author
Cyc Am Bio; Dict Am Auth

8581. Smith, Florence
1845–71
poet
New York, NY
Dict Am Auth

8582. Trafton, Adeline
born 1845
author
Cyc Am Bio

**8583. Upham, Grace le Baron
(Locke);** Grace le Baron
born 1845
children's author
Boston, MA
Dict Am Auth

**8584. Ward, Lydia Arms
(Avery) (Coonley)**
1845–1924

author, poet, patron of the arts,
suffragist, philanthropist
Chicago, IL
Dict Am Auth; Dict Am Bio;
Index t Wom; Nat Cyc Am Bio
v34

8585. Wetherbee, Emily Green
born 1845
author, poet, essayist
Massachusetts
Wom Cent

**8586. Wharton, Anne Hollings-
worth**
1845–1928
author, children's author, biogra-
pher, historian, historical writer
Philadelphia, PA
Cyc Am Bio; Dict Am Auth; Dict
Am Bio; Index t Wom; Nat Cyc
Am Bio v13; Twent Cen Bio
Dict Not Am

8587. Young, Ella (Flagg)
1845–1918
university educator and administrator, writer on education, suffragist
Chicago, IL
Dict Am Auth; Dict Am Bio;
Index t Wom; Nat Cyc Am Bio
v19; Not Am Wom

8588. Banks, Mary Ross
born 1846
author
Georgia
Wom Cent

**8589. Bergen, Fanny (Dicker-
son)**
born 1846/48
educator, botanist, naturalist, science writer
Appl Cyc Am Bio; Cyc Am Bio;
Dict Am Auth

8590. Briggs, Mary Blatchley
born 1846
journalist, poet
Index t Wom

**8591. Chenoweth, Caroline van
Duesen**
born 1846
author, university literary educa-
tor, military clerk during Civil
War, US vice-consul in China
Dict Am Auth; Index t Wom;
Twent Cen Bio Dict Not Am;
Wom Cent

**8592. Cleveland, Rose
Elizabeth**
1846–1918
novelist, writer on literature
Dict Am Auth; Nat Cyc Am Bio
v1; Twent Cen Bio Dict Not
Am; Wom Cent

8593. Evans, Lizzie Phelps Esterbrook; Esta Brooks
born 1846
novelist
Somerville, MA
Dict Am Auth; Wom Cent

8594. Foster, Susie E. (Holland)
born 1846
author, philanthropist
Oregon
Wom Cent

8595. Gilchrist, Fredrika (Beardsley)
born 1846
author
New York, NY
Dict Am Auth

8596. Green, Anna Katherine; Mrs. Charles Rohlfs
1846–1935
author, novelist
Cyc Am Bio and v2 ad; Index t Wom; Wom Lit, More

8597. Hallock, Julia Isabel (Sherman)
born 1846
author
Connecticut
Dict Am Auth

8598. Hewins, Caroline Maria Matilda
1846–1926
librarian, pioneer in library work for children, writer on librarianship
Hartford, CT
Dict Am Auth; Index t Wom; Nat Cyc Am Bio v21; Not Am Wom; Twent Cen Bio Dict Not Am

8599. Hodgkins, Louise Manning
born 1846
author, university educator in literature, writer on literature
Massachusetts
Dict Am Auth; Wom Cent

8600. Lazarus, Josephine
born 1846
author, religious writer
Jewish
Dict Am Auth

8601. Lincoln, Jeannie Gould
born 1846/53
author, poet, children's author
Washington, DC
Dict Am Auth; Index t Wom; Twent Cen Bio Dict Not Am

8602. Mannix, Mary Ellen Walsh
1846–1938

author, poet
Index t Wom

8603. Milne, Frances Margaret
born 1846
author, journalist, poet, political essayist
California
Irish
Wom Cent

8604. Morris, Clara (Morrison)
1846/48–1925
actor, author, children's author, autobiographer
Canadian
Cyc Am Bio and ad; Dict Am Auth; Dict Am Bio; Index t Wom; Nat Cyc Am Bio v11; Not Am Wom; Twent Cen Bio Dict Not Am; Wom Cent

8605. Mosher, Eliza Maria
1846–1928
physician, educator
Index t Wom; Nat Cyc Am Bio v15; Not Am Wom; Twent Cen Bio Dict Not Am

8606. Rohlf, Anora Kathleen (Green) "Anna"
1846–1935
novelist, poet, writer of detective stories
Buffalo, NY
Dict Am Auth; Dict Am Bio supp v1; Nat Cyc Am Bio v9; Twent Cen Bio Dict Not Am; Wom Cent

8607. Shaw, Emma
born 1846
author, traveler, explorer
Wom Cent

8608. Smith, Olive White
born 1846
author, temperance worker
Methodist Episcopal
Vermont
Wom Cent

8609. Summerhayes, Martha
1846–1911
western pioneer, memoirist of the western frontier
Index t Wom; Read Encyc Am West

8610. Tiernan, Frances Christine (Fisher); Christian Reid
1846–1920
author, popular novelist
Catholic
North Carolina
Dict Am Auth; Dict Am Bio; Index t Wom; Nat Cyc Am Bio v20; Not Am Wom; Twent Cen Bio Dict Not Am

8611. Titterington, Sophie (Bronson)
born 1846
children's author, fiction writer
Rochester, IL
Dict Am Auth

8612. Trott, Novella Jewell
born 1846
author, editor
Wom Cent

8613. Waggaman, Mary Teresa McKee
1846–1931
author, Confederate sympathizer
Catholic
Dict Am Bio

8614. Alden, Esther
born 1847
Civil War diarist
Index t Wom

8615. Brown, Emma Elizabeth
born 1847
popular biographer, author
Dict Am Auth; Wom Cent

8616. Catherwood, Mary (Hartwell)
1847–1902
novelist, writer of historical romances, children's author
Universalist
Illinois
Dict Am Auth; Dict Am Bio; Index t Wom; Nat Cyc Am Bio v9; Not Am Wom; Twent Cen Bio Dict Not Am; Wom Cent

8617. Cocke, Zitella
born circa 1847
poet
Dict Am Auth

8618. Foote, Mary Anna (Hallock)
1847–1938
author, novelist, artist, illustrator
Dict Am Auth; Index t Wom; Nat Cyc Am Bio v6; Not Am Wom; Read Encyc Am West; Twent Cen Bio Dict Not Am; Wom Lit, More

8619. Franklin, Christine Ladd; Christine Ladd-Franklin
1847–1930
mathematician; logician; psychologist; writer on math, logic and psychology
Dict Am Bio; Index t Wom; Nat Cyc Am Bio v5 and v26; Not Am Wom; Twent Cen Bio Dict Not Am

8620. Furber, Aurilla
born 1847
poet, temperance worker
Minnesota
Wom Cent

8621. Glynes, Ella Maria (Dietz); Ella Maria (Dietz) Glynes-Clymer
born 1847
author, actor, founder of Sorosis
Nat Cyc Am Bio v13

8622. Goldsmith, Sophia
born circa 1847
author
Bohemian
Index t Wom

8623. Howard, Blanche Willis
1847–98
author
Cyc Am Bio; Dict Am Bio; Nat Cyc Am Bio v1; Not Am Wom; Twent Cen Bio Dict Not Am

8624. Johnson, Virginia Wales; Cousin Virginia
1847/49–1916
novelist
Cyc Am Bio; Dict Am Auth; Dict Am Bio; Nat Cyc Am Bio v13; Twent Cen Bio Dict Not Am

8625. Kimball, Emma Adeline
born 1847
poet, historical sketch writer
Haverville, MA
Dict Am Auth

8626. Lawless, Margaret H. Wynne
born 1847
poet, religious worker, clubwoman
Wom Cent

8627. Martin, Jane (Percy)
born 1847
short story writer
Pendleton, OR
Dict Am Auth

8628. Mitchell, Annie Maria
born 1847
religious writer for children
Dict Am Auth

8629. Porter, Charlotte Endymion
1847/59–1942
writer on literature, magazine editor, poet
Index t Wom; Not Am Wom; Twent Cen Bio Dict Not Am

8630. Rayner, Emily C.
born 1847
author, journalist
Wom Cent

8631. Robinson, Fannie Ruth
born 1847
poet, educator
Index t Wom; Wom Cent

8632. Robinson, Jane Marie Bancroft
1847–1932
Methodist educator, deaconess leader, author, historian, philanthropist
Methodist
Index t Wom; Not Am Wom; Wom Cent

8633. Schulte, Mary Jemima (McColl)
born 1847
poet
Jersey City, NJ
Dict Am Auth

8634. Sheldon, Mary French
born 1847
translator, traveler in Africa, author
Wom Cent

8635. Smith, Jane Luella Dowd
born 1847
educator, author, poet, children's author, suffragist, temperance worker
Hudson, NY
Cyc Am Bio; Dict Am Auth; Nat Cyc Am Bio v1; Twent Cen Bio Dict Not Am; Wom Cent

8636. Sparhawk, Frances Campbell
born 1847/58
author, novelist, philanthropist, Native American welfare worker
Newton, MA
Cyc Am Bio and ad; Dict Am Auth; Nat Cyc Am Bio v10; Wom Cent

8637. Stevenson, Sarah (Yorke)
1847–1921
archaeologist, writer on archaeology
Philadelphia, PA
Dict Am Auth; Dict Am Bio; Index t Wom; Nat Cyc Am Bio v13; Twent Cen Bio Dict Not Am

8638. Teuffel, Blanche Willis (Howard)
1847–98
novelist
German (American expatriate to Germany)
Dict Am Auth

8639. Walker, Rose Kershaw
born 1847
author, journalist
Wom Cent

8640. Whiting, Lilian
1847/55–1942
journalist, essayist, poet, short story writer, biographer, editor

Boston, MA
Dict Am Auth; Index t Wom; Nat Cyc Am Bio v9; Not Am Wom

8641. Winton, Jenevehah Maria (Pray)
born 1847
poet, author
Methodist Episcopal
Wom Cent

8642. Wynne, Madelene (Yale)
born 1847
author, short story writer, silversmith, artist
Index t Wom

8643. Barnum, Frances Courtenay (Baylor)
born 1848
novelist
Dict Am Auth

8644. Bartlett, Alice Eloise; Birch Arnold
1848–1920
journalist, poet
Detroit, MI
Dict Am Auth; Index t Wom; Wom Cent

8645. Bayliss, Clara
born 1848
author
Springfield, IL
Dict Am Auth

8646. Baylor, Frances Courtenay
1848–1911
magazine writer, short story writer
Appl Cyc Am Bio; Cyc Am Bio; Dict Am Bio; Nat Cyc Am Bio v1; Twent Cen Bio Dict Not Am; Wom Cent

8647. Bennett, Adelaide George
born 1848
poet, botanist
Minnesota
Wom Cent; Index t Wom

8648. Black, Mary Fleming
born 1848
religious author, temperance worker
Wom Cent

8649. Carpenter, Esther Bernon
1848–93
short story writer
Rhode Island
Dict Am Auth; Nat Cyc Am Bio v2

8650. Clark, Susanna Rebecca Graham
born 1848
children's author

Maine
Dict Am Auth

8651. Darling, Mary Greenleaf
born 1848
author, novelist
Dict Am Auth

8652. Dayton, Elizabeth; Beth Day
born 1848
poet, author
Wisconsin
English
Wom Cent

8653. Dudley, Lucy (Bronson)
born 1848
miscellaneous writer
Dict Am Auth

8654. Duffey, Eliza Bisbee
18?–1898
writer on sex
Dict Am Auth

8655. Elliott, Sarah Barnwell
1848–1928
author, novelist, dramatist, suffragist
Tennessee
Dict Am Auth; Dict Am Bio; Nat Cyc Am Bio v21; Not Am Wom; Wom Lit, More

8656. Eve, Marie Louise
born 1848
poet
Cyc Am Bio; Wom Cent

8657. Frackleton, Susan Stuart (Goodrich)
born 1848/51
artist, ceramicist, inventor of a gas kiln, writer on ceramic technique
Dict Am Auth; Index t Wom; Twent Cen Bio Dict Not Am; Wom Cent

8658. Gould, Elizabeth Porter
born 1848
author, essayist on education, journalist, lecturer, social critic
Wom Cent

8659. Hatch, Mary R. P.; Mabel Percy
born 1848
poet, storyteller
Wom Cent

8660. Irvine, Julia Josephine (Thomas)
1848–post 1886
classical scholar, fourth president of Wellesley College
Nat Cyc Am Bio v12; Twent Cen Bio Dict Not Am

8661. James, Alice
1848–92

diarist
Index t Wom

8662. Kelly, Florence (Finch)
1848/58–1939
journalist, author
Dict Am Auth; Index t Wom; Not Am Wom

8663. Langford, Laura (Carter) (Holloway)
born 1848
author, biographer, journalist
Cyc Am Bio; Dict Am Auth; Twent Cen Bio Dict Not Am

8664. Norris, Mary Harriot
born 1848
author, novelist, literary editor, university educator
New York; Illinois
Dict Am Auth; Twent Cen Bio Dict Not Am

8665. Peeke, Margaret Bloodgood
born 1848
author
Wom Cent

8666. Perry, Lilla Cabot
1848–1933
artist, painter, poet
Dict Am Auth; Index t Wom; Nat Cyc Am Bio v26

8667. Samuels, Susan Blagge (Caldwell)
born 1848
children's author
Cyc Am Bio; Dict Am Auth

8668. Todd, Mary (Ives)
born 1848
fiction writer
Los Angeles, CA
Dict Am Auth

8669. van Rensselaer, May (King)
born 1848
historical writer on New York City
New York, NY
Dict Am Auth

8670. Woolley, Celia (Parker)
1848–1918
settlement worker, worker for social services for Blacks, Unitarian minister, author, novelist
Chicago, IL
Dict Am Auth; Dict Am Bio; Wom Cent

8671. Andrews, Marie Louise
1849–91
journalist, short story writer
Wom Cent

8672. Atherton, Mary Alderson Chandler
born 1849
suffragist, educator, author
Massachusetts
Nat Cyc Am Bio v18

8673. Babcock, Emma Whitcombe
born 1849
author
Wom Cent

8674. Baer, Libbie C. Riley
born 1849
poet
Wom Cent

8675. Beale, Maria Taylor
born 1849
novelist
North Carolina
Dict Am Auth

8676. Bigelow, Lettie Salina
born 1849
poet, author, lecturer
Nat Cyc Am Bio v6; Wom Cent

8677. Bohan, Elizabeth Baker
born 1849
painter, author, poet
Wom Cent

8678. Burnett, Frances Eliza Hodgson
1849–1924
novelist, children's author
English
Cyc Am Bio and ad; Dict Am Auth; Dict Am Bio; Great Sov Encyc; Index t Wom; Nat Cyc Am Bio v1 and v20; Not Am Wom; Twent Cen Bio Dict Not Am; Wom Cent

8679. Conklin, Viola A. (Peckham)
born 1849
historical writer
Plainfield, NJ
Dict Am Auth

8680. de Graffenreid, Mary Clare
1849–1921
social investigator, writer on social conditions, labor authority
Georgia
Encyc South Hist; Not Am Wom

8681. Gilder, Jeanett Leonard
1849–1916
literary magazine editor, critic, journalist, novelist, autobiographer
New York, NY
Cyc Am Bio and v2 ad; Dict Am Auth; Dict Am Bio; Index t Wom; Nat Cyc Am Bio v8; Not Am Wom; Twent Cen Bio Dict Not Am

8682. Harbee, Lee (Cohen)
born 1849
author, Texas historian, Sorosis member
Texas; New York
Dict Am Auth; Wom Cent

8683. Jewett, Sarah Orne; Alice Eliot
1849–1909
author, short story writer
South Berwick, ME; Boston, MA
Cyc Am Bio; Dict Am Auth; Dict Am Bio; Index t Wom; Nat Cyc Am Bio v1; Not Am Wom; Wom Cent; Wom Lit; Wom Lit, More

8684. Lazarus, Emma
1849–87
author, poet, dramatist, essayist
Jewish
New York
Cyc Am Bio; Dict Am Auth; Dict Am Bio; Index t Wom; Nat Cyc Am Bio v3; Not Am Wom; Twent Cen Bio Dict Not Am; Who Who Jew Hist; Wom Cent

8685. Litchfield, Grace Denio
1849–1944
fiction writer, poet, novelist
Protestant
Washington, DC
Dict Am Auth; Nat Cyc Am Bio v12 and v42, Wom Cent

8686. MacDowell, Katherine Sherwood (Bonner); Sherwood Bonner
1849–1883/84
author, short story writer, novelist
Holly Springs, MS
Cyc Am Bio; Dict Am Auth; Dict Am Bio; Index t Wom; Nat Cyc Am Bio v11; Not Am Wom; Twent Cen Bio Dict Not Am

8687. Marshall, Caroline Louise (Kinsbury)
born 1849
fiction writer
Eldora, IA
Dict Am Auth

8688. Mathews, Joanna Hooe
1849–1901
religious writer for children
Dict Am Auth

8689. Nicholson, Eliza Jane (Poitevent) Holbrook; Pearl Rivers
1849–96
poet, journalist, editor, publisher and owner of the New Orleans *Picayune-Times*

New Orleans, LA
Dict Am Auth; Dict Am Bio; Index t Wom; Nat Cyc Am Bio v1; Not Am Wom; Twent Cen Bio Dict Not Am; Wom Cent

8690. Nowell, Mildred E.
born 1849
author, journalist
South Carolina
Wom Cent

8691. Prescott, Mary Newmarch
1849–88
author, children's author, magazine writer
Newburyport, ME
Cyc Am Bio; Dict Am Auth; Nat Cyc Am Bio v8

8692. Ray, Henrietta Cordelia
1849–1916
poet
Index t Wom

8693. Ray, Rachel Beasley; Kate Carrington
born 1849
poet, author, temperance advocate, feminist
Baptist
Wom Cent

8694. Shoaff, Carrie M.; Carrie Shoff
born 1849
artist, ceramicist, inventor
Index t Wom; Wom Cent

8695. Sprague, Mary Aplin
born 1849
novelist
Newark, OH
Dict Am Auth

8696. Stuart, Ruth McEnery
1849/56/79–1917
short story writer
Dict Am Auth; Dict Am Bio; Index t Wom; Not Am Wom; Twent Cen Bio Dict Not Am

8697. Tuttle, Mary McArthur (Thompson)
born 1849/59
artist, writer and lecturer on art, art historian, novelist
Methodist
Dict Am Bio; Nat Cyc Am Bio v10

8698. Banks, Nancy Huston
born 1850
novelist
Index t Wom

8699. Barker, Ellen Blackmar (Maxwell); Ellen Blackmar Maxwell
born 185?
author

Washington, DC
Dict Am Auth; Index t Wom

8700. Barnes, Mary Downing Sheldon
1850–98
educator, historian, textbook author
California
Dict Am Auth; Dict Am Bio; Not Am Wom; Wom Cent

8701. Braden, Anna Madge; Madge Rile
flourished 1880
author
Presbyterian
Wom Cent

8702. Bruce, Elizabeth M.
flourished 1880s
clergyperson, author, editor
Index t Wom

8703. Bull, Sarah Chapman (Thorpe)
1850–post 1876
temperance worker, biographer
Dict Am Auth; Wom Cent

8704. Burns, Nellie Marie
born circa 1850
poet
Wom Cent

8705. Burt, Mary Elizabeth
1850–1919
primary school educator, author
Dict Am Bio

8706. Cardwill, Mary E.
flourished 1880s
author
Wom Cent

8707. Carpenter, Alice Dimmick
flourished 1880s
traveler, author
Wom Cent

8708. Champney, Elizabeth William; Lizzie Williams
born 1850
children's author
New York
Cyc Am Bio and ad; Dict Am Auth; Nat Cyc Am Bio v11; Twent Cen Bio Dict Not Am; Wom Cent

8709. Chapin, Sallie F.
flourished 1880s
temperance worker, writer on temperance
Wom Cent

8710. Coates, Florence van Leer (Earle) (Nicholson)
1850–1927
poet

Philadelphia, PA
Dict Am Auth; Dict Am Bio;
Index t Wom; Nat Cyc Am Bio
v18; Not Am Wom; Wom Cent

8711. Connelly, Emma M.
flourished 1880s–90s
author
New York, NY
Dict Am Bio; Wom Cent

8712. Cook, Amelia Josephine
flourished 1880s
litterateur, short story writer,
children's author
Wom Cent

8713. Crawford, Alice (Arnold)
1850–74
poet
Milwaukee, WI
Dict Am Auth; Wom Cent

8714. Cruger, S. van Rensselaer
flourished 1880s
novelist
Wom Cent

8715. Dabney, Julia Parker
born 1850
author, artist, novelist
Brookline, MA
Twent Cen Bio Dict Not Am

8716. Darling, Alice O.
flourished 1880s
poet
New Hampshire
Wom Cent

8717. Diehl, Anna Randall
flourished 1880s
author, editor
Index t Wom

8718. Dieudonne, Florence Carpenter
born 1850
litterateur, letter writer
Wom Cent

8719. Fletcher, Julia Constance; George Fleming
born 1850/53
author, novelist, dramatist
Cyc Am Bio; Dict Am Auth; Nat
Cyc Am Bio v13; Twent Cen
Bio Dict Not Am

8720. Flewellyn, Juliette (Colliton)
born 1850
author
Lockport, NY
Dict Am Auth

8721. French, Alice; Octave Thanet
1850–1934
novelist, short story writer

Iowa; Arkansas
Dict Am Auth; Dict Am Bio
supp v1; Index t Wom; Nat Cyc
Am Bio v10 and v25; Not Am
Wom; Twent Cen Bio Dict Not
Am; Wom Cent

8722. Fryatt, Frances Elizabeth
flourished 1880s–90s
author, specialist in household
art, interior decorator
New York
Wom Cent

8723. Graham, Margaret (Collier)
born 1850
author
California
Dict Am Auth

8724. Halvey, Margaret Mary Brophy
flourished 1880s
clubwoman, educator, poet
Irish
Index t Wom

8725. Hapgood, Isabel Florence
1850/51–1928
translator, linguist, writer on
Russian and European literature, journalist
New York, NY
Dict Am Auth; Dict Am Bio; Nat
Cyc Am Bio v21; Not Am
Wom; Twent Cen Bio Dict Not
Am; Wom Cent

8726. Harris, Ethel Hillyer
flourished 1880s
author
Rome, GA
Wom Cent

8727. Hewitt, Emma Churchman
born 1850
miscellaneous writer, journalist
Philadelphia, PA
Dict Am Auth; Wom Cent

8728. Hibbard, Grace
flourished 1880s
author
Wom Cent

8729. Hinman, Ida
flourished 1880s
litterateur, journalist
Wom Cent

8730. Holbrook, Florence
born 185?
textbook author, educator
Chicago, IL
Dict Am Auth

8731. Holmes, Georgina (Klingle); George Klingle
born 185?
poet

Philadelphia, PA
Dict Am Auth; Wom Cent

8732. Housh, Esther T.
flourished 1880s
temperance worker, author
Wom Cent

8733. Huntley, Florence
flourished 1880s; died 1912
journalist, author, humorist
Index t Wom; Wom Cent

8734. Ives, Alice Emma
flourished 1880s
dramatist, journalist
Detroit, MI
Index t Wom; Wom Cent

8735. Jefferis, Marea Wood
flourished 1880s–1900s
poet
Philadelphia, PA
Index t Wom; Wom Cent

8736. Jennison, Lucy White; Owen Innsley
born 1850
poet
Dict Am Auth

8737. Keating, Josephine E.
flourished 1880s–90s
literary critic, musician, music educator
Tennessee
Wom Cent

8738. King, Susan (Petigru)
flourished 1880s
author
Dict Am Bio Men Time

8739. Kingsbury, Elizabeth A.
flourished 1880s
lecturer, poet
Index t Wom

8740. Lauder, Maria Elise Turner
flourished 1880s
author
Canadian
Wom Cent

8741. Lease, Mary Elizabeth (Clyens)
1850/53–1933
Populist orator, politician, Prohibition party worker, suffragist,
evolutionist, birth control advocate, feminist, political author
Kansas
Dict Am Auth; Dict Am Bio
supp v1; Index t Wom; Not Am
Wom; Read Encyc Am West

8742. Logan, Virginia Knight
1850–1940
composer, author
Index t Wom

8743. Mackin, Sarah Maria Spottiswood, Countess
born 1850
author
Index t Wom

8744. Marble, Callie Bonney
flourished 1880s–1910s
author
Illinois
Index t Wom; Wom Cent

8745. McComas, Alice Moore
born 1850
author, editor, lecturer, suffragist
Wom Cent

8746. McLandburgh, Florence
born 1850
short story writer
Cyc Am Bio; Dict Am Auth

8747. Murfree, Fanny Noailles Dickinson
born 185?
novelist
Dict Am Auth

8748. Murfree, Mary Noailles; Charles Egbert Craddock
1850–1922
novelist, short story writer
Tennessee
Cyc Am Bio; Dict Am Auth; Dict
Am Bio; Encyc South Hist; Index t Wom; Not Am Wom;
Twent Cen Bio Dict Not Am;
Wom Cent; Wom Lit; Wom Lit,
More

8749. Pierce, Elizabeth Cumings; Elizabeth Cumings
born 1850
poet, author, children's author
Wom Cent

8750. Pitman, Marie J. (Davis)
1850–88
children's author, journalist,
newspaper foreign correspondent
Boston, MA
Cyc Am Bio; Dict Am Auth

8751. Plassmann, Martha Edgerton
born 1850
author, western pioneer
Index t Wom

8752. Pullen, Elisabeth Jones (Cavazza); E. Cavazza
flourished 1880s–90s
journalist, sketch writer
Portland, ME
Dict Am Auth; Nat Cyc Am Bio
v8

8753. Reifsnider, Anna Cyrene (Porter) Ellis
1850–1932

author
Nat Cyc Am Bio v23

8754. Renfrew, Carrie
flourished 1880s–90s
poet, biographer
Nebraska
Wom Cent

8755. Richards, Laura Elizabeth (Howe)
1850–1943
author, children's author, poet
Dict Am Auth; Dict Am Bio supp v3; Index t Wom; Nat Cyc Am Bio v15 and v39; Not Am Wom; Twent Cen Bio Dict Not Am

8756. Robinson, Mary Dommet (Nauman)
born 185?
novelist
Lancaster, PA
Dict Am Auth

8757. Savage, Minnie Stebbins; Marion Lisle
born 1850
poet, author, Unitarian church worker, temperance worker
Unitarian
Wisconsin
Wom Cent

8758. Schoff, Hannah Kent
1850/53–1940
child welfare worker, juvenile court reformer, child aid leader, editor, author
Philadelphia, PA
Index t Wom; Nat Cyc Am Bio v18; Not Am Wom

8759. Shattuck, Harriette Lucy (Robinson)
born 1850
miscellaneous author, legal clerk, writer on parliamentary law, suffragist
Malden, MA
Dict Am Auth; Index t Wom; Twent Cen Bio Dict Not Am; Wom Cent

8760. Smith, Emily Adella
flourished 1880s
entomologist, author
Index t Wom

8761. Stowell, Louisa Maria (Reed)
born 1850
microscopist, botanist, author on microscopal botany, educator, editor
Cyc Am Bio and ad; Dict Am Auth; Index t Wom; Wom Cent

8762. Sutherland, Evelyn Greenleaf (Baker)
born 185?

playwright
Boston, MA
Dict Am Auth

8763. Thorpe, Rose Alnora (Hartwick)
1850–1939
popular poet, children's author
Cyc Am Bio and ad; Dict Am Auth; Dict Nat Bio supp v2; Index t Wom; Nat Cyc Am Bio v10; Not Am Wom; Twent Cen Bio Dict Not Am; Wom Cent

8764. Todd, Adah J.
flourished 1880s–90s
author, educator, physiologist
Wom Cent

8765. Ward, Anna Lydia
born circa 1850
author
Cyc Am Bio

8766. Weeks-Shaw, Clara
flourished 1880s
nurse, author
Index t Wom

8767. Wilcox, Ella (Wheeler)
1850/55–1919
poet, journalist, novelist
New York, NY
Cyc Am Bio and ad; Dict Am Auth; Dict Am Bio; Index t Wom; Nat Cyc Am Bio v11; Not Am Wom; Wom Lit, More

8768. Wilder, S. Fannie Gerry
born 1850
author, juvenile writer
Wom Cent

8769. Woodruff, Anne Helena
born 1850
children's author
Nat Cyc Am Bio v17

8770. Abbott, Mary Perkins (Ives)
1851–1904
journalist, short story and romance writer
Chicago, IL
Dict Am Auth

8771. Benneson, Cora Agnes
born 1851
lawyer, author
Cyc Am Bio; Nat Cyc Am Bio v17

8772. Best, Eva
born 1851
dramatist, poet, author
Wom Cent

8773. Byers, Margaretta
died 1901
fashion designer, author
Index t Wom

8774. Chopin, Kate O'Flaherty
1851–1904
novelist, short story writer
St. Louis, MO
Dict Am Auth; Cyc Am Bio v25

8775. Clark, Katharine Pickens (Upson)
1851–1935
children's author, journalist, suffragist, temperance worker, lecturer
Dict Am Auth; Nat Cyc Am Bio v30

8776. Crane, Sibylla (Bailey)
1851–1902
vocalist, composer, music educator, writer on music
Boston, MA
Dict Am Auth; Nat Cyc Am Bio v7; Twent Cen Bio Dict Not Am; Wom Cent

8777. Cutting, Mary Stewart (Doubleday)
1851–1924
fiction writer
East Orange, NJ
Dict Am Auth; Index t Wom

8778. Dawes, Anna Laurens
born 1851
author, journalist, essayist
Dict Am Auth; Wom Cent

8779. de Long, Emma J. Wotton
1851–1940
editor, author
Index t Wom

8780. Earle, Alice Morse
1851/53–1911
author, social and domestic historian of colonial New England, writer on history
New England
Dict Am Auth; Dict Am Bio; Index t Wom; Nat Cyc Am Bio v13; Not Am Wom; Twent Cen Bio Dict Not Am

8781. Fraser, Mary Crawford
born 1851
author
Index t Wom

8782. Giles, Ella Augusta
born 1851
author
Madison, WI
Dict Am Auth; Wom Cent

8783. Harper, Ida A. Husted
1851–1931
political journalist, suffragist, feminist, newspaper editor, author
Dict Am Bio; Index t Wom; Nat Cyc Am Bio v25; Not Am Wom; Wom Cent

8784. Hayes, Ellen
born 1851
mathematician, geologist, educator, author
Index t Wom; Twent Cen Bio Dict Not Am

8785. Inglehart, Frances (Chambers) (Gooch)
1851–post 1890
writer on Texas, fiction writer
Austin, TX
Dict Am Auth; Wom Cent

8786. Lathrop, Rose (Hawthorne); Mother Mary Alphonsa; Rose Hawthorne
1851–1926
author, artist, poet, Catholic nun, founder of the Dominican Congregation of St. Rose of Lima, philanthropist
Catholic
Cyc Am Bio; Dict Am Auth; Dict Am Bio; Index t Wom; Nat Cyc Am Bio v9; Not Am Wom; Twent Cen Bio Dict Not Am; Wom Cent

8787. Longyear, Mary Hawley Beecher
born 1851
author, philanthropist
Christian Scientist
Nat Cyc Am Bio csv3

8788. Rimmer, Caroline Hunt
born 1851
writer on artistic technique
Dict Am Auth

8789. Rutherford, Mildred Lewis
1851/52–1928
educator, textbook author, apologist for the Old South
Athens, GA
Dict Am Auth; Nat Cyc Am Bio v10; Not Am Wom; Twent Cen Bio Dict Not Am

8790. van Rensselaer, Mariana Alley (Griswold); Mrs. Schuyler
1851–1934
writer on art, art critic, art historian
Cyc Am Bio and ad; Dict Am Auth; Dict Am Bio; Index t Wom; Not Am Wom

8791. von Teuffel, Blanche Willis Howard; Blanche Willis Howard
born 1851
author
Wom Cent

8792. Winslow, Helen Maria
1851–1938
clubwoman, author, journalist, editor, publisher

Boston, MA
Dict Am Auth; Index t Wom; Nat Cyc Am Bio csv2; Wom Cent

8793. Wright, Mary (Tappan)
born 1851
short story writer
Cambridge, MA
Dict Am Auth

8794. Arrue de Miranda, Luz
born 1852
poet
Guatemalan
Appl Cyc Am Bio

8795. Ballard, Mary Canfield
born 1852
poet
Wom Cent

8796. Daniels, Cora (Linn); Australia
born 1852
author, novelist
Massachusetts
Dict Am Auth; Wom Cent

8797. Davidson, Hannah Amelia
1852–1919
author of study guides, educator, editor, lecturer, publisher
Index t Wom; Nat Cyc Am Bio v19

8798. Davis, Mary Evelyn (Moore)
1852–1909
journalist, novelist, short story writer
New Orleans, LA
Dict Am Auth; Dict Am Bio; Nat Cyc Am Bio v10

8799. Freeman, Mary Eleanor Wilkins
1852–1930
author
Dict Am Bio; Index t Wom; Not Am Wom; Wom Lit; Wom Lit, More

8800. Haswin, Frances R.
born 1852
musician, composer, poet, actor
Wom Cent

8801. Krout, Mary Hannah
1852/57–1927
poet, author, educator, journalist
Denver, CO
Dict Am Auth; Index t Wom; Wom Cent

8802. McGahan, Barbara; Paul Kashirin
born 1852
author, Russian-language journalist, correspondent in the

1874–75 Spanish war, Russo-Turkish Wars correspondent
Wom Cent

8803. Morton, Eliza Happy
1852–1916
author, songwriter, educator, geographer
Maine
Index t Wom; Wom Cent

8804. Myers, Minnie (Walter)
born 1852
writer on the South
Memphis, TN
Dict Am Auth

8805. Ormsby, Mary Frost
born circa 1852
author, journalist, philanthropist, pacifist
New York, NY
Index t Wom; Wom Cent

8806. Roberts, Ada Palmer
born 1852
poet
Wom Cent

8807. Robertson, Georgia Trowbridge; Marcia
born 1852
educator, author
Wom Cent

8808. Skeel, Adelaide
born 1852
children's author
Newburgh, NY
Dict Am Auth

8809. Smith, Genie M.; Maude Meredith; Kit Clover
born 1852
author, magazine writer, short story writer
Dubuque, IA
Dict Am Auth; Wom Cent

8810. St. John, Cynthia Morgan
1852–1919
author, Wordsworthian expert and collector
New York
Index t Wom; Wom Cent

8811. Wheeler, Cora Stuart
born 1852
poet, author, biographer of notable women
Illinois
Wom Cent

8812. Yates, Josephine Silone; R. K. Potter
1852–1912
educator, author
Missouri
Black
Index t Wom; Negro Alman; Prof Negro Wom v1

8813. Birkholz, Eugenie S.
born 1853
author
Wom Cent

8814. Call, Annie Payson
born 1853
author, teacher of nerve training
Dict Am Auth; Index t Wom

8815. Conway, Katherine Eleanor
born 1853
journalist, poet
Catholic
Boston, MA
Dict Am Auth; Twent Cen Bio Dict Not Am; Wom Cent

8816. Dorsey, Ella Loraine
1853–1901
children's author
Washington, DC
Dict Am Auth; Index t Wom; Wom Cent

8817. Field, Caroline Leslie (Whitney)
1853–1902
author
Guilford, CT
Dict Am Auth; Twent Cen Bio Dict Not Am

8818. Fuller, Anna
born 1853
author, novelist
Boston, MA
Dict Am Auth; Twent Cen Bio Dict Not Am

8819. Gardener, Helen Hamilton (Chenoweth)
1853/58–1925
author, novelist, essayist, feminist, suffragist, geneticist, biologist, sociologist, civil service commissioner
Dict Am Bio; Index t Wom; Nat Cyc Am Bio v9; Not Am Wom; Twent Cen Bio Dict Not Am; Wom Cent

8820. Gordon, Anna Adams
1853–1931
temperance reformer, financier, children's author
Index t Wom; Nat Cyc Am Bio csv1; Not Am Wom; Wom Cent

8821. Hager, Lucie Carolyn (Gilson)
born 1853
author, writer on Massachusetts
Massachusetts
Dict Am Auth; Wom Cent

8822. Ide, Frances Otis Ogden; Ruth Ogden
born 1853
children's author

Brooklyn, NY
Dict Am Auth; Twent Cen Bio Dict Not Am

8823. King, Anna (Eichberg)
born 1853
short story writer
Boston, MA
Dict Am Auth

8824. Macchetta d'Allegri, Blanche Roosevelt (Tucker), Marchesa
1853–98
miscellaneous writer
Dict Am Auth

8825. MacClelland, Margaret Greenway
1853–95
author, novelist
Virginia
Dict Am Auth; Nat Cyc Am Bio v2

8826. Mason, Caroline Atwater
born 1853
author
Batavia, NY
Dict Am Auth; Nat Cyc Am Bio v4; Twent Cen Bio Dict Not Am

8827. McMurry, Lida Brown
born 1853
children's author, educator
Nat Cyc Am Bio csv2

8828. Noble, Lucy (Seward)
born 1853
author, traveler, lecturer
Nat Cyc Am Bio v17

8829. Norraikow, Ella, Countess
born 1853
author, journalist, Russian correspondent, traveler
Canadian
Wom Cent

8830. Poulsson, Anne Emilie
1853–1939
children's author, writer on children, editor, illustrator, kindergarten educator
Boston, MA
Dict Am Auth; Index t Wom; Nat Cyc Am Bio v10; Twent Cen Bio Dict Not Am

8831. Read, Jane Maria
born 1853
poet, artist
Colebrook Springs, MA
Dict Am Auth; Wom Cent

8832. Reinertson, Emma May Alexander; Gale Forest
born 1853
short story writer

Wisconsin
Wom Cent

8833. Reynolds, Myra
1853–1936
scholar of English literature, educator
Not Am Wom

8834. Salmon, Lucy Maynard
1853–1927
historian, writer on history, university educator
Dict Am Auth; Dict Am Bio; Not Am Wom

8835. Shuey, Lilian (Hinman)
born 1853
novelist
California
Dict Am Auth

8836. Smart, Helen Hamilton (Gardener)
born 1853
novelist
Boston, MA
Dict Am Auth

8837. Smith, Charlotte Louise
born 1853
poet, author
Maine
Wom Cent

8838. Stephens, Kate
born 1853
history writer
Nat Cyc Am Bio csv2

8839. Sweet, Ada Celeste
1853–1928
journalist, editor, author, social reformer, philanthropist, pension agent
Chicago, IL
Index t Wom; Wom Cent

8840. Trask, Kate (Nichols) "Katrina"
1853/63–1922
magazine author, poet, short story writer, essayist, philanthropist
Saratoga, NY
Dict Am Auth; Nat Cyc Am Bio v11; Not Am Wom

8841. Upton, Harriet Taylor
1853–1945
suffragist, feminist, author, Republican party leader
Index t Wom; Not Am Wom; Obit File

8842. Ward, May (Alden)
born 1853
historical author, biographer, editor, lecturer, club leader, president of the Massachusetts State Federation of Women's Clubs
Dict Am Auth; Index t Wom; Twent Cen Bio Dict Not Am; Wom Cent

8843. Webster, Helen Livermore
1853–post 1890
writer on philology, philologist, university educator
Dict Am Auth; Wom Cent

8844. Wenckebach, Anna Doris Amalie Catharina Carla
born 1853
educator, author on German language and literature
Prussian
Nat Cyc Am Bio v10

8845. Woods, Katharine Pearson
1853–1923
fiction author, educator, social service worker
Dict Am Auth; Not Am Wom

8846. Wright, Marie Robinson
born 1853/60
journalist, travel writer
Georgia; New York
Dict Am Auth; Wom Cent

8847. Archibald, Edith Jessie
born 1854
novelist, temperance reformer
Canadian
Index t Wom; Wom Cent

8848. Burnham, Clara Louise (Root)
1854–1927
poet, novelist, librettist
Chicago, IL
Dict Am Auth; Dict Am Bio; Index t Wom; Nat Cyc Am Bio v9 and v21; Wom Cent

8849. Crow, Martha Emilie Foote
1854–1924
college educator, author
Nat Cyc Am Bio v22; Twent Cen Bio Dict Not Am

8850. Crowninshield, Mary (Bradford)
1854–1913
fiction writer
Washington, DC
Index t Wom

8851. Daggett, Mary (Stewart)
born 1854
novelist
Pasadena, CA
Dict Am Auth; Nat Cyc Am Bio v9

8852. Delatombe, Alice S.
born 1854

poet
Ohio
Wom Cent

8853. Elliott, Maude Howe
1854–1948
author, novelist, suffragist
Unitarian
Chicago, IL
Dict Am Auth; Nat Cyc Am Bio v36; Not Am Wom; Twent Cen Bio Dict Not Am; Wom Cent

8854. Ford, Frances M.
1854–1956
short story writer, children's author
Obit File

8855. French, Lillie Hamilton
born 1854
magazine writer
New York, NY
Dict Am Auth

8856. Griffith, Mary Lillian
born 1854
philanthropist, author on morals, religious writer
Methodist Episcopal
Philadelphia, PA
Wom Cent

8857. Hammond, Henrietta (Hardy); Henri Dange
1854–83
fiction author
Virginia
Dict Am Auth

8858. Keith, Eliza D.; Erie Douglas; Di Vernon
born 1854
author, journalist, worker for the SPCA
California
Nat Cyc Am Bio v2; Wom Cent

8859. Litchfield, Mary Elizabeth
born 1854
author
Index t Wom

8860. Magruder, Julia
1854–1907
author, short story writer, novelist
Cyc Am Bio; Dict Am Auth; Index t Wom; Nat Cyc Am Bio v8; Twent Cen Bio Dict Not Am

8861. Newberry, Julia
1854–76
diarist
Index t Wom

8862. Ober, Sara Endicott
born 1854

missionary in the Tennessee and Kentucky mountains, fiction writer
Tennessee; Kentucky
Dict Am Auth

8863. Palmer, Anna Campbell; Mrs. George Archibald
1854–1928
children's author, poet
Methodist Episcopal
Elmira, NY
Dict Am Auth; Index t Wom; Nat Cyc Am Bio v22; Twent Cen Bio Dict Not Am; Wom Cent

8864. Perry, Mary Alice
1854–83
fiction writer
Dict Am Auth

8865. Reeves, Marian Calhoun Legare; "Fadette"
circa 1854–98
author, novelist
Washington, DC
Cyc Am Bio; Dict Am Auth; Nat Cyc Am Bio v4

8866. Sadlier, Anna Theresa
born 1854/56
author, biographer, translator
Catholic
Cyc Am Bio; Dict Am Auth

8867. Sage, Agnes Carolyn
born 1854
children's author
Dict Am Auth

8868. Tappan, Eva March
1854–1930
educator, children's author, history text writer
Worcester, MA
Dict Am Auth; Dict Am Bio; Not Am Wom; Twent Cen Bio Dict Not Am

8869. Thomas, Edith Matilda
1854–1925
poet, author
New York; Geneva, OH
Cyc Am Bio and ad; Dict Am Auth; Dict Am Bio; Index t Wom; Nat Cyc Am Bio v9; Not Am Wom; Twent Cen Bio Dict Not Am; Wom Cent

8870. Trail, Florence
born 1854
author, translator
Wom Cent

8871. Vaile, Charlotte Marion (White)
1854–1902
children's short story writer
Denver, CO
Dict Am Auth

8872. Wakeman, Antoinette van Hoesen
1854–post 1890
journalist, novelist
Illinois; Hastings, NE
Dict Am Auth; Wom Cent

8873. Breck, Carrie Ellis
1855–1934
author, songwriter
Index t Wom

8874. Davis, Elizabeth Lindsay
born 1855
author, clubwoman
Illinois
Black
Prof Negro Wom v1

8875. Dewing, Elizabeth Bartol
born 1855
author, novelist
New York
Nat Cyc Am Bio csv3

8876. Dodd, Anna Bowman (Blake)
1855–post 1890s
travel writer, essayist
New York
Dict Am Auth; Wom Cent

8877. Dowd, Mary Alice
born 1855
poet, educator
Connecticut
Dict Am Auth; Wom Cent

8878. Dunlap, Laura Comstock
1855–1947
religious writer, textbook author
Obit File

8879. Dye, Eva (Emery)
1855–1947
historian, writer of historical fiction, novelist
Oregon
Dict Am Auth; Index t Wom; Nat Cyc Am Bio v13; Read Encyc Am West

8880. Fairchild, Mary Solome Cutler
1855–1921
librarian for the blind, nonfiction writer
New York
Dict Am Auth; Dict Am Bio; Index t Wom; Nat Cyc Am Bio v20; Not Am Wom; Twent Cen Bio Dict Not Am

8881. Hersey, Heloise Edwina
born 1855
educator, writer on education
Boston, MA
Dict Am Auth

8882. Hogan, Louise E. (Shimer)
born 1855
writer on domestic science
Dict Am Auth

8883. Howe, Maud
born 1855
author
Cyc Am Bio

8884. Lillie, Lucy Cecil (White)
born 1855
children's author
Dict Am Auth

8885. Loughead, Flora (Haines)
born 1855
miscellaneous writer, journalist, novelist, children's author
Santa Barbara, CA
Dict Am Auth; Nat Cyc Am Bio v11; Wom Cent

8886. Manning, Jessie Wilson
born 1855
author, temperance worker, lecturer
Iowa
Index t Wom; Wom Cent

8887. Mossell, Gertrude Bustill
born 1855
newspaper editor, author
Pennsylvania
Black
Negro Alman; Prof Negro Wom v1

8888. Pennell, Elizabeth (Robins)
1855–1936
author, travel writer, biographer, art critic, bicycle tourer
Dict Am Auth; Index t Wom; Nat Cyc Am Bio v10; Not Am Wom

8889. Repplier, Agnes
1855/59–1950
essayist, children's author, biographer
Catholic
Philadelphia, PA
Dict Am Auth; Dict Am Bio supp v4; Index t Wom; Nat Cyc Am Bio v4; Not Am Wom; Obit File; Twent Cen Bio Dict Not Am

8890. Sheldon, Grace Carew
born 1855
journalist, author
Twent Cen Bio Dict Not Am

8891. Smith, Mary Agnes Easby
born 1855
author
Index t Wom

8892. Sweet, Sophia Miriam
1855–1912

author, editor
Index t Wom

8893. Wallace, Mary Ella
1855–1938
author
Index t Wom

8894. Ames, Lucy True
born 1856
author
Dict Am Auth; Wom Cent

8895. Bates, Harriet Leonora (Vose); Eleanor Putnam
1856–86
author
Dict Am Auth; Nat Cyc Am Bio v8

8896. Blanchard, Amy Ella
born 1856
children's author
Philadelphia, PA
Dict Am Auth

8897. Blatch, Harriot Eaton Stanton
1856–1940
leader of the radical wing of the American suffragist movement, author, political activist, Fabian Socialist, lecturer
Dict Am Bio supp v2; Not Am Wom; Obit File

8898. Brown, Alice
1856/57–1948
children's author
Boston, MA
Dict Am Auth; Index t Wom; Nat Cyc Am Bio v15; Not Am Wom; Twent Cen Bio Dict Not Am; Wom Lit; Wom Lit, More

8899. Clymer, Ella Maria (Dietz)
1856–post 1880
poet, actor, president of Sorosis
New York
Dict Am Auth; Wom Cent

8900. Cole, Elizabeth
born 1856
author
Wom Cent

8901. Forbes, Harriette (Merrifield)
born 1856
historical sketch writer
Westborough, MA
Dict Am Auth

8902. Gates, Susa Young
1856–1933
Mormon author, educator, suffragist
Mormon
Nat Cyc Am Bio csv2; Read Encyc Am West

8903. Goodrich, Frances Louisa
born 1856
author, weaver, business executive
Index t Wom

8904. Goodwin, Maud (Wilder)
born 1856
author, historical novelist
New York, NY
Dict Am Auth; Twent Cen Bio Dict Not Am

8905. Grannis, Anna Jane
born 1856
fiction author
Plainville, CT
Dict Am Auth

8906. Greene, Sarah Pratt (McLean)
1856/65–1935
author, novelist
Dict Am Auth; Index t Wom; Nat Cyc Am Bio v13; Not Am Wom; Twent Cen Bio Dict Not Am

8907. Hazard, Caroline
1856–1945
fifth president of Wellesley College, historian, historical author
Congregationalist
Dict Am Auth; Index t Wom; Nat Cyc Am Bio v12, v34, and csv43; Not Am Wom; Twent Cen Bio Dict Not Am

8908. Lamar, Clarinda Huntington Pendleton
1856/77–1943
author, leader of the National Society of Colonial Dames
Nat Cyc Am Bio v32; Obit File

8909. Marbury, Elizabeth
1856–1933
theatrical and author's agent
Dict Am Bio supp v1; Index t Wom

8910. Mead, Lucia True (Ames)
1856–1936
pacifist, internationalist, suffragist, Black welfare and education worker, author
Unitarian
Nat Cyc Am Bio v28; Not Am Wom; Twent Cen Bio Dict Not Am

8911. Merriman, Effie (Woodward)
born 1856
children's writer
Minneapolis, MN
Dict Am Auth

8912. Parker, Elizabeth Lowber (Chandler); Bessie Chandler
born 1856

magazine author
Batavia, NY
Dict Am Auth

8913. Plummer, Mary Wright
1856–1916
librarian, educator, poet, author
Brooklyn, NY
Dict Am Auth; Dict Am Bio; Index t Wom; Nat Cyc Am Bio v21; Not Am Wom; Twent Cen Bio Dict Not Am

8914. Putnam, Ruth
1856–1931
author, history writer
Dict Am Auth; Dict Am Bio

8915. Rathbone, Josephine Adams
1856/64–1941
librarian, editor, educator
Index t Wom; Nat Cyc Am Bio csv4; Not Am Wom

8916. Reese, Lizette Woodworth
1856–1935
lyric poet, English literature teacher
Baltimore, MD
Dict Am Auth; Dict Am Bio supp v1; Index t Wom; Nat Cyc Am Bio csv3; Not Am Wom; Wom Cent; Wom Lit, More

8917. Roe, Nora Ardelia (Metcalf)
born 1856
short story writer
Worcester, MA
Dict Am Auth

8918. Scidmore, Eliza Ruhamah; Eliza Ruhamah
1856–1928
geographer, traveler, travel writer, journalist
Washington, DC
Dict Am Auth; Dict Am Bio; Index t Wom; Twent Cen Bio Dict Not Am

8919. Stephen, Elizabeth (Willisson)
born 1856
author, novelist
Rockport, IL
Dict Am Auth; Wom Cent

8920. Street, Ida Maria
born 1856
educator, art criticism author
Milwaukee, WI
Dict Am Auth

8921. Thompson, Caroline Wadsworth
born 1856
author
Index t Wom

8922. Todd, Mabel Loomis
1856/58–1932
author, editor of Emily Dickinson's books and letters, traveler, lecturer, astronomer
Dict Am Bio; Index t Wom; Nat Cyc Am Bio v9, v28, and v41; Not Am Wom; Twent Cen Bio Dict Not Am; Wom Cent

8923. Train, Elizabeth Phipps
born 1856/57
author, novelist
Duxbury, MA
Dict Am Auth; Twent Cen Bio Dict Not Am

8924. Walter, Carrie Stevens
born 1856
educator, poet
Catholic
California
Wom Cent

8925. Webb, Ella Surtevant
born 1856
author
Wom Cent

8926. White, Eliza Orne; Alex
1856–1947
children's author
Brookline, MA
Dict Am Auth; Nat Cyc Am Bio v13; Not Am Wom; Twent Cen Bio Dict Not Am

8927. Wiggin, Kate Douglas Smith
1856/59–1923
author, children's author, kindergarten educator, philanthropist
California
Dict Am Bio; Index t Wom; Nat Cyc Am Bio v6; Not Am Wom; Wom Cent

8928. Willcox, Mary Alice
1856–1953
zoologist, writer on zoology, college educator
Dict Am Auth; Index t Wom

8929. Atherton, Gertrude Franklin (Horn); Franklin Horne
1857/59–1948
novelist, suffragist, women's rights worker
San Francisco, CA
Dict Am Auth; Dict Am Bio supp v4; Dict Lit Bio v9; Index t Wom; Nat Cyc Am Bio v10, v36, and csv4; Not Am Wom; Obit File; Read Encyc Am West; Twent Cen Bio Dict Not Am; Wom Lit; Wom Lit, More

8930. Barnes, Annie Maria
born 1857
children's author

Methodist
Wom Cent

8931. Belden, Jessie (van Zile)
born 1857
novelist
Syracuse, NY
Dict Am Auth

8932. Benedict, Emma Lee
born 1857
author, educator, temperance worker
New York
Wom Cent

8933. Blackwell, Alice Stone
1857–1950
feminist, suffragist, journalist, editor, author, humanitarian
Dict Am Bio supp v2; Index t Wom; Nat Cyc Am Bio csv6; Not Am Wom; Obit File; Wom Cent

8934. Brown, Helen Dawes
1857–1941
author, lecturer on English literature
Dict Am Auth; Index t Wom

8935. Brown, Katherine "Kate" Louise
1857–1921
children's author, composer, educator
Boston, MA
Dict Am Auth; Index t Wom

8936. Coman, Katharine
1857–1915
economic historian, writer on history, social reformer, educator
Ohio
Dict Am Auth; Index t Wom; Not Am Wom

8937. Davis, Ida May
born 1857
litterateur, author, poet
Terra Haute, IN
Wom Cent

8938. Deland, Margaretta Wade (Campbell)
1857–1945
poet, novelist, short story writer
Presbyterian; Episcopalian
Dict Am Bio supp v3; Index t Wom; Nat Cyc Am Bio v3 and v33; Not Am Wom; Obit File; Twent Cen Bio Dict Not Am; Wom Cent; Wom Lit, More

8939. Delano, Frances Jackson
born 1857
author
Fairhaven, MA
Dict Am Auth

8940. Dey, Haryot Hold; Hattie Hamblin Cahoon Dey
1857–1950
author, editor
Obit File

8941. Farmer, Fannie Merrit
1857–1915
culinary expert, home economist, cookbook author
Dict Am Bio; Index t Wom; Nat Cyc Am Bio v22; Not Am Wom

8942. Gibson, Eva Katherine (Clapp)
born 1857
miscellaneous author
Chicago, IL
Dict Am Auth; Wom Cent

8943. Hall, Adelaide S.
born 1857
art lecturer, author
Index t Wom

8944. Manley, Fanny Louisa
born 1857
educator, history author
Twent Cen Bio Dict Not Am

8945. Moore, Alice Rogers
1857–1928
biologist, children's author
Dict Am Auth; Nat Cyc Am Bio v16

8946. Prince, Helen Choate (Pratt)
born 1857
author, novelist
Dict Am Auth; Twent Cen Bio Dict Not Am

8947. Riggs, Kate Douglas (Wiggin) (Smith)
born 1857/59
children's author
New York, NY
Dict Am Auth; Twent Cen Bio Dict Not Am

8948. Ross, Virginia Evelyn (Conlee)
born 1857
author, pioneer
Nebraska
Wom Cent

8949. Ruffin, Margaret Ellen Henry
born 1857
author
Index t Wom

8950. Sanborn, Helen Josephine
born 1857
travel writer
Dict Am Auth

8951. Searing, Anna Eliza Pidgeon
1857–1942
author, feminist
Index t Wom

8952. Tarbell, Ida Minerva
1857–1944
investigative journalist, muckraker, lecturer, historian, author, biographer of Abraham Lincoln
Dict Am Auth; Dict Am Bio supp v3; Index t Wom; Nat Cyc Am Bio v14; Not Am Wom; Obit File

8953. Thomas, Martha Carey
1857–1935
university educator, second president of Bryn Mawr College, author, feminist
Quaker
Dict Am Auth; Dict Am Bio supp v1; Index t Wom; Nat Cyc Am Bio v13; Not Am Wom; Twent Cen Bio Dict Not Am

8954. Trumbull, Annie Eliot
1857–1949
novelist, poet, playwright, short story writer, first president of the Town and Country Club
Hartford, CT
Dict Am Auth; Obit File

8955. Vannah, Letitia Catharine
born 1857
poet
Gardiner, ME
Dict Am Auth

8956. Warren, Cornelia
born 1857
novelist
Dict Am Auth

8957. Webb, Frances Isabel (Currie)
1857–95
magazine writer
New York, NY
Dict Am Auth

8958. Wheelock, Lucy
1857–1946
kindergarten educator, founder of Wheelock College, lecturer, author
Boston, MA
Dict Am Bio supp v4; Not Am Wom; Wom Cent

8959. Young, Julia Evelyn (Ditto)
born 1857
poet, novelist, magazine writer
Buffalo, NY
Dict Am Auth; Wom Cent

8960. Adams, Juliette Aurelia Graves
born 1858
composer, pianist, music educator, author, lecturer
Index t Wom

8961. Alden, Cynthia May; Sunshine
1858/62–1931
journalist, editor, linguist, author, inventor, social worker, philanthropist, humanitarian
New York, NY
Dict Am Bio supp v1; Index t Wom; Nat Cyc Am Bio v14 and v22

8962. Arnold, Harriet Pritchard; H. E. P.
born 1858
author, poet
Wom Cent

8963. Bacon, Alice Mable
1858–1918
authority on Japan, author on Japanese culture, lecturer, educator of Blacks
Virginia
Dict Am Auth; Dict Am Bio; Not Am Wom

8964. Baker, Julie Keim (Wetherill); J. K. W.
born 1858
journalist, author
New Orleans, LA
Dict Am Auth; Wom Cent

8965. Brisbane, Margaret Hunt
born 1858
poet
Wom Cent

8966. Bush, Jennie Burchfield
born 1858
author
Wichita, KS
Wom Cent

8967. Coombs, Annie (Sheldon)
1858–90
novelist
New York, NY
Dict Am Auth

8968. Corr, Mary Bernadine
born 1858
author, educator
Index t Wom

8969. Dandridge, Danske (Bedinger)
born 1858
poet
West Virginia
Dict Am Auth

8970. Dock, Lavinia Lloyd
1858–1956
nurse, medical author, settlement house worker, suffragist, feminist
Dict Am Bio; Index t Wom; Not Am Wom supp v1

8971. Ely, Helena Rutherfurd
1858–1920
author, landscape gardener
Index t Wom

8972. Fisher, Mary
born 1858
textbook author, educator, novelist
Kansas City, MO
Dict Am Auth; Twent Cen Bio Dict Not Am

8973. Folger, Emily Clara Jordan
1858–1936
Shakespearean scholar and collector
Not Am Wom

8974. Hall, Ruth
born 1858
novelist
Catskill Mountains, NY
Dict Am Auth

8975. Hatcher, Orie Latham
1858–1946
English scholar, pioneer in vocational guidance
Not Am Wom

8976. Lanza, Clara (Hammond), Marchioness
born 1858/59
novelist
New York, NY
Dict Am Auth; Index t Wom; Wom Cent

8977. McLean, Sarah Pratt
born 1858
author
Cyc Am Bio

8978. Melville, Velma Caldwell
born 1858
poet, author
Wisconsin
Wom Cent

8979. Montgomery, Carrie Frances Judd
born 1858
church worker, poet, author, temperance worker, Salvation Army worker, social worker
New York; California
Index t Wom; Wom Cent

8980. Morley, Margaret Warner
1858–1923
educator, author, writer on sex education, naturalist, botanist, zoologist

Boston, MA
Dict Am Auth; Dict Am Bio

8981. Morse, Charlotte Dunning (Wood); Charlotte Dunning
born 1858
novelist
Dict Am Auth

8982. Nutting, Mary Adelaide
1858–1948
leader in professional nursing and nursing education, writer on nursing
Dict Am Bio supp v4; Index t Wom; Not Am Wom; Obit File

8983. Owen, Mary Alicia; Julia Scott
born 1858
folklorist, ethnologist, children's folklore writer, ghost story and short story writer
Dict Am Auth; Index t Wom; Nat Cyc Am Bio v13; Wom Cent

8984. Perry, Charlotte Augusta "Carlotta"
born 1858
poet
Milwaukee, WI
Dict Am Auth; Wom Cent

8985. Robinson, Edith
born 1858
novelist
Boston, MA
Dict Am Auth

8986. Roseboro, Viola
1858–1945
author, magazine writer, literary fiction editor of *McClures Magazine*
New York
Dict Am Auth; Obit File

8987. Seelye, Elizabeth (Eggleston)
born 1858
writer on Native American biography and early American history
New York
Dict Am Auth; Wom Cent

8988. Sharkey, Emma Augusta; Mrs. E. Burke Collins
born 1858
journalist, short story writer, novelist
Louisiana
Wom Cent

8989. Shinn, Milicent Washburn
1858–1940
author, editor, child psychologist

Niles, CA
Dict Am Auth; Index t Wom;
Not Am Wom

8990. Walworth, Ellen Hardin
born 1858
author, artist
Cyc Am Bio and ad; Dict Am
Auth; Index t Wom

**8991. Winterburn, Florence
(Hull) (Brown)**
born 1858
writer on children
New York
Dict Am Auth

8992. Arnold, Sarah Louise
born 1859
educator, education writer
Boston, MA
Dict Am Auth; Index t Wom

8993. Bates, Katharine Lee
1859–1929
poet, author, professor of English
literature
Massachusetts
Dict Am Auth; Dict Am Bio;
Index t Wom; Nat Cyc Am Bio
v1, v9, and v42; Not Am Wom;
Twent Cen Bio Dict Not Am;
Wom Cent

8994. Berry, Adaline Hohp
born 1859
author
Mennonite
Pennsylvania
Wom Cent

8995. Bingham, Jennie M.
born 1859
religious author
Wom Cent

8996. Bishop, Mary Axtell
born 1859
religious worker, author
Index t Wom

8997. Bittinger, Lucy (Forney)
born 1859
historical writer on Pennsylvania
Sweckley, PA
Twent Cen Bio Dict Not Am

8998. Blair, Eliza Nelson
born 1859
novelist
New Hampshire
Dict Am Auth

8999. Blair, Emily Jane Newell
1859/77–1933
suffragist, feminist, author, vice-
president of the Democratic National Committee, chairperson
of the Consumer's Advisory

Board of the National Recovery
Administration
Dict Am Bio supp v5; Not Am
Wom supp v1; Obit File

9000. Brewster, Cora Belle
born 1859
physician, surgeon, medical author
Maryland
Index t Wom; Wom Cent

9001. Brown, Barnetta
1859–1938
author, music writer
Index t Wom

9002. Candee, Helen Churchill
1859/61–1949
novelist, journalist
New York, NY
Dict Am Auth; Obit File

9003. Churchill, Lide A.
born 1859
telegrapher, stenographer, author
Wom Cent

9004. Cone, Helen Gray
1859–1934
educator, poet
New York
Dict Am Auth; Index t Wom;
Wom Cent

9005. Curtis, Georgina Pell
1859–1922
author, social worker
Index t Wom

9006. Dana, Olive Eliza
born 1859
litterateur, poet
Wom Cent

9007. Eastwood, Alice
1859–1953
botanist, author, adventurer
Index t Wom; Not Am Wom
supp v1; Obit File

9008. Ford, Julia Ellsworth
1859–1950
children's author, playwright,
novelist, patron of medicine
Nat Cyc Am Bio csv7; Obit File

**9009. Gilman, Mary Rebecca
Foster**
born 1859
author, religious biographer
Dict Am Auth; Index t Wom

9010. Gummere, Amelia Mott
1859–1937
author
Pennsylvania
Nat Cyc Am Bio v45

**9011. Herrick, Christine Ter-
hune**
1859–1944

writer on household affairs, home
economist, domestic scientist,
Sorosis member
New York, NY; New Jersey
Dict Am Auth; Index t Wom;
Nat Cyc Am Bio v8; Not Am
Wom; Wom Cent

9012. Judson, Jennie S.
born 1859
author
Alabama
Wom Cent

**9013. Kingsley, Florence
(Morse)**
born 1859
religious author
Staten Island, NY
Dict Am Auth; Nat Cyc Am Bio
v11

**9014. Klingelsmith, Margaret
Center**
1859–1931
librarian, author, legal authority,
Democratic political activist,
suffragist
Unitarian
Dict Am Bio

9015. Marr, Jane Barron Hope
born 1859
author, history writer
Twent Cen Bio Dict Not Am

9016. Miller, Annie (Jenness)
born 1859/84
dress reformer, fashion designer,
magazine publisher, author,
novelist, essayist, lecturer
New York, NY
Dict Am Auth; Index t Wom;
Wom Cent

**9017. Moody, Helen (Water-
son)**
1859/60–1928
author, journalist, educator
Ohio; New York, NY
Dict Am Auth; Index t Wom;
Nat Cyc Am Bio v22; Wom
Cent

9018. Ranous, Dora Knowlton
1859–1916
author, editor
Nat Cyc Am Bio v17

**9019. Sheardown, Annie Fill-
more**
born 1859
singer, voice teacher, writer on
voice teaching
Wom Cent

9020. Shorter, Susie
1859–1912
educator, author, businessperson
Black
Index t Wom; Negro Alman

9021. Sivitar, Anna Pierpont
born 1859
religious author
Twent Cen Bio Dict Not Am

9022. Smith, Nora Archibald
1859–1934
kindergarten educator, children's
author
Dict Am Bio; Nat Cyc Am Bio
v26 and csv2

9023. Tilley, Lucy Evangeline
1859–90
poet
Medina, OH
Dict Am Auth; Nat Cyc Am Bio
v4

**9024. van Anderson, Helen
(Van Metre)**
born 1859
minister, lecturer, miscellaneous
author
Boston, MA
Dict Am Auth

9025. Wall, Annie (Carpenter)
born 1859
author, poet, artist
Pueblo, CO
Dict Am Auth; Nat Cyc Am Bio
v5; Wom Cent

9026. Walsworth, Minnie Gow
born 1859
poet
Wom Cent

9027. Whiteley, Isabel (Nixon)
born 1859
romance writer
Philadelphia, PA
Dict Am Auth

**9028. Williamson, Julia May;
Lura Bell**
born 1859
poet
Augusta, ME
Dict Am Auth

9029. Wood, Frances Gilchrist
1859–1944
author, novelist, short story writer
Index t Wom; Obit File

**9030. Workman, Fanny (Bull-
ock)**
1859–1925
traveler, author on travel, explorer of the Himalayas, mountain
climber
Dict Am Auth; Dict Am Bio;
Index t Wom; Not Am Wom

9031. Wright, Mabel (Osgood)
1859–1934

novelist, nature writer, naturalist, bird protectionist
Dict Am Auth; Index t Wom; Nat Cyc Am Bio v12; Not Am Wom

9032. Andrews, Mary Raymond Shipman
1860–1936
novelist
Index t Wom; Not Am Wom

9033. Bancker, Mary E. C. "Betsy"
born 1860
author
Wom Cent

9034. Bevier, Isabel
1860–1942
educator, author, lecturer, home economist
Dict Am Bio supp v3; Index t Wom; Not Am Wom

9035. Brooks, Florence; Mrs. John Marone
1860–1948
artist, author, poet
California
Nat Cyc Am Bio v37

9036. Bryant, Anna Burnham
born 186?
children's author
Dict Am Auth

9037. Bumstead, Eudora Stone
born 1860
poet
Wom Cent

9038. Buttles, Janet
flourished 1890s–1913
author, Egyptologist
Who Who Egypt

9039. Chance, Julie Grinnell; Mrs. Stephen van Rensselaer Cruger
flourished 1890s–1900s
author, poet
Nat Cyc Am Bio v14

9040. Clarke, Helen Archibald
1860–1926
author, magazine editor, cofounder of *Poet Lore Magazine*
Index t Wom; Not Am Wom

9041. Comstock, Harriet Theresa (Nichols)
born 1860
novelist, children's author
Dict Am Auth; Index t Wom

9042. Cruger, Julie Grinnell (Storrow); Julien Gordon
flourished 1890s–1900s
novelist

New York
Dict Am Auth; Twent Cen Bio Dict Not Am

9043. de Koven, Anna Farwell
1860–1953
author, novelist
Episcopalian
New York, NY
Dict Am Auth; Nat Cyc Am Bio v16 and v48; Obit File

9044. Deland, Ellen Douglas
born 1860
children's writer
Dict Am Auth; Twent Cen Bio Dict Not Am

9045. Dromgoole, William Allen
born 1860
short story writer
Murfreesboro, TN
Dict Am Auth

9046. Ellis, Anna M. B.; Max Eliot
1860–1911
author, journalist
Index t Wom

9047. Ewell, Alice Maud
born 1860
historical novelist
Virginia
Dict Am Auth

9048. Gale, Ada Iddings
flourished 1890s
author, educator
Michigan
Wom Cent

9049. Gallatin, Alberta; Alberta Gallatin Jenkins; Mrs. Edwin Ogden Childe
1860–1948
actor, screenwriter, inventor of stage scenery and lighting mechanisms
Nat Cyc Am Bio v39

9050. Gilchrist, Rosetta Luce
flourished 1890s
physician, author, poet, women's rights worker
Cleveland, OH
Wom Cent

9051. Gilman, Charlotte Anna (Perkins) (Stetson)
1860–1935
author, feminist, lecturer, labor worker
San Francisco, CA
Dict Am Auth; Dict Am Bio supp v1; Index t Wom; Nat Cyc Am Bio v13; Not Am Wom; Twent Cen Bio Dict Not Am; Wom Lit, More

9052. Goldthwaite, Lucy Virginia Harmon
flourished 1890s
author
Wom Cent

9053. Greene, Frances Nimmo; Dixie
born 186?
educator, author
Alabama
Wom Cent

9054. Hallam, Julia (Clark)
born 1860
miscellaneous writer
Sioux City, IA
Dict Am Auth

9055. Hughes, Nina Vera B.
flourished 1890s
author, philosopher
Canadian
Wom Cent

9056. Johnson, Margaret
born 1860
miscellaneous writer
New York, NY
Dict Am Auth

9057. Kellogg, Eva Mary (Crosby)
born 1860
children's author
Boston, MA
Dict Am Auth

9058. Knapp, Adeline
born 1860
Household Magazine editor, miscellaneous writer
New York
Dict Am Auth

9059. Lawson, Mary Lockhart
flourished 1890s
poet
Cyc Am Bio

9060. Lee, Jeanette Barbour (Perry)
1860–1951
educator, novelist
Northampton, MA
Dict Am Auth; Index t Wom; Nat Cyc Am Bio csv1; Obit File

9061. Logan, John A., Mrs.
flourished 1890s
editor, author
Index t Wom

9062. Lust, Adelina (Cohenfeldt)
born 1860
novelist
Chicago, IL
Dict Am Auth

9063. Lyon, Anne Bozeman
born 1860

fiction writer
Alabama
Dict Am Auth; Wom Cent

9064. MacKaye, Julia Josephine Gunther
flourished 1890s
author, librarian
Index t Wom

9065. Molineux, Maria Ada
flourished 1890s
bacteriologist, psychologist, author, authority on the Brownings
Twent Cen Bio Dict Not Am

9066. Monroe, Harriet
1860/61–1936
poet, editor
Chicago, IL
Dict Am Auth; Dict Am Bio supp v2; Index t Wom; Nat Cyc Am Bio v28; Not Am Wom

9067. Morgan, Maud
1860/64–1941
harpist, author
Episcopalian
Cyc Am Bio; Index t Wom; Nat Cyc Am Bio v32; Obit File; Wom Cent

9068. Morris, Alice A.
born 186?
fiction writer
New York, NY
Dict Am Auth

9069. Nobles, Catherine
flourished 1890s
club leader, author
Louisiana
Index t Wom; Wom Cent

9070. O'Donnell, Jessie Fremont
1860–post 1890s
miscellaneous author
Lowville, NY
Dict Am Auth; Wom Cent

9071. Perrin, Martha Chamberlain (Drinker)
born 186?
poet
Dict Am Auth

9072. Phelps, Maude Gilette
born 1860
educator, writer of texts on English literature
Dict Am Auth

9073. Rathbun, Mary Jane; Mary Rathbone
1860–1943
marine zoologist, expert on shells, author, government employee
Index t Wom; Not Am Wom

9074. Reed, Florence Campbell
born 1860
author
Wom Cent

9075. Rice, Alice Caldwell (Hegan)
1860/70–1942
author, novelist, children's author, civic worker
New York; Louisville, KY
Dict Am Auth; Dict Am Bio supp v3; Index t Wom; Nat Cyc Am Bio v14; Not Am Wom; Obit File

9076. Robb, Isabella Adams (Hampton)
1860/63–1910
professional nurse, educator, writer on nursing
Cleveland, OH
Index t Wom; Not Am Wom

9077. Rogers, Mary Fletcher
flourished 1890s
author, animal humane worker
Wom Cent

9078. Ryan, Marah Ellis (Martin); Ellis Martin
born 1860
author, novelist, actor
Dict Am Auth; Wom Cent

9079. Seawell, Molly Elliot
1860–1916
author, novelist, children's author, newspaper correspondent
Washington, DC
Dict Am Auth; Dict Am Bio; Index t Wom; Nat Cyc Am Bio v7; Twent Cen Bio Dict Not Am ; Wom Cent

9080. Shepherd, Elizabeth Lee (Kirkland); Odette Tyler
born 1860
actor, author
Dict Am Auth

9081. Skinner, Henrietta Channing (Dana)
186?–1901
author, novelist
Detroit, MI
Dict Am Auth; Twent Cen Bio Dict Not Am

9082. Smith, Ella May
1860–1934
composer, pianist, organist, music educator, author
Index t Wom

9083. Smith, Gertrude
born 1860
short story writer
Boston, MA
Dict Am Auth

9084. Smith, Jeanie Oliver
flourished 1890s
poet, romance writer
New York
Wom Cent

9085. Smith, Minna Caroline
born 1860
journalist, children's author
Boston, MA
Dict Am Auth

9086. Spalding, Susan (Marr)
flourished 1890s
poet
Philadelphia, PA
Dict Am Auth; Wom Cent

9087. Spencer, Josephine
flourished 1890s
poet
Utah
Wom Cent

9088. Spratt, Louise Parker
flourished 1890s
journalist, dialect author
Alabama
Wom Cent

9089. Starkweather, Amelia Minerva
flourished 1890s
educator, author, poet, temperance worker, Methodist Episcopal deaconess
Methodist Episcopal
Wom Cent

9090. Stevens, Alice J.
born 1860
editor, author
Index t Wom

9091. Swafford, Martina; Belle Bremer
flourished 1890s
poet
Indiana
Wom Cent

9092. Swett, Sophia Miriam
born 186?
short story writer, children's author
Arlington, MA
Dict Am Auth

9093. Swett, Susan Hartley
born 186?
short story writer
Arlington, MA
Dict Am Auth

9094. Thomas, Fanny Edgar; 6-5-20
flourished 1890s
author
Wom Cent

9095. Trout, Grace Wilbur
flourished 1890s; died 1955

suffragist, feminist, club leader, author, lecturer
Illinois
Index t Wom; Nat Cyc Am Bio csv2

9096. van Benschoten, Mary Crowell
flourished 1890s
author, writer on industrial education
Illinois
Wom Cent

9097. van Buren, Alicia (Keisker)
1860–1922
composer, singer, poet
Louisville, KY
Dict Am Auth; Index t Wom

9098. Wade, Mary Hazelton Blanchard
born 1860
children's author
Malden, MA
Dict Am Auth

9099. White, Laura Rosamond
flourished 1890s
author
Wom Cent

9100. Wight, Emma Howard
flourished 1890s
magazine writer, theological writer, novelist
Catholic
Wom Cent

9101. Woolman, Mary Raphael Schenck
1860–1940
home economist, textile specialist, vocational educator, author, lecturer
Nat Cyc Am Bio csv1; Not Am Wom

9102. Wylie, Lollie Belle
flourished 1890s
journalist, newspaper editor, poet
Georgia
Wom Cent

9103. Young, Martha; Eli Sheppard
flourished 1890s
author, dialect author, poet
Alabama
Wom Cent

9104. Bacon, Louise Lee (Andrews)
born 1861
travel writer
Dict Am Auth

9105. Bailey, Eliza Randall Simmons
1861–1939

educator, textbook author, education writer
Congregationalist
Nat Cyc Am Bio v29

9106. Bigelow, Edith Evelyn (Jaffray)
born 1861
novelist
Dict Am Auth

9107. Bissell, Emily Perkins; Priscilla Leonard
1861–1948
welfare and child labor worker, author, inventor of Christmas Seals
Nat Cyc Am Bio v38; Not Am Wom; Obit File

9108. Boylan, Grace (Duffie)
born 1861
novelist, journalist, poet
Chicago, IL
Dict Am Auth

9109. Catlin, Louise (Ensign)
born 1861
fiction writer
Brooklyn, NY
Dict Am Auth

9110. Chanler, Margaret Ward Terry
1861–1952
philanthropist, musician, linguist, author
Index t Wom; Obit File

9111. Forney, Tillie May
born 1861
journalist, author
Nat Cyc Am Bio v3; Wom Cent

9112. Green, Julia (Boynton)
born 1861
poet
Rochester, NY
Dict Am Auth; Wom Cent

9113. Guiney, Louise Imogen; The Sunny Young Greek
1861–1920
poet, essayist, fiction author, literary scholar
Newton, MA
Dict Am Auth; Dict Am Bio; Nat Cyc Am Bio v9; Not Am Wom; Twent Cen Bio Dict Not Am; Wom Cent; Wom Lit, More

9114. Hazelrigg, Clara H.
born 1861
author, educator, temperance worker
Wom Cent

9115. Hebard, Grace Raymond
1861–1936
educator, feminist historian, author

Wyoming
Index t Wom; Read Encyc Am
West

9116. Horsford, Cornelia
born 1861
archaeologist, writer on archaeology
Cambridge, MA
Dict Am Auth; Index t Wom;
Twent Cen Bio Dict Not Am

9117. Jackson, Gabrielle Emilie
born 1861
children's author
Dict Am Auth

9118. Jewett, Sophie
born 1861
university educator, writer on literature
Dict Am Auth

9119. Johnson, Emily Pauline;
Tekahionwake
1861–1913
poet
Anglican
Native American (Mohawk)
Great North Am Ind; Wom Cent

9120. Kimball, Hannah Parker
born 1861
poet
Boston, MA
Dict Am Auth

9121. Luce, Alice Hanson
born 1861
dean of women of Oberlin College, English literature professor, educator
Twent Cen Bio Dict Not Am

9122. Mason, Mary Augusta
born 1861
author, poet
Dict Am Auth; Nat Cyc Am Bio
v4

**9123. Montgomery, Helen Bar-
rett**
1861–1934
civic reformer, churchperson, foreign missions worker, translator, author
Baptist
Index t Wom; Nat Cyc Am Bio
csv1; Not Am Wom

**9124. Parsons, Frances Theodo-
ra (Smith) (Dana)**
1861–99
author, nature writer
Albany, NY
Dict Am Auth; Twent Cen Bio
Dict Not Am

9125. Pullen, Sue Vesta; Clyde
St. Claire
born 1861

author, poet
Wom Cent

9126. Richmond, Mary Ellen
1861–1928
social worker, writer on charity
New York
Dict Am Auth; Nat Cyc Am Bio
v21; Not Am Wom

**9127. Robinson, Corinne Roose-
velt**
1861–1933
poet, philanthropist
Index t Wom

**9128. Salyards, Christiana
Stedman**
1861–1951
religious worker, author
Index t Wom

**9129. Saunders, Margaret Mar-
shall;** Marshall Saunders
born 1861
short story writer, novelist
Boston, MA
Canadian (Nova Scotia)
Dict Am Auth

9130. Scudder, Vida Dutton
1861–1954
social reformer, writer on English
literature, author, university ed-
ucator
Christian Scientist
Massachusetts
Cyc Am Bio; Dict Am Auth; Dict
Am Bio supp v5; Index t Wom;
Not Am Wom supp v1; Twent
Cen Bio Dict Not Am; Wom
Lit, More

9131. Siller, Hilda
born 1861
poet
Wom Cent

**9132. Stapleton, Patience
(Tucker)**
1861–93
novelist, short story writer, journalist
Colorado
Dict Am Auth; Nat Cyc Am Bio
v8

9133. Taney, Mary Florence
born 1861
educator, journalist, author, editor
Index t Wom

**9134. Timlow, Elizabeth Wes-
tyn**
born 1861
educator, children's author
Dict Am Auth

9135. Bond, Carrie Jacobs;
Carrie Jacobs-Bond
1862–1946

popular songwriter, composer,
author, publisher
Episcopalian
California
Dict Am Bio supp v4; Index t
Wom; Nat Cyc Am Bio v36 and
csv5; Not Am Wom; Obit File

**9136. Brazza, Cora (Slocomb),
Countess**
born 1862
author
New York, NY
Dict Am Auth

**9137. Chamberlain, Georgia
Louise**
1862–1943
educator, author
Index t Wom

**9138. Cotes, Sara Jeannette
Duncan;** Sara Jeannette Duncan
born 1862
author, journalist
Canadian
Wom Cent

**9139. Dana, William Starr,
Mrs.**
1862–1952
author, gardener
Index t Wom

9140. Higginson, Ella (Rhoads)
born 1862
author, poet, druggist
New Watcom, WA
Dict Am Auth; Twent Cen Bio
Dict Not Am; Wom Cent

9141. Johnson, Sallie M. Mills
born 1862
author
Colorado
Wom Cent

9142. Jonas, Rosalie M.
1862–1953
poet, Black children's welfare
worker
Obit File

9143. Jordan, Kate
1862–1926
novelist, playwright
Dict Am Bio

9144. Libbey, Laura Jean
1862–1924/25
romantic novelist
New York, NY
Dict Am Auth; Index t Wom;
Nat Cyc Am Bio v19; Not Am
Wom

**9145. Logan, Josephine Han-
cock**
1862–1943
patron of the arts, author, poet

Chicago, IL
Nat Cyc Am Bio v35

**9146. Mallon, Isabel Allardice
(Sloan);** Ruth Ashmore
1862–98
writer on deportment
Dict Am Auth

9147. Mason, Harriet Lawrence
born 1862
writer on English language and
English literature
Twent Cen Bio Dict Not Am

9148. Ohl, Maud Andrews
born 1862
journalist, poet
Georgia
Index t Wom; Wom Cent

**9149. O'Malley, Sallie Marga-
ret**
born 1862
poet, author
Index t Wom

9150. Peattie, Elia Wilkerson
born 1862
author, journalist, novelist, travel
writer
Chicago, IL
Dict Am Auth; Wom Cent

**9151. Pickard, Florence [Mar-
tha] Willingham**
1862–1930
author, painter
Georgia
Nat Cyc Am Bio v27 and csv2

9152. Reno, Itti Kinney
born 1862
author, novelist
Washington, DC
Dict Am Auth; Index t Wom;
Wom Cent

**9153. Richardson, Hester Dor-
sey**
born 1862
educator, author
Baltimore, MD
Index t Wom; Wom Cent

9154. Robins, Elizabeth; C. E.
Raymond; C. E. Raimond;
Elizabeth Raymond Parks;
Elizabeth (Robins) Parkes
1862/65–1952
novelist, actor
Dict Am Auth; Index t Wom;
Obit File; Wom Lit; Wom Lit,
More

9155. Seton, Julia Lorinda
born 1862
physician, founder of the New
Thought Church, author
New Thought
Nat Cyc Am Bio v16

9156. Spalding, Harriet Mabel
born 1862
poet
Wom Cent

9157. Stetson, Grace Ellery (Channing)
born 1862
poet, short story writer
Pasadena, CA
Dict Am Auth

9158. Stevens, Susan Sheppard (Pierce)
born 1862
novelist
St. Louis, MO
Dict Am Auth

9159. Thruston, Lucy Meacham
born 1862
novelist
Baltimore, MD
Dict Am Auth; Twent Cen Bio Dict Not Am

9160. Toussaint, Emma; Portia
born 1862
author, translator
Episcopalian
Massachusetts
Wom Cent

9161. Watson, Augusta (Campbell)
born 1862
novelist
Groton, CT
Dict Am Auth

9162. Weir, Irene
1862–1944
painter, art educator, writer on art, founder of the New York School of Design and Liberal Arts
New York
Not Am Wom; Obit File

9163. Wells, Carolyn
1862/69–1942
author, humorist, poet, librarian
Rahway, NJ
Dict Am Auth; Index t Wom; Nat Cyc Am Bio v13; Not Am Wom; Twent Cen Bio Dict Not Am

9164. Wharton, Edith Newbold (Jones)
1862–1937
novelist, short story writer, ghost story writer, autobiographer, travel writer, literary critic
New York, NY

French (American expatriate to Paris)
Dict Am Auth; Dict Am Bio supp v2; Dict Lit Bio v4 and v9; Index t Wom; Nat Cyc Am Bio v14 and csv2; Not Am Wom; Twent Cen Bio Dict Not Am; Wom Lit; Wom Lit, More

9165. Wilkins-Freeman, Mary Eleanor
1862–post 1903
author, novelist
Randolph, MA
Dict Am Auth; Nat Cyc Am Bio v9; Twent Cen Bio Dict Not Am; Wom Cent

9166. Wright, Carrie Douglas
born 1862
music educator, biographer
Chicago, IL
Dict Am Auth

9167. Atkinson, Eleanor Stackhouse
1863–1942
author
Index t Wom

9168. Bailey, Florence Augusta (Merriam)
1863–1948
ornithologist, nature writer, educator
Dict Am Auth; Dict Am Bio supp v4; Index t Wom; Nat Cyc Am Bio v13 and csv1; Not Am Wom

9169. Boyle, Virginia (Frazer)
born 1863
author, poet
Tennessee
Dict Am Bio v13

9170. Calkins, Mary Whiton
1863–1930
philosopher, psychologist, educator, author
Dict Am Bio supp v1; Dict Phil; Index t Wom; Nat Cyc Am Bio v13; Not Am Wom; Who Who Phil

9171. Cartwright, Florence Byrne
born 1863
poet
California
Wom Cent

9172. Chanler, Amelie Rives
born 1863
author
Alabama
Nat Cyc Am Bio v1; Wom Cent

9173. Channing, Blanche Mary
1863–1902
children's author
Brookline, MA

English
Dict Am Auth

9174. Claghorn, Kate Holladay
born 1863
writer on women's education
New York
Dict Am Auth; Twent Cen Bio Dict Not Am

9175. Cooke, Grace MacGowan
born 1863
magazine writer
Chattanooga, TN
Dict Am Auth; Index t Wom

9176. Eastman, Elaine (Goodale); Elaine Hall
1863–1953
educator of Native Americans, poet, short story writer, humorist, editor, scholar of Native American culture
South Dakota
Cyc Am Bio; Dict Am Auth; Index t Wom; Nat Cyc Am Bio v8; Twent Cen Bio Dict Not Am; Wom Cent

9177. Fearing, Lillian Blanche
1863–1901
lawyer, poet
Chicago, IL
blind
Dict Am Auth; Wom Cent

9178. Ford, Harriet (Morgan)
1863/78–1949
playwright
Index t Wom; Obit File

9179. Gerrish-Jones, Abbie
1863–1929
composer, author, critic
Index t Wom

9180. Hall, Gertrude Brownell
born 1863
short story writer, poet, novelist
Boston, MA
Dict Am Auth; Index t Wom

9181. Hitchcock, Caroline Hanks
born 1863
author
Cambridge, MA
Dict Am Auth

9182. Hurll, Estelle May
born 1863
educator, lecturer and writer on art
Dict Am Auth; Index t Wom

9183. Johnston, Annie (Fellows)
1863–1931
children's author
Peewee Valley, KY
Dict Am Auth; Dict Am Bio; Nat Cyc Am Bio v13; Not Am Wom

9184. King, Frances
born 1863
author, landscape gardener
Index t Wom

9185. King, Louisa Boyd Yeomans
1863–1948
writer on gardening, pioneer of the garden club movement
Not Am Wom

9186. Livingston, Margaret Vere (Farrington)
born 1863
author
Episcopalian
Augusta, ME
Dict Am Auth

9187. Merriam, Florence Augusta
born 1863
miscellaneous writer
Washington, DC
Dict Am Auth

9188. Parkhurst, Emelie Tracy Y. Swett
1863–92
poet, author
California
Wom Cent

9189. Peary, Josephine (Diebitsch)
1863–1955
artic explorer, author
Dict Am Auth; Dict Am Bio supp v5; Obit File

9190. Perley, Mary Elizabeth
born 1863
educator, poet
New Hampshire
Wom Cent

9191. Rhoades, Cornelia Harsen
1863–1940
children's author
New York, NY
blind
Dict Am Auth; Index t Wom

9192. Richardson, Emily Tracey Y.
1863–92
translator, poet
Index t Wom

9193. Rives, Amelie Louise (Chanler); Princess Troubetskoy
1863–1945
popular author, novelist
Cyc Am Bio; Dict Am Auth; Index t Wom; Nat Cyc Am Bio csvB; Not Am Wom; Obit File; Twent Cen Bio Dict Not Am

9194. Sears, Clara Endicott
1863–1960
author, antiquarian, cattle breeder
Protestant Episcopal
Massachusetts
Nat Cyc Am Bio v47 and csv1

9195. Semple, Ellen Churchill
1863–1932
geographer, writer on geography, anthropologist, anthropogeographer
Louisville, KY
Dict Am Auth; Dict Am Bio; Encyc South Hist; Index t Wom; Nat Cyc Am Bio v35 and csv1; Not Am Wom

9196. Stein, Evaleen
1863–1923
poet, author, artist
Lafayette, IN
Dict Am Auth; Dict Am Bio; Wom Cent

9197. Stratton-Porter, Gene
1863–1924
novelist
Not Am Wom

9198. Albee, Helen (Ricker)
born 1864
author
Dict Am Auth

9199. Bell, Orelia Key
born 1864
poet
Christian Scientist
Georgia
Wom Cent

9200. Broaker, Julia Anderson Luth
1864–1950
actor, playwright
Danish
Obit File

9201. Brown, Maria J. B.
died post 1914
translator, author
Cyc Am Bio

9202. Brown, Sara H.
died post 1914
author
Cyc Am Bio

9203. Chatham, Kitty Smiley; Catharine Smiley Bugg
1864/69–1946
singer for children, composer, children's author, lecturer
Index t Wom; Obit File; Wom Cent

9204. Davis, Varina Anne Jefferson "Winnie"
1864–98
author

Mississippi
Dict Am Auth; Dict Am Bio; Nat Cyc Am Bio v23; Twent Cen Bio Dict Not Am; Wom Cent

9205. Earle, Mary Trace
born 1864
short story writer, novelist
New York
Dict Am Auth

9206. Fry, Emma V. Sheridan
born 1864
actor, playwright
Wom Cent

9207. Gerson, Virginia
circa 1864–1951
illustrator, author
Index t Wom

9208. Gould, Elizabeth Lincoln
died 1914
author
Index t Wom

9209. Hopkins, Margaret Sutton (Briscoe)
born 1864
short story writer
Amherst, MA
Dict Am Auth

9210. Kohut, Rebekah Bettelheim
1864–1951
social welfare leader, educator, suffragist, lecturer, author, Jewish welfare worker
Jewish
Hungarian
Index t Wom; Nat Cyc Am Bio v41 and csv5; Not Am Wom supp v1

9211. Krause, Lydia Farrington; Barbara Yechton
born 1864
fiction writer, religious writer
New York
Dict Am Auth

9212. la Grange, Magdalene Isadora
born 1864
poet
New York
Wom Cent

9213. Lawrence, Ida Ethel (Eckert)
born 1864
poet, author
Toledo, OH
Dict Am Auth; Nat Cyc Am Bio v4

9214. Lindsay, Anna Robertson Brown
1864–1948
religious author, moral tale writer

Presbyterian
Dict Am Auth; Nat Cyc Am Bio v36

9215. Lippmann, Julie Mathilde
1864–1952
author, playwright, children's author, literary critic
Brooklyn, NY
Dict Am Bio; Index t Wom; Twent Cen Bio Dict Not Am

9216. Marble, Annie Russel
1864–1936
writer on literature
Worcester, MA
Dict Am Auth; Index t Wom; Nat Cyc Am Bio v27

9217. Miller, Marion Mills
born 1864
classical scholar, writer on classical literature
New York, NY
Dict Am Auth

9218. Sherwood, Margaret Pollock; Elizabeth Hastings
1864–1955
writer on literature, college educator
Dict Am Auth; Index t Wom

9219. Smith, Mabell Shippie Clarke
1864–1942
educator, lecturer, author
Index t Wom

9220. Thomas, Edith (Carpenter)
circa 1864–1901
novelist, biographer
Millville, NJ
Dict Am Auth

9221. Voynich, Ethel Lilian
1864–1960
novelist
Irish
Obit File

9222. Woods, Virna
1864–1903
educator, novelist, dramatist
Sacramento, CA
Dict Am Auth

9223. Bell, Lilian; Mrs. Arthur Hoyt Bogue
1865/67–1929
author, novelist
Chicago, IL
Dict Am Auth; Index t Wom; Nat Cyc Am Bio v14

9224. Bergengren, Ann (Farquhar); Margaret Alston
born 1865
novelist, journalist, magazine editor, singer

Boston, MA
Dict Am Auth; Index t Wom; Nat Cyc Am Bio v14

9225. Booth, Evangeline Cory
1865–1950
fourth general of the Salvation Army, orator, musician, poet
Salvationist
English
Dict Am Bio supp v4; Dict Am Rel Bio; Index t Wom; Nat Cyc Am Bio csv2; Not Am Wom; Obit File

9226. Booth, Maud Ballington (Charlesworth)
1865–1948
Salvation Army leader, evangelist, philanthropist, prison reformer, author, founder of PTA
Salvationist
English
Dict Am Auth; Index t Wom; Nat Cyc Am Bio v14 and v38; Not Am Wom; Obit File

9227. Bouvet, Marguerite (Marie)
1865–1915
linguist, children's author
Dict Am Auth; Dict Am Bio

9228. Chase, Jessie Anderson
born 1865
author, textbook writer
Brookline, MA
Dict Am Auth

9229. Crafts, Annetta (Stratford)
born 1865
poet
Austin, IL
Dict Am Auth

9230. Doubleday, Neltje Blanchan de Graff; Neltje Blanchan
1865–1918
science and nature writer, naturalist
Dict Am Bio; Nat Cyc Am Bio v13; Not Am Wom

9231. Douglas, Alice May
born 1865
poet, children's author, temperance worker, pacifist, missionary
Maine
Dict Am Auth; Index t Wom; Wom Cent

9232. Eckstorm, Fannie Pearson Hardy
1865–1946
ornithologist, writer on ornithology, scholar of the Native Americans of Maine, historian of Maine folk songs
Episcopalian

Brewer, ME
Dict Am Auth; Dict Am Bio supp v4; Nat Cyc Am Bio v36; Not Am Wom

9233. Fenollosa, Mary (McNeill); Sidney McCall; Mrs. Rolfs
circa 1865–1954
poet, writer on art
Dict Am Auth; Index t Wom

9234. Fiske, Mary Augusta (Davey); Minnie Madern; Minnie Madern Fiske
1865–1932
actor, author, animal humane worker
Dict Am Bio supp v1; Index t Wom; Nat Cyc Am Bio v10, v35, and csv1; Not Am Wom; Twent Cen Bio Dict Not Am

9235. Hill, Grace (Livingston)
1865–1947
popular novelist, short story writer
Presbyterian
Philadelphia, PA
Dict Am Auth; Dict Am Bio supp v4; Nat Cyc Am Bio v40; Not Am Wom; Obit File

9236. King, Mary (Perry)
born 1865
writer on beauty
New York, NY
Dict Am Auth

9237. Linn, Edith Willis
born 1865
poet
New York
Wom Cent

9238. Madison, Luch (Foster)
born 1865
historical fiction writer
New York, NY
Dict Am Auth

9239. McCabe, Lida Rose
1865–1938
author, lecturer
Index t Wom

9240. Merrill, Helen Maud; Samantha Spriggins
born 1865
litterateur, poet, patriotic writer
Maine
Wom Cent

9241. Morton, Martha
born 1865
author, playwright
New York
Index t Wom; Wom Cent

9242. Moses, Clara Lowenburg
1865–1951

author
Index t Wom

9243. Norton, Morilla M.
born 1865
specialist in French literature
Wom Cent

9244. Palmer, Minnie
born 1865
author
Cyc Am Bio

9245. Perkins, Lucy Fitch
1865–1937
children's author, illustrator
Nat Cyc Am Bio v33; Not Am Wom

9246. Pruit, Willie Franklin; Aylmer Ney
born 1865
philanthropist, poet
Tennessee
Index t Wom; Wom Cent

9247. Ray, Anna Chapin
born 1865
children's author
West Haven, CT
Dict Am Auth; Twent Cen Bio Dict Not Am

9248. Richardson, Anna Steese
1865–1949
magazine editor, author, playwright, feminist
Obit File

9249. Saalfield, Adah Louise (Sutton)
born 1865
children's author
Dict Am Auth

9250. Singleton, Esther
1865–1930
author, writer on music and architecture, writer on art and design, editor, music critic
Dict Am Auth; Dict Am Bio; Twent Cen Bio Dict Not Am

9251. Smith, Helen Grace
born 1865
poet
Index t Wom

9252. Stevens, Augusta de Grasse
1865–94
novelist, art critic
Belgian
Dict Am Auth; Index t Wom

9253. Thomas, Louisa Carroll
born 1865
poet
Nat Cyc Am Bio csv6

9254. Towne, Elizabeth Lois
1865–1960

metaphysical author, editor, lecturer
New Thought
Nat Cyc Am Bio v45 and csv1

9255. Washington, Margaret Murry
1865–1925
women's organizer, Tuskegee College dean of women, author
Black
Index t Wom; Negro Alman; Prof Negro Wom v1

9256. Whitelock, Louise (Clarkson)
born 1865
novelist, short story writer, poet
Baltimore, MD
Dict Am Auth

9257. Willcox, Louise Collier
1865–1929
essayist, literary critic, editor
Dict Am Bio

9258. Williams, Florence B.
born 1865
newspaper editor and publisher, author
Georgia
Wom Cent

9259. Winter, Alice Vivian Ames
1865–1944
women's club leader, author
Not Am Wom

9260. Wolf, Emma
born 1865
fiction writer
San Francisco, CA
Dict Am Auth

9261. Aldrich, Anne Reeve
1866–92
erotic poet, novelist
New York, NY
Dict Am Auth; Index t Wom; Nat Cyc Am Bio v4; Wom Cent

9262. Austin, Mary (Hunter)
1866/68–1934
novelist, folklorist, short story writer, journalist, conservationist, feminist, worker for Native American rights
California
Dict Am Auth; Dict Am Bio supp v1; Dict Lit Bio v9; Not Am Wom; Read Encyc Am West; Wom Lit; Wom Lit, More

9263. Breckinridge, Sophonisba Preston
1866–1948
social worker, social economist, immigrant welfare worker, writer on social issues, educator, lawyer

Presbyterian
Dict Am Bio supp v4; Nat Cyc Am Bio v37; Not Am Wom

9264. Burnham, Bertha H.
born 1866
author, educator
Wom Cent

9265. Chiles, Rosa Pendleton
born 1866
educator, author
Presbyterian
Nat Cyc Am Bio csv4

9266. Flint, Annie Johnson
1866–1932
poet
Index t Wom

9267. Frank, Rachel "Ray"
born 1866
author
Jewish
California
Wom Cent

9268. Goodale, Dora Read
born 1866
poet, author
Massachusetts
Cyc Am Bio; Dict Am Auth; Nat Cyc Am Bio v8; Twent Cen Bio Dict Not Am; Wom Cent

9269. Greene, Marie Louise
graduated 1891
author
Index t Wom

9270. Hensley, Sophie M. (Almon)
born 1866
poet
New York, NY
Dict Am Auth

9271. Johnson, Helen Lossing
1866–1946
artist, children's author
Obit File

9272. Martin, Georgia May; George Madden Martin
1866–1946
author, civil rights and antilynching worker
Episcopalian
Nat Cyc Am Bio v33

9273. Ragsdale, Lulah
born 1866
poet, novelist, actor
Mississippi
Wom Cent

9274. Richmond, Grace Louise Smith
1866–1959
novelist
Index t Wom

9275. **Roma, Caro;** Carey Northey
1866–1937
composer, author, singer
Index t Wom

9276. **Taggart, Marion Ames**
born 1866
children's author
New York
Dict Am Auth

9277. **Waltz, Elizabeth (Cherry)**
1866–1903
journalist, short story writer
Dict Am Auth

9278. **Woodrow, Nancy Mann Waddel;** Mrs. Wilson Woodrow
1866?–1935
author
Not Am Wom

9279. **Armstrong, Margaret Neilson**
1867–1944
author, illustrator
Index t Wom; Obit File

9280. **Carruth, Frances Weston**
born 1867
short story writer
New York
Dict Am Auth

9281. **Carter, Mary Gilmore**
born 1867
author
Index t Wom

9282. **Cary, Elizabeth Luther**
1867–1936
author, art critic, literary critic
Brooklyn, NY
Dict Am Auth; Dict Am Bio supp v2; Wom Lit; Wom Lit, More

9283. **Craigie, Pearl Mary Teresa (Richards);** John Oliver Hobbes
1867–1906
novelist, dramatist, essayist
Index t Wom; Nat Cyc Am Bio v10; Twent Cen Bio Dict Not Am

9284. **Hamilton, Edith**
1867–1963
author, classicist, educator, headmaster of Bryn Mawr College
German
Index t Wom; Nat Cyc Am Bio v52; Not Am Wom supp v1; Obit File

9285. **Hamm, Margharita Arlina**
1867/71–1907
journalist, author, poet, political writer

Canadian
Nat Cyc Am Bio v9; Not Am Wom; Wom Cent

9286. **Mayo, Katherine**
1867–1940
author, novelist
Episcopalian
New York
Index t Wom; Nat Cyc Am Bio v30; Not Am Wom

9287. **Meyer, Annie Florence Nathan**
1867–1950/51
publicist, author, playwright, novelist, educationist, founder of Barnard College, antisuffragist, patron of Black music education, clubwoman
Jewish
New York
Dict Am Auth; Dict Am Bio; Index t Wom; Nat Cyc Am Bio v42; Not Am Wom supp v1; Obit File; Twent Cen Bio Dict Not Am; Wom Cent

9288. **Myers, Harriet Williams**
born 1867
author, ornithologist, founder of California Audubon Society, conservationist, animal humane worker, World War II national defense worker
Los Angeles, CA
Am Bio New Cyc

9289. **O'Dea, Anne Caldwell**
1867–1936
author, librettist
Index t Wom

9290. **Pomeroy, Genie Clark**
born 1867
poet, author
Index t Wom; Wom Cent

9291. **Portuondo, Josephine B. Thomas**
born 1867
author
Index t Wom

9292. **Riley, Alice Cushing Donaldson**
1867–1955
children's playwright and songwriter, librettist
Nat Cyc Am Bio v44 and csv8

9293. **Seymour, Harriet Ayer**
1867/76–1944
pianist, music educator, pioneer of music therapy, music author
Index t Wom; Nat Cyc Am Bio v33; Obit File

9294. **Shelton, Louise**
1867–1934
author, businessperson
Index t Wom

9295. **Sherman, Ellen Burns**
1867–1956
author, suffragist
Unitarian
Massachusetts
Nat Cyc Am Bio v45

9296. **Simkhovich, Mary Melinda Kingsbury**
1867–1951
settlement house worker, housing reformer, social worker, author
New York
Dict Am Bio supp v5; Index t Wom; Not Am Wom supp v1; Obit File

9297. **Talbot, Ellen Bliss**
1867–1968
philosopher, educator, author
Congregationalist
Index t Wom; Nat Cyc Am Bio v54; Who Who Phil

9298. **Tompkins, Elizabeth Knight**
born 1867
novelist
Berkeley, CA
Dict Am Auth

9299. **Turpin, Edna Henry Lee**
1867–1952
author
Index t Wom

9300. **van Vorst, Marie Louise**
1867–1936
author, social reformer, poet
Index t Wom; Not Am Wom; Wom Lit, More

9301. **Wilder, Laura Ingalls**
1867–1957
children's author, educator, editor
Dict Am Bio supp v6; Index t Wom; Not Am Wom supp v1; Obit File; Read Encyc Am West

9302. **Babcock, Bernie (Smade)**
born 1868
novelist
Little Rock, AR
Dict Am Auth

9303. **Bergen, Helen Corinne**
born 1868
author, journalist
Wom Cent

9304. **Buel, Elizabeth Cynthia Barney**
1868–1943
author
Congregationalist
Connecticut
Nat Cyc Am Bio v32

9305. **Chase, Mary Wood**
born 1868

pianist, educator, author
Index t Wom

9306. **Duryea, Nina Larrey Smith**
1868–1951
World War I relief worker, playwright
Obit File

9307. **Follet, Mary Parker**
1868–1933
writer and lecturer on political science, group psychology, and industrial management
Dict Am Auth; Dict Am Bio supp v1; Not Am Wom

9308. **Fryberger, Agnes Moore**
born 1868
music educator, lecturer, author
Index t Wom

9309. **Goldstone, Aline Lewis**
born circa 1868
poet
Index t Wom

9310. **Hayward, Beatrice Herford**
1868–1952
monologuist, author, actor
English
Obit File

9311. **Jackson, Margaret (Doyle)**
born 1868
novelist
New York, NY
Dict Am Auth

9312. **James, Belle Robinson**
1868–1935
religious worker, author
Canadian
Index t Wom

9313. **King, Lida Shaw**
1868–1932
classical scholar, archaeologist, educator, college administrator
Pennsylvania
Nat Cyc Am Bio v23; Not Am Wom

9314. **Lederer, Charlotte**
1868–1955
children's author, illustrator
Hungarian
Obit File

9315. **Martin, Helen Reimensynder**
1868–1939
novelist
Index t Wom; Wom Lit, More

9316. **McCracken, Annie Virginia;** Alma Vivian Mylo
born 1868
author

South Carolina
Wom Cent

9317. Miller, Mary Rogers
born 1868
educator, author
New York, NY
Dict Am Auth

9318. Percival, Olive May Graves
born 1868
underwriter, travel writer
Los Angeles, CA
Dict Am Auth

9319. Porter, Eleanor Hodgman
1868–1920
children's author, novelist
Congregationalist
Dict Lit Bio v9; Index t Wom; Nat Cyc Am Bio v18; Not Am Wom

9320. Porter, Gene Stratton
1868–1924
author, ornithologist
Index t Wom

9321. Sampson, Emma Speed
1868–1947
children's author
Virginia
Nat Cyc Am Bio v37; Obit File

9322. Spurgeon, Caroline Frances Eleanor
1868–1942
authority on Shakespeare and Chaucer, educator, founder of the International Federation of University Women
Obit File

9323. Thurston, Ida B. Treadwell; Marion Thorne
died 1918
author
Index t Wom

9324. Watts, Mary Stanbery
1868–1958
author, novelist
Ohio
Index t Wom; Nat Cyc Am Bio csv3

9325. Young, Ella
1868–1956
poet, authority on Celtic folklore
Irish
Obit File

9326. Arnold, Cornelia Eliza Macmullan
1869–1945
educator, author
Episcopalian
Nat Cyc Am Bio v33

9327. Barker, Elsa
1869–1954

author, poet
Obit File

9328. Bartlett, Alice Hunt
1869–1949
poet, American editor of *London Poetry Review*
Obit File

9329. Blodgett, Mabel Louise Fuller
born 1869
author, novelist, fairy tale writer
Brookline, MA
Dict Am Auth; Nat Cyc Am Bio csv1

9330. Bork, Florence L. Holmes
born 1869
author
Index t Wom

9331. Brower, Harriette
1869–1928
pianist, music educator, author
Index t Wom

9332. Doyle, Martha Claire MacGowan
born 1869
children's author
Boston, MA
Dict Am Auth; Index t Wom

9333. Hamilton, Alice
1869–1970
industrial physician and toxicologist, pioneer in industrial medicine, medical educator, medical author, social reformer
Cur Biog '70; Index t Wom; Nat Cyc Am Bio csv7; Not Am Wom supp v1

9334. Harris, Corra May White
1869–1935
novelist
Georgia
Index t Wom; Nat Cyc Am Bio v26; Not Am Wom; Wom Lit, More

9335. Head, Ozella Shields
born 1869
author
Georgia
Wom Cent

9336. Lipman, Clara
born 1869
actor, playwright
Index t Wom

9337. McGiffert, Gertrude Huntington Boyce
1869–1962
poet
Congregationalist
Nat Cyc Am Bio v51

9338. Niehaus, Regina Armstrong
born 1869
author
Index t Wom

9339. Nielson, Helen Swift; Helen Swift
born 1869
author
Nat Cyc Am Bio csv3

9340. Noyes, Clara Dutton
1869/70–1936
nurse, nursing educator, field nurse in World War I, author
Dict Am Bio supp v2; Index t Wom; Nat Cyc Am Bio csv2

9341. Rittenhouse, Jessie Bell
1869–1948
poet, critic, anthologist
Dict Am Bio supp v4; Index t Wom; Not Am Wom

9342. Tuttle, Florence Guertin (Onertin)
born 1869
author, feminist, birth control advocate, pacifist, League of Nations worker, politician
Index t Wom; Nat Cyc Am Bio csv2 and csv5

9343. Warner, Anne Richmond; Anne Warner French
1869–1913/15
author
Dict Am Bio; Index t Wom

9344. Young, Rida Johnson
1869/75–1926
playwright, author, librettist, actor
Index t Wom

9345. Young, Rose Emmet
1869–1941
editor, journalist, novelist, feminist
New York
Dict Am Auth; Index t Wom

9346. Badcock, Winifred (Eaton); Onoto Watanna
flourished 1900s
writer on Japan
Dict Am Auth

9347. Banks, Elizabeth L.
1870–1938
author, journalist
Index t Wom

9348. Briggs, Margaret Perkins
flourished 1900s–20s
poet
Index t Wom

9349. Chaffee, Allen
flourished 1900s–30s

author
Index t Wom

9350. Chamberlain, Hope Summerhill
born 1870
author
Methodist
North Carolina
Nat Cyc Am Bio csv8

9351. Crothers, Rachel
1870/78–1958
playwright
New York
Dict Am Bio supp v5; Dict Lit Bio v7; Index t Wom; Nat Cyc Am Bio csv3; Not Am Wom supp v1; Obit File; Wom Lit, More

9352. Crowley, Mary Catherine
flourished 1900s
editor, historian, novelist
Detroit, MI
Dict Am Auth; Index t Wom

9353. Daffan, Katie
flourished 1900s–20s
author
Baptist
Texas
Nat Cyc Am Bio csv1

9354. Dargan, Olive Tilford
flourished 1900s–30s
poet, novelist, dramatist
Index t Wom; Nat Cyc Am Bio csv3; Wom Lit, More

9355. Davis, Margaret Ellen (O'Brien)
1870–90
novelist
Birmingham, AL
Dict Am Auth

9356. de Vere, Mary Aigne; Madeline S. Bridges
died 1920
poet, humorist
New York
Dict Am Auth; Nat Cyc Am Bio v8

9357. Donnelly, Lucy Martin
1870–1948
English professor
Not Am Wom

9358. Doyle, Agnes Catherine
flourished 1900s
librarian, author
Index t Wom

9359. Gadsby, James Eakin, Mrs.
flourished 1900s
clubwoman, author
Index t Wom

9360. Gaw, Ethelean Tyson
flourished 1900s–20s
poet, playwright
Index t Wom

9361. Goodsell, Willystine
born 1870
educator, author
Index t Wom

9362. Graham, Nellie Dean;
Vosey
born 1870
short story writer, magazine writer, philanthropist, clubwoman, Republican party worker, Los Angeles civic leader
Los Angeles, CA
Am Bio New Cyc

9363. Haines, Helen Colby
flourished 1900s
author
Index t Wom

9364. Hall, Grace Ethel Adams
flourished 1900s–20s
journalist, author
Portland, OR
Nat Cyc Am Bio csv1

9365. Hall, Sharlott Mabridth
1870–1943
poet
Index t Wom

9366. Hansborough, Mary Berri (Chapman)
born 187?
poet
Dict Am Auth

9367. Hutton, Elizabeth "Bettina" Riddle, Baroness von
born 187?; married 1897
novelist
Bavarian (American expatriate to Bavaria)
Dict Am Auth; Index t Wom

9368. James, Alice Archer (Sewall)
born 1870
artist, poet
Dict Am Auth; Index t Wom

9369. Johnson, Mary
born 1870
novelist
Index t Wom

9370. Johnston, Mary
1870–1936
popular novelist, suffragist, pacifist, internationalist
Birmingham, AL; Virginia
Dict Am Auth; Dict Am Bio supp v2; Dict Lit Bio v9; Index t Wom; Nat Cyc Am Bio v10 and csv3; Not Am Wom; Twent Cen Bio Dict Not Am

9371. Jones, Kate E.
flourished 1900s
clubwoman, poet
Index t Wom

9372. Kahn, Ruth (Ward)
born 1870/72
author, poet
Leadville, CO
Dict Am Auth; Index t Wom; Wom Cent

9373. Keezer, Martha Moulton Wittemore
born 1870
author
Massachusetts
Wom Cent

9374. Kinkhead, Elizabeth Shelby
flourished 1900s
lecturer, author
Index t Wom

9375. Knox, Helen Boardman
1870–1947
author
Index t Wom

9376. Mosher, Edith R.
flourished 1900s–10s
educator, author
Index t Wom

9377. Owens, Vilda Sauvage
flourished 1900s–20s
poet
Welsh
Index t Wom

9378. Patch, Kate; Kate Whiting
born 1870
fiction writer, short story writer
Framington, MA
Dict Am Auth

9379. Quin, Minnie
flourished 1900s
poet
Atlanta, GA
Dict Am Auth

9380. Robertson, Margaret Clyde
born 1870
author, poet
Nat Cyc Am Bio csv2

9381. Schoolcraft, Mary (Howard)
flourished 1900s
author
Dict Am Auth

9382. Seifert, Marjorie Allen
flourished 1900s–20s
poet
Index t Wom

9383. Smith, Jessie Welborn
flourished 1900s–20s
poet
Index t Wom

9384. Tourtillotte, Lillian Adele
born 1870
author
Wom Cent

9385. Wilkinson, Florence
flourished 1900s–20s
poet, novelist
Chicago, IL
Dict Am Auth; Index t Wom

9386. Willis, Pauline
born 1870
religious worker, author
Index t Wom

9387. Wooster, Lizzie E.
born 1870
author, editor
Index t Wom

9388. Allinson, Anne Crosby Emery
1871–1931
educator, college administrator, author
Dict Am Bio supp v1

9389. Bjerkoe, Ethel Hall
1871–1978
antiques authority and author, clubwoman
Connecticut; Maine
Nat Cyc Am Bio v60

9390. Bower, Bertha Muzzy
1871–1940
author
Index t Wom; Wom Lit, More

9391. Brown, Abbie Farwell
1871–1927
poet, author, children's author
Boston, MA
Dict Am Auth; Not Am Wom

9392. Converse, Florence
born 1871
novelist, author
Boston, MA
Dict Am Auth; Nat Cyc Am Bio v13; Wom Lit, More

9393. Crocker, Mary Arnold; Bosworth Crocker
1871–1946
author
Nat Cyc Am Bio v37

9394. Eudy, Mary Cummings Paine
1871–1952
poet, dress manufacturer
Presbyterian
Kentucky
Nat Cyc Am Bio v41; Obit File

9395. Fabbri, Cora Randall
1871–92
poet
Dict Am Auth

9396. Gardner, Mary Sewall
1871–1961
public health nurse, author
Index t Wom; Not Am Wom supp v1

9397. Keen, Dora
born 1871
traveler, author
Index t Wom

9398. Laut, Agnes Christina
1871/72–1936
journalist, novelist, writer on the American West
Canadian
Dict Am Auth; Index t Wom

9399. McChesney, Dora Greenwell
born 1871
novelist
Dict Am Auth

9400. Moore, Anne Carrol
1871–1961
children's author and librarian
Index t Wom; Not Am Wom supp v1

9401. Oskinson, Hildegarde Hawthorne
1871–1952
author, biographer of literary figures, children's author
Obit File

9402. Richardson, Harriet
graduated 1896
biologist, author
Index t Wom

9403. Rickert, Martha Edith
1871–1938
medievalist, professor of English, philologist, novelist
Dict Am Auth; Dict Am Bio supp v2; Not Am Wom

9404. Spicer, Anne Higginson
born 1871
author
Illinois
Nat Cyc Am Bio csv3

9405. Tompkins, Juliet Wilbor
1871–1956
author
Index t Wom

9406. Vermilye, Kate Jordan
1871–1926
author, novelist, short story writer
Irish
Nat Cyc Am Bio v20

9407. Wagnalls, Mabel
born 1871
pianist, writer on music
New York, NY
Dict Am Auth; Twent Cen Bio
Dict Not Am

9408. Wood, Edith (Elmer)
1871–1945
housing reformer, housing economist, novelist
Washington, DC
Dict Am Auth; Dict Am Bio
supp v3; Index t Wom; Not Am
Wom

9409. Abbott, Eleanor Hallowell
1872–1958
novelist, short story writer
Dict Am Bio supp v6, Index t
Wom

9410. Anderson, Audentia Smith
born 1872
religious author, genealogist, pioneer
Mormon
Index t Wom

9411. Bassett, Sara Ware
born 1872
author
Index t Wom

9412. Bryan, Ella Howard;
Clinton Dangerfield
born 1872
poet, author
Nat Cyc Am Bio v13

9413. Busbey, Katharine Graves
1872–1959
author, social reformer
Index t Wom

9414. Charles, Frances
born 1872
author
California
Dict Am Auth

9415. Coburn, Eleanor Habawell Abbot
born 1872
author
Index t Wom

9416. Colton, Elizabeth Avery
1872–1924
professor of English, crusader for
better women's colleges
Dict Am Bio; Not Am Wom

9417. Daviess, Maria Thompson
1872–1924
painter, novelist, author
Dict Am Bio; Index t Wom

9418. Deering, Mabel Craft
born 1872
author, suffragist
Episcopalian
California
Nat Cyc Am Bio csv6

9419. Ewing, Mary Emilie
born 1872
author
Index t Wom

9420. Fuller, Margaret
born 1872
novelist
Index t Wom

9421. Goza, Anne
born 1872
humorist
Alabama
Wom Cent

9422. Haines, Helen Elizabeth
1872–1961
librarian, author, editor, educator
Index t Wom; Not Am Wom
supp v1

9423. Hale, Louise Closser
1872–1933
actor, author
Dict Am Bio supp v1; Index t
Wom

9424. Heller, Helen West
1872–1955
modernist painter, woodcut engraver, poet
Obit File

9425. Howard, Minnie F.
born 1872
author, historian, public welfare
worker
Index t Wom

9426. Kirkland, Winifred Margaretta
1872–1943
author
Index t Wom

9427. Orton, Helen Fuller
1872–1955
children's author
Dict Am Bio supp v5; Index t
Wom; Obit File

9428. Pangborn, Georgia (Wood)
born 1872
novelist
New York, NY
Dict Am Auth

9429. Post, Emily Price
1872/73–1960

author, adviser on etiquette
Dict Am Bio supp v6; Index t
Wom; Nat Cyc Am Bio v44;
Not Am Wom supp v1; Obit
File

9430. Pound, Louise
1872–1958
university educator, writer on literature, folklorist, tennis player,
bicyclist, golfer
Nebraska
Nat Cyc Am Bio v45, csv2, and
csv5; Not Am Wom supp v1;
Obit File

9431. Putnam, Bertha Haven
1872–1960
historian, history writer, authority on medieval history and
criminology, educator
Unitarian
Nat Cyc Am Bio v43; Not Am
Wom supp v1; Obit File

**9432. Seton, Grace Gallatin
Thompson;** Dorothy Dodge
1872–1959
suffragist, feminist, explorer, geographer, author, book designer, bookmaker, composer of
popular songs, historian, cofounder of the Campfire Girls
Dict Am Auth; Dict Am Bio
supp v6; Index t Wom; Nat Cyc
Am Bio v47 and csv5; Not Am
Wom supp v1; Obit File

9433. Smith, Mary Chapin
1872–1950
novelist
Obit File

9434. Smith, Ruth Lyman
1872–1926
child welfare worker, religious
worker, author
Index t Wom

**9435. Speyer, Leonora von
Stosch**
1872–1956
poet
Index t Wom

9436. Bailey, Irene Temple
1873–1953
author
Obit File

9437. Becker, May Lamberton
1873–1958
children's author, children's book
critic, editor, journalist
Index t Wom; Obit File

9438. Bolton, Margaret
1873–1943
religious educator, author
Catholic
Obit File

9439. Borden, Lucille Papin
born 1873
novelist
Index t Wom

9440. Broadhurst, Jean
1873–1954
author, educator, bacteriologist
Index t Wom

9441. Brown, Anna Robeson
born 1873
novelist
Dict Am Auth

9442. Cather, Willa Sibert
1873/74–1944
western novelist
Episcopalian
Nebraska
Dict Am Bio supp v4; Dict Lit
Bio v9; Dict Mex Am Hist;
Index t Wom; Nat Cyc Am Bio
v44 and csv1; Not Am Wom;
Obit File; Read Encyc Am
West; Wom Lit; Wom Lit,
More

9443. Cromwell, Otelia
1873–1972
educator, author
Black
Encyc Black Am

**9444. Dickson, Marguerite
Stockman**
1873–1953
author
Index t Wom

9445. Fisher, Harriet White
married 1898
business manager, author
Index t Wom

9446. Glasgow, Ellen; Anderson
Gholson
1873/74–1945
novelist, Pulitzer Prize winner
Richmond, VA
Dict Am Auth; Dict Am Bio
supp v5; Dict Lit Bio v9; Index
t Wom; Nat Cyc Am Bio v13,
v35, and csv3; Not Am Wom;
Wom Lit; Wom Lit, More

9447. Hartt, Mary Bronson
born 1873
author
Index t Wom

**9448. Hokins, Pauline Bradford
(MacKie)**
born 1873
novelist
Dict Am Auth

**9449. Irwin, Inez Leonore
Haynes Gillmore**
1873–1970
suffragist, feminist, head of the
World Center for Women's Ar-

chives, author, first woman president of the Authors League of America
Brazilian
Index t Wom; Nat Cyc Am Bio csv6; Not Am Wom supp v1; Obit File

9450. Kellor, Frances [Alice]; Frances Kellar
1873–1952
social investigator and reformer, arbitration specialist, immigrant-welfare worker, economist, author, sociologist
Dict Am Bio supp v5; Index t Wom; Nat Cyc Am Bio v15; Not Am Wom supp v1; Obit File

9451. la Motte, Ellen Newbold
1873–1961
nurse, author
Index t Wom

9452. Laidlaw, Harriet Davenport Wright Burton
1873–1949
suffragist, author, educator, lecturer, clubwoman
Presbyterian
Index t Wom; Nat Cyc Am Bio v38; Not Am Wom

9453. Larsen, Hanna A.
1873–1945
author, editor of the *American Scandinavian Review*
Obit File

9454. Laughlin, Clara Elizabeth
1873–1941
miscellaneous author
Chicago, IL
Dict Am Auth; Index t Wom

9455. Leech, Lida Shivers
born 1873
composer, author
Index t Wom

9456. Mackie, Pauline Bradford
born 1873/74
author
Index t Wom

9457. Morrow, Elizabeth Cutter
1873–1955
author, educator
Index t Wom; Obit File

9458. Neilson, Nellie
1873–1947
English historian, first woman president of the American Historical Association, educator, author
Episcopalian
Nat Cyc Am Bio v36; Not Am Wom; Obit File

9459. O'Reilly, Mary Boyle
born 1873
humanitarian, philanthropist, police commissioner, author
Index t Wom

9460. Prentiss, Harriet Doan
flourished 1903
poet, club leader
Index t Wom

9461. Ridge, Lola; Mrs. David Lawson
1873/83–1941
poet
Index t Wom; Not Am Wom; Obit File; Wom Lit, More

9462. Sears, Zelda
born 1873
playwright
Index t Wom

9463. Sedgwick, Anne Douglas; Anne de Selincourt
1873–1935
novelist
Dict Am Auth; Dict Am Bio supp v1; Index t Wom; Nat Cyc Am Bio csv3; Not Am Wom

9464. Spencer, Lilian White
circa 1873–1953
author
Index t Wom

9465. Underwood, Edna Worthley
born 1873
author, linguist, translator
Index t Wom

9466. Woods, Bertha Gerneaux Davis
1873–1952
author
Index t Wom

9467. Wyatt, Edith Franklin
born 1873
novelist
Chicago, IL
Dict Am Auth; Index t Wom

9468. Armer, Laura Adams
1874–1963
author, illustrator
Index t Wom

9469. Blaisdell, Mary Frances
born 1874
author
Index t Wom

9470. Conant, Isabel la Howe Fiske
born 1874
poet
Index t Wom

9471. Cooley, Anna Maria
1874–1955

home economist, author
Index t Wom

9472. Dunbar, Olivia Howard; Olivia Torrence
1874–1953
short story writer
Obit File

9473. Flexner, Anne Crawford
1874–1955
playwright, director of the Institute for Advanced Studies at Princeton University
Princeton, NJ
Index t Wom; Obit File

9474. Frothingham, Eugenia Brooks
born 1874
novelist
Boston, MA
Dict Am Auth

9475. Fulbright, Roberta Waugh
1874–1953
newspaper publisher, political writer, businessperson, banker
Arkansas
Nat Cyc Am Bio v49

9476. Gale, Zona; Mrs. William L. Breese
1874–1938
novelist, playwright, essayist
Wisconsin
Dict Am Bio supp v2; Dict Lit Bio v9; Index t Wom; Nat Cyc Am Bio v30 and csv2; Not Am Wom; Wom Lit, More

9477. Garrison, Theodosia
born 1874
poet
Index t Wom

9478. George, Grace; Mrs. William A. Brady
1874/80–1961
actor, playwright
Index t Wom; Nat Cyc Am Bio v45; Obit File

9479. Gilmore, Elizabeth McCabe
born 1874
author, publisher, critic
Index t Wom

9480. Hare, Maud Cuney
1874–1936
pianist, musicologist, author
Black
Encyc Black Am; Negro Alman; Prof Negro Wom v1

9481. Loeb, Sophia Irene Simon
1874/76–1929

journalist, sponsor of welfare legislation, social reformer, social worker, author
New York
Russian
Dict Am Bio; Index t Wom; Nat Cyc Am Bio v24; Not Am Wom; Slavon Encyc

9482. Lowell, Amy
1874–1925
poet, biographer, lecturer, critic
Dict Am Bio; Index t Wom; Nat Cyc Am Bio v19; Not Am Wom; Wom Lit; Wom Lit, More

9483. MacKenzie, Jean Kenyon
1874–1936
Presbyterian missionary to Cameroun, author
Presbyterian
Nat Cyc Am Bio v28; Not Am Wom

9484. Mather, Winifred Holt
1874–1945
sculptor, patron of welfare of the blind, founder of a school for the blind, author
Episcopalian
Nat Cyc Am Bio v34 and csv6

9485. McCullough, Myrtle Reed; Myrtle Reed
1874–1911
author
Nat Cyc Am Bio v15

9486. Miller, Alice Duer
1874–1942
fiction writer, poet
New York
Dict Am Auth; Index t Wom; Nat Cyc Am Bio csv1; Not Am Wom; Obit File; Wom Lit, More

9487. Monroe, Anne Shannon
1874/77–1942
author, essayist, novelist, magazine writer, Oregon historian, feminist, lecturer, mountain climber
Oregon
Index t Wom; Nat Cyc Am Bio; Obit File

9488. Montgomery, Lucy Maud
1874–1942
novelist
Canadian
Index t Wom

9489. Montgomery, Roselle Mercier
1874–1933
author, poet
Presbyterian
Index t Wom; Nat Cyc Am Bio v24

9490. Nesbitt, Henrietta
1874–1963
author
Obit File

9491. O'Neill, Rose Cecil
1874–1944
illustrator, author, artist, creator
of the Kewpie doll
Dict Am Bio supp v3; Index t
Wom; Not Am Wom; Obit File

9492. Parker, Eleanor R.
born 1874
home economist, editor, author
Index t Wom

9493. Peabody, Josephine Preston; Mrs. Lionel S. Marks
1874/80–1922
poet, dramatist
Cambridge, MA
Dict Am Auth; Dict Am Bio;
Index t Wom; Nat Cyc Am Bio
v19; Not Am Wom; Twent Cen
Bio Dict Not Am

9494. Phillips, Catherine Coffin
1874–1942
author, historian of the Pacific
Coast
California
Nat Cyc Am Bio v32 and csv6

9495. Reed, Myrtle
1874–1911
popular novelist
Chicago, IL
Dict Am Auth; Dict Am Bio;
Index t Wom; Not Am Wom;
Twent Cen Bio Dict Not Am

9496. Rives, Hallie Erminie
1874/76–1956
novelist
New York, NY
Dict Am Auth; Dict Am Bio
supp v6; Index t Wom; Obit
File

9497. Roberts, Ina (Brevoort)
born 1874
novelist
New York, NY
Dict Am Auth

9498. Robinson, Mabel Louise
1874–1962
author, children's author, educator
Index t Wom; Nat Cyc Am Bio
v47

9499. Rollins, Clara Harriot (Sherwood)
born 1874
short story writer
Boston, MA
Dict Am Auth

9500. Stein, Gertrude
1874–1946

author, novelist, literary salon
host, World War I ambulance
driver and supply truck driver
in France
Jewish
French (American expatriate to
Paris)
Dict Am Bio supp v4; Dict Lit
Bio v4; Index t Wom; Nat Cyc
Am Bio v38 and csv4; Not Am
Wom; Obit File; Who Who Jew
Hist; Wom Lit; Wom Lit, More

9501. Vorse, Mary Heaton Marvin
1874/81–1960/66
journalist, novelist, labor activist
Bio Dict Am Lab; Index t Wom;
Not Am Wom supp v1; Obit
File

9502. Yaegle, Marie Tello Phillips
1874–1962
poet, novelist, essayist, founder of
the American Academy of
Poets
Catholic
Pennsylvania
Canadian
Index t Wom; Nat Cyc Am Bio
csv3; Obit File

9503. Adams, Harriet Chalmer
1875–1937
explorer, author, lecturer
Index t Wom; Not Am Wom

9504. Bailey, Carolyn Sherwin
born 1875
author
Index t Wom

9505. Bonnin, Gertrude Simmons; Zitkala-sa
1875–1938
author, Native American rights
worker
Native American (Yankton
Sioux)
Great North Am Ind; Not Am
Wom

9506. Bradley, Lillian Trimble
born 1875
playwright
Index t Wom

9507. Branch, Anna Hempstead
1875–1937
poet, social worker
New London, CT
Dict Am Auth; Index t Wom;
Nat Cyc Am Bio csv3; Not Am
Wom

9508. Brooks, Geraldine
born 1875
colonial historian, author
New York, NY
Dict Am Auth

9509. Brooks, Hildegard
born 1875
novelist
Newburgh, NY
Dict Am Auth

9510. Chanler, Beatrice Ashley Winthrop; Minnie Ashley
1875–1946
actor, sculptor, author, singer
Index t Wom; Nat Cyc Am Bio
v36

9511. Colby, Nathalie Sedgwick
1875–1942
essayist, poet, novelist
Episcopalian
New York
Index t Wom; Nat Cyc Am Bio
v31

9512. Cornell, Sophia S.
born 1875
educator, author
Index t Wom

9513. Delaney, Adelaide Margaret
born 1875
lecturer, editor, author
Index t Wom

9514. Delano, Edith Barnard
1875–1946
novelist, short story writer
Obit File

9515. Denning, Delia; Delia (Denning) Akeley Howe
1875–1970
African explorer, big game hunter, geographer, taxidermist, author, lecturer, World War I
relief worker
Nat Cyc Am Bio v57; Obit File;
Index t Wom

9516. Dickinson, Helena Adall Snyder
1875–1975
nonfiction writer, educator
Presbyterian
Canadian
Nat Cyc Am Bio v54

9517. Downey, June Etta
1875–1932
psychologist, author
Dict Am Bio supp v1; Not Am
Wom

9518. Driscoll, Louise
born 1875
poet
Index t Wom

9519. Fitch, Florency Mary
1875–1959
Biblical literature authority, university educator, religious writer for children

Oberlin, OH
Obit File

9520. Forster, Minnie Jane
born 1875
author
Nat Cyc Am Bio csv9

9521. Gates, Eleonore
1875–1951
author, playwright, novelist
Nat Cyc Am Bio v15; Obit File

9522. Holton, Susan May
circa 1875–1951
business executive, author, educator
Index t Wom

9523. Howe, Delia Akeley (Denning)
1875–1970
African explorer, big game hunter, geographer, taxidermist, author, lecturer, World War I
relief worker
Index t Wom; Nat Cyc Am Bio
v57; Obit File

9524. Hughan, Jessie Wallace
1875–1955
pacifist, Socialist party worker,
politician, educator, author
Index t Wom; Not Am Wom
supp v1

9525. Kelly, Myra
1875/76–1910
author, humorist, social reformer,
educator
Irish
Dict Am Auth; Dict Am Bio;
Index t Wom; Nat Cyc Am Bio
v24; Wom Lit, More

9526. Lacy, Mary Goodwin
1875–1962
librarian, author, government employee
Index t Wom

9527. Livingstone, Belle
1875?–1957
author, actor, adventurer
Dict Am Bio

9528. Marks, Jeannette Augustus
1875–1964
poet, children's author, educator,
Socialist party worker
Index t Wom; Nat Cyc Am Bio
csv2

9529. Martin, Anna Henrietta
1875–1951
suffragist, feminist, author, essayist, social critic, pacifist, politician

Nevada
Dict Am Bio supp v5; Not Am Wom supp v1; Read Encyc Am West

9530. Miller, Nellie Burget
born 1875
poet, lecturer
Index t Wom

9531. Nelson, Alice Ruth Dunbar (Moore)
1875–1935
author, editor, social worker
Louisiana
Black
Encyc Black Am; Negro Alman; Not Am Wom; Prof Negro Wom v1

9532. Parsons, Elsie Clews
1875–1941
sociologist, anthropologist, folklorist, Native American ethnologist, president of the American Anthropology Association
Dict Am Bio supp v3; Index t Wom; Not Am Wom; Obit File; Read Encyc Am West

9533. Rohe, Alice
circa 1875–1957
journalist, magazine writer, UPI Rome bureau head
Index t Wom; Obit File

9534. Winslow, Anna Goodwin
born 1875
author
Index t Wom

9535. Wylie, Ida Alexa Ross
1875–1959
novelist, scenarist, short story writer
Australian
Obit File

9536. Young, Sophie Swanstrom
born 1875
playwright, director of passion plays
Zion, IL
Obit File

9537. Abbott, Edith
1876–1957
social reformer, social work educator, author
Nebraska
Dict Am Bio supp v6; Index t Wom; Nat Cyc Am Bio csv3; Not Am Wom; Obit File

9538. Bacon, Josephine Dodge Daskam
1876–1961
humorist, children's author, short story writer, Girl Scout executive

Stamford, CT
Dict Am Auth; Index t Wom

9539. Barney, Natalie Clifford
1876–1972
novelist, salon host
French (American expatriate to Paris)
Dict Lit Bio v4; Not Am Wom supp v1; Wom Lit

9540. Beard, Mary Ritter
1876–1958
historian, writer on history, feminist
Dict Am Bio supp v6; Index t Wom; Not Am Wom supp v1; Obit File

9541. Beek, Alice D. Engley
born 1876
painter, author, lecturer
Index t Wom

9542. Brown, Katharine Holland
1876–1931
novelist
Index t Wom; Nat Cyc Am Bio v29

9543. Cleghorn, Sarah Norcliffe
1876–1959
poet, novelist, educator, suffragist, civil rights worker, labor worker, pacifist, antivivisectionist, Socialist party member
Vermont
Index t Wom; Nat Cyc Am Bio v46; Obit File; Dict Am Bio supp v5

9544. Comstock, Sarah
1876–1960
editor, novelist
Obit File

9545. Cooke, Marjorie Benton
1876–1920
author, monologuist
Index t Wom; Wom Lit, More

9546. Dix, Beulah Marie
born 1876
historical novelist
Cambridge, MA
Dict Am Auth

9547. Donahey, Mary Dickerson
1876–1962
children's author
Episcopalian
Chicago, IL
Nat Cyc Am Bio v45

9548. Ellis, Edith
1876–1960
playwright, film scenario writer
Index t Wom; Obit File

9549. Flebbe, Beulah Marie Dix
born 1876
playwright, novelist
Index t Wom

9550. Gannon, Anna
born 1876
poet
Philadelphia, PA
Dict Am Auth

9551. Glaspell, Susan Keating; Mrs. George Cram Cook
1876/82–1948
novelist, playwright, feminist
Dict Am Bio supp v4; Dict Lit Bio v7 and v9; Index t Wom; Nat Cyc Am Bio v15 and csv3; Not Am Wom; Wom Lit, More

9552. Hartman, Gertrude
1876–1955
author of school texts, educator, writer on education
Obit File

9553. Leitch, Mary Sinton Lewis
born 1876
poet
Index t Wom

9554. Lowe-Porter, Helen Tracy
1876–1963
translator of Thomas Mann, poet, author
Not Am Wom supp v1; Obit File

9555. Mora, Jo
1876–1947
sculptor, author
Obit File

9556. Norton, Grace Fallow
1876–1926
poet
Index t Wom

9557. Overton, Gwendolen
born 1876
novelist
Los Angeles, CA
Dict Am Auth

9558. Patch, Edith Marion
1876–1954
entomologist, children's author
Index t Wom; Nat Cyc Am Bio v18

9559. Peters, Iva (Lowther)
born 1876
educator, author on education
Methodist Episcopal
Nat Cyc Am Bio csv1

9560. Phelps, Ruth Shepherd; Mme. Paul Morand
born 1876

educator, writer on Romance languages
Nat Cyc Am Bio csv2 and csv5

9561. Rembaugh, Bertha
1876–1950
lawyer, author
Index t Wom

9562. Rinehart, Mary Roberts
1876–1958
novelist, mystery story writer, playwright, suffragist
Episcopalian
Dict Am Bio supp v6; Index t Wom; Nat Cyc Am Bio csv3; Not Am Wom supp v1; Obit File

9563. Sprague, Harriet Chapman
1876–1969
bibliophile, book collector
Congregationalist
Connecticut
Nat Cyc Am Bio v56

9564. Vanamee, Grace Davis
1876–1946
club leader, lecturer, educator, author
Index t Wom

9565. Venable, Mary Elizabeth
died 1926
pianist, music educator, author
Index t Wom

9566. Webster, Alice Jane Chandler "Jean"
1876–1916
author
Dict Am Bio; Index t Wom

9567. Whitney, Helen (Hay)
1876–1944
philanthropist, poet, children's author, financier, equestrian expert, owner of Greentree Racing Stables
Dict Am Auth; Index t Wom; Nat Cyc Am Bio v33; Obit File

9568. Woodbury, Helen Laura Sumner
1876–1933
labor historian, social economist, author, government official
Dict Am Auth; Not Am Wom

9569. Anthony, Katharine Susan
1877–1965
author, biographer
New York
Index t Wom; Nat Cyc Am Bio csv6; Obit File

9570. Brown, Sue M.
1877–1941

clubwoman, educator, author, suffragist, women's rights worker, Black civil rights worker
Black
Negro Alman; Prof Negro Wom

9571. Cannon, Ida Maud
1877–1960
social worker, nurse, medical reformer, author
Dict Am Bio supp v5; Index t Wom; Not Am Wom supp v1

9572. Cooper, Elizabeth
born 1877
author
Index t Wom

9573. Crowell, Grace Noll
born 1877
poet
Index t Wom

9574. Crownfield, Gertrude
1877–1945
children's author
Index t Wom; Obit File

9575. Hard, Anne; Annie Marie Nyhan Scribner
1877–1961
author, radio broadcaster, political journalist
Episcopalian
Washington, DC
Nat Cyc Am Bio v57

9576. Jerome, Maud Nugent
1877–1958
author, actor, composer
Index t Wom

9577. Kruettner, Caroline McAllister
1877–1957
poet, librarian, poetry editor
Obit File

9578. Landowska, Wanda (Lew)
1877/79–1959
harpsichordist, pianist, composer, musicologist, music educator, writer on music
Jewish
Polish
Dict Am Bio supp v6; Obit File; Slavon Encyc; Who Who Jew Hist

9579. Milton, Inez Lopez Seymour
born 1877
author, composer
Episcopalian
Nat Cyc Am Bio csv4

9580. Parmenter, Christine Whiting
1877–1953
author, novelist, magazine writer
Index t Wom; Obit File

9581. Pitkin, E. Winifred
1877–1960
obstetrician, author
Obit File

9582. Redfield, Ethel
born 1877
educator, author
Index t Wom

9583. Richmond, Winifred B.
1877–1945
physician, physiologist, medical author
Obit File

9584. Rombauer, Irma Louise von Starkloff
1877–1962
writer on food, cookbook author
Index t Wom; Not Am Wom supp v1; Obit File

9585. Russell, Edith
1877–1975
fashion writer, World War I correspondent
Obit File

9586. Schwimmer, Rosika
1877–1948
feminist, suffragist, pacifist, author, editor
Jewish
Hungarian
Dict Am Bio supp v4; Not Am Wom; Obit File

9587. Skinner, Constance Lindsay
1877–1939
author, poet, novelist, historian
Canadian
Index t Wom; Nat Cyc Am Bio csv2 and csv5; Not Am Wom

9588. Smith, Fredrika Shumway
1877–1968
children's author
Presbyterian
Illinois
Nat Cyc Am Bio v55

9589. Toklas, Alice Babette
1877/97–1967
writer, cookbook author
Jewish
French (American expatriate to Paris)
Dict Lit Bio v4; Index t Wom; Not Am Wom supp v1; Obit File

9590. Vaka, Demetra; Demetra Vaka Brown
1877–1946
novelist
German
Index t Wom

9591. Akeley, Mary Lee Jobe
1878/86–1966
explorer, photographer, educator, author, botanist
Index t Wom; Not Am Wom

9592. Beach, Cora M.
born 1878
author
Index t Wom

9593. Burr, Amelia Josephine
born 1878
poet
Index t Wom

9594. Coleman, Satis Narrona
born 1878
writer about music
Index t Wom

9595. Conkling, Grace Walcott Hazard
1878–1958
poet
Index t Wom

9596. Corbaley, Kate Alaska Hinckley Cooper
1878–1938
screenplay writer
Los Angeles, CA
Nat Cyc Am Bio v28

9597. Crapssey, Adelaide
1878–1914
poet
Dict Am Bio; Index t Wom; Not Am Wom; Wom Lit, More

9598. Emrick, Jeanette Wallace
born 1878
author, lecturer, humanitarian
Index t Wom

9599. Fairbank, Janet Ayer
1878–1951
author, feminist
Episcopalian
Index t Wom; Nat Cyc Am Bio v39

9600. Finley, Margaret
1878–1909
author
Not Am Wom

9601. Haskell, Helen Eggleston
married 1903
author
Index t Wom

9602. Howard, Alice Sturtevant
1878–1945
library founder, author, Republican party worker
Episcopalian
Index t Wom; Nat Cyc Am Bio v33

9603. Isaacs, Edith Juliet Rich
1878–1956
theater critic, author, editor of *Theater Arts* magazine
Not Am Wom supp v1; Obit File

9604. McQueen, Elizabeth Lippincott
born 1878
author
Christian Scientist
Nat Cyc Am Bio csv1

9605. Mitchell, Lucy Sprague
1878–1967
educator, college administrator, Black education worker, children's author
New York
Nat Cyc Am Bio v53; Not Am Wom supp v1

9606. Montague, Margaret Prescott; Jane Stege
1878–1955
mystic, author
Ill Encyc Myst

9607. Neugass, Miriam Dorothy Newman; Isadora Newman
born 1878
author, artist
Jewish
Louisiana
Nat Cyc Am Bio csv3

9608. Robyn, Louise
circa 1878–1949
composer, author, music educator
Index t Wom

9609. Scarborough, Dorothy
1878–1935
novelist, English teacher, folklorist
Dict Am Bio supp v1; Index t Wom; Wom Lit

9610. Shiber, Etta
circa 1878–1948
author
Index t Wom

9611. Young, Barbara
born 1878
poet
Index t Wom

9612. Belmont, Eleanor Elise Robson
1879–1979
actor, author, nurse, philanthropist, patron of the arts, founder of the Metropolitan Opera Guild
English
Index t Wom; Cur Biog '44 and '80

9613. Brinley, Katherine Gordon Sanger
1879–1966

author
Obit File

9614. Cabot, Ella Lyman
graduated 1904
educator, author
Index t Wom

9615. Drouet, Bessie Clarke
1879–1940
author, painter, sculptor
Index t Wom

9616. Dubois, Mary Constance
1879–1959
author
Index t Wom

9617. Eastman, Mary Huse
1879–1963
librarian, author
Index t Wom

9618. Fisher, Dorothy Canfield;
Dorothea Frances Canfield
1879–1958
novelist, writer on education, essayist
Cyc Am Bio; Dict Am Bio supp
v6; Dict Lit Bio v9; Index t
Wom; Nat Cyc Am Bio v18 and
v44; Not Am Wom supp v1;
Obit File

**9619. Gerould, Katharine
Elizabeth Fullerton**
1879–1944
short story writer, essayist, novelist
Index t Wom; Not Am Wom

**9620. Judson, Clara Ingram
Johnson**
1879–1960
children's author
Index t Wom; Obit File

9621. Lewars, Elsie Singmaster
born 1879
author
Lutheran
Pennsylvania
German
Nat Cyc Am Bio csv3

9622. Luhan, Mabel Dodge
1879–1962
author, patron, salon host
New Mexico
Index t Wom; Not Am Wom
supp v1; Read Encyc Am West

9623. Oemler, Marie Conway
1879–1932
author
Index t Wom

9624. Olcott, Margaret A.
1879–1949
playwright, biographer
Obit File

9625. Ring, Barbara Taylor
1879–1941
psychiatrist, hospital administrator, playwright
Massachusetts
Index t Wom; Obit File

9626. Runkle, Bertha (Brooks)
1879–1958
author, novelist
Index t Wom; Twent Cen Bio
Dict Not Am

9627. Sanger, Margaret Higgins; Mrs. J. Noah H. Slee
1879/83–1966
birth control reformer, lecturer,
author
Episcopalian
Index t Wom; Nat Cyc Am Bio
v52; Not Am Wom supp v1;
Obit File

9628. Sawyer, Josephine Caroline
born 1879
historical novelist
Watertown, NY
Dict Am Auth

**9629. Singmaster, Elsie; Elsie
Lewars**
1879–1958
novelist, children's author
Dict Lit Bio v9; Index t Wom;
Obit File

9630. Stanley, Martha
born 1879
playwright
Index t Wom

**9631. Stokes, Rose Harriet
Pastor**
1879–1933
Socialist and Communist party
leader, feminist, labor leader,
author
Jewish
Polish
Bio Dict Am Lab; Dict Am Bio;
Not Am Wom

9632. Walker, Susan Hunter
married 1904
editor, author
Scottish
Index t Wom

9633. Whitson, Beth Slater
1879–1930
author, poet, songwriter
Index t Wom

9634. Williams, Blanche Colton
1879–1926/44
educator, writer on writing, anthology editor
Index t Wom; Nat Cyc Am Bio
csv2

9635. Avary, Myrta Lockett
flourished 1910s
sociologist, politician, editor, author
Index t Wom

9636. Bailey, Temple (Irene)
188?–1953
novelist, short story writer
Dict Am Bio supp v5; Index t
Wom

9637. Beckley, Zoe
flourished 1910s
journalist, author
Index t Wom; Wom Lit, More

9638. Bernstein, Aline Frankau
1880/82–1955
stage scene and costume designer,
author
Jewish
New York
Dict Am Bio supp v5; Index t
Wom; Nat Cyc Am Bio v47;
Not Am Wom supp v1; Obit
File

9639. Bieber, Margarete
1880–1978
historian, author, archaeologist,
educator, authority on Greek
and Roman art
German
Obit File

9640. Bilbro, Mathilde (Anne)
flourished 1910s–50s
composer, music educator, author
Index t Wom

9641. Bingham, Millicent Todd
1880–1968
geographer, conservationist, author, editor, authority on Emily
Dickinson
Episcopalian
Cur Biog '69; Index t Wom; Nat
Cyc Am Bio csv9

9642. Cutler, Bessie Ingersoll
flourished 1910s–20s
nurse, author
Index t Wom

9643. Donnelly, Dorothy
1880–1928
author, librettist, actor
Index t Wom

9644. Gaines, Ruth
flourished 1910s
social worker, author
Index t Wom

9645. Grabau, Mary Antin
born 188?
autobiographer, translator, writer
in Yiddish

Jewish
Dict Am Auth; Dict Am Bio v4;
Nat Cyc Am Bio v39 and csv3;
Not Am Wom; Obit File

9646. Hemsley, Josephine
born 1880
author, songwriter
Index t Wom

9647. Keller, Helen Adams
1880–1968
author, feminist, suffragist, educator, advocate for the handicapped, pacifist, Socialist party
worker
Swedenborgian
Alabama
blind, deaf
Encyc South Hist; Index t Wom;
Nat Cyc Am Bio v15 and v57;
Not Am Wom supp v1; Obit
File

9648. Kelly, Eleanor Mercein
born 1880
author
Index t Wom

9649. Kerr, Sophie
1880–1965
author
Index t Wom

9650. Kluegel, Anne Jennings
born 1880
author, educator
Index t Wom

9651. Long, Elsie
1880–1946
composer, author
Index t Wom

9652. Lummis, Eliza O'Brien
flourished 1910s
editor, publisher, religious worker, author
Index t Wom

9653. Lupton, Mary Josephine
flourished 1910s
editor, translator, author
Index t Wom

9654. Matthews, Frances Aymar
born 18?; flourished 1910s
playwright, poet, novelist
New York, NY
Dict Am Auth; Index t Wom

**9655. McCormick, Anne
Elizabeth O'Hare**
1880/82–1954
journalist, foreign correspondent,
New York Times editorialist and
writer on world affairs, Pulitzer
Prize winner
Dict Am Bio supp v5; Index t
Wom; Not Am Wom supp v1;
Obit File

9656. Mechtold, Mary Rider
flourished 1910s
playwright
Index t Wom

9657. Mercedes, Mary Antonio Gallagher
flourished 1910s
author, religious worker
Index t Wom

9658. Misch, Caeser, Mrs.
flourished 1910s
religious worker, lecturer, author
Index t Wom

9659. Molloy, Mary Aloysia
born 1880
educator, author, Franciscan nun
Catholic
Nat Cyc Am Bio csv3

9660. Morgan, Agnes
flourished 1910s
playwright
Index t Wom

9661. Morrow, Honore Bryant Willsie
1880–1940
historical novelist
Index t Wom; Nat Cyc Am Bio v29

9662. Nealis, Jean Ursula
flourished 1910s
poet
Index t Wom

9663. Niles, [Mary] Blair Rice
1880/87–1959
author, explorer
Index t Wom; Nat Cyc Am Bio v46

9664. Nitzsche, Else Koenig
1880–1952
artist, author
Unitarian
Pennsylvania
Nat Cyc Am Bio v47

9665. Norris, Kathleen Thompson
1880–1966
author, novelist, magazine writer, pacifist, feminist
Catholic
Index t Wom; Nat Cyc Am Bio csv3; Not Am Wom supp v1; Obit File; Wom Lit, More

9666. Pease, Leonora Elizabeth
flourished 1910s
children's author
Nat Cyc Am Bio v17

9667. Perkins, Edna Brush
1880–1930
author, social worker
Cincinnati, OH
Nat Cyc Am Bio v26

9668. Peterkin, Julia (Mood)
1880–1961
author of books on Black life, Pulitzer Prize winner
South Carolina
Dict Lit Bio v9; Index t Wom; Nat Cyc Am Bio csv3; Obit File; Wom Lit, More

9669. Peyser, Ethel R.
flourished 1910s–30s
author, editor, music critic, lecturer
Index t Wom

9670. Phelps, Pauline
flourished 1910s
playwright
Index t Wom

9671. Poole, Fannie Huntington Runnells
flourished 1910s
poet, book reviewer
Index t Wom

9672. Robins, Julia Gorham
flourished 1910s
author
Index t Wom

9673. Roulet, Mary F. Nixon
flourished 1910s
author, journalist, musician, art critic, linguist
Index t Wom

9674. Sawyer, Ruth
1880–1970
children's author, storyteller
Not Am Wom supp v1

9675. Sherman, Minna E.
flourished 1910s
agriculturist, club leader, lecturer, author
Index t Wom

9676. Short, Marion
flourished 1910s
playwright
Index t Wom

9677. Snow, Ellen
flourished 1910s
author, pacifist, animal humane woker, suffragist
Cyc Am Bio

9678. Tong, Eleanore Elizabeth
flourished 1910s
religious author
Index t Wom

9679. Turner, Nancy Byrd
born 1880
poet, author
Index t Wom

9680. Vail, Stella Boothe
flourished 1910s–20s
nurse, author, social worker
Index t Wom

9681. Walsh, Honor
flourished 1910s
editor, author
Index t Wom

9682. Yezierska, Anzia
1880/85–1970
novelist
Jewish
Polish
Index t Wom; Not Am Wom supp v1; Wom Lit, More

9683. Abbott, Jane Ludlow Drake
born 1881
novelist
Index t Wom

9684. Aldrich, Bess Genevra Streeter
1881–1954
novelist, short story writer
Methodist
Nebraska
Dict Am Bio; Index t Wom; Nat Cyc Am Bio v45 and csv8, Obit File

9685. Bennett, Helen Christine
born 1881
author
Index t Wom

9686. Bianco, Margery Williams
1881–1944
author
Not Am Wom

9687. Black, Margaret Horton (Potter)
born 1881
novelist
Chicago, IL
Dict Am Auth

9688. Branscombe, Gena
born 1881
composer, author, conductor
Canadian
Index t Wom

9689. Burlingame, Anne Elizabeth
born 1881
author, educator
Nat Cyc Am Bio csvl

9690. Deming, Therese O.
1881–1945
children's author
Obit File

9691. Gilmore, Florence MacGruder
born 1881
philanthropist, author
Index t Wom

9692. Glentworth, Marguerite Linton
born 1881
novelist
Newark, NJ
Dict Am Auth

9693. Gruenberg, Sidonie Matsner
1881–1974
parent education leader; director of the Child Study Association of America, specialist in child guidance, parent education, and family relationships; nonfiction writer; lecturer
Austrian
Cur Biog '74; Index t Wom; Not Am Wom supp v1; Obit File

9694. Henderson, Alice Corbin
1881–1949
poet, cofounder of *Poetry Magazine*
Obit File

9695. Loveman, Amy
1881–1955
literary critic, editor, author, cofounder of the !Saturday Review of Literature
Dict Am Bio supp v5; Index t Wom; Nat Cyc Am Bio v44; Not Am Wom supp v1; Obit File

9696. MacLane, Mary
born 1881
autobiographer
Dict Am Auth

9697. Massee, May
1881–1966
editor, children's literature specialist
Not Am Wom supp v1

9698. Phillips, Lena Madesin
1881–1955
feminist, founder of the National and International Federations of Business and Professional Women's Clubs, author, editor, lecturer, politician
Dict Am Bio supp v5; Index t Wom; Not Am Wom supp v1; Obit File

9699. Potter, Margaret Horton
1881–1911
author, novelist
Index t Wom; Twent Cen Bio Dict Not Am

9700. Roberts, Elizabeth Madox
1881/86–1941
poet, novelist

Kentucky
Dict Am Bio supp v3; Dict Lit Bio v9; Encyc South Hist; Index t Wom; Nat Cyc Am Bio csv4; Not Am Wom; Obit File; Wom Lit; Wom Lit, More

9701. Sergeant, Elizabeth Shepley
born 1881
author
Index t Wom

9702. Siegrist, Mary
circa 1881–1953
poet, translator
Index t Wom

9703. Weber, Lois
1881–1939
movie director, writer, actor
Not Am Wom

9704. Block, Anita
born 1882
author, lecturer, Socialist politician
Nat Cyc Am Bio csv9

9705. Burt, Katharine Newlin
born 1882
author
Index t Wom

9706. Colcord, Joanna Carver (Bruno)
1882–1960
social worker, director of the Russell Sage Foundation, author
Index t Wom; Not Am Wom supp v1; Obit File

9707. Cook, Susan Glaspell
1882–1948
novelist, playwright, stage producer, Pulitzer Prize winner
Obit File

9708. Denni, Gwynne
1882–1949
author, actor, musician, songwriter
Index t Wom

9709. Dodd, Katharine
1882–1965
pediatrician, medical educator and author
Episcopalian
Nat Cyc Am Bio v53

9710. Fauset, Jessie Redmon
1882/86–1961
author, novelist, editor, educator
Encyc Black Am; Index t Wom; Negro Alman; Not Am Wom supp v1; Prof Negro Wom v2; Wom Lit; Wom Lit, More

9711. Field, Sarah Bard
1882–1974

poet, suffragist
Not Am Wom supp v1

9712. Flexner, Jennie Maas
1882–1944
librarian, scholar of Black literature, author
Jewish
Dict Am Bio supp v3; Index t Wom; Not Am Wom

9713. Hargreaves, Sheba
born 1882
author
Index t Wom

9714. Hobart, Alice Tisdale Nourse
1882–1967
author, novelist
Index t Wom; Obit File

9715. Humphrey, Grace
born 1882
author
Index t Wom

9716. Laimbeer, Nathalie Schenk
1882–1929
banker, financial writer
Dict Am Bio

9717. Lowe, Corinne Martin
1882–1952
journalist, fashion editor, author
Index t Wom

9718. Loy, Mina
1882–1966
poet
French (American expatriate to Paris)
Dict Lit Bio v4

9719. Mathews, Blanche Dingley
died 1932
composer, author, music educator
Index t Wom

9720. Mayo, Margaret
1882–1951
playwright, author
Index t Wom; Obit File

9721. Miller, Bertha Everett Mahony
1882–1969
bookseller, children's literature specialist, editor
Not Am Wom supp v1

9722. Mitchell, Ruth Comfort; Mrs. Sanborn Young
1882–1954
author, poet, novelist, leader in Republican Organizations for Women
California
Index t Wom; Nat Cyc Am Bio v44; Obit File

9723. Prouty, Olive (Chapin) Higgins
1882–1974
author, novelist
Unitarian
Massachusetts
Index t Wom; Nat Cyc Am Bio v57; Obit File

9724. Richter, Gisela Marie Augusta
1882–1972
classical archaeologist, museum curator, author
English
Index t Wom; Not Am Wom supp v1

9725. Rippen, Jane Parker Deeter
1882–1953
social worker, journalist, Girl Scouts of America executive
Not Am Wom supp v1; Obit File

9726. Scott, Miriam Finn
1882–1944
pioneer child diagnostician, educator, lecturer, author
Russian
Index t Wom; Nat Cyc Am Bio v36

9727. Senn, Margaret Lynch
born 1882
author
Index t Wom

9728. Spencer, Anne
born 1882
poet
Index t Wom; Nort Anth Poet; Wom Lit, More

9729. Strunsky, Manya Gordon
1882–1945
leftist author
Obit File

9730. Wambaugh, Sarah
1882–1955
pacifist, internationalist, authority on plebiscites, author, lecturer, consultant adviser to the League of Nations and the UN
Dict Am Bio supp v5; Index t Wom; Obit File

9731. Wilson, Margaret
1882–1973
novelist
Dict Lit Bio v9

9732. Batchelder, Ann
1883–1955
food editor, poet
Obit File

9733. Bercovici, Naomi Lebrescu
1883–1957
artist, poet

New York
French
Nat Cyc Am Bio v45

9734. Cane, Florence Naumburg
1883–1952
artist, educator, author
Obit File

9735. Cowl, Jane Cowles
1883/84–1950
stage actor, playwright, theatrical producer and director
Dict Am Bio supp v4; Index t Wom; Nat Cyc Am Bio csv2 and csv5; Not Am Wom; Obit File

9736. Frederick, Christine McGaffey
1883–1970
household efficiency expert, home economist, author, businessperson
Index t Wom; Not Am Wom supp v1

9737. Gibbons, Helen Davenport Brown
1883–1960
novelist, founder of Sauvons les Bebes, a World War I orphan aid agency
Obit File

9738. Hauck, Louise Platt
1883–1943
author, novelist
Index t Wom; Obit File

9739. Haynes, Elizabeth A. Ross
1883–1953
YWCA official, social researcher, social worker, author, businessperson, community leader
Index t Wom; Not Am Wom supp v1

9740. la Follette, Fola (Middleton)
1883–1970
actor, author, suffragist
Obit File

9741. Lamson, Armene Tashijian
1883–1970
medical illustrator, physician, UNICEF worker, medical author
Episcopalian
Seattle, WA
Turkish
Nat Cyc Am Bio v56

9742. Miller, Olive Beaupre
1883–1968
children's author, sex education worker

Illinois
Nat Cyc Am Bio v54

9743. Newman, Frances
1883–1928
librarian, author, novelist
Index t Wom; Not Am Wom;
Wom Lit, More

**9744. Spencer, Fleta Jan
Brown**
1883–1938
composer, author
Index t Wom

9745. Strawbridge, Anne West
1883–1941
aviator, author
Index t Wom

9746. Strode, Muriel
married 1908
poet
Index t Wom

**9747. Wilkinson, Marguerite
Ogden Bigelow**
1883–1928
author
Nat Cyc Am Bio v21

9748. Winn, Edith L.
died 1933
violinist, music educator, author
Index t Wom

9749. Wise, Jessie Moore
1883–1949
composer, author
Index t Wom

9750. Woodsmall, Ruth Frances
1883–1963
YWCA leader, government official, author
Index t Wom; Not Am Wom
supp v1

9751. Zunser, Miriam Shomer
1883–1951
novelist, playwright
Russian
Obit File

9752. Arbuthnot, May Hill
1884–1969
educator, specialist in children's
literature
Not Am Wom supp v1

9753. Broadhurst, Lillian Trimble Bradley
1884–1959
Broadway theatrical director,
playwright
Obit File

9754. Darby, Ada Claire
1884–1953
historical author for children
Obit File

9755. Fair, Ethel Marion
born 1884
librarian, editor, author, lecturer
Index t Wom

9756. Fay, Amy
1884–1928
pianist, writer on music
Chicago, IL
Dict Am Auth; Index t Wom;
Not Am Wom; Wom Cent

9757. Finney, Ruth Elbright
1884–1955
journalist, editor, author, clubwoman
Index t Wom

**9758. Gifford, Fannie Stearns
Davis**
born 1884
poet
Index t Wom

9759. Kelley, Edith Summers
1884–1956
novelist, short story writer
Dict Am Bio supp v6; Dict Lit
Bio v9; Wom Lit; Wom Lit,
More

**9760. Marley, Anne Augusta
Bonner**
born 1884
poet, violinist
Christian Scientist
Nat Cyc Am Bio csv9

9761. Miller, Helen Topping
1884–1960
novelist, short story writer
Index t Wom; Obit File

9762. Miller, Mary Britton; Isabel Bolton
1884–1975
novelist, poet
Index t Wom; Obit File

9763. Mountain Wolf Woman;
Kehachiwinga
1884–1960
autobiographer
Native American (Winnebago)
Great North Am Ind

9764. Olcott, Virginia
graduated 1909
social worker, educator, author
Index t Wom

9765. Peck, Anne Marriman
born 1884
illustrator, author
Index t Wom

9766. Roosevelt, [Anna] Eleanor
1884–1962
social reformer, humanitarian,
author, lecturer
Washington, DC

English
Eng Wom; Index t Wom; Nat
Cyc Am Bio v57 and csv4 and
csv6; Not Am Wom supp v1;
Obit File

9767. Swindler, Mary Hamilton
1884–1967
archaeologist, classicist
Nat Cyc Am Bio v54; Not Am
Wom supp v1

9768. Tietjens, Eunice
1884–1944
author, poet
Index t Wom; Not Am Wom

9769. Tolstoy, Mary Koutouzow
1884–1976
author, fashion director, World
War I and II nurse
Obit File

9770. West, Claudine
circa 1884–1943
screenwriter
English
Index t Wom

9771. Bailey, Margaret Emerson
1885–1949
educator, journalist, novelist,
magazine writer, police commissioner
Episcopalian
New Canaan, CT
Nat Cyc Am Bio csv6; Obit File

9772. Bruce, Kathleen Eveleth
1885–1950
historian, author
Nat Cyc Am Bio v42; Obit File

9773. Cromwell, Gladys Louise
1885–1919
poet
Dict Am Bio

9774. Farnham, Mateel Howe
married 1910
novelist
Index t Wom

9775. Ferber, Edna
1885/87–1968
author, playwright
Jewish
Dict Lit Bio v9; Index t Wom;
Nat Cyc Am Bio v60 and csv3;
Not Am Wom supp v1; Obit
File; Read Encyc Am West;
Who Who Jew Hist; Wom Lit,
More

9776. Flexner, Hortense
born 1885
poet
Index t Wom

**9777. Hutchinson, Mary Amory
Hare; Amory Hare**
1885–1969
author, novelist, dramatist, painter, poet, thoroughbred-horse
breeder
Episcopalian
California
Nat Cyc Am Bio v57, Index t
Wom

**9778. Kaup, Elizabeth Bartol
Dewing**
born 1885
author
Index t Wom

**9779. Keyes, Frances Parkinson
Wheeler**
1885–1970
popular novelist
Index t Wom; Obit File

9780. Newsome, Effie Lee
born 1885
poet
Index t Wom

9781. O'Hara, Mary; Mary
Sture-Vasa
1885–1980
composer, novelist, scriptwriter
Cur Biog '81; Index t Wom

9782. Owen, Ruth Bryan; Ruth
Rohde
1885–1954
representative to Congress from
Florida, US diplomat, author,
lecturer
Dict Am Bio v5; Index t Wom;
Nat Cyc Am Bio csv1; Not Am
Wom supp v1; Obit File

9783. Parker, Cornelia Stratton
born 1885
author
Index t Wom

9784. Rourke, Constance Mayfield
1885–1941
student of American culture, historian, folklorist, author, critic,
educator
Dict Am Bio supp v3; Index t
Wom; Nat Cyc Am Bio v32;
Not Am Wom

9785. Rouverol, Aurania
1885–1955
playwright, actor, radio scriptwriter, screenwriter
Index t Wom; Obit File

9786. Strong, Anna Louise
1885–1970
radical journalist,
pro–Communist China advocate, author
Cur Biog '70; Index t Wom; Not
Am Wom supp v1; Obit File

9787. Sturgis, Margaret Castex
1885–1962
gynecologist, cancer researcher, medical author
Episcopalian
Pennsylvania
Nat Cyc Am Bio v49

9788. Winslow, Ola Elizabeth
1885–1977
biographer of Jonathan Edward, historian, Pulitzer Prize winner
Obit File

9789. Wylie, Elinor Morton Hoyt
1885–1928
poet, novelist
Dict Am Bio; Dict Lit Bio v9; Index t Wom; Nat Cyc Am Bio v21; Not Am Wom; Wom Lit

9790. Akins, Zoe
1886–1958
dramatist, poet, novelist, screenwriter, Pulitzer Prize winner
Dict Am Bio supp v5; Index t Wom; Nat Cyc Am Bio csv6; Obit File; Wom Lit, More

9791. Anderson, Margaret Carolyn
1886–1973
editor, author, novelist, autobiographer
French (American expatriate to Paris)
Dict Lit Bio v4; Not Am Wom supp v1

9792. Applegarth, Margaret Tyson
born 1886
playwright, children's author, editor
Index t Wom

9793. Barnes, Margaret Ayer
1886–1967
novelist, Pulitzer Prize winner
Dict Lit Bio v9; Index t Wom

9794. Borden, Mary; Lady Spears
1886–1968
novelist, head of a World War II field hospital in France
English (American expatriate to England)
Index t Wom; Obit File

9795. Bridgman, Olga Louise
born 1886
psychiatrist, medical educator and author
Episcopalian
California
Nat Cyc Am Bio csv6

9796. Brock, Emma Lillian
born 1886
author, illustrator
Index t Wom

9797. Cadilla de Martinez, Maria; Liana
1886–1951
educator, folklorist, author, feminist
Not Am Wom supp v1

9798. Coyle, Kathleen
1886–1952
novelist
Irish
Obit File

9799. Doolittle, Hilda; Hilda Doolittle Aldington; H. D.
1886–1961
poet, leader of the imagist movement in poetry, author, literary magazine editor
Dict Lit Bio v4; Index t Wom; Nat Cyc Am Bio v45 and csv3; Nort Anth Poet; Not Am Wom supp v1; Obit File; Wom Lit; Wom Lit, More

9800. Frost, Elizabeth Hollister
circa 1886–1958
author
Index t Wom

9801. Hall, Hazel
1886–1924
poet
Oregon
Dict Am Bio; Index t Wom; Nat Cyc Am Bio v22

9802. Johnson, Georgia Douglas
1886–1966
poet, composer, author
Black
Encyc Black Am; Index t Wom; Negro Alman; Obit File; Wom Lit, More

9803. Kauffman, Ruth Hammitt
1886–1952
World War I correspondent, children's author
Obit File

9804. Kent, Louise Andrews; Therea Tempest
born 1886
author
Index t Wom

9805. Lane, Rose Wilder
1886/87–1968
novelist, telegrapher, World War I Red Cross worker in Europe, Vietnam war correspondent
Index t Wom; Nat Cyc Am Bio v54

9806. Lindheim, Irma
born 1886

clubwoman, author
Index t Wom

9807. Matthews, Adelaide
born 1886
playwright
Index t Wom

9808. Nicholson, Martha Snell
1886–circa 1951
singer, poet
Index t Wom

9809. Paradis, Marjorie B.; Olive Bartholomew
1886–1970
novelist
Congregationalist
New York
Index t Wom; Nat Cyc Am Bio v57

9810. Parsons, Alice Beal
1886–1962
author, literary critic
New York
Index t Wom; Nat Cyc Am Bio v50

9811. Schmitt, Bernadotte Everly
1886–1969
author on modern European history, educator, historian
Cur Biog '69

9812. Slade, Caroline McCormick
1886–1951
novelist, social worker, civic worker, suffragist, founder of the National League of Women Voters
New York
Index t Wom

9813. Taylor, Lily Ross
1886–1969
classicist
Not Am Wom supp v1

9814. Thompson, Mary Wolfe
born 1886
author
Index t Wom

9815. Treadwell, Sophie
married 1911
playwright, journalist
Index t Wom; Wom Lit, More

9816. Untermeyer, Jean Starr
born 1886
poet
Index t Wom

9817. Watson, Evelyn Mabel Palmer
born 1886
poet
Index t Wom

9818. Allis, Marguerite
1887–1958
historical novelist
Index t Wom; Obit File

9819. Bauer, Marion Eugenia
1887–1955
music educator, writer on music history, composer, editor, music critic
Index t Wom; Nat Cyc Am Bio v43, Not Am Wom supp v1; Obit File

9820. Beach, Sylvia Woodbridge
1887–1962
bookshop proprietor, publisher of James Joyce, lending library owner
French (American expatriate to Paris)
Dict Lit Bio v4; Nat Cyc Am Bio v47; Not Am Wom supp v1; Obit File

9821. Beam, Lura
born 1887
educator, author
Index t Wom

9822. Benedict, Ruth Fulton
1887–1948
anthropologist, author, philosopher, educator
Dict Am Bio supp v4; Index t Wom; Nat Cyc Am Bio v36; Not Am Wom; Who Who Phil

9823. Chase, Mary Ellen
1887–1973
novelist, biographer, short story writer, literary critic, writer on the Bible, university educator
Episcopalian
Cur Biog '73; Index t Wom; Nat Cyc Am Bio csv9; Obit File; Wom Lit, More

9824. Colum, Mary
1887–1957
author, literary critic
Irish
Nat Cyc Am Bio v44

9825. Helburn, Therese (Opdyke)
1887–1959
theatrical producer, dramatist, codirector and administrator of New York City's theater guild
New York, NY
Dict Am Bio supp v6; Index t Wom; Not Am Wom supp v1; Obit File

9826. Hueston, Ethel Powelson
born 1887
author
Index t Wom

9827. Kleeman, Rita Halle
born 1887
author
Index t Wom

9828. Lauferty, Lilian (Wolfe);
Beatrice Fairfax
1887–1958
newspaper journalist, novelist
Index t Wom; Obit File

9829. Madelva, Mary Eveline
Wolff, Sister
1887–1964
president of St. Mary's College,
medievalist, educator, author,
poet, Catholic nun
Catholic
Index t Wom; Nat Cyc Am Bio
v51; Obit File

9830. Marshall, Marguerite
Moers
1887–1964
journalist, author
Index t Wom

9831. Meyer, Agnes Elizabeth
(Ernst)
1887–1970
author, journalist, vice-president
and co-owner of *The Washing-*
ton Post, World War II correspondent, autobiographer,
lecturer, social worker, Republican party worker, crusader for
social services and education
causes
Lutheran
New York
Cur Biog '70; Index t Wom; Nat
Cyc Am Bio v56; Obit File

9832. Moore, Marianne (Craig)
1887–1972
poet, critic, editor, winner of Pu-
litzer Prize and National Book
Award
Presbyterian
New York
Cur Biog '72; Index t Wom; Nat
Cyc Am Bio v57; Nort Anth
Poet; Not Am Wom supp v1;
Obit File; Wom Lit, More

9833. Parker, Lottie (Blair)
died 1937
dramatist, author
Index t Wom; Nat Cyc Am Bio
v10

9834. Parkhurst, Helen
1887–1973
educator, author
Obit File

9835. Pinkerton, Katherine
Sutherland
1887–1967
author
Index t Wom

9836. Ratchford, Fannie
Elizabeth
born 1887
librarian, author, editor
Index t Wom

9837. Snyder, Alice Dorothea
1887–1943
professor of English literature,
author
Index t Wom; Not Am Wom;
Obit File

9838. Stebbins, Lucy Poate
1887–1958
novelist, biographer
Obit File

9839. Strickland, Lily Teresa
born 1887
composer, author
Index t Wom

9840. van Waters, Miriam
1887–1974
penologist, social worker, writer
on penology
Cur Biog '74; Index t Wom; Not
Am Wom supp v1

9841. Waln, Nora
1887/95–1964
author, journalist, antifascist
worker
Index t Wom; Obit File

9842. Wolff, Mary Evaline
"Madelva", Sister
1887–1964
college administrator, Catholic
nun, religious educator, poet
Catholic
Not Am Wom supp v1

9843. Baker, Nina Brown
1888–1957
author
Index t Wom

9844. Barker, Tommie Dora
born 1888
librarian, author, educator
Index t Wom

9845. Bartley, Nalbro
born 1888
novelist
Index t Wom

9846. Baum, Hedwig "Vicki";
Mrs. Richard Lerf
1888–1960/62
novelist, playwright, screenwriter
Jewish
Hollywood, CA
Austrian
Dict Am Bio supp v6; Index t
Wom; Nat Cyc Am Bio v52;
Obit File

9847. Buchanan, Annabel Mor-
ris
born 1888
composer, editor, author
Index t Wom

9848. Butcher, Fanny
born 1888
journalist, poet
Index t Wom

9849. Fergusson, Erna
born 1888
author
Index t Wom

9850. Fletcher, Inglis Clark
born 1888
author
Index t Wom

9851. Fox, Genevieve May
1888–1959
author
Index t Wom; Obit File

9852. Franklin, Pearl
circa 1888–1958
playwright, lawyer, Zionist, Hadassah leader
Jewish
Index t Wom; Obit File

9853. Goodman, Lillian Rose-
dale
born 1888
composer, singer, pianist, critic,
author, linguist
Index t Wom

9854. Gray, Caroline E.
died 1938
author, nurse
Index t Wom

9855. Groves, May Showler
born 1888
author
Index t Wom

9856. Hull, Helen Rose
1888–1971
novelist, short story writer, university educator
New York
Cur Biog '71; Index t Wom; Nat
Cyc Am Bio v60; Obit File

9857. Hyman, Libbie Henrietta
1888–1969
zoologist, author
Index t Wom; Not Am Wom
supp v1

9858. Kilmer, Aline Murray
1888–1941
poet, children's author, lecturer
Index t Wom; Obit File

9859. Kummer, Clare Rodman
Beecher
born 1888

composer, songwriter, playwright
Index t Wom

9860. Lownsbery, Eloise
born 1888
author
Index t Wom

9861. Marion, Frances
1888/1900–1973
screenwriter, playwright, novelist
Hollywood, CA
Index t Wom; Not Am Wom
supp v1; Obit File

9862. McMein, Neysa; Mrs.
John Gordon Baragwanath
1888/90–1949
illustrator, magazine illustrator,
painter, portraitist, commercial
artist, author
Episcopalian
Index t Wom; Nat Cyc Am Bio
v36; Not Am Wom; Obit File

9863. Parrish, Anne (Titzell);
Mrs. Charles A. Corliss
1888–1957
illustrator, novelist, children's author
Index t Wom; Nat Cyc Am Bio
csv4; Obit File

9864. Putnam, Nina Wilcox
1888–1962
author, humorist, novelist, short
story writer, suffragist
Catholic
Nat Cyc Am Bio v45; Obit File

9865. Pyle, Katherine
died 1938
author, illustrator
Index t Wom

9866. Rothery, Agnes Edwards
1888–1954
author
Index t Wom

9867. Sampter, Jessie Ethel
1888–1938
poet, Zionist
Jewish
Not Am Wom

9868. Seifert, Shirley Louise
born 1888/89
novelist
Index t Wom

9869. Seymour, Flora Warren
born 1888
author, lawyer, Native American
scholar
Index t Wom

9870. Solano, Solita
1888–1975
journalist, drama critic, novelist,
poet

French (American expatriate to Paris)
Dict Lit Bio v4

9871. Strahan, Kay Cleaver
born 1888
author
Index t Wom

9872. Turnball, Agnes Sligh
born 1888
author
Index t Wom

9873. Vanderbilt, Amy; Mrs. Hans Knopf
1888/1908–1974
journalist, syndicated columnist, author, etiquette authority
Cur Biog '75; Index t Wom; Obit File

9874. Wagstaff, Blanche Shoemaker
born 1888
poet, editor
Index t Wom

9875. Wawa Calac Chaw; Keep from the Water
1888–1972
author, artist, feminist, lecturer on Native American and feminist matters
Native American (Luiseno)
Great North Am Ind

9876. Akers, Susan Grey
born 1889
librarian, educator, author
Index t Wom

9877. Claytor, Gertrude (Harris) Boatwright
1889–1973
poet, Red Cross worker in World War I
Christian Scientist
Virginia
Nat Cyc Am Bio v57

9878. Cranston, Ruth
1889–1956
religious author, biographer, lecturer
Obit File

9879. de Angeli, Marguerite
born 1889
illustrator, author
Index t Wom

9880. Gaither, Frances (Jones)
1889–1955
author, novelist
Index t Wom; Obit File

9881. Gillespie, Marian
1889–1946
composer, pianist, author, actor, journalist
Index t Wom

9882. Gordon, Dorothy Lerner
1889–1970
radio and television producer, singer, children's author
Cur Biog '70; Index t Wom; Not Am Wom supp v1

9883. Green, Charlotte Hilton
born 1889
naturalist, author
Index t Wom

9884. Hurst, Fannie
1889–1968
novelist, short story writer, women's rights worker, Zionist
Jewish
Index t Wom; Nat Cyc Am Bio csv2 and csv5; Not Am Wom; Obit File; Who Who Jew Hist

9885. Janis, Elisie (Bierbower) (Wilson)
1889/93–1956
mimic, stage actor, singer, dancer, vaudevillian, author, songwriter, World War I entertainer
Dict Am Bio supp v6; Index t Wom; Nat Cyc Am Bio csv1; Obit File

9886. Lillenas, Bertha Mae
1889–1945
composer, author
Index t Wom

9887. Morrison, Adrienne
1889–1940
actor, literary agent
Index t Wom

9888. Page, Elizabeth (Merwin)
born 1889
author, novelist
Quaker
Index t Wom; Nat Cyc Am Bio csv6

9889. Ripperger, Henrietta Sperry
born 1889
novelist
Index t Wom

9890. Rood, Helen Martin
1889–1943
author
Index t Wom

9891. Ryan, Anne
1889–1954
abstract artist specializing in cloth and paper compositions, author, poet
Not Am Wom supp v1; Obit File

9892. Smith, Hannah
died 1939
composer, music educator, author
Index t Wom

9893. Stern, Elizabeth Gertrude Levin; Eleanor Morton; Elsie-Jeab
1889/90–1954
author, editor, social worker, political activist and antiwar worker
Quaker
Nat Cyc Am Bio v39; Obit File

9894. Vance, Marguerite
1889–1965
author
Index t Wom

9895. Wallace, Mildred White
born 1889
composer, singer, publisher, author
Index t Wom

9896. Ward, Maisie
1889–1975
book publisher, author, lecturer, Catholic church worker
Catholic
English
Cur Biog '75; Index t Wom

9897. Weiman, Rita
1889/96–1954
author, playwright, screenwriter
Hollywood, CA
Index t Wom; Obit File

9898. Weiman, Rita
1889/96–1954
author, playwright, screenwriter
Hollywood, CA
Index t Wom; Obit File

9899. Widdemer, Margaret; Mrs. Robert H. Schauffler
born 1889
author, poet
Index t Wom; Nat Cyc Am Bio csv1

9900. Allee, Marjorie Hill
1890–1945
author
Index t Wom

9901. Ashmun, Margaret Eliza
died 1940
author
Index t Wom

9902. Beard, Miriam
flourished 1920s
humorist, feminist
Index t Wom

9903. Best, Molly
flourished 1920s
humorist, journalist, author
Index t Wom

9904. Biddle, Katherine C.; Katherine Garrison Chapin
1890–1977

poet, literary critic
Obit File

9905. Bryant, Louise
1890–1936
journalist, author, Communist party worker
Great Sov Encyc; Index t Wom

9906. Chapin, Katharine Garrison
born 1890
poet
Index t Wom

9907. Dayton, Katherine
1890–1945
journalist, playwright, political satirist, humorist
New York
Index t Wom; Nat Cyc Am Bio v34

9908. Douglas, Marjory Stoneman
born 1890
author
Index t Wom

9909. Douglas, Mary Stoneman
born 1890
poet
Index t Wom

9910. Eliot, Ethel Cook
1890–1972
children's author, religious writer
Catholic
Nat Cyc Am Bio v56

9911. Elliston, George, Miss
flourished 1920s
poet
Index t Wom

9912. Elmendorf, Mary J.
flourished 1920s
poet
Index t Wom

9913. Ferris, Helen Josephine; Mrs. Albert B. Tibbets
1890–1969
author, editor, children's author
Baptist
New York
Index t Wom; Nat Cyc Am Bio v55

9914. Field, Mildred Fowler
flourished 1920s
poet
Index t Wom

9915. Flanagan, Hallie Mae Ferguson (Davis); Hallie Davis
189?–1969
theater educator, theater administrator and director, playwright
Not Am Wom supp v1, Obit File

9916. Goodrich, Frances
born 1890
actor, playwright
Index t Wom

9917. Grant, Blanche C.
flourished 1920s
artist, author
Index t Wom

9918. Griffith, Corinne
flourished 1920s–30s
actor, author
Index t Wom

9919. Grissom, Irene Welch
flourished 1920s
poet
Index t Wom

9920. Hall, Amanda Benjamin
born 1890
poet
Index t Wom

9921. Hart, Frances Noyes
1890–1943
novelist
Obit File

9922. Haste, Gwendolen
flourished 1920s–30s
poet
Index t Wom

9923. Hathway, Katherine Butler
1890–1942
author
Index t Wom

9924. Henderson, Rise
flourished 1920s
poet
Index t Wom

9925. Heyward, Dorothy Hartzell (Kuhns)
1890–1961
playwright, novelist
Dict Lit Bio v7; Index t Wom;
Obit File

9926. Holding, Elizabeth Sanxy
1890–1955
mystery novelist
Obit File

9927. Horan, Kenneth, Mrs.
born 1890
novelist
Index t Wom

9928. Hurd, Muriel Jeffries
1890–1958
poet, editor, president of the National League of American Pen Women
Obit File

9929. Hurst, Vida (Frais)
1890–1958

novelist
California
Nat Cyc Am Bio v43; Obit File

9930. Kennedy, Mary
flourished 1920s–30s
playwright
Index t Wom

9931. Lawrence, Josephine
1890–1978
novelist, children's author
Index t Wom; Obit File

9932. le Cron, Helen Cowles
flourished 1920s
poet
Index t Wom

9933. Leighton, Mary
flourished 1920s–30s
poet
Protestant Episcopal
Nat Cyc Am Bio v26

9934. MacDougal, Violet
flourished 1920s
poet
Index t Wom

9935. McAdoo, Eleanor Wilson
1890–1967
author
Obit File

9936. McClurg, Virginia Donaghe
flourished 1920s
author, lecturer
Index t Wom

9937. McGauley, Minna Hoppe
flourished 1920s
author, dramatic coach
Index t Wom

9938. McKenney, Eileen
died 1940
author
Index t Wom

9939. Morrison, Anne
flourished 1920s
playwright
Index t Wom

9940. Mumford, Ethel Watts
died 1940
playwright, poet, novelist
Index t Wom

9941. Oelrichs, Blanche Marie Louise; Michael Strange; Blanche Twede; Blanche Tweed
1890–1950
actor, poet, playwright, suffragist
Index t Wom; Nat Cyc Am Bio v39; Not Am Wom; Obit File

9942. Pierson, Louise John Randall
born 1890
author
Index t Wom

9943. Porter, Katherine Anne
1890/94–1980
author, short story writer
Texas
French (American expatriate to Paris)
Cur Biog '80; Dict Lit Bio v4 and v9; Encyc South Hist; Index t Wom; Wom Lit; Wom Lit, More

9944. Powers, Rose Mills
flourished 1920s
poet
Index t Wom

9945. Prosper, Joan Dareth
flourished 1920s
poet
Index t Wom

9946. Randolph, Lois
flourished 1920s
educator
Index t Wom

9947. Rothrock, Mary Utopia
born 1890
librarian, editor, author
Index t Wom

9948. Schultz, Sigrid Lillian
flourished 1920s–40s
journalist, author
Index t Wom

9949. Shephard, Esther
flourished 1920s
author
Index t Wom

9950. Sims, Dorothy Rice
1890–1960
bridge expert, sculptor, poet
Obit File

9951. Smith, Marion Couthouy
flourished 1920s
poet
Index t Wom

9952. Stillman, Mildred Margaret Whitney
1890–1950
poet, children's author
Obit File

9953. Sumner, Bertha Cid Ricketts
born 1890
author
Index t Wom

9954. Toor, Frances
1890–1956

anthropologist, scholar of Mexican folklore, children's author
Obit File

9955. Tull, Jewell Bothwell
flourished 1920s
poet
Index t Wom

9956. Unger, Gladys Buchanan
died 1940
playwright
Index t Wom

9957. Weitz, Alice C.
flourished 1920s
poet
Index t Wom

9958. Woodhouse, Margaret Chase Going
born 1890
representative to Congress, economist, educator, author
Index t Wom

9959. Wright, Anna Maria Louisa Perrott Rose
born 1890
author
Index t Wom

9960. Addington, Sarah
1891–1940
author
Index t Wom

9961. Banning, Margaret Culkin
born 1891
novelist
Index t Wom

9962. Barnes, Margaret Campbell
born 1891
author
Index t Wom

9963. Cannell, Kathleen
1891–1974
journalist, fashion editor, ballet critic, autobiographer
French (American expatriate to Paris)
Dict Lit Bio v4

9964. Carrington, Elaine Sterne
1891/92–1958
magazine writer, radio-serial scriptwriter
Dict Am Bio supp v6; Index t Wom; Obit File

9965. Donez, Ian
born 1891
composer, author
Index t Wom

9966. Forbes, Esther; Esther Forbes Hoskins
1891–1967

novelist, children's author, colonial historian, Pulitzer Prize winner
Congregationalist
Massachusetts
Index t Wom; Nat Cyc Am Bio v53; Not Am Wom supp v1; Obit File

9967. Harkness, Georgia Elma
1891–1974
philosopher, theologian, religious educator, author
Dict Am Rel Bio; Index t Wom; Not Am Wom supp v1; Who Who Phil

9968. Holberg, Ruth Langland
born 1891
author
Index t Wom

9969. Lathrop, Dorothy Pulis
born 1891
illustrator, author
Index t Wom

9970. Littledale, Clara Savage
1891–1956
author, magazine editor, journalist
Dict Am Bio supp v6; Index t Wom; Not Am Wom supp v1; Obit File

9971. Mack, Nila; Nila Mac-Laughlin
1891–1953
radio producer, writer, director, actor
Index t Wom; Not Am Wom supp v1; Obit File

9972. McCarroll, Marion Clyde; Beatrice Fairfax
1891–1977
journalist, syndicated advice columnist, author
Nat Cyc Am Bio v60; Obit File

9973. Moore, Elizabeth Evelyn
born 1891
author, songwriter
Index t Wom

9974. Nichols, Anne
1891–1966
playwright, author
Index t Wom; Obit File

9975. Rose, Ann Perrett
1891–1961
children's author
Obit File

9976. Seaver, Blanche Ebert
born 1891
composer, author
Index t Wom

9977. Stewart, Dorothy M.
1891/97–1954

theatrical agent, composer, pianist, author
Australian
Index t Wom

9978. van Doren, Irita (Bradford)
1891–1966
literary editor of *The New York Herald-Tribune* Sunday book review section, journalist
Index t Wom; Not Am Wom supp v1; Obit File

9979. Barber, Edith Michael
1892–1963
home economist, author
Index t Wom

9980. Barnes, Djuna
born 1892
novelist, short story writer, poet, playwright, theatrical columnist, illustrator, portrait painter
French (American expatriate to Paris)
Dict Lit Bio v4 and v9; Wom Lit; Wom Lit, More

9981. Best, Allena Champlin; Anne M. Erick-Berry
born 1892
illustrator, author
Index t Wom

9982. Bromfield, Mary Appleton Wood
1892–1952
author
Obit File

9983. Buck, Pearl Sydenstricker
1892–1973
novelist, Nobel and Pulitzer literary prize winner
Cur Biog '73; Dict Lit Bio v9; Great Sov Encyc; Index t Wom; Nat Cyc Am Bio csv5; Not Am Wom supp v1; Obit File

9984. Carroll, Consolata; Sister Mary Consolata
born 1892
author, educator, Catholic nun
Catholic
Index t Wom

9985. Colver, Alice Mary Ross
born 1892
author
Index t Wom

9986. Crosby, Caresse; Polly Jacob
1892–1970
poet, patron of the arts, cofounder of the Black Sun Press
French (American expatriate to Paris)
Dict Lit Bio v4

9987. Daringer, Helen Fern
born 1892
author
Index t Wom

9988. Davis, Katherine K.
born 1892
composer, author
Index t Wom

9989. Finney, Gertrude Elva Bridgeman
born 1892
author
Index t Wom

9990. Flanner, Janet
1892–1978
journalist, novelist, lecturer, *New Yorker* correspondent from Paris
French (American expatriate to Paris)
Cur Biog '79; Dict Lit Bio v4; Index t Wom; Obit File

9991. Herbst, Josephine Frey; Josephine Herrmann
1892/99–1962
novelist, reporter of radical social and political movements in the 1930s, member of a European avant-garde writers circle in the 1920s
Dict Lit Bio v9; Index t Wom; Not Am Wom supp v1; Obit File; Wom Lit, More

9992. Hill, Helen
died 1942
author
Index t Wom

9993. Holt, Isabella; Mrs. Haldeman Finnie
1892–1962
author, novelist
Index t Wom; Nat Cyc Am Bio v45; Obit File

9994. Houghton, Carolyn Wells
died 1942
children's author, mystery writer
Obit File

9995. Hunt, Mabel Leigh
born 1892
author
Index t Wom

9996. Kaucher, Dorothy Wanita
1892–1972
educator, author, writer on aviation
California
Nat Cyc Am Bio v57

9997. Lewis, Elizabeth Foreman
1892–1958
children's author
Obit File

9998. Lussi, Marie; Mari Mitale
born 1892
songwriter, author
Index t Wom

9999. Lutes, Della Thompson
died 1942
author, novelist, editor
Michigan
Index t Wom

10000. Millay, Edna St. Vincent
1892–1950
poet, Pulitzer Prize winner, women's rights worker
Dict Am Bio supp v4; Index t Wom; Nat Cyc Am Bio v38 and csv2; Nort Anth Poet; Not Am Wom; Obit File; Wom Lit; Wom Lit, More

10001. Nash, Eleanor Arnett
born 1892
author
Index t Wom

10002. Palffy, Eleanor Roelker, Countess
1892–1952
novelist
Obit File

10003. Pinkard, Edna Belle
born 1892
composer, author
Index t Wom

10004. Randall, Ruth Elaine Painter
born 1892
author
Index t Wom

10005. Sachs, Emanie N.
married 1917
author
Index t Wom

10006. Shippen, Katherine Binney
born 1892
author
Index t Wom

10007. Smedley, Agnes
1892/94–1950
author, foreign correspondent, lecturer, champion of revolutionary China, writer on China and the Far East
Dict Am Bio supp v4; Index t Wom; Not Am Wom; Obit File; Wom Lit, More

10008. Stephens, Nan Bagby
born 1892
playwright
Index t Wom

10009. Suckow, Ruth Ann Vivien (Nuhn)
1892–1960
writer, novelist, short story writer
Quaker
Iowa; California
Dict Lit Bio v9; Index t Wom;
Nat Cyc Am Bio v47; Not Am
Wom supp v1; Obit File; Wom
Lit; Wom Lit, More

10010. Trix, Helen
1892–1951
composer, pianist, singer, author,
actor
Index t Wom

10011. Turnbull, Margaret
died 1942
novelist, playwright, movie scenarist
Obit File

10012. West, Mae
1892/93–1980
actor, playwright, screenwriter,
comedian, author
Cur Biog '81; Index t Wom

10013. Wood, Peggy
1892–1978
television and stage actor, novelist, autobiographer
Cur Biog '78; Index t Wom; Obit
File

10014. Alexander, Lillie M.
died 1943
novelist
Obit File

10015. Baldwin, Faith; Mrs.
Hugh H. Cuthrell
1893–1973
novelist
New York
Index t Wom; Nat Cyc Am Bio
csv9; Obit File

10016. Ballaseyus, Virginia
born 1893
composer, author
Index t Wom

10017. Bennett, Dorothy Graham
1893–1959
author
Index t Wom

10018. Brande, Dorothea Thompson
1893–1948
author, editor, journalist
Episcopalian
Chicago, IL
Nat Cyc Am Bio v39

10019. Brockman, Zoe Kincaid
born 1893
poet, journalist
Index t Wom

10020. Chalmers, Audrey
1893/99–1957
illustrator, author
Canadian
Index t Wom

10021. Chatterton, Ruth
1893/1900–1961
actor, novelist
Index t Wom; Obit File

10022. Coatsworth, Elizabeth
born 1893
poet, novelist
Index t Wom

10023. Collins, Dorothea; Dorothea Brande
1893–1948
author
Obit File

10024. Cook, Fannie Bruce
1893–1949
author, social novelist
Index t Wom; Obit File

10025. Curtis, Edith (Goddard) Roelker
1893–1977
author
Episcopalian
New Hampshire; Massachusetts
Nat Cyc Am Bio v60

10026. Dalgliesh, Alice
born 1893
editor, author
Index t Wom

10027. Deming, Dorothy
born 1893
nurse, author
Index t Wom

10028. Doner, Mary Frances
born 1893
author
Index t Wom

10029. Ernst, Jessie
born 1893
playwright
Index t Wom

10030. Fine, Sylvia
born 1893
composer, author
Index t Wom

10031. Gag, Wanda [Hazel]
1893–1946
illustrator, painter, children's author
Dict Am Bio supp v4; Index t
Wom; Not Am Wom; Obit File

10032. Garrett, Eileen Jeanette;
Jean Lyttle
1893–1970
parapsychologist, novelist, founder of the Parapsychology Foundation
Anglican
Irish
Nat Cyc Am Bio v55; Obit File

10033. Hickok, Lorena A.
1893–1968
journalist, author
Index t Wom; Not Am Wom
supp 1

10034. Huntington, Dorothy Phillips; Dorothy Sanburn Phillips
1893–1972
short story writer, magazine writer
Obit File

10035. Kaufman, Agnes Boulton
1893–1968
novelist
Obit File

10036. Kirkus, Virginia
1893–1980
literary critic, book preview company founder, author
Cur Biog '80; Index t Wom

10037. Larson, Nella
1893–1963
author, nurse
Black
Encyc Black Am; Wom Lit; Wom
Lit, More

10038. Leech, Margaret Kernochan; Mrs. Ralph Pulitzer
1893–1974
author, novelist, historian
New York
Cur Biog '74; Index t Wom; Nat
Cyc Am Bio csv6

10039. Lenski, Lois
born 1893
illustrator, author
Index t Wom

10040. Loos, Anita
1893–1981
playwright, screenwriter, novelist,
humorist
Cur Biog '74 and '81; Index t
Wom; Wom Lit, More

10041. Parker, Dorothy Rothschild
1893–1967
author, critic, short story writer,
poet, humorist
Jewish
New York
Index t Wom; Not Am Wom
supp v1; Obit File; Who Who
Jew Hist; Wom Lit, More

10042. Ritter, Margaret Tod
born 1893
poet
Index t Wom

10043. Scott, Evelyn D. (Metcalf)
1893–1963
author, traveler
Dict Lit Bio v9; Index t Wom;
Nat Cyc Am Bio csv3; Wom Lit

10044. Starling, Lynn
born 1893
playwright
Index t Wom

10045. Stevens, Doris
1893–1963
women's rights worker, author,
songwriter
Obit File

10046. Welles, Winifred
1893–1939
poet
Index t Wom

10047. Winslow, Thyra
1893–1961
journalist, novelist, short story
writer
Index t Wom; Obit File; Wom
Lit, More

10048. Anderson, Barbara Tunnell
born 1894
author
Index t Wom

10049. Atkinson, Oriana Torrey
born 1894
author
Index t Wom

10050. Bro, Marguerite Harmon
born 1894
author
Index t Wom

10051. Bushnell, Adelyn
born 1894
actor, author
Index t Wom

10052. Ertz, Susan
born circa 1894
novelist
Index t Wom

10053. Field, Rachel Lyman;
Mrs. Arthur Siegfried Pederson
1894–1942
poet, novelist, children's author
Dict Lit Bio v9; Nat Cyc Am Bio
v33; Not Am Wom

10054. Fyan, Loleta Dawson
born 1894

librarian, author
Index t Wom

10055. Hager, Alice Rogers
born 1894
aviation author
Index t Wom

10056. Harris, Bernice Kelly
born 1894
author
Index t Wom

**10057. Hoisington, May Fol-
well**
born 1894
poet, educator
Index t Wom

**10058. Johnson, Osa Helen
Leighty**
1894–1952/53
explorer, geographer, big game
hunter, filmmaker and film producer, aviator, author
Index t Wom; Nat Cyc Am Bio
v39; Obit File

**10059. Kaufman, Beatrice Bak-
row**
1894–1945
journalist, editor, playwright
Index t Wom; Obit File

10060. Lambert, Janet Snyder
born 1894
author
Index t Wom

10061. M'Cleary, Dorothy
born 1894
author
Index t Wom

**10062. Metzelthin, Pearl Viol-
ette**
1894–1947
dietician, author, editor, health
worker
Index t Wom

**10063. Nicholson, Marjorie
Hope**
1894–1981
university educator, writer on literature
Cur Biog '81; Index t Wom; Nat
Cyc Am Bio csv7

**10064. Osborne, Letitia Os-
borne Preston**
born 1894
author
Index t Wom

10065. Schulze, Margaret
1894–1943
gynecologist, surgeon, pathologist, medical educator, medical
author
California
Nat Cyc Am Bio v34

10066. Shay, Edith Foley
born 1894
author
Index t Wom

10067. St. Johns, Adele Rogers
born 1894
journalist, television personality,
screen writer, novelist, short
story writer
Cur Biog '76; Index t Wom

**10068. Stern, Catherine Brieger
"Kathe"**
1894–1973
educator, child education special-
ist, writer on child education
Lutheran
German
Nat Cyc Am Bio v57; Not Am
Wom supp v1

10069. Taggard, Genevieve
1894–1948
poet, educator, biographer of Emily Dickinson, literature professor
Dict Am Bio supp v4; Index t
Wom; Not Am Wom; Obit File

**10070. Thompson, Dorothy;
Mrs. Sinclair Lewis**
1894–1961
international journalist, newspaper columnist, magazine writer,
anti-Nazi worker, lecturer specializing in foreign affairs, radio
commentator
Encyc Third Reich; Index t
Wom; Nat Cyc Am Bio csv5;
Not Am Wom supp v1; Obit
File

10071. White, Nelia Gardner
1894–1957
author, novelist, short story writer
Index t Wom; Nat Cyc Am Bio
v44; Obit File

10072. Babson, Naomi Lane
born 1895
author
Index t Wom

10073. Bacon, Peggy
born 1895
artist, author
Index t Wom

**10074. Bayliss, Marguerite Far-
leigh**
born 1895
author, scientist
Index t Wom

10075. Bonner, Mary Graham
born 1895
author
Index t Wom

10076. Boyleston, Helen Dore
born 1895
author
Index t Wom

10077. Brink, Carol Ryrie
born 1895
author
Index t Wom

**10078. Chapman, Mary Hamil-
ton Ilsley**
born 1895
novelist
Index t Wom

10079. Deutsch, Babette
born 1895
poet, writer on poetry
Index t Wom

10080. Ets, Marie Hall
born 1895
illustrator, author
Index t Wom

10081. Evatt, Harriet Torrey
born 1895
author, illustrator
Index t Wom

10082. Foster, Edna Abigail
died 1945
author, editor
Index t Wom; Obit File

10083. Franklin, Blanche Ortha
born 1895
composer, author
Index t Wom

10084. Garner, Elvira Carter
born 1895
illustrator, author
Index t Wom

**10085. Gordon, Caroline; Caro-
line Tate**
1895–1981
novelist
French (American expatriate to
Paris)
Dict Lit Bio v4 and v9; Index t
Wom; Wom Lit; Wom Lit,
More

10086. Jackson, Edith Banfield
1895–1977
pediatrician, child psychiatrist,
medical author
Nat Cyc Am Bio csv13; Obit File

**10087. Jamerson, Pauline Thi-
erry; Polly Preyer**
1895–1952
playwright, musical comedy actor
Obit File

**10088. Langer, Susanne Kather-
ina Knauth**
born 1895

philosopher, author, educator
Index t Wom; Who Who Phil

10089. Laramore, Vivian Yeiser
born 1895
poet, songwriter
Index t Wom

10090. Lee, Muna
1895–1965
international affairs specialist,
feminist, US State Department
aide, poet, novelist, translator
Not Am Wom supp v1; Obit File

**10091. McMeekin, Isabel
McLenan**
born 1895/99
author
Index t Wom

**10092. Merrell, Marion Clinch
Calkins; Clinch Calkins; Ma-
jollica Wattles**
1895–1968
poet, journalist, novelist
Nat Cyc Am Bio v54

10093. Pederson, Rachel Fields
1895–1942
popular novelist
Obit File

**10094. Pinckney, Josephine Ly-
ons Scott**
1895–1957
author, poet, novelist
Dict Lit Bio v6; Index t Wom;
Obit File

10095. Quick, Dorothy
circa 1895–1962
poet
Index t Wom

10096. Strang, Ruth [May]
1895–1971
educator, writer on education, education teacher
Cur Biog '71; Index t Wom; Not
Am Wom supp v1

**10097. van de Water, Virginia
Terhune**
died 1945
novelist, short story writer
Obit File

**10098. Bromley, Dorothy Dun-
bar**
born 1896
editor, author, journalist
Index t Wom

**10099. Carraway, Gertrude
Sprague**
born 1896
editor, author
Index t Wom

10100. Chevalier, Elizabeth Picket
born 1896
author
Index t Wom

10101. Clapper, Olive Ewing
1896–1968
author, lecturer, radio commentator, autobiographer, director of the Washington, DC, bureau of CARE
Washington, DC
Cur Biog '69; Index t Wom

10102. Flack, Marjorie
1896–1958
illustrator, children's author
Index t Wom; Obit File

10103. Gordon, Ruth
born 1896
stage and screen character actor, scriptwriter
Cur Biog '72; Index t Wom

10104. Hedden, Worth Tuttle
born 1896
author
Index t Wom

10105. Hersch, Virginia Davis
born 1896
novelist
Index t Wom

10106. Leighton, Margaret Carver
born 1896
author
Index t Wom

10107. Lockridge, Frances Louise Davis
1896–1963
children's author
Nat Cyc Am Bio v47

10108. Morrison, Lucile Gertrude Phillips
born 1896
author
California
Nat Cyc Am Bio csv6

10109. Peltz, Mary Ellie Opdyke
born 1896
journalist, author
Index t Wom

10110. Powdermaker, Hortense
1896/1900–1970
anthropologist, ethnologist, educator, author
California
Cur Biog '70; Index t Wom; Nat Cyc Am Bio v55 and csv10; Not Am Wom supp v1

10111. Pruette, Lorine Livingston
born 1896
psychologist, author
Index t Wom

10112. Rawling, Marjorie Kinnan
1896–1953
novelist, journalist, Pulitzer Prize winner
Dict Am Bio supp v5; Dict Lit Bio v9; Index t Wom; Nat Cyc Am Bio csv7; Not Am Wom supp v1; Obit File

10113. Remsen, Alice
born 1896
composer, author, publisher
English
Index t Wom

10114. Robeson, Eslanda Cardoza Goode
1896–1965
author, civil rights reformer, anthropologist
Black
Index t Wom; Not Am Wom supp v1

10115. Sandoz, Marie Suzette "Mari"
1896/1901–1966
author, novelist, historian
Nebraska
Dict Lit Bio v9; Index t Wom; Not Am Wom supp v1; Read Encyc Am West; Wom Lit, More

10116. Stone, Grace Zaring; Ethel Vance
born 1896
author
Index t Wom

10117. van Doren, Dorothy Graffe
born 1896
novelist
Index t Wom

10118. Worden, Helen
born 1896
author, journalist
Index t Wom

10119. Bogan, Louise
1897–1970
lyric poet, poetry critic, holder of Library of Congress Chair of Poetry, member of the American Academy of Arts and Letters
Index t Wom; Not Am Wom supp v1; Wom Lit; Wom Cent

10120. Bowen, Catherine (Shober) Drinker
1897–1973
biographer, essayist, autobiographer, lecturer
Pennsylvania
Cur Biog '73; Index t Wom; Nat Cyc Am Bio v58; Not Am Wom supp v1; Obit File

10121. Day, Dorothy
1897–1980
journalist, social worker, political activist, fiction writer on Catholic life
Catholic
Cur Biog '82; Index t Wom

10122. Earhart, Amelia May
1897/99–1937
aviator, autobiographer
Dict Am Bio supp v2; Index t Wom; Nat Cyc Am Bio csv4; Not Am Wom

10123. Elliot, Kathleen Morrow
1897–1940
author
Index t Wom

10124. Foley, Martha
1897–!977
short story writer, editor
Cur Biog '77; Index t Wom; Obit File

10125. Goldsmith, Margaret
born 1897
author, journalist
Index t Wom

10126. Jessye, Eva Alberta
1897–post 1930s
music director, educator, writer on music, conductor
Black
Encyc Black Am; Index t Wom

10127. Kenyon, Bernice
born 1897
poet
Index t Wom

10128. Logasa, Hannah
born 1897
librarian, author
Index t Wom

10129. Marshall, Lenore Guinzburg
1897–1971
author, poet, novelist, antinuclear worker, cofounder of the Committee for a Sane Nuclear Policy, worker for Women's International League for Peace and Freedom
Nat Cyc Am Bio v55; Obit File

10130. Montross, Lois Seyster
1897–1961
novelist
Index t Wom

10131. Robertson, Constance Noyes; Dana Scott
born 1897
author
Index t Wom

10132. Robinson, Ophelia
born 1897
educator, poet
Index t Wom

10133. Ross, Isabel
1897–1975
author, novelist, biographer of prominent American women
Scottish
Index t Wom; Obit File

10134. Simon, Charlie May
born 1897
author
Index t Wom

10135. Smith, Betty Wehner
1897/1904–1972
author, novelist, writer of one-act plays
Cur Biog '72; Index t Wom; Obit File

10136. Smith, Harriet Lummis
died 1947
novelist
Obit File

10137. Smith, Lilian Eugenia
1897–1966
novelist, newspaper columnist, writer on race relations, civil rights worker, editor, social worker, educator, lecturer
Florida
Encyc South Hist; Index t Wom; Not Am Wom supp v1; Obit File; Wom Lit; Wom Lit, More

10138. Speare, Dorothy
1897/98–1951
screenwriter, author, novelist, opera singer, labor worker
Index t Wom; Nat Cyc Am Bio v40; Obit File

10139. Sunshine, Marion
born 1897
composer, actor, author
Index t Wom

10140. Turner, Lina Larrimore
born 1897/98
author
Index t Wom

10141. Watkins, Shirley
born 1897
author
Index t Wom

10142. Bell, Margaret Elizabeth
born 1898

author
Index t Wom

10143. Benet, Rosemary Carr
1898–1962
poet
Index t Wom; Obit File

10144. Bloom, Vera
circa 1898–1959
author, lyricist
Index t Wom

10145. Bussiere, Tadema Whaley
born 1898
playwright
Index t Wom

10146. Carlisle, Helen Grace
born 1898
author
Index t Wom

10147. Castle, Marian Johnston
born 1898
author
Index t Wom

10148. Eberle, Irmengarde
born 1898
author
Index t Wom

10149. Fisher, Anne Benson
born 1898
author
Index t Wom

10150. Franken, Rose
born 1898
author, playwright
Index t Wom; Wom Lit, More

10151. Goetz, Delia
born 1898
author
Index t Wom

10152. Govan, Christine Noble
born 1898
author, critic
Index t Wom

10153. Guggenheim, Marguerite "Peggy"
born 1898
patron of modern art and music, art collector, author
Jewish
New York
Cur Biog '80; Index t Wom; Who Who Jew Hist

10154. Jasmyn, Joan
born 1898
composer, author
Index t Wom

10155. Kelly, Regina Zimmerman
born 1898

author, educator
Index t Wom

10156. Knight, Ruth Adams Yingling
born 1898
author
Index t Wom

10157. Langner, Armina Marshall; Isabelle Louden
born 1898
playwright, producer
Index t Wom

10158. MacDonald, Lucile Saunders
born 1898
author, journalist
Index t Wom

10159. Meadowcroft, Enid la Monte
1898–1966
author
Index t Wom

10160. Mudd, Emily Hatshore
born 1898
educator, author, marriage counselor
Index t Wom

10161. Popkins, Zelda
born 1898
novelist
Index t Wom

10162. Schlaugh, Margaret
born 1898
educator, author, philologist
Index t Wom

10163. Seifert, Elizabeth
born 1898
author
Index t Wom

10164. Sifton, Claire
born 1898
playwright
Index t Wom

10165. Soule, Isobel Walker
1898–1972
author, editor, labor leader, suffragist
Obit File

10166. Steward, Ann Schiear
born 1898
novelist
Index t Wom

10167. Tharp, Louise Marshall Hall
born 1898
author, lecturer
Index t Wom

10168. Utley, Freda
1898–1978

author, journalist, foreign correspondent, lecturer
English
Index t Wom; Obit File

10169. Vollmer, Lula; Louisa Smith
1898–1955
playwright, short story writer, radio dramatist
Index t Wom; Obit File

10170. Winter, Ella
1898–1980
journalist, writer on communism, Communist party worker
Australian
Cur Biog '80

10171. Adams, Leonie Fuller
born 1899
poet
Index t Wom

10172. Berg, Gertrude Edelstein
1899–1966
radio, television, and screen writer; playwright; producer
Jewish
New York
Index t Wom; Nat Cyc Am Bio v52; Not Am Wom supp v1; Obit File

10173. Carroll, Ruth Robinson
born 1899
illustrator, author
Index t Wom

10174. Caudill, Rebecca
born 1899
author
Index t Wom

10175. Cavanah, Frances Elizabeth
born 1899
author
Index t Wom

10176. Clark, Dorothy Park; Clark McMeekin
born 1899
author
Index t Wom

10177. Coleman, Emily Holmes
1899–1974
autobiographer, poet
Catholic
French (American expatriate to Paris)
Dict Lit Bio v4

10178. Crawford, Phyllis
born 1899
author, librarian, editor
Index t Wom

10179. Finlay, Lorraine Noel
born 1899

composer, author
Canadian
Index t Wom

10180. Garst, Shannon
born 1899
author
Index t Wom

10181. Green, Anne
born 1899
novelist
Index t Wom

10182. Holt, Rackham
born 1899
author
Index t Wom

10183. Kimbrough, Emily
born 1899
author, editor
Index t Wom

10184. Lewis, Janet
born 1899
novelist, poet
Index t Wom; Wom Lit

10185. McClintock, Katharine Morrison
born 1899
author
Index t Wom

10186. Moser, Edwa Robert
born 1899
author
Index t Wom

10187. Poll, Ruth
born 1899
author, songwriter
Index t Wom

10188. Seredy, Kate
1899–1975
children's author
Cur Biog '75

10189. Sims, Marian McCamy
born 1899
author
Index t Wom

10190. Taber, Gladys; Leonae Bagg
1899–1980
novelist, short story writer, magazine writer
Connecticut
Cur Biog '80; Index t Wom

10191. Talcott, Lucy
1899–1970
archaeologist, archaeological author
Congregationalist
Nat Cyc Am Bio v54

10192. Taylor, Rosemary Drachman
born 1899
author
Index t Wom

10193. Tempski, Armine von
1899–1943
author, lecturer
Index t Wom

10194. White, Olive Bernadine
born 1899
author, educator
Index t Wom

10195. Woolsey, Maryhale
born 1899
songwriter, author
Index t Wom

10196. Yaukey, Grace Sydenstricker; Cornelia Spencer
born 1899
novelist
Index t Wom

10197. Archer, Alma
flourished 1930s
fashion expert, editor, author
Index t Wom

10198. Aylward, Ida
flourished 1930s
author, painter
Index t Wom

10199. Baker, Etta Iva Anthony
flourished 1930s
author
Index t Wom

10200. Barratt, Louise Bascom
flourished 1930s
editor, author
Index t Wom

10201. Bell, Ann
flourished 1930s
author
Index t Wom

10202. Benson, Sally Smith "Sara"
1900–72
author, magazine writer, screenplay writer
Cur Biog '72; Index t Wom; Obit File

10203. Black, Jean Ferguson
born 1900
playwright
Index t Wom

10204. Booth, Alice
flourished 1930s
author
Index t Wom

10205. Bradley, Ora Lewis
flourished 1930s
educator, artist, author
Index t Wom

10206. Brandt, Mary Elizabeth
flourished 1930s
author
Index t Wom

10207. Brooks, G. Anne
flourished 1930s
playwright, stage producer
Index t Wom

10208. Brush, Katherine Ingham
1900/02–1952
author, novelist
Episcopalian
Index t Wom; Nat Cyc Am Bio v43; Obit File

10209. Bryner, Edna
flourished 1930s
author
Index t Wom

10210. Burks, Frances
flourished 1930s
author
Index t Wom

10211. Bussenius, Luellen T.
flourished 1930s
author
Index t Wom

10212. Butler, Lorine Letcher
flourished 1930s
nature writer
Index t Wom

10213. Byard, Dorothy Randolph
flourished 1930s
artist, poet
Index t Wom

10214. Caldwell, Taylor
born 1900
novelist
English
Index t Wom

10215. Carey, Helen A.
flourished 1930s
educator, author
Index t Wom

10216. Carman, Dorothy Walworth
born 1900
novelist
Index t Wom

10217. Carroll, Ruth
flourished 1930s–50s
author
Index t Wom

10218. Coker, Elizabeth Boatwright
born 1900
author
Index t Wom

10219. Cooley, Winnifred Harper
flourished 1930s
author, lecturer, radio personality
Index t Wom

10220. Craig, Mary Marsden Young
flourished 1930s
actor, playwright, director
Index t Wom

10221. Davies, Mary Carolyn
flourished 1930s
poet, songwriter
Index t Wom

10222. Dick, Dorothy
born 1900
author, songwriter
Index t Wom

10223. Dithridge, Rachel L.
flourished 1930s
poet, educator
Index t Wom

10224. Donaldson, Elizabeth W.
flourished 1930s
traveler, author, sportsperson
Index t Wom

10225. Downing, Eleanor
flourished 1930s
author, educator
Index t Wom

10226. Duncan, Rena Buchanan Shore
flourished 1930s
clubwoman, author
Index t Wom

10227. Dyhrenfurth, Hettie
flourished 1930s
educator, author
Index t Wom

10228. Elliott, Grace Loucks
flourished 1930s
editor, author
Index t Wom

10229. Fowler, Marie Louise
flourished 1930s
author
Index t Wom

10230. Giese, Lulu Gable
flourished 1930s
poet
Index t Wom

10231. Gillespie, Marian
flourished 1930s

explorer, photographer, editor, author
Index t Wom

10232. Gilman, Mildred
flourished 1930s
journalist, author
Index t Wom

10233. Golden, Sylvia
born 1900
author, editor, songwriter
Index t Wom

10234. Granville-Barker, Helen Gates
died 1950
author
Index t Wom

10235. Greene, Eleanore D.
flourished 1930s
author
Canadian
Index t Wom

10236. Hamilton, Florence
flourished 1930s
editor, poet
Index t Wom

10237. Hartman, Gustave, Mrs.
born 1900
philanthropist, author
Index t Wom

10238. Hayes, Dorsha
flourished 1930s–40s
novelist
Index t Wom

10239. Hill, Amelia Leavitt
flourished 1930s
editor, author
Index t Wom

10240. Hill, Carol
flourished 1930s
author, literary agent
Index t Wom

10241. Hill, Dedette Lee
1900–50
author, songwriter
Index t Wom

10242. Hiller, Margaret
flourished 1930s
editor, author
Index t Wom

10243. Hillis, Marjorie
flourished 1930s
editor, author
Index t Wom

10244. Hoerle, Helen
flourished 1930s
author
Index t Wom

10245. Hollingsworth, Thekla
flourished 1930s
composer, author
Index t Wom

10246. Hormel, Olive Deane
flourished 1930s
author
Index t Wom

10247. Hough, Maude Clark
flourished 1930s
poet, telegraph operator
Index t Wom

10248. Irwin, Laetitia McDonald
flourished 1930s
author
Index t Wom

10249. Jones, Mary M.
flourished 1930s
author
Index t Wom

10250. Kaghan, Leonora
flourished 1930s
playwright
Index t Wom

10251. Kenyon, Theda
flourished 1930s
novelist
Index t Wom

10252. Landers, Olive Richards
flourished 1930s
editor, author
Index t Wom

10253. Larkin, Margaret
1900–67
author, poet, editor, composer,
    singer
Obit File

10254. Lawrence, Jeanette
flourished 1930s
author, lecturer
Index t Wom

10255. Lowitz, Sadyebeth Heath
flourished 1930s
author
Index t Wom

10256. Lynch, Maude Dutton
flourished 1930s
author
Index t Wom

10257. Madison, Marta
flourished 1930s
playwright
Index t Wom

10258. Mandola, Carol M.
flourished 1930s
metaphysician, lecturer, poet
Index t Wom

10259. Marlatt, Jeanne Steele
flourished 1930s
poet
Index t Wom

10260. Marshall, Rosamond van der Zee
1900/02–1957
author
Index t Wom

10261. McCullough, Esther Morgan
flourished 1930s
artist, author
Index t Wom

10262. Mears, Helen
born 1900
author, lecturer
Index t Wom

10263. Mile, Elizabeth
born 1900
playwright
Index t Wom

10264. Mitchell, Margaret Munnerlyn; Mrs. John Robert Marsh
1900–49
novelist
Georgia
Dict Am Bio supp v4; Dict Lit
    Bio v9; Index t Wom; Nat Cyc
    Am Bio v38 and csv6; Not Am
    Wom; Obit File; Wom Lit,
    More

10265. Miyakawa, Kikuko
flourished 1930s
poet, artist
Japanese
Index t Wom

10266. Moir, Phyllis
flourished 1930s–40s
author, lecturer, editor
English
Index t Wom

10267. Morgan, Charlotte E.
flourished 1930s
educator, author
Index t Wom

10268. Mullins, Edith
flourished 1930s
poet
Index t Wom

10269. Myers, Carlene Brien
flourished 1930s
author
Index t Wom

10270. Mygatt, Tracy Dickinson
flourished 1930s
playwright, author
Index t Wom

10271. Nathan, Adele Gutman
flourished 1930s
theatrical director, author
Index t Wom

10272. Nearing, Elizabeth Custer
born 1900
novelist
Index t Wom

10273. Newman, Isadora
flourished 1930s
artist, author, sculptor
Index t Wom

10274. O'Connor, Mary
1900–64
poet, artist
Obit File

10275. Olcott, Rita
flourished 1930s
playwright
Index t Wom

10276. Olds, Helen Diehl
flourished 1930s
author
Index t Wom

10277. O'Malley, Patricia
flourished 1930s
aviation author
Index t Wom

10278. Ostenso, Martha
1900–63
author, novelist
Norwegian
Index t Wom; Nat Cyc Am Bio
    csv3; Wom Lit, More

10279. Oursler, Grace Perkins
1900–55
novelist, playwright, magazine
    writer and editor
Obit File

10280. Page, Celeste Walker
flourished 1930s
aviation author
Index t Wom

10281. Paxton, Ethel
flourished 1930s
artist, educator, lecturer, author
Index t Wom

10282. Paxton, Jean Gregory
flourished 1930s
editor, author
Index t Wom

10283. Payne-Gaposchkin, Ceilia Helena
born 1900
astronomer, educator, author
English
Index t Wom

10284. Perdue, Virginia
1900–45
mystery novelist
Obit File

10285. Perelman, Laura
flourished 1930s
playwright
Index t Wom

10286. Phelps, Anna Elizabeth
flourished 1930s
author, club leader
Index t Wom

10287. Phillips, Anita
flourished 1930s
playwright
Index t Wom

10288. Powell, Dawn; Mrs. Joseph R. Gousha
born 1900
author
Index t Wom; Wom Lit

10289. Ramsey, Grace Fisher
flourished 1930s
club leader, author
Index t Wom

10290. Richards, Rosa Coates
flourished 1930s
dancer, poet
Index t Wom

10291. Robb, Elizabeth B.
flourished 1930s
poet
Index t Wom

10292. Robinson, Evangeline
flourished 1930s
author
Index t Wom

10293. Samuels, Margaret
flourished 1930s
educator, librarian, author
Index t Wom

10294. Schorr, Esther Brann
flourished 1930s
artist, author
Index t Wom

10295. Shaw, Ellen Eddy
flourished 1930s
naturalist, lecturer, author
Index t Wom

10296. Shedd, Margaret
born 1900
novelist
Index t Wom

10297. Syrkin, Marie
born 1900
editor, educator, author
Swiss
Index t Wom

10298. **Thane, Elswyth**
born 1900
author, playwright
Index t Wom

10299. **Thomas, Dorothy**
flourished 1930s
author
Index t Wom

10300. **Thompson, Eva Bell**
flourished 1930s–60s
author, editor
Black
Encyc Black Am

10301. **Ulmer, Edith Ann**
flourished 1930s
educator, author
Index t Wom

10302. **Vaupel, Ouise**
flourished 1930s
fashion designer, realtor, singer,
author
Index t Wom

10303. **von Hesse, Elizabeth F.**
flourished 1930s
educator, author, lecturer
Index t Wom

10304. **von Klenner, Katherine
E.**
flourished 1930s
author, translator
Index t Wom

10305. **Walker, Jean**
flourished 1930s
musician, poet
Index t Wom

10306. **Walworth, Dorothy; Dorothy Crowell**
born 1900
novelist
Index t Wom

10307. **Watkins, Maurine Dallas**
born 1900
playwright
Index t Wom

10308. **Watson, Virginia Cruse**
flourished 1930s
author
Index t Wom

10309. **Waugh, Dorothy**
flourished 1930s–40s
illustrator, author
Quaker
Index t Wom

10310. **Wayman, Agens R.**
flourished 1930s
author
Index t Wom

10311. **Webster, Barbara**
born 1900
novelist
Index t Wom

10312. **White, Rose Rubin**
flourished 1930s
author, translator
Russian
Index t Wom

10313. **Wilder, Jessie**
flourished 1930s
poet, educator, critic, lecturer
English
Index t Wom

10314. **Wintors, Yvor**
1900–68
poet
Nort Anth Poet

10315. **Winwar, Frances; Mrs.
Bernard Grebanier**
born 1900
author
Sicilian
Nat Cyc Am Bio csv6

10316. **Wood, Ethel Pope**
flourished 1930s
author
Index t Wom

10317. **Bennett, Melba Berry**
1901–68
author; Palm Springs, California,
civic worker
Episcopalian
Palm Springs, CA
Nat Cyc Am Bio v54

10318. **Campbell, Patricia Platt**
born 1901
author
Index t Wom

10319. **Damrosch, Gretchen
Finletter**
born 1901
playwright
Index t Wom

10320. **Delany, Clarissa Scott**
1901–27
poet, educator
Black
Encyc Black Am

10321. **Diamant, Gertrude**
born 1901
author
Index t Wom

10322. **Eyre, Katherine Wig-
more**
born 1901
author
Index t Wom

10323. **Fillmore, Louise Dutton**
died 1951

novelist
Obit File

10324. **Hurston, Zora Neale**
1901/03–1960
author, novelist, folklorist, cultur-
al anthropologist
Black
Dict Am Bio supp v6; Encyc
Black Am; Index t Wom; Negro
Alman; Not Am Wom; Obit
File; Prof Negro Wom v2; Wom
Lit; Wom Lit, More

10325. **Jordan, Mildred**
born 1901
author
Index t Wom

10326. **Kahmann, [Mable]
Chesley**
born 1901
author
Index t Wom

10327. **Loring, Emilie Baker;
Josephine Story**
died 1951
author
Index t Wom

10328. **Mead, Margaret; Margaret Bateson**
1901/02–1978
anthropologist, writer of popular
books on anthropology, autobiographer
Episcopalian
Cur Biog '79; Index t Wom; Nat
Cyc Am Bio csv9; Obit File

10329. **Riding, Laura; Laura
Riding Gottchalk; Barbara
Rich**
born 1901
poet, author
Index t Wom; Nort Anth Poet;
Wom Lit, More

10330. **Skinner, Cornelia Caroline Otis**
1901–79
stage actor, monologuist, poet,
essayist, biographer
Cur Biog '79; Index t Wom; Nat
Cyc Am Bio csv6

10331. **Tarr, Florence**
died 1951
author, radio personality
Index t Wom

10332. **Williams, Bertye Young**
died 1951
poet, editor of *Taleria*
Index t Wom; Obit File

10333. **Biddle, Margret Thompson**
1902–56

author, keeper of a Paris salon for
political and literary personali-
ties
French (American expatriate to
Paris)
Obit File

10334. **Boyle, Kay**
born 1902/03
short story writer
French (American expatriate to
Paris)
Dict Lit Bio v4 and v9; Index t
Wom; Wom Lit, More

10335. **Cushing, Catherine
Chisholm**
died 1952
playwright, lyricist
Index t Wom; Obit File

10336. **de la Torre(-Bueno),
Lillian**
born 1902
author
Index t Wom

10337. **du Jardin, Rosamond
Neal**
born 1902
author
Index t Wom

10338. **Duncan, Vivian**
born 1902
composer, author, publisher
Index t Wom

10339. **Fairbairn, Ann; Dorothy
Tait**
1902–72
author, newspaper reporter and
editor
Obit File

10340. **Finney, Emily Jex**
died 1952
author
Index t Wom

10341. **Flint, Eva Kay**
born 1902
playwright
Russian
Index t Wom

10342. **Fowler-Billings, Katharine**
born 1902
geologist, author, explorer
Index t Wom

10343. **Freudenthal, Elsbeth Estelle**
circa 1902–53
economist, aviation writer
Index t Wom

10344. **Goodnow, Minnie**
died 1952
nurse, author, educator
Index t Wom

10345. Gray, Elizabeth Janet
born 1902
author, librarian, educator
Index t Wom

10346. Henry, Marguerite
born 1902
author
Index t Wom

10347. Howard, Florence Ruth
born 1902
author
Index t Wom

10348. Ilg, Frances Lillian
1902–81
pediatrician, medical educator
and author
Cur Biog '81; Index t Wom

10349. Latham, Jean Lee
born 1902
author
Index t Wom

10350. Mann, Clara Lipman
died 1952
actor, playwright
Obit File

10351. Montgomery, Elizabeth Rider
born 1902
author
Index t Wom

10352. Morris, Edita
born 1902
author
Swedish
Index t Wom

10353. Overstrett, Bonaro Wilkinson
born 1902
educator, lecturer, author
Congregationalist
California
Index t Wom; Nat Cyc Am Bio csv11

10354. Roberts, Edith
born 1902
novelist
Index t Wom

10355. Robinson, Alice Wade
died 1952
author, magazine editor
Obit File

10356. Stone, Winifred Sackville Jr.; Mrs. Charles P. de Bruche
born 1902
children's author
Nat Cyc Am Bio csv2

10357. Thayer, Tiffany
1902–59
novelist, film and advertising writer
Obit File

10358. Tremaine, Marie
born 1902
librarian, author, editor
Index t Wom

10359. Vining, Elizabeth Janet Gray
born 1902
author
Quaker
Index t Wom

10360. West, Jessamyn [Mary]
born 1902/07
short story writer, novelist, poet, autobiographer, operetta librettist, screenplay writer
Quaker
California
Cur Biog '77; Dict Lit Bio v6; Index t Wom

10361. Wheaton, Elizabeth Lee
born 1902
author
Index t Wom

10362. Beer, Lisle; Eloise Crowell Smith
born 1903
artist, author, puppeteer
Unitarian
Nat Cyc Am Bio csv9

10363. Bonelli, Mona Modini
born 1903
author, songwriter
Index t Wom

10364. Bristow, Gwen
born 1903
author
Index t Wom

10365. Caspary, Vera
born 1903/04
author, playwright
Index t Wom

10366. Davenport, Marcie
born 1903
author, music critic
Index t Wom

10367. Dean, Vera Micheles
1903–72
international affairs specialist, editor, author, lecturer
Russian
Cur Biog '72; Index t Wom; Not Am Wom supp v1

10368. Fischer, Marjorie Cone
1903–61
novelist, children's author
Obit File

10369. Hawes, Elizabeth
1903–71
fashion designer, author, feminist
Index t Wom; Not Am Wom supp v1

10370. Holland, Claudia
born 1903
novelist
Index t Wom

10371. Landon, Margaret Dorothea Mortenson
born 1903
author
Index t Wom

10372. Luce, Clare (Boothe)
born 1903
playwright, author, journalist, politician, US ambassador
Episcopalian
Index t Wom; Nat Cyc Am Bio csvF; Wom Lit

10373. McKee, Ruth Eleanor
born 1903
novelist
Index t Wom

10374. Miller, Caroline
born 1903
novelist
Dict Lit Bio v9; Index t Wom

10375. Moore, Ruth
born 1903
author
Index t Wom

10376. Nin, Anais
1903–77
author, novelist, diarist, printer, feminist
French
Cur Biog '75 and '77; Dict Lit Bio v2 and v4; Index t Wom; Wom Lit; Wom Lit, More

10377. Rich, Louise Dickinson
born 1903
author
Index t Wom

10378. Roberts, Dorothy James
born 1903
novelist
Index t Wom

10379. Seeley, Mabel
born 1903
novelist
Index t Wom

10380. Tuve, Rosemond
1903–64
literary scholar, educator
Not Am Wom supp v1

10381. Whitney, Phyllis Ayame
born 1903

author
Index t Wom

10382. Zugsmith, Leane
born 1903
author
Index t Wom

10383. Bard, Mary Ten Eyk
born 1904
author
Index t Wom

10384. Berlin, Ellen Mackay
born 1904
author
Index t Wom

10385. Carroll, Gladys Hasty
born 1904
novelist, children's author
Dict Lit Bio v9; Index t Wom

10386. Casey, Rosemary
1904–76
playwright, screenwriter
Catholic
Pennsylvania
Nat Cyc Am Bio v59

10387. Davis, Adelle
1904–74
food writer, nutritionist
California
Cur Biog '73 and '74; Not Am Wom supp v1; Obit File

10388. Emch, Minna Elizabeth Libman
1904–58
psychiatrist, psychiatric educator and author
Chicago, IL
Lithuanian
Nat Cyc Am Bio v47

10389. Fenner, Beatrice
born 1904
composer, author, publisher
Index t Wom

10390. Fishback, Margaret
born 1904
author, advertiser
Index t Wom

10391. Furnas, Marthedith
born 1904
novelist
Index t Wom

10392. Graham, Shirley
born 1904/07
musical playwright, biographical historian, author, composer
Black
Index t Wom; Negro Alman

10393. Jenkins, Sara
born 1904
author
Index t Wom

10394. Langley, Dorothy
born 1904
novelist
Index t Wom

10395. Lincoln, Victoria
born 1904
novelist
Index t Wom

10396. Mannes, Mary
born 1904
author, journalist, critic
Index t Wom

10397. Morris, Constance Lily
died 1954
clubwoman, author
Index t Wom

10398. Nicholson, Margaret
born 1904
editor, author
Index t Wom

10399. Peterson, Virgilia; Virginia Paulding
1904–66
lecturer, author, literary critic, television moderator, Peabody Award winner
Index t Wom; Obit File

10400. Rand, Ayn
born 1904
author
Russian
Index t Wom

10401. Tucker, Augusta
born 1904
novelist
Index t Wom

10402. Weston, Christine Goutiere
born 1904
author
English
Index t Wom

10403. Wilson, Dorothy Clarke
born 1904
author
Index t Wom

10404. Winnie, Lucille
born 1904
author
Native American (Seneca-Cayuga)
Ind Today

10405. Armstrong, Charlotte
1905–69
playwright, mystery writer
Cur Biog '69; Index t Wom; Obit File

10406. Bartlett, Phyllis (Brooks); Mrs. John A. Pollard
1905–73
educator, scholar of English literature
Episcopalian
New York
Nat Cyc Am Bio v58

10407. Brenner, Anita
1905–74
journalist, writer on Mexico
Obit File

10408. Chase, Ilka
circa 1905–78
stage and screen actor, radio and television personality, novelist, autobiographer
Cur Biog '78; Index t Wom; Obit File

10409. Cooper, Louise Field
born 1905
author
Index t Wom

10410. Cousins, Margaret [Sue]
born 1905
editor, author
Index t Wom

10411. Eastman, Elizabeth
born 1905
novelist
Index t Wom

10412. Frost, Frances May
1905–59
poet, novelist, short story writer
Index t Wom; Obit File

10413. Goertz, Arthemise
born 1905
author
Index t Wom

10414. Hahn, Emily; Mrs. Charles Ralph Boxer
born 1905
geologist, author
Index t Wom; Nat Cyc Am Bio csv8

10415. Hellman, Lillian
1905/06–1984
dramatist, autobiographer
Jewish
Dict Lit Bio v7; Encyc South Hist; Index t Wom; Nat Cyc Am Bio csv7; Who Who Jew Hist; Wom Lit; Wom Lit, More

10416. Howe, Helen; Helen Allen
1905–75
novelist, satiric monologuist
Cur Biog '75; Index t Wom

10417. Kimball, Arie Goebel
died 1955

author and authority on Thomas Jefferson
Obit File

10418. Landi, Elissa
1905–48
stage and screen actor, novelist
Italian
Obit File

10419. Lasswell, Mary
born 1905
novelist
Index t Wom

10420. Lay, Margaret Rebecca
born 1905
author
Index t Wom

10421. Lombard, Helen Carusi
born 1905
author, journalist
Index t Wom

10422. Mann, Erika
1905–69
author, writer on Germany, actor, lecturer
German
Cur Biog '69; Index t Wom

10423. McGinley, Phyllis
1905–78
poet, children's author, Pulitzer Prize winner
Canadian
Cur Biog '78; Index t Wom; Obit File

10424. Pope, Edith Everett Taylor
born 1905
novelist
Index t Wom; Wom Lit, More

10425. Porter, Dorothy B.
born 1905
librarian, library administrator, bibliographer, author
Black
Encyc Black Am; Negro Alman

10426. Slessinger, Tess
1905–45
author
Index t Wom; Wom Lit, More

10427. Trilling, Diana Rubin
born 1905
essayist, book reviewer
Cur Biog '79

10428. Walker, Mildred
born 1905
author
Index t Wom

10429. Ward, Mary Jane
born 1905
novelist
Index t Wom

10430. Webster, Margaret
1905–72
theatrical director, actor, author, producer
Cur Biog '73; Index t Wom; Not Am Wom supp v1

10431. Wicker, Irene
born 1905
singer, actor, radio scriptwriter
Index t Wom

10432. Yates, Elizabeth; Mrs. William McGreal
born 1905
author
New Hampshire
Index t Wom; Nat Cyc Am Bio csv9

10433. Backus, Louise Laidlaw
1906–73
New York civic worker, UNESCO member, international affairs expert, poet
Episcopalian
New York, NY
Nat Cyc Am Bio v57

10434. Baumer, Marie
born 1906
author
Index t Wom

10435. Bennett, Dorothy
born 1906
playwright
Index t Wom

10436. Beranger, Clara
died 1956
screenwriter
Index t Wom

10437. Black, Irma Simonton
1906–72
preschool director, children's author
New York
Nat Cyc Am Bio v58

10438. Carter, Gwendolyn Margaret
born 1906
political scientist, writer on political science, educator
Black
Encyc Black Am

10439. Cheney, Frances Neel
born 1906
librarian, author
Index t Wom

10440. du Bois, Shirley Lola Graham
1906–77
children's author, biographer, composer, stage director, civil rights worker
Black
Cur Biog '77; Encyc Black Am

10441. Erskine, Dorothy
born 1906
novelist
Index t Wom

10442. Estes, Eleanor Ruth Rosenfeld
born 1906
librarian, author
Index t Wom

10443. Faulkner, Nancy
born 1906
author
Index t Wom

10444. Fuller, Iola
born 1906
novelist
Index t Wom

10445. Graham, Elinor Mish
born 1906
author
Index t Wom

10446. Halstead, Anna Roosevelt
1906–75
author, radio broadcaster, journalist
Obit File

10447. Hannum, Alberta Pierson
born 1906
novelist
Index t Wom

10448. Kober, Alice Elizabeth
1906–50
classical scholar, linguist
Not Am Wom

10449. Lindbergh, Anne (Spencer) Morrow
born 1906
aviator, poet, author, autobiographer
Cur Biog '76; Index t Wom; Nat Cyc Am Bio csv6

10450. MacGregor, Ellen
born 1906
author, librarian
Index t Wom

10451. Mayer, Marie Gertrude Goeppert
1906–72
theoretical physicist, Nobel Prize winner in physics, educator, author
German; Polish
Cur Biog '72; Index t Wom; Nat Cyc Am Bio v58; Not Am Wom supp v1; Obit File

10452. Papashvily, Helen Wiate
born 1906
author

Russian
Index t Wom

10453. Patton, Frances Gray
born 1906
author
Index t Wom

10454. Petkere, Bernice
born 1906
composer, author, scenarist
Index t Wom

10455. Ripley, Elizabeth Blake
born 1906
author, illustrator
Index t Wom

10456. Ritner, Ann Gilliland
born 1906
author
Index t Wom

10457. Scott, Natalie Anderson; Natalie B. Sokoloff
born 1906
novelist
Russian
Index t Wom

10458. Tarry, Ellen
born 1906
author, children's author
Catholic
Black
Negro Alman; Prof Negro Wom v2

10459. Waters, Marianne
born 1906
playwright
Index t Wom

10460. Wellman, Margaret
1906–56
author, traveler, explorer
Austrian
Obit File

10461. Whipple, Maureen
born 1906
author
Index t Wom; Wom Lit, More

10462. White, Poppy Cannon
1906–75
food columnist, cookbook author
Obit File

10463. Baker, Dorothy (Dodds)
1907–68
novelist
Index t Wom; Obit File; Wom Lit, More

10464. Carson, Rachel Louise
1907–64
biologist, conservationist, naturalist, nature and conservation writer

Presbyterian
Index t Wom; Nat Cyc Am Bio csv9; Not Am Wom supp v1; Obit File

10465. Chase, Mary Coyle
born 1907
author, playwright
Index t Wom; Nat Cyc Am Bio csv10

10466. Dale, Virginia; Hermina Shirk-Johnstone
1907–57
novelist, short story writer
Obit File

10467. Disney, Doris Miles
born 1907
author
Index t Wom

10468. Emery, Anne Eleanor McGuigan
born 1907
author
Index t Wom

10469. Enters, Angna
born 1907
dancer, painter, author
Index t Wom

10470. Fermi, Laura Capon
born 1907
author
Italian
Index t Wom

10471. Hofmann, Melita Cecelia
1907–76
artist, art educator, book illustrator and designer, author, conservationist
Congregationalist
New York
Nat Cyc Am Bio v60

10472. Howard, Elizabeth Jane
born 1907
author
Index t Wom; Wom Lit, More

10473. Hyde, Madeline
born 1907
composer, author
Index t Wom

10474. Ireland, Norma Olin
born 1907
author, technical indexer, librarian
Index t Wom

10475. Jean, Elsie
born 1907
composer, author
Index t Wom

10476. Lawrence, Mildred
born 1907

author
Index t Wom

10477. MacInnes, Helen Clark; Helen Gilbert Highet
born 1907
author
Scottish
Index t Wom

10478. MacKay, Margaret
born 1907
novelist
Index t Wom

10479. McSwigan, Marie
1907–62
author
Index t Wom

10480. Morgan, Angela
died 1957
poet
Index t Wom

10481. Pearl, Lee
born 1907
author, songwriter
Index t Wom

10482. Ross, Nancy Wilson
born 1907
author
Index t Wom

10483. Steele, Norma Mitchel Talbot
married 1932
playwright
Index t Wom

10484. van Sciver, Esther
born 1907
author, songwriter
Index t Wom

10485. Winchester, Alice
born 1907
editor, author
Index t Wom

10486. Arnow, Harriette
born 1908
novelist
Kentucky
Dict Lit Bio v6; Index t Wom; Wom Lit; Wom Lit, More

10487. Brown, Marion
born 1908
author
Index t Wom

10488. Burnett, Hallie Southgate
born 1908
author, editor
Index t Wom

10489. Carey, Ernestine Moller Gilbreth
born 1908

author, retail executive
Index t Wom

10490. Chastain, Madye Lee
born 1908
author, illustrator
Index t Wom

10491. Dodd, Martha Eccles
born 1908
author
Index t Wom

**10492. Fisher, Mary Frances
Kennedy**
born 1908
author
Index t Wom

10493. Gellhorn, Martha
born 1908
novelist
Index t Wom

10494. Hale, Nancy
born 1908
author
Index t Wom

10495. Hall, Marjory
born 1908
author, businessperson
Index t Wom

10496. Hamilton, Nancy
born 1908
author, singer
Index t Wom

**10497. Hemingway, Mary
Welsh**
born 1908
author, journalist
Index t Wom

10498. MacDonald, Betty; Ann
Elizabeth Campbell Bard
Heskett
1908–58
author, children's author
Dict Am Bio supp v5; Index t
Wom; Obit File

10499. Modell, Merriam; Evelyn Piper
born 1908
author
Index t Wom

**10500. Speare, Elizabeth
George**
born 1908
author
Index t Wom

10501. Tonkonogy, Gertrude
born 1908
playwright
Index t Wom

10502. Wilhelm, Gale
born 1908

novelist
Index t Wom

10503. Baker, Louise Maxwell
born 1909
author
Index t Wom

10504. Buckmaster, Henrietta
born 1909
author, journalist
Index t Wom

10505. Burton, Virginia Lee
1909–68
author, illustrator
Index t Wom

10506. Cavanna, Betty; Betsy
Allen
born 1909
author
Index t Wom

10507. Chute, Marcette Gaylor
born 1909
author
Index t Wom

10508. Cockrell, Marian
born 1909
novelist
Index t Wom

10509. Enright, Elizabeth
born 1909/10
illustrator, author
Index t Wom

10510. Faralla, Dana
born 1909
novelist
Index t Wom

10511. Giles, Janice Holt
born 1909
author
Index t Wom

10512. Hubbard, Margaret Ann
born 1909
author
Index t Wom

**10513. Marlett, Melba Balmat
Grimes**
born 1909
author
Index t Wom

**10514. McLean, Kathryn
(Forbes)**
1909–66
author
Index t Wom; Obit File

10515. O'Donnell, Mary King
born 1909
novelist
Index t Wom

**10516. Schmitt, Gladys Leo-
nore;** Gladys Goldfield
1909–72
author, historical novelist, poet,
editor, university educator
Cur Biog '72; Index t Wom; Obit
File

10517. Strabel, Thelma; Thelma
Godwin
died 1959
novelist, short story writer
Obit File

**10518. Walden, Amelia
Elizabeth**
born 1909
author
Index t Wom

10519. Welty, Eudora Alice
born 1909
novelist
Jackson, MS
Cur Biog '75; Dict Lit Bio v2;
Encyc South Hist; Index t
Wom; Wom Lit; Wom Lit,
More

10520. Wetherell, June
born 1909
novelist
Index t Wom

10521. Brown, Margaret Wise;
Golden MacDonald; Timothy
Hay; Juniper Sage
1910–52
children's author
Dict Am Bio supp v5; Not Am
Wom supp v1; Obit File

10522. Carrick, Jean Warren
flourished 1940s
pianist, music editor, author
Index t Wom

**10523. Clapp, Margaret (An-
toinette)**
1910–74
president of Wellesley College,
historian, biographer, US cultural attaché to India
Nat Cyc Am Bio; Index t Wom

10524. Comfort, Annabel
flourished 1940s
composer, author
Index t Wom

10525. Conkling, Hilda
born 1910
poet
Index t Wom

10526. Cowles, Fleur Fenton
born 1910
painter, editor, author, businessperson
Index t Wom

10527. Cruisinberry, Jane
flourished 1940s
scriptwriter
Index t Wom

10528. Dallam, Helen
flourished 1940s–50s
composer, author
Index t Wom

10529. Gibson, Anna L.
flourished 1940s
nurse, author
Index t Wom

10530. Glenn, Mabelle
flourished 1940s
music educator, author
Index t Wom

10531. Hall, Addye Yeargain
flourished 1940s
musician, lecturer, author
Index t Wom

**10532. Halse, Margaret
Frances**
born 1910
author
Index t Wom

10533. Hathaway, Ann
flourished 1940s
violinist, author, educator
Index t Wom

**10534. Hemingway, Clara Ed-
wards**
flourished 1940s
composer, singer, voice teacher,
author
Index t Wom

10535. Holmes, Marjorie
born 1910
novelist
Index t Wom

**10536. Hood, Marguerite Vivi-
an**
flourished 1940s
pianist, educator, author, editor
Index t Wom

10537. Hudson, Octavia
flourished 1940s
composer, pianist, music educator, author
Index t Wom

10538. Jessey, Cornelia
born 1910
novelist
Index t Wom

**10539. Johnson, Josephine
Winslow;** Josephine Cannon
born 1910
novelist
Congregationalist
Index t Wom; Nat Cyc Am Bio

10540. Leonard, Florence
flourished 1940s
musician, pianist, music educator,
author
Index t Wom

10541. Levien, Sonya (Hovey)
died 1960
screenwriter
Russian
Obit File

10542. McNeilly, Mildred Masterson; James Dewey; Glenn
Kelly
born 1910
novelist
Index t Wom

10543. Moats, Alice-Leone
born 1910/11
journalist, author
Index t Wom

10544. Murray, Paule
born 1910
educator, author, lawyer, civil
rights activist
Black
Encyc Black Am

10545. Niggli, Josephina
born 1910
author
Mexican
Index t Wom

**10546. Oberdorfer, Anne
Faulkner**
flourished 1940s
musician, lecturer, author
Index t Wom

10547. Perfield, Effa Ellis
flourished 1940s
educator, author, organist
Index t Wom

10548. Pinchot, Ann
born 1910
novelist
Index t Wom

10549. Rowe, Fynette
born 1910
novelist
Index t Wom

10550. Runbeck, Margaret Lee
1910–56
author, novelist, short story writer, US Point Four representative to India
Index t Wom; Obit File

10551. Saher, Lilla van
flourished 1940s
novelist
Hungarian
Index t Wom

10552. Simpson, Elizabeth
flourished 1940s
composer, pianist, music educator, lecturer, author
Index t Wom

10553. Sosenko, Anna
born 1910
composer, writer
Index t Wom

10554. Steward, Anna Bird
flourished 1940s
author, lecturer
Index t Wom

10555. Teal, Valentine
flourished 1940s
novelist
Index t Wom

10556. Tomasi, Mari
flourished 1940s
author
Index t Wom

10557. Tracey, Cateau Stegeman
flourished 1940s
pianist, music educator, author, critic, lecturer
Index t Wom

10558. Underwood, Charlotte;
Joan Charles
flourished 1940s–50s
novelist
Index t Wom

10559. Weil, Lisl
born 1910
artist, author
Austrian
Index t Wom

10560. Wollstein, Rose R.
flourished 1940s
pianist, author, linguist
Index t Wom

10561. Albrand, Martha
born 1911
novelist
Index t Wom

10562. Armstrong, Alice Catt
born 1911
biographer, book publisher
Religious Scientist
California
Nat Cyc Am Bio csv10

10563. Bishop, Elizabeth
1911–79
poet
Cur Biog '77 and '79; Dict Lit
Bio v5

10564. Calisher, Hortense
born 1911
novelist
Cur Biog '73; Dict Lit Bio v2;
Wom Lit, More

10565. Green, Eleanor
born 1911
novelist
Index t Wom

**10566. Ingalls, Mildred Dodge
Jeramy**
born 1911
poet, educator
Index t Wom

10567. MacKay, Helen G. Edwards
died 1961
author
Obit File

10568. McKenny, Ruth
1911–72
author, short story writer, humorist, writer on social causes
Cur Biog '72; Index t Wom; Obit
File

10569. Moore, Catherine L.
born 1911
speculative fiction author
Dict Lit Bio v8

10570. Peare, Catherine Ownes
born 1911
author
Index t Wom

10571. Petry, Ann
born 1911
novelist, short story writer, journalist, literary critic
Black
Index t Wom; Negro Alman;
Wom Lit; Wom Lit, More

10572. Roth, Lillian
born 1911
actor, author
Index t Wom

10573. Suess, Dana Nadine
born 1911
composer, pianist, author
Index t Wom

10574. Whitcomb, Catharine
born 1911
novelist
Index t Wom

**10575. Wurdemann, Audrey
May;** Audrey May Auslander
1911–60
poet, novelist, Pulitzer Prize winner
Index t Wom; Obit File

10576. Barnes, Carmen Neal
born 1912
novelist
Index t Wom

10577. Bialk, Elisa
born 1912
author
Index t Wom

10578. Brooks, Gwendolyn
born 1912/17
poet, educator, autobiographer, lecturer, poet laureate of Illinois
Chicago, IL
Black
Cur Biog '77; Dict Lit Bio v5;
Encyc Black Am; Index t Wom;
Negro Alman; Nort Anth Poet;
Prof Negro Wom; Wom Lit;
Wom Lit, More

**10579. Carnegie, Dorothy
Reeder Price**
born 1912
educator, author
Index t Wom

10580. Curry, Peggy Simson
born 1912
author
Scottish
Index t Wom

10581. Kennelly, Ardyth
born 1912
author
Index t Wom

**10582. McCarthy, Mary
Therese**
born 1912
author, novelist, autobiographer, short story writer, essayist, educator
Cur Biog '69; Dict Lit Bio v2;
Index t Wom; Wom Lit; Wom
Lit, More

10583. Neilson, Frances Fullerton Jones
born 1912
author
Index t Wom

**10584. Norton, Alice Mary
"Andre"**
born 1912
speculative fiction writer, children's author, librarian
Dict Lit Bio v8; Index t Wom

10585. Sorenson, Virginia
born 1912
author
Index t Wom

10586. Todd, Helen
1912–63
novelist
Index t Wom

10587. Tuchman, Barbara Wertheim
born 1912
author, historian

Jewish
Index t Wom; Who Who Jew
   Hist

10588. Wason, Betty
born 1912
journalist, author
Index t Wom

10589. Westcott, Jane Vlachos
born 1912
novelist
Index t Wom

10590. Bannon, Laura
died 1963
illustrator, author
Index t Wom

**10591. Bondy, Elizabeth Jeanne
   Hale**
1913–69
literary agent, book editor
Congregationalist
New York
Nat Cyc Am Bio v54

10592. Chute, Beatrice Joy
born 1913
author
Index t Wom

10593. Clark, Eleanor
born 1913
novelist, book reviewer
Cur Biog '78; Dict Lit Bio v6

**10594. Crane, Nathalie Clara
   Ruth**
born 1913
poet
Index t Wom

10595. Janeway, Elizabeth Hall
born 1913
author
Index t Wom

**10596. Johnstone, Margaret
   Blair**
born 1913
clergyperson, author, lecturer
Index t Wom

**10597. Porter, Sylvia Field
   Feldman**
born 1913
economics journalist, financial
   columnist, author
Jewish
Cur Biog '80; Index t Wom

10598. Preminger, Marion Hill;
   Mrs. Albert Mayer
1913–72
social worker, author, African art
   collector, missionary to the
   Congo, philanthropist, screen
   actor
Catholic
New York

Hungarian
Nat Cyc Am Bio v57; Obit File

**10599. Pryce-Jones, Mary
   Kempner;** Mary Jean Kempner
1913–69
author
Obit File

10600. Sinclair, Jo
born 1913
author
Index t Wom

10601. Thompson, Kay
born 1913
actor, singer, author
Index t Wom

10602. Yenni, Julia Truitt
born 1913
novelist
Index t Wom

**10603. Barber, Elsie Marion
   Oakes**
born 1914
author
Index t Wom

10604. Berger, Sylvia (Redman)
1914–58
radio and television scriptwriter
Obit File

10605. Boley, Jean
born 1914
novelist
Index t Wom

10606. Burgos, Julia de
1914?–1953
poet, journalist
Not Am Wom supp v1

**10607. Burgwyn, Mebane Holo-
   man**
born 1914
author
Index t Wom

10608. Crockett, Lucy Herndon
born 1914
author
Index t Wom

10609. Deasy, Mary Margaret
born 1914
author
Index t Wom

10610. Dee, Sylvia
1914–67
author, songwriter
Index t Wom

10611. Downes, Anne Miller
died 1964
novelist, journalist
Index t Wom; Obit File

10612. Fort, Eleanor H.; Hank
born circa 1914
composer, author
Index t Wom

10613. Lee, Gypsy Rose; Rose
   Louise Hovick
1914?–70
burlesque and stage actor, television personality, mystery writer
Cur Biog '70; Index t Wom; Not
   Am Wom supp v1; Obit File

10614. Lowe, Ruth
born 1914
composer, pianist, author
Index t Wom

10615. Luban, Francia
born 1914
musician, songwriter, author
Russian
Index t Wom

**10616. Marshal, Sarah Catha-
   rine**
born 1914
author
Index t Wom

10617. McGrath, Leueen
born 1914
actor, playwright
English
Index t Wom

10618. Montana, Patsy
born 1914
composer, author, musician
Index t Wom

**10619. Philby, Eleanor Carolyn
   Kearns**
1914–68
novelist
Index t Wom

**10620. Saarinen, Aline Milton
   Bernstein (Louchheim)**
1914–72
art critic, television commentator,
   writer on art history
Cur Biog '72; Index t Wom; Not
   Am Wom supp v1

**10621. Twomey, Kathleen
   "Kay"**
born 1914
author, designer, songwriter
Index t Wom

10622. Whitney, Joan
born 1914
composer, singer, music publisher, author
Index t Wom

10623. Wright, Helen
born 1914
astronomer, author
Index t Wom

**10624. Alexander, Margaret
   (Walker)**
born 1915
poet, novelist, college administrator
Black
Encyc Black Am; Encyc South
   Hist; Index t Wom; Negro Alman; Wom Lit; Wom Lit, More

**10625. Bird, Caroline (Maho-
   ney)**
born 1915
lecturer, women's equal rights activist, author
New York
Cur Biog '76

10626. Brackett, Leigh
1915–78
speculative fiction author
Dict Lit Bio v8

10627. Comden, Betty
born 1915/19
author, musician, actor
Index t Wom

10628. Fisher, Doris
born 1915
composer, singer, producer, author
Index t Wom

10629. Frings, Ketti Hartley
1915–81
screenwriter, novelist, playwright
Cur Biog '81; Index t Wom

10630. Goetschius, Marjorie
born 1915
composer, author
Index t Wom

10631. McGraw, Eloise Jarvis
born 1915
author
Index t Wom

10632. Mydans, Shelley Smith
born 1915
journalist, author
Index t Wom

10633. Sheldon, Alice B.;
   James Tiptree, Jr.
born 1915
speculative fiction and short story
   writer, feminist
Dict Lit Bio v8

10634. Stafford, Jean
1915–79
novelist
Cur Biog '79; Dict Lit Bio v2;
   Index t Wom; Wom Lit; Wom
   Lit, More

10635. Weingarten, Violet
1915–76

novelist, newspaper journalist, screenwriter
Obit File

10636. Deming, Louise Mac-Pherson
1916–76
international educator, author, civic worker in Okinawa, Japan
Episcopalian
Nat Cyc Am Bio v58

10637. Eustis, Helen White
born 1916
author
Index t Wom

10638. Hardwick, Elizabeth
born 1916
novelist, essayist, short story writer, literary critic, social critic, editor of the *New York Review of Books*
Cur Biog '81; Dict Lit Bio v6

10639. Jackson, Shirley Hardie
1916/19–1965
short story writer, novelist, ghost story writer, playwright, television scriptwriter, writer on domestic subjects, children's author
Dict Lit Bio v6; Index t Wom; Not Am Wom supp v1; Obit File; Wom Lit; Wom Lit, More

10640. Jacobs, Jane (Butzner)
born 1916
urbanologist, writer on cities
Cur Biog '77

10641. Lennart, Isobel
1916–71
stage and screen writer
Obit File

10642. Marion, Elizabeth
born 1916
novelist
Index t Wom

10643. Seton, Anya; Anya Chase
born 1916
author
Index t Wom

10644. Stanford, Anne
born 1916
poet
California
Dict Lit Bio v5; Wom Lit, More

10645. Windsor, Kathleen
born 1916/19
author
Index t Wom

10646. Chapin, Anne Morrison
died 1967
playwright
Index t Wom

10647. Gibbs, Willa
born 1917
novelist
Index t Wom

10648. Henderson, Zenna (Chlarson)
born 1917
speculative fiction writer
Dict Lit Bio v8

10649. McCullers, Carson Smith
1917–67
novelist, playwright
Georgia
Dict Lit Bio v2 and v7; Encyc South Hist; Index t Wom; Not Am Wom supp v1; Obit File; Wom Lit; Wom Lit, More

10650. Mitford, Jessica Lucy
born 1917
muckraking journalist, autobiographer
English
Cur Biog '74

10651. Ogilvie, Elisabeth May
born 1917
author
Index t Wom

10652. Barton, Betsey
1918–62
author
Index t Wom

10653. Dixon, Jean
born 1918
writer on extrasensory perception and prophecy
Washington, DC
Cur Biog '73

10654. l'Engle, Madeleine
born 1918
novelist, children's author
Index t Wom

10655. Peterson, Betty
born 1918
author
Index t Wom

10656. Rogers, Lettie Hamlett
1918–57
educator, author
Obit File

10657. Rosmond, Babette
born 1918
novelist
Index t Wom

10658. Settle, Mary Lee
born 1918
author
Dict Lit Bio v6; Index t Wom

10659. Shelley, Gladys
born 1918

author, lyricist, actor
Index t Wom

10660. Werner, Kay
born 1918
composer, author, singer
Index t Wom

10661. Werner, Sue
born 1918
composer, author, singer
Index t Wom

10662. Wolff, Marietta M.
born 1918
author
Index t Wom

10663. Chidester, Ann
born 1919
author
Index t Wom

10664. Coit, Margaret Loyise
born 1919
author, journalist
Index t Wom

10665. Early, Eleanor
died 1969
travel guide author
Obit File

10666. Edwards, Joan
1919/20–1981
composer, author, singer, songwriter, radio and screen actor
Cur Biog '82; Index t Wom

10667. Frank, Mary Hughes
born 1919
author, child guidance expert
Irish
Index t Wom

10668. Merchant, Jane
born 1919
poet
Index t Wom

10669. Sone, Monica
born 1919
author
Japanese
Index t Wom

10670. Stevenson, Elizabeth
born 1919
author
Index t Wom

10671. Swenson, May
born 1919
poet
Dict Lit Bio v5; Wom Lit; Wom Lit, More

10672. Childress, Alice
born 1920
playwright, editor, actor

Black
Dict Lit Bio v7; Encyc Black Am; Wom Lit; Wom Lit, More

10673. Dykeman, Wilma
flourished 1950s
author
Index t Wom

10674. Forsee, Aylesa
flourished 1950s
author
Index t Wom

10675. Freedman, Nancy Mars (Lois)
born 1920
author
Index t Wom

10676. Guest, Barbara
born 1920
poet, theatrical producer
New York
Dict Lit Bio v5

10677. Jordan, June
flourished 1950s–1980s
poet, essayist, political writer, civil rights worker, educator
Black
Wom Lit; Wom Lit, More

10678. Mayo, Eleanor R.
born 1920
novelist
Index t Wom

10679. Smart, Alice McGee
flourished 1950s
sociologist, poet, educator
Index t Wom

10680. Spiegel, Clara Gatzert; Clare Jaynes
flourished 1950s
author
Index t Wom

10681. Stinetorf, Louise
flourished 1950s
nurse, author
Index t Wom

10682. Stolz, Mary Slattery
born 1920
author
Index t Wom

10683. Wells, Bernice Young Mitchell
flourished 1950s
author
Black
Index t Wom

10684. Whitney, Julia; Yulya Alexandrovna Zapolskaya
1920–65
composer, musician, singer, author

Russian
Obit File

10685. Witherspoon, Naomi Long
graduated 1945
poet, journalist
Index t Wom

10686. Daly, Maureen Patricia
born 1921
author, editor
Irish
Index t Wom

10687. de Lima, Sigrid
born 1921
author
Index t Wom

10688. Friedan, Betty
born 1921
feminist, founder and president of NOW, writer on the condition of women, women's rights worker
Cur Biog '70

10689. Saxl, Eva R.
born circa 1921
educator, traveler, lecturer, author
Czechoslovak
Index t Wom

10690. Spencer, Elizabeth
born 1921/31
novelist
Mississippi
Dict Lit Bio v6; Index t Wom

10691. Susann, Jacqueline
1921–74
popular novelist, screen actor
Cur Biog '72 and '74; Obit File

10692. van Duyn, Mona
born 1921
poet
Dict Lit Bio v5; Wom Lit; Wom Lit, More

10693. Belle, Barbara
born 1922
composer, author
Index t Wom

10694. Brown, Helen Gurley
born 1922
author, editor of *Cosmopolitan*, lecturer, television personality
Cur Biog '69

10695. Johnston, Patricia
born 1922
author, songwriter
Index t Wom

10696. Leonard, Anita
born 1922
composer, author
Index t Wom

10697. Marsh, Ellen
born 1922
novelist
Index t Wom

10698. Ritchie, Jean
born 1922
folksinger, folklorist, author
Index t Wom

10699. Smith, Anita
born 1922
composer, author
Index t Wom

10700. Goodin, Peggy
born 1923
novelist
Index t Wom

10701. Kerr, Jean Collins
born 1923/24
playwright, humorist
Index t Wom

10702. Kuhn, Rene Leilani
born 1923
novelist
Index t Wom

10703. Levertov, Denise
born 1923
poet
Dict Lit Bio v5; Nort Anth Poet; Wom Lit; Wom Lit, More

10704. Moore, Jenny
1923–73
social activist, author
Obit File

10705. Williams, Lorraine Anderson
born 1923
educator, author
Index t Wom

10706. Bacall, Lauren; Betty Joan Perske
born 1924
screen actor, autobiographer
Cur Biog '70; Index t Wom

10707. Bainbridge, Katherine
born 1924
songwriter, poet
English
Index t Wom

10708. Metalious, Grace de Repentigny
1924–64
author, popular novelist
Index t Wom; Obit File

10709. Edwards, Clara
born 1925
composer, pianist, singer, author
Index t Wom

10710. Johnson, Virginia E. (Shelman)
born 1925
writer on sex, psychologist
Cur Biog '76

10711. Kizer, Carolyn
born 1925
poet
Dict Lit Bio v5; Wom Lit, More

10712. Kumin, Maxine
born 1925
author
Dict Lit Bio v5; Wom Lit, More

10713. MacLean, Katherine Ann
born 1925
speculative fiction author
Dict Lit Bio v8

10714. O'Connor, Flannery [Mary]
1925–64
author, short story writer, novelist
Catholic
Georgia
Dict Lit Bio v2; Encyc South Hist; Index t Wom; Nat Cyc Am Bio v55; Not Am Wom supp v1; Obit File; Wom Lit; Wom Lit, More

10715. Chewiwi, Louise Abeita
born 1926
children's author, educator
Native American (Pueblo-Laguna)
Ind Today

10716. Kubler-Ross, Elisabeth
born 1926
psychiatrist, thanatologist, writer on death and dying
Swiss
Cur Biog '80

10717. Lee, Nelle Harper; Lee Harper
born 1926
author
Index t Wom

10718. Lilly, Doris
born 1926
author, journalist
Index t Wom

10719. Livingstone, Mabel
born 1926
author, poet
Index t Wom

10720. Lurie, Alison (Bishop)
born 1926
novelist
Dict Lit Bio v2; Wom Lit; Wom Lit, More

10721. McCaffrey, Anne Inez
born 1926
speculative fiction writer, novelist, short story writer
Dict Lit Bio v8

10722. Schlein, Miriam
born 1926
author
Index t Wom

10723. Bombeck, Erma
born 1927
humorist, novelist
Cur Biog '79

10724. Jhabvala, Ruth Prawer
born 1927
novelist, short story and screenplay writer, writer of fiction about India
Jewish
Indian; English
Cur Biog '77; Wom Lit; Wom Lit, More

10725. Wojciechowska, Maia [Teresa]
born 1927
children's author, children's book publisher
Catholic
Polish
Cur Biog '76

10726. Angelou, Maya
born 1928
poet, autobiographer, dancer, producer
Black
Cur Biog '74; Encyc Black Am; Wom Lit; Wom Lit, More

10727. Arnez, Nancy Levi
born 1928
educator, poet, author
Black
Encyc Black Am

10728. Sexton, Anne Grey Harvey
1928–74
poet, Pulitzer Prize winner
Dict Lit Bio v5; Nort Anth Poet; Not Am Wom supp v1; Obit File; Wom Lit; Wom Lit, More

10729. Wilhelm, Kate
born 1928
speculative fiction author, short story writer, novelist
Dict Lit Bio v8; Wom Lit, More

10730. Williams, Joan
born 1928
novelist
Dict Lit Bio v6

10731. Couzzins, Phoebe Wilson
1929/45–1913

lawyer, US deputy and marshal in Missouri, political author, suffragist
Index t Wom; Nat Cyc Am Bio v15; Not Am Wom; Wom Cent

10732. Grau, Shirley Ann
born 1929
author, novelist, short story writer
New Orleans, LA
Dict Lit Bio v2; Index t Wom; Wom Lit; Wom Lit, More

10733. le Guin, Ursula K.
born 1929
speculative fiction author, novelist, literary critic
Dict Lit Bio v8; Wom Lit; Wom Lit, More

10734. Marshall, Paule
born 1929
short story writer, novelist
Black
Encyc Black Am; Negro Alman; Wom Lit; Wom Lit, More

10735. Moore, Joan W.
born 1929
sociologist, student of Mexican American culture, author, educator
Dict Mex Am Hist

10736. Rich, Adrienne [Cecile]
born 1929
poet, educator
Cur Biog '76; Dict Lit Bio v5; Nort Anth Poet; Wom Lit; Wom Lit, More

10737. Scott, Ann London
1929–75
feminist, vice-president of NOW, poet
Not Am Wom supp v1; Obit File

10738. Bates, Lila Curtis
flourished 1930s
pianist, poet, educator
Index t Wom

10739. Bennett, Kay Curley
flourished 1960s
author
Native American (Navaho)
Ind Today

10740. Bradley, Marion Zimmer
born 1930
speculative fiction writer
Dict Lit Bio v8

10741. Evans, Mari
flourished 1960s
poet
Black
Negro Alman; Wom Lit; Wom Lit, More

10742. Fornes, Maria Irene
born 1930
playwright, theatrical director
New York
Cuban
Dict Lit Bio v7

10743. Hansberry, Lorraine
1930–65
playwright, civil rights reformer, Socialist party worker
New York
Black
Dict Lit Bio v7; Encyc Black Am; Index t Wom; Nat Cyc Am Bio v60; Negro Alman; Not Am Wom supp v1; Obit File; Prof Negro Wom v2; Wom Lit; Wom Lit, More

10744. McKown, Robin
flourished 1960s
author
Index t Wom

10745. Monture, Ethel Brant
flourished 1960s
author, specialist in Native American culture
Native American (Mohawk)
Ind Today

10746. Morrison, Chloe Anthony Woffard "Toni"
born 1931
author, novelist
Black
Cur Biog '79; Dict Lit Bio v6; Encyc Black Am; Wom Lit; Wom Lit, More

10747. Drake, Debra Bella "Debbie"
born 1932
physical education teacher, author
Index t Wom

10748. Jaffe, Rona
born 1932
author
Index t Wom

10749. Pastan, Linda
born 1932
poet
Dict Lit Bio v5

10750. Plath, Sylvia
1932–63
poet, author
Jewish
Dict Lit Bio v5 and v6; Nort Anth Poet; Not Am Wom supp v1; Wom Lit; Wom Lit, More

10751. Schuyler, Philippa Duke
1932–1967/69
pianist, composer, author, Vietnam war correspondent

Black
Encyc Black Am; Index t Wom; Negro Alman; Obit File

10752. Terry, Megan
born 1932
musical playwright, dramatist, television and radio scriptwriter
Dict Lit Bio v7

10753. Roxon, Lillian
1933–73
rock music authority and author
Obit File

10754. Sontag, Susan
born 1933
cultural and art critic, essayist, novelist, short story writer, filmmaker
Cur Biog '69; Dict Lit Bio v2; Wom Lit, More

10755. di Prima, Diane
born 1934
poet
Dict Lit Bio v5

10756. Didion, Joan
born 1934
novelist, journalist, screenwriter
California
Cur Biog '78; Dict Lit Bio v2; Wom Lit; Wom Lit, More

10757. Giovanni, Nikki; Yolande Cornelia Giovanni, Jr.
born 1934
poet
Black
Cur Biog '73; Dict Lit Bio v5; Encyc Black Am; Negro Alman; Nort Anth Poet; Wom Lit; Wom Lit, More

10758. MacLaine, Shirley
born 1934
stage and screen actor, dancer, autobiographer, feminist, Democratic party worker, political activist, world traveler
Cur Biog '78; Index t Wom

10759. Millett, Kate
born 1934
philosopher, novelist, feminist leader, writer on sex
Cur Biog '71

10760. Murray, Michele [Judith]
1934–74
novelist, poet, critic
Obit File

10761. Brownmiller, Susan
born 1935
feminist leader, writer on rape and social issues, journalist
Cur Biog '78

10762. Drew, Elizabeth (Brenner)
born 1935
political journalist, writer on American politics
Cur Biog '79

10763. Oliver, Mary
born 1935
poet
Dict Lit Bio v5

10764. Rossner, Judith Perelman
born 1935
novelist
Jewish
New York, NY
Dict Lit Bio v6; Wom Lit; Wom Lit, More

10765. Sanchez, Sonia
born 1935
poet, playwright
Black
Negro Alman; Wom Lit; Wom Lit, More

10766. Burroway, Janet
born 1936
novelist
Dict Lit Bio v6; Wom Lit, More

10767. Clifton, Lucille
born 1936
author, poet
Black
Dict Lit Bio v5; Wom Lit, More

10768. Hochman, Sandra
born 1936
poet, novelist, playwright, magazine writer
Jewish
Dict Lit Bio v5

10769. Sherwin, Judith Johnson
born 1936
poet
Nort Anth Poet

10770. Willard, Nancy
born 1936
poet
Dict Lit Bio v5; Wom Lit, More

10771. Godwin, Gail
born 1937
novelist
Dict Lit Bio v6; Wom Lit; Wom Lit, More

10772. Russ, Joanna
born 1937
speculative fiction author, feminist
Dict Lit Bio v8; Wom Lit, More

10773. Wakowski, Diane
born 1937
poet

California
Dict Lit Bio v5; Nort Anth Poet;
  Wom Lit, More

10774. Blume, Judy (Sussman)
born 1938
writer for children and young
  adults
Jewish
Cur Biog '80

10775. Oates, Joyce Carol
born 1938
poet, novelist, short story writer,
  university educator
Cur Biog '70; Dict Lit Bio v2 and
  v5; Wom Lit; Wom Lit, More

10776. Bambara, Toni Cade
born 1939
short story writer, novelist, educator
Black
Encyc Black Am; Wom Lit; Wom
  Lit, More

10777. Chicago, Judy (Cohen)
born 1939
feminist, autobiographer, sculptor, photographer, painter
Cur Biog '81

10778. Brown, Rita Mae
flourished 1970s–80s
novelist, poet
Wom Lit, More

10779. Saunders, Sally; Sally
  Love Saunders Craigie
born 1940
poet, educator
Episcopalian
Pennsylvania
Nat Cyc Am Bio csv12

10780. Tyler, Anne
born 1941
novelist, short story writer
Cur Biog '81; Dict Lit Bio v6;
  Wom Lit, More

10781. Walker, Alice
born 1941/44
poet, novelist, short story writer
Black
Dict Lit Bio v6; Negro Alman;
  Wom Lit; Wom Lit, More

10782. Jong, Erica (Mann)
born 1942
novelist, poet, feminist
Jewish
New York
Cur Biog '75; Dict Lit Bio v2 and
  v5; Wom Lit; Wom Lit, More

10783. Gluck, Louise
born 1943
poet
Dict Lit Bio v5; Wom Lit, More

10784. Davis, Angela [Yvonne]
born 1944
civil rights worker, politician,
  Communist party presidential
  candidate, political writer, university educator
Black
Cur Biog '72; Encyc Black Am;
  Negro Alman

10785. Sargent, Pamela
born 1948
speculative fiction author, novelist, short story writer, story anthologist, feminist
Dict Lit Bio v8

10786. Shange, Ntzoke
born 1948
poet, playwright, novelist
Black
Cur Biog '78; Wom Lit, More

**10787. Breen, May Sighi; Ma-
lia Rosa**
born 1949
composer, author
Index t Wom

10788. Gordon, Mary
born 1949
novelist, writer on Catholic life
Catholic
Cur Biog '81; Dict Lit Bio v6

10789. Forche, Caroline
born 1950
poet
Michigan
Dict Lit Bio v5

10790. Swados, Elizabeth
born 1951
play score writer, avant-garde
  composer, theatrical director,
  playwright
Jewish
New York
Cur Biog '79

10791. Fowler, Jessie Allen
born 1956
phrenologist, medical author
Nat Cyc Am Bio v16

10792. Mercer, Margaret
1771/92–1845
abolitionist, philanthropist, author
Cyc Am Bio; Dict Am Bio; Dict
  Am Bio Men Time; Index t
  Wom

No Dates

10793. Acosta, Mercedes de
author
Index t Wom

10794. Bates, Sylvia Chatfield
author
Index t Wom

10795. Benet, Laura
poet
Index t Wom

10796. Bristol, Margaret
composer, singer, conductor, music educator, writer on music
Index t Wom

10797. Brooks, Rosa Paul
librettist
Index t Wom

10798. Bush, Grace
composer, pianist, poet, lecturer
Index t Wom

10799. Gilchrist, Beth
  Bradford; Elizabeth Drake;
  John Prescott Earl
author, children's author
Congregationalist
Vermont
Nat Cyc Am Bio v47; Obit File

**10800. Parsons, Harriet Oet-
tinger**
motion picture producer, writer
Index t Wom

10801. Sjursen, Helen Schifano
gymnastics coach and sports author
Hall Fame Sport

MEDIA

10802. Stone, Verlinda Cotton
  Burdette Boughton
flourished circa 1650s
colonial journalist, letter writer
Index t Wom

10803. Goddard, Sarah Updike
circa 1700–70
printer, editor, publisher
Index t Wom; Not Am Wom

10804. Zenger, Catherine
  [Anna]
1704–51
publisher
Index t Wom

10805. Timothy, Elizabeth
died 1757
printer, newspaper publisher and
  editor, journalist
Index t Wom; Not Am Wom

10806. Bradford, Cornelia
  Smith
died 1772/75
colonial publisher
Index t Wom; Not Am Wom

10807. Green, Anne Catherine
died 1775
colonial printer, publisher
Index t Wom

10808. Timothy, Ann Donovan
circa 1727–92
printer, newspaper publisher and
  editor, journalist
Index t Wom; Not Am Wom

10809. Draper, Margaret Green
circa 1730–1807
publisher, printer, journalist
Massachusetts
Dict Am Bio; Index t Wom; Who
  Who Dur Am Rev

**10810. Goddard, Mary Kathe-
rine**
1738–1816
printer, newspaper publisher,
  postmaster of Baltimore, merchant
Catholic
Baltimore, MD
Index t Wom; Not Am Wom

10811. Goddard, Anna
flourished 1770s
printer, publisher
Index t Wom

10812. Hoit, Mary
flourished 1770s
publisher
Index t Wom

10813. Rind, Clementina
circa 1740–74
printer, newspaper editor, publisher
Index t Wom; Not Am Wom

10814. Russell, Sarah
flourished 1790s
printer, publisher
Index t Wom

10815. Hillhouse, Sarah Porter
born 1763
colonial editor, publisher
Index t Wom

10816. Royall, Anne Newport
1769–1854
traveler, journalist, newspaper ed-
  itor and publisher, novelist
Washington, DC; Virginia
Am Bio Dict; Cyc Am Bio; Dict
  Am Auth; Dict Am Bio; Dict
  Am Bio Men Time; Encyc
  South Hist; Index t Wom; Not
  Am Wom

10817. Barber, Ann
flourished 1800s
publisher
Index t Wom

10818. Holt, Elizabeth Hunter
1781–85 [*sic*]

printer, publisher
Index t Wom

10819. Leslie, Eliza
1787–1858
cookbook writer, children's author, humorist, short story writer, editor
Philadelphia, PA
Cyc Am Bio; Dict Am Auth; Dict Am Bio; Dict Am Bio Men Time; Index t Wom; Nat Cyc Am Bio v7; Not Am Wom

10820. Hale, Sarah Josepha (Buell)
1788/90–1879/97
magazine editor, author
Philadelphia, PA
Cyc Am Bio; Dict Am Auth; Dict Am Bio; Dict Am Bio Men Time; Dict Lit Bio v1; Index t Wom; Nat Cyc Am Bio v3 and v22; Not Am Wom; Twent Cen Bio Dict Not Am; Wom Lit, More

10821. Whittlesey, Abigail Goodrich
1788–1858
educator, magazine editor, author
Connecticut
Cyc Am Bio; Dict Am Bio; Not Am Wom

10822. Buell, Sarah
flourished 1820s
author, editor
Index t Wom

10823. Parsons, Augustina
flourished 1820s
publisher
Index t Wom

10824. Gilman, Caroline (Howard)
1794–1888
author, poet, editor, domestic novelist
Charleston, SC
Cyc Am Bio; Dict Am Auth; Dict Am Bio; Dict Am Bio Men Time; Dict Lit Bio v3; Index t Wom; Nat Cyc Am Bio v6; Not Am Wom; Twent Cen Bio Dict Not Am

10825. Hutchinson, Ellen MacKay
born 18?
literary journalist
New York, NY
Dict Am Auth

10826. McCracken, Elizabeth
born 18?
journalist
New York, NY
Dict Am Auth

10827. Merrill, Margaret Manton
born 18?
journalist, temperance worker, Sorosis member
English
Wom Cent

10828. White, Sarah Elizabeth [Joy]
born 18?
journalist
Boston, MA
Dict Am Auth

10829. Gibbons, Abigail Hopper "Abby"
1801–93
abolitionist, prison reformer, feminist, women's welfare worker, Civil War nurse, philanthropist, journalist
Quaker
Cyc Am Bio; Dict Am Bio; Index t Wom; Nat Cyc Am Bio v7; Not Am Wom; Twent Cen Bio Dict Not Am; Wom Cent

10830. Kirkland, Caroline Matilda (Stansbury)
1801–64
miscellaneous writer, editor, journalist, writer on pioneering
New York, NY
Cyc Am Bio; Dict Am Auth; Dict Am Bio; Dict Am Bio Men Time; Dict Lit Bio v3; Index t Wom; Nat Cyc Am Bio v5; Not Am Wom; Twent Cen Bio Dict Not Am

10831. Child, Lydia Maria (Francis)
1802–80
author, philanthropist, abolitionist, editor, social reformer
Quaker
Massachusetts
Cyc Am Bio; Dict Am Auth; Dict Am Bio; Dict Am Bio Men Time; Dict Lit Bio v1; Index t Wom; Nat Cyc Am Bio v2; Not Am Wom; Twent Cen Bio Dict Not Am; Wom Cent

10832. Day, Olivia
died 1853
editor
Index t Wom

10833. Martin, Sarah Towne (Smith); Sarah Martyn
1805–79
historian, religious and historical writer for children, editor, abolitionist, temperance worker
New York, NY
Cyc Am Bio; Dict Am Auth; Dict Am Bio; Twent Cen Bio Dict Not Am

10834. Cazneau, Jane Maria Eliza McManus Storms
1807–78
journalist, publicist, expansionist
Not Am Wom

10835. Conant, Hannah O'Brian (Chaplin)
1809–65
religious worker, translator, Oriental scholar and language expert, magazine editor
Cyc Am Bio; Dict Am Auth; Dict Am Bio; Dict Am Bio Men Time; Nat Cyc Am Bio v22; Not Am Wom; Twent Cen Bio Dict Not Am

10836. Fuller, Sarah Margaret; Marchioness Ossoli; Sarah Margaret Fuller Ossoli
1810–50
author, critic, educator, feminist, philosopher, journalist, Transcendentalist revolutionary
Transcendentalist
Boston, MA
Cyc Am Bio; Dict Am Auth; Dict Am Bio; Dict Am Bio Men Time; Dict Lit Bio v1; Index t Wom; Nat Cyc Am Bio v3; Not Am Wom; Twent Cen Bio Dict Not Am; Wom Cent

10837. Nichols, Clarinda Irene Howard
1810–85
newspaper editor, political writer, social reformer, lecturer, women's rights leader, suffragist, feminist
Kansas
Cyc Am Bio; Dict Am Bio; Index t Wom; Nat Cyc Am Bio v5; Not Am Wom

10838. Stephens, Anna Sophia (Winterbotham); Jonathan Slick
1810/13–1886
author, poet, novelist, serial fiction writer, editor
New York, NY
Cyc Am Bio; Dict Am Auth; Dict Am Bio; Dict Am Bio Men Time; Dict Lit Bio v8; Index t Wom; Nat Cyc Am Bio v10; Not Am Wom; Twent Cen Bio Dict Not Am; Wom Lit, More

10839. Parton, Sarah Payson (Willis); Fanny Fern
1811–72

author, newspaper columnist, magazine writer, novelist, club-woman
Cyc Am Bio; Dict Am Auth; Dict Am Bio; Dict Am Bio Men Time; Index t Wom; Nat Cyc Am Bio v1; Not Am Wom; Twent Cen Bio Dict Not Am; Wom Cent; Wom Lit; Wom Lit, More

10840. Whitcher, Frances Miriam (Berry); Widow Bedott
1811/14–1857/67
author, humorist, caricaturist
New York
Cyc Am Bio; Dict Am Auth; Dict Am Bio; Index t Wom; Nat Cyc Am Bio v6; Not Am Wom; Twent Cen Bio Dict Not Am

10841. Bailey, Margaret L.
born 1812
poet, journalist
Index t Wom

10842. Sawyer, Caroline Mehitabel (Fisher)
1812–94
author, editor, poetry anthologist, poet, translator
Dict Am Auth; Index t Wom; Not Am Wom; Twent Cen Bio Dict Not Am

10843. Saxe, Caroline Mehetabel
1812–94
author, editor
Massachusetts
Cyc Am Bio

10844. Curtis, Harriot F.
1813–89
magazine editor, novelist, journalist, club leader
Dict Am Auth; Index t Wom

10845. Davis, Pauline Kellog Wright
1813–76
feminist, women's rights worker, suffragist, abolitionist, temperance worker, journalist, editor, lecturer
Cyc Am Bio; Dict Am Bio; Index t Wom; Nat Cyc Am Bio v22; Not Am Wom

10846. Farley, Harriet
1813/17–1907
millworker, writer on women in the textile mills, children's author, editor
New Hampshire
Cyc Am Bio; Dict Am Auth; Dict Am Bio; Dict Am Bio Men Time; Nat Cyc Am Bio v11; Not Am Wom

10847. Walter, Cornelia Wells
1813?–98

journalist
Not Am Wom

10848. Rea, Julia (de Marguerittes) (Foster)
1814–66
opera singer, drama critic, writer on Europe
Philadelphia, PA
English
Cyc Am Bio; Dict Am Auth; Dict Am Bio Men Time

10849. Wells, Charlotte Fowler
1814–1901
phrenologist, patron of women's medical education, educator, publisher, lecturer, businessperson
New York
Cyc Am Bio; Index t Wom; Not Am Wom; Wom Cent

10850. Cutler, Hannah Maria (Conant) (Tracy)
1815–96
women's rights leader, suffragist, physician, journalist, author, lecturer, pacifist
Illinois
Cyc Am Bio ad; Dict Am Auth; Index t Wom; Not Am Wom; Twent Cen Bio Dict Not Am

10851. Ottendorfer, Anna Sartorius (Behr) Uhl
1815–84
newspaper publisher, philanthropist
Dict Am Bio; Nat Cyc Am Bio v8; Not Am Wom; Twent Cen Bio Dict Not Am

10852. Stanton, Elizabeth Cady
1815/16–1902
feminist, suffragist, women's rights worker, editor, author, social reformer, theologian
Cyc Am Bio; Dict Am Auth; Dict Am Bio; Dict Am Bio Men Time; Dict Am Rel Bio; Index t Wom; Nat Cyc Am Bio v3; Not Am Wom; Twent Cen Bio Dict Not Am; Wom Cent

10853. Swisshelm, Jane (Grey) (Cannon)
1815/16–1884
journalist, author, editor, publisher, abolitionist, women's rights worker, Civil War nurse
Cyc Am Bio; Dict Am Auth; Dict Am Bio; Dict Am Bio Men Time; Index t Wom; Nat Cyc Am Bio v2; Not Am Wom

10854. Thomas, Mary Frame (Myers)
1816–88
physician, suffragist, women's rights worker, prison reformer, temperance worker, editor
Index t Wom; Not Am Wom; Twent Cen Bio Dict Not Am

10855. Johnson, Nancy Cummings; Minnie Myrtle
1818–92
journalist
Index t Wom

10856. Stone, Lucy; Mrs. Henry Brown Blackwell
1818–93
feminist, suffragist, women's rights worker, abolitionist, social reformer, editor, lecturer
Massachusetts
Cyc Am Bio; Dict Am Bio; Dict Am Bio Men Time; Index t Wom; Nat Cyc Am Bio v2 and v29; Not Am Wom; Twent Cen Bio Dict Not Am; Wom Cent

10857. Arey, Harriet Ellen (Grannis)
1819–post 1888
poet, education writer, educator, magazine editor
Appl Cyc Am Bio; Cyc Am Bio; Dict Am Auth; Dict Am Bio Men Time; Wom Cent

10858. Anthony, Susan Brownell
1820–1906
women's suffrage leader, feminist, abolitionist, newspaper publisher, editor
Quaker
Appl Cyc Am Bio; Cyc Am Bio; Dict Am Bio; Dict Am Bio Men Time; Index t Wom; Nat Cyc Am Bio v4; Not Am Wom; Twent Cen Bio Dict Not Am; Wom Cent

10859. Miller, Mary A.
flourished 1850s–80s
editor of a missionary newspaper
Wom Cent

10860. Swain, Adeline Morrison
born 1820
suffragist, politician, newspaper political editor, superintendent of public education, Greenback party worker
Iowa
Wom Cent

10861. Neal, Alice B.
married 1846
author, editor
Index t Wom

10862. Clarke, Mary Bayard (Devereaux)
1822/27–1886
author, editor, poet

North Carolina
Cyc Am Bio; Dict Am Auth; Dict Am Bio; Nat Cyc Am Bio v8; Not Am Wom; Twent Cen Bio Dict Not Am

10863. Cary, Mary Ann Shad
1823–93
educator, lawyer, journalist, editor, abolitionist, Canadian pioneer
Black; Canadian
Index t Wom; Negro Alman; Not Am Wom; Prof Negro Wom

10864. Lippincott, Sarah Jane (Clarke); Grace Greenwood
1823–1904
newspaper journalist, lecturer, author, editor, novelist, feminist, poet, children's author
Philadelphia, PA
Cyc Am Bio; Dict Am Auth; Dict Am Bio; Dict Am Bio Men Time; Index t Wom; Nat Cyc Am Bio v4; Not Am Wom; Twent Cen Bio Dict Not Am; Wom Cent

10865. Stephens, Harriet Marion
1823–1850/58
author, domestic writer, novelist, editor
Cyc Am Bio; Dict Am Auth; Dict Am Bio Men Time

10866. Blake, Euphemia Vale
1824/25–1904
author, historian, literary and art critic
Dict Am Auth; Wom Cent

10867. Larcom, Lucy
1824/26–1893
millworker, author, poet, magazine editor, seminary teacher
Beverly, MA
Cyc Am Bio; Dict Am Auth; Dict Am Bio Men Time; Index t Wom; Nat Cyc Am Bio v1; Not Am Wom; Twent Cen Bio Dict Not Am; Wom Cent

10868. Steele, Rowena Granice
born 1824
journalist, author
California
Wom Cent

10869. French, Lucy Virginia (Smith)
1825/30–1881
poet, author, editor, educator
Memphis, TN
Cyc Am Bio; Dict Am Auth; Dict Am Bio; Nat Cyc Am Bio v7

10870. Robinson, Harriet Jane (Hanson)
1825–1911

suffragist, women's rights worker, feminist, abolitionist, author, poet, dramatist, journalist, merchant
Malden, MA
Cyc Am Bio; Dict Am Auth; Dict Am Bio; Index t Wom; Nat Cyc Am Bio v3; Not Am Wom; Wom Cent

10871. Davis, Varina Howell
1826–1909
Civil War diarist, journalist, Confederate patriot of Civil War
Bio Dict Confed; Encyc South Hist; Index t Wom; Wom Cent

10872. Lamb, Martha Joanna Read (Nash)
1826/29–1893
author, children's author, novelist, New York historian, editor
New York
Cyc Am Bio; Dict Am Auth; Dict Am Bio; Index t Wom; Nat Cyc Am Bio v1; Not Am Wom; Twent Cen Bio Dict Not Am; Wom Cent

10873. McDowell, Anne Elizabeth
1826–1901
editor, journalist
Not Am Wom

10874. Wood, Julia Amanda A. (Sargent); Minnie Mary Lee
born 1826
author, postmaster, pioneer, Minnesota newspaper editor, Catholic novelist
Catholic
Sauk Rapids, MN
Dict Am Auth; Index t Wom; Not Am Wom; Wom Cent

10875. Belcher, Cynthia Holmes
born 1827
journalist, suffragist, temperance worker
Boston, MA
Wom Cent

10876. Doggett, Kate Newell
1827/28–1884
suffragist, educator, art critic, translator
Cyc Am Bio; Index t Wom

10877. Haven, Alice Bradley; Emily Bradley Neal Haven; Alice G. Lee; Cousin Alice
1827/28–1863
author, children's author, magazine editor
Cyc Am Bio; Dict Am Auth; Dict Am Bio; Dict Am Bio Men Time; Nat Cyc Am Bio v5; Not Am Wom; Twent Cen Bio Dict Not Am

10878. Battey, Emily Verdery
born 1828
journalist, women's historian
Wom Cent

10879. Bowen, Eliza Andrews
1828–98
newspaper and magazine writer, writer about astronomy
Georgia
Dict Am Auth

10880. Hemenway, Abby Maria
1828–90
Vermont historian, anthologist, author
Vermont
Dict Am Auth; Not Am Wom; Twent Cen Bio Dict Not Am

10881. Morgan, Maria "Middy"
1828–92
journalist, authority on horses and cattle
Irish
Index t Wom; Wom Cent

10882. Robinson, Abbie C. B.
born 1828
editor, Democratic newspaper publisher, political author
Wisconsin
Index t Wom; Wom Cent

10883. Wells, Emmeline Blanchard Woodward
1828–1921
leader of Mormon women, feminist, suffragist, editor, poet
Mormon
Utah
Cyc Am Bio; Not Am Wom

10884. Brooks, Marie Sears
flourished 1859; died 1893
poet, short story writer, journalist, newspaper editor, suffragist
Index t Wom; Wom Cent

10885. Croly, Jane Cunningham "Jean" "Jennie"; Jennie June
1829/31–1901
journalist, magazine editor, women's club leader, Sorosis member
Cyc Am Bio; Dict Am Auth; Dict Am Bio; Index t Wom; Nat Cyc Am Bio v6; Not Am Wom; Twent Cen Bio Dict Not Am; Wom Cent

10886. Hanaford, Phoebe Ann (Coffin)
1829–1921
Universalist minister, historian, journalist, author, feminist, lecturer, chaplain of the Connecticut state legislature
Universalist

New Haven, CT
Cyc Am Bio; Dict Am Auth; Dict Am Bio; Index t Wom; Nat Cyc Am Bio v13; Not Am Wom; Twent Cen Bio Dict Not Am; Wom Cent

10887. Sherwood, Emily Lee; Jennie Crayon
born 1829/43
journalist, novelist, author
Washington, DC
Dict Am Auth; Index t Wom; Wom Cent

10888. Taylor, Martha Smith
born 1829
author, newspaper correspondent, temperance worker
Wom Cent

10889. Waite, Catharine (Van Valkenburg)
1829–1913
suffragist, women's rights advocate, lawyer, legal journalist, financier, real estate and building executive, writer on Mormonism
Chicago, IL
Cyc Am Bio; Dict Am Auth; Not Am Wom; Wom Cent

10890. Briggs, Emily Pomona Edson; Olivia
1830–1910
journalist
Not Am Wom

10891. Conner, Eliza Archard; "Zig"; E. A.
flourished 1860s–80s
journalist, lecturer, women's rights worker
New York
Wom Cent

10892. Dodge, Mary Abigail "Abby"; Gail Hamilton
1830/36–1896
author, essayist, humorist, magazine writer, editor, abolitionist, suffragist, women's rights worker
Massachusetts
Cyc Am Bio; Dict Am Auth; Dict Am Bio; Dict Am Bio Men Time; Index t Wom; Nat Cyc Am Bio v9; Not Am Wom; Twent Cen Bio Dict Not Am; Wom Cent

10893. Fisher, Rebecca Jane Gilleland
born 183?; married 1848
philanthropist, journalist, pioneer
Austin, TX
Index t Wom; Wom Cent

10894. Miller, Dora Richards
flourished 1860s–80s

author, Civil War diarist, journalist, educator
West Indian (Danish West Indies)
Index t Wom; Wom Cent

10895. Smith, Emily L. Goodrich; Peter Parley
born 1830
club leader, newspaper foreign correspondent
Index t Wom; Wom Cent

10896. Terhune, Mary Virginia (Hawes); Marian Harland
1830/35–1922
popular novelist, writer on household affairs, historian, cookbook author, editor, publisher
New York, NY
Cyc Am Bio; Dict Am Auth; Dict Am Bio Men Time; Index t Wom; Nat Cyc Am Bio v1; Not Am Wom; Twent Cen Bio Dict Not Am; Wom Cent

10897. Townsend, Virginia Frances
1830/36–1914/20
author, novelist, children's author, editor
Cyc Am Bio; Dict Am Auth; Dict Am Bio; Index t Wom; Nat Cyc Am Bio v13; Twent Cen Bio Dict Not Am

10898. Ames, Mary E. Clemmer; Mrs. Hudson
1831/40–1884
journalist, biographer, author
Washington, DC
Appl Cyc Am Bio; Cyc Am Bio; Index t Wom; Nat Cyc Am Bio v7; Not Am Wom; Twent Cen Bio Dict Not Am

10899. Booth, Mary Louisa
1831–89
historian, journalist, translator, author, editor of *Harper's Bazaar*, women's labor worker
Cyc Am Bio; Dict Am Auth; Dict Am Bio; Dict Am Bio Men Time; Index t Wom; Nat Cyc Am Bio v7; Not Am Wom; Twent Cen Bio Dict Not Am; Wom Cent

10900. Bradwell, Myra R. (Colby)
1831–1894/96
lawyer, suffragist, editor, Civil War nurse
Chicago, IL
Dict Am Bio; Index t Wom; Nat Cyc Am Bio v1; Not Am Wom; Twent Cen Bio Dict Not Am; Wom Cent

10901. Dodge, Mary Elizabeth Mapes
1831/38–1905
children's author, poet, editor
New York
Cyc Am Bio; Dict Am Auth; Dict Am Bio; Index t Wom; Nat Cyc Am Bio v1; Not Am Wom; Twent Cen Bio Dict Not Am; Wom Cent

10902. Lockwood, Mary Smith
born 1831
editor, clubwoman, patriot, writer on art and architecture
Dict Am Auth; Index t Wom; Nat Cyc Am Bio v3

10903. Lyman, Laura Elizabeth Baker
born 1831
journalist, business executive
Cyc Am Bio; Index t Wom

10904. Perry, Nora
1831/41–1896
poet, children's author, journalist
Boston, MA
Cyc Am Bio; Dict Am Auth; Dict Am Bio; Index t Wom; Nat Cyc Am Bio v15; Twent Cen Bio Dict Not Am; Wom Cent

10905. Allen, Elizabeth Anne Chase (Akers); Florence Percyips
1832–1911
poet, journalist, author, Sorosis Club member
Appl Cyc Am Bio; Cyc Am Bio; Dict Am Auth; Index t Wom; Nat Cyc Am Bio v6; Not Am Wom; Twent Cen Bio Dict Not Am; Wom Cent

10906. Magill, Mary Tucker
1832–99
fiction writer, journalist, educator
Winchester, VA
Cyc Am Bio; Dict Am Auth; Twent Cen Bio Dict Not Am

10907. Aiken, Amanda L.
1833–92
philanthropist, editor, patron of women's education
Index t Wom; Wom Cent

10908. Churchill, Caroline M.
born 1833
newspaper editor, publisher, journalist, political activist
Wom Cent

10909. Gray, Mary Tenney
born 1833
philanthropist, journalist, editorial writer
Kansas
Wom Cent

10910. Hallowell, Sarah Catherine (Fraley)
born 1833
journalist, newspaper editor
Philadelphia, PA
Dict Am Auth

10911. Miller, Emily Clark Huntington
1833–1913
author, children's author, journalist, editor, poet, semireligious-fiction writer, church worker, temperance worker, educator
Evanston, IL
Dict Am Auth; Dict Am Bio; Index t Wom; Not Am Wom; Twent Cen Bio Dict Not Am; Wom Cent

10912. Poole, Hester Martha (Hunt)
born 1833/43
author, poet, writer on social and domestic issues, art critic, artist, women's rights worker, Sorosis member
Metuchen, NJ
Dict Am Auth; Nat Cyc Am Bio v11; Wom Cent

10913. Duniway, Abigail Jane Scott
1834–1915
pioneer, suffrage leader, feminist, journalist, editor, lecturer
Oregon
Dict Am Bio; Index t Wom; Not Am Wom; Wom Cent

10914. Gregory, Elizabeth Goadby
born 1834
author, translator of French and German literature, journalist, writer on industrial and social topics
Wom Cent

10915. Pollard, Josephine
1834/42–1892
children's author, journalist, poet
Cyc Am Bio; Dict Am Auth; Index t Wom; Twent Cen Bio Dict Not Am; Wom Cent

10916. Read, Elizabeth C. Bunnell "Lizzie B."
born 1834
journalist, suffragist
Methodist
Wom Cent

10917. Rose, Martha E. (Parmelee)
born 1834
women's labor welfare worker, social reformer, sociologist, author, art patron, journalist, Sorosis member

Cleveland, OH
Index t Wom; Nat Cyc Am Bio v11; Wom Cent

10918. Felton, Rebecca Ann Latimer
1835–1930
senator from Georgia, labor welfare worker, journalist, author, orator, feminist, women's rights worker
Georgia
Dict Am Bio; Encyc South Hist; Index t Wom; Nat Cyc Am Bio v13 and v36; Not Am Wom; Wom Cent

10919. Hooper, Lucy Hamilton
1835–93
poet, dramatist, editor, journalist
Cyc Am Bio; Dict Am Bio; Nat Cyc Am Bio v8; Twent Cen Bio Dict Not Am; Wom Cent

10920. Johnston, Maria I.
born 1835
author, newspaper editor, women's rights worker
Mississippi
Index t Wom; Wom Cent

10921. Jordan, Dulcie (Mason)
1835–95
journalist, poet
Richmond, IN
Dict Am Auth

10922. Larned, Augusta
born 1835
author, journalist, poet, women's rights worker
New York, NY
Cyc Am Bio; Dict Am Auth; Nat Cyc Am Bio v13; Twent Cen Bio Dict Not Am

10923. Buchanan, Anna Elizabeth
born 1836
editor
Index t Wom

10924. Duhring, Julia
1836–92
author of critical essays
Dict Am Auth; Twent Cen Bio Dict Not Am

10925. Leslie, Miriam Florence (Folline); Frank K. Leslie
1836/51–1914
magazine editor, publisher, feminist, philanthropist
New York
Cyc Am Bio; Dict Am Bio; Index t Wom; Nat Cyc Am Bio v25; Not Am Wom; Twent Cen Bio Dict Not Am; Wom Cent

10926. Prang, Mary Amelia [Dana] Hicks
1836–1927

art educator, writer on art, editor
Dict Am Bio; Index t Wom; Nat Cyc Am Bio v27; Not Am Wom; Twent Cen Bio Dict Not Am

10927. Preston, Harriet Waters
1836/43–1911
author, literary critic, translator, literary historian
Cyc Am Bio; Dict Am Auth; Dict Am Bio; Nat Cyc Am Bio v8

10928. Scripps, Ellen Browning
1836–1932
philanthropist, newspaper writer and publisher, patron of marine science, founder of Scripps Marine Lab, pacifist, feminist, temperance worker
La Jolla, CA
Dict Am Bio; Index t Wom; Nat Cyc Am Bio v27; Not Am Wom

10929. Herrick, Sophia McIlvaine (Bledsoe)
1837–1919
science editor, natural scientist, microscopist, botanist, science writer
Cyc Am Bio; Dict Am Auth; Dict Am Bio; Twent Cen Bio Dict Not Am

10930. Houghton, Mary Hayes
born 1837
journalist
Ohio
Wom Cent

10931. Logan, Celia (Kellog) (Connelly)
1837/40–1904
journalist, author, dramatist
Washington, DC
Cyc Am Bio; Dict Am Auth; Index t Wom; Twent Cen Bio Dict Not Am; Wom Cent

10932. Pratt, Eliza Ella Anna Farman
1837–1907
children's magazine editor, children's author
Dict Am Auth; Dict Am Bio

10933. West, Mary Allen
1837–92
educator, temperance worker, writer on education and child care, journalist
Illinois
Cyc Am Bio; Dict Am Auth; Index t Wom; Wom Cent

10934. Wyman, Lillie Buffum Chace
born 1837/47
author, muckraking journalist, short story writer, philanthropist, suffragist, labor welfare worker

Georgia
Dict Am Auth; Wom Cent

10935. Bates, Charlotte Fiske; Madame Roge
1838–1916
poet, poetry editor, author
Appl Cyc Am Bio; Cyc Am Bio; Index t Wom; Twent Cen Bio Dict Not Am

10936. Bierce, Sara Elizabeth
born 1838
journalist
Wom Cent

10937. Bryan, Mary (Edwards)
1838/46–1913
journalist, author, editor, poet, clubwoman
Atlanta, GA; New York, NY
Cyc Am Bio; Dict Am Bio; Index t Wom; Nat Cyc Am Bio v8; Not Am Wom; Twent Cen Bio Dict Not Am; Wom Cent

10938. Emery, Sarah Elizabeth van de Vort
1838–95
Greenback party and Populist party worker, political journalist
Not Am Wom

10939. Field, Mary Katherine Kemble "Kate"
1838/54–1896
journalist, actor, playwright, literary critic, lecturer
Washington, DC
Cyc Am Bio; Dict Am Auth; Dict Am Bio; Index t Wom; Nat Cyc Am Bio v6; Not Am Wom; Twent Cen Bio Dict Not Am; Wom Cent

10940. Gordon, Laura de Force
1838/40–1907
lawyer, journalist, suffragist, women's rights worker, Democratic politician, orator
California
Dict Am Bio; Index t Wom; Nat Cyc Am Bio v1; Not Am Wom; Wom Cent

10941. Greene, Aella
1838–1903
journalist, poet
Springfield, MA
Dict Am Auth

10942. Hickman, Mary Catharine
born 1838
journalist, temperance worker
Ohio
Wom Cent

10943. Houghton, Louise Seymour
born 1838

religious magazine editor, translator, religious author
New York, NY
Dict Am Auth

10944. Lincoln, Martha D.;
Bessie Beech
born 1838
author, journalist
Wom Cent

10945. Logan, Mary Simmerson Cunningham
1838–1923
political mover, author, magazine editor, pioneer
Cyc Am Bio; Not Am Wom; Wom Cent

10946. Rawlins, Judy
1838–1974
television actor
Obit File

10947. Roge, Charlotte Fiske (Bates)
born 1838
author, poet, literary critic, educator
New York
Dict Am Auth; Wom Cent

10948. Sangster, Margaret Elizabeth (Munson)
1838–1912
editor of *Harper's Bazaar*, author, poet, journalist
New York, NY
Cyc Am Bio and ad; Dict Am Auth; Index t Wom; Nat Cyc Am Bio v6; Not Am Wom; Twent Cen Bio Dict Not Am; Wom Cent

10949. Stockton, Louise
1838–1914
editor, journalist, novelist, critic, historian, social worker
Philadelphia, PA
Dict Am Auth; Index t Wom; Nat Cyc Am Bio v8; Twent Cen Bio Dict Not Am

10950. Underwood, Sara H. (Francis)
born 1838
free thought journal editor, author
Dict Am Auth

10951. Campbell, Helen (Stuart)
1839–1918
journalist, children's author, social reformer, home economist, educator, philanthropist
New York
Cyc Am Bio; Dict Am Auth; Nat Cyc Am Bio v9; Not Am Wom; Twent Cen Bio Dict Not Am; Wom Cent

10952. Freeman, Mattie A.
born 1839
abolitionist, suffragist, women's rights worker, lecturer, journalist
Chicago, IL
Wom Cent

10953. Hudson, Mary (Clemmer) (Ames)
1839/40–1884
journalist, poet
Washington, DC
Dict Am Auth; Wom Cent

10954. Logan, Olive
1839/41–1909
actor, dramatist, lecturer, women's rights reformer, author, journalist
Cyc Am Bio; Dict Am Bio; Dict Am Bio Men Time; Index t Wom; Nat Cyc Am Bio v6; Not Am Wom; Twent Cen Bio Dict Not Am

10955. Molloy, Emma
born 1839
social reformer, editor, printer
Index t Wom

10956. Palmer, Frances Purdy "Fannie"
1839–1923
author, journalist, lecturer, suffragist, feminist
Providence, RI
Dict Am Auth; Index t Wom; Wom Cent

10957. Smith, Helen Evertson
born 1839
editor, journalist
Index t Wom

10958. Tilton, Lydia H.
born 1839
journalist, temperance worker
Wom Cent

10959. van Marter, Martha
born 1839
editor of Sunday school magazines
Methodist
Dict Am Auth

10960. Willard, Frances Elizabeth Caroline
1839–98
educator, educational philosopher, suffragist, feminist, women's rights worker, temperance leader, naturalist, philanthropist, newspaper editor, traveler
Methodist Episcopal
Cyc Am Bio; Dict Am Auth; Dict Am Bio; Dict Am Bio Men Time; Dict Am Rel Bio; Index t Wom; Nat Cyc Am Bio v1; Not Am Wom; Twent Cen Bio Dict Not Am; Wom Cent

10961. Andrews, Eliza Frances
1840/47–1931
journalist, Civil War diarist, educator, botanist
Georgia
Dict Am Auth; Index t Wom; Nat Cyc Am Bio v6; Not Am Wom; Wom Cent

10962. Bonham, Mildred A.
born 1840
traveler, journalist, social reformer
Index t Wom; Wom Cent

10963. Caldwell, Mira
flourished 1870s–80s
editor
Index t Wom

10964. Cole, Miriam M.
flourished 1870s–80s
lecturer, feminist, author, journalist
Index t Wom

10965. Cory, Fanny Young
flourished 1870s
illustrator, cartoonist
Index t Wom

10966. Dickinson, Susan E.
flourished 1870s–90s
journalist, author
Quaker
Pennsylvania
Index t Wom; Wom Cent

10967. Goodrich, Abigail Whittlesey
flourished 1870s
editor
Index t Wom

10968. Hallowell, R. C.
flourished 1870s–80s
editor
Index t Wom

10969. Hawley, Maria
flourished 1870s
publisher
Index t Wom

10970. Hill, Eliza Trask
born 1840
suffragist, women's welfare worker, journalist, newspaper publisher, political activist, Prohibitionist
Massachusetts
Wom Cent

10971. Joy, Sally
flourished 1870s
journalist
Index t Wom

10972. MacDowell, Annie A. E.
flourished 1870s

editor, publisher
Index t Wom

10973. McPherson, Lydia Starr
flourished 1870s–90s
poet, author, journalist, newspaper publisher
Texas
Wom Cent

10974. Pritchard, Esther Tuttle
born 1840
editor, educator, minister, temperance worker, missionary
Index t Wom; Wom Cent

10975. Pry, Polly
flourished 1870s–90s
journalist
Index t Wom

10976. Rathbun, Harriet M.
born 1840
author, businessperson, journalist, magazine publisher and editor
Wom Cent

10977. Searing, Laura Catherine (Redden); Howard Glyndon
1840–1923
author, war correspondent, journalist, poet
deaf
Cyc Am Bio; Dict Am Auth; Dict Am Bio; Dict Am Bio Men Time; Index t Wom; Nat Cyc Am Bio v9; Wom Cent

10978. Wakefield, Emily Watkins
flourished 1870s–90s
singer, educator, lecturer, musical director
Pennsylvania
English
Wom Cent

10979. Wixon, Susan Helen
flourished 1870s–90s
author, children's editor, educator, feminist
Massachusetts
Wom Cent

10980. Wood, Mary C. Foster; Camilla K. von K.; Mary C. F. Hall-Wood
flourished 1870s–90s
poet, editor, author
California
Wom Cent

10981. Young, Carrie
flourished 1870s
editor
Index t Wom

10982. Moore, Annie Aubertine (Woodward); Aubertine Forestier
1841–1929
pianist, student of Scandinavian music, music critic, lecturer, author, translator of Scandinavian languages
Dict Am Auth; Dict Am Bio; Index t Wom; Twent Cen Bio Dict Not Am; Wom Cent

10983. Pool, Maria Louisa
1841/45–1898
author, novelist, writer for the *New York Tribune*
Rockland, MA
Dict Am Auth; Index t Wom; Nat Cyc Am Bio v6; Twent Cen Bio Dict Not Am

10984. Sherwood, Katharine Margaret (Brownlee) "Kate"
1841/43–1914
journalist, newspaper editor, poet, author, clubwoman, suffragist
Canton, OH
Dict Am Auth; Dict Am Bio; Index t Wom; Nat Cyc Am Bio v1; Not Am Wom; Twent Cen Bio Dict Not Am; Wom Cent

10985. Thomas, Mary Ann (Lane)
born 1841
journalist, newspaper editor and publisher
Tennessee
Wom Cent

10986. Willard, Mary Bannister
born 1841
temperance worker, educator, newspaper editor
Methodist
Wom Cent

10987. Conant, Frances Augusta
born 1842
journalist, businessperson, founder of a women's employment company
Wom Cent

10988. Dare, Ella
born 1842
lecturer, journalist, Civil War relief worker, sanitarian
Wom Cent

10989. Farmer, Lydia (Hoyt)
1842/43–1903
religious author, journalist
Cleveland, OH
Dict Am Auth; Index t Wom; Nat Cyc Am Bio v8; Twent Cen Bio Dict Not Am; Wom Cent

10990. Hill, Agnes Leonard (Scanland); Molly Myrtle
1842–1917
poet, author, newspaper publisher, religious writer, novelist, prisoner's welfare worker, Universalist pastor
Universalist
Colorado
Dict Am Auth; Index t Wom; Nat Cyc Am Bio v17; Wom Cent

10991. Monroe, Harriet Earhart
born 1842
lecturer, educator, journalist
Kansas; Washington, DC
Dict Am Auth; Wom Cent

10992. Rollins, Alice Marland (Wellington)
1842/47–1897
author, poet, muckraking journalist
New York, NY
Cyc Am Bio; Dict Am Auth; Dict Am Bio; Nat Cyc Am Bio v8; Twent Cen Bio Dict Not Am; Wom Cent

10993. Thompson, Eva Griffith
born 1842
temperance worker, Presbyterian missionary worker, newspaper editor and publisher
Presbyterian
Pennsylvania
Wom Cent

10994. Winkler, Angelina Virginia
born 1842
journalist
Texas
Wom Cent

10995. Aldrich, Josephine Cables
born 1843
newspaper publisher, editor, author, philanthropist
Nat Cyc Am Bio v5; Wom Cent

10996. Burt, Mary Towne
flourished 1873
temperance worker, publisher
Protestant Episcopal
New York
Index t Wom; Wom Cent

10997. Johnson, Helen Louise (Kendrick)
1843–1917
miscellaneous writer, children's author, editor
Cyc Am Bio; Dict Am Auth; Dict Am Bio; Nat Cyc Am Bio v1; Twent Cen Bio Dict Not Am

10998. Tileston, Mary Wilder
born 1843

anthologist
Twent Cen Bio Dict Not Am

10999. Ferree, Susan Frances Nelson
born 1844
journalist, temperance worker, suffragist, women's rights worker
Episcopalian
Iowa
Wom Cent

11000. Loud, Hulda Barker
born 1844
editor, publisher, women's rights worker, suffragist, labor worker, lecturer
Index t Wom; Wom Cent

11001. Messenger, Lilian Rozell
born 1844/53
journalist, poet
Dict Am Auth; Twent Cen Bio Dict Not Am; Wom Cent

11002. Stevens, Alzina Parsons
1844/49–1900
labor leader, industrial reformer, settlement house worker, social reformer, newspaper editor and publisher, journalist, author
Chicago, IL
Index t Wom; Not Am Wom; Wom Cent

11003. Towne, Belle Kellogg
born 1844
author, journalist
Wom Cent

11004. Alrich, Emma B.
born 1845
journalist, author, educator
Wom Cent

11005. Barrows, Katherine Isabel Hayes Chapin
1845–1913
ophthalmologist, penologist, editor, travel writer
Dict Am Auth; Index t Wom; Not Am Wom

11006. Charles, Emily Thornton; Emily Thornton
1845–90s
poet, journalist
Dict Am Auth; Twent Cen Bio Dict Not Am; Wom Cent

11007. Claflin, Tennessee Celeste
1845/46–1923
social reformer, feminist, stockbroker, newspaper editor, journalist
Index t Wom; Not Am Wom

11008. Fifield, Stella A. Gaines
born 1845

journalist
Wisconsin
Wom Cent

11009. Richardson, Ellen A.
1845–1911
artist, editor, author, club leader
Index t Wom

11010. Briggs, Mary Blatchley
born 1846
journalist, poet
Index t Wom

11011. Claflin, Adelaide Avery
born 1846
suffragist, journalist
Wom Cent

11012. Krehbiel, Helen Virginia Osborne
1846–94
editor
Twent Cen Bio Dict Not Am

11013. Mallory, Lucy A.
born 1846
editor, educator of Blacks
Oregon
Index t Wom; Wom Cent

11014. Milne, Frances Margaret
born 1846
author, journalist, poet, political essayist
California
Irish
Wom Cent

11015. Moore, Sarah Wool
born 1846
artist, journalist
Nebraska
Index t Wom; Wom Cent

11016. Seymour, Mary Foot
1846–93
stenographer, businessperson, journalist, law reporter, suffragist, women's labor worker
Not Am Wom; Wom Cent

11017. Trott, Novella Jewell
born 1846
author, editor
Wom Cent

11018. Bouton, Emily St. John
flourished 1877
journalist
Wom Cent

11019. Patterson, Flora W.
born 1847
pathologist, botanist, mycologist, editor
Index t Wom

11020. Porter, Charlotte Endymion
1847/59–1942

writer on literature, magazine editor, poet
Index t Wom; Not Am Wom;
  Twent Cen Bio Dict Not Am

11021. Rayner, Emily C.
born 1847
author, journalist
Wom Cent

**11022. Sullivan, Margaret
  Frances (Buchanan)**
1847–1903
journalist
Chicago, IL
Dict Am Auth

11023. Walker, Rose Kershaw
born 1847
author, journalist
Wom Cent

11024. Whiting, Lilian
1847/55–1942
journalist, essayist, poet, short
  story writer, biographer, editor
Boston, MA
Dict Am Auth; Index t Wom;
  Nat Cyc Am Bio v9; Not Am
  Wom

**11025. Bartlett, Alice Eloise;
  Birch Arnold**
1848–1920
journalist, poet
Detroit, MI
Dict Am Auth; Index t Wom;
  Wom Cent

**11026. Cramer, Harriet Laura
  Barker**
1848–1922
journalist, editor, philanthropist
Index t Wom

11027. Diggs, Annie le Porte
1848/53–1916
Populist party leader, orator, poli-
  tician, social reformer, temper-
  ance worker, journalist
Unitarian
Kansas
Canadian
Not Am Wom; Read Encyc Am
  West; Wom Cent

11028. Gould, Elizabeth Porter
born 1848
author, essayist on education,
  journalist, lecturer, social critic
Wom Cent

11029. Kelly, Florence (Finch)
1848/58–1939
journalist, author
Dict Am Auth; Index t Wom;
  Not Am Wom

11030. Lange, Mary T. (Nash)
born 1848
journalist
Wom Cent

**11031. Langford, Laura (Car-
  ter) (Holloway)**
born 1848
author, biographer, journalist
Cyc Am Bio; Dict Am Auth;
  Twent Cen Bio Dict Not Am

**11032. Moore, Susanne Bande-
  grift**
born 1848
editor and publisher
Missouri
Wom Cent

11033. Norris, Mary Harriot
born 1848
author, novelist, literary editor,
  university educator
New York; Illinois
Dict Am Auth; Twent Cen Bio
  Dict Not Am

11034. Troup, Augusta Lewis
circa 1848–1920
labor organizer, journalist
Catholic
Bio Dict Am Lab; Not Am Wom

11035. Andrews, Marie Louise
1849–91
journalist, short story writer
Wom Cent

11036. Ayer, Harriet (Hubbard)
1849/54–1903
businessperson, realtor, manufacturer, journalist, suffragist
Dict Am Auth; Nat Cyc Am Bio
  v43; Not Am Wom; Wom Cent

11037. Clark, Helen Taggart
born 1849
journalist
Pennsylvania
Wom Cent

**11038. Foltz, Clara Shortridge;
  The Portia of the Pacific**
1849–1934
lawyer, political activist, women's
  rights worker, suffragist, newspaper publisher, orator
California
Cyc Am Bio; Nat Cyc Am Bio
  csv3; Not Am Wom; Twent Cen
  Bio Dict Not Am; Wom Cent

11039. Gilder, Jeanett Leonard
1849–1916
literary magazine editor, critic,
  journalist, novelist, autobiogra-
  pher
New York, NY
Cyc Am Bio and v2 ad; Dict Am
  Auth; Dict Am Bio; Index t
  Wom; Nat Cyc Am Bio v8; Not
  Am Wom; Twent Cen Bio Dict
  Not Am

**11040. Nicholson, Eliza Jane
  (Poitevent) Holbrook; Pearl
  Rivers**
1849–96
poet, journalist, editor, publisher
  and owner of the New Orleans
  Picayune-Times
New Orleans, LA
Dict Am Auth; Dict Am Bio;
  Index t Wom; Nat Cyc Am Bio
  v1; Not Am Wom; Twent Cen
  Bio Dict Not Am; Wom Cent

11041. Nowell, Mildred E.
born 1849
author, journalist
South Carolina
Wom Cent

**11042. Thurston, Martha L.
  Poland**
born 1849
philanthropist, journalist
Wom Cent

11043. Bruce, Elizabeth M.
flourished 1880s
clergyperson, author, editor
Index t Wom

11044. Burke, B. Ellen
born 1850
educator, lecturer, editor, publisher
Index t Wom

11045. Butts, Mrs.
flourished 1880s
journalist
Index t Wom

**11046. Crawford, John, Mrs.;
  Maude Moore**
born 1850
newspaper correspondent
Canadian
Wom Cent

11047. Curran, Ida M.
flourished 1880s–90s
journalist, editor
Massachusetts
Wom Cent

11048. Diehl, Anna Randall
flourished 1880s
author, editor
Index t Wom

11049. Durley, Ella Hamilton
flourished 1880s
educator, journalist
Des Moines, IA
Wom Cent

11050. Dwyer, Bessie Agnes
flourished 1880s
journalist
Texas
Wom Cent

11051. Evans, May Garrettson
flourished 1880s
journalist
Index t Wom

**11052. Hapgood, Isabel Flor-
  ence**
1850/51–1928
translator, linguist, writer on
  Russian and European litera-
  ture, journalist
New York, NY
Dict Am Auth; Dict Am Bio; Nat
  Cyc Am Bio v21; Not Am
  Wom; Twent Cen Bio Dict Not
  Am; Wom Cent

**11053. Hewitt, Emma Church-
  man**
born 1850
miscellaneous writer, journalist
Philadelphia, PA
Dict Am Auth; Wom Cent

11054. Hinman, Ida
flourished 1880s
litterateur, journalist
Wom Cent.

11055. Huntley, Florence
flourished 1880s; died 1912
journalist, author, humorist
Index t Wom; Wom Cent

11056. Ives, Alice Emma
flourished 1880s
dramatist, journalist
Detroit, MI
Index t Wom; Wom Cent

11057. Keating, Josephine E.
flourished 1880s–90s
literary critic, musician, music educator
Tennessee
Wom Cent

11058. Marble, Ella M. S.
born 1850
journalist, educator, suffragist,
  temperance worker, dress reformer
Wom Cent

11059. McComas, Alice Moore
born 1850
author, editor, lecturer, suffragist
Wom Cent

**11060. Pitman, Marie J. (Da-
  vis)**
1850–88
children's author, journalist,
  newspaper foreign correspondent
Boston, MA
Cyc Am Bio; Dict Am Auth

**11061. Pullen, Elisabeth Jones
  (Cavazza); E. Cavazza**
flourished 1880s–90s
journalist, sketch writer

Portland, ME
Dict Am Auth; Nat Cyc Am Bio
v8

11062. Schoff, Hannah Kent
1850/53–1940
child welfare worker, juvenile
court reformer, child aid leader,
editor, author
Philadelphia, PA
Index t Wom; Nat Cyc Am Bio
v18; Not Am Wom

11063. Smith, Elizabeth J.
flourished 1880s–90s
editor of a temperance newspaper
Wom Cent

**11064. Stowell, Louisa Maria
(Reed)**
born 1850
microscopist, botanist, author on
microscopal botany, educator,
editor
Cyc Am Bio and ad; Dict Am
Auth; Index t Wom; Wom Cent

11065. Wilcox, Ella (Wheeler)
1850/55–1919
poet, journalist, novelist
New York, NY
Cyc Am Bio and ad; Dict Am
Auth; Dict Am Bio; Index t
Wom; Nat Cyc Am Bio v11;
Not Am Wom; Wom Lit, More

11066. Wilder, S. Fannie Gerry
born 1850
author, juvenile writer
Wom Cent

**11067. Abbott, Mary Perkins
(Ives)**
1851–1904
journalist, short story and romance writer
Chicago, IL
Dict Am Auth

11068. Cameron, Elizabeth
born 1851
editor, temperance worker
Canadian
Wom Cent

**11069. Clark, Katharine Pick-
ens (Upson)**
1851–1935
children's author, journalist, suffragist, temperance worker, lecturer
Dict Am Auth; Nat Cyc Am Bio
v30

11070. Dawes, Anna Laurens
born 1851
author, journalist, essayist
Dict Am Auth; Wom Cent

**11071. de Long, Emma J.
Wotton**
1851–1940

editor, author
Index t Wom

11072. Harper, Ida A. Husted
1851–1931
political journalist, suffragist,
feminist, newspaper editor, author
Dict Am Bio; Index t Wom; Nat
Cyc Am Bio v25; Not Am
Wom; Wom Cent

**11073. Spencer, Anna Carpen-
ter (Garlin)**
1851–1931
Unitarian minister, journalist, educator, temperance worker, suffragist, pacifist, child-labor
reformer, philanthropist
Unitarian
Dict Am Bio; Nat Cyc Am Bio v9
and csv2; Not Am Wom

**11074. van Rensselaer, Mariana
Alley (Griswold); Mrs. Schuyler**
1851–1934
writer on art, art critic, art historian
Cyc Am Bio and ad; Dict Am
Auth; Dict Am Bio; Index t
Wom; Not Am Wom

11075. Wilde, Miriam Leslie
born 1851
publisher
Index t Wom

11076. Winslow, Helen Maria
1851–1938
clubwoman, author, journalist,
editor, publisher
Boston, MA
Dict Am Auth; Index t Wom;
Nat Cyc Am Bio csv2; Wom
Cent

11077. Ballou, Ella Maria
born 1852
court reporter
Index t Wom

**11078. Davidson, Hannah Ame-
lia**
1852–1919
author of study guides, educator,
editor, lecturer, publisher
Index t Wom; Nat Cyc Am Bio
v19

**11079. Davis, Mary Evelyn
(Moore)**
1852–1909
journalist, novelist, short story
writer
New Orleans, LA
Dict Am Auth; Dict Am Bio; Nat
Cyc Am Bio v10

**11080. Doughty, Eva Craig
Graves**
born 1852

journalist, suffragist, temperance
worker
Presbyterian
Wom Cent

11081. Griffith, Eva Kinney
born 1852
journalist, temperance worker
Wom Cent

11082. Krout, Mary Hannah
1852/57–1927
poet, author, educator, journalist
Denver, CO
Dict Am Auth; Index t Wom;
Wom Cent

**11083. McGahan, Barbara;
Paul Kashirin**
born 1852
author, Russian-language journalist, correspondent in the
1874–75 Spanish war, Russo-
Turkish Wars correspondent
Wom Cent

11084. Ormsby, Mary Frost
born circa 1852
author, journalist, philanthropist,
pacifist
New York, NY
Index t Wom; Wom Cent

**11085. Stoddard, Anna
Elizabeth**
born 1852
journalist, anti–secret society agitator, temperance worker, suffragist
Baptist
Wom Cent

**11086. Conway, Katherine El-
eanor**
born 1853
journalist, poet
Catholic
Boston, MA
Dict Am Auth; Twent Cen Bio
Dict Not Am; Wom Cent

11087. Dabbs, Ellen Lawson
born 1853
physician, midwife, women's
rights worker, suffragist, temperance worker, journalist,
Populist party worker
Texas
Wom Cent

11088. Jenkins, Theresa A.
born 1853
suffragist, journalist, women's
rights worker, temperance
worker
Wyoming
Wom Cent

**11089. Norraikow, Ella, Count-
ess**
born 1853

author, journalist, Russian corre-
spondent, traveler
Canadian
Wom Cent

11090. Palmer, Sophia French
1853–1920
professional nurse, nursing editor
Index t Wom; Not Am Wom

11091. Post, Sarah E.
born 1853
physician, nursing-magazine
founder
New York
Wom Cent

11092. Poulsson, Anne Emilie
1853–1939
children's author, writer on children, editor, illustrator, kindergarten educator
Boston, MA
Dict Am Auth; Index t Wom;
Nat Cyc Am Bio v10; Twent
Cen Bio Dict Not Am

11093. Sweet, Ada Celeste
1853–1928
journalist, editor, author, social
reformer, philanthropist, pension agent
Chicago, IL
Index t Wom; Wom Cent

11094. Ward, May (Alden)
born 1853
historical author, biographer, editor, lecturer, club leader, president of the Massachusetts State
Federation of Women's Clubs
Dict Am Auth; Index t Wom;
Twent Cen Bio Dict Not Am;
Wom Cent

11095. Wright, Marie Robinson
born 1853/60
journalist, travel writer
Georgia; New York
Dict Am Auth; Wom Cent

**11096. Brauenlich, Sophia
(Toepken)**
1854–98
journalist, business manager of
Scientific Publishing Co., fellow
of the Imperial Institute of
Great Britain
Nat Cyc Am Bio v9

**11097. Edholm, Mary Gow
Charlton**
born 1854
suffragist, temperance reformer,
journalist
Twent Cen Bio Dict Not Am;
Wom Cent

**11098. Hall, Margaret Thomp-
son**
born 1854

educator, newspaper correspondent
Wom Cent

11099. Ives, Florence C.
born 1854
journalist
New York
Wom Cent

11100. Keith, Eliza D.; Erie Douglas; Di Vernon
born 1854
author, journalist, worker for the SPCA
California
Nat Cyc Am Bio v2; Wom Cent

11101. Porter, Alice Hobbins
born 1854
journalist, newspaper editor
English
Wom Cent

11102. Proctor, Mary Virginia
born 1854
journalist, newspaper publisher, philanthropist
Methodist Episcopal
Virginia
Wom Cent

11103. Wakeman, Antoinette van Hoesen
1854–post 1890
journalist, novelist
Illinois; Hastings, NE
Dict Am Auth; Wom Cent

11104. Ball, Isabel Worrell
born 1855
pioneer, journalist
Index t Wom; Wom Cent

11105. Elmendorf, Theresa Hubbell West
1855–1932
librarian, editor
Buffalo, NY
Index t Wom; Nat Cyc Am Bio v23

11106. Leslie, Amy
1855–1939
light opera singer, drama critic, journalist
Index t Wom; Not Am Wom

11107. Loughead, Flora (Haines)
born 1855
miscellaneous writer, journalist, novelist, children's author
Santa Barbara, CA
Dict Am Auth; Nat Cyc Am Bio v11; Wom Cent

11108. Mossell, Gertrude Bustill
born 1855
newspaper editor, author
Pennsylvania

Black
Negro Alman; Prof Negro Wom v1

11109. Pennell, Elizabeth (Robins)
1855–1936
author, travel writer, biographer, art critic, bicycle tourer
Dict Am Auth; Index t Wom; Nat Cyc Am Bio v10; Not Am Wom

11110. Rogers, Effie Louise Hoffman
born 1855
educator; superintendent of schools of Mahaska County, Iowa; newspaper editor; temperance worker
Mahaska County, IA
Wom Cent

11111. Sheldon, Grace Carew
born 1855
journalist, author
Twent Cen Bio Dict Not Am

11112. Smith, Harriette (Knight)
born 1855
journalist
Boston, MA
Dict Am Auth

11113. Sweet, Sophia Miriam
1855–1912
author, editor
Index t Wom

11114. Bradford, Mary Carroll Craig
born 1856/60
magazine and newspaper correspondent, educator, labor union leader
Christian Scientist
Colorado
Nat Cyc Am Bio csv2; Wom Cent

11115. Field, Martha R.; Catherine Cole
born 1856
journalist
New Orleans, LA
Wom Cent

11116. Huling, Caroline Augusta
born 1856
journalist, suffragist, philanthropist, temperance worker
Illinois
Wom Cent

11117. Rathbone, Josephine Adams
1856/64–1941
librarian, editor, educator
Index t Wom; Nat Cyc Am Bio csv4; Not Am Wom

11118. Scidmore, Eliza Ruhamah; Eliza Ruhamah
1856–1928
geographer, traveler, travel writer, journalist
Washington, DC
Dict Am Auth; Dict Am Bio; Index t Wom; Twent Cen Bio Dict Not Am

11119. Bishop, Mary Agnes Dalrymple
born 1857
journalist
Massachusetts
Wom Cent

11120. Blackwell, Alice Stone
1857–1950
feminist, suffragist, journalist, editor, author, humanitarian
Dict Am Bio supp v2; Index t Wom; Nat Cyc Am Bio csv6; Not Am Wom; Obit File; Wom Cent

11121. Cummings, Alma Carrie
born 1857
journalist, newspaper editor and publisher
New Hampshire
Wom Cent

11122. Dey, Haryot Hold; Hattie Hamblin Cahoon Dey
1857–1950
author, editor
Obit File

11123. Henry, Alice
1857–1943
journalist, women's trade union leader, feminist, suffragist, editor
Unitarian
Australian
Bio Dict Am Lab; Dict Am Bio supp v3; Not Am Wom

11124. Markscheffel, Louise
born 1857
journalist
Ohio
Wom Cent

11125. Tarbell, Ida Minerva
1857–1944
investigative journalist, muckraker, lecturer, historian, author, biographer of Abraham Lincoln
Dict Am Auth; Dict Am Bio supp v3; Index t Wom; Nat Cyc Am Bio v14; Not Am Wom; Obit File

11126. Young, Julia Evelyn (Ditto)
born 1857
poet, novelist, magazine writer
Buffalo, NY
Dict Am Auth; Wom Cent

11127. Alden, Cynthia May; Sunshine
1858/62–1931
journalist, editor, linguist, author, inventor, social worker, philanthropist, humanitarian
New York, NY
Dict Am Bio supp v1; Index t Wom; Nat Cyc Am Bio v14 and v22

11128. Baker, Julie Keim (Wetherill); J. K. W.
born 1858
journalist, author
New Orleans, LA
Dict Am Auth; Wom Cent

11129. Beer, Rachel "Richa"
1858–1927
newspaper editor, publisher, composer
Jewish
Who Who Jew Hist

11130. Byngton, Elia Goode
born 1858
newspaper editor, women's rights worker, journalist
Georgia
Wom Cent

11131. Helmer, Bessie Bradwell
1858–1927
lawyer, editor, publisher
Dict Am Bio; Index t Wom

11132. Roseboro, Viola
1858–1945
author, magazine writer, literary fiction editor of *McClures Magazine*
New York
Dict Am Auth; Obit File

11133. Sharkey, Emma Augusta; Mrs. E. Burke Collins
born 1858
journalist, short story writer, novelist
Louisiana
Wom Cent

11134. Shinn, Milicent Washburn
1858–1940
author, editor, child psychologist
Niles, CA
Dict Am Auth; Index t Wom; Not Am Wom

11135. Candee, Helen Churchill
1859/61–1949
novelist, journalist
New York, NY
Dict Am Auth; Obit File

11136. Miller, Annie (Jenness)
born 1859/84
dress reformer, fashion designer, magazine publisher, author, novelist, essayist, lecturer

New York, NY
Dict Am Auth; Index t Wom;
Wom Cent

11137. Moody, Helen (Waterson)
1859/60–1928
author, journalist, educator
Ohio; New York, NY
Dict Am Auth; Index t Wom;
Nat Cyc Am Bio v22; Wom
Cent

11138. Ranous, Dora Knowlton
1859–1916
author, editor
Nat Cyc Am Bio v17

11139. Smith, Helen Morton
born 1859
journalist
Michigan
Wom Cent

11140. Ahern, Mary Eileen
1860/65–1938
librarian, editor, educator
Index t Wom; Nat Cyc Am Bio
csv1; Not Am Wom

11141. Browne, Nina Eliza
born 1860
librarian, editor
Index t Wom; Nat Cyc Am Bio
csvl

11142. Clarke, Helen Archibald
1860–1926
author, magazine editor, cofounder of *Poet Lore Magazine*
Index t Wom; Not Am Wom

11143. Craft, Mabel
flourished 1890s–1900s
journalist
Index t Wom

11144. Culton, Jessie F.
born 1860
journalist
Wom Cent

11145. Davenport, Esther
flourished 1890s–1930s
journalist
Index t Wom

11146. Donnelly, Norah
flourished 1890s–1900s
journalist
Index t Wom

11147. Ellis, Anna M. B.; Max Eliot
1860–1911
author, journalist
Index t Wom

11148. Hamilton, Anna J.
born 1860
educator, journalist

Kentucky
Wom Cent

11149. Heaton, Eliza Putnam
born 1860
journalist, photojournalist, newspaper editor, Sorosis member
Wom Cent

11150. Hooper, Rebecca Lane
flourished 1890s–1900s
playwright
Index t Wom

11151. Kimball, Kate Fisher
born 1860
editor
Index t Wom

11152. Knapp, Adeline
born 1860
Household Magazine editor, miscellaneous writer
New York
Dict Am Auth

11153. Logan, John A., Mrs.
flourished 1890s
editor, author
Index t Wom

11154. Lummis, Dorothea
born 1860
physician, music critic, journalist, newspaper editor, Native American artifacts collector
Los Angeles, CA
Index t Wom; Wom Cent

11155. Monroe, Harriet
1860/61–1936
poet, editor
Chicago, IL
Dict Am Auth; Dict Am Bio
supp v2; Index t Wom; Nat Cyc
Am Bio v28; Not Am Wom

11156. Orff, Annie L. Y.
flourished 1890s
editor, publisher, women's travel expert
St. Louis, MO
Wom Cent

11157. Owler, Martha Tracy
flourished 1890s
journalist, foreign correspondent
Massachusetts
Wom Cent

11158. Seawell, Molly Elliot
1860–1916
author, novelist, children's author, newspaper correspondent
Washington, DC
Dict Am Auth; Dict Am Bio;
Index t Wom; Nat Cyc Am Bio
v7; Twent Cen Bio Dict Not
Am ; Wom Cent

11159. Smith, Minna Caroline
born 1860

journalist, children's author
Boston, MA
Dict Am Auth

11160. Spratt, Louise Parker
flourished 1890s
journalist, dialect author
Alabama
Wom Cent

11161. Stevens, Alice J.
born 1860
editor, author
Index t Wom

11162. Switzer, Marguerite Birdelle
flourished 1890s
journalist
Index t Wom

11163. Welbron, May Eddins
born 1860
journalist
Wom Cent

11164. Welch, Jane Meade
flourished 1890s
journalist, historical lecturer
New York
Wom Cent

11165. Wight, Emma Howard
flourished 1890s
magazine writer, theological writer, novelist
Catholic
Wom Cent

11166. Willard, Allie C.
born 1860
journalist, newspaper publisher and editor, businessperson, clerk of the Nebraska Senate
Nebraska
Wom Cent

11167. Woodruff, Libbie L.
born 1860
journalist
Nebraska
Wom Cent

11168. Wylie, Lollie Belle
flourished 1890s
journalist, newspaper editor, poet
Georgia
Wom Cent

11169. Ames, Julia A.
1861–91
temperance worker, editor
Twent Cen Bio Dict Not Am;
Wom Cent

11170. Boylan, Grace (Duffie)
born 1861
novelist, journalist, poet
Chicago, IL
Dict Am Auth

11171. Forney, Tillie May
born 1861
journalist, author
Nat Cyc Am Bio v3; Wom Cent

11172. Gilmer, Elizabeth Meriwether; Dorothy Dix
1861/70–1951
journalist, suffragist, advice columnist
Dict Am Bio supp v5; Index t
Wom; Not Am Wom supp v1;
Obit File

11173. Hind, Ella Cora
1861–1942
agriculturist, editor, journalist
Index t Wom

11174. Lawson, Louise
born 1861
sculptor, medical journal editor
Cyc Am Bio; Wom Cent

11175. Roberts, Mary Fantan
1861–1956
art magazine editor, journalist, art patron
Index t Wom; Obit File

11176. Stapleton, Patience (Tucker)
1861–93
novelist, short story writer, journalist
Colorado
Dict Am Auth; Nat Cyc Am Bio
v8

11177. Taney, Mary Florence
born 1861
educator, journalist, author, editor
Index t Wom

11178. Washington, Josephine Turpin
1861–1949
journalist, educator
Black
Negro Alman; Prof Negro Wom
v1

11179. Armbruster, Sara Dary
born 1862
publisher, women's rights worker
Wom Cent

11180. Bloor, Ella Reeve; Ella Omholt
1862–1951
radical labor organizer, journalist, suffragist, Socialist and Communist party leader, a founder of the American Communist party
Bio Dict Am Lab; Dict Am Bio
supp v5; Not Am Wom supp
v1; Obit File

11181. Cotes, Sara Jeannette Duncan; Sara Jeannette Duncan
born 1862
author, journalist
Canadian
Wom Cent

11182. James, Annie Laurie Wilson
born 1862
journalist, editor, horse breeding expert
California
Index t Wom; Wom Cent

11183. Ohl, Maud Andrews
born 1862
journalist, poet
Georgia
Index t Wom; Wom Cent

11184. Peattie, Elia Wilkerson
born 1862
author, journalist, novelist, travel writer
Chicago, IL
Dict Am Auth; Wom Cent

11185. Weir, Irene
1862–1944
painter, art educator, writer on art, founder of the New York School of Design and Liberal Arts
New York
Not Am Wom; Obit File

11186. Wells-Barnett, Ida Bell; Iola
1862/64–1931
Black equal rights advocate, journalist, newspaper publisher, clubwoman, lecturer, antilynching reformer
Black
Encyc Black Am; Encyc South Hist; Eng Wom; Index t Wom; Negro Alman; Not Am Wom; Prof Negro Wom v1 and v2

11187. Wharton, Edith Newbold (Jones)
1862–1937
novelist, short story writer, ghost story writer, autobiographer, travel writer, literary critic
New York, NY
French (American expatriate to Paris)
Dict Am Auth; Dict Am Bio supp v2; Dict Lit Bio v4 and v9; Index t Wom; Nat Cyc Am Bio v14 and csv2; Not Am Wom; Twent Cen Bio Dict Not Am; Wom Lit; Wom Lit, More

11188. Bisland, Elizabeth
born 1863
journalist
Wom Cent

11189. Black, Winifred Sweet
1863–1936
journalist
Index t Wom; Not Am Wom

11190. Cleary, Kate McPhelim
born 1863
newspaper correspondent, journalist
Wom Cent

11191. Crane, Alna
1863–1953
first American newspaper photographer
Obit File

11192. Dwight, Minnie Ryan
1863–1957
editor and publisher of the Holyoke, Massachusetts, *Daily Transcript-Telegraph*
Holyoke, MA
Obit File

11193. Eastman, Elaine (Goodale); Elaine Hall
1863–1953
educator of Native Americans, poet, short story writer, humorist, editor, scholar of Native American culture
South Dakota
Cyc Am Bio; Dict Am Auth; Index t Wom; Nat Cyc Am Bio v8; Twent Cen Bio Dict Not Am; Wom Cent

11194. Gerrish-Jones, Abbie
1863–1929
composer, author, critic
Index t Wom

11195. Jackson, Maria Clopton
1863–1956
chairperson of the board of the Oregon Journal Publishing Co.
Oregon
Obit File

11196. Johnson, Carrie Ashton
born 1863
editor, temperance worker, suffragist
Illinois
Wom Cent

11197. Michel, Nettie Leila
born 1863
editor
New York
Wom Cent

11198. Murphy, Claudia Quigley
born 1863
journalist, suffragist, women's rights worker
Ohio
Wom Cent

11199. Starkey, Jennie O.
born 1863
journalist
Detroit, MI
Wom Cent

11200. Wetmore, Elizabeth (Bisland)
born 1863
journalist, editor, traveler
New York, NY
Dict Am Auth; Index t Wom

11201. Youmans, Theodora Winton
born 1863
journalist
Wisconsin
Wom Cent

11202. Johnston, Frances Benjamin
1864–1952
photojournalist
Dict Am Bio supp v5; Index t Wom; Not Am Wom supp v1; Obit File

11203. Lippmann, Julie Mathilde
1864–1952
author, playwright, children's author, literary critic
Brooklyn, NY
Dict Am Bio; Index t Wom; Twent Cen Bio Dict Not Am

11204. Bergengren, Ann (Farquhar); Margaret Alston
born 1865
novelist, journalist, magazine editor, singer
Boston, MA
Dict Am Auth; Index t Wom; Nat Cyc Am Bio v14

11205. Jordan, Elizabeth Garver
1865/67–1947
journalist, author, adventurer, editor
Catholic
Index t Wom; Nat Cyc Am Bio v40; Not Am Wom; Obit File; Wom Cent

11206. Payne, Winona Wilcox; Mrs. Maxwell
circa 1865–1949
editor
Index t Wom

11207. Richardson, Anna Steese
1865–1949
magazine editor, author, playwright, feminist
Obit File

11208. Seaman, Elizabeth Cochrane; Nellie Bly
1865/67–1922

journalist
Dict Am Bio; Index t Wom; Not Am Wom

11209. Smith, Fannie Douglass
born 1865
journalist
Ohio
Wom Cent

11210. Stevens, Augusta de Grasse
1865–94
novelist, art critic
Belgian
Dict Am Auth; Index t Wom

11211. Towne, Elizabeth Lois
1865–1960
metaphysical author, editor, lecturer
New Thought
Nat Cyc Am Bio v45 and csv1

11212. Tryon, Kate
born 1865
journalist, artist, lecturer
Wom Cent

11213. Willcox, Louise Collier
1865–1929
essayist, literary critic, editor
Dict Am Bio

11214. Williams, Florence B.
born 1865
newspaper editor and publisher, author
Georgia
Wom Cent

11215. Austin, Mary (Hunter)
1866/68–1934
novelist, folklorist, short story writer, journalist, conservationist, feminist, worker for Native American rights
California
Dict Am Auth; Dict Am Bio supp v1; Dict Lit Bio v9; Not Am Wom; Read Encyc Am West; Wom Lit; Wom Lit, More

11216. Dorr, Rheta Childe
1866–1948
World War I correspondent, journalist, feminist
Index t Wom; Not Am Wom; Obit File

11217. Fairbanks, Constance
born 1866
journalist
Wom Cent

11218. Ford, Miriam Chase
born 1866
journalist, vocalist
Wom Cent

11219. Valesh, Eva McDonald
born 1866
printer, journalist, social reformer, feminist, labor leader and activist
Minneapolis, MN
Index t Wom; Wom Cent

11220. Waltz, Elizabeth (Cherry)
1866–1903
journalist, short story writer
Dict Am Auth

11221. Andrews, Fannie Fern (Phillips)
1867–1950
publicist, pacifist, internationalist, suffragist
Nat Cyc Am Bio csv1; Not Am Wom

11222. Cary, Elizabeth Luther
1867–1936
author, art critic, literary critic
Brooklyn, NY
Dict Am Auth; Dict Am Bio supp v2; Wom Lit; Wom Lit, More

11223. Cochrane, Elizabeth; Nellie Bly
born 1867
journalist, traveler
Nat Cyc Am Bio v1; Wom Cent

11224. Flint, Martha Bockee
born 1867
journalist
New York, NY
Dict Am Auth

11225. Hamm, Margharita Arlina
1867/71–1907
journalist, author, poet, political writer
Canadian
Nat Cyc Am Bio v9; Not Am Wom; Wom Cent

11226. Meyer, Annie Florence Nathan
1867–1950/51
publicist, author, playwright, novelist, educationist, founder of Barnard College, antisuffragist, patron of Black music education, clubwoman
Jewish
New York
Dict Am Auth; Dict Am Bio; Index t Wom; Nat Cyc Am Bio v42; Not Am Wom supp v1; Obit File; Twent Cen Bio Dict Not Am; Wom Cent

11227. Wilder, Laura Ingalls
1867–1957

children's author, educator, editor
Dict Am Bio supp v6; Index t Wom; Not Am Wom supp v1; Obit File; Read Encyc Am West

11228. Bergen, Helen Corinne
born 1868
author, journalist
Wom Cent

11229. Dortch, Ellen J.
born 1868
newspaper editor, publisher, Farmers Alliance party worker
Georgia
Wom Cent

11230. Stevens, Helen Norton
born 1868
editor
Index t Wom

11231. Bartlett, Alice Hunt
1869–1949
poet, American editor of *London Poetry Review*
Obit File

11232. Best, Gertrude Delprat
1869–1947
newspaper publisher
Washington
Nat Cyc Am Bio v41

11233. Francis, Louise E.
born 1869
journalist, newspaper editor and publisher
California
Wom Cent

11234. Goldman, Emma
1869–1940
political anarchist, lecturer, publicist, agitator for free speech, popularizer of the arts, feminist, pioneer advocate of birth control, politician
Jewish
Russian
Dict Am Bio supp v2; Index t Wom; Not Am Wom; Who Who Jew Hist

11235. Hatton, Fanny Cottinet Locke
1869–1939
playwright, critic
Episcopalian
Index t Wom; Nat Cyc Am Bio v42

11236. Leslie, Annie Louise Brown; Nancy Brown
1869–1948
journalist
Index t Wom

11237. Miniter, Edith Dowe
born 1869

editor
Index t Wom

11238. O'Hagan, Anne
1869–post 1930s
journalist
New York, NY
Dict Am Auth; Index t Wom

11239. Rittenhouse, Jessie Bell
1869–1948
poet, critic, anthologist
Dict Am Bio supp v4; Index t Wom; Not Am Wom

11240. Simmons, Eleanor Booth
circa 1869–1950
journalist
Index t Wom

11241. Woodbury, Rosa Louise
born 1869
journalist, educator
Georgia
Wom Cent

11242. Young, Rose Emmet
1869–1941
editor, journalist, novelist, feminist
New York
Dict Am Auth; Index t Wom

11243. Banks, Elizabeth L.
1870–1938
author, journalist
Index t Wom

11244. Bowles, A. Lincoln, Mrs.; Nancy Hanks
flourished 1900s
journalist
Index t Wom

11245. Brown, Nancy
circa 1870–1948
journalist
Index t Wom

11246. Crowley, Mary Catherine
flourished 1900s
editor, historian, novelist
Detroit, MI
Dict Am Auth; Index t Wom

11247. Darrach, Marshall, Mrs.
flourished 1900s
journalist
Index t Wom

11248. Hall, Grace Ethel Adams
flourished 1900s–20s
journalist, author
Portland, OR
Nat Cyc Am Bio csv1

11249. Hannah, Persis Dwight
flourished 1900s
journalist
Index t Wom

11250. Harding, Caroline
flourished 1900s
journalist
Index t Wom

11251. Harriman, Florence Jaffray (Hurst)
1870–1967
Democratic party official, diplomat, minister to Norway, politician, journalist, suffragist, clubwoman, social rights worker, Red Cross worker in World War I, World War II relief worker in Norway
Washington, DC
Index t Wom; Nat Cyc Am Bio v53 and csv6; Not Am Wom supp v1; Obit File

11252. Havener, Helen
flourished 1900s–20s
journalist, editor
Index t Wom

11253. Lantz, Emily Emerson
flourished 1900s
journalist, genealogist
Index t Wom

11254. Marble, Anna
flourished 1900s
journalist
Index t Wom

11255. Miller, Sadie Kneller
died 1920
journalist, photographer
Index t Wom

11256. Spring, Agnes Wright
flourished 1900s–20s
journalist
Index t Wom

11257. Woodruff, Susan Harmons
1870–1953
publisher of the Communist newspaper the *Daily Worker*
Obit File

11258. Wooley, Edna K.
flourished 1900s
journalist
Index t Wom

11259. Wooster, Lizzie E.
born 1870
author, editor
Index t Wom

11260. Beasley, Delilah Leontium
1871–1934
historian, journalist, pacifist
California
Black
Encyc Black Am; Negro Alman; Prof Negro Wom

11261. Dooly, Ismay
died 1921
journalist, humanitarian
Index t Wom

11262. Laut, Agnes Christina
1871/72–1936
journalist, novelist, writer on the American West
Canadian
Dict Am Auth; Index t Wom

11263. Smith, Frances Stanton
1871–1931
journalist, suffragist, member of the New York State Civil Service Commission
New York
Nat Cyc Am Bio v27

11264. Stocker, Corinne
born 1871
elocutionist, journalist
Georgia
Wom Cent

11265. Adams, Elizabeth Kemper
1872–1948
educator, editor
Index t Wom

11266. Brastow, Virginia
circa 1872–1952
journalist, editor
Index t Wom

11267. Haines, Helen Elizabeth
1872–1961
librarian, author, editor, educator
Index t Wom; Not Am Wom supp v1

11268. Jones, Jesse Homan
1872–1962
philanthropist, publisher of the *Houston Chronicle*
Houston, TX
Obit File

11269. McComb, Kate
1872–1959
stage, radio, and television character actor
Obit File

11270. Revell, Nellie MacAleney; Nellie Kellar
1872–1958
journalist, circus and theatrical publicist, press agent, *New York World* reporter, radio commentator and personality
Dict Am Bio supp v6; Index t Wom; Obit File

11271. Becker, May Lamberton
1873–1958
children's author, children's book critic, editor, journalist
Index t Wom; Obit File

11272. Coolidge, Emelyn Lincoln
1873–1949
pediatrician, editor
Index t Wom

11273. Garrison, Adele; Nana Springer White
1873–1956
journalist, newspaper serial writer
Index t Wom; Obit File

11274. Larsen, Hanna A.
1873–1945
author, editor of the *American Scandinavian Review*
Obit File

11275. Manning, Marie
1873?–1945
journalist
Dict Am Bio supp v3

11276. Peacock, Virginia Tatnall
born 1873
journalist
Washington, DC
Dict Am Auth

11277. Bloodgood, Edith Holt
1874–1961
cofounder of the New York Association for the Blind and of *Searchlight*, a Braille magazine
New York
Obit File

11278. Bryan, Isabel
1874–1957
publisher of the Greenwich Village, New York, newspaper *The Villager*
Greenwich Village, NY
Obit File

11279. Crawford, Mary Caroline
born 1874
journalist
Boston, MA
Dict Am Auth

11280. Fulbright, Roberta Waugh
1874–1953
newspaper publisher, political writer, businessperson, banker
Arkansas
Nat Cyc Am Bio v49

11281. Gilmore, Elizabeth McCabe
born 1874
author, publisher, critic
Index t Wom

11282. Loeb, Sophia Irene Simon
1874/76–1929
journalist, sponsor of welfare legislation, social reformer, social worker, author
New York
Russian
Dict Am Bio; Index t Wom; Nat Cyc Am Bio v24; Not Am Wom; Slavon Encyc

11283. Lowell, Amy
1874–1925
poet, biographer, lecturer, critic
Dict Am Bio; Index t Wom; Nat Cyc Am Bio v19; Not Am Wom; Wom Lit; Wom Lit, More

11284. Mechlin, Leila
1874–1949
art critic, editor, and administrator
Not Am Wom

11285. Parker, Eleanor R.
born 1874
home economist, editor, author
Index t Wom

11286. Vorse, Mary Heaton Marvin
1874/81–1960/66
journalist, novelist, labor activist
Bio Dict Am Lab; Index t Wom; Not Am Wom supp v1; Obit File

11287. Warren, Sadie
born 1874
newspaper publisher
Black
Encyc Black Am

11288. Wight, Estella
1874–1955
religious worker, journalist
Index t Wom

11289. Brown, Zaidee Mabel
1875–1950
librarian, editor, lecturer
Index t Wom

11290. Delaney, Adelaide Margaret
born 1875
lecturer, editor, author
Index t Wom

11291. Hopkins, Jenny Lind
died 1925
journalist
Index t Wom

11292. Nelson, Alice Ruth Dunbar (Moore)
1875–1935
author, editor, social worker
Louisiana
Black
Encyc Black Am; Negro Alman; Not Am Wom; Prof Negro Wom v1

11293. Rohe, Alice
circa 1875–1957
journalist, magazine writer, UPI Rome bureau head
Index t Wom; Obit File

11294. Bean, Theodora
died 1926
journalist
Index t Wom

11295. Comstock, Sarah
1876–1960
editor, novelist
Obit File

11296. Drayton, Grace (Viola) Gebbie
born 1876
cartoonist, artist
Nat Cyc Am Bio csv2

11297. Bancroft, Jane Wallis Waldron
1877–1949
publisher of the *Wall Street Journal*, president of the Dow Jones & Co. newsgathering organization, Boston civic worker, equestrian
Boston, MA
Nat Cyc Am Bio v38; Obit File

11298. Chase, Edna Woolman
1877–1957
fashion editor, editor of *Vogue*
Dict Am Bio supp v6; Index t Wom; Not Am Wom supp v1; Obit File

11299. Hard, Anne; Annie Marie Nyhan Scribner
1877–1961
author, radio broadcaster, political journalist
Episcopalian
Washington, DC
Nat Cyc Am Bio v57

11300. Miller, Daisy Orr
1877–1955
editor, dog specialist, president of the Animal Protection Union
Index t Wom; Obit File

11301. Roberts, Mary May
1877–1959
nurse, nursing magazine editor, nursing educator, chief nurse of the World War II army nurse corps
Index t Wom; Not Am Wom supp v1; Obit File

11302. Russell, Edith
1877–1975
fashion writer, World War I correspondent
Obit File

11303. Schwimmer, Rosika
1877–1948

feminist, suffragist, pacifist, author, editor
Jewish
Hungarian
Dict Am Bio supp v4; Not Am Wom; Obit File

11304. Thorne, Florence Calvert
1877–1973
labor researcher, editor
Not Am Wom supp v1

11305. Aldrich, Mildred
died 1928
journalist
Index t Wom

11306. Fairfax, Beatrice; Marie M. Gasch
circa 1878–1945
journalist, advice columnist
Index t Wom; Obit File

11307. Isaacs, Edith Juliet Rich
1878–1956
theater critic, author, editor of *Theater Arts* magazine
Not Am Wom supp v1; Obit File

11308. McLeod, Grace
1878–1962
nutritionist, nutrition educator, editor
Congregationalist
Scottish
Index t Wom; Nat Cyc Am Bio v50

11309. Meloney, Mary (Mattingly)
1878–1943
journalist, magazine editor, newspaper editor
Index t Wom; Not Am Wom; Obit File

11310. Pennypacker, Anna Maria Whitaker
1878–1952
co-owner of *The Daily Worker*, Communist party worker
Obit File

11311. Underhill, Harriett
died 1928
journalist, reviewer, critic
Index t Wom

11312. Dunn, Fannie Wyche
1879–1946
editor
Index t Wom

11313. Howard, Kathleen
1879–1956
opera singer, screen actor, fashion editor
Obit File

11314. Mallon, Winifred
1879–1954
journalist
Index t Wom

11315. Walker, Susan Hunter
married 1904
editor, author
Scottish
Index t Wom

11316. Williams, Blanche Colton
1879–1926/44
educator, writer on writing, anthology editor
Index t Wom; Nat Cyc Am Bio csv2

11317. Avary, Myrta Lockett
flourished 1910s
sociologist, politician, editor, author
Index t Wom

11318. Bass, Charlotta A. Spears
1880/90–1969
Progressive party vice-presidential candidate in 1952, civil rights reformer, editor
Black
Negro Alman; Not Am Wom supp v1

11319. Beckley, Zoe
flourished 1910s
journalist, author
Index t Wom; Wom Lit, More

11320. Bingham, Millicent Todd
1880–1968
geographer, conservationist, author, editor, authority on Emily Dickinson
Episcopalian
Cur Biog '69; Index t Wom; Nat Cyc Am Bio csv9

11321. Bodine, Helen K.
flourished 1910s–30s
fashion editor
Index t Wom

11322. Bugbee, Emma
flourished 1910s–20s
journalist
Index t Wom

11323. Byers, Ruth
flourished 1910s
journalist
Index t Wom

11324. Camprubi, Ethel Leaycraft
1880–1955
president of a New York Spanish-language daily newspaper
New York
Obit File

11325. Davis, Frances
flourished 1910s–20s
journalist
Index t Wom

11326. Davis, Nevada Victoria
flourished 1910s
journalist
Index t Wom

11327. Dougherty, Mary
flourished 1910s–20s
journalist
Index t Wom

11328. Doyle, Peggy
flourished 1910s
journalist
Index t Wom

11329. Driscoll, Marjorie
flourished 1910s
journalist
Index t Wom

11330. Evans, Orrena Louise
flourished 1910s
editor, librarian
Index t Wom

11331. Garber, Lucy May (Bradley)
1880–1971
US land commissioner in Oklahoma, newspaper publisher
Oklahoma
Nat Cyc Am Bio v58

11332. Greeley-Smith, Nixola
1880–1919
journalist
Index t Wom; Not Am Wom

11333. Gunterman, Bertha Lisette
flourished 1910s–30s
librarian, editor
Index t Wom

11334. Holf, Nora Douglas
flourished 1910s–60s
musician, composer, singer, music critic
Black
Prof Negro Wom v2

11335. James, Bessie
flourished 1910s
journalist
Index t Wom

11336. King, Fay
flourished 1910s
journalist
Index t Wom

11337. Lummis, Eliza O'Brien
flourished 1910s
editor, publisher, religious worker, author
Index t Wom

11338. Lupton, Mary Josephine
flourished 1910s
editor, translator, author
Index t Wom

11339. McCormick, Anne Elizabeth O'Hare
1880/82–1954
journalist, foreign correspondent, *New York Times* editorialist and writer on world affairs, Pulitzer Prize winner
Dict Am Bio supp v5; Index t Wom; Not Am Wom supp v1; Obit File

11340. McDowell, Rachel Killock
1880–1949
journalist
Index t Wom

11341. Meherin, Elenore
flourished 1910s–20s
journalist
Index t Wom

11342. O'Mahoney, Katherine A.
flourished 1910s
publisher, editor, lecturer, club leader
Irish
Index t Wom

11343. Parsons, Mary L.
flourished 1910s
pioneer journalist
Index t Wom

11344. Patterson, Ada
flourished 1910s–20s
journalist
Index t Wom

11345. Peyser, Ethel R.
flourished 1910s–30s
author, editor, music critic, lecturer
Index t Wom

11346. Phillips, Bessie I.
circa 1880–1954
journalist, society editor of *The New York Times*
Index t Wom; Obit File

11347. Poole, Fannie Huntington Runnells
flourished 1910s
poet, book reviewer
Index t Wom

11348. Rigby, Olga
flourished 1910s–20s
journalist
Index t Wom

11349. Roulet, Mary F. Nixon
flourished 1910s

author, journalist, musician, art critic, linguist
Index t Wom

11350. Scarborough, Katherine
flourished 1910s
journalist
Index t Wom

11351. Standish, Marian Eddy
flourished 1910s–30s
publicity director, journalist
Index t Wom

11352. Stanley, Imogene
flourished 1920s
journalist
Index t Wom

11353. Teichner, Miriam
flourished 1910s
journalist
Index t Wom

11354. Thompson, Charlotte
flourished 1910s
playwright, public relations counsel
Index t Wom

11355. Walsh, Honor
flourished 1910s
editor, author
Index t Wom

11356. Burnham, Mary
born 1881
editor, librarian
Index t Wom

11357. Gardner, Pearl
born 1881
religious worker, editor
Index t Wom

11358. Henderson, Alice Corbin
1881–1949
poet, cofounder of *Poetry Magazine*
Obit File

11359. Lawrence, Mary Viola Tingley
died 1931
journalist
Index t Wom

11360. Loveman, Amy
1881–1955
literary critic, editor, author, cofounder of the !Saturday Review of Literature
Dict Am Bio supp v5; Index t Wom; Nat Cyc Am Bio v44; Not Am Wom supp v1; Obit File

11361. Massee, May
1881–1966
editor, children's literature specialist
Not Am Wom supp v1

11362. Morgan, Jane
1881–1972
vaudeville, radio, and television actor; singer
Index t Wom; Obit File

11363. Parsons, Louella Oettinger
1881/93–1972
journalist, gossip columnist
Hollywood, CA
Cur Biog '73; Index t Wom; Not Am Wom supp v1; Obit File

11364. Patterson, Eleanor Medill "Cissy"
1881/84–1948
newspaper editor, publisher of the Washington, DC, *Times-Herald*
Washington, DC
Dict Am Bio supp v4; Index t Wom; Not Am Wom; Obit File

11365. Phillips, Lena Madesin
1881–1955
feminist, founder of the National and International Federations of Business and Professional Women's Clubs, author, editor, lecturer, politician
Dict Am Bio supp v5; Index t Wom; Not Am Wom supp v1; Obit File

11366. Dixon, Jane
circa 1882–1960
journalist
Index t Wom

11367. Fauset, Jessie Redmon
1882/86–1961
author, novelist, editor, educator
Encyc Black Am; Index t Wom; Negro Alman; Not Am Wom supp v1; Prof Negro Wom v2; Wom Lit; Wom Lit, More

11368. Huck, Winnifred Sprague Mason
1882–1936
representative to Congress, journalist
Index t Wom; Not Am Wom

11369. Kelley, Gertrude; Gertrude B. Gordon
circa 1882–1955
journalist
Index t Wom

11370. Lowe, Corinne Martin
1882–1952
journalist, fashion editor, author
Index t Wom

11371. Mason, Lucy Randolph
1882–1959
labor publicist, public relations officer for the CIO, southern trade union organizer, social worker and reformer, suffragist
Episcopalian

Virginia
Bio Dict Am Lab; Dict Am Bio supp v6; Encyc South Hist; Not Am Wom supp v1; Obit File

11372. McConnell, Lulu
1882–1962
radio, television, and stage comedian
Obit File

11373. Miller, Bertha Everett Mahony
1882–1969
bookseller, children's literature specialist, editor
Not Am Wom supp v1

11374. Ottiano, Rafaela
1882–1942
stage, screen, and radio actor
Obit File

11375. Reid, Helen Miles Rogers
1882–1970
publisher of *The New York Herald-Tribune* newspaper, journalist, suffragist, philanthropist
Episcopalian
New York
Cur Biog '70; Index t Wom; Nat Cyc Am Bio v56; Not Am Wom supp v1; Obit File

11376. Rippen, Jane Parker Deeter
1882–1953
social worker, journalist, Girl Scouts of America executive
Not Am Wom supp v1; Obit File

11377. Rittenhouse, Anne
died 1932
journalist
Index t Wom

11378. Robinson, Elsie (Fremont)
1883–1956
journalist, inspirational columnist for the Hearst newspapers
Index t Wom; Obit File

11379. Secondari, Rita Hume
1883–1953
Seattle Times correspondent in Italy
Washington
Italian
Obit File

11380. Wilson, Maude H. Mellish
died 1933
nurse, editor
Index t Wom

11381. Blanshard, Julia
died 1934
journalist
Index t Wom

11382. Fair, Ethel Marion
born 1884
librarian, editor, author, lecturer
Index t Wom

11383. Finney, Ruth Elbright
1884–1955
journalist, editor, author, clubwoman
Index t Wom

11384. Liebling, Estelle
born 1884/86
composer, singer, music educator, editor
Index t Wom

11385. McAfee, Helen
1884–1956
editor
Congregationalist
New Haven, CT
Nat Cyc Am Bio v43

11386. Bryant, Louise Frances Stevens
1885–1959
social researcher, medical editor, feminist, Socialist party worker, physician, public health worker
Dict Am Bio supp v5

11387. Harding, Margaret Snodgrass
born 1885
editor, publisher
Index t Wom

11388. Hopper, Hedda; Elda Furry
1885/90–1966
actor, journalist, gossip columnist
Hollywood, CA
Index t Wom; Not Am Wom supp v1; Obit File

11389. Kellogg, Elenore
died 1935
journalist
Index t Wom

11390. Patterson, Mary
1885–1975
editor of the New York *Daily Times*
Obit File

11391. Rourke, Constance Mayfield
1885–1941
student of American culture, historian, folklorist, author, critic, educator
Dict Am Bio supp v3; Index t Wom; Nat Cyc Am Bio v32; Not Am Wom

11392. Rouverol, Aurania
1885–1955
playwright, actor, radio scriptwriter, screenwriter
Index t Wom; Obit File

11393. Strong, Anna Louise
1885–1970
radical journalist, pro–Communist China advocate, author
Cur Biog '70; Index t Wom; Not Am Wom supp v1; Obit File

11394. Waldo, Ruth Fanshaw
1885–1975
advertising executive
Not Am Wom supp v1

11395. Anderson, Margaret Carolyn
1886–1973
editor, author, novelist, autobiographer
French (American expatriate to Paris)
Dict Lit Bio v4; Not Am Wom supp v1

11396. Applegarth, Margaret Tyson
born 1886
playwright, children's author, editor
Index t Wom

11397. Beatty, Bessie
1886–1947
radio commentator, journalist, magazine correspondent and editor
Index t Wom; Obit File

11398. Brinkley, Nell [Ethel]; Mrs. Bruce Moir McRae
1886/88–1944
newspaper artist, cartoonist, illustrator, journalist
Presbyterian
Index t Wom; Nat Cyc Am Bio v33; Obit File

11399. Doolittle, Hilda; Hilda Doolittle Aldington; H. D.
1886–1961
poet, leader of the imagist movement in poetry, author, literary magazine editor
Dict Lit Bio v4; Index t Wom; Nat Cyc Am Bio v45 and csv3; Nort Anth Poet; Not Am Wom supp v1; Obit File; Wom Lit; Wom Lit, More

11400. Essary, Helen (Murphy)
1886–1951
syndicated newspaper columnist
Washington, DC
Obit File

11401. Hardwick, Katharine Davis
1886–1974
pianist, newspaper publisher
Christian Scientist
Indiana
Nat Cyc Am Bio v58

11402. Kauffman, Ruth Hammitt
1886–1952
World War I correspondent, children's author
Obit File

11403. Lane, Rose Wilder
1886/87–1968
novelist, telegrapher, World War I Red Cross worker in Europe, Vietnam war correspondent
Index t Wom; Nat Cyc Am Bio v54

11404. Parsons, Alice Beal
1886–1962
author, literary critic
New York
Index t Wom; Nat Cyc Am Bio v50

11405. Paterson, Isabel Bowler
circa 1886–1961
journalist, columnist
Index t Wom

11406. Treadwell, Sophie
married 1911
playwright, journalist
Index t Wom; Wom Lit, More

11407. Bauer, Marion Eugenia
1887–1955
music educator, writer on music history, composer, editor, music critic
Index t Wom; Nat Cyc Am Bio v43, Not Am Wom supp v1; Obit File

11408. Case, Adelaide Teague
1887–1948
Episcopal educator
Episcopalian
Not Am Wom

11409. Chase, Mary Ellen
1887–1973
novelist, biographer, short story writer, literary critic, writer on the Bible, university educator
Episcopalian
Cur Biog '73; Index t Wom; Nat Cyc Am Bio csv9; Obit File; Wom Lit, More

11410. Churchill, Bonnie
died 1937
journalist
Index t Wom

11411. Colum, Mary
1887–1957
author, literary critic
Irish
Nat Cyc Am Bio v44

11412. Comstock, Amy
1887–1944
associate editor of the *Tulsa Tribune*
Tulsa, OK
Obit File

11413. Fawcett, Claire
1887–1960
cofounder of Fawcett Publications, Inc.
Obit File

11414. Lauferty, Lilian (Wolfe); Beatrice Fairfax
1887–1958
newspaper journalist, novelist
Index t Wom; Obit File

11415. Marshall, Marguerite Moers
1887–1964
journalist, author
Index t Wom

11416. Meyer, Agnes Elizabeth (Ernst)
1887–1970
author, journalist, vice-president and co-owner of *The Washington Post*, World War II correspondent, autobiographer, lecturer, social worker, Republican party worker, crusader for social services and education causes
Lutheran
New York
Cur Biog '70; Index t Wom; Nat Cyc Am Bio v56; Obit File

11417. Moore, Marianne (Craig)
1887–1972
poet, critic, editor, winner of Pulitzer Prize and National Book Award
Presbyterian
New York
Cur Biog '72; Index t Wom; Nat Cyc Am Bio v57; Nort Anth Poet; Not Am Wom supp v1; Obit File; Wom Lit, More

11418. Ratchford, Fannie Elizabeth
born 1887
librarian, author, editor
Index t Wom

11419. Robb, Josephine
married 1912
journalist
Index t Wom

11420. Sanderson, Julia
born 1887
radio actor and personality
Index t Wom

11421. Waln, Nora
1887/95–1964
author, journalist, antifascist worker
Index t Wom; Obit File

11422. Bryant, Nana
1888–1955
stage, screen, and television actor
Hollywood, CA
Obit File

11423. Buchanan, Annabel Morris
born 1888
composer, editor, author
Index t Wom

11424. Butcher, Fanny
born 1888
journalist, poet
Index t Wom

11425. Cobb, Beatrice
1888–1959
newspaper editor, publisher of the Morganton, North Carolina, *News-Herald*
Methodist
Morganton, NC
Nat Cyc Am Bio v45; Obit File

11426. Craig, Elisabeth May Adams
1888–1975
political journalist
Cur Biog '75; Index t Wom; Not Am Wom supp v1

11427. Damerel, Myrtle Vail "Murt"
1888–1978
vaudeville and radio actor
Obit File

11428. Drexel, Constance
1888–1952
newspaper reporter
German
Obit File

11429. Goodman, Lillian Rosedale
born 1888
composer, singer, pianist, critic, author, linguist
Index t Wom

11430. Lorne, Marion (Mac-Dougall)
1888–1968
actor, television comedian
Index t Wom; Obit File

11431. Solano, Solita
1888–1975
journalist, drama critic, novelist, poet
French (American expatriate to Paris)
Dict Lit Bio v4

11432. Vanderbilt, Amy; Mrs. Hans Knopf
1888/1908–1974

journalist, syndicated columnist, author, etiquette authority
Cur Biog '75; Index t Wom; Obit File

11433. Wagstaff, Blanche Shoe-maker
born 1888
poet, editor
Index t Wom

11434. Bonfils, Helen Gertrude
1889–1962
newspaper executive, chairperson of the board of the *Denver Post*, theatrical producer
Catholic
Denver, CO
Nat Cyc Am Bio v56; Obit File

11435. Craig, May
1889–1975
Washington, DC, correspondent for a chain of Maine newspapers
Washington, DC
Obit File

11436. de Camp, Rosemary
born 1889
television actor
Index t Wom

11437. Dowd, Alice Casey
circa 1889–1964
fashion consultant, publicist
Index t Wom

11438. Draper, Dorothy Tuck-erman
1889–1969
interior decorator, inventor, newspaper columnist
Cur Biog '69; Index t Wom; Obit File

11439. Gillespie, Marian
1889–1946
composer, pianist, author, actor, journalist
Index t Wom

11440. Gordon, Dorothy Lerner
1889–1970
radio and television producer, singer, children's author
Cur Biog '70; Index t Wom; Not Am Wom supp v1

11441. Roulston, Margorie Hil-lis
1889–1971
editor of *Vogue*
Obit File

11442. Stern, Elizabeth Ger-trude Levin; Eleanor Morton; Elsie-Jeab
1889/90–1954
author, editor, social worker, po-litical activist and antiwar worker

Quaker
Nat Cyc Am Bio v39; Obit File

11443. Taylor, Marion Sayle
1889–1942
radio adviser on domestic affairs
Obit File

11444. Wallace, Lila Bell Ach-eson
born 1889
editor, publisher
Canadian
Index t Wom

11445. Wallace, Mildred White
born 1889
composer, singer, publisher, au-thor
Index t Wom

11446. Waller, Judith Carey
1889–1973
broadcasting executive
Not Am Wom supp v1

11447. Ward, Maisie
1889–1975
book publisher, author, lecturer, Catholic church worker
Catholic
English
Cur Biog '75; Index t Wom

11448. Abrams, Norma
flourished 1920s
journalist
Index t Wom

11449. Best, Molly
flourished 1920s
humorist, journalist, author
Index t Wom

11450. Biddle, Katherine C.; Katherine Garrison Chapin
1890–1977
poet, literary critic
Obit File

11451. Boehringer, Cora Louise
flourished 1920s
educator, journalist
Index t Wom

11452. Brainard, Bertha
flourished 1920s
radio personality
Index t Wom

11453. Bryant, Louise
1890–1936
journalist, author, Communist party worker
Great Sov Encyc; Index t Wom

11454. Butler, Kate Maddux Robinson
circa 1890–1974
publisher, philanthropist, patron of French relief in World War II

Buffalo, NY
Nat Cyc Am Bio v58

11455. Cuthbert, Margaret Ross
1890–1968
program director of NBC
Canadian
Index t Wom; Obit File

11456. Dalrymple, Martha
flourished 1920s
journalist
Index t Wom

11457. Dare, Helen
flourished 1920s
journalist
Index t Wom

11458. Dayton, Dorothy
flourished 1920s
journalist
Index t Wom

11459. Dayton, Katherine
1890–1945
journalist, playwright, political satirist, humorist
New York
Index t Wom; Nat Cyc Am Bio v34

11460. Devereux, Margaret Green
flourished 1920s–30s
interior decorator, editor
Index t Wom

11461. Dougherty, Patricia
flourished 1920s
journalist
Index t Wom

11462. Dragonette, Jessica
flourished 1920s–30s
radio singer
English
Index t Wom

11463. Dumont, Margaret
1890–1965
screen and television actor, comic straight person
Obit File

11464. Ferguson, Edna
flourished 1920s
journalist, parachute jumper
Index t Wom

11465. Ferris, Helen Josephine; Mrs. Albert B. Tibbets
1890–1969
author, editor, children's author
Baptist
New York
Index t Wom; Nat Cyc Am Bio v55

11466. Fish, Helen Dean
1890–1953

book editor at J. B. Lippincott Co.
Obit File

11467. Furbeck, Mary Elizabeth
flourished 1920s–40s
editor, librarian
Index t Wom

11468. Gilliam, Florence
flourished 1920s–40s
journalist, theater critic, maga-zine publisher
French (American expatriate to Paris)
Dict Lit Bio v4

11469. Goss, Margaret
flourished 1920s
journalist, athlete
Index t Wom

11470. Grant, Frances R.
flourished 1920s–30s
museum director, editor
Index t Wom

11471. Greene, Mabel
flourished 1920s
journalist
Index t Wom

11472. Hadakin, Helen
flourished 1920s
journalist
Index t Wom

11473. Harpman, Julia
flourished 1920s
journalist
Index t Wom

11474. Harrison, Marjorie
flourished 1920s–30s
journalist
Index t Wom

11475. Herdman, Ramona
flourished 1920s–30s
journalist
Index t Wom

11476. Hill, Edith Knight
flourished 1920s
journalist
Index t Wom

11477. Hornaday, Mary F.
flourished 1920s
journalist
Index t Wom

11478. Humphrey, Mary
flourished 1920s
journalist, public relations expert
Index t Wom

11479. Hurd, Muriel Jeffries
1890–1958

poet, editor, president of the National League of American Pen Women
Obit File

11480. Jacobson, Pauline
flourished 1920s–30s
journalist
Index t Wom

11481. Jewett, Alice L.
flourished 1920s
librarian, editor
Index t Wom

11482. Keating, Micheline
flourished 1920s–30s
journalist
Index t Wom

11483. King, Mary
flourished 1920s–30s
journalist
Index t Wom

11484. Little, Ethel Holland
flourished 1920s–30s
fashion editor
Index t Wom

11485. Lowry, Judith
1890–1976
stage, screen, and television actor
Obit File

11486. Lynahan, Gertrude
flourished 1920s
journalist
Index t Wom

11487. Mahoney, Mary
flourished 1920s
journalist
Index t Wom

11488. McCarthy, Julia; Margery Rex
flourished 1920s
journalist
Index t Wom

11489. McKernan, Maureen
flourished 1920s
journalist
Index t Wom

11490. McLaughlin, Kathleen
flourished 1920s–30s
journalist
Index t Wom

11491. Mears, Marjorie
flourished 1920s
journalist
Index t Wom

11492. Mitchell, Milley Benett
flourished 1920s
journalist
Index t Wom

11493. Muir, Florabel
1890–1970
newspaper journalist, Hollywood columnist for the New York *Daily News*
Obit File

11494. Nolan, Helen
flourished 1920s–30s
journalist
Index t Wom

11495. Orr, Flora
flourished 1920s
journalist
Index t Wom

11496. Petersen, Agnes J.
flourished 1920s–30s
journalist, librarian
Index t Wom

11497. Pillsbury, Elinor
flourished 1920s–30s
journalist
Index t Wom

11498. Porter, Catherine
flourished 1920s–30s
editor
Index t Wom

11499. Powell, Minna K.
flourished 1920s
journalist
Index t Wom

11500. Prohme, Rayna
flourished 1920s
journalist
Index t Wom

11501. Provines, June
flourished 1920s–30s
journalist
Index t Wom

11502. Read, Elizabeth K.
flourished 1920s–30s
journalist
Index t Wom

11503. Reynolds, Ruth
flourished 1920s–30s
journalist
Index t Wom

11504. Richardson, Florence
flourished 1920s–30s
journalist, editor
Index t Wom

11505. Roe, Dorothy
flourished 1920s–30s
journalist
Index t Wom

11506. Ross, Mary
flourished 1920s–30s
journalist
Index t Wom

11507. Rothrock, Mary Utopia
born 1890
librarian, editor, author
Index t Wom

11508. Sartain, Geraldine
flourished 1920s
journalist
Index t Wom

11509. Schultz, Sigrid Lillian
flourished 1920s–40s
journalist, author
Index t Wom

11510. Seydell, Mildred
flourished 1920s
journalist
Index t Wom

11511. Shipman, Clare
flourished 1920s–30s
journalist
Index t Wom

11512. Shuler, Evelyn
flourished 1920s
journalist
Index t Wom

11513. Shuler, Marjorie
flourished 1920s–30s
journalist, pioneer air traveler
Index t Wom

11514. Smith, Elizabeth
flourished 1920s
journalist
Index t Wom

11515. Snow, Carmel White
1890–1961
editor of *Harper's Bazaar*, journalist, fashion expert
Irish
Index t Wom; Obit File

11516. Susong, Edith (Ingles) O'Keefe
1890–1974
newspaper publisher
Episcopalian
Greenville, TN
Nat Cyc Am Bio v59

11517. Taft, Mary
flourished 1920s
journalist
Index t Wom

11518. Taylor, Alva
flourished 1920s
journalist
Index t Wom

11519. Thomas, Clara Chaplin
flourished 1920s
journalist
Index t Wom

11520. Tinee, Mae
flourished 1920s–30s

journalist
Index t Wom

11521. Tomara, Sonia
flourished 1920s–30s
journalist
Russian
Index t Wom

11522. Watts, Mary
flourished 1920s
journalist
Index t Wom

11523. Wayne, Pinky
flourished 1920s–30s
journalist
Index t Wom

11524. Weekes, Marie
flourished 1920s
publisher, journalist
Index t Wom

11525. Wilson, Louisa
flourished 1920s
journalist
Index t Wom

11526. Woodward, Emily
flourished 1920s–30s
editor, journalist
Index t Wom

11527. Brice, Fanny (Borach)
1891–1951
comedian; stage, screen, and radio actor
Jewish
Brooklyn, NY
Dict Am Bio supp v5; Index t Wom; Not Am Wom supp v1; Obit File

11528. Cannell, Kathleen
1891–1974
journalist, fashion editor, ballet critic, autobiographer
French (American expatriate to Paris)
Dict Lit Bio v4

11529. Carrington, Elaine Sterne
1891/92–1958
magazine writer, radio-serial scriptwriter
Dict Am Bio supp v6; Index t Wom; Obit File

11530. Lane, Gertrude Battles
died 1941
magazine editor, journalist
Index t Wom; Obit File

11531. Littledale, Clara Savage
1891–1956
author, magazine editor, journalist
Dict Am Bio supp v6; Index t Wom; Not Am Wom supp v1; Obit File

11532. Mack, Nila; Nila Mac-Laughlin
1891–1953
radio producer, writer, director, actor
Index t Wom; Not Am Wom supp v1; Obit File

11533. McCarroll, Marion Clyde; Beatrice Fairfax
1891–1977
journalist, syndicated advice columnist, author
Nat Cyc Am Bio v60; Obit File

11534. Mears, Henrietta C.
1891–1963
founder of Gospel Light Church Publications
Obit File

11535. Mills, Marjorie
born 1891
editor
Index t Wom

11536. van Doren, Irita (Bradford)
1891–1966
literary editor of *The New York Herald-Tribune* Sunday book review section, journalist
Index t Wom; Not Am Wom supp v1; Obit File

11537. Barker, Ama
flourished 1922
journalist
Index t Wom

11538. Barnes, Djuna
born 1892
novelist, short story writer, poet, playwright, theatrical columnist, illustrator, portrait painter
French (American expatriate to Paris)
Dict Lit Bio v4 and v9; Wom Lit; Wom Lit, More

11539. Brown, Zara Cully
1892–1978
screen and television actor
Obit File

11540. Flanner, Janet
1892–1978
journalist, novelist, lecturer, *New Yorker* correspondent from Paris
French (American expatriate to Paris)
Cur Biog '79; Dict Lit Bio v4; Index t Wom; Obit File

11541. Grant, Jane
1892–1972
journalist, cofounder of *The New Yorker*, feminist
Index t Wom; Obit File

11542. Herbst, Josephine Frey; Josephine Herrmann
1892/99–1962
novelist, reporter of radical social and political movements in the 1930s, member of a European avant-garde writers circle in the 1920s
Dict Lit Bio v9; Index t Wom; Not Am Wom supp v1; Obit File; Wom Lit, More

11543. Lutes, Della Thompson
died 1942
author, novelist, editor
Michigan
Index t Wom

11544. Mandigo, Pauline Eggleston
1892–1956
journalist, public relations counsel, counsel to the American Association for the United Nations, aide to the US Department of Labor Women's Bureau
Index t Wom; Nat Cyc Am Bio csv7; Obit File

11545. Pattee, Alida Frances
died 1942
dietician, lecturer, publisher, author
Index t Wom

11546. Smedley, Agnes
1892/94–1950
author, foreign correspondent, lecturer, champion of revolutionary China, writer on China and the Far East
Dict Am Bio supp v4; Index t Wom; Not Am Wom; Obit File; Wom Lit, More

11547. Tomkins, Miriam Downing
born 1892
librarian, editor
Index t Wom

11548. Weld, Agnes Vance
1892–1975
newspaper publisher and editor
Episcopalian
Connecticut
Nat Cyc Am Bio v58

11549. Wheaton, Anne (Williams)
1892–1977
journalist, associate press secretary for President Eisenhower, Republican party worker, political activist, public relations expert
Cur Biog '77; Index t Wom; Obit File

11550. Wood, Peggy
1892–1978

television and stage actor, novelist, autobiographer
Cur Biog '78; Index t Wom; Obit File

11551. Brande, Dorothea Thompson
1893–1948
author, editor, journalist
Episcopalian
Chicago, IL
Nat Cyc Am Bio v39

11552. Brockman, Zoe Kincaid
born 1893
poet, journalist
Index t Wom

11553. Byington, Spring
1893–1971
television, stage, and screen character actor
Cur Biog '71; Index t Wom; Obit File

11554. Dalgliesh, Alice
born 1893
editor, author
Index t Wom

11555. Fitz-Gibbon, Bernice; Mrs. Herman Block
graduated 1918
advertising executive
Catholic
New York
Nat Cyc Am Bio csv9

11556. Hickok, Lorena A.
1893–1968
journalist, author
Index t Wom; Not Am Wom supp 1

11557. Hokinson, Helen Elna
1893–1949
cartoonist, artist
Christian Scientist
Dict Nat Bio supp v4; Index t Wom; Nat Cyc Am Bio v41; Not Am Wom

11558. Huntington, Dorothy Phillips; Dorothy Sanburn Phillips
1893–1972
short story writer, magazine writer
Obit File

11559. Kirchwey, Mary Fredrika "Freda"; Mrs. Evans Clark
1893–1976
editor, publisher of *The Nation*, Socialist party worker, feminist
Cur Biog '76; Index t Wom; Obit File

11560. Kirkus, Virginia
1893–1980

literary critic, book preview company founder, author
Cur Biog '80; Index t Wom

11561. Parker, Dorothy Rothschild
1893–1967
author, critic, short story writer, poet, humorist
Jewish
New York
Index t Wom; Not Am Wom supp v1; Obit File; Who Who Jew Hist; Wom Lit, More

11562. White, Katherine S.
1893–1977
first fiction editor of *The New Yorker*
Obit File

11563. Winslow, Thyra
1893–1961
journalist, novelist, short story writer
Index t Wom; Obit File; Wom Lit, More

11564. Armstrong, Bess (Furman)
1894/95–1969
journalist, White House correspondent to the *New York Times*, HEW assistant
Washington, DC
Index t Wom; Not Am Wom; Obit File

11565. Barker, Ellen Frye
died 1944
advertising copywriter, dramatic critic, genealogist, publisher
Index t Wom; Obit File

11566. Dunlap, Anne
married 1919
journalist
Index t Wom

11567. Fuldheim, Dorothy
born 1894
lecturer, radio personality
Nat Cyc Am Bio csv5

11568. Kaufman, Beatrice Bakrow
1894–1945
journalist, editor, playwright
Index t Wom; Obit File

11569. Knopf, Blanche Wolf
1894–1966
editor, publisher, president of Alfred A. Knopf Inc.
New York
Index t Wom; Not Am Wom supp v1; Obit File

11570. McCormick, Elsie
1894–1962
journalist
Index t Wom

11613. Jordan, Marian Driscoll; Mollie McGee
1898–1961
radio actor, comedian
Index t Wom; Obit File

11614. MacDonald, Lucile Saunders
born 1898
author, journalist
Index t Wom

11615. Moore, Grace; Mrs. Valentine Parera
1898/1901–1947
musical comedian, opera and popular soprano singer, screen and radio actor
Dict Am Bio supp v4; Index t Wom; Nat Cyc Am Bio v38; Not Am Wom; Obit File

11616. Soule, Isobel Walker
1898–1972
author, editor, labor leader, suffragist
Obit File

11617. Utley, Freda
1898–1978
author, journalist, foreign correspondent, lecturer
English
Index t Wom; Obit File

11618. Vollmer, Lula; Louisa Smith
1898–1955
playwright, short story writer, radio dramatist
Index t Wom; Obit File

11619. Winter, Ella
1898–1980
journalist, writer on communism, Communist party worker
Australian
Cur Biog '80

11620. Berg, Gertrude Edelstein
1899–1966
radio, television, and screen writer; playwright; producer
Jewish
New York
Index t Wom; Nat Cyc Am Bio v52; Not Am Wom supp v1; Obit File

11621. Crawford, Phyllis
born 1899
author, librarian, editor
Index t Wom

11622. Hansen, Hazel Dorothy
1899–1962
archaeologist, editor
California
Nat Cyc Am Bio v49

11623. Herbert, Elizabeth Sweeney
born 1899
editor, home economist
Index t Wom

11624. Herrick, Genevieve Forbes
married 1924
journalist
Index t Wom

11625. Kimbrough, Emily
born 1899
author, editor
Index t Wom

11626. McBride, Mary Margaret; Martha Deane
1899–1976
journalist, radio personality
Cur Biog '76; Index t Wom; Obit File

11627. Petersen, Anna
1899–1975
newspaper reporter, *New York Times* staff member
New York
Obit File

11628. Seymour, Jane; Jane Lair
1899–1956
stage, screen, and television actor
Obit File

11629. Traubel, Helen Francesca; Mrs. William Bass
1899/1903–1972
Metropolitan Opera soprano concert singer, television and film actor, nightclub entertainer
Cur Biog '72; Index t Wom; Nat Cyc Am Bio csv7; Not Am Wom supp v1; Obit File

11630. Ace, Jane Sherwood
1900/05–1974
radio actor
Cur Biog '75; Index t Wom; Obit File

11631. Adams, Mildred
flourished 1930s
journalist
Index t Wom

11632. Ames, Elinor
flourished 1930s
lecturer, educator, editor
Index t Wom

11633. Anderson, Katherine Watson
flourished 1930s
journalist
Index t Wom

11634. Archer, Alma
flourished 1930s
fashion expert, editor, author
Index t Wom

11635. Austin, Kay
flourished 1930s
journalist
Index t Wom

11636. Babcock, Lucille
flourished 1930s
advertising executive, fashion expert, editor
Index t Wom

11637. Baer, Leone Cass
flourished 1930s
journalist, reviewer, critic
Index t Wom

11638. Bailey, Florence
flourished 1930s
advertising executive, jewelry designer
Index t Wom

11639. Barratt, Louise Bascom
flourished 1930s
editor, author
Index t Wom

11640. Beaupre, Enid
flourished 1930s
advertising executive
Welsh
Index t Wom

11641. Benjamin, Louise Paine
flourished 1930s
editor
Index t Wom

11642. Bennett, Eve
flourished 1930s
fashion designer, editor
Index t Wom

11643. Benson, Clover
flourished 1930s
advertising display designer
Index t Wom

11644. Berwin, Bernice
flourished 1930s
radio actor
Index t Wom

11645. Bevans, Gladys Huntington
flourished 1930s
journalist, editor
Index t Wom

11646. Boardman, Frances
flourished 1930s
journalist
Index t Wom

11647. Bossidy, Mary
flourished 1930s
advertising executive
Index t Wom

11648. Briant, Nila Mack
flourished 1930s
radio director
Index t Wom

11649. Brody, Catherine
flourished 1930s
journalist
Index t Wom

11650. Brosnan, Mary
flourished 1930s
business executive, window display designer
Index t Wom

11651. Brown, Katharine
flourished 1930s
motion picture executive, editor
Index t Wom

11652. Buchanan, Mary Elizabeth
flourished 1930s
editor
Index t Wom

11653. Burke, Mildred
flourished 1930s
journalist, librarian
Index t Wom

11654. Burr, Kate
flourished 1930s
journalist
Index t Wom

11655. Cameron, Kate
flourished 1930s
journalist
Index t Wom

11656. Campbell, Ruth Elizabeth
flourished 1930s
editor
Index t Wom

11657. Carothers, Mina Hall
flourished 1930s
advertising executive
Index t Wom

11658. Cass, Erna W.
flourished 1930s
journalist
Index t Wom

11659. Cattell, Hettie
flourished 1930s
journalist
Index t Wom

11660. Clarahan, Virg Binns
flourished 1930s
public relations worker
Index t Wom

11661. Clayberger, Katharine Marie
flourished 1930s

editor
Index t Wom

11662. Clements, Hall-Kane
flourished 1930s
journalist, publicist
Index t Wom

11663. Coggins, Caroline
flourished 1930s
journalist, editor
Index t Wom

11664. Colburn, Joan
flourished 1930s
fashion commentator, radio
 broadcasting executive
Index t Wom

11665. Connor, Marcia
flourished 1930s
journalist, advertising specialist
Index t Wom

**11666. Cooley, Winnifred
 Harper**
flourished 1930s
author, lecturer, radio personality
Index t Wom

11667. Couch, Hilda Juanita
flourished 1930s
journalist, editor
Index t Wom

11668. Cravens, Kathryn
flourished 1930s
radio commentator
Index t Wom

11669. Crowne, Dorothy
flourished 1930s
public relations expert
Index t Wom

11670. Daggett, Helen M.
flourished 1930s
interior decorator, editor
Index t Wom

11671. Davies, Florence
flourished 1930s
journalist
Index t Wom

11672. Davis, Louise Taylor
flourished 1930s–40s
advertising executive
Index t Wom

11673. Davis, Maxine
flourished 1930s
journalist
Index t Wom

11674. Donner, Vyvyan
flourished 1930s
journalist, fashion designer, artist
Index t Wom

**11675. Duncan, Eleanor Fol-
 liott**
flourished 1930s
editor
Index t Wom

11676. Elliott, Grace Loucks
flourished 1930s
editor, author
Index t Wom

11677. Eskey, Elizabeth
flourished 1930s
journalist
Index t Wom

11678. Fitch, Geraldine
flourished 1930s
journalist
Index t Wom

11679. Fitzwater, Fanny Fern
flourished 1930s
editor, fashion expert
Index t Wom

11680. Flynn, Catherine
flourished 1930s
radio broadcaster
Index t Wom

11681. Foldes, Peggy
flourished 1930s
editor, journalist
Index t Wom

11682. Forbes, Jessica L.
flourished 1930s
publisher
Index t Wom

11683. Franklin, Jane
flourished 1930s
journalist
Index t Wom

11684. Fuller, Tyra Lundberg
flourished 1930s
journalist
Swedish
Index t Wom

11685. Gellhaus, Olga E.
flourished 1930s
journalist
Index t Wom

11686. Genauer, Emily
flourished 1930s
journalist, art critic, editor
Index t Wom

11687. Gillespie, Marian
flourished 1930s
explorer, photographer, editor,
 author
Index t Wom

11688. Gilman, Mildred
flourished 1930s
journalist, author
Index t Wom

11689. Golden, Sylvia
born 1900
author, editor, songwriter
Index t Wom

**11690. Goodbar, Octavia
 Walton**
flourished 1930s
artist, journalist
Index t Wom

11691. Gould, Paula
flourished 1930s
publicist, radio personality
Index t Wom

11692. Greene, Rosaline
flourished 1930s
radio actor
Index t Wom

**11693. Greene, Zula Benning-
 ton**
flourished 1930s
journalist
Index t Wom

11694. Gross, Miriam Zeller
flourished 1930s
educator, public relations worker
Index t Wom

11695. Hall, Kay
flourished 1930s
journalist
Index t Wom

11696. Hamilton, Florence
flourished 1930s
editor, poet
Index t Wom

11697. Hansl, Eva von Baur
flourished 1930s
journalist, editor
Index t Wom

11698. Harrison, Dorothy Ann
flourished 1930s
journalist
Index t Wom

11699. Harvitt, Helene
flourished 1930s
editor, educator
Index t Wom

11700. Hawley, Adelaide
flourished 1930s
radio personality
Index t Wom

11701. Haywood, Rosemary
flourished 1930s
editor, publisher
Index t Wom

11702. Herman, Mollie C.
flourished 1930s
advertising executive
Index t Wom

11703. Hill, Amelia Leavitt
flourished 1930s
editor, author
Index t Wom

11704. Hill, Dorothy Lampe
flourished 1930s
advertising manager
Index t Wom

11705. Hiller, Margaret
flourished 1930s
editor, author
Index t Wom

11706. Hillis, Marjorie
flourished 1930s
editor, author
Index t Wom

11707. Hirst, Anne
flourished 1930s
journalist
Index t Wom

11708. Hooten, Elivira
flourished 1930s–40s
journalist, editor
Index t Wom

11709. Hughes, Alice
flourished 1930s
journalist
Index t Wom

11710. Hull, Peggy
flourished 1930s–40s
journalist
Index t Wom

**11711. Humert, Anne Schu-
 macher**
flourished 1930s–40s
advertising executive, radio producer
Index t Wom

11712. Jeffries, Lila F. S.
flourished 1930s
editor, publicist
Index t Wom

11713. Johnson, Sonya Bortin
flourished 1930s
businessperson, advertising executive
Index t Wom

11714. Jones, Ruth E.
flourished 1930s
journalist
Index t Wom

11715. Keating, Isabelle
flourished 1930s
journalist
Index t Wom

11716. Keep, Mabel Hazlett
flourished 1930s
philanthropist, editor
Index t Wom

11717. Kerr, Adelaide
flourished 1930s
journalist
Index t Wom

11718. King, Frances Rockefeller
flourished 1930s
press agent, radio agent
Index t Wom

11719. Kuhn, Irene Corbally
born 1900
journalist, editor, radio executive, lecturer
Index t Wom

11720. Landers, Olive Richards
flourished 1930s
editor, author
Index t Wom

11721. Lape, Esther Everett
flourished 1930s
educator, editor
Index t Wom

11722. Larkin, Margaret
1900–67
author, poet, editor, composer, singer
Obit File

11723. Law, Helen Lynch
flourished 1930s
radio advertising executive
Index t Wom

11724. Leavitt, Martha
flourished 1930s
editor
Index t Wom

11725. Lee, Rosamond
flourished 1930s
business executive, journalist, advertising director
Index t Wom

11726. Lesser, Margaret Helen
flourished 1930s
editor
Index t Wom

11727. Lindsay, Malvina
flourished 1930s
journalist
Index t Wom

11728. Lobdell, Avis
flourished 1930s
railroad public relations expert, editor
Index t Wom

11729. Loughlin, Mary
flourished 1930s
advertising executive
Index t Wom

11730. Lyman, Esther
flourished 1930s

fashion editor, advertising manager
Index t Wom

11731. Mabry, Beatrice
flourished 1930s
advertising executive
Index t Wom

11732. Macy, Margaret
flourished 1930s
advertising executive
Index t Wom

11733. Mahnkey, Mary Elizabeth
flourished 1930s
journalist
Index t Wom

11734. Marlatt, Frances Knoche
flourished 1930s
lawyer, editor
Index t Wom

11735. Martyn, Marguerite
flourished 1930s
journalist
Index t Wom

11736. Maule, Frances
flourished 1930s
journalist, advertising writer
Index t Wom

11737. McClung, Mary J.
flourished 1930s
journalist, advertising executive, personnel director
Index t Wom

11738. McCulloch, Rhoda E.
flourished 1930s
editor
Index t Wom

11739. Meade, Julia
flourished 1930s
actor, television personality
Index t Wom

11740. Mears, Virginia
flourished 1930s
advertising executive
Index t Wom

11741. Meixell, Louise Granville
flourished 1930s
librarian, editor
Index t Wom

11742. Miles, Allie Lowe
flourished 1930s
cosmetician, radio personality, advertising writer
Index t Wom

11743. Miller, Hope Ridings
born 190?

journalist
Index t Wom

11744. Moir, Phyllis
flourished 1930s–40s
author, lecturer, editor
English
Index t Wom

11745. Moore, Alma Chesnut
flourished 1930s
editor
Index t Wom

11746. Moorehead, Agnes
1900/06–1974
stage, screen, and television actor; character actor
Cur Biog '74; Index t Wom; Not Am Wom supp v1; Obit File

11747. Morgan, Helen
1900?–41
torch singer; stage, screen, and radio actor
Dict Am Bio supp v3; Not Am Wom; Obit File

11748. Morris, Mildred
flourished 1930s
journalist
Index t Wom

11749. Mugglebee, Ruth
flourished 1930s
journalist
Index t Wom

11750. Noyes, Dorothy
flourished 1930s
business executive, advertising writer
Index t Wom

11751. O'Brien, Paulyna J.
flourished 1930s
publicity director
Index t Wom

11752. Olds, Jessie Gouds
flourished 1930s
journalist
Index t Wom

11753. Oursler, Grace Perkins
1900–55
novelist, playwright, magazine writer and editor
Obit File

11754. Ovens, Florence Jane
flourished 1930s
child specialist, editor
English
Index t Wom

11755. Packard, Ruth Mary
flourished 1930s
fashion editor
Index t Wom

11756. Paddleford, Clementine Haskin
1900–67
journalist, food editor
Index t Wom

11757. Palmer, Caroline L.
flourished 1930s
editor
Index t Wom

11758. Paul, Nora Vincent
flourished 1930s
insurance executive, journalist
Index t Wom

11759. Pennock, Grace Lavinia
flourished 1930s
editor
Index t Wom

11760. Pennock, Meta
flourished 1930s
nurse, editor
Index t Wom

11761. Perlman, Phyllis
flourished 1930s
publicity director, journalist
Index t Wom

11762. Phelps, Grace
flourished 1930s
journalist
Index t Wom

11763. Phillips, Frances Lucas
flourished 1930s
editor
Index t Wom

11764. Pinney, Jean Burrows
flourished 1930s
editor, social hygiene worker
Index t Wom

11765. Plummer, Mary Elizabeth
flourished 1930s
journalist
Index t Wom

11766. Polykoff, Shirley
flourished 1930s
advertising executive
Index t Wom

11767. Potter, Hester
flourished 1930s
journalist
Index t Wom

11768. Powell, Cecile V. K.
flourished 1930s
radio personality
Index t Wom

11769. Prim, Mary Elizabeth
flourished 1930s
journalist
Index t Wom

novelist, film and advertising
writer
Obit File

11822. Tremaine, Marie
born 1902
librarian, author, editor
Index t Wom

**11823. Underwood, Agnes May
Wilson**
born 1902
editor
Index t Wom

11824. Davenport, Marcie
born 1903
author, music critic
Index t Wom

11825. Dean, Vera Micheles
1903–72
international affairs specialist, editor, author, lecturer
Russian
Cur Biog '72; Index t Wom; Not
Am Wom supp v1

11826. Delmar, Irene
born 1903
journalist, editor
Index t Wom

11827. Kirkland, Muriel
1903–71
stage, screen, and television actor
Obit File

11828. Luce, Clare (Boothe)
born 1903
playwright, author, journalist,
politician, US ambassador
Episcopalian
Index t Wom; Nat Cyc Am Bio
csvF; Wom Lit

11829. Ryan, Irene
1903–73
screen and television actor
California
Obit File

11830. Shaw, Carolyn Hagner
born circa 1903
publisher
Index t Wom

11831. Talmey, Allene
born 1903
journalist
Index t Wom

11832. Vere, Glenna Collett
born 1903
golfer, sportswriter
Hall Fame Sport

**11833. Vreeland, Diana (Dal-
ziel)**
born circa 1903
fashion editor, journalist, costume museum consultant

French
Cur Biog '79; Index t Wom

**11834. Adair, Marion Hopkin-
son (Barnes)**
1904–65
New York civic leader, World
War II relief worker, cancer-
patient relief worker, patron of
cancer research, radio personality, mimic
New York, NY
Nat Cyc Am Bio v51

11835. Bogdanoff, Rose
1904–57
senior costume designer for NBC,
theatrical designer
Obit File

11836. Bourke-White, Margaret
1904/06–1977
photographer, photojournalist
Cur Biog '71; Index t Wom; Not
Am Wom supp v1

11837. Brittingham, Bettie S.
1904–49
editor of *Methodist Woman*,
Methodist church official
Methodist
Obit File

11838. Fishback, Margaret
born 1904
author, advertiser
Index t Wom

**11839. Hennock, Frieda Barkin
(Simmons)**
1904–60
criminal lawyer, FCC member,
advocate of educational televi-
sion
Jewish
New York
Polish
Index t Wom; Nat Cyc Am Bio
csv8; Not Am Wom supp v1;
Obit File

11840. Mannes, Mary
born 1904
author, journalist, critic
Index t Wom

11841. Nicholson, Margaret
born 1904
editor, author
Index t Wom

**11842. Peterson, Virgilia; Vir-
ginia Paulding**
1904–66
lecturer, author, literary critic,
television moderator, Peabody
Award winner
Index t Wom; Obit File

11843. Poletti, Jean Ellis
1904–74

advertising executive, New York
civic worker, UNICEF worker
Presbyterian
Nat Cyc Am Bio v58

**11844. Zimmerman, Carma
Russell**
born 1904
librarian, editor
Index t Wom

11845. Brenner, Anita
1905–74
journalist, writer on Mexico
Obit File

11846. Cassiday, Claudia
born circa 1905
music, ballet, and drama critic
Index t Wom

11847. Chase, Ilka
circa 1905–78
stage and screen actor, radio and
television personality, novelist,
autobiographer
Cur Biog '78; Index t Wom; Obit
File

11848. Cousins, Margaret [Sue]
born 1905
editor, author
Index t Wom

11849. Ducas, Dorothy
born 1905
journalist
Index t Wom

11850. Hobby, Oveta Culp
born 1905
government official, director of
the Women's Army Auxiliary
Corps, editor, politician
Texas
Index t Wom; Nat Cyc Am Bio
csv6

11851. Landis, Jessie Royce
1905–72
stage, screen, and television actor
Obit File

11852. Lombard, Helen Carusi
born 1905
author, journalist
Index t Wom

11853. Packard, Eleanor
1905–72
journalist, World War II correspondent, Rome correspondent
Cur Biog '72; Index t Wom

11854. Palmer, Gretta Brooker
1905–53
journalist
Index t Wom

11855. Ritter, Thelma
1905–69

stage, screen, and television character actor; first woman to win
the American Academy of Dramatic Arts Achievement Award
Cur Biog '74; Index t Wom; Obit
File

11856. Sergio, Lisa
born 1905
radio personality
Italian
Index t Wom

11857. Tighe, Dixie
circa 1905–46
journalist, foreign correspondent
for the *New York Post*
Index t Wom; Obit File

11858. Trilling, Diana Rubin
born 1905
essayist, book reviewer
Cur Biog '79

11859. Wicker, Irene
born 1905
singer, actor, radio scriptwriter
Index t Wom

**11860. Wurster, Catherine
Bauer**
1905–64
advertising executive, international consultant on housing and
city planning, journalist
Nat Cyc Am Bio v51

**11861. Zorbaugh, Geraldine
Bone**
born 1905
radio and television executive,
lawyer
Index t Wom

11862. Bates, Mary E.
died 1956
librarian, editor
Index t Wom

11863. Benaderet, Bea
1906–68
television actor
Los Angeles, CA
Obit File

11864. Brady, Mildred Edie
1906–65
consumer advocate, editor, journalist
Not Am Wom supp v1

**11865. Cochran, Jacqueline;
Mrs. Floyd B. Odlum**
1906/10–1980
aviator, director of the Women's
Air Force Service Pilots, flight
captain in the US Air Force,
colonel in the Air Force Reserve, World War II correspon-

dent, business executive, cosmetician
Cur Biog '80; Index t Wom; Nat Cyc Am Bio csv10

11866. Dunnigan, Alice Allison
born 1906
journalist, educator, economist
Index t Wom

11867. Halstead, Anna Roosevelt
1906–75
author, radio broadcaster, journalist
Obit File

11868. Haupt, Enid
born 1906
editor
Index t Wom

11869. Messick, Dale
born circa 1906
cartoonist
Index t Wom

11870. Patterson, Alicia; Alice Guggenheim
1906–63
Newsday founder, newspaper editor and publisher
Index t Wom; Not Am Wom supp vl; Obit File

11871. Stewart, Wendy
born 1906
lawyer, law journalist
Los Angeles, CA
English
Nat Cyc Am Bio csv7

11872. White, Poppy Cannon
1906–75
food columnist, cookbook author
Obit File

11873. Lorenz, Ellen Jane
born 1907
composer, editor, educator
Index t Wom

11874. Moran, Lois
born 1907
television actor
Index t Wom

11875. Winchester, Alice
born 1907
editor, author
Index t Wom

11876. Ames, Adrienne
1908–47
actor, radio commentator
Obit File

11877. Burnett, Hallie Southgate
born 1908
author, editor
Index t Wom

11878. Davis, Madonna Josephine "Joan"
1908–61
screen, radio, and television comedian
Obit File

11879. Dixon, Margaret Calder Richardson
1908–70
prison reformer, political journalist, newspaper editor
Episcopalian
Baton Rouge, LA
Nat Cyc Am Bio v58; Obit File

11880. Francis, Arlene
born 1908/12
actor, television personality
Index t Wom

11881. Graham, Sheila
born 1908
journalist, syndicated Hollywood newspaper columnist
English
Cur Biog '69

11882. Hemingway, Mary Welsh
born 1908
author, journalist
Index t Wom

11883. Horwich, Frances Rappaport
born 1908
educator, television personality
Index t Wom

11884. Taylor, Marian Young; Martha Denae
1908–73
interviewer, journalist
Presbyterian
New York
Nat Cyc Am Bio v57

11885. Buckmaster, Henrietta
born 1909
author, journalist
Index t Wom

11886. Coman, Martha
died 1959
journalist
Index t Wom

11887. Kirkpatrick, Helen Paull
born 1909
journalist
Index t Wom

11888. Livingstone, Mary
born 1909
comedian, radio actor
Index t Wom

11889. Schmitt, Gladys Leonore; Gladys Goldfield
1909–72

author, historical novelist, poet, editor, university educator
Cur Biog '72; Index t Wom; Obit File

11890. Smith, Kate
born 1909
singer, radio and television personality
Index t Wom

11891. Young, Marian; Martha Deane
1909–73
radio personality and interviewer
Cur Biog '74; Index t Wom

11892. Cowles, Fleur Fenton
born 1910
painter, editor, author, businessperson
Index t Wom

11893. Dalrymple, Jean
born 1910
theatrical publicist, producer, director
Index t Wom

11894. Edwards, Ester Gordy
flourished 1940s–70s
publishing executive, vice-president of Motown Records
Black
Encyc Black Am

11895. Fitzgerald, Margaret
born 1910
radio commentator
Index t Wom

11896. Fitzgerald, Pegeen
born 1910
advertising, sales, and fashion director
Index t Wom

11897. Hoffa, Portland
born 1910
radio actor
Index t Wom

11898. Hood, Marguerite Vivian
flourished 1940s
pianist, educator, author, editor
Index t Wom

11899. Moats, Alice-Leone
born 1910/11
journalist, author
Index t Wom

11900. Niessen, Gertrude
1910/13–1975
singer; comedian; Broadway stage, screen, nightclub, and radio actor
California
Index t Wom; Obit File

11901. Parker, Gladys
1910–66
fashion designer, cartoonist
Index t Wom; Obit File

11902. Sheppard, Eugenia Benbow
born circa 1910
journalist, columnist
Index t Wom

11903. Tracey, Cateau Stegeman
flourished 1940s
pianist, music educator, author, critic, lecturer
Index t Wom

11904. Ball, Lucille; Lucy Arnaz
born 1911
actor, comedian, television personality, film producer
Cur Biog '78; Index t Wom

11905. Briney, Nancy Wells
born 1911
publisher, editor
Index t Wom

11906. Hagy, Ruth Geri
born 1911
television personality, journalist
Index t Wom

11907. Payne, Virginia
1911–77
radio actor
Obit File

11908. Petry, Ann
born 1911
novelist, short story writer, journalist, literary critic
Black
Index t Wom; Negro Alman; Wom Lit; Wom Lit, More

11909. Wyatt, Jane Waddington
born 1911/12
actor, television personality
Index t Wom

11910. Arden, Eve
born 1912
radio and television actor
Index t Wom

11911. Beale, Betty
born circa 1912
journalist
Index t Wom

11912. Duke, Doris
born 1912
journalist, fashion editor
Index t Wom

11913. Graham, Virginia
born 1912

radio and television personality
Index t Wom

11914. Montgomery, Ruth Shick
born 1912
journalist
Index t Wom

11915. Moore, Lillian
1912–67
ballet dancer, educator, dance historian and critic
Obit File

11916. Powell, Eleanor; Mrs. Glenn Ford
born 1912/13
dancer, actor, television personality
Index t Wom; Nat Cyc Am Bio csv7

11917. Sothern, Ann
born 1912
actor, television personality
Index t Wom

11918. Vance, Vivian
born 1912
television actor
Index t Wom

11919. Wason, Betty
born 1912
journalist, author
Index t Wom

11920. Barrie, Wendy
1913–78
screen and television actor
Index t Wom; Obit File

11921. Bondy, Elizabeth Jeanne Hale
1913–69
literary agent, book editor
Congregationalist
New York
Nat Cyc Am Bio v54

11922. Clark, Eleanor
born 1913
novelist, book reviewer
Cur Biog '78; Dict Lit Bio v6

11923. Hathaway, Joy (Kenny)
1913–54
stage and radio actor
Obit File

11924. Kilgallen, Dorothy Mae
1913–65
journalist, newspaper columnist, television and radio personality
Index t Wom; Obit File

11925. Long, Tania
born 1913
journalist
German; English
Index t Wom

11926. Martin, Mary
born 1913
actor, singer, television personality
Index t Wom

11927. McClendon, Sarah
born 1913
journalist
Index t Wom

11928. Porter, Sylvia Field Feldman
born 1913
economics journalist, financial columnist, author
Jewish
Cur Biog '80; Index t Wom

11929. Reid, Charlotte (Thompson)
born 1913
representative to Congress from Illinois, politician, FCC member
Illinois
Cur Biog '75; Index t Wom

11930. Shields, Helen
died 1963
television character actor
Obit File

11931. Young, Loretta
born 1913/14
actor, television personality
Index t Wom

11932. Berger, Sylvia (Redman)
1914–58
radio and television scriptwriter
Obit File

11933. Burgos, Julia de
1914?–1953
poet, journalist
Not Am Wom supp v1

11934. Cartwright, Marguerite Dorsey
born 1914
educator, journalist
Black
Encyc Black Am

11935. Colby, Anita
born 1914
actor, technical adviser, journalist, editor
Index t Wom

11936. Downes, Anne Miller
died 1964
novelist, journalist
Index t Wom; Obit File

11937. Heap, Jane
died 1964
editor of the *Little Review Magazine*
Obit File

11938. Lee, Gypsy Rose; Rose Louise Hovick
1914?–70
burlesque and stage actor, television personality, mystery writer
Cur Biog '70; Index t Wom; Not Am Wom supp v1; Obit File

11939. May, Catherine Dean
born 1914
representative to Congress, radio commentator, radio producer
Index t Wom

11940. Saarinen, Aline Milton Bernstein (Louchheim)
1914–72
art critic, television commentator, writer on art history
Cur Biog '72; Index t Wom; Not Am Wom supp v1

11941. Smith, Hazel Brannon
born 1914
publisher and editor of Mississippi daily newspapers, Pulitzer Prize winner, civil rights worker
Mississippi
Cur Biog '73

11942. White, Ruth
1914–69
Broadway stage, screen, and television actor
Obit File

11943. Wyman, Jane
born 1914
actor, television personality
Index t Wom

11944. Hudson, Rochelle
1915–72
television and screen actor
Index t Wom; Obit File

11945. Mydans, Shelley Smith
born 1915
journalist, author
Index t Wom

11946. Simms, Virginia E. "Ginny"
born circa 1915
singer, radio personality
Index t Wom

11947. Weingarten, Violet
1915–76
novelist, newspaper journalist, screenwriter
Obit File

11948. Freeman, Lucy Greenbaum
born 1916
journalist
Index t Wom

11949. Furness, Betty
born 1916
actor, television personality, government official
Index t Wom

11950. Hardwick, Elizabeth
born 1916
novelist, essayist, short story writer, literary critic, social critic, editor of the *New York Review of Books*
Cur Biog '81; Dict Lit Bio v6

11951. Havoc, June
born 1916
actor, television personality
Index t Wom

11952. Jackson, Shirley Hardie
1916/19–1965
short story writer, novelist, ghost story writer, playwright, television scriptwriter, writer on domestic subjects, children's author
Dict Lit Bio v6; Index t Wom; Not Am Wom supp v1; Obit File; Wom Lit; Wom Lit, More

11953. Raye, Martha
born 1916
singer, actor, comedian, television personality
Index t Wom

11954. Roundtree, Martha
born 1916
radio and television personality, journalist
Index t Wom

11955. White, Nancy
born 1916
editor, fashion designer
Index t Wom

11956. Clayton, Jan
born 1917
singer, television personality
Index t Wom

11957. Diller, Phyllis
born 1917
television comedian
Index t Wom

11958. Emerson, Faye
born 1917
television actor
Index t Wom

11959. Graham, Katharine (Meyer)
born 1917
president of the Washington Post Co.
Cur Biog '70

11960. McNellis, Maggi
born 1917
radio and television personality
Index t Wom

11961. Mitford, Jessica Lucy
born 1917
muckraking journalist, autobiographer
English
Cur Biog '74

11962. Moss, Elizabeth Murphy
born 1917
business executive, World War II correspondent
Black
Encyc Black Am

11963. Wilson, Marie
1917–72
screen and radio actor, television personality
Hollywood, CA
Index t Wom; Obit File

11964. Landers, Ann
born 1918
advice columnist, journalist
Index t Wom

11965. Lewis, Cathy
1918–68
television actor
Obit File

11966. van Buren, Abigail;
Dear Abby
born 1918/19
journalist, advice columnist
Index t Wom

11967. Bowles, Heloise; Heloise
1919–77
syndicated newspaper columnist on household affairs
Obit File; Index t Wom

11968. Coit, Margaret Loyise
born 1919
author, journalist
Index t Wom

11969. Edwards, Joan
1919/20–1981
composer, author, singer, songwriter, radio and screen actor
Cur Biog '82; Index t Wom

11970. Gillis, Ann; Ann Slocum
1919–57
NBC radio and television producer
Obit File

11971. Jarvis, Lucy (Howard)
born 1919
television documentary producer
Cur Biog '72

11972. Kael, Pauline
born 1919
film critic
Jewish
Cur Biog '74

11973. Carnegie, Mary Elizabeth Lancaster
flourished 1950s–60s
nurse, nursing-magazine editor
Black
Prof Negro Wom v2

11974. Carpenter, Leslie
born 1920
government employee, speechwriter
Index t Wom

11975. Childress, Alice
born 1920
playwright, editor, actor
Black
Dict Lit Bio v7; Encyc Black Am; Wom Lit; Wom Lit, More

11976. Higgins, Marguerite (Hall)
1920–66
journalist, Korean War correspondent, Pulitzer Prize winner
Index t Wom; Not Am Wom supp v1; Obit File

11977. van Horne, Harriet
born 1920
television critic, journalist
Index t Wom

11978. Witherspoon, Naomi Long
graduated 1945
poet, journalist
Index t Wom

11979. Wright, Cobina; Elaine Cobb
died 1970
cabaret singer, society columnist, journalist
Hollywood, CA
Index t Wom; Obit File

11980. Blair, Janet
born 1921
television actor
Index t Wom

11981. Daly, Maureen Patricia
born 1921
author, editor
Irish
Index t Wom

11982. Huxtable, Ada Louise (Landman)
born 1921
architecture critic, journalist
New York, NY
Cur Biog '73

11983. Lee, Judy
1921–58
news and weather television broadcaster
Obit File

11984. Raines, Ella
born 1921
television actor
Index t Wom

11985. Starr, Cecile
born 1921
film critic
Index t Wom

11986. Brown, Helen Gurley
born 1922
author, editor of Cosmopolitan, lecturer, television personality
Cur Biog '69

11987. Fabray, Nanette
born 1922
television actor
Index t Wom

11988. Gray, Coleen
born 1922
television actor
Index t Wom

11989. Meadows, Audrey
born 1922/29
actor, television personality
Index t Wom

11990. Rafferty, Frances
born 1922
television actor
Index t Wom

11991. Ryan, Patricia (Gibson)
1922–49
radio actor
Obit File

11992. Storm, Gale
born 1922/24
actor, singer, television personality
Index t Wom

11993. Allyson, June
born 1923
television and movie actor
Index t Wom

11994. Bentley, Helen Delich
born 1923
newspaper journalist, chairperson of the Federal Maritime Commission, marine shipping expert, television documentary producer
Cur Biog '71

11995. Chandler, Sue Pinkston
flourished 1953–70s
editor, librarian
Black
Encyc Black Am

11996. Dee, Ruby
born 1923
stage, screen, and television actor

Black
Cur Biog '70; Encyc Black Am; Prof Negro Wom v2

11997. Dru, Joanne
born 1923
television personality
Index t Wom

11998. Hart, Dorothy
born circa 1923
television actor
Index t Wom

11999. Jeffreys, Anne
born 1923
television actor
Index t Wom

12000. Stapleton, Jean
born 1923
television character actor, comedian
Cur Biog '72

12001. Saint, Eva Marie
born 1924
actor, television personality
Index t Wom

12002. Torre, Marie
born 1924
journalist, television personality
Index t Wom

12003. Vanocur, Edith C.
1924–75
cookbook author, food columnist for The Washington Post
Obit File

12004. Whiting, Margaret
born 1924
singer, television personality
Index t Wom

12005. Brooks, Geraldine
1925–77
television, screen, and stage actor
Jewish
Index t Wom; Nat Cyc Am Bio v59; Obit File

12006. Cass, Peggy
born 1925
television actor
Index t Wom

12007. Larsen, Lisa (Rasmussen)
1925–59
photojournalist
German
Obit File

12008. Lockhart, June
born 1925
television actor
Index t Wom

12009. Russell, Gail
1925–61

screen and television actor
Obit File

12010. Stritch, Elaine
born 1925
actor, television personality
Index t Wom

12011. Arthur, Beatrice
born 1926
television actor
Cur Biog '73

12012. Ballard, Kay
born 1926
singer; stage, television, and
screen actor; comedian
Cur Biog '69; Index t Wom

12013. Banks, Eloise Hardison
born 1926
publisher, editor
Black
Encyc Black Am

12014. Davis, Anne B.
born 1926
television actor
Index t Wom

12015. Hartline, Mary
born 1926
television personality, orchestra
leader
Index t Wom

**12016. Hernandez, Aileen
Clarke**
born 1926
public affairs consultant; commissioner of Equal Employment
Opportunities Committee, 1965;
president of NOW; labor worker; civil rights worker; feminist
Black
Cur Biog '71; Negro Alman; Negro Her Lib v1

12017. Jackson, Anne
born 1926
stage, screen, and television actor
Cur Biog '80; Index t Wom

12018. Leachman, Cloris
born 1926?
screen and television actor
Cur Biog '75

12019. Leslie, Nan
born 1926
television actor
Index t Wom

12020. Lilly, Doris
born 1926
author, journalist
Index t Wom

12021. Palmer, Betsy
born 1926
actor, television personality
Index t Wom

12022. Reed, Carol
1926–70
television personality
Obit File

12023. Brothers, Joyce
born 1927/28
psychologist, television and radio
personality, newspaper columnist
Cur Biog '71; Index t Wom

12024. Carroll, Pat
born 1927
stage actor, television personality
Cur Biog '80

12025. Cobb, Buff
born 1927
television actor
Index t Wom

12026. MacKenzie, Gisele
born 1927
actor, singer, violinist, television
personality
Canadian
Index t Wom

12027. Page, Patti
born 1927
singer, actor, television personality
Index t Wom

12028. Parsons, Estelle
born 1927
stage, screen, and television actor
Cur Biog '75

12029. Terrington, Lady
married 1927
journalist
Index t Wom

**12030. Wojciechowska, Maia
[Teresa]**
born 1927
children's author, children's book
publisher
Catholic
Polish
Cur Biog '76

12031. Brown, Vanessa
born 1928
television actor
Index t Wom

12032. Johnson, Judy
born 1928
singer, television personality
Index t Wom

**12033. Wells, Mary Georgene
Berg**
born 1928
advertising executive
Index t Wom

12034. Cooney, Joan Ganz
born 1929

television executive, educational-
television programer
Cur Biog '70

12035. Grant, Lee
born 1929?
television and stage actor
Cur Biog '74

**12036. Hanschman, Nancy
Conners**
born circa 1929
journalist
Index t Wom

12037. le Guin, Ursula K.
born 1929
speculative fiction author, novelist, literary critic
Dict Lit Bio v8; Wom Lit; Wom
Lit, More

12038. Lind, Shirley Motter
born 1929
editor, publisher
Black
Encyc Black Am

12039. Brophy, Sallie
born circa 1930
television actor
Index t Wom

12040. Clayton, Xernona
1930/33–post 1952
television producer, television
personality, television host
Black
Encyc Black Am; Negro Alman

**12041. Howard, Lisa; Dorothy
Jean Guggenheim**
1930–65
television actor and reporter
Obit File

12042. Johaneson, Bland
flourished 1930s
journalist
Index t Wom

12043. Millar, Marjie
born 1930
television actor
Index t Wom

**12044. Tankersley, Ruth Mc-
Cormick "Bazy"**
flourished 1960s
editor, journalist, equestrian
Index t Wom

12045. Gorme, Eydie
born 1931/32
singer, television personality
Index t Wom

12046. King, Peggy
born 1931
singer, television personality
Index t Wom

12047. Sanders, Marlene
born 1931
television broadcast journalist,
ABC News executive, director
of television documentaries
Cur Biog '81

12048. Walters, Barbara
born 1931
television broadcaster, interviewer
Cur Biog '71

**12049. Dickinson, Angie; Ange-
line Brown**
born 1932
screen and television actor
Cur Biog '81

12050. Pfeiffer, Jane (Cahill)
born 1932
chairperson of the board of NBC,
IBM executive
Cur Biog '80

12051. Reese, Della
born 1932
popular singer, television variety
show host
Black
Cur Biog '71; Encyc Black Am;
Index t Wom

12052. Schuyler, Philippa Duke
1932–1967/69
pianist, composer, author, Vietnam war correspondent
Black
Encyc Black Am; Index t Wom;
Negro Alman; Obit File

12053. Terry, Megan
born 1932
musical playwright, dramatist,
television and radio scriptwriter
Dict Lit Bio v7

12054. Ball, Suzan
1933–55
screen and television actor
Obit File

12055. Montgomery, Elizabeth
born 1933
television actor
Index t Wom

12056. Sontag, Susan
born 1933
cultural and art critic, essayist,
novelist, short story writer,
filmmaker
Cur Biog '69; Dict Lit Bio v2;
Wom Lit, More

12057. Tyler, Judy; Judy Hess
1933–57
musical comedy actor, television
actor
Obit File

12058. Burnett, Carol
born 1934

singer; stage, screen, and television actor; comedian
Index t Wom

12059. Churchill, Reba
born 1934
journalist
Index t Wom

12060. Didion, Joan
born 1934
novelist, journalist, screenwriter
California
Cur Biog '78; Dict Lit Bio v2; Wom Lit; Wom Lit, More

12061. Henderson, Florence
born 1934
stage, screen, and television actor; singer
Cur Biog '71; Index t Wom

12062. Lewis, Shari
born 1934
television personality, puppeteer, ventriloquist
Index t Wom

12063. Mills, Vicki
born 1934
singer, television personality
Index t Wom

12064. Murray, Michele [Judith]
1934–74
novelist, poet, critic
Obit File

12065. Steinem, Gloria
born 1934/36
journalist, feminist, founder and editor of *Ms.* magazine, political activist
Cur Biog '72

12066. Brownmiller, Susan
born 1935
feminist leader, writer on rape and social issues, journalist
Cur Biog '78

12067. Corey, Jill
born 1935
television actor
Index t Wom

12068. Drew, Elizabeth (Brenner)
born 1935
political journalist, writer on American politics
Cur Biog '79

12069. Garland, Phyllis T.
born 1935
journalist
Black
Negro Alman

12070. Rivers, Joan
born 1935

nightclub entertainer, television comedian
Cur Biog '70

12071. Wright, Mary Kathryn "Mickey"
born 1935
golfer, sportswriter
Hall Fame Sport; Index t Wom

12072. Hochman, Sandra
born 1936
poet, novelist, playwright, magazine writer
Jewish
Dict Lit Bio v5

12073. O'Brien, Joan
born 1936
singer, television personality
Index t Wom

12074. Dennis, Sandy
born 1937
stage, screen, and television actor
Cur Biog '69; Index t Wom

12075. Donahue, Elinor
born 1937
television actor
Index t Wom

12076. Moore, Mary Tyler
born 1937
television and stage actor
Catholic
California
Cur Biog '71; Index t Wom

12077. Provine, Dorothy
born 1937
dancer, singer, television personality
Index t Wom

12078. Turnure, Pamela
born 1937
press secretary
Index t Wom

12079. McNair, Barbara
born 1939
television and screen actor, singer
Cur Biog '71

12080. Tyson, Cicely
born 1939/42
stage, screen, and television actor
Black
Cur Biog '75; Encyc Black Am; Negro Alman

12081. Bryant, Anita
born 1940
singer, television personality, antifeminist, antiabortion worker, antihomosexual crusader; Baptist religious worker
Baptist
Florida
Cur Biog '75

12082. Harper, Valerie
born 1940
television actor
Cur Biog '75

12083. Jenkins, Carol
flourished 1970s
television newscaster
Black
Negro Alman

12084. Lasser, Louise
born 1940?
television and screen actor, comedian
Cur Biog '76

12085. Quarles, Norma
flourished 1970s
television newscaster
New York
Black
Negro Alman

12086. Taylor, Lynette Dobbins
flourished 1970s
editor, executive
Black
Negro Alman

12087. Tolliver, Melba
flourished 1970s
television newscaster
Black
Negro Alman

12088. Zapata, Carman
flourished 1970s–80s
television, stage, and screen actor; director
Los Angeles, CA
Mexican
Dict Mex Am Hist

12089. Murray, Joan
born 1941
television newscaster, advertising executive
Black
Encyc Black Am; Negro Alman

12090. Olsson, Ann-Margret; Ann-Margret
born 1941
television actor, nightclub entertainer
Cur Biog '75

12091. Gault, Charlayne Hunter
born 1942
journalist
Black
Negro Alman

12092. Marshall, Penny [Carole]
born 1942
television actor, comedian
Cur Biog '80

12093. Mason, Marsha
born 1942
stage, screen, and television actor; comedian
Cur Biog '81

12094. Campbell, Toni
born 1944
television actor
Index t Wom

12095. Danner, Blythe
born 1944
stage, screen, and television actor
Cur Biog '81

12096. Chapin, Lauren
born 1945
television actor
Index t Wom

12097. Hawn, Goldie
born 1945
screen and television actor, comedian
Cur Biog '70

12098. Moore, Beatrice "Melba"
born 1945
stage and television actor, singer
Black
Cur Biog '73; Negro Alman

12099. Bergen, Candice
born 1946
screen actor, photojournalist
Cur Biog '75

12100. Bond, Abigail Monique
flourished 1976
television newscaster
Black
Negro Alman

12101. Davis, Christine R.
flourished 1976
publishing executive; staff director, US House Committee on Government Operations, 1949
Black
Negro Alman; Negro Her Lib v1

12102. Duke, Patty
born 1946
screen and television actor
Index t Wom

12103. Duncan, Sandy
born 1946
television actor and personality
Cur Biog '80

12104. Farrow, Mia
born 1946
stage, television, and screen actor
Cur Biog '70

12105. Field, Sally
born 1946
television and screen actor
Cur Biog '79

12106. Radner, Gilda
born 1946
stage, television, and screen comedian
Jewish
Cur Biog '80

12107. Struthers, Sally (Ann)
born 1948
television actor
Cur Biog '74

12108. Streep, Mary Louise "Meryl"
born 1949
stage, screen, and television actor
Cur Biog '80

12109. Pauley, Jane
born 1950
television broadcast journalist
Cur Biog '80

12110. Foster, Jodie; Alicia Foster
born 1962?
screen and television actor
Cur Biog '81

12111. Merande, Doro
died 1975
stage, screen, and television actor
Obit File

No Dates

12112. Allen, Barbara Jo
radio actor
Index t Wom

12113. Allison, Frances "Fran"

television actor
Index t Wom

12114. Battelle, Phyllis
journalist
Index t Wom

12115. Bonney, Therese (Mabel)
photographer, journalist
Index t Wom

12116. Cannon, Poppy
food columnist
South African
Index t Wom

MEDICINE AND LIFE SCIENCES

12117. Capillana
died 1549
author on natural history, historian
Peruvian
Cyc Am Bio

12118. Hawkins, Jane
flourished seventeenth century
pioneer, midwife
Index t Wom

12119. Jonas, Tryntje, Mrs.
flourished 1630s
midwife
Index t Wom

12120. Mance, Jeanne
1606–73
philanthropist, hospital founder and administrator
French Canadian
Cyc Am Bio; Index t Wom

12121. Hebden, Katharine
flourished 1640s
colonial physician
Index t Wom

12122. Wyatt, Mary
circa 1611–1705
colonial midwife
Index t Wom

12123. Bradnox, Mary
flourished 1648
colonial physician
Index t Wom

12124. Hazard, Mary
circa 1639–1739
colonial nurse
Index t Wom

12125. Merian, Marie Sibylle
1647–1717
naturalist, botanist, entomologist, botanical and entomological illustrator
Cyc Am Bio

12126. Hill, "Nurse"
flourished 1680s–1700s
colonial nurse
Index t Wom

12127. Weden, Elizabeth
flourished 1680s
colonial midwife
Index t Wom

12128. Cowell, Hannah
died 1713
colonial nurse
Index t Wom

12129. Tranchepain de Saint Augustine, Marie De, Sister
died 1733
Catholic nun, mother superior and founder of the Ursuline convents, hospital administrator, educator
Catholic
Cyc Am Bio; Index t Wom

12130. Williams, Hannah English
1692–1722

colonial biologist
Index t Wom

12131. Mankin, Widow
flourished 1730s
colonial druggist
Index t Wom

12132. Logan, Martha Daniell
1702/04–1779
educator, gardener, botanist, florist, horticulturist
Am Bio Dict; Index t Wom; Not Am Wom

12133. Beckford, Lydia C.
1703–1804
nurse
Index t Wom

12134. Jacintha do San Jose
1716–68
Catholic nun, school and hospital founder
Catholic
Brazilian
Cyc Am Bio

12135. Browne, Charlotte
flourished circa 1750s
colonial nurse
Index t Wom

12136. Colden, Jane
1724–66
botanist
Dict Am Bio; Index t Wom; Not Am Wom

12137. Farquhar, Jane
1724–60
botanist
New York
Am Bio Dict

12138. Darragh, Lydia Barrington
1728/29–1789
colonial nurse and midwife, hero of American Revolution
Pennsylvania
Cyc Am Bio; Index t Wom; Not Am Wom

12139. Ridgely, Sarah
flourished 1760s
colonial midwife
Index t Wom

12140. Whitmore, Mrs.
flourished 1760s
colonial midwife
Index t Wom

12141. Freeman, Elizabeth; Mum Bett
1732?–1829
litigant who sued for her freedom and won, midwife
Black
Prof Negro Wom v1

12142. Bass, Mary
flourished 1770s
colonial midwife
Index t Wom

12143. Tucker, Lucy Dougherty
flourished 1770s
nurse, pioneer
Index t Wom

12144. Warne, Margaret Violet
flourished 1770s
patriot of American Revolution, physician
Index t Wom

12145. Benjamin, Sara Matthews
circa 1744–1861 [sic]
patriot of American Revolution, nurse
Index t Wom

12146. Bunker, Rachel
died 1796
midwife
Index t Wom

12147. Wyllys, Ruth Belden
1747–1807
patriot of American Revolution
Index t Wom

12148. Penniman, Fanny
1760–1834
pioneer herbalist
Index t Wom

12149. Elliott, Anna
circa 1762–1858
hero of American Revolution, relief worker, nurse
Am Bio Dict; Cyc Am Bio; Index t Wom

12150. Marshall, Elizabeth
flourished 1800s
pharmacist
Index t Wom

12151. Fiske, Catharine
1776–1837
educator, scientist, farmer
New Hampshire
Am Bio Dict; Index t Wom

12152. Dudley, Blandina
1783–1863
patron of science
Cyc Am Bio

12153. Allen, Frances Margaret, Sister
1784–1819
nurse
Catholic
New Cath Encyc

12154. Wirt, Elizabeth Washington (Gamble)
1784–1857

children's author, illustrator, botanist
Cyc Am Bio; Dict Am Auth

12155. Minor, Jane
flourished 1820s
nurse, liberator of slaves
Black
Prof Negro Wom v1

12156. Tytler, Jane
flourished 1820s
pharmacist
Scottish
Index t Wom

12157. Phelps, Almira (Hart) (Lincoln)
1793–1884
educator, botanist, chemist, textbook author
Baltimore, MD
Cyc Am Bio; Dict Am Auth; Dict Am Bio; Dict Am Bio Men Time; Index t Wom; Nat Cyc Am Bio v11; Not Am Wom; Twent Cen Bio Dict Not Am

12158. Dix, Dorothea Lynde
1794/1802–1887
crusader for the welfare of the mentally ill, prison reformer, philanthropist, author, essayist, children's author, superintendent of army nurses in the Civil War
Massachusetts
Cyc Am Bio; Dict Am Auth; Dict Am Bio; Dict Am Bio Men Time; Dict Lit Bio v1; Index t Wom; Nat Cyc Am Bio v3; Not Am Wom; Twent Cen Bio Dict Not Am; Wom Cent

12159. Alexander, Janet
died 1845
midwife
Index t Wom

12160. Martin, Maria
1796–1863
botanical artist
Index t Wom

12161. Butler, Mary Newport
flourished 1830s
physician
Index t Wom

12162. Coxe, Margaret
born 1800
historical author, botanist, feminist, educator
Cyc Am Bio; Dict Am Auth; Dict Am Bio Men Time; Index t Wom

12163. Going, Ellen Maud; E. M. Hardinge
born 18?
nature writer

New York
Dict Am Auth

12164. Grove, Mary
flourished 1830s
lecturer, physiologist
Index t Wom

12165. Johnson, Hallie Tanner
born 18?
physician
Alabama
Black
Prof Negro Wom v1

12166. Lounsberry, Allice
born 18?
botanist, writer on botany
New York
Dict Am Auth

12167. Peter, Sarah Anne (Worthington) King
1800–77
charity worker, philanthropist, founder of art school for women, hospital founder, Civil War nurse, pioneer industrial arts educator, church worker
Catholic
Ohio
Dict Am Bio; Index t Wom; Not Am Wom; Twent Cen Bio Dict Not Am

12168. Redfield, Anna Maria Treadwell
1800–88
botanist, zoologist
Index t Wom; Nat Cyc Am Bio v2; Twent Cen Bio Dict Not Am

12169. Taylor, Rebecca
flourished nineteenth century
nurse
Index t Wom

12170. Gibbons, Abigail Hopper "Abby"
1801–93
abolitionist, prison reformer, feminist, women's welfare worker, Civil War nurse, philanthropist, journalist
Quaker
Cyc Am Bio; Dict Am Bio; Index t Wom; Nat Cyc Am Bio v7; Not Am Wom; Twent Cen Bio Dict Not Am; Wom Cent

12171. Penniman, Adelia
1801–84
pioneer herbalist
Index t Wom

12172. Jackson, Mercy Ruggles Bisbee
1802–77

homeopathic physician, temperance and suffrage worker, educator
Cyc Am Bio; Dict Am Bio; Index t Wom

12173. Powers, Eliza Howard
1802–87
philanthropist, patron of army medicine
Cyc Am Bio

12174. Green, Frances Harriet (Whipple)
1805–78
author, poet, abolitionist, botanist
Cyc Am Bio; Dict Am Bio; Dict Am Bio Men Time

12175. Hunt, Harriot Keziah
1805–75
physician, social reformer, suffragist, lecturer
Boston, MA
Cyc Am Bio; Dict Am Auth; Dict Am Bio; Index t Wom; Nat Cyc Am Bio v9; Not Am Wom; Twent Cen Bio Dict Not Am

12176. Law, Sallie Chapman Gordon; Mother of the Confederacy
1805–94
Civil War hospital organizer, nurse
Dict Am Bio; Index t Wom; Nat Cyc Am Bio

12177. Tyler, Adeline Blanchard, Sister
1805–75
Civil War nurse, Episcopalian deaconess
Episcopalian
Not Am Wom

12178. Taylor, Charlotte de Bernier
1806–61
entomologist, author, illustrator
Dict Am Bio; Nat Cyc Am Bio v1

12179. Hunt, Sarah
born 1808
midwife, physician
Index t Wom

12180. Ladd, Catherine; Minnie Mayflower; Morna; Alida; Arcturus
1809–99
educator, author, Civil War nurse, designer of the Confederate flag
Cyc Am Bio; Dict Am Bio; Nat Cyc Am Bio v24; Twent Cen Bio Dict Not Am

12181. Carrell, Columba
1810–78

founder of the Hospital of Saint Mary and Saint Elizabeth, Catholic nun, mother superior
Catholic
Louisville, KY
Cyc Am Bio

12182. Dircken, Lysbert
flourished 1840s–50s
colonial midwife
Index t Wom

12183. le Vert, Octavia Celeste Walton
1810/11–1877
author, Civil War nurse, travel writer
Mobile, AL
Cyc Am Bio; Dict Am Auth; Dict Am Bio Men Time; Index t Wom; Nat Cyc Am Bio v6; Not Am Wom; Twent Cen Bio Dict Not Am

12184. Maurice, Mrs.
flourished 1840s
healer
Index t Wom

12185. Nichols, Mary Sargent (Neal) Gove
1810–84
women's rights worker, feminist, dress and health reformer, medical author, physician, social reformer, temperance reformer, popular author, novelist
Cyc Am Bio; Dict Am Auth; Dict Am Bio Men Time; Dict Lit Bio v1; Index t Wom; Nat Cyc Am Bio v13; Not Am Wom

12186. Hoge, Jane Currie Blaike; A. H. Hoge
1811–90
Civil War relief leader, church and welfare worker, sanitation commission worker, author
Index t Wom; Not Am Wom

12187. Lohman, Ann Trow
1812–78
abortionist
Not Am Wom

12188. Lozier, Clemence Sophia
1812/13–1888
physician, founder and dean of the New York Women's Medical College and Hospital for Women, suffragist, feminist
Cyc Am Bio; Dict Am Bio; Index t Wom; Not Am Wom; Twent Cen Bio Dict Not Am

12189. Preston, Ann
1813–72
physician, hospital founder, college administrator, educator

Pennsylvania
Cyc Am Bio; Dict Am Bio; Index
t Wom; Nat Cyc Am Bio v10;
Not Am Wom; Twent Cen Bio
Dict Not Am; Wom Cent

12190. Collins, Emily Parmely
born 1814
suffragist, abolitionist, political
writer, Civil War nurse
Hartford, CT
Wom Cent

12191. Hagar, Sarah J.
died 1864
Civil War nurse
Index t Wom

**12192. Howland, Mary Wool-
sey**
died 1864
poet, Civil War nurse
Cyc Am Bio; Index t Wom

**12193. O'Connell, Mary; Sister
Anthony**
1814–97
Catholic nun, Civil War nurse,
orphanage and hospital director
in Cincinnati
Catholic
Cincinnati, OH
Dict Am Bio; Not Am Wom

12194. Seaman, Cleora Augusta
1814–69
physician
Nat Cyc Am Bio v23

12195. Wells, Charlotte Fowler
1814–1901
phrenologist, patron of women's
medical education, educator,
publisher, lecturer, businessperson
New York
Cyc Am Bio; Index t Wom; Not
Am Wom; Wom Cent

12196. Billing, Rose M.
died 1865
Civil War nurse
Index t Wom

**12197. Comstock, Elizabeth
Leslie Rous**
1815–1891/92
social reformer, abolitionist, Underground Railroad worker,
pacifist, freed slave's welfare
worker, temperance reformer,
women's rights worker, Quaker
minister, prison reformer, Civil
War nurse
Quaker
Dict Am Bio; Index t Wom; Nat
Cyc Am Bio v22; Not Am Wom

**12198. Cutler, Hannah Maria
(Conant) (Tracy)**
1815–96

women's rights leader, suffragist,
physician, journalist, author,
lecturer, pacifist
Illinois
Cyc Am Bio ad; Dict Am Auth;
Index t Wom; Not Am Wom;
Twent Cen Bio Dict Not Am

12199. Mason, Emily Virginia
1815–1909
Civil War hospital matron, Confederate army Civil War nurse,
author, biographer, educator
Cyc Am Bio; Dict Am Auth;
Index t Wom; Nat Cyc Am Bio
v5

12200. Remond, Sarah Parker
1815/26–post 1887
abolitionist, antislavery lecturer,
physician
Black
Negro Alman; Not Am Wom;
Prof Negro Wom v1

12201. Sawin, Martha A.
1815–59
physician
Index t Wom

**12202. Swisshelm, Jane (Grey)
(Cannon)**
1815/16–1884
journalist, author, editor, publish-
er, abolitionist, women's rights
worker, Civil War nurse
Cyc Am Bio; Dict Am Auth; Dict
Am Bio; Dict Am Bio Men
Time; Index t Wom; Nat Cyc
Am Bio v2; Not Am Wom

12203. Walker, Adeline
died 1865
Civil War nurse
Index t Wom

12204. Young, M. A. B.
died 1865
Civil War nurse
Index t Wom

**12205. Hopkins, Juliet Ann
Opie**
1816/18–1890
hospital administrator and found-
er, Confederate sympathizer
Alabama
Dict Am Bio; Encyc South Hist;
Not Am Wom

**12206. Thomas, Mary Frame
(Myers)**
1816–88
physician, suffragist, women's
rights worker, prison reformer,
temperance worker, editor
Index t Wom; Not Am Wom;
Twent Cen Bio Dict Not Am

**12207. Tillotson, Mary Ella
(Tillotson)**
1816–190?

writer and lecturer on hygiene,
poet
Vineland, NJ
Dict Am Auth

**12208. Bickerdyke, Mary Ann
Ball; Mother Bickerdyke**
1817–1901
hospital worker, Civil War nurse,
herbalist, philanthropist
Dict Am Bio; Index t Wom; Nat
Cyc Am Bio v21; Not Am
Wom; Wom Cent

**12209. Coleman, Lucy Newhall;
Lucy Colman**
1817–1906
abolitionist, educator of Blacks,
women's rights worker, suffragist, lecturer, health reformer
Universalist
Dict Am Bio; Nat Cyc Am Bio
v4, Wom Cent

**12210. Pomroy, Rebecca Ros-
signol**
1817–84
nurse, war nurse
Massachusetts
Cyc Am Bio

12211. Fales, Almirah L.
died 1868
Civil War relief worker, ambu-
lance nurse, philanthropist
Dict Am Bio Men Time; Index t
Wom

12212. Mowry, Martha H.
born 1818
physician, suffragist
Rhode Island
Wom Cent

**12213. Olnhausen, Mary Phin-
ney von**
1818–1902
Civil War nurse, author
Index t Wom

12214. Cutter, Eunice Powers
1819–93
lecturer, health reformer, abolitionist, historian
Twent Cen Bio Dict Not Am

**12215. Longshore, Hannah E.
Myers**
1819–1901/02
physician
Index t Wom; Nat Cyc Am Bio
v5; Not Am Wom; Wom Cent

12216. Pinkham, Lydia Estes
1819–83
patent medicine proprietor, abolitionist, temperance worker,
women's rights worker
Quaker
Dict Am Bio; Not Am Wom

12217. Davis, Sarah Iliff
born 1820
philanthropist, temperance worker, women's prison reformer,
milliner, sanitation worker for
the Union army during the Civil
War, Freedmen's Aid worker
Wom Cent

12218. Gleason, Rachel Brooks
1820–1905
physician, medical author, abolitionist, patron of freedmen's education, dress reformer,
women's rights worker
Dict Am Auth; Index t Wom;
Wom Cent

**12219. Livermore, Mary
Ashton (Rice)**
1820/21–1905
health reformer, hospital adminis-
trator, suffragist, temperance
worker, abolitionist, Civil War
patriot, miscellaneous author
Universalist
Melrose, MA
Cyc Am Bio; Dict Am Auth; Dict
Am Bio Men Time; Dict Am
Rel Bio; Index t Wom; Nat Cyc
Am Bio v1; Not Am Wom;
Twent Cen Bio Dict Not Am;
Wom Cent

12220. Mason, Biddy
flourished 1850s
pioneer nurse
Index t Wom

12221. Riley, Elizabeth Angela
circa 1820–1927 [sic]
physician, surgeon
Nat Cyc Am Bio v6

12222. Tubman, Harriet Ross
1820/26–1913
hero of the Underground Railroad, liberator of slaves, abolitionist, Union spy during the
Civil War, Civil War nurse, lecturer
Black
Cyc Am Bio; Dict Am Bio; Encyc
Black Am; Encyc South Hist;
Index t Wom; Nat Cyc Am Bio
v9; Negro Alman; Not Am
Wom; Prof Negro Wom v1

**12223. Barton, Clara; Clarissa
Harlowe**
1821/30–1912
founder of the American Red
Cross, Civil War hospital
founder, expert on organizing
military hospitals, philanthro-
pist, nurse
Appl Cyc Am Bio; Cyc Am Bio;
Dict Am Bio; Dict Am Rel Bio;
Index t Wom; Nat Cyc Am Bio
v3 and v15; Not Am Wom;
Twent Cen Bio Dict Not Am;
Wom Cent

12224. Blackwell, Elizabeth
1821–1910
physician, medical author and educator, worker for women's medical education
English
Appl Cyc Am Bio; Cyc Am Bio and ad; Dict Am Auth; Dict Am Bio; Dict Am Bio Men Time; Eng Wom; Nat Cyc Am Bio v9; Not Am Wom; Twent Cen Bio Dict Not Am; Wom Cent

12225. Lewis, Grace Anna
born 1821
naturalist, scientific illustrator, science writer, conservationist, ornithologist, abolitionist, Underground Railroad operator, pacifist, suffragist, philanthropist
Quaker
Index t Wom; Nat Cyc Am Bio v9; Twent Cen Bio Dict Not Am; Wom Cent

12226. Thompson, Elizabeth Rowell
1821–99
philanthropist, temperance worker, patron of science and of women's medical education, suffragist, political philosopher
Cyc Am Bio; Index t Wom; Nat Cyc Am Bio v5; Not Am Wom; Twent Cen Bio Dict Not Am; Wom Cent

12227. Agassiz, Elizabeth Cabot Carrie
1822–1907
founder and president of Radcliffe College, educator, biographer, naturalist, science writer
Boston, MA
Dict Am Auth; Dict Am Bio; Index t Wom; Not Am Wom; Wom Cent

12228. Chase, Mary Maria
1822–1852
botanist, poet
Index t Wom

12229. Dixon, Mary J. Scarlett
born 1822
physician, abolitionist
Pennsylvania
Wom Cent

12230. Fowler, Lydia Folger
1822/23–1979
physician, lecturer, social reformer, author, astronomer, science writer
Cyc Am Bio; Dict Am Auth; Index t Wom; Not Am Wom

12231. Shattuck, Lydia White
1822–89
naturalist, botanist, chemist, teacher of science
Not Am Wom; Wom Cent

12232. Winslow, Caroline B.
born 1822
physician, suffragist
Washington, DC
Wom Cent

12233. Bradley, Amy Morris
1823–1904
educator, Civil War nurse, hospital administrator
Index t Wom; Not Am Wom; Wom Cent

12234. Edson, Susan A.
1823–97
physician
Twent Cen Bio Dict Not Am

12235. Jewell, Catherine Underwood
died 1873
physician
Index t Wom

12236. Kemp, Agnes Nininger
born 1823
physician, abolitionist, temperance worker, lecturer
Wom Cent

12237. Colby, Sarah A.
born 1824
gynecologist
Index t Wom; Wom Cent

12238. Gillespie, Eliza Maria; Mother Mary of St. Angela
1824–87
mother superior and founder of the American Sisters of the Holy Cross, educator, Civil War hospital administrator
Catholic
Cyc Am Bio; Dict Am Bio; Index t Wom; Not Am Wom; Twent Cen Bio Dict Not Am; Wom Cent

12239. Harvey, Cordelia Adelaide Perrine
1824–95
Civil War nurse, relief worker, social welfare leader
Index t Wom

12240. Holstein, Anna
1824–90
author, Civil War nurse
Index t Wom

12241. Parsons, Emily Elizabeth
1824–80
Civil War nurse
Index t Wom; Not Am Wom

12242. Clark, Nancy Talbot
1825–1901
physician
Index t Wom

12243. Barry, Susan E. (Hare)
born 1826
Civil War nurse
Wom Cent

12244. Blackwell, Emily
1826–1910
physician
English
Index t Wom; Nat Cyc Am Bio v9; Not Am Wom; Wom Cent

12245. Denison, Mary Ann Andrews; Mrs. C. W. D.
1826–1911
novelist, short story writer, Civil War nurse
Cyc Am Bio; Dict Am Auth; Dict Am Bio Men Time; Nat Cyc Am Bio v19; Not Am Wom; Twent Cen Bio Dict Not Am

12246. Nash, Mary Louise
born 1826
educator, author, humorist, botanist, geologist
Wom Cent

12247. Plunkett, Harriette Merrick Hodge
born 1826
humanitarian, sanitation reformer
Massachusetts
Index t Wom; Wom Cent

12248. Sherwood, Mary Elizabeth (Wilson); M. E. W. S.
1826/30–1903
short story writer, poet, novelist, miscellaneous writer, patron of literature and science, philanthropist
Washington, DC
Cyc Am Bio; Dict Am Auth; Dict Am Bio; Index t Wom; Nat Cyc Am Bio v5; Wom Cent

12249. Taylor, Esther
1826–post 1872
homeopathic physician
Index t Wom; Wom Cent

12250. Youmans, Eliza Ann
born 1826
botanist, writer on botany, cookbook author
Cyc Am Bio; Dict Am Auth; Nat Cyc Am Bio v5

12251. Bottome, Margaret (McDonald)
1827–1906
health reformer, religious author, founder of King's Daughters, a religious society
Dict Am Bio; Nat Cyc Am Bio v13; Twent Cen Bio Dict Not Am

12252. Holcombe, Elizabeth J.
born 1827
physician
New York
Wom Cent

12253. Jones, Virginia (Smith)
born 1827
naturalist, ornithologist, ornithological illustrator
Dict Am Auth; Twent Cen Bio Dict Not Am

12254. Parker, Helen Eliza Fitch
1827–74
miscellaneous writer, marine naturalist
Cyc Am Bio; Dict Am Auth; Twent Cen Bio Dict Not Am

12255. Cumming, Kate
1828/35–1909
Confederate hospital administrator, diarist, nurse
Alabama
Scottish
Dict Am Auth; Index t Wom; Not Am Wom

12256. Gavitt, Elmina M. Roys
born 1828
physician
Wom Cent

12257. Green, Lucille H.
died 1878
physician
Index t Wom

12258. Pember, Phoebe Yates Levy
1828–1913
Confederate hospital administrator and nurse, diarist
Index t Wom; Not Am Wom

12259. Way, Amanda M.
1828/29–1914
temperance leader, suffrage leader, feminist, clergyperson, nurse
Index t Wom; Not Am Wom

12260. Woolsey, Abby Howland
1828–93
Civil War relief worker, hospital worker, charity and educational worker, author on public health, philanthropist
Dict Am Auth; Index t Wom; Not Am Wom

12261. Cleveland, Emeline Horton
1829–78
surgeon, medical educator, lecturer
Index t Wom; Not Am Wom

12262. Dolley, Sarah Read Adamson
1829–1909

physician, leader of professional
women
Index t Wom; Not Am Wom

**12263. Dorsey, Sarah Anne
(Ellis); Filia Ecclesiae**
1829–79
Civil War nurse, author, novelist,
theologian
Mississippi
Cyc Am Bio; Dict Am Auth;
Index t Wom; Nat Cyc Am Bio
v3; Not Am Wom; Twent Cen
Bio Dict Not Am

**12264. Potts, Anna M. Long-
shore**
born 1829
physician, medical lecturer
Quaker
Index t Wom; Wom Cent

12265. Thompson, Mary Harris
1829–95
surgeon, gynecologist
Index t Wom; Nat Cyc Am Bio
v13; Not Am Wom

**12266. Zakrzewska, Marie
Elizabeth**
1829–1902
physician, hospital founder
Polish; German
Cyc Am Bio; Dict Am Bio; Index
t Wom; Not Am Wom

12267. Adams, Martha
flourished 1860s
Civil War nurse
Index t Wom

12268. Aiken, Lizzie
flourished 1860s
Civil War nurse
Index t Wom

12269. Allen, Phebe
flourished 1860s
Civil War nurse
Index t Wom

12270. Alter, Belle Thompson
flourished 1860s
Civil War nurse
Index t Wom

12271. Aston, Mary A.
flourished 1860s
Civil War nurse
Index t Wom

12272. Baker, Anna H.
flourished 1860s
Civil War nurse
Index t Wom

12273. Baldridge, Elizabeth Lee
flourished 1860s
Civil War nurse
Index t Wom

12274. Ballou, Addie L.
flourished 1860s
Civil War nurse, author, artist,
lawyer
Index t Wom

12275. Barker, Stephen, Mrs.
flourished 1860s
Civil War relief worker, nurse
Index t Wom

12276. Barry, Susan E. Hill
flourished 1860s
Civil War nurse
Index t Wom

12277. Bedell, Leila Gertrude
flourished 1860s
physician
Index t Wom

12278. Bell, Mary E.
flourished 1860s
Civil War nurse
Index t Wom

**12279. Bengless, Catherine H.
Griffith**
flourished 1860s
Civil War nurse
Index t Wom

12280. Bissell, Lucy J.
flourished 1860s
Civil War nurse
Index t Wom

12281. Blackmar, Miss
flourished 1860s
Civil War nurse
Index t Wom

12282. Boyington, Mary K.
flourished 1860s
Civil War nurse
Index t Wom

**12283. Breckinridge, Margaret
Elizabeth**
flourished 1860s
Civil War nurse
Index t Wom

12284. Briggs, M. M., Mrs.
flourished 1860s
Civil War nurse
Index t Wom

**12285. Brown, Nancy M. Nel-
son**
flourished 1860s
Civil War nurse
Index t Wom

**12286. Brown, Susan L.
McLaughlin**
flourished 1860s
Civil War nurse
Index t Wom

12287. Bruson, Mary Blackmar
flourished 1860s

physician
Index t Wom

**12288. Buckley, Lettie E. Co-
vell**
flourished 1860s
Civil War nurse
Index t Wom

12289. Bucklin, Sophronia
flourished 1860s
Civil War relief worker, educator,
nurse
Index t Wom

**12290. Bullard, Jennie Mat-
thewson**
flourished 1860s
Civil War nurse
Index t Wom

12291. Bunnell, Henrietta S. T.
flourished 1860s
Civil War nurse
Index t Wom

12292. Burnell, Helen M.
flourished 1860s
Civil War nurse
Index t Wom

12293. Canfield, Martha
flourished 1860s
Civil War nurse
Index t Wom

**12294. Cartwright, Emily J.
Avery**
flourished 1860s
Civil War nurse
Index t Wom

12295. Chapman, Elizabeth
flourished 1860s
Civil War nurse
Index t Wom

12296. Clark, Bell Vorse
flourished 1860s
Civil War nurse
Index t Wom

12297. Cochran, Nannie M.
flourished 1860s
Civil War nurse
Index t Wom

12298. Cole, Helen Brainard
flourished 1860s
Civil War nurse
Index t Wom

12299. Colfax, Harriet R.
flourished 1860s
Civil War nurse
Index t Wom

12300. Counts, Belle
flourished 1860s
Civil War nurse
Index t Wom

12301. Cross, Sarah B.
flourished 1860s
Civil War nurse
English
Index t Wom

**12302. Crossan, Clarissa Wat-
ter**
flourished 1860s
Civil War nurse
Index t Wom

12303. Curry, Sadie
flourished 1860s
Civil War nurse
Index t Wom

12304. Dada, Hatte A.
flourished 1860s
Civil War nurse
Index t Wom

12305. Dana, Emily W.
flourished 1860s
Civil War nurse
Index t Wom

12306. Danforth, Ruth
flourished 1860s
Civil War nurse
Index t Wom

12307. Daniels, Frances D.
flourished 1860s
Civil War nurse
Index t Wom

12308. Davis, Clara
flourished 1860s
Civil War nurse
Index t Wom

12309. Davis, G. T. M.
flourished 1860s
Civil War nurse, humanitarian
Index t Wom

12310. Day, Juliana
flourished 1860s
Civil War nurse
Index t Wom

**12311. Dieffenbacker, Frances
A.**
flourished 1860s
Civil War nurse
Index t Wom

12312. Divers, Bridget
flourished 1860s
Civil War nurse
Irish
Index t Wom

12313. Dodds, Susanna Way
born 1830
physician
Wom Cent

12314. Dumas, Sarah J. Steady
flourished 1860s

Irish
Index t Wom

12370. Maertz, Louisa
flourished 1860s
Civil War nurse
Index t Wom

12371. Maish, Jennie Gauslin
flourished 1860s
Civil War nurse
Index t Wom

12372. Maxfield, Mary B.
flourished 1860s
Civil War nurse
Index t Wom

12373. McAndrew, Helen Walker
flourished 1860s
physician
Index t Wom

12374. McKay, Charlotte E.
flourished 1860s
Civil War nurse
Index t Wom

12375. McMeens, Anna C.
flourished 1860s
Civil War nurse
Index t Wom

12376. McPeek, Allie
flourished 1860s
Civil War nurse, patriot
Index t Wom

12377. Melton, Joann
flourished 1860s
Civil War nurse
Index t Wom

12378. Mendenhall, Elizabeth S.
flourished 1860s
Civil War relief worker, nurse, philanthropist
Index t Wom

12379. Miller, Adaline
flourished 1860s
Civil War nurse
Index t Wom

12380. Miller, Maria
flourished 1860s
Civil War nurse
Index t Wom

12381. Mills, Susan Carrie
flourished 1860s
Civil War nurse
Index t Wom

12382. Mitchell, Ellen E.
flourished 1860s
Civil War nurse
Index t Wom

12383. Morris, Matilda E.
flourished 1860s
Civil War nurse
Index t Wom

12384. Morton, Jane M.
flourished 1860s
Civil War nurse
Index t Wom

12385. Mott, Mollie C.
flourished 1860s
Civil War nurse
Index t Wom

12386. Munsell, Jane R.
flourished 1860s
Civil War nurse
Index t Wom

12387. Newman, Laura A. Mount
flourished 1860s
Civil War nurse
Index t Wom

12388. Newsome, Ella King
circa 1830–circa 1913
Civil War hospital manager, nurse, Confederate sympathizer
Bio Dict Confed; Index t Wom

12389. Nichols, Elizabeth B.
flourished 1860s
Civil War nurse
Index t Wom

12390. Oleson, Rebecca Lemmon
flourished 1860s
Civil War nurse
Index t Wom

12391. Otis, Rebecca
flourished 1860s
Civil War nurse
Index t Wom

12392. Palmer, Hannah L.
flourished 1860s
Civil War nurse
Index t Wom

12393. Patterson, Sarepta C. McNall
flourished 1860s
Civil War nurse
Index t Wom

12394. Pettes, Mary Dwight
flourished 1860s
Civil War nurse
Index t Wom

12395. Phillips, Emaline
flourished 1860s
Civil War nurse
Index t Wom

12396. Pollard, Carrie Wilkins
flourished 1860s

Civil War nurse
Index t Wom

12397. Pollock, Mary B.
flourished 1860s
Civil War nurse
Index t Wom

12398. Porter, Eliza C.
flourished 1860s
Civil War nurse
Index t Wom

12399. Pratt, Malinda A. Miller
flourished 1860s
Civil War nurse
Index t Wom

12400. Price, Rebecca L.
flourished 1860s
Civil War nurse
Index t Wom

12401. Rathnell, Maria L. Moore
flourished 1860s
Civil War nurse
Index t Wom

12402. Reading, Sarah M.
flourished 1860s
Civil War nurse
Index t Wom

12403. Richards, Maria M. C. Hall
flourished 1860s
Civil War nurse
Index t Wom

12404. Richardson, Mary A. Ransorn
flourished 1860s
Civil War nurse
Index t Wom

12405. Risley, Alice Carey Farmer
flourished 1860s
Civil War nurse
Index t Wom

12406. Ross, Anna Maria
flourished 1860s
Civil War philanthropist, nurse
Index t Wom

12407. Russell, E. J.
flourished 1860s
Civil War nurse, educator
Index t Wom

12408. Sackett, Emma A. French
flourished 1860s
Civil War nurse
Index t Wom

12409. Schram, Ann Maria B.
flourished 1860s

Civil War nurse
Index t Wom

12410. Scott, Harriet M.
flourished 1860s
Civil War nurse
Index t Wom

12411. Scott, Kate M.
flourished 1860s; died 1911
Civil War nurse
Index t Wom

12412. Sharpless, Hattie R.
flourished 1860s
Civil War nurse
Index t Wom

12413. Shelton, A.
flourished 1860s
Civil War nurse
Index t Wom

12414. Small, Jerusha R.
flourished 1860s
Civil War nurse
Index t Wom

12415. Smith, Mary E. Webber
flourished 1860s
Civil War nurse
Index t Wom

12416. Smith, Rebecca S.
flourished 1860s
educator, Civil War nurse
Index t Wom

12417. Smythe, Amanda B.
flourished 1860s
Civil War nurse
Index t Wom

12418. Spaulding, Jennie Tileston
flourished 1860s
Civil War nurse
Index t Wom

12419. Spencer, Emily P.
flourished 1860s
Civil War nurse
Index t Wom

12420. Spencer, R. H., Mrs.
flourished 1860s
Civil War nurse
Index t Wom

12421. Sprague, Sarah J. Milliken
flourished 1860s
Civil War nurse
Index t Wom

12422. Sprague, Susannah
flourished 1860s
Civil War nurse
Index t Wom

12423. Squire, Mary E.
flourished 1860s

Civil War nurse
Index t Wom

12424. Stanley, Cornelia M. Tomkins
flourished 1860s
Civil War nurse
Index t Wom

12425. Starbird, Hannah Judkins
flourished 1860s
Civil War nurse
Index t Wom

12426. Starr, Lucy E.
flourished 1860s
Civil War nurse
Index t Wom

12427. Stevens, Mary O. Townsend
flourished 1860s
Civil War nurse
Index t Wom

12428. Stevenson, Sophie
flourished 1860s
Civil War nurse
Index t Wom

12429. Stewart, Mary E. Pearce
flourished 1860s
Civil War nurse
Index t Wom

12430. Stewart, Salome M.
flourished 1860s
Civil War nurse
Index t Wom

12431. Stubbs, Annie Bell
flourished 1860s
Civil War nurse
Index t Wom

12432. Sturgis, Mother
flourished 1860s
Civil War nurse
Index t Wom

12433. Swartz, Vesta M.
flourished 1860s
Civil War nurse
Index t Wom

12434. Tannehill, Arabella
flourished 1860s
Civil War nurse
Index t Wom

12435. Taylor, Catherine L.
flourished 1860s
Civil War nurse
Index t Wom

12436. Taylor, Nellie Maria
flourished 1860s
Civil War nurse
Index t Wom

12437. Tenney, Abby Amy Grove
flourished 1860s–70s
naturalist, science writer
Cyc Am Bio

12438. Thomas, E., Mrs.
flourished 1860s
Civil War nurse
Index t Wom

12439. Thompson, Charlotte Marson
flourished 1860s
Civil War nurse
Index t Wom

12440. Titcomb, Louise
flourished 1860s
Civil War nurse
Index t Wom

12441. Tomkins, Cornelia M.
flourished 1860s
Civil War nurse
Index t Wom

12442. Townsend, Eliza L.
flourished 1860s
Civil War nurse
Index t Wom

12443. Treat, Mary Lua Adelia (Davis) (Allen)
born 1830/35
scientific author, naturalist
Vineland, NJ
Dict Am Auth; Index t Wom

12444. Tyson, Laura R. Cotton
flourished 1860s
Civil War nurse
Index t Wom

12445. Usher, Rebecca R.
flourished 1860s
Civil War nurse
Index t Wom

12446. Vance, Mary
flourished 1860s
Civil War nurse
Index t Wom

12447. Warnock, Susan Mercer
flourished 1860s
Civil War nurse
Index t Wom

12448. White, Cynthia Elbin
flourished 1860s
Civil War nurse
Index t Wom

12449. Whiteman, Lydia L.
flourished 1860s
Civil War nurse
Index t Wom

12450. Willard, Electra
flourished 1860s

Civil War nurse
Index t Wom

12451. Willets, Georgiana
flourished 1860s
Civil War nurse
Index t Wom

12452. Willson, Mary Eleanor
flourished 1860s
Civil War nurse
Index t Wom

12453. Wiswall, Hattie
flourished 1860s
Civil War nurse
Index t Wom

12454. Witherall, E. C., Mrs.
flourished 1860s
Civil War nurse
Index t Wom

12455. Woodley, Emily E. Wilson
flourished 1860s
Civil War nurse
Index t Wom

12456. Woodworth, Mary A. E. K.
flourished 1860s
Civil War nurse
Index t Wom

12457. Woolsey, Caroline Caisson
flourished 1860s
Civil War nurse, author
Index t Wom

12458. Woolsey, Harriet Roosevelt "Hatty"
flourished 1860s
Civil War nurse, author
Index t Wom

12459. Woolsey, Jane Newton
flourished 1860s
Civil War nurse
Index t Wom

12460. Woolsey, Jane Stuart
1830–91
Civil War relief and hospital worker, charity and educational worker, nurse, author
Index t Wom; Not Am Wom

12461. Wormeley, Katharine Prescott
1830/32–1908
Civil War relief and hospital worker, writer on sanitation, charity worker, philanthropist, translator, biographer
Rhode Island
English
Cyc Am Bio; Dict Am Bio; Index t Wom; Nat Cyc Am Bio v8; Not Am Wom; Twent Cen Bio Dict Not Am; Wom Cent

12462. Wright, Leonore Smith
flourished 1860s
Civil War nurse
Index t Wom

12463. Young, Lucy A. Newton
flourished 1860s
Civil War nurse
Index t Wom

12464. Bodley, Rachel Littler
1831–88
chemist, botanist, physician, naturalist, dean of the Women's Medical College of Pennsylvania
Pennsylvania
Not Am Wom; Wom Cent

12465. Bradwell, Myra R. (Colby)
1831–1894/96
lawyer, suffragist, editor, Civil War nurse
Chicago, IL
Dict Am Bio; Index t Wom; Nat Cyc Am Bio v1; Not Am Wom; Twent Cen Bio Dict Not Am; Wom Cent

12466. Fairbanks, Elizabeth B.
born 1831
philanthropist, mental institution reformer
Wisconsin
Wom Cent

12467. Green, Cordelia A.
born 1831
physician
Index t Wom

12468. Miller, Harriet (Mann); Olive Thorne Miller
1831–1918
author, ornithologist, bird watcher, naturalist, nature writer, conservationist, children's author, magazine writer
Swedenborgian
Brooklyn, NY
Dict Am Auth; Index t Wom; Nat Cyc Am Bio v9; Not Am Wom; Twent Cen Bio Dict Not Am

12469. Seacole, Mary
died 1881
war nurse in the Crimea
Black
World Great Men Col v2

12470. Smith, Adelaide W.
born 1831
Civil War nurse
Index t Wom

12471. Tincker, Mary Agnes
1831/37–1907
novelist, Civil War nurse

Catholic
Cyc Am Bio; Dict Am Bio; Nat
Cyc Am Bio v8; Twent Cen Bio
Dict Not Am

12472. Wilhite, Mary Holloway
1831–92
physician, feminist, philanthropist
Wom Cent

12473. Young, Sarah Graham;
Aunt Betty
born 1831
Civil War army nurse, Union
sympathizer
Wom Cent

12474. Culver, Helen
1832–1925
philanthropist, Black welfare
worker, patron of science, hospital administrator, educator,
real estate businessperson
Index t Wom; Nat Cyc Am Bio
v17; Twent Cen Bio Dict Not
Am

12475. Fussell, Susan
1832–89
educator, army nurse in the Civil
War, Civil War relief worker,
philanthropist
Quaker
Wom Cent

12476. Gordon, S. Anna
born 1832
homeopathic physician, Civil War
doctor, author, temperance
worker, meteorologist
Wom Cent

12477. Hall, Sara C.
born 1832
physician, suffragist
Kansas
Wom Cent

12478. Walker, Mary Edwards
1832–1919
physician, Civil War medical
worker, hospital founder, army
war surgeon, Union spy during
the Civil War; women's rights
worker, suffragist, dress reformer, inventor, lecturer, winner of
the Congressional Medal of
Honor
Dict Am Bio; Index t Wom; Nat
Cyc Am Bio v13; Not Am
Wom; Wom Cent

12479. Walworth, Ellen (Hardin)
1832–1915
author, war nurse, writer on the
history of Saratoga, educator,
poet

Saratoga, NY
Cyc Am Bio and ad; Dict Am
Auth; Index t Wom; Twent Cen
Bio Dict Not Am; Wom Cent

12480. Buckel, Chloe Annette
1833–1912
physician, Civil War nurse
Not Am Wom

12481. Canfield, Corresta T.
born 1833
physician
Chicago, IL
Wom Cent

12482. Pringle, Mary
born 1833
Civil War nurse
Index t Wom

12483. Severance, Juliet H.
born 1833
physician, abolitionist, feminist,
temperance worker, political activist
Spiritualist
Wom Cent

12484. Seward, Sara Cornelia
1833–91
physician, medical missionary
Index t Wom; Twent Cen Bio
Dict Not Am

12485. Stockham, Alice (Bunker)
born 1833
physician, medical author, musician, biographer, suffragist
Dict Am Auth; Wom Cent

12486. Taylor, Lucy Beaman
Hobbs
1833–1910
dentist, dental surgeon
Index t Wom; Not Am Wom

12487. Tompkins, Sally Louisa
1833–1916
Confederate hospital head, captain of cavalry in the Confederate army
Virginia
Bio Dict Confed; Dict Am Bio;
Encyc South Hist; Index t
Wom; Not Am Wom

12488. Wheelock, Julia Susan
born 1833
Civil War nurse, hospital nurse,
author
Cyc Am Bio; Index t Wom

12489. Woolsey, Georgeanne
Muirson
1833–1906
Civil War relief and hospital
worker, charity and educational
worker
Index t Wom; Not Am Wom

12490. Brinton, Emma Southwick
born 1834
Civil War nurse, traveler
Wom Cent

12491. Fairchild, Maria Augusta
born 1834
physician
Swedenborgian
Wom Cent

12492. Furbish, Kate
1834–1931
botanist
Not Am Wom

12493. Safford, Mary Joanna
Jane
1834–91
Civil War nurse, physician, surgeon
Boston, MA
Index t Wom; Not Am Wom;
Wom Cent

12494. Swain, Clara A.
1834–1910
pioneer woman medical missionary to India and the Orient,
physician
Dict Am Bio; Index t Wom; Not
Am Wom

12495. Wilson, Martha Eleanor
Loftin
born 1834
missionary worker, Civil War
nurse
Baptist
Georgia
Wom Cent

12496. Andrews, Annie M.
born 1835
epidemic nurse
Appl Cyc Am Bio

12497. Bristol, Augusta (Cooper)
1835–1910
educator, writer on education, author, poet, sociologist, lecturer
on philosophic and scientific
topics
Cyc Am Bio and ad; Dict Am
Auth; Twent Cen Bio Dict Not
Am; Wom Cent

12498. Cornell, Ellen Frances
born 1835
poet, marine shell collector
Swedenborgian
Massachusetts
Wom Cent

12499. Davis, Minnie S.
born 1835

author, temperance worker, suffragist, women's rights worker,
"mental science" healer
Index t Wom; Wom Cent

12500. Edwards, Anna Cheney
born 1835
geologist, botanist, educator
Wom Cent

12501. Elder, Susan (Blanchard); Hermine
1835–1923
religious author, poet, dramatist,
natural scientist
Catholic
New Orleans, LA
Cyc Am Bio; Dict Am Auth; Dict
Am Bio; Nat Cyc Am Bio v11;
Twent Cen Bio Dict Not Am

12502. Osgood, Helen Louise
(Gibson/Gilson)
1835–68
philanthropist, Civil War hospital
administrator, nurse
Cyc Am Bio; Dict Am Bio Men
Time; Index t Wom; Not Am
Wom

12503. Woolsey, Sarah Chauncy; Susan Coolidge
1835/45–1905
children's author, poet, Civil War
nurse
Newport, RI
Dict Am Auth; Dict Am Bio;
Index t Wom; Nat Cyc Am Bio
v11; Not Am Wom; Wom Cent

12504. Crocker, Susan
Elizabeth Wood
born 1836
physician, surgeon
Twent Cen Bio Dict Not Am

12505. Kalakaua, Emma Kaleleonalani
1836–85
founder of Kamehameha Hospital
Cyc Am Bio

12506. Lemmon, Sarah Allen
(Plummer)
1836–post 1860s
Civil War nurse, botanist, writer
on botany
Dict Am Auth; Index t Wom

12507. Miller, Elizabeth
born 1836
physician, Civil War nurse
Wom Cent

12508. Scripps, Ellen Browning
1836–1932
philanthropist, newspaper writer
and publisher, patron of marine
science, founder of Scripps Marine Lab, pacifist, feminist, temperance worker

La Jolla, CA
Dict Am Bio; Index t Wom; Nat Cyc Am Bio v27; Not Am Wom

12509. Talcott, Eliza
1836–1911
missionary educator and nurse in Japan
Dict Am Bio; Not Am Wom

12510. Wright, Hannah Amelia
born 1836
gynecologist, medical educator
New York
Wom Cent

12511. Cushier, Elizabeth
1837–1932
physician
Index t Wom

12512. Flower, Lucy Louisa (Coues)
1837–1921
social welfare worker, philanthropist, patron of education, president of the Illinois Training School for Nurses, member of the Chicago school board, trustee of the University of Illinois, Republican party worker
Episcopalian
Dict Am Bio; Nat Cyc Am Bio v9; Not Am Wom

12513. Herrick, Sophia McIlvaine (Bledsoe)
1837–1919
science editor, natural scientist, microscopist, botanist, science writer
Cyc Am Bio; Dict Am Auth; Dict Am Bio; Twent Cen Bio Dict Not Am

12514. Keatinge, Harriet Charlotte
born 1837
physician, Sorosis member
New Orleans, LA
Nat Cyc Am Bio v18

12515. Keller, Elizabeth Catharine
born 1837
physician, surgeon
Lutheran
Pennsylvania; Massachusetts
Index t Wom; Wom Cent

12516. Mix, Josephine P. Dexter
born 1837
physician
Index t Wom

12517. Moody, Mary Blair
born 1837
physician
Wom Cent

12518. Schuyler, Louisa Lee
1837/40–1926
leader in welfare work, Civil War philanthropist, patron of nursing, social worker, sanitarian
New York
Dict Am Bio; Index t Wom; Nat Cyc Am Bio v20; Not Am Wom

12519. Sewall, Lucy Ellen
1837–90
physician
Index t Wom; Not Am Wom

12520. Lippincott, Esther J. (Trimble)
1838–88
educator, author on literature, temperance reformer, convalescent-hospital reformer
Quaker
Pennsylvania
Dict Am Auth; Wom Cent

12521. Slosson, Anne (Trumbull)
1838–1926
entomologist, short story writer
New York, NY
Dict Am Auth; Index t Wom

12522. Trader, Ella King Newsom
1838–1919
Confederate hospital administrator, Civil War nurse
Index t Wom; Not Am Wom

12523. Vashon, Susan Paul
1838–1912
educator, nurse, Civil War relief organizer
Black
Index t Wom; Negro Alman; Prof Negro Wom v1

12524. Wait, Phoebe Jane Babcock
1838–1904
physician, temperance worker
Baptist
Nat Cyc Am Bio v2; Wom Cent

12525. Wilcox, Hannah Tyler
born 1838
physician, temperance worker
Wom Cent

12526. Banks, Sarah Gertrude
born 1839
physician, surgeon, suffragist
Unitarian
Michigan
Index t Wom; Nat Cyc Am Bio v18

12527. George, Lydia A.
born 1839
army nurse in Civil War, Women's Relief Corps worker, philanthropist
Wom Cent

12528. Hancock, Cornelia
1839/40–1927
Civil War nurse, educator of freedmen, charity worker, housing reformer
Quaker
Index t Wom; Not Am Wom

12529. Lee, Rebecca
graduated 1864
physician
Index t Wom

12530. Peckham, Mary Chace (Peck)
1839–92
author, fiction writer, poet, Civil War nurse, suffragist, women's rights worker
Unitarian
Providence, RI
Dict Am Auth; Nat Cyc Am Bio v9; Twent Cen Bio Dict Not Am

12531. Smith, Julia Holmes
born 1839
physician, author
Chicago, IL
Index t Wom; Wom Cent

12532. Telford, Mary Jewett
born 1839
army nurse, Civil War nurse, Women's Relief Corps organizer, church worker, children's author
Quaker
Wom Cent

12533. Willard, Frances Elizabeth Caroline
1839–98
educator, educational philosopher, suffragist, feminist, women's rights worker, temperance leader, naturalist, philanthropist, newspaper editor, traveler
Methodist Episcopal
Cyc Am Bio; Dict Am Auth; Dict Am Bio; Dict Am Bio Men Time; Dict Am Rel Bio; Index t Wom; Nat Cyc Am Bio v1; Not Am Wom; Twent Cen Bio Dict Not Am; Wom Cent

12534. Andrews, Eliza Frances
1840/47–1931
journalist, Civil War diarist, educator, botanist
Georgia
Dict Am Auth; Index t Wom; Nat Cyc Am Bio v6; Not Am Wom; Wom Cent

12535. Borden, Helen, Sister
flourished 1870s
nurse, Catholic nun
Catholic
Index t Wom

12536. Crossland, Mary
flourished 1870s
nurse
Index t Wom

12537. Frissell, Seraph
born 1840
physician, temperance worker
Wom Cent

12538. Hamilton, Margaret
born 1840
Civil War nurse
Index t Wom

12539. Hanna, Rebecca
flourished 1870s
physician
Index t Wom

12540. Harding, Evilela
flourished 1870s
physician
Topeka, KS
Nat Cyc Am Bio v21

12541. Hathaway, P. V., Mrs.
flourished 1870s–80s
botanist
Index t Wom

12542. Hazen, Fanny Titus
born 1840
Civil War nurse
Index t Wom

12543. Herson, Jane Lord
born 1840
physician, suffragist
Oregon
Wom Cent

12544. Howard, Leonora (King)
flourished 1870s
physician
Index t Wom

12545. Kimball, Martha Gertrude
1840–94
philanthropist, nurse
Index t Wom

12546. McNutt, Sarah Jane
flourished 1870s–1910s
surgeon, gynecologist
Nat Cyc Am Bio v15

12547. Osborn, William Church, Mrs.
flourished 1870s
nurse
Index t Wom

12548. Owens-Adair, Bethenia Angelina
1840–1926
physician, feminist, social reformer
Index t Wom; Not Am Wom

12549. Reynolds, Belle
born 1840
Civil War nurse, patriot, author
Index t Wom

12550. Rutherford, Frances A.
flourished 1870s
physician
Index t Wom

12551. Salm Salm, Agnes Elizabeth Winona Joy (Leqlerq), Princess
1840/42–1881/1912
circus rider, rope dancer, actor, field hospital worker and organizer, philanthropist
Cyc Am Bio; Dict Am Bio; Twent Cen Bio Dict Not Am

12552. Smallwood, Hannah T.
flourished 1870s
scientific illustrator
Index t Wom

12553. Smith, Sarah E.
flourished 1870s–80s
botanist, linguist
Index t Wom

12554. van Rensselaer, Euphemia; Sister Mary Dolores
born 1840
nurse, Catholic nun
Catholic
Index t Wom

12555. Williams, Clara
flourished 1870s–1910s
physician
Index t Wom

12556. Wright, Laura M.
born 1840
physician, temperance worker
Baptist
Wom Cent

12557. Allen, Mary Wood
born 1841
physician, author, lecturer
Black
Negro Alman

12558. Edmonds, Sarah Emma Evelyn; Franklin Thompson
1841–98
Civil War soldier, spy, nurse
Canadian
Index t Wom; Not Am Wom

12559. Gregory, Emily Lovira
1841–97
botanist
Twent Cen Bio Dict Not Am

12560. Howard, Elmira Y.
born 1841
homeopathic physician
Wom Cent

12561. Jackson, Katherine Johnson
born 1841
physician
Nat Cyc Am Bio v7; Wom Cent

12562. Plimpton, Hannah R. Cope
born 1841
club leader, Women's Relief Corps worker, Civil War nurse
Index t Wom; Wom Cent

12563. Richards, Melinda Ann "Linda"
1841–1930
pioneer nursing educator
Index t Wom; Not Am Wom

12564. Stevenson, Sarah Ann Hackett
1841/49–1909
physician, medical author, science writer
Cyc Am Bio; Dict Am Auth; Index t Wom; Not Am Wom

12565. Walker, Harriet Granger
1841–1917
philanthropist, hospital organizer, temperance worker, suffragist, police reformer
Methodist
Minneapolis, MN
Nat Cyc Am Bio v6; Wom Cent

12566. Wood-Allen, Mary
born 1841
physician, sex education author
Ann Arbor, MI
Dict Am Auth

12567. Cole, Rebecca
graduated 1867
physician
Index t Wom

12568. Dare, Ella
born 1842
lecturer, journalist, Civil War relief worker, sanitarian
Wom Cent

12569. Fowle, Elida Barker Rumsey
1842–1919
Civil War relief worker and nurse, cofounder of a library for Union soldiers in Washington, DC
Index t Wom; Not Am Wom

12570. Haensler, Arminta Victoria Scott
born 1842
gynecologist
Philadelphia, PA
Wom Cent

12571. Henderson, Mary Foote
born 1842/46
suffragist, home economist, cooking and nutrition writer
St. Louis, MO
Dict Am Auth; Twent Cen Bio Dict Not Am

12572. Jacobi, Mary Corinna Putnam
1842–1906
physician, medical author, pharmacist, educator, feminist
New York, NY
Cyc Am Bio; Dict Am Auth; Dict Am Bio; Index t Wom; Nat Cyc Am Bio v8; Not Am Wom; Twent Cen Bio Dict Not Am; Wom Cent

12573. Lathrop, Clarissa Caldwill
died 1892
mental institution reformer
New York
Index t Wom; Wom Cent

12574. Peckham, Lucy Creemer
born 1842
physician, poet
Wom Cent

12575. Pike, Maria Louisa
died 1892
naturalist, illustrator
Twent Cen Bio Dict Not Am

12576. Richards, Ellen Henrietta (Swallow)
1842–1911
sanitation chemist and engineer, mineralogist, leader in applied and domestic science, writer on domestic science, professor at MIT, educator
Massachusetts
Cyc Am Bio; Dict Am Auth; Dict Am Bio; Index t Wom; Nat Cyc Am Bio v7; Not Am Wom; Twent Cen Bio Dict Not Am; Wom Cent

12577. Thayer, Emma (Homan) (Graves)
born 1842
author, novelist, artist, botanical illustrator
Salida, CO
Dict Am Auth; Twent Cen Bio Dict Not Am; Wom Cent

12578. Vale, Euphemia Vale Blake
born 1842
writer on history and science
Cyc Am Bio

12579. Booth, Mary Ann Allard
born 1843
microscopist, biologist
Nat Cyc Am Bio v15

12580. Creevey, Caroline Alathea Stickney
1843–1920
botanist, author, pianist
Nat Cyc Am Bio v30

12581. Leonard, Anna Byford
born 1843
sanitation reformer, Chicago health department officer, sociologist
Chicago, IL
Index t Wom; Wom Cent

12582. Mannon, Mary L.
born 1843
Civil War nurse
Index t Wom

12583. Ripley, Martha George Rogers
1843–1912
physician, humanitarian, feminist, abolitionist, temperance worker, suffragist
Index t Wom; Not Am Wom; Wom Cent

12584. Simonds, Emma E.
died 1893
Civil War nurse
Index t Wom

12585. Brandegee, Mary Catherine Layne Curran
1844–1920
botanist
Not Am Wom

12586. Green, Mary E.
born 1844
physician
Wom Cent

12587. Lozier, Charlotte Irene
1844–70
physician, women's rights worker, suffragist, medical educator
Cyc Am Bio

12588. Lukens, Anna
born 1844
physician
New York
Index t Wom; Wom Cent

12589. Young, Ann Eliza Webb
1844–post 1908
lecturer and writer against Mormon polygamy, feminist, religious worker, pioneer
Index t Wom; Not Am Wom

12590. Barrows, Katherine Isabel Hayes Chapin
1845–1913
ophthalmologist, penologist, editor, travel writer
Dict Am Auth; Index t Wom; Not Am Wom

12591. Brinkman, Mary A.
born 1845
homeopath, gynecologist
Twent Cen Bio Dict Not Am;
Wom Cent

12592. Chapman, Millie Jane
born 1845
physician
Wom Cent

12593. Comfort, Anna (Manning)
born 1845
gynecologist, medical author, suffragist, women's rights worker,
Sorosis member
Dict Am Auth; Nat Cyc Am Bio
v3; Wom Cent

12594. Dodson, Caroline Matilda
born 1845
physician
Baptist
Wom Cent

12595. Mahoney, Mary Elizabeth "Eliza"
1845/53–1923/26
nurse
Black
Encyc Black Am; Index t Wom

12596. Bergen, Fanny (Dickerson)
born 1846/48
educator, botanist, naturalist, science writer
Appl Cyc Am Bio; Cyc Am Bio;
Dict Am Auth

12597. Betts, Helen M.
born 1846
physician
Index t Wom

12598. Brown, Charlotte Amanda Blake
1846–1904
physician, surgeon, founder of the
San Francisco Children's Hospital
Index t Wom; Not Am Wom

12599. Mosher, Eliza Maria
1846–1928
physician, educator
Index t Wom; Nat Cyc Am Bio
v15; Not Am Wom; Twent Cen
Bio Dict Not Am

12600. Pope, Caroline Augusta
born 1846
physician
Cyc Am Bio

12601. Pope, Emily Frances
born 1846
physician
Cyc Am Bio

12602. Sanford, Amanda
graduated 1871
physician
Index t Wom

12603. Broomall, Anna Elizabeth
1847–1931
obstetrician, medical educator
Pennsylvania
Index t Wom; Nat Cyc Am Bio
v24; Not Am Wom

12604. Dimock, Susan
1847–75
physician, surgeon
Cyc Am Bio; Index t Wom; Nat
Cyc Am Bio v19; Not Am Wom

12605. Franklin, Christine Ladd; Christine Ladd-Franklin
1847–1930
mathematician; logician; psychologist; writer on math, logic and
psychology
Dict Am Bio; Index t Wom; Nat
Cyc Am Bio v5 and v26; Not
Am Wom; Twent Cen Bio Dict
Not Am

12606. Lakey, Alice
1847–1935
clubwoman, leader in the pure
food movement
Not Am Wom

12607. Livingston, Nora Gertrude
1847–1927
nurse
Index t Wom

12608. Patterson, Flora W.
born 1847
pathologist, botanist, mycologist,
editor
Index t Wom

12609. Shaw, Anna Howard
1847–1919
minister, lecturer, suffragist,
women's rights worker, physician, temperance worker
Methodist
English
Dict Am Bio; Index t Wom; Nat
Cyc Am Bio v14; Not Am
Wom; Wom Cent

12610. Warr, Emma Louise
circa 1847–1937
nurse
Index t Wom

12611. Bennett, Adelaide George
born 1848
poet, botanist
Minnesota
Wom Cent; Index t Wom

12612. Carroll, Jane Wall
1848–1927
physician, lawyer
Nat Cyc Am Bio v21

12613. Cleaves, Margaret Abagial
born 1848
physician
Wom Cent

12614. Coombs, Lucinda
graduated 1873
physician, medical missionary
Index t Wom

12615. Duffey, Eliza Bisbee
18?–1898
writer on sex
Dict Am Auth

12616. Marshall, Clara
circa 1848–1931
physician, pharmacist, medical
educator
Dict Am Bio; Index t Wom

12617. Murtfieldt, Mary E.
1848–1913
entomologist
Index t Wom

12618. Pettet, Isabella M.
born 1848
physician
Methodist
New York
German
Wom Cent

12619. Steward, Susan S. McKinney
1848–1919
physician
Brooklyn, NY
Black
Index t Wom; Prof Negro Wom
v1

12620. Swallow, Ellen
graduated 1873
chemist
Index t Wom

12621. Taylor, Susie Baker King
born 1848
educator, Civil War nurse
Black
Prof Negro Wom v1

12622. Anderson, Caroline Virginia Still
1849–1919
physician
Philadelphia, PA
Black
Index t Wom; Negro Alman; Prof
Negro Wom

12623. Cady, Helena Maxwell
born 1849

physician, temperance worker,
suffragist
Kentucky
Wom Cent

12624. Clapp, Cornelia Maria
1849–1934
zoologist, educator
Not Am Wom

12625. Knight, Sarah (Harrison)
1849–1928
philanthropist, Minneapolis civic
leader, Methodist church worker, hospital founder, patron of
nurse's training
Methodist
Minneapolis, MN
Am Bio New Cyc

12626. Rorer, Sarah Tyson (Heston)
1849–1937
cooking teacher, cookbook author, home economist, dietician
Dict Am Auth; Nat Cyc Am Bio
v16; Not Am Wom; Twent Cen
Bio Dict Not Am

12627. Anderson, Elizabeth Milbank
1850–1921
World War I relief worker, philanthropist, patron of social
welfare work, patron of Serbian
and Yugoslavian welfare, patron of medical missions
Baptist
New York
Dict Am Bio; Nat Cyc Am Bio
v23; Not Am Wom

12628. Bacon, Rebecca Taylor
flourished 1880s–90s
philanthropist, patron of nursing
education
Appl Cyc Am Bio

12629. Barlow, Arabella Griffith
flourished 1880s
Civil War nurse
Index t Wom

12630. Bonney, Sarah E.
flourished 1880s
ornithologist
Index t Wom

12631. Bromall, Anna E.
flourished 1880s
physician
Index t Wom

12632. Brown, Belle
born 1850
physician, surgeon
New York
Wom Cent

12633. Call, Emma Louise
flourished 1880s
physician
Index t Wom

12634. Fedde, Elizabeth, Sister
1850–1921
Lutheran deacon, nurse, welfare
  worker, Catholic nun
Lutheran; Catholic
Norwegian
Index t Wom; Not Am Wom

12635. Follansbee, Elizabeth A.
flourished 1880s
physician
Index t Wom

12636. Hall, Lucy M.
flourished 1880s–90s
physician, prison doctor
Wom Cent

12637. Holmes, Mary Emilie
born 1850
educator, zoologist, herbalist, educator of Black women
Presbyterian
Illinois
Wom Cent

12638. Hughes, Marietta E.
flourished 1880s–90s
physician
Wom Cent

**12639. Lease, Mary Elizabeth
(Clyens)**
1850/53–1933
Populist orator, politician, Prohibition party worker, suffragist,
  evolutionist, birth control advocate, feminist, political author
Kansas
Dict Am Auth; Dict Am Bio
  supp v1; Index t Wom; Not Am
  Wom; Read Encyc Am West

**12640. Lozier, Jennie de la
Montagnie**
born 1850
physician, president of Sorosis,
  clubwoman, lecturer
Index t Wom; Nat Cyc Am Bio
  v13; Wom Cent

**12641. Mussey, Ellen (Persis)
Spencer**
1850–1936
international lawyer, law educator, feminist, women's rights
  worker, clubwoman, child welfare worker, Red Cross worker,
  social reformer
Swedenborgian
Washington, DC
Dict Am Bio supp v2; Index t
  Wom; Nat Cyc Am Bio v47 and
  csv1; Not Am Wom; Twent Cen
  Bio Dict Not Am

12642. Palmer, Sarah Ellen
flourished 1880s–1930s
surgeon
Congregationalist
Massachusetts
Nat Cyc Am Bio csv5

12643. Smith, Emily Adella
flourished 1880s
entomologist, author
Index t Wom

12644. Stanislaus, Sister
flourished nineteenth to twentieth
  century
Catholic nun, nurse
Catholic
Index t Wom

**12645. Stowell, Louisa Maria
(Reed)**
born 1850
microscopist, botanist, author on
  microscopal botany, educator,
  editor
Cyc Am Bio and ad; Dict Am
  Auth; Index t Wom; Wom Cent

12646. Todd, Adah J.
flourished 1880s–90s
author, educator, physiologist
Wom Cent

12647. Weeks-Shaw, Clara
flourished 1880s
nurse, author
Index t Wom

12648. Bennett, Alice
1851–1925
physician, student of mental
  health, superintendent of a
  women's mental hospital
Pennsylvania
Index t Wom; Not Am Wom;
  Twent Cen Bio Dict Not Am;
  Wom Cent

12649. Martin, Lillian Jane
1851–1943
psychologist, gerontologist, worker for the welfare of the aged,
  suffragist, university educator
Index t Wom; Nat Cyc Am Bio
  v16; Obit File; Twent Cen Bio
  Dict Not Am

12650. Maxwell, Anna Caroline
1851–1929
nurse
Index t Wom

12651. Mergler, Marie Josepha
1851–1901
physician, surgeon, medical educator
Dict Am Bio; Index t Wom; Not
  Am Wom

12652. Searls, Fanny
1851–1939

pioneer naturalist
Index t Wom

**12653. Underwood, Lillian Stir-
ling Horton**
1851–1921
physician, Presbyterian missionary to Korea
Presbyterian
Not Am Wom

12654. Whipple, M. Ella
born 1851
physician, temperance worker,
  suffragist, Methodist Episcopal
  church worker, politician, educator, inventor
Methodist Episcopal
Wom Cent

12655. Conant, Harriet Beecher
born 1852
physician
Wom Cent

12656. Kurt, Katherine
born 1852
homeopathic physician, suffragist, temperance worker, Prohibition party worker
Universalist
Wom Cent

12657. Lankton, Freeda M.
born 1852
physician
Nebraska
Wom Cent

12658. Brooks, Ida Joe
born 1853
physician, surgeon, suffragist
Little Rock, AR
Wom Cent

12659. Call, Annie Payson
born 1853
author, teacher of nerve training
Dict Am Auth; Index t Wom

12660. Dabbs, Ellen Lawson
born 1853
physician, midwife, women's
  rights worker, suffragist, temperance worker, journalist,
  Populist party worker
Texas
Wom Cent

12661. Dunlap, Mary J.
born 1853
physician
New Jersey
Wom Cent

**12662. Gardener, Helen Hamil-
ton (Chenoweth)**
1853/58–1925
author, novelist, essayist, feminist, suffragist, geneticist, biolo-

gist, sociologist, civil service
  commissioner
Dict Am Bio; Index t Wom; Nat
  Cyc Am Bio v9; Not Am Wom;
  Twent Cen Bio Dict Not Am;
  Wom Cent

12663. Linton, Laura Alberta
born 1853
chemist, physician
Index t Wom; Nat Cyc Am Bio
  v12; Wom Cent

12664. Palmer, Sophia French
1853–1920
professional nurse, nursing editor
Index t Wom; Not Am Wom

**12665. Parrish, Celestia Susan-
nah**
1853–1918
educator, psychologist
Dict Am Bio; Not Am Wom;
  Twent Cen Bio Dict Not Am

12666. Post, Sarah E.
born 1853
physician, nursing-magazine
  founder
New York
Wom Cent

12667. Walker, Minerva
born 1853
physician
New York
Wom Cent

**12668. Comstock, Anna (Bots-
ford)**
1854–1930
naturalist, scientific illustrator,
  insect artist, leader in the nature
  study movement, wood engraver, educator
New York
Index t Wom; Nat Cyc Am Bio
  v11 and v22; Not Am Wom;
  Twent Cen Bio Dict Not Am

12669. Fulton, Mary Hannah
1854–1927
medical missionary to China, pioneer in medical education of
  Chinese women
Not Am Wom

12670. Smith, Estelle Turrell
born 1854
naturalist, suffragist
Wom Cent

12671. Straus, Lina Gutherz
1854–1930
patron of Hadassah medical work
  in Palestine
Jewish
German
Nat Cyc Am Bio v22

12717. Ford, Julia Ellsworth
1859–1950
children's author, playwright,
novelist, patron of medicine
Nat Cyc Am Bio csv7; Obit File

12718. Lines, Mary Louise
born 1859
physician, surgeon, suffragist
Nat Cyc Am Bio v16

12719. Pope, Marion (Manville)
born 1859
poet, author
Dict Am Auth; Wom Cent

12720. Roberts, Charlotte Fitch
1859–1917
chemist
Nat Cyc Am Bio v19

12721. Smith, Theodate Louise
1859–1914
genetic psychologist
Dict Am Bio

**12722. Turner, Alice Bellvadore
Sams**
born 1859
physician
Iowa
Wom Cent

12723. Boardman, Mabel Thorp
1860–1946
nurse, Red Cross leader
Dict Am Bio supp v4; Index t
Wom; Not Am Wom; Obit File

12724. Braeunlich, Sophie
born 1860
scientific publisher, government
employee
Index t Wom; Wom Cent

**12725. Coleman, Louise Mac-
Pherson**
flourished 1890s–1900s
nurse
Canadian
Index t Wom

12726. Cutler, Mary M.
flourished 1890s
physician
Index t Wom

12727. Dight, Mary A. G.
born 1860
physician
Wom Cent

12728. Gilchrist, Rosetta Luce
flourished 1890s
physician, author, poet, women's
rights worker
Cleveland, OH
Wom Cent

**12729. Hoyt-Stevens, Jane
Elizabeth**
born 1860

physician
Episcopalian
Nat Cyc Am Bio csv4

12730. Huber, Alice
flourished 1890s
nurse, artist
Index t Wom

12731. Jenkins, Helen Hartley
1860–1935
philanthropist, nurse
Index t Wom; Not Am Wom

12732. Loveridge, Emily L.
born 1860
nurse, hospital administrator
Index t Wom

12733. Lummis, Dorothea
born 1860
physician, music critic, journalist,
newspaper editor, Native American artifacts collector
Los Angeles, CA
Index t Wom; Wom Cent

12734. Maxon, Hannah W.
died 1910
Civil War nurse
Index t Wom

12735. Molineux, Maria Ada
flourished 1890s
bacteriologist, psychologist, author, authority on the
Brownings
Twent Cen Bio Dict Not Am

12736. Ott, Frances M.
flourished 1890s
nurse
Index t Wom

12737. Pope, Amy Elizabeth
flourished 1890s–1900s
nurse
Canadian
Index t Wom

**12738. Rathbun, Mary Jane;
Mary Rathbone**
1860–1943
marine zoologist, expert on shells,
author, government employee
Index t Wom; Not Am Wom

**12739. Robb, Isabella Adams
(Hampton)**
1860/63–1910
professional nurse, educator, writer on nursing
Cleveland, OH
Index t Wom; Not Am Wom

12740. Robbins, Jane Elizabeth
1860–1946
social worker, physician
Not Am Wom

12741. Seymour, Louise
flourished 1890s

nurse
Index t Wom

**12742. Thelberg, Elizabeth
Burr**
1860–1935
physician
Episcopalian
Index t Wom; Nat Cyc Am Bio
v27

12743. Vietor, Agnes Caecilia
flourished 1890s–1920s
surgeon
Nat Cyc Am Bio csv3

**12744. Walcott, Mary Morris
Vaux**
1860–1940
artist, naturalist
Wom Cent

**12745. Ward, Florence Nightin-
gale**
born 1860
surgeon, gynecologist, homeopath
Nat Cyc Am Bio v7

12746. Withington, Alfreda
1860–1951
physician
Index t Wom

12747. Bates, Mary Elizabeth
1861/63–1954
surgeon, child welfare worker,
suffragist
Denver, CO
Index t Wom; Nat Cyc Am Bio
v18

**12748. Bissell, Emily Perkins;
Priscilla Leonard**
1861–1948
welfare and child labor worker,
author, inventor of Christmas
Seals
Nat Cyc Am Bio v38; Not Am
Wom; Obit File

12749. Hobson, Sarah Matilda
born 1861
physician
Nat Cyc Am Bio csv1

12750. Lawson, Louise
born 1861
sculptor, medical journal editor
Cyc Am Bio; Wom Cent

**12751. Magoun, Martha Rob-
erts (Mann)**
born 1861
botanist, biologist, educator
Twent Cen Bio Dict Not Am

**12752. Parsons, Frances Theo-
dora (Smith) (Dana)**
1861–99
author, nature writer

Albany, NY
Dict Am Auth; Twent Cen Bio
Dict Not Am

**12753. Spencer, Caroline
Elizabeth**
1861–1928
suffragist, physician
Nat Cyc Am Bio v21

12754. Stevens, Nettie Maria
1861–1912
biologist, geneticist
Not Am Wom

12755. Bissell, Julia
1862–1928
physician, missionary to India
Congregationalist
Nat Cyc Am Bio v21

12756. Cushman, Emma
born 1862
humanitarian, nurse
Index t Wom

**12757. Davis, Virginia Meri-
wether**
born 1862
physician
New York
Wom Cent

12758. Delano, Jane Arminda
1862–1919
nurse, Red Cross worker, nurse in
the Mexican-American War,
nursing educator
Dict Am Bio; Index t Wom; Nat
Cyc Am Bio v19; Not Am Wom

**12759. Higginson, Ella
(Rhoads)**
born 1862
author, poet, druggist
New Watcom, WA
Dict Am Auth; Twent Cen Bio
Dict Not Am; Wom Cent

**12760. McCreight, Mary Bal-
dwin**
born 1862
pharmacist, plague and epidemic
nurse
Irish
Nat Cyc Am Bio csv1

12761. Seton, Julia Lorinda
born 1862
physician, founder of the New
Thought Church, author
New Thought
Nat Cyc Am Bio v16

**12762. Bailey, Florence Augus-
ta (Merriam)**
1863–1948

ornithologist, nature writer, educator
Dict Am Auth; Dict Am Bio supp v4; Index t Wom; Nat Cyc Am Bio v13 and csv1; Not Am Wom

12763. Bolles, Jeanette Hubbard
1863–1930
osteopath
Congregationalist
Colorado
Nat Cyc Am Bio v28

12764. Breed, Lorena May
born 1863
medical missionary to India, pathologist
California
Nat Cyc Am Bio csv3

12765. Calkins, Mary Whiton
1863–1930
philosopher, psychologist, educator, author
Dict Am Bio supp v1; Dict Phil; Index t Wom; Nat Cyc Am Bio v13; Not Am Wom; Who Who Phil

12766. Elkers, Bertha Kahn
born 1863
Red Cross worker, clubwoman
Index t Wom

12767. Ferguson, Margaret Clay
1863–1951
botanist
Index t Wom; Not Am Wom supp v1

12768. Goldthwaite, Nellie E.
1863–1946
chemist
Obit File

12769. Ladd, Kate Everit Macy
1863–1945
philanthropist, patron of medicine and scientific research
Presbyterian
New York
Dict Am Bio supp v3; Nat Cyc Am Bio v32 and csv4; Not Am Wom

12770. Lockrey, Sarah Hunt
1863–1929
surgeon, suffragist
Dict Am Bio

12771. Miner, Alice Trainer
1863–1950
philanthropist, patron of medicine
Presbyterian
New York
Canadian
Nat Cyc Am Bio v40

12772. Mosher, Clelia
born 1863
physician, educator
Index t Wom

12773. Spink, Mary Angela
1863–1939
physician
Indianapolis, IN
Nat Cyc Am Bio v40

12774. Thoms, Adah B. Samuels
1863?–1943
nursing leader
Black
Index t Wom; Not Am Wom

12775. van Hoosen, Bertha
1863–1952
surgeon, feminist
Index t Wom; Not Am Wom supp v1

12776. Williams, Anna Wessels
1863–1954
physician, bacteriologist noted for research on diphtheria and rabies
Not Am Wom supp v1; Obit File

12777. Wilson, Margaret Barclay
1863–1945
physician, domestic scientist, medical educator
Nat Cyc Am Bio v34

12778. Brant, Cornelia Chase
1864–1959
physician, dean of New York Medical College
Obit File

12779. Cone, Claribel
1864–1929
pathologist, art collector
Nat Cyc Am Bio v4; Not Am Wom

12780. Davis, Minta S. A.
born 1864
physician
Oregon
Wom Cent

12781. Dillon, Halle Tanner
born 1864
physician
Nat Cyc Am Bio v3

12782. Mayo, Hattie Damon
1864–1952
cofounder of the Mayo Medical Clinic
Obit File

12783. McGee, Anita Newcomb
1864–1940

physician, surgeon, founder of the Army Nurse Corps, war doctor, army officer
Index t Wom; Not Am Wom; Twent Cen Bio Dict Not Am

12784. Smith, Charlotte Dodd Stewartson
born 1864
physician
Massachusetts
Nat Cyc Am Bio csv8

12785. Underwood, Lillias
married 1889
missionary, physician, pioneer
Index t Wom

12786. Zabriskie, Louise G.
1864–1963
nurse, social welfare leader
Index t Wom

12787. Baldwin, Helen
1865–1946
physician
Congregationalist
Nat Cyc Am Bio v36

12788. de Bey, Cornelia Barnarda
born 1865
physician, surgeon, pacifist
Dutch
Nat Cyc Am Bio csv3

12789. Doubleday, Neltje Blanchan de Graff; Neltje Blanchan
1865–1918
science and nature writer, naturalist
Dict Am Bio; Nat Cyc Am Bio v13; Not Am Wom

12790. Eckstorm, Fannie Pearson Hardy
1865–1946
ornithologist, writer on ornithology, scholar of the Native Americans of Maine, historian of Maine folk songs
Episcopalian
Brewer, ME
Dict Am Auth; Dict Am Bio supp v4; Nat Cyc Am Bio v36; Not Am Wom

12791. Fearn, Anne Walter
1865/71–1939
physician, surgeon, hospital administrator, medical educator in China
Berkeley, CA
Index t Wom; Nat Cyc Am Bio v31 and csv4; Not Am Wom

12792. Feeney, Mary Ignatius, Sister
died 1915
pharmacist, Catholic nun, nurse

Catholic
Index t Wom

12793. Hall, Rosetta Sherwood
1865–1951
physician, missionary
Index t Wom; Not Am Wom supp v1

12794. Jordan, M. Evangeline
born 1865
dentist
Los Angeles, CA
Nat Cyc Am Bio v17

12795. McKane, Alice Woodby
born 1865
physician, hospital and nursing school founder
Black
Encyc Black Am

12796. Paget, Arthur, Lady
1865–1919
philanthropist, nurse
English
Index t Wom

12797. Peabody, Lucy Evelyn
born 1865
scientist
Index t Wom

12798. Picotte, Susan la Flesche
1865–1915
physician, missionary
Native American (Osage); French
Great North Am Ind; Not Am Wom

12799. Valentine, Lila Hardaway Meade
1865–1921
suffragist, educational reformer, public health worker
Virginia
Encyc South Hist; Not Am Wom

12800. Dellworth, Emma V.
1866–1959
US Army nurse during the Spanish-American War
Obit File

12801. Goodrich, Annie Warburton
1866–1954
World War I nurse, director of the Army School of Nursing, nursing educator, suffragist
Dict Am Bio supp v5; Index t Wom; Nat Cyc Am Bio v42; Not Am Wom supp v1

12802. Guggenheim, Leonie Bernheim
1866–1959
patron of dental clinics, patron of free band concerts in parks
Jewish

New York
Obit File

12803. Hoyt, Minerva Lockhart Hamilton
1866–1945
naturalist, conservationist, botanist, patron of music, president of the Los Angeles Symphony Orchestra
Los Angeles, CA
Am Bio New Cyc; Nat Cyc Am Bio v34

12804. Latham, Vida Annette
1866–1958
physician, dental surgeon, microscopist
Nat Cyc Am Bio v44

12805. Gray, Ida
born 1867
dentist
Black
Negro Alman; Prof Negro Wom v1

12806. Hurd-Mead, Kate Campbell; Kate Mead
1867–1941
physician, historian of women in medicine
Index t Wom; Not Am Wom; Nat Cyc Am Bio v38

12807. Myers, Harriet Williams
born 1867
author, ornithologist, founder of California Audubon Society, conservationist, animal humane worker, World War II national defense worker
Los Angeles, CA
Am Bio New Cyc

12808. Seymour, Harriet Ayer
1867/76–1944
pianist, music educator, pioneer of music therapy, music author
Index t Wom; Nat Cyc Am Bio v33; Obit File

12809. Wald, Lillian D.
1867–1940
public health nurse, physician, social reformer, social worker, settlement house founder
Jewish
Dict Am Bio supp v2; Index t Wom; Nat Cyc Am Bio v29; Not Am Wom

12810. Butler, Ida Fatio
1868–1949
Red Cross nurse
Index t Wom

12811. Chard, Marie L.
1868–1938
physician
Index t Wom

12812. Doane, Marguerite Treat
1868–1954
philanthropist, patron of medical missionaries
Baptist
Nat Cyc Am Bio v41

12813. Follet, Mary Parker
1868–1933
writer and lecturer on political science, group psychology, and industrial management
Dict Am Auth; Dict Am Bio supp v1; Not Am Wom

12814. Hurdon, Elizabeth
1868–1941
gynecologist, pathologist
Not Am Wom

12815. Porter, Gene Stratton
1868–1924
author, ornithologist
Index t Wom

12816. Robinson, Daisy Maude Orleman
1868–1942
dermatologist, surgeon
Nat Cyc Am Bio v32

12817. Strawn, Julia Clark
1868–1942
surgeon, gynecologist
Congregationalist
Chicago, IL
Index t Wom; Nat Cyc Am Bio v31

12818. Wollstein, Martha
1868–1939
pathologist, medical researcher
Not Am Wom

12819. Andrews, Harriet White Fisher
born 1869
disaster relief nurse, dairy farmer, anvil manufacturer
Nat Cyc Am Bio csv2

12820. Chase, [Mary] Agnes
1869–1963
botanist, suffragist
Not Am Wom supp v1, Obit File

12821. Duckering, Florence West
1869–1951
surgeon
Episcopalian
English
Nat Cyc Am Bio v40

12822. Goldman, Emma
1869–1940
political anarchist, lecturer, publicist, agitator for free speech, popularizer of the arts, feminist, pioneer advocate of birth control, politician

Jewish
Russian
Dict Am Bio supp v2; Index t Wom; Not Am Wom; Who Who Jew Hist

12823. Hamilton, Alice
1869–1970
industrial physician and toxicologist, pioneer in industrial medicine, medical educator, medical author, social reformer
Cur Biog '70; Index t Wom; Nat Cyc Am Bio csv7; Not Am Wom supp v1

12824. Lovejoy, Esther Clayson Pohl
1869/70–1967
physician; director of the Portland, Oregon, health department; World War I Red Cross worker in France; feminist
Protestant Episcopal
Portland, OR
Index t Wom; Nat Cyc Am Bio csv1; Not Am Wom supp v1

12825. Mayo, Sarah Tew
1869–1930
physician, surgeon
Not Am Wom

12826. McConnell, Adelaide Dorn
1869–1942
physician, philanthropist
Presbyterian
Nat Cyc Am Bio v31

12827. Noyes, Clara Dutton
1869/70–1936
nurse, nursing educator, field nurse in World War I, author
Dict Am Bio supp v2; Index t Wom; Nat Cyc Am Bio csv2

12828. Parrish, Rebecca
1869–1952
physician
Index t Wom

12829. Slye, Maud [Caroline]
1869/79–1954
pathologist, cancer researcher
Index t Wom; Nat Cyc Am Bio csv6; Not Am Wom supp v1

12830. Tuttle, Florence Guertin (Onertin)
born 1869
author, feminist, birth control advocate, pacifist, League of Nations worker, politician
Index t Wom; Nat Cyc Am Bio csv2 and csv5

12831. Yarros, Rachelle Slobodinsky
1869–1946

obstetrician, birth control and venereal-disease-control advocate, sanitarian
Nat Cyc Am Bio v35; Not Am Wom

12832. Alger, Ellice Murdock
1870–1945
ophthalmologist
Index t Wom

12833. Bragg, Mabel Caroline
1870–1945
health pioneer
Index t Wom

12834. Brockway, Marion T.
flourished 1900s
nurse
Index t Wom

12835. Claypoole, Edith Jane
born 1870
biologist
Nat Cyc Am Bio v13

12836. Dakin, Florence
flourished 1900s–30s
nurse
Index t Wom

12837. Harriman, Florence Jaffray (Hurst)
1870–1967
Democratic party official, diplomat, minister to Norway, politician, journalist, suffragist, clubwoman, social rights worker, Red Cross worker in World War I, World War II relief worker in Norway
Washington, DC
Index t Wom; Nat Cyc Am Bio v53 and csv6; Not Am Wom supp v1; Obit File

12838. Hasson, Esther Vorhees
flourished 1900s
nurse
Index t Wom

12839. Hilyer, Amanda Gray
1870–1957
pharmacist
Black
Encyc Black Am

12840. Hunton, Addie Waites
born 1870
Red Cross worker, World War I relief worker
Black
Prof Negro Wom v2

12841. Keller, Manelva Wylie
flourished 1900s
nurse
Index t Wom

12842. Keyes, Regina Flood
born 1870

physician
Index t Wom

12843. King, Helen
1870–1955
zoologist
Pennsylvania
Obit File

12844. Kinney, Dita H.
flourished 1900s
army nurse
Index t Wom

12845. Lawler, Elsie M.
flourished 1900s
nurse
Index t Wom

12846. Marianne, Sister
flourished 1900s
nurse, Catholic nun
Catholic
Index t Wom

12847. Mexia, Ynes Enriquetta Julietta
1870–1938
botanical explorer
Not Am Wom

12848. Robinson, Ethel Brown Blackwell
1870–1947
physician
Unitarian
Nat Cyc Am Bio v36

12849. Scudder, Ida Sophia
1870–1960
physician, missionary, founder of the American Medical Mission in Veliore, India
Index t Wom; Not Am Wom supp v1; Obit File

12850. Simpson, Cora D.
flourished 1900s–20s
nurse
Index t Wom

12851. Stage, Miriam Kerruish
1870–1929
physician, suffragist
Ohio
Nat Cyc Am Bio v21

12852. Taylor, Euphemia J.
flourished 1900s–20s
nurse
Canadian
Index t Wom

12853. Williams, Mary E.
flourished 1900s
physician
Nat Cyc Am Bio v44

12854. Ackermann, Susan K.
1871–1949
physician

Norwegian
Obit File

12855. Arnold, Alma Cuisian
born 1871
chiropractor
German
Index t Wom

12856. Crandall, Ella Philips
1871–1936/38
leader in public health nursing
Index t Wom; Not Am Wom

12857. Draper, Helen Fidelia
1871–1951
Red Cross nurse, World War I relief worker, social worker
Episcopalian
New York
Index t Wom; Nat Cyc Am Bio v39

12858. Farrar, Lilian Katurah Pond
1871–1962
gynecologist, surgeon
Episcopalian
New York
Nat Cyc Am Bio v48

12859. Gardner, Mary Sewall
1871–1961
public health nurse, author
Index t Wom; Not Am Wom supp v1

12860. Harvey, Kate Benedict Hanna
1871–1936
public health worker, patron of nursing, cattle breeder
Protestant Episcopal
Cleveland, OH
Nat Cyc Am Bio v34

12861. Hawes, Harriet Ann Boyd
1871–1945
classical archaeologist, war nurse in the Greco-Turkish and Spanish-American wars and in World War I
Dict Am Bio supp v3; Not Am Wom

12862. Isham, Mary Keyt
1871–1947
neurologist, psychoanalyst
Obit File

12863. Minnigerode, Lucy
1871–1935
nurse, public health worker
Dict Am Bio supp v1; Index t Wom

12864. Potter, Ellen Culver
1871–1958

physician, public health worker, welfare administrator, social worker
Dict Am Bio supp v6; Index t Wom

12865. Powell, Louise Mathilde
1871–1943
nursing educator
Not Am Wom

12866. Richardson, Harriet
graduated 1896
biologist, author
Index t Wom

12867. Sabin, Florence Rena
1871–1953
physician, medical researcher and educator, anatomist, public health worker, first woman life member of the American Academy of Sciences, author
Colorado
Dict Am Bio supp v5; Index t Wom; Nat Cyc Am Bio v40 and csv3; Not Am Wom supp v1; Obit File

12868. Slagle, Eleonor Clarke
1871–1942
leader in occupational therapy
Not Am Wom

12869. Washburn, Margaret Floy
1871–1939
psychologist
New York
Dict Am Bio supp v2; Nat Cyc Am Bio v30; Not Am Wom

12870. Wood, Louise
1871–1943
Red Cross leader
Obit File

12871. Young, Zina Diantha Huntington
1871–1902
midwife, suffragist, Mormon leader
Mormon
Cyc Am Bio

12872. Carter, Edna
1872–1963
physicist, suffragist
Nat Cyc Am Bio v52

12873. Dennett, Mary Coffin Ware
1872–1947
suffragist, birth control and sex education advocate, founder of the National Birth Control League, pacifist
Not Am Wom; Obit File

12874. Key, Wilhelmine Enteman
born 1872

zoologist, eugenicist
Congregationalist
Nat Cyc Am Bio csv2 and csv5

12875. McCormick, Edith Rockefeller
1872–1932
philanthropist, patron of music and psychiatry
Index t Wom; Nat Cyc Am Bio csv3; Not Am Wom

12876. Moore, Emmeline
1872–1963
biologist, fishery scientist, president of the American Fisheries Association, conservationist
Obit File

12877. Norman, Estelle Gertrude
1872–1959
physician, venereal disease clinic worker
Seventh-Day Adventist
Iowa
Nat Cyc Am Bio v48

12878. Pennington, Mary Engle
1872–1952
chemist, bacteriologist, refrigeration specialist, engineer, inventor
Index t Wom; Not Am Wom supp v1; Obit File

12879. Prescott, Mary
1872–1961
tuberculosis-patient welfare worker
Obit File

12880. Baker, Sarah Josephine
1873–1945
physician, public health administrator, child health pioneer
Unitarian
New York, NY
Dict Am Bio supp v3; Index t Wom; Nat Cyc Am Bio v36; Not Am Wom; Obit File

12881. Broadhurst, Jean
1873–1954
author, educator, bacteriologist
Index t Wom

12882. Coffin, Mary Emma
born 1873
homeopathic physician, temperance worker
Baptist
Nat Cyc Am Bio csv4

12883. Coolidge, Emelyn Lincoln
1873–1949
pediatrician, editor
Index t Wom

12884. Fitzgerald, Alice
1873–1962

chief nurse of the American Red Cross in Europe
Italian
Obit File

12885. Hepburn, Katharine Houghton
1873–1951
suffragist, birth control reform leader
Dict Am Bio supp v5; Obit File

12886. Hickey, Mary A.
circa 1873–1954
nurse, superintendent of Veterans Administration nurses
Index t Wom; Obit File

12887. la Motte, Ellen Newbold
1873–1961
nurse, author
Index t Wom

12888. Long, Margaret
born 1873
physician
Colorado
Nat Cyc Am Bio csv7

12889. Mann, Kristine
1873–1945
psychiatrist, women's labor worker
Nat Cyc Am Bio v34

12890. Seligsberg, Alice Lillie
1873–1940
social worker, developer of Hadassah's medical program, Zionist
Jewish
Who Who Jew Hist

12891. Sidis, Sarah
1873–1959
psychiatrist, founder of the Sidis Institute for Abnormal Psychiatry
Portsmouth, NH
Russian
Obit File

12892. Sloop, Mary T. Martin
1873–1962
physician, educator, social worker
Index t Wom

12893. Stern, Frances
1873–1947
social worker, dietician
Not Am Wom

12894. Urrea, Teresa
1873–1906
folk healer, mystic
Mexican
Dict Mex Am Hist

12895. van Duyn, Sarah Elizabeth
born 1873

physician, medical educator
Nat Cyc Am Bio csv2

12896. Auge, Emily Geary Whitton
1874–1934
surgeon
Presbyterian
Philadelphia, PA
Nat Cyc Am Bio v26

12897. Clayton, S. Lillian
1874–1930
nurse
Index t Wom

12898. Graves, Lulu Grace
1874/78–1949
dietician, home economist
Index t Wom

12899. Hinkle, Beatrice Moses
1874–1953
pioneer psychiatrist, psychoanalyst
Dict Am Bio supp v5; Obit File

12900. Mendenhall, Dorothy Reed
1874–1964
physician
Not Am Wom supp v1

12901. Rose, Mary Davies Swartz
1874–1941
pioneer nutritionist, director of the Bureau of Conservation of the Federal Food Board during World War I
Dict Am Bio supp v3; Index t Wom; Not Am Wom; Obit File

12902. Starr, Sarah Logan Wister
1874–1956
physician, president of the Women's Medical College of Pennsylvania
Pennsylvania
Obit File

12903. Stein, Gertrude
1874–1946
author, novelist, literary salon host, World War I ambulance driver and supply truck driver in France
Jewish
French (American expatriate to Paris)
Dict Am Bio supp v4; Dict Lit Bio v4; Index t Wom; Nat Cyc Am Bio v38 and csv4; Not Am Wom; Obit File; Who Who Jew Hist; Wom Lit; Wom Lit, More

12904. Woolley, Helen Bradford Thompson
1874–1947
psychologist
Not Am Wom

12905. Denning, Delia; Delia (Denning) Akeley Howe
1875–1970
African explorer, big game hunter, geographer, taxidermist, author, lecturer, World War I relief worker
Nat Cyc Am Bio v57; Obit File; Index t Wom

12906. Downey, June Etta
1875–1932
psychologist, author
Dict Am Bio supp v1; Not Am Wom

12907. Gantt, Love Rosa Hirschmann
1875–1935
physician, public health worker
Index t Wom; Not Am Wom

12908. Howe, Delia Akeley (Denning)
1875–1970
African explorer, big game hunter, geographer, taxidermist, author, lecturer, World War I relief worker
Index t Wom; Nat Cyc Am Bio v57; Obit File

12909. Soule, Cora Blanche
1875–1945
missionary, nurse
Bio Dict Sudan

12910. Barringer, Emily Dunning
1876–1961
gynecologist, ambulance surgeon, worker for recognition of women physicians
Protestant Episcopal
Nat Cyc Am Bio v50; Index t Wom; Obit File

12911. Bass, Mary Elizabeth
1876–1956
physician
Baptist
Louisiana
Nat Cyc Am Bio v46; Not Am Wom supp v1

12912. Beard, Mary
1876–1946
administrator and educator in nursing and public health, Rockefeller Foundation administrator, director of American Red Cross Nursing Service
Dict Am Bio supp v4; Index t Wom; Nat Cyc Am Bio v35; Obit File

12913. Blunt, Katharine
1876–1954

college administrator, home economics educator, nutritionist, chemist
Index t Wom; Nat Cyc Am Bio csv2; Not Am Wom supp v1

12914. Bole, Roberta Holden
1876–1950
philanthropist; patron of art, science, and education
Unitarian
Nat Cyc Am Bio v38

12915. Darrow, Anna Labertine Lindstedt
1876–1959
physician, pharmacist
Florida
Nat Cyc Am Bio v48

12916. Maass, Clara Louise
1876/79–1901
nurse
Index t Wom

12917. Mead, Elizabeth Manning Cleveland
1876–1946
patron of cancer research
Episcopalian
New York
Nat Cyc Am Bio v38

12918. Minoka Hill, Lillia Rosa
1876–1952
physician
Not Am Wom supp v1

12919. Morton, Blanche Rosalie Slaughter
born 1876
surgeon, gynecologist, World War I surgeon on Salonica front, major in the US Army
Index t Wom; Nat Cyc Am Bio csv3

12920. Patch, Edith Marion
1876–1954
entomologist, children's author
Index t Wom; Nat Cyc Am Bio v18

12921. Sterling, Lindsay Morris
born 1876
sculptor, scientific sculptor, science illustrator
New York
Nat Cyc Am Bio csv3

12922. Tracy, Martha
1876–1942
physician, public health expert, dean of the Women's Medical College of Pennsylvania
Philadelphia, PA
Index t Wom; Nat Cyc Am Bio v31; Not Am Wom

12923. Tunnicliff, Ruth
1876–1946

bacteriologist, physician
Index t Wom

12924. Upjohn, Elizabeth P.
1876–1910
nurse
Index t Wom

12925. Babcock, Harriet Sprague
1877–1952
psychologist, specialist in the control of mental deficiencies
Index t Wom; Obit File

12926. Breckinridge, Mary
1877/81–1965
nurse, midwife, founder of the Frontier Nursing Service
Index t Wom; Not Am Wom supp v1

12927. Burgess, Elizabeth Chamberlain
1877–1949
nurse, educator
Index t Wom

12928. Cannon, Ida Maud
1877–1960
social worker, nurse, medical reformer, author
Dict Am Bio supp v5; Index t Wom; Not Am Wom supp v1

12929. Leete, Harriet L.
died 1927
nurse
Index t Wom

12930. Norsworthy, Naomi
1877–1916
psychologist, educator
Dict Am Bio

12931. Pitkin, E. Winifred
1877–1960
obstetrician, author
Obit File

12932. Rice, Ethel
born 1877
surgeon, obstetrician/gynecologist
Nat Cyc Am Bio v18

12933. Richmond, Winifred B.
1877–1945
physician, physiologist, medical author
Obit File

12934. Roberts, Mary May
1877–1959
nurse, nursing magazine editor, nursing educator, chief nurse of the World War II army nurse corps
Index t Wom; Not Am Wom supp v1; Obit File

12935. Wheeler, Ruth
1877–1948
home economist, nutritionist, dietician
Not Am Wom

12936. Akeley, Mary Lee Jobe
1878/86–1966
explorer, photographer, educator, author, botanist
Index t Wom; Not Am Wom

12937. Ames, Blanche Ames
1878–1969
botanical illustrator, inventor, feminist, suffragist, birth control advocate
Massachusetts
Nat Cyc Am Bio v53; Not Am Wom; Obit File

12938. Campbell, Eleanor Milbank Anderson
1878–1959
physician, social welfare worker, public health worker, patron of medicine
Baptist
Nat Cyc Am Bio v49 and csv4

12939. Gilbreth, Lillian Evelyn (Moller)
1878–1972
industrial engineer and psychologist, household efficiency and labor efficiency expert, management consultant
Cur Biog '72; Index t Wom; Not Am Wom supp v1; Obit File

12940. Jean, Sally Lucas
born 1878
nurse, educator
Index t Wom

12941. l'Esperance, Elise Depew Strang
1878/79–1959
pathologist, founder of the Kate Depew Strang Tumor Clinic at New York Infirmary
New York
Index t Wom; Not Am Wom supp v1; Obit File

12942. McLeod, Grace
1878–1962
nutritionist, nutrition educator, editor
Congregationalist
Scottish
Index t Wom; Nat Cyc Am Bio v50

12943. Murray, Elsie
1878–1965
psychologist, color blindness expert, museum director
Presbyterian
Pennsylvania
Nat Cyc Am Bio v53

12944. Peele, Grace Darling
1878–1926
physician
New York
Nat Cyc Am Bio v21

12945. South, Lillian H.
born 1878
physician
Index t Wom

12946. Stastny, Olga
1878–1952
physician
Index t Wom

12947. Stewart, Isabel Maitland
1878–1963
nursing educator
Canadian
Index t Wom; Not Am Wom supp v1

12948. Tracy, Susan E.
died 1928
nurse
Index t Wom

12949. Walker, Gertrude A.
died 1928
physician
Index t Wom

12950. Belmont, Eleanor Elise Robson
1879–1979
actor, author, nurse, philanthropist, patron of the arts, founder of the Metropolitan Opera Guild
English
Index t Wom; Cur Biog '44 and '80

12951. Flikke, Julia Otteson
born circa 1879
army nurse
Index t Wom

12952. Parker, Valeria Hopkins
1879–1959
physician, public health worker, Sorosis member
Index t Wom; Nat Cyc Am Bio csv1

12953. Ring, Barbara Taylor
1879–1941
psychiatrist, hospital administrator, playwright
Massachusetts
Index t Wom; Obit File

12954. Roberts, Lydia Jane
1879–1965
nutritionist, home economics educator
Not Am Wom supp v1

12955. Sanger, Margaret Higgins; Mrs. J. Noah H. Slee
1879/83–1966
birth control reformer, lecturer, author
Episcopalian
Index t Wom; Nat Cyc Am Bio v52; Not Am Wom supp v1; Obit File

12956. Spink, Rose Urbana
1879–1952
physician
Indiana
Nat Cyc Am Bio v40

12957. van Blarcom, Carolyn Conant
1879–1960
nurse, midwife
Index t Wom; Not Am Wom supp v1

12958. Voorhees, Florence Edgar
1879–1946
gynecologist
Congregationalist
Nat Cyc Am Bio v36

12959. Carr, Emma Perry
1880–1972
chemist
Methodist
Index t Wom; Nat Cyc Am Bio csv6; Not Am Wom supp v1

12960. Cutler, Bessie Ingersoll
flourished 1910s–20s
nurse, author
Index t Wom

12961. Delfs, Eleanor (Mary)
1880–1977
obstetrician/gynecologist
Presbyterian
Wisconsin
Nat Cyc Am Bio v60

12962. Dunbar, Saidie [Sarah] Orr
1880–1960
patron of nursing and public health, developer of Christmas Seals
Catholic
Oregon
Nat Cyc Am Bio v51

12963. Fernald, Grace M.
1880–1950
educator, psychologist specializing in retarded children
Obit File

12964. Flood, Frances M.
flourished 1910s
physician
Index t Wom

12965. Foerster, Alma
flourished 1910

13006. Meredith, Florence Lyndon
1883–1951
physician, medical educator
Massachusetts
Nat Cyc Am Bio v45 and csv1

13007. Miller, Olive Beaupre
1883–1968
children's author, sex education worker
Illinois
Nat Cyc Am Bio v54

13008. Nice, Margaret Morse
1883–1974
ornithologist
Not Am Wom supp v1

13009. Springs, Lena Joan Jones
1883–1942
Democratic National Committee member, Democratic vice-presidential nominee at the 1924 convention, suffrage leader, World War I Red Cross worker
South Carolina
Nat Cyc Am Bio csv2; Obit File

13010. Wilson, Maude H. Mellish
died 1933
nurse, editor
Index t Wom

13011. Bachrach, Grace Baer
1884–1962
philanthropist, patron of medicine
Jewish
New York
Nat Cyc Am Bio v47

13012. Booth, Ada Pearl Dunlap; Adeline Dunlap
born 1884
actor, World War I nurse
Michigan
Nat Cyc Am Bio v17

13013. Crawford, Mary Merritt; Mrs. Edward Schuster
1884–1972
surgeon, World War I surgeon in France
Episcopalian
New York
Nat Cyc Am Bio v57

13014. Fox, Elizabeth Gordon
1884–1958
nurse, director of the Red Cross Public Health Nursing Program, president of the National Organization for Public Health Nursing
Index t Wom; Obit File

13015. Jordan, Sarah Claudia Murray
1884–1959
gastroenterologist, cofounder of the Lahey Clinic, president of the American Gastroenterological Association
Index t Wom; Not Am Wom supp v1; Obit File

13016. McDaniel, Eugenia L.
born 1884
entomologist
Index t Wom

13017. Morgan, Agnes Fay
1884–1968
biochemist, nutritionist
Index t Wom; Not Am Wom supp v1

13018. Tolstoy, Mary Koutouzow
1884–1976
author, fashion director, World War I and II nurse
Obit File

13019. Zoeckler, Mary Daton Allen
1884–1914
obstetrician/gynecologist, medical missionary to Iran
Presbyterian
Nat Cyc Am Bio v46

13020. Bolton, Frances Payne (Bingham)
1885/86–1977
Republican representative to Congress from Ohio, nurse
Presbyterian
Ohio
Cur Biog '77; Index t Wom; Nat Cyc Am Bio csv11; Obit File

13021. Bryant, Louise Frances Stevens
1885–1959
social researcher, medical editor, feminist, Socialist party worker, physician, public health worker
Dict Am Bio supp v5

13022. Challinor, Mercedes Crimmins (Clara)
1885–1966
Red Cross official, World War I relief worker
Catholic
Nat Cyc Am Bio v52

13023. Curtis, Namahyoke Sockum
died 1935
Des Moines civic leader, nurse
Des Moines, IA
Black
Prof Negro Wom v2

13024. Harvey, Ethel Browne
1885–1965
cell biologist, embryologist
Not Am Wom supp v1

13025. Hazen, Elizabeth Lee
1885–1975
microbiologist, mycologist
Not Am Wom supp v1

13026. Horney, Karen Danielson
1885–1952
psychiatrist, psychoanalyst, dean of the American Institute for Psychoanalysis
German
Dict Am Bio supp v5; Encyc Third Reich; Index t Wom; Not Am Wom supp v1; Obit File

13027. Jackson, Maude Campbell Davison
1885–1956
US Army major, chief of American nurses on Corregidor in World War II, World War II hero
Obit File

13028. Kelman, Sarah R.
circa 1885–1969
psychiatrist, psychoanalyst, founder of the Association for the Advancement of Psychoanalysis, the American Institute for Psychoanalysis, and the American Academy of Psychoanalysis
Russian
Obit File

13029. Lucke, Marion Hague Rea
1885–1946
physician, medical educator
Nat Cyc Am Bio v36

13030. Pearce, Louise
1885/86–1959
pathologist, physician, codiscoverer and codeveloper of tryparsamide as a cure for sleeping sickness
Index t Wom; Not Am Wom supp v1; Obit File

13031. Ray, Rose Carolyn
born 1885
ornithologist
California
Nat Cyc Am Bio csv5

13032. Richards, Esther Loring
born 1885
psychiatrist
Presbyterian
Nat Cyc Am Bio csv7

13033. Sturgis, Margaret Castex
1885–1962
gynecologist, cancer researcher, medical author
Episcopalian
Pennsylvania
Nat Cyc Am Bio v49

13034. Borden, Mary; Lady Spears
1886–1968
novelist, head of a World War II field hospital in France
English (American expatriate to England)
Index t Wom; Obit File

13035. Bridgman, Olga Louise
born 1886
psychiatrist, medical educator and author
Episcopalian
California
Nat Cyc Am Bio csv6

13036. Goodenough, Florence Laura
1886–1959
developmental psychologist
Not Am Wom supp v1

13037. Griggs, Mary Amerman
1886–1962
chemist, chemistry educator
Dutch Reformed
Nat Cyc Am Bio v49

13038. Hollingworth, Leta Anna Stetter
1886–1939
educational psychologist
Dict Am Bio supp v2; Not Am Wom

13039. Kelly, Junea Wangeman
1886–1969
ornithologist, conservationist
California
Nat Cyc Am Bio v55

13040. Lane, Rose Wilder
1886/87–1968
novelist, telegrapher, World War I Red Cross worker in Europe, Vietnam war correspondent
Index t Wom; Nat Cyc Am Bio v54

13041. Rand, Marie Gertrude; Mrs. Clarence Erroll Feree
1886–1970
experimental psychologist
New York
Nat Cyc Am Bio csv7; Not Am Wom supp v1

13042. Riach, May Turner
1886–1946
surgeon, eye doctor, World War I doctor, Spanish Loyalist army physician
Methodist
Nat Cyc Am Bio v34

13043. Sutliffe, Irene
died 1936
nurse
Index t Wom

13044. Ball, Louise C.
1887–1946
dentist
Obit File

13045. Barber, Mary Isabel
circa 1887–1963
dietician
Index t Wom

13046. Calverley, Eleanor Jane Taylor
1887–1968
physician, missionary to Kuwait, nurse in the 1920 Kuwait war, birth control advocate, birth control clinic founder
Dutch Reformed
Connecticut
Nat Cyc Am Bio v57

13047. Dexter, Edith MacBride
1887–1958
ophthalmologist, public health worker
Presbyterian
Pennsylvania
Nat Cyc Am Bio v49

13048. Fairbank, Ruth Eldred
1887–1972
psychiatrist, psychiatric educator
Congregationalist
Massachusetts
Nat Cyc Am Bio v58

13049. Morgan, Barbara Spofford
1887–1971
philosopher, psychologist
Congregationalist
New York
Nat Cyc Am Bio v56; Who Who Phil

13050. Newcomb, Kate Delham
1887–1956
circuit physician, hospital founder
Wisconsin
Obit File

13051. Sellew, Gladys
born 1887
nurse
Index t Wom

13052. Weld, Julia Deforest Tiffany
1887–1973
medical researcher, patron of medicine
New York
Nat Cyc Am Bio v58

13053. Willkie, Julia E.
1887–1943
bacteriologist, educator, linguist
Obit File

13054. Ashton, Dorothy Laing
1888–1958
surgeon, obstetrician/gynecologist, medical educator
Pennsylvania
Nat Cyc Am Bio v49

13055. Branham, Sarah E.
1888–1962
bacteriologist, codiscoverer of the cure for one form of meningitis, chief bacteriologist for the US Public Health Service
Obit File

13056. Dauser, Sue Sophia
born 1888
nurse
Index t Wom

13057. Gowan, M. Olivia, Sister
born 1888
nurse, Catholic nun
Catholic
Index t Wom

13058. Gray, Caroline E.
died 1938
author, nurse
Index t Wom

13059. Hyman, Libbie Henrietta
1888–1969
zoologist, author
Index t Wom; Not Am Wom supp v1

13060. Kenyon, Dorothy
1888–1972
lawyer, feminist, suffragist, women's rights worker, prochoice abortion lobbyist, civil libertarian, director of the ACLU, UN official
New York
Cur Biog '72; Index t Wom; Nat Cyc Am Bio v56; Not Am Wom supp v1

13061. O'Donnell, Mary Agnes
died 1938
nurse
Index t Wom

13062. Rabinoff, Sophie
1888–1957
physician
Russian
Index t Wom

13063. Braun, Emma Lucy
1889–1971
botanist, conservationist
Not Am Wom supp v1

13064. Chung, Margaret Jessie
1889–1959
plastic surgeon, World War II relief worker
California
Chinese
Nat Cyc Am Bio v48

13065. Claytor, Gertrude (Harris) Boatwright
1889–1973
poet, Red Cross worker in World War I
Christian Scientist
Virginia
Nat Cyc Am Bio v57

13066. Fischel, Marguerite Kauffman
1889–1950
composer, worker for the welfare of young cerebral palsy victims
Jewish
Obit File

13067. Fromm-Reichman, Frieda
1889–1957
psychiatrist, psychoanalyst, authority on schizophrenia, faculty chairperson of the Washington School of Psychiatry
Jewish
Washington, DC
German
Dict Am Bio supp v5; Not Am Wom supp v1; Obit File

13068. Gladwin, Mary E.
died 1939
World War I nurse
Index t Wom

13069. Green, Charlotte Hilton
born 1889
naturalist, author
Index t Wom

13070. McHale, Kathryn
1889/90–1956
educator, psychologist, general director of the American Association of University Women
Dict Am Bio supp v6; Index t Wom; Nat Cyc Am Bio v46; Obit File

13071. Mellichamp, Julia St. Lo
died 1939
nurse
Index t Wom

13072. Baker, Bessie
flourished 1920s–30s
nurse
Index t Wom

13073. Bertola, Mariana
flourished 1920s
physician, child welfare worker, educator
Index t Wom

13074. Brokaw, Katherine F.
flourished 1920s–30s
pediatrician
Index t Wom

13075. Charlick, Edith
flourished 1920s–30s
nurse, business executive
Index t Wom

13076. Church, Ellen
flourished 1920s–40s
airline steward, flying nurse
Index t Wom

13077. Corbett, Margaret Darst
born 1890
visual-correction instructor
Nat Cyc Am Bio csv7

13078. Corbin, Hazel
flourished 1920s
nurse
Canadian
Index t Wom

13079. Davis, Elizabeth Greene Upham
born 1890
occupational therapist
Nat Cyc Am Bio csv1

13080. Densford, Katharine Jane
born 1890
nurse, educator
Index t Wom

13081. Deutsche, Naomi
born 1890
nurse
Austrian
Index t Wom

13082. Dreyfus, Berta E.
flourished 1920s
nurse
Index t Wom

13083. Eads, Laura Krieger
flourished 1920s–30s
educator, psychologist
Index t Wom

13084. Elliott, Mabel E.
flourished 1920s
physician
Index t Wom

13085. Foley, Edna
flourished 1920s
nurse
Index t Wom

13086. Graff, Elfie R.
flourished 1920s
physician
Index t Wom

13087. Graham, Helen Tredway
1890–1971
biochemist, air pollution control worker
St. Louis, MO
Nat Cyc Am Bio v56

13088. **Gregg, Elinor D.**
flourished 1920s
nurse
Index t Wom

13089. **Gretter, Lystra E.**
flourished 1920s
nurse
Index t Wom

13090. **Gulett, Lucy E.**
flourished 1920s
physician
Index t Wom

13091. **Hall, Carrie M.**
flourished 1920s–30s
nurse
Index t Wom

13092. **Hawkinson, Nellie X.**
flourished 1920s–30s
nurse, educator
Index t Wom

13093. **Ingersall, Winifred**
1890–1960
physician
Presbyterian
Wyoming
Nat Cyc Am Bio v45

13094. **Joy, Helen N.**
flourished 1920s–30s
nurse
Index t Wom

13095. **Kennedy, Rose (Fitzgerald)**
born 1890
philanthropist, patron of welfare work for the mentally retarded and of research on mental retardation
Catholic
Cur Biog '70

13096. **Kimball, Grace N.**
flourished 1920s
physician
Index t Wom

13097. **Logan, Laura R.**
flourished 1920s–30s
nurse, educator
Index t Wom

13098. **Maria Gratia, Mother**
flourished 1920s
missionary nurse, Catholic nun
Catholic
Index t Wom

13099. **Miller, Elizabeth**
died 1940
nurse
Index t Wom

13100. **Mitchell, Elsie R.**
flourished 1920s
physician
Index t Wom

13101. **Murdoch, Katharine**
flourished 1920s–30s
psychologist
Index t Wom

13102. **Muse, Maude B.**
flourished 1920s–30s
nurse, educator
Index t Wom

13103. **Parmelee, Ruth A.**
flourished 1920s
physician, missionary
Index t Wom

13104. **Randolph, Anne Dillon**
flourished 1920s
nurse
Index t Wom

13105. **Scott, Kate Frances**
born 1890
physician, organization official
Index t Wom

13106. **Sirch, Margaret Frances**
flourished 1920s
nurse
Index t Wom

13107. **Smith, Myrtle Lee**
flourished 1920s–50s
missionary to Africa, physician
Index t Wom

13108. **Staupers, Mabel Keaton**
born 1890
nurse
Barbadian; Black
Encyc Black Am

13109. **Strahan, Elsie T.**
flourished 1920s–30s
dietician, home economist
Index t Wom

13110. **Taylor, Effie J.**
flourished 1920s–30s
nurse, educator
Canadian
Index t Wom

13111. **Wales, Marguerite**
flourished 1920s–30s
public health nurse
Index t Wom

13112. **Wall, Florence Emeline**
flourished 1920s–30s
industrial chemist, cosmetician
Index t Wom

13113. **Woodham, Eva Esther Dowling**
1890–1962
insurance executive, floriculturist
Methodist
South Carolina
Nat Cyc Am Bio v46

13114. **Butler, Sally**
born 1891
lawyer
Index t Wom

13115. **Cockerton, Ina**
1891–1952
nurse
Index t Wom

13116. **Dye, Marie**
born 1891
educator, nutrition researcher
Index t Wom

13117. **Eliot, Martha May**
1891–1978
pediatrician, public health official, president of the American Health Association, UNICEF member, US Children's Bureau official
Unitarian
Massachusetts
Cur Biog '78; Index t Wom; Nat Cyc Am Bio v60

13118. **Lenroot, Katharine Fredrica**
born 1891
government official, social worker, child health worker
Congregationalist
Wisconsin
Index t Wom; Nat Cyc Am Bio csv7

13119. **Mack, Pauline Beery**
born 1891
chemist
Index t Wom

13120. **Quimby, Edith Hinckley**
born 1891
biophysicist, educator
Index t Wom

13121. **Romm, May E.**
1891–1977
psychiatrist, president of the Los Angeles and Southern California psychoanalytic societies, motion picture technical adviser
Los Angeles, CA
Obit File

13122. **Warner, Estella Ford**
born 1891
pioneer public health surgeon
Index t Wom

13123. **Combs, Helen**
1892–1944
physician, physiologist, medical educator
Obit File

13124. **Crump, Jean**
1892–1963
pediatrician
Presbyterian
Pennsylvania
Nat Cyc Am Bio v52

13125. **Gifford, Myrnie Ada**
1892–1966
public health administrator, pediatrician, conservationist
California
Nat Cyc Am Bio v54

13126. **Harrison, Gertrude [Alice] Gordon Grayson**
1892–1961
Washington, DC, civic leader; patron of medicine; racehorse breeder
Episcopalian
Nat Cyc Am Bio v51

13127. **Haupt,. Alma Cecelia**
1892–1956
authority of public health nursing, administrative educator
Dict Am Bio supp v6

13128. **Hiller, Alma Elizabeth**
1892–1958
chemist, biochemist, Rockefeller Institute researcher in protein and amino acid chemistry
Index t Wom; Obit File

13129. **Link, Adeline Desale**
1892–1943
chemist, university educator
Obit File

13130. **Macy, Icie Gertrude; Mrs. Bert Raymon Hoobler**
born 1892
chemist
Presbyterian
Michigan
Nat Cyc Am Bio csv8

13131. **Maher, Aldea**
1892–1959
biochemist, pathologist, cardiologist
Catholic
Louisiana
Nat Cyc Am Bio v51

13132. **O'Driscoll, Hannah**
born 1892
nurse
Irish
Index t Wom

13133. **Pattee, Alida Frances**
died 1942
dietician, lecturer, publisher, author
Index t Wom

13134. **Stone, Hannah Mayer**
1892–1941
gynecologist, medical director of the Margaret Sanger Research Bureau, birth control advocate
Jewish
New York
Index t Wom; Nat Cyc Am Bio v30; Obit File

13135. Buhler, Charlotte Bertha
1893–1974
psychologist
Not Am Wom supp v1

13136. Deming, Dorothy
born 1893
nurse, author
Index t Wom

13137. Garrett, Eileen Jeanette;
Jean Lyttle
1893–1970
parapsychologist, novelist, founder of the Parapsychology Foundation
Anglican
Irish
Nat Cyc Am Bio v55; Obit File

13138. Hill, Justina Hamilton
born 1893
bacteriologist
Index t Wom

13139. Larson, Nella
1893–1963
author, nurse
Black
Encyc Black Am; Wom Lit; Wom Lit, More

13140. Mackie, Janet Welch
1893–1959
physician, tropical medicine expert, US Public Health Service adviser
English
Obit File

13141. Macklin, Madge Thurlow
1893–1962
physician, geneticist
Not Am Wom supp v1

13142. McIver, Pearl
born 1893
public health worker, nurse, government official
Index t Wom

13143. Mintzer, Ida Jessica
1893–1970
dermatologist
Jewish
New York
Nat Cyc Am Bio v55

13144. Peabody, May E.
died 1943
authority on child training
Obit File

13145. Sutley, Margaret Hutchinson
1893–1947
physician, surgeon, medical educator in Japan, venereal disease clinic founder
Nat Cyc Am Bio v35

13146. Thompson, Clara "Mabel"
1893–1958
psychiatrist, psychoanalyst, executive director of the William Allanson White Institute of Psychiatry
Not Am Wom supp v1; Obit File

13147. Wanstrum, Ruth Cecilia
1893–1971
pathologist, medical educator
Episcopalian
Michigan
Nat Cyc Am Bio v57

13148. Groves, Gladys Hoagland
1894–1980
educator, marriage and sex counselor, writer on marriage and sex
Cur Biog '80; Index t Wom

13149. Ireland, Margaret Allen
1894–1961
public health worker, Cleveland civic worker, welfare worker
Episcopalian
Cleveland, OH
Nat Cyc Am Bio v50

13150. Metzelthin, Pearl Violette
1894–1947
dietician, author, editor, health worker
Index t Wom

13151. Porter, Elizabeth Kerr
born 1894
organization official, nurse
Index t Wom

13152. Schulze, Margaret
1894–1943
gynecologist, surgeon, pathologist, medical educator, medical author
California
Nat Cyc Am Bio v34

13153. Stern, Catherine Brieger "Kathe"
1894–1973
educator, child education specialist, writer on child education
Lutheran
German
Nat Cyc Am Bio v57; Not Am Wom supp v1

13154. Todd, Lois Pendleton
1894–1968
physician, medical educator in China
Congregationalist
California
Nat Cyc Am Bio v54

13155. Zachary, Caroline Beaumont
1894–1945
educational psychologist
Not Am Wom

13156. Bayliss, Marguerite Farleigh
born 1895
author, scientist
Index t Wom

13157. Drant, Patricia Hart;
Mrs. James Steffan Collins
1895–1955
dermatologist
Episcopalian
Nat Cyc Am Bio v42

13158. Farr, Wanda Kirkbride
born 1895
biochemist
Index t Wom

13159. Jackson, Edith Banfield
1895–1977
pediatrician, child psychiatrist, medical author
Nat Cyc Am Bio csv13; Obit File

13160. Powdermaker, Florence Bertha
1895–1966
surgeon, psychiatrist, psychoanalyst who helped develop the group psychotherapy theory
Obit File

13161. Adelsberger, Lucie
1896–1971
medical researcher, immunologist
Jewish
Obit File

13162. Beeby, Nell V.
1896–1957
nurse, editor of *American Journal of Nursing*
Index t Wom; Obit File

13163. Birch, Carroll
born 1896
physician
Index t Wom

13164. Chace, Marian
1896–1970
creator of dance therapy, dancer
Not Am Wom supp v1

13165. Cori, Gerty Theresa Radnitz
1896–1957
biochemist, physician, medical educator, Nobel Prize winner
Czechoslovak
Dict Am Bio supp v6; Index t Wom; Nat Cyc Am Bio v48 and csv8; Not Am Wom supp v1; Obit File

13166. Dodge, Eva Francette
born 1896
obstetrician, medical educator, birth control and Planned Parenthood worker, public health worker
Baptist
Nat Cyc Am Bio csv12

13167. Fay, Marion (Spencer)
born 1896
educator, physiological chemist
Episcopalian
Pennsylvania
Nat Cyc Am Bio csv12

13168. Floyd, Theodora A.
born 1896
nurse
Index t Wom

13169. Frantz, Virginia Kneeland
1896–1967
surgical pathologist, medical educator, cancer researcher, dairy farmer
Episcopalian
New York
Nat Cyc Am Bio v53; Not Am Wom supp v1

13170. Pruette, Lorine Livingston
born 1896
psychologist, author
Index t Wom

13171. Stiebeling, Hazel Katherine
born 1896
physical chemist, government official
Index t Wom

13172. Woolley, Alice Stone
died 1946
physician, president of the American Medical Women's Association
New York
Obit File

13173. Bender, Lauretta
born 1897
psychiatrist
Index t Wom

13174. Bernstein, Lotte Kirschner
1897–1971
psychiatrist, psychoanalyst
Jewish
Kentucky
German
Nat Cyc Am Bio v57

13175. Bowman, J. Beatrice
graduated 1922
navy nurse
Index t Wom

13176. Brunswick, Ruth Jane Mack
1897–1946
psychoanalyst
Dict Am Bio supp v5; Not Am Wom

13177. Chappelle, B. F., Mrs.
born 1897
psychologist
Index t Wom

13178. Eichelberger, Lillian (Velma); Mrs. Ralph Cannon
born 1897
biochemist
Baptist
Nat Cyc Am Bio csv13

13179. Heller, Florence Gunsfeld
1897–1966
philanthropist, patron of medicine, Jewish welfare worker
Jewish
Chicago, IL
Nat Cyc Am Bio v51

13180. Prochazka, Anne
born 1897
orthopedic nurse
Index t Wom

13181. Pryor, Helen Brenton
1897–1972
pediatrician, medical educator
Methodist
California
Nat Cyc Am Bio v57

13182. Seibert, Florence Barbara; Florence Seifert
born 1897
biochemist, pioneer scientist
Presbyterian
Index t Wom; Nat Cyc Am Bio csv8

13183. Snow, Kathleyn Smith
born 1897
physician
Episcopalian
Nat Cyc Am Bio csv4

13184. Spencer, Shirley
born 1897
graphologist
Index t Wom

13185. Brown, Rachel Fuller
died 1898
biochemist
Index t Wom

13186. Carter, Lillian "Bessie"
born 1898
nurse, social service worker, peace worker, civil rights worker
Georgia
Cur Biog '78

13187. Craighill, Margaret D.
born 1898
physician, army medical officer
Index t Wom

13188. Daniels, Anna Kleegman
born 1898
gynecologist, medical director of Planned Parenthood
Jewish
Russian
Nat Cyc Am Bio csv11

13189. Mudd, Emily Hatshore
born 1898
educator, author, marriage counselor
Index t Wom

13190. Stimson, Barbara Bartlett
born 1898
physician, orthopedic surgeon
Index t Wom

13191. Taussig, Helen Brooke
born 1898
physician, pediatric cardiologist, president of the American Heart Association
Unitarian
Index t Wom; Nat Cyc Am Bio csv11

13192. van Loon, Emily Lois
born 1898
physician
Index t Wom

13193. Anderson, Elda Emma
1899–1961
health physicist
Congregationalist
Nat Cyc Am Bio v50; Not Am Wom supp v1

13194. Bliss, Eleanor Albert
born 1899
bacteriologist, physician
Index t Wom

13195. Charles, Alta Genevieve
1899–1963
ophthalmologist
Presbyterian
Pennsylvania
Nat Cyc Am Bio v50

13196. Engelbrecht, Mildred Amanda
1899–1973
bacteriologist
Presbyterian
Nat Cyc Am Bio v58

13197. Gardner, Emily
1899–1956
pediatrician
Baptist
Richmond, VA
Nat Cyc Am Bio v42

13198. Nash, Dorothy Klenke
1899–1976
neurosurgeon
Obit File

13199. Sleeper, Ruth
born 1899
organization official, nurse
Index t Wom

13200. Weiss, Soma
1899–1942
physician
Index t Wom

13201. Abelson, Josephine May
flourished 1930s
dental surgeon
Index t Wom

13202. Arkin, Frances S.
flourished 1930s
psychiatrist
Index t Wom

13203. Baer, Louise Andrews
died 1950
patron of heart disease research
Obit File

13204. Bailey, Margaret E.
flourished 1930s–60s
lieutenant colonel in US Army, World War I nurse
Black
Encyc Black Am; Prof Negro Wom v2

13205. Bakwin, Ruth Morris
flourished 1930s
pediatrician
Index t Wom

13206. Ball, Erna D.
flourished 1930s
neurologist
German
Index t Wom

13207. Barnard, Margaret Witter
flourished 1930s
physician
Index t Wom

13208. Baumann, Anny
flourished 1930s
physician
German
Index t Wom

13209. Benjamin, Peggy Haskell
flourished 1930s
naturalist
Index t Wom

13210. Benson, Marguerite
flourished 1930s
social hygiene worker
Index t Wom

13211. Berger, Hulda E.
flourished 1930s
dentist
Index t Wom

13212. Bernheim, Alice Rheinstein
flourished 1930s
surgeon
Index t Wom

13213. Bernie, Rose L.
flourished 1930s
realtor, health expert
Index t Wom

13214. Bogert, L. Jean
flourished 1930s
physiological chemist
Index t Wom

13215. Bruce, Hilde
flourished 1930s
physician
Index t Wom

13216. Bruenn, Anna Rosa
flourished 1930s
dentist
Index t Wom

13217. Butler, Lorine Letcher
flourished 1930s
nature writer
Index t Wom

13218. Caldwell, Mary Letitia
flourished 1930s
chemist
Index t Wom

13219. Carr, Alice G.
flourished 1930s
nurse
Index t Wom

13220. Carrington, Elsie
flourished 1930s–70s
nurse
Black
Encyc Black Am

13221. Clark, Mary Augusta
flourished 1930s
public health worker
Index t Wom

13222. Cooper, Lenna Frances
flourished 1930s
dietician
Index t Wom

13223. Curtis, Maynie Rose
flourished 1930s
research psychologist
Index t Wom

13224. Davis, Nelle
flourished 1930s
pharmacist
English
Index t Wom

13225. Delafield, Ann
flourished 1930s
cosmetician, dietician, educator
Index t Wom

13226. Dunning, Wilhelmina Frances
flourished 1930s
physician
Index t Wom

13227. Edwards, Lena Frances
born 1900
obstetrician
Index t Wom

13228. Fish, Marjorie
flourished 1930s–40s
occupational therapist
Index t Wom

13229. Flager, Alicia Mayre
flourished 1930s
nutritionist
Index t Wom

13230. Flemion, Florence
flourished 1930s
plant physiologist
Index t Wom

13231. Forbes, Grace Springer
flourished 1930s
educator, zoologist
Index t Wom

13232. Fries, Constance
flourished 1930s
physician, educator
Index t Wom

13233. Gans, Bird Stein
flourished 1930s
child study expert
Index t Wom

13234. Gilmore, Marion Sprague
flourished 1930s
dietician
Index t Wom

13235. Goldsmith, C. Elizabeth
flourished 1930s
psychologist
Index t Wom

13236. Hager, Alice Mayre
flourished 1930s
dietician
Index t Wom

13237. Harrington, Helen
flourished 1930s
pediatrician
Index t Wom

13238. Hart, Fanchon
flourished 1930s
bacteriologist
Index t Wom

13239. Hoffman, Myn M.
flourished 1930s–40s
army nurse
Index t Wom

13240. Howland, Ruth B.
flourished 1930s
biologist
Index t Wom

13241. Jamme, Anne C.
flourished 1930s
nurse
Index t Wom

13242. Johnson, Corinne
flourished 1930s
botanist
Index t Wom

13243. Jordan, Alice Boyer
flourished 1930s
nurse, business executive
Index t Wom

13244. Karpeles, Kate B.
flourished 1930s
physician
Index t Wom

13245. Kelner, Sophie
flourished 1930s
dentist
Austrian
Index t Wom

13246. Klumpp, Margaret M.
flourished 1930s
physician
Index t Wom

13247. Kmetz, Annette L.
flourished 1930s
nurse, public health worker
Index t Wom

13248. Kohlhepp, Evelyn Marie
flourished 1930s
dentist
Index t Wom

13249. Krasnow, Frances
flourished 1930s
biochemist
Index t Wom

13250. Kutz, Sally
flourished 1930s
public health worker
Index t Wom

13251. la Roe, Else K.
flourished 1930s
physician
Index t Wom

13252. Lewinson, Thea Stein
flourished 1930s
graphologist
German
Index t Wom

13253. Marmorston, Jessie
flourished 1930s
pathologist
Russian
Index t Wom

13254. McCraken, Mary Isabel
flourished 1930s
entomologist
Index t Wom

13255. McGarvah, Eleanor
flourished 1930s
public health nurse
Index t Wom

13256. Moor, Anne
flourished 1930s
physiologist, dramatic teacher
Index t Wom

13257. Mosher, Edna
flourished 1930s
biologist, entomologist
Canadian
Index t Wom

13258. Murray, Margaret Ransone
flourished 1930s
biologist
Index t Wom

13259. Okama, Kyoko
flourished 1930s
medical missionary
Japanese
Index t Wom

13260. Orcutt, Ruby R. M.
flourished 1930s
chemist
Index t Wom

13261. Ovens, Florence Jane
flourished 1930s
child specialist, editor
English
Index t Wom

13262. Payne, Nelle Maria de Cottrell
born 1900
entomologist
Index t Wom

13263. Pennock, Meta
flourished 1930s
nurse, editor
Index t Wom

13264. Peritz, Edith
flourished 1930s
surgeon
German
Index t Wom

13265. Pinney, Jean Burrows
flourished 1930s
editor, social hygiene worker
Index t Wom

13266. Potter, Marion Craig
flourished 1930s
physician, gynecologist
Index t Wom

13267. Prigosin, Rosa Elizabeth
flourished 1930s
bacteriologist, pediatrician
Index t Wom

13268. Read, Katherine S.
flourished 1930s
public health nurse
Index t Wom

13269. Robbins, Sarah Franklin
flourished 1930s
psychologist, adult education pioneer
Index t Wom

13270. Rowland, Helen
flourished 1930s
journalist
Index t Wom

13271. Sandberg, Marta Ehrlich
flourished 1930s
chemist
German
Index t Wom

13272. Seymour, Frances I.
flourished 1930s
physician
Index t Wom

13273. Shaw, Ellen Eddy
flourished 1930s
naturalist, lecturer, author
Index t Wom

13274. Sheriff, Hilla
flourished 1930s
physician
Index t Wom

13275. Sherven, Betty
flourished 1930s
physiotherapist
Norwegian
Index t Wom

13276. Simecek, Angeline Frances
flourished 1930s
physician
Index t Wom

13277. Snell, Cornelia Tyler
flourished 1930s
chemist
Index t Wom

13278. Stark, Mary B.
flourished 1930s
physician, educator
Index t Wom

13279. Swope, Ethel
flourished 1930s

nurse
Index t Wom

13280. Traver, Ethel K.
flourished 1930s
osteopath
Index t Wom

13281. Wandling, Arlita R.
flourished 1930s
child research worker
Index t Wom

13282. Warner, Marie Pichel
flourished 1930s
gynecologist
Index t Wom

13283. Weill, Blanche C.
flourished 1930s
psychologist
Index t Wom

13284. Willard, Luvia
flourished 1930s
pediatrician
Index t Wom

**13285. Williamson, Pauline
Brooks**
flourished 1930s
health worker
Index t Wom

13286. Wolf, Anna D.
flourished 1930s–40s
nurse
Index t Wom

13287. Wright, Jessie
1900–70
orthopedist, orthopedic inventor,
   medical educator
English
Nat Cyc Am Bio v55

13288. Young, N. Louise
flourished 1930s–40s
physician
Black
Encyc Black Am

13289. Zaidens, Sadie Helene
flourished 1930s
dermatologist
Index t Wom

**13290. Alexander, Hattie
Elizabeth**
1901/08–1968
research pediatrician, microbiolo-
   gist
Congregationalist
New York
Nat Cyc Am Bio csv10; Not Am
   Wom; Obit File

**13291. Anderson, Dorothy
Hansine**
1901–63
pathologist, pediatrician
Not Am Wom supp v1

**13292. Kleegman, Sophia
Josephine**
1901–71
obstetrician/gynecologist
Russian
Index t Wom; Not Am Wom
   supp v1

13293. Osborne, Estelle Massey
1901–post 1976
nurse, nursing educator, army
   nurse in World War II
Black
Negro Alman; Prof Negro Wom
   v2

13294. Travall, Janet Graeme
born 1901
physician
Index t Wom

**13295. Wasson, Valentina Pav-
lovna Guercken**
1901–58
pediatrician, mycologist
New York
Russian
Obit File

**13296. Baumgartner, Leona;
Mrs. Nathaniel M. Elias**
born 1902
pediatrician, public health official
Presbyterian
New York, NY
Index t Wom; Nat Cyc Am Bio
   csv9

13297. Block, Virginia Lee
1902–70
psychologist, educator
California
Nat Cyc Am Bio v56

13298. Cohen, Essie White
1902–63
chemist
Jewish
Denver, CO
Nat Cyc Am Bio v51

13299. Derrick-Swindells, Lucy
died 1952
poet, portrait painter
English
Obit File

13300. Dunbar, Helen Flanders
1902–59
psychiatrist, psychoanalyst, pioneer in psychosomatic medicine
Dict Am Bio supp v5; Not Am
   Wom supp v1; Obit File

13301. Fish, Marie Poland
born 1902
ichthyologist
Index t Wom

13302. Goodnow, Minnie
died 1952

nurse, author, educator
Index t Wom

13303. Ilg, Frances Lillian
1902–81
pediatrician, medical educator
   and author
Cur Biog '81; Index t Wom

13304. Lough, Orpha Maust
born 1902
psychologist
Index t Wom

13305. MacLean, Bernice
1902–46
zoologist, educator
Obit File

13306. Callery, Mary
1903–77
sculptor, ambulance driver in
   France during World War II
Index t Wom; Nat Cyc Am Bio
   v60 and csv9

**13307. Elsome, Katharine
O'Shea**
born 1903
physician, nutritionist
Index t Wom

13308. Emerson, Gladys
born 1903
biochemist
Index t Wom

13309. Levine, Lena
1903–65
gynecologist, psychiatrist
Not Am Wom supp v1

13310. Payson, Joan Whitney
1903–75
philanthropist, race horse breeder, owner of the New York
   Mets, patron of medicine, art
   collector and investor, founder
   of the Museum of Modern Art
   in New York
Episcopalian
New York
Cur Biog '72 and '75; Index t
   Wom; Nat Cyc Am Bio v58 and
   csv10; Obit File

13311. Petry, Lucile
born 1903
nurse, educator
Index t Wom

13312. Quiggle, Dorothy
born 1903
chemical engineer
Index t Wom

13313. Riddle, Estelle Massey
born 1903
nurse
Index t Wom

**13314. Adair, Marion Hopkin-
son (Barnes)**
1904–65
New York civic leader, World
   War II relief worker, cancer-
   patient relief worker, patron of
   cancer research, radio personality, mimic
New York, NY
Nat Cyc Am Bio v51

**13315. Arnstein, Margaret
Gene**
1904–72
public health nurse, nursing educator
Not Am Wom supp v1

**13316. Calderone, Mary Stei-
chen**
born 1904
physician
Index t Wom

13317. Davis, Adelle
1904–74
food writer, nutritionist
California
Cur Biog '73 and '74; Not Am
   Wom supp v1; Obit File

**13318. Emch, Minna Elizabeth
Libman**
1904–58
psychiatrist, psychiatric educator
   and author
Chicago, IL
Lithuanian
Nat Cyc Am Bio v47

**13319. Goldsmith, Grace Ara-
bell**
1904–75
physician, public health educator,
   nutritionist
Episcopalian
Louisiana
Nat Cyc Am Bio csv10; Not Am
   Wom supp v10

13320. Jones, Margaret Holden
born 1904
pediatrician
Methodist
California
Nat Cyc Am Bio csv9

13321. Mann, Marty
born 1904
alcoholism authority
Episcopalian
Nat Cyc Am Bio csv11

**13322. Mauze, Abby
Rockefeller**
1904–76
philanthropist, patron of cancer
   research
Obit File

13366. Wolfenstein, Martha
1911–76
psychiatrist, child psychology
specialist, educator
Jewish
Obit File

13367. Horner, Marjorie Crittenden
married 1938
missionary to Africa, physician
Index t Wom

13368. Pool, Judith Grayham
1913–75
physiologist
Not Am Wom supp v1

13369. Russell, Elizabeth Shull
born 1913
zoologist, geneticist
Index t Wom

13370. van Straaten, Florence Whilhelmina
born 1913
physical chemist
Index t Wom

13371. Andrews, Marie Scherer
1914–73
orthopedic nurse, nursing educator
Catholic
Massachusetts
Nat Cyc Am Bio v57

13372. Graves, Helen (Louise) Pierson
born 1914
physician, medical educator
Methodist
Ohio
Nat Cyc Am Bio csv13

13373. Kelsey, Frances
born 1914
physician, government employee
Index t Wom

13374. Lawrence, Margaret Morgan
born 1914
pediatrician
Black
Encyc Black Am

13375. Ray, Dixie Lee
born 1914
marine biologist, chairperson of the AEC
Cur Biog '73; Index t Wom

13376. Schlotfeldt, Rozella May
born 1914
nurse, nursing educator, women's rights worker, feminist
Nat Cyc Am Bio csv13

13377. Morgan, Edith Galt
1915–68

psychiatric nursing educator
Presbyterian
Nat Cyc Am Bio v55

13378. Fertman, Mildred Been
1916–52
physician, medical researcher
Jewish
California
Nat Cyc Am Bio v49

13379. Shindel, Dorothy Louise; Mrs. Alfred C. LaBoccetta
1916–75
pediatrician
Lutheran
Pennsylvania
Nat Cyc Am Bio v59

13380. Loehrke, Leah Marie
1918–71
psychologist, psychological educator
Lutheran
Ohio
Nat Cyc Am Bio v57

13381. Sager, Ruth
born 1918
geneticist
Index t Wom

13382. Walker, Maggie
born 1918
pediatrician
Black
Encyc Black Am

13383. Brown, Dorothy
born 1919
surgeon, Tennessee state legislator
Tennessee
Black
Encyc Black Am; Negro Alman

13384. Frank, Mary Hughes
born 1919
author, child guidance expert
Irish
Index t Wom

13385. Nyswander, Marie
born 1919
psychiatrist
Index t Wom

13386. Pambrun, Audra Marie
born 1919
nurse
Native American (Blackfoot)
Ind Today

13387. Silverstein, Hannah H.
1919–52
navy nurse, experimental cancer cure volunteer
Obit File

13388. Wright, Jane Cook
born 1919

surgeon, cancer specialist
Black
Encyc Black Am; Index t Wom

13389. Carnegie, Mary Elizabeth Lancaster
flourished 1950s–60s
nurse, nursing-magazine editor
Black
Prof Negro Wom v2

13390. Cushman, Beulah
flourished 1950s
physician, educator
Index t Wom

13391. Duerk, Alene (Bertha)
born 1920
rear admiral in the US Navy, head of the Navy Nurse Corps
Cur Biog '73

13392. Francis, Yvette Fae
flourished 1950s
physician
Black
Encyc Black Am

13393. Hastings, Alicia E.
flourished 1950s–60s
physician, medical educator
Black
Encyc Black Am

13394. MacGuffie, Martha
flourished 1950s
physician
Index t Wom

13395. Ohlson, Agnes
flourished 1950s
nurse, organization official
Index t Wom

13396. Poling, Hazel
born 1920
administrator of Indian Health Service
Native American (Ottawa)
Ind Today

13397. Simmons, Juliette
flourished 1950s–60s
psychiatrist
Black
Prof Negro Wom v2

13398. Stinetorf, Louise
flourished 1950s
nurse, author
Index t Wom

13399. Webster, Augusta
flourished 1950s
physician, educator
Index t Wom

13400. Dougherty, Dora Jean
born 1921
aviator, helicopter pilot, psychologist
Index t Wom

13401. Spurlock, Jeanne
born 1921
psychiatrist, educator
Black
Encyc Black Am

13402. Yalow, Rosalyn Sussman
born 1921
medical physicist, Nobel Prize winner
Jewish
Cur Biog '78

13403. Clark, Eugenie
born 1922
ichthyologist
Index t Wom

13404. Gunter, Laurie Martin
born 1922
nurse, nursing educator
Black
Encyc Black Am

13405. Mitchell-Bateman, Mildred
1922–post 1962
psychiatrist, hospital administrator
Black
Negro Alman; Encyc Black Am

13406. Martin, Julia M.
born 1924
chemist, educator
Black
Encyc Black Am

13407. Johnson, Virginia E. (Shelman)
born 1925
writer on sex, psychologist
Cur Biog '76

13408. Kubler-Ross, Elisabeth
born 1926
psychiatrist, thanatologist, writer on death and dying
Swiss
Cur Biog '80

13409. Lawrence, Annie L.
born 1926
nurse, educator
Black
Encyc Black Am

13410. McBroom, F. Pearl
born 1926
cardiologist
Black
Encyc Black Am

13411. Nettleship, Mae Barnwell
born 1926
physician
Episcopalian
Arkansas
Canadian
Nat Cyc Am Bio csv10

13412. Brothers, Joyce
born 1927/28
psychologist, television and radio personality, newspaper columnist
Cur Biog '71; Index t Wom

13413. Jones, Edith Irby
born 1927
physician, medical educator
Black
Encyc Black Am

13414. Braunwald, Nina Starr
born 1928
surgeon
Index t Wom

13415. Phillips, Mildred E.
born 1928
pathologist
Black
Encyc Black Am

13416. Nash, Gwendolyn V. Brownlee
1929–70
physician
Black
Encyc Black Am

13417. Frankelstein, Beatrice
flourished 1960s
space nutrition expert
Index t Wom

13418. Gaynor, Florence
flourished 1960s–70s
hospital administrator
Black
Encyc Black Am

13419. Harris, Ladonna
flourished 1960s–70s
health reformer, women's rights worker
Native American (Comanche)
Ind Today

13420. Jendritza, Loretta S.
flourished 1960s
air force major, war nurse
Native American (Navaho)
Ind Today

13421. Mary Alma, Sister
flourished 1960s
biochemist, Catholic nun
Catholic
Index t Wom

13422. Mary Benedict, Sister
flourished 1960s
surgeon, Catholic nun
Catholic
Index t Wom

13423. Yellow Rose, Evelyn
flourished 1960s
otolaryngologist
Native American (Dakota-Brule)
Ind Today

13424. Chennault, Madelyn
born 1932
psychologist, educator
Black
Negro Alman

13425. Adams, Clara Isabel
born 1933
chemist
Black
Encyc Black Am

13426. Sinkford, Jeanne Craig
born 1933
dentist, dental educator
Black
Encyc Black Am

13427. Millett, Kate
born 1934
philosopher, novelist, feminist leader, writer on sex
Cur Biog '71

13428. Young, Lois A.
born 1934
ophthalmologist, educator
Black
Encyc Black Am

13429. Mead, Sylvia Alice Earle
born 1935
marine biologist, aquanaut
Los Angeles, CA
Cur Biog '72

13430. O'Hara, Dolores B.
born circa 1935
pioneer space nurse
Index t Wom

13431. Welsing, Frances Cress
born 1935
psychiatrist
Black
Negro Alman; Encyc Black Am

13432. Horner, Matina Souretis
born 1939
psychologist, president of Radcliffe College, college educator
Cur Biog '73

13433. Ferebee, Dorothy B.
flourished 1970s
physician
Black
Negro Alman

13434. Fowler, Jessie Allen
born 1956
phrenologist, medical author
Nat Cyc Am Bio v16

No Dates

13435. Brooks, Matilda Moldenhauer
physiologist, biologist
Index t Wom

MUSIC

13436. Russell, Ezekiel, Mrs.
flourished eighteenth century
colonial printer, ballad writer
Index t Wom

13437. Fletcher, Bridget
1726–70
hymn and spiritual songwriter
Am Bio Dict

13438. Davies, Marianne
1736/44–1792/1816
pianist, harpsichordist, harmonica player
Cyc Am Bio; Dict Nat Bio

13439. Davies, Cecelia
1740/50–1836
vocalist
English
Cyc Am Bio; Index t Wom

13440. Stamper, Mrs.
flourished 1770s
colonial singer
Scottish
Index t Wom

13441. Pownall, Mary Ann; Mary Ann Wrighton
1751–96
actor, singer, composer
Index t Wom

13442. Hodginson, John, Mrs.
died 1803
actor, singer
Index t Wom

13443. Hutchinson, Viola
flourished nineteenth century
social reformer, singer
Index t Wom

13444. Rowson, Charlotte
circa 1779–1855
actor, popular singer
Cyc Am Bio

13445. Oldmixon, Mary (George)
died 1835/36
singer, actor
Dict Am Bio Men Time; Index t Wom

13446. Richings, Caroline Mary
1787–1884
soprano vocalist, pianist
English
Cyc Am Bio; Dict Am Bio Men Time; Nat Cyc Am Bio v9

13447. Moise, Penina
1797–1880
poet, writer of Jewish hymns
Jewish

Charleston, SC
Cyc Am Bio; Dict Am Auth; Dict Am Bio; Index t Wom; Not Am Wom; Wom Lit, More

13448. Caradori-Allan, Maria Caterina Rosabina
1800–65
vocalist
Cyc Am Bio

13449. Smith, Elizabeth N.
flourished nineteenth century
pianist, linguist
Index t Wom

13450. Tennyson, Jean
flourished 1830s
singer
Index t Wom

13451. Hilson, Ellen Augusta (Johnston)
1801–37
actor, singer, harpist
Cyc Am Bio; Dict Am Bio Men Time

13452. Ludnam, Augusta V.
died 1851
pianist
Cincinnati, OH
Am Bio Dict

13453. Judson, Sarah Hall Boardman
1803–45
missionary to Burma, hymn writer, translator
Cyc Am Bio; Dict Am Bio; Index t Wom; Nat Cyc Am Bio v3, Not Am Wom; Twent Cen Bio Dict Not Am

13454. Smith, Eliza Roxey Snow; The Mother of Mormonism
1804–87
Mormon leader, religious poet, hymn writer, women's leader, suffragist, western pioneer
Mormon
Utah
Cyc Am Bio; Dict Am Bio; Index t Wom; Not Am Wom; Read Encyc Am West

13455. Sontag, Henriette
1805–54
opera singer
German
Cyc Am Bio

13456. Greenfield, Elizabeth Taylor; The Black Swan; Elizabeth Taylor-Greenfield
1808/17–1876
singer
Black
Cyc Am Bio; Encyc Black Am; Index t Wom; Not Am Wom; Prof Negro Wom v1

13457. Malibran, Maria Felecia
1808–36
mezzo-soprano vocalist, composer
Cyc Am Bio

13458. Bishop, Anna (Riviere), Madam
1810/14–1884
soprano opera singer
English
Appl Cyc Am Bio; Cyc Am Bio; Dict Am Bio Men Time; Nat Cyc Am Bio v3; Not Am Wom; Twent Cen Bio Dict Not Am; Wom Cent

13459. Hale, Mary Whitwell
1810–62
poet, educator, hymn writer
Massachusetts
Dict Am Auth; Index t Wom

13460. Osgood, Marion
flourished 1840s–90s
composer, violinist, conductor
Boston, MA
Index t Wom; Wom Cent

13461. Fisher, Clara
1811–98
actor, singer
English
Cyc Am Bio; Dict Am Bio; Index t Wom; Not Am Wom

13462. Susini, Isabella (Hinckley)
died 1862
soprano opera singer
Dict Am Bio Men Time

13463. Rea, Julia (de Marguerittes) (Foster)
1814–66
opera singer, drama critic, writer on Europe
Philadelphia, PA
English
Cyc Am Bio; Dict Am Auth; Dict Am Bio Men Time

13464. Seguin, Ann Child (Shelden)
1814–88
opera singer, voice teacher
Cyc Am Bio; Dict Am Bio Men Time; Dict Nat Bio

13465. Cartwright, Ellen M.
1815–73
singer
Index t Wom

13466. Smith, Elizabeth Lee (Allen)
1817–98
biographical editor, poet, hymn writer
Dict Am Auth

13467. Nau, Maria Dolores Benedicta Josephine
1818–91
soprano singer
Index t Wom; Nat Cyc Am Bio v5

13468. Prentiss, Elizabeth (Payson); Elizabeth Prescott
1818–78
children's author, religious fiction writer, hymn writer
Dict Am Bio; Dict Am Bio; Index t Wom; Nat Cyc Am Bio v7; Not Am Wom; Twent Cen Bio Dict Not Am

13469. Howe, Julia Ward
1819–1910
poet, dramatist, songwriter, lecturer, suffrage and women's club leader, feminist, abolitionist, pacifist, prison reformer, Union patriot during the Civil War, philanthropist, traveler
Boston, MA
Cyc Am Bio; Dict Am Auth; Dict Am Bio; Dict Am Bio Men Time; Dict Lit Bio v1; Index t Wom; Nat Cyc Am Bio v1; Not Am Wom; Twent Cen Bio Dict Not Am; Wom Cent

13470. Bowers, Sarah Sedgwick
flourished 1850s
singer
Index t Wom

13471. Crosby, Frances Jane "Fannie"
1820/23–1915
hymn writer
blind
Dict Am Bio; Index t Wom; Not Am Wom; Wom Cent

13472. Lind, Johanna Maria "Jenny"; Jenny Lind-Goldschmidt
1820/21–1887
vocalist
Swedish
Cyc Am Bio; Dict Nat Bio; Index t Wom; Nat Cyc Am Bio v3

13473. van Allstyne, Frances J[ane] (Crosby) "Fanny"
born 1820
hymn writer, poet, songwriter
New York, NY
Dict Am Auth; Nat Cyc Am Bio v7; Twent Cen Bio Dict Not Am

13474. Scudder, Eliza
1821–96
hymn writer
Massachusetts
Dict Am Auth

13475. Caradori, Anna
born 1822

vocalist
Cyc Am Bio

13476. Spencer, Lilly Martin
1822/47–1902
painter
Index t Wom; Not Am Wom

13477. Bisciaccianti, Eliza (Ostinelli)
born 1825
opera singer
Appl Cyc Am Bio; Cyc Am Bio; Dict Am Bio Men Time

13478. Hayes, Catherine (Bushnell)
1825–61
mezzo-soprano opera singer
Irish
Aust Dict Bio; Cyc Am Bio; Dict Irish Bio; Dict Nat Bio; Nat Cyc Am Bio v4

13479. Beers, Ethelinda Eliot; Ethel Lynn
1827–79
poet, children's author, lyricist
Appl Cyc Am Bio; Cyc Am Bio; Bio Dict Am Auth; Dict Am Bio; Index t Wom; Nat Cyc Am Bio v8; Twent Cen Bio Dict Not Am

13480. Taylor, Mary Cecelia
1827–66
actor, opera singer
New York
Cyc Am Bio

13481. Brinkerhoff, Clara M.
born 1828
soprano singer, composer, music educator
English
Wom Cent

13482. Patton, Abigail Jemima; Abby Hutchinson
1829–92
alto singer, composer, poet, social reformer, abolitionist, suffragist, hymn writer, feminist
New York; New Hampshire
Nat Cyc Am Bio v10; Wom Cent; Not Am Wom; Index t Wom

13483. Boteler, Helen
flourished 1860s
Civil War musician
Index t Wom

13484. Cappiani, Luisa
flourished 1860s–80s
opera singer, music educator
Austrian
Wom Cent

13485. Eddy, Sara Hershey
flourished 1860s–70s
music educator, singer
Index t Wom; Wom Cent

13486. Groenevelt, Sara; Stanley M. Bartlett
flourished 1860s
pianist, poet
Wom Cent

13487. Hyers, Anna Madah
flourished 1860s–70s
singer, actor
Black
Index t Wom; Prof Negro Wom v1

13488. Hyers, Emma Louise
flourished 1860s–70s
singer, actor
Black
Index t Wom; Prof Negro Wom v1

13489. Porter, Maggie L.
flourished 1860s
gospel singer
Black
Prof Negro Wom v1

13490. Ritter, Frances Malone (Raymond) "Fannie"
1830–90
writer on music, song compiler, mezzo-soprano vocalist, poet
Cyc Am Bio; Dict Am Auth; Twent Cen Bio Dict Not Am

13491. Sheppard, Ella
flourished 1860s
pianist
Black
Prof Negro Wom v1

13492. Sparrow, Arianna Cooley
flourished 1860s
singer
Black
Index t Wom

13493. van Zandt-Vanzini, Jennie
flourished 1860s–70s
singer
Index t Wom

13494. Boucicault, Agnes Robertson
1832–1916
singer, actor
Scottish
Index t Wom

13495. Gubert, Louise
died 1882
Catholic nun, vocalist
Catholic
Cyc Am Bio

13496. Harrison, Caroline Lavinia Scott
1832–92
musician
Cyc Am Bio; Index t Wom

13497. Hinsdale, Grace Webster (Haddock)
born 1832
hymn writer, religious author
New York, NY
Dict Am Auth; Nat Cyc Am Bio v9

13498. West, Julia E. Houston
born 1832
soprano oratorio singer
Wom Cent

13499. Williams, Louisa Brewster
born 1832
composer, musician
Pennsylvania
Wom Cent

13500. Paul, Isabella Featherstone Howard
1833/35–1879
actor, tenor vocalist
Cyc Am Bio; Dict Nat Bio

13501. Phillips, Adelaide
1833–82
actor, contralto opera singer
English
Cyc Am Bio; Dict Am Bio Men Time; Nat Cyc Am Bio v6; Not Am Wom; Twent Cen Bio Dict Not Am

13502. Stockham, Alice (Bunker)
born 1833
physician, medical author, musician, biographer, suffragist
Dict Am Auth; Wom Cent

13503. Ward, Genevieve; Lucia Genoveva Teresa, Countess Guerbel; Madam Buerrabella
1833/38–1922
actor, tragedian, opera singer
Cyc Am Bio; Dict Am Bio; Nat Cyc Am Bio v9; Wom Cent

13504. Brainard, Kate J.
born 1835
alto vocalist
Wom Cent

13505. Hawks, Annie Sherwood
1835–1918
hymn writer, poet
Baptist
New York
Index t Wom; Nat Cyc Am Bio v17; Wom Cent

13506. Hensler, Eliza; Countess of Edla
born 1835
vocalist
Cyc Am Bio

13507. Patti, Carlotta
1835/40–1889
soprano opera singer

Italian
Cyc Am Bio; Dict Am Bio Men Time; Dict Nat Bio

13508. Wilhorst, Cora de (Withers)
born 1835
concert and opera singer, voice teacher
Cyc Am Bio

13509. Baltimore, Annie E.
1836–1922
musician
Index t Wom

13510. Barry, Flora Elizabeth
born 1836
concert and opera singer
Boston, MA
Wom Cent

13511. Bullock, Helen Louise
born 1836
temperance worker, music educator, women's prison reformer
Wom Cent

13512. Parepa Rosa, Euphrosyne Parepa de Boyesku
1836–74
soprano opera singer
Cyc Am Bio; Dict Nat Bio

13513. Runcie, Constance (Faunt le Roy)
1836–1911
composer, pianist, club leader, poet, children's author, biographer
St. Joseph, MO
Dict Am Auth; Dict Am Bio; Index t Wom; Nat Cyc Am Bio v7; Wom Cent

13514. Smith, Amanda Berry
1836/37–1915
Protestant evangelist, missionary to Africa, faith healer, singer
Protestant
Black
Index t Wom; Negro Alman; Not Am Wom; Prof Negro Wom v1

13515. Smith, Martha Pearson; Mattie May
born 1836
poet, composer
Wom Cent

13516. Chanfrau, Henrietta Baker
1837–1909
singer, actor
Cyc Am Bio; Dict Am Bio; Nat Cyc Am Bio v7

13517. Dike, Jeannie Dean Scott
1837–1920
music educator, Congregationalist missionary

Congregationalist
New York
Twent Cen Bio Dict Not Am; Wom Cent

13518. Fonda, Mary Alice Ives; Octavia Hensel
born 1837
linguist, author, musician, music educator, writer on music
Wom Cent

13519. Bullock, Mary Ann
1838–1918
hymn writer, poet
Nat Cyc Am Bio v19

13520. Fletcher, Alice Cunningham
1838/45–1923
ethnologist, Native American rights worker, writer on Native American music
Dict Am Auth; Dict Am Bio; Index t Wom; Nat Cyc Am Bio v5; Not Am Wom; Twent Cen Bio Dict Not Am; Wom Cent

13521. Straub, Maria
born 1838
songwriter, temperance writer
Wom Cent

13522. Knapp, Phoebe Palmer
born 1839
musician, author, religious composer
Methodist Episcopal
New York
Wom Cent

13523. Thomas, Carrie A.
1839–83
religious worker, poet, hymn writer
Index t Wom

13524. de Fere, A. Litsner
flourished 1870s–80s
classical singer, voice trainer
Hungarian
Wom Cent

13525. Gordon, Georgia
flourished 1870
gospel singer
Black
Prof Negro Wom v1

13526. Hawes, Charlotte W.
flourished 1870s–80s
composer, lecturer, music educator
Wom Cent

13527. Hinckley, Isabella
1840–62
singer
Cyc Am Bio; Nat Cyc Am Bio v1

13528. Hutchinson, Elizabeth Chase
flourished 1870s–80s
social reformer, singer
Index t Wom

13529. Jackson, Jennie
flourished 1870s
gospel singer
Black
Prof Negro Wom v1

13530. Lewis, Mabel
flourished 1870s
gospel singer
Black
Prof Negro Wom v1

13531. Reed, Caroline Keating
flourished 1870s–1910s
musician, pianist, author
Index t Wom; Wom Cent

13532. Selika, Marie
flourished 1870s–80s
singer
Black
Index t Wom

13533. Swenson, Amanda Carlson
flourished 1870s–90s
soprano concert singer
Episcopalian
Swedish
Wom Cent

13534. Tate, Minnie
flourished 1870s
gospel singer
Black
Prof Negro Wom v1

13535. Wakefield, Emily Watkins
flourished 1870s–90s
singer, educator, lecturer, musical director
Pennsylvania
English
Wom Cent

13536. Washington, Rachel M.
flourished 1870s
music educator, pianist
Black
Index t Wom

13537. Cary, Anna Louise; Annie Louise Cary Raymond
1841/42–1921
contralto opera singer
Cyc Am Bio; Dict Am Bio; Index t Wom; Nat Cyc Am Bio v1; Not Am Wom; Twent Cen Bio Dict Not Am

13538. Lathbury, Mary Artemesia; Aunt May
1841–1913

author; psalm, spiritual, and hymn writer; religious writer for children
Dict Am Auth; Dict Am Bio; Nat Cyc Am Bio v10

13539. Moore, Annie Aubertine (Woodward); Aubertine Forestier
1841–1929
pianist, student of Scandinavian music, music critic, lecturer, author, translator of Scandinavian languages
Dict Am Auth; Dict Am Bio; Index t Wom; Twent Cen Bio Dict Not Am; Wom Cent

13540. Barbot, Blanche Hermine
born 1842
musical director, pianist
Belgian
Wom Cent

13541. Garrison, Lucy McKim
1842–77
musician, collector of American slave songs
Not Am Wom

13542. Halcott, Elizabeth Lente
1842–1943
music educator
Obit File

13543. Kellogg, Clara Louise
1842–1916
dramatic soprano opera singer
Cyc Am Bio; Dict Am Bio; Dict Am Bio Men Time; Index t Wom; Not Am Wom; Twent Cen Bio Dict Not Am; Wom Cent

13544. Raymond, Annie Louise Cary
born 1842
contralto opera singer
Wom Cent

13545. Urso, Camilla
1842–1902
violinist
Dict Am Bio; Index t Wom; Not Am Wom

13546. Willson, Mary Elizabeth
born 1842
missionary, gospel singer, songwriter
Pennsylvania
Index t Wom; Wom Cent

13547. Creevey, Caroline Alathea Stickney
1843–1920
botanist, author, pianist
Nat Cyc Am Bio v30

13548. Nilsson, Christine
1843–1921
opera singer, violinist
Swedish
Cyc Am Bio; Index t Wom

13549. Patti, Adelea Juana Maria Clorinda "Adelina"
1843–1903/19
soprano opera singer
Spanish
Cyc Am Bio; Dict Am Bio Men Time; Nat Cyc Am Bio v7; Not Am Wom; Twent Cen Bio Dict Not Am; Wom Cent

13550. Smith, Eva Munson
born 1843
composer, poet
Index t Wom; Wom Cent

13551. Lawton, Henrietta Beebe
born 1844
musician, vocal music educator
Wom Cent

13552. Preston, Frances E. L.
1844–1929
temperance lecturer, organist, elocutionist
Black
Negro Alman; Prof Negro Wom v1

13553. Rogers, Clara Kathleen Barnett
1844–1931
singer, author, composer
English
Dict Am Bio; Index t Wom

13554. Hough, Emma E. (Smith-Payne)
1845–1907
soprano concert and light opera soloist, patron of music education, philanthropist
California
Am Bio New Cyc

13555. Mitchell, Nellie Brown
1845?–1924
singer, music educator
New Hampshire
Black
Index t Wom; Prof Negro Wom v1

13556. Thursby, Emma Cecelia
1845/57–1931
soprano concert singer, music educator
Cyc Am Bio; Dict Am Bio; Index t Wom; Nat Cyc Am Bio v22; Not Am Wom; Twent Cen Bio Dict Not Am

13557. Loud, Annie Frances
born 1846
composer, organist
Nat Cyc Am Bio v8

13558. Hanna, Sarah Jackson
born 1847
musical educator
Georgia
Wom Cent

13559. Blondner, Aline Reese
flourished 1878
pianist, organist, music educator
Wom Cent

13560. Valleria, Alvine Shoening
1848–1925
opera singer
Index t Wom; Nat Cyc Am Bio v1

13561. Abbott, Emma
1849/50–1891
opera singer
Nevada
Dict Am Bio; Index t Wom; Not Am Wom; Twent Cen Bio Dict Not Am; Wom Cent

13562. Bigelow, Ella Augusta
born 1849
singer
Wom Cent

13563. Bohan, Elizabeth Baker
born 1849
painter, author, poet
Wom Cent

13564. Bowen, Ariel Serena Hedges
1849–1904
musician, music educator
Black
Index t Wom; Prof Negro Wom

13565. Johnston, Julia Harriette
1849–1919
hymn writer
Presbyterian
Peoria, IL
Nat Cyc Am Bio v20

13566. Moore, Ella Maude
born 1849
hymn writer
Index t Wom

13567. Oates, Alice
1849–87
actor, singer
Nat Cyc Am Bio v6

13568. Storer, Maria Longworth Nichols
1849–1932
patron of music, ceramicist, sculptor
Index t Wom; Nat Cyc Am Bio v11; Not Am Wom

13569. Wetherell, Emma Abbot
1849–91
vocalist
Nat Cyc Am Bio v3

13570. Ashford, Emma Louise
1850–1930
composer
Index t Wom

13571. Barnes, Hattie Delaro
flourished 1880s–1910s
singer, actor
Index t Wom

13572. Collins, Laura Sedgwick
flourished 1880s–90s
actor, musician, composer, pianist, dancer, dramatic reader
Wom Cent

13573. Crane, Ogden, Mrs.
born 1850
concert singer, music educator
Wom Cent

13574. Decca, Marie
flourished 1880s
soprano opera singer
Wom Cent

13575. Durand, Marie
born 1850
soprano opera singer
Cyc Am Bio

13576. Goodrich, Florence Ada (Backus)
1850–1928
composer, organ teacher
Index t Wom; Nat Cyc Am Bio v23

13577. Hahr, Emma
flourished 1880s
pianist, composer, musical educator
Georgia
Wom Cent

13578. Howard, Mary M.
flourished 1880s
organist, music educator
Wom Cent

13579. Keating, Josephine E.
flourished 1880s–90s
literary critic, musician, music educator
Tennessee
Wom Cent

13580. Logan, Virginia Knight
1850–1940
composer, author
Index t Wom

13581. Peck, Annie Smith
1850–1933/35
mountain climber, musician, archaeologist, lecturer, educator
Rhode Island
Index t Wom; Nat Cyc Am Bio v15; Not Am Wom; Wom Cent

13582. Rosewald, Julie
born 1850
vocalist, vocal teacher, opera
 singer
Wom Cent

13583. Sterling, Antoinette
1850–1904
contralto opera singer
Sterlingville, NY
English
Index t Wom; Wom Cent

**13584. Thurber, Jeannette
 Meyers**
1850–1946
patron of music, founder of the
 National Conservatory of Music
 of America
Dict Am Bio supp v4; Nat Cyc
 Am Bio csv4; Not Am Wom

**13585. Albani, Maria Louise
 Cecilie Emma, Dame; Marie
 Emma Lajeunesse; Marie
 Emma Gye**
1851/52–1930
soprano singer
Canadian (French Canada)
Appl Cyc Am Bio; Index t Wom;
 Nat Cyc Am Bio v9; Not Am
 Wom; Twent Cen Bio Dict Not
 Am; Wom Cent

**13586. Biddulph, Jessie Cather-
 ine Vokes**
1851–84
actor, singer
English
Index t Wom

13587. Crane, Sibylla (Bailey)
1851–1902
vocalist, composer, music educator, writer on music
Boston, MA
Dict Am Auth; Nat Cyc Am Bio
 v7; Twent Cen Bio Dict Not
 Am; Wom Cent

13588. Hauck, Minnie
1851/53–1907/29
soprano opera singer
Cyc Am Bio; Dict Am Bio; Dict
 Am Bio Men Time; Index t
 Wom; Nat Cyc Am Bio v8; Not
 Am Wom; Wom Cent

13589. Stoeckel, Ellen Battell
1851–1939
philanthropist, patron of music
Not Am Wom

**13590. Davenport, Blanche Ma-
 ria**
born 1852
soprano vocalist
Cyc Am Bio

13591. Haswin, Frances R.
born 1852

musician, composer, poet, actor
Wom Cent

13592. Millar, Clara Smart
born 1852
singer, music educator
Wom Cent

13593. Morton, Eliza Happy
1852–1916
author, songwriter, educator, geographer
Maine
Index t Wom; Wom Cent

13594. Osgood, Emma Aline
born circa 1852
soprano vocalist
Cyc Am Bio

13595. Carreno, Teresa
1853–1917
concert pianist
Not Am Wom

13596. Cheney, Abbey Perkins
born 1853
music educator, pianist
Wom Cent

**13597. Kotzschmar, Hermann,
 Mrs.**
born 1853
pianist, music educator
Index t Wom

13598. Pappenheim, Eugenie
born 1853
opera singer and teacher
Wom Cent

**13599. Burnham, Clara Louise
 (Root)**
1854–1927
poet, novelist, librettist
Chicago, IL
Dict Am Auth; Dict Am Bio;
 Index t Wom; Nat Cyc Am Bio
 v9 and v21; Wom Cent

13600. Kirk, Nettie Madora
1854–80
singer
Nat Cyc Am Bio v6

13601. Newell, Laura Emeline
born 1854
songwriter
Wom Cent

13602. Rhodes, Laura Andrews
born 1854
opera singer
Wom Cent

**13603. Rive-King, Julie; Julie
 King**
1854/57–1937
pianist, piano educator
Index t Wom; Not Am Wom;
 Wom Cent

13604. Babcock, Hannah Almy
1855–1931
music educator and director for
 the blind, suffragist, temperance
 worker
Nat Cyc Am Bio v16

13605. Breck, Carrie Ellis
1855–1934
author, songwriter
Index t Wom

13606. Crane, Julia Ettie
1855–1923
musician, music educator
Index t Wom; Nat Cyc Am Bio
 v6

13607. Forman, R. R., Mrs.
1855–1947
composer
Index t Wom

13608. Leslie, Amy
1855–1939
light opera singer, drama critic,
 journalist
Index t Wom; Not Am Wom

13609. Vannah, Kate
1855–1933
composer, pianist, organist
Index t Wom

13610. Black, Fannie de Grasse
born 1856
singer, pianist
Wom Cent

13611. Carrington, Abbie
born 1856
soprano opera singer
Fond du Lac, WI
Wom Cent

**13612. Eames, Emma Hayden;
 Mrs. Julian Story**
1856/67–1952
Metropolitan Opera soprano and
 concert singer
Index t Wom; Nat Cyc Am Bio
 v5 and v42; Not Am Wom supp
 v1; Obit File; Wom Cent

13613. Gobbi, Clothilde Operti
1856–1960
Metropolitan Opera singer
English
Obit File

**13614. Hopekirk, Helene; He-
 lene Wilson**
1856–1945
concert pianist, composer, educator
Not Am Wom; Obit File

**13615. Litta, Marie (von Els-
 ner)**
1856–83
singer
Nat Cyc Am Bio v3

**13616. Northrop, Celestia Jos-
 lin**
born 1856
vocalist
Baptist
Indiana
Wom Cent

13617. Raymond, Emma Marcy
born 1856
composer, opera composer, conductor
New York
Wom Cent

13618. Salter, Mary Turner
1856–1938
composer, singer, songwriter
Index t Wom

**13619. Brown, Katherine
 "Kate" Louise**
1857–1921
children's author, composer, educator
Boston, MA
Dict Am Auth; Index t Wom

13620. Cline, Maggie
1857–1934
vaudeville singer
Not Am Wom

**13621. MacDowell, Marian
 Griswold Nevins**
1857–1956/57
patron of music, musician, pianist, founder of the MacDowell
 Artists Colony, lecturer
New Hampshire
Index t Wom; Not Am Wom
 supp v1; Obit File

13622. Mason, Mary Knight
1857–1944
songwriter, pianist
Index t Wom

**13623. Nordica, Lillian (Nor-
 ton) Gower; Mrs. George W.
 Young; Lillian Dome**
1857/59–1914
soprano opera singer
Cyc Am Bio; Dict Am Bio; Index
 t Wom; Nat Cyc Am Bio v9;
 Not Am Wom; Twent Cen Bio
 Dict Not Am; Wom Cent

**13624. Raymond, Carrie Isa-
 belle Rice**
born 1857
musician, educator, organist, music director, conductor
Nebraska
Wom Cent

**13625. Adams, Juliette Aurelia
 Graves**
born 1858
composer, pianist, music educator, author, lecturer
Index t Wom

13626. Beer, Rachel "Richa"
1858–1927
newspaper editor, publisher, composer
Jewish
Who Who Jew Hist

13627. Hibler, Nellie
born 1858
music educator, soprano singer
Wom Cent

13628. Sage, Florence Eleanor
1858–post 1940
pianist, lecturer
Index t Wom; Wom Cent

13629. Sembrich, Marcella;
Praxede Marcelline Kochanska
1858–1935
soprano opera and concert singer
Polish
Dict Am Bio supp v1; Nat Cyc Am Bio v24; Not Am Wom

13630. Smith, Eleanor
1858–1942
music educator, composer, songwriter
Episcopalian
Index t Wom; Nat Cyc Am Bio v35

13631. van Zandt, Marie
1858/61–1919
soprano opera singer
Cyc Am Bio; Index t Wom; Not Am Wom; Wom Cent

13632. Adams, Carrie B.
1859–1940
composer, music educator, organist
Index t Wom

13633. Brown, Barnetta
1859–1938
author, music writer
Index t Wom

13634. Calve, Emma
1859–1942
Metropolitan Opera singer
Obit File

13635. Dickerman, Julia Elida
born 1859
teacher, organist
Index t Wom

13636. Hill, Mildred J.
1859–1916
composer
Index t Wom

13637. Knowlton, Fanny Snow
1859–1926
composer
Index t Wom

13638. Nevada, Emma (Wixom)
1859/62–1940
soprano opera singer
California
Cyc Am Bio; Dict Am Bio and supp v2; Index t Wom; Not Am Wom; Twent Cen Bio Dict Not Am; Wom Cent

13639. Sheardown, Annie Fillmore
born 1859
singer, voice teacher, writer on voice teaching
Wom Cent

13640. Tapper, Bertha Feiring
1859–1915
pianist, music educator
Norwegian
Dict Am Bio; Index t Wom

13641. Celeste, Marie
flourished 1890s
singer, actor
Index t Wom

13642. Clark, Frances Eliot
1860–1958
music educator
Index t Wom

13643. Clark, Hilda
flourished 1890s
singer, actor
Index t Wom

13644. Davis, Jessie Fremont (Bartlett)
18960/61–1905
contralto opera singer
Index t Wom; Nat Cyc Am Bio v8; Twent Cen Bio Dict Not Am; Wom Cent

13645. Dunning, Carrie Louise
1860–1929
music educator
Index t Wom

13646. Dussuchal, Eugenie
born 1860
musical educator
St. Louis, MO
Wom Cent

13647. Engle, Marie
born circa 1860
singer
Index t Wom

13648. Fonaroff, Vera
flourished 1890s–1930s
violinist
Russian
Index t Wom

13649. Ford, Florrie
flourished 1890s–1920s
singer
Index t Wom

13650. Franklin, Gertrude; Virginia H. Beatty
flourished 1890s
singer, music educator
Wom Cent

13651. Gilman, Mabelle
flourished 1890s
actor, singer
Index t Wom

13652. Hall, Josephine
flourished 1890s
actor, singer
Index t Wom

13653. Heckscher, Celeste de Longpre (Massey)
1860–1928
composer
Index t Wom; Nat Cyc Am Bio v21

13654. Henschel, Lillian June Bailey
1860–1901
vocalist
Index t Wom; Wom Cent

13655. Juch, Emma Antonia Johanna
1860/63–1939
soprano opera singer
Austrian
Index t Wom; Nat Cyc Am Bio v6; Not Am Wom; Wom Cent

13656. Klumpkey, Julia
flourished 1890s–1920s
violinist
San Francisco, CA
Nat Cyc Am Bio v31

13657. Lessing, Madge
flourished 1890s
singer
English
Index t Wom

13658. Lummis, Dorothea
born 1860
physician, music critic, journalist, newspaper editor, Native American artifacts collector
Los Angeles, CA
Index t Wom; Wom Cent

13659. Morgan, Maud
1860/64–1941
harpist, author
Episcopalian
Cyc Am Bio; Index t Wom; Nat Cyc Am Bio v32; Obit File; Wom Cent

13660. Overstolz, Philippine E. von
flourished 1890s
musician, linguist, artist
Wom Cent

13661. Raymond, Maud
flourished 1890s–1900s
singer, actor
Index t Wom

13662. Rice, Isaac L., Mrs.
born 1860
social reformer, musician, linguist
Index t Wom

13663. Serrano, Emelia Benic
flourished 1890s
opera singer
Austrian; Hungarian
Wom Cent

13664. Smith, Ella May
1860–1934
composer, pianist, organist, music educator, author
Index t Wom

13665. Spencer, Fannie M.
born circa 1860
organist, composer, music educator
Nat Cyc Am Bio v11

13666. Steiner, Emma
flourished 1890s–1930s
composer
Index t Wom; Wom Cent

13667. Strong, Susan
flourished 1890s
singer
Index t Wom

13668. van Buren, Alicia (Keisker)
1860–1922
composer, singer, poet
Louisville, KY
Dict Am Auth; Index t Wom

13669. Webb, Bertah
flourished 1890s
violinist
Wom Cent

13670. Williams, Maria Selika
flourished 1880s
coloratura soprano singer
Black
Prof Negro Wom v1

13671. Bagg, Clara B.
born 1861
pianist, music educator
Wom Cent

13672. Berg, Lillie
flourished 1891
pianist, organist, conductor
Wom Cent

13673. Chanler, Margaret Ward Terry
1861–1952
philanthropist, musician, linguist, author
Index t Wom; Obit File

13674. Heinsohn, Dora Henninges
born 1861
opera singer
Wom Cent

13675. Kronold, Selma
1861–1920
soprano opera singer
Not Am Wom

13676. Russell, Lillian
1861/67–1922
actor, musical comedy actor, singer
Dict Am Bio; Index t Wom; Nat Cyc Am Bio v4; Not Am Wom; Wom Cent

13677. Schumann-Heink, Ernestine
1861–1936
opera and concert contralto soprano singer
Dict Am Bio supp v2; Not Am Wom

13678. Stevens, Neally
born 1861
pianist
Nat Cyc Am Bio v8

13679. Taft, Helen Herron
1861–1943
founder and patron of the Cincinnati Orchestra Association, musician, music educator
Index t Wom; Nat Cyc Am Bio v14

13680. Bauer, Bertha
1862–1940
music educator
Cincinnati, OH
German
Index t Wom; Nat Cyc Am Bio v31

13681. Baur, Clara
died 1912
music educator
Ohio
German
Nat Cyc Am Bio v26

13682. Bond, Carrie Jacobs; Carrie Jacobs-Bond
1862–1946
popular songwriter, composer, author, publisher
Episcopalian
California
Dict Am Bio supp v4; Index t Wom; Nat Cyc Am Bio v36 and csv5; Not Am Wom; Obit File

13683. Clayton, Florence Andrews
born 1862
contralto opera singer
Wom Cent

13684. du Bose, Miriam Howard
born 1862
suffragist, composer, pianist
Georgia
Wom Cent

13685. Hall, Pauline
born 1862
opera singer, actor
Index t Wom; Wom Cent

13686. Irwin, May
1862–1938
actor, singer
Dict Am Bio supp v2; Not Am Wom

13687. l'Allemande, Pauline
born 1862
singer
Index t Wom

13688. Saville, Frances
1862–1935
singer
Index t Wom

13689. Sherman, Marietta R.
born 1862
musical educator, orchestral conductor
Wom Cent

13690. Stimson, Harriet Overton
1862–1936
philanthropist, patron of music
Nat Cyc Am Bio v28

13691. Ulmar, Geraldine
1862–1932
actor, singer
Index t Wom; Wom Cent

13692. Woodbury, Hattie
1862–1953
ballad composer
Obit File

13693. Wright, Carrie Douglas
born 1862
music educator, biographer
Chicago, IL
Dict Am Auth

13694. Andrews, Alice A.
flourished 1893
composer
Wom Cent

13695. d'Arville, Camille; Neeltye Dykstra
born 1863
singer, actor
Dutch
Index t Wom

13696. Gaynor, Jessie Lovel
1863–1921
composer, songwriter
Index t Wom

13697. Gerrish-Jones, Abbie
1863–1929
composer, author, critic
Index t Wom

13698. Guggenheim, Florence Shloss
1863–1944
philanthropist, patron of music, Republican party worker
Jewish
New York
Index t Wom; Nat Cyc Am Bio v33; Obit File

13699. Hood, Helen
1863–post 1889
composer
Index t Wom; Nat Cyc Am Bio v8

13700. Huntington, Agnes
born 1863
contralto opera and concert singer
New York
Nat Cyc Am Bio v2; Wom Cent

13701. Lussan, Zelie De
1863–1949
singer
Index t Wom

13702. Orth, Lizette E.
died 1913
composer, pianist
Index t Wom

13703. Sawyer, Antonia (Savage)
born 1863
alto singer, musical talent manager
New York
Nat Cyc Am Bio v16

13704. Zeisler, Fannie Bloomfield
1863/66–1927
concert pianist
Chicago, IL
Austrian
Dict Am Bio; Nat Cyc Am Bio v14; Not Am Wom; Wom Cent

13705. Chatham, Kitty Smiley; Catharine Smiley Bugg
1864/69–1946
singer for children, composer, children's author, lecturer
Index t Wom; Obit File; Wom Cent

13706. Coolidge, Elizabeth Penn Sprague
1864–1953
patron of chamber music, pianist, philanthropist
Dict Am Bio supp v5; Index t Wom; Not Am Wom supp v1

13707. Cravath, Agnes Huntington
1864–1953
concert and opera singer
Obit File

13708. Freer, Eleonor Everest
1864–1942
composer
Episcopalian
Index t Wom; Nat Cyc Am Bio v17 and csv4

13709. Hopper, Edna Wallace
1864?–1959
stage actor, singer, dancer, broker
Dict Am Bio supp v6; Index t Wom; Obit File

13710. Patrick, Fannie Brown
born 1864
musician
Index t Wom

13711. Russell, Ella
1864–1935
singer
Index t Wom

13712. Schoen-Rene, Anna Eugenia
1864–1942
voice teacher
German
Index t Wom

13713. Senkrah, Arma
born 1864
violinist
Index t Wom

13714. Talbott, Katharine Houk
1864–1935
patron of music
Dayton, OH
Nat Cyc Am Bio v28

13715. Wiles, Cora Young
1864–1950
composer
Presbyterian
Nat Cyc Am Bio v39

13716. Bergengren, Ann (Farquhar); Margaret Alston
born 1865
novelist, journalist, magazine editor, singer
Boston, MA
Dict Am Auth; Index t Wom; Nat Cyc Am Bio v14

13717. Booth, Evangeline Cory
1865–1950
fourth general of the Salvation Army, orator, musician, poet
Salvationist
English
Dict Am Bio supp v4; Dict Am Rel Bio; Index t Wom; Nat Cyc Am Bio csv2; Not Am Wom; Obit File

13718. Dow, Maud M. (Jones)
1865–84
pianist
Nat Cyc Am Bio v12

13719. Eckstorm, Fannie Pearson Hardy
1865–1946
ornithologist, writer on ornithology, scholar of the Native Americans of Maine, historian of Maine folk songs
Episcopalian
Brewer, ME
Dict Am Auth; Dict Am Bio supp v4; Nat Cyc Am Bio v36; Not Am Wom

13720. Held, Anna
1865?–1918
musical comedy actor
Not Am Wom

13721. Lorini, Virginia (Whiting)
born 1865
opera singer
Cuban
Dict Am Bio Men Time

13722. Sanderson, Sibyl Swift
1865–1903
operatic soprano
California
Index t Wom; Not Am Wom; Wom Cent

13723. Sapio, Clementine Duchene de Vere
1865–1954
opera and concert soprano singer
Obit File

13724. Savage, Marie Ghislaine Metten (Mamen)
1865–1957
opera singer
Belgian
Obit File

13725. Sheldon, Lillian Taitt
1865–1925
composer, organist
Index t Wom

13726. Singleton, Esther
1865–1930
author, writer on music and architecture, writer on art and design, editor, music critic
Dict Am Auth; Dict Am Bio; Twent Cen Bio Dict Not Am

13727. Sutro, Florence Edith Clinton
1865–1906
musician, composer, lawyer, traveler
Cyc Am Bio; Nat Cyc Am Bio v5

13728. Templeton, Fay
1865–1939
actor, singer
Index t Wom; Not Am Wom

13729. Barbour, Florence Newell
1866–1946
pianist, composer
Rhode Island
Index t Wom; Nat Cyc Am Bio v37

13730. Clary-Squire, Mary Louise
born 1866
contralto singer
Nat Cyc Am Bio v12

13731. Dreier, Christine Nielson
born 1866
concert and oratorio contralto singer
Wom Cent

13732. Esty, Alice May
born 1866
soprano opera singer
Index t Wom

13733. Ford, Miriam Chase
born 1866
journalist, vocalist
Wom Cent

13734. Guggenheim, Leonie Bernheim
1866–1959
patron of dental clinics, patron of free band concerts in parks
Jewish
New York
Obit File

13735. Hilyer, Andrew F., Mrs.
died 1916
musician
Black
Index t Wom

13736. Hoyt, Minerva Lockhart Hamilton
1866–1945
naturalist, conservationist, botanist, patron of music, president of the Los Angeles Symphony Orchestra
Los Angeles, CA
Am Bio New Cyc; Nat Cyc Am Bio v34

13737. Korn, Clara A. (Gerlach)
born 1866
composer
Nat Cyc Am Bio v7

13738. Lanier, Harriet Bishop
1866–1931
patron of music
New York
Nat Cyc Am Bio v34

13739. Marquardt, Alexandria
circa 1866–1943
harpist
Russian
Index t Wom

13740. Reed, Clare Osborn
born 1866
musician, pianist, music educator
Nat Cyc Am Bio csv7

13741. Roma, Caro; Carey Northey
1866–1937
composer, author, singer
Index t Wom

13742. Skinner, Belle
1866–1928
philanthropist, musical instrument collector
Nat Cyc Am Bio v23

13743. Willard, Katherine
born 1866
concert singer
Wom Cent

13744. Amsden, Elizabeth
graduated 1892
singer
Index t Wom

13745. Barnard, Marie Ellen; Marie Barna
1867–post 1899
dramatic soprano opera singer
Nat Cyc Am Bio v10

13746. Beach, Amy Marcy (Cheney); Mrs. H. H. A. Beach
1867–1944
composer, pianist
Dict Am Bio supp v3; Index t Wom; Nat Cyc Am Bio v7, v15, and csv3; Not Am Wom; Obit File; Twent Cen Bio Dict Not Am; Wom Cent

13747. Brown, Gertrude Foster
1867–1956
suffragist, concert pianist, music educator
Dict Am Bio supp v6; Obit File

13748. Bugbee, L. A.
died 1917
composer, music educator
Index t Wom

13749. Densmore, Frances Theresa
1867–1957
ethnomusicologist, musician, scholar of Native American culture
Dict Am Bio supp v6; Index t Wom; Not Am Wom supp v1; Read Encyc Am West

13750. Hackley, Emma Azalia Smith
1867–1922
coloratura soprano singer, composer, choir director, sponsor of Black folk music festivals
Black
Index t Wom; Negro Alman; Not Am Wom; Prof Negro Wom v1

13751. Lang, Margaret Ruthven
born 1867
composer
Index t Wom; Nat Cyc Am Bio v7; Twent Cen Bio Dict Not Am

13752. Meyer, Annie Florence Nathan
1867–1950/51
publicist, author, playwright, novelist, educationist, founder of Barnard College, antisuffragist, patron of Black music education, clubwoman
Jewish
New York
Dict Am Auth; Dict Am Bio; Index t Wom; Nat Cyc Am Bio v42; Not Am Wom supp v1; Obit File; Twent Cen Bio Dict Not Am; Wom Cent

13753. O'Dea, Anne Caldwell
1867–1936
author, librettist
Index t Wom

13754. Powell, Maud
1867/68–1920
violinist
Dict Am Bio; Index t Wom; Nat Cyc Am Bio v13; Not Am Wom; Wom Cent

13755. Riley, Alice Cushing Donaldson
1867–1955
children's playwright and songwriter, librettist
Nat Cyc Am Bio v44 and csv8

13756. Seymour, Harriet Ayer
1867/76–1944
pianist, music educator, pioneer of music therapy, music author
Index t Wom; Nat Cyc Am Bio v33; Obit File

13757. Story, Emma Eames
born 1867
opera singer
Twent Cen Bio Dict Not Am

13758. Walker, Edythe
1867/70–1950
opera singer, voice teacher
Index t Wom; Not Am Wom

13759. Black, Jennie Prince
1868–1945

composer
Index t Wom

13760. Chase, Mary Wood
born 1868
pianist, educator, author
Index t Wom

**13761. Fremstad, Olivia [Anna]
"Olive"**
1868/72–1951
opera singer
Methodist
Swedish
Index t Wom; Nat Cyc Am Bio
v40; Obit File

13762. Fryberger, Agnes Moore
born 1868
music educator, lecturer, author
Index t Wom

**13763. Jones, Matilda Sissier-
ette Joyner; Black Patti**
1868/69–1933
dramatic soprano singer
Black
Encyc Black Am; Index t Wom;
Nat Cyc Am Bio v13; Not Am
Wom; Prof Negro Wom

13764. Lewing, Adele
born 1868
pianist, composer
German
Wom Cent

13765. McAdoo, Martha Allen
1868–1936
singer, social worker
Black
Encyc Black Am

**13766. McAlpin, Margaret
Johnston; Margherita Giollini**
1868–1924
opera singer
Episcopalian
Nat Cyc Am Bio v20

13767. Nielson, Alice
1868/76–1943
soprano singer of light and grand
opera, Metropolitan Opera singer
Dict Am Bio supp v3; Index t
Wom; Not Am Wom; Obit File

13768. Rice, Alice Ary Bates
born 1868
soprano opera singer
Wom Cent

13769. Searing, Florence E.
born 1868
pianist, conductor
Wom Cent

**13770. Yaw, Ellen Beach; Lark
Ellen**
1868/69–1947

soprano opera singer
Nat Cyc Am Bio v13; Not Am
Wom; Obit File

13771. Brower, Harriette
1869–1928
pianist, music educator, author
Index t Wom

13772. Cook, May A.
born 1869
pianist
Portland, OR
Wom Cent

13773. Hughes, Adella Prentiss
1869–1950
concert manager, founder of the
Cleveland Symphony Orchestra
Cleveland, OH
Nat Cyc Am Bio csv3; Not Am
Wom; Obit File

13774. Kelley, Jessie Stillman
born 1869
pianist, piano educator
Nat Cyc Am Bio csv3

**13775. Lowell, Ettie Lois; Mrs.
George Fl.**
born 1869
suffragist, composer, alto singer,
owner and director of the bond
and investment firm of E. L.
Lowell of Boston
Boston, MA
Nat Cyc Am Bio v14

**13776. MacKellar, Gertrude E.
Fritts**
1869–1946
organist
Obit File

**13777. Mannes, Clara Dom-
rosch**
1869–1948
pianist, music educator
Lutheran
German
Dict Am Bio supp v4; Index t
Wom

13778. Marshall, Harriet Gibbs
1869–1941
pianist, music educator
Black
Encyc Black Am; Index t Wom

**13779. Mehan, Caroline Elea-
nore Catharine**
born 1869
singer, music educator, voice
coach
Nat Cyc Am Bio csv2

**13780. Polak, Jessamine; Bar-
oness von Elsner**
born 1869
singer
Index t Wom

13781. Stair, Patty
1869–1926
composer, pianist, organist, music
educator
Index t Wom

**13782. Yohe, May; Lady
Frances White**
circa 1869–1938
actor, singer
Index t Wom

13783. Young, Rida Johnson
1869/75–1926
playwright, author, librettist, actor
Index t Wom

13784. Atwood, Ethel
born 1870
violinist
Wom Cent

13785. Beaton, Isabella
born 1870
pianist, composer
Index t Wom

13786. Bentley, Irene
1870–1940
singer, actor
Index t Wom

13787. Bergen, Flora Batson
1870–1906
singer
Black
Index t Wom

13788. Blye, Birdie
born 187?
pianist
Wom Cent

13789. Davenport, Viola
flourished 1900s
singer
Index t Wom

13790. Doria, Augusta
flourished 1900s–10s
singer
Index t Wom

13791. Europe, Mary L.
flourished 1900s
pianist
Black
Index t Wom

13792. Fox, Della May
1870–1913
light opera comedian
Not Am Wom

13793. Frijsh, Povla
born circa 1870; died 1960
concert soprano singer
Danish
Obit File

13794. Genet, Marianne
flourished 1900s
composer, organist
Index t Wom

**13795. Grenville, Lillian Goert-
ner**
flourished 1900s
singer
Canadian
Index t Wom

13796. Jenkins, Cora W.
circa 1870–1947
composer, music educator
Index t Wom

13797. Lacey, Margaret E.
flourished 1900s–30s
educator, songwriter
Index t Wom

13798. Leveroni, Elvira
flourished 1900s
singer
Index t Wom

13799. Lund, Charlotte
1870–1951
musical director, lecturer
Index t Wom

**13800. Niessen-Stone, Matja
von**
born 1870
singer
Russian
Nat Cyc Am Bio v14

13801. Pasquali, Bernice de
flourished 1900s
opera singer
Index t Wom

13802. Scheider, May
flourished 1900s–10s
singer
Index t Wom

**13803. Stevens, Georgia Lydia,
Mother**
1870–1946
musician, cofounder of the Piux
X School of Liturgical Music,
educator, Catholic nun
Catholic
Not Am Wom; Obit File

13804. Tracey, Minnie
circa 1870–1929
singer
Index t Wom

13805. Villani, Luisa
flourished 1900s
singer
Index t Wom

13806. Wakefield, Henrietta
flourished 1900s
opera singer
Index t Wom

13807. Weed, Marion
1870–1947
opera singer
Index t Wom

13808. Wood-Hill, Mabel
1870–1954
composer
Index t Wom

13809. Brola, Jeanne; Jeanne
Brooks Harrison
1871–1956
opera singer
Obit File

13810. de Moss, Mary Hissem
born 1871
soprano singer
Nat Cyc Am Bio v14

13811. Eberhart, Nelle Richmond
1871–1944
composer, song lyricist
Index t Wom; Obit File

13812. Freeman, Carrie Stone
born 1871
composer
California
Nat Cyc Am Bio csv6

**13813. Greenewalt, Mary
Elizabeth Hallock;** Mary
Greenwalt
1871–1950
pianist, lighting engineer, lecturer
Nat Cyc Am Bio v39; Index t
Wom

**13814. Homer, Louise Dilworth
(Beatty)**
1871/74–1947
Metropolitan Opera contralto
singer
Dict Am Bio supp v4; Index t
Wom; Nat Cyc Am Bio v14;
Not Am Wom; Obit File

13815. Wagnalls, Mabel
born 1871
pianist, writer on music
New York, NY
Dict Am Auth; Twent Cen Bio
Dict Not Am

13816. Adams, Suzanne
1872/74–1953
opera singer
Cyc Am Bio; Index t Wom; Nat
Cyc Am Bio v13, Twent Cen
Bio Dict Not Am

13817. Fox, Delia
born 1872
singer
Index t Wom

13818. Gadski-Tauscher, Johanna Wilhelmine
born 1872

soprano opera singer
German
Nat Cyc Am Bio csv2

13819. Howard, Helen Margaret Willard
born 1872
clubwoman, composer
Massachusetts
Nat Cyc Am Bio v29

**13820. McCormick, Edith
Rockefeller**
1872–1932
philanthropist, patron of music
and psychiatry
Index t Wom; Nat Cyc Am Bio
csv3; Not Am Wom

13821. Preston, Alice
born 1872
concert singer, social worker
Nat Cyc Am Bio csv7

13822. Ring, Blanche
1872–1961
musical comedy actor
Index t Wom; Obit File

**13823. Seton, Grace Gallatin
Thompson;** Dorothy Dodge
1872–1959
suffragist, feminist, explorer, geographer, author, book designer, bookmaker, composer of
popular songs, historian, cofounder of the Campfire Girls
Dict Am Auth; Dict Am Bio
supp v6; Index t Wom; Nat Cyc
Am Bio v47 and csv5; Not Am
Wom supp v1; Obit File

13824. Sutro, Rose Laura
1872–1957
pianist
Index t Wom

13825. Williams, Hattie
1872–1942
musical comedy actor
Obit File

13826. Bates, Blanche Lyon
1873–1941
screen actor, singer
Dict Am Bio supp v3; Index t
Wom; Not Am Wom; Obit File

13827. Blauvelt, Lillian Evans
1873–1947
soprano concert and opera singer
Nat Cyc Am Bio v12; Obit File

13828. Earle, Virginia
born 1873
singer
Index t Wom

13829. Johnson, J. Rosamond
1873–1954

musician, actor, composer of the
Black national anthem "Lift
Every Voice and Sing"
Black
Obit File

13830. Leech, Lida Shivers
born 1873
composer, author
Index t Wom

13831. Moore, Mary Carr
1873–1957
composer, singer
Index t Wom

13832. Osborn-Hannah, Jane
1873–1943
singer
Index t Wom

**13833. Rappold, Marie Bergen
Winteroth**
1873/80–1957
Metropolitan Opera singer
Index t Wom; Obit File

13834. Rio, Anita
born 1873
singer
Index t Wom

13835. White, Elsie Fellows
born 1873
violinist, composer
Index t Wom

13836. Abbott, Clara Barnes
1874–1956
patron of music
Obit File

13837. Clemens, Clara
born circa 1874
singer
Index t Wom

13838. Dufau, Jennie
died 1924
singer
French
Index t Wom

**13839. Firestone, Isabella
Smith**
1874–1954
composer, songwriter
Index t Wom

13840. Garden, Mary
1874/77–1967
soprano opera singer, general director of the Chicago Lyric
Opera
Scottish
Index t Wom; Nat Cyc Am Bio
v15; Not Am Wom supp v1;
Obit File

13841. Glaser, Lulu
1874–1958

comic-opera actor
Index t Wom; Obit File

13842. Hare, Maud Cuney
1874–1936
pianist, musicologist, author
Black
Encyc Black Am; Negro Alman;
Prof Negro Wom v1

13843. Modave, Jeanne
1874–1953
cellist
Obit File

13844. Nugent, Maude; Maude
Jerome
1874–1958
composer, vaudeville entertainer
Obit File

**13845. Powell, Alma Webster
(Hall), Alma Webster-Powell**
1874–1930
musician, economist, linguist,
contralto singer, voice teacher
Cyc Am Bio; Dict Am Bio; Index
t Wom; Nat Cyc Am Bio v14

13846. Burlin, Natalie (Curtis)
1875–1921
ethnomusicologist specializing in
Native American and Afro-
American music, worker for
Native American rights, composer, pianist, lecturer
Dict Am Bio; Not Am Wom;
Index t Wom

**13847. Cahier, Sarah Jane
Layton-Walker**
1875–1951
contralto singer, vocal coach
Index t Wom; Obit File

13848. Chanler, Beatrice Ashley Winthrop; Minnie Ashley
1875–1946
actor, sculptor, author, singer
Index t Wom; Nat Cyc Am Bio
v36

13849. Curran, Pearl Gildersleeve
1875/76–1941
composer, songwriter
Christian Scientist
New York
Index t Wom; Nat Cyc Am Bio
v53

13850. MacDonald, Christie;
Christie Gillespie
1875/77–1962
operetta singer, actor, musical
comedy actor
Presbyterian
Canadian
Index t Wom; Nat Cyc Am Bio
v50; Obit File

of the Metropolitan Opera Guild
English
Index t Wom; Cur Biog '44 and '80

13896. Boyd, Anna Tomlinson
born 1879
pianist, music educator
Index t Wom; Nat Cyc Am Bio v11

13897. Bridewell, Carrie
circa 1879–1955
singer, actor
Index t Wom

13898. Claussen, Julia
1879–1941
Metropolitan Opera contralto and mezzo-soprano singer
Obit File

13899. Howard, Kathleen
1879–1956
opera singer, screen actor, fashion editor
Obit File

13900. Jordan, Mary
1879–1961
singer
Welsh
Index t Wom

13901. Newcomb, Ethel
1879–1959
pianist
Index t Wom

13902. Nichols, Marie
circa 1879–1954
violinist
Index t Wom

13903. Whitson, Beth Slater
1879–1930
author, poet, songwriter
Index t Wom

13904. Zanatello, Maria Gay
1879–1943
opera singer
Obit File

13905. Banks, Margaret
flourished 1910s
singer
Index t Wom

13906. Bayes, Nora
1880–1928
singer
Index t Wom; Not Am Wom

13907. Bilbro, Mathilde (Anne)
flourished 1910s–50s
composer, music educator, author
Index t Wom

13908. Courcy, Florence de
flourished 1910s

opera singer
Index t Wom

13909. de Wolf, Sister
flourished 1910s
singer
Black
Index t Wom

13910. Donnelly, Dorothy
1880–1928
author, librettist, actor
Index t Wom

13911. Dresser, Marcia
flourished 1910s
singer
Index t Wom

13912. Engbergy, Mary Davenport
born 1880
conductor, composer, violinist
Index t Wom

13913. Gainsborg, Lolita Cabrera
flourished 1910s
composer, pianist
Index t Wom

13914. Gates, Lucy
circa 1880–1951
singer
Index t Wom

13915. Green, Ethel
flourished 1910s
vaudeville actor and singer
Index t Wom

13916. Hemsley, Josephine
born 1880
author, songwriter
Index t Wom

13917. Hoffmann, Emma
flourished 1910s
singer
Index t Wom

13918. Holf, Nora Douglas
flourished 1910s–60s
musician, composer, singer, music critic
Black
Prof Negro Wom v2

13919. Kelley, Edgar Stillman, Mrs.
flourished 1910s–30s
pianist, music educator
Index t Wom

13920. Kelly, Elizabeth
flourished 1910s–20s
journalist
Index t Wom

13921. la Croix, Aurore
flourished 1910s

pianist
Index t Wom

13922. Lhevinne, Rosina
1880–1976
classical pianist, piano educator
Russian
Cur Biog '77; Index t Wom; Obit File

13923. Long, Elsie
1880–1946
composer, author
Index t Wom

13924. Maxwell, Margery
flourished 1910s
singer
Index t Wom

13925. Miller, Marie
flourished 1910s–20s
harpist
Index t Wom

13926. Neilson, Alice
flourished 1910s–20s
singer
Index t Wom

13927. Noria, Jana; Josephine Ludwig
flourished 1910s
singer
Index t Wom

13928. Parnell, Evelyn
flourished 1910s
singer
Index t Wom

13929. Peyser, Ethel R.
flourished 1910s–30s
author, editor, music critic, lecturer
Index t Wom

13930. Prentice, Marion
flourished 1910s–20s
composer, director, music educator
Index t Wom

13931. Remy, Egbertina
1880–1956
pianist
Dutch Reformed
Nat Cyc Am Bio v44

13932. Romaine, Margaret
flourished 1910s
singer
Index t Wom

13933. Roulet, Mary F. Nixon
flourished 1910s
author, journalist, musician, art critic, linguist
Index t Wom

13934. Saroya, Bianca
flourished 1910s

singer
Index t Wom

13935. Swartz, Jeska
flourished 1910s–40s
singer
Index t Wom

13936. Talbert, Florence Cole
flourished 1910s
singer
Black
Index t Wom

13937. Tiffany, Marie
flourished 1910s
singer
Index t Wom

13938. van Dresser, Marcia
1880–1937
singer
Index t Wom

13939. van Valkenburg, Catherine E.
born 1880
musician
Index t Wom

13940. Vance, Eunice
flourished 1910s
singer
Index t Wom

13941. Walker, Rachel
flourished 1910s
singer
Black
Index t Wom

13942. Ware, Helen
flourished 1910s
composer, violinist
Index t Wom

13943. Wittkowska, Marta
flourished 1910s
opera singer
Polish
Index t Wom

13944. Aldrich, Mariska
born 1881
singer
Index t Wom

13945. Belcher, Hilda
1881–1963
painter
Index t Wom

13946. Branscombe, Gena
born 1881
composer, author, conductor
Canadian
Index t Wom

13947. Deppen, Jessie L.
born 1881
pianist
Index t Wom

13948. Dillon, Fannie Charles
1881–1947
composer, pianist
Index t Wom

13949. Harrison, Hazel Lucile
1881/83–1969
pianist, music educator
Black
Encyc Black Am; Index t Wom;
Not Am Wom supp v1

13950. Howe, Mary
born 1881/82
composer, pianist
Index t Wom

13951. Lewis, Sarah Masten
died 1931
singer
Black
Index t Wom

13952. Matzenauer, Margaret
1881–1963
opera singer, opera coach
Catholic
Hungarian
Nat Cyc Am Bio v51

13953. Morgan, Jane
1881–1972
vaudeville, radio, and television
actor; singer
Index t Wom; Obit File

**13954. Smith, Gertrude
Robinson**
1881–1963
New York civic worker, World
War I relief worker, founder of
the Tanglewood music festival,
music patron
Nat Cyc Am Bio v48; Obit File

13955. Clayburgh, Alma
1882–1958
concert singer, patron of art, philanthropist
Obit File

13956. de Sousa, May
1882–1968
light opera actor
Obit File

13957. de Treville, Yvonne;
Ediyth le Gierse
1882–1954
soprano opera singer
Obit File

13958. Denni, Gwynne
1882–1949
author, actor, musician, songwriter
Index t Wom

13959. Dresser, Louise (Kerlin)
1882–1965
screen actor, singer
Index t Wom; Obit File

13960. Farrar, Geraldine
1882–1966/67
Metropolitan Opera and concert
singer
Index t Wom; Nat Cyc Am Bio
v16; Not Am Wom supp v1;
Obit File

13961. Guggenheim, Minnie
1882–1966
patron of music, founder and
manager of the Lewisohn Stadium Outdoor Concerts, philanthropist
Jewish
New York
Index t Wom; Obit File

**13962. Mathews, Blanche Ding-
ley**
died 1932
composer, author, music educator
Index t Wom

13963. Samaroff, Olga; Olga
Stokowski
1882–1948
concert pianist, music educator
Dict Am Bio supp v4; Index t
Wom; Not Am Wom; Nat Cyc
Am Bio v36; Obit File

13964. Sanders, Alma M.
1882–1923
composer
Index t Wom

**13965. Sundelius, Marie Louise
Sundborg**
1882–1958
soprano opera singer
Swedish
Obit File

13966. Wickham, Florence
1882–1962
opera singer, composer
Index t Wom

**13967. Alda, Frances Jean Da-
vies**
1883–1952
soprano opera singer
Nat Cyc Am Bio v39; Obit File

13968. Bartlett, Flowy Little
married 1908
composer
Index t Wom

**13969. Morse, [Alfreda] Theo-
dora Strandberg "Dolly"**
1883–1953
popular song lyricist, music publisher
Obit File; Index t Wom

13970. Ross, Ivy
died 1933
journalist
Index t Wom

13971. Simmons, Lydia Avirity
1883–1934
pianist
Index t Wom

**13972. Spencer, Fleta Jan
Brown**
1883–1938
composer, author
Index t Wom

13973. White, Carolina
1883–1961
opera singer
Index t Wom

13974. Winn, Edith L.
died 1933
violinist, music educator, author
Index t Wom

13975. Wise, Jessie Moore
1883–1949
composer, author
Index t Wom

13976. Copp, Laura Remick
died 1934
pianist, music educator
Index t Wom

13977. Ellis, Cecil Osik
born 1884
composer
Index t Wom

13978. Fay, Amy
1884–1928
pianist, writer on music
Chicago, IL
Dict Am Auth; Index t Wom;
Not Am Wom; Wom Cent

13979. Gluck, Anna; Reba
Fiersohn
1884–1938
soprano opera and concert singer
Episcopalian
Rumanian
Dict Am Bio supp v2; Nat Cyc
Am Bio v43; Not Am Wom

13980. Gulesian, Grace Warner
born 1884
composer, pianist, music educator, choral director
Index t Wom

13981. Haake, Gail Martin
born 1884
pianist, music educator
Index t Wom

13982. Hatch, Edith
born 1884
organist, composer, piano educator
Index t Wom

13983. Liebling, Estelle
born 1884/86

composer, singer, music educator,
editor
Index t Wom

**13984. Marley, Anne Augusta
Bonner**
born 1884
poet, violinist
Christian Scientist
Nat Cyc Am Bio csv9

13985. Messenger, Ruth Ellis
1884–1964
hymnologist, educator
Protestant Episcopal
New York
Nat Cyc Am Bio v51

13986. Mitchell, Abbie
1884–1960
singer, actor
Black
Index t Wom; Negro Alman; Not
Am Wom supp v1

13987. Tucker, Sophie; Last of
the Red Hot Mamas
1884–1966
singer, comedian, entertainer
Jewish
Index t Wom; Not Am Wom
supp v1; Obit File; Who Who
Jew Hist

**13988. Clowes, Edith Whitehill
(Hinkel)**
1885–1967
Indianapolis civic leader, patron
of music
Episcopalian
Indianapolis, IN
Nat Cyc Am Bio v53

13989. Easton, Florence; Florence Rogers
1885–1955
Metropolitan Opera dramatic soprano
English
Obit File

13990. Hempel, Frieda
1885–1955
Metropolitan Opera soprano sing-
er
German
Obit File

13991. Hinkle, Florence
1885–1933
singer
Index t Wom

13992. O'Hara, Mary; Mary
Sture-Vasa
1885–1980
composer, novelist, scriptwriter
Cur Biog '81; Index t Wom

13993. Siddall, Louise
died 1935

composer, educator
Index t Wom

13994. Tollefsen, Augusta Schnabel
circa 1885–1955
pianist
Index t Wom

13995. Appleton, Adeline Carola
born 1886
composer, music educator
Index t Wom

13996. Clarke, Rebecca
born 1886
composer
Index t Wom

13997. Fitzu, Anna (Powell)
circa 1886–1967
soprano opera singer, voice teacher
Index t Wom; Obit File

13998. Foster, Fay
1886–1960
composer, pianist, voice teacher
Index t Wom; Nat Cyc Am Bio csv1

13999. Garrison, Mabel
1886–1963
Metropolitan Opera coloratura soprano singer
Index t Wom; Obit File

14000. Hardwick, Katharine Davis
1886–1974
pianist, newspaper publisher
Christian Scientist
Indiana
Nat Cyc Am Bio v58

14001. Johnson, Georgia Douglas
1886–1966
poet, composer, author
Black
Encyc Black Am; Index t Wom; Negro Alman; Obit File; Wom Lit, More

14002. Leginska, Ethel Liggens
1886/90–1970
musician, pianist, conductor, composer
English
Index t Wom; Not Am Wom supp v1

14003. Nicholson, Martha Snell
1886–circa 1951
singer, poet
Index t Wom

14004. Noland, Hampton [Clara]
1886–1960
composer

Episcopalian
Nat Cyc Am Bio v48

14005. Rainey, Gertrude Malissa Nix Pridgett "Ma"
1886–1939
blues singer
Black
Dict Am Bio supp v2; Encyc Black Am; Not Am Wom

14006. Baker, Martha Atwood
1887–1950
soprano opera singer, music educator
Obit File

14007. Bori, Lucrezia; Lucrecia Borja Gonzales de Riancho
1887–1960
Metropolitan Opera soprano singer
Catholic
Spanish
Dict Am Bio supp v5; Nat Cyc Am Bio v44; Obit File

14008. Boulanger, Nadia
1887–1979
composer, pianist, music educator, conductor
French
Cur Biog '80

14009. Bourskaya, Ina
1887–1954
Metropolitan and Chicago Opera soprano singer
Obit File

14010. Brown, Mary Helen
died 1937
composer
Index t Wom

14011. Calloway-Byron, Mayme
flourished 1917
singer
Black
Index t Wom

14012. Fergus, Phyllis; Mrs. Thatcher Hoyt
1887–1964
composer
Illinois
Index t Wom; Nat Cyc Am Bio v52

14013. Holden, Anne Stratton
born 1887
composer
Index t Wom

14014. Lewis, Louise Hills
1887–1948
composer, religious worker, hymn writer
Index t Wom

14015. Marcel, Lucille Wassell
1887–1921

singer
Index t Wom

14016. Spofford, Grace Harriet
1887–1974
music educator, music administrator
Index t Wom; Not Am Wom supp v1

14017. Strickland, Lily Teresa
born 1887
composer, author
Index t Wom

14018. Barnett, Alice
born 1888
composer, songwriter
Index t Wom

14019. Braslau, Sophie
1888/92–1935
concert and opera contralto singer
Dict Am Bio supp v1; Index t Wom; Not Am Wom

14020. Brock, Blanche Kerr
born 1888
composer, hymn writer
Index t Wom

14021. Buchanan, Annabel Morris
born 1888
composer, editor, author
Index t Wom

14022. Ellerman, Amy
circa 1888–1960
concert contralto singer, voice coach
Index t Wom; Obit File

14023. Gentle, Alice
1888–1958
singer
Index t Wom

14024. Goodman, Lillian Rosedale
born 1888
composer, singer, pianist, critic, author, linguist
Index t Wom

14025. Housman, Rosalie Louise
circa 1888–1949
composer, pianist, lecturer, musicologist
Index t Wom

14026. Ingram, Frances
born 1888
contralto singer
Nat Cyc Am Bio v17

14027. Kummer, Clare Rodman Beecher
born 1888

composer, songwriter, playwright
Index t Wom

14028. Lehmann, Lotte
1888–1976
operatic soprano, lieder singer
German
Cur Biog '70 and '76; Obit File

14029. Marsh, Lucille Crews
born 1888
composer
Index t Wom

14030. Peterson, May
1888–1952
soprano opera singer
Index t Wom; Obit File

14031. Pitts, Carol Marhoff
born 1888
composer, conductor, educator
Index t Wom

14032. Price, Florence Beatrice Smith
1888–1953
composer, instrumentalist, pianist, organist, music educator
Black
Index t Wom; Not Am Wom supp v1

14033. Worth, Amy
born 1888
composer, pianist, musical director
Index t Wom

14034. Burns, Annelu
1889–1942
violinist, composer, music educator
Index t Wom

14035. Case, Anna
born 1889
singer
Index t Wom

14036. Cramm, Helen L.
died 1939
composer, music educator
Index t Wom

14037. Davis, Genevieve
1889–1950
composer
Index t Wom

14038. Fischel, Marguerite Kauffman
1889–1950
composer, worker for the welfare of young cerebral palsy victims
Jewish
Obit File

14039. Fisher, Bernice
born 1889
singer
Index t Wom

14040. Freeman, Bettina
born 1889
singer
Index t Wom

14041. Galli-Curci, Amelita
1889–1963
Metropolitan Opera coloratura
    soprano singer
Italian
Obit File

14042. Gillespie, Marian
1889–1946
composer, pianist, author, actor,
    journalist
Index t Wom

14043. Gordon, Dorothy Lerner
1889–1970
radio and television producer,
    singer, children's author
Cur Biog '70; Index t Wom; Not
    Am Wom supp v1

14044. Hier, Ethel Glenn
born 1889
pianist, composer, music educator
Index t Wom

**14045. Janis, Elisie (Bierbower)
    (Wilson)**
1889/93–1956
mimic, stage actor, singer, dancer,
    vaudevillian, author, songwrit-
    er, World War I entertainer
Dict Am Bio supp v6; Index t
    Wom; Nat Cyc Am Bio csv1;
    Obit File

14046. Lillenas, Bertha Mae
1889–1945
composer, author
Index t Wom

**14047. Rosen, Lucie Bigelow
    Dodge**
1889–1968
electronic musician, patron of
    music
Episcopalian
New York
Nat Cyc Am Bio v54

14048. Smith, Hannah
died 1939
composer, music educator, author
Index t Wom

14049. Stanley, Helen
born 1889
singer
Index t Wom

14050. Tas, Helen Teschner
born 1889
violinist
Index t Wom

14051. Virgil, Antha Minerva
died 1939

composer, pianist, educator
Index t Wom

14052. Vreeland, Jeannette
died 1939
singer
Index t Wom

14053. Wallace, Mildred White
born 1889
composer, singer, publisher, au-
    thor
Index t Wom

14054. Alcock, Merle
born 1890
singer
Index t Wom

14055. Bloch, Blanche
flourished 1920s–30s
conductor, pianist
Index t Wom

14056. Burke, Hilda
flourished 1920s–30s
singer
Index t Wom

14057. Corona, Leonora
flourished 1920s
singer
Index t Wom

14058. Davis, Agnes
flourished 1920s–40s
singer
Index t Wom

14059. Dilling, Mildred
flourished 1920s–30s
harpist
Index t Wom

14060. Divine, Grace
flourished 1920s
singer
Index t Wom

14061. Dragonette, Jessica
flourished 1920s–30s
radio singer
English
Index t Wom

**14062. Duckwitz, Dorothy
    Miller**
flourished 1920s
pianist
Index t Wom

14063. Galli-Campi, Amri
flourished 1920s–30s
singer
Index t Wom

14064. George, Anna E.
flourished 1920s
composer, pianist
Index t Wom

14065. Hampton, Hope
flourished 1920s–30s
singer
Index t Wom

14066. Henders, Harriet
flourished 1920s–30s
singer
Index t Wom

14067. Kemper, Ruth
flourished 1920s
violinist
Index t Wom

14068. Kurenko, Maria
flourished 1920s–40s
singer
Russian
Index t Wom

**14069. Lashanska, Hulda; Mrs.
    Harold A. Rosebaum**
1890/93–1974
lyric soprano concert singer
Jewish
New York
Index t Wom; Nat Cyc Am Bio
    v57

14070. Lucchese, Josephine
flourished 1920s
singer
Index t Wom

**14071. Manning, Kathleen
    Lockhart**
1890–1951
composer, pianist, opera singer
Index t Wom; Obit File

14072. Mock, Alice
flourished 1920s–30s
singer
Index t Wom

14073. Morgana, Nina
flourished 1920s–30s
singer
Index t Wom

**14074. Murray, Charlotte
    Wallace**
married 1915
singer, music educator
Black
Index t Wom

14075. Niemack, Ilza
flourished 1920s
violinist, composer
Index t Wom

14076. Redell, Emma
died 1940
singer
Index t Wom

**14077. Reynolds, Libby Hol-
    man**
flourished 1920s–30s

singer
Index t Wom

14078. Roma, Lisa
flourished 1920s
singer
Index t Wom

14079. Shuchari, Sadah
flourished 1920s
violinist
Index t Wom

14080. Simmons, Alberta
flourished 1920s
jazz pianist
Index t Wom

14081. Smith, Mamie
flourished 1920s
jazz musician, singer
Index t Wom

14082. Spencer, Eleanor
born 1890
pianist
Index t Wom

14083. Sundstrom, Ebba
flourished 1920s–30s
conductor, violinist
Index t Wom

14084. Votipka, Thelma
flourished 1920s
opera singer
Index t Wom

14085. Waters, Crystal
flourished 1920s
singer
Index t Wom

14086. Wells, Phradie
flourished 1920s
singer
Index t Wom

14087. Wengerova, Isabella
flourished 1920s
pianist
Jewish
Russian
Index t Wom

14088. Branzell, Karin
1891–1974
Metropolitan Opera contralto
    singer
Cur Biog '75; Obit File

14089. Dawn, Hazel
born 1891/94
actor, singer
Index t Wom

14090. Donez, Ian
born 1891
composer, author
Index t Wom

14091. Hill, Mabel Wood
born 1891
composer
Index t Wom

14092. Kahn, Grace Leboy
born 1891
composer
Index t Wom

14093. Lazzari, Carolina Antoinette
1891–1946
singer
Index t Wom

14094. Lyne, Felice
1891–1935
singer
Index t Wom

14095. MacBeth, Florence
born circa 1891
singer
Index t Wom

14096. Moore, Elizabeth Evelyn
born 1891
author, songwriter
Index t Wom

14097. Painter, Eleanor
1891–1947
opera singer, actor
Nat Cyc Am Bio v44; Obit File

14098. Seaver, Blanche Ebert
born 1891
composer, author
Index t Wom

14099. Stewart, Dorothy M.
1891/97–1954
theatrical agent, composer, pianist, author
Australian
Index t Wom

14100. Zucca, Mana; Madame Manna-Zucca
born 1891/94
composer, pianist, actor, singer
Jewish
Index t Wom

14101. Bassett, Karolyn Wells
1892–1931
composer, pianist
Index t Wom

14102. Davis, Fay Simmons
died 1942
pianist, composer, music educator
Index t Wom

14103. Davis, Katherine K.
born 1892
composer, author
Index t Wom

14104. Gerard, Theodora "Teddie"; Teresa Cabre
1892–1942
musical revue actor
Obit File

14105. Gray-Lhevinne, Estelle
1892–1933
violinist
Index t Wom

14106. Lussi, Marie; Mari Mitale
born 1892
songwriter, author
Index t Wom

14107. McCollin, Frances
1892–1960
composer, educator, lecturer, Socialist party worker
Episcopalian
Pennsylvania
blind
Index t Wom; Nat Cyc Am Bio v45

14108. Meiere, Hildreth
1892–post 1930s
artist, painter, muralist
Catholic
Index t Wom; Nat Cyc Am Bio csv4

14109. Pinkard, Edna Belle
born 1892
composer, author
Index t Wom

14110. Ponselle, Carmela
born 1892
singer
Index t Wom

14111. Steeb, Olga
died 1942
pianist
Index t Wom

14112. Trix, Helen
1892–1951
composer, pianist, singer, author, actor
Index t Wom

14113. Adair, Mildred
died 1943
composer
Index t Wom

14114. Ballaseyus, Virginia
born 1893
composer, author
Index t Wom

14115. Barstow, Vera
born 1893
violinist
Index t Wom

14116. Bordoni, Irene
circa 1893–1953
musical comedy actor
French; Corsican
Index t Wom; Obit File

14117. Fine, Sylvia
born 1893
composer, author
Index t Wom

14118. Gordon, Jeanne
1893–1952
Metropolitan Opera contralto singer
Obit File

14119. Hagan, Helen Eugenia
1893–1964
pianist, music educator
Black
Encyc Black Am; Index t Wom; Prof Negro Wom v2

14120. Hokanson, Margrethe
born 1893
composer
Index t Wom

14121. Krogman, C. W., Mrs.
died 1943
composer
Index t Wom

14122. Mason, Edith Barnes
1893–1973
Metropolitan Opera lyric soprano singer
Index t Wom; Obit File

14123. Raisa, Rosa
1893–1963
soprano opera singer
Chicago, IL
Obit File

14124. Rich, Gladys
born 1893
composer
Index t Wom

14125. Roosevelt, Emily
born 1893
composer, singer
Index t Wom

14126. Stevens, Doris
1893–1963
women's rights worker, author, songwriter
Obit File

14127. Grever, Maria
1894–1951
composer, singer, pianist
Mexican
Index t Wom; Obit File

14128. Ladd, Hattie Belle
died 1944
singer
Obit File

14129. Smith, Bessie
1894–1937
blues singer
Black
Dict Am Bio supp v2; Encyc Black Am; Index t Wom; Negro Alman

14130. Alexander, Ruth Wilbur; Mrs. Raymond L. Redhefer
born 1895
economist, editorial columnist, lecturer, pianist
Buddhist
Index t Wom; Nat Cyc Am Bio csv12

14131. Baker, Belle; Bella Becker
1895/98–1957
vaudeville singer, actor
Index t Wom; Obit File

14132. Copp, Evelyn Fletcher
died 1945
music educator
Index t Wom

14133. Franklin, Blanche Ortha
born 1895
composer, author
Index t Wom

14134. Hunter, Alberta
born 1895
jazz and blues singer and songwriter
Black
Cur Biog '70

14135. Jamerson, Pauline Thierry; Polly Preyer
1895–1952
playwright, musical comedy actor
Obit File

14136. Laramore, Vivian Yeiser
born 1895
poet, songwriter
Index t Wom

14137. Lerch, Louise
circa 1895–1967
singer
Index t Wom

14138. Manski, Dorothee
born circa 1895
singer
Jewish
German
Index t Wom

14139. McDaniel, Hattie
1895/98–1952
radio and television actor, singer
Black
Dict Am Bio supp v5; Encyc Black Am; Index t Wom; Not Am Wom supp v1; Obit File

14140. Merrill, Blanche
born 1895
songwriter
Index t Wom

14141. Mills, Florence
1895–1927
singer, dancer, stage comedian
Black
Encyc Black Am; Index t Wom;
Negro Alman; Not Am Wom

14142. Rethberg, Elizabeth
1895–1976
soprano Wagnerian opera singer
Obit File

14143. Smith, Ada; Bricktop
born 1895
singer, dancer, cabaret owner
Index t Wom

14144. Warton, Elizabeth Hines
1895–1971
musical comedy actor
Obit File

14145. de Leath, Vaughn
1896–1943
singer, songwriter
Index t Wom

14146. MacKown, Marjorie T.
born 1896
composer
Index t Wom

14147. Mario, Queen Tillotson
1896–1951
singer
Index t Wom

14148. Remsen, Alice
born 1896
composer, author, publisher
English
Index t Wom

14149. Rockefeller, Martha Baird
1896–1971
concert pianist, music patron
Obit File

14150. van Emden, Harriet
circa 1896–1953
singer
Index t Wom

14151. van Gordon, Cyrena
born 1896
singer
Index t Wom

14152. Waters, Ethel
1896/1900–1977
gospel and blues singer; stage, screen, and television actor

Black
Cur Biog '77; Encyc Black Am;
Index t Wom; Negro Alman;
Obit File; Prof Negro Wom v2

14153. Bixby, Allene K.
died 1947
organist, composer, music educator
Index t Wom

14154. Bridges, Ethel
born 1897
composer
Index t Wom

14155. Jessye, Eva Alberta
1897–post 1930s
music director, educator, writer
on music, conductor
Black
Encyc Black Am; Index t Wom

14156. Ponselle, Rose Melba
born 1897
singer
Index t Wom

14157. Speare, Dorothy
1897/98–1951
screenwriter, author, novelist,
opera singer, labor worker
Index t Wom; Nat Cyc Am Bio
v40; Obit File

14158. Sunshine, Marion
born 1897
composer, actor, author
Index t Wom

14159. Telva, Marion
1897–1962
singer
Index t Wom

14160. Armstrong, Lillian "Lil" Hardin
1898–1971
jazz pianist
Black
Encyc Black Am

14161. Bloom, Vera
circa 1898–1959
author, lyricist
Index t Wom

14162. Etting, Ruth
1898/1907–1978
singer, radio and screen actor
Index t Wom; Obit File

14163. Given, Thelma
born 1898
violinist
Index t Wom

14164. Guggenheim, Marguerite "Peggy"
born 1898
patron of modern art and music,
art collector, author

Jewish
New York
Cur Biog '80; Index t Wom; Who
Who Jew Hist

14165. Jasmyn, Joan
born 1898
composer, author
Index t Wom

14166. Lawrence, Gertrude (Klassen); Gertrude Alexandra Dagma Lawrence Klassen
1898–1952
Broadway and London stage actor, singer
English
Dict Am Bio supp v5; Dict Nat
Bio 1951–1960; Index t Wom;
Obit File

14167. Lee, Norah
1898–1941
composer
Index t Wom

14168. Meisle, Kathryn
born 1898
singer
Index t Wom

14169. Miller, Maralyn
1898–1936
musical comedy actor
Index t Wom; Not Am Wom

14170. Moore, Grace; Mrs. Valentine Parera
1898/1901–1947
musical comedian, opera and
popular soprano singer, screen
and radio actor
Dict Am Bio supp v4; Index t
Wom; Nat Cyc Am Bio v38;
Not Am Wom; Obit File

14171. Sage, Kay Linn
1898–1963
painter
Not Am Wom supp v1

14172. Wayne, Mabel
born 1898/1904
composer, pianist, songwriter
Index t Wom

14173. Westbrook, Helen Searles
born 1898
composer, organist
Index t Wom

14174. Youse, Glad Robinson
born 1898
composer
Index t Wom

14175. Carreau, Margaret
born 1899
composer
Index t Wom

14176. Finlay, Lorraine Noel
born 1899
composer, author
Canadian
Index t Wom

14177. Gray, Gilda
1899/1901–1959
dancer, singer
Polish
Dict Am Bio supp v6; Index t
Wom; Obit File

14178. Iturbi, Amparo
1899–1969
concert pianist
Spanish
Obit File

14179. Poll, Ruth
born 1899
author, songwriter
Index t Wom

14180. Traubel, Helen Francesca; Mrs. William Bass
1899/1903–1972
Metropolitan Opera soprano concert singer, television and film
actor, nightclub entertainer
Cur Biog '72; Index t Wom; Nat
Cyc Am Bio csv7; Not Am
Wom supp v1; Obit File

14181. Woolsey, Maryhale
born 1899
songwriter, author
Index t Wom

14182. Angelau, Grace
flourished 1930s
singer
Index t Wom

14183. Axman, Gladys
flourished 1930s
singer
Index t Wom

14184. Bary, Gertrude
flourished 1930s
pianist
German
Index t Wom

14185. Beckman, Evelyn
born 1900
composer
Index t Wom

14186. Bodanya, Natalie
flourished 1930s–40s
singer
Index t Wom

14187. Boswell, Connee
flourished 1930s
singer, actor
Index t Wom

14188. Boswell, Vet
flourished 1930s

singer
Index t Wom

14189. Braddock, Amelia
flourished 1930s
singer, music educator
English
Index t Wom

14190. Burford, Beatrice
flourished 1930s
harpist
Index t Wom

14191. Carpara, Clara H.
flourished 1930s
music educator
Index t Wom

14192. Chase, Helen Frances
flourished 1930s
musician, music educator
Index t Wom

14193. Coci, Claire
flourished 1930s–40s
organist
Index t Wom

14194. Crowell, Annie L.
flourished 1930s
pianist, music educator
Index t Wom

14195. Davies, Mary Carolyn
flourished 1930s
poet, songwriter
Index t Wom

14196. Demarco, Sisters
flourished 1930s–50s
singers
Index t Wom

14197. Dethridge, Luvena Wallace
flourished 1930s
singer
Black
Index t Wom

14198. Dick, Dorothy
born 1900
author, songwriter
Index t Wom

14199. Dickey, Annamary
flourished 1930s–40s
singer
Index t Wom

14200. Dike, Victoria
flourished 1930s
musical and art director
Index t Wom

14201. Doe, Doris
flourished 1930s
singer
Index t Wom

14202. Douglas, Helen [Mary] (Gahagan)
1900/05–1980
stage actor, Democratic representative to Congress from California, opera singer
Episcopalian
California
Cur Biog '80; Index t Wom; Nat Cyc Am Bio csvF

14203. du Pre, Grace Annette
flourished 1930s–60s
painter, violinist, tennis player
South Carolina
Nat Cyc Am Bio csv11

14204. Eakin, Vera O.
born 1900
composer, pianist, organist
Index t Wom

14205. Field, Laura
flourished 1930s
ballet dancer, pianist
Index t Wom

14206. Fisher, Susanne
flourished 1930s
singer
Index t Wom

14207. Flagg, Marion
flourished 1930s
music educator
Index t Wom

14208. Gage, Gloria
flourished 1930s
government official, musician
Index t Wom

14209. Galajikian, Florence Grandland
born 1900
composer, pianist, music educator
Index t Wom

14210. Golden, Sylvia
born 1900
author, editor, songwriter
Index t Wom

14211. Gordon, Cyrena Van
flourished 1930s
singer
Index t Wom

14212. Halstead, Margaret
flourished 1930s
singer
Index t Wom

14213. Harris, Hettie
flourished 1930s
singer
Index t Wom

14214. Hill, Dedette Lee
1900–50
author, songwriter
Index t Wom

14215. Hollingsworth, Thekla
flourished 1930s
composer, author
Index t Wom

14216. Jardine, John Alexander, Mrs.
flourished 1930s
musician
Index t Wom

14217. Jenkins, Florence F.
flourished 1930s
singer
Index t Wom

14218. Jones, Abbie Gerrish
flourished 1930s
composer
Index t Wom

14219. Kraeuter, Phyllis Marie
flourished 1930s
cellist
Index t Wom

14220. Larkin, Margaret
1900–67
author, poet, editor, composer, singer
Obit File

14221. Leonard, Myrtle
flourished 1930s
singer
Index t Wom

14222. Lewis, Mary Sybil
1900–41
singer
Index t Wom

14223. Lichtman, Sina
flourished 1930s
pianist
Russian
Index t Wom

14224. Mercer, Mabel
born 1900
nightclub singer
Black
Cur Biog '73

14225. Merrick, C., Mrs.; Edgar Thorn
flourished 1930s
composer
Index t Wom

14226. Monti-Gorsey, Lola
flourished 1930s
singer
Italian
Index t Wom

14227. Moore, Jeanne W. G.
flourished 1930s
hymn writer
Index t Wom

14228. Moore, Mary
flourished 1930s
singer
Index t Wom

14229. Morgan, Helen
1900?–41
torch singer; stage, screen, and radio actor
Dict Am Bio supp v3; Not Am Wom; Obit File

14230. Moten, Etta
flourished 1930s
actor, singer
Black
Index t Wom

14231. Nichols, Edith Elizabeth
flourished 1930s
singer, voice teacher
Index t Wom

14232. Nickerson, Camille L.
flourished 1930s
pianist, music educator
Black
Index t Wom

14233. Norton, Eunice
flourished 1930s–40s
pianist
Index t Wom

14234. Olheim, Helen Marion; Marian Oelheim
flourished 1930s
singer
Index t Wom

14235. Olney, Dorothy McGrayne
flourished 1930s
concert manager
Index t Wom

14236. Park-Lewis, Dorothea
flourished 1930s
cellist
Index t Wom

14237. Pessl, Yella
flourished 1930s–40s
harpsichordist
Index t Wom

14238. Platt, Estelle Gertrude
flourished 1930s
singer, educator, musical director
Index t Wom

14239. Pollock, Muriel
flourished 1930s
composer, pianist, organist
Index t Wom

14240. Potter, Marguerite
flourished 1930s
singer
Index t Wom

14241. Rapoport, Eda
born 1900
composer
Russian
Index t Wom

14242. Rapoport, Ruth
1900/01–1935
composer
Index t Wom

14243. Rea, Virginia
flourished 1930s
singer
Index t Wom

14244. Robinson, Carol
flourished 1930s
pianist
Index t Wom

14245. Ryan, Mary P. van Buren
flourished 1930s
singer, music educator, accountant
Index t Wom

14246. Silberta, Rhea
born 1900
composer, singer, educator
Index t Wom

14247. Smith, Georgina
flourished 1930s
singer, organist
Index t Wom

14248. Speaks, Margaret
flourished 1930s
singer
Index t Wom

14249. Stillings, Kemp
flourished 1930s
violinist, educator
Index t Wom

14250. Tentoni, Rosa
flourished 1930s
singer
Index t Wom

14251. Thomas, Flora
flourished 1930s
pianist
Black
Index t Wom

14252. Tourel, Jennie
1900?–73
opera and concert mezzo-soprano
  singer
Jewish
Cur Biog '74; Not Am Wom supp
  v1; Obit File

14253. Tyson, Mildred Lund
born 1900
composer
Index t Wom

14254. Urbanek, Carolyn
flourished 1930s
singer
Index t Wom

14255. Vaupel, Ouise
flourished 1930s
fashion designer, realtor, singer,
  author
Index t Wom

14256. Villiers, Vera de
flourished 1930s
singer
Index t Wom

14257. Walker, Jean
flourished 1930s
musician, poet
Index t Wom

14258. Welge, Gladys
flourished 1930s
orchestra conductor
Index t Wom

14259. Wysor, Elizabeth
flourished 1930s
singer
Index t Wom

14260. Beebe, Carolyn Harding
died 1951
pianist
Index t Wom

14261. Carter, Maybelle Hunton
1901–70
country music singer, guitarist
Nashville, TN
Obit File

14262. Cary, Mary Harkness Flagler
1901–67
patron of music, conservationist
New York
Nat Cyc Am Bio v55

14263. Cohen, Barbara
born 1901
recording company executive
Index t Wom

14264. Cowles, Cecil
born 1901
composer
Index t Wom

14265. Crawford-Seeger, Ruth Porter
1901–53
composer, folk music scholar,
  music educator, pianist
Index t Wom; Not Am Wom
  supp v1

14266. James, Dorothy
born 1901
composer
Index t Wom

14267. Reed, Ida L.
died 1951
hymn writer
Index t Wom

14268. Anderson, Marian
born 1902/08
contralto concert singer, US alternate delegate to the UN,
  1958–59
Baptist
Black
Encyc Black Am; Index t Wom;
  Nat Cyc Am Bio csv9; Negro
  Alman; Negro Her Lib v1; Prof
  Negro Wom; World Great Men
  Col

14269. Bampton, Ruth
born 1902
composer, choral director
Index t Wom

14270. Bonetti, Mary
born 1902
singer
Index t Wom

14271. Brico, Antonia
born 1902
conductor, pianist, music educator
Index t Wom

14272. Calloway, Blanche
born 1902
conductor
Index t Wom

14273. Cushing, Catherine Chisholm
died 1952
playwright, lyricist
Index t Wom; Obit File

14274. d'Arville, Colette
1902–44
soprano concert and opera singer
French
Obit File

14275. Dawson, Mary Cardwell
1902–62
founder of the National Negro
  Opera Company, soprano concert singer
Black
Obit File

14276. Duncan, Vivian
born 1902
composer, author, publisher
Index t Wom

14277. Eaton, Mary
1902–48
musical comedy actor
Obit File

14278. Giannini, Dusolina
born 1902

singer
Index t Wom

14279. Hall, Juanita
1902/13–1968
musical actor, singer
Index t Wom; Obit File

14280. Jones, Blanche Calloway
1902–78
big-band leader
Obit File

14281. Mielziner, Jo
1902–76
set and lighting designer for dramas, musicals, operas, and ballets
Obit File

14282. Puck, Mabel Withee
died 1952
musical comedy actor
Obit File

14283. West, Jessamyn [Mary]
born 1902/07
short story writer, novelist, poet,
  autobiographer, operetta librettist, screenplay writer
Quaker
California
Cur Biog '77; Dict Lit Bio v6;
  Index t Wom

14284. Williams, Frances; Frances Jelinek
1902–59
musical comedy actor, dancer
  who introduced the Charleston
Obit File

14285. Bailey, Mildred; Mildred Rinker
1903/07–1951
blues and jazz singer
Native American
Dict Am Bio supp v5; Obit File

14286. Bicking, Ada Elizabeth
died 1953
music educator
Index t Wom

14287. Bonelli, Mona Modini
born 1903
author, songwriter
Index t Wom

14288. Britain, Radie
born 1903/04
composer
Index t Wom

14289. Bush, Anita
pre-1903–73
singer, actor
Black
Negro Alman

14290. Davenport, Marcie
born 1903
author, music critic
Index t Wom

14291. Dewey, Frances Eileen Hutt
1903–70
singer
New York
Obit File

14292. Dungan, Olive
born 1903
composer, pianist
Index t Wom

14293. Fairbank, Janet
1903–47
opera and concert singer
Obit File

14294. George, Zelma Watson
1903–post 1960
alternate delegate to the UN, sociologist, singer
Black
Index t Wom; Negro Alman; Negro Her Lib v1

14295. Jarboro, Caterina
born 1903
soprano singer
Black
Encyc Black Am; Index t Wom

14296. MacDonald, Jeanette Anna
1903/07–1965
screen actor, soprano singer, dancer
Index t Wom; Not Am Wom supp v1; Obit File

14297. Monath, Hortense
circa 1903–56
concert pianist
Index t Wom; Obit File

14298. Ross, Margaret Wheeler
died 1953
pianist, music teacher, club leader
Index t Wom

14299. Alter, Martha
born 1904
composer, pianist, music educator
Index t Wom

14300. Anderson, Ivy
1904–49
blues singer
Obit File

14301. de Cevee, Alice
born 1904
composer, pianist
Index t Wom

14302. Fenner, Beatrice
born 1904

composer, author, publisher
Index t Wom

14303. Fields, Dorothy
1904/05–1974
lyricist, librettist
Cur Biog '74; Index t Wom; Not Am Wom supp v1

14304. Gradova, Gitta "Gidda"
born 1904
pianist
Jewish
Index t Wom

14305. Graham, Shirley
born 1904/07
musical playwright, biographical historian, author, composer
Black
Index t Wom; Negro Alman

14306. Kane, Helen; The Boop-a-Doop Girl
1904–66
popular singer
Obit File

14307. Kojis, Harriet Henderson; Harriet Henders
1904–72
Metropolitan Opera soprano singer
Obit File

14308. Pons, Alice Josephina "Lily"; Mrs. Andre Kostelanetz
1904–76
Metropolitan Opera coloratura-soprano singer
French
Cur Biog '76; Index t Wom; Nat Cyc Am Bio csv7; Obit File

14309. Swarthout, Gladys
1904–69
Metropolitan Opera mezzo-soprano singer
Cur Biog '69; Index t Wom; Obit File

14310. Cassiday, Claudia
born circa 1905
music, ballet, and drama critic
Index t Wom

14311. Cole, Ulric
born 1905
composer
Index t Wom

14312. Holman, Libby
1905–71
blues singer, Broadway actor
Index t Wom; Obit File

14313. Kraus, Lili
born 1905?
concert pianist
Jewish

Hungarian
Cur Biog '75

14314. Lawnhurst, Vee
born 1905
composer, pianist, singer
Index t Wom

14315. Roobenian, Amber
born 1905
singer, organist, composer
Index t Wom

14316. Trapp, Maria Augusta
born 1905
singer
Austrian
Index t Wom

14317. Warren, Elinor Remick; Mrs. Zachary Wayne Giffin
born 1905
composer, pianist
Index t Wom; Nat Cyc Am Bio csv6

14318. Wicker, Irene
born 1905
singer, actor, radio scriptwriter
Index t Wom

14319. Baker, Josephine
1906–75
actor, dancer, singer, civil rights worker
Black
Cur Biog '75; Encyc Black Am; Index t Wom; Negro Alman; Not Am Wom

14320. du Bois, Shirley Lola Graham
1906–77
children's author, biographer, composer, stage director, civil rights worker
Black
Cur Biog '77; Encyc Black Am

14321. Gideon, Miriam
born 1906
composer
Index t Wom

14322. Glade, Coe
born 1906
singer
Index t Wom

14323. Grippon, Eva
died 1956
singer
French
Index t Wom

14324. Guilford, Nanette
born 1906
singer
Index t Wom

14325. Jepson, Helen
born 1906

singer
Index t Wom

14326. MacKinstry, Elizabeth
died 1956
illustrator, sculptor, violinist
Index t Wom

14327. Petkere, Bernice
born 1906
composer, author, scenarist
Index t Wom

14328. Talma, Louise
born 1906
composer
Index t Wom

14329. Davis, Ellabelle
1907–60
soprano singer
Black
Obit File

14330. Hyde, Madeline
born 1907
composer, author
Index t Wom

14331. Jean, Elsie
born 1907
composer, author
Index t Wom

14332. Knappen, Betty Compton
1907–44
musical comedy actor
Obit File

14333. Lorenz, Ellen Jane
born 1907
composer, editor, educator
Index t Wom

14334. Monroe, Lucy
born 1907
singer
Index t Wom

14335. Pearl, Lee
born 1907
author, songwriter
Index t Wom

14336. Pierce, Billie Goodson
1907–74
jazz pianist
Obit File

14337. Somigli, Franca
born circa 1907
singer
Index t Wom

14338. Swift, Kay
born 1907
composer, pianist
Index t Wom

14339. Talley, Marion Nevada
born 1907

singer
Index t Wom

14340. van Sciver, Esther
born 1907
author, songwriter
Index t Wom

14341. Antoine, Josephine
born 1908
singer
Index t Wom

14342. Hamilton, Nancy
born 1908
author, singer
Index t Wom

14343. Lawrence, Marjorie
1908–79
Metropolitan Opera soprano singer
Australian
Cur Biog '79

14344. Marlow, Sylvia
born 1908
harpsichordist
Jewish
Index t Wom

14345. Merman, Ethel Agnes Zimmerman
born 1908
stage and screen actor and singer
Index t Wom

14346. Olivette, Nina
1908–71
musical comedy actor
Obit File

14347. Tauber, Doris
born 1908
composer, pianist, singer
Index t Wom

14348. Walker, Bertha "Bee"
born 1908
composer
Index t Wom

14349. Bampton, Rose Elizabeth
born 1909
singer
Index t Wom

14350. Boswell, Martha; Martha Lloyd
circa 1909–58
popular singer, actor
Index t Wom; Obit File

14351. Miranda, Carmen; Maria de Carmo da Cunha
1909/13–1955
singer
Portuguese; Brazilian
Dict Am Bio supp v5; Index t Wom; Obit File

14352. Smith, Kate
born 1909
singer, radio and television personality
Index t Wom

14353. Vronsky, Vitya
born 1909
pianist
Russian
Index t Wom

14354. Altman, Thelma
flourished 1940s
singer
Index t Wom

14355. Arvey, Verna
born 1910
composer, pianist
Index t Wom

14356. Becker, Grace
flourished 1940s
cellist
Index t Wom

14357. Blake, Dorothy Gaynor
flourished 1940s
composer, music educator
Index t Wom

14358. Brown, Annie Williams
flourished 1940s
singer
Black
Index t Wom

14359. Carrick, Jean Warren
flourished 1940s
pianist, music editor, author
Index t Wom

14360. Carroll, Christina
flourished 1940s
singer
Rumanian
Index t Wom

14361. Coit, Lottie Ellsworth
flourished 1940s
music educator, violinist
Index t Wom

14362. Comfort, Annabel
flourished 1940s
composer, author
Index t Wom

14363. Copeland, Bernice Rose
flourished 1940s
composer, music educator
Index t Wom

14364. Cortez, Leonora
flourished 1940s
pianist
Index t Wom

14365. Cotton-Marshall, Grace
flourished 1940s

composer
Index t Wom

14366. Crosby, Marie
flourished 1940s
composer, music educator
Index t Wom

14367. Crowe, Bonita
flourished 1940s
composer, organist, pianist
Index t Wom

14368. Dallam, Helen
flourished 1940s–50s
composer, author
Index t Wom

14369. de Horvath, Cecile
flourished 1940s
pianist
Index t Wom

14370. Dodge, Cynthia Dodge
flourished 1940s
composer
Index t Wom

14371. Dodge, Mary Hewes
flourished 1940s
violinist, pianist, music educator, composer
Index t Wom

14372. Downey, Mary E.
flourished 1940s
organist, composer
Index t Wom

14373. Dutton, Theodora
flourished 1940s
pianist, composer
Index t Wom

14374. Edwards, Ester Gordy
flourished 1940s–70s
publishing executive, vice-president of Motown Records
Black
Encyc Black Am

14375. Elzy, Ruby
circa 1910–43
singer
Index t Wom

14376. Erb, Mae-Aileen Gerhart
flourished 1940s
composer, music educator
Index t Wom

14377. Fisher, Emma Roderick
flourished 1940s
patron of music
Index t Wom

14378. Foster, Bertha M.
flourished 1940s
organist, music educator, choirmaster
Index t Wom

14379. Foster, Harriet
flourished 1940s
singer
Index t Wom

14380. Gere, Florence Parr
flourished 1940s
composer, pianist
Index t Wom

14381. Gescheidt, Adelaide
flourished 1940s
musician, voice teacher
Index t Wom

14382. Gest, Elizabeth
flourished 1940s
composer, pianist
Index t Wom

14383. Glen, Katherine
flourished 1940s
pianist
Index t Wom

14384. Glenn, Mabelle
flourished 1940s
music educator, author
Index t Wom

14385. Gober, Belle Biard
flourished 1940s
composer, pianist, music educator
Index t Wom

14386. Goff, Anna Chandler
flourished 1940s
music educator
Index t Wom

14387. Golson, Florence
flourished 1940s
composer, singer
Index t Wom

14388. Griswold, Henrietta Dippmann
flourished 1940s
composer, pianist
Index t Wom

14389. Hagar, Emily Stokes
flourished 1940s
singer
Index t Wom

14390. Hager, Mina
flourished 1940s
singer
Index t Wom

14391. Hall, Addye Yeargain
flourished 1940s
musician, lecturer, author
Index t Wom

14392. Hamilton, Anna Havermann
flourished 1940s
piano educator
Index t Wom

14393. Hammond, Fanny Reed
flourished 1940s
composer, pianist, music educator
Index t Wom

14394. Harris, Letitia Radcliffe
flourished 1940s
composer
Index t Wom

14395. Hathaway, Ann
flourished 1940s
violinist, author, educator
Index t Wom

14396. Hayden, Ethyl
flourished 1940s
singer
Index t Wom

14397. Hemingway, Clara Edwards
flourished 1940s
composer, singer, voice teacher, author
Index t Wom

14398. Holst, Marie Seuel
flourished 1940s
composer, pianist, music educator
Index t Wom

14399. Hood, Marguerite Vivian
flourished 1940s
pianist, educator, author, editor
Index t Wom

14400. Hotz, Mae Abrey
flourished 1940s
singer
Index t Wom

14401. Howe, Helen
flourished 1940s
music educator
Index t Wom

14402. Hudson, Octavia
flourished 1940s
composer, pianist, music educator, author
Index t Wom

14403. Hunter, Louise
flourished 1940s
singer
Index t Wom

14404. Huss, Hildegarde Hoffman
flourished 1940s
singer, lecturer, music educator
Index t Wom

14405. Inskeep, Alice Carey
flourished 1940s
music educator and director
Index t Wom

14406. Jewitt, Jessie Mae
flourished 1940s
composer, organist, pianist
Index t Wom

14407. Johnson, Christine
flourished 1940s
singer
Index t Wom

14408. Kaskas, Anna
born 1910
singer
Index t Wom

14409. Kinscella, Hazel Gertrude
flourished 1940s
musician, composer, music educator
Index t Wom

14410. Knouss, Isabelle G.
flourished 1940s
composer, pianist, music educator
Index t Wom

14411. Lang, Edith
flourished 1940s
organist, music educator
Index t Wom

14412. Langston, Marie Stone
flourished 1940s
singer
Index t Wom

14413. Lehman, Evangeline
flourished 1940s
composer, singer
Index t Wom

14414. Leonard, Florence
flourished 1940s
musician, pianist, music educator, author
Index t Wom

14415. Lewyn, Helena
flourished 1940s
pianist, music educator
Index t Wom

14416. Liszniewska, Marguerite Melville
flourished 1940s
pianist, music educator, composer
Index t Wom

14417. Lockwood, Charlotte
flourished 1940s
organist, educator
Index t Wom

14418. Madden, Lotta
flourished 1940s
singer
Index t Wom

14419. Marschal-Loepke, Grace
flourished 1940s
composer, pianist
Index t Wom

14420. Maynor, Dorothy; Dorothy Mainor
born 1910
soprano singer
Black
Encyc Black Am; Index t Wom; Negro Alman

14421. McCormic, Mary
flourished 1940s
singer
Index t Wom

14422. Mead, Olive
flourished 1940s
violinist
Index t Wom

14423. Melius, Luella
flourished 1940s
singer
Index t Wom

14424. Moore, Luella Lockwood
flourished 1940s
composer, pianist, music educator
Index t Wom

14425. Morrisey, Marie
flourished 1940s
singer
Index t Wom

14426. Moss, Mary Hissem De
flourished 1940s
singer
Index t Wom

14427. Namara, Marguerite
flourished 1940s
singer
Index t Wom

14428. Nash, Frances
flourished 1940s
pianist
Index t Wom

14429. Niessen, Gertrude
1910/13–1975
singer; comedian; Broadway stage, screen, nightclub, and radio actor
California
Index t Wom; Obit File

14430. Noe, Emma
flourished 1940s
singer
Index t Wom

14431. Norfleet, Helen
flourished 1940s
pianist
Index t Wom

14432. Oberdorfer, Anne Faulkner
flourished 1940s
musician, lecturer, author
Index t Wom

14433. Ottaway, Ruth Haller
flourished 1940s
pianist
Index t Wom

14434. Owen, Julia D.
flourished 1940s
composer, singer, music educator
Index t Wom

14435. Paldi, Mari
flourished 1940s
composer, music educator
Index t Wom

14436. Patterson, Elizabeth Kelso
flourished 1940s
singer, music educator
Index t Wom

14437. Pease, Jessie L.
flourished 1940s
composer, pianist, music educator
Index t Wom

14438. Pelton-Jones, Frances
flourished 1940s
harpsichordist, pianist, organist
Index t Wom

14439. Perfield, Effa Ellis
flourished 1940s
educator, author, organist
Index t Wom

14440. Peterson, Alma
flourished 1940s
singer
Index t Wom

14441. Peterson, Edna Gunnar
flourished 1940s
pianist, music educator
Index t Wom

14442. Phippen, Laud German
flourished 1940s
composer, pianist, music educator
Index t Wom

14443. Polk, Grace Porterfield
flourished 1940s
composer, singer
Index t Wom

14444. Porter, Ruth Stephens
flourished 1940s
composer
Index t Wom

14445. Powers, Ada Weigel
flourished 1940s
composer, pianist
Index t Wom

14446. Pray, Ada Jordan
flourished 1940s
composer, pianist, educator, lecturer
Index t Wom

14447. Preston, Matilee Loeb
flourished 1940s
composer, cornetist
Index t Wom

14448. Ralston, F. Marion
flourished 1940s
composer, pianist, music educator
Index t Wom

14449. Raymondi, Lillian
flourished 1940s
singer
Index t Wom

14450. Rebe, Louise Christine
flourished 1940s
composer, pianist, educator
Index t Wom

14451. Remick, Bertha
flourished 1940s
composer
Index t Wom

14452. Ribla, Gertrude
flourished 1940s
singer
Jewish
Index t Wom

14453. Ritter, Irene Marschand
flourished 1940s
composer, organist, pianist, educator
Index t Wom

14454. Rodgers, Irene
flourished 1940s
composer, pianist
Index t Wom

14455. Rohrer, Gertrude Martin
flourished 1940s
composer, club leader
Index t Wom

14456. Ross, Gertrude
flourished 1940s
composer, pianist
Index t Wom

14457. Ryckoff, Lalla
flourished 1940s
composer, pianist
Index t Wom

14458. Sammis-MacDermid, Sybil
flourished 1940s
singer, educator
Index t Wom

14459. Sarnoff, Dorothy
flourished 1940s
singer
Jewish
Index t Wom

14460. Schmitt, Susan
flourished 1940s
composer, pianist, educator
Index t Wom

14461. Schumann, Meta
flourished 1940s
composer, singer
Index t Wom

14462. Seydel, Irma
flourished 1940s
violinist
Index t Wom

14463. Sharlow, Murna Docia
flourished 1940s
singer
Index t Wom

14464. Showalter, Edna Blanche
flourished 1940s
singer, music educator, pianist, manager
Index t Wom

14465. Simpson, Elizabeth
flourished 1940s
composer, pianist, music educator, lecturer, author
Index t Wom

14466. Snodgrass, Louise Harrison
flourished 1940s
pianist
Index t Wom

14467. Sosenko, Anna
born 1910
composer, writer
Index t Wom

14468. Stairs, Louise E.
flourished 1940s
composer, pianist, organist, music educator
Index t Wom

14469. Stellman, Maxine
flourished 1940s
singer
Index t Wom

14470. Steuber, Lillian
flourished 1940s
singer
Index t Wom

14471. Strong, May A.
flourished 1940s
composer, singer, educator
Index t Wom

14472. Sturkow-Ryder, Theodora
flourished 1940s
composer, pianist
Index t Wom

14473. Sutor, Adele
flourished 1940s

composer, piano educator
Index t Wom

14474. Sutro, Ottilie
flourished 1940s
pianist
Index t Wom

14475. Symons, Charlotte
flourished 1940s
singer
Index t Wom

14476. Tarbox, Frances
flourished 1940s
composer, pianist
Index t Wom

14477. Terhune, Anice Stockton
flourished 1940s
composer, pianist
Index t Wom

14478. Terry, Frances
flourished 1940s
composer, pianist
Index t Wom

14479. Torpadie, Greta
flourished 1940s
singer
Index t Wom

14480. Tracey, Cateau Stegeman
flourished 1940s
pianist, music educator, author, critic, lecturer
Index t Wom

14481. Treville, Yvonne De
flourished 1940s
opera singer
Index t Wom

14482. Troendle, Theodora
flourished 1940s
composer, violinist
Index t Wom

14483. Trumbull, Florence
flourished 1940s
pianist
Index t Wom

14484. Tsianini, Princess
flourished 1940s
singer
Native American
Index t Wom

14485. Tully, Alice
flourished 1940s
singer
Index t Wom

14486. Turner-Maley, Florence
flourished 1940s
composer, singer
Index t Wom

14487. van der Veer, Nevada
flourished 1940s
singer
Index t Wom

14488. van Kirk, Mary
flourished 1940s
singer
Index t Wom

14489. Vandevere, J. Lilian
flourished 1940s
composer, music educator
Index t Wom

14490. Vicarino, Regina
flourished 1940s
singer
Index t Wom

14491. Watson, Mabel Madison
flourished 1940s
composer, pianist, violin teacher
Index t Wom

14492. Wellerson, Mila
born 1910
cellist
Index t Wom

14493. Weston, Mildred
flourished 1940s
composer, music educator
Index t Wom

14494. Wieder, Gertrud
flourished 1940s
singer
Index t Wom

14495. Wilkins, Marie
flourished 1940s
singer
Index t Wom

14496. Williams, Irene
flourished 1940s
singer
Index t Wom

14497. Williams, Mary Lou
1910–81
composer, pianist, jazz music arranger
Cur Biog '81; Index t Wom

14498. Wing, Helen
flourished 1940s
composer, pianist, violinist
Index t Wom

14499. Wollstein, Rose R.
flourished 1940s
pianist, author, linguist
Index t Wom

14500. Wright, N. Louise
flourished 1940s
composer, pianist, music educator
Index t Wom

14501. Andrews, Laverne
1911/16–1967
popular singer
Index t Wom; Obit File

14502. Behrend, Jeanne
born 1911
pianist, composer
Index t Wom

14503. Cornett, Alice
born 1911
composer
Index t Wom

14504. Jackson, Mahalia
1911–72
gospel singer
Black
Cur Biog '72; Encyc Black Am;
Index t Wom; Negro Alman;
Not Am Wom supp v1; Obit
File; Prof Negro Wom v2

14505. Jonas, Mayla
1911–59
concert pianist
Polish
Obit File

14506. Mitchell, Viola
born 1911
violinist
Index t Wom

14507. Rahn, Muriel
1911–61
soprano singer, Broadway musical actor
New York
Black
Obit File

14508. Rockmore, Clara
born 1911
musician
Jewish
Russian
Index t Wom

14509. Smith, Julia
born 1911
composer
Index t Wom

14510. Suess, Dana Nadine
born 1911
composer, pianist, author
Index t Wom

14511. Sullivan, Maxine
born 1911
jazz singer
Black
Encyc Black Am

14512. Castagnetta, Grace
born 1912
pianist, composer
Index t Wom

14513. Colt, Ethel Barrymore
1912–77
actor, singer
Obit File

**14514. Crosby, Dixie Lee; Wil-
ma Wyatt**
1912–52
Broadway singer and dancer
Obit File

14515. Flesch, Ella
1912–57
opera and concert singer
Hungarian
Obit File

14516. Harshaw, Margaret
born circa 1912
singer
Index t Wom

14517. Lev, Ray
born 1912
pianist
Russian
Index t Wom

14518. Rogers, Dale Evans
born 1912
singer, actor, equestrian
Index t Wom

14519. Albanese, Lucia
born 1913
singer
Italian
Index t Wom

14520. Bachaeur, Gina
1913–76
pianist
Obit File

14521. Bonds, Margaret
born 1913
composer, pianist
Black
Negro Alman

14522. Browning, Lucille
born 1913
singer
Index t Wom

14523. Connor, Nadine
born 1913
singer
Index t Wom

14524. Fine, Vivian
born 1913
composer, pianist
Index t Wom

14525. Lane, Leota (Day)
1913–63
big-band and vaudeville singer
Obit File

14526. Logan, Ella
1913–69

stage and screen actor, musical
comedy actor
Scottish
Obit File

14527. Manski, Inge
born circa 1913
singer
Jewish
German
Index t Wom

14528. Martin, Mary
born 1913
actor, singer, television personality
Index t Wom

14529. Powers, Marie
1913–73
opera singer
Cur Biog '74

14530. Sherwood, Roberta
born 1913
singer
Index t Wom

14531. Stevens, Rise
born 1913
opera singer
Index t Wom

14532. Thompson, Kay
born 1913
actor, singer, author
Index t Wom

**14533. Carlisle, Kitty; Kitty
Carlisle Hart**
born 1914
actor, singer
Index t Wom

14534. Clark, Mary Gail
born 1914
composer, music educator
Index t Wom

14535. Dee, Sylvia
1914–67
author, songwriter
Index t Wom

14536. Dickenson, Jean
born 1914
singer
Canadian
Index t Wom

14537. Fenstock, Belle
born 1914
composer, pianist
Index t Wom

14538. Fort, Eleanor H.; Hank
born circa 1914
composer, author
Index t Wom

14539. Lamour, Dorothy
born 1914

actor, singer
Index t Wom

14540. Langford, Frances
born 1914
singer
Index t Wom

14541. Lowe, Ruth
born 1914
composer, pianist, author
Index t Wom

14542. Luban, Francia
born 1914
musician, songwriter, author
Russian
Index t Wom

14543. Montana, Patsy
born 1914
composer, author, musician
Index t Wom

14544. Moorehead, Jean
1914–53
musical comedy actor
Obit File

14545. Tureck, Rosalyn
born 1914
pianist
Jewish
Index t Wom

**14546. Twomey, Kathleen
"Kay"**
born 1914
author, designer, songwriter
Index t Wom

14547. Whitney, Joan
born 1914
composer, singer, music publisher, author
Index t Wom

14548. Comden, Betty
born 1915/19
author, musician, actor
Index t Wom

14549. della Chiesa, Vivian
born circa 1915
singer
Index t Wom

14550. Fisher, Doris
born 1915
composer, singer, producer, author
Index t Wom

14551. Goetschius, Marjorie
born 1915
composer, author
Index t Wom

**14552. Harkness, Rebekah
(West)**
born 1915

patron of dance, semiclassical composer, popular composer
Cur Biog '74

14553. Holiday, Eleanor Fagan (Gough) "Billie"; Lady Day
1915?–59
blues singer
Black
Dict Am Bio supp v2; Encyc Black Am; Index t Wom; Negro Alman; Not Am Wom supp v1; Obit File

14554. Simms, Virginia E. "Ginny"
born circa 1915
singer, radio personality
Index t Wom

14555. Bryner, Vera
1916–67
opera singer
Russian
Obit File

14556. Canova, Judy
born 1916
singer
Index t Wom

14557. Laufer, Beatrice
born 1916
composer
Index t Wom

14558. Morrison, Rosetta Tharpe
1916–73
gospel singer
Black
Obit File

14559. Posselt, Ruth
born 1916
violinist
Index t Wom

14560. Raye, Martha
born 1916
singer, actor, comedian, television personality
Index t Wom

14561. Steber, Eleanor
born 1916
singer
Index t Wom

14562. Arlen, Jeanne Burns
born 1917
composer, author
Index t Wom

14563. Clayton, Jan
born 1917
singer, television personality
Index t Wom

14564. Froman, Jane
born 1917

singer
Index t Wom

14565. Horne, Lena
born 1917
popular singer, actor
Black
Encyc Black Am; Index t Wom; Negro Alman

14566. Kirsten, Dorothy
born 1917/19
singer
Index t Wom

14567. Kullmer, Ann
born 1917
orchestra conductor
Index t Wom

14568. Shore, Frances Rose "Dinah"
born 1917
singer, television personality
Index t Wom

14569. Simms, Alice D.
born 1917
composer
Index t Wom

14570. Andrews, Maxine
born 1918
singer
Index t Wom

14571. Bailey, Pearl (Mae)
born 1918
singer, actor, entertainer
Black
Cur Biog '69

14572. Baker, Bonnie
born 1918
singer
Index t Wom

14573. Fitzgerald, Ella
born 1918
jazz singer, composer
Black
Encyc Black Am; Index t Wom; Negro Alman

14574. Higgenbotham, Irene
born 1918
composer, pianist
Index t Wom

14575. Madeira, Jean (Browning)
1918/24–1972
Metropolitan Opera contralto singer
Cur Biog '72; Index t Wom; Obit File

14576. McGuire, Dorothy
born 1918
actor, singer
Index t Wom

14577. Shelley, Gladys
born 1918
author, lyricist, actor
Index t Wom

14578. Stafford, Jo
born 1918
singer
Index t Wom

14579. Varnay, Astrid
born 1918
opera singer
Swedish
Index t Wom

14580. Werner, Kay
born 1918
composer, author, singer
Index t Wom

14581. Werner, Sue
born 1918
composer, author, singer
Index t Wom

14582. Bustabo, Guila
born 1919
violinist
Index t Wom

14583. Cummings, Victoria "Vicki"
1919–69
musical comedy actor, comedian
New York
Obit File

14584. Edwards, Joan
1919/20–1981
composer, author, singer, songwriter, radio and screen actor
Cur Biog '82; Index t Wom

14585. Osser, Edna
born 1919
composer
Index t Wom

14586. Thebom, Blanche
born 1919
singer
Index t Wom

14587. Brice, Carol
born 1920
singer
Black
Encyc Black Am

14588. Farrell, Eileen
born 1920
singer
Index t Wom

14589. Hale, Mary
born 1920
musician
Index t Wom

14590. Krall, Heidi
flourished 1950s

opera singer
Swiss
Index t Wom

14591. Lee, Peggy; Peggy Lee Barbour
born 1920
singer, composer, actor, businessperson
Index t Wom

14592. McPartland, Marian
flourished 1950s–70s
jazz pianist
English
Cur Biog '76

14593. Ross, Annie
flourished 1950s
jazz singer
Index t Wom

14594. Scott, Hazel Dorothy
1920–81
pianist; jazz singer; stage, screen, and musical actor
West Indian (Trinidad)
Cur Biog '81; Index t Wom

14595. Whitney, Julia; Yulya Alexandrovna Zapolskaya
1920–65
composer, musician, singer, author
Russian
Obit File

14596. Wilson, Dolores
flourished 1950s
opera singer
Index t Wom

14597. Wright, Cobina; Elaine Cobb
died 1970
cabaret singer, society columnist, journalist
Hollywood, CA
Index t Wom; Obit File

14598. Andrews, Patti
born 1921
popular singer
Index t Wom

14599. della Casa, Lisa
born 1921
singer
Swiss
Index t Wom

14600. Grayson, Kathryn
born 1921
singer, actor
Index t Wom

14601. Hillis, Margaret Eleanor
born 1921
conductor
Index t Wom

14602. Hutton, Betty
born 1921
singer
Index t Wom

14603. Lewis, Brenda
born 1921
opera singer
Jewish
Index t Wom

14604. Shay, Dorothy
1921–78
popular singer
Obit File

14605. Solovieff, Miriam
born 1921
violinist
Jewish
Index t Wom

14606. Baker, Laverne
born circa 1922
singer
Index t Wom

14607. Belle, Barbara
born 1922
composer, author
Index t Wom

14608. Curtin, Phyllis
born circa 1922
singer
Index t Wom

14609. Garland, Judy; Frances
Ethel Gumm
1922–69
singer, actor, entertainer
Cur Biog '69; Index t Wom; Not
Am Wom supp v1; Obit File

14610. Glenn, Carroll
born circa 1922
violinist
Index t Wom

14611. Johnston, Patricia
born 1922
author, songwriter
Index t Wom

14612. Leonard, Anita
born 1922
composer, author
Index t Wom

14613. Magnes, Frances
born 1922
violinist
Jewish
Index t Wom

14614. Maxwell, Marilyn
1922–72
screen actor, singer
Hollywood, CA
Index t Wom; Obit File

14615. Resnik, Regina
born 1922
opera singer
Jewish
Index t Wom

14616. Ritchie, Jean
born 1922
folksinger, folklorist, author
Index t Wom

14617. Seay, Virginia
born 1922
composer
Index t Wom

14618. Smith, Anita
born 1922
composer, author
Index t Wom

14619. Storm, Gale
born 1922/24
actor, singer, television personality
Index t Wom

14620. Benzell, Mimi
1923–70
Metropolitan Opera singer,
Broadway stage singer, night-
club singer
Index t Wom; Obit File

14621. Callas, Maria
1923/24–1977
Metropolitan Opera soprano singer
Cur Biog '77; Obit File

14622. Haines, Connie
born 1923
singer
Index t Wom

14623. Lent, Sylvia
born 1923
violinist
Index t Wom

14624. Starr, Kay
born 1923
singer
Index t Wom

14625. Truman, Margaret
[Mary]
born 1923
singer
Index t Wom

14626. Bainbridge, Katherine
born 1924
songwriter, poet
English
Index t Wom

14627. Dandridge, Dorothy
1924–61
screen actor, singer
Hollywood, CA

Black
Index t Wom; Obit File

14628. Day, Doris
born 1924
actor, singer
Index t Wom

14629. Ford, Mary
1924–77
popular singer, guitarist, codeveloper of the recording technique
of multiple harmonies
Index t Wom; Obit File

14630. Miller, Mildred
born 1924
singer
Index t Wom

14631. Nadworney, Devora
born 1924
singer
Index t Wom

14632. Sachs, Evelyn
born 1924
singer
Jewish
Index t Wom

14633. Vaughan, Sarah
born 1924
popular and jazz singer
Black
Cur Biog '80; Index t Wom; Negro Alman

14634. Washington, Dinah
1924–63
jazz and blues singer
Black
Index t Wom; Obit File

14635. Addison, Adele
born 1925
soprano singer
Black
Index t Wom; Negro Alman

14636. Bryant, Felice
born 1925
songwriter
Index t Wom

14637. Darcel, Denise
born 1925
singer, actor
French
Index t Wom

14638. Dobbs, Mattiwilda
born 1925
coloratura-soprano singer
Black
Encyc Black Am; Index t Wom;
Negro Alman

14639. Edwards, Clara
born 1925
composer, pianist, singer, author
Index t Wom

14640. Kirk, Lisa
born 1925
singer
Index t Wom

14641. Munsel, Patricia
born 1925
singer
Index t Wom

14642. Slenczynska, Ruth
born 1925
pianist
Index t Wom

14643. Ward, Clara
1925–73
gospel singer
Obit File

14644. Williams, Camilla
born 1925
soprano singer
Black
Encyc Black Am; Index t Wom

14645. Wilson, Julie
born 1925
singer
Index t Wom

14646. Ballard, Kay
born 1926
singer; stage, television, and
screen actor; comedian
Cur Biog '69; Index t Wom

14647. Fox, Carol
1926–81
producer and manager of the Chicago Opera
Chicago, IL
Cur Biog '78 and '81

14648. Hartline, Mary
born 1926
television personality, orchestra
leader
Index t Wom

14649. London, Julie
born 1926
singer
Index t Wom

14650. Morrow, Doretta (Marano)
1926–68
Broadway and Hollywood stage
and screen musical actor
Obit File

14651. Rankin, Nell
born 1926
opera singer
Index t Wom

14652. Wright, Martha
born 1926
singer, actor
Index t Wom

14653. Carson, Mindy
born 1927
singer, actor
Index t Wom

14654. Hinderas, Natalie
born 1927
concert pianist, music educator
Black
Encyc Black Am

14655. Hurley, Laurel
born 1927
singer
Index t Wom

14656. King, Coretta Scott
born 1927
singer, civil rights leader
Atlanta, GA
Black
Cur Biog '69; Encyc Black Am;
    Negro Alman

14657. MacKenzie, Gisele
born 1927
actor, singer, violinist, television
    personality
Canadian
Index t Wom

14658. Maley, Florence Turner
born 1927
composer, singer, vocal coach
Index t Wom

14659. Page, Patti
born 1927
singer, actor, television personality
Index t Wom

14660. Perry, Julia
born 1927
composer
Black
Negro Alman

14661. Price, Leontyne [Mary]
born 1927/29
Metropolitan Opera lyric-soprano
    singer
Black
Cur Biog '78; Encyc Black Am;
    Index t Wom; Negro Alman

14662. Black, Shirley Temple
born 1928
child actor, singer, UN representative
Cur Biog '70; Index t Wom

14663. Blyth, Anne
born 1928
actor, singer
Index t Wom

14664. Caldwell, Sarah
born 1928
opera director, conductor
Cur Biog '73

14665. Clooney, Rosemary
born 1928
singer
Index t Wom

14666. Francis, Connie
born 1928
singer
Index t Wom

14667. Johnson, Judy
born 1928
singer, television personality
Index t Wom

14668. Kitt, Eartha
born 1928
singer, actor, dancer
Black
Encyc Black Am; Index t Wom

14669. Musgrave, Thea
born 1928
neoclassical composer, conductor
Cur Biog '78

14670. Powell, Jane; Suzanne
    Burce
born circa 1928/29
singer, stage and screen actor
Cur Biog '74; Index t Wom

14671. Raskin, Judith
born 1928
singer
Index t Wom

14672. Stratas, Teresa
born 1928
Metropolitan Opera soprano singer
Cur Biog '80

14673. Lear, Evelyn
born 1929?
soprano opera singer
Jewish
Cur Biog '73

14674. Previn, Dory (Langan)
born 1929?
popular singer, songwriter
Cur Biog '75

14675. Sills, Beverly "Bub-
    bles"; Belle Silverman
born 1929
Metropolitan Opera singer
Jewish
Cur Biog '69

14676. Allen, Betty Lou
born 1930
mezzo-soprano singer
Black
Negro Alman

14677. Bates, Lila Curtis
flourished 1930s
pianist, poet, educator
Index t Wom

14678. Fenn, Jean
born 1930
opera singer
Index t Wom

14679. Gordon, Odetta Holmes
    Felious Gordon; Odetta
flourished 1960s–70s
singer, guitarist
Black
Index t Wom

14680. Gray, Dolores
born 1930
singer, actor
Index t Wom

14681. James, Joni
born 1930
singer
Index t Wom

14682. Martinez, Mescal
flourished 1960s
opera singer
Native American (Algonquin-
    Apache)
Ind Today

14683. Peters, Roberta
born 1930
opera singer
Index t Wom

14684. Rivera, Chita
flourished 1960s–80s
singer, dancer, stage and screen
    comedian
Puerto Rican
Index t Wom

14685. Umeki, Miyoshi
born 1930
singer, actor
Japanese
Index t Wom

14686. Bancroft, Anne
born 1931
singer, actor
Italian
Index t Wom

14687. Brewer, Theresa
born 1931
singer
Index t Wom

14688. Elias, Rosalind
born 1931
singer
Index t Wom

14689. Gorme, Eydie
born 1931/32
singer, television personality
Index t Wom

14690. King, Peggy
born 1931
singer, television personality
Index t Wom

14691. Rodgers, Mary
born 1931
composer
Index t Wom

14692. Suzuki, Pat
born 1931
singer, actor
Index t Wom

14693. Lane, Abbe
born 1932/35
singer
Index t Wom

14694. Lynn, Loretta
born 1932?
country and western singer, songwriter
Cur Biog '73

14695. Malbin, Elaine
born 1932
singer
Index t Wom

14696. Morgan, Jayne P.
born 1932
popular singer
Index t Wom

14697. Moyland, Marianne
born 1932
singer
Index t Wom

14698. Reese, Della
born 1932
popular singer, television variety
    show host
Black
Cur Biog '71; Encyc Black Am;
    Index t Wom

14699. Schuyler, Philippa Duke
1932–1967/69
pianist, composer, author, Vietnam war correspondent
Black
Encyc Black Am; Index t Wom;
    Negro Alman; Obit File

14700. Smith, Keely
born 1932
singer, comedian
Index t Wom

14701. Terry, Megan
born 1932
musical playwright, dramatist,
    television and radio scriptwriter
Dict Lit Bio v7

14702. de Gaetani, Jane; Janice
    Reutz
born 1933
classical and chamber music singer
Cur Biog '77

14703. Ono, Yoko
born 1933

modern and conceptual artist, musician
Japanese
Cur Biog '72

14704. Roxon, Lillian
1933–73
rock music authority and author
Obit File

14705. Tyler, Judy; Judy Hess
1933–57
musical comedy actor, television actor
Obit File

14706. Verrett, Shirley
circa 1933–post 1976
mezzo-soprano opera singer
Black
Index t Wom; Negro Alman

14707. Burnett, Carol
born 1934
singer; stage, screen, and television actor; comedian
Index t Wom

14708. Henderson, Florence
born 1934
stage, screen, and television actor; singer
Cur Biog '71; Index t Wom

14709. Horne, Marilyn
born 1934
opera singer
Index t Wom

14710. Lawrence, Carol
born 1934
actor, singer, dancer
Index t Wom

14711. Mills, Vicki
born 1934
singer, television personality
Index t Wom

14712. Moylan, Peggy Joan
born 1934
singer
Index t Wom

14713. Carroll, Diahann
born 1935
singer, film and stage actor
Black
Encyc Black Am; Index t Wom; Negro Alman

14714. Moffo, Anna
born circa 1935
singer
Index t Wom

14715. Simone, Nina; Eunice Kathleen Waymon
born 1935
singer, pianist, composer
Black
Negro Alman

14716. Arroyo, Martina
born 1936/39
Metropolitan Opera soprano singer
Black
Cur Biog '71; Encyc Black Am; Negro Alman

14717. O'Brien, Joan
born 1936
singer, television personality
Index t Wom

14718. Queler, Eve
born 1936
orchestra conductor, pianist
Cur Biog '72

14719. Scotto, Renata
born 1936?
Metropolitan Opera soprano singer
Cur Biog '78

14720. Bumbry, Grace
born 1937
mezzo-soprano singer
Black
Index t Wom; Negro Alman

14721. Provine, Dorothy
born 1937
dancer, singer, television personality
Index t Wom

14722. Wilson, Nancy
born 1937
singer
Index t Wom

14723. Troyanos, Tatiana
born 1938
Metropolitan Opera singer
Cur Biog '79

14724. Bryant, Hazel J.
born 1939
singer, actor, producer
Black
Encyc Black Am

14725. Collins, Judy
born 1939
folk singer, composer
Colorado
Cur Biog '69

14726. McNair, Barbara
born 1939
television and screen actor, singer
Cur Biog '71

14727. Bryant, Anita
born 1940
singer, television personality, antifeminist, antiabortion worker, antihomosexual crusader; Baptist religious worker
Baptist
Florida
Cur Biog '75

14728. Carr, Vicki; Florencia Bicenta de Casillas Martinez Cardona
born 1940
popular singer
Mexican
Dict Mex Am Hist

14729. Flack, Roberta
born 1940
popular and jazz singer, composer, musician
Black
Cur Biog '73; Negro Alman

14730. Forsyth, Josephine
born 1940
singer
Index t Wom

14731. Grist, Beri
flourished 1970s
coloratura soprano opera singer
Black
Negro Alman

14732. Lincoln, Abby
flourished 1970s
jazz singer
Black
Negro Alman

14733. Warwick, Dionne; Marie Dionne Warrick
born 1940
popular singer
Black
Cur Biog '69

14734. Baez, Joan
born 1941
folk and popular singer, anti–Vietnam war activist, pacifist, worker for Amnesty International
Mexican
Dict Mex Am Hist; Index t Wom

14735. Blegan, Judith Eyer
born 1941
Metropolitan Opera soprano singer
Cur Biog '77

14736. Elliot, Cass; Mama Cass
1941–74
popular and folk singer
Obit File

14737. King, Carole
born 1941
popular singer, songwriter
Cur Biog '74

14738. Reddy, Helen
born 1941
popular singer, feminist
Australian
Cur Biog '75

14739. Carey, Annie Louise
born 1942
singer
Index t Wom

14740. Franklin, Aretha
born 1942
popular singer
Black
Encyc Black Am; Index t Wom; Negro Alman

14741. Funicello, Annette
born 1942
singer, actor, dancer
Index t Wom

14742. Kahn, Madeline Gail
born 1942
screen actor, singer, comedian
Cur Biog '77

14743. Sainte-Marie, Beverley "Buffie"
born 1942
folk singer, composer
Native American (Cree)
Cur Biog '69; Ind Today

14744. Streisand, Barbra
born 1942
singer, actor
Index t Wom

14745. Joplin, Janis Lyn
1943–70
rock and blues singer
Cur Biog '70; Not Am Wom supp v1; Obit File

14746. Mitchell, Joni; Roberta Joan Anderson
born 1943
popular singer, songwriter
California
Cur Biog '76

14747. Uggams, Leslie
born 1943
singer, actor
Black
Index t Wom; Negro Alman

14748. Ballard, Florence
1944–76
popular singer
Black
Obit File

14749. Lee, Brenda
born 1944
singer
Index t Wom

14750. Richter, Ada
born 1944
composer, educator, lecturer
Index t Wom

14751. Ross, Diana
born 1944
popular singer, actor, entertainer

Black
Cur Biog '73; Encyc Black Am;
  Negro Alman

14752. Midler, Bette
born 1945?
popular singer, actor, comedian
Jewish
Cur Biog '73

14753. Moore, Beatrice "Melba"
born 1945
stage and television actor, singer
Black
Cur Biog '73; Negro Alman

14754. Norman, Jessy
born 1945
soprano opera singer
Black
Cur Biog '76

14755. Simon, Carly
born 1945
popular singer, songwriter
Cur Biog '76

14756. von Stade, Frederica
born 1945
mezzo-soprano opera and concert
  singer
Cur Biog '77

14757. Bassey, Shirley
flourished 1976
jazz singer
Black
Negro Alman

14758. Bono, Cherilyn (Lapiere); Cher
born 1946
popular singer, actor, television
  entertainer
California
Native American (Cherokee)
Cur Biog '74

14759. Harry, Deborah
born 1946?
New Wave singer
Cur Biog '81

14760. Minelli, Liza May
born 1946
stage and screen actor, singer
Cur Biog '70

14761. Parton, Dolly Rebecca
born 1946
country music singer, songwriter,
  screen actor
Native American (Cherokee)
Cur Biog '77

14762. Rondstadt, Linda
born 1946
popular and country music singer
Los Angeles, CA
Mexican
Cur Biog '78; Dict Mex Am Hist

14763. Te Kanawa, Kiri
born 1946?
Metropolitan Opera mezzo-soprano singer
New Zealand; Maori
Cur Biog '78

**14764. Terrell, Tammi; Tammy
  Montgomery**
1946–70
rhythm and blues singer
Obit File

14765. Dale, Clemma
born 1948
soprano opera singer
Black
Cur Biog '79

14766. Summer, Donna
born 1948
disco singer
Black
Cur Biog '79

**14767. Breen, May Sighi; Malia
  Rosa**
born 1949
composer, author
Index t Wom

14768. Swados, Elizabeth
born 1951
play score writer, avant-garde
  composer, theatrical director,
  playwright
Jewish
New York
Cur Biog '79

No Dates

14769. Aborn, Lora
composer
Index t Wom

14770. Becker, Angela
pianist, composer, music educator, organist
Index t Wom

14771. Breton, Ruth
violinist
Index t Wom

14772. Briggs, Cora S.
composer, organist, music educator
Index t Wom

14773. Briggs, Dorothy Bell
composer
Index t Wom

14774. Bristol, Margaret
composer, singer, conductor, music educator, writer on music
Index t Wom

14775. Brooks, Rosa Paul
librettist
Index t Wom

14776. Broughton, Julia
organist, music educator
Index t Wom

14777. Bush, Grace
composer, pianist, poet, lecturer
Index t Wom

14778. Carter, Artie Mason
musician, patron of music
Index t Wom

14779. Graudan, Joanna Freudberg
pianist
Jewish
Russian
Index t Wom

14780. Patti-Brown, Anita
singer
Black
Index t Wom

14781. Williams, Frances
composer
Welsh
Index t Wom

ORATORY

**14782. Drummond, Sarah
  Prescott**
flourished 1670s
patriot, politician, lecturer
Cyc Am Bio; Index t Wom

14783. Gardner, Anna
flourished 1770s–80s
lecturer, poet
Index t Wom

14784. Flintham, Lydia Stirling
flourished 1780s–90s
author, lecturer
Index t Wom

**14785. Sampson, Deborah;
  Robert Shirtliffe; Deborah
  Gannett**
1760–1827
soldier and hero of American
  Revolution, lecturer
Massachusetts
Am Bio Dict; Cyc Am Bio; Dict
  Am Bio Men Time; Index t
  Wom; Nat Cyc Am Bio v8; Not
  Am Wom

**14786. Truth, Sojourner; Isabel
  Baumfree**
1775/97–1883/85
social reformer, abolitionist, feminist, lecturer, temperance writer

Black
Cyc Am Bio; Dict Am Rel Bio;
  Encyc Black Am; Index t Wom;
  Negro Alman; Not Am Wom;
  Prof Negro Wom v1

14787. Grimke, Sarah Moore
1792/93–1873
abolitionist, women's rights worker, writer on social problems,
  political author, lecturer
Quaker
Cyc Am Bio; Dict Am Auth; Dict
  Am Bio; Dict Am Rel Bio;
  Index t Wom; Nat Cyc Am Bio
  v2; Twent Cen Bio Dict Not
  Am; Wom Cent

**14788. Wright, Frances
  (d'Arusmont) "Fanny"; Fanny
  d'Arusmont**
1795–1852
author, abolitionist, feminist, philanthropist, lecturer
Scottish
Am Bio Dict; Cyc Am Bio; Dict
  Am Bio; Dict Am Bio Men
  Time; Index t Wom; Nat Cyc
  Am Bio v2; Not Am Wom

14789. Foster, Mabel G.
born 18?
author, lecturer
Boston, MA
Dict Am Auth

14790. Grove, Mary
flourished 1830s
lecturer, physiologist
Index t Wom

**14791. Stewart, Maria
  [Frances] W. Miller**
1803–79
educator, lecturer, social reformer
Black
Index t Wom; Not Am Wom

**14792. Grimke, Angelina Emily; Angelina Emily Grimke
  Weld**
1805/38–1879
abolitionist, feminist, lecturer
Quaker
Cyc Am Bio; Dict Am Auth; Dict
  Am Rel Bio; Index t Wom; Nat
  Cyc Am Bio v2; Twent Cen Bio
  Dict Not Am

14793. Hunt, Harriot Keziah
1805–75
physician, social reformer, suffragist, lecturer
Boston, MA
Cyc Am Bio; Dict Am Auth; Dict
  Am Bio; Index t Wom; Nat Cyc
  Am Bio v9; Not Am Wom;
  Twent Cen Bio Dict Not Am

**14794. Smith, Elizabeth Oakes
  (Prince)**
1806–93

poet, novelist, lecturer, suffragist, women's rights worker, feminist
Cyc Am Bio; Dict Am Auth; Dict Am Bio; Dict Am Bio Men Time; Dict Lit Bio v1; Index t Wom; Nat Cyc Am Bio v9; Not Am Wom; Twent Cen Bio Dict Not Am; Wom Cent; Wom Lit, More

14795. Gage, Frances Dana (Barker); Aunt Fanny
1808–84
lecturer, author, temperance worker, abolitionist, suffragist, women's rights worker, Civil War relief worker
Cyc Am Bio; Dict Am Auth; Dict Am Bio; Dict Am Bio Men Time; Index t Wom; Nat Cyc Am Bio v2; Not Am Wom; Twent Cen Bio Dict Not Am; Wom Cent

14796. Doolittle, Mary Antoinette
1810–86
lecturer on religious subjects, Shaker eldress, author
Shaker
New York
Cyc Am Bio

14797. Foster, Abigail (Kelley) "Abby"
1810/11–1887
abolitionist, feminist, Prohibitionist, lecturer, suffragist, temperance worker
Quaker
Cyc Am Bio; Dict Am Bio; Index t Wom; Nat Cyc Am Bio v2; Not Am Wom; Twent Cen Bio Dict Not Am

14798. Nichols, Clarinda Irene Howard
1810–85
newspaper editor, political writer, social reformer, lecturer, women's rights leader, suffragist, feminist
Kansas
Cyc Am Bio; Dict Am Bio; Index t Wom; Nat Cyc Am Bio v5; Not Am Wom

14799. Bacon, Delia Salter
1811–95
author, lecturer, originator of the Bacon/Shakespeare theory
Appl Cyc Am Bio; Cyc Am Bio; Dict Am Bio; Dict Am Bio; Dict Lit Bio v1; Index t Wom; Nat Cyc Am Bio v1; Not Am Wom; Twent Cen Bio Dict Not Am

14800. Davis, Pauline Kellog Wright
1813–76

feminist, women's rights worker, suffragist, abolitionist, temperance worker, journalist, editor, lecturer
Cyc Am Bio; Dict Am Bio; Index t Wom; Nat Cyc Am Bio v22; Not Am Wom

14801. Grew, Mary
1813–96
abolitionist, suffragist, feminist, Unitarian preacher, lecturer
Unitarian
Index t Wom; Not Am Wom; Wom Cent

14802. Jones, Jane Elizabeth Hitchcock
1813–96
antislavery and women's rights advocate, lecturer
Index t Wom; Not Am Wom

14803. Wells, Charlotte Fowler
1814–1901
phrenologist, patron of women's medical education, educator, publisher, lecturer, businessperson
New York
Cyc Am Bio; Index t Wom; Not Am Wom; Wom Cent

14804. Cutler, Hannah Maria (Conant) (Tracy)
1815–96
women's rights leader, suffragist, physician, journalist, author, lecturer, pacifist
Illinois
Cyc Am Bio ad; Dict Am Auth; Index t Wom; Not Am Wom; Twent Cen Bio Dict Not Am

14805. Farnham, Eliza Woodson (Burhans)
1815–64
prison reformer, author, lecturer, feminist, suffragist, philanthropist
New York; California
Cyc Am Bio; Dict Am Auth; Dict Am Bio; Dict Am Bio Men Time; Index t Wom; Nat Cyc Am Bio v4; Not Am Wom; Twent Cen Bio Dict Not Am

14806. Phelps, Elizabeth Wooster (Stuart); H. Trusta
1815–1852/53
novelist, lecturer
Am Bio Dict; Cyc Am Bio; Dict Am Auth; Dict Am Bio Men Time; Index t Wom; Nat Cyc Am Bio v9; Not Am Wom; Twent Cen Bio Dict Not Am

14807. Remond, Sarah Parker
1815/26–post 1887
abolitionist, antislavery lecturer, physician

Black
Negro Alman; Not Am Wom; Prof Negro Wom v1

14808. Tillotson, Mary Ella (Tillotson)
1816–190?
writer and lecturer on hygiene, poet
Vineland, NJ
Dict Am Auth

14809. Coleman, Lucy Newhall; Lucy Colman
1817–1906
abolitionist, educator of Blacks, women's rights worker, suffragist, lecturer, health reformer
Universalist
Dict Am Bio; Nat Cyc Am Bio v4, Wom Cent

14810. de Kroyft, Sarah Susan Helen (Aldrich)
1818–1915
author, lecturer
New York
blind
Cyc Am Bio; Dict Am Auth; Index t Wom; Nat Cyc Am Bio v11

14811. Holley, Sallie
1818–93
abolitionist, educator of freedmen, feminist, lecturer
Index t Wom; Not Am Wom

14812. Stone, Lucy; Mrs. Henry Brown Blackwell
1818–93
feminist, suffragist, women's rights worker, abolitionist, social reformer, editor, lecturer
Massachusetts
Cyc Am Bio; Dict Am Bio; Dict Am Bio Men Time; Index t Wom; Nat Cyc Am Bio v2 and v29; Not Am Wom; Twent Cen Bio Dict Not Am; Wom Cent

14813. Cutter, Eunice Powers
1819–93
lecturer, health reformer, abolitionist, historian
Twent Cen Bio Dict Not Am

14814. Howe, Julia Ward
1819–1910
poet, dramatist, songwriter, lecturer, suffrage and women's club leader, feminist, abolitionist, pacifist, prison reformer, Union patriot during the Civil War, philanthropist, traveler
Boston, MA
Cyc Am Bio; Dict Am Auth; Dict Am Bio; Dict Am Bio Men Time; Dict Lit Bio v1; Index t Wom; Nat Cyc Am Bio v1; Not Am Wom; Twent Cen Bio Dict Not Am; Wom Cent

14815. Coe, Emma Robinson
flourished 1850s–60s
lawyer, feminist, lecturer
Index t Wom

14816. Jenkins, Lydia A.
flourished 1850s
clergyperson, feminist, lecturer
Index t Wom

14817. Thomas, Mary
flourished 1850s
lecturer
Index t Wom

14818. Tubman, Harriet Ross
1820/26–1913
hero of the Underground Railroad, liberator of slaves, abolitionist, Union spy during the Civil War, Civil War nurse, lecturer
Black
Cyc Am Bio; Dict Am Bio; Encyc Black Am; Encyc South Hist; Index t Wom; Nat Cyc Am Bio v9; Negro Alman; Not Am Wom; Prof Negro Wom v1

14819. Diaz, Abby (Morton)
1821–1904
author, children's author, essayist, social reformer, suffragist, abolitionist, lecturer
Boston, MA
Dict Am Auth; Nat Cyc Am Bio v11; Not Am Wom; Twent Cen Bio Dict Not Am; Wom Cent

14820. Richards, Maria Tolman
born 1821
author, educator, lecturer
Providence, RI
Cyc Am Bio; Dict Am Auth

14821. Fowler, Lydia Folger
1822/23–1979
physician, lecturer, social reformer, author, astronomer, science writer
Cyc Am Bio; Dict Am Auth; Index t Wom; Not Am Wom

14822. Hooker, Isabella Beecher
1822–1907
suffragist, feminist, philanthropist, lecturer, essayist
Spiritualist
Hartford, CT
Cyc Am Bio; Dict Am Auth; Dict Am Bio; Index t Wom; Not Am Wom; Twent Cen Bio Dict Not Am; Wom Cent

14823. Kemp, Agnes Nininger
born 1823
physician, abolitionist, temperance worker, lecturer
Wom Cent

14824. Lippincott, Sarah Jane (Clarke); Grace Greenwood
1823–1904
newspaper journalist, lecturer, author, editor, novelist, feminist, poet, children's author
Philadelphia, PA
Cyc Am Bio; Dict Am Auth; Dict Am Bio; Dict Am Bio Men Time; Index t Wom; Nat Cyc Am Bio v4; Not Am Wom; Twent Cen Bio Dict Not Am; Wom Cent

14825. Cheney, Endah Dow (Littlehale)
1824–1904
philanthropist, author, abolitionist, suffragist, women's rights worker, Black civil rights worker, lecturer, philosopher
Transcendentalist
Boston, MA
Cyc Am Bio; Dict Am Auth; Dict Am Bio; Dict Lit Bio v1; Index t Wom; Nat Cyc Am Bio v9; Not Am Wom; Twent Cen Bio Dict Not Am; Wom Cent

14826. Davis, Mary Fenn
1824–86
Spiritualist lecturer, reformer
Spiritualist
Not Am Wom

14827. Ketchum, Annie Chambers
1824–1904
poet, novelist, educator, lecturer
Cyc Am Bio; Dict Am Auth

14828. Perkins, Sarah Maria Clinton
born 1824
lecturer, clergyperson, temperance worker, suffragist
Index t Wom; Wom Cent

14829. Soule, Caroline Augusta (White)
1824–1903/04
author, publisher, editor, church worker, Universalist minister, foreign missionary, social reformer, lecturer
Universalist
Cyc Am Bio; Dict Am Auth; Dict Am Bio Men Time; Index t Wom; Not Am Wom; Twent Cen Bio Dict Not Am

14830. Starr, Eliza Allen
1824–1901
writer and lecturer on art and religion, poet, author, artist, educator
Chicago, IL
Cyc Am Bio; Dict Am Auth; Dict Am Bio; Nat Cyc Am Bio v13; Not Am Wom; Twent Cen Bio Dict Not Am; Wom Cent

14831. Walton, Electa Noble Lincoln
born 1824
educator, lecturer, suffragist, feminist
Massachusetts
Wom Cent

14832. Adsit, Mary H.
born 1825
art lecturer
Wom Cent

14833. Blackwell, Antoinette Louisa (Brown)
1825–1921
Universalist minister, author, lecturer, temperance worker, abolitionist, suffragist, women's rights worker, philosopher, poet, novelist
Unitarian; Congregationalist
Appl Cyc Am Bio; Cyc Am Bio; Dict Am Bio; Dict Am Bio Men Time; Index t Wom; Nat Cyc Am Bio v9 and v29; Not Am Wom; Twent Cen Bio Dict Not Am; Wom Cent

14834. Harper, Frances Ellen Watkins
1825–1911
poet, lecturer, author, abolitionist
Black
Dict Am Rel Bio; Encyc Black Am; Index t Wom; Negro Alman; Not Am Wom; Prof Negro Wom v1

14835. Craft, Ellen
circa 1826–circa 1897
fugitive slave, abolitionist, lecturer
Black
Index t Wom; Not Am Wom

14836. Gage, Matilda Joslyn
1826–98
feminist, suffragist, abolitionist, author, lecturer
Cyc Am Bio; Dict Am Auth; Dict Am Bio; Index t Wom; Nat Cyc Am Bio v2; Not Am Wom; Twent Cen Bio Dict Not Am; Wom Cent

14837. Gorton, Cynthia M. R.; Ida Glenwood; The Sweet Singer; The Blind Bard of Michigan
born 1826
poet, author, lecturer
Michigan
blind
Wom Cent

14838. Rice, Rosella; Pipsissiway Pobbs
1827–18?
author, lecturer, novelist
Cyc Am Bio; Dict Am Auth; Nat Cyc Am Bio v5

14839. Wittenmyer, Annie (Turner)
1827–1900
Civil War relief worker, leader in church and charitable work, philanthropist, temperance worker, lecturer, author
Ohio
Index t Wom; Nat Cyc Am Bio v12; Not Am Wom; Wom Cent

14840. Cleveland, Emeline Horton
1829–78
surgeon, medical educator, lecturer
Index t Wom; Not Am Wom

14841. Hanaford, Phoebe Ann (Coffin)
1829–1921
Universalist minister, historian, journalist, author, feminist, lecturer, chaplain of the Connecticut state legislature
Universalist
New Haven, CT
Cyc Am Bio; Dict Am Auth; Dict Am Bio; Index t Wom; Nat Cyc Am Bio v13; Not Am Wom; Twent Cen Bio Dict Not Am; Wom Cent

14842. Meriwether, Lide
born 1829
author, lecturer, temperance worker, suffragist
Tennessee
Wom Cent

14843. Potts, Anna M. Longshore
born 1829
physician, medical lecturer
Quaker
Index t Wom; Wom Cent

14844. Warren, Mary Evalin
born 1829
author, lecturer, temperance worker, suffragist
Baptist
Wisconsin
Wom Cent

14845. Benton, Mrs.
flourished 1860s
missionary, lecturer
Index t Wom

14846. Conner, Eliza Archard; "Zig"; E. A.
flourished 1860s–80s
journalist, lecturer, women's rights worker
New York
Wom Cent

14847. Couzzins, Adaline
flourished 1860s
humanitarian, lecturer
Index t Wom

14848. Benton, Louisa Dow
born 1831
linguist, lecturer
Index t Wom; Wom Cent

14849. Ripley, Mary A.
born 1831
poet, educator, lecturer, author
Index t Wom; Wom Cent

14850. Saxon, Elizabeth Lyle
1832–1915
suffragist, temperance worker, lecturer
Congregationalist
Memphis, TN
Nat Cyc Am Bio v16; Wom Cent

14851. Walker, Mary Edwards
1832–1919
physician, Civil War medical worker, hospital founder, army war surgeon, Union spy during the Civil War; women's rights worker, suffragist, dress reformer, inventor, lecturer, winner of the Congressional Medal of Honor
Dict Am Bio; Index t Wom; Nat Cyc Am Bio v13; Not Am Wom; Wom Cent

14852. Wilbour, Charlotte Beebee
1833–1914
women's rights worker, dress reformer, lecturer, president of Sorosis
Cyc Am Bio and ad; Index t Wom; Nat Cyc Am Bio v13

14853. Duniway, Abigail Jane Scott
1834–1915
pioneer, suffrage leader, feminist, journalist, editor, lecturer
Oregon
Dict Am Bio; Index t Wom; Not Am Wom; Wom Cent

14854. Willing, Jennie Fowler
1834–1916
Methodist local preacher, church worker, temperance reformer, lecturer, author, educator
Methodist
Canadian
Index t Wom; Not Am Wom; Wom Cent

14855. Bristol, Augusta (Cooper)
1835–1910
educator, writer on education, author, poet, sociologist, lecturer on philosophic and scientific topics
Cyc Am Bio and ad; Dict Am Auth; Twent Cen Bio Dict Not Am; Wom Cent

14856. Brown, Olympia; Mrs. John H. Willis
1835–1926
Universalist minister, suffragist, lecturer, feminist
Universalist; Unitarian
Cyc Am Bio and ad; Dict Am Bio; Index t Wom; Nat Cyc Am Bio v20; Not Am Wom; Wom Cent; Index t Wom

14857. Coppin, Fanny Marion Jackson
1835/37–1912/18
educator, foreign missionary, social worker, lecturer, women's rights worker
Black
Encyc Black Am; Index t Wom; Negro Alman; Not Am Wom; Prof Negro Wom

14858. Felton, Rebecca Ann Latimer
1835–1930
senator from Georgia, labor welfare worker, journalist, author, orator, feminist, women's rights worker
Georgia
Dict Am Bio; Encyc South Hist; Index t Wom; Nat Cyc Am Bio v13 and v36; Not Am Wom; Wom Cent

14859. Chapin, Augusta Jane
1836–1905
Universalist minister, lecturer
Universalist
Index t Wom; Not Am Wom; Wom Cent

14860. Reignolds, Catherine Mary "Kate"
1836–1911
actor, dramatic reader, educator
Not Am Wom

14861. Mountcastle, Clara H.
born 1837
author, elocutionist
Canadian
Cyc Am Bio; Wom Cent

14862. Newman, Angelia Louise French Thurston
1837–1910
church worker, missionary, Mormon women's relief worker, lecturer, reformer
Mormon
Utah
Index t Wom; Not Am Wom; Wom Cent

14863. Richardson, Abby (Sage)
1837–1900

author, actor, historian, lecturer on history, writer on literature, educator
Dict Am Auth; Index t Wom; Nat Cyc Am Bio v5; Twent Cen Bio Dict Not Am

14864. Brown, Martha McClellen
1838–1916
founder of the Prohibition party, temperance reformer, suffragist, lecturer
Methodist
Ohio
Index t Wom; Nat Cyc Am Bio v27; Not Am Wom; Wom Cent

14865. Field, Mary Katherine Kemble "Kate"
1838/54–1896
journalist, actor, playwright, literary critic, lecturer
Washington, DC
Cyc Am Bio; Dict Am Auth; Dict Am Bio; Index t Wom; Nat Cyc Am Bio v6; Not Am Wom; Twent Cen Bio Dict Not Am; Wom Cent

14866. Gordon, Laura de Force
1838/40–1907
lawyer, journalist, suffragist, women's rights worker, Democratic politician, orator
California
Dict Am Bio; Index t Wom; Nat Cyc Am Bio v1; Not Am Wom; Wom Cent

14867. Nichols, Josephine Ralston
born 1838
lecturer, temperance reformer
Wom Cent

14868. Shoemaker, Rachel H.
born 1838
dramatic elocutionist, Shakespearean reciter
Wom Cent

14869. Walling, Mary Cole; The Banished Heroine of the South
born 1838
lecturer, Union patriot during the Civil War
Texas
Index t Wom; Wom Cent

14870. Woolson, Abba Louisa (Goold)
1838–1921
educator, author, lecturer, dress reformer
Boston, MA
Cyc Am Bio; Dict Am Auth; Dict Am Bio; Index t Wom; Nat Cyc Am Bio v9; Not Am Wom; Wom Cent

14871. Freeman, Mattie A.
born 1839
abolitionist, suffragist, women's rights worker, lecturer, journalist
Chicago, IL
Wom Cent

14872. Graves, Mary H.
born 1839
Unitarian minister, author, lecturer
Unitarian
Index t Wom; Wom Cent

14873. Logan, Olive
1839/41–1909
actor, dramatist, lecturer, women's rights reformer, author, journalist
Cyc Am Bio; Dict Am Bio; Dict Am Bio Men Time; Index t Wom; Nat Cyc Am Bio v6; Not Am Wom; Twent Cen Bio Dict Not Am

14874. Palmer, Frances Purdy "Fannie"
1839–1923
author, journalist, lecturer, suffragist, feminist
Providence, RI
Dict Am Auth; Index t Wom; Wom Cent

14875. Sanborn, Katharine Abbott "Kate"
1839–1917
miscellaneous author, educator, lecturer, essayist, literary professor, agriculturist
New Hampshire
Cyc Am Bio; Dict Am Auth; Dict Am Bio; Index t Wom; Nat Cyc Am Bio v9; Twent Cen Bio Dict Not Am

14876. Sunderland, Eliza Jane (Read)
1839–1910
lecturer, author, educator, temperance worker, women's rights worker, philosopher
Universalist
Michigan
Dict Am Bio; Nat Cyc Am Bio v10; Wom Cent

14877. Tuttle, Emma Rood
born 1839/59
author, poet, lecturer
Berlin Heights, OH
Cyc Am Bio; Dict Am Auth; Wom Cent

14878. Callanan, Mrs.
flourished 1870s–80s
lecturer, feminist
Index t Wom

14879. Churchill, Elizabeth K.
flourished 1870s–80s

lecturer
Index t Wom

14880. Clark, Mary S.
flourished 1870s–80s
lecturer
Index t Wom

14881. Cole, Miriam M.
flourished 1870s–80s
lecturer, feminist, author, journalist
Index t Wom

14882. Cowell, S. Emma
flourished 1870s–80s
dramatic reader
Index t Wom

14883. Foss, Louise Woodworth
flourished 1870s–80s
orator
Index t Wom

14884. Foster, Judith Ellen (Horton)
1840–1910
temperance leader, lawyer, Republican party worker, Prohibitionist, suffragist, political writer, lecturer
Iowa
Cyc Am Bio; Dict Am Auth; Dict Am Bio; Index t Wom; Nat Cyc Am Bio v22; Not Am Wom; Twent Cen Bio Dict Not Am; Wom Cent

14885. French, Anna Densmore
flourished 1870s–80s
lecturer
Index t Wom

14886. Hawes, Charlotte W.
flourished 1870s–80s
composer, lecturer, music educator
Wom Cent

14887. Hoyt, Deristha Lavinta
born 184?
lecturer on the history of painting, writer on art
Massachusetts
Dict Am Auth

14888. Imen, Loraine
born 1840
elocutionist, clubwoman
Wom Cent

14889. O'Keefe, Katharine A.
flourished 1870s–90s
educator, lecturer
Massachusetts
Irish
Wom Cent

14890. Pollard, Marie Antoinette Nathalie Granier-Dowell
flourished 1870s

lecturer, temperance reformer, political activist
Cyc Am Bio

14891. Stetson, Martha A.
flourished 1870s–80s
lecturer
Index t Wom

14892. Stevens, E. Hebert, Mrs.
flourished 1870s–1910s
agricultural librarian, lecturer
Washington, DC
Index t Wom; Wom Cent

14893. Stoddard, Dora V.
flourished 1870s
lecturer
Index t Wom

14894. Strickland, S. E.
flourished 1870s
feminist, lecturer, educator
Index t Wom

14895. Wakefield, Emily Watkins
flourished 1870s–90s
singer, educator, lecturer, musical director
Pennsylvania
English
Wom Cent

14896. Allen, Mary Wood
born 1841
physician, author, lecturer
Black
Negro Alman

14897. McAvoy, Emma
born 1841
author, lecturer
Ohio
Wom Cent

14898. Moore, Annie Aubertine (Woodward); Aubertine Forestier
1841–1929
pianist, student of Scandinavian music, music critic, lecturer, author, translator of Scandinavian languages
Dict Am Auth; Dict Am Bio; Index t Wom; Twent Cen Bio Dict Not Am; Wom Cent

14899. Sikes, Olive (Logan)
born 1841
actor, lecturer, author, novelist, autobiographer
Dict Am Auth

14900. Todd, Marion Marsh
1841–post 1913
lawyer, Greenback party worker, political economist, labor leader, author, lecturer
Not Am Wom; Wom Cent

14901. Custer, Elizabeth Bacon
1842–1933
author, western pioneer, lecturer on frontier life
Cyc Am Bio; Dict Am Auth; Index t Wom; Wom Cent

14902. Dare, Ella
born 1842
lecturer, journalist, Civil War relief worker, sanitarian
Wom Cent

14903. Dickinson, Anna Elizabeth
1842–1932
Civil War orator, lyceum lecturer, abolitionist, women's rights worker, suffragist, political activist, Republican party worker, author, actor, philanthropist
Quaker
Cyc Am Bio; Dict Am Auth; Dict Am Bio supp v1; Dict Am Bio Men Time; Index t Wom; Nat Cyc Am Bio v3; Not Am Wom; Twent Cen Bio Dict Not Am; Wom Cent

14904. Monroe, Harriet Earhart
born 1842
lecturer, educator, journalist
Kansas; Washington, DC
Dict Am Auth; Wom Cent

14905. Watson, Elizabeth Lowe
born 1842
lecturer, pastor of the San Francisco Religious and Philosophical Society, fruit farmer
California
Wom Cent

14906. Boyd, Belle; Belle Hardinge
1843/44–1900
Confederate spy, actor, lecturer
Episcopalian
Bio Dict Confed; Dict Am Bio; Index t Wom; Not Am Wom

14907. Gougar, Helen Mar Jackson
1843–1907
suffrage and temperance reformer, orator, author
Index t Wom; Not Am Wom; Wom Cent

14908. Harbert, Elizabeth Boynton "Lizzie"
born 1843
author, lecturer, suffragist
Index t Wom; Wom Cent

14909. Parloa, Maria
1843–1909

home economics educator, writer on cooking and domestic economy, lecturer
Dict Am Auth; Index t Wom; Not Am Wom

14910. Pickett, Lasalle Carbell
born 1843
Civil War patriot, hero, diarist, lecturer
Index t Wom; Wom Cent

14911. Howell, Mary Seymour
born 1844
lecturer, suffragist
New York
Wom Cent

14912. Lincoln, Mary Johnson (Bailey)
1844–1921
educator, writer and lecturer on cookery, culinary educator, home economist
Boston, MA
Dict Am Auth; Dict Am Bio; Index t Wom; Nat Cyc Am Bio v24; Not Am Wom

14913. Loud, Hulda Barker
born 1844
editor, publisher, women's rights worker, suffragist, labor worker, lecturer
Index t Wom; Wom Cent

14914. Orum, Julia Anna
born 1844
educator, elocutionist
Pennsylvania
Wom Cent

14915. Phelps, Elizabeth Stuart; Mrs. Ward
1844–1911
author, lecturer, women's rights worker, temperance worker
Cyc Am Bio and ad; Dict Am Bio Men Time

14916. Preston, Frances E. L.
1844–1929
temperance lecturer, organist, elocutionist
Black
Negro Alman; Prof Negro Wom v1

14917. Stevens, Lillian Marion Norton Ames
1844–1914
temperance reformer, women's rights worker, lecturer, philanthropist
Maine
Index t Wom; Nat Cyc Am Bio v13; Not Am Wom; Wom Cent

14918. Young, Ann Eliza Webb
1844–post 1908

lecturer and writer against Mormon polygamy, feminist, religious worker, pioneer
Index t Wom; Not Am Wom

14919. Bailey, Lepha Eliza (Dunton)
born 1845
temperance worker, Prohibitionist, suffragist, lecturer, author
Wom Cent

14920. Brown, Hallie Quinn
1845/50–1949
educator, elocutionist, lecturer, Black women's leader
Index t Wom; Negro Alman; Not Am Wom; Prof Negro Wom v1

14921. Hall, Florence Marion Howe
1845–1922
author, essayist, writer on etiquette, lecturer, suffragist
Unitarian
Plainfield, NJ
Dict Am Auth; Dict Am Bio; Nat Cyc Am Bio v19

14922. Noble, Edna Chaffee
born 1846
educator, elocutionist
Michigan
Index t Wom; Wom Cent

14923. Stone, Ellen Maria
1846–1927
missionary, temperance worker, lecturer
Dict Am Bio

14924. Shaw, Anna Howard
1847–1919
minister, lecturer, suffragist, women's rights worker, physician, temperance worker
Methodist
English
Dict Am Bio; Index t Wom; Nat Cyc Am Bio v14; Not Am Wom; Wom Cent

14925. Diggs, Annie le Porte
1848/53–1916
Populist party leader, orator, politician, social reformer, temperance worker, journalist
Unitarian
Kansas
Canadian
Not Am Wom; Read Encyc Am West; Wom Cent

14926. Gould, Elizabeth Porter
born 1848
author, essayist on education, journalist, lecturer, social critic
Wom Cent

14927. Mee, Cassie Ward
born 1848

labor leader, Knights of Labor worker, temperance worker, lecturer
Quaker
Canadian
Index t Wom; Wom Cent

14928. Barry, Leonore Marie Kearney
1849–1930
labor organizer, lecturer
Not Am Wom

14929. Bigelow, Lettie Salina
born 1849
poet, author, lecturer
Nat Cyc Am Bio v6; Wom Cent

14930. Devoe, Emma Smith
born 1849
suffragist, lecturer
South Dakota
Wom Cent

14931. Foltz, Clara Shortridge; The Portia of the Pacific
1849–1934
lawyer, political activist, women's rights worker, suffragist, newspaper publisher, orator
California
Cyc Am Bio; Nat Cyc Am Bio csv3; Not Am Wom; Twent Cen Bio Dict Not Am; Wom Cent

14932. Moore, Marguerite
born 1849
orator, patriot, pacifist
Irish
Wom Cent

14933. Tuttle, Mary McArthur (Thompson)
born 1849/59
artist, writer and lecturer on art, art historian, novelist
Methodist
Dict Am Bio; Nat Cyc Am Bio v10

14934. Baxter, Marion Babcock
born 1850
temperance worker, lecturer
Twent Cen Bio Dict Not Am; Wom Cent

14935. Beauchamp, Frances E.
flourished 1880s
social reformer, lecturer
Index t Wom

14936. Burke, B. Ellen
born 1850
educator, lecturer, editor, publisher
Index t Wom

14937. Collins, Laura Sedgwick
flourished 1880s–90s
actor, musician, composer, pianist, dancer, dramatic reader
Wom Cent

14938. Deforrest, Jane O.
flourished 1880s
lecturer
Index t Wom

14939. Eastman, Mary F.
flourished 1880s
lecturer
Index t Wom

14940. Jenkins, Helen P.
flourished 1880s
lecturer
Index t Wom

14941. Kingsbury, Elizabeth A.
flourished 1880s
lecturer, poet
Index t Wom

14942. Lease, Mary Elizabeth (Clyens)
1850/53–1933
Populist orator, politician, Prohibition party worker, suffragist, evolutionist, birth control advocate, feminist, political author
Kansas
Dict Am Auth; Dict Am Bio supp v1; Index t Wom; Not Am Wom; Read Encyc Am West

14943. Lozier, Jennie de la Montagnie
born 1850
physician, president of Sorosis, clubwoman
Index t Wom; Nat Cyc Am Bio v13; Wom Cent

14944. Lyman, Walter C., Mrs.
flourished 1880s
lecturer
Index t Wom

14945. McComas, Alice Moore
born 1850
author, editor, lecturer, suffragist
Wom Cent

14946. Peck, Annie Smith
1850–1933/35
mountain climber, musician, archaeologist, lecturer, educator
Rhode Island
Index t Wom; Nat Cyc Am Bio v15; Not Am Wom; Wom Cent

14947. Wood, Frances Fisher
flourished 1880s–90s
educator, lecturer, scientist, dress reformer, dairy farmer, businessperson
Wom Cent

14948. Clark, Katharine Pickens (Upson)
1851–1935

children's author, journalist, suffragist, temperance worker, lecturer
Dict Am Auth; Nat Cyc Am Bio v30

14949. Gause, Nora Trueblood
born 1851
humane worker, lecturer
Indiana
Wom Cent

14950. Morgan, Anna
1851–1936
speech teacher, drama coach, elocutionist
Chicago, IL
Nat Cyc Am Bio v17; Not Am Wom

14951. Safford, Mary Augusta
born 1851
Unitarian minister, lecturer, suffragist, philanthropist
Unitarian

Index t Wom; Nat Cyc Am Bio v14

14952. Davidson, Hannah Amelia
1852–1919
author of study guides, educator, editor, lecturer, publisher
Index t Wom; Nat Cyc Am Bio v19

14953. Noble, Lucy (Seward)
born 1853
author, traveler, lecturer
Nat Cyc Am Bio v17

14954. Strickland, Martha
born 1853
lawyer, feminist, orator
Michigan
Wom Cent

14955. Ward, May (Alden)
born 1853
historical author, biographer, editor, lecturer, club leader, president of the Massachusetts State Federation of Women's Clubs
Dict Am Auth; Index t Wom; Twent Cen Bio Dict Not Am; Wom Cent

14956. Manning, Jessie Wilson
born 1855
author, temperance worker, lecturer
Iowa
Index t Wom; Wom Cent

14957. Williams, Fannie Barrier
1855–1944
lecturer, civic leader, librarian, clubwoman
Chicago, IL

Black
Dict Am Bio supp v3; Not Am Wom; Prof Negro Wom v1

14958. Blatch, Harriot Eaton Stanton
1856–1940
leader of the radical wing of the American suffragist movement, author, political activist, Fabian Socialist, lecturer
Dict Am Bio supp v2; Not Am Wom; Obit File

14959. Todd, Mabel Loomis
1856/58–1932
author, editor of Emily Dickinson's books and letters, traveler, lecturer, astronomer
Dict Am Bio; Index t Wom; Nat Cyc Am Bio v9, v28, and v41; Not Am Wom; Twent Cen Bio Dict Not Am; Wom Cent

14960. Barrett, Kate Harwood Waller
1857/59–1925/29
social reformer, philanthropist, lecturer, social worker, suffragist, women's welfare worker
Virginia
Dict Am Bio; Encyc South Hist; Index t Wom; Not Am Wom

14961. Brown, Helen Dawes
1857–1941
author, lecturer on English literature
Dict Am Auth; Index t Wom

14962. Hall, Adelaide S.
born 1857
art lecturer, author
Index t Wom

14963. Howard, Belle
born 1857
dramatic reader
Kansas
Wom Cent

14964. MacDowell, Marian Griswold Nevins
1857–1956/57
patron of music, musician, pianist, founder of the MacDowell Artists Colony, lecturer
New Hampshire
Index t Wom; Not Am Wom supp v1; Obit File

14965. Peirce, Frances Elizabeth
born 1857
elocutionist, educator
Wom Cent

14966. Tarbell, Ida Minerva
1857–1944

investigative journalist, muckraker, lecturer, historian, author, biographer of Abraham Lincoln
Dict Am Auth; Dict Am Bio supp v3; Index t Wom; Nat Cyc Am Bio v14; Not Am Wom; Obit File

14967. Wheelock, Lucy
1857–1946
kindergarten educator, founder of Wheelock College, lecturer, author
Boston, MA
Dict Am Bio supp v4; Not Am Wom; Wom Cent

14968. Yates, Elizabeth U.
born 1857
lecturer, Methodist Episcopal preacher
Methodist Episcopal
Maine
Wom Cent

14969. Adams, Juliette Aurelia Graves
born 1858
composer, pianist, music educator, author, lecturer
Index t Wom

14970. Bacon, Alice Mable
1858–1918
authority on Japan, author on Japanese culture, lecturer, educator of Blacks
Virginia
Dict Am Auth; Dict Am Bio; Not Am Wom

14971. Bishop, Emily Mulkin Montague
born 1858
Delsartean lecturer and instructor in dress, expression, and physical culture
Index t Wom; Wom Cent

14972. Pond, Nella Brown
born 1858
actor, dramatic reader
Index t Wom; Wom Cent

14973. Sage, Florence Eleanor
1858–post 1940
pianist, lecturer
Index t Wom; Wom Cent

14974. Miller, Annie (Jenness)
born 1859/84
dress reformer, fashion designer, magazine publisher, author, novelist, essayist, lecturer
New York, NY
Dict Am Auth; Index t Wom; Wom Cent

14975. Thompson, Mary Sophia
born 1859

Delsartean acting-method instructor, elocutionist
Wom Cent

14976. van Anderson, Helen (Van Metre)
born 1859
minister, lecturer, miscellaneous author
Boston, MA
Dict Am Auth

14977. Bevier, Isabel
1860–1942
educator, author, lecturer, home economist
Dict Am Bio supp v3; Index t Wom; Not Am Wom

14978. Furman, Myrtie E.
born 1860
professor of elocution, orator
blind
Wom Cent

14979. Gilman, Charlotte Anna (Perkins) (Stetson)
1860–1935
author, feminist, lecturer, labor worker
San Francisco, CA
Dict Am Auth; Dict Am Bio supp v1; Index t Wom; Nat Cyc Am Bio v13; Not Am Wom; Twent Cen Bio Dict Not Am; Wom Lit, More

14980. Goessmann, Helena Theresa
flourished 1890s–1900s
educator, lecturer
Index t Wom

14981. Parker, Helen Almena
graduated 1885
educator, dramatic reader, impersonator
Index t Wom; Wom Cent

14982. Trout, Grace Wilbur
flourished 1890s; died 1955
suffragist, feminist, club leader, author, lecturer
Illinois
Index t Wom; Nat Cyc Am Bio csv2

14983. Welch, Jane Meade
flourished 1890s
journalist, historical lecturer
New York
Wom Cent

14984. Woolman, Mary Raphael Schenck
1860–1940
home economist, textile specialist, vocational educator, author, lecturer
Nat Cyc Am Bio csv1; Not Am Wom

14985. Nichols, Minerva Parker
1861/63–1949
architect, lecturer
Index t Wom; Not Am Wom; Wom Cent

14986. American, Sadie
1862–1944
lecturer, clubwoman, founder of the National Council of Jewish Women
Jewish
Index t Wom; Obit File

14987. Wells-Barnett, Ida Bell; Iola
1862/64–1931
Black equal rights advocate, journalist, newspaper publisher, clubwoman, lecturer, antilynching reformer
Black
Encyc Black Am; Encyc South Hist; Eng Wom; Index t Wom; Negro Alman; Not Am Wom; Prof Negro Wom v1 and v2

14988. Hurll, Estelle May
born 1863
educator, lecturer and writer on art
Dict Am Auth; Index t Wom

14989. Terrell, Mary Eliza Church
1863–1954
community leader, social reformer, suffragist, feminist, civil rights leader, NAACP organizer, lecturer, educator
Congregationalist
Washington, DC
Dict Am Bio supp v5; Encyc Black Am; Encyc South Hist; Index t Wom; Nat Cyc Am Bio v52; Negro Alman; Not Am Wom; Prof Negro Wom v1; World Great Men Col v2

14990. Chatham, Kitty Smiley; Catharine Smiley Bugg
1864/69–1946
singer for children, composer, children's author, lecturer
Index t Wom; Obit File; Wom Cent

14991. Kohut, Rebekah Bettelheim
1864–1951
social welfare leader, educator, suffragist, lecturer, author, Jewish welfare worker
Jewish
Hungarian
Index t Wom; Nat Cyc Am Bio v41 and csv5; Not Am Wom supp v1

14992. Smith, Mabell Shippie Clarke
1864–1942
educator, lecturer, author
Index t Wom

14993. Booth, Evangeline Cory
1865–1950
fourth general of the Salvation Army, orator, musician, poet
Salvationist
English
Dict Am Bio supp v4; Dict Am Rel Bio; Index t Wom; Nat Cyc Am Bio csv2; Not Am Wom; Obit File

14994. McCabe, Lida Rose
1865–1938
author, lecturer
Index t Wom

14995. Putnam, Emily James Smith
1865–1944
author, educator, first dean of Barnard College, lecturer
Index t Wom; Not Am Wom; Obit File; Twent Cen Bio Dict Not Am

14996. Towne, Elizabeth Lois
1865–1960
metaphysical author, editor, lecturer
New Thought
Nat Cyc Am Bio v45 and csv1

14997. Tryon, Kate
born 1865
journalist, artist, lecturer
Wom Cent

14998. Dowd, Mary Hickey
born 1866
educator, lecturer
Index t Wom

14999. Stearns, Lutie Eugenia
1866–1943
librarian, lecturer, social reformer
Index t Wom; Not Am Wom

15000. Potter, Jennie O'Neill
born 1867
actor, dramatic reader
Wom Cent

15001. Follet, Mary Parker
1868–1933
writer and lecturer on political science, group psychology, and industrial management
Dict Am Auth; Dict Am Bio supp v1; Not Am Wom

15002. Fryberger, Agnes Moore
born 1868
music educator, lecturer, author
Index t Wom

15003. Hayward, Beatrice Herford
1868–1952
monologuist, author, actor
English
Obit File

15004. Goldman, Emma
1869–1940
political anarchist, lecturer, publicist, agitator for free speech, popularizer of the arts, feminist, pioneer advocate of birth control, politician
Jewish
Russian
Dict Am Bio supp v2; Index t Wom; Not Am Wom; Who Who Jew Hist

15005. Hardy, Jennie Law
born 1869
temperance worker, lecturer
Nat Cyc Am Bio csv2

15006. Schoonhoven, Helen Butterfield
born 1869
lecturer, educator
Index t Wom

15007. Kinkhead, Elizabeth Shelby
flourished 1900s
lecturer, author
Index t Wom

15008. Lund, Charlotte
1870–1951
musical director, lecturer
Index t Wom

15009. Chase, Kate Fowler
1871–1951
educator, lecturer, clubwoman
Index t Wom

15010. Greenewalt, Mary Elizabeth Hallock; Mary Greenwalt
1871–1950
pianist, lighting engineer, lecturer
Nat Cyc Am Bio v39; Index t Wom

15011. Stocker, Corinne
born 1871
elocutionist, journalist
Georgia
Wom Cent

15012. Laidlaw, Harriet Davenport Wright Burton
1873–1949
suffragist, author, educator, lecturer, clubwoman
Presbyterian
Index t Wom; Nat Cyc Am Bio v38; Not Am Wom

15013. Lowell, Amy
1874–1925
poet, biographer, lecturer, critic
Dict Am Bio; Index t Wom; Nat Cyc Am Bio v19; Not Am Wom; Wom Lit; Wom Lit, More

15014. Monroe, Anne Shannon
1874/77–1942
author, essayist, novelist, magazine writer, Oregon historian, feminist, lecturer, mountain climber
Oregon
Index t Wom; Nat Cyc Am Bio; Obit File

15015. Adams, Harriet Chalmer
1875–1937
explorer, author, lecturer
Index t Wom; Not Am Wom

15016. Brown, Zaidee Mabel
1875–1950
librarian, editor, lecturer
Index t Wom

15017. Burlin, Natalie (Curtis)
1875–1921
ethnomusicologist specializing in Native American and Afro-American music, worker for Native American rights, composer, pianist, lecturer
Dict Am Bio; Not Am Wom; Index t Wom

15018. Delaney, Adelaide Margaret
born 1875
lecturer, editor, author
Index t Wom

15019. Denning, Delia; Delia (Denning) Akeley Howe
1875–1970
African explorer, big game hunter, geographer, taxidermist, author, lecturer, World War I relief worker
Nat Cyc Am Bio v57; Obit File; Index t Wom

15020. Howe, Delia Akeley (Denning)
1875–1970
African explorer, big game hunter, geographer, taxidermist, author, lecturer, World War I relief worker
Index t Wom; Nat Cyc Am Bio v57; Obit File

15021. Miller, Nellie Burget
born 1875
poet, lecturer
Index t Wom

15022. Beek, Alice D. Engley
born 1876
painter, author, lecturer
Index t Wom

15023. Vanamee, Grace Davis
1876–1946
club leader, lecturer, educator, author
Index t Wom

15024. Cunningham, Kate (Richards) (O'Hare)
1877–1948
Socialist party presidential nominee, community organizer, prison reformer, anti–World War I activist, lecturer, educator
Index t Wom; Not Am Wom; Obit File; Dict Am Bio v4

15025. Center, Stella Steward
born 1878
educator, lecturer
Index t Wom

15026. Emrick, Jeanette Wallace
born 1878
author, lecturer, humanitarian
Index t Wom

15027. Sanger, Margaret Higgins; Mrs. J. Noah H. Slee
1879/83–1966
birth control reformer, lecturer, author
Episcopalian
Index t Wom; Nat Cyc Am Bio v52; Not Am Wom supp v1; Obit File

15028. Misch, Caeser, Mrs.
flourished 1910s
religious worker, lecturer, author
Index t Wom

15029. O'Mahoney, Katherine A.
flourished 1910s
publisher, editor, lecturer, club leader
Irish
Index t Wom

15030. Peyser, Ethel R.
flourished 1910s–30s
author, editor, music critic, lecturer
Index t Wom

15031. Prentiss, Henrietta
1880–1940
educator, speech authority
Index t Wom

15032. Sawyer, Ruth
1880–1970
children's author, storyteller
Not Am Wom supp v1

15033. Sherman, Minna E.
flourished 1910s
agriculturist, club leader, lecturer, author
Index t Wom

15034. Wellington, Violet Irene
flourished 1910s
dramatic reader, drama teacher, suffragist, pacifist
Nat Cyc Am Bio v19

15035. Gruenberg, Sidonie Matsner
1881–1974
parent education leader; director of the Child Study Association of America, specialist in child guidance, parent education, and family relationships; nonfiction writer; lecturer
Austrian
Cur Biog '74; Index t Wom; Not Am Wom supp v1; Obit File

15036. Phillips, Lena Madesin
1881–1955
feminist, founder of the National and International Federations of Business and Professional Women's Clubs, author, editor, lecturer, politician
Dict Am Bio supp v5; Index t Wom; Not Am Wom supp v1; Obit File

15037. Stewart, Sallie W.
1881–1951
educator, clubwoman, realtor, lecturer, Black women's welfare worker
Indiana
Black
Negro Alman; Prof Negro Wom v1

15038. Block, Anita
born 1882
author, lecturer, Socialist politician
Nat Cyc Am Bio csv9

15039. Scott, Miriam Finn
1882–1944
pioneer child diagnostician, educator, lecturer, author
Russian
Index t Wom; Nat Cyc Am Bio v36

15040. Wambaugh, Sarah
1882–1955
pacifist, internationalist, authority on plebiscites, author, lecturer, consultant adviser to the League of Nations and the UN
Dict Am Bio supp v5; Index t Wom; Obit File

15041. Fair, Ethel Marion
born 1884
librarian, editor, author, lecturer
Index t Wom

15042. Roosevelt, [Anna] Eleanor
1884–1962

social reformer, humanitarian, author, lecturer
Washington, DC
English
Eng Wom; Index t Wom; Nat Cyc Am Bio v57 and csv4 and csv6; Not Am Wom supp v1; Obit File

15043. Brooker, Mary Isaphene Ives
born 1885
elocutionist
Nat Cyc Am Bio csv3

15044. Owen, Ruth Bryan; Ruth Rohde
1885–1954
representative to Congress from Florida, US diplomat, author, lecturer
Dict Am Bio v5; Index t Wom; Nat Cyc Am Bio csvl; Not Am Wom supp v1; Obit File

15045. Roche, Josephine Aspinwall
1886–1976
industrialist, lecturer, UMW executive
Index t Wom; Obit File

15046. Meyer, Agnes Elizabeth (Ernst)
1887–1970
author, journalist, vice-president and co-owner of *The Washington Post*, World War II correspondent, autobiographer, lecturer, social worker, Republican party worker, crusader for social services and education causes
Lutheran
New York
Cur Biog '70; Index t Wom; Nat Cyc Am Bio v56; Obit File

15047. Deloria, Ella Carla; Anpetu Wastewin
1888–1971
interpreter, linguist, ethnologist, anthropologist, lecturer
Native American (Yankton Sioux-Dakota)
Great North Am Ind; Ind Today; Not Am Wom supp v1

15048. Housman, Rosalie Louise
circa 1888–1949
composer, pianist, lecturer, musicologist
Index t Wom

15049. Kilmer, Aline Murray
1888–1941
poet, children's author, lecturer
Index t Wom; Obit File

15050. Wawa Calac Chaw; Keep from the Water
1888–1972
author, artist, feminist, lecturer on Native American and feminist matters
Native American (Luiseno)
Great North Am Ind

15051. Cranston, Ruth
1889–1956
religious author, biographer, lecturer
Obit File

15052. Ward, Maisie
1889–1975
book publisher, author, lecturer, Catholic church worker
Catholic
English
Cur Biog '75; Index t Wom

15053. Brooks, Erica May
flourished 1920s–30s
athlete, lecturer
English
Index t Wom

15054. McClurg, Virginia Donaghe
flourished 1920s
author, lecturer
Index t Wom

15055. Orth, Jane Davis
flourished 1920s–30s
lecturer, traveler
Index t Wom

15056. Shinn, Florence Scovel
died 1940
illustrator, lecturer, metaphysicist
Index t Wom

15057. Flanner, Janet
1892–1978
journalist, novelist, lecturer, *New Yorker* correspondent from Paris
French (American expatriate to Paris)
Cur Biog '79; Dict Lit Bio v4; Index t Wom; Obit File

15058. McCollin, Frances
1892–1960
composer, educator, lecturer, Socialist party worker
Episcopalian
Pennsylvania
blind
Index t Wom; Nat Cyc Am Bio v45

15059. Pattee, Alida Frances
died 1942
dietician, lecturer, publisher, author
Index t Wom

15060. Smedley, Agnes
1892/94–1950
author, foreign correspondent, lecturer, champion of revolutionary China, writer on China and the Far East
Dict Am Bio supp v4; Index t Wom; Not Am Wom; Obit File; Wom Lit, More

15061. Fuldheim, Dorothy
born 1894
lecturer, radio personality
Nat Cyc Am Bio csv5

15062. Thompson, Dorothy; Mrs. Sinclair Lewis
1894–1961
international journalist, newspaper columnist, magazine writer, anti-Nazi worker, lecturer specializing in foreign affairs, radio commentator
Encyc Third Reich; Index t Wom; Nat Cyc Am Bio csv5; Not Am Wom supp v1; Obit File

15063. Alexander, Ruth Wilbur; Mrs. Raymond L. Redhefer
born 1895
economist, editorial columnist, lecturer, pianist
Buddhist
Index t Wom; Nat Cyc Am Bio csv12

15064. Vormelker, Rose Lillian
born 1895
librarian, editor, lecturer
Index t Wom

15065. Clapper, Olive Ewing
1896–1968
author, lecturer, radio commentator, autobiographer, director of the Washington, DC, bureau of CARE
Washington, DC
Cur Biog '69; Index t Wom

15066. Bowen, Catherine (Shober) Drinker
1897–1973
biographer, essayist, autobiographer, lecturer
Pennsylvania
Cur Biog '73; Index t Wom; Nat Cyc Am Bio v58; Not Am Wom supp v1; Obit File

15067. Smith, Lilian Eugenia
1897–1966
novelist, newspaper columnist, writer on race relations, civil rights worker, editor, social worker, educator, lecturer
Florida
Encyc South Hist; Index t Wom; Not Am Wom supp v1; Obit File; Wom Lit; Wom Lit, More

15068. Richards, Janet Elizabeth Hosmer
died 1948
lecturer, feminist
Index t Wom

15069. Tharp, Louise Marshall Hall
born 1898
author, lecturer
Index t Wom

15070. Utley, Freda
1898–1978
author, journalist, foreign correspondent, lecturer
English
Index t Wom; Obit File

15071. Tempski, Armine von
1899–1943
author, lecturer
Index t Wom

15072. Ames, Elinor
flourished 1930s
lecturer, educator, editor
Index t Wom

15073. Bader, Golda Maude
flourished 1930s
lecturer
Index t Wom

15074. Cooley, Winnifred Harper
flourished 1930s
author, lecturer, radio personality
Index t Wom

15075. Gasaway, Alice Elizabeth
flourished 1930s
lecturer
Index t Wom

15076. Kelley, Marion Booth
flourished 1930s
lecturer
Index t Wom

15077. Kuhn, Irene Corbally
born 1900
journalist, editor, radio executive, lecturer
Index t Wom

15078. Lawrence, Jeanette
flourished 1930s
author, lecturer
Index t Wom

15079. Mandola, Carol M.
flourished 1930s
metaphysician, lecturer, poet
Index t Wom

15080. McLean, Margaret
flourished 1930s
dramatic coach, speech teacher
Index t Wom

15081. Mears, Helen
born 1900
author, lecturer
Index t Wom

15082. Moir, Phyllis
flourished 1930s–40s
author, lecturer, editor
English
Index t Wom

15083. Paxton, Ethel
flourished 1930s
artist, educator, lecturer, author
Index t Wom

15084. Reavis, Babs H.
flourished 1930s
lecturer, politician, club leader
Index t Wom

15085. Seacombe, Charles M., Mrs.
flourished 1930s
critic, translator, lecturer, actor
Index t Wom

15086. Shaw, Ellen Eddy
flourished 1930s
naturalist, lecturer, author
Index t Wom

15087. Soper, Luella Hartt
flourished 1930s
club leader, lecturer
Index t Wom

15088. Stuerm, Ruza Lukavaska
flourished 1930s
railroad executive, lecturer
Czechoslovak
Index t Wom

15089. von Hesse, Elizabeth F.
flourished 1930s
educator, author, lecturer
Index t Wom

15090. Wilder, Jessie
flourished 1930s
poet, educator, critic, lecturer
English
Index t Wom

15091. Sampson, Edith (Spurlock)
1901–79
lawyer, judge, alternate delegate to the UN, lecturer
Illinois
Black
Cur Biog '80; Encyc Black Am; Index t Wom; Negro Alman; Negro Her Lib v1

15092. Hardy, Kay
born 1902
artist, lecturer, educator
Index t Wom

15093. Overstrett, Bonaro Wilkinson
born 1902
educator, lecturer, author
Congregationalist
California
Index t Wom; Nat Cyc Am Bio csv11

15094. Dean, Vera Micheles
1903–72
international affairs specialist, editor, author, lecturer
Russian
Cur Biog '72; Index t Wom; Not Am Wom supp v1

15095. Peterson, Virgilia; Virginia Paulding
1904–66
lecturer, author, literary critic, television moderator, Peabody Award winner
Index t Wom; Obit File

15096. Howe, Helen; Helen Allen
1905–75
novelist, satiric monologuist
Cur Biog '75; Index t Wom

15097. Mann, Erika
1905–69
author, writer on Germany, actor, lecturer
German
Cur Biog '69; Index t Wom

15098. Schuell, Hildred Magdalene
1906–70
speech pathologist
Minnesota
Nat Cyc Am Bio v55

15099. Hall, Addye Yeargain
flourished 1940s
musician, lecturer, author
Index t Wom

15100. Huss, Hildegarde Hoffman
flourished 1940s
singer, lecturer, music educator
Index t Wom

15101. Oberdorfer, Anne Faulkner
flourished 1940s
musician, lecturer, author
Index t Wom

15102. Pray, Ada Jordan
flourished 1940s
composer, pianist, educator, lecturer
Index t Wom

15103. Schain, Josephine
flourished 1940s
consultant, social worker, lecturer
Index t Wom

15104. Simpson, Elizabeth
flourished 1940s
composer, pianist, music educator, lecturer, author
Index t Wom

15105. Steward, Anna Bird
flourished 1940s
author, lecturer
Index t Wom

15106. Tracey, Cateau Stegeman
flourished 1940s
pianist, music educator, author, critic, lecturer
Index t Wom

15107. Brooks, Gwendolyn
born 1912/17
poet, educator, autobiographer, lecturer, poet laureate of Illinois
Chicago, IL
Black
Cur Biog '77; Dict Lit Bio v5; Encyc Black Am; Index t Wom; Negro Alman; Nort Anth Poet; Prof Negro Wom; Wom Lit; Wom Lit, More

15108. Johnstone, Margaret Blair
born 1913
clergyperson, author, lecturer
Index t Wom

15109. Bird, Caroline (Mahoney)
born 1915
lecturer, women's equal rights activist, author
New York
Cur Biog '76

15110. Abzug, Bella (Savitsky)
born 1920
representative to Congress from New York, lawyer with specialty in labor law, lecturer, peace worker
Jewish
New York
Cur Biog '71

15111. Carpenter, Leslie
born 1920
government employee, speechwriter
Index t Wom

15112. Howey, Ella Mae
flourished 1950s
deaf lecturer
deaf
Index t Wom

15113. Rombeau, Anne M.
flourished 1950s
aviator, lecturer, traveler
Index t Wom

15114. Trulock, Mussette Langford
flourished 1950s
organization official, lecturer
Index t Wom

15115. Saxl, Eva R.
born circa 1921
educator, traveler, lecturer, author
Czechoslovak
Index t Wom

15116. Brown, Helen Gurley
born 1922
author, editor of *Cosmopolitan*, lecturer, television personality
Cur Biog '69

15117. Larkin, Moscelyne
born 1925
ballet dancer and teacher, choreographer, lecturer
Native American (Shawnee-Ploria)
Ind Today

15118. Costanza, Margaret "Midge"
born 1932
special assistant on women's affairs to President Carter, feminist, human rights worker
Cur Biog '78

15119. Richter, Ada
born 1944
composer, educator, lecturer
Index t Wom

No Dates

15120. Bush, Grace
composer, pianist, poet, lecturer
Index t Wom

PACIFISM AND INTERNATIONALISM

15121. Mott, Lucretia (Coffin)
1793–1880
abolitionist, feminist, Quaker minister, pacifist
Quaker
Cyc Am Bio; Dict Am Bio; Dict Am Bio Men Time; Dict Am Rel Bio; Index t Wom; Nat Cyc Am Bio v2; Not Am Wom; Twent Cen Bio Dict Not Am; Wom Cent

15122. Cox, Hannah
1796/97–1876
abolitionist, temperance worker, pacifist, women's rights worker
Quaker
Cyc Am Bio; Dict Am Bio; Index t Wom

15123. Comstock, Elizabeth Leslie Rous
1815–1891/92
social reformer, abolitionist, Underground Railroad worker, pacifist, freed slave's welfare worker, temperance reformer, women's rights worker, Quaker minister, prison reformer, Civil War nurse
Quaker
Dict Am Bio; Index t Wom; Nat Cyc Am Bio v22; Not Am Wom

15124. Cutler, Hannah Maria (Conant) (Tracy)
1815–96
women's rights leader, suffragist, physician, journalist, author, lecturer, pacifist
Illinois
Cyc Am Bio ad; Dict Am Auth; Index t Wom; Not Am Wom; Twent Cen Bio Dict Not Am

15125. Howe, Julia Ward
1819–1910
poet, dramatist, songwriter, lecturer, suffrage and women's club leader, feminist, abolitionist, pacifist, prison reformer, Union patriot during the Civil War, philanthropist, traveler
Boston, MA
Cyc Am Bio; Dict Am Auth; Dict Am Bio; Dict Am Bio Men Time; Dict Lit Bio v1; Index t Wom; Nat Cyc Am Bio v1; Not Am Wom; Twent Cen Bio Dict Not Am; Wom Cent

15126. Lewis, Grace Anna
born 1821
naturalist, scientific illustrator, science writer, conservationist, ornithologist, abolitionist, Underground Railroad operator, pacifist, suffragist, philanthropist
Quaker
Index t Wom; Nat Cyc Am Bio v9; Twent Cen Bio Dict Not Am; Wom Cent

15127. Howland, Emily
1827–1929
educator, educator of Blacks, abolitionist, suffragist, pacifist, temperance worker, philanthropist
Quaker
New York
Dict Am Bio; Nat Cyc Am Bio v25; Not Am Wom; Wom Cent

15128. Lockwood, Belva Ann Bennett McNall
1830/54–1917
lawyer, politician, women's rights worker, suffragist, pacifist
Dict Am Bio; Index t Wom; Nat Cyc Am Bio v1; Not Am Wom; Twent Cen Bio Dict Not Am; Wom Cent

15129. Smith, Hannah Whitall
1832–1911
religious author, evangelist, pacifist, temperance worker, women's rights worker
Quaker
Dict Am Bio; Index t Wom; Not Am Wom

15130. Scripps, Ellen Browning
1836–1932
philanthropist, newspaper writer and publisher, patron of marine science, founder of Scripps Marine Lab, pacifist, feminist, temperance worker
La Jolla, CA
Dict Am Bio; Index t Wom; Nat Cyc Am Bio v27; Not Am Wom

15131. Deyo, Amanda
born 1838
Universalist minister, pacifist
Universalist
Wom Cent

15132. Bailey, Hannah Clark Johnston
1839–1923
peace worker, temperance reformer, suffragist, philanthropist
Maine
Index t Wom; Nat Cyc Am Bio v10; Not Am Wom; Wom Cent

15133. Bond, Elizabeth Powell
1841–1926
abolitionist, educator of Blacks, women's rights worker, pacifist, civil rights and temperance worker, dean of Swarthmore College
Pennsylvania
Dict Am Bio; Index t Wom; Nat Cyc Am Bio v6; Wom Cent

15134. Sewall, Mary Eliza Wright
1844–1920
educator, suffragist, women's rights worker, feminist, Sorosis member, clubwoman, pacifist
Dict Am Bio; Index t Wom; Nat Cyc Am Bio v19; Not Am Wom; Wom Cent

15135. Villard, Helen Frances Garrison "Fanny"
1844–1928
philanthropist, suffragist, pacifist, worker for Black civil rights
Dict Am Bio; Not Am Wom

15136. Tingley, Katherine Augusta Westcott
1847/52–1929
founder of the Point Loma Community in California, pacifist
Theosophist
Point Loma, CA
Dict Am Bio; Index t Wom; Nat Cyc Am Bio v15; Not Am Wom

15137. Benham, Ida Whipple
born 1849
pacifist
Index t Wom; Wom Cent

15138. Moore, Marguerite
born 1849
orator, patriot, pacifist
Irish
Wom Cent

15139. Spencer, Anna Carpenter (Garlin)
1851–1931
Unitarian minister, journalist, educator, temperance worker, suffragist, pacifist, child-labor reformer, philanthropist
Unitarian
Dict Am Bio; Nat Cyc Am Bio v9 and csv2; Not Am Wom

15140. Moore, Eva Perry
1852–post 1900
club leader, pacifist
Index t Wom; Nat Cyc Am Bio csv1

15141. Ormsby, Mary Frost
born circa 1852
author, journalist, philanthropist, pacifist
New York, NY
Index t Wom; Wom Cent

15142. Mead, Lucia True (Ames)
1856–1936
pacifist, internationalist, suffragist, Black welfare and education worker, author
Unitarian
Nat Cyc Am Bio v28; Not Am Wom; Twent Cen Bio Dict Not Am

15143. Blake, Katherine Devereux
1857–1950
educator, suffragist, international peace movement leader
New York
Index t Wom; Obit File

15144. Boole, Ella Alexander
1858–1952
temperance leader, president of WCTU, suffragist, pacifist, Presbyterian deacon
Presbyterian
Dict Am Bio supp v5; Index t Wom; Nat Cyc Am Bio v38 and csv2; Not Am Wom supp v1; Obit File

15145. Dudley, Helena Stuart
1858/98–1932
settlement house worker, social reformer, pacifist
Index t Wom; Not Am Wom

15146. Catt, Carrie Clinton Lane Champman
1859–1947
suffragist, women's rights worker, peace worker
Dict Am Bio supp v3; Index t Wom; Nat Cyc Am Bio v15 and v38; Not Am Wom; Obit File; Wom Cent

15147. Addams, Jane
1860–1935
political activist, social reformer, sociologist, social welfare worker, settlement house founder, peace worker
Chicago, IL
Dict Am Auth; Dict Am Bio supp v1; Index t Wom; Nat Cyc Am Bio v13 and v27; Not Am Wom

15148. Nathan, Maud
1862–1946
social welfare leader, social worker, consumer advocate, suffragist, feminist, pacifist
Jewish
Dict Am Bio supp v4; Index t Wom; Nat Cyc Am Bio v15; Not Am Wom; Obit File

15149. Woolley, Mary Emma
1863–1947
second president of Mt. Holyoke College, educator, pacifist, suffragist
Congregationalist
Dict Am Bio supp v4; Index t Wom; Nat Cyc Am Bio v13, v37, and csv4; Not Am Wom

15150. de Bey, Cornelia Barnarda
born 1865
physician, surgeon, pacifist
Dutch
Nat Cyc Am Bio csv3

15151. Douglas, Alice May
born 1865
poet, children's author, temperance worker, pacifist, missionary
Maine
Dict Am Auth; Index t Wom; Wom Cent

15152. Hilles, Florence Bayard
1865–1954

suffragist, feminist, ERA worker, pacifist, golfer
Episcopalian
Delaware
Nat Cyc Am Bio v46

15153. Hooper, Jessie Annette Jack
1865–1935
suffragist, Democratic politician, peace advocate
Wisconsin
Dict Am Bio supp v1; Nat Cyc Am Bio csv1; Not Am Wom

15154. Blaine, Anita [Eugenie] McCormick
1866–1954
philanthropist, pacifist, patron of education and child welfare, patron of the League of Nations
Chicago, IL
Dict Am Bio supp v5; Nat Cyc Am Bio v44; Not Am Wom supp v1; Obit File

15155. Andrews, Fannie Fern (Phillips)
1867–1950
publicist, pacifist, internationalist, suffragist
Nat Cyc Am Bio csv1; Not Am Wom

15156. Balch, Emily Greene
1867–1961
pacifist, social reformer, sociologist, economist, winner of the Nobel Peace Prize
Quaker
Index t Wom; Nat Cyc Am Bio csv7; Not Am Wom; Obit File

15157. Tuttle, Florence Guertin (Onertin)
born 1869
author, feminist, birth control advocate, pacifist, League of Nations worker, politician
Index t Wom; Nat Cyc Am Bio csv2 and csv5

15158. Johnston, Mary
1870–1936
popular novelist, suffragist, pacifist, internationalist
Birmingham, AL; Virginia
Dict Am Auth; Dict Am Bio supp v2; Dict Lit Bio v9; Index t Wom; Nat Cyc Am Bio v10 and csv3; Not Am Wom; Twent Cen Bio Dict Not Am

15159. Park, Maud May Wood; C. J. Maywood
1871–1955
suffragist, feminist, civic leader, social worker, police reformer, pacifist
Dict Am Bio supp v5; Index t Wom; Nat Cyc Am Bio csv1; Not Am Wom supp v1

15160. Wold, Emma
1871–1950
lawyer, suffragist, women's rights worker, pacifist
Nat Cyc Am Bio v38

15161. Dennett, Mary Coffin Ware
1872–1947
suffragist, birth control and sex education advocate, founder of the National Birth Control League, pacifist
Not Am Wom; Obit File

15162. Hull, Hannah Hallowell Clothier
1872–1958
pacifist, suffragist
Not Am Wom supp v1

15163. Edwards, Edith
born 1873
social worker, suffragist, pacifist
Nat Cyc Am Bio v17

15164. Hughan, Jessie Wallace
1875–1955
pacifist, Socialist party worker, politician, educator, author
Index t Wom; Not Am Wom supp v1

15165. Lloyd, Lola Maverick
1875–1944
pacifist, feminist, suffragist
Nat Cyc Am Bio v33; Obit File

15166. Martin, Anna Henrietta
1875–1951
suffragist, feminist, author, essayist, social critic, pacifist, politician
Nevada
Dict Am Bio supp v5; Not Am Wom supp v1; Read Encyc Am West

15167. Weed, Helen Hill
1875–1958
suffrage leader, pacifist, child labor reformer
Obit File

15168. Cleghorn, Sarah Norcliffe
1876–1959
poet, novelist, educator, suffragist, civil rights worker, labor worker, pacifist, antivivisectionist, Socialist party member
Vermont
Index t Wom; Nat Cyc Am Bio v46; Obit File; Dict Am Bio supp v5

15169. Cunningham, Kate (Richards) (O'Hare)
1877–1948
Socialist party presidential nominee, community organizer, pris-

on reformer, anti–World War I activist, lecturer, educator
Index t Wom; Not Am Wom; Obit File; Dict Am Bio v4

15170. Gildersleeve, Virginia Crocheron
1877–1965
educator, dean emeritus of Barnard College, US delegate to the 1945 San Francisco conference to draft the UN charter, creator of UNESCO
New York
Index t Wom; Nat Cyc Am Bio csv1 and csv7; Not Am Wom supp v1; Obit File

15171. Schwimmer, Rosika
1877–1948
feminist, suffragist, pacifist, author, editor
Jewish
Hungarian
Dict Am Bio supp v4; Not Am Wom; Obit File

15172. Warbasse, Agnes Louise Dyer
1877–1945
cooperative manufacturer, cooperative housing expert, suffragist, pacifist
Nat Cyc Am Bio v34

15173. Keller, Helen Adams
1880–1968
author, feminist, suffragist, educator, advocate for the handicapped, pacifist, Socialist party worker
Swedenborgian
Alabama
blind, deaf
Encyc South Hist; Index t Wom; Nat Cyc Am Bio v15 and v57; Not Am Wom supp v1; Obit File

15174. Norris, Kathleen Thompson
1880–1966
author, novelist, magazine writer, pacifist, feminist
Catholic
Index t Wom; Nat Cyc Am Bio csv3; Not Am Wom supp v1; Obit File; Wom Lit, More

15175. Rankin, Jeannette Pickering
1880–1973
suffragist, feminist, first woman elected to Congress, pacifist
Index t Wom; Not Am Wom supp v1; Obit File

15176. Snow, Ellen
flourished 1910s
author, pacifist, animal humane woker, suffragist
Cyc Am Bio

15177. Wellington, Violet Irene
flourished 1910s
dramatic reader, drama teacher, suffragist, pacifist
Nat Cyc Am Bio v19

15178. Eastman, Crystal
1881–1928
social investigator, peace worker, feminist, suffragist
Not Am Wom

15179. Traphagen, Ethel; Mrs. William R. Leigh
1882–1963
fashion designer, founder of the first school of fashion design in the United States, pacifist
Index t Wom; Nat Cyc Am Bio v54 and csv9; Obit File

15180. Wambaugh, Sarah
1882–1955
pacifist, internationalist, authority on plebiscites, author, lecturer, consultant adviser to the League of Nations and the UN
Dict Am Bio supp v5; Index t Wom; Obit File

15181. Vernon, Mabel
1883–1975
suffragist, feminist, pacifist
Not Am Wom supp v1

15182. Bremer, Edith Terry
1885–1964
social worker, founder of the International Institute movement
Not Am Wom supp v1

15183. Stokes, Lilia Woodruff
1885–1973
Philadelphia civic worker, worker for Women's International League for Peace and Freedom, conservationist
Quaker
Pennsylvania
Nat Cyc Am Bio v58

15184. Bussey, Gertrude C.
1888–1961
president of the Women's International League for Peace and Freedom, philosopher, educator
Obit File

15185. Bussey, Ruth Carman
1888–1961
educator, worker for Women's International League for Peace and Freedom party
Episcopalian
Maryland
Nat Cyc Am Bio v49

15186. Stern, Elizabeth Gertrude Levin; Eleanor Morton; Elsie-Jeab
1889/90–1954

author, editor, social worker, political activist and antiwar worker
Quaker
Nat Cyc Am Bio v39; Obit File

15187. Eliot, Martha May
1891–1978
pediatrician, public health official, president of the American Health Association, UNICEF member, US Children's Bureau official
Unitarian
Massachusetts
Cur Biog '78; Index t Wom; Nat Cyc Am Bio v60

15188. Barus, Jane Garey
1892–1977
suffragist; political activist; prison reformer; Montclair, New Jersey, civic worker; antinuclear activist; anti–Vietnam war worker
Unitarian
Montclair, NJ
Nat Cyc Am Bio v60

15189. White, Helen Constance
1896–1967
educator, historial novelist, religious historian, UNESCO member
Catholic
Index t Wom; Nat Cyc Am Bio v53; Not Am Wom supp v1

15190. Marshall, Lenore Guinzburg
1897–1971
author, poet, novelist, antinuclear worker, cofounder of the Committee for a Sane Nuclear Policy, worker for Women's International League for Peace and Freedom
Nat Cyc Am Bio v55; Obit File

15191. Carter, Lillian "Bessie"
born 1898
nurse, social service worker, peace worker, civil rights worker
Georgia
Cur Biog '78

15192. Strauss, Anna Lord
1899–1979
editor, club leader, feminist, political activist, New York civic worker, internationalist
Quaker
New York
Cur Biog '79; Index t Wom; Nat Cyc Am Bio csv10

15193. Brunauer, Esther Delia Caukin
1901–59

international affairs specialist, UN official, textbook editor
Index t Wom; Not Am Wom supp v1

15194. Reid, Helen Dwight
1901–65
international political scientist, educator, pacifist
Christian Scientist
Washington, DC
Scottish
Nat Cyc Am Bio v51

15195. Hamer, Fannie Lou
1917–77
civil rights worker, founder of the Mississippi Freedom Democratic party, worker for Student Nonviolent Coordinating Committee, farmer
Mississippi
Black
Encyc Black Am; Obit File

15196. Abzug, Bella (Savitsky)
born 1920
representative to Congress from New York, lawyer with specialty in labor law, lecturer, peace worker
Jewish
New York
Cur Biog '71

15197. Black, Shirley Temple
born 1928
child actor, singer, UN representative
Cur Biog '70; Index t Wom

15198. Gaston, Gloria Laureha
flourished 1960s–70s
development officer for the Agency for International Development's Bureau of Latin America
Black
Negro Alman; Negro Her Lib v1

15199. Fonda, Jane
born 1937
actor, political activist, antinuclear worker
Index t Wom

15200. Baez, Joan
born 1941
folk and popular singer, anti–Vietnam war activist, pacifist, worker for Amnesty International
Mexican
Dict Mex Am Hist; Index t Wom

15201. Holtzman, Elizabeth
born 1941
lawyer, Democratic representative to Congress from New York, feminist, anti–Vietnam war protester

New York
Cur Biog '73

15202. Robinson, Ruby Doris Smith
1942–67
civil rights reformer, founder and executive of the Student Nonviolent Coordinating Committee
Black
Not Am Wom supp v1; Obit File

15203. Silkwood, Karen
1946–74
critic of the procedures of an Oklahoma nuclear facility
Oklahoma
Obit File

PHILANTHROPY

15204. Bradford, Alice
circa 1590–1670
Pilgrim, Plymouth Colony civic worker, patron of education
Puritan
Massachusetts
English
Am Bio Dict; Index t Wom

15205. Mance, Jeanne
1606–73
philanthropist, hospital founder and administrator
French Canadian
Cyc Am Bio; Index t Wom

15206. Philipse, Catharine Duval van Cortland
flourished 1690s
colonial property manager, philanthropist
Index t Wom

15207. Brittano, Susannah
died 1764
colonial educator, philanthropist
Index t Wom

15208. Perkins, Elizabeth Peck
1735/36–1807
businessperson, philanthropist, merchant
Index t Wom; Not Am Wom

15209. Ledyard, Mary
flourished 1770s
hero of American Revolution, philanthropist
Index t Wom

15210. Putnam, Susannah French
flourished 1770s
humanitarian of American Revolution
Index t Wom

15211. Graham, Isabella Marshall
1742–1814/15
educator, charity worker, philanthropist
New York
Scottish
Am Bio Dict; Cyc Am Bio; Dict Am Bio; Dict Am Bio Men Time; Index t Wom; Nat Cyc Am Bio v4; Not Am Wom; Our Count; Who Who Dur Am Rev

15212. Hoffman, Sarah C.
born 1742
philanthropist
Cyc Am Bio; Index t Wom

15213. Bache, Sarah Franklin
1743/44–1808
relief worker in American Revolution, philanthropist
Philadelphia, PA
Appl Cyc Am Bio; Cyc Am Bio; Dict Am Bio Men Time; Index t Wom; Nat Cyc Am Bio v7; Not Am Wom; Twent Cen Bio Dict Not Am

15214. Adams, Abigail Smith
1744–1818
patriot and relief worker of American Revolution, political mover, letter writer, feminist
Am Bio Dict; Appl Cyc Am Bio; Cyc Am Bio; Dict Am Auth; Dict Am Bio; Dict Am Bio Men Time; Index t Wom; Nat Cyc Am Bio v1; Not Am Wom; Twent Cen Bio Dict Not Am; Wom Cent

15215. Reed, Esther de Berdt
1746–80
leader of women's relief work during the American Revolution, hero of American Revolution, patriot, philanthropist
Index t Wom; Not Am Wom

15216. Alford, Joanna
flourished 1785
philanthropist
Index t Wom

15217. Parrish, Anne
1760–1800
colonial philanthropist for women's causes, educator
Pennsylvania
Dict Am Bio; Index t Wom; Who Who Dur Am Rev

15218. Elliott, Anna
circa 1762–1858
hero of American Revolution, relief worker, nurse
Am Bio Dict; Cyc Am Bio; Index t Wom

15219. Bradford, Susan
1764–1854

philanthropist
Burlington, NJ
Index t Wom

15220. Lum, Mary
died 1815
philanthropist
Index t Wom

15221. Rotch, Charity (Rodman)
1765/66–1824
philanthropist
Cyc Am Bio; Index t Wom

15222. Phillips, Phoebe Foxcraft
died 1818
cofounder of the Andover Theological Seminary, philanthropist
Cyc Am Bio; Index t Wom

15223. Roach, Elizabeth Greenfield
flourished 1800s
philanthropist
Index t Wom

15224. Prior, Margaret Barrett Allen
1773–1842
charitable worker, philanthropist
Index t Wom; Not Am Wom

15225. Seton, Elizabeth Ann (Bayley), Saint; Mother Seton
1774–1821
Catholic nun, founder and superior of the American Sisters of Charity of St. Vincent de Paul (the first American sisterhood), philanthropist, autobiographer
Catholic
Maryland
Cyc Am Bio; Dict Am Auth; Dict Am Bio; Dict Am Rel Bio; Encyc South Hist; Index t Wom; Nat Cyc Am Bio v2; Not Am Wom; Twent Cen Bio Dict Not Am

15226. Outein, Nancy C.
1778–1814
philanthropist
Massachusetts
Am Bio Dict

15227. Reed, Hannah
1778–1855
missionary worker, philanthropist
Marblehead, MA
Am Bio Dict

15228. Hunter, M. A., Mrs.
flourished 1810s
philanthropist
Index t Wom

15229. Gratz, Rebecca
1781/82–1869
charity worker, philanthropist, educator
Jewish
Dict Am Bio; Index t Wom; Nat Cyc Am Bio v10; Not Am Wom

15230. Kaahumanu
died 1832
Hawaiian ruler, patron of Christianity
Not Am Wom

15231. van Ness, Marcia Burns
1782–1832
philanthropist, patriot
Washington, DC
Cyc Am Bio; Index t Wom

15232. Dudley, Blandina
1783–1863
patron of science
Cyc Am Bio

15233. Jenkins, Anna Almy
1790–1849
philanthropist
Quaker
Providence, RI
Cyc Am Bio; Dict Am Bio Men Time

15234. Huntington, Susan Mansfield
1791–1823
religious writer, philanthropist, diarist, poet
Am Bio Dict; Cyc Am Bio; Index t Wom

15235. Sigourney, Lydia Howard (Huntley)
1791–1865
author, poet, philanthropist
Connecticut
Cyc Am Bio; Dict Am Auth; Dict Am Bio; Dict Am Bio Men Time; Dict Lit Bio v1; Index t Wom; Nat Cyc Am Bio v1; Not Am Wom; Twent Cen Bio Dict Not Am; Wom Cent; Wom Lit, More

15236. Dix, Dorothea Lynde
1794/1802–1887
crusader for the welfare of the mentally ill, prison reformer, philanthropist, author, essayist, children's author, superintendent of army nurses in the Civil War
Massachusetts
Cyc Am Bio; Dict Am Auth; Dict Am Bio; Dict Am Bio Men Time; Dict Lit Bio v1; Index t Wom; Nat Cyc Am Bio v3; Not Am Wom; Twent Cen Bio Dict Not Am; Wom Cent

15237. Tubman, Emily H.
1794–1885
philanthropist, religious worker
Index t Wom

15238. Wright, Frances (d'Arusmont) "Fanny"; Fanny d'Arusmont
1795–1852
author, abolitionist, feminist, philanthropist, lecturer
Scottish
Am Bio Dict; Cyc Am Bio; Dict Am Bio; Dict Am Bio Men Time; Index t Wom; Nat Cyc Am Bio v2; Not Am Wom

15239. Otis, Eliza Henderson (Boardman)
1796–1873
philanthropist, novelist
Boston, MA
Dict Am Auth; Twent Cen Bio Dict Not Am

15240. Smith, Sophia
1796–1870
founder of Smith College, educationist, philanthropist
Dict Am Bio; Index t Wom; Nat Cyc Am Bio v7; Not Am Wom; Twent Cen Bio Dict Not Am

15241. Townsend, Mira Sharpless
1798–1859
philanthropist
Dict Am Bio

15242. Cadwise, David, Mrs.
flourished nineteenth century
humanitarian, philanthropist
Index t Wom

15243. Peter, Sarah Anne (Worthington) King
1800–77
charity worker, philanthropist, founder of art school for women, hospital founder, Civil War nurse, pioneer industrial arts educator, church worker
Catholic
Ohio
Dict Am Bio; Index t Wom; Not Am Wom; Twent Cen Bio Dict Not Am

15244. Rouse, Benjamin, Mrs.
born 1800
Civil War humanitarian, social reformer
Index t Wom

15245. Sibley, George C., Mrs.
flourished 1830s
humanitarian
Index t Wom

15246. Simpson, Martha Ritchie
flourished nineteenth century
humanitarian
Index t Wom

15247. White, Rhoda Elizabeth (Waterman)
flourished 1830s–50s
humanitarian, philanthropist, miscellaneous writer
Dict Am Auth; Index t Wom

15248. Gibbons, Abigail Hopper "Abby"
1801–93
abolitionist, prison reformer, feminist, women's welfare worker, Civil War nurse, philanthropist, journalist
Quaker
Cyc Am Bio; Dict Am Bio; Index t Wom; Nat Cyc Am Bio v7; Not Am Wom; Twent Cen Bio Dict Not Am; Wom Cent

15249. Child, Lydia Maria (Francis)
1802–80
author, philanthropist, abolitionist, editor, social reformer
Quaker
Massachusetts
Cyc Am Bio; Dict Am Auth; Dict Am Bio; Dict Am Bio Men Time; Dict Lit Bio v1; Index t Wom; Nat Cyc Am Bio v2; Not Am Wom; Twent Cen Bio Dict Not Am; Wom Cent

15250. Doremus, Sarah Platt Haines
1802–77
foreign missionary, founder of foreign missions, charity organizer, philanthropist, social worker
Cyc Am Bio; Dict Am Bio; Index t Wom; Nat Cyc Am Bio v6; Not Am Wom; Twent Cen Bio Dict Not Am

15251. Powers, Eliza Howard
1802–87
philanthropist, patron of army medicine
Cyc Am Bio

15252. Robert, Ann Maria
1802–82
philanthropist
Cyc Am Bio

15253. Thompson, Sarah; Countess Rumford
died 1852
philanthropist
Index t Wom

15254. Crandall, Prudence (Philles)
1803–1889/90
educator of Blacks, abolitionist, philanthropist
Quaker

English
Cyc Am Bio; Dict Am Bio; Eng
Wom; Index t Wom; Nat Cyc
Am Bio v2; Not Am Wom;
Twent Cen Bio Dict Not Am

**15255. Donovan, Caroline
(Soulsby)**
1803–90
philanthropist
Twent Cen Bio Dict Not Am

15256. Garrett, Eliza Clark
1805–55
philanthropist
Index t Wom

**15257. Chapman, Maria We-
ston**
1806–85
abolitionist, feminist, philanthropist
Dict Am Bio; Index t Wom; Nat
Cyc Am Bio v2; Not Am Wom;
Twent Cen Bio Dict Not Am

**15258. Cook, Martha Elizabeth
Duncan Walker**
1806–74
magazine editor, author, linguist,
translator, abolitionist, patron
of Polish arts and artists
Cyc Am Bio; Dict Am Bio

**15259. Wright, Martha Coffin
Pelham**
1806–75
women's rights leader, philanthropist
Index t Wom; Not Am Wom

**15260. Porter, Eliza Emily
Chappell**
1807–88
educator, Civil War relief worker
Not Am Wom

**15261. Gage, Frances Dana
(Barker); Aunt Fanny**
1808–84
lecturer, author, temperance
worker, abolitionist, suffragist,
women's rights worker, Civil
War relief worker
Cyc Am Bio; Dict Am Auth; Dict
Am Bio; Dict Am Bio Men
Time; Index t Wom; Nat Cyc
Am Bio v2; Not Am Wom;
Twent Cen Bio Dict Not Am;
Wom Cent

15262. Haviland, Laura Smith
1808–98
abolitionist, freedmen's welfare
worker, philanthropist
Quaker
Cyc Am Bio; Not Am Wom

**15263. James, Julia Bradford
Huntington**
1810–97

philanthropist
Twent Cen Bio Dict Not Am

**15264. Sever, Anne Elizabeth
Parsons**
1810–79
benefactor
Cyc Am Bio

15265. Ball, Martha Violet
born 1811
abolitionist, philanthropist, educator of Black women
Baptist
Wom Cent

**15266. Hoge, Jane Currie
Blaikie; A. H. Hoge**
1811–90
Civil War relief leader, church
and welfare worker, sanitation
commission worker, author
Index t Wom; Not Am Wom

**15267. Colt, Henrietta L.
Peckham**
1812–post 1860s
Civil War relief worker
Index t Wom

**15268. Cooper, Susan Augusta
Fenimore**
1813/15–1894
author, philanthropist
Cyc Am Bio; Dict Am Auth; Dict
Am Bio; Dict Am Bio Men
Time; Index t Wom; Nat Cyc
Am Bio v6; Not Am Wom;
Twent Cen Bio Dict Not Am

**15269. Haughery, Margaret
Gaffney; The Bread Woman
of New Orleans**
1813/25–1882
charitable worker, philanthropist,
dairy farmer, bakery operator
and owner
Cyc Am Bio; Dict Am Bio; Index
t Wom; Not Am Wom; Twent
Cen Bio Dict Not Am

15270. Pomeroy, Lucy Gaylord
died 1863
Civil War humanitarian
Index t Wom

15271. Wells, Charlotte Fowler
1814–1901
phrenologist, patron of women's
medical education, educator,
publisher, lecturer, businessperson
New York
Cyc Am Bio; Index t Wom; Not
Am Wom; Wom Cent

**15272. Farnham, Eliza Wood-
son (Burhans)**
1815–64
prison reformer, author, lecturer,
feminist, suffragist, philanthropist

New York; California
Cyc Am Bio; Dict Am Auth; Dict
Am Bio; Dict Am Bio Men
Time; Index t Wom; Nat Cyc
Am Bio v4; Not Am Wom;
Twent Cen Bio Dict Not Am

15273. Miner, Myrtilla
1815–64
educator, pioneer in teacher education for Black women, abolitionist, philanthropist
Cyc Am Bio; Dict Am Bio; Not
Am Wom

**15274. Ottendorfer, Anna Sar-
torius (Behr) Uhl**
1815–84
newspaper publisher, philanthropist
Dict Am Bio; Nat Cyc Am Bio
v8; Not Am Wom; Twent Cen
Bio Dict Not Am

15275. Palmer, Mary E.
died 1865
Civil War humanitarian
Index t Wom

**15276. Vanderpoel, Ann Priscil-
la**
1815–70
philanthropist
Cyc Am Bio

15277. Ayres, Anne
1816–96
pioneer in American Episcopal
Sisterhoods, religious author,
philanthropist
Dict Am Auth; Dict Am Bio; Not
Am Wom

15278. Bradley, Lydia Moss
1816–1908
philanthropist
Dict Am Bio

15279. Bruce, Catherine Wolfe
1816–1900
philanthropist, patron of astronomy
Not Am Wom

**15280. Newcomb, Josephine
Louise le Monnier**
1816–1901
philanthropist, patron of women's
education
Dict Am Bio; Not Am Wom

**15281. Stewart, Eliza Daniel
"Mother"**
1816–1908
temperance reformer, suffragist,
Civil War relief worker
Illinois
Dict Am Bio; Nat Cyc Am Bio
v7; Not Am Wom; Wom Cent

15282. Stone, Martha Elvira
born 1816

postmaster of North Oxford,
Massachusetts; genealogist; Civ-
il War relief worker
North Oxford, MA
Wom Cent

**15283. Bickerdyke, Mary Ann
Ball; Mother Bickerdyke**
1817–1901
hospital worker, Civil War nurse,
herbalist, philanthropist
Dict Am Bio; Index t Wom; Nat
Cyc Am Bio v21; Not Am
Wom; Wom Cent

15284. Mercer, Ann Jane
1817–86
philanthropist
Cyc Am Bio

15285. Fales, Almirah L.
died 1868
Civil War relief worker, ambu-
lance nurse, philanthropist
Dict Am Bio Men Time; Index t
Wom

15286. Mitchell, Martha Reed
born 1818
patron of art, traveler, philanthropist
Index t Wom; Wom Cent

15287. Esmond, Rhoda Anna
born 1819
philanthropist, temperance worker
Wom Cent

15288. Greene, Louisa Morton
born 1819
author, abolitionist, suffragist,
women's rights worker, temperance worker, Civil War relief
worker
Wom Cent

15289. Howe, Julia Ward
1819–1910
poet, dramatist, songwriter, lec-
turer, suffrage and women's
club leader, feminist, abolition-
ist, pacifist, prison reformer,
Union patriot during the Civil
War, philanthropist, traveler
Boston, MA
Cyc Am Bio; Dict Am Auth; Dict
Am Bio; Dict Am Bio Men
Time; Dict Lit Bio v1; Index t
Wom; Nat Cyc Am Bio v1; Not
Am Wom; Twent Cen Bio Dict
Not Am; Wom Cent

**15290. Lord, Elizabeth W.
Russell**
born 1819
educator, philanthropist, educator of the blind
Index t Wom; Wom Cent

15291. Lynde, Mary Elizabeth Blanchard
born 1819
philanthropist
Milwaukee, WI
Index t Wom; Wom Cent

15292. Coit, Elizabeth
born 1820
suffragist, temperance worker, humanitarian
Ohio
Irish
Wom Cent

15293. Davis, Sarah Iliff
born 1820
philanthropist, temperance worker, women's prison reformer, milliner, sanitation worker for the Union army during the Civil War, Freedmen's Aid worker
Wom Cent

15294. Gleason, Rachel Brooks
1820–1905
physician, medical author, abolitionist, patron of freedmen's education, dress reformer, women's rights worker
Dict Am Auth; Index t Wom; Wom Cent

15295. Harlan, James, Mrs.
married 1845/46
Civil War relief worker
Index t Wom

15296. Hemenway, Mary Porter (Tileston)
1820/22–1894
philanthropist, patron of archaeology and education
Dict Am Bio; Index t Wom; Not Am Wom; Twent Cen Bio Dict Not Am

15297. Henderson, Frances Cox
born 1820
linguist, translator, traveler, philanthropist, suffragist
Episcopalian
Wom Cent

15298. Mather, Sarah Ann
born 1820
philanthropist, patron of Black education, educator, author
South Carolina
Index t Wom; Wom Cent

15299. McHenry, Mary
flourished 1850s–70s
philanthropist, sponsor of Native American children's education
Cyc Am Bio

15300. Moore, Kate
flourished 1850s
philanthropist, pioneer
Index t Wom

15301. Shields, Mary
1820–80
philanthropist
Pennsylvania
Cyc Am Bio; Nat Cyc Am Bio v3

15302. Barton, Clara; Clarissa Harlowe
1821/30–1912
founder of the American Red Cross, Civil War hospital founder, expert on organizing military hospitals, philanthropist, nurse
Appl Cyc Am Bio; Cyc Am Bio; Dict Am Bio; Dict Am Rel Bio; Index t Wom; Nat Cyc Am Bio v3 and v15; Not Am Wom; Twent Cen Bio Dict Not Am; Wom Cent

15303. Brady, Mary A.
1821–64
philanthropist, Civil War relief worker
Irish
Index t Wom

15304. Farrand, Olive M.
born 1821
philanthropist
Nat Cyc Am Bio v10

15305. Lewis, Grace Anna
born 1821
naturalist, scientific illustrator, science writer, conservationist, ornithologist, abolitionist, Underground Railroad operator, pacifist, suffragist, philanthropist
Quaker
Index t Wom; Nat Cyc Am Bio v9; Twent Cen Bio Dict Not Am; Wom Cent

15306. Morse, Rebecca A.; Ruth Moza; R. A. Kidder; R. A. K.
born 1821
clubwoman, Sorosis member, suffragist, patron of art, abolitionist, author
New York
Index t Wom; Wom Cent

15307. Richmond, Sarah
1821–66
philanthropist
Cyc Am Bio

15308. Thompson, Elizabeth Rowell
1821–99
philanthropist, temperance worker, patron of science and of women's medical education, suffragist, political philosopher
Cyc Am Bio; Index t Wom; Nat Cyc Am Bio v5; Not Am Wom; Twent Cen Bio Dict Not Am; Wom Cent

15309. Ewing, Catherine A. Fay
born 1822
educator, philanthropist, missionary to the Choctaw people
Wom Cent

15310. Hooker, Isabella Beecher
1822–1907
suffragist, feminist, philanthropist, lecturer, essayist
Spiritualist
Hartford, CT
Cyc Am Bio; Dict Am Auth; Dict Am Bio; Index t Wom; Not Am Wom; Twent Cen Bio Dict Not Am; Wom Cent

15311. Jeanes, Anne T.
1822–1907
philanthropist
Quaker
Dict Am Bio

15312. Smith, Bathsheba (Bigler)
1822–1910
philanthropist
Mormon
Cyc Am Bio

15313. Williams, Mary Ann
1822–74
philanthropist, Civil War relief worker, Confederate sympathizer
Georgia
Nat Cyc Am Bio v7

15314. Farmer, Hannah Tobey Sharpleigh
1823–91
philanthropist, author, poet, religious worker
Dict Am Bio; Index t Wom; Nat Cyc Am Bio v7; Twent Cen Bio Dict Not Am

15315. Fitzgibbon, Mary Catherine Irene; Sister Irene
1823–96
Catholic nun, philanthropist
Catholic
Dict Am Bio; Twent Cen Bio Dict Not Am

15316. Hendricks, Eliza C. Morgan
born 1823
philanthropist, women's prison welfare worker
Episcopalian
Wom Cent

15317. Cheney, Endah Dow (Littlehale)
1824–1904
philanthropist, author, abolitionist, suffragist, women's rights worker, Black civil rights worker, lecturer, philosopher

Transcendentalist
Boston, MA
Cyc Am Bio; Dict Am Auth; Dict Am Bio; Dict Lit Bio v1; Index t Wom; Nat Cyc Am Bio v9; Not Am Wom; Twent Cen Bio Dict Not Am; Wom Cent

15318. Harvey, Cordelia Adelaide Perrine
1824–95
Civil War nurse, relief worker, social welfare leader
Index t Wom

15319. Minor, Virginia Louisa
1824–94
Civil War relief worker, suffrage leader, women's rights worker
Missouri
Cyc Am Bio; Dict Am Bio; Encyc South Hist; Nat Cyc Am Bio v25; Not Am Wom; Twent Cen Bio Dict Not Am

15320. Moore, Clara Sophia (Jessup); Clara Moreton; Clara Sophia (Jessup) Bloomfield-Moore
1824–99
author, poet, novelist, philanthropist, Civil War relief worker
Philadelphia, PA
Cyc Am Bio; Dict Am Auth; Index t Wom; Nat Cyc Am Bio v9; Not Am Wom; Twent Cen Bio Dict Not Am; Wom Cent

15321. Astor, Charlotte Augusta
1825–87
philanthropist
Cyc Am Bio

15322. Cooper, Sarah Brown Ingersoll
1825/36–1896
kindergartner, Bible teacher, philanthropist
California
Dict Am Bio; Nat Cyc Am Bio v3; Not Am Wom; Wom Cent

15323. Gaffney, Margaret
1825–82
philanthropist, dairy farmer
Nat Cyc Am Bio v2

15324. Gould, Emily Bliss
circa 1825–75
philanthropist
Cyc Am Bio

15325. Hoffman, Sophia Curtiss
born 1825
philanthropist, Sorosis member
Index t Wom; Wom Cent

15326. Stanford, Jane Eliza Lathrop
1825/28–1905

cofounder of Stanford University, patron of education, philanthropist
Index t Wom; Nat Cyc Am Bio v24; Not Am Wom; Twent Cen Bio Dict Not Am; Wom Cent

15327. Andrews, Judith Walker
born 1826
philanthropist
Index t Wom; Wom Cent

15328. Hazard, Rebecca N.
born 1826
philanthropist, suffragist, Civil War relief worker
Missouri
Wom Cent

15329. Plunkett, Harriette Merrick Hodge
born 1826
humanitarian, sanitation reformer
Massachusetts
Index t Wom; Wom Cent

15330. Sherwood, Mary Elizabeth (Wilson); M. E. W. S.
1826/30–1903
short story writer, poet, novelist, miscellaneous writer, patron of literature and science, philanthropist
Washington, DC
Cyc Am Bio; Dict Am Auth; Dict Am Bio; Index t Wom; Nat Cyc Am Bio v5; Wom Cent

15331. Howland, Emily
1827–1929
educator, educator of Blacks, abolitionist, suffragist, pacifist, temperance worker, philanthropist
Quaker
New York
Dict Am Bio; Nat Cyc Am Bio v25; Not Am Wom; Wom Cent

15332. Hussey, Cornelia Collins
born 1827
philanthropist, suffragist
New Jersey
Wom Cent

15333. McCabe, Harriet Calista Clark
1827–1919
philanthropist, temperance worker
Ohio
Index t Wom; Wom Cent

15334. Wittenmyer, Annie (Turner)
1827–1900
Civil War relief worker, leader in church and charitable work, philanthropist, temperance worker, lecturer, author

Ohio
Index t Wom; Nat Cyc Am Bio v12; Not Am Wom; Wom Cent

15335. Baker, Delphine P.
born 1828
Civil War relief worker
Index t Wom

15336. Collins, Ellen
1828–1912
philanthropist, housing reformer, Civil War patriot
Index t Wom; Not Am Wom

15337. Collins, Jennie
1828–87
labor reformer, welfare worker, philanthropist, suffragist
Massachusetts
Bio Dict Am Lab; Index t Wom; Not Am Wom; Twent Cen Bio Dict Not Am

15338. Leonard, Cynthia H. van Name
born 1828
philanthropist, author
Illinois
Index t Wom; Wom Cent

15339. Rand, Caroline Amanda Sherfey
1828–1905
philanthropist
Not Am Wom

15340. Sage, Margaret Olivia (Slocum)
1828–1918
philanthropist
Dict Am Bio; Index t Wom; Nat Cyc Am Bio v16; Not Am Wom

15341. Wolfe, Catharine Lorillard
1828–87
philanthropist, patron of the Metropolitan Museum of Art, art collector
New York
Cyc Am Bio; Dict Am Bio; Index t Wom; Nat Cyc Am Bio v10; Not Am Wom; Wom Cent

15342. Woolsey, Abby Howland
1828–93
Civil War relief worker, hospital worker, charity and educational worker, author on public health, philanthropist
Dict Am Auth; Index t Wom; Not Am Wom

15343. Dyer, Julia Knowlton
born 1829
philanthropist
Methodist
Wom Cent

15344. May, Abigail Williams
1829–88

Boston social reformer, abolitionist, suffragist, education commissioner, Civil War relief worker
Boston, MA
Index t Wom; Not Am Wom; Twent Cen Bio Dict Not Am

15345. Andrews, Emma
flourished 1860s
Civil War relief worker
Index t Wom

15346. Barker, Stephen, Mrs.
flourished 1860s
Civil War relief worker, nurse
Index t Wom

15347. Bigelow, R. M.
flourished 1860s
Civil War relief worker
Index t Wom

15348. Bradford, Charlotte
flourished 1860s
Civil War humanitarian
Index t Wom

15349. Brayton, Mary Clark
flourished 1860s–80s
Civil War relief worker, social reformer
Index t Wom

15350. Bucklin, Sophronia
flourished 1860s
Civil War relief worker, educator, nurse
Index t Wom

15351. Campbell, Valeria
flourished 1860s
Civil War relief worker, author
Index t Wom

15352. Clapp, Anna L.
flourished 1860s
Civil War relief worker, educator
Index t Wom

15353. Collins, Delia
born 1830
educator, temperance worker, philanthropist, welfare worker
Wom Cent

15354. Couzzins, Adaline
flourished 1860s
humanitarian, lecturer
Index t Wom

15355. Davis, G. T. M.
flourished 1860s
Civil War nurse, humanitarian
Index t Wom

15356. Eaton, J. S., Mrs.
flourished 1860s
Civil War relief worker
Index t Wom

15357. Etheridge, Annie
flourished 1860s
Civil War hero, nurse, humanitarian
Index t Wom

15358. Fenn, Curtis T., Mrs.
flourished 1860s
Civil War relief worker
Index t Wom

15359. Fisher, Rebecca Jane Gilleland
born 183?; married 1848
philanthropist, journalist, pioneer
Austin, TX
Index t Wom; Wom Cent

15360. Fletcher, Martha Mary
1830–85
philanthropist
Twent Cen Bio Dict Not Am

15361. Fogg, Isabella
flourished 1860s
Civil War nurse, philanthropist
Index t Wom

15362. Forbes, Arethusa L.
flourished 1860s
humanitarian
Index t Wom

15363. George, E. E., Mrs.
flourished 1860s
Civil War nurse, relief worker
Index t Wom

15364. Greble, Susan Virginia
flourished 1860s
Civil War relief worker
Index t Wom

15365. Grier, Maria C.
flourished 1860s
Civil War relief worker
Index t Wom

15366. Griffin, Josephine R.
flourished 1860s
Civil War relief worker, hero, philanthropist
Index t Wom

15367. Hadley, Piety Lucretia
flourished 1860s
Civil War relief worker
Index t Wom

15368. Hallowell, M. M., Mrs.
flourished 1860s
Civil War humanitarian and relief worker
Index t Wom

15369. Harris, Eliza
flourished 1860s
Civil War humanitarian, nurse
Index t Wom

15370. Harris, John, Mrs.
flourished 1860s

Civil War relief worker, nurse
Index t Wom

15371. Hosmer, O. E., Mrs.
flourished 1860s
Civil War relief worker
Index t Wom

15372. Jackson, Helen Maria (Fiske) (Hunt); Saxe Holme; H. H.
1830/31–1881/85
author, poet, novelist, crusader for Native American rights, philanthropist
Quaker
Cyc Am Bio; Dict Am Auth; Dict Am Bio; Index t Wom; Nat Cyc Am Bio v1; Not Am Wom; Read Encyc Am West; Twent Cen Bio Dict Not Am; Wom Cent; Wom Lit, More

15373. Johnston, Sarah R.
flourished 1860s
Civil War relief worker
Index t Wom

15374. Lee, Mary W.
flourished 1860s
Civil War nurse, patriot, philanthropist
Irish
Index t Wom

15375. Mann, Maria R.
flourished 1860s
Civil War philanthropist, educator
Index t Wom

15376. Marsh, M. M., Mrs.
flourished 1860s
Civil War relief worker
Index t Wom

15377. Mendenhall, Elizabeth S.
flourished 1860s
Civil War relief worker, nurse, philanthropist
Index t Wom

15378. Moore, Jane Boswell
flourished 1860s
Civil War relief worker
Index t Wom

15379. Parrish, Lydia G.
flourished 1860s
Civil War humanitarian
Index t Wom

15380. Phelps, John S., Mrs.
flourished 1860s
Civil War humanitarian
Index t Wom

15381. Powers, Lucy Gaylord
flourished 1860s
Civil War patriot, humanitarian
Index t Wom

15382. Ricketts, Fanny L.
flourished 1860s
Civil War humanitarian
English
Index t Wom

15383. Ross, Anna Maria
flourished 1860s
Civil War philanthropist, nurse
Index t Wom

15384. Rullmann, Maria
flourished 1860s
educator, philanthropist
Index t Wom

15385. Salomon, Eliza
flourished 1860s
Civil War philanthropist
Index t Wom

15386. Semmes, Myra E.
flourished 1860s
Civil War philanthropist
Index t Wom

15387. Seymour, Horatio, Mrs.
flourished 1860s
Civil War humanitarian
Index t Wom

15388. Shelton, Mary E.
flourished 1860s
Civil War philanthropist
Index t Wom

15389. Springer, C. R., Mrs.
flourished 1860s
Civil War humanitarian, educator
Index t Wom

15390. Stranahan, Marianne F.
flourished 1860s
Civil War humanitarian
Index t Wom

15391. Streeter, Elizabeth M.
flourished 1860s
Civil War humanitarian
Index t Wom

15392. Terry, Ellen F.
flourished 1860s
Civil War humanitarian
Index t Wom

15393. Wallace, Susan (Arnold) (Elston)
1830–1907
miscellaneous author, poet, religious writer, philanthropist
Indiana
Cyc Am Bio and ad; Dict Am Auth; Index t Wom; Nat Cyc Am Bio v10; Twent Cen Bio Dict Not Am; Wom Cent

15394. Wells, Mary Fletcher
flourished 1860s–90s
philanthropist, educator of freedmen

Alabama
Wom Cent

15395. Wells, Shepard, Mrs.
flourished 1860s
Civil War humanitarian
Index t Wom

15396. White, Armenia
flourished 1860s
philanthropist, social reformer, Civil War patriot
Index t Wom

15397. Woolsey, Jane Stuart
1830–91
Civil War relief and hospital worker, charity and educational worker, nurse, author
Index t Wom; Not Am Wom

15398. Wormeley, Katharine Prescott
1830/32–1908
Civil War relief and hospital worker, writer on sanitation, charity worker, philanthropist, translator, biographer
Rhode Island
English
Cyc Am Bio; Dict Am Bio; Index t Wom; Nat Cyc Am Bio v8; Not Am Wom; Twent Cen Bio Dict Not Am; Wom Cent

15399. Wright, Crafts J., Mrs.
flourished 1860s
Civil War humanitarian
Index t Wom

15400. Bishop, Bernice Pauahi
1831–84
philanthropist
Not Am Wom

15401. Calkins, Adelaide Augusta Hosmer
1831–1909
philanthropist, children's welfare worker
Congregationalist
Massachusetts
Nat Cyc Am Bio v28

15402. Clark, Susan Carrington
1831–1895
philanthropist
Index t Wom

15403. Fairbanks, Elizabeth B.
born 1831
philanthropist, mental institution reformer
Wisconsin
Wom Cent

15404. Wilhite, Mary Holloway
1831–92
physician, feminist, philanthropist
Wom Cent

15405. Blackall, Emily Lucas
1832–92
philanthropist, temperance worker
Baptist
Wom Cent

15406. Cadwallader, Allice A. W.
born 1832
philanthropist, Civil War relief worker, temperance worker
Wom Cent

15407. Culver, Helen
1832–1925
philanthropist, Black welfare worker, patron of science, hospital administrator, educator, real estate businessperson
Index t Wom; Nat Cyc Am Bio v17; Twent Cen Bio Dict Not Am

15408. Doolittle, Lucy Salisbury
born 1832
philanthropist, reformer of women's prisons, suffragist, educator of freedwomen
Wom Cent

15409. Eddy, Eliza Jackson
died circa 1882
philanthropist
Index t Wom

15410. Fussell, Susan
1832–89
educator, army nurse in the Civil War, Civil War relief worker, philanthropist
Quaker
Wom Cent

15411. Hiles, Osia Joslyn
born 1832
philanthropist, poet, Native American welfare worker
Wisconsin
Wom Cent

15412. Reese, Mary Bynon
born 1832
temperance worker, poet, Civil War humanitarian, Union sympathizer
Wom Cent

15413. Russell, Elizabeth Augusta
born 1832
philanthropist, Freedmen's Bureau worker, temperance worker
Wom Cent

15414. Aiken, Amanda L.
1833–92
philanthropist, editor, patron of women's education
Index t Wom; Wom Cent

15415. Carey, Emma Forbes
born 1833
humanitarian, author
Index t Wom

15416. Freeman, Julia S. (Wheelock)
1833–1900
philanthropist, Civil War relief worker
Nat Cyc Am Bio v7

15417. Gray, Mary Tenney
born 1833
philanthropist, journalist, editorial writer
Kansas
Wom Cent

15418. Quinton, Amelia Stone
1833–1926
Native American reform and rights worker, temperance worker, club leader, humanitarian
Index t Wom; Not Am Wom; Twent Cen Bio Dict Not Am; Wom Cent

15419. White, Carolina Earle
1833–1916
philanthropist
Index t Wom

15420. Woolsey, Georgeanne Muirson
1833–1906
Civil War relief and hospital worker, charity and educational worker
Index t Wom; Not Am Wom

15421. Cary, Mary Stockley
born 1834
businessperson, investor, philanthropist
Cleveland, OH
Wom Cent

15422. Rose, Martha E. (Parmelee)
born 1834
women's labor welfare worker, social reformer, sociologist, author, art patron, journalist, Sorosis member
Cleveland, OH
Index t Wom; Nat Cyc Am Bio v11; Wom Cent

15423. Talbot, Emily Fairbanks
1834–1900
philanthropist
Dict Am Bio

15424. Brown, Mary Frank
born 1835
philanthropist, Chinese and Japanese women's welfare worker, temperance worker
Oakland, CA
Wom Cent

15425. Carse, Matilda Bradley
1835–1917
temperance worker, child care worker, welfare worker, philanthropist, financier
Chicago, IL
Index t Wom; Not Am Wom; Twent Cen Bio Dict Not Am; Wom Cent

15426. Howe, Mary Ann
1835–70
educator of Blacks, philanthropist
Nat Cyc Am Bio v8

15427. McCormick, Nancy Maria Fowler "Nettie"
1835–1923
patron of education in China, philanthropist, businessperson
Presbyterian
Index t Wom; Nat Cyc Am Bio v21; Not Am Wom

15428. Newberry, Helen Parmelee Handy
1835–1912
philanthropist
Presbyterian
Detroit, MI
Nat Cyc Am Bio v41

15429. Osgood, Helen Louise (Gibson/Gilson)
1835–68
philanthropist, Civil War hospital administrator, nurse
Cyc Am Bio; Dict Am Bio Men Time; Index t Wom; Not Am Wom

15430. Ahrens, Mary A.
born 1836
philanthropist, suffragist, lawyer
Index t Wom

15431. Clark, Frances P.
born 1836
philanthropist, temperance worker
Omaha, NE
Wom Cent

15432. Leslie, Miriam Florence (Folline); Frank K. Leslie
1836/51–1914
magazine editor, publisher, feminist, philanthropist
New York
Cyc Am Bio; Dict Am Bio; Index t Wom; Nat Cyc Am Bio v25; Not Am Wom; Twent Cen Bio Dict Not Am; Wom Cent

15433. Scripps, Ellen Browning
1836–1932
philanthropist, newspaper writer and publisher, patron of marine science, founder of Scripps Marine Lab, pacifist, feminist, temperance worker

La Jolla, CA
Dict Am Bio; Index t Wom; Nat Cyc Am Bio v27; Not Am Wom

15434. Smith, Virginia Trall
1836–1903
mission and charity worker, pioneer in child care
Not Am Wom

15435. Stearns, Sarah Burger
1836–post 1899
suffragist, women's rights worker, philanthropist, Civil War humanitarian, temperance worker, social reformer, educator of freedmen
Unitarian
Cyc Am Bio; Index t Wom; Nat Cyc Am Bio v10; Twent Cen Bio Dict Not Am; Wom Cent

15436. Alexander, Esther Frances "Francesca"
1837–1917
artist, illustrator, author, translator, philanthropist
Italian (American expatriate to Italy)
Dict Am Auth; Not Am Wom

15437. Bergen, Cornelia M.
born 1837
philanthropist
Wom Cent

15438. Flower, Lucy Louisa (Coues)
1837–1921
social welfare worker, philanthropist, patron of education, president of the Illinois Training School for Nurses, member of the Chicago school board, trustee of the University of Illinois, Republican party worker
Episcopalian
Dict Am Bio; Nat Cyc Am Bio v9; Not Am Wom

15439. Harkness, Anna Richardson
1837–1926
philanthropist
Not Am Wom

15440. Keim, Jane Sumner Owen
graduated 1862
social reformer, humanitarian
Index t Wom

15441. Langworthy, Elizabeth
born 1837
philanthropist; civic worker in Monticello, Iowa, and Seward, Nebraska; clubwoman
Monticello, IA; Seward, NE
Index t Wom; Wom Cent

15442. Schuyler, Louisa Lee
1837/40–1926

leader in welfare work, Civil War philanthropist, patron of nursing, social worker, sanitarian
New York
Dict Am Bio; Index t Wom; Nat Cyc Am Bio v20; Not Am Wom

15443. Truitt, Anna Augusta
born 1837
temperance reformer, suffragist, patron of industrial education
Muncie, IN
Wom Cent

15444. Wing, Amelia Kempshall
born 1837
author, philanthropist
New York
Wom Cent

15445. Wyman, Lillie Buffum Chace
born 1837/47
author, muckraking journalist, short story writer, philanthropist, suffragist, labor welfare worker
Georgia
Dict Am Auth; Wom Cent

15446. Brown, Charlotte Emerson
1838–95
president of the General Federation of Women's Literary Clubs, patron of missionaries
Dict Am Bio; Wom Cent

15447. Cobb, Mary Emilie
born 1838
educator, philanthropist, juvenile-prison reformer
Wom Cent

15448. Johnson, Electa Amanda
born 1838
philanthropist
Wisconsin
Index t Wom; Wom Cent

15449. Palmer, Lizzie Pitts Merrill
1838–1916
philanthropist
Not Am Wom

15450. Sullivan, Mary Mildred Hammond
1838–1933
philanthropist, Civil War patriot, New York civic leader
Presbyterian
New York
Index t Wom; Nat Cyc Am Bio v31

15451. Vashon, Susan Paul
1838–1912
educator, nurse, Civil War relief organizer

Black
Index t Wom; Negro Alman; Prof
Negro Wom v1

**15452. Bailey, Hannah Clark
Johnston**
1839–1923
peace worker, temperance reformer, suffragist, philanthropist
Maine
Index t Wom; Nat Cyc Am Bio
v10; Not Am Wom; Wom Cent

15453. Battels, Sarah M. E.
born 1839
philanthropist
Wom Cent

15454. Campbell, Helen (Stuart)
1839–1918
journalist, children's author, social reformer, home economist,
educator, philanthropist
New York
Cyc Am Bio; Dict Am Auth; Nat
Cyc Am Bio v9; Not Am Wom;
Twent Cen Bio Dict Not Am;
Wom Cent

**15455. Draper, Mary Anna
Palmer**
1839–1914
philanthropist, benefactor of astronomy
Index t Wom; Not Am Wom

15456. George, Lydia A.
born 1839
army nurse in Civil War, Women's Relief Corps worker, philanthropist
Wom Cent

15457. Hancock, Cornelia
1839/40–1927
Civil War nurse, educator of
freedmen, charity worker, housing reformer
Quaker
Index t Wom; Not Am Wom

**15458. Willard, Frances
Elizabeth Caroline**
1839–98
educator, educational philosopher, suffragist, feminist, women's rights worker, temperance
leader, naturalist, philanthropist, newspaper editor, traveler
Methodist Episcopal
Cyc Am Bio; Dict Am Auth; Dict
Am Bio; Dict Am Bio Men
Time; Dict Am Rel Bio; Index t
Wom; Nat Cyc Am Bio v1; Not
Am Wom; Twent Cen Bio Dict
Not Am; Wom Cent

15459. Ames, Fanny Baker
1840–1931

industrial reformer in public institutions, charity organizer
Index t Wom; Not Am Wom;
Wom Cent

15460. Bell, Caroline Horton
born 1840
philanthropist
Presbyterian
Milwaukee, WI
Wom Cent

15461. Casseday, Jennie
born 1840
philanthropist, temperance worker
Kentucky
Wom Cent

15462. Chase, Elizabeth B.
flourished 1870s–80s
philanthropist
Index t Wom

15463. Coffin, C. F., Mrs.
flourished 1870s
philanthropist
Index t Wom

15464. Colt, Mrs.
flourished 1870s–80s
philanthropist
Index t Wom

**15465. Coolidge, Harriet Abbot
Lincoln**
flourished 1870s–80s
philanthropist, sanitary educator,
worker for women's education,
author
Wom Cent

15466. Endicott, Annie T.
flourished 1870s–80s
philanthropist
Index t Wom

15467. Hudlun, Anna Elizabeth
1840–1914
social worker, welfare worker,
philanthropist
African Methodist Episcopal
Zion
Black
Index t Wom; Negro Alman; Prof
Negro Wom v1

15468. Kimball, Martha Gertrude
1840–94
philanthropist, nurse
Index t Wom

15469. Leland, Caroline Weaver
born 1840
philanthropist, educator
Presbyterian
Michigan
Wom Cent

15470. Phelps, Aurora
flourished 1870s–80s
philanthropist
Index t Wom

15471. Potter, Isabella Abbe
flourished 1870s
philanthropist
Massachusetts
Nat Cyc Am Bio v14

**15472. Salm Salm, Agnes
Elizabeth Winona Joy
(Leqlerq), Princess**
1840/42–1881/1912
circus rider, rope dancer, actor,
field hospital worker and organizer, philanthropist
Cyc Am Bio; Dict Am Bio;
Twent Cen Bio Dict Not Am

15473. Trott, Lois E.
flourished 1870s–90s
educator, philanthropist, temperance worker
Wom Cent

15474. Woodbury, Anna Lowell
flourished 1870s–80s
humanitarian, educator
Index t Wom

15475. Catlin, Laura Wood
born 1841
philanthropist, author
Wom Cent

**15476. Conklin, Jennie Maria
(Drinkwater); Maria Drinkwater**
1841–1900
children's author, philanthropist,
clubwoman, founder of the
Shut-in Society for Invalids
Dict Am Auth; Index t Wom;
Dict Am Bio

15477. Pullman, Harriet Sanger
married 1866
humanitarian, philanthropist
Index t Wom

15478. Shaw, Pauline Agassiz
1841–1917
educational philanthropist
Swiss
Dict Am Bio; Nat Cyc Am Bio
v27; Not Am Wom

15479. Walker, Harriet Granger
1841–1917
philanthropist, hospital organizer,
temperance worker, suffragist,
police reformer
Methodist
Minneapolis, MN
Nat Cyc Am Bio v6; Wom Cent

15480. Wallace, Emma R. (Gilson)
1841–1911

club leader, philanthropist
Universalist
Chicago, IL
Index t Wom; Wom Cent

**15481. Ziegler, Electra Matilda
Curtis**
1841–1932
patron of welfare of the blind
Christian Scientist
New York
Index t Wom; Nat Cyc Am Bio
v37

15482. Dare, Ella
born 1842
lecturer, journalist, Civil War relief worker, sanitarian
Wom Cent

**15483. Dickinson, Anna
Elizabeth**
1842–1932
Civil War orator, lyceum lecturer,
abolitionist, women's rights
worker, suffragist, political activist, Republican party worker,
author, actor, philanthropist
Quaker
Cyc Am Bio; Dict Am Auth; Dict
Am Bio supp v1; Dict Am Bio
Men Time; Index t Wom; Nat
Cyc Am Bio v3; Not Am Wom;
Twent Cen Bio Dict Not Am;
Wom Cent

15484. Dow, Cornelia M.
born 1842
temperance worker, philanthropist
Congregationalist
Portland, OR
Wom Cent

**15485. Fowle, Elida Barker
Rumsey**
1842–1919
Civil War relief worker and
nurse, cofounder of a library for
Union soldiers in Washington,
DC
Index t Wom; Not Am Wom

15486. Fry, Elizabeth Turner
born 1842
philanthropist, Prohibitionist, humane worker, suffragist
San Antonio, TX
Wom Cent

15487. Hearst, Phoebe Apperson
1842–1919
philanthropist, patron of education and anthropology, Egyptologist
Dict Am Bio; Index t Wom; Nat
Cyc Am Bio v25; Not Am
Wom; Who Who Egypt

15488. Hunt, Augusta Merrill
born 1842

philanthropist, temperance worker, suffragist, prison reformer
Universalist
Wom Cent

15489. Lautz, Katherine Bardol
born 1842
philanthropist
Index t Wom

15490. Reed, Elizabeth (Armstrong)
1842–1915
theologist, religious author, philosopher, historian of India and Persia, writer on Oriental literature, temperance worker, philanthropist
Chicago, IL
Dict Am Auth; Dict Am Bio; Index t Wom; Nat Cyc Am Bio v1 and v15; Twent Cen Bio Dict Not Am

15491. Westinghouse, Marguerite Erskine Walker
1842–1914
sculptor, philanthropist
Nat Cyc Am Bio v15

15492. Aldrich, Josephine Cables
born 1843
newspaper publisher, editor, author, philanthropist
Nat Cyc Am Bio v5; Wom Cent

15493. Jacobs, Frances Wisebart; Mother of the Charities
1843–92
welfare worker, charity worker
Colorado
Not Am Wom

15494. Lowell, Josephine (Shaw)
1843–1905
charitable worker, philanthropist, social worker, prison reformer, labor reformer, writer on philanthropy
New York, NY
Cyc Am Bio; Dict Am Auth; Dict Am Bio; Index t Wom; Nat Cyc Am Bio v8; Not Am Wom; Twent Cen Bio Dict Not Am

15495. Ripley, Martha George Rogers
1843–1912
physician, humanitarian, feminist, abolitionist, temperance worker, suffragist
Index t Wom; Not Am Wom; Wom Cent

15496. Roebling, Emily Warren
1843–1903
Civil War patriot, philanthropist, club leader, author, lawyer
Index t Wom

15497. Spurlock, Isabella Smiley Davis
born 1843
philanthropist, temperance worker, Mormon women's welfare worker
Nebraska
Wom Cent

15498. Stevens, Lillian Marion Norton Ames
1844–1914
temperance reformer, women's rights worker, lecturer, philanthropist
Maine
Index t Wom; Nat Cyc Am Bio v13; Not Am Wom; Wom Cent

15499. Tanner, Mero L. White
born 1844
educator, humanitarian
Index t Wom

15500. Villard, Helen Frances Garrison "Fanny"
1844–1928
philanthropist, suffragist, pacifist, worker for Black civil rights
Dict Am Bio; Not Am Wom

15501. Ward, Elizabeth Stuart (Phelps)
1844–1911
author, popular novelist, women's rights worker, temperance worker, philanthropist
Massachusetts
Cyc Am Bio; Dict Am Auth; Dict Am Bio; Dict Am Bio Men Time; Index t Wom; Nat Cyc Am Bio v9; Not Am Wom; Twent Cen Bio Dict Not Am; Wom Cent; Wom Lit, More

15502. Buell, Caroline Brown
flourished 1875
temperance worker, philanthropist
Wom Cent

15503. Cheney, Armilla Amanda
born 1845
Civil War relief worker
Detroit, MI
Wom Cent

15504. Gilman, Mary L.
married 1870
philanthropist
Index t Wom

15505. Hough, Emma E. (Smith-Payne)
1845–1907
soprano concert and light opera soloist, patron of music education, philanthropist
California
Am Bio New Cyc

15506. Jones, Irma Theoda
born 1845
philanthropist, temperance worker
Lansing, MI
Index t Wom; Wom Cent

15507. Shaw, Cornelia Dean
born 1845
suffragist, philanthropist, Congregationalist missionary worker
Congregationalist
Toledo, OH
Wom Cent

15508. Ward, Lydia Arms (Avery) (Coonley)
1845–1924
author, poet, patron of the arts, suffragist, philanthropist
Chicago, IL
Dict Am Auth; Dict Am Bio; Index t Wom; Nat Cyc Am Bio v34

15509. Cole, Anna Virginia Russell
1846–1926
philanthropist
Not Am Wom

15510. Foster, Susie E. (Holland)
born 1846
author, philanthropist
Oregon
Wom Cent

15511. McCoy, Mary Eleanora
born 1846
philanthropist
Detroit, MI
Black
Prof Negro Wom v1

15512. Woody, Mary Williams Chawner
born 1846
philanthropist, educator, temperance worker
Wom Cent

15513. Barker, E. Florence
died 1897
officer in Women's Relief Corps
Index t Wom

15514. Gilbert, Linda
1847–95
prison welfare worker, philanthropist
Cyc Am Bio; Index t Wom; Not Am Wom; Twent Cen Bio Dict Not Am; Wom Cent

15515. Henrotin, Ellen M. Martin
1847–1922
women's club leader, labor and social reformer, philanthropist
Index t Wom; Not Am Wom

15516. Robinson, Jane Marie Bancroft
1847–1932
Methodist educator, deaconess leader, author, historian, philanthropist
Methodist
Index t Wom; Not Am Wom; Wom Cent

15517. Sparhawk, Frances Campbell
born 1847/58
author, novelist, philanthropist, Native American welfare worker
Newton, MA
Cyc Am Bio and ad; Dict Am Auth; Nat Cyc Am Bio v10; Wom Cent

15518. Stokes, Olivia Egleston Phelps
1847–1927
philanthropist
Dict Am Bio; Not Am Wom

15519. Adams, Helen Balfour
1848–1950
Civil War relief worker
Index t Wom

15520. Cramer, Harriet Laura Barker
1848–1922
journalist, editor, philanthropist
Index t Wom

15521. Gould, Ellen M.
born 1848
philanthropist, suffragist
Unitarian
Rhode Island
Wom Cent

15522. Kerens, Frances Jones
1848–1914
patron of Catholicism, philanthropist
St. Louis, MO
Nat Cyc Am Bio v31

15523. Roby, Lelia P.
born 1848
philanthropist, founder of the Ladies of the Grand Army of the Republic, veteran's welfare worker
Index t Wom; Wom Cent

15524. Spray, Ruth Hinshaw
born 1848
educator, philanthropist
Index t Wom

15525. East, Edward H., Mrs.
born 1849
philanthropist, temperance worker
Tennessee
Wom Cent

15526. Knight, Sarah (Harrison)
1849–1928
philanthropist, Minneapolis civic leader, Methodist church worker, hospital founder, patron of nurse's training
Methodist
Minneapolis, MN
Am Bio New Cyc

15527. Palmer, Bertha Honore
1849/51–1918
clubwoman, philanthropist, women's rights worker, art collector
Chicago, IL
Dict Am Bio; Index t Wom; Twent Cen Bio Dict Not Am; Wom Cent

15528. Speyer, Ellen Leslie Prince Lowery
1849/62–1921
philanthropist
Index t Wom; Not Am Wom

15529. Storer, Maria Longworth Nichols
1849–1932
patron of music, ceramicist, sculptor
Index t Wom; Nat Cyc Am Bio v11; Not Am Wom

15530. Thurston, Martha L. Poland
born 1849
philanthropist, journalist
Wom Cent

15531. Anderson, Elizabeth Milbank
1850–1921
World War I relief worker, philanthropist, patron of social welfare work, patron of Serbian and Yugoslavian welfare, patron of medical missions
Baptist
New York
Dict Am Bio; Nat Cyc Am Bio v23; Not Am Wom

15532. Bacon, Rebecca Taylor
flourished 1880s–90s
philanthropist, patron of nursing education
Appl Cyc Am Bio

15533. Guirado, Luz (Sanchez)
flourished 1880s–1930s
patron of the Catholic church
Catholic
Los Angeles, CA
Mexican
Am Bio New Cyc

15534. Horton, John Miller, Mrs.
flourished 1880s–1900s
philanthropist, clubwoman
Index t Wom

15535. Hughes, Caroline
flourished 1880s–90s
philanthropist, realtor
Chicago, IL
Wom Cent

15536. Jones, Melodia Blackmarr
1850–1931
philanthropist, Republican party worker
Episcopalian
Buffalo, NY
Nat Cyc Am Bio v32

15537. Quinby, Cordelia Adeline
flourished 1880s
philanthropist
Index t Wom

15538. Thurber, Jeannette Meyers
1850–1946
patron of music, founder of the National Conservatory of Music of America
Dict Am Bio supp v4; Nat Cyc Am Bio csv4; Not Am Wom

15539. Craig, Charity Rusk
born 1851
soldier's relief worker
Wom Cent

15540. Harriman, Mary Williamson (Averall)
1851–1932
philanthropist, businessperson
New York
Index t Wom; Nat Cyc Am Bio v23; Not Am Wom

15541. Johnston, Lizzie Johnston Evans
1851–1934
philanthropist, juvenile-prison reformer, Democratic party worker
Presbyterian
Alabama
Nat Cyc Am Bio v31

15542. Lathrop, Rose (Hawthorne); Mother Mary Alphonsa; Rose Hawthorne
1851–1926
author, artist, poet, Catholic nun, founder of the Dominican Congregation of St. Rose of Lima, philanthropist
Catholic
Cyc Am Bio; Dict Am Auth; Dict Am Bio; Index t Wom; Nat Cyc Am Bio v9; Not Am Wom; Twent Cen Bio Dict Not Am; Wom Cent

15543. Longyear, Mary Hawley Beecher
born 1851
author, philanthropist

Christian Scientist
Nat Cyc Am Bio csv3

15544. Safford, Mary Augusta
born 1851
Unitarian minister, lecturer, suffragist, philanthropist
Unitarian

Index t Wom; Nat Cyc Am Bio v14

15545. Spencer, Anna Carpenter (Garlin)
1851–1931
Unitarian minister, journalist, educator, temperance worker, suffragist, pacifist, child-labor reformer, philanthropist
Unitarian
Dict Am Bio; Nat Cyc Am Bio v9 and csv2; Not Am Wom

15546. Stoeckel, Ellen Battell
1851–1939
philanthropist, patron of music
Not Am Wom

15547. Balbach, Julia Anna
born 1852
inventor, philanthropist, suffragist
Nat Cyc Am Bio v17

15548. Bell, Mabel Gardner; Mrs. Alexander Graham Bell
married 1877
patron of aviation
Index t Wom

15549. Mather, Flora Stone
1852–1909
philanthropist
Cleveland, OH
Nat Cyc Am Bio v44

15550. Ormsby, Mary Frost
born circa 1852
author, journalist, philanthropist, pacifist
New York, NY
Index t Wom; Wom Cent

15551. Taft, Anne Sinton; Mrs. Charles Phelps
1852–1931
philanthropist
Cincinnati, OH
Nat Cyc Am Bio v23

15552. White, Emily Thorn Vanderbilt Sloane
1852–1946
philanthropist
Nat Cyc Am Bio v35

15553. Belmont, Alva Erskin Smith Vanderbilt
1853–1933
suffragist, feminist, politician, philanthropist
Index t Wom; Not Am Wom

15554. Noyes, Ida E. Smith
1853–1912
artist, photographer, philanthropist, club leader
Index t Wom; Nat Cyc Am Bio v17

15555. Sweet, Ada Celeste
1853–1928
journalist, editor, author, social reformer, philanthropist, pension agent
Chicago, IL
Index t Wom; Wom Cent

15556. Trask, Kate (Nichols) "Katrina"
1853/63–1922
magazine author, poet, short story writer, essayist, philanthropist
Saratoga, NY
Dict Am Auth; Nat Cyc Am Bio v11; Not Am Wom

15557. Williams, Theresa Amelia
born 1853
philanthropist, social reformer
Index t Wom

15558. Boughton, Caroline Greenbank
born 1854
educator, suffragist, philanthropist
Wom Cent

15559. Garrett, Mary Elizabeth
1854–1915
philanthropist, suffragist
Index t Wom; Not Am Wom

15560. Griffith, Mary Lillian
born 1854
philanthropist, author on morals, religious writer
Methodist Episcopal
Philadelphia, PA
Wom Cent

15561. Perkins, Angie Villette
1854–1921
educator, clubwoman, philanthropist
Nat Cyc Am Bio v19

15562. Proctor, Mary Virginia
born 1854
journalist, newspaper publisher, philanthropist
Methodist Episcopal
Virginia
Wom Cent

15563. Stokes, Caroline Phelps
1854–1909
philanthropist
Dict Am Bio; Not Am Wom

15564. Burdette, Clara Bradley
1855–1954

clubwoman, founder of women's clubs, philanthropist
Los Angeles, CA
Index t Wom; Nat Cyc Am Bio csv2; Obit File

15565. Cutting, Olivia Murray
1855–1949
philanthropist
New York
Nat Cyc Am Bio v38

15566. Havemeyer, Louisine Waldron Elder
1855–1929
art collector, philanthropist, suffragist
Not Am Wom

15567. Laws, Annie
1855–1927
kindergarten and education worker, clubwoman, civic leader, patron of nursing
Ohio
Nat Cyc Am Bio v22; Not Am Wom

15568. Richards, Mary Virginia
born 1855
philanthropist
Index t Wom

15569. Dodge, Grace Hoadley
1856–1914
social welfare and charity worker, philanthropist, educator
New York
Cyc Am Bio; Dict Am Bio; Index t Wom; Nat Cyc Am Bio v18; Not Am Wom; Wom Cent

15570. Gill, Emily Frances Lombard Abbey
1856–1950
patron of college education
Obit File

15571. Huling, Caroline Augusta
born 1856
journalist, suffragist, philanthropist, temperance worker
Illinois
Wom Cent

15572. Pond, Cora Scott
born 1856
philanthropist
Index t Wom

15573. Wiggin, Kate Douglas Smith
1856/59–1923
author, children's author, kindergarten educator, philanthropist
California
Dict Am Bio; Index t Wom; Nat Cyc Am Bio v6; Not Am Wom; Wom Cent

15574. Barrett, Kate Harwood Waller
1857/59–1925/29
social reformer, philanthropist, lecturer, social worker, suffragist, women's welfare worker
Virginia
Dict Am Bio; Encyc South Hist; Index t Wom; Not Am Wom

15575. Blackwell, Alice Stone
1857–1950
feminist, suffragist, journalist, editor, author, humanitarian
Dict Am Bio supp v2; Index t Wom; Nat Cyc Am Bio csv6; Not Am Wom; Obit File; Wom Cent

15576. Carnegie, Louise Whitfield
1857–1946
philanthropist
Not Am Wom

15577. MacDowell, Marian Griswold Nevins
1857–1956/57
patron of music, musician, pianist, founder of the MacDowell Artists Colony, lecturer
New Hampshire
Index t Wom; Not Am Wom supp v1; Obit File

15578. Alden, Cynthia May; Sunshine
1858/62–1931
journalist, editor, linguist, author, inventor, social worker, philanthropist, humanitarian
New York, NY
Dict Am Bio supp v1; Index t Wom; Nat Cyc Am Bio v14 and v22

15579. Doane, Ida Frances
1858–1942
philanthropist
Baptist
Nat Cyc Am Bio v41

15580. Dodge, Grace Parish
1858–1949
philanthropist
Obit File

15581. Drexel, Katharine Mary; Mother Mary Katharine
1858–1955
founder of the Catholic Sisters of the Most Blessed Sacrament for Indians and Colored People, educator of Blacks, missionary, philanthropist
Catholic
Dict Am Bio supp v5; Dict Am Rel Bio; Index t Wom; Not Am Wom supp v1; Obit File; Read Encyc Am West

15582. Hoel, Libbie Beach
born 1858
philanthropist
Wom Cent

15583. Morrison, May Treat
1858–1939
patron of the University of California, philanthropist
San Francisco, CA
Nat Cyc Am Bio v31

15584. Murdock, Louise Caldwell
1858–1915
interior designer, art patron
Kansas
Not Am Wom

15585. Osborne, Susan M.
1858–1918
philanthropist
Index t Wom

15586. Reid, Elizabeth Mills
1858–1931
philanthropist
Nat Cyc Am Bio v22; Not Am Wom

15587. Schofield, Mary Lyon Cheney
1858–1943
philanthropist
New Hampshire
Nat Cyc Am Bio v36

15588. Bowen, Louise Hadduck de Koven
1859–1953
philanthropist, welfare leader, Chicago social worker, president of Hull House, suffragist
Chicago, IL
Dict Am Bio supp v5; Index t Wom; Not Am Wom supp v1; Obit File

15589. Ford, Julia Ellsworth
1859–1950
children's author, playwright, novelist, patron of medicine
Nat Cyc Am Bio csv7; Obit File

15590. Bliss, George, Mrs.
flourished 1890s
philanthropist
Index t Wom

15591. Brackenridge, M. Eleanor
flourished 1890s
feminist, humanitarian
Index t Wom

15592. Davis, Katherine Bement
1860–1935
penologist, prison reformer, sociologist, social worker, philan-

thropist, disaster relief worker in Italy
Dict Am Bio ad; Index t Wom; Nat Cyc Am Bio csv1; Not Am Wom

15593. Emig, Lelia Dromgold
flourished 1890s–1900s
social reformer, philanthropist
Index t Wom

15594. Jenkins, Helen Hartley
1860–1935
philanthropist, nurse
Index t Wom; Not Am Wom

15595. Leary, Anne
born 1860
philanthropist
Cyc Am Bio; Index t Wom

15596. Nevins, Georgia Marquis
flourished 1890s–1910s
philanthropist
Index t Wom

15597. Smith, Sarah Rozet
flourished 1890s–1920s
philanthropist
Index t Wom

15598. Chanler, Margaret Ward Terry
1861–1952
philanthropist, musician, linguist, author
Index t Wom; Obit File

15599. Hammond, Natalie Harris
1861–1931
social worker, philanthropist
Index t Wom; Nat Cyc Am Bio v24

15600. Kaufman, Betty Wolf
1861–1942
philanthropist, welfare worker
Jewish
Philadelphia, PA
Nat Cyc Am Bio v32

15601. Lang, Florence Osgood Rand
1861–1943
patron of art, philanthropist
Congregationalist
Massachusetts
Nat Cyc Am Bio v32 and csv5

15602. Pfeiffer, Annie M.
1861–1946
philanthropist
Obit File

15603. Rice, Eleanor Elkins
1861–1937
philanthropist
Nat Cyc Am Bio v29

15604. Richmond, Mary Ellen
1861–1928
social worker, writer on charity
New York
Dict Am Auth; Nat Cyc Am Bio
v21; Not Am Wom

15605. Roberts, Mary Fantan
1861–1956
art magazine editor, journalist,
art patron
Index t Wom; Obit File

15606. Robinson, Corinne Roosevelt
1861–1933
poet, philanthropist
Index t Wom

15607. Taft, Helen Herron
1861–1943
founder and patron of the Cincinnati Orchestra Association, musician, music educator
Index t Wom; Nat Cyc Am Bio
v14

15608. Blodgett, Daisy Albertine Peck
1862–1947
philanthropist, equestrian
Washington, DC
Nat Cyc Am Bio v37

15609. Cushman, Emma
born 1862
humanitarian, nurse
Index t Wom

15610. Jones, Elizabeth Dickson
born 1862
philanthropist
Index t Wom

15611. Logan, Josephine Hancock
1862–1943
patron of the arts, author, poet
Chicago, IL
Nat Cyc Am Bio v35

15612. McCormick, Harriet Hammond
1862–1917
philanthropist, suffragist, patron
of child welfare
Episcopalian
Nat Cyc Am Bio v21

15613. Stimson, Harriet Overton
1862–1936
philanthropist, patron of music
Nat Cyc Am Bio v28

15614. Teresa, M. Imelda, Sister
born 1862
philanthropist, Catholic nun
Catholic
Index t Wom

15615. Wilson, Alice
1862–1948
philanthropist
Obit File

15616. Booth, Ellen Warren Scripps
1863–1948
philanthropist
Not Am Wom

15617. Caldwell, Mary Gwendolin
1863–1909
philanthropist
Not Am Wom

15618. Guggenheim, Florence Shloss
1863–1944
philanthropist, patron of music,
Republican party worker
Jewish
New York
Index t Wom; Nat Cyc Am Bio
v33; Obit File

15619. Ladd, Kate Everit Macy
1863–1945
philanthropist, patron of medicine and scientific research
Presbyterian
New York
Dict Am Bio supp v3; Nat Cyc
Am Bio v32 and csv4; Not Am
Wom

15620. Miner, Alice Trainer
1863–1950
philanthropist, patron of medicine
Presbyterian
New York
Canadian
Nat Cyc Am Bio v40

15621. Roberts, Dora
1863–1953
rancher, philanthropist
Texas
Obit File

15622. Bliss, Lizzie Plummer
1864–1931
art collector, philanthropist
Not Am Wom

15623. Coolidge, Elizabeth Penn Sprague
1864–1953
patron of chamber music, pianist,
philanthropist
Dict Am Bio supp v5; Index t
Wom; Not Am Wom supp v1

15624. Fuld, Carrie Bamberger Frank
1864–1944
philanthropist, cofounder of the
Institute for Advanced Study at
Princeton University

Princeton, NJ
Not Am Wom

15625. Talbott, Katharine Houk
1864–1935
patron of music
Dayton, OH
Nat Cyc Am Bio v28

15626. Booth, Maud Ballington (Charlesworth)
1865–1948
Salvation Army leader, evangelist, philanthropist, prison reformer, author, founder of PTA
Salvationist
English
Dict Am Auth; Index t Wom;
Nat Cyc Am Bio v14 and v38;
Not Am Wom; Obit File

15627. de Wolfe, Elsie Anderson; Lady Mendl
1865/70–1950
actor, stage producer, interior
decorator, World War I relief
worker
Dict Am Bio supp v4; Index t
Wom; Nat Cyc Am Bio csv6;
Not Am Wom

15628. Gleason, Kate
1865–1933
business promoter, community
developer, philanthropist
Dict Am Bio supp v1; Not Am
Wom

15629. Hepburn, Emily [Louisa] Eaton
1865–1956
clubwoman, philanthropist
New York
Index t Wom; Nat Cyc Am Bio
v46

15630. McFadden, Margaret Bischell
married 1890
philanthropist
Index t Wom

15631. Osborn, Alice Dodge
1865–1946
philanthropist, foe of Tammany
Hall
New York
Obit File

15632. Paget, Arthur, Lady
1865–1919
philanthropist, nurse
English
Index t Wom

15633. Pruit, Willie Franklin; Aylmer Ney
born 1865
philanthropist, poet
Tennessee
Index t Wom; Wom Cent

15634. Berry, Martha McChesney; Sunday Lady of the Possum Trot
1866–1942
educator, founder of the Berry
School for underprivileged
mountain children, philanthropist
Episcopalian
Georgia
Dict Am Bio supp v3; Encyc
South Hist; Index t Wom; Nat
Cyc Am Bio csv3; Not Am
Wom; Obit File

15635. Blaine, Anita [Eugenie] McCormick
1866–1954
philanthropist, pacifist, patron of
education and child welfare, patron of the League of Nations
Chicago, IL
Dict Am Bio supp v5; Nat Cyc
Am Bio v44; Not Am Wom
supp v1; Obit File

15636. Guggenheim, Leonie Bernheim
1866–1959
patron of dental clinics, patron of
free band concerts in parks
Jewish
New York
Obit File

15637. Hoyt, Minerva Lockhart Hamilton
1866–1945
naturalist, conservationist, botanist, patron of music, president
of the Los Angeles Symphony
Orchestra
Los Angeles, CA
Am Bio New Cyc; Nat Cyc Am
Bio v34

15638. Lanier, Harriet Bishop
1866–1931
patron of music
New York
Nat Cyc Am Bio v34

15639. Merrick, Mary Virginia
1866–1955
social worker, philanthropist,
founder of the Christ Child Society to aid crippled children
Index t Wom; Obit File

15640. Skinner, Belle
1866–1928
philanthropist, musical instrument collector
Nat Cyc Am Bio v23

15641. Young, Mary Vance
1866–1946
educator, linguist, World War I
relief worker
Presbyterian
Index t Wom; Nat Cyc Am Bio
v33

15642. Bingham, Mary Lily Kenan
1867–1917
philanthropist
Nat Cyc Am Bio v38

15643. Fisher, Elizabeth Holmes
born 1867
philanthropist
Methodist
California
Nat Cyc Am Bio csv6

15644. Herron, Carrie Rand
1867–1914
patron of socialist causes
Not Am Wom

15645. Meyer, Annie Florence Nathan
1867–1950/51
publicist, author, playwright, novelist, educationist, founder of Barnard College, antisuffragist, patron of Black music education, clubwoman
Jewish
New York
Dict Am Auth; Dict Am Bio; Index t Wom; Nat Cyc Am Bio v42; Not Am Wom supp v1; Obit File; Twent Cen Bio Dict Not Am; Wom Cent

15646. Randall, Minnie Josephine Smith
1867–1955
industrialist, founder of the Vacuum Can Co., philanthropist
Catholic
Chicago, IL
Nat Cyc Am Bio v42; Obit File

15647. Robertson, Ina Law
1867–1916
educator, philanthropist
Nat Cyc Am Bio v17

15648. Rogers, Grace Rainey
1867–1943
art collector, philanthropist
Not Am Wom

15649. Doane, Marguerite Treat
1868–1954
philanthropist, patron of medical missionaries
Baptist
Nat Cyc Am Bio v41

15650. Duryea, Nina Larrey Smith
1868–1951
World War I relief worker, playwright
Obit File

15651. Gould, Helen Miller
born 1868

philanthropist
Index t Wom; Nat Cyc Am Bio v13; Twent Cen Bio Dict Not Am

15652. Guggenheim, Irene Rothschild
1868–1954
patron of child welfare, philanthropist
Jewish
New York
Nat Cyc Am Bio v44

15653. Kittredge, Mabel
1868–1955
World War I relief worker, school lunch crusader
Obit File

15654. Lowden, Florence Pullman
born 1868
philanthropist
Index t Wom

15655. Bullowa, Emilie M.
1869–1942
lawyer, World War II relief worker, Sorosis member
Jewish
New York
Nat Cyc Am Bio v31

15656. Evans, Anne
1869/71–1941
civil leader, patron of the arts
Colorado
Index t Wom; Not Am Wom

15657. McConnell, Adelaide Dorn
1869–1942
physician, philanthropist
Presbyterian
Nat Cyc Am Bio v31

15658. Pratt, Helen Sherman
1869–1923
philanthropist
Nat Cyc Am Bio v6

15659. Clews, Mary Else Whelen
1870–1959
patron of art
French
Obit File

15660. Conger, Al, Mrs.
flourished 1900s
humanitarian, clubwoman
Index t Wom

15661. Graham, Nellie Dean; Vosey
born 1870
short story writer, magazine writer, philanthropist, clubwoman, Republican party worker, Los Angeles civic leader

Los Angeles, CA
Am Bio New Cyc

15662. Grouitch, Slavko, Madame
flourished 1900s
philanthropist
Index t Wom

15663. Harriman, Florence Jaffray (Hurst)
1870–1967
Democratic party official, diplomat, minister to Norway, politician, journalist, suffragist, clubwoman, social rights worker, Red Cross worker in World War I, World War II relief worker in Norway
Washington, DC
Index t Wom; Nat Cyc Am Bio v53 and csv6; Not Am Wom supp v1; Obit File

15664. Hunton, Addie Waites
born 1870
Red Cross worker, World War I relief worker
Black
Prof Negro Wom v2

15665. Lillie, Frances Crane
1870–1958
philanthropist
Chicago, IL
Obit File

15666. Mallone, Annie M. Turnbo; Annie Turnbo-Mallone
1870–1957
business executive, philanthropist
Black
Encyc Black Am; Not Am Wom supp v1

15667. Penrose, Julie Villers Lewis
1870–1956
philanthropist
Catholic
Colorado Springs, CO
Nat Cyc Am Bio v44

15668. Rubenstein, Helena
1870/71–1965
cosmetics manufacturer, entrepreneur, art collector, philanthropist
Jewish
Polish
Index t Wom; Nat Cyc Am Bio v50; Not Am Wom supp v1; Obit File; Who Who Jew Hist

15669. Spurr, Elizabeth Albright
1870–1934
rubber manufacturer, philanthropist
Newark, NJ
Nat Cyc Am Bio v27

15670. Strachan, Grace Charlotte
flourished 1900s
educator, philanthropist
Index t Wom

15671. Wollman, Kate
1870–1955
philanthropist
New York
Obit File

15672. Adler, Sophie Rosenwald
1871–1955
philanthropist, patron of the blind
Jewish
Obit File

15673. Dooly, Ismay
died 1921
journalist, humanitarian
Index t Wom

15674. Draper, Helen Fidelia
1871–1951
Red Cross nurse, World War I relief worker, social worker
Episcopalian
New York
Index t Wom; Nat Cyc Am Bio v39

15675. Harvey, Kate Benedict Hanna
1871–1936
public health worker, patron of nursing, cattle breeder
Protestant Episcopal
Cleveland, OH
Nat Cyc Am Bio v34

15676. Hauberg, Susanne Christine Denkmann
1872–1942
philanthropist
Presbyterian
Rock Island, IL
Nat Cyc Am Bio v42

15677. Hubbard, Helen Fahnestock
1872–1955
philanthropist, historical collector
Nat Cyc Am Bio v46

15678. Jones, Jesse Homan
1872–1962
philanthropist, publisher of the *Houston Chronicle*
Houston, TX
Obit File

15679. McCormick, Edith Rockefeller
1872–1932
philanthropist, patron of music and psychiatry
Index t Wom; Nat Cyc Am Bio csv3; Not Am Wom

15680. Patino, Albina Rodriguez
1872–1953
mine owner and operator, dairy farmer, philanthropist
Bolivian
Nat Cyc Am Bio v40

15681. Schoenfeld, Julia
graduated 1897
philanthropist
Index t Wom

15682. Clubb, Laura Abigail Rutherford
1873–1952
art collector, rare book collector, philanthropist, cattle rancher
Methodist
Oklahoma
Nat Cyc Am Bio v38

15683. Crane, Josephine (Porter) Boardman
1873–1972
New York civic leader, patron of the arts
Episcopalian
New York
Nat Cyc Am Bio v57

15684. Harriman, Grace Carley
1873–1950
humanitarian
Index t Wom

15685. Morgan, Anne Tracy
1873–1952
philanthropist, organizer of relief work in France during World War II, World War I relief worker, social worker
Dict Am Bio supp v5; Index t Wom; Nat Cyc Am Bio csv2 and csv5; Not Am Wom supp v1; Obit File

15686. O'Reilly, Mary Boyle
born 1873
humanitarian, philanthropist, police commissioner, author
Index t Wom

15687. Smith, Georgine Northrop Wetherill
1873–1955
artist, art patron
Unitarian
Philadelphia, PA
Nat Cyc Am Bio v48

15688. Abbott, Clara Barnes
1874–1956
patron of music
Obit File

15689. Hammand, Emily Vanderbilt Sloane
1874–1907
philanthropist, social worker, Moral Rearmament Society member

Presbyterian
New York
Nat Cyc Am Bio v55 and csv8

15690. Harkness, Mary Emma Stillman
1874–1950
philanthropist
Index t Wom; Not Am Wom

15691. Mather, Winifred Holt
1874–1945
sculptor, patron of welfare of the blind, founder of a school for the blind, author
Episcopalian
Nat Cyc Am Bio v34 and csv6

15692. Pouch, Helena R. Hellwig
1874–1960
humanitarian, president of DAR, tennis champion
Index t Wom; Obit File

15693. Rockefeller, Abby Green Aldrich
1874/75–1948
philanthropist, art patron
New York
Dict Am Bio supp v4; Index t Wom; Nat Cyc Am Bio v45; Not Am Wom

15694. Wise, Louise Waterman
1874–1947
charitable worker, founder and president of the women's division of the American Jewish Congress, Zionist
Jewish
New York
Not Am Wom

15695. Wright, Katherine
1874–1929
patron of aviation
Index t Wom

15696. Ball, Bertha
born 1875
philanthropist, civic worker
Universalist
Muncie, IN
Nat Cyc Am Bio csv6

15697. Barnard, Kate
1875–1930
Democratic political reformer, Native American rights advocate, child welfare leader, philanthropist
Oklahoma
Index t Wom; Nat Cyc Am Bio v15, Not Am Wom; Read Encyc Am West

15698. Denning, Delia; Delia (Denning) Akeley Howe
1875–1970
African explorer, big game hunter, geographer, taxidermist, au-

thor, lecturer, World War I relief worker
Nat Cyc Am Bio v57; Obit File; Index t Wom

15699. Howe, Delia Akeley (Denning)
1875–1970
African explorer, big game hunter, geographer, taxidermist, author, lecturer, World War I relief worker
Index t Wom; Nat Cyc Am Bio v57; Obit File

15700. McCormick, Katharine Dexter
1875–1967
philanthropist
Not Am Wom supp v1

15701. Tusch, Mary E. Hall "Mother"
circa 1875–1960
aviation patron
Index t Wom

15702. Whitney, Gertrude Vanderbilt
1875–1942
sculptor, patron of art, patron of opera, museum founder
Dict Am Bio supp v3; Index t Wom; Nat Cyc Am Bio v17, csv2, and csv5; Not Am Wom; Obit File

15703. Bellingrath, Mary Nesbitt Elmore
1876–1955
philanthropist, president of the Coca-Cola Bottling Co.
Alabama
Nat Cyc Am Bio v47

15704. Bole, Roberta Holden
1876–1950
philanthropist; patron of art, science, and education
Unitarian
Nat Cyc Am Bio v38

15705. Carr, Edith Adele
1876–1965
philanthropist, diplomatic and consular officer
Washington, DC
Nat Cyc Am Bio v51

15706. Cornish, Nellie Centennial
1876–1956
music educator, patron of music, music school founder
Washington
Index t Wom; Read Encyc Am West

15707. Ellinwood, Henrietta Elizabeth (Schneider)
born 1876
philanthropist, suffragist

Illinois
Nat Cyc Am Bio v16

15708. Huntington, Ann (Vaughan) Hyatt
1876–1973
sculptor, patron of the arts
Cur Biog '73; Index t Wom; Nat Cyc Am Bio v18 and 59; Not Am Wom supp v1; Obit File

15709. Kahn, Addie Wolff
1876–1949
patron of the arts
Obit File

15710. Mead, Elizabeth Manning Cleveland
1876–1946
patron of cancer research
Episcopalian
New York
Nat Cyc Am Bio v38

15711. Warburg, Frieda Schiff
1876–1958
philanthropist, Jewish welfare worker
Jewish
New York
Nat Cyc Am Bio v44; Obit File

15712. Whitney, Helen (Hay)
1876–1944
philanthropist, poet, children's author, financier, equestrian expert, owner of Greentree Racing Stables
Dict Am Auth; Index t Wom; Nat Cyc Am Bio v33; Obit File

15713. Zimbalist, Mary Louise Curtis Bok
1876–1970
music patron, philanthropist
Index t Wom; Not Am Wom supp v1; Obit File

15714. Balsan, Consuelo Vanderbilt
born 1877
philanthropist
Index t Wom

15715. de Kotzebue, Alene Tew; Countess Paul
1877–1955
philanthropist
Obit File

15716. Dreier, Katherine Sophie
1877–1952
patron of art, painter, early promoter of abstract and surrealist art
Dict Am Bio supp v5; Not Am Wom supp v1; Obit File

15717. Hutchison, Ida Jones Seymour
1877–1950

educator, philanthropist
Index t Wom

15718. Bartlett, Florence Dibell
1878–1954
patron of art
Obit File

15719. Borg, Madeleine Beer
1878–1956
social worker, humanitarian
Index t Wom

15720. Campbell, Eleanor Milbank Anderson
1878–1959
physician, social welfare worker, public health worker, patron of medicine
Baptist
Nat Cyc Am Bio v49 and csv4

15721. Emrick, Jeanette Wallace
born 1878
author, lecturer, humanitarian
Index t Wom

15722. Gindhart, Mary Wilhelmina (Simon)
1878–1969
music patron
Methodist
Philadelphia, PA
Nat Cyc Am Bio v57

15723. Guggenheim, Olga Hersh
1878–1970
philanthropist, patron of the arts
Jewish
New York
Obit File

15724. Manville, Henrietta Estelle
1878–1947
patron of floriculture and horticulture, philanthropist
New York
Nat Cyc Am Bio v56 and csv6

15725. Pugsley, Emma Catherine Gregory
died 1928
philanthropist, investor, entrepreneur
Presbyterian
New York
Nat Cyc Am Bio v22

15726. Belmont, Eleanor Elise Robson
1879–1979
actor, author, nurse, philanthropist, patron of the arts, founder of the Metropolitan Opera Guild
English
Index t Wom; Cur Biog '44 and '80

15727. Reilly, Marion
1879–1928
educator, suffragist, philanthropist
Dict Am Bio

15728. Dunbar, Saidie [Sarah] Orr
1880–1960
patron of nursing and public health, developer of Christmas Seals
Catholic
Oregon
Nat Cyc Am Bio v51

15729. Glass, Meta
1880–1967
president of Sweet Briar College, educator, YWCA executive, World War I and II relief worker, defense worker
Episcopalian
Virginia
Nat Cyc Am Bio v53 and csv7; Obit File

15730. McGill, Sarah
flourished 1910s
linguist, translator, philanthropist
Index t Wom

15731. McShane, Agnes
flourished 1910s
philanthropist
Index t Wom

15732. Miliken, D. A., Mrs.
flourished 1910s
philanthropist
Index t Wom

15733. Rosenbery, Millie R. M.
flourished 1910s
club leader, philanthropist
Index t Wom

15734. Ryan, Ida Barry
flourished 1910s
philanthropist
Index t Wom

15735. Schweppe, Laura Shedd
1880–1937
philanthropist, art patron
Chicago, IL
Nat Cyc Am Bio v50

15736. Shapiro, Dora Monness
1880–1952
philanthropist, Jewish welfare worker
Jewish
Obit File

15737. Spalding, Anne
flourished 1910s
philanthropist
Index t Wom

15738. Trader, Georgia
flourished 1910s
philanthropist, humanitarian
Index t Wom

15739. Welsh, Andrews, Sr., Mrs.
flourished 1910s
philanthropist
Index t Wom

15740. Blossom, Elizabeth Beardsley Bingham
1881–1970
Cleveland civic worker, philanthropist
Cleveland, OH
Nat Cyc Am Bio v58

15741. Boardman, Queen Walker
born 1881
horticulturist, philanthropist
Religious Scientist
Los Angeles, CA
Nat Cyc Am Bio csv7

15742. Driscoll, Clara
1881–1945
clubwoman, philanthropist, politician, political activist
Texas
Not Am Wom; Obit File

15743. Gilmore, Florence MacGruder
born 1881
philanthropist, author
Index t Wom

15744. Jones, Eleanor Dwight
circa 1881–1965
humanitarian
Index t Wom

15745. McClellan, Irene Moulton Ward
1881–1967
philanthropist, World War I Red Cross relief worker in England, patent medicine manufacturer, dairy and chicken farmer
Episcopalian
New York
Nat Cyc Am Bio v53

15746. Sears, Eleanora Randolph
1881–1968
tennis player, squash champion, patron of equestrian sports and figure skating
Hall Fame Sport; Index t Wom; Not Am Wom supp v1; Obit File

15747. Smith, Gertrude Robinson
1881–1963
New York civic worker, World War I relief worker, founder of the Tanglewood music festival, music patron
Nat Cyc Am Bio v48; Obit File

15748. Spreckels, Alma Emma Charlotte Corday le Normand de Bretteville
1881–1968
patron of art
San Francisco, CA
Obit File

15749. Stein, Beatrice Borg
1881–1958
welfare leader, philanthropist, founder of the Play School Association
Jewish
New York
Nat Cyc Am Bio v47; Obit File

15750. Clayburgh, Alma
1882–1958
concert singer, patron of art, philanthropist
Obit File

15751. Guggenheim, Minnie
1882–1966
patron of music, founder and manager of the Lewisohn Stadium Outdoor Concerts, philanthropist
Jewish
New York
Index t Wom; Obit File

15752. Harris, Mary Ormerod
born 1882
philanthropist, patron of the University of Southern California
Congregationalist
California
Nat Cyc Am Bio csv6

15753. Hogg, Ima
1882–1975
philanthropist
Not Am Wom supp v1

15754. Meagher, Katherine Kelly
married 1907
philanthropist
Index t Wom

15755. Reid, Helen Miles Rogers
1882–1970
publisher of *The New York Herald-Tribune* newspaper, journalist, suffragist, philanthropist
Episcopalian
New York
Cur Biog '70; Index t Wom; Nat Cyc Am Bio v56; Not Am Wom supp v1; Obit File

15756. Walsh, Carrie Belle Reed
died 1932
philanthropist

Washington, DC
Nat Cyc Am Bio v26

15757. Cameron, Helen de Young
1883–1969
philanthropist
San Francisco, CA
Obit File

15758. Carter, Alice (Olin) Draper
born 1883
YWCA executive, world war relief worker, welfare worker
Episcopalian
New York
Nat Cyc Am Bio v55

15759. Gibbons, Helen Davenport Brown
1883–1960
novelist, founder of Sauvons les Bebes, a World War I orphan aid agency
Obit File

15760. Lamson, Armene Tashijian
1883–1970
medical illustrator, physician, UNICEF worker, medical author
Episcopalian
Seattle, WA
Turkish
Nat Cyc Am Bio v56

15761. Pew, Helen Jennings Thopson
1883–1963
philanthropist
Pittsburgh, PA
Nat Cyc Am Bio v57

15762. Watson, Jeannette Kittredge
1883–1966
philanthropist, founder and director of International Business Machines
Nat Cyc Am Bio v51

15763. Wilson, Matilda Rausch
1883–1967
philanthropist, Detroit civic worker, chairperson of the board of directors of Fidelity Bank & Trust, member of the state board of agriculture, lieutenant governor of Michigan, Salvation Army worker
Presbyterian
Detroit, MI
Nat Cyc Am Bio v59

15764. Bachrach, Grace Baer
1884–1962
philanthropist, patron of medicine
Jewish

New York
Nat Cyc Am Bio v47

15765. Emery, Mary Muhlenberk Hopkins
1884–1927
philanthropist, founder of Mariemont, a model town near Cincinnati
Protestant Episcopal
Ohio
Nat Cyc Am Bio v24

15766. Roosevelt, [Anna] Eleanor
1884–1962
social reformer, humanitarian, author, lecturer
Washington, DC
English
Eng Wom; Index t Wom; Nat Cyc Am Bio v57 and csv4 and csv6; Not Am Wom supp v1; Obit File

15767. Challinor, Mercedes Crimmins (Clara)
1885–1966
Red Cross official, World War I relief worker
Catholic
Nat Cyc Am Bio v52

15768. Clowes, Edith Whitehill (Hinkel)
1885–1967
Indianapolis civic leader, patron of music
Episcopalian
Indianapolis, IN
Nat Cyc Am Bio v53

15769. Greenfield, Edith Mary
died 1935
patron of Egyptology
Who Who Egypt

15770. Woerishoffer, Emma Carola
1885–1911
philanthropist, social worker
Not Am Wom

15771. Couvent, Bernard, Madame
died 1936
philanthropist
Index t Wom

15772. Draper, Muriel Gordon Sanders
1886–1952
feminist, humanitarian, founder of the Pro-Soviet Congress of American Women
Index t Wom; Obit File

15773. Dummer, Ethel Sturges
1886–1954
philanthropist
Not Am Wom supp v1

15774. Eustis, Dorothy Leib Harrison Wood
1886–1946
philanthropist, patron of agriculture, founder and president of the Seeing-Eye Association, dog breeder
Dict Am Bio supp v4; Index t Wom; Nat Cyc Am Bio csv5; Not Am Wom; Obit File

15775. Sternberger, Estelle Miller
born 1886
humanitarian
Index t Wom

15776. Auerbach, Beatrice
1887–1968
philanthropist, businessperson
Not Am Wom supp v1

15777. Biddle, Mary Duke
1887–1960
humanitarian, philanthropist, patron of Duke University
Methodist Episcopal
North Carolina
Index t Wom; Nat Cyc Am Bio v49

15778. Drake, Dula Heisel Rae
born 1887
philanthropist, patron of World War I relief in Italy
Nat Cyc Am Bio csv2

15779. MacNeil, Marie Stevens Hicks
1887–1952
developer of the British plan for evacuation of bombed-out children in World War II
Obit File

15780. Post, Marjorie Merriweather
1887–1973
philanthropist, antique collector, suffragist, director of National Savings and Trust, founder and director of General Foods
Christian Scientist
Washington, DC
Nat Cyc Am Bio v58; Not Am Wom supp v1; Obit File

15781. Weld, Julia Deforest Tiffany
1887–1973
medical researcher, patron of medicine
New York
Nat Cyc Am Bio v58

15782. Aldrich, Harriet Alexander
1888–1972
New York civic worker, World War II relief worker
New York, NY
Nat Cyc Am Bio v60

15783. Brandstrom-Ulrich, Elsa; The Angel of Siberia
1889–1948
World War I prisoner of war relief worker in Russia and Siberia
Obit File

15784. Chung, Margaret Jessie
1889–1959
plastic surgeon, World War II relief worker
California
Chinese
Nat Cyc Am Bio v48

15785. Neese, Laura Janvrin Aldrich
1889–1967
artist, philanthropist
Congregationalist
Wisconsin
Nat Cyc Am Bio v53

15786. Rosen, Lucie Bigelow Dodge
1889–1968
electronic musician, patron of music
Episcopalian
New York
Nat Cyc Am Bio v54

15787. Burdick, Nellie Follis
flourished 1920s–30s
actor, feminist, philanthropist
Index t Wom

15788. Butler, Kate Maddux Robinson
circa 1890–1974
publisher, philanthropist, patron of French relief in World War II
Buffalo, NY
Nat Cyc Am Bio v58

15789. Dreier, Ethel E.
flourished 1920s–30s
humanitarian, club leader
Index t Wom

15790. Kennedy, Rose (Fitzgerald)
born 1890
philanthropist, patron of welfare work for the mentally retarded and of research on mental retardation
Catholic
Cur Biog '70

15791. Merrill, Eleanor Brown
flourished 1920s–30s
humanitarian, worker with the blind
Index t Wom

15792. Rex, Peggy
flourished 1920s
patron of aviation
Index t Wom

15793. Ford, Eleanor Clay
graduated 1916
philanthropist
Index t Wom

15794. Lilly, Ruth Allison
1891–1973
philanthropist
Episcopalian
Indianapolis, IN
Nat Cyc Am Bio v58

15795. Mather, Elizabeth Ring Ireland
1891–1957
philanthropist, patron of horticulture
Cleveland, OH
Nat Cyc Am Bio v43

15796. Crosby, Caresse; Polly Jacob
1892–1970
poet, patron of the arts, cofounder of the Black Sun Press
French (American expatriate to Paris)
Dict Lit Bio v4

15797. Field, Mary Hickson Matthews
married 1917
artist, philanthropist
Nat Cyc Am Bio v23

15798. Grossinger, Jennie
1892–1972
philanthropist; hotel executive, owner, and manager; country club owner
Jewish
Catskill Mountains, NY
Austrian
Cur Biog '73; Index t Wom; Not Am Wom supp v1; Obit File

15799. Harrison, Gertrude [Alice] Gordon Grayson
1892–1961
Washington, DC, civic leader; patron of medicine; racehorse breeder
Episcopalian
Nat Cyc Am Bio v51

15800. Lewisohn, Alice Irene
1892–1944
social worker, theatrical patron and innovator
Index t Wom; Not Am Wom

15801. Dodge, Pauline Morgan
1893–1971
YWCA executive, philanthropist
Presbyterian
New York
Nat Cyc Am Bio v56

15802. Levy, Adele Rosenwald
1893–1960
philanthropist, chairperson of the United Jewish Appeal National Women's Division, art collector
Jewish
New York
Obit File

15803. Lewisohn, Margaret Seligman
1895–1954
educator, art patron, clubwoman
New York
Index t Wom; Nat Cyc Am Bio v44

15804. Rockefeller, Martha Baird
1896–1971
concert pianist, music patron
Obit File

15805. Russell, Helen Victoria Crocker
1896–1966
bank director, UNESCO executive, philanthropist
Episcopalian
San Francisco, CA
Nat Cyc Am Bio v53

15806. Heller, Florence Gunsfeld
1897–1966
philanthropist, patron of medicine, Jewish welfare worker
Jewish
Chicago, IL
Nat Cyc Am Bio v51

15807. Rosenstein, Nettie
born 1897
fashion designer, philanthropist, business executive
Australian
Index t Wom

15808. Danzig, Allison
born 1898
patron of tennis
Hall Fame Sport

15809. Guggenheim, Marguerite "Peggy"
born 1898
patron of modern art and music, art collector, author
Jewish
New York
Cur Biog '80; Index t Wom; Who Who Jew Hist

15810. Newhall, Jannette E.
born 1898
philosopher
Who Who Phil

15811. Abbott, Helen Probst
flourished 1930s
feminist, humanitarian
Index t Wom

15812. Baer, Louise Andrews
died 1950
patron of heart disease research
Obit File

15813. Bay, Josephine Holt Perfect
born 1900
financier, philanthropist
Index t Wom

15814. Coffey, Phyllis C.
flourished 1930s
educator, humanitarian
Index t Wom

15815. Colby, Marie F.
flourished 1930s
humanitarian
Index t Wom

15816. Connors, Grace
born 1900
philanthropist
Index t Wom

15817. Dublin, Mary
flourished 1930s
economist, humanitarian
Index t Wom

15818. Dunn, Hilda S.
flourished 1930s
humanitarian
Index t Wom

15819. Eddy, Olive Tyndale
flourished 1930s
humanitarian
Index t Wom

15820. Hartman, Gustave, Mrs.
born 1900
philanthropist, author
Index t Wom

15821. Hartman, May Weisser
born circa 1900
humanitarian, social welfare leader
Index t Wom

15822. Holden, Miriam Young
flourished 1930s
humanitarian, clubwoman
Index t Wom

15823. Hunton, Hazel
flourished 1930s
patriot, humanitarian
Index t Wom

15824. Ingersoll, Marion Crary
flourished 1930s
humanitarian
Index t Wom

15825. Keep, Mabel Hazlett
flourished 1930s
philanthropist, editor
Index t Wom

15826. Kraft, Lucile L.
flourished 1930s
humanitarian
Index t Wom

15827. Kubie, Matilda Steinam
flourished 1930s
humanitarian, philanthropist, clubwoman
Index t Wom

15828. Lasker, Mary Woodward
born 1900
philanthropist
Index t Wom

15829. Leach, Agnes Brown
flourished 1930s
humanitarian, clubwoman
Index t Wom

15830. Lehman, Edith
flourished 1930s
humanitarian
Index t Wom

15831. Lynn, Meda C.
flourished 1930s
educator, humanitarian
Index t Wom

15832. Maxfield, Kathryn Erroll
flourished 1930s
humanitarian
Index t Wom

15833. McDougal, Irene G.
flourished 1930s
clubwoman, philanthropist
Index t Wom

15834. Miller, Rose
flourished 1930s
humanitarian
Index t Wom

15835. Pratt, Gladys Lynwall
flourished 1930s
explorer, museum patron
Index t Wom

15836. Purdy, Grace Bronson
flourished 1930s
humanitarian
Index t Wom

15837. Randall, Ollie Annette
flourished 1930s
social worker, humanitarian
Index t Wom

15838. Sheppard, Jeanie R.
flourished 1930s
social worker, humanitarian
Index t Wom

15839. Thurber, Louise Lockwood
flourished 1930s

humanitarian, feminist, social worker
Index t Wom

15840. Vanderlip, Candace Alig
flourished 1930s
humanitarian, business executive
Index t Wom

15841. White, Edith Hamilton
flourished 1930s
humanitarian
Index t Wom

15842. Bruce, Ailsa Mellon
1901–69
philanthropist, patron of art, conservationist
Episcopalian
New York
Nat Cyc Am Bio v55; Obit File

15843. Menken, Helen (Richard)
1901–66
actor, president of the American Theater Wing, humanitarian
Index t Wom; Obit File

15844. Abbell, Fannie Edelman
born 1902
business executive, philanthropist
Jewish
Chicago, IL
Nat Cyc Am Bio csv11

15845. Koussevitzky, Olga
1902–78
patron of the arts
Obit File

15846. Lamont, Florence Corliss
died 1952
patron of education
Obit File

15847. Pleydel-Bouverie, Ava Alice Muriel Astor
1902–56
patron of art, patron of ballet
Obit File

15848. Hubbard, Muriel McCormick
1903–59
philanthropist
Obit File

15849. Payson, Joan Whitney
1903–75
philanthropist, race horse breeder, owner of the New York Mets, patron of medicine, art collector and investor, founder of the Museum of Modern Art in New York
Episcopalian
New York
Cur Biog '72 and '75; Index t Wom; Nat Cyc Am Bio v58 and csv10; Obit File

15850. Adair, Marion Hopkinson (Barnes)
1904–65
New York civic leader, World War II relief worker, cancer-patient relief worker, patron of cancer research, radio personality, mimic
New York, NY
Nat Cyc Am Bio v51

15851. Lewisohn, Adele Guggenheimer
died 1954
philanthropist
Jewish
New York
Obit File

15852. Lord, Mary Stimson Pillsbury
born 1904
social welfare worker, UN representative, humanitarian
Index t Wom

15853. Mauze, Abby Rockefeller
1904–76
philanthropist, patron of cancer research
Obit File

15854. Fosburgh, Mary Cushing
1906–78
patron of the arts
Obit File

15855. Allison, Ruth Jones
died 1957
philanthropist
Chicago, IL
Obit File

15856. Medinger, Elizabeth Eudora
1907–77
Catholic church worker, philanthropist
Catholic
Washington, DC
Nat Cyc Am Bio v60

15857. Crowinshield, Louise E. du Pont
died 1958
philanthropist, patron of historical monuments
Obit File

15858. Resnick, Rose
graduated 1934
educator of the blind, humanitarian
Index t Wom

15859. Fisher, Emma Roderick
flourished 1940s
patron of music
Index t Wom

15860. Latham, Natalie Wales
born 1911
humanitarian
Index t Wom

15861. Allen, Vivian Beaumont
died 1962
philanthropist
Index t Wom; Obit File

15862. Preminger, Marion Hill; Mrs. Albert Mayer
1913–72
social worker, author, African art collector, missionary to the Congo, philanthropist, screen actor
Catholic
New York
Hungarian
Nat Cyc Am Bio v57; Obit File

15863. Harkness, Rebekah (West)
born 1915
patron of dance, semiclassical composer, popular composer
Cur Biog '74

15864. Paley, Barbara Cushing
born circa 1917
philanthropist
Index t Wom

15865. Smith, Mary Elizabeth Leinen
born 1917
business executive, worker for the welfare of the handicapped, philanthropist
Nat Cyc Am Bio csv13

15866. Olivarez, Graciela
born 1928
lawyer, United Way executive, civil rights worker
Mexican
Dict Mex Am Hist

15867. Castleman, Alice Barbee
born 1943
philanthropist, women's rights worker
Episcopalian
Louisville, KY
Wom Cent

15868. Nave, Anna Eliza Seamans
born 1948
philanthropist
Index t Wom

15869. Mercer, Margaret
1771/92–1845
abolitionist, philanthropist, author
Cyc Am Bio; Dict Am Bio; Dict Am Bio Men Time; Index t Wom

No Dates

15870. Carter, Artie Mason
musician, patron of music
Index t Wom

15871. King, Louise Woodward
founder of the Georgia SPCA, philanthropist
Georgia
Cyc Am Bio

PHOTOGRAPHY

15872. Adams, Marian Hooper
1843–85
photographer
Not Am Wom

15873. Barnes, Catharine Wee
born 1851
artist, photographer
Nat Cyc Am Bio; Wom Cent

15874. Kasebier, Gertrude Stanton
1852–1943
photographer
Not Am Wom

15875. Noyes, Ida E. Smith
1853–1912
artist, photographer, philanthropist, club leader
Index t Wom; Nat Cyc Am Bio v17

15876. Cobb, Sarah M. Maxson
born 1858
artist, art educator, photographer, microscopist
Wom Cent

15877. Heaton, Eliza Putnam
born 1860
journalist, photojournalist, newspaper editor, Sorosis member
Wom Cent

15878. Billwiller, Henrietta Hudson
1863–1942
pioneer in color photography; inventor of the Hudetta process, an early method of making color prints
Obit File

15879. Crane, Alna
1863–1953
first American newspaper photographer
Obit File

15880. Johnston, Frances Benjamin
1864–1952

photojournalist
Dict Am Bio supp v5; Index t
  Wom; Not Am Wom supp v1;
  Obit File

**15881. Austen, Alice
  (Elizabeth)**
1866–1952
photographer
Dict Am Bio supp v5; Index t
  Wom; Obit File

**15882. Dupont, Aime; Etta A.
  Greer**
flourished 1900s
photographer
Nat Cyc Am Bio v15

15883. Miller, Sadie Kneller
died 1920
journalist, photographer
Index t Wom

15884. Akeley, Mary Lee Jobe
1878/86–1966
explorer, photographer, educator,
  author, botanist
Index t Wom; Not Am Wom

15885. Sipprell, Clara
flourished 1920s
photographer
Index t Wom

15886. Hudson, Henrietta
died 1942
photographer
Index t Wom

15887. Kanaga, Consuelo
1894–1978
photographer
New York
Nat Cyc Am Bio v60; Obit File

15888. Lange, Dorothea
1895–1965
photographer
Not Am Wom supp v1; Obit File

15889. Abbott, Berenice
born 1898
photographer
Index t Wom

**15890. Breckinridge, Mary
  Marvin**
flourished 1930s
photographer, politician
Index t Wom

15891. Gillespie, Marian
flourished 1930s
explorer, photographer, editor,
  author
Index t Wom

15892. Helvarg, Sue
flourished 1930s
photographer's agent
Russian
Index t Wom

15893. Jacobi, Lotte J.
flourished 1930s
photographer
German
Index t Wom

15894. Light, Mary
flourished 1930s
aeronautical photographer
Index t Wom

15895. Pote, Louise
flourished 1930s
aviator, aerial photographer
Index t Wom

15896. Richards, Wynn
flourished 1930s
photographer
Index t Wom

15897. Martin, Jackie [Cecelia]
born 1903
photographer
Index t Wom

15898. Bourke-White, Margaret
1904/06–1977
photographer, photojournalist
Cur Biog '71; Index t Wom; Not
  Am Wom supp v1

**15899. Cummings, Marion
  Morehouse**
1906–69
photographer
Obit File

15900. Frissell, Toni
born 1907
photographer
Index t Wom

15901. Koffler, Ylla "Camilla"

1911–55
photographer, animal photographer
Austrian
Obit File

**15902. Anderson, Erica Kellnor
  Collier**
born 1914
photographer
Australian
Index t Wom

15903. Bannister, Constance
born 1919
photographer
Index t Wom

15904. Arbus, Diane Nemerov
1923–71
photographer
Not Am Wom supp v1

**15905. Larsen, Lisa (Rasmus-
  sen)**
1925–59
photojournalist

German
Obit File

15906. Chicago, Judy (Cohen)
born 1939
feminist, autobiographer, sculptor, photographer, painter
Cur Biog '81

15907. Bergen, Candice
born 1946
screen actor, photojournalist
Cur Biog '75

No Dates

**15908. Bonney, Therese
  (Mabel)**
photographer, journalist
Index t Wom

PHYSICS, MATHEMATICS, AND EARTH SCIENCES

15909. Mitchell, Maria
1791/1818–1889
astronomer, women's rights
  worker, educator, novelist, poet
Quaker
Massachusetts
Cyc Am Bio; Dict Am Bio; Dict
  Am Bio Men Time; Index t
  Wom; Nat Cyc Am Bio v5; Not
  Am Wom; Twent Cen Bio Dict
  Not Am; Wom Cent

**15910. Peterson, Hannah Mary
  (Bouvier)**
1811–70
astronomer, author, illustrator,
  writer on astronomy
Cyc Am Bio; Dict Am Auth

15911. Bruce, Catherine Wolfe
1816–1900
philanthropist, patron of astronomy
Not Am Wom

15912. Burnham, Sarah Maria
1818–1901
educator, historical author, writer
  on geology and travel
Cambridge, MA
Dict Am Auth

15913. Fowler, Lydia Folger
1822/23–1979
physician, lecturer, social reformer, author, astronomer, science
  writer
Cyc Am Bio; Dict Am Auth;
  Index t Wom; Not Am Wom

**15914. Thomas, Mary von Er-
  den**
born 1825
author, novelist, statistician

Washington, DC
Cyc Am Bio; Dict Am Bio

15915. Nash, Mary Louise
born 1826
educator, author, humorist, botanist, geologist
Wom Cent

15916. Bowen, Eliza Andrews
1828–98
newspaper and magazine writer,
  writer about astronomy
Georgia
Dict Am Auth

15917. Gordon, S. Anna
born 1832
homeopathic physician, Civil War
  doctor, author, temperance
  worker, meteorologist
Wom Cent

**15918. Bristol, Augusta (Coo-
  per)**
1835–1910
educator, writer on education, author, poet, sociologist, lecturer
  on philosophic and scientific
  topics
Cyc Am Bio and ad; Dict Am
  Auth; Twent Cen Bio Dict Not
  Am; Wom Cent

15919. Edwards, Anna Cheney
born 1835
geologist, botanist, educator
Wom Cent

**15920. Smith, Erminnie Adele
  (Platt)**
1836/37–1886
ethnologist, geologist, geographer
Cyc Am Bio; Dict Am Auth; Dict
  Am Bio; Index t Wom; Nat Cyc
  Am Bio v13; Not Am Wom

**15921. Draper, Mary Anna
  Palmer**
1839–1914
philanthropist, benefactor of astronomy
Index t Wom; Not Am Wom

15922. Shafer, Helen Almira
1839–94
mathematician, educator, third
  president of Wellesley College
Cyc Am Bio; Dict Am Bio; Index
  t Wom; Nat Cyc Am Bio v7;
  Twent Cen Bio Dict Not Am;
  Wom Cent

15923. Homer, Ella
flourished 1870s–80s
mineralogist
Index t Wom

**15924. Cunningham, Susan
  Jane**
1842–1921

suffragist, educator, mathematician, astronomer
Pennsylvania
Nat Cyc Am Bio v6; Wom Cent

15925. Richards, Ellen Henrietta (Swallow)
1842–1911
sanitation chemist and engineer, mineralogist, leader in applied and domestic science, writer on domestic science, professor at MIT, educator
Massachusetts
Cyc Am Bio; Dict Am Auth; Dict Am Bio; Index t Wom; Nat Cyc Am Bio v7; Not Am Wom; Twent Cen Bio Dict Not Am; Wom Cent

15926. Strong, Harriet Williams Russell
1844–1926/29
agriculturist, student of water supply problems, horticulturist, engineer, civic leader
Los Angeles, CA
Dict Am Bio; Nat Cyc Am Bio v17; Not Am Wom

15927. Swarthout, M. French
born 1844
educator, mathematics textbook author
Illinois
Wom Cent

15928. Franklin, Christine Ladd; Christine Ladd-Franklin
1847–1930
mathematician; logician; psychologist; writer on math, logic and psychology
Dict Am Bio; Index t Wom; Nat Cyc Am Bio v5 and v26; Not Am Wom; Twent Cen Bio Dict Not Am

15929. Whiting, Sarah Frances
1847–1927
physicist, astronomer
Not Am Wom

15930. Whitney, Mary Watson
1847–1920/21
astronomer, educator
Dict Am Bio; Not Am Wom

15931. Graffenrief, Mary Clare de
born 1849
statistician
Index t Wom

15932. Proctor, Mary
flourished 1880s–1910s
astronomer
Irish
Index t Wom; Nat Cyc Am Bio v9; Twent Cen Bio Dict Not Am

15933. Wood, Frances Fisher
flourished 1880s–90s
educator, lecturer, scientist, dress reformer, dairy farmer, businessperson
Wom Cent

15934. Hayes, Ellen
born 1851
mathematician, geologist, educator, author
Index t Wom; Twent Cen Bio Dict Not Am

15935. Brauenlich, Sophia (Toepken)
1854–98
journalist, business manager of Scientific Publishing Co., fellow of the Imperial Institute of Great Britain
Nat Cyc Am Bio v9

15936. Carr, Deborah Edith Wallbridge
born 1854
librarian, statistician
Index t Wom

15937. Todd, Mabel Loomis
1856/58–1932
author, editor of Emily Dickinson's books and letters, traveler, lecturer, astronomer
Dict Am Bio; Index t Wom; Nat Cyc Am Bio v9, v28, and v41; Not Am Wom; Twent Cen Bio Dict Not Am; Wom Cent

15938. Fleming, Williamina Patron Stevens "Mina"; M. Fleming
1857–1911
astronomer
Dict Am Bio; Index t Wom; Nat Cyc Am Bio v7; Not Am Wom; Twent Cen Bio Dict Not Am

15939. Scott, Charlotte Angas
1858–1931
mathematician
Index t Wom; Not Am Wom

15940. Westover, Cynthia M.
born 1858
scientist, naturalist, inventor, businessperson, linguist
Wom Cent

15941. Braeunlich, Sophie
born 1860
scientific publisher, government employee
Index t Wom; Wom Cent

15942. Maltby, Margaret E.
born 1860
physicist
Index t Wom

15943. Roberts, Dorothea (Klumpke)
1861–1942
astronomer
San Francisco, CA
Index t Wom; Nat Cyc Am Bio v13 and v31

15944. Bascom, Florence
1862–1945
geologist
Dict Am Bio supp v3; Index t Wom; Not Am Wom

15945. Cannon, Annie Jump
1863–1941
astronomer
Methodist; Congregationalist
Cambridge, MA
Dict Lit Bio supp v3; Index t Wom; Nat Cyc Am Bio csv2; Not Am Wom; Obit File

15946. Merrill, Helen Abbot
1864–1949
educator, mathematician
Congregationalist
Nat Cyc Am Bio v42

15947. Smith, Clara Eliza
circa 1865–1943
mathematician, educator
Index t Wom

15948. Maury, Antonia Caetana de Paiva Pereira
1866/86–1952
astronomer
Index t Wom; Not Am Wom supp v1

15949. Leavitt, Henrietta Swan
1868–1921
research astronomer
Dict Am Bio; Index t Wom; Nat Cyc Am Bio v25; Not Am Wom

15950. Donald, Mary Jane
flourished 1900s
geologist
Index t Wom

15951. Greenewalt, Mary Elizabeth Hallock; Mary Greenwalt
1871–1950
pianist, lighting engineer, lecturer
Nat Cyc Am Bio v39; Index t Wom

15952. Pennington, Mary Engle
1872–1952
chemist, bacteriologist, refrigeration specialist, engineer, inventor
Index t Wom; Not Am Wom supp v1; Obit File

15953. Fisher, Elizabeth Florette
born 1873

field geologist
Nat Cyc Am Bio csv3

15954. Maury, Carlotta Joaquina
1874–1938
paleontologist
Episcopalian
New York
Nat Cyc Am Bio v28

15955. Ogilvie, Ida Helen
born 1874
geologist, educator
Nat Cyc Am Bio v16

15956. Wick, Frances Gertrude
1875–1941
physicist, educator
Presbyterian
Index t Wom; Nat Cyc Am Bio v34; Obit File

15957. Hahn, Dorothy Anna
1876–1950
organic chemist
Not Am Wom

15958. Wells, Agnes Ermina
1876–1959
mathematician, astronomer, educator
Index t Wom

15959. Gilbreth, Lillian Evelyn (Moller)
1878–1972
industrial engineer and psychologist, household efficiency and labor efficiency expert, management consultant
Cur Biog '72; Index t Wom; Not Am Wom supp v1; Obit File

15960. Bingham, Millicent Todd
1880–1968
geographer, conservationist, author, editor, authority on Emily Dickinson
Episcopalian
Cur Biog '69; Index t Wom; Nat Cyc Am Bio csv9

15961. Gardner, Julia Anne
1882–1960
geologist, stratigraphic paleontologist
Not Am Wom supp v1

15962. Barney, Nora Stanton Blatch
1883–1971
civil engineer, architect, suffragist
Not Am Wom supp v1

15963. Clarke, Edith
1883–1959
electrical engineer
Index t Wom; Not Am Wom supp v1

15964. Knopf, Eleanora Frances Bliss
1883–1974
geologist
Not Am Wom supp v1

15965. Wheeler, Anna Johnson Pell
1883–1966
mathematician
Not Am Wom supp v1

15966. Dennis, Olive Wetzel
1885–1957
engineer, inventor, railroad executive
Index t Wom

15967. Boyd, Louise Arner
1887–1972
scientific polar explorer, geographer, technical expert for the War Department and the National Bureau of Standards
Episcopalian
Cur Biog '72; Index t Wom; Nat Cyc Am Bio csv7; Obit File

15968. Deardorff, Neva R.
1887–1958
social welfare statistical expert, president of the Child Welfare League of America, cofounder of the Health Insurance Plan of Greater New York
New York
Obit File

15969. Goldring, Winifred
1888–1971
paleontologist
Not Am Wom supp v1

15970. Quick, Hazel Irene
graduated 1915
engineer
Index t Wom

15971. Wall, Florence Emeline
flourished 1920s–30s
industrial chemist, cosmetician
Index t Wom

15972. Ingels, Margaret
graduated 1916
mechanical engineer
Index t Wom

15973. Makemsen, Maud Worcester
born 1891
astronomer
Index t Wom

15974. Quimby, Edith Hinckley
born 1891
biophysicist, educator
Index t Wom

15975. Geiringer, Hilda
1893–1973

applied mathematician, statistician, space scientist
Index t Wom; Not Am Wom supp v1

15976. Friedman, Elizabeth Smith
born 1894
cryptanalyst in World War I
Nat Cyc Am Bio csv5

15977. Gardner, Maude Elsa
born 1894
aeronautical engineer
Index t Wom

15978. Kellems, Vivien
1896–1975
industrialist, engineer, president of the Kellems Co.
Connecticut
Cur Biog '69; Index t Wom

15979. Stiebeling, Hazel Katherine
born 1896
physical chemist, government official
Index t Wom

15980. Stinson, Katherine
born 1896
aviator, aeronautical engineer
Index t Wom

15981. Blodgett, Katherine Burr (Seibert)
1897/98–1979
physicist, chemist, inventor of scientific equipment
Cur Biog '80; Eng Wom; Index t Wom

15982. Edinger, Tilly
1897–1967
vertebrate paleontologist, paleoneurologist
Not Am Wom supp v1

15983. Eaves, Elsie
born 1898
civil engineer
Index t Wom

15984. Sitterly, Charlotte Moore
born 1898
astrophysicist
Index t Wom

15985. Anderson, Elda Emma
1899–1961
health physicist
Congregationalist
Nat Cyc Am Bio v50; Not Am Wom supp v1

15986. Carlin, Dorothy A.
flourished 1930s
civil engineer
Index t Wom

15987. Clark, Frances Hurd
flourished 1930s
metallurgist
Index t Wom

15988. Gardner, Elsa
flourished 1930s–40s
navy aeronautical engineer
Index t Wom

15989. Gillette, Martha Taylor
flourished 1930s
engineer, draftsperson
Index t Wom

15990. Hale, Evelyn Wickham
flourished 1930s
astronomer
Index t Wom

15991. Hoff, Madeline
flourished 1930s
engineer, aviator
Index t Wom

15992. Johnson, Dorothy B.
flourished 1930s
entomologist
Index t Wom

15993. Lewis, Jean Satterlee
flourished 1930s
meteorologist
Index t Wom

15994. McNally, Margaret
flourished 1930s
civil engineer
Index t Wom

15995. Payne-Gaposchkin, Cecilia Helena
born 1900
astronomer, educator, author
English
Index t Wom

15996. Rusk, Evelyn Carroll
1900–64
mathematician, educator
Catholic
New York
Nat Cyc Am Bio v51

15997. Scofield, Edna May
flourished 1930s
meteorologist
Index t Wom

15998. Walker, Helen M.
flourished 1930s
mathematician
Index t Wom

15999. Walsh, Betty
flourished 1930s
meteorologist
Index t Wom

16000. Weisner, Dorothy E.
flourished 1930s

statistician, social worker
Index t Wom

16001. Wilson, Frances Seydel
flourished 1930s
astronomer
Index t Wom

16002. Fowler-Billings, Katharine
born 1902
geologist, author, explorer
Index t Wom

16003. Rees, Mina S.
born 1902
mathematician, educator, government official
Index t Wom

16004. Rockwell, Mabel MacFerran
born 1902
electrical engineer
Index t Wom

16005. Wills, Doris Margaret Wood
1902–63
astronomer, research engineer
Unitarian
Pennsylvania
Nat Cyc Am Bio v53

16006. Flugge-Lotz, Irmgard
1903–74
engineer, mathematician
Not Am Wom supp v1

16007. Meyer, Editha Paula Chartkoff
born 1903
engineer
Index t Wom

16008. Quiggle, Dorothy
born 1903
chemical engineer
Index t Wom

16009. McGill, Elizabeth Gregory
graduated 1929
aeronautical engineer
Index t Wom

16010. Hahn, Emily; Mrs. Charles Ralph Boxer
born 1905
geologist, author
Index t Wom; Nat Cyc Am Bio csv8

16011. Bishop, Hazel
born 1906
industrial chemist, manufacturer
Index t Wom

16012. Mayer, Marie Gertrude Goeppert
1906–72

theoretical physicist, Nobel Prize winner in physics, educator, author
German; Polish
Cur Biog '72; Index t Wom; Nat Cyc Am Bio v58; Not Am Wom supp v1; Obit File

16013. Hagood, Margaret Lloyd Jarman
1907–63
sociologist, statistician, demographer
Not Am Wom supp v1

16014. Ebel, Isabel Caroline
born 1908
aeronautical engineer
Index t Wom

16015. Jordan, Louise
born 1908
paleontologist, geologist
Index t Wom

16016. Kahane, Melanie
born 1910
interior decorator, industrial engineer
Index t Wom

16017. MacIntyre, Sheila Scott
1910–60
mathematician
Presbyterian
Scottish
Nat Cyc Am Bio v48

16018. Palmer, Bernice
flourished 1940s
aircraft inventor
Index t Wom

16019. Stewart, Sylvia
flourished 1940s
aircraft engine instructor
Index t Wom

16020. Sink, Mary Virginia
born 1913
engineer, organization official
Index t Wom

16021. Straten, Florence Van
born 1913
meteorologist
Index t Wom

16022. van Straaten, Florence Whilhelmina
born 1913
physical chemist
Index t Wom

16023. Wright, Helen
born 1914
astronomer, author
Index t Wom

16024. Hicks, Beatrice A.
born 1919

engineer
Index t Wom

16025. Eckles, Ann
flourished 1950s
space scientist
Index t Wom

16026. van der Wal, Franki
flourished 1950s–60s
space scientist, designer
Index t Wom

16027. Collins, Evelyn Boyd
born 1924
mathematician, educator
Black
Prof Negro Wom v2

16028. Roman, Nancy Grace
born 1925
astronomer, space scientist
Index t Wom

16029. Glennon, Nan
flourished 1960s
space scientist, rocket designer, mechanical engineer
Index t Wom

16030. Mann, Helen
flourished 1960s
tracking engineer
Index t Wom

16031. Romic, Mary
flourished 1960s
space scientist
Index t Wom

16032. Steinberg, Maria Alice
flourished 1960s
aeronautical research engineer
Index t Wom

No Dates

16033. Clinton, Doris
mechanical and aeronautical engineer
Index t Wom

16034. Davis, Ninetta
swimmer, mining engineer
Hall Fame Sport

16035. Gill, Jocelyn R.
space scientist
Index t Wom

16036. Olson, Edith
electronics and miniaturization expert
Index t Wom

PIONEERING, ADVENTURE, AND FOLK HEROES

16037. Mendoza, Ana de Zaldivar y
flourished sixteenth century
colonial pioneer
Index t Wom

16038. Hinestrosa, Francisca
died 1534
pioneer
Index t Wom

16039. Penalosa, Eufemia
flourished circa 1590s
American colony cosponsor
Spanish
Index t Wom

16040. Brewster, Mary
circa 1569–1627
Pilgrim, pioneer
Puritan
Index t Wom

16041. Allerton, Mary Norris
flourished 1600s
Pilgrim
Puritan
Index t Wom

16042. Billington, Helen
flourished 1600s
Pilgrim
Index t Wom

16043. Burroughs, Ann
flourished 1600s
pioneer
Index t Wom

16044. Carpenter, Mary
flourished 1600s
pioneer
Index t Wom

16045. Carver, Katherin
flourished 1600s
Pilgrim
Puritan
Index t Wom

16046. Cooper, Humility
flourished 1600s
Pilgrim
Puritan
Index t Wom

16047. Hawkins, Jane
flourished seventeenth century
pioneer, midwife
Index t Wom

16048. Hicks, Margaret
flourished 1600s
colonial educator, pioneer
Index t Wom

16049. Hopkins, Elizabeth
flourished 1600s
Pilgrim
Puritan
Index t Wom

16050. Laydon, Annie Burras
flourished seventeenth century
pioneer
Index t Wom

16051. Mack, Mrs.
flourished seventeenth century
pioneer hero
Index t Wom

16052. Maverick, Amias Thomson
flourished seventeenth century
pioneer
Index t Wom

16053. Minter, Desire
flourished 1600s
Pilgrim
Puritan
Index t Wom

16054. More, Ellen
flourished 1600s
pioneer
Index t Wom

16055. Mullens, Alice
flourished 1600s
pioneer
Index t Wom

16056. Standish, Rose
died 1620
Pilgrim
Puritan
Index t Wom

16057. Storey, Widow
flourished 1600s
pioneer
Index t Wom

16058. Tilley, Ann
flourished 1600s
Pilgrim
Puritan
Index t Wom

16059. Tilley, Bridget
flourished 1600s
Pilgrim
Puritan
Index t Wom

16060. Winslow, Elizabeth Barker
died 1621
Pilgrim
Puritan
Index t Wom

16061. Eaton, Sarah
flourished 1610s–20s
Pilgrim

Puritan
Index t Wom

16062. Johnson, Arabella
died 1630
colonist
Cyc Am Bio

16063. Warren, Elizabeth
1583–1673
Pilgrim
Puritan
Index t Wom

16064. Allerton, Fear Brewster
died 1634
Pilgrim
Puritan
Index t Wom

16065. Brewster, Patience
died 1634
Pilgrim, pioneer
Index t Wom

16066. Pole, Elizabeth;
Elizabeth Poole
1588–1654
pioneer; founder of the town of
Taunton, New Jersey
Taunton, NJ; Massachusetts
English
Am Bio Dict; Index t Wom; Nat
Cyc Am Bio v4

16067. Bradford, Alice
circa 1590–1670
Pilgrim, Plymouth Colony civic
worker, patron of education
Puritan
Massachusetts
English
Am Bio Dict; Index t Wom

16068. Lyford, Sarah
flourished 1620s
pioneer
Index t Wom

16069. Bradford, Dorothy
circa 1597–1602
Pilgrim
Puritan
Index t Wom

**16070. Bogardus, Annetje Jan-
sen; Annekke Jans**
circa 1600–circa 1663
settler of New Amsterdam
New York
Dutch
Index t Wom; Nat Cyc Am Bio
v9

16071. Dudley, Mary
flourished 1630s–50s
pioneer
Index t Wom

16072. Eliot, Anne Mumford
flourished 1630s–40s

pioneer
Index t Wom

**16073. Tayloe, Ann; Ann
Taylor**
flourished seventeenth century
pioneer
Index t Wom

16074. Alden, Priscilla Mullins
born 1602; married 1621
Pilgrim hero of American folklore
Puritan
Index t Wom; Not Am Wom

16075. Brent, Mary
flourished 1638–50s
colonial land proprietor, colonizer
Index t Wom

**16076. Howland, Elizabeth Til-
ley**
1608–87
Pilgrim
Puritan
Index t Wom

16077. Winslow, Mary Chilton
circa 1608–79
Pilgrim
Puritan
Index t Wom

16078. Standish, Barbara
died circa 1659
Pilgrim
Puritan
Index t Wom

16079. Nash, Deborah
flourished 1640s
pioneer
Index t Wom

16080. Nash, Elizabeth
flourished 1640s
pioneer
Index t Wom

16081. Nash, Hannah
flourished 1640s
pioneer
Index t Wom

16082. Nash, Mehitabel
flourished 1640s
pioneer
Index t Wom

**16083. Stout, Penelope van
Princes**
circa 1612–1712
pioneer
Index t Wom

16084. Allerton, Remember
circa 1614–1652/56
Pilgrim
Puritan
Index t Wom

16085. Fuller, Bridget Lee
married 1641
Pilgrim
Puritan
Index t Wom

**16086. van Cortlandt, Annetje
Lockermans**
married 1642
pioneer
Index t Wom

16087. Paybody, Elizabeth
flourished 1650s
pioneer
Index t Wom

**16088. Cooke, Demaris Hop-
kins**
married 1647; died pre-1669
Pilgrim
Puritan
Index t Wom

**16089. Rapelje, Cataline de
Trice**
born 1624
pioneer
Index t Wom

**16090. Bogaert, Sarah Rapelje
Bergen**
1625–1685/1700
pioneer
Index t Wom

**16091. Winslow, Susanna
Fuller White**
died pre–1675
Pilgrim
Puritan
Index t Wom

16092. Snow, Constantia
died 1679
pioneer
Index t Wom

16093. Hard, Eliza
flourished 1660s–80s
pioneer
Index t Wom

16094. Hoyt, Mrs.
flourished 1660s
pioneer, hero
Index t Wom

16095. Noble, Frank, Mrs.
flourished circa 1660s
pioneer
Index t Wom

16096. Chilton, Susanna
1634–circa 1676
Pilgrim, pioneer
Puritan
Index t Wom

**16097. Rowlandson, Mary
(White)**
circa 1635–circa 1682

author, autobiographer, colonial
pioneer
Lancaster, MA
Dict Am Auth; Dict Am Bio;
Dict Am Bio Men Time; Index t
Wom; Nat Cyc Am Bio v8

16098. Standish, Sarah Alden
died circa 1688
Pilgrim
Puritan
Index t Wom

16099. Wolcott, Martha Pitkins
circa 1639–1719
pioneer
Index t Wom

16100. Pentry, Edward, Mrs.
flourished circa 1670s
pioneer
Index t Wom

16101. Shute, James, Mrs.
flourished circa 1670s
pioneer
Index t Wom

16102. Heard, Mrs.
flourished circa 1680s
pioneer
Index t Wom

**16103. Scott, Catharine Mar-
bury**
flourished seventeenth to eighteenth century
pioneer
Index t Wom

16104. Walling, Harriet
flourished 1680s
pioneer
Puritan
Index t Wom

16105. Wyllys, Ruth
flourished 1680s
pioneer
Index t Wom

16106. Smith, Priscilla Allen
married 1682
pioneer
Index t Wom

**16107. Manigault, Judith Giton
Royer**
died 1711
colonial agronomist, pioneer
Index t Wom

16108. Knight, Sarah Kemble
1666–1725/27
diarist, educator, hotel keeper,
traveler, merchant
Boston, MA
Cyc Am Bio; Dict Am Auth; Dict
Am Bio; Dict Am Bio Men
Time; Index t Wom; Not Am
Wom; Wom Lit, More

16109. Bonum, Elizabeth Johnson
flourished 1700s
pioneer
Index t Wom

16110. Brett, Catheryna
flourished 1700s–20s
pioneer
Index t Wom

16111. Chapin, Hannah; Hannah Sheldon
flourished 1700s
American pioneer, hero
Index t Wom

16112. Cook, Miss
flourished 1700s
pioneer
Index t Wom

16113. Dennis, Hannah
flourished 1700s
pioneer
Index t Wom

16114. Eliott, Susannah Smith
flourished 1700s
pioneer
Index t Wom

16115. Linn, Nancy Hunter
flourished eighteenth century
pioneer
Index t Wom

16116. Williams, Esther
flourished 1700s
pioneer
Index t Wom

16117. Wolcott, Sara Drake
married 1702
pioneer
Index t Wom

16118. Irwing, Mary Katie
1678–1721
adventurer
English
Cyc Am Bio

16119. Vercheres, Mary Madeline de
1678–post 1700
hero
Canadian
Cyc Am Bio

16120. Estaugh, Elizabeth Haddon
1680/83–1762
colonial proprietor; founder of Haddonfield, New Jersey; pioneer
Quaker
New Jersey
Cyc Am Bio; Dict Am Bio; Index t Wom; Nat Cyc Am Bio v17; Not Am Wom

16121. Williams, Abigail
flourished 1710s–40s
pioneer
Index t Wom

16122. Brown, Frances Fowke
married 1710
pioneer
Index t Wom

16123. Amy
1686–1826 [sic]
pioneer, slave
Charleston, SC
Black
Appl Cyc Am Bio

16124. Franks, Abigail Levy
1696–1756
pioneer
Index t Wom

16125. Wright, Susanna
1697–1784
poet, colonial frontiersperson, businessperson
Index t Wom; Not Am Wom

16126. Brett, Margaret
flourished 1730s
pioneer
Index t Wom

16127. Lewis, Margaret
flourished 1730s–70s
pioneer
Index t Wom

16128. Richardson, Sarah
flourished eighteenth century
pioneer
Index t Wom

16129. Rutledge, Sarah Hert
flourished 1730s
pioneer
Index t Wom

16130. St. Clair, Phoebe Bayard
flourished eighteenth century
pioneer
Index t Wom

16131. Willis, Mildred Washington
flourished eighteenth century
pioneer
Index t Wom

16132. Hall, Abigail Burr
died 1753
pioneer
Index t Wom

16133. Byrd, Lucy Parke
born circa 1704
pioneer
Index t Wom

16134. Braxton, Judith Robinson
died 1757
pioneer, patriot of American Revolution
Index t Wom

16135. Zellers, Christine
flourished 1740s
colonial hero
Index t Wom

16136. Hayward, Ruth Rutter
died 1761
pioneer
Index t Wom

16137. Middleton, Mary Williams
died 1761
pioneer
Index t Wom

16138. Hart, Deborah Scudder
married 1740
pioneer, patriot
Index t Wom

16139. Thomas, Jane; Jane
Black
married 1740
hero of American Revolution
Cyc Am Bio; Index t Wom

16140. Allen, Elizabeth
born 1716
patriot, western pioneer
Index t Wom

16141. Draper, Mary Aldis
circa 1718–1810
hero of American Revolution, patriot
Index t Wom

16142. Ingles, Mary Draper
circa 1718–1810
pioneer
Index t Wom

16143. Corbin, Elizabeth T.
flourished 1750s
pioneer
Index t Wom

16144. Draper, Betty
flourished 1750s
pioneer
Index t Wom

16145. Hall, Mary
flourished 1750s
pioneer
Index t Wom

16146. Hartman, Regina
flourished 1750s
pioneer
Index t Wom

16147. Heilein, Matheis, Mrs.
flourished 1750s

pioneer
Index t Wom

16148. Howe, Jemima
flourished 1750s
pioneer
Index t Wom

16149. Morton, Anne Justis
married 1745/46
patriot, pioneer
Index t Wom

16150. MacDonald, Flora
1722–90
Scottish hero who assisted in the escape of pretender to the throne Charles Edward in 1746, pioneer
Fayetteville, NC
Scottish
Am Bio Dict; Cyc Am Bio; Dict Am Bio Men Time; Index t Wom

16151. Steel, Katharine Fisher
circa 1724–85
pioneer hero
Index t Wom

16152. Ward, Sarah Trowbridge
circa 1724–88
pioneer
Index t Wom

16153. Bailey, Ann; Mad Anne
1725/42–1825
frontier scout and messenger on the Virginia border, soldier, Indian fighter, American patriot
Ohio; Virginia
British
Appl Cyc Am Bio; Dict Am Bio; Encyc South Hist; Who Who Dur Am Rev; Wom Cent

16154. Ellery, Ann Ramington
married 1750
patriot, pioneer
Index t Wom

16155. Wright, Patience Lovell
1725–1785/86
wax modeler, spy during American Revolution
Quaker
New Jersey
Dict Am Bio; Dict Nat Bio; Index t Wom; Nat Cyc Am Bio v8; Not Am Wom; Who Who Dur Am Rev

16156. Darragh, Lydia Barrington
1728/29–1789
colonial nurse and midwife, hero of American Revolution
Pennsylvania
Cyc Am Bio; Index t Wom; Not Am Wom

16157. Philipse, Mary
circa 1728/30–1822
Tory loyalist in the American
  Revolution, hero
Index t Wom; Our Count

**16158. Smith, Elizabeth Mart-
  ing "Betty"**
died 1778
pioneer
Index t Wom

16159. Inglis, Mary
1729–1813
Kentucky settler
Kentucky
Cyc Am Bio

16160. Brandt, Molly
flourished 1760s
pioneer
Index t Wom

16161. Chappel, Mrs.
flourished 1760s–80s
western pioneer
Index t Wom

16162. Clendenin, Mrs.
flourished 1760s–70s
western pioneer
Index t Wom

16163. Denis, Mrs.
flourished 1760s
western pioneer
Index t Wom

16164. Glendenning, Mrs.
flourished circa 1760s
pioneer
Index t Wom

16165. Gore, Hannah Park
flourished 1760s
pioneer
Index t Wom

16166. Ivans, Martha
flourished 1780s
western pioneer
Index t Wom

**16167. Morris, Mary Philipse
  "Polly"**
1730–1825
pioneer
Index t Wom

16168. Robertson, Ann Lewis
flourished 1770s
pioneer
Index t Wom

16169. Rouse, Anna
flourished 1760s
pioneer
Index t Wom

**16170. Whitmore, Thomas,
  Mrs.**
flourished 1760s

colonial pioneer
Index t Wom

**16171. Jackson, Elizabeth
  Hutchinson**
died 1781
hero of American Revolution
Index t Wom

16172. van Alstine, Nancy
born circa 1733
patriot of American Revolution,
  hero
Index t Wom

**16173. Hart, Nancy; Ann
  Morgan**
1735/55–1830
hero of American Revolution
Georgia
Cyc Am Bio; Encyc South Hist;
  Index t Wom; Nat Cyc Am Bio
  v13; Not Am Wom

**16174. Moor, Eunice Farns-
  worth**
1735–1822
pioneer
Index t Wom

**16175. Wyman, Margaret
  Holmes**
married circa 1760
pioneer
Index t Wom

**16176. Morgan, Abigail Bailey
  "Abbie"**
1736–1802
pioneer, patriot
Index t Wom

16177. Sillman, Mary Fish
1736–1818
hero of American Revolution
Index t Wom

16178. Chase, Ann Baldwin
married 1762
pioneer, American patriot
Index t Wom

**16179. Keith, Mary Isham
  (Marshall)**
1737–1809
patriot of American Revolution,
  pioneer
Index t Wom

**16180. Breckinridge, Mary
  Hopkins Cabell**
flourished circa 1768
pioneer
Index t Wom

16181. Motte, Rebecca Brewton
1738–1815
hero of American Revolution, patriot
Dict Am Bio Men Time; Index t
  Wom; Our Count

16182. Allen, Maria
flourished 1770s
hero of American Revolution
Index t Wom

**16183. Barrett, Meliscent
  "Milly"**
flourished 1770s
hero of American Revolution
Index t Wom

16184. Beckham, Mrs.
flourished 1770s
hero of American Revolution
Index t Wom

**16185. Braxton, Elizabeth Cor-
  bin**
flourished 1770s
pioneer, patriot of American Revolution
Index t Wom

16186. Braxton, Mary Carter
flourished 1770s
pioneer, patriot of American Revolution
Index t Wom

16187. Brevard, Mrs.
flourished 1770s
hero of American Revolution
Index t Wom

16188. Brown, Jane Gillespie
born 1740
western pioneer
Index t Wom

16189. Brown, Mary Buckman
1740–1824
hero of American Revolution
Index t Wom

**16190. Cadwalader, Elizabeth
  Lloyd**
flourished 1770s
pioneer
Index t Wom

16191. Captain Molly
flourished 1770s
hero of American Revolution
Index t Wom

16192. Channing, Mrs.
flourished 1770s
hero of American Revolution
Index t Wom

16193. Clyde, Mrs.
flourished 1770s
pioneer
Index t Wom

16194. Cunningham, Mrs.
flourished 1770s
western pioneer
Index t Wom

16195. Cutbert, Susan Stockton
flourished 1770s

patriot, pioneer
Index t Wom

16196. Daggett, Polly
flourished 1770s
hero of American Revolution
Index t Wom

16197. Daviess, Mrs.
flourished 1770s
hero of American Revolution
Index t Wom

16198. Denne, Elizabeth
flourished 1770s
pioneer
Index t Wom

16199. Dillard, Mrs.
flourished 1770s
hero of American Revolution
Index t Wom

16200. Edgar, Rachel
flourished 1770s
hero of American Revolution
Index t Wom

16201. Franks, Rebecca
flourished 1770s; died 1823
hero of American Revolution
Index t Wom

16202. Fulton, Sarah Bradlee
1740–1835
hero of American Revolution
Index t Wom

16203. Goddard, Hannah
flourished 1770s
patriot, pioneer
Index t Wom

16204. Gore, Ann Avery
flourished 1770s
pioneer
Index t Wom

16205. Gower, Nancy
flourished 1770s–80s
pioneer
Index t Wom

16206. Haynes, Ann
died 1790
western pioneer
Index t Wom

16207. Jack, Mary Barnett
flourished 1770s
pioneer
Index t Wom

16208. Jackson, Mrs.
flourished 1770s
hero of American Revolution
Index t Wom

16209. Jarboe, Elizabeth
flourished 1770s
pioneer
Index t Wom

16210. Jennings, Mrs.
flourished 1770s
pioneer
Index t Wom

16211. Johnson, Isabella
flourished 1770s
pioneer
Index t Wom

16212. Jones, Willie, Mrs.
flourished 1770s; died 1828
hero of American Revolution
Index t Wom

16213. Ledyard, Mary
flourished 1770s
hero of American Revolution,
   philanthropist
Index t Wom

16214. Lee, Hannah Ludwell
flourished 1770s
pioneer
Index t Wom

16215. Livingston, Susan
flourished 1770s
hero of American Revolution
Index t Wom

16216. Mammy Kate
flourished 1770s
hero of American Revolution
Index t Wom

16217. Manter, Parnel
flourished 1770s
hero of American Revolution
Index t Wom

16218. Marshall, Christopher,
   Mrs.
flourished 1770s
pioneer, patriot of American Revolution
Index t Wom

16219. Martin, Elizabeth Marshall
flourished 1770s
patriot of American Revolution,
   hero
Index t Wom

16220. Martin, Grace
flourished 1770s
hero of American Revolution, patriot
Index t Wom

16221. Martin, Rachel; Rachel
   Clay
flourished 1770s
hero of American Revolution
Index t Wom

16222. McCalla, Mrs.
flourished 1770s
hero of American Revolution
Index t Wom

16223. McClure, Mary
flourished 1770s
pioneer hero
Index t Wom

16224. Merrill, John, Mrs.
flourished 1770s–80s
hero of American Revolution, pioneer
Index t Wom

16225. Moultrie, Elizabeth St.
   Julien
flourished 1770s
pioneer
Index t Wom

16226. Ogden, Robert, Mrs.
flourished 1770s
pioneer
Index t Wom

16227. Otterson, Mrs.
flourished 1770s
hero of American Revolution
Index t Wom

16228. Potter, Mrs.
flourished 1770s
hero of American Revolution
Index t Wom

16229. Redmond, Mary
flourished 1770s
hero of American Revolution, patriot
Index t Wom

16230. Simms, Sarah Dickinson
flourished 1770s
hero of American Revolution
Index t Wom

16231. Sims, Isabella
flourished 1770s
hero of American Revolution
Index t Wom

16232. Spalding, Mrs.
flourished 1770s
hero of American Revolution
Index t Wom

16233. Steele, Elizabeth Maxwell
flourished 1770s
hero of American Revolution
Index t Wom

16234. Sullivan, Lydia Wooster
married 1765
pioneer
Index t Wom

16235. Swain, Meliscent Barrett
flourished 1770s
pioneer
Index t Wom

16236. Tucker, Lucy Dougherty
flourished 1770s

nurse, pioneer
Index t Wom

16237. Vrooman, Angelica
flourished 1770s
hero of American Revolution
Index t Wom

16238. Wilkinson, Eliza
flourished 1770s
hero of American Revolution
Index t Wom

16239. Wright, David, Mrs.
flourished 1770s
hero of American Revolution
Index t Wom

16240. Richardson, Dorcas Nelson
circa 1741–1834
hero of American Revolution
Index t Wom

16241. Jemison, Mary Dehe-
   wamis; White Woman of the
   Genessee
1742/43–1833
pioneer
New York
English
Index t Wom; Who Who Dur Am
   Rev

16242. Lake, Mary
1742–1802
western pioneer, religious worker,
   educator
English
Am Bio Dict; Index t Wom

16243. Mercer, Isabella Gordon
married 1767
pioneer
Index t Wom

16244. Story, Ann; Ann Goodrich
1742–1817
hero of American Revolution
Index t Wom

16245. Ellery, Abigail Carey
died 1793
patriot, pioneer
Index t Wom

16246. Israel, Hannah Erwin
circa 1743–1821
hero of American Revolution
Index t Wom

16247. Wayne, Polly; Mary
   Penrose
died 1793
pioneer
Index t Wom

16248. Kirkland, Jerusha [Jem-
   ima] Bingham
married 1769

pioneer missionary
Index t Wom

16249. McCauley, Mary (Lud-
   wig) Hays; Molly Pitcher
1744/54–1832
sergeant in the US Army, hero of
   American Revolution
Pennsylvania
Dict Am Bio; Index t Wom; Nat
   Cyc Am Bio v9; Not Am Wom;
   Twent Cen Bio Dict Not Am;
   Who Who Dur Am Rev

16250. Philips, Abigail
married 1769
pioneer
Index t Wom

16251. Gaylord, Katherine Cole
1745–1840
patriot, hero of American Revolution
Index t Wom

16252. Pickens, Rebecca; Rebecca Calhoun
1745–1815
pioneer
Index t Wom

16253. Gibbes, Sarah Reeve
1746–1825
hero of American Revolution
Index t Wom

16254. Reed, Esther de Berdt
1746–80
leader of women's relief work
   during the American Revolution, hero of American Revolution, patriot, philanthropist
Index t Wom; Not Am Wom

16255. Riedesel, Frederica
   Charlotte Louisa Massow,
   Baroness de
1746–1808
hero of American Revolution
Index t Wom

16256. Bache, Sarah
died 1798
hero of American Revolution
Index t Wom

16257. Lynch, Elizabeth Shubrick
married 1773
pioneer
Index t Wom

16258. Bartholomew, Elizabeth
1749–1833
pioneer
Index t Wom

16259. Bozarth, Mrs.
flourished 1779
pioneer, hero of American Revolution
Index t Wom

16260. Genet, Cornelia
married 1774
pioneer
Index t Wom

16261. Iredel, Hannah
flourished 1779
pioneer
Index t Wom

16262. Dagget, Mrs.
flourished 1780s
pioneer
Index t Wom

16263. Daviess, Samuel, Mrs.
flourished 1780s
pioneer
Index t Wom

16264. Edwards, Mrs.
flourished 1780s–90s
western pioneer
Index t Wom

**16265. Fages, Eulalia de Callis
y**
flourished circa 1780s
colonial pioneer
Index t Wom

16266. Glass, Mrs.
flourished 1780s
western pioneer
Index t Wom

16267. Herbeson, Massy
flourished 1780s–90s
American hero
Index t Wom

16268. Jameson, Edward, Mrs.
flourished 1780s
pioneer
Index t Wom

16269. Juggins, Elizabeth
flourished 1780s
western pioneer
Index t Wom

16270. Lee, Lucy Grymes
flourished 1780s
pioneer
Index t Wom

16271. Morris, Deborah
died 1800
pioneer
Index t Wom

16272. Plumer, Sally Fowler
flourished 1780s
pioneer
Index t Wom

16273. Porter, Mrs.
flourished 1780s
pioneer hero
Index t Wom

16274. Rouse, Rebecca
flourished 1780s
western pioneer
Index t Wom

16275. Scott, Mrs.
flourished 1780s
western pioneer
Index t Wom

16276. Wilson, Sarah; Marchioness de Waldegrave
born 1750
adventurer
Not Am Wom

16277. Aylett, Mary Macon
married 1776
pioneer
Index t Wom

16278. Corbin, Margaret Cochran
1751–circa 1800
hero of American Revolution, soldier
Pennsylvania
Dict Am Bio; Index t Wom; Nat Cyc Am Bio v6; Not Am Wom; Twent Cen Bio Dict Not Am; Who Who Dur Am Rev

16279. Dana, Elizabeth
born 1751
pioneer
Index t Wom

16280. Robertson, Charlotte Reeves
1751–1814/43
western pioneer
Cyc Am Bio; Index t Wom; Nat Cyc Am Bio v1

16281. Crocker, Hannah (Mather)
1752/65–1829/47
author, women's rights worker, pioneer, essayist
Cyc Am Bio; Dict Am Auth; Dict Am Bio; Dict Am Bio Men Time; Index t Wom; Not Am Wom

16282. Wilkinson, Jemima
1752/53–1819/21
evangelist, religious leader, founder of a pioneer community in western New York
New York
Am Bio Dict; Dict Am Bio; Dict Am Bio Men Time; Dict Am Rel Bio; Index t Wom; Nat Cyc Am Bio v1; Not Am Wom

16283. Champion, Deborah
born 1753
pioneer, American hero
Index t Wom

16284. Greene, Catharine Littlefield
1753–1814
hero of American Revolution, patriot
Index t Wom

16285. Johnson, Jemima Suggett
1753–1814
American hero
Index t Wom

16286. Cadwalader, Wilhelmina Bond
married 1779
pioneer
Index t Wom

16287. Hendee, Mrs.
1754–post 1818
western hero
Cyc Am Bio; Twent Cen Bio Dict Not Am

16288. Knox, Lucy Flucker
circa 1754/56–1824
political mover, hero of American Revolution, patriot
Cyc Am Bio; Index t Wom

16289. Moulton, Hannah Lynch
married 1779
pioneer
Index t Wom

16290. Peters, Fannie Ledyard
circa 1754–1816
hero of American Revolution
Index t Wom

16291. Sevier, Catherine Sherrill; Bonny Kate
circa 1754–1836
western pioneer
Index t Wom

16292. Williams, Rebecca
born 1754
western pioneer
Index t Wom

16293. Lemon, Catharine
flourished circa 1786
western pioneer
Index t Wom

16294. Bartlett, Hanna Gray
died 1807
pioneer
Index t Wom

16295. Bailey, Anna Warner; Mother Bailey
1758–1850/51
patriot of American Revolution, colonial hero
Connecticut
Appl Cyc Am Bio; Cyc Am Bio; Dict Am Bio; Index t Wom; Wom Cent

16296. Bledsoe, Mary
died 1808
western pioneer
Index t Wom

16297. Chase, Hannah Kilty
married 1783
pioneer
Index t Wom

16298. van Rensselaer, Margaret
married 1783
pioneer
Index t Wom

16299. Weston, Hannah Watts
1758–1885
hero of American Revolution, patriot
Index t Wom

16300. Chinn, Sarah Bryan
married circa 1784
western pioneer, American patriot
Index t Wom

16301. Humaston, Abi
circa 1759–1847
hero of American Revolution
Index t Wom

16302. Knight, Mary Worrell
circa 1759–1849
hero of American Revolution
Index t Wom

16303. Marion, Mary Vidaue
married 1784
pioneer
Index t Wom

16304. Shelby, Sarah Bledsoe
married 1784
western pioneer
Index t Wom

16305. Smith, Susan Hayes
married 1784
pioneer, telegraph operator
Index t Wom

16306. Zane, Elizabeth "Betty"

1759/66–1831/47
frontier hero, hero of American Revolution
Cyc Am Bio; Index t Wom; Not Am Wom

16307. Carroll, Harriet Chew
flourished 1790s
pioneer
Index t Wom

16308. Cook, Hosea, Mrs.
flourished circa 1790s
pioneer, hero
Index t Wom

16309. Cook, Jessie
flourished 1790s
pioneer, hero
Index t Wom

16310. Dick, Jane
flourished 1790s
western pioneer
Index t Wom

16311. Dunham, Mrs.
flourished 1790s
western pioneer
Index t Wom

16312. Geiger, Emily
born 1760
hero of American Revolution
Cyc Am Bio; Index t Wom

16313. Greene, Ruhama
married 1785
western pioneer
Index t Wom

**16314. Hamilton, Anne
Kennedy**
circa 1760–1836
hero of American Revolution
Index t Wom

16315. Mason, Mrs.
flourished 1790s
pioneer
Index t Wom

16316. Owen, James, Mrs.
flourished 1790s
western pioneer
Index t Wom

16317. Robbins, Nancy
flourished 1790s
pioneer hero
Index t Wom

**16318. Sampson, Deborah;
Robert Shirtliffe; Deborah
Gannett**
1760–1827
soldier and hero of American
Revolution, lecturer
Massachusetts
Am Bio Dict; Cyc Am Bio; Dict
Am Bio Men Time; Index t
Wom; Nat Cyc Am Bio v8; Not
Am Wom

16319. Schenck, Hannah Brett
flourished 1790s
pioneer
Index t Wom

16320. Slocum, Mary Hooks
1760–1836
hero of American Revolution
Index t Wom

**16321. Springfield, Laodicia
Langston ''Dicey''**
born 1760

hero of American Revolution
Index t Wom

16322. Thorp, Sarah
flourished 1790s–1800s
western pioneer
Index t Wom

16323. Thorpe, Sarah
flourished 1790s
pioneer
Index t Wom

16324. Threrwitz, Emily Geiger
born circa 1760
hero of American Revolution
Index t Wom

16325. Townsend, Sally
1760–1842
hero of American Revolution
Index t Wom

16326. Warth, Sally Fleehart
flourished 1790s
western pioneer
Index t Wom

16327. Wilson, Sarah
flourished 1790s
western pioneer
Index t Wom

16328. Cranch, Mary
died 1811
pioneer
Index t Wom

16329. Ludington, Sybil
1761–1839
hero of American Revolution
Index t Wom

16330. Norris, Deborah
1761–1839
colonial pioneer
Index t Wom

**16331. Smart, Susannah Bar-
nett**
born 1761
pioneer, hero
Index t Wom

16332. Boone, Jemima
born circa 1762
pioneer
Index t Wom

16333. Elliott, Anna
circa 1762–1858
hero of American Revolution, relief worker, nurse
Am Bio Dict; Cyc Am Bio; Index
t Wom

16334. Gerry, Ann Thompson
1763–1849
patriot, pioneer
Irish
Index t Wom

16335. Allen, Sarah
1764–1849
missionary, pioneer
Black
Index t Wom; Negro Alman; Prof
Negro Wom

16336. Dunlevy, Mary Craig
born 1765
western pioneer
Index t Wom

**16337. Goodrich, Mary Ann;
Mary Ann Wolcott**
born 1765
patriot, pioneer
Index t Wom

16338. Teller, Alice Schenck
married 1790
pioneer
Index t Wom

16339. Bratton, Martha
died 1816
hero of American Revolution, patriot
Cyc Am Bio; Index t Wom

16340. Frietchie, Barbara
1766–1862/65
Union Civil War hero
Maryland
German
Index t Wom; Who Who Dur Am
Rev

**16341. Rutledge, Mary Shu-
brick Eveleigh**
married 1792
pioneer
Index t Wom

**16342. Sumter, Mary Canty
Jeimesson**
died 1818
pioneer
Index t Wom

**16343. Duchesne, Rose Philip-
pine**
1769–1852
missionary, Catholic nun, founder
of the American Convents of
the Sacred Heart, pioneer, educator
Catholic
Kansas
Cyc Am Bio; Dict Am Rel Bio;
Not Am Wom; Read Encyc Am
West; Twent Cen Bio Dict Not
Am

16344. Royall, Anne Newport
1769–1854
traveler, journalist, newspaper editor and publisher, novelist

Washington, DC; Virginia
Am Bio Dict; Cyc Am Bio; Dict
Am Auth; Dict Am Bio; Dict
Am Bio Men Time; Encyc
South Hist; Index t Wom; Not
Am Wom

16345. Anderson, Mrs.
flourished 1800s
western pioneer
Index t Wom

**16346. Bledsoe, Katherine
Montgomery**
flourished 1800s
western pioneer
Index t Wom

16347. Brown, Maria Foster
flourished 1800s
western pioneer
Index t Wom

16348. Carter, Mrs.
flourished 1800s
western pioneer
Index t Wom

16349. Carter, Sisters
flourished 1800s
western pioneers
Index t Wom

16350. Chapin, Lucy
flourished 1800s
western pioneer
Index t Wom

16351. Clark, Charlotte A.
flourished 1800s
western pioneer
Index t Wom

**16352. Combs, Sarah Richard-
son**
flourished 1800s
western pioneer
Index t Wom

16353. Comstock, Mrs.
flourished 1800s
western pioneer
Index t Wom

16354. Ellery, Mary Goddard
flourished 1800s
pioneer
Index t Wom

16355. Fox, Hannah
flourished 1800s
pioneer
Index t Wom

16356. Gates, Mary Valence
flourished 1800s
pioneer
English
Index t Wom

16357. Geer, Charlotte Clark
flourished 1800s

western pioneer
Index t Wom

16358. Heald, Rebecca
flourished 1800s
western pioneer
Index t Wom

16359. Lovejoy, Julia
flourished 1800s
western pioneer
Index t Wom

16360. McMillan, Mary
flourished 1800s
western pioneer
Index t Wom

16361. Paine, Eliza Baker
married 1795
pioneer
Index t Wom

16362. Trask, Frances
flourished nineteenth century
western pioneer
Index t Wom

16363. Walworth, John, Mrs.
flourished 1800s
western pioneer
Index t Wom

16364. White, Tryphena
flourished 1800s
pioneer, diarist
Index t Wom

16365. Ames, Nabby Lee
born 1771
pioneer
Index t Wom

16366. Robb, Louisa St. Clair
born 1773
western pioneer, patriot
Index t Wom

**16367. Slocum, Frances; Maco-
naquah**
1773–1847
pioneer
Index t Wom

16368. Taylor, Keturah Leitch
born 1773
pioneer
Index t Wom

16369. Sitgreaves, Mary
born 1774
pioneer
Index t Wom

16370. Spark, Ruth Sevier
died 1824
western pioneer
Index t Wom

16371. Boone, Rebecca B.
circa 1775–1813

pioneer
Index t Wom

16372. Jumel, Eliza Bowen
1775–1865
adventurer
Not Am Wom

**16373. de Casa Yrujo, Sarah
McKean, Marchioness**
born 1777
pioneer
Index t Wom

16374. Moore, Mary
1777–90
western pioneer
Index t Wom

16375. Sibley, Sarah Sproat
married 1802
western pioneer
Index t Wom

**16376. Montgomery, Janet Liv-
ingston**
died 1828
pioneer
Index t Wom

16377. Ellet, Mary
born 1779
war hero
Index t Wom

16378. Barnes, Jane
flourished 1810s
western pioneer
Index t Wom

16379. Brown, Tabitha Moffat
born 1780
western pioneer
Index t Wom

16380. Derby, Mary
flourished 1810s
pioneer, artist
Index t Wom

**16381. Jameson, Hannah Tag-
gart**
died 1830
pioneer
Index t Wom

16382. Buchanan, Sarah
died 1831
pioneer, western hero
Cyc Am Bio

16383. Heckewelder, Mary
born 1781
western pioneer
Index t Wom

**16384. Marshall, Nancy Stin-
nett**
died 1831
pioneer
Index t Wom

16385. Harper, Elizabeth
died 1833
western pioneer
Index t Wom

16386. Sacajawea; Bird Woman
1784/87–1812
interpreter, pioneer, guide
Native American (Shoshone)
Dict Am Bio; Great North Am
Ind; Index t Wom; Not Am
Wom; Read Encyc Am West

**16387. Tappen, Elizabeth Harp-
er**
born 1784
western pioneer
Index t Wom

16388. Dorion, Marie
1786/91–1850
explorer; participant in 1811–12
overland expedition to Astoria,
at the mouth of the Columbia
River; pioneer; hero
Index t Wom; Not Am Wom

**16389. Blennerhassett, Marga-
ret Agnew**
circa 1788–1892
pioneer
Irish
Index t Wom

16390. Judson, Ann Hasseltine
1789–1826
missionary to Burma, pioneer
Am Bio Dict; Cyc Am Bio; Dict
Am Bio; Dict Am Bio Men
Time; Dict Ind Bio; Index t
Wom; Nat Cyc Am Bio v3; Not
Am Wom; Our Count; Twent
Cen Bio Dict Not Am

16391. Arthur, William, Mrs.
flourished 1820s
frontier reformer
Index t Wom

16392. Goodrich, Mrs.
flourished 1820s
western pioneer
Index t Wom

16393. Mann, Pamela
died 1840
pioneer
Index t Wom

16394. Rumsey, Mary Ann
flourished 1820s
western pioneer
Index t Wom

**16395. Arguello, Concha Maria
de Concepcion**
1791–1857
pioneer, Catholic nun
Catholic
Spanish
Index t Wom

**16396. Kenton, Elizabeth Jar-
boe**
died 1842
western pioneer
Index t Wom

16397. Allen, Ann
flourished 1824
western pioneer
Index t Wom

**16398. Helm, Lina J. Helm
McKillip**
died 1844
western pioneer
Index t Wom

16399. Snelling, Abigail Hunt
born circa 1797/98
western pioneer
Index t Wom

**16400. Winslow, Catherine Wa-
tersbury Carman**
1799–1837
traveler
Cyc Am Bio

16401. Ballard, Emily
flourished 1830s
sea hero
Index t Wom

16402. Dickerson, Susanna
flourished 1830s
pioneer, hero
English
Index t Wom

16403. Marks, Jane
flourished nineteenth century
pioneer scout
Index t Wom

16404. Pettigrew, Susan
flourished 1830s
traveler
Index t Wom

16405. Plummer, Rachel
flourished 1830s
western pioneer
Index t Wom

16406. Scott, Hector, Mrs.
flourished 1830s
western pioneer
Index t Wom

**16407. van Kleeck, Margaret
Teller**
flourished nineteenth century
pioneer
Index t Wom

16408. Wharton, Sarah Grace
flourished 1830s
pioneer
Index t Wom

16409. White, Mrs.
flourished 1830s

western pioneer
Index t Wom

16455. Gross, Elizabeth West
born 1817
pioneer
Index t Wom

16456. Chapman, Caroline
1818?–76
actor, western pioneer
Index t Wom; Not Am Wom

16457. Mitchell, Martha Reed
born 1818
patron of art, traveler, philanthropist
Index t Wom; Wom Cent

16458. Montez, Maria "Lola" Dolores Eliza Rosanna Gilbert Porris y; Marie Dolores Eliza Rosanna Gilbert; Countess of Landsfeld
1818/24–1861
dancer, western pioneer, adventurer
Irish
Aust Dict Bio; Cyc Am Bio; Dict Am Bio Men Time; Dict Irish Bio; Dict Nat Bio; Index t Wom; Read Encyc Am West

16459. van Lew, Elizabeth L.
1818–1900
unionist and federal agent during the Civil War, Civil War spy
Virginia
Index t Wom; Not Am Wom

16460. Clapp, Louise Amelia Knapp Smith; Dame Shirley; Amelia Knapp Smith
1819–1906
author, educator, letter writer during the California gold rush, gold rush pioneer
California
Index t Wom; Not Am Wom; Read Encyc Am West

16461. Howe, Julia Ward
1819–1910
poet, dramatist, songwriter, lecturer, suffrage and women's club leader, feminist, abolitionist, pacifist, prison reformer, Union patriot during the Civil War, philanthropist, traveler
Boston, MA
Cyc Am Bio; Dict Am Auth; Dict Am Bio; Dict Am Bio Men Time; Dict Lit Bio v1; Index t Wom; Nat Cyc Am Bio v1; Not Am Wom; Twent Cen Bio Dict Not Am; Wom Cent

16462. Preston, Margaret Wickliffe
born 1819
pioneer
Index t Wom

16463. Royce, Sarah Eleonor Bayliss
1819–91
California pioneer, author
California
English
Index t Wom; Not Am Wom

16464. Banfield, Mary
flourished 1850s
pioneer
Index t Wom

16465. Barber, Thomas, Mrs.
flourished 1850s
pioneer
Index t Wom

16466. Fair, Laura D.
flourished 1850s–70s
western pioneer
Index t Wom

16467. Gautier, Madame
flourished 1850s
western pioneer
Index t Wom

16468. Henderson, Frances Cox
born 1820
linguist, translator, traveler, philanthropist, suffragist
Episcopalian
Wom Cent

16469. Lee, Lillie
flourished 1850s
western pioneer
Index t Wom

16470. Longmire, Mrs.
flourished 1850s
western pioneer
Index t Wom

16471. Magoffin, Susan Shelby
married 1845
western pioneer
Index t Wom

16472. Moore, Kate
flourished 1850s
philanthropist, pioneer
Index t Wom

16473. Neal, Frances [Jean]
flourished 1850s
western pioneer
Index t Wom

16474. Simpson, Lucretia Harper
born 1820
pioneer
Index t Wom

16475. Thompson, Mrs.
flourished 1850s
western pioneer
Index t Wom

16476. Tubman, Harriet Ross
1820/26–1913
hero of the Underground Railroad, liberator of slaves, abolitionist, Union spy during the Civil War, Civil War nurse, lecturer
Black
Cyc Am Bio; Dict Am Bio; Encyc Black Am; Encyc South Hist; Index t Wom; Nat Cyc Am Bio v9; Negro Alman; Not Am Wom; Prof Negro Wom v1

16477. Washburn, Florinda
flourished 1850s
pioneer, milliner, businessperson
Index t Wom

16478. Waters, Lydia
flourished 1850s
western pioneer
Index t Wom

16479. Bowser, Mary Elizabeth
flourished 1851
Union spy
Black
Prof Negro Wom

16480. Lamar, Mirebean B.
died 1871
pioneer
Index t Wom

16481. Lee, Sarah Gould
1821–1905
pioneer
Index t Wom

16482. Tupper, Ellen Smith
born 1822
apiarist, writer on beekeeping, pioneer
Index t Wom; Wom Cent

16483. Cary, Mary Ann Shad
1823–93
educator, lawyer, journalist, editor, abolitionist, Canadian pioneer
Black; Canadian
Index t Wom; Negro Alman; Not Am Wom; Prof Negro Wom

16484. Bowers, Eilley Orrum
1826–1903
western pioneer
Index t Wom

16485. Craft, Ellen
circa 1826–circa 1897
fugitive slave, abolitionist, lecturer
Black
Index t Wom; Not Am Wom

16486. Turchin, Nadine
1826–1904
Civil War patriot, soldier, hero
Russian
Index t Wom

16487. Wood, Julia Amanda A. (Sargent); Minnie Mary Lee
born 1826
author, postmaster, pioneer, Minnesota newspaper editor, Catholic novelist
Catholic
Sauk Rapids, MN
Dict Am Auth; Index t Wom; Not Am Wom; Wom Cent

16488. Ball, Frances
flourished 1857
pioneer
Index t Wom

16489. Parker, Cynthia Ann
1827–64
pioneer
Index t Wom

16490. Moon, Charlotte
1829–1912
Civil War spy, hero
Index t Wom

16491. Baker, E. H., Mrs.
flourished 1860s
Civil War spy, Pinkerton detective
Index t Wom

16492. Bayley, Gertrude Arthur
flourished 1860s
western pioneer, mountain climber
Index t Wom

16493. Bradford, Mary
flourished 1860s
Civil War hero
Index t Wom

16494. Burks, Amanda
flourished 1860s
western pioneer
Index t Wom

16495. Cox, Lucy Ann
flourished 1860s
Civil War hero
Index t Wom

16496. Dalton, Mrs.
flourished 1860s
pioneer
Index t Wom

16497. Duckett, Elizabeth Waring
flourished 1860s
author, Civil War spy
Index t Wom

16498. Duvall, Betty
flourished 1860s
Civil War spy
Index t Wom

16499. Etheridge, Annie
flourished 1860s

Civil War hero, nurse, humanitarian
Index t Wom

16500. Fisher, Rebecca Jane Gilleland
born 183?; married 1848
philanthropist, journalist, pioneer
Austin, TX
Index t Wom; Wom Cent

16501. Ford, Antonia
flourished 1860s
Civil War spy, hero
Index t Wom

16502. Griffin, Josephine R.
flourished 1860s
Civil War relief worker, hero, philanthropist
Index t Wom

16503. Grummond, Frances
flourished 1860s
western pioneer
Index t Wom

16504. Harland, Elizabeth Carraway
flourished 1860s
spy
Index t Wom

16505. Harmon, Amelia
flourished 1860s
Civil War hero, patriot
Index t Wom

16506. Holmes, Emma E.
flourished 1860s
Civil War hero
Index t Wom

16507. Hook, Frances
flourished 1860s–70s
soldier, frontier scout
Nat Cyc Am Bio v6

16508. Hull, Rose Mitchell
flourished 1860s
western pioneer
Index t Wom

16509. Jackson, Eleanor Noyes
flourished 1860s
Civil War hero
Index t Wom

16510. Kirby, William, Mrs.
flourished 1860s
Civil War hero
Index t Wom

16511. Kollock, Augusta J.
flourished 1860s
Civil War hero
Index t Wom

16512. Lawton, Hattie
flourished 1860s
Civil War spy
Index t Wom

16513. Leavitt, Mary Greenleaf Clement
1830–1912
educator, temperance missionary, traveler
Dict Am Bio; Nat Cyc Am Bio v5; Not Am Wom; Twent Cen Bio Dict Not Am; Wom Cent

16514. Love, Mary
flourished 1860s
Civil War hero
Index t Wom

16515. MacKall, Lillie
flourished 1860s
Civil War spy
Index t Wom

16516. Mary of the Infant Jesus, Sister
circa 1830–1917
western pioneer, Catholic nun
Catholic
Index t Wom

16517. McEwen, Hettie M.
flourished 1860s
Civil War hero, patriot
Index t Wom

16518. Meekins, A. M., Mrs.
flourished 1860s
Civil War spy
Index t Wom

16519. Morrison, Mary Anna
flourished 1860s
Civil War hero
Index t Wom

16520. Park, Lucia Darling
flourished 1860s
western pioneer, educator, vigilante
Index t Wom

16521. Pearson, Flora
flourished 1860s
western pioneer
Index t Wom

16522. Pickens, Lucy Holcombe
flourished 1860s
Civil War hero
Index t Wom

16523. Pigott, Emeline
flourished 1860s
Civil War hero, spy
Dict Am Auth; Index t Wom

16524. Pollock, Roberta
flourished 1860s
Civil War hero
Index t Wom

16525. Pryor, Sara Agnes Rice
1830–1912
author, Civil War hero
Index t Wom; Not Am Wom

16526. Russell, Lenie
flourished 1860s
Civil War hero
Index t Wom

16527. Russell, Tillie
flourished 1860s
Civil War hero
Index t Wom

16528. Sansom, Emma
flourished 1860s; died 1900
Civil War hero, diarist
Index t Wom

16529. Sheads, Carrie
flourished 1860s
Civil War hero
Index t Wom

16530. Shover, Felicia Lee Carey Thornton
flourished 1860s
Civil War hero
Index t Wom

16531. Slade, Maria Virginia Dale "Molly"
flourished 1860s
western pioneer, vigilante
Index t Wom

16532. Sokalski, Annie Blanche
flourished 1860s
western pioneer
Index t Wom

16533. Stuart, Flora Cooke
flourished 1860s
Civil War hero
Index t Wom

16534. Titlow, Effie
flourished 1860s
Civil War hero
Index t Wom

16535. Tynes, Mary Elizabeth "Molly"
flourished 1860s
Civil War hero
Index t Wom

16536. Windsor, Mary Catherine
1830–1914
Civil War hero, spy
Index t Wom

16537. Wister, Annis Lee Furness "Anna"
1830–1908
traveler, translator of German novels
Cyc Am Bio; Dict Am Auth; Index t Wom

16538. Grant, Bridget
1831–1923
pioneer, innkeeper
Irish
Index t Wom

16539. Hutchings, Augusta Ladd Sweetland
died 1881
western pioneer
Index t Wom

16540. Vestal, Belle; Belle Siddons
died circa 1881
western pioneer
Index t Wom

16541. Bulette, Julia
1832–67
western pioneer
Index t Wom

16542. Hurd, P. B., Mrs.
married 1857
Civil War hero
Index t Wom

16543. Walker, Mary Edwards
1832–1919
physician, Civil War medical worker, hospital founder, army war surgeon, Union spy during the Civil War; women's rights worker, suffragist, dress reformer, inventor, lecturer, winner of the Congressional Medal of Honor
Dict Am Bio; Index t Wom; Nat Cyc Am Bio v13; Not Am Wom; Wom Cent

16544. Carson, Delia E.
born 1833
educator of women, traveler
Madison, WI
Wom Cent

16545. Cushman, Pauline
1833/35–1895
Union spy during the Civil War, actor
Cyc Am Bio; Dict Am Bio; Index t Wom; Nat Cyc Am Bio v23; Twent Cen Bio Dict Not Am

16546. Reed, Virginia
born 1833
western pioneer, realtor
Index t Wom

16547. Tabor, Augusta Pierce
1833–95
western pioneer
Index t Wom

16548. Brinton, Emma Southwick
born 1834
Civil War nurse, traveler
Wom Cent

16549. Duniway, Abigail Jane Scott
1834–1915
pioneer, suffrage leader, feminist, journalist, editor, lecturer

Oregon
Dict Am Bio; Index t Wom; Not Am Wom; Wom Cent

16550. Sanders, Harriet Fenn
1834–1909
pioneer
Index t Wom

16551. Waters, Clara (Erskine) (Clement); Clara Clement
1834–1916
author, writer on art, art historian, world traveler
Boston, MA
Dict Am Auth; Index t Wom; Not Am Wom; Wom Cent; Wom Lit, More

16552. Ragozin, Zenaide Alexievna
1835–post 1906
traveler, writer of Russian histories
Russian
Cyc Am Bio; Dict Am Auth

16553. Foster, Annette Hotchkiss Dimsdale
circa 1836–74
western pioneer, vigilante
Index t Wom

16554. Horton, Abbie Augusta Wingate
1836–1925
pioneer, religious worker
Index t Wom

16555. Logan, Mary Simmerson Cunningham
1838–1923
political mover, author, magazine editor, pioneer
Cyc Am Bio; Not Am Wom; Wom Cent

16556. Velasquez, Loretta Janeta
born 1838
western pioneer, Civil War diarist, Civil War spy
Index t Wom

16557. Velazquez, Louta Janita; Velasquez, Loretta Janeta; Harry T. Buford
born 1838/42
Civil War autobiographer, western pioneer, Civil War spy
Encyc South Hist; Index t Wom

16558. Woolson, Constanta Fennimore
1838/48–1894
author, novelist, poet, traveler
Cyc Am Bio; Dict Am Auth; Dict Am Bio; Index t Wom; Nat Cyc Am Bio v1; Not Am Wom; Twent Cen Bio Dict Not Am; Wom Cent; Wom Lit, More

16559. Wright, Rebecca McPherson
born 1838
Union spy during the Civil War, Civil War hero
Quaker
Cyc Am Bio; Index t Wom

16560. Willard, Frances Elizabeth Caroline
1839–98
educator, educational philosopher, suffragist, feminist, women's rights worker, temperance leader, naturalist, philanthropist, newspaper editor, traveler
Methodist Episcopal
Cyc Am Bio; Dict Am Auth; Dict Am Bio; Dict Am Bio Men Time; Dict Am Rel Bio; Index t Wom; Nat Cyc Am Bio v1; Not Am Wom; Twent Cen Bio Dict Not Am; Wom Cent

16561. Bonham, Mildred A.
born 1840
traveler, journalist, social reformer
Index t Wom; Wom Cent

16562. Clark, Isabella P.
flourished 1870s
western pioneer
Index t Wom

16563. Clifford, Mrs.
flourished 1870s
traveler
Index t Wom

16564. di Gallotti, Stephanie, Baroness
born 1840
western pioneer
Index t Wom

16565. Dutcher, Sally L.
flourished 1870s
western pioneer
Index t Wom

16566. Howard, Ida Tinsley
flourished 1870s
pioneer, educator
Index t Wom

16567. Kitty the Schemer
flourished 1870s
western pioneer
Index t Wom

16568. le Roy, Kitty
flourished 1870s
western pioneer
Index t Wom

16569. McCauley, Barbara
flourished 1870s
western pioneer
German
Index t Wom

16570. Moore, Huldah Traxler
flourished 1870s
western pioneer
Index t Wom

16571. Preston, Lizzie
flourished 1870s
western pioneer
Index t Wom

16572. Ragan, John, Mrs.
flourished 1870s
pioneer
Index t Wom

16573. Snow, Emily Topple
flourished 1870s–90s
western pioneer
Index t Wom

16574. Swain, Louisa Ann
flourished 1870s
western pioneer, feminist
Index t Wom

16575. Wallis, Mary D.
flourished 1870s
traveler, author
Index t Wom

16576. Edmonds, Sarah Emma Evelyn; Franklin Thompson
1841–98
Civil War soldier, spy, nurse
Canadian
Index t Wom; Not Am Wom

16577. Lewis, Ida Walley; Ida Walley
1841/42–1911
lighthouse keeper, sea rescuer and hero
Cyc Am Bio; Index t Wom; Nat Cyc Am Bio v5; Not Am Wom; Wom Cent

16578. Brownell, Kady
born 1842
Civil War soldier, hero
Index t Wom

16579. Chipeta
circa 1842–1924
Native American hero
Native American
Index t Wom

16580. Custer, Elizabeth Bacon
1842–1933
author, western pioneer, lecturer on frontier life
Cyc Am Bio; Dict Am Auth; Index t Wom; Wom Cent

16581. Hutchings, Elvira Bonney Sproat
born 1842
western pioneer
Index t Wom

16582. Plummer, Electa Bryan
circa 1842–1912

western pioneer, vigilante
Index t Wom

16583. Silcott, Jane
1842–95
hero
Native American
Index t Wom

16584. Boyd, Belle; Belle Hardinge
1843/44–1900
Confederate spy, actor, lecturer
Episcopalian
Bio Dict Confed; Dict Am Bio; Index t Wom; Not Am Wom

16585. Isely, Elise Dubach
born circa 1843
pioneer
Swiss
Index t Wom

16586. Pickett, Lasalle Carbell
born 1843
Civil War patriot, hero, diarist, lecturer
Index t Wom; Wom Cent

16587. Thorp, Mandana Coleman
born 1843
Union patriot during the Civil War, pioneer, deputy clerk and register of deeds in northern Michigan, sheep and wool farmer
Michigan
Wom Cent

16588. Wade, Mary Virginia "Jenny"
born 1843
Union hero during the Civil War
Cyc Am Bio v1

16589. Collins, Libby Smith
1844–1921
western pioneer, cattle rancher
Index t Wom

16590. Winnemucca, Sarah (Thocmetony)
circa 1844–91
hero, Native American rights worker
Native American (Paviotsu Paiute)
Dict Am Bio; Eng Wom; Great North Am Ind; Not Am Wom

16591. Young, Ann Eliza Webb
1844–post 1908
lecturer and writer against Mormon polygamy, feminist, religious worker, pioneer
Index t Wom; Not Am Wom

16592. Kelly, Fanny Wiggins
circa 1845–1904
pioneer
Index t Wom

16593. Moon, Virginia
1845–1926
Civil War spy, hero
Index t Wom

16594. Bradford, Susan
born circa 1846
Civil War hero
Index t Wom

16595. Fiske, Myra Morrow
died circa 1896
western pioneer
Index t Wom

16596. Shaw, Emma
born 1846
author, traveler, explorer
Wom Cent

16597. Silks, Mattie "Martha"

1846/48–1929
western pioneer
Index t Wom

16598. Summerhayes, Martha
1846–1911
western pioneer, memoirist of the western frontier
Index t Wom; Read Encyc Am West

16599. Sheldon, Mary French
born 1847
translator, traveler in Africa, author
Wom Cent

16600. Starr, Myra Belle Shirley
1848/49–1889
western pioneer, outlaw
Index t Wom; Read Encyc Am West

16601. Bruce, Azealia
flourished 1880s
western pioneer
Index t Wom

16602. Canary, Martha Jane;
Mary Jane Burke; Calamity Jane
1850/52–1903
western pioneer, frontiersperson
Index t Wom; Not Am Wom; Read Encyc Am West

16603. Carpenter, Alice Dimmick
flourished 1880s
traveler, author
Wom Cent

16604. Chapin, Sylvia
flourished 1880s
western pioneer
Index t Wom

16605. Hall, Frances M.
flourished 1880s

western pioneer, educator
Index t Wom

16606. Leidig, Isabela Dobie "Belle"
flourished 1880s
western pioneer
Index t Wom

16607. Noble, Harriet L.
flourished 1880s
western pioneer
Index t Wom

16608. Peck, Annie Smith
1850–1933/35
mountain climber, musician, archaeologist, lecturer, educator
Rhode Island
Index t Wom; Nat Cyc Am Bio v15; Not Am Wom; Wom Cent

16609. Peregoy, Mary Cochran
flourished 1880s
western pioneer
Index t Wom

16610. Plassmann, Martha Edgerton
born 1850
author, western pioneer
Index t Wom

16611. Rogers, Sara Jane "Jennie"
flourished 1880s
western pioneer
Index t Wom

16612. Weldon, Catherine S.
flourished 1880s
western pioneer
Index t Wom

16613. Woodward, Mary D.
flourished 1880s
western pioneer
Index t Wom

16614. Ivers, Alice
1851–1930
pioneer
English
Index t Wom

16615. le Plongeon, Alice (Dixon)
born 1851
explorer, traveler, antiquarian
Dict Am Auth; Index t Wom

16616. Tubbs, Alice Ivers; Poker Alice
1851–1930
pioneer
Index t Wom

16617. Bemis, Lalu Nathoy;
China Polly
1852–1933
western pioneer

Chinese
Index t Wom

16618. Baldwin, Verona
flourished 1883–87
western pioneer
Index t Wom

16619. Meeker, Josephine
graduated 1878
western pioneer
Index t Wom

16620. Monoghan, Josephine;
Little Jo
died 1903
pioneer, rancher
Index t Wom

16621. Noble, Lucy (Seward)
born 1853
author, traveler, lecturer
Nat Cyc Am Bio v17

16622. Norraikow, Ella, Countess
born 1853
author, journalist, Russian correspondent, traveler
Canadian
Wom Cent

16623. Wright, Marie Robinson
born 1853/60
journalist, travel writer
Georgia; New York
Dict Am Auth; Wom Cent

16624. Glynn, Elizabeth E.
died 1904
western pioneer
Index t Wom

16625. Tabor, Elizabeth Bonduel McCourt; Baby Doe
1854–1935
pioneer
Index t Wom

16626. Ball, Isabel Worrell
born 1855
pioneer, journalist
Index t Wom; Wom Cent

16627. Everson, Mary Dah
born 1855
western pioneer
Norwegian
Index t Wom

16628. Meagher, Mary
born circa 1855
western pioneer, agriculturist
Index t Wom

16629. Scidmore, Eliza Ruhamah; Eliza Ruhamah
1856–1928
geographer, traveler, travel writer, journalist

Washington, DC
Dict Am Auth; Dict Am Bio; Index t Wom; Twent Cen Bio
Dict Not Am

16630. Todd, Mabel Loomis
1856/58–1932
author, editor of Emily Dickinson's books and letters, traveler, lecturer, astronomer
Dict Am Bio; Index t Wom; Nat Cyc Am Bio v9, v28, and v41; Not Am Wom; Twent Cen Bio
Dict Not Am; Wom Cent

16631. Ross, Virginia Evelyn (Conlee)
born 1857
author, pioneer
Nebraska
Wom Cent

16632. Eastwood, Alice
1859–1953
botanist, author, adventurer
Index t Wom; Not Am Wom supp v1; Obit File

16633. Sanders, Wilbur, Mrs.
died circa 1909
western pioneer, vigilante
Index t Wom

16634. Thompson, Sarah
died 1909
Civil War spy
Index t Wom

16635. Workman, Fanny (Bullock)
1859–1925
traveler, author on travel, explorer of the Himalayas, mountain climber
Dict Am Auth; Dict Am Bio; Index t Wom; Not Am Wom

16636. Alderson, Nannie Tiffany
1860–1946
western pioneer
Index t Wom

16637. Crippen, Abbie
born 1860
western pioneer
Index t Wom

16638. Crockett, Elizabeth
born 1860
western pioneer
Index t Wom

16639. Ely, Gertrude S.
flourished 1890s; died 1970
two-time recipient of the French Croix de Guerre for bravery in operating a YWCA canteen in World War I while under fire
Obit File

author, explorer
Index t Wom; Nat Cyc Am Bio v46

16685. Woodstock, Lenoir Carpenter
born 1882
religious worker, pioneer
Index t Wom

16686. Orstein, Honora;
Diamond Tooth Lil
1883–1975
dance hall actor during the Alaska gold rush
Alaska
Obit File

16687. Jackson, Maude Campbell Davison
1885–1956
US Army major, chief of American nurses on Corregidor in World War II, World War II hero
Obit File

16688. Boyd, Louise Arner
1887–1972
scientific polar explorer, geographer, technical expert for the War Department and the National Bureau of Standards
Episcopalian
Cur Biog '72; Index t Wom; Nat Cyc Am Bio csv7; Obit File

16689. Degnan, Mary Ellen
born circa 1887
western pioneer
Index t Wom

16690. Lebel, Margaret
1887–1951
World War I hero
Obit File

16691. Baldwin, Tillie
circa 1888–1958
western pioneer, cowhand
Index t Wom

16692. Byrd, Marie A.
1889–1974
explorer
Obit File

16693. Callender, Bessie Stough
1889–1951
sculptor, mountain climber
Presbyterian
Nat Cyc Am Bio v38

16694. Burr, Frances; Mrs.
John Reynolds
1890–post 1930s
artist, mountaineer, suffragist
Index t Wom; Nat Cyc Am Bio csv12

16695. Degnan, Bridget Dixon
died 1940

western pioneer
Irish
Index t Wom

16696. Kirk, Henrietta
flourished 1920s
swimmer, hero
Index t Wom

16697. Orth, Jane Davis
flourished 1920s–30s
lecturer, traveler
Index t Wom

16698. Starr, Harold, Mrs.
flourished 1920s
hero
Index t Wom

16699. Atkinson, Dorothy
born 1892
western pioneer
Index t Wom

16700. Dickinson, Velvalee
born circa 1893
Japanese spy
Index t Wom

16701. Kiaer, Alice Damrosch Wolfe
1893–1967
skiing promoter, Olympic skier, mountain climber, first woman to scale the Matterhorn
Hall Fame Sport; Obit File

16702. Scott, Evelyn D. (Metcalf)
1893–1963
author, traveler
Dict Lit Bio v9; Index t Wom; Nat Cyc Am Bio csv3; Wom Lit

16703. Cutting, Helen McMahon
1894–1961
worker for the welfare of the blind, traveler
New York
Nat Cyc Am Bio v47

16704. Johnson, Osa Helen Leighty
1894–1952/53
explorer, geographer, big game hunter, filmmaker and film producer, aviator, author
Index t Wom; Nat Cyc Am Bio v39; Obit File

16705. Grandma
died 1946
spy
Index t Wom

16706. Nelson, Klondy Esmerelda
born 1897
Alaskan hero
Alaska
Index t Wom

16707. Curry, Jennie Foster
died 1948
western pioneer
Index t Wom

16708. Dudley, Anne
born 1898
pioneer
Index t Wom

16709. Donaldson, Elizabeth W.
flourished 1930s
traveler, author, sportsperson
Index t Wom

16710. Gillespie, Marian
flourished 1930s
explorer, photographer, editor, author
Index t Wom

16711. Harkness, William, Mrs.
flourished 1930s
explorer
Index t Wom

16712. Harris, Jane Davenport
flourished 1930s
sculptor, explorer
French
Index t Wom

16713. Pratt, Gladys Lynwall
flourished 1930s
explorer, museum patron
Index t Wom

16714. Singer, Ava Hamilton
flourished 1930s
explorer, geographer
Index t Wom

16715. Pell, Isabel Townsend;
Frederika; The Girl with Blonde Hair
1901–52
leader of Maquis resistance groups on the French Riviera during World War II
Obit File

16716. Fowler-Billings, Katharine
born 1902
geologist, author, explorer
Index t Wom

16717. Strassmann, Antonie
1902–52
aviator, World War II hero, anti-Nazi worker
German
Obit File

16718. Brooks, Virginia Field Walton
born 1904
traveler, explorer
Christian Scientist
Nat Cyc Am Bio csv13

16719. Parent, Jeanne
1904–57
US Medal of Freedom winner for hiding Allied aviators shot down in Belgium during World War II
Obit File

16720. Wellman, Margaret
1906–56
author, traveler, explorer
Austrian
Obit File

16721. Bentley, Elizabeth Terrill
1908–63
spy for the Soviet Union during World War II
Obit File

16722. Cushing, Lily (Dulany)
1909–69
artist, traveler
Nat Cyc Am Bio v60

16723. Bradley, Mary Hastings
flourished 1940s
explorer
Index t Wom

16724. Engelhard, Georgia
flourished 1940s
mountaineer
Index t Wom

16725. Rombeau, Anne M.
flourished 1950s
aviator, lecturer, traveler
Index t Wom

16726. Saxl, Eva R.
born circa 1921
educator, traveler, lecturer, author
Czechoslovak
Index t Wom

16727. Hart, Janey
flourished 1960s
aviator, helicopter pilot, astronaut
Index t Wom

16728. Funk, Mary Wallace
graduated 1958
aviator, astronaut
Index t Wom

16729. MacLaine, Shirley
born 1934
stage and screen actor, dancer, autobiographer, feminist, Democratic party worker, political activist, world traveler
Cur Biog '78; Index t Wom

16730. Duperault, Terry Jo
born circa 1950
sea hero
Index t Wom

No Dates

16731. Bates, D. B.
western pioneer
Index t Wom

PRISON AND INDUSTRIAL REFORM

16732. Dudley, Blandina
1783–1863
patron of science
Cyc Am Bio

16733. Dix, Dorothea Lynde
1794/1802–1887
crusader for the welfare of the mentally ill, prison reformer, philanthropist, author, essayist, children's author, superintendent of army nurses in the Civil War
Massachusetts
Cyc Am Bio; Dict Am Auth; Dict Am Bio; Dict Am Bio Men Time; Dict Lit Bio v1; Index t Wom; Nat Cyc Am Bio v3; Not Am Wom; Twent Cen Bio Dict Not Am; Wom Cent

16734. Gibbons, Abigail Hopper "Abby"
1801–93
abolitionist, prison reformer, feminist, women's welfare worker, Civil War nurse, philanthropist, journalist
Quaker
Cyc Am Bio; Dict Am Bio; Index t Wom; Nat Cyc Am Bio v7; Not Am Wom; Twent Cen Bio Dict Not Am; Wom Cent

16735. Chace, Elizabeth Buffum
1806–99
abolitionist, suffragist, women's rights worker, prison reformer, temperance worker
Quaker
Dict Am Bio; Not Am Wom; Twent Cen Bio Dict Not Am; Wom Cent

16736. Johnson, Mary Anne
1808–72
prison reformer
Cyc Am Bio

16737. Day, Martha
1813–33
scholar of mathematics and language, author
New Haven, CT
Cyc Am Bio; Dict Am Bio Men Time; Index t Wom

16738. Spear, Catherine Swan Brown
born 1814

educator, abolitionist, Underground Railroad worker, prison reformer, suffragist
Wom Cent

16739. Comstock, Elizabeth Leslie Rous
1815–1891/92
social reformer, abolitionist, Underground Railroad worker, pacifist, freed slave's welfare worker, temperance reformer, women's rights worker, Quaker minister, prison reformer, Civil War nurse
Quaker
Dict Am Bio; Index t Wom; Nat Cyc Am Bio v22; Not Am Wom

16740. Farnham, Eliza Woodson (Burhans)
1815–64
prison reformer, author, lecturer, feminist, suffragist, philanthropist
New York; California
Cyc Am Bio; Dict Am Auth; Dict Am Bio; Dict Am Bio Men Time; Index t Wom; Nat Cyc Am Bio v4; Not Am Wom; Twent Cen Bio Dict Not Am

16741. Thomas, Mary Frame (Myers)
1816–88
physician, suffragist, women's rights worker, prison reformer, temperance worker, editor
Index t Wom; Not Am Wom; Twent Cen Bio Dict Not Am

16742. Howe, Julia Ward
1819–1910
poet, dramatist, songwriter, lecturer, suffrage and women's club leader, feminist, abolitionist, pacifist, prison reformer, Union patriot during the Civil War, philanthropist, traveler
Boston, MA
Cyc Am Bio; Dict Am Auth; Dict Am Bio; Dict Am Bio Men Time; Dict Lit Bio v1; Index t Wom; Nat Cyc Am Bio v1; Not Am Wom; Twent Cen Bio Dict Not Am; Wom Cent

16743. Johnson, Ellen Cheney
1819/29–1899
prison reformer, prison superintendent, educator
Dict Am Bio; Not Am Wom; Twent Cen Bio Dict Not Am

16744. Davis, Sarah Iliff
born 1820
philanthropist, temperance worker, women's prison reformer, milliner, sanitation worker for the Union army during the Civil War, Freedmen's Aid worker
Wom Cent

16745. Hendricks, Eliza C. Morgan
born 1823
philanthropist, women's prison welfare worker
Episcopalian
Wom Cent

16746. Barney, Susan Hammond
flourished 1854–90s
evangelist, Prohibitionist, temperance worker, prison reformer
Rhode Island
Index t Wom; Wom Cent

16747. Goff, Harriet Newell (Kneeland)
born 1828
temperance reformer, author, suffragist, women's prison reformer, essayist
Brooklyn, NY
Dict Am Auth; Wom Cent

16748. Doolittle, Lucy Salisbury
born 1832
philanthropist, reformer of women's prisons, suffragist, educator of freedwomen
Wom Cent

16749. Gregory, Elizabeth Goadby
born 1834
author, translator of French and German literature, journalist, writer on industrial and social topics
Wom Cent

16750. Tutwiler, Julia Strudwick
1835/41–1916
educator, women's educator, temperance worker, prison reformer
Alabama
Dict Am Bio; Encyc South Hist; Index t Wom; Nat Cyc Am Bio v15; Not Am Wom; Wom Cent

16751. Bullock, Helen Louise
born 1836
temperance worker, music educator, women's prison reformer
Wom Cent

16752. Hall, Emma Amelia
1837–84
prison reformer, prison administrator
Not Am Wom

16753. Cobb, Mary Emilie
born 1838
educator, philanthropist, juvenile-prison reformer
Wom Cent

16754. Ames, Fanny Baker
1840–1931
industrial reformer in public institutions, charity organizer
Index t Wom; Not Am Wom; Wom Cent

16755. Ricker, Marilla Marks Young
1840–1920
lawyer, suffragist, prison reformer, politician, author, political writer
New Hampshire
Index t Wom; Nat Cyc Am Bio v17; Not Am Wom; Wom Cent

16756. Walker, Harriet Granger
1841–1917
philanthropist, hospital organizer, temperance worker, suffragist, police reformer
Methodist
Minneapolis, MN
Nat Cyc Am Bio v6; Wom Cent

16757. Hill, Agnes Leonard (Scanland); Molly Myrtle
1842–1917
poet, author, newspaper publisher, religious writer, novelist, prisoner's welfare worker, Universalist pastor
Universalist
Colorado
Dict Am Auth; Index t Wom; Nat Cyc Am Bio v17; Wom Cent

16758. Hunt, Augusta Merrill
born 1842
philanthropist, temperance worker, suffragist, prison reformer
Universalist
Wom Cent

16759. Lowell, Josephine (Shaw)
1843–1905
charitable worker, philanthropist, social worker, prison reformer, labor reformer, writer on philanthropy
New York, NY
Cyc Am Bio; Dict Am Auth; Dict Am Bio; Index t Wom; Nat Cyc Am Bio v8; Not Am Wom; Twent Cen Bio Dict Not Am

16760. Barrows, Katherine Isabel Hayes Chapin
1845–1913
ophthalmologist, penologist, editor, travel writer
Dict Am Auth; Index t Wom; Not Am Wom

16761. Gilbert, Linda
1847–95

prison welfare worker, philanthropist
Cyc Am Bio; Index t Wom; Not Am Wom; Twent Cen Bio Dict Not Am; Wom Cent

16762. Hall, Lucy M.
flourished 1880s–90s
physician, prison doctor
Wom Cent

16763. Schoff, Hannah Kent
1850/53–1940
child welfare worker, juvenile court reformer, child aid leader, editor, author
Philadelphia, PA
Index t Wom; Nat Cyc Am Bio v18; Not Am Wom

16764. Johnston, Lizzie Johnston Evans
1851–1934
philanthropist, juvenile-prison reformer, Democratic party worker
Presbyterian
Alabama
Nat Cyc Am Bio v31

16765. Davis, Katherine Bement
1860–1935
penologist, prison reformer, sociologist, social worker, philanthropist, disaster relief worker in Italy
Dict Am Bio ad; Index t Wom; Nat Cyc Am Bio csv1; Not Am Wom

16766. Schaffner, Ernestine;
The Prisoner's Friend
flourished 1890s
prison reformer and prison relief worker
New York, NY
Wom Cent

16767. Talbert, Mary Burnett
1862/66–1923
educator, social reformer, prison reformer, Black rights worker, club leader
Black
Index t Wom; Negro Alman; Prof Negro Wom v1

16768. Booth, Maud Ballington (Charlesworth)
1865–1948
Salvation Army leader, evangelist, philanthropist, prison reformer, author, founder of PTA
Salvationist
English
Dict Am Auth; Index t Wom; Nat Cyc Am Bio v14 and v38; Not Am Wom; Obit File

16769. Bartelme, Mary Margaret
1866/69–1954
lawyer, judge, juvenile prison reformer, Chicago juvenile court judge
Illinois
Index t Wom; Nat Cyc Am Bio; Not Am Wom; Obit File

16770. Hodder, Jessie Donaldson
1867–1931
prison reformer
Not Am Wom

16771. Follet, Mary Parker
1868–1933
writer and lecturer on political science, group psychology, and industrial management
Dict Am Auth; Dict Am Bio supp v1; Not Am Wom

16772. Grenfell, Helen Loring
born 1868
educator, penologist
Index t Wom

16773. Hamilton, Alice
1869–1970
industrial physician and toxicologist, pioneer in industrial medicine, medical educator, medical author, social reformer
Cur Biog '70; Index t Wom; Nat Cyc Am Bio csv7; Not Am Wom supp v1

16774. Beasley, Delilah Leontium
1871–1934
historian, journalist, pacifist
California
Black
Encyc Black Am; Negro Alman; Prof Negro Wom

16775. Harris, Mary Belle
1874–1957
prison administrator
Not Am Wom supp v1

16776. Jacobs, Pattie Ruffner
1875–1935
Alabama suffrage leader, child labor welfare worker, prison reformer, Prohibition party worker
Encyc South Hist; Not Am Wom

16777. Cunningham, Kate (Richards) (O'Hare)
1877–1948
Socialist party presidential nominee, community organizer, prison reformer, anti–World War I activist, lecturer, educator
Index t Wom; Not Am Wom; Obit File; Dict Am Bio v4

16778. Burwell, Mary E.
flourished 1913
hospital founder, prison reformer
Richmond, VA
Prof Negro Wom

16779. van Waters, Miriam
1887–1974
penologist, social worker, writer on penology
Cur Biog '74; Index t Wom; Not Am Wom supp v1

16780. Barus, Jane Garey
1892–1977
suffragist; political activist; prison reformer; Montclair, New Jersey, civic worker; antinuclear activist; anti–Vietnam war worker
Unitarian
Montclair, NJ
Nat Cyc Am Bio v60

16781. Harbeson, Georgiana Brown
born 1894
industrial artist, designer
Index t Wom

16782. Baker, Helen
1900–55
industrial relations expert, university educator
Obit File

16783. Eddy, Lillian E.
circa 1902–66
industrial designer
New Zealand
Index t Wom

16784. Dixon, Margaret Calder Richardson
1908–70
prison reformer, political journalist, newspaper editor
Episcopalian
Baton Rouge, LA
Nat Cyc Am Bio v58; Obit File

RANCHING, FARMING, HUSBANDRY, AND ECOLOGY

16785. Pearce, Mistress
1607–27
pioneer gardener
Index t Wom

16786. Fenwick, Lady
flourished 1639–45
gardener
Index t Wom

16787. Coming, Affra Harleston
died 1699
colonial agronomist
Index t Wom

16788. Diggs, Elizabeth
died 1699
colonial planter, plantation owner and manager
Index t Wom

16789. Manigault, Judith Giton Royer
died 1711
colonial agronomist, pioneer
Index t Wom

16790. Axtell, Rebecca, Lady
flourished 1700s
colonial planter
Index t Wom

16791. Byrd, Mary Willing
flourished eighteenth century
colonial business executive, plantation manager
Index t Wom

16792. Minis, Abigail
1701–94
planter
Jewish
Index t Wom

16793. Logan, Martha Daniell
1702/04–1779
educator, gardener, botanist, florist, horticulturist
Am Bio Dict; Index t Wom; Not Am Wom

16794. Blakeway, Sarah
flourished 1741
colonial planter, businessperson
Index t Wom

16795. Dubre, Hannah; Hanna Dubrey; Hanna Duberry
flourished 1750s
colonial agriculturist
Index t Wom

16796. Pinckney, Elizabeth Lucas "Eliza"
1722/23–1793
plantation manager identified with the development of indigo as a staple of the colonial South, textile manufacturer, agriculturist, author
South Carolina
Dict Am Bio; Encyc South Hist; Index t Wom; Not Am Wom; Who Who Dur Am Rev

16797. Carter, Frances Ann Tasker
1737–97
agriculturist
Index t Wom

16798. Downs, Jane Douglas
flourished 1770s
planter
Index t Wom

16799. Harnet, Mary
died 1792
colonial plantation manager
Index t Wom

16800. Ramsay, Martha Laurens
1759–1811
missionary, colonial horticulturist, author, autobiographer
Am Bio Dict; Cyc Am Bio; Index t Wom

16801. Fiske, Catharine
1776–1837
educator, scientist, farmer
New Hampshire
Am Bio Dict; Index t Wom

16802. Eldridge, Elleonor
1785–1845
author, amateur lawyer, dairy farmer
Black
Negro Alman; Prof Negro Wom v1

16803. King, Anna Page
1798–1859
gardener
Index t Wom

16804. McCord, Louisa Susannah (Cheves)
1810–1879/80
miscellaneous author, poet, political writer, translator, Confederate essayist, Black welfare worker, feminist, plantation manager
South Carolina
Cyc Am Bio; Dict Am Auth; Dict Am Bio; Dict Am Bio Men Time; Index t Wom; Nat Cyc Am Bio v9; Not Am Wom; Twent Cen Bio Dict Not Am

16805. Haughery, Margaret Gaffney; The Bread Woman of New Orleans
1813/25–1882
charitable worker, philanthropist, dairy farmer, bakery operator and owner
Cyc Am Bio; Dict Am Bio; Index t Wom; Not Am Wom; Twent Cen Bio Dict Not Am

16806. Daviess, Maria (Thompson)
1814–96
writer on agriculture
Kentucky
Cyc Am Bio; Dict Am Auth; Nat Cyc Am Bio v3

16807. Riggs, Mary
1818–52
gardener, pioneer missionary
Index t Wom

16808. Filley, Mary A. Powers
born 1821
suffragist, dairy stock farmer
New Hampshire
Wom Cent

16809. Lewis, Grace Anna
born 1821
naturalist, scientific illustrator, science writer, conservationist, ornithologist, abolitionist, Underground Railroad operator, pacifist, suffragist, philanthropist
Quaker
Index t Wom; Nat Cyc Am Bio v9; Twent Cen Bio Dict Not Am; Wom Cent

16810. Thomas, M. Louise (Palmer)
born 1822
president of Sorosis, farmer, agriculturist, apiarist
Index t Wom; Nat Cyc Am Bio v13

16811. Tupper, Ellen Smith
born 1822
apiarist, writer on beekeeping, pioneer
Index t Wom; Wom Cent

16812. Gaffney, Margaret
1825–82
philanthropist, dairy farmer
Nat Cyc Am Bio v2

16813. Long, Ellen Call
1825–1905
civic leader, author, planter
Florida
Read Encyc Am West

16814. Blackwell, Sarah Ellen
born 1828
artist, author, suffragist, land and labor reformer, antivivisectionist
Nat Cyc Am Bio v9; Wom Cent

16815. Morgan, Maria "Middy"
1828–92
journalist, authority on horses and cattle
Irish
Index t Wom; Wom Cent

16816. Austin, Helen Vickroy
born 1829
horticulturist, temperance worker, suffragist
Wom Cent

16817. Dulany, Ida
flourished 1860s
plantation manager, Civil War patriot
Index t Wom

16818. Elmore, Ellen
flourished 1860s
plantation manager
Index t Wom

16819. Elmore, Grace
flourished 1860s
plantation manager
Index t Wom

16820. Gillett, Sisters
flourished 1860s–80s
farm managers, businesspeople
Index t Wom

16821. Miller, Harriet (Mann); Olive Thorne Miller
1831–1918
author, ornithologist, bird watcher, naturalist, nature writer, conservationist, children's author, magazine writer
Swedenborgian
Brooklyn, NY
Dict Am Auth; Index t Wom; Nat Cyc Am Bio v9; Not Am Wom; Twent Cen Bio Dict Not Am

16822. King, Henrietta Maria Morse Chamberlain
1832–1925
cattle rancher
Texas
Nat Cyc Am Bio v20

16823. McCrackin, Josephine Woempner Clifford
1838/46–1920
author, journalist, clubwoman, conservationist
German
Index t Wom; Not Am Wom

16824. Clay, Mary Barr
born 1839
suffragist, women's rights worker, farmer
Kentucky
Wom Cent

16825. Jack, Annie L. Hayr; Loyal Janet
born 1839
horticulturist, author
Wom Cent

16826. Sanborn, Katharine Abbott "Kate"
1839–1917
miscellaneous author, educator, lecturer, essayist, literary professor, agriculturist
New Hampshire
Cyc Am Bio; Dict Am Auth; Dict Am Bio; Index t Wom; Nat Cyc Am Bio v9; Twent Cen Bio Dict Not Am

16827. Fuller, Electa
flourished 1870s–80s

agriculturist
Index t Wom

16828. Fuller, Laura
flourished 1870s–80s
agriculturist
Index t Wom

16829. Stevens, E. Hebert, Mrs.
flourished 1870s–1910s
agricultural librarian, lecturer
Washington, DC
Index t Wom; Wom Cent

16830. Watson, Jennie
flourished 1870s–80s
botanist
Index t Wom

16831. Wilson, Mary
flourished 1870s
agriculturist
Index t Wom

16832. Fry, Elizabeth Turner
born 1842
philanthropist, Prohibitionist, humane worker, suffragist
San Antonio, TX
Wom Cent

16833. Watson, Elizabeth Lowe
born 1842
lecturer, pastor of the San Francisco Religious and Philosophical Society, fruit farmer
California
Wom Cent

16834. Everhard, Caroline McCullough
born 1843
suffragist, feminist, humane society worker
Ohio
Wom Cent

16835. Rose, Ellen Alida
born 1843
feminist, agriculturist, businessperson, Grange worker, suffragist
Index t Wom; Wom Cent

16836. Thorp, Mandana Coleman
born 1843
Union patriot during the Civil War, pioneer, deputy clerk and register of deeds in northern Michigan, sheep and wool farmer
Michigan
Wom Cent

16837. Collins, Libby Smith
1844–1921
western pioneer, cattle rancher
Index t Wom

16838. Strong, Harriet Williams Russell
1844–1926/29
agriculturist, student of water supply problems, horticulturist, engineer, civic leader
Los Angeles, CA
Dict Am Bio; Nat Cyc Am Bio v17; Not Am Wom

16839. Mayo, Mary Anne Bryant
1845–1903
Grange and Farmers Institute worker
Dict Am Bio

16840. Pringle, Elizabeth Waties Allston
1845–1921
rice planter, author
Not Am Wom

16841. Clapp, Cornelia Maria
1849–1934
zoologist, educator
Not Am Wom

16842. Maxwell, Kate; Cattle Kate
flourished 1880s–90s
western cattle rancher
Index t Wom

16843. Wood, Frances Fisher
flourished 1880s–90s
educator, lecturer, scientist, dress reformer, dairy farmer, businessperson
Wom Cent

16844. Gause, Nora Trueblood
born 1851
humane worker, lecturer
Indiana
Wom Cent

16845. Monoghan, Josephine; Little Jo
died 1903
pioneer, rancher
Index t Wom

16846. Keith, Eliza D.; Erie Douglas; Di Vernon
born 1854
author, journalist, worker for the SPCA
California
Nat Cyc Am Bio v2; Wom Cent

16847. Miller, Louise Klein
1854–1943
horticulturist, landscape architect, educator
Index t Wom

16848. Bush, Katharine Jeanette
born 1855
zoologist
Index t Wom

16849. Meagher, Mary
born circa 1855
western pioneer, agriculturist
Index t Wom

16850. Sessions, Kate Olivia
1857–1940
horticulturist, nurseryperson
California
Not Am Wom

16851. Ely, Helena Rutherfurd
1858–1920
author, landscape gardener
Index t Wom

16852. Wright, Mabel (Osgood)
1859–1934
novelist, nature writer, naturalist, bird protectionist
Dict Am Auth; Index t Wom; Nat Cyc Am Bio v12; Not Am Wom

16853. Rogers, Mary Fletcher
flourished 1890s
author, animal humane worker
Wom Cent

16854. Worley, Laura Davis
flourished 1890s
dairy farmer
Indiana
Wom Cent

16855. Hind, Ella Cora
1861–1942
agriculturist, editor, journalist
Index t Wom

16856. Dana, William Starr, Mrs.
1862–1952
author, gardener
Index t Wom

16857. James, Annie Laurie Wilson
born 1862
journalist, editor, horse breeding expert
California
Index t Wom; Wom Cent

16858. Sherman, Mary Belle King
1862–1935
clubwoman, champion of national parks
Not Am Wom

16859. King, Frances
born 1863
author, landscape gardener
Index t Wom

16860. King, Louisa Boyd Yeomans
1863–1948
writer on gardening, pioneer of the garden club movement
Not Am Wom

16861. Roberts, Dora
1863–1953
rancher, philanthropist
Texas
Obit File

16862. Sears, Clara Endicott
1863–1960
author, antiquarian, cattle breeder
Protestant Episcopal
Massachusetts
Nat Cyc Am Bio v47 and csv1

16863. Fiske, Mary Augusta (Davey); Minnie Madern; Minnie Madern Fiske
1865–1932
actor, author, animal humane worker
Dict Am Bio supp v1; Index t Wom; Nat Cyc Am Bio v10, v35, and csv1; Not Am Wom; Twent Cen Bio Dict Not Am

16864. Austin, Mary (Hunter)
1866/68–1934
novelist, folklorist, short story writer, journalist, conservationist, feminist, worker for Native American rights
California
Dict Am Auth; Dict Am Bio supp v1; Dict Lit Bio v9; Not Am Wom; Read Encyc Am West; Wom Lit; Wom Lit, More

16865. Freshel, Maud Hammer
1866–1948
antivivisectionist, animal humane worker
Christian Scientist
Obit File

16866. Hoyt, Minerva Lockhart Hamilton
1866–1945
naturalist, conservationist, botanist, patron of music, president of the Los Angeles Symphony Orchestra
Los Angeles, CA
Am Bio New Cyc; Nat Cyc Am Bio v34

16867. Brown, Helen
1867–1942
president of the Women's Land Army (volunteer farm labor workers) during World War I
Obit File

16868. Hoffman, Zelia Kumbhaar
1867–1929
horticulturist
Nat Cyc Am Bio v32

16869. Myers, Harriet Williams
born 1867
author, ornithologist, founder of California Audubon Society, conservationist, animal humane worker, World War II national defense worker
Los Angeles, CA
Am Bio New Cyc

16870. Andrews, Harriet White Fisher
born 1869
disaster relief nurse, dairy farmer, anvil manufacturer
Nat Cyc Am Bio csv2

16871. Williston, Anne Robson Sterling
born 1869
conservationist
Methodist
Canadian
Nat Cyc Am Bio csv2

16872. Harvey, Kate Benedict Hanna
1871–1936
public health worker, patron of nursing, cattle breeder
Protestant Episcopal
Cleveland, OH
Nat Cyc Am Bio v34

16873. Farrand, Beatrix Cadwalader Jones
1872–1959
landscape architect
Dict Am Bio supp v5; Not Am Wom supp v1

16874. Kibbe, Flora Harriet d'Aubry Jenkins
1872–1943
animal humane worker
New York
Nat Cyc Am Bio v37

16875. Moore, Emmeline
1872–1963
biologist, fishery scientist, president of the American Fisheries Association, conservationist
Obit File

16876. Patino, Albina Rodriguez
1872–1953
mine owner and operator, dairy farmer, philanthropist
Bolivian
Nat Cyc Am Bio v40

16877. Clements, Edith Gertrude Schwartz
graduated 1898
ecologist
Nat Cyc Am Bio csv7

16878. Clubb, Laura Abigail Rutherford
1873–1952
art collector, rare book collector, philanthropist, cattle rancher

Methodist
Oklahoma
Nat Cyc Am Bio v38

16879. Atwater, Helen Woodard
1876–1947
US Department of Agriculture official, home economist
Nat Cyc Am Bio v46 and csv12; Not Am Wom; Obit File

16880. Cleghorn, Sarah Norcliffe
1876–1959
poet, novelist, educator, suffragist, civil rights worker, labor worker, pacifist, antivivisectionist, Socialist party member
Vermont
Index t Wom; Nat Cyc Am Bio v46; Obit File; Dict Am Bio supp v5

16881. Edge, Rosalie Barrow
1877–1962
conservationist
Index t Wom

16882. Miller, Daisy Orr
1877–1955
editor, dog specialist, president of the Animal Protection Union
Index t Wom; Obit File

16883. Fox, Gertrude Elizabeth Wilbur
1878–1947
animal breeder
Index t Wom

16884. Manville, Henrietta Estelle
1878–1947
patron of floriculture and horticulture, philanthropist
New York
Nat Cyc Am Bio v56 and csv6

16885. Bingham, Millicent Todd
1880–1968
geographer, conservationist, author, editor, authority on Emily Dickinson
Episcopalian
Cur Biog '69; Index t Wom; Nat Cyc Am Bio csv9

16886. Garber, Lucy May (Bradley)
1880–1971
US land commissioner in Oklahoma, newspaper publisher
Oklahoma
Nat Cyc Am Bio v58

16887. Mowat, Vivia A.
flourished 1910s
agriculturist, businessperson
Index t Wom

16888. Pratt, Harriet Barnes
flourished 1910s–30s
horticulturist
Index t Wom

16889. Ross, Rita
flourished 1910s–30s
animal humane worker
Index t Wom

16890. Sherman, Minna E.
flourished 1910s
agriculturist, club leader, lecturer, author
Index t Wom

16891. Simms, Ruth Hanna McCormick
1880–1944
representative to Congress from Illinois, political leader, Republican National Committee member from New Mexico, dairy farmer
Quaker
Illinois; New Mexico
Dict Am Bio supp v3; Index t Wom; Nat Cyc Am Bio v34; Not Am Wom; Obit File

16892. Snow, Ellen
flourished 1910s
author, pacifist, animal humane woker, suffragist
Cyc Am Bio

16893. Boardman, Queen Walker
born 1881
horticulturist, philanthropist
Religious Scientist
Los Angeles, CA
Nat Cyc Am Bio csv7

16894. McClellan, Irene Moulton Ward
1881–1967
philanthropist, World War I Red Cross relief worker in England, patent medicine manufacturer, dairy and chicken farmer
Episcopalian
New York
Nat Cyc Am Bio v53

16895. Sewell, Edna Belle Scott
1881–1967
farm women's leader
Not Am Wom supp v1

16896. Benchley, Belle Jennings
born 1882
zoo director
Index t Wom

16897. Morgan, Anne Haven
1882–1966
zoologist, ecologist
Not Am Wom supp v1

16898. Goode, Edith J.
1883–1970
suffragist, animal humane worker, cofounder of the National Women's party
Obit File

16899. Hutchinson, Mary Amory Hare; Amory Hare
1885–1969
author, novelist, dramatist, painter, poet, thoroughbred-horse breeder
Episcopalian
California
Nat Cyc Am Bio v57, Index t Wom

16900. Stokes, Lilia Woodruff
1885–1973
Philadelphia civic worker, worker for Women's International League for Peace and Freedom, conservationist
Quaker
Pennsylvania
Nat Cyc Am Bio v58

16901. Eustis, Dorothy Leib Harrison Wood
1886–1946
philanthropist, patron of agriculture, founder and president of the Seeing-Eye Association, dog breeder
Dict Am Bio supp v4; Index t Wom; Nat Cyc Am Bio csv5; Not Am Wom; Obit File

16902. Kelly, Junea Wangeman
1886–1969
ornithologist, conservationist
California
Nat Cyc Am Bio v55

16903. Hubbard, Theodora Kimball
1887–1935
landscape architect, city planner
Unitarian
Massachusetts
Nat Cyc Am Bio v28 and csv3

16904. Baldwin, Tillie
circa 1888–1958
western pioneer, cowhand
Index t Wom

16905. Braun, Emma Lucy
1889–1971
botanist, conservationist
Not Am Wom supp v1

16906. Graham, Helen Tredway
1890–1971
biochemist, air pollution control worker
St. Louis, MO
Nat Cyc Am Bio v56

16907. Maltby, Esther Stark
flourished 1920s

park board member
Index t Wom

16908. Mather, Elizabeth Ring Ireland
1891–1957
philanthropist, patron of horticulture
Cleveland, OH
Nat Cyc Am Bio v43

16909. Street, Margaret Berry
1891–1967
cattle farmer, lawyer, Civil Air Regulations executive, suffragist, Black welfare worker
Presbyterian
North Carolina
Nat Cyc Am Bio v54

16910. Gifford, Myrnie Ada
1892–1966
public health administrator, pediatrician, conservationist
California
Nat Cyc Am Bio v54

16911. Harrison, Gertrude [Alice] Gordon Grayson
1892–1961
Washington, DC, civic leader; patron of medicine; racehorse breeder
Episcopalian
Nat Cyc Am Bio v51

16912. Stark, Mabel
born 1892
animal trainer
Canadian
Index t Wom

16913. Castle, Irene (Foote)
1893–1969
ballroom dancer, animal welfare worker
Index t Wom; Not Am Wom supp v1; Obit File

16914. Frantz, Virginia Kneeland
1896–1967
surgical pathologist, medical educator, cancer researcher, dairy farmer
Episcopalian
New York
Nat Cyc Am Bio v53; Not Am Wom supp v1

16915. Stoehr, Edith
died 1946
sportswoman, first woman to be a US game warden
Obit File

16916. Sloane, Isabel Dodge
circa 1897–1962
racehorse breeder, owner of Brookemeade Stables
Obit File

16917. van Deman, Ruth
died 1948
information director of the Agriculture Department's Nutrition and Home Economics Bureau
Obit File

16918. Westcott, Cynthia
born 1898
plant pathologist
Index t Wom

16919. Wolle, Muriel Sibell
1898–1977
artist, art educator, Native American art scholar and collector, western history writer, conservationist
Episcopalian
Boulder, CO
Nat Cyc Am Bio v60

16920. Bonaparte, Jerome Napoleon, Mrs.
flourished 1930s
dog breeder and expert
Index t Wom

16921. Jones, Helen Swift
flourished 1930s
landscape architect
Index t Wom

16922. Sellers, Marie
flourished 1930s
agriculturist, editor
Index t Wom

16923. Wright, Lucille Voorhies Parker
flourished 1930s–50s
sportsperson, horse breeder
Christian Scientist
Nat Cyc Am Bio csv8

16924. Austin, Madalaine Horne
died 1951
dog breeder
Obit File

16925. Bruce, Ailsa Mellon
1901–69
philanthropist, patron of art, conservationist
Episcopalian
New York
Nat Cyc Am Bio v55; Obit File

16926. Cary, Mary Harkness Flagler
1901–67
patron of music, conservationist
New York
Nat Cyc Am Bio v55

16927. Daingerfield, Elizabeth
died 1951
thoroughbred-racehorse breeder
Obit File

16928. Payson, Joan Whitney
1903–75
philanthropist, race horse breeder, owner of the New York Mets, patron of medicine, art collector and investor, founder of the Museum of Modern Art in New York
Episcopalian
New York
Cur Biog '72 and '75; Index t Wom; Nat Cyc Am Bio v58 and csv10; Obit File

16929. Carson, Rachel Louise
1907–64
biologist, conservationist, naturalist, nature and conservation writer
Presbyterian
Index t Wom; Nat Cyc Am Bio csv9; Not Am Wom supp v1; Obit File

16930. Hofmann, Melita Cecelia
1907–76
artist, art educator, book illustrator and designer, author, conservationist
Congregationalist
New York
Nat Cyc Am Bio v60

16931. Johnston, Velma B.; Wild Horse Annie
1912–77
animal humane worker, wildhorse-protection worker
Index t Wom; Obit File

16932. Martin, Helen Frances Theresa
born 1912
animal keeper
Index t Wom

16933. Waller, Wilhelmine Stewart Kirby
born 1914
conservationist, horsewoman
Episcopalian
New York
Nat Cyc Am Bio csv13

16934. Hamer, Fannie Lou
1917–77
civil rights worker, founder of the Mississippi Freedom Democratic party, worker for Student Nonviolent Coordinating Committee, farmer
Mississippi
Black
Encyc Black Am; Obit File

16935. Stevens, Christine
born 1918
antivivisectionist
Index t Wom

16936. Lee, Frances Marron
flourished 1950s–60s
rancher, politician
Index t Wom

16937. Rogers, Anne Hone
born 1929
animal handler
Index t Wom

16938. Marvel, Louise; Cattle Lady
flourished 1960s
cattle rancher
Index t Wom

16939. Burke, Yvonne Watson Brathwaite
born 1932
lawyer, representative to Congress from California, regent of the University of California, environmentalist, feminist
California
Black
Cur Biog '75; Encyc Black Am; Negro Alman

No Dates

16940. Brown, Charlotte Coudrey
gardener
Index t Wom

16941. Jewett, Mildred; Madaket Millie
dog trainer
Index t Wom

16942. King, Louise Woodward
founder of the Georgia SPCA, philanthropist
Georgia
Cyc Am Bio

RELIGIOUS AND CHURCH WORK

16943. Eliot, Ann
flourished 1600s
missionary
Index t Wom

16944. Hutchinson, Anne (Marbury)
1590/91–1642/43
religious and political leader, founder of the Antinomian sect of Puritanism
Puritan
Rhode Island; Massachusetts
English
Am Bio Dict; Cyc Am Bio; Dict Am Bio; Dict Am Bio Men Time; Dict Am Rel Bio; Dict Nat Bio; Index t Wom; Nat Cyc Am Bio v9; Not Am Wom; Twent Cen Bio Dict Not Am

16945. l'Incarnation, Maria de, Mother
1599–1672
Catholic nun, educator, founder of the Ursuline Convent in Quebec, student of Native American languages
Catholic
Canadian
Cyc Am Bio

16946. Fox, Margaret Fell
1614–1702
religious leader
Index t Wom

16947. Austin, Ann
died 1665
colonial missionary
Index t Wom

16948. Bourgeois, Margaret, Sister
1620–1700
founder of the Congregation of Notre Dame, Catholic nun
Catholic
Cyc Am Bio

16949. Clark, Mary
flourished 1650s
colonial religious worker
Quaker
English
Index t Wom

16950. Godby, Ann
flourished 1650s
religious leader
Quaker
Index t Wom

16951. Harris, Elizabeth
flourished 1650s
religious worker
Quaker
English
Index t Wom

16952. Prince, Mary
flourished 1650s
colonial religious worker
Quaker
Index t Wom

16953. Tilton, Mary
flourished 1650s
colonial religious worker
Quaker
Index t Wom

16954. Wetherhead, Mary
flourished 1650s
religious worker
Quaker
Index t Wom

16955. Fisher, Mary
flourished 1652; died 1697
Quaker preacher, missionary

Quaker
Dict Nat Bio; Index t Wom; Not Am Wom

16956. Ganneaktena, Catharine
died 1673
founder of a Christian village for Native Americans
Native American
Cyc Am Bio

16957. Crosse, Mary Fisher Byaley
1624–90
colonial missionary
Index t Wom

16958. Ambrose, Alice
flourished 1660s
colonial religious worker
Puritan
Index t Wom

16959. Coleman, Ann
flourished 1660s
colonial religious worker
Quaker
Index t Wom

16960. Smith, Margaret
flourished 1660s–70s
colonial religious worker
Quaker
Index t Wom

16961. Wardel, Elizabeth
flourished 1660s
religious worker
Quaker
Index t Wom

16962. Wardell, Lydia
flourished 1660s
religious worker
Quaker
Index t Wom

16963. Wilson, Deborah
flourished 1660s
religious worker
Index t Wom

16964. Pennington, Mary Proude Springett
died 1682
religious leader
Index t Wom

16965. Dyer, Mary
born pre-1638; died 1660
religious leader, Quaker martyr
Quaker
Massachusetts
Am Bio Dict; Cyc Am Bio; Dict Am Bio; Dict Am Bio Men Time; Dict Am Rel Bio; Index t Wom; Nat Cyc Am Bio v11; Not Am Wom

16966. Brewster, Margaret
flourished 1670s
colonial religious worker

Quaker
Index t Wom

16967. Starbuck, Mary Coffyn
circa 1644/45–circa 1717
Quaker minister, religious leader
Quaker
Index t Wom; Not Am Wom

16968. Tekakwitha, Catherine "Kateri"
1656?–80
Catholic leader
Catholic
Native American
Dict Am Rel Bio; Great North Am Ind; Index t Wom; Not Am Wom

16969. Wilkinson, Ruth
flourished 1690s–1700s
religious worker
Quaker
Index t Wom

16970. Duncan, Margaret
flourished eighteenth century
colonial merchant, church builder
Index t Wom

16971. Hachard, Marie-Madeliene, Sister
flourished 1710s
pioneer, Catholic nun
Catholic
Index t Wom

16972. Tranchepain de Saint Augustine, Marie De, Sister
died 1733
Catholic nun, mother superior and founder of the Ursuline convents, hospital administrator, educator
Catholic
Cyc Am Bio; Index t Wom

16973. Lancastle, Lydia
1684–1761
Quaker preacher
Quaker
Cyc Am Bio

16974. Hoskens, Jane
born 1694
colonial clergyperson, educator
Index t Wom

16975. Timothy, Mary
flourished 1730s–40s
colonial religious worker
Quaker
Index t Wom

16976. Scott, Sarah
married 1726
colonial religious worker
Quaker
Index t Wom

16977. Hume, Sophia Wiginton
1702–74

Quaker minister, religious writer
Index t Wom; Not Am Wom

16978. Morris, Sarah
1704–75
Quaker preacher
Quaker
Cyc Am Bio; Dict Am Bio Men Time

16979. Edwards, Sarah Pierpont
1710–58
Puritan mystic
Puritan
Am Bio Dict; Not Am Wom

16980. Osborn, Sarah
born circa 1714
religious worker
Index t Wom

16981. Jacintha do San Jose
1716–68
Catholic nun, school and hospital founder
Catholic
Brazilian
Cyc Am Bio

16982. Levis, Elizabeth
flourished 1750s
colonial clergyperson
Index t Wom

16983. Neale, Mary Peasley
flourished 1750s
colonial religious worker
Quaker
Index t Wom

16984. Paisley, Mary Neale
flourished 1750s
colonial evangelist
Index t Wom

16985. Peyton, Catherine
flourished 1750s
colonial religious worker
Quaker
Index t Wom

16986. Watteville, Benigna [Henrietta] Justine Zinzendorf von
1725–89
educator, a founder of the Moravian Seminary and College for Women
Moravian
Moravian
Index t Wom; Not Am Wom

16987. Anthony, Susanna
1726–91
theologian, religious author
Quaker
Rhode Island
Am Bio Dict; Appl Cyc Am Bio; Cyc Am Bio; Dict Am Bio Men Time

16988. Fletcher, Bridget
1726–70
hymn and spiritual songwriter
Am Bio Dict

16989. Phillips, Catherine Payton
1727–94
colonial evangelist
English
Index t Wom

16990. Terrell, Ann
married 1755
religious worker
Quaker
Index t Wom

16991. Heck, Barbara Ruckle; The Mother of American Methodism
1734/44–1804
missionary, religious founder
Methodist
New York
Irish
Cyc Am Bio; Dict Am Bio; Index t Wom; Nat Cyc Am Bio v13; Not Am Wom; Who Who Dur Am Rev

16992. Lee, Ann; Ann Lee Standerin; Mother Ann
1736–84
founder of the American Society of Shakers
Shaker
New York
English
Am Bio Dict; Cyc Am Bio; Dict Am Bio; Dict Am Bio Men Time; Dict Am Rel Bio; Dict Nat Bio; Index t Wom; Nat Cyc Am Bio v5; Not Am Wom; Our Count; Twent Cen Bio Dict Not Am; Who Who Dur Am Rev

16993. Jones, Rebecca
1739–1818
Quaker minister
Quaker
Index t Wom

16994. Galloway, Anne
flourished 1770s
colonial religious worker
Quaker
Index t Wom

16995. Lake, Mary
1742–1802
western pioneer, religious worker, educator
English
Am Bio Dict; Index t Wom

16996. Bingham, Jemima
married 1769
missionary
Index t Wom

16997. Kirkland, Jerusha [Jemima] Bingham
married 1769
pioneer missionary
Index t Wom

16998. Harrison, Sarah
1748–1812
Quaker preacher
Quaker
Cyc Am Bio

16999. Ferguson, Catherine
circa 1749–1854
religious and welfare worker, baker
New York
Black
Index t Wom; Our Count

17000. Prince, Joanna
flourished eighteenth to nineteenth century
religious worker
Index t Wom

17001. Welch, Nancy
flourished eighteenth to nineteenth century
religious worker
Index t Wom

17002. Wilkinson, Jemima
1752/53–1819/21
evangelist, religious leader, founder of a pioneer community in western New York
New York
Am Bio Dict; Dict Am Bio; Dict Am Bio Men Time; Dict Am Rel Bio; Index t Wom; Nat Cyc Am Bio v1; Not Am Wom

17003. Barnard, Hannah Jenkins
1754–1825
Quaker minister
Quaker
Index t Wom; Not Am Wom

17004. Adams, Hannah
1755–1831/32
historian, compiler of historical data, religious author
Massachusetts
Am Bio Dict; Appl Cyc Am Bio; Cyc Am Bio; Dict Am Auth; Dict Am Bio; Dict Am Bio Men Time; Index t Wom; Nat Cyc Am Bio v5; Not Am Wom; Wom Cent

17005. Dickinson, Mary Clare
1755–1830
superior of the Carmelite nuns
Catholic
Cyc Am Bio

17006. Ramsay, Martha Laurens
1759–1811

missionary, colonial horticulturist, author, autobiographer
Am Bio Dict; Cyc Am Bio; Index t Wom

17007. Savage, Mary
flourished 1790s
clergyperson
Index t Wom

17008. Wright, Lucy
1760–1821
Shaker leader
Shaker
Index t Wom; Not Am Wom

17009. Hall, Sarah (Ewing); Constantia; Florepha
1761–1830
author, essayist, religious writer
Philadelphia, PA
Cyc Am Bio; Dict Am Auth; Dict Am Bio; Index t Wom; Nat Cyc Am Bio v11

17010. Allen, Sarah
1764–1849
missionary, pioneer
Black
Index t Wom; Negro Alman; Prof Negro Wom

17011. Lalor, Alice Teresa; Mother Teresa
1766–1846
mother superior and founder of the Convent and Academy of the Visitation, the first Roman Catholic female academy in the United States, educator
Catholic
Irish
Cyc Am Bio; Twent Cen Bio Dict Not Am; Who Who Dur Am Rev

17012. Teresa, Mother; Alice Labor
circa 1766–1846
founder of the Visitation Order in the United States, Catholic nun
Catholic
Dict Nat Bio

17013. Ripley, Dorothea
1767–1832
preacher
Am Bio Dict

17014. Phillips, Phoebe Foxcraft
died 1818
cofounder of the Andover Theological Seminary, philanthropist
Cyc Am Bio; Index t Wom

17015. Duchesne, Rose Philippine
1769–1852
missionary, Catholic nun, founder of the American Convents of

the Sacred Heart, pioneer, educator
Catholic
Kansas
Cyc Am Bio; Dict Am Rel Bio; Not Am Wom; Read Encyc Am West; Twent Cen Bio Dict Not Am

17016. Graham, Margaret
1770–1853
Christian evangelist
Am Bio Dict

17017. Davis, Hannah
1771–1856
missionary worker
Am Bio Dict

17018. Newton, Mrs.
died 1821
missionary to the Osage people
Am Bio Dict

17019. Hubbs, Rebecca
1772–1852
Quaker preacher
Quaker
Dict Am Bio

17020. Seton, Elizabeth Ann (Bayley), Saint; Mother Seton
1774–1821
Catholic nun, founder and superior of the American Sisters of Charity of St. Vincent de Paul (the first American sisterhood), philanthropist, autobiographer
Catholic
Maryland
Cyc Am Bio; Dict Am Auth; Dict Am Bio; Dict Am Rel Bio; Encyc South Hist; Index t Wom; Nat Cyc Am Bio v2; Not Am Wom; Twent Cen Bio Dict Not Am

17021. Collins, Elizabeth Ballinger
1775–1831
Quaker minister
Quaker
Cyc Am Bio

17022. Smith, Lucy Mack
1776–1855
religious worker
Index t Wom

17023. de Witt, Susan Linn
1778–1824
author, religious poet
Am Bio Dict; Cyc Am Bio

17024. Reed, Hannah
1778–1855
missionary worker, philanthropist
Marblehead, MA
Am Bio Dict

17025. Buttrick, Elizabeth
1780–1847

missionary to the Cherokee people
Am Bio Dict

17026. Cram, Nancy Gore
flourished 1810s
clergyperson
Index t Wom

17027. Brace, Lucy Collins
1782–1854
religious worker, missionary society leader
Am Bio Dict

17028. Kaahumanu
died 1832
Hawaiian ruler, patron of Christianity
Not Am Wom

17029. Rhodes, Mary, Mother
1782?–1853
Catholic nun, founder of the Sisters of Loretto
Catholic
Index t Wom; Not Am Wom

17030. Brown, Phoebe (Hinsdale)
1783–1861
hymn writer, poet
Dict Am Auth; Dict Am Bio; Nat Cyc Am Bio v11

17031. Stetson, Ellen
1783–1848
missionary to the Cherokee people, educator
Am Bio Dict

17032. Wilson, Mary J. (Smithey)
died 1836
missionary to Africa
Am Bio Dict

17033. Todd, Clarissa (Emerson)
died 1837
missionary to India
Am Bio Dict

17034. Feller, Henrietta
1788–1868
missionary
Cyc Am Bio

17035. Livermore, Harriet
1788–1868
preacher, evangelist, religious writer
Index t Wom; Not Am Wom; Twent Cen Bio Dict Not Am

17036. Barber, Jerusha
1789–1860
religious worker
Index t Wom

17037. Barber, Mary Augustine
1789–1860

educator, convent founder
Catholic
Appl Cyc Am Bio; Cyc Am Bio;
Wom Cent

17038. Johnson, Maria Preston
died 1839
missionary to Siam
Am Bio Dict

17039. Judson, Ann Hasseltine
1789–1826
missionary to Burma, pioneer
Am Bio Dict; Cyc Am Bio; Dict
Am Bio; Dict Am Bio Men
Time; Dict Ind Bio; Index t
Wom; Nat Cyc Am Bio v3; Not
Am Wom; Our Count; Twent
Cen Bio Dict Not Am

**17040. Sedgwick, Catharine
Maria**
1789–1867
novelist, writer of moral tales for
juveniles, educator
Stockbridge, MA
Cyc Am Bio; Dict Am Auth; Dict
Am Bio; Dict Am Bio Men
Time; Dict Lit Bio v1; Index t
Wom; Nat Cyc Am Bio v1; Not
Am Wom; Twent Cen Bio Dict
Not Am; Wom Cent; Wom Lit;
Wom Lit, More

17041. Cook, Maria
flourished 1820s
clergyperson
Index t Wom

**17042. Hebard, Rebecca W.
(Williams)**
died 1840
missionary to Beirut
Am Bio Dict

17043. Jones, Mrs.
flourished 1820s
missionary, seafarer
Index t Wom

17044. Allen, Sarah Johnson
1791–1848
missionary to the Mohegan people
Norwich, MA
Am Bio Dict

**17045. Arguello, Concha Maria
de Concepcion**
1791–1857
pioneer, Catholic nun
Catholic
Spanish
Index t Wom

**17046. Huntington, Susan
Mansfield**
1791–1823
religious writer, philanthropist,
diarist, poet
Am Bio Dict; Cyc Am Bio; Index
t Wom

17047. Roberts, Abigail Hoag
died 1841
clergyperson
Index t Wom

**17048. Sedgwick, Elizabeth
Buckminster (Dwight)**
1791–1864
educator, writer of Sunday school
tales
Dict Am Auth

17049. Wolcott, Mrs.
died 1841
missionary to Syria
Am Bio Dict

17050. Locke, Rowell, Mrs.
died 1842
missionary to the Sandwich Islands
Am Bio Dict

17051. Newell, Harriet Atwood
1792/93–1812
pioneer American missionary
worker in India
Am Bio Dict; Cyc Am Bio; Index
t Wom; Not Am Wom; Our
Count; Wom Cent

**17052. Putnam, Katharine
Hunt (Palmer)**
1792–1861
religious textbook writer
Boston, MA
Dict Am Auth

17053. Smith, Julia Evelina
1792–1886/92
suffragist, women's rights worker,
abolitionist, Biblical translator
Connecticut
Cyc Am Bio; Dict Am Bio; Nat
Cyc Am Bio v7; Not Am Wom

17054. Bingham, Sibyl M.
1793–1848
missionary to the Sandwich Islands
Am Bio Dict

17055. Dubost, Marie Louise
born 1793
Catholic nun, mother superior
and founder of the Sisters of
Charity in Brazil
Catholic
Cyc Am Bio

17056. Laurie, Mrs.
died 1843
missionary to Mosul [Iraq]
Am Bio Dict

17057. Mott, Lucretia (Coffin)
1793–1880
abolitionist, feminist, Quaker
minister, pacifist

Quaker
Cyc Am Bio; Dict Am Bio; Dict
Am Bio Men Time; Dict Am
Rel Bio; Index t Wom; Nat Cyc
Am Bio v2; Not Am Wom;
Twent Cen Bio Dict Not Am;
Wom Cent

**17058. Spalding, Catherine,
Mother**
1793–1858
Catholic nun, founder and first
superior of the Sisters of Charity of Nazareth
Catholic
Cyc Am Bio; Dict Am Bio; Index
t Wom; Not Am Wom

17059. Winslow, Anne (Spiers)
died 1843
missionary to Madras
Am Bio Dict

17060. Tubman, Emily H.
1794–1885
philanthropist, religious worker
Index t Wom

17061. Farrar, Cynthia
1795–1862
missionary
Not Am Wom

**17062. Gallitzin, Elizabeth,
Princess**
1795–1843
Catholic nun, convent and mis-
sion founder
Catholic
Cyc Am Bio

17063. Heinemann, Barbara
1795–1883
spiritual leader of the Community
of True Inspiration
Amanist
Not Am Wom

**17064. Page, Elizabeth Whi-
tredge**
died 1845
educator, religious worker
Index t Wom

**17065. Sansbury, Angela,
Mother**
1795–1839
convent founder, Catholic nun
Catholic
Index t Wom

**17066. Scudder, Harriet (Wa-
terbury)**
1795–1849
missionary to Madras [India]
Am Bio Dict

17067. Thurston, Lucy Goodall
1795–1876
missionary
Cyc Am Bio; Index t Wom

17068. Thomas, Sally
1796–1813
religious worker
Index t Wom

**17069. Winslow, Harriet W.
(Lathrop)**
1796–1833
missionary and educator in Ceylon
Am Bio Dict; Cyc Am Bio

17070. Danforth, Clarissa H.
married 1822
clergyperson
Index t Wom

17071. Millett, Deborah D.
1797–1869
religious worker
Index t Wom

17072. Moise, Penina
1797–1880
poet, writer of Jewish hymns
Jewish
Charleston, SC
Cyc Am Bio; Dict Am Auth; Dict
Am Bio; Index t Wom; Not Am
Wom; Wom Lit, More

**17073. Guerin, Anne-Theresa;
Mother Theodore**
1798–1856
educator, Catholic nun, founder
of the Sisters of Providence of
St. Mary-of-the-Woods
Indiana
French
Dict Am Bio; Nat Cyc Am Bio
v23

**17074. Hervey, Elizabeth
(Smith)**
1798–1831
missionary to Bombay
Am Bio Dict

**17075. Tuthill, Louisa Cornelia
Caroline (Huggins)**
1798/99–1879
author, popular writer of moral
tales for children
Princeton, NJ
Cyc Am Bio; Dict Am Auth; Dict
Am Bio Men Time; Index t
Wom; Not Am Wom

17076. Griswold, Mary H.
died 1849
missionary to Africa
Am Bio Dict

**17077. Hill, Frances Maria
Mulligan**
1799/1807–1884
Episcopal missionary and pioneer
educator of women in Greece
Episcopalian
Cyc Am Bio; Index t Wom; Not
Am Wom

17078. Scudder, Katherine
died 1849
missionary at Arcot, India
Am Bio Dict

17079. Tucker, Sarah
1799–1840
Quaker preacher
Quaker
Cyc Am Bio

17080. Walker, Mrs.
died 1849
missionary to West Africa
Am Bio Dict

17081. Brown, Catherine
1800–23
Moravian religious worker
Moravian
Alabama
Moravian; Native American (Cherokee)
Am Bio Dict

17082. Bugg, Lelia Hardin
born 18?
novelist, religious author
Catholic
Wichita, KS
Dict Am Auth

17083. Comstock, Sarah Davis
flourished 1830s
missionary
Index t Wom

17084. Dow, Betsy
flourished 1830s
religious educator
Index t Wom

17085. Jacobs, Phebe Ann
died 1850
church worker
Brunswick, ME
Black
Am Bio Dict

17086. Loughbridge, Mary
died 1850
missionary to the Creek people
Am Bio Dict

17087. Lund, Mary Dwinnell (Chellis)
born 18?
religious fiction author
Dict Am Auth

17088. Meeker, Eleanor Richardson
flourished 1830s–50s
missionary, educator
Index t Wom

17089. Peter, Sarah Anne (Worthington) King
1800–77
charity worker, philanthropist, founder of art school for women, hospital founder, Civil War

nurse, pioneer industrial arts educator, church worker
Catholic
Ohio
Dict Am Bio; Index t Wom; Not Am Wom; Twent Cen Bio Dict Not Am

17090. St. Augustine, Mother
flourished 1830s
Catholic nun
Catholic
French
Index t Wom

17091. Thompson, Eliza N.
1800–34
Christian missionary to Jerusalem
Am Bio Dict

17092. White, Mrs.
flourished 1830s
pioneer missionary
Index t Wom

17093. Wood, (Johnston), Mrs.
flourished nineteenth century
missionary to Singapore
Morristown, NJ
Am Bio Dict

17094. Allen, Myra
1801–31
missionary to Bombay
Am Bio Dict

17095. Burgess, N. M. Hall, Mrs.
died 1851
missionary to Native Americans on the Allegheny reservation
Allegheny, NY
Am Bio Dict

17096. Hancock, Martha M.
died 1851
missionary to the Sioux people
Minnesota
Am Bio Dict

17097. Macomber, Eleonor
1801–40
missionary
Cyc Am Bio; Index t Wom

17098. Doremus, Sarah Platt Haines
1802–77
foreign missionary, founder of foreign missions, charity organizer, philanthropist, social worker
Cyc Am Bio; Dict Am Bio; Index t Wom; Nat Cyc Am Bio v6; Not Am Wom; Twent Cen Bio Dict Not Am

17099. Newton, Mrs.
1802–35
missionary to the Cherokee people

Arkansas
Am Bio Dict

17100. Whittlesey, Anna L.
died 1852
missionary educator to Beirut
Am Bio Dict

17101. Burgess, Mrs.
died 1853
missionary to Satara, India
Am Bio Dict

17102. Clarke, Mary Francis
1803–87
Catholic nun, founder of the Sisters of the Blessed Virgin Mary
Catholic
Dict Am Bio

17103. Gurney, Eliza Paul Kirkbride
1803–81
Quaker minister
Quaker
Not Am Wom

17104. Judson, Sarah Hall Boardman
1803–45
missionary to Burma, hymn writer, translator
Cyc Am Bio; Dict Am Bio; Index t Wom; Nat Cyc Am Bio v3, Not Am Wom; Twent Cen Bio Dict Not Am

17105. Pumpelly, Mary Hollenback (Welles)
1803–79
poet, religious history writer
Cyc Am Bio; Dict Am Auth

17106. Smith, Sarah Lanman Huntington
1803–36
missionary to the Mohegan people at Mohegan, New York; missionary to Syria
New York
Am Bio Dict; Index t Wom

17107. Everett, Seraphina Sarah
died 1854
missionary to Constantinople
Am Bio Dict

17108. Smith, Eliza Roxey Snow; The Mother of Mormonism
1804–87
Mormon leader, religious poet, hymn writer, women's leader, suffragist, western pioneer
Mormon
Utah
Cyc Am Bio; Dict Am Bio; Index t Wom; Not Am Wom; Read Encyc Am West

17109. Smith, Emma Hale
1804–79
prominent figure in early Mormonism, religious worker
Mormon
Cyc Am Bio; Index t Wom; Not Am Wom

17110. Tanner, Sarah Elizabeth
1804–1914
educator, religious worker
Index t Wom

17111. Williams, Sarah P.
died 1854
missionary to Mosul, Iraq
Am Bio Dict

17112. Becroft, Ann Marie; Sister Aloysius
1805–33
educator, Catholic nun
Catholic
Black
Negro Alman; Prof Negro Wom

17113. Bridgman, Eliza Jane Gilbert
1805–71
missionary educator in China
Not Am Wom

17114. Foote, Roxana
died 1855
missionary to Tripoli
Am Bio Dict

17115. Grout, Hannah Davis
1805–36
missionary to Africa
Am Bio Dict

17116. Lyman, Sarah Joiner
1805–85
missionary
Cyc Am Bio

17117. Martin, Sarah Towne (Smith); Sarah Martyn
1805–79
historian, religious and historical writer for children, editor, abolitionist, temperance worker
New York, NY
Cyc Am Bio; Dict Am Auth; Dict Am Bio; Twent Cen Bio Dict Not Am

17118. Pierce, Susan
died 1855
missionary to Gabon
Am Bio Dict

17119. Powers, Harriet (Goulding)
1805–42
missionary to Broosa [Turkey]
Am Bio Dict

17120. Ramsey, Mary (Wire)
1805–34

missionary to Bombay
Am Bio Dict

17121. Tyler, Adeline Blanchard, Sister
1805–75
Civil War nurse, Episcopalian deaconess
Episcopalian
Not Am Wom

17122. Dwight, Elizabeth Baker
1806/08–1936
missionary to Constantinople, autobiographer
Am Bio Dict; Index t Wom

17123. Munger, Maria (Andrews)
1806–46
missionary to India
Am Bio Dict

17124. Wilkins, Ann
born 1806
missionary
Index t Wom

17125. Agnew, Eliza
1807–83
missionary
Dict Am Bio

17126. Andrews, Parnelly (Pierce)
1807–46
missionary to the Sandwich Islands
Am Bio Dict

17127. Ball, Lucy
1807–44
missionary to China
Am Bio Dict

17128. Palmer, Phoebe Worrall
1807–74
social reformer, religious writer, Methodist leader, Wesleyan evangelist
Wesleyan
New York, NY
Cyc Am Bio; Dict Am Auth; Dict Am Rel Bio; Index t Wom; Not Am Wom

17129. Spalding, Eliza Hart
1807–51
pioneer missionary to Oregon
Oregon
Index t Wom; Not Am Wom

17130. Jones, Sybil
1808/13–1873
Quaker minister, missionary
Quaker
Dict Am Bio; Index t Wom; Nat Cyc Am Bio v2; Not Am Wom

17131. Muzzy, Samantha
1808–46

missionary to Madurai, India
Am Bio Dict

17132. Whitman, Narcissa Prentiss
1808–47
missionary to the Native Americans of Northwest America, pioneer
Dict Am Rel Bio; Index t Wom; Not Am Wom

17133. Baxter, Lydia
1809–74
poet, hymn writer
Appl Cyc Am Bio; Cyc Am Bio; Dict Am Auth; Twent Cen Bio Dict Not Am

17134. Conant, Hannah O'Brian (Chaplin)
1809–65
religious worker, translator, Oriental scholar and language expert, magazine editor
Cyc Am Bio; Dict Am Auth; Dict Am Bio; Dict Am Bio Men Time; Nat Cyc Am Bio v22; Not Am Wom; Twent Cen Bio Dict Not Am

17135. Connelly, Cornelia Augusta Peacock, Mother
1809–79
Catholic nun, founder of the Society of the Holy Child Jesus
Catholic
English
Dict Am Bio; Index t Wom; Nat Cyc Am Bio v23; Not Am Wom

17136. Hardey, Mary Aloysia Hawley; Mother Mary Aloysia
1809/10–1886
Catholic nun, founder of the Sacred Heart convents and schools in the New World, educator
Catholic
Cyc Am Bio; Dict Am Bio; Index t Wom; Not Am Wom; Twent Cen Bio Dict Not Am

17137. Munn, Louisa
1809–41
missionary to the Sandwich Islands
Am Bio Dict

17138. Vinton, Calesta Holman
1809–64
missionary
Cyc Am Bio

17139. Wright, Laura Marie Sheldon
1809–86
missionary to the Seneca people in western New York
New York
Not Am Wom

17140. Aloysia, Sister
flourished 1840s
western pioneer, Catholic nun
Catholic
Index t Wom

17141. Carrell, Columba
1810–78
founder of the Hospital of Saint Mary and Saint Elizabeth, Catholic nun, mother superior
Catholic
Louisville, KY
Cyc Am Bio

17142. Craigin, Mary
flourished 1840s
religious cult leader
Index t Wom

17143. Doolittle, Mary Antoinette
1810–86
lecturer on religious subjects, Shaker eldress, author
Shaker
New York
Cyc Am Bio

17144. Eckard, Margaret Esther Bayard
1810–72
missionary
Cyc Am Bio

17145. Hale, Mary Whitwell
1810–62
poet, educator, hymn writer
Massachusetts
Dict Am Auth; Index t Wom

17146. Hallock, Mary Angeline A. (Ray) (Lathrop)
born 1810
author of religious tales for children
Cyc Am Bio; Dict Am Auth

17147. Loyola, Sister
flourished 1840s
Catholic nun, western pioneer
Catholic
Index t Wom

17148. Mary Loyola, Sister
flourished 1840s
western pioneer, Catholic nun
Catholic
Index t Wom

17149. Noyes, Charlotte
flourished 1840s
religious worker
Index t Wom

17150. Noyes, Harriet
flourished 1840s
religious worker
Index t Wom

17151. Shindler, Mary Stanley Bunce (Palmer) (Dana)
1810–83
author, poet, religious writer
Unitarian; Episcopalian
Nacogdoches, TX
Cyc Am Bio; Dict Am Auth; Dict Am Bio Men Time; Index t Wom

17152. Warde, Frances
1810–84
Catholic nun, sister of mercy, religious worker
Catholic
Dict Am Rel Bio

17153. Baldwin, Mary Briscoe
1811–77
missionary
Index t Wom

17154. Bradley, Emilie
1811–45
missionary to Siam
Am Bio Dict

17155. Bushnell, Mrs.
1811–50
Methodist missionary to West Africa
Methodist
Am Bio Dict

17156. Castle, Angelina
1811–41
missionary to Hawaii
Honolulu, HI
Am Bio Dict

17157. Cherry, Charlotte H. (Lathrop)
1811–1937 [*sic*]
missionary to Ceylon
Am Bio Dict

17158. Condee, Andelucia (Lee)
1811–55
missionary to the Sandwich Islands
Am Bio Dict

17159. Cutts, Maria
1811–53
Catholic nun, sister superior of all Convents of the Sacred Heart in the western United States
Catholic
Cyc Am Bio

17160. Hamlin, Henrietta Anna Loraine
1811–50
missionary to Turkey
Am Bio Dict

17161. Hoge, Jane Currie Blaike; A. H. Hoge
1811–90

Civil War relief leader, church and welfare worker, sanitation commission worker, author
Index t Wom; Not Am Wom

17162. Pohlman, Theodosia R. (Scudder)
1811–45
missionary to Borneo
Am Bio Dict

17163. Rankin, Melinda
1811–88
missionary
Index t Wom

17164. Stowe, Harriet Elizabeth Beecher
1811/12–1896
author, abolitionist, social reformer, theologian
Connecticut
Cyc Am Bio; Dict Am Auth; Dict Am Bio; Dict Am Bio Men Time; Dict Am Rel Bio; Dict Lit Bio v1; Nat Cyc Am Bio v1; Not Am Wom; Twent Cen Bio Dict Not Am; Wom Cent; Wom Lit; Wom Lit, More

17165. Tracy, Adeline (White)
1811–51
missionary to China
Am Bio Dict

17166. Hopkins, Louisa Payson
1812–62
religious writer for children
Cyc Am Bio; Dict Am Auth; Nat Cyc Am Bio v5

17167. Grew, Mary
1813–96
abolitionist, suffragist, feminist, Unitarian preacher, lecturer
Unitarian
Index t Wom; Not Am Wom; Wom Cent

17168. Reed, Rebecca Theresa
born 1813
proselyte
Cyc Am Bio

17169. Schriek, Louise van der, Sister
1813–86
founder of the Sisters of Notre Dame de Namur in America, Catholic nun
Catholic
Dict Am Bio

17170. Thomson, Catharine
1813–39
missionary to Borneo and India
Am Bio Dict

17171. Hayden, Mary Bridget, Mother
1814–90

Catholic nun, missionary, educator of Native Americans
Not Am Wom

17172. O'Connell, Mary; Sister Anthony
1814–97
Catholic nun, Civil War nurse, orphanage and hospital director in Cincinnati
Catholic
Cincinnati, OH
Dict Am Bio; Not Am Wom

17173. Olin, Julia Matilda
1814–79
religious author
Cyc Am Bio; Dict Am Auth; Twent Cen Bio Dict Not Am

17174. Perkins, Elmira Johnson
1814–96
missionary to Native Americans in Oregon, poet
Oregon; Boston, MA
Dict Am Auth

17175. Baker, Harriette Newell Woods; Mrs. Madeline Leslie; Aunt Hattie
1815–93
religious author, novelist
Appl Cyc Am Bio; Cyc Am Bio; Dict Am Auth; Index t Wom; Nat Cyc Am Bio v14; Wom Cent

17176. Cheney, Harriet Vaughan (Foster)
born 1815
religious author, historian
Cyc Am Bio; Dict Am Auth; Dict Am Bio Men Time; Index t Wom

17177. Comstock, Elizabeth Leslie Rous
1815–1891/92
social reformer, abolitionist, Underground Railroad worker, pacifist, freed slave's welfare worker, temperance reformer, women's rights worker, Quaker minister, prison reformer, Civil War nurse
Quaker
Dict Am Bio; Index t Wom; Nat Cyc Am Bio v22; Not Am Wom

17178. Desiree
1815–79
Catholic nun, sister superior
Catholic
Cyc Am Bio

17179. Hubbell, Martha Elizabeth (Stone)
1815–56
author, religious writer for children
Am Bio Dict; Cyc Am Bio; Dict Am Auth

17180. Stanton, Elizabeth Cady
1815/16–1902
feminist, suffragist, women's rights worker, editor, author, social reformer, theologian
Cyc Am Bio; Dict Am Auth; Dict Am Bio; Dict Am Bio Men Time; Dict Am Rel Bio; Index t Wom; Nat Cyc Am Bio v3; Not Am Wom; Twent Cen Bio Dict Not Am; Wom Cent

17181. Whittier, Elizabeth Hussey
1815–64
poet, abolitionist, religious worker
Quaker
Cyc Am Bio; Index t Wom; Nat Cyc Am Bio v8

17182. Ayres, Anne
1816–96
pioneer in American Episcopal Sisterhoods, religious author, philanthropist
Dict Am Auth; Dict Am Bio; Not Am Wom

17183. Euphemia
1816–87
mother superior of the Sisters of Charity
Catholic
Cyc Am Bio

17184. Fiske, Fidelia
1816–1864/84
Congregationalist missionary to Persia, educator
Congregationalist
Cyc Am Bio; Dict Am Bio; Dict Am Bio Men Time; Index t Wom; Nat Cyc Am Bio v3; Not Am Wom; Wom Cent

17185. Pierce, Mary E.
1816–44
missionary to Siam
Am Bio Dict

17186. Bishop, Harriet E.
1817–83
educator, missionary
Index t Wom; Not Am Wom

17187. Judson, Emily (Chubbuck); Fanny Forrester
1817–54
popular author, missionary
Am Bio Dict; Dict Am Auth; Dict Am Bio; Dict Am Bio Men Time; Index t Wom; Nat Cyc Am Bio v3; Not Am Wom; Twent Cen Bio Dict Not Am

17188. Paris, (Grant), Mrs.
1817–47
missionary to the Sandwich Islands
Am Bio Dict

17189. Shuck, Henrietta (Hall)
1817–44
missionary to China, writer on China
Cyc Am Bio; Dict Am Auth; Index t Wom

17190. Smith, Elizabeth Lee (Allen)
1817–98
biographical editor, poet, hymn writer
Dict Am Auth

17191. Stewart, Electra Maria (Sheldon); Electra Maria Sheldon
born 1817
writer on Michigan history, writer of religious tales for children
Detroit, MI
Cyc Am Bio; Dict Am Auth

17192. Torrey, Mary (Ide)
1817–69
religious and nonfiction writer
Vermont
Dict Am Auth

17193. Fox, Ana Leah
1818?–90
spiritual medium
Spiritualist
Not Am Wom

17194. Prentiss, Elizabeth (Payson); Elizabeth Prescott
1818–78
children's author, religious fiction writer, hymn writer
Dict Am Auth; Dict Am Bio; Index t Wom; Nat Cyc Am Bio v7; Not Am Wom; Twent Cen Bio Dict Not Am

17195. Riggs, Mary
1818–52
gardener, pioneer missionary
Index t Wom

17196. Warner, Susan Bogart; Elizabeth Wetherell
1818/19–1885
author, novelist, religious writer
Highland Falls, NY
Cyc Am Bio; Dict Am Auth; Dict Am Bio; Index t Wom; Nat Cyc Am Bio v5; Not Am Wom; Twent Cen Bio Dict Not Am; Wom Lit; Wom Lit, More

17197. Chaplin, Jane Dunbar
1819–84
children's author, religious writer
Dict Am Auth; Twent Cen Bio Dict Not Am

17198. Pike, Frances West (Atherton)
born 1819
religious author, magazine writer
Cyc Am Bio; Dict Am Bio

17199. Sewall, Harriet (Winslow)
1819–89
suffragist, poet, religious poet, abolitionist
Transcendentalist
Boston, MA
Dict Am Auth; Nat Cyc Am Bio v10

17200. Smith, Maria Ward
1819–42
missionary to Syria
Am Bio Dict

17201. Bailey, Urania Locke (Stoughton); Una Locke
1820–82
children's author, religious poet
Providence, RI
Dict Am Auth

17202. Blavatsky, Helena Petrovna (Hahn-Hahn)
1820/31–1891
occultist, mystic, founder of the semireligious Theosophical Society
Theosophist
Russian
Appl Cyc Am Bio; Cyc Am Bio; Dict Am Auth; Dict Am Bio; Dict Am Rel Bio; Nat Cyc Am Bio v15; Not Am Wom; Twent Cen Bio Dict Not Am; Wom Cent

17203. Butler, William, Mrs.
flourished 1850s
missionary
Index t Wom

17204. Claflin, Roxie
flourished 1850s–60s
feminist, religious worker
Index t Wom

17205. Clement, Annie W.
flourished 1850s
missionary
Index t Wom

17206. Crosby, Frances Jane "Fannie"
1820/23–1915
hymn writer
blind
Dict Am Bio; Index t Wom; Not Am Wom; Wom Cent

17207. Fay, Lydia Mary
flourished 1850s
missionary
Index t Wom

17208. Haynes, Lorenza
born 1820
Universalist minister
Universalist
Index t Wom; Wom Cent

17209. Horan, Mary Austin
1820–74
Catholic nun, superior of the Sisters of Mercy
Catholic
Cyc Am Bio

17210. Ingersoll, Julia Harriet (Pratt)
182?–98
religious author, religious poet
New Haven, CT
Dict Am Auth

17211. Jenkins, Lydia A.
flourished 1850s
clergyperson, feminist, lecturer
Index t Wom

17212. Livingstone, Mary Moffat
1820–62
missionary
English
Index t Wom

17213. Miller, Mary A.
flourished 1850s–80s
editor of a missionary newspaper
Wom Cent

17214. Pierson, Cornelia (Tuthill)
1820–70
moral and religious tale writer
Dict Am Auth

17215. Sadlier, Mary Anne (Madden)
1820–1903
novelist, author, Sunday school story writer
Catholic
Irish
Cyc Am Bio; Dict Am Auth; Dict Am Bio; Dict Am Bio Men Time; Dict Irish Bio; Index t Wom; Not Am Wom

17216. Scroggins, Eliza Anna Clark
1820–1912
religious worker
Index t Wom

17217. Warner, Anna Bartlett; Amy Lothrop
1820/27–1915
author, novelist, children's author, religious writer
Cyc Am Bio; Dict Am Auth; Dict Am Bio; Index t Wom; Nat Cyc Am Bio v4; Not Am Wom

17218. Wilson, Harriet M. Howe
died 1870
religious worker
Index t Wom

17219. Eddy, Mary Morse (Baker) (Glover) (Patterson)
1821/27–1910
founder of Christian Science
Christian Scientist
Concord, NH
Dict Am Auth; Dict Am Rel Bio; Index t Wom; Nat Cyc Am Bio v3; Not Am Wom; Twent Cen Bio Dict Not Am

17220. Hilderburn, Mary Jane (Reed); Marie Roseau
1821–82
author, children's author, religious author
Philadelphia, PA
Cyc Am Bio; Dict Am Auth; Nat Cyc Am Bio v13

17221. Scudder, Eliza
1821–96
hymn writer
Massachusetts
Dict Am Auth

17222. van Lennep, Mary Elizabeth
1821–44
missionary to Smyrna
Am Bio Dict; Cyc Am Bio; Index t Wom

17223. Ewing, Catherine A. Fay
born 1822
educator, philanthropist, missionary to the Choctaw people
Wom Cent

17224. Stoddard, Harriet B.
1822–48
missionary to Persia
Am Bio Dict; Index t Wom

17225. Weston, Mary Catharine (North)
1822–82
religious writer
Cyc Am Bio; Dict Am Auth

17226. Willard, Cordelia Young
born 1822
missionary worker
Methodist Episcopal
New York
Wom Cent

17227. Brittan, Harriet G.
1823–97
missionary to India, writer on India and Africa
Dict Am Auth

17228. Cannon, Harriet Star
1823–96
first mother superior of the Episcopal Community of St. Mary
Episcopalian
Dict Am Bio; Not Am Wom

17229. Farmer, Hannah Tobey Sharpleigh
1823–91
philanthropist, author, poet, religious worker
Dict Am Bio; Index t Wom; Nat Cyc Am Bio v7; Twent Cen Bio Dict Not Am

17230. Fitzgibbon, Mary Catherine Irene; Sister Irene
1823–96
Catholic nun, philanthropist
Catholic
Dict Am Bio; Twent Cen Bio Dict Not Am

17231. Shuck, Eliza G.
1823–51
missionary to China
Baptist
Am Bio Dict

17232. Barney, Susan Hammond
flourished 1854–90s
evangelist, Prohibitionist, temperance worker, prison reformer
Rhode Island
Index t Wom; Wom Cent

17233. Davis, Mary Fenn
1824–86
Spiritualist lecturer, reformer
Spiritualist
Not Am Wom

17234. Gillespie, Eliza Maria; Mother Mary of St. Angela
1824–87
mother superior and founder of the American Sisters of the Holy Cross, educator, Civil War hospital administrator
Catholic
Cyc Am Bio; Dict Am Bio; Index t Wom; Not Am Wom; Twent Cen Bio Dict Not Am; Wom Cent

17235. Harris, Amanda Bartlett
born 1824
author, children's author, magazine writer, religious author
Warner, NH
Dict Am Auth; Twent Cen Bio Dict Not Am

17236. Kimball, Harriet MacEwen
born 1824/34
religious poet
Portsmouth, NH
Cyc Am Bio; Dict Am Auth; Nat Cyc Am Bio v11; Wom Cent

17237. Packard, Sophia B.
1824–91
founder of Spelman College, church worker, educator of Blacks
Baptist

Atlanta, GA
Nat Cyc Am Bio v2; Not Am
Wom

**17238. Perkins, Sarah Maria
Clinton**
born 1824
lecturer, clergyperson, temperance worker, suffragist
Index t Wom; Wom Cent

**17239. Soule, Caroline Augusta
(White)**
1824–1903/04
author, publisher, editor, church worker, Universalist minister, foreign missionary, social reformer, lecturer
Universalist
Cyc Am Bio; Dict Am Auth; Dict Am Bio Men Time; Index t Wom; Not Am Wom; Twent Cen Bio Dict Not Am

17240. Starr, Eliza Allen
1824–1901
writer and lecturer on art and religion, poet, author, artist, educator
Chicago, IL
Cyc Am Bio; Dict Am Auth; Dict Am Bio; Nat Cyc Am Bio v13; Not Am Wom; Twent Cen Bio Dict Not Am; Wom Cent

**17241. Beauchamp, Mary
Elizabeth; Filia Ecclesiae**
born 1825
religious author, educator
Wom Cent

**17242. Blackwell, Antoinette
Louisa (Brown)**
1825–1921
Universalist minister, author, lecturer, temperance worker, abolitionist, suffragist, women's rights worker, philosopher, poet, novelist
Unitarian; Congregationalist
Appl Cyc Am Bio; Cyc Am Bio; Dict Am Bio; Dict Am Bio Men Time; Index t Wom; Nat Cyc Am Bio v9 and v29; Not Am Wom; Twent Cen Bio Dict Not Am; Wom Cent

**17243. Cooper, Sarah Brown
Ingersoll**
1825/36–1896
kindergartner, Bible teacher, philanthropist
California
Dict Am Bio; Nat Cyc Am Bio v3; Not Am Wom; Wom Cent

17244. James, Annie P.
born 1825
missionary
Index t Wom

**17245. Mills, Susan Lincoln
Tolman**
1825/26–1912
missionary educator, college president
Dict Am Bio; Index t Wom; Not Am Wom; Twent Cen Bio Dict Not Am

17246. Riepp, Benedicta, Mother
1825–62
Catholic nun, founder of the Sisters of St. Benedict in the United States
Catholic
Not Am Wom

17247. Tefft, Eliza
1825–51
missionary to Africa
Am Bio Dict

17248. White, Catherine Ann
1825–78
writer on religions, superior of the Convent of the Sacred Heart, Catholic nun, classicist
Catholic
Dict Am Auth

**17249. Dubose, Catherine Anne
(Richards)**
born 1826
poet, Sunday school story writer
Georgia
Cyc Am Bio; Dict Am Auth

**17250. Griswold, Frances Irene
(Burge); F. Burge Smith**
1826–1900
author, religious writer for children
Brooklyn, NY
Dict Am Auth; Wom Cent

17251. Jenkins, Frances C.
born 1826
evangelist, temperance worker
Quaker
Wom Cent

**17252. Robertson, Ann Eliza
Worcester**
1826–1905
missionary, educator, student of Native American languages
Not Am Wom

**17253. Bottome, Margaret
(McDonald)**
1827–1906
health reformer, religious author, founder of King's Daughters, a religious society
Dict Am Bio; Nat Cyc Am Bio v13; Twent Cen Bio Dict Not Am

**17254. Gillette, Lucia Fidelia
(Woolley); Lyra; Carrie
Russell**
born 1827
Universalist minister, author, poet
Universalist
Dict Am Auth; Index t Wom; Wom Cent

17255. Guild, Caroline Snowden (Whitmarsh)
1827–98
religious author
Boston, MA
Dict Am Auth

17256. McGroarty, Julia, Sister
1827–1901
Catholic nun, educator
Catholic
Not Am Wom

**17257. White, Ellen Gould
Harmon**
1827–1915
cofounder of the Seventh-Day Adventists, theologian, religious writer
Seventh-Day Adventist
Dict Am Auth; Dict Am Bio; Dict Am Rel Bio; Index t Wom; Not Am Wom

**17258. Wittenmyer, Annie
(Turner)**
1827–1900
Civil War relief worker, leader in church and charitable work, philanthropist, temperance worker, lecturer, author
Ohio
Index t Wom; Nat Cyc Am Bio v12; Not Am Wom; Wom Cent

**17259. Finley, Martha; Martha
Farquharson**
1828–1909
poet, author, children's author, writer of religious and moral tales
Maryland
Cyc Am Bio; Dict Am Auth; Dict Am Bio; Index t Wom; Nat Cyc Am Bio v11; Twent Cen Bio Dict Not Am; Wom Cent

17260. Ingalls, Marilla Baker
1828–1902
missionary
Baptist
Dict Am Bio; Index t Wom

17261. O'Daniels, A. M.
born 1828
clergyperson
Index t Wom

17262. Way, Amanda M.
1828/29–1914

temperance leader, suffrage leader, feminist, clergyperson, nurse
Index t Wom; Not Am Wom

**17263. Wells, Emmeline
Blanchard Woodward**
1828–1921
leader of Mormon women, feminist, suffragist, editor, poet
Mormon
Utah
Cyc Am Bio; Not Am Wom

17264. Woolston, Beulah
1828–86
missionary
Index t Wom

**17265. Bateham, Josephine
Abiah Penfield Cushman**
1829–1901
temperance reformer, Sabbatarian reformer
Not Am Wom; Wom Cent

**17266. Dorsey, Sarah Anne
(Ellis); Filia Ecclesiae**
1829–79
Civil War nurse, author, novelist, theologian
Mississippi
Cyc Am Bio; Dict Am Auth; Index t Wom; Nat Cyc Am Bio v3; Not Am Wom; Twent Cen Bio Dict Not Am

**17267. Hanaford, Phoebe Ann
(Coffin)**
1829–1921
Universalist minister, historian, journalist, author, feminist, lecturer, chaplain of the Connecticut state legislature
Universalist
New Haven, CT
Cyc Am Bio; Dict Am Auth; Dict Am Bio; Index t Wom; Nat Cyc Am Bio v13; Not Am Wom; Twent Cen Bio Dict Not Am; Wom Cent

**17268. Rogers, Elizabeth Ann;
Sister Beatrice**
1829–1921
educator, Anglican nun
Anglican
Not Am Wom

**17269. Russell, Mary Baptist,
Mother**
1829–98
Catholic nun, superior of Sisters of Mercy in San Francisco, founder of the Sisters of Mercy in California
Catholic
San Francisco, CA
Irish
Dict Am Bio; Not Am Wom

17270. van Deusen, Mary (Westbrook)
born 1829
religious writer, novelist, poet
Rondout, NY
Dict Am Auth; Wom Cent

17271. Waite, Catharine (Van Valkenburg)
1829–1913
suffragist, women's rights advocate, lawyer, legal journalist, financier, real estate and building executive, writer on Mormonism
Chicago, IL
Cyc Am Bio; Dict Am Auth; Not Am Wom; Wom Cent

17272. Benton, Mrs.
flourished 1860s
missionary, lecturer
Index t Wom

17273. Bixby, Susan
1830–1956
missionary to Maulmain [Burma]
Baptist
Am Bio Dict

17274. Damon, Ruth Augusta
flourished 1860s–70s
clergyperson
Index t Wom

17275. Hosmer, Margaret (Kerr)
1830–97
novelist, religious writer for children
Philadelphia, PA
Cyc Am Bio; Dict Am Auth

17276. Kalopathakes, Martha Hooper Blackler
1830–71
missionary
Cyc Am Bio

17277. Louis, Minnie Dessau
flourished 1860s–90s
Jewish welfare worker, educator
Jewish
New York
Nat Cyc Am Bio v18

17278. Lynch, Joseph, Mother
flourished 1860s
Catholic nun, nurse
Catholic
Irish
Index t Wom

17279. Mary of the Infant Jesus, Sister
circa 1830–1917
western pioneer, Catholic nun
Catholic
Index t Wom

17280. Mathews, Julia A.
born 183?

writer of Sunday school fiction
Dict Am Auth

17281. McBeth, Susan Law
1830–93
Presbyterian missionary to Native Americans
Presbyterian
Not Am Wom

17282. Porter, Maggie L.
flourished 1860s
gospel singer
Black
Prof Negro Wom v1

17283. Smiley, Sarah Frances
born 1830
clergyperson, author
Index t Wom

17284. van Cott, Margaret Ann Newton "Maggie"
1830–1914
Methodist evangelist, clergyperson
Methodist
Index t Wom; Not Am Wom

17285. Wallace, Susan (Arnold) (Elston)
1830–1907
miscellaneous author, poet, religious writer, philanthropist
Indiana
Cyc Am Bio and ad; Dict Am Auth; Index t Wom; Nat Cyc Am Bio v10; Twent Cen Bio Dict Not Am; Wom Cent

17286. Clark, Mary (Latham)
born 1831
Sunday school story writer
Maine
Dict Am Auth

17287. Conklin, Jane Elizabeth Dexter
born 1831
poet, religious writer
Binghamton, NY
Wom Cent

17288. Cooley, Emily M. J.
born 1831
temperance and church worker, evangelical preacher
Methodist Episcopal
Wom Cent

17289. Cunnyngham, Elizabeth Litchfield
born 1831
missionary to China, Methodist Episcopal church worker
Methodist Episcopal
Wom Cent

17290. Davis, Caroline E.
born 1831
children's author, religious writer
Cyc Am Bio; Dict Am Auth

17291. Dunning, Annie Ketchum; Nellie Grahame
born 1831
author, Sunday school story writer
Presbyterian
Cyc Am Bio; Dict Am Auth; Twent Cen Bio Dict Not Am

17292. White, Anna
1831–1910
Shaker eldress, social reformer
Shaker
Not Am Wom

17293. Cunningham, Annie Sinclair
born 1832
Presbyterian church and mission society worker
Presbyterian
Scottish
Wom Cent

17294. Cusack, Margaret Anne; Sister Mary Frances Clare; Nun of Kenmare
1832–99
welfare worker, founder of the Sisters of Peace in America, Catholic nun
Catholic
Index t Wom

17295. Gubert, Louise
died 1882
Catholic nun, vocalist
Catholic
Cyc Am Bio

17296. Hinsdale, Grace Webster (Haddock)
born 1832
hymn writer, religious author
New York, NY
Dict Am Auth; Nat Cyc Am Bio v9

17297. Huntley, Mary Sutton
born 1832
Christian religious worker
Nebraska
Wom Cent

17298. Ingham, Mary Bigelow; Anne Hathaway
born 1832
author, temperance worker, Methodist Episcopal missionary and religious worker
Methodist Episcopal
Wom Cent

17299. Janes, Martha Waldron
born 1832
Baptist minister, suffragist, temperance worker
Baptist
Iowa
Index t Wom; Wom Cent

17300. Nevius, Helen S. (Coan)
born 1832
religious author
Dict Am Auth

17301. Shelley, Mary Jane
born 1832
temperance worker, missionary worker
Methodist
Nebraska
Wom Cent

17302. Smith, Hannah Whitall
1832–1911
religious author, evangelist, pacifist, temperance worker, women's rights worker
Quaker
Dict Am Bio; Index t Wom; Not Am Wom

17303. Boya, Ellen Wright
born 1833
educator, author on religious education, writer on art and architecture
Albany, NY
Dict Am Auth

17304. Drake, Mary Eveline
born 1833
temperance worker, Congregationalist minister, home missionary
Congregationalist
Wom Cent

17305. Fox, Margaret
1833/36–1893
spiritual medium
Spiritualist
Cyc Am Bio; Index t Wom; Not Am Wom

17306. Isaac, Hannah M. Underhill
born 1833
evangelist, temperance worker
New York
Wom Cent

17307. Miller, Emily Clark Huntington
1833–1913
author, children's author, journalist, editor, poet, semireligious-fiction writer, church worker, temperance worker, educator
Evanston, IL
Dict Am Auth; Dict Am Bio; Index t Wom; Not Am Wom; Twent Cen Bio Dict Not Am; Wom Cent

17308. Morrison, Sarah Parke
born 1833
temperance worker, Quaker minister
Quaker
Twent Cen Bio Dict Not Am

17309. Peebles, Mary Louise (Parmelee); Lynde Palmer
1833/34–1915
author of religious tales for children
Cyc Am Bio; Dict Am Auth; Index t Wom; Nat Cyc Am Bio v4

17310. Seward, Sara Cornelia
1833–91
physician, medical missionary
Index t Wom; Twent Cen Bio Dict Not Am

17311. Beasley, Matilda, Mother
1834–1903
educator, social worker, Catholic nun
Catholic
Georgia
Black
Negro Alman; Prof Negro Wom

17312. Leonowens, Anna Harriette (Crawford)
born 1834
author on Siam, kindergarten educator, missionary educator in Siam
New York
English
Cyc Am Bio; Dict Am Bio

17313. MacConaughy, Julia E. (Loomis)
born 1834
religious fiction writer for children
Dict Am Auth

17314. Swain, Clara A.
1834–1910
pioneer woman medical missionary to India and the Orient, physician
Dict Am Bio; Index t Wom; Not Am Wom

17315. Walker, Marietta Hodges
1834–1930
religious worker
Index t Wom

17316. Willing, Jennie Fowler
1834–1916
Methodist local preacher, church worker, temperance reformer, lecturer, author, educator
Methodist
Canadian
Index t Wom; Not Am Wom; Wom Cent

17317. Wilson, Martha Eleanor Loftin
born 1834
missionary worker, Civil War nurse
Baptist

Georgia
Wom Cent

17318. Brown, Olympia; Mrs. John H. Willis
1835–1926
Universalist minister, suffragist, lecturer, feminist
Universalist; Unitarian
Cyc Am Bio and ad; Dict Am Bio; Index t Wom; Nat Cyc Am Bio v20; Not Am Wom; Wom Cent; Index t Wom

17319. Coppin, Fanny Marion Jackson
1835/37–1912/18
educator, foreign missionary, social worker, lecturer, women's rights worker
Black
Encyc Black Am; Index t Wom; Negro Alman; Not Am Wom; Prof Negro Wom

17320. Davis, Minnie S.
born 1835
author, temperance worker, suffragist, women's rights worker, "mental science" healer
Index t Wom; Wom Cent

17321. Elder, Susan (Blanchard); Hermine
1835–1923
religious author, poet, dramatist, natural scientist
Catholic
New Orleans, LA
Cyc Am Bio; Dict Am Auth; Dict Am Bio; Nat Cyc Am Bio v11; Twent Cen Bio Dict Not Am

17322. Hamilton, Kate Waterman; Fleeta
born 1835/41
religious author for children, novelist
Illinois
Cyc Am Bio; Dict Am Auth; Nat Cyc Am Bio v4; Twent Cen Bio Dict Not Am

17323. Hawks, Annie Sherwood
1835–1918
hymn writer, poet
Baptist
New York
Index t Wom; Nat Cyc Am Bio v17; Wom Cent

17324. Meech, Jeannette du Bois
born 1835
evangelist, missionary worker, Baptist preacher, temperance worker, industrial educator of women
Baptist
New Jersey
Index t Wom; Wom Cent

17325. Wheeler, Mary Sparks
born 1835
poet, religious author
Philadelphia, PA
Dict Am Auth

17326. Bowles, Ada Christina
born 1836
Universalist minister, suffragist
Universalist
Index t Wom; Wom Cent

17327. Burlingame, Emeline S.
born 1836
Baptist evangelist, temperance worker
Baptist
Wom Cent

17328. Chapin, Augusta Jane
1836–1905
Universalist minister, lecturer
Universalist
Index t Wom; Not Am Wom; Wom Cent

17329. Danforth, Abbie Ellsworth
born 1836
clergyperson
Index t Wom

17330. Horton, Abbie Augusta Wingate
1836–1925
pioneer, religious worker
Index t Wom

17331. Smith, Amanda Berry
1836/37–1915
Protestant evangelist, missionary to Africa, faith healer, singer
Protestant
Black
Index t Wom; Negro Alman; Not Am Wom; Prof Negro Wom v1

17332. Smith, Virginia Trall
1836–1903
mission and charity worker, pioneer in child care
Not Am Wom

17333. Talcott, Eliza
1836–1911
missionary educator and nurse in Japan
Dict Am Bio; Not Am Wom

17334. Dike, Jeannie Dean Scott
1837–1920
music educator, Congregationalist missionary
Congregationalist
New York
Twent Cen Bio Dict Not Am; Wom Cent

17335. Hunt, Louise Frances
born 1837

religious worker
Index t Wom

17336. McFarland, Amanda R.
1837–98
missionary
Cyc Am Bio

17337. Newman, Angelia Louise French Thurston
1837–1910
church worker, missionary, Mormon women's relief worker, lecturer, reformer
Mormon
Utah
Index t Wom; Not Am Wom; Wom Cent

17338. Norton, Minerva (Brace)
born 1837
educator, author, missionary worker
Beloit, WI
Dict Am Auth; Wom Cent

17339. Swift, Frances Laura
born 1837
church worker, temperance worker
Presbyterian
Pennsylvania
Wom Cent

17340. Brown, Charlotte Emerson
1838–95
president of the General Federation of Women's Literary Clubs, patron of missionaries
Dict Am Bio; Wom Cent

17341. Bullock, Mary Ann
1838–1918
hymn writer, poet
Nat Cyc Am Bio v19

17342. Deyo, Amanda
born 1838
Universalist minister, pacifist
Universalist
Wom Cent

17343. Donnelly, Eleonor Cecilia
1838/48–1917
poet, religious author
Catholic
Cyc Am Bio; Dict Am Auth; Dict Am Bio; Nat Cyc Am Bio v2; Twent Cen Bio Dict Not Am

17344. Houghton, Louise Seymour
born 1838
religious magazine editor, translator, religious author
New York, NY
Dict Am Auth

17345. Lathrap, Mary Torrans; The Daniel Webster of Prohibition
born 1838
poet, temperance reformer, Congregationalist preacher
Congregationalist
Wom Cent

17346. Ward, Susan Hayes
born 1838
author, religious writer
New York, NY
Dict Am Auth

17347. Wells, Catharine Boott (Gannett)
born 1838
author, religious writer, essayist, novelist, educator
Boston, MA
Dict Am Auth; Twent Cen Bio Dict Not Am

17348. Fielde, Adele Marion
born 1839
missionary to Siam and China, writer on China, writer in Chinese
Dict Am Auth

17349. Fox, Catherine "Kate"
1839?–92
spiritual medium
Spiritualist
Index t Wom; Not Am Wom

17350. Graves, Mary H.
born 1839
Unitarian minister, author, lecturer
Unitarian
Index t Wom; Wom Cent

17351. Grinnell, Katherine van Allen; Adasha
born 1839
theologian
Wom Cent

17352. Helm, Lucinda Barbour; Lucile
1839–97
author, religious writer
Methodist Episcopal
Kentucky
Twent Cen Bio Dict Not Am; Wom Cent

17353. Henry, Sarepta Myrenda (Irish)
1839–1900/01
author, religious writer, poet, children's author, temperance worker, evangelist
Evanston, IL
Dict Am Auth; Nat Cyc Am Bio v4; Twent Cen Bio Dict Not Am; Wom Cent

17354. Knapp, Phoebe Palmer
born 1839

musician, author, religious composer
Methodist Episcopal
New York
Wom Cent

17355. Mordecai, Rose
born 1839
author, religious leader
Index t Wom

17356. Telford, Mary Jewett
born 1839
army nurse, Civil War nurse, Women's Relief Corps organizer, church worker, children's author
Quaker
Wom Cent

17357. Thomas, Carrie A.
1839–83
religious worker, poet, hymn writer
Index t Wom

17358. van Marter, Martha
born 1839
editor of Sunday school magazines
Methodist
Dict Am Auth

17359. Baldwin, Esther E.
born 1840
missionary to China, worker for the rights of Chinese Americans, temperance worker
Wom Cent

17360. Bartlett, Ella Elizabeth
flourished 1870s
clergyperson
Index t Wom

17361. Benjamin, Elizabeth Dundas (Bedell)
died 1890
religious author
Stratford, CT
Dict Am Auth

17362. Borden, Helen, Sister
flourished 1870s
nurse, Catholic nun
Catholic
Index t Wom

17363. Creemer, Lucy M.
flourished 1870s–80s
poet, religious worker
Index t Wom

17364. Drake, Lucy R.
flourished 1870s
religious worker
Index t Wom

17365. Folsom, Mariana Thompson
flourished 1870s

clergyperson
Index t Wom

17366. Frame, Esther Gordon
born 1840
minister and evangelist
Quaker
Wom Cent

17367. Gordon, Georgia
flourished 1870
gospel singer
Black
Prof Negro Wom v1

17368. Gustin, Ellen G.
flourished 1870s
clergyperson
Index t Wom

17369. Hardin, Julia Carlin
flourished 1870s
religious educator
Index t Wom

17370. Hovey, Augusta M.
flourished 1870s–80s
religious worker
Index t Wom

17371. Hoyt, Lucy
flourished 1870s–80s
religious worker
Index t Wom

17372. Joyce, Eliza le Brun Miller
born 1840
religious worker
Index t Wom

17373. Lyth, R. B., Mrs.
died 1890
missionary
Index t Wom

17374. Moon, Lottie Diggs; Lottie Clark
1840–1912
Southern Baptist missionary to China
Baptist
Index t Wom; Not Am Wom

17375. Newman, E. E.
flourished 1870s–80s
clergyperson
Index t Wom

17376. Papin, Theophile Emily Carlin
married 1865
religious worker
Index t Wom

17377. Patterson, Jane C.
flourished 1870s–80s
clergyperson
Index t Wom

17378. Polyblank, Ellen Albertina; Sister Albertina
1840–1930
Anglican sister, educator
Anglican
Not Am Wom

17379. Powell, Elizabeth M.
flourished 1870s
clergyperson
Index t Wom

17380. Pritchard, Esther Tuttle
born 1840
editor, educator, minister, temperance worker, missionary
Index t Wom; Wom Cent

17381. Roberts, Fannie
flourished 1870s
clergyperson
Index t Wom

17382. Sawyer, Lucy Sargent
born 1840
Methodist missionary, church worker
Nat Cyc Am Bio v5; Wom Cent

17383. Smedes, Susan (Dabney)
born 1840
author, missionary to the Sioux people, educator, historian of the antebellum South
Mississippi
Cyc Am Bio; Dict Am Auth; Wom Cent

17384. Smith, Helen
1840–91
missionary
Index t Wom

17385. Tate, Minnie
flourished 1870s
gospel singer
Black
Prof Negro Wom v1

17386. Thoburn, Isabella
1840–1901
Methodist missionary to India, educator
Canadian
Dict Am Bio; Index t Wom; Nat Cyc Am Bio v19; Not Am Wom

17387. van Rensselaer, Euphemia; Sister Mary Dolores
born 1840
nurse, Catholic nun
Catholic
Index t Wom

17388. Walker, Katherine Kent (Child)
born 1840
religious author
Cyc Am Bio; Dict Am Auth

17389. Webster, Mary C.
flourished 1870s

clergyperson, author
Index t Wom

17390. West, Maria A.
flourished 1870s–80s
missionary, author
Index t Wom

17391. Whittier, Abigail H.
flourished 1870s
religious worker
Index t Wom

17392. Wilson, Augustus
flourished 1870s–90s
suffragist, temperance worker,
   Methodist Episcopal church
   worker, missionary worker
Methodist Episcopal
Kansas
Wom Cent

17393. Wilson, Zara A.
born 1840
lawyer, suffragist, feminist, temperance worker, missionary
   worker
Methodist Episcopal
Nebraska
Wom Cent

17394. Wright, Julia MacNair
1840–1930
author, novelist, temperance writer, temperance worker, anti-
   Catholic writer
Cyc Am Bio; Dict Am Auth;
   Index t Wom; Wom Cent

**17395. Alden, Isabella (Mac-
Donald); Pansy**
1841–1930
religious author, children's au-
   thor
Appl Cyc Am Bio; Cyc Am Bio;
   Dict Am Auth; Dict Am Bio;
   Index t Wom; Nat Cyc Am Bio
   v10; Not Am Wom; Twent Cen
   Bio Dict Not Am; Wom Cent

**17396. Lathbury, Mary Ar-
temesia; Aunt May**
1841–1913
author; psalm, spiritual, and
   hymn writer; religious writer for
   children
Dict Am Auth; Dict Am Bio; Nat
   Cyc Am Bio v10

**17397. Baker, Sarah Schoon-
maker (Tuthill); Aunt
   Friendly**
born 1842
Sunday school story writer
Dict Am Auth

17398. Chaplin, Ada C.
1842–83
author, Sunday school story writer
Massachusetts
Cyc Am Bio; Dict Am Auth

**17399. Dunham, Marion
Howard**
born 1842
temperance worker, suffragist,
   Christian Socialist party worker
Wom Cent

17400. Farmer, Lydia (Hoyt)
1842/43–1903
religious author, journalist
Cleveland, OH
Dict Am Auth; Index t Wom;
   Nat Cyc Am Bio v8; Twent Cen
   Bio Dict Not Am; Wom Cent

17401. Haines, Sarah Platt
born 1842
missionary
Index t Wom

**17402. Hill, Agnes Leonard
(Scanland); Molly Myrtle**
1842–1917
poet, author, newspaper publish-
   er, religious writer, novelist,
   prisoner's welfare worker, Uni-
   versalist pastor
Universalist
Colorado
Dict Am Auth; Index t Wom;
   Nat Cyc Am Bio v17; Wom
   Cent

17403. Jones, Mary C. "May"

born 1842
Baptist minister, evangelist
Baptist
Washington
Index t Wom; Wom Cent

**17404. Kearney, Martha Elea-
nor**
1842–1930
religious worker, author
Index t Wom

17405. Mims, Sue Harper
born 1842
Christian Science leader
Christian Scientist
Georgia
Index t Wom; Wom Cent

17406. Moody, Emma Revell
1842–1902
religious worker
Index t Wom

**17407. Reed, Elizabeth
(Armstrong)**
1842–1915
theologist, religious author, philosopher, historian of India and
   Persia, writer on Oriental literature, temperance worker, philanthropist
Chicago, IL
Dict Am Auth; Dict Am Bio;
   Index t Wom; Nat Cyc Am Bio
   v1 and v15; Twent Cen Bio Dict
   Not Am

**17408. Stetson, Augusta Emma
Simmons**
1842–1928
Christian Science leader
Christian Scientist
Dict Am Bio; Nat Cyc Am Bio
   v18; Not Am Wom

17409. Thompson, Eva Griffith
born 1842
temperance worker, Presbyterian
   missionary worker, newspaper
   editor and publisher
Presbyterian
Pennsylvania
Wom Cent

17410. Watson, Elizabeth Lowe
born 1842
lecturer, pastor of the San Francisco Religious and Philosophical Society, fruit farmer
California
Wom Cent

17411. Watson, Ellen Maria
born 1842
church worker, temperance worker
Methodist Episcopal
Wom Cent

17412. Willson, Mary Elizabeth
born 1842
missionary, gospel singer, songwriter
Pennsylvania
Index t Wom; Wom Cent

**17413. Bond, Rosalie B. de
Dolms**
born 1843
religious worker
Index t Wom

17414. Crawford, Mary J.
born 1843
Episcopal church worker and or-
   ganizer
Episcopalian
Wom Cent

**17415. Moots, Cornelia Moore
Chillison**
born 1843
temperance evangelist, suffragist,
   women's rights worker
Methodist Episcopal
Michigan
Wom Cent

17416. Oliver, Anna
died 1893
clergyperson, feminist
Index t Wom

17417. Smith, Bertha Madison
1843–96
religious worker
Index t Wom

17418. Burton, Emma
1844–1927
missionary, author
Index t Wom

17419. Huntley, Amelia Almore
born 1844
missionary
Index t Wom

**17420. Merrick, Sarah New-
comb**
born 1844
educator, educational missionary
   to Nova Scotia
Texas
Canadian
Wom Cent

**17421. Merriman, Helen (Bige-
low)**
born 1844
artist, writer on art, religious author
Worcester, MA
Dict Am Auth; Index t Wom;
   Twent Cen Bio Dict Not Am

17422. Wilkes, Eliza Tupper
born 1844
clergyperson, missionary
Unitarian
Index t Wom; Wom Cent

17423. Young, Ann Eliza Webb
1844–post 1908
lecturer and writer against Mormon polygamy, feminist, religious worker, pioneer
Index t Wom; Not Am Wom

17424. Barboza, Mary (Garnet)
1845–90
educator, missionary
Black
Nat Cyc Am Bio v5

17425. Case, Marietta Stanley
born 1845
author, poet, temperance worker,
   home and foreign mission worker
Manchester, OH
Wom Cent

17426. Fillmore, Myrtle Page
1845–1931/48
founder of the Unity School of
   Christianity
Dict Am Rel Bio; Index t Wom;
   Not Am Wom

**17427. Gestefield, Ursula Ne-
well**
1845–1921
New Thought leader
Index t Wom; Not Am Wom

17428. Haygood, Laura Askew
1845–1900

educator, school administrator, missionary educator in China
Dict Am Bio; Not Am Wom

17429. Miller, Minnie (Willis) (Baines)
born 1845
religious author, temperance worker
Springfield, OH
Dict Am Auth; Wom Cent

17430. Peters, Alice E. H.
born 1845
church and temperance worker, suffragist, author
Methodist Episcopal
Ohio
Wom Cent

17431. Porter, Rose
1845–1906
author, religious novelist, compiler
New Haven, CT
Dict Am Auth; Nat Cyc Am Bio v10; Wom Cent

17432. Shaw, Cornelia Dean
born 1845
suffragist, philanthropist, Congregationalist missionary worker
Congregationalist
Toledo, OH
Wom Cent

17433. Baker, Louise S.
born 1846
Congregationalist minister
Congregationalist
Wom Cent

17434. Dunne, Sarah Theresa; Amadeus; Mother Mary of the Heart of Jesus
1846–1917
convent founder
Catholic
Index t Wom

17435. Lazarus, Josephine
born 1846
author, religious writer
Jewish
Dict Am Auth

17436. McCabe, Margaret
born 1846
religious worker
Index t Wom

17437. Prosser, Anna Weed
born 1846/66
evangelist, missionary
Index t Wom; Wom Cent

17438. Stone, Ellen Maria
1846–1927
missionary, temperance worker, lecturer
Dict Am Bio

17439. Gulick, Alice Winfield Gordon
1847–1903
missionary to Spain, temperance worker
Not Am Wom; Wom Cent

17440. Kepley, Ada Miser
born 1847
lawyer, temperance agitator, Unitarian minister
Unitarian
Index t Wom; Wom Cent

17441. Lawless, Margaret H. Wynne
born 1847
poet, religious worker, clubwoman
Wom Cent

17442. Mitchell, Annie Maria
born 1847
religious writer for children
Dict Am Auth

17443. Robinson, Jane Marie Bancroft
1847–1932
Methodist educator, deaconess leader, author, historian, philanthropist
Methodist
Index t Wom; Not Am Wom; Wom Cent

17444. Shaw, Anna Howard
1847–1919
minister, lecturer, suffragist, women's rights worker, physician, temperance worker
Methodist
English
Dict Am Bio; Index t Wom; Nat Cyc Am Bio v14; Not Am Wom; Wom Cent

17445. Smith, Emma Elizabeth
1847–1918
religious worker
Index t Wom

17446. Taylor, Sarah Katherine Paine
born 1847
evangelist, temperance worker
Wom Cent

17447. Black, Mary Fleming
born 1848
religious author, temperance worker
Wom Cent

17448. Coombs, Lucinda
graduated 1873
physician, medical missionary
Index t Wom

17449. Kerens, Frances Jones
1848–1914

patron of Catholicism, philanthropist
St. Louis, MO
Nat Cyc Am Bio v31

17450. Kollock, Florence E.
born 1848
Universalist minister, suffragist, temperance worker, kindergarten educator, missionary
Index t Wom; Wom Cent

17451. Shattuck, Corinna
born 1848
missionary
Twent Cen Bio Dict Not Am

17452. Smith, Emma Pow
born 1848
evangelist
Wom Cent

17453. Woolley, Celia (Parker)
1848–1918
settlement worker, worker for social services for Blacks, Unitarian minister, author, novelist
Chicago, IL
Dict Am Auth; Dict Am Bio; Wom Cent

17454. Devore, Ella
1849–1920
missionary
Index t Wom

17455. Johnston, Julia Harriette
1849–1919
hymn writer
Presbyterian
Peoria, IL
Nat Cyc Am Bio v20

17456. Knight, Sarah (Harrison)
1849–1928
philanthropist, Minneapolis civic leader, Methodist church worker, hospital founder, patron of nurse's training
Methodist
Minneapolis, MN
Am Bio New Cyc

17457. Mathews, Joanna Hooe
1849–1901
religious writer for children
Dict Am Auth

17458. Meyer, Lucy Jane Rider
1849–1922
pioneer in Methodist urban social work and in the Methodist deaconess movement
Methodist
Not Am Wom

17459. Moore, Ella Maude
born 1849

hymn writer
Index t Wom

17460. Murdoch, Marion
born 1849
Unitarian minister
Index t Wom; Wom Cent

17461. Babcock, Clara Maria
flourished 1880s
clergyperson
Index t Wom

17462. Bruce, Elizabeth M.
flourished 1880s
clergyperson, author, editor
Index t Wom

17463. Burleigh, Celia
flourished 1880s
clergyperson
Index t Wom

17464. Cabrini, Francis Xavier, St.
1850–1917
founder of the Missionary Sisters of the Sacred Heart, Catholic nun
Catholic
Italian
Dict Am Bio supp v1; Dict Am Rel Bio; Index t Wom; Nat Cyc Am Bio v27; Not Am Wom

17465. Cobb, Zoe Desloge
born 1850
religious worker
Index t Wom

17466. Fedde, Elizabeth, Sister
1850–1921
Lutheran deacon, nurse, welfare worker, Catholic nun
Lutheran; Catholic
Norwegian
Index t Wom; Not Am Wom

17467. Guirado, Luz (Sanchez)
flourished 1880s–1930s
patron of the Catholic church
Catholic
Los Angeles, CA
Mexican
Am Bio New Cyc

17468. le Brun, Adele
flourished 1880s–90s
religious worker
Index t Wom

17469. Lowrie, Mrs.
flourished 1880s
actor, clergyperson
Index t Wom

17470. Moore, Henrietta G.
flourished 1880s–90s
Universalist minister, temperance worker
Ohio
Wom Cent

17471. Pettey, Sarah Dudley
flourished 1880
missionary leader
African Methodist Episcopal
   Zion
Black
Prof Negro Wom v1

17472. Savage, Minnie Stebbins; Marion Lisle
born 1850
poet, author, Unitarian church
   worker, temperance worker
Unitarian
Wisconsin
Wom Cent

17473. Sommerfield, Rose
flourished 1880s–90s
religious worker, educator
Index t Wom

17474. Stanislaus, Sister
flourished nineteenth to twentieth
   century
Catholic nun, nurse
Catholic
Index t Wom

17475. Townsley, Frances Eleanor
born 1850
Baptist minister, evangelist, temperance worker
Baptist
Nebraska
Wom Cent

17476. Avery, Martha Gallison Moore
1851–1929
Socialist, Catholic lay apostle
Catholic
Not Am Wom

17477. Keister, Lillie Resler
born 1851
Christian church worker and organizer, missionary
Index t Wom; Wom Cent

17478. Lathrop, Rose (Hawthorne); Mother Mary Alphonsa; Rose Hawthorne
1851–1926
author, artist, poet, Catholic nun,
   founder of the Dominican Congregation of St. Rose of Lima,
   philanthropist
Catholic
Cyc Am Bio; Dict Am Auth; Dict
   Am Bio; Index t Wom; Nat Cyc
   Am Bio v9; Not Am Wom;
   Twent Cen Bio Dict Not Am;
   Wom Cent

17479. Safford, Mary Augusta
born 1851
Unitarian minister, lecturer, suffragist, philanthropist
Unitarian

Index t Wom; Nat Cyc Am Bio
   v14

17480. Spencer, Anna Carpenter (Garlin)
1851–1931
Unitarian minister, journalist, educator, temperance worker, suffragist, pacifist, child-labor
   reformer, philanthropist
Unitarian
Dict Am Bio; Nat Cyc Am Bio v9
   and csv2; Not Am Wom

17481. Underwood, Lillian Stirling Horton
1851–1921
physician, Presbyterian missionary to Korea
Presbyterian
Not Am Wom

17482. Whipple, M. Ella
born 1851
physician, temperance worker,
   suffragist, Methodist Episcopal
   church worker, politician, educator, inventor
Methodist Episcopal
Wom Cent

17483. Andrews, Mary Garard
born 1852
Universalist minister
Universalist
Index t Wom; Wom Cent

17484. Bennett, Belle Harris
1852–1922
Southern Methodist lay leader
Methodist
Not Am Wom

17485. Eastman, Annie Bertha Ford
1852–1910
Congregationalist minister
Congregationalist
Not Am Wom

17486. Leggett, Mary Lydia
born 1852
Liberal minister
Massachusetts
Index t Wom; Wom Cent

17487. van Hook, Loretta C.
born 1852
missionary, educator in Persia
Wom Cent

17488. Whitney, Mary Traffarn
born 1852
minister
Unitarian
Wom Cent

17489. Day, Emma V.
1853–94
missionary
Index t Wom

17490. Hollister, Lilian
born 1853
temperance worker, suffragist,
   Methodist Episcopal church
   worker
Methodist Episcopal
Michigan
Wom Cent

17491. Hopkins, Emma Curtis
1853–1925
Spiritualist teacher, mystic, leader
   in the New Thought movement
Spiritualist
Dict Am Rel Bio; Not Am Wom

17492. Kelley, Catherine Bishop
1853–1944
educator, religious worker
Index t Wom

17493. Mossell, Mary Ella
1853–86
educator, missionary to Haiti
Black
Index t Wom; Negro Alman; Prof
   Negro Wom v1

17494. Williams, Annie Frances Day
1853–1931
missionary leader
Congregationalist
Nat Cyc Am Bio v31

17495. Dancer, Alice
1854–1944
religious worker
Index t Wom

17496. Eagle, Mary Kavanaugh
born 1854
Baptist church worker
Baptist
Arkansas
Wom Cent

17497. Fulton, Mary Hannah
1854–1927
medical missionary to China, pioneer in medical education of
   Chinese women
Not Am Wom

17498. Griffith, Mary Lillian
born 1854
philanthropist, author on morals,
   religious writer
Methodist Episcopal
Philadelphia, PA
Wom Cent

17499. Ober, Sara Endicott
born 1854
missionary in the Tennessee and
   Kentucky mountains, fiction
   writer
Tennessee; Kentucky
Dict Am Auth

17500. Pratt, Hannah T.
born 1854
evangelist, temperance worker,
   chaplain of the Maine Senate
Maine
Wom Cent

17501. Reed, Mary
1854–1943
Methodist missionary to lepers in
   India
Methodist
Dict Am Bio supp v3; Index t
   Wom; Not Am Wom; Obit File

17502. Battle, Laura Elizabeth Lee
1855
religious worker
Index t Wom

17503. Bennett, Ella May
born 1855
Universalist minister
Universalist
Wom Cent

17504. Dunlap, Laura Comstock
1855–1947
religious writer, textbook author
Obit File

17505. Militz, Annie Rix
1855–1924
religious author, New Thought
   minister, faith healer
New Thought
Nat Cyc Am Bio v21

17506. Bushnell, Kate
born 1856
physician, temperance reformer,
   evangelist
Wom Cent

17507. Dempsey, Mary Joseph, Sister
1856–1939
Catholic nun, hospital administrator, surgical assistant
Catholic
Not Am Wom

17508. Gates, Susa Young
1856–1933
Mormon author, educator, suffragist
Mormon
Nat Cyc Am Bio csv2; Read
   Encyc Am West

17509. Kugler, Anna Sara "Annie"
1856–1930
Lutheran medical missionary to
   India, physician
Lutheran
Index t Wom; Not Am Wom

17510. MacLeish, Martha Hillard
1856–1947
educator, leader in church and community work, second president of Rockford College
Not Am Wom; Obit File

17511. Culbertson, Belle Caldwell
born 1857
missionary
Index t Wom

17512. Denton, Mary Florence
1857–1947
missionary educator in Japan
Not Am Wom

17513. Oldham, Marie Augusta
born 1857
missionary to India, educator, temperance worker
Methodist Episcopal
Wom Cent

17514. Yates, Elizabeth U.
born 1857
lecturer, Methodist Episcopal preacher
Methodist Episcopal
Maine
Wom Cent

17515. Bagley, Blanche Pentecost
born 1858
Unitarian minister, suffragist
Unitarian
British
Wom Cent

17516. Bartlett, Caroline Julia
born 1858
Unitarian minister, suffragist
Unitarian
Wom Cent

17517. Boole, Ella Alexander
1858–1952
temperance leader, president of WCTU, suffragist, pacifist, Presbyterian deacon
Presbyterian
Dict Am Bio supp v5; Index t Wom; Nat Cyc Am Bio v38 and csv2; Not Am Wom supp v1; Obit File

17518. Chapellin, Emilia, Mother
1858–90
convent founder, Catholic nun
Catholic
Index t Wom

17519. Coleman, Alice Blanchard
born 1858
missionary
Index t Wom

17520. Crane, Caroline Julia Bartlett
1858–1935
Unitarian minister, People's Church minister, urban reformer, suffragist, city planner, sanitation expert
Unitarian
Index t Wom; Nat Cyc Am Bio v15; Not Am Wom

17521. Drexel, Katharine Mary; Mother Mary Katharine
1858–1955
founder of the Catholic Sisters of the Most Blessed Sacrament for Indians and Colored People, educator of Blacks, missionary, philanthropist
Catholic
Dict Am Bio supp v5; Dict Am Rel Bio; Index t Wom; Not Am Wom supp v1; Obit File; Read Encyc Am West

17522. Montgomery, Carrie Frances Judd
born 1858
church worker, poet, author, temperance worker, Salvation Army worker, social worker
New York; California
Index t Wom; Wom Cent

17523. Solomon, Hannah Greenebaum
1858–1942
clubwoman, founder of the National Council of Jewish Women, welfare worker
Jewish
Chicago, IL
Nat Cyc Am Bio v36; Not Am Wom

17524. Stebbins, Clara B. "Callie"
1858–1958
religious worker
Index t Wom

17525. Bingham, Jennie M.
born 1859
religious author
Wom Cent

17526. Bishop, Mary Axtell
born 1859
religious worker, author
Index t Wom

17527. Gilman, Mary Rebecca Foster
born 1859
author, religious biographer
Dict Am Auth; Index t Wom

17528. Kingsley, Florence (Morse)
born 1859
religious author
Staten Island, NY
Dict Am Auth; Nat Cyc Am Bio v11

17529. Moreland, Mary L.
born 1859
Congregationalist minister, temperance worker
Congregationalist
Illinois

Wom Cent

17530. Piper, Leonor Evelina Simonds
1859–1950
medium
Spiritualist
Not Am Wom

17531. Sivitar, Anna Pierpont
born 1859
religious author
Twent Cen Bio Dict Not Am

17532. van Anderson, Helen (Van Metre)
born 1859
minister, lecturer, miscellaneous author
Boston, MA
Dict Am Auth

17533. Booth-Tucker, Emma Moss
1860–1903
consul of the Salvation Army
Salvationist
Dict Am Bio

17534. Butler, Marie Joseph, Mother
1860–1940
founder of Marymount Schools, Catholic nun
Catholic
Not Am Wom

17535. Knox, Louise Chambers
circa 1860–1942
religious worker
Index t Wom

17536. Rogers, Emma Winner
flourished 1890s–1910s
missionary
Methodist
Index t Wom; Wom Cent

17537. Starkweather, Amelia Minerva
flourished 1890s
educator, author, poet, temperance worker, Methodist Episcopal deaconess
Methodist Episcopal
Wom Cent

17538. Szold, Henrietta
1860–1945
Zionist leader

Jewish
Dict Am Bio supp v3; Dict Am Rel Bio; Index t Wom; Not Am Wom; Obit File; Who Who Jew Hist

17539. West, Annie Blythe
1860–1941
missionary
Index t Wom

17540. Wight, Emma Howard
flourished 1890s
magazine writer, theological writer, novelist
Catholic
Wom Cent

17541. Fensham, Florence Amanda
born 1861
religious educator
Index t Wom

17542. Miner, Sarah Luella
1861–1935
Congregationalist missionary and educator in China
Congregationalist
Not Am Wom

17543. Montgomery, Helen Barrett
1861–1934
civic reformer, churchperson, foreign missions worker, translator, author
Baptist
Index t Wom; Nat Cyc Am Bio csv1; Not Am Wom

17544. Morgan, Mary Kimball
1861–1948
Christian Science educator
Christian Scientist
Not Am Wom

17545. Peabody, Lucy Whitehead McGill Waterbury
1861–1949
Baptist lay leader, pioneer in ecumenical women's foreign missions programs
Dict Am Bio supp v4; Not Am Wom

17546. Salyards, Christiana Stedman
1861–1951
religious worker, author
Index t Wom

17547. Wood, Mary Elizabeth
1861–1931
missionary, librarian in China
Episcopalian
Dict Am Bio; Not Am Wom

17548. American, Sadie
1862–1944

lecturer, clubwoman, founder of the National Council of Jewish Women
Jewish
Index t Wom; Obit File

17549. Bissell, Julia
1862–1928
physician, missionary to India
Congregationalist
Nat Cyc Am Bio v21

17550. Booth, Florence Eleanor Soper
1862–1957
Salvation Army leader
Salvationist
Obit File

17551. Brewster, Elizabeth Fisher; Shepherdess Mother of Hinghwa
1862–1955
Methodist missionary to China
Methodist
Obit File

17552. Butler, Clementina
born 1862
evangelist
Wom Cent

17553. Eldred, Edith Lillia Byers
died 1912
missionary to Africa
Index t Wom

17554. Seton, Julia Lorinda
born 1862
physician, founder of the New Thought Church, author
New Thought
Nat Cyc Am Bio v16

17555. Teresa, M. Imelda, Sister
born 1862
philanthropist, Catholic nun
Catholic
Index t Wom

17556. White, Alma Bridwell "Mollie"
1862–1946
founder of the Pillar of Fire Church, bishop, preacher
Pillar of Fire
Dict Am Bio supp v4; Dict Am Rel Bio; Nat Cyc Am Bio v35 and csv2 and csv5; Not Am Wom; Obit File

17557. Angelini, Arabella
born 1863
evangelical worker
Wom Cent

17558. Blow, Mary Elizabeth Thomas
born 1863

religious worker
Index t Wom

17559. Breed, Lorena May
born 1863
medical missionary to India, pathologist
California
Nat Cyc Am Bio csv3

17560. Fels, Mary
born 1863
Zionist
Jewish
German
Nat Cyc Am Bio csv1

17561. Krause, Lydia Farrington; Barbara Yechton
born 1864
fiction writer, religious writer
New York
Dict Am Auth

17562. Lindsay, Anna Robertson Brown
1864–1948
religious author, moral tale writer
Presbyterian
Dict Am Auth; Nat Cyc Am Bio v36

17563. Mason, Lena
born 1864
Methodist evangelist
Methodist
Black
Prof Negro Wom v1

17564. Tupper, Mila Frances
born 1864
Unitarian minister
Unitarian
Wom Cent

17565. Underwood, Lillias
married 1889
missionary, physician, pioneer
Index t Wom

17566. Booth, Evangeline Cory
1865–1950
fourth general of the Salvation Army, orator, musician, poet
Salvationist
English
Dict Am Bio supp v4; Dict Am Rel Bio; Index t Wom; Nat Cyc Am Bio csv2; Not Am Wom; Obit File

17567. Booth, Maud Ballington (Charlesworth)
1865–1948
Salvation Army leader, evangelist, philanthropist, prison reformer, author, founder of PTA
Salvationist
English
Dict Am Auth; Index t Wom; Nat Cyc Am Bio v14 and v38; Not Am Wom; Obit File

17568. Douglas, Alice May
born 1865
poet, children's author, temperance worker, pacifist, missionary
Maine
Dict Am Auth; Index t Wom; Wom Cent

17569. Feeney, Mary Ignatius, Sister
died 1915
pharmacist, Catholic nun, nurse
Catholic
Index t Wom

17570. Hall, Rosetta Sherwood
1865–1951
physician, missionary
Index t Wom; Not Am Wom supp v1

17571. Harvey, Maud Clark
born 1865
religious worker
Index t Wom

17572. Towne, Elizabeth Lois
1865–1960
metaphysical author, editor, lecturer
New Thought
Nat Cyc Am Bio v45 and csv1

17573. Gordon, Nora Antonia
1866–1901
educator, missionary to Africa
Black
Negro Alman; Prof Negro Wom v1

17574. Merrick, Mary Virginia
1866–1955
social worker, philanthropist, founder of the Christ Child Society to aid crippled children
Index t Wom; Obit File

17575. Newport, Elfreda Louisa Shaffer
born 1866
Universalist minister
Universalist
Wom Cent

17576. Bennett, Mary Katherine Jones
1867–1950
church worker, leader in home mission and interdenominational work
Not Am Wom

17577. Pfohl, Katherine Laughlin
born 1867
religious worker
Index t Wom

17578. Adams, Evangeline Smith; Mrs. George E. Jordan, Jr.
1868/72–1932
astrologer
Index t Wom; Nat Cyc Am Bio v25 and csv3

17579. Doane, Marguerite Treat
1868–1954
philanthropist, patron of medical missionaries
Baptist
Nat Cyc Am Bio v41

17580. Jaggard, Annella
died 1918
missionary to Africa
Index t Wom

17581. James, Belle Robinson
1868–1935
religious worker, author
Canadian
Index t Wom

17582. Cameron, Donaldina MacKenzie
1869–1968
missionary, social reformer
Not Am Wom supp v1

17583. Gurney, Marion Francis; Marianne of Jesus
1869–1957
founder and mother general of the Sisters of Our Lady of Christian Doctrine
Catholic
Obit File

17584. Higgins, Edward J., Mrs.
1869–1952
Salvation Army pioneer
Obit File

17585. Kennedy, Minnie "Ma"
1869–1947
evangelist
Obit File

17586. Regan, Agnes Gertrude
1869–1943
Catholic social welfare leader, educator, women's rights worker
Catholic
Dict Am Bio supp v3; Not Am Wom

17587. Roper, Janet Lord "Mother"
1869–1943
founder of the Missing Seaman's Bureau, manager of the Seaman's Church Institute of New York
New York
Obit File

17588. Abell, Edwin F., Mrs.
flourished 1900s
religious worker
Index t Wom

17589. Blackburn, Katherine
flourished 1900s
missionary
Index t Wom

17590. Case, Alice Montague
born 1870
missionary, pioneer
Index t Wom

17591. Edwards, Edna Eck
flourished 1900s–50s
missionary to Africa
Index t Wom

**17592. Eutropia McMahon,
Mother**
flourished 1900s
Catholic nun
Catholic
Index t Wom

17593. Ewing, Ella Campbell
flourished 1900s
missionary to Africa
Index t Wom

17594. Mann, Rowena Morse
born 1870
Unitarian minister
Nat Cyc Am Bio csv2

17595. Marianne, Sister
flourished 1900s
nurse, Catholic nun
Catholic
Index t Wom

17596. Mary Agnes
1870–1962
founder of the Order of Francis-
can Nuns of the Most Blessed
Sacrament in the United States,
Catholic nun
Catholic
Obit File

**17597. McLaughlin, Sarah,
Marchioness**
flourished 1900s
religious worker
Index t Wom

**17598. Moon, Bessie
Huntington**
flourished 1900s–40s
missionary to Africa
Index t Wom

17599. Page, Fannie Pender
1870–1942
missionary, educator
Index t Wom

17600. Scudder, Ida Sophia
1870–1960

physician, missionary, founder of
the American Medical Mission
in Veliore, India
Index t Wom; Not Am Wom
supp v1; Obit File

**17601. Smith, Mary Hopkins
"Sis"**
flourished 1900s–40s
missionary to Africa
Index t Wom

**17602. Stevens, Georgia Lydia,
Mother**
1870–1946
musician, cofounder of the Piux
X School of Liturgical Music,
educator, Catholic nun
Catholic
Not Am Wom; Obit File

17603. Willis, Pauline
born 1870
religious worker, author
Index t Wom

17604. de Lima, Rose
1871–1945
Catholic nun
Catholic
Obit File

17605. Lea, Frank T., Mrs.
married 1896
missionary to Africa
Index t Wom

17606. Smith, Ada Clark
1871–1915
religious worker
Canadian
Index t Wom

**17607. Young, Zina Diantha
Huntington**
1871–1902
midwife, suffragist, Mormon
leader
Mormon
Cyc Am Bio

**17608. Anderson, Audentia
Smith**
born 1872
religious author, genealogist, pioneer
Mormon
Index t Wom

**17609. Etzenhouser, Ida
Pearson**
1872–1936
religious worker
English
Index t Wom

17610. Phelan, Marie Gerard
1872–1960
superior general of the Institute of
the Religious of the Sacred
Heart of Mary, cofounder of
Marymount College

Catholic
California
Obit File

17611. Smith, Ruth Lyman
1872–1926
child welfare worker, religious
worker, author
Index t Wom

17612. Bolton, Margaret
1873–1943
religious educator, author
Catholic
Obit File

**17613. Dammann, Grace Cow-
ardin**
1873–1945
president of Manhattanville College of the Sacred Heart
Catholic
Obit File

17614. Pitt, Rosa Parks
1873–1959
missionary
Index t Wom

17615. Seligsberg, Alice Lillie
1873–1940
social worker, developer of Hadassah's medical program, Zionist
Jewish
Who Who Jew Hist

17616. Urrea, Teresa
1873–1906
folk healer, mystic
Mexican
Dict Mex Am Hist

**17617. Casey, Margaret
Elizabeth**
born 1874
religious worker
Index t Wom

**17618. Hyde, Violet McDougall
Buel**
married 1899
religious worker
Index t Wom

**17619. MacKenzie, Jean Ken-
yon**
1874–1936
Presbyterian missionary to Cam-
eroun, author
Presbyterian
Nat Cyc Am Bio v28; Not Am
Wom

**17620. Tillinghast, Anna Chur-
chill Moulton**
1874–1951
temperance worker, women's and
children's welfare worker, Universalist pastor, suffragist
Universalist

Massachusetts
Nat Cyc Am Bio v45

17621. Wight, Estella
1874–1955
religious worker, journalist
Index t Wom

17622. Wise, Louise Waterman
1874–1947
charitable worker, founder and
president of the women's division of the American Jewish
Congress, Zionist
Jewish
New York
Not Am Wom

17623. Fitch, Florency Mary
1875–1959
Biblical literature authority, university educator, religious writer for children
Oberlin, OH
Obit File

**17624. Goodrich, Nelle Chat-
burn**
born 1875
religious worker, pioneer
Index t Wom

17625. Soule, Cora Blanche
1875–1945
missionary, nurse
Bio Dict Sudan

**17626. Thurston, Matilda Smy-
nell Calder**
1875–1958
missionary educator in Turkey
and China, founder and president of Ginling College in Nanking, China
Congregationalist
Not Am Wom supp v1; Obit File

**17627. Dewhirst, Susan Lucre-
tia**
born 1876
missionary
Index t Wom

17628. Dickenson, Helena A.
1876–1957
cofounder of the Sacred Heart
Music School at Union Theological Seminary
Catholic
Obit File

17629. Faris, Bessie Homan
married 1901
missionary to Africa
Index t Wom

17630. Warburg, Frieda Schiff
1876–1958
philanthropist, Jewish welfare
worker
Jewish

New York
Nat Cyc Am Bio v44; Obit File

17631. Homer, Frances T., Mrs.
married 1902
religious worker
Index t Wom

17632. Piltz, Maria Puuohau
1877–1932
religious worker
Index t Wom

17633. Reinhardt, Aurelia Isabelle Henry
1877–1948
president of Mills College, educator, religious worker, Unitarian minister
Unitarian
Oakland, CA
Dict Am Bio supp v4; Index t Wom; Not Am Wom; Obit File

17634. Frame, Alice Seymour Browne
1878–1941
Congregationalist missionary and educator in China
Congregationalist
Dict Am Bio supp v3; Not Am Wom

17635. Montague, Margaret Prescott; Jane Stege
1878–1955
mystic, author
Ill Encyc Myst

17636. Neenan, Mary Pius, Sister
born 1878
philosopher, Catholic nun
Catholic
Who Who Phil

17637. Fisher, Welthy (Blakesley) Honsinger
1879/80–1980
Methodist missionary to India and China, social worker, educator, president of World Education, Inc.
Methodist
Cur Biog '69 and '81; Index t Wom

17638. Barger, Myrtle King
flourished 1910s–30s
missionary
Index t Wom

17639. Brownson, Josephine van Dyke
1880–1942
educator, catechist
Index t Wom

17640. Clews, James Blanchard, Mrs.
flourished 1910s

religious worker
Index t Wom

17641. Frymire, Josephine
flourished 1910s–20s
missionary to Africa
Index t Wom

17642. Hedges, Lillie Bowyer
flourished 1910s–40s
missionary to Africa
Index t Wom

17643. Holder, Myrtle Avery
flourished 1910s–50s
missionary to Africa
Index t Wom

17644. Jaggard, Wilhelmina Zoe Smith
flourished 1910s–50s
missionary to Africa
Index t Wom

17645. Lummis, Eliza O'Brien
flourished 1910s
editor, publisher, religious worker, author
Index t Wom

17646. Mary de Sales, Mother; Wilhelmina Tredow
flourished 1910s
educator, Catholic nun
Catholic
Index t Wom

17647. Mary Madalene, Sister; Sarah C. Cox
flourished 1910s
translator, Catholic nun
Catholic
Index t Wom

17648. Mercedes, Mary Antonio Gallagher
flourished 1910s
author, religious worker
Index t Wom

17649. Misch, Caeser, Mrs.
flourished 1910s
religious worker, lecturer, author
Index t Wom

17650. Molloy, Mary Aloysia
born 1880
educator, author, Franciscan nun
Catholic
Nat Cyc Am Bio csv3

17651. Morison, Rebecca Newell
flourished 1910s
religious worker
Index t Wom

17652. Mosher, Edith Apperson
flourished 1910s–40s
missionary to Africa
Index t Wom

17653. Musgrave, Ruth
flourished 1910s–40s
missionary to Africa
Index t Wom

17654. Palms, Marie Martin
flourished 1910s
religious worker
Index t Wom

17655. Pearson, Evelyn Utter
flourished 1910s–50s
missionary to Africa
Index t Wom

17656. Shapiro, Dora Monness
1880–1952
philanthropist, Jewish welfare worker
Jewish
Obit File

17657. Smith, Lulu Gestis
flourished 1910s–50s
missionary to Africa
Index t Wom

17658. Tong, Eleanore Elizabeth
flourished 1910s
religious author
Index t Wom

17659. Walter, Mary Jane
flourished 1910s
social reformer, evangelist
Index t Wom

17660. Wells, Goldie Ruth
flourished 1910s–40s
missionary to Africa
Index t Wom

17661. Gardner, Pearl
born 1881
religious worker, editor
Index t Wom

17662. Cummins, Grace
1882–1953
Presbyterian leader, religious educator, social worker
Presbyterian
Obit File

17663. Rogers, Mary Josephine; Mother Mary Joseph
1882–1955
founder of the Maryknoll Sisters of St. Dominic, missionary
Catholic
Dict Am Bio supp v5; Not Am Wom supp v1; Obit File

17664. Woodstock, Lenoir Carpenter
born 1882
religious worker, pioneer
Index t Wom

17665. James, Mary Latimer
1883–1963
medical missionary to the Ute people in Utah, medical missionary to China, obstetrician/gynecologist, psychiatrist
Protestant Episcopal
Utah
Nat Cyc Am Bio v51

17666. Joseph, Mary, Sister
born 1883
educator, Catholic nun
Catholic
Index t Wom

17667. Robinson, Elsie (Fremont)
1883–1956
journalist, inspirational columnist for the Hearst newspapers
Index t Wom; Obit File

17668. Wilson, Matilda Rausch
1883–1967
philanthropist, Detroit civic worker, chairperson of the board of directors of Fidelity Bank & Trust, member of the state board of agriculture, lieutenant governor of Michigan, Salvation Army worker
Presbyterian
Detroit, MI
Nat Cyc Am Bio v59

17669. Kenyon, Helen
born 1884
religious worker
Index t Wom

17670. Layton, Jessie Trunkey
died 1934
missionary to Africa
Index t Wom

17671. Messenger, Ruth Ellis
1884–1964
hymnologist, educator
Protestant Episcopal
New York
Nat Cyc Am Bio v51

17672. Wilson, Bess K. Kidston
married 1909
missionary to Africa
Canadian
Index t Wom

17673. Zoeckler, Mary Daton Allen
1884–1914
obstetrician/gynecologist, medical missionary to Iran
Presbyterian
Nat Cyc Am Bio v46

17674. Cort, Mabel Gibson
flourished 1915
missionary
Index t Wom

17675. Coltman, Constance M.
graduated 1911
clergyperson
Index t Wom

17676. Maher, Frances
1886–1958
supreme regent of the Catholic
  Daughters of America
Catholic
Obit File

17677. Mary Julia, Sister;
  Elizabeth Ann Dullea
born 1886
educator, Catholic nun
Catholic
Index t Wom

17678. Rowley, M. Rita
1886–1963
superior general of the Roman
  Catholic Institute of the Reli-
  gious of the Sacred Heart of
  Mary, provincial superior of the
  Eastern Province of North
  America
Catholic
Obit File

17679. Smith, Nina G.
1886–1950
religious worker
Index t Wom

17680. Vautrin, Minnie
1886–1941
missionary educator in China
Not Am Wom

17681. Calverley, Eleanor Jane
  Taylor
1887–1968
physician, missionary to Kuwait,
  nurse in the 1920 Kuwait war,
  birth control advocate, birth
  control clinic founder
Dutch Reformed
Connecticut
Nat Cyc Am Bio v57

17682. Case, Adelaide Teague
1887–1948
Episcopal educator
Episcopalian
Not Am Wom

17683. Chase, Mary Ellen
1887–1973
novelist, biographer, short story
  writer, literary critic, writer on
  the Bible, university educator
Episcopalian
Cur Biog '73; Index t Wom; Nat
  Cyc Am Bio csv9; Obit File;
  Wom Lit, More

17684. Lewis, Louise Hills
1887–1948
composer, religious worker, hymn
  writer
Index t Wom

17685. Lyman, Mary Ely
1887–1975
theologian, university educator
Not Am Wom supp v1; Obit File

17686. Madelva, Mary Eveline
  Wolff, Sister
1887–1964
president of St. Mary's College,
  medievalist, educator, author,
  poet, Catholic nun
Catholic
Index t Wom; Nat Cyc Am Bio
  v51; Obit File

17687. Verda, Mary (Dorsch),
  Sister
born 1887
philosopher, Catholic nun
Catholic
Who Who Phil

17688. Wolff, Mary Evaline
  "Madelva", Sister
1887–1964
college administrator, Catholic
  nun, religious educator, poet
Catholic
Not Am Wom supp v1

17689. Brock, Blanche Kerr
born 1888
composer, hymn writer
Index t Wom

17690. Franklin, Pearl
circa 1888–1958
playwright, lawyer, Zionist, Hadassah leader
Jewish
Index t Wom; Obit File

17691. Garvey, Mary Patricia,
  Sister
born 1888
Catholic nun, philosopher
Who Who Phil

17692. Gowan, M. Olivia, Sis-
  ter
born 1888
nurse, Catholic nun
Catholic
Index t Wom

17693. Lasker, Loula Davis
1888–1961
New York civic worker, Zionist,
  Hadassah member
Jewish
New York
Nat Cyc Am Bio v48

17694. McCune, Vesta Marie
died 1938
missionary to Africa
Index t Wom

17695. Sampter, Jessie Ethel
1888–1938
poet, Zionist

Jewish
Not Am Wom

17696. Bateman, Martha
flourished 1919–50s
missionary
Index t Wom

17697. Cranston, Ruth
1889–1956
religious author, biographer, lecturer
Obit File

17698. Hayward, Mildred Mar-
  shal
1889–1967
artist, Moral Rearmament worker
Nat Cyc Am Bio v53

17699. Hurst, Fannie
1889–1968
novelist, short story writer, wom-
  en's rights worker, Zionist
Jewish
Index t Wom; Nat Cyc Am Bio
  csv2 and csv5; Not Am Wom;
  Obit File; Who Who Jew Hist

17700. Ward, Maisie
1889–1975
book publisher, author, lecturer,
  Catholic church worker
Catholic
English
Cur Biog '75; Index t Wom

17701. Alumbaugh, Godie P.
flourished 1920s–50s
missionary
Index t Wom

17702. Atherton, Eva Havens
flourished 1920s–50s
missionary
Index t Wom

17703. Bateman, Georgia
flourished 1920s–50s
missionary
Index t Wom

17704. Byerlee, Victoria Ann
flourished 1920s–50s
missionary
Index t Wom

17705. Clarke, Virginia
flourished 1920s–50s
missionary to Africa
Index t Wom

17706. Davis, Newell Trimble
flourished 1920s–50s
missionary to Africa
Index t Wom

17707. Eccles, George E., Mrs.
flourished 1920s
missionary to Africa
Index t Wom

17708. Eliot, Ethel Cook
1890–1972
children's author, religious writer
Catholic
Nat Cyc Am Bio v56

17709. Learned, Grace Utter
flourished 1920s–50s
missionary to Africa
Index t Wom

17710. Maria Gratia, Mother
flourished 1920s
missionary nurse, Catholic nun
Catholic
Index t Wom

17711. McCraken, Faith A.
flourished 1920s–50s
missionary to Africa
Index t Wom

17712. McPherson, Aimee Sem-
  ple
1890–1944
religious leader, evangelist
Spiritualist
Dict Am Bio supp v3; Dict Am
  Rel Bio; Index t Wom; Nat Cyc
  Am Bio v34; Obit File

17713. Mitchell, Hattie Poley
flourished 1920s–50s
missionary to Africa
Index t Wom

17714. Noah, Myrtle Whaley
flourished 1920s–50s
missionary to Africa
Index t Wom

17715. Parmelee, Ruth A.
flourished 1920s
physician, missionary
Index t Wom

17716. Shinn, Florence Scovel
died 1940
illustrator, lecturer, metaphysicist
Index t Wom

17717. Shoemaker, Gertrude
  Mae
flourished 1920s–50s
missionary to Africa
Index t Wom

17718. Smith, Elizabeth Baker
flourished 1920s–50s
missionary to Africa
Index t Wom

17719. Smith, Myrtle Lee
flourished 1920s–50s
missionary to Africa, physician
Index t Wom

17720. Snipes, Esther
flourished 1920s–50s
missionary to Africa
Index t Wom

17721. Stober, Buena Rose
flourished 1920s–50s
missionary to Africa
Index t Wom

17722. Ward, Myrle Olive
flourished 1920s–50s
missionary to Africa
Index t Wom

17723. Watts, Hazel Biven
flourished 1920s
missionary to Africa
Index t Wom

17724. Weaver, Maurine Barr
flourished 1920s–30s
missionary to Africa
Index t Wom

17725. Williams, Tessie
flourished 1920s–50s
missionary to Africa
Index t Wom

17726. Harkness, Georgia Elma
1891–1974
philosopher, theologian, religious
  educator, author
Dict Am Rel Bio; Index t Wom;
  Not Am Wom supp v1; Who
  Who Phil

17727. Hobgood, Tabitha Aldersen
married 1916
missionary to Africa
Index t Wom

17728. Hurt, Ambra Halsey
married 1916
missionary to Africa
Index t Wom

17729. Mears, Henrietta C.
1891–1963
founder of Gospel Light Church
  Publications
Obit File

17730. Carroll, Consolata; Sister Mary Consolata
born 1892
author, educator, Catholic nun
Catholic
Index t Wom

17731. Galassi, Josephine
1892–1958
provincial superior of the Salesian
  Sisters of the United States
Catholic
Italian
Obit File

17732. Healy, Emma Therese, Sister
born 1892
philosopher, Catholic nun
Catholic
Who Who Phil

17733. Ross, Myrta Pearson
married 1917
missionary to Africa
Index t Wom

17734. Garrett, Eileen Jeanette; Jean Lyttle
1893–1970
parapsychologist, novelist, founder of the Parapsychology Foundation
Anglican
Irish
Nat Cyc Am Bio v55; Obit File

17735. Levy, Adele Rosenwald
1893–1960
philanthropist, chairperson of the
  United Jewish Appeal National
  Women's Division, art collector
Jewish
New York
Obit File

17736. Boyer, Beatrice Alexander
married 1919
missionary
Index t Wom

17737. McCartney, Sadie Kissak
died 1944
missionary to China
Methodist
Obit File

17738. Russell, Lois Hasselvander
married 1920
missionary to Africa
Index t Wom

17739. Halprin, Rose
1896–1978
president of Hadassah, Zionist
Jewish
Obit File

17740. Johnston, Lillian Proefrock
died 1946
missionary to Africa
Index t Wom

17741. Rowe, Lucretia Olin
born 1896
missionary to Africa, educator
Index t Wom

17742. Waters, Ethel
1896/1900–1977
gospel and blues singer; stage,
  screen, and television actor
Black
Cur Biog '77; Encyc Black Am;
  Index t Wom; Negro Alman;
  Obit File; Prof Negro Wom v2

17743. White, Helen Constance
1896–1967
educator, historial novelist, religious historian, UNESCO
  member
Catholic
Index t Wom; Nat Cyc Am Bio
  v53; Not Am Wom supp v1

17744. Day, Dorothy
1897–1980
journalist, social worker, political
  activist, fiction writer on Catholic life
Catholic
Cur Biog '82; Index t Wom

17745. Heller, Florence Gunsfeld
1897–1966
philanthropist, patron of medicine, Jewish welfare worker
Jewish
Chicago, IL
Nat Cyc Am Bio v51

17746. Kingsley, Myra
born 1897
astrologer
Index t Wom

17747. Lowry, Edith Elizabeth
1897–1970
religious leader, Protestant Organization executive of the Council of Women
Protestant
Not Am Wom supp v1

17748. Brooks, Juanita
born 1898
historian of Mormonism
Mormon
Read Encyc Am West

17749. Baker, Lelia Barber
flourished 1930s–50s
missionary
Index t Wom

17750. Brooks, Nona L.
flourished 1930s
clergyperson
Index t Wom

17751. Cobbe, Alice Dunning
flourished 1930s–50s
missionary to Africa
Index t Wom

17752. Danser, Fanny Root
flourished 1930s
clubwoman, missionary, social reformer
Index t Wom

17753. Havens, Mary Sue McDonald
flourished 1930s–50s
missionary to Africa
Index t Wom

17754. Hensey, Alice Ferrin
died 1950
missionary to Africa
Index t Wom

17755. Hixon, Evalyn Willard
flourished 1930s–50s
missionary to Africa
Index t Wom

17756. Horton, Constance Smith
flourished 1930s–50s
missionary to Africa
Index t Wom

17757. MacLeod, Dorothy Shaw
born 1900
religious leader, social worker
Index t Wom

17758. Mandola, Carol M.
flourished 1930s
metaphysician, lecturer, poet
Index t Wom

17759. McGuigan, Gertrude St. George Congregation de Notre Dame, Sister
born 1900
Catholic nun, philosopher
Catholic
Who Who Phil

17760. Moore, Jeanne W. G.
flourished 1930s
hymn writer
Index t Wom

17761. Okama, Kyoko
flourished 1930s
medical missionary
Japanese
Index t Wom

17762. Poole, Edna
flourished 1930s–50s
missionary to Africa
Index t Wom

17763. Watkins, Carolyn Ellen
flourished 1930s–50s
missionary to Africa
Index t Wom

17764. Wolfe, Joan of Arc, Sister
born 1900
philosopher, Catholic nun
Catholic
Who Who Phil

17765. Demjanovich, Miriam Teresa
1901–27
religious worker
Catholic
Index t Wom

17766. Dye, Royal J., Mrs.
died 1951
missionary to Africa
Index t Wom

17767. Reed, Ida L.
died 1951
hymn writer
Index t Wom

17768. Schwartz, Bertha
1901–61
judge, lawyer, Zionist
Jewish
Austrian
Index t Wom; Nat Cyc Am Bio
v51

17769. Green, Blanche Tucker
1903–49
religious worker
Index t Wom

17770. Brittingham, Bettie S.
1904–49
editor of *Methodist Woman*,
Methodist church official
Methodist
Obit File

17771. Ross, Mabel Hughes
married 1929
missionary to Africa
Index t Wom

17772. Stam, Elizabeth "Betty"
born 1906
missionary
Index t Wom

17773. Tobin, Mary; Mother
Mary Maurice
1906–59
mother general of the Catholic
Sisters of Mercy, executive
chairperson of the National
Conference of Major Religious
Superiors, Catholic nun
Catholic
Obit File

**17774. Chatfield, Ena Lyle
Brown**
married 1932
missionary
Index t Wom

**17775. Medinger, Elizabeth Eu-
dora**
1907–77
Catholic church worker, philan-
thropist
Catholic
Washington, DC
Nat Cyc Am Bio v60

**17776. Tucker, Margaret
Emmeline**
1907–75
radiologist, medical missionary to
China and India
Congregationalist
Nat Cyc Am Bio v59

17777. Wedel, Cynthia Clark
born 1908

Episcopalian church worker,
president of the National Council of the Churches of Christ in
the United States
Episcopalian
Cur Biog '70

**17778. Roberts, Jewell
Elizabeth Owen**
married 1934
missionary to Africa
Index t Wom

17779. Brinton, Mary Williams
flourished 1940s–50s
missionary, nurse
Index t Wom

17780. Cardwell, Sue Webb
flourished 1940s–50s
missionary
Index t Wom

17781. Coates, Ruth Keezel
flourished 1940s–50s
missionary and nurse in Africa
Index t Wom

**17782. Cuppy, Vera Grace
Negley**
flourished 1940s–50s
missionary to Africa
Index t Wom

17783. Davis, Jane
flourished 1940s–50s
missionary to Africa
Index t Wom

**17784. Edwards, Ruth Hamil-
ton**
flourished 1940s–50s
missionary to Africa
Index t Wom

17785. Johnson, Eva Marie
flourished 1940s–50s
missionary to Africa
Index t Wom

17786. Kuhlman, Kathryn
1910?–76
Protestant evangelist, minister,
faith healer
Protestant
Cur Biog '74 and '76; Obit File

17787. Lewis, Lillian Callis
flourished 1940s–50s
missionary to Africa
Index t Wom

17788. McMillan, Hazel Fern
flourished 1940s–50s
missionary to Africa
Index t Wom

**17789. Milligan, Lucy Richard-
son**
flourished 1940s–50s

New York civic leader, antifascist, Jewish welfare worker, Hadassah worker, cancer worker
Nat Cyc Am Bio v53

17790. Miriam Michael, Sister
flourished 1940s–60s
scientist, Catholic nun
Catholic
Index t Wom

17791. Paget, della Mae Dale
flourished 1940s–50s
missionary to Africa
Index t Wom

17792. Paul, Helen
flourished 1940s
astrologist
Index t Wom

17793. Rosalita, Sister
flourished 1940s
missionary, Catholic nun
Catholic
Index t Wom

17794. Seymour, Agnes Rogers
flourished 1940s
missionary to Africa
Index t Wom

**17795. Shaw, Margaret
Elizabeth**
flourished 1940s–50s
missionary to Africa
Index t Wom

17796. Sibley, Harper, Mrs.
flourished 1940s
religious worker, educator
Index t Wom

17797. Tillery, Merle Gulley
flourished 1940s–50s
missionary to Africa
Index t Wom

17798. Watson, Glenda Sawyer
flourished 1940s–50s
missionary to Africa
Index t Wom

17799. Weeks, Helen Weeks
flourished 1940s–50s
missionary to Africa
Index t Wom

17800. Waddles, Charloezetta
born 1912
clergyperson
Black
Negro Alman

**17801. Horner, Marjorie Crit-
tenden**
married 1938
missionary to Africa, physician
Index t Wom

**17802. Johnstone, Margaret
Blair**
born 1913
clergyperson, author, lecturer
Index t Wom

17803. Praxedes Carty, Mother
died 1963
Catholic nun
Catholic
Irish
Index t Wom

17804. Preminger, Marion Hill;
Mrs. Albert Mayer
1913–72
social worker, author, African art
collector, missionary to the
Congo, philanthropist, screen
actor
Catholic
New York
Hungarian
Nat Cyc Am Bio v57; Obit File

**17805. Henderson, Allison Jam-
ison**
married 1939
missionary to Africa
Index t Wom

**17806. Whitmer, Veneta Fern
Viers**
married 1939
missionary to Africa
Index t Wom

17807. Luahine, Iolana
1915–78
traditional sacred hula dancer
Hawaii
Polynesian
Obit File

17808. Dade, Barbara Bates
married 1941
missionary to Africa
Index t Wom

**17809. Morrison, Rosetta
Tharpe**
1916–73
gospel singer
Black
Obit File

17810. Dixon, Jean
born 1918
writer on extrasensory perception
and prophecy
Washington, DC
Cur Biog '73

17811. Nawkins, Angelina
born 1918
Salvation Army worker
Index t Wom

17812. Bowers, Gladys Irene
married 1944
missionary
Index t Wom

17813. Cloud, Roe, Mrs.
flourished 1950s
missionary
Native American
Index t Wom

17814. Mary Aquinas, Sister
flourished 1950s
aviator, jet pilot, Catholic nun
Catholic
Index t Wom

17815. Williams, Kathryn Taylor
flourished 1950s
missionary to Africa
Index t Wom

17816. Harris, Ula Moulton
married 1946
missionary to Africa
Index t Wom

17817. McMillan, Lucile Short
married 1946
missionary to Africa
Index t Wom

17818. Branch, Dorothy Sutton
born 1922
Baptist clergyperson
Baptist
Black
Encyc Black Am

17819. Davis, Julia Margaret Hubman
married 1948
missionary to Africa
Index t Wom

17820. Heimer, Ruth Loretta Duggins
married 1948
missionary to Africa
Index t Wom

17821. Johnson, Ava Dale Plummer
married 1949
missionary to Africa
Index t Wom

17822. Dodson, Wilma Joy Livingston
married 1950
missionary to Africa
Index t Wom

17823. Ward, Clara
1925–73
gospel singer
Obit File

17824. Barron, Marjorie Wilson
married 1952
missionary
Index t Wom

17825. Mary Alma, Sister
flourished 1960s
biochemist, Catholic nun
Catholic
Index t Wom

17826. Mary Benedict, Sister
flourished 1960s
surgeon, Catholic nun
Catholic
Index t Wom

17827. Veronica, M., Sister
flourished 1960s
educator, Catholic nun
Catholic
Index t Wom

17828. Davis, Gloria Ann, Sister
born 1933
Catholic nun, educator
Catholic
Native American (Navaho-Chocktaw)
Ind Today

17829. Bryant, Anita
born 1940
singer, television personality, antifeminist, antiabortion worker, antihomosexual crusader; Baptist religious worker
Baptist
Florida
Cur Biog '75

17830. Gordon, Mary
born 1949
novelist, writer on Catholic life
Catholic
Cur Biog '81; Dict Lit Bio v6

SEAFARING, AVIATION, ASTRONAUTICS, AND RAILROADS

17831. Philipse, Margaret Hardenbrook de Vries
flourished 1659; died 1690
colonial merchant, ship owner
Index t Wom; Not Am Wom

17832. Alice
1686–1802 [*sic*]
ferry captain, slave
Philadelphia, PA
Black
Am Bio Dict

17833. West, Lydia
married 1770
whaling voyager
Index t Wom

17834. Longfellow, Margaret Bigelow
1747–1842
seafarer
Index t Wom

17835. Haswell, Susanna Haswell
circa 1763–1824
seafarer
Index t Wom

17836. Barker, Sarah
flourished 1800s
pioneer steamboat passenger
Index t Wom

17837. Page, Julia
flourished 1800s
pioneer
Index t Wom

17838. Wise, Louisa
flourished nineteenth century
balloonist
Index t Wom

17839. Porter, Fidelia
1771–1847
seamen's welfare worker
Am Bio Dict

17840. Jones, Mrs.
flourished 1820s
missionary, seafarer
Index t Wom

17841. Lukens, Rebecca Webb Pennock
1794–1854
iron manufacturer, shipwright
Pennsylvania
Dict Am Bio; Index t Wom; Nat Cyc Am Bio v15; Not Am Wom

17842. Ballard, Emily
flourished 1830s
sea hero
Index t Wom

17843. Dexter, Clarissa L.
died 1856
whaling voyager
Index t Wom

17844. Folger, Susan
married 1831
whaling voyager
Index t Wom

17845. Mayhew, Caroline
married 1834
whaling voyager
Index t Wom

17846. Dawes, James H., Mrs.
flourished 1840s
seafarer
Index t Wom

17847. Owen, Jane Grafton Luce
flourished 1840s–70s
whaling voyager
Index t Wom

17848. Colt, Susan
died 1863
whaling voyager
Index t Wom

17849. Bradley, Lucretia
flourished 1850s
balloonist
Index t Wom

17850. Osborn, Desire Allen
flourished 1850s–60s
whaling voyager
Index t Wom

17851. Ripley, Lucy Norton
flourished 1850s
whaling voyager
Index t Wom

17852. Vincent, Abigail S.
flourished 1850s
whaling voyager
Index t Wom

17853. Lewis, Grace Anna
born 1821
naturalist, scientific illustrator, science writer, conservationist, ornithologist, abolitionist, Underground Railroad operator, pacifist, suffragist, philanthropist
Quaker
Index t Wom; Nat Cyc Am Bio v9; Twent Cen Bio Dict Not Am; Wom Cent

17854. Randall, Charity
circa 1822–1905
whaling voyager
Index t Wom

17855. Carlin, Mary
married 1851
whaling voyager
Index t Wom

17856. Cleveland, Harriet
married 1841
whaling voyager
Index t Wom

17857. Mayhew, Eliza
married 1851
whaling voyager
Index t Wom

17858. Smith, Phebe Ann
married 1851
whaling voyager
Index t Wom

17859. Harding, Jane
married 1852
whaling voyager
Index t Wom

17860. Coston, Martha J.
1828–86
inventor of navy night signals from ship to ship
Twent Cen Bio Dict Not Am

17861. Dunham, Charlotte Corday
born circa 1829
whaling voyager
Index t Wom

17862. Hillman, Charlotte
flourished 1860s–90s
whaling voyager
Index t Wom

17863. Luce, Sarah Reynolds
flourished 1860s–70s
whaling voyager
Index t Wom

17864. Vincent, Ellen M.
flourished 1860s–70s
whaling voyager
Index t Wom

17865. Luce, Almira E.
born circa 1832
whaling voyager
Index t Wom

17866. Claghorn, Ethelinda;
Ethelinda Lewis
married 1858
whaling voyager
Index t Wom

17867. Burgess, Hannah Rebecca Crowell
born circa 1835
sea navigator
Index t Wom

17868. Clark, Helen
married 1862
whaling voyager
Index t Wom

17869. Courtney, Kate
married 1862
whaling voyager
Index t Wom

17870. Burgess, Abbie
born 1839
lighthouse keeper
Index t Wom

17871. Hobart, Lucy M. P.;
Lucy Osborn
flourished 1870s
whaling voyager
Index t Wom

17872. Matthews, Rebecca
flourished 1870s–80s
whaling voyager
Index t Wom

17873. Mellen, Laura
flourished 1870s
whaling voyager
Index t Wom

17874. Lewis, Ida Walley; Ida Walley
1841/42–1911

lighthouse keeper, sea rescuer and hero
Cyc Am Bio; Index t Wom; Nat Cyc Am Bio v5; Not Am Wom; Wom Cent

17875. Stone, Mary Perry
born 1842
businessperson, railroad station agent, suffragist
Oregon
Wom Cent

17876. Vincent, Lucy P.
1842–1933
whaling voyager
Index t Wom

17877. Cannon, Mary H.
married 1871
whaling voyager
Index t Wom

17878. Dow, Mary E. H. G.
born 1848
financier, president of the Dover Horse Railway
Wom Cent

17879. Manchester, Virginia
flourished 1880s
whaling voyager
Index t Wom

17880. Snow, Alice Rowe
flourished 1880s
seafarer
Index t Wom

17881. Bell, Mabel Gardner;
Mrs. Alexander Graham Bell
married 1877
patron of aviation
Index t Wom

17882. Lipei Naij; Elizabeth Worth
married 1880
whaling voyager
Index t Wom

17883. Kelly, Ella Maynard
born 1857
railroad operator, telegrapher
Index t Wom

17884. Thayer, Lizzie E. D.
born 1857
train dispatcher, telegraph operator
Connecticut
Index t Wom; Wom Cent

17885. Marchant, Mabel
flourished 1890s
whaling voyager
Index t Wom

17886. Matthews, Honor
flourished 1890s–1900s
whaling voyager
Index t Wom

17887. Millenchamps, Henry, Mrs.
flourished 1890s
whaling voyager
Index t Wom

17888. Pease, Parnell Smith
married 1885
whaling voyager
Index t Wom

17889. Crowell, Mary
married 1886
whaling voyager
Index t Wom

17890. Clark, Julia
died 1912
aviator
Index t Wom

17891. Jernegan, Amy Chase
born 1863
whaling voyager
Index t Wom

17892. Eager, Gertrude
married 1893
whaling voyager
Index t Wom

17893. Roper, Janet Lord "Mother"
1869–1943
founder of the Missing Seaman's Bureau, manager of the Seaman's Church Institute of New York
New York
Obit File

17894. Cody, S. F., Mrs.
flourished 1900s
pioneer air passenger
Index t Wom

17895. Martin, Mrs.
flourished 1900s–10s
aviator
English
Index t Wom

17896. Mayhew, Adelaide
flourished 1900s–10s
whaling voyager
Index t Wom

17897. Converse, Mary Parker
1872–1961
sea captain
Obit File

17898. Harmon, Louise Benedict
1872–1944
balloon racer
Obit File

17899. Wright, Katherine
1874–1929
patron of aviation
Index t Wom

17900. James, Anna (Cleveland)
1875–1954
pioneer aviator, actor
Obit File

17901. Tusch, Mary E. Hall "Mother"
circa 1875–1960
aviation patron
Index t Wom

17902. Bancroft, Elizabeth McQueen
1878–1958
founder of the Women's International Association of Aeronautics
Obit File

17903. Moisant, Mathilde
circa 1878–1964
pioneer aviator
Index t Wom; Obit File

17904. Broadwick, Tiny
flourished 1910s
parachutist
Index t Wom

17905. Miller, Bernetta
flourished 1910s
aviator
Index t Wom

17906. Raiche, Bessica Faith
flourished 1910s
pioneer aviator
Index t Wom

17907. Rufus, Maud Squire; Flying Grandma
born 1880
aviator
Index t Wom

17908. Smith, Hilder Florentina
flourished 1910s
parachutist
Index t Wom

17909. Cohoe, Edith Rubidge
1881–1956
aviator
Obit File

17910. Hyde, Elizabeth [Carrie]
1881–1957
lawyer, corporate lawyer for a railroad
Presbyterian
Iowa
Nat Cyc Am Bio v47

17911. Strawbridge, Anne West
1883–1941
aviator, author
Index t Wom

17912. Quimby, Harriet
1884–1912
pioneer aviator
Index t Wom

17913. Godfrey, Daisy May
married 1911
seafarer
Index t Wom

17914. Scott, Blanche Stuart "Betty"
1886–1970
pioneer aviator
Index t Wom; Obit File

17915. Bunker, Zaddie
born 1887
aviator
Index t Wom

17916. Law, Ruth Bancroft
born 1887
aviator
Index t Wom

17917. Phillips, Luba Galanchikoff (Philpoff)
1888–1959
pioneer aviator, pre–World War I test pilot, early altitude and distance record holder, taxi driver
New York
Russian
Obit File

17918. Adams, Clara
flourished 1920s–30s
aviator
Index t Wom

17919. Church, Ellen
flourished 1920s–40s
airline steward, flying nurse
Index t Wom

17920. Cooper, Edna May
flourished 1920s
aviator
Index t Wom

17921. Davis, Maxine
flourished 1920s
aviator
Index t Wom

17922. Denny, Edith Litchfield
flourished 1920s–30s
airship pilot
Index t Wom

17923. Doran, Mildred
flourished 1920s
aviator
Index t Wom

17924. Ferguson, Edna
flourished 1920s
journalist, parachute jumper
Index t Wom

17925. Fisher, Wayne H., Mrs.
flourished 1920s
aviator
Index t Wom

17926. Gillies, Betty Huyler
flourished 1920s–30s
aviator
Index t Wom

17927. Gillis, Fay
flourished 1920s
aviator
Index t Wom

17928. Grayson, Francis W.
flourished 1920s
aviator
Index t Wom

17929. Griffin, Clementina de Forest
born 1890
high school educator, aviator
Los Angeles, CA
Nat Cyc Am Bio csv9

17930. Ingalls, Laura
flourished 1920s–40s
pioneer aviator
Index t Wom

17931. Lemon, Dot
flourished 1920s–30s
aviator
Index t Wom

17932. MacFarland, Irene
flourished 1920s
parachutist
Index t Wom

17933. O'Donnell, Gladys
flourished 1920s–30s
aviator
Index t Wom

17934. Perry, Margaret
flourished 1920s
aviator, airport operator
Index t Wom

17935. Rex, Peggy
flourished 1920s
patron of aviation
Index t Wom

17936. Rogner, Arveta
flourished 1920s
parachutist
Index t Wom

17937. Shuler, Marjorie
flourished 1920s–30s
journalist, pioneer air traveler
Index t Wom

17938. Hart, Marion Rice
born 1891
aviator
Index t Wom

17939. Vestey, Evelyn
died 1941

executive of Union Cold Storage and Blue Star Steamship companies
Obit File

17940. Bevins, Okey, Mrs.
died 1942
glider pilot
Index t Wom

17941. Eaton, Genevieve
died 1942
aviator, glider pilot
Index t Wom

17942. Kaucher, Dorothy Wanita
1892–1972
educator, author, writer on aviation
California
Nat Cyc Am Bio v57

17943. Geiringer, Hilda
1893–1973
applied mathematician, statistician, space scientist
Index t Wom; Not Am Wom supp v1

17944. Gardner, Maude Elsa
born 1894
aeronautical engineer
Index t Wom

17945. Hager, Alice Rogers
born 1894
aviation author
Index t Wom

17946. Johnson, Osa Helen Leighty
1894–1952/53
explorer, geographer, big game hunter, filmmaker and film producer, aviator, author
Index t Wom; Nat Cyc Am Bio v39; Obit File

17947. Streeter, Ruth Cheney
born 1895
aviator, marines officer
Index t Wom

17948. Stinson, Katherine
born 1896
aviator, aeronautical engineer
Index t Wom

17949. Stinson, Marjorie
born circa 1896
aviator
Index t Wom

17950. Earhart, Amelia May
1897/99–1937
aviator, autobiographer
Dict Am Bio supp v2; Index t Wom; Nat Cyc Am Bio csv4; Not Am Wom

17951. Hancock, Joy Bright
born 1898
aviator, lieutenant commander in the US Navy, director of the WAVES
Index t Wom; Nat Cyc Am Bio csv7

17952. Borden, Sylvia
born 1899
parachutist
Index t Wom

17953. Beechman, Maria A.
flourished 1930s
railroad worker
Index t Wom

17954. Brown, Justine
flourished 1930s–40s
mariner
Index t Wom

17955. Brown, Willa B.
flourished 1930s–40s
aviator
Index t Wom

17956. Brunton, Laura May
flourished 1930s
aviator, glider pilot
Index t Wom

17957. Burke, Marion E.
flourished 1930s
aviator, flying school owner
Index t Wom

17958. Burleson, Evelyn
flourished 1930s
aviator
Index t Wom

17959. Cavis, Helen
flourished 1930s
aviator, aviation instructor
Index t Wom

17960. Coppege, Ione
flourished 1930s
aviator
Index t Wom

17961. Crawford, Connie
flourished 1930s
aviation radio operator
Index t Wom

17962. Davis, "Bun"
flourished 1930s
airline steward
Index t Wom

17963. de Tuscan, Bela
flourished 1930s
aviator, "gyro-cycle" (type of helicopter) pilot, fencer
Index t Wom

17964. Downsbrough, Margaret
flourished 1930s

glider pilot
Index t Wom

17965. du Pont, Allaire
flourished 1930s
glider pilot
Index t Wom

17966. Erickson, Barbara Jane
flourished 1930s
aviator, flying instructor
Index t Wom

17967. Farr, Virginia
flourished 1930s
aviation instructor
Index t Wom

17968. Gentry, Viola
born 1900
aviator
Index t Wom

17969. Gipson, Elsie
flourished 1930s
aviation instructor
Index t Wom

17970. Granger, Nellie
flourished 1930s
airline host
Index t Wom

17971. Gray, Phyllis
flourished 1930s
aviator
Index t Wom

17972. Hager, Carol
flourished 1930s
aviation instructor
Index t Wom

17973. Haizlip, Mae
flourished 1930s–40s
aviator
Index t Wom

17974. Hallady, Bessie G.
flourished 1930s
aviation instructor
Index t Wom

17975. Hamilton, Cecile
flourished 1930s–40s
aviator
Index t Wom

17976. Harmon, Ruth J.
flourished 1930s
aviation instructor
Index t Wom

17977. Hester, Dorothy
flourished 1930s
aviator
Index t Wom

17978. Hoff, Madeline
flourished 1930s
engineer, aviator
Index t Wom

17979. Holderman, Dorothy
flourished 1930s
glider pilot
Index t Wom

17980. Huntington, Grace
flourished 1930s
aviator
Index t Wom

17981. Kauffman, Mildred
flourished 1930s
aviator
Index t Wom

17982. Keene, Mona
flourished 1930s
airline host
Index t Wom

**17983. Kenyon, Cecil
MacGlashan "Teddy"**
flourished 1930s–40s
pioneer aviator, test pilot, helicopter pilot
Index t Wom

17984. Kidd, Edna Gardner
flourished 1930s
aviator
Index t Wom

17985. Kilgore, Evelyn
flourished 1930s
aviator, head of a training school
for aviators
Index t Wom

17986. Lennox, Peggy
flourished 1930s–40s
aviator, flying instructor
Index t Wom

17987. Light, Mary
flourished 1930s
aeronautical photographer
Index t Wom

17988. Livingston, Clara E.
flourished 1930s–60s
aviator
Index t Wom

17989. Lobdell, Avis
flourished 1930s
railroad public relations expert,
editor
Index t Wom

17990. MacKay, Dorothy A.
flourished 1930s
aviator
Index t Wom

**17991. Marsalis, Frances Har-
rell**
flourished 1930s–40s
aviator
Index t Wom

17992. McCloskey, Helen
flourished 1930s

aviator
Index t Wom

17993. McElroy, Lenore
flourished 1930s
aviator instructor
Index t Wom

17994. Monasterio, Lillian
flourished 1930s
aviation instructor
Index t Wom

17995. Moore, Terris, Mrs.
flourished 1930s
aviator
Index t Wom

17996. Noyes, Blanche Wilcox
born 1900
aviator
Index t Wom

17997. O'Malley, Patricia
flourished 1930s
aviation author
Index t Wom

17998. Owen, Bessie
flourished 1930s
aviator
Index t Wom

17999. Page, Celeste Walker
flourished 1930s
aviation author
Index t Wom

18000. Paul, Josephine Bay
1900–62
brokerage and shipping business
executive
Reformed Church
Nat Cyc Am Bio csv9; Obit File

18001. Plant, Jane
flourished 1930s
aviation instructor
Index t Wom

18002. Poole, Barbara
flourished 1930s
aviator
Index t Wom

18003. Pote, Louise
flourished 1930s
aviator, aerial photographer
Index t Wom

18004. Pusey, Katrina
flourished 1930s
aviator
Index t Wom

18005. Rogers, N.
flourished 1930s
aviator
Index t Wom

18006. Ross, Betsy
flourished 1930s

aviator
Index t Wom

18007. Scharr, Adela Rick
flourished 1930s
aviation instructor
Index t Wom

18008. Schimmoler, Laurette
flourished 1930s
aviator
Index t Wom

**18009. Slocum, Catherine Lu-
den**
flourished 1930s
aviator
Index t Wom

18010. Snook, Neta
flourished 1930s
aviator
Index t Wom

18011. Spicer, Dorothy
flourished 1930s
aviator
Index t Wom

18012. Spirito, Yolanda
flourished 1930s–40s
aviation instructor
Index t Wom

18013. Stilson, Ruth
flourished 1930s
aviation instructor
Index t Wom

**18014. Stuerm, Ruza Lukavas-
ka**
flourished 1930s
railroad executive, lecturer
Czechoslovak
Index t Wom

18015. Sullivan, Marie
flourished 1930s
aviation inspector, decorator
Index t Wom

18016. Sutton, Kate "Ma"
flourished 1930s–50s
seafarer
Index t Wom

18017. Tanner, Margo
flourished 1930s
aviator
Index t Wom

18018. Thomas, Patricia
flourished 1930s
aviation instructor
Index t Wom

18019. Tier, Nancy Hopkins
flourished 1930s
aviator
Index t Wom

18020. Ulm, Mary Josephine
flourished 1930s
aviator, mail pilot
Index t Wom

18021. Wadsworth, Mary Ann
flourished 1930s
aviator
Index t Wom

18022. Waterhouse, Helen
flourished 1930s
journalist, aviation editor
Index t Wom

18023. Whyte, Edna Gardner
flourished 1930s
nurse, aviator
Index t Wom

18024. Wiggin, Mary
flourished 1930s–40s
aviator, stunt flyer
Index t Wom

18025. Wilson, Mabel K.
flourished 1930s
aviator, airport manager
Index t Wom

18026. Young, Dorothy Lamb
flourished 1930s–50s
aviator, helicopter pilot
Index t Wom

18027. Young, Pearl
flourished 1930s
aviator, aviation technical editor
Index t Wom

18028. Nichols, Ruth Rowland
1901–60
pioneer aviator, first woman sea-
plane and airline pilot
Dict Am Bio supp v6; Index t
   Wom; Not Am Wom supp v1;
   Obit File

**18029. Freudenthal, Elsbeth Es-
telle**
circa 1902–53
economist, aviation writer
Index t Wom

**18030. Omlie, Phoebe Jane
Fairgrave**
1902–75
aviator, aviation instructor
Index t Wom; Not Am Wom
   supp v1

18031. Pugh, Jessie
1902–72
aviator, record holder for number
   of flights across the US
Obit File

**18032. Shelley, Mary
J[osephine]**
1902–76
aviator, air force colonel, head of
   the navy education program for

women during World War II,
commander of women in the air
force during the Korean War
Cur Biog '76; Index t Wom; Obit
   File

18033. Strassmann, Antonie
1902–52
aviator, World War II hero, anti-
Nazi worker
German
Obit File

**18034. Beech, Olive Ann Mel-
lor**
born 1903
aviation executive, industrialist
Index t Wom

18035. Elder, Ruth
1904–77
aviator
Index t Wom; Obit File

**18036. McGill, Elizabeth
Gregory**
graduated 1929
aeronautical engineer
Index t Wom

18037. Cochran, Jacqueline;
Mrs. Floyd B. Odlum
1906/10–1980
aviator, director of the Women's
   Air Force Service Pilots, flight
   captain in the US Air Force,
   colonel in the Air Force Reserve, World War II correspondent, business executive,
   cosmetician
Cur Biog '80; Index t Wom; Nat
   Cyc Am Bio csv10

**18038. Lindbergh, Anne (Spen-
cer) Morrow**
born 1906
aviator, poet, author, autobiographer
Cur Biog '76; Index t Wom; Nat
   Cyc Am Bio csv6

**18039. Thaden, Louise McPhe-
tridge**
born 1906
pioneer aviator
Index t Wom

18040. Trout, Evelyn "Bobby"
born 1906
pioneer aviator
Index t Wom

18041. Ebel, Isabel Caroline
born 1908
aeronautical engineer
Index t Wom

18042. Smith, Elinor
born 1908
aviator
Index t Wom

**18043. Barnes, Florence Lowe
"Pancho"**
1909–75
aviator, motion-picture stunt pilot, resort owner
Index t Wom; Obit File

18044. Rhonie, Aline
born 1909
painter, aviator
Index t Wom

18045. Bennis, Virginia
flourished 1940s
glider pilot
Index t Wom

18046. Boswell, Florence
flourished 1940s
aviator
Index t Wom

18047. Carl, Ann Baumgartner
flourished 1940s
aviator
Index t Wom

18048. Carter, Ann Shaw
flourished 1940s
aviator, pioneer helicopter pilot
Index t Wom

18049. Cyrus, Diana
flourished 1940s–50s
aviator
Index t Wom

18050. Fairweather, Margie
flourished 1940s
aviator, navigator
Index t Wom

18051. Fort, Cornelia
flourished 1940s
aviator
Index t Wom

18052. Gore, Margot
flourished 1940s
aviator
Index t Wom

18053. Gray, Adeline
flourished 1940s
parachutist
Index t Wom

18054. Heard, Marilyn Grover
flourished 1940s–50s
aviator, helicopter pilot
Index t Wom

18055. Heberding, Dolly
flourished 1940s
aviator
Index t Wom

18056. Hooker, Elizabeth
flourished 1940s
aviator
Index t Wom

**18057. Howard, Maxine
"Mike"**
flourished 1940s
aviator
Index t Wom

18058. Jayne, Barbara
flourished 1940s
aviator, test pilot
Index t Wom

18059. Lind, Paula
flourished 1940s
aviator
Index t Wom

18060. Loufek, Betty
flourished 1940s
glider pilot
Index t Wom

18061. McBride, Helen
flourished 1940s
aviator
Index t Wom

18062. Nolde, Frances
flourished 1940s
aviator
Index t Wom

18063. O'Shea, G. Leona
flourished 1940s
aviator
Index t Wom

18064. Palmer, Bernice
flourished 1940s
aircraft inventor
Index t Wom

18065. Rees, Rosemary
flourished 1940s
ballet dancer, aviator
Index t Wom

18066. Richey, Helen
1910–47
pioneer aviator, wartime ferry pilot
Index t Wom; Obit File

18067. Roth, Vita F.
flourished 1940s
aviator
Index t Wom

18068. Rudnick, Elynor
flourished 1940s–60s
aviator, helicopter pilot
Index t Wom

18069. Smith, Quincy
flourished 1940s
aircraft inventor
Index t Wom

18070. Stein, Camille L.
flourished 1940s
airline executive
Index t Wom

18071. Stewart, Sylvia
flourished 1940s
aircraft engine instructor
Index t Wom

18072. Stites, Mabel M.
flourished 1940s
aviator
Index t Wom

18073. Stroup, Leora
flourished 1940s
aviator, nurse
Index t Wom

18074. Tonkin, Lois Coots
flourished 1940s
aviator
Index t Wom

18075. Wilson, Elva
flourished 1940s
aircraft inventor
Index t Wom

**18076. Montgomery, Helen
Marie**
born 1911
aviator, glider pilot
Index t Wom

18077. Barnato, Diana
flourished 1944
aviator
Index t Wom

18078. Davis, Arlene Palsgraff
died 1964
aviator, business executive
Index t Wom

18079. Love, Nancy
born 1914
aviator
Index t Wom

**18080. Hurlburt, Margaret
"Marge"**
circa 1915–47
aviator, speed flyer, educator
Index t Wom; Obit File

18081. White, Ann
married 1943
seafarer
Index t Wom

18082. Bera, Frances
flourished 1950s
aviator
Index t Wom

18083. Brick, Katherine
flourished 1950s
aviator
Index t Wom

**18084. Deveau, Harvey J.,
Mrs.; Tugboat Mary**
flourished 1950s
seafarer
Index t Wom

18085. Eckles, Ann
flourished 1950s
space scientist
Index t Wom

18086. Gillies, Pat
flourished 1950s
aviator
Index t Wom

18087. Hixon, Jean
flourished 1950s
educator, aviator
Index t Wom

18088. Howard, Jean Ross
flourished 1950s
aviator, helicopter pilot
Index t Wom

18089. Kiernan, Barbara
flourished 1950s
helicopter test pilot
Index t Wom

18090. Mary Aquinas, Sister
flourished 1950s
aviator, jet pilot, Catholic nun
Catholic
Index t Wom

18091. Morse, Louisa Spruance
flourished 1950s
aviator
Index t Wom

18092. Murphy, Florence Jones
flourished 1950s
aviator
Index t Wom

18093. Reading, Martha Ann
flourished 1950s–60s
aviator
Index t Wom

18094. Rombeau, Anne M.
flourished 1950s
aviator, lecturer, traveler
Index t Wom

18095. Saunders, Aileen
flourished 1950s–60s
aviator
Index t Wom

18096. Spears, Nanette M.
flourished 1950s
aviator
Index t Wom

18097. Sproull, Lillian R.
flourished 1950s
aviator
Index t Wom

18098. Thompson, Myrtle Grey
flourished 1950s–60s
aviator, airport operator
Index t Wom

18099. van der Wal, Franki
flourished 1950s–60s
space scientist, designer
Index t Wom

**18100. Woodward, Elizabeth
W. "Betsy"**
flourished 1950s–60s
glider pilot
Hall Fame Sport; Index t Wom

18101. Dougherty, Dora Jean
born 1921
aviator, helicopter pilot, psychologist
Index t Wom

18102. Luckenbach, Andrea
1921–62
vice-president of the Luckenbach
Steamship Co.
Obit File

18103. Bentley, Helen Delich
born 1923
newspaper journalist, chairperson
of the Federal Maritime Commission, marine shipping expert, television documentary
producer
Cur Biog '71

18104. Bixby, Diana
1923–55
aviator
Index t Wom; Obit File

18105. Roman, Nancy Grace
born 1925
astronomer, space scientist
Index t Wom

18106. Skelton, Betty
born 1926
aviator
Index t Wom

18107. Abrescia, Donna
flourished 1960s
parachutist
Index t Wom

18108. Anderson, Dorothy L.
flourished 1960s
air traffic controller
Native American (Flathead)
Ind Today

18109. Dietrich, Jan
flourished 1960s
astronaut
Index t Wom

18110. Dietrich, Marion
flourished 1960s
astronaut
Index t Wom

18111. Edwards, June
flourished 1960s
aviator, helicopter pilot
Index t Wom

18112. Frankelstein, Beatrice
flourished 1960s
space nutrition expert
Index t Wom

18113. Gilmour
flourished 1960s
helicopter pilot
Index t Wom

18114. Glennon, Nan
flourished 1960s
space scientist, rocket designer,
mechanical engineer
Index t Wom

18115. Hart, Janey
flourished 1960s
aviator, helicopter pilot, astronaut
Index t Wom

18116. Hastings, Margaret
flourished 1960s
glider pilot
Index t Wom

18117. Hicks, Betty
flourished 1960s
aviator
Index t Wom

18118. Kimball, Yeffe
flourished 1960s
pioneer painter of outer space
Native American (Osage)
Ind Today

18119. Mowry, Crystal
flourished 1960s
aviator
Index t Wom

18120. Nicks, Diana
flourished 1960s
glider pilot
Index t Wom

18121. Romic, Mary
flourished 1960s
space scientist
Index t Wom

18122. Sandell, Viola T.
flourished 1960s
aviator
Index t Wom

18123. Steinberg, Maria Alice
flourished 1960s
aeronautical research engineer
Index t Wom

18124. Wilson, Jane
flourished 1960s
helicopter pilot
Index t Wom

**18125. Cobb, Geraldine M.
"Jerrie"**
born 1931
aviator
Index t Wom

18126. Funk, Mary Wallace
graduated 1958
aviator, astronaut
Index t Wom

18127. Mead, Sylvia Alice Earle
born 1935
marine biologist, aquanaut
Los Angeles, CA
Cur Biog '72

18128. O'Hara, Dolores B.
born circa 1935
pioneer space nurse
Index t Wom

18129. Smith, Joan Merriam
1937–65
aviator
Obit File

18130. Guthrie, Janet
born 1938
race car driver, aviator
Cur Biog '78

18131. Duperault, Terry Jo
born circa 1950
sea hero
Index t Wom

18132. Onassis, Christina
born 1950
shipping magnate
Cur Biog '76

No Dates

18133. Beales, Iris
air traffic controller
Index t Wom

18134. Carter, Amy
aircraft factory instructor
Index t Wom

18135. Clark, Helen Mary
aviator
Index t Wom

18136. Cull, Betty
army aerial observer, bomb tester
Index t Wom

18137. Dick, Helen N.
soarer
Hall Fame Sport

18138. Gill, Jocelyn R.
space scientist
Index t Wom

18139. Gudzin, Margaret S.
aviator
Index t Wom

18140. Hall, Ilizabeth
aviation instructor
Index t Wom

18141. Iverson, Caroline
aviator
Index t Wom

18142. Jorgensen, Evelyn
aircraft instructor
Index t Wom

18143. Kellet, Charlotte
aviator, airline host
Index t Wom

18144. Mallette, Dorothy
aircraft instructor
Index t Wom

18145. Mark, Joyce
pioneer airline radio operator
Index t Wom

18146. Robinson, Pearle Thurber "Perry"
preflight aviation instructor
Index t Wom

18147. Schweizer, Virginia M.
soarer
Hall Fame Sport

SOCIAL WORK AND REFORM

18148. Ferguson, Catherine
circa 1749–1854
religious and welfare worker, baker
New York
Black
Index t Wom; Our Count

18149. Sanders, Elizabeth (Elkins)
1762–1851/54
social critic, pamphleteer, author, history writer on Massachusetts, Native American rights worker
Salem, MA
Cyc Am Bio; Dict Am Auth; Dict Am Bio; Dict Am Bio Men Time; Not Am Wom

18150. Bethune, Joanna Graham
1770–1860
social reformer
Not Am Wom

18151. Hutchinson, Viola
flourished nineteenth century
social reformer, singer
Index t Wom

18152. Porter, Fidelia
1771–1847
seamen's welfare worker
Am Bio Dict

18153. Truth, Sojourner; Isabel Baumfree
1775/97–1883/85
social reformer, abolitionist, feminist, lecturer, temperance writer
Black
Cyc Am Bio; Dict Am Rel Bio; Encyc Black Am; Index t Wom; Negro Alman; Not Am Wom; Prof Negro Wom v1

18154. Arthur, William, Mrs.
flourished 1820s
frontier reformer
Index t Wom

18155. Grimke, Sarah Moore
1792/93–1873
abolitionist, women's rights worker, writer on social problems, political author, lecturer
Quaker
Cyc Am Bio; Dict Am Auth; Dict Am Bio; Dict Am Rel Bio; Index t Wom; Nat Cyc Am Bio v2; Twent Cen Bio Dict Not Am; Wom Cent

18156. Dix, Dorothea Lynde
1794/1802–1887
crusader for the welfare of the mentally ill, prison reformer, philanthropist, author, essayist, children's author, superintendent of army nurses in the Civil War
Massachusetts
Cyc Am Bio; Dict Am Auth; Dict Am Bio; Dict Am Bio Men Time; Dict Lit Bio v1; Index t Wom; Nat Cyc Am Bio v3; Not Am Wom; Twent Cen Bio Dict Not Am; Wom Cent

18157. Beecher, Catherine Esther
1800–78
educator of women, education writer, social reformer, poet
Episcopalian
New York
Appl Cyc Am Bio; Cyc Am Bio; Dict Am Bio; Dict Am Bio Men Time; Dict Lit Bio v1; Index t Wom; Nat Cyc Am Bio v3; Not Am Wom; Twent Cen Bio Dict Not Am; Wom Cent

18158. Rouse, Benjamin, Mrs.
born 1800
Civil War humanitarian, social reformer
Index t Wom

18159. Gibbons, Abigail Hopper "Abby"
1801–93
abolitionist, prison reformer, feminist, women's welfare worker, Civil War nurse, philanthropist, journalist
Quaker
Cyc Am Bio; Dict Am Bio; Index t Wom; Nat Cyc Am Bio v7; Not Am Wom; Twent Cen Bio Dict Not Am; Wom Cent

18160. Child, Lydia Maria (Francis)
1802–80
author, philanthropist, abolitionist, editor, social reformer
Quaker
Massachusetts
Cyc Am Bio; Dict Am Auth; Dict Am Bio; Dict Am Bio Men Time; Dict Lit Bio v1; Index t Wom; Nat Cyc Am Bio v2; Not Am Wom; Twent Cen Bio Dict Not Am; Wom Cent

18161. Doremus, Sarah Platt Haines
1802–77
foreign missionary, founder of foreign missions, charity organizer, philanthropist, social worker
Cyc Am Bio; Dict Am Bio; Index t Wom; Nat Cyc Am Bio v6; Not Am Wom; Twent Cen Bio Dict Not Am

18162. Stewart, Maria [Frances] W. Miller
1803–79
educator, lecturer, social reformer
Black
Index t Wom; Not Am Wom

18163. Hunt, Harriot Keziah
1805–75
physician, social reformer, suffragist, lecturer
Boston, MA
Cyc Am Bio; Dict Am Auth; Dict Am Bio; Index t Wom; Nat Cyc Am Bio v9; Not Am Wom; Twent Cen Bio Dict Not Am

18164. Pyles, Charlotta Gordon
1806–80
abolitionist, social reformer
Black
Index t Wom; Negro Alman

18165. Palmer, Phoebe Worrall
1807–74
social reformer, religious writer, Methodist leader, Wesleyan evangelist
Wesleyan
New York, NY
Cyc Am Bio; Dict Am Auth; Dict Am Rel Bio; Index t Wom; Not Am Wom

18166. Haviland, Laura Smith
1808–98
abolitionist, freedmen's welfare worker, philanthropist
Quaker
Cyc Am Bio; Not Am Wom

18167. McCord, Louisa Susannah (Cheves)
1810–1879/80
miscellaneous author, poet, political writer, translator, Confederate essayist, Black welfare worker, feminist, plantation manager
South Carolina
Cyc Am Bio; Dict Am Auth; Dict Am Bio; Dict Am Bio Men Time; Index t Wom; Nat Cyc Am Bio v9; Not Am Wom; Twent Cen Bio Dict Not Am

18168. Nichols, Clarinda Irene Howard
1810–85
newspaper editor, political writer, social reformer, lecturer, women's rights leader, suffragist, feminist
Kansas
Cyc Am Bio; Dict Am Bio; Index t Wom; Nat Cyc Am Bio v5; Not Am Wom

18169. Nichols, Mary Sargent (Neal) Gove
1810–84
women's rights worker, feminist, dress and health reformer, medical author, physician, social reformer, temperance reformer, popular author, novelist
Cyc Am Bio; Dict Am Auth; Dict Am Bio Men Time; Dict Lit Bio v1; Index t Wom; Nat Cyc Am Bio v13; Not Am Wom

18170. Phillips, Anna Greene
flourished 1840s
social reformer
Index t Wom

18171. Stuart, Sarah M.
flourished 1840s
social reformer
Index t Wom

18172. Hoge, Jane Currie Blaikie; A. H. Hoge
1811–90
Civil War relief leader, church and welfare worker, sanitation commission worker, author
Index t Wom; Not Am Wom

18173. Stowe, Harriet Elizabeth Beecher
1811/12–1896
author, abolitionist, social reformer, theologian
Connecticut
Cyc Am Bio; Dict Am Auth; Dict Am Bio; Dict Am Bio Men Time; Dict Am Rel Bio; Dict Lit Bio v1; Nat Cyc Am Bio v1; Not Am Wom; Twent Cen Bio Dict Not Am; Wom Cent; Wom Lit; Wom Lit, More

18174. Bayer, Adele Parmentier
1814–92
social welfare worker
Not Am Wom

18175. Griffing, Josephine Sophia White
1814–72
abolitionist, feminist, suffragist, welfare worker
Dict Am Bio; Index t Wom; Not Am Wom

18176. O'Connell, Mary; Sister Anthony
1814–97
Catholic nun, Civil War nurse, orphanage and hospital director in Cincinnati
Catholic
Cincinnati, OH
Dict Am Bio; Not Am Wom

18177. Comstock, Elizabeth Leslie Rous
1815–1891/92
social reformer, abolitionist, Underground Railroad worker, pacifist, freed slave's welfare worker, temperance reformer, women's rights worker, Quaker minister, prison reformer, Civil War nurse
Quaker
Dict Am Bio; Index t Wom; Nat Cyc Am Bio v22; Not Am Wom

18178. Stanton, Elizabeth Cady
1815/16–1902
feminist, suffragist, women's rights worker, editor, author, social reformer, theologian
Cyc Am Bio; Dict Am Auth; Dict Am Bio; Dict Am Bio Men Time; Dict Am Rel Bio; Index t Wom; Nat Cyc Am Bio v3; Not Am Wom; Twent Cen Bio Dict Not Am; Wom Cent

18179. Packard, Elizabeth Parsons Ware
1816–97
social reformer
Not Am Wom

18180. Coleman, Lucy Newhall; Lucy Colman
1817–1906
abolitionist, educator of Blacks, women's rights worker, suffragist, lecturer, health reformer
Universalist
Dict Am Bio; Nat Cyc Am Bio v4, Wom Cent

18181. Stone, Lucy; Mrs. Henry Brown Blackwell
1818–93
feminist, suffragist, women's rights worker, abolitionist, social reformer, editor, lecturer

Massachusetts
Cyc Am Bio; Dict Am Bio; Dict Am Bio Men Time; Index t Wom; Nat Cyc Am Bio v2 and v29; Not Am Wom; Twent Cen Bio Dict Not Am; Wom Cent

18182. Brown, Frances Jane
1819–1914
social reformer
Index t Wom

18183. Cutter, Eunice Powers
1819–93
lecturer, health reformer, abolitionist, historian
Twent Cen Bio Dict Not Am

18184. Lord, Elizabeth W. Russell
born 1819
educator, philanthropist, educator of the blind
Index t Wom; Wom Cent

18185. Lewis, Delecta Barbour
flourished 1850s
social reformer
Index t Wom

18186. Livermore, Mary Ashton (Rice)
1820/21–1905
health reformer, hospital administrator, suffragist, temperance worker, abolitionist, Civil War patriot, miscellaneous author
Universalist
Melrose, MA
Cyc Am Bio; Dict Am Auth; Dict Am Bio Men Time; Dict Am Rel Bio; Index t Wom; Nat Cyc Am Bio v1; Not Am Wom; Twent Cen Bio Dict Not Am; Wom Cent

18187. Pellet, Miss
flourished 1850s
social reformer
Index t Wom

18188. Severance, Carolina Maria (Seymour)
1820–1914
social reformer, women's club leader, women's rights worker, feminist, abolitionist
Dict Am Bio; Index t Wom; Nat Cyc Am Bio v8; Not Am Wom; Wom Cent

18189. Diaz, Abby (Morton)
1821–1904
author, children's author, essayist, social reformer, suffragist, abolitionist, lecturer
Boston, MA
Dict Am Auth; Nat Cyc Am Bio v11; Not Am Wom; Twent Cen Bio Dict Not Am; Wom Cent

18190. Fowler, Lydia Folger
1822/23–1979
physician, lecturer, social reformer, author, astronomer, science writer
Cyc Am Bio; Dict Am Auth; Index t Wom; Not Am Wom

18191. Lamson, Mary (Swift)
born 1822
educator of the blind and deaf, biographer
Dict Am Auth

18192. Miller, Elizabeth Smith
1822–1911
social reformer, feminist
Index t Wom; Not Am Wom

18193. Hendricks, Eliza C. Morgan
born 1823
philanthropist, women's prison welfare worker
Episcopalian
Wom Cent

18194. Stebbins, Catherine A. F.
1823–post 1880
social reformer, abolitionist, feminist, suffragist
Index t Wom; Wom Cent

18195. Davis, Mary Fenn
1824–86
Spiritualist lecturer, reformer
Spiritualist
Not Am Wom

18196. Harvey, Cordelia Adelaide Perrine
1824–95
Civil War nurse, relief worker, social welfare leader
Index t Wom

18197. Soule, Caroline Augusta (White)
1824–1903/04
author, publisher, editor, church worker, Universalist minister, foreign missionary, social reformer, lecturer
Universalist
Cyc Am Bio; Dict Am Auth; Dict Am Bio Men Time; Index t Wom; Not Am Wom; Twent Cen Bio Dict Not Am

18198. Estes, Huldah
died 1875
social reformer
Index t Wom

18199. Gifford, Susan A.
born 1826
social reformer
Index t Wom

18200. Plunkett, Harriette Merrick Hodge
born 1826
humanitarian, sanitation reformer
Massachusetts
Index t Wom; Wom Cent

18201. Bottome, Margaret (McDonald)
1827–1906
health reformer, religious author, founder of King's Daughters, a religious society
Dict Am Bio; Nat Cyc Am Bio v13; Twent Cen Bio Dict Not Am

18202. Collins, Ellen
1828–1912
philanthropist, housing reformer, Civil War patriot
Index t Wom; Not Am Wom

18203. Collins, Jennie
1828–87
labor reformer, welfare worker, philanthropist, suffragist
Massachusetts
Bio Dict Am Lab; Index t Wom; Not Am Wom; Twent Cen Bio Dict Not Am

18204. May, Abigail Williams
1829–88
Boston social reformer, abolitionist, suffragist, education commissioner, Civil War relief worker
Boston, MA
Index t Wom; Not Am Wom; Twent Cen Bio Dict Not Am

18205. Patton, Abigail Jemima; Abby Hutchinson
1829–92
alto singer, composer, poet, social reformer, abolitionist, suffragist, hymn writer, feminist
New York; New Hampshire
Nat Cyc Am Bio v10; Wom Cent; Not Am Wom; Index t Wom

18206. Brayton, Mary Clark
flourished 1860s–80s
Civil War relief worker, social reformer
Index t Wom

18207. Collins, Delia
born 1830
educator, temperance worker, philanthropist, welfare worker
Wom Cent

18208. Louis, Minnie Dessau
flourished 1860s–90s
Jewish welfare worker, educator
Jewish
New York
Nat Cyc Am Bio v18

18209. White, Armenia
flourished 1860s
philanthropist, social reformer, Civil War patriot
Index t Wom

18210. Calkins, Adelaide Augusta Hosmer
1831–1909
philanthropist, children's welfare worker
Congregationalist
Massachusetts
Nat Cyc Am Bio v28

18211. Eyster, Nellie Blessing
born 1831
author, children's author, temperance reformer, worker for Chinese American welfare
Pennsylvania; California
Cyc Am Bio; Dict Am Auth; Nat Cyc Am Bio v10; Twent Cen Bio Dict Not Am; Wom Cent

18212. Fairbanks, Elizabeth B.
born 1831
philanthropist, mental institution reformer
Wisconsin
Wom Cent

18213. Hallowell, Anna
1831–1905
welfare worker, educational reformer, kindergarten leader
Not Am Wom

18214. Hobson, Elizabeth Christophers Kimball
1831–1912
social welfare worker
Not Am Wom

18215. White, Anna
1831–1910
Shaker eldress, social reformer
Shaker
Not Am Wom

18216. Culver, Helen
1832–1925
philanthropist, Black welfare worker, patron of science, hospital administrator, educator, real estate businessperson
Index t Wom; Nat Cyc Am Bio v17; Twent Cen Bio Dict Not Am

18217. Cusack, Margaret Anne; Sister Mary Frances Clare; Nun of Kenmare
1832–99
welfare worker, founder of the Sisters of Peace in America, Catholic nun
Catholic
Index t Wom

18218. Hiles, Osia Joslyn
born 1832

philanthropist, poet, Native American welfare worker
Wisconsin
Wom Cent

18219. Poole, Hester Martha (Hunt)
born 1833/43
author, poet, writer on social and domestic issues, art critic, artist, women's rights worker, Sorosis member
Metuchen, NJ
Dict Am Auth; Nat Cyc Am Bio v11; Wom Cent

18220. Quinton, Amelia Stone
1833–1926
Native American reform and rights worker, temperance worker, club leader, humanitarian
Index t Wom; Not Am Wom; Twent Cen Bio Dict Not Am; Wom Cent

18221. Beasley, Matilda, Mother
1834–1903
educator, social worker, Catholic nun
Catholic
Georgia
Black
Negro Alman; Prof Negro Wom

18222. Gregory, Elizabeth Goadby
born 1834
author, translator of French and German literature, journalist, writer on industrial and social topics
Wom Cent

18223. Grubb, Sophronia Farrington Naylor
born 1834
temperance worker, freedmen's welfare worker
Wom Cent

18224. Rogers, Harriet Burbank
1834–1919
educator of the deaf
Not Am Wom

18225. Rose, Martha E. (Parmelee)
born 1834
women's labor welfare worker, social reformer, sociologist, author, art patron, journalist, Sorosis member
Cleveland, OH
Index t Wom; Nat Cyc Am Bio v11; Wom Cent

18226. Bristol, Augusta (Cooper)
1835–1910

educator, writer on education, author, poet, sociologist, lecturer on philosophic and scientific topics
Cyc Am Bio and ad; Dict Am Auth; Twent Cen Bio Dict Not Am; Wom Cent

18227. Brown, Mary Frank
born 1835
philanthropist, Chinese and Japanese women's welfare worker, temperance worker
Oakland, CA
Wom Cent

18228. Carse, Matilda Bradley
1835–1917
temperance worker, child care worker, welfare worker, philanthropist, financier
Chicago, IL
Index t Wom; Not Am Wom; Twent Cen Bio Dict Not Am; Wom Cent

18229. Coppin, Fanny Marion Jackson
1835/37–1912/18
educator, foreign missionary, social worker, lecturer, women's rights worker
Black
Encyc Black Am; Index t Wom; Negro Alman; Not Am Wom; Prof Negro Wom

18230. Fuller, Sarah
1836–1927
educator of the deaf
Not Am Wom

18231. Smith, Virginia Trall
1836–1903
mission and charity worker, pioneer in child care
Not Am Wom

18232. Stearns, Sarah Burger
1836–post 1899
suffragist, women's rights worker, philanthropist, Civil War humanitarian, temperance worker, social reformer, educator of freedmen
Unitarian
Cyc Am Bio; Index t Wom; Nat Cyc Am Bio v10; Twent Cen Bio Dict Not Am; Wom Cent

18233. Dye, Mary Irene Clark
born 1837
telegrapher, welfare worker, temperance worker
Wom Cent

18234. Flower, Lucy Louisa (Coues)
1837–1921
social welfare worker, philanthropist, patron of education, president of the Illinois Training

School for Nurses, member of the Chicago school board, trustee of the University of Illinois, Republican party worker
Episcopalian
Dict Am Bio; Nat Cyc Am Bio v9; Not Am Wom

18235. Keim, Jane Sumner Owen
graduated 1862
social reformer, humanitarian
Index t Wom

18236. Newman, Angelia Louise French Thurston
1837–1910
church worker, missionary, Mormon women's relief worker, lecturer, reformer
Mormon
Utah
Index t Wom; Not Am Wom; Wom Cent

18237. Schuyler, Louisa Lee
1837/40–1926
leader in welfare work, Civil War philanthropist, patron of nursing, social worker, sanitarian
New York
Dict Am Bio; Index t Wom; Nat Cyc Am Bio v20; Not Am Wom

18238. Wyman, Lillie Buffum Chace
born 1837/47
author, muckraking journalist, short story writer, philanthropist, suffragist, labor welfare worker
Georgia
Dict Am Auth; Wom Cent

18239. Lippincott, Esther J. (Trimble)
1838–88
educator, author on literature, temperance reformer, convalescent-hospital reformer
Quaker
Pennsylvania
Dict Am Auth; Wom Cent

18240. Little, Sarah F. Cowles
born 1838
educator of the blind
Index t Wom; Wom Cent

18241. Stockton, Louise
1838–1914
editor, journalist, novelist, critic, historian, social worker
Philadelphia, PA
Dict Am Auth; Index t Wom; Nat Cyc Am Bio v8; Twent Cen Bio Dict Not Am

18242. Wells, Kate Gannet
1838–1911
social reformer
Not Am Wom

18243. Woodhull, Victoria Claflin; Victoria Martin
1838–1927
social reformer, political reformer, stockbroker, feminist
English (American expatriate to England)
Dict Am Auth; Dict Am Bio; Index t Wom; Not Am Wom

18244. Campbell, Helen (Stuart)
1839–1918
journalist, children's author, social reformer, home economist, educator, philanthropist
New York
Cyc Am Bio; Dict Am Auth; Nat Cyc Am Bio v9; Not Am Wom; Twent Cen Bio Dict Not Am; Wom Cent

18245. Garrett, Mary Smith
1839–1925
educator of the deaf, child welfare worker
Not Am Wom

18246. Hancock, Cornelia
1839/40–1927
Civil War nurse, educator of freedmen, charity worker, housing reformer
Quaker
Index t Wom; Not Am Wom

18247. Molloy, Emma
born 1839
social reformer, editor, printer
Index t Wom

18248. Morse, Lucy (Gibbons)
1839–1936
author, novelist, abolitionist, Black welfare worker
New York, NY
Dict Am Auth; Nat Cyc Am Bio

18249. Ames, Fanny Baker
1840–1931
industrial reformer in public institutions, charity organizer
Index t Wom; Not Am Wom; Wom Cent

18250. Bonham, Mildred A.
born 1840
traveler, journalist, social reformer
Index t Wom; Wom Cent

18251. Coolidge, Harriet Abbot Lincoln
flourished 1870s–80s
philanthropist, sanitary educator, worker for women's education, author
Wom Cent

18252. Darlington, Hannah
flourished 1870s–80s
social reformer
Index t Wom

18253. Ellis, Margaret Dye
flourished 1870s
social reformer
Index t Wom

18254. Greeley, Mary Y. C.
flourished 1870s
social reformer
Index t Wom

18255. Herrick, Mary Elizabeth
flourished 1870s–80s
lawyer, social reformer
Index t Wom

18256. Hill, Eliza Trask
born 1840
suffragist, women's welfare worker, journalist, newspaper publisher, political activist, Prohibitionist
Massachusetts
Wom Cent

18257. Hudlun, Anna Elizabeth
1840–1914
social worker, welfare worker, philanthropist
African Methodist Episcopal Zion
Black
Index t Wom; Negro Alman; Prof Negro Wom v1

18258. Hutchinson, Elizabeth Chase
flourished 1870s–80s
social reformer, singer
Index t Wom

18259. Johnson, Mary C.
flourished 1870s
social reformer
Index t Wom

18260. Owens-Adair, Bethenia Angelina
1840–1926
physician, feminist, social reformer
Index t Wom; Not Am Wom

18261. Pennock, Deborah
flourished 1870s
social reformer
Index t Wom

18262. Reed, Catherine S.
flourished 1870s–80s
social reformer
Index t Wom

18263. Woodbridge, Mary Ann
flourished 1870s
social reformer
Index t Wom

18264. Conklin, Jennie Maria (Drinkwater); Maria Drinkwater
1841–1900
children's author, philanthropist, clubwoman, founder of the Shut-in Society for Invalids
Dict Am Auth; Index t Wom; Dict Am Bio

18265. Huntington, Emily
1841–1909
welfare worker, founder of the kitchen garden movement
Not Am Wom

18266. Plumb, L. H.
born 1841
social reformer, temperance worker, financier, banker
Illinois
Index t Wom; Wom Cent

18267. Ziegler, Electra Matilda Curtis
1841–1932
patron of welfare of the blind
Christian Scientist
New York
Index t Wom; Nat Cyc Am Bio v37

18268. Dare, Ella
born 1842
lecturer, journalist, Civil War relief worker, sanitarian
Wom Cent

18269. Hill, Agnes Leonard (Scanland); Molly Myrtle
1842–1917
poet, author, newspaper publisher, religious writer, novelist, prisoner's welfare worker, Universalist pastor
Universalist
Colorado
Dict Am Auth; Index t Wom; Nat Cyc Am Bio v17; Wom Cent

18270. Lathrop, Clarissa Caldwill
died 1892
mental institution reformer
New York
Index t Wom; Wom Cent

18271. Ruffin, Josephine St. Pierre
1842–1924
clubwoman, Black leader, Black welfare and rights worker, president of the National Federation of Afro-American Women, Union patriot in the Civil War
Black
Index t Wom; Negro Alman; Not Am Wom; Prof Negro Wom v1

18272. Eliot, Charlotte Champe Stearns
1843–1929
author, welfare worker
Not Am Wom

18273. Jacobs, Frances Wisebart; Mother of the Charities
1843–92
welfare worker, charity worker
Colorado
Not Am Wom

18274. Leonard, Anna Byford
born 1843
sanitation reformer, Chicago health department officer, sociologist
Chicago, IL
Index t Wom; Wom Cent

18275. Lowell, Josephine (Shaw)
1843–1905
charitable worker, philanthropist, social worker, prison reformer, labor reformer, writer on philanthropy
New York, NY
Cyc Am Bio; Dict Am Auth; Dict Am Bio; Index t Wom; Nat Cyc Am Bio v8; Not Am Wom; Twent Cen Bio Dict Not Am

18276. Spurlock, Isabella Smiley Davis
born 1843
philanthropist, temperance worker, Mormon women's welfare worker
Nebraska
Wom Cent

18277. Leiter, Fannie W.
born 1844
social reformer
Index t Wom

18278. Stevens, Alzina Parsons
1844/49–1900
labor leader, industrial reformer, settlement house worker, social reformer, newspaper editor and publisher, journalist, author
Chicago, IL
Index t Wom; Not Am Wom; Wom Cent

18279. Claflin, Tennessee Celeste
1845/46–1923
social reformer, feminist, stockbroker, newspaper editor, journalist
Index t Wom; Not Am Wom

18280. Cushing, Juliet Clannon
1845–1934
welfare worker
Presbyterian
New Jersey
Nat Cyc Am Bio v28

18281. Osburn, Mary
born 1845
social reformer
Index t Wom

18282. Garrett, Emma
circa 1846–93
educator of the deaf
Not Am Wom

18283. Bradford, Cornelia Foster
1847–1935
social worker
Not Am Wom

18284. Henrotin, Ellen M. Martin
1847–1922
women's club leader, labor and social reformer, philanthropist
Index t Wom; Not Am Wom

18285. Lakey, Alice
1847–1935
clubwoman, leader in the pure food movement
Not Am Wom

18286. Payott, Annie Eliza (Fredenbur) Evens
1847–1927
welfare worker
Unitarian
San Francisco, CA
Nat Cyc Am Bio v21

18287. Sparhawk, Frances Campbell
born 1847/58
author, novelist, philanthropist, Native American welfare worker
Newton, MA
Cyc Am Bio and ad; Dict Am Auth; Nat Cyc Am Bio v10; Wom Cent

18288. Alexander, Grace
born 1848
social reformer
Index t Wom

18289. Diggs, Annie le Porte
1848/53–1916
Populist party leader, orator, politician, social reformer, temperance worker, journalist
Unitarian
Kansas
Canadian
Not Am Wom; Read Encyc Am West; Wom Cent

18290. Gould, Elizabeth Porter
born 1848
author, essayist on education, journalist, lecturer, social critic
Wom Cent

18291. Roby, Lelia P.
born 1848
philanthropist, founder of the Ladies of the Grand Army of the Republic, veteran's welfare worker
Index t Wom; Wom Cent

18292. Woolley, Celia (Parker)
1848–1918
settlement worker, worker for social services for Blacks, Unitarian minister, author, novelist
Chicago, IL
Dict Am Auth; Dict Am Bio; Wom Cent

18293. Yale, Caroline Ardelia
1848–1933
educator of the deaf
Congregationalist
Vermont
Dict Am Bio; Nat Cyc Am Bio v31; Not Am Wom

18294. Brown, Corinne Stubbs
born 1849
Socialist party member, labor activist, sociologist, educator
Index t Wom; Wom Cent

18295. de Graffenreid, Mary Clare
1849–1921
social investigator, writer on social conditions, labor authority
Georgia
Encyc South Hist; Not Am Wom

18296. Hammond, Lily Hardy
1849–1925
social reformer
Dict Am Rel Bio

18297. Meyer, Lucy Jane Rider
1849–1922
pioneer in Methodist urban social work and in the Methodist deaconess movement
Methodist
Not Am Wom

18298. Shelton, Emma Sanford
born 1849
social reformer
Index t Wom

18299. Thurman, Lucy Smith
1849–1918
social worker, club leader
Index t Wom

18300. Anderson, Elizabeth Milbank
1850–1921
World War I relief worker, philanthropist, patron of social welfare work, patron of Serbian and Yugoslavian welfare, patron of medical missions
Baptist

New York
Dict Am Bio; Nat Cyc Am Bio v23; Not Am Wom

18301. Beauchamp, Frances E.
flourished 1880s
social reformer, lecturer
Index t Wom

18302. Fedde, Elizabeth, Sister
1850–1921
Lutheran deacon, nurse, welfare worker, Catholic nun
Lutheran; Catholic
Norwegian
Index t Wom; Not Am Wom

18303. Joy, Charlotte Austin
flourished 1880s
social reformer
Index t Wom

18304. Mussey, Ellen (Persis) Spencer
1850–1936
international lawyer, law educator, feminist, women's rights worker, clubwoman, child welfare worker, Red Cross worker, social reformer
Swedenborgian
Washington, DC
Dict Am Bio supp v2; Index t Wom; Nat Cyc Am Bio v47 and csv1; Not Am Wom; Twent Cen Bio Dict Not Am

18305. Pugh, Esther
flourished 1880s
social reformer, temperance reformer, publisher
Index t Wom; Wom Cent

18306. Schoff, Hannah Kent
1850/53–1940
child welfare worker, juvenile court reformer, child aid leader, editor, author
Philadelphia, PA
Index t Wom; Nat Cyc Am Bio v18; Not Am Wom

18307. Johnston, Lizzie Johnston Evans
1851–1934
philanthropist, juvenile-prison reformer, Democratic party worker
Presbyterian
Alabama
Nat Cyc Am Bio v31

18308. Lane, Amanda
married 1876
social reformer
Index t Wom

18309. Martin, Lillian Jane
1851–1943

psychologist, gerontologist, worker for the welfare of the aged, suffragist, university educator
Index t Wom; Nat Cyc Am Bio v16; Obit File; Twent Cen Bio Dict Not Am

18310. Spencer, Anna Carpenter (Garlin)
1851–1931
Unitarian minister, journalist, educator, temperance worker, suffragist, pacifist, child-labor reformer, philanthropist
Unitarian
Dict Am Bio; Nat Cyc Am Bio v9 and csv2; Not Am Wom

18311. Decker, Sarah Sophia Chase Platt
1852–1912
civic and social reformer, educator
Index t Wom; Not Am Wom

18312. Smith, Zilpah Drew
1852?–1926
social worker
Not Am Wom

18313. Gardener, Helen Hamilton (Chenoweth)
1853/58–1925
author, novelist, essayist, feminist, suffragist, geneticist, biologist, sociologist, civil service commissioner
Dict Am Bio; Index t Wom; Nat Cyc Am Bio v9; Not Am Wom; Twent Cen Bio Dict Not Am; Wom Cent

18314. Sweet, Ada Celeste
1853–1928
journalist, editor, author, social reformer, philanthropist, pension agent
Chicago, IL
Index t Wom; Wom Cent

18315. Williams, Theresa Amelia
born 1853
philanthropist, social reformer
Index t Wom

18316. Woods, Katharine Pearson
1853–1923
fiction author, educator, social service worker
Dict Am Auth; Not Am Wom

18317. McDowell, Mary Eliza
1854–1936
settlement house director and founder, social welfare reformer and worker, NAACP member
Methodist
Dict Am Bio supp v2; Index t Wom; Nat Cyc Am Bio csv2; Not Am Wom

18318. Robertson, Alice Mary
1854–1931
educator of Native Americans, representative to Congress from Oklahoma, educator, social worker, postmaster
Oklahoma
Dict Am Bio; Index t Wom; Not Am Wom

18319. Streeter, Lilian Carpenter
born 1854
social worker
Nat Cyc Am Bio v17

18320. Babcock, Hannah Almy
1855–1931
music educator and director for the blind, suffragist, temperance worker
Nat Cyc Am Bio v16

18321. Fairchild, Mary Solome Cutler
1855–1921
librarian for the blind, nonfiction writer
New York
Dict Am Auth; Dict Am Bio; Index t Wom; Nat Cyc Am Bio v20; Not Am Wom; Twent Cen Bio Dict Not Am

18322. Iams, Lucy Virginia Dorsey
1855–1924
welfare worker, leader in reform legislation
Not Am Wom

18323. Jones, Minona Stearns Fitts
born 1855
politician, feminist, social reformer
Index t Wom

18324. Story, Daisy Allen
born 1855
social reformer
Nat Cyc Am Bio v16

18325. Dodge, Grace Hoadley
1856–1914
social welfare and charity worker, philanthropist, educator
New York
Cyc Am Bio; Dict Am Bio; Index t Wom; Nat Cyc Am Bio v18; Not Am Wom; Wom Cent

18326. Evans, Elizabeth Glendower
1856–1937
social reformer
Not Am Wom

18327. Mead, Lucia True (Ames)
1856–1936

pacifist, internationalist, suffragist, Black welfare and education worker, author
Unitarian
Nat Cyc Am Bio v28; Not Am Wom; Twent Cen Bio Dict Not Am

18328. Willard, Mary Hatch
1856–1926
businessperson, chef, social worker
Dict Am Bio

18329. Barrett, Kate Harwood Waller
1857/59–1925/29
social reformer, philanthropist, lecturer, social worker, suffragist, women's welfare worker
Virginia
Dict Am Bio; Encyc South Hist; Index t Wom; Not Am Wom

18330. Coman, Katharine
1857–1915
economic historian, writer on history, social reformer, educator
Ohio
Dict Am Auth; Index t Wom; Not Am Wom

18331. Gerberding, Elizabeth
born 1857
social reformer, sociologist
Index t Wom

18332. Hopkins, Archibald, Mrs.
born 1857
sociologist, social reformer
Index t Wom

18333. Mears, Mary Grinnell
1857–1935
child welfare worker
Nat Cyc Am Bio v31

18334. Alden, Cynthia May; Sunshine
1858/62–1931
journalist, editor, linguist, author, inventor, social worker, philanthropist, humanitarian
New York, NY
Dict Am Bio supp v1; Index t Wom; Nat Cyc Am Bio v14 and v22

18335. Birney, Alice Josephine McLellan
1858–1907
social welfare worker
Not Am Wom

18336. Crane, Caroline Julia Bartlett
1858–1935
Unitarian minister, People's Church minister, urban reformer, suffragist, city planner, sanitation expert

Unitarian
Index t Wom; Nat Cyc Am Bio v15; Not Am Wom

18337. Daniel, Annie Sturgis
1858–1944
physician, public health reformer, medical social worker
Not Am Wom; Obit File

18338. Dock, Lavinia Lloyd
1858–1956
nurse, medical author, settlement house worker, suffragist, feminist
Dict Am Bio; Index t Wom; Not Am Wom supp v1

18339. Dudley, Helena Stuart
1858/98–1932
settlement house worker, social reformer, pacifist
Index t Wom; Not Am Wom

18340. Kander, Lizzie Black
1858–1950
settlement house founder, cookbook author, social worker
Index t Wom; Not Am Wom

18341. Lathrop, Julia Edward Clifford
1858–1932
social worker, social reformer, chief of the US Children's Bureau
Dict Am Bio supp v1; Index t Wom; Nat Cyc Am Bio v24 and csv3; Not Am Wom

18342. Montgomery, Carrie Frances Judd
born 1858
church worker, poet, author, temperance worker, Salvation Army worker, social worker
New York; California
Index t Wom; Wom Cent

18343. Solomon, Hannah Greenebaum
1858–1942
clubwoman, founder of the National Council of Jewish Women, welfare worker
Jewish
Chicago, IL
Nat Cyc Am Bio v36; Not Am Wom

18344. Bowen, Louise Hadduck de Koven
1859–1953
philanthropist, welfare leader, Chicago social worker, president of Hull House, suffragist
Chicago, IL
Dict Am Bio supp v5; Index t Wom; Not Am Wom supp v1; Obit File

18345. Curtis, Georgina Pell
1859–1922
author, social worker
Index t Wom

18346. Davis, Edith Smith
married 1884
social reformer
Index t Wom

18347. Kehew, Mary Morton Kimball
1859–1918
social reformer in education and employment for women, labor organizer, worker for the welfare of children and the blind
Dict Am Bio; Not Am Wom

18348. Kelley, Florence
1859–1932
social reformer, social worker
Quaker
Dict Am Bio supp v1; Index t Wom; Nat Cyc Am Bio v23; Not Am Wom

18349. Starr, Ellen Gates
1859–1940
social reformer, settlement house worker, cofounder of Hull House
Dict Am Rel Bio; Not Am Wom

18350. Wittpenn, Caroline Bayard Stevens
1859–1932
welfare worker
New Jersey
Not Am Wom

18351. Addams, Jane
1860–1935
political activist, social reformer, sociologist, social welfare worker, settlement house founder, peace worker
Chicago, IL
Dict Am Auth; Dict Am Bio supp v1; Index t Wom; Nat Cyc Am Bio v13 and v27; Not Am Wom

18352. Armor, Mary Harris
flourished 1890s–1910s
social reformer
Index t Wom

18353. Coolidge, Mary Elizabeth Burroughs Roberts Smith
born 1860
sociologist
Index t Wom

18354. Davis, Katherine Bement
1860–1935
penologist, prison reformer, sociologist, social worker, philan-thropist, disaster relief worker in Italy
Dict Am Bio ad; Index t Wom; Nat Cyc Am Bio csv1; Not Am Wom

18355. Emig, Lelia Dromgold
flourished 1890s–1900s
social reformer, philanthropist
Index t Wom

18356. Goldmark, Pauline Dorothea
flourished 1890s–1930s
welfare worker, business research worker
Index t Wom

18357. Grandfield, Jennie McKee
married 1885
social reformer
Index t Wom

18358. Gregory, Ida Leona Sturdavent
born 1860
social worker, juvenile justice worker
Nat Cyc Am Bio v18

18359. Harvey, Jenny Dow
flourished 1890s–1920s
social worker
Index t Wom

18360. Rice, Isaac L., Mrs.
born 1860
social reformer, musician, linguist
Index t Wom

18361. Robbins, Jane Elizabeth
1860–1946
social worker, physician
Not Am Wom

18362. Stewart, Mary E. (Smith); Sun-saing Poo-in
flourished 1890s–1930s
worker for the welfare of Koreans in Southern California
California
Am Bio New Cyc

18363. Thacher, Ella Hoover
flourished 1890s
social reformer
Index t Wom

18364. Willmarth, Mary Hawes
flourished 1890s–1920s
social worker
Index t Wom

18365. Wilson, Ellen Louise Axson; Mrs. Woodrow Wilson
1860–1914
welfare worker, education worker for southern mountain people
Nat Cyc Am Bio v19

18366. Bates, Mary Elizabeth
1861/63–1954
surgeon, child welfare worker, suffragist
Denver, CO
Index t Wom; Nat Cyc Am Bio v18

18367. Bissell, Emily Perkins; Priscilla Leonard
1861–1948
welfare and child labor worker, author, inventor of Christmas Seals
Nat Cyc Am Bio v38; Not Am Wom; Obit File

18368. Hammond, Natalie Harris
1861–1931
social worker, philanthropist
Index t Wom; Nat Cyc Am Bio v24

18369. Kaufman, Betty Wolf
1861–1942
philanthropist, welfare worker
Jewish
Philadelphia, PA
Nat Cyc Am Bio v32

18370. Matthews, Victoria Earle
1861–98
social worker, mission society founder, clubwoman
Fort Valley, GA
Black
Index t Wom; Negro Alman; Prof Negro Wom v1

18371. Richmond, Mary Ellen
1861–1928
social worker, writer on charity
New York
Dict Am Auth; Nat Cyc Am Bio v21; Not Am Wom

18372. Scudder, Vida Dutton
1861–1954
social reformer, writer on English literature, author, university educator
Christian Scientist
Massachusetts
Cyc Am Bio; Dict Am Auth; Dict Am Bio supp v5; Index t Wom; Not Am Wom supp v1; Twent Cen Bio Dict Not Am; Wom Lit, More

18373. Einstein, Hannah Backman
1862–1929
social welfare worker
Not Am Wom

18374. Falconer, Martha Platt
1862–1941
social worker
Not Am Wom

18375. Jonas, Rosalie M.
1862–1953
poet, Black children's welfare worker
Obit File

18376. McCormick, Harriet Hammond
1862–1917
philanthropist, suffragist, patron of child welfare
Episcopalian
Nat Cyc Am Bio v21

18377. Moore, Helen
1862–1954
social worker, editor of the research publications of the Russell Sage Foundation
Obit File

18378. Nathan, Maud
1862–1946
social welfare leader, social worker, consumer advocate, suffragist, feminist, pacifist
Jewish
Dict Am Bio supp v4; Index t Wom; Nat Cyc Am Bio v15; Not Am Wom; Obit File

18379. Talbert, Mary Burnett
1862/66–1923
educator, social reformer, prison reformer, Black rights worker, club leader
Black
Index t Wom; Negro Alman; Prof Negro Wom v1

18380. Danner, Louise Rutledge
circa 1863–1943
welfare worker, YWCA official
Index t Wom

18381. Giffin, Etta Josselyn
1863–1932
librarian for the blind
Index t Wom

18382. Terrell, Mary Eliza Church
1863–1954
community leader, social reformer, suffragist, feminist, civil rights leader, NAACP organizer, lecturer, educator
Congregationalist
Washington, DC
Dict Am Bio supp v5; Encyc Black Am; Encyc South Hist; Index t Wom; Nat Cyc Am Bio v52; Negro Alman; Not Am Wom; Prof Negro Wom v1; World Great Men Col v2

18383. Brown, Ida Prescott Bigelow Eldredge
circa 1864–1950
social welfare leader
Index t Wom

18384. Kohut, Rebekah Bettelheim
1864–1951
social welfare leader, educator, suffragist, lecturer, author, Jewish welfare worker
Jewish
Hungarian
Index t Wom; Nat Cyc Am Bio v41 and csv5; Not Am Wom supp v1

18385. Peixotto, Jessica Blanche
1864–1941
social economist, university educator
Not Am Wom

18386. Zabriskie, Louise G.
1864–1963
nurse, social welfare leader
Index t Wom

18387. Bacon, Albion Fellows
1865–1933
housing reformer
Methodist
Indiana
Index t Wom; Nat Cyc Am Bio v34 and csv4; Not Am Wom

18388. Barrett, Janie Porter
1865–1948
social welfare leader, educator
Virginia
Black
Dict Am Bio supp v4; Negro Alman; Index t Wom; Not Am Wom; Prof Negro Wom

18389. Gordon, Jean Margaret
1865–1931
social welfare leader, suffrage leader
Not Am Wom

18390. Valentine, Lila Hardaway Meade
1865–1921
suffragist, educational reformer, public health worker
Virginia
Encyc South Hist; Not Am Wom

18391. Barnum, Gertrude
1866–1919/48
social worker, labor leader and reformer, government official
Bio Dict Am Lab; Not Am Wom

18392. Berry, Martha McChesney; Sunday Lady of the Possum Trot
1866–1942
educator, founder of the Berry School for underprivileged mountain children, philanthropist
Episcopalian

Georgia
Dict Am Bio supp v3; Encyc South Hist; Index t Wom; Nat Cyc Am Bio csv3; Not Am Wom; Obit File

18393. Blaine, Anita [Eugenie] McCormick
1866–1954
philanthropist, pacifist, patron of education and child welfare, patron of the League of Nations
Chicago, IL
Dict Am Bio supp v5; Nat Cyc Am Bio v44; Not Am Wom supp v1; Obit File

18394. Breckinridge, Sophonisba Preston
1866–1948
social worker, social economist, immigrant welfare worker, writer on social issues, educator, lawyer
Presbyterian
Dict Am Bio supp v4; Nat Cyc Am Bio v37; Not Am Wom

18395. Ingham, Mary Hall
1866–1937
reformer, suffragist
Not Am Wom

18396. McMain, Eleonor Laura
1866–1934
New Orleans settlement house worker and social reformer
New Orleans, LA
Not Am Wom

18397. Merrick, Mary Virginia
1866–1955
social worker, philanthropist, founder of the Christ Child Society to aid crippled children
Index t Wom; Obit File

18398. Stallings, Olive Andrews
born 1866
welfare worker
Catholic
New Orleans, LA
Nat Cyc Am Bio csv5

18399. Stearns, Lutie Eugenia
1866–1943
librarian, lecturer, social reformer
Index t Wom; Not Am Wom

18400. Sullivan, Anne; Anne Sullivan Macy
1866–1936
educator of the blind
Index t Wom; Not Am Wom

18401. Valesh, Eva McDonald
born 1866
printer, journalist, social reformer, feminist, labor leader and activist
Minneapolis, MN
Index t Wom; Wom Cent

18402. Wright, Sophie Bell
1866–1912
educator, night school founder, welfare worker, temperance worker
Nat Cyc Am Bio v10; Not Am Wom

18403. Balch, Emily Greene
1867–1961
pacifist, social reformer, sociologist, economist, winner of the Nobel Peace Prize
Quaker
Index t Wom; Nat Cyc Am Bio csv7; Not Am Wom; Obit File

18404. Gillespie, Mabel [Edna]
1867/77–1923
women's labor reformer, labor leader, social worker
Dict Am Bio; Nat Cyc Am Bio v23; Not Am Wom

18405. Gilman, Elizabeth
1867–1950
Socialist party worker, social reformer
Not Am Wom

18406. Hathaway, Maggie Smith
born 1867
educator, welfare worker, politician
Index t Wom

18407. Pratt, Anna Beach
1867–1932
social worker
Not Am Wom

18408. Simkhovich, Mary Melinda Kingsbury
1867–1951
settlement house worker, housing reformer, social worker, author
New York
Dict Am Bio supp v5; Index t Wom; Not Am Wom supp v1; Obit File

18409. van Vorst, Marie Louise
1867–1936
author, social reformer, poet
Index t Wom; Not Am Wom; Wom Lit, More

18410. Wald, Lillian D.
1867–1940
public health nurse, physician, social reformer, social worker, settlement house founder
Jewish
Dict Am Bio supp v2; Index t Wom; Nat Cyc Am Bio v29; Not Am Wom

18411. Cratty, Mabel
1868–1928
YWCA leader, social worker

Methodist
Dict Am Bio; Nat Cyc Am Bio v22; Not Am Wom

18412. Fuller, Minnie Ursula Oliver Scott Rutherford
1868–1946
temperance and child labor worker, suffragist
Arkansas
Encyc South Hist; Not Am Wom

18413. Guggenheim, Irene Rothschild
1868–1954
patron of child welfare, philanthropist
Jewish
New York
Nat Cyc Am Bio v44

18414. Kittredge, Mabel
1868–1955
World War I relief worker, school lunch crusader
Obit File

18415. McAdoo, Martha Allen
1868–1936
singer, social worker
Black
Encyc Black Am

18416. Pettit, Katherine
1868–1936
settlement house worker
Kentucky
Encyc South Hist; Not Am Wom

18417. Robins, Margaret Dreier
1868/69–1945
labor reformer, woman- and child-labor welfare worker, suffragist, feminist, social economist, founder of the Municipal League
Bio Dict Am Lab; Dict Am Bio supp v3; Index t Wom; Nat Cyc Am Bio v33; Not Am Wom; Obit File

18418. Barnum, Mary Gilmore
born 1869
educator, social worker, Los Angeles civic worker
Congregationalist
Los Angeles, CA
Nat Cyc Am Bio csv7

18419. Cameron, Donaldina MacKenzie
1869–1968
missionary, social reformer
Not Am Wom supp v1

18420. Eaves, Lucile
1869–1953
sociologist, labor relations expert
Unitarian
San Francisco, CA
Nat Cyc Am Bio v41 and csv1

18421. Glenn, Mary Wilcox Brown
1869–1940
social worker
Index t Wom; Not Am Wom

18422. Hamilton, Alice
1869–1970
industrial physician and toxicologist, pioneer in industrial medicine, medical educator, medical author, social reformer
Cur Biog '70; Index t Wom; Nat Cyc Am Bio csv7; Not Am Wom supp v1

18423. Hertz, Laura B.
born 1869
social reformer, sociologist
Index t Wom

18424. O'Day, Caroline Love Goodwin
1869/75–1943
social welfare worker, Democratic representative to Congress from New York, New Deal supporter, artist
Episcopalian
New York
Index t Wom; Nat Cyc Am Bio csv6; Not Am Wom; Obit File

18425. Regan, Agnes Gertrude
1869–1943
Catholic social welfare leader, educator, women's rights worker
Catholic
Dict Am Bio supp v3; Not Am Wom

18426. Williams, Elizabeth Sprague
1869–1922
social worker
Not Am Wom

18427. Yarros, Rachelle Slobodinsky
1869–1946
obstetrician, birth control and venereal-disease-control advocate, sanitarian
Nat Cyc Am Bio v35; Not Am Wom

18428. Arms, Julia
flourished 1900s
social reformer
Index t Wom

18429. Belias, Diana
flourished 1900s
social reformer, sociologist
Index t Wom

18430. Buell, Edith May
born 1870
educator of the deaf
Congregationalist
Nat Cyc Am Bio csv6

18431. Byington, Margaret
born 1870s; died 1952
educator, social worker
Bulgarian
Obit File

18432. Chapman, Wood-Allen, Mrs.
graduated 1895
social reformer
Index t Wom

18433. Edson, Katherine Philips
1870–1933
social reformer, government official
Not Am Wom

18434. Harriman, Florence Jaffray (Hurst)
1870–1967
Democratic party official, diplomat, minister to Norway, politician, journalist, suffragist, clubwoman, social rights worker, Red Cross worker in World War I, World War II relief worker in Norway
Washington, DC
Index t Wom; Nat Cyc Am Bio v53 and csv6; Not Am Wom supp v1; Obit File

18435. Hathaway, Winifred Phillips
circa 1870–1954
educator of the partially blind
Index t Wom; Obit File

18436. Hitchcock, Helen Sanborn (Sargent)
born 1870
social welfare worker, creator of social welfare programs to promote the arts
Episcopalian
Nat Cyc Am Bio v18

18437. Holt, Winifred
1870–1945
leader in work for the blind, sculptor
Dict Am Bio supp v3; Index t Wom; Not Am Wom

18438. Kingsbury, Susan Myra
1870–1949
social investigator, social work educator, social economist, feminist
Pennsylvania
Not Am Wom; Obit File

18439. Lothrop, Alice Louise Higgins
1870–1920
social worker
Dict Am Bio; Not Am Wom

18440. Robbins, Margaret Dreier
flourished 1900s–10s
sociologist
Index t Wom

18441. Swartz, Nelle
flourished 1900s–30s
social worker
Index t Wom

18442. Adler, Sophie Rosenwald
1871–1955
philanthropist, patron of the blind
Jewish
Obit File

18443. Crandall, Ella Philips
1871–1936/38
leader in public health nursing
Index t Wom; Not Am Wom

18444. Draper, Helen Fidelia
1871–1951
Red Cross nurse, World War I relief worker, social worker
Episcopalian
New York
Index t Wom; Nat Cyc Am Bio v39

18445. Fitzgerald, Susan Grimes Walker
1871–1943
labor worker, trade unionist, suffragist
Unitarian
Boston, MA
Nat Cyc Am Bio v32

18446. Gardner, Mary Sewall
1871–1961
public health nurse, author
Index t Wom; Not Am Wom supp v1

18447. Harvey, Kate Benedict Hanna
1871–1936
public health worker, patron of nursing, cattle breeder
Protestant Episcopal
Cleveland, OH
Nat Cyc Am Bio v34

18448. Minnigerode, Lucy
1871–1935
nurse, public health worker
Dict Am Bio supp v1; Index t Wom

18449. Park, Maud May Wood; C. J. Maywood
1871–1955
suffragist, feminist, civic leader, social worker, police reformer, pacifist
Dict Am Bio supp v5; Index t Wom; Nat Cyc Am Bio csv1; Not Am Wom supp v1

18450. Potter, Ellen Culver
1871–1958
physician, public health worker, welfare administrator, social worker
Dict Am Bio supp v6; Index t Wom

18451. Sabin, Florence Rena
1871–1953
physician, medical researcher and educator, anatomist, public health worker, first woman life member of the American Academy of Sciences, author
Colorado
Dict Am Bio supp v5; Index t Wom; Nat Cyc Am Bio v40 and csv3; Not Am Wom supp v1; Obit File

18452. Swope, Mary Paton
1871–1955
welfare worker
Obit File

18453. Wood, Edith (Elmer)
1871–1945
housing reformer, housing economist, novelist
Washington, DC
Dict Am Auth; Dict Am Bio supp v3; Index t Wom; Not Am Wom

18454. Breckinridge, Madeline McDowell
1872–1920
social reformer, social worker
Kentucky
Nat Cyc Am Bio v29; Not Am Wom

18455. Busbey, Katharine Graves
1872–1959
author, social reformer
Index t Wom

18456. Howard, Minnie F.
born 1872
author, historian, public welfare worker
Index t Wom

18457. Lyman, Amy Brown
born 1872
social worker
Index t Wom

18458. Prescott, Mary
1872–1961
tuberculosis-patient welfare worker
Obit File

18459. Preston, Alice
born 1872
concert singer, social worker
Nat Cyc Am Bio csv7

18460. Salomon, Alice
1872–1948
sociologist
Obit File

18461. Smith, Ruth Lyman
1872–1926
child welfare worker, religious worker, author
Index t Wom

18462. Vittum, Harriet E.
1872–1953
social worker, suffrage worker
Chicago, IL
Obit File

18463. Ward, Hortense Sparks Malsch
1872–1944
lawyer, social reformer
Texas
Not Am Wom

18464. Baker, Sarah Josephine
1873–1945
physician, public health administrator, child health pioneer
Unitarian
New York, NY
Dict Am Bio supp v3; Index t Wom; Nat Cyc Am Bio v36; Not Am Wom; Obit File

18465. Edwards, Edith
born 1873
social worker, suffragist, pacifist
Nat Cyc Am Bio v17

18466. Ickes, Anna Willmarth Thompson
1873–1935
reformer, Illinois state legislator
Illinois
Not Am Wom

18467. Kellor, Frances [Alice]; Frances Kellar
1873–1952
social investigator and reformer, arbitration specialist, immigrant-welfare worker, economist, author, sociologist
Dict Am Bio supp v5; Index t Wom; Nat Cyc Am Bio v15; Not Am Wom supp v1; Obit File

18468. Lamkin, Nina Belle
born 1873
educator, child welfare worker
Nat Cyc Am Bio v18

18469. Morgan, Anne Tracy
1873–1952
philanthropist, organizer of relief work in France during World War II, World War I relief worker, social worker
Dict Am Bio supp v5; Index t Wom; Nat Cyc Am Bio csv2 and csv5; Not Am Wom supp v1; Obit File

18470. Seligsberg, Alice Lillie
1873–1940
social worker, developer of Hadassah's medical program, Zionist
Jewish
Who Who Jew Hist

18471. Sloop, Mary T. Martin
1873–1962
physician, educator, social worker
Index t Wom

18472. Stern, Frances
1873–1947
social worker, dietician
Not Am Wom

18473. Bloodgood, Edith Holt
1874–1961
cofounder of the New York Association for the Blind and of *Searchlight*, a Braille magazine
New York
Obit File

18474. Dewson, Mary Williams
1874–1962
social worker, social reformer, suffragist, economist, politician, Democratic party official
Index t Wom; Not Am Wom supp v1

18475. Greaves, Jessie Royer
1874–1967
educator of the blind
United Church of Christ
Pennsylvania
Nat Cyc Am Bio v53

18476. Hammand, Emily Vanderbilt Sloane
1874–1907
philanthropist, social worker, Moral Rearmament Society member
Presbyterian
New York
Nat Cyc Am Bio v55 and csv8

18477. Loeb, Sophia Irene Simon
1874/76–1929
journalist, sponsor of welfare legislation, social reformer, social worker, author
New York
Russian
Dict Am Bio; Index t Wom; Nat Cyc Am Bio v24; Not Am Wom; Slavon Encyc

18478. Mather, Winifred Holt
1874–1945
sculptor, patron of welfare of the blind, founder of a school for the blind, author
Episcopalian
Nat Cyc Am Bio v34 and csv6

18479. Randolph, Virginia Estelle
1874/76–1958
social worker, educator
Virginia
Black
Index t Wom; Negro Alman; Prof Negro Wom v1

18480. Tillinghast, Anna Churchill Moulton
1874–1951
temperance worker, women's and children's welfare worker, Universalist pastor, suffragist
Universalist
Massachusetts
Nat Cyc Am Bio v45

18481. Tompers, Lucie Margaret
1874–1938
social worker
Baptist
New York
Canadian
Nat Cyc Am Bio v29

18482. Williams, Lulu Margaret Roberts
1874/75–1945
educator, social reformer, Black student aid worker
Black
Negro Alman; Prof Negro Wom v1

18483. Barnard, Kate
1875–1930
Democratic political reformer, Native American rights advocate, child welfare leader, philanthropist
Oklahoma
Index t Wom; Nat Cyc Am Bio v15, Not Am Wom; Read Encyc Am West

18484. Branch, Anna Hempstead
1875–1937
poet, social worker
New London, CT
Dict Am Auth; Index t Wom; Nat Cyc Am Bio csv3; Not Am Wom

18485. Gantt, Love Rosa Hirschmann
1875–1935
physician, public health worker
Index t Wom; Not Am Wom

18486. Jacobs, Pattie Ruffner
1875–1935
Alabama suffrage leader, child labor welfare worker, prison reformer, Prohibition party worker
Encyc South Hist; Not Am Wom

18487. Kelly, Myra
1875/76–1910
author, humorist, social reformer, educator
Irish
Dict Am Auth; Dict Am Bio; Index t Wom; Nat Cyc Am Bio v24; Wom Lit, More

18488. Kryszak, Mary Olszewski
1875–1945
Polish American welfare worker, Wisconsin state legislator
Wisconsin
Polish
Not Am Wom

18489. Martin, Anna Henrietta
1875–1951
suffragist, feminist, author, essayist, social critic, pacifist, politician
Nevada
Dict Am Bio supp v5; Not Am Wom supp v1; Read Encyc Am West

18490. Nelson, Alice Ruth Dunbar (Moore)
1875–1935
author, editor, social worker
Louisiana
Black
Encyc Black Am; Negro Alman; Not Am Wom; Prof Negro Wom v1

18491. Parsons, Elsie Clews
1875–1941
sociologist, anthropologist, folklorist, Native American ethnologist, president of the American Anthropology Association
Dict Am Bio supp v3; Index t Wom; Not Am Wom; Obit File; Read Encyc Am West

18492. Weed, Helen Hill
1875–1958
suffrage leader, pacifist, child labor reformer
Obit File

18493. Abbott, Edith
1876–1957
social reformer, social work educator, author
Nebraska
Dict Am Bio supp v6; Index t Wom; Nat Cyc Am Bio csv3; Not Am Wom; Obit File

18494. Beard, Mary
1876–1946

administrator and educator in nursing and public health, Rockefeller Foundation administrator, director of American Red Cross Nursing Service
Dict Am Bio supp v4; Index t Wom; Nat Cyc Am Bio v35; Obit File

18495. Campbell, Mary Dranga
1876–1957
welfare worker for the blind
Obit File

18496. Dunk, Edith Watkins
born 1876
consumer advocate, suffragist, welfare worker
Nat Cyc Am Bio v17

18497. Tracy, Martha
1876–1942
physician, public health expert, dean of the Women's Medical College of Pennsylvania
Philadelphia, PA
Index t Wom; Nat Cyc Am Bio v31; Not Am Wom

18498. Warburg, Frieda Schiff
1876–1958
philanthropist, Jewish welfare worker
Jewish
New York
Nat Cyc Am Bio v44; Obit File

18499. White, Eartha Mary Magdalene
1876–1974
social welfare worker, community leader, businessperson
Black
Not Am Wom supp v1

18500. Woodbury, Helen Laura Sumner
1876–1933
labor historian, social economist, author, government official
Dict Am Auth; Not Am Wom

18501. Cannon, Ida Maud
1877–1960
social worker, nurse, medical reformer, author
Dict Am Bio supp v5; Index t Wom; Not Am Wom supp v1

18502. Goldmark, Josephine
1877–1950
social legislation leader
Obit File

18503. Jarrett, Mary Cromwell
1877–1961
social worker, social work educator
Not Am Wom supp v1

18504. Moskowitz, Belle Lindner Israels
1877–1933
social worker, welfare worker, political leader, clubwoman, political adviser to New York governor Alfred E. Smith
Jewish
New York
Dict Am Bio supp v1; Index t Wom; Not Am Wom

18505. Riis, Mary Phillips
1877–1967
businessperson, social worker, financier
Index t Wom; Obit File

18506. Walrath, Florence Dahl
1877–1958
founder of adoption societies
Obit File

18507. Warbasse, Agnes Louise Dyer
1877–1945
cooperative manufacturer, cooperative housing expert, suffragist, pacifist
Nat Cyc Am Bio v34

18508. Abbott, Grace
1878–1939
public administrator, child welfare worker, social worker
Unitarian
Dict Am Bio supp v2; Index t Wom; Nat Cyc Am Bio v29 and csv3; Not Am Wom

18509. Borg, Madeleine Beer
1878–1956
social worker, humanitarian
Index t Wom

18510. Campbell, Eleanor Milbank Anderson
1878–1959
physician, social welfare worker, public health worker, patron of medicine
Baptist
Nat Cyc Am Bio v49 and csv4

18511. Chapin, Alice Delafield
1879–1964
educator, social welfare leader
Episcopalian
New York
Index t Wom; Nat Cyc Am Bio v52

18512. Dinwiddie, Emily Wayland
1879–1949
social worker, housing reformer
Not Am Wom

18513. Fisher, Welthy (Blakesley) Honsinger
1879/80–1980
Methodist missionary to India and China, social worker, educator, president of World Education, Inc.
Methodist
Cur Biog '69 and '81; Index t Wom

18514. Parker, Valeria Hopkins
1879–1959
physician, public health worker, Sorosis member
Index t Wom; Nat Cyc Am Bio csv1

18515. Thayer, Mary Appleton Shute
married 1904
social worker
Index t Wom

18516. Avary, Myrta Lockett
flourished 1910s
sociologist, politician, editor, author
Index t Wom

18517. Bernardy, Amy Allemand
born 1880
social reformer
Italian
Index t Wom

18518. Dunbar, Saidie [Sarah] Orr
1880–1960
patron of nursing and public health, developer of Christmas Seals
Catholic
Oregon
Nat Cyc Am Bio v51

18519. Gaines, Ruth
flourished 1910s
social worker, author
Index t Wom

18520. Hall, Helen
flourished 1910s–30s
social worker
Index t Wom

18521. Keller, Helen Adams
1880–1968
author, feminist, suffragist, educator, advocate for the handicapped, pacifist, Socialist party worker
Swedenborgian
Alabama
blind, deaf
Encyc South Hist; Index t Wom; Nat Cyc Am Bio v15 and v57; Not Am Wom supp v1; Obit File

18522. Mayer, Harriet Wilbur
flourished 1910s–30s
public welfare worker, translator
Index t Wom

18523. McKissick, Margaret Smith
flourished 1910s
sociologist, social reformer
Index t Wom

18524. Page, Lucy Gaston
flourished 1910s
social reformer, club leader
Index t Wom

18525. Palmer, A. M.
flourished 1910s
social reformer, sociologist
Index t Wom

18526. Perkins, Edna Brush
1880–1930
author, social worker
Cincinnati, OH
Nat Cyc Am Bio v26

18527. Perkins, Frances; Mrs. Paul C. Wilson
1880/82–1965
social worker and reformer, US secretary of labor
Index t Wom; Nat Cyc Am Bio csv4 and csv6; Not Am Wom supp v1; Obit File

18528. Sargent, Ellen C.
flourished 1910s
social reformer
Index t Wom

18529. Shapiro, Dora Monness
1880–1952
philanthropist, Jewish welfare worker
Jewish
Obit File

18530. Vail, Stella Boothe
flourished 1910s–20s
nurse, author, social worker
Index t Wom

18531. van Winkle, Mina Ginger
born 1880
social worker, lieutenant in the police force, suffragist
Nat Cyc Am Bio csv3

18532. Walter, Mary Jane
flourished 1910s
social reformer, evangelist
Index t Wom

18533. Windsor, Helen Howell
1880–1926
social welfare worker
Episcopalian
Iowa
Nat Cyc Am Bio v20

18534. Bailey, Elizabeth Donovan
1881–post 1930
social welfare worker
Catholic

New York
Index t Wom; Nat Cyc Am Bio
csv5

18535. Eastman, Crystal
1881–1928
social investigator, peace worker,
feminist, suffragist
Not Am Wom

18536. Lundberg, Emma Octavia
1881–1954
social worker
Not Am Wom supp v1

18537. Pinchot, Cornelia Elizabeth Bryce
1881–1960
politician, suffragist, women's
rights worker, worker for the
welfare of women and children,
advocate of social welfare legislation
Dict Am Bio supp v6; Not Am
Wom supp v1

18538. Rumsey, Mary Harriman
1881–1934
social welfare leader, New York
civic worker, spokesperson for
consumer interests, chairperson
of the Consumer Advisory
Board, defense worker during
World War I
New York
Dict Am Bio supp v1; Nat Cyc
Am Bio v24 and csv4; Not Am
Wom

18539. Stein, Beatrice Borg
1881–1958
welfare leader, philanthropist,
founder of the Play School Association
Jewish
New York
Nat Cyc Am Bio v47; Obit File

18540. Stewart, Sallie W.
1881–1951
educator, clubwoman, realtor,
lecturer, Black women's welfare
worker
Indiana
Black
Negro Alman; Prof Negro Wom
v1

18541. Colcord, Joanna Carver (Bruno)
1882–1960
social worker, director of the
Russell Sage Foundation, author
Index t Wom; Not Am Wom
supp v1; Obit File

18542. Cummins, Grace
1882–1953

Presbyterian leader, religious educator, social worker
Presbyterian
Obit File

18543. Gulliver, Lucile
born 1882
social studies text author
Nat Cyc Am Bio csv2

18544. Hunter, Jane Edna
1882–1971
social worker, nurse, educator,
clubwoman
Cleveland, OH
Black
Index t Wom; Negro Alman; Prof
Negro Wom v1

18545. Mason, Lucy Randolph
1882–1959
labor publicist, public relations
officer for the CIO, southern
trade union organizer, social
worker and reformer, suffragist
Episcopalian
Virginia
Bio Dict Am Lab; Dict Am Bio
supp v6; Encyc South Hist; Not
Am Wom supp v1; Obit File

18546. Rippen, Jane Parker Deeter
1882–1953
social worker, journalist, Girl
Scouts of America executive
Not Am Wom supp v1; Obit File

18547. Schneiderman, Rose
1882/84–1972
labor organizer, Women's Trade
Union leader, secretary of the
New York State Labor Department, social reformer, suffragist
Jewish
Polish; Russian
Bio Dict Am Lab; Cur Biog '72;
Index t Wom; Not Am Wom
supp v1; Obit File

18548. Taft, Jessie
1882–1960
psychologist, social work educator
Not Am Wom supp v1

18549. Gibbons, Helen Davenport Brown
1883–1960
novelist, founder of Sauvons les
Bebes, a World War I orphan
aid agency
Obit File

18550. Haynes, Elizabeth A. Ross
1883–1953
YWCA official, social researcher,
social worker, author, businessperson, community leader
Index t Wom; Not Am Wom
supp v1

18551. Porter, Delia Lyman
died 1933
social reformer
Index t Wom

18552. van Kleeck, Mary Abby
1883–1972
social researcher, social reformer
Index t Wom; Not Am Wom
supp v1

18553. Fox, Elizabeth Gordon
1884–1958
nurse, director of the Red Cross
Public Health Nursing Program, president of the National
Organization for Public Health
Nursing
Index t Wom; Obit File

18554. Olcott, Virginia
graduated 1909
social worker, educator, author
Index t Wom

18555. Roosevelt, [Anna] Eleanor
1884–1962
social reformer, humanitarian,
author, lecturer
Washington, DC
English
Eng Wom; Index t Wom; Nat
Cyc Am Bio v57 and csv4 and
csv6; Not Am Wom supp v1;
Obit File

18556. Bremer, Edith Terry
1885–1964
social worker, founder of the International Institute movement
Not Am Wom supp v1

18557. Bryant, Louise Frances Stevens
1885–1959
social researcher, medical editor,
feminist, Socialist party worker,
physician, public health worker
Dict Am Bio supp v5

18558. Hutchins, Grace
1885–1969
labor researcher, social reformer
Not Am Wom supp v1

18559. Woerishoffer, Emma Carola
1885–1911
philanthropist, social worker
Not Am Wom

18560. Eustis, Dorothy Leib Harrison Wood
1886–1946
philanthropist, patron of agriculture, founder and president of
the Seeing-Eye Association, dog
breeder
Dict Am Bio supp v4; Index t
Wom; Nat Cyc Am Bio csv5;
Not Am Wom; Obit File

18561. Slade, Caroline McCormick
1886–1951
novelist, social worker, civic
worker, suffragist, founder of
the National League of Women
Voters
New York
Index t Wom

18562. Addition, Henrietta Silvis
born 1887
social worker, educator
Index t Wom

18563. Deardorff, Neva R.
1887–1958
social welfare statistical expert,
president of the Child Welfare
League of America, cofounder
of the Health Insurance Plan of
Greater New York
New York
Obit File

18564. Dexter, Edith MacBride
1887–1958
ophthalmologist, public health
worker
Presbyterian
Pennsylvania
Nat Cyc Am Bio v49

18565. Ladd, Mary Babbott
1887–1964
New York civic worker, worker
for the welfare of the aged
Nat Cyc Am Bio v51

18566. Meyer, Agnes Elizabeth (Ernst)
1887–1970
author, journalist, vice-president
and co-owner of *The Washington Post*, World War II correspondent, autobiographer,
lecturer, social worker, Republican party worker, crusader for
social services and education
causes
Lutheran
New York
Cur Biog '70; Index t Wom; Nat
Cyc Am Bio v56; Obit File

18567. van Waters, Miriam
1887–1974
penologist, social worker, writer
on penology
Cur Biog '74; Index t Wom; Not
Am Wom supp v1

18568. Woodward, Ellen Sullivan
1887–1971
federal official, state legislator,
public welfare worker
Encyc South Hist; Not Am Wom
supp v1

18569. Blakeslee, Myra Allen
circa 1888–1953
advertising executive, social welfare worker
Index t Wom

18570. Peck, Lillie
1888–1957
leader in the settlement house movement, social worker, president of the International Federation of Settlements, German welfare worker after World War II
Dict Am Bio supp v6; Obit File

18571. Denison, Elsa
born 1889
social reformer
Index t Wom

18572. Fischel, Marguerite Kauffman
1889–1950
composer, worker for the welfare of young cerebral palsy victims
Jewish
Obit File

18573. Magee, Elizabeth Stewart
born 1889
social worker, labor leader
Index t Wom

18574. Routzahn, Mary Swain
married 1914
social worker
Index t Wom

18575. Stern, Elizabeth Gertrude Levin; Eleanor Morton; Elsie-Jeab
1889/90–1954
author, editor, social worker, political activist and antiwar worker
Quaker
Nat Cyc Am Bio v39; Obit File

18576. Bertola, Mariana
flourished 1920s
physician, child welfare worker, educator
Index t Wom

18577. Carr, Charlotte E.
1890–1956
personnel manager, social worker, settlement house director
Dict Nat Bio supp v6; Index t Wom; Obit File

18578. Dawley, Almira
1890–1956
sociologist, educator
Dict Nat Bio supp v6

18579. Kennedy, Rose (Fitzgerald)
born 1890

18580. Merrill, Eleanor Brown
flourished 1920s–30s
humanitarian, worker with the blind
Index t Wom

18581. Mulliner, Gabrielle
flourished 1920s
lawyer, sociologist
Index t Wom

18582. Stuart, Cora Wilson
flourished 1920s
educator, social reformer
Index t Wom

18583. Wales, Marguerite
flourished 1920s–30s
public health nurse
Index t Wom

18584. Williams, Fannie Ransom
flourished 1920s
constitutionalist, World War I soldier's welfare worker
Presbyterian
North Carolina
Nat Cyc Am Bio v21

18585. Eliot, Martha May
1891–1978
pediatrician, public health official, president of the American Health Association, UNICEF member, US Children's Bureau official
Unitarian
Massachusetts
Cur Biog '78; Index t Wom; Nat Cyc Am Bio v60

18586. Lenroot, Katharine Fredrica
born 1891
government official, social worker, child health worker
Congregationalist
Wisconsin
Index t Wom; Nat Cyc Am Bio csv7

18587. Street, Margaret Berry
1891–1967
cattle farmer, lawyer, Civil Air Regulations executive, suffragist, Black welfare worker
Presbyterian
North Carolina
Nat Cyc Am Bio v54

18588. Warner, Estella Ford
born 1891
pioneer public health surgeon
Index t Wom

philanthropist, patron of welfare work for the mentally retarded and of research on mental retardation
Catholic
Cur Biog '70

18589. Coyle, Grace Longwell
1892–1962
social work educator
Not Am Wom supp v1

18590. Gifford, Myrnie Ada
1892–1966
public health administrator, pediatrician, conservationist
California
Nat Cyc Am Bio v54

18591. Hamilton, Gordon
1892–1967
social worker, educator
Not Am Wom supp v1

18592. Haupt, Alma Cecelia
1892–1956
authority of public health nursing, administrative educator
Dict Am Bio supp v6

18593. Herbst, Josephine Frey; Josephine Herrmann
1892/99–1962
novelist, reporter of radical social and political movements in the 1930s, member of a European avant-garde writers circle in the 1920s
Dict Lit Bio v9; Index t Wom; Not Am Wom supp v1; Obit File; Wom Lit, More

18594. Hoey, Jane Margueretta
1892–1968
social worker, federal official
Index t Wom; Not Am Wom supp v1

18595. Lewisohn, Alice Irene
1892–1944
social worker, theatrical patron and innovator
Index t Wom; Not Am Wom

18596. Cook, Fannie Bruce
1893–1949
author, social novelist
Index t Wom; Obit File

18597. Kahn, Dorothy C.
1893–1955
chief of the social services section of the UN Secretariat
Obit File

18598. McIver, Pearl
born 1893
public health worker, nurse, government official
Index t Wom

18599. Reeves, Margaret
born 1893
child welfare worker
Index t Wom

18600. Smith, Caroline E.
died 1943

early proponent of Braille
Obit File

18601. Bellanca, Dorothy Jacobs
1894–1946
trade union organizer, founder and only woman vice-president of the Amalgamated Clothing Workers union, social reformer, politician
Jewish
Russian
Bio Dict Am Lab; Dict Am Bio supp v3; Not Am Wom; Obit File

18602. Cutting, Helen McMahon
1894–1961
worker for the welfare of the blind, traveler
New York
Nat Cyc Am Bio v47

18603. Ireland, Margaret Allen
1894–1961
public health worker, Cleveland civic worker, welfare worker
Episcopalian
Cleveland, OH
Nat Cyc Am Bio v50

18604. Kuhne, Marie Peary
1894–1978
authority on Arctic history, Inuit welfare worker
Obit File

18605. Kiser, Louise Venable Kennedy
1895–1954
sociologist, demographer
Presbyterian
Nat Cyc Am Bio v42

18606. Robinson, Gladys Lloyd Cassell
born 1895
actor, social worker
New York
Nat Cyc Am Bio csv6

18607. Dodge, Eva Francette
born 1896
obstetrician, medical educator, birth control and Planned Parenthood worker, public health worker
Baptist
Nat Cyc Am Bio csv12

18608. Towle, Charlotte Helen
1896–1966
social work educator
Not Am Wom supp v1

18609. Bronson, Ruth Muskrat
born 1897
Cherokee government official, field representative of Save the Children Federation

Oklahoma
Native American (Cherokee)
Ind Today; Read Encyc Am West

18610. Coolidge, Grace Anna Goodhue
1897–1957
worker for welfare of the deaf
Index t Wom; Not Am Wom supp v1

18611. Day, Dorothy
1897–1980
journalist, social worker, political activist, fiction writer on Catholic life
Catholic
Cur Biog '82; Index t Wom

18612. Goldthwaite, Lucy A.
1897–1957
librarian in the New York Public Library for the Blind, founder of the *Braille Book Review*
New York
Obit File

18613. Heller, Florence Gunsfeld
1897–1966
philanthropist, patron of medicine, Jewish welfare worker
Jewish
Chicago, IL
Nat Cyc Am Bio v51

18614. Prince, Mildred Mallon
1897–1961
lawyer, social legislation agitator, San Francisco civic worker
Catholic
San Francisco, CA
Nat Cyc Am Bio v47

18615. Smith, Lilian Eugenia
1897–1966
novelist, newspaper columnist, writer on race relations, civil rights worker, editor, social worker, educator, lecturer
Florida
Encyc South Hist; Index t Wom; Not Am Wom supp v1; Obit File; Wom Lit; Wom Lit, More

18616. Carter, Lillian "Bessie"
born 1898
nurse, social service worker, peace worker, civil rights worker
Georgia
Cur Biog '78

18617. Glueck, Eleanor (Touroff)
1898–1972
research criminologist, Harvard Law School criminologist, pioneer in the study of juvenile delinquency, social worker

New York; Massachusetts
Cur Biog '72; Index t Wom; Nat Cyc Am Bio v57; Not Am Wom supp v1; Obit File

18618. Barrett, S. Ruth
1899–1961
educator of the blind
Obit File

18619. Carter, Eunice Hunton
1899–1970
lawyer, community leader, social worker
New York
Black
Not Am Wom supp v1; Obit File

18620. Arnold, Mary
flourished 1930s
social worker
Index t Wom

18621. Benson, Marguerite
flourished 1930s
social hygiene worker
Index t Wom

18622. Broido, Lucy Kaufmann
1900–69
welfare agency leader
Jewish
New York, NY
Nat Cyc Am Bio v55

18623. Clark, Mary Augusta
flourished 1930s
public health worker
Index t Wom

18624. Danser, Fanny Root
flourished 1930s
clubwoman, missionary, social reformer
Index t Wom

18625. Estelle, Helen G. H.
flourished 1930s
educator, social reformer
Index t Wom

18626. Hartman, May Weisser
born circa 1900
humanitarian, social welfare leader
Index t Wom

18627. Kmetz, Annette L.
flourished 1930s
nurse, public health worker
Index t Wom

18628. Kutz, Sally
flourished 1930s
public health worker
Index t Wom

18629. MacLeod, Dorothy Shaw
born 1900
religious leader, social worker
Index t Wom

18630. McGarvah, Eleanor
flourished 1930s
public health nurse
Index t Wom

18631. Pinney, Jean Burrows
flourished 1930s
editor, social hygiene worker
Index t Wom

18632. Randall, Ollie Annette
flourished 1930s
social worker, humanitarian
Index t Wom

18633. Read, Katherine S.
flourished 1930s
public health nurse
Index t Wom

18634. Reyner, Rebecca Hourwich
flourished 1930s
social worker, journalist
Index t Wom

18635. Rosenman, Dorothy Reuben
born 1900
housing expert
Index t Wom

18636. Sheppard, Jeanie R.
flourished 1930s
social worker, humanitarian
Index t Wom

18637. Switzer, Mary Elizabeth
1900–71
commissioner of welfare and rehabilitation programs for HEW, welfare worker for the disabled
Episcopalian
Index t Wom; Nat Cyc Am Bio v56; Not Am Wom supp v1; Obit File

18638. Thurber, Louise Lockwood
flourished 1930s
humanitarian, feminist, social worker
Index t Wom

18639. Todd, Jane Hedges
flourished 1930s
social worker, politician
Index t Wom

18640. Weisner, Dorothy E.
flourished 1930s
statistician, social worker
Index t Wom

18641. Baumgartner, Leona; Mrs. Nathaniel M. Elias
born 1902
pediatrician, public health official
Presbyterian
New York, NY
Index t Wom; Nat Cyc Am Bio csv9

18642. Blue, Edna
1902–41
founder and international chairperson of the Foster Parents' Plan for War Children
Obit File

18643. George, Zelma Watson
1903–post 1960
alternate delegate to the UN, sociologist, singer
Black
Index t Wom; Negro Alman; Negro Her Lib v1

18644. Moore, Elisabeth Luce
born 1903
social worker
Index t Wom

18645. Arnstein, Margaret Gene
1904–72
public health nurse, nursing educator
Not Am Wom supp v1

18646. Goldsmith, Grace Arabell
1904–75
physician, public health educator, nutritionist
Episcopalian
Louisiana
Nat Cyc Am Bio csv10; Not Am Wom supp v10

18647. Lee, Rose Hum
1904–64
sociologist
Chinese
Not Am Wom supp v1

18648. Lord, Mary Stimson Pillsbury
born 1904
social welfare worker, UN representative, humanitarian
Index t Wom

18649. Mann, Marty
born 1904
alcoholism authority
Episcopalian
Nat Cyc Am Bio csv11

18650. McGeachy, Mary Agnes Craig
born 1904
social worker, administrator
Index t Wom

18651. Bauer, Catherine Krouse
1905–64
housing expert, planner
Not Am Wom supp v1

18652. Wurster, Catherine Bauer
1905–64

advertising executive, international consultant on housing and city planning, journalist
Nat Cyc Am Bio v51

18653. Duvall, Evelyn Ruth Millis
born 1906
social counselor
Index t Wom

18654. Hayman, Charlotte Law
born 1906
social worker
Index t Wom

18655. Komarovsky, Mirra
born 1906
educator, sociologist
Russian
Index t Wom

18656. Taeuber, Irene Barnes
1906–74
demographer
Not Am Wom supp v1

18657. Taueber, Irene Barnes
1906–74
demographer, sociologist, UNESCO member
Nat Cyc Am Bio v58; Not Am Wom supp v1

18658. Weed, Ethel Berenice
1906–75
military officer, Japanese women's rights advocate
Not Am Wom supp v1

18659. Hagood, Margaret Lloyd Jarman
1907–63
sociologist, statistician, demographer
Not Am Wom supp v1

18660. Resnick, Rose
graduated 1934
educator of the blind, humanitarian
Index t Wom

18661. Milligan, Lucy Richardson
flourished 1940s–50s
New York civic leader, antifascist, Jewish welfare worker, Hadassah worker, cancer worker
Nat Cyc Am Bio v53

18662. Schain, Josephine
flourished 1940s
consultant, social worker, lecturer
Index t Wom

18663. Gayl, Jeannette Orleans
born 1911
president of the Women's American Organization for Rehabilitation through Training
Obit File

18664. McKenny, Ruth
1911–72
author, short story writer, humorist, writer on social causes
Cur Biog '72; Index t Wom; Obit File

18665. Height, Dorothy Irene
born 1912/13
social worker, YWCA executive, civil rights worker, president of the National Council of Negro Women
Cur Biog '72; Encyc Black Am; Negro Alman

18666. Holbrook, Sabra Rollins
born 1912
educator, youth worker
Index t Wom

18667. Preminger, Marion Hill; Mrs. Albert Mayer
1913–72
social worker, author, African art collector, missionary to the Congo, philanthropist, screen actor
Catholic
New York
Hungarian
Nat Cyc Am Bio v57; Obit File

18668. Hardwick, Elizabeth
born 1916
novelist, essayist, short story writer, literary critic, social critic, editor of the *New York Review of Books*
Cur Biog '81; Dict Lit Bio v6

18669. Jacobs, Jane (Butzner)
born 1916
urbanologist, writer on cities
Cur Biog '77

18670. Smith, Mary Elizabeth Leinen
born 1917
business executive, worker for the welfare of the handicapped, philanthropist
Nat Cyc Am Bio csv13

18671. Hewell, Grace
born 1918
educator; social worker; HEW official; chief of education, House Committee on Education and Labor
Washington, DC
Black
Encyc Black Am; Negro Her Lib v1

18672. Smart, Alice McGee
flourished 1950s
sociologist, poet, educator
Index t Wom

18673. Moore, Jenny
1923–73

social activist, author
Obit File

18674. Rapoport, Lydia
1923–71
social work educator
Not Am Wom supp v1

18675. Smith, Elizabeth Bacheler "Isabel"
born 1924
founder of AYH
Not Am Wom

18676. Moore, Joan W.
born 1929
sociologist, student of Mexican American culture, author, educator
Dict Mex Am Hist

18677. Harris, Ladonna
flourished 1960s–70s
health reformer, women's rights worker
Native American (Comanche)
Ind Today

18678. Hastings, Lucille Ahnawake
flourished 1960s
social worker
Native American (Cherokee)
Ind Today

18679. Lindsay, Inabel Burns
flourished 1930s–50s
social worker
Black
Prof Negro Wom v2

18680. Manning, Leah Hicks
flourished 1960s
social worker
Native American (Shoshone-Paiute-Cherokee)
Ind Today

18681. Jackson, Jaquelyn Johnson
born 1932
sociologist, educator
Black
Encyc Black Am

18682. Morris, Christine
born 1932
sociologist, anthropologist
Native American (Blackfoot)
Ind Today

18683. Brownmiller, Susan
born 1935
feminist leader, writer on rape and social issues, journalist
Cur Biog '78

18684. Deer, Ada
born 1935
social worker, worker for Native American rights

Native American (Menominee)
Ind Today

18685. Baca-Barragan, Polly
born 1941
Colorado state senator, housing reformer
Colorado
Mexican
Dict Mex Am Hist

SPORTS, GAMES, AND ATHLETICS

18686. Walworth, Julianna Morgan
1769–1853
equestrian
Cyc Am Bio

18687. Davene, William, Mrs.
flourished 1800s
circus acrobat
Index t Wom

18688. Bayley, Gertrude Arthur
flourished 1860s
western pioneer, mountain climber
Index t Wom

18689. Mather, Margaret Morgan (Herbert)
184?–1900
writer on polo and fox hunting
Dict Am Auth

18690. Salm Salm, Agnes Elizabeth Winona Joy (Leqlerq), Princess
1840/42–1881/1912
circus rider, rope dancer, actor, field hospital worker and organizer, philanthropist
Cyc Am Bio; Dict Am Bio; Twent Cen Bio Dict Not Am

18691. Homans, Amy Morris
1848–1933
educator, physical education director
Index t Wom

18692. Peck, Annie Smith
1850–1933/35
mountain climber, musician, archaeologist, lecturer, educator
Rhode Island
Index t Wom; Nat Cyc Am Bio v15; Not Am Wom; Wom Cent

18693. Pennell, Elizabeth (Robins)
1855–1936
author, travel writer, biographer, art critic, bicycle tourer
Dict Am Auth; Index t Wom; Nat Cyc Am Bio v10; Not Am Wom

18694. Workman, Fanny (Bullock)
1859–1925
traveler, author on travel, explorer of the Himalayas, mountain climber
Dict Am Auth; Dict Am Bio; Index t Wom; Not Am Wom

18695. Brown, Charles S., Mrs.
flourished 1890s
golfer
Index t Wom

18696. Oakley, Annie; Phoebe Anne Oakley Mozee
1860–1926
trapshooter, sharpshooter, marksperson
Dict Am Bio; Hall Fame Sport; Not Am Wom; Read Encyc Am West

18697. Blodgett, Daisy Albertine Peck
1862–1947
philanthropist, equestrian
Washington, DC
Nat Cyc Am Bio v37

18698. James, Annie Laurie Wilson
born 1862
journalist, editor, horse breeding expert
California
Index t Wom; Wom Cent

18699. Hilles, Florence Bayard
1865–1954
suffragist, feminist, ERA worker, pacifist, golfer
Episcopalian
Delaware
Nat Cyc Am Bio v46

18700. Robinson, Josephine de Mott
1865–1948
circus performer, equestrian
Index t Wom; Obit File

18701. Bancroft, Jessie Hubbell
1867–1952
physical education specialist
Not Am Wom supp v1

18702. Berenson, Senda
1868–1954
basketball player, gymnast, physical education authority
Jewish
Lithuanian
Dict Am Bio supp v5

18703. Toulmin, Bertha Townsend
1869–1909
tennis player
Hall Fame Sport

18704. Sutton, Mary G.
flourished 1900s
tennis player
Index t Wom

18705. Taylor, Anna
flourished 1900s
stuntperson
Index t Wom

18706. Kingsley, Elizabeth Seelman
1871–1957
crossword puzzle maker, inventor of the double-crostic literary puzzle
Dict Am Bio supp v46; Obit File

18707. Perrin, Ethel
1871–1962
physical education specialist
Not Am Wom supp v1

18708. Varden, Dolly
1871–1955
circus aerialist and equestrian
Obit File

18709. Wallach, Maud Barger
1871–1954
tennis player
Hall Fame Sport

18710. Dreyfuss, Florence Wolf
1872–1958
owner of the Pittsburgh Pirates baseball team
Obit File

18711. Pound, Louise
1872–1958
university educator, writer on literature, folklorist, tennis player, bicyclist, golfer
Nebraska
Nat Cyc Am Bio v45, csv2, and csv5; Not Am Wom supp v1; Obit File

18712. Monroe, Anne Shannon
1874/77–1942
author, essayist, novelist, magazine writer, Oregon historian, feminist, lecturer, mountain climber
Oregon
Index t Wom; Nat Cyc Am Bio; Obit File

18713. Pouch, Helena R. Hellwig
1874–1960
humanitarian, president of DAR, tennis champion
Index t Wom; Obit File

18714. Dunn, Mary A.
1875–1963
owner of the Baltimore Orioles baseball team
Obit File

18715. Whitney, Helen (Hay)
1876–1944
philanthropist, poet, children's author, financier, equestrian expert, owner of Greentree Racing Stables
Dict Am Auth; Index t Wom; Nat Cyc Am Bio v33; Obit File

18716. Bancroft, Jane Wallis Waldron
1877–1949
publisher of the *Wall Street Journal*, president of the Dow Jones & Co. newsgathering organization, Boston civic worker, equestrian
Boston, MA
Nat Cyc Am Bio v38; Obit File

18717. Moore, Elizabeth H.
1877–1959
tennis player
Hall Fame Sport

18718. Arden, Elizabeth; Florence Nightingale Graham
1878/84–1966
cosmetician, entrepreneur, founder of Elizabeth Arden Inc., owner of Main Chance racing stables
Canadian
Index t Wom; Not Am Wom supp v1; Obit File

18719. Barnard, Tissayac
born 1878
pioneer, mountain climber
Index t Wom

18720. McKinstry, Helen May
1878–1949
president of Russell Sage College, physical education expert
Presbyterian
New York
Nat Cyc Am Bio v37; Obit File

18721. Bigsby, Helene Hathaway Robinson
1879–1950
first woman to own a major league baseball club, the St. Louis Cardinals
Obit File

18722. Bradna, Ella
1879–1957
circus bareback equestrian
Bohemian
Obit File

18723. Charmon; The Perfect Woman
flourished 1910s
actor, acrobat
Index t Wom

18724. Hoyt, Beatrix "Trixie"
1880–1963

18715. Whitney, Helen (Hay) — golfer
Hall Fame Sport; Obit File

18725. Sears, Eleanora Randolph
1881–1968
tennis player, squash champion, patron of equestrian sports and figure skating
Hall Fame Sport; Index t Wom; Not Am Wom supp v1; Obit File

18726. Burright, Neva "Grandma"
1883–1958
harness racing driver
Obit File

18727. Curtis, Margaret
1883–1965
golfer
Hall Fame Sport

18728. Hurd, Dorothy Iona Campbell
1883–1945
golfer
Hall Fame Sport

18729. Patterson, Myra Doremus
1883–1957
golf champion
Obit File

18730. Phipps, Henry Carnegie, Mrs.
1883–1970
owner of Wheatly Racing Stables
Obit File

18731. Wagner, Mara
1883–1975
tennis player
Hall Fame Sport

18732. Sandwina, Kati
1884–1952
circus strongperson
Obit File

18733. Hutchinson, Mary Amory Hare; Amory Hare
1885–1969
author, novelist, dramatist, painter, poet, thoroughbred-horse breeder
Episcopalian
California
Nat Cyc Am Bio v57, Index t Wom

18734. Mulhall, Lucille
1885–1940
equestrian
Obit File

18735. Clothier, Anita Porter
1886–1955
Philadelphia civic worker, equestrian

Philadelphia, PA
Nat Cyc Am Bio v50

18736. Wightman, Hazel Hotchkiss; Hazel Whiteman
1886/96–1974
tennis, squash and badminton player
Hall Fame Sport; Index t Wom; Not Am Wom supp v1; Obit File

18737. Allerdice, Ellen Hansell
died 1937
tennis player
Hall Fame Sport

18738. Bundy, May Sutton
1887–1975
tennis player, Wimbledon champion
Hall Fame Sport; Obit File

18739. McCutcheon, Floretta Doty
1888–1967
bowler
Hall Fame Sport; Index t Wom

18740. Callender, Bessie Stough
1889–1951
sculptor, mountain climber
Presbyterian
Nat Cyc Am Bio v38

18741. Andrews, Emily Russell
1890–1973
physical education authority
Congregationalist
Nat Cyc Am Bio v57

18742. Brooks, Erica May
flourished 1920s–30s
athlete, lecturer
English
Index t Wom

18743. Burr, Frances; Mrs. John Reynolds
1890–post 1930s
artist, mountaineer, suffragist
Index t Wom; Nat Cyc Am Bio csv12

18744. Cummings, Edith
flourished 1920s
golfer
Index t Wom

18745. Fletcher, Jennie
1890–1968
swimmer
Hall Fame Sport

18746. Goss, Margaret
flourished 1920s
journalist, athlete
Index t Wom

18747. Hawley, Gertrude
flourished 1920s

athlete, coach
Index t Wom

18748. Kirk, Henrietta
flourished 1920s
swimmer, hero
Index t Wom

18749. Sims, Dorothy Rice
1890–1960
bridge expert, sculptor, poet
Obit File

18750. Smith, Helen Sobel
1890–1969
champion bridge player
Obit File

18751. Wortman, Doris Nash
1890–1967
puzzle writer
Obit File

18752. Greenwald, Goldie
1891–1926
bowler
Hall Fame Sport

18753. King, Anita
1891–63
silent-screen actor, racehorse owner
Obit File

18754. Tuthill, Elaine Mae Golding
1891–1951
swimming champion, first woman to swim the Panama Canal
Obit File

18755. Harrison, Gertrude [Alice] Gordon Grayson
1892–1961
Washington, DC, civic leader; patron of medicine; racehorse breeder
Episcopalian
Nat Cyc Am Bio v51

18756. Leitzel, Lillian
1892–1931
circus aerial gymnast
Not Am Wom

18757. MacKenzie, Ada
1892–1973
golfer
Hall Fame Sport

18758. Mallory, Ann Margrethe Bjurstedt "Molla"
1892–1959
tennis player
Norwegian
Dict Am Bio supp v6; Hall Fame Sport; Obit File

18759. Ryan, Elizabeth "Bunny"
born 1892

lawn tennis player
Hall Fame Sport; Index t Wom

18760. Comiskey, Grace Elizabeth Reidy
1893–1956
co-owner of the Chicago White Sox baseball team
Obit File

18761. Kiaer, Alice Damrosch Wolfe
1893–1967
skiing promoter, Olympic skier, mountain climber, first woman to scale the Matterhorn
Hall Fame Sport; Obit File

18762. Weld, Theresa; Theresa Blanchard
born 1893
ice skater
Index t Wom

18763. Ainsworth, Dorothy Sears
born 1894
physical education authority
Congregationalist
Nat Cyc Am Bio csv12

18764. Branaster, Greta Johanson
born 1895
diver
Hall Fame Sport

18765. Grant, Anita
flourished 1925
tennis and basketball player, promoter of women's sports
Black
Encyc Black Am

18766. McLane, Elsie Muller
born 1895
speed skater
Hall Fame Sport

18767. Topperwein, Elizabeth "Plinky"
died 1945
trapshooter
Hall Fame Sport

18768. Stoehr, Edith
died 1946
sportswoman, first woman to be a US game warden
Obit File

18769. Browne, Mary K.
1897–1971
tennis player
Hall Fame Sport

18770. Farrar, Margaret Petherbridge
1897–1967
crossword puzzle editor
Index t Wom

18771. Fraser, Alexa Stirling
born 1897
golfer
Hall Fame Sport

18772. Marlowe, Helen
died 1947
tennis player, US Marine Corps captain in World War II
Obit File

18773. Sloane, Isabel Dodge
circa 1897–1962
racehorse breeder, owner of Brookemeade Stables
Obit File

18774. Danzig, Allison
born 1898
patron of tennis
Hall Fame Sport

18775. Culbertson, Josephine Murphy
1899–1956
contract bridge expert, bridge strategist
Dict Am Bio supp v6; Obit File

18776. Clark, Florence Stokes
died 1950
steeplechase racehorse owner, equestrian
Obit File

18777. de Tuscan, Bela
flourished 1930s
aviator, "gyro-cycle" (type of helicopter) pilot, fencer
Index t Wom

18778. Donaldson, Elizabeth W.
flourished 1930s
traveler, author, sportsperson
Index t Wom

18779. du Pre, Grace Annette
flourished 1930s–60s
painter, violinist, tennis player
South Carolina
Nat Cyc Am Bio csv11

18780. Ederle, Gertrude
born 1900/08
competitive and English Channel swimmer
Hall Fame Sport; Index t Wom

18781. Hymes, Lula
flourished 1930s
track athlete
Black
Encyc Black Am

18782. Wright, Lucille Voorhies Parker
flourished 1930s–50s
sportsperson, horse breeder
Christian Scientist
Nat Cyc Am Bio csv8

18783. Daingerfield, Elizabeth
died 1951
thoroughbred-racehorse breeder
Obit File

18784. Wethered, Joyce; Lady
Heathcoat Amory
born 1901
golfer, sports author
Hall Fame Sport

18785. Bitzenberger, "Babe"
born 1903
archer
Hall Fame Sport

18786. Collett, Glenna
born 1903
golfer
Index t Wom

**18787. Cummings, Dorothy
Smith**
born 1903
archer
Hall Fame Sport

18788. Payson, Joan Whitney
1903–75
philanthropist, race horse breeder, owner of the New York Mets, patron of medicine, art collector and investor, founder of the Museum of Modern Art in New York
Episcopalian
New York
Cur Biog '72 and '75; Index t Wom; Nat Cyc Am Bio v58 and csv10; Obit File

18789. Pinkston, Betty Becker
born 1903
diver
Hall Fame Sport

18790. Rosenfeld, Fanny "Bobbie"
1903–69
track and field athlete
Hall Fame Sport

18791. Vere, Glenna Collett
born 1903
golfer, sportswriter
Hall Fame Sport

18792. Copeland, Lillian
1904–64
discus thrower
Hall Fame Sport

**18793. Roark, Helen (Wills)
(Moody)**
born 1905/06
tennis player
Hall Fame Sport; Index t Wom

18794. Gordon, Agnes (Wilson)
1906–67
contract bridge champion

Canadian
Obit File

18795. Riggin, Aileen; Aileen
Soule
born 1906
swimmer, diver
Hall Fame Sport; Index t Wom

18796. Brock, Holly
born 1907
volleyball player
Hall Fame Sport

18797. Geraghty, Agnes
1907–74
Olympic and world-record-holding breast stroke swimmer
Obit File

18798. Wachtel, Erna
born 1907
gymnastics coach
Hall Fame Sport

18799. Brooks, Lela
born 1908
speed skater
Hall Fame Sport

18800. Jacobs, Helen Hull
born 1908
tennis player
Hall Fame Sport; Index t Wom

18801. Neitzel, Loretta
born 1908
speed skater
Hall Fame Sport

18802. van Wie, Virginia
born 1909
golfer
Hall Fame Sport

18803. Engelhard, Georgia
flourished 1940s
mountaineer
Index t Wom

18804. Norelius, Martha; Martha Brown
1910–55
Olympic swimming champion
Hall Fame Sport; Obit File

18805. Outland, Kit Klein
born 1910
speed skater
Hall Fame Sport

18806. Souther, Marguerite
flourished 1940s
basketball coach, dance teacher
Index t Wom

18807. Horne, Madeline
born 1911
speed skater
Hall Fame Sport

18808. Newhouse, Jean Shiley
born 1911
high jumper
Hall Fame Sport

**18809. Swartz, Elizabeth
Robinson "Betty"**
born 1911
track athlete, sprinter
Hall Fame Sport

18810. Walsh, Stella
born 1911
track and field athlete, sprinter, broad jumper, discus thrower
Polish
Hall Fame Sport; Index t Wom

18811. Coleman, Georgia
1912–40
diver
Hall Fame Sport; Index t Wom

18812. Danzig, Sarah Palfrey
born 1912
tennis player
Hall Fame Sport

18813. Henie, Sonja
1912–69
figure skater, film actor
Norwegian
Cur Biog '70; Hall Fame Sport; Index t Wom; Not Am Wom supp v1; Obit File

18814. Rogers, Dale Evans
born 1912
singer, actor, equestrian
Index t Wom

18815. Holm, Eleanor
born 1913
swimmer
Hall Fame Sport; Index t Wom

18816. Madison, Helene
1913–70
Olympic swimming champion
Hall Fame Sport; Obit File

18817. Marble, Alice
born 1913
tennis player
Hall Fame Sport; Index t Wom

18818. Carter, Hannah Looke
born 1914
skier
Hall Fame Sport

**18819. Waller, Wilhelmine
Stewart Kirby**
born 1914
conservationist, horsewoman
Episcopalian
New York
Nat Cyc Am Bio csv13

18820. Zaharias, Mildred Didrikson "Babe"
1914–56

golfer, track and field athlete, high jumper, hurdler, runner, javelin thrower, basketball player
Dict Am Bio supp v6; Hall Fame Sport; Index t Wom; Not Am Wom supp v1; Obit File

18821. Lengkop, Dorothy Franey
born 1915
speed skater
Hall Fame Sport

18822. Bernard, Carmelita Landry
born 1917
speed skater
Hall Fame Sport

18823. Berg, Patricia Jane
born 1918
golfer
Hall Fame Sport; Index t Wom

18824. Chadwick, Florence
born 1918/19
English Channel swimmer
Hall Fame Sport; Index t Wom

18825. Dupont, Margaret Osborne
born 1918
tennis player
Hall Fame Sport; Index t Wom

18826. Addie, Pauline (Betz)
born 1919
tennis player
Hall Fame Sport; Index t Wom

18827. Fraser, Gretchen Kunigh
born 1919
skier
Hall Fame Sport; Index t Wom

18828. Hamar, Irene; Mrs.
Henry Peter de Vries
1919–73
sculptor, skier
New York
Brazilian
Nat Cyc Am Bio v57

**18829. Jameson, Elizabeth
"Betty"**
born 1919
golfer
Hall Fame Sport

18830. Watson, Virginia
1919–51
swimming instructor, swimmer
Hollywood, CA
Obit File

18831. Comiskey, Grace Lou
1921–52
co-owner of the Chicago White Sox baseball team
Chicago, IL
Obit File

18832. Gestring, Marjorie
born 1922
diver
Hall Fame Sport

18833. Brough, Louise Althea;
Louise Clapp
born 1923
tennis player
Index t Wom; Hall Fame Sport

18834. Davis, Alice Coachman
born 1923
high jumper
Black
Encyc Black Am; Hall Fame
Sport

18835. Suggs, Louise
born 1923
golfer
Hall Fame Sport; Index t Wom

18836. Williams, Esther
born 1923
aquacade and screen swimmer,
actor, businessperson
Hall Fame Sport; Index t Wom

18837. Draves, Victoria Manolo
born 1924
diver
Philippine
Hall Fame Sport; Index t Wom

18838. Garms, Shirley
born 1924
bowler
Hall Fame Sport; Index t Wom

18839. Haraughty, Lois Ellen
born 1924
volleyball player
Hall Fame Sport

18840. Harup, Karen
born 1924
swimmer
Hall Fame Sport

18841. Hart, Doris
born 1925
tennis player
Hall Fame Sport

18842. Cuneo, Ann (Curtis)
born 1926
swimmer
Index t Wom; Hall Fame Sport

18843. Merki, Nancy Lees
born 1926
swimmer
Index t Wom

18844. Merrill, Gretchen Van-
zandt
1926–65
Olympic skater
Obit File

18845. Owen, Maribel Vinson
1926–61
figure skater
Hall Fame Sport

18846. Shedd, Marjorie
born 1926
badminton player
Hall Fame Sport

18847. Gibson, Althea; Althea
Gibson Darben
born 1927
tennis player, golfer
Black
Encyc Black Am; Hall Fame
Sport; Index t Wom; Negro Al-
man; Prof Negro Wom v2

18848. Irvin, Shirley Fry
born 1927
tennis player
Hall Fame Sport

18849. Szekeley, Eva
born 1927
swimmer
Hall Fame Sport

18850. Varner, Margaret
born 1927
tennis player
Index t Wom

18851. Andersen, Greta
born 1928
swimmer
Hall Fame Sport

18852. Rawls, Elizabeth Earle
"Betsy"
born 1928
golfer
Hall Fame Sport

18853. Scott, Barbara Ann
born 1928
figure skater
Hall Fame Sport

18854. Grant, Gloria
flourished 1960s
rodeo trick rider
Native American (Navaho-Omaha)
Ind Today

18855. Grant, Joy
flourished 1960s
rodeo trick rider
Native American (Navaho-Omaha)
Ind Today

18856. Grant, Ruth
flourished 1960s
rodeo trick rider
Native American (Navaho-Omaha)
Ind Today

18857. MacFarland, Zoann
Neff
born 1930
volleyball player
Hall Fame Sport

18858. McCormick, Patricia
Keller
born 1930
swimmer, diver
Hall Fame Sport; Index t Wom

18859. Tankersley, Ruth Mc-
Cormick "Bazy"
flourished 1960s
editor, journalist, equestrian
Index t Wom

18860. Trabert, Marion
"Tony"
born 1930
tennis player
Hall Fame Sport

18861. Connolly, Olga Fikotova
born 1932
discus thrower
Hall Fame Sport

18862. Drake, Debra Bella
"Debbie"
born 1932
physical education teacher, author
Index t Wom

18863. Ward, Jane
born 1932
volleyball player
Hall Fame Sport

18864. Lawrence, Andrea Mead
born 1933
skier
Index t Wom

18865. McDaniel, Mildred
born 1933
high jumper, track athlete
Hall Fame Sport; Index t Wom

18866. Brinker, Maureen Con-
nolly; Little Mo
1934–69
tennis player
Hall Fame Sport

18867. Connolly, Maureen
Catherine (Brinker)
1934–69
tennis player
Cur Biog '69; Index t Wom; Obit
File

18868. Albright, Tenley E.
born 1935
figure skater
Hall Fame Sport; Index t Wom

18869. Brown, Earlene
born 1935

shot putter, discus thrower
Hall Fame Sport

18870. Conrad, Carolyn
Gregory
born 1935
volleyball player
Hall Fame Sport

18871. Hashman, Judy M.
Devlin
born 1935
badminton champion
Hall Fame Sport

18872. Marshall, Patricia
Gibson
born 1935
speed skater
Hall Fame Sport

18873. Vaughn, Lucile Wheeler
born 1935
skier
Hall Fame Sport

18874. Wright, Mary Kathryn
"Mickey"
born 1935
golfer, sportswriter
Hall Fame Sport; Index t Wom

18875. Hard, Darlene R.
born 1936
tennis player
Hall Fame Sport; Index t Wom

18876. Bell, Marilyn
born 1937
marathon swimmer
Canadian
Hall Fame Sport; Index t Wom

18877. Fraser, Dawn
born 1937
swimmer
Hall Fame Sport

18878. Larney, Marjorie
born 1937
javelin thrower
Hall Fame Sport

18879. Crapp, Lorraine
born 1938
swimmer
Hall Fame Sport

18880. Gaertner, Jean K.
born 1938
volleyball player
Hall Fame Sport

18881. Guthrie, Janet
born 1938
race car driver, aviator
Cur Biog '78

18882. Sand, Mary Novak
born 1938
speed skater
Hall Fame Sport

18883. Zimmerman, Penelope
Pitou
born 1938
skier
Hall Fame Sport

18884. Carner, Jo Anne Gunderson
born 1939
golfer
Hall Fame Sport

18885. White, Willye
born 1939
track and field athlete, long jumper
Hall Fame Sport

18886. Whitworth, Kathy
born 1939
golfer
Cur Biog '76

18887. Heiss, Carol
born 1940
figure skater
Hall Fame Sport; Index t Wom

18888. Kusner, Kathy
born 1940
equestrian, jockey
Cur Biog '73

18889. Rudolph, Wilma Glodean
born 1940
runner, track athlete
Black
Hall Fame Sport; Index t Wom;
Negro Alman

18890. Tyus, Wyomia
flourished 1970s
track athlete, sprinter
Black
Hall Fame Sport

18891. Vare, Glenna Collett
born 1940
golfer
Index t Wom

18892. Gunter, Nancy Richey
born 1942
tennis player
Hall Fame Sport

18893. Konrad, Ilsa
born 1942
swimmer
Hall Fame Sport

18894. McWilliams, Lou Sara
Clark
born 1942
volleyball player
Hall Fame Sport

18895. Susman, Karen
born 1942
tennis player
Index t Wom

18896. King, Billie Jean Moffit
born 1943
tennis player, women's rights
worker, feminist
Hall Fame Sport; Index t Wom

18897. Kramer, Ingrid
born 1943
swimmer
Hall Fame Sport

18898. McElmury, Audrey
born 1943
cyclist
Hall Fame Sport

18899. Murphy, Linda
born 1943
volleyball player
Hall Fame Sport

18900. Owen, Nancy
born 1943
volleyball player
Hall Fame Sport

18901. Duvall, Edith McGuire
born 1944
track sprinter
Hall Fame Sport

18902. Saltza, Chris von
born 1944
swimmer
Index t Wom

18903. Smith, Robyn
born 1944
jockey
Cur Biog '76

18904. Perry, Barbara Beverley
born 1945
volleyball player
Hall Fame Sport

18905. Ferrell, Barbara
born 1947
track sprinter
Hall Fame Sport

18906. Fleming, Peggy Gale
born 1948
figure skater
Hall Fame Sport; Index t Wom

18907. Stouder, Sharon
born 1948
swimmer
Hall Fame Sport

18908. Kolb, Claudia
born 1949
swimmer
Hall Fame Sport

18909. Nyad, Diana (Sneed)
born 1949
marathon swimmer
Cur Biog '79

18910. Redmond, Carol
born 1949
swimmer
Hall Fame Sport

18911. Rubin, Barbara Jo
born 1949
professional jockey
Cur Biog '69

18912. McGrath, Margo
born 1950
swimmer
Hall Fame Sport

18913. Young, Sheila
born 1950/51
cyclist, Olympic speed skater
Cur Biog '77; Hall Fame Sport

18914. Cochran, Barbara Ann
born 1951
skier
Hall Fame Sport

18915. Zoberski, Susan Corrock
born 1951
skier
Hall Fame Sport

18916. Magnussen, Karen D.
born 1952
figure skater
Hall Fame Sport

18917. Meyer, Deborah
Elizabeth
born 1952
Olympic swimmer
California
Cur Biog '69; Hall Fame Sport

18918. Evert, Christine Marie
"Chrissie"; Chris Evert Lloyd
born 1954
tennis player
Cur Biog '73

18919. Ball, Catherine
born 1955
swimmer
Hall Fame Sport

18920. Hamill, Dorothy
born 1956?
figure skater, Olympic champion
Cur Biog '76

18921. Lopez, Nancy
born 1957
golfer
Mexican
Cur Biog '78; Dict Mex Am Hist

18922. Atwood, Donna
born 1962
ice skater
Index t Wom

18923. Austin, Tracy
born 1962
tennis player
Cur Biog '81

No Dates

18924. Anderson, Teresa W.
swimmer
Hall Fame Sport

18925. Aspedon, Carole Phillips
basketball player
Hall Fame Sport

18926. Atkinson, Juliette
tennis player
Hall Fame Sport

18927. Banks, Alline
basketball player
Hall Fame Sport

18928. Barham, Leota
basketball player
Hall Fame Sport

18929. Barone, Marian Twining
gymnast
Hall Fame Sport

18930. Bauer, Sybil
swimmer
Hall Fame Sport

18931. Blanchard, Theresa
Weld
figure skater
Hall Fame Sport

18932. Bleibtrey, Ethel
swimmer
Hall Fame Sport

18933. Blenn, Loretta
basketball player
Hall Fame Sport

18934. Boeckmann, Dolores;
Dee Beckman
track coach and runner
Hall Fame Sport

18935. Bohlen, Philena
bowler
Hall Fame Sport

18936. Braun, "Ma"
swimming coach
Hall Fame Sport

18937. Bright, Clarita Heath
skier, promoter of skiing
Hall Fame Sport

18938. Burling, Catherine
bowler
Hall Fame Sport

18939. Burns, Nina van Camp
bowler
Hall Fame Sport

18940. Bush, Lesley
diver
Hall Fame Sport

18941. Busick, Virginia "Ginny"
softball pitcher
Hall Fame Sport

18942. Buzona, Gail Johnson
swimmer
Hall Fame Sport

18943. Cahill, Mabel
tennis player
Hall Fame Sport

18944. Caito, Estelle "Ricki"
softball second base player
Hall Fame Sport

18945. Carter, Laverne
bowler
Hall Fame Sport

18946. Catherwood, Ethel
high jumper
Hall Fame Sport

18947. Chapman, Emily
bowler
Hall Fame Sport

18948. Close, Amy
shuffleboard champion
Hall Fame Sport

18949. Coburn, Doris
bowler
Hall Fame Sport

18950. Cone, Carin
swimmer
Hall Fame Sport

18951. Contel, Jeanne
softball third-base player
Hall Fame Sport

18952. Cooke, Nancy Reynolds
skiing promoter
Hall Fame Sport

18953. Cox, Alberta Lee
basketball player
Hall Fame Sport

18954. Crawford, Joan
basketball player
Hall Fame Sport

18955. Curtis, Katherine
creator of the sport of synchronized swimming
Hall Fame Sport

18956. Cushman, Joy
synchronized-swimming coach
Hall Fame Sport

18957. Davis, Ninetta
swimmer, mining engineer
Hall Fame Sport

18958. Dick, Helen N.
soarer
Hall Fame Sport

18959. Dobson, Margaret
softball third-base player
Hall Fame Sport

18960. Dodson, Dorothy
shotput, javelin, discus, and field
event athlete
Hall Fame Sport

18961. Durack, Fanny
swimmer
Hall Fame Sport

18962. Durbrown, Margaret
swimmer
Hall Fame Sport

18963. Duval, Helen
bowler
Hall Fame Sport

18964. Easton, Mary
archer
Hall Fame Sport

18965. Elste, Meta Nuemann
gymnast
Hall Fame Sport

18966. Fellmeth, Catherine
bowler
Hall Fame Sport

18967. Ferguson, Cathy Jean
swimmer
Hall Fame Sport

18968. Fiete, Sandra
basketball player
Hall Fame Sport

18969. Frank, Lela Hall
trapshooter
Hall Fame Sport

18970. Fritz, Deane
bowler
Hall Fame Sport

18971. Fullard-Leo, Ellen; Ma
Leo
swimming organizer
Hall Fame Sport

18972. Galligan, Claire
swimmer
Hall Fame Sport

18973. Garlington, Frances
King
trapshooter
Hall Fame Sport

18974. Gaustad, Josephine
shuffleboard player
Hall Fame Sport

18975. Georgian, Carolyn Ann
"Papsie"
synchronized swimmer
Hall Fame Sport

18976. Gibson, Helen
badminton player
Hall Fame Sport

18977. Gillis, Rhona Wurtele
skier
Hall Fame Sport

18978. Gloor, Olga
bowler
Hall Fame Sport

18979. Gorham, Roberta
Armstrong
synchronized-swimming coach
Hall Fame Sport

18980. Gossik, Sue
diver
Hall Fame Sport

18981. Grayson, Betty Evans
"Bullet"
softball pitcher
Hall Fame Sport

18982. Green, Carolyn
swimmer
Hall Fame Sport

18983. Greer, Lurlyne
basketball player
Hall Fame Sport

18984. Gregory, June Taylor
synchronized swimmer
Hall Fame Sport

18985. Gregson, Kathi
horseshoe pitcher
Hall Fame Sport

18986. Gunling, Beulah
synchronized swimmer
Hall Fame Sport

18987. Haley, Audrey
shuffleboard player
Hall Fame Sport

18988. Hall, Evelyn
track hurdler
Hall Fame Sport

18989. Hall, Mal
shuffleboard player
Hall Fame Sport

18990. Hammond, Kathy B.
track athlete
Hall Fame Sport

18991. Hanger, Ruth
horseshoe pitcher
Hall Fame Sport

18992. Harrison, Pat
softball outfielder
Hall Fame Sport

18993. Hart, Carolyn Thome
softball outfielder
Hall Fame Sport

18994. Hartrick, Stella
bowler
Hall Fame Sport

18995. Hatch, Grace
bowler
Hall Fame Sport

18996. Hawkins, Elsie
shuffleboard player
Hall Fame Sport

18997. Henderson, Bess
shuffleboard player
Hall Fame Sport

18998. Hilton, Alice S.
archer
Hall Fame Sport

18999. Hines, Nancy
swimmer
Hall Fame Sport

19000. Hochstaater, Madalene
bowler
Hall Fame Sport

19001. Hoelzle, Ruth Allen
horseshoe pitcher
Hall Fame Sport

19002. Hoffay, Mary Winslow
basketball player
Hall Fame Sport

19003. Holm, Joan
bowler
Hall Fame Sport

19004. Holmes, Lucille
shuffleboard player
Hall Fame Sport

19005. Horky, Rita
basketball player
Hall Fame Sport

19006. Howell, M. C. Lydia
Scott
archer
Hall Fame Sport

19007. Hoyt, Anne Marie
Webster
archer
Hall Fame Sport

19008. Hudson, Sally Neidling-er
skier
Hall Fame Sport

19009. Irwin, Juno Strover
diver
Hall Fame Sport

19010. Jaax, Corine
basketball player
Hall Fame Sport

19011. Jaeger, Emma
bowler
Hall Fame Sport

19012. Jarvis, Iva Pembridge
trapshooter
Hall Fame Sport

19013. Johnson, Janette Burr
skier
Hall Fame Sport

19014. Jones, Frances L.
swimming coach
Hall Fame Sport

19015. Jordan, Evelyn
basketball player
Hall Fame Sport

19016. Kane, Marion Olson
synchronized-swimming coach
Hall Fame Sport

19017. Kaszubski, Frances
shotputter, discus thrower
Hall Fame Sport

19018. King, Harriet
fencer
Hall Fame Sport

19019. King, Kathryn "Sis"
softball catcher, outfielder
Hall Fame Sport

19020. King, Micki
diver
Hall Fame Sport

19021. Kinsella, Esther
shuffleboard player
Hall Fame Sport

19022. Kint, Cor
swimmer
Hall Fame Sport

19023. Knipprath, Jeanette
bowler
Hall Fame Sport

19024. Kok, Ada
swimmer
Hall Fame Sport

19025. Korgan, Nina
softball pitcher
Hall Fame Sport

19026. Kretschmer, Katherine
swimmer
Hall Fame Sport

19027. Kuchinski, Sue
horseshoe pitcher
Hall Fame Sport

19028. Lackie, Ethel
swimmer
Hall Fame Sport

19029. Ladewig, Marion von Oosten
bowler
Hall Fame Sport

19030. Landry, Mabel
broad jumper, sprinter
Hall Fame Sport

19031. Larham, C., Mrs.
horseshoe pitcher
Hall Fame Sport

19032. Lasher, Iolia
bowler
Hall Fame Sport

19033. Laurence, Andrea Mead "Andy"
skier
Hall Fame Sport

19034. Law, Marjorie
softball pitcher, outfielder, in-fielder
Hall Fame Sport

19035. Lessard, Lucille
field archer
Hall Fame Sport

19036. Lomady, Clara Schroth
gymnast
Hall Fame Sport

19037. Lombardo, Jean Lee
archer
Hall Fame Sport

19038. MacKellar, Lillian "Bil-lie"
synchronized-swimming coach
Hall Fame Sport

19039. Mandel, Carola Panerai
sportsperson
Cuban
Index t Wom

19040. Mann, Shelley
swimmer
Hall Fame Sport

19041. Manning, Madeline Johnson
track athlete
Hall Fame Sport

19042. Marker, Dorothy
trapshooter
Hall Fame Sport

19043. Marshall, Ethel
badminton player
Hall Fame Sport

19044. Marshall, Mary
basketball player
Hall Fame Sport

19045. Martin, Sylvia Wene
bowler
Hall Fame Sport

19046. Martorella, Mildred
bowler
Hall Fame Sport

19047. May, Amy Peralta
softball pitcher
Hall Fame Sport

19048. May, Gloria
softball first-base player
Hall Fame Sport

19049. McAlpin, Helen Bende-lari Goughton-Leigh
skier
Hall Fame Sport

19050. McEvoy, Elsie Hanne-man
diver
Hall Fame Sport

19051. McGinnis, Ruth
billiards player
Hall Fame Sport

19052. McKnight, Grace Carter Lindley
skier
Hall Fame Sport

19053. Meadows, Mary
trapshooter
Hall Fame Sport

19054. Meany, Helen
diver
Hall Fame Sport

19055. Miller, Dorothy
bowler
Hall Fame Sport

19056. Mitchell, Maxine
fencer
Hall Fame Sport

19057. Morris, Pamela
synchronized swimmer
Hall Fame Sport

19058. Murchison, Loren
track athlete, sprinter
Hall Fame Sport

19059. Myers, Paula Jean Pope
diver
Hall Fame Sport

19060. Nelson, Cindy
skier
Hall Fame Sport

19061. Nibel, Dorothy Hoyt
skier
Hall Fame Sport

19062. Norris, Natalie
dog musher
Hall Fame Sport

19063. Novak, Eva
swimmer
Hall Fame Sport

19064. Novak, Ilona
swimmer
Hall Fame Sport

19065. Odom, Lometa
basketball player
Hall Fame Sport

19066. Olsen, Zoe Ann
diver
Hall Fame Sport

19067. O'Rourke, Heidi
swimmer
Hall Fame Sport

19068. Ortner, Beverly
bowler
Hall Fame Sport

19069. Patterson, Inez
pioneer Black woman athlete
Black
Encyc Black Am

19070. Powers, Connie
bowler
Hall Fame Sport

19071. Poynton, Dorothy
diver
Hall Fame Sport

19072. Prchal, Mildred
gymnastics coach
Hall Fame Sport

19073. Pugliese, Julia Jones
fencer
Hall Fame Sport

19074. Raine, Nancy Greene
skier
Hall Fame Sport

19075. Rawls, Katherine "Peg-gy"
swimmer, diver
Hall Fame Sport

19076. Ray, Joie
track athlete, runner
Hall Fame Sport

19077. Reilly, Betsy Snite
skier
Hall Fame Sport

19078. Rich, Kay
softball outfielder and infielder
Hall Fame Sport

19079. Robinson, Leona
bowler
Hall Fame Sport

19080. Romary, Janice-Lee York
fencer
Hall Fame Sport

19081. Roosevelt, Ellen
tennis player
Hall Fame Sport

19082. Ruble, Olan
basketball player
Hall Fame Sport

19083. Rump, Anita
bowler
Hall Fame Sport

19084. Ruschmeyer, Addie
bowler
Hall Fame Sport

19085. Ruuska, Sylvia
swimmer
Hall Fame Sport

19086. Ryan, Esther
bowler
Hall Fame Sport

19087. Sanborn, Thelma Payne
diver
Hall Fame Sport

19088. Saubert, Jean
skier, skiing promoter
Hall Fame Sport

19089. Scalise, Mary
shuffleboard player
Hall Fame Sport

19090. Schulte, Myrtle
bowler
Hall Fame Sport

19091. Schweizer, Virginia M.
soarer
Hall Fame Sport

19092. Sears, Ruth
softball first-base player
Hall Fame Sport

19093. Seeley, Eva B.
dog musher
Hall Fame Sport

19094. Sexton, Margaret
basketball player
Hall Fame Sport

19095. Shablis, Helen
bowler
Hall Fame Sport

19096. Simon, Violet E. "Billy"
bowler
Hall Fame Sport

19097. Sims, Alberta Kohls
softball outfielder
Hall Fame Sport

19098. Sipes, Barbara
basketball player
Hall Fame Sport

19099. Sjursen, Helen Schifano
gymnastics coach and sports author
Hall Fame Sport

19100. Small, Tess Morris
bowler
Hall Fame Sport

19101. Smith, Grace
bowler
Hall Fame Sport

19102. Smith, Janet
shuffleboard player
Hall Fame Sport

19103. Soutar, Judy
bowler
Hall Fame Sport

19104. Starr, Heriwentha Mae Faggs
track athlete, runner
Hall Fame Sport

19105. Stephens, Helen
track and field athlete, runner, javelin thrower
Hall Fame Sport

19106. Stockdale, Louise
bowler
Hall Fame Sport

19107. Sutton, Marie
shuffleboard player
Hall Fame Sport

19108. Thomas, Lorraine
horseshoe pitcher
Hall Fame Sport

19109. Thurman, Lucille
basketball player
Hall Fame Sport

19110. Tickey, Bertha
softball pitcher
Hall Fame Sport

19111. Tishman, Maria Cerra
fencer
Hall Fame Sport

19112. Toepler, Elvira
bowler
Hall Fame Sport

19113. Toutman, Marie
shuffleboard player
Hall Fame Sport

19114. Trantina, Barbara "Bede"
swimmer
Hall Fame Sport

19115. Twyford, Sally
bowler
Hall Fame Sport

19116. Valar, Paula Kann
skier
Hall Fame Sport

19117. Varona, Donna De
swimmer
Hall Fame Sport

19118. Verner, Margaret (Bloss)
badminton player
Hall Fame Sport

19119. Vida, Clair
swimmer
Hall Fame Sport

19120. Vilen, Kay
swimming coach
Hall Fame Sport

19121. Vince, Marion Lloyd
fencer
Hall Fame Sport

19122. von Saltza, Susan Christine
swimmer
Hall Fame Sport

19123. Wadlow, M. Maria "Waddy"
softball pitcher
Hall Fame Sport

19124. Wainwright, Helen
swimmer and diver
Hall Fame Sport

19125. Walker, Hazel
basketball player
Hall Fame Sport

19126. Walker, Pat
softball outfielder
Hall Fame Sport

19127. Warmbiu, Marie
bowler
Hall Fame Sport

19128. Washington, Katherine
basketball player
Hall Fame Sport

19129. Watson, Lilian Debra "Pokey"
swimmer
Hall Fame Sport

19130. Wegeman, Kathy Rudolph Wyatt "Katy"
skier
Hall Fame Sport

19131. Welcome, Thelma Kinsbury
badminton player
Hall Fame Sport

19132. Welshons, Kim
swimmer
Hall Fame Sport

19133. White, Nera
basketball player
Hall Fame Sport

19134. Wigglesworth, Margaret McKean "Marian"
skier
Hall Fame Sport

19135. Wilkinson, Dot
softball catcher
Hall Fame Sport

19136. Willard, Patty
swimmer
Hall Fame Sport

19137. Williams, Alberta
basketball player
Hall Fame Sport

19138. Wilson, Lura K.
archer
Hall Fame Sport

19139. Windsor, Vicki
horseshoe pitcher
Hall Fame Sport

19140. Wirandy, Cecelia
bowler
Hall Fame Sport

19141. Wise, Dorothy
billiards player
Hall Fame Sport

19142. Wylie, Mina
swimmer
Hall Fame Sport

TEMPERANCE MOVEMENT

19143. Truth, Sojourner; Isabel Baumfree
1775/97–1883/85

social reformer, abolitionist, feminist, lecturer, temperance writer
Black
Cyc Am Bio; Dict Am Rel Bio; Encyc Black Am; Index t Wom; Negro Alman; Not Am Wom; Prof Negro Wom v1

19144. Cox, Hannah
1796/97–1876
abolitionist, temperance worker, pacifist, women's rights worker
Quaker
Cyc Am Bio; Dict Am Bio; Index t Wom

19145. Merrill, Margaret Manton
born 18?
journalist, temperance worker, Sorosis member
English
Wom Cent

19146. Jackson, Mercy Ruggles Bisbee
1802–77
homeopathic physician, temperance and suffrage worker, educator
Cyc Am Bio; Dict Am Bio; Index t Wom

19147. Martin, Sarah Towne (Smith); Sarah Martyn
1805–79
historian, religious and historical writer for children, editor, abolitionist, temperance worker
New York, NY
Cyc Am Bio; Dict Am Auth; Dict Am Bio; Twent Cen Bio Dict Not Am

19148. Chace, Elizabeth Buffum
1806–99
abolitionist, suffragist, women's rights worker, prison reformer, temperance worker
Quaker
Dict Am Bio; Not Am Wom; Twent Cen Bio Dict Not Am; Wom Cent

19149. Gage, Frances Dana (Barker); Aunt Fanny
1808–84
lecturer, author, temperance worker, abolitionist, suffragist, women's rights worker, Civil War relief worker
Cyc Am Bio; Dict Am Auth; Dict Am Bio; Dict Am Bio Men Time; Index t Wom; Nat Cyc Am Bio v2; Not Am Wom; Twent Cen Bio Dict Not Am; Wom Cent

19150. Foster, Abigail (Kelley) "Abby"
1810/11–1887

abolitionist, feminist, Prohibitionist, lecturer, suffragist, temperance worker
Quaker
Cyc Am Bio; Dict Am Bio; Index t Wom; Nat Cyc Am Bio v2; Not Am Wom; Twent Cen Bio Dict Not Am

19151. Nichols, Mary Sargent (Neal) Gove
1810–84
women's rights worker, feminist, dress and health reformer, medical author, physician, social reformer, temperance reformer, popular author, novelist
Cyc Am Bio; Dict Am Auth; Dict Am Bio Men Time; Dict Lit Bio v1; Index t Wom; Nat Cyc Am Bio v13; Not Am Wom

19152. Rose, Ernestine Louise Lasmond Siismondi Potowski
1810–92
feminist, women's rights worker, temperance worker, abolitionist
Jewish
Polish
Cyc Am Bio; Dict Am Bio; Not Am Wom

19153. Davis, Pauline Kellog Wright
1813–76
feminist, women's rights worker, suffragist, abolitionist, temperance worker, journalist, editor, lecturer
Cyc Am Bio; Dict Am Bio; Index t Wom; Nat Cyc Am Bio v22; Not Am Wom

19154. Thompson, Eliza Jane Trimble
1813/16–1905
temperance reformer
Ohio
Index t Wom; Not Am Wom; Wom Cent

19155. Comstock, Elizabeth Leslie Rous
1815–1891/92
social reformer, abolitionist, Underground Railroad worker, pacifist, freed slave's welfare worker, temperance reformer, women's rights worker, Quaker minister, prison reformer, Civil War nurse
Quaker
Dict Am Bio; Index t Wom; Nat Cyc Am Bio v22; Not Am Wom

19156. Stewart, Eliza Daniel "Mother"
1816–1908
temperance reformer, suffragist, Civil War relief worker

Illinois
Dict Am Bio; Nat Cyc Am Bio v7; Not Am Wom; Wom Cent

19157. Thomas, Mary Frame (Myers)
1816–88
physician, suffragist, women's rights worker, prison reformer, temperance worker, editor
Index t Wom; Not Am Wom; Twent Cen Bio Dict Not Am

19158. Wallace, Zerelda Gray Sanders
1817–1909
temperance worker, suffrage leader, women's rights worker
Index t Wom; Nat Cyc Am Bio v5; Not Am Wom; Wom Cent

19159. Bloomer, Amelia (Jenks)
1818–94
temperance reformer, women's rights worker, suffragist, dress reformer
Cyc Am Bio; Dict Am Auth; Dict Am Bio; Index t Wom; Nat Cyc Am Bio v8; Not Am Wom; Twent Cen Bio Dict Not Am; Wom Cent

19160. Esmond, Rhoda Anna
born 1819
philanthropist, temperance worker
Wom Cent

19161. Greene, Louisa Morton
born 1819
author, abolitionist, suffragist, women's rights worker, temperance worker, Civil War relief worker
Wom Cent

19162. Pinkham, Lydia Estes
1819–83
patent medicine proprietor, abolitionist, temperance worker, women's rights worker
Quaker
Dict Am Bio; Not Am Wom

19163. Coit, Elizabeth
born 1820
suffragist, temperance worker, humanitarian
Ohio
Irish
Wom Cent

19164. Davis, Sarah Iliff
born 1820
philanthropist, temperance worker, women's prison reformer, milliner, sanitation worker for the Union army during the Civil War, Freedmen's Aid worker
Wom Cent

19165. Livermore, Mary Ashton (Rice)
1820/21–1905
health reformer, hospital administrator, suffragist, temperance worker, abolitionist, Civil War patriot, miscellaneous author
Universalist
Melrose, MA
Cyc Am Bio; Dict Am Auth; Dict Am Bio Men Time; Dict Am Rel Bio; Index t Wom; Nat Cyc Am Bio v1; Not Am Wom; Twent Cen Bio Dict Not Am; Wom Cent

19166. Dodge, Hannah P.
born 1821
educator, temperance worker
Wom Cent

19167. Thompson, Elizabeth Rowell
1821–99
philanthropist, temperance worker, patron of science and of women's medical education, suffragist, political philosopher
Cyc Am Bio; Index t Wom; Nat Cyc Am Bio v5; Not Am Wom; Twent Cen Bio Dict Not Am; Wom Cent

19168. Kemp, Agnes Nininger
born 1823
physician, abolitionist, temperance worker, lecturer
Wom Cent

19169. Barney, Susan Hammond
flourished 1854–90s
evangelist, Prohibitionist, temperance worker, prison reformer
Rhode Island
Index t Wom; Wom Cent

19170. Lowe, Martha Ann (Perry)
1824/29–1902
poet, temperance worker, suffragist, author
Somerville, MA
Cyc Am Bio; Dict Am Auth; Index t Wom; Nat Cyc Am Bio v10; Twent Cen Bio Dict Not Am; Wom Cent

19171. Perkins, Sarah Maria Clinton
born 1824
lecturer, clergyperson, temperance worker, suffragist
Index t Wom; Wom Cent

19172. Blackwell, Antoinette Louisa (Brown)
1825–1921
Universalist minister, author, lecturer, temperance worker, abolitionist, suffragist, women's

rights worker, philosopher, poet, novelist
Unitarian; Congregationalist
Appl Cyc Am Bio; Cyc Am Bio; Dict Am Bio; Dict Am Bio Men Time; Index t Wom; Nat Cyc Am Bio v9 and v29; Not Am Wom; Twent Cen Bio Dict Not Am; Wom Cent

19173. Merrick, Caroline Elizabeth (Thomas)
1825–1908
suffragist, temperance leader, author on the South
New Orleans, LA
Dict Am Auth; Nat Cyc Am Bio v10; Not Am Wom; Wom Cent

19174. Richmond, Euphemia Johnson (Guernsey)
born 1825
fiction author, temperance advocate
Upton, NY
Dict Am Auth; Nat Cyc Am Bio v4; Wom Cent

19175. Frazier, Martha M.
born 1826
educator, temperance worker
Wisconsin
Wom Cent

19176. Jenkins, Frances C.
born 1826
evangelist, temperance worker
Quaker
Wom Cent

19177. Belcher, Cynthia Holmes
born 1827
journalist, suffragist, temperance worker
Boston, MA
Wom Cent

19178. Blair, Ellen A. Dayton
born 1827
temperance worker
Wom Cent

19179. Crane, Mary Helen Peck
born 1827
temperance worker
Methodist Episcopal
Wom Cent

19180. Douglas, Lavantia Densmore
born 1827
temperance worker
Wom Cent

19181. Howland, Emily
1827–1929
educator, educator of Blacks, abolitionist, suffragist, pacifist, temperance worker, philanthropist
Quaker

New York
Dict Am Bio; Nat Cyc Am Bio v25; Not Am Wom; Wom Cent

19182. McCabe, Harriet Calista Clark
1827–1919
philanthropist, temperance worker
Ohio
Index t Wom; Wom Cent

19183. Wittenmyer, Annie (Turner)
1827–1900
Civil War relief worker, leader in church and charitable work, philanthropist, temperance worker, lecturer, author
Ohio
Index t Wom; Nat Cyc Am Bio v12; Not Am Wom; Wom Cent

19184. Youmans, Letitia Creighton
1827–96
temperance reformer
Canadian
Cyc Am Bio; Wom Cent

19185. Bascom, Emma Curtiss
born 1828
suffragist, temperance worker
Wom Cent

19186. Chandler, Lucinda Banister
born 1828
political author, temperance worker, political economist
Wom Cent

19187. Colman, Julia
1828–1909
temperance writer
Methodist Episcopal
Index t Wom; Not Am Wom; Wom Cent

19188. Goff, Harriet Newell (Kneeland)
born 1828
temperance reformer, author, suffragist, women's prison reformer, essayist
Brooklyn, NY
Dict Am Auth; Wom Cent

19189. Austin, Helen Vickroy
born 1829
horticulturist, temperance worker, suffragist
Wom Cent

19190. Bateham, Josephine Abiah Penfield Cushman
1829–1901
temperance reformer, Sabbatarian reformer
Not Am Wom; Wom Cent

19191. Cornelius, Mary A.
born 1829
temperance reformer
Wom Cent

19192. Elmore, Lucie Ann Morrison
born 1829
temperance reformer
Episcopalian
Wom Cent

19193. Fawcett, Mary S.
born 1829
temperance reformer
Canadian
Wom Cent

19194. Meriwether, Lide
born 1829
author, lecturer, temperance worker, suffragist
Tennessee
Wom Cent

19195. Taylor, Martha Smith
born 1829
author, newspaper correspondent, temperance worker
Wom Cent

19196. Warren, Mary Evalin
born 1829
author, lecturer, temperance worker, suffragist
Baptist
Wisconsin
Wom Cent

19197. Carter, Mary Adaline Edwards
flourished 1860s–80s
industrial arts instructor and designer, embroiderer, painter, china painter, plastics artist, temperance worker
Wom Cent

19198. Chapin, Sarah Flournoy Moor
1830?–96
temperance reformer
Not Am Wom

19199. Charpiot, Mary Russell
1830–1908
temperance reformer
Nat Cyc Am Bio v14

19200. Collins, Delia
born 1830
educator, temperance worker, philanthropist, welfare worker
Wom Cent

19201. Hunt, Mary Hannah Hanchett
1830–1906

leader of the campaign for temperance education in the schools, educator
Dict Am Bio; Not Am Wom; Wom Cent

19202. Leavitt, Mary Greenleaf Clement
1830–1912
educator, temperance missionary, traveler
Dict Am Bio; Nat Cyc Am Bio v5; Not Am Wom; Twent Cen Bio Dict Not Am; Wom Cent

19203. Stevens, Emily Pitt
flourished 1860s–90s
educator, temperance worker, feminist, suffragist
Presbyterian
California
Wom Cent

19204. Cooley, Emily M. J.
born 1831
temperance and church worker, evangelical preacher
Methodist Episcopal
Wom Cent

19205. Eyster, Nellie Blessing
born 1831
author, children's author, temperance reformer, worker for Chinese American welfare
Pennsylvania; California
Cyc Am Bio; Dict Am Auth; Nat Cyc Am Bio v10; Twent Cen Bio Dict Not Am; Wom Cent

19206. Hayes, Lucy Ware Webb
1831–1879/89
temperance worker
Index t Wom; Wom Cent

19207. Hoffman, Clara Cleghorn
born 1831
temperance worker
Wom Cent

19208. Blackall, Emily Lucas
1832–92
philanthropist, temperance worker
Baptist
Wom Cent

19209. Cadwallader, Allice A. W.
born 1832
philanthropist, Civil War relief worker, temperance worker
Wom Cent

19210. Gordon, S. Anna
born 1832
homeopathic physician, Civil War doctor, author, temperance worker, meteorologist
Wom Cent

19211. Ingham, Mary Bigelow; Anne Hathaway
born 1832
author, temperance worker, Methodist Episcopal missionary and religious worker
Methodist Episcopal
Wom Cent

19212. Janes, Martha Waldron
born 1832
Baptist minister, suffragist, temperance worker
Baptist
Iowa
Index t Wom; Wom Cent

19213. McKinney, Jane Army
born 1832
educator, temperance worker, suffragist, kindergartner
Wom Cent

19214. Reese, Mary Bynon
born 1832
temperance worker, poet, Civil War humanitarian, Union sympathizer
Wom Cent

19215. Russell, Elizabeth Augusta
born 1832
philanthropist, Freedmen's Bureau worker, temperance worker
Wom Cent

19216. Saxon, Elizabeth Lyle
1832–1915
suffragist, temperance worker, lecturer
Congregationalist
Memphis, TN
Nat Cyc Am Bio v16; Wom Cent

19217. Shelley, Mary Jane
born 1832
temperance worker, missionary worker
Methodist
Nebraska
Wom Cent

19218. Smith, Hannah Whitall
1832–1911
religious author, evangelist, pacifist, temperance worker, women's rights worker
Quaker
Dict Am Bio; Index t Wom; Not Am Wom

19219. Watts, Margaret Anderson
born 1832
temperance worker, feminist, suffragist
Kentucky
Wom Cent

19220. Aldrich, Mary Jane
born 1833
temperance worker
Wom Cent

19221. Cole, Cordelia Throop
born 1833
temperance reformer
Wom Cent

19222. Drake, Mary Eveline
born 1833
temperance worker, Congregationalist minister, home missionary
Congregationalist
Wom Cent

19223. Isaac, Hannah M. Underhill
born 1833
evangelist, temperance worker
New York
Wom Cent

19224. Miller, Emily Clark Huntington
1833–1913
author, children's author, journalist, editor, poet, semireligious-fiction writer, church worker, temperance worker, educator
Evanston, IL
Dict Am Auth; Dict Am Bio; Index t Wom; Not Am Wom; Twent Cen Bio Dict Not Am; Wom Cent

19225. Morrison, Sarah Parke
born 1833
temperance worker, Quaker minister
Quaker
Twent Cen Bio Dict Not Am

19226. Quinton, Amelia Stone
1833–1926
Native American reform and rights worker, temperance worker, club leader, humanitarian
Index t Wom; Not Am Wom; Twent Cen Bio Dict Not Am; Wom Cent

19227. Severance, Juliet H.
born 1833
physician, abolitionist, feminist, temperance worker, political activist
Spiritualist
Wom Cent

19228. Benjamin, Anna Smeed
born 1834
temperance worker
Michigan
Wom Cent

19229. Bradley, Ann Weaver
born 1834

temperance worker
Wom Cent

19230. Grubb, Sophronia Farrington Naylor
born 1834
temperance worker, freedmen's welfare worker
Wom Cent

19231. Hitchcock, Mary Antoinette
born 1834
temperance reformer
Wom Cent

19232. Willing, Jennie Fowler
1834–1916
Methodist local preacher, church worker, temperance reformer, lecturer, author, educator
Methodist
Canadian
Index t Wom; Not Am Wom; Wom Cent

19233. Brown, Mary Frank
born 1835
philanthropist, Chinese and Japanese women's welfare worker, temperance worker
Oakland, CA
Wom Cent

19234. Carse, Matilda Bradley
1835–1917
temperance worker, child care worker, welfare worker, philanthropist, financier
Chicago, IL
Index t Wom; Not Am Wom; Twent Cen Bio Dict Not Am; Wom Cent

19235. Davis, Minnie S.
born 1835
author, temperance worker, suffragist, women's rights worker, "mental science" healer
Index t Wom; Wom Cent

19236. Meech, Jeannette du Bois
born 1835
evangelist, missionary worker, Baptist preacher, temperance worker, industrial educator of women
Baptist
New Jersey
Index t Wom; Wom Cent

19237. Taylor, Hannah E.
born 1835
poet, temperance worker
Baptist
Wom Cent

19238. Tutwiler, Julia Strudwick
1835/41–1916

educator, women's educator, temperance worker, prison reformer
Alabama
Dict Am Bio; Encyc South Hist; Index t Wom; Nat Cyc Am Bio v15; Not Am Wom; Wom Cent

19239. Washington, Lucy Hall (Walker)
born 1835
poet, temperance reformer
Port Jervis, NY
Dict Am Auth; Wom Cent

19240. Boyd, Kate Parker (Scott)
born 1836
artist, temperance worker
Wom Cent

19241. Bullock, Helen Louise
born 1836
temperance worker, music educator, women's prison reformer
Wom Cent

19242. Burlingame, Emeline S.
born 1836
Baptist evangelist, temperance worker
Baptist
Wom Cent

19243. Clark, Frances P.
born 1836
philanthropist, temperance worker
Omaha, NE
Wom Cent

19244. Doe, Mary L.
born 1836
suffragist, temperance reformer, merchant
Methodist
Iowa
Wom Cent

19245. Holley, Marietta; Josiah Allen's Wife; Jemyma
1836/44–1926
author, humorist, poet, essayist, novelist, popularizer of women's rights and temperance doctrines, feminist
Ellisburg, NY
Dict Am Auth; Dict Am Bio; Index t Wom; Nat Cyc Am Bio v9; Not Am Wom; Twent Cen Bio Dict Not Am; Wom Cent; Wom Lit, More

19246. Scripps, Ellen Browning
1836–1932
philanthropist, newspaper writer and publisher, patron of marine science, founder of Scripps Marine Lab, pacifist, feminist, temperance worker

La Jolla, CA
Dict Am Bio; Index t Wom; Nat
Cyc Am Bio v27; Not Am Wom

19247. Stearns, Sarah Burger
1836–post 1899
suffragist, women's rights worker,
philanthropist, Civil War humanitarian, temperance worker,
social reformer, educator of
freedmen
Unitarian
Cyc Am Bio; Index t Wom; Nat
Cyc Am Bio v10; Twent Cen
Bio Dict Not Am; Wom Cent

19248. Dye, Mary Irene Clark
born 1837
telegrapher, welfare worker, temperance worker
Wom Cent

**19249. O'Donnell, Martha Bar-
num**
born 1837
temperance worker
New York
Wom Cent

19250. Swift, Frances Laura
born 1837
church worker, temperance worker
Presbyterian
Pennsylvania
Wom Cent

19251. Truitt, Anna Augusta
born 1837
temperance reformer, suffragist,
patron of industrial education
Muncie, IN
Wom Cent

19252. West, Mary Allen
1837–92
educator, temperance worker,
writer on education and child
care, journalist
Illinois
Cyc Am Bio; Dict Am Auth;
Index t Wom; Wom Cent

**19253. Brown, Martha McClel-
len**
1838–1916
founder of the Prohibition party,
temperance reformer, suffragist,
lecturer
Methodist
Ohio
Index t Wom; Nat Cyc Am Bio
v27; Not Am Wom; Wom Cent

**19254. Hickman, Mary Catha-
rine**
born 1838
journalist, temperance worker
Ohio
Wom Cent

**19255. Hodgin, Emily Caroline
Chandler**
born 1838
temperance reformer, suffragist
Quaker
Indiana
Wom Cent

19256. Lathrap, Mary Torrans;
The Daniel Webster of Prohibition
born 1838
poet, temperance reformer, Congregationalist preacher
Congregationalist
Wom Cent

**19257. Lippincott, Esther J.
(Trimble)**
1838–88
educator, author on literature,
temperance reformer, convalescent-hospital reformer
Quaker
Pennsylvania
Dict Am Auth; Wom Cent

**19258. Nichols, Josephine Ral-
ston**
born 1838
lecturer, temperance reformer
Wom Cent

19259. Rude, Ellen (Sargent)
born 1838
poet, author, temperance worker,
Worthy Chief Templar of the
Order of Good Templars
Duluth, MN
Dict Am Auth; Index t Wom;
Wom Cent

19260. Sibley, Jane Eliza
born 1838
temperance worker
Nat Cyc Am Bio v1

19261. Stokes, Missouri H.
1838–post 1860
Civil War diarist, educator, tem-
perance worker
Presbyterian
Georgia
Index t Wom; Wom Cent

19262. Straub, Maria
born 1838
songwriter, temperance writer
Wom Cent

**19263. Wait, Phoebe Jane Bab-
cock**
1838–1904
physician, temperance worker
Baptist
Nat Cyc Am Bio v2; Wom Cent

19264. Wilcox, Hannah Tyler
born 1838
physician, temperance worker
Wom Cent

**19265. Bailey, Hannah Clark
Johnston**
1839–1923
peace worker, temperance reformer, suffragist, philanthropist
Maine
Index t Wom; Nat Cyc Am Bio
v10; Not Am Wom; Wom Cent

**19266. Henry, Sarepta Myren-
da (Irish)**
1839–1900/01
author, religious writer, poet,
children's author, temperance
worker, evangelist
Evanston, IL
Dict Am Auth; Nat Cyc Am Bio
v4; Twent Cen Bio Dict Not
Am; Wom Cent

19267. Holmes, Mary Emma
born 1839
suffragist, temperance worker
Illinois
Wom Cent

19268. Hurd, Helen Marr
born 1839
poet, temperance worker
Maine
Wom Cent

**19269. Sunderland, Eliza Jane
(Read)**
1839–1910
lecturer, author, educator, temperance worker, women's rights
worker, philosopher
Universalist
Michigan
Dict Am Bio; Nat Cyc Am Bio
v10; Wom Cent

19270. Tilton, Lydia H.
born 1839
journalist, temperance worker
Wom Cent

**19271. Willard, Frances
Elizabeth Caroline**
1839–98
educator, educational philoso-
pher, suffragist, feminist, wom-
en's rights worker, temperance
leader, naturalist, philanthro-
pist, newspaper editor, traveler
Methodist Episcopal
Cyc Am Bio; Dict Am Auth; Dict
Am Bio; Dict Am Bio Men
Time; Dict Am Rel Bio; Index t
Wom; Nat Cyc Am Bio v1; Not
Am Wom; Twent Cen Bio Dict
Not Am; Wom Cent

19272. Baldwin, Esther E.
born 1840
missionary to China, worker for
the rights of Chinese Americans, temperance worker
Wom Cent

19273. Burnett, Cynthia S.
born 1840
educator, temperance worker
Index t Wom; Wom Cent

19274. Casseday, Jennie
born 1840
philanthropist, temperance worker
Kentucky
Wom Cent

19275. Chase, Louise
born 1840
temperance worker
Rhode Island
Wom Cent

**19276. Foster, Judith Ellen
(Horton)**
1840–1910
temperance leader, lawyer, Re-
publican party worker, Prohibi-
tionist, suffragist, political
writer, lecturer
Iowa
Cyc Am Bio; Dict Am Auth; Dict
Am Bio; Index t Wom; Nat Cyc
Am Bio v22; Not Am Wom;
Twent Cen Bio Dict Not Am;
Wom Cent

19277. Frissell, Seraph
born 1840
physician, temperance worker
Wom Cent

**19278. Hammer, Anna Maria
Nichols**
born 1840
temperance worker
Pennsylvania
Wom Cent

19279. Hill, Eliza Trask
born 1840
suffragist, women's welfare worker, journalist, newspaper publisher, political activist,
Prohibitionist
Massachusetts
Wom Cent

**19280. Pollard, Marie Antoin-
ette Nathalie Granier-Dowell**
flourished 1870s
lecturer, temperance reformer,
political activist
Cyc Am Bio

19281. Pritchard, Esther Tuttle
born 1840
editor, educator, minister, temperance worker, missionary
Index t Wom; Wom Cent

19282. Trott, Lois E.
flourished 1870s–90s
educator, philanthropist, temperance worker
Wom Cent

19283. Wilson, Augustus
flourished 1870s–90s
suffragist, temperance worker, Methodist Episcopal church worker, missionary worker
Methodist Episcopal
Kansas
Wom Cent

19284. Wilson, Zara A.
born 1840
lawyer, suffragist, feminist, temperance worker, missionary worker
Methodist Episcopal
Nebraska
Wom Cent

19285. Woodbridge, Mary A. Brayton
flourished 1870s–90s
temperance reformer
Ohio
Wom Cent

19286. Woodward, Caroline M. Clark
born 1840
temperance worker
Wom Cent

19287. Wright, Julia MacNair
1840–1930
author, novelist, temperance writer, temperance worker, anti-Catholic writer
Cyc Am Bio; Dict Am Auth; Index t Wom; Wom Cent

19288. Wright, Laura M.
born 1840
physician, temperance worker
Baptist
Wom Cent

19289. Amies, Olive Pond
flourished 1871
temperance worker, educator
Universalist
Wom Cent

19290. Bolton, Sarah Knowles
1841–1916
author, temperance worker
Cleveland, OH
Cyc Am Bio and ad; Dict Am Auth; Dict Am Bio; Nat Cyc Am Bio v1; Twent Cen Bio Dict Not Am; Wom Cent

19291. Bond, Elizabeth Powell
1841–1926
abolitionist, educator of Blacks, women's rights worker, pacifist, civil rights and temperance worker, dean of Swarthmore College
Pennsylvania
Dict Am Bio; Index t Wom; Nat Cyc Am Bio v6; Wom Cent

19292. Oberholtzer, Sara Louisa (Vikers)
1841–1930
poet, author, novelist, temperance worker, leader in school savings movement, economist
Quaker
Norristown, PA
Cyc Am Bio; Dict Am Auth; Dict Am Bio; Index t Wom; Nat Cyc Am Bio v7; Wom Cent

19293. Plumb, L. H.
born 1841
social reformer, temperance worker, financier, banker
Illinois
Index t Wom; Wom Cent

19294. Rittenhouse, Laura Jacinta
born 1841
temperance worker, author, poet
Cairo, IL
Wom Cent

19295. Walker, Harriet Granger
1841–1917
philanthropist, hospital organizer, temperance worker, suffragist, police reformer
Methodist
Minneapolis, MN
Nat Cyc Am Bio v6; Wom Cent

19296. Willard, Mary Bannister
born 1841
temperance worker, educator, newspaper editor
Methodist
Wom Cent

19297. Bones, Marietta M.
born 1842
suffragist, temperance worker
Wom Cent

19298. Dow, Cornelia M.
born 1842
temperance worker, philanthropist
Congregationalist
Portland, OR
Wom Cent

19299. Dunham, Marion Howard
born 1842
temperance worker, suffragist, Christian Socialist party worker
Wom Cent

19300. Fry, Elizabeth Turner
born 1842
philanthropist, Prohibitionist, humane worker, suffragist
San Antonio, TX
Wom Cent

19301. Holmes, Jennie Florella
born 1842

temperance worker, suffragist, women's rights worker
Nebraska
Wom Cent

19302. Hunt, Augusta Merrill
born 1842
philanthropist, temperance worker, suffragist, prison reformer
Universalist
Wom Cent

19303. Neblett, Ann Viola
born 1842
temperance worker, suffragist
South Carolina; Georgia
Index t Wom

19304. Reed, Elizabeth (Armstrong)
1842–1915
theologist, religious author, philosopher, historian of India and Persia, writer on Oriental literature, temperance worker, philanthropist
Chicago, IL
Dict Am Auth; Dict Am Bio; Index t Wom; Nat Cyc Am Bio v1 and v15; Twent Cen Bio Dict Not Am

19305. Skelton, Henriette
born 1842
temperance worker
California
German
Wom Cent

19306. Thompson, Eva Griffith
born 1842
temperance worker, Presbyterian missionary worker, newspaper editor and publisher
Presbyterian
Pennsylvania
Wom Cent

19307. Watson, Ellen Maria
born 1842
church worker, temperance worker
Methodist Episcopal
Wom Cent

19308. Wintermute, Martha (Vandermark)
born 1842
poet, temperance writer
Ohio
Wom Cent

19309. Adkinson, Mary Osburn
born 1843
temperance worker
Wom Cent

19310. Burt, Mary Towne
flourished 1873
temperance worker, publisher
Protestant Episcopal

New York
Index t Wom; Wom Cent

19311. Campbell, Eugenia Steele
born 1843
temperance reformer
Methodist Episcopal
Michigan
Wom Cent

19312. Gougar, Helen Mar Jackson
1843–1907
suffrage and temperance reformer, orator, author
Index t Wom; Not Am Wom; Wom Cent

19313. la Fetra, Sarah Doan
born 1843
temperance worker
Washington, DC
Index t Wom; Wom Cent

19314. Moots, Cornelia Moore Chillison
born 1843
temperance evangelist, suffragist, women's rights worker
Methodist Episcopal
Michigan
Wom Cent

19315. Palmer, Hannah Borden
born 1843
temperance reformer
Wom Cent

19316. Ripley, Martha George Rogers
1843–1912
physician, humanitarian, feminist, abolitionist, temperance worker, suffragist
Index t Wom; Not Am Wom; Wom Cent

19317. Spurlock, Isabella Smiley Davis
born 1843
philanthropist, temperance worker, Mormon women's welfare worker
Nebraska
Wom Cent

19318. Weatherby, Delia L.
born 1843
temperance reformer, author, politician, educator
Kansas
Wom Cent

19319. Wickens, Margaret R.
born 1843
Women's Relief Corps worker, temperance worker, clubwoman
Wom Cent

19320. Acheson, Sarah C.
born 1844

temperance worker
Index t Wom; Wom Cent

19321. Berry, Martia L. Davis
born 1844
suffragist, temperance worker, politician, political reformer
Index t Wom; Wom Cent

19322. Colby, H. Maria George; H. Maria George
born 1844
children's author, domestic writer, women's rights and temperance worker
Wom Cent

19323. Ferree, Susan Frances Nelson
born 1844
journalist, temperance worker, suffragist, women's rights worker
Episcopalian
Iowa
Wom Cent

19324. Harrell, Sarah Carmichael
born 1844
educator, temperance worker
Indiana
Wom Cent

19325. Howe, Emeline Harriet (Siggins)
born 1844
poet, temperance worker
Pennsylvania
Wom Cent

19326. Phelps, Elizabeth Stuart; Mrs. Ward
1844–1911
author, lecturer, women's rights worker, temperance worker
Cyc Am Bio and ad; Dict Am Bio Men Time

19327. Preston, Frances E. L.
1844–1929
temperance lecturer, organist, elocutionist
Black
Negro Alman; Prof Negro Wom v1

19328. Stevens, Lillian Marion Norton Ames
1844–1914
temperance reformer, women's rights worker, lecturer, philanthropist
Maine
Index t Wom; Nat Cyc Am Bio v13; Not Am Wom; Wom Cent

19329. Switzer, Lucy Robbins Messer
born 1844

temperance worker, feminist, suffragist, politician
Wom Cent

19330. Ward, Elizabeth Stuart (Phelps)
1844–1911
author, popular novelist, women's rights worker, temperance worker, philanthropist
Massachusetts
Cyc Am Bio; Dict Am Auth; Dict Am Bio; Dict Am Bio Men Time; Index t Wom; Nat Cyc Am Bio v9; Not Am Wom; Twent Cen Bio Dict Not Am; Wom Cent; Wom Lit, More

19331. Bailey, Lepha Eliza (Dunton)
born 1845
temperance worker, Prohibitionist, suffragist, lecturer, author
Wom Cent

19332. Buell, Caroline Brown
flourished 1875
temperance worker, philanthropist
Wom Cent

19333. Carhart, Clara Sully
born 1845
educator, temperance worker, women's labor welfare worker
Methodist Episcopal
New York
Canadian
Wom Cent

19334. Case, Marietta Stanley
born 1845
author, poet, temperance worker, home and foreign mission worker
Manchester, OH
Wom Cent

19335. Henry, Josephine Kirby Williamson
born 1845
suffragist, politician, political writer, Prohibitionist
Kentucky
Wom Cent

19336. Jones, Irma Theoda
born 1845
philanthropist, temperance worker
Lansing, MI
Index t Wom; Wom Cent

19337. Knox, Janette Hill
born 1845
temperance reformer
New Hampshire
Wom Cent

19338. Miller, Minnie (Willis) (Baines)
born 1845

religious author, temperance worker
Springfield, OH
Dict Am Auth; Wom Cent

19339. Peters, Alice E. H.
born 1845
church and temperance worker, suffragist, author
Methodist Episcopal
Ohio
Wom Cent

19340. Barnes, Frances Julia (Allis)
born 1846
temperance reformer
Index t Wom; Twent Cen Bio Dict Not Am; Wom Cent

19341. Black, Sarah Hearst
born 1846
temperance worker
Wom Cent

19342. Bourne, Emma
born 1846
temperance worker
Newark, NJ
Wom Cent

19343. Morris, Ellen Douglas
born 1846
temperance worker
Wom Cent

19344. Nation, Carry Amelia Moore
1846–1911
direct action temperance reformer
Kansas
Dict Am Bio; Index t Wom; Not Am Wom; Read Encyc Am West

19345. Smith, Olive White
born 1846
author, temperance worker
Methodist Episcopal
Vermont
Wom Cent

19346. Stone, Ellen Maria
1846–1927
missionary, temperance worker, lecturer
Dict Am Bio

19347. Woody, Mary Williams Chawner
born 1846
philanthropist, educator, temperance worker
Wom Cent

19348. Albright, Eliza Downing
born 1847
temperance worker
Wom Cent

19349. Furber, Aurilla
born 1847

poet, temperance worker
Minnesota
Wom Cent

19350. Gulick, Alice Winfield Gordon
1847–1903
missionary to Spain, temperance worker
Not Am Wom; Wom Cent

19351. Kepley, Ada Miser
born 1847
lawyer, temperance agitator, Unitarian minister
Unitarian
Index t Wom; Wom Cent

19352. Shaw, Anna Howard
1847–1919
minister, lecturer, suffragist, women's rights worker, physician, temperance worker
Methodist
English
Dict Am Bio; Index t Wom; Nat Cyc Am Bio v14; Not Am Wom; Wom Cent

19353. Smith, Jane Luella Dowd
born 1847
educator, author, poet, children's author, suffragist, temperance worker
Hudson, NY
Cyc Am Bio; Dict Am Auth; Nat Cyc Am Bio v1; Twent Cen Bio Dict Not Am; Wom Cent

19354. Taylor, Sarah Katherine Paine
born 1847
evangelist, temperance worker
Wom Cent

19355. Wheelock, Dora V.
born 1847
temperance worker, suffragist
Nebraska
Wom Cent

19356. Bittenbender, Ada Matilda Cole
1848–1925
suffragist, temperance leader, political reformer, lawyer admitted to practice before the Supreme Court
Presbyterian
Nebraska
Not Am Wom; Wom Cent

19357. Black, Mary Fleming
born 1848
religious author, temperance worker
Wom Cent

19358. Diggs, Annie le Porte
1848/53–1916

Populist party leader, orator, politician, social reformer, temperance worker, journalist
Unitarian
Kansas
Canadian
Not Am Wom; Read Encyc Am West; Wom Cent

19359. Kollock, Florence E.
born 1848
Universalist minister, suffragist, temperance worker, kindergarten educator, missionary
Index t Wom; Wom Cent

19360. Mee, Cassie Ward
born 1848
labor leader, Knights of Labor worker, temperance worker, lecturer
Quaker
Canadian
Index t Wom; Wom Cent

19361. Cady, Helena Maxwell
born 1849
physician, temperance worker, suffragist
Kentucky
Wom Cent

19362. East, Edward H., Mrs.
born 1849
philanthropist, temperance worker
Tennessee
Wom Cent

19363. Greenwood, Elizabeth W.
born 1849
temperance reformer
Wom Cent

19364. Kendrick, Ella Bagnell
born 1849
temperance worker, Prohibition party worker
Wom Cent

19365. Ray, Rachel Beasley; Kate Carrington
born 1849
poet, author, temperance advocate, feminist
Baptist
Wom Cent

19366. Armstrong, Ruth Alice
born 1850
suffragist, temperance worker
Index t Wom; Wom Cent

19367. Baxter, Marion Babcock
born 1850
temperance worker, lecturer
Twent Cen Bio Dict Not Am; Wom Cent

19368. Bull, Sarah Chapman (Thorpe)
1850–post 1876
temperance worker, biographer
Dict Am Auth; Wom Cent

19369. Chapin, Sallie F.
flourished 1880s
temperance worker, writer on temperance
Wom Cent

19370. Holman, Silena Moore
1850–1915
temperance worker
Tennessee
Nat Cyc Am Bio v17

19371. Housh, Esther T.
flourished 1880s
temperance worker, author
Wom Cent

19372. Hutchinson, Elizabeth P.
1850–1915
temperance worker
Methodist Episcopal
Nat Cyc Am Bio v16

19373. Ingalls, Eliza B.
flourished 1880s
temperance worker
Missouri
Wom Cent

19374. Lease, Mary Elizabeth (Clyens)
1850/53–1933
Populist orator, politician, Prohibition party worker, suffragist, evolutionist, birth control advocate, feminist, political author
Kansas
Dict Am Auth; Dict Am Bio supp v1; Index t Wom; Not Am Wom; Read Encyc Am West

19375. Marble, Ella M. S.
born 1850
journalist, educator, suffragist, temperance worker, dress reformer
Wom Cent

19376. Moore, Henrietta G.
flourished 1880s–90s
Universalist minister, temperance worker
Ohio
Wom Cent

19377. Pitblado, Eupemia Wilson
flourished 1880s–90s
temperance worker, suffragist
Wom Cent

19378. Pugh, Esther
flourished 1880s

social reformer, temperance reformer, publisher
Index t Wom; Wom Cent

19379. Ramsey, Lula A.
flourished 1880s
temperance worker
South Dakota
Wom Cent

19380. Riggs, Anna Rankin
flourished 1880s–90s
temperance reformer
Oregon
Wom Cent

19381. Savage, Minnie Stebbins; Marion Lisle
born 1850
poet, author, Unitarian church worker, temperance worker
Unitarian
Wisconsin
Wom Cent

19382. Smith, Elizabeth J.
flourished 1880s–90s
editor of a temperance newspaper
Wom Cent

19383. Townsley, Frances Eleanor
born 1850
Baptist minister, evangelist, temperance worker
Baptist
Nebraska
Wom Cent

19384. Bigelow, Belle G.
born 1851
suffragist, Prohibitionist
Wom Cent

19385. Cameron, Elizabeth
born 1851
editor, temperance worker
Canadian
Wom Cent

19386. Clark, Katharine Pickens (Upson)
1851–1935
children's author, journalist, suffragist, temperance worker, lecturer
Dict Am Auth; Nat Cyc Am Bio v30

19387. Gilbert, Ruby I.
born 1851
temperance worker, businessperson
Wom Cent

19388. Spencer, Anna Carpenter (Garlin)
1851–1931
Unitarian minister, journalist, educator, temperance worker, suffragist, pacifist, child-labor reformer, philanthropist

Unitarian
Dict Am Bio; Nat Cyc Am Bio v9 and csv2; Not Am Wom

19389. Whipple, M. Ella
born 1851
physician, temperance worker, suffragist, Methodist Episcopal church worker, politician, educator, inventor
Methodist Episcopal
Wom Cent

19390. Chapin, Clara Christiana; La Petite
born 1852
suffragist, temperance worker
English
Wom Cent

19391. Doughty, Eva Craig Graves
born 1852
journalist, suffragist, temperance worker
Presbyterian
Wom Cent

19392. Griffith, Eva Kinney
born 1852
journalist, temperance worker
Wom Cent

19393. Kurt, Katherine
born 1852
homeopathic physician, suffragist, temperance worker, Prohibition party worker
Universalist
Wom Cent

19394. Leader, Olive Moorman
born 1852
temperance reformer, suffragist
Christian Scientist
Wom Cent

19395. Stoddard, Anna Elizabeth
born 1852
journalist, anti–secret society agitator, temperance worker, suffragist
Baptist
Wom Cent

19396. Dabbs, Ellen Lawson
born 1853
physician, midwife, women's rights worker, suffragist, temperance worker, journalist, Populist party worker
Texas
Wom Cent

19397. Gordon, Anna Adams
1853–1931
temperance reformer, financier, children's author
Index t Wom; Nat Cyc Am Bio csv1; Not Am Wom; Wom Cent

19398. Hollister, Lilian
born 1853
temperance worker, suffragist, Methodist Episcopal church worker
Methodist Episcopal
Michigan
Wom Cent

19399. Jenkins, Theresa A.
born 1853
suffragist, journalist, women's rights worker, temperance worker
Wyoming
Wom Cent

19400. Porter, Florence Collins
born 1853
temperance worker
Wom Cent

19401. Williams, Alice
born 1853
temperance reformer
Missouri
Wom Cent

19402. Archibald, Edith Jessie
born 1854
novelist, temperance reformer
Canadian
Index t Wom; Wom Cent

19403. Cummins, Mary Stuart
born 1854
educator, temperance worker
Presbyterian
Montana
Wom Cent

19404. Edholm, Mary Gow Charlton
born 1854
suffragist, temperance reformer, journalist
Twent Cen Bio Dict Not Am; Wom Cent

19405. Kinney, Narcissa Edith White
born 1854
temperance worker
Wom Cent

19406. Pratt, Hannah T.
born 1854
evangelist, temperance worker, chaplain of the Maine Senate
Maine
Wom Cent

19407. Stille, Mary Ingram
born 1854
temperance worker
Pennsylvania
Wom Cent

19408. Babcock, Hannah Almy
1855–1931

music educator and director for the blind, suffragist, temperance worker
Nat Cyc Am Bio v16

19409. Baker, Charlotte Johnson
born 1855
ophthalmologist, suffragist, temperance worker
Wom Cent

19410. Manning, Jessie Wilson
born 1855
author, temperance worker, lecturer
Iowa
Index t Wom; Wom Cent

19411. Martin, Angie Starr
1855–1944
temperance leader
Obit File

19412. Rogers, Effie Louise Hoffman
born 1855
educator; superintendent of schools of Mahaska County, Iowa; newspaper editor; temperance worker
Mahaska County, IA
Wom Cent

19413. Bushnell, Kate
born 1856
physician, temperance reformer, evangelist
Wom Cent

19414. Huling, Caroline Augusta
born 1856
journalist, suffragist, philanthropist, temperance worker
Illinois
Wom Cent

19415. Jones, Harriet B.
born 1856
physician, temperance worker
Virginia
Index t Wom; Wom Cent

19416. Benedict, Emma Lee
born 1857
author, educator, temperance worker
New York
Wom Cent

19417. Butin, Mary Ryerson
born 1857
physician, temperance worker
Nebraska
Wom Cent

19418. Gray, Jennie T.
born 1857
temperance worker
Wom Cent

19419. Hay, Mary Garret
1857–1928
suffragist, temperance worker, New York civic worker
New York, NY
Dict Am Bio; Index t Wom; Not Am Wom

19420. Mark, Nellie V.
born 1857
physician, suffragist, temperance worker
Wom Cent

19421. Oldham, Marie Augusta
born 1857
missionary to India, educator, temperance worker
Methodist Episcopal
Wom Cent

19422. Boole, Ella Alexander
1858–1952
temperance leader, president of WCTU, suffragist, pacifist, Presbyterian deacon
Presbyterian
Dict Am Bio supp v5; Index t Wom; Nat Cyc Am Bio v38 and csv2; Not Am Wom supp v1; Obit File

19423. Cranmer, Emma A.
born 1858
temperance reformer, suffragist
South Dakota
Wom Cent

19424. Granger, Lottie E.
born 1858
temperance worker, educator
Wom Cent

19425. Montgomery, Carrie Frances Judd
born 1858
church worker, poet, author, temperance worker, Salvation Army worker, social worker
New York; California
Index t Wom; Wom Cent

19426. Baker, Ida Wickoff
born 1859
stock company owner, temperance worker, women's rights worker
Wom Cent

19427. Brain, Belle M.
born 1859
temperance author, educator
Springfield, OH
Dict Am Auth

19428. Miller, Addie Dickman
born 1859
educator, temperance worker, inventor of the dishwasher
Oregon
Wom Cent

19429. Moreland, Mary L.
born 1859
Congregationalist minister, temperance worker
Congregationalist
Illinois
Wom Cent

19430. Ackermann, Jessie A.
born 1860
temperance worker
Wom Cent

19431. Gordon, Elizabeth P.
flourished 1890s
temperance reformer
Wom Cent

19432. Sibley, Jennie E.
flourished 1890s
temperance worker
Georgia
Wom Cent

19433. Starkweather, Amelia Minerva
flourished 1890s
educator, author, poet, temperance worker, Methodist Episcopal deaconess
Methodist Episcopal
Wom Cent

19434. Ames, Julia A.
1861–91
temperance worker, editor
Twent Cen Bio Dict Not Am; Wom Cent

19435. Hazelrigg, Clara H.
born 1861
author, educator, temperance worker
Wom Cent

19436. McCulloch, Catharine Gouger Waugh
1862–1945
lawyer, judge, suffragist, temperance worker
Illinois
Not Am Wom; Obit File; Wom Cent

19437. Smith, Mary Belle
born 1862
educator, temperance worker
Methodist Episcopal
Connecticut
Wom Cent

19438. Johnson, Carrie Ashton
born 1863
editor, temperance worker, suffragist
Illinois
Wom Cent

19439. Kearney, Belle
1863–1939

temperance reformer, suffragist, Mississippi state legislator
Mississippi
Nat Cyc Am Bio v11; Not Am Wom

19440. Douglas, Alice May
born 1865
poet, children's author, temperance worker, pacifist, missionary
Maine
Dict Am Auth; Index t Wom; Wom Cent

19441. Hart, Mary Ward
born 1865
suffragist, temperance worker
Illinois
Nat Cyc Am Bio v18

19442. Wright, Sophie Bell
1866–1912
educator, night school founder, welfare worker, temperance worker
Nat Cyc Am Bio v10; Not Am Wom

19443. Fuller, Minnie Ursula Oliver Scott Rutherford
1868–1946
temperance and child labor worker, suffragist
Arkansas
Encyc South Hist; Not Am Wom

19444. Hardy, Jennie Law
born 1869
temperance worker, lecturer
Nat Cyc Am Bio csv2

19445. Smith, Ida B. Wise
1871–1952
president of WCTU, educator, businessperson
Index t Wom; Obit File

19446. Stoddard, Cora Frances
1872–1936
temperance educator
Not Am Wom

19447. Coffin, Mary Emma
born 1873
homeopathic physician, temperance worker
Baptist
Nat Cyc Am Bio csv4

19448. Tillinghast, Anna Churchill Moulton
1874–1951
temperance worker, women's and children's welfare worker, Universalist pastor, suffragist
Universalist
Massachusetts
Nat Cyc Am Bio v45

19449. Jacobs, Pattie Ruffner
1875–1935

Alabama suffrage leader, child labor welfare worker, prison reformer, Prohibition party worker
Encyc South Hist; Not Am Wom

19450. Astor, Nancy Witcher Langhorne Shaw, Lady; Dowager Viscountess
1879–1964
politician, member of the English House of Commons, women's rights worker, temperance worker
British (American expatriate to England)
Index t Wom; Nat Cyc Am Bio csv1; Obit File

19451. Colvin, Mamie White
1883–1955
WCTU president
Obit File

19452. Gross, M. Louise
1884–1951
founder and president of the Women's Moderation Unit, an anti-Prohibition group
Obit File

19453. Davis, Pauline Morton Sabin
1887–1955
Republican party women's leader, anti-Prohibition worker
Dict Am Bio supp v5

19454. Sabin, Pauline Morton; Mrs. Charles
1887–1955
Prohibition repeal leader, Republican party official, interior decorator
Index t Wom; Not Am Wom supp v1

19455. Potter, Rose Saltonstall
1892–1946
leader in the fight to repeal Prohibition
Obit File

THEATER AND FILM

19456. Centlivre, Susannah
circa 1667–1723
playwright, actor
Index t Wom

19457. Rosehill, Margaret Cheer, Lady
flourished eighteenth century
colonial actor
English
Index t Wom

19458. Stagg, Mary
flourished 1710s–30s

colonial actor, dancer, dancing teacher
Index t Wom

19459. Morris, Mrs.
died 1767
colonial actor
Index t Wom

19460. Lennox, Charlotte Ramsey
1720–1804
novelist, dramatist, translator
Dict Am Bio; Dict Nat Bio; Index t Wom; Nat Cyc Am Bio v6; Twent Cen Bio Dict Not Am; Wom Lit; Wom Lit, More

19461. Douglass, Sarah Hallam
died 1773
colonial actor
Index t Wom

19462. Harman, Catharine Maria
died 1775
colonial actor
Index t Wom

19463. Warren, Mercy Otis
1727/28–1814
poet, author, dramatist, political author and satirist, historian, patriot
Massachusetts
Am Bio Dict; Cyc Am Bio; Dict Am Auth; Dict Am Bio; Dict Am Bio Men Time; Index t Wom; Nat Cyc Am Bio v7; Not Am Wom; Our Count; Who Who Dur Am Rev; Wom Lit, More

19464. Hallam, Nancy
flourished 1759; died 1775
colonial actor
Index t Wom

19465. Hallam, Sarah
flourished 1760s–70s
actor, dancer
Index t Wom

19466. Keith, Franklin, Mrs.
flourished 1770s–80s
theater operator
Index t Wom

19467. Cheer, Margaret
married 1768
colonial actor
Index t Wom

19468. Storer, Maria
died 1795
actor
Index t Wom

19469. Murray, Judith Sargent Stevens; The Gleaner; Constantia
1751–1820

author, essayist, poet, dramatist, feminist
Massachusetts
Cyc Am Bio; Dict Am Bio; Index t Wom; Not Am Wom; Who Who Dur Am Rev

19470. Pownall, Mary Ann; Mary Ann Wrighton
1751–96
actor, singer, composer
Index t Wom

19471. Hodginson, John, Mrs.
died 1803
actor, singer
Index t Wom

19472. Morris, Elizabeth
circa 1753–1826
actor
Pennsylvania
English
Dict Am Bio; Index t Wom; Who Who Dur Am Rev

19473. Fontenelle, Miss; Mrs. John Brown Williamson
flourished 1790s
actor
Index t Wom

19474. Johnson, John, Mrs.
flourished 1790s
actor
Index t Wom

19475. Storer, Fanny
flourished 1790s
actor
Index t Wom

19476. Kemble, Elizabeth; Elizabeth Kemble Whitlock
1761/62–1836
actor
Index t Wom

19477. Rowson, Susanna (Haswell)
1762/67–1824
novelist, dramatist, poet, educator, actor
Boston, MA
English
Cyc Am Bio; Dict Am Auth; Dict Am Bio; Dict Am Bio Men Time; Dict Nat Bio; Index t Wom; Nat Cyc Am Bio v9; Not Am Wom; Wom Lit; Wom Lit, More

19478. Hallam, Lewis, Mrs.
married circa 1793/94
actor
Index t Wom

19479. Merry, Ann Brunton
1769–1808
actor, tragedian, theater manager
Cyc Am Bio; Dict Am Bio; Index t Wom; Not Am Wom

19480. Davene, William, Mrs.
flourished 1800s
circus acrobat
Index t Wom

19481. Warren, Anne Brunton (Merry) (Wignell)
born 1770
actor
English
Dict Am Bio Men Time

19482. Wheatley, Ross, Mrs.
flourished 1800s–20s
actor
Index t Wom

19483. Williams, Cecelia
flourished 1800s
actor, poet
Index t Wom

19484. Faugeres, Margaretta V. (Bleeker)
1771–1801
dramatist, poet
Am Bio Dict; Dict Am Bio Men Time; Index t Wom; Nat Cyc Am Bio v9

19485. Storer, Ann
married 1798
actor
Index t Wom

19486. Hallam, Mrs.
died 1774
actor
Not Am Wom

19487. Morris, Owen, Mrs.
died circa 1825
actor
Index t Wom

19488. Douvillier, Suzanne Theodore Vaillande; Madame Placide
1778–1826
dancer, pantomimist
Not Am Wom

19489. Wood, Juliana Westray
1778–1836
actor
Cyc Am Bio; Index t Wom

19490. Darley, Ellen Westray
1779–1848/49
stage actor
Dict Am Bio Men Time; Index t Wom

19491. Rowson, Charlotte
circa 1779–1855
actor, popular singer
Cyc Am Bio

19492. Oldmixon, Mary (George)
died 1835/36
singer, actor
Dict Am Bio Men Time; Index t Wom

19493. Poe, Elizabeth Arnold Hopkins
1787?–1811
actor
Index t Wom; Not Am Wom

19494. Jefferson, Mary Anne
flourished 1820s
actor
Index t Wom

19495. Wheatley, Sarah
1790–1854
actor, comedian
Cyc Am Bio; Nat Cyc Am Bio v1

19496. Golfert, Agnes Holman
1793–1833
actor
Index t Wom; Nat Cyc Am Bio v2

19497. Pelby, Rosalie (French)
1793–1855/57
actor
Cyc Am Bio; Dict Am Bio Men Time

19498. Duff, Mary Ann Dyke
1794/95–1857
actor
Cyc Am Bio; Dict Am Bio; Nat Cyc Am Bio v6; Not Am Wom

19499. Sugg, Catharine Lee
married 1819
actor
Index t Wom

19500. Vernon, Jane Marchant (Fisher)
1796/1827–1869
actor
English
Cyc Am Bio; Dict Am Bio Men Time; Nat Cyc Am Bio v10

19501. Denny, Mary Frances
born 1797
actor
Index t Wom

19502. Drake, Frances Ann Denny; Mary Frances Denny
1797–1875
actor
Dict Am Bio; Not Am Wom

19503. Feron, Madame
born 1797
actor
Index t Wom

19504. Hackett, Katherine
1797–1847
actor
Cyc Am Bio

19505. Barker, Widow
flourished 1830s
actor
Index t Wom

19506. Barrett, Ann Henry
married 1825
actor
Index t Wom

19507. Crane, Elizabeth Green
born 18?
poet, dramatist
Dict Am Auth

19508. Farren, Maria Ann Russell
flourished 1830s
actor
Index t Wom

19509. Hentz, Caroline Lee (Whiting)
1800–56
novelist, dramatist, poet, romance writer, educator
Episcopalian
Am Bio Dict; Cyc Am Bio; Dict Am Bio; Dict Am Bio Men Time; Dict Lit Bio v3; Index t Wom; Nat Cyc Am Bio v6; Not Am Wom; Twent Cen Bio Dict Not Am; Wom Lit, More

19510. Merington, Marguerite
born 18?
playwright
New York, NY
Dict Am Auth

19511. Ryley, Madeleine Lucette
born 18?
dramatist
Dict Am Auth

19512. Vos, Elizabeth
flourished 1830s
actor
Index t Wom

19513. Gilbert, Mrs.
1801–66
stage actor
Dict Am Bio Men Time

19514. Hilson, Ellen Augusta (Johnston)
1801–37
actor, singer, harpist
Cyc Am Bio; Dict Am Bio Men Time

19515. Wray, Mary A. (Retan)
1805–92
actor
Wom Cent

19516. Kemble, Frances Anne "Fanny"; Fanny Kemble Butler
1809/11–1893
actor, diarist, author, abolitionist
Georgia
English
Cyc Am Bio; Dict Am Bio; Dict Am Bio Men Time; Dict Nat Bio supp; Encyc South Hist; Index t Wom; Nat Cyc Am Bio v3; Not Am Wom

19517. MacKenzie, Hettie
circa 1810–45
actor
Cyc Am Bio

19518. Read, Henrietta Fanning
flourished 1840s
actor, poet
Dict Am Bio Men Time; Wom Lit, More

19519. Fisher, Clara
1811–98
actor, singer
English
Cyc Am Bio; Dict Am Bio; Index t Wom; Not Am Wom

19520. Maeder, Clara (Fisher)
1811–98
actor
Nat Cyc Am Bio v10

19521. Anderson, Ophelia Brown
1813–52
stage actor
Boston, MA
Appl Cyc Am Bio; Dict Am Bio

19522. Clifton, Josephine
1813–47
actor
Dict Am Bio; Index t Wom; Nat Cyc Am Bio v6

19523. Celeste, Madame; Celeste-Elliott
1814?–82
actor, dancer
Cyc Am Bio

19524. Rea, Julia (de Marguerittes) (Foster)
1814–66
opera singer, drama critic, writer on Europe
Philadelphia, PA
English
Cyc Am Bio; Dict Am Auth; Dict Am Bio Men Time

19525. Dorsey, Annah Hanson McKenney
1815/16–1896
author, dramatist, poet, novelist, essayist, short story writer, political writer
Catholic

Washington, DC
Cyc Am Bio; Dict Am Auth; Dict
Am Bio; Index t Wom; Nat Cyc
Am Bio v11 Twent Cen Bio
Dict Not Am; Wom Cent

19526. Marble, Anna Warren
born 1815
actor
Cyc Am Bio

**19527. Avellanada, Gertrudis
Gomez de**
1816–64/76
poet, dramatist
Cuban
Appl Cyc Am Bio; Cyc Am Bio

19528. Barnes, John, Mrs.
born 1816
actor
Index t Wom

**19529. Cushman, Charlotte
Saunders**
1816–76
actor, author
Cyc Am Bio; Dict Am Bio; Dict
Am Bio Men Time; Index t
Wom; Nat Cyc Am Bio v4; Not
Am Wom; Twent Cen Bio Dict
Not Am; Wom Cent

19530. Tyler, Priscilla Cooper
1816–89
actor
Not Am Wom

**19531. Forrest, Catherine Nor-
ton Sinclair**
1817/18–1891
actor
Not Am Wom; Twent Cen Bio
Dict Not Am

**19532. Barnes, Charlotte Mary
Sanford**
1818–63
actor, dramatist
Twent Cen Bio Dict Not Am

19533. Chapman, Caroline
1818?–76
actor, western pioneer
Index t Wom; Not Am Wom

**19534. Vincent, Mary Anne
Farley "J. R."; Mary Farley**
1818–87
actor, comedian
Cyc Am Bio; Dict Am Bio; Index
t Wom; Nat Cyc Am Bio v10;
Not Am Wom

19535. Howe, Julia Ward
1819–1910
poet, dramatist, songwriter, lecturer, suffrage and women's
club leader, feminist, abolitionist, pacifist, prison reformer,
Union patriot during the Civil
War, philanthropist, traveler

Boston, MA
Cyc Am Bio; Dict Am Auth; Dict
Am Bio; Dict Am Bio Men
Time; Dict Lit Bio v1; Index t
Wom; Nat Cyc Am Bio v1; Not
Am Wom; Twent Cen Bio Dict
Not Am; Wom Cent

**19536. Mowatt, Anna Cora
Ogden (Ritchie); Helen Berk-
ley; Ann Cora Ogden (Mow-
att) Ritchie**
1819/22–70
author, actor, dramatist, novelist,
autobiographer
French
Cyc Am Bio; Dict Am Auth; Dict
Am Bio; Dict Am Bio Men
Time; Index t Wom; Nat Cyc
Am Bio v3 and csvB; Not Am
Wom; Obit File; Twent Cen Bio
Dict Not Am; Wom Lit, More

19537. Baker, Alexina Fisher
flourished 1850s
actor
Index t Wom

19538. Blake, Caroline Placide
flourished 1850s
actor
Appl Cyc Am Bio

19539. Drew, Louisa Lane
1820–97
actor, theater manager
English
Cyc Am Bio; Dict Am Bio; Index
t Wom; Nat Cyc Am Bio v8;
Not Am Wom; Twent Cen Bio
Dict Not Am; Wom Cent

19540. Keene, Laura
1820/26–1873
actor, theater manager
English
Cyc Am Bio; Dict Am Bio; Dict
Am Bio Men Time; Index t
Wom; Nat Cyc Am Bio v8; Not
Am Wom; Twent Cen Bio Dict
Not Am

19541. Lane, Louisa
1820–97
actor
Index t Wom

19542. St. Clair, Catherine N.
flourished 1850s
actor, theatrical builder, manager
Index t Wom

19543. Waller, Emma
circa 1820–99
actor
Dict Am Bio; Nat Cyc Am Bio
v11

**19544. Gilbert, Anne Jane
Hartley**
1821–1904

dancer, actor, autobiographer
Dict Am Auth; Dict Am Bio;
Index t Wom; Not Am Wom;
Twent Cen Bio Dict Not Am

19545. Cushman, Susan Webb
1822–59
actor
Cyc Am Bio; Dict Am Bio; Index
t Wom; Nat Cyc Am Bio v23

**19546. Gilbert, G. H. "Grand-
ma", Mrs.**
1822–1904
actor
Index t Wom

**19547. Muspratt, Susan Webb;
Susan Cushman**
1822–59
stage actor
Dict Am Bio Men Time

19548. Ristori, Adelaide
1822–1906
actor
Italian
Cyc Am Bio

**19549. Bateman, Sidney
Frances Cowell**
1823–81
dramatist, theater manager, actor
Dict Am Bio

**19550. France, Rachel Ann
Noah**
1824–1925
actor
Nat Cyc Am Bio v20

19551. Hoey, Josephine (Shaw)
1824–96
actor
English
Cyc Am Bio; Dict Am Bio Men
Time

**19552. Lewis, Estelle Anna
Blanche (Robinson); Stella**
1824–80
author, dramatist, poet
Brooklyn, NY
Cyc Am Bio; Dict Am Auth; Dict
Am Bio; Dict Am Bio Men
Time; Index t Wom; Nat Cyc
Am Bio v10

**19553. Robinson, Harriet Jane
(Hanson)**
1825–1911
suffragist, women's rights worker,
feminist, abolitionist, author,
poet, dramatist, journalist, mer-
chant
Malden, MA
Cyc Am Bio; Dict Am Auth; Dict
Am Bio; Index t Wom; Nat Cyc
Am Bio v3; Not Am Wom;
Wom Cent

**19554. Jeffrey, Rosa Vertner
(Griffith) (Johnson); Rosa**
1826/28–1894
poet, novelist, dramatist
Lexington, KY
Cyc Am Bio; Dict Am Auth; Dict
Am Bio; Nat Cyc Am Bio v11;
Wom Cent

19555. Butler, Benjamin, Mrs.
died 1877
actor
Index t Wom

19556. Logan, Eliza
1827/30–1872
actor
Cyc Am Bio; Dict Am Bio Men
Time; Twent Cen Bio Dict Not
Am

19557. Taylor, Mary Cecelia
1827–66
actor, opera singer
New York
Cyc Am Bio

**19558. Williams, Maria Pray
Mestayer**
born 1828
dancer, actor
Cyc Am Bio; Index t Wom

**19559. Davenport, Fanny
Elizabeth Vining**
1829–91
actor
Cyc Am Bio

19560. Gannon, Margaret Mary
1829–68
comedian, actor
Cyc Am Bio; Index t Wom; Nat
Cyc Am Bio v11

19561. Hepburn, Audrey
born 1829
actor
Belgian
Index t Wom

**19562. Janauschek, Francesca
Romance Magdalena; Fanny**
1829/30–1904
actor
German
Dict Nat Bio; Index t Wom; Nat
Cyc Am Bio v10; Not Am Wom

**19563. Lander, Jean Margaret
Davenport**
1829–1903
actor
English
Cyc Am Bio; Dict Am Bio; Dict
Am Bio Men Time; Index t
Wom; Nat Cyc Am Bio v8;
Twent Cen Bio Dict Not Am

**19564. Bowers, Elizabeth
Crocker; Elizabeth Crocker**

McCollum; Mrs. D. P. Bowers
1830–95
actor
Dict Am Bio; Index t Wom; Twent Cen Bio Dict Not Am; Wom Cent

19565. Dean, Julia
1830–1868/69
stage actor
New York
Cyc Am Bio; Dict Am Bio; Dict Am Bio Men Time; Index t Wom; Nat Cyc Am Bio v3; Not Am Wom

19566. Florence, Malvina Pray
1830–1906
dancer, comic actor
Index t Wom; Not Am Wom

19567. Heron, Matilda Agnes
1830/31–1877
actor
Irish
Cyc Am Bio; Dict Am Bio; Dict Am Bio Men Time; Index t Wom; Nat Cyc Am Bio v8; Not Am Wom; Twent Cen Bio Dict Not Am

19568. Hyers, Anna Madah
flourished 1860s–70s
singer, actor
Black
Index t Wom; Prof Negro Wom v1

19569. Hyers, Emma Louise
flourished 1860s–70s
singer, actor
Black
Index t Wom; Prof Negro Wom v1

19570. Menken, la Belle
flourished 1860s
actor
Jewish
Index t Wom

19571. Siddons, Mary Frances Scott
flourished 1860s–90s
actor
Wom Cent

19572. Wood, Charlotte Matilda (Vining)
1831/36–1915
actor
English
Cyc Am Bio; Dict Am Bio Men Time; Index t Wom; Not Am Wom

19573. Boucicault, Agnes Robertson
1832–1916
singer, actor

Scottish
Index t Wom

19574. Manchester, Albertine
1832–89
actor
Nat Cyc Am Bio v9

19575. Mitchell, Margaret Julia "Maggie"
1832/37–1918
light comedy actor
Cyc Am Bio; Dict Am Bio; Index t Wom; Nat Cyc Am Bio v25; Not Am Wom; Twent Cen Bio Dict Not Am

19576. Cushman, Pauline
1833/35–1895
Union spy during the Civil War, actor
Cyc Am Bio; Dict Am Bio; Index t Wom; Nat Cyc Am Bio v23; Twent Cen Bio Dict Not Am

19577. Paul, Isabella Featherstone Howard
1833/35–1879
actor, tenor vocalist
Cyc Am Bio; Dict Nat Bio

19578. Phillips, Adelaide
1833–82
actor, contralto opera singer
English
Cyc Am Bio; Dict Am Bio Men Time; Nat Cyc Am Bio v6; Not Am Wom; Twent Cen Bio Dict Not Am

19579. Robertson, Agnes Kelly
1833–1916
actor
Not Am Wom

19580. Ward, Genevieve; Lucia Genoveva Teresa, Countess Guerbel; Madam Buerrabella
1833/38–1922
actor, tragedian, opera singer
Cyc Am Bio; Dict Am Bio; Nat Cyc Am Bio v9; Wom Cent

19581. Conway, Sarah G. Crocker
1834–1874/75
actor, theater manager
Cyc Am Bio; Nat Cyc Am Bio v11

19582. Clare, Ada; Jane McEthenrey
1835/36–1874
author, actor
Nat Cyc Am Bio v6; Not Am Wom

19583. Denin, Susan
1835–75
actor
Cyc Am Bio

19584. Elder, Susan (Blanchard); Hermine
1835–1923
religious author, poet, dramatist, natural scientist
Catholic
New Orleans, LA
Cyc Am Bio; Dict Am Auth; Dict Am Bio; Nat Cyc Am Bio v11; Twent Cen Bio Dict Not Am

19585. Eytinge, Rose
1835/38–1911
actor, author, drama teacher
Cyc Am Bio; Dict Am Bio; Index t Wom; Not Am Wom; Twent Cen Bio Dict Not Am

19586. Hooper, Lucy Hamilton
1835–93
poet, dramatist, editor, journalist
Cyc Am Bio; Dict Am Bio; Nat Cyc Am Bio v8; Twent Cen Bio Dict Not Am; Wom Cent

19587. Jefferson, Cornelia Burke
1835–99
actor
Index t Wom; Twent Cen Bio Dict Not Am

19588. Menken, Adah Isaachs; Dolores Adios Fuertes
1835/37–1868
actor, poet
Jewish
English
Cyc Am Bio; Dict Am Auth; Dict Am Bio; Index t Wom; Nat Cyc Am Bio v5; Not Am Wom; Wom Lit, More

19589. Wormeley, Arianna Randolph
born 1835
author, dramatist
Cyc Am Bio

19590. Reignolds, Catherine Mary "Kate"
1836–1911
actor, dramatic reader, educator
Not Am Wom

19591. Winslow, Catherine Mary (Reignolds) "Kate"
1836–1911
actor, dramatic reader
Boston, MA
English
Dict Am Auth; Nat Cyc Am Bio v23

19592. Chanfrau, Henrietta Baker
1837–1909
singer, actor
Cyc Am Bio; Dict Am Bio; Nat Cyc Am Bio v7

19593. Denin, Kate
born 1837
actor
Cyc Am Bio

19594. Logan, Celia (Kellog) (Connelly)
1837/40–1904
journalist, author, dramatist
Washington, DC
Cyc Am Bio; Dict Am Auth; Index t Wom; Twent Cen Bio Dict Not Am; Wom Cent

19595. Richardson, Abby (Sage)
1837–1900
author, actor, historian, lecturer on history, writer on literature, educator
Dict Am Auth; Index t Wom; Nat Cyc Am Bio v5; Twent Cen Bio Dict Not Am

19596. Ewen, Mary Cecelia
1838–66
actor
New York
Cyc Am Bio

19597. Field, Mary Katherine Kemble "Kate"
1838/54–1896
journalist, actor, playwright, literary critic, lecturer
Washington, DC
Cyc Am Bio; Dict Am Auth; Dict Am Bio; Index t Wom; Nat Cyc Am Bio v6; Not Am Wom; Twent Cen Bio Dict Not Am; Wom Cent

19598. McCrackin, Josephine Woempner Clifford
1838/46–1920
author, journalist, clubwoman, conservationist
German
Index t Wom; Not Am Wom

19599. Shoemaker, Rachel H.
born 1838
dramatic elocutionist, Shakespearean reciter
Wom Cent

19600. Jones, Avonia Stanhope
1839–67
actor
Dict Am Bio Men Time; Index t Wom

19601. Logan, Olive
1839/41–1909
actor, dramatist, lecturer, women's rights reformer, author, journalist
Cyc Am Bio; Dict Am Bio; Dict Am Bio Men Time; Index t Wom; Nat Cyc Am Bio v6; Not Am Wom; Twent Cen Bio Dict Not Am

19602. Bennett, Laura
flourished 1870s–90s
actor
Index t Wom

19603. Booth, Mary Devlin
1840–63
actor
Index t Wom

19604. Irwin, Flora
flourished 1870s
actor
Index t Wom

19605. Modjeska, Helena
1840/44–1909
actor
Polish
Cyc Am Bio; Dict Am Bio; Index
t Wom; Nat Cyc Am Bio v10;
Not Am Wom; Wom Cent

19606. Morant, Fanny
flourished 1870s
actor
Index t Wom

**19607. Salm Salm, Agnes
Elizabeth Winona Joy
(Leqlerq), Princess**
1840/42–1881/1912
circus rider, rope dancer, actor,
field hospital worker and organizer, philanthropist
Cyc Am Bio; Dict Am Bio;
Twent Cen Bio Dict Not Am

**19608. Booth, Agnes; Marian
Agnes Land Rookes**
1841/46–1910
actor
Australian
Dict Am Bio; Index t Wom; Nat
Cyc Am Bio v1; Not Am Wom;
Wom Cent

19609. Sinclair, Catherine
died 1891
actor, manager
English
Index t Wom

**19610. Bateman, Kate
Josephine**
1842/43–1917
actor
Appl Cyc Am Bio; Cyc Am Bio;
Dict Am Bio; Dict Am Bio Men
Time; Index t Wom; Nat Cyc
Am Bio v10; Not Am Wom;
Twent Cen Bio Dict Not Am;
Wom Cent

19611. Claire, Ina Fagan
died 1892/95
actor
Index t Wom

**19612. Dickinson, Anna
Elizabeth**
1842–1932

Civil War orator, lyceum lecturer,
abolitionist, women's rights
worker, suffragist, political ac-
tivist, Republican party worker,
author, actor, philanthropist
Quaker
Cyc Am Bio; Dict Am Auth; Dict
Am Bio supp v1; Dict Am Bio
Men Time; Index t Wom; Nat
Cyc Am Bio v3; Not Am Wom;
Wom Cent

19613. Fox, Mary Hewins
born 1842
actor, dramatist, poet
Cyc Am Bio

**19614. Hosmer, Jean; Jean
Stanley**
1842–90
actor
Cyc Am Bio; Dict Am Bio Men
Time; Nat Cyc Am Bio v4

**19615. Boyd, Belle; Belle
Hardinge**
1843/44–1900
Confederate spy, actor, lecturer
Episcopalian
Bio Dict Confed; Dict Am Bio;
Index t Wom; Not Am Wom

**19616. Harrison, Constance
Cary**
1843/46–1920
author, novelist, miscellaneous
writer, dramatist
New York, NY
Cyc Am Bio; Dict Am Auth; Dict
Am Bio; Index t Wom; Nat Cyc
Am Bio v4; Not Am Wom;
Twent Cen Bio Dict Not Am;
Wom Cent; Wom Lit, More

19617. Western, Pauline Lucille
1843–77
actor
Cyc Am Bio; Dict Am Bio

19618. Whiffen, Blanche Galton
1845–1936
actor
English
Index t Wom; Not Am Wom

**19619. Morris, Clara
(Morrison)**
1846/48–1925
actor, author, children's author,
autobiographer
Canadian
Cyc Am Bio and ad; Dict Am
Auth; Dict Am Bio; Index t
Wom; Nat Cyc Am Bio v11;
Not Am Wom; Twent Cen Bio
Dict Not Am; Wom Cent

19620. Crabtree, Lotta Mignon
1847/54–1924

actor
Cyc Am Bio; Dict Am Bio; Index
t Wom; Nat Cyc Am Bio v9;
Twent Cen Bio Dict Not Am;
Wom Cent

**19621. Glynes, Ella Maria
(Dietz); Ella Maria (Dietz)
Glynes-Clymer**
born 1847
author, actor, founder of Sorosis
Nat Cyc Am Bio v13

19622. Jewett, Sarah
1847–99
actor
Nat Cyc Am Bio v11; Twent Cen
Bio Dict Not Am

**19623. Claxton, Catherine
Elizabeth "Kate"**
1848/49–1924
actor
Cyc Am Bio; Dict Am Bio; Index
t Wom; Nat Cyc Am Bio v22;
Not Am Wom; Wom Cent

19624. Elliott, Sarah Barnwell
1848–1928
author, novelist, dramatist, suf-
fragist
Tennessee
Dict Am Auth; Dict Am Bio; Nat
Cyc Am Bio v21; Not Am
Wom; Wom Lit, More

19625. Howard, Cordelia
1848–1941
actor
Not Am Wom

19626. MacDonald, Cordelia
1848–1941
actor
Index t Wom

**19627. Neilson, Adelaide [Lilli-
an]; Elizabeth Ann Brown**
1848/50–1880
actor
English
Cyc Am Bio; Dict Nat Bio; Index
t Wom

**19628. Booth, Mary F.
McVicker**
1849–81
actor
Index t Wom

19629. Lazarus, Emma
1849–87
author, poet, dramatist, essayist
Jewish
New York
Cyc Am Bio; Dict Am Auth; Dict
Am Bio; Index t Wom; Nat Cyc
Am Bio v3; Not Am Wom;
Twent Cen Bio Dict Not Am;
Who Who Jew Hist; Wom Cent

19630. Oates, Alice
1849–87
actor, singer
Nat Cyc Am Bio v6

19631. Weathersby, Eliza
1849–87
actor
Nat Cyc Am Bio v5

19632. Banks, Maude
flourished 1880s
stage actor
Appl Cyc Am Bio

19633. Barnes, Hattie Delaro
flourished 1880s–1910s
singer, actor
Index t Wom

19634. Chapman, Blanche
circa 1850–1941
actor
Index t Wom

19635. Coghlan, Rose
1850/52–1932
actor
English
Dict Am Bio supp v1; Index t
Wom; Nat Cyc Am Bio v13;
Not Am Wom; Wom Cent

19636. Collins, Laura Sedgwick
flourished 1880s–90s
actor, musician, composer, pianist, dancer, dramatic reader
Wom Cent

19637. Comstock, Nanette
flourished 1880s–90s
actor
Index t Wom

**19638. Davenport, Fanny Lily
Gypsy**
1850–98
actor
English
Cyc Am Bio; Dict Am Bio; Index
t Wom; Nat Cyc Am Bio v4;
Not Am Wom; Twent Cen Bio
Dict Not Am; Wom Cent

**19639. Fletcher, Julia Con-
stance; George Fleming**
born 1850/53
author, novelist, dramatist
Cyc Am Bio; Dict Am Auth; Nat
Cyc Am Bio v13; Twent Cen
Bio Dict Not Am

19640. Ives, Alice Emma
flourished 1880s
dramatist, journalist
Detroit, MI
Index t Wom; Wom Cent

19641. Lowrie, Mrs.
flourished 1880s
actor, clergyperson
Index t Wom

19642. McMillan, Lida
flourished 1880s–1930s
actor
Index t Wom

19643. Potter, Cora Urquhart
flourished 1880s–90s
actor
Wom Cent

19644. Robinson, Margaret A.
flourished nineteenth to twentieth
century
actor
Canadian
Index t Wom

19645. Sutherland, Evelyn Greenleaf (Baker)
born 185?
playwright
Boston, MA
Dict Am Auth

19646. Tyler, Odette
flourished 1880s
actor
Index t Wom

19647. Best, Eva
born 1851
dramatist, poet, author
Wom Cent

19648. Biddulph, Jessie Catherine Vokes
1851–84
actor, singer
English
Index t Wom

19649. Kimball, Jennie
born 1851
actor, theatrical manager
Index t Wom; Wom Cent

19650. Morgan, Anna
1851–1936
speech teacher, drama coach, elocutionist
Chicago, IL
Nat Cyc Am Bio v17; Not Am Wom

19651. Brace, Maria Porter
born 1852
educator, elocutionist
New York
Wom Cent

19652. Ethel, Agnes
1852–1903
actor
Index t Wom

19653. Haswin, Frances R.
born 1852
musician, composer, poet, actor
Wom Cent

19654. Langtry, Lillie Emilie Charlotte le Breton
1852–1929
actor
English
Cyc Am Bio; Index t Wom

19655. Herne, Katherine Corcoran
married 1878
actor
Index t Wom

19656. Mayhew, Kate
1853–1944
stage actor
Obit File

19657. Noyes, Ida E. Smith
1853–1912
artist, photographer, philanthropist, club leader
Index t Wom; Nat Cyc Am Bio v17

19658. Barrymore, Georgianna Emma Drew
1854/56–93
actor
Dict Am Bio; Index t Wom; Not Am Wom

19659. Bateman, Isabel
born 1854
actor
Wom Cent

19660. Davenport, Lily Antoinette
1854–78
actor
Cyc Am Bio

19661. Ellsler, Effie
1854/65–1942
stage and screen actor
Not Am Wom; Obit File; Wom Cent

19662. Shaw, Mary G.
1854/60–1929
actor
Dict Am Bio; Index t Wom; Not Am Wom

19663. Leslie, Amy
1855–1939
light opera singer, drama critic, journalist
Index t Wom; Not Am Wom

19664. Weaver, Affie
1855–1940
actor
Index t Wom

19665. Bailey, Sarah Lord
born 1856
elocutionist
Massachusetts
British
Wom Cent

19666. Clymer, Ella Maria (Dietz)
1856–post 1880
poet, actor, president of Sorosis
New York
Dict Am Auth; Wom Cent

19667. Conner, Elizabeth Marney; Paul Veronique
born 1856
dramatic reader, educator, actor
Wom Cent

19668. Marbury, Elizabeth
1856–1933
theatrical and author's agent
Dict Am Bio supp v1; Index t Wom

19669. Cayvan, Georgia Eva
1857/58–1906
actor
Dict Am Bio; Index t Wom; Nat Cyc Am Bio v1 and v2; Not Am Wom; Wom Cent

19670. Cline, Maggie
1857–1934
vaudeville singer
Not Am Wom

19671. Davenport, Marion Caroline "May"
born 1857
actor
Cyc Am Bio

19672. Trumbull, Annie Eliot
1857–1949
novelist, poet, playwright, short story writer, first president of the Town and Country Club
Hartford, CT
Dict Am Auth; Obit File

19673. Adler, Sara Levitzka
1858–1953
actor in Yiddish theater
Jewish
New York, NY
Dict Am Bio supp v5; Obit File

19674. Bishop, Emily Mulkin Montague
born 1858
Delsartean lecturer and instructor in dress, expression, and physical culture
Index t Wom; Wom Cent

19675. Pond, Nella Brown
born 1858
actor, dramatic reader
Index t Wom; Wom Cent

19676. Robson, May; May Robison
1858/65–1942
stage and screen actor
Australian
Dict Am Bio supp v3; Index t Wom; Not Am Wom; Obit File

19677. Anderson, Mary Antoinette; Mrs. Antonio F. de Navarro
1859–1939/40
actor
British
Appl Cyc Am Bio; Cyc Am Bio; Dict Am Auth; Dict Am Bio supp v2; Index t Wom; Nat Cyc Am Bio v1; Not Am Wom; Twent Cen Bio Dict Not Am; Wom Cent

19678. Brown-Potter, Cora Urquhart
born 1859
actor
Index t Wom

19679. Cherry, Addie Rose Alma
circa 1859–1942
vaudeville actor
Index t Wom; Obit File

19680. Dauvray, Helen; Little Nell; The California Diamond
born 1859
actor, theatrical manager
Cyc Am Bio; Index t Wom; Wom Cent

19681. Ford, Julia Ellsworth
1859–1950
children's author, playwright, novelist, patron of medicine
Nat Cyc Am Bio csv7; Obit File

19682. le Moyne, Sarah (Cowell)
born 1859
actor
Index t Wom; Nat Cyc Am Bio v13

19683. Mather, Margaret
1859/62–1898
actor
Canadian
Index t Wom; Nat Cyc Am Bio v9; Wom Cent

19684. Rehan, Ada (Crehan)
1859/60–1916
actor
New York
Irish
Cyc Am Bio; Dict Am Bio; Dict Irish Bio; Index t Wom; Nat Cyc Am Bio v1; Not Am Wom; Twent Cen Bio Dict Not Am; Wom Cent

19685. Thompson, Mary Sophia
born 1859
Delsartean acting-method instructor, elocutionist
Wom Cent

19686. Baker, Anna Auer
1860–1944

screen actor
Index t Wom; Obit File

19687. Celeste, Marie
flourished 1890s
singer, actor
Index t Wom

19688. Clark, Hilda
flourished 1890s
singer, actor
Index t Wom

19689. Edwardes, Paula
flourished 1890s
actor
Index t Wom

19690. Gallatin, Alberta; Alberta Gallatin Jenkins; Mrs. Edwin Ogden Childe
1860–1948
actor, screenwriter, inventor of stage scenery and lighting mechanisms
Nat Cyc Am Bio v39

19691. Gilman, Mabelle
flourished 1890s
actor, singer
Index t Wom

19692. Hall, Josephine
flourished 1890s
actor, singer
Index t Wom

19693. Hooper, Rebecca Lane
flourished 1890s–1900s
playwright
Index t Wom

19694. Lawrence, Lillian
flourished 1890s
stage actor
Index t Wom

19695. Parker, Helen Almena
graduated 1885
educator, dramatic reader, impersonator
Index t Wom; Wom Cent

19696. Raymond, Maud
flourished 1890s–1900s
singer, actor
Index t Wom

19697. Riccardo, Corona
flourished 1890s
actor
Italian
Index t Wom

19698. Ryan, Marah Ellis (Martin); Ellis Martin
born 1860
author, novelist, actor
Dict Am Auth; Wom Cent

19699. Shepherd, Elizabeth Lee (Kirkland); Odette Tyler
born 1860
actor, author
Dict Am Auth

19700. Westray, Elizabeth
flourished 1890s
actor
Index t Wom

19701. Biggart, Mabelle
born 1861
educator, dramatic reader
Wom Cent

19702. Crosman, Henrietta Foster
1861–1944
stage and screen actor
Index t Wom; Not Am Wom; Obit File

19703. Martinot, Sarah Frances Marie "Sadie"
born 1861
actor
Nat Cyc Am Bio v12

19704. Roberts, Florence
1861–1940
actor
Index t Wom

19705. Russell, Lillian
1861/67–1922
actor, musical comedy actor, singer
Dict Am Bio; Index t Wom; Nat Cyc Am Bio v4; Not Am Wom; Wom Cent

19706. Bert, Mabel
born 1862
actor
Australian
Wom Cent

19707. Carter, Caroline Louise Dudley; Mrs. Leslie Carter
1862–1937
actor
Dict Am Bio supp v2; Index t Wom; Not Am Wom

19708. Fuller, Loie
1862–1928
actor, dancer, innovator in stage lighting
Dict Am Bio; Index t Wom; Not Am Wom

19709. Hall, Pauline
born 1862
opera singer, actor
Index t Wom; Wom Cent

19710. Irwin, May
1862–1938
actor, singer
Dict Am Bio supp v2; Not Am Wom

19711. Robins, Elizabeth; C. E. Raymond; C. E. Raimond; Elizabeth Raymond Parks; Elizabeth (Robins) Parkes
1862/65–1952
novelist, actor
Dict Am Auth; Index t Wom; Obit File; Wom Lit; Wom Lit, More

19712. Ulmar, Geraldine
1862–1932
actor, singer
Index t Wom; Wom Cent

19713. Adams, Florence Adelaide Fowle
born 1863
dramatic reader
Wom Cent

19714. d'Arville, Camille; Neeltye Dykstra
born 1863
singer, actor
Dutch
Index t Wom

19715. Fitzgerald, Cissy
circa 1863–1941
actor
Index t Wom

19716. Ford, Harriet (Morgan)
1863/78–1949
playwright
Index t Wom; Obit File

19717. Reynolds, Adeline de Walt
1863–1961
screen actor
Obit File

19718. Russell, Ada Dwyer
1863–1952
Broadway and London stage actor
New York
Obit File

19719. Broaker, Julia Anderson Luth
1864–1950
actor, playwright
Danish
Obit File

19720. Collins, Miriam O'Leary
born 1864
actor
Wom Cent

19721. Fry, Emma V. Sheridan
born 1864
actor, playwright
Wom Cent

19722. Harris, Renee
1864–1969

theatrical producer
Obit File

19723. Hopper, Edna Wallace
1864?–1959
stage actor, singer, dancer, broker
Dict Am Bio supp v6; Index t Wom; Obit File

19724. Lippmann, Julie Mathilde
1864–1952
author, playwright, children's author, literary critic
Brooklyn, NY
Dict Am Bio; Index t Wom; Twent Cen Bio Dict Not Am

19725. Russell, Annie
1864–1936
actor
English
Dict Am Bio supp v2; Nat Cyc Am Bio v13; Not Am Wom

19726. Skipworth, Alison
1864–1952
stage and screen actor
English
Obit File

19727. Woods, Virna
1864–1903
educator, novelist, dramatist
Sacramento, CA
Dict Am Auth

19728. de Wolfe, Elsie Anderson; Lady Mendl
1865/70–1950
actor, stage producer, interior decorator, World War I relief worker
Dict Am Bio supp v4; Index t Wom; Nat Cyc Am Bio csv6; Not Am Wom

19729. Douglas, Blanche MacDonald
1865–1952
vaudeville actor
Obit File

19730. Fiske, Mary Augusta (Davey); Minnie Madern; Minnie Madern Fiske
1865–1932
actor, author, animal humane worker
Dict Am Bio supp v1; Index t Wom; Nat Cyc Am Bio v10, v35, and csv1; Not Am Wom; Twent Cen Bio Dict Not Am

19731. Held, Anna
1865?–1918
musical comedy actor
Not Am Wom

19732. Lazarovich-Hrebelianovich, Eleanor (Calhoun), Princess
1865–1957
classical actor, Serbian freedom fighter
Serbian
Index t Wom; Obit File

19733. Marlowe, Julia; Sarah Frances "Fannie" Frost
1865/70–1950
Shakespearean actor
English
Dict Am Bio supp v4; Index t Wom; Nat Cyc Am Bio v13; Obit File; Wom Cent

19734. Morton, Martha
born 1865
author, playwright
New York
Index t Wom; Wom Cent

19735. Richardson, Anna Steese
1865–1949
magazine editor, author, playwright, feminist
Obit File

19736. Robinson, Josephine de Mott
1865–1948
circus performer, equestrian
Index t Wom; Obit File

19737. Templeton, Fay
1865–1939
actor, singer
Index t Wom; Not Am Wom

19738. Burroughs, Marie; Lillie Arrington
born 1866
actor
Index t Wom; Nat Cyc Am Bio v13

19739. Ragsdale, Lulah
born 1866
poet, novelist, actor
Mississippi
Wom Cent

19740. Smith, Jessie Earnestine Shirley
1866–1918
actor
Nat Cyc Am Bio v18

19741. Whitty, May Webster
1866–1948
stage and screen actor
English
Obit File

19742. Wolfe, Elsie De; Lady Mendl
1866–1950
actor, interior decorator
Index t Wom; Obit File

19743. Allen, Viola Emily; Mrs. Peter Edward Cornel Duryea
1867/69–1948
actor
Episcopalian
Dict Am Bio supp v4; Index t Wom; Nat Cyc Am Bio v34; Not Am Wom; Obit File

19744. Babcock, Helen Louise (Bailey)
born 1867
dramatic reader
Wom Cent

19745. Craigie, Pearl Mary Teresa (Richards); John Oliver Hobbes
1867–1906
novelist, dramatist, essayist
Index t Wom; Nat Cyc Am Bio v10; Twent Cen Bio Dict Not Am

19746. Hearne, Mercedes Leigh
born 1867
actor
Wom Cent

19747. Meyer, Annie Florence Nathan
1867–1950/51
publicist, author, playwright, novelist, educationist, founder of Barnard College, antisuffragist, patron of Black music education, clubwoman
Jewish
New York
Dict Am Auth; Dict Am Bio; Index t Wom; Nat Cyc Am Bio v42; Not Am Wom supp v1; Obit File; Twent Cen Bio Dict Not Am; Wom Cent

19748. Potter, Jennie O'Neill
born 1867
actor, dramatic reader
Wom Cent

19749. Riley, Alice Cushing Donaldson
1867–1955
children's playwright and songwriter, librettist
Nat Cyc Am Bio v44 and csv8

19750. Shannon, Effie
1867–1941/54
stage actor
Index t Wom; Obit File

19751. Sitgreaves, Beverley
1867–1943
actor, dramatic coach
Index t Wom; Obit File

19752. Sutherland, Anne
1867–1942
stage actor
Index t Wom; Obit File

19753. Campbell, Evelyn
born 1868
actor
English
Wom Cent

19754. Duryea, Nina Larrey Smith
1868–1951
World War I relief worker, playwright
Obit File

19755. Elliott, Maxine; Jessie Dermot
1868/73–1948
actor
Dict Am Bio supp v2; Index t Wom; Nat Cyc Am Bio v14; Not Am Wom

19756. Harned, Virginia
1868/72–1946
stage actor
Index t Wom; Obit File

19757. Hayward, Beatrice Herford
1868–1952
monologuist, author, actor
English
Obit File

19758. Howell, Ida
1868–1944
stage comedian
Obit File

19759. Kidder, Kathryn
circa 1868–1939
actor, vaudevillian
Index t Wom

19760. Moscowitz, Jennie
1868–1935
actor
Jewish
Rumanian
Obit File

19761. Arthur, Julia; Julia Cheney; Ida Lewis
1869–1950
actor
Canadian
Index t Wom; Nat Cyc Am Bio v10; Not Am Wom; Obit File

19762. Bingham, Amelia
1869–1927
actor
Dict Am Bio; Nat Cyc Am Bio v21

19763. Dressler, Marie; Leila von Koerber
1869/73–1934
stage and screen actor, comedian, suffragist

Canadian
Dict Am Bio supp v1; Index t Wom; Nat Cyc Am Bio v27; Not Am Wom

19764. Finch, Flora
1869–1940
actor
Index t Wom

19765. Fisher, Alice
born 1869
actor
Nat Cyc Am Bio v13

19766. Hatton, Fanny Cottinet Locke
1869–1939
playwright, critic
Episcopalian
Index t Wom; Nat Cyc Am Bio v42

19767. Lipman, Clara
born 1869
actor, playwright
Index t Wom

19768. Ringling, Edith Conway
1869–1953
chairperson of the Ringling Bros. and Barnum and Bailey Circus
Obit File

19769. Yohe, May; Lady Frances White
circa 1869–1938
actor, singer
Index t Wom

19770. Young, Rida Johnson
1869/75–1926
playwright, author, librettist, actor
Index t Wom

19771. Bentley, Irene
1870–1940
singer, actor
Index t Wom

19772. Busley, Jessie
1870–1950
actor
Obit File

19773. Cahill, Marie
1870–1933
actor
Index t Wom; Not Am Wom

19774. Crothers, Rachel
1870/78–1958
playwright
New York
Dict Am Bio supp v5; Dict Lit Bio v7; Index t Wom; Nat Cyc Am Bio csv3; Not Am Wom supp v1; Obit File; Wom Lit, More

19775. Dargan, Olive Tilford
flourished 1900s–30s
poet, novelist, dramatist
Index t Wom; Nat Cyc Am Bio
csv3; Wom Lit, More

19776. Fox, Della May
1870–1913
light opera comedian
Not Am Wom

19777. Gaw, Ethelean Tyson
flourished 1900s–20s
poet, playwright
Index t Wom

19778. Gordon, Julia Swayne
flourished 1900s–10s
actor
Index t Wom

19779. Mercer, Beryl
flourished 1900s–30s
actor
Index t Wom

19780. Taber, Julia Marlowe
born 1870
actor
Twent Cen Bio Dict Not Am

19781. Taylor, Anna
flourished 1900s
stuntperson
Index t Wom

**19782. Barnell, Jane; Lady
Olga**
born 1871
circus personality
Index t Wom

**19783. Bonstelle, Justine Laura
"Jessie"**
1871–1932
stage actor, director, producer,
theater manager
Dict Am Bio supp v1; Nat Cyc
Am Bio v25; Not Am Wom

**19784. Greenewalt, Mary
Elizabeth Hallock; Mary
Greenwalt**
1871–1950
pianist, lighting engineer, lecturer
Nat Cyc Am Bio v39; Index t
Wom

19785. Irving, Isabel
1871–1944
stage actor
Index t Wom; Obit File

19786. Varden, Dolly
1871–1955
circus aerialist and equestrian
Obit File

19787. Adams, Maud
1872–1953
actor
Dict Am Bio supp v5; Index t
Wom; Nat Cyc Am Bio v13;
Not Am Wom; Obit File; Twent
Cen Bio Dict Not Am

19788. Belasco, Genevieve
1872–1956
stage and silent-screen actor
Obit File

19789. Davis, Fay
1872/83–1945
Shakespearean actor
Index t Wom; Obit File

**19790. Friganza, Tixie; Brigid
O'Callaghan**
1872–1955
vaudeville actor
Obit File

19791. Kruger, Alma
1872–1960
actor
Obit File

19792. Langworthy, Mary Lewis
born 1872
clubwoman, drama director
Nat Cyc Am Bio csv2

19793. Matthison, Edith Wynne
1872/75–1955
stage actor
English
Index t Wom; Obit File

19794. McComb, Kate
1872–1959
stage, radio, and television character actor
Obit File

19795. Revell, Nellie MacAleney; Nellie Kellar
1872–1958
journalist, circus and theatrical
publicist, press agent, *New York
World* reporter, radio commentator and personality
Dict Am Bio supp v6; Index t
Wom; Obit File

19796. Ring, Blanche
1872–1961
musical comedy actor
Index t Wom; Obit File

19797. Tyler, Helen
1872–1950
Broadway stage producer
New York
Obit File

19798. Ward, Fannie
1872–1952
Broadway stage actor
New York
Index t Wom; Obit File

19799. Williams, Hattie
1872–1942
musical comedy actor
Obit File

19800. Adair, Jean
1873–1953
actor
Obit File

19801. Bates, Blanche Lyon
1873–1941
screen actor, singer
Dict Am Bio supp v3; Index t
Wom; Not Am Wom; Obit File

19802. Grey, Katherine
1873–1950
actor
Obit File

19803. Insull, Gladys Wallis
1873–1953
Broadway stage actor
Obit File

19804. Johnson, J. Rosamond
1873–1954
musician, actor, composer of the
Black national anthem "Lift
Every Voice and Sing"
Black
Obit File

19805. Kimball, Corinne; Corinne
born 1873
actor
Index t Wom; Wom Cent

19806. la Verne, Lucille
1873–1945
stage actor
Obit File

19807. Sears, Zelda
born 1873
playwright
Index t Wom

19808. Smock, Rose Melville
born 1873
actor
Index t Wom

19809. Walsh, Blanche
1873–1915
actor, vaudevillian
Dict Am Bio; Index t Wom; Nat
Cyc Am Bio v12

**19810. Best, Marjorie Ayres;
Mrs. A. Starr Best**
born 1874
founder of the Drama League of
America
Nat Cyc Am Bio v16

19811. Brinker, Una Abell
1874–1952
stage actor

New York, NY
Obit File

19812. Elliott, Gertrude
1874–1950
actor
Not Am Wom

19813. Flexner, Anne Crawford
1874–1955
playwright, director of the Institute for Advanced Studies at
Princeton University
Princeton, NJ
Index t Wom; Obit File

19814. Gale, Zona; Mrs. William L. Breese
1874–1938
novelist, playwright, essayist
Wisconsin
Dict Am Bio supp v2; Dict Lit
Bio v9; Index t Wom; Nat Cyc
Am Bio v30 and csv2; Not Am
Wom; Wom Lit, More

**19815. George, Grace; Mrs.
William A. Brady**
1874/80–1961
actor, playwright
Index t Wom; Nat Cyc Am Bio
v45; Obit File

19816. Glaser, Lulu
1874–1958
comic-opera actor
Index t Wom; Obit File

19817. Kalich, Bertha
1874–1939
actor
Not Am Wom

**19818. Nugent, Maude; Maude
Jerome**
1874–1958
composer, vaudeville entertainer
Obit File

19819. O'Neill, Nance; Gertrude Lamson
1874–1965
stage and screen tragedian,
Shakespearean and Greek tragedy actor
Index t Wom; Obit File

**19820. Peabody, Josephine
Preston; Mrs. Lionel S.
Marks**
1874/80–1922
poet, dramatist
Cambridge, MA
Dict Am Auth; Dict Am Bio;
Index t Wom; Nat Cyc Am Bio
v19; Not Am Wom; Twent Cen
Bio Dict Not Am

19821. Bradley, Lillian Trimble
born 1875
playwright
Index t Wom

actor, author, nurse, philanthropist, patron of the arts, founder of the Metropolitan Opera Guild
English
Index t Wom; Cur Biog '44 and '80

19866. Bradna, Ella
1879–1957
circus bareback equestrian
Bohemian
Obit File

19867. Bridewell, Carrie
circa 1879–1955
singer, actor
Index t Wom

19868. Carus, Emma
1879–1927
vaudeville actor
German
Index t Wom

19869. Cherry, Effie
1879–1944
vaudeville actor
Obit File

19870. Coughland, Gertrude
1879–1952
actor
Obit File

19871. Crews, Laura Hope
1879/80–1942
stage and screen character actor, comedian
Index t Wom; Not Am Wom; Obit File

19872. Howard, Kathleen
1879–1956
opera singer, screen actor, fashion editor
Obit File

19873. Illington, Margaret
1879/81–1934
actor
Dict Am Bio supp v1; Index t Wom

19874. Olcott, Margaret A.
1879–1949
playwright, biographer
Obit File

19875. Ring, Barbara Taylor
1879–1941
psychiatrist, hospital administrator, playwright
Massachusetts
Index t Wom; Obit File

19876. Stanley, Martha
born 1879
playwright
Index t Wom

19877. Watson, Lucile
1879–1962
character actor
Index t Wom; Obit File

19878. Armond, Isabel d'
flourished 1910
actor
Index t Wom

19879. Barnard, Sophye
flourished 1910s
actor
Index t Wom

19880. Barnes, Gertrude
flourished 1910s
actor
Index t Wom

19881. Bernstein, Aline Frankau
1880/82–1955
stage scene and costume designer, author
Jewish
New York
Dict Am Bio supp v5; Index t Wom; Nat Cyc Am Bio v47; Not Am Wom supp v1; Obit File

19882. Charlesworth, Violet
flourished 1910s
actor
Index t Wom

19883. Charmon; The Perfect Woman
flourished 1910s
actor, acrobat
Index t Wom

19884. Dare, Violet
flourished 1910s
vaudeville actor
Index t Wom

19885. Darwell, Jane; Patti Woodward
circa 1880–1967
screen actor
Hollywood, CA
Index t Wom; Obit File

19886. Donnelly, Dorothy
1880–1928
author, librettist, actor
Index t Wom

19887. Eis, Alice
flourished 1910s
actor
Index t Wom

19888. Green, Ethel
flourished 1910s
vaudeville actor and singer
Index t Wom

19889. Joy, Leatrice
flourished 1910s–20s

actor
Index t Wom

19890. Kate, Elinor
flourished 1910s
vaudeville actor
Index t Wom

19891. Matthews, Frances Aymar
born 18?; flourished 1910s
playwright, poet, novelist
New York, NY
Dict Am Auth; Index t Wom

19892. Mechtold, Mary Rider
flourished 1910s
playwright
Index t Wom

19893. Morgan, Agnes
flourished 1910s
playwright
Index t Wom

19894. Paige, Mabel
1880–1954
actor
California
Obit File

19895. Phelps, Pauline
flourished 1910s
playwright
Index t Wom

19896. Pierpont, Laura
flourished 1910s
actor
Index t Wom

19897. Shaw, Lilian
flourished 1910s
vaudeville actor
Index t Wom

19898. Short, Marion
flourished 1910s
playwright
Index t Wom

19899. Thompson, Charlotte
flourished 1910s
playwright, public relations counsel
Index t Wom

19900. Wallace, Grace
flourished 1910s
vaudeville actor, ventriloquist
Index t Wom

19901. Wellington, Violet Irene
flourished 1910s
dramatic reader, drama teacher, suffragist, pacifist
Nat Cyc Am Bio v19

19902. Bauchens, Anne
1881–1967
film editor
Not Am Wom supp v1

19903. Durnell, Fannie Dafflon; Nitta Jo
born 1881
actor
French
Nat Cyc Am Bio csv1

19904. Fulton, Maud
1881–1950
vaudeville and Broadway stage actor, playwright
Index t Wom; Obit File

19905. John, Alice
1881–1956
Broadway stage actor
New York
Welsh
Obit File

19906. Lee, Auriol
1881–1941
stage director, actor
Obit File

19907. Morgan, Jane
1881–1972
vaudeville, radio, and television actor; singer
Index t Wom; Obit File

19908. O'Connor, Una; Agnes Teresa McGlade
1881–1959
character actor
Irish
Obit File

19909. Weber, Lois
1881–1939
movie director, writer, actor
Not Am Wom

19910. Conquest, Ida
1882–1937
actor
Index t Wom

19911. Cook, Susan Glaspell
1882–1948
novelist, playwright, stage producer, Pulitzer Prize winner
Obit File

19912. de Sousa, May
1882–1968
light opera actor
Obit File

19913. Denni, Gwynne
1882–1949
author, actor, musician, songwriter
Index t Wom

19914. Doro, Marie
1882–1956
actor
Index t Wom

19915. Dresser, Louise (Kerlin)
1882–1965

screen actor, singer
Index t Wom; Obit File

19916. Herne, Chrystal Katharine; Chrystal Pollard
1882–1950
actor
Dict Am Bio supp v4; Not Am Wom; Obit File

19917. Jasie, Tillie Leblang
1882–1945
theater ticket agent
New York
Obit File

19918. Levey, Ethel; Queen of Ragtime
1882–1955
international vaudeville actor
Obit File

19919. Mayo, Margaret
1882–1951
playwright, author
Index t Wom; Obit File

19920. McConnell, Lulu
1882–1962
radio, television, and stage comedian
Obit File

19921. Ottiano, Rafaela
1882–1942
stage, screen, and radio actor
Obit File

19922. Patterson, Nan
born circa 1882
actor, dancer
Index t Wom

19923. Stevens, Emily
1882–1928
actor
Dict Am Bio; Index t Wom

19924. Vokes, May
circa 1882–1957
Broadway stage comedian
New York
Obit File

19925. Clark, Marguerite; Mrs. Harry Palmerston Williams
1883/87–1940
stage and screen actor
Index t Wom; Nat Cyc Am Bio v30; Not Am Wom

19926. Cowl, Jane Cowles
1883/84–1950
stage actor, playwright, theatrical producer and director
Dict Am Bio supp v4; Index t Wom; Nat Cyc Am Bio csv2 and csv5; Not Am Wom; Obit File

19927. Ferguson, Elsie
1883–1961

actor
Index t Wom; Obit File

19928. Frederick, Pauline
1883/86–1938
stage and screen actor
Index t Wom; Not Am Wom

19929. la Follette, Fola (Middleton)
1883–1970
actor, author, suffragist
Obit File

19930. Oliver, Edna May
1883–1942
character actor, comedian
Unitarian
California
Index t Wom; Nat Cyc Am Bio csv6; Obit File

19931. Orstein, Honora; Diamond Tooth Lil
1883–1975
dance hall actor during the Alaska gold rush
Alaska
Obit File

19932. Reed, Florence
born 1883
actor
Index t Wom

19933. Zunser, Miriam Shomer
1883–1951
novelist, playwright
Russian
Obit File

19934. Allgood, Sara
1884–1950
actor
Irish
Obit File

19935. Booth, Ada Pearl Dunlap; Adeline Dunlap
born 1884
actor, World War I nurse
Michigan
Nat Cyc Am Bio v17

19936. Broadhurst, Lillian Trimble Bradley
1884–1959
Broadway theatrical director, playwright
Obit File

19937. Draper, Ruth
1884–1956
actor, monologuist
Dict Am Bio supp v6; Index t Wom; Not Am Wom supp v1; Obit File

19938. Guinan, Mary Louise Cecelia "Texas"
1884–1933

actor, circus performer
Index t Wom; Not Am Wom

19939. McClendon, Rose
1884–1936
actor
Black
Encyc Black Am; Not Am Wom

19940. Miller, Izetta Jewel
1884–1978
feminist, actor
Obit File

19941. Mitchell, Abbie
1884–1960
singer, actor
Black
Index t Wom; Negro Alman; Not Am Wom supp v1

19942. Moran, Pauline Therese "Polly"
1884–1952
movie comedian
Obit File

19943. Prevost, Marie
died 1934
actor
Canadian
Index t Wom

19944. Sandwina, Kati
1884–1952
circus strongperson
Obit File

19945. Taylor, Laurette; Loretta Cooney
1884–1946
actor
Dict Am Bio supp v4; Index t Wom; Not Am Wom; Obit File

19946. Tucker, Sophie; Last of the Red Hot Mamas
1884–1966
singer, comedian, entertainer
Jewish
Index t Wom; Not Am Wom supp v1; Obit File; Who Who Jew Hist

19947. Ward, Winifred Louise
1884–1975
children's theater specialist
Not Am Wom supp v1

19948. West, Claudine
circa 1884–1943
screenwriter
English
Index t Wom

19949. Wycherley, Margaret
circa 1884–1956
stage and screen actor
English
Index t Wom; Obit File

19950. Bara, Theda; Theodosia Goodman
1885/90–1955
silent-screen actor
Jewish
Dict Am Bio supp v5; Index t Wom; Not Am Wom supp v1; Obit File

19951. Burke, Billie
1885–1970
stage and screen actor and comedian
Index t Wom; Obit File

19952. Cecil, Mary
1885–1940
actor
Index t Wom

19953. Ferber, Edna
1885/87–1968
author, playwright
Jewish
Dict Lit Bio v9; Index t Wom; Nat Cyc Am Bio v60 and csv3; Not Am Wom supp v1; Obit File; Read Encyc Am West; Who Who Jew Hist; Wom Lit, More

19954. Hopper, Hedda; Elda Furry
1885/90–1966
actor, journalist, gossip columnist
Hollywood, CA
Index t Wom; Not Am Wom supp v1; Obit File

19955. Hutchinson, Mary Amory Hare; Amory Hare
1885–1969
author, novelist, dramatist, painter, poet, thoroughbred-horse breeder
Episcopalian
California
Nat Cyc Am Bio v57, Index t Wom

19956. Keane, Doris
1885–1945
stage actor
Index t Wom; Obit File

19957. Nash, Mary
born 1885
actor
Index t Wom

19958. O'Hara, Mary; Mary Sture-Vasa
1885–1980
composer, novelist, scriptwriter
Cur Biog '81; Index t Wom

19959. Rouverol, Aurania
1885–1955
playwright, actor, radio scriptwriter, screenwriter
Index t Wom; Obit File

19960. Varden, Evelyn
1885–1958
character actor
Obit File

19961. Akins, Zoe
1886–1958
dramatist, poet, novelist, screenwriter, Pulitzer Prize winner
Dict Am Bio supp v5; Index t
Wom; Nat Cyc Am Bio csv6;
Obit File; Wom Lit, More

**19962. Applegarth, Margaret
Tyson**
born 1886
playwright, children's author, editor
Index t Wom

19963. Boland, Mary
1886–1965
stage and screen actor
Index t Wom; Obit File

19964. Cahill, Lily
1886–1955
stage and screen actor
Texas
Obit File

19965. Clark, Pearl Franklin
1886–1962
dramatist, international management consultant, business executive
Christian Scientist
New York
Nat Cyc Am Bio v47

19966. Fealey, Maude
born 1886
actor
Index t Wom

**19967. Hull, Josephine Sher-
wood; Mary Josephine Sherwood**
1886?–1957
character actor
Dict Am Bio supp v6; Index t
Wom; Obit File

19968. Lawrence, Florence
1886–1938
screen actor
Index t Wom; Not Am Wom

19969. Matthews, Adelaide
born 1886
playwright
Index t Wom

19970. Starr, France
born circa 1886
actor
Index t Wom

19971. Treadwell, Sophie
married 1911
playwright, journalist
Index t Wom; Wom Lit, More

19972. Astor, Gertrude
1887–1977
screen actor
Obit File

19973. Gates, Ruth
1887–1966
actor
Obit File

**19974. Helburn, Therese (Op-
dyke)**
1887–1959
theatrical producer, dramatist,
codirector and administrator of
New York City's theater guild
New York, NY
Dict Am Bio supp v6; Index t
Wom; Not Am Wom supp v1;
Obit File

19975. Kimball, Grace
born 1887
actor
Index t Wom

19976. Parker, Lottie (Blair)
died 1937
dramatist, author
Index t Wom; Nat Cyc Am Bio
v10

19977. Valdo, Pat
born 1887
circus personnel director
Index t Wom

**19978. Yurka, Blanche; Bela
Yurkova**
1887–1974
actor
Not Am Wom supp v1; Obit File;
Slavon Encyc

**19979. Baum, Hedwig "Vicki";
Mrs. Richard Lerf**
1888–1960/62
novelist, playwright, screenwriter
Jewish
Hollywood, CA
Austrian
Dict Am Bio supp v6; Index t
Wom; Nat Cyc Am Bio v52;
Obit File

19980. Bryant, Nana
1888–1955
stage, screen, and television actor
Hollywood, CA
Obit File

**19981. Damerel, Myrtle Vail
"Murt"**
1888–1978
vaudeville and radio actor
Obit File

19982. Dean, Julia
1888–1952
stage and screen actor
Hollywood, CA
Obit File

19983. Franklin, Pearl
circa 1888–1958
playwright, lawyer, Zionist, Hadassah leader
Jewish
Index t Wom; Obit File

**19984. Gleason, Lucille Web-
ster**
1888–1947
stage and screen actor
Hollywood, CA
Obit File

19985. Grey, Jane
1888–1944
stage actor
Obit File

**19986. Kummer, Clare Rodman
Beecher**
born 1888
composer, songwriter, playwright
Index t Wom

**19987. Lorne, Marion (Mac-
Dougall)**
1888–1968
actor, television comedian
Index t Wom; Obit File

19988. Marion, Frances
1888/1900–1973
screenwriter, playwright, novelist
Hollywood, CA
Index t Wom; Not Am Wom
supp v1; Obit File

**19989. O'Neil, Carlotta Monte-
rey**
1888–1970
actor
Obit File

**19990. Perry, Antoinette
(Frueauff)**
1888–1946
actor, theatrical director and pro-
ducer
Dict Am Bio supp v4; Index t
Wom; Nat Cyc Am Bio v37;
Not Am Wom

19991. Solano, Solita
1888–1975
journalist, drama critic, novelist,
poet
French (American expatriate to
Paris)
Dict Lit Bio v4

19992. Starr, Muriel
1888–1950
actor
Obit File

**19993. Turner, Florence E.;
The Vitagraph Girl**
1888?–1946
screen actor
Index t Wom; Not Am Wom;
Obit File

19994. Bates, Florence
1889–1954
movie character actor
Obit File

19995. Bonfils, Helen Gertrude
1889–1962
newspaper executive, chairperson
of the board of the *Denver Post*,
theatrical producer
Catholic
Denver, CO
Nat Cyc Am Bio v56; Obit File

19996. Coit, Dorothy
born 1889
drama coach, director, educator
Index t Wom

19997. Gillespie, Marian
1889–1946
composer, pianist, author, actor,
journalist
Index t Wom

**19998. Janis, Elisie (Bierbower)
(Wilson)**
1889/93–1956
mimic, stage actor, singer, dancer,
vaudevillian, author, songwriter, World War I entertainer
Dict Am Bio supp v6; Index t
Wom; Nat Cyc Am Bio csv1;
Obit File

19999. Morrison, Adrienne
1889–1940
actor, literary agent
Index t Wom

20000. Nilsson, Anna Q.
1889–1974
silent-screen actor
Swedish
Obit File

20001. Rambeau, Marjorie
1889–1970
stage and screen actor
Index t Wom; Obit File

20002. Weiman, Rita
1889/96–1954
author, playwright, screenwriter
Hollywood, CA
Index t Wom; Obit File

20003. White, Pearl Fay
1889–1938
screen actor
Dict Am Bio supp v2; Index t
Wom; Not Am Wom

20004. Arbuckle, Minta Durfee
1890–1975
silent-screen actor, comedian
Obit File

20005. Banky, Vilma
flourished 1920s–30s
actor

Hungarian
Index t Wom

20006. Bellamy, Madge
flourished 1920s
actor
Index t Wom

20007. Brian, Mary
flourished 1920s
actor
Index t Wom

20008. Bronson, Betty
flourished 1920s
actor
Index t Wom

20009. Burdick, Nellie Follis
flourished 1920s–30s
actor, feminist, philanthropist
Index t Wom

20010. Dayton, Katherine
1890–1945
journalist, playwright, political
    satirist, humorist
New York
Index t Wom; Nat Cyc Am Bio
    v34

20011. Dove, Billie
flourished 1920s
actor
Index t Wom

20012. Dumont, Margaret
1890–1965
screen and television actor, comic
    straight person
Obit File

20013. Eagels, Jeanne
1890/94–1929
actor
Dict Am Bio; Index t Wom; Not
    Am Wom

20014. Felton, Verna
1890–1966
actor
California
Index t Wom; Obit File

**20015. Flanagan, Hallie Mae
    Ferguson (Davis); Hallie Da-
    vis**
189?–1969
theater educator, theater adminis-
    trator and director, playwright
Not Am Wom supp v1, Obit File

20016. Gilliam, Florence
flourished 1920s–40s
journalist, theater critic, maga-
    zine publisher
French (American expatriate to
    Paris)
Dict Lit Bio v4

20017. Goodner, Carol
flourished 1920s–30s

actor
Index t Wom

20018. Goodrich, Frances
born 1890
actor, playwright
Index t Wom

20019. Griffith, Corinne
flourished 1920s–30s
actor, author
Index t Wom

**20020. Heyward, Dorothy
    Hartzell (Kuhns)**
1890–1961
playwright, novelist
Dict Lit Bio v7; Index t Wom;
    Obit File

20021. Joyce, Alice
1890–1955
silent-screen actor
Hollywood, CA
Index t Wom; Obit File

20022. Kennedy, Mary
flourished 1920s–30s
playwright
Index t Wom

20023. la Plante, Laura
flourished 1920s
actor
Index t Wom

20024. Linley, Betty
1890–1951
actor
English
Obit File

20025. Logan, Jacqueline
flourished 1920s
actor
Index t Wom

20026. Lord, Pauline
1890–1950
stage actor
Dict Am Bio supp v4; Index t
    Wom; Not Am Wom; Obit File

20027. Lowry, Judith
1890–1976
stage, screen, and television actor
Obit File

**20028. Main, Marjorie; Ma
    Kettle**
1890–1975
screen and stage actor
Cur Biog '75; Index t Wom; Obit
    File

20029. McAvoy, Mary
flourished 1920s
actor
Index t Wom

**20030. McGauley, Minna Hop-
    pe**
flourished 1920s
author, dramatic coach
Index t Wom

20031. Morrison, Anne
flourished 1920s
playwright
Index t Wom

20032. Mumford, Ethel Watts
died 1940
playwright, poet, novelist
Index t Wom

**20033. Murray, Mae; Marie
    Andrienne Koenig**
circa 1890–1965
dancer, silent-screen actor
Index t Wom; Obit File

20034. Nash, Comedien
1890–1950
comedian
Obit File

20035. Natwick, Mildred
flourished 1920s
actor
Index t Wom

20036. Nissen, Greta
flourished 1920s–30s
actor
Norwegian
Index t Wom

**20037. Oelrichs, Blanche Marie
    Louise; Michael Strange;
    Blanche Twede; Blanche
    Tweed**
1890–1950
actor, poet, playwright, suffragist
Index t Wom; Nat Cyc Am Bio
    v39; Not Am Wom; Obit File

20038. Philbin, Mary
flourished 1920s
actor
Index t Wom

**20039. Riddle, Elizabeth "Eli-
    za"**
flourished 1920s
actor
Index t Wom

20040. Sondergand, Gale
flourished 1920s–30s
actor
Index t Wom

**20041. Unger, Gladys Buchan-
    an**
died 1940
playwright
Index t Wom

20042. White, Alice
flourished 1920s–30s

actor
Index t Wom

20043. Wilson, Lois
flourished 1920s
actor
Index t Wom

20044. Witherspoon, Cora
1890–1957
actor
Obit File

20045. Young, Clara Kimball
1890–1960
silent-screen actor
California
Obit File

**20046. Bainter, Fay; Mrs. Re-
    ginald S. H. Venable**
1891/93–1968
stage and screen actor
California
Index t Wom; Nat Cyc Am Bio
    csv6; Obit File

20047. Brice, Fanny (Borach)
1891–1951
comedian; stage, screen, and ra-
    dio actor
Jewish
Brooklyn, NY
Dict Am Bio supp v5; Index t
    Wom; Not Am Wom supp v1;
    Obit File

20048. Broderick, Helen
1891–1959
actor
Obit File

20049. Dawn, Hazel
born 1891/94
actor, singer
Index t Wom

**20050. Kershaw, Willette (La-
    mar)**
1891–1960
actor
Obit File

20051. King, Anita
1891–63
silent-screen actor, racehorse
    owner
Obit File

**20052. Mack, Nila; Nila Mac-
    Laughlin**
1891–1953
radio producer, writer, director,
    actor
Index t Wom; Not Am Wom
    supp v1; Obit File

20053. Nichols, Anne
1891–1966
playwright, author
Index t Wom; Obit File

20054. Painter, Eleanor
1891–1947
opera singer, actor
Nat Cyc Am Bio v44; Obit File

20055. Rich, Irene
born 1891/1917
actor
Index t Wom

20056. Romm, May E.
1891–1977
psychiatrist, president of the Los Angeles and Southern California psychoanalytic societies, motion picture technical adviser
Los Angeles, CA
Obit File

20057. Stewart, Dorothy M.
1891/97–1954
theatrical agent, composer, pianist, author
Australian
Index t Wom

20058. Zucca, Mana; Madame Manna-Zucca
born 1891/94
composer, pianist, actor, singer
Jewish
Index t Wom

20059. Barnes, Djuna
born 1892
novelist, short story writer, poet, playwright, theatrical columnist, illustrator, portrait painter
French (American expatriate to Paris)
Dict Lit Bio v4 and v9; Wom Lit; Wom Lit, More

20060. Brady, Alice
1892–1939
actor
Dict Am Bio supp v2; Index t Wom; Not Am Wom

20061. Brown, Zara Cully
1892–1978
screen and television actor
Obit File

20062. Cotton, Lucy
1892–1948
actor
Obit File

20063. Gerard, Theodora "Teddie"; Teresa Cabre
1892–1942
musical revue actor
Obit File

20064. Gombell, Minna
1892–1973
Broadway stage and screen actor
Obit File

20065. Leitzel, Lillian
1892–1931
circus aerial gymnast
Not Am Wom

20066. Lewisohn, Alice Irene
1892–1944
social worker, theatrical patron and innovator
Index t Wom; Not Am Wom

20067. Lorraine, Lillian
1892–1955
stage actor
Obit File

20068. Preston, Edna
1892–1960
actor
Obit File

20069. Shepley, Ruth
1892–1951
Broadway stage actor
New York
Obit File

20070. Stephens, Nan Bagby
born 1892
playwright
Index t Wom

20071. Trix, Helen
1892–1951
composer, pianist, singer, author, actor
Index t Wom

20072. Turnbull, Margaret
died 1942
novelist, playwright, movie scenarist
Obit File

20073. West, Mae
1892/93–1980
actor, playwright, screenwriter, comedian, author
Cur Biog '81; Index t Wom

20074. Windsor, Claire
1892–1972
silent-screen actor
Hollywood, CA
Obit File

20075. Wood, Peggy
1892–1978
television and stage actor, novelist, autobiographer
Cur Biog '78; Index t Wom; Obit File

20076. Acker, Jean
1893–1978
silent-screen actor
Obit File

20077. Bordoni, Irene
circa 1893–1953
musical comedy actor
French; Corsican
Index t Wom; Obit File

20078. Bush, Marian Spore
1893–1946
philanthropist
Obit File

20079. Byington, Spring
1893–1971
television, stage, and screen character actor
Cur Biog '71; Index t Wom; Obit File

20080. Chatterton, Ruth
1893/1900–1961
actor, novelist
Index t Wom; Obit File

20081. Cornell, Katharine
1893/98–1973
stage actor, theatrical producer
Cur Biog '74; Index t Wom; Nat Cyc Am Bio csv4; Not Am Wom supp v1; Obit File

20082. Ernst, Jessie
born 1893
playwright
Index t Wom

20083. Greenwood, Charlotte
1893–1978
actor, stage and screen comedian
Index t Wom; Obit File

20084. Joyce, Peggy Hopkins
1893/95–1957
actor
Index t Wom; Obit File

20085. Loos, Anita
1893–1981
playwright, screenwriter, novelist, humorist
Cur Biog '74 and '81; Index t Wom; Wom Lit, More

20086. MacMillan, Violet
1893–1953
stage and silent-screen actor
Obit File

20087. Manner, Jane; Jennie Mannheimer
died 1943
dramatic coach
Index t Wom

20088. Normand, Mabel Ethelreid
1893?–1930
silent-screen comedian
Index t Wom; Not Am Wom

20089. Pickford, Mary Smith; Mrs. Douglas Fairbanks
1893–1978
silent-screen actor
Canadian
Cur Biog '79; Index t Wom; Nat Cyc Am Bio csv1

20090. Starling, Lynn
born 1893
playwright
Index t Wom

20091. Barker, Ellen Frye
died 1944
advertising copywriter, dramatic critic, genealogist, publisher
Index t Wom; Obit File

20092. Bushnell, Adelyn
born 1894
actor, author
Index t Wom

20093. Cunard, Grace; Harriet Mildred Jeffries
1894–1967
silent-screen actor
California
Obit File

20094. Ellis, Evelyn
1894–1958
actor
Black
Obit File

20095. Johnson, Osa Helen Leighty
1894–1952/53
explorer, geographer, big game hunter, filmmaker and film producer, aviator, author
Index t Wom; Nat Cyc Am Bio v39; Obit File

20096. O'Hara, Joyce
circa 1894–1953
executive vice-president of the Motion Picture Association of America
Obit File

20097. St. Johns, Adele Rogers
born 1894
journalist, television personality, screen writer, novelist, short story writer
Cur Biog '76; Index t Wom

20098. Ulric, Lenore
1894–1970
stage and screen actor
Index t Wom; Obit File

20099. Allen, Grace Ethel Cecile Rosalie "Gracie"
1895/1905–1964
comedian; radio, movie, and television actor
Index t Wom; Not Am Wom supp v1; Obit File

20100. Baker, Belle; Bella Becker
1895/98–1957
vaudeville singer, actor
Index t Wom; Obit File

20101. Barry, Iris
1895–1969
film historian and critic
Not Am Wom supp v1

20102. Cody, Ethel Sack
1895–1957
Broadway stage actor
Obit File

20103. Eakin, Mary
1895–1947
actor
Obit File

20104. Fazenda, Louise
1895–1962
screen comedian
California
Obit File

20105. Gordon, Mazie P.
born circa 1895
theater owner
Index t Wom

20106. Hansen, Juanita
1895–1961
silent-screen actor
Obit File

20107. Hibbard, Edna
circa 1895–1942
actor, comedian
Index t Wom; Obit File

20108. Jamerson, Pauline Thierry; Polly Preyer
1895–1952
playwright, musical comedy actor
Obit File

20109. MacGill, Moyna
1895–1975
stage and screen actor
Obit File

20110. Mills, Florence
1895–1927
singer, dancer, stage comedian
Black
Encyc Black Am; Index t Wom; Negro Alman; Not Am Wom

20111. Robinson, Gladys Lloyd Cassell
born 1895
actor, social worker
New York
Nat Cyc Am Bio csv6

20112. Smith, Ada; Bricktop
born 1895
singer, dancer, cabaret owner
Index t Wom

20113. Sweet, Blanche
born 1895/96
actor
Index t Wom

20114. Vidor, Florence
1895–1977
silent-screen actor
California
Obit File

20115. Warton, Elizabeth Hines
1895–1971
musical comedy actor
Obit File

20116. Day, Edith
born 1896
actor
Index t Wom

20117. Dickson, Dorothy
born 1896
actor
Index t Wom

20118. Fontanne, Lynn; Mrs. Alfred Lunt
born 1896
actor
English
Nat Cyc Am Bio csv4

20119. Gerston, Berta
1896?–1972
actor
Not Am Wom supp v1

20120. Gish, Lillian
born 1896
screen actor
Cur Biog '78; Index t Wom

20121. Gordon, Ruth
born 1896
stage and screen character actor, scriptwriter
Cur Biog '72; Index t Wom

20122. Marsh, Mae
1896–1968
silent-screen actor
Not Am Wom supp v1; Obit File

20123. McDevitt, Ruth
1896–1976
Broadway stage actor
Obit File

20124. Stewart, Anita
1896–1961
silent-screen actor
Obit File

20125. Waters, Ethel
1896/1900–1977
gospel and blues singer; stage, screen, and television actor
Black
Cur Biog '77; Encyc Black Am; Index t Wom; Negro Alman; Obit File; Prof Negro Wom v2

20126. Chadwick, Helene
1897–1940
actor
Index t Wom

20127. Compson, Betty
1897–1974
silent-screen actor
Index t Wom; Obit File

20128. Foster, Lillian Benson
1897–1949
stage actor
Obit File

20129. Giles, Julia Robbins; Julia Hoyt
1897–1955
actor
Obit File

20130. Godowsky, Dagmar
born 1897
actor
Austrian
Index t Wom

20131. Goldstein, Jennie; Jennie Groll
1897–1960
actor in Yiddish theater
Jewish
New York
Obit File

20132. Mabley, Jackie "Moms"
1897–1975
comedian, vaudevillian
Black
Cur Biog '75; Negro Alman; Obit File

20133. Purviance, Edna (Squires)
1897–1958
silent-screen actor, comedian
Obit File

20134. Smith, Betty Wehner
1897/1904–1972
author, novelist, writer of one-act plays
Cur Biog '72; Index t Wom; Obit File

20135. Speare, Dorothy
1897/98–1951
screenwriter, author, novelist, opera singer, labor worker
Index t Wom; Nat Cyc Am Bio v40; Obit File

20136. Sunshine, Marion
born 1897
composer, actor, author
Index t Wom

20137. Talmadge, Norma
1897–1957
silent-screen actor, producer
California
Dict Am Bio supp v6; Index t Wom; Nat Cyc Am Bio v48; Obit File

20138. Vaughn, Hilda; Hilda Strouse
1897–1957
Broadway stage character actor
New York
Obit File

20139. Ayres, Agnes
1898–1940
silent-screen actor
Index t Wom; Obit File

20140. Bussiere, Tadema Whaley
born 1898
playwright
Index t Wom

20141. Clayton, Bessie
died 1948
vaudeville dancer
Index t Wom

20142. Eager, Helen
1898–1952
drama and film critic
Boston, MA
Obit File

20143. Emerson, Hope
1898–1960
screen actor
Hollywood, CA
Obit File

20144. Etting, Ruth
1898/1907–1978
singer, radio and screen actor
Index t Wom; Obit File

20145. Franken, Rose
born 1898
author, playwright
Index t Wom; Wom Lit, More

20146. Gish, Dorothy
1898–1968
stage and screen actor
Index t Wom; Not Am Wom supp v1; Obit File

20147. Langner, Armina Marshall; Isabelle Louden
born 1898
playwright, producer
Index t Wom

20148. Larrimore, Francine
born 1898
actor
French
Index t Wom

20149. Lawrence, Gertrude (Klassen); Gertrude Alexandra Dagma Lawrence Klassen
1898–1952

Broadway and London stage actor, singer
English
Dict Am Bio supp v5; Dict Nat Bio 1951–1960; Index t Wom; Obit File

20150. Lenihan, Winifred (Wheeler)
1898–1964
actor, theatrical director
Index t Wom; Obit File

20151. Miller, Maralyn
1898–1936
musical comedy actor
Index t Wom; Not Am Wom

20152. Moore, Grace; Mrs. Valentine Parera
1898/1901–1947
musical comedian, opera and popular soprano singer, screen and radio actor
Dict Am Bio supp v4; Index t Wom; Nat Cyc Am Bio v38; Not Am Wom; Obit File

20153. Naldi, Nita; Nonna Dooley
1898–1961
stage and silent-screen actor
Obit File

20154. Picon, Molly
born 1898
actor
Index t Wom

20155. Pitts, Zasu
1898/1900–1963
actor
Santa Cruz, CA
Index t Wom; Not Am Wom supp v1; Obit File

20156. Sifton, Claire
born 1898
playwright
Index t Wom

20157. Vollmer, Lula; Louisa Smith
1898–1955
playwright, short story writer, radio dramatist
Index t Wom; Obit File

20158. Berg, Gertrude Edelstein
1899–1966
radio, television, and screen writer; playwright; producer
Jewish
New York
Index t Wom; Nat Cyc Am Bio v52; Not Am Wom supp v1; Obit File

20159. Francis, Kay; Katherine Gibbs
1899/1905–1968

screen actor
Index t Wom; Obit File

20160. Kaminska, Ida
1899–1980
stage actor, producer, director of Yiddish theater
Jewish
New York, NY
Cur Biog '69 and '80

20161. Langner, Ruth Livingston
1899–1959
play translator
Obit File

20162. le Gallienne, Eva
born 1899
stage actor and producer
English
Nat Cyc Am Bio csv3

20163. MacMahon, Aline
born 1899
actor
Index t Wom

20164. Negri, Pola
born 1899
screen actor
Polish
Index t Wom; Slavon Encyc

20165. Seymour, Jane; Jane Lair
1899–1956
stage, screen, and television actor
Obit File

20166. Swanson, Gloria
born 1899
silent-screen actor
Index t Wom

20167. Talmadge, Natalie
1899–1969
silent-screen actor
California
Obit File

20168. Taylor, Estelle [Ida]
circa 1899–1958
Broadway stage and screen actor
California
Index t Wom; Obit File

20169. Traubel, Helen Francesca; Mrs. William Bass
1899/1903–1972
Metropolitan Opera soprano concert singer, television and film actor, nightclub entertainer
Cur Biog '72; Index t Wom; Nat Cyc Am Bio csv7; Not Am Wom supp v1; Obit File

20170. Vanderbilt, Gertrude
circa 1899–1960
actor, dancer, vaudevillian
Index t Wom

20171. Ace, Jane Sherwood
1900/05–1974
radio actor
Cur Biog '75; Index t Wom; Obit File

20172. Ackley, Edith Flack
flourished 1930s
marionette expert
Index t Wom

20173. Allen, Judith
flourished 1930s
actor
Index t Wom

20174. Axelson, Mary Macdougal
flourished 1930s
playwright
Index t Wom

20175. Benson, Sally Smith "Sara"
1900–72
author, magazine writer, screenplay writer
Cur Biog '72; Index t Wom; Obit File

20176. Best, Edna
1900–74
stage and screen actor
Cur Biog '74

20177. Black, Jean Ferguson
born 1900
playwright
Index t Wom

20178. Blythe, Betty
1900–72
silent-screen and screen actor
Obit File

20179. Boswell, Connee
flourished 1930s
singer, actor
Index t Wom

20180. Brant, Evelyn
1900–75
screen actor
Los Angeles, CA
Obit File

20181. Brooks, G. Anne
flourished 1930s
playwright, stage producer
Index t Wom

20182. Brown, Katharine
flourished 1930s
motion picture executive, editor
Index t Wom

20183. Christians, Mady
1900–51
Broadway stage actor
Austrian
Obit File

20184. Craig, Mary Marsden Young
flourished 1930s
actor, playwright, director
Index t Wom

20185. Davies, Marion; Marion Cecelia Douras
1900–61
screen actor
California
Index t Wom; Obit File

20186. Douglas, Helen [Mary] (Gahagan)
1900/05–1980
stage actor, Democratic representative to Congress from California, opera singer
Episcopalian
California
Cur Biog '80; Index t Wom; Nat Cyc Am Bio csvF

20187. Ellen, Minetta
flourished 1930s
actor
Index t Wom

20188. Feigenblatt, Ann
flourished 1930s
actor, retailer
Polish
Index t Wom

20189. Grew, Agnes Mengel
flourished 1930s
motion picture executive
Index t Wom

20190. Haver, Phyllis
1900/26–1960
silent-screen actor
Index t Wom; Obit File

20191. Hayes, Helen; Mrs. Charles G. MacArthur
born 1900
actor
Catholic
Index t Wom; Nat Cyc Am Bio csv5

20192. Hilder, Vera Gertrude
flourished 1930s
actor, business executive
English
Index t Wom

20193. Irvine, Theodore Ursula
flourished 1930s; died 1952
educator, dramatic coach
Canadian
Index t Wom; Obit File

20194. Kaghan, Leonora
flourished 1930s
playwright
Index t Wom

20195. Kelly, Patsy
flourished 1930s–40s

actor, comedian
Index t Wom

20196. Madison, Marta
flourished 1930s
playwright
Index t Wom

20197. Malloch, Elizabeth
flourished 1930s
actor
Index t Wom

20198. Maxwell, Vera K.
died 1950
Broadway stage actor
Obit File

20199. McLean, Margaret
flourished 1930s
dramatic coach, speech teacher
Index t Wom

20200. Meade, Julia
flourished 1930s
actor, television personality
Index t Wom

20201. Mendelssohn, Eleonora
1900–51
actor
German
Obit File

20202. Mile, Elizabeth
born 1900
playwright
Index t Wom

20203. Moor, Anne
flourished 1930s
physiologist, dramatic teacher
Index t Wom

20204. Moorehead, Agnes
1900/06–1974
stage, screen, and television actor;
  character actor
Cur Biog '74; Index t Wom; Not
  Am Wom supp v1; Obit File

20205. Morgan, Helen
1900?–41
torch singer; stage, screen, and
  radio actor
Dict Am Bio supp v3; Not Am
  Wom; Obit File

20206. Moten, Etta
flourished 1930s
actor, singer
Black
Index t Wom

**20207. Mygatt, Tracy
  Dickinson**
flourished 1930s
playwright, author
Index t Wom

20208. Nathan, Adele Gutman
flourished 1930s

theatrical director, author
Index t Wom

20209. Olcott, Rita
flourished 1930s
playwright
Index t Wom

20210. Oursler, Grace Perkins
1900–55
novelist, playwright, magazine
  writer and editor
Obit File

20211. Perelman, Laura
flourished 1930s
playwright
Index t Wom

20212. Phillips, Anita
flourished 1930s
playwright
Index t Wom

**20213. Seacombe, Charles M.,
  Mrs.**
flourished 1930s
critic, translator, lecturer, actor
Index t Wom

20214. Stickney, Dorothy
born 1900
actor
Index t Wom

20215. Talmadge, Constance
1900–73
silent-screen actor, comedian
California
Index t Wom; Obit File

20216. Thane, Elswyth
born 1900
author, playwright
Index t Wom

20217. van Cleve, Edith
flourished 1930s
dancer, actor
Index t Wom

20218. Verrill, Virginia
flourished 1930s
actor, radio actor
Index t Wom

**20219. Watkins, Maurine Dal-
  las**
born 1900
playwright
Index t Wom

20220. Willard, Catherine
1900–54
actor
Obit File

20221. Wilson, Kathleen
flourished 1930s
radio actor
Index t Wom

20222. Wolter, Annett
flourished 1930s
dramatics educator
Index t Wom

**20223. Damrosch, Gretchen
  Finletter**
born 1901
playwright
Index t Wom

20224. Daniels, Bebe
1901–71
screen actor
Index t Wom; Obit File

20225. Duncan, Rosetta
1901–59
vaudeville actor
Obit File

20226. Eldridge, Florence
born 1901
actor
Index t Wom

20227. Hastings, Mary Hay
1901–57
screen dancer
Obit File

20228. King, Muriel
1901–77
fashion and costume designer
Cur Biog '77; Index t Wom

20229. Lee, Lila
1901/14–1973
silent-screen actor
Index t Wom; Obit File

**20230. Menken, Helen (Rich-
  ard)**
1901–66
actor, president of the American
  Theater Wing, humanitarian
Index t Wom; Obit File

20231. Nillson, Carlotta
died 1951
Broadway stage actor
Swedish
Obit File

**20232. Skinner, Cornelia Caro-
  line Otis**
1901–79
stage actor, monologuist, poet,
  essayist, biographer
Cur Biog '79; Index t Wom; Nat
  Cyc Am Bio csv6

20233. Walker, June
1901–66
screen actor
Hollywood, CA
Obit File

20234. Algase, Julia Cohn
1902–75
lawyer, AFL-CIO worker, actor
Jewish

New York, NY
Nat Cyc Am Bio v58

**20235. Bankhead, Tallulah
  Brockman**
1902–68
screen actor
Cur Biog '69; Index t Wom; Not
  Am Wom supp v12; Obit File

20236. Beavers, Louise
1902–62
screen and television actor
Black
Obit File

20237. Busch, Mae
1902–46
silent-screen actor
California
Obit File

20238. Crawford, Cheryl
born 1902
theatrical producer
Index t Wom

**20239. Cushing, Catherine
  Chisholm**
died 1952
playwright, lyricist
Index t Wom; Obit File

20240. Darvas, Lili
1902–74
Broadway stage actor
Obit File

20241. Eaton, Mary
1902–48
musical comedy actor
Obit File

20242. Flint, Eva Kay
born 1902
playwright
Russian
Index t Wom

20243. Gilbert, Mercedes
died 1952
radio, television, and stage actor
Black
Obit File

20244. Hall, Juanita
1902/13–1968
musical actor, singer
Index t Wom; Obit File

20245. Hamilton, Margaret
born 1902
stage and screen actor
Cur Biog '79

20246. Harding, Ann
born 1902
actor
Index t Wom

20247. Hopkins, Miriam
1902–72

Broadway stage and screen actor
Index t Wom; Obit File

20248. Lessey, Mary E. (Abbey)
died 1952
actor
Obit File

20249. Mann, Clara Lipman
died 1952
actor, playwright
Obit File

20250. Mielziner, Jo
1902–76
set and lighting designer for dramas, musicals, operas, and ballets
Obit File

20251. Minter, Mary Miles
born 1902
actor
Index t Wom

20252. Moore, Colleen
born 1902
actor
Index t Wom

20253. Puck, Mabel Withee
died 1952
musical comedy actor
Obit File

20254. Ralston, Esther
born 1902
actor
Index t Wom

20255. Thayer, Tiffany
1902–59
novelist, film and advertising writer
Obit File

20256. West, Jessamyn [Mary]
born 1902/07
short story writer, novelist, poet, autobiographer, operetta librettist, screenplay writer
Quaker
California
Cur Biog '77; Dict Lit Bio v6; Index t Wom

20257. Williams, Frances;
Frances Jelinek
1902–59
musical comedy actor, dancer who introduced the Charleston
Obit File

20258. Beer, Lisle; Eloise Crowell Smith
born 1903
artist, author, puppeteer
Unitarian
Nat Cyc Am Bio csv9

20259. Bush, Anita
pre-1903–73
singer, actor
Black
Negro Alman

20260. Caspary, Vera
born 1903/04
author, playwright
Index t Wom

20261. Harris, Mildred
1903–44
silent-screen actor
Obit File

20262. Kirkland, Muriel
1903–71
stage, screen, and television actor
Obit File

20263. Luce, Clare (Boothe)
born 1903
playwright, author, journalist, politician, US ambassador
Episcopalian
Index t Wom; Nat Cyc Am Bio csvF; Wom Lit

20264. MacDonald, Jeanette Anna
1903/07–1965
screen actor, soprano singer, dancer
Index t Wom; Not Am Wom supp v1; Obit File

20265. Mitchell, Esther (Wilson)
died 1953
Broadway stage actor
Obit File

20266. Revere, Anne
born 1903
actor
Index t Wom

20267. Ryan, Irene
1903–73
screen and television actor
California
Obit File

20268. Adair, Marion Hopkinson (Barnes)
1904–65
New York civic leader, World War II relief worker, cancer-patient relief worker, patron of cancer research, radio personality, mimic
New York, NY
Nat Cyc Am Bio v51

20269. Bogdanoff, Rose
1904–57
senior costume designer for NBC, theatrical designer
Obit File

20270. Casey, Rosemary
1904–76
playwright, screenwriter
Catholic
Pennsylvania
Nat Cyc Am Bio v59

20271. Costello, Helene
1904–57
silent-screen actor
California
Obit File

20272. de la Motte, Marguerite
1904–50
silent-screen actor
Obit File

20273. Dietrich, Marlene
born 1904
actor
German
Index t Wom

20274. Dunne, Irene; Mrs. Francis Dennis Griffin
born 1904
screen actor
Index t Wom; Nat Cyc Am Bio csv6

20275. George, Gladys; Gladys Clare
1904–54
stage and screen actor
Dict Am Bio supp v5; Obit File

20276. Graham, Shirley
born 1904/07
musical playwright, biographical historian, author, composer
Black
Index t Wom; Negro Alman

20277. Methot, Mayo
1904–51
actor
Obit File

20278. Shearer, Norma
born 1904
actor
Canadian
Index t Wom

20279. Singleton, Catherine Moylen
1904–69
silent-screen actor
Obit File

20280. Anderson, Gertrude Maynard
1905–53
actor, theatrical trainer
Obit File

20281. Armstrong, Charlotte
1905–69
playwright, mystery writer
Cur Biog '69; Index t Wom; Obit File

20282. Bennett, Constance
1905/06–1965
screen actor
Index t Wom; Obit File

20283. Bow, Clara, The "It" Girl
1905–1965
silent-screen actor
Index t Wom; Obit File

20284. Cassiday, Claudia
born circa 1905
music, ballet, and drama critic
Index t Wom

20285. Chase, Ilka
circa 1905–78
stage and screen actor, radio and television personality, novelist, autobiographer
Cur Biog '78; Index t Wom; Obit File

20286. Garbo, Greta
born 1905
actor
Swedish
Index t Wom

20287. Hellman, Lillian
1905/06–1984
dramatist, autobiographer
Jewish
Dict Lit Bio v7; Encyc South Hist; Index t Wom; Nat Cyc Am Bio csv7; Who Who Jew Hist; Wom Lit; Wom Lit, More

20288. Holman, Libby
1905–71
blues singer, Broadway actor
Index t Wom; Obit File

20289. Hyams, Leila
1905–77
silent-screen actor
Obit File

20290. Landi, Elissa
1905–48
stage and screen actor, novelist
Italian
Obit File

20291. Landis, Jessie Royce
1905–72
stage, screen, and television actor
Obit File

20292. Losch, Tilly
1905/07–1975
stage and screen dancer, choreographer
Austrian
Cur Biog '76; Obit File

20293. Loy, Myrna
born 1905
actor
Index t Wom

20294. Mann, Erika
1905–69
author, writer on Germany, actor, lecturer
German
Cur Biog '69; Index t Wom

20295. Miller, Patsy Ruth
born 1905
actor
Index t Wom

20296. Ritter, Thelma
1905–69
stage, screen, and television character actor; first woman to win the American Academy of Dramatic Arts Achievement Award
Cur Biog '74; Index t Wom; Obit File

20297. Webster, Margaret
1905–72
theatrical director, actor, author, producer
Cur Biog '73; Index t Wom; Not Am Wom supp v1

20298. Wicker, Irene
born 1905
singer, actor, radio scriptwriter
Index t Wom

20299. Wong, Anna May; Wong Lu Tsong
1905/07–1961
screen actor
Chinese
Index t Wom; Not Am Wom supp v1; Obit File

20300. Astor, Mary
born 1906
actor
Index t Wom

20301. Baker, Josephine
1906–75
actor, dancer, singer, civil rights worker
Black
Cur Biog '75; Encyc Black Am; Index t Wom; Negro Alman; Not Am Wom

20302. Bennett, Dorothy
born 1906
playwright
Index t Wom

20303. Beranger, Clara
died 1956
screenwriter
Index t Wom

20304. Carroll, Nancy; Ann Veronica La-Hiff
1906–65
stage and screen actor
Index t Wom; Obit File

20305. Costello, Dolores
born 1906
actor
Index t Wom

20306. du Bois, Shirley Lola Graham
1906–77
children's author, biographer, composer, stage director, civil rights worker
Black
Cur Biog '77; Encyc Black Am

20307. Dunnock, Mildred
born 1906
actor
Index t Wom

20308. Gaynor, Janet
born 1906
actor
Index t Wom

20309. Hall, Dorothy
1906–53
Broadway stage actor
Obit File

20310. Munson, Ona
1906–55
stage and screen actor
Obit File

20311. Nolan, Mary; Mary Robertson
1906–48
screen actor
Obit File

20312. Petkere, Bernice
born 1906
composer, author, scenarist
Index t Wom

20313. Sebastien, Dorothy; Dorothy Shapiro
1906–57
silent-screen actor
Obit File

20314. Waters, Marianne
born 1906
playwright
Index t Wom

20315. Booth, Shirley
born 1907/09
actor
Index t Wom

20316. Borden, Olive
circa 1907–47
screen actor
Los Angeles, CA
Index t Wom; Obit File

20317. Chase, Mary Coyle
born 1907
author, playwright
Index t Wom; Nat Cyc Am Bio csv10

20318. Colbert, Claudette
born 1907
actor
French
Index t Wom

20319. Collyer, June; Dorothea Heermance
1907–68
actor
California
Obit File

20320. Knappen, Betty Compton
1907–44
musical comedy actor
Obit File

20321. Rosenstein, Sophie
1907–52
drama coach
Hollywood, CA
Obit File

20322. Shannon, Peggy
1907/10–1941
screen actor, dancer
Index t Wom; Obit File

20323. Stanwyk, Barbara
born 1907
actor
Index t Wom

20324. Steele, Norma Mitchel Talbot
married 1932
playwright
Index t Wom

20325. Ames, Adrienne
1908–47
actor, radio commentator
Obit File

20326. Arthur, Jean
born 1908
actor
Index t Wom

20327. Bonner, Isabelle (Kramm)
1908–55
actor
Obit File

20328. Coca, Imogene
born 1908
actor
Index t Wom

20329. Crawford, Joan
1908–77
screen actor, director of the Pepsi-Cola Co.
Hollywood, CA
Cur Biog '77; Index t Wom; Obit File

20330. Davis, Madonna Josephine "Joan"
1908–61
screen, radio, and television comedian
Obit File

20331. Eilers, Sally
born 1908
actor
Index t Wom

20332. Francis, Arlene
born 1908/12
actor, television personality
Index t Wom

20333. Garson, Greer
born 1908
actor
Irish
Index t Wom

20334. Harrison, Joan Mary
circa 1908
producer, scenarist
English
Index t Wom

20335. Lombard, Carole; Jane Alice Peters
1908–42
screen actor
Dict Am Bio supp v3; Index t Wom; Not Am Wom; Obit File

20336. Merman, Ethel Agnes Zimmerman
born 1908
stage and screen actor and singer
Index t Wom

20337. Olivette, Nina
1908–71
musical comedy actor
Obit File

20338. Rosenthal, Jean
1908/12–1969
theatrical lighting designer, specialist and consultant
Index t Wom; Not Am Wom supp v1; Obit File

20339. Tonkonogy, Gertrude
born 1908
playwright
Index t Wom

20340. Twelvetrees, Helen (Jurgen)
1908–58
screen actor
Obit File

20341. van Riper, Kay
1908–48
movie scenarist
Hollywood, CA
Obit File

20342. Barnes, Florence Lowe "Pancho"
1909–75
aviator, motion-picture stunt pilot, resort owner
Index t Wom; Obit File

20343. Blondell, Joan
born 1909
actor
Index t Wom

20344. Boswell, Martha; Martha Lloyd
circa 1909–58
popular singer, actor
Index t Wom; Obit File

20345. Dodd, Claire
1909–73
screen actor
California
Obit File

20346. Hepburn, Katharine
born 1909
stage and screen actor
Cur Biog '69; Index t Wom

20347. Keeler, Ruby
born 1909/10
Broadway stage actor and dancer, screen actor
Canadian
Cur Biog '71; Index t Wom

20348. Kennedy, Myrna
1909–44
silent-screen actor
Obit File

20349. Sullavan, Margaret (Brooke)
1909/11–1960
screen and stage actor
Dict Am Bio supp v6; Index t Wom; Nat Cyc Am Bio v44

20350. Bennett, Joan; Mrs. Walker Wanger
born 1910
stage actor
Episcopalian
Index t Wom; Nat Cyc Am Bio csv7

20351. Cruisinberry, Jane
flourished 1940s
scriptwriter
Index t Wom

20352. Cullman, Marguerite
married 1935
theatrical producer
Index t Wom

20353. Cummings, Constance
born 1910
actor
Index t Wom

20354. Dalrymple, Jean
born 1910
theatrical publicist, producer, director
Index t Wom

20355. Jewell, Isabel
1910–72
screen and stage character actor
Obit File

20356. la Planche, Rosemary
flourished 1940s
actor
Index t Wom

20357. Levien, Sonya (Hovey)
died 1960
screenwriter
Russian
Obit File

20358. Lynn, Sharon
1910–63
screen actor
Hollywood, CA
Obit File

20359. Niessen, Gertrude
1910/13–1975
singer; comedian; Broadway stage, screen, nightclub, and radio actor
California
Index t Wom; Obit File

20360. Selznick, Irene
born 1910
theatrical producer
Index t Wom

20361. Sidney, Sylvia; Sylvia Kosow
born 1910
stage and screen actor
Cur Biog '81; Index t Wom

20362. Stewart, Ellen
flourished 1940s–70s
off-off-Broadway theatrical producer
Black
Cur Biog '73

20363. Ball, Lucille; Lucy Arnaz
born 1911
actor, comedian, television personality, film producer
Cur Biog '78; Index t Wom

20364. Goddard, Paulette
born 1911
actor
Index t Wom

20365. Harlow, Jean; Harlean Carpenter
1911–37

screen actor
Dict Am Bio supp v2; Index t Wom; Nat Cyc Am Bio v27; Not Am Wom

20366. Oberon, Merle
1911–79
screen actor
Cur Biog '80

20367. O'Sullivan, Maureen
born 1911
actor
Irish
Index t Wom

20368. Rahn, Muriel
1911–61
soprano singer, Broadway musical actor
New York
Black
Obit File

20369. Rogers, Ginger; Virginia Katherine McMath
born 1911
screen actor, dancer
Index t Wom; Nat Cyc Am Bio csv6

20370. Roth, Lillian
born 1911
actor, author
Index t Wom

20371. Russell, Rosalind
1911–76
stage and screen actor
California
Cur Biog '77; Index t Wom; Nat Cyc Am Bio v60; Obit File

20372. Strasberg, Paula; Paula Miller
1911–66
actor, drama coach
Obit File

20373. Weston, Ruth
1911–55
actor
Obit File

20374. Wyatt, Jane Waddington
born 1911/12
actor, television personality
Index t Wom

20375. Allen, Rita
1912–68
theatrical producer
Obit File

20376. Arden, Eve
born 1912
radio and television actor
Index t Wom

20377. Baird, Cora Eisenberg; Cora Burlar
1912–67
puppeteer
Index t Wom; Obit File

20378. Cherrill, Virginia
married 1937
actor
Index t Wom

20379. Colt, Ethel Barrymore
1912–77
actor, singer
Obit File

20380. Crosby, Dixie Lee; Wilma Wyatt
1912–52
Broadway singer and dancer
Obit File

20381. Damarel, Donna
1912–41
actor
Index t Wom

20382. Davis, Joan
1912–61
actor, comedian
Index t Wom

20383. Gibbons, Irene
died 1962
movie fashion designer
Hollywood, CA
Obit File

20384. Henie, Sonja
1912–69
figure skater, film actor
Norwegian
Cur Biog '70; Hall Fame Sport; Index t Wom; Not Am Wom supp v1; Obit File

20385. Jones, Margo
1912–55
Broadway stage producer and director, founder of the modern American concept of theater-in-the-round
Not Am Wom supp v1; Obit File

20386. Kitchell, Iva
born 1912
dancer, comedian
Index t Wom

20387. Massey, Ilona
1912–74
screen actor
Hungarian
Index t Wom; Obit File

20388. Morgan, Claudia
1912–74
Broadway stage actor
Obit File

20389. Powell, Eleanor; Mrs. Glenn Ford
born 1912/13
dancer, actor, television personality
Index t Wom; Nat Cyc Am Bio csv7

20390. Rogers, Dale Evans
born 1912
singer, actor, equestrian
Index t Wom

20391. Sothern, Ann
born 1912
actor, television personality
Index t Wom

20392. Barrett, Edith
1913–77
stage and screen actor
Obit File

20393. Barrie, Wendy
1913–78
screen and television actor
Index t Wom; Obit File

20394. Bevans, Philippa
1913–68
actor
English
Obit File

20395. Evelyn, Judith
1913–67
actor
Index t Wom; Obit File

20396. Gerlette, Anne
1913–58
actor, director, producer, dramatics teacher
Canadian
Obit File

20397. Hathaway, Joy (Kenny)
1913–54
stage and radio actor
Obit File

20398. Larose, Rose
1913–72
burlesque actor
Obit File

20399. Logan, Ella
1913–69
stage and screen actor, musical comedy actor
Scottish
Obit File

20400. Mankiewicz, Rose Stradner
1913–58
actor
Austrian
Obit File

20401. Martin, Mary
born 1913

actor, singer, television personality
Index t Wom

20402. Preminger, Marion Hill; Mrs. Albert Mayer
1913–72
social worker, author, African art collector, missionary to the Congo, philanthropist, screen actor
Catholic
New York
Hungarian
Nat Cyc Am Bio v57; Obit File

20403. Stoddard, Haila
born 1913
actor
Index t Wom

20404. Thompson, Kay
born 1913
actor, singer, author
Index t Wom

20405. Young, Loretta
born 1913/14
actor, television personality
Index t Wom

20406. Carlisle, Kitty; Kitty Carlisle Hart
born 1914
actor, singer
Index t Wom

20407. Colby, Anita
born 1914
actor, technical adviser, journalist, editor
Index t Wom

20408. Farmer, Frances
1914–70
screen and stage actor
Obit File

20409. Lamour, Dorothy
born 1914
actor, singer
Index t Wom

20410. Lee, Gypsy Rose; Rose Louise Hovick
1914?–70
burlesque and stage actor, television personality, mystery writer
Cur Biog '70; Index t Wom; Not Am Wom supp v1; Obit File

20411. McGrath, Leueen
born 1914
actor, playwright
English
Index t Wom

20412. Moorehead, Jean
1914–53
musical comedy actor
Obit File

20413. Scott, Martha
born 1914
actor
Index t Wom

20414. White, Ruth
1914–69
Broadway stage, screen, and television actor
Obit File

20415. Wyman, Jane
born 1914
actor, television personality
Index t Wom

20416. Cashin, Bonnie
born 1915
fashion designer, costume designer
Cur Biog '70; Index t Wom

20417. Comden, Betty
born 1915/19
author, musician, actor
Index t Wom

20418. Faye, Alice
born 1915
actor
Index t Wom

20419. Fisher, Doris
born 1915
composer, singer, producer, author
Index t Wom

20420. Frings, Ketti Hartley
1915–81
screenwriter, novelist, playwright
Cur Biog '81; Index t Wom

20421. Hudson, Rochelle
1915–72
television and screen actor
Index t Wom; Obit File

20422. Lamarr, Hedy
born 1915
actor
Austrian
Index t Wom

20423. Sheridan, Clara Lou "Ann"
1915–67
actor
California
Index t Wom; Obit File

20424. Vickers, Martha
1915–71
screen actor
Obit File

20425. Weingarten, Violet
1915–76
novelist, newspaper journalist, screenwriter
Obit File

20426. Conway, Shirl
born 1916
actor
Index t Wom

20427. Dehavilland, Olivia [Mary]
born 1916
actor
Episcopalian
English
Index t Wom; Nat Cyc Am Bio csv9

20428. Furness, Betty
born 1916
actor, television personality, government official
Index t Wom

20429. Grable, Betty
1916–73
screen actor
California
Dict Am Auth; Index t Wom; Not Am Wom supp v1

20430. Havoc, June
born 1916
actor, television personality
Index t Wom

20431. Henry, Charlotte V.
born circa 1916
actor
Index t Wom

20432. Jackson, Shirley Hardie
1916/19–1965
short story writer, novelist, ghost story writer, playwright, television scriptwriter, writer on domestic subjects, children's author
Dict Lit Bio v6; Index t Wom; Not Am Wom supp v1; Obit File; Wom Lit; Wom Lit, More

20433. Lennart, Isobel
1916–71
stage and screen writer
Obit File

20434. Raye, Martha
born 1916
singer, actor, comedian, television personality
Index t Wom

20435. Stone, Carol
born 1916
actor
Index t Wom

20436. Worth, Irene
born 1916
actor
Index t Wom

20437. Chapin, Anne Morrison
died 1967

playwright
Index t Wom

20438. Deren, Maya
1917–61
filmmaker
Not Am Wom supp v1

20439. Fontaine, Joan
born 1917
actor
Index t Wom

20440. Hayward, Susan
1917/19–1975
film actor
Cur Biog '75; Index t Wom; Not
   Am Wom supp v1; Obit File

20441. Horne, Lena
born 1917
popular singer, actor
Black
Encyc Black Am; Index t Wom;
   Negro Alman

20442. Louise, Anita
1917–70
screen actor
Hollywood, CA
Obit File

**20443. McCullers, Carson
Smith**
1917–67
novelist, playwright
Georgia
Dict Lit Bio v2 and v7; Encyc
   South Hist; Index t Wom; Not
   Am Wom supp v1; Obit File;
   Wom Lit; Wom Lit, More

**20444. Raedler, Dorothy Flor-
ence**
born 1917
theatrical producer
Index t Wom

**20445. Shore, Frances Rose
"Dinah"**
born 1917
singer, television personality
Index t Wom

20446. Wilson, Marie
1917–72
screen and radio actor, television
   personality
Hollywood, CA
Index t Wom; Obit File

20447. Andrews, Lois; Lorraine
   Gourley
died 1968
actor
Obit File

20448. Bailey, Pearl (Mae)
born 1918
singer, actor, entertainer
Black
Cur Biog '69

20449. Field, Betty
1918–73
stage and screen character actor
Cur Biog '73; Index t Wom; Obit
   File

20450. Gabor, Magda
born circa 1918
actor
Hungarian
Index t Wom

20451. Healy, Mary
born 1918
television actor
Index t Wom

20452. Holm, Celeste
born 1918
actor
Index t Wom

20453. Lupino, Ida
born 1918
actor
English
Index t Wom

20454. McCambridge, Mercedes
born 1918
actor
Index t Wom

20455. McGuire, Dorothy
born 1918
actor, singer
Index t Wom

20456. Shelley, Gladys
born 1918
author, lyricist, actor
Index t Wom

20457. Wright, Teresa
born 1918
actor
Index t Wom

**20458. Cummings, Victoria
"Vicki"**
1919–69
musical comedy actor, comedian
New York
Obit File

20459. Edwards, Joan
1919/20–1981
composer, author, singer, songwriter, radio and screen actor
Cur Biog '82; Index t Wom

20460. Falkenburg, Jinx
born 1919
actor
Index t Wom

20461. Hayworth, Rita
born 1919
actor
Index t Wom

20462. Heckart, Eileen
born 1919
actor
Index t Wom

20463. Jones, Jennifer
born 1919
actor
Index t Wom

20464. Kael, Pauline
born 1919
film critic
Jewish
Cur Biog '74

20465. Lake, Veronica
1919–73
screen actor
Hollywood, CA
Index t Wom; Obit File

20466. Miller, Ann; Lucille
   Ann Collier
born 1919/23
tap dancer, stage actor.
Cur Biog '80; Index t Wom

20467. Montgomery, Peggy;
   Baby Peggy
born 1919
actor
Index t Wom

20468. Morison, Patricia
born 1919
actor
Index t Wom

20469. Osato, Sono
born 1919
dancer, actor
Japanese
Index t Wom

20470. Pearce, Alice
1919–67
comedian
Obit File

20471. Childress, Alice
born 1920
playwright, editor, actor
Black
Dict Lit Bio v7; Encyc Black Am;
   Wom Lit; Wom Lit, More

**20472. Dagmar, [Virginia Ruth
Egnor]**
born circa 1920
actor
Index t Wom

20473. Day, Laraine
born 1920/29
actor
Index t Wom

20474. Gabor, Eva
flourished 1950s–60s
actor

Hungarian
Index t Wom

20475. Gabor, Zsa Zsa
born circa 1920
actor
Hungarian
Index t Wom

20476. Guest, Barbara
born 1920
poet, theatrical producer
New York
Dict Lit Bio v5

20477. Lee, Peggy; Peggy Lee
   Barbour
born 1920
singer, composer, actor, businessperson
Index t Wom

**20478. Lindfors, Elsa Viveca
Torstensdotter**
born 1920
actor
Swedish
Index t Wom

**20479. McDonald, Marie
(Frye);** The Body
1920/23–1965
Hollywood screen actor
Hollywood, CA
Index t Wom; Obit File

20480. Pearson, Beatrice
born 1920
actor
Index t Wom

20481. Scott, Hazel Dorothy
1920–81
pianist; jazz singer; stage, screen,
   and musical actor
West Indian (Trinidad)
Cur Biog '81; Index t Wom

20482. Simms, Hilda
born 1920
actor
Black
Index t Wom; Negro Alman

20483. St. Cyr, Lily
born 1920
burlesque queen
Index t Wom

20484. Tierney, Gene
born 1920
actor
Index t Wom

20485. Turner, Lana
born 1920
actor
Index t Wom

**20486. Barrymore, Diana
Blanche Blythe**
1921–60

actor
Index t Wom; Obit File

20487. Channing, Carol
born 1921
film and stage actor
Index t Wom

20488. Grayson, Kathryn
born 1921
singer, actor
Index t Wom

20489. Green, Mitzi
1921–69
Broadway and screen child actor
Obit File

20490. Holliday, Judy; Judith
Tuvim
1921/23–1965
actor
Index t Wom; Not Am Wom
supp v1; Obit File

20491. Kelly, Nancy
born 1921
actor
Index t Wom

20492. Kerr, Deborah
born 1921
actor
Scottish
Index t Wom

20493. McClendon, Ernestine
born 1921
theatrical agent
Black
Negro Alman

20494. O'Hara, Maureen
born 1921
actor
Irish
Index t Wom

20495. Peters, Susan; Suzanne
Carnahan
1921–52
actor
physically handicapped
Obit File

20496. Reed, Donna
born 1921
actor
Index t Wom

20497. Russell, Jane
born 1921
actor
Index t Wom

20498. Starr, Cecile
born 1921
film critic
Index t Wom

20499. Susann, Jacqueline
1921–74

popular novelist, screen actor
Cur Biog '72 and '74; Obit File

20500. Walker, Helen
1921–68
screen actor
Hollywood, CA
Obit File

**20501. Caulfield, Joan [Be-
atrice]**
born 1922
television actor
Index t Wom

20502. de Carlo, Yvonne
born 1922
actor
Canadian
Index t Wom

20503. Garland, Judy; Frances
Ethel Gumm
1922–69
singer, actor, entertainer
Cur Biog '69; Index t Wom; Not
Am Wom supp v1; Obit File

20504. Geddes, Barbara Bel
born 1922
actor
Index t Wom

20505. Grayson, Bette
1922–54
actor
Obit File

20506. Hunter, Kim
born 1922
actor
Index t Wom

20507. Maxwell, Marilyn
1922–72
screen actor, singer
Hollywood, CA
Index t Wom; Obit File

20508. McCraken, Joan
1922–61
actor, dancer
Index t Wom; Obit File

20509. Meadows, Audrey
born 1922/29
actor, television personality
Index t Wom

20510. Storm, Gale
born 1922/24
actor, singer, television personality
Index t Wom

20511. van Fleet, Jo
born 1922
actor
Index t Wom

20512. Walker, Nancy
born 1922

actor
Index t Wom

20513. Winters, Shelley
born 1922
screen actor
Index t Wom

20514. Allyson, June
born 1923
television and movie actor
Index t Wom

20515. Baxter, Anne
born 1923
screen actor
Cur Biog '72; Index t Wom

20516. Benzell, Mimi
1923–70
Metropolitan Opera singer,
Broadway stage singer, night-
club singer
Index t Wom; Obit File

20517. Christian, Linda
born 1923
actor
Mexican
Index t Wom

20518. Darnell, Linda; Monette
Eloyse
1923–65
screen actor
Index t Wom; Obit File

20519. Dee, Ruby
born 1923
stage, screen, and television actor
Black
Cur Biog '70; Encyc Black Am;
Prof Negro Wom v2

20520. Fleming, Rhonda
born 1923
actor
Index t Wom

20521. Gardner, Ava
born 1923
actor
Index t Wom

20522. Kerr, Jean Collins
born 1923/24
playwright, humorist
Index t Wom

20523. Paige, Janis
born 1923
dancer, actor, comedian
Index t Wom

20524. Sterling, Jan
born 1923
actor
Index t Wom

20525. Welch, Mary; Mary
White
1923–58

actor
Index t Wom

20526. Williams, Esther
born 1923
aquacade and screen swimmer,
actor, businessperson
Hall Fame Sport; Index t Wom

**20527. Adams, Abigail (Tom-
mye)**
1924–55
actor
Obit File

20528. Avery, Phyllis
born 1924
actor
Index t Wom

20529. Bacall, Lauren; Betty
Joan Perske
born 1924
screen actor, autobiographer
Cur Biog '70; Index t Wom

20530. Blaine, Vivian
born 1924
television and stage actor
Index t Wom

20531. Dandridge, Dorothy
1924–61
screen actor, singer
Hollywood, CA
Black
Index t Wom; Obit File

20532. Day, Doris
born 1924
actor, singer
Index t Wom

20533. Foch, Nina
born 1924
actor
Dutch
Index t Wom

20534. Haney, Carol
1924–64
dancer, choreographer, musical
stage and screen actor
Index t Wom; Obit File

20535. Page, Geraldine
born 1924
actor
Index t Wom

20536. Saint, Eva Marie
born 1924
actor, television personality
Index t Wom

20537. Brooks, Geraldine
1925–77
television, screen, and stage actor
Jewish
Index t Wom; Nat Cyc Am Bio
v59; Obit File

Broadway stage actor
New York
Obit File

20538. Calvet, Corinne
born 1925
actor
French
Index t Wom

20539. Crain, Jeanne
born 1925
actor
Index t Wom

20540. Darcel, Denise
born 1925
singer, actor
French
Index t Wom

20541. Harris, Julie Ann
born 1925
stage actor
Cur Biog '77; Index t Wom

20542. Lansbury, Angela
born 1925
actor
English
Index t Wom

20543. Leslie, Joan
born 1925
actor
Index t Wom

20544. Meadows, Jayne Cotter
born 1925
actor
Index t Wom

20545. Merrill, Dina
born 1925
actor
Index t Wom

20546. Russell, Gail
1925–61
screen and television actor
Obit File

20547. Stanley, Kim
born 1925
actor
Index t Wom

20548. Stapleton, Maureen
born circa 1925
actor
Index t Wom

20549. Stritch, Elaine
born 1925
actor, television personality
Index t Wom

20550. Verdon, Gwen
born 1925
dancer, actor
Index t Wom

20551. Baggett, Lynne
1926–60
actor
Obit File

20552. Ballard, Kay
born 1926
singer; stage, television, and
    screen actor; comedian
Cur Biog '69; Index t Wom

20553. Dewhurst, Coleen
born 1926?
stage actor
Cur Biog '74

20554. Garroway, Pamela
1926–61
actor, ballet dancer
Obit File

20555. Jackson, Anne
born 1926
stage, screen, and television actor
Cur Biog '80; Index t Wom

20556. Leachman, Cloris
born 1926?
screen and television actor
Cur Biog '75

20557. Lynn, Diana
1926–71
stage and screen actor, comedian
Cur Biog '72; Obit File

20558. Monroe, Marilyn
1926–62
screen actor, comedian
Index t Wom; Not Am Wom
    supp v1; Obit File

20559. Morrow, Doretta (Marano)
1926–68
Broadway and Hollywood stage
    and screen musical actor
Obit File

20560. Neal, Patricia
born 1926
actor
Index t Wom

20561. Palmer, Betsy
born 1926
actor, television personality
Index t Wom

**20562. Rowlands, Virginia
Cathryn "Gena"**
born 1926
screen actor
Cur Biog '75

20563. Vera-Ellen; Vera-Ellen
    Rohe
1926–81
stage actor, dancer
Cur Biog '81; Index t Wom

20564. Wickwire, Nancy
1926–74
stage actor
Obit File

20565. Withers, Jane
circa 1926
actor
Index t Wom

20566. Wright, Martha
born 1926
singer, actor
Index t Wom

20567. Adams, Edith "Edie"
born 1927
actor
Index t Wom

20568. Carroll, Pat
born 1927
stage actor, television personality
Cur Biog '80

20569. Carson, Mindy
born 1927
singer, actor
Index t Wom

20570. Cook, Barbara
born 1927
actor
Index t Wom

20571. Dahl, Arlene
born 1927
actor
Index t Wom

20572. Jhabvala, Ruth Prawer
born 1927
novelist, short story and screen-
    play writer, writer of fiction
    about India
Jewish
Indian; English
Cur Biog '77; Wom Lit; Wom
    Lit, More

20573. Leigh, Janet
born 1927
actor
Index t Wom

20574. MacKenzie, Gisele
born 1927
actor, singer, violinist, television
    personality
Canadian
Index t Wom

20575. Page, Patti
born 1927
singer, actor, television personali-
    ty
Index t Wom

20576. Parsons, Estelle
born 1927
stage, screen, and television actor
Cur Biog '75

20577. Angelou, Maya
born 1928
poet, autobiographer, dancer,
    producer
Black
Cur Biog '74; Encyc Black Am;
    Wom Lit; Wom Lit, More

20578. Black, Shirley Temple
born 1928
child actor, singer, UN represen-
    tative
Cur Biog '70; Index t Wom

20579. Blyth, Anne
born 1928
actor, singer
Index t Wom

20580. Gam, Rita
born 1928
actor
Index t Wom

20581. Kitt, Eartha
born 1928
singer, actor, dancer
Black
Encyc Black Am; Index t Wom

20582. Payton, Barbara
1928–67
screen actor
Obit File

20583. Powell, Jane; Suzanne
    Burce
born circa 1928/29
singer, stage and screen actor
Cur Biog '74; Index t Wom

20584. Grant, Lee
born 1929?
television and stage actor
Cur Biog '74

20585. Kelly, Grace Patricia;
    Princess Grace of Monaco
born 1929
actor
Index t Wom

20586. Moore, Terry
born 1929
actor
Index t Wom

20587. Nichols, Barbara
1929–76
stage and screen actor
California
Obit File

**20588. Thompson, Sada Caro-
lyn**
born 1929
stage actor
Cur Biog '73

20589. Bowen, Ruth
born 1930
businessperson, founder of a tal-
    ent booking agency
Black
Encyc Black Am; Negro Alman

20590. Califano, Grace Marsh
flourished 1960s
actor
Native American (Piscataway)
Ind Today

20591. Calkin, Laurie Archer
flourished 1960s
dancer, choreographer, costume
designer, actor
Native American (Cherokee)
Ind Today

20592. d'Annunzio, Lola
1930–56
stage actor
Obit File

20593. Davis, Bette; Ruth
Elizabeth Davis; Mrs. Arthur
Farnsworth
died 1980
screen actor, character actor
Index t Wom; Nat Cyc Am Bio
csv6

20594. Fields, Totie; Sophie
Feldman
1930–78
nightclub comedian
Jewish
Obit File

20595. Fisher, Gail
flourished 1960s
actor
Black
Negro Alman

20596. Fornes, Maria Irene
born 1930
playwright, theatrical director
New York
Cuban
Dict Lit Bio v7

20597. Gray, Dolores
born 1930
singer, actor
Index t Wom

20598. Hansberry, Lorraine
1930–65
playwright, civil rights reformer,
Socialist party worker
New York
Black
Dict Lit Bio v7; Encyc Black Am;
Index t Wom; Nat Cyc Am Bio
v60; Negro Alman; Not Am
Wom supp v1; Obit File; Prof
Negro Wom v2; Wom Lit;
Wom Lit, More

20599. Henderson, Marcia
born 1930
actor
Index t Wom

20600. Kirk, Phyllis
born 1930

actor
Index t Wom

20601. MacArthur, Mary
1930–49
actor
Obit File

20602. Rivera, Chita
flourished 1960s–80s
singer, dancer, stage and screen
comedian
Puerto Rican
Index t Wom

20603. Umeki, Miyoshi
born 1930
singer, actor
Japanese
Index t Wom

20604. Baker, Carroll
born 1931
dancer, actor
Index t Wom

20605. Bancroft, Anne
born 1931
singer, actor
Italian
Index t Wom

20606. Gaynor, Mitzi
born 1931
actor
Index t Wom

20607. Rule, Janice
born 1931
actor
Index t Wom

20608. Suzuki, Pat
born 1931
singer, actor
Index t Wom

20609. Burstyn, Ellen
born 1932
screen actor
Cur Biog '75

20610. Dickinson, Angie; Angeline Brown
born 1932
screen and television actor
Cur Biog '81

20611. Laurie, Piper
born 1932
actor
Index t Wom

20612. May, Elaine
born 1932
actor
Index t Wom

20613. North, Sheree
born circa 1932
dancer, actor
Index t Wom

20614. Reynolds, Debbie
born 1932
actor
Index t Wom

20615. Smith, Keely
born 1932
singer, comedian
Index t Wom

20616. Terry, Megan
born 1932
musical playwright, dramatist,
television and radio scriptwriter
Dict Lit Bio v7

20617. Angeli, Pier
born 1933
actor
Italian (Sardinia)
Index t Wom

20618. Ball, Suzan
1933–55
screen and television actor
Obit File

20619. Collins, Joan
born 1933
actor
English
Index t Wom

**20620. Grant, Kathryn "Ka-
thy"**
born 1933
actor
Index t Wom

20621. Jones, Carolyn
born 1933
actor
Index t Wom

20622. Lange, Hope
born 1933
actor
Index t Wom

20623. Mansfield, Jayne; Vera
Jayne Palmer
1933–67
stage and screen actor
Index t Wom; Obit File

20624. Novak, Kim
born 1933
actor
Index t Wom

20625. Paget, Dera
born 1933
actor
Index t Wom

20626. Sontag, Susan
born 1933
cultural and art critic, essayist,
novelist, short story writer,
filmmaker
Cur Biog '69; Dict Lit Bio v2;
Wom Lit, More

20627. Tyler, Judy; Judy Hess
1933–57
musical comedy actor, television
actor
Obit File

20628. van Doren, Mamie
born 1933
actor
Index t Wom

20629. Anders, Merry
born 1934
actor
Index t Wom

20630. Burnett, Carol
born 1934
singer; stage, screen, and television actor; comedian
Index t Wom

20631. Didion, Joan
born 1934
novelist, journalist, screenwriter
California
Cur Biog '78; Dict Lit Bio v2;
Wom Lit; Wom Lit, More

20632. Henderson, Florence
born 1934
stage, screen, and television actor;
singer
Cur Biog '71; Index t Wom

20633. Jones, Shirley
born 1934
actor
Index t Wom

20634. Lawrence, Carol
born 1934
actor, singer, dancer
Index t Wom

20635. Lewis, Shari
born 1934
television personality, puppeteer,
ventriloquist
Index t Wom

20636. Louise, Tina
born 1934
actor
Index t Wom

20637. MacLaine, Shirley
born 1934
stage and screen actor, dancer,
autobiographer, feminist, Democratic party worker, political
activist, world traveler
Cur Biog '78; Index t Wom

20638. Sands, Diana
1934–73
stage actor
Encyc Black Am; Obit File

20639. Scala, Gia; Giovanna
Scoglio
1934–72

screen actor
California
Italian
Obit File

20640. Stevens, Inger
1934–70
actor
Swedish
Index t Wom

20641. Woodward, Joanne
born 1934
screen actor
Index t Wom

20642. Carroll, Diahann
born 1935
singer, film and stage actor
Black
Encyc Black Am; Index t Wom;
  Negro Alman

20643. Harris, Barbara
born 1935/37
actor
Index t Wom

20644. Lansing, Joi
1935–72
screen actor
Hollywood, CA
Obit File

20645. Newmar, Julie
born 1935
dancer, director
Index t Wom

20646. Remick, Lee
born 1935
actor
Index t Wom

20647. Rivers, Joan
born 1935
nightclub entertainer, television
  comedian
Cur Biog '70

20648. Sanchez, Sonia
born 1935
poet, playwright
Black
Negro Alman; Wom Lit; Wom
  Lit, More

20649. Hochman, Sandra
born 1936
poet, novelist, playwright, magazine writer
Jewish
Dict Lit Bio v5

20650. Balin, Ina
born 1937
actor
Index t Wom

20651. Dennis, Sandy
born 1937

stage, screen, and television actor
Cur Biog '69; Index t Wom

20652. Fonda, Jane
born 1937
actor, political activist, antinuclear worker
Index t Wom

20653. Moore, Mary Tyler
born 1937
television and stage actor
Catholic
California
Cur Biog '71; Index t Wom

20654. O'Brien, Margaret
born 1937
actor
Index t Wom

20655. Pleshette, Suzanne
born 1937
actor
Index t Wom

20656. Varsi, Diane
born 1937
actor
Index t Wom

**20657. Strasberg, Susan
  Elizabeth**
born 1938
actor
Index t Wom

20658. Wood, Natalie
1938–82
actor
Index t Wom

**20659. Alexander, Jane (Quig-
  ley)**
born 1939
Broadway stage actor
Cur Biog '77

20660. Ashley, Elizabeth
born 1939
stage actor
Cur Biog '78

20661. Bryant, Hazel J.
born 1939
singer, actor, producer
Black
Encyc Black Am

20662. McNair, Barbara
born 1939
television and screen actor, singer
Cur Biog '71

20663. Prentiss, Paula
born 1939
actor
Index t Wom

20664. Seberg, Jean
1939–79

screen actor
Cur Biog '79; Index t Wom

20665. Tomlin, Lily
born 1939?
comedian, stage and screen actor
Cur Biog '73

20666. Tyson, Cicely
born 1939/42
stage, screen, and television actor
Black
Cur Biog '75; Encyc Black Am;
  Negro Alman

**20667. Graves, Nancy Steven-
  son**
born 1940
sculptor, painter, filmmaker
Cur Biog '81

20668. Lasser, Louise
born 1940?
television and screen actor, comedian
Cur Biog '76

20669. Welch, Raquel
born 1940
screen actor
Cur Biog '71

20670. Zapata, Carman
flourished 1970s–80s
television, stage, and screen actor;
  director
Los Angeles, CA
Mexican
Dict Mex Am Hist

20671. Dunaway, Faye
born 1941
screen actor
Cur Biog '72; Index t Wom

20672. Mimieux, Yvette
born 1941
actor
Index t Wom

**20673. Olsson, Ann-Margret;
  Ann-Margret**
born 1941
television actor, nightclub entertainer
Cur Biog '75

**20674. Black, Karen Blanche
  (Zeigler)**
born 1942
screen actor
Scientologist
Cur Biog '76

20675. Dee, Sandra
born 1942
actor
Index t Wom

20676. Funicello, Annette
born 1942

singer, actor, dancer
Index t Wom

20677. Kahn, Madeline Gail
born 1942
screen actor, singer, comedian
Cur Biog '77

20678. Mason, Marsha
born 1942
stage, screen, and television actor;
  comedian
Cur Biog '81

20679. Streisand, Barbra
born 1942
singer, actor
Index t Wom

20680. Tiffin, Pamela
born 1942
actor
Index t Wom

20681. Church, Sandra
born 1943
actor
Index t Wom

20682. Lynley, Carol
born 1943
actor
Index t Wom

20683. Perrine, Valerie
born 1943
stage actor, dancer
Cur Biog '75

**20684. Post, Edith Sedgwick;
  Edie**
1943–71
underground-film actor
California
Obit File

20685. Uggams, Leslie
born 1943
singer, actor
Black
Index t Wom; Negro Alman

20686. Weld, Tuesday
born 1943
actor
Index t Wom

20687. Chaplin, Geraldine
born 1944
screen actor
Cur Biog '79

20688. Clayburgh, Jill
born 1944
stage and screen actor
Cur Biog '79

20689. Danner, Blythe
born 1944
stage, screen, and television actor
Cur Biog '81

20690. Heinkel, Susan
born circa 1944
television actor
Index t Wom

20691. Lansing, Sherry
born 1944
president of production at Twentieth Century–Fox
Cur Biog '81

20692. Ross, Diana
born 1944
popular singer, actor, entertainer
Black
Cur Biog '73; Encyc Black Am; Negro Alman

20693. Hawn, Goldie
born 1945
screen and television actor, comedian
Cur Biog '70

20694. Midler, Bette
born 1945?
popular singer, actor, comedian
Jewish
Cur Biog '73

20695. Moore, Beatrice "Melba"
born 1945
stage and television actor, singer
Black
Cur Biog '73; Negro Alman

20696. Spacek, Mary Elizabeth "Sissy"
born 1945
screen actor
Cur Biog '78

20697. Bergen, Candice
born 1946
screen actor, photojournalist
Cur Biog '75

20698. Duke, Patty
born 1946
screen and television actor
Index t Wom

20699. Farrow, Mia
born 1946
stage, television, and screen actor
Cur Biog '70

20700. Field, Sally
born 1946
television and screen actor
Cur Biog '79

20701. Keaton, Diane
born 1946
screen actor
Cur Biog '78

20702. Lyon, Sue
born 1946
actor
Index t Wom

20703. Minelli, Liza May
born 1946
stage and screen actor, singer
Cur Biog '70

20704. Parton, Dolly Rebecca
born 1946
country music singer, songwriter, screen actor
Native American (Cherokee)
Cur Biog '77

20705. Radner, Gilda
born 1946
stage, television, and screen comedian
Jewish
Cur Biog '80

20706. Shange, Ntzoke
born 1948
poet, playwright, novelist
Black
Cur Biog '78; Wom Lit, More

20707. Streep, Mary Louise "Meryl"
born 1949
stage, screen, and television actor
Cur Biog '80

20708. Swados, Elizabeth
born 1951
play score writer, avant-garde composer, theatrical director, playwright
Jewish
New York
Cur Biog '79

20709. Hemingway, Margaux
born 1955
screen actor
Cur Biog '78

20710. Foster, Jodie; Alicia Foster
born 1962?
screen and television actor
Cur Biog '81

20711. Merande, Doro
died 1975
stage, screen, and television actor
Obit File

No Dates

20712. Ate, Te
traditional Native American actor
Native American (Chickasaw)
Ind Today

20713. Parsons, Harriet Oettinger
motion picture producer, writer
Index t Wom

20714. Woolsey, Betty
skier and skisport builder
Hall Fame Sport

WOMEN'S RIGHTS AND WOMEN'S ISSUES

20715. Adams, Abigail Smith
1744–1818
patriot and relief worker of American Revolution, political mover, letter writer, feminist
Am Bio Dict; Appl Cyc Am Bio; Cyc Am Bio; Dict Am Auth; Dict Am Bio; Dict Am Bio Men Time; Index t Wom; Nat Cyc Am Bio v1; Not Am Wom; Twent Cen Bio Dict Not Am; Wom Cent

20716. Murray, Judith Sargent Stevens; The Gleaner; Constantia
1751–1820
author, essayist, poet, dramatist, feminist
Massachusetts
Cyc Am Bio; Dict Am Bio; Index t Wom; Not Am Wom; Who Who Dur Am Rev

20717. Crocker, Hannah (Mather)
1752/65–1829/47
author, women's rights worker, pioneer, essayist
Cyc Am Bio; Dict Am Auth; Dict Am Bio; Dict Am Bio Men Time; Index t Wom; Not Am Wom

20718. Parrish, Anne
1760–1800
colonial philanthropist for women's causes, educator
Pennsylvania
Dict Am Bio; Index t Wom; Who Who Dur Am Rev

20719. Hinsdale, Nancy
1769–1851
educator of women
Am Bio Dict

20720. Greenwood, Mary Langdon
1775–1855
writer on women's education
Am Bio Dict

20721. Truth, Sojourner; Isabel Baumfree
1775/97–1883/85
social reformer, abolitionist, feminist, lecturer, temperance writer
Black
Cyc Am Bio; Dict Am Rel Bio; Encyc Black Am; Index t Wom; Negro Alman; Not Am Wom; Prof Negro Wom v1

20722. Mitchell, Maria
1791/1818–1889
astronomer, women's rights worker, educator, novelist, poet

Quaker
Massachusetts
Cyc Am Bio; Dict Am Bio; Dict Am Bio Men Time; Index t Wom; Nat Cyc Am Bio v5; Not Am Wom; Twent Cen Bio Dict Not Am; Wom Cent

20723. Grimke, Sarah Moore
1792/93–1873
abolitionist, women's rights worker, writer on social problems, political author, lecturer
Quaker
Cyc Am Bio; Dict Am Auth; Dict Am Bio; Dict Am Rel Bio; Index t Wom; Nat Cyc Am Bio v2; Twent Cen Bio Dict Not Am; Wom Cent

20724. Smith, Julia Evelina
1792–1886/92
suffragist, women's rights worker, abolitionist, Biblical translator
Connecticut
Cyc Am Bio; Dict Am Bio; Nat Cyc Am Bio v7; Not Am Wom

20725. Mott, Lucretia (Coffin)
1793–1880
abolitionist, feminist, Quaker minister, pacifist
Quaker
Cyc Am Bio; Dict Am Bio; Dict Am Bio Men Time; Dict Am Rel Bio; Index t Wom; Nat Cyc Am Bio v2; Not Am Wom; Twent Cen Bio Dict Not Am; Wom Cent

20726. Wright, Frances (d'Arusmont) "Fanny"; Fanny d'Arusmont
1795–1852
author, abolitionist, feminist, philanthropist, lecturer
Scottish
Am Bio Dict; Cyc Am Bio; Dict Am Bio; Dict Am Bio Men Time; Index t Wom; Nat Cyc Am Bio v2; Not Am Wom

20727. Cox, Hannah
1796/97–1876
abolitionist, temperance worker, pacifist, women's rights worker
Quaker
Cyc Am Bio; Dict Am Bio; Index t Wom

20728. Smith, Abigail Hadassah "Abby"
1796/97–1878
suffragist, women's rights worker, abolitionist
Connecticut
Cyc Am Bio; Dict Am Bio; Nat Cyc Am Bio v7; Not Am Wom

20729. Beecher, Catherine Esther
1800–78

educator of women, education writer, social reformer, poet
Episcopalian
New York
Appl Cyc Am Bio; Cyc Am Bio; Dict Am Bio; Dict Am Bio Men Time; Dict Lit Bio v1; Index t Wom; Nat Cyc Am Bio v3; Not Am Wom; Twent Cen Bio Dict Not Am; Wom Cent

20730. Coxe, Margaret
born 1800
historical author, botanist, feminist, educator
Cyc Am Bio; Dict Am Auth; Dict Am Bio Men Time; Index t Wom

20731. Pugh, Sarah
1800–84
educator, abolitionist, suffragist
Not Am Wom

20732. Seward, Maria
flourished 1830s; died 188?
Black women's rights worker
Black
Index t Wom

20733. Umphreville, Lucina
flourished 1830s
feminist
Index t Wom

20734. Gibbons, Abigail Hopper "Abby"
1801–93
abolitionist, prison reformer, feminist, women's welfare worker, Civil War nurse, philanthropist, journalist
Quaker
Cyc Am Bio; Dict Am Bio; Index t Wom; Nat Cyc Am Bio v7; Not Am Wom; Twent Cen Bio Dict Not Am; Wom Cent

20735. Jackson, Mercy Ruggles Bisbee
1802–77
homeopathic physician, temperance and suffrage worker, educator
Cyc Am Bio; Dict Am Bio; Index t Wom

20736. Whitman, Sarah Helen (Power)
1803/13–1878
poet, essayist, feminist
Spiritualist
Providence, RI
Cyc Am Bio; Dict Am Auth; Dict Am Bio; Dict Am Bio Men Time; Dict Lit Bio v1; Nat Cyc Am Bio v8; Not Am Wom; Wom Cent

20737. Smith, Eliza Roxey Snow; The Mother of Mormonism
1804–87
Mormon leader, religious poet, hymn writer, women's leader, suffragist, western pioneer
Mormon
Utah
Cyc Am Bio; Dict Am Bio; Index t Wom; Not Am Wom; Read Encyc Am West

20738. Grimke, Angelina Emily; Angelina Emily Grimke Weld
1805/38–1879
abolitionist, feminist, lecturer
Quaker
Cyc Am Bio; Dict Am Auth; Dict Am Rel Bio; Index t Wom; Nat Cyc Am Bio v2; Twent Cen Bio Dict Not Am

20739. Hunt, Harriot Keziah
1805–75
physician, social reformer, suffragist, lecturer
Boston, MA
Cyc Am Bio; Dict Am Auth; Dict Am Bio; Index t Wom; Nat Cyc Am Bio v9; Not Am Wom; Twent Cen Bio Dict Not Am

20740. McDougal, Frances Harriet (Whipple) (Greene)
1805–75
poet, miscellaneous writer, suffragist
Rhode Island; California
Dict Am Auth; Cyc Am Bio

20741. Chace, Elizabeth Buffum
1806–99
abolitionist, suffragist, women's rights worker, prison reformer, temperance worker
Quaker
Dict Am Bio; Not Am Wom; Twent Cen Bio Dict Not Am; Wom Cent

20742. Chapman, Maria Weston
1806–85
abolitionist, feminist, philanthropist
Dict Am Bio; Index t Wom; Nat Cyc Am Bio v2; Not Am Wom; Twent Cen Bio Dict Not Am

20743. Embury, Emma Catherine (Manly)
1806–63
author, poet, writer on women's education
Brooklyn, NY
Cyc Am Bio; Dict Am Auth; Dict Am Bio; Dict Am Bio Men Time; Index t Wom; Nat Cyc Am Bio v9

20744. Smith, Elizabeth Oakes (Prince)
1806–93
poet, novelist, lecturer, suffragist, women's rights worker, feminist
Cyc Am Bio; Dict Am Auth; Dict Am Bio; Dict Am Bio Men Time; Dict Lit Bio v1; Index t Wom; Nat Cyc Am Bio v9; Not Am Wom; Twent Cen Bio Dict Not Am; Wom Cent; Wom Lit, More

20745. Wright, Martha Coffin Pelham
1806–75
women's rights leader, philanthropist
Index t Wom; Not Am Wom

20746. Taylor, Susan Lucy Barry
1807–81
feminist, pioneer
Index t Wom

20747. Gage, Frances Dana (Barker); Aunt Fanny
1808–84
lecturer, author, temperance worker, abolitionist, suffragist, women's rights worker, Civil War relief worker
Cyc Am Bio; Dict Am Auth; Dict Am Bio; Dict Am Bio Men Time; Index t Wom; Nat Cyc Am Bio v2; Not Am Wom; Twent Cen Bio Dict Not Am; Wom Cent

20748. Ferrin, Mary Upton
1810–81
women's legal rights advocate, feminist
Index t Wom; Not Am Wom

20749. Foster, Abigail (Kelley) "Abby"
1810/11–1887
abolitionist, feminist, Prohibitionist, lecturer, suffragist, temperance worker
Quaker
Cyc Am Bio; Dict Am Bio; Index t Wom; Nat Cyc Am Bio v2; Not Am Wom; Twent Cen Bio Dict Not Am

20750. Fuller, Sarah Margaret; Marchioness Ossoli; Sarah Margaret Fuller Ossoli
1810–50
author, critic, educator, feminist, philosopher, journalist, Transcendentalist revolutionary
Transcendentalist

Boston, MA
Cyc Am Bio; Dict Am Auth; Dict Am Bio; Dict Am Bio Men Time; Dict Lit Bio v1; Index t Wom; Nat Cyc Am Bio v3; Not Am Wom; Twent Cen Bio Dict Not Am; Wom Cent

20751. McCord, Louisa Susannah (Cheves)
1810–1879/80
miscellaneous author, poet, political writer, translator, Confederate essayist, Black welfare worker, feminist, plantation manager
South Carolina
Cyc Am Bio; Dict Am Auth; Dict Am Bio; Dict Am Bio Men Time; Index t Wom; Nat Cyc Am Bio v9; Not Am Wom; Twent Cen Bio Dict Not Am

20752. Nichols, Clarinda Irene Howard
1810–85
newspaper editor, political writer, social reformer, lecturer, women's rights leader, suffragist, feminist
Kansas
Cyc Am Bio; Dict Am Bio; Index t Wom; Nat Cyc Am Bio v5; Not Am Wom

20753. Nichols, Mary Sargent (Neal) Gove
1810–84
women's rights worker, feminist, dress and health reformer, medical author, physician, social reformer, temperance reformer, popular author, novelist
Cyc Am Bio; Dict Am Auth; Dict Am Bio Men Time; Dict Lit Bio v1; Index t Wom; Nat Cyc Am Bio v13; Not Am Wom

20754. Rose, Ernestine Louise Lasmond Siismondi Potowski
1810–92
feminist, women's rights worker, temperance worker, abolitionist
Jewish
Polish
Cyc Am Bio; Dict Am Bio; Not Am Wom

20755. Drake, Priscilla Holmes
born 1812
suffragist
Wom Cent

20756. Lozier, Clemence Sophia
1812/13–1888
physician, founder and dean of the New York Women's Medical College and Hospital for Women, suffragist, feminist
Cyc Am Bio; Dict Am Bio; Index t Wom; Not Am Wom; Twent Cen Bio Dict Not Am

20757. Davis, Pauline Kellog Wright
1813–76
feminist, women's rights worker, suffragist, abolitionist, temperance worker, journalist, editor, lecturer
Cyc Am Bio; Dict Am Bio; Index t Wom; Nat Cyc Am Bio v22; Not Am Wom

20758. Grew, Mary
1813–96
abolitionist, suffragist, feminist, Unitarian preacher, lecturer
Unitarian
Index t Wom; Not Am Wom; Wom Cent

20759. Jones, Jane Elizabeth Hitchcock
1813–96
antislavery and women's rights advocate, lecturer
Index t Wom; Not Am Wom

20760. Morris, Esther Hobart McQuigg Slack
1813/14–1902
suffragist, feminist, judge, western pioneer, justice of the peace
Wyoming
Index t Wom; Not Am Wom; Read Encyc Am West; Wom Cent

20761. Collins, Emily Parmely
born 1814
suffragist, abolitionist, political writer, Civil War nurse
Hartford, CT
Wom Cent

20762. Griffing, Josephine Sophia White
1814–72
abolitionist, feminist, suffragist, welfare worker
Dict Am Bio; Index t Wom; Not Am Wom

20763. Spear, Catherine Swan Brown
born 1814
educator, abolitionist, Underground Railroad worker, prison reformer, suffragist
Wom Cent

20764. Stone, Lucinda Hinsdale
1814–1900
educator, clubwoman, women's club organizer, women's educator, feminist
Index t Wom; Nat Cyc Am Bio v13; Not Am Wom; Wom Cent

20765. Comstock, Elizabeth Leslie Rous
1815–1891/92
social reformer, abolitionist, Underground Railroad worker, pacifist, freed slave's welfare worker, temperance reformer, women's rights worker, Quaker minister, prison reformer, Civil War nurse
Quaker
Dict Am Bio; Index t Wom; Nat Cyc Am Bio v22; Not Am Wom

20766. Cutler, Hannah Maria (Conant) (Tracy)
1815–96
women's rights leader, suffragist, physician, journalist, author, lecturer, pacifist
Illinois
Cyc Am Bio ad; Dict Am Auth; Index t Wom; Not Am Wom; Twent Cen Bio Dict Not Am

20767. Farnham, Eliza Woodson (Burhans)
1815–64
prison reformer, author, lecturer, feminist, suffragist, philanthropist
New York; California
Cyc Am Bio; Dict Am Auth; Dict Am Bio; Dict Am Bio Men Time; Index t Wom; Nat Cyc Am Bio v4; Not Am Wom; Twent Cen Bio Dict Not Am

20768. Stanton, Elizabeth Cady
1815/16–1902
feminist, suffragist, women's rights worker, editor, author, social reformer, theologian
Cyc Am Bio; Dict Am Auth; Dict Am Bio; Dict Am Bio Men Time; Dict Am Rel Bio; Index t Wom; Nat Cyc Am Bio v3; Not Am Wom; Twent Cen Bio Dict Not Am; Wom Cent

20769. Swisshelm, Jane (Grey) (Cannon)
1815/16–1884
journalist, author, editor, publisher, abolitionist, women's rights worker, Civil War nurse
Cyc Am Bio; Dict Am Auth; Dict Am Bio; Dict Am Bio Men Time; Index t Wom; Nat Cyc Am Bio v2; Not Am Wom

20770. Gardner, Anna
born 1816
abolitionist, educator of freedmen, women's rights worker
Wom Cent

20771. Mortimer, Mary
1816/18–1877
educator, women's educator, founder of the Milwaukee Female College
Wisconsin
English
Dict Am Bio; Index t Wom; Nat Cyc Am Bio v7; Not Am Wom; Wom Cent

20772. Newcomb, Josephine Louise le Monnier
1816–1901
philanthropist, patron of women's education
Dict Am Bio; Not Am Wom

20773. Stewart, Eliza Daniel "Mother"
1816–1908
temperance reformer, suffragist, Civil War relief worker
Illinois
Dict Am Bio; Nat Cyc Am Bio v7; Not Am Wom; Wom Cent

20774. Thomas, Mary Frame (Myers)
1816–88
physician, suffragist, women's rights worker, prison reformer, temperance worker, editor
Index t Wom; Not Am Wom; Twent Cen Bio Dict Not Am

20775. Anneke, Mathilde Franziska Giesler
1817–84
author, educator, women's rights worker
Dict Am Bio; Nat Cyc Am Bio v4; Not Am Wom

20776. Coleman, Lucy Newhall; Lucy Colman
1817–1906
abolitionist, educator of Blacks, women's rights worker, suffragist, lecturer, health reformer
Universalist
Dict Am Bio; Nat Cyc Am Bio v4; Wom Cent

20777. Wallace, Zerelda Gray Sanders
1817–1909
temperance worker, suffrage leader, women's rights worker
Index t Wom; Nat Cyc Am Bio v5; Not Am Wom; Wom Cent

20778. Bloomer, Amelia (Jenks)
1818–94
temperance reformer, women's rights worker, suffragist, dress reformer
Cyc Am Bio; Dict Am Auth; Dict Am Bio; Index t Wom; Nat Cyc Am Bio v8; Not Am Wom; Twent Cen Bio Dict Not Am; Wom Cent

20779. Holley, Sallie
1818–93
abolitionist, educator of freedmen, feminist, lecturer
Index t Wom; Not Am Wom

20780. Kirby, Georgiana (Bruce)
born 1818
feminist, prison matron, autobiographer
Santa Cruz, CA
English
Dict Am Auth

20781. Mowry, Martha H.
born 1818
physician, suffragist
Rhode Island
Wom Cent

20782. Stone, Lucy; Mrs. Henry Brown Blackwell
1818–93
feminist, suffragist, women's rights worker, abolitionist, social reformer, editor, lecturer
Massachusetts
Cyc Am Bio; Dict Am Bio; Dict Am Bio Men Time; Index t Wom; Nat Cyc Am Bio v2 and v29; Not Am Wom; Twent Cen Bio Dict Not Am; Wom Cent

20783. Greene, Louisa Morton
born 1819
author, abolitionist, suffragist, women's rights worker, temperance worker, Civil War relief worker
Wom Cent

20784. Howe, Julia Ward
1819–1910
poet, dramatist, songwriter, lecturer, suffrage and women's club leader, feminist, abolitionist, pacifist, prison reformer, Union patriot during the Civil War, philanthropist, traveler
Boston, MA
Cyc Am Bio; Dict Am Auth; Dict Am Bio; Dict Am Bio Men Time; Dict Lit Bio v1; Index t Wom; Nat Cyc Am Bio v1; Not Am Wom; Twent Cen Bio Dict Not Am; Wom Cent

20785. Pinkham, Lydia Estes
1819–83
patent medicine proprietor, abolitionist, temperance worker, women's rights worker
Quaker
Dict Am Bio; Not Am Wom

20786. Sewall, Harriet (Winslow)
1819–89
suffragist, poet, religious poet, abolitionist
Transcendentalist
Boston, MA
Dict Am Auth; Nat Cyc Am Bio v10

20787. Anthony, Susan Brownell
1820–1906

women's suffrage leader, feminist, abolitionist, newspaper publisher, editor
Quaker
Appl Cyc Am Bio; Cyc Am Bio; Dict Am Bio; Dict Am Bio Men Time; Index t Wom; Nat Cyc Am Bio v4; Not Am Wom; Twent Cen Bio Dict Not Am; Wom Cent

20788. Claflin, Roxie
flourished 1850s–60s
feminist, religious worker
Index t Wom

20789. Coe, Emma Robinson
flourished 1850s–60s
lawyer, feminist, lecturer
Index t Wom

20790. Coit, Elizabeth
born 1820
suffragist, temperance worker, humanitarian
Ohio
Irish
Wom Cent

20791. Gleason, Rachel Brooks
1820–1905
physician, medical author, abolitionist, patron of freedmen's education, dress reformer, women's rights worker
Dict Am Auth; Index t Wom; Wom Cent

20792. Henderson, Frances Cox
born 1820
linguist, translator, traveler, philanthropist, suffragist
Episcopalian
Wom Cent

20793. Jenkins, Lydia A.
flourished 1850s
clergyperson, feminist, lecturer
Index t Wom

20794. Livermore, Mary Ashton (Rice)
1820/21–1905
health reformer, hospital administrator, suffragist, temperance worker, abolitionist, Civil War patriot, miscellaneous author
Universalist
Melrose, MA
Cyc Am Bio; Dict Am Auth; Dict Am Bio Men Time; Dict Am Rel Bio; Index t Wom; Nat Cyc Am Bio v1; Not Am Wom; Twent Cen Bio Dict Not Am; Wom Cent

20795. Severance, Carolina Maria (Seymour)
1820–1914

social reformer, women's club leader, women's rights worker, feminist, abolitionist
Dict Am Bio; Index t Wom; Nat Cyc Am Bio v8; Not Am Wom; Wom Cent

20796. Swain, Adeline Morrison
born 1820
suffragist, politician, newspaper political editor, superintendent of public education, Greenback party worker
Iowa
Wom Cent

20797. Blackwell, Elizabeth
1821–1910
physician, medical author and educator, worker for women's medical education
English
Appl Cyc Am Bio; Cyc Am Bio and ad; Dict Am Auth; Dict Am Bio; Dict Am Bio Men Time; Eng Wom; Nat Cyc Am Bio v9; Not Am Wom; Twent Cen Bio Dict Not Am; Wom Cent

20798. Diaz, Abby (Morton)
1821–1904
author, children's author, essayist, social reformer, suffragist, abolitionist, lecturer
Boston, MA
Dict Am Auth; Nat Cyc Am Bio v11; Not Am Wom; Twent Cen Bio Dict Not Am; Wom Cent

20799. Filley, Mary A. Powers
born 1821
suffragist, dairy stock farmer
New Hampshire
Wom Cent

20800. Lewis, Grace Anna
born 1821
naturalist, scientific illustrator, science writer, conservationist, ornithologist, abolitionist, Underground Railroad operator, pacifist, suffragist, philanthropist
Quaker
Index t Wom; Nat Cyc Am Bio v9; Twent Cen Bio Dict Not Am; Wom Cent

20801. Morse, Rebecca A.; Ruth Moza; R. A. Kidder; R. A. K.
born 1821
clubwoman, Sorosis member, suffragist, patron of art, abolitionist, author
New York
Index t Wom; Wom Cent

20802. Thompson, Elizabeth Rowell
1821–99
philanthropist, temperance worker, patron of science and of women's medical education, suffragist, political philosopher
Cyc Am Bio; Index t Wom; Nat Cyc Am Bio v5; Not Am Wom; Twent Cen Bio Dict Not Am; Wom Cent

20803. Whitney, Anne
1821–1915
sculptor, artist, poet, abolitionist, suffragist
Boston, MA
Cyc Am Bio; Dict Am Auth; Dict Am Bio; Index t Wom; Nat Cyc Am Bio v7; Not Am Wom; Wom Cent

20804. Dall, Caroline Wells (Healey)
1822–1912
author, essayist, women's rights worker, women's labor reformer, educator
Boston, MA
Cyc Am Bio; Dict Am Auth; Dict Am Bio; Dict Lit Bio v1; Index t Wom; Nat Cyc Am Bio v9; Not Am Wom; Twent Cen Bio Dict Not Am; Wom Cent

20805. Hooker, Isabella Beecher
1822–1907
suffragist, feminist, philanthropist, lecturer, essayist
Spiritualist
Hartford, CT
Cyc Am Bio; Dict Am Auth; Dict Am Bio; Index t Wom; Not Am Wom; Twent Cen Bio Dict Not Am; Wom Cent

20806. Miller, Elizabeth Smith
1822–1911
social reformer, feminist
Index t Wom; Not Am Wom

20807. Winslow, Caroline B.
born 1822
physician, suffragist
Washington, DC
Wom Cent

20808. Lippincott, Sarah Jane (Clarke); Grace Greenwood
1823–1904
newspaper journalist, lecturer, author, editor, novelist, feminist, poet, children's author
Philadelphia, PA
Cyc Am Bio; Dict Am Auth; Dict Am Bio; Dict Am Bio Men Time; Index t Wom; Nat Cyc Am Bio v4; Not Am Wom; Twent Cen Bio Dict Not Am; Wom Cent

20809. Stebbins, Catherine A. F.
1823–post 1880
social reformer, abolitionist, feminist, suffragist
Index t Wom; Wom Cent

20810. Cheney, Endah Dow (Littlehale)
1824–1904
philanthropist, author, abolitionist, suffragist, women's rights worker, Black civil rights worker, lecturer, philosopher
Transcendentalist
Boston, MA
Cyc Am Bio; Dict Am Auth; Dict Am Bio; Dict Lit Bio v1; Index t Wom; Nat Cyc Am Bio v9; Not Am Wom; Twent Cen Bio Dict Not Am; Wom Cent

20811. Lowe, Martha Ann (Perry)
1824/29–1902
poet, temperance worker, suffragist, author
Somerville, MA
Cyc Am Bio; Dict Am Auth; Index t Wom; Nat Cyc Am Bio v10; Twent Cen Bio Dict Not Am; Wom Cent

20812. Meriwether, Elizabeth (Avery)
1824/32–1916
novelist, women's rights worker, suffragist, Prohibition party worker
Memphis, TN
Dict Am Auth; Encyc South Hist

20813. Minor, Virginia Louisa
1824–94
Civil War relief worker, suffrage leader, women's rights worker
Missouri
Cyc Am Bio; Dict Am Bio; Encyc South Hist; Nat Cyc Am Bio v25; Not Am Wom; Twent Cen Bio Dict Not Am

20814. Perkins, Sarah Maria Clinton
born 1824
lecturer, clergyperson, temperance worker, suffragist
Index t Wom; Wom Cent

20815. Blackwell, Antoinette Louisa (Brown)
1825–1921
Universalist minister, author, lecturer, temperance worker, abolitionist, suffragist, women's rights worker, philosopher, poet, novelist

Unitarian; Congregationalist
Appl Cyc Am Bio; Cyc Am Bio; Dict Am Bio; Dict Am Bio Men Time; Index t Wom; Nat Cyc Am Bio v9 and v29; Not Am Wom; Twent Cen Bio Dict Not Am; Wom Cent

20816. Clay-Clopton, Virginia Caroline Tunstall
1825–1915
suffragist
Not Am Wom

20817. Dahlgren, Madeleine Vinton [Sara] (Goodard); Corinne; Cornelia
1825/35–1898
novelist, translator, antisuffragist
Catholic
Washington, DC
Cyc Am Bio; Dict Am Auth; Dict Am Bio; Index t Wom; Nat Cyc Am Bio v22; Twent Cen Bio Dict Not Am; Wom Cent

20818. Merrick, Caroline Elizabeth (Thomas)
1825–1908
suffragist, temperance leader, author on the South
New Orleans, LA
Dict Am Auth; Nat Cyc Am Bio v10; Not Am Wom; Wom Cent

20819. Robinson, Harriet Jane (Hanson)
1825–1911
suffragist, women's rights worker, feminist, abolitionist, author, poet, dramatist, journalist, merchant
Malden, MA
Cyc Am Bio; Dict Am Auth; Dict Am Bio; Index t Wom; Nat Cyc Am Bio v3; Not Am Wom; Wom Cent

20820. Gage, Matilda Joslyn
1826–98
feminist, suffragist, abolitionist, author, lecturer
Cyc Am Bio; Dict Am Auth; Dict Am Bio; Index t Wom; Nat Cyc Am Bio v2; Not Am Wom; Twent Cen Bio Dict Not Am; Wom Cent

20821. Hazard, Rebecca N.
born 1826
philanthropist, suffragist, Civil War relief worker
Missouri
Wom Cent

20822. Penny, Virginia
born 1826
author, educator, women's labor reform worker, feminist
Cyc Am Bio; Dict Am Auth; Dict Am Bio Men Time

20823. Turner, Eliza L. Sproat Randolph
1826–1903
author, poet, suffragist, women's club leader
Pennsylvania
Dict Am Auth; Not Am Wom

20824. Belcher, Cynthia Holmes
born 1827
journalist, suffragist, temperance worker
Boston, MA
Wom Cent

20825. Doggett, Kate Newell
1827/28–1884
suffragist, educator, art critic, translator
Cyc Am Bio; Index t Wom

20826. Howland, Emily
1827–1929
educator, educator of Blacks, abolitionist, suffragist, pacifist, temperance worker, philanthropist
Quaker
New York
Dict Am Bio; Nat Cyc Am Bio v25; Not Am Wom; Wom Cent

20827. Hussey, Cornelia Collins
born 1827
philanthropist, suffragist
New Jersey
Wom Cent

20828. Kennedy, Kate
1827–90
educator, educational reformer, champion of equal pay for women, women's rights worker, women's labor worker
Oakland, CA
Irish
Nat Cyc Am Bio v30; Not Am Wom

20829. Rich, Helen (Hinsdale); The Poet of the Adirondacks
born 1827
poet, suffragist
Chicago, IL
Dict Am Auth; Index t Wom; Wom Cent

20830. Bascom, Emma Curtiss
born 1828
suffragist, temperance worker
Wom Cent

20831. Battey, Emily Verdery
born 1828
journalist, women's historian
Wom Cent

20832. Blackwell, Sarah Ellen
born 1828

artist, author, suffragist, land and labor reformer, antivivisectionist
Nat Cyc Am Bio v9; Wom Cent

20833. Collins, Jennie
1828–87
labor reformer, welfare worker, philanthropist, suffragist
Massachusetts
Bio Dict Am Lab; Index t Wom; Not Am Wom; Twent Cen Bio Dict Not Am

20834. Goff, Harriet Newell (Kneeland)
born 1828
temperance reformer, author, suffragist, women's prison reformer, essayist
Brooklyn, NY
Dict Am Auth; Wom Cent

20835. Way, Amanda M.
1828/29–1914
temperance leader, suffrage leader, feminist, clergyperson, nurse
Index t Wom; Not Am Wom

20836. Wells, Emmeline Blanchard Woodward
1828–1921
leader of Mormon women, feminist, suffragist, editor, poet
Mormon
Utah
Cyc Am Bio; Not Am Wom

20837. Austin, Helen Vickroy
born 1829
horticulturist, temperance worker, suffragist
Wom Cent

20838. Brooks, Marie Sears
flourished 1859; died 1893
poet, short story writer, journalist, newspaper editor, suffragist
Index t Wom; Wom Cent

20839. Dolley, Sarah Read Adamson
1829–1909
physician, leader of professional women
Index t Wom; Not Am Wom

20840. Hanaford, Phoebe Ann (Coffin)
1829–1921
Universalist minister, historian, journalist, author, feminist, lecturer, chaplain of the Connecticut state legislature
Universalist
New Haven, CT
Cyc Am Bio; Dict Am Auth; Dict Am Bio; Index t Wom; Nat Cyc Am Bio v13; Not Am Wom; Twent Cen Bio Dict Not Am; Wom Cent

20841. May, Abigail Williams
1829–88
Boston social reformer, abolitionist, suffragist, education commissioner, Civil War relief worker
Boston, MA
Index t Wom; Not Am Wom; Twent Cen Bio Dict Not Am

20842. Meriwether, Lide
born 1829
author, lecturer, temperance worker, suffragist
Tennessee
Wom Cent

20843. Patton, Abigail Jemima; Abby Hutchinson
1829–92
alto singer, composer, poet, social reformer, abolitionist, suffragist, hymn writer, feminist
New York; New Hampshire
Nat Cyc Am Bio v10; Wom Cent; Not Am Wom; Index t Wom

20844. Waite, Catharine (Van Valkenburg)
1829–1913
suffragist, women's rights advocate, lawyer, legal journalist, financier, real estate and building executive, writer on Mormonism
Chicago, IL
Cyc Am Bio; Dict Am Auth; Not Am Wom; Wom Cent

20845. Warren, Mary Evalin
born 1829
author, lecturer, temperance worker, suffragist
Baptist
Wisconsin
Wom Cent

20846. Avery, Rosa Miller; Sue Smith
1830–94
author, abolitionist, suffragist
Index t Wom; Nat Cyc Am Bio v6; Wom Cent

20847. Conner, Eliza Archard; "Zig"; E. A.
flourished 1860s–80s
journalist, lecturer, women's rights worker
New York
Wom Cent

20848. Dodge, Mary Abigail "Abby"; Gail Hamilton
1830/36–1896
author, essayist, humorist, magazine writer, editor, abolitionist, suffragist, women's rights worker

Massachusetts
Cyc Am Bio; Dict Am Auth; Dict
Am Bio; Dict Am Bio Men
Time; Index t Wom; Nat Cyc
Am Bio v9; Not Am Wom;
Twent Cen Bio Dict Not Am;
Wom Cent

20849. Doyle, Sarah Elizabeth
1830–1922
educator, clubwoman, women's
rights worker
Dict Am Bio; Not Am Wom

**20850. Humphreys, Sarah
Gibson**
born 1830
author, suffragist
Kentucky
Wom Cent

**20851. Lockwood, Belva Ann
Bennett McNall**
1830/54–1917
lawyer, politician, women's rights
worker, suffragist, pacifist
Dict Am Bio; Index t Wom; Nat
Cyc Am Bio v1; Not Am Wom;
Twent Cen Bio Dict Not Am;
Wom Cent

20852. Stevens, Emily Pitt
flourished 1860s–90s
educator, temperance worker,
feminist, suffragist
Presbyterian
California
Wom Cent

**20853. Bradwell, Myra R.
(Colby)**
1831–1894/96
lawyer, suffragist, editor, Civil
War nurse
Chicago, IL
Dict Am Bio; Index t Wom; Nat
Cyc Am Bio v1; Not Am Wom;
Twent Cen Bio Dict Not Am;
Wom Cent

20854. Eddy, Sarah Stoddard
born 1831
suffragist
Universalist
Wom Cent

20855. Wilhite, Mary Holloway
1831–92
physician, feminist, philanthropist
Wom Cent

**20856. Doolittle, Lucy Salis-
bury**
born 1832
philanthropist, reformer of wom-
en's prisons, suffragist, educator
of freedwomen
Wom Cent

20857. Fray, Ellen Sulley
born 1832

suffragist, feminist, women's la-
bor reformer
Ohio
Wom Cent

20858. Greenleaf, Jean Brooks
born 1832
suffragist
Wom Cent

20859. Hall, Sara C.
born 1832
physician, suffragist
Kansas
Wom Cent

20860. Janes, Martha Waldron
born 1832
Baptist minister, suffragist, tem-
perance worker
Baptist
Iowa
Index t Wom; Wom Cent

20861. McKinney, Jane Army
born 1832
educator, temperance worker,
suffragist, kindergartner
Wom Cent

20862. Saxon, Elizabeth Lyle
1832–1915
suffragist, temperance worker,
lecturer
Congregationalist
Memphis, TN
Nat Cyc Am Bio v16; Wom Cent

20863. Smith, Hannah Whitall
1832–1911
religious author, evangelist, pacifist, temperance worker, wom-
en's rights worker
Quaker
Dict Am Bio; Index t Wom; Not
Am Wom

20864. Walker, Mary Edwards
1832–1919
physician, Civil War medical
worker, hospital founder, army
war surgeon, Union spy during
the Civil War; women's rights
worker, suffragist, dress reformer, inventor, lecturer, winner of
the Congressional Medal of
Honor
Dict Am Bio; Index t Wom; Nat
Cyc Am Bio v13; Not Am
Wom; Wom Cent

**20865. Watts, Margaret Ander-
son**
born 1832
temperance worker, feminist, suffragist
Kentucky
Wom Cent

**20866. Blake, Lillie Devereaux
(Umstead)**
1833/35–1913

suffragist, women's rights worker,
magazine writer, short story
writer
Appl Cyc Am Bio; Cyc Am Bio;
Dict Am Auth; Dict Am Bio;
Index t Wom; Nat Cyc Am Bio
v11; Not Am Wom; Twent Cen
Bio Dict Not Am; Wom Cent

20867. Carson, Delia E.
born 1833
educator of women, traveler
Madison, WI
Wom Cent

**20868. Poole, Hester Martha
(Hunt)**
born 1833/43
author, poet, writer on social and
domestic issues, art critic, artist,
women's rights worker, Sorosis
member
Metuchen, NJ
Dict Am Auth; Nat Cyc Am Bio
v11; Wom Cent

20869. Segur, Rosa L.
born 1833
suffragist
Ohio
Wom Cent

20870. Severance, Juliet H.
born 1833
physician, abolitionist, feminist,
temperance worker, political activist
Spiritualist
Wom Cent

**20871. Stockham, Alice (Bun-
ker)**
born 1833
physician, medical author, musician, biographer, suffragist
Dict Am Auth; Wom Cent

**20872. Wilbour, Charlotte Bee-
bee**
1833–1914
women's rights worker, dress reformer, lecturer, president of
Sorosis
Cyc Am Bio and ad; Index t
Wom; Nat Cyc Am Bio v13

**20873. Duniway, Abigail Jane
Scott**
1834–1915
pioneer, suffrage leader, feminist,
journalist, editor, lecturer
Oregon
Dict Am Bio; Index t Wom; Not
Am Wom; Wom Cent

**20874. Read, Elizabeth C. Bun-
nell "Lizzie B."**
born 1834
journalist, suffragist
Methodist
Wom Cent

**20875. Rose, Martha E. (Par-
melee)**
born 1834
women's labor welfare worker,
social reformer, sociologist, author, art patron, journalist, Sorosis member
Cleveland, OH
Index t Wom; Nat Cyc Am Bio
v11; Wom Cent

**20876. Brown, Olympia; Mrs.
John H. Willis**
1835–1926
Universalist minister, suffragist,
lecturer, feminist
Universalist; Unitarian
Cyc Am Bio and ad; Dict Am
Bio; Index t Wom; Nat Cyc Am
Bio v20; Not Am Wom; Wom
Cent; Index t Wom

**20877. Coppin, Fanny Marion
Jackson**
1835/37–1912/18
educator, foreign missionary, so-
cial worker, lecturer, women's
rights worker
Black
Encyc Black Am; Index t Wom;
Negro Alman; Not Am Wom;
Prof Negro Wom

**20878. Coues, Mary Emily
Bennett**
born 1835
suffragist, women's rights worker
Philadelphia, PA
Wom Cent

20879. Davis, Minnie S.
born 1835
author, temperance worker, suffragist, women's rights worker,
"mental science" healer
Index t Wom; Wom Cent

**20880. Felton, Rebecca Ann
Latimer**
1835–1930
senator from Georgia, labor welfare worker, journalist, author,
orator, feminist, women's rights
worker
Georgia
Dict Am Bio; Encyc South Hist;
Index t Wom; Nat Cyc Am Bio
v13 and v36; Not Am Wom;
Wom Cent

20881. Johnston, Maria I.
born 1835
author, newspaper editor, wom-
en's rights worker
Mississippi
Index t Wom; Wom Cent

20882. Larned, Augusta
born 1835
author, journalist, poet, women's
rights worker

New York, NY
Cyc Am Bio; Dict Am Auth; Nat Cyc Am Bio v13; Twent Cen Bio Dict Not Am

20883. Meech, Jeannette du Bois
born 1835
evangelist, missionary worker, Baptist preacher, temperance worker, industrial educator of women
Baptist
New Jersey
Index t Wom; Wom Cent

20884. Tutwiler, Julia Strudwick
1835/41–1916
educator, women's educator, temperance worker, prison reformer
Alabama
Dict Am Bio; Encyc South Hist; Index t Wom; Nat Cyc Am Bio v15; Not Am Wom; Wom Cent

20885. Ahrens, Mary A.
born 1836
philanthropist, suffragist, lawyer
Index t Wom

20886. Bowles, Ada Christina
born 1836
Universalist minister, suffragist
Universalist
Index t Wom; Wom Cent

20887. Brackett, Anna Callender
1836–1911
women's educator, women's rights worker, author
Dict Am Auth; Dict Am Bio; Nat Cyc Am Bio v21; Not Am Wom

20888. Bullock, Helen Louise
born 1836
temperance worker, music educator, women's prison reformer
Wom Cent

20889. Doe, Mary L.
born 1836
suffragist, temperance reformer, merchant
Methodist
Iowa
Wom Cent

20890. Holley, Marietta; Josiah Allen's Wife; Jemyma
1836/44–1926
author, humorist, poet, essayist, novelist, popularizer of women's rights and temperance doctrines, feminist

Ellisburg, NY
Dict Am Auth; Dict Am Bio; Index t Wom; Nat Cyc Am Bio v9; Not Am Wom; Twent Cen Bio Dict Not Am; Wom Cent; Wom Lit, More

20891. Kilgore, Caroline Burnham "Carrie"
1836/38–1909
educator, lawyer, women's rights advocate
Index t Wom; Nat Cyc Am Bio v5; Not Am Wom

20892. Leslie, Miriam Florence (Folline); Frank K. Leslie
1836/51–1914
magazine editor, publisher, feminist, philanthropist
New York
Cyc Am Bio; Dict Am Bio; Index t Wom; Nat Cyc Am Bio v25; Not Am Wom; Twent Cen Bio Dict Not Am; Wom Cent

20893. Post, Amalia Barney Simons
born 1836
feminist, suffragist
Wyoming
Index t Wom; Wom Cent

20894. Scripps, Ellen Browning
1836–1932
philanthropist, newspaper writer and publisher, patron of marine science, founder of Scripps Marine Lab, pacifist, feminist, temperance worker
La Jolla, CA
Dict Am Bio; Index t Wom; Nat Cyc Am Bio v27; Not Am Wom

20895. Stearns, Sarah Burger
1836–post 1899
suffragist, women's rights worker, philanthropist, Civil War humanitarian, temperance worker, social reformer, educator of freedmen
Unitarian
Cyc Am Bio; Index t Wom; Nat Cyc Am Bio v10; Twent Cen Bio Dict Not Am; Wom Cent

20896. Spencer, Sara Andrews
born 1837
suffragist, women's rights worker, business educator, author
Washington, DC
Cyc Am Bio; Dict Am Auth

20897. Truitt, Anna Augusta
born 1837
temperance reformer, suffragist, patron of industrial education
Muncie, IN
Wom Cent

20898. Wait, Anna C.
born 1837

suffragist, educator, politician
Kansas
Wom Cent

20899. Wyman, Lillie Buffum Chace
born 1837/47
author, muckraking journalist, short story writer, philanthropist, suffragist, labor welfare worker
Georgia
Dict Am Auth; Wom Cent

20900. Brown, Martha McClellen
1838–1916
founder of the Prohibition party, temperance reformer, suffragist, lecturer
Methodist
Ohio
Index t Wom; Nat Cyc Am Bio v27; Not Am Wom; Wom Cent

20901. Gordon, Laura de Force
1838/40–1907
lawyer, journalist, suffragist, women's rights worker, Democratic politician, orator
California
Dict Am Bio; Index t Wom; Nat Cyc Am Bio v1; Not Am Wom; Wom Cent

20902. Hodgin, Emily Caroline Chandler
born 1838
temperance reformer, suffragist
Quaker
Indiana
Wom Cent

20903. Woodhull, Victoria Claflin; Victoria Martin
1838–1927
social reformer, political reformer, stockbroker, feminist
English (American expatriate to England)
Dict Am Auth; Dict Am Bio; Index t Wom; Not Am Wom

20904. Bailey, Hannah Clark Johnston
1839–1923
peace worker, temperance reformer, suffragist, philanthropist
Maine
Index t Wom; Nat Cyc Am Bio v10; Not Am Wom; Wom Cent

20905. Banks, Sarah Gertrude
born 1839
physician, surgeon, suffragist
Unitarian
Michigan
Index t Wom; Nat Cyc Am Bio v18

20906. Clay, Mary Barr
born 1839
suffragist, women's rights worker, farmer
Kentucky
Wom Cent

20907. Freeman, Mattie A.
born 1839
abolitionist, suffragist, women's rights worker, lecturer, journalist
Chicago, IL
Wom Cent

20908. Holmes, Mary Emma
born 1839
suffragist, temperance worker
Illinois
Wom Cent

20909. Logan, Olive
1839/41–1909
actor, dramatist, lecturer, women's rights reformer, author, journalist
Cyc Am Bio; Dict Am Bio; Dict Am Bio Men Time; Index t Wom; Nat Cyc Am Bio v6; Not Am Wom; Twent Cen Bio Dict Not Am

20910. Palmer, Frances Purdy "Fannie"
1839–1923
author, journalist, lecturer, suffragist, feminist
Providence, RI
Dict Am Auth; Index t Wom; Wom Cent

20911. Peckham, Mary Chace (Peck)
1839–92
author, fiction writer, poet, Civil War nurse, suffragist, women's rights worker
Unitarian
Providence, RI
Dict Am Auth; Nat Cyc Am Bio v9; Twent Cen Bio Dict Not Am

20912. Sunderland, Eliza Jane (Read)
1839–1910
lecturer, author, educator, temperance worker, women's rights worker, philosopher
Universalist
Michigan
Dict Am Bio; Nat Cyc Am Bio v10; Wom Cent

20913. Willard, Frances Elizabeth Caroline
1839–98
educator, educational philosopher, suffragist, feminist, women's rights worker, temperance leader, naturalist, philanthropist, newspaper editor, traveler

Methodist Episcopal
Cyc Am Auth; Dict Am Bio; Dict Am Bio Men Time; Dict Am Rel Bio; Index t Wom; Nat Cyc Am Bio v1; Not Am Wom; Twent Cen Bio Dict Not Am; Wom Cent

20914. Callanan, Mrs.
flourished 1870s–80s
lecturer, feminist
Index t Wom

20915. Cole, Miriam M.
flourished 1870s–80s
lecturer, feminist, author, journalist
Index t Wom

20916. Coolidge, Harriet Abbot Lincoln
flourished 1870s–80s
philanthropist, sanitary educator, worker for women's education, author
Wom Cent

20917. Foster, Judith Ellen (Horton)
1840–1910
temperance leader, lawyer, Republican party worker, Prohibitionist, suffragist, political writer, lecturer
Iowa
Cyc Am Bio; Dict Am Auth; Dict Am Bio; Index t Wom; Nat Cyc Am Bio v22; Not Am Wom; Twent Cen Bio Dict Not Am; Wom Cent

20918. Herson, Jane Lord
born 1840
physician, suffragist
Oregon
Wom Cent

20919. Hill, Eliza Trask
born 1840
suffragist, women's welfare worker, journalist, newspaper publisher, political activist, Prohibitionist
Massachusetts
Wom Cent

20920. Mason, Amelia (Gere)
184?–1923
author on women's history
Chicago, IL
Dict Am Auth; Index t Wom

20921. Owens-Adair, Bethenia Angelina
1840–1926
physician, feminist, social reformer
Index t Wom; Not Am Wom

20922. Ricker, Marilla Marks Young
1840–1920
lawyer, suffragist, prison reformer, politician, author, political writer
New Hampshire
Index t Wom; Nat Cyc Am Bio v17; Not Am Wom; Wom Cent

20923. Strickland, S. E.
flourished 1870s
feminist, lecturer, educator
Index t Wom

20924. Swain, Louisa Ann
flourished 1870s
western pioneer, feminist
Index t Wom

20925. Wilson, Augustus
flourished 1870s–90s
suffragist, temperance worker, Methodist Episcopal church worker, missionary worker
Methodist Episcopal
Kansas
Wom Cent

20926. Wilson, Zara A.
born 1840
lawyer, suffragist, feminist, temperance worker, missionary worker
Methodist Episcopal
Nebraska
Wom Cent

20927. Wixon, Susan Helen
flourished 1870s–90s
author, children's editor, educator, feminist
Massachusetts
Wom Cent

20928. Bond, Elizabeth Powell
1841–1926
abolitionist, educator of Blacks, women's rights worker, pacifist, civil rights and temperance worker, dean of Swarthmore College
Pennsylvania
Dict Am Bio; Index t Wom; Nat Cyc Am Bio v6; Wom Cent

20929. Gamble, Eliza Burt
1841–1920
suffragist, women's rights worker, writer on women's rights
Nat Cyc Am Bio v18

20930. Sherwood, Katharine Margaret (Brownlee) "Kate"
1841/43–1914
journalist, newspaper editor, poet, author, clubwoman, suffragist
Canton, OH
Dict Am Auth; Dict Am Bio; Index t Wom; Nat Cyc Am Bio v1; Not Am Wom; Twent Cen Bio Dict Not Am; Wom Cent

20931. Walker, Harriet Granger
1841–1917
philanthropist, hospital organizer, temperance worker, suffragist, police reformer
Methodist
Minneapolis, MN
Nat Cyc Am Bio v6; Wom Cent

20932. Bones, Marietta M.
born 1842
suffragist, temperance worker
Wom Cent

20933. Conant, Frances Augusta
born 1842
journalist, businessperson, founder of a women's employment company
Wom Cent

20934. Cunningham, Susan Jane
1842–1921
suffragist, educator, mathematician, astronomer
Pennsylvania
Nat Cyc Am Bio v6; Wom Cent

20935. Dickinson, Anna Elizabeth
1842–1932
Civil War orator, lyceum lecturer, abolitionist, women's rights worker, suffragist, political activist, Republican party worker, author, actor, philanthropist
Quaker
Cyc Am Bio; Dict Am Auth; Dict Am Bio supp v1; Dict Am Bio Men Time; Index t Wom; Nat Cyc Am Bio v3; Not Am Wom; Twent Cen Bio Dict Not Am; Wom Cent

20936. Dunham, Marion Howard
born 1842
temperance worker, suffragist, Christian Socialist party worker
Wom Cent

20937. Fry, Elizabeth Turner
born 1842
philanthropist, Prohibitionist, humane worker, suffragist
San Antonio, TX
Wom Cent

20938. Henderson, Mary Foote
born 1842/46
suffragist, home economist, cooking and nutrition writer
St. Louis, MO
Dict Am Auth; Twent Cen Bio Dict Not Am

20939. Holmes, Jennie Florella
born 1842

temperance worker, suffragist, women's rights worker
Nebraska
Wom Cent

20940. Hunt, Augusta Merrill
born 1842
philanthropist, temperance worker, suffragist, prison reformer
Universalist
Wom Cent

20941. Jacobi, Mary Corinna Putnam
1842–1906
physician, medical author, pharmacist, educator, feminist
New York, NY
Cyc Am Bio; Dict Am Auth; Dict Am Bio; Index t Wom; Nat Cyc Am Bio v8; Not Am Wom; Twent Cen Bio Dict Not Am; Wom Cent

20942. Neblett, Ann Viola
born 1842
temperance worker, suffragist
South Carolina; Georgia
Index t Wom

20943. Ruffin, Josephine St. Pierre
1842–1924
clubwoman, Black leader, Black welfare and rights worker, president of the National Federation of Afro-American Women, Union patriot in the Civil War
Black
Index t Wom; Negro Alman; Not Am Wom; Prof Negro Wom v1

20944. Stone, Mary Perry
born 1842
businessperson, railroad station agent, suffragist
Oregon
Wom Cent

20945. Everhard, Caroline McCullough
born 1843
suffragist, feminist, humane society worker
Ohio
Wom Cent

20946. Gougar, Helen Mar Jackson
1843–1907
suffrage and temperance reformer, orator, author
Index t Wom; Not Am Wom; Wom Cent

20947. Harbert, Elizabeth Boynton "Lizzie"
born 1843
author, lecturer, suffragist
Index t Wom; Wom Cent

20948. Moots, Cornelia Moore Chillison
born 1843
temperance evangelist, suffragist, women's rights worker
Methodist Episcopal
Michigan
Wom Cent

20949. Oliver, Anna
died 1893
clergyperson, feminist
Index t Wom

20950. Ripley, Martha George Rogers
1843–1912
physician, humanitarian, feminist, abolitionist, temperance worker, suffragist
Index t Wom; Not Am Wom; Wom Cent

20951. Rose, Ellen Alida
born 1843
feminist, agriculturist, businessperson, Grange worker, suffragist
Index t Wom; Wom Cent

20952. Spurlock, Isabella Smiley Davis
born 1843
philanthropist, temperance worker, Mormon women's welfare worker
Nebraska
Wom Cent

20953. Austin, Harriet Bunker
born 1844
women's rights worker, author
Wom Cent

20954. Berry, Martia L. Davis
born 1844
suffragist, temperance worker, politician, political reformer
Index t Wom; Wom Cent

20955. Colby, H. Maria George; H. Maria George
born 1844
children's author, domestic writer, women's rights and temperance worker
Wom Cent

20956. Ferree, Susan Frances Nelson
born 1844
journalist, temperance worker, suffragist, women's rights worker
Episcopalian
Iowa
Wom Cent

20957. Howell, Mary Seymour
born 1844
lecturer, suffragist

New York
Wom Cent

20958. Loud, Hulda Barker
born 1844
editor, publisher, women's rights worker, suffragist, labor worker, lecturer
Index t Wom; Wom Cent

20959. Lozier, Charlotte Irene
1844–70
physician, women's rights worker, suffragist, medical educator
Cyc Am Bio

20960. Phelps, Elizabeth Stuart; Mrs. Ward
1844–1911
author, lecturer, women's rights worker, temperance worker
Cyc Am Bio and ad; Dict Am Bio Men Time

20961. Sewall, Mary Eliza Wright
1844–1920
educator, suffragist, women's rights worker, feminist, Sorosis member, clubwoman, pacifist
Dict Am Bio; Index t Wom; Nat Cyc Am Bio v19; Not Am Wom; Wom Cent

20962. Stevens, Lillian Marion Norton Ames
1844–1914
temperance reformer, women's rights worker, lecturer, philanthropist
Maine
Index t Wom; Nat Cyc Am Bio v13; Not Am Wom; Wom Cent

20963. Switzer, Lucy Robbins Messer
born 1844
temperance worker, feminist, suffragist, politician
Wom Cent

20964. Todd, Minnie J. Terrell
born 1844
suffragist
Nebraska
Wom Cent

20965. Villard, Helen Frances Garrison "Fanny"
1844–1928
philanthropist, suffragist, pacifist, worker for Black civil rights
Dict Am Bio; Not Am Wom

20966. Ward, Elizabeth Stuart (Phelps)
1844–1911
author, popular novelist, women's rights worker, temperance worker, philanthropist

Massachusetts
Cyc Am Bio; Dict Am Auth; Dict Am Bio; Dict Am Bio Men Time; Index t Wom; Nat Cyc Am Bio v9; Not Am Wom; Twent Cen Bio Dict Not Am; Wom Cent; Wom Lit, More

20967. Young, Ann Eliza Webb
1844–post 1908
lecturer and writer against Mormon polygamy, feminist, religious worker, pioneer
Index t Wom; Not Am Wom

20968. Bailey, Lepha Eliza (Dunton)
born 1845
temperance worker, Prohibitionist, suffragist, lecturer, author
Wom Cent

20969. Blankenburg, Lucretia M. Longshore
1845–1937
suffragist, women's rights worker, clubwoman, civic worker
Pennsylvania
Nat Cyc Am Bio csv2; Not Am Wom

20970. Carhart, Clara Sully
born 1845
educator, temperance worker, women's labor welfare worker
Methodist Episcopal
New York
Canadian
Wom Cent

20971. Claflin, Tennessee Celeste
1845/46–1923
social reformer, feminist, stockbroker, newspaper editor, journalist
Index t Wom; Not Am Wom

20972. Comfort, Anna (Manning)
born 1845
gynecologist, medical author, suffragist, women's rights worker, Sorosis member
Dict Am Auth; Nat Cyc Am Bio v3; Wom Cent

20973. Gannett, Abbie M.
born 1845
author, women's rights worker
Unitarian
Wom Cent

20974. Hall, Florence Marion Howe
1845–1922
author, essayist, writer on etiquette, lecturer, suffragist
Unitarian
Plainfield, NJ
Dict Am Auth; Dict Am Bio; Nat Cyc Am Bio v19

20975. Henry, Josephine Kirby Williamson
born 1845
suffragist, politician, political writer, Prohibitionist
Kentucky
Wom Cent

20976. Peters, Alice E. H.
born 1845
church and temperance worker, suffragist, author
Methodist Episcopal
Ohio
Wom Cent

20977. Pier, Kate Hamilton
1845–1925
lawyer, feminist
Wisconsin
Index t Wom; Nat Cyc Am Bio v21; Wom Cent

20978. Shaw, Cornelia Dean
born 1845
suffragist, philanthropist, Congregationalist missionary worker
Congregationalist
Toledo, OH
Wom Cent

20979. Ward, Lydia Arms (Avery) (Coonley)
1845–1924
author, poet, patron of the arts, suffragist, philanthropist
Chicago, IL
Dict Am Auth; Dict Am Bio; Index t Wom; Nat Cyc Am Bio v34

20980. Young, Ella (Flagg)
1845–1918
university educator and administrator, writer on education, suffragist
Chicago, IL
Dict Am Auth; Dict Am Bio; Index t Wom; Nat Cyc Am Bio v19; Not Am Wom

20981. Claflin, Adelaide Avery
born 1846
suffragist, journalist
Wom Cent

20982. Colby, Clara Dorothy Bewick
1846–1916
suffragist
Not Am Wom

20983. Seymour, Mary Foot
1846–93
stenographer, businessperson, journalist, law reporter, suffragist, women's labor worker
Not Am Wom; Wom Cent

20984. Henrotin, Ellen M. Martin
1847–1922

women's club leader, labor and social reformer, philanthropist
Index t Wom; Not Am Wom

20985. Johnson, Adelaide
1847/49–1955
sculptor, feminist, women's rights worker
Index t Wom; Not Am Wom supp v1; Obit File

20986. Shaw, Anna Howard
1847–1919
minister, lecturer, suffragist, women's rights worker, physician, temperance worker
Methodist
English
Dict Am Bio; Index t Wom; Nat Cyc Am Bio v14; Not Am Wom; Wom Cent

20987. Smith, Jane Luella Dowd
born 1847
educator, author, poet, children's author, suffragist, temperance worker
Hudson, NY
Cyc Am Bio; Dict Am Auth; Nat Cyc Am Bio v1; Twent Cen Bio Dict Not Am; Wom Cent

20988. Wheelock, Dora V.
born 1847
temperance worker, suffragist
Nebraska
Wom Cent

20989. Bittenbender, Ada Matilda Cole
1848–1925
suffragist, temperance leader, political reformer, lawyer admitted to practice before the Supreme Court
Presbyterian
Nebraska
Not Am Wom; Wom Cent

20990. Elliott, Sarah Barnwell
1848–1928
author, novelist, dramatist, suffragist
Tennessee
Dict Am Auth; Dict Am Bio; Nat Cyc Am Bio v21; Not Am Wom; Wom Lit, More

20991. Gould, Ellen M.
born 1848
philanthropist, suffragist
Unitarian
Rhode Island
Wom Cent

20992. Kollock, Florence E.
born 1848
Universalist minister, suffragist, temperance worker, kindergarten educator, missionary
Index t Wom; Wom Cent

20993. Atherton, Mary Alderson Chandler
born 1849
suffragist, educator, author
Massachusetts
Nat Cyc Am Bio v18

20994. Ayer, Harriet (Hubbard)
1849/54–1903
businessperson, realtor, manufacturer, journalist, suffragist
Dict Am Auth; Nat Cyc Am Bio v43; Not Am Wom; Wom Cent

20995. Beckwith, Emma (Knight)
born 1849
suffragist, politician
Brooklyn, NY
Wom Cent

20996. Cady, Helena Maxwell
born 1849
physician, temperance worker, suffragist
Kentucky
Wom Cent

20997. Clay, Laura
1849–1941
women's suffrage leader, women's rights worker
Kentucky
Encyc South Hist; Index t Wom; Not Am Wom

20998. Devoe, Emma Smith
born 1849
suffragist, lecturer
South Dakota
Wom Cent

20999. Foltz, Clara Shortridge; The Portia of the Pacific
1849–1934
lawyer, political activist, women's rights worker, suffragist, newspaper publisher, orator
California
Cyc Am Bio; Nat Cyc Am Bio csv3; Not Am Wom; Twent Cen Bio Dict Not Am; Wom Cent

21000. Hayward, Mary E. Smith
born 1849
oil and mercantile businessperson, suffragist
Nebraska
Wom Cent

21001. Johns, Laura M.
born 1849
suffragist
Kansas
Wom Cent

21002. Palmer, Bertha Honore
1849/51–1918
clubwoman, philanthropist, women's rights worker, art collector

Chicago, IL
Dict Am Bio; Index t Wom; Twent Cen Bio Dict Not Am; Wom Cent

21003. Ray, Rachel Beasley; Kate Carrington
born 1849
poet, author, temperance advocate, feminist
Baptist
Wom Cent

21004. Armstrong, Ruth Alice
born 1850
suffragist, temperance worker
Index t Wom; Wom Cent

21005. Iliohan, Henrica
born 1850
suffragist
Nebraska
Dutch
Wom Cent

21006. Lease, Mary Elizabeth (Clyens)
1850/53–1933
Populist orator, politician, Prohibition party worker, suffragist, evolutionist, birth control advocate, feminist, political author
Kansas
Dict Am Auth; Dict Am Bio supp v1; Index t Wom; Not Am Wom; Read Encyc Am West

21007. Marble, Ella M. S.
born 1850
journalist, educator, suffragist, temperance worker, dress reformer
Wom Cent

21008. McComas, Alice Moore
born 1850
author, editor, lecturer, suffragist
Wom Cent

21009. Mussey, Ellen (Persis) Spencer
1850–1936
international lawyer, law educator, feminist, women's rights worker, clubwoman, child welfare worker, Red Cross worker, social reformer
Swedenborgian
Washington, DC
Dict Am Bio supp v2; Index t Wom; Nat Cyc Am Bio v47 and csv1; Not Am Wom; Twent Cen Bio Dict Not Am

21010. Pitblado, Eupemia Wilson
flourished 1880s–90s
temperance worker, suffragist
Wom Cent

21011. Shattuck, Harriette Lucy (Robinson)
born 1850
miscellaneous author, legal clerk, writer on parliamentary law, suffragist
Malden, MA
Dict Am Auth; Index t Wom; Twent Cen Bio Dict Not Am; Wom Cent

21012. Trix, Harriet Phelps
born 1850
suffragist
Swedenborgian
Detroit, MI
Nat Cyc Am Bio v18

21013. Bigelow, Belle G.
born 1851
suffragist, Prohibitionist
Wom Cent

21014. Clark, Katharine Pickens (Upson)
1851–1935
children's author, journalist, suffragist, temperance worker, lecturer
Dict Am Auth; Nat Cyc Am Bio v30

21015. Harper, Ida A. Husted
1851–1931
political journalist, suffragist, feminist, newspaper editor, author
Dict Am Bio; Index t Wom; Nat Cyc Am Bio v25; Not Am Wom; Wom Cent

21016. Martin, Lillian Jane
1851–1943
psychologist, gerontologist, worker for the welfare of the aged, suffragist, university educator
Index t Wom; Nat Cyc Am Bio v16; Obit File; Twent Cen Bio Dict Not Am

21017. Safford, Mary Augusta
born 1851
Unitarian minister, lecturer, suffragist, philanthropist
Unitarian

Index t Wom; Nat Cyc Am Bio v14

21018. Spencer, Anna Carpenter (Garlin)
1851–1931
Unitarian minister, journalist, educator, temperance worker, suffragist, pacifist, child-labor reformer, philanthropist
Unitarian
Dict Am Bio; Nat Cyc Am Bio v9 and csv2; Not Am Wom

21019. Whipple, M. Ella
born 1851

physician, temperance worker, suffragist, Methodist Episcopal church worker, politician, educator, inventor
Methodist Episcopal
Wom Cent

21020. Babcock, Elnora Monroe
born 1852
suffragist
Wom Cent

21021. Balbach, Julia Anna
born 1852
inventor, philanthropist, suffragist
Nat Cyc Am Bio v17

21022. Ballore, Ella Maria
born 1852
stenographer, women's rights worker
Wom Cent

21023. Chapin, Clara Christiana; La Petite
born 1852
suffragist, temperance worker
English
Wom Cent

21024. Doughty, Eva Craig Graves
born 1852
journalist, suffragist, temperance worker
Presbyterian
Wom Cent

21025. Edey, Birdsall Otis
1852–1940
feminist
Index t Wom

21026. Gillett, Emma Millinda
1852–1927
lawyer, educator, feminist
Nat Cyc Am Bio v17; Not Am Wom

21027. Gonzales Parsons, Lucia
circa 1852–1942
feminist, labor leader, a founder of International Labor Defense and of Industrial Workers of the World, Socialist party worker
Mexican
Dict Mex Am Hist

21028. Kurt, Katherine
born 1852
homeopathic physician, suffragist, temperance worker, Prohibition party worker
Universalist
Wom Cent

21029. Leader, Olive Moorman
born 1852
temperance reformer, suffragist

Christian Scientist
Wom Cent

21030. Mattingly, Sarah Irwin
1852–1934
educator of Blacks, suffragist
Nat Cyc Am Bio v30

21031. Stoddard, Anna Elizabeth
born 1852
journalist, anti–secret society agitator, temperance worker, suffragist
Baptist
Wom Cent

21032. Belmont, Alva Erskin Smith Vanderbilt
1853–1933
suffragist, feminist, politician, philanthropist
Index t Wom; Not Am Wom

21033. Brooks, Ida Joe
born 1853
physician, surgeon, suffragist
Little Rock, AR
Wom Cent

21034. Dabbs, Ellen Lawson
born 1853
physician, midwife, women's rights worker, suffragist, temperance worker, journalist, Populist party worker
Texas
Wom Cent

21035. Gardener, Helen Hamilton (Chenoweth)
1853/58–1925
author, novelist, essayist, feminist, suffragist, geneticist, biologist, sociologist, civil service commissioner
Dict Am Bio; Index t Wom; Nat Cyc Am Bio v9; Not Am Wom; Twent Cen Bio Dict Not Am; Wom Cent

21036. Hollister, Lilian
born 1853
temperance worker, suffragist, Methodist Episcopal church worker
Methodist Episcopal
Michigan
Wom Cent

21037. Jenkins, Theresa A.
born 1853
suffragist, journalist, women's rights worker, temperance worker
Wyoming
Wom Cent

21038. Strickland, Martha
born 1853
lawyer, feminist, orator

Michigan
Wom Cent

21039. Upton, Harriet Taylor
1853–1945
suffragist, feminist, author, Republican party leader
Index t Wom; Not Am Wom; Obit File

21040. Ward, May (Alden)
born 1853
historical author, biographer, editor, lecturer, club leader, president of the Massachusetts State Federation of Women's Clubs
Dict Am Auth; Index t Wom; Twent Cen Bio Dict Not Am; Wom Cent

21041. Boughton, Caroline Greenbank
born 1854
educator, suffragist, philanthropist
Wom Cent

21042. Edholm, Mary Gow Charlton
born 1854
suffragist, temperance reformer, journalist
Twent Cen Bio Dict Not Am; Wom Cent

21043. Elliott, Maude Howe
1854–1948
author, novelist, suffragist
Unitarian
Chicago, IL
Dict Am Auth; Nat Cyc Am Bio v36; Not Am Wom; Twent Cen Bio Dict Not Am; Wom Cent

21044. Garrett, Mary Elizabeth
1854–1915
philanthropist, suffragist
Index t Wom; Not Am Wom

21045. Smith, Estelle Turrell
born 1854
naturalist, suffragist
Wom Cent

21046. Babcock, Hannah Almy
1855–1931
music educator and director for the blind, suffragist, temperance worker
Nat Cyc Am Bio v16

21047. Baker, Charlotte Johnson
born 1855
ophthalmologist, suffragist, temperance worker
Wom Cent

21048. Havemeyer, Louisine Waldron Elder
1855–1929

art collector, philanthropist, suffragist
Not Am Wom

21049. Jones, Minona Stearns Fitts
born 1855
politician, feminist, social reformer
Index t Wom

21050. Bird, Anna Child
born 1856
suffragist, Republican political leader
Nat Cyc Am Bio csv4

21051. Blatch, Harriot Eaton Stanton
1856–1940
leader of the radical wing of the American suffragist movement, author, political activist, Fabian Socialist, lecturer
Dict Am Bio supp v2; Not Am Wom; Obit File

21052. Gates, Susa Young
1856–1933
Mormon author, educator, suffragist
Mormon
Nat Cyc Am Bio csv2; Read Encyc Am West

21053. Huling, Caroline Augusta
born 1856
journalist, suffragist, philanthropist, temperance worker
Illinois
Wom Cent

21054. Mead, Lucia True (Ames)
1856–1936
pacifist, internationalist, suffragist, Black welfare and education worker, author
Unitarian
Nat Cyc Am Bio v28; Not Am Wom; Twent Cen Bio Dict Not Am

21055. Pope, Cora Scott Pond
born 1856
suffragist, suffrage leader
Chicago, IL
Wom Cent

21056. Atherton, Gertrude Franklin (Horn); Franklin Horne
1857/59–1948
novelist, suffragist, women's rights worker

San Francisco, CA
Dict Am Auth; Dict Am Bio supp v4; Dict Lit Bio v9; Index t Wom; Nat Cyc Am Bio v10, v36, and csv4; Not Am Wom; Obit File; Read Encyc Am West; Twent Cen Bio Dict Not Am; Wom Lit; Wom Lit, More

21057. Barrett, Kate Harwood Waller
1857/59–1925/29
social reformer, philanthropist, lecturer, social worker, suffragist, women's welfare worker
Virginia
Dict Am Bio; Encyc South Hist; Index t Wom; Not Am Wom

21058. Blackwell, Alice Stone
1857–1950
feminist, suffragist, journalist, editor, author, humanitarian
Dict Am Bio supp v2; Index t Wom; Nat Cyc Am Bio csv6; Not Am Wom; Obit File; Wom Cent

21059. Blake, Katherine Devereux
1857–1950
educator, suffragist, international peace movement leader
New York
Index t Wom; Obit File

21060. Hay, Mary Garret
1857–1928
suffragist, temperance worker, New York civic worker
New York, NY
Dict Am Bio; Index t Wom; Not Am Wom

21061. Henry, Alice
1857–1943
journalist, women's trade union leader, feminist, suffragist, editor
Unitarian
Australian
Bio Dict Am Lab; Dict Am Bio supp v3; Not Am Wom

21062. Mark, Nellie V.
born 1857
physician, suffragist, temperance worker
Wom Cent

21063. Mills, Harriet May
born 1857
suffragist
Nat Cyc Am Bio v15

21064. Putnam, Helen Cordelia
1857–1951
physician, health educator, suffragist
Dict Am Bio supp v5

21065. Searing, Anna Eliza Pidgeon
1857–1942
author, feminist
Index t Wom

21066. Thomas, Martha Carey
1857–1935
university educator, second president of Bryn Mawr College, author, feminist
Quaker
Dict Am Auth; Dict Am Bio supp v1; Index t Wom; Nat Cyc Am Bio v13; Not Am Wom; Twent Cen Bio Dict Not Am

21067. Arthur, Clara Blanche
born 1858
suffragist
Canadian
Nat Cyc Am Bio v17

21068. Avery, Rachel G. Foster
1858–1919
suffragist, feminist
Index t Wom; Not Am Wom; Wom Cent

21069. Bagley, Blanche Pentecost
born 1858
Unitarian minister, suffragist
Unitarian
British
Wom Cent

21070. Bartlett, Caroline Julia
born 1858
Unitarian minister, suffragist
Unitarian
Wom Cent

21071. Boole, Ella Alexander
1858–1952
temperance leader, president of WCTU, suffragist, pacifist, Presbyterian deacon
Presbyterian
Dict Am Bio supp v5; Index t Wom; Nat Cyc Am Bio v38 and csv2; Not Am Wom supp v1; Obit File

21072. Byngton, Elia Goode
born 1858
newspaper editor, women's rights worker, journalist
Georgia
Wom Cent

21073. Crane, Caroline Julia Bartlett
1858–1935
Unitarian minister, People's Church minister, urban reformer, suffragist, city planner, sanitation expert
Unitarian
Index t Wom; Nat Cyc Am Bio v15; Not Am Wom

21074. Cranmer, Emma A.
born 1858
temperance reformer, suffragist
South Dakota
Wom Cent

21075. Curtis, Martha E.
born 1858
suffragist, women's rights worker
Massachusetts
Wom Cent

21076. Dock, Lavinia Lloyd
1858–1956
nurse, medical author, settlement house worker, suffragist, feminist
Dict Am Bio; Index t Wom; Not Am Wom supp v1

21077. Slosson, May Genevieve Preston
1858–1943
educator, suffragist
Congregationalist
Nat Cyc Am Bio v35

21078. Baker, Ida Wickoff
born 1859
stock company owner, temperance worker, women's rights worker
Wom Cent

21079. Bass, George, Mrs.
1859–1950
suffragist, first woman to preside over a national political convention
Obit File

21080. Blair, Emily Jane Newell
1859/77–1933
suffragist, feminist, author, vice-president of the Democratic National Committee, chairperson of the Consumer's Advisory Board of the National Recovery Administration
Dict Am Bio supp v5; Not Am Wom supp v1; Obit File

21081. Bowen, Louise Hadduck de Koven
1859–1953
philanthropist, welfare leader, Chicago social worker, president of Hull House, suffragist
Chicago, IL
Dict Am Bio supp v5; Index t Wom; Not Am Wom supp v1; Obit File

21082. Catt, Carrie Clinton Lane Champman
1859–1947

suffragist, women's rights worker, peace worker
Dict Am Bio supp v3; Index t Wom; Nat Cyc Am Bio v15 and v38; Not Am Wom; Obit File; Wom Cent

21083. Kehew, Mary Morton Kimball
1859–1918
social reformer in education and employment for women, labor organizer, worker for the welfare of children and the blind
Dict Am Bio; Not Am Wom

21084. Lines, Mary Louise
born 1859
physician, surgeon, suffragist
Nat Cyc Am Bio v16

21085. Miller, Annie (Jenness)
born 1859/84
dress reformer, fashion designer, magazine publisher, author, novelist, essayist, lecturer
New York, NY
Dict Am Auth; Index t Wom; Wom Cent

21086. Stevens, Anna Evans (Shipman)
1859–1939
women's club worker
Detroit, MI
Nat Cyc Am Bio v17 and v32

21087. Thompson, Adaline Emerson
born 1859
educational worker, women's education reformer
Wom Cent

21088. Brackenridge, M. Eleanor
flourished 1890s
feminist, humanitarian
Index t Wom

21089. Gilchrist, Rosetta Luce
flourished 1890s
physician, author, poet, women's rights worker
Cleveland, OH
Wom Cent

21090. Gilman, Charlotte Anna (Perkins) (Stetson)
1860–1935
author, feminist, lecturer, labor worker
San Francisco, CA
Dict Am Auth; Dict Am Bio supp v1; Index t Wom; Nat Cyc Am Bio v13; Not Am Wom; Twent Cen Bio Dict Not Am; Wom Lit, More

21091. Haskell, Ella Louisa (Knowles)
1860/62–1911

lawyer, attorney general of Montana, politician, women's rights advocate, suffragist, Populist party worker
Theosophist
Dict Am Bio; Nat Cyc Am Bio v11

21092. Orff, Annie L. Y.
flourished 1890s
editor, publisher, women's travel expert
St. Louis, MO
Wom Cent

21093. Trout, Grace Wilbur
flourished 1890s; died 1955
suffragist, feminist, club leader, author, lecturer
Illinois
Index t Wom; Nat Cyc Am Bio csv2

21094. Anthony, Lucy E.
1861–1944
women's suffrage leader
Obit File

21095. Bates, Mary Elizabeth
1861/63–1954
surgeon, child welfare worker, suffragist
Denver, CO
Index t Wom; Nat Cyc Am Bio v18

21096. Gilmer, Elizabeth Meriwether; Dorothy Dix
1861/70–1951
journalist, suffragist, advice columnist
Dict Am Bio supp v5; Index t Wom; Not Am Wom supp v1; Obit File

21097. Gordon, Kate M.
1861–1932
suffrage leader, civic leader
Not Am Wom

21098. Spencer, Caroline Elizabeth
1861–1928
suffragist, physician
Nat Cyc Am Bio v21

21099. Armbruster, Sara Dary
born 1862
publisher, women's rights worker
Wom Cent

21100. Buckland, Fanny
1862–1939
pioneer in women's education, first headmistress of the Witwatersrand School in South Africa
Not Am Wom supp v1

21101. du Bose, Miriam Howard
born 1862
suffragist, composer, pianist
Georgia
Wom Cent

21102. McCormick, Harriet Hammond
1862–1917
philanthropist, suffragist, patron of child welfare
Episcopalian
Nat Cyc Am Bio v21

21103. McCulloch, Catharine Gouger Waugh
1862–1945
lawyer, judge, suffragist, temperance worker
Illinois
Not Am Wom; Obit File; Wom Cent

21104. Merrill, Winifred Edgerton
1862–1951
women's educator
Episcopalian
Nat Cyc Am Bio v41

21105. Nathan, Maud
1862–1946
social welfare leader, social worker, consumer advocate, suffragist, feminist, pacifist
Jewish
Dict Am Bio supp v4; Index t Wom; Nat Cyc Am Bio v15; Not Am Wom; Obit File

21106. Shuler, Nettie Rogers
1862–1939
suffragist, clubwoman
Not Am Wom

21107. Spence, Clara Beebe
1862–1923
educator of women, World War I patriot
Nat Cyc Am Bio v20

21108. Claghorn, Kate Holladay
born 1863
writer on women's education
New York
Dict Am Auth; Twent Cen Bio Dict Not Am

21109. Johnson, Carrie Ashton
born 1863
editor, temperance worker, suffragist
Illinois
Wom Cent

21110. Kearney, Belle
1863–1939
temperance reformer, suffragist, Mississippi state legislator
Mississippi
Nat Cyc Am Bio v11; Not Am Wom

21111. Lockrey, Sarah Hunt
1863–1929
surgeon, suffragist
Dict Am Bio

21112. Murphy, Claudia Quigley
born 1863
journalist, suffragist, women's rights worker
Ohio
Wom Cent

21113. Somerville, Nellie Nugent
1863–1952
suffragist, representative to Congress
Not Am Wom supp v1

21114. Terrell, Mary Eliza Church
1863–1954
community leader, social reformer, suffragist, feminist, civil rights leader, NAACP organizer, lecturer, educator
Congregationalist
Washington, DC
Dict Am Bio supp v5; Encyc Black Am; Encyc South Hist; Index t Wom; Nat Cyc Am Bio v52; Negro Alman; Not Am Wom; Prof Negro Wom v1; World Great Men Col v2

21115. van Hoosen, Bertha
1863–1952
surgeon, feminist
Index t Wom; Not Am Wom supp v1

21116. Woolley, Mary Emma
1863–1947
second president of Mt. Holyoke College, educator, pacifist, suffragist
Congregationalist
Dict Am Bio supp v4; Index t Wom; Nat Cyc Am Bio v13, v37, and csv4; Not Am Wom

21117. Boswell, Helen Varick
1864–1942
suffrage leader, founder and president of the Women's Forum
New York
Obit File

21118. Gannett, Mary Thorn Lewis
1864–1952
suffragist, civil rights worker
Obit File

21119. Kohut, Rebekah Bettelheim
1864–1951
social welfare leader, educator, suffragist, lecturer, author, Jewish welfare worker
Jewish

Hungarian
Index t Wom; Nat Cyc Am Bio v41 and csv5; Not Am Wom supp v1

21120. Parker, Alice
born 1864
lawyer, feminist
Massachusetts
Index t Wom; Wom Cent

21121. Clarke, Grace Giddings Julian
1865–1938
suffragist
Not Am Wom

21122. Gordon, Jean Margaret
1865–1931
social welfare leader, suffrage leader
Not Am Wom

21123. Hart, Mary Ward
born 1865
suffragist, temperance worker
Illinois
Nat Cyc Am Bio v18

21124. Hilles, Florence Bayard
1865–1954
suffragist, feminist, ERA worker, pacifist, golfer
Episcopalian
Delaware
Nat Cyc Am Bio v46

21125. Hooper, Jessie Annette Jack
1865–1935
suffragist, Democratic politician, peace advocate
Wisconsin
Dict Am Bio supp v1; Nat Cyc Am Bio csv1; Not Am Wom

21126. Richardson, Anna Steese
1865–1949
magazine editor, author, playwright, feminist
Obit File

21127. Valentine, Lila Hardaway Meade
1865–1921
suffragist, educational reformer, public health worker
Virginia
Encyc South Hist; Not Am Wom

21128. Washington, Margaret Murry
1865–1925
women's organizer, Tuskegee College dean of women, author
Black
Index t Wom; Negro Alman; Prof Negro Wom v1

21129. Austin, Mary (Hunter)
1866/68–1934

21200. Tillinghast, Anna Churchill Moulton
1874–1951
temperance worker, women's and children's welfare worker, Universalist pastor, suffragist
Universalist
Massachusetts
Nat Cyc Am Bio v45

21201. Bethune, Mary McLeod
1875–1955
educator, founder and president of Bethune-Cookman College, director of the Negro Affairs National Youth Council, civil rights worker, women's rights worker
Daytona Beach, FL
Black
Dict Am Bio supp v5; Dict Am Rel Bio; Encyc Black Am; Encyc South Hist; Index t Wom; Nat Cyc Am Bio v49; Negro Alman; Negro Her Lib v1; Not Am Wom supp v1; Prof Negro Wom; Obit File

21202. Cotten, Elizabeth Brownrigg Henderson
born 1875
suffragist
North Carolina
Nat Cyc Am Bio csv1

21203. Dreier, Mary Elisabeth
1875–1963
labor reformer, suffragist, New York civic leader, Bull Moose party politician
Presbyterian
New York
Nat Cyc Am Bio csv9; Not Am Wom supp v1

21204. Jacobs, Pattie Ruffner
1875–1935
Alabama suffrage leader, child labor welfare worker, prison reformer, Prohibition party worker
Encyc South Hist; Not Am Wom

21205. Lloyd, Lola Maverick
1875–1944
pacifist, feminist, suffragist
Nat Cyc Am Bio v33; Obit File

21206. Martin, Anna Henrietta
1875–1951
suffragist, feminist, author, essayist, social critic, pacifist, politician
Nevada
Dict Am Bio supp v5; Not Am Wom supp v1; Read Encyc Am West

21207. Tiffany, Katrina Brandes Ely
1875–1927

civic worker, suffragist
Dict Am Bio

21208. Weed, Helen Hill
1875–1958
suffrage leader, pacifist, child labor reformer
Obit File

21209. Barringer, Emily Dunning
1876–1961
gynecologist, ambulance surgeon, worker for recognition of women physicians
Protestant Episcopal
Nat Cyc Am Bio v50; Index t Wom; Obit File

21210. Beard, Mary Ritter
1876–1958
historian, writer on history, feminist
Dict Am Bio supp v6; Index t Wom; Not Am Wom supp v1; Obit File

21211. Cleghorn, Sarah Norcliffe
1876–1959
poet, novelist, educator, suffragist, civil rights worker, labor worker, pacifist, antivivisectionist, Socialist party member
Vermont
Index t Wom; Nat Cyc Am Bio v46; Obit File; Dict Am Bio supp v5

21212. Dunk, Edith Watkins
born 1876
consumer advocate, suffragist, welfare worker
Nat Cyc Am Bio v17

21213. Ellinwood, Henrietta Elizabeth (Schneider)
born 1876
philanthropist, suffragist
Illinois
Nat Cyc Am Bio v16

21214. Glaspell, Susan Keating; Mrs. George Cram Cook
1876/82–1948
novelist, playwright, feminist
Dict Am Bio supp v4; Dict Lit Bio v7 and v9; Index t Wom; Nat Cyc Am Bio v15 and csv3; Not Am Wom; Wom Lit, More

21215. Rinehart, Mary Roberts
1876–1958
novelist, mystery story writer, playwright, suffragist
Episcopalian
Dict Am Bio supp v6; Index t Wom; Nat Cyc Am Bio csv3; Not Am Wom supp v1; Obit File

21216. Brown, Sue M.
1877–1941
clubwoman, educator, author, suffragist, women's rights worker, Black civil rights worker
Black
Negro Alman; Prof Negro Wom

21217. Schwimmer, Rosika
1877–1948
feminist, suffragist, pacifist, author, editor
Jewish
Hungarian
Dict Am Bio supp v4; Not Am Wom; Obit File

21218. Warbasse, Agnes Louise Dyer
1877–1945
cooperative manufacturer, cooperative housing expert, suffragist, pacifist
Nat Cyc Am Bio v34

21219. Ames, Blanche Ames
1878–1969
botanical illustrator, inventor, feminist, suffragist, birth control advocate
Massachusetts
Nat Cyc Am Bio v53; Not Am Wom; Obit File

21220. Burroughs, Nannie Helen
1878/83–1961
educator, founder of the National Trade and Professional School for Women and Girls, women's rights worker
Baptist
Black
Index t Wom; Negro Alman; Not Am Wom supp v1; Prof Negro Wom

21221. Fairbank, Janet Ayer
1878–1951
author, feminist
Episcopalian
Index t Wom; Nat Cyc Am Bio v39

21222. Gellhorn, Edna Fischel
1878–1970
community leader, suffragist
Not Am Wom supp v1

21223. Raugh, Ida; Ida Eastman
1878–1970
feminist, sculptor, painter
Obit File

21224. Wiley, Anna Campbel Kelton
1878–1964
women's rights worker
Obit File

21225. Astor, Nancy Witcher Langhorne Shaw, Lady; Dowager Viscountess
1879–1964
politician, member of the English House of Commons, women's rights worker, temperance worker
British (American expatriate to England)
Index t Wom; Nat Cyc Am Bio csv1; Obit File

21226. Burns, Lucy
1879–1966
suffragist, feminist
Index t Wom; Not Am Wom supp v1

21227. Morrisson, Mary (Taylor) Foulke
1879–1971
political economist and activist, suffragist, women's rights worker
Nat Cyc Am Bio v17 and v56

21228. Patterson, Hannah Jane
1879–1937
suffragist, World War I defense official
Not Am Wom

21229. Reilly, Marion
1879–1928
educator, suffragist, philanthropist
Dict Am Bio

21230. Sanger, Margaret Higgins; Mrs. J. Noah H. Slee
1879/83–1966
birth control reformer, lecturer, author
Episcopalian
Index t Wom; Nat Cyc Am Bio v52; Not Am Wom supp v1; Obit File

21231. Stokes, Rose Harriet Pastor
1879–1933
Socialist and Communist party leader, feminist, labor leader, author
Jewish
Polish
Bio Dict Am Lab; Dict Am Bio; Not Am Wom

21232. Keller, Helen Adams
1880–1968
author, feminist, suffragist, educator, advocate for the handicapped, pacifist, Socialist party worker
Swedenborgian
Alabama

blind, deaf
Encyc South Hist; Index t Wom;
Nat Cyc Am Bio v15 and v57;
Not Am Wom supp v1; Obit
File

21233. Lewis, Lawrence, Mrs.
flourished 1910s
feminist
Index t Wom

21234. McBride, Lucia McCurdy
1880–1970
Cleveland civic leader, suffragist
Episcopalian
Cleveland, OH
Nat Cyc Am Bio v57 and csv7

21235. Miller, Lucy Kennedy
born 1880
suffrage leader
Pennsylvania
Nat Cyc Am Bio csv4

21236. Norris, Kathleen Thompson
1880–1966
author, novelist, magazine writer,
pacifist, feminist
Catholic
Index t Wom; Nat Cyc Am Bio
csv3; Not Am Wom supp v1;
Obit File; Wom Lit, More

21237. Pyke, Bernice S.
1880–1964
suffragist, first woman delegate to
a national political convention
Obit File

21238. Rankin, Jeannette Pickering
1880–1973
suffragist, feminist, first woman
elected to Congress, pacifist
Index t Wom; Not Am Wom
supp v1; Obit File

21239. Smith, Doris
flourished 1910s
feminist
Index t Wom

21240. van Winkle, Mina Ginger
born 1880
social worker, lieutenant in the
police force, suffragist
Nat Cyc Am Bio csv3

21241. Wadsworth, Alice Hay
born 1880
New York civic worker, suffragist
Presbyterian
New York
Nat Cyc Am Bio csv8

21242. Wellington, Violet Irene
flourished 1910s

dramatic reader, drama teacher,
suffragist, pacifist
Nat Cyc Am Bio v19

21243. Eastman, Crystal
1881–1928
social investigator, peace worker,
feminist, suffragist
Not Am Wom

21244. Phillips, Lena Madesin
1881–1955
feminist, founder of the National
and International Federations
of Business and Professional
Women's Clubs, author, editor,
lecturer, politician
Dict Am Bio supp v5; Index t
Wom; Not Am Wom supp v1;
Obit File

21245. Pinchot, Cornelia Elizabeth Bryce
1881–1960
politician, suffragist, women's
rights worker, worker for the
welfare of women and children,
advocate of social welfare legislation
Dict Am Bio supp v6; Not Am
Wom supp v1

21246. Sewell, Edna Belle Scott
1881–1967
farm women's leader
Not Am Wom supp v1

21247. Cunningham, Minnie Fisher
1882–1964
suffragist, politician, community
leader
Not Am Wom supp v1

21248. Field, Sarah Bard
1882–1974
poet, suffragist
Not Am Wom supp v1

21249. Mason, Lucy Randolph
1882–1959
labor publicist, public relations
officer for the CIO, southern
trade union organizer, social
worker and reformer, suffragist
Episcopalian
Virginia
Bio Dict Am Lab; Dict Am Bio
supp v6; Encyc South Hist; Not
Am Wom supp v1; Obit File

21250. Reid, Helen Miles Rogers
1882–1970
publisher of *The New York Herald-Tribune* newspaper, journalist, suffragist, philanthropist
Episcopalian

New York
Cur Biog '70; Index t Wom; Nat
Cyc Am Bio v56; Not Am Wom
supp v1; Obit File

21251. Schneiderman, Rose
1882/84–1972
labor organizer, Women's Trade
Union leader, secretary of the
New York State Labor Depart-
ment, social reformer, suffragist
Jewish
Polish; Russian
Bio Dict Am Lab; Cur Biog '72;
Index t Wom; Not Am Wom
supp v1; Obit File

21252. Townshend, Anna Draper
born 1882
suffragist, Connecticut state legis-
lator from New Haven, New
Haven civic worker
Unitarian
New Haven, CT
Nat Cyc Am Bio csv6

21253. Ames, Jessie Daniel
1883–1972
Progressive party politician,
Black civil rights worker, anti-
lynching reformer, suffragist
Texas
Encyc South Hist; Not Am Wom
supp v1

21254. Barney, Nora Stanton Blatch
1883–1971
civil engineer, architect, suffragist
Not Am Wom supp v1

21255. Gomper, Gertrude
1883–1953
labor union worker, campaigner
for liberal divorce laws
Obit File

21256. Goode, Edith J.
1883–1970
suffragist, animal humane worker, cofounder of the National
Women's party
Obit File

21257. Goode, Edith J.
1883–1970
suffragist, animal humane worker, cofounder of the National
Women's party
Obit File

21258. la Follette, Fola (Middleton)
1883–1970
actor, author, suffragist
Obit File

21259. Lampkin, Daisy Elizabeth Adams
1883?–1965

civil rights reformer, suffragist,
community leader
Not Am Wom supp v1

21260. McCreery, Maria Maud Leonard
1883–1938
Wisconsin suffragist, Socialist
party worker, labor organizer
Wisconsin
Not Am Wom

21261. Miller, Olive Beaupre
1883–1968
children's author, sex education
worker
Illinois
Nat Cyc Am Bio v54

21262. Rorke, Margaret Hayden
1883–1967
color standards expert, suffragist
Catholic
Nat Cyc Am Bio v54

21263. Springs, Lena Joan Jones
1883–1942
Democratic National Committee
member, Democratic vice-presidential nominee at the 1924
convention, suffrage leader,
World War I Red Cross worker
South Carolina
Nat Cyc Am Bio csv2; Obit File

21264. Vanderbilt, Alva Smith Belmont
died 1933
feminist
Index t Wom

21265. Vernon, Mabel
1883–1975
suffragist, feminist, pacifist
Not Am Wom supp v1

21266. Allen, Florence Ellinwood
1884–1966
lawyer, US Court of Appeals
judge, suffragist
Congregationalist
Ohio
Index t Wom; Nat Cyc Am Bio
v52 and csv3; Not Am Wom;
Obit File

21267. Elliott, Harriet Wiseman
1884–1947
educator, dean of women's college at the University of North
Carolina, suffragist, women's
rights worker, political organizer, public official
North Carolina
Encyc South Hist; Index t Wom;
Not Am Wom; Obit File

editor, publisher of *The Nation*, Socialist party worker, feminist
Cur Biog '76; Index t Wom; Obit File

21304. Stevens, Doris
1893–1963
women's rights worker, author, songwriter
Obit File

21305. Sutley, Margaret Hutchinson
1893–1947
physician, surgeon, medical educator in Japan, venereal disease clinic founder
Nat Cyc Am Bio v35

21306. Swing, Betty Gram
1893–1969
feminist, leader of the National Women's Party
Obit File

21307. Groves, Gladys Hoagland
1894–1980
educator, marriage and sex counselor, writer on marriage and sex
Cur Biog '80; Index t Wom

21308. Pollitzer, Anita Lily
1894–1975
suffragist, feminist
Not Am Wom supp v1

21309. Lee, Muna
1895–1965
international affairs specialist, feminist, US State Department aide, poet, novelist, translator
Not Am Wom supp v1; Obit File

21310. Bowman, Geline MacDonald
died 1946
women's business worker, head of the National Federation of Business and Professional Women
Obit File

21311. Dodge, Eva Francette
born 1896
obstetrician, medical educator, birth control and Planned Parenthood worker, public health worker
Baptist
Nat Cyc Am Bio csv12

21312. Ross, Isabel
1897–1975
author, novelist, biographer of prominent American women
Scottish
Index t Wom; Obit File

21313. Ainge, Edith
died 1948

feminist
Obit File

21314. Daniels, Anna Kleegman
born 1898
gynecologist, medical director of Planned Parenthood
Jewish
Russian
Nat Cyc Am Bio csv11

21315. Mudd, Emily Hatshore
born 1898
educator, author, marriage counselor
Index t Wom

21316. Richards, Janet Elizabeth Hosmer
died 1948
lecturer, feminist
Index t Wom

21317. Soule, Isobel Walker
1898–1972
author, editor, labor leader, suffragist
Obit File

21318. Strauss, Anna Lord
1899–1979
editor, club leader, feminist, political activist, New York civic worker, internationalist
Quaker
New York
Cur Biog '79; Index t Wom; Nat Cyc Am Bio csv10

21319. Abbott, Helen Probst
flourished 1930s
feminist, humanitarian
Index t Wom

21320. Durlach, Theresa Mayer
flourished 1930s
feminist, politician
Index t Wom

21321. Taylor, Kathleen Devere
flourished 1930s
feminist, stockbroker
Index t Wom

21322. Thurber, Louise Lockwood
flourished 1930s
humanitarian, feminist, social worker
Index t Wom

21323. Wilson, Justina Leavitt
flourished 1930s
feminist
Index t Wom

21324. Mills, Louise Morris
1901–76
Girl Scout executive, YWCA executive, Planned Parenthood executive

New York
Nat Cyc Am Bio v59

21325. Milholland, Vida
died 1952
suffragist
Obit File

21326. Hawes, Elizabeth
1903–71
fashion designer, author, feminist
Index t Wom; Not Am Wom supp v1

21327. Nin, Anais
1903–77
author, novelist, diarist, printer, feminist
French
Cur Biog '75 and '77; Dict Lit Bio v2 and v4; Index t Wom; Wom Lit; Wom Lit, More

21328. Peterson, Esther Eggertsen
born 1906
labor leader, director of the US Department of Labor Women's Bureau
Mormon
Washington, DC
Bio Dict Am Lab; Index t Wom; Nat Cyc Am Bio csv10

21329. Gayl, Jeannette Orleans
born 1911
president of the Women's American Organization for Rehabilitation through Training
Obit File

21330. Schlotfeldt, Rozella May
born 1914
nurse, nursing educator, women's rights worker, feminist
Nat Cyc Am Bio csv13

21331. Bird, Caroline (Mahoney)
born 1915
lecturer, women's equal rights activist, author
New York
Cur Biog '76

21332. Sheldon, Alice B.; James Tiptree, Jr.
born 1915
speculative fiction and short story writer, feminist
Dict Lit Bio v8

21333. Wolfgang, Myra K.
1915–76
women's labor worker, trade union leader
Obit File

21334. Calloway, Deverne Lee
born 1916

Missouri state legislator, Black civil rights worker, women's rights worker
Encyc Black Am

21335. Koontz, Elizabeth Duncan
born 1919
director of the US Department of Labor Women's Bureau, US delegate to the Commission on the Status of Women, labor organizer, educator
Black
Cur Biog '69; Encyc Black Am; Index t Wom; Negro Alman

21336. Tobolowsky, Hermine D.
flourished 1950s–60s
feminist, lawyer
Index t Wom

21337. Friedan, Betty
born 1921
feminist, founder and president of NOW, writer on the condition of women, women's rights worker
Cur Biog '70

21338. Schlafly, Phyllis (Stewart)
born 1924
anti-ERA campaigner, antifeminist
Cur Biog '78

21339. Hernandez, Aileen Clarke
born 1926
public affairs consultant; commissioner of Equal Employment Opportunities Committee, 1965; president of NOW; labor worker; civil rights worker; feminist
Black
Cur Biog '71; Negro Alman; Negro Her Lib v1

21340. Couzzins, Phoebe Wilson
1929/45–1913
lawyer, US deputy and marshal in Missouri, political author, suffragist
Index t Wom; Nat Cyc Am Bio v15; Not Am Wom; Wom Cent

21341. Scott, Ann London
1929–75
feminist, vice-president of NOW, poet
Not Am Wom supp v1; Obit File

21342. Harris, Ladonna
flourished 1960s–70s
health reformer, women's rights worker
Native American (Comanche)
Ind Today

21343. Burke, Yvonne Watson Brathwaite
born 1932
lawyer, representative to Congress from California, regent of the University of California, environmentalist, feminist
California
Black
Cur Biog '75; Encyc Black Am; Negro Alman

21344. Costanza, Margaret "Midge"
born 1932
special assistant on women's affairs to President Carter, feminist, human rights worker
Cur Biog '78

21345. Krupsak, Mary Anne
born 1932
Democratic lieutenant governor of New York, lawyer, feminist, women's rights worker
New York
Cur Biog '75

21346. MacLaine, Shirley
born 1934
stage and screen actor, dancer, autobiographer, feminist, Democratic party worker, political activist, world traveler
Cur Biog '78; Index t Wom

21347. Millett, Kate
born 1934
philosopher, novelist, feminist leader, writer on sex
Cur Biog '71

21348. Steinem, Gloria
born 1934/36
journalist, feminist, founder and editor of *Ms.* magazine, political activist
Cur Biog '72

21349. Brownmiller, Susan
born 1935
feminist leader, writer on rape and social issues, journalist
Cur Biog '78

21350. Russ, Joanna
born 1937
speculative fiction author, feminist
Dict Lit Bio v8; Wom Lit, More

21351. Chicago, Judy (Cohen)
born 1939
feminist, autobiographer, sculptor, photographer, painter
Cur Biog '81

21352. Smeal, Eleanor [Marie] Cutri
born 1939
president of NOW
Cur Biog '80

21353. Bryant, Anita
born 1940
singer, television personality, antifeminist, antiabortion worker, antihomosexual crusader; Baptist religious worker
Baptist
Florida
Cur Biog '75

21354. Schroeder, Patricia (Scott)
born 1940
representative to Congress from Colorado, feminist
Colorado
Cur Biog '78

21355. Washington, Bennetta Bullock
flourished 1970s
special assistant, US Department of Commerce; director of the Women's Job Corps of the Office of Economic Opportunity
Black
Negro Alman; Negro Her Lib v1

21356. Holtzman, Elizabeth
born 1941
lawyer, Democratic representative to Congress from New York, feminist, anti–Vietnam war protester
New York
Cur Biog '73

21357. Reddy, Helen
born 1941
popular singer, feminist
Australian
Cur Biog '75

21358. Jong, Erica (Mann)
born 1942
novelist, poet, feminist
Jewish
New York
Cur Biog '75; Dict Lit Bio v2 and v5; Wom Lit; Wom Lit, More

21359. Castleman, Alice Barbee
born 1943
philanthropist, women's rights worker
Episcopalian
Louisville, KY
Wom Cent

21360. King, Billie Jean Moffit
born 1943
tennis player, women's rights worker, feminist
Hall Fame Sport; Index t Wom

21361. Sargent, Pamela
born 1948
speculative fiction author, novelist, short story writer, story anthologist, feminist
Dict Lit Bio v8

II. Religious Affiliation Index

ADVENTIST

1. White, Ellen Gould Harmon
1827–1915
cofounder of the Seventh-Day
Adventists, theologian, religious
writer
Seventh-Day Adventist
Dict Am Auth; Dict Am Bio;
Dict Am Rel Bio; Index t Wom;
Not Am Wom

2. Norman, Estelle Gertrude
1872–1959
physician, venereal disease clinic
worker
Seventh-Day Adventist
Iowa
Nat Cyc Am Bio v48

AMANA CHURCH SOCIETY

3. Heinemann, Barbara
1795–1883
spiritual leader of the Community
of True Inspiration
Amanist
Not Am Wom

AMERICAN SOCIETY OF SHAKERS

4. Lee, Ann; Ann Lee
Standerin; Mother Ann
1736–84
founder of the American Society
of Shakers
Shaker
New York
English
Am Bio Dict; Cyc Am Bio; Dict
Am Bio; Dict Am Bio Men
Time; Dict Am Rel Bio; Dict
Nat Bio; Index t Wom; Nat Cyc
Am Bio v5; Not Am Wom; Our
Count; Twent Cen Bio Dict Not
Am; Who Who Dur Am Rev

5. Wright, Lucy
1760–1821
Shaker leader
Shaker
Index t Wom; Not Am Wom

6. Doolittle, Mary Antoinette
1810–86
lecturer on religious subjects,
Shaker eldress, author
Shaker
New York
Cyc Am Bio

7. White, Anna
1831–1910
Shaker eldress, social reformer
Shaker
Not Am Wom

BAPTIST

8. Ball, Martha Violet
born 1811
abolitionist, philanthropist, educator of Black women
Baptist
Wom Cent

**9. Rambaut, Mary Lucinda
Bonney**
1816–1900
Native American rights worker,
educator
Baptist
Dict Am Bio; Index t Wom; Nat
Cyc Am Bio v6; Twent Cen Bio
Dict Not Am; Wom Cent

10. Shuck, Eliza G.
1823–51
missionary to China
Baptist
Am Bio Dict

11. Packard, Sophia B.
1824–91
founder of Spelman College,
church worker, educator of
Blacks
Baptist

Atlanta, GA
Nat Cyc Am Bio v2; Not Am
Wom

12. Ingalls, Marilla Baker
1828–1902
missionary
Baptist
Dict Am Bio; Index t Wom

**13. Lincoln, Jane Elizabeth
(Larcombe); Kate Campbell**
born 1829
author
Baptist
Cyc Am Bio

14. Warren, Mary Evalin
born 1829
author, lecturer, temperance
worker, suffragist
Baptist
Wisconsin
Wom Cent

15. Bixby, Susan
1830–1956
missionary to Maulmain [Burma]
Baptist
Am Bio Dict

**16. Clarke, Mary Basset; Ida
Fairfield**
born 1831
author, poet
Seventh-Day Baptist
Wom Cent

17. Blackall, Emily Lucas
1832–92
philanthropist, temperance worker
Baptist
Wom Cent

18. Janes, Martha Waldron
born 1832
Baptist minister, suffragist, temperance worker
Baptist
Iowa
Index t Wom; Wom Cent

**19. Wilson, Martha Eleanor
Loftin**
born 1834
missionary worker, Civil War
nurse
Baptist
Georgia
Wom Cent

20. Hawks, Annie Sherwood
1835–1918
hymn writer, poet
Baptist
New York
Index t Wom; Nat Cyc Am Bio
v17; Wom Cent

21. Meech, Jeannette du Bois
born 1835
evangelist, missionary worker,
Baptist preacher, temperance
worker, industrial educator of
women
Baptist
New Jersey
Index t Wom; Wom Cent

22. Taylor, Hannah E.
born 1835
poet, temperance worker
Baptist
Wom Cent

23. Burlingame, Emeline S.
born 1836
Baptist evangelist, temperance
worker
Baptist
Wom Cent

24. Wait, Phoebe Jane Babcock
1838–1904
physician, temperance worker
Baptist
Nat Cyc Am Bio v2; Wom Cent

25. Moon, Lottie Diggs; Lottie
Clark
1840–1912
Southern Baptist missionary to
China

Baptist
Index t Wom; Not Am Wom

26. Robinson, Leora (Bettison)
born 1840
fiction writer, educator
Baptist
Tallahassee, TN
Dict Am Auth; Wom Cent

27. Wright, Laura M.
born 1840
physician, temperance worker
Baptist
Wom Cent

28. Jones, Mary C. "May"
born 1842
Baptist minister, evangelist
Baptist
Washington
Index t Wom; Wom Cent

29. Dodson, Caroline Matilda
born 1845
physician
Baptist
Wom Cent

30. Ray, Rachel Beasley; Kate Carrington
born 1849
poet, author, temperance advocate, feminist
Baptist
Wom Cent

31. Anderson, Elizabeth Milbank
1850–1921
World War I relief worker, philanthropist, patron of social welfare work, patron of Serbian and Yugoslavian welfare, patron of medical missions
Baptist
New York
Dict Am Bio; Nat Cyc Am Bio v23; Not Am Wom

32. Townsley, Frances Eleanor
born 1850
Baptist minister, evangelist, temperance worker
Baptist
Nebraska
Wom Cent

33. Stoddard, Anna Elizabeth
born 1852
journalist, anti–secret society agitator, temperance worker, suffragist
Baptist
Wom Cent

34. Eagle, Mary Kavanaugh
born 1854
Baptist church worker
Baptist
Arkansas
Wom Cent

35. Cocke, Martha Louise
1855–1938
president of Hollins College
Enon Baptist
Virginia
Nat Cyc Am Bio v29

36. Northrop, Celestia Joslin
born 1856
vocalist
Baptist
Indiana
Wom Cent

37. Doane, Ida Frances
1858–1942
philanthropist
Baptist
Nat Cyc Am Bio v41

38. Montgomery, Helen Barrett
1861–1934
civic reformer, churchperson, foreign missions worker, translator, author
Baptist
Index t Wom; Nat Cyc Am Bio csv1; Not Am Wom

39. Calvin, Henrietta Willard
1865–1947
home economist
Baptist
Nat Cyc Am Bio v41

40. Doane, Marguerite Treat
1868–1954
philanthropist, patron of medical missionaries
Baptist
Nat Cyc Am Bio v41

41. Daffan, Katie
flourished 1900s–20s
author
Baptist
Texas
Nat Cyc Am Bio csvl

42. Coffin, Mary Emma
born 1873
homeopathic physician, temperance worker
Baptist
Nat Cyc Am Bio csv4

43. Tompers, Lucie Margaret
1874–1938
social worker
Baptist
New York
Canadian
Nat Cyc Am Bio v29

44. Bass, Mary Elizabeth
1876–1956
physician
Baptist
Louisiana
Nat Cyc Am Bio v46; Not Am Wom supp v1

45. Burroughs, Nannie Helen
1878/83–1961
educator, founder of the National Trade and Professional School for Women and Girls, women's rights worker
Baptist
Black
Index t Wom; Negro Alman; Not Am Wom supp v1; Prof Negro Wom

46. Campbell, Eleanor Milbank Anderson
1878–1959
physician, social welfare worker, public health worker, patron of medicine
Baptist
Nat Cyc Am Bio v49 and csv4

47. Sutton, Mary Wooster Munson
born 1886
lawyer
Baptist
Nat Cyc Am Bio csv2

48. Starbuck, Kathryn Helene
1887–1965
lawyer, women's rights worker, educator
Baptist
New York
Nat Cyc Am Bio v53

49. Ferris, Helen Josephine; Mrs. Albert B. Tibbets
1890–1969
author, editor, children's author
Baptist
New York
Index t Wom; Nat Cyc Am Bio v55

50. Dodge, Eva Francette
born 1896
obstetrician, medical educator, birth control and Planned Parenthood worker, public health worker
Baptist
Nat Cyc Am Bio csv12

51. Eichelberger, Lillian (Velma); Mrs. Ralph Cannon
born 1897
biochemist
Baptist
Nat Cyc Am Bio csv13

52. Gardner, Emily
1899–1956
pediatrician
Baptist
Richmond, VA
Nat Cyc Am Bio v42

53. Anderson, Marian
born 1902/08

contralto concert singer, US alternate delegate to the UN, 1958–59
Baptist
Black
Encyc Black Am; Index t Wom; Nat Cyc Am Bio csv9; Negro Alman; Negro Her Lib v1; Prof Negro Wom; World Great Men Col

54. Davis, Rachel [Kathryn]; Sarah Rebecca (Darden) Speight
born 1905
gynecologist, cancer researcher, eugenicist
Baptist
North Carolina
Nat Cyc Am Bio supp vK

55. Branch, Dorothy Sutton
born 1922
Baptist clergyperson
Baptist
Black
Encyc Black Am

56. Bryant, Anita
born 1940
singer, television personality, antifeminist, antiabortion worker, antihomosexual crusader; Baptist religious worker
Baptist
Florida
Cur Biog '75

BLACK MUSLIM

57. Shabazz, Betty
born 1936
community activist
Black Muslim
Black
Negro Alman

BUDDHIST

58. Alexander, Ruth Wilbur; Mrs. Raymond L. Redhefer
born 1895
economist, editorial columnist, lecturer, pianist
Buddhist
Index t Wom; Nat Cyc Am Bio csv12

CATHOLIC

59. l'Incarnation, Maria de, Mother
1599–1672
Catholic nun, educator, founder of the Ursuline Convent in Que-

bec, student of Native American languages
Catholic
Canadian
Cyc Am Bio

60. Bourgeois, Margaret, Sister
1620–1700
founder of the Congregation of Notre Dame, Catholic nun
Catholic
Cyc Am Bio

61. Tekakwitha, Catherine "Kateri"
1656?–80
Catholic leader
Catholic
Native American
Dict Am Rel Bio; Great North Am Ind; Index t Wom; Not Am Wom

62. Hachard, Marie-Madeliene, Sister
flourished 1710s
pioneer, Catholic nun
Catholic
Index t Wom

63. Tranchepain de Saint Augustine, Marie De, Sister
died 1733
Catholic nun, mother superior and founder of the Ursuline convents, hospital administrator, educator
Catholic
Cyc Am Bio; Index t Wom

64. Jacintha do San Jose
1716–68
Catholic nun, school and hospital founder
Catholic
Brazilian
Cyc Am Bio

65. Goddard, Mary Katherine
1738–1816
printer, newspaper publisher, postmaster of Baltimore, merchant
Catholic
Baltimore, MD
Index t Wom; Not Am Wom

66. Dickinson, Mary Clare
1755–1830
superior of the Carmelite nuns
Catholic
Cyc Am Bio

67. Lalor, Alice Teresa; Mother Teresa
1766–1846
mother superior and founder of the Convent and Academy of the Visitation, the first Roman Catholic female academy in the United States, educator
Catholic

Irish
Cyc Am Bio; Twent Cen Bio Dict Not Am; Who Who Dur Am Rev

68. Teresa, Mother; Alice Labor
circa 1766–1846
founder of the Visitation Order in the United States, Catholic nun
Catholic
Dict Nat Bio

69. Duchesne, Rose Philippine
1769–1852
missionary, Catholic nun, founder of the American Convents of the Sacred Heart, pioneer, educator
Catholic
Kansas
Cyc Am Bio; Dict Am Rel Bio; Not Am Wom; Read Encyc Am West; Twent Cen Bio Dict Not Am

70. Seton, Elizabeth Ann (Bayley), Saint; Mother Seton
1774–1821
Catholic nun, founder and superior of the American Sisters of Charity of St. Vincent de Paul (the first American sisterhood), philanthropist, autobiographer
Catholic
Maryland
Cyc Am Bio; Dict Am Auth; Dict Am Bio; Dict Am Rel Bio; Encyc South Hist; Index t Wom; Nat Cyc Am Bio v2; Not Am Wom; Twent Cen Bio Dict Not Am

71. Rhodes, Mary, Mother
1782?–1853
Catholic nun, founder of the Sisters of Loretto
Catholic
Index t Wom; Not Am Wom

72. Allen, Frances Margaret, Sister
1784–1819
nurse
Catholic
New Cath Encyc

73. Barber, Mary Augustine
1789–1860
educator, convent founder
Catholic
Appl Cyc Am Bio; Cyc Am Bio; Wom Cent

74. Arguello, Concha Maria de Concepcion
1791–1857
pioneer, Catholic nun
Catholic
Spanish
Index t Wom

75. Dubost, Marie Louise
born 1793
Catholic nun, mother superior and founder of the Sisters of Charity in Brazil
Catholic
Cyc Am Bio

76. Spalding, Catherine, Mother
1793–1858
Catholic nun, founder and first superior of the Sisters of Charity of Nazareth
Catholic
Cyc Am Bio; Dict Am Bio; Index t Wom; Not Am Wom

77. Gallitzin, Elizabeth, Princess
1795–1843
Catholic nun, convent and mission founder
Catholic
Cyc Am Bio

78. Sansbury, Angela, Mother
1795–1839
convent founder, Catholic nun
Catholic
Index t Wom

79. Bugg, Lelia Hardin
born 18?
novelist, religious author
Catholic
Wichita, KS
Dict Am Auth

80. Peter, Sarah Anne (Worthington) King
1800–77
charity worker, philanthropist, founder of art school for women, hospital founder, Civil War nurse, pioneer industrial arts educator, church worker
Catholic
Ohio
Dict Am Bio; Index t Wom; Not Am Wom; Twent Cen Bio Dict Not Am

81. St. Augustine, Mother
flourished 1830s
Catholic nun
Catholic
French
Index t Wom

82. Chouteau, Berenice
1801–88
pioneer
Catholic
Twent Cen Bio Dict Not Am

83. Clarke, Mary Francis
1803–87
Catholic nun, founder of the Sisters of the Blessed Virgin Mary
Catholic
Dict Am Bio

84. Maury, Sarah Mytton (Hughes)
1803/08–1948/49
miscellaneous writer
Catholic
Cyc Am Bio; Dict Am Auth; Dict Am Bio Men Time

85. Becroft, Ann Marie; Sister Aloysius
1805–33
educator, Catholic nun
Catholic
Black
Negro Alman; Prof Negro Wom

86. Connelly, Cornelia Augusta Peacock, Mother
1809–79
Catholic nun, founder of the Society of the Holy Child Jesus
Catholic
English
Dict Am Bio; Index t Wom; Nat Cyc Am Bio v23; Not Am Wom

87. Hardey, Mary Aloysia Hawley; Mother Mary Aloysia
1809/10–1886
Catholic nun, founder of the Sacred Heart convents and schools in the New World, educator
Catholic
Cyc Am Bio; Dict Am Bio; Index t Wom; Not Am Wom; Twent Cen Bio Dict Not Am

88. Aloysia, Sister
flourished 1840s
western pioneer, Catholic nun
Catholic
Index t Wom

89. Carrell, Columba
1810–78
founder of the Hospital of Saint Mary and Saint Elizabeth, Catholic nun, mother superior
Catholic
Louisville, KY
Cyc Am Bio

90. Loyola, Sister
flourished 1840s
Catholic nun, western pioneer
Catholic
Index t Wom

91. Mary Loyola, Sister
flourished 1840s
western pioneer, Catholic nun
Catholic
Index t Wom

92. Warde, Frances
1810–84
Catholic nun, sister of mercy, religious worker
Catholic
Dict Am Rel Bio

93. Cutts, Maria
1811–53
Catholic nun, sister superior of all Convents of the Sacred Heart in the western United States
Catholic
Cyc Am Bio

94. Schriek, Louise van der, Sister
1813–86
founder of the Sisters of Notre Dame de Namur in America, Catholic nun
Catholic
Dict Am Bio

95. O'Connell, Mary; Sister Anthony
1814–97
Catholic nun, Civil War nurse, orphanage and hospital director in Cincinnati
Catholic
Cincinnati, OH
Dict Am Bio; Not Am Wom

96. Desiree
1815–79
Catholic nun, sister superior
Catholic
Cyc Am Bio

97. Dorsey, Annah Hanson McKenney
1815/16–1896
author, dramatist, poet, novelist, essayist, short story writer, political writer
Catholic
Washington, DC
Cyc Am Bio; Dict Am Auth; Dict Am Bio; Index t Wom; Nat Cyc Am Bio v11 Twent Cen Bio Dict Not Am; Wom Cent

98. Greenhow, Rose O'Neal
1815/17–1864
Confederate spy
Catholic
Washington, DC
Bio Dict Confed; Index t Wom; Not Am Wom; Read Encyc Am West

99. Euphemia
1816–87
mother superior of the Sisters of Charity
Catholic
Cyc Am Bio

100. Horan, Mary Austin
1820–74
Catholic nun, superior of the Sisters of Mercy
Catholic
Cyc Am Bio

101. Sadlier, Mary Anne (Madden)
1820–1903
novelist, author, Sunday school story writer
Catholic
Irish
Cyc Am Bio; Dict Am Auth; Dict Am Bio; Dict Am Bio Men Time; Dict Irish Bio; Index t Wom; Not Am Wom

102. Fitzgibbon, Mary Catherine Irene; Sister Irene
1823–96
Catholic nun, philanthropist
Catholic
Dict Am Bio; Twent Cen Bio Dict Not Am

103. Gillespie, Eliza Maria; Mother Mary of St. Angela
1824–87
mother superior and founder of the American Sisters of the Holy Cross, educator, Civil War hospital administrator
Catholic
Cyc Am Bio; Dict Am Bio; Index t Wom; Not Am Wom; Twent Cen Bio Dict Not Am; Wom Cent

104. Dahlgren, Madeleine Vinton [Sara] (Goddard); Corinne; Cornelia
1825/35–1898
novelist, translator, antisuffragist
Catholic
Washington, DC
Cyc Am Bio; Dict Am Auth; Dict Am Bio; Index t Wom; Nat Cyc Am Bio v22; Twent Cen Bio Dict Not Am; Wom Cent

105. Riepp, Benedicta, Mother
1825–62
Catholic nun, founder of the Sisters of St. Benedict in the United States
Catholic
Not Am Wom

106. White, Catherine Ann
1825–78
writer on religions, superior of the Convent of the Sacred Heart, Catholic nun, classicist
Catholic
Dict Am Auth

107. Wood, Julia Amanda A. (Sargent); Minnie Mary Lee
born 1826
author, postmaster, pioneer, Minnesota newspaper editor, Catholic novelist
Catholic
Sauk Rapids, MN
Dict Am Auth; Index t Wom; Not Am Wom; Wom Cent

108. McGroarty, Julia, Sister
1827–1901
Catholic nun, educator

Catholic
Not Am Wom

109. Russell, Mary Baptist, Mother
1829–98
Catholic nun, superior of Sisters of Mercy in San Francisco, founder of the Sisters of Mercy in California
Catholic
San Francisco, CA
Irish
Dict Am Bio; Not Am Wom

110. Lynch, Joseph, Mother
flourished 1860s
Catholic nun, nurse
Catholic
Irish
Index t Wom

111. Mary of the Infant Jesus, Sister
circa 1830–1917
western pioneer, Catholic nun
Catholic
Index t Wom

112. Tincker, Mary Agnes
1831/37–1907
novelist, Civil War nurse
Catholic
Cyc Am Bio; Dict Am Bio; Nat Cyc Am Bio v8; Twent Cen Bio Dict Not Am

113. Cusack, Margaret Anne; Sister Mary Frances Clare; Nun of Kenmare
1832–99
welfare worker, founder of the Sisters of Peace in America, Catholic nun
Catholic
Index t Wom

114. Gubert, Louise
died 1882
Catholic nun, vocalist
Catholic
Cyc Am Bio

115. Beasley, Matilda, Mother
1834–1903
educator, social worker, Catholic nun
Catholic
Georgia
Black
Negro Alman; Prof Negro Wom

116. Elder, Susan (Blanchard); Hermine
1835–1923
religious author, poet, dramatist, natural scientist
Catholic
New Orleans, LA
Cyc Am Bio; Dict Am Auth; Dict Am Bio; Nat Cyc Am Bio v11; Twent Cen Bio Dict Not Am

117. Hughes, Kate Duval
born 1837
author, inventor
Catholic
Washington, DC
Wom Cent

118. Donnelly, Eleonor Cecilia
1838/48–1917
poet, religious author
Catholic
Cyc Am Bio; Dict Am Auth; Dict Am Bio; Nat Cyc Am Bio v2; Twent Cen Bio Dict Not Am

119. Blake, Mary Elizabeth McGrath
1840–1907
author, poet
Catholic
Boston, MA
Irish
Dict Am Auth; Dict Am Bio; Wom Cent

120. Borden, Helen, Sister
flourished 1870s
nurse, Catholic nun
Catholic
Index t Wom

121. Cecil, Elizabeth Frances
flourished 1870s–1900s
author
Catholic
Nat Cyc Am Bio v3

122. Turnbull, Frances Hubbard (Litchfield)
born 184?
novelist
Catholic
Baltimore, MD
Dict Am Auth

123. van Rensselaer, Euphemia; Sister Mary Dolores
born 1840
nurse, Catholic nun
Catholic
Index t Wom

124. Dunne, Sarah Theresa; Amadeus; Mother Mary of the Heart of Jesus
1846–1917
convent founder
Catholic
Index t Wom

125. Tiernan, Frances Christine (Fisher); Christian Reid
1846–1920
author, popular novelist
Catholic
North Carolina
Dict Am Auth; Dict Am Bio; Index t Wom; Nat Cyc Am Bio v20; Not Am Wom; Twent Cen Bio Dict Not Am

126. Waggaman, Mary Teresa McKee
1846–1931
author, Confederate sympathizer
Catholic
Dict Am Bio

127. Troup, Augusta Lewis
circa 1848–1920
labor organizer, journalist
Catholic
Bio Dict Am Lab; Not Am Wom

128. Cabrini, Francis Xavier, St.
1850–1917
founder of the Missionary Sisters of the Sacred Heart, Catholic nun
Catholic
Italian
Dict Am Bio supp v1; Dict Am Rel Bio; Index t Wom; Nat Cyc Am Bio v27; Not Am Wom

129. Fedde, Elizabeth, Sister
1850–1921
Lutheran deacon, nurse, welfare worker, Catholic nun
Lutheran; Catholic
Norwegian
Index t Wom; Not Am Wom

130. Guirado, Luz (Sanchez)
flourished 1880s–1930s
patron of the Catholic church
Catholic
Los Angeles, CA
Mexican
Am Bio New Cyc

131. Stanislaus, Sister
flourished nineteenth to twentieth century
Catholic nun, nurse
Catholic
Index t Wom

132. Avery, Martha Gallison Moore
1851–1929
Socialist, Catholic lay apostle
Catholic
Not Am Wom

133. Lathrop, Rose (Hawthorne); Mother Mary Alphonsa; Rose Hawthorne
1851–1926
author, artist, poet, Catholic nun, founder of the Dominican Congregation of St. Rose of Lima, philanthropist
Catholic
Cyc Am Bio; Dict Am Auth; Dict Am Bio; Index t Wom; Nat Cyc Am Bio v9; Not Am Wom; Twent Cen Bio Dict Not Am; Wom Cent

134. Conway, Katherine Eleanor
born 1853
journalist, poet
Catholic
Boston, MA
Dict Am Auth; Twent Cen Bio Dict Not Am; Wom Cent

135. Sadlier, Anna Theresa
born 1854/56
author, biographer, translator
Catholic
Cyc Am Bio; Dict Am Auth

136. Repplier, Agnes
1855/59–1950
essayist, children's author, biographer
Catholic
Philadelphia, PA
Dict Am Auth; Dict Am Bio supp v4; Index t Wom; Nat Cyc Am Bio v4; Not Am Wom; Obit File; Twent Cen Bio Dict Not Am

137. Dempsey, Mary Joseph, Sister
1856–1939
Catholic nun, hospital administrator, surgical assistant
Catholic
Not Am Wom

138. Walter, Carrie Stevens
born 1856
educator, poet
Catholic
California
Wom Cent

139. Chapellin, Emilia, Mother
1858–90
convent founder, Catholic nun
Catholic
Index t Wom

140. Drexel, Katharine Mary; Mother Mary Katharine
1858–1955
founder of the Catholic Sisters of the Most Blessed Sacrament for Indians and Colored People, educator of Blacks, missionary, philanthropist
Catholic
Dict Am Bio supp v5; Dict Am Rel Bio; Index t Wom; Not Am Wom supp v1; Obit File; Read Encyc Am West

141. Butler, Marie Joseph, Mother
1860–1940
founder of Marymount Schools, Catholic nun
Catholic
Not Am Wom

142. Wight, Emma Howard
flourished 1890s
magazine writer, theological writer, novelist
Catholic
Wom Cent

143. Haley, Margaret Angela
1861–1939
educator, civic reformer, labor leader
Catholic
Illinois
Bio Dict Am Lab; Not Am Wom

144. Teresa, M. Imelda, Sister
born 1862
philanthropist, Catholic nun
Catholic
Index t Wom

145. Feeney, Mary Ignatius, Sister
died 1915
pharmacist, Catholic nun, nurse
Catholic
Index t Wom

146. Jordan, Elizabeth Garver
1865/67–1947
journalist, author, adventurer, editor
Catholic
Index t Wom; Nat Cyc Am Bio v40; Not Am Wom; Obit File; Wom Cent

147. Stallings, Olive Andrews
born 1866
welfare worker
Catholic
New Orleans, LA
Nat Cyc Am Bio csv5

148. Randall, Minnie Josephine Smith
1867–1955
industrialist, founder of the Vacuum Can Co., philanthropist
Catholic
Chicago, IL
Nat Cyc Am Bio v42; Obit File

149. Bates, Eda Tibbles
1868–1950
suffragist, economist
Catholic
Nat Cyc Am Bio v37

150. Gurney, Marion Francis; Marianne of Jesus
1869–1957
founder and mother general of the Sisters of Our Lady of Christian Doctrine
Catholic
Obit File

151. Regan, Agnes Gertrude
1869–1943
Catholic social welfare leader, educator, women's rights worker
Catholic
Dict Am Bio supp v3; Not Am Wom

152. Eutropia McMahon, Mother
flourished 1900s
Catholic nun
Catholic
Index t Wom

153. Marianne, Sister
flourished 1900s
nurse, Catholic nun
Catholic
Index t Wom

154. Mary Agnes
1870–1962
founder of the Order of Franciscan Nuns of the Most Blessed Sacrament in the United States, Catholic nun
Catholic
Obit File

155. Penrose, Julie Villers Lewis
1870–1956
philanthropist
Catholic
Colorado Springs, CO
Nat Cyc Am Bio v44

156. Stevens, Georgia Lydia, Mother
1870–1946
musician, cofounder of the Piux X School of Liturgical Music, educator, Catholic nun
Catholic
Not Am Wom; Obit File

157. de Lima, Rose
1871–1945
Catholic nun
Catholic
Obit File

158. Phelan, Marie Gerard
1872–1960
superior general of the Institute of the Religious of the Sacred Heart of Mary, cofounder of Marymount College
Catholic
California
Obit File

159. Bolton, Margaret
1873–1943
religious educator, author
Catholic
Obit File

160. Dammann, Grace Cowardin
1873–1945
president of Manhattanville College of the Sacred Heart
Catholic
Obit File

161. Yaegle, Marie Tello Phillips
1874–1962
poet, novelist, essayist, founder of the American Academy of Poets
Catholic
Pennsylvania
Canadian
Index t Wom; Nat Cyc Am Bio csv3; Obit File

162. Dickenson, Helena A.
1876–1957
cofounder of the Sacred Heart Music School at Union Theological Seminary
Catholic
Obit File

163. Good, Alice Campbell
1878–1956
Democratic party worker, New York civic worker
Catholic
New York
Nat Cyc Am Bio v42

164. Neenan, Mary Pius, Sister
born 1878
philosopher, Catholic nun
Catholic
Who Who Phil

165. Scheff, Fritzi
1878–1954
singer
Catholic
Nat Cyc Am Bio v40

166. Barrymore, Ethel
1879–1959
actor
Catholic
Dict Am Bio supp v6; Index t Wom; Nat Cyc Am Bio v60, csv2, and csv5; Not Am Wom supp v1; Obit File

167. Swartz, Maud O'Farrell
1879–1937
labor leader
Catholic
New York
Irish
Bio Dict Am Lab; Not Am Wom

168. Dunbar, Saidie [Sarah] Orr
1880–1960
patron of nursing and public health, developer of Christmas Seals
Catholic
Oregon
Nat Cyc Am Bio v51

169. Mary de Sales, Mother; Wilhelmina Tredow
flourished 1910s
educator, Catholic nun
Catholic
Index t Wom

170. Mary Madalene, Sister; Sarah C. Cox
flourished 1910s
translator, Catholic nun
Catholic
Index t Wom

171. Molloy, Mary Aloysia
born 1880
educator, author, Franciscan nun
Catholic
Nat Cyc Am Bio csv3

172. Norris, Kathleen Thompson
1880–1966
author, novelist, magazine writer, pacifist, feminist
Catholic
Index t Wom; Nat Cyc Am Bio csv3; Not Am Wom supp v1; Obit File; Wom Lit, More

173. Bailey, Elizabeth Donovan
1881–post 1930
social welfare worker
Catholic
New York
Index t Wom; Nat Cyc Am Bio csv5

174. Matzenauer, Margaret
1881–1963
opera singer, opera coach
Catholic
Hungarian
Nat Cyc Am Bio v51

175. Rogers, Mary Josephine; Mother Mary Joseph
1882–1955
founder of the Maryknoll Sisters of St. Dominic, missionary
Catholic
Dict Am Bio supp v5; Not Am Wom supp v1; Obit File

176. Joseph, Mary, Sister
born 1883
educator, Catholic nun
Catholic
Index t Wom

177. Rorke, Margaret Hayden
1883–1967
color standards expert, suffragist
Catholic
Nat Cyc Am Bio v54

178. Challinor, Mercedes Crimmins (Clara)
1885–1966
Red Cross official, World War I relief worker
Catholic
Nat Cyc Am Bio v52

179. Maher, Frances
1886–1958
supreme regent of the Catholic Daughters of America
Catholic
Obit File

180. Mary Julia, Sister; Elizabeth Ann Dullea
born 1886
educator, Catholic nun
Catholic
Index t Wom

181. Rowley, M. Rita
1886–1963
superior general of the Roman Catholic Institute of the Religious of the Sacred Heart of Mary, provincial superior of the Eastern Province of North America
Catholic
Obit File

182. Schaefer, Gertrude Rose Keegan
1886–1944
suffragist, lawyer
Catholic
New York
Nat Cyc Am Bio v34

183. Westropp, Clara Elizabeth
1886–1965
banker
Catholic
Ohio
Nat Cyc Am Bio v51

184. Bori, Lucrezia; Lucrecia Borja Gonzales de Riancho
1887–1960
Metropolitan Opera soprano singer
Catholic
Spanish
Dict Am Bio supp v5; Nat Cyc Am Bio v44; Obit File

185. Madelva, Mary Eveline Wolff, Sister
1887–1964
president of St. Mary's College, medievalist, educator, author, poet, Catholic nun
Catholic
Index t Wom; Nat Cyc Am Bio v51; Obit File

186. Verda, Mary (Dorsch), Sister
born 1887
philosopher, Catholic nun
Catholic
Who Who Phil

187. Wolff, Mary Evaline "Madelva", Sister
1887–1964
college administrator, Catholic nun, religious educator, poet
Catholic
Not Am Wom supp v1

188. Gowan, M. Olivia, Sister
born 1888
nurse, Catholic nun
Catholic
Index t Wom

189. Putnam, Nina Wilcox
1888–1962
author, humorist, novelist, short story writer, suffragist
Catholic
Nat Cyc Am Bio v45; Obit File

190. Bonfils, Helen Gertrude
1889–1962
newspaper executive, chairperson of the board of the *Denver Post*, theatrical producer
Catholic
Denver, CO
Nat Cyc Am Bio v56; Obit File

191. Ward, Maisie
1889–1975
book publisher, author, lecturer, Catholic church worker
Catholic
English
Cur Biog '75; Index t Wom

192. Eliot, Ethel Cook
1890–1972
children's author, religious writer
Catholic
Nat Cyc Am Bio v56

193. Kennedy, Rose (Fitzgerald)
born 1890
philanthropist, patron of welfare work for the mentally retarded and of research on mental retardation
Catholic
Cur Biog '70

194. Maria Gratia, Mother
flourished 1920s
missionary nurse, Catholic nun
Catholic
Index t Wom

195. Carroll, Consolata; Sister Mary Consolata
born 1892
author, educator, Catholic nun
Catholic
Index t Wom

196. Galassi, Josephine
1892–1958
provincial superior of the Salesian Sisters of the United States
Catholic
Italian
Obit File

197. Healy, Emma Therese, Sister
born 1892
philosopher, Catholic nun
Catholic
Who Who Phil

198. Maher, Aldea
1892–1959
biochemist, pathologist, cardiologist
Catholic
Louisiana
Nat Cyc Am Bio v51

199. Meiere, Hildreth
1892–post 1930s
artist, painter, muralist
Catholic
Index t Wom; Nat Cyc Am Bio csv4

200. Fitz-Gibbon, Bernice; Mrs. Herman Block
graduated 1918
advertising executive
Catholic
New York
Nat Cyc Am Bio csv9

201. White, Helen Constance
1896–1967
educator, historial novelist, religious historian, UNESCO member
Catholic
Index t Wom; Nat Cyc Am Bio v53; Not Am Wom supp v1

202. Day, Dorothy
1897–1980
journalist, social worker, political activist, fiction writer on Catholic life
Catholic
Cur Biog '82; Index t Wom

203. Prince, Mildred Mallon
1897–1961
lawyer, social legislation agitator, San Francisco civic worker
Catholic
San Francisco, CA
Nat Cyc Am Bio v47

204. Coleman, Emily Holmes
1899–1974
autobiographer, poet
Catholic
French (American expatriate to Paris)
Dict Lit Bio v4

205. Hayes, Helen; Mrs. Charles G. MacArthur
born 1900
actor
Catholic
Index t Wom; Nat Cyc Am Bio csv5

206. McGuigan, Gertrude St. George Congregation de Notre Dame, Sister
born 1900
Catholic nun, philosopher
Catholic
Who Who Phil

207. Rusk, Evelyn Carroll
1900–64
mathematician, educator
Catholic
New York
Nat Cyc Am Bio v51

208. Wolfe, Joan of Arc, Sister
born 1900
philosopher, Catholic nun
Catholic
Who Who Phil

209. Demjanovich, Miriam Teresa
1901–27
religious worker
Catholic
Index t Wom

210. Casey, Rosemary
1904–76
playwright, screenwriter
Catholic
Pennsylvania
Nat Cyc Am Bio v59

211. Murphy, Rosemary Ann
1906–69
physician, medical researcher, zoologist
Catholic
Indiana
Nat Cyc Am Bio v54

212. Tarry, Ellen
born 1906
author, children's author
Catholic
Black
Negro Alman; Prof Negro Wom v2

213. Tobin, Mary; Mother Mary Maurice
1906–59
mother general of the Catholic Sisters of Mercy, executive chairperson of the National Conference of Major Religious Superiors, Catholic nun
Catholic
Obit File

214. Medinger, Elizabeth Eudora
1907–77
Catholic church worker, philanthropist
Catholic
Washington, DC
Nat Cyc Am Bio v60

215. Miriam Michael, Sister
flourished 1940s–60s
scientist, Catholic nun
Catholic
Index t Wom

216. Rosalita, Sister
flourished 1940s
missionary, Catholic nun
Catholic
Index t Wom

217. Milligan, Mary Louise
born 1911
colonel in the US army, Women's Army Air Corps director
Catholic
Index t Wom; Nat Cyc Am Bio csv9

218. Praxedes Carty, Mother
died 1963
Catholic nun
Catholic
Irish
Index t Wom

219. Preminger, Marion Hill; Mrs. Albert Mayer
1913–72
social worker, author, African art collector, missionary to the Congo, philanthropist, screen actor
Catholic
New York
Hungarian
Nat Cyc Am Bio v57; Obit File

220. Andrews, Marie Scherer
1914–73
orthopedic nurse, nursing educator
Catholic
Massachusetts
Nat Cyc Am Bio v57

221. Kent, Corita
born 1918
"op-pop" artist
Catholic
Cur Biog '69

222. Mary Aquinas, Sister
flourished 1950s
aviator, jet pilot, Catholic nun
Catholic
Index t Wom

223. O'Connor, Flannery [Mary]
1925–64
author, short story writer, novelist
Catholic
Georgia
Dict Lit Bio v2; Encyc South Hist; Index t Wom; Nat Cyc Am Bio v55; Not Am Wom supp v1; Obit File; Wom Lit; Wom Lit, More

224. Wexler, Jacqueline Grennan
born 1926
president of Hunter College
Catholic
New York
Cur Biog '70

225. Wojciechowska, Maia [Teresa]
born 1927
children's author, children's book publisher
Catholic
Polish
Cur Biog '76

226. Huerta, Dolores Fernandez
1930–post 1970
United Farm Workers executive
Catholic
California
Mexican
Bio Dict Am Lab; Dict Mex Am Hist

227. Mary Alma, Sister
flourished 1960s
biochemist, Catholic nun
Catholic
Index t Wom

228. Mary Benedict, Sister
flourished 1960s
surgeon, Catholic nun
Catholic
Index t Wom

229. Veronica, M., Sister
flourished 1960s
educator, Catholic nun
Catholic
Index t Wom

230. Davis, Gloria Ann, Sister
born 1933
Catholic nun, educator
Catholic
Native American (Navaho-Chocktaw)
Ind Today

231. Moore, Mary Tyler
born 1937
television and stage actor
Catholic
California
Cur Biog '71; Index t Wom

232. Gordon, Mary
born 1949
novelist, writer on Catholic life
Catholic
Cur Biog '81; Dict Lit Bio v6

CHRISTIAN SCIENCE

233. Eddy, Mary Morse (Baker) (Glover) (Patterson)
1821/27–1910
founder of Christian Science
Christian Scientist
Concord, NH
Dict Am Auth; Dict Am Rel Bio; Index t Wom; Nat Cyc Am Bio v3; Not Am Wom; Twent Cen Bio Dict Not Am

234. Whitney, Adeline Dutton (Train)
1824–1906
writer of popular didactic verse and fiction
Christian Scientist
Milton, MA
Cyc Am Bio; Dict Am Auth; Dict Am Bio Men Time; Index t Wom; Nat Cyc Am Bio v1; Not Am Wom; Twent Cen Bio Dict Not Am; Wom Cent

235. Coman, Charlotte Buell
1833/45–1924
painter
Christian Scientist
New York
Cyc Am Bio; Dict Am Bio; Index t Wom; Nat Cyc Am Bio v22

236. Norton, Della Whitney
born 1840
poet, author
Christian Scientist
Wom Cent

237. Ziegler, Electra Matilda Curtis
1841–1932
patron of welfare of the blind
Christian Scientist
New York
Index t Wom; Nat Cyc Am Bio v37

238. Mims, Sue Harper
born 1842
Christian Science leader
Christian Scientist
Georgia
Index t Wom; Wom Cent

239. Stetson, Augusta Emma Simmons
1842–1928
Christian Science leader
Christian Scientist
Dict Am Bio; Nat Cyc Am Bio v18; Not Am Wom

240. Longyear, Mary Hawley Beecher
born 1851
author, philanthropist
Christian Scientist
Nat Cyc Am Bio csv3

241. Leader, Olive Moorman
born 1852
temperance reformer, suffragist
Christian Scientist
Wom Cent

242. Bradford, Mary Carroll Craig
born 1856/60
magazine and newspaper correspondent, educator, labor union leader
Christian Scientist

Colorado
Nat Cyc Am Bio csv2; Wom Cent

243. Morgan, Mary Kimball
1861–1948
Christian Science educator
Christian Scientist
Not Am Wom

244. Scudder, Vida Dutton
1861–1954
social reformer, writer on English literature, author, university educator
Christian Scientist
Massachusetts
Cyc Am Bio; Dict Am Auth; Dict Am Bio supp v5; Index t Wom; Not Am Wom supp v1; Twent Cen Bio Dict Not Am; Wom Lit, More

245. Bell, Orelia Key
born 1864
poet
Christian Scientist
Georgia
Wom Cent

246. Freshel, Maud Hammer
1866–1948
antivivisectionist, animal humane worker
Christian Scientist
Obit File

247. Baxter, Martha Wheeler
born 1869
sculptor, painter
Christian Scientist
Index t Wom; Nat Cyc Am Bio csv8

248. Curran, Pearl Gildersleeve
1875/76–1941
composer, songwriter
Christian Scientist
New York
Index t Wom; Nat Cyc Am Bio v53

249. McQueen, Elizabeth Lippincott
born 1878
author
Christian Scientist
Nat Cyc Am Bio csv1

250. Marley, Anne Augusta Bonner
born 1884
poet, violinist
Christian Scientist
Nat Cyc Am Bio csv9

251. Clark, Pearl Franklin
1886–1962
dramatist, international management consultant, business executive
Christian Scientist

New York
Nat Cyc Am Bio v47

252. Hardwick, Katharine Davis
1886–1974
pianist, newspaper publisher
Christian Scientist
Indiana
Nat Cyc Am Bio v58

253. Post, Marjorie Merriweather
1887–1973
philanthropist, antique collector, suffragist, director of National Savings and Trust, founder and director of General Foods
Christian Scientist
Washington, DC
Nat Cyc Am Bio v58; Not Am Wom supp v1; Obit File

254. Steere, Lora Woodhead
born 1888
sculptor
Christian Scientist
Los Angeles, CA
Nat Cyc Am Bio csv7

255. Claytor, Gertrude (Harris) Boatwright
1889–1973
poet, Red Cross worker in World War I
Christian Scientist
Virginia
Nat Cyc Am Bio v57

256. Hokinson, Helen Elna
1893–1949
cartoonist, artist
Christian Scientist
Dict Nat Bio supp v4; Index t Wom; Nat Cyc Am Bio v41; Not Am Wom

257. Hughes, Arleen Florence Wilson
born 1897
investment counselor
Christian Scientist
Colorado
Nat Cyc Am Bio csv9

258. Thompson, Helen Victoria Veale
born 1897
artist
Christian Scientist
Detroit, MI
Nat Cyc Am Bio csv9

259. Wright, Lucille Voorhies Parker
flourished 1930s–50s
sportsperson, horse breeder
Christian Scientist
Nat Cyc Am Bio csv8

260. Reid, Helen Dwight
1901–65

international political scientist, educator, pacifist
Christian Scientist
Washington, DC
Scottish
Nat Cyc Am Bio v51

261. Forman, Julie (Rose) Ripley
1902–75
educator
Christian Scientist
Connecticut
Nat Cyc Am Bio v59

262. Brooks, Virginia Field Walton
born 1904
traveler, explorer
Christian Scientist
Nat Cyc Am Bio csv13

CHURCH OF ENGLAND

263. Lawson, Mary J.; M. J. K.; M. J. K. L.
born 1828
author
Anglican
Wom Cent

264. Rogers, Elizabeth Ann; Sister Beatrice
1829–1921
educator, Anglican nun
Anglican
Not Am Wom

265. Polyblank, Ellen Albertina; Sister Albertina
1840–1930
Anglican sister, educator
Anglican
Not Am Wom

266. Johnson, Emily Pauline; Tekahionwake
1861–1913
poet
Anglican
Native American (Mohawk)
Great North Am Ind; Wom Cent

267. Garrett, Eileen Jeanette; Jean Lyttle
1893–1970
parapsychologist, novelist, founder of the Parapsychology Foundation
Anglican
Irish
Nat Cyc Am Bio v55; Obit File

CHURCH OF JESUS CHRIST OF THE LATTER-DAY SAINTS

268. Smith, Eliza Roxey Snow;
The Mother of Mormonism
1804–87
Mormon leader, religious poet, hymn writer, women's leader, suffragist, western pioneer
Mormon
Utah
Cyc Am Bio; Dict Am Bio; Index t Wom; Not Am Wom; Read Encyc Am West

269. Smith, Emma Hale
1804–79
prominent figure in early Mormonism, religious worker
Mormon
Cyc Am Bio; Index t Wom; Not Am Wom

270. Smith, Bathsheba (Bigler)
1822–1910
philanthropist
Mormon
Cyc Am Bio

271. Wells, Emmeline Blanchard Woodward
1828–1921
leader of Mormon women, feminist, suffragist, editor, poet
Mormon
Utah
Cyc Am Bio; Not Am Wom

272. Newman, Angelia Louise French Thurston
1837–1910
church worker, missionary, Mormon women's relief worker, lecturer, reformer
Mormon
Utah
Index t Wom; Not Am Wom; Wom Cent

273. Gates, Susa Young
1856–1933
Mormon author, educator, suffragist
Mormon
Nat Cyc Am Bio csv2; Read Encyc Am West

274. Young, Zina Diantha Huntington
1871–1902
midwife, suffragist, Mormon leader
Mormon
Cyc Am Bio

275. Anderson, Audentia Smith
born 1872
religious author, genealogist, pioneer
Mormon
Index t Wom

276. MacDonald, Lillie Ann Neal
1884–1966
candy manufacturer
Mormon
Utah
Nat Cyc Am Bio v53

277. Brooks, Juanita
born 1898
historian of Mormonism
Mormon
Read Encyc Am West

278. Priest, Ivy [Maud] Baker;
Ivy Maud Baker
1905–75
Republican party worker, US treasurer, politician, treasurer of California
Mormon
California
Cur Biog '75; Index t Wom; Nat Cyc Am Bio v59 and csv9; Not Am Wom supp v1; Obit File

279. Peterson, Esther Eggertsen
born 1906
labor leader, director of the US Department of Labor Women's Bureau
Mormon
Washington, DC
Bio Dict Am Lab; Index t Wom; Nat Cyc Am Bio csv10

CHURCHES OF THE NEW JERUSALEM

280. Miller, Harriet (Mann);
Olive Thorne Miller
1831–1918
author, ornithologist, bird watcher, naturalist, nature writer, conservationist, children's author, magazine writer
Swedenborgian
Brooklyn, NY
Dict Am Auth; Index t Wom; Nat Cyc Am Bio v9; Not Am Wom; Twent Cen Bio Dict Not Am

281. Fairchild, Maria Augusta
born 1834
physician
Swedenborgian
Wom Cent

282. Cornell, Ellen Frances
born 1835
poet, marine shell collector
Swedenborgian
Massachusetts
Wom Cent

283. Mussey, Ellen (Persis) Spencer
1850–1936
international lawyer, law educator, feminist, women's rights worker, clubwoman, child welfare worker, Red Cross worker, social reformer
Swedenborgian
Washington, DC
Dict Am Bio supp v2; Index t Wom; Nat Cyc Am Bio v47 and csv1; Not Am Wom; Twent Cen Bio Dict Not Am

284. Trix, Harriet Phelps
born 1850
suffragist
Swedenborgian
Detroit, MI
Nat Cyc Am Bio v18

285. Keller, Helen Adams
1880–1968
author, feminist, suffragist, educator, advocate for the handicapped, pacifist, Socialist party worker
Swedenborgian
Alabama
blind, deaf
Encyc South Hist; Index t Wom; Nat Cyc Am Bio v15 and v57; Not Am Wom supp v1; Obit File

CONGREGATIONALIST

286. Fiske, Fidelia
1816–1864/84
Congregationalist missionary to Persia, educator
Congregationalist
Cyc Am Bio; Dict Am Bio; Dict Am Bio Men Time; Index t Wom; Nat Cyc Am Bio v3; Not Am Wom; Wom Cent

287. Blackwell, Antoinette Louisa (Brown)
1825–1921
Universalist minister, author, lecturer, temperance worker, abolitionist, suffragist, women's rights worker, philosopher, poet, novelist
Unitarian; Congregationalist
Appl Cyc Am Bio; Cyc Am Bio; Dict Am Bio; Dict Am Bio Men Time; Index t Wom; Nat Cyc Am Bio v9 and v29; Not Am Wom; Twent Cen Bio Dict Not Am; Wom Cent

288. Calkins, Adelaide Augusta Hosmer
1831–1909
philanthropist, children's welfare worker
Congregationalist
Massachusetts
Nat Cyc Am Bio v28

289. Saxon, Elizabeth Lyle
1832–1915
suffragist, temperance worker, lecturer
Congregationalist
Memphis, TN
Nat Cyc Am Bio v16; Wom Cent

290. Drake, Mary Eveline
born 1833
temperance worker, Congregationalist minister, home missionary
Congregationalist
Wom Cent

291. Dike, Jeannie Dean Scott
1837–1920
music educator, Congregationalist missionary
Congregationalist
New York
Twent Cen Bio Dict Not Am; Wom Cent

292. Lathrap, Mary Torrans;
The Daniel Webster of Prohibition
born 1838
poet, temperance reformer, Congregationalist preacher
Congregationalist
Wom Cent

293. Dow, Cornelia M.
born 1842
temperance worker, philanthropist
Congregationalist
Portland, OR
Wom Cent

294. Shaw, Cornelia Dean
born 1845
suffragist, philanthropist, Congregationalist missionary worker
Congregationalist
Toledo, OH
Wom Cent

295. Baker, Louise S.
born 1846
Congregationalist minister
Congregationalist
Wom Cent

296. Yale, Caroline Ardelia
1848–1933
educator of the deaf
Congregationalist
Vermont
Dict Am Bio; Nat Cyc Am Bio v31; Not Am Wom

297. Hall, Mary
born 185?
lawyer, notary public
Congregationalist

Connecticut
Wom Cent

298. le Valley, Laura A. Woodin
flourished 1880s
lawyer
Congregationalist
New York
Wom Cent

299. Palmer, Sarah Ellen
flourished 1880s–1930s
surgeon
Congregationalist
Massachusetts
Nat Cyc Am Bio csv5

300. Eastman, Annie Bertha Ford
1852–1910
Congregationalist minister
Congregationalist
Not Am Wom

301. Williams, Annie Frances Day
1853–1931
missionary leader
Congregationalist
Nat Cyc Am Bio v31

302. Hazard, Caroline
1856–1945
fifth president of Wellesley College, historian, historical author
Congregationalist
Dict Am Auth; Index t Wom; Nat Cyc Am Bio v12, v34, and csv43; Not Am Wom; Twent Cen Bio Dict Not Am

303. Slosson, May Genevieve Preston
1858–1943
educator, suffragist
Congregationalist
Nat Cyc Am Bio v35

304. Moreland, Mary L.
born 1859
Congregationalist minister, temperance worker
Congregationalist
Illinois

Wom Cent

305. Bailey, Eliza Randall Simmons
1861–1939
educator, textbook author, education writer
Congregationalist
Nat Cyc Am Bio v29

306. Lang, Florence Osgood Rand
1861–1943
patron of art, philanthropist
Congregationalist

Massachusetts
Nat Cyc Am Bio v32 and csv5

307. Miner, Sarah Luella
1861–1935
Congregationalist missionary and educator in China
Congregationalist
Not Am Wom

308. Bissell, Julia
1862–1928
physician, missionary to India
Congregationalist
Nat Cyc Am Bio v21

309. Bolles, Jeanette Hubbard
1863–1930
osteopath
Congregationalist
Colorado
Nat Cyc Am Bio v28

310. Cannon, Annie Jump
1863–1941
astronomer
Methodist; Congregationalist
Cambridge, MA
Dict Lit Bio supp v3; Index t Wom; Nat Cyc Am Bio csv2; Not Am Wom; Obit File

311. Terrell, Mary Eliza Church
1863–1954
community leader, social reformer, suffragist, feminist, civil rights leader, NAACP organizer, lecturer, educator
Congregationalist
Washington, DC
Dict Am Bio supp v5; Encyc Black Am; Encyc South Hist; Index t Wom; Nat Cyc Am Bio v52; Negro Alman; Not Am Wom; Prof Negro Wom v1; World Great Men Col v2

312. Woolley, Mary Emma
1863–1947
second president of Mt. Holyoke College, educator, pacifist, suffragist
Congregationalist
Dict Am Bio supp v4; Index t Wom; Nat Cyc Am Bio v13, v37, and csv4; Not Am Wom

313. Merrill, Helen Abbot
1864–1949
educator, mathematician
Congregationalist
Nat Cyc Am Bio v42

314. Baldwin, Helen
1865–1946
physician
Congregationalist
Nat Cyc Am Bio v36

315. Talbot, Ellen Bliss
1867–1968

philosopher, educator, author
Congregationalist
Index t Wom; Nat Cyc Am Bio v54; Who Who Phil

316. Buel, Elizabeth Cynthia Barney
1868–1943
author
Congregationalist
Connecticut
Nat Cyc Am Bio v32

317. Porter, Eleanor Hodgman
1868–1920
children's author, novelist
Congregationalist
Dict Lit Bio v9; Index t Wom; Nat Cyc Am Bio v18; Not Am Wom

318. Strawn, Julia Clark
1868–1942
surgeon, gynecologist
Congregationalist
Chicago, IL
Index t Wom; Nat Cyc Am Bio v31

319. Barnum, Mary Gilmore
born 1869
educator, social worker, Los Angeles civic worker
Congregationalist
Los Angeles, CA
Nat Cyc Am Bio csv7

320. McGiffert, Gertrude Huntington Boyce
1869–1962
poet
Congregationalist
Nat Cyc Am Bio v51

321. Buell, Edith May
born 1870
educator of the deaf
Congregationalist
Nat Cyc Am Bio csv6

322. Brosseau, Grace Lincoln Hall
1872–1959
president general of DAR
Congregationalist
Illinois
Nat Cyc Am Bio csv4; Obit File

323. Key, Wilhelmine Enteman
born 1872
zoologist, eugenicist
Congregationalist
Nat Cyc Am Bio csv2 and csv5

324. Thurston, Matilda Smynell Calder
1875–1958
missionary educator in Turkey and China, founder and president of Ginling College in Nanking, China

Congregationalist
Not Am Wom supp v1; Obit File

325. Sprague, Harriet Chapman
1876–1969
bibliophile, book collector
Congregationalist
Connecticut
Nat Cyc Am Bio v56

326. Marvin, Adelaide Camilla Hoffman
born 1877
New York civic leader
Congregationalist
New York, NY
Nat Cyc Am Bio csv8

327. Sapp, Ruth Bent
1877–1951
clubwoman
Congregationalist
Illinois
Nat Cyc Am Bio v47

328. Frame, Alice Seymour Browne
1878–1941
Congregationalist missionary and educator in China
Congregationalist
Dict Am Bio supp v3; Not Am Wom

329. McLeod, Grace
1878–1962
nutritionist, nutrition educator, editor
Congregationalist
Scottish
Index t Wom; Nat Cyc Am Bio v50

330. Voorhees, Florence Edgar
1879–1946
gynecologist
Congregationalist
Nat Cyc Am Bio v36

331. Wilcox, Elsie Hart
1879–1954
Kauai, Hawaii, civic worker; territorial senator from Hawaii; politician; business executive
Congregationalist
Hawaii
Nat Cyc Am Bio v48

332. Harris, Mary Ormerod
born 1882
philanthropist, patron of the University of Southern California
Congregationalist
California
Nat Cyc Am Bio csv6

333. Allen, Florence Ellinwood
1884–1966
lawyer, US Court of Appeals judge, suffragist
Congregationalist

Ohio
Index t Wom; Nat Cyc Am Bio
v52 and csv3; Not Am Wom;
Obit File

334. McAfee, Helen
1884–1956
editor
Congregationalist
New Haven, CT
Nat Cyc Am Bio v43

335. Magna, Edith Scott
1885–1960
executive of DAR
Congregationalist
Massachusetts
Nat Cyc Am Bio v49

336. Paradis, Marjorie B.; Olive Bartholomew
1886–1970
novelist
Congregationalist
New York
Index t Wom; Nat Cyc Am Bio
v57

337. Fairbank, Ruth Eldred
1887–1972
psychiatrist, psychiatric educator
Congregationalist
Massachusetts
Nat Cyc Am Bio v58

338. Morgan, Barbara Spofford
1887–1971
philosopher, psychologist
Congregationalist
New York
Nat Cyc Am Bio v56; Who Who
Phil

339. Neese, Laura Janvrin Aldrich
1889–1967
artist, philanthropist
Congregationalist
Wisconsin
Nat Cyc Am Bio v53

340. Abee, Grace Arnold (Thurston)
born 1890
artist
Congregationalist
Rhode Island
Nat Cyc Am Bio csvll

341. Andrews, Emily Russell
1890–1973
physical education authority
Congregationalist
Nat Cyc Am Bio v57

342. Forbes, Esther; Esther Forbes Hoskins
1891–1967
novelist, children's author, colonial historian, Pulitzer Prize
winner
Congregationalist

Massachusetts
Index t Wom; Nat Cyc Am Bio
v53; Not Am Wom supp v1;
Obit File

343. Lenroot, Katharine Fredrica
born 1891
government official, social worker, child health worker
Congregationalist
Wisconsin
Index t Wom; Nat Cyc Am Bio
csv7

344. Ochtman, Dorothy; Mrs. William A. del Mar
1892–1971
artist
Congregationalist
Connecticut
Nat Cyc Am Bio v56

345. Ainsworth, Dorothy Sears
born 1894
physical education authority
Congregationalist
Nat Cyc Am Bio csv12

346. Smith, Blanche Hixson
1894–1974
newspaper publisher and editor
Congregationalist
Connecticut
Nat Cyc Am Bio v58

347. Todd, Lois Pendleton
1894–1968
physician, medical educator in
China
Congregationalist
California
Nat Cyc Am Bio v54

348. Anderson, Elda Emma
1899–1961
health physicist
Congregationalist
Nat Cyc Am Bio v50; Not Am
Wom supp v1

349. Talcott, Lucy
1899–1970
archaeologist, archaeological author
Congregationalist
Nat Cyc Am Bio v54

350. Alexander, Hattie Elizabeth
1901/08–1968
research pediatrician, microbiologist
Congregationalist
New York
Nat Cyc Am Bio csv10; Not Am
Wom; Obit File

351. Overstrett, Bonaro Wilkinson
born 1902
educator, lecturer, author

Congregationalist
California
Index t Wom; Nat Cyc Am Bio
csv11

352. Hofmann, Melita Cecelia
1907–76
artist, art educator, book illustrator and designer, author, conservationist
Congregationalist
New York
Nat Cyc Am Bio v60

353. Park, Rosemary
born 1907
educator, president of Barnard
College
Congregationalist
Connecticut
Index t Wom; Nat Cyc Am Bio
csv10

354. Tucker, Margaret Emmeline
1907–75
radiologist, medical missionary to
China and India
Congregationalist
Nat Cyc Am Bio v59

355. Johnson, Josephine Winslow; Josephine Cannon
born 1910
novelist
Congregationalist
Index t Wom; Nat Cyc Am Bio
csv8

356. Bondy, Elizabeth Jeanne Hale
1913–69
literary agent, book editor
Congregationalist
New York
Nat Cyc Am Bio v54

357. Culver, Agnes Moe
1914–75
illustration dealer, historian
Congregationalist
New York
Nat Cyc Am Bio v58 and v59

No Dates

358. Gilchrist, Beth Bradford; Elizabeth Drake; John Prescott Earl
author, children's author
Congregationalist
Vermont
Nat Cyc Am Bio v47; Obit File

EASTERN CHURCHES

359. Nazimova, Alla
1878/79–1945
stage and screen actor

Jewish; Greek-Russian Orthodox
California
Russian
Dict Am Bio supp v3; Index t
Wom; Nat Cyc Am Bio v36;
Not Am Wom; Obit File

FOUNDER'S CHURCH OF RELIGIOUS SCIENCE

360. Boardman, Queen Walker
born 1881
horticulturist, philanthropist
Religious Scientist
Los Angeles, CA
Nat Cyc Am Bio csv7

361. Armstrong, Alice Catt
born 1911
biographer, book publisher
Religious Scientist
California
Nat Cyc Am Bio csv10

JEWISH

362. Minis, Abigail
1701–94
planter
Jewish
Index t Wom

363. Gratz, Rebecca
1781/82–1869
charity worker, philanthropist,
educator
Jewish
Dict Am Bio; Index t Wom; Nat
Cyc Am Bio v10; Not Am Wom

364. Moise, Penina
1797–1880
poet, writer of Jewish hymns
Jewish
Charleston, SC
Cyc Am Bio; Dict Am Auth; Dict
Am Bio; Index t Wom; Not Am
Wom; Wom Lit, More

365. Rose, Ernestine Louise Lasmond Siismondi Potowski
1810–92
feminist, women's rights worker,
temperance worker, abolitionist
Jewish
Polish
Cyc Am Bio; Dict Am Bio; Not
Am Wom

366. Handlin, Mary Flug
1813–1976
economist, American historian
Jewish
Nat Cyc Am Bio v59

367. Louis, Minnie Dessau
flourished 1860s–90s

Jewish welfare worker, educator
Jewish
New York
Nat Cyc Am Bio v18

368. Menken, la Belle
flourished 1860s
actor
Jewish
Index t Wom

369. Menken, Adah Isaachs;
Dolores Adios Fuertes
1835/37–1868
actor, poet
Jewish
English
Cyc Am Bio; Dict Am Auth; Dict
Am Bio; Index t Wom; Nat Cyc
Am Bio v5; Not Am Wom;
Wom Lit, More

370. Lazarus, Josephine
born 1846
author, religious writer
Jewish
Dict Am Auth

371. Lazarus, Emma
1849–87
author, poet, dramatist, essayist
Jewish
New York
Cyc Am Bio; Dict Am Auth; Dict
Am Bio; Index t Wom; Nat Cyc
Am Bio v3; Not Am Wom;
Twent Cen Bio Dict Not Am;
Who Who Jew Hist; Wom Cent

372. Cohen, Mary M.
born 1854
social economist
Jewish
Wom Cent

373. Straus, Lina Gutherz
1854–1930
patron of Hadassah medical work
in Palestine
Jewish
German
Nat Cyc Am Bio v22

374. Adler, Sara Levitzka
1858–1953
actor in Yiddish theater
Jewish
New York, NY
Dict Am Bio supp v5; Obit File

375. Beer, Rachel "Richa"
1858–1927
newspaper editor, publisher, composer
Jewish
Who Who Jew Hist

**376. Solomon, Hannah Green-
ebaum**
1858–1942

clubwoman, founder of the Na-
tional Council of Jewish Wom-
en, welfare worker
Jewish
Chicago, IL
Nat Cyc Am Bio v36; Not Am
Wom

377. Szold, Henrietta
1860–1945
Zionist leader
Jewish
Dict Am Bio supp v3; Dict Am
Rel Bio; Index t Wom; Not Am
Wom; Obit File; Who Who Jew
Hist

378. Kaufman, Betty Wolf
1861–1942
philanthropist, welfare worker
Jewish
Philadelphia, PA
Nat Cyc Am Bio v32

379. American, Sadie
1862–1944
lecturer, clubwoman, founder of
the National Council of Jewish
Women
Jewish
Index t Wom; Obit File

380. Nathan, Maud
1862–1946
social welfare leader, social worker, consumer advocate, suffragist, feminist, pacifist
Jewish
Dict Am Bio supp v4; Index t
Wom; Nat Cyc Am Bio v15;
Not Am Wom; Obit File

381. Fels, Mary
born 1863
Zionist
Jewish
German
Nat Cyc Am Bio csv1

**382. Guggenheim, Florence
Shloss**
1863–1944
philanthropist, patron of music,
Republican party worker
Jewish
New York
Index t Wom; Nat Cyc Am Bio
v33; Obit File

**383. Kohut, Rebekah Bettel-
heim**
1864–1951
social welfare leader, educator,
suffragist, lecturer, author, Jewish welfare worker
Jewish
Hungarian
Index t Wom; Nat Cyc Am Bio
v41 and csv5; Not Am Wom
supp v1

384. Frank, Rachel "Ray"
born 1866
author
Jewish
California
Wom Cent

**385. Guggenheim, Leonie Bern-
heim**
1866–1959
patron of dental clinics, patron of
free band concerts in parks
Jewish
New York
Obit File

**386. Meyer, Annie Florence
Nathan**
1867–1950/51
publicist, author, playwright,
novelist, educationist, founder
of Barnard College, antisuffragist, patron of Black music education, clubwoman
Jewish
New York
Dict Am Auth; Dict Am Bio;
Index t Wom; Nat Cyc Am Bio
v42; Not Am Wom supp v1;
Obit File; Twent Cen Bio Dict
Not Am; Wom Cent

387. Wald, Lillian D.
1867–1940
public health nurse, physician, social reformer, social worker, settlement house founder
Jewish
Dict Am Bio supp v2; Index t
Wom; Nat Cyc Am Bio v29;
Not Am Wom

388. Berenson, Senda
1868–1954
basketball player, gymnast, physical education authority
Jewish
Lithuanian
Dict Am Bio supp v5

**389. Guggenheim, Irene Roth-
schild**
1868–1954
patron of child welfare, philanthropist
Jewish
New York
Nat Cyc Am Bio v44

390. Moscowitz, Jennie
1868–1935
actor
Jewish
Rumanian
Obit File

391. Bullowa, Emilie M.
1869–1942
lawyer, World War II relief worker, Sorosis member
Jewish

New York
Nat Cyc Am Bio v31

392. Goldman, Emma
1869–1940
political anarchist, lecturer, publicist, agitator for free speech,
popularizer of the arts, feminist,
pioneer advocate of birth control, politician
Jewish
Russian
Dict Am Bio supp v2; Index t
Wom; Not Am Wom; Who
Who Jew Hist

393. Kussy, Sarah
1869–1956
cofounder of Hadassah
Jewish
Obit File

394. Rubenstein, Helena
1870/71–1965
cosmetics manufacturer, entrepreneur, art collector, philanthropist
Jewish
Polish
Index t Wom; Nat Cyc Am Bio
v50; Not Am Wom supp v1;
Obit File; Who Who Jew Hist

395. Adler, Sophie Rosenwald
1871–1955
philanthropist, patron of the blind
Jewish
Obit File

396. Seligsberg, Alice Lillie
1873–1940
social worker, developer of Hadassah's medical program, Zionist
Jewish
Who Who Jew Hist

397. Stein, Gertrude
1874–1946
author, novelist, literary salon
host, World War I ambulance
driver and supply truck driver
in France
Jewish
French (American expatriate to
Paris)
Dict Am Bio supp v4; Dict Lit
Bio v4; Index t Wom; Nat Cyc
Am Bio v38 and csv4; Not Am
Wom; Obit File; Who Who Jew
Hist; Wom Lit; Wom Lit, More

398. Wise, Louise Waterman
1874–1947
charitable worker, founder and
president of the women's division of the American Jewish
Congress, Zionist
Jewish
New York
Not Am Wom

399. Warburg, Frieda Schiff
1876–1958
philanthropist, Jewish welfare
worker
Jewish
New York
Nat Cyc Am Bio v44; Obit File

400. Landowska, Wanda (Lew)
1877/79–1959
harpsichordist, pianist, composer,
musicologist, music educator,
writer on music
Jewish
Polish
Dict Am Bio supp v6; Obit File;
Slavon Encyc; Who Who Jew
Hist

401. Mero-Iron, Yolanda
1877/87–1963
pianist
Jewish
Hungarian
Index t Wom

402. Moskowitz, Belle Lindner
Israels
1877–1933
social worker, welfare worker, political leader, clubwoman, political adviser to New York
governor Alfred E. Smith
Jewish
New York
Dict Am Bio supp v1; Index t
Wom; Not Am Wom

403. Rolland, Pauline Hoffman
1877–1952
actor in Yiddish and American
theater
Jewish
New York
Obit File

404. Schwimmer, Rosika
1877–1948
feminist, suffragist, pacifist, au-
thor, editor
Jewish
Hungarian
Dict Am Bio supp v4; Not Am
Wom; Obit File

405. Toklas, Alice Babette
1877/97–1967
writer, cookbook author
Jewish
French (American expatriate to
Paris)
Dict Lit Bio v4; Index t Wom;
Not Am Wom supp v1; Obit
File

406. Guggenheim, Olga Hersh
1878–1970
philanthropist, patron of the arts
Jewish
New York
Obit File

407. Nazimova, Alla
1878/79–1945
stage and screen actor
Jewish; Greek-Russian Orthodox
California
Russian
Dict Am Bio supp v3; Index t
Wom; Nat Cyc Am Bio v36;
Not Am Wom; Obit File

408. Neugass, Miriam Dorothy
Newman; Isadora Newman
born 1878
author, artist
Jewish
Louisiana
Nat Cyc Am Bio csv3

409. Stokes, Rose Harriet Pas-
tor
1879–1933
Socialist and Communist party
leader, feminist, labor leader,
author
Jewish
Polish
Bio Dict Am Lab; Dict Am Bio;
Not Am Wom

410. Bernstein, Aline Frankau
1880/82–1955
stage scene and costume designer,
author
Jewish
New York
Dict Am Bio supp v5; Index t
Wom; Nat Cyc Am Bio v47;
Not Am Wom supp v1; Obit
File

411. Bernstein, Theresa; Mrs.
William Meyerowitz
flourished 1910s–60s
artist
Jewish
Index t Wom; Nat Cyc Am Bio
csv11

412. Fromenson, Ruth Bernard
1880–1953
cofounder of Hadassah
Jewish
Obit File

413. Grabau, Mary Antin
born 188?
autobiographer, translator, writer
in Yiddish
Jewish
Dict Am Auth; Dict Am Bio v4;
Nat Cyc Am Bio v39 and csv3;
Not Am Wom; Obit File

414. Shapiro, Dora Monness
1880–1952
philanthropist, Jewish welfare
worker
Jewish
Obit File

415. Yezierska, Anzia
1880/85–1970

novelist
Jewish
Polish
Index t Wom; Not Am Wom
supp v1; Wom Lit, More

416. Goldman, Hettie
1881–1972
archaeologist, nurse in the Greek-
Balkan war
Jewish
Nat Cyc Am Bio v56; Not Am
Wom supp v1

417. Stein, Beatrice Borg
1881–1958
welfare leader, philanthropist,
founder of the Play School Association
Jewish
New York
Nat Cyc Am Bio v47; Obit File

418. Flexner, Jennie Maas
1882–1944
librarian, scholar of Black literature, author
Jewish
Dict Am Bio supp v3; Index t
Wom; Not Am Wom

419. Guggenheim, Minnie
1882–1966
patron of music, founder and
manager of the Lewisohn Stadium Outdoor Concerts, philanthropist
Jewish
New York
Index t Wom; Obit File

420. Schneiderman, Rose
1882/84–1972
labor organizer, Women's Trade
Union leader, secretary of the
New York State Labor Depart-
ment, social reformer, suffragist
Jewish
Polish; Russian
Bio Dict Am Lab; Cur Biog '72;
Index t Wom; Not Am Wom
supp v1; Obit File

421. Bachrach, Grace Baer
1884–1962
philanthropist, patron of medicine
Jewish
New York
Nat Cyc Am Bio v47

422. Tucker, Sophie; Last of
the Red Hot Mamas
1884–1966
singer, comedian, entertainer
Jewish
Index t Wom; Not Am Wom
supp v1; Obit File; Who Who
Jew Hist

423. Bara, Theda; Theodosia
Goodman
1885/90–1955
silent-screen actor
Jewish
Dict Am Bio supp v5; Index t
Wom; Not Am Wom supp v1;
Obit File

424. Cohn, Fannie Mary
1885/88–1962
labor leader and organizer, labor
educator
Jewish
Russian
Cyc Am Bio; Bio Dict Am Lab;
Not Am Wom supp v1

425. Ferber, Edna
1885/87–1968
author, playwright
Jewish
Dict Lit Bio v9; Index t Wom;
Nat Cyc Am Bio v60 and csv3;
Not Am Wom supp v1; Obit
File; Read Encyc Am West;
Who Who Jew Hist; Wom Lit,
More

426. Kaplan, Lena
1885–1958
cofounder of Hadassah
Jewish
Obit File

427. Natelson, Rachel
1885–1943
cofounder of Hadassah
Jewish
Obit File

428. Rosenthal, Ida Cohen
1886–1973
manufacturing executive, director
of Maidenform Co., inventor of
the brassiere
Jewish
New York
Nat Cyc Am Bio v57; Not Am
Wom supp v1

429. Baum, Hedwig "Vicki";
Mrs. Richard Lerf
1888–1960/62
novelist, playwright, screenwriter
Jewish
Hollywood, CA
Austrian
Dict Am Bio supp v6; Index t
Wom; Nat Cyc Am Bio v52;
Obit File

430. Franklin, Pearl
circa 1888–1958
playwright, lawyer, Zionist, Hadassah leader
Jewish
Index t Wom; Obit File

431. Lasker, Loula Davis
1888–1961

New York civic worker, Zionist,
Hadassah member
Jewish
New York
Nat Cyc Am Bio v48

432. Sampter, Jessie Ethel
1888–1938
poet, Zionist
Jewish
Not Am Wom

**433. Fischel, Marguerite Kauff-
man**
1889–1950
composer, worker for the welfare
of young cerebral palsy victims
Jewish
Obit File

434. Fromm-Reichman, Frieda
1889–1957
psychiatrist, psychoanalyst, au-
thority on schizophrenia, facul-
ty chairperson of the
Washington School of Psychia-
try
Jewish
Washington, DC
German
Dict Am Bio supp v5; Not Am
Wom supp v1; Obit File

**435. Hillman, Bessie Abramow-
itz**
1889–1970
labor leader, president of the
Amalgamated Clothing Work-
ers of America
Jewish
New York, NY
Russian
Nat Cyc Am Bio v56; Obit File

436. Hurst, Fannie
1889–1968
novelist, short story writer, wom-
en's rights worker, Zionist
Jewish
Index t Wom; Nat Cyc Am Bio
csv2 and csv5; Not Am Wom;
Obit File; Who Who Jew Hist

**437. Lashanska, Hulda; Mrs.
Harold A. Rosebaum**
1890/93–1974
lyric soprano concert singer
Jewish
New York
Index t Wom; Nat Cyc Am Bio
v57

438. Wengerova, Isabella
flourished 1920s
pianist
Jewish
Russian
Index t Wom

439. Brice, Fanny (Borach)
1891–1951

comedian; stage, screen, and ra-
dio actor
Jewish
Brooklyn, NY
Dict Am Bio supp v5; Index t
Wom; Not Am Wom supp v1;
Obit File

440. Newman, Pauline M.
1891–post 1940s
labor leader, Socialist party work-
er
Jewish
New York
Russian
Bio Dict Am Lab; Index t Wom

**441. Zucca, Mana; Madame
Manna-Zucca**
born 1891/94
composer, pianist, actor, singer
Jewish
Index t Wom

442. Grossinger, Jennie
1892–1972
philanthropist; hotel executive,
owner, and manager; country
club owner
Jewish
Catskill Mountains, NY
Austrian
Cur Biog '73; Index t Wom; Not
Am Wom supp v1; Obit File

443. Stone, Hannah Mayer
1892–1941
gynecologist, medical director of
the Margaret Sanger Research
Bureau, birth control advocate
Jewish
New York
Index t Wom; Nat Cyc Am Bio
v30; Obit File

444. Levy, Adele Rosenwald
1893–1960
philanthropist, chairperson of the
United Jewish Appeal National
Women's Division, art collector
Jewish
New York
Obit File

445. Mintzer, Ida Jessica
1893–1970
dermatologist
Jewish
New York
Nat Cyc Am Bio v55

**446. Parker, Dorothy Roth-
schild**
1893–1967
author, critic, short story writer,
poet, humorist
Jewish
New York
Index t Wom; Not Am Wom
supp v1; Obit File; Who Who
Jew Hist; Wom Lit, More

447. Bellanca, Dorothy Jacobs
1894–1946
trade union organizer, founder
and only woman vice-president
of the Amalgamated Clothing
Workers union, social reformer,
politician
Jewish
Russian
Bio Dict Am Lab; Dict Am Bio
supp v3; Not Am Wom; Obit
File

**448. Bryant, Lane; Lena Him-
melstein; Mrs. Albert Malsin**
1881/1895–1951
dress merchant, mail order businessperson, maternity and special sizes designer
Jewish
New York
Lithuanian
Nat Cyc Am Bio v47; Index t
Wom; Who Who Jew Hist

449. Manski, Dorothee
born circa 1895
singer
Jewish
German
Index t Wom

450. Victor, Sally (Josephs)
1895/1905–1977
hat designer
Jewish
New York
Cur Biog '77; Index t Wom; Nat
Cyc Am Bio v49

451. Adelsberger, Lucie
1896–1971
medical researcher, immunologist
Jewish
Obit File

452. Halprin, Rose
1896–1978
president of Hadassah, Zionist
Jewish
Obit File

453. Bernstein, Lotte Kirschner
1897–1971
psychiatrist, psychoanalyst
Jewish
Kentucky
German
Nat Cyc Am Bio v57

**454. Goldstein, Jennie; Jennie
Groll**
1897–1960
actor in Yiddish theater
Jewish
New York
Obit File

455. Heller, Florence Gunsfeld
1897–1966
philanthropist, patron of medicine, Jewish welfare worker

Jewish
Chicago, IL
Nat Cyc Am Bio v51

456. Daniels, Anna Kleegman
born 1898
gynecologist, medical director of
Planned Parenthood
Jewish
Russian
Nat Cyc Am Bio csv11

**457. Guggenheim, Marguerite
"Peggy"**
born 1898
patron of modern art and music,
art collector, author
Jewish
New York
Cur Biog '80; Index t Wom; Who
Who Jew Hist

458. Berg, Gertrude Edelstein
1899–1966
radio, television, and screen writer; playwright; producer
Jewish
New York
Index t Wom; Nat Cyc Am Bio
v52; Not Am Wom supp v1;
Obit File

459. Kaminska, Ida
1899–1980
stage actor, producer, director of
Yiddish theater
Jewish
New York, NY
Cur Biog '69 and '80

460. Broido, Lucy Kaufmann
1900–69
welfare agency leader
Jewish
New York, NY
Nat Cyc Am Bio v55

461. Lipschitz, Sylvia Steinberg
flourished 1930s
lawyer
Jewish
Index t Wom

462. Tourel, Jennie
1900?–73
opera and concert mezzo-soprano
singer
Jewish
Cur Biog '74; Not Am Wom supp
v1; Obit File

463. Lewis, Tillie [Myrtle]
1901–77
cannery owner and executive
Jewish
California
Nat Cyc Am Bio v60

464. Schwartz, Bertha
1901–61
judge, lawyer, Zionist
Jewish

Austrian
Index t Wom; Nat Cyc Am Bio
v51

465. Abbell, Fannie Edelman
born 1902
business executive, philanthropist
Jewish
Chicago, IL
Nat Cyc Am Bio csv11

466. Algase, Julia Cohn
1902–75
lawyer, AFL-CIO worker, actor
Jewish
New York, NY
Nat Cyc Am Bio v58

467. Cohen, Essie White
1902–63
chemist
Jewish
Denver, CO
Nat Cyc Am Bio v51

468. Rosenberg, Anna Marie
born 1902
US assistant secretary of defense
Jewish
Hungarian
Index t Wom; Who Who Jew
Hist

469. Atkin, Mildred Tommy;
Mrs. Fisher Winston
1903–69
artist
Jewish
New York
Nat Cyc Am Bio v53 and csv9

470. Gradova, Gitta "Gidda"
born 1904
pianist
Jewish
Index t Wom

**471. Hennock, Frieda Barkin
(Simmons)**
1904–60
criminal lawyer, FCC member,
advocate of educational televi-
sion
Jewish
New York
Polish
Index t Wom; Nat Cyc Am Bio
csv8; Not Am Wom supp v1;
Obit File

**472. Lewisohn, Adele Guggen-
heimer**
died 1954
philanthropist
Jewish
New York
Obit File

473. Hellman, Lillian
1905/06–1984
dramatist, autobiographer

Jewish
Dict Lit Bio v7; Encyc South
Hist; Index t Wom; Nat Cyc
Am Bio csv7; Who Who Jew
Hist; Wom Lit; Wom Lit, More

474. Klein, Anne; Hannah Golofsky
1905/23–1974
fashion designer
Jewish
New York
Nat Cyc Am Bio v58; Obit File

475. Kraus, Lili
born 1905?
concert pianist
Jewish
Hungarian
Cur Biog '75

476. Arendt, Hannah
1906–1975
political theorist, philosopher
Jewish
German
Cur Biog '76; Not Am Wom supp
v1; Obit File

477. Krasner, Lenore "Lee"
born 1908
abstract expressionist painter
Jewish
Cur Biog '74

478. Marlow, Sylvia
born 1908
harpsichordist
Jewish
Index t Wom

**479. Konheim, Beatrice Gold-
stein**
1909–73
science educator, member of the
ACLU
Jewish
New York
Nat Cyc Am Bio v58

480. Ribla, Gertrude
flourished 1940s
singer
Jewish
Index t Wom

481. Sarnoff, Dorothy
flourished 1940s
singer
Jewish
Index t Wom

482. Rockmore, Clara
born 1911
musician
Jewish
Russian
Index t Wom

483. Wolfenstein, Martha
1911–76

psychiatrist, child psychology
specialist, educator
Jewish
Obit File

**484. Tuchman, Barbara Wer-
theim**
born 1912
author, historian
Jewish
Index t Wom; Who Who Jew
Hist

485. Manski, Inge
born circa 1913
singer
Jewish
German
Index t Wom

**486. Porter, Sylvia Field Feld-
man**
born 1913
economics journalist, financial
columnist, author
Jewish
Cur Biog '80; Index t Wom

487. Tureck, Rosalyn
born 1914
pianist
Jewish
Index t Wom

488. Sokolow, Anna
born 1915
choreographer, director, dancer,
dance educator
Jewish
Cur Biog '69

489. Fertman, Mildred Been
1916–52
physician, medical researcher
Jewish
California
Nat Cyc Am Bio v49

490. Kael, Pauline
born 1919
film critic
Jewish
Cur Biog '74

491. Abzug, Bella (Savitsky)
born 1920
representative to Congress from
New York, lawyer with specialty in labor law, lecturer, peace
worker
Jewish
New York
Cur Biog '71

492. Lewis, Brenda
born 1921
opera singer
Jewish
Index t Wom

493. Solovieff, Miriam
born 1921

violinist
Jewish
Index t Wom

494. Yalow, Rosalyn Sussman
born 1921
medical physicist, Nobel Prize
winner
Jewish
Cur Biog '78

495. Magnes, Frances
born 1922
violinist
Jewish
Index t Wom

496. Resnik, Regina
born 1922
opera singer
Jewish
Index t Wom

497. Sachs, Evelyn
born 1924
singer
Jewish
Index t Wom

498. Brooks, Geraldine
1925–77
television, screen, and stage actor
Jewish
Index t Wom; Nat Cyc Am Bio
v59; Obit File

499. Jhabvala, Ruth Prawer
born 1927
novelist, short story and screenplay writer, writer of fiction
about India
Jewish
Indian; English
Cur Biog '77; Wom Lit; Wom
Lit, More

500. Lear, Evelyn
born 1929?
soprano opera singer
Jewish
Cur Biog '73

501. Sills, Beverly "Bubbles";
Belle Silverman
born 1929
Metropolitan Opera singer
Jewish
Cur Biog '69

502. Fields, Totie; Sophie Feldman
1930–78
nightclub comedian
Jewish
Obit File

503. Plath, Sylvia
1932–63
poet, author

Jewish
Dict Lit Bio v5 and v6; Nort
Anth Poet; Not Am Wom supp
v1; Wom Lit; Wom Lit, More

504. Rossner, Judith Perelman
born 1935
novelist
Jewish
New York, NY
Dict Lit Bio v6; Wom Lit; Wom
Lit, More

505. Hochman, Sandra
born 1936
poet, novelist, playwright, magazine writer
Jewish
Dict Lit Bio v5

506. Blume, Judy (Sussman)
born 1938
writer for children and young
adults
Jewish
Cur Biog '80

507. Jong, Erica (Mann)
born 1942
novelist, poet, feminist
Jewish
New York
Cur Biog '75; Dict Lit Bio v2 and
v5; Wom Lit; Wom Lit, More

508. Midler, Bette
born 1945?
popular singer, actor, comedian
Jewish
Cur Biog '73

509. Radner, Gilda
born 1946
stage, television, and screen comedian
Jewish
Cur Biog '80

510. Swados, Elizabeth
born 1951
play score writer, avant-garde
composer, theatrical director,
playwright
Jewish
New York
Cur Biog '79

No Dates

**511. Graudan, Joanna
Freudberg**
pianist
Jewish
Russian
Index t Wom

LUTHERAN

**512. Keller, Elizabeth
Catharine**
born 1837
physician, surgeon
Lutheran
Pennsylvania; Massachusetts
Index t Wom; Wom Cent

513. Fedde, Elizabeth, Sister
1850–1921
Lutheran deacon, nurse, welfare
worker, Catholic nun
Lutheran; Catholic
Norwegian
Index t Wom; Not Am Wom

**514. Kugler, Anna Sara "An-
nie"**
1856–1930
Lutheran medical missionary to
India, physician
Lutheran
Index t Wom; Not Am Wom

515. Mannes, Clara Domrosch
1869–1948
pianist, music educator
Lutheran
German
Dict Am Bio supp v4; Index t
Wom

516. Lewars, Elsie Singmaster
born 1879
author
Lutheran
Pennsylvania
German
Nat Cyc Am Bio csv3

**517. Meyer, Agnes Elizabeth
(Ernst)**
1887–1970
author, journalist, vice-president
and co-owner of *The Washington Post*, World War II correspondent, autobiographer,
lecturer, social worker, Republican party worker, crusader for
social services and education
causes
Lutheran
New York
Cur Biog '70; Index t Wom; Nat
Cyc Am Bio v56; Obit File

**518. Stern, Catherine Brieger
"Kathe"**
1894–1973
educator, child education special-
ist, writer on child education
Lutheran
German
Nat Cyc Am Bio v57; Not Am
Wom supp v1

**519. Roseborough, Melanie
Rohrer; Mrs. Adolph J. Ra-
dosta**
born 1898
German language educator
Lutheran
Florida
Nat Cyc Am Bio csv13

**520. Neuschaefer, Helen Ah-
rens**
1903–61
inventor of colored nail polish,
business executive
Lutheran
New York
Nat Cyc Am Bio v46

521. Braucher, Pela Fay
1905–66
nutritionist, educator
Evangelical Lutheran
Nat Cyc Am Bio v52

**522. Shindel, Dorothy Louise;
Mrs. Alfred C. LaBoccetta**
1916–75
pediatrician
Lutheran
Pennsylvania
Nat Cyc Am Bio v59

523. Loehrke, Leah Marie
1918–71
psychologist, psychological educator
Lutheran
Ohio
Nat Cyc Am Bio v57

MENNONITE

524. Berry, Adaline Hohp
born 1859
author
Mennonite
Pennsylvania
Wom Cent

**525. Musselman, Emma Good
Sweigert**
1880–1966
canner
Mennonite
Pennsylvania
Nat Cyc Am Bio v52

METHODIST

**526. Heck, Barbara Ruckle;
The Mother of American
Methodism**
1734/44–1804
missionary, religious founder
Methodist
New York

Irish
Cyc Am Bio; Dict Am Bio; Index
t Wom; Nat Cyc Am Bio v13;
Not Am Wom; Who Who Dur
Am Rev

**527. Willard, Mary Thompson
Hill**
1805–92
pioneer
Methodist
Wisconsin
Wom Cent

528. Bushnell, Mrs.
1811–50
Methodist missionary to West Af-
rica
Methodist
Am Bio Dict

529. Willard, Cordelia Young
born 1822
missionary worker
Methodist Episcopal
New York
Wom Cent

530. Crane, Mary Helen Peck
born 1827
temperance worker
Methodist Episcopal
Wom Cent

531. Colman, Julia
1828–1909
temperance writer
Methodist Episcopal
Index t Wom; Not Am Wom;
Wom Cent

532. Dyer, Julia Knowlton
born 1829
philanthropist
Methodist
Wom Cent

**533. van Cott, Margaret Ann
Newton "Maggie"**
1830–1914
Methodist evangelist, clergyper-
son
Methodist
Index t Wom; Not Am Wom

534. Cooley, Emily M. J.
born 1831
temperance and church worker,
evangelical preacher
Methodist Episcopal
Wom Cent

**535. Cunnyngham, Elizabeth
Litchfield**
born 1831
missionary to China, Methodist
Episcopal church worker
Methodist Episcopal
Wom Cent

536. Ingham, Mary Bigelow; Anne Hathaway
born 1832
author, temperance worker, Methodist Episcopal missionary and religious worker
Methodist Episcopal
Wom Cent

537. Shelley, Mary Jane
born 1832
temperance worker, missionary worker
Methodist
Nebraska
Wom Cent

538. Read, Elizabeth C. Bunnell "Lizzie B."
born 1834
journalist, suffragist
Methodist
Wom Cent

539. Willing, Jennie Fowler
1834–1916
Methodist local preacher, church worker, temperance reformer, lecturer, author, educator
Methodist
Canadian
Index t Wom; Not Am Wom; Wom Cent

540. Wilson, Augusta C. Jane (Evans)
1835/36–1909
novelist, Confederate author
Methodist
Mobile, AL
Cyc Am Bio; Dict Am Auth; Dict Am Bio; Dict Am Bio Men Time; Encyc South Hist; Index t Wom; Nat Cyc Am Bio v4; Not Am Wom; Wom Cent; Wom Lit, More

541. Doe, Mary L.
born 1836
suffragist, temperance reformer, merchant
Methodist
Iowa
Wom Cent

542. Brown, Martha McClellen
1838–1916
founder of the Prohibition party, temperance reformer, suffragist, lecturer
Methodist
Ohio
Index t Wom; Nat Cyc Am Bio v27; Not Am Wom; Wom Cent

543. Helm, Lucinda Barbour; Lucile
1839–97
author, religious writer
Methodist Episcopal
Kentucky
Twent Cen Bio Dict Not Am; Wom Cent

544. Knapp, Phoebe Palmer
born 1839
musician, author, religious composer
Methodist Episcopal
New York
Wom Cent

545. van Marter, Martha
born 1839
editor of Sunday school magazines
Methodist
Dict Am Auth

546. Willard, Frances Elizabeth Caroline
1839–98
educator, educational philosopher, suffragist, feminist, women's rights worker, temperance leader, naturalist, philanthropist, newspaper editor, traveler
Methodist Episcopal
Cyc Am Bio; Dict Am Auth; Dict Am Bio; Dict Am Bio Men Time; Dict Am Rel Bio; Index t Wom; Nat Cyc Am Bio v1; Not Am Wom; Twent Cen Bio Dict Not Am; Wom Cent

547. Hudlun, Anna Elizabeth
1840–1914
social worker, welfare worker, philanthropist
African Methodist Episcopal Zion
Black
Index t Wom; Negro Alman; Prof Negro Wom v1

548. Wilson, Augustus
flourished 1870s–90s
suffragist, temperance worker, Methodist Episcopal church worker, missionary worker
Methodist Episcopal
Kansas
Wom Cent

549. Wilson, Zara A.
born 1840
lawyer, suffragist, feminist, temperance worker, missionary worker
Methodist Episcopal
Nebraska
Wom Cent

550. McClain, Louise Bowman
born 1841
author
Methodist Episcopal
Indiana
Wom Cent

551. Walker, Harriet Granger
1841–1917

philanthropist, hospital organizer, temperance worker, suffragist, police reformer
Methodist
Minneapolis, MN
Nat Cyc Am Bio v6; Wom Cent

552. Willard, Mary Bannister
born 1841
temperance worker, educator, newspaper editor
Methodist
Wom Cent

553. Watson, Ellen Maria
born 1842
church worker, temperance worker
Methodist Episcopal
Wom Cent

554. Campbell, Eugenia Steele
born 1843
temperance reformer
Methodist Episcopal
Michigan
Wom Cent

555. Moots, Cornelia Moore Chillison
born 1843
temperance evangelist, suffragist, women's rights worker
Methodist Episcopal
Michigan
Wom Cent

556. Carhart, Clara Sully
born 1845
educator, temperance worker, women's labor welfare worker
Methodist Episcopal
New York
Canadian
Wom Cent

557. Peters, Alice E. H.
born 1845
church and temperance worker, suffragist, author
Methodist Episcopal
Ohio
Wom Cent

558. Smith, Olive White
born 1846
author, temperance worker
Methodist Episcopal
Vermont
Wom Cent

559. Robinson, Jane Marie Bancroft
1847–1932
Methodist educator, deaconess leader, author, historian, philanthropist
Methodist
Index t Wom; Not Am Wom; Wom Cent

560. Shaw, Anna Howard
1847–1919
minister, lecturer, suffragist, women's rights worker, physician, temperance worker
Methodist
English
Dict Am Bio; Index t Wom; Nat Cyc Am Bio v14; Not Am Wom; Wom Cent

561. Winton, Jenevehah Maria (Pray)
born 1847
poet, author
Methodist Episcopal
Wom Cent

562. Pettet, Isabella M.
born 1848
physician
Methodist
New York
German
Wom Cent

563. Knight, Sarah (Harrison)
1849–1928
philanthropist, Minneapolis civic leader, Methodist church worker, hospital founder, patron of nurse's training
Methodist
Minneapolis, MN
Am Bio New Cyc

564. Meyer, Lucy Jane Rider
1849–1922
pioneer in Methodist urban social work and in the Methodist deaconess movement
Methodist
Not Am Wom

565. Tuttle, Mary McArthur (Thompson)
born 1849/59
artist, writer and lecturer on art, art historian, novelist
Methodist
Dict Am Bio; Nat Cyc Am Bio v10

566. Hutchinson, Elizabeth P.
1850–1915
temperance worker
Methodist Episcopal
Nat Cyc Am Bio v16

567. Pettey, Sarah Dudley
flourished 1880
missionary leader
African Methodist Episcopal Zion
Black
Prof Negro Wom v1

568. Whipple, M. Ella
born 1851
physician, temperance worker, suffragist, Methodist Episcopal

church worker, politician, educator, inventor
Methodist Episcopal
Wom Cent

569. Bennett, Belle Harris
1852–1922
Southern Methodist lay leader
Methodist
Not Am Wom

570. Durrell, Irene Clark
born 1852
educator
Methodist
New Hampshire
Wom Cent

571. Hollister, Lilian
born 1853
temperance worker, suffragist, Methodist Episcopal church worker
Methodist Episcopal
Michigan
Wom Cent

572. Griffith, Mary Lillian
born 1854
philanthropist, author on morals, religious writer
Methodist Episcopal
Philadelphia, PA
Wom Cent

573. McDowell, Mary Eliza
1854–1936
settlement house director and founder, social welfare reformer and worker, NAACP member
Methodist
Dict Am Bio supp v2; Index t Wom; Nat Cyc Am Bio csv2; Not Am Wom

574. Palmer, Anna Campbell;
Mrs. George Archibald
1854–1928
children's author, poet
Methodist Episcopal
Elmira, NY
Dict Am Auth; Index t Wom; Nat Cyc Am Bio v22; Twent Cen Bio Dict Not Am; Wom Cent

575. Proctor, Mary Virginia
born 1854
journalist, newspaper publisher, philanthropist
Methodist Episcopal
Virginia
Wom Cent

576. Reed, Mary
1854–1943
Methodist missionary to lepers in India
Methodist
Dict Am Bio supp v3; Index t Wom; Not Am Wom; Obit File

577. Barnes, Annie Maria
born 1857
children's author
Methodist
Wom Cent

578. Oldham, Marie Augusta
born 1857
missionary to India, educator, temperance worker
Methodist Episcopal
Wom Cent

579. Yates, Elizabeth U.
born 1857
lecturer, Methodist Episcopal preacher
Methodist Episcopal
Maine
Wom Cent

580. Rogers, Emma Winner
flourished 1890s–1910s
missionary
Methodist
Index t Wom; Wom Cent

581. Starkweather, Amelia Minerva
flourished 1890s
educator, author, poet, temperance worker, Methodist Episcopal deaconess
Methodist Episcopal
Wom Cent

582. Baker, Joanna
born 1862
linguist
Methodist
Wom Cent

583. Brewster, Elizabeth Fisher; Shepherdess Mother of Hinghwa
1862–1955
Methodist missionary to China
Methodist
Obit File

584. Smith, Mary Belle
born 1862
educator, temperance worker
Methodist Episcopal
Connecticut
Wom Cent

585. Cannon, Annie Jump
1863–1941
astronomer
Methodist; Congregationalist
Cambridge, MA
Dict Lit Bio supp v3; Index t Wom; Nat Cyc Am Bio csv2; Not Am Wom; Obit File

586. Smith, Minnie Louise
1863–1927
educator, Sorosis member
Methodist Episcopal
Illinois
Nat Cyc Am Bio v21

587. Mason, Lena
born 1864
Methodist evangelist
Methodist
Black
Prof Negro Wom v1

588. van Rensselaer, Martha
1864–1932
home economist, educator
Methodist
New York
Dict Am Bio; Nat Cyc Am Bio v23; Not Am Wom

589. Bacon, Albion Fellows
1865–1933
housing reformer
Methodist
Indiana
Index t Wom; Nat Cyc Am Bio v34 and csv4; Not Am Wom

590. Bartlett, Maud Whitehead
born 1865
educator
Methodist Episcopal
Colorado
Index t Wom

591. Foote, Elizabeth Louisa
born 1866
librarian
Methodist Episcopal
Nat Cyc Am Bio csv3

592. Fisher, Elizabeth Holmes
born 1867
philanthropist
Methodist
California
Nat Cyc Am Bio csv6

593. Cratty, Mabel
1868–1928
YWCA leader, social worker
Methodist
Dict Am Bio; Nat Cyc Am Bio v22; Not Am Wom

594. Fremstad, Olivia [Anna] "Olive"
1868/72–1951
opera singer
Methodist
Swedish
Index t Wom; Nat Cyc Am Bio v40; Obit File

595. Williston, Anne Robson Sterling
born 1869
conservationist
Methodist
Canadian
Nat Cyc Am Bio csv2

596. Chamberlain, Hope Summerhill
born 1870
author
Methodist

North Carolina
Nat Cyc Am Bio csv8

597. Conkling, Mabel Viola Harrs
1871–1966
sculptor
Methodist
Maine
Index t Wom; Nat Cyc Am Bio v53

598. Clubb, Laura Abigail Rutherford
1873–1952
art collector, rare book collector, philanthropist, cattle rancher
Methodist
Oklahoma
Nat Cyc Am Bio v38

599. Bradley, Alice
born 1875
home economics educator
Methodist
Massachusetts
Nat Cyc Am Bio csv2

600. Peters, Iva (Lowther)
born 1876
educator, author on education
Methodist Episcopal
Nat Cyc Am Bio csv1

601. Franklin, Lucy Jenkins
born 1877
university educator
Methodist Episcopal
Boston, MA
Nat Cyc Am Bio csv4

602. Caraway, Hattie Ophelia Wyatt
1878–1950
Democratic US senator from Arkansas
Methodist
Arkansas
Australian
Dict Am Bio supp v4; Dict Aust Bio; Encyc South Hist; Eng Wom; Index t Wom; Nat Cyc Am Bio v44 and csv4; Not Am Wom; Obit File

603. Gindhart, Mary Wilhelmina (Simon)
1878–1969
music patron
Methodist
Philadelphia, PA
Nat Cyc Am Bio v57

604. Fisher, Welthy (Blakesley) Honsinger
1879/80–1980
Methodist missionary to India and China, social worker, educator, president of World Education, Inc.

Methodist
Cur Biog '69 and '81; Index t
Wom

605. Carr, Emma Perry
1880–1972
chemist
Methodist
Index t Wom; Nat Cyc Am Bio
csv6; Not Am Wom supp v1

**606. Aldrich, Bess Genevra
Streeter**
1881–1954
novelist, short story writer
Methodist
Nebraska
Dict Am Bio; Index t Wom; Nat
Cyc Am Bio v45 and csv8, Obit
File

607. Baker, Edna Dean
1883–1956
kindergarten educator
Methodist
Nat Cyc Am Bio v43

608. Balz, Arcada Stark
1883–1973
Indiana state senator, Indianapolis civic worker
Methodist
Indianapolis, IN
Nat Cyc Am Bio v57

609. Riach, May Turner
1886–1946
surgeon, eye doctor, World War I
doctor, Spanish Loyalist army
physician
Methodist
Nat Cyc Am Bio v34

610. Biddle, Mary Duke
1887–1960
humanitarian, philanthropist, patron of Duke University
Methodist Episcopal
North Carolina
Index t Wom; Nat Cyc Am Bio
v49

611. Dobie, Edith
1887–1975
historian, educator
Methodist
Washington
Nat Cyc Am Bio v58

612. Cobb, Beatrice
1888–1959
newspaper editor, publisher of the
Morganton, North Carolina,
News-Herald
Methodist
Morganton, NC
Nat Cyc Am Bio v45; Obit File

**613. Woodham, Eva Esther
Dowling**
1890–1962
insurance executive, floriculturist

Methodist
South Carolina
Nat Cyc Am Bio v46

614. Boothe, Viva Belle
1893–1964
business researcher, economist,
educator
Methodist
Ohio
Nat Cyc Am Bio v51

615. Bradley, Florence Kauffman Thacker
born 1893
lawyer, political activist
Methodist
Indiana
Nat Cyc Am Bio csv7

616. McCartney, Sadie Kissak
died 1944
missionary to China
Methodist
Obit File

617. Cheney, Margaret Aneline
born 1895
banker
Methodist Episcopal
Lafayette, IN
Nat Cyc Am Bio csv2

618. Pryor, Helen Brenton
1897–1972
pediatrician, medical educator
Methodist
California
Nat Cyc Am Bio v57

619. Smith, Margaret Chase
born 1897
US senator from Maine, lieutenant colonel in the US Air Force
Reserve
Methodist
Maine
Index t Wom; Nat Cyc Am Bio
csv9

620. Tauch, Waldine
born 1898
sculptor
Methodist
Texas
Index t Wom; Nat Cyc Am Bio
csv12

621. Brittingham, Bettie S.
1904–49
editor of *Methodist Woman*,
Methodist church official
Methodist
Obit File

622. Jones, Margaret Holden
born 1904
pediatrician
Methodist
California
Nat Cyc Am Bio csv9

623. Black, Marian Watkins
1905–75
educator
Methodist
Florida
Twent Cen Bio Dict Not Am

624. Covalt, Nila (Gale) Kirkpatrick
born 1905
physician, physical therapist
Methodist
Nat Cyc Am Bio csv11

**625. Duncan, Catherine (la
Vanche) Gross**
1908–68
phytopathologist
Methodist
Wisconsin
Nat Cyc Am Bio v54

626. Apgar, Virginia
1909–74
medical researcher, pediatrician,
anesthesiologist
Methodist
Cur Biog '74; Nat Cyc Am Bio
csv9; Not Am Wom; Obit File

627. Graves, Helen (Louise) Pierson
born 1914
physician, medical educator
Methodist
Ohio
Nat Cyc Am Bio csv13

MORAVIAN

**628. Watteville, Benigna
[Henrietta] Justine
Zinzendorf von**
1725–89
educator, a founder of the Moravian Seminary and College for
Women
Moravian
Moravian
Index t Wom; Not Am Wom

629. Brown, Catherine
1800–23
Moravian religious worker
Moravian
Alabama
Moravian; Native American
(Cherokee)
Am Bio Dict

630. Fleshman, Mina Pepper
1879–1965
realtor, developer
Moravian
North Carolina
Moravian
Nat Cyc Am Bio v50

PILLAR OF FIRE

**631. White, Alma Bridwell
"Mollie"**
1862–1946
founder of the Pillar of Fire
Church, bishop, preacher
Pillar of Fire
Dict Am Bio supp v4; Dict Am
Rel Bio; Nat Cyc Am Bio v35
and csv2 and csv5; Not Am
Wom; Obit File

PRESBYTERIAN

632. McBeth, Susan Law
1830–93
Presbyterian missionary to Native
Americans
Presbyterian
Not Am Wom

633. Stevens, Emily Pitt
flourished 1860s–90s
educator, temperance worker,
feminist, suffragist
Presbyterian
California
Wom Cent

**634. Dunning, Annie Ketchum;
Nellie Grahame**
born 1831
author, Sunday school story writer
Presbyterian
Cyc Am Bio; Dict Am Auth;
Twent Cen Bio Dict Not Am

635. Cunningham, Annie Sinclair
born 1832
Presbyterian church and mission
society worker
Presbyterian
Scottish
Wom Cent

**636. McCormick, Nancy Maria
Fowler "Nettie"**
1835–1923
patron of education in China,
philanthropist, businessperson
Presbyterian
Index t Wom; Nat Cyc Am Bio
v21; Not Am Wom

**637. Newberry, Helen Parmelee
Handy**
1835–1912
philanthropist
Presbyterian
Detroit, MI
Nat Cyc Am Bio v41

638. Swift, Frances Laura
born 1837
church worker, temperance worker

Presbyterian
Pennsylvania
Wom Cent

639. Stokes, Missouri H.
1838–post 1860
Civil War diarist, educator, temperance worker
Presbyterian
Georgia
Index t Wom; Wom Cent

640. Sullivan, Mary Mildred Hammond
1838–1933
philanthropist, Civil War patriot, New York civic leader
Presbyterian
New York
Index t Wom; Nat Cyc Am Bio v31

641. Bell, Caroline Horton
born 1840
philanthropist
Presbyterian
Milwaukee, WI
Wom Cent

642. Leland, Caroline Weaver
born 1840
philanthropist, educator
Presbyterian
Michigan
Wom Cent

643. Edgar, Elizabeth
born 1842
educator
Presbyterian
Pennsylvania
Wom Cent

644. Lowman, Mary D.
born 1842
educator of Blacks; deputy register of deeds and mayor of Oskaloosa, Kansas
Presbyterian
Oskaloosa, KS
Index t Wom; Wom Cent

645. Thompson, Eva Griffith
born 1842
temperance worker, Presbyterian missionary worker, newspaper editor and publisher
Presbyterian
Pennsylvania
Wom Cent

646. Cushing, Juliet Clannon
1845–1934
welfare worker
Presbyterian
New Jersey
Nat Cyc Am Bio v28

647. Bittenbender, Ada Matilda Cole
1848–1925
suffragist, temperance leader, political reformer, lawyer admitted to practice before the Supreme Court
Presbyterian
Nebraska
Not Am Wom; Wom Cent

648. Johnston, Julia Harriette
1849–1919
hymn writer
Presbyterian
Peoria, IL
Nat Cyc Am Bio v20

649. Braden, Anna Madge; Madge Rile
flourished 1880
author
Presbyterian
Wom Cent

650. Holmes, Mary Emilie
born 1850
educator, zoologist, herbalist, educator of Black women
Presbyterian
Illinois
Wom Cent

651. Johnston, Lizzie Johnston Evans
1851–1934
philanthropist, juvenile-prison reformer, Democratic party worker
Presbyterian
Alabama
Nat Cyc Am Bio v31

652. Underwood, Lillian Stirling Horton
1851–1921
physician, Presbyterian missionary to Korea
Presbyterian
Not Am Wom

653. Doughty, Eva Craig Graves
born 1852
journalist, suffragist, temperance worker
Presbyterian
Wom Cent

654. Cummins, Mary Stuart
born 1854
educator, temperance worker
Presbyterian
Montana
Wom Cent

655. Deland, Margaretta Wade (Campbell)
1857–1945
poet, novelist, short story writer
Presbyterian; Episcopalian
Dict Am Bio supp v3; Index t Wom; Nat Cyc Am Bio v3 and v33; Not Am Wom; Obit File; Twent Cen Bio Dict Not Am; Wom Cent; Wom Lit, More

656. Parry, Angenette
1857–1939
obstetrician/gynecologist
Presbyterian
Index t Wom; Nat Cyc Am Bio v29

657. Boole, Ella Alexander
1858–1952
temperance leader, president of WCTU, suffragist, pacifist, Presbyterian deacon
Presbyterian
Dict Am Bio supp v5; Index t Wom; Nat Cyc Am Bio v38 and csv2; Not Am Wom supp v1; Obit File

658. Giles, Anne H.
born 1860
philanthropist
Presbyterian
Wom Cent

659. Ladd, Kate Everit Macy
1863–1945
philanthropist, patron of medicine and scientific research
Presbyterian
New York
Dict Am Bio supp v3; Nat Cyc Am Bio v32 and csv4; Not Am Wom

660. Miner, Alice Trainer
1863–1950
philanthropist, patron of medicine
Presbyterian
New York
Canadian
Nat Cyc Am Bio v40

661. Lindsay, Anna Robertson Brown
1864–1948
religious author, moral tale writer
Presbyterian
Dict Am Auth; Nat Cyc Am Bio v36

662. Wiles, Cora Young
1864–1950
composer
Presbyterian
Nat Cyc Am Bio v39

663. Hill, Grace (Livingston)
1865–1947
popular novelist, short story writer
Presbyterian

Philadelphia, PA
Dict Am Auth; Dict Am Bio supp v4; Nat Cyc Am Bio v40; Not Am Wom; Obit File

664. Breckinridge, Sophonisba Preston
1866–1948
social worker, social economist, immigrant welfare worker, writer on social issues, educator, lawyer
Presbyterian
Dict Am Bio supp v4; Nat Cyc Am Bio v37; Not Am Wom

665. Chiles, Rosa Pendleton
born 1866
educator, author
Presbyterian
Nat Cyc Am Bio csv4

666. Young, Mary Vance
1866–1946
educator, linguist, World War I relief worker
Presbyterian
Index t Wom; Nat Cyc Am Bio v33

667. McConnell, Adelaide Dorn
1869–1942
physician, philanthropist
Presbyterian
Nat Cyc Am Bio v31

668. Adams, Winifred Brady
born 1871
painter
Presbyterian
Indiana
Nat Cyc Am Bio csv6

669. Eudy, Mary Cummings Paine
1871–1952
poet, dress manufacturer
Presbyterian
Kentucky
Nat Cyc Am Bio v41; Obit File

670. Hauberg, Susanne Christine Denkmann
1872–1942
philanthropist
Presbyterian
Rock Island, IL
Nat Cyc Am Bio v42

671. Speers, Emma (Doll) Bailey
1872–1961
YWCA executive
Presbyterian
Pennsylvania
Nat Cyc Am Bio v52

672. Laidlaw, Harriet Davenport Wright Burton
1873–1949
suffragist, author, educator, lecturer, clubwoman

Presbyterian
Index t Wom; Nat Cyc Am Bio
v38; Not Am Wom

673. Lingelbach, Anna Lane
1873–1954
historian, educator, civic leader,
feminist
Presbyterian
Pennsylvania
Dict Am Bio supp v5; Nat Cyc
Am Bio v44; Obit File

674. Auge, Emily Geary Whitton
1874–1934
surgeon
Presbyterian
Philadelphia, PA
Nat Cyc Am Bio v26

675. Hammand, Emily Vanderbilt Sloane
1874–1907
philanthropist, social worker,
Moral Rearmament Society
member
Presbyterian
New York
Nat Cyc Am Bio v55 and csv8

676. MacKenzie, Jean Kenyon
1874–1936
Presbyterian missionary to Cameroun, author
Presbyterian
Nat Cyc Am Bio v28; Not Am
Wom

677. Montgomery, Roselle Mercier
1874–1933
author, poet
Presbyterian
Index t Wom; Nat Cyc Am Bio
v24

678. Dickinson, Helena Adall Snyder
1875–1975
nonfiction writer, educator
Presbyterian
Canadian
Nat Cyc Am Bio v54

679. Dreier, Mary Elisabeth
1875–1963
labor reformer, suffragist, New
York civic leader, Bull Moose
party politician
Presbyterian
New York
Nat Cyc Am Bio csv9; Not Am
Wom supp v1

680. MacDonald, Christie;
Christie Gillespie
1875/77–1962
operetta singer, actor, musical
comedy actor
Presbyterian

Canadian
Index t Wom; Nat Cyc Am Bio
v50; Obit File

681. Paige, Mabeth Hurd
born 1875
Minnesota state legislator, lawyer
Presbyterian
Minnesota
Nat Cyc Am Bio csv2

682. Wick, Frances Gertrude
1875–1941
physicist, educator
Presbyterian
Index t Wom; Nat Cyc Am Bio
v34; Obit File

683. Eckel, Berenice Long
born 1876
pianist, violinist, music educator
Presbyterian
Nat Cyc Am Bio csv5

684. Williams, Amelia Worthington
1876–1958
educator, historian of Texas
Presbyterian
Texas
Nat Cyc Am Bio v44

685. Smith, Fredrika Shumway
1877–1968
children's author
Presbyterian
Illinois
Nat Cyc Am Bio v55

686. Lawson, Roberta Campbell
1878–1940
clubwoman, student of Native
American music and culture,
ethnologist, Native American
leader, singer, songwriter
Presbyterian
Native American (Delaware)
Great North Am Ind; Nat Cyc
Am Bio v36; Not Am Wom

687. McKinstry, Helen May
1878–1949
president of Russell Sage College,
physical education expert
Presbyterian
New York
Nat Cyc Am Bio v37; Obit File

688. Murray, Elsie
1878–1965
psychologist, color blindness expert, museum director
Presbyterian
Pennsylvania
Nat Cyc Am Bio v53

689. Pugsley, Emma Catherine Gregory
died 1928
philanthropist, investor, entrepreneur
Presbyterian

New York
Nat Cyc Am Bio v22

690. Parke, Jessie Burns
1879–1964
artist
Presbyterian
Nat Cyc Am Bio v50

691. Coulter, Edith Margaret
1880–1963
librarian, library educator
Presbyterian
California
Nat Cyc Am Bio v50

692. Delfs, Eleanor (Mary)
1880–1977
obstetrician/gynecologist
Presbyterian
Wisconsin
Nat Cyc Am Bio v60

693. Schall, Nina Dennis
1880–1961
physician
Presbyterian
New York; Pennsylvania
Nat Cyc Am Bio v49

694. Wadsworth, Alice Hay
born 1880
New York civic worker, suffragist
Presbyterian
New York
Nat Cyc Am Bio csv8

695. Hyde, Elizabeth [Carrie]
1881–1957
lawyer, corporate lawyer for a
railroad
Presbyterian
Iowa
Nat Cyc Am Bio v47

696. Cummins, Grace
1882–1953
Presbyterian leader, religious educator, social worker
Presbyterian
Obit File

697. Wilson, Matilda Rausch
1883–1967
philanthropist, Detroit civic
worker, chairperson of the
board of directors of Fidelity
Bank & Trust, member of the
state board of agriculture, lieutenant governor of Michigan,
Salvation Army worker
Presbyterian
Detroit, MI
Nat Cyc Am Bio v59

698. Miller, Evylena Nunn
born 1884
artist
Presbyterian
California
Nat Cyc Am Bio csv6

699. Zoeckler, Mary Daton Allen
1884–1914
obstetrician/gynecologist, medical missionary to Iran
Presbyterian
Nat Cyc Am Bio v46

700. Bolton, Frances Payne (Bingham)
1885/86–1977
Republican representative to
Congress from Ohio, nurse
Presbyterian
Ohio
Cur Biog '77; Index t Wom; Nat
Cyc Am Bio csv11; Obit File

701. Richards, Esther Loring
born 1885
psychiatrist
Presbyterian
Nat Cyc Am Bio csv7

702. Brinkley, Nell [Ethel];
Mrs. Bruce Moir McRae
1886/88–1944
newspaper artist, cartoonist, illustrator, journalist
Presbyterian
Index t Wom; Nat Cyc Am Bio
v33; Obit File

703. Conrad, Elisabeth Whiting
1886–1964
educator
Presbyterian
Nat Cyc Am Bio v52

704. Dexter, Edith MacBride
1887–1958
ophthalmologist, public health
worker
Presbyterian
Pennsylvania
Nat Cyc Am Bio v49

705. Franklin, Elizabeth Jennings
1887–1967
founder of Bennington College
and chairperson of the board of
trustees
Presbyterian
Vermont; New York
Nat Cyc Am Bio v53; Obit File

706. Moore, Marianne (Craig)
1887–1972
poet, critic, editor, winner of Pulitzer Prize and National Book
Award
Presbyterian
New York
Cur Biog '72; Index t Wom; Nat
Cyc Am Bio v57; Nort Anth
Poet; Not Am Wom supp v1;
Obit File; Wom Lit, More

707. Callender, Bessie Stough
1889–1951
sculptor, mountain climber

Presbyterian
Nat Cyc Am Bio v38

708. Myrin, Mabel (Anderson) Pew
1889–1972
Philadelphia civic leader
Presbyterian
Philadelphia, PA
Nat Cyc Am Bio v57

709. Ingersall, Winifred
1890–1960
physician
Presbyterian
Wyoming
Nat Cyc Am Bio v45

710. Williams, Fannie Ransom
flourished 1920s
constitutionalist, World War I soldier's welfare worker
Presbyterian
North Carolina
Nat Cyc Am Bio v21

711. Street, Margaret Berry
1891–1967
cattle farmer, lawyer, Civil Air Regulations executive, suffragist, Black welfare worker
Presbyterian
North Carolina
Nat Cyc Am Bio v54

712. Crump, Jean
1892–1963
pediatrician
Presbyterian
Pennsylvania
Nat Cyc Am Bio v52

713. Macy, Icie Gertrude; Mrs. Bert Raymon Hoobler
born 1892
chemist
Presbyterian
Michigan
Nat Cyc Am Bio csv8

714. Dodge, Pauline Morgan
1893–1971
YWCA executive, philanthropist
Presbyterian
New York
Nat Cyc Am Bio v56

715. Stover, Clara [Mae] Lewis
born 1893
candy manufacturer
Presbyterian
Nat Cyc Am Bio csv12

716. Kiser, Louise Venable Kennedy
1895–1954
sociologist, demographer
Presbyterian
Nat Cyc Am Bio v42

717. Seibert, Florence Barbara; Florence Seifert
born 1897
biochemist, pioneer scientist
Presbyterian
Index t Wom; Nat Cyc Am Bio csv8

718. Gambrell, Mary Latimer
1898–1974
educator, president of Hunter College
Presbyterian
New York
Nat Cyc Am Bio v59; Obit File

719. Charles, Alta Genevieve
1899–1963
ophthalmologist
Presbyterian
Pennsylvania
Nat Cyc Am Bio v50

720. Engelbrecht, Mildred Amanda
1899–1973
bacteriologist
Presbyterian
Nat Cyc Am Bio v58

721. Horton, Mildred Helen McAfee
born 1900
president of Wellesley College, director of the WAVES
Presbyterian
Index t Wom

722. Baumgartner, Leona; Mrs. Nathaniel M. Elias
born 1902
pediatrician, public health official
Presbyterian
New York, NY
Index t Wom; Nat Cyc Am Bio csv9

723. Barber, Muriel Virginia (Kozlay)
1904–71
artist
Presbyterian
New Jersey
Nat Cyc Am Bio v57

724. Poletti, Jean Ellis
1904–74
advertising executive, New York civic worker, UNICEF worker
Presbyterian
Nat Cyc Am Bio v58

725. Carson, Rachel Louise
1907–64
biologist, conservationist, naturalist, nature and conservation writer
Presbyterian
Index t Wom; Nat Cyc Am Bio csv9; Not Am Wom supp v1; Obit File

726. Taylor, Marian Young; Martha Denae
1908–73
interviewer, journalist
Presbyterian
New York
Nat Cyc Am Bio v57

727. Winters, Jeannette Epler McPheeters
born 1908
manufacturer
Presbyterian
Indiana
Nat Cyc Am Bio csv8

728. Crary, Catherine Snell
1909–74
historian, educator
Presbyterian
New York
Nat Cyc Am Bio v58

729. MacIntyre, Sheila Scott
1910–60
mathematician
Presbyterian
Scottish
Nat Cyc Am Bio v48

730. Morgan, Edith Galt
1915–68
psychiatric nursing educator
Presbyterian
Nat Cyc Am Bio v55

PROTESTANT EPISCOPAL

731. Hill, Frances Maria Mulligan
1799/1807–1884
Episcopal missionary and pioneer educator of women in Greece
Episcopalian
Cyc Am Bio; Index t Wom; Not Am Wom

732. Beecher, Catherine Esther
1800–78
educator of women, education writer, social reformer, poet
Episcopalian
New York
Appl Cyc Am Bio; Cyc Am Bio; Dict Am Bio; Dict Am Bio Men Time; Dict Lit Bio v1; Index t Wom; Nat Cyc Am Bio v3; Not Am Wom; Twent Cen Bio Dict Not Am; Wom Cent

733. Hentz, Caroline Lee (Whiting)
1800–56
novelist, dramatist, poet, romance writer, educator

726. Taylor, Marian Young;

Episcopalian
Am Bio Dict; Cyc Am Bio; Dict Am Bio; Dict Am Bio Men Time; Dict Lit Bio v3; Index t Wom; Nat Cyc Am Bio v6; Not Am Wom; Twent Cen Bio Dict Not Am; Wom Lit, More

734. Tyler, Adeline Blanchard, Sister
1805–75
Civil War nurse, Episcopalian deaconess
Episcopalian
Not Am Wom

735. Shindler, Mary Stanley Bunce (Palmer) (Dana)
1810–83
author, poet, religious writer
Unitarian; Episcopalian
Nacogdoches, TX
Cyc Am Bio; Dict Am Auth; Dict Am Bio Men Time; Index t Wom

736. Henderson, Frances Cox
born 1820
linguist, translator, traveler, philanthropist, suffragist
Episcopalian
Wom Cent

737. Cannon, Harriet Star
1823–96
first mother superior of the Episcopal Community of St. Mary
Episcopalian
Dict Am Bio; Not Am Wom

738. Hendricks, Eliza C. Morgan
born 1823
philanthropist, women's prison welfare worker
Episcopalian
Wom Cent

739. Elmore, Lucie Ann Morrison
born 1829
temperance reformer
Episcopalian
Wom Cent

740. Parker, Jane Marsh
1836–1913
author, novelist
Episcopalian
Dict Am Bio; Nat Cyc Am Bio v10; Twent Cen Bio Dict Not Am

741. Smith, Amanda Berry
1836/37–1915
Protestant evangelist, missionary to Africa, faith healer, singer
Protestant
Black
Index t Wom; Negro Alman; Not Am Wom; Prof Negro Wom v1

742. Flower, Lucy Louisa (Coues)
1837–1921
social welfare worker, philanthropist, patron of education, president of the Illinois Training School for Nurses, member of the Chicago school board, trustee of the University of Illinois, Republican party worker
Episcopalian
Dict Am Bio; Nat Cyc Am Bio v9; Not Am Wom

743. Ransford, Nettie
born 1838
clubleader, general grand matron of the Order of the Eastern Star
Episcopalian
Index t Wom; Wom Cent

744. Swenson, Amanda Carlson
flourished 1870s–90s
soprano concert singer
Episcopalian
Swedish
Wom Cent

745. Watson, Annah Robinson
flourished 1870s–90s
author
Episcopalian
Wom Cent

746. Dawson, Sarah; Ida Fowler
1842–1909
author, Civil War diarist
Episcopalian
Index t Wom; Nat Cyc Am Bio v23

747. Boyd, Belle; Belle Hardinge
1843/44–1900
Confederate spy, actor, lecturer
Episcopalian
Bio Dict Confed; Dict Am Bio; Index t Wom; Not Am Wom

748. Burt, Mary Towne
flourished 1873
temperance worker, publisher
Protestant Episcopal
New York
Index t Wom; Wom Cent

749. Crawford, Mary J.
born 1843
Episcopal church worker and organizer
Episcopalian
Wom Cent

750. Ferree, Susan Frances Nelson
born 1844
journalist, temperance worker, suffragist, women's rights worker
Episcopalian
Iowa
Wom Cent

751. Walton, Sarah Stokes
born 1844
poet, artist
Protestant Episcopal
Wom Cent

752. Litchfield, Grace Denio
1849–1944
fiction writer, poet, novelist
Protestant
Washington, DC
Dict Am Auth; Nat Cyc Am Bio v12 and v42, Wom Cent

753. Jones, Melodia Blackmarr
1850–1931
philanthropist, Republican party worker
Episcopalian
Buffalo, NY
Nat Cyc Am Bio v32

754. Day, Mary Gage; Mary Hannah Gage-Day
1857–1935
physician
Episcopalian
New York
Nat Cyc Am Bio csv2 and v26

755. Deland, Margaretta Wade (Campbell)
1857–1945
poet, novelist, short story writer
Presbyterian; Episcopalian
Dict Am Bio supp v3; Index t Wom; Nat Cyc Am Bio v3 and v33; Not Am Wom; Obit File; Twent Cen Bio Dict Not Am; Wom Cent; Wom Lit, More

756. Smith, Eleanor
1858–1942
music educator, composer, songwriter
Episcopalian
Index t Wom; Nat Cyc Am Bio v35

757. de Koven, Anna Farwell
1860–1953
author, novelist
Episcopalian
New York, NY
Dict Am Auth; Nat Cyc Am Bio v16 and v48; Obit File

758. Hoyt-Stevens, Jane Elizabeth
born 1860
physician
Episcopalian
Nat Cyc Am Bio csv4

759. Low, Juliette Magill Kinzie (Gordon)
1860–1927
founder of the Girl Scouts of America, clubwoman
Protestant Episcopal
Dict Am Bio; Index t Wom; Nat Cyc Am Bio v24; Not Am Wom

760. Morgan, Maud
1860/64–1941
harpist, author
Episcopalian
Cyc Am Bio; Index t Wom; Nat Cyc Am Bio v32; Obit File; Wom Cent

761. Thelberg, Elizabeth Burr
1860–1935
physician
Episcopalian
Index t Wom; Nat Cyc Am Bio v27

762. Sorin, Sarah Inslee Herring
1861–1914
lawyer
Episcopalian
Arizona
Nat Cyc Am Bio v36

763. Wood, Mary Elizabeth
1861–1931
missionary, librarian in China
Episcopalian
Dict Am Bio; Not Am Wom

764. Bond, Carrie Jacobs; Carrie Jacobs-Bond
1862–1946
popular songwriter, composer, author, publisher
Episcopalian
California
Dict Am Bio supp v4; Index t Wom; Nat Cyc Am Bio v36 and csv5; Not Am Wom; Obit File

765. McCormick, Harriet Hammond
1862–1917
philanthropist, suffragist, patron of child welfare
Episcopalian
Nat Cyc Am Bio v21

766. Merrill, Winifred Edgerton
1862–1951
women's educator
Episcopalian
Nat Cyc Am Bio v41

767. Toussaint, Emma; Portia
born 1862
author, translator
Episcopalian
Massachusetts
Wom Cent

768. Livingston, Margaret Vere (Farrington)
born 1863
author
Episcopalian
Augusta, ME
Dict Am Auth

769. Sears, Clara Endicott
1863–1960
author, antiquarian, cattle breeder
Protestant Episcopal
Massachusetts
Nat Cyc Am Bio v47 and csv1

770. Freer, Eleanor Everest
1864–1942
composer
Episcopalian
Index t Wom; Nat Cyc Am Bio v17 and csv4

771. Eckstorm, Fannie Pearson Hardy
1865–1946
ornithologist, writer on ornithology, scholar of the Native Americans of Maine, historian of Maine folk songs
Episcopalian
Brewer, ME
Dict Am Auth; Dict Am Bio supp v4; Nat Cyc Am Bio v36; Not Am Wom

772. Hilles, Florence Bayard
1865–1954
suffragist, feminist, ERA worker, pacifist, golfer
Episcopalian
Delaware
Nat Cyc Am Bio v46

773. Berry, Martha McChesney; Sunday Lady of the Possum Trot
1866–1942
educator, founder of the Berry School for underprivileged mountain children, philanthropist
Episcopalian
Georgia
Dict Am Bio supp v3; Encyc South Hist; Index t Wom; Nat Cyc Am Bio csv3; Not Am Wom; Obit File

774. Emmet, Lydia Field
1866–1952
artist, painter of children's portraits, suffragist, women's rights worker
Episcopalian
Index t Wom; Nat Cyc Am Bio v15, cv42, and csv6; Obit File

775. Martin, Georgia May; George Madden Martin
1866–1946
author, civil rights and antilynching worker
Episcopalian
Nat Cyc Am Bio v33

776. **Allen, Viola Emily; Mrs.
Peter Edward Cornel Duryea**
1867/69–1948
actor
Episcopalian
Dict Am Bio supp v4; Index t
Wom; Nat Cyc Am Bio v34;
Not Am Wom; Obit File

777. **Mayo, Katherine**
1867–1940
author, novelist
Episcopalian
New York
Index t Wom; Nat Cyc Am Bio
v30; Not Am Wom

778. **McVea, Emilie Watts**
1867–1928
president of Sweet Briar College
Episcopalian
Virginia
Nat Cyc Am Bio v21

779. **McAlpin, Margaret Johnston; Margherita Giollini**
1868–1924
opera singer
Episcopalian
Nat Cyc Am Bio v20

780. **Arnold, Cornelia Eliza
Macmullan**
1869–1945
educator, author
Episcopalian
Nat Cyc Am Bio v33

781. **Caddy, Alice; Mrs. Ben
Lucien Burman**
1869–1977
artist, illustrator, traveler
Episcopalian
Nat Cyc Am Bio v59

782. **Duckering, Florence West**
1869–1951
surgeon
Episcopalian
English
Nat Cyc Am Bio v40

783. **Hatton, Fanny Cottinet
Locke**
1869–1939
playwright, critic
Episcopalian
Index t Wom; Nat Cyc Am Bio
v42

784. **Lovejoy, Esther Clayson
Pohl**
1869/70–1967
physician; director of the
Portland, Oregon, health de-
partment; World War I Red
Cross worker in France; femi-
nist
Protestant Episcopal
Portland, OR
Index t Wom; Nat Cyc Am Bio
csv1; Not Am Wom supp v1

785. **O'Day, Caroline Love
Goodwin**
1869/75–1943
social welfare worker, Democratic representative to Congress
from New York, New Deal supporter, artist
Episcopalian
New York
Index t Wom; Nat Cyc Am Bio
csv6; Not Am Wom; Obit File

786. **Bogle, Sarah Comly
Norris**
1870–1932
librarian
Protestant Episcopal
New York
Index t Wom; Nat Cyc Am Bio
csv3; Not Am Wom

787. **Braddock, Katherine**
born 1870
Democratic political leader
Episcopalian
California
Nat Cyc Am Bio csv2

788. **Hitchcock, Helen Sanborn
(Sargent)**
born 1870
social welfare worker, creator of
social welfare programs to promote the arts
Episcopalian
Nat Cyc Am Bio v18

789. **Draper, Helen Fidelia**
1871–1951
Red Cross nurse, World War I
relief worker, social worker
Episcopalian
New York
Index t Wom; Nat Cyc Am Bio
v39

790. **Farrar, Lilian Katurah
Pond**
1871–1962
gynecologist, surgeon
Episcopalian
New York
Nat Cyc Am Bio v48

791. **Harvey, Kate Benedict
Hanna**
1871–1936
public health worker, patron of
nursing, cattle breeder
Protestant Episcopal
Cleveland, OH
Nat Cyc Am Bio v34

792. **Torrey, Lillie Gay**
born 1871
artist
Episcopalian
Hawaii
Nat Cyc Am Bio csv8

793. **Deering, Mabel Craft**
born 1872
author, suffragist
Episcopalian
California
Nat Cyc Am Bio csv6

794. **Cather, Willa Sibert**
1873/74–1944
western novelist
Episcopalian
Nebraska
Dict Am Bio supp v4; Dict Lit
Bio v9; Dict Mex Am Hist;
Index t Wom; Nat Cyc Am Bio
v44 and csv1; Not Am Wom;
Obit File; Read Encyc Am
West; Wom Lit; Wom Lit,
More

795. **Crane, Josephine (Porter)
Boardman**
1873–1972
New York civic leader, patron of
the arts
Episcopalian
New York
Nat Cyc Am Bio v57

796. **Hanks, Mary Esther Vilas**
1873–1959
Madison civic leader
Episcopalian
Madison, WI
Nat Cyc Am Bio v49

797. **Neilson, Nellie**
1873–1947
English historian, first woman
president of the American Historical Association, educator,
author
Episcopalian
Nat Cyc Am Bio v36; Not Am
Wom; Obit File

798. **Mather, Winifred Holt**
1874–1945
sculptor, patron of welfare of the
blind, founder of a school for
the blind, author
Episcopalian
Nat Cyc Am Bio v34 and csv6

799. **Maury, Carlotta Joaquina**
1874–1938
paleontologist
Episcopalian
New York
Nat Cyc Am Bio v28

800. **Miller, Emma Guffey**
1874–1970
Democratic party official, suffrag-
ist, feminist
Episcopalian
Pennsylvania
Index t Wom; Nat Cyc Am Bio
v55; Not Am Wom supp v1

801. **Colby, Nathalie Sedgwick**
1875–1942
essayist, poet, novelist
Episcopalian

New York
Index t Wom; Nat Cyc Am Bio
v31

802. **Ferguson, Miriam Amanda
Wallace "Ma"**
1875–1961
twenty-eighth governor of Texas
Episcopalian
Texas
Index t Wom; Nat Cyc Am Bio
csv1; Not Am Wom supp v1;
Obit File; Encyc South Hist

803. **Stanwood, Cornelia Terry
McKinne**
born 1875
educator
Episcopalian
California
Nat Cyc Am Bio csv7

804. **Barringer, Emily Dunning**
1876–1961
gynecologist, ambulance surgeon,
worker for recognition of wom-
en physicians
Protestant Episcopal
Nat Cyc Am Bio v50; Index t
Wom; Obit File

805. **Donahey, Mary Dickerson**
1876–1962
children's author
Episcopalian
Chicago, IL
Nat Cyc Am Bio v45

806. **Mead, Elizabeth Manning
Cleveland**
1876–1946
patron of cancer research
Episcopalian
New York
Nat Cyc Am Bio v38

807. **Rinehart, Mary Roberts**
1876–1958
novelist, mystery story writer,
playwright, suffragist
Episcopalian
Dict Am Bio supp v6; Index t
Wom; Nat Cyc Am Bio csv3;
Not Am Wom supp v1; Obit
File

808. **Tanzer, Helen Henrietta**
born 1876
archaeologist
Episcopalian
Nat Cyc Am Bio csv7

809. **Hard, Anne; Annie Marie
Nyhan Scribner**
1877–1961
author, radio broadcaster, politi-
cal journalist
Episcopalian
Washington, DC
Nat Cyc Am Bio v57

810. Milton, Inez Lopez Seymour
born 1877
author, composer
Episcopalian
Nat Cyc Am Bio csv4

811. Pratt, Ruth (Sears) Baker
1877–1965
representative to Congress from New York
Episcopalian
New York
Index t Wom; Nat Cyc Am Bio v51

812. Fairbank, Janet Ayer
1878–1951
author, feminist
Episcopalian
Index t Wom; Nat Cyc Am Bio v39

813. Howard, Alice Sturtevant
1878–1945
library founder, author, Republican party worker
Episcopalian
Index t Wom; Nat Cyc Am Bio v33

814. Jackson, Leonora; Mrs. W. Duncan McKim
born 1878
violinist
Episcopalian
Nat Cyc Am Bio csv7, Index t Wom

815. MacLane, Jean; Mrs. John C. Johansen
1878–1964
artist, painter
Episcopalian
Index t Wom; Nat Cyc Am Bio v52

816. Muhlhofer, Mary Elizabeth
1878–1950
painter
Episcopalian
Washington, DC
Nat Cyc Am Bio v38

817. Chapin, Alice Delafield
1879–1964
educator, social welfare leader
Episcopalian
New York
Index t Wom; Nat Cyc Am Bio v52

818. Dodge, Lillian Sefton
1879–1960
cosmetics manufacturer
Episcopalian
Nat Cyc Am Bio v47

819. Sanger, Margaret Higgins; Mrs. J. Noah H. Slee
1879/83–1966
birth control reformer, lecturer, author
Episcopalian
Index t Wom; Nat Cyc Am Bio v52; Not Am Wom supp v1; Obit File

820. Taylor, Anna Heyward
1879–1956
artist
Episcopalian
South Carolina
Nat Cyc Am Bio v42

821. Bingham, Millicent Todd
1880–1968
geographer, conservationist, author, editor, authority on Emily Dickinson
Episcopalian
Cur Biog '69; Index t Wom; Nat Cyc Am Bio csv9

822. Glass, Meta
1880–1967
president of Sweet Briar College, educator, YWCA executive, World War I and II relief worker, defense worker
Episcopalian
Virginia
Nat Cyc Am Bio v53 and csv7; Obit File

823. McBride, Lucia McCurdy
1880–1970
Cleveland civic leader, suffragist
Episcopalian
Cleveland, OH
Nat Cyc Am Bio v57 and csv7

824. Windsor, Helen Howell
1880–1926
social welfare worker
Episcopalian
Iowa
Nat Cyc Am Bio v20

825. Martin, Mabel Agnes; Mrs. Harry N. Totten
1881–1957
physician
Episcopalian
New York
Nat Cyc Am Bio v45

826. McClellan, Irene Moulton Ward
1881–1967
philanthropist, World War I Red Cross relief worker in England, patent medicine manufacturer, dairy and chicken farmer
Episcopalian
New York
Nat Cyc Am Bio v53

827. Dodd, Katharine
1882–1965
pediatrician, medical educator and author
Episcopalian
Nat Cyc Am Bio v53

828. Mason, Lucy Randolph
1882–1959
labor publicist, public relations officer for the CIO, southern trade union organizer, social worker and reformer, suffragist
Episcopalian
Virginia
Bio Dict Am Lab; Dict Am Bio supp v6; Encyc South Hist; Not Am Wom supp v1; Obit File

829. Reid, Helen Miles Rogers
1882–1970
publisher of *The New York Herald-Tribune* newspaper, journalist, suffragist, philanthropist
Episcopalian
New York
Cur Biog '70; Index t Wom; Nat Cyc Am Bio v56; Not Am Wom supp v1; Obit File

830. Carter, Alice (Olin) Draper
born 1883
YWCA executive, world war relief worker, welfare worker
Episcopalian
New York
Nat Cyc Am Bio v55

831. James, Mary Latimer
1883–1963
medical missionary to the Ute people in Utah, medical missionary to China, obstetrician/gynecologist, psychiatrist
Protestant Episcopal
Utah
Nat Cyc Am Bio v51

832. Lamson, Armene Tashijian
1883–1970
medical illustrator, physician, UNICEF worker, medical author
Episcopalian
Seattle, WA
Turkish
Nat Cyc Am Bio v56

833. Verner, Elizabeth O'Neill
born 1883
etcher, painter
Episcopalian
South Carolina
Nat Cyc Am Bio csv12

834. Brown, Margaret Fitzhugh
1884–1972
artist
Episcopalian
Massachusetts
Nat Cyc Am Bio v57

835. Crawford, Mary Merritt; Mrs. Edward Schuster
1884–1972
surgeon, World War I surgeon in France
Episcopalian
New York
Nat Cyc Am Bio v57

836. Emery, Mary Muhlenberk Hopkins
1884–1927
philanthropist, founder of Mariemont, a model town near Cincinnati
Protestant Episcopal
Ohio
Nat Cyc Am Bio v24

837. Gluck, Anna; Reba Fiersohn
1884–1938
soprano opera and concert singer
Episcopalian
Rumanian
Dict Am Bio supp v2; Nat Cyc Am Bio v43; Not Am Wom

838. Messenger, Ruth Ellis
1884–1964
hymnologist, educator
Protestant Episcopal
New York
Nat Cyc Am Bio v51

839. Bailey, Margaret Emerson
1885–1949
educator, journalist, novelist, magazine writer, police commissioner
Episcopalian
New Canaan, CT
Nat Cyc Am Bio csv6; Obit File

840. Clowes, Edith Whitehill (Hinkel)
1885–1967
Indianapolis civic leader, patron of music
Episcopalian
Indianapolis, IN
Nat Cyc Am Bio v53

841. Everett, Flora Pierce Morris
born 1885
Cleveland civic worker
Episcopalian
Cleveland, OH
Nat Cyc Am Bio csv6

842. Hutchinson, Mary Amory Hare; Amory Hare
1885–1969
author, novelist, dramatist, painter, poet, thoroughbred-horse breeder
Episcopalian
California
Nat Cyc Am Bio v57, Index t Wom

843. Randolph, Bessie Carter
1885–1966

political scientist, international
law and affairs expert, president
of Hollins College
Episcopalian
Virginia
Nat Cyc Am Bio v52 and csv6

844. Sturgis, Margaret Castex
1885–1962
gynecologist, cancer researcher,
medical author
Episcopalian
Pennsylvania
Nat Cyc Am Bio v49

845. Bridgman, Olga Louise
born 1886
psychiatrist, medical educator
and author
Episcopalian
California
Nat Cyc Am Bio csv6

846. Noland, Hampton [Clara]
1886–1960
composer
Episcopalian
Nat Cyc Am Bio v48

847. Allison, Marjorie
1887–1961
banker
Episcopalian
Pennsylvania
Nat Cyc Am Bio v49

848. Boyd, Louise Arner
1887–1972
scientific polar explorer, geographer, technical expert for the
War Department and the National Bureau of Standards
Episcopalian
Cur Biog '72; Index t Wom; Nat
Cyc Am Bio csv7; Obit File

849. Case, Adelaide Teague
1887–1948
Episcopal educator
Episcopalian
Not Am Wom

850. Chase, Mary Ellen
1887–1973
novelist, biographer, short story
writer, literary critic, writer on
the Bible, university educator
Episcopalian
Cur Biog '73; Index t Wom; Nat
Cyc Am Bio csv9; Obit File;
Wom Lit, More

**851. Pedder, Alice Pratt Ber-
dell**
1887–1947
realtor, business executive
Episcopalian
California
Nat Cyc Am Bio v36

852. Bussey, Ruth Carman
1888–1961

educator, worker for Women's
International League for Peace
and Freedom party
Episcopalian
Maryland
Nat Cyc Am Bio v49

**853. McMein, Neysa; Mrs.
John Gordon Baragwanath**
1888/90–1949
illustrator, magazine illustrator,
painter, portraitist, commercial
artist, author
Episcopalian
Index t Wom; Nat Cyc Am Bio
v36; Not Am Wom; Obit File

**854. Rosen, Lucie Bigelow
Dodge**
1889–1968
electronic musician, patron of
music
Episcopalian
New York
Nat Cyc Am Bio v54

855. Leighton, Mary
flourished 1920s–30s
poet
Protestant Episcopal
Nat Cyc Am Bio v26

**856. Susong, Edith (Ingles)
O'Keefe**
1890–1974
newspaper publisher
Episcopalian
Greenville, TN
Nat Cyc Am Bio v59

857. Lilly, Ruth Allison
1891–1973
philanthropist
Episcopalian
Indianapolis, IN
Nat Cyc Am Bio v58

**858. Mudd, Mildred Hardy
Esterbrook**
1891–1958
national president of the Girl
Scouts of America
Episcopalian
Nat Cyc Am Bio csv8; Obit File

**859. Harrison, Gertrude [Alice]
Gordon Grayson**
1892–1961
Washington, DC, civic leader; pa-
tron of medicine; racehorse
breeder
Episcopalian
Nat Cyc Am Bio v51

860. McCollin, Frances
1892–1960
composer, educator, lecturer, Socialist party worker
Episcopalian
Pennsylvania

blind
Index t Wom; Nat Cyc Am Bio
v45

**861. Rienecke, Mabel Eunice
(Gilmore)**
born 1892
suffragist, internal revenue collec-
tor
Protestant
Illinois
Nat Cyc Am Bio csv3

862. Weld, Agnes Vance
1892–1975
newspaper publisher and editor
Episcopalian
Connecticut
Nat Cyc Am Bio v58

**863. Brande, Dorothea Thomp-
son**
1893–1948
author, editor, journalist
Episcopalian
Chicago, IL
Nat Cyc Am Bio v39

**864. Curtis, Edith (Goddard)
Roelker**
1893–1977
author
Episcopalian
New Hampshire; Massachusetts
Nat Cyc Am Bio v60

865. Wanstrum, Ruth Cecilia
1893–1971
pathologist, medical educator
Episcopalian
Michigan
Nat Cyc Am Bio v57

866. Ireland, Margaret Allen
1894–1961
public health worker, Cleveland
civic worker, welfare worker
Episcopalian
Cleveland, OH
Nat Cyc Am Bio v50

867. Moore, Elizabeth Finley
1894–1976
South Carolina historical worker
Episcopalian
South Carolina
Nat Cyc Am Bio v60

**868. Drant, Patricia Hart; Mrs.
James Steffan Collins**
1895–1955
dermatologist
Episcopalian
Nat Cyc Am Bio v42

869. Boyd, Katharine Lamont
1896–1974
newspaper editor
Episcopalian
North Carolina
Nat Cyc Am Bio v59

870. Dole, Margaret Fernald
1896–1970
portrait painter
Episcopalian
New York
Nat Cyc Am Bio v56

871. Fay, Marion (Spencer)
born 1896
educator, physiological chemist
Episcopalian
Pennsylvania
Nat Cyc Am Bio csv12

872. Frantz, Virginia Kneeland
1896–1967
surgical pathologist, medical educator, cancer researcher, dairy
farmer
Episcopalian
New York
Nat Cyc Am Bio v53; Not Am
Wom supp v1

**873. Russell, Helen Victoria
Crocker**
1896–1966
bank director, UNESCO execu-
tive, philanthropist
Episcopalian
San Francisco, CA
Nat Cyc Am Bio v53

**874. Clark, Mary Chase; Mrs.
Raymond S. Darrenougue**
1897–1945
lawyer
Episcopalian
New York
Index t Wom; Nat Cyc Am Bio
v32

875. Hayden, Saint Clare Okie
born 1897
industrialist
Episcopalian
Colorado
Nat Cyc Am Bio csv7

876. Lowry, Edith Elizabeth
1897–1970
religious leader, Protestant Organization executive of the Council of Women
Protestant
Not Am Wom supp v1

877. Shaver, Dorothy (Yeiser)
1897–1959
business executive, merchandising
executive, president of Lord and
Taylor department stores
Episcopalian
New York
Index t Wom; Nat Cyc Am Bio
v56 and csv8; Not Am Wom
supp v1; Obit File

878. Snow, Kathleyn Smith
born 1897
physician

Episcopalian
Nat Cyc Am Bio csv4

879. Wolle, Muriel Sibell
1898–1977
artist, art educator, Native American art scholar and collector,
western history writer, conservationist
Episcopalian
Boulder, CO
Nat Cyc Am Bio v60

880. Bailey, Consuelo Northrop
born 1899
lieutenant governor of Vermont,
lawyer
Episcopalian
Vermont
Index t Wom; Nat Cyc Am Bio
csv12

881. Brush, Katherine Ingham
1900/02–1952
author, novelist
Episcopalian
Index t Wom; Nat Cyc Am Bio
v43; Obit File

**882. Douglas, Helen [Mary]
(Gahagan)**
1900/05–1980
stage actor, Democratic represen-
tative to Congress from Califor-
nia, opera singer
Episcopalian
California
Cur Biog '80; Index t Wom; Nat
Cyc Am Bio csvF

883. Switzer, Mary Elizabeth
1900–71
commissioner of welfare and rehabilitation programs for HEW,
welfare worker for the disabled
Episcopalian
Index t Wom; Nat Cyc Am Bio
v56; Not Am Wom supp v1;
Obit File

884. Bennett, Melba Berry
1901–68
author; Palm Springs, California,
civic worker
Episcopalian
Palm Springs, CA
Nat Cyc Am Bio v54

885. Bruce, Ailsa Mellon
1901–69
philanthropist, patron of art, conservationist
Episcopalian
New York
Nat Cyc Am Bio v55; Obit File

886. Mead, Margaret; Margaret
Bateson
1901/02–1978
anthropologist, writer of popular
books on anthropology, autobiographer

Episcopalian
Cur Biog '79; Index t Wom; Nat
Cyc Am Bio csv9; Obit File

887. Luce, Clare (Boothe)
born 1903
playwright, author, journalist,
politician, US ambassador
Episcopalian
Index t Wom; Nat Cyc Am Bio
csvF; Wom Lit

888. Payson, Joan Whitney
1903–75
philanthropist, race horse breeder, owner of the New York
Mets, patron of medicine, art
collector and investor, founder
of the Museum of Modern Art
in New York
Episcopalian
New York
Cur Biog '72 and '75; Index t
Wom; Nat Cyc Am Bio v58 and
csv10; Obit File

889. Spain, Frances Lander
born 1903
librarian, organization official
Episcopalian
Florida
Index t Wom; Nat Cyc Am Bio
csv10

890. Goldsmith, Grace Arabell
1904–75
physician, public health educator,
nutritionist
Episcopalian
Louisiana
Nat Cyc Am Bio csv10; Not Am
Wom supp v10

891. Mann, Marty
born 1904
alcoholism authority
Episcopalian
Nat Cyc Am Bio csv11

892. Bartlett, Phyllis (Brooks);
Mrs. John A. Pollard
1905–73
educator, scholar of English liter-
ature
Episcopalian
New York
Nat Cyc Am Bio v58

**893. Darnault, Florence Mal-
colm**
born 1905
sculptor
Episcopalian
Nat Cyc Am Bio

894. Jackson, Beatrice; Mrs.
David Humphreys
born 1905
artist
Episcopalian
New York

English
Nat Cyc Am Bio csv13

895. Pitkin, Winifred Mercer;
Winifred Smith
born 1905
physician
Episcopalian
English
Nat Cyc Am Bio csv7

896. Roebling, Mary Gindhart
born 1905/06
banker
Episcopalian
Trenton, NJ
Index t Wom; Nat Cyc Am Bio
csv9

897. Backus, Louise Laidlaw
1906–73
New York civic worker, UNES-
CO member, international af-
fairs expert, poet
Episcopalian
New York, NY
Nat Cyc Am Bio v57

**898. Darlington, Alice (Nelson)
Benning**
1906–73
New York civic worker
Episcopalian
New York, NY
Twent Cen Bio Dict Not Am

899. Mobley, Eleanor Smith
1906–64
Girl Scout executive
Episcopalian
Nat Cyc Am Bio v51

900. Baldwin, Janet Sterling;
Mrs. Herbert C. Maier
1908–58
pediatrician, medical educator
Episcopalian
New York
Nat Cyc Am Bio v59

**901. Dixon, Margaret Calder
Richardson**
1908–70
prison reformer, political journal-
ist, newspaper editor
Episcopalian
Baton Rouge, LA
Nat Cyc Am Bio v58; Obit File

**902. Shepard, Marguerite Dun-
bar**
1908–57
physician
Episcopalian
Connecticut
Nat Cyc Am Bio v47

903. Wedel, Cynthia Clark
born 1908
Episcopalian church worker,
president of the National Coun-

cil of the Churches of Christ in
the United States
Episcopalian
Cur Biog '70

**904. Jones, Sarah [Frances]
Roddis**
1909–75
president general of DAR
Episcopalian
Wisconsin
Nat Cyc Am Bio v59

905. Beeuwkes, Adelia Marie
1910–66
nutritionist, educator
Episcopalian
Michigan
Nat Cyc Am Bio v52

906. Bennett, Joan; Mrs. Walker Wanger
born 1910
stage actor
Episcopalian
Index t Wom; Nat Cyc Am Bio
csv7

907. Guion, Molly
born 1910
artist
Episcopalian
Nat Cyc Am Bio csv9

908. Kuhlman, Kathryn
1910?–76
Protestant evangelist, minister,
faith healer
Protestant
Cur Biog '74 and '76; Obit File

**909. Pannell, Anne Thomas
Gary**
born 1910
educator, president of Sweet Briar
College
Protestant Episcopal
Virginia
Index t Wom; Nat Cyc Am Bio
csv10

910. Lucas, Martha Bob
born 1912
educator, president of Sweet Briar
College
Episcopalian
Virginia
Index t Wom; Nat Cyc Am Bio
csv7

**911. Waller, Wilhelmine
Stewart Kirby**
born 1914
conservationist, horsewoman
Episcopalian
New York
Nat Cyc Am Bio csv13

**912. Dehavilland, Olivia
[Mary]**
born 1916
actor

Episcopalian
English
Index t Wom; Nat Cyc Am Bio
csv9

913. Deming, Louise MacPherson
1916–76
international educator, author,
civic worker in Okinawa, Japan
Episcopalian
Nat Cyc Am Bio v58

**914. Smith, Constance
Elizabeth**
1922–70
college educator and administrator
Episcopalian
Massachusetts
Nat Cyc Am Bio

915. Nettleship, Mae Barnwell
born 1926
physician
Episcopalian
Arkansas
Canadian
Nat Cyc Am Bio csv10

**916. Saunders, Sally; Sally
Love Saunders Craigie**
born 1940
poet, educator
Episcopalian
Pennsylvania
Nat Cyc Am Bio csv12

917. Castleman, Alice Barbee
born 1943
philanthropist, women's rights
worker
Episcopalian
Louisville, KY
Wom Cent

PURITAN

918. Brewster, Mary
circa 1569–1627
Pilgrim, pioneer
Puritan
Index t Wom

919. Allerton, Mary Norris
flourished 1600s
Pilgrim
Puritan
Index t Wom

920. Carver, Katherin
flourished 1600s
Pilgrim
Puritan
Index t Wom

921. Cooper, Humility
flourished 1600s
Pilgrim

Puritan
Index t Wom

922. Hopkins, Elizabeth
flourished 1600s
Pilgrim
Puritan
Index t Wom

923. Minter, Desire
flourished 1600s
Pilgrim
Puritan
Index t Wom

924. Standish, Rose
died 1620
Pilgrim
Puritan
Index t Wom

925. Tilley, Ann
flourished 1600s
Pilgrim
Puritan
Index t Wom

926. Tilley, Bridget
flourished 1600s
Pilgrim
Puritan
Index t Wom

927. Winslow, Elizabeth Barker
died 1621
Pilgrim
Puritan
Index t Wom

928. Eaton, Sarah
flourished 1610s–20s
Pilgrim
Puritan
Index t Wom

929. Warren, Elizabeth
1583–1673
Pilgrim
Puritan
Index t Wom

930. Allerton, Fear Brewster
died 1634
Pilgrim
Puritan
Index t Wom

931. Bradford, Alice
circa 1590–1670
Pilgrim, Plymouth Colony civic
worker, patron of education
Puritan
Massachusetts
English
Am Bio Dict; Index t Wom

932. Hutchinson, Anne (Marbury)
1590/91–1642/43
religious and political leader,
founder of the Antinomian sect
of Puritanism

Puritan
Rhode Island; Massachusetts
English
Am Bio Dict; Cyc Am Bio; Dict
Am Bio; Dict Am Bio Men
Time; Dict Am Rel Bio; Dict
Nat Bio; Index t Wom; Nat Cyc
Am Bio v9; Not Am Wom;
Twent Cen Bio Dict Not Am

933. Bradford, Dorothy
circa 1597–1602
Pilgrim
Puritan
Index t Wom

934. Alden, Priscilla Mullins
born 1602; married 1621
Pilgrim hero of American folklore
Puritan
Index t Wom; Not Am Wom

935. Howland, Elizabeth Tilley
1608–87
Pilgrim
Puritan
Index t Wom

936. Winslow, Mary Chilton
circa 1608–79
Pilgrim
Puritan
Index t Wom

937. Standish, Barbara
died circa 1659
Pilgrim
Puritan
Index t Wom

938. Bradstreet, Anne Dudley
1612–72
poet
Puritan
English
Am Bio Dict; Cyc Am Bio; Dict
Am Auth; Dict Am Bio; Dict
Am Bio Men Time; Index t
Wom; Nat Cyc Am Bio v7; Not
Am Wom; Twent Cen Bio Dict
Not Am; Wom Lit; Wom Lit,
More

939. Allerton, Remember
circa 1614–1652/56
Pilgrim
Puritan
Index t Wom

940. Fuller, Bridget Lee
married 1641
Pilgrim
Puritan
Index t Wom

941. Cooke, Demaris Hopkins
married 1647; died pre-1669
Pilgrim
Puritan
Index t Wom

**942. Winslow, Susanna Fuller
White**
died pre-1675
Pilgrim
Puritan
Index t Wom

943. Ambrose, Alice
flourished 1660s
colonial religious worker
Puritan
Index t Wom

944. Chilton, Susanna
1634–circa 1676
Pilgrim, pioneer
Puritan
Index t Wom

945. Standish, Sarah Alden
died circa 1688
Pilgrim
Puritan
Index t Wom

946. Walling, Harriet
flourished 1680s
pioneer
Puritan
Index t Wom

947. Edwards, Sarah Pierpont
1710–58
Puritan mystic
Puritan
Am Bio Dict; Not Am Wom

REFORMED BODIES

948. Remy, Egbertina
1880–1956
pianist
Dutch Reformed
Nat Cyc Am Bio v44

949. Griggs, Mary Amerman
1886–1962
chemist, chemistry educator
Dutch Reformed
Nat Cyc Am Bio v49

**950. Calverley, Eleanor Jane
Taylor**
1887–1968
physician, missionary to Kuwait,
nurse in the 1920 Kuwait war,
birth control advocate, birth
control clinic founder
Dutch Reformed
Connecticut
Nat Cyc Am Bio v57

951. Paul, Josephine Bay
1900–62
brokerage and shipping business
executive
Reformed Church
Nat Cyc Am Bio csv9; Obit File

SALVATION ARMY

952. Booth-Tucker, Emma Moss
1860–1903
consul of the Salvation Army
Salvationist
Dict Am Bio

953. Booth, Florence Eleanor Soper
1862–1957
Salvation Army leader
Salvationist
Obit File

954. Booth, Evangeline Cory
1865–1950
fourth general of the Salvation Army, orator, musician, poet
Salvationist
English
Dict Am Bio supp v4; Dict Am Rel Bio; Index t Wom; Nat Cyc Am Bio csv2; Not Am Wom; Obit File

955. Booth, Maud Ballington (Charlesworth)
1865–1948
Salvation Army leader, evangelist, philanthropist, prison reformer, author, founder of PTA
Salvationist
English
Dict Am Auth; Index t Wom; Nat Cyc Am Bio v14 and v38; Not Am Wom; Obit File

SCIENTOLOGY

956. Black, Karen Blanche (Zeigler)
born 1942
screen actor
Scientologist
Cur Biog '76

SOCIETY FOR ETHICAL CULTURE

957. Hyde, Ida Henrietta
1857–1945
research physiologist
Ethical Culture
Nat Cyc Am Bio csv2; Not Am Wom

SOCIETY OF FRIENDS

958. Clark, Mary
flourished 1650s
colonial religious worker
Quaker

English
Index t Wom

959. Godby, Ann
flourished 1650s
religious leader
Quaker
Index t Wom

960. Harris, Elizabeth
flourished 1650s
religious worker
Quaker
English
Index t Wom

961. Prince, Mary
flourished 1650s
colonial religious worker
Quaker
Index t Wom

962. Tilton, Mary
flourished 1650s
colonial religious worker
Quaker
Index t Wom

963. Wetherhead, Mary
flourished 1650s
religious worker
Quaker
Index t Wom

964. Fisher, Mary
flourished 1652; died 1697
Quaker preacher, missionary
Quaker
Dict Nat Bio; Index t Wom; Not Am Wom

965. Coleman, Ann
flourished 1660s
colonial religious worker
Quaker
Index t Wom

966. Smith, Margaret
flourished 1660s–70s
colonial religious worker
Quaker
Index t Wom

967. Wardel, Elizabeth
flourished 1660s
religious worker
Quaker
Index t Wom

968. Wardell, Lydia
flourished 1660s
religious worker
Quaker
Index t Wom

969. Dyer, Mary
born pre-1638; died 1660
religious leader, Quaker martyr
Quaker

Massachusetts
Am Bio Dict; Cyc Am Bio; Dict Am Bio; Dict Am Bio Men Time; Dict Am Rel Bio; Index t Wom; Nat Cyc Am Bio v11; Not Am Wom

970. Brewster, Margaret
flourished 1670s
colonial religious worker
Quaker
Index t Wom

971. Starbuck, Mary Coffyn
circa 1644/45–circa 1717
Quaker minister, religious leader
Quaker
Index t Wom; Not Am Wom

972. Wilkinson, Ruth
flourished 1690s–1700s
religious worker
Quaker
Index t Wom

973. Penn, Hannah Callowhill
1671–1726
executor of William Penn
Quaker
Pennsylvania
Cyc Am Bio; Index t Wom; Not Am Wom

974. Estaugh, Elizabeth Haddon
1680/83–1762
colonial proprietor; founder of Haddonfield, New Jersey; pioneer
Quaker
New Jersey
Cyc Am Bio; Dict Am Bio; Index t Wom; Nat Cyc Am Bio v17; Not Am Wom

975. Lancastle, Lydia
1684–1761
Quaker preacher
Quaker
Cyc Am Bio

976. Sargent, Mary Forward Kooser
flourished eighteenth century
artist
Quaker
Nat Cyc Am Bio v50

977. Timothy, Mary
flourished 1730s–40s
colonial religious worker
Quaker
Index t Wom

978. Scott, Sarah
married 1726
colonial religious worker
Quaker
Index t Wom

979. Morris, Sarah
1704–75

Quaker preacher
Quaker
Cyc Am Bio; Dict Am Bio Men Time

980. Neale, Mary Peasley
flourished 1750s
colonial religious worker
Quaker
Index t Wom

981. Peyton, Catherine
flourished 1750s
colonial religious worker
Quaker
Index t Wom

982. Wright, Patience Lovell
1725–1785/86
wax modeler, spy during American Revolution
Quaker
New Jersey
Dict Am Bio; Dict Nat Bio; Index t Wom; Nat Cyc Am Bio v8; Not Am Wom; Who Who Dur Am Rev

983. Anthony, Susanna
1726–91
theologian, religious author
Quaker
Rhode Island
Am Bio Dict; Appl Cyc Am Bio; Cyc Am Bio; Dict Am Bio Men Time

984. Terrell, Ann
married 1755
religious worker
Quaker
Index t Wom

985. Jones, Rebecca
1739–1818
Quaker minister
Quaker
Index t Wom

986. Galloway, Anne
flourished 1770s
colonial religious worker
Quaker
Index t Wom

987. Drinker, Elizabeth Sandwith
1743–1807
colonial diarist
Quaker
Index t Wom

988. Harrison, Sarah
1748–1812
Quaker preacher
Quaker
Cyc Am Bio

989. Barnard, Hannah Jenkins
1754–1825
Quaker minister

Quaker
Index t Wom; Not Am Wom

990. Wister, Sarah "Sally"
1761/62–1804
diarist, patriot of American Revolution
Quaker
Pennsylvania
Dict Am Bio; Index t Wom; Who Who Dur Am Rev

991. Hubbs, Rebecca
1772–1852
Quaker preacher
Quaker
Dict Am Bio

992. Collins, Elizabeth Ballinger
1775–1831
Quaker minister
Quaker
Cyc Am Bio

993. Jenkins, Anna Almy
1790–1849
philanthropist
Quaker
Providence, RI
Cyc Am Bio; Dict Am Bio Men Time

994. Mitchell, Maria
1791/1818–1889
astronomer, women's rights worker, educator, novelist, poet
Quaker
Massachusetts
Cyc Am Bio; Dict Am Bio; Dict Am Bio Men Time; Index t Wom; Nat Cyc Am Bio v5; Not Am Wom; Twent Cen Bio Dict Not Am; Wom Cent

995. Grimke, Sarah Moore
1792/93–1873
abolitionist, women's rights worker, writer on social problems, political author, lecturer
Quaker
Cyc Am Bio; Dict Am Auth; Dict Am Bio; Dict Am Rel Bio; Index t Wom; Nat Cyc Am Bio v2; Twent Cen Bio Dict Not Am; Wom Cent

996. Mott, Lucretia (Coffin)
1793–1880
abolitionist, feminist, Quaker minister, pacifist
Quaker
Cyc Am Bio; Dict Am Bio; Dict Am Bio Men Time; Dict Am Rel Bio; Index t Wom; Nat Cyc Am Bio v2; Not Am Wom; Twent Cen Bio Dict Not Am; Wom Cent

997. Cox, Hannah
1796/97–1876

abolitionist, temperance worker, pacifist, women's rights worker
Quaker
Cyc Am Bio; Dict Am Bio; Index t Wom

998. Tucker, Sarah
1799–1840
Quaker preacher
Quaker
Cyc Am Bio

999. Gibbons, Abigail Hopper "Abby"
1801–93
abolitionist, prison reformer, feminist, women's welfare worker, Civil War nurse, philanthropist, journalist
Quaker
Cyc Am Bio; Dict Am Bio; Index t Wom; Nat Cyc Am Bio v7; Not Am Wom; Twent Cen Bio Dict Not Am; Wom Cent

1000. Case, Mary
died 1852
magazine writer
Quaker
New York
Am Bio Dict

1001. Child, Lydia Maria (Francis)
1802–80
author, philanthropist, abolitionist, editor, social reformer
Quaker
Massachusetts
Cyc Am Bio; Dict Am Auth; Dict Am Bio; Dict Am Bio Men Time; Dict Lit Bio v1; Index t Wom; Nat Cyc Am Bio v2; Not Am Wom; Twent Cen Bio Dict Not Am; Wom Cent

1002. Crandall, Prudence (Philles)
1803–1889/90
educator of Blacks, abolitionist, philanthropist
Quaker
English
Cyc Am Bio; Dict Am Bio; Eng Wom; Index t Wom; Nat Cyc Am Bio v2; Not Am Wom; Twent Cen Bio Dict Not Am

1003. Gurney, Eliza Paul Kirkbride
1803–81
Quaker minister
Quaker
Not Am Wom

1004. Grimke, Angelina Emily; Angelina Emily Grimke Weld
1805/38–1879
abolitionist, feminist, lecturer

Quaker
Cyc Am Bio; Dict Am Auth; Dict Am Rel Bio; Index t Wom; Nat Cyc Am Bio v2; Twent Cen Bio Dict Not Am

1005. Chace, Elizabeth Buffum
1806–99
abolitionist, suffragist, women's rights worker, prison reformer, temperance worker
Quaker
Dict Am Bio; Not Am Wom; Twent Cen Bio Dict Not Am; Wom Cent

1006. Haviland, Laura Smith
1808–98
abolitionist, freedmen's welfare worker, philanthropist
Quaker
Cyc Am Bio; Not Am Wom

1007. Jones, Sybil
1808/13–1873
Quaker minister, missionary
Quaker
Dict Am Bio; Index t Wom; Nat Cyc Am Bio v2; Not Am Wom

1008. Foster, Abigail (Kelley) "Abby"
1810/11–1887
abolitionist, feminist, Prohibitionist, lecturer, suffragist, temperance worker
Quaker
Cyc Am Bio; Dict Am Bio; Index t Wom; Nat Cyc Am Bio v2; Not Am Wom; Twent Cen Bio Dict Not Am

1009. Comstock, Elizabeth Leslie Rous
1815–1891/92
social reformer, abolitionist, Underground Railroad worker, pacifist, freed slave's welfare worker, temperance reformer, women's rights worker, Quaker minister, prison reformer, Civil War nurse
Quaker
Dict Am Bio; Index t Wom; Nat Cyc Am Bio v22; Not Am Wom

1010. Whittier, Elizabeth Hussey
1815–64
poet, abolitionist, religious worker
Quaker
Cyc Am Bio; Index t Wom; Nat Cyc Am Bio v8

1011. Pinkham, Lydia Estes
1819–83
patent medicine proprietor, abolitionist, temperance worker, women's rights worker
Quaker
Dict Am Bio; Not Am Wom

1012. Anthony, Susan Brownell
1820–1906
women's suffrage leader, feminist, abolitionist, newspaper publisher, editor
Quaker
Appl Cyc Am Bio; Cyc Am Bio; Dict Am Bio; Dict Am Bio Men Time; Index t Wom; Nat Cyc Am Bio v4; Not Am Wom; Twent Cen Bio Dict Not Am; Wom Cent

1013. Lewis, Grace Anna
born 1821
naturalist, scientific illustrator, science writer, conservationist, ornithologist, abolitionist, Underground Railroad operator, pacifist, suffragist, philanthropist
Quaker
Index t Wom; Nat Cyc Am Bio v9; Twent Cen Bio Dict Not Am; Wom Cent

1014. Jeanes, Anne T.
1822–1907
philanthropist
Quaker
Dict Am Bio

1015. Jenkins, Frances C.
born 1826
evangelist, temperance worker
Quaker
Wom Cent

1016. Howland, Emily
1827–1929
educator, educator of Blacks, abolitionist, suffragist, pacifist, temperance worker, philanthropist
Quaker
New York
Dict Am Bio; Nat Cyc Am Bio v25; Not Am Wom; Wom Cent

1017. Potts, Anna M. Longshore
born 1829
physician, medical lecturer
Quaker
Index t Wom; Wom Cent

1018. Jackson, Helen Maria (Fiske) (Hunt); Saxe Holme; H. H.
1830/31–1881/85
author, poet, novelist, crusader for Native American rights, philanthropist
Quaker
Cyc Am Bio; Dict Am Auth; Dict Am Bio; Index t Wom; Nat Cyc Am Bio v1; Not Am Wom; Read Encyc Am West; Twent Cen Bio Dict Not Am; Wom Cent; Wom Lit, More

1019. Fussell, Susan
1832–89

educator, army nurse in the Civil War, Civil War relief worker, philanthropist
Quaker
Wom Cent

1020. Smith, Hannah Whitall
1832–1911
religious author, evangelist, pacifist, temperance worker, women's rights worker
Quaker
Dict Am Bio; Index t Wom; Not Am Wom

1021. Morrison, Sarah Parke
born 1833
temperance worker, Quaker minister
Quaker
Twent Cen Bio Dict Not Am

1022. Hodgin, Emily Caroline Chandler
born 1838
temperance reformer, suffragist
Quaker
Indiana
Wom Cent

1023. Lippincott, Esther J. (Trimble)
1838–88
educator, author on literature, temperance reformer, convalescent-hospital reformer
Quaker
Pennsylvania
Dict Am Auth; Wom Cent

1024. Wright, Rebecca McPherson
born 1838
Union spy during the Civil War, Civil War hero
Quaker
Cyc Am Bio; Index t Wom

1025. Hancock, Cornelia
1839/40–1927
Civil War nurse, educator of freedmen, charity worker, housing reformer
Quaker
Index t Wom; Not Am Wom

1026. Schofield, Martha
1839–1916
educator of freedmen
Quaker
Not Am Wom

1027. Telford, Mary Jewett
born 1839
army nurse, Civil War nurse, Women's Relief Corps organizer, church worker, children's author
Quaker
Wom Cent

1028. Dickinson, Susan E.
flourished 1870s–90s
journalist, author
Quaker
Pennsylvania
Index t Wom; Wom Cent

1029. Frame, Esther Gordon
born 1840
minister and evangelist
Quaker
Wom Cent

1030. Oberholtzer, Sara Louisa (Vikers)
1841–1930
poet, author, novelist, temperance worker, leader in school savings movement, economist
Quaker
Norristown, PA
Cyc Am Bio; Dict Am Auth; Dict Am Bio; Index t Wom; Nat Cyc Am Bio v7; Wom Cent

1031. Dickinson, Anna Elizabeth
1842–1932
Civil War orator, lyceum lecturer, abolitionist, women's rights worker, suffragist, political activist, Republican party worker, author, actor, philanthropist
Quaker
Cyc Am Bio; Dict Am Auth; Dict Am Bio supp v1; Dict Am Bio Men Time; Index t Wom; Nat Cyc Am Bio v3; Not Am Wom; Twent Cen Bio Dict Not Am; Wom Cent

1032. Mee, Cassie Ward
born 1848
labor leader, Knights of Labor worker, temperance worker, lecturer
Quaker
Canadian
Index t Wom; Wom Cent

1033. Thomas, Martha Carey
1857–1935
university educator, second president of Bryn Mawr College, author, feminist
Quaker
Dict Am Auth; Dict Am Bio supp v1; Index t Wom; Nat Cyc Am Bio v13; Not Am Wom; Twent Cen Bio Dict Not Am

1034. Kelley, Florence
1859–1932
social reformer, social worker
Quaker
Dict Am Bio supp v1; Index t Wom; Nat Cyc Am Bio v23; Not Am Wom

1035. Marot, Helen
1865–1940
labor leader

Quaker
Bio Dict Am Lab; Index t Wom

1036. Balch, Emily Greene
1867–1961
pacifist, social reformer, sociologist, economist, winner of the Nobel Peace Prize
Quaker
Index t Wom; Nat Cyc Am Bio csv7; Not Am Wom; Obit File

1037. Baker, Caroline Tilden
1873–1931
educator
Quaker
New York
Nat Cyc Am Bio v22

1038. Simms, Ruth Hanna Mc-Cormick
1880–1944
representative to Congress from Illinois, political leader, Republican National Committee member from New Mexico, dairy farmer
Quaker
Illinois; New Mexico
Dict Am Bio supp v3; Index t Wom; Nat Cyc Am Bio v34; Not Am Wom; Obit File

1039. Paul, Alice
1885–1977
feminist, founder of the National Women's Party, co-author of the ERA, suffragist, lawyer
Quaker
Cur Biog '77; Index t Wom; Obit File

1040. Stokes, Lilia Woodruff
1885–1973
Philadelphia civic worker, worker for Women's International League for Peace and Freedom, conservationist
Quaker
Pennsylvania
Nat Cyc Am Bio v58

1041. Page, Elizabeth (Merwin)
born 1889
author, novelist
Quaker
Index t Wom; Nat Cyc Am Bio csv6

1042. Stern, Elizabeth Gertrude Levin; Eleanor Morton; Elsie-Jeab
1889/90–1954
author, editor, social worker, political activist and antiwar worker
Quaker
Nat Cyc Am Bio v39; Obit File

1043. Suckow, Ruth Ann Vivien (Nuhn)
1892–1960

writer, novelist, short story writer
Quaker
Iowa; California
Dict Lit Bio v9; Index t Wom; Nat Cyc Am Bio v47; Not Am Wom supp v1; Obit File; Wom Lit; Wom Lit, More

1044. Blanshard, Frances Bradshaw
1895–1966
educator
Quaker
Connecticut
Nat Cyc Am Bio v54

1045. Strauss, Anna Lord
1899–1979
editor, club leader, feminist, political activist, New York civic worker, internationalist
Quaker
New York
Cur Biog '79; Index t Wom; Nat Cyc Am Bio csv10

1046. Waugh, Dorothy
flourished 1930s–40s
illustrator, author
Quaker
Index t Wom

1047. Vining, Elizabeth Janet Gray
born 1902
author
Quaker
Index t Wom

1048. West, Jessamyn [Mary]
born 1902/07
short story writer, novelist, poet, autobiographer, operetta librettist, screenplay writer
Quaker
California
Cur Biog '77; Dict Lit Bio v6; Index t Wom

SPIRITUALIST

1049. Whitman, Sarah Helen (Power)
1803/13–1878
poet, essayist, feminist
Spiritualist
Providence, RI
Cyc Am Bio; Dict Am Auth; Dict Am Bio; Dict Am Bio Men Time; Dict Lit Bio v1; Nat Cyc Am Bio v8; Not Am Wom; Wom Cent

1050. Fox, Ana Leah
1818?–90
spiritual medium
Spiritualist
Not Am Wom

1051. Hooker, Isabella Beecher
1822–1907
suffragist, feminist, philanthropist, lecturer, essayist
Spiritualist
Hartford, CT
Cyc Am Bio; Dict Am Auth; Dict Am Bio; Index t Wom; Not Am Wom; Twent Cen Bio Dict Not Am; Wom Cent

1052. Davis, Mary Fenn
1824–86
Spiritualist lecturer, reformer
Spiritualist
Not Am Wom

1053. Doten, Lizzie
born 1829
poet
Spiritualist
Boston, MA
Cyc Am Bio; Dict Am Auth

1054. Fox, Margaret
1833/36–1893
spiritual medium
Spiritualist
Cyc Am Bio; Index t Wom; Not Am Wom

1055. Severance, Juliet H.
born 1833
physician, abolitionist, feminist, temperance worker, political activist
Spiritualist
Wom Cent

1056. Jones, Amanda Theodosia
1835–1914
author, inventor of an improved process for canning food, poet, educator
Spiritualist
Chicago, IL
Cyc Am Bio; Dict Am Auth; Dict Am Bio; Nat Cyc Am Bio v7; Not Am Wom; Wom Cent

1057. Fox, Catherine "Kate"
1839?–92
spiritual medium
Spiritualist
Index t Wom; Not Am Wom

1058. Hopkins, Emma Curtis
1853–1925
Spiritualist teacher, mystic, leader in the New Thought movement
Spiritualist
Dict Am Rel Bio; Not Am Wom

1059. Militz, Annie Rix
1855–1924
religious author, New Thought minister, faith healer
New Thought
Nat Cyc Am Bio v21

1060. Piper, Leonor Evelina Simonds
1859–1950
medium
Spiritualist
Not Am Wom

1061. Seton, Julia Lorinda
born 1862
physician, founder of the New Thought Church, author
New Thought
Nat Cyc Am Bio v16

1062. Towne, Elizabeth Lois
1865–1960
metaphysical author, editor, lecturer
New Thought
Nat Cyc Am Bio v45 and csv1

1063. McPherson, Aimee Semple
1890–1944
religious leader, evangelist
Spiritualist
Dict Am Bio supp v3; Dict Am Rel Bio; Index t Wom; Nat Cyc Am Bio v34; Obit File

THEOSOPHICAL SOCIETY

1064. Blavatsky, Helena Petrovna (Hahn-Hahn)
1820/31–1891
occultist, mystic, founder of the semireligious Theosophical Society
Theosophist
Russian
Appl Cyc Am Bio; Cyc Am Bio; Dict Am Auth; Dict Am Bio; Dict Am Rel Bio; Nat Cyc Am Bio v15; Not Am Wom; Twent Cen Bio Dict Not Am; Wom Cent

1065. Tingley, Katherine Augusta Westcott
1847/52–1929
founder of the Point Loma Community in California, pacifist
Theosophist
Point Loma, CA
Dict Am Bio; Index t Wom; Nat Cyc Am Bio v15; Not Am Wom

1066. Haskell, Ella Louisa (Knowles)
1860/62–1911
lawyer, attorney general of Montana, politician, women's rights advocate, suffragist, Populist party worker
Theosophist
Dict Am Bio; Nat Cyc Am Bio v11

TRANSCENDENTALIST

1067. Ripley, Sophia Willard
1803–61
leading spirit in the Brook Farm commune experiment
Transcendentalist
Not Am Wom

1068. Peabody, Elizabeth Palmer
1804–94
educator, writer on education, educational reformer, kindergartner
Transcendentalist
Boston, MA
Cyc Am Bio; Dict Am Auth; Dict Am Bio; Dict Am Bio Men Time; Dict Lit Bio v1; Index t Wom; Not Am Wom; Twent Cen Bio Dict Not Am; Wom Cent

1069. Fuller, Sarah Margaret; Marchioness Ossoli; Sarah Margaret Fuller Ossoli
1810–50
author, critic, educator, feminist, philosopher, journalist, Transcendentalist revolutionary
Transcendentalist
Boston, MA
Cyc Am Bio; Dict Am Auth; Dict Am Bio; Dict Am Bio Men Time; Dict Lit Bio v1; Index t Wom; Nat Cyc Am Bio v3; Not Am Wom; Twent Cen Bio Dict Not Am; Wom Cent

1070. Hooper, Ellen Strugis
1812–48
Transcendentalist poet
Transcendentalist
Not Am Wom

1071. Sewall, Harriet (Winslow)
1819–89
suffragist, poet, religious poet, abolitionist
Transcendentalist
Boston, MA
Dict Am Auth; Nat Cyc Am Bio v10

1072. Tappan, Caroline Sturgis
1819–88
poet
Transcendentalist
Not Am Wom

1073. Cheney, Endah Dow (Littlehale)
1824–1904
philanthropist, author, abolitionist, suffragist, women's rights worker, Black civil rights worker, lecturer, philosopher
Transcendentalist

Boston, MA
Cyc Am Bio; Dict Am Auth; Dict Am Bio; Dict Lit Bio v1; Index t Wom; Nat Cyc Am Bio v9; Not Am Wom; Twent Cen Bio Dict Not Am; Wom Cent

UNITARIAN/ UNIVERSALIST

1074. Townsend, Eliza
1789–1854
poet
Unitarian
Boston, MA
Am Bio Dict; Cyc Am Bio; Dict Am Bio

1075. Shindler, Mary Stanley Bunce (Palmer) (Dana)
1810–83
author, poet, religious writer
Unitarian; Episcopalian
Nacogdoches, TX
Cyc Am Bio; Dict Am Auth; Dict Am Bio Men Time; Index t Wom

1076. Grew, Mary
1813–96
abolitionist, suffragist, feminist, Unitarian preacher, lecturer
Unitarian
Index t Wom; Not Am Wom; Wom Cent

1077. Coleman, Lucy Newhall; Lucy Colman
1817–1906
abolitionist, educator of Blacks, women's rights worker, suffragist, lecturer, health reformer
Universalist
Dict Am Bio; Nat Cyc Am Bio v4, Wom Cent

1078. Cary, Alice
1820–71
poet, novelist
Universalist
New York; Ohio
Cyc Am Bio; Dict Am Auth; Dict Am Bio; Dict Am Bio Men Time; Index t Wom; Nat Cyc Am Bio v1; Not Am Wom; Twent Cen Bio Dict Not Am; Wom Cent; Wom Lit, More

1079. Haynes, Lorenza
born 1820
Universalist minister
Universalist
Index t Wom; Wom Cent

1080. Livermore, Mary Ashton (Rice)
1820/21–1905
health reformer, hospital administrator, suffragist, temperance

worker, abolitionist, Civil War patriot, miscellaneous author
Universalist
Melrose, MA
Cyc Am Bio; Dict Am Auth; Dict Am Bio Men Time; Dict Am Rel Bio; Index t Wom; Nat Cyc Am Bio v1; Not Am Wom; Twent Cen Bio Dict Not Am; Wom Cent

1081. Soule, Caroline Augusta (White)
1824–1903/04
author, publisher, editor, church worker, Universalist minister, foreign missionary, social reformer, lecturer
Universalist
Cyc Am Bio; Dict Am Auth; Dict Am Bio Men Time; Index t Wom; Not Am Wom; Twent Cen Bio Dict Not Am

1082. Blackwell, Antoinette Louisa (Brown)
1825–1921
Universalist minister, author, lecturer, temperance worker, abolitionist, suffragist, women's rights worker, philosopher, poet, novelist
Unitarian; Congregationalist
Appl Cyc Am Bio; Cyc Am Bio; Dict Am Bio; Dict Am Bio Men Time; Index t Wom; Nat Cyc Am Bio v9 and v29; Not Am Wom; Twent Cen Bio Dict Not Am; Wom Cent

1083. Dunham, Emma Bedelia
born 1826
poet
Universalist
Wom Cent

1084. Gillette, Lucia Fidelia (Woolley); Lyra; Carrie Russell
born 1827
Universalist minister, author, poet
Universalist
Dict Am Auth; Index t Wom; Wom Cent

1085. Hanaford, Phoebe Ann (Coffin)
1829–1921
Universalist minister, historian, journalist, author, feminist, lecturer, chaplain of the Connecticut state legislature
Universalist
New Haven, CT
Cyc Am Bio; Dict Am Auth; Dict Am Bio; Index t Wom; Nat Cyc Am Bio v13; Not Am Wom; Twent Cen Bio Dict Not Am; Wom Cent

1086. Eddy, Sarah Stoddard
born 1831
suffragist
Universalist
Wom Cent

1087. Brown, Olympia; Mrs. John H. Willis
1835–1926
Universalist minister, suffragist, lecturer, feminist
Universalist; Unitarian
Cyc Am Bio and ad; Dict Am Bio; Index t Wom; Nat Cyc Am Bio v20; Not Am Wom; Wom Cent; Index t Wom

1088. Brown, Olympia; Mrs. John H. Willis
1835–1926
Universalist minister, suffragist, lecturer, feminist
Universalist; Unitarian
Cyc Am Bio and ad; Dict Am Bio; Index t Wom; Nat Cyc Am Bio v20; Not Am Wom; Wom Cent; Index t Wom

1089. Bowles, Ada Christina
born 1836
Universalist minister, suffragist
Universalist
Index t Wom; Wom Cent

1090. Chapin, Augusta Jane
1836–1905
Universalist minister, lecturer
Universalist
Index t Wom; Not Am Wom; Wom Cent

1091. Stearns, Sarah Burger
1836–post 1899
suffragist, women's rights worker, philanthropist, Civil War humanitarian, temperance worker, social reformer, educator of freedmen
Unitarian
Cyc Am Bio; Index t Wom; Nat Cyc Am Bio v10; Twent Cen Bio Dict Not Am; Wom Cent

1092. Deyo, Amanda
born 1838
Universalist minister, pacifist
Universalist
Wom Cent

1093. Banks, Sarah Gertrude
born 1839
physician, surgeon, suffragist
Unitarian
Michigan
Index t Wom; Nat Cyc Am Bio v18

1094. Graves, Mary H.
born 1839
Unitarian minister, author, lecturer

Unitarian
Index t Wom; Wom Cent

1095. Peckham, Mary Chace (Peck)
1839–92
author, fiction writer, poet, Civil War nurse, suffragist, women's rights worker
Unitarian
Providence, RI
Dict Am Auth; Nat Cyc Am Bio v9; Twent Cen Bio Dict Not Am

1096. Sunderland, Eliza Jane (Read)
1839–1910
lecturer, author, educator, temperance worker, women's rights worker, philosopher
Universalist
Michigan
Dict Am Bio; Nat Cyc Am Bio v10; Wom Cent

1097. Griswold, Harriet (Tyng) "Hattie"
1840/42–1910
author, poet
Unitarian
Cyc Am Bio and v3 ad; Dict Am Auth; Nat Cyc Am Bio v10; Twent Cen Bio Dict Not Am; Wom Cent

1098. Amies, Olive Pond
flourished 1871
temperance worker, educator
Universalist
Wom Cent

1099. Wallace, Emma R. (Gilson)
1841–1911
club leader, philanthropist
Universalist
Chicago, IL
Index t Wom; Wom Cent

1100. Hill, Agnes Leonard (Scanland); Molly Myrtle
1842–1917
poet, author, newspaper publisher, religious writer, novelist, prisoner's welfare worker, Universalist pastor
Universalist
Colorado
Dict Am Auth; Index t Wom; Nat Cyc Am Bio v17; Wom Cent

1101. Hunt, Augusta Merrill
born 1842
philanthropist, temperance worker, suffragist, prison reformer
Universalist
Wom Cent

1102. Utter, Rebecca (Palfrey)
born 1844

poet
Unitarian
Dict Am Auth

1103. Wilkes, Eliza Tupper
born 1844
clergyperson, missionary
Unitarian
Index t Wom; Wom Cent

1104. Gannett, Abbie M.
born 1845
author, women's rights worker
Unitarian
Wom Cent

1105. Hall, Florence Marion Howe
1845–1922
author, essayist, writer on etiquette, lecturer, suffragist
Unitarian
Plainfield, NJ
Dict Am Auth; Dict Am Bio; Nat Cyc Am Bio v19

1106. Catherwood, Mary (Hartwell)
1847–1902
novelist, writer of historical romances, children's author
Universalist
Illinois
Dict Am Auth; Dict Am Bio; Index t Wom; Nat Cyc Am Bio v9; Not Am Wom; Twent Cen Bio Dict Not Am; Wom Cent

1107. Kepley, Ada Miser
born 1847
lawyer, temperance agitator, Unitarian minister
Unitarian
Index t Wom; Wom Cent

1108. Payott, Annie Eliza (Fredenbur) Evens
1847–1927
welfare worker
Unitarian
San Francisco, CA
Nat Cyc Am Bio v21

1109. Diggs, Annie le Porte
1848/53–1916
Populist party leader, orator, politician, social reformer, temperance worker, journalist
Unitarian
Kansas
Canadian
Not Am Wom; Read Encyc Am West; Wom Cent

1110. Gould, Ellen M.
born 1848
philanthropist, suffragist
Unitarian
Rhode Island
Wom Cent

1111. Savage, Minnie Stebbins;
  Marion Lisle
born 1850
poet, author, Unitarian church
  worker, temperance worker
Unitarian
Wisconsin
Wom Cent

1112. Safford, Mary Augusta
born 1851
Unitarian minister, lecturer, suffragist, philanthropist
Unitarian

Index t Wom; Nat Cyc Am Bio
  v14

1113. Spencer, Anna Carpenter
  (Garlin)
1851–1931
Unitarian minister, journalist, educator, temperance worker, suffragist, pacifist, child-labor
  reformer, philanthropist
Unitarian
Dict Am Bio; Nat Cyc Am Bio v9
  and csv2; Not Am Wom

1114. Andrews, Mary Garard
born 1852
Universalist minister
Universalist
Index t Wom; Wom Cent

1115. Kurt, Katherine
born 1852
homeopathic physician, suffragist, temperance worker, Prohibition party worker
Universalist
Wom Cent

1116. Whitney, Mary Traffarn
born 1852
minister
Unitarian
Wom Cent

1117. Elliott, Maude Howe
1854–1948
author, novelist, suffragist
Unitarian
Chicago, IL
Dict Am Auth; Nat Cyc Am Bio
  v36; Not Am Wom; Twent Cen
  Bio Dict Not Am; Wom Cent

1118. Bennett, Ella May
born 1855
Universalist minister
Universalist
Wom Cent

1119. Mead, Lucia True
  (Ames)
1856–1936
pacifist, internationalist, suffragist, Black welfare and education
  worker, author

Unitarian
Nat Cyc Am Bio v28; Not Am
  Wom; Twent Cen Bio Dict Not
  Am

1120. Henry, Alice
1857–1943
journalist, women's trade union
  leader, feminist, suffragist, editor
Unitarian
Australian
Bio Dict Am Lab; Dict Am Bio
  supp v3; Not Am Wom

1121. Bagley, Blanche Pente-
  cost
born 1858
Unitarian minister, suffragist
Unitarian
British
Wom Cent

1122. Bartlett, Caroline Julia
born 1858
Unitarian minister, suffragist
Unitarian
Wom Cent

1123. Crane, Caroline Julia
  Bartlett
1858–1935
Unitarian minister, People's
  Church minister, urban reform-
  er, suffragist, city planner, sani-
  tation expert
Unitarian
Index t Wom; Nat Cyc Am Bio
  v15; Not Am Wom

1124. Steedman, Mary Balch
  Lippitt
born 1858
Providence, Rhode Island, civic
  worker
Unitarian
Providence, RI
Nat Cyc Am Bio csv2

1125. Klingelsmith, Margaret
  Center
1859–1931
librarian, author, legal authority,
  Democratic political activist,
  suffragist
Unitarian
Dict Am Bio

1126. Tupper, Mila Frances
born 1864
Unitarian minister
Unitarian
Wom Cent

1127. Newport, Elfreda Louisa
  Shaffer
born 1866
Universalist minister
Universalist
Wom Cent

1128. Sherman, Ellen Burns
1867–1956
author, suffragist
Unitarian
Massachusetts
Nat Cyc Am Bio v45

1129. Talbot, Anna Charlotte
  Hedges
born 1868
women's educator
Unitarian
New York
Nat Cyc Am Bio v30

1130. Eaves, Lucile
1869–1953
sociologist, labor relations expert
Unitarian
San Francisco, CA
Nat Cyc Am Bio v41 and csv1

1131. Robinson, Ethel Brown
  Blackwell
1870–1947
physician
Unitarian
Nat Cyc Am Bio v36

1132. Fitzgerald, Susan Grimes
  Walker
1871–1943
labor worker, trade unionist, suf-
  fragist
Unitarian
Boston, MA
Nat Cyc Am Bio v32

1133. Putnam, Bertha Haven
1872–1960
historian, history writer, authority on medieval history and
  criminology, educator
Unitarian
Nat Cyc Am Bio v43; Not Am
  Wom supp v1; Obit File

1134. Baker, Sarah Josephine
1873–1945
physician, public health adminis-
  trator, child health pioneer
Unitarian
New York, NY
Dict Am Bio supp v3; Index t
  Wom; Nat Cyc Am Bio v36;
  Not Am Wom; Obit File

1135. Smith, Georgine Nor-
  throp Wetherill
1873–1955
artist, art patron
Unitarian
Philadelphia, PA
Nat Cyc Am Bio v48

1136. Tillinghast, Anna Chur-
  chill Moulton
1874–1951
temperance worker, women's and
  children's welfare worker, Universalist pastor, suffragist
Universalist

Massachusetts
Nat Cyc Am Bio v45

1137. Ball, Bertha
born 1875
philanthropist, civic worker
Universalist
Muncie, IN
Nat Cyc Am Bio csv6

1138. Humphrey, Caroline Lou-
  ise
born 1875
educator
Unitarian
Boston, MA
Nat Cyc Am Bio csv2 and csv5

1139. Bole, Roberta Holden
1876–1950
philanthropist; patron of art, science, and education
Unitarian
Nat Cyc Am Bio v38

1140. Reinhardt, Aurelia Isa-
  belle Henry
1877–1948
president of Mills College, educator, religious worker, Unitarian
  minister
Unitarian
Oakland, CA
Dict Am Bio supp v4; Index t
  Wom; Not Am Wom; Obit File

1141. Abbott, Grace
1878–1939
public administrator, child welfare worker, social worker
Unitarian
Dict Am Bio supp v2; Index t
  Wom; Nat Cyc Am Bio v29 and
  csv3; Not Am Wom

1142. Nitzsche, Else Koenig
1880–1952
artist, author
Unitarian
Pennsylvania
Nat Cyc Am Bio v47

1143. Prouty, Olive (Chapin)
  Higgins
1882–1974
author, novelist
Unitarian
Massachusetts
Index t Wom; Nat Cyc Am Bio
  v57; Obit File

1144. Townshend, Anna Draper
born 1882
suffragist, Connecticut state legis-
  lator from New Haven, New
  Haven civic worker
Unitarian
New Haven, CT
Nat Cyc Am Bio csv6

1145. Oliver, Edna May
1883–1942

character actor, comedian
Unitarian
California
Index t Wom; Nat Cyc Am Bio csv6; Obit File

1146. Hubbard, Theodora Kimball
1887–1935
landscape architect, city planner
Unitarian
Massachusetts
Nat Cyc Am Bio v28 and csv3

1147. Eliot, Martha May
1891–1978
pediatrician, public health official, president of the American Health Association, UNICEF member, US Children's Bureau official
Unitarian
Massachusetts
Cur Biog '78; Index t Wom; Nat Cyc Am Bio v60

1148. Warner, Nell Walker;
Mrs. Emil Shostrum
born 1891
artist
Unitarian
Los Angeles, CA
Nat Cyc Am Bio csv8

1149. Barus, Jane Garey
1892–1977
suffragist; political activist; prison reformer; Montclair, New Jersey, civic worker; antinuclear activist; anti–Vietnam war worker
Unitarian
Montclair, NJ
Nat Cyc Am Bio v60

1150. Taussig, Helen Brooke
born 1898
physician, pediatric cardiologist, president of the American Heart Association
Unitarian
Index t Wom; Nat Cyc Am Bio csv11

1151. Warburton, Amber Arthun
1898–1976
economist, educational guidance consultant
Unitarian
Nat Cyc Am Bio v59

1152. Wills, Doris Margaret Wood
1902–63
astronomer, research engineer
Unitarian
Pennsylvania
Nat Cyc Am Bio v53

1153. Beer, Lisle; Eloise Crowell Smith
born 1903
artist, author, puppeteer
Unitarian
Nat Cyc Am Bio csv9

1154. Neuberger, Maurine
born 1907
US senator from Oregon, politician
Unitarian
Oregon
Index t Wom; Nat Cyc Am Bio csv10

UNITED CHURCH OF CHRIST

1155. Greaves, Jessie Royer
1874–1967
educator of the blind
United Church of Christ
Pennsylvania
Nat Cyc Am Bio v53

WESLEYAN

1156. Palmer, Phoebe Worrall
1807–74
social reformer, religious writer, Methodist leader, Wesleyan evangelist
Wesleyan
New York, NY
Cyc Am Bio; Dict Am Auth; Dict Am Rel Bio; Index t Wom; Not Am Wom

III. Ethnic and Racial Index

1. Nitsch, Helen Alice (Matthews); Catherine Owen
18?–1889
domestic scientist, writer on domestic science
Plainfield, NJ

Dict Am Auth

2. Safford, Mary Augusta
born 1851
Unitarian minister, lecturer, suffragist, philanthropist
Unitarian

Index t Wom; Nat Cyc Am Bio v14

3. Moreland, Mary L.
born 1859
Congregationalist minister, temperance worker
Congregationalist
Illinois

Wom Cent

AFRICAN

4. Wheatley, Phillis
1735/53–1784
poet
Boston, MA
Black; African
Am Bio Dict; Cyc Am Bio; Dict Am Bio Men Time; Encyc Black Am; Encyc South Hist; Index t Wom; Negro Alman; Nat Cyc Am Bio v1; Not Am Wom; Prof Negro Wom v1; Wom Lit; Wom Lit, More

5. Morier
flourished 1780s
baker, confectioner
Black; African
Prof Negro Wom v1

AUSTRALIAN

6. Booth, Agnes; Marian Agnes Land Rookes
1841/46–1910
actor
Australian
Dict Am Bio; Index t Wom; Nat Cyc Am Bio v1; Not Am Wom; Wom Cent

7. Henry, Alice
1857–1943
journalist, women's trade union leader, feminist, suffragist, editor
Unitarian
Australian
Bio Dict Am Lab; Dict Am Bio supp v3; Not Am Wom

8. Robson, May; May Robison
1858/65–1942
stage and screen actor
Australian
Dict Am Bio supp v3; Index t Wom; Not Am Wom; Obit File

9. Bert, Mabel
born 1862
actor
Australian
Wom Cent

10. Wylie, Ida Alexa Ross
1875–1959
novelist, scenarist, short story writer
Australian
Obit File

11. Caraway, Hattie Ophelia Wyatt
1878–1950
Democratic US senator from Arkansas
Methodist
Arkansas

Australian
Dict Am Bio supp v4; Dict Aust Bio; Encyc South Hist; Eng Wom; Index t Wom; Nat Cyc Am Bio v44 and csv4; Not Am Wom; Obit File

12. Stewart, Dorothy M.
1891/97–1954
theatrical agent, composer, pianist, author
Australian
Index t Wom

13. Rosenstein, Nettie
born 1897
fashion designer, philanthropist, business executive
Australian
Index t Wom

14. Winter, Ella
1898–1980
journalist, writer on communism, Communist party worker
Australian
Cur Biog '80

15. Binner, Madam
flourished 1930s
business executive
Australian
Index t Wom

16. Lawrence, Marjorie
1908–79
Metropolitan Opera soprano singer
Australian
Cur Biog '79

17. Rogers, Vesta Marie
born 1909
physician
Australian
Index t Wom

18. Anderson, Erica Kellnor Collier
born 1914
photographer
Australian
Index t Wom

19. Reddy, Helen
born 1941
popular singer, feminist
Australian
Cur Biog '75

AUSTRIAN

20. Harazthy, Mrs.
flourished 1840s
western pioneer
Austrian
Index t Wom

21. Cappiani, Luisa
flourished 1860s–80s
opera singer, music educator
Austrian
Wom Cent

22. Juch, Emma Antonia Johanna
1860/63–1939
soprano opera singer
Austrian
Index t Wom; Nat Cyc Am Bio v6; Not Am Wom; Wom Cent

23. Serrano, Emelia Benic
flourished 1890s
opera singer
Austrian; Hungarian
Wom Cent

24. Zeisler, Fannie Bloomfield
1863/66–1927
concert pianist
Chicago, IL
Austrian
Dict Am Bio; Nat Cyc Am Bio v14; Not Am Wom; Wom Cent

25. Carnegie, Hattie (Zanft)
1877/89–1956
fashion designer, entrepreneur, clothing retailer
Austrian
Dict Am Bio supp v6; Index t Wom; Not Am Wom supp v1; Obit File

26. Gruenberg, Sidonie Matsner
1881–1974
parent education leader; director of the Child Study Association of America, specialist in child guidance, parent education, and family relationships; nonfiction writer; lecturer
Austrian
Cur Biog '74; Index t Wom; Not Am Wom supp v1; Obit File

27. Baum, Hedwig "Vicki"; Mrs. Richard Lerf
1888–1960/62
novelist, playwright, screenwriter
Jewish
Hollywood, CA
Austrian
Dict Am Bio supp v6; Index t Wom; Nat Cyc Am Bio v52; Obit File

28. Brummer, Ethel Serly
1888–1952
vaudeville dancer
Austrian
Obit File

29. Deutsche, Naomi
born 1890
nurse
Austrian
Index t Wom

30. Grossinger, Jennie
1892–1972
philanthropist; hotel executive, owner, and manager; country club owner
Jewish
Catskill Mountains, NY
Austrian
Cur Biog '73; Index t Wom; Not Am Wom supp v1; Obit File

31. Godowski, Dagmar
born 1897
actor
Austrian
Index t Wom

32. Christians, Mady
1900–51
Broadway stage actor
Austrian
Obit File

33. Kelner, Sophie
flourished 1930s
dentist
Austrian
Index t Wom

34. Schwartz, Bertha
1901–61
judge, lawyer, Zionist
Jewish
Austrian
Index t Wom; Nat Cyc Am Bio v51

35. Kayne, Hilde
born 1903
artist
Austrian
Index t Wom

36. Losch, Tilly
1905/07–1975
stage and screen dancer, choreographer
Austrian
Cur Biog '76; Obit File

37. Trapp, Maria Augusta
born 1905
singer
Austrian
Index t Wom

38. Wellman, Margaret
1906–56
author, traveler, explorer
Austrian
Obit File

39. Weil, Lisl
born 1910
artist, author
Austrian
Index t Wom

40. Koffler, Ylla "Camilla"
1911–55
photographer, animal photographer
Austrian
Obit File

41. Horvath, Stephanie
1913–60
police officer, undercover agent
Austrian
Obit File

42. Mankiewicz, Rose Stradner
1913–58
actor
Austrian
Obit File

43. Lamarr, Hedy
born 1915
actor
Austrian
Index t Wom

BARBADIAN

44. Staupers, Mabel Keaton
born 1890
nurse
Barbadian; Black
Encyc Black Am

BAVARIAN

45. Hutton, Elizabeth "Bettina" Riddle, Baroness von
born 187?; married 1897
novelist
Bavarian (American expatriate to Bavaria)
Dict Am Auth; Index t Wom

BELGIAN

46. Hepburn, Audrey
born 1829
actor
Belgian
Index t Wom

47. Barbot, Blanche Hermine
born 1842
musical director, pianist
Belgian
Wom Cent

48. Savage, Marie Ghislaine Metten (Mamen)
1865–1957
opera singer
Belgian
Obit File

49. Stevens, Augusta de Grasse
1865–94
novelist, art critic
Belgian
Dict Am Auth; Index t Wom

50. Sylvia, Marguerite; Marguerite Alice Helen Smith Mann Smith
1875–1957
opera singer
Belgian
Obit File

51. Hare, Jeannette R.
born 1898
sculptor
Belgian
Index t Wom

52. Sardeau, Helen; Mrs. George Biddle
1899–1969
sculptor
New York
Belgian
Nat Cyc Am Bio v55

BLACK

53. Charlotte
flourished 1708

litigant who challenged the legality of slavery in court
Black; Canadian
Prof Negro Wom v1

54. Alice
1686–1802 [sic]
ferry captain, slave
Philadelphia, PA
Black
Am Bio Dict

55. Amy
1686–1826 [sic]
pioneer, slave
Charleston, SC
Black
Appl Cyc Am Bio

56. Terry, Lucy
1730–1821
poet
Black
Negro Alman; Prof Negro Wom v1

57. Freeman, Elizabeth; Mum Bett
1732?–1829
litigant who sued for her freedom and won, midwife
Black
Prof Negro Wom v1

58. Wheatley, Phillis
1735/53–1784
poet
Boston, MA
Black; African
Am Bio Dict; Cyc Am Bio; Dict Am Bio Men Time; Encyc Black Am; Encyc South Hist; Index t Wom; Negro Alman; Nat Cyc Am Bio v1; Not Am Wom; Prof Negro Wom v1; Wom Lit; Wom Lit, More

59. Slew, Jenney
flourished 1766
litigant who sued for her freedom from slavery and won
Black
Prof Negro Wom v1

60. Ferguson, Catherine
circa 1749–1854
religious and welfare worker, baker
New York
Black
Index t Wom; Our Count

61. Morier
flourished 1780s
baker, confectioner
Black; African
Prof Negro Wom v1

62. Allen, Sarah
1764–1849
missionary, pioneer

Black
Index t Wom; Negro Alman; Prof
Negro Wom v1

101. Beasley, Matilda, Mother
1834–1903
educator, social worker, Catholic
nun
Catholic
Georgia
Black
Negro Alman; Prof Negro Wom

102. Allerton, Ellen Palmer
1835–93
poet
Black
Dict Am Auth; Negro Alman

**103. Coppin, Fanny Marion
Jackson**
1835/37–1912/18
educator, foreign missionary, so-
cial worker, lecturer, women's
rights worker
Black
Encyc Black Am; Index t Wom;
Negro Alman; Not Am Wom;
Prof Negro Wom

104. Smith, Amanda Berry
1836/37–1915
Protestant evangelist, missionary
to Africa, faith healer, singer
Protestant
Black
Index t Wom; Negro Alman; Not
Am Wom; Prof Negro Wom v1

**105. Grimke, Charlotte L. For-
ten**
1837/38–1914
educator, author, poet
Black
Index t Wom; Negro Alman; Not
Am Wom; Prof Negro Wom v1

106. Vashon, Susan Paul
1838–1912
educator, nurse, Civil War relief
organizer
Black
Index t Wom; Negro Alman; Prof
Negro Wom v1

**107. Putnam, Georgianna
Frances**
1839–1914
educator, school principal
Black
Index t Wom; Negro Alman; Prof
Negro Wom v1

108. Gordon, Georgia
flourished 1870
gospel singer
Black
Prof Negro Wom v1

109. Hudlun, Anna Elizabeth
1840–1914

social worker, welfare worker,
philanthropist
African Methodist Episcopal
Zion
Black
Index t Wom; Negro Alman; Prof
Negro Wom v1

110. Jackson, Jennie
flourished 1870s
gospel singer
Black
Prof Negro Wom v1

111. Lewis, Mabel
flourished 1870s
gospel singer
Black
Prof Negro Wom v1

112. Patterson, Mary Jane
1840–94
educator
Philadelphia, PA
Black
Index t Wom; Negro Alman; Prof
Negro Wom vl

113. Selika, Marie
flourished 1870s–80s
singer
Black
Index t Wom

114. Tate, Minnie
flourished 1870s
gospel singer
Black
Prof Negro Wom v1

115. Washington, Rachel M.
flourished 1870s
music educator, pianist
Black
Index t Wom

116. Allen, Mary Wood
born 1841
physician, author, lecturer
Black
Negro Alman

**117. Ruffin, Josephine St.
Pierre**
1842–1924
clubwoman, Black leader, Black
welfare and rights worker, president of the National Federation
of Afro-American Women,
Union patriot in the Civil War
Black
Index t Wom; Negro Alman; Not
Am Wom; Prof Negro Wom v1

118. Preston, Frances E. L.
1844–1929
temperance lecturer, organist, elocutionist
Black
Negro Alman; Prof Negro Wom
v1

119. Barboza, Mary (Garnet)
1845–90
educator, missionary
Black
Nat Cyc Am Bio v5

120. Lewis, Edmonia [Mary]
1845–90
sculptor
Native American (Chippewa);
Black
Cyc Am Bio; Encyc Black Am;
Index t Wom; Nat Cyc Am Bio
v5; Negro Alman; Not Am
Wom; Prof Negro Wom v1;
Twent Cen Bio Dict Not Am

**121. Mahoney, Mary Elizabeth
"Eliza"**
1845/53–1923/26
nurse
Black
Encyc Black Am; Index t Wom

122. Mitchell, Nellie Brown
1845?–1924
singer, music educator
New Hampshire
Black
Index t Wom; Prof Negro Wom
v1

123. McCoy, Mary Eleanora
born 1846
philanthropist
Detroit, MI
Black
Prof Negro Wom v1

**124. Steward, Susan S. McKin-
ney**
1848–1919
physician
Brooklyn, NY
Black
Index t Wom; Prof Negro Wom
v1

125. Taylor, Susie Baker King
born 1848
educator, Civil War nurse
Black
Prof Negro Wom v1

**126. Anderson, Caroline Virgin-
ia Still**
1849–1919
physician
Philadelphia, PA
Black
Index t Wom; Negro Alman; Prof
Negro Wom

**127. Bowen, Ariel Serena
Hedges**
1849–1904
musician, music educator
Black
Index t Wom; Prof Negro Wom

128. Pettey, Sarah Dudley
flourished 1880

missionary leader
African Methodist Episcopal
Zion
Black
Prof Negro Wom v1

**129. Yates, Josephine Silone;
R. K. Potter**
1852–1912
educator, author
Missouri
Black
Index t Wom; Negro Alman; Prof
Negro Wom v1

130. Mossell, Mary Ella
1853–86
educator, missionary to Haiti
Black
Index t Wom; Negro Alman; Prof
Negro Wom v1

131. Laney, Lucy Craft
1854–1933
educator, founder of the Haines
Normal Institute
Georgia
Black
Index t Wom; Negro Alman; Not
Am Wom; Prof Negro Wom v1

**132. Washington, Olivia David-
son**
1854/59–1889
fund-raiser
Black
Negro Alman; Prof Negro Wom
v1

133. Davis, Elizabeth Lindsay
born 1855
author, clubwoman
Illinois
Black
Prof Negro Wom v1

134. Mossell, Gertrude Bustill
born 1855
newspaper editor, author
Pennsylvania
Black
Negro Alman; Prof Negro Wom
v1

135. Williams, Fannie Barrier
1855–1944
lecturer, civic leader, librarian,
clubwoman
Chicago, IL
Black
Dict Am Bio supp v3; Not Am
Wom; Prof Negro Wom v1

**136. Baldwin, Mary Louise
"Maria Louisa"**
1856–1919/22
educator, civic leader
Massachusetts
Black
Index t Wom; Negro Alman; Not
Am Wom; Prof Negro Wom

137. Cooper, Anna Julia Haywood
1858/68–1964
educator, scholar
Black
Negro Alman; Not Am Wom supp v1; Prof Negro Wom v1

138. Shorter, Susie
1859–1912
educator, author, businessperson
Black
Index t Wom; Negro Alman

139. Merritt, Emma Frances Grayson
1860–1933
educator
Black
Encyc Black Am; Negro Alman; Prof Negro Wom v1

140. Plummer, Nellie Arnold
1860–1924
educator
Black
Encyc Black Am

141. Williams, Maria Selika
flourished 1880s
coloratura soprano singer
Black
Prof Negro Wom v1

142. Matthews, Victoria Earle
1861–98
social worker, mission society founder, clubwoman
Fort Valley, GA
Black
Index t Wom; Negro Alman; Prof Negro Wom v1

143. Washington, Josephine Turpin
1861–1949
journalist, educator
Black
Negro Alman; Prof Negro Wom v1

144. Talbert, Mary Burnett
1862/66–1923
educator, social reformer, prison reformer, Black rights worker, club leader
Black
Index t Wom; Negro Alman; Prof Negro Wom v1

145. Wells-Barnett, Ida Bell; Iola
1862/64–1931
Black equal rights advocate, journalist, newspaper publisher, clubwoman, lecturer, antilynching reformer
Black
Encyc Black Am; Encyc South Hist; Eng Wom; Index t Wom; Negro Alman; Not Am Wom; Prof Negro Wom v1 and v2

146. Logan, Adelle Hunt
1863–1915
educator, a founder of Tuskegee Institute
Black
Negro Alman; Prof Negro Wom v1

147. Thoms, Adah B. Samuels
1863?–1943
nursing leader
Black
Index t Wom; Not Am Wom

148. Frazier, Susan Elizabeth
1864/66–1909/24
educator, president of the 369th Infantry of the New York National Guard's Women's Auxiliary
Black
Index t Wom; Negro Alman; Prof Negro Wom v1

149. Mason, Lena
born 1864
Methodist evangelist
Methodist
Black
Prof Negro Wom v1

150. Barrett, Janie Porter
1865–1948
social welfare leader, educator
Virginia
Black
Dict Am Bio supp v4; Negro Alman; Index t Wom; Not Am Wom; Prof Negro Wom

151. McKane, Alice Woodby
born 1865
physician, hospital and nursing school founder
Black
Encyc Black Am

152. Walker, Maggie Lena
1865/67–1934
insurance and banking executive, president of the Consolidated Bank and Trust Co.
Richmond, VA
Black
Encyc Black Am; Index t Wom; Not Am Wom; Prof Negro Wom v1

153. Washington, Margaret Murry
1865–1925
women's organizer, Tuskegee College dean of women, author
Black
Index t Wom; Negro Alman; Prof Negro Wom v1

154. Gordon, Nora Antonia
1866–1901
educator, missionary to Africa

Black
Negro Alman; Prof Negro Wom v1

155. Hilyer, Andrew F., Mrs.
died 1916
musician
Black
Index t Wom

156. Simpson, Georgianna R.
1866–1944
professor, linguist
Black
Negro Alman; Prof Negro Wom v1

157. Gray, Ida
born 1867
dentist
Black
Negro Alman; Prof Negro Wom v1

158. Hackley, Emma Azalia Smith
1867–1922
coloratura soprano singer, composer, choir director, sponsor of Black folk music festivals
Black
Index t Wom; Negro Alman; Not Am Wom; Prof Negro Wom v1

159. Walker, Sarah McWilliams Breedlove "Madame C. J."
1867/69–1919
cosmetics executive and manufacturer, millionaire entrepreneur
Black
Dict Am Bio; Encyc Black Am; Index t Wom; Negro Alman; Not Am Wom; Prof Negro Wom v1

160. Jones, Matilda Sissierette Joyner; Black Patti
1868/69–1933
dramatic soprano singer
Black
Encyc Black Am; Index t Wom; Nat Cyc Am Bio v13; Not Am Wom; Prof Negro Wom

161. McAdoo, Martha Allen
1868–1936
singer, social worker
Black
Encyc Black Am

162. Wesley, Rachel Parker
died 1918
litigant who sued for her freedom from slavery and won
Maryland
Black
Prof Negro Wom v1

163. Marshall, Harriet Gibbs
1869–1941
pianist, music educator

Black
Encyc Black Am; Index t Wom

164. Bergen, Flora Batson
1870–1906
singer
Black
Index t Wom

165. Cook, Myrtle Foster
1870–1951
educator, civic leader, financier, Black civil rights worker
Kansas City, KS
Black; Canadian
Negro Alman; Prof Negro Wom

166. Europe, Mary L.
flourished 1900s
pianist
Black
Index t Wom

167. Hilyer, Amanda Gray
1870–1957
pharmacist
Black
Encyc Black Am

168. Hunton, Addie Waites
born 1870
Red Cross worker, World War I relief worker
Black
Prof Negro Wom v2

169. Jackson, May Howard
1870/77–1931
sculptor
Black
Index t Wom; Negro Alman; Prof Negro Wom v1

170. Mallone, Annie M. Turnbo; Annie Turnbo-Mallone
1870–1957
business executive, philanthropist
Black
Encyc Black Am; Not Am Wom supp v1

171. Williams, Molly
flourished pre–1900
fire fighter
New York
Black
Prof Negro Wom v1

172. Beasley, Delilah Leontium
1871–1934
historian, journalist, pacifist
California
Black
Encyc Black Am; Negro Alman; Prof Negro Wom

173. Holland, Annie Wealthy
1871–1934
educator
North Carolina

Black
Negro Alman; Prof Negro Wom v1

174. Butler, Selena Sloan
1872?–1964
community leader, founder of the National Congress of Colored Parents and Teachers Association
Black
Not Am Wom supp v1

175. Cromwell, Otelia
1873–1972
educator, author
Black
Encyc Black Am

176. Johnson, J. Rosamond
1873–1954
musician, actor, composer of the Black national anthem "Lift Every Voice and Sing"
Black
Obit File

177. Hare, Maud Cuney
1874–1936
pianist, musicologist, author
Black
Encyc Black Am; Negro Alman; Prof Negro Wom v1

178. Randolph, Virginia Estelle
1874/76–1958
social worker, educator
Virginia
Black
Index t Wom; Negro Alman; Prof Negro Wom v1

179. Warren, Sadie
born 1874
newspaper publisher
Black
Encyc Black Am

180. Williams, Lulu Margaret Roberts
1874/75–1945
educator, social reformer, Black student aid worker
Black
Negro Alman; Prof Negro Wom v1

181. Bethune, Mary McLeod
1875–1955
educator, founder and president of Bethune-Cookman College, director of the Negro Affairs National Youth Council, civil rights worker, women's rights worker
Daytona Beach, FL

Black
Dict Am Bio supp v5; Dict Am Rel Bio; Encyc Black Am; Encyc South Hist; Index t Wom; Nat Cyc Am Bio v49; Negro Alman; Negro Her Lib v1; Not Am Wom supp v1; Prof Negro Wom; Obit File

182. Huntington, Addie D. Waites
1875–1943
civil rights worker, YWCA official
Black
Not Am Wom

183. Nelson, Alice Ruth Dunbar (Moore)
1875–1935
author, editor, social worker
Louisiana
Black
Encyc Black Am; Negro Alman; Not Am Wom; Prof Negro Wom v1

184. White, Eartha Mary Magdalene
1876–1974
social welfare worker, community leader, businessperson
Black
Not Am Wom supp v1

185. Brown, Sue M.
1877–1941
clubwoman, educator, author, suffragist, women's rights worker, Black civil rights worker
Black
Negro Alman; Prof Negro Wom

186. Fuller, Meta Vaux Warrick
1877–1967/68
sculptor
Black
Encyc Black Am; Index t Wom; Negro Alman; Not Am Wom supp v1; Prof Negro Wom v2

187. Burroughs, Nannie Helen
1878/83–1961
educator, founder of the National Trade and Professional School for Women and Girls, women's rights worker
Baptist
Black
Index t Wom; Negro Alman; Not Am Wom supp v1; Prof Negro Wom

188. Bass, Charlotta A. Spears
1880/90–1969
Progressive party vice-presidential candidate in 1952, civil rights reformer, editor
Black
Negro Alman; Not Am Wom supp v1

189. de Wolf, Sister
flourished 1910s
singer
Black
Index t Wom

190. Holf, Nora Douglas
flourished 1910s–60s
musician, composer, singer, music critic
Black
Prof Negro Wom v2

191. Talbert, Florence Cole
flourished 1910s
singer
Black
Index t Wom

192. Walker, Rachel
flourished 1910s
singer
Black
Index t Wom

193. Harrison, Hazel Lucile
1881/83–1969
pianist, music educator
Black
Encyc Black Am; Index t Wom; Not Am Wom supp v1

194. Lewis, Sarah Masten
died 1931
singer
Black
Index t Wom

195. Stewart, Sallie W.
1881–1951
educator, clubwoman, realtor, lecturer, Black women's welfare worker
Indiana
Black
Negro Alman; Prof Negro Wom v1

196. Anderson, Violette
born 1882
lawyer
Chicago, IL
English; Black
Encyc Black Am

197. Branch, Mary E.
1882–1945
educator
Black
Encyc Black Am

198. Brown, Charlotte Eugenia Hawkins
1882/83–1961
educator, founder of the Palmer Memorial Institute, YWCA national board member
North Carolina

Black
Encyc Black Am; Index t Wom; Negro Alman; Not Am Wom supp v1; Obit File; Prof Negro Wom v1 and v2

199. Hunter, Jane Edna
1882–1971
social worker, nurse, educator, clubwoman
Cleveland, OH
Black
Index t Wom; Negro Alman; Prof Negro Wom v1

200. McClendon, Rose
1884–1936
actor
Black
Encyc Black Am; Not Am Wom

201. Mitchell, Abbie
1884–1960
singer, actor
Black
Index t Wom; Negro Alman; Not Am Wom supp v1

202. Bowser, Rosa Dixon
1885–1931
educator, clubwoman
Richmond, VA
Black
Negro Alman; Prof Negro Wom

203. Curtis, Namahyoke Sockum
died 1935
Des Moines civic leader, nurse
Des Moines, IA
Black
Prof Negro Wom v2

204. Gafford, Alice
born 1886
painter
Black
Negro Alman

205. Johnson, Georgia Douglas
1886–1966
poet, composer, author
Black
Encyc Black Am; Index t Wom; Negro Alman; Obit File; Wom Lit, More

206. Rainey, Gertrude Malissa Nix Pridgett "Ma"
1886–1939
blues singer
Black
Dict Am Bio supp v2; Encyc Black Am; Not Am Wom

207. Calloway-Byron, Mayme
flourished 1917
singer
Black
Index t Wom

208. Waring, Laura Wheeler
1887–1948
painter, educator
Black
Encyc Black Am; Negro Alman

209. Price, Florence Beatrice Smith
1888–1953
composer, instrumentalist, pianist, organist, music educator
Black
Index t Wom; Not Am Wom supp v1

210. Smith, Lucy Harth
1888–1955
educator, educational administrator
Kentucky
Black
Dict Am Bio supp v5

211. Clark, Septima Poinsette
flourished 1920s–80s
civil rights leader
Black
Prof Negro Wom v2

212. Murray, Charlotte Wallace
married 1915
singer, music educator
Black
Index t Wom

213. Rollins, Charlemae Hill
flourished 1920s–40s
librarian
Black
Encyc Black Am; Index t Wom

214. Staupers, Mabel Keaton
born 1890
nurse
Barbadian; Black
Encyc Black Am

215. Bearden, Bessye J.
1891–1943
educator, first female member of the New York City school board, clubwoman
New York, NY
Black
Encyc Black Am; Index t Wom

216. Savage, Augusta Christine
1892/1900–1962
sculptor
Black
Encyc Black Am; Index t Wom; Negro Alman; Not Am Wom supp v1

217. Fauset, Crystal Dreda Bird
1893–1965
race relations specialist, state legislator
Black
Not Am Wom supp v1

218. Hagan, Helen Eugenia
1893–1964
pianist, music educator
Black
Encyc Black Am; Index t Wom; Prof Negro Wom v2

219. Larson, Nella
1893–1963
author, nurse
Black
Encyc Black Am; Wom Lit; Wom Lit, More

220. Ellis, Evelyn
1894–1958
actor
Black
Obit File

221. Harsh, Vivian
1894–1960
librarian
Black
Encyc Black Am

222. Smith, Bessie
1894–1937
blues singer
Black
Dict Am Bio supp v2; Encyc Black Am; Index t Wom; Negro Alman

223. Grant, Anita
flourished 1925
tennis and basketball player, promoter of women's sports
Black
Encyc Black Am

224. Hunter, Alberta
born 1895
jazz and blues singer and songwriter
Black
Cur Biog '70

225. McDaniel, Hattie
1895/98–1952
radio and television actor, singer
Black
Dict Am Bio supp v5; Encyc Black Am; Index t Wom; Not Am Wom supp v1; Obit File

226. Mills, Florence
1895–1927
singer, dancer, stage comedian
Black
Encyc Black Am; Index t Wom; Negro Alman; Not Am Wom

227. Robeson, Eslanda Cardoza Goode
1896–1965
author, civil rights reformer, anthropologist
Black
Index t Wom; Not Am Wom supp v1

228. Waters, Ethel
1896/1900–1977
gospel and blues singer; stage, screen, and television actor
Black
Cur Biog '77; Encyc Black Am; Index t Wom; Negro Alman; Obit File; Prof Negro Wom v2

229. Derricotte, Juliette
1897–1931
educator, dean of women at Fiske University
Black
Encyc Black Am; Prof Negro Wom v1

230. Jessye, Eva Alberta
1897–post 1930s
music director, educator, writer on music, conductor
Black
Encyc Black Am; Index t Wom

231. Mabley, Jackie "Moms"
1897–1975
comedian, vaudevillian
Black
Cur Biog '75; Negro Alman; Obit File

232. Thomas, Anna Perry
born 1897
educator
Black
Encyc Black Am

233. Alexander, Sadie Tanner Mossell
born 1898
lawyer
Black
Encyc Black Am; Negro Alman; Prof Negro Wom

234. Armstrong, Lillian "Lil" Hardin
1898–1971
jazz pianist
Black
Encyc Black Am

235. Carter, Eunice Hunton
1899–1970
lawyer, community leader, social worker
New York
Black
Not Am Wom supp v1; Obit File

236. Hedgeman, Anna Arnold
born 1899
New York civic leader, New York mayor's cabinet member, consultant on urban affairs and Afro-American studies, assistant to the administrator of the Federal Security Agency
Black
Encyc Black Am; Negro Alman; Negro Her Lib v1

237. Bailey, Margaret E.
flourished 1930s–60s
lieutenant colonel in US Army, World War I nurse
Black
Encyc Black Am; Prof Negro Wom v2

238. Carrington, Elsie
flourished 1930s–70s
nurse
Black
Encyc Black Am

239. Dethridge, Luvena Wallace
flourished 1930s
singer
Black
Index t Wom

240. Freeman, Frankie Muse
flourished 1930s–60s
lawyer, Black civil rights leader
Black
Encyc Black Am

241. Hubbard, Charlotte Moton
flourished 1930s–70s
US deputy assistant secretary of state for public affairs, educator
Black
Encyc Black Am; Negro Alman; Negro Her Lib v1

242. Hymes, Lula
flourished 1930s
track athlete
Black
Encyc Black Am

243. Jackson, Juanita A.
flourished 1930s–60s
lawyer, civil rights worker
Black
Encyc Black Am

244. Kidd, Mae Street
flourished 1930s–70s
Kentucky state legislator
Kentucky
Black
Encyc Black Am

245. Mercer, Mabel
born 1900
nightclub singer
Black
Cur Biog '73

246. Moten, Etta
flourished 1930s
actor, singer
Black
Index t Wom

247. Nickerson, Camille L.
flourished 1930s
pianist, music educator
Black
Index t Wom

248. Thomas, Flora
flourished 1930s
pianist
Black
Index t Wom

249. Thompson, Eva Bell
flourished 1930s–60s
author, editor
Black
Encyc Black Am

250. Welcome, Verda Freeman
flourished 1930s–60s
educator, Maryland state legislator
Maryland
Black
Encyc Black Am

251. Young, N. Louise
flourished 1930s–40s
physician
Black
Encyc Black Am

252. Delany, Clarissa Scott
1901–27
poet, educator
Black
Encyc Black Am

253. Hurston, Zora Neale
1901/03–1960
author, novelist, folklorist, cultural anthropologist
Black
Dict Am Bio supp v6; Encyc Black Am; Index t Wom; Negro Alman; Not Am Wom; Obit File; Prof Negro Wom v2; Wom Lit; Wom Lit, More

254. Osborne, Estelle Massey
1901–post 1976
nurse, nursing educator, army nurse in World War II
Black
Negro Alman; Prof Negro Wom v2

255. Sampson, Edith (Spurlock)
1901–79
lawyer, judge, alternate delegate to the UN, lecturer
Illinois
Black
Cur Biog '80; Encyc Black Am; Index t Wom; Negro Alman; Negro Her Lib v1

256. Whaley, Ruth Whitehead
born 1901
lawyer
Black
Encyc Black Am

257. Anderson, Marian
born 1902/08
contralto concert singer, US alternate delegate to the UN, 1958–59
Baptist
Black
Encyc Black Am; Index t Wom; Nat Cyc Am Bio csv9; Negro Alman; Negro Her Lib v1; Prof Negro Wom; World Great Men Col

258. Beavers, Louise
1902–62
screen and television actor
Black
Obit File

259. Dawson, Mary Cardwell
1902–62
founder of the National Negro Opera Company, soprano concert singer
Black
Obit File

260. Gilbert, Mercedes
died 1952
radio, television, and stage actor
Black
Obit File

261. Bush, Anita
pre-1903–73
singer, actor
Black
Negro Alman

262. George, Zelma Watson
1903–post 1960
alternate delegate to the UN, sociologist, singer
Black
Index t Wom; Negro Alman; Negro Her Lib v1

263. Jarboro, Caterina
born 1903
soprano singer
Black
Encyc Black Am; Index t Wom

264. Baker, Augusta (Alexander)
flourished 1934–68
children's librarian
Black
Encyc Black Am; Negro Alman

265. Graham, Shirley
born 1904/07
musical playwright, biographical historian, author, composer
Black
Index t Wom; Negro Alman

266. Jones, Lois Mailore
born 1905
painter, art educator
Black
Index t Wom; Negro Alman

267. Porter, Dorothy B.
born 1905
librarian, library administrator, bibliographer, author
Black
Encyc Black Am; Negro Alman

268. Tate, Merze
born 1905
historian of the Pacific
Black
Encyc Black Am

269. Baker, Josephine
1906–75
actor, dancer, singer, civil rights worker
Black
Cur Biog '75; Encyc Black Am; Index t Wom; Negro Alman; Not Am Wom

270. Carter, Gwendolyn Margaret
born 1906
political scientist, writer on political science, educator
Black
Encyc Black Am

271. du Bois, Shirley Lola Graham
1906–77
children's author, biographer, composer, stage director, civil rights worker
Black
Cur Biog '77; Encyc Black Am

272. Tarry, Ellen
born 1906
author, children's author
Catholic
Black
Negro Alman; Prof Negro Wom v2

273. Byrd, Hannah Elizabeth
1907–68
judge
Pennsylvania
Black
Encyc Black Am

274. Davis, Ellabelle
1907–60
soprano singer
Black
Obit File

275. Hamilton, Grace Towns
born 1907
educator, Georgia state legislator from Atlanta
Atlanta, GA
Black
Encyc Black Am

276. Bolin, Jane Matilda; Mrs. Walter P. Offutt, Jr.
born 1908
lawyer, judge
Black
Encyc Black Am; Index t Wom

277. Jones, Ruth Holoway
born 1908
US customs collector
Black
Negro Her Lib v1

278. Mallory, Arenia Cornelia
born 1908
educator
Black
Encyc Black Am

279. Perkins, Marion Marche
1908–61
sculptor
Black
Encyc Black Am

280. Dickens, Helen Octavia
born 1909
obstetrician/gynecologist, medical educator
Black
Encyc Black Am; Prof Negro Wom v2

281. Player, Willa Beatrice
born 1909
educator
Black
Encyc Black Am; Index t Wom

282. Williams, Ethel
born 1909
librarian, bibliographer, biographer
Black
Encyc Black Am

283. Brown, Annie Williams
flourished 1940s
singer
Black
Index t Wom

284. Dargans, Louise M.
flourished 1940s–70s
chief clerk, US House Committee on Education and Labor, 1946
Black
Negro Alman; Negro Her Lib v1

285. Dunham, Katherine
born 1910
dancer, choreographer, anthropologist
Black
Encyc Black Am; Index t Wom; Negro Alman; Prof Negro Wom v2

286. Edwards, Ester Gordy
flourished 1940s–70s
publishing executive, vice-president of Motown Records
Black
Encyc Black Am

287. Ford, Geraldine Bledsoe
flourished 1940s–70s
lawyer, judge

Black
Encyc Black Am

288. Franklin, Eleonor I.
flourished 1940s–70s
endocrinologist, educator
Black
Encyc Black Am

289. Freeman, Elizabeth
flourished 1940s
World War II army nurse
Black
Prof Negro Wom v2

290. Kemp, Maida Springer
born 1910
labor leader
Black
Negro Alman

291. Maynor, Dorothy; Dorothy Mainor
born 1910
soprano singer
Black
Encyc Black Am; Index t Wom; Negro Alman

292. McGuire, Rosalie J.
born 1910
educator
Black
Negro Alman

293. Murray, Paule
born 1910
educator, author, lawyer, civil rights activist
Black
Encyc Black Am

294. Stewart, Ellen
flourished 1940s–70s
off-off-Broadway theatrical producer
Black
Cur Biog '73

295. Yergan, Laura H.
flourished 1940s–70s
nurse
Black
Encyc Black Am

296. Edmonds, Helen Grey
born 1911
historian, educator
Black
Encyc Black Am

297. Jackson, Mahalia
1911–72
gospel singer
Black
Cur Biog '72; Encyc Black Am; Index t Wom; Negro Alman; Not Am Wom supp v1; Obit File; Prof Negro Wom v2

298. Petry, Ann
born 1911
novelist, short story writer, journalist, literary critic
Black
Index t Wom; Negro Alman; Wom Lit; Wom Lit, More

299. Rahn, Muriel
1911–61
soprano singer, Broadway musical actor
New York
Black
Obit File

300. Sullivan, Maxine
born 1911
jazz singer
Black
Encyc Black Am

301. Brooks, Gwendolyn
born 1912/17
poet, educator, autobiographer, lecturer, poet laureate of Illinois
Chicago, IL
Black
Cur Biog '77; Dict Lit Bio v5; Encyc Black Am; Index t Wom; Negro Alman; Nort Anth Poet; Prof Negro Wom; Wom Lit; Wom Lit, More

302. Fortune, Hilda O.
born circa 1912
educator
Black
Encyc Black Am

303. Jones, Virginia Lacy
born 1912/14
librarian, educator
Black
Encyc Black Am; Index t Wom

304. Robinson, Wilhelmina S.
born 1912
educator, historian
Black
Encyc Black Am

305. Waddles, Charloezetta
born 1912
clergyperson
Black
Negro Alman

306. Bonds, Margaret
born 1913
composer, pianist
Black
Negro Alman

307. Jones, Clara Stanton
born 1913
librarian, president of the American Library Association
Detroit, MI
Black
Cur Biog '76; Encyc Black Am

308. Cartwright, Marguerite Dorsey
born 1914
educator, journalist
Black
Encyc Black Am

309. Hudson, Jean Blackwell
born 1914
curator of the Schomburg Collection
Black
Negro Alman

310. Hutson, Jean Blackwell
born 1914
librarian, curator of the Schomburg Center for Research and Black Culture
New York
Black
Encyc Black Am

311. Lawrence, Margaret Morgan
born 1914
pediatrician
Black
Encyc Black Am

312. Alexander, Margaret (Walker)
born 1915
poet, novelist, college administrator
Black
Encyc Black Am; Encyc South Hist; Index t Wom; Negro Alman; Wom Lit; Wom Lit, More

313. Brown, Letitia Woods
1915–76
historian, educator
Black
Encyc Black Am

314. Catlett, Elizabeth
born 1915
sculptor, painter
Black
Encyc Black Am

315. Holiday, Eleanor Fagan (Gough) "Billie"; Lady Day
1915?–59
blues singer
Black
Dict Am Bio supp v2; Encyc Black Am; Index t Wom; Negro Alman; Not Am Wom supp v1; Obit File

316. Parks, Rosa
born 1915
civil rights activist
Black
Negro Alman; Prof Negro Wom v2

317. Diggs, Estella B.
born 1916
New York State legislator
New York
Black
Encyc Black Am

318. Morrison, Rosetta Tharpe
1916–73
gospel singer
Black
Obit File

319. Putney, Martha Settle
born 1916
historian, educator
Black
Encyc Black Am

320. Smith, Ruth Camp
born 1916
librarian, director of the scientific document division of the Naval Ship Systems Command
Black
Encyc Black Am

321. Burke, Lillian W.
born 1917
lawyer, judge
Ohio
Black
Encyc Black Am

322. Burroughs, Margaret
born 1917
painter, sculptor
Black
Negro Alman

323. Goff, Regina
born 1917
educator; consultant to the Ministry of Education of Iran, 1955; assistant commissioner of HEW's Office of Education
Black
Negro Alman; Negro Her Lib v1

324. Hamer, Fannie Lou
1917–77
civil rights worker, founder of the Mississippi Freedom Democratic party, worker for Student Nonviolent Coordinating Committee, farmer
Mississippi
Black
Encyc Black Am; Obit File

325. Horne, Lena
born 1917
popular singer, actor
Black
Encyc Black Am; Index t Wom; Negro Alman

326. Moss, Elizabeth Murphy
born 1917
business executive, World War II correspondent
Black
Encyc Black Am

327. Bailey, Pearl (Mae)
born 1918
singer, actor, entertainer
Black
Cur Biog '69

328. Fitzgerald, Ella
born 1918
jazz singer, composer
Black
Encyc Black Am; Index t Wom;
Negro Alman

329. Guzman, Jessie P.
born 1918
educator
Black
Negro Alman

330. Hewell, Grace
born 1918
educator; social worker; HEW of-
ficial; chief of education, House
Committee on Education and
Labor
Washington, DC
Black
Encyc Black Am; Negro Her Lib
v1

331. Walker, Maggie
born 1918
pediatrician
Black
Encyc Black Am

332. Brown, Dorothy
born 1919
surgeon, Tennessee state legislator
Tennessee
Black
Encyc Black Am; Negro Alman

333. Elliott, Daisy
born 1919
Michigan state legislator from
Detroit, civil rights worker
Detroit, MI
Black
Encyc Black Am

334. Gadsden, Marie Davis
born 1919
Peace Corps training officer
Black
Index t Wom

335. Koontz, Elizabeth Duncan
born 1919
director of the US Department of
Labor Women's Bureau, US
delegate to the Commission on
the Status of Women, labor organizer, educator
Black
Cur Biog '69; Encyc Black Am;
Index t Wom; Negro Alman

336. Lawson, Marjorie
born 1919
lawyer, judge

Pittsburgh, PA
Black
Encyc Black Am; Negro Alman

337. Primus, Pearl
born 1919
dancer
Black; West Indian (Trinidad)
Negro Alman

338. Stout, Juanita Kidd
1919–post 1976
municipal court judge
Black
Index t Wom; Negro Alman; Prof
Negro Wom v2

**339. Wilson, Margaret Berenice
Bush**
born 1919
lawyer, civic leader, chairperson
of the national board of the
NAACP
St. Louis, MO
Black
Cur Biog '75; Encyc Black Am

340. Wright, Jane Cook
born 1919
surgeon, cancer specialist
Black
Encyc Black Am; Index t Wom

341. Brice, Carol
born 1920
singer
Black
Encyc Black Am

**342. Carnegie, Mary Elizabeth
Lancaster**
flourished 1950s–60s
nurse, nursing-magazine editor
Black
Prof Negro Wom v2

**343. Chambers, Yolande Har-
grave**
flourished 1950s–60s
lawyer, business executive
Black
Encyc Black Am

344. Childress, Alice
born 1920
playwright, editor, actor
Black
Dict Lit Bio v7; Encyc Black Am;
Wom Lit; Wom Lit, More

345. Crosson, Wilhelmina
flourished 1950s
educator, president of Palmer
Memorial Institute
Black
Prof Negro Wom v2

346. Drewry, Cecelia Hodges
flourished 1950s–60s
educator
New Jersey

Black
Prof Negro Wom v2

347. Ferguson, Rosetta
born 1920
Michigan state legislator
Michigan
Black
Encyc Black Am

348. Francis, Yvette Fae
flourished 1950s
physician
Black
Encyc Black Am

349. Hastings, Alicia E.
flourished 1950s–60s
physician, medical educator
Black
Encyc Black Am

350. Jordan, June
flourished 1950s–1980s
poet, essayist, political writer, civil rights worker, educator
Black
Wom Lit; Wom Lit, More

351. Rose, Lucille Mason
born 1920
New York City commissioner of
employment
New York, NY
Black
Negro Alman

352. Simmons, Juliette
flourished 1950s–60s
psychiatrist
Black
Prof Negro Wom v2

353. Simms, Hilda
born 1920
actor
Black
Index t Wom; Negro Alman

354. Southern, Eileen Jackson
born 1920
musicologist, educator
Black
Encyc Black Am

355. Spaulding, Jane M.
flourished 1950s
assistant to the secretary of HEW
Black
Negro Her Lib v1

**356. Wells, Bernice Young
Mitchell**
flourished 1950s
author
Black
Index t Wom

357. Willis, Gertrude Geddes
died 1970
business executive

Black
Encyc Black Am

358. Marr, Carmell Carrington
born 1921
lawyer, New York State Public
Service commissioner, legal adviser to the United Mission of
the UN
Black
Encyc Black Am; Negro Alman;
Negro Her Lib v1

359. McClendon, Ernestine
born 1921
theatrical agent
Black
Negro Alman

360. Motley, Constance Baker
born 1921
lawyer, federal judge, US senator
Black
Encyc Black Am; Index t Wom;
Prof Negro Wom v2

361. Spurlock, Jeanne
born 1921
psychiatrist, educator
Black
Encyc Black Am

362. Bailey, Minnie T.
born 1922
historian
Black
Encyc Black Am

363. Bates, Daisy Lee Gatson
born 1922
civil rights leader
Little Rock, AR
Black
Encyc Black Am; Index t Wom;
Negro Alman; Prof Negro
Wom v2

364. Branch, Dorothy Sutton
born 1922
Baptist clergyperson
Baptist
Black
Encyc Black Am

365. Gaines, Edyth J.
born 1922
educator
Black
Encyc Black Am

366. Gunter, Laurie Martin
born 1922
nurse, nursing educator
Black
Encyc Black Am

**367. Lafontant, Jewell Strad-
ford**
born 1922
lawyer, US deputy soliciter general

Black
Encyc Black Am; Negro Alman

368. Mitchell-Bateman, Mildred
1922–post 1962
psychiatrist, hospital administrator
Black
Negro Alman; Encyc Black Am

369. Richardson, Gloria Hays
born 1922
civil rights activist
Black
Encyc Black Am

370. Atkins, Hannah D.
born 1923
librarian
Black
Encyc Black Am

371. Chandler, Sue Pinkston
flourished 1953–70s
editor, librarian
Black
Encyc Black Am

372. Collins, Janet
born 1923
dancer
Black
Encyc Black Am

373. Davis, Alice Coachman
born 1923
high jumper
Black
Encyc Black Am; Hall Fame
Sport

374. Davis, Georgia M.
born 1923
business executive, Kentucky
state senator, Black civil rights
worker
Kentucky
Black
Encyc Black Am

375. Dee, Ruby
born 1923
stage, screen, and television actor
Black
Cur Biog '70; Encyc Black Am;
Prof Negro Wom v2

**376. Chisholm, Shirley [Anita]
(St. Hill)**
born 1924/26
New York State legislator, representative to Congress from New
York, 1972 presidential candidate in New York Democratic
primary
New York
Black
Cur Biog '69; Encyc Black Am;
Negro Alman

377. Collins, Evelyn Boyd
born 1924

mathematician, educator
Black
Prof Negro Wom v2

378. Cook, Celestine Strode
born 1924
business executive, civic leader
New Orleans, LA
Black
Encyc Black Am

379. Dandridge, Dorothy
1924–61
screen actor, singer
Hollywood, CA
Black
Index t Wom; Obit File

380. Harris, Patricia Roberts
born 1924
lawyer, educator, ambassador to
Luxembourg
Black
Encyc Black Am; Index t Wom;
Negro Alman; Negro Her Lib
v1; Prof Negro Wom v2

381. Martin, Julia M.
born 1924
chemist, educator
Black
Encyc Black Am

382. Sipuel, Ada Lois
born 1924
lawyer, educator, civil rights activist
Black
Encyc Black Am

383. Vaughan, Sarah
born 1924
popular and jazz singer
Black
Cur Biog '80; Index t Wom; Negro Alman

384. Washington, Dinah
1924–63
jazz and blues singer
Black
Index t Wom; Obit File

385. Addison, Adele
born 1925
soprano singer
Black
Index t Wom; Negro Alman

386. Dobbs, Mattiwilda
born 1925
coloratura-soprano singer
Black
Encyc Black Am; Index t Wom;
Negro Alman

387. Williams, Camilla
born 1925
soprano singer
Black
Encyc Black Am; Index t Wom

388. Banks, Eloise Hardison
born 1926
publisher, editor
Black
Encyc Black Am

389. Hernandez, Aileen Clarke
born 1926
public affairs consultant; commissioner of Equal Employment
Opportunities Committee, 1965;
president of NOW; labor worker; civil rights worker; feminist
Black
Cur Biog '71; Negro Alman; Negro Her Lib v1

390. Lawrence, Annie L.
born 1926
nurse, educator
Black
Encyc Black Am

391. McBroom, F. Pearl
born 1926
cardiologist
Black
Encyc Black Am

392. Walker, Cora T.
born 1926
lawyer, civic leader, co-op founder
Harlem, NY
Black
Encyc Black Am; Negro Alman;
Prof Negro Wom v2

393. Walker, Ernestine
born 1926
historian of England
Black
Encyc Black Am

394. Whiting, Willie M.
born 1926
lawyer, judge
Black
Encyc Black Am

**395. Gibson, Althea; Althea
Gibson Darben**
born 1927
tennis player, golfer
Black
Encyc Black Am; Hall Fame
Sport; Index t Wom; Negro Alman; Prof Negro Wom v2

396. Hinderas, Natalie
born 1927
concert pianist, music educator
Black
Encyc Black Am

397. Jones, Edith Irby
born 1927
physician, medical educator
Black
Encyc Black Am

398. King, Coretta Scott
born 1927
singer, civil rights leader
Atlanta, GA
Black
Cur Biog '69; Encyc Black Am;
Negro Alman

399. Perry, Julia
born 1927
composer
Black
Negro Alman

400. Price, Leontyne [Mary]
born 1927/29
Metropolitan Opera lyric-soprano
singer
Black
Cur Biog '78; Encyc Black Am;
Index t Wom; Negro Alman

**401. Tucker, Cynthia Delores
Nottage**
born 1927
secretary of the Commonwealth
of Pennsylvania
Pennsylvania
Black
Encyc Black Am

402. Angelou, Maya
born 1928
poet, autobiographer, dancer,
producer
Black
Cur Biog '74; Encyc Black Am;
Wom Lit; Wom Lit, More

403. Arnez, Nancy Levi
born 1928
educator, poet, author
Black
Encyc Black Am

404. Kitt, Eartha
born 1928
singer, actor, dancer
Black
Encyc Black Am; Index t Wom

405. McCullough, Geraldine
born 1928
sculptor
Black
Negro Alman; Prof Negro Wom
v2

406. Phillips, Mildred E.
born 1928
pathologist
Black
Encyc Black Am

407. Lind, Shirley Motter
born 1929
editor, publisher
Black
Encyc Black Am

408. Marshall, Paule
born 1929

short story writer, novelist
Black
Encyc Black Am; Negro Alman;
Wom Lit; Wom Lit, More

**409. Nash, Gwendolyn V.
Brownlee**
1929–70
physician
Black
Encyc Black Am

410. Allen, Betty Lou
born 1930
mezzo-soprano singer
Black
Negro Alman

411. Billops, Camille
flourished 1960s
ceramic sculptor
Black
Negro Alman

412. Bowen, Ruth
born 1930
businessperson, founder of a talent booking agency
Black
Encyc Black Am; Negro Alman

413. Clayton, Xernona
1930/33–post 1952
television producer, television
personality, television host
Black
Encyc Black Am; Negro Alman

414. Evans, Mari
flourished 1960s
poet
Black
Negro Alman; Wom Lit; Wom
Lit, More

415. Fisher, Gail
flourished 1960s
actor
Black
Negro Alman

416. Gaston, Gloria Laureha
flourished 1960s–70s
development officer for the Agency for International Development's Bureau of Latin
America
Black
Negro Alman; Negro Her Lib v1

417. Gaynor, Florence
flourished 1960s–70s
hospital administrator
Black
Encyc Black Am

**418. Gordon, Odetta Holmes
Felious Gordon; Odetta**
flourished 1960s–70s
singer, guitarist
Black
Index t Wom

419. Hansberry, Lorraine
1930–65
playwright, civil rights reformer,
Socialist party worker
New York
Black
Dict Lit Bio v7; Encyc Black Am;
Index t Wom; Nat Cyc Am Bio
v60; Negro Alman; Not Am
Wom supp v1; Obit File; Prof
Negro Wom v2; Wom Lit;
Wom Lit, More

420. Lindsay, Inabel Burns
flourished 1930s–50s
social worker
Black
Prof Negro Wom v2

421. Miller, Edith
born 1930
lawyer, judge
Black
Encyc Black Am

422. Smith, Jessie Carney
born 1930
librarian, educator
Black
Encyc Black Am

**423. Morrison, Chloe Anthony
Woffard "Toni"**
born 1931
author, novelist
Black
Cur Biog '79; Dict Lit Bio v6;
Encyc Black Am; Wom Lit;
Wom Lit, More

**424. Whittington, Geraldine
Delores**
born 1931
secretary to Lyndon Johnson
Black
Negro Alman; Negro Her Lib v1

425. Barrett, Brenetta H.
born 1932
director of the federal Human
Resources Administration
Illinois
Black
Negro Alman

**426. Burke, Yvonne Watson
Brathwaite**
born 1932
lawyer, representative to Congress from California, regent of
the University of California, environmentalist, feminist
California
Black
Cur Biog '75; Encyc Black Am;
Negro Alman

427. Chennault, Madelyn
born 1932
psychologist, educator
Black
Negro Alman

428. Crockett, Gwendolyn
born 1932
lawyer, educator
Louisiana
Black
Encyc Black Am

**429. Jackson, Jaquelyn John-
son**
born 1932
sociologist, educator
Black
Encyc Black Am

430. Reese, Della
born 1932
popular singer, television variety
show host
Black
Cur Biog '71; Encyc Black Am;
Index t Wom

431. Schuyler, Philippa Duke
1932–1967/69
pianist, composer, author, Vietnam war correspondent
Black
Encyc Black Am; Index t Wom;
Negro Alman; Obit File

432. Adams, Clara Isabel
born 1933
chemist
Black
Encyc Black Am

433. Sinkford, Jeanne Craig
born 1933
dentist, dental educator
Black
Encyc Black Am

434. Verrett, Shirley
circa 1933–post 1976
mezzo-soprano opera singer
Black
Index t Wom; Negro Alman

**435. Giovanni, Nikki; Yolande
Cornelia Giovanni, Jr.**
born 1934
poet
Black
Cur Biog '73; Dict Lit Bio v5;
Encyc Black Am; Negro Al-
man; Nort Anth Poet; Wom
Lit; Wom Lit, More

436. Ringgold, Faith
born 1934
painter
Black
Negro Alman

437. Young, Lois A.
born 1934
ophthalmologist, educator
Black
Encyc Black Am

438. Carroll, Diahann
born 1935

singer, film and stage actor
Black
Encyc Black Am; Index t Wom;
Negro Alman

439. Garland, Phyllis T.
born 1935
journalist
Black
Negro Alman

440. Sanchez, Sonia
born 1935
poet, playwright
Black
Negro Alman; Wom Lit; Wom
Lit, More

**441. Simone, Nina; Eunice
Kathleen Waymon**
born 1935
singer, pianist, composer
Black
Negro Alman

442. Welsing, Frances Cress
born 1935
psychiatrist
Black
Negro Alman; Encyc Black Am

443. Arroyo, Martina
born 1936/39
Metropolitan Opera soprano sing-
er
Black
Cur Biog '71; Encyc Black Am;
Negro Alman

444. Clifton, Lucille
born 1936
author, poet
Black
Dict Lit Bio v5; Wom Lit, More

445. Jordan, Barbara
born 1936
lawyer, Texas state senator, representative to Congress from Texas
Texas
Black
Cur Biog '74; Encyc Black Am;
Negro Alman

446. Shabazz, Betty
born 1936
community activist
Black Muslim
Black
Negro Alman

447. Bumbry, Grace
born 1937
mezzo-soprano singer
Black
Index t Wom; Negro Alman

448. Norton, Eleanor Holmes
born 1937
lawyer, chairperson of the Equal
Opportunities Committee, New

York City Human Rights commissioner, civil rights worker
New York
Black
Cur Biog '76; Encyc Black Am; Negro Alman

449. Berry, Mary Frances
born 1938
historian, educator
Black
Encyc Black Am

450. Bambara, Toni Cade
born 1939
short story writer, novelist, educator
Black
Encyc Black Am; Wom Lit; Wom Lit, More

451. Bryant, Hazel J.
born 1939
singer, actor, producer
Black
Encyc Black Am

452. Edelman, Marian Wright
born 1939
lawyer, member of the Yale University board of trustees
Black
Encyc Black Am; Negro Alman

453. Tyson, Cicely
born 1939/42
stage, screen, and television actor
Black
Cur Biog '75; Encyc Black Am; Negro Alman

454. Ferebee, Dorothy B.
flourished 1970s
physician
Black
Negro Alman

455. Flack, Roberta
born 1940
popular and jazz singer, composer, musician
Black
Cur Biog '73; Negro Alman

456. Grist, Beri
flourished 1970s
coloratura soprano opera singer
Black
Negro Alman

457. Jenkins, Carol
flourished 1970s
television newscaster
Black
Negro Alman

458. Lincoln, Abby
flourished 1970s
jazz singer
Black
Negro Alman

459. Noble, Jeanne
flourished 1970s
educator
Black
Negro Alman

460. Quarles, Norma
flourished 1970s
television newscaster
New York
Black
Negro Alman

461. Rudolph, Wilma Glodean
born 1940
runner, track athlete
Black
Hall Fame Sport; Index t Wom; Negro Alman

462. Taylor, Lynette Dobbins
flourished 1970s
editor, executive
Black
Negro Alman

463. Tolliver, Melba
flourished 1970s
television newscaster
Black
Negro Alman

464. Tyus, Wyomia
flourished 1970s
track athlete, sprinter
Black
Hall Fame Sport

465. Warwick, Dionne; Marie Dionne Warrick
born 1940
popular singer
Black
Cur Biog '69

466. Washington, Bennetta Bullock
flourished 1970s
special assistant, US Department of Commerce; director of the Women's Job Corps of the Office of Economic Opportunity
Black
Negro Alman; Negro Her Lib v1

467. Barry, Mary Treadwell
born 1941
executive and cofounder of Pride Corp.
Black
Negro Alman

468. Murray, Joan
born 1941
television newscaster, advertising executive
Black
Encyc Black Am; Negro Alman

469. Walker, Alice
born 1941/44
poet, novelist, short story writer

Black
Dict Lit Bio v6; Negro Alman; Wom Lit; Wom Lit, More

470. Franklin, Aretha
born 1942
popular singer
Black
Encyc Black Am; Index t Wom; Negro Alman

471. Gault, Charlayne Hunter
born 1942
journalist
Black
Negro Alman

472. Robinson, Ruby Doris Smith
1942–67
civil rights reformer, founder and executive of the Student Nonviolent Coordinating Committee
Black
Not Am Wom supp v1; Obit File

473. Jamison, Judith
born 1943/44
modern dancer
Black
Cur Biog '73; Encyc Black Am; Negro Alman

474. Uggams, Leslie
born 1943
singer, actor
Black
Index t Wom; Negro Alman

475. Ballard, Florence
1944–76
popular singer
Black
Obit File

476. Davis, Angela [Yvonne]
born 1944
civil rights worker, politician, Communist party presidential candidate, political writer, university educator
Black
Cur Biog '72; Encyc Black Am; Negro Alman

477. Ross, Diana
born 1944
popular singer, actor, entertainer
Black
Cur Biog '73; Encyc Black Am; Negro Alman

478. Moore, Beatrice "Melba"

born 1945
stage and television actor, singer
Black
Cur Biog '73; Negro Alman

479. Norman, Jessy
born 1945
soprano opera singer

Black
Cur Biog '76

480. Bassey, Shirley
flourished 1976
jazz singer
Black
Negro Alman

481. Bolden, Dorothy
flourished 1976
labor leader
Black
Negro Alman

482. Bond, Abigail Monique
flourished 1976
television newscaster
Black
Negro Alman

483. Davis, Christine R.
flourished 1976
publishing executive; staff director, US House Committee on Government Operations, 1949
Black
Negro Alman; Negro Her Lib v1

484. Dale, Clemma
born 1948
soprano opera singer
Black
Cur Biog '79

485. Shange, Ntzoke
born 1948
poet, playwright, novelist
Black
Cur Biog '78; Wom Lit, More

486. Summer, Donna
born 1948
disco singer
Black
Cur Biog '79

No Dates

487. Patterson, Inez
pioneer Black woman athlete
Black
Encyc Black Am

488. Patti-Brown, Anita
singer
Black
Index t Wom

BOHEMIAN

489. Goldsmith, Sophia
born circa 1847
author
Bohemian
Index t Wom

490. Bradna, Ella
1879–1957

circus bareback equestrian
Bohemian
Obit File

BOLIVIAN

491. Patino, Albina Rodriguez
1872–1953
mine owner and operator, dairy
    farmer, philanthropist
Bolivian
Nat Cyc Am Bio v40

BRAZILIAN

492. Jacintha do San Jose
1716–68
Catholic nun, school and hospital
    founder
Catholic
Brazilian
Cyc Am Bio

**493. Irwin, Inez Leonore
    Haynes Gillmore**
1873–1970
suffragist, feminist, head of the
    World Center for Women's Ar-
    chives, author, first woman
    president of the Authors League
    of America
Brazilian
Index t Wom; Nat Cyc Am Bio
    csv6; Not Am Wom supp v1;
    Obit File

494. Miranda, Carmen; Maria
    de Carmo da Cunha
1909/13–1955
singer
Portuguese; Brazilian
Dict Am Bio supp v5; Index t
    Wom; Obit File

495. Hamar, Irene; Mrs. Henry
    Peter de Vries
1919–73
sculptor, skier
New York
Brazilian
Nat Cyc Am Bio v57

BRITISH

496. Aubrey, Leticia; Lady
    Worminghurst
flourished 1730s–40s
owner and ruler of the Barony of
    Nazareth, a tract of 5,000 acres
    in Northampton County, Penn-
    sylvania
Pennsylvania
British
Appl Cyc Am Bio

497. Bailey, Ann; Mad Anne
1725/42–1825
frontier scout and messenger on
    the Virginia border, soldier,
    Indian fighter, American patri-
    ot
Ohio; Virginia
British
Appl Cyc Am Bio; Dict Am Bio;
    Encyc South Hist; Who Who
    Dur Am Rev; Wom Cent

498. Bailey, Sarah Lord
born 1856
elocutionist
Massachusetts
British
Wom Cent

499. Bagley, Blanche Pentecost
born 1858
Unitarian minister, suffragist
Unitarian
British
Wom Cent

**500. Anderson, Mary Antoin-
    ette;** Mrs. Antonio F. de Na-
    varro
1859–1939/40
actor
British
Appl Cyc Am Bio; Cyc Am Bio;
    Dict Am Auth; Dict Am Bio
    supp v2; Index t Wom; Nat Cyc
    Am Bio v1; Not Am Wom;
    Twent Cen Bio Dict Not Am;
    Wom Cent

**501. Astor, Nancy Witcher
    Langhorne Shaw, Lady;** Dow-
    ager Viscountess
1879–1964
politician, member of the English
    House of Commons, women's
    rights worker, temperance
    worker
British (American expatriate to
    England)
Index t Wom; Nat Cyc Am Bio
    csv1; Obit File

BULGARIAN

502. Byington, Margaret
born 1870s; died 1952
educator, social worker
Bulgarian
Obit File

CANADIAN

**503. l'Incarnation, Maria de,
    Mother**
1599–1672
Catholic nun, educator, founder
    of the Ursuline Convent in Que-

bec, student of Native Ameri-
    can languages
Catholic
Canadian
Cyc Am Bio

**504. la Peltrie, Marie Made-
    leine de**
1603–71
educator
Canadian (French Canada)
Cyc Am Bio

505. Charlotte
flourished 1708
litigant who challenged the legali-
    ty of slavery in court
Black; Canadian
Prof Negro Wom v1

**506. Vercheres, Mary Madeline
    de**
1678–post 1700
hero
Canadian
Cyc Am Bio

507. Picken, Joanna Belfrage
1748/98–1859
poet
Canadian; Scottish
Cyc Am Bio; Dict Nat Bio

**508. Traill, Catherine Parr
    (Strickland)**
1802–99
author
Canadian
Cyc Am Bio; Dict Am Bio Men
    Time

509. Davis, Ann Scott
1805–91
pioneer, hero
Irish; Canadian
Index t Wom

510. Cary, Mary Ann Shad
1823–93
educator, lawyer, journalist, edi-
    tor, abolitionist, Canadian pio-
    neer
Black; Canadian
Index t Wom; Negro Alman; Not
    Am Wom; Prof Negro Wom

**511. Youmans, Letitia Creigh-
    ton**
1827–96
temperance reformer
Canadian
Cyc Am Bio; Wom Cent

512. Fawcett, Mary S.
born 1829
temperance reformer
Canadian
Wom Cent

**513. Leprohan, Rosanna Eleo-
    nora**
1832–79

poet, novelist
Canadian
Cyc Am Bio; Wom Cent

514. Willing, Jennie Fowler
1834–1916
Methodist local preacher, church
    worker, temperance reformer,
    lecturer, author, educator
Methodist
Canadian
Index t Wom; Not Am Wom;
    Wom Cent

515. Mountcastle, Clara H.
born 1837
author, elocutionist
Canadian
Cyc Am Bio; Wom Cent

516. Rothwell, Annie
born 1837
poet
English; Canadian
Wom Cent

517. Thoburn, Isabella
1840–1901
Methodist missionary to India,
    educator
Canadian
Dict Am Bio; Index t Wom; Nat
    Cyc Am Bio v19; Not Am Wom

**518. Edmonds, Sarah Emma
    Evelyn;** Franklin Thompson
1841–98
Civil War soldier, spy, nurse
Canadian
Index t Wom; Not Am Wom

519. Merrick, Sarah Newcomb
born 1844
educator, educational missionary
    to Nova Scotia
Texas
Canadian
Wom Cent

520. Carhart, Clara Sully
born 1845
educator, temperance worker,
    women's labor welfare worker
Methodist Episcopal
New York
Canadian
Wom Cent

521. Morris, Clara (Morrison)
1846/48–1925
actor, author, children's author,
    autobiographer
Canadian
Cyc Am Bio and ad; Dict Am
    Auth; Dict Am Bio; Index t
    Wom; Nat Cyc Am Bio v11;
    Not Am Wom; Twent Cen Bio
    Dict Not Am; Wom Cent

522. Diggs, Annie le Porte
1848/53–1916

Populist party leader, orator, politician, social reformer, temperance worker, journalist
Unitarian
Kansas
Canadian
Not Am Wom; Read Encyc Am West; Wom Cent

523. Mee, Cassie Ward
born 1848
labor leader, Knights of Labor worker, temperance worker, lecturer
Quaker
Canadian
Index t Wom; Wom Cent

524. Crawford, John, Mrs.; Maude Moore
born 1850
newspaper correspondent
Canadian
Wom Cent

525. Lauder, Maria Elise Turner
flourished 1880s
author
Canadian
Wom Cent

526. Robinson, Margaret A.
flourished nineteenth to twentieth century
actor
Canadian
Index t Wom

527. Albani, Maria Louise Cecilie Emma, Dame; Marie Emma Lajeunesse; Marie Emma Gye
1851/52–1930
soprano singer
Canadian (French Canada)
Appl Cyc Am Bio; Index t Wom; Nat Cyc Am Bio v9; Not Am Wom; Twent Cen Bio Dict Not Am; Wom Cent

528. Cameron, Elizabeth
born 1851
editor, temperance worker
Canadian
Wom Cent

529. Norraikow, Ella, Countess
born 1853
author, journalist, Russian correspondent, traveler
Canadian
Wom Cent

530. Archibald, Edith Jessie
born 1854
novelist, temperance reformer
Canadian
Index t Wom; Wom Cent

531. Arthur, Clara Blanche
born 1858

suffragist
Canadian
Nat Cyc Am Bio v17

532. Mather, Margaret
1859/62–1898
actor
Canadian
Index t Wom; Nat Cyc Am Bio v9; Wom Cent

533. Coleman, Louise MacPherson
flourished 1890s–1900s
nurse
Canadian
Index t Wom

534. Hughes, Nina Vera B.
flourished 1890s
author, philosopher
Canadian
Wom Cent

535. Pope, Amy Elizabeth
flourished 1890s–1900s
nurse
Canadian
Index t Wom

536. Saunders, Margaret Marshall; Marshall Saunders
born 1861
short story writer, novelist
Boston, MA
Canadian (Nova Scotia)
Dict Am Auth

537. Cotes, Sara Jeannette Duncan; Sara Jeannette Duncan
born 1862
author, journalist
Canadian
Wom Cent

538. Miner, Alice Trainer
1863–1950
philanthropist, patron of medicine
Presbyterian
New York
Canadian
Nat Cyc Am Bio v40

539. Buck, Henriette
born 1864
educator
French; English; Canadian
Wom Cent

540. Hamm, Margharita Arlina
1867/71–1907
journalist, author, poet, political writer
Canadian
Nat Cyc Am Bio v9; Not Am Wom; Wom Cent

541. James, Belle Robinson
1868–1935
religious worker, author

Canadian
Index t Wom

542. Arthur, Julia; Julia Cheney; Ida Lewis
1869–1950
actor
Canadian
Index t Wom; Nat Cyc Am Bio v10; Not Am Wom; Obit File

543. Dressler, Marie; Leila von Koerber
1869/73–1934
stage and screen actor, comedian, suffragist
Canadian
Dict Am Bio supp v1; Index t Wom; Nat Cyc Am Bio v27; Not Am Wom

544. Graser, Hilda Regina
born 1869
customhouse broker
Chicago, IL
Canadian
Wom Cent

545. Williston, Anne Robson Sterling
born 1869
conservationist
Methodist
Canadian
Nat Cyc Am Bio csv2

546. Cook, Myrtle Foster
1870–1951
educator, civic leader, financier, Black civil rights worker
Kansas City, KS
Black; Canadian
Negro Alman; Prof Negro Wom

547. Grenville, Lillian Goertner
flourished 1900s
singer
Canadian
Index t Wom

548. Taylor, Euphemia J.
flourished 1900s–20s
nurse
Canadian
Index t Wom

549. Laut, Agnes Christina
1871/72–1936
journalist, novelist, writer on the American West
Canadian
Dict Am Auth; Index t Wom

550. Smith, Ada Clark
1871–1915
religious worker
Canadian
Index t Wom

551. Montgomery, Lucy Maud
1874–1942
novelist

Canadian
Index t Wom

552. Tompers, Lucie Margaret
1874–1938
social worker
Baptist
New York
Canadian
Nat Cyc Am Bio v29

553. Yaegle, Marie Tello Phillips
1874–1962
poet, novelist, essayist, founder of the American Academy of Poets
Catholic
Pennsylvania
Canadian
Index t Wom; Nat Cyc Am Bio csv3; Obit File

554. Dickinson, Helena Adall Snyder
1875–1975
nonfiction writer, educator
Presbyterian
Canadian
Nat Cyc Am Bio v54

555. MacDonald, Christie; Christie Gillespie
1875/77–1962
operetta singer, actor, musical comedy actor
Presbyterian
Canadian
Index t Wom; Nat Cyc Am Bio v50; Obit File

556. Anglin, Margaret Mary; Margaret Hull
1876–1958
Broadway stage actor
Canadian
Dict Am Bio supp v6; Index t Wom; Obit File

557. Skinner, Constance Lindsay
1877–1939
author, poet, novelist, historian
Canadian
Index t Wom; Nat Cyc Am Bio csv2 and csv5; Not Am Wom

558. Arden, Elizabeth; Florence Nightingale Graham
1878/84–1966
cosmetician, entrepreneur, founder of Elizabeth Arden Inc., owner of Main Chance racing stables
Canadian
Index t Wom; Not Am Wom supp v1; Obit File

559. Stewart, Isabel Maitland
1878–1963
nursing educator

Canadian
Index t Wom; Not Am Wom
supp v1

560. Branscombe, Gena
born 1881
composer, author, conductor
Canadian
Index t Wom

561. Prevost, Marie
died 1934
actor
Canadian
Index t Wom

562. Wilson, Bess K. Kidston
married 1909
missionary to Africa
Canadian
Index t Wom

563. Carter, Helene
1887–1961
illustrator
Canadian
Index t Wom

564. Wallace, Lila Bell Acheson
born 1889
editor, publisher
Canadian
Index t Wom

565. Corbin, Hazel
flourished 1920s
nurse
Canadian
Index t Wom

566. Cuthbert, Margaret Ross
1890–1968
program director of NBC
Canadian
Index t Wom; Obit File

567. Taylor, Effie J.
flourished 1920s–30s
nurse, educator
Canadian
Index t Wom

568. Stark, Mabel
born 1892
animal trainer
Canadian
Index t Wom

569. Chalmers, Audrey
1893/99–1957
illustrator, author
Canadian
Index t Wom

570. Pickford, Mary Smith;
Mrs. Douglas Fairbanks
1893–1978
silent-screen actor
Canadian
Cur Biog '79; Index t Wom; Nat
Cyc Am Bio csv1

571. Stewart, Isabella Hilda
born 1894
educator
Massachusetts
Canadian
Nat Cyc Am Bio csv8

572. Thorne, Diana
born 1895
painter
Canadian
Index t Wom

573. Finlay, Lorraine Noel
born 1899
composer, author
Canadian
Index t Wom

574. Dingman, Margaret Christian
flourished 1930s
retail buyer
Canadian
Index t Wom

575. Greene, Eleanore D.
flourished 1930s
author
Canadian
Index t Wom

576. Holland, Clara Helena
flourished 1930s
personnel director
Canadian
Index t Wom

577. Irvine, Theodore Ursula
flourished 1930s; died 1952
educator, dramatic coach
Canadian
Index t Wom; Obit File

578. MacMullen, Frances A.
flourished 1930s
cosmetician
Canadian
Index t Wom

579. Mosher, Edna
flourished 1930s
biologist, entomologist
Canadian
Index t Wom

580. Schuyler, Margaretta
flourished 1930s
retail manager
Canadian
Index t Wom

581. Sparks, Sarah
flourished 1930s
personnel director
Canadian
Index t Wom

582. von Kettler, Wanda
flourished 1930s
journalist

Canadian
Index t Wom

583. Shearer, Norma
born 1904
actor
Canadian
Index t Wom

584. McGinley, Phyllis
1905–78
poet, children's author, Pulitzer
Prize winner
Canadian
Cur Biog '78; Index t Wom; Obit
File

585. Gordon, Agnes (Wilson)
1906–67
contract bridge champion
Canadian
Obit File

586. Fisher, Katherine A.
died 1958
home economist, director of the
Good Housekeeping Institute
Canadian
Obit File

587. Keeler, Ruby
born 1909/10
Broadway stage actor and dancer,
screen actor
Canadian
Cur Biog '71; Index t Wom

588. Gerlette, Anne
1913–58
actor, director, producer, dramatics teacher
Canadian
Obit File

589. Dickenson, Jean
born 1914
singer
Canadian
Index t Wom

590. de Carlo, Yvonne
born 1922
actor
Canadian
Index t Wom

591. Nettleship, Mae Barnwell
born 1926
physician
Episcopalian
Arkansas
Canadian
Nat Cyc Am Bio csv10

592. MacKenzie, Gisele
born 1927
actor, singer, violinist, television
personality
Canadian
Index t Wom

593. Bell, Marilyn
born 1937
marathon swimmer
Canadian
Hall Fame Sport; Index t Wom

CHILEAN

**594. Solar, Mercedes Marin
De**
1804–66
poet
Chilean
Cyc Am Bio

CHINESE

595. Bemis, Lalu Nathoy;
China Polly
1852–1933
western pioneer
Chinese
Index t Wom

596. Look, Lilly Chin
born 1873
western pioneer
Chinese
Index t Wom

597. Chung, Margaret Jessie
1889–1959
plastic surgeon, World War II
relief worker
California
Chinese
Nat Cyc Am Bio v48

598. Lee, Rose Hum
1904–64
sociologist
Chinese
Not Am Wom supp v1

**599. Wong, Anna May; Wong
Lu Tsong**
1905/07–1961
screen actor
Chinese
Index t Wom; Not Am Wom
supp v1; Obit File

600. Wong, Jeanyee
born 1920
illustrator
Chinese
Index t Wom

CORSICAN

601. Bordoni, Irene
circa 1893–1953
musical comedy actor
French; Corsican
Index t Wom; Obit File

CUBAN

602. Santa Cruz, Maria de las Mercedes; Countess of Merlin
1789–1852
author
Cuban
Cyc Am Bio

603. Avellanada, Gertrudis Gomez de
1816–64/76
poet, dramatist
Cuban
Appl Cyc Am Bio; Cyc Am Bio

604. Auber, Virginia Felicia; Felicia
born 1825
poet
Cuban
Appl Cyc Am Bio

605. Perez de Zambrana, Luisa
born 1837
author
Cuban
Cyc Am Bio

606. Lorini, Virginia (Whiting)
born 1865
opera singer
Cuban
Dict Am Bio Men Time

607. Alonso, Alicia; Alicia Ernestina de la Caridad del Cobre Martinez
born 1921?
ballet dancer
Cuban
Cur Biog '77

608. Fornes, Maria Irene
born 1930
playwright, theatrical director
New York
Cuban
Dict Lit Bio v7

No Dates

609. Mandel, Carola Panerai
sportsperson
Cuban
Index t Wom

CZECHOSLOVAK

610. Cori, Gerty Theresa Radnitz
1896–1957
biochemist, physician, medical educator, Nobel Prize winner

Czechoslovak
Dict Am Bio supp v6; Index t Wom; Nat Cyc Am Bio v48 and csv8; Not Am Wom supp v1; Obit File

611. Stuerm, Ruza Lukavaska
flourished 1930s
railroad executive, lecturer
Czechoslovak
Index t Wom

612. Saxl, Eva R.
born circa 1921
educator, traveler, lecturer, author
Czechoslovak
Index t Wom

DANISH

613. Broaker, Julia Anderson Luth
1864–1950
actor, playwright
Danish
Obit File

614. Frijsh, Povla
born circa 1870s; died 1960
concert soprano singer
Danish
Obit File

DUTCH

615. Bogardus, Annetje Jansen; Annekke Jans
circa 1600–circa 1663
settler of New Amsterdam
New York
Dutch
Index t Wom; Nat Cyc Am Bio v9

616. Iliohan, Henrica
born 1850
suffragist
Nebraska
Dutch
Wom Cent

617. d'Arville, Camille; Neeltye Dykstra
born 1863
singer, actor
Dutch
Index t Wom

618. de Bey, Cornelia Barnarda
born 1865
physician, surgeon, pacifist
Dutch
Nat Cyc Am Bio csv3

619. Zilve, Alida
flourished 1920s
sculptor

Dutch
Index t Wom

620. Foch, Nina
born 1924
actor
Dutch
Index t Wom

621. van Hamel, Martine
born 1945
ballet dancer
Dutch
Cur Biog '79

ENGLISH

622. Pole, Elizabeth; Elizabeth Poole
1588–1654
pioneer; founder of the town of Taunton, New Jersey
Taunton, NJ; Massachusetts
English
Am Bio Dict; Index t Wom; Nat Cyc Am Bio v4

623. Bradford, Alice
circa 1590–1670
Pilgrim, Plymouth Colony civic worker, patron of education
Puritan
Massachusetts
English
Am Bio Dict; Index t Wom

624. Hutchinson, Anne (Marbury)
1590/91–1642/43
religious and political leader, founder of the Antinomian sect of Puritanism
Puritan
Rhode Island; Massachusetts
English
Am Bio Dict; Cyc Am Bio; Dict Am Bio; Dict Am Bio Men Time; Dict Am Rel Bio; Dict Nat Bio; Index t Wom; Nat Cyc Am Bio v9; Not Am Wom; Twent Cen Bio Dict Not Am

625. Bradstreet, Anne Dudley
1612–72
poet
Puritan
English
Am Bio Dict; Cyc Am Bio; Dict Am Auth; Dict Am Bio; Dict Am Bio Men Time; Index t Wom; Nat Cyc Am Bio v7; Not Am Wom; Twent Cen Bio Dict Not Am; Wom Lit; Wom Lit, More

626. Clark, Mary
flourished 1650s
colonial religious worker
Quaker

English
Index t Wom

627. Harris, Elizabeth
flourished 1650s
religious worker
Quaker
English
Index t Wom

628. Berkeley, Frances, Lady
1634–post 1695
politician
English
Not Am Wom

629. Rosehill, Margaret Cheer, Lady
flourished eighteenth century
colonial actor
English
Index t Wom

630. Irwing, Mary Katie
1678–1721
adventurer
English
Cyc Am Bio

631. Phillips, Catherine Payton
1727–94
colonial evangelist
English
Index t Wom

632. Lee, Ann; Ann Lee Standerin; Mother Ann
1736–84
founder of the American Society of Shakers
Shaker
New York
English
Am Bio Dict; Cyc Am Bio; Dict Am Bio; Dict Am Bio Men Time; Dict Am Rel Bio; Dict Nat Bio; Index t Wom; Nat Cyc Am Bio v5; Not Am Wom; Our Count; Twent Cen Bio Dict Not Am; Who Who Dur Am Rev

633. Davies, Cecelia
1740/50–1836
vocalist
English
Cyc Am Bio; Index t Wom

634. Jemison, Mary Dehewamis; White Woman of the Genessee
1742/43–1833
pioneer
New York
English
Index t Wom; Who Who Dur Am Rev

635. Lake, Mary
1742–1802
western pioneer, religious worker, educator

English
Am Bio Dict; Index t Wom

636. Morris, Elizabeth
circa 1753–1826
actor
Pennsylvania
English
Dict Am Bio; Index t Wom; Who
Who Dur Am Rev

637. Rowson, Susanna (Haswell)
1762/67–1824
novelist, dramatist, poet, educator, actor
Boston, MA
English
Cyc Am Bio; Dict Am Auth; Dict
Am Bio; Dict Am Bio Men
Time; Dict Nat Bio; Index t
Wom; Nat Cyc Am Bio v9; Not
Am Wom; Wom Lit; Wom Lit,
More

638. Gates, Mary Valence
flourished 1800s
pioneer
English
Index t Wom

639. Warren, Anne Brunton (Merry) (Wignell)
born 1770
actor
English
Dict Am Bio Men Time

640. Trollope, Frances Milton
1780/90–1863
author
English
Cyc Am Bio; Dict Am Bio Men
Time

641. Richings, Caroline Mary
1787–1884
soprano vocalist, pianist
English
Cyc Am Bio; Dict Am Bio Men
Time; Nat Cyc Am Bio v9

642. Vernon, Jane Marchant (Fisher)
1796/1827–1869
actor
English
Cyc Am Bio; Dict Am Bio Men
Time; Nat Cyc Am Bio v10

643. Dickerson, Susanna
flourished 1830s
pioneer, hero
English
Index t Wom

644. Merrill, Margaret Manton
born 18?
journalist, temperance worker,
Sorosis member
English
Wom Cent

645. Crandall, Prudence (Philles)
1803–1889/90
educator of Blacks, abolitionist,
philanthropist
Quaker
English
Cyc Am Bio; Dict Am Bio; Eng
Wom; Index t Wom; Nat Cyc
Am Bio v2; Not Am Wom;
Twent Cen Bio Dict Not Am

646. Connelly, Cornelia Augusta Peacock, Mother
1809–79
Catholic nun, founder of the Society of the Holy Child Jesus
Catholic
English
Dict Am Bio; Index t Wom; Nat
Cyc Am Bio v23; Not Am Wom

647. Kemble, Frances Anne "Fanny"; Fanny Kemble Butler
1809/11–1893
actor, diarist, author, abolitionist
Georgia
English
Cyc Am Bio; Dict Am Bio; Dict
Am Bio Men Time; Dict Nat
Bio supp; Encyc South Hist;
Index t Wom; Nat Cyc Am Bio
v3; Not Am Wom

648. Bishop, Anna (Riviere), Madam
1810/14–1884
soprano opera singer
English
Appl Cyc Am Bio; Cyc Am Bio;
Dict Am Bio Men Time; Nat
Cyc Am Bio v3; Not Am Wom;
Twent Cen Bio Dict Not Am;
Wom Cent

649. Fisher, Clara
1811–98
actor, singer
English
Cyc Am Bio; Dict Am Bio; Index
t Wom; Not Am Wom

650. Rea, Julia (de Marguerittes) (Foster)
1814–66
opera singer, drama critic, writer
on Europe
Philadelphia, PA
English
Cyc Am Bio; Dict Am Auth; Dict
Am Bio Men Time

651. Mortimer, Mary
1816/18–1877
educator, women's educator,
founder of the Milwaukee Female College
Wisconsin

English
Dict Am Bio; Index t Wom; Nat
Cyc Am Bio v7; Not Am Wom;
Wom Cent

652. Kirby, Georgiana (Bruce)
born 1818
feminist, prison matron, autobiographer
Santa Cruz, CA
English
Dict Am Auth

653. Royce, Sarah Eleonor Bayliss
1819–91
California pioneer, author
California
English
Index t Wom; Not Am Wom

654. Drew, Louisa Lane
1820–97
actor, theater manager
English
Cyc Am Bio; Dict Am Bio; Index
t Wom; Nat Cyc Am Bio v8;
Not Am Wom; Twent Cen Bio
Dict Not Am; Wom Cent

655. Keene, Laura
1820/26–1873
actor, theater manager
English
Cyc Am Bio; Dict Am Bio; Dict
Am Bio Men Time; Index t
Wom; Nat Cyc Am Bio v8; Not
Am Wom; Twent Cen Bio Dict
Not Am

656. Livingstone, Mary Moffat
1820–62
missionary
English
Index t Wom

657. Blackwell, Elizabeth
1821–1910
physician, medical author and educator, worker for women's
medical education
English
Appl Cyc Am Bio; Cyc Am Bio
and ad; Dict Am Auth; Dict
Am Bio; Dict Am Bio Men
Time; Eng Wom; Nat Cyc Am
Bio v9; Not Am Wom; Twent
Cen Bio Dict Not Am; Wom
Cent

658. Latimer, [Mary] Elizabeth (Wormeley)
1822–1904
novelist, educator, historian, writer on history
Baltimore, MD
English
Cyc Am Bio; Dict Am Auth; Dict
Am Bio; Dict Am Bio Men
Time; Index t Wom; Nat Cyc
Am Bio v9; Wom Cent

659. Burnz, Eliza Boardman
1823–1903
educator, phoneticist, stenographic educator, spelling reformer
English
Nat Cyc Am Bio v6; Wom Cent

660. Hoey, Josephine (Shaw)
1824–96
actor
English
Cyc Am Bio; Dict Am Bio Men
Time

661. Blackwell, Emily
1826–1910
physician
English
Index t Wom; Nat Cyc Am Bio
v9; Not Am Wom; Wom Cent

662. Brinkerhoff, Clara M.
born 1828
soprano singer, composer, music
educator
English
Wom Cent

663. Lander, Jean Margaret Davenport
1829–1903
actor
English
Cyc Am Bio; Dict Am Bio; Dict
Am Bio Men Time; Index t
Wom; Nat Cyc Am Bio v8;
Twent Cen Bio Dict Not Am

664. Cross, Sarah B.
flourished 1860s
Civil War nurse
English
Index t Wom

665. Ricketts, Fanny L.
flourished 1860s
Civil War humanitarian
English
Index t Wom

666. Wormeley, Katharine Prescott
1830/32–1908
Civil War relief and hospital
worker, writer on sanitation,
charity worker, philanthropist,
translator, biographer
Rhode Island
English
Cyc Am Bio; Dict Am Bio; Index
t Wom; Nat Cyc Am Bio v8;
Not Am Wom; Twent Cen Bio
Dict Not Am; Wom Cent

667. Barr, Amelia Edith Huddleston
1831/32–1919
novelist

English
Appl Cyc Am Bio; Cyc Am Bio;
Dict Am Auth; Dict Am Bio;
Index t Wom; Nat Cyc Am Bio
v4; Not Am Wom; Twent Cen
Bio Dict Not Am; Wom Cent

**668. Wood, Charlotte Matilda
(Vining)**
1831/36–1915
actor
English
Cyc Am Bio; Dict Am Bio Men
Time; Index t Wom; Not Am
Wom

669. Alcott, Louisa May
1832–88
novelist, children's author, mystery story writer
English
Appl Cyc Am Bio; Cyc Am Bio;
Dict Am Auth; Dict Am Bio;
Dict Lit Bio; Index t Wom; Nat
Cyc Am Bio v1; Not Am Wom;
Wom Lit; Wom Lit, More;
Wom Cent

670. Phillips, Adelaide
1833–82
actor, contralto opera singer
English
Cyc Am Bio; Dict Am Bio Men
Time; Nat Cyc Am Bio v6; Not
Am Wom; Twent Cen Bio Dict
Not Am

671. Leonowens, Anna Harriette (Crawford)
born 1834
author on Siam, kindergarten educator, missionary educator in
Siam
New York
English
Cyc Am Bio; Dict Am Bio

672. Booth, Emma Scarr
born 1835
author
English
Wom Cent

**673. Menken, Adah Isaachs;
Dolores Adios Fuertes**
1835/37–1868
actor, poet
Jewish
English
Cyc Am Bio; Dict Am Auth; Dict
Am Bio; Index t Wom; Nat Cyc
Am Bio v5; Not Am Wom;
Wom Lit, More

**674. Winslow, Catherine Mary
(Reignolds) "Kate"**
1836–1911
actor, dramatic reader
Boston, MA
English
Dict Am Auth; Nat Cyc Am Bio
v23

675. Rothwell, Annie
born 1837
poet
English; Canadian
Wom Cent

**676. Woodhull, Victoria Claflin;
Victoria Martin**
1838–1927
social reformer, political reformer, stockbroker, feminist
English (American expatriate to
England)
Dict Am Auth; Dict Am Bio;
Index t Wom; Not Am Wom

677. Spencer, Bella Zilfa
born 1840–67
author, novelist
English
Cyc Am Bio; Dict Am Auth; Dict
Am Bio Men Time

678. Wakefield, Emily Watkins
flourished 1870s–90s
singer, educator, lecturer, musical
director
Pennsylvania
English
Wom Cent

679. Sartain, Emily
1841–1927
painter, mezzotint engraver, etcher, illustrator, art educator
Philadelphia, PA
English
Cyc Am Bio; Dict Am Bio; Index
t Wom; Nat Cyc Am Bio v13;
Not Am Wom; Twent Cen Bio
Dict Not Am; Wom Cent

680. Sinclair, Catherine
died 1891
actor, manager
English
Index t Wom

**681. Rogers, Clara Kathleen
Barnett**
1844–1931
singer, author, composer
English
Dict Am Bio; Index t Wom

**682. Murphy, Blanche
Elizabeth Mary Annunciata
Noel, Lady**
1845/50–1881
author, magazine writer
English
Cyc Am Bio; Dict Am Auth; Nat
Cyc Am Bio v11

683. Whiffen, Blanche Galton
1845–1936
actor
English
Index t Wom; Not Am Wom

684. Wright, Emma Scholfield
born 1845

artist
English
Index t Wom

685. Donlevy, Alice Heighes
1846–1929
artist, illuminator, china painter,
wood engraver
English
Index t Wom; Wom Cent

686. Shaw, Anna Howard
1847–1919
minister, lecturer, suffragist,
women's rights worker, physician, temperance worker
Methodist
English
Dict Am Bio; Index t Wom; Nat
Cyc Am Bio v14; Not Am
Wom; Wom Cent

**687. Dayton, Elizabeth; Beth
Day**
born 1848
poet, author
Wisconsin
English
Wom Cent

**688. Neilson, Adelaide [Lillian];
Elizabeth Ann Brown**
1848/50–1880
actor
English
Cyc Am Bio; Dict Nat Bio; Index
t Wom

**689. Burnett, Frances Eliza
Hodgson**
1849–1924
novelist, children's author
English
Cyc Am Bio and ad; Dict Am
Auth; Dict Am Bio; Great Sov
Encyc; Index t Wom; Nat Cyc
Am Bio v1 and v20; Not Am
Wom; Twent Cen Bio Dict Not
Am; Wom Cent

690. Coghlan, Rose
1850/52–1932
actor
English
Dict Am Bio supp v1; Index t
Wom; Nat Cyc Am Bio v13;
Not Am Wom; Wom Cent

**691. Davenport, Fanny Lily
Gypsy**
1850–98
actor
English
Cyc Am Bio; Dict Am Bio; Index
t Wom; Nat Cyc Am Bio v4;
Not Am Wom; Twent Cen Bio
Dict Not Am; Wom Cent

692. Sterling, Antoinette
1850–1904
contralto opera singer
Sterlingville, NY

English
Index t Wom; Wom Cent

**693. Biddulph, Jessie Catherine
Vokes**
1851–84
actor, singer
English
Index t Wom

694. Ivers, Alice
1851–1930
pioneer
English
Index t Wom

**695. Chapin, Clara Christiana;
La Petite**
born 1852
suffragist, temperance worker
English
Wom Cent

**696. Langtry, Lillie Emilie
Charlotte le Breton**
1852–1929
actor
English
Cyc Am Bio; Index t Wom

697. Nicholls, Rhoda Holmes
1854–1930
artist, educator, painter
English
Dict Am Bio; Index t Wom; Nat
Cyc Am Bio v7; Wom Cent

698. Porter, Alice Hobbins
born 1854
journalist, newspaper editor
English
Wom Cent

699. Gobbi, Clothilde Operti
1856–1960
Metropolitan Opera singer
English
Obit File

700. Lessing, Madge
flourished 1890s
singer
English
Index t Wom

701. Channing, Blanche Mary
1863–1902
children's author
Brookline, MA
English
Dict Am Auth

702. Buck, Henriette
born 1864
educator
French; English; Canadian
Wom Cent

703. Russell, Annie
1864–1936
actor

English
Dict Am Bio supp v2; Nat Cyc
Am Bio v13; Not Am Wom

704. Skipworth, Alison
1864–1952
stage and screen actor
English
Obit File

705. Booth, Evangeline Cory
1865–1950
fourth general of the Salvation
Army, orator, musician, poet
Salvationist
English
Dict Am Bio supp v4; Dict Am
Rel Bio; Index t Wom; Nat Cyc
Am Bio csv2; Not Am Wom;
Obit File

**706. Booth, Maud Ballington
(Charlesworth)**
1865–1948
Salvation Army leader, evange-
list, philanthropist, prison re-
former, author, founder of PTA
Salvationist
English
Dict Am Auth; Index t Wom;
Nat Cyc Am Bio v14 and v38;
Not Am Wom; Obit File

707. Marlowe, Julia; Sarah
Frances "Fannie" Frost
1865/70–1950
Shakespearean actor
English
Dict Am Bio supp v4; Index t
Wom; Nat Cyc Am Bio v13;
Obit File; Wom Cent

708. Paget, Arthur, Lady
1865–1919
philanthropist, nurse
English
Index t Wom

**709. Meyer, Elizabeth Stuart
McCauley**
1866–1952
western pioneer
English
Index t Wom

710. Whitty, May Webster
1866–1948
stage and screen actor
English
Obit File

711. Campbell, Evelyn
born 1868
actor
English
Wom Cent

**712. Hayward, Beatrice Her-
ford**
1868–1952
monologuist, author, actor

English
Obit File

713. Duckering, Florence West
1869–1951
surgeon
Episcopalian
English
Nat Cyc Am Bio v40

714. Martin, Mrs.
flourished 1900s–10s
aviator
English
Index t Wom

715. Etzenhouser, Ida Pearson
1872–1936
religious worker
English
Index t Wom

716. Matthison, Edith Wynne
1872/75–1955
stage actor
English
Index t Wom; Obit File

717. Mannering, Mary; Flor-
ence Friend
1876–1953
Broadway stage actor
English
Nat Cyc Am Bio v42 and csv4;
Obit File

718. Collier, Constance; Laura
Constance Hardie
1878–1955
stage and screen actor, drama
coach
English
Dict Am Bio supp v5; Obit File

**719. Belmont, Eleanor Elise
Robson**
1879–1979
actor, author, nurse, philanthropist, patron of the arts, founder
of the Metropolitan Opera
Guild
English
Index t Wom; Cur Biog '44 and
'80

720. Anderson, Violette
born 1882
lawyer
Chicago, IL
English; Black
Encyc Black Am

721. Green, Florence Topping
circa 1882–1945
painter, portraitist
English
Index t Wom; Obit File

**722. Richter, Gisela Marie Au-
gusta**
1882–1972

classical archaeologist, museum
curator, author
English
Index t Wom; Not Am Wom
supp v1

723. Roosevelt, [Anna] Eleanor
1884–1962
social reformer, humanitarian,
author, lecturer
Washington, DC
English
Eng Wom; Index t Wom; Nat
Cyc Am Bio v57 and csv4 and
csv6; Not Am Wom supp v1;
Obit File

724. West, Claudine
circa 1884–1943
screenwriter
English
Index t Wom

725. Wycherley, Margaret
circa 1884–1956
stage and screen actor
English
Index t Wom; Obit File

726. Easton, Florence; Florence
Rogers
1885–1955
Metropolitan Opera dramatic so-
prano
English
Obit File

727. Kirmse, Marguerite
1885–1954
illustrator, etcher
English
Index t Wom

728. Borden, Mary; Lady
Spears
1886–1968
novelist, head of a World War II
field hospital in France
English (American expatriate to
England)
Index t Wom; Obit File

729. Leginska, Ethel Liggens
1886/90–1970
musician, pianist, conductor,
composer
English
Index t Wom; Not Am Wom
supp v1

730. Stirling, Mrs.; Lady Cholmondeley
married 1911
dancer
English
Index t Wom

731. Ward, Maisie
1889–1975
book publisher, author, lecturer,
Catholic church worker
Catholic

English
Cur Biog '75; Index t Wom

732. Bromhall, Winifred
flourished 1920s–40s
illustrator
English
Index t Wom

733. Brooks, Erica May
flourished 1920s–30s
athlete, lecturer
English
Index t Wom

734. Dragonette, Jessica
flourished 1920s–30s
radio singer
English
Index t Wom

735. Linley, Betty
1890–1951
actor
English
Obit File

736. Mackie, Janet Welch
1893–1959
physician, tropical medicine expert, US Public Health Service
adviser
English
Obit File

737. Fontanne, Lynn; Mrs. Alfred Lunt
born 1896
actor
English
Nat Cyc Am Bio csv4

738. Remsen, Alice
born 1896
composer, author, publisher
English
Index t Wom

**739. Lawrence, Gertrude (Klas-
sen);** Gertrude Alexandra
Dagma Lawrence Klassen
1898–1952
Broadway and London stage ac-
tor, singer
English
Dict Am Bio supp v5; Dict Nat
Bio 1951–1960; Index t Wom;
Obit File

740. Utley, Freda
1898–1978
author, journalist, foreign correspondent, lecturer
English
Index t Wom; Obit File

741. le Gallienne, Eva
born 1899
stage actor and producer
English
Nat Cyc Am Bio csv3

742. Braddock, Amelia
flourished 1930s
singer, music educator
English
Index t Wom

743. Caldwell, Taylor
born 1900
novelist
English
Index t Wom

744. Davis, Nelle
flourished 1930s
pharmacist
English
Index t Wom

745. Hilder, Vera Gertrude
flourished 1930s
actor, business executive
English
Index t Wom

746. Moir, Phyllis
flourished 1930s–40s
author, lecturer, editor
English
Index t Wom

747. Ovens, Florence Jane
flourished 1930s
child specialist, editor
English
Index t Wom

748. Payne-Gaposchkin, Ceilia Helena
born 1900
astronomer, educator, author
English
Index t Wom

749. Wilder, Jessie
flourished 1930s
poet, educator, critic, lecturer
English
Index t Wom

750. Wright, Jessie
1900–70
orthopedist, orthopedic inventor, medical educator
English
Nat Cyc Am Bio v55

751. Derrick-Swindells, Lucy
died 1952
poet, portrait painter
English
Obit File

752. Weston, Christine Goutiere
born 1904
author
English
Index t Wom

753. Jackson, Beatrice; Mrs. David Humphreys
born 1905

artist
Episcopalian
New York
English
Nat Cyc Am Bio csv13

754. Pitkin, Winifred Mercer; Winifred Smith
born 1905
physician
Episcopalian
English
Nat Cyc Am Bio csv7

755. Stewart, Wendy
born 1906
lawyer, law journalist
Los Angeles, CA
English
Nat Cyc Am Bio csv7

756. Graham, Sheila
born 1908
journalist, syndicated Hollywood newspaper columnist
English
Cur Biog '69

757. Harrison, Joan Mary
circa 1908
producer, scenarist
English
Index t Wom

758. Bevans, Philippa
1913–68
actor
English
Obit File

759. Long, Tania
born 1913
journalist
German; English
Index t Wom

760. McGrath, Leueen
born 1914
actor, playwright
English
Index t Wom

761. Dehavilland, Olivia [Mary]
born 1916
actor
Episcopalian
English
Index t Wom; Nat Cyc Am Bio csv9

762. Mitford, Jessica Lucy
born 1917
muckraking journalist, autobiographer
English
Cur Biog '74

763. Lupino, Ida
born 1918
actor

English
Index t Wom

764. McPartland, Marian
flourished 1950s–70s
jazz pianist
English
Cur Biog '76

765. Bainbridge, Katherine
born 1924
songwriter, poet
English
Index t Wom

766. Lansbury, Angela
born 1925
actor
English
Index t Wom

767. Jhabvala, Ruth Prawer
born 1927
novelist, short story and screenplay writer, writer of fiction about India
Jewish
Indian; English
Cur Biog '77; Wom Lit; Wom Lit, More

768. Collins, Joan
born 1933
actor
English
Index t Wom

ESTONIAN

769. Taba, Hilda
1902–67
educator, UNESCO consultant
Estonian
Nat Cyc Am Bio v54; Not Am Wom supp v1

FRENCH

770. Young, Poyner, Mrs.
flourished 1770s
patriot of American Revolution
French
Index t Wom

771. Guerin, Anne-Theresa; Mother Theodore
1798–1856
educator, Catholic nun, founder of the Sisters of Providence of St. Mary-of-the-Woods
Indiana
French
Dict Am Bio; Nat Cyc Am Bio v23

772. St. Augustine, Mother
flourished 1830s
Catholic nun

Catholic
French
Index t Wom

773. Mowatt, Anna Cora Ogden (Ritchie); Helen Berkley; Ann Cora Ogden (Mowatt) Ritchie
1819/22–70
author, actor, dramatist, novelist, autobiographer
French
Cyc Am Bio; Dict Am Auth; Dict Am Bio; Dict Am Bio Men Time; Index t Wom; Nat Cyc Am Bio v3 and csvB; Not Am Wom; Obit File; Twent Cen Bio Dict Not Am; Wom Lit, More

774. Clerc, Henrietta Fannie Virginie
born 1841
educator
French
Wom Cent

775. Tibbles, Susette Laflesche; Inshtatheumba; Bright Eyes
1854–1903
spokesperson for Native American rights
Native American (Osage); French
Great North Am Ind; Not Am Wom

776. Wharton, Edith Newbold (Jones)
1862–1937
novelist, short story writer, ghost story writer, autobiographer, travel writer, literary critic
New York, NY
French (American expatriate to Paris)
Dict Am Auth; Dict Am Bio supp v2; Dict Lit Bio v4 and v9; Index t Wom; Nat Cyc Am Bio v14 and csv2; Not Am Wom; Twent Cen Bio Dict Not Am; Wom Lit; Wom Lit, More

777. Buck, Henriette
born 1864
educator
French; English; Canadian
Wom Cent

778. Picotte, Susan la Flesche
1865–1915
physician, missionary
Native American (Osage); French
Great North Am Ind; Not Am Wom

779. Clews, Mary Else Whelen
1870–1959
patron of art
French
Obit File

780. Dufau, Jennie
died 1924

singer
French
Index t Wom

781. Stein, Gertrude
1874–1946
author, novelist, literary salon host, World War I ambulance driver and supply truck driver in France
Jewish
French (American expatriate to Paris)
Dict Am Bio supp v4; Dict Lit Bio v4; Index t Wom; Nat Cyc Am Bio v38 and csv4; Not Am Wom; Obit File; Who Who Jew Hist; Wom Lit; Wom Lit, More

782. Cowles, Sophia Esther
born 1875
toy manufacturer, fire escape manufacturer
Illinois
French
Nat Cyc Am Bio csv2

783. Barney, Natalie Clifford
1876–1972
novelist, salon host
French (American expatriate to Paris)
Dict Lit Bio v4; Not Am Wom supp v1; Wom Lit

784. Toklas, Alice Babette
1877/97–1967
writer, cookbook author
Jewish
French (American expatriate to Paris)
Dict Lit Bio v4; Index t Wom; Not Am Wom supp v1; Obit File

785. Durnell, Fannie Dafflon; Nitta Jo
born 1881
actor
French
Nat Cyc Am Bio csv1

786. Loy, Mina
1882–1966
poet
French (American expatriate to Paris)
Dict Lit Bio v4

787. Bercovici, Naomi Lebrescu
1883–1957
artist, poet
New York
French
Nat Cyc Am Bio v45

788. Anderson, Margaret Carolyn
1886–1973
editor, author, novelist, autobiographer

French (American expatriate to Paris)
Dict Lit Bio v4; Not Am Wom supp v1

789. Beach, Sylvia Woodbridge
1887–1962
bookshop proprietor, publisher of James Joyce, lending library owner
French (American expatriate to Paris)
Dict Lit Bio v4; Nat Cyc Am Bio v47; Not Am Wom supp v1; Obit File

790. Boulanger, Nadia
1887–1979
composer, pianist, music educator, conductor
French
Cur Biog '80

791. Solano, Solita
1888–1975
journalist, drama critic, novelist, poet
French (American expatriate to Paris)
Dict Lit Bio v4

792. Gilliam, Florence
flourished 1920s–40s
journalist, theater critic, magazine publisher
French (American expatriate to Paris)
Dict Lit Bio v4

793. Porter, Katherine Anne
1890/94–1980
author, short story writer
Texas
French (American expatriate to Paris)
Cur Biog '80; Dict Lit Bio v4 and v9; Encyc South Hist; Index t Wom; Wom Lit; Wom Lit, More

794. Cannell, Kathleen
1891–1974
journalist, fashion editor, ballet critic, autobiographer
French (American expatriate to Paris)
Dict Lit Bio v4

795. Barnes, Djuna
born 1892
novelist, short story writer, poet, playwright, theatrical columnist, illustrator, portrait painter
French (American expatriate to Paris)
Dict Lit Bio v4 and v9; Wom Lit; Wom Lit, More

796. Crosby, Caresse; Polly Jacob
1892–1970

poet, patron of the arts, cofounder of the Black Sun Press
French (American expatriate to Paris)
Dict Lit Bio v4

797. Flanner, Janet
1892–1978
journalist, novelist, lecturer, *New Yorker* correspondent from Paris
French (American expatriate to Paris)
Cur Biog '79; Dict Lit Bio v4; Index t Wom; Obit File

798. Bordoni, Irene
circa 1893–1953
musical comedy actor
French; Corsican
Index t Wom; Obit File

799. Gordon, Caroline; Caroline Tate
1895–1981
novelist
French (American expatriate to Paris)
Dict Lit Bio v4 and v9; Index t Wom; Wom Lit; Wom Lit, More

800. Larrimore, Francine
born 1898
actor
French
Index t Wom

801. Coleman, Emily Holmes
1899–1974
autobiographer, poet
Catholic
French (American expatriate to Paris)
Dict Lit Bio v4

802. Harris, Jane Davenport
flourished 1930s
sculptor, explorer
French
Index t Wom

803. Biddle, Margret Thompson
1902–56
author, keeper of a Paris salon for political and literary personalities
French (American expatriate to Paris)
Obit File

804. Boyle, Kay
born 1902/03
short story writer
French (American expatriate to Paris)
Dict Lit Bio v4 and v9; Index t Wom; Wom Lit, More

805. d'Arville, Colette
1902–44
soprano concert and opera singer

French
Obit File

806. Nin, Anais
1903–77
author, novelist, diarist, printer, feminist
French
Cur Biog '75 and '77; Dict Lit Bio v2 and v4; Index t Wom; Wom Lit; Wom Lit, More

807. Vreeland, Diana (Dalziel)
born circa 1903
fashion editor, journalist, costume museum consultant
French
Cur Biog '79; Index t Wom

808. Dache, Lilly
born 1904
milliner, fashion designer
French
Index t Wom

809. Pons, Alice Josephina "Lily"; Mrs. Andre Kostelanetz
1904–76
Metropolitan Opera coloratura-soprano singer
French
Cur Biog '76; Index t Wom; Nat Cyc Am Bio csv7; Obit File

810. Grippon, Eva
died 1956
singer
French
Index t Wom

811. Colbert, Claudette
born 1907
actor
French
Index t Wom

812. Trigere, Pauline
born 1912
fashion designer
French
Index t Wom

813. Calvet, Corinne
born 1925
actor
French
Index t Wom

814. Darcel, Denise
born 1925
singer, actor
French
Index t Wom

815. Verdy, Violette
born 1933
ballet dancer, manager of the Boston Ballet
French
Cur Biog '69 and '80

FRENCH CANADIAN

816. Mance, Jeanne
1606–73
philanthropist, hospital founder
and administrator
French Canadian
Cyc Am Bio; Index t Wom

GERMAN

817. Frietchie, Barbara
1766–1862/65
Union Civil War hero
Maryland
German
Index t Wom; Who Who Dur Am
Rev

**818. Robinson, Therese Alber-
tine Louise (von Jakob); Mrs.
Edward; Talvi; Talvj**
1797–1869/70
author, short story writer, historical writer, translator, linguist,
philologist
German
Cyc Am Bio; Dict Am Bio; Dict
Am Bio Men Time; Index t
Wom; Nat Cyc Am Bio v1

819. Sontag, Henriette
1805–54
opera singer
German
Cyc Am Bio

820. Dassel, Herminie
died 1857
painter
German
Index t Wom

821. Ullmann, Amelia
flourished 1850s
author
German
Index t Wom

822. Bloede, Marie
1821–70
author
German
Appl Cyc Am Bio; Cyc Am Bio

**823. Janauschek, Francesca Ro-
mance Magdalena; Fanny**
1829/30–1904
actor
German
Dict Nat Bio; Index t Wom; Nat
Cyc Am Bio v10; Not Am Wom

**824. Zakrzewska, Marie
Elizabeth**
1829–1902
physician, hospital founder

Polish; German
Cyc Am Bio; Dict Am Bio; Index
t Wom; Not Am Wom

825. Baum, A.
flourished 1860s; died 1910
Civil War patriot
German
Index t Wom

826. Gardner, Adaline
flourished 1860s
Civil War patriot
German
Index t Wom

827. Ney, Elizabeth
1833/45–1907
sculptor
German
Dict Am Bio; Index t Wom; Nat
Cyc Am Bio v13; Not Am Wom

828. Kraus-Boelte, Maria
1836–1918
kindergarten educator
German
Dict Am Bio; Nat Cyc Am Bio
v13; Not Am Wom

**829. McCrackin, Josephine
Woempner Clifford**
1838/46–1920
author, journalist, clubwoman,
conservationist
German
Index t Wom; Not Am Wom

830. McCauley, Barbara
flourished 1870s
western pioneer
German
Index t Wom

831. Skelton, Henriette
born 1842
temperance worker
California
German
Wom Cent

**832. Bloede, Gertrude; Stuart
Sterne**
1845–1905
poet
Brooklyn, NY
German
Dict Am Auth; Dict Nat Bio; Nat
Cyc Am Bio v10; Wom Cent

**833. Teuffel, Blanche Willis
(Howard)**
1847–98
novelist
German (American expatriate to
Germany)
Dict Am Auth

834. Pettet, Isabella M.
born 1848
physician
Methodist

New York
German
Wom Cent

835. Straus, Lina Gutherz
1854–1930
patron of Hadassah medical work
in Palestine
Jewish
German
Nat Cyc Am Bio v22

836. Bauer, Bertha
1862–1940
music educator
Cincinnati, OH
German
Index t Wom; Nat Cyc Am Bio
v31

837. Baur, Clara
died 1912
music educator
Ohio
German
Nat Cyc Am Bio v26

838. Fels, Mary
born 1863
Zionist
Jewish
German
Nat Cyc Am Bio csv1

**839. Schoen-Rene, Anna Euge-
nia**
1864–1942
voice teacher
German
Index t Wom

840. Collitz, Klara Hechtenbert
circa 1865–1944
German philologist
German
Index t Wom; Nat Cyc Am Bio
csv1

841. Hamilton, Edith
1867–1963
author, classicist, educator, head-
master of Bryn Mawr College
German
Index t Wom; Nat Cyc Am Bio
v52; Not Am Wom supp v1;
Obit File

842. Lewing, Adele
born 1868
pianist, composer
German
Wom Cent

843. Mannes, Clara Domrosch
1869–1948
pianist, music educator
Lutheran
German
Dict Am Bio supp v4; Index t
Wom

844. Arnold, Alma Cuisian
born 1871
chiropractor
German
Index t Wom

**845. Gadski-Tauscher, Johanna
Wilhelmine**
born 1872
soprano opera singer
German
Nat Cyc Am Bio csv2

**846. MacDonald, Marie Bruck-
mann**
1875–1954
Socialist party leader
German
Obit File

**847. Vaka, Demetra; Demetra
Vaka Brown**
1877–1946
novelist
German
Index t Wom

848. Carus, Emma
1879–1927
vaudeville actor
German
Index t Wom

849. Lewars, Elsie Singmaster
born 1879
author
Lutheran
Pennsylvania
German
Nat Cyc Am Bio csv3

850. Bieber, Margarete
1880–1978
historian, author, archaeologist,
educator, authority on Greek
and Roman art
German
Obit File

**851. Bostelmann, Else W. von
Roder**
circa 1882–1961
illustrator
German
Index t Wom

852. Hempel, Frieda
1885–1955
Metropolitan Opera soprano sing-
er
German
Obit File

853. Horney, Karen Danielson
1885–1952
psychiatrist, psychoanalyst, dean
of the American Institute for
Psychoanalysis
German
Dict Am Bio supp v5; Encyc
Third Reich; Index t Wom; Not
Am Wom supp v1; Obit File

854. Drexel, Constance
1888–1952
newspaper reporter
German
Obit File

855. Lehmann, Lotte
1888–1976
operatic soprano, lieder singer
German
Cur Biog '70 and '76; Obit File

856. Sender, Toni
born 1888
labor leader
German
Index t Wom

857. Fromm-Reichman, Frieda
1889–1957
psychiatrist, psychoanalyst, authority on schizophrenia, faculty chairperson of the Washington School of Psychiatry
Jewish
Washington, DC
German
Dict Am Bio supp v5; Not Am Wom supp v1; Obit File

858. Stern, Catherine Brieger "Kathe"
1894–1973
educator, child education specialist, writer on child education
Lutheran
German
Nat Cyc Am Bio v57; Not Am Wom supp v1

859. Manski, Dorothee
born circa 1895
singer
Jewish
German
Index t Wom

860. Bernstein, Lotte Kirschner
1897–1971
psychiatrist, psychoanalyst
Jewish
Kentucky
German
Nat Cyc Am Bio v57

861. Duncan, Irma
1897–1977
modern dancer
German
Index t Wom; Obit File

862. Ball, Erna D.
flourished 1930s
neurologist
German
Index t Wom

863. Bary, Gertrude
flourished 1930s
pianist
German
Index t Wom

864. Baumann, Anny
flourished 1930s
physician
German
Index t Wom

865. Jacobi, Lotte J.
flourished 1930s
photographer
German
Index t Wom

866. Lewinson, Thea Stein
flourished 1930s
graphologist
German
Index t Wom

867. McFadden, Dorothy L.
flourished 1930s
business executive
German
Index t Wom

868. Mendelssohn, Eleonora
1900–51
actor
German
Obit File

869. Niswonger, Ilse W.
born 1900
sculptor
German
Index t Wom

870. Peritz, Edith
flourished 1930s
surgeon
German
Index t Wom

871. Sandberg, Marta Ehrlich
flourished 1930s
chemist
German
Index t Wom

872. Strassmann, Antonie
1902–52
aviator, World War II hero, anti-Nazi worker
German
Obit File

873. Dietrich, Marlene
born 1904
actor
German
Index t Wom

874. Mann, Erika
1905–69
author, writer on Germany, actor, lecturer
German
Cur Biog '69; Index t Wom

875. Arendt, Hannah
1906–1975
political theorist, philosopher
Jewish
German
Cur Biog '76; Not Am Wom supp v1; Obit File

876. Mayer, Marie Gertrude Goeppert
1906–72
theoretical physicist, Nobel Prize winner in physics, educator, author
German; Polish
Cur Biog '72; Index t Wom; Nat Cyc Am Bio v58; Not Am Wom supp v1; Obit File

877. Long, Tania
born 1913
journalist
German; English
Index t Wom

878. Manski, Inge
born circa 1913
singer
Jewish
German
Index t Wom

879. Zorina, Vera
born 1917
dancer
German
Index t Wom

880. Larsen, Lisa (Rasmussen)
1925–59
photojournalist
German
Obit File

881. Gray, Hannah Holborn
born 1930
president of the University of Chicago, historian
Chicago, IL
German
Cur Biog '79

GREEK

882. Chryssa (Vardea)
born 1933
sculptor
Greek
Cur Biog '78

GUATEMALAN

883. Arrue de Miranda, Luz
born 1852
poet
Guatemalan
Appl Cyc Am Bio

HUNGARIAN

884. de Fere, A. Litsner
flourished 1870s–80s
classical singer, voice trainer
Hungarian
Wom Cent

885. Serrano, Emelia Benic
flourished 1890s
opera singer
Austrian; Hungarian
Wom Cent

886. Kohut, Rebekah Bettelheim
1864–1951
social welfare leader, educator, suffragist, lecturer, author, Jewish welfare worker
Jewish
Hungarian
Index t Wom; Nat Cyc Am Bio v41 and csv5; Not Am Wom supp v1

887. Lederer, Charlotte
1868–1955
children's author, illustrator
Hungarian
Obit File

888. Mero-Iron, Yolanda
1877/87–1963
pianist
Jewish
Hungarian
Index t Wom

889. Schwimmer, Rosika
1877–1948
feminist, suffragist, pacifist, author, editor
Jewish
Hungarian
Dict Am Bio supp v4; Not Am Wom; Obit File

890. Matzenauer, Margaret
1881–1963
opera singer, opera coach
Catholic
Hungarian
Nat Cyc Am Bio v51

891. Petersham, Miska
1888–1960
illustrator
Hungarian
Index t Wom

892. Banky, Vilma
flourished 1920s–30s
actor
Hungarian
Index t Wom

893. Gabor, Jolie
born 1896
businessperson

Irish
Cyc Am Bio; Dict Am Bio; Dict
Am Bio Men Time; Index t
Wom; Nat Cyc Am Bio v8; Not
Am Wom; Twent Cen Bio Dict
Not Am

928. Jones, Mary Harris;
Mother Jones
1830–1930
labor leader, union organizer
Irish
Bio Dict Am Lab; Dict Am Bio;
Eng Wom; Index t Wom; Nat
Cyc Am Bio v23

929. Lee, Mary W.
flourished 1860s
Civil War nurse, patriot, philan-
thropist
Irish
Index t Wom

930. Lynch, Joseph, Mother
flourished 1860s
Catholic nun, nurse
Catholic
Irish
Index t Wom

931. Grant, Bridget
1831–1923
pioneer, innkeeper
Irish
Index t Wom

932. Adams, Mary (Mathews)
1840–1902
educator, poet
Madison, WI
Irish
Dict Am Auth; Wom Cent

933. Blake, Mary Elizabeth
McGrath
1840–1907
author, poet
Catholic
Boston, MA
Irish
Dict Am Auth; Dict Am Bio;
Wom Cent

934. O'Keefe, Katharine A.
flourished 1870s–90s
educator, lecturer
Massachusetts
Irish
Wom Cent

935. Milne, Frances Margaret
born 1846
author, journalist, poet, political
essayist
California
Irish
Wom Cent

936. Moore, Marguerite
born 1849
orator, patriot, pacifist

Irish
Wom Cent

937. Halvey, Margaret Mary
Brophy
flourished 1880s
clubwoman, educator, poet
Irish
Index t Wom

938. Proctor, Mary
flourished 1880s–1910s
astronomer
Irish
Index t Wom; Nat Cyc Am Bio
v9; Twent Cen Bio Dict Not
Am

939. Rehan, Ada (Crehan)
1859/60–1916
actor
New York
Irish
Cyc Am Bio; Dict Am Bio; Dict
Irish Bio; Index t Wom; Nat
Cyc Am Bio v1; Not Am Wom;
Twent Cen Bio Dict Not Am;
Wom Cent

940. McCreight, Mary Baldwin
born 1862
pharmacist, plague and epidemic
nurse
Irish
Nat Cyc Am Bio csv1

941. Voynich, Ethel Lilian
1864–1960
novelist
Irish
Obit File

942. Young, Ella
1868–1956
poet, authority on Celtic folklore
Irish
Obit File

943. Vermilye, Kate Jordan
1871–1926
author, novelist, short story writer
Irish
Nat Cyc Am Bio v20

944. O'Toole, Mary
born 1874
judge, suffragist, banker
Washington, DC
Irish
Nat Cyc Am Bio csv2

945. Kelly, Myra
1875/76–1910
author, humorist, social reformer,
educator
Irish
Dict Am Auth; Dict Am Bio;
Index t Wom; Nat Cyc Am Bio
v24; Wom Lit, More

946. Swartz, Maud O'Farrell
1879–1937
labor leader
Catholic
New York
Irish
Bio Dict Am Lab; Not Am Wom

947. O'Mahoney, Katherine A.
flourished 1910s
publisher, editor, lecturer, club
leader
Irish
Index t Wom

948. O'Connor, Una; Agnes
Teresa McGlade
1881–1959
charactor actor
Irish
Obit File

949. Allgood, Sara
1884–1950
actor
Irish
Obit File

950. Coyle, Kathleen
1886–1952
novelist
Irish
Obit File

951. Colum, Mary
1887–1957
author, literary critic
Irish
Nat Cyc Am Bio v44

952. Degnan, Bridget Dixon
died 1940
western pioneer
Irish
Index t Wom

953. Snow, Carmel White
1890–1961
editor of *Harper's Bazaar*, journalist, fashion expert
Irish
Index t Wom; Obit File

954. O'Driscoll, Hannah
born 1892
nurse
Irish
Index t Wom

955. Garrett, Eileen Jeanette;
Jean Lyttle
1893–1970
parapsychologist, novelist, founder of the Parapsychology Foundation
Anglican
Irish
Nat Cyc Am Bio v55; Obit File

956. Parnell, Eileen
born 1902
sculptor

Irish
Index t Wom

957. Garson, Greer
born 1908
actor
Irish
Index t Wom

958. O'Sullivan, Maureen
born 1911
actor
Irish
Index t Wom

959. Praxedes Carty, Mother
died 1963
Catholic nun
Catholic
Irish
Index t Wom

960. Frank, Mary Hughes
born 1919
author, child guidance expert
Irish
Index t Wom

961. Daly, Maureen Patricia
born 1921
author, editor
Irish
Index t Wom

962. O'Hara, Maureen
born 1921
actor
Irish
Index t Wom

ITALIAN

963. Brewster, Anne M.
Hampton
1818–92
author
Italian (American expatriate to
Rome)
Dict Am Auth

964. Ristori, Adelaide
1822–1906
actor
Italian
Cyc Am Bio

965. Patti, Carlotta
1835/40–1889
soprano opera singer
Italian
Cyc Am Bio; Dict Am Bio Men
Time; Dict Nat Bio

966. Alexander, Esther Frances
"Francesca"
1837–1917
artist, illustrator, author, translator, philanthropist

Italian (American expatriate to
Italy)
Dict Am Auth; Not Am Wom

967. Solari, Mary M.
born 1849
artist
Memphis, TN
Italian
Wom Cent

**968. Cabrini, Francis Xavier,
St.**
1850–1917
founder of the Missionary Sisters
of the Sacred Heart, Catholic
nun
Catholic
Italian
Dict Am Bio supp v1; Dict Am
Rel Bio; Index t Wom; Nat Cyc
Am Bio v27; Not Am Wom

969. Riccardo, Corona
flourished 1890s
actor
Italian
Index t Wom

970. MacKubin, Florence
1861–1918
portrait and miniature painter
Italian
Dict Am Bio; Index t Wom; Nat
Cyc Am Bio v15

971. Fitzgerald, Alice
1873–1962
chief nurse of the American Red
Cross in Europe
Italian
Obit File

972. Carreras, Maria Avani
1877–1966
concert pianist
Italian
Obit File

973. Bernardy, Amy Allemand
born 1880
social reformer
Italian
Index t Wom

974. Secondari, Rita Hume
1883–1953
Seattle Times correspondent in
Italy
Washington
Italian
Obit File

975. Galli-Curci, Amelita
1889–1963
Metropolitan Opera coloratura
soprano singer
Italian
Obit File

976. Galassi, Josephine
1892–1958

provincial superior of the Salesian
Sisters of the United States
Catholic
Italian
Obit File

**977. Corte, Fausta Vitorio
Mengarini**
1893–1952
sculptor
Italian
Obit File

**978. Whitman, Lucile Mara de
Vescovi, Countess**
born 1893
fashion designer, businessperson
Italian
Index t Wom

979. Monti-Gorsey, Lola
flourished 1930s
singer
Italian
Index t Wom

980. Landi, Elissa
1905–48
stage and screen actor, novelist
Italian
Obit File

981. Sergio, Lisa
born 1905
radio personality
Italian
Index t Wom

982. Fermi, Laura Capon
born 1907
author
Italian
Index t Wom

983. Albanese, Lucia
born 1913
singer
Italian
Index t Wom

984. Bancroft, Anne
born 1931
singer, actor
Italian
Index t Wom

985. Angeli, Pier
born 1933
actor
Italian (Sardinia)
Index t Wom

**986. Scala, Gia; Giovanna
Scoglio**
1934–72
screen actor
California
Italian
Obit File

JAPANESE

987. Miyakawa, Kikuko
flourished 1930s
poet, artist
Japanese
Index t Wom

988. Okama, Kyoko
flourished 1930s
medical missionary
Japanese
Index t Wom

989. Osato, Sono
born 1919
dancer, actor
Japanese
Index t Wom

990. Sone, Monica
born 1919
author
Japanese
Index t Wom

991. Mink, Patsy Takemoto
born 1927
representative to Congress
Japanese
Index t Wom

992. Umeki, Miyoshi
born 1930
singer, actor
Japanese
Index t Wom

993. Ono, Yoko
born 1933
modern and conceptual artist,
musician
Japanese
Cur Biog '72

LEBANESE

994. Khoury, Marie Azeez El
1883–1957
jewelry designer
Lebanese
Obit File

LITHUANIAN

995. Berenson, Senda
1868–1954
basketball player, gymnast, physical education authority
Jewish
Lithuanian
Dict Am Bio supp v5

**996. Bryant, Lane; Lena Him-
melstein; Mrs. Albert Malsin**
1881/1895–1951

dress merchant, mail order busi-
nessperson, maternity and spe-
cial sizes designer
Jewish
New York
Lithuanian
Nat Cyc Am Bio v47; Index t
Wom; Who Who Jew Hist

**997. Emch, Minna Elizabeth
Libman**
1904–58
psychiatrist, psychiatric educator
and author
Chicago, IL
Lithuanian
Nat Cyc Am Bio v47

MAORI

998. Te Kanawa, Kiri
born 1946?
Metropolitan Opera mezzo-sopra-
no singer
New Zealand; Maori
Cur Biog '78

MEXICAN

999. Cruz, Juana Inez de la
1651–95
poet
Mexican
Cyc Am Bio; Wom Cour

**1000. Ord, Augustias de la Gu-
erra**
1815–80
historian of California
California
Mexican
Dict Mex Am Hist

1001. Guirado, Luz (Sanchez)
flourished 1880s–1930s
patron of the Catholic church
Catholic
Los Angeles, CA
Mexican
Am Bio New Cyc

1002. Gonzales Parsons, Lucia
circa 1852–1942
feminist, labor leader, a founder
of International Labor Defense
and of Industrial Workers of the
World, Socialist party worker
Mexican
Dict Mex Am Hist

1003. Zavala, Adina Emila de
1861–1955
historian of Texas, historical
worker
Mexican
Dict Mex Am Hist

1004. Urrea, Teresa
1873–1906
folk healer, mystic
Mexican
Dict Mex Am Hist

1005. Esparza, Francisca
1883–1962
litigant
Texas
Mexican
Dict Mex Am Hist

1006. Grever, Maria
1894–1951
composer, singer, pianist
Mexican
Index t Wom; Obit File

1007. Moreno, Luisa
flourished 1930s–50s
union organizer
Mexican
Dict Mex Am Hist

1008. Niggli, Josephina
born 1910
author
Mexican
Index t Wom

1009. Tenayuca (Brooks), Emma
born 1916
civil rights worker, labor leader, Communist party worker
Mexican
Dict Mex Am Hist

1010. Christian, Linda
born 1923
actor
Mexican
Index t Wom

1011. Banuelos, Ramona Acosta
born 1925
US treasurer, banker
Los Angeles, CA
Mexican
Dict Mex Am Hist

1012. Jaramillo, Mari-Luci
born 1928
educator, US ambassador to Honduras
Mexican
Dict Mex Am Hist

1013. Olivarez, Graciela
born 1928
lawyer, United Way executive, civil rights worker
Mexican
Dict Mex Am Hist

1014. Huerta, Dolores Fernandez
1930–post 1970
United Farm Workers executive
Catholic
California
Mexican
Bio Dict Am Lab; Dict Mex Am Hist

1015. Carr, Vicki; Florencia Bicenta de Casillas Martinez Cardona
born 1940
popular singer
Mexican
Dict Mex Am Hist

1016. Hernandez, Maria L.
flourished 1970s–80s
Mexican American community leader, civil rights worker
Texas
Mexican
Dict Mex Am Hist

1017. Zapata, Carman
flourished 1970s–80s
television, stage, and screen actor; director
Los Angeles, CA
Mexican
Dict Mex Am Hist

1018. Baca-Barragan, Polly
born 1941
Colorado state senator, housing reformer
Colorado
Mexican
Dict Mex Am Hist

1019. Baez, Joan
born 1941
folk and popular singer, anti–Vietnam war activist, pacifist, worker for Amnesty International
Mexican
Dict Mex Am Hist; Index t Wom

1020. Rondstadt, Linda
born 1946
popular and country music singer
Los Angeles, CA
Mexican
Cur Biog '78; Dict Mex Am Hist

1021. Lopez, Nancy
born 1957
golfer
Mexican
Cur Biog '78; Dict Mex Am Hist

MORAVIAN

1022. Watteville, Benigna [Henrietta] Justine Zinzendorf von
1725–89
educator, a founder of the Moravian Seminary and College for Women
Moravian
Moravian
Index t Wom; Not Am Wom

1023. Brown, Catherine
1800–23
Moravian religious worker
Moravian
Alabama
Moravian; Native American (Cherokee)
Am Bio Dict

1024. Fleshman, Mina Pepper
1879–1965
realtor, developer
Moravian
North Carolina
Moravian
Nat Cyc Am Bio v50

NATIVE AMERICAN

1025. Squaw, Sachem
flourished 1640s
Queen of the Indians in New England
Native American
Am Bio Dict

1026. Ganneaktena, Catharine
died 1673
founder of a Christian village for Native Americans
Native American
Cyc Am Bio

1027. Weetamoo
circa 1650–76
tribal leader
Native American (Pocasset)
Great North Am Ind

1028. Tekakwitha, Catherine "Kateri"
1656?–80
Catholic leader
Catholic
Native American
Dict Am Rel Bio; Great North Am Ind; Index t Wom; Not Am Wom

1029. Martha
1685–1805 [sic]
agent of the Mohegan people
Connecticut
Native American (Mohegan)
Am Bio Dict

1030. Musgrove, Mary; Coosaponakeesa
circa 1770–circa 1763
Native American leader in colonial Georgia, interpreter, trader
Georgia
Native American (Creek)
Great North Am Ind; Not Am Wom

1031. Brant, Mary; Molly Brant; Deganiwadonte
circa 1736–96

British advocate, worker for Native American rights
Native American (Mohawk-Iroquois)
Great North Am Ind; Not Am Wom; Read Encyc Am West

1032. Ward, Nancy; Nanye hi; The Pocahontas of the West
circa 1738/40–1822
Native American leader and civil rights advocate
Native American (Cherokee)
Cyc Am Bio; Great North Am Ind; Not Am Wom; Who Who Dur Am Rev

1033. Gedney, Rachel
1741–1848
last of the Mohegan people
New York
Native American (Mohegan)
Am Bio Dict

1034. Montour, Esther
flourished 1778
Seneca leader
Native American (Seneca)
Cyc Am Bio

1035. Burr, Mary
1751–1852
last of the Punkapaug Indians
Native American (Punkapaug)
Am Bio Dict

1036. Howdee, Sarah
died 1827
last of the Queen Awashunk people
Rhode Island
Native American (Queen Awashunk)
Am Bio Dict

1037. Sacajawea; Bird Woman
1784/87–1812
interpreter, pioneer, guide
Native American (Shoshone)
Dict Am Bio; Great North Am Ind; Index t Wom; Not Am Wom; Read Encyc Am West

1038. Brown, Catherine
1800–23
Moravian religious worker
Moravian
Alabama
Moravian; Native American (Cherokee)
Am Bio Dict

1039. Homer, Elmira
died 1852
last of the Turkey Hill people
New Milford, CT
Native American (Turkey Hill)
Am Bio Dict

1040. Converse, Harriet Maxwell; Ya-ie-wah-no; Salome; Musidora
1836–1903
Seneca rights advocate, Seneca tribal leader, author, folklorist, Native American scholar, poet
New York
Native American (Seneca by adoption)
Dict Am Auth; Not Am Wom; Twent Cen Bio Dict Not Am; Wom Cent

1041. Chipeta
circa 1842–1924
Native American hero
Native American
Index t Wom

1042. Silcott, Jane
1842–95
hero
Native American
Index t Wom

1043. Winnemucca, Sarah (Thocmetony)
circa 1844–91
hero, Native American rights worker
Native American (Paviotsu Paiute)
Dict Am Bio; Eng Wom; Great North Am Ind; Not Am Wom

1044. Lewis, Edmonia [Mary]
1845–90
sculptor
Native American (Chippewa); Black
Cyc Am Bio; Encyc Black Am; Index t Wom; Nat Cyc Am Bio v5; Negro Alman; Not Am Wom; Prof Negro Wom v1; Twent Cen Bio Dict Not Am

1045. Winema, Kaitchkona; Toby Riddle
circa 1848–1932
arbitrator
Native American (Modoc)
Great North Am Ind

1046. Davis, Alice Brown
1852–1935
leader of Seminole people
Native American (Seminole)
Not Am Wom

1047. Tibbles, Susette Laflesche; Inshtatheumba; Bright Eyes
1854–1903
spokesperson for Native American rights
Native American (Osage); French
Great North Am Ind; Not Am Wom

1048. Johnson, Emily Pauline; Tekahionwake
1861–1913
poet
Anglican
Native American (Mohawk)
Great North Am Ind; Wom Cent

1049. Picotte, Susan la Flesche
1865–1915
physician, missionary
Native American (Osage); French
Great North Am Ind; Not Am Wom

1050. Dietz, Angel de Cora; Hinookmahiw-kilinaka; Fleecy Cloud Floating into Place
circa 1871–1919
artist
Native American (Winnebago)
Great North Am Ind

1051. Bonnin, Gertrude Simmons; Zitkala-sa
1875–1938
author, Native American rights worker
Native American (Yankton Sioux)
Great North Am Ind; Not Am Wom

1052. Lawson, Roberta Campbell
1878–1940
clubwoman, student of Native American music and culture, ethnologist, Native American leader, singer, songwriter
Presbyterian
Native American (Delaware)
Great North Am Ind; Nat Cyc Am Bio v36; Not Am Wom

1053. Martinez, Maria Montoya
born 1881/87
ceramicist
New Mexico
Native American (Pueblo-San Ildefonso)
Ind Today; Read Encyc Am West

1054. Mountain Wolf Woman; Kehachiwinga
1884–1960
autobiographer
Native American (Winnebago)
Great North Am Ind

1055. Deloria, Ella Carla; Anpetu Wastewin
1888–1971
interpreter, linguist, ethnologist, anthropologist, lecturer
Native American (Yankton Sioux-Dakota)
Great North Am Ind; Ind Today; Not Am Wom supp v1

1056. Wawa Calac Chaw; Keep from the Water
1888–1972
author, artist, feminist, lecturer on Native American and feminist matters
Native American (Luiseno)
Great North Am Ind

1057. Bronson, Ruth Muskrat
born 1897
Cherokee government official, field representative of Save the Children Federation
Oklahoma
Native American (Cherokee)
Ind Today; Read Encyc Am West

1058. George, Lucy Squirrel
born 1897
basket weaver
Native American (Cherokee)
Ind Today

1059. Tantaquidgeon, Gladys
born 1899
anthropologist
Native American (Mohegan)
Ind Today

1060. Wright, Muriel Hazel
1899–1975
historian, community leader
Native American (Choctaw)
Ind Today; Not Am Wom supp v1

1061. Akers, Dolly Smith
born 1902
tribal leader
Native American (Assiniboine)
Ind Today

1062. Bailey, Mildred; Mildred Rinker
1903/07–1951
blues and jazz singer
Native American
Dict Am Bio supp v5; Obit File

1063. Winnie, Lucille
born 1904
author
Native American (Seneca-Cayuga)
Ind Today

1064. Hall, Ina Beauchamp
born 1905
community leader
Native American (Arikara)
Ind Today

1065. Horne, Esther Burnett
born 1909
educator
Native American (Shoshone)
Ind Today

1066. Menard, Nellie Star Boy
born 1910
craft artist, featherworker

Native American (Dakota-Brule)
Ind Today

1067. Penn, Jane Pablo
born 1910
historian, museum director
Native American (Wana-Kik-Cahuilla)
Ind Today

1068. Tsianini, Princess
flourished 1940s
singer
Native American
Index t Wom

1069. Rickard, Montana Hopkins
born 1913
professor of humanities
Native American (Cherokee)
Ind Today

1070. Peterson, Helen White
born 1915
assistant to the commissioner of the Bureau of Indian affairs, race relations worker
Colorado
Native American (Dakota-Oglala)
Ind Today; Read Encyc Am West

1071. Walz, Erma Hicks
born 1915
chief of tribal relations of the Bureau of Indian Affairs
Native American (Cherokee)
Ind Today

1072. Velarde, Pablita
born 1918
artist
Native American (Pueblo-Santa Clara)
Ind Today

1073. Pambrun, Audra Marie
born 1919
nurse
Native American (Blackfoot)
Ind Today

1074. Cloud, Roe, Mrs.
flourished 1950s
missionary
Native American
Index t Wom

1075. Hightower, Rosella
born 1920
ballet dancer, choreographer
Native American (Choctaw)
Index t Wom; Ind Today

1076. Paddock, Constance Harper
born 1920
chief clerk of the Alaska House of Representatives
Alaska

Native American (Athabascan)
Ind Today

1077. Poling, Hazel
born 1920
administrator of Indian Health
Service
Native American (Ottawa)
Ind Today

1078. Ricklefs, Elsie Gardner
born 1920
tribal leader
Native American (Hoopa)
Ind Today

1079. Jumper, Betty Mae Tiger
born 1923
tribal chairperson
Native American (Seminole)
Ind Today

1080. Medicine, Beatrice
born 1924
anthropologist
Native American (Dakota-Standing Rock)
Ind Today

1081. Larkin, Moscelyne
born 1925
ballet dancer and teacher, choreographer, lecturer
Native American (Shawnee-Ploria)
Ind Today

1082. Tallchief, Maria
born 1925
ballet dancer
Native American (Osage)
Index t Wom; Ind Today

1083. Chewiwi, Louise Abeita
born 1926
children's author, educator
Native American (Pueblo-Laguna)
Ind Today

1084. Tallchief, Marjorie
born 1927
ballet dancer
Native American (Osage)
Index t Wom; Ind Today

1085. Crowe, Amanda M.
born 1928
wood sculptor, carving teacher
Native American (Cherokee)
Ind Today

1086. Lallmang, Sue Sillaway
born 1929
Native American adviser, Republican party worker
Native American (Seneca)
Ind Today

1087. Walker, Tillie
born 1929

specialist in Native American education
North Dakota
Native American (Mandan-Hidatsa)
Read Encyc Am West

1088. Anderson, Dorothy L.
flourished 1960s
air traffic controller
Native American (Flathead)
Ind Today

1089. Bennett, Kay Curley
flourished 1960s
author
Native American (Navaho)
Ind Today

1090. Caldwell, Leticia
flourished 1960s
Chippewa tribal leader
Native American (Chippewa)
Ind Today

1091. Califano, Grace Marsh
flourished 1960s
actor
Native American (Piscataway)
Ind Today

1092. Calkin, Laurie Archer
flourished 1960s
dancer, choreographer, costume designer, actor
Native American (Cherokee)
Ind Today

1093. Davids, Dorothy W.
flourished 1960s
educator
Native American (Stockbridge-Munsee)
Ind Today

1094. Grant, Gloria
flourished 1960s
rodeo trick rider
Native American (Navaho-Omaha)
Ind Today

1095. Grant, Joy
flourished 1960s
rodeo trick rider
Native American (Navaho-Omaha)
Ind Today

1096. Grant, Ruth
flourished 1960s
rodeo trick rider
Native American (Navaho-Omaha)
Ind Today

1097. Harris, Ladonna
flourished 1960s–70s
health reformer, women's rights worker
Native American (Comanche)
Ind Today

1098. Hastings, Lucille Ahnawake
flourished 1960s
social worker
Native American (Cherokee)
Ind Today

1099. Hill, Joan
flourished 1960s
artist
Native American (Cherokee)
Ind Today

1100. Jendritza, Loretta S.
flourished 1960s
air force major, war nurse
Native American (Navaho)
Ind Today

1101. Kimball, Yeffe
flourished 1960s
pioneer painter of outer space
Native American (Osage)
Ind Today

1102. Loloma, Otellie Sequafenema
flourished 1960s
ceramic sculptor, painter
Native American (Hopi)
Ind Today

1103. Manning, Leah Hicks
flourished 1960s
social worker
Native American (Shoshone-Paiute-Cherokee)
Ind Today

1104. Martinez, Mescal
flourished 1960s
opera singer
Native American (Algonquin-Apache)
Ind Today

1105. Massey, Edna Hogner
flourished 1960s
interior designer, arts and crafts specialist
Native American (Cherokee)
Ind Today

1106. Monture, Ethel Brant
flourished 1960s
author, specialist in Native American culture
Native American (Mohawk)
Ind Today

1107. Savilla, Agnes
flourished 1960s
tribal leader
Native American (Mohave)
Ind Today

1108. Victor, Wilma L.
flourished 1960s
educational administrator
Native American (Choctaw)
Ind Today

1109. Waano-Gano, Nunny
flourished 1960s
floral artist
Native American (Karok)
Ind Today

1110. Wallace, Gladys Sky
flourished 1960s
stockbroker
Native American (Peoria)
Ind Today

1111. Wauneka, Annie Dodge
flourished 1960s
tribal leader
Native American (Navaho)
Ind Today

1112. Widmark, Emma G.
flourished 1960s
home economist
Native American (Tlinget)
Ind Today

1113. Yellow Rose, Evelyn
flourished 1960s
otolaryngologist
Native American (Dakota-Brule)
Ind Today

1114. Morris, Christine
born 1932
sociologist, anthropologist
Native American (Blackfoot)
Ind Today

1115. Davis, Gloria Ann, Sister
born 1933
Catholic nun, educator
Catholic
Native American (Navaho-Chocktaw)
Ind Today

1116. Nelson, Mary
born 1933
educator, sculptor
Native American (Colville-Cree-Mohawk)
Ind Today

1117. Hayden, Iola Pohucsucut
born 1934
Native American rights worker, educator
Native American (Comanche)
Ind Today

1118. Deer, Ada
born 1935
social worker, worker for Native American rights
Native American (Menominee)
Ind Today

1119. Scheirbeck, Helen Maynor
born 1935
director of the Education for American Indians Office of HEW

Native American (Lumbee)
Ind Today

1120. Sainte-Marie, Beverley "Buffie"
born 1942
folk singer, composer
Native American (Cree)
Cur Biog '69; Ind Today

1121. Maas, Caroline Orr
born 1943
artist
Native American (Colville)
Ind Today

1122. Natches, Millicent Maxine
born 1943
tribal secretary
Native American (Ute)
Ind Today

1123. Biddleman, Marcia Ann
born 1945
first lieutenant in the US Marine Corps
Native American (Seneca)
Ind Today

1124. Bono, Cherilyn (Lapiere); Cher
born 1946
popular singer, actor, television entertainer
California
Native American (Cherokee)
Cur Biog '74

1125. Hardin, Helen; Tsa-sah-wee-eh; Little Standing Spruce
born 1946
artist
Native American (Pueblo-Santa Clara)
Ind Today

1126. Parton, Dolly Rebecca
born 1946
country music singer, songwriter, screen actor
Native American (Cherokee)
Cur Biog '77

No Dates

1127. Ate, Te
traditional Native American actor
Native American (Chickasaw)
Ind Today

NEW ZEALAND

1128. Eddy, Lillian E.
circa 1902–66
industrial designer
New Zealand
Index t Wom

1129. Te Kanawa, Kiri
born 1946?
Metropolitan Opera mezzo-soprano singer
New Zealand; Maori
Cur Biog '78

NORWEGIAN

1130. Fedde, Elizabeth, Sister
1850–1921
Lutheran deacon, nurse, welfare worker, Catholic nun
Lutheran; Catholic
Norwegian
Index t Wom; Not Am Wom

1131. Everson, Mary Dah
born 1855
western pioneer
Norwegian
Index t Wom

1132. Tapper, Bertha Feiring
1859–1915
pianist, music educator
Norwegian
Dict Am Bio; Index t Wom

1133. Ackermann, Susan K.
1871–1949
physician
Norwegian
Obit File

1134. Nissen, Greta
flourished 1920s–30s
actor
Norwegian
Index t Wom

1135. Mallory, Ann Margrethe Bjurstedt "Molla"
1892–1959
tennis player
Norwegian
Dict Am Bio supp v6; Hall Fame Sport; Obit File

1136. Ostenso, Martha
1900–63
author, novelist
Norwegian
Index t Wom; Nat Cyc Am Bio csv3; Wom Lit, More

1137. Sherven, Betty
flourished 1930s
physiotherapist
Norwegian
Index t Wom

1138. Henie, Sonja
1912–69
figure skater, film actor
Norwegian
Cur Biog '70; Hall Fame Sport; Index t Wom; Not Am Wom supp v1; Obit File

PERUVIAN

1139. Capillana
died 1549
author on natural history, historian
Peruvian
Cyc Am Bio

PHILIPPINE

1140. Draves, Victoria Manolo
born 1924
diver
Philippine
Hall Fame Sport; Index t Wom

POLISH

1141. Rose, Ernestine Louise Lasmond Siismondi Potowski
1810–92
feminist, women's rights worker, temperance worker, abolitionist
Jewish
Polish
Cyc Am Bio; Dict Am Bio; Not Am Wom

1142. Zakrzewska, Marie Elizabeth
1829–1902
physician, hospital founder
Polish; German
Cyc Am Bio; Dict Am Bio; Index t Wom; Not Am Wom

1143. Modjeska, Helena
1840/44–1909
actor
Polish
Cyc Am Bio; Dict Am Bio; Index t Wom; Nat Cyc Am Bio v10; Not Am Wom; Wom Cent

1144. Sembrich, Marcella; Praxede Marcelline Kochanska
1858–1935
soprano opera and concert singer
Polish
Dict Am Bio supp v1; Nat Cyc Am Bio v24; Not Am Wom

1145. Rubenstein, Helena
1870/71–1965
cosmetics manufacturer, entrepreneur, art collector, philanthropist
Jewish
Polish
Index t Wom; Nat Cyc Am Bio v50; Not Am Wom supp v1; Obit File; Who Who Jew Hist

1146. Kryszak, Mary Olszewski
1875–1945

Polish American welfare worker, Wisconsin state legislator
Wisconsin
Polish
Not Am Wom

1147. Landowska, Wanda (Lew)
1877/79–1959
harpsichordist, pianist, composer, musicologist, music educator, writer on music
Jewish
Polish
Dict Am Bio supp v6; Obit File; Slavon Encyc; Who Who Jew Hist

1148. Stokes, Rose Harriet Pastor
1879–1933
Socialist and Communist party leader, feminist, labor leader, author
Jewish
Polish
Bio Dict Am Lab; Dict Am Bio; Not Am Wom

1149. Wittkowska, Marta
flourished 1910s
opera singer
Polish
Index t Wom

1150. Yezierska, Anzia
1880/85–1970
novelist
Jewish
Polish
Index t Wom; Not Am Wom supp v1; Wom Lit, More

1151. Schneiderman, Rose
1882/84–1972
labor organizer, Women's Trade Union leader, secretary of the New York State Labor Department, social reformer, suffragist
Jewish
Polish; Russian
Bio Dict Am Lab; Cur Biog '72; Index t Wom; Not Am Wom supp v1; Obit File

1152. Eastman, Eliena Krylenko
1895–1956
painter
Polish
Obit File

1153. Gray, Gilda
1899/1901–1959
dancer, singer
Polish
Dict Am Bio supp v6; Index t Wom; Obit File

1154. Negri, Pola
born 1899
screen actor

New York State Labor Department, social reformer, suffragist
Jewish
Polish; Russian
Bio Dict Am Lab; Cur Biog '72; Index t Wom; Not Am Wom supp v1; Obit File

1188. Scott, Miriam Finn
1882–1944
pioneer child diagnostician, educator, lecturer, author
Russian
Index t Wom; Nat Cyc Am Bio v36

1189. Zunser, Miriam Shomer
1883–1951
novelist, playwright
Russian
Obit File

1190. Cohn, Fannie Mary
1885/88–1962
labor leader and organizer, labor educator
Jewish
Russian
Cyc Am Bio; Bio Dict Am Lab; Not Am Wom supp v1

1191. Kelman, Sarah R.
circa 1885–1969
psychiatrist, psychoanalyst, founder of the Association for the Advancement of Psychoanalysis, the American Institute for Psychoanalysis, and the American Academy of Psychoanalysis
Russian
Obit File

1192. Karinska, Barbara
born 1886
ballet costume designer and maker
Russian
Cur Biog '71

1193. Phillips, Luba Galanchikoff (Philpoff)
1888–1959
pioneer aviator, pre–World War I test pilot, early altitude and distance record holder, taxi driver
New York
Russian
Obit File

1194. Rabinoff, Sophie
1888–1957
physician
Russian
Index t Wom

1195. Hillman, Bessie Abramowitz
1889–1970
labor leader, president of the Amalgamated Clothing Workers of America

Jewish
New York, NY
Russian
Nat Cyc Am Bio v56; Obit File

1196. Kurenko, Maria
flourished 1920s–40s
singer
Russian
Index t Wom

1197. Mideladze, Ketto
flourished 1920s–30s
dancer, fashion designer
Russian
Index t Wom

1198. Tomara, Sonia
flourished 1920s–30s
journalist
Russian
Index t Wom

1199. Wengerova, Isabella
flourished 1920s
pianist
Jewish
Russian
Index t Wom

1200. Kross, Anna Moscowitz
1891–1979
municipal court judge, feminist
New York, NY
Russian
Cur Biog '79; Index t Wom

1201. Newman, Pauline M.
1891–post 1940s
labor leader, Socialist party worker
Jewish
New York
Russian
Bio Dict Am Lab; Index t Wom

1202. Nijinska, Bronislava
1891–1972
choreographer, ballet dancer
Russian
Obit File

1203. Paeff, Bashka
born 1893
sculptor
Russian
Index t Wom

1204. Bellanca, Dorothy Jacobs
1894–1946
trade union organizer, founder and only woman vice-president of the Amalgamated Clothing Workers union, social reformer, politician
Jewish
Russian
Bio Dict Am Lab; Dict Am Bio supp v3; Not Am Wom; Obit File

1205. Daniels, Anna Kleegman
born 1898
gynecologist, medical director of Planned Parenthood
Jewish
Russian
Nat Cyc Am Bio csv11

1206. Halpert, Edith Gregor
1900?–70
art dealer and collector
Russian
Cur Biog '70; Index t Wom; Not Am Wom supp v1

1207. Helvarg, Sue
flourished 1930s
photographer's agent
Russian
Index t Wom

1208. Lichtman, Sina
flourished 1930s
pianist
Russian
Index t Wom

1209. Marmorston, Jessie
flourished 1930s
pathologist
Russian
Index t Wom

1210. Nevelson, Louise
born 1900
sculptor
Russian
Index t Wom

1211. Rapoport, Eda
born 1900
composer
Russian
Index t Wom

1212. White, Rose Rubin
flourished 1930s
author, translator
Russian
Index t Wom

1213. Zachs, Anna H.
flourished 1930s
lawyer
Russian
Index t Wom

1214. Kleegman, Sophia Josephine
1901–71
obstetrician/gynecologist
Russian
Index t Wom; Not Am Wom supp v1

1215. Wasson, Valentina Pavlovna Guercken
1901–58
pediatrician, mycologist
New York
Russian
Obit File

1216. Flint, Eva Kay
born 1902
playwright
Russian
Index t Wom

1217. Dean, Vera Micheles
1903–72
international affairs specialist, editor, author, lecturer
Russian
Cur Biog '72; Index t Wom; Not Am Wom supp v1

1218. Rand, Ayn
born 1904
author
Russian
Index t Wom

1219. Valentina
born 1904
fashion designer
Russian
Index t Wom

1220. Komarovsky, Mirra
born 1906
educator, sociologist
Russian
Index t Wom

1221. Papashvily, Helen Wiate
born 1906
author
Russian
Index t Wom

1222. Scott, Natalie Anderson; Natalie B. Sokoloff
born 1906
novelist
Russian
Index t Wom

1223. Vronsky, Vitya
born 1909
pianist
Russian
Index t Wom

1224. Levien, Sonya (Hovey)
died 1960
screenwriter
Russian
Obit File

1225. Rockmore, Clara
born 1911
musician
Jewish
Russian
Index t Wom

1226. Lev, Ray
born 1912
pianist
Russian
Index t Wom

1227. Luban, Francia
born 1914

musician, songwriter, author
Russian
Index t Wom

1228. Bryner, Vera
1916–67
opera singer
Russian
Obit File

1229. Whitney, Julia; Yulya Alexandrovna Zapolskaya
1920–65
composer, musician, singer, author
Russian
Obit File

1230. Makarova, Natalia
born 1940
ballet dancer
Russian
Cur Biog '72

No Dates

1231. Graudan, Joanna Freudberg
pianist
Jewish
Russian
Index t Wom

SCOTTISH

1232. MacDonald, Flora
1722–90
Scottish hero who assisted in the escape of pretender to the throne Charles Edward in 1746, pioneer
Fayetteville, NC
Scottish
Am Bio Dict; Cyc Am Bio; Dict Am Bio Men Time; Index t Wom

1233. Stamper, Mrs.
flourished 1770s
colonial singer
Scottish
Index t Wom

1234. Graham, Isabella Marshall
1742–1814/15
educator, charity worker, philanthropist
New York
Scottish
Am Bio Dict; Cyc Am Bio; Dict Am Bio; Dict Am Bio Men Time; Index t Wom; Nat Cyc Am Bio v4; Not Am Wom; Our Count; Who Who Dur Am Rev

1235. Picken, Joanna Belfrage
1748/98–1859
poet

Canadian; Scottish
Cyc Am Bio; Dict Nat Bio

1236. Grant, Anne
1755–1838
author
Scottish
Cyc Am Bio; Dict Am Bio Men Time; Dict Nat Bio

1237. d'Arusmont, Frances Wright
1789–1852
abolitionist, political essayist, author
Scottish
Am Bio Dict; Dict Am Auth

1238. Tytler, Jane
flourished 1820s
pharmacist
Scottish
Index t Wom

1239. Wright, Frances (d'Arusmont) "Fanny"; Fanny d'Arusmont
1795–1852
author, abolitionist, feminist, philanthropist, lecturer
Scottish
Am Bio Dict; Cyc Am Bio; Dict Am Bio; Dict Am Bio Men Time; Index t Wom; Nat Cyc Am Bio v2; Not Am Wom

1240. Cumming, Kate
1828/35–1909
Confederate hospital administrator, diarist, nurse
Alabama
Scottish
Dict Am Auth; Index t Wom; Not Am Wom

1241. Boucicault, Agnes Robertson
1832–1916
singer, actor
Scottish
Index t Wom

1242. Cunningham, Annie Sinclair
born 1832
Presbyterian church and mission society worker
Presbyterian
Scottish
Wom Cent

1243. Washburn, Jean Linsey Bruce
1838–1904
poet
Scottish
Index t Wom

1244. Moran, Mary Nimmo
1842–99
painter, etcher

Scottish
Cyc Am Bio; Index t Wom; Nat Cyc Am Bio v22; Not Am Wom; Twent Cen Bio Dict Not Am

1245. Gutelius, Jean Harrower
born 1846
artist, bookstore proprietor
Scottish
Wom Cent

1246. Sandes, Margaret Isabelle
born 1849
industrial reformer, club leader
Scottish
Wom Cent

1247. Garden, Mary
1874/77–1967
soprano opera singer, general director of the Chicago Lyric Opera
Scottish
Index t Wom; Nat Cyc Am Bio v15; Not Am Wom supp v1; Obit File

1248. Loftus, Mare Cecilia "Cissie"
1876–1943
Broadway and London stage actor, impersonator
Scottish
Not Am Wom; Obit File

1249. McLeod, Grace
1878–1962
nutritionist, nutrition educator, editor
Congregationalist
Scottish
Index t Wom; Nat Cyc Am Bio v50

1250. Walker, Susan Hunter
married 1904
editor, author
Scottish
Index t Wom

1251. Ross, Isabel
1897–1975
author, novelist, biographer of prominent American women
Scottish
Index t Wom; Obit File

1252. Reid, Helen Dwight
1901–65
international political scientist, educator, pacifist
Christian Scientist
Washington, DC
Scottish
Nat Cyc Am Bio v51

1253. MacInnes, Helen Clark; Helen Gilbert Highet
born 1907
author

Scottish
Index t Wom

1254. MacIntyre, Sheila Scott
1910–60
mathematician
Presbyterian
Scottish
Nat Cyc Am Bio v48

1255. Curry, Peggy Simson
born 1912
author
Scottish
Index t Wom

1256. Logan, Ella
1913–69
stage and screen actor, musical comedy actor
Scottish
Obit File

1257. Kerr, Deborah
born 1921
actor
Scottish
Index t Wom

SERBIAN

1258. Lazarovich-Hrebelianovich, Eleanor (Calhoun), Princess
1865–1957
classical actor, Serbian freedom fighter
Serbian
Index t Wom; Obit File

SICILIAN

1259. Winwar, Frances; Mrs. Bernard Grebanier
born 1900
author
Sicilian
Nat Cyc Am Bio csv6

SOUTH AFRICAN

No Dates

1260. Cannon, Poppy
food columnist
South African
Index t Wom

SPANISH

1261. Penalosa, Eufemia
flourished circa 1590s
American colony cosponsor

Spanish
Index t Wom

1262. Arguello, Concha Maria de Concepcion
1791–1857
pioneer, Catholic nun
Catholic
Spanish
Index t Wom

1263. Patti, Adelea Juana Maria Clorinda "Adelina"
1843–1903/19
soprano opera singer
Spanish
Cyc Am Bio; Dict Am Bio Men Time; Nat Cyc Am Bio v7; Not Am Wom; Twent Cen Bio Dict Not Am; Wom Cent

1264. Bori, Lucrezia; Lucrecia Borja Gonzales de Riancho
1887–1960
Metropolitan Opera soprano singer
Catholic
Spanish
Dict Am Bio supp v5; Nat Cyc Am Bio v44; Obit File

1265. Marcial-Dorado, Caroline
1889–1941
educator
Spanish
Index t Wom

1266. Iturbi, Amparo
1899–1969
concert pianist
Spanish
Obit File

SWEDISH

1267. Printz, Aregot
died 1695
landowner
Swedish
Index t Wom

1268. Bremer, Fredrika
1801–65
novelist
Swedish
Dict Am Bio Men Time

1269. Lind, Johanna Maria "Jenny"; Jenny Lind-Goldschmidt
1820/21–1887
vocalist
Swedish
Cyc Am Bio; Dict Nat Bio; Index t Wom; Nat Cyc Am Bio v3

1270. Swenson, Amanda Carlson
flourished 1870s–90s
soprano concert singer

Episcopalian
Swedish
Wom Cent

1271. Nilsson, Christine
1843–1921
opera singer, violinist
Swedish
Cyc Am Bio; Index t Wom

1272. Wallin, Mathilda K.
1858–1955
physician
Swedish
Index t Wom

1273. Fremstad, Olivia [Anna] "Olive"
1868/72–1951
opera singer
Methodist
Swedish
Index t Wom; Nat Cyc Am Bio v40; Obit File

1274. Fromen, Agnes Valborg Erica
1869–1956
sculptor
Swedish
Obit File

1275. Anderson, Mary
1872–1964
director of the US Labor Department Women's Bureau, labor union official
Swedish
Bio Dict Am Lab; Index t Wom; Not Am Wom supp v1; Obit File

1276. Sundelius, Marie Louise Sundborg
1882–1958
soprano opera singer
Swedish
Obit File

1277. Totten, Vichen von P.
born 1886
sculptor
Swedish
Index t Wom

1278. Nilsson, Anna Q.
1889–1974
silent-screen actor
Swedish
Obit File

1279. Fuller, Tyra Lundberg
flourished 1930s
journalist
Swedish
Index t Wom

1280. Nillson, Carlotta
died 1951
Broadway stage actor
Swedish
Obit File

1281. Morris, Edita
born 1902
author
Swedish
Index t Wom

1282. Garbo, Greta
born 1905
actor
Swedish
Index t Wom

1283. Varnay, Astrid
born 1918
opera singer
Swedish
Index t Wom

1284. Lindfors, Elsa Viveca Torstensdotter
born 1920
actor
Swedish
Index t Wom

1285. Stevens, Inger
1934–70
actor
Swedish
Index t Wom

SWISS

1286. Shaw, Pauline Agassiz
1841–1917
educational philanthropist
Swiss
Dict Am Bio; Nat Cyc Am Bio v27; Not Am Wom

1287. Isely, Elise Dubach
born circa 1843
pioneer
Swiss
Index t Wom

1288. Kempin, Emile
flourished 1880s–90s
lawyer, educator
Swiss
Index t Wom

1289. Brupbacher, Alice
flourished 1930s
business executive
Swiss
Index t Wom

1290. Syrkin, Marie
born 1900
editor, educator, author
Swiss
Index t Wom

1291. Krall, Heidi
flourished 1950s
opera singer
Swiss
Index t Wom

1292. della Casa, Lisa
born 1921
singer
Swiss
Index t Wom

1293. Kubler-Ross, Elisabeth
born 1926
psychiatrist, thanatologist, writer on death and dying
Swiss
Cur Biog '80

TURKISH

1294. Hinman, Alice Hamlin
1867–1934
educator
Turkish
Nat Cyc Am Bio v26

1295. Lamson, Armene Tashijian
1883–1970
medical illustrator, physician, UNICEF worker, medical author
Episcopalian
Seattle, WA
Turkish
Nat Cyc Am Bio v56

VENEZUALAN

1296. de Pina, May Frances
flourished 1930s
modeling-school director
Venezualan
Index t Wom

1297. Marisol (Escobar)
born 1930
sculptor, painter
Venezualan
Index t Wom

WELSH

1298. Owens, Vilda Sauvage
flourished 1900s–20s
poet
Welsh
Index t Wom

1299. Jordan, Mary
1879–1961
singer
Welsh
Index t Wom

1300. John, Alice
1881–1956
Broadway stage actor
New York
Welsh
Obit File

1301. Beaupre, Enid
flourished 1930s
advertising executive
Welsh
Index t Wom

No Dates

1302. Williams, Frances
composer

Welsh
Index t Wom

WEST INDIAN

1303. Miller, Dora Richards
flourished 1860s–80s
author, Civil War diarist, journalist, educator

West Indian (Danish West Indies)
Index t Wom; Wom Cent

1304. Primus, Pearl
born 1919
dancer
Black; West Indian (Trinidad)
Negro Alman

1305. Scott, Hazel Dorothy
1920–81
pianist; jazz singer; stage, screen, and musical actor
West Indian (Trinidad)
Cur Biog '81; Index t Wom

IV. Geographical Index

ALABAMA

1. Brown, Catherine
1800–23
Moravian religious worker
Moravian
Alabama
Moravian; Native American (Cherokee)
Am Bio Dict

2. Cruse, Mary Anne
born 18?
author, educator
Alabama
Dict Am Auth

3. Johnson, Hallie Tanner
born 18?
physician
Alabama
Black
Prof Negro Wom v1

4. Weeden, Howard
born 18?
artist, poet
Huntsville, AL
Dict Am Auth

5. Stafford, Maria Brewster Brooks
born 1809
educator
Alabama
Wom Cent

6. le Vert, Octavia Celeste Walton
1810/11–1877
author, Civil War nurse, travel writer
Mobile, AL
Cyc Am Bio; Dict Am Auth; Dict Am Bio Men Time; Index t Wom; Nat Cyc Am Bio v6; Not Am Wom; Twent Cen Bio Dict Not Am

7. Hopkins, Juliet Ann Opie
1816/18–1890
hospital administrator and founder, Confederate sympathizer
Alabama
Dict Am Bio; Encyc South Hist; Not Am Wom

8. Creswell, Julia (Pleasants)
1827–86
poet, novelist
Alabama
Cyc Am Bio; Dict Am Bio

9. Cumming, Kate
1828/35–1909
Confederate hospital administrator, diarist, nurse
Alabama
Scottish
Dict Am Auth; Index t Wom; Not Am Wom

10. Ware, Mary (Harris)
born 1828
poet
Alabama
Wom Cent

11. Wells, Mary Fletcher
flourished 1860s–90s
philanthropist, educator of freedmen
Alabama
Wom Cent

12. Tutwiler, Julia Strudwick
1835/41–1916
educator, women's educator, temperance worker, prison reformer
Alabama
Dict Am Bio; Encyc South Hist; Index t Wom; Nat Cyc Am Bio v15; Not Am Wom; Wom Cent

13. Wilson, Augusta C. Jane (Evans)
1835/36–1909
novelist, Confederate author
Methodist

Mobile, AL
Cyc Am Bio; Dict Am Auth; Dict Am Bio; Dict Am Bio Men Time; Encyc South Hist; Index t Wom; Nat Cyc Am Bio v4; Not Am Wom; Wom Cent; Wom Lit, More

14. Bellamy, Emily Elizabeth Whitfield (Croom); A Southern Lady; Kamba Thorpe
1837/39–1900
author, novelist
Mobile, AL; Florida
Appl Cyc Am Bio; Cyc Am Bio; Dict Am Auth; Dict Am Bio; Nat Cyc Am Bio v12; Wom Cent

15. Duffel, Mary Gordon; Mary Duff Gordon
born 1840
poet, writer on the history and geography of Alabama
Alabama
Cyc Am Bio; Dict Am Auth

16. Gibbs, Eleanor Churchill
flourished 1870s–90s
educator
Alabama
Wom Cent

17. Moore, Idora McClellan (Plowman)
1843–1929
author
Alabama
Index t Wom; Wom Cent

18. Johnston, Lizzie Johnston Evans
1851–1934
philanthropist, juvenile-prison reformer, Democratic party worker
Presbyterian
Alabama
Nat Cyc Am Bio v31

19. Judson, Jennie S.
born 1859
author
Alabama
Wom Cent

20. Greene, Frances Nimmo; Dixie
born 186?
educator, author
Alabama
Wom Cent

21. Lyon, Anne Bozeman
born 1860
fiction writer
Alabama
Dict Am Auth; Wom Cent

22. Spratt, Louise Parker
flourished 1890s
journalist, dialect author
Alabama
Wom Cent

23. Young, Martha; Eli Sheppard
flourished 1890s
author, dialect author, poet
Alabama
Wom Cent

24. Chanler, Amelie Rives
born 1863
author
Alabama
Nat Cyc Am Bio v1; Wom Cent

25. Davis, Margaret Ellen (O'Brien)
1870–90
novelist
Birmingham, AL
Dict Am Auth

26. Johnston, Mary
1870–1936
popular novelist, suffragist, pacifist, internationalist
Birmingham, AL; Virginia
Dict Am Auth; Dict Am Bio supp v2; Dict Lit Bio v9; Index t Wom; Nat Cyc Am Bio v10 and csv3; Not Am Wom; Twent Cen Bio Dict Not Am

27. Goza, Anne
born 1872
humorist
Alabama
Wom Cent

28. Bellingrath, Mary Nesbitt Elmore
1876–1955
philanthropist, president of the Coca-Cola Bottling Co.
Alabama
Nat Cyc Am Bio v47

29. Keller, Helen Adams
1880–1968
author, feminist, suffragist, educator, advocate for the handicapped, pacifist, Socialist party worker
Swedenborgian
Alabama
blind, deaf
Encyc South Hist; Index t Wom; Nat Cyc Am Bio v15 and v57; Not Am Wom supp v1; Obit File

30. Wallace, Lurleen Burns
1926–68
governor of Alabama, politician
Alabama
Index t Wom; Obit File

ALASKA

31. van Duren, Kate Rockwell Waner Matson; Klondike Kate
1881–1957
dancer, Alaska financier
Alaska
Obit File

32. Orstein, Honora; Diamond Tooth Lil
1883–1975
dance hall actor during the Alaska gold rush
Alaska
Obit File

33. Nelson, Klondy Esmerelda
born 1897
Alaskan hero
Alaska
Index t Wom

34. Dalacea Kasudluk
born 1906
sculptor
Port Harrison, AK
Inuit
Esk Art

35. Annie Weetaluktuk
born 1919
carver
Port Harrison, AK

Inuit
Esk Art

36. Guinn, Nora
born 1920
Alaska district judge
Alaska
Inuit
Ind Today

37. Paddock, Constance Harper
born 1920
chief clerk of the Alaska House of Representatives
Alaska
Native American (Athabascan)
Ind Today

ARIZONA

38. Sorin, Sarah Inslee Herring
1861–1914
lawyer
Episcopalian
Arizona
Nat Cyc Am Bio v36

39. King, Isabella Greenway
1885–1953
Democratic representative to Congress from Arizona
Arizona
Obit File

ARKANSAS

40. Newton, Mrs.
1802–35
missionary to the Cherokee people
Arkansas
Am Bio Dict

41. Loughborough, Mary Ann Webster
1836–87
author, Civil War diarist
Little Rock, AR
Cyc Am Bio; Dict Am Auth; Index t Wom

42. French, Alice; Octave Thanet
1850–1934
novelist, short story writer
Iowa; Arkansas
Dict Am Auth; Dict Am Bio supp v1; Index t Wom; Nat Cyc Am Bio v10 and v25; Not Am Wom; Twent Cen Bio Dict Not Am; Wom Cent

43. Brooks, Ida Joe
born 1853
physician, surgeon, suffragist
Little Rock, AR
Wom Cent

44. Eagle, Mary Kavanaugh
born 1854
Baptist church worker
Baptist
Arkansas
Wom Cent

45. Hawes, Flora Harrod
born 1863
postmaster
Arkansas
Wom Cent

46. Smith, Lura Eugenie (Brown)
born 1864
journalist
Little Rock, AR
Dict Am Auth; Wom Cent

47. Babcock, Bernie (Smade)
born 1868
novelist
Little Rock, AR
Dict Am Auth

48. Fuller, Minnie Ursula Oliver Scott Rutherford
1868–1946
temperance and child labor worker, suffragist
Arkansas
Encyc South Hist; Not Am Wom

49. Fulbright, Roberta Waugh
1874–1953
newspaper publisher, political writer, businessperson, banker
Arkansas
Nat Cyc Am Bio v49

50. Caraway, Hattie Ophelia Wyatt
1878–1950
Democratic US senator from Arkansas
Methodist
Arkansas
Australian
Dict Am Bio supp v4; Dict Aust Bio; Encyc South Hist; Eng Wom; Index t Wom; Nat Cyc Am Bio v44 and csv4; Not Am Wom; Obit File

51. Bates, Daisy Lee Gatson
born 1922
civil rights leader
Little Rock, AR
Black
Encyc Black Am; Index t Wom; Negro Alman; Prof Negro Wom v2

52. Nettleship, Mae Barnwell
born 1926
physician
Episcopalian
Arkansas
Canadian
Nat Cyc Am Bio csv10

CALIFORNIA

53. Smith, Alice (Prescott)
born 18?
novelist
California
Dict Am Auth

54. McDougal, Frances Harriet (Whipple) (Greene)
1805–75
poet, miscellaneous writer, suffragist
Rhode Island; California
Dict Am Auth; Cyc Am Bio

55. Pleasant, Mary Ellen "Mammy"
1814?–1904
pioneer, boardinghouse keeper, civil rights advocate
California
Black
Not Am Wom

56. Farnham, Eliza Woodson (Burhans)
1815–64
prison reformer, author, lecturer, feminist, suffragist, philanthropist
New York; California
Cyc Am Bio; Dict Am Auth; Dict Am Bio; Dict Am Bio Men Time; Index t Wom; Nat Cyc Am Bio v4; Not Am Wom; Twent Cen Bio Dict Not Am

57. Ord, Augustias de la Guerra
1815–80
historian of California
California
Mexican
Dict Mex Am Hist

58. Kirby, Georgiana (Bruce)
born 1818
feminist, prison matron, autobiographer
Santa Cruz, CA
English
Dict Am Auth

59. Clapp, Louise Amelia Knapp Smith; Dame Shirley; Amelia Knapp Smith
1819–1906
author, educator, letter writer during the California gold rush, gold rush pioneer
California
Index t Wom; Not Am Wom; Read Encyc Am West

60. Royce, Sarah Eleanor Bayliss
1819–91
California pioneer, author
California

English
Index t Wom; Not Am Wom

61. Fremont, Jessie Ann (Benton)
1824/25–1902
writer
Los Angeles, CA
Dict Am Auth; Dict Am Bio; Index t Wom; Nat Cyc Am Bio v4; Not Am Wom; Read Encyc Am West; Twent Cen Bio Dict Not Am; Wom Cent

62. Steele, Rowena Granice
born 1824
journalist, author
California
Wom Cent

63. Cooper, Sarah Brown Ingersoll
1825/36–1896
kindergartner, Bible teacher, philanthropist
California
Dict Am Bio; Nat Cyc Am Bio v3; Not Am Wom; Wom Cent

64. Victor, Frances Auretta (Fuller) (Barrett); Florence Fane
1826–1902
author, historian of the Pacific Northwest
Oregon; California
Cyc Am Bio; Dict Am Auth; Dict Am Bio; Nat Cyc Am Bio v13; Not Am Wom; Twent Cen Bio Dict Not Am; Wom Cent

65. Kennedy, Kate
1827–90
educator, educational reformer, champion of equal pay for women, women's rights worker, women's labor worker
Oakland, CA
Irish
Nat Cyc Am Bio v30; Not Am Wom

66. Russell, Mary Baptist, Mother
1829–98
Catholic nun, superior of Sisters of Mercy in San Francisco, founder of the Sisters of Mercy in California
Catholic
San Francisco, CA
Irish
Dict Am Bio; Not Am Wom

67. Stevens, Emily Pitt
flourished 1860s–90s
educator, temperance worker, feminist, suffragist
Presbyterian
California
Wom Cent

68. Eyster, Nellie Blessing
born 1831
author, children's author, temperance reformer, worker for Chinese American welfare
Pennsylvania; California
Cyc Am Bio; Dict Am Auth; Nat Cyc Am Bio v10; Twent Cen Bio Dict Not Am; Wom Cent

69. Brown, Mary Frank
born 1835
philanthropist, Chinese and Japanese women's welfare worker, temperance worker
Oakland, CA
Wom Cent

70. Mace, Frances Parker (Laughton)
1836–99
poet
Maine; San Jose, CA
Cyc Am Bio; Dict Am Auth; Index t Wom; Nat Cyc Am Bio v10; Wom Cent

71. Scripps, Ellen Browning
1836–1932
philanthropist, newspaper writer and publisher, patron of marine science, founder of Scripps Marine Lab, pacifist, feminist, temperance worker
La Jolla, CA
Dict Am Bio; Index t Wom; Nat Cyc Am Bio v27; Not Am Wom

72. Pittsinger, Eliza A.
born 1837
poet
San Francisco, CA
Dict Am Auth; Wom Cent

73. Gordon, Laura de Force
1838/40–1907
lawyer, journalist, suffragist, women's rights worker, Democratic politician, orator
California
Dict Am Bio; Index t Wom; Nat Cyc Am Bio v1; Not Am Wom; Wom Cent

74. Wood, Mary C. Foster; Camilla K. von K.; Mary C. F. Hall-Wood
flourished 1870s–90s
poet, editor, author
California
Wom Cent

75. Coolbrith, Ina Donna
1841/42–1928
poet, librarian
California
Dict Am Auth; Dict Am Bio; Nat Cyc Am Bio v13; Not Am Wom; Twent Cen Bio Dict Not Am; Wom Cent; Wom Lit, More

76. Skelton, Henriette
born 1842
temperance worker
California
German
Wom Cent

77. Watson, Elizabeth Lowe
born 1842
lecturer, pastor of the San Francisco Religious and Philosophical Society, fruit farmer
California
Wom Cent

78. Strong, Harriet Williams Russell
1844–1926/29
agriculturist, student of water supply problems, horticulturist, engineer, civic leader
Los Angeles, CA
Dict Am Bio; Nat Cyc Am Bio v17; Not Am Wom

79. Hough, Emma E. (Smith-Payne)
1845–1907
soprano concert and light opera soloist, patron of music education, philanthropist
California
Am Bio New Cyc

80. Milne, Frances Margaret
born 1846
author, journalist, poet, political essayist
California
Irish
Wom Cent

81. Payott, Annie Eliza (Fredenbur) Evens
1847–1927
welfare worker
Unitarian
San Francisco, CA
Nat Cyc Am Bio v21

82. Tingley, Katherine Augusta Westcott
1847/52–1929
founder of the Point Loma Community in California, pacifist
Theosophist
Point Loma, CA
Dict Am Bio; Index t Wom; Nat Cyc Am Bio v15; Not Am Wom

83. Todd, Mary (Ives)
born 1848
fiction writer
Los Angeles, CA
Dict Am Auth

84. Foltz, Clara Shortridge; The Portia of the Pacific
1849–1934
lawyer, political activist, women's rights worker, suffragist, newspaper publisher, orator
California
Cyc Am Bio; Nat Cyc Am Bio csv3; Not Am Wom; Twent Cen Bio Dict Not Am; Wom Cent

85. Barnes, Mary Downing Sheldon
1850–98
educator, historian, textbook author
California
Dict Am Auth; Dict Am Bio; Not Am Wom; Wom Cent

86. Graham, Margaret (Collier)
born 1850
author
California
Dict Am Auth

87. Guirado, Luz (Sanchez)
flourished 1880s–1930s
patron of the Catholic church
Catholic
Los Angeles, CA
Mexican
Am Bio New Cyc

88. Coronel, Mariana W. de, Senora
born 1851
collector of Native American artifacts
Los Angeles, CA
Wom Cent

89. Shuey, Lilian (Hinman)
born 1853
novelist
California
Dict Am Auth

90. Daggett, Mary (Stewart)
born 1854
novelist
Pasadena, CA
Dict Am Auth; Nat Cyc Am Bio v9

91. Keith, Eliza D.; Erie Douglas; Di Vernon
born 1854
author, journalist, worker for the SPCA
California
Nat Cyc Am Bio v2; Wom Cent

92. Burdette, Clara Bradley
1855–1954
clubwoman, founder of women's clubs, philanthropist
Los Angeles, CA
Index t Wom; Nat Cyc Am Bio csv2; Obit File

93. Loughead, Flora (Haines)
born 1855
miscellaneous writer, journalist, novelist, children's author
Santa Barbara, CA
Dict Am Auth; Nat Cyc Am Bio v11; Wom Cent

94. Klumpke, Anna Elizabeth
1856–1942
painter
San Francisco, CA
Index t Wom; Nat Cyc Am Bio
v31

95. Walter, Carrie Stevens
born 1856
educator, poet
Catholic
California
Wom Cent

**96. Wiggin, Kate Douglas
Smith**
1856/59–1923
author, children's author, kindergarten educator, philanthropist
California
Dict Am Bio; Index t Wom; Nat
Cyc Am Bio v6; Not Am Wom;
Wom Cent

**97. Atherton, Gertrude
Franklin (Horn); Franklin
Horne**
1857/59–1948
novelist, suffragist, women's
rights worker
San Francisco, CA
Dict Am Auth; Dict Am Bio
supp v4; Dict Lit Bio v9; Index
t Wom; Nat Cyc Am Bio v10,
v36, and csv4; Not Am Wom;
Obit File; Read Encyc Am
West; Twent Cen Bio Dict Not
Am; Wom Lit; Wom Lit, More

98. Sessions, Kate Olivia
1857–1940
horticulturist, nurseryperson
California
Not Am Wom

**99. Montgomery, Carrie
Frances Judd**
born 1858
church worker, poet, author, temperance worker, Salvation
Army worker, social worker
New York; California
Index t Wom; Wom Cent

100. Morrison, May Treat
1858–1939
patron of the University of California, philanthropist
San Francisco, CA
Nat Cyc Am Bio v31

101. Shinn, Milicent Washburn
1858–1940
author, editor, child psychologist
Niles, CA
Dict Am Auth; Index t Wom;
Not Am Wom

102. Nevada, Emma (Wixom)
1859/62–1940
soprano opera singer
California
Cyc Am Bio; Dict Am Bio and
supp v2; Index t Wom; Not Am
Wom; Twent Cen Bio Dict Not
Am; Wom Cent

**103. Brooks, Florence; Mrs.
John Marone**
1860–1948
artist, author, poet
California
Nat Cyc Am Bio v37

**104. Gilman, Charlotte Anna
(Perkins) (Stetson)**
1860–1935
author, feminist, lecturer, labor
worker
San Francisco, CA
Dict Am Auth; Dict Am Bio
supp v1; Index t Wom; Nat Cyc
Am Bio v13; Not Am Wom;
Twent Cen Bio Dict Not Am;
Wom Lit, More

105. Klumpkey, Julia
flourished 1890s–1920s
violinist
San Francisco, CA
Nat Cyc Am Bio v31

106. Lummis, Dorothea
born 1860
physician, music critic, journalist,
newspaper editor, Native American artifacts collector
Los Angeles, CA
Index t Wom; Wom Cent

**107. Stewart, Mary E. (Smith);
Sun-saing Poo-in**
flourished 1890s–1930s
worker for the welfare of Koreans
in Southern California
California
Am Bio New Cyc

**108. Roberts, Dorothea
(Klumpke)**
1861–1942
astronomer
San Francisco, CA
Index t Wom; Nat Cyc Am Bio
v13 and v31

109. Bond, Carrie Jacobs; Carrie Jacobs-Bond
1862–1946
popular songwriter, composer,
author, publisher
Episcopalian
California
Dict Am Bio supp v4; Index t
Wom; Nat Cyc Am Bio v36 and
csv5; Not Am Wom; Obit File

110. James, Annie Laurie Wilson
born 1862
journalist, editor, horse breeding
expert

California
Index t Wom; Wom Cent

**111. Stetson, Grace Ellery
(Channing)**
born 1862
poet, short story writer
Pasadena, CA
Dict Am Auth

112. Beaver, Mary (Miller)
died 1913
San Francisco civic leader
San Francisco, CA
Am Bio New Cyc

113. Breed, Lorena May
born 1863
medical missionary to India, pathologist
California
Nat Cyc Am Bio csv3

**114. Cartwright, Florence
Byrne**
born 1863
poet
California
Wom Cent

**115. Parkhurst, Emelie Tracy
Y. Swett**
1863–92
poet, author
California
Wom Cent

**116. Thorp, Louisa Elizabeth
Garden McLeod**
1864–1944
artist, founder of the first recognized art school in Los Angeles
Los Angeles, CA
Obit File

117. Woods, Virna
1864–1903
educator, novelist, dramatist
Sacramento, CA
Dict Am Auth

118. Fearn, Anne Walter
1865/71–1939
physician, surgeon, hospital administrator, medical educator in
China
Berkeley, CA
Index t Wom; Nat Cyc Am Bio
v31 and csv4; Not Am Wom

119. Jordan, M. Evangeline
born 1865
dentist
Los Angeles, CA
Nat Cyc Am Bio v17

120. Sanderson, Sibyl Swift
1865–1903
operatic soprano
California
Index t Wom; Not Am Wom;
Wom Cent

121. Wolf, Emma
born 1865
fiction writer
San Francisco, CA
Dict Am Auth

122. Austin, Mary (Hunter)
1866/68–1934
novelist, folklorist, short story
writer, journalist, conservationist, feminist, worker for Native
American rights
California
Dict Am Auth; Dict Am Bio
supp v1; Dict Lit Bio v9; Not
Am Wom; Read Encyc Am
West; Wom Lit; Wom Lit,
More

123. Frank, Rachel "Ray"
born 1866
author
Jewish
California
Wom Cent

**124. Hoyt, Minerva Lockhart
Hamilton**
1866–1945
naturalist, conservationist, botanist, patron of music, president
of the Los Angeles Symphony
Orchestra
Los Angeles, CA
Am Bio New Cyc; Nat Cyc Am
Bio v34

125. Kahn, Florence Prag
1866/68–1948
Republican representative to
Congress from California
California
Dict Am Bio supp v4; Index t
Wom; Not Am Wom; Obit File

126. Capps, Effa Caroline
born 1867
San Diego civic worker
San Diego, CA
Nat Cyc Am Bio csv6

127. Fisher, Elizabeth Holmes
born 1867
philanthropist
Methodist
California
Nat Cyc Am Bio csv6

128. Myers, Harriet Williams
born 1867
author, ornithologist, founder of
California Audubon Society,
conservationist, animal humane
worker, World War II national
defense worker
Los Angeles, CA
Am Bio New Cyc

**129. Tompkins, Elizabeth
Knight**
born 1867
novelist

Berkeley, CA
Dict Am Auth

130. Percival, Olive May Graves
born 1868
underwriter, travel writer
Los Angeles, CA
Dict Am Auth

131. Barnum, Mary Gilmore
born 1869
educator, social worker, Los Angeles civic worker
Congregationalist
Los Angeles, CA
Nat Cyc Am Bio csv7

132. Eaves, Lucile
1869–1953
sociologist, labor relations expert
Unitarian
San Francisco, CA
Nat Cyc Am Bio v41 and csv1

133. Francis, Louise E.
born 1869
journalist, newspaper editor and publisher
California
Wom Cent

134. Braddock, Katherine
born 1870
Democratic political leader
Episcopalian
California
Nat Cyc Am Bio csv2

135. Graham, Nellie Dean; Vosey
born 1870
short story writer, magazine writer, philanthropist, clubwoman, Republican party worker, Los Angeles civic leader
Los Angeles, CA
Am Bio New Cyc

136. Beasley, Delilah Leontium
1871–1934
historian, journalist, pacifist
California
Black
Encyc Black Am; Negro Alman; Prof Negro Wom

137. Freeman, Carrie Stone
born 1871
composer
California
Nat Cyc Am Bio csv6

138. Morse, Ednah Anne Rich
1871–1945
educator
California
Nat Cyc Am Bio v38

139. Charles, Frances
born 1872
author

California
Dict Am Auth

140. Deering, Mabel Craft
born 1872
author, suffragist
Episcopalian
California
Nat Cyc Am Bio csv6

141. Morgan, Julia
1872–1957
architect
California
Dict Am Bio supp v6; Nat Cyc Am Bio csv7; Not Am Wom supp v1

142. Phelan, Marie Gerard
1872–1960
superior general of the Institute of the Religious of the Sacred Heart of Mary, cofounder of Marymount College
Catholic
California
Obit File

143. Phillips, Catherine Coffin
1874–1942
author, historian of the Pacific Coast
California
Nat Cyc Am Bio v32 and csv6

144. Lloyd, Caroline Alma
1875–1945
sculptor
Los Angeles, CA
Nat Cyc Am Bio v33

145. Stanwood, Cornelia Terry McKinne
born 1875
educator
Episcopalian
California
Nat Cyc Am Bio csv7

146. Overton, Gwendolen
born 1876
novelist
Los Angeles, CA
Dict Am Auth

147. Patterson, Elizabeth
1876–1966
character actor
California
Obit File

148. Adams, Annette Abbot
1877–1956
lawyer, judge
California
Dict Am Bio supp v6; Index t Wom; Nat Cyc Am Bio v43 and csvl; Not Am Wom supp v1

149. Reinhardt, Aurelia Isabelle Henry
1877–1948

president of Mills College, educator, religious worker, Unitarian minister
Unitarian
Oakland, CA
Dict Am Bio supp v4; Index t Wom; Not Am Wom; Obit File

150. Boyle, Gertrude; Gertrude Boyle Kanno; Gertrude Farquharson
1878–1937
sculptor
San Francisco, CA
Nat Cyc Am Bio v34

151. Corbaley, Kate Alaska Hinckley Cooper
1878–1938
screenplay writer
Los Angeles, CA
Nat Cyc Am Bio v28

152. Nazimova, Alla
1878/79–1945
stage and screen actor
Jewish; Greek-Russian Orthodox
California
Russian
Dict Am Bio supp v3; Index t Wom; Nat Cyc Am Bio v36; Not Am Wom; Obit File

153. van Buren, Mabel
1878–1947
stage and screen actor
California
Obit File

154. Coulter, Edith Margaret
1880–1963
librarian, library educator
Presbyterian
California
Nat Cyc Am Bio v50

155. Darwell, Jane; Patti Woodward
circa 1880–1967
screen actor
Hollywood, CA
Index t Wom; Obit File

156. Paige, Mabel
1880–1954
actor
California
Obit File

157. Boardman, Queen Walker
born 1881
horticulturist, philanthropist
Religious Scientist
Los Angeles, CA
Nat Cyc Am Bio csv7

158. Parsons, Louella Oettinger
1881/93–1972
journalist, gossip columnist
Hollywood, CA
Cur Biog '73; Index t Wom; Not Am Wom supp v1; Obit File

159. Spreckels, Alma Emma Charlotte Corday le Normand de Bretteville
1881–1968
patron of art
San Francisco, CA
Obit File

160. Harris, Mary Ormerod
born 1882
philanthropist, patron of the University of Southern California
Congregationalist
California
Nat Cyc Am Bio csv6

161. Mitchell, Ruth Comfort; Mrs. Sanborn Young
1882–1954
author, poet, novelist, leader in Republican Organizations for Women
California
Index t Wom; Nat Cyc Am Bio v44; Obit File

162. Cameron, Helen de Young
1883–1969
philanthropist
San Francisco, CA
Obit File

163. Oliver, Edna May
1883–1942
character actor, comedian
Unitarian
California
Index t Wom; Nat Cyc Am Bio csv6; Obit File

164. Miller, Evylena Nunn
born 1884
artist
Presbyterian
California
Nat Cyc Am Bio csv6

165. Raulston, Marion Churchill
born 1884
painter
California
Nat Cyc Am Bio csv7

166. Hopper, Hedda; Elda Furry
1885/90–1966
actor, journalist, gossip columnist
Hollywood, CA
Index t Wom; Not Am Wom supp v1; Obit File

167. Hutchinson, Mary Amory Hare; Amory Hare
1885–1969
author, novelist, dramatist, painter, poet, thoroughbred-horse breeder
Episcopalian
California
Nat Cyc Am Bio v57, Index t Wom

168. Ray, Rose Carolyn
born 1885
ornithologist
California
Nat Cyc Am Bio csv5

169. Bridgman, Olga Louise
born 1886
psychiatrist, medical educator
and author
Episcopalian
California
Nat Cyc Am Bio csv6

170. Kelly, Junea Wangeman
1886–1969
ornithologist, conservationist
California
Nat Cyc Am Bio v55

171. Pedder, Alice Pratt Berdell
1887–1947
realtor, business executive
Episcopalian
California
Nat Cyc Am Bio v36

172. Baum, Hedwig "Vicki";
Mrs. Richard Lerf
1888–1960/62
novelist, playwright, screenwriter
Jewish
Hollywood, CA
Austrian
Dict Am Bio supp v6; Index t
Wom; Nat Cyc Am Bio v52;
Obit File

173. Bryant, Nana
1888–1955
stage, screen, and television actor
Hollywood, CA
Obit File

174. Dean, Julia
1888–1952
stage and screen actor
Hollywood, CA
Obit File

175. Gleason, Lucille Webster
1888–1947
stage and screen actor
Hollywood, CA
Obit File

176. Marion, Frances
1888/1900–1973
screenwriter, playwright, novelist
Hollywood, CA
Index t Wom; Not Am Wom
supp v1; Obit File

177. Steere, Lora Woodhead
born 1888
sculptor
Christian Scientist
Los Angeles, CA
Nat Cyc Am Bio csv7

178. Chung, Margaret Jessie
1889–1959
plastic surgeon, World War II
relief worker
California
Chinese
Nat Cyc Am Bio v48

179. Weiman, Rita
1889/96–1954
author, playwright, screenwriter
Hollywood, CA
Index t Wom; Obit File

180. Willebrandt, Mabel Walker
1889–1963
lawyer, US assistant attorney general
California
Index t Wom; Nat Cyc Am Bio
csv2 and csv5; Not Am Wom
supp v1

181. Felton, Verna
1890–1966
actor
California
Index t Wom; Obit File

182. Griffin, Clementina de Forest
born 1890
high school educator, aviator
Los Angeles, CA
Nat Cyc Am Bio csv9

183. Hurst, Vida (Frais)
1890–1958
novelist
California
Nat Cyc Am Bio v43; Obit File

184. Joyce, Alice
1890–1955
silent-screen actor
Hollywood, CA
Index t Wom; Obit File

185. Young, Clara Kimball
1890–1960
silent-screen actor
California
Obit File

186. Bainter, Fay; Mrs. Reginald S. H. Venable
1891/93–1968
stage and screen actor
California
Index t Wom; Nat Cyc Am Bio
csv6; Obit File

187. Romm, May E.
1891–1977
psychiatrist, president of the Los
Angeles and Southern California psychoanalytic societies,
motion picture technical adviser
Los Angeles, CA
Obit File

188. Warner, Nell Walker;
Mrs. Emil Shostrum
born 1891
artist
Unitarian
Los Angeles, CA
Nat Cyc Am Bio csv8

189. Dolly, Jenny
1892–1941
dancer
California
Index t Wom; Obit File

190. Gifford, Myrnie Ada
1892–1966
public health administrator, pediatrician, conservationist
California
Nat Cyc Am Bio v54

191. Kaucher, Dorothy Wanita
1892–1972
educator, author, writer on aviation
California
Nat Cyc Am Bio v57

**192. Suckow, Ruth Ann Vivien
(Nuhn)**
1892–1960
writer, novelist, short story writer
Quaker
Iowa; California
Dict Lit Bio v9; Index t Wom;
Nat Cyc Am Bio v47; Not Am
Wom supp v1; Obit File; Wom
Lit; Wom Lit, More

193. Windsor, Claire
1892–1972
silent-screen actor
Hollywood, CA
Obit File

194. Cunard, Grace; Harriet
Mildred Jeffries
1894–1967
silent-screen actor
California
Obit File

195. Schulze, Margaret
1894–1943
gynecologist, surgeon, pathologist, medical educator, medical
author
California
Nat Cyc Am Bio v34

196. Todd, Lois Pendleton
1894–1968
physician, medical educator in
China
Congregationalist
California
Nat Cyc Am Bio v54

197. Fazenda, Louise
1895–1962
screen comedian

198. Vidor, Florence
1895–1977
silent-screen actor
California
Obit File

**199. Morrison, Lucile Gertrude
Phillips**
born 1896
author
California
Nat Cyc Am Bio csv6

200. Powdermaker, Hortense
1896/1900–1970
anthropologist, ethnologist, educator, author
California
Cur Biog '70; Index t Wom; Nat
Cyc Am Bio v55 and csv10; Not
Am Wom supp v1

**201. Russell, Helen Victoria
Crocker**
1896–1966
bank director, UNESCO executive, philanthropist
Episcopalian
San Francisco, CA
Nat Cyc Am Bio v53

202. Prince, Mildred Mallon
1897–1961
lawyer, social legislation agitator,
San Francisco civic worker
Catholic
San Francisco, CA
Nat Cyc Am Bio v47

203. Pryor, Helen Brenton
1897–1972
pediatrician, medical educator
Methodist
California
Nat Cyc Am Bio v57

204. Talmadge, Norma
1897–1957
silent-screen actor, producer
California
Dict Am Bio supp v6; Index t
Wom; Nat Cyc Am Bio v48;
Obit File

205. Emerson, Hope
1898–1960
screen actor
Hollywood, CA
Obit File

206. Pitts, Zasu
1898/1900–1963
actor
Santa Cruz, CA
Index t Wom; Not Am Wom
supp v1; Obit File

207. Hansen, Hazel Dorothy
1899–1962

California
Obit File

archaeologist, editor
California
Nat Cyc Am Bio v49

208. Talmadge, Natalie
1899–1969
silent-screen actor
California
Obit File

209. Taylor, Estelle [Ida]
circa 1899–1958
Broadway stage and screen actor
California
Index t Wom; Obit File

210. Brant, Evelyn
1900–75
screen actor
Los Angeles, CA
Obit File

211. Davies, Marion; Marion
Cecelia Douras
1900–61
screen actor
California
Index t Wom; Obit File

212. Douglas, Helen [Mary] (Gahagan)
1900/05–1980
stage actor, Democratic representative to Congress from California, opera singer
Episcopalian
California
Cur Biog '80; Index t Wom; Nat Cyc Am Bio csvF

213. Gilmore, George Davidson, Mrs.
flourished 1930s
Los Angeles civic leader, clubwoman
Los Angeles, CA
Am Bio New Cyc

214. Talmadge, Constance
1900–73
silent-screen actor, comedian
California
Index t Wom; Obit File

215. Bennett, Melba Berry
1901–68
author; Palm Springs, California, civic worker
Episcopalian
Palm Springs, CA
Nat Cyc Am Bio v54

216. Lewis, Tillie [Myrtle]
1901–77
cannery owner and executive
Jewish
California
Nat Cyc Am Bio v60

217. Walker, June
1901–66
screen actor

Hollywood, CA
Obit File

218. Block, Virginia Lee
1902–70
psychologist, educator
California
Nat Cyc Am Bio v56

219. Busch, Mae
1902–46
silent-screen actor
California
Obit File

220. Overstrett, Bonaro Wilkinson
born 1902
educator, lecturer, author
Congregationalist
California
Index t Wom; Nat Cyc Am Bio csv11

221. West, Jessamyn [Mary]
born 1902/07
short story writer, novelist, poet, autobiographer, operetta librettist, screenplay writer
Quaker
California
Cur Biog '77; Dict Lit Bio v6; Index t Wom

222. Chambers, Eleanor
1903–72
deputy mayor of Los Angeles
Los Angeles, CA
Obit File

223. Ryan, Irene
1903–73
screen and television actor
California
Obit File

224. Costello, Helene
1904–57
silent-screen actor
California
Obit File

225. Davis, Adelle
1904–74
food writer, nutritionist
California
Cur Biog '73 and '74; Not Am Wom supp v1; Obit File

226. Jones, Margaret Holden
born 1904
pediatrician
Methodist
California
Nat Cyc Am Bio csv9

227. Priest, Ivy [Maud] Baker; Ivy Maud Baker
1905–75
Republican party worker, US treasurer, politician, treasurer of California

Mormon
California
Cur Biog '75; Index t Wom; Nat Cyc Am Bio v59 and csv9; Not Am Wom supp v1; Obit File

228. Benaderet, Bea
1906–68
television actor
Los Angeles, CA
Obit File

229. Stewart, Wendy
born 1906
lawyer, law journalist
Los Angeles, CA
English
Nat Cyc Am Bio csv7

230. Borden, Olive
circa 1907–47
screen actor
Los Angeles, CA
Index t Wom; Obit File

231. Collyer, June; Dorothea Heermance
1907–68
actor
California
Obit File

232. Rosenstein, Sophie
1907–52
drama coach
Hollywood, CA
Obit File

233. Crawford, Joan
1908–77
screen actor, director of the Pepsi-Cola Co.
Hollywood, CA
Cur Biog '77; Index t Wom; Obit File

234. Halgarten, Katherine MacArthur Drew
born 1908
government attorney, international lawyer
California
Nat Cyc Am Bio csv13

235. van Riper, Kay
1908–48
movie scenarist
Hollywood, CA
Obit File

236. Dodd, Claire
1909–73
screen actor
California
Obit File

237. Laich, Katherine; Wilhelmina Schlegel
born 1910
librarian, president of the American Library Association, library science educator

California
Cur Biog '72

238. Lynn, Sharon
1910–63
screen actor
Hollywood, CA
Obit File

239. Niessen, Gertrude
1910/13–1975
singer; comedian; Broadway stage, screen, nightclub, and radio actor
California
Index t Wom; Obit File

240. Armstrong, Alice Catt
born 1911
biographer, book publisher
Religious Scientist
California
Nat Cyc Am Bio csv10

241. Russell, Rosalind
1911–76
stage and screen actor
California
Cur Biog '77; Index t Wom; Nat Cyc Am Bio v60; Obit File

242. Gibbons, Irene
died 1962
movie fashion designer
Hollywood, CA
Obit File

243. Sheridan, Clara Lou "Ann"
1915–67
actor
California
Index t Wom; Obit File

244. Fertman, Mildred Been
1916–52
physician, medical researcher
Jewish
California
Nat Cyc Am Bio v49

245. Grable, Betty
1916–73
screen actor
California
Dict Am Auth; Index t Wom; Not Am Wom supp v1

246. Stanford, Anne
born 1916
poet
California
Dict Lit Bio v5; Wom Lit, More

247. Louise, Anita
1917–70
screen actor
Hollywood, CA
Obit File

248. Wilson, Marie
1917–72

screen and radio actor, television
 personality
Hollywood, CA
Index t Wom; Obit File

249. Lake, Veronica
1919–73
screen actor
Hollywood, CA
Index t Wom; Obit File

250. Watson, Virginia
1919–51
swimming instructor, swimmer
Hollywood, CA
Obit File

251. McDonald, Marie (Frye);
 The Body
1920/23–1965
Hollywood screen actor
Hollywood, CA
Index t Wom; Obit File

252. Wright, Cobina; Elaine
 Cobb
died 1970
cabaret singer, society columnist,
 journalist
Hollywood, CA
Index t Wom; Obit File

253. Walker, Helen
1921–68
screen actor
Hollywood, CA
Obit File

254. Maxwell, Marilyn
1922–72
screen actor, singer
Hollywood, CA
Index t Wom; Obit File

255. Dandridge, Dorothy
1924–61
screen actor, singer
Hollywood, CA
Black
Index t Wom; Obit File

256. Banuelos, Ramona Acosta
born 1925
US treasurer, banker
Los Angeles, CA
Mexican
Dict Mex Am Hist

257. Nichols, Barbara
1929–76
stage and screen actor
California
Obit File

258. Huerta, Dolores Fernan-
dez
1930–post 1970
United Farm Workers executive
Catholic
California

Mexican
Bio Dict Am Lab; Dict Mex Am
 Hist

259. Burke, Yvonne Watson
Brathwaite
born 1932
lawyer, representative to Congress from California, regent of
 the University of California, environmentalist, feminist
California
Black
Cur Biog '75; Encyc Black Am;
 Negro Alman

260. Feinstein, Dianne
born 1933
mayor of San Francisco
San Francisco, CA
Cur Biog '79

261. Didion, Joan
born 1934
novelist, journalist, screenwriter
California
Cur Biog '78; Dict Lit Bio v2;
 Wom Lit; Wom Lit, More

262. Scala, Gia; Giovanna
 Scoglio
1934–72
screen actor
California
Italian
Obit File

263. Lansing, Joi
1935–72
screen actor
Hollywood, CA
Obit File

264. Mead, Sylvia Alice Earle
born 1935
marine biologist, aquanaut
Los Angeles, CA
Cur Biog '72

265. Moore, Mary Tyler
born 1937
television and stage actor
Catholic
California
Cur Biog '71; Index t Wom

266. Wakowski, Diane
born 1937
poet
California
Dict Lit Bio v5; Nort Anth Poet;
 Wom Lit, More

267. Zapata, Carman
flourished 1970s–80s
television, stage, and screen actor;
 director
Los Angeles, CA
Mexican
Dict Mex Am Hist

268. Mitchell, Joni; Roberta
 Joan Anderson
born 1943
popular singer, songwriter
California
Cur Biog '76

269. Post, Edith Sedgwick;
 Edie
1943–71
underground-film actor
California
Obit File

270. Bono, Cherilyn (Lapiere);
 Cher
born 1946
popular singer, actor, television
 entertainer
California
Native American (Cherokee)
Cur Biog '74

271. Rondstadt, Linda
born 1946
popular and country music singer
Los Angeles, CA
Mexican
Cur Biog '78; Dict Mex Am Hist

272. Meyer, Deborah Elizabeth
born 1952
Olympic swimmer
California
Cur Biog '69; Hall Fame Sport

COLORADO

273. Hill, Agnes Leonard
(Scanland); Molly Myrtle
1842–1917
poet, author, newspaper publish-
 er, religious writer, novelist,
 prisoner's welfare worker, Uni-
 versalist pastor
Universalist
Colorado
Dict Am Auth; Index t Wom;
 Nat Cyc Am Bio v17; Wom
 Cent

274. Thayer, Emma (Homan)
(Graves)
born 1842
author, novelist, artist, botanical
 illustrator
Salida, CO
Dict Am Auth; Twent Cen Bio
 Dict Not Am; Wom Cent

275. Jacobs, Frances Wisebart;
 Mother of the Charities
1843–92
welfare worker, charity worker
Colorado
Not Am Wom

276. Krout, Mary Hannah
1852/57–1927
poet, author, educator, journalist

Denver, CO
Dict Am Auth; Index t Wom;
 Wom Cent

277. Vaile, Charlotte Marion
(White)
1854–1902
children's short story writer
Denver, CO
Dict Am Auth

278. Bradford, Mary Carroll
Craig
born 1856/60
magazine and newspaper correspondent, educator, labor union
 leader
Christian Scientist
Colorado
Nat Cyc Am Bio csv2; Wom Cent

279. Wall, Annie (Carpenter)
born 1859
author, poet, artist
Pueblo, CO
Dict Am Auth; Nat Cyc Am Bio
 v5; Wom Cent

280. Bates, Mary Elizabeth
1861/63–1954
surgeon, child welfare worker,
 suffragist
Denver, CO
Index t Wom; Nat Cyc Am Bio
 v18

281. Stapleton, Patience (Tuck-
er)
1861–93
novelist, short story writer, journalist
Colorado
Dict Am Auth; Nat Cyc Am Bio
 v8

282. Johnson, Sallie M. Mills
born 1862
author
Colorado
Wom Cent

283. Bolles, Jeanette Hubbard
1863–1930
osteopath
Congregationalist
Colorado
Nat Cyc Am Bio v28

284. Bartlett, Maud Whitehead
born 1865
educator
Methodist Episcopal
Colorado
Index t Wom

285. Evans, Anne
1869/71–1941
civil leader, patron of the arts
Colorado
Index t Wom; Not Am Wom

286. Kahn, Ruth (Ward)
born 1870/72
author, poet
Leadville, CO
Dict Am Auth; Index t Wom; Wom Cent

287. Penrose, Julie Villers Lewis
1870–1956
philanthropist
Catholic
Colorado Springs, CO
Nat Cyc Am Bio v44

288. Sabin, Florence Rena
1871–1953
physician, medical researcher and educator, anatomist, public health worker, first woman life member of the American Academy of Sciences, author
Colorado
Dict Am Bio supp v5; Index t Wom; Nat Cyc Am Bio v40 and csv3; Not Am Wom supp v1; Obit File

289. Long, Margaret
born 1873
physician
Colorado
Nat Cyc Am Bio csv7

290. Bonfils, Helen Gertrude
1889–1962
newspaper executive, chairperson of the board of the *Denver Post*, theatrical producer
Catholic
Denver, CO
Nat Cyc Am Bio v56; Obit File

291. Hayden, Saint Clare Okie
born 1897
industrialist
Episcopalian
Colorado
Nat Cyc Am Bio csv7

292. Hughes, Arleen Florence Wilson
born 1897
investment counselor
Christian Scientist
Colorado
Nat Cyc Am Bio csv9

293. Wolle, Muriel Sibell
1898–1977
artist, art educator, Native American art scholar and collector, western history writer, conservationist
Episcopalian
Boulder, CO
Nat Cyc Am Bio v60

294. Schneider, Alma Kittredge
1901–75
superintendent of the Denver Mint
Denver, CO
Index t Wom; Obit File

295. Cohen, Essie White
1902–63
chemist
Jewish
Denver, CO
Nat Cyc Am Bio v51

296. Peterson, Helen White
born 1915
assistant to the commissioner of the Bureau of Indian affairs, race relations worker
Colorado
Native American (Dakota-Oglala)
Ind Today; Read Encyc Am West

297. Collins, Judy
born 1939
folk singer, composer
Colorado
Cur Biog '69

298. Schroeder, Patricia (Scott)
born 1940
representative to Congress from Colorado, feminist
Colorado
Cur Biog '78

299. Baca-Barragan, Polly
born 1941
Colorado state senator, housing reformer
Colorado
Mexican
Dict Mex Am Hist

CONNECTICUT

300. Martha
1685–1805 [*sic*]
agent of the Mohegan people
Connecticut
Native American (Mohegan)
Am Bio Dict

301. Bailey, Anna Warner; Mother Bailey
1758–1850/51
patriot of American Revolution, colonial hero
Connecticut
Appl Cyc Am Bio; Cyc Am Bio; Dict Am Bio; Index t Wom; Wom Cent

302. Whittlesey, Abigail Goodrich
1788–1858
educator, magazine editor, author
Connecticut
Cyc Am Bio; Dict Am Bio; Not Am Wom

303. Sigourney, Lydia Howard (Huntley)
1791–1865
author, poet, philanthropist
Connecticut
Cyc Am Bio; Dict Am Auth; Dict Am Bio; Dict Am Bio Men Time; Dict Lit Bio v1; Index t Wom; Nat Cyc Am Bio v1; Not Am Wom; Twent Cen Bio Dict Not Am; Wom Cent; Wom Lit, More

304. Hyde, Nancy Maria
1792–1816
educator, author
Connecticut
Am Bio Dict; Cyc Am Bio; Dict Am Bio Men Time

305. Smith, Julia Evelina
1792–1886/92
suffragist, women's rights worker, abolitionist, Biblical translator
Connecticut
Cyc Am Bio; Dict Am Bio; Nat Cyc Am Bio v7; Not Am Wom

306. Caulkins, Frances Manwaring
1795/96–1869
historian, historical author
Connecticut
Cyc Am Bio; Dict Am Bio Men Time; Not Am Wom; Twent Cen Bio Dict Not Am

307. Smith, Abigail Hadassah "Abby"
1796/97–1878
suffragist, women's rights worker, abolitionist
Connecticut
Cyc Am Bio; Dict Am Bio; Nat Cyc Am Bio v7; Not Am Wom

308. du Bois, Constance Goddard
born 18?
novelist
Waterbury, CT
Dict Am Auth

309. Homer, Elmira
died 1852
last of the Turkey Hill people
New Milford, CT
Native American (Turkey Hill)
Am Bio Dict

310. Stowe, Harriet Elizabeth Beecher
1811/12–1896
author, abolitionist, social reformer, theologian

Connecticut
Cyc Am Bio; Dict Am Auth; Dict Am Bio; Dict Am Bio Men Time; Dict Am Rel Bio; Dict Lit Bio v1; Nat Cyc Am Bio v1; Not Am Wom; Twent Cen Bio Dict Not Am; Wom Cent; Wom Lit; Wom Lit, More

311. Day, Martha
1813–33
scholar of mathematics and language, author
New Haven, CT
Cyc Am Bio; Dict Am Bio Men Time; Index t Wom

312. Collins, Emily Parmely
born 1814
suffragist, abolitionist, political writer, Civil War nurse
Hartford, CT
Wom Cent

313. Trowbridge, Catherine Maria
born 1818
children's author
South Manchester, CT
Dict Am Auth

314. Ingersoll, Julia Harriet (Pratt)
182?–98
religious author, religious poet
New Haven, CT
Dict Am Auth

315. Hooker, Isabella Beecher
1822–1907
suffragist, feminist, philanthropist, lecturer, essayist
Spiritualist
Hartford, CT
Cyc Am Bio; Dict Am Auth; Dict Am Bio; Index t Wom; Not Am Wom; Twent Cen Bio Dict Not Am; Wom Cent

316. Hale, Anne Gardner
born 1823
poet, author
Newburyport, CT
Dict Am Auth

317. Cooke, Rose (Terry)
1827–92
author, poet
Connecticut
Cyc Am Bio; Dict Am Auth; Dict Am Bio; Index t Wom; Nat Cyc Am Bio v6; Not Am Wom; Twent Cen Bio Dict Not Am; Wom Cent; Wom Lit; Wom Lit, More

318. Cady, Sarah Louise (Ensign)
1829–1912
educator, kindergartner, founder of Mrs. Cady's School for Girls (now the West End Institute)

New Haven, CT
Dict Am Bio; Nat Cyc Am Bio v9

319. Hanaford, Phoebe Ann (Coffin)
1829–1921
Universalist minister, historian, journalist, author, feminist, lecturer, chaplain of the Connecticut state legislature
Universalist
New Haven, CT
Cyc Am Bio; Dict Am Auth; Dict Am Bio; Index t Wom; Nat Cyc Am Bio v13; Not Am Wom; Twent Cen Bio Dict Not Am; Wom Cent

320. Prichard, Sarah Johnson
born 1830
children's author, fiction writer
Waterbury, CT
Dict Am Auth; Twent Cen Bio Dict Not Am

321. Morris, Eugenia Laura (Tuttle); Alyn Yates Keith
born 1833
miscellaneous writer
New Haven, CT
Dict Am Auth

322. Seymour, Mary Harrison (Browne)
born 1835
children's author
Hartford, CT
Cyc Am Bio; Dict Am Auth; Nat Cyc Am Bio v4; Twent Cen Bio Dict Not Am

323. Todd, Letitia Willey; Alice Afton; Enola
born 1835
poet
Connecticut
Wom Cent

324. Benjamin, Elizabeth Dundas (Bedell)
died 1890
religious author
Stratford, CT
Dict Am Auth

325. Bennett, Mary E.; Elizabeth Glover
born 1841
miscellaneous author, children's author
New Haven, CT
Dict Am Auth

326. Hawley, Frances Mallette
born 1843
poet, author
Bridgeport, CT
Wom Cent

327. Porter, Rose
1845–1906

author, religious novelist, compiler
New Haven, CT
Dict Am Auth; Nat Cyc Am Bio v10; Wom Cent

328. Hallock, Julia Isabel (Sherman)
born 1846
author
Connecticut
Dict Am Auth

329. Hewins, Caroline Maria Matilda
1846–1926
librarian, pioneer in library work for children, writer on librarianship
Hartford, CT
Dict Am Auth; Index t Wom; Nat Cyc Am Bio v21; Not Am Wom; Twent Cen Bio Dict Not Am

330. Hall, Mary
born 185?
lawyer, notary public
Congregationalist
Connecticut
Wom Cent

331. Holcombe, Emily Seymour Goodwin
1852–1923
civic worker
Connecticut
Nat Cyc Am Bio v16 and v18

332. Field, Caroline Leslie (Whitney)
1853–1902
author
Guilford, CT
Dict Am Auth; Twent Cen Bio Dict Not Am

333. Dowd, Mary Alice
born 1855
poet, educator
Connecticut
Dict Am Auth; Wom Cent

334. Grannis, Anna Jane
born 1856
fiction author
Plainville, CT
Dict Am Auth

335. Thayer, Lizzie E. D.
born 1857
train dispatcher, telegraph operator
Connecticut
Index t Wom; Wom Cent

336. Trumbull, Annie Eliot
1857–1949
novelist, poet, playwright, short story writer, first president of the Town and Country Club

Hartford, CT
Dict Am Auth; Obit File

337. Smith, Mary Belle
born 1862
educator, temperance worker
Methodist Episcopal
Connecticut
Wom Cent

338. Watson, Augusta (Campbell)
born 1862
novelist
Groton, CT
Dict Am Auth

339. Ray, Anna Chapin
born 1865
children's author
West Haven, CT
Dict Am Auth; Twent Cen Bio Dict Not Am

340. Buel, Elizabeth Cynthia Barney
1868–1943
author
Congregationalist
Connecticut
Nat Cyc Am Bio v32

341. Bjerkoe, Ethel Hall
1871–1978
antiques authority and author, clubwoman
Connecticut; Maine
Nat Cyc Am Bio v60

342. Branch, Anna Hempstead
1875–1937
poet, social worker
New London, CT
Dict Am Auth; Index t Wom; Nat Cyc Am Bio csv3; Not Am Wom

343. Bacon, Josephine Dodge Daskam
1876–1961
humorist, children's author, short story writer, Girl Scout executive
Stamford, CT
Dict Am Auth; Index t Wom

344. Sprague, Harriet Chapman
1876–1969
bibliophile, book collector
Congregationalist
Connecticut
Nat Cyc Am Bio v56

345. Townshend, Anna Draper
born 1882
suffragist, Connecticut state legislator from New Haven, New Haven civic worker
Unitarian
New Haven, CT
Nat Cyc Am Bio csv6

346. McAfee, Helen
1884–1956
editor
Congregationalist
New Haven, CT
Nat Cyc Am Bio v43

347. Bailey, Margaret Emerson
1885–1949
educator, journalist, novelist, magazine writer, police commissioner
Episcopalian
New Canaan, CT
Nat Cyc Am Bio csv6; Obit File

348. Calverley, Eleanor Jane Taylor
1887–1968
physician, missionary to Kuwait, nurse in the 1920 Kuwait war, birth control advocate, birth control clinic founder
Dutch Reformed
Connecticut
Nat Cyc Am Bio v57

349. Alexander, Mary Louise
1889–1976
librarian
Connecticut
Nat Cyc Am Bio v59

350. Ochtman, Dorothy; Mrs. William A. del Mar
1892–1971
artist
Congregationalist
Connecticut
Nat Cyc Am Bio v56

351. Weld, Agnes Vance
1892–1975
newspaper publisher and editor
Episcopalian
Connecticut
Nat Cyc Am Bio v58

352. Smith, Blanche Hixson
1894–1974
newspaper publisher and editor
Congregationalist
Connecticut
Nat Cyc Am Bio v58

353. Blanshard, Frances Bradshaw
1895–1966
educator
Quaker
Connecticut
Nat Cyc Am Bio v54

354. Kellems, Vivien
1896–1975
industrialist, engineer, president of the Kellems Co.
Connecticut
Cur Biog '69; Index t Wom

355. Taber, Gladys; Leonae
Bagg
1899–1980
novelist, short story writer, magazine writer
Connecticut
Cur Biog '80; Index t Wom

356. Forman, Julie (Rose) Ripley
1902–75
educator
Christian Scientist
Connecticut
Nat Cyc Am Bio v59

357. Park, Rosemary
born 1907
educator, president of Barnard College
Congregationalist
Connecticut
Index t Wom; Nat Cyc Am Bio csv10

358. Shepard, Marguerite Dunbar
1908–57
physician
Episcopalian
Connecticut
Nat Cyc Am Bio v47

359. Wright, Mary Clabaugh
1917–70
historian, scholar of Chinese history, university educator
Connecticut
Not Am Wom supp v1; Obit File

360. Grasso, Ella Tambussi
1919–81
Democratic governor of Connecticut, politician
Connecticut
Cur Biog '75; Index t Wom

DELAWARE

361. Pyle, Katherine
born 18?
children's author
Wilmington, DE
Dict Am Auth

362. Chandler, Elizabeth Margaret
1807–1834/35
author, poet, abolitionist
Delaware
Cyc Am Bio; Dict Am Auth; Dict Am Bio; Dict Am Bio Men Time; Index t Wom; Not Am Wom; Twent Cen Bio Dict Not Am

363. Hilles, Florence Bayard
1865–1954
suffragist, feminist, ERA worker, pacifist, golfer

Episcopalian
Delaware
Nat Cyc Am Bio v46

DISTRICT OF COLUMBIA

364. Royall, Anne Newport
1769–1854
traveler, journalist, newspaper editor and publisher, novelist
Washington, DC; Virginia
Am Bio Dict; Cyc Am Bio; Dict Am Auth; Dict Am Bio; Dict Am Bio Men Time; Encyc South Hist; Index t Wom; Not Am Wom

365. van Ness, Marcia Burns
1782–1832
philanthropist, patriot
Washington, DC
Cyc Am Bio; Index t Wom

366. Taylor, Mary Imlay
born 18?
novelist
Washington, DC
Dict Am Auth

367. Dorsey, Annah Hanson McKenney
1815/16–1896
author, dramatist, poet, novelist, essayist, short story writer, political writer
Catholic
Washington, DC
Cyc Am Bio; Dict Am Auth; Dict Am Bio; Index t Wom; Nat Cyc Am Bio v11 Twent Cen Bio Dict Not Am; Wom Cent

368. Greenhow, Rose O'Neal
1815/17–1864
Confederate spy
Catholic
Washington, DC
Bio Dict Confed; Index t Wom; Not Am Wom; Read Encyc Am West

369. Southworth, Emma Dorothy Eliza (Nevitte); Dorothy Eliza Nevitte
1818/19–1899
romance novelist
Washington, DC
Cyc Am Bio; Dict Am Auth; Dict Am Bio; Dict Am Bio Men Time; Index t Wom; Nat Cyc Am Bio v1; Not Am Wom; Twent Cen Bio Dict Not Am; Wom Cent; Wom Lit, More

370. Winslow, Caroline B.
born 1822
physician, suffragist
Washington, DC
Wom Cent

371. Dahlgren, Madeleine Vinton [Sara] (Goodard); Corinne; Cornelia
1825/35–1898
novelist, translator, antisuffragist
Catholic
Washington, DC
Cyc Am Bio; Dict Am Auth; Dict Am Bio; Index t Wom; Nat Cyc Am Bio v22; Twent Cen Bio Dict Not Am; Wom Cent

372. Thomas, Mary von Erden
born 1825
author, novelist, statistician
Washington, DC
Cyc Am Bio; Dict Am Bio

373. Sherwood, Mary Elizabeth (Wilson); M. E. W. S.
1826/30–1903
short story writer, poet, novelist, miscellaneous writer, patron of literature and science, philanthropist
Washington, DC
Cyc Am Bio; Dict Am Auth; Dict Am Bio; Index t Wom; Nat Cyc Am Bio v5; Wom Cent

374. Sherwood, Emily Lee; Jennie Crayon
born 1829/43
journalist, novelist, author
Washington, DC
Dict Am Auth; Index t Wom; Wom Cent

375. Ames, Mary E. Clemmer; Mrs. Hudson
1831/40–1884
journalist, biographer, author
Washington, DC
Appl Cyc Am Bio; Cyc Am Bio; Index t Wom; Nat Cyc Am Bio v7; Not Am Wom; Twent Cen Bio Dict Not Am

376. Ireland, Mary E. (Haines)
born 1834
children's author
Washington, DC
Dict Am Auth; Wom Cent

377. Festetitts, Kate (Neely)
born 1837
children's author
Washington, DC
Dict Am Auth

378. Hughes, Kate Duval
born 1837
author, inventor
Catholic
Washington, DC
Wom Cent

379. Logan, Celia (Kellog) (Connelly)
1837/40–1904
journalist, author, dramatist

Washington, DC
Cyc Am Bio; Dict Am Auth; Index t Wom; Twent Cen Bio Dict Not Am; Wom Cent

380. Spencer, Sara Andrews
born 1837
suffragist, women's rights worker, business educator, author
Washington, DC
Cyc Am Bio; Dict Am Auth

381. Field, Mary Katherine Kemble "Kate"
1838/54–1896
journalist, actor, playwright, literary critic, lecturer
Washington, DC
Cyc Am Bio; Dict Am Auth; Dict Am Bio; Index t Wom; Nat Cyc Am Bio v6; Not Am Wom; Twent Cen Bio Dict Not Am; Wom Cent

382. Hudson, Mary (Clemmer) (Ames)
1839/40–1884
journalist, poet
Washington, DC
Dict Am Auth; Wom Cent

383. Schayer, Julia (Thompson) (Von Storch)
born 1840
short story writer
Washington, DC
Dict Am Auth

384. Stevens, E. Hebert, Mrs.
flourished 1870s–1910s
agricultural librarian, lecturer
Washington, DC
Index t Wom; Wom Cent

385. White, Nettie L.
flourished 1870s–90s
stenographer, government employee
Washington, DC
Index t Wom; Wom Cent

386. Monroe, Harriet Earhart
born 1842
lecturer, educator, journalist
Kansas; Washington, DC
Dict Am Auth; Wom Cent

387. la Fetra, Sarah Doan
born 1843
temperance worker
Washington, DC
Index t Wom; Wom Cent

388. Cleveland, Cynthia Eloise
born 1845
political writer and activist, lawyer, civil service worker, novelist
Washington, DC
Dict Am Auth; Twent Cen Bio Dict Not Am

389. Lincoln, Jeannie Gould
born 1846/53
author, poet, children's author
Washington, DC
Dict Am Auth; Index t Wom; Twent Cen Bio Dict Not Am

390. Houghton, Alice
born 1849
real estate broker, insurance and investment counselor
Washington, DC
Wom Cent

391. Litchfield, Grace Denio
1849–1944
fiction writer, poet, novelist
Protestant
Washington, DC
Dict Am Auth; Nat Cyc Am Bio v12 and v42, Wom Cent

392. Barker, Ellen Blackmar (Maxwell); Ellen Blackmar Maxwell
born 185?
author
Washington, DC
Dict Am Auth; Index t Wom

393. Mussey, Ellen (Persis) Spencer
1850–1936
international lawyer, law educator, feminist, women's rights worker, clubwoman, child welfare worker, Red Cross worker, social reformer
Swedenborgian
Washington, DC
Dict Am Bio supp v2; Index t Wom; Nat Cyc Am Bio v47 and csv1; Not Am Wom; Twent Cen Bio Dict Not Am

394. Dorsey, Ella Loraine
1853–1901
children's author
Washington, DC
Dict Am Auth; Index t Wom; Wom Cent

395. Crowninshield, Mary (Bradford)
1854–1913
fiction writer
Washington, DC
Index t Wom

396. Reeves, Marian Calhoun Legare; "Fadette"
circa 1854–98
author, novelist
Washington, DC
Cyc Am Bio; Dict Am Auth; Nat Cyc Am Bio v4

397. Scidmore, Eliza Ruhamah; Eliza Ruhamah
1856–1928
geographer, traveler, travel writer, journalist

Washington, DC
Dict Am Auth; Dict Am Bio; Index t Wom; Twent Cen Bio Dict Not Am

398. Seawell, Molly Elliot
1860–1916
author, novelist, children's author, newspaper correspondent
Washington, DC
Dict Am Auth; Dict Am Bio; Index t Wom; Nat Cyc Am Bio v7; Twent Cen Bio Dict Not Am ; Wom Cent

399. Blodgett, Daisy Albertine Peck
1862–1947
philanthropist, equestrian
Washington, DC
Nat Cyc Am Bio v37

400. Reno, Itti Kinney
born 1862
author, novelist
Washington, DC
Dict Am Auth; Index t Wom; Wom Cent

401. Merriam, Florence Augusta
born 1863
miscellaneous writer
Washington, DC
Dict Am Auth

402. Terrell, Mary Eliza Church
1863–1954
community leader, social reformer, suffragist, feminist, civil rights leader, NAACP organizer, lecturer, educator
Congregationalist
Washington, DC
Dict Am Bio supp v5; Encyc Black Am; Encyc South Hist; Index t Wom; Nat Cyc Am Bio v52; Negro Alman; Not Am Wom; Prof Negro Wom v1; World Great Men Col v2

403. Harriman, Florence Jaffray (Hurst)
1870–1967
Democratic party official, diplomat, minister to Norway, politician, journalist, suffragist, clubwoman, social rights worker, Red Cross worker in World War I, World War II relief worker in Norway
Washington, DC
Index t Wom; Nat Cyc Am Bio v53 and csv6; Not Am Wom supp v1; Obit File

404. Wood, Edith (Elmer)
1871–1945
housing reformer, housing economist, novelist

Washington, DC
Dict Am Auth; Dict Am Bio supp v3; Index t Wom; Not Am Wom

405. Peacock, Virginia Tatnall
born 1873
journalist
Washington, DC
Dict Am Auth

406. Helm, Edith Benham
1874–1962
White House social secretary
Washington, DC
Obit File

407. O'Toole, Mary
born 1874
judge, suffragist, banker
Washington, DC
Irish
Nat Cyc Am Bio csv2

408. Carr, Edith Adele
1876–1965
philanthropist, diplomatic and consular officer
Washington, DC
Nat Cyc Am Bio v51

409. Hard, Anne; Annie Marie Nyhan Scribner
1877–1961
author, radio broadcaster, political journalist
Episcopalian
Washington, DC
Nat Cyc Am Bio v57

410. Muhlhofer, Mary Elizabeth
1878–1950
painter
Episcopalian
Washington, DC
Nat Cyc Am Bio v38

411. Patterson, Eleanor Medill "Cissy"
1881/84–1948
newspaper editor, publisher of the Washington, DC, *Times-Herald*
Washington, DC
Dict Am Bio supp v4; Index t Wom; Not Am Wom; Obit File

412. Walsh, Carrie Belle Reed
died 1932
philanthropist
Washington, DC
Nat Cyc Am Bio v26

413. Roosevelt, [Anna] Eleanor
1884–1962
social reformer, humanitarian, author, lecturer
Washington, DC

English
Eng Wom; Index t Wom; Nat Cyc Am Bio v57 and csv4 and csv6; Not Am Wom supp v1; Obit File

414. Essary, Helen (Murphy)
1886–1951
syndicated newspaper columnist
Washington, DC
Obit File

415. Post, Marjorie Merriweather
1887–1973
philanthropist, antique collector, suffragist, director of National Savings and Trust, founder and director of General Foods
Christian Scientist
Washington, DC
Nat Cyc Am Bio v58; Not Am Wom supp v1; Obit File

416. Craig, May
1889–1975
Washington, DC, correspondent for a chain of Maine newspapers
Washington, DC
Obit File

417. Fromm-Reichman, Frieda
1889–1957
psychiatrist, psychoanalyst, authority on schizophrenia, faculty chairperson of the Washington School of Psychiatry
Jewish
Washington, DC
German
Dict Am Bio supp v5; Not Am Wom supp v1; Obit File

418. Armstrong, Bess (Furman)
1894/95–1969
journalist, White House correspondent to the *New York Times*, HEW assistant
Washington, DC
Index t Wom; Not Am Wom; Obit File

419. Borchardt, Selma Munter
1895/1900–1968
educator, lawyer, labor leader, lobbyist
Washington, DC
Bio Dict Am Lab; Not Am Wom supp v1

420. Clapper, Olive Ewing
1896–1968
author, lecturer, radio commentator, autobiographer, director of the Washington, DC, bureau of CARE
Washington, DC
Cur Biog '69; Index t Wom

421. Reid, Helen Dwight
1901–65

international political scientist, educator, pacifist
Christian Scientist
Washington, DC
Scottish
Nat Cyc Am Bio v51

422. Peterson, Esther Eggertsen
born 1906
labor leader, director of the US Department of Labor Women's Bureau
Mormon
Washington, DC
Bio Dict Am Lab; Index t Wom; Nat Cyc Am Bio csv10

423. Medinger, Elizabeth Eudora
1907–77
Catholic church worker, philanthropist
Catholic
Washington, DC
Nat Cyc Am Bio v60

424. Kabis, Dorothy Andrews
1917–71
US treasurer, Republican party activist, president of the National Federation of Republican Women
Washington, DC
Obit File

425. Dixon, Jean
born 1918
writer on extrasensory perception and prophecy
Washington, DC
Cur Biog '73

426. Hewell, Grace
born 1918
educator; social worker; HEW official; chief of education, House Committee on Education and Labor
Washington, DC
Black
Encyc Black Am; Negro Her Lib v1

FLORIDA

427. Long, Ellen Call
1825–1905
civic leader, author, planter
Florida
Read Encyc Am West

428. Bellamy, Emily Elizabeth Whitfield (Croom); A Southern Lady; Kamba Thorpe
1837/39–1900
author, novelist

Mobile, AL; Florida
Appl Cyc Am Bio; Cyc Am Bio; Dict Am Auth; Dict Am Bio; Nat Cyc Am Bio v12; Wom Cent

429. Hague, Parthenia Antoinette (Vardaman)
born 1838; flourished 1860s
Civil War diarist
Florida
Dict Am Auth; Index t Wom

430. Bethune, Mary McLeod
1875–1955
educator, founder and president of Bethune-Cookman College, director of the Negro Affairs National Youth Council, civil rights worker, women's rights worker
Daytona Beach, FL
Black
Dict Am Bio supp v5; Dict Am Rel Bio; Encyc Black Am; Encyc South Hist; Index t Wom; Nat Cyc Am Bio v49; Negro Alman; Negro Her Lib v1; Not Am Wom supp v1; Prof Negro Wom; Obit File

431. Darrow, Anna Labertine Lindstedt
1876–1959
physician, pharmacist
Florida
Nat Cyc Am Bio v48

432. Smith, Lilian Eugenia
1897–1966
novelist, newspaper columnist, writer on race relations, civil rights worker, editor, social worker, educator, lecturer
Florida
Encyc South Hist; Index t Wom; Not Am Wom supp v1; Obit File; Wom Lit; Wom Lit, More

433. Roseborough, Melanie Rohrer; Mrs. Adolph J. Radosta
born 1898
German language educator
Lutheran
Florida
Nat Cyc Am Bio csv13

434. Spain, Frances Lander
born 1903
librarian, organization official
Episcopalian
Florida
Index t Wom; Nat Cyc Am Bio csv10

435. Black, Marian Watkins
1905–75
educator
Methodist
Florida
Twent Cen Bio Dict Not Am

436. Bryant, Anita
born 1940
singer, television personality, antifeminist, antiabortion worker, antihomosexual crusader; Baptist religious worker
Baptist
Florida
Cur Biog '75

GEORGIA

437. Musgrove, Mary; Coosaponakeesa
circa 1770–circa 1763
Native American leader in colonial Georgia, interpreter, trader
Georgia
Native American (Creek)
Great North Am Ind; Not Am Wom

438. Hart, Nancy; Ann Morgan
1735/55–1830
hero of American Revolution
Georgia
Cyc Am Bio; Encyc South Hist; Index t Wom; Nat Cyc Am Bio v13; Not Am Wom

439. McLaws, [Emily] Lafayette
born 18?
novelist
Augusta, GA
Dict Am Auth

440. Kemble, Frances Anne "Fanny"; Fanny Kemble Butler
1809/11–1893
actor, diarist, author, abolitionist
Georgia
English
Cyc Am Bio; Dict Am Bio; Dict Am Bio Men Time; Dict Nat Bio supp; Encyc South Hist; Index t Wom; Nat Cyc Am Bio v3; Not Am Wom

441. Williams, Mary Ann
1822–74
philanthropist, Civil War relief worker, Confederate sympathizer
Georgia
Nat Cyc Am Bio v7

442. McCoy, Catherine (Webb) (Towles)
born 1823
fiction writer
Columbus, GA
Dict Am Auth

443. Packard, Sophia B.
1824–91

founder of Spelman College, church worker, educator of Blacks
Baptist
Atlanta, GA
Nat Cyc Am Bio v2; Not Am Wom

444. Dubose, Catherine Anne (Richards)
born 1826
poet, Sunday school story writer
Georgia
Cyc Am Bio; Dict Am Auth

445. Bowen, Eliza Andrews
1828–98
newspaper and magazine writer, writer about astronomy
Georgia
Dict Am Auth

446. Beasley, Matilda, Mother
1834–1903
educator, social worker, Catholic nun
Catholic
Georgia
Black
Negro Alman; Prof Negro Wom

447. Wilson, Martha Eleanor Loftin
born 1834
missionary worker, Civil War nurse
Baptist
Georgia
Wom Cent

448. Felton, Rebecca Ann Latimer
1835–1930
senator from Georgia, labor welfare worker, journalist, author, orator, feminist, women's rights worker
Georgia
Dict Am Bio; Encyc South Hist; Index t Wom; Nat Cyc Am Bio v13 and v36; Not Am Wom; Wom Cent

449. Tiernana, Mary Spear (Nicholas)
1836–91
novelist
Georgia
Dict Am Auth

450. Wyman, Lillie Buffum Chace
born 1837/47
author, muckraking journalist, short story writer, philanthropist, suffragist, labor welfare worker
Georgia
Dict Am Auth; Wom Cent

451. Bryan, Mary (Edwards)
1838/46–1913

journalist, author, editor, poet, clubwoman
Atlanta, GA; New York, NY
Cyc Am Bio; Dict Am Bio; Index t Wom; Nat Cyc Am Bio v8; Not Am Wom; Twent Cen Bio Dict Not Am; Wom Cent

452. Stokes, Missouri H.
1838–post 1860
Civil War diarist, educator, temperance worker
Presbyterian
Georgia
Index t Wom; Wom Cent

453. Andrews, Eliza Frances
1840/47–1931
journalist, Civil War diarist, educator, botanist
Georgia
Dict Am Auth; Index t Wom; Nat Cyc Am Bio v6; Not Am Wom; Wom Cent

454. Mims, Sue Harper
born 1842
Christian Science leader
Christian Scientist
Georgia
Index t Wom; Wom Cent

455. Neblett, Ann Viola
born 1842
temperance worker, suffragist
South Carolina; Georgia
Index t Wom

456. Wynne, Emma (Moffett)
born 1844
novelist
Georgia
Dict Am Auth

457. Banks, Mary Ross
born 1846
author
Georgia
Wom Cent

458. Hanna, Sarah Jackson
born 1847
musical educator
Georgia
Wom Cent

459. de Graffenreid, Mary Clare
1849–1921
social investigator, writer on social conditions, labor authority
Georgia
Encyc South Hist; Not Am Wom

460. Hahr, Emma
flourished 1880s
pianist, composer, musical educator
Georgia
Wom Cent

461. Harris, Ethel Hillyer
flourished 1880s
author
Rome, GA
Wom Cent

462. Rutherford, Mildred Lewis
1851/52–1928
educator, textbook author, apologist for the Old South
Athens, GA
Dict Am Auth; Nat Cyc Am Bio v10; Not Am Wom; Twent Cen Bio Dict Not Am

463. Wright, Marie Robinson
born 1853/60
journalist, travel writer
Georgia; New York
Dict Am Auth; Wom Cent

464. Laney, Lucy Craft
1854–1933
educator, founder of the Haines Normal Institute
Georgia
Black
Index t Wom; Negro Alman; Not Am Wom; Prof Negro Wom v1

465. Byngton, Elia Goode
born 1858
newspaper editor, women's rights worker, journalist
Georgia
Wom Cent

466. Sibley, Jennie E.
flourished 1890s
temperance worker
Georgia
Wom Cent

467. Wylie, Lollie Belle
flourished 1890s
journalist, newspaper editor, poet
Georgia
Wom Cent

468. Matthews, Victoria Earle
1861–98
social worker, mission society founder, clubwoman
Fort Valley, GA
Black
Index t Wom; Negro Alman; Prof Negro Wom v1

469. Beck, Leonora
born 1862
educator, founder of Leonora Beck College
Atlanta, GA
Wom Cent

470. du Bose, Miriam Howard
born 1862
suffragist, composer, pianist
Georgia
Wom Cent

471. Ohl, Maud Andrews
born 1862
journalist, poet
Georgia
Index t Wom; Wom Cent

472. Pickard, Florence [Martha] Willingham
1862–1930
author, painter
Georgia
Nat Cyc Am Bio v27 and csv2

473. Bell, Orelia Key
born 1864
poet
Christian Scientist
Georgia
Wom Cent

474. Roach, Aurelia
born 1865
educator
Atlanta, GA
Wom Cent

475. Williams, Florence B.
born 1865
newspaper editor and publisher, author
Georgia
Wom Cent

476. Berry, Martha McChesney; Sunday Lady of the Possum Trot
1866–1942
educator, founder of the Berry School for underprivileged mountain children, philanthropist
Episcopalian
Georgia
Dict Am Bio supp v3; Encyc South Hist; Index t Wom; Nat Cyc Am Bio csv3; Not Am Wom; Obit File

477. Dortch, Ellen J.
born 1868
newspaper editor, publisher, Farmers Alliance party worker
Georgia
Wom Cent

478. Harris, Corra May White
1869–1935
novelist
Georgia
Index t Wom; Nat Cyc Am Bio v26; Not Am Wom; Wom Lit, More

479. Head, Ozella Shields
born 1869
author
Georgia
Wom Cent

480. Woodbury, Rosa Louise
born 1869
journalist, educator

Georgia
Wom Cent

481. Pape, Nina
1870–1944
educator
Savannah, GA
Obit File

482. Quin, Minnie
flourished 1900s
poet
Atlanta, GA
Dict Am Auth

483. Stocker, Corinne
born 1871
elocutionist, journalist
Georgia
Wom Cent

484. Whitener, Catherine Evans
1880–1964
textile industry pioneer
Georgia
Nat Cyc Am Bio v51

485. Thompson, Clara Mildred
born 1881
Reconstruction historian
Georgia
Encyc South Hist

486. Carter, Lillian "Bessie"
born 1898
nurse, social service worker, peace worker, civil rights worker
Georgia
Cur Biog '78

487. Mitchell, Margaret Munnerlyn; Mrs. John Robert Marsh
1900–49
novelist
Georgia
Dict Am Bio supp v4; Dict Lit Bio v9; Index t Wom; Nat Cyc Am Bio v38 and csv6; Not Am Wom; Obit File; Wom Lit, More

488. Hamilton, Grace Towns
born 1907
educator, Georgia state legislator from Atlanta
Atlanta, GA
Black
Encyc Black Am

489. McCullers, Carson Smith
1917–67
novelist, playwright
Georgia
Dict Lit Bio v2 and v7; Encyc South Hist; Index t Wom; Not Am Wom supp v1; Obit File; Wom Lit; Wom Lit, More

490. Henderson, Vivian
1924–76

author, religious writer, poet, children's author, temperance worker, evangelist
Evanston, IL
Dict Am Auth; Nat Cyc Am Bio v4; Twent Cen Bio Dict Not Am; Wom Cent

523. Holmes, Mary Emma
born 1839
suffragist, temperance worker
Illinois
Wom Cent

524. Smith, Julia Holmes
born 1839
physician, author
Chicago, IL
Index t Wom; Wom Cent

525. Jeffery, Isador Gilbert
born 184?
poet, stenographer
Chicago, IL
Wom Cent

526. Mason, Amelia (Gere)
184?–1923
author on women's history
Chicago, IL
Dict Am Auth; Index t Wom

527. Starrett, Helen (Ekin)
born 1840
nonfiction author, educator
Chicago, IL
Dict Am Auth; Twent Cen Bio Dict Not Am

528. Plumb, L. H.
born 1841
social reformer, temperance worker, financier, banker
Illinois
Index t Wom; Wom Cent

529. Rittenhouse, Laura Jacinta
born 1841
temperance worker, author, poet
Cairo, IL
Wom Cent

530. Wallace, Emma R. (Gilson)
1841–1911
club leader, philanthropist
Universalist
Chicago, IL
Index t Wom; Wom Cent

531. Reed, Elizabeth (Armstrong)
1842–1915
theologist, religious author, philosopher, historian of India and Persia, writer on Oriental literature, temperance worker, philanthropist
Chicago, IL
Dict Am Auth; Dict Am Bio; Index t Wom; Nat Cyc Am Bio v1 and v15; Twent Cen Bio Dict Not Am

532. Leonard, Anna Byford
born 1843
sanitation reformer, Chicago health department officer, sociologist
Chicago, IL
Index t Wom; Wom Cent

533. Stevens, Alzina Parsons
1844/49–1900
labor leader, industrial reformer, settlement house worker, social reformer, newspaper editor and publisher, journalist, author
Chicago, IL
Index t Wom; Not Am Wom; Wom Cent

534. Swarthout, M. French
born 1844
educator, mathematics textbook author
Illinois
Wom Cent

535. Knowles, Mary Henrietta
1845–1926
educator
Chicago, IL
Nat Cyc Am Bio v22

536. Oliver, Martha Capps
born 1845
children's poet
Jacksonville, IL
Dict Am Auth; Wom Cent

537. Ward, Lydia Arms (Avery) (Coonley)
1845–1924
author, poet, patron of the arts, suffragist, philanthropist
Chicago, IL
Dict Am Auth; Dict Am Bio; Index t Wom; Nat Cyc Am Bio v34

538. Young, Ella (Flagg)
1845–1918
university educator and administrator, writer on education, suffragist
Chicago, IL
Dict Am Auth; Dict Am Bio; Index t Wom; Nat Cyc Am Bio v19; Not Am Wom

539. Titterington, Sophie (Bronson)
born 1846
children's author, fiction writer
Rochester, IL
Dict Am Auth

540. Catherwood, Mary (Hartwell)
1847–1902
novelist, writer of historical romances, children's author
Universalist
Illinois
Dict Am Auth; Dict Am Bio; Index t Wom; Nat Cyc Am Bio v9; Not Am Wom; Twent Cen Bio Dict Not Am; Wom Cent

541. Sullivan, Margaret Frances (Buchanan)
1847–1903
journalist
Chicago, IL
Dict Am Auth

542. Bayliss, Clara
born 1848
author
Springfield, IL
Dict Am Auth

543. Norris, Mary Harriot
born 1848
author, novelist, literary editor, university educator
New York; Illinois
Dict Am Auth; Twent Cen Bio Dict Not Am

544. Woolley, Celia (Parker)
1848–1918
settlement worker, worker for social services for Blacks, Unitarian minister, author, novelist
Chicago, IL
Dict Am Auth; Dict Am Bio; Wom Cent

545. Johnston, Julia Harriette
1849–1919
hymn writer
Presbyterian
Peoria, IL
Nat Cyc Am Bio v20

546. Palmer, Bertha Honore
1849/51–1918
clubwoman, philanthropist, women's rights worker, art collector
Chicago, IL
Dict Am Bio; Index t Wom; Twent Cen Bio Dict Not Am; Wom Cent

547. Holbrook, Florence
born 185?
textbook author, educator
Chicago, IL
Dict Am Auth

548. Holmes, Mary Emilie
born 1850
educator, zoologist, herbalist, educator of Black women
Presbyterian
Illinois
Wom Cent

549. Hughes, Caroline
flourished 1880s–90s
philanthropist, realtor
Chicago, IL
Wom Cent

550. Marble, Callie Bonney
flourished 1880s–1910s
author
Illinois
Index t Wom; Wom Cent

551. Richmond, Lizzie R.
born 1850
businessperson, insurance agent
Illinois
Wom Cent

552. Abbott, Mary Perkins (Ives)
1851–1904
journalist, short story and romance writer
Chicago, IL
Dict Am Auth

553. Morgan, Anna
1851–1936
speech teacher, drama coach, elocutionist
Chicago, IL
Nat Cyc Am Bio v17; Not Am Wom

554. Wheeler, Cora Stuart
born 1852
poet, author, biographer of notable women
Illinois
Wom Cent

555. Copp, Helen Rankin
born 1853
sculptor
Chicago, IL
Wom Cent

556. Sweet, Ada Celeste
1853–1928
journalist, editor, author, social reformer, philanthropist, pension agent
Chicago, IL
Index t Wom; Wom Cent

557. Burnham, Clara Louise (Root)
1854–1927
poet, novelist, librettist
Chicago, IL
Dict Am Auth; Dict Am Bio; Index t Wom; Nat Cyc Am Bio v9 and v21; Wom Cent

558. Elliott, Maude Howe
1854–1948
author, novelist, suffragist
Unitarian
Chicago, IL
Dict Am Auth; Nat Cyc Am Bio v36; Not Am Wom; Twent Cen Bio Dict Not Am; Wom Cent

559. Wakeman, Antoinette van Hoesen
1854–post 1890
journalist, novelist
Illinois; Hastings, NE
Dict Am Auth; Wom Cent

560. Davis, Elizabeth Lindsay
born 1855
author, clubwoman
Illinois
Black
Prof Negro Wom v1

561. Williams, Fannie Barrier
1855–1944
lecturer, civic leader, librarian, clubwoman
Chicago, IL
Black
Dict Am Bio supp v3; Not Am Wom; Prof Negro Wom v1

562. Huling, Caroline Augusta
born 1856
journalist, suffragist, philanthropist, temperance worker
Illinois
Wom Cent

563. Pope, Cora Scott Pond
born 1856
suffragist, suffrage leader
Chicago, IL
Wom Cent

564. Stephen, Elizabeth (Willisson)
born 1856
author, novelist
Rockport, IL
Dict Am Auth; Wom Cent

565. Gibson, Eva Katherine (Clapp)
born 1857
miscellaneous author
Chicago, IL
Dict Am Auth; Wom Cent

566. Roby, Ida Hall
born 1857/67
pharmacist
Chicago, IL
Index t Wom; Wom Cent

567. Solomon, Hannah Greenebaum
1858–1942
clubwoman, founder of the National Council of Jewish Women, welfare worker
Jewish
Chicago, IL
Nat Cyc Am Bio v36; Not Am Wom

568. Talbot, Marion
1858–1948
first dean of women of the University of Chicago, professor of household administration

Chicago, IL
Not Am Wom; Obit File

569. Bowen, Louise Hadduck de Koven
1859–1953
philanthropist, welfare leader, Chicago social worker, president of Hull House, suffragist
Chicago, IL
Dict Am Bio supp v5; Index t Wom; Not Am Wom supp v1; Obit File

570. Moreland, Mary L.
born 1859
Congregationalist minister, temperance worker
Congregationalist
Illinois

Wom Cent

571. Addams, Jane
1860–1935
political activist, social reformer, sociologist, social welfare worker, settlement house founder, peace worker
Chicago, IL
Dict Am Auth; Dict Am Bio supp v1; Index t Wom; Nat Cyc Am Bio v13 and v27; Not Am Wom

572. Lust, Adelina (Cohenfeldt)
born 1860
novelist
Chicago, IL
Dict Am Auth

573. Monroe, Harriet
1860/61–1936
poet, editor
Chicago, IL
Dict Am Auth; Dict Am Bio supp v2; Index t Wom; Nat Cyc Am Bio v28; Not Am Wom

574. Trout, Grace Wilbur
flourished 1890s; died 1955
suffragist, feminist, club leader, author, lecturer
Illinois
Index t Wom; Nat Cyc Am Bio csv2

575. van Benschoten, Mary Crowell
flourished 1890s
author, writer on industrial education
Illinois
Wom Cent

576. Boylan, Grace (Duffie)
born 1861
novelist, journalist, poet
Chicago, IL
Dict Am Auth

577. Haley, Margaret Angela
1861–1939
educator, civic reformer, labor leader
Catholic
Illinois
Bio Dict Am Lab; Not Am Wom

578. Logan, Josephine Hancock
1862–1943
patron of the arts, author, poet
Chicago, IL
Nat Cyc Am Bio v35

579. McCulloch, Catharine Gouger Waugh
1862–1945
lawyer, judge, suffragist, temperance worker
Illinois
Not Am Wom; Obit File; Wom Cent

580. Peattie, Elia Wilkerson
born 1862
author, journalist, novelist, travel writer
Chicago, IL
Dict Am Auth; Wom Cent

581. Wright, Carrie Douglas
born 1862
music educator, biographer
Chicago, IL
Dict Am Auth

582. Fearing, Lillian Blanche
1863–1901
lawyer, poet
Chicago, IL
blind
Dict Am Auth; Wom Cent

583. Johnson, Carrie Ashton
born 1863
editor, temperance worker, suffragist
Illinois
Wom Cent

584. Smith, Minnie Louise
1863–1927
educator, Sorosis member
Methodist Episcopal
Illinois
Nat Cyc Am Bio v21

585. Zeisler, Fannie Bloomfield
1863/66–1927
concert pianist
Chicago, IL
Austrian
Dict Am Bio; Nat Cyc Am Bio v14; Not Am Wom; Wom Cent

586. Bell, Lilian; Mrs. Arthur Hoyt Bogue
1865/67–1929
author, novelist
Chicago, IL
Dict Am Auth; Index t Wom; Nat Cyc Am Bio v14

587. Crafts, Annetta (Stratford)
born 1865
poet
Austin, IL
Dict Am Auth

588. Hart, Mary Ward
born 1865
suffragist, temperance worker
Illinois
Nat Cyc Am Bio v18

589. Bartelme, Mary Margaret
1866/69–1954
lawyer, judge, juvenile prison reformer, Chicago juvenile court judge
Illinois
Index t Wom; Nat Cyc Am Bio; Not Am Wom; Obit File

590. Blaine, Anita [Eugenie] McCormick
1866–1954
philanthropist, pacifist, patron of education and child welfare, patron of the League of Nations
Chicago, IL
Dict Am Bio supp v5; Nat Cyc Am Bio v44; Not Am Wom supp v1; Obit File

591. Miner, Jean Pond
born 1866
sculptor
Illinois; Wisconsin
Wom Cent

592. Newbury, Mollie Netcher; Mollie Neuberger
1867–1954
owner and operator of the Boston Store
Chicago, IL
Obit File

593. Randall, Minnie Josephine Smith
1867–1955
industrialist, founder of the Vacuum Can Co., philanthropist
Catholic
Chicago, IL
Nat Cyc Am Bio v42; Obit File

594. Strawn, Julia Clark
1868–1942
surgeon, gynecologist
Congregationalist
Chicago, IL
Index t Wom; Nat Cyc Am Bio v31

595. Graser, Hilda Regina
born 1869
customhouse broker
Chicago, IL
Canadian
Wom Cent

596. Lillie, Frances Crane
1870–1958

philanthropist
Chicago, IL
Obit File

597. Wilkinson, Florence
flourished 1900s–20s
poet, novelist
Chicago, IL
Dict Am Auth; Index t Wom

598. Spicer, Anne Higginson
born 1871
author
Illinois
Nat Cyc Am Bio csv3

599. Brosseau, Grace Lincoln Hall
1872–1959
president general of DAR
Congregationalist
Illinois
Nat Cyc Am Bio csv4; Obit File

600. Hauberg, Susanne Christine Denkmann
1872–1942
philanthropist
Presbyterian
Rock Island, IL
Nat Cyc Am Bio v42

601. Vittum, Harriet E.
1872–1953
social worker, suffrage worker
Chicago, IL
Obit File

602. Ickes, Anna Willmarth Thompson
1873–1935
reformer, Illinois state legislator
Illinois
Not Am Wom

603. Laughlin, Clara Elizabeth
1873–1941
miscellaneous author
Chicago, IL
Dict Am Auth; Index t Wom

604. Wyatt, Edith Franklin
born 1873
novelist
Chicago, IL
Dict Am Auth; Index t Wom

605. Reed, Myrtle
1874–1911
popular novelist
Chicago, IL
Dict Am Auth; Dict Am Bio; Index t Wom; Not Am Wom; Twent Cen Bio Dict Not Am

606. Cowles, Sophia Esther
born 1875
toy manufacturer, fire escape manufacturer
Illinois
French
Nat Cyc Am Bio csv2

607. Young, Sophie Swanstrom
born 1875
playwright, director of passion plays
Zion, IL
Obit File

608. Donahey, Mary Dickerson
1876–1962
children's author
Episcopalian
Chicago, IL
Nat Cyc Am Bio v45

609. Ellinwood, Henrietta Elizabeth (Schneider)
born 1876
philanthropist, suffragist
Illinois
Nat Cyc Am Bio v16

610. Sapp, Ruth Bent
1877–1951
clubwoman
Congregationalist
Illinois
Nat Cyc Am Bio v47

611. Smith, Fredrika Shumway
1877–1968
children's author
Presbyterian
Illinois
Nat Cyc Am Bio v55

612. Schweppe, Laura Shedd
1880–1937
philanthropist, art patron
Chicago, IL
Nat Cyc Am Bio v50

613. Simms, Ruth Hanna McCormick
1880–1944
representative to Congress from Illinois, political leader, Republican National Committee member from New Mexico, dairy farmer
Quaker
Illinois; New Mexico
Dict Am Bio supp v3; Index t Wom; Nat Cyc Am Bio v34; Not Am Wom; Obit File

614. Black, Margaret Horton (Potter)
born 1881
novelist
Chicago, IL
Dict Am Auth

615. Dick, Gladys Rowena Henry
1881–1963
microbiologist, pathologist
Chicago, IL
Index t Wom; Nat Cyc Am Bio v51; Not Am Wom supp v1

616. Anderson, Violette
born 1882

lawyer
Chicago, IL
English; Black
Encyc Black Am

617. Miller, Olive Beaupre
1883–1968
children's author, sex education worker
Illinois
Nat Cyc Am Bio v54

618. Fay, Amy
1884–1928
pianist, writer on music
Chicago, IL
Dict Am Auth; Index t Wom; Not Am Wom; Wom Cent

619. Mars, Ethel Veronica
1884–1945
president of the Mars Candy Co.
Chicago, IL
Obit File

620. Bane, Juliet Lita
1887–1957
home economics educator
Illinois
Nat Cyc Am Bio v43

621. Fergus, Phyllis; Mrs. Thatcher Hoyt
1887–1964
composer
Illinois
Index t Wom; Nat Cyc Am Bio v52

622. Rienecke, Mabel Eunice (Gilmore)
born 1892
suffragist, internal revenue collector
Protestant
Illinois
Nat Cyc Am Bio csv3

623. Brande, Dorothea Thompson
1893–1948
author, editor, journalist
Episcopalian
Chicago, IL
Nat Cyc Am Bio v39

624. Raisa, Rosa
1893–1963
soprano opera singer
Chicago, IL
Obit File

625. Heller, Florence Gunsfeld
1897–1966
philanthropist, patron of medicine, Jewish welfare worker
Jewish
Chicago, IL
Nat Cyc Am Bio v51

626. Mullen, Frances Vedder Buell
born 1901
artist
Chicago, IL
Nat Cyc Am Bio csv10

627. Sampson, Edith (Spurlock)
1901–79
lawyer, judge, alternate delegate to the UN, lecturer
Illinois
Black
Cur Biog '80; Encyc Black Am; Index t Wom; Negro Alman; Negro Her Lib v1

628. Abbell, Fannie Edelman
born 1902
business executive, philanthropist
Jewish
Chicago, IL
Nat Cyc Am Bio csv11

629. Dodds, Bernice Lee
1903–59
dean of the University of Illinois College of Education, head of the education department of Purdue University
Illinois
Obit File

630. Emch, Minna Elizabeth Libman
1904–58
psychiatrist, psychiatric educator and author
Chicago, IL
Lithuanian
Nat Cyc Am Bio v47

631. Allison, Ruth Jones
died 1957
philanthropist
Chicago, IL
Obit File

632. Brooks, Gwendolyn
born 1912/17
poet, educator, autobiographer, lecturer, poet laureate of Illinois
Chicago, IL
Black
Cur Biog '77; Dict Lit Bio v5; Encyc Black Am; Index t Wom; Negro Alman; Nort Anth Poet; Prof Negro Wom; Wom Lit; Wom Lit, More

633. Reid, Charlotte (Thompson)
born 1913
representative to Congress from Illinois, politician, FCC member
Illinois
Cur Biog '75; Index t Wom

634. Comiskey, Grace Lou
1921–52

co-owner of the Chicago White
  Sox baseball team
Chicago, IL
Obit File

635. Fox, Carol
1926–81
producer and manager of the Chicago Opera
Chicago, IL
Cur Biog '78 and '81

636. Gray, Hannah Holborn
born 1930
president of the University of
  Chicago, historian
Chicago, IL
German
Cur Biog '79

637. Barrett, Brenetta H.
born 1932
director of the federal Human
  Resources Administration
Illinois
Black
Negro Alman

**638. Byrne, Jane; Margaret
  Burke**
born 1934
Republican mayor of Chicago
Chicago, IL
Cur Biog '80

INDIANA

**639. Dumont, Julia Louisa
  (Carey)**
1794–1857
poet, author, educator
Vevay, IN
Cyc Am Bio; Dict Am Auth

**640. Guerin, Anne-Theresa;
  Mother Theodore**
1798–1856
educator, Catholic nun, founder
  of the Sisters of Providence of
  St. Mary-of-the-Woods
Indiana
French
Dict Am Bio; Nat Cyc Am Bio
  v23

641. Krout, Caroline Virginia
born 18?
novelist
Crawfordsville, IN
Dict Am Auth

642. Merrill, Catherine
1824–1900
educator, writer on Indiana
Indianapolis, IN
Dict Am Auth

**643. Woodward, Caroline Mar-
  shall**
1828–90

author, artist
Indiana
Wom Cent

**644. Wallace, Susan (Arnold)
  (Elston)**
1830–1907
miscellaneous author, poet, reli-
  gious writer, philanthropist
Indiana
Cyc Am Bio and ad; Dict Am
  Auth; Index t Wom; Nat Cyc
  Am Bio v10; Twent Cen Bio
  Dict Not Am; Wom Cent

**645. Banta, Melissa Elizabeth
  Riddle**
born 1834
poet
Indiana
Wom Cent

646. Jordan, Dulcie (Mason)
1835–95
journalist, poet
Richmond, IN
Dict Am Auth

647. Truitt, Anna Augusta
born 1837
temperance reformer, suffragist,
  patron of industrial education
Muncie, IN
Wom Cent

**648. Hodgin, Emily Caroline
  Chandler**
born 1838
temperance reformer, suffragist
Quaker
Indiana
Wom Cent

649. McClain, Louise Bowman
born 1841
author
Methodist Episcopal
Indiana
Wom Cent

650. Harrell, Sarah Carmichael
born 1844
educator, temperance worker
Indiana
Wom Cent

**651. Hammond, Mary Virginia
  Spitler**
born 1847; flourished 1890s
manager of the 1899 Chicago
  World's Fair
Indiana
Wom Cent

652. Gause, Nora Trueblood
born 1851
humane worker, lecturer
Indiana
Wom Cent

653. Northrop, Celestia Joslin
born 1856

vocalist
Baptist
Indiana
Wom Cent

654. Davis, Ida May
born 1857
litterateur, author, poet
Terra Haute, IN
Wom Cent

**655. Swafford, Martina; Belle
  Bremer**
flourished 1890s
poet
Indiana
Wom Cent

656. Worley, Laura Davis
flourished 1890s
dairy farmer
Indiana
Wom Cent

657. Spink, Mary Angela
1863–1939
physician
Indianapolis, IN
Nat Cyc Am Bio v40

658. Stein, Evaleen
1863–1923
poet, author, artist
Lafayette, IN
Dict Am Auth; Dict Am Bio;
  Wom Cent

659. Bacon, Albion Fellows
1865–1933
housing reformer
Methodist
Indiana
Index t Wom; Nat Cyc Am Bio
  v34 and csv4; Not Am Wom

660. Adams, Winifred Brady
born 1871
painter
Presbyterian
Indiana
Nat Cyc Am Bio csv6

661. Ball, Bertha
born 1875
philanthropist, civic worker
Universalist
Muncie, IN
Nat Cyc Am Bio csv6

662. Jenckes, Virginia Ellis
1878–1975
representative to Congress from
  Indiana, anticommunist activist
Indiana
Index t Wom; Obit File

663. Spink, Rose Urbana
1879–1952
physician
Indiana
Nat Cyc Am Bio v40

664. Stewart, Sallie W.
1881–1951
educator, clubwoman, realtor,
  lecturer, Black women's welfare
  worker
Indiana
Black
Negro Alman; Prof Negro Wom
  v1

665. Balz, Arcada Stark
1883–1973
Indiana state senator, Indianapo-
  lis civic worker
Methodist
Indianapolis, IN
Nat Cyc Am Bio v57

**666. Clowes, Edith Whitehill
  (Hinkel)**
1885–1967
Indianapolis civic leader, patron
  of music
Episcopalian
Indianapolis, IN
Nat Cyc Am Bio v53

**667. Hardwick, Katharine Da-
  vis**
1886–1974
pianist, newspaper publisher
Christian Scientist
Indiana
Nat Cyc Am Bio v58

668. Lilly, Ruth Allison
1891–1973
philanthropist
Episcopalian
Indianapolis, IN
Nat Cyc Am Bio v58

**669. Bradley, Florence Kauff-
  man Thacker**
born 1893
lawyer, political activist
Methodist
Indiana
Nat Cyc Am Bio csv7

670. Cheney, Margaret Aneline
born 1895
banker
Methodist Episcopal
Lafayette, IN
Nat Cyc Am Bio csv2

671. Murphy, Rosemary Ann
1906–69
physician, medical researcher, zoologist
Catholic
Indiana
Nat Cyc Am Bio v54

**672. Winters, Jeannette Epler
  McPheeters**
born 1908
manufacturer
Presbyterian
Indiana
Nat Cyc Am Bio csv8

IOWA

673. Swain, Adeline Morrison
born 1820
suffragist, politician, newspaper
political editor, superintendent
of public education, Greenback
party worker
Iowa
Wom Cent

674. Janes, Martha Waldron
born 1832
Baptist minister, suffragist, temperance worker
Baptist
Iowa
Index t Wom; Wom Cent

675. Doe, Mary L.
born 1836
suffragist, temperance reformer,
merchant
Methodist
Iowa
Wom Cent

676. Langworthy, Elizabeth
born 1837
philanthropist; civic worker in
Monticello, Iowa, and Seward,
Nebraska; clubwoman
Monticello, IA; Seward, NE
Index t Wom; Wom Cent

677. Foster, Judith Ellen (Horton)
1840–1910
temperance leader, lawyer, Republican party worker, Prohibitionist, suffragist, political
writer, lecturer
Iowa
Cyc Am Bio; Dict Am Auth; Dict
Am Bio; Index t Wom; Nat Cyc
Am Bio v22; Not Am Wom;
Twent Cen Bio Dict Not Am;
Wom Cent

678. Collier, Ada (Langworthy)
born 1843
poet
Dubuque, IA
Dict Am Auth; Wom Cent

**679. Ferree, Susan Frances
Nelson**
born 1844
journalist, temperance worker,
suffragist, women's rights worker
Episcopalian
Iowa
Wom Cent

**680. Marshall, Caroline Louise
(Kinsbury)**
born 1849
fiction writer
Eldora, IA
Dict Am Auth

681. Durley, Ella Hamilton
flourished 1880s
educator, journalist
Des Moines, IA
Wom Cent

**682. French, Alice; Octave
Thanet**
1850–1934
novelist, short story writer
Iowa; Arkansas
Dict Am Auth; Dict Am Bio
supp v1; Index t Wom; Nat Cyc
Am Bio v10 and v25; Not Am
Wom; Twent Cen Bio Dict Not
Am; Wom Cent

**683. Smith, Genie M.; Maude
Meredith; Kit Clover**
born 1852
author, magazine writer, short
story writer
Dubuque, IA
Dict Am Auth; Wom Cent

684. Manning, Jessie Wilson
born 1855
author, temperance worker, lecturer
Iowa
Index t Wom; Wom Cent

685. Rogers, Effie Louise Hoffman
born 1855
educator; superintendent of
schools of Mahaska County, Iowa; newspaper editor; temperance worker
Mahaska County, IA
Wom Cent

**686. Turner, Alice Bellvadore
Sams**
born 1859
physician
Iowa
Wom Cent

687. Hallam, Julia (Clark)
born 1860
miscellaneous writer
Sioux City, IA
Dict Am Auth

688. Norman, Estelle Gertrude
1872–1959
physician, venereal disease clinic
worker
Seventh-Day Adventist
Iowa
Nat Cyc Am Bio v48

689. Windsor, Helen Howell
1880–1926
social welfare worker
Episcopalian
Iowa
Nat Cyc Am Bio v20

690. Hyde, Elizabeth [Carrie]
1881–1957

lawyer, corporate lawyer for a
railroad
Presbyterian
Iowa
Nat Cyc Am Bio v47

691. Curtis, Namahyoke Sockum
died 1935
Des Moines civic leader, nurse
Des Moines, IA
Black
Prof Negro Wom v2

**692. Suckow, Ruth Ann Vivien
(Nuhn)**
1892–1960
writer, novelist, short story writer
Quaker
Iowa; California
Dict Lit Bio v9; Index t Wom;
Nat Cyc Am Bio v47; Not Am
Wom supp v1; Obit File; Wom
Lit; Wom Lit, More

KANSAS

693. Duchesne, Rose Philippine
1769–1852
missionary, Catholic nun, founder
of the American Convents of
the Sacred Heart, pioneer, educator
Catholic
Kansas
Cyc Am Bio; Dict Am Rel Bio;
Not Am Wom; Read Encyc Am
West; Twent Cen Bio Dict Not
Am

694. Bugg, Lelia Hardin
born 18?
novelist, religious author
Catholic
Wichita, KS
Dict Am Auth

**695. Nichols, Clarinda Irene
Howard**
1810–85
newspaper editor, political writer,
social reformer, lecturer, women's rights leader, suffragist,
feminist
Kansas
Cyc Am Bio; Dict Am Bio; Index
t Wom; Nat Cyc Am Bio v5;
Not Am Wom

**696. Robinson, Sarah Tappan
Doolittle (Lawrence)**
born 1827
author, historian of Kansas
Lawrence, KS
Cyc Am Bio; Dict Am Auth;
Twent Cen Bio Dict Not Am

697. Hall, Sara C.
born 1832
physician, suffragist

Kansas
Wom Cent

698. Gray, Mary Tenney
born 1833
philanthropist, journalist, editorial writer
Kansas
Wom Cent

699. Wait, Anna C.
born 1837
suffragist, educator, politician
Kansas
Wom Cent

700. Harding, Evilela
flourished 1870s
physician
Topeka, KS
Nat Cyc Am Bio v21

701. Wilson, Augustus
flourished 1870s–90s
suffragist, temperance worker,
Methodist Episcopal church
worker, missionary worker
Methodist Episcopal
Kansas
Wom Cent

702. Lowman, Mary D.
born 1842
educator of Blacks; deputy register of deeds and mayor of Oskaloosa, Kansas
Presbyterian
Oskaloosa, KS
Index t Wom; Wom Cent

703. Monroe, Harriet Earhart
born 1842
lecturer, educator, journalist
Kansas; Washington, DC
Dict Am Auth; Wom Cent

704. Weatherby, Delia L.
born 1843
temperance reformer, author, politician, educator
Kansas
Wom Cent

**705. Nation, Carry Amelia
Moore**
1846–1911
direct action temperance reformer
Kansas
Dict Am Bio; Index t Wom; Not
Am Wom; Read Encyc Am
West

706. Diggs, Annie le Porte
1848/53–1916
Populist party leader, orator, politician, social reformer, temperance worker, journalist
Unitarian
Kansas
Canadian
Not Am Wom; Read Encyc Am
West; Wom Cent

707. Johns, Laura M.
born 1849
suffragist
Kansas
Wom Cent

708. Lease, Mary Elizabeth (Clyens)
1850/53–1933
Populist orator, politician, Prohibition party worker, suffragist, evolutionist, birth control advocate, feminist, political author
Kansas
Dict Am Auth; Dict Am Bio supp v1; Index t Wom; Not Am Wom; Read Encyc Am West

709. Howard, Belle
born 1857
dramatic reader
Kansas
Wom Cent

710. Bush, Jennie Burchfield
born 1858
author
Wichita, KS
Wom Cent

711. Murdock, Louise Caldwell
1858–1915
interior designer, art patron
Kansas
Not Am Wom

712. Grisham, Sadie Park
born 1859
educator; city councilperson in Cottonwood Falls, Kansas
Cottonwood Falls, KS
Wom Cent

713. Black, Martha Louise Munger Purdy
1866–1957
member of Canadian Parliament, participant in the Klondike gold rush
Kansas
Obit File

714. Diehl, Cora Victoria
born 1869
register of deeds in Great Bend, Kansas; register of deeds for Logan County, Oklahoma; Populist party politician with Democratic endorsement; Farmer's Alliance party worker; Greenback party worker
Kansas; Oklahoma
Wom Cent

715. Young, Jennie B.
born 1869
artist
Kansas
Wom Cent

716. Cook, Myrtle Foster
1870–1951

educator, civic leader, financier, Black civil rights worker
Kansas City, KS
Black; Canadian
Negro Alman; Prof Negro Wom

KENTUCKY

717. Inglis, Mary
1729–1813
Kentucky settler
Kentucky
Cyc Am Bio

718. Carrell, Columba
1810–78
founder of the Hospital of Saint Mary and Saint Elizabeth, Catholic nun, mother superior
Catholic
Louisville, KY
Cyc Am Bio

719. Daviess, Maria (Thompson)
1814–96
writer on agriculture
Kentucky
Cyc Am Bio; Dict Am Auth; Nat Cyc Am Bio v3

720. Dupuy, Eliza Ann
1814–1880/81
popular author
Kentucky
Cyc Am Bio; Dict Am Auth; Dict Am Bio; Dict Am Bio Men Time; Nat Cyc Am Bio v6; Not Am Wom

721. Warfield, Catharine Ann (Ware)
1816/17–1877
author, novelist, poet
Kentucky
Cyc Am Bio; Dict Am Auth; Dict Am Bio; Dict Am Bio Men Time; Nat Cyc Am Bio v5; Twent Cen Bio Dict Not Am

722. Cross, Jane Tandy (Chinn) (Harding)
1817–70
author, poet, translator
Kentucky
Cyc Am Bio; Dict Am Auth

723. Welby, Amelia Ball (Coppuck); Amelie
1819–52
poet, author
Louisville, KY
Am Bio Dict; Cyc Am Bio; Dict Am Bio; Dict Am Bio Men Time; Index t Wom; Nat Cyc Am Bio v6; Wom Cent

724. Jeffrey, Rosa Vertner (Griffith) (Johnson); Rosa
1826/28–1894

poet, novelist, dramatist
Lexington, KY
Cyc Am Bio; Dict Am Auth; Dict Am Bio; Nat Cyc Am Bio v11; Wom Cent

725. Dixon, Susan (Bullitt)
born 1829
American historian, writer on history
Kentucky
Dict Am Auth; Nat Cyc Am Bio v13

726. Humphreys, Sarah Gibson
born 1830
author, suffragist
Kentucky
Wom Cent

727. Watts, Margaret Anderson
born 1832
temperance worker, feminist, suffragist
Kentucky
Wom Cent

728. Piatt, Sarah Morgan (Bryan)
1836–1919
poet
Kentucky
Cyc Am Bio; Dict Am Auth; Dict Am Bio; Index t Wom; Nat Cyc Am Bio v8; Not Am Wom; Twent Cen Bio Dict Not Am; Wom Cent

729. Clay, Mary Barr
born 1839
suffragist, women's rights worker, farmer
Kentucky
Wom Cent

730. Helm, Lucinda Barbour; Lucile
1839–97
author, religious writer
Methodist Episcopal
Kentucky
Twent Cen Bio Dict Not Am; Wom Cent

731. Casseday, Jennie
born 1840
philanthropist, temperance worker
Kentucky
Wom Cent

732. Rollston, Adelaide Day
flourished 1870s–90s
author, poet
Kentucky
Wom Cent

733. Henry, Josephine Kirby Williamson
born 1845
suffragist, politician, political writer, Prohibitionist

Kentucky
Wom Cent

734. MacAfee, Nelly Nichol (Marshal)
born 1845
fiction writer
Kentucky
Dict Am Auth

735. Cady, Helena Maxwell
born 1849
physician, temperance worker, suffragist
Kentucky
Wom Cent

736. Clay, Laura
1849–1941
women's suffrage leader, women's rights worker
Kentucky
Encyc South Hist; Index t Wom; Not Am Wom

737. Ober, Sara Endicott
born 1854
missionary in the Tennessee and Kentucky mountains, fiction writer
Tennessee; Kentucky
Dict Am Auth

738. Hamilton, Anna J.
born 1860
educator, journalist
Kentucky
Wom Cent

739. Rice, Alice Caldwell (Hegan)
1860/70–1942
author, novelist, children's author, civic worker
New York; Louisville, KY
Dict Am Auth; Dict Am Bio supp v3; Index t Wom; Nat Cyc Am Bio v14; Not Am Wom; Obit File

740. van Buren, Alicia (Keisker)
1860–1922
composer, singer, poet
Louisville, KY
Dict Am Auth; Index t Wom

741. Johnston, Annie (Fellows)
1863–1931
children's author
Peewee Valley, KY
Dict Am Auth; Dict Am Bio; Nat Cyc Am Bio v13; Not Am Wom

742. Semple, Ellen Churchill
1863–1932
geographer, writer on geography, anthropologist, anthropogeographer

Louisville, KY
Dict Am Auth; Dict Am Bio;
Encyc South Hist; Index t
Wom; Nat Cyc Am Bio v35 and
csv1; Not Am Wom

743. Pettit, Katherine
1868–1936
settlement house worker
Kentucky
Encyc South Hist; Not Am Wom

**744. Eudy, Mary Cummings
Paine**
1871–1952
poet, dress manufacturer
Presbyterian
Kentucky
Nat Cyc Am Bio v41; Obit File

**745. Breckinridge, Madeline
McDowell**
1872–1920
social reformer, social worker
Kentucky
Nat Cyc Am Bio v29; Not Am
Wom

746. Roberts, Elizabeth Madox
1881/86–1941
poet, novelist
Kentucky
Dict Am Bio supp v3; Dict Lit
Bio v9; Encyc South Hist; Index
t Wom; Nat Cyc Am Bio csv4;
Not Am Wom; Obit File; Wom
Lit; Wom Lit, More

747. Smith, Lucy Harth
1888–1955
educator, educational administrator
Kentucky
Black
Dict Am Bio supp v5

748. Bernstein, Lotte Kirschner
1897–1971
psychiatrist, psychoanalyst
Jewish
Kentucky
German
Nat Cyc Am Bio v57

749. Kidd, Mae Street
flourished 1930s–70s
Kentucky state legislator
Kentucky
Black
Encyc Black Am

750. Cromwell, Emma Guy
died 1952
secretary of state and treasurer of
Kentucky
Kentucky
Obit File

751. Arnow, Harriette
born 1908
novelist

Kentucky
Dict Lit Bio v6; Index t Wom;
Wom Lit; Wom Lit, More

752. Davis, Georgia M.
born 1923
business executive, Kentucky
state senator, Black civil rights
worker
Kentucky
Black
Encyc Black Am

753. Castleman, Alice Barbee
born 1943
philanthropist, women's rights
worker
Episcopalian
Louisville, KY
Wom Cent

754. Lagace, Sherry
1944–75
strip miner
Kentucky
Obit File

LOUISIANA

755. Thayer, Caroline Matilda
died 1844
magazine writer, poet
Louisiana
Am Bio Dict

756. Pitkin, Helen
born 18?
novelist
New Orleans, LA
Index t Wom

**757. Robinson, Suzanne (Antro-
bus)**
born 18?
novelist
New Orleans, LA
Dict Am Auth

**758. Dinnies, Anna Peyre
(Shackelford); Moina**
1805/16–1886
poet
New Orleans, LA
Cyc Am Bio; Dict Am Auth;
Index t Wom; Nat Cyc Am Bio
v13

**759. Whitaker, Mary Scrimze-
our (Furman) (Miller)**
1820–post 1867
author, poet, novelist
New Orleans, LA
Cyc Am Bio; Dict Am Auth; Nat
Cyc Am Bio v1

**760. Merrick, Caroline
Elizabeth (Thomas)**
1825–1908
suffragist, temperance leader, author on the South

New Orleans, LA
Dict Am Auth; Nat Cyc Am Bio
v10; Not Am Wom; Wom Cent

**761. Holmes, Mary Sophia
(Shaw) (Rogers)**
born 1830
author, poet
New Orleans, LA
Dict Am Auth

**762. Townsend, Mary Ashley
(van Voorhees); Xariffa**
1832/36–1901
author, poet
New Orleans, LA
Cyc Am Bio; Dict Am Auth; Dict
Am Bio; Nat Cyc Am Bio v11;
Twent Cen Bio Dict Not Am;
Wom Cent

**763. Elder, Susan (Blanchard);
Hermine**
1835–1923
religious author, poet, dramatist,
natural scientist
Catholic
New Orleans, LA
Cyc Am Bio; Dict Am Auth; Dict
Am Bio; Nat Cyc Am Bio v11;
Twent Cen Bio Dict Not Am

**764. Keatinge, Harriet Char-
lotte**
born 1837
physician, Sorosis member
New Orleans, LA
Nat Cyc Am Bio v18

765. Nixon, Jennie Caldwell
born 1839
educator
Louisiana
Wom Cent

**766. Pugh, Eliza Lofton (Phil-
lips)**
born 1841
author, novelist
Assumption Parish, LA
Cyc Am Bio; Dict Am Auth

767. Dalsheimer, Alice
1845–80
poet
Louisiana
Cyc Am Bio

**768. Nicholson, Eliza Jane
(Poitevent) Holbrook; Pearl
Rivers**
1849–96
poet, journalist, editor, publisher
and owner of the New Orleans
Picayune-Times
New Orleans, LA
Dict Am Auth; Dict Am Bio;
Index t Wom; Nat Cyc Am Bio
v1; Not Am Wom; Twent Cen
Bio Dict Not Am; Wom Cent

769. King, Grace Elizabeth
1851/53–1932
historian of New Orleans
New Orleans, LA
Dict Am Auth; Dict Am Bio;
Index t Wom; Nat Cyc Am Bio
v2; Not Am Wom; Twent Cen
Bio Dict Not Am; Wom Lit,
More

**770. Davis, Mary Evelyn
(Moore)**
1852–1909
journalist, novelist, short story
writer
New Orleans, LA
Dict Am Auth; Dict Am Bio; Nat
Cyc Am Bio v10

771. Campbell, Georgine
flourished 1883
artist
New Orleans, LA
Wom Cent

**772. Field, Martha R.; Cather-
ine Cole**
born 1856
journalist
New Orleans, LA
Wom Cent

**773. Baker, Julie Keim
(Wetherill); J. K. W.**
born 1858
journalist, author
New Orleans, LA
Dict Am Auth; Wom Cent

**774. Sharkey, Emma Augusta;
Mrs. E. Burke Collins**
born 1858
journalist, short story writer, novelist
Louisiana
Wom Cent

775. Nobles, Catherine
flourished 1890s
club leader, author
Louisiana
Index t Wom; Wom Cent

776. McMain, Eleanor Laura
1866–1934
New Orleans settlement house
worker and social reformer
New Orleans, LA
Not Am Wom

777. Stallings, Olive Andrews
born 1866
welfare worker
Catholic
New Orleans, LA
Nat Cyc Am Bio csv5

778. Culver, Essae Martha
flourished 1900s–30s
librarian

Louisiana
Index t Wom; Nat Cyc Am Bio
csv6

779. Nelson, Alice Ruth Dunbar (Moore)
1875–1935
author, editor, social worker
Louisiana
Black
Encyc Black Am; Negro Alman;
Not Am Wom; Prof Negro
Wom v1

780. Bass, Mary Elizabeth
1876–1956
physician
Baptist
Louisiana
Nat Cyc Am Bio v46; Not Am
Wom supp v1

781. Neugass, Miriam Dorothy Newman; Isadora Newman
born 1878
author, artist
Jewish
Louisiana
Nat Cyc Am Bio csv3

782. Werlein, Elizabeth Thomas
1883–1946
leader in preserving the New Orleans French Quarter
New Orleans, LA
Not Am Wom

783. Maher, Aldea
1892–1959
biochemist, pathologist, cardiologist
Catholic
Louisiana
Nat Cyc Am Bio v51

784. Goldsmith, Grace Arabell
1904–75
physician, public health educator, nutritionist
Episcopalian
Louisiana
Nat Cyc Am Bio csv10; Not Am
Wom supp v10

785. Dixon, Margaret Calder Richardson
1908–70
prison reformer, political journalist, newspaper editor
Episcopalian
Baton Rouge, LA
Nat Cyc Am Bio v58; Obit File

786. Cook, Celestine Strode
born 1924
business executive, civic leader
New Orleans, LA
Black
Encyc Black Am

787. Grau, Shirley Ann
born 1929

author, novelist, short story writer
New Orleans, LA
Dict Lit Bio v2; Index t Wom;
Wom Lit; Wom Lit, More

788. Crockett, Gwendolyn
born 1932
lawyer, educator
Louisiana
Black
Encyc Black Am

MAINE

789. Wood, Sarah Sayward (Barrell) (Keating)
1759–1855
writer of sentimental novels
Maine
Am Bio Dict; Dict Am Auth;
Dict Am Bio; Not Am Wom

790. Jacobs, Phebe Ann
died 1850
church worker
Brunswick, ME
Black
Am Bio Dict

791. Weston, Roxana
1800–91
poet
Skowhegan, ME
Dict Am Auth

792. Whitehouse, Florence Brooks
born 18?
novelist
Portland, ME
Dict Am Auth

793. Howe, Caroline Dana
born 183?
poet
Portland, ME
Dict Am Auth

794. Clark, Mary (Latham)
born 1831
Sunday school story writer
Maine
Dict Am Auth

795. Clarke, Rebecca Sophia; Sophie May
1833–1906
children's author
Maine
Dict Am Auth; Dict Am Bio;
Index t Wom; Nat Cyc Am Bio
v8; Not Am Wom; Twent Cen
Bio Dict Not Am; Wom Cent

796. Dole, Phebe Cobb Larry
born 1835
poet
Maine
Wom Cent

797. Rowe, Henrietta Gould
born 1835
short story writer
Bangor, ME
Dict Am Auth

798. Mace, Frances Parker (Laughton)
1836–99
poet
Maine; San Jose, CA
Cyc Am Bio; Dict Am Auth;
Index t Wom; Nat Cyc Am Bio
v10; Wom Cent

799. Simpson, Corelli C. W.
born 1837
poet
Maine
Wom Cent

800. Bailey, Hannah Clark Johnston
1839–1923
peace worker, temperance reformer, suffragist, philanthropist
Maine
Index t Wom; Nat Cyc Am Bio
v10; Not Am Wom; Wom Cent

801. Hurd, Helen Marr
born 1839
poet, temperance worker
Maine
Wom Cent

802. Nash, Clara Holmes Hapgood
born 1839
lawyer
Maine
Index t Wom; Wom Cent

803. Gifford, Augusta (Hale)
born 1842
historical author
Portland, ME
Dict Am Auth

804. Stevens, Lillian Marion Norton Ames
1844–1914
temperance reformer, women's rights worker, lecturer, philanthropist
Maine
Index t Wom; Nat Cyc Am Bio
v13; Not Am Wom; Wom Cent

805. Nason, Emma (Huntington)
born 1845
translator, author, poet, children's writer
Augusta, ME
Dict Am Auth; Index t Wom;
Wom Cent

806. Clark, Susanna Rebecca Graham
born 1848

children's author
Maine
Dict Am Auth

807. Jewett, Sarah Orne; Alice Eliot
1849–1909
author, short story writer
South Berwick, ME; Boston, MA
Cyc Am Bio; Dict Am Auth; Dict
Am Bio; Index t Wom; Nat Cyc
Am Bio v1; Not Am Wom;
Wom Cent; Wom Lit; Wom Lit,
More

808. Prescott, Mary Newmarch
1849–88
author, children's author, magazine writer
Newburyport, ME
Cyc Am Bio; Dict Am Auth; Nat
Cyc Am Bio v8

809. Pullen, Elisabeth Jones (Cavazza); E. Cavazza
flourished 1880s–90s
journalist, sketch writer
Portland, ME
Dict Am Auth; Nat Cyc Am Bio
v8

810. Morton, Eliza Happy
1852–1916
author, songwriter, educator, geographer
Maine
Index t Wom; Wom Cent

811. Smith, Charlotte Louise
born 1853
poet, author
Maine
Wom Cent

812. Pratt, Hannah T.
born 1854
evangelist, temperance worker, chaplain of the Maine Senate
Maine
Wom Cent

813. Vannah, Letitia Catharine
born 1857
poet
Gardiner, ME
Dict Am Auth

814. Yates, Elizabeth U.
born 1857
lecturer, Methodist Episcopal preacher
Methodist Episcopal
Maine
Wom Cent

815. Williamson, Julia May; Lura Bell
born 1859
poet
Augusta, ME
Dict Am Auth

816. Moulton, Frances Estelle (Mason)
1861–1919
bank president
Maine
Nat Cyc Am Bio v22

817. Livingston, Margaret Vere (Farrington)
born 1863
author
Episcopalian
Augusta, ME
Dict Am Auth

818. Douglas, Alice May
born 1865
poet, children's author, temperance worker, pacifist, missionary
Maine
Dict Am Auth; Index t Wom; Wom Cent

819. Eckstorm, Fannie Pearson Hardy
1865–1946
ornithologist, writer on ornithology, scholar of the Native Americans of Maine, historian of Maine folk songs
Episcopalian
Brewer, ME
Dict Am Auth; Dict Am Bio supp v4; Nat Cyc Am Bio v36; Not Am Wom

820. Merrill, Helen Maud; Samantha Spriggins
born 1865
litterateur, poet, patriotic writer
Maine
Wom Cent

821. Bjerkoe, Ethel Hall
1871–1978
antiques authority and author, clubwoman
Connecticut; Maine
Nat Cyc Am Bio v60

822. Conkling, Mabel Viola Harrs
1871–1966
sculptor
Methodist
Maine
Index t Wom; Nat Cyc Am Bio v53

823. Hale, Florence
1880–1959
president of the National Education Association, rural education director of Maine
Maine
Obit File

824. Smith, Margaret Chase
born 1897

US senator from Maine, lieutenant colonel in the US Air Force Reserve
Methodist
Maine
Index t Wom; Nat Cyc Am Bio csv9

MARYLAND

825. Brent, Margaret
1600/01–1670/71
landowner, business agent, executor for the governor of Maryland
Maryland
Dict Am Bio; Index t Wom; Not Am Wom

826. Goddard, Mary Katherine
1738–1816
printer, newspaper publisher, postmaster of Baltimore, merchant
Catholic
Baltimore, MD
Index t Wom; Not Am Wom

827. Frietchie, Barbara
1766–1862/65
Union Civil War hero
Maryland
German
Index t Wom; Who Who Dur Am Rev

828. Seton, Elizabeth Ann (Bayley), Saint; Mother Seton
1774–1821
Catholic nun, founder and superior of the American Sisters of Charity of St. Vincent de Paul (the first American sisterhood), philanthropist, autobiographer
Catholic
Maryland
Cyc Am Bio; Dict Am Auth; Dict Am Bio; Dict Am Rel Bio; Encyc South Hist; Index t Wom; Nat Cyc Am Bio v2; Not Am Wom; Twent Cen Bio Dict Not Am

829. Phelps, Almira (Hart) (Lincoln)
1793–1884
educator, botanist, chemist, textbook author
Baltimore, MD
Cyc Am Bio; Dict Am Auth; Dict Am Bio; Dict Am Bio Men Time; Nat Cyc Am Bio v11; Not Am Wom; Twent Cen Bio Dict Not Am

830. McLeod, Georgiana A. (Hulse)
18?–1890
educator, short story writer

Baltimore, MD
Dict Am Auth

831. Latimer, [Mary] Elizabeth (Wormeley)
1822–1904
novelist, educator, historian, writer on history
Baltimore, MD
English
Cyc Am Bio; Dict Am Auth; Dict Am Bio; Dict Am Bio Men Time; Index t Wom; Nat Cyc Am Bio v9; Wom Cent

832. Marshall, Joanna
born 1822
poet
Maryland
Wom Cent

833. Finley, Martha; Martha Farquharson
1828–1909
poet, author, children's author, writer of religious and moral tales
Maryland
Cyc Am Bio; Dict Am Auth; Dict Am Bio; Index t Wom; Nat Cyc Am Bio v11; Twent Cen Bio Dict Not Am; Wom Cent

834. Easter, Marguerite Elizabeth (Miller)
1839–94
poet
Baltimore, MD
Dict Am Auth

835. Randolph, Sarah Nicholas (Jefferson)
1839–92
author, educator, biographer
Baltimore, MD
Cyc Am Bio; Dict Am Auth; Dict Am Bio; Twent Cen Bio Dict Not Am

836. Turnbull, Frances Hubbard (Litchfield)
born 184?
novelist
Catholic
Baltimore, MD
Dict Am Auth

837. Raymond, Evelyn (Hunt)
born 1843
children's author
Baltimore, MD
Dict Am Auth; Twent Cen Bio Dict Not Am

838. Reese, Lizette Woodworth
1856–1935
lyric poet, English literature teacher

Baltimore, MD
Dict Am Auth; Dict Am Bio supp v1; Index t Wom; Nat Cyc Am Bio csv3; Not Am Wom; Wom Cent; Wom Lit, More

839. Brewster, Cora Belle
born 1859
physician, surgeon, medical author
Maryland
Index t Wom; Wom Cent

840. Richardson, Hester Dorsey
born 1862
educator, author
Baltimore, MD
Index t Wom; Wom Cent

841. Thruston, Lucy Meacham
born 1862
novelist
Baltimore, MD
Dict Am Auth; Twent Cen Bio Dict Not Am

842. Whitelock, Louise (Clarkson)
born 1865
novelist, short story writer, poet
Baltimore, MD
Dict Am Auth

843. Wesley, Rachel Parker
died 1918
litigant who sued for her freedom from slavery and won
Maryland
Black
Prof Negro Wom v1

844. Bussey, Ruth Carman
1888–1961
educator, worker for Women's International League for Peace and Freedom party
Episcopalian
Maryland
Nat Cyc Am Bio v49

845. Welcome, Verda Freeman
flourished 1930s–60s
educator, Maryland state legislator
Maryland
Black
Encyc Black Am

846. Byron, Katharine Edgar
1902–76
Democratic representative to Congress from Maryland
Maryland
Index t Wom; Obit File

MASSACHUSETTS

847. Pole, Elizabeth; Elizabeth Poole
1588–1654

pioneer; founder of the town of
   Taunton, New Jersey
Taunton, NJ; Massachusetts
English
Am Bio Dict; Index t Wom; Nat
   Cyc Am Bio v4

848. Bradford, Alice
circa 1590–1670
Pilgrim, Plymouth Colony civic
   worker, patron of education
Puritan
Massachusetts
English
Am Bio Dict; Index t Wom

849. Hutchinson, Anne (Marbury)
1590/91–1642/43
religious and political leader,
   founder of the Antinomian sect
   of Puritanism
Puritan
Rhode Island; Massachusetts
English
Am Bio Dict; Cyc Am Bio; Dict
   Am Bio; Dict Am Bio Men
   Time; Dict Am Rel Bio; Dict
   Nat Bio; Index t Wom; Nat Cyc
   Am Bio v9; Not Am Wom;
   Twent Cen Bio Dict Not Am

850. Rowlandson, Mary (White)
circa 1635–circa 1682
author, autobiographer, colonial
   pioneer
Lancaster, MA
Dict Am Auth; Dict Am Bio;
   Dict Am Bio Men Time; Index t
   Wom; Nat Cyc Am Bio v8

851. Dyer, Mary
born pre-1638; died 1660
religious leader, Quaker martyr
Quaker
Massachusetts
Am Bio Dict; Cyc Am Bio; Dict
   Am Bio; Dict Am Bio Men
   Time; Dict Am Rel Bio; Index t
   Wom; Nat Cyc Am Bio v11;
   Not Am Wom

852. Knight, Sarah Kemble
1666–1725/27
diarist, educator, hotel keeper,
   traveler, merchant
Boston, MA
Cyc Am Bio; Dict Am Auth; Dict
   Am Bio; Dict Am Bio Men
   Time; Index t Wom; Not Am
   Wom; Wom Lit, More

853. Warren, Mercy Otis
1727/28–1814
poet, author, dramatist, political
   author and satirist, historian,
   patriot

Massachusetts
Am Bio Dict; Cyc Am Bio; Dict
   Am Auth; Dict Am Bio; Dict
   Am Bio Men Time; Index t
   Wom; Nat Cyc Am Bio v7; Not
   Am Wom; Our Count; Who
   Who Dur Am Rev; Wom Lit,
   More

854. Draper, Margaret Green
circa 1730–1807
publisher, printer, journalist
Massachusetts
Dict Am Bio; Index t Wom; Who
   Who Dur Am Rev

855. Wheatley, Phillis
1735/53–1784
poet
Boston, MA
Black; African
Am Bio Dict; Cyc Am Bio; Dict
   Am Bio Men Time; Encyc
   Black Am; Encyc South Hist;
   Index t Wom; Negro Alman;
   Nat Cyc Am Bio v1; Not Am
   Wom; Prof Negro Wom v1;
   Wom Lit; Wom Lit, More

**856. Murray, Judith Sargent
Stevens; The Gleaner; Constantia**
1751–1820
author, essayist, poet, dramatist,
   feminist
Massachusetts
Cyc Am Bio; Dict Am Bio; Index
   t Wom; Not Am Wom; Who
   Who Dur Am Rev

857. Adams, Hannah
1755–1831/32
historian, compiler of historical
   data, religious author
Massachusetts
Am Bio Dict; Appl Cyc Am Bio;
   Cyc Am Bio; Dict Am Auth;
   Dict Am Bio; Dict Am Bio Men
   Time; Index t Wom; Nat Cyc
   Am Bio v5; Not Am Wom;
   Wom Cent

858. Foster, Hannah (Webster)
1758/90–1840
author, novelist, biographer
Massachusetts
Am Bio Dict; Cyc Am Bio; Dict
   Am Auth; Dict Am Bio; Dict
   Am Bio Men Time; Index t
   Wom; Not Am Wom; Who
   Who Dur Am Rev

**859. Morton, Sarah Wentworth
(Apthorp); Philenia**
1759–1846
poet, author
Quincy, MA
Cyc Am Bio; Dict Am Auth; Dict
   Am Bio; Dict Am Bio Men
   Time; Nat Cyc Am Bio v8; Not
   Am Wom; Who Who Dur Am
   Rev

**860. Sampson, Deborah; Robert
Shirtliffe; Deborah Gannett**
1760–1827
soldier and hero of American
   Revolution, lecturer
Massachusetts
Am Bio Dict; Cyc Am Bio; Dict
   Am Bio Men Time; Index t
   Wom; Nat Cyc Am Bio v8; Not
   Am Wom

861. Rowson, Susanna (Haswell)
1762/67–1824
novelist, dramatist, poet, educator, actor
Boston, MA
English
Cyc Am Bio; Dict Am Auth; Dict
   Am Bio; Dict Am Bio Men
   Time; Dict Nat Bio; Index t
   Wom; Nat Cyc Am Bio v9; Not
   Am Wom; Wom Lit; Wom Lit,
   More

862. Sanders, Elizabeth (Elkins)
1762–1851/54
social critic, pamphleteer, author,
   history writer on Massachusetts, Native American rights
   worker
Salem, MA
Cyc Am Bio; Dict Am Auth; Dict
   Am Bio; Dict Am Bio Men
   Time; Not Am Wom

863. Outein, Nancy C.
1778–1814
philanthropist
Massachusetts
Am Bio Dict

864. Reed, Hannah
1778–1855
missionary worker, philanthropist
Marblehead, MA
Am Bio Dict

**865. Lee, Hannah Farnham
(Sawyer)**
1780/89–1865
writer on history and art
Boston, MA
Cyc Am Bio; Dict Am Auth; Dict
   Am Bio; Dict Am Bio Men
   Time; Index t Wom; Nat Cyc
   Am Bio v25

866. Savage, Sarah
1785–1837
author, story writer
Salem, MA
Am Bio Dict

867. Robbins, Eliza
1786–1853
educator, historian, author
Boston, MA
Dict Am Auth

868. Lee, Eliza Buckminster
1788/94–1864

novelist, translator
Boston, MA
Cyc Am Bio; Dict Am Auth; Dict
   Am Bio; Dict Am Bio Men
   Time; Index t Wom; Nat Cyc
   Am Bio v25

869. Sedgwick, Catharine Maria
1789–1867
novelist, writer of moral tales for
   juveniles, educator
Stockbridge, MA
Cyc Am Bio; Dict Am Auth; Dict
   Am Bio; Dict Am Bio Men
   Time; Dict Lit Bio v1; Index t
   Wom; Nat Cyc Am Bio v1; Not
   Am Wom; Twent Cen Bio Dict
   Not Am; Wom Cent; Wom Lit;
   Wom Lit, More

870. Townsend, Eliza
1789–1854
poet
Unitarian
Boston, MA
Am Bio Dict; Cyc Am Bio; Dict
   Am Bio

871. Allen, Sarah Johnson
1791–1848
missionary to the Mohegan people
Norwich, MA
Am Bio Dict

872. Farrar, Eliza Ware Rotch
1791/1815–1870
children's author
Cambridge, MA
Cyc Am Bio; Dict Am Auth; Dict
   Am Bio Men Time; Index t
   Wom; Nat Cyc Am Bio v13;
   Not Am Wom

873. Mitchell, Maria
1791/1818–1889
astronomer, women's rights
   worker, educator, novelist, poet
Quaker
Massachusetts
Cyc Am Bio; Dict Am Bio; Dict
   Am Bio Men Time; Index t
   Wom; Nat Cyc Am Bio v5; Not
   Am Wom; Twent Cen Bio Dict
   Not Am; Wom Cent

**874. Putnam, Katharine Hunt
(Palmer)**
1792–1861
religious textbook writer
Boston, MA
Dict Am Auth

**875. Brooks, Maria (Gowen);
Maria del Occidente**
1794/95–1845
poet

Massachusetts
Am Bio Dict; Cyc Am Bio; Dict Am Auth; Dict Am Auth; Dict Am Bio Men Time; Index t Wom; Nat Cyc Am Bio v8; Not Am Wom; Twent Cen Bio Dict Not Am

876. Dix, Dorothea Lynde
1794/1802–1887
crusader for the welfare of the mentally ill, prison reformer, philanthropist, author, essayist, children's author, superintendent of army nurses in the Civil War
Massachusetts
Cyc Am Bio; Dict Am Auth; Dict Am Bio; Dict Am Bio Men Time; Dict Lit Bio v1; Index t Wom; Nat Cyc Am Bio v3; Not Am Wom; Twent Cen Bio Dict Not Am; Wom Cent

877. Otis, Eliza Henderson (Boardman)
1796–1873
philanthropist, novelist
Boston, MA
Dict Am Auth; Twent Cen Bio Dict Not Am

878. Lyon, Mary
1797–1844/49
educator and founder of Mt. Holyoke Female Seminary (now Mt. Holyoke College)
Mt. Holyoke, MA
Am Bio Dict; Cyc Am Bio; Dict Am Bio; Dict Am Bio Men Time; Index t Wom; Nat Cyc Am Bio v4; Not Am Wom; Twent Cen Bio Dict Not Am; Wom Cent

879. Aspinwall, Alicia (Towne)
born 18?
children's author
Brookline, MA
Dict Am Auth

880. Bouve, Pauline Carrington (Rust)
born 18?
author
Boston, MA
Dict Am Auth

881. Devereux, Mary (Watson)
born 18?
novelist
Marblehead, MA
Dict Am Auth

882. Dickinson, Martha Gilbert
born 18?
poet
Amherst, MA
Dict Am Auth

883. Foster, Mabel G.
born 18?
author, lecturer
Boston, MA
Dict Am Auth

884. Lee, Mary Catherine (Jenkins)
born 18?
novelist
Springfield, MA
Dict Am Auth

885. Noble, Lucretia Gray
born 18?
novelist
Wilbraham, MA
Dict Am Auth

886. Plympton, Almira George
born 18?
children's author
Massachusetts
Dict Am Auth

887. Potter, Mary Knight
born 18?
writer on art, author
Boston, MA
Dict Am Auth

888. Rayner, Emma
born 18?
novelist
Boston, MA
Dict Am Auth

889. Sanborn, Mary (Farley)
born 18?
novelist
Boston, MA
Dict Am Auth

890. Sibley, Louise Florence Maria (Lyndon)
born 18?
author
Malden, MA
Dict Am Auth

891. Ticknor, Caroline
born 18?
short story writer
Boston, MA
Dict Am Auth

892. Urbino, Lavinia Buoncuore
born 18?
biographer, autobiographer, translator
Boston, MA
Dict Am Auth

893. Walker, Mary Spring
born 18?
miscellaneous author
Boston, MA
Dict Am Auth

894. Warner, Eliza A.
born 18?
children's author
Northampton, MA
Dict Am Auth

895. White, Sarah Elizabeth [Joy]
born 18?
journalist
Boston, MA
Dict Am Auth

896. Child, Lydia Maria (Francis)
1802–80
author, philanthropist, abolitionist, editor, social reformer
Quaker
Massachusetts
Cyc Am Bio; Dict Am Auth; Dict Am Bio; Dict Am Bio Men Time; Dict Lit Bio v1; Index t Wom; Nat Cyc Am Bio v2; Not Am Wom; Twent Cen Bio Dict Not Am; Wom Cent

897. Hall, Arethusa
1802–91
literary educator, author
Massachusetts
Cyc Am Bio; Dict Am Auth; Dict Am Bio; Nat Cyc Am Bio v22; Twent Cen Bio Dict Not Am

898. Dwight, Margarette
1804–45
educator
Northampton, MA
Am Bio Dict

899. Peabody, Elizabeth Palmer
1804–94
educator, writer on education, educational reformer, kindergartner
Transcendentalist
Boston, MA
Cyc Am Bio; Dict Am Auth; Dict Am Bio; Dict Am Bio Men Time; Dict Lit Bio v1; Index t Wom; Not Am Wom; Twent Cen Bio Dict Not Am; Wom Cent

900. Hunt, Harriot Keziah
1805–75
physician, social reformer, suffragist, lecturer
Boston, MA
Cyc Am Bio; Dict Am Auth; Dict Am Bio; Index t Wom; Nat Cyc Am Bio v9; Not Am Wom; Twent Cen Bio Dict Not Am

901. Locke, Jane Ermina (Starkweather)
1805–59
author, poet
Boston, MA
Cyc Am Bio; Dict Am Auth; Dict Am Bio Men Time; Twent Cen Bio Dict Not Am

902. Fuller, Sarah Margaret; Marchioness Ossoli; Sarah Margaret Fuller Ossoli
1810–50
author, critic, educator, feminist, philosopher, journalist, Transcendentalist revolutionary
Transcendentalist
Boston, MA
Cyc Am Bio; Dict Am Auth; Dict Am Bio; Dict Am Bio Men Time; Dict Lit Bio v1; Index t Wom; Nat Cyc Am Bio v3; Not Am Wom; Twent Cen Bio Dict Not Am; Wom Cent

903. Hale, Mary Whitwell
1810–62
poet, educator, hymn writer
Massachusetts
Dict Am Auth; Index t Wom

904. Lander, Sarah West
1810/19–1872
author of travel books for children
Salem, MA
Cyc Am Bio; Dict Am Auth

905. Osgood, Marion
flourished 1840s–90s
composer, violinist, conductor
Boston, MA
Index t Wom; Wom Cent

906. Putnam, Mary Traill Spence (Lowell)
1810–98
author, history writer, translator, linguist, traveler
Boston, MA
Cyc Am Bio; Dict Am Auth; Dict Am Bio Men Time; Index t Wom; Twent Cen Bio Dict Not Am

907. Saxe, Caroline Mehetabel
1812–94
author, editor
Massachusetts
Cyc Am Bio

908. Silsbee, Marianne Cabot (Devereux)
1812–89
historian of Salem, Massachusetts, poet
Boston, MA
Dict Am Auth

909. Anderson, Ophelia Brown
1813–52
stage actor
Boston, MA
Appl Cyc Am Bio; Dict Am Bio

910. Jacobs, Sarah Sprague
born 1813
children's author, historical author
Cambridge, MA
Cyc Am Bio; Dict Am Auth

911. Goodrich, Mary Hopkins
born 1814

originator of village improvement
association cooperatives
Massachusetts
Wom Cent

912. Perkins, Elmira Johnson
1814–96
missionary to Native Americans
in Oregon, poet
Oregon; Boston, MA
Dict Am Auth

913. Eames, Jane Anthony
1816–94
author, traveler
New Hampshire; Massachusetts
Cyc Am Bio; Dict Am Auth;
Index t Wom; Twent Cen Bio
Dict Not Am

914. Stone, Martha Elvira
born 1816
postmaster of North Oxford,
Massachusetts; genealogist; Civil War relief worker
North Oxford, MA
Wom Cent

**915. Pomroy, Rebecca Rossig-
nol**
1817–84
nurse, war nurse
Massachusetts
Cyc Am Bio

916. Burnham, Sarah Maria
1818–1901
educator, historical author, writer
on geology and travel
Cambridge, MA
Dict Am Auth

917. Orne, Caroline Francis
1818–1906
poet, children's author
Cambridge, MA
Dict Am Auth; Nat Cyc Am Bio
v6

**918. Stone, Lucy; Mrs. Henry
Brown Blackwell**
1818–93
feminist, suffragist, women's
rights worker, abolitionist, so-
cial reformer, editor, lecturer
Massachusetts
Cyc Am Bio; Dict Am Bio; Dict
Am Bio Men Time; Index t
Wom; Nat Cyc Am Bio v2 and
v29; Not Am Wom; Twent Cen
Bio Dict Not Am; Wom Cent

919. Yale, Catharine (Brooks)
1818–1900
short story writer
Deerfield, MA
Dict Am Auth

920. Howe, Julia Ward
1819–1910
poet, dramatist, songwriter, lecturer, suffrage and women's

club leader, feminist, abolition-
ist, pacifist, prison reformer,
Union patriot during the Civil
War, philanthropist, traveler
Boston, MA
Cyc Am Bio; Dict Am Auth; Dict
Am Bio; Dict Am Bio Men
Time; Dict Lit Bio v1; Index t
Wom; Nat Cyc Am Bio v1; Not
Am Wom; Twent Cen Bio Dict
Not Am; Wom Cent

921. Sewall, Harriet (Winslow)
1819–89
suffragist, poet, religious poet, abolitionist
Transcendentalist
Boston, MA
Dict Am Auth; Nat Cyc Am Bio
v10

**922. Livermore, Mary Ashton
(Rice)**
1820/21–1905
health reformer, hospital adminis-
trator, suffragist, temperance
worker, abolitionist, Civil War
patriot, miscellaneous author
Universalist
Melrose, MA
Cyc Am Bio; Dict Am Auth; Dict
Am Bio Men Time; Dict Am
Rel Bio; Index t Wom; Nat Cyc
Am Bio v1; Not Am Wom;
Twent Cen Bio Dict Not Am;
Wom Cent

923. Diaz, Abby (Morton)
1821–1904
author, children's author, essayist, social reformer, suffragist,
abolitionist, lecturer
Boston, MA
Dict Am Auth; Nat Cyc Am Bio
v11; Not Am Wom; Twent Cen
Bio Dict Not Am; Wom Cent

924. Emery, Sarah Anna
born 1821
novelist
West Newbury, MA
Dict Am Auth

925. Scudder, Eliza
1821–96
hymn writer
Massachusetts
Dict Am Auth

926. Whitney, Anne
1821–1915
sculptor, artist, poet, abolitionist,
suffragist
Boston, MA
Cyc Am Bio; Dict Am Auth; Dict
Am Bio; Index t Wom; Nat Cyc
Am Bio v7; Not Am Wom;
Wom Cent

**927. Agassiz, Elizabeth Cabot
Carrie**
1822–1907

founder and president of Rad-
cliffe College, educator, biogra-
pher, naturalist, science writer
Boston, MA
Dict Am Auth; Dict Am Bio;
Index t Wom; Not Am Wom;
Wom Cent

**928. Dall, Caroline Wells
(Healey)**
1822–1912
author, essayist, women's rights
worker, women's labor reform-
er, educator
Boston, MA
Cyc Am Bio; Dict Am Auth; Dict
Am Bio; Dict Lit Bio v1; Index
t Wom; Nat Cyc Am Bio v9;
Not Am Wom; Twent Cen Bio
Dict Not Am; Wom Cent

**929. Mason, Caroline Atherton
(Briggs)**
1823–90
poet
Fitchburg, MA
Cyc Am Bio; Dict Am Auth

**930. Palfrey, Sarah H. Ham-
mond Hamilton; E. Foxton**
1823–post 1886
author, poet, novelist
Cambridge, MA
Cyc Am Bio; Dict Am Auth; Nat
Cyc Am Bio v7; Twent Cen Bio
Dict Not Am

931. Very, Lydia Louise Ann
1823–1901/07
poet, children's author, illustra-
tor, educator
Salem, MA
Cyc Am Bio; Dict Am Auth; Dict
Am Bio; Index t Wom; Nat Cyc
Am Bio v6; Wom Cent

**932. Cheney, Endah Dow (Lit-
tlehale)**
1824–1904
philanthropist, author, abolitionist, suffragist, women's rights
worker, Black civil rights worker, lecturer, philosopher
Transcendentalist
Boston, MA
Cyc Am Bio; Dict Am Auth; Dict
Am Bio; Dict Lit Bio v1; Index
t Wom; Nat Cyc Am Bio v9;
Not Am Wom; Twent Cen Bio
Dict Not Am; Wom Cent

933. Larcom, Lucy
1824/26–1893
millworker, author, poet, maga-
zine editor, seminary teacher
Beverly, MA
Cyc Am Bio; Dict Am Auth; Dict
Am Bio Men Time; Index t
Wom; Nat Cyc Am Bio v1; Not
Am Wom; Twent Cen Bio Dict
Not Am; Wom Cent

**934. Lowe, Martha Ann (Per-
ry)**
1824/29–1902
poet, temperance worker, suffragist, author
Somerville, MA
Cyc Am Bio; Dict Am Auth;
Index t Wom; Nat Cyc Am Bio
v10; Twent Cen Bio Dict Not
Am; Wom Cent

**935. Walton, Electa Noble Lin-
coln**
born 1824
educator, lecturer, suffragist, feminist
Massachusetts
Wom Cent

**936. Whitney, Adeline Dutton
(Train)**
1824–1906
writer of popular didactic verse
and fiction
Christian Scientist
Milton, MA
Cyc Am Bio; Dict Am Auth; Dict
Am Bio Men Time; Index t
Wom; Nat Cyc Am Bio v1; Not
Am Wom; Twent Cen Bio Dict
Not Am; Wom Cent

**937. Claflin, Mary Bucklin
(Davenport)**
1825–96
author
Boston, MA
Dict Am Auth; Twent Cen Bio
Dict Not Am

**938. Robinson, Harriet Jane
(Hanson)**
1825–1911
suffragist, women's rights worker,
feminist, abolitionist, author,
poet, dramatist, journalist, mer-
chant
Malden, MA
Cyc Am Bio; Dict Am Auth; Dict
Am Bio; Index t Wom; Nat Cyc
Am Bio v3; Not Am Wom;
Wom Cent

**939. Plunkett, Harriette Mer-
rick Hodge**
born 1826
humanitarian, sanitation reformer
Massachusetts
Index t Wom; Wom Cent

940. Belcher, Cynthia Holmes
born 1827
journalist, suffragist, temperance
worker
Boston, MA
Wom Cent

941. Cummins, Maria Susanna
1827/28–1866
novelist

Massachusetts
Cyc Am Bio; Dict Am Auth; Dict
Am Bio; Dict Am Bio Men
Time; Index t Wom; Nat Cyc
Am Bio v6; Twent Cen Bio Dict
Not Am; Wom Lit; Wom Lit,
More

**942. Curtis, Caroline Gardiner
(Cary); Carroll Winchester**
born 1827
novelist
Boston, MA
Dict Am Auth

**943. Goodwin, Hannah
Elizabeth (Bradbury)**
1827–93
children's author
Boston, MA
Dict Am Auth; Wom Cent

**944. Guild, Caroline Snowden
(Whitmarsh)**
1827–98
religious author
Boston, MA
Dict Am Auth

945. Collins, Jennie
1828–87
labor reformer, welfare worker,
philanthropist, suffragist
Massachusetts
Bio Dict Am Lab; Index t Wom;
Not Am Wom; Twent Cen Bio
Dict Not Am

946. Doten, Lizzie
born 1829
poet
Spiritualist
Boston, MA
Cyc Am Bio; Dict Am Auth

947. May, Abigail Williams
1829–88
Boston social reformer, abolitionist, suffragist, education commissioner, Civil War relief
worker
Boston, MA
Index t Wom; Not Am Wom;
Twent Cen Bio Dict Not Am

948. Carpenter, Ellen M.
born 1830/36
artist
Boston, MA
Cyc Am Bio; Twent Cen Bio Dict
Not Am; Wom Cent

**949. Dickinson, Emily
Elizabeth**
1830–86
poet, letter writer
Amherst, MA
Dict Am Auth; Dict Lit Bio v1;
Index t Wom; Nat Cyc Am Bio
v11 and v23; Nort Anth Poet;
Not Am Wom; Twent Cen Bio
Dict Not Am

**950. Dodge, Mary Abigail
"Abby"; Gail Hamilton**
1830/36–1896
author, essayist, humorist, maga-
zine writer, editor, abolitionist,
suffragist, women's rights work-
er
Massachusetts
Cyc Am Bio; Dict Am Auth; Dict
Am Bio; Dict Am Bio Men
Time; Index t Wom; Nat Cyc
Am Bio v9; Not Am Wom;
Twent Cen Bio Dict Not Am;
Wom Cent

**951. MacKaye, Maria Ellery
(Goodwin)**
born 1830
educator, author
Cambridge, MA
Dict Am Auth

**952. Stickney, Julia Granby
(Noyes)**
born 1830
poet
Groveland, MA
Dict Am Auth

953. Stranahan, Clara Harrison
183?–post 1890
writer on art
Boston, MA
Dict Am Auth; Wom Cent

**954. Thompson, Ella Mason
(Williams)**
183?–75
author
Newton, MA
Dict Am Auth

955. Austin, Jane Goodwin
1831–94
historical novelist
Boston, MA
Dict Am Auth; Dict Am Bio;
Index t Wom; Nat Cyc Am Bio
v6; Twent Cen Bio Dict Not
Am; Wom Cent

**956. Calkins, Adelaide Augusta
Hosmer**
1831–1909
philanthropist, children's welfare
worker
Congregationalist
Massachusetts
Nat Cyc Am Bio v28

957. Perry, Nora
1831/41–1896
poet, children's author, journalist
Boston, MA
Cyc Am Bio; Dict Am Auth; Dict
Am Bio; Index t Wom; Nat Cyc
Am Bio v15; Twent Cen Bio
Dict Not Am; Wom Cent

958. Knowlton, Helen Mary
1832–1918

painter, art educator, writer on
art and art technique
Boston, MA
Cyc Am Bio; Dict Am Auth; Not
Am Wom; Twent Cen Bio Dict
Not Am

**959. Morrison, Mary Jane
(Whitney)**
1832–1904
short story writer
Waltham, MA
Dict Am Auth

960. Fields, Annie (Adams)
1834–1915
author, poet, literary host
Boston, MA
Dict Am Auth; Dict Am Bio;
Index t Wom; Nat Cyc Am Bio
v1; Not Am Wom; Twent Cen
Bio Dict Not Am

**961. Hopkins, Louisa Parsons
(Stone)**
1834–95
educator, writer on education,
poet
Boston, MA
Dict Am Auth

**962. Safford, Mary Joanna
Jane**
1834–91
Civil War nurse, physician, sur-
geon
Boston, MA
Index t Wom; Not Am Wom;
Wom Cent

**963. Waters, Clara (Erskine)
(Clement); Clara Clement**
1834–1916
author, writer on art, art histori-
an, world traveler
Boston, MA
Dict Am Auth; Index t Wom;
Not Am Wom; Wom Cent;
Wom Lit, More

964. Cornell, Ellen Frances
born 1835
poet, marine shell collector
Swedenborgian
Massachusetts
Wom Cent

965. Frothingham, Ellen
1835–1902
scholar of German literature,
translator, linguist
Boston, MA
Cyc Am Bio; Dict Am Auth;
Index t Wom

**966. Moulton, [Ellen] Louise
(Chandler)**
1835–1908
magazine writer, children's author, poet

Boston, MA
Cyc Am Bio; Dict Am Auth; Dict
Am Bio Men Time; Index t
Wom; Nat Cyc Am Bio v3; Not
Am Wom; Twent Cen Bio Dict
Not Am; Wom Cent

**967. Spofford, Harriet
Elizabeth (Prescott)**
1835–1921
author, novelist, poet
Newburyport, MA
Cyc Am Bio and ad; Dict Am
Auth; Dict Am Bio; Dict Am
Bio Men Time; Index t Wom;
Nat Cyc Am Bio v4; Not Am
Wom; Twent Cen Bio Dict Not
Am; Wom Cent

968. Barry, Flora Elizabeth
born 1836
concert and opera singer
Boston, MA
Wom Cent

**969. Tucker, Margaretta
(Ames); Margaret May**
born 1836
poet
Boston, MA
Dict Am Auth

**970. Wakefield, Nancy Amelia
Woodbury (Priest) "A. C."**
1836–70
poet
Massachusetts
Cyc Am Bio; Dict Am Auth; Dict
Am Bio Men Time

**971. Winslow, Catherine Mary
(Reignolds) "Kate"**
1836–1911
actor, dramatic reader
Boston, MA
English
Dict Am Auth; Nat Cyc Am Bio
v23

972. Eastman, Julia Arabella
1837–1911
children's author, novelist
Massachusetts
Cyc Am Bio; Dict Am Auth;
Index t Wom

973. Emerson, Ellen (Russell)
1837–1907
author, ethnologist, writer on Native American art and mythology
Boston, MA
Dict Am Auth; Dict Am Bio;
Twent Cen Bio Dict Not Am;
Wom Cent

**974. Keller, Elizabeth Catha-
rine**
born 1837
physician, surgeon
Lutheran

Pennsylvania; Massachusetts
Index t Wom; Wom Cent

975. Greene, Aella
1838–1903
journalist, poet
Springfield, MA
Dict Am Auth

976. Wells, Catharine Boott (Gannett)
born 1838
author, religious writer, essayist, novelist, educator
Boston, MA
Dict Am Auth; Twent Cen Bio Dict Not Am

977. Woods, Kate Tannatt
1838–1910
club leader, editor, poet, children's author
Salem, MA
Dict Am Auth; Index t Wom; Wom Cent

978. Woolson, Abba Louisa (Goold)
1838–1921
educator, author, lecturer, dress reformer
Boston, MA
Cyc Am Bio; Dict Am Auth; Dict Am Bio; Index t Wom; Nat Cyc Am Bio v9; Not Am Wom; Wom Cent

979. Blake, Mary Elizabeth McGrath
1840–1907
author, poet
Catholic
Boston, MA
Irish
Dict Am Auth; Dict Am Bio; Wom Cent

980. Hill, Eliza Trask
born 1840
suffragist, women's welfare worker, journalist, newspaper publisher, political activist, Prohibitionist
Massachusetts
Wom Cent

981. Hoyt, Deristha Lavinta
born 184?
lecturer on the history of painting, writer on art
Massachusetts
Dict Am Auth

982. O'Keefe, Katharine A.
flourished 1870s–90s
educator, lecturer
Massachusetts
Irish
Wom Cent

983. Potter, Isabella Abbe
flourished 1870s

philanthropist
Massachusetts
Nat Cyc Am Bio v14

984. Wesselhoeft, Elizabeth Foster (Pope)
born 1840
children's author
Boston, MA
Dict Am Auth

985. Williams, Anne (Bolles); Jak
born 1840
children's author
Springfield, MA
Dict Am Auth

986. Wixon, Susan Helen
flourished 1870s–90s
author, children's editor, educator, feminist
Massachusetts
Wom Cent

987. Pool, Maria Louisa
1841/45–1898
author, novelist, writer for the *New York Tribune*
Rockland, MA
Dict Am Auth; Index t Wom; Nat Cyc Am Bio v6; Twent Cen Bio Dict Not Am

988. Chaplin, Ada C.
1842–83
author, Sunday school story writer
Massachusetts
Cyc Am Bio; Dict Am Auth

989. Poor, Agnes Blake; Dorothy Prescott
1842–1922
author
Brookline, MA
Dict Am Auth; Nat Cyc Am Bio v19

990. Richards, Ellen Henrietta (Swallow)
1842–1911
sanitation chemist and engineer, mineralogist, leader in applied and domestic science, writer on domestic science, professor at MIT, educator
Massachusetts
Cyc Am Bio; Dict Am Auth; Dict Am Bio; Index t Wom; Nat Cyc Am Bio v7; Not Am Wom; Twent Cen Bio Dict Not Am; Wom Cent

991. Lincoln, Mary Johnson (Bailey)
1844–1921
educator, writer and lecturer on cookery, culinary educator, home economist

Boston, MA
Dict Am Auth; Dict Am Bio; Index t Wom; Nat Cyc Am Bio v24; Not Am Wom

992. Lothrop, Harriett Mulford (Stone); Margaret Sydney
1844–1924
author, children's author
Concord, MA
Cyc Am Bio; Dict Am Auth; Dict Am Bio; Index t Wom; Nat Cyc Am Bio v8; Not Am Wom; Twent Cen Bio Dict Not Am; Wom Cent

993. Merriman, Helen (Bigelow)
born 1844
artist, writer on art, religious author
Worcester, MA
Dict Am Auth; Index t Wom; Twent Cen Bio Dict Not Am

994. Oliver, Grace Atkinson (Little) (Ellis)
1844–99
author, biographer, story editor
Salem, MA
Cyc Am Bio; Dict Am Auth; Index t Wom; Twent Cen Bio Dict Not Am; Wom Cent

995. Ward, Elizabeth Stuart (Phelps)
1844–1911
author, popular novelist, women's rights worker, temperance worker, philanthropist
Massachusetts
Cyc Am Bio; Dict Am Auth; Dict Am Bio; Dict Am Bio Men Time; Index t Wom; Nat Cyc Am Bio v9; Not Am Wom; Twent Cen Bio Dict Not Am; Wom Cent; Wom Lit, More

996. Paine, Harriet Eliza; Eliza Chester
1845–1910
author, educator
Boston, MA
Dict Am Auth; Index t Wom; Twent Cen Bio Dict Not Am

997. Upham, Grace le Baron (Locke); Grace le Baron
born 1845
children's author
Boston, MA
Dict Am Auth

998. Wetherbee, Emily Green
born 1845
author, poet, essayist
Massachusetts
Wom Cent

999. Evans, Lizzie Phelps Esterbrook; Esta Brooks
born 1846

novelist
Somerville, MA
Dict Am Auth; Wom Cent

1000. Hodgkins, Louise Manning
born 1846
author, university educator in literature, writer on literature
Massachusetts
Dict Am Auth; Wom Cent

1001. Kimball, Emma Adeline
born 1847
poet, historical sketch writer
Haverville, MA
Dict Am Auth

1002. Leonard, Mary Hall
1847–1921
educator
Massachusetts
Nat Cyc Am Bio v20

1003. Sparhawk, Frances Campbell
born 1847/58
author, novelist, philanthropist, Native American welfare worker
Newton, MA
Cyc Am Bio and ad; Dict Am Auth; Nat Cyc Am Bio v10; Wom Cent

1004. Whiting, Lilian
1847/55–1942
journalist, essayist, poet, short story writer, biographer, editor
Boston, MA
Dict Am Auth; Index t Wom; Nat Cyc Am Bio v9; Not Am Wom

1005. Atherton, Mary Alderson Chandler
born 1849
suffragist, educator, author
Massachusetts
Nat Cyc Am Bio v18

1006. Jewett, Sarah Orne; Alice Eliot
1849–1909
author, short story writer
South Berwick, ME; Boston, MA
Cyc Am Bio; Dict Am Auth; Dict Am Bio; Index t Wom; Nat Cyc Am Bio v1; Not Am Wom; Wom Cent; Wom Lit; Wom Lit, More

1007. Curran, Ida M.
flourished 1880s–90s
journalist, editor
Massachusetts
Wom Cent

1008. Dabney, Julia Parker
born 1850
author, artist, novelist

Brookline, MA
Twent Cen Bio Dict Not Am

1009. Palmer, Sarah Ellen
flourished 1880s–1930s
surgeon
Congregationalist
Massachusetts
Nat Cyc Am Bio csv5

1010. Pitman, Marie J. (Davis)
1850–88
children's author, journalist,
 newspaper foreign correspondent
Boston, MA
Cyc Am Bio; Dict Am Auth

**1011. Shattuck, Harriette Lucy
(Robinson)**
born 1850
miscellaneous author, legal clerk,
 writer on parliamentary law,
 suffragist
Malden, MA
Dict Am Auth; Index t Wom;
 Twent Cen Bio Dict Not Am;
 Wom Cent

**1012. Smith, Emma Adelia
Flint**
1850–1946
last executor of the estate of Samuel J. Tilden
Massachusetts
Obit File

**1013. Sutherland, Evelyn
Greenleaf (Baker)**
born 185?
playwright
Boston, MA
Dict Am Auth

1014. Crane, Sibylla (Bailey)
1851–1902
vocalist, composer, music educator, writer on music
Boston, MA
Dict Am Auth; Nat Cyc Am Bio
 v7; Twent Cen Bio Dict Not
 Am; Wom Cent

1015. Winslow, Helen Maria
1851–1938
clubwoman, author, journalist,
 editor, publisher
Boston, MA
Dict Am Auth; Index t Wom;
 Nat Cyc Am Bio csv2; Wom
 Cent

1016. Wright, Mary (Tappan)
born 1851
short story writer
Cambridge, MA
Dict Am Auth

**1017. Daniels, Cora (Linn);
Australia**
born 1852
author, novelist

Massachusetts
Dict Am Auth; Wom Cent

1018. Leggett, Mary Lydia
born 1852
Liberal minister
Massachusetts
Index t Wom; Wom Cent

**1019. Conway, Katherine Elea-
nor**
born 1853
journalist, poet
Catholic
Boston, MA
Dict Am Auth; Twent Cen Bio
 Dict Not Am; Wom Cent

1020. Fuller, Anna
born 1853
author, novelist
Boston, MA
Dict Am Auth; Twent Cen Bio
 Dict Not Am

**1021. Hager, Lucie Carolyn
(Gilson)**
born 1853
author, writer on Massachusetts
Massachusetts
Dict Am Auth; Wom Cent

1022. King, Anna (Eichberg)
born 1853
short story writer
Boston, MA
Dict Am Auth

1023. Poulsson, Anne Emilie
1853–1939
children's author, writer on children, editor, illustrator, kindergarten educator
Boston, MA
Dict Am Auth; Index t Wom;
 Nat Cyc Am Bio v10; Twent
 Cen Bio Dict Not Am

1024. Read, Jane Maria
born 1853
poet, artist
Colebrook Springs, MA
Dict Am Auth; Wom Cent

**1025. Smart, Helen Hamilton
(Gardener)**
born 1853
novelist
Boston, MA
Dict Am Auth

1026. Tappan, Eva March
1854–1930
educator, children's author, histo-
 ry text writer
Worcester, MA
Dict Am Auth; Dict Am Bio; Not
 Am Wom; Twent Cen Bio Dict
 Not Am

1027. Fall, Anna Christy
born 1855

lawyer
Massachusetts
Wom Cent

1028. Hersey, Heloise Edwina
born 1855
educator, writer on education
Boston, MA
Dict Am Auth

1029. Smith, Harriette (Knight)
born 1855
journalist
Boston, MA
Dict Am Auth

1030. Bailey, Sarah Lord
born 1856
elocutionist
Massachusetts
British
Wom Cent

**1031. Baldwin, Mary Louise
"Maria Louisa"**
1856–1919/22
educator, civic leader
Massachusetts
Black
Index t Wom; Negro Alman; Not
 Am Wom; Prof Negro Wom

1032. Brown, Alice
1856/57–1948
children's author
Boston, MA
Dict Am Auth; Index t Wom;
 Nat Cyc Am Bio v15; Not Am
 Wom; Twent Cen Bio Dict Not
 Am; Wom Lit; Wom Lit, More

**1033. Forbes, Harriette (Merri-
field)**
born 1856
historical sketch writer
Westborough, MA
Dict Am Auth

**1034. Roe, Nora Ardelia (Met-
calf)**
born 1856
short story writer
Worcester, MA
Dict Am Auth

1035. Train, Elizabeth Phipps
born 1856/57
author, novelist
Duxbury, MA
Dict Am Auth; Twent Cen Bio
 Dict Not Am

1036. White, Eliza Orne; Alex
1856–1947
children's author
Brookline, MA
Dict Am Auth; Nat Cyc Am Bio
 v13; Not Am Wom; Twent Cen
 Bio Dict Not Am

**1037. Bishop, Mary Agnes Dal-
rymple**
born 1857
journalist
Massachusetts
Wom Cent

**1038. Brown, Katherine "Kate"
Louise**
1857–1921
children's author, composer, educator
Boston, MA
Dict Am Auth; Index t Wom

1039. Delano, Frances Jackson
born 1857
author
Fairhaven, MA
Dict Am Auth

1040. Wheelock, Lucy
1857–1946
kindergarten educator, founder of
 Wheelock College, lecturer, au-
 thor
Boston, MA
Dict Am Bio supp v4; Not Am
 Wom; Wom Cent

1041. Curtis, Martha E.
born 1858
suffragist, women's rights worker
Massachusetts
Wom Cent

**1042. Morley, Margaret War-
ner**
1858–1923
educator, author, writer on sex
 education, naturalist, botanist,
 zoologist
Boston, MA
Dict Am Auth; Dict Am Bio

1043. Robinson, Edith
born 1858
novelist
Boston, MA
Dict Am Auth

1044. Arnold, Sarah Louise
born 1859
educator, education writer
Boston, MA
Dict Am Auth; Index t Wom

1045. Bates, Katharine Lee
1859–1929
poet, author, professor of English
 literature
Massachusetts
Dict Am Auth; Dict Am Bio;
 Index t Wom; Nat Cyc Am Bio
 v1, v9, and v42; Not Am Wom;
 Twent Cen Bio Dict Not Am;
 Wom Cent

**1046. van Anderson, Helen
(Van Metre)**
born 1859

minister, lecturer, miscellaneous
author
Boston, MA
Dict Am Auth

**1047. Kellogg, Eva Mary
(Crosby)**
born 1860
children's author
Boston, MA
Dict Am Auth

**1048. Lee, Jeanette Barbour
(Perry)**
1860–1951
educator, novelist
Northampton, MA
Dict Am Auth; Index t Wom;
Nat Cyc Am Bio csv1; Obit File

1049. Owler, Martha Tracy
flourished 1890s
journalist, foreign correspondent
Massachusetts
Wom Cent

1050. Smith, Gertrude
born 1860
short story writer
Boston, MA
Dict Am Auth

1051. Smith, Minna Caroline
born 1860
journalist, children's author
Boston, MA
Dict Am Auth

1052. Swett, Sophia Miriam
born 186?
short story writer, children's author
Arlington, MA
Dict Am Auth

1053. Swett, Susan Hartley
born 186?
short story writer
Arlington, MA
Dict Am Auth

**1054. Wade, Mary Hazelton
Blanchard**
born 1860
children's author
Malden, MA
Dict Am Auth

1055. Guiney, Louise Imogen;
The Sunny Young Greek
1861–1920
poet, essayist, fiction author, liter-
ary scholar
Newton, MA
Dict Am Auth; Dict Am Bio; Nat
Cyc Am Bio v9; Not Am Wom;
Twent Cen Bio Dict Not Am;
Wom Cent; Wom Lit, More

1056. Horsford, Cornelia
born 1861

archaeologist, writer on archaeol-
ogy
Cambridge, MA
Dict Am Auth; Index t Wom;
Twent Cen Bio Dict Not Am

1057. Kimball, Hannah Parker
born 1861
poet
Boston, MA
Dict Am Auth

**1058. Lang, Florence Osgood
Rand**
1861–1943
patron of art, philanthropist
Congregationalist
Massachusetts
Nat Cyc Am Bio v32 and csv5

1059. Macomber, Mary Lizzie
1861–1916
painter of decorative symbolic
panels, portraitist
Massachusetts
Dict Am Bio; Index t Wom; Nat
Cyc Am Bio v24

**1060. Saunders, Margaret Mar-
shall; Marshall Saunders**
born 1861
short story writer, novelist
Boston, MA
Canadian (Nova Scotia)
Dict Am Auth

1061. Scudder, Vida Dutton
1861–1954
social reformer, writer on English
literature, author, university ed-
ucator
Christian Scientist
Massachusetts
Cyc Am Bio; Dict Am Auth; Dict
Am Bio supp v5; Index t Wom;
Not Am Wom supp v1; Twent
Cen Bio Dict Not Am; Wom
Lit, More

1062. Toussaint, Emma; Portia
born 1862
author, translator
Episcopalian
Massachusetts
Wom Cent

**1063. Wilkins-Freeman, Mary
Eleanor**
1862–post 1903
author, novelist
Randolph, MA
Dict Am Auth; Nat Cyc Am Bio
v9; Twent Cen Bio Dict Not
Am; Wom Cent

1064. Cannon, Annie Jump
1863–1941
astronomer
Methodist; Congregationalist

Cambridge, MA
Dict Lit Bio supp v3; Index t
Wom; Nat Cyc Am Bio csv2;
Not Am Wom; Obit File

1065. Channing, Blanche Mary
1863–1902
children's author
Brookline, MA
English
Dict Am Auth

1066. Dwight, Minnie Ryan
1863–1957
editor and publisher of the Holyoke, Massachusetts, *Daily
Transcript-Telegraph*
Holyoke, MA
Obit File

1067. Hall, Gertrude Brownell
born 1863
short story writer, poet, novelist
Boston, MA
Dict Am Auth; Index t Wom

**1068. Hitchcock, Caroline
Hanks**
born 1863
author
Cambridge, MA
Dict Am Auth

1069. Sears, Clara Endicott
1863–1960
author, antiquarian, cattle breeder
Protestant Episcopal
Massachusetts
Nat Cyc Am Bio v47 and csv1

**1070. Hopkins, Margaret Sut-
ton (Briscoe)**
born 1864
short story writer
Amherst, MA
Dict Am Auth

1071. Marble, Annie Russel
1864–1936
writer on literature
Worcester, MA
Dict Am Auth; Index t Wom;
Nat Cyc Am Bio v27

1072. Parker, Alice
born 1864
lawyer, feminist
Massachusetts
Index t Wom; Wom Cent

**1073. Smith, Charlotte Dodd
Stewartson**
born 1864
physician
Massachusetts
Nat Cyc Am Bio csv8

**1074. Bergengren, Ann (Far-
quhar); Margaret Alston**
born 1865

novelist, journalist, magazine edi-
tor, singer
Boston, MA
Dict Am Auth; Index t Wom;
Nat Cyc Am Bio v14

1075. Chase, Jessie Anderson
born 1865
author, textbook writer
Brookline, MA
Dict Am Auth

1076. Emerson, Mary Alice
1865–1922
educator
Boston, MA
Nat Cyc Am Bio v20

1077. Goodale, Dora Read
born 1866
poet, author
Massachusetts
Cyc Am Bio; Dict Am Auth; Nat
Cyc Am Bio v8; Twent Cen Bio
Dict Not Am; Wom Cent

1078. Sherman, Ellen Burns
1867–1956
author, suffragist
Unitarian
Massachusetts
Nat Cyc Am Bio v45

**1079. Blodgett, Mabel Louise
Fuller**
born 1869
author, novelist, fairy tale writer
Brookline, MA
Dict Am Auth; Nat Cyc Am Bio
csv1

**1080. Doyle, Martha Claire
MacGowan**
born 1869
children's author
Boston, MA
Dict Am Auth; Index t Wom

1081. Lowell, Ettie Lois; Mrs.
George Fl.
born 1869
suffragist, composer, alto singer,
owner and director of the bond
and investment firm of E. L.
Lowell of Boston
Boston, MA
Nat Cyc Am Bio v14

1082. Page, Marie Danforth
1869/70–1940
painter, artist
Boston, MA
Index t Wom; Nat Cyc Am Bio
v29

**1083. Keezer, Martha Moulton
Wittemore**
born 1870
author
Massachusetts
Wom Cent

1084. Patch, Kate; Kate Whiting
born 1870
fiction writer, short story writer
Framington, MA
Dict Am Auth

1085. Brown, Abbie Farwell
1871–1927
poet, author, children's author
Boston, MA
Dict Am Auth; Not Am Wom

1086. Converse, Florence
born 1871
novelist, author
Boston, MA
Dict Am Auth; Nat Cyc Am Bio
v13; Wom Lit, More

1087. Fitzgerald, Susan Grimes Walker
1871–1943
labor worker, trade unionist, suffragist
Unitarian
Boston, MA
Nat Cyc Am Bio v32

1088. Kitson, Theo Alice (Ruggles)
1871–1932
sculptor
Massachusetts
Index t Wom; Wom Cent

1089. Howard, Helen Margaret Willard
born 1872
clubwoman, composer
Massachusetts
Nat Cyc Am Bio v29

1090. Bolton, Ethel (Stanwood)
born 1873
genealogist
Brookline, MA
Dict Am Auth

1091. Crawford, Mary Caroline
born 1874
journalist
Boston, MA
Dict Am Auth

1092. Frothingham, Eugenia Brooks
born 1874
novelist
Boston, MA
Dict Am Auth

1093. Peabody, Josephine Preston; Mrs. Lionel S. Marks
1874/80–1922
poet, dramatist
Cambridge, MA
Dict Am Auth; Dict Am Bio;
Index t Wom; Nat Cyc Am Bio
v19; Not Am Wom; Twent Cen
Bio Dict Not Am

1094. Rollins, Clara Harriot (Sherwood)
born 1874
short story writer
Boston, MA
Dict Am Auth

1095. Tillinghast, Anna Churchill Moulton
1874–1951
temperance worker, women's and children's welfare worker, Universalist pastor, suffragist
Universalist
Massachusetts
Nat Cyc Am Bio v45

1096. Bradley, Alice
born 1875
home economics educator
Methodist
Massachusetts
Nat Cyc Am Bio csv2

1097. Humphrey, Caroline Louise
born 1875
educator
Unitarian
Boston, MA
Nat Cyc Am Bio csv2 and csv5

1098. Comstock, Ada Louise;
Ada Notestein
1876–1973
college administrator, president of Radcliffe College
Boston, MA
Nat Cyc Am Bio csv3; Not Am
Wom supp v1; Obit File

1099. Dix, Beulah Marie
born 1876
historical novelist
Cambridge, MA
Dict Am Auth

1100. Bancroft, Jane Wallis Waldron
1877–1949
publisher of the *Wall Street Journal*, president of the Dow Jones & Co. newsgathering organization, Boston civic worker, equestrian
Boston, MA
Nat Cyc Am Bio v38; Obit File

1101. Franklin, Lucy Jenkins
born 1877
university educator
Methodist Episcopal
Boston, MA
Nat Cyc Am Bio csv4

1102. Ames, Blanche Ames
1878–1969
botanical illustrator, inventor, feminist, suffragist, birth control advocate
Massachusetts
Nat Cyc Am Bio v53; Not Am
Wom; Obit File

1103. Daniels, Mabel Wheeler
1878/79–1971
composer, conductor
Boston and Wheeler, MA
Index t Wom; Nat Cyc Am Bio
csv1 and csv6; Not Am Wom
supp v1

1104. Fiske, Gertrude Horsford
born 1879
artist
Massachusetts
Nat Cyc Am Bio csv2

1105. Ring, Barbara Taylor
1879–1941
psychiatrist, hospital administrator, playwright
Massachusetts
Index t Wom; Obit File

1106. Rogers, Edith Nourse
1881–1960
Republican representative to Congress from Massachusetts, sponsor of a bill creating the Women's Army Air Corps, co-author of a bill of rights for World War II veterans, World War I military hospital observer
Massachusetts
Dict Am Bio supp v6; Index t
Wom; Nat Cyc Am Bio v44;
Not Am Wom supp v1; Obit
File

1107. Prouty, Olive (Chapin) Higgins
1882–1974
author, novelist
Unitarian
Massachusetts
Index t Wom; Nat Cyc Am Bio
v57; Obit File

1108. Meredith, Florence Lyndon
1883–1951
physician, medical educator
Massachusetts
Nat Cyc Am Bio v45 and csv1

1109. Brown, Margaret Fitzhugh
1884–1972
artist
Episcopalian
Massachusetts
Nat Cyc Am Bio v57

1110. Bulfinch, Ellen Susan
born 1884
artist
Massachusetts
Dict Am Auth

1111. Ilsley, Marjorie [Louise] Henry
1885–1961
educator
Massachusetts
Nat Cyc Am Bio v52

1112. Magna, Edith Scott
1885–1960
executive of DAR
Congregationalist
Massachusetts
Nat Cyc Am Bio v49

1113. Fairbank, Ruth Eldred
1887–1972
psychiatrist, psychiatric educator
Congregationalist
Massachusetts
Nat Cyc Am Bio v58

1114. Hubbard, Theodora Kimball
1887–1935
landscape architect, city planner
Unitarian
Massachusetts
Nat Cyc Am Bio v28 and csv3

1115. Coolidge, Mary Lowell
1891–1958
philosopher, educator, dean of Wellesley College
Massachusetts
Obit File; Who Who Phil

1116. Eliot, Martha May
1891–1978
pediatrician, public health official, president of the American Health Association, UNICEF member, US Children's Bureau official
Unitarian
Massachusetts
Cur Biog '78; Index t Wom; Nat
Cyc Am Bio v60

1117. Forbes, Esther; Esther Forbes Hoskins
1891–1967
novelist, children's author, colonial historian, Pulitzer Prize winner
Congregationalist
Massachusetts
Index t Wom; Nat Cyc Am Bio
v53; Not Am Wom supp v1;
Obit File

1118. Johnson, Edith Christina
1891–1954
educator
Massachusetts
Nat Cyc Am Bio v41

1119. Curtis, Edith (Goddard) Roelker
1893–1977
author
Episcopalian

New Hampshire; Massachusetts
Nat Cyc Am Bio v60

1120. Stewart, Isabella Hilda
born 1894
educator
Massachusetts
Canadian
Nat Cyc Am Bio csv8

1121. Eager, Helen
1898–1952
drama and film critic
Boston, MA
Obit File

1122. Glueck, Eleonor (Touroff)
1898–1972
research criminologist, Harvard Law School criminologist, pioneer in the study of juvenile delinquency, social worker
New York; Massachusetts
Cur Biog '72; Index t Wom; Nat Cyc Am Bio v57; Not Am Wom supp v1; Obit File

1123. Bunting, Mary Ingraham
born 1910
microbiologist, bacteriologist, educator, president of Radcliffe College
Massachusetts
Index t Wom; Nat Cyc Am Bio csv10

1124. Andrews, Marie Scherer
1914–73
orthopedic nurse, nursing educator
Catholic
Massachusetts
Nat Cyc Am Bio v57

1125. Smith, Constance Elizabeth
1922–70
college educator and administrator
Episcopalian
Massachusetts
Nat Cyc Am Bio

MICHIGAN

1126. Peirson, Lydia Jane (Wheeler)
1802–62
author, poet
Adrian, MI; Pennsylvania
Cyc Am Bio; Dict Am Auth; Dict Am Bio Men Time

1127. Stewart, Electra Maria (Sheldon); Electra Maria Sheldon
born 1817
writer on Michigan history, writer of religious tales for children

Detroit, MI
Cyc Am Bio; Dict Am Auth

1128. Gorton, Cynthia M. R.; Ida Glenwood; The Sweet Singer; The Blind Bard of Michigan
born 1826
poet, author, lecturer
Michigan
blind
Wom Cent

1129. Patterson, Minnie Ward; Zinobar Green
flourished 1860s–90s
poet, author
Michigan
Wom Cent

1130. Benjamin, Anna Smeed
born 1834
temperance worker
Michigan
Wom Cent

1131. Newberry, Helen Parmelee Handy
1835–1912
philanthropist
Presbyterian
Detroit, MI
Nat Cyc Am Bio v41

1132. Whiting, Mary Collins
born 1835
lawyer, businessperson
Michigan
Wom Cent

1133. Banks, Sarah Gertrude
born 1839
physician, surgeon, suffragist
Unitarian
Michigan
Index t Wom; Nat Cyc Am Bio v18

1134. Sunderland, Eliza Jane (Read)
1839–1910
lecturer, author, educator, temperance worker, women's rights worker, philosopher
Universalist
Michigan
Dict Am Bio; Nat Cyc Am Bio v10; Wom Cent

1135. Dudley, Sarah Marie
flourished 1870s–90s
merchant, investor, inventor, architect, designer, builder
Detroit, MI
Wom Cent

1136. Leland, Caroline Weaver
born 1840
philanthropist, educator
Presbyterian
Michigan
Wom Cent

1137. Wood-Allen, Mary
born 1841
physician, sex education author
Ann Arbor, MI
Dict Am Auth

1138. Campbell, Eugenia Steele
born 1843
temperance reformer
Methodist Episcopal
Michigan
Wom Cent

1139. Moots, Cornelia Moore Chillison
born 1843
temperance evangelist, suffragist, women's rights worker
Methodist Episcopal
Michigan
Wom Cent

1140. Thorp, Mandana Coleman
born 1843
Union patriot during the Civil War, pioneer, deputy clerk and register of deeds in northern Michigan, sheep and wool farmer
Michigan
Wom Cent

1141. Cheney, Armilla Amanda
born 1845
Civil War relief worker
Detroit, MI
Wom Cent

1142. Jones, Irma Theoda
born 1845
philanthropist, temperance worker
Lansing, MI
Index t Wom; Wom Cent

1143. McCoy, Mary Eleanora
born 1846
philanthropist
Detroit, MI
Black
Prof Negro Wom v1

1144. Noble, Edna Chaffee
born 1846
educator, elocutionist
Michigan
Index t Wom; Wom Cent

1145. Bartlett, Alice Eloise; Birch Arnold
1848–1920
journalist, poet
Detroit, MI
Dict Am Auth; Index t Wom; Wom Cent

1146. Ives, Alice Emma
flourished 1880s
dramatist, journalist
Detroit, MI
Index t Wom; Wom Cent

1147. Trix, Harriet Phelps
born 1850
suffragist
Swedenborgian
Detroit, MI
Nat Cyc Am Bio v18

1148. Hollister, Lilian
born 1853
temperance worker, suffragist, Methodist Episcopal church worker
Methodist Episcopal
Michigan
Wom Cent

1149. Strickland, Martha
born 1853
lawyer, feminist, orator
Michigan
Wom Cent

1150. Bishop, Ella Matilda Clark
1856–1926
clubwoman
Michigan
Nat Cyc Am Bio v21

1151. Smith, Helen Morton
born 1859
journalist
Michigan
Wom Cent

1152. Stevens, Anna Evans (Shipman)
1859–1939
women's club worker
Detroit, MI
Nat Cyc Am Bio v17 and v32

1153. Gale, Ada Iddings
flourished 1890s
author, educator
Michigan
Wom Cent

1154. Skinner, Henrietta Channing (Dana)
186?–1901
author, novelist
Detroit, MI
Dict Am Auth; Twent Cen Bio Dict Not Am

1155. Starkey, Jennie O.
born 1863
journalist
Detroit, MI
Wom Cent

1156. Hopkins, Florence May
born 1865
librarian
Detroit, MI
Nat Cyc Am Bio v18

1157. Dyar, Clara
born 1869
suffragist, Detroit civic worker

Detroit, MI
Nat Cyc Am Bio csv1

1158. Crowley, Mary Catherine
flourished 1900s
editor, historian, novelist
Detroit, MI
Dict Am Auth; Index t Wom

1159. Wilson, Matilda Rausch
1883–1967
philanthropist, Detroit civic
worker, chairperson of the
board of directors of Fidelity
Bank & Trust, member of the
state board of agriculture, lieutenant governor of Michigan,
Salvation Army worker
Presbyterian
Detroit, MI
Nat Cyc Am Bio v59

**1160. Booth, Ada Pearl Dun-
lap;** Adeline Dunlap
born 1884
actor, World War I nurse
Michigan
Nat Cyc Am Bio v17

1161. Lutes, Della Thompson
died 1942
author, novelist, editor
Michigan
Index t Wom

1162. Macy, Icie Gertrude;
Mrs. Bert Raymon Hoobler
born 1892
chemist
Presbyterian
Michigan
Nat Cyc Am Bio csv8

1163. Wanstrum, Ruth Cecilia
1893–1971
pathologist, medical educator
Episcopalian
Michigan
Nat Cyc Am Bio v57

1164. Lloyd, Alice C.
1894–1950
dean of women of the University
of Michigan, president of the
National Association of Deans
of Women
Michigan
Obit File

**1165. Thompson, Helen Victo-
ria Veale**
born 1897
artist
Christian Scientist
Detroit, MI
Nat Cyc Am Bio csv9

1166. Johnson, Marguerite C.
1902–59
public safety director of Dearborn, Michigan; police commissioner

Dearborn, MI
Obit File

1167. Beeuwkes, Adelia Marie
1910–66
nutritionist, educator
Episcopalian
Michigan
Nat Cyc Am Bio v52

1168. Jones, Clara Stanton
born 1913
librarian, president of the American Library Association
Detroit, MI
Black
Cur Biog '76; Encyc Black Am

1169. Elliott, Daisy
born 1919
Michigan state legislator from
Detroit, civil rights worker
Detroit, MI
Black
Encyc Black Am

1170. Ferguson, Rosetta
born 1920
Michigan state legislator
Michigan
Black
Encyc Black Am

1171. Forche, Caroline
born 1950
poet
Michigan
Dict Lit Bio v5

MINNESOTA

1172. Tiffany, Nina Moore
born 18?
historical author
St. Paul, MN
Dict Am Auth

1173. Hancock, Martha M.
died 1851
missionary to the Sioux people
Minnesota
Am Bio Dict

**1174. Wood, Julia Amanda A.
(Sargent);** Minnie Mary Lee
born 1826
author, postmaster, pioneer, Min-
nesota newspaper editor, Catho-
lic novelist
Catholic
Sauk Rapids, MN
Dict Am Auth; Index t Wom;
Not Am Wom; Wom Cent

1175. Rude, Ellen (Sargent)
born 1838
poet, author, temperance worker,
Worthy Chief Templar of the
Order of Good Templars

Duluth, MN
Dict Am Auth; Index t Wom;
Wom Cent

1176. Walker, Harriet Granger
1841–1917
philanthropist, hospital organizer,
temperance worker, suffragist,
police reformer
Methodist
Minneapolis, MN
Nat Cyc Am Bio v6; Wom Cent

1177. Furber, Aurilla
born 1847
poet, temperance worker
Minnesota
Wom Cent

1178. Bennett, Adelaide George
born 1848
poet, botanist
Minnesota
Wom Cent; Index t Wom

1179. Knight, Sarah (Harrison)
1849–1928
philanthropist, Minneapolis civic
leader, Methodist church worker, hospital founder, patron of
nurse's training
Methodist
Minneapolis, MN
Am Bio New Cyc

**1180. Merriman, Effie (Wood-
ward)**
born 1856
children's writer
Minneapolis, MN
Dict Am Auth

1181. Countryman, Gratia Alta
1866–1953
librarian
Minnesota
Index t Wom; Nat Cyc Am Bio
csv5

1182. Valesh, Eva McDonald
born 1866
printer, journalist, social reformer, feminist, labor leader and
activist
Minneapolis, MN
Index t Wom; Wom Cent

1183. Paige, Mabeth Hurd
born 1875
Minnesota state legislator, lawyer
Presbyterian
Minnesota
Nat Cyc Am Bio csv2

1184. Kempfer, Hannah Jensen
1880–1943
Minnesota state legislator
Minnesota
Not Am Wom

1185. Nute, Grace Lee
born 1895

historian
Minnesota
Read Encyc Am West

**1186. Schuell, Hildred Magda-
lene**
1906–70
speech pathologist
Minnesota
Nat Cyc Am Bio v55

MISSISSIPPI

**1187. Dorsey, Sarah Anne
(Ellis);** Filia Ecclesiae
1829–79
Civil War nurse, author, novelist,
theologian
Mississippi
Cyc Am Bio; Dict Am Auth;
Index t Wom; Nat Cyc Am Bio
v3; Not Am Wom; Twent Cen
Bio Dict Not Am

1188. Granson, Milla
flourished pre-1860s
educator of slaves
Mississippi
Black
Prof Negro Wom v1

1189. Johnston, Maria I.
born 1835
author, newspaper editor, wom-
en's rights worker
Mississippi
Index t Wom; Wom Cent

1190. Smedes, Susan (Dabney)
born 1840
author, missionary to the Sioux
people, educator, historian of
the antebellum South
Mississippi
Cyc Am Bio; Dict Am Auth;
Wom Cent

**1191. MacDowell, Katherine
Sherwood (Bonner);** Sherwood
Bonner
1849–1883/84
author, short story writer, novel-
ist
Holly Springs, MS
Cyc Am Bio; Dict Am Auth; Dict
Am Bio; Index t Wom; Nat Cyc
Am Bio v11; Not Am Wom;
Twent Cen Bio Dict Not Am

1192. Kearney, Belle
1863–1939
temperance reformer, suffragist,
Mississippi state legislator
Mississippi
Nat Cyc Am Bio v11; Not Am
Wom

**1193. Davis, Varina Anne Jef-
ferson "Winnie"**
1864–98

author
Mississippi
Dict Am Auth; Dict Am Bio; Nat Cyc Am Bio v23; Twent Cen Bio Dict Not Am; Wom Cent

1194. Ragsdale, Lulah
born 1866
poet, novelist, actor
Mississippi
Wom Cent

1195. Tucker, Rosa Lee
born 1868
state librarian of Mississippi
Mississippi
Wom Cent

1196. Welty, Eudora Alice
born 1909
novelist
Jackson, MS
Cur Biog '75; Dict Lit Bio v2; Encyc South Hist; Index t Wom; Wom Lit; Wom Lit, More

1197. Smith, Hazel Brannon
born 1914
publisher and editor of Mississippi daily newspapers, Pulitzer Prize winner, civil rights worker
Mississippi
Cur Biog '73

1198. Hamer, Fannie Lou
1917–77
civil rights worker, founder of the Mississippi Freedom Democratic party, worker for Student Nonviolent Coordinating Committee, farmer
Mississippi
Black
Encyc Black Am; Obit File

1199. Spencer, Elizabeth
born 1921/31
novelist
Mississippi
Dict Lit Bio v6; Index t Wom

MISSOURI

1200. Minor, Virginia Louisa
1824–94
Civil War relief worker, suffrage leader, women's rights worker
Missouri
Cyc Am Bio; Dict Am Bio; Encyc South Hist; Nat Cyc Am Bio v25; Not Am Wom; Twent Cen Bio Dict Not Am

1201. Hazard, Rebecca N.
born 1826
philanthropist, suffragist, Civil War relief worker
Missouri
Wom Cent

1202. Ford, Sally Rochester
born 1828
author
St. Louis, MO
Cyc Am Bio; Dict Am Auth; Twent Cen Bio Dict Not Am

1203. Runcie, Constance (Faunt le Roy)
1836–1911
composer, pianist, club leader, poet, children's author, biographer
St. Joseph, MO
Dict Am Auth; Dict Am Bio; Index t Wom; Nat Cyc Am Bio v7; Wom Cent

1204. Stone, Margaret Manson (Barbour)
born 1841
nonfiction writer
St. Louis, MO
Dict Am Auth

1205. Veeder, Emily Elizabeth (Ferris)
1841–post 1890
author, poet, novelist
Pennsylvania; St. Louis, MO
Dict Am Auth; Wom Cent

1206. Henderson, Mary Foote
born 1842/46
suffragist, home economist, cooking and nutrition writer
St. Louis, MO
Dict Am Auth; Twent Cen Bio Dict Not Am

1207. Knox, Adeline (Trafton)
born 1845
author, novelist
St. Louis, MO
Dict Am Auth; Index t Wom; Wom Cent

1208. Kerens, Frances Jones
1848–1914
patron of Catholicism, philanthropist
St. Louis, MO
Nat Cyc Am Bio v31

1209. Moore, Susanne Bandegrift
born 1848
editor and publisher
Missouri
Wom Cent

1210. Ingalls, Eliza B.
flourished 1880s
temperance worker
Missouri
Wom Cent

1211. Chopin, Kate O'Flaherty
1851–1904
novelist, short story writer
St. Louis, MO
Dict Am Auth; Cyc Am Bio v25

1212. Yates, Josephine Silone; R. K. Potter
1852–1912
educator, author
Missouri
Black
Index t Wom; Negro Alman; Prof Negro Wom v1

1213. Williams, Alice
born 1853
temperance reformer
Missouri
Wom Cent

1214. Fisher, Mary
born 1858
textbook author, educator, novelist
Kansas City, MO
Dict Am Auth; Twent Cen Bio Dict Not Am

1215. Dussuchal, Eugenie
born 1860
musical educator
St. Louis, MO
Wom Cent

1216. Orff, Annie L. Y.
flourished 1890s
editor, publisher, women's travel expert
St. Louis, MO
Wom Cent

1217. Stevens, Susan Sheppard (Pierce)
born 1862
novelist
St. Louis, MO
Dict Am Auth

1218. Baxter, Annie White
born 1864
county clerk of court, politician
Missouri
Twent Cen Bio Dict Not Am; Wom Cent

1219. Murphy, Martha Alice
1871–1909
modern artist
Missouri
Nat Cyc Am Bio v55

1220. Graham, Helen Tredway
1890–1971
biochemist, air pollution control worker
St. Louis, MO
Nat Cyc Am Bio v56

1221. Wilson, Margaret Berenice Bush
born 1919
lawyer, civic leader, chairperson of the national board of the NAACP
St. Louis, MO
Black
Cur Biog '75; Encyc Black Am

MONTANA

1222. Barbour, A. (Maynard)
born 18?
novelist
Helena, MT
Dict Am Auth

1223. Cummins, Mary Stuart
born 1854
educator, temperance worker
Presbyterian
Montana
Wom Cent

1224. Knowles, Ella L.
born 1870
lawyer, notary public, candidate for attorney general of Montana on the Alliance ticket
Montana
Index t Wom; Wom Cent

NEBRASKA

1225. Huntley, Mary Sutton
born 1832
Christian religious worker
Nebraska
Wom Cent

1226. Shelley, Mary Jane
born 1832
temperance worker, missionary worker
Methodist
Nebraska
Wom Cent

1227. Clark, Frances P.
born 1836
philanthropist, temperance worker
Omaha, NE
Wom Cent

1228. Langworthy, Elizabeth
born 1837
philanthropist; civic worker in Monticello, Iowa, and Seward, Nebraska; clubwoman
Monticello, IA; Seward, NE
Index t Wom; Wom Cent

1229. Wilson, Zara A.
born 1840
lawyer, suffragist, feminist, temperance worker, missionary worker
Methodist Episcopal
Nebraska
Wom Cent

1230. Holmes, Jennie Florella
born 1842
temperance worker, suffragist, women's rights worker
Nebraska
Wom Cent

1231. Spurlock, Isabella Smiley Davis
born 1843
philanthropist, temperance worker, Mormon women's welfare worker
Nebraska
Wom Cent

1232. Todd, Minnie J. Terrell
born 1844
suffragist
Nebraska
Wom Cent

1233. Moore, Sarah Wool
born 1846
artist, journalist
Nebraska
Index t Wom; Wom Cent

1234. Wheelock, Dora V.
born 1847
temperance worker, suffragist
Nebraska
Wom Cent

1235. Bittenbender, Ada Matilda Cole
1848–1925
suffragist, temperance leader, political reformer, lawyer admitted to practice before the Supreme Court
Presbyterian
Nebraska
Not Am Wom; Wom Cent

1236. Hayward, Mary E. Smith
born 1849
oil and mercantile businessperson, suffragist
Nebraska
Wom Cent

1237. Iliohan, Henrica
born 1850
suffragist
Nebraska
Dutch
Wom Cent

1238. Renfrew, Carrie
flourished 1880s–90s
poet, biographer
Nebraska
Wom Cent

1239. Townsley, Frances Eleanor
born 1850
Baptist minister, evangelist, temperance worker
Baptist
Nebraska
Wom Cent

1240. Lankton, Freeda M.
born 1852
physician

Nebraska
Wom Cent

1241. Wakeman, Antoinette van Hoesen
1854–post 1890
journalist, novelist
Illinois; Hastings, NE
Dict Am Auth; Wom Cent

1242. Butin, Mary Ryerson
born 1857
physician, temperance worker
Nebraska
Wom Cent

1243. Raymond, Carrie Isabelle Rice
born 1857
musician, educator, organist, music director, conductor
Nebraska
Wom Cent

1244. Ross, Virginia Evelyn (Conlee)
born 1857
author, pioneer
Nebraska
Wom Cent

1245. Phillips, L. Vance
born 1858
artist
Nebraska
Wom Cent

1246. Keysor, Jennie Ellis
born 1860
educator
Omaha, NE
Wom Cent

1247. Mumaugh, Frances Miller
born 1860
artist
Nebraska
Wom Cent

1248. Willard, Allie C.
born 1860
journalist, newspaper publisher and editor, businessperson, clerk of the Nebraska Senate
Nebraska
Wom Cent

1249. Woodruff, Libbie L.
born 1860
journalist
Nebraska
Wom Cent

1250. Pound, Louise
1872–1958
university educator, writer on literature, folklorist, tennis player, bicyclist, golfer

Nebraska
Nat Cyc Am Bio v45, csv2, and csv5; Not Am Wom supp v1; Obit File

1251. Cather, Willa Sibert
1873/74–1944
western novelist
Episcopalian
Nebraska
Dict Am Bio supp v4; Dict Lit Bio v9; Dict Mex Am Hist; Index t Wom; Nat Cyc Am Bio v44 and csv1; Not Am Wom; Obit File; Read Encyc Am West; Wom Lit; Wom Lit, More

1252. Abbott, Edith
1876–1957
social reformer, social work educator, author
Nebraska
Dict Am Bio supp v6; Index t Wom; Nat Cyc Am Bio csv3; Not Am Wom; Obit File

1253. Aldrich, Bess Genevra Streeter
1881–1954
novelist, short story writer
Methodist
Nebraska
Dict Am Bio; Index t Wom; Nat Cyc Am Bio v45 and csv8, Obit File

1254. Sandoz, Marie Suzette "Mari"
1896/1901–1966
author, novelist, historian
Nebraska
Dict Lit Bio v9; Index t Wom; Not Am Wom supp v1; Read Encyc Am West; Wom Lit, More

NEVADA

1255. Abbott, Emma
1849/50–1891
opera singer
Nevada
Dict Am Bio; Index t Wom; Not Am Wom; Twent Cen Bio Dict Not Am; Wom Cent

1256. Wier, Jeanne Elizabeth
1870–1950
historian of Nevada and the state's Native Americans, educator, suffragist
Nevada
Nat Cyc Am Bio v51 and csv1; Obit File; Read Encyc Am West

1257. Martin, Anna Henrietta
1875–1951

suffragist, feminist, author, essayist, social critic, pacifist, politician
Nevada
Dict Am Bio supp v5; Not Am Wom supp v1; Read Encyc Am West

NEW ENGLAND

1258. Emerson, Mary Moody
1774–1863
New England intellectual
New England
Not Am Wom

1259. Cate, Eliza Jane
1812–84
author on New England
New England
Dict Am Auth

1260. Earle, Alice Morse
1851/53–1911
author, social and domestic historian of colonial New England, writer on history
New England
Dict Am Auth; Dict Am Bio; Index t Wom; Nat Cyc Am Bio v13; Not Am Wom; Twent Cen Bio Dict Not Am

1261. Carpenter, Fanny Hallock (Rouse)
flourished 1896–1900s
lawyer, Sorosis member
New England
Nat Cyc Am Bio v14

NEW HAMPSHIRE

1262. Tenney, Tabitha (Gilman)
1762–1837
satirical novelist
Exeter, NH
Am Bio Dict; Cyc Am Bio; Dict Am Auth; Dict Am Bio; Not Am Wom

1263. Fiske, Catharine
1776–1837
educator, scientist, farmer
New Hampshire
Am Bio Dict; Index t Wom

1264. Farley, Harriet
1813/17–1907
millworker, writer on women in the textile mills, children's author, editor
New Hampshire
Cyc Am Bio; Dict Am Auth; Dict Am Bio; Dict Am Bio Men Time; Nat Cyc Am Bio v11; Not Am Wom

1265. Eames, Jane Anthony
1816–94
author, traveler
New Hampshire; Massachusetts
Cyc Am Bio; Dict Am Auth; Index t Wom; Twent Cen Bio Dict Not Am

1266. Eddy, Mary Morse (Baker) (Glover) (Patterson)
1821/27–1910
founder of Christian Science
Christian Scientist
Concord, NH
Dict Am Auth; Dict Am Rel Bio; Index t Wom; Nat Cyc Am Bio v3; Not Am Wom; Twent Cen Bio Dict Not Am

1267. Filley, Mary A. Powers
born 1821
suffragist, dairy stock farmer
New Hampshire
Wom Cent

1268. Worthen, Augusta Harvey
born 1823
educator, author, historian of New Hampshire
New Hampshire
Wom Cent

1269. Harris, Amanda Bartlett
born 1824
author, children's author, magazine writer, religious author
Warner, NH
Dict Am Auth; Twent Cen Bio Dict Not Am

1270. Kimball, Harriet MacEwen
born 1824/34
religious poet
Portsmouth, NH
Cyc Am Bio; Dict Am Auth; Nat Cyc Am Bio v11; Wom Cent

1271. Patton, Abigail Jemima; Abby Hutchinson
1829–92
alto singer, composer, poet, social reformer, abolitionist, suffragist, hymn writer, feminist
New York; New Hampshire
Nat Cyc Am Bio v10; Wom Cent; Not Am Wom; Index t Wom

1272. Thaxter, Celia (Laighton)
1835/36–1894
poet, author
New Hampshire
Cyc Am Bio; Dict Am Auth; Dict Am Bio; Index t Wom; Nat Cyc Am Bio v1; Not Am Wom; Twent Cen Bio Dict Not Am; Wom Cent

1273. Sanborn, Katharine Abbott "Kate"
1839–1917

miscellaneous author, educator, lecturer, essayist, literary professor, agriculturist
New Hampshire
Cyc Am Bio; Dict Am Auth; Dict Am Bio; Index t Wom; Nat Cyc Am Bio v9; Twent Cen Bio Dict Not Am

1274. Ricker, Marilla Marks Young
1840–1920
lawyer, suffragist, prison reformer, politician, author, political writer
New Hampshire
Index t Wom; Nat Cyc Am Bio v17; Not Am Wom; Wom Cent

1275. Robinson, Annie Douglass Green; Marian Douglas
born 1842
poet, author, children's poet
Briston, NH
Cyc Am Bio; Dict Am Auth; Nat Cyc Am Bio v3

1276. Fletcher, Lisa Anne
born 1844
poet, flower painter
New Hampshire
Wom Cent

1277. Greene, Isabella Catherine (Colton)
born 1844
novelist, children's author
Nashua, NH
Dict Am Auth

1278. Knox, Janette Hill
born 1845
temperance reformer
New Hampshire
Wom Cent

1279. Mitchell, Nellie Brown
1845?–1924
singer, music educator
New Hampshire
Black
Index t Wom; Prof Negro Wom v1

1280. Darling, Alice O.
flourished 1880s
poet
New Hampshire
Wom Cent

1281. Durrell, Irene Clark
born 1852
educator
Methodist
New Hampshire
Wom Cent

1282. Stearns, Nellie George
born 1855
artist
New Hampshire
Wom Cent

1283. Cummings, Alma Carrie
born 1857
journalist, newspaper editor and publisher
New Hampshire
Wom Cent

1284. MacDowell, Marian Griswold Nevins
1857–1956/57
patron of music, musician, pianist, founder of the MacDowell Artists Colony, lecturer
New Hampshire
Index t Wom; Not Am Wom supp v1; Obit File

1285. Schofield, Mary Lyon Cheney
1858–1943
philanthropist
New Hampshire
Nat Cyc Am Bio v36

1286. Blair, Eliza Nelson
born 1859
novelist
New Hampshire
Dict Am Auth

1287. Perley, Mary Elizabeth
born 1863
educator, poet
New Hampshire
Wom Cent

1288. Sidis, Sarah
1873–1959
psychiatrist, founder of the Sidis Institute for Abnormal Psychiatry
Portsmouth, NH
Russian
Obit File

1289. Curtis, Edith (Goddard) Roelker
1893–1977
author
Episcopalian
New Hampshire; Massachusetts
Nat Cyc Am Bio v60

1290. Yates, Elizabeth; Mrs. William McGreal
born 1905
author
New Hampshire
Index t Wom; Nat Cyc Am Bio csv9

NEW JERSEY

1291. Pole, Elizabeth; Elizabeth Poole
1588–1654
pioneer; founder of the town of Taunton, New Jersey
Taunton, NJ; Massachusetts

English
Am Bio Dict; Index t Wom; Nat Cyc Am Bio v4

1292. Estaugh, Elizabeth Haddon
1680/83–1762
colonial proprietor; founder of Haddonfield, New Jersey; pioneer
Quaker
New Jersey
Cyc Am Bio; Dict Am Bio; Index t Wom; Nat Cyc Am Bio v17; Not Am Wom

1293. Wright, Patience Lovell
1725–1785/86
wax modeler, spy during American Revolution
Quaker
New Jersey
Dict Am Bio; Dict Nat Bio; Index t Wom; Nat Cyc Am Bio v8; Not Am Wom; Who Who Dur Am Rev

1294. Bradford, Susan
1764–1854
philanthropist
Burlington, NJ
Index t Wom

1295. Ricord, Elizabeth (Stryker)
1788–1865
educator, poet
New York; New Jersey
Cyc Am Bio; Dict Am Auth; Dict Am Bio Men Time

1296. Tuthill, Louisa Cornelia Caroline (Huggins)
1798/99–1879
author, popular writer of moral tales for children
Princeton, NJ
Cyc Am Bio; Dict Am Auth; Dict Am Bio Men Time; Index t Wom; Not Am Wom

1297. Gates, Ellen M. (Huntington)
born 18?
poet
East Orange, NJ
Dict Am Auth

1298. Mason, Agnes Louisa (Carter)
born 18?
poet
Montclair, NJ
Dict Am Auth

1299. Nitsch, Helen Alice (Matthews); Catherine Owen
18?–1889
domestic scientist, writer on domestic science
Plainfield, NJ

Dict Am Auth

1300. Wood, (Johnston), Mrs.
flourished nineteenth century
missionary to Singapore
Morristown, NJ
Am Bio Dict

1301. Kinney, Elizabeth Clementine (Dodge) (Stedman)
1810–89
poet, essayist
Newark, NJ
Cyc Am Bio; Dict Am Auth; Dict Am Bio; Dict Am Bio Men Time; Nat Cyc Am Bio v13

1302. Tillotson, Mary Ella (Tillotson)
1816–190?
writer and lecturer on hygiene, poet
Vineland, NJ
Dict Am Auth

1303. Howarth, Ellen Clementine (Doran)
1827–99
poet
Trenton, NJ
Dict Am Auth; Nat Cyc Am Bio v7

1304. Hussey, Cornelia Collins
born 1827
philanthropist, suffragist
New Jersey
Wom Cent

1305. Treat, Mary Lua Adelia (Davis) (Allen)
born 1830/35
scientific author, naturalist
Vineland, NJ
Dict Am Auth; Index t Wom

1306. Douglas, Amanda Minnie
1831/38–1916
short story writer, novelist, children's author
Newark, NJ
Cyc Am Bio; Dict Am Auth; Dict Am Bio; Index t Wom; Twent Cen Bio Dict Not Am; Wom Cent

1307. Poole, Hester Martha (Hunt)
born 1833/43
author, poet, writer on social and domestic issues, art critic, artist, women's rights worker, Sorosis member
Metuchen, NJ
Dict Am Auth; Nat Cyc Am Bio v11; Wom Cent

1308. Meech, Jeannette du Bois
born 1835

evangelist, missionary worker, Baptist preacher, temperance worker, industrial educator of women
Baptist
New Jersey
Index t Wom; Wom Cent

1309. Cushing, Juliet Clannon
1845–1934
welfare worker
Presbyterian
New Jersey
Nat Cyc Am Bio v28

1310. Hall, Florence Marion Howe
1845–1922
author, essayist, writer on etiquette, lecturer, suffragist
Unitarian
Plainfield, NJ
Dict Am Auth; Dict Am Bio; Nat Cyc Am Bio v19

1311. Bourne, Emma
born 1846
temperance worker
Newark, NJ
Wom Cent

1312. Schulte, Mary Jemima (McColl)
born 1847
poet
Jersey City, NJ
Dict Am Auth

1313. Conklin, Viola A. (Peckham)
born 1849
historical writer
Plainfield, NJ
Dict Am Auth

1314. Cutting, Mary Stewart (Doubleday)
1851–1924
fiction writer
East Orange, NJ
Dict Am Auth; Index t Wom

1315. Dunlap, Mary J.
born 1853
physician
New Jersey
Wom Cent

1316. Herrick, Christine Terhune
1859–1944
writer on household affairs, home economist, domestic scientist, Sorosis member
New York, NY; New Jersey
Dict Am Auth; Index t Wom; Nat Cyc Am Bio v8; Not Am Wom; Wom Cent

1317. Wittpenn, Caroline Bayard Stevens
1859–1932

welfare worker
New Jersey
Not Am Wom

1318. Wells, Carolyn
1862/69–1942
author, humorist, poet, librarian
Rahway, NJ
Dict Am Auth; Index t Wom; Nat Cyc Am Bio v13; Not Am Wom; Twent Cen Bio Dict Not Am

1319. Fuld, Carrie Bamberger Frank
1864–1944
philanthropist, cofounder of the Institute for Advanced Study at Princeton University
Princeton, NJ
Not Am Wom

1320. Thomas, Edith (Carpenter)
circa 1864–1901
novelist, biographer
Millville, NJ
Dict Am Auth

1321. Spurr, Elizabeth Albright
1870–1934
rubber manufacturer, philanthropist
Newark, NJ
Nat Cyc Am Bio v27

1322. Flexner, Anne Crawford
1874–1955
playwright, director of the Institute for Advanced Studies at Princeton University
Princeton, NJ
Index t Wom; Obit File

1323. Norton, Mary Teresa Hopkins
1875–1959
representative to Congress from New Jersey, Labor Department aide, first woman Democrat elected to Congress
New Jersey
Dict Am Bio supp v6; Index t Wom; Nat Cyc Am Bio v45; Not Am Wom supp v1; Obit File

1324. Douglass, Mabel Smith
1877–1933
founder and dean of the New Jersey College for Women (Douglass College)
New Jersey
Not Am Wom

1325. Glentworth, Marguerite Linton
born 1881
novelist
Newark, NJ
Dict Am Auth

welfare worker
New Jersey
Not Am Wom

1326. Barus, Jane Garey
1892–1977
suffragist; political activist; prison reformer; Montclair, New Jersey, civic worker; antinuclear activist; anti–Vietnam war worker
Unitarian
Montclair, NJ
Nat Cyc Am Bio v60

1327. Williams, Madaline A.
born 1895
register of deeds in Essex County, New Jersey; politician; Democratic party worker
New Jersey
Prof Negro Wom v2

1328. Barber, Muriel Virginia (Kozlay)
1904–71
artist
Presbyterian
New Jersey
Nat Cyc Am Bio v57

1329. Roebling, Mary Gindhart
born 1905/06
banker
Episcopalian
Trenton, NJ
Index t Wom; Nat Cyc Am Bio csv9

1330. Fenwick, Millicent Vernon (Hammond)
born 1910
representative to Congress from New Jersey
New Jersey
Cur Biog '77

1331. Drewry, Cecelia Hodges
flourished 1950s–60s
educator
New Jersey
Black
Prof Negro Wom v2

NEW MEXICO

1332. Luhan, Mabel Dodge
1879–1962
author, patron, salon host
New Mexico
Index t Wom; Not Am Wom supp v1; Read Encyc Am West

1333. Simms, Ruth Hanna McCormick
1880–1944
representative to Congress from Illinois, political leader, Republican National Committee member from New Mexico, dairy farmer
Quaker

Illinois; New Mexico
Dict Am Bio supp v3; Index t
Wom; Nat Cyc Am Bio v34;
Not Am Wom; Obit File

**1334. Martinez, Maria Monto-
ya**
born 1881/87
ceramicist
New Mexico
Native American (Pueblo-San Ildefonso)
Ind Today; Read Encyc Am West

1335. Lusk, Georgia Lee Witt
1893–1971
educator, Democratic representa-
tive to Congress from New
Mexico
New Mexico
Cur Biog '71; Index t Wom; Not
Am Wom supp v1

NEW YORK

**1336. Bogardus, Annetje
Jansen;** Annekke Jans
circa 1600–circa 1663
settler of New Amsterdam
New York
Dutch
Index t Wom; Nat Cyc Am Bio
v9

1337. Moody, Deborah, Lady
died 1659?
founder of a colony on Long
Island, politician
Long Island, NY
Index t Wom; Not Am Wom

**1338. Schuyler, Margaretta
Schuyler**
1701–82
colonial administrator, Tory politician with military influence
New York
Encyc South Hist; Index t Wom

1339. Farquhar, Jane
1724–60
botanist
New York
Am Bio Dict

1340. Heck, Barbara Ruckle;
The Mother of American
Methodism
1734/44–1804
missionary, religious founder
Methodist
New York
Irish
Cyc Am Bio; Dict Am Bio; Index
t Wom; Nat Cyc Am Bio v13;
Not Am Wom; Who Who Dur
Am Rev

1341. Lee, Ann; Ann Lee
Standerin; Mother Ann
1736–84
founder of the American Society
of Shakers
Shaker
New York
English
Am Bio Dict; Cyc Am Bio; Dict
Am Bio; Dict Am Bio Men
Time; Dict Am Rel Bio; Dict
Nat Bio; Index t Wom; Nat Cyc
Am Bio v5; Not Am Wom; Our
Count; Twent Cen Bio Dict Not
Am; Who Who Dur Am Rev

1342. Gedney, Rachel
1741–1848
last of the Mohegan people
New York
Native American (Mohegan)
Am Bio Dict

**1343. Graham, Isabella Mar-
shall**
1742–1814/15
educator, charity worker, philan-
thropist
New York
Scottish
Am Bio Dict; Cyc Am Bio; Dict
Am Bio; Dict Am Bio Men
Time; Index t Wom; Nat Cyc
Am Bio v4; Not Am Wom; Our
Count; Who Who Dur Am Rev

**1344. Jemison, Mary Dehe-
wamis;** White Woman of the
Genessee
1742/43–1833
pioneer
New York
English
Index t Wom; Who Who Dur Am
Rev

1345. Ferguson, Catherine
circa 1749–1854
religious and welfare worker,
baker
New York
Black
Index t Wom; Our Count

**1346. Bleecker, Ann Eliza
(Schuyler)**
1752–83
author, poet
New York, NY
Am Bio Dict; Appl Cyc Am Bio;
Cyc Am Bio; Dict Am Auth;
Dict Am Bio; Dict Am Bio Men
Time; Index t Wom; Nat Cyc
Am Bio v8; Not Am Wom;
Twent Cen Bio Dict Not Am;
Wom Lit, More

1347. Wilkinson, Jemima
1752/53–1819/21
evangelist, religious leader, founder of a pioneer community in
western New York

New York
Am Bio Dict; Dict Am Bio; Dict
Am Bio Men Time; Dict Am
Rel Bio; Index t Wom; Nat Cyc
Am Bio v1; Not Am Wom

1348. Willard, Emma C. (Hart)
1787–1870/76
educator, textbook writer, poet
Troy, NY
Cyc Am Bio; Dict Am Auth; Dict
Am Bio; Dict Am Bio Men
Time; Index t Wom; Nat Cyc
Am Bio v1; Not Am Wom;
Twent Cen Bio Dict Not Am;
Wom Cent

**1349. Ricord, Elizabeth (Stryk-
er)**
1788–1865
educator, poet
New York; New Jersey
Cyc Am Bio; Dict Am Auth; Dict
Am Bio Men Time

**1350. Beecher, Catherine Es-
ther**
1800–78
educator of women, education
writer, social reformer, poet
Episcopalian
New York
Appl Cyc Am Bio; Cyc Am Bio;
Dict Am Bio; Dict Am Bio Men
Time; Dict Lit Bio v1; Index t
Wom; Nat Cyc Am Bio v3; Not
Am Wom; Twent Cen Bio Dict
Not Am; Wom Cent

**1351. Brine, Mary Dow (Nort-
ham)**
born 18?
children's poet
New York, NY
Dict Am Auth

1352. Colton, Julia M.
born 18?
historical writer
Brooklyn, NY
Dict Am Auth

1353. Going, Ellen Maud; E.
M. Hardinge
born 18?
nature writer
New York
Dict Am Auth

1354. Guerber, Helen Adeline
born 18?
educator, textbook writer, historical author
Nyack, NY
Dict Am Auth

1355. Hall, Violette
born 18?
novelist
Catskill Mountains, NY
Dict Am Auth

**1356. Hutchinson, Ellen MacK-
ay**
born 18?
literary journalist
New York, NY
Dict Am Auth

1357. Lounsberry, Allice
born 18?
botanist, writer on botany
New York
Dict Am Auth

1358. MacKubin, Ellen
born 18?
novelist
New York
Dict Am Auth

1359. McCracken, Elizabeth
born 18?
journalist
New York, NY
Dict Am Auth

1360. Merington, Marguerite
born 18?
playwright
New York, NY
Dict Am Auth

**1361. Moore, Susan Teakle
(Smith)**
born 18?
novelist
Brooklyn, NY
Dict Am Auth

**1362. Burgess, N. M. Hall,
Mrs.**
died 1851
missionary to Native Americans
on the Allegheny reservation
Allegheny, NY
Am Bio Dict

**1363. Kirkland, Caroline Matil-
da (Stansbury)**
1801–64
miscellaneous writer, editor, jour-
nalist, writer on pioneering
New York, NY
Cyc Am Bio; Dict Am Auth; Dict
Am Bio; Dict Am Bio Men
Time; Dict Lit Bio v3; Index t
Wom; Nat Cyc Am Bio v5; Not
Am Wom; Twent Cen Bio Dict
Not Am

1364. Case, Mary
died 1852
magazine writer
Quaker
New York
Am Bio Dict

1365. McIntosh, Maria Jane;
Aunt Kitty
1803–78
author, children's author, novelist

New York
Cyc Am Bio; Dict Am Auth; Dict Am Bio Men Time; Index t Wom; Nat Cyc Am Bio v6; Not Am Wom; Twent Cen Bio Dict Not Am

1366. Smith, Sarah Lanman Huntington
1803–36
missionary to the Mohegan people at Mohegan, New York; missionary to Syria
New York
Am Bio Dict; Index t Wom

1367. Martin, Sarah Towne (Smith); Sarah Martyn
1805–79
historian, religious and historical writer for children, editor, abolitionist, temperance worker
New York, NY
Cyc Am Bio; Dict Am Auth; Dict Am Bio; Twent Cen Bio Dict Not Am

1368. Bogart, Elizabeth; Estelle
1806–18?
poet
New York, NY
Cyc Am Bio; Dict Am Auth; Dict Am Bio Men Time; Wom Lit, More

1369. Dwight, Mary Ann
1806–58
textbook author, writer on art, artist
New York, NY
Cyc Am Bio; Dict Am Auth; Dict Am Bio Men Time

1370. Embury, Emma Catherine (Manly)
1806–63
author, poet, writer on women's education
Brooklyn, NY
Cyc Am Bio; Dict Am Auth; Dict Am Bio; Dict Am Bio Men Time; Index t Wom; Nat Cyc Am Bio v9

1371. Palmer, Phoebe Worrall
1807–74
social reformer, religious writer, Methodist leader, Wesleyan evangelist
Wesleyan
New York, NY
Cyc Am Bio; Dict Am Auth; Dict Am Rel Bio; Index t Wom; Not Am Wom

1372. Davidson, Lucretia Maria
1808–1825/38
poet

New York
Am Bio Dict; Cyc Am Bio; Dict Am Auth; Dict Am Bio; Dict Am Bio Men Time; Index t Wom; Nat Cyc Am Bio v7; Our Count; Twent Cen Bio Dict Not Am; Wom Lit, More

1373. Wright, Laura Marie Sheldon
1809–86
missionary to the Seneca people in western New York
New York
Not Am Wom

1374. Doolittle, Mary Antoinette
1810–86
lecturer on religious subjects, Shaker eldress, author
Shaker
New York
Cyc Am Bio

1375. Sleight, Mary Breck
flourished 1840s–90s
short story writer
Sag Harbor, NY
Dict Am Auth; Twent Cen Bio Dict Not Am

1376. Stephens, Anna Sophia (Winterbotham); Jonathan Slick
1810/13–1886
author, poet, novelist, serial fiction writer, editor
New York, NY
Cyc Am Bio; Dict Am Auth; Dict Am Bio; Dict Am Bio Men Time; Dict Lit Bio v8; Index t Wom; Nat Cyc Am Bio v10; Not Am Wom; Twent Cen Bio Dict Not Am; Wom Lit, More

1377. Whitcher, Frances Miriam (Berry); Widow Bedott
1811/14–1857/67
author, humorist, caricaturist
New York
Cyc Am Bio; Dict Am Auth; Dict Am Bio; Index t Wom; Nat Cyc Am Bio v6; Not Am Wom; Twent Cen Bio Dict Not Am

1378. Wells, Charlotte Fowler
1814–1901
phrenologist, patron of women's medical education, educator, publisher, lecturer, businessperson
New York
Cyc Am Bio; Index t Wom; Not Am Wom; Wom Cent

1379. Botta, Anne Charlotte Lynch
1815/20–1891
author, literary host, educator, poet

New York
Cyc Am Bio; Dict Am Auth; Dict Am Bio; Dict Am Bio Men Time; Dict Lit Bio v3; Nat Cyc Am Bio v7; Not Am Wom; Twent Cen Bio Dict Not Am; Wom Cent

1380. Farnham, Eliza Woodson (Burhans)
1815–64
prison reformer, author, lecturer, feminist, suffragist, philanthropist
New York; California
Cyc Am Bio; Dict Am Auth; Dict Am Bio; Dict Am Bio Men Time; Index t Wom; Nat Cyc Am Bio v4; Not Am Wom; Twent Cen Bio Dict Not Am

1381. Stebbins, Emma
1815–82
painter, sculptor, biographer of Charlotte Cushman
New York
Cyc Am Bio; Dict Am Auth; Index t Wom; Nat Cyc Am Bio v8; Not Am Wom; Twent Cen Bio Dict Not Am

1382. Hooper, Lucy
1816–41
poet
Brooklyn, NY
Am Bio Dict; Cyc Am Bio; Dict Am Bio Men Time; Index t Wom

1383. de Kroyft, Sarah Susan Helen (Aldrich)
1818–1915
author, lecturer
New York
blind
Cyc Am Bio; Dict Am Auth; Index t Wom; Nat Cyc Am Bio v11

1384. Warner, Susan Bogart; Elizabeth Wetherell
1818/19–1885
author, novelist, religious writer
Highland Falls, NY
Cyc Am Bio; Dict Am Auth; Dict Am Bio; Index t Wom; Nat Cyc Am Bio v5; Not Am Wom; Twent Cen Bio Dict Not Am; Wom Lit; Wom Lit, More

1385. Cary, Alice
1820–71
poet, novelist
Universalist
New York; Ohio
Cyc Am Bio; Dict Am Auth; Dict Am Bio; Dict Am Bio Men Time; Index t Wom; Nat Cyc Am Bio v1; Not Am Wom; Twent Cen Bio Dict Not Am; Wom Cent; Wom Lit, More

1386. van Allstyne, Frances J[ane] (Crosby) "Fanny"
born 1820
hymn writer, poet, songwriter
New York, NY
Dict Am Auth; Nat Cyc Am Bio v7; Twent Cen Bio Dict Not Am

1387. Morse, Rebecca A.; Ruth Moza; R. A. Kidder; R. A. K.
born 1821
clubwoman, Sorosis member, suffragist, patron of art, abolitionist, author
New York
Index t Wom; Wom Cent

1388. Barrow, Frances Elizabeth (Mease); Aunt Fanny
1822–94
children's author
New York, NY
Appl Cyc Am Bio; Dict Am Auth; Index t Wom; Nat Cyc Am Bio v4; Twent Cen Bio Dict Not Am; Wom Cent

1389. Willard, Cordelia Young
born 1822
missionary worker
Methodist Episcopal
New York
Wom Cent

1390. Berard, Augusta Blanche
1824–1901
writer on the history of West Point, history text author, historian
West Point, NY
Appl Cyc Am Bio; Cyc Am Bio; Dict Am Auth

1391. Lewis, Estelle Anna Blanche (Robinson); Stella
1824–80
author, dramatist, poet
Brooklyn, NY
Cyc Am Bio; Dict Am Auth; Dict Am Bio; Dict Am Bio Men Time; Index t Wom; Nat Cyc Am Bio v10

1392. Chesebro, Caroline; Chesebrough, Caroline
1825/28–1873
short story writer, novelist, college educator
New York
Cyc Am Bio; Dict Am Auth; Dict Am Bio; Dict Am Bio Men Time; Nat Cyc Am Bio v22; Twent Cen Bio Dict Not Am

1393. Holmes, Mary Jane (Hawes)
1825–1902/07
writer of sentimental novels

New York
Cyc Am Bio; Dict Am Auth; Dict Am Bio; Index t Wom; Nat Cyc Am Bio v8; Not Am Wom; Wom Cent; Wom Lit, More

1394. Johnson, Laura Winthrop
1825–18?
poet, miscellaneous writer
New York, NY
Dict Am Auth

1395. Olmstead, Elizabeth Martha
born 1825
poet
New York
Index t Wom; Wom Cent

1396. Richmond, Euphemia Johnson (Guernsey)
born 1825
fiction author, temperance advocate
Upton, NY
Dict Am Auth; Nat Cyc Am Bio v4; Wom Cent

1397. Ford, Emily Ellsworth (Fowler)
1826–93
author, poet
Brooklyn, NY
Dict Am Auth; Nat Cyc Am Bio v13

1398. Griswold, Frances Irene (Burge); F. Burge Smith
1826–1900
author, religious writer for children
Brooklyn, NY
Dict Am Auth; Wom Cent

1399. Lamb, Martha Joanna Read (Nash)
1826/29–1893
author, children's author, novelist, New York historian, editor
New York
Cyc Am Bio; Dict Am Auth; Dict Am Bio; Index t Wom; Nat Cyc Am Bio v1; Not Am Wom; Twent Cen Bio Dict Not Am; Wom Cent

1400. Holcombe, Elizabeth J.
born 1827
physician
New York
Wom Cent

1401. Howland, Emily
1827–1929
educator, educator of Blacks, abolitionist, suffragist, pacifist, temperance worker, philanthropist
Quaker
New York
Dict Am Bio; Nat Cyc Am Bio v25; Not Am Wom; Wom Cent

1402. Taylor, Mary Cecelia
1827–66
actor, opera singer
New York
Cyc Am Bio

1403. Wheeler, Candace (Thurber)
1827–1923
pioneer in American textile design, interior decorator, artist, needleworker, writer on artistic technique, fairy tale writer
New York, NY
Dict Am Auth; Index t Wom; Not Am Wom

1404. Goff, Harriet Newell (Kneeland)
born 1828
temperance reformer, author, suffragist, women's prison reformer, essayist
Brooklyn, NY
Dict Am Auth; Wom Cent

1405. Sturges, Mary Jane (Upshur) (Stith); Fanny Fielding
born 1828
novelist, poet
New York, NY
Cyc Am Bio; Dict Am Auth

1406. Wolfe, Catharine Lorillard
1828–87
philanthropist, patron of the Metropolitan Museum of Art, art collector
New York
Cyc Am Bio; Dict Am Bio; Index t Wom; Nat Cyc Am Bio v10; Not Am Wom; Wom Cent

1407. Oakey, Emily Sullivan
1829–83
author, poet, educator
Albany, NY
Cyc Am Bio; Dict Am Auth

1408. Patton, Abigail Jemima; Abby Hutchinson
1829–92
alto singer, composer, poet, social reformer, abolitionist, suffragist, hymn writer, feminist
New York; New Hampshire
Nat Cyc Am Bio v10; Wom Cent; Not Am Wom; Index t Wom

1409. van Deusen, Mary (Westbrook)
born 1829
religious writer, novelist, poet
Rondout, NY
Dict Am Auth; Wom Cent

1410. Ames, Eleanor Maria Easterbrook; Eleanor Kirkips
born 1830
author

New York
Dict Am Auth; Wom Cent

1411. Conner, Eliza Archard; "Zig"; E. A.
flourished 1860s–80s
journalist, lecturer, women's rights worker
New York
Wom Cent

1412. Dean, Julia
1830–1868/69
stage actor
New York
Cyc Am Bio; Dict Am Bio; Dict Am Bio Men Time; Index t Wom; Nat Cyc Am Bio v3; Not Am Wom

1413. Louis, Minnie Dessau
flourished 1860s–90s
Jewish welfare worker, educator
Jewish
New York
Nat Cyc Am Bio v18

1414. Terhune, Mary Virginia (Hawes); Marian Harland
1830/35–1922
popular novelist, writer on household affairs, historian, cookbook author, editor, publisher
New York, NY
Cyc Am Bio; Dict Am Auth; Dict Am Bio; Dict Am Bio Men Time; Index t Wom; Nat Cyc Am Bio v1; Not Am Wom; Twent Cen Bio Dict Not Am; Wom Cent

1415. Conklin, Jane Elizabeth Dexter
born 1831
poet, religious writer
Binghamton, NY
Wom Cent

1416. Cutler, Lizzie Petit
1831/36–1902
novelist
New York, NY
Cyc Am Bio; Dict Am Auth; Dict Am Bio

1417. Dodge, Mary Elizabeth Mapes
1831/38–1905
children's author, poet, editor
New York
Cyc Am Bio; Dict Am Auth; Dict Am Bio; Index t Wom; Nat Cyc Am Bio v1; Not Am Wom; Twent Cen Bio Dict Not Am; Wom Cent

1418. Garnett, Sarah J. Smith Thompson
1831–1911
educator, civic worker
New York

Black
Index t Wom; Not Am Wom; Prof Negro Wom v1

1419. Miller, Harriet (Mann); Olive Thorne Miller
1831–1918
author, ornithologist, bird watcher, naturalist, nature writer, conservationist, children's author, magazine writer
Swedenborgian
Brooklyn, NY
Dict Am Auth; Index t Wom; Nat Cyc Am Bio v9; Not Am Wom; Twent Cen Bio Dict Not Am

1420. Victor, Metta Victoria (Fuller); Seeley Register; The Singing Sibyl
1831/51–1885/86
popular author, novelist, poet
New York, NY
Cyc Am Bio; Dict Am Auth; Dict Am Bio Men Time; Index t Wom; Nat Cyc Am Bio v4; Not Am Wom; Twent Cen Bio Dict Not Am; Wom Cent

1421. Hinsdale, Grace Webster (Haddock)
born 1832
hymn writer, religious author
New York, NY
Dict Am Auth; Nat Cyc Am Bio v9

1422. Walworth, Ellen (Hardin)
1832–1915
author, war nurse, writer on the history of Saratoga, educator, poet
Saratoga, NY
Cyc Am Bio and ad; Dict Am Auth; Index t Wom; Twent Cen Bio Dict Not Am; Wom Cent

1423. Woodruff, Julia Louisa Matilda (Curtiss); W. M. L. Jan
born 1832
author, compiler
New York, NY
Dict Am Auth

1424. Boya, Ellen Wright
born 1833
educator, author on religious education, writer on art and architecture
Albany, NY
Dict Am Auth

1425. Coman, Charlotte Buell
1833/45–1924
painter
Christian Scientist
New York
Cyc Am Bio; Dict Am Bio; Index t Wom; Nat Cyc Am Bio v22

1426. Isaac, Hannah M. Underhill
born 1833
evangelist, temperance worker
New York
Wom Cent

1427. Jones, Jennie E.
born 1833
poet, short story writer
New York
Wom Cent

1428. Cruger, Mary
born 1834
novelist
New York
Dict Am Auth; Wom Cent

1429. Harris, Miriam (Coles)
1834–1925
novelist
New York
Cyc Am Bio; Dict Am Auth; Dict
Am Bio; Nat Cyc Am Bio v11;
Twent Cen Bio Dict Not Am

1430. Leonowens, Anna Harriette (Crawford)
born 1834
author on Siam, kindergarten educator, missionary educator in
Siam
New York
English
Cyc Am Bio; Dict Am Bio

1431. Dana, Katherine (Floyd)
1835–86
author
New York
Dict Am Auth

1432. Hawks, Annie Sherwood
1835–1918
hymn writer, poet
Baptist
New York
Index t Wom; Nat Cyc Am Bio
v17; Wom Cent

1433. Larned, Augusta
born 1835
author, journalist, poet, women's
rights worker
New York, NY
Cyc Am Bio; Dict Am Auth; Nat
Cyc Am Bio v13; Twent Cen
Bio Dict Not Am

1434. Walworth, Jeanette Ritchie (Hadermann)
1835/37–1906/18
author, novelist
New York, NY
Cyc Am Bio and ad; Dict Am
Auth; Dict Am Bio; Nat Cyc
Am Bio v8; Wom Cent

1435. Washington, Lucy Hall (Walker)
born 1835

poet, temperance reformer
Port Jervis, NY
Dict Am Auth; Wom Cent

1436. Weiss, Susan Archer (Talley)
born 1835
poet, artist
Virginia; New York, NY
Cyc Am Bio; Dict Am Auth;
Wom Cent

1437. Comfort, Lucy Randall
1836–1914
novelist
New York
Nat Cyc Am Bio v18

1438. Converse, Harriet Maxwell; Ya-ie-wah-no; Salome; Musidora
1836–1903
Seneca rights advocate, Seneca
tribal leader, author, folklorist,
Native American scholar, poet
New York
Native American (Seneca by
adoption)
Dict Am Auth; Not Am Wom;
Twent Cen Bio Dict Not Am;
Wom Cent

1439. Holley, Marietta; Josiah Allen's Wife; Jemyma
1836/44–1926
author, humorist, poet, essayist,
novelist, popularizer of women's rights and temperance doctrines, feminist
Ellisburg, NY
Dict Am Auth; Dict Am Bio;
Index t Wom; Nat Cyc Am Bio
v9; Not Am Wom; Twent Cen
Bio Dict Not Am; Wom Cent;
Wom Lit, More

1440. Leslie, Miriam Florence (Folline); Frank K. Leslie
1836/51–1914
magazine editor, publisher, feminist, philanthropist
New York
Cyc Am Bio; Dict Am Bio; Index
t Wom; Nat Cyc Am Bio v25;
Not Am Wom; Twent Cen Bio
Dict Not Am; Wom Cent

1441. Mitchell, Marion Juliet
born 1836
poet
New York
Wom Cent

1442. Nourse, Laura A. Sunderlin
born 1836
poet
New York
Wom Cent

1443. Parker, Permelia Jane Marsh
born 1836
children's author, novelist
Rochester, NY
Cyc Am Bio; Dict Am Auth

1444. Wright, Hannah Amelia
born 1836
gynecologist, medical educator
New York
Wom Cent

1445. Dike, Jeannie Dean Scott
1837–1920
music educator, Congregationalist missionary
Congregationalist
New York
Twent Cen Bio Dict Not Am;
Wom Cent

1446. O'Donnell, Martha Barnum
born 1837
temperance worker
New York
Wom Cent

1447. Schuyler, Louisa Lee
1837/40–1926
leader in welfare work, Civil War
philanthropist, patron of nursing, social worker, sanitarian
New York
Dict Am Bio; Index t Wom; Nat
Cyc Am Bio v20; Not Am Wom

1448. Wing, Amelia Kempshall
born 1837
author, philanthropist
New York
Wom Cent

1449. Bryan, Mary (Edwards)
1838/46–1913
journalist, author, editor, poet,
clubwoman
Atlanta, GA; New York, NY
Cyc Am Bio; Dict Am Bio; Index
t Wom; Nat Cyc Am Bio v8;
Not Am Wom; Twent Cen Bio
Dict Not Am; Wom Cent

1450. Ewen, Mary Cecelia
1838–66
actor
New York
Cyc Am Bio

1451. Houghton, Louise Seymour
born 1838
religious magazine editor, translator, religious author
New York, NY
Dict Am Auth

1452. Roge, Charlotte Fiske (Bates)
born 1838

author, poet, literary critic, educator
New York
Dict Am Auth; Wom Cent

1453. Sangster, Margaret Elizabeth (Munson)
1838–1912
editor of *Harper's Bazaar*, author,
poet, journalist
New York, NY
Cyc Am Bio and ad; Dict Am
Auth; Index t Wom; Nat Cyc
Am Bio v6; Not Am Wom;
Twent Cen Bio Dict Not Am;
Wom Cent

1454. Seemuller, Annie Moncure (Crane)
1838–72
novelist
New York, NY
Dict Am Auth

1455. Slosson, Anne (Trumbull)
1838–1926
entomologist, short story writer
New York, NY
Dict Am Auth; Index t Wom

1456. Sullivan, Mary Mildred Hammond
1838–1933
philanthropist, Civil War patriot,
New York civic leader
Presbyterian
New York
Index t Wom; Nat Cyc Am Bio
v31

1457. Ward, Susan Hayes
born 1838
author, religious writer
New York, NY
Dict Am Auth

1458. Campbell, Helen (Stuart)
1839–1918
journalist, children's author, social reformer, home economist,
educator, philanthropist
New York
Cyc Am Bio; Dict Am Auth; Nat
Cyc Am Bio v9; Not Am Wom;
Twent Cen Bio Dict Not Am;
Wom Cent

1459. Dickinson, Mary Lowe
1839–1914
author, educator, short story
writer, poet
New York, NY
Dict Am Auth; Index t Wom

1460. Fenner, Mary Galentine
born 1839
author, poet
New York
Wom Cent

1461. Knapp, Phoebe Palmer
born 1839

musician, author, religious composer
Methodist Episcopal
New York
Wom Cent

1462. Morse, Lucy (Gibbons)
1839–1936
author, novelist, abolitionist, Black welfare worker
New York, NY
Dict Am Auth; Nat Cyc Am Bio

1463. Branch, Mary Lydia Bolles
1840–1922
poet, children's author
New York
Cyc Am Bio; Dict Am Auth; Nat Cyc Am Bio v21; Twent Cen Bio Dict Not Am

1464. Hall, Sarah Elizabeth
flourished 1870s–80s
educator
New York
Wom Cent

1465. Higginson, Sarah Jane (Hatfield)
born 1840
novelist
New York, NY
Dict Am Auth

1466. Lee, Margaret
1840–1914
novelist
Brooklyn, NY
Dict Am Auth; Nat Cyc Am Bio v15

1467. Loop, Jennette Shepherd (Harrison)
1840–1909
artist, painter
New York
Cyc Am Bio; Index t Wom; Twent Cen Bio Dict Not Am; Wom Cent

1468. Putnam, Sarah A. Brock "Sallie"; Virginia Madison
1840/45–post 1900
author, novelist, Civil War writer
New York, NY
Cyc Am Bio; Dict Am Auth; Nat Cyc Am Bio v10; Twent Cen Bio Dict Not Am; Wom Cent

1469. Corson, Juliet
1841/42–1897
culinary educator, cookbook writer
New York
Cyc Am Bio; Dict Am Auth; Dict Am Bio; Index t Wom; Nat Cyc Am Bio v8; Not Am Wom; Twent Cen Bio Dict Not Am

1470. Gustafson, Zadel Barnes (Buddington); Axel Carl Johan Gustafson
born 1841
author, poet, novelist
New York
Cyc Am Bio; Dict Am Auth; Wom Cent

1471. Lemcke, Gesine
born 1841
domestic science educator, cookbook author
New York
Dict Am Auth

1472. Winter, Elizabeth (Campbell)
born 1841
novelist
Staten Island, NY
Dict Am Auth

1473. Ziegler, Electra Matilda Curtis
1841–1932
patron of welfare of the blind
Christian Scientist
New York
Index t Wom; Nat Cyc Am Bio v37

1474. Jacobi, Mary Corinna Putnam
1842–1906
physician, medical author, pharmacist, educator, feminist
New York, NY
Cyc Am Bio; Dict Am Auth; Dict Am Bio; Index t Wom; Nat Cyc Am Bio v8; Not Am Wom; Twent Cen Bio Dict Not Am; Wom Cent

1475. Lathrop, Clarissa Caldwill
died 1892
mental institution reformer
New York
Index t Wom; Wom Cent

1476. Rollins, Alice Marland (Wellington)
1842/47–1897
author, poet, muckraking journalist
New York, NY
Cyc Am Bio; Dict Am Auth; Dict Am Bio; Nat Cyc Am Bio v8; Twent Cen Bio Dict Not Am; Wom Cent

1477. Smith, Mary Louise (Riley)
born 1842/52
author, poet
New York, NY
Cyc Am Bio; Dict Am Auth; Wom Cent

1478. Vanderpoel, Emily Caroline Noyes
1842–1939
painter, author
New York
Nat Cyc Am Bio v29

1479. Burt, Mary Towne
flourished 1873
temperance worker, publisher
Protestant Episcopal
New York
Index t Wom; Wom Cent

1480. Harrison, Constance Cary
1843/46–1920
author, novelist, miscellaneous writer, dramatist
New York, NY
Cyc Am Bio; Dict Am Auth; Dict Am Bio; Index t Wom; Nat Cyc Am Bio v4; Not Am Wom; Twent Cen Bio Dict Not Am; Wom Cent; Wom Lit, More

1481. le Row, Caroline Bigelow
born 1843
educator, writer on education
Brooklyn, NY
Dict Am Auth

1482. Lowell, Josephine (Shaw)
1843–1905
charitable worker, philanthropist, social worker, prison reformer, labor reformer, writer on philanthropy
New York, NY
Cyc Am Bio; Dict Am Auth; Dict Am Bio; Index t Wom; Nat Cyc Am Bio v8; Not Am Wom; Twent Cen Bio Dict Not Am

1483. Arnold, Augusta Foote
born 1844
cookbook writer, author
New York
Dict Am Auth

1484. Howell, Mary Seymour
born 1844
lecturer, suffragist
New York
Wom Cent

1485. Lukens, Anna
born 1844
physician
New York
Index t Wom; Wom Cent

1486. Noble, Annette Lucile
born 1844
fiction writer
Albion, NY
Cyc Am Bio and ad; Dict Am Auth; Twent Cen Bio Dict Not Am

1487. Bloede, Gertrude; Stuart Sterne
1845–1905
poet
Brooklyn, NY
German
Dict Am Auth; Dict Nat Bio; Nat Cyc Am Bio v10; Wom Cent

1488. Carhart, Clara Sully
born 1845
educator, temperance worker, women's labor welfare worker
Methodist Episcopal
New York
Canadian
Wom Cent

1489. Kipp, Josephine
born 1845
author
New York
Wom Cent

1490. Smith, Florence
1845–71
poet
New York, NY
Dict Am Auth

1491. Gilchrist, Fredrika (Beardsley)
born 1846
author
New York, NY
Dict Am Auth

1492. Rohlf, Anora Kathleen (Green) "Anna"
1846–1935
novelist, poet, writer of detective stories
Buffalo, NY
Dict Am Auth; Dict Am Bio supp v1; Nat Cyc Am Bio v9; Twent Cen Bio Dict Not Am; Wom Cent

1493. Smith, Jane Luella Dowd
born 1847
educator, author, poet, children's author, suffragist, temperance worker
Hudson, NY
Cyc Am Bio; Dict Am Auth; Nat Cyc Am Bio v1; Twent Cen Bio Dict Not Am; Wom Cent

1494. Norris, Mary Harriot
born 1848
author, novelist, literary editor, university educator
New York; Illinois
Dict Am Auth; Twent Cen Bio Dict Not Am

1495. Pettet, Isabella M.
born 1848
physician
Methodist
New York

German
Wom Cent

1496. Steward, Susan S. McKinney
1848–1919
physician
Brooklyn, NY
Black
Index t Wom; Prof Negro Wom
v1

1497. van Rensselaer, May (King)
born 1848
historical writer on New York City
New York, NY
Dict Am Auth

1498. Beckwith, Emma (Knight)
born 1849
suffragist, politician
Brooklyn, NY
Wom Cent

1499. Gilder, Jeanett Leonard
1849–1916
literary magazine editor, critic, journalist, novelist, autobiographer
New York, NY
Cyc Am Bio and v2 ad; Dict Am Auth; Dict Am Bio; Index t Wom; Nat Cyc Am Bio v8; Not Am Wom; Twent Cen Bio Dict Not Am

1500. Harbee, Lee (Cohen)
born 1849
author, Texas historian, Sorosis member
Texas; New York
Dict Am Auth; Wom Cent

1501. Lazarus, Emma
1849–87
author, poet, dramatist, essayist
Jewish
New York
Cyc Am Bio; Dict Am Auth; Dict Am Bio; Index t Wom; Nat Cyc Am Bio v3; Not Am Wom; Twent Cen Bio Dict Not Am; Who Who Jew Hist; Wom Cent

1502. Saunders, Mary A.
born 1849
inventor, businessperson
New York
Index t Wom; Wom Cent

1503. Anderson, Elizabeth Milbank
1850–1921
World War I relief worker, philanthropist, patron of social welfare work, patron of Serbian and Yugoslavian welfare, patron of medical missions
Baptist

New York
Dict Am Bio; Nat Cyc Am Bio v23; Not Am Wom

1504. Braman, Ella Frances
born 1850
lawyer, government official
New York
Index t Wom; Wom Cent

1505. Brown, Belle
born 1850
physician, surgeon
New York
Wom Cent

1506. Champney, Elizabeth William; Lizzie Williams
born 1850
children's author
New York
Cyc Am Bio and ad; Dict Am Auth; Nat Cyc Am Bio v11; Twent Cen Bio Dict Not Am; Wom Cent

1507. Connelly, Emma M.
flourished 1880s–90s
author
New York, NY
Dict Am Bio; Wom Cent

1508. Flewellyn, Juliette (Colliton)
born 1850
author
Lockport, NY
Dict Am Auth

1509. Fryatt, Frances Elizabeth
flourished 1880s–90s
author, specialist in household art, interior decorator
New York
Wom Cent

1510. Hapgood, Isabel Florence
1850/51–1928
translator, linguist, writer on Russian and European literature, journalist
New York, NY
Dict Am Auth; Dict Am Bio; Nat Cyc Am Bio v21; Not Am Wom; Twent Cen Bio Dict Not Am; Wom Cent

1511. Jones, Melodia Blackmarr
1850–1931
philanthropist, Republican party worker
Episcopalian
Buffalo, NY
Nat Cyc Am Bio v32

1512. le Valley, Laura A. Woodin
flourished 1880s
lawyer
Congregationalist

New York
Wom Cent

1513. Sterling, Antoinette
1850–1904
contralto opera singer
Sterlingville, NY
English
Index t Wom; Wom Cent

1514. Wilcox, Ella (Wheeler)
1850/55–1919
poet, journalist, novelist
New York, NY
Cyc Am Bio and ad; Dict Am Auth; Dict Am Bio; Index t Wom; Nat Cyc Am Bio v11; Not Am Wom; Wom Lit, More

1515. Harriman, Mary Williamson (Averall)
1851–1932
philanthropist, businessperson
New York
Index t Wom; Nat Cyc Am Bio v23; Not Am Wom

1516. Wupperman, Josephine Wright (Hancox)
1851–1936
manufacturer
New York
Nat Cyc Am Bio v27

1517. Brace, Maria Porter
born 1852
educator, elocutionist
New York
Wom Cent

1518. Ormsby, Mary Frost
born circa 1852
author, journalist, philanthropist, pacifist
New York, NY
Index t Wom; Wom Cent

1519. Skeel, Adelaide
born 1852
children's author
Newburgh, NY
Dict Am Auth

1520. St. John, Cynthia Morgan
1852–1919
author, Wordsworthian expert and collector
New York
Index t Wom; Wom Cent

1521. Ide, Frances Otis Ogden; Ruth Ogden
born 1853
children's author
Brooklyn, NY
Dict Am Auth; Twent Cen Bio Dict Not Am

1522. Mason, Caroline Atwater
born 1853
author

Batavia, NY
Dict Am Auth; Nat Cyc Am Bio v4; Twent Cen Bio Dict Not Am

1523. Post, Sarah E.
born 1853
physician, nursing-magazine founder
New York
Wom Cent

1524. Scribner, Lucy Skidmore
1853–1931
founder of Skidmore College, educator
New York
Nat Cyc Am Bio v23

1525. Trask, Kate (Nichols) "Katrina"
1853/63–1922
magazine author, poet, short story writer, essayist, philanthropist
Saratoga, NY
Dict Am Auth; Nat Cyc Am Bio v11; Not Am Wom

1526. Walker, Minerva
born 1853
physician
New York
Wom Cent

1527. Wright, Marie Robinson
born 1853/60
journalist, travel writer
Georgia; New York
Dict Am Auth; Wom Cent

1528. Comstock, Anna (Botsford)
1854–1930
naturalist, scientific illustrator, insect artist, leader in the nature study movement, wood engraver, educator
New York
Index t Wom; Nat Cyc Am Bio v11 and v22; Not Am Wom; Twent Cen Bio Dict Not Am

1529. French, Lillie Hamilton
born 1854
magazine writer
New York, NY
Dict Am Auth

1530. Ives, Florence C.
born 1854
journalist
New York
Wom Cent

1531. Palmer, Anna Campbell; Mrs. George Archibald
1854–1928
children's author, poet
Methodist Episcopal

Elmira, NY
Dict Am Auth; Index t Wom;
Nat Cyc Am Bio v22; Twent
Cen Bio Dict Not Am; Wom
Cent

1532. Thomas, Edith Matilda
1854–1925
poet, author
New York; Geneva, OH
Cyc Am Bio and ad; Dict Am
Auth; Dict Am Bio; Index t
Wom; Nat Cyc Am Bio v9; Not
Am Wom; Twent Cen Bio Dict
Not Am; Wom Cent

1533. Cutting, Olivia Murray
1855–1949
philanthropist
New York
Nat Cyc Am Bio v38

1534. Dewing, Elizabeth Bartol
born 1855
author, novelist
New York
Nat Cyc Am Bio csv3

1535. Dodd, Anna Bowman (Blake)
1855–post 1890s
travel writer, essayist
New York
Dict Am Auth; Wom Cent

1536. Elmendorf, Theresa Hubbell West
1855–1932
librarian, editor
Buffalo, NY
Index t Wom; Nat Cyc Am Bio
v23

1537. Fairchild, Mary Solome Cutler
1855–1921
librarian for the blind, nonfiction
writer
New York
Dict Am Auth; Dict Am Bio;
Index t Wom; Nat Cyc Am Bio
v20; Not Am Wom; Twent Cen
Bio Dict Not Am

1538. Clymer, Ella Maria (Dietz)
1856–post 1880
poet, actor, president of Sorosis
New York
Dict Am Auth; Wom Cent

1539. Dodge, Grace Hoadley
1856–1914
social welfare and charity worker,
philanthropist, educator
New York
Cyc Am Bio; Dict Am Bio; Index
t Wom; Nat Cyc Am Bio v18;
Not Am Wom; Wom Cent

1540. Goodwin, Maud (Wilder)
born 1856

author, historical novelist
New York, NY
Dict Am Auth; Twent Cen Bio
Dict Not Am

1541. Parker, Elizabeth Lowber (Chandler); Bessie Chandler
born 1856
magazine author
Batavia, NY
Dict Am Auth

1542. Plummer, Mary Wright
1856–1916
librarian, educator, poet, author
Brooklyn, NY
Dict Am Auth; Dict Am Bio;
Index t Wom; Nat Cyc Am Bio
v21; Not Am Wom; Twent Cen
Bio Dict Not Am

1543. Raymond, Emma Marcy
born 1856
composer, opera composer, conductor
New York
Wom Cent

1544. Belden, Jessie (van Zile)
born 1857
novelist
Syracuse, NY
Dict Am Auth

1545. Benedict, Emma Lee
born 1857
author, educator, temperance
worker
New York
Wom Cent

1546. Blake, Katherine Devereux
1857–1950
educator, suffragist, international
peace movement leader
New York
Index t Wom; Obit File

1547. Case, Mary Emily
born 1857
university educator, classical languages scholar
New York
Dict Am Auth

1548. Day, Mary Gage; Mary Hannah Gage-Day
1857–1935
physician
Episcopalian
New York
Nat Cyc Am Bio csv2 and v26

1549. Hay, Mary Garret
1857–1928
suffragist, temperance worker,
New York civic worker
New York, NY
Dict Am Bio; Index t Wom; Not
Am Wom

1550. Riggs, Kate Douglas (Wiggin) (Smith)
born 1857/59
children's author
New York, NY
Dict Am Auth; Twent Cen Bio
Dict Not Am

1551. Rowe, Anna Forrest
1857–1920
physician, surgeon
New York
Nat Cyc Am Bio v20

1552. Webb, Frances Isabel (Currie)
1857–95
magazine writer
New York, NY
Dict Am Auth

1553. Young, Julia Evelyn (Ditto)
born 1857
poet, novelist, magazine writer
Buffalo, NY
Dict Am Auth; Wom Cent

1554. Adler, Sara Levitzka
1858–1953
actor in Yiddish theater
Jewish
New York, NY
Dict Am Bio supp v5; Obit File

1555. Alden, Cynthia May; Sunshine
1858/62–1931
journalist, editor, linguist, author,
inventor, social worker, philanthropist, humanitarian
New York, NY
Dict Am Bio supp v1; Index t
Wom; Nat Cyc Am Bio v14 and
v22

1556. Bender, Ida Catherine
1858–1916
educator
Buffalo, NY
Nat Cyc Am Bio v21

1557. Britton, Elizabeth Gertrude Knight
1858–1934
botanist
New York
Nat Cyc Am Bio v25; Not Am
Wom

1558. Coombs, Annie (Sheldon)
1858–90
novelist
New York, NY
Dict Am Auth

1559. Hall, Ruth
born 1858
novelist
Catskill Mountains, NY
Dict Am Auth

1560. Lanza, Clara (Hammond), Marchioness
born 1858/59
novelist
New York, NY
Dict Am Auth; Index t Wom;
Wom Cent

1561. Montgomery, Carrie Frances Judd
born 1858
church worker, poet, author, temperance worker, Salvation
Army worker, social worker
New York; California
Index t Wom; Wom Cent

1562. Roseboro, Viola
1858–1945
author, magazine writer, literary
fiction editor of *McClures Magazine*
New York
Dict Am Auth; Obit File

1563. Seelye, Elizabeth (Eggleston)
born 1858
writer on Native American biography and early American history
New York
Dict Am Auth; Wom Cent

1564. Wheeler, Doris
born 1858/60
artist, needleworker, designer,
decorator
New York
Cyc Am Bio; Nat Cyc Am Bio v1;
Wom Cent

1565. Winterburn, Florence (Hull) (Brown)
born 1858
writer on children
New York
Dict Am Auth

1566. Baker, Charlotte Sanford
1859–1932
educator
New York
Nat Cyc Am Bio v23

1567. Candee, Helen Churchill
1859/61–1949
novelist, journalist
New York, NY
Dict Am Auth; Obit File

1568. Cone, Helen Gray
1859–1934
educator, poet
New York
Dict Am Auth; Index t Wom;
Wom Cent

1569. Herrick, Christine Terhune
1859–1944

writer on household affairs, home economist, domestic scientist, Sorosis member
New York, NY; New Jersey
Dict Am Auth; Index t Wom; Nat Cyc Am Bio v8; Not Am Wom; Wom Cent

1570. Kingsley, Florence (Morse)
born 1859
religious author
Staten Island, NY
Dict Am Auth; Nat Cyc Am Bio v11

1571. Miller, Annie (Jenness)
born 1859/84
dress reformer, fashion designer, magazine publisher, author, novelist, essayist, lecturer
New York, NY
Dict Am Auth; Index t Wom; Wom Cent

1572. Moody, Helen (Waterson)
1859/60–1928
author, journalist, educator
Ohio; New York, NY
Dict Am Auth; Index t Wom; Nat Cyc Am Bio v22; Wom Cent

1573. Rehan, Ada (Crehan)
1859/60–1916
actor
New York
Irish
Cyc Am Bio; Dict Am Bio; Dict Irish Bio; Index t Wom; Nat Cyc Am Bio v1; Not Am Wom; Twent Cen Bio Dict Not Am; Wom Cent

1574. Cruger, Julie Grinnell (Storrow); Julien Gordon
flourished 1890s–1900s
novelist
New York
Dict Am Auth; Twent Cen Bio Dict Not Am

1575. de Koven, Anna Farwell
1860–1953
author, novelist
Episcopalian
New York, NY
Dict Am Auth; Nat Cyc Am Bio v16 and v48; Obit File

1576. Johnson, Margaret
born 1860
miscellaneous writer
New York, NY
Dict Am Auth

1577. Knapp, Adeline
born 1860
Household Magazine editor, miscellaneous writer

New York
Dict Am Auth

1578. Morris, Alice A.
born 186?
fiction writer
New York, NY
Dict Am Auth

1579. Moses, Anna Mary Robertson "Grandma"
1860–1961
primitive painter
New York
Index t Wom; Nat Cyc Am Bio v45; Not Am Wom supp v1

1580. O'Donnell, Jessie Fremont
1860–post 1890s
miscellaneous author
Lowville, NY
Dict Am Auth; Wom Cent

1581. Rice, Alice Caldwell (Hegan)
1860/70–1942
author, novelist, children's author, civic worker
New York; Louisville, KY
Dict Am Auth; Dict Am Bio supp v3; Index t Wom; Nat Cyc Am Bio v14; Not Am Wom; Obit File

1582. Schaffner, Ernestine; The Prisoner's Friend
flourished 1890s
prison reformer and prison relief worker
New York, NY
Wom Cent

1583. Smith, Jeanie Oliver
flourished 1890s
poet, romance writer
New York
Wom Cent

1584. Welch, Jane Meade
flourished 1890s
journalist, historical lecturer
New York
Wom Cent

1585. Benjamin, Caroline Shevelson
1861–1951
founder of the Benjamin Dean School for Girls, educator
New York
Obit File

1586. Catlin, Louise (Ensign)
born 1861
fiction writer
Brooklyn, NY
Dict Am Auth

1587. Green, Julia (Boynton)
born 1861
poet

Rochester, NY
Dict Am Auth; Wom Cent

1588. Marshall, Nina (Caroline) Lovering
born 1861
educator
New York, NY
Dict Am Auth

1589. Parsons, Frances Theodora (Smith) (Dana)
1861–99
author, nature writer
Albany, NY
Dict Am Auth; Twent Cen Bio Dict Not Am

1590. Richmond, Mary Ellen
1861–1928
social worker, writer on charity
New York
Dict Am Auth; Nat Cyc Am Bio v21; Not Am Wom

1591. Brazza, Cora (Slocomb), Countess
born 1862
author
New York, NY
Dict Am Auth

1592. Davis, Virginia Meriwether
born 1862
physician
New York
Wom Cent

1593. Libbey, Laura Jean
1862–1924/25
romantic novelist
New York, NY
Dict Am Auth; Index t Wom; Nat Cyc Am Bio v19; Not Am Wom

1594. Morse, Alice Cordelia
born 1862
artist, stained glass designer, book designer
New York
Index t Wom; Wom Cent

1595. Weir, Irene
1862–1944
painter, art educator, writer on art, founder of the New York School of Design and Liberal Arts
New York
Not Am Wom; Obit File

1596. Wharton, Edith Newbold (Jones)
1862–1937
novelist, short story writer, ghost story writer, autobiographer, travel writer, literary critic
New York, NY

French (American expatriate to Paris)
Dict Am Auth; Dict Am Bio supp v2; Dict Lit Bio v4 and v9; Index t Wom; Nat Cyc Am Bio v14 and csv2; Not Am Wom; Twent Cen Bio Dict Not Am; Wom Lit; Wom Lit, More

1597. Claghorn, Kate Holladay
born 1863
writer on women's education
New York
Dict Am Auth; Twent Cen Bio Dict Not Am

1598. Guggenheim, Florence Shloss
1863–1944
philanthropist, patron of music, Republican party worker
Jewish
New York
Index t Wom; Nat Cyc Am Bio v33; Obit File

1599. Huntington, Agnes
born 1863
contralto opera and concert singer
New York
Nat Cyc Am Bio v2; Wom Cent

1600. Ladd, Kate Everit Macy
1863–1945
philanthropist, patron of medicine and scientific research
Presbyterian
New York
Dict Am Bio supp v3; Nat Cyc Am Bio v32 and csv4; Not Am Wom

1601. Margareten, Regina
1863–1959
treasurer and director of Horowitz Bros. & Margareten
New York
Obit File

1602. Michel, Nettie Leila
born 1863
editor
New York
Wom Cent

1603. Miner, Alice Trainer
1863–1950
philanthropist, patron of medicine
Presbyterian
New York
Canadian
Nat Cyc Am Bio v40

1604. Rhoades, Cornelia Harsen
1863–1940
children's author
New York, NY
blind
Dict Am Auth; Index t Wom

1605. Russell, Ada Dwyer
1863–1952
Broadway and London stage actor
New York
Obit File

1606. Sawyer, Antonia (Savage)
born 1863
alto singer, musical talent manager
New York
Nat Cyc Am Bio v16

1607. Wetmore, Elizabeth (Bisland)
born 1863
journalist, editor, traveler
New York, NY
Dict Am Auth; Index t Wom

1608. Boswell, Helen Varick
1864–1942
suffrage leader, founder and president of the Women's Forum
New York
Obit File

1609. Earle, Mary Trace
born 1864
short story writer, novelist
New York
Dict Am Auth

1610. Kellas, Eliza
1864–1943
educator, cofounder and president of Russell Sage College, president of the Emma Willard School
New York
Index t Wom; Not Am Wom; Obit File

1611. Krause, Lydia Farrington; Barbara Yechton
born 1864
fiction writer, religious writer
New York
Dict Am Auth

1612. la Grange, Magdalene Isadora
born 1864
poet
New York
Wom Cent

1613. Lippmann, Julie Mathilde
1864–1952
author, playwright, children's author, literary critic
Brooklyn, NY
Dict Am Bio; Index t Wom; Twent Cen Bio Dict Not Am

1614. Miller, Marion Mills
born 1864
classical scholar, writer on classical literature
New York, NY
Dict Am Auth

1615. van Rensselaer, Martha
1864–1932
home economist, educator
Methodist
New York
Dict Am Bio; Nat Cyc Am Bio v23; Not Am Wom

1616. Hepburn, Emily [Louisa] Eaton
1865–1956
clubwoman, philanthropist
New York
Index t Wom; Nat Cyc Am Bio v46

1617. King, Mary (Perry)
born 1865
writer on beauty
New York, NY
Dict Am Auth

1618. Linn, Edith Willis
born 1865
poet
New York
Wom Cent

1619. Madison, Luch (Foster)
born 1865
historical fiction writer
New York, NY
Dict Am Auth

1620. Morton, Martha
born 1865
author, playwright
New York
Index t Wom; Wom Cent

1621. Osborn, Alice Dodge
1865–1946
philanthropist, foe of Tammany Hall
New York
Obit File

1622. Aldrich, Anne Reeve
1866–92
erotic poet, novelist
New York, NY
Dict Am Auth; Index t Wom; Nat Cyc Am Bio v4; Wom Cent

1623. Guggenheim, Leonie Bernheim
1866–1959
patron of dental clinics, patron of free band concerts in parks
Jewish
New York
Obit File

1624. Hensley, Sophie M. (Almon)
born 1866
poet
New York, NY
Dict Am Auth

1625. Lanier, Harriet Bishop
1866–1931
patron of music
New York
Nat Cyc Am Bio v34

1626. Taggart, Marion Ames
born 1866
children's author
New York
Dict Am Auth

1627. Carruth, Frances Weston
born 1867
short story writer
New York
Dict Am Auth

1628. Cary, Elizabeth Luther
1867–1936
author, art critic, literary critic
Brooklyn, NY
Dict Am Auth; Dict Am Bio supp v2; Wom Lit; Wom Lit, More

1629. Flint, Martha Bockee
born 1867
journalist
New York, NY
Dict Am Auth

1630. MacDougall, Alice Foote
1867–1945
businessperson, restaurateur, entrepreneur
New York
Index t Wom; Obit File

1631. Mayo, Katherine
1867–1940
author, novelist
Episcopalian
New York
Index t Wom; Nat Cyc Am Bio v30; Not Am Wom

1632. Meyer, Annie Florence Nathan
1867–1950/51
publicist, author, playwright, novelist, educationist, founder of Barnard College, antisuffragist, patron of Black music education, clubwoman
Jewish
New York
Dict Am Auth; Dict Am Bio; Index t Wom; Nat Cyc Am Bio v42; Not Am Wom supp v1; Obit File; Twent Cen Bio Dict Not Am; Wom Cent

1633. Simkhovich, Mary Melinda Kingsbury
1867–1951
settlement house worker, housing reformer, social worker, author
New York
Dict Am Bio supp v5; Index t Wom; Not Am Wom supp v1; Obit File

1634. Whitney, Charlotte Anita
1867–1955
suffragist, political activist, Communist party worker, treasurer of the New York Communist party
New York
Dict Am Bio supp v5; Obit File

1635. Guggenheim, Irene Rothschild
1868–1954
patron of child welfare, philanthropist
Jewish
New York
Nat Cyc Am Bio v44

1636. Jackson, Margaret (Doyle)
born 1868
novelist
New York, NY
Dict Am Auth

1637. Miller, Mary Rogers
born 1868
educator, author
New York, NY
Dict Am Auth

1638. Talbot, Anna Charlotte Hedges
born 1868
women's educator
Unitarian
New York
Nat Cyc Am Bio v30

1639. Bullowa, Emilie M.
1869–1942
lawyer, World War II relief worker, Sorosis member
Jewish
New York
Nat Cyc Am Bio v31

1640. O'Day, Caroline Love Goodwin
1869/75–1943
social welfare worker, Democratic representative to Congress from New York, New Deal supporter, artist
Episcopalian
New York
Index t Wom; Nat Cyc Am Bio csv6; Not Am Wom; Obit File

1641. O'Hagan, Anne
1869–post 1930s
journalist
New York, NY
Dict Am Auth; Index t Wom

1642. Roper, Janet Lord "Mother"
1869–1943
founder of the Missing Seaman's Bureau, manager of the Seaman's Church Institute of New York

New York
Obit File

1643. Young, Rose Emmet
1869–1941
editor, journalist, novelist, feminist
New York
Dict Am Auth; Index t Wom

1644. Bogle, Sarah Comly Norris
1870–1932
librarian
Protestant Episcopal
New York
Index t Wom; Nat Cyc Am Bio csv3; Not Am Wom

1645. Crothers, Rachel
1870/78–1958
playwright
New York
Dict Am Bio supp v5; Dict Lit Bio v7; Index t Wom; Nat Cyc Am Bio csv3; Not Am Wom supp v1; Obit File; Wom Lit, More

1646. de Vere, Mary Aigne; Madeline S. Bridges
died 1920
poet, humorist
New York
Dict Am Auth; Nat Cyc Am Bio v8

1647. Mack, Harriet Belle Taggart
flourished 1900s–30s
Democratic presidential elector
New York
Nat Cyc Am Bio csv5

1648. Williams, Molly
flourished pre-1900
fire fighter
New York
Black
Prof Negro Wom v1

1649. Wollman, Kate
1870–1955
philanthropist
New York
Obit File

1650. Draper, Helen Fidelia
1871–1951
Red Cross nurse, World War I relief worker, social worker
Episcopalian
New York
Index t Wom; Nat Cyc Am Bio v39

1651. Farrar, Lilian Katurah Pond
1871–1962
gynecologist, surgeon
Episcopalian

New York
Nat Cyc Am Bio v48

1652. Smith, Frances Stanton
1871–1931
journalist, suffragist, member of the New York State Civil Service Commission
New York
Nat Cyc Am Bio v27

1653. Wagnalls, Mabel
born 1871
pianist, writer on music
New York, NY
Dict Am Auth; Twent Cen Bio Dict Not Am

1654. Washburn, Margaret Floy
1871–1939
psychologist
New York
Dict Am Bio supp v2; Nat Cyc Am Bio v30; Not Am Wom

1655. Jackson, Alice Hooker Day
1872–1926
labor welfare worker
New York
Nat Cyc Am Bio v21

1656. Kibbe, Flora Harriet d'Aubry Jenkins
1872–1943
animal humane worker
New York
Nat Cyc Am Bio v37

1657. Pangborn, Georgia (Wood)
born 1872
novelist
New York, NY
Dict Am Auth

1658. Tyler, Helen
1872–1950
Broadway stage producer
New York
Obit File

1659. Ward, Fannie
1872–1952
Broadway stage actor
New York
Index t Wom; Obit File

1660. Baker, Caroline Tilden
1873–1931
educator
Quaker
New York
Nat Cyc Am Bio v22

1661. Baker, Sarah Josephine
1873–1945
physician, public health administrator, child health pioneer
Unitarian

New York, NY
Dict Am Bio supp v3; Index t Wom; Nat Cyc Am Bio v36; Not Am Wom; Obit File

1662. Crane, Josephine (Porter) Boardman
1873–1972
New York civic leader, patron of the arts
Episcopalian
New York
Nat Cyc Am Bio v57

1663. Bloodgood, Edith Holt
1874–1961
cofounder of the New York Association for the Blind and of *Searchlight*, a Braille magazine
New York
Obit File

1664. Brinker, Una Abell
1874–1952
stage actor
New York, NY
Obit File

1665. Bryan, Isabel
1874–1957
publisher of the Greenwich Village, New York, newspaper *The Villager*
Greenwich Village, NY
Obit File

1666. Hammand, Emily Vanderbilt Sloane
1874–1907
philanthropist, social worker, Moral Rearmament Society member
Presbyterian
New York
Nat Cyc Am Bio v55 and csv8

1667. Knapp, Florence Elizabeth Smith
1874–1949
New York secretary of state
New York
Obit File

1668. Loeb, Sophia Irene Simon
1874/76–1929
journalist, sponsor of welfare legislation, social reformer, social worker, author
New York
Russian
Dict Am Bio; Index t Wom; Nat Cyc Am Bio v24; Not Am Wom; Slavon Encyc

1669. Maury, Carlotta Joaquina
1874–1938
paleontologist
Episcopalian
New York
Nat Cyc Am Bio v28

1670. Miller, Alice Duer
1874–1942
fiction writer, poet
New York
Dict Am Auth; Index t Wom; Nat Cyc Am Bio csv1; Not Am Wom; Obit File; Wom Lit, More

1671. Rives, Hallie Erminie
1874/76–1956
novelist
New York, NY
Dict Am Auth; Dict Am Bio supp v6; Index t Wom; Obit File

1672. Roberts, Ina (Brevoort)
born 1874
novelist
New York, NY
Dict Am Auth

1673. Rockefeller, Abby Green Aldrich
1874/75–1948
philanthropist, art patron
New York
Dict Am Bio supp v4; Index t Wom; Nat Cyc Am Bio v45; Not Am Wom

1674. Tompers, Lucie Margaret
1874–1938
social worker
Baptist
New York
Canadian
Nat Cyc Am Bio v29

1675. Wise, Louise Waterman
1874–1947
charitable worker, founder and president of the women's division of the American Jewish Congress, Zionist
Jewish
New York
Not Am Wom

1676. Brooks, Geraldine
born 1875
colonial historian, author
New York, NY
Dict Am Auth

1677. Brooks, Hildegard
born 1875
novelist
Newburgh, NY
Dict Am Auth

1678. Colby, Nathalie Sedgwick
1875–1942
essayist, poet, novelist
Episcopalian
New York
Index t Wom; Nat Cyc Am Bio v31

1679. Curran, Pearl Gildersleeve
1875/76–1941
composer, songwriter
Christian Scientist
New York
Index t Wom; Nat Cyc Am Bio v53

1680. Dreier, Mary Elisabeth
1875–1963
labor reformer, suffragist, New York civic leader, Bull Moose party politician
Presbyterian
New York
Nat Cyc Am Bio csv9; Not Am Wom supp v1

1681. Rand, Ellen Gertrude Emmet
1875/76–1941
portrait painter
New York
Index t Wom; Nat Cyc Am Bio v40 and csv5; Not Am Wom; Obit File

1682. Burchenal, Elizabeth
1876–1959
folklorist, folk dance educator, cofounder of the American Folk Dance Society, originator of the New York Folk Dance Festival
New York
Index t Wom; Not Am Wom supp v1; Obit File

1683. Farnham, Sally James
1876–1943
sculptor
New York
Index t Wom; Nat Cyc Am Bio v37

1684. Mead, Elizabeth Manning Cleveland
1876–1946
patron of cancer research
Episcopalian
New York
Nat Cyc Am Bio v38

1685. Sterling, Lindsay Morris
born 1876
sculptor, scientific sculptor, science illustrator
New York
Nat Cyc Am Bio csv3

1686. Warburg, Frieda Schiff
1876–1958
philanthropist, Jewish welfare worker
Jewish
New York
Nat Cyc Am Bio v44; Obit File

1687. Anthony, Katharine Susan
1877–1965
author, biographer

New York
Index t Wom; Nat Cyc Am Bio csv6; Obit File

1688. Gildersleeve, Virginia Crocheron
1877–1965
educator, dean emeritus of Barnard College, US delegate to the 1945 San Francisco conference to draft the UN charter, creator of UNESCO
New York
Index t Wom; Nat Cyc Am Bio csv1 and csv7; Not Am Wom supp v1; Obit File

1689. Marvin, Adelaide Camilla Hoffman
born 1877
New York civic leader
Congregationalist
New York, NY
Nat Cyc Am Bio csv8

1690. Moskowitz, Belle Lindner Israels
1877–1933
social worker, welfare worker, political leader, clubwoman, political adviser to New York governor Alfred E. Smith
Jewish
New York
Dict Am Bio supp v1; Index t Wom; Not Am Wom

1691. Norris, Jean Hortense
born 1877
jurist, international lawyer
New York
Nat Cyc Am Bio csv3

1692. Pratt, Ruth (Sears) Baker
1877–1965
representative to Congress from New York
Episcopalian
New York
Index t Wom; Nat Cyc Am Bio v51

1693. Rolland, Pauline Hoffman
1877–1952
actor in Yiddish and American theater
Jewish
New York
Obit File

1694. Sahler, Helen Gertrude
1877–1950
sculptor
New York
Index t Wom; Nat Cyc Am Bio v39

1695. Chess, Mary Grace; Mrs. Avery Robinson
1878–1964

perfumer, flower sculptor
New York
Nat Cyc Am Bio v52

1696. Good, Alice Campbell
1878–1956
Democratic party worker, New York civic worker
Catholic
New York
Nat Cyc Am Bio v42

1697. Guggenheim, Olga Hersh
1878–1970
philanthropist, patron of the arts
Jewish
New York
Obit File

1698. l'Esperance, Elise Depew Strang
1878/79–1959
pathologist, founder of the Kate Depew Strang Tumor Clinic at New York Infirmary
New York
Index t Wom; Not Am Wom supp v1; Obit File

1699. Manville, Henrietta Estelle
1878–1947
patron of floriculture and horticulture, philanthropist
New York
Nat Cyc Am Bio v56 and csv6

1700. McKinstry, Helen May
1878–1949
president of Russell Sage College, physical education expert
Presbyterian
New York
Nat Cyc Am Bio v37; Obit File

1701. Mitchell, Lucy Sprague
1878–1967
educator, college administrator, Black education worker, children's author
New York
Nat Cyc Am Bio v53; Not Am Wom supp v1

1702. Peele, Grace Darling
1878–1926
physician
New York
Nat Cyc Am Bio v21

1703. Pugsley, Emma Catherine Gregory
died 1928
philanthropist, investor, entrepreneur
Presbyterian
New York
Nat Cyc Am Bio v22

1704. Chapin, Alice Delafield
1879–1964
educator, social welfare leader

Episcopalian
New York
Index t Wom; Nat Cyc Am Bio v52

1705. Sawyer, Josephine Caroline
born 1879
historical novelist
Watertown, NY
Dict Am Auth

1706. Swartz, Maud O'Farrell
1879–1937
labor leader
Catholic
New York
Irish
Bio Dict Am Lab; Not Am Wom

1707. Bernstein, Aline Frankau
1880/82–1955
stage scene and costume designer, author
Jewish
New York
Dict Am Bio supp v5; Index t Wom; Nat Cyc Am Bio v47; Not Am Wom supp v1; Obit File

1708. Camprubi, Ethel Leaycraft
1880–1955
president of a New York Spanish-language daily newspaper
New York
Obit File

1709. Matthews, Frances Aymar
born 18?; flourished 1910s
playwright, poet, novelist
New York, NY
Dict Am Auth; Index t Wom

1710. Naumbergy, Elsie Margaret Binger
1880–1953
ornithologist
New York
Index t Wom; Nat Cyc Am Bio v41

1711. Schall, Nina Dennis
1880–1961
physician
Presbyterian
New York; Pennsylvania
Nat Cyc Am Bio v49

1712. Wadsworth, Alice Hay
born 1880
New York civic worker, suffragist
Presbyterian
New York
Nat Cyc Am Bio csv8

1713. Bailey, Elizabeth Donovan
1881–post 1930
social welfare worker

1745. Starbuck, Kathryn Helene
1887–1965
lawyer, women's rights worker, educator
Baptist
New York
Nat Cyc Am Bio v53

1746. Weld, Julia Deforest Tiffany
1887–1973
medical researcher, patron of medicine
New York
Nat Cyc Am Bio v58

1747. Aldrich, Harriet Alexander
1888–1972
New York civic worker, World War II relief worker
New York, NY
Nat Cyc Am Bio v60

1748. Hull, Helen Rose
1888–1971
novelist, short story writer, university educator
New York
Cur Biog '71; Index t Wom; Nat Cyc Am Bio v60; Obit File

1749. Kenyon, Dorothy
1888–1972
lawyer, feminist, suffragist, women's rights worker, prochoice abortion lobbyist, civil libertarian, director of the ACLU, UN official
New York
Cur Biog '72; Index t Wom; Nat Cyc Am Bio v56; Not Am Wom supp v1

1750. Lasker, Loula Davis
1888–1961
New York civic worker, Zionist, Hadassah member
Jewish
New York
Nat Cyc Am Bio v48

1751. Phillips, Luba Galanchikoff (Philpoff)
1888–1959
pioneer aviator, pre–World War I test pilot, early altitude and distance record holder, taxi driver
New York
Russian
Obit File

1752. Hillman, Bessie Abramowitz
1889–1970
labor leader, president of the Amalgamated Clothing Workers of America
Jewish
New York, NY

Russian
Nat Cyc Am Bio v56; Obit File

1753. Rosen, Lucie Bigelow Dodge
1889–1968
electronic musician, patron of music
Episcopalian
New York
Nat Cyc Am Bio v54

1754. Butler, Kate Maddux Robinson
circa 1890–1974
publisher, philanthropist, patron of French relief in World War II
Buffalo, NY
Nat Cyc Am Bio v58

1755. Dayton, Katherine
1890–1945
journalist, playwright, political satirist, humorist
New York
Index t Wom; Nat Cyc Am Bio v34

1756. Ferris, Helen Josephine; Mrs. Albert B. Tibbets
1890–1969
author, editor, children's author
Baptist
New York
Index t Wom; Nat Cyc Am Bio v55

1757. Hume, Jessie Fremont
flourished 1920s–30s
librarian
New York
Nat Cyc Am Bio csv1

1758. Lashanska, Hulda; Mrs. Harold A. Rosebaum
1890/93–1974
lyric soprano concert singer
Jewish
New York
Index t Wom; Nat Cyc Am Bio v57

1759. Bearden, Bessye J.
1891–1943
educator, first female member of the New York City school board, clubwoman
New York, NY
Black
Encyc Black Am; Index t Wom

1760. Brice, Fanny (Borach)
1891–1951
comedian; stage, screen, and radio actor
Jewish
Brooklyn, NY
Dict Am Bio supp v5; Index t Wom; Not Am Wom supp v1; Obit File

1761. Kross, Anna Moscowitz
1891–1979
municipal court judge, feminist
New York, NY
Russian
Cur Biog '79; Index t Wom

1762. Newman, Pauline M.
1891–post 1940s
labor leader, Socialist party worker
Jewish
New York
Russian
Bio Dict Am Lab; Index t Wom

1763. Grossinger, Jennie
1892–1972
philanthropist; hotel executive, owner, and manager; country club owner
Jewish
Catskill Mountains, NY
Austrian
Cur Biog '73; Index t Wom; Not Am Wom supp v1; Obit File

1764. Shepley, Ruth
1892–1951
Broadway stage actor
New York
Obit File

1765. Stone, Hannah Mayer
1892–1941
gynecologist, medical director of the Margaret Sanger Research Bureau, birth control advocate
Jewish
New York
Index t Wom; Nat Cyc Am Bio v30; Obit File

1766. Baldwin, Faith; Mrs. Hugh H. Cuthrell
1893–1973
novelist
New York
Index t Wom; Nat Cyc Am Bio csv9; Obit File

1767. Dodge, Pauline Morgan
1893–1971
YWCA executive, philanthropist
Presbyterian
New York
Nat Cyc Am Bio v56

1768. Fitz-Gibbon, Bernice; Mrs. Herman Block
graduated 1918
advertising executive
Catholic
New York
Nat Cyc Am Bio csv9

1769. Leech, Margaret Kernochan; Mrs. Ralph Pulitzer
1893–1974
author, novelist, historian

New York
Cur Biog '74; Index t Wom; Nat Cyc Am Bio csv6

1770. Levy, Adele Rosenwald
1893–1960
philanthropist, chairperson of the United Jewish Appeal National Women's Division, art collector
Jewish
New York
Obit File

1771. Mintzer, Ida Jessica
1893–1970
dermatologist
Jewish
New York
Nat Cyc Am Bio v55

1772. Parker, Dorothy Rothschild
1893–1967
author, critic, short story writer, poet, humorist
Jewish
New York
Index t Wom; Not Am Wom supp v1; Obit File; Who Who Jew Hist; Wom Lit, More

1773. Cutting, Helen McMahon
1894–1961
worker for the welfare of the blind, traveler
New York
Nat Cyc Am Bio v47

1774. Donlon, Mary (Honor)
1894?–1977
US customs court judge, lawyer
New York
Cur Biog '77; Index t Wom

1775. Kanaga, Consuelo
1894–1978
photographer
New York
Nat Cyc Am Bio v60; Obit File

1776. Knopf, Blanche Wolf
1894–1966
editor, publisher, president of Alfred A. Knopf Inc.
New York
Index t Wom; Not Am Wom supp v1; Obit File

1777. Alexander, Helen M.
died 1945
New York civic leader
New York, NY
Obit File

1778. Bryant, Lane; Lena Himmelstein; Mrs. Albert Malsin
1881/1895–1951
dress merchant, mail order businessperson, maternity and special sizes designer
Jewish
New York

Lithuanian
Nat Cyc Am Bio v47; Index t
Wom; Who Who Jew Hist

1779. Lewisohn, Margaret Seligman
1895–1954
educator, art patron, clubwoman
New York
Index t Wom; Nat Cyc Am Bio
v44

1780. Robinson, Gladys Lloyd Cassell
born 1895
actor, social worker
New York
Nat Cyc Am Bio csv6

1781. Victor, Sally (Josephs)
1895/1905–1977
hat designer
Jewish
New York
Cur Biog '77; Index t Wom; Nat
Cyc Am Bio v49

1782. Dole, Margaret Fernald
1896–1970
portrait painter
Episcopalian
New York
Nat Cyc Am Bio v56

1783. Frantz, Virginia Kneeland
1896–1967
surgical pathologist, medical educator, cancer researcher, dairy farmer
Episcopalian
New York
Nat Cyc Am Bio v53; Not Am
Wom supp v1

1784. Woolley, Alice Stone
died 1946
physician, president of the American Medical Women's Association
New York
Obit File

1785. Clark, Mary Chase; Mrs. Raymond S. Darrenougue
1897–1945
lawyer
Episcopalian
New York
Index t Wom; Nat Cyc Am Bio
v32

1786. Goldstein, Jennie; Jennie Groll
1897–1960
actor in Yiddish theater
Jewish
New York
Obit File

1787. Goldthwaite, Lucy A.
1897–1957
librarian in the New York Public Library for the Blind, founder of the *Braille Book Review*
New York
Obit File

1788. Shaver, Dorothy (Yeiser)
1897–1959
business executive, merchandising executive, president of Lord and Taylor department stores
Episcopalian
New York
Index t Wom; Nat Cyc Am Bio
v56 and csv8; Not Am Wom
supp v1; Obit File

1789. Vaughn, Hilda; Hilda Strouse
1897–1957
Broadway stage character actor
New York
Obit File

1790. Gambrell, Mary Latimer
1898–1974
educator, president of Hunter College
Presbyterian
New York
Nat Cyc Am Bio v59; Obit File

1791. Glueck, Eleanor (Touroff)
1898–1972
research criminologist, Harvard Law School criminologist, pioneer in the study of juvenile delinquency, social worker
New York; Massachusetts
Cur Biog '72; Index t Wom; Nat
Cyc Am Bio v57; Not Am Wom
supp v1; Obit File

1792. Guggenheim, Marguerite "Peggy"
born 1898
patron of modern art and music, art collector, author
Jewish
New York
Cur Biog '80; Index t Wom; Who
Who Jew Hist

1793. Pickel, Mary Barnard
1898–1955
educator, dean of women at Columbia University
New York
Obit File

1794. Berg, Gertrude Edelstein
1899–1966
radio, television, and screen writer; playwright; producer
Jewish
New York
Index t Wom; Nat Cyc Am Bio
v52; Not Am Wom supp v1;
Obit File

1795. Carter, Eunice Hunton
1899–1970
lawyer, community leader, social worker
New York
Black
Not Am Wom supp v1; Obit File

1796. Kaminska, Ida
1899–1980
stage actor, producer, director of Yiddish theater
Jewish
New York, NY
Cur Biog '69 and '80

1797. Petersen, Anna
1899–1975
newspaper reporter, *New York Times* staff member
New York
Obit File

1798. Sardeau, Helen; Mrs. George Biddle
1899–1969
sculptor
New York
Belgian
Nat Cyc Am Bio v55

1799. Strauss, Anna Lord
1899–1979
editor, club leader, feminist, political activist, New York civic worker, internationalist
Quaker
New York
Cur Biog '79; Index t Wom; Nat
Cyc Am Bio csv10

1800. Broido, Lucy Kaufmann
1900–69
welfare agency leader
Jewish
New York, NY
Nat Cyc Am Bio v55

1801. Rusk, Evelyn Carroll
1900–64
mathematician, educator
Catholic
New York
Nat Cyc Am Bio v51

1802. Scaravaglione, Concetta Maria
1900–75
sculptor
New York
Nat Cyc Am Bio v59

1803. Alexander, Hattie Elizabeth
1901/08–1968
research pediatrician, microbiologist
Congregationalist
New York
Nat Cyc Am Bio csv10; Not Am
Wom; Obit File

1804. Bruce, Ailsa Mellon
1901–69
philanthropist, patron of art, conservationist
Episcopalian
New York
Nat Cyc Am Bio v55; Obit File

1805. Cary, Mary Harkness Flagler
1901–67
patron of music, conservationist
New York
Nat Cyc Am Bio v55

1806. de Lany, Dorothy Celia
1901–60
home economics educator
Ithaca, NY
Nat Cyc Am Bio v47

1807. Mills, Louise Morris
1901–76
Girl Scout executive, YWCA executive, Planned Parenthood executive
New York
Nat Cyc Am Bio v59

1808. Wasson, Valentina Pavlovna Guercken
1901–58
pediatrician, mycologist
New York
Russian
Obit File

1809. Algase, Julia Cohn
1902–75
lawyer, AFL-CIO worker, actor
Jewish
New York, NY
Nat Cyc Am Bio v58

1810. Baumgartner, Leona; Mrs. Nathaniel M. Elias
born 1902
pediatrician, public health official
Presbyterian
New York, NY
Index t Wom; Nat Cyc Am Bio
csv9

1811. Serge, Anne Brooks McAdoo
1902–53
chief auditing clerk of the Third District, Internal Revenue Service
New York
Obit File

1812. Atkin, Mildred Tommy; Mrs. Fisher Winston
1903–69
artist
Jewish
New York
Nat Cyc Am Bio v53 and csv9

1813. Dewey, Frances Eileen Hutt
1903–70
singer

New York
Obit File

1814. Neuschaefer, Helen Ahrens
1903–61
inventor of colored nail polish, business executive
Lutheran
New York
Nat Cyc Am Bio v46

1815. Payson, Joan Whitney
1903–75
philanthropist, race horse breeder, owner of the New York Mets, patron of medicine, art collector and investor, founder of the Museum of Modern Art in New York
Episcopalian
New York
Cur Biog '72 and '75; Index t Wom; Nat Cyc Am Bio v58 and csv10; Obit File

1816. Adair, Marion Hopkinson (Barnes)
1904–65
New York civic leader, World War II relief worker, cancer-patient relief worker, patron of cancer research, radio personality, mimic
New York, NY
Nat Cyc Am Bio v51

1817. Greene, Gertrude Glass
1904–56
sculptor, abstract painter
New York
Nat Cyc Am Bio v47; Obit File

1818. Hennock, Frieda Barkin (Simmons)
1904–60
criminal lawyer, FCC member, advocate of educational television
Jewish
New York
Polish
Index t Wom; Nat Cyc Am Bio csv8; Not Am Wom supp v1; Obit File

1819. Lewisohn, Adele Guggenheimer
died 1954
philanthropist
Jewish
New York
Obit File

1820. Bartlett, Phyllis (Brooks); Mrs. John A. Pollard
1905–73
educator, scholar of English literature
Episcopalian
New York
Nat Cyc Am Bio v58

1821. Jackson, Beatrice; Mrs. David Humphreys
born 1905
artist
Episcopalian
New York
English
Nat Cyc Am Bio csv13

1822. Klein, Anne; Hannah Golofsky
1905/23–1974
fashion designer
Jewish
New York
Nat Cyc Am Bio v58; Obit File

1823. Backus, Louise Laidlaw
1906–73
New York civic worker, UNESCO member, international affairs expert, poet
Episcopalian
New York, NY
Nat Cyc Am Bio v57

1824. Black, Irma Simonton
1906–72
preschool director, children's author
New York
Nat Cyc Am Bio v58

1825. Darlington, Alice (Nelson) Benning
1906–73
New York civic worker
Episcopalian
New York, NY
Twent Cen Bio Dict Not Am

1826. Hofmann, Melita Cecelia
1907–76
artist, art educator, book illustrator and designer, author, conservationist
Congregationalist
New York
Nat Cyc Am Bio v60

1827. Adams, Eva Bertrand
born 1908
director of the US Mint, New York politician, lawyer
New York
Index t Wom; Read Encyc Am West

1828. Baldwin, Janet Sterling; Mrs. Herbert C. Maier
1908–58
pediatrician, medical educator
Episcopalian
New York
Nat Cyc Am Bio v59

1829. Taylor, Marian Young; Martha Denae
1908–73
interviewer, journalist
Presbyterian

New York
Nat Cyc Am Bio v57

1830. Brooks, Ruth Walker; Mrs. Kenneth L. Hoffman
born 1909
sculptor
New York
Nat Cyc Am Bio csv5

1831. Crary, Catherine Snell
1909–74
historian, educator
Presbyterian
New York
Nat Cyc Am Bio v58

1832. Konheim, Beatrice Goldstein
1909–73
science educator, member of the ACLU
Jewish
New York
Nat Cyc Am Bio v58

1833. Wilson, Frances M.
1910–59
director of child guidance for the New York City board of education
New York
Obit File

1834. Rahn, Muriel
1911–61
soprano singer, Broadway musical actor
New York
Black
Obit File

1835. Bondy, Elizabeth Jeanne Hale
1913–69
literary agent, book editor
Congregationalist
New York
Nat Cyc Am Bio v54

1836. Preminger, Marion Hill; Mrs. Albert Mayer
1913–72
social worker, author, African art collector, missionary to the Congo, philanthropist, screen actor
Catholic
New York
Hungarian
Nat Cyc Am Bio v57; Obit File

1837. Culver, Agnes Moe
1914–75
illustration dealer, historian
Congregationalist
New York
Nat Cyc Am Bio v58 and v59

1838. Hutson, Jean Blackwell
born 1914

librarian, curator of the Schomburg Center for Research and Black Culture
New York
Black
Encyc Black Am

1839. Waller, Wilhelmine Stewart Kirby
born 1914
conservationist, horsewoman
Episcopalian
New York
Nat Cyc Am Bio csv13

1840. Bird, Caroline (Mahoney)
born 1915
lecturer, women's equal rights activist, author
New York
Cur Biog '76

1841. Diggs, Estella B.
born 1916
New York State legislator
New York
Black
Encyc Black Am

1842. Cummings, Victoria "Vicki"
1919–69
musical comedy actor, comedian
New York
Obit File

1843. Hamar, Irene; Mrs. Henry Peter de Vries
1919–73
sculptor, skier
New York
Brazilian
Nat Cyc Am Bio v57

1844. Abzug, Bella (Savitsky)
born 1920
representative to Congress from New York, lawyer with specialty in labor law, lecturer, peace worker
Jewish
New York
Cur Biog '71

1845. Guest, Barbara
born 1920
poet, theatrical producer
New York
Dict Lit Bio v5

1846. Rose, Lucille Mason
born 1920
New York City commissioner of employment
New York, NY
Black
Negro Alman

1847. Huxtable, Ada Louise (Landman)
born 1921
architecture critic, journalist

New York, NY
Cur Biog '73

1848. McWhinney, Adeline H(ouston)
born 1922
banking executive, founder and president of the First Women's Bank
New York, NY
Cur Biog '76

1849. Welch, Mary; Mary White
1923–58
Broadway stage actor
New York
Obit File

1850. Chisholm, Shirley [Anita] (St. Hill)
born 1924/26
New York State legislator, representative to Congress from New York, 1972 presidential candidate in New York Democratic primary
New York
Black
Cur Biog '69; Encyc Black Am; Negro Alman

1851. Walker, Cora T.
born 1926
lawyer, civic leader, co-op founder
Harlem, NY
Black
Encyc Black Am; Negro Alman; Prof Negro Wom v2

1852. Wexler, Jacqueline Grennan
born 1926
president of Hunter College
Catholic
New York
Cur Biog '70

1853. Fornes, Maria Irene
born 1930
playwright, theatrical director
New York
Cuban
Dict Lit Bio v7

1854. Hansberry, Lorraine
1930–65
playwright, civil rights reformer, Socialist party worker
New York
Black
Dict Lit Bio v7; Encyc Black Am; Index t Wom; Nat Cyc Am Bio v60; Negro Alman; Not Am Wom supp v1; Obit File; Prof Negro Wom v2; Wom Lit; Wom Lit, More

1855. Krupsak, Mary Anne
born 1932

Democratic lieutenant governor of New York, lawyer, feminist, women's rights worker
New York
Cur Biog '75

1856. Rossner, Judith Perelman
born 1935
novelist
Jewish
New York, NY
Dict Lit Bio v6; Wom Lit; Wom Lit, More

1857. Norton, Eleonor Holmes
born 1937
lawyer, chairperson of the Equal Opportunities Committee, New York City Human Rights commissioner, civil rights worker
New York
Black
Cur Biog '76; Encyc Black Am; Negro Alman

1858. Quarles, Norma
flourished 1970s
television newscaster
New York
Black
Negro Alman

1859. Holtzman, Elizabeth
born 1941
lawyer, Democratic representative to Congress from New York, feminist, anti-Vietnam war protester
New York
Cur Biog '73

1860. Jong, Erica (Mann)
born 1942
novelist, poet, feminist
Jewish
New York
Cur Biog '75; Dict Lit Bio v2 and v5; Wom Lit; Wom Lit, More

1861. Swados, Elizabeth
born 1951
play score writer, avant-garde composer, ᵒ⁻ᵃⁱ director, playwright
Jewish
New York
Cur Biog '79

NORTH CAROLINA

1862. MacDonald, Flora
1722–90
Scottish hero who assisted in the escape of pretender to the throne Charles Edward in 1746, pioneer
Fayetteville, NC

Scottish
Am Bio Dict; Cyc Am Bio; Dict Am Bio Men Time; Index t Wom

1863. Clarke, Mary Bayard (Devereaux)
1822/27–1886
author, editor, poet
North Carolina
Cyc Am Bio; Dict Am Auth; Dict Am Bio; Nat Cyc Am Bio v8; Not Am Wom; Twent Cen Bio Dict Not Am

1864. Spencer, Cornelia Ann (Phillips)
1825–1908
historian, history writer, writer on the Civil War era
North Carolina
Dict Am Auth; Dict Am Bio; Not Am Wom

1865. Downing, Frances Murdaugh "Fanny"; Frank Dashmore; Viola
1835–94
poet, author, novelist
Charlottesville, VA; North Carolina
Cyc Am Bio; Dict Am Auth; Nat Cyc Am Bio v7

1866. Cotten, Sallie Sims Southall
1846–1929
leader in North Carolina women's club movement
North Carolina
Encyc South Hist; Not Am Wom

1867. Tiernan, Frances Christine (Fisher); Christian Reid
1846–1920
author, popular novelist
Catholic
North Carolina
Dict Am Auth; Dict Am Bio; Index t Wom; Nat Cyc Am Bio v20; Not Am Wom; Twent Cen Bio Dict Not Am

1868. Beale, Maria Taylor
born 1849
novelist
North Carolina
Dict Am Auth

1869. Chamberlain, Hope Summerhill
born 1870
author
Methodist
North Carolina
Nat Cyc Am Bio csv8

1870. Holland, Annie Wealthy
1871–1934
educator
North Carolina

Black
Negro Alman; Prof Negro Wom v1

1871. Cotten, Elizabeth Brownrigg Henderson
born 1875
suffragist
North Carolina
Nat Cyc Am Bio csv1

1872. Fleshman, Mina Pepper
1879–1965
realtor, developer
Moravian
North Carolina
Moravian
Nat Cyc Am Bio v50

1873. Brown, Charlotte Eugenia Hawkins
1882/83–1961
educator, founder of the Palmer Memorial Institute, YWCA national board member
North Carolina
Black
Encyc Black Am; Index t Wom; Negro Alman; Not Am Wom supp v1; Obit File; Prof Negro Wom v1 and v2

1874. Elliott, Harriet Wiseman
1884–1947
educator, dean of women's college at the University of North Carolina, suffragist, women's rights worker, political organizer, public official
North Carolina
Encyc South Hist; Index t Wom; Not Am Wom; Obit File

1875. Biddle, Mary Duke
1887–1960
humanitarian, philanthropist, patron of Duke University
Methodist Episcopal
North Carolina
Index t Wom; Nat Cyc Am Bio v49

1876. Cobb, Beatrice
1888–1959
newspaper editor, publisher of the Morganton, North Carolina, *News-Herald*
Methodist
Morganton, NC
Nat Cyc Am Bio v45; Obit File

1877. Williams, Fannie Ransom
flourished 1920s
constitutionalist, World War I soldier's welfare worker
Presbyterian
North Carolina
Nat Cyc Am Bio v21

1878. Street, Margaret Berry
1891–1967

cattle farmer, lawyer, Civil Air Regulations executive, suffragist, Black welfare worker
Presbyterian
North Carolina
Nat Cyc Am Bio v54

1879. Boyd, Katharine Lamont
1896–1974
newspaper editor
Episcopalian
North Carolina
Nat Cyc Am Bio v59

1880. Davis, Rachel [Kathryn]; Sarah Rebecca (Darden) Speight
born 1905
gynecologist, cancer researcher, eugenicist
Baptist
North Carolina
Nat Cyc Am Bio supp vK

NORTH DAKOTA

1881. Walker, Tillie
born 1929
specialist in Native American education
North Dakota
Native American (Mandan-Hidatsa)
Read Encyc Am West

OHIO

1882. Bailey, Ann; Mad Anne
1725/42–1825
frontier scout and messenger on the Virginia border, soldier, Indian fighter, American patriot
Ohio; Virginia
British
Appl Cyc Am Bio; Dict Am Bio; Encyc South Hist; Who Who Dur Am Rev; Wom Cent

1883. Brodhead, Eva Wilder (McGlasson)
born 18?
poet, magazine writer
Cincinnati, OH
Dict Am Auth

1884. Peter, Sarah Anne (Worthington) King
1800–77
charity worker, philanthropist, founder of art school for women, hospital founder, Civil War nurse, pioneer industrial arts educator, church worker
Catholic

Ohio
Dict Am Bio; Index t Wom; Not Am Wom; Twent Cen Bio Dict Not Am

1885. Pratt, Anna Marie
born 18?
children's author
Cleveland, OH
Dict Am Auth

1886. Wolfenstein, Martha
born 18?
short story writer
Columbus, OH
Dict Am Auth

1887. Ludnam, Augusta V.
died 1851
pianist
Cincinnati, OH
Am Bio Dict

1888. Smith, Sarah Louisa P. (Hickman)
1811–32
poet
Cincinnati, OH
Cyc Am Bio; Dict Am Auth; Dict Am Bio Men Time; Index t Wom

1889. Thompson, Eliza Jane Trimble
1813/16–1905
temperance reformer
Ohio
Index t Wom; Not Am Wom; Wom Cent

1890. O'Connell, Mary; Sister Anthony
1814–97
Catholic nun, Civil War nurse, orphanage and hospital director in Cincinnati
Catholic
Cincinnati, OH
Dict Am Bio; Not Am Wom

1891. Cary, Alice
1820–71
poet, novelist
Universalist
New York; Ohio
Cyc Am Bio; Dict Am Auth; Dict Am Bio; Dict Am Bio Men Time; Index t Wom; Nat Cyc Am Bio v1; Not Am Wom; Twent Cen Bio Dict Not Am; Wom Cent; Wom Lit, More

1892. Coit, Elizabeth
born 1820
suffragist, temperance worker, humanitarian
Ohio
Irish
Wom Cent

1893. Bostwick, Helen Louise (Barrow)
born 1826
poet
Ohio
Dict Am Auth; Dict Am Bio Men Time

1894. McCabe, Harriet Calista Clark
1827–1919
philanthropist, temperance worker
Ohio
Index t Wom; Wom Cent

1895. Wittenmyer, Annie (Turner)
1827–1900
Civil War relief worker, leader in church and charitable work, philanthropist, temperance worker, lecturer, author
Ohio
Index t Wom; Nat Cyc Am Bio v12; Not Am Wom; Wom Cent

1896. Fray, Ellen Sulley
born 1832
suffragist, feminist, women's labor reformer
Ohio
Wom Cent

1897. Segur, Rosa L.
born 1833
suffragist
Ohio
Wom Cent

1898. Cary, Mary Stockley
born 1834
businessperson, investor, philanthropist
Cleveland, OH
Wom Cent

1899. Rose, Martha E. (Parmelee)
born 1834
women's labor welfare worker, social reformer, sociologist, author, art patron, journalist, Sorosis member
Cleveland, OH
Index t Wom; Nat Cyc Am Bio v11; Wom Cent

1900. Houghton, Mary Hayes
born 1837
journalist
Ohio
Wom Cent

1901. Brown, Martha McClellen
1838–1916
founder of the Prohibition party, temperance reformer, suffragist, lecturer
Methodist

Ohio
Index t Wom; Nat Cyc Am Bio v27; Not Am Wom; Wom Cent

1902. Hickman, Mary Catharine
born 1838
journalist, temperance worker
Ohio
Wom Cent

1903. Tuttle, Emma Rood
born 1839/59
author, poet, lecturer
Berlin Heights, OH
Cyc Am Bio; Dict Am Auth; Wom Cent

1904. Warner, Marion E. Knowlton
born 1839
poet, story writer
Ohio
Wom Cent

1905. Brotherton, Alice William
flourished 1870s; died 1930
author, poet, lecturer, magazine writer
Cincinnati, OH
Dict Am Auth; Index t Wom; Wom Cent

1906. McLaughlin, Mary Louise M.
flourished 1870s–1900s
ceramic artist, writer on art techniques
Cincinnati, OH
Dict Am Auth; Index t Wom

1907. Ruprecht, Jenny Terrill
born 1840
author, children's author, Sorosis member
Cleveland, OH
Wom Cent

1908. Smith, Mary Prudence (Wells); P. Thorne
born 1840
children's author
Cincinnati, OH
Cyc Am Bio and ad; Dict Am Auth

1909. Woodbridge, Mary A. Brayton
flourished 1870s–90s
temperance reformer
Ohio
Wom Cent

1910. Bolton, Sarah Knowles
1841–1916
author, temperance worker
Cleveland, OH
Cyc Am Bio and ad; Dict Am Auth; Dict Am Bio; Nat Cyc Am Bio v1; Twent Cen Bio Dict Not Am; Wom Cent

1911. McAvoy, Emma
born 1841
author, lecturer
Ohio
Wom Cent

1912. Patterson, Virginia Sharpe
born 1841
author
Ohio
Wom Cent

1913. Sherwood, Katharine Margaret (Brownlee) "Kate"
1841/43–1914
journalist, newspaper editor, poet, author, clubwoman, suffragist
Canton, OH
Dict Am Auth; Dict Am Bio; Index t Wom; Nat Cyc Am Bio v1; Not Am Wom; Twent Cen Bio Dict Not Am; Wom Cent

1914. Farmer, Lydia (Hoyt)
1842/43–1903
religious author, journalist
Cleveland, OH
Dict Am Auth; Index t Wom; Nat Cyc Am Bio v8; Twent Cen Bio Dict Not Am; Wom Cent

1915. Wintermute, Martha (Vandermark)
born 1842
poet, temperance writer
Ohio
Wom Cent

1916. Everhard, Caroline McCullough
born 1843
suffragist, feminist, humane society worker
Ohio
Wom Cent

1917. Strohm, Gertrude
born 1843
miscellaneous author, compiler of information
Dayton, OH
Dict Am Auth; Wom Cent

1918. Treat, Anna Elizabeth
born 1843
author, poet
Ohio
Wom Cent

1919. Baines-Miller, Minnie (Willis)
born 1845
author
Springfield, OH
Dict Am Auth

1920. Case, Marietta Stanley
born 1845

author, poet, temperance worker, home and foreign mission worker
Manchester, OH
Wom Cent

1921. Miller, Minnie (Willis) (Baines)
born 1845
religious author, temperance worker
Springfield, OH
Dict Am Auth; Wom Cent

1922. Peters, Alice E. H.
born 1845
church and temperance worker, suffragist, author
Methodist Episcopal
Ohio
Wom Cent

1923. Shaw, Cornelia Dean
born 1845
suffragist, philanthropist, Congregationalist missionary worker
Congregationalist
Toledo, OH
Wom Cent

1924. Smith, Isabel Elizabeth
1845–1938
painter
Ohio
Index t Wom; Wom Cent

1925. Sprague, Mary Aplin
born 1849
novelist
Newark, OH
Dict Am Auth

1926. Moore, Henrietta G.
flourished 1880s–90s
Universalist minister, temperance worker
Ohio
Wom Cent

1927. Mather, Flora Stone
1852–1909
philanthropist
Cleveland, OH
Nat Cyc Am Bio v44

1928. Taft, Anne Sinton; Mrs. Charles Phelps
1852–1931
philanthropist
Cincinnati, OH
Nat Cyc Am Bio v23

1929. Delatombe, Alice S.
born 1854
poet
Ohio
Wom Cent

1930. Thomas, Edith Matilda
1854–1925
poet, author

New York; Geneva, OH
Cyc Am Bio and ad; Dict Am Auth; Dict Am Bio; Index t Wom; Nat Cyc Am Bio v9; Not Am Wom; Twent Cen Bio Dict Not Am; Wom Cent

1931. Laws, Annie
1855–1927
kindergarten and education worker, clubwoman, civic leader, patron of nursing
Ohio
Nat Cyc Am Bio v22; Not Am Wom

1932. Coman, Katharine
1857–1915
economic historian, writer on history, social reformer, educator
Ohio
Dict Am Auth; Index t Wom; Not Am Wom

1933. Fry, Laura Ann
born 1857
artist, ceramicist
Ohio
Wom Cent

1934. Markscheffel, Louise
born 1857
journalist
Ohio
Wom Cent

1935. Brain, Belle M.
born 1859
temperance author, educator
Springfield, OH
Dict Am Auth

1936. Moody, Helen (Waterson)
1859/60–1928
author, journalist, educator
Ohio; New York, NY
Dict Am Auth; Index t Wom; Nat Cyc Am Bio v22; Wom Cent

1937. Tilley, Lucy Evangeline
1859–90
poet
Medina, OH
Dict Am Auth; Nat Cyc Am Bio v4

1938. Gilchrist, Rosetta Luce
flourished 1890s
physician, author, poet, women's rights worker
Cleveland, OH
Wom Cent

1939. Robb, Isabella Adams (Hampton)
1860/63–1910
professional nurse, educator, writer on nursing
Cleveland, OH
Index t Wom; Not Am Wom

1940. Bauer, Bertha
1862–1940
music educator
Cincinnati, OH
German
Index t Wom; Nat Cyc Am Bio v31

1941. Baur, Clara
died 1912
music educator
Ohio
German
Nat Cyc Am Bio v26

1942. Murphy, Claudia Quigley
born 1863
journalist, suffragist, women's rights worker
Ohio
Wom Cent

1943. Lawrence, Ida Ethel (Eckert)
born 1864
poet, author
Toledo, OH
Dict Am Auth; Nat Cyc Am Bio v4

1944. Talbott, Katharine Houk
1864–1935
patron of music
Dayton, OH
Nat Cyc Am Bio v28

1945. Smith, Fannie Douglass
born 1865
journalist
Ohio
Wom Cent

1946. Eastman, Linda Anne
1867–1963
librarian
Cleveland, OH
Index t Wom; Nat Cyc Am Bio csv3; Not Am Wom supp v1

1947. Sherwin, Belle
1868–1955
suffragist, president of the National League of Women Voters, civic leader
Ohio
Nat Cyc Am Bio csv3; Not Am Wom supp v1; Obit File

1948. Watts, Mary Stanbery
1868–1958
author, novelist
Ohio
Index t Wom; Nat Cyc Am Bio csv3

1949. Hughes, Adella Prentiss
1869–1950
concert manager, founder of the Cleveland Symphony Orchestra
Cleveland, OH
Nat Cyc Am Bio csv3; Not Am Wom; Obit File

1950. Stage, Miriam Kerruish
1870–1929
physician, suffragist
Ohio
Nat Cyc Am Bio v21

1951. Harvey, Kate Benedict Hanna
1871–1936
public health worker, patron of nursing, cattle breeder
Protestant Episcopal
Cleveland, OH
Nat Cyc Am Bio v34

1952. Fitch, Florency Mary
1875–1959
Biblical literature authority, university educator, religious writer for children
Oberlin, OH
Obit File

1953. McKesson, Martha Fredrika
born 1878
business executive
Toledo, OH
Nat Cyc Am Bio csv7

1954. McBride, Lucia McCurdy
1880–1970
Cleveland civic leader, suffragist
Episcopalian
Cleveland, OH
Nat Cyc Am Bio v57 and csv7

1955. Perkins, Edna Brush
1880–1930
author, social worker
Cincinnati, OH
Nat Cyc Am Bio v26

1956. Blossom, Elizabeth Beardsley Bingham
1881–1970
Cleveland civic worker, philanthropist
Cleveland, OH
Nat Cyc Am Bio v58

1957. Hunter, Jane Edna
1882–1971
social worker, nurse, educator, clubwoman
Cleveland, OH
Black
Index t Wom; Negro Alman; Prof Negro Wom v1

1958. Allen, Florence Ellinwood
1884–1966
lawyer, US Court of Appeals judge, suffragist
Congregationalist
Ohio
Index t Wom; Nat Cyc Am Bio v52 and csv3; Not Am Wom; Obit File

1959. Emery, Mary Muhlenberk Hopkins
1884–1927
philanthropist, founder of Mariemont, a model town near Cincinnati
Protestant Episcopal
Ohio
Nat Cyc Am Bio v24

1960. Bolton, Frances Payne (Bingham)
1885/86–1977
Republican representative to Congress from Ohio, nurse
Presbyterian
Ohio
Cur Biog '77; Index t Wom; Nat Cyc Am Bio csv11; Obit File

1961. Everett, Flora Pierce Morris
born 1885
Cleveland civic worker
Episcopalian
Cleveland, OH
Nat Cyc Am Bio csv6

1962. Westropp, Clara Elizabeth
1886–1965
banker
Catholic
Ohio
Nat Cyc Am Bio v51

1963. Grooms, Jessie Macy Roberts
1891–1955
artist, art educator
Ohio
Nat Cyc Am Bio v46

1964. Mather, Elizabeth Ring Ireland
1891–1957
philanthropist, patron of horticulture
Cleveland, OH
Nat Cyc Am Bio v43

1965. Boothe, Viva Belle
1893–1964
business researcher, economist, educator
Methodist
Ohio
Nat Cyc Am Bio v51

1966. Ireland, Margaret Allen
1894–1961
public health worker, Cleveland civic worker, welfare worker
Episcopalian
Cleveland, OH
Nat Cyc Am Bio v50

1967. Graves, Helen (Louise) Pierson
born 1914
physician, medical educator
Methodist

Ohio
Nat Cyc Am Bio csv13

1968. Burke, Lillian W.
born 1917
lawyer, judge
Ohio
Black
Encyc Black Am

1969. Loehrke, Leah Marie
1918–71
psychologist, psychological educator
Lutheran
Ohio
Nat Cyc Am Bio v57

OKLAHOMA

1970. Robertson, Alice Mary
1854–1931
educator of Native Americans, representative to Congress from Oklahoma, educator, social worker, postmaster
Oklahoma
Dict Am Bio; Index t Wom; Not Am Wom

1971. Diehl, Cora Victoria
born 1869
register of deeds in Great Bend, Kansas; register of deeds for Logan County, Oklahoma; Populist party politician with Democratic endorsement; Farmer's Alliance party worker; Greenback party worker
Kansas; Oklahoma
Wom Cent

1972. Clubb, Laura Abigail Rutherford
1873–1952
art collector, rare book collector, philanthropist, cattle rancher
Methodist
Oklahoma
Nat Cyc Am Bio v38

1973. Barnard, Kate
1875–1930
Democratic political reformer, Native American rights advocate, child welfare leader, philanthropist
Oklahoma
Index t Wom; Nat Cyc Am Bio v15, Not Am Wom; Read Encyc Am West

1974. Garber, Lucy May (Bradley)
1880–1971
US land commissioner in Oklahoma, newspaper publisher
Oklahoma
Nat Cyc Am Bio v58

1975. Comstock, Amy
1887–1944
associate editor of the *Tulsa Tribune*
Tulsa, OK
Obit File

1976. Bronson, Ruth Muskrat
born 1897
Cherokee government official, field representative of Save the Children Federation
Oklahoma
Native American (Cherokee)
Ind Today; Read Encyc Am West

1977. Silkwood, Karen
1946–74
critic of the procedures of an Oklahoma nuclear facility
Oklahoma
Obit File

OREGON

1978. Eliot, Henrietta Robins (Mack)
born 18?
author
Portland, OR
Dict Am Auth

1979. Spalding, Eliza Hart
1807–51
pioneer missionary to Oregon
Oregon
Index t Wom; Not Am Wom

1980. Bailey, Margaret Jewett
circa 1812–82
pioneer, author
Oregon
Read Encyc Am West

1981. Perkins, Elmira Johnson
1814–96
missionary to Native Americans in Oregon, poet
Oregon; Boston, MA
Dict Am Auth

1982. Victor, Frances Auretta (Fuller) (Barrett); Florence Fane
1826–1902
author, historian of the Pacific Northwest
Oregon; California
Cyc Am Bio; Dict Am Auth; Dict Am Bio; Nat Cyc Am Bio v13; Not Am Wom; Twent Cen Bio Dict Not Am; Wom Cent

1983. Duniway, Abigail Jane Scott
1834–1915
pioneer, suffrage leader, feminist, journalist, editor, lecturer

Oregon
Dict Am Bio; Index t Wom; Not
Am Wom; Wom Cent

1984. Herson, Jane Lord
born 1840
physician, suffragist
Oregon
Wom Cent

1985. Dow, Cornelia M.
born 1842
temperance worker, philanthropist
Congregationalist
Portland, OR
Wom Cent

1986. Stone, Mary Perry
born 1842
businessperson, railroad station
agent, suffragist
Oregon
Wom Cent

1987. Foster, Susie E. (Holland)
born 1846
author, philanthropist
Oregon
Wom Cent

1988. Mallory, Lucy A.
born 1846
editor, educator of Blacks
Oregon
Index t Wom; Wom Cent

1989. Martin, Jane (Percy)
born 1847
short story writer
Pendleton, OR
Dict Am Auth

1990. Riggs, Anna Rankin
flourished 1880s–90s
temperance reformer
Oregon
Wom Cent

1991. Dye, Eva (Emery)
1855–1947
historian, writer of historical fiction, novelist
Oregon
Dict Am Auth; Index t Wom;
Nat Cyc Am Bio v13; Read
Encyc Am West

1992. Miller, Addie Dickman
born 1859
educator, temperance worker, inventor of the dishwasher
Oregon
Wom Cent

1993. Jackson, Maria Clopton
1863–1956
chairperson of the board of the
Oregon Journal Publishing Co.
Oregon
Obit File

1994. Davis, Minta S. A.
born 1864
physician
Oregon
Wom Cent

1995. Cook, May A.
born 1869
pianist
Portland, OR
Wom Cent

1996. Lovejoy, Esther Clayson Pohl
1869/70–1967
physician; director of the
Portland, Oregon, health department; World War I Red
Cross worker in France; feminist
Protestant Episcopal
Portland, OR
Index t Wom; Nat Cyc Am Bio
csv1; Not Am Wom supp v1

1997. Hall, Grace Ethel Adams
flourished 1900s–20s
journalist, author
Portland, OR
Nat Cyc Am Bio csv1

1998. Monroe, Anne Shannon
1874/77–1942
author, essayist, novelist, magazine writer, Oregon historian,
feminist, lecturer, mountain
climber
Oregon
Index t Wom; Nat Cyc Am Bio;
Obit File

1999. Dunbar, Saidie [Sarah] Orr
1880–1960
patron of nursing and public
health, developer of Christmas
Seals
Catholic
Oregon
Nat Cyc Am Bio v51

2000. Hall, Hazel
1886–1924
poet
Oregon
Dict Am Bio; Index t Wom; Nat
Cyc Am Bio v22

2001. Neuberger, Maurine
born 1907
US senator from Oregon, politician
Unitarian
Oregon
Index t Wom; Nat Cyc Am Bio
csv10

PENNSYLVANIA

2002. Penn, Hannah Callowhill
1671–1726
executor of William Penn
Quaker
Pennsylvania
Cyc Am Bio; Index t Wom; Not
Am Wom

2003. Alice
1686–1802 [sic]
ferry captain, slave
Philadelphia, PA
Black
Am Bio Dict

2004. Aubrey, Leticia; Lady
Worminghurst
flourished 1730s–40s
owner and ruler of the Barony of
Nazareth, a tract of 5,000 acres
in Northampton County, Pennsylvania
Pennsylvania
British
Appl Cyc Am Bio

2005. Darragh, Lydia Barrington
1728/29–1789
colonial nurse and midwife, hero
of American Revolution
Pennsylvania
Cyc Am Bio; Index t Wom; Not
Am Wom

**2006. Ferguson, Elizabeth
(Graeme)**
1737/39–1801
litterateur, poet, translator, letter
writer, diarist, hero of American Revolution
Philadelphia, PA
Am Bio Dict; Cyc Am Bio; Dict
Am Auth; Dict Am Bio; Dict
Am Bio Men Time; Index t
Wom; Nat Cyc Am Bio v7; Not
Am Wom; Who Who Dur Am
Rev

2007. Bache, Sarah Franklin
1743/44–1808
relief worker in American Revolution, philanthropist
Philadelphia, PA
Appl Cyc Am Bio; Cyc Am Bio;
Dict Am Bio Men Time; Index t
Wom; Nat Cyc Am Bio v7; Not
Am Wom; Twent Cen Bio Dict
Not Am

2008. McCauley, Mary (Ludwig) Hays; Molly Pitcher
1744/54–1832
sergeant in the US Army, hero of
American Revolution

Pennsylvania
Dict Am Bio; Index t Wom; Nat
Cyc Am Bio v9; Not Am Wom;
Twent Cen Bio Dict Not Am;
Who Who Dur Am Rev

2009. Corbin, Margaret Cochran
1751–circa 1800
hero of American Revolution, soldier
Pennsylvania
Dict Am Bio; Index t Wom; Nat
Cyc Am Bio v6; Not Am Wom;
Twent Cen Bio Dict Not Am;
Who Who Dur Am Rev

2010. Ross, Betsy Griscom;
Elizabeth Claypool; Elizabeth
Grimke
1752–1832/36
flag maker
Pennsylvania
Dict Am Bio; Index t Wom; Not
Am Wom; Who Who Dur Am
Rev

2011. Morris, Elizabeth
circa 1753–1826
actor
Pennsylvania
English
Dict Am Bio; Index t Wom; Who
Who Dur Am Rev

2012. Parrish, Anne
1760–1800
colonial philanthropist for women's causes, educator
Pennsylvania
Dict Am Bio; Index t Wom; Who
Who Dur Am Rev

2013. Hall, Sarah (Ewing);
Constantia; Florepha
1761–1830
author, essayist, religious writer
Philadelphia, PA
Cyc Am Bio; Dict Am Auth; Dict
Am Bio; Index t Wom; Nat Cyc
Am Bio v11

2014. Logan, Deborah Norris
1761–1839
collector of historical records, historian
Pennsylvania
Am Bio Dict; Dict Am Bio; Index
t Wom; Nat Cyc Am Bio v25;
Not Am Wom

2015. Wister, Sarah "Sally"
1761/62–1804
diarist, patriot of American Revolution
Quaker
Pennsylvania
Dict Am Bio; Index t Wom; Who
Who Dur Am Rev

2016. Bingham, Anne Willing
1764–1801

Federalist political activist
Pennsylvania
Not Am Wom; Who Who Dur
Am Rev

2017. Pierce, Sarah "Sally"
1767–1852
educator
Litchfield, PA
Am Bio Dict; Index t Wom; Not
Am Wom

2018. Leslie, Eliza
1787–1858
cookbook writer, children's au-
thor, humorist, short story writ-
er, editor
Philadelphia, PA
Cyc Am Bio; Dict Am Auth; Dict
Am Bio; Dict Am Bio Men
Time; Index t Wom; Nat Cyc
Am Bio v7; Not Am Wom

**2019. Hale, Sarah Josepha
(Buell)**
1788/90–1879/97
magazine editor, author
Philadelphia, PA
Cyc Am Bio; Dict Am Auth; Dict
Am Bio; Dict Am Bio Men
Time; Dict Lit Bio v1; Index t
Wom; Nat Cyc Am Bio v3 and
v22; Not Am Wom; Twent Cen
Bio Dict Not Am; Wom Lit,
More

**2020. Lukens, Rebecca Webb
Pennock**
1794–1854
iron manufacturer, shipwright
Pennsylvania
Dict Am Bio; Index t Wom; Nat
Cyc Am Bio v15; Not Am Wom

2021. Forten, Harriet
flourished 1830s
abolitionist
Philadelphia, PA
Black
Prof Negro Wom v1

2022. Forten, Margaretta
flourished 1830s
abolitionist
Philadelphia, PA
Black
Prof Negro Wom v1

2023. Forten, Sarah Louisa
flourished 1830s
abolitionist
Philadelphia, PA
Black
Prof Negro Wom v1

**2024. Loud, Marguerite St.
Leon (Barstow)**
born circa 1800
poet
Philadelphia, PA
Cyc Am Bio; Dict Am Auth

**2025. Morrison, Sarah
Elizabeth**
born 18?
children's author
Philadelphia, PA
Dict Am Auth

**2026. Myers, Sarah Ann (Ir-
win)**
1800–76
children's author, artist
Carlisle, PA
Cyc Am Bio; Dict Am Auth

**2027. Robinson, Martha
Harrison**
born 18?
novelist, translator
Philadelphia, PA
Dict Am Auth

**2028. Peirson, Lydia Jane
(Wheeler)**
1802–62
author, poet
Adrian, MI; Pennsylvania
Cyc Am Bio; Dict Am Auth; Dict
Am Bio Men Time

2029. Canfield, Francesca Anna
1803–23
poet, translator, linguist
Philadelphia, PA
Cyc Am Bio; Dict Am Bio Men
Time

**2030. Douglass, Sarah Mapps
Douglass**
1806–82
educator, abolitionist
Philadelphia, PA
Black
Negro Alman; Not Am Wom;
Prof Negro Wom v1

2031. McKeever, Harriet Burn
1807–86
educator
Pennsylvania
Cyc Am Bio

2032. Scott, Julia H. (Kinney)
1809–42
poet
Towanda, PA
Dict Am Auth; Dict Am Bio Men
Time; Index t Wom

**2033. Esling, Catherine Harbe-
son (Waterman)**
born 1812
poet
Philadelphia, PA
Cyc Am Bio; Dict Am Auth

2034. Preston, Ann
1813–72
physician, hospital founder, college administrator, educator

Pennsylvania
Cyc Am Bio; Dict Am Bio; Index
t Wom; Nat Cyc Am Bio v10;
Not Am Wom; Twent Cen Bio
Dict Not Am; Wom Cent

**2035. Rea, Julia (de Marguer-
ittes) (Foster)**
1814–66
opera singer, drama critic, writer
on Europe
Philadelphia, PA
English
Cyc Am Bio; Dict Am Auth; Dict
Am Bio Men Time

2036. Shields, Mary
1820–80
philanthropist
Pennsylvania
Cyc Am Bio; Nat Cyc Am Bio v3

2037. Gibbons, Phoebe (Earle)
1821–190?
essayist
Lancaster County, PA
Dict Am Auth

**2038. Gillespie, Elizabeth
(Duane)**
1821–1901
autobiographer
Philadelphia, PA
Dict Am Auth

**2039. Hilderburn, Mary Jane
(Reed); Marie Roseau**
1821–82
author, children's author, reli-
gious author
Philadelphia, PA
Cyc Am Bio; Dict Am Auth; Nat
Cyc Am Bio v13

2040. Dixon, Mary J. Scarlett
born 1822
physician, abolitionist
Pennsylvania
Wom Cent

**2041. Lippincott, Sarah Jane
(Clarke); Grace Greenwood**
1823–1904
newspaper journalist, lecturer,
author, editor, novelist, femi-
nist, poet, children's author
Philadelphia, PA
Cyc Am Bio; Dict Am Auth; Dict
Am Bio; Dict Am Bio Men
Time; Index t Wom; Nat Cyc
Am Bio v4; Not Am Wom;
Twent Cen Bio Dict Not Am;
Wom Cent

**2042. Moore, Clara Sophia
(Jessup); Clara Moreton;
Clara Sophia (Jessup) Bloomfield-Moore**
1824–99
author, poet, novelist, philanthropist, Civil War relief worker

Philadelphia, PA
Cyc Am Bio; Dict Am Auth;
Index t Wom; Nat Cyc Am Bio
v9; Not Am Wom; Twent Cen
Bio Dict Not Am; Wom Cent

**2043. Turner, Eliza L. Sproat
Randolph**
1826–1903
author, poet, suffragist, women's
club leader
Pennsylvania
Dict Am Auth; Not Am Wom

**2044. Drinker, Anne; Edith
May**
born 1827
poet
Montrose, PA
Dict Am Auth; Dict Am Bio Men
Time; Nat Cyc Am Bio v11

2045. Dallas, Mary (Kyle)
1830–97
fiction writer
Philadelphia, PA
Dict Am Auth

2046. Hosmer, Margaret (Kerr)
1830–97
novelist, religious writer for children
Philadelphia, PA
Cyc Am Bio; Dict Am Auth

2047. Bodley, Rachel Littler
1831–88
chemist, botanist, physician, naturalist, dean of the Women's
Medical College of Pennsylvania
Pennsylvania
Not Am Wom; Wom Cent

2048. Eyster, Nellie Blessing
born 1831
author, children's author, temperance reformer, worker for Chinese American welfare
Pennsylvania; California
Cyc Am Bio; Dict Am Auth; Nat
Cyc Am Bio v10; Twent Cen
Bio Dict Not Am; Wom Cent

**2049. Rollins, Ellen Chapman
(Hobbs); E. H. Arr**
1831–81
writer on history
Philadelphia, PA
Cyc Am Bio; Dict Am Auth

**2050. Williams, Louisa Brew-
ster**
born 1832
composer, musician
Pennsylvania
Wom Cent

**2051. Hallowell, Sarah Cather-
ine (Fraley)**
born 1833
journalist, newspaper editor

Philadelphia, PA
Dict Am Auth

2052. Coues, Mary Emily Bennett
born 1835
suffragist, women's rights worker
Philadelphia, PA
Wom Cent

2053. Wheeler, Mary Sparks
born 1835
poet, religious author
Philadelphia, PA
Dict Am Auth

2054. Wister, Sarah (Butler)
born 1835
poet, translator
Philadelphia, PA
Dict Am Auth

2055. Keller, Elizabeth Catharine
born 1837
physician, surgeon
Lutheran
Pennsylvania; Massachusetts
Index t Wom; Wom Cent

2056. Swift, Frances Laura
born 1837
church worker, temperance worker
Presbyterian
Pennsylvania
Wom Cent

2057. Lambert, Mary Eliza (Perine) (Tucker)
born 1838
poet, author
Philadelphia, PA
Dict Am Auth

2058. Lippincott, Esther J. (Trimble)
1838–88
educator, author on literature, temperance reformer, convalescent-hospital reformer
Quaker
Pennsylvania
Dict Am Auth; Wom Cent

2059. Stockton, Louise
1838–1914
editor, journalist, novelist, critic, historian, social worker
Philadelphia, PA
Dict Am Auth; Index t Wom; Nat Cyc Am Bio v8; Twent Cen Bio Dict Not Am

2060. Sinclair, Carrie Bell
born 1839
poet
Philadelphia, PA
Cyc Am Bio; Dict Am Auth

2061. Dickinson, Susan E.
flourished 1870s–90s

journalist, author
Quaker
Pennsylvania
Index t Wom; Wom Cent

2062. Hammer, Anna Maria Nichols
born 1840
temperance worker
Pennsylvania
Wom Cent

2063. Killikelly, Sarah Hutchins
1840–1912
author
Pittsburgh, PA
Nat Cyc Am Bio v19

2064. Patterson, Mary Jane
1840–94
educator
Philadelphia, PA
Black
Index t Wom; Negro Alman; Prof Negro Wom vl

2065. Wakefield, Emily Watkins
flourished 1870s–90s
singer, educator, lecturer, musical director
Pennsylvania
English
Wom Cent

2066. Bond, Elizabeth Powell
1841–1926
abolitionist, educator of Blacks, women's rights worker, pacifist, civil rights and temperance worker, dean of Swarthmore College
Pennsylvania
Dict Am Bio; Index t Wom; Nat Cyc Am Bio v6; Wom Cent

2067. Oberholtzer, Sara Louisa (Vikers)
1841–1930
poet, author, novelist, temperance worker, leader in school savings movement, economist
Quaker
Norristown, PA
Cyc Am Bio; Dict Am Auth; Dict Am Bio; Index t Wom; Nat Cyc Am Bio v7; Wom Cent

2068. Sartain, Emily
1841–1927
painter, mezzotint engraver, etcher, illustrator, art educator
Philadelphia, PA
English
Cyc Am Bio; Dict Am Bio; Index t Wom; Nat Cyc Am Bio v13; Not Am Wom; Twent Cen Bio Dict Not Am; Wom Cent

2069. Veeder, Emily Elizabeth (Ferris)
1841–post 1890
author, poet, novelist
Pennsylvania; St. Louis, MO
Dict Am Auth; Wom Cent

2070. Cunningham, Susan Jane
1842–1921
suffragist, educator, mathematician, astronomer
Pennsylvania
Nat Cyc Am Bio v6; Wom Cent

2071. Edgar, Elizabeth
born 1842
educator
Presbyterian
Pennsylvania
Wom Cent

2072. Haensler, Arminta Victoria Scott
born 1842
gynecologist
Philadelphia, PA
Wom Cent

2073. Kirk, Ellen Warner (Olney); Henry Hayes
born 1842/46
author, novelist
Germantown, PA
Cyc Am Bio; Dict Am Auth; Index t Wom; Nat Cyc Am Bio vl; Twent Cen Bio Dict Not Am; Wom Cent

2074. Mumford, Mary Eno Bassett
1842–1935
education and civic leader, clubwoman
Philadelphia, PA
Not Am Wom

2075. Thompson, Eva Griffith
born 1842
temperance worker, Presbyterian missionary worker, newspaper editor and publisher
Presbyterian
Pennsylvania
Wom Cent

2076. Willson, Mary Elizabeth
born 1842
missionary, gospel singer, songwriter
Pennsylvania
Index t Wom; Wom Cent

2077. Howe, Emeline Harriet (Siggins)
born 1844
poet, temperance worker
Pennsylvania
Wom Cent

2078. Janvier, Margaret Thompson; Margaret Vandegrift
1844/45–1913
children's author
Philadelphia, PA
Dict Am Auth; Dict Am Bio; Nat Cyc Am Bio v12

2079. Orum, Julia Anna
born 1844
educator, elocutionist
Pennsylvania
Wom Cent

2080. Blankenburg, Lucretia M. Longshore
1845–1937
suffragist, women's rights worker, clubwoman, civic worker
Pennsylvania
Nat Cyc Am Bio csv2; Not Am Wom

2081. Wharton, Anne Hollingsworth
1845–1928
author, children's author, biographer, historian, historical writer
Philadelphia, PA
Cyc Am Bio; Dict Am Auth; Dict Am Bio; Index t Wom; Nat Cyc Am Bio v13; Twent Cen Bio Dict Not Am

2082. Broomall, Anna Elizabeth
1847–1931
obstetrician, medical educator
Pennsylvania
Index t Wom; Nat Cyc Am Bio v24; Not Am Wom

2083. Stevenson, Sarah (Yorke)
1847–1921
archaeologist, writer on archaeology
Philadelphia, PA
Dict Am Auth; Dict Am Bio; Index t Wom; Nat Cyc Am Bio v13; Twent Cen Bio Dict Not Am

2084. Anderson, Caroline Virginia Still
1849–1919
physician
Philadelphia, PA
Black
Index t Wom; Negro Alman; Prof Negro Wom

2085. Clark, Helen Taggart
born 1849
journalist
Pennsylvania
Wom Cent

2086. Coates, Florence van Leer (Earle) (Nicholson)
1850–1927
poet

Philadelphia, PA
Dict Am Auth; Dict Am Bio;
Index t Wom; Nat Cyc Am Bio
v18; Not Am Wom; Wom Cent

2087. Dillaye, Blanche
flourished 1880s; died 1931
artist, painter, etcher, sculptor
Philadelphia, PA
Index t Wom; Wom Cent

2088. Hewitt, Emma Churchman
born 1850
miscellaneous writer, journalist
Philadelphia, PA
Dict Am Auth; Wom Cent

2089. Holmes, Georgina (Klingle); George Klingle
born 185?
poet
Philadelphia, PA
Dict Am Auth; Wom Cent

2090. Jefferis, Marea Wood
flourished 1880s–1900s
poet
Philadelphia, PA
Index t Wom; Wom Cent

2091. Robinson, Mary Dommet (Nauman)
born 185?
novelist
Lancaster, PA
Dict Am Auth

2092. Schoff, Hannah Kent
1850/53–1940
child welfare worker, juvenile
court reformer, child aid leader,
editor, author
Philadelphia, PA
Index t Wom; Nat Cyc Am Bio
v18; Not Am Wom

2093. Bennett, Alice
1851–1925
physician, student of mental
health, superintendent of a
women's mental hospital
Pennsylvania
Index t Wom; Not Am Wom;
Twent Cen Bio Dict Not Am;
Wom Cent

2094. Griffith, Mary Lillian
born 1854
philanthropist, author on morals,
religious writer
Methodist Episcopal
Philadelphia, PA
Wom Cent

2095. Stille, Mary Ingram
born 1854
temperance worker
Pennsylvania
Wom Cent

2096. Mossell, Gertrude Bustill
born 1855
newspaper editor, author
Pennsylvania
Black
Negro Alman; Prof Negro Wom
v1

2097. Repplier, Agnes
1855/59–1950
essayist, children's author, biographer
Catholic
Philadelphia, PA
Dict Am Auth; Dict Am Bio
supp v4; Index t Wom; Nat Cyc
Am Bio v4; Not Am Wom; Obit
File; Twent Cen Bio Dict Not
Am

2098. Blanchard, Amy Ella
born 1856
children's author
Philadelphia, PA
Dict Am Auth

2099. Berry, Adaline Hohp
born 1859
author
Mennonite
Pennsylvania
Wom Cent

2100. Bittinger, Lucy (Forney)
born 1859
historical writer on Pennsylvania
Sweckley, PA
Twent Cen Bio Dict Not Am

2101. Gummere, Amelia Mott
1859–1937
author
Pennsylvania
Nat Cyc Am Bio v45

2102. Whiteley, Isabel (Nixon)
born 1859
romance writer
Philadelphia, PA
Dict Am Auth

2103. Spalding, Susan (Marr)
flourished 1890s
poet
Philadelphia, PA
Dict Am Auth; Wom Cent

2104. Taylor, Emily Drayton
1860–1952
miniature painter, founder of the
Philadelphia Arts Alliance
Philadelphia, PA
Obit File

2105. Kaufman, Betty Wolf
1861–1942
philanthropist, welfare worker
Jewish
Philadelphia, PA
Nat Cyc Am Bio v32

2106. Smith, Jessie Wilcox
1863–1935
painter, illustrator
Philadelphia, PA
Index t Wom; Nat Cyc Am Bio
v26; Not Am Wom

2107. Martin, Elizabeth Price
1864–1932
civic leader
Philadelphia, PA
Dict Am Bio supp v1

2108. Wilson, Lucy Langdon Williams
1864–1937
educator
Philadelphia, PA
Nat Cyc Am Bio v29

2109. Hill, Grace (Livingston)
1865–1947
popular novelist, short story writer
Presbyterian
Philadelphia, PA
Dict Am Auth; Dict Am Bio
supp v4; Nat Cyc Am Bio v40;
Not Am Wom; Obit File

2110. Shipley, Katherine Morris
1867–1929
educator
Pennsylvania
Nat Cyc Am Bio v23

2111. King, Lida Shaw
1868–1932
classical scholar, archaeologist,
educator, college administrator
Pennsylvania
Nat Cyc Am Bio v23; Not Am
Wom

2112. McGee, Alice G.
born 1869
lawyer
Pennsylvania
Wom Cent

2113. King, Helen
1870–1955
zoologist
Pennsylvania
Obit File

2114. Kingsbury, Susan Myra
1870–1949
social investigator, social work
educator, social economist, feminist
Pennsylvania
Not Am Wom; Obit File

2115. Speers, Emma (Doll) Bailey
1872–1961
YWCA executive
Presbyterian
Pennsylvania
Nat Cyc Am Bio v52

2116. Lingelbach, Anna Lane
1873–1954
historian, educator, civic leader,
feminist
Presbyterian
Pennsylvania
Dict Am Bio supp v5; Nat Cyc
Am Bio v44; Obit File

2117. Smith, Georgine Northrop Wetherill
1873–1955
artist, art patron
Unitarian
Philadelphia, PA
Nat Cyc Am Bio v48

2118. Auge, Emily Geary Whitton
1874–1934
surgeon
Presbyterian
Philadelphia, PA
Nat Cyc Am Bio v26

2119. Greaves, Jessie Royer
1874–1967
educator of the blind
United Church of Christ
Pennsylvania
Nat Cyc Am Bio v53

2120. Miller, Emma Guffey
1874–1970
Democratic party official, suffragist, feminist
Episcopalian
Pennsylvania
Index t Wom; Nat Cyc Am Bio
v55; Not Am Wom supp v1

2121. Starr, Sarah Logan Wister
1874–1956
physician, president of the Women's Medical College of Pennsylvania
Pennsylvania
Obit File

2122. Yaegle, Marie Tello Phillips
1874–1962
poet, novelist, essayist, founder of
the American Academy of
Poets
Catholic
Pennsylvania
Canadian
Index t Wom; Nat Cyc Am Bio
csv3; Obit File

2123. Benedict, Mary Kendrick
1875–1956
president of Sweet Briar College
Pennsylvania
Obit File

2124. Gannon, Anna
born 1876
poet

Philadelphia, PA
Dict Am Auth

2125. Tracy, Martha
1876–1942
physician, public health expert, dean of the Women's Medical College of Pennsylvania
Philadelphia, PA
Index t Wom; Nat Cyc Am Bio v31; Not Am Wom

2126. Gindhart, Mary Wilhelmina (Simon)
1878–1969
music patron
Methodist
Philadelphia, PA
Nat Cyc Am Bio v57

2127. Harcum, Edith H.
1878–1958
cofounder and president of Harcum Junior College
Philadelphia, PA
Obit File

2128. Murray, Elsie
1878–1965
psychologist, color blindness expert, museum director
Presbyterian
Pennsylvania
Nat Cyc Am Bio v53

2129. Cleophas, Mary
1879–1946
president of Rosemont College
Pennsylvania
Obit File

2130. Henius, Lillian Grace (Beck)
1879–1926
artist
Pittsburgh, PA
Nat Cyc Am Bio v21

2131. Lewars, Elsie Singmaster
born 1879
author
Lutheran
Pennsylvania
German
Nat Cyc Am Bio csv3

2132. Miller, Lucy Kennedy
born 1880
suffrage leader
Pennsylvania
Nat Cyc Am Bio csv4

2133. Musselman, Emma Good Sweigert
1880–1966
canner
Mennonite
Pennsylvania
Nat Cyc Am Bio v52

2134. Nitzsche, Else Koenig
1880–1952

artist, author
Unitarian
Pennsylvania
Nat Cyc Am Bio v47

2135. Schall, Nina Dennis
1880–1961
physician
Presbyterian
New York; Pennsylvania
Nat Cyc Am Bio v49

2136. Lewis, Margaret Adaline Reed
1881–1970
biologist, cytologist, medical researcher
Pennsylvania
Index t Wom; Nat Cyc Am Bio v58

2137. Pew, Helen Jennings Thompson
1883–1963
philanthropist
Pittsburgh, PA
Nat Cyc Am Bio v57

2138. Stokes, Lilia Woodruff
1885–1973
Philadelphia civic worker, worker for Women's International League for Peace and Freedom, conservationist
Quaker
Pennsylvania
Nat Cyc Am Bio v58

2139. Sturgis, Margaret Castex
1885–1962
gynecologist, cancer researcher, medical author
Episcopalian
Pennsylvania
Nat Cyc Am Bio v49

2140. Clothier, Anita Porter
1886–1955
Philadelphia civic worker, equestrian
Philadelphia, PA
Nat Cyc Am Bio v50

2141. Allison, Marjorie
1887–1961
banker
Episcopalian
Pennsylvania
Nat Cyc Am Bio v49

2142. Dexter, Edith MacBride
1887–1958
ophthalmologist, public health worker
Presbyterian
Pennsylvania
Nat Cyc Am Bio v49

2143. Fenton, Beatrice
born 1887
sculptor

Pennsylvania
Index t Wom; Nat Cyc Am Bio csv6

2144. Ashton, Dorothy Laing
1888–1958
surgeon, obstetrician/gynecologist, medical educator
Pennsylvania
Nat Cyc Am Bio v49

2145. Myrin, Mabel (Anderson) Pew
1889–1972
Philadelphia civic leader
Presbyterian
Philadelphia, PA
Nat Cyc Am Bio v57

2146. Sternbergh, Katharine Eleanor Cornell
1890–1950
Reading, Pennsylvania, civic worker; owner and manager of the American Tool and Die Co.
Reading, PA
Nat Cyc Am Bio v39

2147. Crump, Jean
1892–1963
pediatrician
Presbyterian
Pennsylvania
Nat Cyc Am Bio v52

2148. Keast, Susette Schultz
1892–1932
artist
Pennsylvania
Nat Cyc Am Bio v25

2149. McCollin, Frances
1892–1960
composer, educator, lecturer, Socialist party worker
Episcopalian
Pennsylvania
blind
Index t Wom; Nat Cyc Am Bio v45

2150. Godfrey, Grace
1893–1944
home economics educator
Philadelphia, PA
Obit File

2151. Fay, Marion (Spencer)
born 1896
educator, physiological chemist
Episcopalian
Pennsylvania
Nat Cyc Am Bio csv12

2152. Bowen, Catherine (Shober) Drinker
1897–1973
biographer, essayist, autobiographer, lecturer

Pennsylvania
Cur Biog '73; Index t Wom; Nat Cyc Am Bio v58; Not Am Wom supp v1; Obit File

2153. Charles, Alta Genevieve
1899–1963
ophthalmologist
Presbyterian
Pennsylvania
Nat Cyc Am Bio v50

2154. Buchanan, Vera D.
1902–55
representative to Congress from Pennsylvania
Pennsylvania
Obit File

2155. Wills, Doris Margaret Wood
1902–63
astronomer, research engineer
Unitarian
Pennsylvania
Nat Cyc Am Bio v53

2156. Casey, Rosemary
1904–76
playwright, screenwriter
Catholic
Pennsylvania
Nat Cyc Am Bio v59

2157. McBride, Katharine Elizabeth
1904–76
psychologist, university educator, president of Bryn Mawr College
Bryn Mawr, PA
Cur Biog '76; Index t Wom; Obit File

2158. Byrd, Hannah Elizabeth
1907–68
judge
Pennsylvania
Black
Encyc Black Am

2159. Sartain, Harriet
died 1957
artist, dean of Moore Institute of Art, Science and Industry, educator
Philadelphia, PA
Index t Wom; Obit File

2160. Shindel, Dorothy Louise; Mrs. Alfred C. LaBoccetta
1916–75
pediatrician
Lutheran
Pennsylvania
Nat Cyc Am Bio v59

2161. Lawson, Marjorie
born 1919
lawyer, judge
Pittsburgh, PA
Black
Encyc Black Am; Negro Alman

2162. Tucker, Cynthia Delores Nottage
born 1927
secretary of the Commonwealth of Pennsylvania
Pennsylvania
Black
Encyc Black Am

2163. Saunders, Sally; Sally Love Saunders Craigie
born 1940
poet, educator
Episcopalian
Pennsylvania
Nat Cyc Am Bio csv12

RHODE ISLAND

2164. Hutchinson, Anne (Marbury)
1590/91–1642/43
religious and political leader, founder of the Antinomian sect of Puritanism
Puritan
Rhode Island; Massachusetts
English
Am Bio Dict; Cyc Am Bio; Dict Am Bio; Dict Am Bio Men Time; Dict Am Rel Bio; Dict Nat Bio; Index t Wom; Nat Cyc Am Bio v9; Not Am Wom; Twent Cen Bio Dict Not Am

2165. Anthony, Susanna
1726–91
theologian, religious author
Quaker
Rhode Island
Am Bio Dict; Appl Cyc Am Bio; Cyc Am Bio; Dict Am Bio Men Time

2166. Stoneman, Abigail
flourished 1760s; died 1777
innkeeper of colonial Rhode Island
Rhode Island
Not Am Wom

2167. Howdee, Sarah
died 1827
last of the Queen Awashunk people
Rhode Island
Native American (Queen Awashunk)
Am Bio Dict

2168. Williams, Catherine Read (Arnold)
1787/90–1872
author, poet, novelist, biographer, historical author
Providence, RI
Cyc Am Bio; Dict Am Auth; Dict Am Bio; Dict Am Bio Men Time

2169. Jenkins, Anna Almy
1790–1849
philanthropist
Quaker
Providence, RI
Cyc Am Bio; Dict Am Bio Men Time

2170. Little, Sophia Louise (Robbins)
born 1799
poet, author
Newport, RI
Cyc Am Bio; Dict Am Auth; Dict Am Bio Men Time

2171. Taggart, Cynthia
1801–49
poet
Rhode Island
Am Bio Dict; Dict Am Bio Men Time

2172. Hall, Louisa Jane Park
1802–92
poet, author
Providence, RI
Cyc Am Bio; Dict Am Auth; Dict Am Bio Men Time; Index t Wom

2173. Whitman, Sarah Helen (Power)
1803/13–1878
poet, essayist, feminist
Spiritualist
Providence, RI
Cyc Am Bio; Dict Am Auth; Dict Am Bio; Dict Am Bio Men Time; Dict Lit Bio v1; Nat Cyc Am Bio v8; Not Am Wom; Wom Cent

2174. McDougal, Frances Harriet (Whipple) (Greene)
1805–75
poet, miscellaneous writer, suffragist
Rhode Island; California
Dict Am Auth; Cyc Am Bio

2175. Mowry, Martha H.
born 1818
physician, suffragist
Rhode Island
Wom Cent

2176. Bailey, Urania Locke (Stoughton); Una Locke
1820–82
children's author, religious poet
Providence, RI
Dict Am Auth

2177. Richards, Maria Tolman
born 1821
author, educator, lecturer
Providence, RI
Cyc Am Bio; Dict Am Auth

2178. Barney, Susan Hammond
flourished 1854–90s
evangelist, Prohibitionist, temperance worker, prison reformer
Rhode Island
Index t Wom; Wom Cent

2179. Wormeley, Katharine Prescott
1830/32–1908
Civil War relief and hospital worker, writer on sanitation, charity worker, philanthropist, translator, biographer
Rhode Island
English
Cyc Am Bio; Dict Am Bio; Index t Wom; Nat Cyc Am Bio v8; Not Am Wom; Twent Cen Bio Dict Not Am; Wom Cent

2180. Evans, Elizabeth Edson (Gibson)
born 1833
essayist, short story writer
Rhode Island
Cyc Am Bio; Dict Am Auth; Twent Cen Bio Dict Not Am

2181. Woolsey, Sarah Chauncy; Susan Coolidge
1835/45–1905
children's author, poet, Civil War nurse
Newport, RI
Dict Am Auth; Dict Am Bio; Index t Wom; Nat Cyc Am Bio v11; Not Am Wom; Wom Cent

2182. Peirce, Melusina [Fay]
born 1836
author, community organizer, co-op advocate, writer on domestic science
Newport, RI
Dict Am Auth; Twent Cen Bio Dict Not Am

2183. Palmer, Frances Purdy "Fannie"
1839–1923
author, journalist, lecturer, suffragist, feminist
Providence, RI
Dict Am Auth; Index t Wom; Wom Cent

2184. Peckham, Mary Chace (Peck)
1839–92
author, fiction writer, poet, Civil War nurse, suffragist, women's rights worker
Unitarian
Providence, RI
Dict Am Auth; Nat Cyc Am Bio v9; Twent Cen Bio Dict Not Am

2185. Chase, Louise
born 1840
temperance worker
Rhode Island
Wom Cent

2186. Carpenter, Esther Bernon
1848–93
short story writer
Rhode Island
Dict Am Auth; Nat Cyc Am Bio v2

2187. Gould, Ellen M.
born 1848
philanthropist, suffragist
Unitarian
Rhode Island
Wom Cent

2188. Peck, Annie Smith
1850–1933/35
mountain climber, musician, archaeologist, lecturer, educator
Rhode Island
Index t Wom; Nat Cyc Am Bio v15; Not Am Wom; Wom Cent

2189. Greene, Mary A.
born 1857
lawyer, law educator
Rhode Island
Index t Wom; Wom Cent

2190. Steedman, Mary Balch Lippitt
born 1858
Providence, Rhode Island, civic worker
Unitarian
Providence, RI
Nat Cyc Am Bio csv2

2191. Barbour, Florence Newell
1866–1946
pianist, composer
Rhode Island
Index t Wom; Nat Cyc Am Bio v37

2192. Abee, Grace Arnold (Thurston)
born 1890
artist
Congregationalist
Rhode Island
Nat Cyc Am Bio csv11

2193. McLaughlin, Agnes Winifred
flourished 1920s–30s
lawyer
Rhode Island
Nat Cyc Am Bio csv3

SOUTH CAROLINA

2194. Amy
1686–1826 [*sic*]
pioneer, slave
Charleston, SC
Black
Appl Cyc Am Bio

2195. Pinckney, Elizabeth Lucas "Eliza"
1722/23–1793
plantation manager identified with the development of indigo as a staple of the colonial South, textile manufacturer, agriculturist, author
South Carolina
Dict Am Bio; Encyc South Hist; Index t Wom; Not Am Wom; Who Who Dur Am Rev

2196. Gilman, Caroline (Howard)
1794–1888
author, poet, editor, domestic novelist
Charleston, SC
Cyc Am Bio; Dict Am Auth; Dict Am Bio; Dict Am Bio Men Time; Dict Lit Bio v3; Index t Wom; Nat Cyc Am Bio v6; Not Am Wom; Twent Cen Bio Dict Not Am

2197. Moise, Penina
1797–1880
poet, writer of Jewish hymns
Jewish
Charleston, SC
Cyc Am Bio; Dict Am Auth; Dict Am Bio; Index t Wom; Not Am Wom; Wom Lit, More

2198. Martin, Margaret Maxwell
born 1807
author, educator, poet
Columbia, SC
Cyc Am Bio; Dict Am Auth

2199. McCord, Louisa Susannah (Cheves)
1810–1879/80
miscellaneous author, poet, political writer, translator, Confederate essayist, Black welfare worker, feminist, plantation manager
South Carolina
Cyc Am Bio; Dict Am Auth; Dict Am Bio; Dict Am Bio Men Time; Index t Wom; Nat Cyc Am Bio v9; Not Am Wom; Twent Cen Bio Dict Not Am

2200. Lee, Mary Elizabeth
1813–49
poet, children's author
Charleston, SC
Cyc Am Bio; Dict Am Auth; Index t Wom; Nat Cyc Am Bio v6

2201. Poyas, Catherine Gendron
1813–82
poet
Charleston, SC
Dict Am Auth

2202. Mather, Sarah Ann
born 1820
philanthropist, patron of Black education, educator, author
South Carolina
Index t Wom; Wom Cent

2203. Bowen, Sue (Petrigru) (King)
1824–75
novelist
South Carolina
Dict Am Auth

2204. Ravenel, Harriot Horry (Rutledge)
1832–1912
author, biographer
Charleston, SC
Dict Am Auth; Dict Am Bio

2205. Dargan, Clara Victoria (MacLean); Claudia
born 1840
poet, fiction writer, educator
South Carolina
Cyc Am Bio; Dict Am Auth; Nat Cyc Am Bio v7

2206. Neblett, Ann Viola
born 1842
temperance worker, suffragist
South Carolina; Georgia
Index t Wom

2207. Garner, Eliza A.
born 1845
educator, politician
South Carolina
Wom Cent

2208. Nowell, Mildred E.
born 1849
author, journalist
South Carolina
Wom Cent

2209. McCracken, Annie Virginia; Alma Vivian Mylo
born 1868
author
South Carolina
Wom Cent

2210. Taylor, Anna Heyward
1879–1956
artist
Episcopalian
South Carolina
Nat Cyc Am Bio v42

2211. Peterkin, Julia (Mood)
1880–1961
author of books on Black life, Pulitzer Prize winner
South Carolina
Dict Lit Bio v9; Index t Wom; Nat Cyc Am Bio csv3; Obit File; Wom Lit, More

2212. Springs, Lena Joan Jones
1883–1942
Democratic National Committee member, Democratic vice-presidential nominee at the 1924 convention, suffrage leader, World War I Red Cross worker
South Carolina
Nat Cyc Am Bio csv2; Obit File

2213. Verner, Elizabeth O'Neill
born 1883
etcher, painter
Episcopalian
South Carolina
Nat Cyc Am Bio csv12

2214. Beasley, Victoria Louise Dowling
1888–1956
Hartsville, South Carolina, civic worker
Hartsville, SC
Nat Cyc Am Bio v46

2215. Woodham, Eva Esther Dowling
1890–1962
insurance executive, floriculturist
Methodist
South Carolina
Nat Cyc Am Bio v46

2216. Moore, Elizabeth Finley
1894–1976
South Carolina historical worker
Episcopalian
South Carolina
Nat Cyc Am Bio v60

2217. du Pre, Grace Annette
flourished 1930s–60s
painter, violinist, tennis player
South Carolina
Nat Cyc Am Bio csv11

SOUTH DAKOTA

2218. Devoe, Emma Smith
born 1849
suffragist, lecturer
South Dakota
Wom Cent

2219. Ramsey, Lula A.
flourished 1880s
temperance worker
South Dakota
Wom Cent

2220. Cranmer, Emma A.
born 1858
temperance reformer, suffragist
South Dakota
Wom Cent

2221. Eastman, Elaine (Goodale); Elaine Hall
1863–1953
educator of Native Americans, poet, short story writer, humorist, editor, scholar of Native American culture
South Dakota
Cyc Am Bio; Dict Am Auth; Index t Wom; Nat Cyc Am Bio v8; Twent Cen Bio Dict Not Am; Wom Cent

TENNESSEE

2222. Kennedy, Sarah Beaumont (Cannon)
born 18?
novelist
Memphis, TN
Dict Am Auth

2223. Graves, Adelia Cleopatra (Spencer); Aunt Alice
1821–95
author, children's author, rhetorician, linguist, educator, president of Mary Sharp College
Tennessee
Cyc Am Bio; Dict Am Auth; Twent Cen Bio Dict Not Am; Wom Cent

2224. Meriwether, Elizabeth (Avery)
1824/32–1916
novelist, women's rights worker, suffragist, Prohibition party worker
Memphis, TN
Dict Am Auth; Encyc South Hist

2225. French, Lucy Virginia (Smith)
1825/30–1881
poet, author, editor, educator
Memphis, TN
Cyc Am Bio; Dict Am Auth; Dict Am Bio; Nat Cyc Am Bio v7

2226. Meriwether, Lide
born 1829
author, lecturer, temperance worker, suffragist
Tennessee
Wom Cent

2227. Saxon, Elizabeth Lyle
1832–1915
suffragist, temperance worker, lecturer
Congregationalist
Memphis, TN
Nat Cyc Am Bio v16; Wom Cent

2228. Robinson, Leora (Bettison)
born 1840
fiction writer, educator
Baptist
Tallahassee, TN
Dict Am Auth; Wom Cent

2229. Thomas, Mary Ann (Lane)
born 1841
journalist, newspaper editor and publisher
Tennessee
Wom Cent

2230. Elliott, Sarah Barnwell
1848–1928
author, novelist, dramatist, suffragist
Tennessee
Dict Am Auth; Dict Am Bio; Nat Cyc Am Bio v21; Not Am Wom; Wom Lit, More

2231. East, Edward H., Mrs.
born 1849
philanthropist, temperance worker
Tennessee
Wom Cent

2232. Solari, Mary M.
born 1849
artist
Memphis, TN
Italian
Wom Cent

2233. Conway, Clara
flourished 1880s
founder of the Clara Conway School
Tennessee
Wom Cent

2234. Holman, Silena Moore
1850–1915
temperance worker
Tennessee
Nat Cyc Am Bio v17

2235. Keating, Josephine E.
flourished 1880s–90s
literary critic, musician, music educator
Tennessee
Wom Cent

2236. Murfree, Mary Noailles; Charles Egbert Craddock
1850–1922
novelist, short story writer
Tennessee
Cyc Am Bio; Dict Am Auth; Dict Am Bio; Encyc South Hist; Index t Wom; Not Am Wom; Twent Cen Bio Dict Not Am; Wom Cent; Wom Lit; Wom Lit, More

2237. Foxworthy, Alice S.
born 1852
educator
Tennessee
Wom Cent

2238. Myers, Minnie (Walter)
born 1852
writer on the South

Memphis, TN
Dict Am Auth

2239. Ober, Sara Endicott
born 1854
missionary in the Tennessee and Kentucky mountains, fiction writer
Tennessee; Kentucky
Dict Am Auth

2240. Lutz, Edelia Armstrong
born 1859
artist, art educator
Knoxville, TN
Wom Cent

2241. Dromgoole, William Allen
born 1860
short story writer
Murfreesboro, TN
Dict Am Auth

2242. Boyle, Virginia (Frazer)
born 1863
author, poet
Tennessee
Dict Am Bio v13

2243. Cooke, Grace MacGowan
born 1863
magazine writer
Chattanooga, TN
Dict Am Auth; Index t Wom

2244. Pruit, Willie Franklin; Aylmer Ney
born 1865
philanthropist, poet
Tennessee
Index t Wom; Wom Cent

2245. O'Donnell, Nellie
born 1867
educator
Tennessee
Index t Wom; Wom Cent

2246. Slaughter, Elizabeth Vanuxem Kennedy
1876–1960
Confederate historian
Tennessee
Nat Cyc Am Bio v44

2247. Susong, Edith (Ingles) O'Keefe
1890–1974
newspaper publisher
Episcopalian
Greenville, TN
Nat Cyc Am Bio v59

2248. Carter, Maybelle Hunton
1901–70
country music singer, guitarist
Nashville, TN
Obit File

2249. Brown, Dorothy
born 1919

surgeon, Tennessee state legislator
Tennessee
Black
Encyc Black Am; Negro Alman

TEXAS

2250. Holley, Mary Phelps Austin
1784–1846
Texas historian, historical author, biographer, miscellaneous writer, land speculator
Texas
Am Bio Dict; Dict Am Auth; Not Am Wom

2251. Shindler, Mary Stanley Bunce (Palmer) (Dana)
1810–83
author, poet, religious writer
Unitarian; Episcopalian
Nacogdoches, TX
Cyc Am Bio; Dict Am Auth; Dict Am Bio Men Time; Index t Wom

2252. Fisher, Rebecca Jane Gilleland
born 183?; married 1848
philanthropist, journalist, pioneer
Austin, TX
Index t Wom; Wom Cent

2253. King, Henrietta Maria Morse Chamberlain
1832–1925
cattle rancher
Texas
Nat Cyc Am Bio v20

2254. Bedford, Lou Singletary
born 1837
poet
Texas
Wom Cent

2255. Dannelly, Elizabeth Otis (Marshall)
born 1838
poet
Texas
Dict Am Auth; Wom Cent

2256. Walling, Mary Cole; The Banished Heroine of the South
born 1838
lecturer, Union patriot during the Civil War
Texas
Index t Wom; Wom Cent

2257. Kidd, Lucy Ann
1839–1916
educator, president of the North Texas Female College

Texas
Index t Wom; Nat Cyc Am Bio v117; Wom Cent

2258. McPherson, Lydia Starr
flourished 1870s–90s
poet, author, journalist, newspaper publisher
Texas
Wom Cent

2259. Fry, Elizabeth Turner
born 1842
philanthropist, Prohibitionist, humane worker, suffragist
San Antonio, TX
Wom Cent

2260. Whitten, Martha Elizabeth Hotchkiss
born 1842
author, poet
Texas
Wom Cent

2261. Winkler, Angelina Virginia
born 1842
journalist
Texas
Wom Cent

2262. Merrick, Sarah Newcomb
born 1844
educator, educational missionary to Nova Scotia
Texas
Canadian
Wom Cent

2263. Harbee, Lee (Cohen)
born 1849
author, Texas historian, Sorosis member
Texas; New York
Dict Am Auth; Wom Cent

2264. Dwyer, Bessie Agnes
flourished 1880s
journalist
Texas
Wom Cent

2265. Inglehart, Frances (Chambers) (Gooch)
1851–post 1890
writer on Texas, fiction writer
Austin, TX
Dict Am Auth; Wom Cent

2266. Dabbs, Ellen Lawson
born 1853
physician, midwife, women's rights worker, suffragist, temperance worker, journalist, Populist party worker
Texas
Wom Cent

2267. Roberts, Dora
1863–1953
rancher, philanthropist

Texas
Obit File

2268. Daffan, Katie
flourished 1900s–20s
author
Baptist
Texas
Nat Cyc Am Bio csvl

2269. Jones, Jesse Homan
1872–1962
philanthropist, publisher of the
Houston Chronicle
Houston, TX
Obit File

**2270. Ward, Hortense Sparks
Malsch**
1872–1944
lawyer, social reformer
Texas
Not Am Wom

2271. Ferguson, Miriam Amanda Wallace "Ma"
1875–1961
twenty-eighth governor of Texas
Episcopalian
Texas
Index t Wom; Nat Cyc Am Bio
csvl; Not Am Wom supp v1;
Obit File; Encyc South Hist

2272. Hockaday, Ela
1876–1956
educator
Texas
Nat Cyc Am Bio v42

2273. Williams, Amelia Worthington
1876–1958
educator, historian of Texas
Presbyterian
Texas
Nat Cyc Am Bio v44

2274. Driscoll, Clara
1881–1945
clubwoman, philanthropist, politician, political activist
Texas
Not Am Wom; Obit File

2275. Ames, Jessie Daniel
1883–1972
Progressive party politician,
Black civil rights worker, antilynching reformer, suffragist
Texas
Encyc South Hist; Not Am Wom
supp v1

2276. Esparza, Francisca
1883–1962
litigant
Texas
Mexican
Dict Mex Am Hist

2277. Neiman, Carrie
1884–1953
cofounder of Neiman Marcus department stores
Dallas, TX
Obit File

2278. Cahill, Lily
1886–1955
stage and screen actor
Texas
Obit File

2279. Porter, Katherine Anne
1890/94–1980
author, short story writer
Texas
French (American expatriate to Paris)
Cur Biog '80; Dict Lit Bio v4 and
v9; Encyc South Hist; Index t
Wom; Wom Lit; Wom Lit,
More

2280. Tauch, Waldine
born 1898
sculptor
Methodist
Texas
Index t Wom; Nat Cyc Am Bio
csv12

2281. Hobby, Oveta Culp
born 1905
government official, director of
the Women's Army Auxiliary
Corps, editor, politician
Texas
Index t Wom; Nat Cyc Am Bio
csv6

2282. Waggoner, Electra
born 1914
sculptor
Texas
Index t Wom; Nat Cyc Am Bio
csv6

2283. Jordan, Barbara
born 1936
lawyer, Texas state senator, representative to Congress from Texas
Texas
Black
Cur Biog '74; Encyc Black Am;
Negro Alman

2284. Hernandez, Maria L.
flourished 1970s–80s
Mexican American community
leader, civil rights worker
Texas
Mexican
Dict Mex Am Hist

UTAH

**2285. Smith, Eliza Roxey
Snow; The Mother of
Mormonism**
1804–87
Mormon leader, religious poet,
hymn writer, women's leader,
suffragist, western pioneer
Mormon
Utah
Cyc Am Bio; Dict Am Bio; Index
t Wom; Not Am Wom; Read
Encyc Am West

2286. Wells, Emmeline Blanchard Woodward
1828–1921
leader of Mormon women, feminist, suffragist, editor, poet
Mormon
Utah
Cyc Am Bio; Not Am Wom

**2287. Newman, Angelia Louise
French Thurston**
1837–1910
church worker, missionary, Mormon women's relief worker, lecturer, reformer
Mormon
Utah
Index t Wom; Not Am Wom;
Wom Cent

2288. Spencer, Josephine
flourished 1890s
poet
Utah
Wom Cent

2289. James, Mary Latimer
1883–1963
medical missionary to the Ute
people in Utah, medical missionary to China, obstetrician/
gynecologist, psychiatrist
Protestant Episcopal
Utah
Nat Cyc Am Bio v51

**2290. MacDonald, Lillie Ann
Neal**
1884–1966
candy manufacturer
Mormon
Utah
Nat Cyc Am Bio v53

VERMONT

2291. Gould, Hannah Flagg
1789–1865
poet
Newburyport, VT
Cyc Am Bio; Dict Am Auth; Dict
Am Bio; Dict Am Bio Men
Time; Index t Wom; Nat Cyc
Am Bio v8

2292. Porter, Lydia Ann (Emerson)
born 1816
author, educator
Springfield, VT
Cyc Am Bio; Dict Am Auth

2293. Torrey, Mary (Ide)
1817–69
religious and nonfiction writer
Vermont
Dict Am Auth

2294. Dorr, Julia Caroline Ripley
1825–1913
poet, author, novelist, essayist
Vermont
Cyc Am Bio; Dict Am Auth; Dict
Am Bio; Index t Wom; Nat Cyc
Am Bio v6; Twent Cen Bio Dict
Not Am; Wom Cent

2295. Hemenway, Abby Maria
1828–90
Vermont historian, anthologist,
author
Vermont
Dict Am Auth; Not Am Wom;
Twent Cen Bio Dict Not Am

2296. Page, Emily Rebecca
1834–62
poet
Vermont
Cyc Am Bio; Dict Am Auth

**2297. Foster, Theodosia Maria
(Toll); Faye Huntington**
born 1838
author, children's author, educator
Vermont
Twent Cen Bio Dict Not Am

2298. Ward, Mary E.
born 1843
poet
Vermont
Wom Cent

2299. Smith, Olive White
born 1846
author, temperance worker
Methodist Episcopal
Vermont
Wom Cent

2300. Yale, Caroline Ardelia
1848–1933
educator of the deaf
Congregationalist
Vermont
Dict Am Bio; Nat Cyc Am Bio
v31; Not Am Wom

2301. Owen, Ella Seaver
born 1852
artist, decorator
Vermont
Wom Cent

2302. Cleghorn, Sarah Norcliffe
1876–1959
poet, novelist, educator, suffragist, civil rights worker, labor worker, pacifist, antivivisectionist, Socialist party member
Vermont
Index t Wom; Nat Cyc Am Bio v46; Obit File; Dict Am Bio supp v5

2303. Franklin, Elizabeth Jennings
1887–1967
founder of Bennington College and chairperson of the board of trustees
Presbyterian
Vermont; New York
Nat Cyc Am Bio v53; Obit File

2304. Bailey, Consuelo Northrop
born 1899
lieutenant governor of Vermont, lawyer
Episcopalian
Vermont
Index t Wom; Nat Cyc Am Bio csv12

No Dates

2305. Gilchrist, Beth Bradford; Elizabeth Drake; John Prescott Earl
author, children's author
Congregationalist
Vermont
Nat Cyc Am Bio v47; Obit File

VIRGINIA

2306. Bailey, Ann; Mad Anne
1725/42–1825
frontier scout and messenger on the Virginia border, soldier, Indian fighter, American patriot
Ohio; Virginia
British
Appl Cyc Am Bio; Dict Am Bio; Encyc South Hist; Who Who Dur Am Rev; Wom Cent

2307. Wood, Jean (Moncure)
1754–1823
poet
Virginia
Dict Am Auth

2308. Royall, Anne Newport
1769–1854
traveler, journalist, newspaper editor and publisher, novelist

Washington, DC; Virginia
Am Bio Dict; Cyc Am Bio; Dict Am Auth; Dict Am Bio; Dict Am Bio Men Time; Encyc South Hist; Index t Wom; Not Am Wom

2309. Moseby, Mary Webster
1791–1844
magazine writer, author
Virginia
Cyc Am Bio; Dict Am Bio Men Time

2310. Tidball, Mary Langdon
18?–1904
novelist
Virginia
Dict Am Auth

2311. Eastman, Mary (Henderson)
1817/18–1887
author, scholar of Native American life and culture, ethnologist, Native American folklorist
Virginia
Cyc Am Bio; Dict Am Auth; Dict Am Bio Men Time; Not Am Wom; Twent Cen Bio Dict Not Am

2312. van Lew, Elizabeth L.
1818–1900
unionist and federal agent during the Civil War, Civil War spy
Virginia
Index t Wom; Not Am Wom

2313. Preston, Margaret (Junkin)
1820/25–1897
poet, author, novelist, Civil War letter writer
Lexington, VA
Cyc Am Bio; Dict Am Auth; Dict Am Bio; Index t Wom; Nat Cyc Am Bio v7; Not Am Wom; Twent Cen Bio Dict Not Am; Wom Cent

2314. Slenker, Elmina (Drake); Aunt Elmina
born 1827
miscellaneous author, abolitionist
Snowville, VA
Cyc Am Bio; Dict Am Auth; Nat Cyc Am Bio v7

2315. Jordan, Conrelia Jane (Matthews)
1830–98
poet, Confederate sympathizer
Virginia
Cyc Am Bio; Dict Am Auth; Index t Wom; Wom Cent

2316. Magill, Mary Tucker
1832–99
fiction writer, journalist, educator

Winchester, VA
Cyc Am Bio; Dict Am Auth; Twent Cen Bio Dict Not Am

2317. Tompkins, Sally Louisa
1833–1916
Confederate hospital head, captain of cavalry in the Confederate army
Virginia
Bio Dict Confed; Dict Am Bio; Encyc South Hist; Index t Wom; Not Am Wom

2318. Smith, Mary Stewart (Harrison)
born 1834
author, translator, children's author
Virginia
Dict Am Auth; Wom Cent

2319. Downing, Frances Murdaugh "Fanny"; Frank Dashmore; Viola
1835–94
poet, author, novelist
Charlottesville, VA; North Carolina
Cyc Am Bio; Dict Am Auth; Nat Cyc Am Bio v7

2320. Weiss, Susan Archer (Talley)
born 1835
poet, artist
Virginia; New York, NY
Cyc Am Bio; Dict Am Auth; Wom Cent

2321. de Jarnette, Evelyn Magruder
born 1842
author
Virginia
Wom Cent

2322. Moran, Jane Warmly (Blackburn)
born 1842
novelist
Charlottesville, VA
Dict Am Auth

2323. Jackson, Lily Irene
flourished 1880s–90s
sculptor, artist, designer, clubwoman
Virginia
Index t Wom; Wom Cent

2324. MacClelland, Margaret Greenway
1853–95
author, novelist
Virginia
Dict Am Auth; Nat Cyc Am Bio v2

2325. Hammond, Henrietta (Hardy); Henri Dange
1854–83

fiction author
Virginia
Dict Am Auth

2326. Proctor, Mary Virginia
born 1854
journalist, newspaper publisher, philanthropist
Methodist Episcopal
Virginia
Wom Cent

2327. Cocke, Martha Louise
1855–1938
president of Hollins College
Enon Baptist
Virginia
Nat Cyc Am Bio v29

2328. Jones, Harriet B.
born 1856
physician, temperance worker
Virginia
Index t Wom; Wom Cent

2329. Barrett, Kate Harwood Waller
1857/59–1925/29
social reformer, philanthropist, lecturer, social worker, suffragist, women's welfare worker
Virginia
Dict Am Bio; Encyc South Hist; Index t Wom; Not Am Wom

2330. Bacon, Alice Mable
1858–1918
authority on Japan, author on Japanese culture, lecturer, educator of Blacks
Virginia
Dict Am Auth; Dict Am Bio; Not Am Wom

2331. Ewell, Alice Maud
born 1860
historical novelist
Virginia
Dict Am Auth

2332. Barrett, Janie Porter
1865–1948
social welfare leader, educator
Virginia
Black
Dict Am Bio supp v4; Negro Alman; Index t Wom; Not Am Wom; Prof Negro Wom

2333. Munford, Mary Cooke Branch
1865–1938
education reformer, civic leader
Virginia
Index t Wom; Not Am Wom

2334. Stanard, Mary Mann Page Newton
1865–1929
historian of Virginia
Virginia
Dict Am Bio

2335. Valentine, Lila Hardaway Meade
1865–1921
suffragist, educational reformer, public health worker
Virginia
Encyc South Hist; Not Am Wom

2336. Walker, Maggie Lena
1865/67–1934
insurance and banking executive, president of the Consolidated Bank and Trust Co.
Richmond, VA
Black
Encyc Black Am; Index t Wom; Not Am Wom; Prof Negro Wom v1

2337. McVea, Emilie Watts
1867–1928
president of Sweet Briar College
Episcopalian
Virginia
Nat Cyc Am Bio v21

2338. Sampson, Emma Speed
1868–1947
children's author
Virginia
Nat Cyc Am Bio v37; Obit File

2339. Johnston, Mary
1870–1936
popular novelist, suffragist, pacifist, internationalist
Birmingham, AL; Virginia
Dict Am Auth; Dict Am Bio supp v2; Dict Lit Bio v9; Index t Wom; Nat Cyc Am Bio v10 and csv3; Not Am Wom; Twent Cen Bio Dict Not Am

2340. Glasgow, Ellen; Anderson Gholson
1873/74–1945
novelist, Pulitzer Prize winner
Richmond, VA
Dict Am Auth; Dict Am Bio supp v5; Dict Lit Bio v9; Index t Wom; Nat Cyc Am Bio v13, v35, and csv3; Not Am Wom; Wom Lit; Wom Lit, More

2341. Randolph, Virginia Estelle
1874/76–1958
social worker, educator
Virginia
Black
Index t Wom; Negro Alman; Prof Negro Wom v1

2342. Glass, Meta
1880–1967
president of Sweet Briar College, educator, YWCA executive, World War I and II relief worker, defense worker
Episcopalian

Virginia
Nat Cyc Am Bio v53 and csv7; Obit File

2343. Mason, Lucy Randolph
1882–1959
labor publicist, public relations officer for the CIO, southern trade union organizer, social worker and reformer, suffragist
Episcopalian
Virginia
Bio Dict Am Lab; Dict Am Bio supp v6; Encyc South Hist; Not Am Wom supp v1; Obit File

2344. Burwell, Mary E.
flourished 1913
hospital founder, prison reformer
Richmond, VA
Prof Negro Wom

2345. Bowser, Rosa Dixon
1885–1931
educator, clubwoman
Richmond, VA
Black
Negro Alman; Prof Negro Wom

2346. Randolph, Bessie Carter
1885–1966
political scientist, international law and affairs expert, president of Hollins College
Episcopalian
Virginia
Nat Cyc Am Bio v52 and csv6

2347. Williamson, Pauline Brooks
1887–1972
educator
Virginia
Nat Cyc Am Bio v56

2348. Claytor, Gertrude (Harris) Boatwright
1889–1973
poet, Red Cross worker in World War I
Christian Scientist
Virginia
Nat Cyc Am Bio v57

2349. Gardner, Emily
1899–1956
pediatrician
Baptist
Richmond, VA
Nat Cyc Am Bio v42

2350. Pannell, Anne Thomas Gary
born 1910
educator, president of Sweet Briar College
Protestant Episcopal
Virginia
Index t Wom; Nat Cyc Am Bio csv10

2351. Lucas, Martha Bob
born 1912
educator, president of Sweet Briar College
Episcopalian
Virginia
Index t Wom; Nat Cyc Am Bio csv7

2352. Cabell, Mary Virginia Ellet
born 1939
educator
Virginia
Wom Cent

WASHINGTON

2353. Jones, Mary C. "May"
born 1842
Baptist minister, evangelist
Baptist
Washington
Index t Wom; Wom Cent

2354. Lamson, Lucy Stedman
born 1857
educator, realtor
Washington
Index t Wom; Wom Cent

2355. Higginson, Ella (Rhoads)
born 1862
author, poet, druggist
New Watcom, WA
Dict Am Auth; Twent Cen Bio Dict Not Am; Wom Cent

2356. Landes, Bertha Ethel Knight
1868–1943
clubwoman, civic reformer, mayor of Seattle
Seattle, WA
Index t Wom; Not Am Wom; Obit File

2357. Best, Gertrude Delprat
1869–1947
newspaper publisher
Washington
Nat Cyc Am Bio v41

2358. Reeves, Belle
1871–1948
secretary of state of Washington
Washington
Obit File

2359. Cornish, Nellie Centennial
1876–1956
music educator, patron of music, music school founder
Washington
Index t Wom; Read Encyc Am West

2360. Lamson, Armene Tashijian
1883–1970
medical illustrator, physician, UNICEF worker, medical author
Episcopalian
Seattle, WA
Turkish
Nat Cyc Am Bio v56

2361. Secondari, Rita Hume
1883–1953
Seattle Times correspondent in Italy
Washington
Italian
Obit File

2362. Dobie, Edith
1887–1975
historian, educator
Methodist
Washington
Nat Cyc Am Bio v58

WEST VIRGINIA

2363. Dandridge, Danske (Bedinger)
born 1858
poet
West Virginia
Dict Am Auth

WISCONSIN

2364. Willard, Mary Thompson Hill
1805–92
pioneer
Methodist
Wisconsin
Wom Cent

2365. Mortimer, Mary
1816/18–1877
educator, women's educator, founder of the Milwaukee Female College
Wisconsin
English
Dict Am Bio; Index t Wom; Nat Cyc Am Bio v7; Not Am Wom; Wom Cent

2366. Lynde, Mary Elizabeth Blanchard
born 1819
philanthropist
Milwaukee, WI
Index t Wom; Wom Cent

2367. Curtiss, Abby (Allin)
born 1820
poet

Madison, WI
Cyc Am Bio; Dict Am Auth; Dict
Am Bio Men Time

2368. Frazier, Martha M.
born 1826
educator, temperance worker
Wisconsin
Wom Cent

2369. Robinson, Abbie C. B.
born 1828
editor, Democratic newspaper
publisher, political author
Wisconsin
Index t Wom; Wom Cent

2370. Warren, Mary Evalin
born 1829
author, lecturer, temperance
worker, suffragist
Baptist
Wisconsin
Wom Cent

2371. Fairbanks, Elizabeth B.
born 1831
philanthropist, mental institution
reformer
Wisconsin
Wom Cent

2372. Hiles, Osia Joslyn
born 1832
philanthropist, poet, Native
American welfare worker
Wisconsin
Wom Cent

2373. Carson, Delia E.
born 1833
educator of women, traveler
Madison, WI
Wom Cent

2374. Norton, Minerva (Brace)
born 1837
educator, author, missionary
worker
Beloit, WI
Dict Am Auth; Wom Cent

2375. Johnson, Electa Amanda
born 1838
philanthropist
Wisconsin
Index t Wom; Wom Cent

**2376. Manville, Helen Adelia
(Wood) "Nellie"**
born 1839
poet
La Crosse, WI
Dict Am Auth; Index t Wom;
Nat Cyc Am Bio v4

2377. Adams, Mary (Mathews)
1840–1902
educator, poet
Madison, WI
Irish
Dict Am Auth; Wom Cent

2378. Bell, Caroline Horton
born 1840
philanthropist
Presbyterian
Milwaukee, WI
Wom Cent

**2379. Reed, Rebecca Perley
(Page)**
born 1840
children's writer
Milwaukee, WI
Dict Am Auth

2380. Fifield, Stella A. Gaines
born 1845
journalist
Wisconsin
Wom Cent

2381. Hobart, Sarah Dyer
born 1845
poet, author
Wisconsin
Wom Cent

2382. Pier, Kate Hamilton
1845–1925
lawyer, feminist
Wisconsin
Index t Wom; Nat Cyc Am Bio
v21; Wom Cent

**2383. Dayton, Elizabeth; Beth
Day**
born 1848
poet, author
Wisconsin
English
Wom Cent

2384. Crawford, Alice (Arnold)
1850–74
poet
Milwaukee, WI
Dict Am Auth; Wom Cent

**2385. Savage, Minnie Stebbins;
Marion Lisle**
born 1850
poet, author, Unitarian church
worker, temperance worker
Unitarian
Wisconsin
Wom Cent

2386. Giles, Ella Augusta
born 1851
author
Madison, WI
Dict Am Auth; Wom Cent

**2387. Reinertson, Emma May
Alexander; Gale Forest**
born 1853
short story writer
Wisconsin
Wom Cent

2388. Carrington, Abbie
born 1856
soprano opera singer

Fond du Lac, WI
Wom Cent

2389. Street, Ida Maria
born 1856
educator, art criticism author
Milwaukee, WI
Dict Am Auth

2390. Frisby, Almah J.
born 1857
physician
Wisconsin
Wom Cent

2391. Melville, Velma Caldwell
born 1858
poet, author
Wisconsin
Wom Cent

**2392. Perry, Charlotte Augusta
"Carlotta"**
born 1858
poet
Milwaukee, WI
Dict Am Auth; Wom Cent

2393. la Follette, Belle Case
1859–1931
leader in Wisconsin Progressive
movement
Wisconsin
Index t Wom; Not Am Wom;
Wom Cent

**2394. Youmans, Theodora Win-
ton**
born 1863
journalist
Wisconsin
Wom Cent

**2395. Hooper, Jessie Annette
Jack**
1865–1935
suffragist, Democratic politician,
peace advocate
Wisconsin
Dict Am Bio supp v1; Nat Cyc
Am Bio csv1; Not Am Wom

2396. Miner, Jean Pond
born 1866
sculptor
Illinois; Wisconsin
Wom Cent

2397. Pier, Kate Hamilton
born 1868
lawyer, feminist
Wisconsin
Wom Cent

2398. Pier, Caroline Hamilton
born 1870
lawyer, feminist
Wisconsin
Wom Cent

**2399. Hanks, Mary Esther Vi-
las**
1873–1959
Madison civic leader
Episcopalian
Madison, WI
Nat Cyc Am Bio v49

**2400. Gale, Zona; Mrs. Wil-
liam L. Breese**
1874–1938
novelist, playwright, essayist
Wisconsin
Dict Am Bio supp v2; Dict Lit
Bio v9; Index t Wom; Nat Cyc
Am Bio v30 and csv2; Not Am
Wom; Wom Lit, More

**2401. Kryszak, Mary Olszew-
ski**
1875–1945
Polish American welfare worker,
Wisconsin state legislator
Wisconsin
Polish
Not Am Wom

2402. Delfs, Eleanor (Mary)
1880–1977
obstetrician/gynecologist
Presbyterian
Wisconsin
Nat Cyc Am Bio v60

**2403. McCreery, Maria Maud
Leonard**
1883–1938
Wisconsin suffragist, Socialist
party worker, labor organizer
Wisconsin
Not Am Wom

2404. Newcomb, Kate Delham
1887–1956
circuit physician, hospital founder
Wisconsin
Obit File

**2405. Neese, Laura Janvrin Al-
drich**
1889–1967
artist, philanthropist
Congregationalist
Wisconsin
Nat Cyc Am Bio v53

**2406. Lenroot, Katharine Fre-
drica**
born 1891
government official, social worker, child health worker
Congregationalist
Wisconsin
Index t Wom; Nat Cyc Am Bio
csv7

2407. Hoan, Gladys
1901–52
Wisconsin Democratic National
Committee member
Wisconsin
Obit File

2408. Duncan, Catherine (la Vanche) Gross
1908–68
phytopathologist
Methodist
Wisconsin
Nat Cyc Am Bio v54

2409. Jones, Sarah [Frances] Roddis
1909–75
president general of DAR
Episcopalian
Wisconsin
Nat Cyc Am Bio v59

WYOMING

2410. Morris, Esther Hobart McQuigg Slack
1813/14–1902
suffragist, feminist, judge, western pioneer, justice of the peace
Wyoming
Index t Wom; Not Am Wom; Read Encyc Am West; Wom Cent

2411. Post, Amalia Barney Simons
born 1836
feminist, suffragist
Wyoming
Index t Wom; Wom Cent

2412. Jenkins, Theresa A.
born 1853
suffragist, journalist, women's rights worker, temperance worker
Wyoming
Wom Cent

2413. Hebard, Grace Raymond
1861–1936
educator, feminist historian, author
Wyoming
Index t Wom; Read Encyc Am West

2414. Ross, Nellie (Tayloe)
1876/80–1977
thirteenth governor of Wyoming (Democrat)
Wyoming
Cur Biog '78; Index t Wom; Nat Cyc Am Bio csv2 and csv5; Obit File

2415. Ingersall, Winifred
1890–1960
physician
Presbyterian
Wyoming
Nat Cyc Am Bio v45

V. Alphabetical Index

Bonaparte, Jerome Napoleon, Mrs., **I** 16920

Bond, Abigail Monique, **I** 12100, **III** 482

Bond, Carrie Jacobs; Carrie Jacobs-Bond, **I** 431, 9135, 13682, **II** 764, **IV** 109

Bond, Elizabeth Powell, **I** 1188, 2494, 15133, 19291, 20928, **IV** 2066

Bond, Helen Judy, **I** 2107

Bond, Rosalie B. de Dolms, **I** 17413

Bonds, Margaret, **I** 14521, **III** 306

Bondy, Elizabeth Jeanne Hale, **I** 995, 10591, 11921, **II** 356, **IV** 1835

Bonelli, Mona Modini, **I** 10363, 14287

Bones, Marietta M., **I** 19297, 20932

Bonetti, Mary, **I** 14270

Bonfanti, Marie, **I** 1906

Bonfield, Lida, **I** 729

Bonfils, Helen Gertrude, **I** 626, 11434, 19995, **II** 190, **IV** 290

Bonham, Mildred A., **I** 10962, 16561, 18250

Bonner, Isabelle (Kramm), **I** 20327

Bonner, Mary Graham, **I** 10075

Bonner, Sherwood. *See* MacDowell, Katherine Sherwood (Bonner).

Bonney, Mary Lucinda, **I** 1127, 2257

Bonney, Sarah E., **I** 12630

Bonney, Therese (Mabel), **I** 12115, 15908

Bonnin, Gertrude Simmons; Zitkala-sa, **I** 1216, 9505, **III** 1051

Bonny Kate. *See* Sevier, Catherine Sherrill.

Bono, Cherilyn (Lapiere); Cher, **I** 14758, **III** 1124, **IV** 270

Bonsall, Mary M., **I** 4197

Bonstelle, Justine Laura "Jessie", **I** 483, 19783

Bonum, Elizabeth Johnson, **I** 16109

Boole, Ella Alexander, **I** 1413, 15144, 17517, 19422, 21071, **II** 657

Boone, Jemima, **I** 16332

Boone, Rebecca B., **I** 16371

Booth, Ada Pearl Dunlap; Adeline Dunlap, **I** 5662, 13012, 19935, **IV** 1160

Booth, Agnes; Marian Agnes Land Rookes, **I** 19608, **III** 6

Booth, Alice, **I** 10204

Booth, Almida, **I** 2587

Booth, Ellen Warren Scripps, **I** 15616

Booth, Emma Scarr, **I** 8179, **III** 672

Booth, Evangeline Cory, **I** 1475, 9225, 13717, 14993, 17566, **II** 954, **III** 705

Booth, Florence Eleanor Soper, **I** 1453, 17550, **II** 953

Booth, Mary Ann Allard, **I** 12579

Booth, Mary Devlin, **I** 19603

Booth, Mary F. McVicker, **I** 19628

Booth, Mary H. C., **I** 8091

Booth, Mary Louisa, **I** 5887, 6399, 6552, 10899

Booth, Maud Ballington (Charlesworth), **I** 1476, 2871, 9226, 15626, 16768, 17567, **II** 955, **III** 706

Booth, Mrs., **I** 5182

Booth, Shirley, **I** 20315

Boothe, Clare. *See* Luce, Clare Boothe.

Boothe, Viva Belle, **I** 662, 3268, **II** 614, **IV** 1965

Booth-Tucker, Emma Moss, **I** 1424, 17533, **II** 952

Boott, Elizabeth, **I** 3940

Boozer, Mary, **I** 5183

Borchardt, Selma Munter, **I** 3290, 6485, 7104, **IV** 419

Borden, Helen, Sister, **I** 12535, 17362, **II** 120

Borden, Lucille Papin, **I** 9439

Borden, Mary; Lady Spears, **I** 5668, 9794, 13034, **III** 728

Borden, Mrs., **I** 4880

Borden, Olive, **I** 20316, **IV** 230

Borden, Sylvia, **I** 17952

Bordoni, Irene, **I** 14116, 20077, **III** 601, 798

Borg, Madeleine Beer, **I** 15719, 18509

Bori, Lucrezia; Lucrecia Borja Gonzales de Riancho, **I** 14007, **II** 184, **III** 1264

Boris, Ruthanna, **I** 1990

Bork, Florence L. Holmes, **I** 9330

Bosomworth, Mary Musgrove, **I** 113

Bosone, Reva Beck, **I** 7400

Bossidy, Mary, **I** 730, 11647

Bostelmann, Else W. von Roder, **I** 4374, **III** 851

Bostwick, Helen Louise, **I** 7913

Bostwick, Helen Louise (Barrow), **I** 7914, **IV** 1893

Boswell, Connee, **I** 14187, 20179

Boswell, Florence, **I** 18046

Boswell, Helen Varick, **I** 1468, 21117, **IV** 1608

Boswell, Martha; Martha Lloyd, **I** 14350, 20344

Boswell, Vet, **I** 14188

Boteler, Helen, **I** 5184, 13483

Botta, Anne Charlotte Lynch, **I** 2254, 7720, **IV** 1379

Bottome, Margaret (McDonald), **I** 1291, 12251, 17253, 18201

Bottomshaw, Mrs., **I** 137

Botume, Elizabeth Hyde, **I** 2337, 5185

Boucicault, Agnes Robertson, **I** 13494, 19573, **III** 1241

Boughton, Caroline Greenbank, **I** 2661, 15558, 21041

Bougureau, Elizabeth Jane, **I** 4031

Boulanger, Nadia, **I** 3191, 14008, **III** 790

Bourgeois, Florence, **I** 4656

Bourgeois, Margaret, Sister, **I** 16948, **II** 60

Bourke-White, Margaret, **I** 11836, 15898

Bourne, Emma, **I** 19342, **IV** 1311

Bourskaya, Ina, **I** 14009

Boutillier, Cornelia Geer le. *See* le Boutillier, Cornelia Geer.

Bouton, Emily St. John, **I** 11018

Bouve, Pauline Carrington (Rust), **I** 7523, **IV** 880

Bouverie, Ava Alice Muriel Astor Pleydel. *See* Pleydel-Bouverie, Ava Alice Muriel Astor.

Bouvet, Marguerite (Marie), **I** 6589, 9227

Bouvier, Hannah Mary. *See* Peterson, Hannah Mary (Bouvier).

Boves, Josefina, **I** 7401

Bow, Clara, The "It" Girl, **I** 20283

Bowen, Ariel Serena Hedges, **I** 2579, 13564, **III** 127

Bowen, Catherine (Shober) Drinker, **I** 6205, 10120, 15066, **IV** 2152

Bowen, Eliza Andrews, **I** 7963, 10879, 15916, **IV** 445

Bowen, Louise Hadduck de Koven, **I** 15588, 18344, 21081, **IV** 569

Bowen, Mary, **I** 4881

Bowen, Ruth, **I** 1050, 20589, **III** 412

Bowen, Sue (Petrigru) (King), **I** 7866, **IV** 2203

Bower, Bertha Muzzy, **I** 9390

Bowers, Eilley Orrum, **I** 16484

Bowers, Elizabeth Crocker; Elizabeth Crocker McCollum; Mrs. D. P. Bowers, **I** 19564

Bowers, Gladys Irene, **I** 17812

Bowers, Sarah Sedgwick, **I** 13470

Bowles, A. Lincoln, Mrs.; Nancy Hanks, **I** 11244

Bowles, Ada Christina, **I** 17326, 20886, **II** 1089

Bowles, Eva Del Vakia, **I** 1572

Bowles, Heloise; Heloise, **I** 2133, 11967

Bowman, Geline MacDonald, **I** 686, 1749, 21310

Bowman, J. Beatrice, **I** 5693, 13175

Bowne, Eliza Southgate, **I** 7443

Bowser, Mary Elizabeth, **I** 5127, 16479, **III** 84

Bowser, Rosa Dixon, **I** 1676, 3160, **III** 202, **IV** 2345

Boxer, Mrs. Charles Ralph. *See* Hahn, Emily.

Boya, Ellen Wright, **I** 2381, 3922, 8138, 17303, **IV** 1424

Boyce, Westray Battle, **I** 5710

Boyd, Anna Tomlinson, **I** 3084, 13896

Boyd, Belle; Belle Hardinge, **I** 5573, 14906, 16584, 19615, **II** 747

Boyd, Kate Parker (Scott), **I** 3933, 19240

Boyd, Katharine Lamont, **I** 11590, **II** 869, **IV** 1879

Boyd, Louise Arner, **I** 5672, 15967, 16688, **II** 848

Boyd, Louise Esther Vickroy, **I** 7936

Boyer, Beatrice Alexander, **I** 17736

Boyer, Margaret, **I** 5186

Boyer, Sophia Ames, **I** 1715

Boyington, Mary K., **I** 5187, 12282

Boylan, Grace (Duffie), **I** 9108, 11170, **IV** 576

Boyle, Gertrude; Gertrude Boyle Kanno;- Gertrude Farquharson, **I** 4324, **IV** 150

Boyle, Kay, **I** 10334, **III** 804

Boyle, Virginia (Frazer), **I** 9169, **IV** 2242

Boyleston, Helen Dore, **I** 10076

Boyleston, Sarah, **I** 157

Bozarth, Mrs., **I** 5008, 16259

Brace, Lucy Collins, **I** 17027

Brace, Maria Porter, **I** 2628, 19651, **IV** 1517

Bracken, Clio Hinton Huneker, **I** 4198

Brackenridge, M. Eleanor, **I** 15591, 21088

Brackenridge, Marian, **I** 4647

Brackett, Anna Callender, **I** 2406, 8225, 20887

Brackett, Leigh, **I** 10626

Braddock, Amelia, **I** 3338, 14189, **III** 742

Braddock, Katherine, **I** 6869, **II** 787, **IV** 134

Braden, Anna Madge; Madge Rile, **I** 8701, **II** 649

Bradford, Alice, **I** 1269, 2138, 15204, 16067, **II** 931, **III** 623, **IV** 848

Bradford, Charlotte, **I** 5188, 15348

Bradford, Cornelia Foster, **I** 18283

Bradford, Cornelia Smith, **I** 148, 10806

Bradford, Dorothy, **I** 16069, **II** 933

Bradford, Mary, **I** 5189, 16493

Bradford, Mary Carroll Craig, **I** 2689, 6423, 11114, **II** 242, **IV** 278

Bradford, Susan, **I** 5585, 15219, 16594, **IV** 1294

Bradley, Alice, **I** 2086, 3008, **II** 599, **IV** 1096

Bradley, Amy Morris, I 2295, 5131, 12233
Bradley, Ann Weaver, I 19229
Bradley, Emilie, I 17154
Bradley, Florence Kauffman Thacker, I 7086, II 615, IV 669
Bradley, Lillian Trimble, I 9506, 19821
Bradley, Lucretia, I 17849
Bradley, Lydia Moss, I 15278
Bradley, Marion Zimmer, I 10740
Bradley, Mary Emily (Neeley), I 8180
Bradley, Mary Hastings, I 16723
Bradley, Ora Lewis, I 3339, 4554, 10205
Bradna, Ella, I 18722, 19866, III 490
Bradnox, Mary, I 12123
Bradshaw, Lillian Moore, I 1860, 6294
Bradstreet, Anne Dudley, I 7406, II 938, III 625
Bradstreet, Martha, I 205
Bradwell, Myra R. (Colby), I 5504, 6696, 10900, 12465, 20853, IV 511
Brady, Alice, I 20060
Brady, Mary A., I 5128, 15303, III 921
Brady, Mildred Edie, I 950, 11864
Brady, Mrs. William A. See George, Grace.
Braeunlich, Sophie, I 416, 6816, 12724, 15941
Bragdon, Helen Dalton, I 3291
Bragg, Mabel Caroline, I 12833
Brain, Belle M., I 2751, 19427, IV 1935
Brainard, Bertha, I 11452
Brainard, Kate J., I 13504
Braithwaite-Burke, Yvonne Watson. See Burke, Yvonne Watson Braithwaite.
Brall, Ruth Hirsch, I 4636
Braman, Ella Frances, I 6766, IV 1504
Branaster, Greta Johanson, I 18764
Branch, Anna Hempstead, I 9507, 18484, IV 342
Branch, Dorothy Sutton, I 17818, II 55, III 364
Branch, Hazel E., I 3098, 6604
Branch, Mary E., I 3129, III 197
Branch, Mary Lydia Bolles, I 8360, IV 1463
Brande, Dorothea. See Collins, Dorothea.
Brande, Dorothea Thompson, I 10018, 11551, II 863, IV 623
Brandegee, Mary Catherine Layne Curran, I 12585
Brandstrom-Ulrich, Elsa; The Angel of Siberia, I 5681, 15783

Brandt, Mary Elizabeth, I 10206
Brandt, Mary Largent, I 4533
Brandt, Molly, I 16160
Brandwein, Gertrude, I 731
Branham, Sarah E., I 7034, 13055
Brannan, Sophie Marston, I 4555
Branscombe, Gena, I 9688, 13946, III 560
Brant, Cornelia Chase, I 2850, 12778
Brant, Evelyn, I 20180, IV 210
Brant, Mary; Molly Brant; Deganiwadonte, I 1076, 6650, III 1031
Brant, Molly. See Brant, Mary.
Branzell, Karin, I 14088
Brasher, Judith, I 124
Braslau, Sophie, I 14019
Brastow, Virginia, I 11266
Bratton, Martha, I 5060, 16339
Braucher, Pela Fay, I 2126, 3479, 13326, II 521
Brauenlich, Sophia (Toepken), I 386, 1394, 11096, 15935
Braumuller, Luetta Elmina, I 4062
Braun, Annette Frances, I 6613
Braun, Emma Lucy, I 13063, 16905
Braun, "Ma", I 18936
Braunwald, Nina Starr, I 13414
Braxton, Elizabeth Corbin, I 4882, 16185
Braxton, Judith Robinson, I 4782, 16134
Braxton, Mary Carter, I 4883, 16186
Brayton, Mary Clark, I 5190, 15349, 18206
Brazza, Cora (Slocomb), Countess, I 9136, IV 1591
Bread Woman of New Orleans, The. See Haughery, Margaret Gaffney.
Breck, Carrie Ellis, I 8873, 13605
Breckinridge, Madeline McDowell, I 18454, IV 745
Breckinridge, Margaret Elizabeth, I 5191, 12283
Breckinridge, Mary, I 523, 12926
Breckinridge, Mary Hopkins Cabell, I 16180
Breckinridge, Mary Marvin, I 7147, 15890
Breckinridge, Sophonisba Preston, I 453, 2889, 6845, 9263, 18394, II 664
Breed, Lorena May, I 12764, 17559, IV 113
Breedlove, Sarah McWilliams. See Walker, Sarah McWilliams Breedlove.
Breen, May Sighi; Malia Rosa, I 10787, 14767
Breen, Patrick, Mrs., I 16425
Breese, Mrs. William L. See Gale, Zona.

Breintnall, Hannah, I 138
Bremer, Belle. See Swafford, Martina.
Bremer, Edith Terry, I 1677, 15182, 18556
Bremer, Fredrika, I 7600, III 1268
Brennan, Ella, I 1042
Brenner, Anita, I 6253, 10407, 11845
Brenner, Dora, I 1770
Brent, Margaret, I 82, 6633, IV 825
Brent, Mary, I 85, 16075
Breton, Ruth, I 14771
Brett, Catheryna, I 16110
Brett, Margaret, I 16126
Brevard, Mrs., I 4884, 16187
Brewer, Theresa, I 14687
Brewster, Anne M. Hampton, I 7755, III 963
Brewster, Cora Belle, I 9000, 12713, IV 839
Brewster, Elizabeth Fisher; Shepherdess Mother of Hinghwa, I 17551, II 583
Brewster, Margaret, I 16966, II 970
Brewster, Mary, I 16040, II 918
Brewster, Patience, I 16065
Brewton, Robert, Mrs., I 4885
Brian, Mary, I 20007
Briant, Nila Mack, I 732, 11648
Brice, Carol, I 14587, III 341
Brice, Fanny (Borach), I 11527, 20047, II 439, IV 1760
Brick, Katherine, I 18083
Bricktop. See Smith, Ada.
Brico, Antonia, I 3448, 14271
Bridewell, Carrie, I 13897, 19867
Bridge, Edith McKenney, I 1771
Bridges, Ethel, I 14154
Bridges, Fidelia, I 3927
Bridges, Madeline S. See de Vere, Mary Aigne.
Bridgman, Eliza Jane Gilbert, I 17113
Bridgman, Olga Louise, I 3174, 9795, 13035, II 845, IV 169
Briggs, Berta N., I 4556
Briggs, Cora S., I 3691, 14772
Briggs, Dorothy Bell, I 14773
Briggs, Emily Pomona Edson; Olivia, I 10890
Briggs, M. M., Mrs., I 5192, 12284
Briggs, Margaret Perkins, I 9348
Briggs, Mary Blatchley, I 8590, 11010
Brigham, Mary Ann, I 2302
Brigham, Sarah J. (Lathbury), I 3931, 8181
Brigham, Sarah Prentice, I 8139
Brigham, Susan S., I 5089
Bright, Clarita Heath, I 18937

Bright Eyes. See Tibbles, Susette Laflesche.
Brill, Jeanette Goodman, I 7035
Brine, Mary Dow (Northam), I 7524, IV 1351
Briney, Nancy Wells, I 990, 11905
Brink, Carol Ryrie, I 10077
Brinker, Maureen Catherine. See Connolly, Maureen Catherine (Brinker).
Brinker, Maureen Connolly; Little Mo, I 18866
Brinker, Una Abell, I 19811, IV 1664
Brinkerhoff, Clara M., I 2326, 13481, III 662
Brinkley, Nell [Ethel]; Mrs. Bruce Moir McRae, I 4403, 11398, II 702
Brinkman, Mary A., I 12591
Brinley, Katherine Gordon Sanger, I 9613
Brinton, Emma Southwick, I 5524, 12490, 16548
Brinton, Mary Williams, I 13350, 17779
Brisbane, Margaret Hunt, I 8965
Bristol, Augusta (Cooper), I 2394, 6318, 8182, 12497, 14855, 15918, 18226
Bristol, Margaret, I 3692, 10796, 14774
Bristow, Gwen, I 10364
Britain, Radie, I 14288
Brittan, Harriet G., I 5822, 7843, 17227
Brittano, Susannah, I 2155, 15207
Brittingham, Bettie S., I 11837, 17770, II 621
Britton, Elizabeth Gertrude Knight, I 12698, IV 1557
Britts, Mattie (Dyer), I 8458
Bro, Marguerite Harmon, I 10050
Broadbent, Bessie May, I 6617
Broadhurst, Jean, I 2986, 9440, 12881
Broadhurst, Lillian Trimble Bradley, I 586, 9753, 19936
Broadwick, Tiny, I 17904
Broaker, Julia Anderson Luth, I 9200, 19719, III 613
Brochester, Ruth, I 7148
Brock, Blanche Kerr, I 14020, 17689
Brock, Emma Lillian, I 4404, 9796
Brock, Holly, I 18796
Brockman, Zoe Kincaid, I 10019, 11552
Brockway, Marion T., I 12834
Brode, Mildred Hooker, I 1772, 6220
Broderick, Helen, I 20048
Brodhead, Eva Wilder (McGlasson), I 7525, IV 1883
Brodie, Helen, I 6384

Carpenter, Harlean. *See*
Harlow, Jean.
Carpenter, Leslie, I 7318,
11974, 15111
Carpenter, Mary, I 16044
Carpenter, Mildred Carver, I
6222
Carpenter, Phillip, Mrs., I
1515, 6870
Carr, Alice G., I 13219
Carr, Charlotte E., I 637,
18577
Carr, Deborah Edith
Wallbridge, I 5984, 15936
Carr, Edith Adele, I 6923,
15705, IV 408
Carr, Emma Perry, I 12959, II
605
Carr, Geraldine Wildon, I 6331
Carr, Vicki; Florencia Bicenta
de Casillas Martinez
Cardona, I 14728, III 1015
Carraway, Gertrude Sprague, I
10099, 11592
Carreau, Margaret, I 14175
Carrell, Columba, I 12181,
17141, II 89, IV 718
Carreno, Teresa, I 13595
Carreras, Maria Avani, I
13867, III 972
Carrick, Jean Warren, I 3516,
10522, 14359
Carrington, Abbie, I 13611, IV
2388
Carrington, Elaine Sterne, I
9964, 11529
Carrington, Elsie, I 13220, III
238
Carrington, Kate. *See* Ray,
Rachel Beasley.
Carrington, Margaret Irwin, I
16454
Carroll, Anna Ella, I 5100,
6671, 7721
Carroll, Christina, I 14360, III
1173
Carroll, Consolata; Sister Mary
Consolata, I 3259, 9984,
17730, II 195
Carroll, Diahann, I 14713,
20642, III 438
Carroll, Gladys Hasty, I 10385
Carroll, Harriet Chew, I 16307
Carroll, Jane Wall, I 6759,
12612
Carroll, Mary Darnell, I 5001
Carroll, Nancy; Ann Veronica
La-Hiff, I 20304
Carroll, Pat, I 12024, 20568
Carroll, Ruth, I 10217
Carroll, Ruth Robinson, I
4545, 10173
Carruth, Frances Weston, I
9280, IV 1627
Carse, Matilda Bradley, I 280,
15425, 18228, 19234, IV 516
Carson, Delia E., I 2382,
16544, 20867, IV 2373
Carson, Luella Clay, I 2690
Carson, Mindy, I 14653, 20569
Carson, Rachel Louise, I
10464, 13336, 16929, II 725

Carter, Alice (Olin) Draper, I
1662, 5659, 15758, II 830,
IV 1725
Carter, Amy, I 1072, 3694,
18134
Carter, Ann Shaw, I 18048
Carter, Artie Mason, I 14778,
15870
Carter, Caroline Louise Dudley;
Mrs. Leslie Carter, I 19707
Carter, Cora C. C., I 1776
Carter, Edna, I 12872, 21178
Carter, Eunice Hunton, I 1763,
7135, 18619, III 235, IV
1795
Carter, Frances Ann Tasker, I
16797
Carter, Gwendolyn Margaret, I
3484, 7240, 10438, III 270
Carter, Hannah Benedict, I
4835
Carter, Hannah Johnson, I
2341, 3910
Carter, Hannah Looke, I 18818
Carter, Helene, I 4410, III 563
Carter, Laverne, I 18945
Carter, Lillian "Bessie", I
1235, 13186, 15191, 18616,
IV 486
Carter, Mabel Ogilvie, I 743,
3766
Carter, Mary Adaline Edwards,
I 261, 2342, 3911, 19197
Carter, Mary Gilmore, I 9281
Carter, Maybelle Hunton, I
14261, IV 2248
Carter, Mrs., I 16348
Carter, Sisters, I 16349
Cartwright, Ellen M., I 13465
Cartwright, Emily J. Avery, I
5206, 12294
Cartwright, Florence Byrne, I
9171, IV 114
Cartwright, Marguerite Dorsey,
I 3596, 11934, III 308
Carus, Emma, I 19868, III 848
Carver, Katherin, I 16045, II
920
Cary, Alice, I 7789, II 1078,
IV 1385, 1891
Cary, Anna Louise; Annie
Louise Cary Raymond, I
13537
Cary, Constance, I 5207, 5849,
8010
Cary, Elizabeth Luther, I 9282,
11222, IV 1628
Cary, Mary Ann Shad, I 1149,
2297, 6681, 10863, 16483,
III 86, 510
Cary, Mary Harkness Flagler, I
14262, 16926, IV 1805
Cary, Mary Stockley, I 276,
15421, IV 1898
Cary, Phoebe, I 7867
Casa, Lisa della. *See* della
Casa, Lisa.
Case, Adelaide Teague, I
11408, 17682, II 849
Case, Alice Montague, I 16664,
17590
Case, Anna, I 14035

Case, Marietta Stanley, I 8556,
17425, 19334, IV 1920
Case, Mary, I 7603, II 1000,
IV 1364
Case, Mary Emily, I 2709,
6576, IV 1547
Case, Mary Sophia, I 2662
Casey, Margaret Elizabeth, I
17617
Casey, Rosemary, I 10386,
20270, II 210, IV 2156
Cashin, Bonnie, I 3833, 20416
Caspary, Vera, I 10365, 20260
Cass, Erna W., I 11658
Cass, Peggy, I 12006
Cassat, Marie (Stevenson), I
3976
Casseday, Jennie, I 15461,
19274, IV 731
Cassiday, Claudia, I 1964,
11846, 14310, 20284
Cassiday, Mary, I 3348
Castagnetta, Grace, I 14512
Castle, Angelina, I 17156, IV
494
Castle, Irene (Foote), I 1931,
16913
Castle, Marian Johnston, I
10147
Castleman, Alice Barbee, I
15867, 21359, II 917, IV 753
Caswell, Mary McIlweane, I
4808
Cate, Eliza Jane, I 5793, 7684,
IV 1259
Cather, Willa Sibert, I 9442, II
794, IV 1251
Catherine, Mother. *See*
Spalding, Catherine.
Catherine, Sister, I 16427
Catherwood, Ethel, I 18946
Catherwood, Mary (Hartwell),
I 5952, 8616, II 1106, IV
540
Catlett, Elizabeth, I 4718, III
314
Catlin, Laura Wood, I 8429,
15475
Catlin, Louise (Ensign), I 9109,
IV 1586
Catt, Carrie Clinton Lane
Champman, I 15146, 21082
Cattell, Hettie, I 11659
Cattle Kate. *See* Watson, Ella
and Maxwell, Kate.
Cattle Lady. *See* Marvel,
Louise.
Caudill, Rebecca, I 10174
Caulfield, Joan [Beatrice], I
20501
Caulkins, Frances Manwaring,
I 5773, 7505, IV 306
Cavanah, Frances Elizabeth, I
10175
Cavanna, Betty; Betsy Allen, I
10506
Cavazza, E. *See* Pullen,
Elisabeth Jones (Cavazza).
Cavis, Helen, I 3349, 17959
Cayvan, Georgia Eva, I 19669

Cazneau, Jane Maria Eliza
McManus Storms, I 227,
6664, 10834
Cecil, Elizabeth Frances, I
8362, II 121
Cecil, Mary, I 19952
Celeste, Madame; Celeste-
Elliott, I 1897, 19523
Celeste, Marie, I 13641, 19687
Celeste-Elliott. *See* Celeste,
Madame.
Center, Stella Steward, I 3069,
15025
Centlivre, Susannah, I 7412,
19456
Cevee, Alice de. *See* de Cevee,
Alice.
Chace, Elizabeth Buffum, I
1102, 16735, 19148, 20741,
II 1005
Chace, Marian, I 1939, 13164
Chadwick, Florence, I 18824
Chadwick, Helene, I 20126
Chaffee, Allen, I 9349
Chaffee, Lucy Morris. *See*
Alden, Lucy Morris Chaffee.
Challinor, Mercedes Crimmins
(Clara), I 1678, 5665, 13022,
15767, II 178
Chalmers, Audrey, I 4491,
10020, III 569
Chamberlain, Georgia Louise, I
2824, 9137
Chamberlain, Hope Summerhill,
I 9350, II 596, IV 1869
Chambers, Eleanor, I 7217, IV
222
Chambers, Yolande Hargrave, I
1017, 7319, III 343
Chamie, Tatiana, I 1959
Champion, Deborah, I 16283
Champion, Marge Celeste;
Marjorie Celeste Belcher, I
2005
Champney, Elizabeth William;
Lizzie Williams, I 8708, IV
1506
Chance, Julie Grinnell; Mrs.
Stephen van Rensselaer
Cruger, I 9039
Chandler, Anna Curtis, I 3100
Chandler, Bessie. *See* Parker,
Elizabeth Lowber (Chandler).
Chandler, Dorothey Buffum, I
11805
Chandler, Elizabeth Margaret, I
1107, 7636, IV 362
Chandler, Lucinda Banister, I
257, 6685, 7964, 19186
Chandler, Mary Alderson. *See*
Atherton, Mary Alderson
Chandler.
Chandler, Mary Alderson, I
352, 2581
Chandler, Mary Greene. *See*
Ware, Mary Greene
(Chandler).
Chandler, Sue Pinkston, I
6307, 11995, III 371
Chandor, Valentine, I 3233
Chanfrau, Henrietta Baker, I
13516, 19592

Dwight, Minnie Ryan, **I** 437, 11192, **IV** 1066

Dwyer, Bessie Agnes, **I** 11050, **IV** 2264

Dwyer, Florence P., **I** 7209

Dyar, Clara, **I** 1508, 21154, **IV** 1157

Dye, Clarissa F., **I** 5241, 12316

Dye, Eva (Emery), **I** 5990, 8879, **IV** 1991

Dye, Marie, **I** 2105, 3253, 13116

Dye, Mary Irene Clark, **I** 287, 18233, 19248

Dye, Royal J., Mrs., **I** 17766

Dyer, Catherine Cornelia [Joy], **I** 5808, 7745

Dyer, Clara L. Brown, **I** 4008

Dyer, Julia Knowlton, **I** 15343, **II** 532

Dyer, Mary, **I** 16965, **II** 969, **IV** 851

Dyer, Mattie. *See* Britts, Mattie (Dyer).

Dyer, Mattie, **I** 8465

Dyhrenfurth, Hettie, **I** 3363, 10227

Dykeman, Wilma, **I** 10673

Dykstra, Neeltye. *See* d'Arville, Camille.

E. A. *See* Conner, Eliza Archard.

Eads, Laura Krieger, **I** 3237, 13083

Eagels, Jeanne, **I** 20013

Eager, Gertrude, **I** 17892

Eager, Helen, **I** 11610, 20142, **IV** 1121

Eagle, Mary Kavanaugh, **I** 17496, **II** 34, **IV** 44

Eakin, Mary, **I** 20103

Eakin, Vera O., **I** 14204

Eames, Elizabeth Jessup, **I** 7685

Eames, Emma Hayden; Mrs. Julian Story, **I** 13612

Eames, Jane Anthony, **I** 7736, 16453, **IV** 913, 1265

Earhart, Amelia May, **I** 10122, 17950

Earl, John Prescott. *See* Gilchrist, Beth Bradford.

Earle, Alice Morse, **I** 5969, 8780, **IV** 1260

Earle, Florence van Leer. *See* Coates, Florence van Leer (Earle) (Nicholson).

Earle, Genevieve Beavers, **I** 6990

Earle, Mary Orr, **I** 1414

Earle, Mary Trace, **I** 9205, **IV** 1609

Earle, Virginia, **I** 13828

Early, Eleanor, **I** 6302, 10665

East, Edward H., Mrs., **I** 15525, 19362, **IV** 2231

East, Henrietta Maria, **I** 161, 3851

Easter, Marguerite Elizabeth (Miller), **I** 8328, **IV** 834

Eastman, Annie Bertha Ford, **I** 17485, **II** 300

Eastman, Crystal, **I** 15178, 18535, 21243

Eastman, Elaine (Goodale); Elaine Hall, **I** 25, 2841, 9176, 11193, **IV** 2221

Eastman, Eliena Krylenko, **I** 4510, **III** 1152

Eastman, Elizabeth, **I** 10411

Eastman, Ida. *See* Raugh, Ida.

Eastman, Julia Arabella, **I** 8254, **IV** 972

Eastman, Linda Anne, **I** 6061, **IV** 1946

Eastman, Mary F., **I** 14939

Eastman, Mary (Henderson), **I** 3, 7746, **IV** 2311

Eastman, Mary Huse, **I** 6134, 9617

Easton, Florence; Florence Rogers, **I** 13989, **III** 726

Easton, Mary, **I** 18964

Eastwood, Alice, **I** 9007, 12716, 16632

Eaton, Genevieve, **I** 17941

Eaton, J. S., Mrs., **I** 5242, 15356

Eaton, Mary, **I** 14277, 20241

Eaton, Sarah, **I** 16061, **II** 928

Eaton, Winifred. *See* Badcock, Winifred (Eaton).

Eaves, Elsie, **I** 15983

Eaves, Lucile, **I** 6438, 18420, **II** 1130, **IV** 132

Ebel, Isabel Caroline, **I** 16014, 18041

Eberhart, Nelle Richmond, **I** 13811

Eberle, Abastenia [Mary] St. Leger, **I** 4520

Eberle, Irmengarde, **I** 10148

Eccles, George E., Mrs., **I** 17707

Eccleston, Sarah Chamberlain, **I** 5243, 12317

Eckard, Margaret Esther Bayard, **I** 17144

Eckel, Berenice Long, **I** 3034, 13859, **II** 683

Eckert, Ida Ethel. *See* Lawrence, Ida Ethel (Eckert).

Eckles, Ann, **I** 16025, 18085

Eckstorm, Fannie Pearson Hardy, **I** 27, 9232, 12790, 13719, **II** 771, **IV** 819

Eddy, Eliza Jackson, **I** 15409

Eddy, Lillian E., **I** 923, 16783, **III** 1128

Eddy, Mary Morse (Baker) (Glover) (Patterson), **I** 17219, **II** 233, **IV** 1266

Eddy, Olive Tyndale, **I** 15819

Eddy, Sara Hershey, **I** 2346, 13485

Eddy, Sarah James, **I** 4032

Eddy, Sarah Stoddard, **I** 20854, **II** 1086

Edelman, Marian Wright, **I** 3684, 7390, **III** 452

Ederle, Gertrude, **I** 18780

Edey, Birdsall Otis, **I** 21025

Edgar, Elizabeth, **I** 2506, **II** 643, **IV** 2071

Edgar, Rachel, **I** 4900, 16200

Edgarton, Sarah Carter. *See* Mayo, Sarah Carter (Edgarton).

Edge, Rosalie Barrow, **I** 16881

Edgerly, Anne R., **I** 773

Edgerly, Mira; Countess Korzybska, **I** 4341

Edholm, Mary Gow Charlton, **I** 11097, 19404, 21042

Edie. *See* Post, Edith Sedgwick.

Edinger, Tilly, **I** 15982

Edith May. *See* Drinker, Anne.

Edla, Countess of. *See* Hensler, Eliza.

Edmonds, Helen Grey, **I** 3578, 6279, **III** 296

Edmonds, Sarah Emma Evelyn; Franklin Thompson, **I** 5563, 12558, 16576, **III** 518

Edmondson, Belle, **I** 5244, 5851, 8017

Edmondston, Catherine Ann, **I** 5245, 5852, 8018

Edson, Katherine Philips, **I** 6871, 18433

Edson, Sarah P., **I** 5246, 8019, 12318

Edson, Susan A., **I** 12234

Edward, Mrs. *See* Robinson, Therese Albertine Louise (von Jakob).

Edwardes, Paula, **I** 19689

Edwards, Anna Cheney, **I** 2396, 12500, 15919

Edwards, Clara, **I** 10709, 14639

Edwards, Edith, **I** 15163, 18465, 21188

Edwards, Edna Eck, **I** 17591

Edwards, Emma Atwood, **I** 2434

Edwards, Ester Gordy, **I** 973, 11894, 14374, **III** 286

Edwards, India, **I** 7106, 11580

Edwards, Joan, **I** 10666, 11969, 14584, 20459

Edwards, June, **I** 18111

Edwards, Lena Frances, **I** 13227

Edwards, Mrs., **I** 16264

Edwards, Ruth Hamilton, **I** 17784

Edwards, Sarah Pierpont, **I** 16979, **II** 947

Eells, Myra Fairbanks, **I** 16415

Eggleston, Allegra, **I** 4096

Eggleston, Marjorie E., **I** 774

Eggleston, Sarah Dabney, **I** 5538

Eichelberger, Lillian (Velma); Mrs. Ralph Cannon, **I** 13178, **II** 51

Eigenmann, Rosa Smith, **I** 12703

Eilers, Sally, **I** 20331

Einstein, Hannah Backman, **I** 18373

Eis, Alice, **I** 19887

Ekin, Helen. *See* Starrett, Helen (Ekin).

El Khoury, Marie Azeez. *See* Khoury, Marie Azeez El.

Elder, Ruth, **I** 18035

Elder, Susan (Blanchard); Hermine, **I** 8192, 12501, 17321, 19584, **II** 116, **IV** 763

Elderkin, Anne Wood, **I** 4801

Eldred, Edith Lillia Byers, **I** 17553

Eldred, Maria Olmstead, **I** 5247, 12319

Eldridge, Elleonor, **I** 215, 6660, 7469, 16802, **III** 64

Eldridge, Florence, **I** 20226

Elias, Mrs. Nathaniel M. *See* Baumgartner, Leona.

Elias, Rosalind, **I** 14688

Eliasoph, Paula, **I** 4573

Eliot, Alice. *See* Jewett, Sarah Orne.

Eliot, Ann, **I** 16943

Eliot, Anne Mumford, **I** 16072

Eliot, Charlotte Champe Stearns, **I** 8496, 18272

Eliot, Ethel Cook, **I** 9910, 17708, **II** 192

Eliot, Frances, **I** 4632

Eliot, Henrietta Robins (Mack), **I** 7541, **IV** 1978

Eliot, Martha May, **I** 1726, 7068, 13117, 15187, 18585, **II** 1147, **IV** 1116

Eliot, Max. *See* Ellis, Anna M. B.

Eliott, Susannah Smith, **I** 16114

Elizabeth, Sister. *See* Fedde, Elizabeth.

Elkers, Bertha Kahn, **I** 1463, 12766

Elkins, Elizabeth. *See* Sanders, Elizabeth (Elkins).

Elkus, Savilla, **I** 6335

Ellen, Minetta, **I** 20187

Ellerman, Amy, **I** 14022

Ellery, Abigail Carey, **I** 4983, 16245

Ellery, Ann Ramington, **I** 4810, 16154

Ellery, Mary Goddard, **I** 16354

Ellet, Mary, **I** 5066, 16377

Ellett, Elizabeth Fries (Lummis), **I** 5794, 7686

Ellinwood, Henrietta Elizabeth (Schneider), **I** 15707, 21213, **IV** 609

Elliot, Cass; Mama Cass, **I** 14736

Elliot, Elizabeth. *See* Green, Elizabeth Shippen.

Elliot, Kathleen Morrow, **I** 10123

Elliot, Rebekah Ward, **I** 775

Elliott, Anna, **I** 5052, 12149, 15218, 16333

Elliott, Daisy, **I** 1250, 7309, **III** 333, **IV** 1169

Elliott, Gertrude, **I** 19812

Elliott, Grace Loucks, **I** 10228, 11676

Elliott, Harriet Wiseman, **I** 3151, 7003, 21267, **IV** 1874

Fishback, Margaret, **I** 10390, 11838
Fisher, Alice, **I** 19765
Fisher, Anna A., **I** 2733
Fisher, Anne Benson, **I** 10149
Fisher, Bernice, **I** 14039
Fisher, Clara, **I** 13461, 19519, **III** 649
Fisher, Doris, **I** 1005, 10628, 14550, 20419
Fisher, Dorothy Canfield; Dorothea Frances Canfield, **I** 3088, 9618
Fisher, Elizabeth Florette, **I** 15953
Fisher, Elizabeth Holmes, **I** 15643, **II** 592, **IV** 127
Fisher, Emma Roderick, **I** 14377, 15859
Fisher, Gail, **I** 20595, **III** 415
Fisher, Harriet White. *See* Andrews, Harriet White Fisher.
Fisher, Harriet White, **I** 497, 9445
Fisher, Jane Marchant. *See* Vernon, Jane Marchant (Fisher).
Fisher, Katherine A., **I** 960, 1840, 2128, **III** 586
Fisher, Mary, **I** 2734, 8972, 16955, **II** 964, **IV** 1214
Fisher, Mary Frances Kennedy, **I** 10492
Fisher, Mrs. Thomas Hart. *See* Page, Ruth.
Fisher, Rebecca Jane Gilleland, **I** 10893, 15359, 16500, **IV** 2252
Fisher, Susanne, **I** 14206
Fisher, Wayne H., Mrs., **I** 17925
Fisher, Welthy (Blakesley) Honsinger, **I** 540, 3089, 17637, 18513, **II** 604
Fiske, Caroline Paull, **I** 16659
Fiske, Catharine, **I** 2182, 12151, 16801, **IV** 1263
Fiske, Fidelia, **I** 2258, 17184, **II** 286
Fiske, Gertrude Horsford, **I** 4342, **IV** 1104
Fiske, Mary Augusta (Davey); Minnie Madern; Minnie Madern Fiske, **I** 9234, 16863, 19730
Fiske, Minnie Madern. *See* Fiske, Mary Augusta (Davey).
Fiske, Myra Morrow, **I** 16595
Fitch, Florency Mary, **I** 3012, 9519, 17623, **IV** 1952
Fitch, Geraldine, **I** 11678
Fitzgerald, Alice, **I** 1552, 12884, **III** 971
Fitzgerald, Cissy, **I** 19715
Fitzgerald, Ella, **I** 14573, **III** 328
Fitzgerald, Margaret, **I** 11895
Fitzgerald, Pegeen, **I** 975, 3825, 11896

Fitzgerald, Susan Grimes Walker, **I** 6442, 18445, 21172, **II** 1132, **IV** 1087
Fitz-Gibbon, Bernice; Mrs. Herman Block, **I** 666, 11555, **II** 200, **IV** 1768
Fitzgibbon, Mary Catherine Irene; Sister Irene, **I** 15315, 17230, **II** 102
Fitzhugh, Anne, **I** 4815
Fitzu, Anna (Powell), **I** 3177, 13997
Fitzwater, Fanny Fern, **I** 3780, 11679
Fl. , Mrs. George. *See* Lowell, Ettie Lois.
Flack, Marjorie, **I** 4521, 10102
Flack, Roberta, **I** 14729, **III** 455
Flager, Alicia Mayre, **I** 2114, 13229
Flagg, Ella. *See* Young, Ella (Flagg).
Flagg, Marion, **I** 3368, 14207
Flanagan, Hallie Mae Ferguson (Davis); Hallie Davis, **I** 641, 3238, 9915, 20015
Flanner, Janet, **I** 9990, 11540, 15057, **III** 797
Flebbe, Beulah Marie Dix, **I** 9549, 19836
Fleecy Cloud Floating into Place. *See* Dietz, Angel de Cora.
Fleeson, Doris, **I** 7190, 11806
Fleeta. *See* Hamilton, Kate Waterman.
Fleming, Elizabeth, **I** 7416
Fleming, George. *See* Fletcher, Julia Constance.
Fleming, M. *See* Fleming, Williamina Patron Stevens.
Fleming, May Agnes (Early); Cousin May Carleton, **I** 8373
Fleming, Peggy Gale, **I** 18906
Fleming, Rhonda, **I** 20520
Fleming, Williamina Patron Stevens "Mina"; M. Fleming, **I** 15938
Flemion, Florence, **I** 13230
Flesch, Ella, **I** 14515, **III** 900
Flesche, Susan la. *See* Picotte, Susan la Flesche.
Fleshman, Mina Pepper, **I** 541, **II** 630, **III** 1024, **IV** 1872
Fletcher, Alice Cunningham, **I** 10, 1182, 8292, 13520
Fletcher, Bridget, **I** 13437, 16988
Fletcher, Inglis Clark, **I** 9850
Fletcher, Jennie, **I** 18745
Fletcher, Julia Constance; George Fleming, **I** 8719, 19639
Fletcher, Lisa Anne, **I** 3977, 8524, **IV** 1276
Fletcher, Martha Mary, **I** 15360
Flewellyn, Juliette (Colliton), **I** 8720, **IV** 1508
Flexner, Anne Crawford, **I** 2998, 9473, 19813, **IV** 1322

Flexner, Hortense, **I** 9776
Flexner, Jennie Maas, **I** 6148, 9712, **II** 418
Flikke, Julia Otteson, **I** 5645, 12951
Flint, Annie Johnson, **I** 9266
Flint, Eva Kay, **I** 10341, 20242, **III** 1216
Flint, Martha Bockee, **I** 11224, **IV** 1629
Flintham, Lydia Stirling, **I** 7435, 14784
Flood, Frances M., **I** 12964
Florence, Malvina Pray, **I** 1904, 19566
Florepha. *See* Hall, Sarah (Ewing).
Flower, Elizabeth, **I** 6383
Flower, Lucy Louisa (Coues), **I** 2421, 6705, 12512, 15438, 18234, **II** 742
Floyd, Hannah Jones, **I** 4830
Floyd, Joanna Strong, **I** 4903
Floyd, Theodora A., **I** 13168
Flugge-Lotz, Irmgard, **I** 16006
Flying Grandma. *See* Rufus, Maud Squire.
Flynn, Catherine, **I** 11680
Flynn, Elizabeth Gurley, **I** 6479, 7049
Fobes, Philena, **I** 2244
Foch, Nina, **I** 20533, **III** 620
Foerster, Alma, **I** 1609, 12965
Fogarty, Anne, **I** 1014, 3836
Fogg, Isabella, **I** 5257, 12326, 15361
Foldes, Peggy, **I** 11681
Foley, Edna, **I** 13085
Foley, Margaret E., **I** 3901
Foley, Martha, **I** 10124, 11604
Folger, Emily Clara Jordan, **I** 6016, 8973
Folger, Susan, **I** 17844
Follansbee, Elizabeth A., **I** 12635
Follen, Eliza Lee (Cabot), **I** 1080, 7472
Follet, Mary Parker, **I** 464, 6855, 9307, 12813, 15001, 16771
Follette, Fola (Middletown) la. *See* la Follette, Fola (Middletown).
Folsom, Abby, **I** 1083
Folsom, Mariana Thompson, **I** 17365
Foltz, Clara Shortridge; The Portia of the Pacific, **I** 353, 6764, 11038, 14931, 20999, **IV** 84
Fonaroff, Vera, **I** 13648, **III** 1178
Fonda, Jane, **I** 7388, 15199, 20652
Fonda, Mary Alice Ives; Octavia Hensel, **I** 2422, 6560, 8257, 13518
Fontaine, Joan, **I** 20439
Fontanne, Lynn; Mrs. Alfred Lunt, **I** 20118, **III** 737
Fontenelle, Miss; Mrs. John Brown Williamson, **I** 19473

Foote, Elizabeth Louisa, **I** 6057, **II** 591
Foote, Mary Anna (Hallock), **I** 3999, 8618
Foote, Roxana, **I** 17114
Forbes, Arethusa L., **I** 15362
Forbes, Esther; Esther Forbes Hoskins, **I** 6182, 9966, **II** 342, **IV** 1117
Forbes, Grace Springer, **I** 3369, 13231
Forbes, Harriette (Merrifield), **I** 5998, 8901, **IV** 1033
Forbes, Jessica L., **I** 778, 11682
Force, Juliana Rieser, **I** 6120
Forche, Caroline, **I** 10789, **IV** 1171
Ford, Antonia, **I** 5258, 16501
Ford, Eileen (Otte), **I** 1031, 3837
Ford, Eleanor Clay, **I** 15793
Ford, Emily Ellsworth (Fowler), **I** 7919, **IV** 1397
Ford, Florrie, **I** 13649
Ford, Frances M., **I** 8854
Ford, Geraldine Bledsoe, **I** 7269, 13733
Ford, Gertrude H., **I** 779
Ford, Harriet (Morgan), **I** 9178, 19716
Ford, Irene de Pendall, **I** 4576
Ford, Julia Ellsworth, **I** 9008, 12717, 15589, 19681
Ford, Kathryn, **I** 780, 1785
Ford, Lauren, **I** 4474
Ford, Mary, **I** 1037, 14629
Ford, Miriam Chase, **I** 11218, 13733
Ford, Mrs. Glenn. *See* Powell, Eleanor.
Ford, Sally Rochester, **I** 7967, **IV** 1202
Forest, Gale. *See* Reinertson, Emma May Alexander.
Forestier, Aubertine. *See* Moore, Annie Aubertine (Woodward).
Forge, Margaret Getchell la. *See* la Forge, Margaret Getchell.
Forman, Julie (Rose) Ripley, **I** 3449, **II** 261, **IV** 356
Forman, R. R., Mrs., **I** 13607
Fornes, Maria Irene, **I** 1052, 10742, 20596, **III** 608, **IV** 1853
Forney, Lucy. *See* Bittinger, Lucy (Forney).
Forney, Tillie May, **I** 9111, 11171
Fornia-Labey, Rita, **I** 13884
Forrest, Catherine Norton Sinclair, **I** 19531
Forrester, Fanny. *See* Judson, Emily (Chubbuck).
Forsee, Aylesa, **I** 10674
Forster, Minnie Jane, **I** 9520
Forsyth, Josephine, **I** 14730
Fort, Cornelia, **I** 18051
Fort, Eleanor H.; Hank, **I** 10612, 14538

Forten, Charlotte L. *See*
Grimke, Charlotte L. Forten.
Forten, Harriet, I 1090, III 66,
IV 2021
Forten, Margaretta, I 1091, III
67, IV 2022
Forten, Sarah Louisa, I 1092,
III 68, IV 2023
Fortune, Hilda O., I 3585, III
302
Fortune, Jennie, I 7107
Fosburgh, Mary Cushing, I
4674, 15854
Foss, Louise Woodworth, I
14883
Foster, Abigail (Kelley)
"Abby", I 1111, 6666,
14797, 19150, 20749, II 1008
Foster, Alicia. *See* Foster,
Jodie.
Foster, Annette Hotchkiss
Dimsdale, I 16553
Foster, Bertha M., I 3524,
14378
Foster, Edna Abigail, I 10082,
11581
Foster, Fay, I 13998
Foster, Hannah (Webster), I
5760, 7442, IV 858
Foster, Harriet, I 14379
Foster, Jodie; Alicia Foster, I
12110, 20710
Foster, John W., Mrs., I 1326
Foster, Judith Ellen (Horton), I
6718, 14884, 19276, 20917,
IV 677
Foster, Julia (de Marguerittes).
See Rea, Julia (de
Marguerittes) (Foster).
Foster, Lillian Benson, I 20128
Foster, Mabel G., I 7544,
14789, IV 883
Foster, Susie E. (Holland), I
8594, 15510, IV 1987
Foster, Theodosia Maria (Toll);
Faye Huntington, I 2436,
8293, IV 2297
Fowle, Elida Barker Rumsey, I
5570, 5934, 12569, 15485
Fowler, Jessie Allen, I 10791,
13434
Fowler, Lydia Folger, I 7836,
12230, 14821, 15913, 18190
Fowler, Marie Louise, I 10229
Fowler-Billings, Katharine, I
10342, 16002, 16716
Fox, Ana Leah, I 17193, II
1050
Fox, Carol, I 1044, 14647, IV
635
Fox, Catherine "Kate", I
17349, II 1057
Fox, Delia, I 13817
Fox, Della May, I 13792,
19776
Fox, Elizabeth Gordon, I 1672,
13014, 18553
Fox, Genevieve May, I 9851
Fox, Gertrude Elizabeth
Wilbur, I 16883
Fox, Hannah, I 16355

Fox, Margaret, I 17305, II
1054
Fox, Margaret Fell, I 16946
Fox, Mary Hewins, I 8467,
19613
Fox, Mary Jane, I 5259, 12327
Foxton, E. *See* Palfrey, Sarah
H. Hammond Hamilton.
Foxworthy, Alice S., I 2632,
IV 2237
Frackleton, Susan Stuart
(Goodrich), I 347, 4005,
8657
Frame, Alice Seymour Browne,
I 3071, 17634, II 328
Frame, Esther Gordon, I
17366, II 1029
France, Rachel Ann Noah, I
19550
Francis, Arlene, I 11880, 20332
Francis, Connie, I 14666
Francis, Kay; Katherine Gibbs,
I 20159
Francis, Louise E., I 469,
11233, IV 133
Francis, Yvette Fae, I 13392,
III 348
Frank, Lela Hall, I 18969
Frank, Mary Hughes, I 10667,
13384, III 960
Frank, Rachel "Ray", I 9267,
II 384, IV 123
Frankau, Aline. *See* Bernstein,
Aline Frankau.
Frankelstein, Beatrice, I 13417,
18112
Franken, Rose, I 10150, 20145
Frankenthaler, Helen, I 4739
Frankfurt, Elsie, I 1013, 3834
Franklin, Ann Smith, I 111
Franklin, Aretha, I 14740, III
470
Franklin, Blanche Ortha, I
10083, 14133
Franklin, Christine Ladd;
Christine Ladd-Franklin, I
8619, 12605, 15928
Franklin, Eleanor I., I 3525,
13354, III 288
Franklin, Elizabeth, I 140
Franklin, Elizabeth Jennings, I
3195, II 705, IV 1740, 2303
Franklin, Gertrude; Virginia H.
Beatty, I 2775, 13650
Franklin, Irene, I 19837
Franklin, Jane, I 11683
Franklin, Lucy Jenkins, I 3056,
II 601, IV 1101
Franklin, Pearl, I 1703, 7039,
9852, 17690, 19983, II 430
Franks, Abigail Levy, I 16124
Franks, Rebecca, I 4904, 16201
Frantz, Virginia Kneeland, I
687, 3300, 13169, 16914, II
872, IV 1783
Fraser, Alexa Stirling, I 18771
Fraser, Dawn, I 18877
Fraser, Gretchen Kunigh, I
18827
Fraser, Laura Gardin, I 4432
Fraser, Mary Crawford, I 8781
Fraser, Matilda, I 2159

Fray, Ellen Sulley, I 6401,
20857, IV 1896
Frazier, Martha M., I 2318,
19175, IV 2368
Frazier, Maude, I 3121, 6971
Frazier, Susan Elizabeth, I
1469, 2853, 6834, III 148
Frederick, Christine McGaffey,
I 578, 2097, 9736
Frederick, Pauline, I 19928
Frederika. *See* Pell, Isabel
Townsend.
Freedman, Nancy Mars (Lois),
I 10675
Freeman, Bettina, I 14040
Freeman, Carrie Stone, I
13812, IV 137
Freeman, Elizabeth, I 5731,
13355, III 289
Freeman, Elizabeth; Mum Bett,
I 6648, 12141, III 57
Freeman, Florence, I 3934
Freeman, Frankie Muse, I
1236, 7157, III 240
Freeman, Horatia Augusta
Latilla, I 3898
Freeman, Julia S. (Wheelock),
I 5519, 15416
Freeman, Lucy Greenbaum, I
11948
Freeman, Margaret, I 4493
Freeman, Mary Eleanor
Wilkins, I 8799
Freeman, Mattie A., I 1183,
10952, 14871, 20907, IV 521
Freer, Eleonor Everest, I
13708, II 770
Fremont, Jessie Ann (Benton),
I 7870, IV 61
Fremstad, Olivia [Anna]
"Olive", I 13761, II 594, III
1273
French, Alice; Octave Thanet,
I 8721, IV 42, 682
French, Anna Densmore, I
14885
French, Anne Warner. *See*
Warner, Anne Richmond.
French, Lillie Hamilton, I
8855, IV 1529
French, Lucy Virginia (Smith),
I 2313, 7897, 10869, IV
2225
Frenkel-Brunswick, Else, I
13341
Freshel, Maud Hammer, I
16865, II 246
Freudenthal, Elsbeth Estelle, I
924, 10343, 18029
Frick, Helen Clay, I 4577
Frick, Rebecca E., I 5260,
12328
Friedan, Betty, I 1878, 10688,
21337
Friedman, Elizabeth Smith, I
5689, 15976
Friend, Florence. *See*
Mannering, Mary.
Friendly, Aunt. *See* Baker,
Sarah Schoonmaker (Tuthill).
Fries, Constance, I 3370, 13232

Frietchie, Barbara, I 5061,
16340, III 817, IV 827
Friganza, Tixie; Brigid
O'Callaghan, I 19790
Frijsh, Povla, I 13793, III 614
Frings, Ketti Hartley, I 10629,
20420
Frisby, Almah J., I 12687, IV
2390
Frishmuth, Harriet Whitney, I
4352
Frissell, Seraph, I 12537, 19277
Frissell, Toni, I 15900
Fritcher, Elizabeth L., I 5261,
12329
Fritz, Deane, I 18970
Froman, Jane, I 14564
Fromen, Agnes Valborg Erica,
I 4185, III 1274
Fromenson, Ruth Bernard, I
1610, II 412
Fromm-Reichman, Frieda, I
3222, 13067, II 434, III 857,
IV 417
Frooks, Dorothy, I 7158
Frost, Elizabeth Hollister, I
9800
Frost, Frances May, I 10412
Frost, Sarah Frances. *See*
Marlowe, Julia.
Frothingham, Ellen, I 6556,
8195, IV 965
Frothingham, Eugenia Brooks,
I 9474, IV 1092
Frueauff, Antoinette. *See* Perry,
Antoinette (Frueauff).
Fry, Elizabeth Turner, I 6738,
15486, 16832, 19300, 20937,
IV 2259
Fry, Emma V. Sheridan, I
9206, 19721
Fry, Laura Ann, I 4069, IV
1933
Fryatt, Frances Elizabeth, I
364, 4019, 8722, IV 1509
Fryberger, Agnes Moore, I
2921, 9308, 13762, 15002
Frymire, Josephine, I 17641
Fuchs, Henriette J., I 781
Fuertes, Dolores Adios. *See*
Menken, Adah Isaacs.
Fulbright, Roberta Waugh, I
503, 6898, 9475, 11280, IV
49
Fuld, Carrie Bamberger Frank,
I 2854, 15624, IV 1319
Fuldheim, Dorothy, I 11567,
15061
Fullard-Leo, Ellen; Ma Leo, I
18971
Fuller, Anna, I 8818, IV 1020
Fuller, Bridget Lee, I 16085, II
940
Fuller, Clara Cornelia, I 2633
Fuller, Electa, I 16827
Fuller, Frances. *See* Barrit,
Frances (Fuller).
Fuller, Frances Auretta. *See*
Victor, Frances Auretta
(Fuller) (Barrett).
Fuller, Iola, I 10444
Fuller, Laura, I 16828

Gellhaus, Olga E., **I** 11685
Gellhorn, Edna Fischel, **I** 1599, 6942, 21222
Gellhorn, Martha, **I** 10493
Genauer, Emily, **I** 4578, 11686
Genet, Cornelia, **I** 16260
Genet, Marianne, **I** 13794
Genth, Lillian Matilde, **I** 4306
Gentle, Alice, **I** 14023
Gentry, Helen, **I** 694
Gentry, Viola, **I** 17968
George, Anna E., **I** 14064
George, E. E., Mrs., **I** 5265, 12331, 15363
George, Gladys; Gladys Clare, **I** 20275
George, Grace; Mrs. William A. Brady, **I** 9478, 19815
George, H. Maria. *See* Colby, H. Maria George.
George, Lucy Squirrel, **I** 4529, **III** 1058
George, Lydia A., **I** 1321, 5549, 12527, 15456
George, Zelma Watson, **I** 7219, 14294, 18643, **III** 262
Georgia Lydia, Mother. *See* Stevens, Georgia Lydia.
Georgian, Carolyn Ann "Papsie", **I** 18975
Geraghty, Agnes, **I** 18797
Gerard, Theodora "Teddie"; Teresa Cabre, **I** 14104, 20063
Gerberding, Elizabeth, **I** 18331
Gere, Florence Parr, **I** 14380
Gerlette, Anne, **I** 996, 3593, 20396, **III** 588
Gerould, Katharine Elizabeth Fullerton, **I** 9619
Gerrish-Jones, Abbie, **I** 9179, 11194, 13697
Gerry, Ann Thompson, **I** 5053, 16334, **III** 913
Gerson, Virginia, **I** 4143, 9207
Gerston, Berta, **I** 20119
Gertrude St. George Congregation de Notre Dame, Sister. *See* McGuigan, Gertrude St. George Congregation de Notre Dame.
Gescheidt, Adelaide, **I** 14381
Gest, Elizabeth, **I** 14382
Gestefield, Ursula Newell, **I** 17427
Gestring, Marjorie, **I** 18832
Getchell, Donnie Campbell, **I** 3373
Gholson, Anderson. *See* Glasgow, Ellen.
Giannini, Dusolina, **I** 14278
Gibbes, Sarah Reeve, **I** 4995, 16253
Gibbons, Abigail Hopper "Abby", **I** 1095, 5073, 10829, 12170, 15248, 16734, 18159, 20734, **II** 999
Gibbons, Helen Davenport Brown, **I** 5660, 9737, 15759, 18549
Gibbons, Irene, **I** 991, 3830, 20383, **IV** 242

Gibbons, Lucy. *See* Morse, Lucy (Gibbons).
Gibbons, Marie Raymond, **I** 1352
Gibbons, Phoebe (Earle), **I** 7819, **IV** 2037
Gibbs, Eleanor Churchill, **I** 2467, **IV** 16
Gibbs, Florence R., **I** 7270
Gibbs, Katherine. *See* Francis, Kay.
Gibbs, Willa, **I** 10647
Gibson, Althea; Althea Gibson Darben, **I** 18847, **III** 395
Gibson, Anna L., **I** 10529, 13356
Gibson, E. O., Mrs., **I** 5266, 12332
Gibson, Eva Katherine (Clapp), **I** 8942, **IV** 565
Gibson, Helen, **I** 18976
Gideon, Miriam, **I** 14321
Gierse, Ediyth le. *See* de Treville, Yvonne.
Giese, Lulu Gable, **I** 10230
Giesler, Mathilde Franziska. *See* Anneke, Mathilde Franziska Giesler.
Giffin, Etta Josselyn, **I** 6042, 18381
Giffin, Mrs. Zachary Wayne. *See* Warren, Elinor Remick.
Gifford, Augusta (Hale), **I** 5936, 8468, **IV** 803
Gifford, Fannie Stearns Davis, **I** 9758
Gifford, Myrnie Ada, **I** 7076, 13125, 16910, 18590, **IV** 190
Gifford, Susan A., **I** 18199
Gilbert, Anne Jane Hartley, **I** 1899, 7820, 19544
Gilbert, G. H. "Grandma", Mrs., **I** 19546
Gilbert, Helen. *See* MacInnes, Helen Clark.
Gilbert, Katharine Everett, **I** 3178, 6342
Gilbert, Linda, **I** 15514, 16761
Gilbert, Maria Dolorez Eliza Rosanna. *See* Montez, Maria Dolorez Eliza Rosanna Gilbert Porris y.
Gilbert, Mercedes, **I** 11817, 20243, **III** 260
Gilbert, Mrs., **I** 19513
Gilbert, Ruby I., **I** 375, 19387
Gilbreth, Lillian Evelyn (Moller), **I** 531, 2092, 6456, 12939, 15959
Gilchrist, Anne, **I** 7968
Gilchrist, Beth Bradford; Elizabeth Drake; John Prescott Earl, **I** 10799, **II** 358, **IV** 2305
Gilchrist, Fredrika (Beardsley), **I** 8595, **IV** 1491
Gilchrist, Rosetta Luce, **I** 9050, 12728, 21089, **IV** 1938
Gildemeister, Theda, **I** 6332
Gilder, Jeanett Leonard, **I** 8681, 11039, **IV** 1499

Gildersleeve, Virginia Crocheron, **I** 1590, 3057, 6932, 15170, **IV** 1688
Giles, Anne H., **I** 6326, **II** 658
Giles, Ella Augusta, **I** 8782, **IV** 2386
Giles, Janice Holt, **I** 10511
Giles, Julia Robbins; Julia Hoyt, **I** 20129
Gill, Elizabeth Mary, **I** 297
Gill, Emily Frances Lombard Abbey, **I** 2694, 15570
Gill, Jocelyn R., **I** 16035, 18138
Gill, Laura Drake, **I** 2778
Gill, Rosalie Lorraine, **I** 4165
Gillespie, Christie. *See* MacDonald, Christie.
Gillespie, Eliza Maria; Mother Mary of St. Angela, **I** 2303, 5134, 12238, 17234, **II** 103
Gillespie, Elizabeth (Duane), **I** 7821, **IV** 2038
Gillespie, Mabel [Edna], **I** 6434, 18404, 21137
Gillespie, Marian, **I** 9881, 10231, 11439, 11687, 14042, 15891, 16710, 19997
Gillett, Emma Millinda, **I** 2634, 6786, 21026
Gillett, Sisters, **I** 265, 16820
Gillette, Lucia Fidelia (Woolley); Lyra; Carrie Russell, **I** 7942, 17254, **II** 1084
Gillette, Martha Taylor, **I** 15989
Gilliam, Florence, **I** 643, 11468, 20016, **III** 792
Gillies, Betty Huyler, **I** 17926
Gillies, Pat, **I** 18086
Gillis, Ann; Ann Slocum, **I** 1015, 11970
Gillis, Fay, **I** 17927
Gillis, Rhona Wurtele, **I** 18977
Gilman, Caroline Howard. *See* Jervey, Caroline Howard (Gilman) Glover.
Gilman, Caroline (Howard), **I** 2046, 7502, 10824, **IV** 2196
Gilman, Charlotte Anna (Perkins) (Stetson), **I** 6426, 9051, 14979, 21090, **IV** 104
Gilman, Elizabeth, **I** 6848, 18405
Gilman, Mabelle, **I** 13651, 19691
Gilman, Mary C., **I** 1520
Gilman, Mary L., **I** 15504
Gilman, Mary Rebecca Foster, **I** 6019, 9009, 17527
Gilman, Mildred, **I** 10232, 11688
Gilman, Stella (Scott), **I** 2524, 8525
Gilman, Tabitha. *See* Tenney, Tabitha (Gilman).
Gilmer, Elizabeth Meriwether; Dorothy Dix, **I** 3720, 11172, 21096
Gilmer, Louisa Fredericka, **I** 5267, 5853, 8021

Gilmer, Loulie, **I** 5268, 5854, 8022
Gilmore, Elizabeth McCabe, **I** 505, 9479, 11281
Gilmore, Florence MacGruder, **I** 9691, 15743
Gilmore, George Davidson, Mrs., **I** 1786, **IV** 213
Gilmore, Gladys Chase, **I** 783, 3374
Gilmore, Marion Sprague, **I** 2115, 13234
Gilmour, **I** 18113
Gilson, Mary Barnett, **I** 525
Gimbel, Sophie, **I** 925, 3810
Gindhart, Mary Wilhelmina (Simon), **I** 13885, 15722, **II** 603, **IV** 2126
Giollini, Margherita. *See* McAlpin, Margaret Johnston.
Giovanni, Nikki; Yolande Cornelia Giovanni, Jr., **I** 10757, **III** 435
Giovanni, Yolande Cornelia Jr. *See* Giovanni, Nikki.
Gipson, Elsie, **I** 3375, 17969
Girl with Blonde Hair, The. *See* Pell, Isabel Townsend.
Gish, Dorothy, **I** 20146
Gish, Lillian, **I** 20120
Gist, Malvina Black, **I** 5571, 5937, 8469
Given, Thelma, **I** 14163
Glade, Coe, **I** 14322
Gladwin, Mary E., **I** 5684, 13068
Glantzberg, Pinckney L., **I** 7050
Glaser, Lulu, **I** 13841, 19816
Glasgow, Ellen; Anderson Gholson, **I** 9446, **IV** 2340
Glaspell, Susan Keating; Mrs. George Cram Cook, **I** 9551, 19838, 21214
Glass, Meta, **I** 1611, 3103, 5647, 15729, **II** 822, **IV** 2342
Glass, Mrs., **I** 16266
Gleaner, The. *See* Murray, Judith Sargent Stevens.
Gleason, Kate, **I** 449, 15628
Gleason, Lucille Webster, **I** 19984, **IV** 175
Gleason, Rachel Brooks, **I** 1139, 2278, 3707, 7793, 12218, 15294, 20791
Glen, Katherine, **I** 14383
Glendenning, Mrs., **I** 16164
Glenn, Carroll, **I** 14610
Glenn, Mabelle, **I** 3526, 10530, 14384
Glenn, Mary Wilcox Brown, **I** 18421
Glennon, Nan, **I** 16029, 18114
Glentworth, Marguerite Linton, **I** 9692, **IV** 1325
Glenwood, Ida. *See* Gorton, Cynthia M. R.
Gloor, Olga, **I** 18978
Gloria Ann, Sister. *See* Davis, Gloria Ann.
Glover, Anna, **I** 5922, 8374

Glover, Caroline Howard (Gilman). *See* Jervey, Caroline Howard (Gilman) Glover.

Glover, Elizabeth. *See* Bennett, Mary E.

Glover, Elizabeth, I 84

Glover, Mildred S., I 1787

Gluck, Anna; Reba Fiersohn, I 13979, II 837, III 1172

Gluck, Louise, I 10783

Glueck, Eleanor (Touroff), I 3317, 7128, 18617, IV 1122, 1791

Glyndon, Howard. *See* Searing, Laura Catherine (Redden).

Glynes, Ella Maria (Dietz); Ella Maria (Dietz) Glynes-Clymer, I 1355, 8621, 19621

Glynes-Clymer, Ella Maria. *See* Glynes, Ella Maria.

Glynn, Elizabeth E., I 16624

Gobbi, Clothilde Operti, I 13613, III 699

Gober, Belle Biard, I 3527, 14385

Godby, Ann, I 16950, II 959

Goddard, Anna, I 175, 10811

Goddard, Hannah, I 4907, 16203

Goddard, Mary Katherine, I 171, 6652, 10810, II 65, IV 826

Goddard, Paulette, I 20364

Goddard, Sarah Updike, I 117, 10803

Godfrey, Daisy May, I 17913

Godfrey, Grace, I 2109, 3269, IV 2150

Godowski, Dagmar, I 20130, III 31

Godwin, Frances Bryant, I 4485

Godwin, Gail, I 10771

Godwin, Thelma. *See* Strabel, Thelma.

Goertz, Arthemise, I 10413

Goessmann, Helena Theresa, I 2779, 14980

Goetschius, Marjorie, I 10630, 14551

Goetz, Delia, I 10151

Goff, Anna Chandler, I 3528, 14386

Goff, Eugenia Wheeler, I 3978, 5943

Goff, Harriet Newell (Kneeland), I 7969-70, 16747, 19188, 20834, IV 1404

Goff, Hazel A., I 12966

Goff, Regina, I 3609, 7302, III 323

Going, Ellen Maud; E. M. Hardinge, I 7546, 12163, IV 1353

Golden, Sylvia, I 10233, 11689, 14210

Goldfield, Gladys. *See* Schmitt, Gladys Leonore.

Goldman, Emma, I 470, 4186, 6864, 11234, 12822, 15004, 21155, II 392, III 1180

Goldman, Hettie, I 47, 5651, 12984, II 416

Goldmark, Josephine, I 6933, 18502

Goldmark, Pauline Dorothea, I 419, 18356

Goldring, Winifred, I 15969

Goldsmith, C. Elizabeth, I 13235

Goldsmith, Deborah, I 3877

Goldsmith, Grace Arabell, I 2125, 3472, 13319, 18646, II 890, IV 784

Goldsmith, Margaret, I 10125, 11605

Goldsmith, Sophia, I 8622, III 489

Goldstein, Jennie; Jennie Groll, I 20131, II 454, IV 1786

Goldstein, Kate Arlene, I 3781

Goldstone, Aline Lewis, I 9309

Goldthwaite, Anne Wilson, I 4187

Goldthwaite, Lucy A., I 6206, 11606, 18612, IV 1787

Goldthwaite, Lucy Virginia Harmon, I 9052

Goldthwaite, Nellie E., I 12768

Golfert, Agnes Holman, I 19496

Gollner, Nana, I 1995

Golofsky, Hannah. *See* Klein, Anne.

Golson, Florence, I 14387

Gombell, Minna, I 20064

Gomper, Gertrude, I 6466, 6992, 21255

Gonzales Parsons, Lucia, I 1387, 6787, 21027, III 1002

Gooch, Frances (Chambers). *See* Inglehart, Frances (Chambers)(Gooch).

Good, Alice Campbell, I 1600, 6943, II 163, IV 1696

Goodale, Dora Read, I 9268, IV 1077

Goodale, Elaine. *See* Eastman, Elaine (Goodale).

Goodard, Sara. *See* Dahlgren, Madeleine Vinton [Sara] (Goodard).

Goodbar, Octavia Walton, I 4579, 11690

Goode, Edith J., I 6993, 16898, 21256-57

Goodell, Lavinia, I 6719

Goodenough, Florence Laura, I 13036

Goodin, Peggy, I 10700

Goodman, Lillian Rosedale, I 6616, 9853, 11429, 14024

Goodman, Theodosia. *See* Bara, Theda.

Goodner, Carol, I 20017

Goodnow, Minnie, I 3450, 10344, 13302

Goodrich, Abigail Whittlesey, I 10967

Goodrich, Ann. *See* Story, Ann.

Goodrich, Annie Warburton, I 2893, 5616, 12801, 21132

Goodrich, Florence Ada (Backus), I 2596, 13576

Goodrich, Frances, I 9916, 20018

Goodrich, Frances Louisa, I 390, 4063, 8903

Goodrich, Mary Ann; Mary Ann Wolcott, I 5059, 16337

Goodrich, Mary Hopkins, I 1277, IV 911

Goodrich, Mrs., I 16392

Goodrich, Nelle Chatburn, I 16677, 17624

Goodridge, Ellen, I 5269

Goodridge, Sarah, I 3860

Goodsell, Willystine, I 2948, 9361

Goodwin, Hannah Elizabeth (Bradbury), I 7943, IV 943

Goodwin, Lavinia Stella (Tyler), I 2383, 8143

Goodwin, Maud (Wilder), I 5999, 8904, IV 1540

Goodwin, Sarah, I 127

Goold, Abba Louisa. *See* Woolson, Abba Louisa (Goold).

Goose, Mrs., I 88

Gordon, Agnes (Wilson), I 18794, III 585

Gordon, Anna Adams, I 383, 8820, 19397

Gordon, Caroline; Caroline Tate, I 10085, III 799

Gordon, Cyrena Van, I 14211

Gordon, Dorothy Lerner, I 9882, 11440, 14043

Gordon, Edith Frances, I 784

Gordon, Elizabeth P., I 19431

Gordon, Georgia, I 13525, 17367, III 108

Gordon, Gertrude B. *See* Kelley, Gertrude.

Gordon, Jean Margaret, I 18389, 21122

Gordon, Jeanne, I 14118

Gordon, Julia Swayne, I 19778

Gordon, Julien. *See* Cruger, Julie Grinnell (Storrow).

Gordon, Kate, I 6337

Gordon, Kate M., I 1446, 21097

Gordon, Kitty, I 19855

Gordon, Laura de Force, I 6710-11, 10940, 14866, 20901, IV 73

Gordon, Mary, I 10788, 17830, II 232

Gordon, Mary Duff. *See* Duffel, Mary Gordon.

Gordon, Mazie P., I 683, 20105

Gordon, Nora Antonia, I 2894, 17573, III 154

Gordon, Odetta Holmes Felious Gordon; Odetta, I 14679, III 418

Gordon, Ruth, I 10103, 20121

Gordon, S. Anna, I 8117, 12476, 15917, 19210

Gordon, Sallie Chapman. *See* Law, Sally Chapman Gordon.

Gordon, Sallie Chapman, I 5075

Gordon-Cumming, Constance, I 8375

Gore, Ann Avery, I 16204

Gore, Hannah Park, I 16165

Gore, Margot, I 18052

Gorham, Roberta Armstrong, I 18979

Gorme, Eydie, I 12045, 14689

Gorton, Cynthia M. R.; Ida Glenwood; The Sweet Singer; The Blind Bard of Michigan, I 7921, 14837, IV 1128

Goss, Margaret, I 11469, 18746

Gossik, Sue, I 18980

Gottchalk, Laura Riding. *See* Riding, Laura.

Goudy, Bertha M., I 450

Gougar, Helen Mar Jackson, I 8497, 14907, 19312, 20946

Gould, Beulah H., I 219, 3702

Gould, Elizabeth Lincoln, I 9208

Gould, Elizabeth Porter, I 2568, 8658, 11028, 14926, 18290

Gould, Ellen M., I 15521, 20991, II 1110, IV 2187

Gould, Emily Bliss, I 15324

Gould, Hannah Flagg, I 7483, IV 2291

Gould, Helen Miller, I 15651

Gould, M. Woodbridge, I 2186, 6521

Gould, Paula, I 11691

Gousha, Mrs. Joseph R. *See* Powell, Dawn.

Govan, Christine Noble, I 10152, 11612

Gowan, M. Olivia, Sister, I 13057, 17692, II 188

Gower, Nancy, I 16205

Goya, Carola, I 1948

Goza, Anne, I 9421, IV 27

Grabau, Mary Antin, I 6606, 9645, II 413

Grable, Betty, I 20429, IV 245

Grace of Monaco, Princess. *See* Kelly, Grace Patricia.

Gradova, Gitta "Gidda", I 14304, II 470

Graff, Elfie R., I 13086

Graffenreid, Mary Clare de. *See* de Graffenreid, Mary Clare.

Graffenrief, Mary Clare de, I 15931

Graham, Aubry Lee, I 6224

Graham, Cecelia B., I 4452

Graham, Elinor Mish, I 10445

Graham, Florence Nightingale. *See* Arden, Elizabeth.

Graham, Helen Tredway, I 13087, 16906, IV 1220

Graham, Isabella Marshall, I 2166, 15211, III 1234, IV 1343

Graham, Katharine (Meyer), I 1009, 11959

Graham, Margaret, I 17016

Graham, Margaret (Collier), I 8723, IV 86

Graham, Martha, I 1934

Graham, Nellie Dean; Vosey, I 1521, 6872, 9362, 15661, IV 135

Graham, Sheila, I 11881, III 756

Graham, Shirley, I 6249, 10392, 14305, 20276, III 265

Graham, Virginia, I 11913

Grahame, Nellie. See Dunning, Annie Ketchum.

Granahan, Kathryn Elizabeth, I 7112

Granberry, Virginia, I 3947

Grand, Julia le. See le Grand, Julia.

Grandfield, Jennie McKee, I 18357

Grandma, I 5692, 16705

Grandstaff, Grace M., I 785

Grange, Ann le. See le Grange, Ann.

Grange, Magdalene Isadora la. See la Grange, Magdalene Isadora.

Granger, Euphrasia Smith, I 5626

Granger, Lottie E., I 2735, 19424

Granger, Nellie, I 17970

Grannis, Anna Jane, I 8905, IV 334

Grannis, Harriet Ellen. See Arey, Harriet Ellen (Grannis).

Granson, Milla, I 1169, 2347, III 91, IV 1188

Grant, Anita, I 11582, 18765, III 223

Grant, Anne, I 7441, III 1236

Grant, Blanche C., I 4453, 9917

Grant, Bridget, I 269, 16538, III 931

Grant, Frances R., I 6173, 11470

Grant, Gloria, I 18854, III 1094

Grant, Hannah Tracy, I 4772

Grant, Jane, I 659, 11541, 21298

Grant, Joy, I 18855, III 1095

Grant, Kathryn "Kathy", I 20620

Grant, Lee, I 12035, 20584

Grant, Ruth, I 18856, III 1096

Grant, Sueton, I 128

Grant, Zilpah Polly, I 2201

Granville-Barker, Helen Gates, I 10234

Graser, Hilda Regina, I 471, III 544, IV 595

Grass, Elizabeth, I 5270, 12333

Grasso, Ella Tambussi, I 7311, IV 360

Gratz, Rebecca, I 2183, 15229, II 363

Grau, Shirley Ann, I 10732, IV 787

Graudan, Joanna Freudberg, I 14779, II 511, III 1231

Graves, Adelia Cleopatra (Spencer); Aunt Alice, I 2286, 6543, 7822, IV 2223

Graves, Dixie Bibb, I 7161

Graves, Emma (Homan). See Thayer, Emma (Homan) (Graves).

Graves, Helen (Louise) Pierson, I 3598, 13372, II 627, IV 1967

Graves, Julia Aurelia. See Adams, Juliette Aurelia Graves.

Graves, Lulu Grace, I 2083, 12898

Graves, Marion Coates, I 3163

Graves, Mary H., I 8332, 14872, 17350, II 1094

Graves, Nancy Stevenson, I 4758, 20667

Gray, Adeline, I 18053

Gray, Caroline E., I 9854, 13058

Gray, Coleen, I 11988

Gray, Dolores, I 14680, 20597

Gray, Elizabeth Janet, I 3451, 6240, 10345

Gray, Etta, I 12967

Gray, Gilda, I 1944, 14177, III 1153

Gray, Hannah Holborn, I 3664, 6309, III 881, IV 636

Gray, Ida, I 12805, III 157

Gray, Jennie T., I 19418

Gray, Mary Augusta Fox, I 16432

Gray, Mary Tenney, I 10909, 15417, IV 698

Gray, Nina. See Clarke, Mary Hannah (Gray).

Gray, Phyllis, I 17971

Gray, Sophie de Butts, I 4097

Graydon, Mrs., I 4908

Gray-Lhevinne, Estelle, I 14105

Grayson, Bette, I 20505

Grayson, Betty Evans "Bullet", I 18981

Grayson, Francis W., I 17928

Grayson, Kathryn, I 14600, 20488

Greaney, Helen F., I 12704

Greathouse, Matilda. See Alexander, Matilda (Greathouse).

Greatorex, Eliza (Pratt), I 3889, III 918

Greatorex, Elizabeth Eleanor, I 4049

Greatorex, Kathleen Honora, I 4033

Greaves, Jessie Royer, I 2999, 18475, II 1155, IV 2119

Grebanier, Mrs. Bernard. See Winwar, Frances.

Greble, Susan Virginia, I 5271, 15364

Greeley, Mary Y. C., I 18254

Greeley-Smith, Nixola, I 11332

Green, Alice Kollock, I 4826

Green, Anna Catherine Hoof, I 141

Green, Anna Katherine; Mrs. Charles Rohlfs, I 8596

Green, Anne, I 10181

Green, Anne Catherine, I 153, 10807

Green, Blanche Tucker, I 17769

Green, Carolyn, I 18982

Green, Charlotte Hilton, I 9883, 13069

Green, Constance Winsor McLaughlin, I 6207

Green, Cordelia A., I 12467

Green, Edith Starrett, I 7271

Green, Eleanor, I 10565

Green, Elizabeth Shippen; Elizabeth Elliott, I 4242

Green, Ethel, I 13915, 19888

Green, Florence Topping, I 4376, III 721

Green, Frances Harriet (Whipple), I 1099, 7622, 12174

Green, Henrietta Howland (Robinson) "Hettie", I 278

Green, Julia (Boynton), I 9112, IV 1587

Green, Lucille H., I 12257

Green, Mary, I 2160

Green, Mary E., I 12586

Green, Mitzi, I 20489

Green, Zinobar. See Patterson, Minnie Ward.

Greene, Aella, I 8294, 10941, IV 975

Greene, Belle Colton, I 8526

Greene, Belle da Costa, I 6151, IV 1726

Greene, Catharine Littlefield, I 5025, 16284

Greene, Catherine, I 168

Greene, Eleanore D., I 10235, III 575

Greene, Frances Harriet (Whipple). See McDougal, Frances Harriet (Whipple) (Greene).

Greene, Frances Nimmo; Dixie, I 2780, 9053, IV 20

Greene, Gertrude Glass, I 4657, IV 1817

Greene, Isabella Catherine (Colton), I 8527, IV 1277

Greene, Louisa Morton, I 1134, 5118, 7775, 15288, 19161, 20783

Greene, Mabel, I 11471

Greene, Marie Louise, I 9269

Greene, Mary A., I 2712, 6804, IV 2189

Greene, Mary Hayden. See Pike, Mary Hayden (Greene).

Greene, Rosaline, I 11692

Greene, Ruhama, I 16313

Greene, Sarah Pratt (McLean), I 8906

Greene, Zula Bennington, I 11693

Greenewalt, Mary Elizabeth Hallock; Mary Greenwalt, I 13813, 15010, 15951, 19784

Greenfield, Edith Mary, I 51, 15769

Greenfield, Elizabeth Taylor; The Black Swan; Elizabeth Taylor-Greenfield, I 13456, III 79

Greenhow, Rose O'Neal, I 5102, 16449, II 98, IV 368

Greenleaf, Jean Brooks, I 20858

Greenough, Sara Dana (Loring), I 7944

Greenwald, Goldie, I 18752

Greenwalt, Mary. See Greenewalt, Mary Elizabeth Hallock.

Greenway, Isabella, I 7162

Greenwood, Charlotte, I 20083

Greenwood, Elizabeth W., I 19363

Greenwood, Gertrude B., I 4454

Greenwood, Grace. See Lippincott, Sarah Jane (Clarke).

Greenwood, Marion, I 4697

Greenwood, Mary Langdon, I 2181, 7459, 20720

Greer, Lurlyne, I 18983

Gregg, Elinor D., I 13088

Gregory, Angela, I 4649

Gregory, Cynthia, I 2040

Gregory, Elizabeth Goadby, I 279, 6554, 8162, 10914, 16749, 18222

Gregory, Emily Lovira, I 12559

Gregory, Ida Leona Sturdavent, I 6817, 18358

Gregory, June Taylor, I 18984

Gregory, Mary Rogers, I 3992

Gregson, Kathi, I 18985

Grenfell, Helen Loring, I 2922, 6856, 16772

Grenville, Lillian Goertner, I 13795, III 547

Gretter, Lystra E., I 13089

Grever, Maria, I 14127, III 1006

Grew, Agnes Mengel, I 786, 20189

Grew, Mary, I 1116, 14801, 17167, 20758, II 1076

Grey, Jane, I 19985

Grey, Katherine, I 19802

Gridley, Ann Eliza, I 12334

Grier, Maria C., I 5272, 15365

Griffin, Clementina de Forest, I 3239, 17929, IV 182

Griffin, Josephine R., I 5273, 15366, 16502

Griffin, Marion Lucy Mahony, I 4243

Griffin, Mrs. Francis Dennis. See Dunne, Irene.

Griffin, William Preston, Mrs., I 5274

Griffing, Josephine Sophia White, I 1119, 18175, 20762

Griffith, Corinne, I 9918, 20019

Griffith, Emily, I 3104

Griffith, Eva Kinney, I 11081, 19392

Griffith, Harriet Pomroy (Roelofson), I 8470

Griffith, Mary Lillian, I 8856, 15560, 17498, II 572, IV 2094

Griffith, Nora Christina Cobban, I 37

Griffith, Rosa Vertner. *See* Jeffrey, Rosa Vertner (Griffith) (Johnson).

Griffiths, Martha, I 7280

Griggs, Mary Amerman, I 3179, 13037, II 949

Grimes, Frances, I 4188

Grimke, Angelina Emily; Angelina Emily Grimke Weld, I 1100, 14792, 20738, II 1004

Grimke, Charlotte L. Forten, I 2423, 8259, III 105

Grimke, Elizabeth. *See* Ross, Betsy Griscom.

Grimke, Sarah Moore, I 1084, 6662, 7494, 14787, 18155, 20723, II 995

Grinnell, Katherine van Allen; Adasha, I 17351

Grippon, Eva, I 14323, III 810

Grisham, Sadie Park, I 2755, 6811, IV 712

Grissom, Irene Welch, I 9919

Grist, Beri, I 14731, III 456

Griswold, Frances Irene (Burge); F. Burge Smith, I 7922, 17250, IV 1398

Griswold, Harriet (Tyng) "Hattie", I 8376, II 1097

Griswold, Henrietta Dippmann, I 14388

Griswold, Mariana Alley. *See* van Rensselaer, Marianna Alley (Griswold).

Griswold, Mary H., I 17076

Griswold, Ursula Wolcott, I 4909

Groenevelt, Sara; Stanley M. Bartlett, I 8023, 13486

Groll, Jennie. *See* Goldstein, Jennie.

Grooms, Jessie Macy Roberts, I 3254, 4475, IV 1963

Grose, Helen Mason, I 4353

Gross, Elizabeth West, I 16455

Gross, M. Louise, I 1673, 7005, 19452

Gross, Miriam Zeller, I 3376, 11694

Grosse, Juliet Mary White, I 4377

Grossinger, Jennie, I 660, 15798, II 442, III 30, IV 1763

Grouitch, Slavko, Madame, I 15662

Grout, Hannah Davis, I 17115

Grove, Mary, I 12164, 14790

Groves, Gladys Hoagland, I 3278, 3756, 13148, 21307

Groves, May Showler, I 9855

Grubb, Sophronia Farrington Naylor, I 1177, 18223, 19230

Gruenberg, Sidonie Matsner, I 1643, 3122, 9693, 12985, 15035, III 26

Grummond, Frances, I 16503

Gscheidle, Gertrude E., I 6254

Gubert, Louise, I 13495, 17295, II 114

Gudzin, Margaret S., I 18139

Guerbel, Countess. *See* Ward, Genevieve.

Guerber, Helen Adeline, I 2214, 5778, 7547, IV 1354

Guerin, Anne-Theresa; Mother Theodore, I 2207, 17073, III 771, IV 640

Guernsey, Lucy Ellen, I 7923

Guerrier, Edith, I 6077

Guest, Barbara, I 1018, 10676, 20476, IV 1845

Guggenheim, Alice. *See* Patterson, Alicia.

Guggenheim, Dorothy Jean. *See* Howard, Lisa.

Guggenheim, Florence Shloss, I 6827, 13698, 15618, II 382, IV 1598

Guggenheim, Irene Rothschild, I 15652, 18413, II 389, IV 1635

Guggenheim, Leonie Bernheim, I 12802, 13734, 15636, II 385, IV 1623

Guggenheim, Marguerite "Peggy", I 4534, 6211, 10153, 14164, 15809, II 457, IV 1792

Guggenheim, Minnie, I 569, 13961, 15751, II 419, IV 1720

Guggenheim, Olga Hersh, I 4328, 15723, II 406, IV 1697

Guild, Caroline Snowden (Whitmarsh), I 7945, 17255, IV 944

Guild, Emma. *See* Cadwalader-Guild, Emma Marie.

Guilford, Nanette, I 14324

Guin, Ursula K. le. *See* le Guin, Ursula K.

Guinan, Mary Louise Cecelia "Texas", I 19938

Guiney, Louise Imogen; The Sunny Young Greek, I 9113, IV 1055

Guinn, Nora, I 7322, III 909, IV 36

Guion, Connie Myers, I 12994

Guion, Molly, I 4702, II 907

Guirado, Luz (Sanchez), I 15533, 17467, II 130, III 1001, IV 87

Gulesian, Grace Warner, I 3152, 13980

Gulett, Lucy E., I 13090

Gulick, Alice Winfield Gordon, I 17439, 19350

Gulliver, Julia Henrietta, I 2695, 6324

Gulliver, Lucile, I 3133, 18543

Gumm, Frances Ethel. *See* Garland, Judy.

Gummere, Amelia Mott, I 9010, IV 2101

Gunderson, Barbara Bates, I 7296

Gunling, Beulah, I 18986

Gunter, Laurie Martin, I 3635, 13404, III 366

Gunter, Nancy Richey, I 18892

Gunterman, Bertha Lisette, I 6142, 11333

Gurney, Eliza Paul Kirkbride, I 17103, II 1003

Gurney, Marion Francis; Marianne of Jesus, I 17583, II 150

Gustafson, Axel Carl Johan. *See* Gustafson, Zadel Barnes (Buddington).

Gustafson, Zadel Barnes (Buddington); Axel Carl Johan Gustafson, I 8432, IV 1470

Gustin, Ellen G., I 17368

Gutelius, Jean Harrower, I 338, 3993, III 1245

Guthrie, Janet, I 18130, 18881

Guzman, Jessie P., I 3611, III 329

Gwinnett, Button, Mrs., I 4840

Gye, Marie Emma. *See* Albani, Maria Louisa Cecilie Emma.

H. D. *See* Doolittle, Hilda.

H. E. P. *See* Arnold, Harriet Pritchard.

H. H. *See* Jackson, Helen Maria (Fiske) (Hunt).

Haake, Gail Martin, I 3153, 13981

Haas, Alice Preble Tucker de. *See* de Haas, Alice Preble Tucker.

Hachard, Marie-Madeliene, Sister, I 4774, 16971, II 62

Hackett, Katherine, I 19504

Hackley, Emma Azalia Smith, I 13750, III 158

Hadakin, Helen, I 11472

Haddock, Emma, I 6720

Hader, Berta Hoerner, I 4455

Hadley, Piety Lucretia, I 5275, 15367

Haensler, Arminta Victoria Scott, I 12570, IV 2072

Hafkesbrink, Hanna, I 6370

Hagan, Helen Eugenia, I 3270, 14119, III 218

Hagar, Emily Stokes, I 14389

Hagar, Sarah J., I 5096, 12191

Hager, Alice Mayre, I 2116, 13236

Hager, Alice Rogers, I 10055, 17945

Hager, Carol, I 3377, 17972

Hager, Lucie Carolyn (Gilson), I 5980, 8821, IV 1021

Hager, Mina, I 14390

Hagidorn, Mary, I 4910

Hagood, Margaret Lloyd Jarman, I 16013, 18659

Hague, Parthenia Antoinette (Vardaman), I 5539, 5910, 8295, IV 429

Hagy, Ruth Geri, I 11906

Hahn, Anna, I 5276, 12335

Hahn, Dorothy Anna, I 15957

Hahn, Emily; Mrs. Charles Ralph Boxer, I 10414, 16010

Hahn-Hahn, Helena Petrovna. *See* Blavatsky, Helena Petrovna (Hahn-Hahn).

Hahr, Emma, I 2597, 13577, IV 460

Haines, Connie, I 14622

Haines, Edith Key, I 2117

Haines, Frances E., I 12968

Haines, Helen Colby, I 9363

Haines, Helen Elizabeth, I 2978, 6093, 9422, 11267

Haines, Sarah Platt, I 17401

Haizlip, Mae, I 17973

Halcott, Elizabeth Lente, I 2507, 13542

Hale, Anne Gardner, I 7847, IV 316

Hale, Ellen Day, I 4056

Hale, Evelyn Wickham, I 15990

Hale, Florence, I 1612, 3105, 6957, IV 823

Hale, Lilian Westcott, I 4369

Hale, Louise Closser, I 4257, 9423

Hale, Lucretia Peabody, I 7794

Hale, Mary, I 14589

Hale, Mary Whitwell, I 2242, 7652, 13459, 17145, IV 903

Hale, Nancy, I 10494

Hale, Sarah Josepha (Buell), I 7476, 10820, IV 2019

Hale, Susan, I 3924, 5894, 8144

Haley, Audrey, I 18987

Haley, Margaret Angela, I 1447, 2803, 6428, II 143, IV 577

Halgarten, Katherine MacArthur Drew, I 7257, IV 234

Hall, Abigail Burr, I 16132

Hall, Addye Yeargain, I 10531, 14391, 15099

Hall, Adelaide S., I 4070, 8943, 14962

Hall, Alma Webster. *See* Powell, Alma Webster (Hall).

Hall, Amanda Benjamin, I 9920

Hall, Anne, I 3862

Hall, Arethusa, I 2220, 7605, IV 897

Hall, Carrie M., I 13091

Hall, Daniel, Mrs., I 4911

Hall, Dorian, Mrs., I 5277, 5855, 8024

Hall, Dorothy, I 20309

Hall, Elaine. *See* Eastman, Elaine (Goodale).
Hall, Emma Amelia, I 6706, 16752
Hall, Evelyn, I 18988
Hall, Florence Louise, I 1704, 5679, 21281
Hall, Florence Marion Howe, I 3712, 8563, 14921, 20974, II 1105, IV 1310
Hall, Frances M., I 2598, 16605
Hall, Gertrude Brownell, I 9180, IV 1067
Hall, Grace Ethel Adams, I 9364, 11248, IV 1997
Hall, Hazel, I 9801, IV 2000
Hall, Helen, I 18520
Hall, Henrietta. *See* Shuck, Henrietta (Hall).
Hall, Herman J., Mrs., I 1376
Hall, Ilizabeth, I 3695, 18140
Hall, Ina Beauchamp, I 1832, 7229, III 1064
Hall, Josephine, I 13652, 19692
Hall, Juanita, I 14279, 20244
Hall, Kay, I 11695
Hall, Louisa Jane Park, I 7606, IV 2172
Hall, Lucy M., I 12636, 16762
Hall, Mal, I 18889
Hall, Margaret Thompson, I 2667, 11098
Hall, Maria M. C., I 5278, 12336
Hall, Marian Wells, I 787, 4580
Hall, Marjory, I 961, 10495
Hall, Mary, I 6767, 16145, II 297, IV 330
Hall, Mary, Dame, I 1360
Hall, Pauline, I 13685, 19709
Hall, Rosetta Sherwood, I 12793, 17570
Hall, Ruth, I 8974, IV 1559
Hall, Sara C., I 12477, 20859, IV 697
Hall, Sarah Elizabeth, I 2468, IV 1464
Hall, Sarah (Ewing); Constantia; Florepha, I 7447, 17009, IV 2013
Hall, Sharlott Mabridth, I 9365
Hall, Susan E., I 5279, 12337
Hall, Violette, I 7548, IV 1355
Hallady, Bessie G., I 3378, 17974
Hallam, Julia (Clark), I 9054, IV 687
Hallam, Lewis, Mrs., I 19478
Hallam, Mrs., I 19486
Hallam, Nancy, I 19464
Hallam, Sarah, I 1894, 19465
Hallaren, Mary Agnes, I 5727
Hallock, Julia Isabel (Sherman), I 8597, IV 328
Hallock, Mary Angeline A. (Ray) (Lathrop), I 7653, 17146
Hallowell, Anna, I 2367, 18213
Hallowell, Anna Coffin (Davis), I 5911, 8296

Hallowell, M. M., Mrs., I 5280, 15368
Hallowell, R. C., I 10968
Hallowell, Sarah Catherine (Fraley), I 10910, IV 2051
Hall-Wood, Mary C. F. *See* Wood, Mary C. Foster.
Hally, Lydia S., I 6721
Halpert, Edith Gregor, I 788, 4581, 6225, III 1206
Halprin, Rose, I 1751, 17739, II 452
Halse, Margaret Frances, I 10532
Halstead, Anna Roosevelt, I 10446, 11867
Halstead, Margaret, I 14212
Halvey, Margaret Mary Brophy, I 1377, 2599, 8724, III 937
Hamar, Irene; Mrs. Henry Peter de Vries, I 4728, 18828, III 495, IV 1843
Hamblet, Julia E., I 5648
Hamburger, Bessie Snow, I 6958
Hamer, Fannie Lou, I 1249, 7303, 15195, 16934, III 324, IV 1198
Hamill, Dorothy, I 18920
Hamill, Virginia, I 789, 4582
Hamilton, Alice, I 2932, 9333, 12823, 16773, 18422
Hamilton, Alice King, I 7549
Hamilton, Anna Havermann, I 3529, 14392
Hamilton, Anna J., I 2781, 11148, IV 738
Hamilton, Anne Kennedy, I 5043, 16314
Hamilton, Cecile, I 17975
Hamilton, Edith, I 2904, 9284, III 841
Hamilton, Elizabeth Schuyler, I 5030
Hamilton, Florence, I 10236, 11696
Hamilton, Gail. *See* Dodge, Mary Abigail.
Hamilton, Gordon, I 3263, 18591
Hamilton, Grace Towns, I 3493, 7250, III 275, IV 488
Hamilton, Kate Waterman; Fleeta, I 8196, 17322, IV 518
Hamilton, Margaret, I 5555, 12538, 20245
Hamilton, Nancy, I 10496, 14342
Hamlin, Frances Bacon, I 1361
Hamlin, Genevieve Karr, I 4522
Hamlin, Henrietta Anna Loraine, I 17160
Hamm, Margharita Arlina, I 6849, 9285, 11225, III 540
Hammand, Emily Vanderbilt Sloane, I 1565, 15689, 18476, II 675, IV 1666
Hammer, Anna Maria Nichols, I 19278, IV 2062

Hammond, Fanny Reed, I 3530, 14393
Hammond, Henrietta (Hardy); Henri Dange, I 8857, IV 2325
Hammond, Kathy B., I 18990
Hammond, Lily Hardy, I 18296
Hammond, Mary Virginia Spitler, I 342, IV 651
Hammond, Natalie Harris, I 15599, 18368
Hammond, Natalie Hays, I 3818, 4666
Hampton, Hope, I 14065
Hanaford, Phoebe Ann (Coffin), I 5844, 6687, 7987, 10886, 14841, 17267, 20840, II 1085, IV 319
Hancock, Cornelia, I 1184, 2449, 5550, 12528, 15457, 18246, II 1025
Hancock, Dorothy Quincy, I 5013
Hancock, Joy Bright, I 5697, 17951
Hancock, Martha M., I 17096, IV 1173
Hand, Marguerite Alice le. *See* le Hand, Marguerite Alice.
Handlin, Mary Flug, I 232, 5796, II 366
Haney, Carol, I 2004, 20534
Hanger, Ruth, I 18991
Hank. *See* Fort, Eleanor H.
Hanks, Mary Esther Vilas, I 1553, II 796, IV 2399
Hanks, Nancy. *See* Bowles, A. Lincoln.
Hanks, Nancy, I 4737, 7355
Hanna, Rebecca, I 12539
Hanna, Sarah Jackson, I 2561, 13558, IV 458
Hannah, Jane Osborn, I 13860
Hannah, Persis Dwight, I 11249
Hannum, Alberta Pierson, I 10447
Hansberry, Lorraine, I 1260, 7366, 10743, 20598, III 419, IV 1854
Hansborough, Mary Berri (Chapman), I 9366
Hanschman, Nancy Conners, I 12036
Hansen, Hazel Dorothy, I 63, 11622, IV 207
Hansen, Juanita, I 20106
Hansen, Julia Butler, I 7251
Hansl, Eva von Baur, I 11697
Hanson, Eliza Rice, I 7898
Hanson, Harriet Jane. *See* Robinson, Harriet Jane (Hanson).
Hanssen, Hertha I., I 790
Hapgood, Isabel Florence, I 6570, 8725, 11052, IV 1510
Haraughty, Lois Ellen, I 18839
Harazthy, Mrs., I 16433, III 20
Harbee, Lee (Cohen), I 1365, 5959, 8682, IV 1500, 2263

Harbert, Elizabeth Boynton "Lizzie", I 8498, 14908, 20947
Harbeson, Georgiana Brown, I 4500, 16781
Harcum, Edith H., I 3073, IV 2127
Hard, Anne; Annie Marie Nyhan Scribner, I 6934, 9575, 11299, II 809, IV 409
Hard, Darlene R., I 18875
Hard, Eliza, I 16093
Harden, Cecil Murray, Mrs., I 7099
Hardey, Mary Aloysia Hawley; Mother Mary Aloysia, I 2237, 17136, II 87
Hardin, Ellen. *See* Walworth, Ellen (Hardin).
Hardin, Helen; Tsa-sah-wee-eh; Little Standing Spruce, I 4760, III 1125
Hardin, Julia Carlin, I 2469, 17369
Hardin, Lillian. *See* Armstrong, Lillian Hardin.
Harding, Ann, I 20246
Harding, Caroline, I 11250
Harding, Charlotte, I 4269
Harding, Elizabeth McGavock, I 5115, 5813, 7759
Harding, Evilela, I 12540, IV 700
Harding, Jane, I 17859
Harding, Margaret Snodgrass, I 596, 11387
Hardinge, E. M. *See* Going, Ellen Maud.
Hardwick, Elizabeth, I 10638, 11950, 18668
Hardwick, Katharine Davis, I 600, 11401, 14000, II 252, IV 667
Hardy, Anna Eliza, I 3939
Hardy, Jennie Law, I 15005, 19444
Hardy, Kay, I 3452, 4640, 15092
Hare, Amory. *See* Hutchinson, Mary Amory Hare.
Hare, Emily. *See* Winthrop, Laura.
Hare, Jeannette R., I 4535, III 51
Hare, Maud Cuney, I 9480, 13842, III 177
Hargreaves, Sheba, I 9713
Harkness, Anna Richardson, I 15439
Harkness, Georgia Elma, I 3255, 6354, 9967, 17726
Harkness, Mary Emma Stillman, I 15690
Harkness, Rebekah (West), I 1985, 14552, 15863
Harkness, William, Mrs., I 16711
Harlan, James, Mrs., I 5122, 15295
Harland, Elizabeth Carraway, I 5281, 16504

Harland, Marian. *See* Terhune, Mary Virginia (Hawes).

Harlow, Jean; Harlean Carpenter, **I** 20365

Harlowe, Clarissa. *See* Barton, Clara.

Harman, Catharine Maria, **I** 19462

Harmon, Amelia, **I** 5282, 16505

Harmon, Lily, **I** 4711

Harmon, Louise Benedict, **I** 17898

Harmon, Ruth J., **I** 3379, 17976

Harned, Virginia, **I** 19756

Harnet, Mary, **I** 182, 16799

Harper, Elizabeth, **I** 16385

Harper, Frances Ellen Watkins, **I** 1157, 7899, 14834, **III** 88

Harper, Ida A. Husted, **I** 6781, 8783, 11072, 21015

Harper, Lee. *See* Lee, Nelle Harper.

Harper, Martha Matilda; Mrs. Robert Arthur MacBain, **I** 395, 3716

Harper, Olive, **I** 8377

Harper, Valerie, **I** 12082

Harpman, Julia, **I** 11473

Harrell, Sarah Carmichael, **I** 2525, 19324, **IV** 650

Harriman, Florence Jaffray (Hurst), **I** 1522, 5627, 6873, 11251, 12837, 15663, 18434, 21163, **IV** 403

Harriman, Grace Carley, **I** 15684

Harriman, Mary Williamson (Averall), **I** 376, 15540, **IV** 1515

Harrington, Cornelia, **I** 5283, 12338

Harrington, Helen, **I** 13237

Harris, Amanda Bartlett, **I** 7871, 17235, **IV** 1269

Harris, Barbara, **I** 20643

Harris, Belle C., **I** 1430

Harris, Bernice Kelly, **I** 10056

Harris, Christina Phelps, **I** 6241

Harris, Claire. *See* McCardell, Claire (Harris).

Harris, Corra May White, **I** 9334, **IV** 478

Harris, Eliza, **I** 12339, 15369

Harris, Elizabeth, **I** 16951, **II** 960, **III** 627

Harris, Ethel Hillyer, **I** 8726, **IV** 461

Harris, Hettie, **I** 14213

Harris, Jane Davenport, **I** 4583, 16712, **III** 802

Harris, John, Mrs., **I** 5284, 12340, 15370

Harris, Julie Ann, **I** 20541

Harris, Ladonna, **I** 13419, 18677, 21342, **III** 1097

Harris, Letitia Radcliffe, **I** 14394

Harris, Marjorie Silliman, **I** 6351

Harris, Mary Belle, **I** 6899, 16775

Harris, Mary Ormerod, **I** 3134, 15752, **II** 332, **IV** 160

Harris, Mildred, **I** 20261

Harris, Miriam (Coles), **I** 8163, **IV** 1429

Harris, Patricia Roberts, **I** 3639, 7344, **III** 380

Harris, Renee, **I** 443, 19722

Harris, Selima, **I** 6, **III** 92

Harris, Ula Moulton, **I** 17816

Harris, W. F., Mrs., **I** 5285, 12341

Harrison, Caroline Lavinia Scott, **I** 13496

Harrison, Constance Cary, **I** 8499, 19616, **IV** 1480

Harrison, Dorothy Ann, **I** 11698

Harrison, Elizabeth, **I** 2582

Harrison, Elizabeth Bassett, **I** 4970

Harrison, Gertrude [Alice] Gordon Grayson, **I** 1733, 13126, 15799, 16911, 18755, **II** 859

Harrison, Hazel Lucile, **I** 3123, 13949, **III** 193

Harrison, Jeanne Brooks. *See* Brola, Jeanne.

Harrison, Joan Mary, **I** 962, 20334, **III** 757

Harrison, Margaret, **I** 201

Harrison, Margaritta Willetts, **I** 3948

Harrison, Marjorie, **I** 11474

Harrison, Pat, **I** 18992

Harrison, Sarah, **I** 16998, **II** 988

Harron, Marion Janet, **I** 7220

Harry, Deborah, **I** 14759

Harsh, Vivian, **I** 6191, **III** 221

Harshaw, Margaret, **I** 14516

Hart, Almira. *See* Phelps, Almira (Hart) (Lincoln).

Hart, Carolyn Thome, **I** 18993

Hart, Deborah Scudder, **I** 4787, 16138

Hart, Doris, **I** 18841

Hart, Dorothy, **I** 11998

Hart, Emma C. *See* Willard, Emma C. (Hart).

Hart, Fanchon, **I** 13238

Hart, Frances Noyes, **I** 9921

Hart, Janey, **I** 16727, 18115

Hart, Kitty Carlisle. *See* Carlisle, Kitty.

Hart, Letitia Bennet, **I** 4166

Hart, Marion Rice, **I** 17938

Hart, Mary Ward, **I** 19441, 21123, **IV** 588

Hart, Nancy; Ann Morgan, **I** 4841, 16173, **IV** 438

Hart, Pearl, **I** 16671

Hart, Ruth Cole, **I** 4975

Hartigan, Grace, **I** 4733

Hartline, Mary, **I** 12015, 14648

Hartman, Gertrude, **I** 3035, 9552

Hartman, Grace (Abbott), **I** 1912, 19839

Hartman, Gustave, Mrs., **I** 10237, 15820

Hartman, May Weisser, **I** 15821, 18626

Hartman, Regina, **I** 16146

Hartrick, Stella, **I** 18994

Hartt, Mary Bronson, **I** 9447

Hartwick, Rose Alnora. *See* Thorpe, Rose Alnora (Hartwick).

Harup, Karen, **I** 18840

Harvey, Cordelia Adelaide Perrine, **I** 5135, 12239, 15318, 18196

Harvey, Ethel Browne, **I** 13024

Harvey, Jenny Dow, **I** 18359

Harvey, Kate Benedict Hanna, **I** 485, 12860, 15675, 16872, 18447, **II** 791, **IV** 1951

Harvey, Maud Clark, **I** 17571

Harvey, Mrs., **I** 4912

Harvitt, Helene, **I** 3380, 11699

Hashman, Judy M. Devlin, **I** 18871

Haskell, Ella Louisa (Knowles), **I** 6818, 21091, **II** 1066

Haskell, Harriet Newell, **I** 2398

Haskell, Helen Eggleston, **I** 9601

Haskell, Parola, **I** 5923

Hasson, Esther Vorhees, **I** 12838

Haste, Gwendolen, **I** 9922

Hastings, Alicia E., **I** 3624, 13393, **III** 349

Hastings, Elizabeth. *See* Sherwood, Margaret Pollock.

Hastings, Lucille Ahnawake, **I** 18678, **III** 1098

Hastings, Margaret, **I** 18116

Hastings, Mary Hay, **I** 1954, 20227

Haswell, Susanna. *See* Rowson, Susanna (Haswell).

Haswell, Susanna Haswell, **I** 17835

Haswin, Frances R., **I** 8800, 13591, 19653

Hatch, Edith, **I** 3154, 13982

Hatch, Grace, **I** 18995

Hatch, Mary R. P.; Mabel Percy, **I** 8659

Hatcher, Georgia H. Stockton, **I** 1470

Hatcher, Orie Latham, **I** 2736, 8975

Hathaway, Ann, **I** 3531, 10533, 14395

Hathaway, Anne. *See* Ingham, Mary Bigelow.

Hathaway, Joy (Kenny), **I** 11923, 20397

Hathaway, Maggie Smith, **I** 2905, 6850, 18406

Hathaway, P. V., Mrs., **I** 12541

Hathaway, Winifred Phillips, **I** 2949, 18435

Hathorne, Mary, **I** 187

Hathway, Katherine Butler, **I** 9923

Hartman, Gustave, Mrs., **I** 10237, 15820

Hattie, Aunt. *See* Baker, Harriette Newell Woods.

Hatton, Fanny Cottinet Locke, **I** 11235, 19766, **II** 783

Hauberg, Susanne Christine Denkmann, **I** 15676, **II** 670, **IV** 600

Hauck, Louise Platt, **I** 9738

Hauck, Minnie, **I** 13588

Haughery, Margaret Gaffney; The Bread Woman of New Orleans, **I** 233, 15269, 16805

Haupt, Alma Cecelia, **I** 3264, 13127, 18592

Haupt, Enid, **I** 11868

Havemeyer, Louisine Waldron Elder, **I** 4057, 5993, 15566, 21048

Haven, Alice Bradley; Emily Bradley Neal Haven; Alice G. Lee; Cousin Alice, **I** 7946, 10877

Haven, Emily Bradley Neal. *See* Haven, Alice Bradley.

Haven, Mary Emerson, **I** 2275

Havener, Helen, **I** 11252

Havens, Belle, **I** 4204

Havens, Mary Sue McDonald, **I** 17753

Haver, Phyllis, **I** 20190

Haviland, Laura Smith, **I** 1109, 15262, 18166, **II** 1006

Havoc, June, **I** 11951, 20430

Hawes, Charlotte W., **I** 2470, 13526, 14886

Hawes, Elizabeth, **I** 931, 3812, 10369, 21326

Hawes, Flora Harrod, **I** 6828, **IV** 45

Hawes, Franc P., **I** 4020

Hawes, Harriet Ann Boyd, **I** 35, 5632, 12861

Hawes, Mary Virginia. *See* Terhune, Mary Virginia (Hawes).

Hawkes, Anna Lorette Rose, **I** 3240

Hawkins, Elsie, **I** 18996

Hawkins, Jane, **I** 12118, 16047

Hawkinson, Nellie X., **I** 3241, 13092

Hawks, Annie Sherwood, **I** 8197, 13505, 17323, **II** 20, **IV** 1432

Hawks, Rachel Marshall, **I** 4343

Hawley, Adelaide, **I** 11700

Hawley, Frances Mallette, **I** 8500, **IV** 326

Hawley, Gertrude, **I** 18747

Hawley, Harriet Foote, **I** 5286, 12342

Hawley, Laura M., **I** 7688

Hawley, Margaret Foote, **I** 3879

Hawley, Maria, **I** 298, 10969

Hawn, Goldie, **I** 12097, 20693

Hawthorn, Mrs., **I** 4021

Hawthorne, Hildegarde, **I** 7550

Hawthorne, Rose. *See* Lathrop, Rose (Hawthorne).

Howe, Emeline Harriet (Siggins), **I** 8529, 19325, **IV** 2077

Howe, Helen, **I** 3533, 14401

Howe, Helen; Helen Allen, **I** 10416, 15096

Howe, Jemima, **I** 16148

Howe, Julia Romana. *See* Anagnos, Julia Romana (Howe).

Howe, Julia Romana, **I** 2527

Howe, Julia Ward, **I** 1135, 1280, 5120, 7777, 13469, 14814, 15125, 15289, 16461, 16742, 19535, 20784, **IV** 920

Howe, Laura Elizabeth. *See* Richards, Laura Elizabeth (Howe).

Howe, Mary, **I** 13950

Howe, Mary Ann, **I** 1178, 2399, 15426

Howe, Maud, **I** 8883

Howell, Elizabeth (Lloyd), **I** 7796

Howell, Ida, **I** 19758

Howell, M. C. Lydia Scott, **I** 19006

Howell, Mary Seymour, **I** 14911, 20957, **IV** 1484

Howey, Ella Mae, **I** 15112

Howland, Edith, **I** 4136

Howland, Eliza W., **I** 5296, 8028, 12349

Howland, Elizabeth Tilley, **I** 16076, **II** 935

Howland, Emily, **I** 1162, 2323, 15127, 15331, 19181, 20826, **II** 1016, **IV** 1401

Howland, Mary Woolsey, **I** 5097, 7714, 12192

Howland, Ruth B., **I** 13240

Howorth, Lucy Somerville, **I** 1747, 7108

Hoxie, Vinnie (Ream), **I** 3994

Hoyle, Ethel, **I** 1020

Hoyt, Anne Marie Webster, **I** 19007

Hoyt, Beatrix "Trixie", **I** 18724

Hoyt, Deristha Lavinta, **I** 3950, 5924, 8380, 14887, **IV** 981

Hoyt, Elizabeth Orpha, **I** 8165

Hoyt, Julia. *See* Giles, Julia Robbins.

Hoyt, Lucy, **I** 17371

Hoyt, Minerva Lockhart Hamilton, **I** 12803, 13736, 15637, 16866, **IV** 124

Hoyt, Mrs., **I** 16094

Hoyt, Mrs. Thatcher. *See* Fergus, Phyllis.

Hoyt, Peggy, **I** 807, 4587

Hoyt-Stevens, Jane Elizabeth, **I** 12729, **II** 758

Hrebelianovich, Eleanor (Calhoun) Lazarovich. *See* Lazarovich-Hrebelianovich, Eleanor (Calhoun).

Hubbard, Charlotte Moton, **I** 3384, 7165, **III** 241

Hubbard, Emma, **I** 2473, 6725

Hubbard, Harriet. *See* Ayer, Harriet (Hubbard).

Hubbard, Helen Fahnestock, **I** 6095, 15677

Hubbard, Margaret Ann, **I** 10512

Hubbard, Muriel McCormick, **I** 15848

Hubbard, Theodora Kimball, **I** 4412, 7024, 16903, **II** 1146, **IV** 1114

Hubbell, Martha Elizabeth (Stone), **I** 7726, 17179

Hubbell, Mary Elizabeth; Lelia Linwood, **I** 8232

Hubbs, Rebecca, **I** 17019, **II** 991

Huber, Alice, **I** 4099, 12730

Huck, Winnifred Sprague Mason, **I** 6981, 11368

Huddleston, Amelia Edith. *See* Barr, Amelia Edith Huddleston.

Hudlun, Anna Elizabeth, **I** 15467, 18257, **II** 547, **III** 109

Hudson, Grace, **I** 4210

Hudson, Henrietta. *See* Billwiller, Henrietta Hudson.

Hudson, Henrietta, **I** 15886

Hudson, Hester, **I** 183

Hudson, Hortense Imboden, **I** 808

Hudson, Jean Blackwell, **I** 6289, **III** 309

Hudson, Mary (Clemmer) (Ames), **I** 8335, 10953, **IV** 382

Hudson, Mrs. *See* Ames, Mary E. Clemmer.

Hudson, Octavia, **I** 3534, 10537, 14402

Hudson, Rochelle, **I** 11944, 20421

Hudson, Sally Neidlinger, **I** 19008

Huerta, Dolores Fernandez, **I** 1887, 6509, **II** 226, **III** 1014, **IV** 258

Hueston, Ethel Powelson, **I** 9826

Hufstedler, Shirley [Ann] Mount, **I** 3644, 7347

Huggins, Louisa Cornelia Caroline. *See* Tuthill, Louisa Cornelia Caroline (Huggins).

Hughan, Jessie Wallace, **I** 3014, 6911, 9524, 15164

Hughes, Adella Prentiss, **I** 472, 13773, **IV** 1949

Hughes, Alice, **I** 11709

Hughes, Arleen Florence Wilson, **I** 696, **II** 257, **IV** 292

Hughes, Bernice Gaines, **I** 5720

Hughes, Caroline, **I** 365, 15535, **IV** 549

Hughes, Kate Duval, **I** 288, 8261, **II** 117, **IV** 378

Hughes, Marietta E., **I** 12638

Hughes, Nina Vera B., **I** 6327, 9055, **III** 534

Hughes, Sarah Mytton. *See* Maury, Sarah Mytton (Hughes).

Hughes, Sarah Tilghman, **I** 7113

Hulbert, Katharine Allmond, **I** 4211

Hulett, Alta M., **I** 6795

Huling, Caroline Augusta, **I** 11116, 15571, 19414, 21053, **IV** 562

Hull, Elizabeth Clarke, **I** 4833

Hull, Hannah Hallowell Clothier, **I** 15162, 21182

Hull, Helen Rose, **I** 3214, 9856, **IV** 1748

Hull, Josephine Sherwood; Mary Josephine Sherwood, **I** 19967

Hull, Margaret. *See* Anglin, Margaret Mary.

Hull, Peggy, **I** 11710

Hull, Rose Frances Witz Whitney, **I** 1574, 6912

Hull, Rose Mitchell, **I** 16508

Hull, Sarah, **I** 5028

Hulse, Anne Elizabeth, **I** 809, 3385

Hulton, Ann, **I** 5756, 7423

Humaston, Abi, **I** 5036, 16301

Hume, Jessie Fremont, **I** 6174, **IV** 1757

Hume, Sophia Wiginton, **I** 7414, 16977

Humert, Anne Schumacher, **I** 810, 11711

Humphrey, Caroline Louise, **I** 3015, **II** 1138, **IV** 1097

Humphrey, Doris, **I** 1936

Humphrey, Elizabeth B., **I** 4022

Humphrey, Grace, **I** 9715

Humphrey, Helen Florence, **I** 7260

Humphrey, Mary, **I** 11478

Humphrey, Maud, **I** 4174

Humphreys, Marie Champney, **I** 4168

Humphreys, Mrs. David. *See* Jackson, Beatrice.

Humphreys, Sara Riggs, **I** 4785

Humphreys, Sarah Gibson, **I** 8029, 20850, **IV** 726

Hunt, Augusta Merrill, **I** 15488, 16758, 19302, 20940, **II** 1101

Hunt, Elizabeth Pickard, **I** 5297, 12350

Hunt, Harriot Keziah, **I** 12175, 14793, 18163, 20739, **IV** 900

Hunt, Helen Fiske, **I** 8103

Hunt, Helen Maria (Fiske). *See* Jackson, Helen Maria (Fiske) (Hunt).

Hunt, Hester Martha. *See* Poole, Hester Martha (Hunt).

Hunt, Louise Frances, **I** 17335

Hunt, Mabel Leigh, **I** 9995

Hunt, Mary Hannah Hanchett, **I** 2348, 19201

Hunt, Sarah, **I** 12179

Hunter, Alberta, **I** 14134, **III** 224

Hunter, Jane Edna, **I** 1655, 3135, 12996, 18544, **III** 199, **IV** 1957

Hunter, Kim, **I** 20506

Hunter, Louise, **I** 14403

Hunter, M. A., Mrs., **I** 15228

Hunter, Mary. *See* Austin, Mary (Hunter).

Huntington, Addie D. Waites, **I** 1218, 1575, **III** 182

Huntington, Agnes, **I** 13700, **IV** 1599

Huntington, Ann (Vaughan) Hyatt, **I** 4307, 15708

Huntington, Clara, **I** 4330

Huntington, Dorothy Phillips; Dorothy Sanburn Phillips, **I** 10034, 11558

Huntington, Emily, **I** 18265

Huntington, Emily Clark. *See* Miller, Emily Clark Huntington.

Huntington, Faye. *See* Foster, Theodosia Maria (Toll).

Huntington, Grace, **I** 17980

Huntington, Margaret Jane Evans, **I** 2509

Huntington, Martha Devotion, **I** 4987

Huntington, Susan Mansfield, **I** 5771, 7490, 15234, 17046

Huntley, Amelia Almore, **I** 17419

Huntley, Florence, **I** 8733, 11055

Huntley, Lydia Howard. *See* Sigourney, Lydia Howard (Huntley).

Huntley, Mary Sutton, **I** 17297, **IV** 1225

Hunton, Addie Waites, **I** 1523, 5628, 12840, 15664, **III** 168

Hunton, Hazel, **I** 5705, 15823

Hurd, Dorothy Iona Campbell, **I** 18728

Hurd, Helen Marr, **I** 8336, 19268, **IV** 801

Hurd, Muriel Jeffries, **I** 1719, 9928, 11479

Hurd, P. B., Mrs., **I** 5512, 16542

Hurd-Mead, Kate Campbell; Kate Mead, **I** 6062, 12806

Hurdon, Elizabeth, **I** 12814

Hurlburt, Margaret "Marge", **I** 3602, 18080

Hurlbut, Harriette Persis, **I** 4127

Hurley, Catharine, **I** 2179

Hurley, Laurel, **I** 14655

Hurll, Estelle May, **I** 2842, 4137, 9182, 14988

Hurst, Fannie, **I** 9884, 17699, 21286, **II** 436

Hurst, Vida (Frais), **I** 9929, **IV** 183

Hurston, Zora Neale, **I** 67, 10324, **III** 253

Hurt, Ambra Halsey, **I** 17728

Jamerson, Pauline Thierry;
Polly Preyer, **I** 10087, 14135,
20108
James, Alice, **I** 5955, 8661
James, Alice Archer (Sewall), **I**
4213, 9368
James, Anna (Cleveland), **I**
17900, 19826
James, Annie Laurie Wilson, **I**
11182, 16857, 18698, **IV** 110
James, Annie P., **I** 17244
James, Belle Robinson, **I** 9312,
17581, **III** 541
James, Bessie, **I** 11335
James, Dorothy, **I** 14266
James, Hannah Packard, **I**
5899
James, Joni, **I** 14681
James, Julia Bradford
Huntington, **I** 15263
James, Maria, **I** 7497
James, Mary Latimer, **I** 13004,
17665, **II** 831, **IV** 2289
Jameson, Edward, Mrs., **I**
16268
Jameson, Elizabeth "Betty", **I**
18829
Jameson, Hannah Taggart, **I**
16381
Jamison, Cecelia Viets (Dakin)
(Hamilton), **I** 3938, 8262
Jamison, Judith, **I** 2036, **III**
473
Jamme, Anne C., **I** 13241
Jan, W. M. L. *See* Woodruff,
Julia Louisa Matilda
(Curtiss).
Janauschek, Francesca Romance
Magdalena; Fanny, **I** 19562,
III 823
Janes, Martha Waldron, **I**
17299, 19212, 20860, **II** 18,
IV 674
Janeway, Elizabeth Hall, **I**
10595
Janis, Elsie (Bierbower)
(Wilson), **I** 1924, 5685, 9885,
14045, 19998
Janowszky, Bela, **I** 4589, **III**
895
Jans, Annekke. *See* Bogardus,
Annetje Jansen.
Janvier, Catharine Ann, **I** 3964,
8433
Janvier, Margaret Thompson;
Margaret Vandegrift, **I** 8530,
IV 2078
Janvrin, Mary W. (Ellsworth),
I 8031
Jaramillo, Mari-Luci, **I** 3656,
7359, **III** 1012
Jarboe, Elizabeth, **I** 16209
Jarboro, Caterina, **I** 14295, **III**
263
Jardine, John Alexander, Mrs.,
I 14216
Jarnette, Evelyn Magruder de.
See de Jarnette, Evelyn
Magruder.
Jarrell, Helen Ira, **I** 3301,
6487, 7114

Jarrett, Mary Cromwell, **I**
3059, 18503
Jarvis, Anna M., **I** 1471
Jarvis, Iva Pembridge, **I** 19012
Jarvis, Lucy (Howard), **I** 11971
Jasie, Tillie Leblang, **I** 570,
19917, **IV** 1721
Jasmyn, Joan, **I** 10154, 14165
Jayne, Barbara, **I** 18058
Jaynes, Clare. *See* Spiegel,
Clara Gatzert.
Jean, Elsie, **I** 10475, 14331
Jean, Sally Lucas, **I** 3074,
12940
Jeanes, Anne T., **I** 15311, **II**
1014
Jeanette, Sister. *See* Roesch,
Jeanette.
Jebb, Caroline Lane Reynolds
Slemmer, **I** 8381
Jebb, Lady. *See* Slemmer,
Caroline Lane Reynolds.
Jefferis, Marea Wood, **I** 8735,
IV 2090
Jefferson, Cornelia Burke, **I**
19587
Jefferson, Mary Anne, **I** 19494
Jeffery, Harriet, **I** 6381
Jeffery, Isador Gilbert, **I** 300,
8382, **IV** 525
Jeffrey, Rosa Vertner (Griffith)
(Johnson); Rosa, **I** 7924,
19554, **IV** 724
Jeffreys, Anne, **I** 11999
Jeffries, Harriet Mildred. *See*
Cunard, Grace.
Jeffries, Lila F. S., **I** 11712
Jemison, Alice Mae Lee, **I**
7192, 11807
Jemison, Mary Dehewamis;
White Woman of the
Genessee, **I** 16241, **III** 634,
IV 1344
Jemne, Elsa Laubach, **I** 4417
Jemyma. *See* Holley, Marietta.
Jenckes, Virginia Ellis, **I** 1221,
6945, **IV** 662
Jendritza, Loretta S., **I** 5742,
13420, **III** 1100
Jenkins, Alberta Gallatin. *See*
Gallatin, Alberta.
Jenkins, Anna Almy, **I** 15233,
II 993, **IV** 2169
Jenkins, Carol, **I** 12083, **III**
457
Jenkins, Cora W., **I** 2950,
13796
Jenkins, Florence F., **I** 14217
Jenkins, Frances C., **I** 17251,
19176, **II** 1015
Jenkins, Helen Hartley, **I**
12731, 15594
Jenkins, Helen P., **I** 14940
Jenkins, Lydia A., **I** 14816,
17211, 20793
Jenkins, Mary Catherine. *See*
Lee, Mary Catherine
(Jenkins).
Jenkins, Sara, **I** 10393
Jenkins, Theresa A., **I** 11088,
19399, 21037, **IV** 2412

Jenks, Amelia. *See* Bloomer,
Amelia (Jenks).
Jenks, Phoebe A. Pickering
Hoyt, **I** 4001
Jennings, Mrs., **I** 16210
Jennison, Lucy White; Owen
Innsley, **I** 8736
Jennison, Mary, **I** 206
Jepson, Helen, **I** 14325
Jernegan, Amy Chase, **I** 17891
Jerome, Irene Elizabeth, **I** 4074
Jerome, Maud Nugent, **I** 9576,
13870, 19847
Jerome, Maude. *See* Nugent,
Maude.
Jervey, Caroline Howard
(Gilman) Glover, **I** 7848
Jessey, Cornelia, **I** 10538
Jessup, Clara Sophia. *See*
Bloomfield-Moore, Clara
Sophia (Jessup).
Jessye, Eva Alberta, **I** 3309,
10126, 14155, **III** 230
Jewell, Catherine Underwood, **I**
12235
Jewell, Isabel, **I** 20355
Jewett, Alice L., **I** 6175, 11481
Jewett, Maude Sherwood, **I**
4271
Jewett, Mildred; Madaket
Millie, **I** 16941
Jewett, Sarah, **I** 19622
Jewett, Sarah Orne; Alice Eliot,
I 8683, **IV** 807, 1006
Jewett, Sophie, **I** 2806, 9118
Jewett, Susan W., **I** 7654
Jewitt, Jessie Mae, **I** 14406
Jhabvala, Ruth Prawer, **I**
10724, 20572, **II** 499, **III**
767, 906
Joan of Arc, Sister. *See* Wolfe,
Joan of Arc.
Jobe, Mary Lee. *See* Akeley,
Mary Lee (Jobe).
Jobes, Mary Adelaide
Daugherty, **I** 5301, 12353
Johaneson, Bland, **I** 12042
Johansen, Mrs. John C. *See*
MacLane, Jean.
John, Alice, **I** 19905, **III** 1300,
IV 1714
Johns, Annie E., **I** 5302
Johns, Laura M., **I** 21001, **IV**
707
Johnson, Ada, **I** 5303, 12354
Johnson, Adelaide, **I** 4002,
20985
Johnson, Alison Heart, **I** 6380
Johnson, Anne Jennings, **I**
4971
Johnson, Arabella, **I** 16062
Johnson, Ava Dale Plummer, **I**
17821
Johnson, Carrie Ashton, **I**
11196, 19438, 21109, **IV** 583
Johnson, Christine, **I** 14407
Johnson, Clara Ingram. *See*
Judson, Clara Ingram
Johnson.
Johnson, Corinne, **I** 13242
Johnson, Dorothy B., **I** 15992

Johnson, Edith Christina, **I**
3256, **IV** 1118
Johnson, Electa Amanda, **I**
15448, **IV** 2375
Johnson, Ellen Cheney, **I** 2276,
6675, 16743
Johnson, Emily Pauline;
Tekahionwake, **I** 9119, **II**
266, **III** 1048
Johnson, Eva Marie, **I** 17785
Johnson, Evangeline Maria, **I**
5925, 6565, 8383
Johnson, Florence Merriam, **I**
1613, 12971
Johnson, Georgia Douglas, **I**
9802, 14001, **III** 205
Johnson, Grace Mott, **I** 4378
Johnson, Hallie Tanner, **I**
12165, **III** 70, **IV** 3
Johnson, Helen Lossing, **I**
4158, 9271
Johnson, Helen Louise
(Kendrick), **I** 8501, 10997
Johnson, Isabella, **I** 16211
Johnson, J. Rosamond, **I**
13829, 19804, **III** 176
Johnson, Janette Burr, **I** 19013
Johnson, Jemima Suggett, **I**
16285
Johnson, John, Mrs., **I** 19474
Johnson, Josephine Winslow;
Josephine Cannon, **I** 10539,
II 355
Johnson, Judy, **I** 12032, 14667
Johnson, Laura Winthrop, **I**
7901, **IV** 1394
Johnson, Lucy, **I** 216
Johnson, Lydia S., **I** 5304,
12355
Johnson, Margaret, **I** 9056, **IV**
1576
Johnson, Marguerite C., **I**
7211, **IV** 1166
Johnson, Maria Preston, **I**
17038
Johnson, Mary, **I** 9369
Johnson, Mary Anne, **I** 16736
Johnson, Mary C., **I** 18259
Johnson, Mary Katharine, **I**
1524
Johnson, Nancy Cummings;
Minnie Myrtle, **I** 10855
Johnson, Olivia, **I** 1871
Johnson, Osa Helen Leighty, **I**
674, 10058, 16704, 17946,
20095
Johnson, Rosa Vertner, **I** 7798
Johnson, Rosa Vertner
(Griffith). *See* Jeffrey, Rosa
Vertner (Griffith) (Johnson).
Johnson, Sallie M. Mills, **I**
9141, **IV** 282
Johnson, Sarah (Barclay), **I**
5908, 8263
Johnson, Sonya Bortin, **I** 812,
11713
Johnson, Thomasina Walker, **I**
7276
Johnson, Virginia E. (Shelman),
I 10710, 13407
Johnson, Virginia Wales;
Cousin Virginia, **I** 8624

Keast, Susette Schultz, I 4486, IV 2148

Keating, Isabelle, I 11715

Keating, Josephine E., I 2603, 8737, 11057, 13579, IV 2235

Keating, Micheline, I 11482

Keating, Sarah. See Wood, Sarah Sayward (Barrell) (Keating).

Keatinge, Harriet Charlotte, I 1312, 12514, IV 764

Keaton, Diane, I 20701

Keck, Lucile Liebermann, I 6212

Keckley, Elizabeth Hobbs, I 238, 3706, 7761, III 82

Kee, Elizabeth Frazier, I 7138

Keeler, Ruby, I 1972, 20347, III 587

Keen, Dora, I 9397, 16669

Keene, Laura, I 242, 19540, III 655

Keene, Mona, I 17982

Keeney, Ana, I 4536

Keep, Mabel Hazlett, I 11716, 15825

Keep from the Water. See Wawa Calac Chaw.

Keezer, Martha Moulton Wittemore, I 9373, IV 1083

Kehachiwinga. See Mountain Wolf Woman.

Kehew, Mary Morton Kimball, I 2756, 6425, 18347, 21083

Keim, Jane Sumner Owen, I 15440, 18235

Keister, Lillie Resler, I 17477

Keith, Alyn Yates. See Morris, Eugenia Laura (Tuttle).

Keith, Dora Wheeler, I 4071

Keith, Eliza D.; Erie Douglas; Di Vernon, I 1395, 8858, 11100, 16846, IV 91

Keith, Franklin, Mrs., I 177, 19466

Keith, Mary Isham (Marshall), I 4851, 16179

Kellar, Frances. See Kellor, Frances [Alice].

Kellar, Nellie. See Revell, Nellie MacAleney.

Kellas, Eliza, I 2855, IV 1610

Kellems, Vivien, I 689, 15978, IV 354

Keller, Elizabeth Catharine, I 12515, II 512, IV 974, 2055

Keller, Helen Adams, I 3108, 6960, 9647, 15173, 18521, 21232, II 285, IV 29

Keller, Manelva Wylie, I 12841

Kellet, Charlotte, I 18143

Kelley, Catherine Bishop, I 2646, 17492

Kelley, Edgar Stillman, Mrs., I 3109, 13919

Kelley, Edith Summers, I 9759

Kelley, Ella Maynard, I 411

Kelley, Florence, I 18348, II 1034

Kelley, Gertrude; Gertrude B. Gordon, I 11369

Kelley, Jessie Stillman, I 2933, 13774

Kelley, Marion Booth, I 15076

Kellog, Celia. See Logan, Celia (Kellog) (Connelly).

Kellogg, Clara Louise, I 13543

Kellogg, Elenore, I 11389

Kellogg, Eva Mary (Crosby), I 9057, IV 1047

Kellor, Frances [Alice]; Frances Kellar, I 498, 9450, 18467

Kelly, Amie, I 5313, 5857, 8035

Kelly, Edna Flannery, I 7241

Kelly, Eleanor Mercein, I 9648

Kelly, Elizabeth, I 13920

Kelly, Ella Maynard, I 396, 17883

Kelly, Fanny Wiggins, I 16592

Kelly, Florence (Finch), I 8662, 11029

Kelly, Glenn. See McNeilly, Mildred Masterson.

Kelly, Grace Patricia; Princess Grace of Monaco, I 20585

Kelly, Junea Wangeman, I 13039, 16902, IV 170

Kelly, Margaret V., I 6874

Kelly, Myra, I 3016, 9525, 18487, III 945

Kelly, Nancy, I 20491

Kelly, Patsy, I 20195

Kelly, Regina Zimmerman, I 3318, 10155

Kelman, Sarah R., I 1683, 3165, 13028, III 1191

Kelner, Sophie, I 13245, III 33

Kelsey, Frances, I 7285, 13373

Kemble, Elizabeth; Elizabeth Kemble Whitlock, I 19476

Kemble, Frances Anne "Fanny"; Fanny Kemble Butler, I 1110, 5788, 7646, 19516, III 647, IV 440

Kemp, Agnes Nininger, I 1151, 12236, 14823, 19168

Kemp, Maida Springer, I 6500, III 290

Kemper, Ruth, I 14067

Kempfer, Hannah Jensen, I 6961, IV 1184

Kempin, Emile, I 2604, 6769, III 1288

Kempner, Mary Jean. See Prycet Jones, Mary Jean Kempner

Kendall, Elizabeth Kemball, I 2876, 6051, 16653

Kendall, Margaret Stickney, I 4245

Kendrick, Ella Bagnell, I 6765, 19364

Kennedy, Gail, I 6366

Kennedy, Kate, I 2324, 6395, 20828, III 923, IV 65

Kennedy, Mary, I 9930, 20022

Kennedy, Minnie "Ma", I 17585

Kennedy, Myrna, I 20348

Kennedy, Rose (Fitzgerald), I 13095, 15790, 18579, II 193

Kennedy, Sarah Beaumont (Cannon), I 7553, IV 2222

Kennelly, Ardyth, I 10581

Kent, Allegra, I 2031

Kent, Corita, I 4725, II 221

Kent, Louise Andrews; Therea Tempest, I 9804

Kent, Rachel Fitch, I 4537

Kenton, Elizabeth Jarboe, I 16396

Kenyon, Bernice, I 10127

Kenyon, Cecil MacGlashan "Teddy", I 17983

Kenyon, Dorothy, I 1228, 1705, 7040, 13060, 21282, IV 1749

Kenyon, Helen, I 17669

Kenyon, Jean. See MacKenzie, Jean Kenyon.

Kenyon, Theda, I 10251

Kepley, Ada Miser, I 6756, 17440, 19351, II 1107

Kerby, Marion, I 6126, 13871, 19848

Kerens, Frances Jones, I 15522, 17449, IV 1208

Kerfoot, Annie Warfield, I 1293

Kerr, Adelaide, I 11717

Kerr, Deborah, I 20492, III 1257

Kerr, Jean Collins, I 10701, 20522

Kerr, Sophie, I 9649

Kershaw, Willette (Lamar), I 20050

Ketcham, Harriet Ann (McDivitt), I 3995

Ketchum, Annie Chambers, I 2304, 7874, 14827

Key, Wilhelmine Enteman, I 12874, II 323

Keyes, Bessie. See Vonnoh, Bessie Onahotema (Potter).

Keyes, Frances Parkinson Wheeler, I 9779

Keyes, Regina Flood, I 12842

Keysor, Jennie Ellis, I 2783, IV 1246

Khoury, Marie Azeez El, I 4384, III 994

Kiaer, Alice Damrosch Wolfe, I 16701, 18761

Kibbe, Flora Harriet d'Aubry Jenkins, I 16874, IV 1656

Kidd, Edna Gardner, I 17984

Kidd, Lucy Ann, I 2450, IV 2257

Kidd, Mae Street, I 7167, III 244, IV 749

Kidder, Kathryn, I 19759

Kidder, R. A. See Morse, Rebecca A.

Kiernan, Barbara, I 18089

Kies, Mary, I 202

Kilgallen, Dorothy Mae, I 11924

Kilgore, Caroline Burnham "Carrie", I 2410, 6703, 20891

Kilgore, Evelyn, I 3388, 17985

Killikelly, Sarah Hutchins, I 8384, IV 2063

Kilmer, Aline Murray, I 9858, 15049

Kimball, Arie Goebel, I 6255, 10417

Kimball, Corinne; Corinne, I 19805

Kimball, Emma Adeline, I 5953, 8625, IV 1001

Kimball, Grace, I 19975

Kimball, Grace N., I 13096

Kimball, Hannah Parker, I 9120, IV 1057

Kimball, Harriet MacEwen, I 7875, 17236, IV 1270

Kimball, Jennie, I 377, 19649

Kimball, Josephine, I 816

Kimball, Kate Fisher, I 11151

Kimball, Martha Gertrude, I 12545, 15468

Kimball, Yeffe, I 4744, 18118, III 1101

Kimbrough, Emily, I 10183, 11625

Kinder, Katharine Louise, I 6281

King, Anita, I 18753, 20051

King, Anna (Eichberg), I 8823, IV 1022

King, Anna Page, I 16803

King, Billie Jean Moffit, I 18896, 21360

King, Carol Weiss, I 1232, 7109

King, Carole, I 14737

King, Coretta Scott, I 1257, 14656, III 398, IV 492

King, E. M., I 5314, 12359

King, Fay, I 11336

King, Frances, I 9184, 16859

King, Frances Rockefeller, I 817, 11718

King, Grace Elizabeth, I 5971, IV 769

King, Harriet, I 19018

King, Helen, I 12843, IV 2113

King, Henrietta Maria Morse Chamberlain, I 272, 16822, IV 2253

King, Isabella Greenway, I 7010, IV 39

King, Julie. See Rive-King, Julie.

King, Kathryn "Sis", I 19019

King, Lida Shaw, I 30, 2924, 9313, IV 2111

King, Louisa Boyd Yeomans, I 1465, 9185, 16860

King, Louise Woodward, I 1892, 15871, 16942, IV 493

King, Marion P., I 4502

King, Mary, I 11483

King, Mary (Perry), I 3722, 9236, IV 1617

King, Micki, I 19020

King, Muriel, I 3806, 20228

King, Peggy, I 12046, 14690

King, Sue. See Bowen, Sue (Petigru) (King).

King, Susan, I 366

King, Susan (Petigru), I 8738

Lathbury, Mary Artemesia; Aunt May, **I** 8435, 13538, 17396

Lathbury, Sarah J. *See* Brigham, Sarah J. (Lathbury).

Lathrap, Mary Torrans; The Daniel Webster of Prohibition, **I** 8299, 17345, 19256, **II** 292

Lathrop, Clarissa Caldwell, **I** 12573, 18270, **IV** 1475

Lathrop, Dorothy Pulis, **I** 4476, 9969

Lathrop, Gertrude K., **I** 4524

Lathrop, Julia Edward Clifford, **I** 6807, 18341

Lathrop, Mary Florence, **I** 6839

Lathrop, Rose (Hawthorne); Mother Mary Alphonsa; Rose Hawthorne, **I** 4034, 8786, 15542, 17478, **II** 133

Latimer, [Mary] Elizabeth (Wormeley), **I** 2293, 5821, 7837, **III** 658, **IV** 831

Lattimore, Eleanor Frances, **I** 4659

Lauder, Maria Elise Turner, **I** 8740, **III** 525

Laufer, Beatrice, **I** 14557

Lauferty, Lilian (Wolfe); Beatrice Fairfax, **I** 9828, 11414

Laughlin, Alice Denniston, **I** 4515

Laughlin, Clara Elizabeth, **I** 9454, **IV** 603

Laughlin, Gail, **I** 1502, 6858, 21146

Laurence, Andrea Mead "Andy", **I** 19033

Laurie, Mrs., **I** 17056

Laurie, Piper, **I** 20611

Laut, Agnes Christina, **I** 6085, 9398, 11262, **III** 549

Lautz, Katherine Bardol, **I** 15489

Lavallade, Carmen de. *See* de Lavallade, Carmen.

Law, Helen Lynch, **I** 825, 11723

Law, Marjorie, **I** 19034

Law, Ruth Bancroft, **I** 17916

Law, Sallie Chapman Gordon; Mother of the Confederacy, **I** 5076, 12176

Lawler, Elsie M., **I** 12845

Lawless, Margaret H. Wynne, **I** 1358, 8626, 17441

Lawnhurst, Vee, **I** 14314

Lawrence, Andrea Mead, **I** 18864

Lawrence, Annie L., **I** 3649, 13409, **III** 390

Lawrence, Carol, **I** 2027, 14710, 20634

Lawrence, Charlotte Louise, **I** 1614

Lawrence, Florence, **I** 19968

Lawrence, Gertrude (Klassen); Gertrude Alexandra Dagma Lawrence Klassen, **I** 14166, 20149, **III** 739

Lawrence, Ida Ethel (Eckert), **I** 9213, **IV** 1943

Lawrence, Jeanette, **I** 10254, 15078

Lawrence, Josephine, **I** 9931

Lawrence, Lillian, **I** 19694

Lawrence, Margaret Morgan, **I** 13374, **III** 311

Lawrence, Margaret Oliver (Woods); Meta Lander, **I** 7703

Lawrence, Marjorie, **I** 14343, **III** 16

Lawrence, Mary Viola Tingley, **I** 11359

Lawrence, Mildred, **I** 10476

Lawrence, Mrs. *See* Wilson, Jane Delaplaine.

Lawrence, Ruth Woodhull, **I** 1488, 5617, 6058

Lawrence, Sarah Tappan Doolittle. *See* Robinson, Sarah Tappan Doolittle (Lawrence).

Laws, Annie, **I** 1402, 2682, 12675, 15567, **IV** 1931

Lawson, Deborah, **I** 4918

Lawson, Katherine Stewart, **I** 4401

Lawson, Louise, **I** 4118, 11174, 12750

Lawson, Marjorie, **I** 7313, **III** 336, **IV** 2161

Lawson, Mary J.; M. J. K.; M. J. K. L., **I** 7973, **II** 263

Lawson, Mary Lockhart, **I** 9059

Lawson, Mrs. David. *See* Ridge, Lola.

Lawson, Roberta Campbell, **I** 43, 1222, 1602, 6946, 13887, **II** 686, **III** 1052

Lawton, Elizabeth Tillinghast, **I** 2374

Lawton, Hattie, **I** 5322, 16512

Lawton, Henrietta Beebe, **I** 2528, 13551

Lawton, Sarah Alexander, **I** 5323, 5859, 8037

Lawton, Thais, **I** 3075, 19858

Lay, Julia, **I** 5324, 8038

Lay, Margaret Rebecca, **I** 10420

Laydon, Annie Burras, **I** 16050

Layton, Jessie Trunkey, **I** 17670

Layton, Olivia (Cameron) Higgins, **I** 1757

Layton-Walker, Sarah Jane. *See* Cahier, Sarah Jane Layton-Walker.

Lazarovich-Hrebelianovich, Eleanor (Calhoun), Princess, **I** 5612, 16654, 19732, **III** 1258

Lazarus, Emma, **I** 8684, 19629, **II** 371, **IV** 1501

Lazarus, Josephine, **I** 8600, 17435, **II** 370

Lazzari, Carolina Antoinette, **I** 14093

le Baron, Grace. *See* Upham, Grace le Baron (Locke).

le Boutillier, Cornelia Geer, **I** 6362

le Brun, Adele, **I** 17468

le Conte, Emma Florence, **I** 5325, 5860, 8039

le Cron, Helen Cowles, **I** 9932

le Gallienne, Eva, **I** 710, 20162, **III** 741

le Gierse, Ediyth. *See* de Treville, Yvonne.

le Grand, Julia, **I** 5326, 5861, 8040

le Grange, Ann, **I** 826, 3784

le Guin, Ursula K., **I** 10733, 12037

le Hand, Marguerite Alice, **I** 7130

le Moyne, Sarah (Cowell), **I** 19682

le Plongeon, Alice (Dixon), **I** 5972, 16615

le Porte, Annie. *See* Diggs, Annie le Porte.

le Row, Caroline Bigelow, **I** 2517, 8502, **IV** 1481

le Roy, Kitty, **I** 16568

le Valley, Laura A. Woodin, **I** 6770, **II** 298, **IV** 1512

le Vert, Octavia Celeste Walton, **I** 5086, 5791, 7657, 12183, **IV** 6

Lea, Anna M., **I** 4024

Lea, Fanny Heaslip, **I** 8147

Lea, Frank T., Mrs., **I** 17605

Leach, Abby, **I** 2683, 6575

Leach, Agnes Brown, **I** 1794, 15829

Leach, Ruth Marian, **I** 1008

Leachman, Cloris, **I** 12018, 20556

Leader, Olive Moorman, **I** 19394, 21029, **II** 241

Leahy, Agnes Berkeley, **I** 827

Lear, Evelyn, **I** 14673, **II** 500

Learned, Grace Utter, **I** 17709

Leary, Anne, **I** 15595

Lease, Mary Elizabeth (Clyens), **I** 6771, 8741, 12639, 14942, 19374, 21006, **IV** 708

Leath, Vaughn de. *See* de Leath, Vaughn.

Leaveitt, Adelia, **I** 5327, 12364

Leavenworth, Harriet, **I** 5063

Leavitt, Henrietta Swan, **I** 15949

Leavitt, Martha, **I** 11724

Leavitt, Mary Greenleaf Clement, **I** 2349, 16513, 19202

Lebel, Margaret, **I** 5675, 16690

Lederer, Charlotte, **I** 4175, 9314, **III** 887

Ledyard, Mary, **I** 4919, 15209, 16213

Lee, Alice G. *See* Haven, Alice Bradley.

Lee, Ann; Ann Lee Standerin; Mother Ann, **I** 16992, **II** 4, **III** 632, **IV** 1341

Lee, Auriol, **I** 19906

Lee, Brenda, **I** 14749

Lee, Doris Emrick, **I** 4669

Lee, Dorothy McCullough, **I** 7193

Lee, Eleanor Percy (Ware), **I** 7799

Lee, Eliza Buckminster, **I** 6522, 7477, **IV** 868

Lee, Frances Marron, **I** 1021, 7324, 16936

Lee, Gypsy Rose; Rose Louise Hovick, **I** 10613, 11938, 20410

Lee, Hannah Farnham (Sawyer), **I** 3856, 5766, 7462, **IV** 865

Lee, Hannah Ludwell, **I** 16214

Lee, Henrietta Bedinger, **I** 5328, 5862, 8041

Lee, Jeanette Barbour (Perry), **I** 2784, 9060, **IV** 1048

Lee, Judy, **I** 11983

Lee, Lila, **I** 20229

Lee, Lillie, **I** 16469

Lee, Lucy Grymes, **I** 16270

Lee, Margaret, **I** 8385, **IV** 1466

Lee, Mary Ann, **I** 1901

Lee, Mary Catherine (Jenkins), **I** 7555, **IV** 884

Lee, Mary Elizabeth, **I** 7704, **IV** 2200

Lee, Mary Randolph Custis, **I** 5079, 16420

Lee, Mary W., **I** 5329, 12365, 15374, **III** 929

Lee, Minnie Mary. *See* Wood, Julia Amanda A. (Sargent).

Lee, Muna, **I** 6619, 7110, 10090, 21309

Lee, Nelle Harper; Lee Harper, **I** 10717

Lee, Norah, **I** 14167

Lee, Peggy; Peggy Lee Barbour, **I** 1022, 14591, 20477

Lee, Rebecca, **I** 12529

Lee, Rebecca Tayloe, **I** 5002

Lee, Rosamond, **I** 828, 11725

Lee, Rose Hum, **I** 18647, **III** 598

Lee, Sarah Gould, **I** 16481

Leech, Lida Shivers, **I** 9455, 13830

Leech, Margaret Kernochan; Mrs. Ralph Pulitzer, **I** 6187, 10038, **IV** 1769

Leese, Mary Elizabeth, **I** 6792

Leete, Harriet L., **I** 12929

Legare, Mary Swinton, **I** 3880

Legedre, Anne. *See* Armstrong, Anne (Legedre).

Leggett, Mary Lydia, **I** 17486, **IV** 1018

Leginska, Ethel Liggens, **I** 14002, **III** 729

Lehman, Edith, **I** 15830

Lehman, Evangeline, **I** 14413

Lippmann, Julie Mathilde, **I** 9215, 11203, 19724, **IV** 1613

Lippner, Sally Nemerover, **I** 7168

Lipschitz, Sylvia Steinberg, **I** 7169, **II** 461

Lipscomb, Mary Ann (Rutherford), **I** 2572

Liquiens, Elizabeth May Bell Kill, **I** 4332

Lisle, Marion. *See* Savage, Minnie Stebbins.

List, Harriet Winslow, **I** 7778

Liszniewska, Marguerite Melville, **I** 3543, 14416

Litchfield, Grace Denio, **I** 8685, **II** 752, **IV** 391

Litchfield, Mary Elizabeth, **I** 8859

Litta, Marie (von Elsner), **I** 13615

Little, Ethel Holland, **I** 3748, 11484

Little, Grace Atkinson. *See* Oliver, Grace Atkinson (Little) (Ellis).

Little, Sarah F. Cowles, **I** 2438, 18240

Little, Sophia Louise (Robbins), **I** 7518, **IV** 2170

Little Jo. *See* Monoghan, Josephine.

Little Mo. *See* Brinker, Maureen Connolly.

Little Nell. *See* Dauvray, Helen.

Little Standing Spruce. *See* Hardin, Helen.

Littledale, Clara Savage, **I** 9970, 11531

Littlefield, Catherine, **I** 1962

Littleton, Martin N., Mrs., **I** 6096

Liuzzo, Viola Gregg, **I** 1258

Livermore, Harriet, **I** 7478, 17035

Livermore, Mary Ashton (Rice), **I** 1140, 5123, 7800, 12219, 18186, 19165, 20794, **II** 1080, **IV** 922

Livermore, Sarah White, **I** 7484

Livingston, Bell; Isabelle Hutchins, **I** 499

Livingston, Christina Ten Broeck, **I** 4920

Livingston, Clara E., **I** 17988

Livingston, Margaret Beekman, **I** 4792

Livingston, Margaret Vere (Farrington), **I** 9186, **II** 768, **IV** 817

Livingston, Nora Gertrude, **I** 12607

Livingston, Susan, **I** 4921, 16215

Livingston, Susannah French, **I** 4865

Livingstone, Belle, **I** 9527, 16679, 19827

Livingstone, Mabel, **I** 10719

Livingstone, Mary, **I** 11888

Livingstone, Mary Moffat, **I** 17212, 15128

Lloyd, Alice C., **I** 1741, 3280, **IV** 1164

Lloyd, Alice Spencer Geddes, **I** 3037

Lloyd, Caroline Alma, **I** 4293, **IV** 144

Lloyd, Chris Evert. *See* Evert, Christine Marie.

Lloyd, Lola Maverick, **I** 15165, 21205

Lloyd, Martha. *See* Boswell, Martha.

Lobdell, Avis, **I** 835, 11728, 17989

Locke, Bessie, **I** 1480, 2877

Locke, Jane Ermina (Starkweather), **I** 7623, **IV** 901

Locke, Rowell, Mrs., **I** 17050

Locke, Una. *See* Bailey, Urania Locke (Stoughton).

Lockhart, June, **I** 12008

Lockrey, Sarah Hunt, **I** 12770, 21111

Lockridge, Frances Louise Davis, **I** 10107

Lockwood, Belva Ann Bennett McNall, **I** 6693, 15128, 20851

Lockwood, Charlotte, **I** 3544, 14417

Lockwood, Mary Smith, **I** 1300, 3918, 5505, 8104, 10902

Loeb, Sophia Irene Simon, **I** 6902, 9481, 11282, 18477, **III** 1183, **IV** 1668

Loeber, L. Elsa, **I** 3393, 6227

Loehrke, Leah Marie, **I** 3613, 13380, **II** 523, **IV** 1969

Loepke, Grace Marschal. *See* Marschal-Loepke, Grace.

Loftus, Mare Cecilia "Cissie", **I** 19840, **III** 1248

Logan, Adelle Hunt, **I** 2843, **III** 146

Logan, Celia (Kellog) (Connelly), **I** 8264, 10931, 19594, **IV** 379

Logan, Charlotte, **I** 836, 3785, 4593

Logan, Deborah Norris, **I** 5761, **IV** 2014

Logan, Eliza, **I** 19556

Logan, Ella, **I** 14526, 20399, **III** 1256

Logan, Jacqueline, **I** 20025

Logan, John A., Mrs., **I** 9061, 11153

Logan, Josephine Hancock, **I** 4129, 9145, 15611, **IV** 578

Logan, Laura R., **I** 3242, 13097

Logan, Martha Daniell, **I** 2152, 12132, 16793

Logan, Mary Simmerson Cunningham, **I** 6712, 8303, 10945, 16555

Logan, Olive, **I** 8339, 10954, 14873, 19601, 20909

Logan, Sallie, **I** 1391

Logan, Virginia Knight, **I** 8742, 13580

Logasa, Hannah, **I** 6208, 10128

Lohman, Ann Trow, **I** 12187

Loloma, Otellie Sequafenema, **I** 4745, **III** 1102

Lomady, Clara Schroth, **I** 19036

Lombard, Carole; Jane Alice Peters, **I** 20335

Lombard, Helen Carusi, **I** 10421, 11852

Lombardo, Jean Lee, **I** 19037

London, Julie, **I** 14649

Long, Ellen Call, **I** 252, 1289, 7902, 16813, **IV** 427

Long, Elsie, **I** 9651, 13923

Long, Emma J. Wotton de. *See* de Long, Emma J. Wotton.

Long, Lois, **I** 3808, 11808

Long, Margaret, **I** 12888, **IV** 289

Long, Mary M'Kinney, **I** 4922

Long, Rose McConnell, **I** 7079

Long, Tania, **I** 11925, **III** 759, 877

Longfellow, Margaret Bigelow, **I** 17834

Longman, Evelyn [Mary] Beatrice; Mrs. Nathanial Horton Batchelder, **I** 4279

Longmire, Mrs., **I** 16470

Longshore, Hannah E. Myers, **I** 12215

Longyear, Mary Hawley Beecher, **I** 8787, 15543, **II** 240

Look, Lilly Chin, **I** 16673, **III** 596

Loomis, Mary A., **I** 5330, 12366

Loop, Jennette Shepherd (Harrison), **I** 3952, **IV** 1467

Loos, Anita, **I** 10040, 20085

Lopez, Nancy, **I** 18921, **III** 1021

Lord, Eleanor Louise, **I** 2785

Lord, Elizabeth W. Russell, **I** 2277, 15290, 18184

Lord, Isabel Ely, **I** 2118, 6228

Lord, Mary Stimson Pillsbury, **I** 7226, 15852, 18648

Lord, Pauline, **I** 20026

Lorenz, Ellen Jane, **I** 3496, 11873, 14333

Lorimer, Mrs. Frank W. *See* Williams, Faith Moors.

Loring, Emilie Baker; Josephine Story, **I** 10327

Lorini, Virginia (Whiting), **I** 13721, **III** 606

Lorne, Marion (MacDougall), **I** 11430, 19987

Lorraine, Lillian, **I** 20067

Losch, Tilly, **I** 1966, 20292, **III** 36

Lothrop, Alice Louise Higgins, **I** 18439

Lothrop, Amy. *See* Warner, Anna Bartlett.

Lothrop, Harriett Mulford (Stone); Margaret Sydney, **I** 8531, **IV** 992

Lotz, Matilda, **I** 4216

Loucheim, Katie Scofield, **I** 7221

Louchheim, Aline Milton Bernstein. *See* Saarinen, Aline Milton Bernstein (Louchheim).

Loud, Annie Frances, **I** 13557

Loud, Hulda Barker, **I** 331, 6410, 11000, 14913, 20958

Loud, Marguerite St. Leon (Barstow), **I** 7556, **IV** 2024

Loud, Mary Hallowell, **I** 4102

Louden, Isabelle. *See* Langner, Armina Marshall.

Loufek, Betty, **I** 18060

Lough, Orpha Maust, **I** 13304

Loughborough, Mary Ann Webster, **I** 5533, 5902, 8234, **IV** 41

Loughbridge, Mary, **I** 17086

Loughead, Flora (Haines), **I** 8885, 11107, **IV** 93

Loughlin, Mary, **I** 837, 11729

Louis, Minnie Dessau, **I** 2350, 17277, 18208, **II** 367, **IV** 1413

Louise, Anita, **I** 20442, **IV** 247

Louise, Sister. *See* Schriek, Louise van der.

Louise, Tina, **I** 20636

Lounsberry, Allice, **I** 7557, 12166, **IV** 1357

Love, Mary, **I** 5331, 16514

Love, Nancy, **I** 18079

Lovejoy, Esther Clayson Pohl, **I** 1512, 5624, 6865, 12824, 21156, **II** 784, **IV** 1996

Lovejoy, Julia, **I** 16359

Loveman, Amy, **I** 9695, 11360

Loveridge, Emily L., **I** 12732

Low, Esther, **I** 209

Low, Juliette Magill Kinzie (Gordon), **I** 1435, **II** 759

Low, Mary Fairchild, **I** 4076

Lowden, Florence Pullman, **I** 15654

Lowe, Corinne Martin, **I** 3739, 9717, 11370

Lowe, Lucy, **I** 5332, 5863, 8042

Lowe, Martha Ann (Perry), **I** 7878, 19170, 20811, **IV** 934

Lowe, Ruth, **I** 10614, 14541

Lowell, Amy, **I** 6105, 9482, 11283, 15013

Lowell, Anna, **I** 5333

Lowell, Anna Cabot (Jackson), **I** 2245, 3705, 7672

Lowell, Ettie Lois; Mrs. George Fl., **I** 473, 13775, 21157, **IV** 1081

Lowell, Josephine (Shaw), **I** 6409, 8503, 15494, 16759, 18275, **IV** 1482

Lowell, Maria (White), **I** 7825

Lowell, Susan R., **I** 5334, 12367

MacLeod, Dorothy Shaw, **I** 17757, 18629
MacMahon, Aline, **I** 20163
MacManus Mansfield, Blanche, **I** 4217
MacMillan, Violet, **I** 20086
MacMonnies, Mary Fairchild, **I** 4104
MacMullen, Frances A., **I** 3787, **III** 578
MacNeil, Carol Brooks, **I** 4247
MacNeil, Marie Stevens Hicks, **I** 5676, 15779
Macomber, Eleanor, **I** 17097
Macomber, Mary Lizzie, **I** 4120, **IV** 1059
Maconaquah. *See* Slocum, Frances.
MacRae, Emma Fordyce; Mrs. Homer F. Swift, **I** 4355
MacUrm, Adeline, **I** 6229
MacVay, Anna Pearl, **I** 3395
Macy, Anne Sullivan. *See* Sullivan, Anne.
Macy, Icie Gertrude; Mrs. Bert Raymon Hoobler, **I** 13130, **II** 713, **IV** 1162
Macy, Margaret, **I** 840, 11732
Mad Anne. *See* Bailey, Ann.
Madaket Millie. *See* Jewett, Mildred.
Madden, Lotta, **I** 14418
Madden, Mary Anne. *See* Sadlier, Mary Anne (Madden).
Madeira, Jean (Browning), **I** 14575
Madelva, Mary Eveline Wolff, Sister, **I** 3197, 6165, 9829, 17686, **II** 185
Madelva, Sister. *See* Wolff, Mary Evaline.
Madern, Minnie. *See* Fiske, Mary Augusta (Davey).
Madison, Helene, **I** 18816
Madison, Luch (Foster), **I** 6052, 9238, **IV** 1619
Madison, Marta, **I** 10257, 20196
Madison, Virginia. *See* Putnam, Sarah A. Brock.
Maeder, Clara (Fisher), **I** 19520
Maertz, Louisa, **I** 5337, 12370
Magee, Elizabeth Stewart, **I** 6476, 18573
Magill, Mary Tucker, **I** 2375, 8124, 10906, **IV** 2316
Magna, Edith Scott, **I** 1684, 5667, **II** 335, **IV** 1112
Magnes, Frances, **I** 14613, **II** 495
Magnussen, Karen D., **I** 18916
Magoffin, Susan Shelby, **I** 16471
Magonigle, Edith Marian Day, **I** 4319
Magoon, Mary E., **I** 6694
Magoun, Martha Roberts (Mann), **I** 2808, 12751
Magruder, Julia, **I** 8860

Maher, Aldea, **I** 13131, **II** 198, **IV** 783
Maher, Frances, **I** 1691, 17676, **II** 179
Mahnkey, Mary Elizabeth, **I** 11733
Mahoney, Mary, **I** 11487
Mahoney, Mary Elizabeth "Eliza", **I** 12595, **III** 121
Maier, Mrs. Herbert C. *See* Baldwin, Janet Sterling.
Main, Charlotte Emerson, **I** 1436
Main, Marjorie; Ma Kettle, **I** 20028
Mainor, Dorothy. *See* Maynor, Dorothy.
Maish, Jennie Gauslin, **I** 5338, 12371
Makarova, Natalia, **I** 2032, **III** 1230
Makemsen, Maud Worcester, **I** 15973
Malbin, Elaine, **I** 14695
Maley, Florence Turner, **I** 14658
Malia Rosa. *See* Breen, May Sighi.
Malibran, Maria Felecia, **I** 13457
Malintzin. *See* Marian Malintzin.
Mallette, Dorothy, **I** 3697, 18144
Malloch, Elizabeth, **I** 20197
Mallon, Isabel Allardice (Sloan); Ruth Ashmore, **I** 3721, 9146
Mallon, Winifred, **I** 11314
Mallone, Annie M. Turnbo; Annie Turnbo-Mallone, **I** 478, 15666, **III** 170
Mallory, Ann Margrethe Bjurstedt "Molla", **I** 18758, **III** 1135
Mallory, Arenia Cornelia, **I** 3504, **III** 278
Mallory, Lucy A., **I** 1197, 2556, 11013, **IV** 1988
Malloy, Louise [Marie]; Josh Wink, **I** 11607
Malsin, Mrs. Albert. *See* Bryant, Lane
Maltby, Esther Stark, **I** 7054, 16907
Maltby, Margaret E., **I** 15942
Mammy Kate, **I** 4923, 16216
Mance, Jeanne, **I** 12120, 15205, **III** 816
Manchester, Albertine, **I** 19574
Manchester, Virginia, **I** 17879
Mandel, Carola Panerai, **I** 19039, **III** 609
Mandigo, Pauline Eggleston, **I** 6482, 7080, 11544, 21299
Mandola, Carol M., **I** 10258, 15079, 17758
Maneck, Margaret Brown, **I** 841
Manigault, Ann, **I** 5753, 7418
Manigault, Judith Giton Royer, **I** 16107, 16789

Mankiewicz, Rose Stradner, **I** 20400, **III** 42
Mankin, Helen Douglas, **I** 7100
Mankin, Widow, **I** 12131
Manley, Fanny Louisa, **I** 2714, 6009, 8944
Manley, Marian C., **I** 6184
Mann, Clara Lipman, **I** 10350, 20249
Mann, Elizabeth, **I** 940
Mann, Erika, **I** 6257, 10422, 15097, 20294, **III** 874
Mann, Harriet. *See* Miller, Harriet (Mann).
Mann, Helen, **I** 16030
Mann, Kristine, **I** 6445, 12889, 21193
Mann, Maria R., **I** 2352, 5339, 15375
Mann, Marty, **I** 13321, 18649, **II** 891
Mann, Mary Tyler (Peabody), **I** 2232, 7633
Mann, Pamela, **I** 16393
Mann, Rowena Morse, **I** 17594
Mann, Shelley, **I** 19040
Manna-Zucca, Madame. *See* Zucca, Mana.
Manner, Jane; Jennie Mannheimer, **I** 3272, 20087
Mannering, Mary; Florence Friend, **I** 19841, **III** 717
Manners, Mrs. *See* Richards, Cornelia Holroyd (Bradley).
Mannes, Clara Domrosch, **I** 2934, 13777, **II** 515, **III** 843
Mannes, Mary, **I** 10396, 11840
Manney, Henrietta Remsen Meserole. *See* Westley, Helen.
Mannheimer, Jennie. *See* Manner, Jane.
Manning, Jessie Wilson, **I** 8886, 14956, 19410, **IV** 684
Manning, Kathleen Lockhart, **I** 14071
Manning, Leah Hicks, **I** 18680, **III** 1103
Manning, Madeline Johnson, **I** 19041
Manning, Marie, **I** 11275
Manning, Mary Margaret Fryer, **I** 1421
Manning, Rosalie H., **I** 4356
Mannix, Mary Ellen Walsh, **I** 8602
Mannon, Mary L., **I** 5574, 12582
Mansfield, Arabella A., **I** 6822
Mansfield, Blanche (McManus), **I** 7560
Mansfield, Jayne; Vera Jayne Palmer, **I** 20623
Manski, Dorothee, **I** 14138, **II** 449, **III** 859
Manski, Inge, **I** 14527, **II** 485, **III** 878
Manter, Parnel, **I** 4924, 16217
Manville, Helen Adelia (Wood) "Nellie", **I** 8340, **IV** 2376
Manville, Henrietta Estelle, **I** 15724, 16884, **IV** 1699

Marble, Alice, **I** 18817
Marble, Anna, **I** 11254
Marble, Anna Warren, **I** 19526
Marble, Annie Russel, **I** 9216, **IV** 1071
Marble, Callie Bonney, **I** 8744, **IV** 550
Marble, Ella M. S., **I** 2605, 3713, 11058, 19375, 21007
Marbury, Elizabeth, **I** 391, 8909, 19668
Marcci, Carmelia, **I** 1982
Marcel, Lucille Wasself, **I** 14015
Marchant, Mabel, **I** 17885
Marcia. *See* Robertson, Georgia Trowbridge.
Marcial-Dorado, Caroline, **I** 3224, **III** 1265
Marco, Renee de. *See* de Marco, Renee.
Margareten, Regina, **I** 439, **IV** 1601
Marguerittes, Julia de. *See* Rea, Julia (de Marguerittes) (Foster).
Maria de l'Incarnation, Mother. *See* l'Incarnation, Maria de.
Maria Gratia, Mother, **I** 13098, 17710, **II** 194
Marian, Malintzin, **I** 6631
Marianne, Sister, **I** 12846, 17595, **II** 153
Marianne of Jesus. *See* Gurney, Marion Francis.
Marie de Tranchepain de Saint Augustine, Sister. *See* Tranchepain de Saint Augustine, Marie de.
Marie-Madeleine, Sister. *See* Hachard, Marie-Madeliene.
Mario, Queen Tillotson, **I** 14147
Marion, Elizabeth, **I** 10642
Marion, Frances, **I** 9861, 19988, **IV** 176
Marion, Mary Vidaue, **I** 16303
Marisol (Escobar), **I** 4746, **III** 1297
Mark, Joyce, **I** 1073, 18145
Mark, Nellie V., **I** 12691, 19420, 21062
Marker, Dorothy, **I** 19042
Marks, Jane, **I** 16403
Marks, Jeannette Augustus, **I** 3017, 6917, 9528
Marks, Mrs. Lionel S. *See* Peabody, Josephine Preston.
Markscheffel, Louise, **I** 11124, **IV** 1934
Marlatt, Aby Lillian, **I** 2080
Marlatt, Frances Knoche, **I** 7170, 11734
Marlatt, Jeanne Steele, **I** 10259
Marlett, Melba Balmat Grimes, **I** 10513
Marley, Anne Augusta Bonner, **I** 9760, 13984, **II** 250
Marlow, Sylvia, **I** 14344, **II** 478
Marlowe, Helen, **I** 5694, 18772

Marlowe, Julia; Sarah Frances "Fannie" Frost, **I** 19733, **III** 707

Marmorston, Jessie, **I** 13253, **III** 1209

Marohn, Irma Elaine, **I** 4594

Marot, Helen, **I** 6431, **II** 1035

Marquardt, Alexandria, **I** 13739, **III** 1179

Marr, Carmell Carrington, **I** 7335, **III** 358

Marr, Frances Harrison, **I** 8203

Marr, Jane Barron Hope, **I** 6021, 9015

Marriott, Alice Lee, **I** 70

Marriott, Elizabeth, **I** 123

Mars, Ethel Veronica, **I** 589, **IV** 619

Marsalis, Frances Harrell, **I** 17991

Marschal-Loepke, Grace, **I** 14419

Marsh, Alice Randall, **I** 4595

Marsh, Caroline Crane, **I** 5805, 6539, 7738

Marsh, Ellen, **I** 10697

Marsh, Lucille, **I** 1950, 3396

Marsh, Lucille Crews, **I** 14029

Marsh, M. M., Mrs., **I** 5340, 15376

Marsh, Mae, **I** 20122

Marsh, Mrs. John Robert. *See* Mitchell, Margaret Munnerlyn.

Marshal, Sarah Catharine, **I** 10616

Marshall, Bernice C., **I** 1720

Marshall, Caroline Louise (Kinsbury), **I** 8687, **IV** 680

Marshall, Christopher, Mrs., **I** 4925, 16218

Marshall, Clara, **I** 348, 2573, 12616

Marshall, Elizabeth, **I** 203, 12150

Marshall, Ethel, **I** 19043

Marshall, Florence M., **I** 2955

Marshall, Harriet Gibbs, **I** 2935, 13778, **III** 163

Marshall, Joanna, **I** 7839, **IV** 832

Marshall, Lenore Guinzburg, **I** 1759, 7123, 10129, 15190

Marshall, Marguerite Moers, **I** 9830, 11415

Marshall, Mary, **I** 19044

Marshall, Nancy Stinnett, **I** 16384

Marshall, Nelly Nichol, **I** 8532

Marshall, Nina (Caroline) Lovering, **I** 2809, **IV** 1588

Marshall, Patricia Gibson, **I** 18872

Marshall, Paule, **I** 10734, **III** 408

Marshall, Penny [Carole], **I** 12092

Marshall, Rosamond van der Zee, **I** 10260

Martha, **I** 6643, **III** 1029, **IV** 300

Martin, Allie Beth (Dent), **I** 1858, 6291

Martin, Angie Starr, **I** 19411

Martin, Anna Henrietta, **I** 6918, 9529, 15166, 18489, 21206, **IV** 1257

Martin, Elizabeth Gilbert, **I** 6561, 8265

Martin, Elizabeth Marshall, **I** 4926, 16219

Martin, Elizabeth Price, **I** 1472, **IV** 2107

Martin, Ellis. *See* Ryan, Marah Ellis (Martin).

Martin, George Madden. *See* Martin, Georgia May.

Martin, Georgia May; George Madden Martin, **I** 1210, 9272, **II** 775

Martin, Gertrude, **I** 3112

Martin, Grace, **I** 4927, 16220

Martin, Helen Frances Theresa, **I** 16932

Martin, Helen Reimensynder, **I** 9315

Martin, Jackie [Cecelia], **I** 15897

Martin, Jane (Percy), **I** 8627, **IV** 1989

Martin, Julia M., **I** 3641, 13406, **III** 381

Martin, Lillian Jane, **I** 2620, 12649, 18309, 21016

Martin, Mabel Agnes; Mrs. Harry N. Totten, **I** 12987, **II** 825, **IV** 1715

Martin, Margaret Maxwell, **I** 2233, 7637, **IV** 2198

Martin, Maria, **I** 3864, 12160

Martin, Mary, **I** 11926, 14528, 20401

Martin, Mrs., **I** 17895, **III** 714

Martin, Myra Belle, **I** 427, 2810

Martin, Rachel; Rachel Clay, **I** 4928, 16221

Martin, Sarah J., **I** 1328

Martin, Sarah Towne (Smith); Sarah Martyn, **I** 1101, 5783, 7624, 10833, 17117, 19147, **IV** 1367

Martin, Sylvia Wene, **I** 19045

Martin, Victoria. *See* Woodhull, Victoria Claflin.

Martinez, Alicia Ernestina de la Caridad del Cobre. *See* Alonso, Alicia.

Martinez, Maria Cadilla de. *See* Cadilla de Martinez, Maria.

Martinez, Maria Montoya, **I** 4370, **III** 1053, **IV** 1334

Martinez, Mescal, **I** 14682, **III** 1104

Martinot, Sarah Frances Marie "Sadie", **I** 19703

Martorella, Mildred, **I** 19046

Martyn, Marguerite, **I** 11735

Martyn, Sarah. *See* Martin, Sarah Towne (Smith).

Marvel, Louise; Cattle Lady, **I** 16938

Marvin, Adelaide Camilla Hoffman, **I** 1592, **II** 326, **IV** 1689

Marwedel, Emma Jacobina Christiana, **I** 2272

Mary, Mother. *See* Rhodes, Mary.

Mary Agnes, **I** 17596, **II** 154

Mary Alma, Sister, **I** 13421, 17825, **II** 227

Mary Aloysia, Mother. *See* Hardey, Mary Aloysia Hawley.

Mary Alphonsa, Mother. *See* Lathrop, Rose (Hawthorne).

Mary Aquinas, Sister, **I** 17814, 18090, **II** 222

Mary Baptist, Mother. *See* Russell, Mary Baptist.

Mary Benedict, Sister, **I** 13422, 17826, **II** 228

Mary Bridget, Mother. *See* Hayden, Mary Bridget.

Mary Consolata, Sister. *See* Carroll, Consolata.

Mary de Sales, Mother; Wilhelmina Tredow, **I** 3113, 17646, **II** 169

Mary Dolores, Sister. *See* van Rensselaer, Euphemia.

Mary Eveline, Sister. *See* Madelva, Mary Eveline Wolff.

Mary Frances Clare, Sister. *See* Cusack, Margaret Anne.

Mary Ignatius, Sister. *See* Feeney, Mary Ignatius.

Mary Joseph, Mother. *See* Rogers, Mary Josephine.

Mary Joseph, Sister. *See* Dempsey, Mary Joseph.

Mary Julia, Sister; Elizabeth Ann Dullea, **I** 3181, 17677, **II** 180

Mary Katharine, Mother. *See* Drexel, Katharine Mary.

Mary Loyola, Sister, **I** 16436, 17148, **II** 91

Mary Madalene, Sister; Sarah C. Cox, **I** 6608, 17647, **II** 170

Mary Maurice, Mother. *See* Tobin, Mary.

Mary of St. Angela, Mother. *See* Gillespie, Eliza Maria.

Mary of the Heart of Jesus, Mother. *See* Dunne, Sarah Theresa.

Mary of the Infant Jesus, Sister, **I** 16516, 17279, **II** 111

Mary Patricia, Sister. *See* Garvey, Mary Patricia.

Mary Pius, Sister. *See* Neenan, Mary Pius.

Masha. *See* Stern, Mary Simchow.

Masland, Mary Elizabeth, **I** 3114

Mason, Agnes Louisa (Carter), **I** 7561, **IV** 1298

Mason, Amelia (Gere), **I** 5926, 8386, 20920, **IV** 526

Mason, Biddy, **I** 12220

Mason, Caroline Atherton (Briggs), **I** 7851, **IV** 929

Mason, Caroline Atwater, **I** 8826, **IV** 1522

Mason, Clara, **I** 4596

Mason, Clara Stevens Arthur, **I** 8533

Mason, Edith Barnes, **I** 14122

Mason, Emily Virginia, **I** 2255, 5103, 5801, 7727, 12199

Mason, Harriet Lawrence, **I** 1455, 9147

Mason, Lena, **I** 17563, **II** 587, **III** 149

Mason, Lucy Randolph, **I** 572, 1656, 6464, 11371, 18545, 21249, **II** 828, **IV** 2343

Mason, Marsha, **I** 12093, 20678

Mason, Mary Augusta, **I** 9122

Mason, Mary Knight, **I** 13622

Mason, Maud M., **I** 1493, 4169

Mason, Mrs., **I** 16315

Massee, May, **I** 9697, 11361

Massey, Edna Hogner, **I** 1053, 4747, **III** 1105

Massey, Ilona, **I** 20387, **III** 901

Massow, Frederica Charlotte Louisa. *See* Riedesel, Frederica Charlotte Louisa Massow.

Masters, Sybilla, **I** 108

Mathebat, Ruth Harriet, **I** 1838

Mather, Elizabeth Ring Ireland, **I** 15795, 16908, **IV** 1964

Mather, Flora Stone, **I** 15549, **IV** 1927

Mather, Margaret, **I** 19683, **III** 532

Mather, Margaret Morgan (Herbert), **I** 8387, 18689

Mather, Sarah Ann, **I** 1141, 2280, 7801, 15298, **IV** 2202

Mather, Winifred Holt, **I** 3000, 4280, 9484, 15691, 18478, **II** 798

Mathews, Blanche Dingley, **I** 3136, 9719, 13962

Mathews, Joanna Hooe, **I** 8688, 17457

Mathews, Julia A., **I** 8044, 17280

Mathews, Mary. *See* Adams, Mary (Mathews).

Mathias, Mildred E., **I** 13332

Matthews, Adelaide, **I** 9807, 19969

Matthews, Anne, **I** 142

Matthews, Burnita Shelton, **I** 7101

Matthews, Frances Aymar, **I** 9654, 19891, **IV** 1709

Matthews, Honor, **I** 17886

Matthews, Rebecca, **I** 17872

Matthews, Victoria Earle, **I** 1448, 18370, **III** 142, **IV** 468

Mills, Susan Carrie, **I** 5357, 12381

Mills, Susan Lincoln Tolman, **I** 2314, 17245

Mills, Vicki, **I** 12063, 14711

Milne, Frances Margaret, **I** 6754, 8603, 11014, **III** 935, **IV** 80

Milton, Inez Lopez Seymour, **I** 9579, 13875, **II** 810

Mimieux, Yvette, **I** 20672

Mims, Sue Harper, **I** 17405, **II** 238, **IV** 454

Minelli, Liza May, **I** 14760, 20703

Miner, Alice Trainer, **I** 12771, 15620, **II** 660, **III** 538, **IV** 1603

Miner, Dorothy Eugenia, **I** 4660, 6250

Miner, Jean Pond, **I** 4160, **IV** 591, 2396

Miner, Myrtilla, **I** 1123, 2256, 15273

Miner, Sarah Luella, **I** 2811, 17542, **II** 307

Minis, Abigail, **I** 122, 16792, **II** 362

Minister's Wife, A. *See* Beecher, Eunice White (Bullard).

Miniter, Edith Dowe, **I** 11237

Mink, Patsy Takemoto, **I** 7356, **III** 991

Mink, Sarah C., **I** 1353

Minnie, **I** 16666

Minnigerode, Lucy, **I** 12863, 18448

Minoka Hill, Lillia Rosa, **I** 12918

Minor, Anne Rogers, **I** 1473, 5610

Minor, Jane, **I** 1082, 12155, **III** 65

Minor, Virginia Louisa, **I** 5137, 15319, 20813, **IV** 1200

Minot, Fannie E., **I** 1367

Minter, Desire, **I** 16053, **II** 923

Minter, Mary Miles, **I** 20251

Mintzer, Ida Jessica, **I** 13143, **II** 445, **IV** 1771

Miranda, Carmen; Maria de Carmo da Cunha, **I** 14351, **III** 494, 1166

Mirenburg, Mary, **I** 7173

Miriam Michael, Sister, **I** 13358, 17790, **II** 215

Misch, Caeser, Mrs., **I** 9658, 15028, 17649

Mistrot, Ethel Reed, **I** 853

Mitale, Mari. *See* Lussi, Marie.

Mitchell, Abbie, **I** 13986, 19941, **III** 201

Mitchell, Annie Maria, **I** 8628, 17442

Mitchell, Ellen E., **I** 5358, 12382

Mitchell, Elsie R., **I** 13100

Mitchell, Esther (Wilson), **I** 20265

Mitchell, Hattie Poley, **I** 17713

Mitchell, Joni; Roberta Joan Anderson, **I** 14746, **IV** 268

Mitchell, Lucy Myers Wright, **I** 12, 3985, 5945, 8570

Mitchell, Lucy Sprague, **I** 1223, 3078, 9605, **IV** 1701

Mitchell, Margaret Julia "Maggie", **I** 19575

Mitchell, Margaret Munnerlyn; Mrs. John Robert Marsh, **I** 10264, **IV** 487

Mitchell, Maria, **I** 2194, 7491, 15909, 20722, **II** 994, **IV** 873

Mitchell, Marion Juliet, **I** 8236, **IV** 1441

Mitchell, Martha Reed, **I** 3888, 15286, 16457

Mitchell, Maxine, **I** 19056

Mitchell, Milley Benett, **I** 11492

Mitchell, Nellie Brown, **I** 2546, 13555, **III** 122, **IV** 1279

Mitchell, Ruth Comfort; Mrs. Sanborn Young, **I** 1657, 6982, 9722, **IV** 161

Mitchell, Viola, **I** 14506

Mitchell-Bateman, Mildred, **I** 13405, **III** 368

Mitford, Jessica Lucy, **I** 10650, 11961, **III** 762

Mix, Josephine P. Dexter, **I** 12516

Miyakawa, Kikuko, **I** 4600, 10265, **III** 987

Moats, Alice-Leone, **I** 10543, 11899

Mobley, Eleanor Smith, **I** 1835, **II** 899

Mock, Alice, **I** 14072

Modave, Jeanne, **I** 13843

Modell, Merriam; Evelyn Piper, **I** 10499

Modjeska, Helena, **I** 19605, **III** 1143

Moffo, Anna, **I** 14714

Moina. *See* Dinnies, Anna Peyre (Shackelford).

Moir, Phyllis, **I** 10266, 11744, 15082, **III** 746

Moisant, Mathilde, **I** 17903

Moise, Penina, **I** 7510, 13447, 17072, **II** 364, **IV** 2197

Molineux, Maria Ada, **I** 9065, 12735

Molloy, Emma, **I** 293, 10955, 18247

Molloy, Mary Aloysia, **I** 3115, 9659, 17650, **II** 171

Monasterio, Lillian, **I** 3399, 17994

Monath, Hortense, **I** 14297

Mondale, Joan (Adams), **I** 4748, 6310, 7368

Monmouth, L. N., Mrs., **I** 369

Monoghan, Josephine; Little Jo, **I** 384, 16620, 16845

Monroe, Anne Shannon, **I** 6106, 9487, 15014, 16674, 18712, 21197, **IV** 1998

Monroe, Harriet, **I** 9066, 11155, **IV** 573

Monroe, Harriet Earhart, **I** 2512, 10991, 14904, **IV** 386, 703

Monroe, Lucy, **I** 14334

Monroe, Marilyn, **I** 20558

Montague, Margaret Prescott; Jane Stege, **I** 9606, 17635

Montana, Patsy, **I** 10618, 14543

Montez, Maria "Lola" Dolores Eliza Rosanna Gilbert Porris y; Marie Dolores Eliza Rosanna Gilbert; Countess of Landsfeld, **I** 1898, 16458, **III** 917

Montgomery, Carrie Frances Judd, **I** 8979, 17522, 18342, 19425, **IV** 99, 1561

Montgomery, Elizabeth, **I** 12055

Montgomery, Elizabeth Rider, **I** 10351

Montgomery, Helen Barrett, **I** 1449, 6584, 9123, 17543, **II** 38

Montgomery, Helen Marie, **I** 18076

Montgomery, Janet Livingston, **I** 16376

Montgomery, Lucy Maud, **I** 9488, **III** 551

Montgomery, Peggy; Baby Peggy, **I** 20467

Montgomery, Roselle Mercier, **I** 9489, **II** 677

Montgomery, Ruth Shick, **I** 11914

Montgomery, Tammy. *See* Terrell, Tammi.

Monti-Gorsey, Lola, **I** 14226, **III** 979

Montour, Catherine, Madame, **I** 6514, 6642

Montour, Esther, **I** 6655, **III** 1034

Montross, Lois Seyster, **I** 10130

Monture, Ethel Brant, **I** 77, 10745, **III** 1106

Mood, Julia. *See* Peterkin, Julia (Mood).

Moody, Deborah, Lady, **I** 6634, **IV** 1337

Moody, Emma Revell, **I** 17406

Moody, Helen (Waterson), **I** 2759, 9017, 11137, **IV** 1572, 1936

Moody, Helen (Wills). *See* Roark, Helen (Wills) (Moody).

Moody, Mary Blair, **I** 12517

Moon, Bessie Huntington, **I** 17598

Moon, Charlotte, **I** 5156, 16490

Moon, Lottie Diggs; Lottie Clark, **I** 17374, **II** 25

Moon, Virginia, **I** 5583, 16593

Mooney, Hannah Gaunt, **I** 4934

Moor, Anne, **I** 3400, 13256, 20203

Moor, Eunice Farnsworth, **I** 16174

Moore, Alice Rogers, **I** 8945, 12692

Moore, Alice Ruth Dunbar. *See* Nelson, Alice Ruth Dunbar (Moore).

Moore, Alma Chesnut, **I** 11745

Moore, Anne Carrol, **I** 6086, 9400

Moore, Annie Aubertine (Woodward); Aubertine Forestier, **I** 5931, 6567, 8439, 10982, 13539, 14898

Moore, Beatrice "Melba", **I** 12098, 14753, 20695, **III** 478

Moore, Catherine L., **I** 10569

Moore, Clara Sophia (Jessup); Clara Moreton; Clara Sophia (Jessup) Bloomfield-Moore, **I** 5138, 7881, 15320, **IV** 2042

Moore, Colleen, **I** 20252

Moore, Elisabeth Luce, **I** 18644

Moore, Elizabeth Evelyn, **I** 9973, 14096

Moore, Elizabeth Finley, **I** 6193, **II** 867, **IV** 2216

Moore, Elizabeth H., **I** 18717

Moore, Ella Maude, **I** 13566, 17459

Moore, Emmeline, **I** 1546, 12876, 16875

Moore, Eva Perry, **I** 1389, 15140

Moore, Grace; Mrs. Valentine Parera, **I** 11615, 14170, 20152

Moore, Helen, **I** 18377

Moore, Henrietta G., **I** 17470, 19376, **IV** 1926

Moore, Huldah Traxler, **I** 16570

Moore, Idora McClellan (Plowman), **I** 8504, **IV** 17

Moore, Jane Boswell, **I** 5359, 15378

Moore, Jeanne W. G., **I** 14227, 17760

Moore, Jenny, **I** 10704, 18673

Moore, Joan W., **I** 76, 3659, 10735, 18676

Moore, Kate, **I** 15300, 16472

Moore, Lillian, **I** 1983, 3591, 6282, 11915

Moore, Lizzie, **I** 2518

Moore, Luella Lockwood, **I** 3546, 14424

Moore, Marguerite, **I** 5593, 14932, 15138, **III** 936

Moore, Marianne (Craig), **I** 9832, 11417, **II** 706, **IV** 1743

Moore, Martha Gallison. *See* Avery, Martha Gallison Moore.

Moore, Mary, **I** 14228, 16374

Moore, Mary Carr, **I** 13831

Moore, Mary E., **I** 4460

Moore, Mary Evelyn. *See* Davis, Mary Evelyn (Moore).

Moore, Mary Tyler, **I** 12076, 20653, **II** 231, **IV** 265

Moore, Maude. *See* Crawford, Mrs. John.

Moore, Ruth, **I** 10375

Moore, Sarah Wool, I 3996, 11015, IV 1233

Moore, Susan Teakle (Smith), I 7566, IV 1361

Moore, Susanne Bandegrift, I 349, 11032, IV 1209

Moore, Terris, Mrs., I 17995

Moore, Terry, I 20586

Moorehead, Agnes, I 11746, 20204

Moorehead, Jean, I 14544, 20412

Moorland, Jane; Jane Morland, I 163

Moots, Cornelia Moore Chillison, I 17415, 19314, 20948, II 555, IV 1139

Mora, Jo, I 4309, 9555

Moran, Jane Warmly (Blackburn), I 8477, IV 2322

Moran, Lois, I 11874

Moran, Mary Nimmo, I 3969, III 1244

Moran, Pauline Therese "Polly", I 19942

Morand, Mme. Paul. *See* Phelps, Ruth Shepherd.

Morant, Fanny, I 19606

Morcomb, Mary, I 164, 3700

Mordecai, Rose, I 8341, 17355

More, Ellen, I 16054

Moreland, Mary L., I 17529, 19429, II 304, III 3, IV 570

Morell, Imogene Robinson, I 4077

Morena, Berta, I 13889

Moreno, Luisa, I 6494, III 1007

Moreton, Clara. *See* Moore, Clara Sophia (Jessup).

Morgan, Abigail Bailey "Abbie", I 4843, 16176

Morgan, Agnes, I 9660, 19893

Morgan, Agnes Fay, I 2100, 13017

Morgan, Alice Bell, I 490, 2979

Morgan, Angela, I 10480

Morgan, Ann. *See* Hart, Nancy.

Morgan, Anna, I 2622, 14950, 19650, IV 553

Morgan, Anne Eugenia Felicia, I 2547, 6323, 8571

Morgan, Anne Haven, I 12997, 16897

Morgan, Anne Tracy, I 5634, 15685, 18469

Morgan, Barbara Spofford, I 6344, 13049, II 338, IV 1744

Morgan, Caroline (Starr), I 8391

Morgan, Charlotte E., I 3401, 10267

Morgan, Claudia, I 20388

Morgan, Edith Galt, I 3603, 13377, II 730

Morgan, Helen, I 11747, 14229, 20205

Morgan, Helen Clarissa, I 2548

Morgan, Henrietta Hunt, I 5077, 5784, 7626, 16416

Morgan, Jane, I 11362, 13953, 19907

Morgan, Jayne P., I 14696

Morgan, Julia, I 4262, IV 141

Morgan, Lucy Calista, I 3226

Morgan, Maria "Middy", I 10881, 16815, III 924

Morgan, Martha Ready, I 5360, 5866, 8047

Morgan, Mary Kimball, I 2812, 17544, II 243

Morgan, Maud, I 9067, 13659, II 760

Morgan, Norma Gloria, I 4741

Morgan, Sarah, I 5564, 5932, 8440

Morgan, Sarah Berrien Casey, I 1620

Morgan, Therese E., I 854

Morgana, Nina, I 14073

Morier, I 186, III 5, 61

Morison, Patricia, I 20468

Morison, Rebecca Newell, I 17651

Morlacchi, Giuseppina, I 1905

Morley, Margaret Warner, I 2740, 8980, 12706, IV 1042

Morna. *See* Ladd, Catherine.

Morrell, Imogene Robinson, I 3891

Morris, Alice A., I 9068, IV 1578

Morris, Alice V. Shepard, I 1721

Morris, Ann Eliott, I 4935

Morris, Christine, I 78, 18682, III 1114

Morris, Clara (Morrison), I 8604, 19619, III 521

Morris, Constance Lily, I 1830, 10397

Morris, Dave Hennen, Mrs., I 1576, 6599

Morris, Deborah, I 16271

Morris, Edita, I 10352, III 1281

Morris, Elizabeth, I 19472, III 636, IV 2011

Morris, Ellen Douglas, I 19343

Morris, Esther Hobart McQuigg Slack, I 6669, 16446, 20760, IV 2410

Morris, Eugenia Laura (Tuttle); Alyn Yates Keith, I 8149, IV 321

Morris, Margaret, I 5062, 7453

Morris, Mary Philipse "Polly", I 16167

Morris, Matilda E., I 5361, 12383

Morris, Mildred, I 11748

Morris, Mrs., I 19459

Morris, Owen, Mrs., I 19487

Morris, Pamela, I 19057

Morris, Sarah, I 16978, II 979

Morrisey, Marie, I 14425

Morrison, Adrienne, I 630, 9887, 19999

Morrison, Anne, I 9939, 20031

Morrison, Chloe Anthony Wofford "Toni", I 10746, III 423

Morrison, Lucile Gertrude Phillips, I 10108, IV 199

Morrison, Mary Anna, I 5362, 16519

Morrison, Mary Jane (Whitney), I 8125, IV 959

Morrison, May Treat, I 2741, 15583, IV 100

Morrison, Rosetta Tharpe, I 14558, 17809, III 318

Morrison, Sarah Elizabeth, I 7567, IV 2025

Morrison, Sarah Parke, I 17308, 19225, II 1021

Morrisson, Mary (Taylor) Foulke, I 542, 6949, 21227

Morrow, Doretta (Marano), I 14650, 20559

Morrow, Elizabeth Cutter, I 2992, 9457

Morrow, Honore Bryant Willsie, I 6143, 9661

Morsch, Lucile M., I 1836, 6268

Morse, Alice Cordelia, I 4130, IV 1594

Morse, Charlotte Dunning (Wood); Charlotte Dunning, I 8981

Morse, Ednah Anne Rich, I 2966, IV 138

Morse, Fanny, I 855

Morse, Louisa Spruance, I 18091

Morse, Lucy (Gibbons), I 1185, 8342, 18248, IV 1462

Morse, Rebecca A.; Ruth Moza; R. A. Kidder; R. A. K., I 1145, 1285, 3893, 7826, 15306, 20801, IV 1387

Morse, Ruth V., I 856, 6231

Morse, [Alfreda] Theodora Strandberg "Dolly", I 581, 13969

Mortimer, Mary, I 2260, 20771, III 651, IV 2365

Morton, Anne Justis, I 4797, 16149

Morton, Blanche Rosalie Slaughter, I 5641, 12919

Morton, Eleanor. *See* Stern, Elizabeth Gertrude Levin.

Morton, Eliza Happy, I 2638, 5975, 8803, 13593, IV 810

Morton, Florrinell Frances, I 3475, 6251

Morton, Jane M., I 5363, 12384

Morton, Martha, I 9241, 19734, IV 1620

Morton, Sarah Wentworth (Apthorp); Philenia, I 7444, IV 859

Moscowitz, Jennie, I 19760, II 390, III 1171

Moseby, Mary Webster, I 7492, IV 2309

Mosely, Mrs., I 16642

Moser, Edwa Robert, I 10186

Moses, Anna Mary Robertson "Grandma", I 4105, IV 1579

Moses, Clara Lowenburg, I 9242

Moses, Mary Frances Hoyt, I 6808

Mosher, Clelia, I 2844, 12772

Mosher, Edith Apperson, I 17652

Mosher, Edith R., I 2957, 9376

Mosher, Edna, I 13257, III 579

Mosher, Eliza Maria, I 8605, 12599

Moskowitz, Belle Lindner Israels, I 6936, 18504, II 402, IV 1690

Moss, Elizabeth Murphy, I 1010, 5738, 11962, III 326

Moss, Mary Hissem de. *See* de Moss, Mary Hissem.

Moss, Mary Hissem De, I 14426

Mossell, Gertrude Bustill, I 8887, 11108, III 134, IV 2096

Mossell, Mary Ella, I 2649, 17493, III 130

Mossell, Sadie Tanner. *See* Alexander, Sadie Tanner Mossell.

Moten, Etta, I 14230, 20206, III 246

Moten, Lucy Ella, I 2623

Mother of American Methodism, The. *See* Heck, Barbara Ruckle.

Mother of Flag Day, The. *See* Prisk, Laura B.

Mother of Mormonism, The. *See* Smith, Eliza Roxey Snow.

Mother of the Charities. *See* Jacobs, Frances Wisebart.

Mother of the Confederacy. *See* Law, Sallie Chapman Gordon.

Motley, Constance Baker, I 7336, III 360

Mott, Lucretia (Coffin), I 1086, 15121, 17057, 20725, II 996

Mott, Marjorie Mahon de. *See* de Mott, Marjorie Mahon.

Mott, Mollie C., I 5364, 12385

Motte, Ellen Newbold la. *See* la Motte, Ellen Newbold.

Motte, Marguerite de la. *See* de la Motte, Marguerite.

Motte, Rebecca Brewton, I 4859, 16181

Moulton, Frances Estelle (Mason), I 428, IV 816

Moulton, Hannah Lynch, I 16289

Moulton, [Ellen] Louise (Chandler), I 8206, IV 966

Moultrie, Elizabeth St. Julien, I 16225

Mountain Wolf Woman; Kehachiwinga, I 9763, III 1054

Mountcastle, Clara H., I 2425, 8266, 14861, III 515

Rogers, Ginger; Virginia Katherine McMath, **I** 1979, 20369

Rogers, Grace Rainey, **I** 4170, 6063, 15648

Rogers, Harriet Burbank, **I** 2392, 18224

Rogers, Lettie Hamlett, **I** 3615, 10656

Rogers, Loula Kendall, **I** 5407

Rogers, Mary Fletcher, **I** 9077, 16853

Rogers, Mary Josephine; Mother Mary Joseph, **I** 17663, **II** 175

Rogers, Mrs., **I** 2171

Rogers, N., **I** 18005

Rogers, Sara Jane "Jennie", **I** 16611

Rogers, Vesta Marie, **I** 13347, **III** 17

Rogner, Arveta, **I** 17936

Rohde, Ruth. *See* Owen, Ruth Bryan.

Rohe, Alice, **I** 9533, 11293

Rohe, Vera-Ellen. *See* Vera-Ellen.

Rohlf, Anora Kathleen (Green) "Anna", **I** 8606, **IV** 1492

Rohlfs, Mrs. Charles. *See* Green, Anna Katherine.

Rohrer, Gertrude Martin, **I** 1849, 14455

Rolfs, Mrs. *See* Fenollosa, Mary (McNeill).

Rolland, Pauline Hoffman, **I** 19851, **II** 403, **IV** 1693

Rollins, Alice Marland (Wellington), **I** 8483, 10992, **IV** 1476

Rollins, Charlemae Hill, **I** 6178, **III** 213

Rollins, Clara Harriot (Sherwood), **I** 9499, **IV** 1094

Rollins, Ellen Chapman (Hobbs); E. H. Arr, **I** 5889, 8109, **IV** 2049

Rollston, Adelaide Day, **I** 8403, **IV** 732

Roma, Caro; Carey Northey, **I** 9275, 13741

Roma, Lisa, **I** 14078

Romaine, Margaret, **I** 13932

Roman, Mae, **I** 882, 3798

Roman, Nancy Grace, **I** 16028, 18105

Romary, Janice-Lee York, **I** 19080

Rombauer, Irma Louise von Starkloff, **I** 2089, 9584

Rombeau, Anne M., **I** 15113, 16725, 18094

Romic, Mary, **I** 16031, 18121

Romm, May E., **I** 1729, 13121, 20056, **IV** 187

Rondstadt, Linda, **I** 14762, **III** 1020, **IV** 271

Roobenian, Amber, **I** 14315

Rood, Helen Martin, **I** 9890

Rookes, Marian Agnes Land. *See* Booth, Agnes.

Rooney, Miriam Theresa, **I** 6389

Roosevelt, Ellen, **I** 19081

Roosevelt, Emily, **I** 14125

Roosevelt, [Anna] Eleanor, **I** 9766, 15042, 15766, 18555, **III** 723, **IV** 413

Root, Clara Louise. *See* Burnham, Clara Louise (Root).

Root, Eliza H., **I** 12696

Roper, Janet Lord "Mother", **I** 17587, 17893, **IV** 1642

Rorer, Sarah Tyson (Heston), **I** 2067, 2584, 12626

Rorke, Margaret Hayden, **I** 4387, 21262, **II** 177

Rosa. *See* Jeffrey, Rosa Vertner (Griffith) (Johnson).

Rosalita, Sister, **I** 17793, **II** 216

Rose, Ann Perrett, **I** 9975

Rose, Ellen Alida, **I** 327, 1341, 16835, 20951

Rose, Ernestine Louise Lasmond Siismondi Potowski, **I** 1112, 19152, 20754, **II** 365, **III** 1141

Rose, Laura Martin, **I** 1456

Rose, Lucille Mason, **I** 6506, 7330, **III** 351, **IV** 1846

Rose, Martha E. (Parmelee), **I** 1306, 3928, 6402, 8172, 10917, 15422, 18225, 20875, **IV** 1899

Rose, Mary Davies Swartz, **I** 2085, 5636, 6905, 12901

Rose de Lima. *See* de Lima, Rose.

Rose Marie, "Baby", **I** 11773

Rose of the Cimarron. *See* Dunn, Rose.

Roseau, Marie. *See* Hilderburn, Mary Jane (Reed).

Rosebaum, Mrs. Harold A. *See* Lashanska, Hulda.

Roseboro, Viola, **I** 8986, 11132, **IV** 1562

Roseborough, Melanie Rohrer; Mrs. Adolph J. Radosta, **I** 3322, 6621, **II** 519, **IV** 433

Rosehill, Margaret Cheer, Lady, **I** 19457, **III** 629

Rosen, Lucie Bigelow Dodge, **I** 14047, 15786, **II** 854, **IV** 1753

Rosenberg, Anna Marie, **I** 5714, 7213, **II** 468, **III** 897

Rosenberg, Beatrice, **I** 883

Rosenbery, Millie R. M., **I** 1630, 15733

Rosenblatt, Louise M., **I** 6373

Rosenfeld, Fanny "Bobbie", **I** 18790

Rosenman, Dorothy Reuben, **I** 7178, 18635

Rosenstein, Nettie, **I** 699, 3760, 15807, **III** 13

Rosenstein, Sophie, **I** 3498, 20321, **IV** 232

Rosenthal, Doris, **I** 4707

Rosenthal, Ida Cohen, **I** 604, 3744, **II** 428, **IV** 1736

Rosenthal, Jean, **I** 963, 20338

Rosewald, Julie, **I** 13582

Rosmond, Babette, **I** 10657

Ross, Anna Maria, **I** 5408, 12406, 15383

Ross, Anne Lawler, **I** 4812

Ross, Annie, **I** 14593

Ross, Betsy, **I** 18006

Ross, Betsy Griscom; Elizabeth Claypool; Elizabeth Grimke, **I** 188, 5022, **IV** 2010

Ross, Diana, **I** 14751, 20692, **III** 477

Ross, Gertrude, **I** 14456

Ross, Isabel, **I** 6209, 10133, 21312, **III** 1251

Ross, Ivy, **I** 13970

Ross, Letitia Roano Dowdell, **I** 1823

Ross, Mabel Hughes, **I** 17771

Ross, Margaret Wheeler, **I** 1827, 3465, 14298

Ross, Mary, **I** 11506

Ross, Myrta Pearson, **I** 17733

Ross, Nancy Wilson, **I** 10482

Ross, Nellie (Tayloe), **I** 6926, **IV** 2414

Ross, Rita, **I** 16889

Ross, Virginia Evelyn (Conlee), **I** 8948, 16631, **IV** 1244

Rossner, Judith Perelman, **I** 10764, **II** 504, **IV** 1856

Rotch, Charity (Rodman), **I** 15221

Roth, Frank C., Mrs., **I** 11774

Roth, Lillian, **I** 10572, 20370

Roth, Vita F., **I** 18067

Rothenberg, Rose, **I** 7179

Rothery, Agnes Edwards, **I** 9866

Rothrock, Mary Utopia, **I** 6179, 9947, 11507

Rothwell, Annie, **I** 8272, **III** 516, 675

Roulet, Mary F. Nixon, **I** 4360, 6611, 9673, 11349, 13933

Roulston, Margorie Hillis, **I** 3747, 11441

Roundtree, Martha, **I** 11954

Rourke, Constance Mayfield, **I** 52, 3170, 6158, 9784, 11391

Rouse, Anna, **I** 16169

Rouse, Benjamin, Mrs., **I** 5072, 15244, 18158

Rouse, Rebecca, **I** 16274

Routzahn, Mary Swain, **I** 18574

Rouverol, Aurania, **I** 9785, 11392, 19959

Rowe, Anna Forrest, **I** 12697, **IV** 1551

Rowe, Fynette, **I** 10549

Rowe, Henrietta Gould, **I** 8208, **IV** 797

Rowe, Lucretia Olin, **I** 3304, 17741

Rowland, Helen, **I** 13270

Rowland, Kate Mason, **I** 8404

Rowlands, Virginia Cathryn "Gena", **I** 20562

Rowlandson, Mary (White), **I** 7409, 16097, **IV** 850

Rowley, M. Rita, **I** 17678, **II** 181

Rowson, Charlotte, **I** 13444, 19491

Rowson, Susanna (Haswell), **I** 2172, 7449, 19477, **III** 637, **IV** 861

Roxon, Lillian, **I** 10753, 14704

Royall, Anne Newport, **I** 199, 7454, 10816, 16344, **IV** 364, 2308

Royce, Sarah Eleonor Bayliss, **I** 7783, 16463, **III** 653, **IV** 60

Rubenstein, Helena, **I** 479, 3724, 4222, 6079, 15668, **II** 394, **III** 1145

Rubin, Barbara Jo, **I** 18911

Ruble, Olan, **I** 19082

Rude, Ellen (Sargent), **I** 1318, 8307, 19259, **IV** 1175

Rudkin, Margaret Fogarty, **I** 700

Rudnick, Dorothea, **I** 13337

Rudnick, Elynor, **I** 18068

Rudolph, Wilma Glodean, **I** 18889, **III** 461

Ruellan, Andree, **I** 4670

Ruffin, Josephine St. Pierre, **I** 1191, 1338, 5572, 18271, 20943, **III** 117

Ruffin, Margaret Ellen Henry, **I** 8949

Rufus, Maud Squire; Flying Grandma, **I** 17907

Ruggles, Emily, **I** 254

Ruggles, Theo Alice. *See* Kitson, Theo Alice (Ruggles).

Ruhamah, Eliza. *See* Scidmore, Eliza Ruhamah.

Rukeyser, Muriel, **I** 7707

Rule, Janice, **I** 20607

Rullmann, Maria, **I** 2356, 15384

Rumford, Countess. *See* Thompson, Sarah.

Rump, Anita, **I** 19083

Rumsey, Mary Ann, **I** 16394

Rumsey, Mary Harriman, **I** 563, 1646, 5655, 6976, 18538, **IV** 1718

Runbeck, Margaret Lee, **I** 10550

Runcie, Constance (Faunt le Roy), **I** 1310, 5904, 8244, 13513, **IV** 1203

Runkle, Bertha (Brooks), **I** 9626

Runkle, Lucia Isabella, **I** 8540

Ruprecht, Jenny Terrill, **I** 1329, 8405, **IV** 1907

Ruschmeyer, Addie, **I** 19084

Rush, Julia Stockton, **I** 5038

Rush, Phoebe Ann Ridgway, **I** 6525

Rusk, Evelyn Carroll, **I** 3414, 15996, **II** 207, **IV** 1801

Russ, Joanna, **I** 10772, 21350

Russell, Ada Dwyer, **I** 19718, **IV** 1605

Russell, Annie, **I** 19725, **III** 703

Russell, Carrie. *See* Gillette, Lucia Fidelia (Woolley).

Russell, E. J., **I** 2357, 5409, 12407

Russell, Edith, **I** 3731, 5644, 9585, 11302

Russell, Elizabeth Augusta, **I** 1174, 15413, 19215

Russell, Elizabeth Shull, **I** 13369

Russell, Ella, **I** 13711

Russell, Ezekiel, Mrs., **I** 120, 13436

Russell, Gail, **I** 12009, 20546

Russell, Helen Victoria Crocker, **I** 691, 7115, 15805, **II** 873, **IV** 201

Russell, Jane, **I** 20497

Russell, Jane Anne, **I** 13364

Russell, Joseph, Mrs., **I** 4945

Russell, Lenie, **I** 5410, 16526

Russell, Lillian, **I** 13676, 19705

Russell, Lois Hasselvander, **I** 17738

Russell, Martha M., **I** 12977

Russell, Mary Baptist, Mother, **I** 17269, **II** 109, **III** 925, **IV** 66

Russell, Penelope, **I** 180

Russell, Rosalind, **I** 20371, **IV** 241

Russell, Sarah, **I** 192, 10814

Russell, Tillie, **I** 5411, 16527

Ruter, Rebecca. *See* Springer, Rebecca (Ruter).

Rutherford, Frances A., **I** 12550

Rutherford, Mildred Lewis, **I** 2624, 5973, 8789, **IV** 462

Rutledge, Elizabeth Grimke, **I** 4978

Rutledge, Henrietta Middleton, **I** 5017

Rutledge, Mary Shubrick Eveleigh, **I** 16341

Rutledge, Sarah Hert, **I** 16129

Ruuska, Sylvia, **I** 19085

Ryan, Anne, **I** 4439, 9891

Ryan, Elizabeth "Bunny", **I** 18759

Ryan, Esther, **I** 19086

Ryan, Harriet, **I** 193, 3701

Ryan, Ida Barry, **I** 15734

Ryan, Irene, **I** 11829, 20267, **IV** 223

Ryan, Marah Ellis (Martin); Ellis Martin, **I** 9078, 19698

Ryan, Mary M., **I** 429, 2813

Ryan, Mary P. van Buren, **I** 884, 3415, 14245

Ryan, Patricia (Gibson), **I** 11991

Ryckoff, Lalla, **I** 14457

Ryder, Theodora Sturkow, **I** 3044, 13863

Ryerson, Margery Austen, **I** 4406

Ryley, Madeleine Lucette, **I** 19511

Saalfield, Adah Louise (Sutton), **I** 9249

Saarinen, Aline Milton Bernstein (Louchheim), **I** 4716, 6292, 10620, 11940

Sabin, Ellen Clara, **I** 2609

Sabin, Florence Rena, **I** 1537, 2972, 12867, 18451, **IV** 288

Sabin, Pauline Morton; Mrs. Charles, **I** 617, 4415, 7027, 19454

Sacajawea; Bird Woman, **I** 6520, 16386, **III** 1037

Sachs, Emanie N., **I** 10005

Sachs, Evelyn, **I** 14632, **II** 497

Sackett, Emma A. French, **I** 5412, 12408

Sadlier, Anna Theresa, **I** 5987, 6573, 8866, **II** 135

Sadlier, Mary Anne (Madden), **I** 7807, 17215, **II** 101, **III** 920

Safford, Mary Augusta, **I** 14951, 15544, 17479, 21017, **II** 1112, **III** 2

Safford, Mary Joanna Jane, **I** 5526, 12493, **IV** 962

Sage, Abby. *See* Richardson, Abby (Sage).

Sage, Agnes Carolyn, **I** 8867

Sage, Cornelia B., **I** 4361, 6145

Sage, Florence Eleanor, **I** 13628, 14973

Sage, Juniper. *See* Brown, Margaret Wise.

Sage, Kay Linn, **I** 14171

Sage, Margaret Olivia (Slocum), **I** 15340

Sager, Ruth, **I** 13381

Saher, Lilla van, **I** 10551, **III** 899

Sahler, Helen Gertrude, **I** 4320, **IV** 1694

Saint, Eva Marie, **I** 12001, 20536

Sainte-Marie, Beverley "Buffie", **I** 14743, **III** 1120

Salm Salm, Agnes Elizabeth Winona Joy (Leqlerq), Princess, **I** 5559, 12551, 15472, 18690, 19607

Salmon, Lucy Maynard, **I** 2653, 5981, 8834

Salmon, Mary, **I** 145

Salome. *See* Converse, Harriet Maxwell.

Salomon, Alice, **I** 18460

Salomon, Eliza, **I** 5413, 15385

Salomonsky, Verna Cook, **I** 4616

Salter, Mary Turner, **I** 13618

Saltza, Chris von, **I** 18902

Saltzman-Stevens, Minnie, **I** 13891

Salyards, Christiana Stedman, **I** 9128, 17546

Samaroff, Olga; Olga Stokowski, **I** 3137, 13963

Sammis-MacDermid, Sybil, **I** 3560, 14458

Sampson, Deborah; Robert Shirtliffe; Deborah Gannett, **I** 5044, 14785, 16318, **IV** 860

Sampson, Edith (Spurlock), **I** 7196, 15091, **III** 255, **IV** 627

Sampson, Emma Speed, **I** 9321, **IV** 2338

Sampter, Jessie Ethel, **I** 9867, 17695, **II** 432

Samuels, Adelaide Florence Frances, **I** 8580

Samuels, Margaret, **I** 3416, 6234, 10293

Samuels, Susan Blagge (Caldwell), **I** 8667

Sanborn, Helen Josephine, **I** 6011, 8950

Sanborn, Katharine Abbott "Kate", **I** 2454, 8347, 14875, 16826, **IV** 1273

Sanborn, Mary (Farley), **I** 7582, **IV** 889

Sanborn, Thelma Payne, **I** 19087

Sanchez, Sonia, **I** 10765, 20648, **III** 440

Sand, Mary Novak, **I** 18882

Sandberg, Marta Ehrlich, **I** 13271, **III** 871

Sandell, Viola T., **I** 18122

Sanders, Alma M., **I** 13964

Sanders, Elizabeth (Elkins), **I** 1078, 5763, 7450, 18149, **IV** 862

Sanders, Harriet Fenn, **I** 16550

Sanders, Marlene, **I** 1055, 12047

Sanders, Sue A. Pike, **I** 1287, 5140, **IV** 506

Sanders, Wilbur, Mrs., **I** 16633

Sanderson, Julia, **I** 11420

Sanderson, Sibyl Swift, **I** 13722, **IV** 120

Sandes, Margaret Isabelle, **I** 357, 1369, 6421, **III** 1246

Sandoz, Marie Suzette "Mari", **I** 6202, 10115, **IV** 1254

Sands, Diana, **I** 20638

Sandwina, Kati, **I** 18732, 19944

Sanford, Amanda, **I** 12602

Sanford, Maria Louise, **I** 2415

Sanger, Margaret Higgins; Mrs. J. Noah H. Slee, **I** 9627, 12955, 15027, 21230, **II** 819

Sangster, Margaret Elizabeth (Munson), **I** 3710, 8308, 10948, **IV** 1453

Sansbury, Angela, Mother, **I** 17065, **II** 78

Sansom, Emma, **I** 5414, 5874, 8059, 16528

Santa Cruz, Maria de las Mercedes; Countess of Merlin, **I** 7485, **III** 602

Sapio, Clementine Duchene de Vere, **I** 13723

Sapp, Ruth Bent, **I** 1594, **II** 327, **IV** 610

Sardeau, Helen; Mrs. George Biddle, **I** 4549, **III** 52, **IV** 1798

Sargent, Ellen. *See* Rude, Ellen (Sargent).

Sargent, Ellen C., **I** 18528

Sargent, Helen Durham, **I** 13325

Sargent, Julia Amanda A. *See* Wood, Julia Amanda A. (Sargent).

Sargent, Mary Forward Kooser, **I** 3845, **II** 976

Sargent, Pamela, **I** 10785, 21361

Sarnoff, Dorothy, **I** 14459, **II** 481

Saroya, Bianca, **I** 13934

Sartain, Emily, **I** 2501, 3966, **III** 679, **IV** 2068

Sartain, Geraldine, **I** 11508

Sartain, Harriet, **I** 3499, 4687, **IV** 2159

Saruya, Julia Salinger, **I** 885, 3799

Saubert, Jean, **I** 19088

Saunders, Agnes Kelly, **I** 6180

Saunders, Aileen, **I** 18095

Saunders, Margaret Marshall; Marshall Saunders, **I** 9129, **III** 536, **IV** 1060

Saunders, Marshall. *See* Saunders, Margaret Marshall.

Saunders, Mary A., **I** 358, **IV** 1502

Saunders, Sally; Sally Love Saunders Craigie, **I** 3687, 10779, **II** 916, **IV** 2163

Savage, Augusta Christine, **I** 4489, **III** 216

Savage, Marie Ghislaine Metten (Mamen), **I** 13724, **III** 48

Savage, Mary, **I** 17007

Savage, Minnie Stebbins; Marion Lisle, **I** 8757, 17472, 19381, **II** 1111, **IV** 2385

Savage, Sarah, **I** 7470, **IV** 866

Savilla, Agnes, **I** 7369, **III** 1107

Saville, Frances, **I** 13688

Savitzky, Bella. *See* Abzug, Bella (Savitzky).

Savord, Ruth, **I** 6195

Sawin, Martha A., **I** 12201

Sawtelle, Lelia Robinson, **I** 6774

Sawyer, A. R., **I** 3959

Sawyer, Antonia (Savage), **I** 441, 13703, **IV** 1606

Sawyer, Caroline Mehitabel (Fisher), **I** 6535, 7691, 10842

Sawyer, Hannah Farnham. *See* Lee, Hannah Farnham (Sawyer).

Sawyer, Helen Alice, **I** 3627, 4729

Sawyer, Josephine Caroline, **I** 6136, 9628, **IV** 1705

Sawyer, Lucy, **I** 309

Sawyer, Lucy Sargent, **I** 17382

Sawyer, Ruth, **I** 9674, 15032

Sawyers, Martha, **I** 4617

Smith, Virginia Beatrice, I 1039, 3643

Smith, Virginia Trall, I 15434, 17332, 18231

Smith, Winifred. *See* Pitkin, Winifred Mercer.

Smith, Zilpah Drew, I 18312

Smock, Rose Melville, I 19808

Smythe, Amanda B., I 5434, 12417

Snead, Nell, I 11783

Snell, Cornelia Tyler, I 13277

Snelling, Abigail Hunt, I 16399

Snipes, Esther, I 17720

Snodgrass, Louise Harrison, I 14466

Snook, Neta, I 18010

Snow, Alice Rowe, I 17880

Snow, Anna Rablen, I 16645

Snow, C. Georgie, I 6728

Snow, Carmel White, I 3750, 11515, III 953

Snow, Constantia, I 16092

Snow, Ellen, I 9677, 15176, 16892

Snow, Emily Topple, I 16573

Snow, Kathleyn Smith, I 13183, II 878

Snyder, Alice Dorothea, I 3201, 9837

Snyder, Grace McCance, I 7466

Sokalski, Annie Blanche, I 16532

Sokoloff, Natalie B. *See* Scott, Natalie Anderson.

Sokolow, Anna, I 1007, 1987, 3604, II 488

Solano, Solita, I 9870, 11431, 19991, III 791

Solar, Mercedes Marin De, I 7620, III 594

Solari, Mary M., I 4011, III 967, IV 2232

Solomon, Hannah Greenebaum, I 1416, 17523, 18343, II 376, IV 567

Solovieff, Miriam, I 14605, II 493

Somerville, Nellie Nugent, I 6830, 21113

Somigli, Franca, I 14337

Sommerfield, Rose, I 2612, 17473

Sondergand, Gale, I 20040

Sone, Monica, I 10669, III 990

Sontag, Henriette, I 13455, III 819

Sontag, Susan, I 4754, 10754, 12056, 20626

Soper, Eileen A., I 4671

Soper, Luella Hartt, I 1809, 15087

Sorenson, Virginia, I 10585

Sorin, Sarah Inslee Herring, I 6823, II 762, IV 38

Sosenko, Anna, I 10553, 14467

Soss, Wilma Porter, I 927, 1825, 11820

Sothern, Ann, I 11917, 20391

Souder, Emily Bliss, I 5435, 8066

Soule, Aileen. *See* Riggin, Aileen.

Soule, Caroline Augusta (White), I 249, 7885, 14829, 17239, 18197, II 1081

Soule, Cora Blanche, I 12909, 17625

Soule, Isobel Walker, I 6492, 10165, 11616, 21317

Sousa, May de. *See* de Sousa, May.

Soutar, Judy, I 19103

South, Lillian H., I 12945

Souther, Marguerite, I 1978, 3565, 18806

Southern, Eileen Jackson, I 3629, 4730, III 354

Southern Lady, A. *See* Bellamy, Emily Elizabeth Whitfield (Croom).

Southgate, Eliza, I 2168

Southwick, Elsie Whitmore, I 4469

Southworth, Ella, I 4265

Southworth, Emma Dorothy Eliza (Nevitte); Dorothy Eliza Nevitte, I 7766, IV 369

Spacek, Mary Elizabeth "Sissy", I 20696

Spaford, Emily Maria. *See* Scott, Emily Maria (Spaford).

Spain, Frances Lander, I 1828, 6245, II 889, IV 434

Spalding, Anne, I 15737

Spalding, Catherine, Mother, I 17058, II 76

Spalding, Eliza Hart, I 17129, IV 1979

Spalding, Harriet Mabel, I 9156

Spalding, Mrs., I 4951, 16232

Spalding, Susan (Marr), I 9086, IV 2103

Sparhawk, Frances Campbell, I 8636, 15517, 18287, IV 1003

Spark, Ruth Sevier, I 16370

Sparks, Sarah, I 896, III 581

Sparrow, Arianna Cooley, I 13492, III 97

Spaulding, Jane M., I 7331, III 355

Spaulding, Jennie Tileston, I 5436, 12418

Speaks, Margaret, I 14248

Spear, Catherine Swan Brown, I 1121, 2251, 16738, 20763

Speare, Dorothy, I 6489, 10138, 14157, 20135

Speare, Elizabeth George, I 10500

Spears, Charlotta A. *See* Bass, Charlotta A. Spears.

Spears, Lady. *See* Borden, Mary.

Spears, Nanette M., I 18096

Speers, Emma (Doll) Bailey, I 1548, II 671, IV 2115

Speers, Helen Barrett, I 1737

Speight, Sarah Rebecca (Darden). *See* Davis, Rachel [Kathryn].

Spence, Clara Beebe, I 2833, 5608, 21107

Spencer, Anna Carpenter (Garlin), I 2625, 6422, 11073, 15139, 15545, 17480, 18310, 19388, 21018, II 1113

Spencer, Anne, I 9728

Spencer, Bella Zilfa, I 8411, III 677

Spencer, Caroline Elizabeth, I 12753, 21098

Spencer, Cornelia. *See* Yaukey, Grace Sydenstricker.

Spencer, Cornelia Ann (Phillips), I 5832, 7907, IV 1864

Spencer, Eleanor, I 14082

Spencer, Elizabeth, I 10690, IV 1199

Spencer, Emily P., I 5437, 12419

Spencer, Ethel, I 7181

Spencer, Fannie M., I 2793, 13665

Spencer, Fleta Jan Brown, I 9744, 13972

Spencer, Josephine, I 9087, IV 2288

Spencer, Lilian White, I 9464

Spencer, Lilly Martin, I 13476

Spencer, R. H., Mrs., I 5438, 12420

Spencer, Sara Andrews, I 289, 2428, 8274, 20896, IV 380

Spencer, Shirley, I 13184

Spencer, William Loring (Nunez), Mrs., I 7586

Speyer, Ellen Leslie Prince Lowery, I 15528

Speyer, Leonora von Stosch, I 9435

Spicer, Anne Higginson, I 9404, IV 598

Spicer, Dorothy, I 18011

Spiegel, Clara Gatzert; Clare Jaynes, I 10680

Spilman, Baldwin Day, Mrs., I 1635

Spink, Mary Angela, I 12773, IV 657

Spink, Rose Urbana, I 12956, IV 663

Spirito, Yolanda, I 3421, 18012

Spitz, Sophie; Mrs. Arthur C. Allen, I 13359

Spitzer, Marian, I 11784

Spofford, Grace Harriet, I 3202, 14016

Spofford, Harriet Elizabeth (Prescott), I 8210, IV 967

Sporborg, Constance Amberg, I 1605

Spottiswood, Sarah Maria. *See* Mackin, Sarah Maria Spottiswood.

Sprague, Harriet Chapman, I 6122, 9563, II 325, IV 344

Sprague, Mary Aplin, I 8695, IV 1925

Sprague, Sarah J. Milliken, I 5439, 12421

Sprague, Susannah, I 5440, 12422

Spratt, Louise Parker, I 9088, 11160, IV 22

Spratt, Maria. *See* Provoost, Maria de Peyster Schrick Spratt.

Spray, Ruth Hinshaw, I 2575, 15524

Spreckels, Alma Emma Charlotte Corday le Normand de Bretteville, I 4372, 15748, IV 159

Spriggins, Samantha. *See* Merrill, Helen Maud.

Spring, Agnes Wright, I 11256

Springer, Adele I., I 1839, 7253

Springer, C. R., Mrs., I 2359, 5441, 15389

Springer, Rebecca (Ruter), I 8131, IV 512

Springfield, Laodicia Langston "Dicey", I 5046, 16321

Springs, Lena Joan Jones, I 1667, 5661, 6998, 13009, 21263, IV 2212

Sproat, Florantha Thompson, I 230, 16443

Sproull, Lillian R., I 18097

Spurgeon, Caroline Frances Eleanor, I 1505, 2926, 6066, 9322, 21150

Spurlock, Isabella Smiley Davis, I 15497, 18276, 19317, 20952, IV 1231

Spurlock, Jeanne, I 3633, 13401, III 361

Spurr, Elizabeth Albright, I 480, 15669, IV 1321

Squaw, Sachem, III 1025

Squaw Sachem of Pocasset. *See* Weetamoo.

Squire, Mary E., I 5442, 12423

St. Augustine, Mother, I 17090, II 81, III 772

St. Clair, Catherine N., I 243, 19542

St. Clair, Phoebe Bayard, I 16130

St. Claire, Clyde. *See* Pullen, Sue Vesta.

St. Cyr, Lily, I 20483

St. Denis, Ruth, I 536, 1914

St. Gaudens, Annetta Johnson, I 4193

St. George, Katharine, I 692, 7116

St. John, Cynthia Morgan, I 5978, 8810, IV 1520

St. Johns, Adele Rogers, I 10067, 11573, 20097

Stacey, Anna Lee, I 4224

Stafford, Jean, I 10634

Stafford, Jo, I 14578

Stafford, Maria Brewster Brooks, I 2239, IV 5

Stage, Miriam Kerruish, I 12851, 21168, IV 1950

Stagg, Jessie A., I 4470

Stagg, Mary, I 1893, 2144, 19458

Stewart, Mary E. (Smith); Sun-saing Poo-in, I 18362, IV 107

Stewart, Priscilla, I 7809

Stewart, Sallie W., I 564, 1650, 3126, 15037, 18540, III 195, IV 664

Stewart, Salome M., I 5449, 12430

Stewart, Sylvia, I 3567, 16019, 18071

Stewart, Wendy, I 5725, 11871, III 755, IV 229

Stickney, Dorothy, I 20214

Stickney, Julia Granby (Noyes), I 8067, IV 952

Stiebeling, Hazel Katherine, I 7117, 13171, 15979

Still, Caroline Virginia. *See* Anderson, Caroline Virginia Still.

Stille, Mary Ingram, I 19407, IV 2095

Stillings, Kemp, I 3423, 14249

Stillman, Mildred Margaret Whitney, I 9952

Stillman, Sarah S., I 4471

Stilson, Ruth, I 3424, 18013

Stimson, Barbara Bartlett, I 13190

Stimson, Harriet Overton, I 13690, 15613

Stimson, Julia Catherine, I 3127, 5657, 12990

Stinetorf, Louise, I 10681, 13398

Stinson, Katherine, I 15980, 17948

Stinson, Marjorie, I 17949

Stinson, Virginia McCollum, I 5450, 5878, 8068

Stirling, Mrs.; Lady Cholmondeley, I 1922, III 730

Stites, Mabel M., I 18072

Stober, Buena Rose, I 17721

Stockdale, Louise, I 19106

Stocker, Corinne, I 2974, 11264, 15011, IV 483

Stockham, Alice (Bunker), I 5895, 8153, 12485, 13502, 20871

Stockton, Annis Boudinot, I 7426

Stockton, Louise, I 5913, 8312, 10949, 18241, IV 2059

Stoddard, Anna Elizabeth, I 1390, 11085, 19395, 21031, II 33

Stoddard, Cora Frances, I 19446

Stoddard, Dora V., I 14893

Stoddard, Elizabeth Drew (Barstow), I 7858

Stoddard, Haila, I 20403

Stoddard, Harriet B., I 17224

Stoeckel, Ellen Battell, I 13589, 15546

Stoehr, Edith, I 7118, 16915, 18768

Stokes, Caroline Phelps, I 15563

Stokes, Ella Harrison, I 6329

Stokes, Lilia Woodruff, I 1687, 7015, 15183, 16900, II 1040, IV 2138

Stokes, Missouri H., I 2440, 5541, 5914, 8313, 19261, II 639, IV 452

Stokes, Olivia Egleston Phelps, I 15518

Stokes, Rose Harriet Pastor, I 6459, 6950, 9631, 21231, II 409, III 1148

Stokowski, Olga. *See* Samaroff, Olga.

Stolz, Mary Slattery, I 10682

Stone, Alice. *See* Blackwell, Alice Stone.

Stone, Carol, I 20435

Stone, Cornelia Branch, I 1330, 5562

Stone, Ellen Maria, I 14923, 17438, 19346

Stone, Grace Zaring; Ethel Vance, I 10116

Stone, Hannah Mayer, I 13134, 21302, II 443, IV 1765

Stone, Helen, I 4661

Stone, Lucinda Hinsdale, I 1278, 2252, 20764

Stone, Lucy; Mrs. Henry Brown Blackwell, I 1132, 10856, 14812, 18181, 20782, IV 918

Stone, Margaret Brown, I 4857

Stone, Margaret Manson (Barbour), I 8451, IV 1204

Stone, Martha Elvira, I 5110, 5806, 6673, 15282, IV 914

Stone, Mary Perry, I 324, 6740, 17875, 20944, IV 1986

Stone, Verlinda Cotton Burdette Boughton, I 5750, 7408, 10802

Stone, Winifred Sackville Jr.; Mrs. Charles P. de Bruche, I 10356

Stoneman, Abigail, I 165, IV 2166

Stoothoff, Saartze Kierstede von Borsum, I 6513

Storer, Ann, I 19485

Storer, Fanny, I 19475

Storer, Maria, I 19468

Storer, Maria Longworth Nichols, I 4012, 13568, 15529

Storey, Widow, I 16057

Storm, Gale, I 11992, 14619, 20510

Story, Ann; Ann Goodrich, I 4979, 16244

Story, Daisy Allen, I 18324

Story, Emma Eames, I 13757

Story, Josephine. *See* Loring, Emilie Baker.

Story, Mrs. Julian. *See* Eames, Emma Hayden.

Stouder, Sharon, I 18907

Stoughton, Urania Locke. *See* Bailey, Urania Locke (Stoughton).

Stout, Juanita Kidd, I 7315, III 338

Stout, Penelope van Princes, I 16083

Stout, Ruth Albertine, I 3568, 7274

Stovall, Kate Bradley, I 1606

Stover, Clara [Mae] Lewis, I 669, II 715

Stover, Sarah, I 5451

Stow, Freelove Baldwin, I 4820

Stowe, Harriet Elizabeth Beecher, I 1114, 7678, 17164, 18173, IV 310

Stowell, Louisa Maria (Reed), I 2613, 8761, 11064, 12645

Strabel, Thelma; Thelma Godwin, I 10517

Strachan, Grace Charlotte, I 2961, 15670

Strahan, Elsie T., I 2104, 13109

Strahan, Kay Cleaver, I 9871

Stranahan, Clara Harrison, I 3915, 8069, IV 953

Stranahan, Marianne F., I 5452, 15390

Strang, Elise Depew. *See* l'Esperance, Elise Depew Strang.

Strang, Ruth [May], I 3296, 10096

Strange, Michael. *See* Oelrichs, Blanche Marie Louise.

Strasberg, Paula; Paula Miller, I 3580, 20372

Strasberg, Susan Elizabeth, I 20657

Strassmann, Antonie, I 5716, 7215, 16717, 18033, III 872

Stratas, Teresa, I 14672

Straten, Florence Van, I 16021

Stratton, Dorothy Constance, I 5699

Stratton-Porter, Gene, I 9197

Straub, Maria, I 13521, 19262

Straus, Flora B. S., I 1810

Straus, Lina Gutherz, I 1398, 12671, II 373, III 835

Strauss, Anna Lord, I 1766, 3329, 7140, 15192, 21318, II 1045, IV 1799

Strawbridge, Anne West, I 9745, 17911

Strawn, Julia Clark, I 12817, II 318, IV 594

Streep, Mary Louise "Meryl", I 12108, 20707

Street, Ida Maria, I 2702, 4067, 8920, IV 2389

Street, Margaret Berry, I 656, 1730, 7072, 16909, 18587, 21296, II 711, IV 1878

Streeter, Bess Genevra. *See* Aldrich, Bess Genevra Streeter.

Streeter, Elizabeth M., I 5453, 15391

Streeter, Lilian Carpenter, I 18319

Streeter, Ruth Cheney, I 5691, 17947

Streisand, Barbra, I 14744, 20679

Strickland, Lily Teresa, I 9839, 14017

Strickland, Martha, I 6793, 14954, 21038, IV 1149

Strickland, S. E., I 2487, 14894, 20923

Stritch, Elaine, I 12010, 20549

Strode, Muriel, I 9746

Strohm, Gertrude, I 5942, 8511, IV 1917

Strong, Anna Louise, I 7016, 9786, 11393

Strong, Betsy, I 11785

Strong, Harriet Williams Russell, I 1345, 15926, 16838, IV 78

Strong, May A., I 3569, 14471

Strong, Susan, I 13667

Stroup, Leora, I 13360, 18073

Strouse, Hilda. *See* Vaughn, Hilda.

Strunsky, Manya Gordon, I 6984, 9729

Struthers, Sally (Ann), I 12107

Stryker, Elizabeth. *See* Ricord, Elizabeth (Stryker).

Stryker, Helen, I 11786

Stuart, Cora Wilson, I 3247, 18582

Stuart, Elizabeth Wooster. *See* Phelps, Elizabeth Wooster (Stuart).

Stuart, Flora Cooke, I 5454, 16533

Stuart, Jane, I 3881

Stuart, Ruth McEnery, I 8696

Stuart, Sarah M., I 18171

Stubbs, Annie Bell, I 5455, 12431

Studebaker, Mabel, I 1819, 3445

Stuerm, Ruza Lukavaska, I 897, 15088, 18014, III 611

Stumm, Maud, I 4225

Sture-Vasa, Mary. *See* O'Hara, Mary.

Sturges, Mary Jane (Upshur) (Stith); Fanny Fielding, I 7977, IV 1405

Sturgis, Margaret Castex, I 9787, 13033, II 844, IV 2139

Sturgis, Mother, I 5456, 12432

Sturkow-Ryder, Theodora, I 14472

Stutz, Geraldine, I 1040, 3838

Suckow, Ruth Ann Vivien (Nuhn), I 10009, II 1043, IV 192, 692

Suess, Dana Nadine, I 10573, 14510

Sugg, Catharine Lee, I 19499

Suggs, Louise, I 18835

Sullavan, Margaret (Brooke), I 20349

Sullivan, Anne; Anne Sullivan Macy, I 2898, 18400

Sullivan, Betsy "Mother", I 5457

Sullivan, Leonore Alice Kretzger, I 7332

Taussig, Helen Brooke, **I** 1762, 13191, **II** 1150
Tayloe, Ann; Ann Taylor, **I** 16073
Tayloe, Nellie. *See* Ross, Nellie (Tayloe).
Taylor, Alice, **I** 5461
Taylor, Alva, **I** 11518
Taylor, Ann. *See* Tayloe, Ann.
Taylor, Anna, **I** 18705, 19781
Taylor, Anna Heyward, **I** 4347, **II** 820, **IV** 2210
Taylor, Catherine L., **I** 5462, 12435
Taylor, Charlotte de Bernier, **I** 3874, 7635, 12178
Taylor, Effie J., **I** 3248, 13110, **III** 567
Taylor, Elizabeth, **I** 311
Taylor, Emily Drayton, **I** 1443, 4111, **IV** 2104
Taylor, Estelle [Ida], **I** 20168, **IV** 209
Taylor, Esther, **I** 12249
Taylor, Euphemia J., **I** 12852, **III** 548
Taylor, Hannah E., **I** 8212, 19237, **II** 22
Taylor, Kathleen Devere, **I** 901, 21321
Taylor, Keturah Leitch, **I** 16368
Taylor, Laurette; Loretta Cooney, **I** 19945
Taylor, Lily Ross, **I** 9813
Taylor, Lodusky J., Mrs., **I** 1408
Taylor, Lucy Beaman Hobbs, **I** 12486
Taylor, Lynette Dobbins, **I** 1062, 12086, **III** 462
Taylor, Marian Young; Martha Denae, **I** 11884, **II** 726, **IV** 1829
Taylor, Marion Sayle, **I** 2103, 11443
Taylor, Martha Smith, **I** 7994, 10888, 19195
Taylor, Mary Cecelia, **I** 13480, 19557, **IV** 1402
Taylor, Mary Imlay, **I** 7587, **IV** 366
Taylor, Nancy Savage, **I** 4786
Taylor, Nellie Maria, **I** 5463, 12436
Taylor, Pauline, **I** 3426
Taylor, Peggy Hammond, **I** 3803
Taylor, Rebecca, **I** 12169
Taylor, Rosemary Drachman, **I** 10192
Taylor, Sarah Katherine Paine, **I** 17446, 19354
Taylor, Susan Lucy Barry, **I** 16421, 20746
Taylor, Susie Baker King, **I** 2576, 5592, 12621, **III** 125
Taylor-Greenfield, Elizabeth. *See* Greenfield, Elizabeth Taylor.
Te Kanawa, Kiri, **I** 14763, **III** 998, 1129

Tead, Ordway, Mrs., **I** 3427
Teal, Valentine, **I** 10555
Teasdale, Sara; Mrs. Ernst B. Filsinger, **I** 8542
Tee-Van, Helen Damrosch, **I** 4363
Tefft, Eliza, **I** 17247
Teichner, Miriam, **I** 11353
Tekakwitha, Catherine "Kateri", **I** 16968, **II** 61, **III** 1028
Telford, Mary Jewett, **I** 1322, 5552, 12532, 17356, **II** 1027
Teller, Alice Schenck, **I** 16338
Telva, Marion, **I** 14159
Tempest, Therea. *See* Kent, Louise Andrews.
Templeton, Fay, **I** 13728, 19737
Tempski, Armine von, **I** 10193, 15071
Tenayuca (Brooks), Emma, **I** 1248, 6502, 7298, **III** 1009
Tenney, Abby Amy Grove, **I** 8071, 12437
Tenney, Sarah (Brownsen), **I** 8351
Tenney, Tabitha (Gilman), **I** 7451, **IV** 1262
Tennyson, Jean, **I** 13450
Tentoni, Rosa, **I** 14250
Teresa, M. Imelda, Sister, **I** 15614, 17555, **II** 144
Teresa, Mother. *See* Lalor, Alice Teresa.
Teresa, Mother; Alice Labor, **I** 17012, **II** 68
Terhune, Anice Stockton, **I** 14477
Terhune, Mary Virginia (Hawes); Marian Harland, **I** 268, 2053, 5880, 8072, 10896, **IV** 1414
Terrell, Alexander W., Mrs., **I** 16667
Terrell, Ann, **I** 16990, **II** 984
Terrell, Mary Eliza Church, **I** 1206, 1467, 2847, 6831, 14989, 18382, 21114, **II** 311, **IV** 402
Terrell, Tammi; Tammy Montgomery, **I** 14764
Terrington, Lady, **I** 12029
Terry, Ellen F., **I** 5464, 15392
Terry, Frances, **I** 14478
Terry, Lucy, **I** 7424, **III** 56
Terry, Megan, **I** 10752, 12053, 14701, 20616
Terry, Rose, **I** 7954
Teuffel, Blanche Willis (Howard), **I** 8638, **III** 833
Thacher, Ella Hoover, **I** 18363
Thackrey, Dorothy (Schiff), **I** 937, 3466
Thaden, Louise McPhetridge, **I** 18039
Thal, Augusta, **I** 902
Thane, Elswyth, **I** 10298, 20216
Thanet, Octave. *See* French, Alice.

Tharp, Louise Marshall Hall, **I** 10167, 15069
Tharp, Twyla, **I** 2033
Thaw, Evelyn. *See* Nesbit, Evelyn.
Thaxter, Celia (Laighton), **I** 8213, **IV** 1272
Thayer, Caroline Matilda, **I** 7503, **IV** 755
Thayer, Emma (Homan) (Graves), **I** 3971, 8485, 12577, **IV** 274
Thayer, Lizzie E. D., **I** 401, 17884, **IV** 335
Thayer, Mary Appleton Shute, **I** 18515
Thayer, Theodora Willard, **I** 4177
Thayer, Tiffany, **I** 10357, 11821, 20255
Thebom, Blanche, **I** 14586
Thelberg, Elizabeth Burr, **I** 12742, **II** 761
Theodore, Mother. *See* Guerin, Anne-Theresa.
Thoburn, Isabella, **I** 2488, 17386, **III** 517
Thocmetony, Sarah. *See* Winnemucca.
Thomas, Anna Perry, **I** 3313, **III** 232
Thomas, Carrie A., **I** 8352, 13523, 17357
Thomas, Clara Chaplin, **I** 11519
Thomas, Clara Fargo, **I** 4623
Thomas, Dorothy, **I** 10299
Thomas, E., Mrs., **I** 5465, 12438
Thomas, Edith (Carpenter), **I** 6048, 9220, **IV** 1320
Thomas, Edith Matilda, **I** 8869, **IV** 1532, 1930
Thomas, Elizabeth Finley, **I** 4285
Thomas, Fanny Edgar; 6-5-20, **I** 9094
Thomas, Flora, **I** 14251, **III** 248
Thomas, Jane; Jane Black, **I** 4788, 16139
Thomas, Lorraine, **I** 19108
Thomas, Louisa Carroll, **I** 9253
Thomas, M. Louise (Palmer), **I** 246, 1286, 16810
Thomas, Martha Carey, **I** 2719, 8953, 21066, **II** 1033
Thomas, Martha McCannon, **I** 7860
Thomas, Mary, **I** 14817
Thomas, Mary Ann (Lane), **I** 320, 10985, **IV** 2229
Thomas, Mary Frame (Myers), **I** 10854, 12206, 16741, 19157, 20774
Thomas, Mary von Erden, **I** 7908, 15914, **IV** 372
Thomas, Patricia, **I** 3428, 18018
Thomas, Sally, **I** 17068
Thompson, Adaline Emerson, **I** 2765, 21087

Thompson, Alleen, **I** 6303
Thompson, Caroline Wadsworth, **I** 8921
Thompson, Charlotte, **I** 557, 11354, 19899
Thompson, Charlotte Marson, **I** 5466, 12439
Thompson, Clara "Mabel", **I** 13146
Thompson, Clara Mildred, **I** 6147, **IV** 485
Thompson, Dorothy; Mrs. Sinclair Lewis, **I** 7103, 10070, 11574, 15062
Thompson, Eliza Jane Trimble, **I** 19154, **IV** 1889
Thompson, Eliza N., **I** 17091
Thompson, Elizabeth Rowell, **I** 2288, 6315, 6680, 12226, 15308, 19167, 20802
Thompson, Ella Mason (Williams), **I** 8073, **IV** 954
Thompson, Eva Bell, **I** 10300, 11789, **III** 249
Thompson, Eva Griffith, **I** 325, 10993, 17409, 19306, **II** 645, **IV** 2075
Thompson, Franklin. *See* Edmonds, Sarah Emma Evelyn.
Thompson, Helen Muford, **I** 965, 1841, 4692
Thompson, Helen Victoria Veale, **I** 4532, **II** 258, **IV** 1165
Thompson, Kay, **I** 10601, 14532, 20404
Thompson, Mary Harris, **I** 12265
Thompson, Mary Sophia, **I** 2766, 14975, 19685
Thompson, Mary Wolfe, **I** 9814
Thompson, Mrs., **I** 16475
Thompson, Myrtle Grey, **I** 1024, 18098
Thompson, Ruth, **I** 7029
Thompson, Sada Carolyn, **I** 20588
Thompson, Sarah, **I** 5603, 16634
Thompson, Sarah; Countess Rumford, **I** 15253
Thoms, Adah B. Samuels, **I** 12774, **III** 147
Thomson, Catharine, **I** 17170
Thorn, Edgar. *See* Merrick, Mrs. C.
Thorne, Diana, **I** 4517, **III** 572
Thorne, Florence Calvert, **I** 6454, 11304
Thorne, Marion. *See* Thurston, Ida B. Treadwell.
Thorne, P. *See* Smith, Mary Prudence (Wells).
Thornton, Eliza B., **I** 7506
Thornton, Emily. *See* Charles, Emily Thornton.
Thornton, Hannah Jack, **I** 4842
Thorp, Louisa Elizabeth Garden McLeod, **I** 2864, 4144, **IV** 116

Weaver, Anna K., I 312
Weaver, Maurine Barr, I 17724
Webb, Aileen Osborn, I 4490
Webb, Bertah, I 13669
Webb, Ella Surtevant, I 8925
Webb, Frances Isabel (Currie), I 8957, IV 1552
Webber, Irma Eleanor Schmidt, I 4662
Webber, Mary T., I 8080
Webel, Janet Darling, I 4714
Weber, Lois, I 9703, 19909
Webster, Abigail Eastman, I 4858
Webster, Alice Jane Chandler "Jean", I 9566
Webster, Augusta, I 3630, 13399
Webster, Barbara, I 10311
Webster, Helen Livermore, I 2655, 6571, 8843
Webster, Margaret, I 946, 10430, 20297
Webster, Mary C., I 8417, 17389
Webster-Powell, Alma. *See* Powell, Alma Webster (Hall).
Wedel, Cynthia Clark, I 1842, 17777, II 903
Weden, Elizabeth, I 12127
Weed, Ella, I 2656
Weed, Ethel Berenice, I 1241, 5726, 18658
Weed, Helen Hill, I 6450, 15167, 18492, 21208
Weed, Marion, I 13807
Weeden, Howard, I 3870, 7594, IV 4
Weekes, Marie, I 649, 11524
Weeks, Helen Weeks, I 17799
Weeks-Shaw, Clara, I 8766, 12647
Weetamoo, I 6639, III 1027
Wegeman, Kathy Rudolph Wyatt "Katy", I 19130
Weick, Louise, I 11795
Weil, Lisl, I 4708, 10559, III 39
Weill, Blanche C., I 13283
Weiman, Rita, I 9897-98, 20002, IV 179
Weingarten, Violet, I 10635, 11947, 20425
Weir, Irene, I 2835, 4134, 6037, 9162, 11185, IV 1595
Weis, Jessica McCullough, I 1820, 7198
Weisner, Dorothy E., I 16000, 18640
Weiss, Soma, I 13200
Weiss, Susan Archer (Talley), I 3932, 8217, IV 1436, 2320
Weitz, Alice C., I 9957
Weitzel, Sophie Winthrop (Shepherd), I 8418
Welbron, May Eddins, I 11163
Welby, Amelia Ball (Coppuck); Amelie, I 7786, IV 723
Welch, Fannie Alma Dixon, I 6894, 21194
Welch, Jane Meade, I 6030, 11164, 14983, IV 1584

Welch, Mabel R., I 4251
Welch, Mary; Mary White, I 20525, IV 1849
Welch, Nancy, I 17001
Welch, Raquel, I 20669
Welcome, Thelma Kinsbury, I 19131
Welcome, Verda Freeman, I 3433, 7186, III 250, IV 845
Weld, Agnes Vance, I 11548, II 862, IV 351
Weld, Angelina Emily Grimke. *See* Grimke, Angelina Emily.
Weld, Julia Deforest Tiffany, I 13052, 15781, IV 1746
Weld, Theresa; Theresa Blanchard, I 18762
Weld, Tuesday, I 20686
Weldon, Catherine S., I 16612
Welge, Gladys, I 14258
Wellerson, Mila, I 14492
Welles, Winifred, I 10046
Wellington, Margaret, I 313
Wellington, Violet Irene, I 3119, 15034, 15177, 19901, 21242
Wellman, Louisa, I 5481
Wellman, Margaret, I 10460, 16720, III 38
Wells, Agnes Ermina, I 3048, 15958
Wells, Ann Maria, I 7514
Wells, Bernice Young Mitchell, I 10683, III 356
Wells, Carolyn, I 6038, 9163, IV 1318
Wells, Catharine Boott (Gannett), I 2442, 8320, 17347, IV 976
Wells, Charlotte Fowler, I 235, 2253, 10849, 12195, 14803, 15271, IV 1378
Wells, Emmeline Blanchard Woodward, I 7979, 10883, 17263, 20836, II 271, IV 2286
Wells, Goldie Ruth, I 17660
Wells, Ida B. *See* Wells-Barnett, Ida Bell.
Wells, Kate Gannet, I 18242
Wells, Margaret Elizabeth, I 3434
Wells, Marguerite Milton, I 1550, 21186
Wells, Mary Fletcher, I 1171, 2361, 15394, IV 11
Wells, Mary Georgene Berg, I 1047, 12033
Wells, Phradie, I 14086
Wells, Rebecca, I 147
Wells, Shepard, Mrs., I 5482, 15395
Wells-Barnett, Ida Bell; Iola, I 1205, 1460, 11186, 14987, III 145
Welsch, Lilian, I 2746, 12710
Welsh, Andrews, Sr., Mrs., I 15739
Welshons, Kim, I 19132
Welsing, Frances Cress, I 13431, III 442

Welty, Eudora Alice, I 10519, IV 1196
Wenckebach, Anna Doris Amalie Catharina Carla, I 2657, 6572, 8844, III 1168
Wendt, Julia M. Bracken, I 4252
Wengerova, Isabella, I 14087, II 438, III 1199
Wentworth, Cecile (Smith) De, I 4046
Wergeland, Agnes Mathilde, I 2720, 6013
Werlein, Elizabeth Thomas, I 6154, IV 782
Werner, Kay, I 10660, 14580
Werner, Sue, I 10661, 14581
Wertman, Sarah Killgore, I 6745
Wesley, Rachel Parker, I 1211, III 162, IV 843
Wesselhoeft, Elizabeth Foster (Pope), I 8419, IV 984
West, Annie Blythe, I 17539
West, Berenice Delemar; Berenice Delemar Beyers, I 4682
West, Claudine, I 9770, 19948, III 724
West, Jessamyn [Mary], I 10360, 14283, 20256, II 1048, IV 221
West, Julia E. Houston, I 13498
West, Lydia, I 17833
West, Mae, I 10012, 20073
West, Maria A., I 8420, 17390
West, Mary Allen, I 2431, 8277, 10933, 19252, IV 520
Westbrook, Helen Searles, I 14173
Westcott, Cynthia, I 16918
Westcott, Jane Vlachos, I 10589
Western, Pauline Lucille, I 19617
Westgate, Elizabeth, I 909
Westinghouse, Marguerite Erskine Walker, I 3973, 15491
Westley, Helen; Henrietta Remsen Meserole Manney, I 1580, 19830
Weston, Bertine Emma, I 6237
Weston, Christine Goutiere, I 10402, III 752
Weston, Hannah Watts, I 5033, 16299
Weston, Mary Catharine (North), I 7842, 17225
Weston, Mary Pillsbury, I 3962
Weston, Mildred, I 3574, 14493
Weston, Roxana, I 7595, IV 791
Weston, Ruth, I 20373
Westover, Cynthia M., I 406, 6579, 12711, 15940
Westray, Elizabeth, I 19700
Westropp, Clara Elizabeth, I 605, II 183, IV 1962

Wetherbee, Emily Green, I 8585, IV 998
Wethered, Joyce; Lady Heathcoat Amory, I 11813, 18784
Wetherell, Elizabeth. *See* Warner, Susan Bogart.
Wetherell, Emma Abbot, I 13569
Wetherell, June, I 10520
Wetherhead, Mary, I 16954, II 963
Wetherill, Julia Keim. *See* Baker, Julia Keim (Wetherill).
Wetherill, Louisa, I 16668
Wetmore, Elizabeth (Bisland), I 11200, 16649, IV 1607
Wexler, Jacqueline Grennan, I 3651, II 224, IV 1852
Whaley, Ruth Whitehead, I 7199, III 256
Wharton, Anne Hollingsworth, I 5948, 8586, IV 2081
Wharton, Edith Newbold (Jones), I 6039, 9164, 11187, III 776, IV 1596
Wharton, Sarah Grace, I 16408
Wharton, Susannah Lloyd, I 4803
Wheatley, Phillis, I 7425, III 4, 58, IV 855
Wheatley, Ross, Mrs., I 19482
Wheatley, Sarah, I 19495
Wheaton, Anne (Williams), I 7085, 11549
Wheaton, Elizabeth Lee, I 10361
Wheeler, Anna Johnson Pell, I 15965
Wheeler, Candace (Thurber), I 255, 3903, 7955, IV 1403
Wheeler, Cora Stuart, I 5979, 8811, IV 554
Wheeler, Doris, I 4083, IV 1564
Wheeler, Ella. *See* Wilcox, Ella Wheeler.
Wheeler, Janet D., I 4229
Wheeler, Lydia Jane. *See* Peirson, Lydia Jane (Wheeler).
Wheeler, Mary Sparks, I 8218, 17325, IV 2053
Wheeler, Ruth, I 2091, 12935
Wheelock, Deborah Thayer, I 4980
Wheelock, Dora V., I 19355, 20988, IV 1234
Wheelock, Julia Susan, I 5522, 8154, 12488
Wheelock, Lucy, I 2721, 8958, 14967, IV 1040
Wheelwright, Mary Cabot, I 45
Whetton, Harriet Douglas, I 5483
Whetton, Margaret Todd, I 5039
Whiffen, Blanche Galton, I 19618, III 683